The National Hockey League

Official Guide & Record Book

1998-99

Published by the National Hockey League.
Compiled by the NHL Public Relations Department
and the 27 NHL Club Public Relations Directors.

THE NATIONAL HOCKEY LEAGUE
Official Guide & Record Book/1998-99

Staff

For the NHL: David McConnachie; Supervising Editor: Greg Inglis; Statistician: Benny Ercolani; Editorial Staff: David Keon, Sherry McKeown, Jackie Rinaldi, Kelley Rosset, Chris Tredree

Managing Editors: Ralph Dinger, James Duplacey

Contributing Editor: Igor Kuperman

Production Editors: John Pasternak, Alex Dubiel

Assistant Editors: Paul Bontje, Eric Zweig

Contributors: Jim Anderson (IHL), Mike Berger, Joe Bertagna, Mike A. Boland, Bob Borgen, Tim Bryant, Kevin Cahill, Paul R. Carroll Jr., Denis Demers (QMJHL), Mark "Dewey" De Wit, Bob Duff, Gene Dupras, Jeff Fanter (ECAC) Peter Fillman, Ernie Fitzsimmons, Marlene Fitzsimmons, Mel Foster, Pierre Genest, Dan Hamill, Lloyd Hamshaw (WHL), Martin Hill, C. David Johnson, Lori Kessel (UHL), Robert Kirk, Edward Kulperger, Zhenia Kuperman, Eric Lavigne, W.D. Lighthall, Doug Lord (CHL), Rich MacEwen, Roy W. Mackie, John MacKinnon (CHA), Al Mason, Penny McEwen, Herb Morrell (OHL), NHL Broadcasters' Association, NHL Central Registry, NHL Players' Association, Mark Paddock, John D. Painter (NCAA), John Paton, Gary J. Pearce, Andrew Podnieks, Valentina Riazanova, Dennis M. Riggin, Jason Rothwell (ECHL), Ed Saunders (Hockey East), Doug Spencer (WCHA), Matt Steinke (CHL), Tony Techko, Sammy Wallace (WCHL), Jeff Weiss (CCHA), William Wolper (AHL), Scott Woods, (IHL), Jonathan Zweig.

Consulting Editor: Dan Diamond

Photo Credits

Historical and special event photos: Bruce Bennett, David Bier, Michael Burns, Graphic Artists Collection, NHL Images/Allsport, New York Rangers, Rice Studio, Robert Shaver, Imperial Oil Turofsky Collection, Hockey Hall of Fame.

Current photos: Graig Abel, Toronto; Marc Archambault, Montreal; Steve Babineau, Boston; Andrew D. Bernstein, Los Angeles; Bruce Bennett Studios; Mark Buckner, St. Louis; Steve Crandall, New Jersey; Edmonton Northlands; Bob Fisher, Montreal; Gregg Forwerck, Carolina; Tim De Frisco, Colorado; Ray Grabowski, Chicago; John Hartman, Detroit; Jonathan Tayt, Tampa Bay; Mark Hicks, Detroit; David Klutho, St. Louis; Robert Laberge, Montreal; Richard C. Lewis, Florida; V.J. Lovero, Anaheim; Dale MacMillan, Edmonton; McElligott-Teckles Sports Focus Imaging, Ottawa; NHL Images; Orca Bay Sports and Entertainment, Vancouver;Tim Parker, St. Louis; Andre Pichette, Montreal; Len Redkoles, Philadelphia; Debora Robinson, Anaheim; Harry Scull, Jr., Buffalo; Slapshot Photo, Chicago; Don Smith, San Jose; Diane Sobelewski, Hartford; Gerry Thomas, Calgary and Edmonton; Brad Watson, Calgary; Brian Winkler, New Jersey; Bill Wippert, Buffalo.

Distribution

Canadian representatives:

North 49 Books, 35 Prince Andrew Drive, Toronto, Ontario M3C 2H2
416/449-4000; FAX 416/449-9924
NHL Publishing, 194 Dovercourt Road, Toronto, Ontario M6J 3C8
416/531-6535; FAX 416/531-3939

U.S. representatives: Benchmark Press, a division of Triumph Books,
601 South LaSalle, Suite 500, Chicago, Illinois 60605 312/939-3330; FAX 312/663-3557

International representatives: Barkers Worldwide Publications,
155 Maybury Road, Working, Surrey, England GU21 5JR
Tel: 011/441/483/776-161 and FAX: 011/441/483/725-161

Data Management and Typesetting: Caledon Data Management, Hillsburgh, Ontario
Film Output and Scanning: Stafford Graphics, Toronto, Ontario
Printing: Moore Data Management Services, Scarborough, Ontario
Production Management: Dan Diamond and Associates, Inc., Toronto Ontario

The National Hockey League
1251 Avenue of the Americas, 47th Floor, New York, New York 10020-1198
1800 McGill College Ave., Suite 2600, Montreal, Quebec H3A 3J6
75 International Boulevard, Suite 300, Toronto, Ontario M9W 6L9

Table of Contents

Table of Contents *continued*

(1998-99 NHL Schedule begins inside front cover)

Introduction

WELCOME TO *THE NHL OFFICIAL GUIDE & RECORD BOOK FOR 1998-99.* This 67th edition of the *Guide* continues to provide comprehensive statistical coverage of the National Hockey League, its players and top prospects in minor pro, European, junior or college leagues and conferences.

Special features in this edition include a list of NHL league and team websites is found on page 120. A detailed diagram of the newly-configured NHL ice surface is found on page 12.

Also included in this edition are overviews of the two Olympic hockey tournaments played in Nagano, Japan in February of 1998. These Winter Olympics were unique from hockey's perspective because, for the first time, the NHL structured its schedule to enable many of the world's best players to play for their national teams. Six "dream teams" resulted—Canada, the Czech Republic, Finland, Russia, Slovakia and Sweden—with the Czech Republic winning gold behind the sensational goaltending of Dominik Hasek. Russia won the silver medal; Finland, the bronze. Hasek, who is a two-time winner of the Hart Trophy as the NHL player judged to be most valuable to his team, was named the top goaltender at Nagano as well. The other award winners were also NHL superstars: Pavel Bure was named top forward; Rob Blake was top defenseman. A highlight of this Olympics was the talent on some teams from lesser hockey nations. Strong showings by players from Belarus, Kazakhstan and others demonstrate that scouting and drafting for NHL clubs will become increasingly complex in the millennium. Women's hockey made its Olympic debut at Nagano as well. The U.S. women's team played well enroute to the gold medal game where it defeated Canada for the first time at a world event. The *NHL Guide*'s coverage of men's Olympic hockey begins on page 129. Women's coverage is found on page 132.

Complete Olympic hockey statistics are an important addition to the *Guide*'s "best-in-the-business" player and goaltender registers. Other changes to the register include simplified notation for all-star selections and awards and the addition of special notes to supply additional information about a player's career. These notes are highlighted with a bullet (•).

The Player Register begins on page 259. As the NHL grows, so does this section of the *NHL Guide*, in this instance by ten pages or approximately eighty players from last year to this. A key to abbreviations and symbols used in the individual player and goaltender data panels that make up the Registers as well as a list of NHL clubs' minor-league affiliates are found on page 257. The Retired Player Index, beginning on page 419, contains more new statistical research, particularly relating to the NHL's first four seasons when statistics weren't accurately tabulated. Bob Duff, a reporter for the Windsor Star and a gifted hockey historian, has used detailed newspaper accounts of the day to compile a complete statistical package for the early NHL. These numbers have resulted in amendments to the scoring totals of many early players. These changes have rippled through the *NHL Guide*, affecting features such as Individual Scoring Records – History (page 152) and Goals-per-game Leaders, One Season (page 181).

For 1998-99, the NHL welcomes the Nashville Predators who will play in the Central Division of the Western Conference. Three additional franchises (Atlanta Thrashers, Columbus Blue Jackets and Minnesota Wild) will begin play in 1999-2000 or 2000-01. These new franchises are listed on page 119. With the addition of these clubs, the NHL will become a 30-team league, organized in two conferences, each of which will be made up of three five-team divisions. This six-division set-up begins with the 1998-99 season. Divisional alignment and scheduling are described on the inside front cover.

We would also be remiss if we didn't draw attention to our new (big) sister publication, *Total Hockey*. This 1,888-page encyclopedia covers the game with a breadth and depth never seen before and is sure to be of interest to *NHL Guide & Record Book* readers. More information is found at the end of this book on page 480.

As always, our thanks to readers, correspondents and members of the media who take the time to comment on the *Guide & Record Book*. Thanks as well to the people working in the communications departments of the NHL's member clubs and to their counterparts in the AHL, IHL, ECHL, Central, United, West Coast and Western Professional and junior leagues as well as in college athletic conferences and European hockey federations.

Best wishes for an enjoyable 1998-99 NHL season.

ACCURACY REMAINS THE *GUIDE & RECORD BOOK*'S TOP PRIORITY.

We appreciate comments and clarification from our readers. Please direct these to:

Greg Inglis 47th floor, 1251 Avenue of the Americas, New York, New York 10020-1198 . . . or . . .

David Keon 75 International Blvd., Suite 300, Rexdale, Ontario M9W 6L9.

Your involvement makes a better book.

NATIONAL HOCKEY LEAGUE

Established November 22, 1917

New York – 1251 Avenue of the Americas, 47th Floor, New York, NY 10020-1198, (212)789-2000, Fax: (212)789-2020
Montréal – 1800 McGill College Avenue, Suite 2600, Montréal, Québec H3A 3J6, (514)288-9220, Fax: (514)284-0300
Toronto – 75 International Blvd., Suite 300, Rexdale, Ontario M9W 6L9, (416)798-0809, Fax: (416)798-0819
NHL Enterprises – 1251 Avenue of the Americas, 47th Floor, New York, NY 10020-1198, (212)789-2000, Fax: (212)789-2020
NHL Enterprises Canada – 75 International Blvd., Suite 301, Rexdale, Ontario M9W 6L9, 416/798-9388, Fax: 416/798-9395
NHL Europe – Signaustrasse 1, 8008 Zurich – Switzerland, 41-1-389-8080, Fax: 41-1-389-8090
NHL Productions – 183 Oak Tree Road, Tappan, NY 10983-2809, (914)365-6701, Fax: (914)365-6010

Executive

Commissioner....Gary B. Bettman
Senior Vice President and Chief Operating Officer....Stephen J. Solomon
Senior Vice President, Legal Affairs....William L. Daly
Senior Vice President and Director of Hockey Operations....Colin Campbell
Executive Assistant to the Commissioner....Debbie Jordan

Administration

Director of Administration....Debbie Jordan
Director, Human Resources....Janet Meyers

Broadcasting/NHL Productions

Vice President, Broadcasting....Glenn Adamo
Executive Producer....Ken Rosen
Senior Producer....Darryl Lepik
Director, Broadcasting....Adam Acone
Director, Broadcast Business Affairs....Samuel Esposito, Jr.
Director, Broadcast Operations/NHLP....Patti Fallick
Director, Scheduling and Operations....Steve HatzePetros
Manager, Broadcasting....Todd Goodman
Manager, Broadcasting....Anthony Triano
Manager, NHL Productions....Peg Walsh

New Business Development

Vice President, New Business Development....Bryant McBride
Director, Youth Development NHL/USA Diversity Task Force....Willie O'Ree

Communications

Vice President, Communications....Bernadette Mansur
Vice President, Media Relations....Frank Brown
Vice President, Public Relations and Media Services (Toronto)....Gary Meagher
Vice President, Public Relations....Arthur Pincus
Chief Statistician (Toronto)....Benny Ercolani
Director, Corporate Communications....Mary Pat Clarke
Director, Creative Services....David Haney
Director, Public Relations....Andrew McGowan
Associate Director, Creative Services....Kathy Drew
Manager, Media Services....Susan Aglietti
Manager, NHL Images....Anita Cechowski
Manager, Community Relations....Adrienne Drennan
Manager, News Services....Greg Inglis
Manager, Corporate Communications....Tracey Warshaw

Finance

Group Vice President and Chief Financial Officer....Craig Harnett
Vice President, Finance....Joseph DeSousa
Controller, Broadcasting and Special Projects....Megan O'Donnell
Controller and Office Manager (Montreal)....Olivia Pietrantonio

Hockey Operations

Vice President, Hockey Operations (Toronto)....Jim Gregory
Managing Director, Central Registry (Montreal)....Garry Lovegrove
Director, Central Registry (Montreal)....Steve Pellegrini
Assistant Director, Central Registry (Montreal)....Madeleine Supino
Director of Central Scouting (Toronto)....Frank Bonello
Director of Officiating (Toronto)....Bryan Lewis
Director, Alumni Relations (Toronto)....Pat Flatley
Assistant Director of Officiating (Toronto)....Charlie Banfield
Manager, Hockey Operations (New York)....Claude Loiselle
Technical Manager, Officiating (Toronto)....Dave Baker
Consultant (Montreal)....Brian F. O'Neill
Video Director, Hockey Operations (Tappan)....Rob Schoenbach

Information Technology

Director....Peter DelGiacco
Assistant Director (Montreal)....Luc Coulombe
Manager, Network Communication....Patrick Powers
Senior Project Manager....Lee Reichman

Legal

Vice President and General Counsel....David Zimmerman
Assistant General Counsel....Katherine Jones

Pension

Director (Montreal)....Yvon Chamberland
Controller, Pension (Montreal)....Mary Skiadopoulos
Manager, Pension (Montreal)....Lise de Jocas

Security

Vice President and Director....Dennis Cunningham
Assistant Director....Joseph Caporicci

Special Events

Vice President, Special Events....Frank Supovitz
Director, Special Events....Karen Ayoub
Director, Special Events....Lori Boesch

Special Events *(continued)*

Director, Special Events....Anne I. Grotefeld
Manager, Special Events....Ken Chin
Manager, Special Events....Patricia L. Conrad
Manager, Special Events....Debbie Hodkinson
Manager, Special Events....Bill Miller
Manager, Special Events....Sally Printz

Television and Business Affairs

Vice President Television and Business Affairs....Ellis T. "Skip" Prince
Manager, Satellite Television....Kenneth Gelman
Manager, NHL Video....David Levy
Manager, Television and Business Affairs, International....Susanna Mandel-Mantello
Manager, Team Television....John Tortora

NHL Enterprises, L.P.

Consumer Products/Retail Sales Marketing

Vice President....Brian Jennings
Vice President, NHLE, Canada....Glenn Wakefield
Group Director, Special Projects and Promotional Services....Glenn Horine
Director, Center Ice Program and Sporting Goods....Lloyd Haymes
Director, Consumer Products Marketing, Canada....Karen Hanson
Director, Apparel and Headwear....Jim Haskins
Director, Non-Apparel....Judith Salsberg
Sales Manager, Eastern Region....Adam Blinderman
Sales Manager, Midwest Region....Cathy Groves
Manager, Retail Sales and Marketing, Canada....Barry Monahan

Marketing

Group Vice President, Marketing....Ed Horne

Corporate Marketing

Director, Corporate Marketing....Tim Conway
Director, Corporate Marketing....Mark Donovan
Director, Corporate Marketing....Andrew Judelson
Director, Corporate Marketing, Canada....Laurie Kepron
Manager, Corporate Marketing....David Abrutyn
Manager, Corporate Marketing....Janet Shimberg

Club Marketing

Director, Club Marketing....Scott Carmichael
Director, Club Marketing....Susan Cohig

Youth Marketing

Vice President, Youth Marketing....Dina Gilbertie
Director, Youth Marketing....Elle Farrell

Printed Products Marketing

Director, Printed Products Marketing....David McConnachie

Marketing Services and Special Projects

Group Director, Marketing Services and Special Projects....Glenn Horine
Manager, Marketing Services and Special Projects....Mary Ellen Curran
Manager, Marketing Services and Special Projects....Eva Collins

Fan Development

Vice President, Fan Development....Ken Yaffe
Director, Off-Ice Programs....Brian Mullen
Director, Fan Development....Alysse Soll
Manager, Fan Development....Peter London
Manager, Fan Development....Kamini Sharma

International Marketing

Managing Director, NHLE Europe....Brad Kwong
Director, International Marketing, Asia/Pacific Rim....Frank Nakano

Finance

Controller, Consumer Products Marketing....Mary McCarthy
Controller, Marketing and NHL ICE....Pam Wakoff
Director, Accounting Operations....Belinda Haeberlein
Finance Manager, Events....Scott Weinfeld

Legal

Senior Vice President and General Counsel....Richard Zahnd
Vice President, Legal and Associate General Counsel....Mary Sotis
Senior Counsel, Legal and Business Affairs....Leslie Gittess
Senior Counsel, Legal and Business Affairs....Douglas Perlman
Associate Counsel....Robert Hawkins
Staff Attorney....Anita Andrade
Director, Consumer Products Marketing and Trademark Compliance....Ruth Gruhin
Director, Contract Administration....Heather Bell

NHL Interactive CyberEnterprises (NHL ICE)

General Manager....Tom Richardson
Director, Editorial and Production....Refet Kaplan
Director, Sales and Marketing....Kenny Nova
Manager, Sales and Marketing....Tom Leyden

BOARD OF GOVERNORS

Chairman of the Board – Harley N. Hotchkiss

Mighty Ducks of Anaheim
Disney Sports Enterprises, Inc,

Tony Tavares .... Governor
Michael D. Eisner .... Alternate Governor
Jack Ferreira .... Alternate Governor

Boston Bruins
Boston Professional Hockey Association, Inc.

Jeremy M. Jacobs .... Governor
Louis Jacobs .... Alternate Governor
Harry J. Sinden .... Alternate Governor

Buffalo Sabres
Niagara Frontier Hockey, L.P.

Seymour H. Knox, IV .... Alternate Governor
John J. Rigas .... Alternate Governor
Michael J. Rigas .... Alternate Governor
Timothy J. Rigas .... Alternate Governor
Robert O. Swados .... Alternate Governor

Calgary Flames
Calgary Flames Limited Partnership

Harley N. Hotchkiss .... Governor
Al Coates .... Alternate Governor
Ron Bremner .... Alternate Governor
Grant Bartlett .... Alternate Governor
Byron J. Seaman .... Alternate Governor
N. Murray Edwards .... Alternate Governor

Carolina Hurricanes
KTR Hockey Limited Partnership

Peter Karmanos, Jr. .... Governor
Jim Rutherford .... Alternate Governor
Dean Jordan .... Alternate Governor

Chicago Blackhawks
Chicago Blackhawks Hockey Team, Inc.

William W. Wirtz .... Governor
Gene Gozdecki .... Alternate Governor
Thomas N. Ivan .... Alternate Governor
Robert J. Pulford .... Alternate Governor
W. Rockwell Wirtz .... Alternate Governor

Colorado Avalanche
Colorado Avalanche, LLC

Charlie Lyons .... Governor
Pierre Lacroix .... Alternate Governor

Dallas Stars
Dallas Stars, L.P.

Tom Hicks .... Governor
James R. Lites .... Alternate Governor

Detroit Red Wings
Detroit Red Wings, Inc.

Michael Ilitch .... Governor
Jay A. Bielfield .... Alternate Governor
Jim Devellano .... Alternate Governor
Atanas Ilitch .... Alternate Governor
Christopher Ilitch .... Alternate Governor

Edmonton Oilers
Edmonton Investors Group Limited Partnership

James F. Hole .... Governor
Glen Sather .... Alternate Governor

Florida Panthers
Florida Panthers Hockey Club, Ltd.

William A. Torrey .... Governor
H. Wayne Huizenga .... Alternate Governor
Bryan Murray .... Alternate Governor

Los Angeles Kings
Los Angeles Kings Hockey Club, L.P.

Robert Sanderman .... Governor
Philip F. Anschutz .... Alternate Governor
Timothy J. Leiweke .... Alternate Governor
Edward Roski, Jr. .... Alternate Governor
David Taylor .... Alternate Governor

Montréal Canadiens
Le Club de Hockey Canadien, Inc.

Ronald L. Corey .... Governor
Rejean Houle .... Alternate Governor
Fred Steer .... Alternate Governor

Nashville Predators
Nashville Hockey Club, L.P.

Craig Leipold .... Governor
David Poile .... Alternate Governor
Jack Diller .... Alternate Governor

New Jersey Devils
Meadowlanders, Inc.

Dr. John J. McMullen .... Governor
Lou A. Lamoriello .... Alternate Governor
Peter McMullen .... Alternate Governor

New York Islanders
New York Islanders Hockey Club, L.P.

Steven Gluckstern .... Governor
Howard Milstein .... Alternate Governor
Edward Milstein .... Alternate Governor
David Seldin .... Alternate Governor
William Skehan .... Alternate Governor

New York Rangers
Madison Square Garden, L.P.

David W. Checketts .... Governor
Marc Lustgarten .... Alternate Governor
Kenneth W. Munoz .... Alternate Governor
Neil Smith .... Alternate Governor

Ottawa Senators
Ottawa Senators Hockey Club Limited Partnership

Roderick M. Bryden .... Governor
Roy Mlakar .... Alternate Governor
David Ferguson .... Alternate Governor

Philadelphia Flyers
Comcast Spectacor L.P.

Edward M. Snider .... Governor
Bob Clarke .... Alternate Governor
Ronald K. Ryan .... Alternate Governor
Philip I. Weinberg .... Alternate Governor

Phoenix Coyotes
BG Hockey Ventures

Richard T. Burke .... Governor
Shawn Hunter .... Alternate Governor
Robert D. Smith .... Alternate Governor

Pittsburgh Penguins
Pittsburgh Hockey Associates

Roger Marino .... Governor
Craig Patrick .... Alternate Governor
Howard Baldwin .... Alternate Governor

St. Louis Blues
St. Louis Blues Hockey Club, L.P.

Jerry E. Ritter .... Governor
Larry Pleau .... Alternate Governor
Mark Sauer .... Alternate Governor

San Jose Sharks
San Jose Sharks, L.P.

George Gund III .... Governor
Gordon Gund .... Alternate Governor
Greg Jamison .... Alternate Governor
Irvin A. Leonard .... Alternate Governor
Dean Lombardi .... Alternate Governor

Tampa Bay Lightning
ALW Sports Management

Bill McGehee .... Governor
Phil Esposito .... Alternate Governor
Jeff Gaines .... Alternate Governor

Toronto Maple Leafs
Maple Leaf Gardens Limited

Steve A. Stavro .... Governor
Brian P. Bellmore .... Alternate Governor
Ken Dryden .... Alternate Governor

Vancouver Canucks
Vancouver Hockey Club Ltd.

John E. McCaw, Jr. .... Governor
Steve Bellringer .... Alternate Governor
Stanley McCammon .... Alternate Governor
Brian Burke .... Alternate Governor

Washington Capitals
Washington Capitals, L.P.

Abe Pollin .... Governor
Richard M. Patrick .... Alternate Governor
Peter O'Malley .... Alternate Governor
David Osnos .... Alternate Governor

Commissioner and League Presidents

Gary B. Bettman

Gary B. Bettman took office as the NHL's first Commissioner on February 1, 1993. Since the League was formed in 1917, there have been five League Presidents.

NHL President	Years in Office
Frank Calder	1917-1943
Mervyn "Red" Dutton	1943-1946
Clarence Campbell	1946-1977
John A. Ziegler, Jr.	1977-1992
Gil Stein	1992-1993

NHL Europe, B.V.

Signaustrasse 1
8008 Zurich – Switzerland
Phone: 41(0)1 389-8080
Fax: 41(0)1 389-8090

Brad Kwong – Managing Director
J.D. Kershaw – Co-ordinator
Carla Galley – Assistant

Hockey Hall of Fame

BCE Place
30 Yonge Street
Toronto, Ontario M5E 1X8
Phone: 416/360-7735
Executive Fax: 416/360-1501
Resource Center/Retail Fax: 416/360-1316
www.hhof.com

William C. Hay – Chairman
Jeff Denomme – President
Bryan Black – Senior Vice President, Marketing
Craig Baines – Director, Business Development and Facilities
Jan Barrina – Manager, Special Events and Facility Sales
Craig Beckim – Associate Manager, Merchandising
Sandra Buffone – Controller and Office Manager
Craig Campbell – Manager, Resource Center
Ron Ellis – Director, Public Affairs
Barry Eversley – Manager, Building Services
Anthony Fusco – Manager, Information Systems
Jeff Graham – Manager, Guest Services
Kelly Massé – Executive Assistant, Marketing
Tim McWilliams – Associate Manager, Retail Operations
Ray Paquet – Creative Director, Exhibits
Phil Pritchard – Director, Information and Acquisitions
Pearl Rajwanth – Executive Assistant

National Hockey League Players' Association

777 Bay Street, Suite 2400
Toronto, Ontario M5G 2C8
Phone: 416/408-4040
Fax: 416/408-3685
E-mail: media@nhlpa.com Internet: http://www.nhlpa.com

Robert W. Goodenow – Executive Director and General Counsel
JP Barry, Jeff Citron, Chris DiFrancesco, Ian Pulver – Associate Counsels
Ted Saskin – Senior Director, Business Affairs and Licensing
Jordan Banks, David Kleiman, Mike Ouellet – Associate Counsels, Licensing
Ken Kim – Marketing Manager, "Be A Player" and Promotional Licensing
Michael Merhab – Director, Trading Cards and Collectibles
Alison McDonald – Television and Media Projects Director
Chris Allard – Communications Co-ordinator
David Silverman – Webmaster
Barbara Larcina – Director of Business Operations
Kim Murdoch – Manager, Pensions and Benefits
Devin Smith – Manager, Media Relations at ext. 279 or e-mail: dsmith@nhlpa.com

NHL On-Ice Officials

Total NHL Games and 97-98 Games columns count regular-season games only.

Referees

#	Name	Birthplace	Birthdate	First NHL Game	Total NHL Games	97-98 Games
9	Blaine Angus	Shawville, Que	9/25/61	10/17/92	75	21
30	Bernard DeGrace	Lameque, N.B.	5/1/67	10/15/91	*158	1
10	Paul Devorski	Guelph, Ont.	8/18/58	10/14/89	458	68
11	Mark Faucette	Springfield, MA	6/9/58	12/23/87	567	60
2	Kerry Fraser	Sarnia, Ont.	5/30/52	4/6/75	1106	63
4	Terry Gregson	Erin, Ont.	11/7/53	12/19/81	1003	69
95	Conrad Haché	Sudbury, Ont.	5/15/72	2/27/95	**24	0
8	Dave Jackson	Montreal, Que.	11/28/64	12/23/90	315	60
33	Marc Joannette	Verdun, Que.	11/3/68			
18	Greg Kimmerly	Toronto, Ont.	12/8/64	11/30/96	6	5
12	Don Koharski	Halifax, N.S.	12/2/55	10/14/77	*1132	66
32	Tom Kowal	Vernon, B.C.	11/2/67			
14	Dennis LaRue	Savannah, GA	7/14/59	3/26/91	146	63
28	Mike Leggo	North Bay, Ont.	10/7/64		2	2
27	Kevin Maguire	Toronto, Ont.	5/1/63		2	2
6	Dan Marouelli	Edmonton, Alta.	7/16/55	11/2/84	829	62
26	Rob Martell	Winnipeg, Man.	10/21/63	3/14/84	*6	3
7	Bill McCreary	Guelph, Ont.	11/17/55	11/3/84	863	67
19	Mick McGeough	Regina, Sask.	6/20/57	1/19/89	453	67
40	Brad Meier	Dayton, OH	4/11/67			
15	Dan O'Halloran	Leamington, Ont.	3/25/64	10/14/95	42	16
37	Tim Peel	Toronto, Ont.	4/27/66			
20	Lance Roberts	Edmonton, Alta.	5/28/57	11/3/89	334	62
31	Lyle Seitz	Brooks, Alta.	1/22/69	10/6/92	**0	102
16	Rob Shick	Port Alberni, B.C.	12/4/57	4/6/86	646	55
22	Paul Stewart	Boston, MA	3/21/55	3/27/87	692	68
17	Richard Trottier	Laval, Que.	2/28/57	12/13/89	332	44
21	Don Van Massenhoven	London, Ont.	7/17/60	11/11/93	250	68
24	Stephen Walkom	North Bay, Ont.	8/8/63	10/18/92	248	65
23	Brad Watson	Regina, Sask.	10/4/61	2/5/94	9	6
29	Scott Zelkin	Wilmette, IL	9/12/68	4/13/97	2	1

* Includes some games worked as a linesman. ** All games worked as a linesman

Linesmen

#	Name	Birthplace	Birthdate	First NHL Game	Total NHL Games	97-98 Games
75	Derek Amell	Port Colborne, Ont.	9/16/68		23	23
94	Wayne Bonney	Ottawa, Ont.	5/27/53	10/10/79	1309	74
55	Gord Broseker	Baltimore, MD	7/8/50	1/14/75	1659	63
74	Lonnie Cameron	Victoria, B.C.	7/15/64	10/5/96	134	69
35	Pierre Champoux	Ville St-Pierre, Que.	4/18/63	10/8/88	643	77
50	Kevin Collins	Springfield, MA	12/15/50	10/13/77	1614	67
88	Mike Cvik	Calgary, Alta.	7/6/62	10/8/87	716	72
33	Pat Dapuzzo	Hoboken, NJ	12/29/58	12/5/84	1001	70
44	Greg Devorski	Guelph, Ont.	8/3/69	10/9/93	308	67
68	Scott Driscoll	Seaforth, Ont.	5/2/68	10/10/92	364	67
70	Francois Gagnon	Montreal, Que.	3/16/70			
36	Gerard Gauthier	Montreal, Que.	9/5/48	10/16/71	2009	65
66	Darren Gibbs	Edmonton, Alta.	9/30/66		34	34
91	Don Henderson	Calgary, Alta.	9/23/68	3/10/95	126	70
64	Shane Heyer	Summerland, B.C.	2/7/64	10/5/88	712	79
48	Swede Knox	Edmonton, Alta.	3/2/48	10/14/72	1917	71
71	Brad Kovachik	Woodstock, Ont.	3/7/71	10/10/96	93	66
86	Brad Lazarowich	Vancouver, B.C.	8/4/62	10/9/86	821	70
46	Dan McCourt	Falconbridge, Ont.	8/14/54	12/27/80	1215	73
90	Andy McElman	Chicago Heights, IL	8/4/61	10/7/93	296	63
39	Randy Mitton	Fredericton, N.B.	9/22/50	2/2/74	1701	58
41	Jean Morin	Sorel, Que.	8/10/63	10/5/91	426	78
93	Brian Murphy	Dover, NH	12/13/64	10/7/88	648	66
40	Thor Nelson	Westminister, CA	1/6/68	2/16/95	105	66
43	Tim Nowak	Buffalo, NY	9/6/67	10/8/93	304	71
79	Mark Paré	Windsor, Ont.	7/26/57	10/11/79	1398	71
51	Baron Parker	Vancouver, B.C.	3/5/67	1/25/95	237	63
72	Stephane Provost	Montreal, Que.	5/5/67	1/25/95	252	68
34	Pierre Racicot	Verdun, Que.	2/15/67	10/12/93	312	75
32	Ray Scapinello	Guelph, Ont.	11/5/46	10/17/71	2090	71
47	Dan Schachte	Madison, WI	7/13/58	10/6/82	1116	63
84	Anthony Sericolo	Troy, NY	7/17/68			
57	Jay Sharrers	Jamaica, West Indies	7/3/67	10/6/90	507	75
56	Mark Wheler	North Battleford, Sask.	9/20/65	10/10/92	384	68

NHL History

1917 — National Hockey League organized November 22 in Montreal following suspension of operations by the National Hockey Association of Canada Limited (NHA). Montreal Canadiens, Montreal Wanderers, Ottawa Senators and Quebec Bulldogs attended founding meeting. Delegates decided to use NHA rules.

Toronto Arenas were later admitted as fifth team; Quebec decided not to operate during the first season. Quebec players allocated to remaining four teams.

Frank Calder elected president and secretary-treasurer.

First NHL games played December 19, with Toronto only arena with artificial ice. Clubs played 22-game split schedule.

1918 — Emergency meeting held January 3 due to destruction by fire of Montreal Arena which was home ice for both Canadiens and Wanderers.

Wanderers withdrew, reducing the NHL to three teams; Canadiens played remaining home games at 3,250-seat Jubilee rink.

Quebec franchise sold to P.J. Quinn of Toronto on October 18 on the condition that the team operate in Quebec City for 1918-19 season. Quinn did not attend the November League meeting and Quebec did not play in 1918-19.

1919-20 — NHL reactivated Quebec Bulldogs franchise. Former Quebec players returned to the club. New Mount Royal Arena became home of Canadiens. Toronto Arenas changed name to St. Patricks. Clubs played 24-game split schedule.

1920-21 — H.P. Thompson of Hamilton, Ontario made application for the purchase of an NHL franchise. Quebec franchise shifted to Hamilton with other NHL teams providing players to strengthen the club.

1921-22 — Split schedule abandoned. First and second place teams at the end of full schedule to play for championship.

1922-23 — Clubs agreed that players could not be sold or traded to clubs in any other league without first being offered to all other clubs in the NHL. In March, Foster Hewitt broadcasts radio's first hockey game.

1923-24 — Ottawa's new 10,000-seat arena opened. First U.S. franchise granted to Boston for following season.

Dr. Cecil Hart Trophy donated to NHL to be awarded to the player judged most useful to his team.

1924-25 — Canadian Arena Company of Montreal granted a franchise to operate Montreal Maroons. NHL now six team league with two clubs in Montreal. Inaugural game in new Montreal Forum played November 29, 1924 as Canadiens defeated Toronto 7-1. Forum was home rink for the Maroons, but no ice was available in the Canadiens arena November 29, resulting in shift to Forum.

Hamilton finished first in the standings, receiving a bye into the finals. But Hamilton players, demanding $200 each for additional games in the playoffs, went on strike. The NHL suspended all players, fining them $200 each. Stanley Cup finalist to be the winner of NHL semi-final between Toronto and Canadiens.

Prince of Wales and Lady Byng trophies donated to NHL.

Clubs played 30-game schedule.

1925-26 — Hamilton club dropped from NHL. Players signed by new New York Americans franchise. Franchise granted to Pittsburgh.

Clubs played 36-game schedule.

1926-27 — New York Rangers granted franchise May 15, 1926. Chicago Black Hawks and Detroit Cougars granted franchises September 25, 1926. NHL now ten-team league with an American and a Canadian Division.

Stanley Cup came under the control of NHL. In previous seasons, winners of the now-defunct Western or Pacific Coast leagues would play NHL champion in Cup finals.

Toronto franchise sold to a new company controlled by Hugh Aird and Conn Smythe. Name changed from St. Patricks to Maple Leafs.

Clubs played 44-game schedule.

The Montreal Canadiens donated the Vezina Trophy to be awarded to the team allowing the fewest goals-against in regular season play. The winning team would, in turn, present the trophy to the goaltender playing in the greatest number of games during the season.

1930-31 — Detroit franchise changed name from Cougars to Falcons. Pittsburgh transferred to Philadelphia for one season. Pirates changed name to Philadelphia Quakers. Trading deadline for teams set at February 15 of each year. NHL approved operation of farm teams by Rangers, Americans, Falcons and Bruins. Four-sided electric arena clock first demonstrated.

1931-32 — Philadelphia dropped out. Ottawa withdrew for one season. New Maple Leaf Gardens completed.

Clubs played 48-game schedule

1932-33 — Detroit franchise changed name from Falcons to Red Wings. Franchise application received from St. Louis but refused because of additional travel costs. Ottawa team resumed play.

1933-34 — First All-Star Game played as a benefit for injured player Ace Bailey. Leafs defeated All-Stars 7-3 in Toronto.

1934-35 — Ottawa franchise transferred to St. Louis. Team called St. Louis Eagles and consisted largely of Ottawa's players.

1935-36 — Ottawa-St. Louis franchise terminated. Montreal Canadiens finished season with very poor record. To strengthen the club, NHL gave Canadiens first call on the services of all French-Canadian players for three seasons.

1937-38 — Second benefit all-star game staged November 2 in Montreal in aid of the family of the late Canadiens star Howie Morenz.

Montreal Maroons withdrew from the NHL on June 22, 1938, leaving seven clubs in the League.

1938-39 — Expenses for each club regulated at $5 per man per day for meals and $2.50 per man per day for accommodation.

1939-40 — Benefit All-Star Game played October 29, 1939 in Montreal for the children of the late Albert (Babe) Siebert.

1940-41 — Ross-Tyer puck adopted as the official puck of the NHL. Early in the season it was apparent that this puck was too soft. The Spalding puck was adopted in its place.

After the playoffs, Arthur Ross, NHL governor from Boston, donated a perpetual trophy to be awarded annually to the player voted outstanding in the league.

1941-42 — New York Americans changed name to Brooklyn Americans.

1942-43 — Brooklyn Americans withdrew from NHL, leaving six teams: Boston, Chicago, Detroit, Montreal, New York and Toronto. Playoff format saw first-place team play third-place team and second play fourth.

Clubs played 50-game schedule.

Frank Calder, president of the NHL since its inception, died in Montreal. Meryn "Red" Dutton, former manager of the New York Americans, became president. The NHL commissioned the Calder Memorial Trophy to be awarded to the League's outstanding rookie each year.

1945-46 — Philadelphia, Los Angeles and San Francisco applied for NHL franchises.

The Philadelphia Arena Company of the American Hockey League applied for an injunction to prevent the possible operation of an NHL franchise in that city.

1946-47 — Mervyn Dutton retired as president of the NHL prior to the start of the season. He was succeeded by Clarence S. Campbell.

Individual trophy winners and all-star team members to receive $1,000 awards.

Playoff guarantees for players introduced.

Clubs played 60-game schedule.

1947-48 — The first annual All-Star Game for the benefit of the players' pension fund was played when the All-Stars defeated the Stanley Cup Champion Toronto Maple Leafs 4-3 in Toronto on October 13, 1947.

Ross Trophy, awarded to the NHL's outstanding player since 1941, to be awarded annually to the League's scoring leader.

Philadelphia and Los Angeles franchise applications refused.

National Hockey League Pension Society formed.

1949-50 — Clubs played 70-game schedule.

First intra-league draft held April 30, 1950. Clubs allowed to protect 30 players. Remaining players available for $25,000 each.

1951-52 — Referees included in the League's pension plan.

1952-53 — In May of 1952, City of Cleveland applied for NHL franchise. Application denied. In March of 1953, the Cleveland Barons of the AHL challenged the NHL champions for the Stanley Cup. The NHL governors did not accept this challenge.

1953-54 — The James Norris Memorial Trophy presented to the NHL for annual presentation to the League's best defenseman.

Intra-league draft rules amended to allow teams to protect 18 skaters and two goaltenders, claiming price reduced to $15,000.

1954-55 — Each arena to operate an "out-of-town" scoreboard. Referees and linesmen to wear shirts of black and white vertical stripes.

1956-57 — Standardized signals for referees and linesmen introduced.

1960-61 — Canadian National Exhibition, City of Toronto and NHL reach agreement for the construction of a Hockey Hall of Fame on the CNE grounds. Hall opens on August 26, 1961.

1963-64 — Player development league established with clubs operated by NHL franchises located in Minneapolis, St. Paul, Indianapolis, Omaha and, beginning in 1964-65, Tulsa. First universal amateur draft took place. All players of qualifying age (17) unaffected by sponsorship of junior teams available to be drafted.

1964-65 — Conn Smythe Trophy presented to the NHL to be awarded annually to the outstanding player in the Stanley Cup playoffs.

Minimum age of players subject to amateur draft changed to 18.

1965-66 — NHL announced expansion plans for a second six-team division to begin play in 1967-68.

1966-67 — Fourteen applications for NHL franchises received.

Lester Patrick Trophy presented to the NHL to be awarded annually for outstanding service to hockey in the United States.

NHL sponsorship of junior teams ceased, making all players of qualifying age not already on NHL-sponsored lists eligible for the amateur draft.

1967-68 — Six new teams added: California Seals, Los Angeles Kings, Minnesota North Stars, Philadelphia Flyers, Pittsburgh Penguins, St. Louis Blues. New teams to play in West Division. Remaining six teams to play in East Division.

Minimum age of players subject to amateur draft changed to 20.

Clubs played 74-game schedule.

Clarence S. Campbell Trophy awarded to team finishing the regular season in first place in West Division.

California Seals changed name to Oakland Seals on December 8, 1967.

1968-69 — Clubs played 76-game schedule.

Amateur draft expanded to cover any amateur player of qualifying age throughout the world.

1970-71 — Two new teams added: Buffalo Sabres and Vancouver Canucks. These teams joined East Division: Chicago switched to West Division.

Clubs played 78-game schedule.

1971-72 — Playoff format amended. In each division, first to play fourth; second to play third.

1972-73 — Soviet Nationals and Canadian NHL stars play eight-game pre-season series. Canadians win 4-3-1.

Two new teams added. Atlanta Flames join West Division; New York Islanders join East Division.

1974-75 — Two new teams added: Kansas City Scouts and Washington Capitals. Teams realigned into two nine-team conferences, the Prince of Wales made up of the Norris and Adams Divisions, and the Clarence Campbell made up of the Smythe and Patrick Divisions.

Clubs played 80-game schedule.

NHL History — *continued*

1976-77 — California franchise transferred to Cleveland. Team named Cleveland Barons. Kansas City franchise transferred to Denver. Team named Colorado Rockies.

1977-78 — Clarence S. Campbell retires as NHL president. Succeeded by John A. Ziegler, Jr.

1978-79 — Cleveland and Minnesota franchises merge, leaving NHL with 17 teams. Merged team placed in Adams Division, playing home games in Minnesota.
Minimum age of players subject to amateur draft changed to 19.

1979-80 — Four new teams added: Edmonton Oilers, Hartford Whalers, Quebec Nordiques and Winnipeg Jets.
Minimum age of players subject to entry draft changed to 18.

1980-81 — Atlanta franchise shifted to Calgary, retaining "Flames" name.

1981-82 — Teams realigned within existing divisions. New groupings based on geographical areas. Unbalanced schedule adopted.

1982-83 — Colorado Rockies franchise shifted to East Rutherford, New Jersey. Team named New Jersey Devils. Franchise moved to Patrick Division from Smythe; Winnipeg moved to Smythe Division from Norris.

1991-92 — San Jose Sharks added, making the NHL a 22-team league. NHL celebrates 75th Anniversary Season. The 1991-92 regular season suspended due to a strike by members of the NHL Players' Association on April 1, 1992. Play resumed April 12, 1992.

1992-93 — Gil Stein named NHL president (October, 1992). Gary Bettman named first NHL Commissioner (February, 1993). Ottawa Senators and Tampa Bay Lightning added, making the NHL a 24-team league. NHL celebrates Stanley Cup Centennial. Clubs played 84-game schedule.

1993-94 — Mighty Ducks of Anaheim and Florida Panthers added, making the NHL a 26-team league. Minnesota franchise shifted to Dallas, team named Dallas Stars. Prince of Wales and Clarence Campbell Conferences renamed Eastern and Western. Adams, Patrick, Norris and Smythe Divisions renamed Northeast, Atlantic, Central and Pacific. Winnipeg moved to Central Division from Pacific; Tampa Bay moved to Atlantic Division from Central; Pittsburgh moved to Northeast Division from Atlantic.

1994-95 — A labor disruption forced the cancellation of 468 games from October 1, 1994 to January 19, 1995. Clubs played a 48-game schedule that began January 20, 1995 and ended May 3, 1995. No inter-conference games were played.

1995-96 — Quebec franchise transferred to Denver. Team named Colorado Avalanche and placed in Pacific Division of Western Conference. Clubs to play 82-game schedule.

1996-97 — Winnipeg franchise transferred to Phoenix. Team named Phoenix Coyotes and placed in Central Division of Western Conference.

1997-98 — Hartford franchise transferred to Raleigh. Team named Carolina Hurricanes and remains in Northeast Division of Eastern Conference.

1998-99 — The addition of the Nashville Predators made the NHL a 27-team league and brought about the creation of two new divisions and a League-wide realignment in preparation for further expansion to 30 teams by 2000-2001. Nashville was added to the Central Division of the Western Conference, while Toronto moved into the Northeast Division of the Eastern Conference. Pittsburgh was shifted from the Northeast to the Atlantic, while Carolina left the Northeast for the newly created Southeast Division of the Eastern Conference. Florida, Tampa Bay and Washington also joined the Southeast. In the Western Conference, Calgary, Colorado, Edmonton and Vancouver make up the new Northwest Division. Dallas and Phoenix moved from the Central to the Pacific Division.

NHL Attendance

	Regular Season		Playoffs		Total
Season	Games	Attendance	Games	Attendance	Attendance
1960-61	210	2,317,142	17	242,000	2,559,142
1961-62	210	2,435,424	18	277,000	2,712,424
1962-63	210	2,590,574	16	220,906	2,811,480
1963-64	210	2,732,642	21	309,149	3,041,791
1964-65	210	2,822,635	20	303,859	3,126,494
1965-66	210	2,941,164	16	249,000	3,190,184
1966-67	210	3,084,759	16	248,336	3,333,095
1967-68[1]	444	4,938,043	40	495,089	5,433,132
1968-69	456	5,550,613	33	431,739	5,982,352
1969-70	456	5,992,065	34	461,694	6,453,759
1970-71[2]	546	7,257,677	43	707,633	7,965,310
1971-72	546	7,609,368	36	582,666	8,192,034
1972-73[3]	624	8,575,651	38	624,637	9,200,288
1973-74	624	8,640,978	38	600,442	9,241,420
1974-75[4]	720	9,521,536	51	784,181	10,305,717
1975-76	720	9,103,761	48	726,279	9,830,040
1976-77	720	8,563,890	44	646,279	9,210,169
1977-78	720	8,526,564	45	686,634	9,213,198
1978-79	680	7,758,053	45	694,521	8,452,574
1979-80[5]	840	10,533,623	63	976,699	11,510,322
1980-81	840	10,726,198	68	966,390	11,692,588
1981-82	840	10,710,894	71	1,058,948	11,769,842
1982-83	840	11,020,610	66	1,088,222	12,028,832
1983-84	840	11,359,386	70	1,107,400	12,466,786
1984-85	840	11,633,730	70	1,107,500	12,741,230
1985-86	840	11,621,000	72	1,152,503	12,773,503
1986-87	840	11,855,880	87	1,383,967	13,239,847
1987-88	840	12,117,512	83	1,336,901	13,454,413
1988-89	840	12,417,969	83	1,327,214	13,745,183
1989-90	840	12,579,651	85	1,355,593	13,935,244
1990-91	840	12,343,897	92	1,442,203	13,786,100
1991-92[6]	880	12,769,676	86	1,327,920	14,097,596
1992-93[7]	1,008	14,158,177[8]	83	1,346,034	15,504,211
1993-94[9]	1,092	16,105,604[10]	90	1,440,095	17,545,699
1994-95	624[11]	9,233,884	81	1,329,130	10,563,014
1995-96	1,066	17,041,614	86	1,540,140	18,581,754
1996-97	1,066	17,640,529	82	1,494,878	19,135,407
1997-98	1,066	17,264,678	82	1,507,416	18,772,094

[1] First expansion: Los Angeles, Pittsburgh, California (Cleveland),Philadelphia, St. Louis and Minnesota (Dallas)
[2] Second expansion: Buffalo and Vancouver
[3] Third expansion: Atlanta (Calgary) and New York Islanders
[4] Fourth expansion: Kansas City (Colorado, New Jersey) and Washington
[5] Fifth expansion: Edmonton, Hartford, Quebec (Colorado) and Winnipeg
[6] Sixth expansion: San Jose
[7] Seventh expansion: Ottawa and Tampa Bay
[8] Includes 24 neutral site games
[9] Eighth expansion: Anaheim and Florida
[10] Includes 26 neutral site games
[11] Lockout resulted in the cancellation of 468 regular-season games.

Major Rule Changes

1910-11 — Game changed from two 30-minute periods to three 20-minute periods.

1911-12 — National Hockey Association (forerunner of the NHL) originated six-man hockey, replacing seven-man game.

1917-18 — Goalies permitted to fall to the ice to make saves. Previously a goaltender was penalized for dropping to the ice.

1918-19 — Penalty rules amended. For minor fouls, substitutes not allowed until penalized player had served three minutes. For major fouls, no substitutes for five minutes. For match fouls, no substitutes allowed for the remainder of the game.
With the addition of two lines painted on the ice twenty feet from center, three playing zones were created, producing a forty-foot neutral center ice area in which forward passing was permitted. Kicking the puck was permitted in this neutral zone.
Tabulation of assists began.

1921-22 — Goaltenders allowed to pass the puck forward up to their own blue line.
Overtime limited to twenty minutes.
Minor penalties changed from three minutes to two minutes.

1923-24 — Match foul defined as actions deliberately injuring or disabling an opponent. For such actions, a player was fined not less than $50 and ruled off the ice for the balance of the game. A player assessed a match penalty may be replaced by a substitute at the end of 20 minutes. Match penalty recipients must meet with the League president who can assess additional punishment.

1925-26 — Delayed penalty rules introduced. Each team must have a minimum of four players on the ice at all times.
Two rules were amended to encourage offense: No more than two defensemen permitted to remain inside a team's own blue line when the puck has left the defensive zone. A faceoff to be called for ragging the puck unless short-handed.
Team captains only players allowed to talk to referees.
Goaltender's leg pads limited to 12-inch width.
Timekeeper's gong to mark end of periods rather than referee's whistle. Teams to dress a maximum of 12 players for each game from a roster of no more than 14 players.

1926-27 — Blue lines repositioned to sixty feet from each goal-line, thereby enlarging the neutral zone and standardizing distance from blueline to goal.
Uniform goal nets adopted throughout NHL with goal posts securely fastened to the ice.

1927-28 — To further encourage offense, forward passes allowed in defending and neutral zones and goaltender's pads reduced in width from 12 to 10 inches.
Game standardized at three twenty-minute periods of stop-time separated by ten-minute intermissions.
Teams to change ends after each period.
Ten minutes of sudden-death overtime to be played if the score is tied after regulation time.
Minor penalty to be assessed to any player other than a goaltender for deliberately picking up the puck while it is in play. Minor penalty to be assessed for deliberately shooting the puck out of play.
The Art Ross goal net adopted as the official net of the NHL.
Maximum length of hockey sticks limited to 53 inches measured from heel of blade to end of handle. No minimum length stipulated.
Home teams given choice of goals to defend at start of game.

1928-29 — Forward passing permitted in defensive and neutral zones and into attacking zone if pass receiver is in neutral zone when pass is made. No forward passing allowed inside attacking zone.
Minor penalty to be assessed to any player who delays the game by passing the puck back into his defensive zone.
Ten-minute overtime without sudden-death provision to be played in games tied after regulation time. Games tied after this overtime period declared a draw.
Exclusive of goaltenders, team to dress at least 8 and no more than 12 skaters.

Major Rule Changes — *continued*

1929-30 — Forward passing permitted inside all three zones but not permitted across either blue line.

Kicking the puck allowed, but a goal cannot be scored by kicking the puck in.

No more than three players including the goaltender may remain in their defensive zone when the puck has gone up ice. Minor penalties to be assessed for the first two violations of this rule in a game; major penalties thereafter.

Goaltenders forbidden to hold the puck. Pucks caught must be cleared immediately. For infringement of this rule, a faceoff to be taken ten feet in front of the goal with no player except the goaltender standing between the faceoff spot and the goal-line.

Highsticking penalties introduced.

Maximum number of players in uniform increased from 12 to 15.

December 21, 1929 — Forward passing rules instituted at the beginning of the 1929-30 season more than doubled number of goals scored. Partway through the season, these rules were further amended to read, "No attacking player allowed to precede the play when entering the opposing defensive zone." This is similar to modern offside rule.

1930-31 — A player without a complete stick ruled out of play and forbidden from taking part in further action until a new stick is obtained. A player who has broken his stick must obtain a replacement at his bench.

A further refinement of the offside rule stated that the puck must first be propelled into the attacking zone before any player of the attacking side can enter that zone; for infringement of this rule a faceoff to take place at the spot where the infraction took place.

1931-32 — Though there is no record of a team attempting to play with two goaltenders on the ice, a rule was instituted which stated that each team was allowed only one goaltender on the ice at one time.

Attacking players forbidden to impede the movement or obstruct the vision of opposing goaltenders.

Defending players with the exception of the goaltender forbidden from falling on the puck within 10 feet of the net.

1932-33 — Each team to have captain on the ice at all times.

If the goaltender is removed from the ice to serve a penalty, the manager of the club to appoint a substitute.

Match penalty with substitution after five minutes instituted for kicking another player.

1933-34 — Number of players permitted to stand in defensive zone restricted to three including goaltender.

Visible time clocks required in each rink.

Two referees replace one referee and one linesman.

1934-35 — Penalty shot awarded when a player is tripped and thus prevented from having a clear shot on goal, having no player to pass to other than the offending player. Shot taken from inside a 10-foot circle located 38 feet from the goal. The goaltender must not advance more than one foot from his goal-line when the shot is taken.

1937-38 — Rules introduced governing icing the puck.

Penalty shot awarded when a player other than a goaltender falls on the puck within 10 feet of the goal.

1938-39 — Penalty shot modified to allow puck carrier to skate in before shooting.

One referee and one linesman replace two referee system.

Blue line widened to 12 inches.

Maximum number of players in uniform increased from 14 to 15.

1939-40 — A substitute replacing a goaltender removed from ice to serve a penalty may use a goaltender's stick and gloves but no other goaltending equipment.

1940-41 — Flooding ice surface between periods made obligatory.

1941-42 — Penalty shots classified as minor and major. Minor shot to be taken from a line 28 feet from the goal. Major shot, awarded when a player is tripped with only the goaltender to beat, permits the player taking the penalty shot to skate right into the goalkeeper and shoot from point-blank range.

One referee and two linesmen employed to officiate games.

For playoffs, standby minor league goaltenders employed by NHL as emergency substitutes.

1942-43 — Because of wartime restrictions on train scheduling, regular-season overtime was discontinued on November 21, 1942.

Player limit reduced from 15 to 14. Minimum of 12 men in uniform abolished.

1943-44 — Red line at center ice introduced to speed up the game and reduce offside calls. This rule is considered to mark the beginning of the modern era in the NHL.

Delayed penalty rules introduced.

1945-46 — Goal indicator lights synchronized with official time clock required at all rinks.

1946-47 — System of signals by officials to indicate infractions introduced.

Linesmen from neutral cities employed for all games.

1947-48 — Goal awarded when a player with the puck has an open net to shoot at and a thrown stick prevents the shot on goal. Major penalty to any player who throws his stick in any zone other than defending zone. If a stick is thrown by a player in his defending zone but the thrown stick is not considered to have prevented a goal, a penalty shot is awarded.

All playoff games played until a winner determined, with 20-minute sudden-death overtime periods separated by 10-minute intermissions.

1949-50 — Ice surface painted white.

Clubs allowed to dress 17 players exclusive of goaltenders.

Major penalties incurred by goaltenders served by a member of the goaltender's team instead of resulting in a penalty shot.

1950-51 — Each team required to provide an emergency goaltender in attendance with full equipment at each game for use by either team in the event of illness or injury to a regular goaltender.

1951-52 — Home teams to wear basic white uniforms; visiting teams basic colored uniforms.

Goal crease enlarged from 3 × 7 feet to 4 × 8 feet.

Number of players in uniform reduced to 15 plus goaltenders.

Faceoff circles enlarged from 10-foot to 15-foot radius.

1952-53 — Teams permitted to dress 15 skaters on the road and 16 at home.

1953-54 — Number of players in uniform set at 16 plus goaltenders.

1954-55 — Number of players in uniform set at 18 plus goaltenders up to December 1 and 16 plus goaltenders thereafter. Teams agree to wear colored uniforms at home and white uniforms on the road.

1956-57 — Player serving a minor penalty allowed to return to ice when a goal is scored by opposing team.

1959-60 — Players prevented from leaving their benches to enter into an altercation. Substitutions permitted providing substitutes do not enter into altercation.

1960-61 — Number of players in uniform set at 16 plus goaltenders.

1961-62 — Penalty shots to be taken by the player against whom the foul was committed. In the event of a penalty shot called in a situation where a particular player hasn't been fouled, the penalty shot to be taken by any player on the ice when the foul was committed.

1964-65 — No bodily contact on faceoffs.

In playoff games, each team to have its substitute goaltender dressed in his regular uniform except for leg pads and body protector. All previous rules governing standby goaltenders terminated.

1965-66 — Teams required to dress two goaltenders for each regular-season game. Maximum stick length increased to 55 inches.

1966-67 — Substitution allowed on coincidental major penalties.

Between-periods intermissions fixed at 15 minutes.

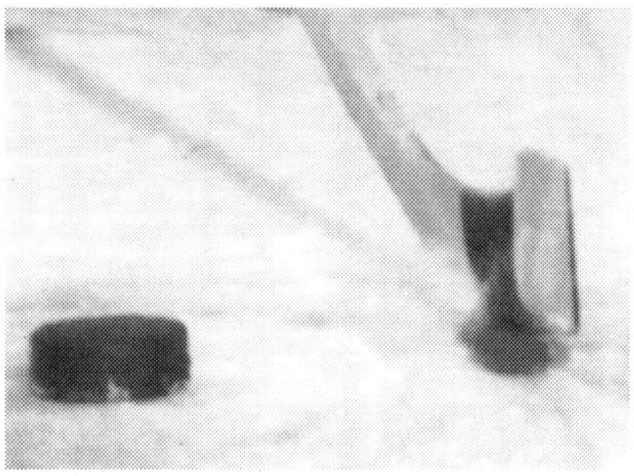

Banana-bladed sticks like this one ended the era of the maskless goaltender in the late 1960s and early 1970s. League rules first established a limit on blade curvature in 1967-68.

1967-68 — If a penalty incurred by a goaltender is a co-incident major, the penalty to be served by a player of the goaltender's team on the ice at the time the penalty was called. Limit of curvature of hockey stick blade set at 1-$^1/_2$ inches.

1969-70 — Limit of curvature of hockey stick blade set at 1 inch.

1970-71 — Home teams to wear basic white uniforms; visiting teams basic colored uniforms.

Limit of curvature of hockey stick blade set at $^1/_2$ inch.

Minor penalty for deliberately shooting the puck out of the playing area.

1971-72 — Number of players in uniform set at 17 plus 2 goaltenders.

Third man to enter an altercation assessed an automatic game misconduct penalty.

1972-73 — Minimum width of stick blade reduced to 2 inches from 2-$^1/_2$ inches.

1974-75 — Bench minor penalty imposed if a penalized player does not proceed directly and immediately to the penalty box.

1976-77 — Rule dealing with fighting amended to provide a major and game misconduct penalty for any player who is clearly the instigator of a fight.

1977-78 — Teams requesting a stick measurement to be assessed a minor penalty in the event that the measured stick does not violate the rules.

1979-80 — Wearing of helmets made mandatory for players entering the NHL.

1980-81 — Maximum stick length increased to 58 inches.

1981-82 — If both of a team's listed goaltenders are incapacitated, the team can dress and play any eligible goaltender who is available.

1982-83 — Number of players in uniform set at 18 plus 2 goaltenders.

1983-84 — Five-minute sudden-death overtime to be played in regular-season games that are tied at the end of regulation time.

1985-86 — Substitutions allowed in the event of co-incidental minor penalties. Maximum stick length increased to 60 inches.

1986-87 — Delayed off-side is no longer in effect once the players of the offending team have cleared the opponents' defensive zone.

1990-91 — The goal lines, blue lines, defensive zone face-off circles and markings all moved one foot out from the end boards, creating 11 feet of room behind the nets and shrinking the neutral zone from 60 to 58 feet.

1991-92 — Video replays employed to assist referees in goal/no goal situations. Size of goal crease increased. Crease changed to semi-circular configuration. Time clock to record tenths of a second in last minute of each period and overtime. Major and game misconduct penalty for checking from behind into boards. Penalties added for crease infringement and unnecessary contact with goaltender. Goal disallowed if puck enters net while a player of the attacking team is standing on the goal crease line, is in the goal crease or places his stick in the goal crease.

1992-93 — No substitutions allowed in the event of coincidental minor penalties called when both teams are at full strength. Wearing of helmets made optional for forwards and defensemen. Minor penalty for attempting to draw a penalty ("diving"). Major and game misconduct penalty for checking from behind into goal frame. Game misconduct penalty for instigating a fight. Highsticking redefined to include any use of the stick above waist-height. Previous rule stipulated shoulder-height.

1993-94 — High sticking redefined to allow goals scored with a high stick below the height of the crossbar of the goal frame.

1996-97 — Maximum stick length increased to 63 inches.

1998-99 — The league instituted a two-referee system with each team to play 20 regular-season games with two referees and a pair of linesmen. Also, the goal lines, blue lines, defensive zone face-off circles and markings all moved two feet closer to center, creating 13 feet of room behind the nets and cutting the neutral zone from 58 to 54 feet. The goal crease was altered so that it extends only one foot beyond each goal post (eight feet across in total) and has square sides for the first 4'6". Only the top of the crease remains rounded.

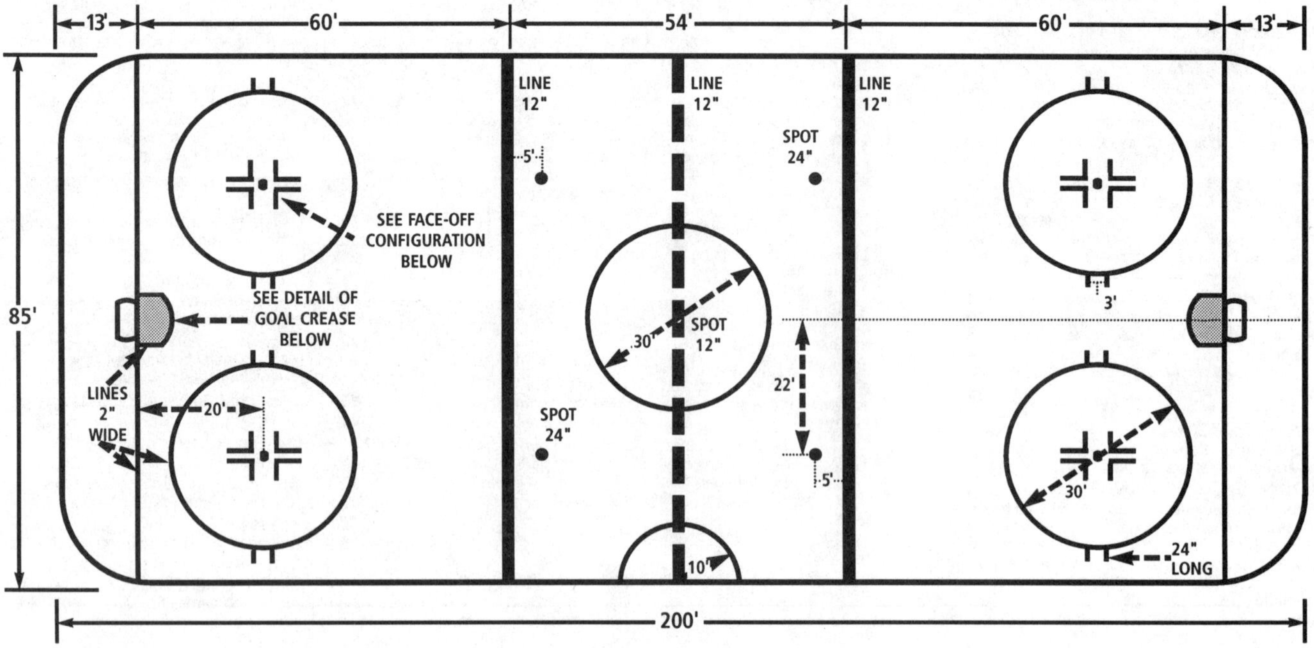

NHL RINK DIMENSIONS

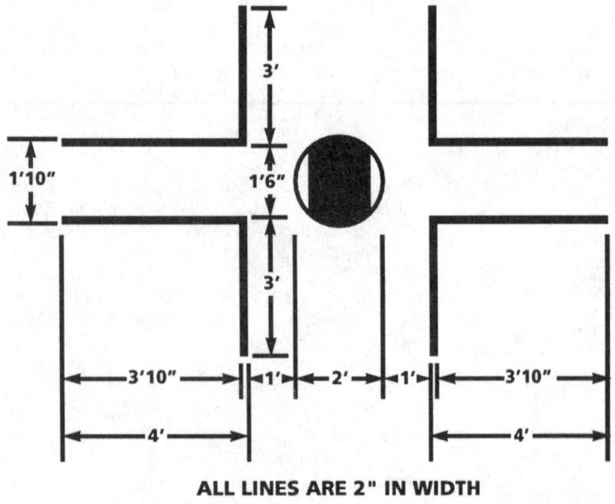

FACE-OFF CONFIGURATION

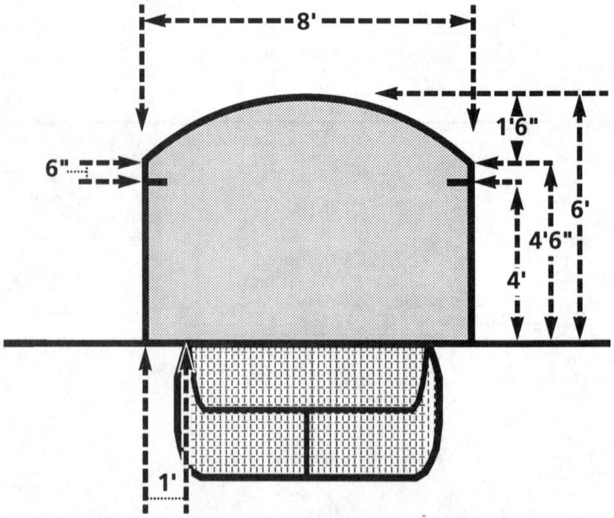

CREASE DIMENSIONS

Mighty Ducks of Anaheim

1997-98 Results: 26W-43L-13T 65PTS. Sixth, Pacific Division

Year-by-Year Record

Season	GP	Home W	Home L	Home T	Road W	Road L	Road T	Overall W	Overall L	Overall T	GF	GA	Pts.	Finished	Playoff Result
1997-98	82	12	23	6	14	20	7	26	43	13	205	261	65	6th, Pacific Div.	Out of Playoffs
1996-97	82	23	12	6	13	21	7	36	33	13	245	233	85	2nd, Pacific Div.	Lost Conf. Semi-Final
1995-96	82	22	15	4	13	24	4	35	39	8	234	247	78	4th, Pacific Div.	Out of Playoffs
1994-95	48	11	9	4	5	18	1	16	27	5	125	164	37	6th, Pacific Div.	Out of Playoffs
1993-94	84	14	26	2	19	20	3	33	46	5	229	251	71	4th, Pacific Div.	Out of Playoffs

1998-99 Schedule

Oct.	Sat.	10	at Washington
	Sun.	11	at Philadelphia
	Tue.	13	at Montreal
	Thu.	15	at Chicago
	Wed.	21	Boston
	Sun.	25	Phoenix
	Wed.	28	Tampa Bay
	Fri.	30	at Dallas
	Sat.	31	at St. Louis
Nov.	Wed.	4	St. Louis
	Fri.	6	San Jose
	Sun.	8	Detroit
	Wed.	11	Carolina
	Fri.	13	at Vancouver
	Sat.	14	at Calgary
	Mon.	16	Los Angeles
	Wed.	18	NY Rangers
	Fri.	20	Edmonton
	Sun.	22	Chicago
	Wed.	25	at Detroit
	Fri.	27	at Nashville
	Sun.	29	at Carolina
Dec.	Tue.	1	at Pittsburgh
	Thu.	3	at Chicago
	Sun.	6	at San Jose
	Wed.	9	Vancouver
	Fri.	11	Washington
	Sun.	13	Los Angeles
	Wed.	16	Nashville
	Fri.	18	NY Islanders
	Mon.	21	Colorado
	Tue.	22	at Colorado
	Mon.	28	at Ottawa
	Wed.	30	at Toronto
Jan.	Fri.	1	at Buffalo*
	Sat.	2	at Boston
	Mon.	4	at Nashville
	Wed.	6	Buffalo
	Fri.	8	Phoenix
	Sun.	10	Edmonton
	Wed.	13	Calgary
	Fri.	15	Dallas
	Mon.	18	Pittsburgh
	Wed.	20	New Jersey
	Thu.	21	at Phoenix
	Wed.	27	Colorado
	Thu.	28	at Colorado
	Sat.	30	at Edmonton
Feb.	Wed.	3	Chicago
	Fri.	5	at Tampa Bay
	Sat.	6	at St. Louis
	Wed.	10	Philadelphia
	Fri.	12	Dallas
	Sun.	14	at Phoenix
	Mon.	15	at Los Angeles
	Wed.	17	Edmonton
	Fri.	19	at Calgary
	Sat.	20	at Vancouver
	Wed.	24	at Edmonton
	Fri.	26	San Jose
	Sat.	27	at San Jose
Mar.	Wed.	3	Los Angeles
	Fri.	5	Nashville
	Sun.	7	Detroit
	Wed.	10	Vancouver
	Fri.	12	at Dallas
	Sat.	13	at Phoenix
	Wed.	17	Ottawa
	Thu.	18	at Los Angeles
	Sun.	21	Florida
	Fri.	26	Dallas
	Sun.	28	Calgary
	Wed.	31	at New Jersey
Apr.	Fri.	2	at NY Rangers
	Sat.	3	at NY Islanders
	Mon.	5	at Detroit
	Wed.	7	at Dallas
	Fri.	9	San Jose
	Sun.	11	Phoenix
	Wed.	14	St. Louis
	Thu.	15	at Los Angeles
	Sat.	17	at San Jose

* Denotes afternoon game.

With Paul Kariya sidelined for most of the 1997-98 season, it was up to Teemu Selanne to provide the offense in Anaheim. He responded with 52 goals to tie Washington's Peter Bondra for the NHL lead and had the league's longest scoring streak when he recorded goals in 11 straight games from October 21st to November 10th. Selanne had 17 goals during that stretch. His excellent season earned him a nomination for the Hart Trophy as the NHL's most valuable player.

Franchise date: June 15, 1993

PACIFIC DIVISION

6th NHL Season

1998-99 Player Personnel

FORWARDS	HT	WT	S	Place of Birth	Date	1997-98 Club
AALTO, Antti	6-2	195	L	Lappeenranta, Finland	3/4/75	Anaheim-Cincinatti (AHL)
BANHAM, Frank	6-0	190	R	Calahoo, Alta.	4/14/75	Anaheim-Cincinatti (AHL)
BERNIER, David	6-3	205	R	St-Hyacinthe, Que.	1/9/78	Quebec (QMJHL)
CHOUINARD, Marc	6-5	200	R	Charlesbourg, Ont.	5/5/77	Cincinatti (AHL)
CULLEN, Matt	6-1	195	L	Virginia, MN	11/2/76	Anaheim-Cincinatti (AHL)
DAVIDSSON, Johan	6-1	190	R	Jonkoping, Sweden	1/6/76	Helsinki
DRURY, Ted	6-0	208	L	Boston, MA	9/13/71	Anaheim-United States
GREEN, Travis	6-1	193	R	Castlegar, B.C.	12/20/70	NY Islanders-Anaheim-Canada
GRIMSON, Stu	6-5	227	L	Kamloops, B.C.	5/20/65	Carolina
KARIYA, Paul	5-11	180	L	Vancouver, B.C.	10/16/74	Anaheim
LeBOUTILLIER, Peter	6-1	205	R	Neepawa, Man.	1/11/75	Anaheim-Cincinatti (AHL)
LECLERC, Mike	6-1	205	L	Winnipeg, Man.	11/10/76	Anaheim-Cincinatti (AHL)
LeCOMPTE, Eric	6-4	190	L	Montreal, Que.	4/4/75	Indianapolis-Cincinatti (AHL)
LEGAULT, Jay	6-4	205	L	Peterborough, Ont.	5/15/79	London
MARHA, Josef	6-0	176	L	Havlickuv Brod, Czech.	6/2/76	Colorado-Hershey-Anaheim
McKENZIE, Jim	6-3	205	L	Gull Lake, Sask.	11/3/69	Phoenix
MOHAGEN, Tony	6-4	220	L	Regina, Sask.	7/13/78	Swift Current
NIELSEN, Jeff	6-0	200	L	Grand Rapids, MN	9/20/71	Anaheim-Cincinatti (AHL)
NIKULIN, Igor	6-1	200	L	Cherepovets, USSR	8/26/72	Cincinatti (AHL)
REICHERT, Craig	6-1	200	R	Winnipeg, Man.	5/11/74	Cincinatti (AHL)
RUCCHIN, Steve	6-3	215	L	Thunder Bay, Ont.	7/4/71	Anaheim-Canada
SANDSTROM, Tomas	6-2	205	L	Jakobstad, Finland	9/4/64	Anaheim-Sweden
SELANNE, Teemu	6-0	200	R	Helsinki, Finland	7/3/70	Anaheim-Finland
STEVENSON, Jeremy	6-2	220	L	San Bernadino, CA	7/28/74	Anaheim-Cincinatti (AHL)
TUZZOLINO, Tony	6-2	190	R	Buffalo, NY	10/9/75	Kentucky-Ana-Cincinatti (AHL)
WREN, Bob	5-10	185	L	Preston, Ont.	9/16/74	Anaheim-Cincinatti (AHL)
DEFENSEMEN						
BANNISTER, Drew	6-2	200	R	Belleville, Ont.	9/4/74	Edmonton-Anaheim
BRISKE, Byron	6-3	200	R	Humboldt, Sask.	1/23/76	Cincinatti (AHL)
CROWLEY, Mike	5-11	190	L	Bloomington, MN	7/4/75	Ana-Cin (AHL)-United States
FERGUSON, Scott	6-1	195	L	Camrose, Alta.	1/6/73	Edmonton-Hamilton
HALLER, Kevin	6-2	195	L	Trochu, Alta.	12/5/70	Carolina
HOUDA, Doug	6-2	190	R	Blairmore, Alta.	6/3/66	NY Islanders-Anaheim
KWIATKOWSKI, Joel	6-2	200	L	Maymont, Sask.	3/22/77	Prince George
MARSHALL, Jason	6-2	200	R	Cranbrook, B.C.	2/22/71	Anaheim
MORO, Marc	6-1	225	L	Toronto, Ont.	7/17/77	Anaheim-Cincinatti (AHL)
OLAUSSON, Fredrik	6-2	198	R	Dadesjo, Sweden	10/5/66	Pittsburgh
PUSHOR, Jamie	6-3	225	R	Lethbridge, Alta.	2/11/73	Detroit-Anaheim
SALEI, Ruslan	6-2	205	L	Minsk, USSR	11/2/74	Ana-Cin (AHL)-Belarus
SANDWITH, Terran	6-4	210	L	Edmonton, Alta.	4/17/72	Edmonton-Hamilton
SHAW, Lloyd	6-3	220	R	Regina, Sask.	9/26/76	Cin (AHL)-Colum. (ECHL)
TREBIL, Daniel	6-3	210	R	Bloomington, MN	4/10/74	Ana-Cin (AHL)-United States
TRNKA, Pavel	6-3	200	L	Plzen, Czech.	7/27/76	Anaheim-Cincinatti (AHL)

GOALTENDERS	HT	WT	C	Place of Birth	Date	1997-98 Club
ASKEY, Tom	6-2	185	L	Kenmore, NY	10/4/74	Anaheim-Cincinatti (AHL)
HEBERT, Guy	5-11	185	L	Troy, NY	1/7/67	Anaheim
LALIME, Patrick	6-2	170	L	St. Bonaventure, Que.	7/7/74	Grand Rapids
MASON, Chris	6-0	200	L	Red Deer, Alta.	4/20/76	Cincinatti (AHL)
RAM, Jamie	5-11	175	L	Scarborough, Ont.	1/18/71	Kentucky-Utica
RUSSELL, Blaine	5-11	180	L	Wetaskawin, Sask.	1/11/77	Colum. (ECHL)-Cin (AHL)-Huntington-New Orleans

1997-98 Scoring

* – rookie

Regular Season

Pos	#	Player	Team	GP	G	A	Pts	+/–	PIM	PP	SH	GW	GT	S	%
R	8	Teemu Selanne	ANA	73	52	34	86	12	30	10	1	10	3	268	19.4
C	20	Steve Rucchin	ANA	72	17	36	53	8	13	8	1	3	0	131	13.0
C	39	Travis Green	NYI	54	14	12	26	-19	66	8	0	2	1	99	14.1
			ANA	22	5	11	16	-10	16	1	0	0	1	42	11.9
			TOTAL	76	19	23	42	-29	82	9	0	2	2	141	13.5
R	48	Scott Young	ANA	73	13	20	33	-13	22	4	2	1	0	187	7.0
L	9	Paul Kariya	ANA	22	17	14	31	12	23	3	0	2	1	103	16.5
C	45	* Matt Cullen	ANA	61	6	21	27	-4	23	2	0	0	0	75	8.0
C	10	* Josef Marha	COL	11	2	5	7	0	4	0	0	0	0	10	20.0
			ANA	12	7	4	11	4	0	3	0	0	0	21	33.3
			TOTAL	23	9	9	18	4	4	3	0	0	0	31	29.0
R	17	Tomas Sandstrom	ANA	77	9	8	17	-25	64	2	1	0	1	136	6.6
C	13	Ted Drury	ANA	73	6	10	16	-10	82	0	1	0	0	110	5.5
D	24	Ruslan Salei	ANA	66	5	10	15	7	70	1	0	0	1	104	4.8
D	33	Dave Karpa	ANA	78	1	11	12	-3	217	0	0	0	0	64	1.6
R	29	* Frank Banham	ANA	21	9	2	11	-6	12	1	0	0	2	43	20.9
C	12	Kevin Todd	ANA	27	4	7	11	-5	12	3	0	1	0	30	13.3
R	19	* Jeff Nielsen	ANA	32	4	5	9	-1	16	0	0	0	0	36	11.1
D	23	Jason Marshall	ANA	72	3	6	9	-8	189	1	0	0	0	68	4.4
D	4	Jamie Pushor	DET	54	2	5	7	2	71	0	0	0	0	43	4.7
			ANA	10	0	2	2	1	10	0	0	0	0	8	0.0
			TOTAL	64	2	7	9	3	81	0	0	0	0	51	3.9
L	40	* Jeremy Stevenson	ANA	45	3	5	8	-4	101	0	0	1	0	43	7.0
D	5	Drew Bannister	EDM	34	0	2	2	-7	42	0	0	0	0	27	0.0
			ANA	27	0	6	6	-2	47	0	0	0	0	23	0.0
			TOTAL	61	0	8	8	-9	89	0	0	0	0	50	0.0
D	7	* Pavel Trnka	ANA	48	3	4	7	-4	40	1	0	0	1	46	6.5
D	6	Doug Houda	NYI	31	1	2	3	-6	47	0	0	0	0	15	6.7
			ANA	24	1	2	3	-5	52	0	1	0	0	9	11.1
			TOTAL	55	2	4	6	-11	99	0	1	0	0	24	8.3
D	38	* Mike Crowley	ANA	8	2	2	4	0	8	0	0	1	0	17	11.8
R	46	Jean-Francois Jomphe	ANA	9	1	3	4	1	8	0	0	0	0	8	12.5
R	22	Brent Severyn	ANA	37	1	3	4	-3	133	0	0	0	0	27	3.7
C	21	* Espen Knutsen	ANA	19	3	0	3	-10	6	1	0	0	1	21	14.3
R	52	* Peter LeBoutillier	ANA	12	1	1	2	-1	55	0	0	0	0	6	16.7
C	32	Richard Park	ANA	15	0	2	2	-3	8	0	0	0	0	14	0.0
L	11	Shawn Antoski	ANA	9	1	0	1	1	18	0	0	0	0	6	16.7
D	34	Daniel Trebil	ANA	21	0	1	1	-8	2	0	0	0	0	11	0.0
G	35	M. Shtalenkov	ANA	40	0	1	1	0	0	0	0	0	0	0	0.0
G	31	Guy Hebert	ANA	46	0	1	1	0	4	0	0	0	0	0	0.0
L	42	Barry Nieckar	ANA	1	0	0	0	0	2	0	0	0	0	0	0.0
R	36	* Tony Tuzzolino	ANA	1	0	0	0	-2	2	0	0	0	0	0	0.0
D	37	* Marc Moro	ANA	1	0	0	0	0	0	0	0	0	0	0	0.0
L	50	* Bob Wren	ANA	3	0	0	0	0	0	0	0	0	0	4	0.0
C	44	* Antti Aalto	ANA	3	0	0	0	-1	0	0	0	0	0	1	0.0
G	67	* Tom Askey	ANA	7	0	0	0	0	0	0	0	0	0	0	0.0
L	27	* Mike Leclerc	ANA	7	0	0	0	-6	6	0	0	0	0	11	0.0

Goaltending

No.	Goaltender	GPI	Mins	Avg	W	L	T	EN	SO	GA	SA	S%
67	* Tom Askey	7	273	2.64	0	1	2	2	0	12	113	.894
31	Guy Hebert	46	2660	2.93	13	24	6	4	3	130	1339	.903
35	M. Shtalenkov	40	2049	3.22	13	18	5	3	1	110	1031	.893
	Totals	**82**	**5007**	**3.13**	**26**	**43**	**13**	**9**	**4**	**261**	**2492**	**.895**

President and General Manager

GAUTHIER, PIERRE
President and General Manager, Mighty Ducks of Anaheim.
Born in Montreal, Que., May 28, 1953.

Following his resignation from the Ottawa Senators in June, Pierre Gauthier returned to the Mighty Ducks of Anaheim on July 16, 1998 when he was named club president. Three weeks later, on August 6, Gauthier succeeded Jack Ferreira as the second general manager in franchise history.

Gauthier, 45, returns to the Mighty Ducks after spending two-and-a-half seasons as general manager in Ottawa. The Senators qualified for the Stanley Cup Playoffs in each of Gauthier's two full seasons, reaching the postseason for the first time in 1997 and advancing to the second round in May of 1998. Gauthier served as assistant general manager of the Mighty Ducks from 1993 to 1995 before joining the Senators. He was a key part of management in starting up the Anaheim franchise in 1993.

Prior to his first stint with the Mighty Ducks, Gauthier had spent 12 seasons in the scouting department with the Quebec Nordiques. He had joined the club as a scout in 1983 and worked in that capacity for three seasons before being named assistant director of scouting in 1986. Gauthier was promoted to chief scout in 1988, serving at that capacity until he joined Anaheim in 1993.

Gauthier received a master's degree in sports administration in 1983 from the University of Minnesota, where he also served as a teaching associate in physical education. He is also a graduate of Syracuse University, where he earned a bachelor of science degree in physical education.

A native of Montreal, Gauthier and his wife, Manon Roberge, have a daughter, Catherine, and a son Vincent. The family resides in Irvine, California.

Guy Hebert topped 100 wins in a Ducks uniform in 1997-98 and enters the 1998-99 season with 102 victories in Anaheim and 115 in his career.

Club Records

Team

(Figures in brackets for season records are games played; records for fewest points, wins, ties, losses, goals, goals against are for 70 or more games)

Most Points	**85**	1996-97 (82)
Most Wins	**36**	1996-97 (82)
Most Ties	**13**	1996-97 (82); 1997-98 (82)
Most Losses	**46**	1993-94 (84)
Most Goals	**245**	1996-97 (82)
Most Goals Against	**261**	1997-98 (82)
Fewest Points	**65**	1997-98 (82)
Fewest Wins	**26**	1997-98 (82)
Fewest Ties	**5**	1993-94 (84)
Fewest Losses	**33**	1996-97 (82)
Fewest Goals	**205**	1997-98 (82)
Fewest Goals Against	**233**	1996-97 (82)
Longest Winning Streak		
Overall	**6**	Mar. 8-22/96
Home	**5**	Twice
Away	**4**	Nov. 19-24/93
Longest Undefeated Streak		
Overall	**12**	Feb. 22-Mar. 19/97 (7 wins, 5 ties)
Home	**14**	Feb. 12-Apr. 9/97 (10 wins, 4 ties)
Away	**5**	Three times
Longest Losing Streak		
Overall	**8**	Oct. 12-30/96
Home	**6**	Feb. 7-Mar. 11/98
Away	**6**	Four times
Longest Winless Streak		
Overall	**9**	Twice
Home	**6**	Feb. 7-Mar. 11/98 (6 losses)
Away	**10**	Mar. 26-Oct. 11/95 (9 losses, 1 tie)
Most Shutouts, Season	**6**	1996-97 (82)
Most PIM, Season	**1,843**	1997-98 (82)
Most Goals, Game	**8**	Jan. 21/98 (Ana. 8, Fla. 3)

Individual

Most Seasons	**5**	Guy Hebert, Mikhail Shtalenkov, Bobby Dollas, Joe Sacco
Most Games	**333**	Joe Sacco
Most Goals, Career	**129**	Paul Kariya
Most Assists, Career	**148**	Paul Kariya
Most Points, Career	**277**	Paul Kariya (129G, 148A)
Most PIM, Career	**788**	Dave Karpa
Most Shutouts, Career	**15**	Guy Hebert
Longest Consecutive Games Streak	**159**	Bobby Dollas
Most Goals, Season	**52**	Teemu Selanne (1997-98)
Most Assists, Season	**58**	Paul Kariya (1995-96), Teemu Selanne (1996-97)
Most Points, Season	**109**	Teemu Selanne (1996-97; 51G, 58A)
Most PIM, Season	**285**	Todd Ewen (1995-96)
Most Points, Defenseman, Season	**46**	Dmitri Mironov (1996-97; 12G, 34A)
Most Points, Center, Season	**67**	Steve Rucchin (1996-97; 19G, 48A)
Most Points, Right Wing, Season	**109**	Teemu Selanne (1996-97; 51G, 58A)
Most Points, Left Wing, Season	**108**	Paul Kariya (1995-96; 50G, 58A)
Most Points, Rookie, Season	**39**	Paul Kariya (1994-95; 18G, 21A)
Most Shutouts, Season	**4**	Guy Hebert (1995-96, 1996-97)
Most Goals, Game	**3**	Eleven times
Most Assists, Game	**5**	Dmitri Mironov (Dec. 12/97)
Most Points, Game	**5**	Four times

General Managers' History

Jack Ferreira, 1993-94 to 1997-98; Pierre Gauthier, 1998-99.

Coaching History

Ron Wilson, 1993-94 to 1996-97; Pierre Page, 1997-98; Craig Hartsburg, 1998-99.

Captains' History

Troy Loney, 1993-94; Randy Ladouceur, 1994-95, 1995-96; Paul Kariya, 1996-97; Paul Kariya and Teemu Selanne, 1997-98; Paul Kariya, 1998-99.

All-time Record vs. Other Clubs

Regular Season

	At Home							On Road							Total						
	GP	W	L	T	GF	GA	PTS	GP	W	L	T	GF	GA	PTS	GP	W	L	T	GF	GA	PTS
Boston	4	1	2	1	6	12	3	4	2	2	0	13	14	4	8	3	4	1	19	26	7
Buffalo	4	2	2	0	10	10	4	4	1	2	1	7	10	3	8	3	4	1	17	20	7
Calgary	14	5	6	3	41	38	13	13	5	8	0	32	38	10	27	10	14	3	73	76	23
Carolina	4	2	2	0	16	13	4	4	1	3	0	7	11	2	8	3	5	0	23	24	6
Chicago	10	3	6	1	21	29	7	11	4	6	1	19	27	9	21	7	12	2	40	56	16
Colorado	9	4	3	2	23	18	10	9	2	5	2	30	36	6	18	6	8	4	53	54	16
Dallas	11	5	6	0	25	31	10	10	1	9	0	18	45	2	21	6	15	0	43	76	12
Detroit	10	2	6	2	21	38	6	10	1	6	3	26	39	5	20	3	12	5	47	77	11
Edmonton	13	9	3	1	40	31	19	13	7	6	0	33	26	14	26	16	9	1	73	57	33
Florida	4	2	2	0	16	12	4	4	1	1	2	11	10	4	8	3	3	2	27	22	8
Los Angeles	13	6	4	3	47	37	15	14	4	8	2	33	42	10	27	10	12	5	80	79	25
Montreal	4	1	3	0	15	17	2	4	2	1	1	15	16	5	8	3	4	1	30	33	7
New Jersey	4	3	1	0	14	8	6	4	1	3	0	7	14	2	8	4	4	0	21	22	8
NY Islanders	4	1	2	1	9	12	3	4	2	2	0	13	10	4	8	3	4	1	22	22	7
NY Rangers	4	4	0	0	18	10	8	4	1	2	1	10	13	3	8	5	2	1	28	23	11
Ottawa	4	3	0	1	14	5	7	4	3	1	0	13	11	6	8	6	1	1	27	16	13
Philadelphia	4	1	2	1	13	13	3	4	1	1	2	8	10	4	8	2	3	3	21	23	7
Phoenix	10	7	3	0	33	25	14	10	5	5	0	36	40	10	20	12	8	0	69	65	24
Pittsburgh	4	1	3	0	13	18	2	4	0	3	1	9	17	1	8	1	6	1	22	35	3
St. Louis	10	3	6	1	28	32	7	10	4	5	1	32	35	9	20	7	11	2	60	67	16
San Jose	14	5	9	0	39	52	10	13	6	6	1	42	43	13	27	11	15	1	81	95	23
Tampa Bay	4	2	1	1	12	9	5	4	2	2	0	11	7	4	8	4	3	1	23	16	9
Toronto	10	4	5	1	29	27	9	10	1	5	4	22	32	6	20	5	10	5	51	59	15
Vancouver	13	4	7	2	30	40	10	14	5	9	0	35	50	10	27	9	16	2	65	90	20
Washington	4	2	1	1	15	15	5	4	2	2	0	8	8	4	8	4	3	1	23	23	9
Totals	**189**	**82**	**85**	**22**	**548**	**552**	**186**	**189**	**64**	**103**	**22**	**490**	**604**	**150**	**378**	**146**	**188**	**44**	**1038**	**1156**	**336**

Playoffs

	Series	W	L	GP	W	L	T	GF	GA	Last Mtg.	Round	Result
Detroit	1	0	1	4	0	4	0	8	13	1997	CSF	L 0-4
Phoenix	1	1	0	7	4	3	0	17	17	1997	CQF	W 4-3
Totals	**2**	**1**	**1**	**11**	**4**	**7**	**0**	**25**	**30**			

Playoff Results 1998-94

Year	Round	Opponent	Result	GF	GA
1997	CSF	Detroit	L 0-4	8	13
	CQF	Phoenix	W 4-3	17	17

Abbreviations: Round: CQF – conference quarter-final; **CSF** – conference semi-final

Carolina totals include Hartford, 1993-94 to 1996-97. Colorado totals include Quebec, 1993-94 to 1994-95. Phoenix totals include Winnipeg, 1993-94 to 1995-96.

1997-98 Results

Oct.	3	at	Vancouver	2-3		3	at	Tampa Bay	4-1
	4		Vancouver	3-2		4	at	Florida	3-3
	10		Ottawa	1-1		7		Buffalo	2-3
	13		Boston	0-3		9		Edmonton	1-5
	15		Philadelphia	2-2		11		Dallas	2-1
	17		Edmonton	2-1		12	at	Los Angeles	2-3
	19		NY Islanders	2-5		14		Colorado	0-2
	21	at	Phoenix	4-3		21		Florida	8-3
	22		Detroit	1-4		22	at	Colorado	4-3
	25	at	NY Islanders	4-2		24		Los Angeles	3-3
	26	at	NY Rangers	3-3		27	at	San Jose	2-4
	28	at	Toronto	2-2		28		Calgary	2-5
	30	at	Boston	3-0	**Feb.**	1		Chicago	4-3
Nov.	2	at	Detroit	3-4		4		NY Rangers	3-2
	5		Tampa Bay	5-2		7		Los Angeles	2-5
	7	at	Calgary	4-3		25	at	Vancouver	2-5
	8	at	Vancouver	3-2		27	at	Edmonton	4-0
	10		San Jose	4-6	**Mar.**	1		St. Louis	2-6
	12		Montreal	3-4		4		Detroit	0-2
	14		Vancouver	3-3		6		San Jose	0-3
	16		Dallas	0-4		8		Carolina	1-3
	18	at	San Jose	2-4		9	at	Los Angeles	3-4
	19		Chicago	0-4		11		Toronto	1-3
	22	at	St. Louis	2-0		13	at	Dallas	3-6
	24	at	Dallas	0-5		15		Colorado	5-3
	26		New Jersey	2-0		18	at	New Jersey	0-3
	28	at	Edmonton	3-1		19	at	Philadelphia	3-3
	29	at	Calgary	2-3		21	at	Montreal	5-4
Dec.	2	at	Toronto	3-3		22	at	Ottawa	5-2
	3	at	Buffalo	0-4		25	at	Chicago	3-2
	6	at	Pittsburgh	2-5		26	at	Detroit	3-3
	10		Pittsburgh	0-3		28	at	Colorado	3-5
	12		Washington	6-4	**Apr.**	1		Phoenix	1-5
	17		Toronto	2-6		3	at	Phoenix	3-6
	19		Phoenix	2-6		5		Calgary	3-3
	21		San Jose	2-4		8		Edmonton	4-2
	22		Calgary	5-1		9	at	San Jose	2-5
	27	at	St. Louis	5-5		13		Colorado	2-2
	28	at	Chicago	0-2		15	at	Edmonton	3-5
	30	at	Carolina	1-2		18	at	Los Angeles	4-1
Jan.	1	at	Washington	2-3		19		St. Louis	3-5

Entry Draft Selections 1998-93

1998

Pick	
5	Vitaly Vishnevsky
32	Stephen Peat
112	Viktor Wallin
150	Trent Hunter
178	Jesse Fibiger
205	David Bernier
233	Pelle Prestberg
245	Andreas Andersson

1997

Pick	
18	Mikael Holmqvist
45	Maxim Balmochnykh
72	Jay Legault
125	Luc Vaillancourt
178	Tony Mohagen
181	Mat Snesrud
209	Rene Stussi
235	Tommi Degerman

1996

Pick	
9	Ruslan Salei
35	Matt Cullen
117	Brendan Buckley
149	Blaine Russell
172	Timo Ahmaoja
198	Kevin Kellett
224	Tobias Johansson

1995

Pick	
4	Chad Kilger
29	Brian Wesenberg
55	Mike Leclerc
107	Igor Nikulin
133	Peter Leboutillier
159	Mike Laplante
185	Igor Karpenko

1994

Pick	
2	Oleg Tverdovsky
28	Johan Davidsson
67	Craig Reichert
80	Byron Briske
106	Pavel Trnka
132	Jon Battaglia
158	Mark (Rocky) Welsing
184	John Brad Englehart
236	Tommi Miettinen
262	Jeremy Stevenson

1993

Pick	
4	Paul Kariya
30	Nikolai Tsulygin
56	Valeri Karpov
82	Joel Gagnon
108	Mikhail Shtalenkov
134	Antti Aalto
160	Matt Peterson
186	Tom Askey
212	Vitaly Kozel
238	Anatoli Fedotov
264	David Penney

Coach

HARTSBURG, CRAIG
Coach, Mighty Ducks of Anaheim. Born in Stratford, Ont., June 29, 1959.

On July 21, 1998, Craig Hartsburg signed a three-year contract to become the third head coach in the history of the Mighty Ducks of Anaheim. The 39-year-old Hartsburg comes to the Mighty Ducks after serving the last three seasons as head coach of the Chicago Blackhawks. During his tenure with Chicago, Hartsburg compiled a 104-102-40 record. He was the 30th head coach in Chicago Blackhawks history.

The Blackhawks posted a 40-28-14 record in Hartsburg's first season behind the bench in Chicago (1995-96), finishing second in the Central Division and third overall in the Western Conference. After a sweep of the Calgary Flames in the opening round of the playoffs, the Blackhawks fell to the eventual Stanley Cup champion Colorado Avalanche. Hartsburg led Chicago back to the Stanley Cup Playoffs in 1997, pushing the top-seeded Avalanche to six games in the first round before falling, four games to two. In 1997-98, Chicago stayed in contention for postseason play until the last week of the season, finishing just five points out of a playoff spot. Hartsburg's Blackhawks had the seventh-most rookie man-games played in the league (230) last year.

Before joining the Blackhawks, Hartsburg received his first head coaching job in 1994 with the Guelph Storm of the Ontario Hockey League. He was named OHL coach of the year after leading the Storm to a 47-14-5 record for a .750 winning percentage in 1994-95. Hartsburg also spent four years as an assistant coach with the Philadelphia Flyers from 1990 to 1994 and one season as an assistant coach with the Minnesota North Stars in 1989-90.

Hartsburg played his entire 10-year NHL career with Minnesota from 1979 to 1989. Known as an offensive defenseman, he was the North Stars' captain for six seasons until injuries forced him to retire from active play on January 13, 1989. Hartsburg was Minnesota's first round selection (sixth overall) in the 1979 NHL Entry Draft and immediately made an impact on the North Stars' blueline, scoring 44 points in 79 games during his rookie season. Hartsburg led all Minnesota defensemen in scoring each of his first four seasons. During the 1981 playoffs, he was a key player for the North Stars, scoring three goals and 12 assists to help lead the club to its first appearance in the Stanley Cup finals. Hartsburg also became the first North Stars defenseman to record a hat trick, netting three goals on November 1, 1986 vs. Chicago.

Hartsburg played in 570 games during his NHL career, scoring 98 goals and 315 assists for 413 points with 818 penalty minutes. He also appeared in 61 playoff games during his career, posting 15 goals and 27 assists for 42 points. Hartsburg holds or shares seven Stars' team records, including most assists (60) and most points (77) by a defenseman in one season. In February of 1992, he was voted to the North Stars' 25th Anniversary Dream Team by Minnesota fans.

A participant in three NHL All-Star Games (1980, 1982 and 1983), Hartsburg also competed in three World championship tournaments for Team Canada, including being chosen as best defenseman of the 1987 World Championships. He lists winning the Canada Cup championship in 1987 as his most memorable moment in hockey.

Hartsburg and his wife Peggy have two children, Christopher and Katie.

Coaching Record

		Regular Season					Playoffs			
Season	Team	Games	W	L	T	%	Games	W	L	%
1994-95	Guelph (OHL)	66	47	14	5	.750	14	10	4	.714
1995-96	**Chicago (NHL)**	**82**	**40**	**28**	**14**	**.573**	**10**	**6**	**4**	**.600**
1996-97	**Chicago (NHL)**	**82**	**34**	**35**	**13**	**.494**	**6**	**2**	**4**	**.333**
1997-98	**Chicago (NHL)**	**82**	**30**	**39**	**13**	**.455**	....	....	....	....
	NHL Totals	**246**	**104**	**102**	**40**	**.504**	**16**	**8**	**8**	**.500**

Club Directory

Anaheim Sports, Inc.
Arrowhead Pond of Anaheim
2695 Katella Ave.
Anaheim, CA 92806
Phone **714/940-2900**
FAX 714/940-2953
Ticket Information 714/704-2701
Website: www.mightyducks.com
Capacity: 17,174

Executive Management	
Chairman and Governor	Tony Tavares
President and General Manager	Pierre Gauthier
Assistant General Manager	David McNab
Vice President, Finance/Administration	Andy Roundtree
Vice President, Business Operations	Spencer Neumann
Vice President, Advertising Sales and Broadcasting	Bob Wagner
Vice President, Communications	Tim Mead
Vice President, Business and Legal Affairs	Rick Schlesinger
Vice President, Hockey Operations	Jack Ferreira
Administrative Assistant, Chairman	Jennifer Mitchell
Administrative Assistant, President and General Manager	Maureen Nyehott
Administrative Assistant, Finance/Administration	Monica Campanis
Administrative Assistant, Advertising Sales and Broadcasting	Sonia Salem
Administrative Assistant, Business Affairs	Tia Wood
Administrative Assistant, Communications	TBA
Coaching Staff	
Head Coach	Craig Hartsburg
Assistant Coaches	Newell Brown, George Burnett
Goaltending Consultant	Franois Allaire
Hockey Club Operations	
Chief Amateur Scout	Alain Chainey
Scouting Coordinator	Neal Latman
Scouts	Richard Green, Mark Odnokon
Scouting Staff	Jan Danielsson, Donald Marier, Mike McGraw, David McNamara, Konstantin Krylov
Pro Scout	Lucien DeBlois
Head Athletic Trainer	Greg Smith
Equipment Manager	Mark O'Neill
Assistant Equipment Manager	John Allaway
Cincinnati Mighty Ducks (AHL) Head Coach	Moe Mantha
Team Physicians	Dr. Ronald Glousman, Dr. Craig Milhouse
Oral Surgeon	Dr. Jeff Pulver
Visiting Team Equipment Attendant	Chris Kincaid
Communications Department	
Manager, Communications and Team Services	Rob Scichili
Manager, Publications	Doug Ward
Media Relations Representative	Luis Garcia
Community Relations Representative	Paul Desaulniers
Media Relations Coordinator	Alex Gilchrist
Team Photographer	V.J. Lovero (Lovero Group)
Finance and Administration Department	
Director, Finance	John Rinehart
Sr. Financial Analyst	Amy Langdale
Business Development Analyst	Marc Kolin
Manager, Human Resources	Jenny Price
Manager, Information Services	Al Castro
Assistant Controller	Melody Martin
Accountants	Jean Ouyang, Roseanna Sitzman
Accounting Assistants	Rob Dumlao, Trang Nguyen
Administrative Assistant, Human Resources	Cindy Williams
Human Resources Assistant	Lisa Giancanelli
Event Supervisor	John Drum
Administrative Assistant, Operations	Leslie Flammini
General Manager, Disney ICE	Art Trottier
Office Assistant	Paul Zessau
Sales & Marketing Department	
Director, Sales and Marketing	Bill Holford
Manager, Premium Ticket Services	Anne McNiff
Manager, Marketing	Lisa Manning
Manager, Ticket Operations	Kevin Gidden
Manager, Group Sales	Andy Silverman
Ticketing Supervisor	Chad Canez
Account Executives	Ron Campbell, Kent Chantung, Mike Gullo
Group Ticket Sales Executives	Kristen Atkinson, Ken Bamberg, Matt Cohen, Joe Furmanski
Administrative Assistants	Christi Le Narz, Pat Lissy
Advertising Sales and Broadcasting Department	
Director, Broadcasting	Mark Vittorio
Manager, Advertising and Broadcast Sales	John Covarrubias
Manager, Sponsorship Services	Sue O'Shea
Advertising Sales Managers	Hap Deneen, Richard McClemmy, Jennifer Flaa
Broadcast Advertising Sales Managers	Victor Camino, John Davis, AnneMarie du LeBohn, Tracey Hall
Web Site Editor	Rick Capstraw
Sponsorship Services Representatives	Chris Sinta, Brian Strohecker
Broadcast Manager	Aaron Teats
Production Assistant	Mike Levy
Television, KCAL (Ch. 9) & Fox Sports West 2 (Cable)	Chris Madsen, Brian Hayward
Radio, XTRA Sports (690 AM) & Mighty Ducks Radio Network	Brian Hamilton, Darren Eliot
Administrative Assistant, Advertising	Janine Martin
Director, Entertainment	Marty Berg
Receptionist	Sue Felix
Miscellaneous	
Team Colors	Purple (PMS 518C), Jade (PMS 329C), Silver (PMS 429C) and White
Practice Facilities	Disney ICE (300 W. Lincoln Ave.) and the Arrowhead Pond (2695 Katella Ave.)
Press Box Phone	714/704-2623
Press Room	714/704-2514 or 2517

Boston Bruins

1997-98 Results: 39W-30L-13T 91PTS. Second, Northeast Division

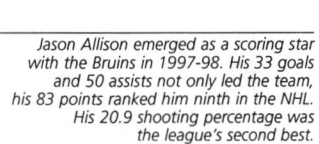

Jason Allison emerged as a scoring star with the Bruins in 1997-98. His 33 goals and 50 assists not only led the team, his 83 points ranked him ninth in the NHL. His 20.9 shooting percentage was the league's second best.

1998-99 Schedule

Month	Day	Date	Opponent
Oct.	Sat.	10	St. Louis
	Mon.	12	NY Islanders*
	Wed.	14	at Colorado
	Fri.	16	at Los Angeles
	Sun.	18	at San Jose
	Mon.	19	at Phoenix
	Wed.	21	at Anaheim
	Sat.	24	at New Jersey
	Wed.	28	at Montreal
	Thu.	29	Montreal
	Sat.	31	Carolina
Nov.	Tue.	3	at Buffalo
	Thu.	5	Toronto
	Sat.	7	at Pittsburgh*
	Sun.	8	at Carolina
	Fri.	13	at NY Rangers
	Sat.	14	Dallas
	Thu.	19	Florida
	Sat.	21	Washington
	Tue.	24	at Tampa Bay
	Wed.	25	at Florida
	Fri.	27	Montreal*
Dec.	Tue.	1	Vancouver
	Sat.	5	Pittsburgh
	Thu.	10	at Carolina
	Sat.	12	Buffalo
	Wed.	16	at Detroit
	Thu.	17	Ottawa
	Sat.	19	Detroit
	Mon.	21	Tampa Bay
	Wed.	23	Philadelphia
	Sat.	26	at NY Islanders
	Mon.	28	at Washington
	Wed.	30	at Nashville
	Thu.	31	at Dallas
Jan.	Sat.	2	Anaheim
	Mon.	4	Calgary
	Thu.	7	Toronto
	Sat.	9	at Toronto
	Fri.	15	at Buffalo
	Sat.	16	Tampa Bay
	Mon.	18	Nashville*
	Thu.	21	Ottawa
	Tue.	26	at NY Islanders
	Thu.	28	New Jersey
	Sat.	30	at Pittsburgh*
	Sun.	31	Carolina*
Feb.	Tue.	2	Colorado
	Thu.	4	NY Islanders
	Sat.	6	at Philadelphia*
	Sun.	7	NY Rangers*
	Tue.	9	at Edmonton
	Fri.	12	at Calgary
	Sat.	13	at Vancouver
	Thu.	18	at Ottawa
	Sun.	21	at Chicago*
	Tue.	23	Ottawa
	Thu.	25	New Jersey
	Sat.	27	Washington*
Mar.	Tue.	2	Phoenix
	Wed.	3	at Carolina
	Fri.	5	at New Jersey
	Sun.	7	NY Rangers*
	Tue.	9	Florida
	Fri.	12	at NY Rangers
	Sat.	13	at Buffalo
	Wed.	17	at Toronto
	Sat.	20	San Jose*
	Sun.	21	at Washington
	Wed.	24	at Ottawa
	Thu.	25	Chicago
	Sat.	27	at Toronto
	Tue.	30	Los Angeles
Apr.	Thu.	1	at Montreal
	Sat.	3	Philadelphia*
	Mon.	5	Montreal
	Wed.	7	at Florida
	Thu.	8	at Tampa Bay
	Sat.	10	Tampa Bay*
	Thu.	15	Pittsburgh
	Sat.	17	Buffalo*
	Sun.	18	at Philadelphia*

* Denotes afternoon game.

Franchise date: November 1, 1924

NORTHEAST DIVISION

75th NHL Season

Year-by-Year Record

		Home			Road			Overall							
Season	GP	W	L	T	W	L	T	W	L	T	GF	GA	Pts.	Finished	Playoff Result
1997-98	82	19	16	6	20	14	7	39	30	13	221	194	91	2nd, Northeast Div.	Lost Conf. Quarter-Final
1996-97	82	14	20	7	12	27	2	26	47	9	234	300	61	6th, Northeast Div.	Out of Playoffs
1995-96	82	22	14	5	18	17	6	40	31	11	282	269	91	2nd, Northeast Div.	Lost Conf. Quarter-Final
1994-95	48	15	7	2	12	11	1	27	18	3	150	127	57	3rd, Northeast Div.	Lost Conf. Quarter-Final
1993-94	84	20	14	8	22	15	5	42	29	13	289	252	97	2nd, Northeast Div.	Lost Conf. Semi-Final
1992-93	84	29	10	3	22	16	4	51	26	7	332	268	109	1st, Adams Div.	Lost Div. Semi-Final
1991-92	80	23	11	6	13	21	6	36	32	12	270	275	84	2nd, Adams Div.	Lost Conf. Championship
1990-91	80	26	9	5	18	15	7	44	24	12	299	264	100	1st, Adams Div.	Lost Conf. Championship
1989-90	80	23	13	4	23	12	5	46	25	9	289	232	101	1st, Adams Div.	Lost Final
1988-89	80	17	15	8	20	14	6	37	29	14	289	256	88	2nd, Adams Div.	Lost Div. Final
1987-88	80	24	13	3	20	17	3	44	30	6	300	251	94	2nd, Adams Div.	Lost Final
1986-87	80	25	11	4	14	23	3	39	34	7	301	276	85	3rd, Adams Div.	Lost Div. Semi-Final
1985-86	80	24	9	7	13	22	5	37	31	12	311	288	86	3rd, Adams Div.	Lost Div. Semi-Final
1984-85	80	21	15	4	15	19	6	36	34	10	303	287	82	4th, Adams Div.	Lost Div. Semi-Final
1983-84	80	25	12	3	24	13	3	49	25	6	336	261	104	1st, Adams Div.	Lost Div. Semi-Final
1982-83	80	28	6	6	22	14	4	50	20	10	327	228	110	1st, Adams Div.	Lost Conf. Championship
1981-82	80	24	12	4	19	15	6	43	27	10	323	285	96	2nd, Adams Div.	Lost Div. Final
1980-81	80	26	10	4	11	20	9	37	30	13	316	272	87	2nd, Adams Div.	Lost Prelim. Round
1979-80	80	27	9	4	19	12	9	46	21	13	310	234	105	2nd, Adams Div.	Lost Quarter-Final
1978-79	80	25	10	5	18	13	9	43	23	14	316	270	100	1st, Adams Div.	Lost Semi-Final
1977-78	80	29	6	5	22	12	6	51	18	11	333	218	113	1st, Adams Div.	Lost Final
1976-77	80	27	7	6	22	16	2	49	23	8	312	240	106	1st, Adams Div.	Lost Final
1975-76	80	27	5	8	21	10	9	48	15	17	313	237	113	1st, Adams Div.	Lost Semi-Final
1974-75	80	29	5	6	11	21	8	40	26	14	345	245	94	2nd, Adams Div.	Lost Prelim. Round
1973-74	78	33	4	2	19	13	7	52	17	9	349	221	113	1st, East Div.	Lost Final
1972-73	78	27	10	2	24	12	3	51	22	5	330	235	107	2nd, East Div.	Lost Quarter-Final
1971-72	**78**	**28**	**4**	**7**	**26**	**9**	**4**	**54**	**13**	**11**	**330**	**204**	**119**	**1st, East Div.**	**Won Stanley Cup**
1970-71	78	33	4	2	24	10	5	57	14	7	399	207	121	1st, East Div.	Lost Quarter-Final
1969-70	**76**	**27**	**3**	**8**	**13**	**14**	**11**	**40**	**17**	**19**	**277**	**216**	**99**	**2nd, East Div.**	**Won Stanley Cup**
1968-69	76	29	3	6	13	15	10	42	18	16	303	221	100	2nd, East Div.	Lost Semi-Final
1967-68	74	22	9	6	15	18	4	37	27	10	259	216	84	3rd, East Div.	Lost Quarter-Final
1966-67	70	10	21	4	7	22	6	17	43	10	182	253	44	6th,	Out of Playoffs
1965-66	70	15	17	3	6	26	3	21	43	6	174	275	48	5th,	Out of Playoffs
1964-65	70	12	17	6	9	26	0	21	43	6	166	253	48	6th,	Out of Playoffs
1963-64	70	13	15	7	5	25	5	18	40	12	170	212	48	6th,	Out of Playoffs
1962-63	70	7	18	10	7	21	7	14	39	17	198	281	45	6th,	Out of Playoffs
1961-62	70	9	22	4	6	25	4	15	47	8	177	306	38	6th,	Out of Playoffs
1960-61	70	13	17	5	2	25	8	15	42	13	176	254	43	6th,	Out of Playoffs
1959-60	70	21	11	3	7	23	5	28	34	8	220	241	64	5th,	Out of Playoffs
1958-59	70	21	11	3	11	18	6	32	29	9	205	215	73	2nd,	Lost Semi-Final
1957-58	70	15	14	6	12	14	9	27	28	15	199	194	69	4th,	Lost Final
1956-57	70	20	9	6	14	15	6	34	24	12	195	174	80	3rd,	Lost Final
1955-56	70	14	14	7	9	20	6	23	34	13	147	185	59	5th,	Out of Playoffs
1954-55	70	16	10	9	7	16	12	23	26	21	169	188	67	4th,	Lost Semi-Final
1953-54	70	22	8	5	10	20	5	32	28	10	177	181	74	4th,	Lost Semi-Final
1952-53	70	19	10	6	9	19	7	28	29	13	152	172	69	3rd,	Lost Final
1951-52	70	15	12	8	10	17	8	25	29	16	162	176	66	4th,	Lost Semi-Final
1950-51	70	13	12	10	9	18	8	22	30	18	178	197	62	4th,	Lost Semi-Final
1949-50	70	15	12	8	7	20	8	22	32	16	198	228	60	5th,	Out of Playoffs
1948-49	60	18	10	2	11	13	6	29	23	8	178	163	66	2nd,	Lost Semi-Final
1947-48	60	12	8	10	11	16	3	23	24	13	167	168	59	3rd,	Lost Semi-Final
1946-47	60	18	7	5	8	16	6	26	23	11	190	175	63	3rd,	Lost Semi-Final
1945-46	50	11	5	4	13	13	4	24	18	8	167	156	56	2nd,	Lost Final
1944-45	50	11	12	2	5	18	2	16	30	4	179	219	36	4th,	Lost Semi-Final
1943-44	50	15	8	2	4	18	3	19	26	5	223	268	43	5th,	Out of Playoffs
1942-43	50	17	3	5	7	14	4	24	17	9	195	176	57	2nd,	Lost Final
1941-42	48	17	4	3	8	13	3	25	17	6	160	118	56	3rd,	Lost Semi-Final
1940-41	**48**	**15**	**4**	**5**	**12**	**4**	**8**	**27**	**8**	**13**	**168**	**102**	**67**	**1st,**	**Won Stanley Cup**
1939-40	48	20	3	1	11	9	4	31	12	5	170	98	67	1st,	Lost Semi-Final
1938-39	**48**	**20**	**2**	**2**	**16**	**8**	**0**	**36**	**10**	**2**	**156**	**76**	**74**	**1st,**	**Won Stanley Cup**
1937-38	48	18	3	3	12	8	4	30	11	7	142	89	67	1st, Amn. Div.	Lost Semi-Final
1936-37	48	9	11	4	14	7	3	23	18	7	120	110	53	2nd, Amn. Div.	Lost Quarter-Final
1935-36	48	15	8	1	7	12	5	22	20	6	92	83	50	2nd, Amn. Div.	Lost Quarter-Final
1934-35	48	17	7	0	9	9	6	26	16	6	129	112	58	1st, Amn. Div.	Lost Semi-Final
1933-34	48	11	11	2	7	14	3	18	25	5	111	130	41	4th, Amn. Div.	Out of Playoffs
1932-33	48	19	2	3	6	13	5	25	15	8	124	88	58	1st, Amn. Div.	Lost Semi-Final
1931-32	48	11	10	3	4	11	9	15	21	12	122	117	42	4th, Amn. Div.	Out of Playoffs
1930-31	44	16	1	5	12	9	1	28	10	6	143	90	62	1st, Amn. Div.	Lost Semi-Final
1929-30	44	21	1	0	17	4	1	38	5	1	179	98	77	1st, Amn. Div.	Lost Final
1928-29	**44**	**15**	**6**	**1**	**11**	**7**	**4**	**26**	**13**	**5**	**89**	**52**	**57**	**1st, Amn. Div.**	**Won Stanley Cup**
1927-28	44	13	4	5	7	9	6	20	13	11	77	70	51	1st, Amn. Div.	Lost Semi-Final
1926-27	44	15	7	0	6	13	3	21	20	3	97	89	45	2nd, Amn. Div.	Lost Final
1925-26	36	10	7	1	7	8	3	17	15	4	92	85	38	4th,	Out of Playoffs
1924-25	30	3	12	0	3	12	0	6	24	0	49	119	12	6th,	Out of Playoffs

1998-99 Player Personnel

FORWARDS	HT	WT	S	Place of Birth	Date	1997-98 Club
ALLISON, Jason	6-3	205	R	North York, Ont.	5/29/75	Boston
ALVEY, Matt	6-5	200	R	Troy, NY	5/15/75	Charlotte
AXELSSON, Per-Johan	6-1	174	L	Kungalv, Sweden	2/26/75	Boston
BATES, Shawn	5-11	205	R	Melrose, MA	4/3/75	Boston-Providence (AHL)
BAUMGARTNER, Ken	6-1	205	L	Flin Flon, Man.	3/11/66	Boston
CARTER, Anson	6-1	185	R	Toronto, Ont.	6/6/74	Boston
DiMAIO, Rob	5-10	190	R	Calgary, Alta.	2/19/68	Boston
DONATO, Ted	5-10	181	L	Boston, MA	4/28/69	Boston
DOWNEY, Aaron	6-0	210	R	Shelburne, Ont.	8/27/74	Providence (AHL)
FERRARO, Peter	5-10	180	R	Port Jefferson, NY	1/24/73	Pittsburgh-NY Rangers-Hartford
HEINZE, Stephen	5-11	202	R	Lawrence, MA	1/30/70	Boston
HENDERSON, Jay	5-11	188	L	Edmonton, Alta.	9/17/78	Edmonton (WHL)
KHRISTICH, Dmitri	6-2	195	R	Kiev, USSR	7/23/69	Boston
LAAKSONEN, Antti	6-0	180	L	Tammela, Finland	10/3/73	Providence (AHL)-Charlotte
MANN, Cameron	6-0	194	R	Thompson, Man.	4/20/77	Boston-Providence (AHL)
MILANOVIC, Ryan	6-2	201	L	Toronto, Ont.	9/3/80	Kitchener
NORDSTROM, Peter	6-1	200	L	Munkfors, Sweden	7/26/74	Farjestad
PRPIC, Joel	6-7	225	L	Sudbury, Ont.	9/25/74	Boston-Providence (AHL)
ROBITAILLE, Randy	5-11	190	L	Ottawa, Ont.	10/12/75	Boston-Providence (AHL)
SAMSONOV, Sergei	5-8	184	R	Moscow, USSR	10/27/78	Boston
SAVAGE, Andre	6-0	195	R	Ottawa, Ont.	5/27/75	Michigan Tech
TAYLOR, Chris	6-0	189	L	Stratford, Ont.	3/6/72	Utah
TAYLOR, Tim	6-1	185	L	Stratford, Ont.	2/6/69	Boston
THORNTON, Joe	6-4	225	L	London, Ont.	7/2/79	Boston
TROTTIER, Joel	6-0	190	R	Alexandria, Ont.	2/11/77	Plymouth-Belleville
WILSON, Landon	6-2	216	R	St. Louis, MO	3/13/75	Boston-Providence (AHL)
DEFENSEMEN						
ABRAHAMSSON, Elias	6-3	240	L	Uppsala, Sweden	6/15/77	Providence (AHL)
AITKEN, Johnathan	6-4	215	L	Edmonton, Alta.	5/24/78	Brandon
BAXTER, Jim	6-2	186	R	Brantford, Ont.	8/24/79	Oshawa
BELTER, Shane	6-1	205	R	Swift Current, Sask.	10/5/77	Lethbridge-Kamloops
BOURQUE, Ray	5-11	219	L	Montreal, Que.	12/28/60	Boston-Canada
ELLETT, Dave	6-2	205	L	Cleveland, OH	3/30/64	Boston
GILL, Hal	6-7	240	L	Concord, MA	4/6/75	Boston-Providence (AHL)
GIRARD, Jonathan	5-11	192	R	Joliette, Que.	5/27/80	Laval
LEDYARD, Grant	6-2	195	L	Winnipeg, Man.	11/19/61	Vancouver-Boston
McLAREN, Kyle	6-4	219	L	Humboldt, Sask.	6/18/77	Boston
SHALDYBIN, Yevgeny	6-2	198	L	Novosibirsk, USSR	7/29/75	Providence (AHL)
SMITH, Brandon	6-1	196	L	Hazelton, B.C.	2/25/73	Adirondack
SWEENEY, Don	5-10	184	L	St. Stephen, N.B.	8/17/66	Boston
TIMANDER, Mattias	6-3	210	L	Solleftea, Sweden	4/16/74	Boston-Providence (AHL)
VAN ACKER, Eric	6-5	220	L	St. Jean, Que.	3/1/79	Chicoutimi
VAN IMPE, Darren	6-1	205	L	Saskatoon, Sask.	5/18/73	Anaheim-Boston

GOALTENDERS	HT	WT	C	Place of Birth	Date	1997-98 Club
CAREY, Jim	6-2	205	L	Dorchester, MA	5/31/74	Boston-Providence (AHL)
DAFOE, Byron	5-11	190	L	Sussex, England	2/25/71	Boston
GRAHAME, John	6-2	210	L	Denver, CO	8/31/75	Providence (AHL)
RAYCROFT, Andrew	6-0	150	L	Belleville, Ont.	5/4/80	Sudbury
SCHAFER, Paxton	5-9	164	L	Medicine Hat, Alta.	2/26/76	Providence (AHL)-Charlotte
TALLAS, Robbie	6-0	163	L	Edmonton, Alta.	3/20/73	Boston-Providence (AHL)

Coaching History

Art Ross, 1924-25 to 1927-28; Cy Denneny, 1928-29; Art Ross, 1929-30 to 1933-34; Frank Patrick, 1934-35, 1935-36; Art Ross, 1936-37 to 1938-39; Cooney Weiland, 1939-40, 1940-41; Art Ross, 1941-42 to 1944-45; Dit Clapper, 1945-46 to 1948-49; George Boucher, 1949-50; Lynn Patrick, 1950-51 to 1953-54; Lynn Patrick and Milt Schmidt, 1954-55; Milt Schmidt, 1955-56 to 1960-61; Phil Watson, 1961-62; Phil Watson and Milt Schmidt, 1962-63; Milt Schmidt, 1963-64 to 1965-66; Harry Sinden, 1966-67 to 1969-70; Tom Johnson, 1970-71, 1971-72; Tom Johnson and Bep Guidolin, 1972-73; Bep Guidolin, 1973-74; Don Cherry, 1974-75 to 1978-79; Fred Creighton and Harry Sinden, 1979-80; Gerry Cheevers, 1980-81 to 1983-84; Gerry Cheevers and Harry Sinden, 1984-85; Butch Goring, 1985-86; Butch Goring and Terry O'Reilly, 1986-87; Terry O'Reilly, 1987-88, 1988-89; Mike Milbury, 1989-90, 1990-91; Rick Bowness, 1991-92; Brian Sutter, 1992-93 to 1994-95; Steve Kasper, 1995-96, 1996-97; Pat Burns, 1997-98 to date.

Coach

BURNS, PAT
Coach, Boston Bruins. Born in St-Henri, Que., April 4, 1952.

Pat Burns led the Bruins back into the playoffs in his first season behind the Bruins bench in 1997-98. The club's 30-point improvement saw Burns honored with the Jack Adams Award, making him the first man to be named coach of the year on three occasions. The three victories have come with three different clubs.

Burns began his coaching career with the Hull Olympiques of the QMJHL. During his four seasons behind the Hull bench, he compiled a 138-136-6 record and a berth in the 1986 Memorial Cup finals. In 1987-88, he moved to the professional ranks, assuming the head coaching position with Montreal's AHL affiliate in Sherbrooke. After leading that team to a 42-34-4 record, he was named as the head coach in Montreal.

He was the NHL's winningest coach over his four-year tenure in Montreal, with a 174-104-42 record and .609 winning percentage from 1988-89 through 1991-92.

On May 29, 1992, Burns was named as the head coach for the Toronto Maple Leafs. In his first season with Toronto, he led the team to the highest single-season turnaround in club history with club records in regular season wins, points and home wins and playoff games and victories. Their 44-29-11 record in 1992-93 was a 32-point improvement from their 1991-92 campaign. His second season behind the Toronto bench earned the team consecutive 40-win seasons for the first time in club history.

1997-98 Scoring

* – rookie

Regular Season

Pos	#	Player	Team	GP	G	A	Pts	+/–	PIM	PP	SH	GW	GT	S	%
C	41	Jason Allison	BOS	81	33	50	83	33	60	5	0	8	2	158	20.9
R	12	Dmitri Khristich	BOS	82	29	37	66	25	42	13	2	1	0	144	20.1
D	77	Ray Bourque	BOS	82	13	35	48	2	80	9	0	3	1	264	4.9
L	14 *	Sergei Samsonov	BOS	81	22	25	47	9	8	7	0	3	0	159	13.8
R	23	Steve Heinze	BOS	61	26	20	46	8	54	9	0	6	0	160	16.3
C	33	Anson Carter	BOS	78	16	27	43	7	31	6	0	4	0	179	8.9
L	21	Ted Donato	BOS	79	16	23	39	6	54	3	0	5	1	129	12.4
C	26	Tim Taylor	BOS	79	20	11	31	-16	57	1	3	0	1	127	15.7
L	19	Rob Dimaio	BOS	79	10	17	27	-13	82	0	0	4	1	112	8.9
R	11 *	Per Axelsson	BOS	82	8	19	27	-14	38	2	0	1	0	144	5.6
D	18	Kyle McLaren	BOS	66	5	20	25	13	56	2	0	0	0	101	5.0
D	36	Grant Ledyard	VAN	49	2	13	15	-2	14	1	0	0	0	57	3.5
			BOS	22	2	7	9	-2	6	1	0	0	0	33	6.1
			TOTAL	71	4	20	24	-4	20	2	0	0	0	90	4.4
D	44	Dave Ellett	BOS	82	3	20	23	3	67	2	0	1	0	129	2.3
L	42	Mike Sullivan	BOS	77	5	13	18	-1	34	0	0	2	0	83	6.0
D	32	Don Sweeney	BOS	59	1	15	16	12	24	0	0	0	0	55	1.8
D	20	Darren Van Impe	ANA	19	1	3	4	-10	4	0	0	0	0	21	4.8
			BOS	50	2	8	10	4	36	2	0	0	0	50	4.0
			TOTAL	69	3	11	14	-6	40	2	0	0	0	71	4.2
C	6 *	Joe Thornton	BOS	55	3	4	7	-6	19	0	0	1	0	33	9.1
D	25 *	Hal Gill	BOS	68	2	4	6	4	47	0	0	0	0	56	3.6
R	27	Landon Wilson	BOS	28	1	5	6	3	7	0	0	0	0	26	3.8
G	34	Byron Dafoe	BOS	65	0	3	3	0	2	0	0	0	0	0	0.0
C	17 *	Shawn Bates	BOS	13	2	0	2	-3	2	0	0	0	0	12	16.7
D	37	Mattias Timander	BOS	23	1	1	2	-9	6	0	0	0	0	17	5.9
D	29	Dean Malkoc	BOS	40	1	0	1	-12	86	0	0	0	0	15	6.7
R	10 *	Cameron Mann	BOS	9	0	1	1	1	4	0	0	0	0	6	0.0
L	22	Ken Baumgartner	BOS	82	0	1	1	-14	199	0	0	0	0	28	0.0
C	39 *	Joel Prpic	BOS	1	0	0	0	0	2	0	0	0	0	0	0.0
D	28	Dean Chynoweth	BOS	2	0	0	0	-4	0	0	0	0	0	1	0.0
R	43	Jean-Yves Roy	BOS	2	0	0	0	0	0	0	0	0	0	1	0.0
C	16 *	Randy Robitaille	BOS	4	0	0	0	-2	0	0	0	0	0	5	0.0
R	60 *	Kirk Nielsen	BOS	6	0	0	0	-1	0	0	0	0	0	1	0.0
G	30	Jim Carey	BOS	10	0	0	0	0	0	0	0	0	0	0	0.0
G	35	Robbie Tallas	BOS	14	0	0	0	0	0	0	0	0	0	0	0.0

Goaltending

No.	Goaltender	GPI	Mins	Avg	W	L	T	EN	SO	GA	SA	S%
35	Robbie Tallas	14	788	1.83	6	3	3	0	1	24	326	.926
34	Byron Dafoe	65	3693	2.24	30	25	9	8	6	138	1602	.914
30	Jim Carey	10	496	2.90	3	2	1	0	2	24	225	.893
	Totals	**82**	**4995**	**2.33**	**39**	**30**	**13**	**8**	**9**	**194**	**2161**	**.910**

Playoffs

Pos	#	Player	Team	GP	G	A	Pts	+/–	PIM	PP	SH	GW	OT	S	%
C	41	Jason Allison	BOS	6	2	6	8	0	4	1	0	0	0	13	15.4
L	14 *	Sergei Samsonov	BOS	6	2	5	7	1	0	0	0	1	0	18	11.1
D	77	Ray Bourque	BOS	6	1	4	5	-2	2	1	0	0	0	42	2.4
R	12	Dmitri Khristich	BOS	6	2	2	4	1	2	2	0	0	0	15	13.3
D	20	Darren Van Impe	BOS	6	2	1	3	0	0	1	0	1	1	19	10.5
C	33	Anson Carter	BOS	6	1	1	2	-3	0	0	0	0	0	19	5.3
L	19	Rob Dimaio	BOS	6	1	0	1	-3	8	0	0	0	0	14	7.1
D	18	Kyle McLaren	BOS	6	1	0	1	-3	4	1	0	0	0	21	4.8
R	11 *	Per Axelsson	BOS	6	1	0	1	-3	0	0	0	0	0	13	7.7
D	44	Dave Ellett	BOS	6	0	1	1	-1	6	0	0	0	0	11	0.0
L	42	Mike Sullivan	BOS	6	0	1	1	0	2	0	0	0	0	10	0.0
R	27	Landon Wilson	BOS	1	0	0	0	0	0	0	0	0	0	1	0.0
L	21	Ted Donato	BOS	5	0	0	0	-3	2	0	0	0	0	3	0.0
L	22	Ken Baumgartner	BOS	6	0	0	0	0	14	0	0	0	0	1	0.0
D	36	Grant Ledyard	BOS	6	0	0	0	-3	2	0	0	0	0	8	0.0
G	34	Byron Dafoe	BOS	6	0	0	0	0	0	0	0	0	0	0	0.0
R	23	Steve Heinze	BOS	6	0	0	0	-4	6	0	0	0	0	15	0.0
C	26	Tim Taylor	BOS	6	0	0	0	-2	10	0	0	0	0	10	0.0
D	25 *	Hal Gill	BOS	6	0	0	0	-1	4	0	0	0	0	3	0.0
C	6 *	Joe Thornton	BOS	6	0	0	0	0	9	0	0	0	0	3	0.0

Goaltending

No.	Goaltender	GPI	Mins	Avg	W	L	EN	SO	GA	SA	S%
34	Byron Dafoe	6	422	1.99	2	4	1	1	14	159	.912
	Totals	**6**	**423**	**2.13**	**2**	**4**	**1**	**1**	**15**	**160**	**.906**

Coaching Record

		Regular Season					Playoffs			
Season	Team	Games	W	L	T	%	Games	W	L	%
1983-84	Hull (QMJHL)	70	25	45	0	.357	....	....	....	....
1984-85	Hull (QMJHL)	68	33	34	1	.493	5	1	4	.200
1985-86	Hull (QMJHL)	72	54	18	0	.750	15	15	0	1.000
1986-87	Hull (QMJHL)	70	26	39	5	.407	8	4	4	.500
1987-88	Sherbrooke (AHL)	80	42	34	4	.550	6	2	4	.333
1988-89	**Montreal (NHL)**	**80**	**53**	**18**	**9**	**.719**	**21**	**14**	**7**	**.667**
1989-90	**Montreal (NHL)**	**80**	**41**	**28**	**11**	**.581**	**11**	**5**	**6**	**.455**
1990-91	**Montreal (NHL)**	**80**	**39**	**30**	**11**	**.556**	**13**	**7**	**6**	**.538**
1991-92	**Montreal (NHL)**	**80**	**41**	**28**	**11**	**.581**	**11**	**4**	**7**	**.364**
1992-93	**Toronto (NHL)**	**84**	**44**	**29**	**11**	**.589**	**21**	**11**	**10**	**.524**
1993-94	**Toronto (NHL)**	**84**	**43**	**29**	**12**	**.583**	**18**	**9**	**9**	**.500**
1994-95	**Toronto (NHL)**	**48**	**21**	**19**	**8**	**.521**	**7**	**3**	**4**	**.429**
1995-96	**Toronto (NHL)**	**65**	**25**	**30**	**10**	**.462**	....	....	....	....
1997-98	**Boston (NHL)**	**82**	**39**	**30**	**13**	**.555**	**6**	**2**	**4**	**.333**
	NHL Totals	**683**	**346**	**241**	**96**	**.577**	**108**	**55**	**53**	**.509**

Club Records

Team

(Figures in brackets for season records are games played; records for fewest points, wins, ties, losses, goals, goals against are for 70 or more games)

Most Points 121 1970-71 (78)
Most Wins 57 1970-71 (78)
Most Ties 21 1954-55 (70)
Most Losses 47 1961-62 (70), 1996-97 (82)
Most Goals 399 1970-71 (78)
Most Goals Against 306 1961-62 (70)
Fewest Points 38 1961-62 (70)
Fewest Wins 14 1962-63 (70)
Fewest Ties 5 1972-73 (78)
Fewest Losses 13 1971-72 (78)
Fewest Goals 147 1955-56 (70)
Fewest Goals Against 172 1952-53 (70)

Longest Winning Streak
Overall .... 14 Dec. 3/29-Jan. 9/30
Home .... *20 Dec. 3/29-Mar. 18/30
Away .... 8 Feb. 17-Mar. 8/72, Mar. 15-Apr. 14/93

Longest Undefeated Streak
Overall .... 23 Dec. 22/40-Feb. 23/41 (15 wins, 8 ties)
Home .... 27 Nov. 22/70-Mar. 20/71 (26 wins, 1 tie)
Away .... 15 Dec. 22/40-Mar. 16/41 (9 wins, 6 ties)

Longest Losing Streak
Overall .... 11 Dec. 3/24-Jan. 5/25
Home .... *11 Dec. 8/24-Feb. 17/25
Away .... 14 Dec. 27/64-Feb. 21/65

Longest Winless Streak
Overall .... 20 Jan. 28-Mar. 11/62 (16 losses, 4 ties)
Home .... 11 Dec. 8/24-Feb. 17/25 (11 losses)
Away .... 14 Three times

Most Shutouts, Season 15 1927-28 (44)
Most PIM, Season 2,443 1987-88 (80)
Most Goals, Game .... 14 Jan. 21/45 (NYR 3 at Bos. 14)

Individual

Most Seasons .... 21 John Bucyk
Most Games .... 1,436 John Bucyk
Most Goals, Career .... 545 John Bucyk
Most Assists, Career .... 1,036 Ray Bourque
Most Points, Career .... 1,411 Ray Bourque (375G, 1,036A)
Most PIM, Career .... 2,095 Terry O'Reilly
Most Shutouts, Career .... 74 Tiny Thompson
Longest Consecutive Games Streak .... 418 John Bucyk (Jan. 23/69-Mar. 2/75)
Most Goals, Season .... 76 Phil Esposito (1970-71)
Most Assists, Season .... 102 Bobby Orr (1970-71)
Most Points, Season .... 152 Phil Esposito (1970-71; 76G, 76A)
Most PIM, Season .... 304 Jay Miller (1987-88)
Most Points, Defenseman, Season .... *139 Bobby Orr (1970-71; 37G, 102A)
Most Points, Center, Season .... 152 Phil Esposito (1970-71; 76G, 76A)
Most Points, Right Wing, Season .... 105 Ken Hodge (1970-71; 43G, 62A), (1973-74; 50G, 55A), Rick Middleton (1983-84; 47G, 58A)
Most Points, Left Wing, Season .... 116 John Bucyk (1970-71; 51G, 65A)
Most Points, Rookie, Season .... 102 Joe Juneau (1992-93; 32G, 70A)
Most Shutouts, Season .... 15 Hal Winkler (1927-28)
Most Goals, Game .... 4 Nineteen times
Most Assists, Game .... 6 Ken Hodge (Feb. 9/71), Bobby Orr (Jan. 1/73)
Most Points, Game .... 7 Bobby Orr (Nov. 15/73; 3G, 4A), Phil Esposito (Dec. 19/74; 3G, 4A), Barry Pederson (Apr. 4/82; 3G, 4A), Cam Neely (Oct. 16/88; 3G, 4A)

* NHL Record.

Retired Numbers

2	Eddie Shore	1926-1940
3	Lionel Hitchman	1925-1934
4	Bobby Orr	1966-1976
5	Dit Clapper	1927-1947
7	Phil Esposito	1967-1975
9	John Bucyk	1957-1978
15	Milt Schmidt	1936-1955

All-time Record vs. Other Clubs

Regular Season

	At Home							On Road							Total						
	GP	W	L	T	GF	GA	PTS	GP	W	L	T	GF	GA	PTS	GP	W	L	T	GF	GA	PTS
Anaheim	4	2	2	0	14	13	4	4	2	1	1	12	6	5	8	4	3	1	26	19	9
Buffalo	92	52	28	12	362	281	116	92	32	45	15	283	343	79	184	84	73	27	645	624	195
Calgary	42	25	11	6	147	116	56	41	22	16	3	146	150	47	83	47	27	9	293	266	103
Carolina	66	44	16	6	257	174	94	63	28	28	7	221	220	63	129	72	44	13	478	394	157
Chicago	279	159	87	33	1009	788	351	281	93	144	44	748	905	230	560	252	231	77	1757	1693	581
Colorado	58	31	19	8	231	179	70	60	33	21	6	257	217	72	118	64	40	14	488	396	142
Dallas	56	40	7	9	248	133	89	56	29	15	12	210	160	70	112	69	22	21	458	293	159
Detroit	282	151	88	43	994	751	345	281	77	152	52	708	941	206	563	228	240	95	1702	1692	551
Edmonton	26	18	6	2	113	74	38	25	13	9	3	88	85	29	51	31	15	5	201	159	67
Florida	10	3	5	2	25	28	8	9	5	4	0	27	28	10	19	8	9	2	52	56	18
Los Angeles	57	43	10	4	273	159	90	56	31	19	6	213	195	68	113	74	29	10	486	354	158
Montreal	319	146	119	54	943	869	346	319	90	184	45	747	1085	225	638	236	303	99	1690	1954	571
New Jersey	44	27	12	5	187	137	59	41	22	10	9	139	108	53	85	49	22	14	326	245	112
NY Islanders	47	26	11	10	184	135	62	49	24	19	6	165	163	54	96	50	30	16	349	298	116
NY Rangers	286	153	92	41	1038	803	347	290	110	126	54	816	881	274	576	263	218	95	1854	1684	621
Ottawa	17	12	3	2	74	46	26	16	13	1	2	60	30	28	33	25	4	4	134	76	54
Philadelphia	64	42	14	8	260	183	92	61	27	27	7	180	206	61	125	69	41	15	440	389	153
Phoenix	25	18	4	3	117	81	39	26	14	10	2	98	93	30	51	32	14	5	215	174	69
Pittsburgh	66	47	13	6	305	195	100	68	27	29	12	253	245	66	134	74	42	18	558	440	166
St. Louis	54	34	12	8	234	146	76	55	23	23	9	192	175	55	109	57	35	17	426	321	131
San Jose	6	5	0	1	24	15	11	6	3	1	2	26	18	8	12	8	1	3	50	33	19
Tampa Bay	10	7	1	2	37	23	16	11	5	4	2	31	29	12	21	12	5	4	68	52	28
Toronto	283	152	84	47	930	754	351	283	86	148	49	736	963	221	566	238	232	96	1666	1717	572
Vancouver	46	36	6	4	203	110	76	47	25	14	8	198	154	58	93	61	20	12	401	264	134
Washington	44	25	13	6	169	120	56	43	22	11	10	159	126	54	87	47	24	16	328	246	110
Defunct Clubs	164	112	39	13	525	306	237	164	79	67	18	496	440	176	328	191	106	31	1021	746	413
Totals	**2447**	**1410**	**702**	**335**	**8903**	**6619**	**3155**	**2447**	**935**	**1128**	**384**	**7209**	**7966**	**2254**	**4894**	**2345**	**1830**	**719**	**16112**	**14585**	**5409**

Playoffs

	Series	W	L	GP	W	L	T	GF	GA	Last Mtg.	Round	Result
Buffalo	6	5	1	33	19	14	0	132	113	1993	DSF	L 0-4
Chicago	6	5	1	22	16	5	1	97	63	1978	QF	W 4-0
Colorado	2	1	1	11	6	5	0	37	36	1983	DSF	W 3-1
Dallas	1	0	1	3	0	3	0	13	20	1981	PR	L 0-3
Detroit	7	4	3	33	19	14	0	96	98	1957	SF	W 4-1
Edmonton	2	0	2	9	1	8	0	20	41	1990	F	L 1-4
Florida	1	0	1	5	1	4	0	16	22	1996	CQF	L 1-4
Hartford	2	2	0	13	8	5	0	24	17	1991	DSF	W 4-2
Los Angeles	2	2	0	13	8	5	0	56	38	1977	QF	W 4-2
Montreal	28	7	21	139	52	87	0	339	430	1994	CQF	W 4-3
New Jersey	3	1	2	18	7	11	0	52	55	1995	CQF	L 1-4
NY Islanders	2	0	2	11	3	8	0	35	49	1983	CF	L 2-4
NY Rangers	9	6	3	42	22	18	2	114	104	1973	QF	L 1-4
Philadelphia	4	2	2	20	11	9	0	60	57	1978	SF	W 4-1
Pittsburgh	4	2	2	19	9	10	0	62	67	1992	CF	L 0-4
St. Louis	2	2	0	8	8	0	0	48	15	1972	SF	W 4-0
Toronto	13	5	8	62	30	31	1	153	150	1974	QF	W 4-0
Washington	2	1	1	10	6	4	0	28	21	1998	CQF	L 2-4
Defunct Clubs	3	1	2	11	4	5	2	20	20			
Totals	**99**	**46**	**53**	**482**	**230**	**246**	**6**	**1418**	**1437**			

Calgary totals include Atlanta, 1972-73 to 1979-80. Carolina totals include Hartford, 1979-80 to 1996-97.
Colorado totals include Quebec, 1979-80 to 1994-95. Dallas totals include Minnesota, 1967-68 to 1992-93.
New Jersey totals include Kansas City, 1974-75 to 1975-76, and Colorado Rockies, 1976-77 to 1981-82.
Phoenix totals include Winnipeg, 1979-80 to 1995-96.

Playoff Results 1998-94

Year	Round	Opponent	Result	GF	GA
1998	CQF	Washington	L 2-4	13	15
1996	CQF	Florida	L 1-4	16	22
1995	CQF	New Jersey	L 1-4	5	14
1994	CSF	New Jersey	L 2-4	17	22
	CQF	Montreal	W 4-3	22	20

Abbreviations: Round: F – Final;
CF – conference final; **CQF** – conference quarter-final;
CSF – conference semi-final;
DSF – division semi-final; **SF** – semi-final;
QF – quarter-final; **PR** – preliminary round.

1997-98 Results

Oct.	2		Los Angeles	6-5		3		San Jose	3-0
	4		Montreal	1-4		7	at	Montreal	2-1
	7	at	Colorado	2-3		8		Phoenix	5-2
	8	at	Phoenix	3-2		12		New Jersey	1-1
	11	at	San Jose	2-5		14		Pittsburgh	5-2
	13	at	Anaheim	3-0		21	at	Montreal	2-4
	15	at	Los Angeles	5-3		24	at	Pittsburgh	2-4
	17	at	Vancouver	2-0		25	at	Washington	1-4
	18	at	Calgary	3-0		27		Ottawa	6-1
	21	at	Edmonton	2-1		29		Pittsburgh	2-4
	23		Tampa Bay	2-2		31		NY Rangers	4-2
	25		Florida	4-5	**Feb.**	1	at	NY Islanders	2-2
	30		Anaheim	0-3		4	at	Buffalo	2-2
Nov.	1		Edmonton	3-1		5		St. Louis	1-3
	2	at	Ottawa	3-1		7		Carolina	1-3
	6		Washington	2-0		26		Buffalo	1-1
	8	at	New Jersey	0-2		28		Pittsburgh	6-2
	12	at	Dallas	3-3	**Mar.**	1	at	NY Islanders	5-4
	13	at	St. Louis	2-4		3	at	Washington	3-0
	15		Ottawa	3-3		5	at	New Jersey	1-1
	17	at	Ottawa	4-2		7		Chicago	1-2
	19	at	Pittsburgh	3-3		10	at	Detroit	6-3
	20		Buffalo	0-5		12		Calgary	2-5
	22		Dallas	0-2		14		NY Rangers	5-1
	26	at	Florida	5-10		16		Tampa Bay	4-3
	28		Vancouver	2-5		19		Toronto	4-0
	29		Washington	1-1		21	at	Buffalo	2-1
Dec.	1	at	Carolina	1-3		22	at	Chicago	0-1
	3	at	Philadelphia	3-0		26		Philadelphia	4-2
	6		Carolina	4-1		28		Florida	2-3
	11		Buffalo	2-1		30		Colorado	4-1
	13		Montreal	4-2	**Apr.**	1	at	NY Rangers	4-2
	15	at	Florida	6-2		3	at	Buffalo	4-5
	17	at	Tampa Bay	0-2		6		Carolina	0-3
	18	at	Philadelphia	2-2		7	at	Ottawa	4-2
	20		NY Islanders	3-4		9		NY Islanders	4-1
	22		Detroit	2-4		11		New Jersey	2-3
	27	at	Tampa Bay	3-1		13	at	Carolina	3-2
	28	at	NY Rangers	3-4		15	at	Montreal	6-2
	31	at	Toronto	2-2		18	at	Pittsburgh	2-5
Jan.	1		Ottawa	0-0		19		Philadelphia	2-1

Entry Draft Selections 1998-84

1998

Pick	
48	Jonathon Girard
52	Bobby Allen
78	Peter Nordstrom
135	Andrew Raycroft
165	Ryan Milanovic

1997

Pick	
1	Joe Thornton
8	Sergei Samsonov
27	Ben Clymer
54	Mattias Karlin
63	Lee Goren
81	Karol Bartanus
135	Denis Timofeev
162	Joel Trottier
180	Jim Baxter
191	Antti Laaksonen
218	Eric Van Acker
246	Jay Henderson

1996

Pick	
8	Johnathan Aitken
45	Henry Kuster
53	Eric Naud
80	Jason Doyle
100	Trent Whitfield
132	Elias Abrahamsson
155	Chris Lane
182	Thomas Brown
208	Bob Prier
234	Anders Soderberg

1995

Pick	
9	Kyle McLaren
21	Sean Brown
47	Paxton Schafer
73	Bill McCauley
99	Cameron Mann
151	Yevgeny Shaldybin
177	Per Johan Axelsson
203	Sergei Zhukov
229	Jonathan Murphy

1994

Pick	
21	Evgeni Ryabchikov
47	Daniel Goneau
99	Eric Nickulas
125	Darren Wright
151	Andre Roy
177	Jeremy Schaefer
229	John Grahame
255	Neil Savary
281	Andrei Yakhanov

1993

Pick	
25	Kevyn Adams
51	Matt Alvey
88	Charles Paquette
103	Shawn Bates
129	Andrei Sapozhnikov
155	Milt Mastad
181	Ryan Golden
207	Hal Gill
233	Joel Prpic
259	Joakim Persson

1992

Pick	
16	Dmitri Kvartalnov
55	Sergei Zholtok
112	Scott Bailey
133	Jiri Dopita
136	Grigori Panteleev
184	Kurt Seher
208	Mattias Timander
232	Chris Crombie
256	Denis Chervyakov
257	Evgeny Pavlov

1991

Pick	
18	Glen Murray
40	Jozef Stumpel
62	Marcel Cousineau
84	Brad Tiley
106	Mariusz Czerkawski
150	Gary Golczewski
172	John Moser
194	Daniel Hodge
216	Steve Norton
238	Stephen Lombardi
260	Torsten Kienass

1990

Pick	
21	Bryan Smolinski
63	Cameron Stewart
84	Jerome Buckley
105	Mike Bales
126	Mark Woolf
147	Jim Mackey
168	John Gruden
189	Darren Wetherill
210	Dean Capuano
231	Andy Bezeau
252	Ted Miskolczi

1989

Pick	
17	Shayne Stevenson
38	Mike Parson
57	Wes Walz
80	Jackson Penney
101	Mark Montanari
122	Stephen Foster
143	Otto Hascak
164	Rick Allain
185	James Lavish
206	Geoff Simpson
227	David Franzosa

1988

Pick	
18	Robert Cimetta
60	Stephen Heinze
81	Joe Juneau
102	Daniel Murphy
123	Derek Geary
165	Mark Krys
186	Jon Rohloff
228	Eric Reisman
249	Doug Jones

1987

Pick	
3	Glen Wesley
14	Stephane Quintal
56	Todd Lalonde
67	Darwin McPherson
77	Matt Delguidice
98	Ted Donato
119	Matt Glennon
140	Rob Cheevers
161	Chris Winnes
182	Paul Ohman
203	Casey Jones
224	Eric Lemarque
245	Sean Gorman

1986

Pick	
13	Craig Janney
34	Pekka Tirkkonen
76	Dean Hall
97	Matt Pesklewis
118	Garth Premak
139	Paul Beraldo
160	Brian Ferreira
181	Jeff Flaherty
202	Greg Hawgood
223	Staffan Malmqvist
244	Joel Gardner

1985

Pick	
31	Alain Cote
52	Bill Ranford
73	Jaime Kelly
94	Steve Moore
115	Gord Hynes
136	Per Martinelle
157	Randy Burridge
178	Gord Cruickshank
199	Dave Buda
210	Bob Beers
220	John Byce
241	Marc West

1984

Pick	
19	Dave Pasin
40	Ray Podloski
61	Jeff Cornelius
82	Robert Joyce
103	Mike Bishop
124	Randy Oswald
145	Mark Thietke
166	Don Sweeney
186	Kevin Heffernan
207	J.D. Urbanic
227	Bill Kopecky
248	Jim Newhouse

President and General Manager

SINDEN, HARRY
President and General Manager, Boston Bruins.
Born in Toronto, Ont., September 14, 1932.

Harry Sinden enters his tenth season as the Bruins' president and his 27th season as the club's general manager.

Sinden's name has been synonymous with the Bruins organization for over 36 years. He has been instrumental in bringing a Stanley Cup, six Conference titles and ten Division championships to Boston. On October 17, 1995 with a 7-4 Boston win at St. Louis, he became the first general manager in the history of the NHL to record 1,000 victories as a g.m.

His many accomplishments, in addition to his knowledge and experience, led to his 1983 induction into the Hockey Hall of Fame in the Builder's category as he became the 23rd Bruin enshrined.

Sinden was a top amateur player in Canada as a defenseman who captained his Whitby Dunlops team to both the 1957 Allan Cup as Canada's Senior Amateur Champions and the 1958 World Championship title. He also competed in the 1960 Olympics in Squaw Valley, bringing a silver medal home to Canada.

He came to the Bruins organization in 1961 as he assumed the position of player-coach in Kingston, Ontario. After coaching Boston's minor league affiliate in Minneapolis, he became a player-coach in Oklahoma City and led that team to the 1966 CHL championship with eight consecutive victories. He moved to Boston to assume the Bruins head coaching reins in 1966-67.

In 1972 he served as coach of Team Canada in the classic series between NHL players and the Soviet Union.

Sinden and his wife, Eleanor, reside in Winchester, MA. They have four daughters.

NHL Coaching Record

		Regular Season					Playoffs			
Season	Team	Games	W	L	T	%	Games	W	L	%
1966-67	Boston	70	17	43	10	.314				
1967-68	Boston	74	37	27	10	.568	4	0	4	.000
1968-69	Boston	76	42	18	16	.658	10	6	4	.600
1969-70	Boston	76	40	17	19	.651	14	12	2	.857*
1979-80	Boston	7	6	1	0	.857	10	4	6	.400
1984-85	Boston	24	11	10	3	.521	5	2	3	.400
	NHL Totals	**327**	**153**	**116**	**58**	**.557**	**43**	**24**	**19**	**.558**

* Stanley Cup win.

Club Directory

FleetCenter
One FleetCenter, Suite 250
Boston, Massachusetts
02114-1303
Phone **617/624-1900**
FAX 617/523-7184
Capacity: 17,565

Executive	
Owner and Governor	Jeremy M. Jacobs
Alternate Governor	Louis Jacobs
President, General Manager and Alternate Governor	Harry Sinden
Vice President	Tom Johnson
Assistant General Manager	Mike O'Connell
Senior Assistant to the President	Nate Greenberg
General Counsel	Michael Wall
Director of Administration	Dale Hamilton
Assistant to the President	Joe Curnane
Team Travel Coordinator/Administrative Assistant	Carol Gould
Receptionist	Karen Ondo
Coaching Staff	
Coach	Pat Burns
Assistant Coaches	Jacques Laperriere, Bobby Francis
Coach, Providence Bruins	Peter Laviolette
Scouting Staff	
Director of Scouting	Scott Bradley
Director of Development	Bob Tindall
Director of Scouting Information	Jeff Gorton
Scouting Staff	Don Saatzer, Jean Ratelle, Daniel Dore, Scott McLellan, Don Matheson, Ernie Gare, Svenake Svensson, Yuri Karmanov, Gerry Cheevers, Jim Morrison, Tim O'Connell, Tom McVie
Communications Staff	
Director of Media Relations	Heidi Holland
Media Relations Assistant	Greg Post
Director of Marketing and Community Relations	Sue Byrne
Corporate Marketing Manager	Brian Oates
Community Relations Coordinator	Heather Wright
Director of Alumni Community Relations	John Bucyk
Administrative Assistant, Alumni Office	Mal Viola
Medical and Training Staff	
Athletic Trainer	Don Del Negro
Physical Therapist	Scott Waugh
Equipment Manager	Peter Henderson
Assistant Equipment Manager	Keith Robinson
Team Physicians	Dr. Bertram Zarins, Dr. Ashby Moncure, Dr. John J. Boyle
Team Dentists	Dr. Edwin Riley, DMD; Dr. Bruce Donoff, DMD, MD; Dr. Robert Amato, DMD
Team Opthalmic Consultant	Dr. Bradford Shingleton
Team Psychologist	Dr. Fred Neff
Ticketing and Finance Staff	
Director of Ticket Operations	Matt Brennan
Assistant Director of Ticket Operations	Jim Foley
Ticket Office Assistant	Justin Brennan
Ticket Office Receptionist	Jo-Ann Connolly-White
Controller	Richard McGlinchey
Payroll Manager	Barbara Johnson
Accounts Payable	Linda Bartlett
Television and Radio	
Broadcasters	(UPN38 WSBK-TV) Dave Shea and Andy Brickley (NESN) Dale Arnold and Gord Kluzak (Radio) Bob Neumeier and Bob Beers
TV Channels	New England Sports Network (NESN) and UPN38 WSBK-TV
Radio Station	WBZ (1030 AM) and Bruins Radio Network

General Managers' History

Art Ross, 1924-25 to 1953-54; Lynn Patrick, 1954-55 to 1964-65; Hap Emms, 1965-66, 1966-67; Milt Schmidt, 1967-68 to 1971-72; Harry Sinden, 1972-73 to date.

Captains' History

No captain, 1924-25 to 1926-27; Lionel Hitchman, 1927-28 to 1930-31; George Owen, 1931-32; Dit Clapper, 1932-33 to 1937-38; Cooney Weiland, 1938-39; Dit Clapper, 1939-40 to 1945-46; Dit Clapper and John Crawford, 1946-47; John Crawford 1947-48 to 1949-50; Milt Schmidt, 1950-51 to 1953-54; Milt Schmidt, Ed Sanford, 1954-55; Fern Flaman, 1955-56 to 1960-61; Don McKenney, 1961-62, 1962-63; Leo Boivin, 1963-64 to 1965-66; John Bucyk, 1966-67; no captain, 1967-68 to 1972-73; John Bucyk, 1973-74 to 1976-77; Wayne Cashman, 1977-78 to 1982-83; Terry O'Reilly, 1983-84, 1984-85; Ray Bourque, Rick Middleton (co-captains) 1985-86 to 1987-88; Ray Bourque, 1988-89 to date.

Buffalo Sabres

1997-98 Results: 36W-29L-17T 89PTS. Third, Northeast Division

Dominik Hasek's 13 shutouts in 1997-98 were the most in the NHL since Tony Esposito had 15 in 1969-70. Hasek earned the Vezina Trophy for the fourth time in his career and became the first goalie to win the Hart Trophy in back-to-back seasons.

1998-99 Schedule

Oct.	Sat.	10	at Dallas		Mon.	18	at Florida
	Mon.	12	at Colorado		Tue.	19	at Tampa Bay
	Fri.	16	Florida		Tue.	26	Phoenix
	Sat.	17	at Montreal		Thu.	28	Nashville
	Fri.	23	Washington		Sat.	30	Los Angeles
	Sat.	24	at NY Islanders	**Feb.**	Tue.	2	at Pittsburgh
	Tue.	27	at NY Rangers		Wed.	3	Colorado
	Fri.	30	Toronto		Sat.	6	at Montreal
	Sat.	31	at Toronto		Sun.	7	at Washington
Nov.	Tue.	3	Boston		Tue.	9	at Ottawa
	Sat.	7	at Philadelphia*		Thu.	11	Montreal
	Tue.	10	Ottawa		Sat.	13	NY Islanders
	Thu.	12	at Washington		Mon.	15	Carolina
	Sat.	14	Chicago		Wed.	17	Toronto
	Fri.	20	Toronto		Fri.	19	San Jose
	Sat.	21	at Toronto		Sun.	21	Detroit*
	Wed.	25	NY Rangers		Wed.	24	at Calgary
	Sat.	28	at Florida		Fri.	26	at Edmonton
	Sun.	29	at Tampa Bay		Sun.	28	at Vancouver
Dec.	Wed.	2	Florida	**Mar.**	Wed.	3	Edmonton
	Fri.	4	Philadelphia		Fri.	5	Dallas
	Sat.	5	at Nashville		Sun.	7	Philadelphia
	Tue.	8	at St. Louis		Mon.	8	at Carolina
	Fri.	11	NY Rangers		Thu.	11	Tampa Bay
	Sat.	12	at Boston		Sat.	13	Boston
	Fri.	18	Montreal		Mon.	15	NY Islanders
	Sat.	19	Carolina		Fri.	19	at NY Rangers
	Mon.	21	at Carolina		Tue.	23	at New Jersey
	Wed.	23	Tampa Bay		Wed.	24	at Detroit
	Sat.	26	at New Jersey		Sat.	27	at Pittsburgh*
	Mon.	28	New Jersey		Sun.	28	Pittsburgh*
	Wed.	30	Ottawa		Wed.	31	at Chicago
Jan.	Fri.	1	Anaheim*	**Apr.**	Sat.	3	at Montreal
	Sat.	2	Calgary		Mon.	5	Pittsburgh
	Wed.	6	at Anaheim		Tue.	6	at NY Islanders
	Thu.	7	at Los Angeles		Fri.	9	Florida
	Sat.	9	at San Jose		Sat.	10	at Ottawa
	Mon.	11	at Phoenix		Tue.	13	at Philadelphia
	Wed.	13	St. Louis		Wed.	14	New Jersey
	Fri.	15	Boston		Sat.	17	at Boston*
	Sat.	16	at Ottawa		Sun.	18	Washington*

* Denotes afternoon game.

Franchise date: May 22, 1970

29th NHL Season

NORTHEAST DIVISION

Year-by-Year Record

		Home			Road			Overall							
Season	**GP**	**W**	**L**	**T**	**W**	**L**	**T**	**W**	**L**	**T**	**GF**	**GA**	**Pts.**	**Finished**	**Playoff Result**
1997-98	82	20	13	8	16	16	9	36	29	17	211	187	89	3rd, Northeast Div.	Lost Conf. Final
1996-97	82	24	11	6	16	19	6	40	30	12	237	208	92	1st, Northeast Div.	Lost Conf. Semi-Final
1995-96	82	19	17	5	14	25	2	33	42	7	247	262	73	5th, Northeast Div.	Out of Playoffs
1994-95	48	15	8	1	7	11	6	22	19	7	130	119	51	4th, Northeast Div.	Lost Conf. Quarter-Final
1993-94	84	22	17	3	21	15	6	43	32	9	282	218	95	4th, Northeast Div.	Lost Conf. Quarter-Final
1992-93	84	25	15	2	13	21	8	38	36	10	335	297	86	4th, Adams Div.	Lost Div. Final
1991-92	80	22	13	5	9	24	7	31	37	12	289	299	74	3rd, Adams Div.	Lost Div. Semi-Final
1990-91	80	15	13	12	16	17	7	31	30	19	292	278	81	3rd, Adams Div.	Lost Div. Semi-Final
1989-90	80	27	11	2	18	16	6	45	27	8	286	248	98	2nd, Adams Div.	Lost Div. Semi-Final
1988-89	80	25	12	3	13	23	4	38	35	7	291	299	83	3rd, Adams Div.	Lost Div. Semi-Final
1987-88	80	19	14	7	18	18	4	37	32	11	283	305	85	3rd, Adams Div.	Lost Div. Semi-Final
1986-87	80	18	18	4	10	26	4	28	44	8	280	308	64	5th, Adams Div.	Out of Playoffs
1985-86	80	23	16	1	14	21	5	37	37	6	296	291	80	5th, Adams Div.	Out of Playoffs
1984-85	80	23	10	7	15	18	7	38	28	14	290	237	90	3rd, Adams Div.	Lost Div. Semi-Final
1983-84	80	25	9	6	23	16	1	48	25	7	315	257	103	2nd, Adams Div.	Lost Div. Semi-Final
1982-83	80	25	7	8	13	22	5	38	29	13	318	285	89	3rd, Adams Div.	Lost Div. Final
1981-82	80	23	8	9	16	18	6	39	26	15	307	273	93	3rd, Adams Div.	Lost Div. Semi-Final
1980-81	80	21	7	12	18	13	9	39	20	21	327	250	99	1st, Adams Div.	Lost Quarter-Final
1979-80	80	27	5	8	20	12	8	47	17	16	318	201	110	1st, Adams Div.	Lost Semi-Final
1978-79	80	19	13	8	17	15	8	36	28	16	280	263	88	2nd, Adams Div.	Lost Prelim. Round
1977-78	80	25	7	8	19	12	9	44	19	17	288	215	105	2nd, Adams Div.	Lost Quarter-Final
1976-77	80	27	8	5	21	16	3	48	24	8	301	220	104	2nd, Adams Div.	Lost Quarter-Final
1975-76	80	28	7	5	18	14	8	46	21	13	339	240	105	2nd, Adams Div.	Lost Quarter-Final
1974-75	80	28	6	6	21	10	9	49	16	15	354	240	113	1st, Adams Div.	Lost Final
1973-74	78	23	10	6	9	24	6	32	34	12	242	250	76	5th, East Div.	Out of Playoffs
1972-73	78	30	6	3	7	21	11	37	27	14	257	219	88	4th, East Div.	Lost Quarter-Final
1971-72	78	11	19	9	5	24	10	16	43	19	203	289	51	6th, East Div.	Out of Playoffs
1970-71	78	16	13	10	8	26	5	24	39	15	217	291	63	5th, East Div.	Out of Playoffs

1998-99 Player Personnel

FORWARDS	HT	WT	S	Place of Birth	Date	1997-98 Club
AUDETTE, Donald	5-8	184	R	Laval, Que.	9/23/69	Buffalo
BARNABY, Matthew	6-0	188	L	Ottawa, Ont.	5/4/73	Buffalo
BIENVENUE, Daniel	6-0	196	L	Val d'Or, Que.	6/10/77	Rochester-South Carolina
BROWN, Curtis	6-0	190	L	Unity, Sask.	2/12/76	Buffalo
CUNNEYWORTH, Randy	6-0	198	L	Etobicoke, Ont.	5/10/61	Ottawa
DAVIDSON, Matt	6-2	190	R	Flin Flon, Man.	8/9/77	Rochester
DUTIAUME, Mark	6-0	200	L	Winnipeg, Man.	1/31/77	Rochester-South Carolina
FISHER, Craig	6-3	180	L	Oshawa, Ont.	6/30/70	Kolner Haie
GOLDADE, Aaron	6-0	180	L	Prince Albert, Sask.	7/30/80	Brandon
GROSEK, Michal	6-2	207	R	Vyskov, Czech.	6/1/75	Buffalo
HAMEL, Denis	6-2	200	L	Lachute, Que.	5/10/77	Rochester
HOLZINGER, Brian	5-11	190	R	Parma, OH	10/10/72	Buffalo
KOTALIK, Ales	6-1	198	R	Jindrichuv Hradec, Czech.	12/23/78	HC Budejovice
KRISTEK, Jaroslav	6-0	183	L	Zlin, Czechoslovakia	3/16/80	ZPS Zlin-Prostejov
KRUSE, Paul	6-0	202	L	Merritt, B.C.	3/15/70	NY Islanders-Buffalo
MILLEY, Norman	5-11	185	R	Toronto, Ont.	2/14/80	Sudbury
NICHOL, Scott	5-8	160	R	Edmonton, Alta.	12/31/74	Buffalo-Rochester
PANDOLFO, Mike	6-3	226	L	Winchester, MA	9/15/79	St. Sebastians
PECA, Michael	5-11	181	R	Toronto, Ont.	3/26/74	Buffalo
PETERS, Andrew	6-4	195	L	St. Catharines, Ont.	5/5/80	Oshawa
PITTIS, Domenic	5-11	190	L	Calgary, Alta.	10/1/74	Syracuse
PLANTE, Derek	5-11	181	L	Cloquet, MN	1/17/71	Buffalo
PRIMEAU, Wayne	6-3	220	L	Scarborough, Ont.	6/4/76	Buffalo
RASMUSSEN, Erik	6-2	205	L	Minneapolis, MN	3/28/77	Buffalo-Rochester
RAY, Rob	6-0	203	L	Stirling, Ont.	6/8/68	Buffalo
SANDERSON, Geoff	6-0	190	L	Hay River, N.W.T.	2/1/72	Carolina-Vancouver-Buffalo
SATAN, Miroslav	6-1	195	L	Topolcany, Czech.	10/22/74	Buffalo
VARADA, Vaclav	6-0	200	L	Vsetin, Czech.	4/26/76	Buffalo-Rochester
WALBY, Steffon	6-1	198	R	Madison, WI	11/22/72	Fort Wayne
WARD, Dixon	6-0	200	R	Leduc, Alta.	9/23/68	Buffalo
ZANUTTO, Mike	6-0	190	L	Burlington, Ont.	1/1/77	Rochester-South Carolina
DEFENSEMEN						
GRAND PIERRE, Jean-Luc	6-3	207	R	Montreal, Que.	2/2/77	Rochester
HOLLAND, Jason	6-2	193	R	Morinville, Alta.	4/30/76	NY Islanders-Kentucky-Rochester
HURLBUT, Mike	6-2	200	L	Massena, NY	10/7/66	Buffalo-Rochester
KALININ, Dmitri	6-2	198	L	Chelyabinsk, USSR	7/22/80	Chelyabinsk
McKEE, Jay	6-3	195	L	Kingston, Ont.	9/8/77	Buffalo-Rochester
NDUR, Rumun	6-2	200	L	Zaria, Nigeria	7/7/75	Buffalo-Rochester
SARICH, Cory	6-3	175	R	Saskatoon, Sask.	8/16/78	Saskatoon-Canada-Seattle
SHANNON, Darryl	6-2	208	L	Barrie, Ont.	6/21/68	Buffalo
SMEHLIK, Richard	6-3	222	L	Ostrava, Czech.	1/23/70	Buffalo-Czech Republic
WILSON, Mike	6-6	212	L	Brampton, Ont.	2/26/75	Buffalo
WOOLLEY, Jason	6-1	188	L	Toronto, Ont.	7/27/69	Buffalo
ZHITNIK, Alexei	5-11	204	L	Kiev, USSR	10/10/72	Buffalo-Russia

GOALTENDERS	HT	WT	C	Place of Birth	Date	1997-98 Club
BIRON, Martin	6-1	154	L	Lac St. Charles, Que.	8/15/77	South Carolina-Rochester
HASEK, Dominik	5-11	168	L	Pardubice, Czech.	1/29/65	Buffalo-Czech Republic
ROLOSON, Dwayne	6-1	190	L	Simcoe, Ont.	10/12/69	Calgary-Saint John

General Manager

REGIER, DARCY
General Manager, Buffalo Sabres. Born in Swift Current, Sask., Nov. 27, 1957.

Darcy Regier became the sixth general manager of the Buffalo Sabres on June 11, 1997 after a lengthy management apprenticeship in the New York Islanders organization. As a player, Regier played eight pro seasons, including parts of the 1982-83 and 1983-84 campaigns with the New York Islanders.

He began his career as an administrator with the Islanders in 1984-85 and went on to serve in a variety of capacities including director of administration, assistant director of hockey operations, assistant coach and assistant general manager. He also served as an assistant coach with Hartford in 1991-92.

While with the Islanders, Regier benefitted from working with talented managers and coaches including Bill Torrey and Al Arbour. As a minor pro player with Indianapolis of the CHL he became associated with another important influence on his hockey career, current Detroit Red Wing executive Jim Devellano.

Regier and his wife Kathy have three sons: Jonathan, 17; Justin, 13; and Jarrett, 5.

Head Coach

RUFF, LINDY
Head Coach, Buffalo Sabres. Born in Warburg, Alta., February, 17, 1960.

A former captain of the Sabres, Lindy Ruff was appointed as the club's 15th head coach on July 21, 1997. As a player, Ruff was drafted 32nd overall by the Sabres in the 1979 Entry Draft. He played both defense and left wing in an NHL career that spanned 12 seasons including 608 regular-season games with Buffalo. He became a playing assistant coach with Rochester of the AHL in 1991-92 and San Diego of the IHL in 1992-93. Ruff's San Diego club set a pro hockey record with 62 wins. In 1993-94 he became an NHL assistant coach for the Florida Panthers, handling the defense and penalty killing units for coach Roger Neilson.

Ruff and his wife Gaye have four children: Brett, 9; Eryn, 7; and twins Brian and Madeleine, 4.

Coaching Record

		Regular Season					Playoffs			
Season	**Team**	**Games**	**W**	**L**	**T**	**%**	**Games**	**W**	**L**	**%**
1997-98	Buffalo (NHL)	82	36	29	17	.543	15	10	5	.667

1997-98 Scoring

* – rookie

Regular Season

Pos	#	Player	Team	GP	G	A	Pts	+/–	PIM	PP	SH	GW	GT	S	%
L	81	Miroslav Satan	BUF	79	22	24	46	2	34	9	0	4	0	139	15.8
D	44	Alexei Zhitnik	BUF	78	15	30	45	19	102	2	3	3	2	191	7.9
R	28	Donald Audette	BUF	75	24	20	44	10	59	10	0	5	1	198	12.1
C	27	Michael Peca	BUF	61	18	22	40	12	57	6	5	1	1	132	13.6
C	19	Brian Holzinger	BUF	69	14	21	35	-2	36	4	2	1	1	116	12.1
D	5	Jason Woolley	BUF	71	9	26	35	8	35	3	0	2	1	129	7.0
C	26	Derek Plante	BUF	72	13	21	34	8	26	5	0	1	0	150	8.7
L	18	Michal Grosek	BUF	67	10	20	30	9	60	2	0	1	0	114	8.8
L	80	Geoff Sanderson	CAR	40	7	10	17	-4	14	2	0	0	1	96	7.3
			VAN	9	0	3	3	-1	4	0	0	0	0	29	0.0
			BUF	26	4	5	9	6	20	0	0	2	0	72	5.6
			TOTAL	75	11	18	29	1	38	2	0	2	1	197	5.6
R	36	Matthew Barnaby	BUF	72	5	20	25	8	289	0	0	2	0	96	5.2
L	37	Curtis Brown	BUF	63	12	12	24	11	34	1	1	2	1	91	13.2
R	15	Dixon Ward	BUF	71	10	13	23	9	42	0	2	3	1	99	10.1
D	8	Darryl Shannon	BUF	76	3	19	22	26	56	1	0	1	0	85	3.5
D	42	Richard Smehlik	BUF	72	3	17	20	11	62	0	1	0	0	90	3.3
D	74	Jay McKee	BUF	56	1	13	14	-1	42	0	0	0	0	55	1.8
C	22	Wayne Primeau	BUF	69	6	6	12	9	87	2	0	1	0	51	11.8
R	25 *	Vaclav Varada	BUF	27	5	6	11	0	15	0	0	1	1	27	18.5
L	12	Randy Burridge	BUF	30	4	6	10	0	0	1	0	1	0	40	10.0
L	24	Paul Kruse	NYI	62	6	1	7	-12	138	0	0	2	1	44	13.6
			BUF	12	1	1	2	1	49	0	0	0	0	8	12.5
			TOTAL	74	7	2	9	-11	187	0	0	2	1	52	13.5
D	4	Mike Wilson	BUF	66	4	4	8	13	48	0	0	1	0	52	7.7
R	32	Rob Ray	BUF	63	2	4	6	2	234	1	0	1	0	19	10.5
C	9 *	Erik Rasmussen	BUF	21	2	3	5	2	14	0	0	0	0	28	7.1
D	6	Bob Boughner	BUF	69	1	3	4	5	165	0	0	0	0	26	3.8
G	39	Dominik Hasek	BUF	72	0	2	2	0	12	0	0	0	0	0	0.0
D	40 *	Rumun Ndur	BUF	1	0	0	0	-1	2	0	0	0	0	0	0.0
D	21	Mike Hurlbut	BUF	3	0	0	0	-1	2	0	0	0	0	3	0.0
C	45 *	Scott Nichol	BUF	3	0	0	0	0	4	0	0	0	0	5	0.0
G	31 *	Steve Shields	BUF	16	0	0	0	0	17	0	0	0	0	0	0.0

Goaltending

No.	Goaltender	GPI	Mins	Avg	W	L	T	EN	SO	GA	SA	S%
39	Dominik Hasek	72	4220	2.09	33	23	13	3	13	147	2149	.932
31	* Steve Shields	16	785	2.83	3	6	4	0	0	37	408	.909
	Totals	**82**	**5019**	**2.24**	**36**	**29**	**17**	**3**	**13**	**187**	**2560**	**.927**

Playoffs

Pos	#	Player	Team	GP	G	A	Pts	+/–	PIM	PP	SH	GW	OT	S	%
R	36	Matthew Barnaby	BUF	15	7	6	13	6	22	3	0	1	0	25	28.0
R	28	Donald Audette	BUF	15	5	8	13	-4	10	3	0	2	0	31	16.1
C	19	Brian Holzinger	BUF	15	4	7	11	-2	18	1	1	0	0	24	16.7
R	15	Dixon Ward	BUF	15	3	8	11	8	6	0	0	0	0	29	10.3
D	5	Jason Woolley	BUF	15	2	9	11	8	12	1	0	1	0	32	6.3
L	18	Michal Grosek	BUF	15	6	4	10	5	28	2	0	3	1	40	15.0
L	81	Miroslav Satan	BUF	14	5	4	9	-9	4	4	0	1	0	20	25.0
R	25 *	Vaclav Varada	BUF	15	3	4	7	3	18	0	0	0	0	24	12.5
D	8	Darryl Shannon	BUF	15	2	4	6	0	8	0	1	0	0	15	13.3
C	27	Michael Peca	BUF	13	3	2	5	4	8	0	0	1	1	24	12.5
L	80	Geoff Sanderson	BUF	14	3	1	4	0	4	1	0	1	1	25	12.0
C	22	Wayne Primeau	BUF	14	1	3	4	-1	6	0	0	0	0	10	10.0
D	6	Bob Boughner	BUF	14	0	4	4	9	15	0	0	0	0	7	0.0
L	37	Curtis Brown	BUF	13	1	2	3	6	10	1	0	0	0	23	4.3
C	26	Derek Plante	BUF	11	0	3	3	1	10	0	0	0	0	13	0.0
D	44	Alexei Zhitnik	BUF	15	0	3	3	1	36	0	0	0	0	24	0.0
D	42	Richard Smehlik	BUF	15	0	2	2	3	6	0	0	0	0	12	0.0
L	24	Paul Kruse	BUF	1	1	0	1	1	4	0	0	0	0	2	50.0
D	4	Mike Wilson	BUF	15	0	1	1	-4	13	0	0	0	0	16	0.0
D	74	Jay McKee	BUF	1	0	0	0	-1	0	0	0	0	0	0	0.0
R	32	Rob Ray	BUF	10	0	0	0	-2	24	0	0	0	0	2	0.0
G	39	Dominik Hasek	BUF	15	0	0	0	0	4	0	0	0	0	0	0.0

Goaltending

No.	Goaltender	GPI	Mins	Avg	W	L	EN	SO	GA	SA	S%
39	Dominik Hasek	15	948	2.03	10	5	0	1	32	514	.938
	Totals	**15**	**949**	**2.02**	**10**	**5**	**0**	**1**	**32**	**514**	**.938**

General Managers' History

Punch Imlach, 1970-71 to 1977-78; John Anderson, 1978-79; Scotty Bowman, 1979-80 to 1985-86; Scotty Bowman and Gerry Meehan, 1986-87; Gerry Meehan, 1987-88 to 1992-93; John Muckler, 1993-94 to 1996-97; Darcy Regier, 1997-98 to date.

Coaching History

Punch Imlach, 1970-71; Punch Imlach, Floyd Smith and Joe Crozier, 1971-72; Joe Crozier, 1972-73, 1973-74; Floyd Smith, 1974-75 to 1976-77; Marcel Pronovost, 1977-78; Marcel Pronovost and Billy Inglis, 1978-79; Scotty Bowman, 1979-80; Roger Neilson, 1980-81; Jim Roberts and Scotty Bowman, 1981-82; Scotty Bowman 1982-83 to 1984-85; Jim Schoenfeld and Scotty Bowman, 1985-86; Scotty Bowman, Craig Ramsay and Ted Sator, 1986-87; Ted Sator, 1987-88, 1988-89; Rick Dudley, 1989-90, 1990-91; Rick Dudley and John Muckler, 1991-92; John Muckler, 1992-93 to 1994-95; Ted Nolan, 1995-96, 1996-97; Lindy Ruff, 1997-98 to date.

Club Records

Team

(Figures in brackets for season records are games played; records for fewest points, wins, ties, losses, goals, goals against are for 70 or more games)

Most Points	**113**	1974-75 (80)
Most Wins	**49**	1974-75 (80)
Most Ties	**21**	1980-81 (80)
Most Losses	**44**	1986-87 (80)
Most Goals	**354**	1974-75 (80)
Most Goals Against	**308**	1986-87 (80)
Fewest Points	**51**	1971-72 (78)
Fewest Wins	**16**	1971-72 (78)
Fewest Ties	**6**	1985-86 (80)
Fewest Losses	**16**	1974-75 (80)
Fewest Goals	**203**	1971-72 (78)
Fewest Goals Against	**187**	1997-98 (82)
Longest Winning Streak		
Overall	**10**	Jan. 4-23/84
Home	**12**	Nov. 12/72-Jan. 7/73, Oct. 13-Dec. 10/89
Away	***10**	Dec. 10/83-Jan. 23/84
Longest Undefeated Streak		
Overall	**14**	Mar. 6-Apr. 6/80 (8 wins, 6 ties)
Home	**21**	Oct. 8/72-Jan. 7/73 (18 wins, 3 ties)
Away	***10**	Dec. 10/83-Jan. 23/84 (10 wins)
Longest Losing Streak		
Overall	**7**	Oct. 25-Nov. 8/70, Apr. 3-15/93, Oct. 9-22/93
Home	**6**	Oct. 10-Nov. 10/93, Mar. 3-Apr. 3/96
Away	**7**	Oct. 14-Nov. 7/70, Feb. 6-27/71, Jan. 10-Feb. 3/96
Longest Winless Streak		
Overall	**12**	Nov. 23-Dec. 20/91 (8 losses, 4 ties)
Home	**12**	Jan. 27-Mar. 10/91 (7 losses, 5 ties)
Away	**23**	Oct. 30/71-Feb. 19/72 (15 losses, 8 ties)
Most Shutouts, Season	**13**	1997-98 (82)
Most PIM, Season	**2,712**	1991-92 (80)
Most Goals, Game	**14**	Jan. 21/75 (Wsh. 2 at Buf. 14), Mar. 19/81 (Tor. 4 at Buf. 14)

Individual

Most Seasons	**17**	Gilbert Perreault
Most Games	**1,191**	Gilbert Perreault
Most Goals, Career	**512**	Gilbert Perreault
Most Assists, Career	**814**	Gilbert Perreault
Most Points, Career	**1,326**	Gilbert Perreault
Most PIM, Career	**2,268**	Rob Ray
Most Shutouts, Career	**32**	Dominik Hasek
Longest Consecutive Games Streak	**776**	Craig Ramsay (Mar. 27/73-Feb. 10/83)
Most Goals, Season	**76**	Alexander Mogilny (1992-93)
Most Assists, Season	**95**	Pat LaFontaine (1992-93)
Most Points, Season	**148**	Pat LaFontaine (1992-93; 53G, 95A)
Most PIM, Season	**354**	Rob Ray (1991-92)
Most Points, Defenseman, Season	**81**	Phil Housley (1989-90; 21G, 60A)
Most Points, Center, Season	**148**	Pat LaFontaine (1992-93; 53G, 95A)
Most Points, Right Wing, Season	**127**	Alexander Mogilny (1992-93; 76G, 51A)
Most Points, Left Wing, Season	**95**	Rick Martin (1974-75; 52G, 43A)
Most Points, Rookie, Season	**74**	Rick Martin (1971-72; 44G, 30A)
Most Shutouts, Season	**13**	Dominik Hasek (1997-98)
Most Goals, Game	**5**	Dave Andreychuk (Feb. 6/86)
Most Assists, Game	**5**	Gilbert Perreault (Feb. 1/76, Mar. 9/80, Jan. 4/84), Dale Hawerchuk (Jan. 15/92), Pat LaFontaine (Dec. 31/92, Feb. 10/93)
Most Points, Game	**7**	Gilbert Perreault (Feb. 1/76; 2G, 5A)

* NHL Record.

Retired Numbers

2	Tim Horton	1972-1974
7	Rick Martin	1971-1981
11	Gilbert Perreault	1970-1987
14	Rene Robert	1971-1979

Captains' History

Floyd Smith, 1970-71; Gerry Meehan, 1971-72 to 1973-74; Gerry Meehan and Jim Schoenfeld, 1974-75; Jim Schoenfeld, 1975-76, 1976-77; Danny Gare, 1977-78 to 1980-81; Danny Gare and Gilbert Perreault, 1981-82; Gilbert Perreault, 1982-83 to 1985-86; Gilbert Perreault and Lindy Ruff, 1986-87; Lindy Ruff, 1987-88; Lindy Ruff and Mike Foligno, 1988-89; Mike Foligno, 1989-90; Mike Foligno and Mike Ramsey, 1990-91; Mike Ramsey, 1991-92; Mike Ramsey and Pat LaFontaine, 1992-93; Pat LaFontaine and Alexander Mogilny, 1993-94; Pat LaFontaine, 1994-95 to 1996-97; Michael Peca and Donald Audette, 1997-98; Michael Peca, 1998-99.

All-time Record vs. Other Clubs

Regular Season

	At Home							On Road							Total						
	GP	W	L	T	GF	GA	PTS	GP	W	L	T	GF	GA	PTS	GP	W	L	T	GF	GA	PTS
Anaheim	4	2	1	1	10	7	5	4	2	2	0	10	10	4	8	4	3	1	20	17	9
Boston	92	45	32	15	343	283	105	92	28	52	12	281	362	68	184	73	84	27	624	645	173
Calgary	41	23	13	5	170	124	51	41	16	15	10	136	143	42	82	39	28	15	306	267	93
Carolina	65	38	20	7	266	199	83	66	30	26	10	202	200	70	131	68	46	17	468	399	153
Chicago	48	29	13	6	181	127	64	46	15	25	6	127	152	36	94	44	38	12	308	279	100
Colorado	59	34	16	9	237	191	77	59	18	30	11	184	221	47	118	52	46	20	421	412	124
Dallas	48	25	13	10	175	130	60	49	20	23	6	148	157	46	97	45	36	16	323	287	106
Detroit	48	32	9	7	213	134	71	50	18	27	5	150	186	41	98	50	36	12	363	320	112
Edmonton	26	10	10	6	104	98	26	25	5	18	2	67	106	12	51	15	28	8	171	204	38
Florida	10	7	2	1	38	14	15	9	4	5	0	28	27	8	19	11	7	1	66	41	23
Los Angeles	48	24	15	9	195	145	57	49	22	18	9	173	168	53	97	46	33	18	368	313	110
Montreal	87	43	25	19	271	239	105	87	26	49	12	264	351	64	174	69	74	31	535	590	169
New Jersey	42	27	10	5	181	131	59	42	22	12	8	154	130	52	84	49	22	13	335	261	111
NY Islanders	49	26	16	7	174	141	59	49	20	21	8	136	142	48	98	46	37	15	310	283	107
NY Rangers	56	33	16	7	243	180	73	54	17	24	13	146	183	47	110	50	40	20	389	363	120
Ottawa	16	12	4	0	62	22	24	17	10	4	3	56	37	23	33	22	8	3	118	59	47
Philadelphia	51	25	20	6	179	157	56	55	13	32	10	145	200	36	106	38	52	16	324	357	92
Phoenix	25	20	2	3	115	61	43	25	12	11	2	87	83	26	50	32	13	5	202	144	69
Pittsburgh	59	30	13	16	247	159	76	59	16	29	14	194	229	46	118	46	42	30	441	388	122
St. Louis	47	29	12	6	193	145	64	46	14	26	6	120	168	34	93	43	38	12	313	313	98
San Jose	7	7	0	0	37	21	14	6	1	3	2	23	24	4	13	8	3	2	60	45	18
Tampa Bay	11	5	5	1	29	36	11	11	9	1	1	38	20	19	22	14	6	2	67	56	30
Toronto	53	33	16	4	223	151	70	52	24	19	9	192	159	57	105	57	35	13	415	310	127
Vancouver	48	24	16	8	176	142	56	47	15	22	10	155	176	40	95	39	38	18	331	318	96
Washington	44	29	9	6	182	121	64	44	26	11	7	164	118	59	88	55	20	13	346	239	123
Defunct Clubs	23	13	5	5	94	63	31	23	12	8	3	97	76	27	46	25	13	8	191	139	58
Totals	**1107**	**625**	**313**	**169**	**4338**	**3221**	**1419**	**1107**	**415**	**513**	**179**	**3477**	**3828**	**1009**	**2214**	**1040**	**826**	**348**	**7815**	**7049**	**2428**

Playoffs

	Series	W	L	GP	W	L	T	GF	GA	Last Mtg.	Round	Result
Boston	6	1	5	33	14	19	0	113	132	1993	DSF	W 4-0
Chicago	2	2	0	9	8	1	0	36	17	1980	QF	W 4-0
Colorado	2	0	2	8	2	6	0	27	35	1985	DSF	L 2-3
Dallas	2	1	1	7	3	4	0	28	26	1981	QF	L 1-4
Montreal	7	3	4	35	17	18	0	111	124	1998	CSF	W 4-0
New Jersey	1	0	1	7	3	4	0	14	14	1994	CQF	L 3-4
NY Islanders	3	0	3	16	4	12	0	45	59	1980	SF	L 2-4
NY Rangers	1	1	0	3	2	1	0	11	6	1978	PR	W 2-1
Ottawa	1	1	0	7	4	3	0	14	13	1997	CQF	W 4-3
Philadelphia	5	1	4	26	9	17	0	67	83	1998	CQF	W 4-1
Pittsburgh	1	0	1	3	1	2	0	9	9	1979	PR	L 1-2
St. Louis	1	1	0	3	2	1	0	7	8	1976	PR	W 2-1
Vancouver	2	2	0	7	6	1	0	28	14	1981	PR	W 3-0
Washington	1	0	1	6	2	4	0	11	13	1998	CF	L 2-4
Totals	**35**	**13**	**22**	**170**	**77**	**93**	**0**	**521**	**546**			

Calgary totals include Atlanta, 1972-73 to 1979-80. Carolina totals include Hartford, 1979-80 to 1996-97.
Colorado totals include Quebec, 1979-80 to 1994-95. Dallas totals include Minnesota, 1970-71 to 1992-93.
New Jersey totals include Kansas City, 1974-75 to 1975-76, and Colorado Rockies, 1976-77 to 1981-82.
Phoenix totals include Winnipeg, 1979-80 to 1995-96.

Playoff Results 1998-94

Year	Round	Opponent	Result	GF	GA
1998	CF	Washington	L 2-4	11	13
	CSF	Montreal	W 4-0	17	10
	CQF	Philadelphia	W 4-1	18	9
1997	CSF	Philadelphia	L 1-4	13	21
	CQF	Ottawa	W 4-3	14	13
1995	CQF	Philadelphia	L 1-4	13	18
1994	CQF	New Jersey	L 3-4	14	14

Abbreviations: Round: CF – conference final; **CQF** – conference quarter-final; **CSF** – conference semi-final; **DSF** – division semi-final; **SF** – semi-final; **QF** – quarter-final; **PR** – preliminary round.

1997-98 Results

Oct.	1	at	St. Louis	3-1
	3	at	Washington	2-6
	5	at	Tampa Bay	1-1
	7		Dallas	2-4
	9		Washington	5-2
	11	at	New Jersey	2-3
	15	at	Carolina	3-3
	17		Montreal	1-5
	19	at	Chicago	2-5
	22		Calgary	4-1
	26	at	Phoenix	1-6
	28	at	Colorado	2-3
	31	at	Carolina	3-2
Nov.	1	at	Florida	4-3
	6		Florida	2-4
	8	at	Pittsburgh	2-2
	10		Edmonton	4-4
	13		Washington	2-3
	15		New Jersey	2-3
	20	at	Boston	5-0
	22		NY Islanders	6-1
	24	at	Pittsburgh	1-5
	26		Philadelphia	1-3
	28		NY Rangers	3-3
Dec.	1	at	Philadelphia	1-1
	3		Anaheim	4-0
	5		Tampa Bay	4-0
	6	at	Ottawa	0-3
	11	at	Boston	1-2
	12		Carolina	3-2
	15	at	Dallas	4-8
	17	at	NY Islanders	0-4
	19		Montreal	1-0
	21	at	NY Rangers	2-0
	23		Detroit	1-3
	26		NY Rangers	3-0
	27	at	Carolina	1-4
	29		New Jersey	1-3
	31		Ottawa	3-0
Jan.	2		Colorado	2-2
	7	at	Anaheim	3-2
	8	at	Los Angeles	2-2
	10	at	San Jose	2-5
	14	at	Toronto	4-1
	15		Vancouver	6-2
	20	at	Philadelphia	0-3
	21		Carolina	2-1
	23		Tampa Bay	4-1
	27		St. Louis	3-3
	30		Phoenix	3-3
Feb.	1	at	Florida	5-2
	2	at	Tampa Bay	7-3
	4		Boston	2-2
	6		Pittsburgh	2-2
	7	at	Montreal	4-1
	25		Toronto	2-2
	26	at	Boston	1-1
Mar.	1	at	Washington	3-0
	2	at	NY Rangers	1-0
	6		NY Islanders	2-4
	7	at	Montreal	2-1
	10	at	NY Islanders	2-2
	12		San Jose	3-1
	14	at	Pittsburgh	1-2
	15		Pittsburgh	3-0
	17		Chicago	3-5
	19		Florida	6-1
	21		Boston	1-2
	24	at	Calgary	2-0
	26	at	Vancouver	5-2
	27	at	Edmonton	1-0
	29	at	Detroit	2-4
Apr.	1		Los Angeles	4-0
	3		Boston	5-4
	5		Ottawa	0-1
	8		Carolina	3-1
	10		Montreal	2-1
	11	at	Ottawa	4-4
	13		Philadelphia	2-1
	15	at	New Jersey	4-5
	18	at	Montreal	3-3
	19		Ottawa	1-2

Entry Draft Selections 1998-84

1998
Pick	
18	Dimitri Kalinin
34	Andrew Peters
47	Norman Milley
50	Jaroslav Kristek
77	Mike Pandolfo
137	Aaron Goldade
164	Ales Kotalik
191	Brad Moran
218	David Moravec
249	Edo Terglav

1997
Pick	
21	Mika Noronen
48	Henrik Tallinder
69	Maxim Afinogenov
75	Jeff Martin
101	Luc Theoret
128	Torrey Diroberto
156	Brian Campbell
184	Jeremy Adduono
212	Kamil Piros
238	Dylan Kemp

1996
Pick	
7	Erik Rasmussen
27	Cory Sarich
33	Darren Van Oene
54	Francois Methot
87	Kurt Walsh
106	Mike Martone
115	Alexei Tezikov
142	Ryan Davis
161	Darren Mortier
222	Scott Buhler

1995
Pick	
14	Jay McKee
16	Martin Biron
42	Mark Dutiaume
68	Mathieu Sunderland
94	Matt Davidson
111	Marian Menhart
119	Kevin Popp
123	Daniel Bienvenue
172	Brian Scott
198	Mike Zanutto
224	Rob Skrlac

1994
Pick	
17	Wayne Primeau
43	Curtis Brown
69	Rumun Ndur
121	Sergei Klimentjev
147	Cal Benazic
168	Steve Plouffe
173	Shane Hnidy
176	Steve Webb
199	Bob Westerby
225	Craig Millar
251	Mark Polak
277	Shayne Wright

1993
Pick	
38	Denis Tsygurov
64	Ethan Philpott
116	Richard Safarik
142	Kevin Pozzo
168	Sergei Petrenko
194	Mike Barrie
220	Barrie Moore
246	Chris Davis
272	Scott Nichol

1992
Pick	
11	David Cooper
35	Jozef Cierny
59	Ondrej Steiner
80	Dean Melanson
83	Matthew Barnaby
107	Markus Ketterer
108	Yuri Khmylev
131	Paul Rushforth
179	Dean Tiltgen
203	Todd Simon
227	Rick Kowalsky
251	Chris Clancy

1991
Pick	
13	Philippe Boucher
35	Jason Dawe
57	Jason Young
72	Peter Ambroziak
101	Steve Shields
123	Sean O'Donnell
124	Brian Holzinger
145	Chris Snell
162	Jiri Kuntos
189	Tony Iob
211	Spencer Meany
233	Mikhail Volkov
255	Michael Smith

1990
Pick	
14	Brad May
82	Brian McCarthy
97	Richard Smehlik
100	Todd Bojcun
103	Brad Pascall
142	Viktor Gordiyuk
166	Milan Nedoma
187	Jason Winch
208	Sylvain Naud
229	Kenneth Martin
250	Brad Rubachuk

1989
Pick	
14	Kevin Haller
56	John (Scott) Thomas
77	Doug MacDonald
98	Ken Sutton
107	Bill Pye
119	Mike Barkley
161	Derek Plante
183	Donald Audette
194	Mark Astley
203	John Nelson
224	Todd Henderson
245	Michael Bavis

1988
Pick	
13	Joel Savage
55	Darcy Loewen
76	Keith E. Carney
89	Alexander Mogilny
97	Robert Ray
106	David Di Vita
118	Mike McLaughlin
139	Mike Griffith
160	Daniel Ruoho
181	Wade Flaherty
223	Thomas Nieman
244	Robert Wallwork

1987
Pick	
1	Pierre Turgeon
22	Brad Miller
53	Andrew MacVicar
84	John Bradley
85	David Pergola
106	Chris Marshall
127	Paul Flanagan
148	Sean Dooley
153	Tim Roberts
169	Grant Tkachuk
190	Ian Herbers
211	David Littman
232	Allan MacIsaac

1986
Pick	
5	Shawn Anderson
26	Greg Brown
47	Bob Corkum
56	Kevin Kerr
68	David Baseggio
89	Larry Rooney
110	Miguel Baldris
131	Mike Hartman
152	Francois Guay
173	Shawn Whitham
194	Kenton Rein
215	Troy Arndt

1985
Pick	
14	Calle Johansson
35	Benoit Hogue
56	Keith Gretzky
77	Dave Moylan
98	Ken Priestlay
119	Joe Reekie
140	Petri Matikainen
161	Trent Kaese
182	Jiri Sejba
203	Boyd Sutton
224	Guy Larose
245	Ken Baumgartner

1984
Pick	
18	Mikael Andersson
39	Doug Trapp
60	Ray Sheppard
81	Bob Halkidis
102	Joey Rampton
123	James Gasseau
144	Darcy Wakaluk
165	Orvar Stambert
206	Brian McKinnon
226	Grant Delcourt
247	Sean Baker

Club Directory

Marine Midland Arena
One Seymour H. Knox III Plaza
Buffalo, NY 14203
Phone **716/855-4100**
Fax 716/855-4110
Ticket Office: 716/888-4000
Capacity: 18,595

Board of Niagara Frontier Hockey Management Corp. – General Partner

Chairman of the Board	John J. Rigas
Vice Chairman of the Board & Counsel	Robert O. Swados
Vice Chairman of the Board	Robert E. Rich Jr.
Chief Executive Officer	Timothy J. Rigas
Director	Michael J. Rigas
Director	George Strawbridge Jr.
Director	Seymour H. Knox IV

Partnership Board of Niagara Frontier Hockey L.P.
(includes above-listed Executives and Directors)
Edwin C. Andrews, Peter C. Andrews, William C. Cox III, John B. Fisher, George T. Gregory, John E. Houghton, Richard W. Rupp, Howard T. Saperston Jr., Paul A. Schoellkopf, William H. Weeks

Executive Department

Interim Vice President/Administration	Ron Bertovich
Senior Vice President/Legal & Business Affairs	Kevin Billet
Vice President/Corporate Relations	Seymour H. Knox IV
Vice President/Marketing	Christye Peterson
Vice President/Ticket Sales & Operations	John Sinclair
Assistant to the President	Chris Schoepflin
Special Consultant to the President	Joe Crozier
Executive Assistants	Debbie Driscoll, Eleanore MacKenzie

Hockey Department

General Manager	Darcy Regier
Assistant to the General Manager	Larry Carriere
Director of Player Personnel	Don Luce
Director of Team Operations	Jeff Holbrook
Professional Scout	Terry Martin
Scouting Staff	Don Barrie, Jim Benning, Paul Merritt, Mike Racicot, Rudy Migay, David Volek
Head Coach	Lindy Ruff
Associate Coach	Don Lever
Assistant Coach	Mike Ramsey
Strength & Conditioning Coach	Doug McKenney
Administrative Assistant Coach	Jon Christiano
Head Trainer/Massage Therapist	Jim Pizzutelli
Physical Therapist	Joe Acquino
Equipment Manager	Rip Simonick
Assistant Equipment Manager	George Babcock
Administrative Assistant	Elaine Burzynski
Team Travel Coordinator	Verna Wojcik

Medical

Club Doctor	John L. Butsch, M.D.
Orthopedic Consultant	John Marzo, M.D.
Club Dentist	Daniel Yustin, DDS, M.S.
Oral Surgeon	Steven Jensen, DDS
Team Psychologists	Max Offenberger, Ph.D., Dan Smith, Ph.D.

Legal

Associate Counsel	Richard Mugel

Administration

Human Resources Coordinator	Vanessa Barrons
Management Information Systems Manager	Ken Bass
Distribution Manager	Gerry Magill
Receptionists	Olive Anticola, Roza Barker

Broadcast Production

Director of Broadcast & Production Services	Joe Guarnieri
Broadcast Coordinator	Lisa Tzetzo
Editor/Technical Director	Eric Grossman
Producer	Lowell MacDonald
Feature Producer/Avid Editor	Martin McCreary
Director	Phil Mollica
Senior Commercial Producer/Editor	Joe Pinter
Broadcast Team:	Rick Jeanneret (play-by-play), Jim Lorentz (color commentary), Danny Gare (reporter)

Communications

Director of Communications	Michael Gilbert
Media Relations Director	Gil Chorbajian
Director of Information	Bob Schranz
Director of Alumni Relations	Larry Playfair
Corporate & Community Relations Liaison	Gilbert Perreault
Team Photographer	Bill Wippert

Empire Sports Sales

Director of Corporate Sales	Dan Rozanski
National Sales Manager	Nick DiVico
Senior Account Managers	Steve Cuccia, Mark Kennedy
Vendor Programs Manager	Jim Harrington
Account Manager	Mike Jones
Sales Support Account Executive	Len Synor
Traffic Coordinator	Corinne Moyer
Administrative Assistant	Krista Argeros

Finance

Controller	Chuck LaMattina
Financial Analyst	Elizabeth McPartland
Accounting Manager – Buffalo Sabres	Chris Ivansitz
Accounting Manager – Marine Midland Arena	Scott Haima
Payroll Manager	Birgid Haensel
Finance Assistant	Mary Jones
Finance Assistant	Sally Lippert
Staff Accountant	Dave Eisenreid

Marketing

Director of Canadian Marketing	Steve Katzman
Director of Promotions & Advertising	Tanya Isherwood
Director of Game Presentation & Special Events	Kathy Manley
Promotions & Advertising Coordinator	Tara Doster
Game Presentation Coordinator	Mark Mashiotta
Game Presentation/Matrix Coordinator	Dawn Reed
Rochester Area Representative	Gary Sajdak
Director of Community Relations	Ken Martin Jr.
Community Relations Coordinator	Deidre Daniels
Administrative Assistant	Donna Webb

Ticket Sales & Operations

Director of Ticket Sales	Gary Rabinowitz
Director of New Business Development	Nick Turano
Season & Group Account Representatives	Dan Carroll, Dave Forman Jr., Don Fornier, Keri Francis, Grant Weber
Sales Associate	Todd Langdon
Account Services Manager	Rose Thompson
Account Service Representatives	Roxanne Anderson, Gretchen Huzinec, Elaine Fredo
Box Office Manager	Mike Tout
Assistant Box Office Manager	Christopher Makowski
Group Sales Coordinator	Paul Barker
Ticket Administrators	Lisa Jacobs, Andrea Giambra, Marty Maloney, Cindi Reuther, Pete Riedy
Cash & Settlement Administrator	Jennifer Glowny
Database Manager	Mark Wittman

Merchandise

Director of Merchandise	Julie Regan
Merchandise Manager	Mike Kaminska
Store Manager	Tammy Preteroti
Inventory Control Manager	Glenn Barker
Administrative Assistant	Brenda Hawkins

Marine Midland Arena

Director of Facilities Management	Stan Makowski
Director of Event Booking	Jennifer Stich
Asst. Dir. of Event Booking	Bridgette Cassidy
Event Managers	Matt Rabinowitz, John Faso
Communications Engineer	Al Weissman
Utility Crew Manager	Bud Redding
Director of Suite Sales & Special Services	Mark Stone
Suite Services Manager	Sue Smith
Coordinator of Suite Services	Michelle Mitchell
Director of Lacrosse & Amateur Athletics	Kurt Silcott
Assistant Manager Lacrosse & Amateur Sports	Joe Baldini
Assistant Manager Lacrosse & Amateur Sports	Chris Colleary
Web site	www.sabres.com
Broadcasts	TV: Empire Sports Network, Radio: WHTT 104.1 FM

Calgary Flames

1997-98 Results: 26W-41L-15T 67PTS. Fifth, Pacific Division

Defenseman Derek Morris corrals a loose puck beside goalie Dwayne Roloson. Morris led all Flames rookies with 29 points (nine goals, 20 assists) in 1997-98 and was one of few Calgary players with a plus rating (+1).

1998-99 Schedule

Oct.	Fri.	9	San Jose
	Sat.	10	at San Jose
	Fri.	16	Toronto
	Sun.	18	at Detroit*
	Tue.	20	at Dallas
	Fri.	23	at Nashville
	Sat.	24	at St. Louis
	Wed.	28	Pittsburgh
	Fri.	30	Washington
Nov.	Sun.	1	at Chicago
	Tue.	3	at Detroit
	Fri.	6	Nashville
	Sun.	8	Colorado*
	Tue.	10	Los Angeles
	Thu.	12	Vancouver
	Sat.	14	Anaheim
	Mon.	16	Detroit
	Thu.	19	at Montreal
	Sat.	21	at Ottawa
	Mon.	23	at Toronto
	Wed.	25	at Nashville
	Fri.	27	Edmonton
	Sat.	28	Chicago
Dec.	Thu.	3	Tampa Bay
	Sat.	5	Phoenix
	Mon.	7	Dallas
	Fri.	11	at Tampa Bay
	Sat.	12	at Florida
	Mon.	14	at NY Rangers
	Thu.	17	at Philadelphia
	Fri.	18	at New Jersey
	Tue.	22	Vancouver
	Wed.	23	at Vancouver
	Sun.	27	Colorado
	Tue.	29	Philadelphia
	Thu.	31	Montreal
Jan.	Sat.	2	at Buffalo
	Mon.	4	at Boston
	Tue.	5	at Pittsburgh
	Fri.	8	Dallas
	Sun.	10	Florida*
	Wed.	13	at Anaheim
	Thu.	14	at Los Angeles
	Sat.	16	at San Jose
	Tue.	19	Detroit
	Thu.	21	at Colorado
	Thu.	28	Chicago
	Sat.	30	St. Louis
Feb.	Mon.	1	at Dallas
	Tue.	2	at Phoenix
	Thu.	4	Nashville
	Sat.	6	Ottawa
	Mon.	8	Edmonton
	Tue.	9	at Colorado
	Fri.	12	Boston
	Fri.	19	Anaheim
	Sat.	20	Los Angeles
	Mon.	22	NY Rangers
	Wed.	24	Buffalo
	Fri.	26	St. Louis
Mar.	Mon.	1	San Jose
	Fri.	5	at Vancouver
	Sat.	6	at Los Angeles
	Tue.	9	at St. Louis
	Fri.	12	at Carolina
	Sat.	13	at Washington
	Tue.	16	at Nashville
	Wed.	17	at Chicago
	Sun.	21	NY Islanders*
	Mon.	22	at Edmonton
	Thu.	25	Montreal
	Sat.	27	at Phoenix
	Sun.	28	at Anaheim
	Tue.	30	at Colorado
Apr.	Thu.	1	Phoenix
	Sat.	3	Toronto
	Wed.	7	at Edmonton
	Fri.	9	Edmonton
	Mon.	12	Vancouver
	Wed.	14	at Vancouver
	Thu.	15	Colorado
	Sat.	17	at Edmonton

* Denotes afternoon game.

Franchise date: June 6, 1972
Transferred from Atlanta to Calgary, June 24, 1980.

NORTHWEST DIVISION

27th NHL Season

Year-by-Year Record

		Home			Road			Overall							
Season	GP	W	L	T	W	L	T	W	L	T	GF	GA	Pts.	Finished	Playoff Result
1997-98	82	18	17	6	8	24	9	26	41	15	217	252	67	5th, Pacific Div.	Out of Playoffs
1996-97	82	21	18	2	11	23	7	32	41	9	214	239	73	5th, Pacific Div.	Out of Playoffs
1995-96	82	18	18	5	16	19	6	34	37	11	241	240	79	2nd, Pacific Div.	Lost Conf. Quarter-Final
1994-95	48	15	7	2	9	10	5	24	17	7	163	135	55	1st, Pacific Div.	Lost Conf. Quarter-Final
1993-94	84	25	12	5	17	17	8	42	29	13	302	256	97	1st, Pacific Div.	Lost Conf. Quarter-Final
1992-93	84	23	14	5	20	16	6	43	30	11	322	282	97	2nd, Smythe Div.	Lost Div. Semi-Final
1991-92	80	19	14	7	12	23	5	31	37	12	296	305	74	5th, Smythe Div.	Out of Playoffs
1990-91	80	29	8	3	17	18	5	46	26	8	344	263	100	2nd, Smythe Div.	Lost Div. Semi-Final
1989-90	80	28	7	5	14	16	10	42	23	15	348	265	99	1st, Smythe Div.	Lost Div. Semi-Final
1988-89	**80**	**32**	**4**	**4**	**22**	**13**	**5**	**54**	**17**	**9**	**354**	**226**	**117**	**1st, Smythe Div.**	**Won Stanley Cup**
1987-88	80	26	11	3	22	12	6	48	23	9	397	305	105	1st, Smythe Div.	Lost Div. Final
1986-87	80	25	13	2	21	18	1	46	31	3	318	289	95	2nd, Smythe Div.	Lost Div. Semi-Final
1985-86	80	23	11	6	17	20	3	40	31	9	354	315	89	2nd, Smythe Div.	Lost Final
1984-85	80	23	11	6	18	16	6	41	27	12	363	302	94	3rd, Smythe Div.	Lost Div. Semi-Final
1983-84	80	22	11	7	12	21	7	34	32	14	311	314	82	2nd, Smythe Div.	Lost Div. Final
1982-83	80	21	12	7	11	22	7	32	34	14	321	317	78	2nd, Smythe Div.	Lost Div. Final
1981-82	80	20	11	9	9	23	8	29	34	17	334	345	75	3rd, Smythe Div.	Lost Div. Semi-Final
1980-81	80	25	5	10	14	22	4	39	27	14	329	298	92	3rd, Patrick Div.	Lost Semi-Final
1979-80*	80	18	15	7	17	17	6	35	32	13	282	269	83	4th, Patrick Div.	Lost Prelim. Round
1978-79*	80	25	11	4	16	20	4	41	31	8	327	280	90	4th, Patrick Div.	Lost Prelim. Round
1977-78*	80	20	13	7	14	14	12	34	27	19	274	252	87	3rd, Patrick Div.	Lost Prelim. Round
1976-77*	80	22	11	7	12	23	5	34	34	12	264	265	80	3rd, Patrick Div.	Lost Prelim. Round
1975-76*	80	19	14	7	16	19	5	35	33	12	262	237	82	3rd, Patrick Div.	Lost Prelim. Round
1974-75*	80	24	9	7	10	22	8	34	31	15	243	233	83	4th, Patrick Div.	Out of Playoffs
1973-74*	78	17	15	7	13	19	7	30	34	14	214	238	74	4th, West Div.	Lost Quarter-Final
1972-73*	78	16	16	7	9	22	8	25	38	15	191	239	65	7th, West Div.	Out of Playoffs

* Atlanta Flames

1998-99 Player Personnel

FORWARDS	HT	WT	S	Place of Birth	Date	1997-98 Club
ANDERSSON, Erik	6-3	210	L	Stockholm, Sweden	8/19/71	Calgary-Saint John
BASSEN, Bob	5-10	185	L	Calgary, Alta.	5/6/65	Dallas
BEGIN, Steve	5-11	185	L	Trois-Rivieres, Que.	6/14/78	Val D'Or-Canada-Calgary
BETTS, Blair	6-1	183	L	Edmonton, Alta.	2/16/80	Prince George (WHL)
BRIGLEY, Travis	6-1	195	L	Coronation, Alta.	6/16/77	Calgary-Saint John
BROWN, Bobby	6-0	200	R	Winnipeg, Man.	9/26/75	Saint John-Dayton
BURE, Valeri	5-11	179	R	Moscow, USSR	6/13/74	Montreal-Calgary-Russia
CASSELS, Andrew	6-1	185	L	Bramalea, Ont.	7/23/69	Calgary
CLARK, Chris	6-0	200	R	Manchester, CT	3/8/76	Clarkson
COWAN, Jeff	6-2	185	L	Scarborough, Ont.	9/27/76	Saint John
DINGMAN, Chris	6-4	245	L	Edmonton, Alta.	7/6/76	Calgary
DOMENICHELLI, Hnat	6-0	190	L	Edmonton, Alta.	2/17/76	Calgary-Saint John
FATA, Rico	5-11	202	L	Sault Ste. Marie, Ont.	2/12/80	London
FLEURY, Theoren	5-6	180	R	Oxbow, Sask.	6/29/68	Calgary-Canada
HEALEY, Eric	6-0	195	L	Hull, MA	1/20/75	RPI
IGINLA, Jarome	6-1	202	R	Edmonton, Alta.	7/1/77	Calgary
IRVING, Joel	6-3	210	R	Lumsden, Sask.	1/2/76	Western Michigan
LANDRY, Eric	5-11	190	L	Gatineau, Que.	1/20/75	Calgary-Saint John
McINNIS, Marty	5-11	190	R	Hingham, MA.	6/2/70	Calgary
MURRAY, Marty	5-9	178	L	Deloraine, Man.	2/16/75	Calgary-Saint John
NYLANDER, Michael	5-11	195	L	Stockholm, Sweden	10/3/72	Calgary-Sweden
PANKEWIEZ, Greg	6-0	185	R	Drayton Valley, Alta.	6/13/75	Manitoba
PETROVICKY, Ronald	5-11	185	R	Zilina, Czech.	2/15/77	Regina
READY, Ryan	6-2	185	L	Peterborough, Ont.	11/7/78	Belleville
ROCHE, Dave	6-4	234	L	Lindsay, Ont.	6/13/75	Syracuse
St. LOUIS, Martin	5-9	180	L	Laval, Que.	8/9/71	Saint John-Cleveland
SHELLEY, Jody	6-3	228	L	Yarmouth, N.S.	2/7/76	Saint John-Dalhousie
STILLMAN, Cory	6-0	190	L	Peterborough, Ont.	12/20/73	Calgary
THOMPSON, Rocky	6-2	205	R	Calgary, Alta.	8/8/77	Calgary-Saint John
TKACZUK, Daniel	6-0	190	L	Toronto, Ont.	6/10/79	Barrie
TRIPP, John	6-2	207	R	Kingston, Ont.	5/4/77	Roanoke-Saint John
VARLAMOV, Sergei	5-11	190	L	Kiev, USSR	7/21/78	Swift Current-Cgy-Saint John
WARD, Ed	6-3	215	R	Edmonton, Alta.	11/10/69	Calgary
WIEMER, Jason	6-2	219	L	Kimberley, B.C.	4/14/76	Tampa Bay-Calgary
WILM, Clarke	6-0	202	L	Central Butte, Sask.	10/24/76	Saint John
DEFENSEMEN						
ALBELIN, Tommy	6-1	200	L	Stockholm, Sweden	5/21/64	Calgary-Sweden
ALLISON, Jamie	6-1	195	L	Lindsay, Ont.	5/13/75	Calgary-Saint John
BANCROFT, Steve	6-1	215	L	Toronto, Ont.	10/6/70	Saint John-Las Vegas
CHARRON, Eric	6-3	195	L	Verdun, Que.	1/14/70	Calgary-Saint John
COOPER, David	6-2	204	L	Ottawa, Ont.	11/2/73	Toronto-St. John's
ELICK, Mickey	6-1	200	L	Calgary, Alta.	3/17/74	Canada
GAUTHIER, Denis	6-2	220	L	Montreal, Que.	10/1/76	Calgary-Saint John
HELENIUS, Sami	6-5	225	L	Helsinki, Finland	1/22/74	Saint John-Las Vegas
HOUSLEY, Phil	5-10	185	L	St. Paul, MN	3/9/64	Washington
HULSE, Cale	6-3	215	R	Edmonton, Alta.	11/10/73	Calgary
MORRIS, Derek	6-0	200	R	Edmonton, Alta.	8/24/78	Calgary
O'DETTE, Matt	6-5	220	R	Oshawa, Ont.	11/9/75	Saint John-Roanoke
O'SULLIVAN, Chris	6-2	205	L	Dorchester, MA	5/15/74	Calgary-Saint John
SCOVILLE, Darrel	6-3	205	L	Regina, Sask.	10/13/75	Merrimack
SIMPSON, Todd	6-3	215	L	North Vancouver, B.C.	5/28/73	Calgary
SMITH, Steve	6-4	215	L	Glasgow, Scotland	4/30/63	
VELLINGA, Mike	6-1	218	R	Chatham, Ont.	8/19/78	Guelph

GOALTENDERS	HT	WT	C	Place of Birth	Date	1997-98 Club
GARNER, Tyrone	6-1	170	L	Stoney Creek, Ont.	7/27/78	Oshawa
GIGUERE, Jean-Sebastien	6-0	175	L	Montreal, Que.	5/16/77	Saint John
KARPENKO, Igor	5-8	158	L	Kiev, Ukraine	7/23/76	Port Huron-Saint John
LINDSAY, Evan	6-1	180	L	Calgary, Alta.	5/5/79	Prince Albert
MOSS, Tyler	6-0	184	R	Ottawa, Ont.	6/29/75	Calgary-Saint John
WREGGET, Ken	6-1	201	L	Brandon, Man.	3/25/64	Pittsburgh

1997-98 Scoring

* – rookie

Regular Season

Pos	#	Player	Team	GP	G	A	Pts	+/–	PIM	PP	SH	GW	GT	S	%
R	14	Theoren Fleury	CGY	82	27	51	78	0	197	3	2	4	1	282	9.6
C	16	Cory Stillman	CGY	72	27	22	49	-9	40	9	4	1	1	178	15.2
L	18	Marty McInnis	CGY	75	19	25	44	1	34	5	4	0	0	128	14.8
C	21	Andrew Cassels	CGY	81	17	27	44	-7	32	6	1	2	1	138	12.3
L	13	German Titov	CGY	68	18	22	40	-1	38	6	1	2	0	133	13.5
R	8	Valeri Bure	MTL	50	7	22	29	-5	33	2	0	1	0	134	5.2
			CGY	16	5	4	9	0	2	0	0	1	0	45	11.1
			TOTAL	66	12	26	38	-5	35	2	0	2	0	179	6.7
C	92	Michael Nylander	CGY	65	13	23	36	10	24	0	0	2	0	117	11.1
R	12	Jarome Iginla	CGY	70	13	19	32	-10	29	0	2	1	0	154	8.4
D	53	* Derek Morris	CGY	82	9	20	29	1	88	5	1	1	1	120	7.5
D	32	Cale Hulse	CGY	79	5	22	27	1	169	1	1	0	0	117	4.3
L	24	Jason Wiemer	T.B.	67	8	9	17	-9	132	2	0	0	0	106	7.5
			CGY	12	4	1	5	-1	28	1	0	2	0	16	25.0
			TOTAL	79	12	10	22	-10	160	3	0	2	0	122	9.8
D	5	Tommy Albelin	CGY	69	2	17	19	9	32	1	0	2	0	88	2.3
D	3	James Patrick	CGY	60	6	11	17	-2	26	1	0	1	0	57	10.5
C	17	* Hnat Domenichelli	CGY	31	9	7	16	4	6	1	0	1	2	70	12.9
C	34	Jim Dowd	CGY	48	6	8	14	10	12	0	1	0	0	58	10.3
D	6	Joel Bouchard	CGY	44	5	7	12	0	57	0	1	1	0	51	9.8
D	2	* Jamie Allison	CGY	43	3	8	11	3	104	0	0	1	0	27	11.1
L	42	Ed Ward	CGY	64	4	5	9	-1	122	0	0	0	1	52	7.7
L	7	* Chris Dingman	CGY	70	3	3	6	-11	149	1	0	0	0	47	6.4
D	27	Todd Simpson	CGY	53	1	5	6	-10	109	0	0	1	0	51	2.0
C	23	Aaron Gavey	CGY	26	2	3	5	-5	24	0	0	1	0	27	7.4
G	30	Dwayne Roloson	CGY	39	0	4	4	0	10	0	0	0	0	0	0.0
R	29	Erik Andersson	CGY	12	2	1	3	-4	8	0	0	0	0	11	18.2
D	19	* Chris O'Sullivan	CGY	12	0	2	2	4	10	0	0	0	0	12	0.0
C	11	* Eric Landry	CGY	12	1	0	1	-2	4	0	0	0	0	7	14.3
R	26	* Ladislav Kohn	CGY	4	0	1	1	2	0	0	0	0	0	2	0.0
L	20	Todd Hlushko	CGY	13	0	1	1	0	27	0	0	0	0	7	0.0
D	4	Kevin Dahl	CGY	19	0	1	1	-3	6	0	0	0	0	17	0.0
G	31	Rick Tabaracci	CGY	42	0	1	1	0	14	0	0	0	0	0	0.0
L	58	* Sergei Varlamov	CGY	1	0	0	0	0	0	0	0	0	0	0	0.0
D	38	Eric Charron	CGY	2	0	0	0	0	4	0	0	0	0	1	0.0
C	28	* Marty Murray	CGY	2	0	0	0	1	2	0	0	0	0	2	0.0
L	43	* Travis Brigley	CGY	2	0	0	0	0	2	0	0	0	0	1	0.0
C	57	* Steve Begin	CGY	5	0	0	0	0	23	0	0	0	0	2	0.0
G	1	* Tyler Moss	CGY	6	0	0	0	0	0	0	0	0	0	0	0.0
D	24	* Denis Gauthier	CGY	10	0	0	0	-5	16	0	0	0	0	3	0.0
D	55	* Rocky Thompson	CGY	12	0	0	0	0	61	0	0	0	0	3	0.0
L	8	Mike Peluso	CGY	23	0	0	0	-6	113	0	0	0	0	8	0.0

Goaltending

No.	Goaltender	GPI	Mins	Avg	W	L	T	EN	SO	GA	SA	S%
31	Rick Tabaracci	42	2419	2.88	13	22	6	2	0	116	1087	.893
30	Dwayne Roloson	39	2205	2.99	11	16	8	4	0	110	997	.890
1	* Tyler Moss	6	367	3.27	2	3	1	0	0	20	186	.892
	Totals	**82**	**5016**	**3.01**	**26**	**41**	**15**	**6**	**0**	**252**	**2276**	**.889**

Right winger Valeri Bure joined the Flames on February 1, 1998 after a trade with the Montreal Canadiens. The former WHL all-star also played for Russia at the 1998 Winter Olympics.

General Manager

COATES, AL
Executive Vice President/General Manager, Calgary Flames.
Born in Listowel, Ont., December 3, 1945.

Al Coates was named executive vice president of the Calgary Flames on June 22, 1995. On November 3, he was designated the interim general manager, replacing Doug Risebrough. Coates' appointment as general manager became official on May 31, 1996. In this role, he is responsible for all aspects of hockey operations for the club.

Coates had been a member of the Flames senior management team since the club's arrival in Calgary in 1980. He has over 27 years of professional hockey experience, including 18 years of service with the Calgary Flames.

Following a playing career in Europe, Coates joined the Detroit Red Wings organization in 1971. He spent nine seasons with the Red Wings, working in various capacities. In the summer of 1980, he joined the Flames as the team's director of public relations. In August, 1982, Coates was named as the assistant to the president, working directly with then president and general manager Cliff Fletcher in a number of hockey administrative capacities. Later, on August 1, 1989, he was promoted to director of hockey administration. He continued his progression through the organization when, on September 8, 1991, he was named the team's assistant general manager, a position he held until his promotion to executive vice president and general manager.

Coates' work has involved player contracts, coordinating professional scouting, and working with the Flames development team in Saint John (AHL). Coates also now serves as the chairman of the executive committee of the American Hockey League. His progressive management and leadership style has helped shape the Flames franchise into a successful, respected organization both on and off the ice.

Coaching History

Bernie Geoffrion, 1972-73, 1973-74; Bernie Geoffrion and Fred Creighton, 1974-75; Fred Creighton, 1975-76 to 1978-79; Al MacNeil, 1979-80 to 1981-82; Bob Johnson, 1982-83 to 1986-87; Terry Crisp, 1987-88 to 1989-90; Doug Risebrough, 1990-91; Doug Risebrough and Guy Charron, 1991-92; Dave King, 1992-93 to 1994-95; Pierre Page, 1995-96, 1996-97; Brian Sutter, 1997-98 to date.

Club Records

Team

(Figures in brackets for season records are games played; records for fewest points, wins, ties, losses, goals, goals against are for 70 or more games)

Most Points	**117**	1988-89 (80)
Most Wins	**54**	1988-89 (80)
Most Ties	**19**	1977-78 (80)
Most Losses	**41**	1996-97 (82), 1997-98 (82)
Most Goals	**397**	1987-88 (80)
Most Goals Against	**345**	1981-82 (80)
Fewest Points	**65**	1972-73 (78)
Fewest Wins	**25**	1972-73 (78)
Fewest Ties	**3**	1986-87 (80)
Fewest Losses	**17**	1988-89 (80)
Fewest Goals	**191**	1972-73 (78)
Fewest Goals Against	**226**	1988-89 (80)
Longest Winning Streak		
Overall	**10**	Oct. 14-Nov. 3/78
Home	**9**	Oct. 17-Nov. 15/78, Jan. 3-Feb. 5/89, Mar. 3-Apr. 1/90, Feb. 21-Mar. 14/91
Away	**7**	Nov. 10-Dec. 4/88
Longest Undefeated Streak		
Overall	**13**	Nov. 10-Dec. 8/88 (12 wins, 1 tie)
Home	**18**	Dec. 29/90-Mar. 14/91 (17 wins, 1 tie)
Away	**9**	Feb. 20-Mar. 21/88 (6 wins, 3 ties), Nov. 11-Dec. 16/90 (6 wins, 3 ties)
Longest Losing Streak		
Overall	**11**	Dec. 14/85-Jan. 7/86
Home	**4**	Eight times
Away	**9**	Dec. 1/85-Jan. 12/86
Longest Winless Streak		
Overall	**11**	Dec. 14/85-Jan. 7/86 (11 losses), Jan. 5-26/93 (9 losses, 2 ties)
Home	**6**	Nov. 25-Dec. 18/82 (5 losses, 1 tie), Nov. 18-Dec. 9/95 (4 losses, 2 ties)
Away	**13**	Feb. 3-Mar. 29/73 (10 losses, 3 ties)
Most Shutouts, Season	**8**	1974-75 (80)
Most PIM, Season	**2,655**	1991-92 (80)
Most Goals, Game	**13**	Feb. 10/93 (S.J. 1 at Cgy. 13)

Individual

Most Seasons	**13**	Al MacInnis
Most Games	**803**	Al MacInnis
Most Goals, Career	**334**	Theoren Fleury
Most Assists, Career	**609**	Al MacInnis
Most Points, Career	**822**	Al MacInnis (213G, 609A)
Most PIM, Career	**2,405**	Tim Hunter
Most Shutouts, Career	**20**	Dan Bouchard
Longest Consecutive Games Streak	**257**	Brad Marsh (Oct. 11/78-Nov. 10/81)
Most Goals, Season	**66**	Lanny McDonald (1982-83)
Most Assists, Season	**82**	Kent Nilsson (1980-81)
Most Points, Season	**131**	Kent Nilsson (1980-81) (49G, 82A)
Most PIM, Season	**375**	Tim Hunter (1988-89)
Most Points, Defenseman, Season	**103**	Al MacInnis (1990-91; 28G, 75A)
Most Points, Center, Season	**131**	Kent Nilsson (1980-81; 49G, 82A)
Most Points, Right Wing, Season	**110**	Joe Mullen (1988-89; 51G, 59A)
Most Points, Left Wing, Season	**90**	Gary Roberts (1991-92; 53G, 37A)
Most Points, Rookie, Season	**92**	Joe Nieuwendyk (1987-88; 51G, 41A)
Most Shutouts, Season	**5**	Dan Bouchard (1973-74), Phil Myre (1974-75)
Most Goals, Game	**5**	Joe Nieuwendyk (Jan. 11/89)
Most Assists, Game	**6**	Guy Chouinard (Feb. 25/81), Gary Suter (Apr. 4/86)
Most Points, Game	**7**	Sergei Makarov (Feb. 25/90; 2G, 5A)

Records include Atlanta Flames, 1972-73 through 1979-80.

Retired Numbers

9	Lanny McDonald	1981-1989

Captains' History

Keith McCreary, 1972-73 to 1974-75; Pat Quinn, 1975-76, 1976-77; Tom Lysiak, 1977-78, 1978-79; Jean Pronovost, 1979-80; Brad Marsh, 1980-81; Phil Russell, 1981-82, 1982-83; Lanny McDonald, Doug Risebrough (co-captains), 1983-84; Lanny McDonald, Doug Risebrough, Jim Peplinski (tri-captains), 1984-85 to 1986-87; Lanny McDonald, Jim Peplinski (co-captains), 1987-88; Lanny McDonald, Jim Peplinski, Tim Hunter (tri-captains), 1988-89; Brad McCrimmon, 1989-90; alternating captains, 1990-91; Joe Nieuwendyk, 1991-92 to 1994-95; Theoren Fleury, 1995-96, 1996-97; Todd Simpson, 1997-98 to date.

General Managers' History

Cliff Fletcher, 1972-73 to 1990-91; Doug Risebrough, 1991-92 to 1994-95; Doug Risebrough and Al Coates, 1995-96; Al Coates, 1996-97 to date.

All-time Record vs. Other Clubs

Regular Season

	At Home							On Road							Total						
	GP	W	L	T	GF	GA	PTS	GP	W	L	T	GF	GA	PTS	GP	W	L	T	GF	GA	PTS
Anaheim	13	8	5	0	38	32	16	14	6	5	3	38	41	15	27	14	10	3	76	73	31
Boston	41	16	22	3	150	146	35	42	11	25	6	116	147	28	83	27	47	9	266	293	63
Buffalo	41	15	16	10	143	136	40	41	13	23	5	124	170	31	82	28	39	15	267	306	71
Carolina	25	19	5	1	126	83	39	25	13	8	4	96	82	30	50	32	13	5	222	165	69
Chicago	51	23	19	9	160	153	55	49	15	21	13	143	167	43	100	38	40	22	303	320	98
Colorado	31	17	8	6	128	97	40	30	11	11	8	111	121	30	61	28	19	14	239	218	70
Dallas	50	29	10	11	191	131	69	50	18	25	7	168	189	43	100	47	35	18	359	320	112
Detroit	48	26	16	6	193	153	58	47	14	24	9	147	181	37	95	40	40	15	340	334	95
Edmonton	64	36	22	6	291	234	78	65	22	34	9	231	266	53	129	58	56	15	522	500	131
Florida	4	2	1	1	10	9	5	4	2	2	0	9	8	4	8	4	3	1	19	17	9
Los Angeles	82	50	23	9	380	272	109	79	30	40	9	290	309	69	161	80	63	18	670	581	178
Montreal	40	12	23	5	125	144	29	41	11	23	7	100	147	29	81	23	46	12	225	291	58
New Jersey	39	27	5	7	175	101	61	40	24	13	3	148	114	51	79	51	18	10	323	215	112
NY Islanders	46	22	13	11	166	139	55	46	12	25	9	124	185	33	92	34	38	20	290	324	88
NY Rangers	46	26	10	10	205	139	62	47	21	21	5	170	166	47	93	47	31	15	375	305	109
Ottawa	5	4	0	1	28	11	9	5	1	2	2	12	10	4	10	5	2	3	40	21	13
Philadelphia	48	24	15	9	197	157	57	47	13	32	2	125	187	28	95	37	47	11	322	344	85
Phoenix	59	36	16	7	273	193	79	58	21	27	10	206	232	52	117	57	43	17	479	425	131
Pittsburgh	41	25	9	7	183	125	57	41	10	21	10	129	154	30	82	35	30	17	312	279	87
St. Louis	50	25	21	4	175	149	54	51	20	23	8	159	179	48	101	45	44	12	334	328	102
San Jose	20	13	6	1	90	55	27	22	15	6	1	74	61	31	42	28	12	2	164	116	58
Tampa Bay	5	3	2	0	18	11	6	6	2	3	1	23	22	5	11	5	5	1	41	33	11
Toronto	50	30	15	5	212	156	65	48	17	24	7	177	185	41	98	47	39	12	389	341	106
Vancouver	82	54	16	12	358	235	120	82	35	30	17	278	288	87	164	89	46	29	636	523	207
Washington	35	24	6	5	152	85	53	36	13	18	5	126	137	31	71	37	24	10	278	222	84
Defunct Clubs	13	8	4	1	51	34	17	13	7	3	3	43	33	17	26	15	7	4	94	67	34
Totals	**1029**	**574**	**308**	**147**	**4218**	**3180**	**1295**	**1029**	**377**	**489**	**163**	**3367**	**3781**	**917**	**2058**	**951**	**797**	**310**	**7585**	**6961**	**2212**

Playoffs

	Series	W	L	GP	W	L	T	GF	GA	Last Mtg.	Round	Result
Chicago	3	2	1	12	7	5	0	37	33	1996	CQF	L 0-4
Dallas	1	0	1	6	2	4	0	18	25	1981	SF	L 2-4
Detroit	1	0	1	2	0	2	0	5	8	1978	PR	L 0-2
Edmonton	5	1	4	30	11	19	0	96	132	1991	DSF	L 3-4
Los Angeles	6	2	4	26	13	13	0	102	105	1993	DSF	L 2-4
Montreal	2	1	1	11	5	6	0	32	31	1989	F	W 4-2
NY Rangers	1	0	1	4	1	3	0	8	14	1980	PR	L 1-3
Philadelphia	2	1	1	11	4	7	0	28	43	1981	QF	W 4-3
St. Louis	1	1	0	7	4	3	0	28	22	1986	CF	W 4-3
San Jose	1	0	1	7	3	4	0	35	26	1995	CQF	L 3-4
Toronto	1	0	1	2	0	2	0	5	9	1979	PR	L 0-2
Vancouver	5	3	2	25	13	12	0	82	80	1994	CQF	L 3-4
Winnipeg	3	1	2	13	6	7	0	43	45	1987	DSF	L 2-4
Totals	**32**	**12**	**20**	**156**	**69**	**87**	**0**	**529**	**590**			

Calgary totals include Atlanta, 1972-73 to 1979-80. Carolina totals include Hartford, 1979-80 to 1996-97.
Colorado totals include Quebec, 1979-80 to 1994-95. Dallas totals include Minnesota, 1972-73 to 1992-93.
New Jersey totals include Kansas City, 1974-75 to 1975-76, and Colorado Rockies, 1976-77 to 1981-82.
Phoenix totals include Winnipeg, 1979-80 to 1995-96.

Playoff Results 1998-94

Year	Round	Opponent	Result	GF	GA
1996	CQF	Chicago	L 0-4	7	16
1995	CQF	San Jose	L 3-4	35	26
1994	CQF	Vancouver	L 3-4	20	23

Abbreviations: Round: F – Final; **CF** – conference final; **CQF** – conference quarter-final; **DSF** – division semi-final; **SF** – semi-final; **QF** – quarter-final; **PR** – preliminary round.

1997-98 Results

Oct.	1		Detroit	1-3		31		Montreal	2-3
	3		Colorado	1-4	**Jan.**	3	at	St. Louis	3-4
	7		Toronto	1-2		5	at	Chicago	1-1
	9		NY Rangers	1-1		6	at	Colorado	3-1
	12	at	Detroit	4-4		9		Florida	3-3
	14	at	Dallas	4-5		10		St. Louis	1-5
	17		Colorado	6-5		14	at	Edmonton	2-5
	18		Boston	0-3		20	at	Los Angeles	3-4
	22	at	Buffalo	1-4		21	at	San Jose	1-7
	23	at	Philadelphia	3-4		24		Vancouver	5-2
	25	at	Toronto	3-4		28	at	Anaheim	5-2
	28		Pittsburgh	6-3		29	at	Los Angeles	3-5
	30		Phoenix	4-2		31		New Jersey	2-2
Nov.	1	at	Colorado	3-3	**Feb.**	3		Los Angeles	3-6
	2	at	Phoenix	1-3		5		San Jose	4-2
	5		Toronto	3-4		7		Edmonton	4-2
	7		Anaheim	3-4		27		Vancouver	4-4
	9	at	Detroit	3-6	**Mar.**	1		Ottawa	2-1
	10	at	Chicago	1-1		3		Tampa Bay	2-1
	13		Carolina	2-4		5	at	Vancouver	6-2
	15	at	Edmonton	2-2		7	at	Ottawa	1-2
	18	at	New Jersey	1-2		9	at	Washington	2-5
	20	at	Florida	2-1		11	at	Pittsburgh	1-4
	22	at	Tampa Bay	3-4		12	at	Boston	5-2
	23	at	Carolina	3-3		14	at	Toronto	1-2
	27		Chicago	2-2		16	at	Montreal	3-3
	29		Anaheim	3-2		20		NY Islanders	4-1
Dec.	1		San Jose	3-2		22		St. Louis	5-3
	3		Detroit	3-4		24		Buffalo	0-2
	5	at	Dallas	1-4		26		Washington	3-2
	6	at	St. Louis	3-4		28		Los Angeles	5-2
	9	at	NY Islanders	3-1		30	at	Edmonton	1-3
	10	at	NY Rangers	4-1	**Apr.**	1		Dallas	3-1
	12		Colorado	3-1		5	at	Anaheim	3-3
	16		Chicago	4-3		7	at	San Jose	0-6
	18		Dallas	1-2		9		Vancouver	3-6
	20		Los Angeles	1-4		11		Edmonton	4-5
	22	at	Anaheim	1-5		13	at	Los Angeles	2-4
	23	at	Phoenix	2-2		15		San Jose	3-3
	27		Philadelphia	5-2		17	at	Vancouver	4-2
	29		Phoenix	3-5		18	at	San Jose	1-4

Entry Draft Selections 1998-84

1998
Pick
6 Rico Fata
33 Blair Betts
62 Paul Manning
102 Shaun Sutter
108 Dany Sabourin
120 Brent Gauvreau
192 Radek Duda
206 Jonas Frogren
234 Kevin Mitchell

1997
Pick
6 Daniel Tkaczuk
32 Evan Lindsay
42 John Tripp
51 Dimitri Kokorev
60 Derek Schutz
70 Erik Andersson
92 Chris St. Croix
100 Ryan Ready
113 Martin Moise
140 Ilja Demidov
167 Jeremy Rondeau
223 Dustin Paul

1996
Pick
13 Derek Morris
39 Travis Brigley
40 Steve Begin
73 Dmitri Vlasenkov
89 Toni Lydman
94 Christian Lefebvre
122 Josef Straka
202 Ryan Wade
228 Ronald Petrovicky

1995
Pick
20 Denis Gauthier Jr.
46 Pavel Smirnov
72 Rocky Thompson
98 Jan Labraaten
150 Clarke Wilm
176 Ryan Gillis
233 Steve Shirreffs

1994
Pick
19 Chris Dingman
45 Dmitri Ryabykin
77 Chris Clark
91 Ryan Duthie
97 Johan Finnstrom
107 Nils Ekman
123 Frank Appel
149 Patrick Haltia
175 Ladislav Kohn
201 Keith McCambridge
227 Jorgen Jonsson
253 Mike Peluso
279 Pavel Torgayev

1993
Pick
18 Jesper Mattsson
44 Jamie Allison
70 Dan Tompkins
95 Jason Smith
96 Marty Murray
121 Darryl Lafrance
122 John Emmons
148 Andreas Karlsson
200 Derek Sylvester
252 German Titov
278 Burke Murphy

1992
Pick
6 Cory Stillman
30 Chris O'Sullivan
54 Mathias Johansson
78 Robert Svehla
102 Sami Helenius
126 Ravil Yakubov
129 Joel Bouchard
150 Pavel Rajnoha
174 Ryan Mulhern
198 Brandon Carper
222 Jonas Hoglund
246 Andrei Potaichuk

1991
Pick
19 Niklas Sundblad
41 Francois Groleau
52 Sandy McCarthy
63 Brian Caruso
85 Steven Magnusson
107 Jerome Butler
129 Bobby Marshall
140 Matt Hoffman
151 Kelly Harper
173 David St. Pierre
195 David Struch
217 Sergei Zolotov
239 Marko Jantunen
261 Andrei Trefilov

1990
Pick
11 Trevor Kidd
26 Nicolas P. Perreault
32 Vesa Viitakoski
41 Etienne Belzile
62 Glen Mears
83 Paul Kruse
125 Chris Tschupp
146 Dmitri Frolov
167 Shawn Murray
188 Mike Murray
209 Rob Sumner
230 invalid claim
251 Leo Gudas

1989
Pick
24 Kent Manderville
42 Ted Drury
50 Veli-Pekka Kautonen
63 Corey Lyons
70 Robert Reichel
84 Ryan O'Leary
105 F. (Toby) Kearney
147 Alex Nikolic
168 Kevin Wortman
189 Sergei Gomolyako
210 Dan Sawyer
231 Alexander Yudin
252 Kenneth Kennholt

1988
Pick
21 Jason Muzzatti
42 Todd Harkins
84 Gary Socha
85 Thomas Forslund
90 Scott Matusovich
126 Jonas Bergqvist
147 Stefan Nilsson
168 Troy Kennedy
189 Brett Peterson
210 Guy Darveau
231 Dave Tretowicz
252 Sergei Priakhan

1987
Pick
19 Bryan Deasley
25 Stephane Matteau
40 Kevin Grant
61 Scott Mahoney
70 Tim Harris
103 Tim Corkery
124 Joe Aloi
145 Peter Ciavaglia
166 Theoren Fleury
187 Mark Osiecki
208 William Sedergren
229 Peter Hasselblad
250 Magnus Svensson

1986
Pick
16 George Pelawa
37 Brian Glynn
79 Tom Quinlan
100 Scott Bloom
121 John Parker
142 Rick Lessard
163 Mark Olsen
184 Warren Sharples
205 Doug Pickell
226 Anders Lindstrom
247 Antonin Stavjana

1985
Pick
17 Chris Biotti
27 Joe Nieuwendyk
38 Jeff Wenaas
59 Lane MacDonald
80 Roger Johansson
101 Esa Keskinen
122 Tim Sweeney
143 Stu Grimson
164 Nate Smith
185 Darryl Olsen
206 Peter Romberg
227 Alexander Kozhevnikov
248 Bill Gregoire

1984
Pick
12 Gary Roberts
33 Ken Sabourin
38 Paul Ranheim
75 Petr Rosol
96 Joel Paunio
117 Brett Hull
138 Kevan Melrose
159 Jiri Hrdina
180 Gary Suter
200 Petr Rucka
221 Stefan Jonsson
241 Rudolf Suchanek

Coach

SUTTER, BRIAN
Coach, Calgary Flames. Born in Viking, Alta., October 7, 1956.

Brian Sutter enters his second season as head coach of the Calgary Flames after recording a 26-41-15 record and a .409 winning percentage last year with a young rebuilding club. The Alberta-born Sutter is one of six Sutter brothers involved in hockey but the first to have either played or coached at the NHL level in their native province. Brian is the tenth head coach in Flames franchise history, and eighth in the 19 year history of the team in Calgary.

Following a 12 season playing career (1976-1988) with St. Louis, Sutter immediately joined the NHL coaching ranks as head coach of the team he captained for nine of his twelve seasons. He coached the Blues for four years (1988-92), before moving on to coach the Boston Bruins between 1992-95.

During his three seasons as head coach of the Boston Bruins, Sutter led the Bruins to the third best record in the NHL (120-73-23). During the 1992-93 season, Sutter coached his team to the second best overall record in the league (51-26-7, 109 points). The 1992-93 season marked the first time in ten years the Bruins posted a 50-win season and earned Sutter runner-up honors in the balloting for the Jack Adams Trophy as the league's top coach. In his second season behind the Bruins bench, Sutter coached one of the league's youngest rosters, including Bryan Smolinski and Joe Juneau, to 42 wins. Sutter's win percentage during his tenure with the Bruins was an impressive .609.

Sutter spent four seasons (1988-92) behind the bench of the St. Louis Blues where he exceeded Scotty Bowman's record to become the winningest coach in Blues history, posting a Blues' career record of 153-124-43 and .545 winning percentage. Sutter won coach-of-the-year honors in 1990-91 after leading his charges to a 47-22-11 record, second overall in the league.

Following his junior career with Lethbridge (WHL), Sutter was drafted by the St. Louis Blues as their second pick, 20th overall, in the 1976 Amateur Draft. Sutter played his entire twelve year NHL career with the Blues. His number 11 was retired by the Blues on December 30, 1988. Sutter ranks second all-time among Blues players in games played and assists and third all-time in goals and points.

Sutter and his wife, Judy, return to "Sutter Country" Alberta in the Sylvan Lake area during the off-season. They have one son, Shaun and one daughter, Abigail. Shaun was drafted by the Flames from the Lethbridge Hurricanes in the 1998 NHL Entry Draft.

Club Directory

Canadian Airlines Saddledome
P.O. Box 1540 Station M
Calgary, Alberta T2P 3B9
Phone **403/777-2177**
FAX 403/777-2195
Website: www.calgaryflames.com
Capacity: 17,104

Owners Grant A. Bartlett (Alt. Governor), N. Murray Edwards (Alt. Governor), Harley N. Hotchkiss (Governor), Ronald V. Joyce, Alvin G. Libin, Allan P. Markin, J.R. (Bud) McCaig, Byron J. Seaman, Daryl K. Seaman

Management	
President & Chief Executive Officer – Alternate Governor	Ron Bremner
Executive Vice-President & General Manager – Alternate Governor	Al Coates
Vice-President, Finance & Administration	Michael Holditch
Vice-President, Corporate Development	Lanny McDonald
Vice-President, Marketing & Sales	Garry McKenzie
Hockey Club Personnel	
Director, Player Personnel	Nick Polano
Director, Hockey Operations	Al MacNeil
Head Coach	Brian Sutter
Assistant Coach	Rich Preston
Development Coordinator	Jamie Hislop
Director, Hockey Administration	Mike Burke
Video Coordinator	Gary Taylor
Pro Scout	Tod Button
Saint John Flames Head Coach	Rick Vaive
Saint John Assistant Coach	Jeff Perry
Amateur Scouting Coordinator	Mike Kelly
Scouts	Ian McKenzie, Guy Lapointe
Scouting Staff	Glen Giovanucci, Jiri Hrdina, Larry Johnston, Nikolai Ladigan, Lars Norrman, Mike Polano, Jarmo Tolvanen
Exec. Asst. to President/CEO	Yvette Mutcheson
Exec. Asst. to GM and Hockey Operations	Brenda Koyich
Exec. Asst. to VP, Finance & Corporate Development	Nancy Nelson
Administration	
Controller	Jackie Manwaring
Assistant Controller	Karen Kingham
Communications	
Director, Communications	Peter Hanlon
Assistant Director, Communications	Kathy Gieck
Community Relations Representative	Jim 'Bearcat' Murray
Secretary, Communications	Bernie Doenz
Communications Assistant	Sean O'Brien
Human Resources	
Director, Human Resources	Eleanor Culver
Marketing	
Director, Advertising and Promotions	John Vidalin
Retail Operations Manager	Dean Borle
Director, Advertising and Publishing	Pat Halls
Director, Executive Suites	Bob White
Business Development Manager	Al Molnar
Director, Game Presentation	Peter Sorcoff
Sales/Customer Services	
Director, Sales & Ticket Operations	Jack Maloney
Manager, Ticket Office	Brad Andrews
Manager, Customer Relations	Craig Fisher
Medical/Training Staff	
Equipment Manager	Bobby Stewart
Physiotherapist	Terry Kane
Athletic Trainer	Morris Boyer
Strength & Conditioning	Rich Hesketh
Head Physician – Sport Medicine	Dr. Willem Meeuwisse
Orthopedic Surgeon	Dr. Nicholas Mohtadi
Internal Medicine	Dr. Terry Groves
Team Dentist	Dr. Bill Blair
Spoerts Psychologist	Dr. Cal Botterill
Dressing Room Attendant	Les Jarvis, Jules Carriere
Canadian Airlines Saddledome	
GM, Building Operations	Libby Raines
Operations Manager	George Greenwood
Food Services Asst. Manager	Art Hernandez
Concessions Manager	Sheila Parisien
Maintenance Superintendant	Ron Leopold
Facility	
Location of Media Boxes	Print – north side TV & Radio – south side
Dimensions of Rink	200 feet by 85 feet
Broadcast Stations	
Radio	66 CFR Radio (660 AM)
Television	Calgary 7 (Channels 2 & 7)

Coaching Record

		Regular Season					Playoffs			
Season	Team	Games	W	L	T	%	Games	W	L	%
1988-89	St. Louis (NHL)	80	33	35	12	.488	10	5	5	.500
1989-90	St. Louis (NHL)	80	37	34	9	.519	12	7	5	.583
1990-91	St. Louis (NHL)	80	47	22	11	.656	13	6	7	.462
1991-92	St. Louis (NHL)	80	36	33	11	.519	6	2	4	.333
1992-93	Boston (NHL)	84	51	26	7	.649	4	0	4	.000
1993-94	Boston (NHL)	84	42	29	13	.577	13	6	7	.462
1994-95	Boston (NHL)	48	27	18	3	.594	5	1	4	.200
1997-98	Calgary (NHL)	82	26	41	15	.409	....	....	....	....
	NHL Totals	618	299	238	81	.549	63	27	36	.429

Carolina Hurricanes

1997-98 Results: 33W-41L-8T 74PTS. Sixth, Northeast Division

Year-by-Year Record

Season	GP	Home W	Home L	Home T	Road W	Road L	Road T	Overall W	Overall L	Overall T	GF	GA	Pts.	Finished		Playoff Result
1997-98	82	16	18	7	17	23	1	33	41	8	200	219	74	6th,	Northeast Div.	Out of Playoffs
1996-97*	82	23	15	3	9	24	8	32	39	11	226	256	75	5th,	Northeast Div.	Out of Playoffs
1995-96*	82	22	15	4	12	24	5	34	39	9	237	259	77	4th,	Northeast Div.	Out of Playoffs
1994-95*	48	12	10	2	7	14	3	19	24	5	127	141	43	5th,	Northeast Div.	Out of Playoffs
1993-94*	84	14	22	6	13	26	3	27	48	9	227	288	63	6th,	Northeast Div.	Out of Playoffs
1992-93*	84	12	25	5	14	27	1	26	52	6	284	369	58	5th,	Adams Div.	Out of Playoffs
1991-92*	80	13	17	10	13	24	3	26	41	13	247	283	65	4th,	Adams Div.	Lost Div. Semi-Final
1990-91*	80	18	16	6	13	22	5	31	38	11	238	276	73	4th,	Adams Div.	Lost Div. Semi-Final
1989-90*	80	17	18	5	21	15	4	38	33	9	275	268	85	4th,	Adams Div.	Lost Div. Semi-Final
1988-89*	80	21	17	2	16	21	3	37	38	5	299	290	79	4th,	Adams Div.	Lost Div. Semi-Final
1987-88*	80	21	14	5	14	24	2	35	38	7	249	267	77	4th,	Adams Div.	Lost Div. Semi-Final
1986-87*	80	26	9	5	17	21	2	43	30	7	287	270	93	1st,	Adams Div.	Lost Div. Semi-Final
1985-86*	80	21	17	2	19	19	2	40	36	4	332	302	84	4th,	Adams Div.	Lost Div. Final
1984-85*	80	17	18	5	13	23	4	30	41	9	268	318	69	5th,	Adams Div.	Out of Playoffs
1983-84*	80	19	16	5	9	26	5	28	42	10	288	320	66	5th,	Adams Div.	Out of Playoffs
1982-83*	80	13	22	5	6	32	2	19	54	7	261	403	45	5th,	Adams Div.	Out of Playoffs
1981-82*	80	13	17	10	8	24	8	21	41	18	264	351	60	5th,	Adams Div.	Out of Playoffs
1980-81*	80	14	17	9	7	24	9	21	41	18	292	372	60	4th,	Norris Div.	Out of Playoffs
1979-80*	80	22	12	6	5	22	13	27	34	19	303	312	73	4th,	Norris Div.	Lost Prelim. Round

* Hartford Whalers

1998-99 Schedule

Oct.	Sat.	10	Tampa Bay
	Tue.	13	at Nashville
	Thu.	15	Dallas
	Sat.	17	Philadelphia
	Tue.	20	Vancouver
	Sat.	24	at Ottawa
	Sun.	25	Los Angeles
	Wed.	28	Chicago
	Fri.	30	at NY Rangers
	Sat.	31	at Boston
Nov.	Mon.	2	Colorado
	Thu.	5	at NY Islanders
	Fri.	6	at Washington
	Sun.	8	Boston
	Wed.	11	at Anaheim
	Thu.	12	at San Jose
	Sat.	14	at Los Angeles
	Tue.	17	Montreal
	Thu.	19	at New Jersey
	Fri.	20	Philadelphia
	Sun.	22	New Jersey*
	Wed.	25	San Jose
	Sat.	28	at NY Islanders*
	Sun.	29	Anaheim
Dec.	Wed.	2	Montreal
	Fri.	4	Pittsburgh
	Sat.	5	at Florida
	Thu.	10	Boston
	Sat.	12	Detroit
	Tue.	15	Edmonton
	Fri.	18	at Ottawa
	Sat.	19	at Buffalo
	Mon.	21	Buffalo
	Wed.	23	at NY Rangers
	Sat.	26	NY Rangers
	Wed.	30	Tampa Bay
Jan.	Fri.	1	at Florida*
	Sat.	2	Nashville*
	Mon.	4	Ottawa
	Thu.	7	at Pittsburgh
	Sat.	9	at Philadelphia
	Thu.	14	Florida
	Sat.	16	Washington
	Mon.	18	Toronto
	Thu.	21	at Detroit
	Tue.	26	at Pittsburgh
	Thu.	28	NY Rangers
	Sat.	30	at Montreal*
	Sun.	31	at Boston*
Feb.	Wed.	3	New Jersey
	Fri.	5	at Washington
	Sat.	6	Florida
	Wed.	10	at Toronto
	Fri.	12	at NY Rangers
	Sat.	13	at New Jersey
	Mon.	15	at Buffalo
	Thu.	18	Washington
	Sat.	20	at Tampa Bay
	Sun.	21	NY Islanders
	Wed.	24	at Toronto
	Fri.	26	at Vancouver
	Sat.	27	at Edmonton
Mar.	Wed.	3	Boston
	Sat.	6	at Florida
	Mon.	8	Buffalo
	Wed.	10	Pittsburgh
	Fri.	12	Calgary
	Mon.	15	at Phoenix
	Thu.	18	at Colorado
	Sun.	21	at Dallas
	Mon.	22	at St. Louis
	Wed.	24	NY Islanders
	Fri.	26	Toronto
	Sun.	28	Tampa Bay*
	Tue.	30	at Philadelphia
Apr.	Sat.	3	at Chicago
	Tue.	6	New Jersey
	Wed.	7	at Montreal
	Sat.	10	at NY Islanders
	Wed.	14	Washington
	Fri.	16	at Tampa Bay
	Sat.	17	Ottawa

* Denotes afternoon game.

Jeff O'Neill established career highs with 19 goals, 20 assists and 39 points in 1997-98. The former junior star with the Ontario Hockey League's Guelph Storm had seven goals on the power-play, tying Keith Primeau for the team lead.

Franchise date: June 22, 1979
Transferred from Hartford to Carolina, June 25, 1997.

EASTERN NHL CONFERENCE

SOUTHEAST DIVISION

20th NHL Season

1998-99 Player Personnel

FORWARDS	HT	WT	S	Place of Birth	Date	1997-98 Club
BATTAGLIA, Bates	6-2	185	L	Chicago, IL	12/13/75	Car-New Haven-United States
BUCKLEY, Tom	6-1	204	L	Buffalo, NY	5/26/76	New Haven-Richmond
DINEEN, Kevin	5-11	190	R	Quebec City, Que.	10/28/63	Carolina
EMERSON, Nelson	5-11	175	R	Hamilton, Ont.	8/17/67	Carolina-Canada
FITZGERALD, Randy	5-9	175	L	Toronto, Ont.	9/5/79	Plymouth
FRANCIS, Ron	6-3	200	L	Sault Ste. Marie, Ont.	3/1/63	Pittsburgh
GELINAS, Martin	5-11	195	L	Shawinigan, Que.	6/5/70	Vancouver-Carolina-Canada
KAPANEN, Sami	5-10	170	L	Vantaa, Finland	6/14/73	Carolina-Finland
KOEHLER, Greg	6-2	195	L	Scarborough, Ont.	2/27/75	U. Mass.-Lowell-New Haven
KRON, Robert	5-11	185	L	Brno, Czech.	2/27/67	Carolina
LEACH, Stephen	5-11	197	R	Cambridge, MA	1/16/66	Carolina
LEVINS, Scott	6-4	210	R	Spokane, WA	1/30/70	Phoenix-Springfield
MacDONALD, Craig	6-2	180	L	Antigonish, N.S.	4/7/77	Canada
MacNEIL, Ian	6-2	171	L	Halifax, N.S.	4/27/77	New Haven
MANDERVILLE, Kent	6-3	210	L	Edmonton, Alta.	4/12/71	Carolina
MCDONELL, Kent	6-0	175	R	Cornwall, Ont.	3/1/79	Guelph
MORRONE, Mike	5-11	215	L	Windsor, Ont.	1/3/76	Richmond-New Haven
O'NEILL, Jeff	6-1	190	R	Richmond Hill, Ont.	2/23/76	Carolina
PETRUNIN, Andrei	5-9	169	L	Moscow, USSR	2/2/78	CSKA Moscow
PRIMEAU, Keith	6-4	210	L	Toronto, Ont.	11/24/71	Carolina-Canada
RANHEIM, Paul	6-1	210	R	St. Louis, MO	1/25/66	Carolina
RITCHIE, Byron	5-10	180	L	Burnaby, B.C.	4/24/77	New Haven
ROBERTS, Gary	6-1	190	L	North York, Ont.	5/23/66	Carolina
SHEPPARD, Ray	6-1	195	R	Pembroke, Ont.	5/27/66	Florida-Carolina
VASICEK, Josef	6-4	189	L	Havlickuv Brod, Czech.	9/12/80	Slavia Praha
WESTLUND, Tommy	6-0	210	R	Fors, Sweden	12/29/74	Brynas Gavle
WILLIS, Shane	6-0	176	R	Edmonton, Alta.	6/13/77	Lethbridge-New Haven
DEFENSEMEN						
BURT, Adam	6-2	207	L	Detroit, MI	1/15/69	Carolina-United States
CHIASSON, Steve	6-1	205	L	Barrie, Ont.	4/14/67	Carolina
FEDOTOV, Sergei	6-1	185	L	Moscow, USSR	1/24/77	Plymouth-New Haven-Richmond
HALKO, Steven	6-1	195	R	Etobicoke, Ont.	3/8/74	Carolina-New Haven
HAMILTON, Hugh	6-1	175	L	Saskatoon, Sask.	2/11/77	New Haven
HILL, Sean	6-0	203	R	Duluth, MN	2/14/70	Ottawa-Carolina
KARPA, Dave	6-1	210	R	Regina, Sask.	5/7/71	Anaheim
LESCHYSHYN, Curtis	6-1	205	L	Thompson, Man.	9/21/69	Carolina
MALIK, Marek	6-5	190	L	Ostrava, Czech.	6/24/75	Malmo IF
McMAHON, Mark	6-1	179	L	Geralton, Ont.	2/10/78	Kitchener-New Haven
PRATT, Nolan	6-2	195	L	Fort McMurray, Alta.	8/14/75	Carolina-New Haven
RUCINSKI, Mike	5-11	179	L	Trenton, MI	3/30/75	Carolina-New Haven-Cleveland
TSELIOS, Nikos	6-4	187	L	Oak Park, IL	1/20/79	Belv'le-Plymouth-United States
WESLEY, Glen	6-1	197	L	Red Deer, Alta.	10/2/68	Carolina

GOALTENDERS	HT	WT	C	Place of Birth	Date	1997-98 Club
FOUNTAIN, Mike	6-1	176	L	North York, Ont.	1/26/72	Carolina-New Haven
JABLONSKI, Pat	6-0	180	R	Toledo, OH	6/20/67	Carolina-Cleveland-Quebec (IHL)
KIDD, Trevor	6-2	190	L	Dugald, Man.	3/29/72	Carolina
MADDEN, Chris	6-0	177	L	Syracuse, NY	3/10/79	Guelph
PETRUK, Randy	5-9	178	R	Cranbrook, B.C.	4/23/78	Kamloops

1997-98 Scoring

* – rookie

Regular Season

Pos	#	Player	Team	GP	G	A	Pts	+/–	PIM	PP	SH	GW	GT	S	%
C	55	Keith Primeau	CAR	81	26	37	63	19	110	7	3	2	0	180	14.4
R	24	Sami Kapanen	CAR	81	26	37	63	9	16	4	0	5	0	190	13.7
L	10	Gary Roberts	CAR	61	20	29	49	3	103	4	0	2	1	106	18.9
R	19	Nelson Emerson	CAR	81	21	24	45	-17	50	6	0	4	1	203	10.3
C	92	Jeff O'Neill	CAR	74	19	20	39	-8	67	7	1	4	1	114	16.7
R	26	Ray Sheppard	FLA	61	14	17	31	-13	21	5	0	1	0	136	10.3
			CAR	10	4	2	6	2	2	2	0	1	0	33	12.1
			TOTAL	71	18	19	37	-11	23	7	0	2	0	169	10.7
R	18	Robert Kron	CAR	81	16	20	36	-8	12	4	0	2	1	175	9.1
L	23	Martin Gelinas	VAN	24	4	4	8	-6	10	1	1	1	0	49	8.2
			CAR	40	12	14	26	1	30	2	1	4	0	98	12.2
			TOTAL	64	16	18	34	-5	40	3	2	5	0	147	10.9
D	3	Steve Chiasson	CAR	66	7	27	34	-2	65	6	0	0	0	173	4.0
D	2	Glen Wesley	CAR	82	6	19	25	7	36	1	0	1	0	121	5.0
R	11	Kevin Dineen	CAR	54	7	16	23	-7	105	0	0	1	0	96	7.3
L	28	Paul Ranheim	CAR	73	5	9	14	-11	28	0	1	2	0	77	6.5
D	7	Curtis Leschyshyn	CAR	73	2	10	12	-2	45	1	0	1	0	53	3.8
D	6	Adam Burt	CAR	76	1	11	12	-6	106	0	1	0	0	51	2.0
R	27	Stephen Leach	CAR	45	4	5	9	-19	42	1	1	2	0	60	6.7
C	44	Kent Manderville	CAR	77	4	4	8	-6	31	0	0	0	0	80	5.0
D	5	Kevin Haller	CAR	65	3	5	8	-5	94	0	0	0	0	67	4.5
L	32	Stu Grimson	CAR	82	3	4	7	0	204	0	0	1	0	17	17.6
D	22	Sean Hill	OTT	13	1	1	2	-3	6	0	0	0	0	16	6.3
			CAR	42	0	5	5	-2	48	0	0	0	0	37	0.0
			TOTAL	55	1	6	7	-5	54	0	0	0	0	53	1.9
L	33	* Jon Battaglia	CAR	33	2	4	6	-1	10	0	0	1	0	21	9.5
R	12	Steven Rice	CAR	47	2	4	6	-16	38	0	0	0	0	39	5.1
D	14	* Steven Halko	CAR	18	0	2	2	-1	10	0	0	0	0	7	0.0
D	4	* Nolan Pratt	CAR	23	0	2	2	-2	44	0	0	0	0	11	0.0
D	46	* Mike Rucinski	CAR	9	0	1	1	0	2	0	0	0	0	3	0.0
L	3	Jeff Daniels	CAR	2	0	0	0	0	0	0	0	0	0	1	0.0
G	30	* Michael Fountain	CAR	3	0	0	0	0	2	0	0	0	0	0	0.0
C	34	Steve Martins	CAR	3	0	0	0	0	0	0	0	0	0	0	0.0
R	29	Kevin Brown	CAR	4	0	0	0	-2	0	0	0	0	0	0	0.0
G	39	Pat Jablonski	CAR	5	0	0	0	0	0	0	0	0	0	0	0.0
G	37	Trevor Kidd	CAR	47	0	0	0	0	2	0	0	0	0	0	0.0

Goaltending

No.	Goaltender	GPI	Mins	Avg	W	L	T	EN	SO	GA	SA	S%
37	Trevor Kidd	47	2685	2.17	21	21	3	7	3	97	1237	.922
33	Sean Burke	25	1415	2.80	7	11	5	2	1	66	655	.899
39	Pat Jablonski	5	279	3.01	1	4	0	1	0	14	115	.878
1	Kirk McLean	8	401	3.29	4	2	0	0	0	22	181	.878
30	* Michael Fountain	3	163	3.68	0	3	0	0	0	10	68	.853
	Totals	**82**	**4973**	**2.64**	**33**	**41**	**8**	**10**	**4**	**219**	**2266**	**.903**

General Managers' History

Jack Kelly, 1979-80, 1980-81; Larry Pleau, 1981-82, 1982-83; Emile Francis, 1983-84 to 1988-89; Ed Johnston, 1989-90 to 1991-92; Brian Burke, 1992-93; Paul Holmgren, 1993-94; Jim Rutherford, 1994-95 to date.

Coaching History

Don Blackburn, 1979-80; Don Blackburn and Larry Pleau, 1980-81; Larry Pleau, 1981-82; Larry Kish, Larry Pleau and John Cuniff, 1982- 83; Jack Evans, 1983-84 to 1986-87; Jack Evans and Larry Pleau, 1987-88; Larry Pleau, 1988-89; Rick Ley, 1989-90, 1990-91; Jim Roberts, 1991-92; Paul Holmgren, 1992-93; Paul Holmgren and Pierre Maguire, 1993-94; Paul Holmgren, 1994-95; Paul Holmgren and Paul Maurice, 1995-96; Paul Maurice, 1996-97 to date.

Captains' History

Rick Ley, 1979-80; Rick Ley and Mike Rogers, 1980-81; Dave Keon, 1981-82; Russ Anderson, 1982-83; Mark Johnson, 1983-84; Mark Johnson and Ron Francis, 1984-85; Ron Francis, 1985-86 to 1990-91; Randy Ladouceur, 1991-92; Pat Verbeek, 1992-93 to 1994-95; Brendan Shanahan, 1995-96; Kevin Dineen, 1996-97 to date.

Coach

MAURICE, PAUL

Coach, Carolina Hurricanes. Born in Sault Ste. Marie, Ont., January 30, 1967.

Paul Maurice is entering his fourth year as the franchise's head coach and is the first head coach of the Carolina Hurricanes. Maurice became the tenth coach in the 18-year history of the franchise on November 6, 1995, just 12 games into the 1995-96 season. Maurice stepped in as the youngest coach in the National Hockey League and remains the youngest head coach in the NHL despite ranking in the top five in tenure among NHL head coaches. In franchise history, Maurice ranks second in all-time wins (94) and second in games coached (234). In the 1996-97 season, Maurice was chosen to coach in the 1997 NHL All-Star Game.

Maurice joined the Whalers in June of 1995 as an assistant coach after serving as the head coach of the Detroit Junior Red Wings for two seasons. The Junior Wings won the OHL Western Division regular season title and played for the 1995 Memorial Cup by winning the OHL playoffs. The Wings lost in the Cup finals to Kamloops. For his efforts, Maurice was the runner-up for OHL coach of the year honors in 1995. In the 1993-94 season, Maurice's squad won the OHL Hap Emms Division title and advanced to the finals of the OHL playoffs before losing in seven games to North Bay.

Maurice began his coaching career in 1986 as an assistant coach for the Detroit Junior Red Wings after an eye injury ended his junior playing career. He served six seasons in that capacity before taking over the head coaching responsibilities in the 1993-94 season.

Coaching Record

		Regular Season					Playoffs			
Season	Team	Games	W	L	T	%	Games	W	L	%
1993-94	Detroit (OHL)	66	42	20	4	.697	17	11	6	.647
1994-95	Detroit (OHL)	66	44	18	4	.727	21	16	5	.762
1995-96	**Hartford (NHL)**	**70**	**29**	**33**	**8**	**.471**	....	....	....	....
1996-97	**Hartford (NHL)**	**82**	**32**	**39**	**11**	**.457**	....	....	....	....
1997-98	**Carolina (NHL)**	**82**	**33**	**41**	**8**	**.451**	....	....	....	....
	NHL Totals	**234**	**94**	**113**	**27**	**.459**	....	....	....	....

Club Records

Team

(Figures in brackets for season records are games played; records for fewest points, wins, ties, losses, goals, goals against are for 70 or more games)

Most Points	93	1986-87 (80)
Most Wins	43	1986-87 (80)
Most Ties	19	1979-80 (80)
Most Losses	54	1982-83 (80)
Most Goals	332	1985-86 (80)
Most Goals Against	403	1982-83 (80)
Fewest Points	45	1982-83 (80)
Fewest Wins	19	1982-83 (80)
Fewest Ties	4	1985-86 (80)
Fewest Losses	30	1986-87 (80)
Fewest Goals	200	1997-98 (82)
Fewest Goals Against	219	1997-98 (82)
Longest Winning Streak		
Overall	7	Mar. 16-29/85
Home	5	Mar. 17-29/85
Away	6	Nov. 10-Dec. 7/90
Longest Undefeated Streak		
Overall	10	Jan. 20-Feb. 10/82 (6 wins, 4 ties)
Home	7	Mar. 15-Apr. 5/86 (5 wins, 2 ties)
Away	8	Nov. 11-Dec. 5/96 (4 wins, 4 ties)
Longest Losing Streak		
Overall	9	Feb. 19-Mar. 8/83
Home	6	Feb. 19-Mar. 12/83, Feb. 10-Mar. 3/85
Away	13	Dec. 18/82-Feb. 5/83
Longest Winless Streak		
Overall	14	Jan. 4-Feb. 9/92 (8 losses, 6 ties)
Home	13	Jan. 15-Mar. 10/85 (11 losses, 2 ties)
Away	15	Nov. 11/79-Jan. 9/80 (11 losses, 4 ties)
Most Shutouts, Season	6	1995-96 (82)
Most PIM, Season	2,354	1992-93 (84)
Most Goals, Game	11	Feb. 12/84 (Edm. 0 at Hfd. 11), Oct. 19/85 (Mtl. 6 at Hfd. 11), Jan. 17/86 (Que. 6 at Hfd. 11), Mar. 15/86 (Chi. 4 at Hfd. 11)

Individual

Most Seasons	11	Kevin Dineen
Most Games	714	Ron Francis
Most Goals, Career	264	Ron Francis
Most Assists, Career	557	Ron Francis
Most Points, Career	821	Ron Francis (264G, 557A)
Most PIM, Career	1,368	Torrie Robertson
Most Shutouts, Career	13	Mike Liut
Longest Consecutive Games Streak	419	Dave Tippett (Mar. 3/84-Oct. 7/89)
Most Goals, Season	56	Blaine Stoughton (1979-80)
Most Assists, Season	69	Ron Francis (1989-90)
Most Points, Season	105	Mike Rogers (1979-80; 44G, 61A), (1980-81; 40G, 65A)
Most PIM, Season	358	Torrie Robertson (1985-86)
Most Points, Defenseman, Season	69	Dave Babych (1985-86; 14G, 55A)
Most Points, Center, Season	105	Mike Rogers (1979-80; 44G, 61A), (1980-81; 40G, 65A)
Most Points, Right Wing, Season	100	Blaine Stoughton (1979-80; 56G, 44A)
Most Points, Left Wing, Season	89	Geoff Sanderson (1992-93; 46G, 43A)
Most Points, Rookie, Season	72	Sylvain Turgeon (1983-84; 40G, 32A)
Most Shutouts, Season	4	Mike Liut (1986-87), Peter Sidorkiewicz (1988-89), Sean Burke (1995-96, 1996-97)
Most Goals, Game	4	Jordy Douglas (Feb. 3/80), Ron Francis (Feb. 12/84)
Most Assists, Game	6	Ron Francis (Mar. 5/87)
Most Points, Game	6	Paul Lawless (Jan. 4/87; 2G, 4A), Ron Francis (Mar. 5/87; 6A) (Oct. 8/89; 3G, 3A)

Records include Hartford Whalers, 1979-80 through 1996-97.

All-time Record vs. Other Clubs

Regular Season

	At Home							On Road							Total						
	GP	W	L	T	GF	GA	PTS	GP	W	L	T	GF	GA	PTS	GP	W	L	T	GF	GA	PTS
Anaheim	4	3	1	0	11	7	6	4	2	2	0	13	16	4	8	5	3	0	24	23	10
Boston	63	28	28	7	220	221	63	66	16	44	6	174	257	38	129	44	72	13	394	478	101
Buffalo	66	26	30	10	200	202	62	65	20	38	7	199	266	47	131	46	68	17	399	468	109
Calgary	25	8	13	4	82	96	20	25	5	19	1	83	126	11	50	13	32	5	165	222	31
Chicago	26	11	12	3	86	88	25	25	7	15	3	71	109	17	51	18	27	6	157	197	42
Colorado	58	24	23	11	195	202	59	60	17	34	9	183	255	43	118	41	57	20	378	457	102
Dallas	26	9	14	3	88	103	21	25	10	14	1	78	104	21	51	19	28	4	166	207	42
Detroit	25	15	9	1	91	69	31	26	7	13	6	73	100	20	51	22	22	7	164	169	51
Edmonton	25	10	10	5	104	92	25	26	5	18	3	79	109	13	51	15	28	8	183	201	38
Florida	10	4	6	0	30	30	8	10	3	5	2	19	29	8	20	7	11	2	49	59	16
Los Angeles	26	13	9	4	103	102	30	25	8	14	3	98	110	19	51	21	23	7	201	212	49
Montreal	66	25	32	9	200	238	59	63	14	42	7	186	275	35	129	39	74	16	386	513	94
New Jersey	31	14	10	7	109	95	35	33	12	18	3	108	118	27	64	26	28	10	217	213	62
NY Islanders	33	15	13	5	122	120	35	31	10	17	4	82	112	24	64	25	30	9	204	232	59
NY Rangers	31	17	11	3	115	103	37	32	9	20	3	93	139	21	63	26	31	6	208	242	58
Ottawa	15	14	1	0	54	29	28	17	9	5	3	55	42	21	32	23	6	3	109	71	49
Philadelphia	32	10	16	6	116	132	26	31	8	21	2	84	124	18	63	18	37	8	200	256	44
Phoenix	25	12	7	6	97	78	30	27	14	12	1	98	93	29	52	26	19	7	195	171	59
Pittsburgh	36	17	17	2	142	140	36	34	10	19	5	132	161	25	70	27	36	7	274	301	61
St. Louis	27	11	14	2	85	86	24	26	8	16	2	82	104	18	53	19	30	4	167	190	42
San Jose	7	3	4	0	23	18	6	6	3	3	0	23	31	6	13	6	7	0	46	49	12
Tampa Bay	11	8	2	1	37	26	17	11	4	6	1	30	34	9	22	12	8	2	67	60	26
Toronto	25	15	6	4	117	81	34	25	13	9	3	96	88	29	50	28	15	7	213	169	63
Vancouver	25	11	10	4	83	88	26	26	9	11	6	75	94	24	51	20	21	10	158	182	50
Washington	33	11	17	5	92	113	27	32	10	20	2	88	109	22	65	21	37	7	180	222	49
Totals	**751**	**334**	**315**	**102**	**2602**	**2559**	**770**	**751**	**233**	**435**	**83**	**2302**	**3005**	**549**	**1502**	**567**	**750**	**185**	**4904**	**5564**	**1319**

Playoffs

	Series	W	L	GP	W	L	T	GF	GA	Last Mtg.	Round	Result
Boston	2	0	2	13	5	8	0	38	47	1991	DSF	L 2-4
Colorado	2	1	1	9	5	4	0	35	34	1987	DSF	L 2-4
Montreal	5	0	5	27	8	19	0	70	96	1992	DSF	L 3-4
Totals	**9**	**1**	**8**	**49**	**18**	**31**	**0**	**143**	**177**			

Playoff Results 1998-94

Year	Round	Opponent	Result	GF	GA

(Last playoff appearance: 1992)

Abbreviations: Round: DSF – division semi-final.

Calgary totals include Atlanta, 1979-80.
Dallas totals include Minnesota, 1979-80 to 1992-93.
Phoenix totals include Winnipeg, 1979-80 to 1995-96.
Colorado totals include Quebec, 1979-80 to 1994-95.
New Jersey totals include Colorado Rockies, 1979-80 to 1981-82.

1997-98 Results

Oct.	1	at	Tampa Bay	2-4	**Jan.**	3		Dallas	1-6
	3		Pittsburgh	3-4		5		Ottawa	4-1
	4	at	Ottawa	2-3		6	at	NY Rangers	2-4
	7		Los Angeles	3-3		8		Philadelphia	3-3
	10		New Jersey	2-1		10	at	NY Islanders	2-1
	11	at	Pittsburgh	1-4		12		Pittsburgh	1-4
	13	at	St. Louis	1-3		14		Chicago	1-4
	15		Buffalo	3-3		21	at	Buffalo	1-2
	18	at	Detroit	2-4		22	at	Ottawa	4-2
	20	at	NY Rangers	2-4		24	at	Montreal	4-3
	22		St. Louis	4-3		27	at	Florida	0-3
	24	at	Colorado	3-3		28	at	Tampa Bay	3-2
	26	at	Chicago	3-2		30	at	NY Islanders	0-2
	31		Buffalo	2-3	**Feb.**	1		Montreal	3-6
Nov.	3		Vancouver	5-3		4		Tampa Bay	3-3
	5		Detroit	3-1		7	at	Boston	3-1
	7		NY Islanders	2-3		28	at	New Jersey	3-4
	9		Ottawa	4-1	**Mar.**	2	at	San Jose	3-1
	12	at	Edmonton	6-4		5	at	Los Angeles	2-1
	13	at	Calgary	4-2		6	at	Phoenix	5-4
	16	at	Vancouver	1-4		8	at	Anaheim	3-1
	19		Montreal	2-1		12		New Jersey	0-2
	21		NY Rangers	3-4		14		San Jose	1-2
	23		Calgary	3-3		15		Edmonton	4-1
	26	at	Pittsburgh	2-3		18	at	Washington	0-1
	28		Tampa Bay	2-0		20	at	Dallas	1-6
	29		Colorado	2-3		23	at	Florida	5-3
Dec.	1		Boston	3-1		26		NY Rangers	4-1
	3		NY Islanders	5-3		28	at	Philadelphia	4-2
	5		Phoenix	2-2		29		Philadelphia	1-3
	6	at	Boston	1-4		31		Montreal	3-3
	10		Florida	2-5	**Apr.**	1	at	New Jersey	4-0
	12	at	Buffalo	2-3		4	at	Montreal	1-0
	16		Ottawa	2-1		6	at	Boston	3-0
	18	at	Ottawa	2-3		8	at	Buffalo	1-3
	20		Washington	1-2		9		Toronto	5-2
	23	at	Philadelphia	2-4		11	at	Toronto	1-5
	26		Florida	2-5		13		Boston	2-3
	27		Buffalo	4-1		16		Pittsburgh	1-4
	30		Anaheim	2-1		18		Washington	3-4
	31	at	Pittsburgh	2-3		19	at	Washington	1-2

Entry Draft Selections 1998-84

1998

Pick	
11	Jeff Heerema
70	Kevin Holdridge
71	Erik Cole
91	Josef Vasicek
93	Tommy Westlund
97	Chris Madden
184	Donald Smith
208	Jaroslav Svoboda
211	Mark Kosick
239	Brent McDonald

1997

Pick	
22	Nikos Tselios
28	Brad Defauw
80	Francis Lessard
88	Shane Willis
142	Kyle Dafoe
169	Andrew Merrick
195	Niklas Nordgren
199	Randy Fitzgerald
225	Kent McDonell

1996

Pick	
34	Trevor Wasyluk
61	Andrei Petrunin
88	Craig MacDonald
104	Steve Wasylko
116	Mark McMahon
143	Aaron Baker
171	Greg Kuznik
197	Kevin Marsh
223	Craig Adams
231	Askhat Rakhmatullin

1995

Pick	
13	J-Sebastien Giguere
35	Sergei Fedotov
85	Ian MacNeil
87	Sami Kapanen
113	Hugh Hamilton
165	Byron Ritchie
191	Milan Kostolny
217	Mike Rucinski

1994

Pick	
5	Jeff O'Neill
83	Hnat Domenichelli
109	Ryan Risidore
187	Tom Buckley
213	Ashlin Halfnight
230	Matt Ball
239	Brian Regan
265	Steve Nimigon

1993

Pick	
2	Chris Pronger
72	Marek Malik
84	Trevor Roenick
115	Nolan Pratt
188	Emmanuel Legace
214	Dmitri Gorenko
240	Wes Swinson
266	Igor Chibirev

1992

Pick	
9	Robert Petrovicky
47	Andrei Nikolishin
57	Jan Vopat
79	Kevin Smyth
81	Jason McBain
143	Jarret Reid
153	Ken Belanger
177	Konstantin Korotkov
201	Greg Zwakman
225	Steven Halko
249	Joacim Esbjors

1991

Pick	
9	Patrick Poulin
31	Martin Hamrlik
53	Todd Hall
59	Mikael Nylander
75	Jim Storm
119	Mike Harding
141	Brian Mueller
163	Steve Yule
185	Chris Belanger
207	Jason Currie
229	Mike Santonelli
251	Rob Peters

1990

Pick	
15	Mark Greig
36	Geoff Sanderson
57	Mike Lenarduzzi
78	Chris Bright
120	Cory Keenan
141	Jergus Baca
162	Martin D'Orsonnens
183	Corey Osmak
204	Espen Knutsen
225	Tommie Eriksen
246	Denis Chalifoux

1989

Pick	
10	Robert Holik
52	Blair Atcheynum
73	Jim McKenzie
94	James Black
115	Jerome Bechard
136	Scott Daniels
157	Raymond Saumier
178	Michel Picard
199	Trevor Buchanan
220	John Battice
241	Peter Kasowski

1988

Pick	
11	Chris Govedaris
32	Barry Richter
74	Dean Dyer
95	Scott Morrow
116	Corey Beaulieu
137	Kerry Russell
158	Jim Burke
179	Mark Hirth
200	Wayde Bucsis
221	Rob White
242	Dan Slatalla

1987

Pick	
18	Jody Hull
39	Adam Burt
81	Terry Yake
102	Marc Rousseau
123	Jeff St. Cyr
144	Greg Wolf
165	John Moore
186	Joe Day
228	Kevin Sullivan
249	Steve Laurin

1986

Pick	
11	Scott Young
32	Marc Laforge
74	Brian Chapman
95	Bill Horn
116	Joe Quinn
137	Steve Torrel
158	Ron Hoover
179	Robert Glasgow
200	Sean Evoy
221	Cal Brown
242	Brian Verbeek

1985

Pick	
5	Dana Murzyn
26	Kay Whitmore
68	Gary Callaghan
110	Shane Churla
131	Chris Brant
152	Brian Puhalsky
173	Greg Dornbach
194	Paul Tory
215	Jerry Pawlowski
236	Bruce Hill

1984

Pick	
11	Sylvain Cote
110	Mike Millar
131	Mike Vellucci
173	John Devereaux
193	Brent Regan
214	Jim Culhane
234	Pete Abric

Club Directory

Greensboro Coliseum

Carolina Hurricanes
5000 Aerial Center Parkway
Suite 1000
Morrisville, NC 27560
Phone **919/467-7825**
FAX 919/462-7030
Capacity: TBA

Executive Management	
Chief Executive Officer/Governor	Peter Karmanos Jr.
General Partner	Thomas Thewes
President and Chief Operating Officer, Gale Force Holdings, LLP.	Dean Jordan
President and General Manager	Jim Rutherford
Hockey Operations	
Assistant General Manager	Jason Karmanos
Vice President of Hockey Operations	Terry McDonnell
Head Coach	Paul Maurice
Assistant Coaches	Randy Ladouceur, Tom Webster
Director of Amateur Scouting	Sheldon Ferguson
Amateur Scouts	Laurence Ferguson, Willy Langer, Willy Lindstrom, Bert Marshall, Tony MacDonald, Terry E. McDonnell, Doug Woods
Pro Scouts	Claude Larose, Sam McMaster
Goaltender Coach/Pro Scout	Steve Weeks
Head Athletic Therapist/Strength and Conditioning Coach	Peter Friesen
Assistant Athletic Therapist	Scott Green
Equipment Managers	Skip Cunningham, Wally Tatomir
Assistant Equipment Managers	Bob Gorman, Rick Szuber
Broadcasters	
Television Play-by-Play	John Forslund
Television Analyst	Bill Gardner
Radio Play-by-Play	Chuck Kaiton
TV	Hurricanes Television Network
Radio	Hurricanes Radio Network
Media Relations	
Director of Media Relations	Chris Brown
Media Relations Manager/Travel Coordinator	Jerry Peters
Media Relations Phone	(919) 467-7825, exts. 351, 354
Press Box Phone	(919) 280-5620

Keith Primeau's total of 63 points in 1997-98 was the second-best of his career. With 26 goals and 37 assists, he tied Sami Kapanen for the team lead in all three categories.

President and General Manager

RUTHERFORD, JIM
President and General Manager, Carolina Hurricanes.
Born in Beeton, Ont., February 17, 1949.

Jim Rutherford, a former NHL goaltender, is the franchise's seventh general manager and the first general manager of the Carolina Hurricanes. Entering his fifth season, Rutherford has taken an aggressive approach towards improving the fortunes of the franchise through trades and the NHL draft.

A veteran of 13 NHL seasons, Rutherford began his professional goaltending career in 1969 as a first-round selection of the Detroit Red Wings. While playing for Detroit, Pittsburgh, Toronto and Los Angeles, Rutherford collected 14 career shutouts. For five seasons he also served as the Red Wings' player representative. Rutherford also played for Team Canada in the IIHF World Championships in Vienna in 1977 and Moscow in 1979.

After his playing days with the Red Wings, Rutherford joined Compuware to serve as the director of hockey operations for Compuware Sports Corporation. Rutherford gained a wealth of experience in youth hockey and junior programs. As a former player, coach, and general manager, his ability to develop players and produce winning programs is widely respected throughout the hockey community.

He started his management career by guiding Compuware Sports Corporation's purchase of the Windsor Spitfires of the Ontario Hockey League in April of 1984. During the next four years, Rutherford acted as general manager of the Spitfires. After the Spitfires advanced to the 1988 Memorial Cup finals, Rutherford led Compuware's efforts to bring the first American-based OHL franchise to Detroit on December 11, 1989. Rutherford was voted the 1987 executive of the year in both the OHL and the CHL and won the OHL executive of the year award again in 1988.

Chicago Blackhawks

1997-98 Results: 30W-39L-13T 73PTS. Fifth, Central Division

Rugged defenseman Chris Chelios led the Blackhawks with 151 penalty minutes in 1997-98, but still finished in a three-way tie for third in team scoring with 42 points. His 39 assists trailed only Tony Amonte (42) for the lead in Chicago.

1998-99 Schedule

Oct.	Sat.	10	New Jersey		Tue.	12	at Colorado
	Tue.	13	at Dallas		Fri.	15	at NY Rangers
	Thu.	15	Anaheim		Sun.	17	Phoenix
	Sat.	17	Dallas		Thu.	21	Montreal
	Mon.	19	at Montreal		Wed.	27	at Edmonton
	Thu.	22	San Jose		Thu.	28	at Calgary
	Sat.	24	Nashville		Sat.	30	at Vancouver
	Wed.	28	at Carolina	**Feb.**	Mon.	1	at San Jose
	Fri.	30	Florida		Wed.	3	at Anaheim
Nov.	Sun.	1	Calgary		Thu.	4	at Los Angeles
	Wed.	4	at Florida		Sat.	6	at Phoenix*
	Fri.	6	at Tampa Bay		Wed.	10	San Jose
	Sun.	8	Edmonton		Fri.	12	Detroit
	Tue.	10	at St. Louis		Sat.	13	at Toronto
	Thu.	12	Toronto		Mon.	15	at Ottawa
	Sat.	14	at Buffalo		Wed.	17	Vancouver
	Sun.	15	Ottawa		Fri.	19	at Dallas
	Tue.	17	at Nashville		Sun.	21	Boston*
	Sat.	21	at Los Angeles		Wed.	24	at St. Louis
	Sun.	22	at Anaheim		Fri.	26	Los Angeles
	Tue.	24	at Phoenix		Sun.	28	St. Louis
	Sat.	28	at Calgary	**Mar.**	Sat.	6	at San Jose*
	Sun.	29	at Edmonton		Sun.	7	at Vancouver
Dec.	Thu.	3	Anaheim		Wed.	10	Nashville
	Sun.	6	Tampa Bay		Fri.	12	at Nashville
	Tue.	8	at Detroit		Sun.	14	St. Louis*
	Wed.	9	Edmonton		Wed.	17	Calgary
	Fri.	11	Toronto		Sat.	20	at Colorado*
	Sun.	13	Dallas		Sun.	21	Colorado*
	Thu.	17	Washington		Tue.	23	at Pittsburgh
	Sat.	19	at Philadelphia*		Thu.	25	at Boston
	Sun.	20	Los Angeles		Sat.	27	at New Jersey*
	Wed.	23	Phoenix		Sun.	28	St. Louis*
	Sat.	26	Philadelphia		Wed.	31	Buffalo
	Thu.	31	NY Islanders	**Apr.**	Fri.	2	at Detroit
Jan.	Sat.	2	at Detroit		Sat.	3	Carolina
	Sun.	3	Detroit		Mon.	5	Vancouver
	Tue.	5	at NY Islanders		Thu.	8	NY Rangers
	Thu.	7	at St. Louis		Mon.	12	at Washington
	Sat.	9	at Nashville		Thu.	15	Nashville
	Sun.	10	Colorado		Sat.	17	Detroit

* Denotes afternoon game.

Year-by-Year Record

		Home			Road			Overall							
Season	**GP**	**W**	**L**	**T**	**W**	**L**	**T**	**W**	**L**	**T**	**GF**	**GA**	**Pts.**	**Finished**	**Playoff Result**
1997-98	82	14	19	8	16	20	5	30	39	13	192	199	73	5th, Central Div.	Out of Playoffs
1996-97	82	16	21	4	18	14	9	34	35	13	223	210	81	5th, Central Div.	Lost Conf. Quarter-Final
1995-96	82	22	13	6	18	15	8	40	28	14	273	220	94	2nd, Central Div.	Lost Conf. Semi-Final
1994-95	48	11	10	3	13	9	2	24	19	5	156	115	53	3rd, Central Div.	Lost Conf. Championship
1993-94	84	21	16	5	18	20	4	39	36	9	254	240	87	5th, Central Div.	Lost Conf. Quarter-Final
1992-93	84	25	11	6	22	14	6	47	25	12	279	230	106	1st, Norris Div.	Lost Div. Semi-Final
1991-92	80	23	9	8	13	20	7	36	29	15	257	236	87	2nd, Norris Div.	Lost Final
1990-91	80	28	8	4	21	15	4	49	23	8	284	211	106	1st, Norris Div.	Lost Div. Semi-Final
1989-90	80	25	13	2	16	20	4	41	33	6	316	294	88	1st, Norris Div.	Lost Conf. Championship
1988-89	80	16	14	10	11	27	2	27	41	12	297	335	66	4th, Norris Div.	Lost Conf. Championship
1987-88	80	21	17	2	9	24	7	30	41	9	284	328	69	3rd, Norris Div.	Lost Div. Semi-Final
1986-87	80	18	13	9	11	24	5	29	37	14	290	310	72	3rd, Norris Div.	Lost Div. Semi-Final
1985-86	80	23	12	5	16	21	3	39	33	8	351	349	86	1st, Norris Div.	Lost Div. Semi-Final
1984-85	80	22	16	2	16	19	5	38	35	7	309	299	83	2nd, Norris Div.	Lost Conf. Championship
1983-84	80	25	13	2	5	29	6	30	42	8	277	311	68	4th, Norris Div.	Lost Div. Semi-Final
1982-83	80	29	8	3	18	15	7	47	23	10	338	268	104	1st, Norris Div.	Lost Conf. Championship
1981-82	80	20	13	7	10	25	5	30	38	12	332	363	72	4th, Norris Div.	Lost Conf. Championship
1980-81	80	21	11	8	10	22	8	31	33	16	304	315	78	2nd, Smythe Div.	Lost Prelim. Round
1979-80	80	21	12	7	13	15	12	34	27	19	241	250	87	1st, Smythe Div.	Lost Quarter-Final
1978-79	80	18	12	10	11	24	5	29	36	15	244	277	73	1st, Smythe Div.	Lost Quarter-Final
1977-78	80	20	9	11	12	20	8	32	29	19	230	220	83	1st, Smythe Div.	Lost Quarter-Final
1976-77	80	19	16	5	7	27	6	26	43	11	240	298	63	3rd, Smythe Div.	Lost Prelim. Round
1975-76	80	17	15	8	15	15	10	32	30	18	254	261	82	1st, Smythe Div.	Lost Quarter-Final
1974-75	80	24	12	4	13	23	4	37	35	8	268	241	82	3rd, Smythe Div.	Lost Quarter-Final
1973-74	78	20	6	13	21	8	10	41	14	23	272	164	105	2nd, West Div.	Lost Semi-Final
1972-73	78	26	9	4	16	18	5	42	27	9	284	225	93	1st, West Div.	Lost Final
1971-72	78	28	3	8	18	14	7	46	17	15	256	166	107	1st, West Div.	Lost Semi-Final
1970-71	78	30	6	3	19	14	6	49	20	9	277	184	107	1st, West Div.	Lost Final
1969-70	76	26	7	5	19	15	4	45	22	9	250	170	99	1st, East Div.	Lost Semi-Final
1968-69	76	20	14	4	14	19	5	34	33	9	280	246	77	6th, East Div.	Out of Playoffs
1967-68	74	20	13	4	12	13	12	32	26	16	212	222	80	4th, East Div.	Lost Semi-Final
1966-67	70	24	5	6	17	12	6	41	17	12	264	170	94	1st,	Lost Semi-Final
1965-66	70	21	8	6	16	17	2	37	25	8	240	187	82	2nd,	Lost Semi-Final
1964-65	70	20	13	2	14	15	6	34	28	8	224	176	76	3rd,	Lost Final
1963-64	70	26	4	5	10	18	7	36	22	12	218	169	84	2nd,	Lost Semi-Final
1962-63	70	17	9	9	15	12	8	32	21	17	194	178	81	2nd,	Lost Semi-Final
1961-62	70	20	10	5	11	16	8	31	26	13	217	186	75	3rd,	Lost Final
1960-61	**70**	**20**	**6**	**9**	**9**	**18**	**8**	**29**	**24**	**17**	**198**	**180**	**75**	**3rd,**	**Won Stanley Cup**
1959-60	70	18	11	6	10	18	7	28	29	13	191	180	69	3rd,	Lost Semi-Final
1958-59	70	14	12	9	14	17	4	28	29	13	197	208	69	3rd,	Lost Semi-Final
1957-58	70	15	17	3	9	22	4	24	39	7	163	202	55	5th,	Out of Playoffs
1956-57	70	12	15	8	4	24	7	16	39	15	169	225	47	6th,	Out of Playoffs
1955-56	70	9	19	7	10	20	5	19	39	12	155	216	50	6th,	Out of Playoffs
1954-55	70	6	21	8	7	19	9	13	40	17	161	235	43	6th,	Out of Playoffs
1953-54	70	8	21	6	4	30	1	12	51	7	133	242	31	6th,	Out of Playoffs
1952-53	70	14	11	10	13	17	5	27	28	15	169	175	69	4th,	Lost Semi-Final
1951-52	70	9	19	7	8	25	2	17	44	9	158	241	43	6th,	Out of Playoffs
1950-51	70	8	22	5	5	25	5	13	47	10	171	280	36	6th,	Out of Playoffs
1949-50	70	13	18	4	9	20	6	22	38	10	203	244	54	6th,	Out of Playoffs
1948-49	60	13	12	5	8	19	3	21	31	8	173	211	50	5th,	Out of Playoffs
1947-48	60	10	17	3	10	17	3	20	34	6	195	225	46	6th,	Out of Playoffs
1946-47	60	10	17	3	9	20	1	19	37	4	193	274	42	6th,	Out of Playoffs
1945-46	50	15	5	5	8	15	2	23	20	7	200	178	53	3rd,	Lost Semi-Final
1944-45	50	9	14	2	4	16	5	13	30	7	141	194	33	5th,	Out of Playoffs
1943-44	50	15	6	4	7	17	1	22	23	5	178	187	49	4th,	Lost Final
1942-43	50	14	3	8	3	15	7	17	18	15	179	180	49	5th,	Out of Playoffs
1941-42	48	15	8	1	7	15	2	22	23	3	145	155	47	4th,	Lost Quarter-Final
1940-41	48	11	10	3	5	15	4	16	25	7	112	139	39	5th,	Lost Semi-Final
1939-40	48	15	7	2	8	12	4	23	19	6	112	120	52	4th,	Lost Quarter-Final
1938-39	48	5	13	6	7	15	2	12	28	8	91	132	32	7th,	Out of Playoffs
1937-38	**48**	**10**	**10**	**4**	**4**	**15**	**5**	**14**	**25**	**9**	**97**	**139**	**37**	**3rd, Amn. Div.**	**Won Stanley Cup**
1936-37	48	8	13	3	6	14	4	14	27	7	99	131	35	4th, Amn. Div.	Out of Playoffs
1935-36	48	15	7	2	6	12	6	21	19	8	93	92	50	3rd, Amn. Div.	Lost Quarter-Final
1934-35	48	12	9	3	14	8	2	26	17	5	118	88	57	2nd, Amn. Div.	Lost Quarter-Final
1933-34	**48**	**13**	**4**	**7**	**7**	**13**	**4**	**20**	**17**	**11**	**88**	**83**	**51**	**2nd, Amn. Div.**	**Won Stanley Cup**
1932-33	48	12	7	5	4	13	7	16	20	12	88	101	44	4th, Amn. Div.	Out of Playoffs
1931-32	48	13	5	6	5	14	5	18	19	11	86	101	47	2nd, Amn. Div.	Lost Quarter-Final
1930-31	44	13	8	1	11	9	2	24	17	3	108	78	51	2nd, Amn. Div.	Lost Final
1929-30	44	12	9	1	9	9	4	21	18	5	117	111	47	2nd, Amn. Div.	Lost Quarter-Final
1928-29	44	3	13	6	4	16	2	7	29	8	33	85	22	5th, Amn. Div.	Out of Playoffs
1927-28	44	2	18	2	5	16	1	7	34	3	68	134	17	5th, Amn. Div.	Out of Playoffs
1926-27	44	12	8	2	7	14	1	19	22	3	115	116	41	3rd, Amn. Div.	Lost Quarter-Final

Franchise date: September 25, 1926

CENTRAL DIVISION

73rd NHL Season

1998-99 Player Personnel

FORWARDS	HT	WT	S	Place of Birth	Date	1997-98 Club
AMONTE, Tony	6-0	195	L	Hingham, MA	8/2/70	Chicago-United States
BELL, Mark	6-3	185	L	St. Paul's, Ont.	8/5/80	Ottawa (OHL)
BLACK, James	6-0	202	L	Regina, Sask.	8/15/69	Chicago
CALDER, Kyle	5-11	180	L	Mannville, Alta.	1/5/79	Regina
CLEARY, Daniel	6-0	203	L	Carbonear, Nfld.	12/18/78	Belleville-Chicago-Indianapolis
CLOUTIER, Sylvain	6-0	195	L	Mont-Laurier, Que.	2/13/74	Adirondack-Detroit (IHL)
COUTURE, Alexandre	6-4	217		Sorel, Quebec	9/14/80	Sherbrooke
DAZE, Eric	6-6	220	L	Montreal, Que.	7/2/75	Chicago-Canada
DUBINSKY, Steve	6-0	190	L	Montreal, Que.	7/9/70	Chicago
DUMONT, Jean-Pierre	6-1	187	L	Montreal, Que.	4/1/78	Val D'Or-Canada
GILMOUR, Doug	5-11	175	L	Kingston, Ont.	6/25/63	New Jersey
HANKINSON, Casey	6-1	187	L	Edina, MN	5/8/76	U. of Minnesota
HERPERGER, Chris	6-0	190	L	Esterhazy, Sask.	2/24/74	Canada
JANSSENS, Mark	6-3	212	L	Surrey, B.C.	5/19/68	Anaheim-NY Islanders-Phoenix
JONES, Ty	6-3	218	R	Richland, WA	2/22/79	Spokane-United States
KILGER, Chad	6-3	204	L	Cornwall, Ont.	11/27/76	Phoenix-Springfield-Chicago
LEROUX, Jean-Yves	6-2	211	L	Montreal, Que.	6/24/76	Chicago
MAKINEN, Marko	6-5	200	R	Turku, Finland	3/31/77	Kentucky-Louisville
MARA, Rob	6-1	175	R	Boston, MA	9/25/75	Colgate
MILLS, Craig	6-0	190	R	Toronto, Ont.	8/27/76	Chicago-Indianapolis
MOREAU, Ethan	6-2	205	L	Huntsville, Ont.	9/22/75	Chicago
OLCZYK, Ed	6-1	205	L	Chicago, IL	8/16/66	Pittsburgh
PEPPERALL, Colin	5-11	160	L	Niagara Falls, Ont.	4/28/78	Erie (OHL)-Hartford
PERROTT, Nathan	6-0	215	R	Owen Sound, Ont.	12/8/76	Indianapolis-Jacksonville
PETERS, Geoff	6-0	174	L	Hamilton, Ont.	4/30/78	Erie (OHL)-N.B.-Ind
PROBERT, Bob	6-3	225	L	Windsor, Ont.	6/5/65	Chicago
REICH, Jeremy	6-1	198	L	Craik, Sask.	2/11/79	Seattle-Swift Current
SHANTZ, Jeff	6-0	195	R	Duchess, Alta.	10/10/73	Chicago
SIMPSON, Reid	6-2	220	L	Flin Flon, Man.	5/21/69	New Jersey-Chicago
TARDIF, Steve	5-11	178	L	St-Agnes, Que.	3/29/77	Jacksonville-Indianapolis
VANDENBUSSCHE, Ryan	5-11	187	R	Simcoe, Ont.	2/28/73	NYR-Hartford-Chi-Indianapolis
WHITE, Todd	5-10	181	L	Kanata, Ont.	5/21/75	Chicago-Indianapolis
ZHAMNOV, Alexei	6-1	195	L	Moscow, USSR	10/1/70	Chicago-Russia
DEFENSEMEN						
CHELIOS, Chris	6-1	190	R	Chicago, IL	1/25/62	Chicago-United States
COFFEY, Paul	6-0	190	L	Weston, Ont.	6/1/61	Philadelphia
FEIL, Chris	6-2	180	L	Orland Park, IL	4/25/78	Barrie
FOGARTY, Bryan	6-2	206	L	Brantford, Ont.	6/11/69	Hannover
HAMILTON, Jason	6-2	218	R	Montreal, Que.	1/25/77	Shawinigan
HOCKING, Justin	6-4	205	R	Stettler, Alta.	1/9/74	Worcester
JOHNSON, Andy	6-3	188	L	Fredericton, N.B.	3/6/78	Peterborough
KOZYREV, Andrei	6-1	200	L	Cherepovets, USSR	6/17/73	Indianapolis
LAFLAMME, Christian	6-1	202	R	St. Charles, Que.	11/24/76	Chicago
NASREDDINE, Alain	6-1	201	L	Montreal, Que.	7/10/75	Indianapolis
PAUL, Jeff	6-3	196	R	London, Ont.	3/1/78	Erie (OHL)
ROHLOFF, Todd	6-3	213	L	Grand Rapids, MN	1/16/74	Miami-Ohio-Indianapolis
ROYER, Remi	6-1	183	R	Donnacona, Que.	2/12/78	Rouyn-Noranda-Indianapolis
RUSSELL, Cam	6-4	200	L	Halifax, N.S.	1/12/69	Chicago
SMITH, Jerad	6-3	205	R	Lethbridge, Alta.	1/5/79	Portland (WHL)
WEINRICH, Eric	6-1	210	L	Roanoke, VA	12/19/66	United States-Chicago
WILFORD, Marty	6-0	207	L	Cobourg, Ont.	4/17/77	Columbus (ECHL)-Indianapolis
YAWNEY, Trent	6-3	195	L	Hudson Bay, Sask.	9/29/65	Chicago
ZMOLEK, Doug	6-2	222	L	Rochester, MN	11/3/70	Los Angeles

GOALTENDERS	HT	WT	C	Place of Birth	Date	1997-98 Club
DAUBENSPECK, Kirk	6-0	190		Madison, WI	7/16/74	Indianapolis-Jacksonville
FITZPATRICK, Mark	6-2	198	L	Toronto, Ont.	11/13/68	Florida-Fort Wayne-Tampa Bay
HACKETT, Jeff	6-1	195	L	London, Ont.	6/1/68	Chicago-Canada
LAMOTHE, Marc	6-1	204	L	New Liskeard, Ont.	2/27/74	Indianapolis
PELLETIER, Jonathan	5-11	165	L	Riviere-du-loop, Que.	4/15/80	Victoriaville-Drummondville
TREFILOV, Andrei	6-0	190	L	Kirovo-Chepetsk, USSR	8/31/69	Roch-Chi-Ind-Russia

1997-98 Scoring

* – rookie

Regular Season

Pos	#	Player	Team	GP	G	A	Pts	+/–	PIM	PP	SH	GW	GT	S	%
R	10	Tony Amonte	CHI	82	31	42	73	21	66	7	3	5	0	296	10.5
C	36	Alexei Zhamnov	CHI	70	21	28	49	16	61	6	2	3	1	193	10.9
L	55	Eric Daze	CHI	80	31	11	42	4	22	10	0	7	1	216	14.4
D	20	Gary Suter	CHI	73	14	28	42	1	74	5	2	0	0	199	7.0
D	7	Chris Chelios	CHI	81	3	39	42	-7	151	1	0	0	0	205	1.5
C	22	Greg Johnson	PIT	5	1	0	1	0	2	0	0	0	0	4	25.0
			CHI	69	11	22	33	-2	38	4	0	3	0	85	12.9
			TOTAL	74	12	22	34	-2	40	4	0	3	0	89	13.5
C	11	Jeff Shantz	CHI	61	11	20	31	0	36	1	2	2	0	69	15.9
R	25	Sergei Krivokrasov	CHI	58	10	13	23	-1	33	1	0	2	0	127	7.9
D	2	Eric Weinrich	CHI	82	2	21	23	10	106	0	0	0	0	85	2.4
L	19	Ethan Moreau	CHI	54	9	9	18	0	73	2	0	0	0	87	10.3
C	14	Steve Dubinsky	CHI	82	5	13	18	-6	57	0	1	0	0	112	4.5
L	38	James Black	CHI	52	10	5	15	-8	8	2	1	3	1	90	11.1
L	23 *	Jean-Yves Leroux	CHI	66	6	7	13	-2	55	0	0	0	0	57	10.5
D	4	Jay More	PHX	41	5	5	10	0	53	0	1	0	0	40	12.5
			CHI	17	0	2	2	7	8	0	0	0	0	17	0.0
			TOTAL	58	5	7	12	7	61	0	1	0	0	57	8.8
C	15	Chad Kilger	PHX	10	0	1	1	-2	4	0	0	0	0	9	0.0
			CHI	22	3	8	11	2	6	2	0	1	0	23	13.0
			TOTAL	32	3	9	12	0	10	2	0	1	0	32	9.4
C	46 *	Dmitri Nabokov	CHI	25	7	4	11	-1	10	3	0	2	0	34	20.6
C	16	Jarrod Skalde	S.J.	22	4	6	10	-2	14	0	0	0	0	30	13.3
			CHI	4	0	1	1	0	2	0	0	0	0	4	0.0
			DAL	1	0	0	0	0	0	0	0	0	0	0	0.0
			CHI	3	0	0	0	0	2	0	0	0	0	0	0.0
			TOTAL	30	4	7	11	-2	18	0	0	0	0	34	11.8
R	17	Kevin Miller	CHI	37	4	7	11	-4	8	0	0	1	0	37	10.8
D	3 *	Christian Laflamme	CHI	72	0	11	11	14	59	0	0	0	0	75	0.0
C	12	Brent Sutter	CHI	52	2	6	8	-6	28	0	1	0	0	43	4.7
L	33	Reid Simpson	N.J.	6	0	0	0	-2	16	0	0	0	0	5	0.0
			CHI	38	3	2	5	-1	102	1	0	0	0	19	15.8
			TOTAL	44	3	2	5	-3	118	1	0	0	0	24	12.5
L	14 *	Brian Felsner	CHI	12	1	3	4	0	12	0	0	0	0	14	7.1
D	6	Michal Sykora	CHI	28	1	3	4	-10	12	0	0	0	0	35	2.9
L	24	Bob Probert	CHI	14	2	1	3	-7	48	2	0	0	0	18	11.1
R	39 *	Craig Mills	CHI	20	0	3	3	1	34	0	0	0	0	5	0.0
R	34 *	Ryan Vandenbussche	NYR	16	1	0	1	-2	38	0	0	0	0	2	50.0
			CHI	4	0	1	1	0	5	0	0	0	0	0	0.0
			TOTAL	20	1	1	2	-2	43	0	0	0	0	2	50.0
D	8	Cam Russell	CHI	41	1	1	2	3	79	0	0	1	0	18	5.6
C	26 *	Todd White	CHI	7	1	0	1	0	2	0	0	0	0	3	33.3
D	5	Trent Yawney	CHI	45	1	0	1	-5	76	0	0	0	0	19	5.3
G	40	Chris Terreri	CHI	21	0	1	1	0	2	0	0	0	0	0	0.0
L	31 *	Ryan Huska	CHI	1	0	0	0	0	0	0	0	0	0	0	0.0
L	29 *	Peri Varis	CHI	1	0	0	0	0	0	0	0	0	0	0	0.0
R	14	Martin Gendron	CHI	2	0	0	0	-1	0	0	0	0	0	3	0.0
G	29	Andrei Trefilov	CHI	6	0	0	0	0	0	0	0	0	0	0	0.0
L	7 *	Daniel Cleary	CHI	6	0	0	0	-2	0	0	0	0	0	4	0.0
G	31	Jeff Hackett	CHI	58	0	0	0	0	8	0	0	0	0	0	0.0

Goaltending

No.	Goaltender	GPI	Mins	Avg	W	L	T	EN	SO	GA	SA	S%
31	Jeff Hackett	58	3441	2.20	21	25	11	3	8	126	1520	.917
40	Chris Terreri	21	1222	2.41	8	10	2	4	2	49	519	.906
29	Andrei Trefilov	6	299	3.41	1	4	0	0	0	17	145	.883
	Totals	**82**	**4999**	**2.39**	**30**	**39**	**13**	**7**	**10**	**199**	**2191**	**.909**

Coach

GRAHAM, DIRK
Coach, Chicago Blackhawks. Born in Regina, Sask., July 29, 1959

Dirk Graham, who played parts of eight seasons as a player in Chicago between 1988 and 1995, was named the 31st coach in Blackhawks history on June 29, 1998. During his time in Chicago Graham played a hard-hitting brand of hockey that epitomized the Blackhawks' style of play. Following his retirement from active play in 1995, Graham served as an assistant coach under Craig Hartsburg during the 1995-96 season. After taking a year off from hockey in 1996-97, Graham returned to the Blackhawks as a pro scout last season.

Graham was originally Vancouvers 5th choice (89th overall) in the 1979 Entry Draft. He spent four seasons in the minor leagues with Dallas (CHL), Fort Wayne (IHL) and Toledo (IHL) before breaking into the NHL with Minnesota in 1983-84. Graham was a member of Turner Cup championship teams with Toledo in 1982 and 1983. After scoring 70 goals and 55 assists for 125 points in 78 games with Toledo during the 1982-83 season Graham was signed as a free agent by the Minnesota North Stars on August 17, 1983.

Minnesota traded Graham to Chicago on January 2, 1988 and he enjoyed his best NHL season in 1988-89, his first full season with the Blackhawks, as he recorded NHL career-highs in goals (33), assists (45) and points (78). He also recorded a Blackhawk record 10 shorthanded goals that season. Graham was named team captain of the Blackhawks midway through the 1988-89 season, a position he held until his retirement following the 1994-95 season.

Known as an excellent two-way player, Graham was the recipient of the 1991 Frank Selke Trophy, as the forward who best excels at the defensive aspects of the game. Graham was a key member of the 1991-92 Blackhawk team that won 11 consecutive playoff games to advance to the Stanley Cup finals. He recorded seven goals and 12 points in 18 playoff games. Graham recorded a hat trick in the first period of game four of the Stanley Cup finals to tie a record for most goals by one player in one period of a Stanley Cup finals game.

Captains' History

Dick Irvin, 1926-27 to 1928-29; Duke Dukowski, 1929-30; Ty Arbour, 1930-31; Cy Wentworth, 1931-32; Helge Bostrom, 1932-33; Chuck Gardiner, 1933-34; no captain, 1934-35; Johnny Gottselig, 1935-36 to 1939-40; Earl Seibert, 1940-41, 1941-42; Doug Bentley, 1942-43, 1943-44; Clint Smith 1944-45; John Mariucci, 1945-46; Red Hamill, 1946-47; John Mariucci, 1947-48; Gaye Stewart, 1948-49; Doug Bentley, 1949-50; Jack Stewart, 1950-51, 1951-52; Bill Gadsby, 1952-53, 1953-54; Gus Mortson, 1954-55 to 1956-57; no captain, 1957-58; Ed Litzenberger, 1958-59 to 1960-61; Pierre Pilote, 1961-62 to 1967-68, no captain, 1968-69; Pat Stapleton, 1969-70; no captain, 1970-71 to 1974-75; Stan Mikita and Pit Martin, 1975-76; Stan Mikita, Pit Martin and Keith Magnuson, 1976-77; Keith Magnuson, 1977-78, 1978-79; Keith Magnuson and Terry Ruskowski, 1979-80; Terry Ruskowski, 1980-81, 1981-82; Darryl Sutter, 1982-83 to 1984-85; Darryl Sutter and Bob Murray, 1985-86; Darryl Sutter, 1986-87; no captain, 1987-88; Denis Savard and Dirk Graham, 1988-89; Dirk Graham, 1989-90 to 1994-95; Chris Chelios, 1995-96 to date.

Club Records

Team

(Figures in brackets for season records are games played; records for fewest points, wins, ties, losses, goals, goals against are for 70 or more games)

Most Points	107	1970-71 (78), 1971-72 (78)
Most Wins	49	1970-71 (78), 1990-91 (80)
Most Ties	23	1973-74 (78)
Most Losses	51	1953-54 (70)
Most Goals	351	1985-86 (80)
Most Goals Against	363	1981-82 (80)
Fewest Points	31	1953-54 (70)
Fewest Wins	12	1953-54 (70)
Fewest Ties	6	1989-90 (80)
Fewest Losses	14	1973-74 (78)
Fewest Goals	*133	1953-54 (70)
Fewest Goals Against	164	1973-74 (78)
Longest Winning Streak		
Overall	8	Dec. 9-26/71, Jan. 4-21/81
Home	13	Nov. 11-Dec. 20/70
Away	7	Dec. 9-29/64
Longest Undefeated Streak		
Overall	15	Jan. 14-Feb. 16/67 (12 wins, 3 ties)
Home	18	Oct. 11-Dec. 20/70 (16 wins, 2 ties)
Away	12	Nov. 2-Dec. 16/67 (6 wins, 6 ties)
Longest Losing Streak		
Overall	13	Feb. 25-Oct. 11/51
Home	11	Feb. 8-Nov. 22/28
Away	17	Jan. 2-Oct. 7/54
Longest Winless Streak		
Overall	21	Dec. 17/50-Jan. 28/51 (18 losses, 3 ties)
Home	15	Dec. 16/28-Feb. 28/29 (11 losses, 4 ties)
Away	23	Dec. 19/50-Oct. 11/51 (21 losses, 2 ties)
Most Shutouts, Season	15	1969-70 (76)
Most PIM, Season	2,663	1991-92 (80)
Most Goals, Game	12	Jan. 30/69 (Chi. 12 at Phi. 0)

Individual

Most Seasons	22	Stan Mikita
Most Games	1,394	Stan Mikita
Most Goals, Career	604	Bobby Hull
Most Assists, Career	926	Stan Mikita
Most Points, Career	1,467	Stan Mikita (541G, 926A)
Most PIM, Career	1,442	Keith Magnuson
Most Shutouts, Career	74	Tony Esposito
Longest Consecutive Games Streak	884	Steve Larmer (1982-83 to 1992-93)
Most Goals, Season	58	Bobby Hull (1968-69)
Most Assists, Season	87	Denis Savard (1981-82, 1987-88)
Most Points, Season	131	Denis Savard (1987-88; 44G, 87A)
Most PIM, Season	408	Mike Peluso (1991-92)
Most Points, Defenseman, Season	85	Doug Wilson (1981-82; 39G, 46A)
Most Points, Center, Season	131	Denis Savard (1987-88; 44G, 87A)
Most Points, Right Wing, Season	101	Steve Larmer (1990-91; 44G, 57A)
Most Points, Left Wing, Season	107	Bobby Hull (1968-69; 58G, 49A)
Most Points, Rookie, Season	90	Steve Larmer (1982-83; 43G, 47A)
Most Shutouts, Season	15	Tony Esposito (1969-70)
Most Goals, Game	5	Grant Mulvey (Feb. 3/82)
Most Assists, Game	6	Pat Stapleton (Mar. 30/69)
Most Points, Game	7	Max Bentley (Jan. 28/43; 4G, 3A), Grant Mulvey (Feb. 3/82; 5G, 2A)

* NHL Record.

Retired Numbers

1	Glenn Hall	1957-1967
9	Bobby Hull	1957-1972
18	Denis Savard	1980-1990, 1995-1997
21	Stan Mikita	1958-1980
35	Tony Esposito	1969-1984

All-time Record vs. Other Clubs

Regular Season

	At Home							On Road							Total						
	GP	W	L	T	GF	GA	PTS	GP	W	L	T	GF	GA	PTS	GP	W	L	T	GF	GA	PTS
Anaheim	11	6	4	1	27	19	13	10	6	3	1	29	21	13	21	12	7	2	56	40	26
Boston	281	144	93	44	905	748	332	279	87	159	33	788	1009	207	560	231	252	77	1693	1757	539
Buffalo	46	25	15	6	152	127	56	48	13	29	6	127	181	32	94	38	44	12	279	308	88
Calgary	49	21	15	13	167	143	55	51	19	23	9	153	160	47	100	40	38	22	320	303	102
Carolina	25	15	7	3	109	71	33	26	12	11	3	88	86	27	51	27	18	6	197	157	60
Colorado	29	16	11	2	105	93	34	28	11	13	4	105	113	26	57	27	24	6	210	206	60
Dallas	97	61	25	11	390	252	133	100	42	43	15	316	334	99	197	103	68	26	706	586	232
Detroit	321	147	123	51	968	895	345	319	93	196	30	782	1093	216	640	240	319	81	1750	1988	561
Edmonton	32	17	10	5	132	118	39	33	14	15	4	122	127	32	65	31	25	9	254	245	71
Florida	4	1	2	1	13	15	3	4	3	1	0	19	12	6	8	4	3	1	32	27	9
Los Angeles	63	31	24	8	237	192	70	62	29	27	6	218	212	64	125	60	51	14	455	404	134
Montreal	270	92	123	55	725	754	239	270	51	171	48	636	1049	150	540	143	294	103	1361	1803	389
New Jersey	42	23	10	9	171	117	55	41	16	15	10	128	121	42	83	39	25	19	299	238	97
NY Islanders	44	23	16	5	150	150	51	42	12	17	13	127	150	37	86	35	33	18	277	300	88
NY Rangers	281	126	113	42	854	780	294	282	111	116	55	798	833	277	563	237	229	97	1652	1613	571
Ottawa	5	3	1	1	13	11	7	5	4	1	0	18	11	8	10	7	2	1	31	22	15
Philadelphia	56	25	12	19	200	159	69	57	16	30	11	153	185	43	113	41	42	30	353	344	112
Phoenix	37	23	10	4	159	107	50	38	13	21	4	125	140	30	75	36	31	8	284	247	80
Pittsburgh	55	38	8	9	231	147	85	54	23	25	6	180	191	52	109	61	33	15	411	338	137
St. Louis	102	58	30	14	396	310	130	98	34	47	17	307	326	85	200	92	77	31	703	636	215
San Jose	13	8	4	1	47	35	17	14	7	7	0	41	34	14	27	15	11	1	88	69	31
Tampa Bay	8	3	3	2	18	19	8	7	2	4	1	17	19	5	15	5	7	3	35	38	13
Toronto	310	154	114	42	950	806	350	310	94	163	53	802	1059	241	620	248	277	95	1752	1865	591
Vancouver	59	39	14	6	226	137	84	60	19	27	14	176	181	52	119	58	41	20	402	318	136
Washington	35	21	9	5	141	105	47	36	12	20	4	113	133	28	71	33	29	9	254	238	75
Defunct Clubs	139	79	40	20	408	268	178	140	52	67	21	316	346	125	279	131	107	41	724	614	303
Totals	**2414**	**1199**	**836**	**379**	**7894**	**6578**	**2777**	**2414**	**795**	**1251**	**368**	**6684**	**8126**	**1958**	**4828**	**1994**	**2087**	**747**	**14578**	**14704**	**4735**

Playoffs

	Series	W	L	GP	W	L	T	GF	GA	Last Mtg.	Round	Result
Boston	6	1	5	22	5	16	1	63	97	1978	QF	L 0-4
Buffalo	2	0	2	9	1	8	0	17	36	1980	QF	L 0-4
Calgary	3	1	2	12	5	7	0	33	37	1996	CQF	W 4-0
Colorado	2	0	2	12	4	8	0	28	49	1997	CQF	L 2-4
Dallas	6	4	2	33	19	14	0	119	119	1991	DSF	L 2-4
Detroit	14	8	6	69	38	31	0	210	190	1995	CF	L 1-4
Edmonton	4	1	3	20	8	12	0	77	102	1992	CF	W 4-0
Los Angeles	1	1	0	5	4	1	0	10	7	1974	QF	W 4-1
Montreal	17	5	12	81	29	50	2	185	261	1976	QF	L 0-4
NY Islanders	2	0	2	6	0	6	0	6	21	1979	QF	L 0-4
NY Rangers	5	4	1	24	14	10	0	66	54	1973	SF	W 4-1
Philadelphia	1	1	0	4	4	0	0	20	8	1971	QF	W 4-0
Pittsburgh	2	1	1	8	4	4	0	24	23	1992	F	L 0-4
St. Louis	9	7	2	45	27	18	0	166	129	1993	DSF	L 0-4
Toronto	9	3	6	38	15	22	1	89	111	1995	CQF	W 4-3
Vancouver	2	1	1	9	5	4	0	24	24	1995	CSF	W 4-0
Defunct Clubs	4	2	2	9	5	3	1	16	15			
Totals	**89**	**40**	**49**	**406**	**187**	**214**	**5**	**1153**	**1283**			

Calgary totals include Atlanta, 1972-73 to 1979-80. Carolina totals include Hartford, 1979-80 to 1996-97.
Colorado totals include Quebec, 1979-80 to 1994-95. Dallas totals include Minnesota, 1967-68 to 1992-93.
New Jersey totals include Kansas City, 1974-75 to 1975-76, and Colorado Rockies, 1976-77 to 1981-82.
Phoenix totals include Winnipeg, 1979-80 to 1995-96.

Playoff Results 1998-94

Year	Round	Opponent	Result	GF	GA
1997	CQF	Colorado	L 2-4	14	28
1996	CSF	Colorado	L 2-4	14	21
	CQF	Calgary	W 4-0	16	7
1995	CF	Detroit	L 1-4	12	13
	CSF	Vancouver	W 4-0	11	6
	CQF	Toronto	W 4-3	22	20
1994	CQF	Toronto	L 2-4	10	15

Abbreviations: Round: F – Final; **CF** – conference final; **CQF** – conference quarter-final; **CSF** – conference semi-final; **DSF** – division semi-final; **SF** – semi-final; **QF** – quarter-final.

1997-98 Results

Oct.	1	at	Phoenix	2-6		5		Calgary	1-1
	4	at	San Jose	2-3		9		Phoenix	2-4
	9		Tampa Bay	1-4		10	at	Toronto	4-3
	10	at	Dallas	0-7		12		Vancouver	3-2
	13	at	Phoenix	1-2		14	at	Carolina	4-1
	15		Washington	0-2		15	at	Washington	2-3
	17		St. Louis	0-2		20		NY Islanders	5-2
	19		Buffalo	5-2		22		Toronto	0-3
	22	at	NY Rangers	1-0		24		St. Louis	5-4
	24		Dallas	0-2		29	at	San Jose	3-0
	26		Carolina	2-3		31	at	Los Angeles	0-3
	27	at	Montreal	2-4	**Feb.**	1	at	Anaheim	3-4
	29		Vancouver	3-0		3	at	Phoenix	4-2
	31		San Jose	5-3		5	at	Colorado	2-4
Nov.	2		Pittsburgh	3-1		7	at	Dallas	1-3
	6		St. Louis	2-1		26		Los Angeles	4-7
	8	at	NY Islanders	4-2		28	at	Colorado	4-0
	10		Calgary	1-1	**Mar.**	1		Dallas	2-2
	11	at	Toronto	2-5		3	at	St. Louis	3-5
	13		Toronto	1-2		5	at	Pittsburgh	2-2
	16		Detroit	3-3		7	at	Boston	2-1
	19	at	Anaheim	4-0		9		Edmonton	3-4
	20	at	Los Angeles	3-4		12	at	Detroit	0-3
	22	at	Vancouver	5-4		14	at	Tampa Bay	0-1
	25	at	Edmonton	2-2		15	at	Florida	8-4
	27	at	Calgary	2-2		17	at	Buffalo	5-3
	29	at	Ottawa	3-2		19		Montreal	1-0
Dec.	4		Colorado	1-2		22		Boston	1-0
	7		Edmonton	3-3		23	at	Detroit	5-5
	10		Phoenix	3-3		25		Anaheim	2-3
	12		Philadelphia	2-3		27		Ottawa	2-1
	14		San Jose	1-2		29		Florida	0-4
	16	at	Calgary	3-4		31	at	Philadelphia	2-3
	17	at	Edmonton	0-0	**Apr.**	2		Colorado	2-1
	20	at	Vancouver	5-0		4		Detroit	2-3
	22		Los Angeles	0-1		5		NY Rangers	1-2
	26	at	St. Louis	4-1		9	at	St. Louis	2-3
	28		Anaheim	2-0		12		Phoenix	1-2
	30	at	New Jersey	6-2		15	at	Toronto	2-3
Jan.	1		Toronto	3-3		16		New Jersey	1-1
	4		Detroit	3-1		18	at	Dallas	1-3

Entry Draft Selections 1998-84

1998

Pick	
8	Mark Bell
94	Matthias Trattnig
156	Kent Huskins
158	Jari Viuhkola
166	Jonathan Pelletier
183	Tyler Arnason
210	Sean Griffin
238	Alexandre Couture
240	Andrei Yershov

1997

Pick	
13	Daniel Cleary
16	Ty Jones
39	Jeremy Reich
67	Mike Souza
110	Benjamin Simon
120	Peter Gardiner
130	Kyle Calder
147	Heath Gordon
174	Jerad Smith
204	Sergei Shikhanov
230	Chris Feil

1996

Pick	
31	Remi Royer
42	Jeff Paul
46	Geoff Peters
130	Andy Johnson
184	Mike Vellinga
210	Chris Twerdun
236	Alexei Kozyrev

1995

Pick	
19	Dimitri Nabokov
45	Christian Laflamme
71	Kevin McKay
82	Chris Van Dyk
97	Pavel Kriz
146	Marc Magliarditi
149	Marty Wilford
175	Steve Tardif
201	Casey Hankinson
227	Mike Pittman

1994

Pick	
14	Ethan Moreau
40	Jean-Yves Leroux
85	Steve McLaren
118	Marc Dupuis
144	Jim Enson
170	Tyler Prosofsky
196	Mike Josephson
222	Lubomir Jandera
248	Lars Weibel
263	Rob Mara

1993

Pick	
24	Eric Lecompte
50	Eric Manlow
54	Bogdan Savenko
76	Ryan Huska
90	Eric Daze
102	Patrik Pysz
128	Jonni Vauhkonen
180	Tom White
206	Sergei Petrov
232	Mike Rusk
258	Mike McGhan
284	Tom Noble

1992

Pick	
12	Sergei Krivokrasov
36	Jeff Shantz
41	Sergei Klimovich
89	Andy MacIntyre
113	Tim Hogan
137	Gerry Skrypec
161	Mike Prokopec
185	Layne Roland
209	David Hymovitz
233	Richard Raymond

1991

Pick	
22	Dean McAmmond
39	Michael Pomichter
44	Jamie Matthews
66	Bobby House
71	Igor Kravchuk
88	Zac Boyer
110	Maco Balkovec
112	Kevin St. Jacques
132	Jacques Auger
154	Scott Kirton
176	Roch Belley
198	Scott MacDonald
220	A. Andriyevsky
242	Mike Larkin
264	Scott Dean

1990

Pick	
16	Karl Dykhuis
37	Ivan Droppa
79	Chris Tucker
121	Brett Stickney
124	Derek Edgerly
163	Hugo Belanger
184	Owen Lessard
205	Erik Peterson
226	Steve Dubinsky
247	Dino Grossi

1989

Pick	
6	Adam Bennett
27	Michael Speer
48	Bob Kellogg
111	Tommi Pullola
132	Tracy Egeland
153	Milan Tichy
174	Jason Greyerbiehl
195	Matt Saunders
216	Mike Kozak
237	Michael Doneghey

1988

Pick	
8	Jeremy Roenick
50	Trevor Dam
71	Stefan Elvenas
92	Joe Cleary
113	Justin Lafayette
134	Craig Woodcroft
155	Jon Pojar
176	Mathew Hentges
197	Daniel Maurice
218	Dirk Tenzer
239	Andreas Lupzig

1987

Pick	
8	Jimmy Waite
29	Ryan McGill
50	Cam Russell
60	Mike Dagenais
92	Ulf Sandstrom
113	Mike McCormick
134	Stephen Tepper
155	John Reilly
176	Lance Werness
197	Dale Marquette
218	Bill Lacouture
239	Mike Lappin

1986

Pick	
14	Everett Sanipass
35	Mark Kurzawski
77	Frantisek Kucera
98	Lonnie Loach
119	Mario Doyon
140	Mike Hudson
161	Marty Nanne
182	Geoff Benic
203	Glen Lowes
224	Chris Thayer
245	Sean Williams

1985

Pick	
11	Dave Manson
53	Andy Helmuth
74	Dan Vincelette
87	Rick Herbert
95	Brad Belland
116	Jonas Heed
137	Victor Posa
158	John Reid
179	Richard LaPlante
200	Brad Hamilton
221	Ian Pound
242	Rick Braccia

1984

Pick	
3	Ed Olczyk
45	Trent Yawney
66	Tommy Eriksson
90	Timo Lehkonen
101	Darin Sceviour
111	Chris Clifford
132	Mike Stapleton
153	Glen Greenough
174	Ralph DiFiorie
194	Joakim Persson
215	Bill Brown
224	David Mackey
235	Dan Williams

General Manager

MURRAY, BOB
General Manager, Chicago Blackhawks.
Born in Kingston, Ont., November 26, 1954.

Bob Murray was named as the sixth general manager in the history of the Chicago Blackhawks on July 3, 1997. Murray has been with the Blackhawk organization for more than 24 years, dating back to 1974 when he was drafted by the Blackhawks.

Murray spent his entire NHL playing career in Chicago, playing 1,008 games in a Blackhawk uniform. He became only the fourth player in team history to reach the 1,000-game plateau and during the 1990 Stanley Cup Playoffs, he became the first defenseman in team history to play over 100 playoff games.

He ranks first among all-time Blackhawk defensemen in games played and ranks second among all-time Blackhawk defensemen in career points with 514. During his 15-year Blackhawk career, Murray scored 132 goals (26th overall) and 382 assists (8th overall) totalling 514 points (12th overall). He played in two NHL All-Star Games (1981 and 1983) and recorded an assist.

Murray's playing career was marked by tremendous skill, endurance and determination. His great effort and preparation were well noted by the organization, along with his organization and management skills. All these traits convinced the Blackhawks to sign Murray as a pro scout in 1990. Within a year he was appointed director of player personnel, mastering the computerized system which keeps tabs on all players observed by the scouting staff.

Murray has directed the Blackhawks in the NHL Entry Draft since 1992, and his selections over the last six drafts have provided a solid foundation for the future of the organization. Murray's keen eye for talent has brought young NHL players like Eric Daze, Ethan Moreau and Jeff Shantz into the Blackhawks organization.

Prior to the 1995-96 season Murray was named as the club's assistant general manager.

Club Directory

United Center

Chicago Blackhawk Hockey Team, Inc.
1901 W. Madison Street
Chicago, IL 60612
Phone **312/455-7000**
FAX 312/455-7041
Internet Address
www.chicagoblackhawks.com
Capacity: 20,500

President	William W. Wirtz
Vice President & Assistant to the President	Thomas N. Ivan
Senior Vice President	Robert J. Pulford
Vice President	Jack Davison
General Manager	Bob Murray
Head Coach	Dirk Graham
Assistant Coach	Denis Savard
Assistant Coach	Lorne Molleken
Goaltending Consultant	Vladislav Tretiak
Director of Player Personnel	Dale Tallon
Pro Scout	Phil Russell
Chief Amateur Scout	Michel Dumas
Amateur Scout	Bruce Franklin
Amateur Scout	Tim Higgins
Amateur Scout	Dave Lucas
Amateur Scout	Steve Richmond
European Scout	Jan Blomgren
Executive Assistant	Cindy Brueck
Assistant to the General Manager	Steve Williams
Manager of Team Services	David Stensby
Medical Staff	
Club Doctors	Mark Bowen, Gordon Nuber
Team Dentist	Dr. Daniel Mackey, Dr. Dean Sana
Oral Surgeon	Dr. Eric Pulver
Eye Doctor	Dr. Robert Stein
Head Trainer	Michael Gapski
Equipment Manager	Troy Parchman
Asst. Equipment Mgr.	Lou Varga
Massage Therapist	Pawel Prylinski
Public Relations/Marketing	
Vice President of Marketing	Peter R. Wirtz
Executive Director of Public Relations	Jim DeMaria
Director of Community Relations/PR Assistant	Barbara Davidson
Director of Publications/PR Assistant	Brad Freeman
Executive Director of Marketing/Merchandising	Jim Sofranko
Dir. of Corporate Partnerships	Elliot Bell
Manager, Client Services	Kelly Bodnarchuk
Dir. of Projects & Development	Carol Kolbus
Manager, Special Events	Matt Colleran
Manager, Game Operations	Kellett McConville
Marketing Associate	Alison Tragesser
Administrative Assistant	Kelly Higginbotham
Finance	
Controller	Robert Rinkus
Assistant Controller	Penny Swenson
Assistant to the Controller	Deb Kulir
Staff Accountant	Jennifer Aspan
Ticketing	
Director of Ticket Operations	James K. Bare
Sales Manager	Doug Ryan
Sr. Season & Group Sales Rep.	Danny Lucier
Season & Group Sales Rep.	Steve Rigney
Sr. Ticket Operations Rep.	Kathie Ralmondi
Ticket Operations Rep.	Martha Webster
Miscellaneous Information	
Team Photographers	Ray Grabowski, Rob Grabowski
Organist	Frank Pellico
Public Address Announcer	Harvey Wittenberg
Executive Offices/Home Ice	United Center
Location of Press Box	South Side of United Center
Dimensions of Rink	200 feet by 85 feet
Ends of Rink	Plexi-glass extends above boards all around rink
Club Colors	Red, White & Black
Radio Station	WMAQ (AM 670)
Television Station	Fox Sports Chicago
Broadcasters	Pat Foley, Dave Pasch, Billy Jaffe

Coaching History

Pete Muldoon, 1926-27; Barney Stanley and Hugh Lehman, 1927-28; Herb Gardiner, 1928-29; Tom Shaughnessy and Bill Tobin, 1929-30; Dick Irvin, 1930-31; Dick Irvin and Bill Tobin, 1931-32; Emil Iverson, Godfrey Matheson and Tommy Gorman, 1932-33; Tommy Gorman, 1933-34; Clem Loughlin, 1934-35 to 1936-37; Bill Stewart, 1937-38; Bill Stewart and Paul Thompson, 1938-39; Paul Thompson, 1939-40 to 1943-44; Paul Thompson and Johnny Gottselig, 1944-45; Johnny Gottselig, 1945-46, 1946-47; Johnny Gottselig and Charlie Conacher, 1947-48; Charlie Conacher, 1948-49, 1949-50; Ebbie Goodfellow, 1950-51, 1951-52; Sid Abel, 1952-53, 1953-54; Frank Eddolls, 1954-55; Dick Irvin, 1955-56; Tommy Ivan, 1956-57; Tommy Ivan and Rudy Pilous, 1957-58; Rudy Pilous, 1958-59 to 1962-63; Billy Reay, 1963-64 to 1975-76; Billy Reay and Bill White, 1976-77; Bob Pulford, 1977-78, 1978-79; Eddie Johnston, 1979-80; Keith Magnuson, 1980-81; Keith Magnuson and Bob Pulford, 1981-82; Orval Tessier, 1982-83, 1983-84; Orval Tessier and Bob Pulford, 1984-85; Bob Pulford, 1985-86, 1986-87; Bob Murdoch, 1987-88; Mike Keenan, 1988-89 to 1991-92; Darryl Sutter, 1992-93 to 1994-95; Craig Hartsburg, 1995-96 to 1997-98; Dirk Graham, 1998-99.

General Managers' History

Major Frederic McLaughlin, 1926-27 to 1941-42; Bill Tobin, 1942-43 to 1953-54; Tommy Ivan, 1954-55 to 1976-77; Bob Pulford, 1977-78 to 1989-90; Mike Keenan, 1990-91, 1991-92; Mike Keenan and Bob Pulford, 1992-93; Bob Pulford, 1993-94 to 1996-97; Bob Murray, 1997-98 to date.

Colorado Avalanche

1997-98 Results: 39W-26L-17T 95PTS. First, Pacific Division

Though he played just 64 games in 1997-98, captain Joe Sakic still led the Avalanche in goals (27) and power-play goals (12). His 63 points trailed only Peter Forsberg (91) and Valeri Kamensky (66).

1998-99 Schedule

Month	Day	Date	Opponent	Month	Day	Date	Opponent
Oct.	Sat.	10	Ottawa		Tue.	12	Chicago
	Mon.	12	Buffalo		Sat.	16	St. Louis*
	Wed.	14	Boston		Tue.	19	at Los Angeles
	Thu.	15	at Phoenix		Thu.	21	Calgary
	Sun.	18	at Los Angeles		Wed.	27	at Anaheim
	Sat.	24	Edmonton		Thu.	28	Anaheim
	Mon.	26	Phoenix		Sat.	30	San Jose
	Thu.	29	San Jose	**Feb.**	Tue.	2	at Boston
	Sat.	31	at Nashville		Wed.	3	at Buffalo
Nov.	Mon.	2	at Carolina		Fri.	5	at Detroit
	Wed.	4	at Toronto		Sun.	7	at Dallas*
	Fri.	6	at Edmonton		Tue.	9	Calgary
	Sun.	8	at Calgary*		Sat.	13	Phoenix*
	Tue.	10	at Phoenix		Sun.	14	Philadelphia*
	Fri.	13	Tampa Bay		Fri.	19	at Nashville
	Sun.	15	at Vancouver		Sun.	21	at Dallas*
	Tue.	17	NY Islanders		Tue.	23	Vancouver
	Thu.	19	Vancouver		Thu.	25	Pittsburgh
	Sat.	21	at Montreal		Sat.	27	Nashville
	Wed.	25	at Edmonton	**Mar.**	Mon.	1	Edmonton
	Sat.	28	New Jersey		Wed.	3	at Florida
Dec.	Wed.	2	Detroit		Thu.	4	at Tampa Bay
	Fri.	4	St. Louis		Sun.	7	at Pittsburgh*
	Sat.	5	at St. Louis		Tue.	9	at Washington
	Tue.	8	at NY Islanders		Thu.	11	at Philadelphia
	Wed.	9	at NY Rangers		Sun.	14	Detroit*
	Sat.	12	at New Jersey*		Thu.	18	Carolina
	Mon.	14	St. Louis		Sat.	20	Chicago*
	Thu.	17	at Vancouver		Sun.	21	at Chicago*
	Sat.	19	at San Jose		Wed.	24	Vancouver
	Mon.	21	at Anaheim		Fri.	26	Washington
	Tue.	22	Anaheim		Sun.	28	Los Angeles*
	Sat.	26	Dallas		Tue.	30	Calgary
	Sun.	27	at Calgary		Wed.	31	at San Jose
	Tue.	29	at Vancouver	**Apr.**	Sat.	3	Edmonton
	Thu.	31	NY Rangers		Mon.	5	Los Angeles
Jan.	Sat.	2	at Los Angeles		Wed.	7	Nashville
	Mon.	4	Montreal		Sun.	11	at St. Louis*
	Wed.	6	Florida		Thu.	15	at Calgary
	Sat.	9	at Detroit*		Fri.	16	at Edmonton
	Sun.	10	at Chicago		Sun.	18	Dallas*

* Denotes afternoon game.

Franchise date: June 22, 1979
Transferred from Quebec to Denver, June 21, 1995

NORTHWEST DIVISION

20th NHL Season

Year-by-Year Record

Season	GP	Home W	Home L	Home T	Road W	Road L	Road T	Overall W	Overall L	Overall T	GF	GA	Pts.	Finished		Playoff Result
1997-98	82	21	10	10	18	16	7	39	26	17	231	205	95	1st,	Pacific Div.	Lost Conf. Quarter-Final
1996-97	82	26	10	5	23	14	4	49	24	9	277	205	107	1st,	Pacific Div.	Lost Conf. Championship
1995-96	**82**	**24**	**10**	**7**	**23**	**15**	**3**	**47**	**25**	**10**	**326**	**240**	**104**	**1st,**	**Pacific Div.**	**Won Stanley Cup**
1994-95*	48	19	1	4	11	12	1	30	13	5	185	134	65	1st,	Northeast Div.	Lost Conf. Quarter-Final
1993-94*	84	19	17	6	15	25	2	34	42	8	277	292	76	5th,	Northeast Div.	Out of Playoffs
1992-93*	84	23	17	2	24	10	8	47	27	10	351	300	104	2nd,	Adams Div.	Lost Div. Semi-Final
1991-92*	80	18	19	3	2	29	9	20	48	12	255	318	52	5th,	Adams Div.	Out of Playoffs
1990-91*	80	9	23	8	7	27	6	16	50	14	236	354	46	5th,	Adams Div.	Out of Playoffs
1989-90*	80	8	26	6	4	35	1	12	61	7	240	407	31	5th,	Adams Div.	Out of Playoffs
1988-89*	80	16	20	4	11	26	3	27	46	7	269	342	61	5th,	Adams Div.	Out of Playoffs
1987-88*	80	15	23	2	17	20	3	32	43	5	271	306	69	5th,	Adams Div.	Out of Playoffs
1986-87*	80	20	13	7	11	26	3	31	39	10	267	276	72	4th,	Adams Div.	Lost Div. Final
1985-86*	80	23	13	4	20	18	2	43	31	6	330	289	92	1st,	Adams Div.	Lost Div. Semi-Final
1984-85*	80	24	12	4	17	18	5	41	30	9	323	275	91	2nd,	Adams Div.	Lost Conf. Championship
1983-84*	80	24	11	5	18	17	5	42	28	10	360	278	94	3th,	Adams Div.	Lost Div. Final
1982-83*	80	23	10	7	11	24	5	34	34	12	343	336	80	4th,	Adams Div.	Lost Div. Semi-Final
1981-82*	80	24	13	3	9	18	13	33	31	16	356	345	82	4th,	Adams Div.	Lost Conf. Championship
1980-81*	80	18	11	11	12	21	7	30	32	18	314	318	78	4th,	Adams Div.	Lost Prelim. Round
1979-80*	80	17	16	7	8	28	4	25	44	11	248	313	61	5th,	Adams Div.	Out of Playoffs

* Quebec Nordiques

1998-99 Player Personnel

FORWARDS	HT	WT	S	Place of Birth	Date	1997-98 Club
ABID, Ramzi	6-2	195	L	Montreal, Que.	3/24/80	Chicoutimi
BEAUDOIN, Nic	6-3	205	L	Ottawa, Ont.	12/25/76	
BOOTLAND, Nick	6-0	210	L	Shelbourne, Ont.	7/31/78	Guelph
CORBET, Rene	6-0	187	L	St-Hyacinthe, Que.	6/25/73	Colorado
DEADMARSH, Adam	6-0	195	R	Trail, B.C.	5/10/75	Colorado-United States
DONOVAN, Shean	6-3	210	R	Timmins, Ont.	1/22/75	San Jose-Colorado
DRURY, Chris	5-10	180	R	Trumbull, CT	8/20/76	Boston U.-United States
FORSBERG, Peter	6-0	190	L	Ornskoldsvik, Sweden	7/20/73	Colorado-Sweden
JOHANSSON, Mikael	5-10	185	L	Stockholm, Swe.	6/12/66	Djurgarden
JONES, Keith	6-2	200	L	Brantford, Ont.	11/8/68	Colorado-Hershey
KAMENSKY, Valeri	6-2	198	R	Voskresensk, USSR	4/18/66	Colorado-Russia
KIDNEY, Kyle	6-2	223	L	Ithaca, NY	1/11/78	U-Mass.-Lowell
LACROIX, Eric	6-2	210	L	Montreal, Que.	7/15/71	Colorado
LAMARCHE, Martin	6-1	205	L	Ste. Justine, Que.	10/2/75	Binghamton-Hershey
LARSEN, Brad	5-11	212	L	Nakusp, B.C.	1/28/77	Colorado-Hershey
LAZAREV, Yevgeny	6-2	215	L	Kharkov, USSR	4/25/80	Kitchener
LEMIEUX, Claude	6-1	215	R	Buckingham, Que.	7/16/65	Colorado
MATTE, Christian	5-11	170	R	Hull, Que.	1/20/75	Colorado-Hershey
MOORE, Steve	6-2	190	R	Windsor, Ont.	9/22/78	Harvard
NIEMINEN, Ville	5-11	205	L	Tampere, Finland	4/6/77	Hershey
ODGERS, Jeff	6-0	200	R	Spy Hill, Sask.	5/31/69	Providence (AHL)-Colorado
PARKER, Scott	6-4	220	R	Hanford, CA	1/29/78	Kelowna
RYCHEL, Warren	6-0	205	L	Tecumseh, Ont.	5/12/67	Anaheim-Colorado
SAKIC, Joe	5-11	185	L	Burnaby, B.C.	7/7/69	Colorado-Canada
SHEARER, Rob	5-10	190	R	Kitchener, Ont.	10/19/76	Hershey
TANGUAY, Alex	6-0	180	L	Ste-Justine, Que.	11/21/79	Halifax
TIMMONS, K.C.	6-2	205	L	Victoria, B.C.	4/6/80	Tri-City
YELLE, Stephane	6-1	190	L	Ottawa, Ont.	5/9/74	Colorado
DEFENSEMEN						
BELAK, Wade	6-4	213	R	Saskatoon, Sask.	7/3/76	Colorado-Hershey
BUCHANAN, Jeff	6-2	200	R	Swift Current, Sask.	5/23/71	Orlando-Kansas City
CROWLEY, Ted	6-2	188	R	Concord, MA	5/3/70	Springfield
FOOTE, Adam	6-1	205	R	Toronto, Ont.	7/10/71	Colorado-Canada
GUSAROV, Alexei	6-3	185	L	Leningrad, USSR	7/8/64	Colorado-Russia
KLEMM, Jon	6-3	200	R	Cranbrook, B.C.	1/8/70	Colorado
LEFEBVRE, Sylvain	6-2	205	L	Richmond, Que.	10/14/67	Colorado
MESSIER, Eric	6-2	200	L	Drummondville, Que.	10/29/73	Colorado
MILLER, Aaron	6-3	200	R	Buffalo, NY	8/11/71	Colorado
OZOLINSH, Sandis	6-3	205	L	Riga, Latvia	8/3/72	Colorado
REGEHR, Robyn	6-2	210	L	Recife, Brazil	4/19/80	Kamloops
RYAZANTSEV, Alexander	5-11	200	R	Moscow, USSR	3/15/80	Spartak-2-Victoriaville
SCHMIDT, Doug	5-10	205	R	Pompton Plains, NJ	1/19/78	Northern Michigan
SKOULA, Martin	6-2	195	L	Litvinov, Czechoslovakia	10/28/79	Barrie
SMITH, Dan	6-2	195	L	Fernie, B.C.	10/19/76	Hershey
TREPANIER, Pascal	6-0	205	R	Gaspe, Que.	4/9/73	Colorado-Hershey

GOALTENDERS	HT	WT	C	Place of Birth	Date	1997-98 Club
BILLINGTON, Craig	5-10	170	L	London, Ont.	9/11/66	Colorado
DENIS, Marc	6-0	188	L	Montreal, Que.	8/1/77	Hershey
FISCHER, Kai	5-11	176	L	Forst, Germany	3/25/77	Germany
ROY, Patrick	6-0	192	L	Quebec City, Que.	10/5/65	Colorado-Canada
SAUVE, Phillipe	6-0	175	L	Buffalo, NY	2/27/80	Rimouski

General Managers' History

Maurice Filion, 1979-80 to 1987-88; Martin Madden, 1988-89; Martin Madden and Maurice Filion, 1989-90; Pierre Page, 1990-91 to 1993-94; Pierre Lacroix, 1994-95 to date.

Coaching History

Jacques Demers, 1979-80; Maurice Filion and Michel Bergeron, 1980-81; Michel Bergeron, 1981-82 to 1986-87; Andre Savard and Ron Lapointe, 1987-88; Ron Lapointe and Jean Perron, 1988-89; Michel Bergeron, 1989-90; Dave Chambers, 1990-91; Dave Chambers and Pierre Page, 1991-92; Pierre Page, 1992-93, 1993-94; Marc Crawford, 1994-95 to 1997-98; Bob Hartley, 1998-99.

Coach

HARTLEY, BOB
Coach, Colorado Avalanche. Born in Hawkesbury, Ont., September 7, 1960.

Bob Hartley became the second coach of the Colorado Avalanche and the 11th coach in the club's overall history when he was named to the position on June 30, 1998. Hartley has spent four years as a head coach with the organization's American Hockey League affiliates in Cornwall and Hershey compiling a record of 151-136-33 for a .523 winning percentage.

Hartley began his coaching career with the Hawksbury Hawks, where he won two Junior A championships in four seasons. In 1992 he became head coach of the Laval Titans of the Quebec Major Junior Hockey League, where he won another championship prior to becoming an assistant coach with the Cornwall Aces in 1993. He became head coach in Cornwall the following year and remained with the Avalanche affiliate after it relocated to Hershey for the 1996-97 season. Hartley coached Hershey to the Calder Cup championship that year. In addition to his on-ice success in Hershey, Hartley was known for his summer hockey camps and volunteer work within the community.

Hartley and his wife Micheline have two children, Kristin and Steve.

Coaching Record

		Regular Season					Playoffs			
Season	Team	Games	W	L	T	%	Games	W	L	%
1992-93	Laval (QMJHL)	70	43	25	2	.629	13	12	1	.923
1994-95	Cornwall (AHL)	80	38	33	9	.531	15	8	7	.533
1995-96	Cornwall (AHL)	80	34	39	7	.469	8	3	5	.375
1996-97	Hershey (AHL)	80	43	27	10	.600	23	15	8	.652
1997-98	Hershey (AHL)	80	36	37	7	.494	7	3	4	.429

1997-98 Scoring

* – rookie

Regular Season

Pos	#	Player	Team	GP	G	A	Pts	+/–	PIM	PP	SH	GW	GT	S	%
C	21	Peter Forsberg	COL	72	25	66	91	6	94	7	3	7	1	202	12.4
L	13	Valeri Kamensky	COL	75	26	40	66	-2	60	8	0	4	0	173	15.0
C	19	Joe Sakic	COL	64	27	36	63	0	50	12	1	2	1	254	10.6
R	22	Claude Lemieux	COL	78	26	27	53	-7	115	11	1	1	1	261	10.0
D	8	Sandis Ozolinsh	COL	66	13	38	51	-12	65	9	0	2	1	135	9.6
R	18	Adam Deadmarsh	COL	73	22	21	43	0	125	10	0	6	3	187	11.8
L	28	Eric Lacroix	COL	82	16	15	31	0	84	5	0	6	0	126	12.7
D	4	Uwe Krupp	COL	78	9	22	31	21	38	5	0	2	0	149	6.0
L	20	Rene Corbet	COL	68	16	12	28	8	133	4	0	4	2	117	13.7
C	26	Stephane Yelle	COL	81	7	15	22	-10	48	0	1	0	0	93	7.5
C	17	Jari Kurri	COL	70	5	17	22	6	12	2	0	0	0	61	8.2
R	14	Tom Fitzgerald	FLA	69	10	5	15	-4	57	0	1	1	0	105	9.5
			COL	11	2	1	3	0	22	0	1	0	0	14	14.3
			TOTAL	80	12	6	18	-4	79	0	2	1	0	119	10.1
R	12	Shean Donovan	S.J.	20	3	3	6	3	22	0	0	0	0	24	12.5
			COL	47	5	7	12	3	48	0	0	0	0	57	8.8
			TOTAL	67	8	10	18	6	70	0	0	0	0	81	9.9
D	52	Adam Foote	COL	77	3	14	17	-3	124	0	0	1	0	64	4.7
D	29	* Eric Messier	COL	62	4	12	16	4	20	0	0	0	0	66	6.1
D	24	Jon Klemm	COL	67	6	8	14	-3	30	0	0	0	1	60	10.0
D	5	Alexei Gusarov	COL	72	4	10	14	9	42	0	1	1	0	47	8.5
R	16	Jeff Odgers	COL	68	5	8	13	5	213	0	0	0	0	47	10.6
L	10	Warren Rychel	ANA	63	5	6	11	-10	198	1	0	0	0	62	8.1
			COL	8	0	0	0	-1	23	0	0	0	0	4	0.0
			TOTAL	71	5	6	11	-11	221	1	0	0	0	66	7.6
R	11	Keith Jones	COL	23	3	7	10	-4	22	1	0	2	0	31	9.7
D	2	Sylvain Lefebvre	COL	81	0	10	10	2	48	0	0	0	0	66	0.0
D	3	Aaron Miller	COL	55	2	2	4	0	51	0	0	0	0	29	6.9
D	27	Francois Leroux	COL	50	1	2	3	-3	140	0	0	0	0	14	7.1
G	33	Patrick Roy	COL	65	0	3	3	0	39	0	0	0	0	1	0.0
D	6	* Wade Belak	COL	8	1	1	2	-3	27	0	0	1	0	2	50.0
L	15	Yves Sarault	COL	2	1	0	1	1	0	0	0	0	0	1	100.0
D	7	* Pascal Trepanier	COL	15	0	1	1	-2	18	0	0	0	0	9	0.0
L	40	* Brad Larsen	COL	1	0	0	0	0	0	0	0	0	0	0	0.0
R	14	* Christian Matte	COL	5	0	0	0	0	6	0	0	0	0	5	0.0
G	1	Craig Billington	COL	23	0	0	0	0	2	0	0	0	0	0	0.0

Goaltending

No.	Goaltender	GPI	Mins	Avg	W	L	T	EN	SO	GA	SA	S%
1	Craig Billington	23	1162	2.32	8	7	4	2	1	45	588	.923
33	Patrick Roy	65	3835	2.39	31	19	13	5	4	153	1825	.916
	Totals	**82**	**5017**	**2.45**	**39**	**26**	**17**	**7**	**5**	**205**	**2420**	**.915**

Playoffs

Pos	#	Player	Team	GP	G	A	Pts	+/–	PIM	PP	SH	GW	OT	S	%
C	21	Peter Forsberg	COL	7	6	5	11	3	12	2	0	0	0	18	33.3
D	8	Sandis Ozolinsh	COL	7	0	7	7	-3	14	0	0	0	0	19	0.0
R	22	Claude Lemieux	COL	7	3	3	6	2	8	1	0	1	0	29	10.3
C	19	Joe Sakic	COL	6	2	3	5	0	6	0	1	2	1	24	8.3
L	13	Valeri Kamensky	COL	7	2	3	5	1	18	1	0	0	0	17	11.8
R	18	Adam Deadmarsh	COL	7	2	0	2	-1	4	1	0	0	0	14	14.3
C	26	Stephane Yelle	COL	7	1	0	1	-3	12	0	0	0	0	7	14.3
R	14	Tom Fitzgerald	COL	7	0	1	1	-2	20	0	0	0	0	8	0.0
D	5	Alexei Gusarov	COL	7	0	1	1	1	6	0	0	0	0	3	0.0
D	4	Uwe Krupp	COL	7	0	1	1	2	4	0	0	0	0	18	0.0
G	33	Patrick Roy	COL	7	0	1	1	0	0	0	0	0	0	0	0.0
G	1	Craig Billington	COL	1	0	0	0	0	0	0	0	0	0	0	0.0
L	20	Rene Corbet	COL	2	0	0	0	0	2	0	0	0	0	5	0.0
C	17	Jari Kurri	COL	4	0	0	0	-1	0	0	0	0	0	2	0.0
D	24	Jon Klemm	COL	4	0	0	0	1	0	0	0	0	0	1	0.0
L	10	Warren Rychel	COL	6	0	0	0	-2	24	0	0	0	0	4	0.0
R	16	Jeff Odgers	COL	6	0	0	0	-1	25	0	0	0	0	4	0.0
D	2	Sylvain Lefebvre	COL	7	0	0	0	-1	4	0	0	0	0	4	0.0
D	52	Adam Foote	COL	7	0	0	0	-1	23	0	0	0	0	12	0.0
R	11	Keith Jones	COL	7	0	0	0	-1	13	0	0	0	0	12	0.0
L	28	Eric Lacroix	COL	7	0	0	0	-2	6	0	0	0	0	5	0.0
D	3	Aaron Miller	COL	7	0	0	0	0	8	0	0	0	0	6	0.0

Goaltending

No.	Goaltender	GPI	Mins	Avg	W	L	EN	SO	GA	SA	S%
1	Craig Billington	1	1	0.00	0	0	0	0	0	0	.000
33	Patrick Roy	7	430	2.51	3	4	1	0	18	191	.906
	Totals	**7**	**435**	**2.62**	**3**	**4**	**1**	**0**	**19**	**192**	**.901**

President and General Manager

LACROIX, PIERRE
President and General Manager, Colorado Avalanche.
Born in Montreal, Que., August 3, 1948.

Pierre Lacroix was appointed to the general manager's post on May 24, 1994 after 21 years as a respected player agent. In his first season as general manager, his leadership was instrumental in moving the team from 11th to second place in the NHL. Lacroix's second season began with the club's move to Denver. He set out to improve the team and did so through acquisitions that brought Claude Lemieux, Sandis Ozolinsh, Patrick Roy and Mike Keane to Colorado. The revamped Avs finished atop the Pacific Division and went on to win the Stanley Cup. He was named NHL executive of the year by *The Hockey News* and became president of the club's hockey operations in August, 1995.

Lacroix and his wife Colombe have two children. Martin (28) is a player agent, Eric (27) plays left wing for the Avalanche.

Club Records

Team

(Figures in brackets for season records are games played; records for fewest points, wins, ties, losses, goals, goals against are for 70 or more games)

Most Points	**107**	1996-97 (82)
Most Wins	**49**	1996-97 (82)
Most Ties	**18**	1980-81 (80)
Most Losses	**61**	1989-90 (80)
Most Goals	**360**	1983-84 (80)
Most Goals Against	**407**	1989-90 (80)
Fewest Points	**31**	1989-90 (80)
Fewest Wins	**12**	1989-90 (80)
Fewest Ties	**5**	1987-88 (80)
Fewest Losses	**24**	1996-97 (82)
Fewest Goals	**231**	1997-98 (82)
Fewest Goals Against	**205**	1996-97 (82), 1997-98 (82)
Longest Winning Streak		
Overall	**8**	Oct. 18-Nov. 5/95
Home	**10**	Nov. 26/83-Jan. 10/84, Mar. 6-Apr. 16/95
Away	**5**	Feb. 28-Mar. 24/86, Oct. 25-Nov. 11/95
Longest Undefeated Streak		
Overall	**12**	Dec. 23/96-Jan. 20/97 (9 wins, 3 ties)
Home	**14**	Nov. 19/83-Jan. 21/84 (11 wins, 3 ties)
Away	**8**	Feb. 17-Mar. 22/81 (6 wins, 2 ties), Dec. 23/96-Jan. 20/97 (5 wins, 3 ties)
Longest Losing Streak		
Overall	**14**	Oct. 21-Nov. 19/90
Home	**8**	Oct. 21-Nov. 24/90
Away	**18**	Jan. 18-Apr. 1/90
Longest Winless Streak		
Overall	**17**	Oct. 21-Nov. 25/90 (15 losses, 2 ties)
Home	**11**	Nov. 14-Dec. 26/89 (7 losses, 4 ties)
Away	**33**	Oct. 8/91-Feb. 27/92 (25 losses, 8 ties)
Most Shutouts, Season	**8**	1996-97 (82)
Most PIM, Season	**2,104**	1989-90 (80)
Most Goals, Game	**12**	Three times

Individual

Most Seasons	**11**	Michel Goulet
Most Games	**813**	Michel Goulet
Most Goals, Career	**456**	Michel Goulet
Most Assists, Career	**668**	Peter Stastny
Most Points, Career	**1,048**	Peter Stastny (380G, 668A)
Most PIM, Career	**1,545**	Dale Hunter
Most Shutouts, Career	**12**	Patrick Roy
Longest Consecutive Games Streak	**312**	Dale Hunter (Oct. 9/80-Mar. 13/84)
Most Goals, Season	**57**	Michel Goulet (1982-83)
Most Assists, Season	**93**	Peter Stastny (1981-82)
Most Points, Season	**139**	Peter Stastny (1981-82; 46G, 93A)
Most PIM, Season	**301**	Gord Donnelly (1987-88)
Most Points, Defenseman, Season	**82**	Steve Duchesne (1992-93; 20G, 62A)
Most Points, Center, Season	**139**	Peter Stastny (1981-82; 46G, 93A)
Most Points, Right Wing, Season	**103**	Jacques Richard (1980-81; 52G, 51A)
Most Points, Left Wing, Season	**121**	Michel Goulet (1983-84; 56G, 65A)
Most Points, Rookie, Season	**109**	Peter Stastny (1980-81; 39G, 70A)
Most Shutouts, Season	**7**	Patrick Roy (1996-97)
Most Goals, Game	**5**	Mats Sundin (Mar. 5/92), Mike Ricci (Feb. 17/94)
Most Assists, Game	**5**	Six times
Most Points, Game	**8**	Peter Stastny (Feb. 22/81; 4G, 4A), Anton Stastny (Feb. 22/81; 3G, 5A)

Records include Quebec Nordiques, 1979-80 through 1994-95.

Quebec Nordiques Retired Numbers

3	J.C. Tremblay	1972-1979
8	Marc Tardif	1979-1983
16	Michel Goulet	1979-1990

Captains' History

Marc Tardif, 1979-80, 1980-81; Robbie Ftorek and Andre Dupont, 1981-82; Mario Marois, 1982-83 to 1984-85; Mario Marois and Peter Stastny, 1985-86; Peter Stastny, 1986-87 to 1989-90; Joe Sakic and Steven Finn, 1990-91; Mike Hough, 1991-92; Joe Sakic, 1992-93 to date.

All-time Record vs. Other Clubs

Regular Season

	At Home							On Road							Total						
	GP	W	L	T	GF	GA	PTS	GP	W	L	T	GF	GA	PTS	GP	W	L	T	GF	GA	PTS
Anaheim	9	5	2	2	36	30	12	9	3	4	2	18	23	8	18	8	6	4	54	53	20
Boston	60	21	33	6	217	257	48	58	19	31	8	179	231	46	118	40	64	14	396	488	94
Buffalo	59	30	18	11	221	184	71	59	16	34	9	191	237	41	118	46	52	20	412	421	112
Calgary	30	11	11	8	121	111	30	31	8	17	6	97	128	22	61	19	28	14	218	239	52
Carolina	60	34	17	9	255	183	77	58	23	24	11	202	195	57	118	57	41	20	457	378	134
Chicago	28	13	11	4	113	105	30	29	11	16	2	93	105	24	57	24	27	6	206	210	54
Dallas	29	17	8	4	123	83	38	28	10	16	2	88	101	22	57	27	24	6	211	184	60
Detroit	29	16	9	4	115	101	36	28	11	16	1	90	107	23	57	27	25	5	205	208	59
Edmonton	30	13	15	2	125	128	28	30	11	17	2	99	141	24	60	24	32	4	224	269	52
Florida	6	2	2	2	17	17	6	7	6	1	0	28	17	12	13	8	3	2	45	34	18
Los Angeles	30	14	13	3	122	112	31	30	10	18	2	99	128	22	60	24	31	5	221	240	53
Montreal	60	29	26	5	201	212	63	59	13	37	9	187	251	35	119	42	63	14	388	463	98
New Jersey	29	15	11	3	108	87	33	31	12	16	3	107	127	27	60	27	27	6	215	214	60
NY Islanders	29	17	10	2	110	90	36	28	12	15	1	100	115	25	57	29	25	3	210	205	61
NY Rangers	30	15	12	3	125	117	33	28	6	18	4	77	118	16	58	21	30	7	202	235	49
Ottawa	11	10	0	1	58	29	21	13	7	4	2	60	40	16	24	17	4	3	118	69	37
Philadelphia	29	10	9	10	108	105	30	30	7	21	2	78	112	16	59	17	30	12	186	217	46
Phoenix	29	14	11	4	114	106	32	28	13	10	5	112	106	31	57	27	21	9	226	212	63
Pittsburgh	28	14	12	2	129	113	30	31	12	15	4	128	134	28	59	26	27	6	257	247	58
St. Louis	28	14	11	3	103	91	31	28	6	19	3	88	123	15	56	20	30	6	191	214	46
San Jose	11	8	2	1	53	26	17	12	7	5	0	53	42	14	23	15	7	1	106	68	31
Tampa Bay	8	5	2	1	34	20	11	8	1	6	1	21	29	3	16	6	8	2	55	49	14
Toronto	29	17	7	5	111	87	39	29	14	12	3	121	99	31	58	31	19	8	232	186	70
Vancouver	31	14	11	6	105	88	34	30	14	11	5	128	114	33	61	28	22	11	233	202	67
Washington	29	13	12	4	95	106	30	29	9	16	4	96	122	22	58	22	28	8	191	228	52
Totals	**751**	**371**	**275**	**105**	**2919**	**2588**	**847**	**751**	**261**	**399**	**91**	**2540**	**2945**	**613**	**1502**	**632**	**674**	**196**	**5459**	**5533**	**1460**

Playoffs

	Series	W	L	GP	W	L	T	GF	GA	Last Mtg.	Round	Result
Boston	2	1	1	11	5	6	0	36	37	1983	DSF	L 1-3
Buffalo	2	2	0	8	6	2	0	35	27	1985	DSF	W 3-2
Chicago	2	2	0	12	8	4	0	49	28	1997	CQF	W 4-2
Detroit	2	1	1	12	6	6	0	32	32	1997	CF	L 2-4
Edmonton	2	1	1	12	7	5	0	35	30	1998	CQF	W 3-4
Florida	1	1	0	4	4	0	0	15	4	1996	F	W 4-0
Hartford	2	1	1	9	4	5	0	34	35	1987	DSF	W 4-2
Montreal	5	2	3	31	14	17	0	85	105	1993	DSF	L 2-4
NY Islanders	1	0	1	4	0	4	0	9	18	1982	CF	L 0-4
NY Rangers	1	0	1	6	2	4	0	19	25	1995	CQF	L 2-4
Philadelphia	2	0	2	11	4	7	0	29	39	1985	CF	L 2-4
Vancouver	1	1	0	6	4	2	0	24	17	1996	CQF	W 4-2
Totals	**23**	**12**	**11**	**126**	**64**	**62**	**0**	**402**	**397**			

Playoff Results 1998-94

Year	Round	Opponent	Result	GF	GA
1998	CQF	Edmonton	L 3-4	16	19
1997	CF	Detroit	L 2-4	12	16
	CSF	Edmonton	W 4-1	19	11
	CQF	Chicago	W 4-2	28	14
1996	**F**	**Florida**	**W 4-0**	**15**	**4**
	CF	Detroit	W 4-2	20	16
	CSF	Chicago	W 4-2	21	14
	CQF	Vancouver	W 4-2	24	17
1995	CQF	NY Rangers	L 2-4	19	25

Abbreviations: Round: F – Final; **CF** – conference final; **CQF** – conference quarter-final; **CSF** – conference semi-final; **DSF** – division semi-final.

Calgary totals include Atlanta, 1979-80.
Colorado totals include Quebec, 1979-80 to 1994-95.
New Jersey totals include Colorado Rockies, 1979-80 to 1981-82.
Carolina totals include Hartford, 1979-80 to 1996-97.
Dallas totals include Minnesota, 1979-80 to 1992-93.
Phoenix totals include Winnipeg, 1979-80 to 1995-96.

1997-98 Results

Oct.	1		Dallas	2-2	**Jan.**	2	at	Buffalo	2-2
	3	at	Calgary	4-1		3	at	Pittsburgh	5-4
	5	at	Edmonton	3-0		6		Calgary	1-3
	7		Boston	3-2		8		Vancouver	4-4
	9		San Jose	3-2		10		Ottawa	3-3
	11		Phoenix	3-3		12		Florida	3-1
	15	at	Edmonton	6-2		14	at	Anaheim	2-0
	17	at	Calgary	5-6		15		San Jose	2-2
	19	at	Vancouver	4-4		21	at	Dallas	2-3
	22		Washington	4-3		22		Anaheim	3-4
	24		Carolina	3-3		24		Dallas	2-3
	25	at	Dallas	1-3		26		Edmonton	2-1.
	28		Buffalo	3-2		28		Vancouver	6-1
	30	at	St. Louis	2-2		31	at	San Jose	2-5
Nov.	1		Calgary	3-3	**Feb.**	2	at	Vancouver	2-1
	5		NY Rangers	2-4		5		Chicago	4-2
	8		St. Louis	4-1		7		Philadelphia	3-2
	11	at	Detroit	2-0		25	at	Phoenix	4-2
	13	at	Philadelphia	2-1		26		Phoenix	3-0
	14	at	New Jersey	1-4		28		Chicago	0-4
	16	at	NY Rangers	1-4	**Mar.**	2		Edmonton	4-5
	18	at	Washington	6-6		4	at	Toronto	5-3
	21		Toronto	3-1		5	at	Ottawa	2-4
	23		Los Angeles	1-2		7	at	NY Islanders	4-2
	26	at	Tampa Bay	3-3		9		Tampa Bay	1-2
	28	at	Florida	3-2		11		St. Louis	3-2
	29	at	Carolina	3-2		14	at	Los Angeles	2-5
Dec.	2		Edmonton	4-2		15	at	Anaheim	3-5
	4	at	Chicago	2-1		19	at	Phoenix	4-3
	6		Vancouver	6-4		21	at	San Jose	2-0
	8	at	Montreal	2-4		26		New Jersey	0-2
	10	at	Toronto	2-2		28		Anaheim	5-3
	12	at	Calgary	1-3		30	at	Boston	1-4
	13	at	Vancouver	5-2	**Apr.**	1	at	Detroit	0-2
	15		Toronto	3-2		2	at	Chicago	1-2
	17		Detroit	2-2		4	at	St. Louis	1-4
	19		Pittsburgh	3-3		6		Los Angeles	1-3
	23		Los Angeles	5-1		11	at	Los Angeles	3-4
	27	at	Edmonton	5-1		13	at	Anaheim	2-2
	29		Montreal	1-1		16		San Jose	4-1
	31		NY Islanders	3-1		18		Detroit	4-3

Entry Draft Selections 1998-84

1998
Pick
12 Alex Tanguay
17 Martin Skoula
19 Robyn Regeher
20 Scott Parker
28 Ramzi Abid
38 Philippe Sauve
53 Steve Moore
79 Yevgeny Lazarev
141 Kristinn Timmons
167 Alexander Ryazantsev

1997
Pick
26 Kevin Grimes
53 Graham Belak
55 Rick Berry
78 Ville Nieminen
87 Brad Larsen
133 Aaron Miskovich
161 David Aebischer
217 Doug Schmidt
243 Kyle Kidney
245 Stephen Lafleur

1996
Pick
25 Peter Ratchuk
51 Yuri Babenko
79 Mark Parrish
98 Ben Storey
107 Randy Petruk
134 Luke Curtin
146 Brian Willsie
160 Kai Fischer
167 Dan Hinote
176 Samuel Pahlsson
188 Roman Pylner
214 Matthew Scorsune
240 Justin Clark

1995
Pick
25 Marc Denis
51 Nic Beaudoin
77 John Tripp
81 Tomi Kallio
159 Brent Johnson
155 John Cirjak
181 Dan Smith
207 Tomi Hirvonen
228 Chris George

1994
Pick
12 Wade Belak
22 Jeffrey Kealty
35 Josef Marha
61 Sebastien Bety
72 Chris Drury
87 Milan Hejduk
113 Tony Tuzzolino
139 Nicholas Windsor
165 Calvin Elfring
191 Jay Bertsch
217 Tim Thomas
243 Chris Pittman
285 Steven Low

1993
Pick
10 Jocelyn Thibault
14 Adam Deadmarsh
49 Ashley Buckberger
75 Bill Pierce
101 Ryan Tocher
127 Anders Myrvold
137 Nicholas Checco
153 Christian Matte
179 David Ling
205 Petr Franek
231 Vincent Auger
257 Mark Pivetz
283 John Hillman

1992
Pick
4 Todd Warriner
28 Paul Brousseau
29 Tuomas Gronman
52 Emmanuel Fernandez
76 Ian McIntyre
100 Charlie Wasley
124 Paxton Schulte
148 Martin LePage
172 Mike Jickling
196 Steve Passmore
220 Anson Carter
244 Aaron Ellis

1991
Pick
1 Eric Lindros
24 Rene Corbet
46 Richard Brennan
68 Dave Karpa
90 Patrick Labrecque
103 Bill Lindsay
134 Mikael Johansson
156 Janne Laukkanen
157 Aaron Asp
178 Adam Bartell
188 Brent Brekke
200 Paul Koch
222 Doug Friedman
244 Eric Meloche

1990
Pick
1 Owen Nolan
22 Ryan Hughes
43 Bradley Zavisha
106 Jeff Parrott
127 Dwayne Norris
148 Andrei Kovalenko
158 Alexander Karpovtsev
169 Pat Mazzoli
190 Scott Davis
211 Mika Stromberg
232 Wade Klippenstein

1989
Pick
1 Mats Sundin
22 Adam Foote
43 Stephane Morin
54 John Tanner
68 Niklas Andersson
76 Eric Dubois
85 Kevin Kaiser
106 Dan Lambert
127 Sergei Mylnikov
148 Paul Krake
169 Viacheslav Bykov
190 Andrei Khomutov
211 Byron Witkowski
232 Noel Rahn

1988
Pick
3 Curtis Leschyshyn
5 Daniel Dore
24 Stephane Fiset
45 Petri Aaltonen
66 Darin Kimble
87 Stephane Venne
108 Ed Ward
129 Valeri Kamensky
150 Sakari Lindfors
171 Dan Wiebe
213 Alexei Gusarov
234 Claude Lapointe

1987
Pick
9 Bryan Fogarty
15 Joe Sakic
51 Jim Sprott
72 Kip Miller
93 Rob Mendel
114 Garth Snow
135 Tim Hanus
156 Jake Enebak
177 Jaroslav Sevcik
183 Ladislav Tresl
198 Darren Nauss
219 Mike Williams

1986
Pick
18 Ken McRae
39 Jean-Marc Routhier
41 Stephane Guerard
81 Ron Tugnutt
102 Gerald Bzdel
117 Scott White
123 Morgan Samuelsson
134 Mark Vermette
144 Jean-Francois Nault
165 Keith Miller
186 Pierre Millier
207 Chris Lappin
228 Martin Latreille
249 Sean Boudreault

1985
Pick
15 David Latta
36 Jason Lafreniere
57 Max Middendorf
65 Peter Massey
78 David Espe
99 Bruce Major
120 Andy Akervik
141 Mike Oliverio
162 Mario Brunetta
183 Brit Peer
204 Tom Sasso
225 Gary Murphy
246 Jean Bois

1984
Pick
15 Trevor Stienburg
36 Jeff Brown
57 Steve Finn
78 Terry Perkins
120 Darren Cota
141 Henrik Cedergren
162 Jyrki Maki
183 Guy Ouellette
203 Ken Quinney
244 Peter Loob

Sandis Ozolinsh was Colorado's top-scoring defenseman in 1997-98. He was one of only nine defensemen in the NHL to finish with 50-or-more points in the regular season.

Club Directory

McNichols Arena
1635 Clay Street
Denver, CO 80204
Phone **303/893-6700**
FAX 303/893-0614
Capacity: 16,061

Owner	Ascent Entertainment Group, Inc.
Governor and Chairman	Charlie Lyons
Alternate Governor, President and General Manager	Pierre Lacroix
Assistant General Manager	Francois Giguere
Director of Player Personnel	Michel Goulet
Head Coach	Bob Hartley
Assistant Coaches	Jacques Cloutier, Bryan Trottier
Equipment Manager	Rob McLean
Athletic Trainer	Pat Karns
Director of Media Relations and Team Services	Jean Martineau
Assistant Director of Media Relations	Damen Zier
Media Relations Assistant	Hayne Ellis
Team Colors	Burgundy, Silver, Black and Blue
Minor League Affiliate	Hershey Bears (AHL)
Television	FOX Sports Rocky Mountain, KTVD UPN-20
Play-by-Play	John Kelly
Analyst	Peter McNab
Radio	KKFN AM-950
Play-by-Play	Mike Haynes
Analyst	Norm Jones
Web Site	www.coloradoavalanche.com

Dallas Stars

1997-98 Results: 49W-22L-11T 109PTS. First, Central Division

1998-99 Schedule

Oct.	Sat.	10	Buffalo
	Tue.	13	Chicago
	Thu.	15	at Carolina
	Sat.	17	at Chicago
	Tue.	20	Calgary
	Thu.	22	Phoenix
	Sat.	24	San Jose
	Fri.	30	Anaheim
	Sat.	31	Detroit
Nov.	Wed.	4	at San Jose
	Sat.	7	at Los Angeles
	Wed.	11	Phoenix
	Fri.	13	at Detroit
	Sat.	14	at Boston
	Fri.	20	NY Islanders
	Sat.	21	at St. Louis
	Mon.	23	San Jose
	Wed.	25	New Jersey
	Fri.	27	Washington
Dec.	Wed.	2	at San Jose
	Fri.	4	at Vancouver
	Sun.	6	at Edmonton
	Mon.	7	at Calgary
	Wed.	9	San Jose
	Fri.	11	Montreal
	Sun.	13	at Chicago
	Tue.	15	St. Louis
	Fri.	18	at Detroit
	Sun.	20	at Ottawa*
	Mon.	21	at Montreal
	Wed.	23	at Toronto
	Sat.	26	at Colorado
	Mon.	28	Nashville
	Thu.	31	Boston
Jan.	Fri.	1	at Phoenix
	Wed.	6	Vancouver
	Fri.	8	at Calgary
	Sun.	10	at Vancouver
	Tue.	12	at Edmonton
	Wed.	13	at San Jose
	Fri.	15	at Anaheim
	Mon.	18	Vancouver
	Wed.	20	Toronto
	Wed.	27	Los Angeles
	Fri.	29	at Tampa Bay
	Sat.	30	at Florida
Feb.	Mon.	1	Calgary
	Sun.	7	Colorado*
	Fri.	12	at Anaheim
	Sat.	13	at Los Angeles
	Mon.	15	Edmonton
	Wed.	17	Florida
	Fri.	19	Chicago
	Sun.	21	Colorado*
	Tue.	23	at Nashville
	Wed.	24	Nashville
	Fri.	26	Pittsburgh
	Sun.	28	Los Angeles*
Mar.	Tue.	2	at NY Rangers
	Thu.	4	at NY Islanders
	Fri.	5	at Buffalo
	Sun.	7	St. Louis*
	Wed.	10	Edmonton
	Fri.	12	Anaheim
	Sun.	14	at Philadelphia
	Tue.	16	at Pittsburgh
	Wed.	17	at Washington
	Fri.	19	Ottawa
	Sun.	21	Carolina
	Tue.	23	at Phoenix
	Thu.	25	at Los Angeles
	Fri.	26	at Anaheim
	Sun.	28	at Nashville*
	Wed.	31	Tampa Bay
Apr.	Sat.	3	at St. Louis*
	Sun.	4	Detroit*
	Wed.	7	Anaheim
	Fri.	9	NY Rangers
	Sun.	11	Los Angeles*
	Wed.	14	Phoenix
	Sat.	17	at Phoenix*
	Sun.	18	at Colorado*

* Denotes afternoon game.

Franchise date: June 5, 1967
Transferred from Minnesota to Dallas, June 9, 1993.

PACIFIC DIVISION

32nd NHL Season

In his first season with Dallas, Ed Belfour set a franchise record with 37 wins and lead the Stars to the Presidents' Trophy for the first time. Belfour's 1.88 goals-against average was the best in the NHL.

Year-by-Year Record

		Home			Road			Overall								
Season	GP	W	L	T	W	L	T	W	L	T	GF	GA	Pts.	Finished		Playoff Result
1997-98	82	26	8	7	23	14	4	49	22	11	242	167	109	1st,	Central Div.	Lost Conf. Final
1996-97	82	25	13	3	23	13	5	48	26	8	252	198	104	1st,	Central Div.	Lost Conf. Quarter-Final
1995-96	82	14	18	9	12	24	5	26	42	14	227	280	66	6th,	Central Div.	Out of Playoffs
1994-95	48	9	10	5	8	13	3	17	23	8	136	135	42	5th,	Central Div.	Lost Conf. Quarter-Final
1993-94	84	23	12	7	19	17	6	42	29	13	286	265	97	3rd,	Central Div.	Lost Conf. Semi-Final
1992-93*	84	18	17	7	18	21	3	36	38	10	272	293	82	5th,	Norris Div.	Out of Playoffs
1991-92*	80	20	16	4	12	26	2	32	42	6	246	278	70	4th,	Norris Div.	Lost Div. Semi-Final
1990-91*	80	19	15	6	8	24	8	27	39	14	256	266	68	4th,	Norris Div.	Lost Final
1989-90*	80	26	12	2	10	28	2	36	40	4	284	291	76	4th,	Norris Div.	Lost Div. Semi-Final
1988-89*	80	17	15	8	10	22	8	27	37	16	258	278	70	3rd,	Norris Div.	Lost Div. Semi-Final
1987-88*	80	10	24	6	9	24	7	19	48	13	242	349	51	5th,	Norris Div.	Out of Playoffs
1986-87*	80	17	20	3	13	20	7	30	40	10	296	314	70	5th,	Norris Div.	Out of Playoffs
1985-86*	80	21	15	4	17	18	5	38	33	9	327	305	85	2nd,	Norris Div.	Lost Div. Semi-Final
1984-85*	80	14	19	7	11	24	5	25	43	12	268	321	62	4th,	Norris Div.	Lost Div. Final
1983-84*	80	22	14	4	17	17	6	39	31	10	345	344	88	1st,	Norris Div.	Lost Conf. Championship
1982-83*	80	23	6	11	17	18	5	40	24	16	321	290	96	2nd,	Norris Div.	Lost Div. Final
1981-82*	80	21	7	12	16	16	8	37	23	20	346	288	94	1st,	Norris Div.	Lost Div. Semi-Final
1980-81*	80	23	10	7	12	18	10	35	28	17	291	263	87	3rd,	Adams Div.	Lost Final
1979-80*	80	25	8	7	11	20	9	36	28	16	311	253	88	3rd,	Adams Div.	Lost Semi-Final
1978-79*	80	19	15	6	9	25	6	28	40	12	257	289	68	4th,	Adams Div.	Out Of Playoffs
1977-78*	80	12	24	4	6	29	5	18	53	9	218	325	45	5th,	Smythe Div.	Out of Playoffs
1976-77*	80	17	14	9	6	25	9	23	39	18	240	310	64	2nd,	Smythe Div.	Lost Prelim. Round
1975-76*	80	15	22	3	5	31	4	20	53	7	195	303	47	4th,	Smythe Div.	Out of Playoffs
1974-75*	80	17	20	3	6	30	4	23	50	7	221	341	53	4th,	Smythe Div.	Out of Playoffs
1973-74*	78	18	15	6	5	23	11	23	38	17	235	275	63	7th,	West Div.	Out of Playoffs
1972-73*	78	26	8	5	11	22	6	37	30	11	254	230	85	3rd,	West Div.	Lost Quarter-Final
1971-72*	78	22	11	6	15	18	6	37	29	12	212	191	86	2nd,	West Div.	Lost Quarter-Final
1970-71*	78	16	15	8	12	19	8	28	34	16	191	223	72	4th,	West Div.	Lost Semi-Final
1969-70*	76	11	16	11	8	19	11	19	35	22	224	257	60	3rd,	West Div.	Lost Quarter-Final
1968-69*	76	11	21	6	7	22	9	18	43	15	189	270	51	6th,	West Div.	Out of Playoffs
1967-68*	74	17	12	8	10	20	7	27	32	15	191	226	69	4th,	West Div.	Lost Semi-Final

* Minnesota North Stars

1998-99 Player Personnel

FORWARDS	HT	WT	S	Place of Birth	Date	1997-98 Club
BOTTERILL, Jason	6-3	205	L	Edmonton, Alta.	5/19/76	Dallas-Michigan
CARBONNEAU, Guy	5-11	186	R	Sept-Iles, Que.	3/18/60	Dallas
FAIRCHILD, Kelly	5-11	180	L	Hibbing, MN	4/9/73	St. John's-Orlando-Milwaukee
GAVEY, Aaron	6-2	200	L	Sudbury, Ont.	2/22/74	Calgary-Saint John
HRKAC, Tony	5-11	170	L	Thunder Bay, Ont.	7/7/66	Dallas-Michigan-Edmonton
HULL, Brett	5-10	201	R	Belleville, Ont.	8/9/64	St. Louis-United States
KEANE, Mike	6-0	185	R	Winnipeg, Man.	5/29/67	NY Rangers-Dallas
LANGENBRUNNER, Jamie	5-11	185	R	Duluth, MN	7/24/75	Dallas-United States
LEHTINEN, Jere	6-0	192	R	Espoo, Finland	6/24/73	Dallas-Finland
MARSHALL, Grant	6-1	193	R	Mississauga, Ont.	6/9/73	Dallas
MITCHELL, Jeff	6-1	190	R	Wayne, MI	5/16/75	Dallas-Michigan
MODANO, Mike	6-3	200	L	Livonia, MI	6/7/70	Dallas-United States
NIEUWENDYK, Joe	6-1	195	L	Oshawa, Ont.	9/10/66	Dallas
REID, David	6-1	217	L	Toronto, Ont.	5/15/64	Dallas
ROBERTS, David	6-0	185	L	Alameda, CA	5/28/70	Vancouver-Syracuse
SEVERYN, Brent	6-2	211	L	Vegreville, Alta.	2/22/66	Anaheim
SIM, Jonathan	5-9	175	L	New Glasgow, N.S.	9/29/77	Sarnia
SKRUDLAND, Brian	6-0	195	L	Peace River, Alta.	7/31/63	NY Rangers-Dallas
VERBEEK, Pat	5-9	192	R	Sarnia, Ont.	5/24/64	Dallas
WRIGHT, Jamie	6-0	172	L	Kitchener, Ont.	5/13/76	Dallas-Michigan
DEFENSEMEN						
BUZEK, Petr	6-0	205	L	Jihlava, Czech.	4/26/77	Dallas-Michigan
CHAMBERS, Shawn	6-2	200	L	Sterling Hts., MI	10/11/66	Dallas
GUSEV, Sergey	6-1	195	L	Nizhny Tagil, USSR	7/31/75	Dallas-Michigan
HATCHER, Derian	6-5	225	L	Sterling Heights, MI	6/4/72	Dallas-United States
JACKMAN, Richard	6-2	180	R	Toronto, Ont.	6/28/78	S.S. Marie-Michigan
KECZMER, Dan	6-1	190	L	Mt. Clemens, MI	5/25/68	Dallas-Michigan
LUDWIG, Craig	6-3	220	L	Rhinelander, WI	3/15/61	Dallas
LUKOWICH, Brad	6-1	170	L	Cranbrook, B.C.	8/12/76	Dallas-Michigan
MARTIN, Matt	6-3	205	L	Hamden, CT	4/30/71	Chicago (IHL)
MATVICHUK, Richard	6-2	200	L	Edmonton, Alta.	2/5/73	Dallas
SYDOR, Darryl	6-0	195	L	Edmonton, Alta.	5/13/72	Dallas
ZUBOV, Sergei	6-1	200	R	Moscow, USSR	7/22/70	Dallas

GOALTENDERS	HT	WT	C	Place of Birth	Date	1997-98 Club
BALES, Mike	6-1	180	L	Prince Albert, Sask.	8/6/71	Rochester
BELFOUR, Ed	5-11	182	L	Carman, Man.	4/21/65	Dallas
FERNANDEZ, Manny	6-0	185	L	Etobicoke, Ont.	8/27/74	Dallas-Michigan
TUREK, Roman	6-3	190	R	Pisek, Czech.	5/21/70	Dallas-Michigan

Coaching History

Wren Blair, 1967-68; Wren Blair and John Muckler, 1968-69; Wren Blair and Charlie Burns, 1969-70; Jackie Gordon, 1970-71 to 1972-73; Jackie Gordon and Parker MacDonald, 1973-74; Jackie Gordon and Charlie Burns, 1974-75; Ted Harris, 1975-76, 1976-77; Ted Harris, André Beaulieu and Lou Nanne, 1977-78; Harry Howell and Glen Sonmor, 1978-79; Glen Sonmor, 1979-80 to 1981-82; Glen Sonmor and Murray Oliver, 1982-83; Bill Mahoney, 1983-84, 1984-85; Lorne Henning, 1985-86; Lorne Henning and Glen Sonmor, 1986-87; Herb Brooks, 1987-88; Pierre Page, 1988-89, 1989-90; Bob Gainey, 1990-91 to 1994-95; Bob Gainey and Ken Hitchcock, 1995-96; Ken Hitchcock, 1996-97 to date.

Coach

HITCHCOCK, KEN
Coach, Dallas Stars. Born in Edmonton, Alberta, December 17, 1951.

Ken Hitchcock earned his second straight nomination for the Jack Adams Award as coach of the year in 1997-98 after leading the Dallas Stars to the Presidents' Trophy for the first time in franchise history. The Stars led the NHL with 49 victories and 109 points (49-22-11), breaking the club marks for wins and points established under Hitchcock the year before.

Named to his current position on January 8, 1996, Hitchcock had previously enjoyed winning seasons in every year at every level at which he had coached. He posted an incredible 575-69 mark in 10 seasons of Canadian Triple A midget hockey with Sherwood Park in suburban Edmonton, and then went on to record-breaking success with a .693 winning percentage in six seasons with Kamloops of the Western Hockey League. Hitchcock was the WHL coach of the year in 1986-87 and again in 1989-90, when he also added honors as Canadian Major Junior coach of the year.

After a three-year stint (1990-93) as an assistant coach for the Philadelphia Flyers, Hitchcock returned to head coaching duties in the International Hockey League before earning his promotion to Dallas.

Coaching Record

		Regular Season					Playoffs			
Season	Team	Games	W	L	T	%	Games	W	L	%
1984-85	Kamloops (WHL)	71	52	17	2	.746	15	10	5	.667
1985-86	Kamloops (WHL)	72	49	19	4	.708	16	14	2	.875
1986-87	Kamloops (WHL)	72	55	14	3	.785	13	8	5	.615
1987-88	Kamloops (WHL)	72	45	26	1	.632	18	12	6	.667
1988-89	Kamloops (WHL)	72	34	33	5	.507	16	8	8	.500
1989-90	Kamloops (WHL)	72	56	16	0	.778	17	14	3	.824
1993-94	Kalamazoo (IHL)	81	48	26	7	.636	5	1	4	.200
1994-95	Kalamazoo (IHL)	81	43	24	14	.617	16	10	6	.625
1995-96	Michigan (IHL)	40	19	10	11	.613	....	....	....	....
	Dallas (NHL)	**43**	**15**	**23**	**5**	**.407**	....	....	....	....
1996-97	**Dallas (NHL)**	**82**	**48**	**26**	**8**	**.634**	**7**	**3**	**4**	**.429**
1997-98	**Dallas (NHL)**	**82**	**49**	**22**	**11**	**.665**	**17**	**10**	**7**	**.588**
	NHL Totals	**207**	**112**	**71**	**24**	**.599**	**24**	**13**	**11**	**.542**

1997-98 Scoring

* – rookie

Regular Season

Pos	#	Player	Team	GP	G	A	Pts	+/–	PIM	PP	SH	GW	GT	S	%
C	25	Joe Nieuwendyk	DAL	73	39	30	69	16	30	14	0	11	0	203	19.2
C	9	Mike Modano	DAL	52	21	38	59	25	32	7	5	2	1	191	11.0
R	16	Pat Verbeek	DAL	82	31	26	57	15	170	9	0	8	1	190	16.3
D	56	Sergei Zubov	DAL	73	10	47	57	16	16	5	1	2	1	148	6.8
L	15	Jamie Langenbrunner	DAL	81	23	29	52	9	61	8	0	6	1	159	14.5
D	5	Darryl Sydor	DAL	79	11	35	46	17	51	4	1	1	0	166	6.6
R	26	Jere Lehtinen	DAL	72	23	19	42	19	20	7	2	6	1	201	11.4
L	23	Greg Adams	DAL	49	14	18	32	11	20	7	0	1	0	75	18.7
D	2	Derian Hatcher	DAL	70	6	25	31	9	132	3	0	2	0	74	8.1
C	21	Guy Carbonneau	DAL	77	7	17	24	3	40	0	1	1	0	81	8.6
D	27	Shawn Chambers	DAL	57	2	22	24	11	26	1	1	0	0	73	2.7
R	12	Mike Keane	NYR	70	8	10	18	-12	47	2	0	0	0	113	7.1
			DAL	13	2	3	5	0	5	0	0	1	0	15	13.3
			TOTAL	83	10	13	23	-12	52	2	0	1	0	128	7.8
L	33	Benoit Hogue	DAL	53	6	16	22	7	35	3	0	1	0	55	10.9
R	10	Todd Harvey	DAL	59	9	10	19	5	104	0	0	1	0	88	10.2
R	29	Grant Marshall	DAL	72	9	10	19	-2	96	3	0	1	0	91	9.9
L	14	Dave Reid	DAL	65	6	12	18	-15	14	3	0	1	0	90	6.7
D	24	Richard Matvichuk	DAL	74	3	15	18	7	63	0	0	0	0	71	4.2
C	10	Brian Skrudland	NYR	59	5	6	11	-4	39	0	0	1	0	42	11.9
			DAL	13	2	0	2	-2	10	0	0	0	0	13	15.4
			TOTAL	72	7	6	13	-6	49	0	0	1	0	55	12.7
C	28	Bob Bassen	DAL	58	3	4	7	-4	57	0	0	1	0	40	7.5
D	3	Craig Ludwig	DAL	80	0	7	7	21	131	0	0	0	0	46	0.0
L	46 *	Jamie Wright	DAL	21	4	2	6	8	2	0	0	2	0	15	26.7
L	11 *	Juha Lind	DAL	39	2	3	5	4	6	0	0	0	0	27	7.4
D	6	Dan Keczmer	DAL	17	1	2	3	5	26	0	0	0	0	9	11.1
D	22	Craig Muni	DAL	40	1	1	2	0	25	0	0	1	0	12	8.3
R	18	Chris Tancill	DAL	2	0	1	1	-1	0	0	0	0	0	1	0.0
D	37 *	Brad Lukowich	DAL	4	0	1	1	-2	2	0	0	0	0	2	0.0
C	39	Mike Kennedy	TOR	13	0	1	1	-2	14	0	0	0	0	12	0.0
			DAL	2	0	0	0	1	2	0	0	0	0	0	0.0
			TOTAL	15	0	1	1	-1	16	0	0	0	0	12	0.0
R	39	Peter Douris	DAL	1	0	0	0	-1	0	0	0	0	0	3	0.0
G	30 *	Manny Fernandez	DAL	2	0	0	0	0	0	0	0	0	0	0	0.0
D	34 *	Petr Buzek	DAL	2	0	0	0	1	2	0	0	0	0	0	0.0
L	17 *	Patrick Cote	DAL	3	0	0	0	-1	15	0	0	0	0	3	0.0
L	38 *	Jason Botterill	DAL	4	0	0	0	-1	19	0	0	0	0	2	0.0
R	36 *	Jeffrey Mitchell	DAL	7	0	0	0	0	7	0	0	0	0	3	0.0
D	4 *	Sergey Gusev	DAL	9	0	0	0	-5	2	0	0	0	0	5	0.0
G	1	Roman Turek	DAL	23	0	0	0	0	2	0	0	0	0	0	0.0
G	20	Ed Belfour	DAL	61	0	0	0	0	18	0	0	0	0	0	0.0

Goaltending

No.	Goaltender	GPI	Mins	Avg	W	L	T	EN	SO	GA	SA	S%
30	* Manny Fernandez	2	69	1.74	1	0	0	0	0	2	35	.943
20	Ed Belfour	61	3581	1.88	37	12	10	1	9	112	1335	.916
1	Roman Turek	23	1324	2.22	11	10	1	3	1	49	496	.901
	Totals	**82**	**4986**	**2.01**	**49**	**22**	**11**	**4**	**10**	**167**	**1870**	**.911**

Playoffs

Pos	#	Player	Team	GP	G	A	Pts	+/–	PIM	PP	SH	GW	OT	S	%
C	9	Mike Modano	DAL	17	4	10	14	4	12	1	0	1	0	49	8.2
D	56	Sergei Zubov	DAL	17	4	5	9	3	2	3	0	1	0	34	11.8
R	12	Mike Keane	DAL	17	4	4	8	7	0	0	1	1	1	23	17.4
R	26	Jere Lehtinen	DAL	12	3	5	8	0	2	1	0	0	0	31	9.7
L	33	Benoit Hogue	DAL	17	4	2	6	0	16	1	0	2	1	23	17.4
D	2	Derian Hatcher	DAL	17	3	3	6	-1	39	2	0	0	0	22	13.6
R	16	Pat Verbeek	DAL	17	3	2	5	-3	26	2	0	1	0	25	12.0
L	15	Jamie Langenbrunner	DAL	16	1	4	5	-5	14	0	0	1	1	35	2.9
D	5	Darryl Sydor	DAL	17	0	5	5	5	14	0	0	0	0	38	0.0
C	21	Guy Carbonneau	DAL	16	3	1	4	0	6	0	0	0	0	19	15.8
L	23	Greg Adams	DAL	12	2	2	4	4	0	0	0	2	0	14	14.3
L	11 *	Juha Lind	DAL	15	2	2	4	4	8	0	0	1	0	15	13.3
L	14	Dave Reid	DAL	5	0	3	3	-2	2	0	0	0	0	8	0.0
D	27	Shawn Chambers	DAL	14	0	3	3	5	20	0	0	0	0	16	0.0
D	24	Richard Matvichuk	DAL	16	1	1	2	2	14	0	0	0	0	20	5.0
R	29	Grant Marshall	DAL	17	0	2	2	0	47	0	0	0	0	8	0.0
C	25	Joe Nieuwendyk	DAL	1	1	0	1	1	0	0	0	0	0	1	100.0
C	28	Bob Bassen	DAL	17	1	0	1	-3	12	0	0	0	0	13	7.7
D	3	Craig Ludwig	DAL	17	0	1	1	0	22	0	0	0	0	10	0.0
C	10	Brian Skrudland	DAL	17	0	1	1	0	16	0	0	0	0	14	0.0
G	30 *	Manny Fernandez	DAL	1	0	0	0	0	0	0	0	0	0	0	0.0
D	6	Dan Keczmer	DAL	2	0	0	0	0	2	0	0	0	0	2	0.0
D	22	Craig Muni	DAL	5	0	0	0	-2	4	0	0	0	0	1	0.0
L	46 *	Jamie Wright	DAL	5	0	0	0	3	0	0	0	0	0	6	0.0
G	20	Ed Belfour	DAL	17	0	0	0	0	18	0	0	0	0	0	0.0

Goaltending

No.	Goaltender	GPI	Mins	Avg	W	L	EN	SO	GA	SA	S%
30	* Manny Fernandez	1	2	0.00	0	0	0	0	0	0	.000
20	Ed Belfour	17	1039	1.79	10	7	1	1	31	399	.922
	Totals	**17**	**1044**	**1.84**	**10**	**7**	**1**	**1**	**32**	**400**	**.920**

Captains' History

Bob Woytowich, 1967-68; Elmer Vasko, 1968-69; Claude Larose, 1969-70; Ted Harris, 1970-71 to 1973-74; Bill Goldsworthy, 1974-75, 1975-76; Bill Hogaboam, 1976-77; Nick Beverley, 1977-78; J.P. Parise, 1978-79; Paul Shmyr, 1979-80, 1980-81; Tim Young, 1981-82; Craig Hartsburg, 1982-83; Craig Hartsburg and Brian Bellows, 1983-84; Craig Hartsburg, 1984-85 to 1987-88; Curt Fraser, Bob Rouse and Curt Giles, 1988-89; Curt Giles, 1989-90, 1990-91; Mark Tinordi, 1991-92 to 1993-94; Neal Broten and Derian Hatcher, 1994-95; Derian Hatcher, 1995-96 to date.

Club Records

Team

(Figures in brackets for season records are games played; records for fewest points, wins, ties, losses, goals, goals against are for 70 or more games)

Most Points	**109**	1997-98 (82)
Most Wins	**49**	1997-98 (82)
Most Ties	**22**	1969-70 (76)
Most Losses	**53**	1975-76, 1977-78 (80)
Most Goals	**346**	1981-82 (80)
Most Goals Against	**349**	1987-88 (80)
Fewest Points	**45**	1977-78 (80)
Fewest Wins	**18**	1968-69 (76), 1977-78 (80)
Fewest Ties	**4**	1989-90 (80)
Fewest Losses	**22**	1997-98 (82)
Fewest Goals	**189**	1968-69 (76)
Fewest Goals Against	**167**	1997-98 (82)
Longest Winning Streak		
Overall	**7**	Mar. 16-28/80, Mar. 16-Apr. 2/97, Nov. 22-Dec. 5/97
Home	**11**	Nov. 4-Dec. 27/72
Away	**7**	Nov. 18-Dec. 5/92, Jan. 26-Feb. 21/94
Longest Undefeated Streak		
Overall	**12**	Feb. 18-Mar. 15/82 (9 wins, 3 ties)
Home	**13**	Oct. 28-Dec. 27/72 (12 wins, 1 tie), Nov. 21/79-Jan. 9/80 (10 wins, 3 ties), Jan. 17-Mar. 17/91 (11 wins, 2 ties)
Away	**8**	Jan. 26-Feb. 23/94 (7 wins, 1 tie)
Longest Losing Streak		
Overall	**10**	Feb. 1-20/76
Home	**6**	Jan. 17-Feb. 4/70
Away	**8**	Oct. 19-Nov. 13/75, Jan. 28-Mar. 3/88
Longest Winless Streak		
Overall	**20**	Jan. 15-Feb. 28/70 (15 losses, 5 ties)
Home	**12**	Jan. 17-Feb. 25/70 (8 losses, 4 ties)
Away	**23**	Oct. 25/74-Jan. 28/75 (19 losses, 4 ties)
Most Shutouts, Season	**10**	1997-98 (82)
Most PIM, Season	**2,313**	1987-88 (80)
Most Goals, Game	**15**	Nov. 11/81 (Wpg. 2 at Min. 15)

Individual

Most Seasons	**16**	Neal Broten
Most Games	**992**	Neal Broten
Most Goals, Career	**342**	Brian Bellows
Most Assists, Career	**593**	Neal Broten
Most Points, Career	**867**	Neal Broten (274G, 593A)
Most PIM, Career	**1,883**	Shane Churla
Most Shutouts, Career	**26**	Cesare Maniago
Longest Consecutive Games Streak	**442**	Danny Grant (Dec. 4/68-Apr. 7/74)
Most Goals, Season	**55**	Dino Ciccarelli (1981-82), Brian Bellows (1989-90)
Most Assists, Season	**76**	Neal Broten (1985-86)
Most Points, Season	**114**	Bobby Smith (1981-82; 43G, 71A)
Most PIM, Season	**382**	Basil McRae (1987-88)
Most Points, Defenseman, Season	**77**	Craig Hartsburg (1981-82; 17G, 60A)
Most Points, Center, Season	**114**	Bobby Smith (1981-82; 43G, 71A)
Most Points, Right Wing, Season	**107**	Dino Ciccarelli (1981-82; 55G, 52A)
Most Points, Left Wing, Season	**99**	Brian Bellows (1989-90; 55G, 44A)
Most Points, Rookie, Season	**98**	Neal Broten (1981-82; 38G, 60A)
Most Shutouts, Season	**9**	Ed Belfour (1997-98)
Most Goals, Game	**5**	Tim Young (Jan. 15/79)
Most Assists, Game	**5**	Murray Oliver (Oct. 24/71), Larry Murphy (Oct. 17/89)
Most Points, Game	**7**	Bobby Smith (Nov. 11/81; 4G, 3A)

Records include Minnesota North Stars, 1967-68 through 1992-93.

General Managers' History

Wren Blair, 1967-68 to 1973-74; Jack Gordon, 1974-75 to 1976-77; Lou Nanne, 1977-78 to 1987-88; Jack Ferreira, 1988-89, 1989-90; Bob Clarke 1990-91, 1991-92; Bob Gainey, 1992-93 to date.

Minnesota North Stars Retired Numbers

8	Bill Goldsworthy	1967-1976
19	Bill Masterton	1967-1968

All-time Record vs. Other Clubs

Regular Season

	At Home							On Road							Total						
	GP	W	L	T	GF	GA	PTS	GP	W	L	T	GF	GA	PTS	GP	W	L	T	GF	GA	PTS
Anaheim	10	9	1	0	45	18	18	11	6	5	0	31	25	12	21	15	6	0	76	43	30
Boston	56	15	29	12	160	210	42	56	7	40	9	133	248	23	112	22	69	21	293	458	65
Buffalo	49	23	20	6	157	148	52	48	13	25	10	130	175	36	97	36	45	16	287	323	88
Calgary	50	25	18	7	189	168	57	50	10	29	11	131	191	31	100	35	47	18	320	359	88
Carolina	25	14	10	1	104	78	29	26	14	9	3	103	88	31	51	28	19	4	207	166	60
Chicago	100	43	42	15	334	316	101	97	25	61	11	252	390	61	197	68	103	26	586	706	162
Colorado	28	16	10	2	101	88	34	29	8	17	4	83	123	20	57	24	27	6	184	211	54
Detroit	94	49	30	15	344	281	113	94	31	49	14	306	377	76	188	80	79	29	650	658	189
Edmonton	33	14	13	6	121	106	34	32	9	17	6	107	141	24	65	23	30	12	228	247	58
Florida	4	1	1	2	15	12	4	4	1	2	1	12	14	3	8	2	3	3	27	26	7
Los Angeles	67	39	16	12	274	186	90	66	21	27	18	200	230	60	133	60	43	30	474	416	150
Montreal	55	14	30	11	142	199	39	54	10	37	7	132	241	27	109	24	67	18	274	440	66
New Jersey	40	24	10	6	157	104	54	40	18	19	3	125	135	39	80	42	29	9	282	239	93
NY Islanders	42	16	19	7	124	156	39	42	11	23	8	121	162	30	84	27	42	15	245	318	69
NY Rangers	56	16	30	10	167	211	42	57	13	34	10	155	200	36	113	29	64	20	322	411	78
Ottawa	6	4	2	0	25	13	8	5	3	2	0	15	13	6	11	7	4	0	40	26	14
Philadelphia	62	25	23	14	205	206	64	62	9	41	12	143	247	30	124	34	64	26	348	453	94
Phoenix	39	21	13	5	160	124	47	37	17	18	2	131	130	36	76	38	31	7	291	254	83
Pittsburgh	60	33	21	6	225	199	72	59	18	36	5	166	225	41	119	51	57	11	391	424	113
St. Louis	103	46	38	19	349	311	111	106	29	58	19	300	388	77	209	75	96	38	649	699	188
San Jose	13	6	6	1	41	35	13	13	8	5	0	43	32	16	26	14	11	1	84	67	29
Tampa Bay	7	5	1	1	25	15	11	8	5	1	2	22	13	12	15	10	2	3	47	28	23
Toronto	94	49	34	11	358	296	109	97	33	48	16	306	345	82	191	82	82	27	664	641	191
Vancouver	59	32	16	11	227	176	75	59	22	27	10	183	223	54	118	54	43	21	410	399	129
Washington	35	16	11	8	132	102	40	36	15	14	7	115	113	37	71	31	25	15	247	215	77
Defunct Clubs	33	19	8	6	123	86	44	32	10	16	6	84	105	26	65	29	24	12	207	191	70
Totals	**1220**	**574**	**452**	**194**	**4304**	**3844**	**1342**	**1220**	**366**	**660**	**194**	**3529**	**4574**	**926**	**2440**	**940**	**1112**	**388**	**7833**	**8418**	**2268**

Playoffs

	Series	W	L	GP	W	L	T	GF	GA	Last Mtg.	Round	Result
Boston	1	1	0	3	3	0	0	20	13	1981	PR	W 3-0
Buffalo	2	1	1	7	4	3	0	26	28	1981	QF	W 4-1
Calgary	1	1	0	6	4	2	0	25	18	1981	SF	W 4-2
Chicago	6	2	4	33	14	19	0	119	119	1991	DSF	W 4-2
Detroit	3	0	3	18	6	12	0	40	55	1998	CF	L 2-4
Edmonton	4	2	2	21	11	10	0	57	62	1998	CSF	W 4-1
Los Angeles	1	1	0	7	4	3	0	26	21	1968	QF	W 4-3
Montreal	2	1	1	13	6	7	0	37	48	1980	QF	W 4-3
NY Islanders	1	0	1	5	1	4	0	16	26	1981	F	L 1-4
Philadelphia	2	0	2	11	3	8	0	26	41	1980	SF	L 1-4
Pittsburgh	1	0	1	6	2	4	0	16	28	1991	F	L 2-4
St. Louis	10	5	5	56	30	26	0	174	162	1994	CQF	W 4-0
San Jose	1	1	0	6	4	2	0	16	12	1998	CQF	W 4-2
Toronto	2	2	0	7	6	1	0	35	26	1983	DSF	W 3-1
Vancouver	1	0	1	5	1	4	0	11	18	1994	CSF	L 1-4
Totals	**38**	**17**	**21**	**204**	**99**	**105**	**0**	**644**	**677**			

Playoff Results 1998-94

Year	Round	Opponent	Result	GF	GA
1998	CF	Detroit	L 2-4	11	15
	CSF	Edmonton	W 4-1	9	5
	CQF	San Jose	W 4-2	16	12
1997	CQF	Edmonton	L 3-4	18	21
1995	CQF	Detroit	L 1-4	10	17
1994	CSF	Vancouver	L 1-4	11	18
	CQF	St. Louis	W 4-0	16	10

Abbreviations: Round: F – Final; **CF** – conference final; **CQF** – conference quarter-final; **CSF** – conference semi-final; **DSF** – division semi-final; **SF** – semi-final; **QF** – quarter-final; **PR** – preliminary round.

Calgary totals include Atlanta, 1972-73 to 1979-80. Carolina totals include Hartford, 1979-80 to 1996-97.
Colorado totals include Quebec, 1979-80 to 1994-95. Dallas totals include Minnesota, 1967-68 to 1992-93.
New Jersey totals include Kansas City, 1974-75 to 1975-76, and Colorado Rockies, 1976-77 to 1981-82.
Phoenix totals include Winnipeg, 1979-80 to 1995-96.

1997-98 Results

Oct.	1	at	Colorado	2-2	**Jan.**	2		NY Islanders	2-1
	4		St. Louis	1-2		3	at	Carolina	6-1
	7	at	Buffalo	4-2		5	at	New Jersey	4-3
	8	at	Detroit	1-3		7		Ottawa	0-2
	10		Chicago	7-0		9		Detroit	3-3
	14		Calgary	5-4		11	at	Anaheim	1-2
	16		Florida	4-0		12	at	San Jose	3-1
	18	at	Toronto	5-4		14	at	St. Louis	2-1
	19	at	Ottawa	1-3		21		Colorado	3-2
	21		Vancouver	1-5		24	at	Colorado	3-2
	24	at	Chicago	2-0		26		Toronto	5-1
	25		Colorado	3-1		29	at	Florida	2-3
	28	at	NY Rangers	3-2		31	at	St. Louis	3-6
	29	at	Washington	4-3	**Feb.**	2	at	Toronto	5-1
Nov.	2	at	Philadelphia	3-3		4		Philadelphia	1-0
	3	at	Montreal	4-6		7		Chicago	3-1
	5	at	Pittsburgh	5-2		25	at	NY Islanders	4-1
	7		NY Rangers	2-2		28		Phoenix	4-0
	10		St. Louis	1-7	**Mar.**	1	at	Chicago	2-2
	12		Boston	3-3		4		Montreal	1-3
	15	at	Los Angeles	5-1		7	at	St. Louis	1-2
	16	at	Anaheim	4-0		8		Phoenix	1-1
	19		Edmonton	3-2		12	at	Phoenix	4-5
	21	at	Detroit	2-4		13		Anaheim	6-3
	22	at	Boston	2-0		17	at	Los Angeles	4-3
	24		Anaheim	5-0		18	at	San Jose	3-1
	26		Los Angeles	4-1		20		Carolina	6-1
	27	at	Phoenix	4-1		22		Pittsburgh	0-0
	29		Phoenix	5-2		26		Toronto	0-1
Dec.	3		Edmonton	4-1		28		San Jose	1-4
	5		Calgary	4-1		29		New Jersey	3-1
	8	at	Toronto	0-3	**Apr.**	1	at	Calgary	1-3
	10		Tampa Bay	3-0		3	at	Edmonton	1-4
	12		San Jose	0-1		4	at	Vancouver	3-5
	15		Buffalo	8-4		6		Toronto	4-2
	18	at	Calgary	2-1		8		Washington	2-1
	20	at	Edmonton	2-1		11	at	Tampa Bay	5-1
	23	at	Vancouver	3-1		12		St. Louis	4-3
	27		Vancouver	3-3		15		Detroit	3-1
	29	at	Detroit	2-2		16	at	Phoenix	2-3
	31		Los Angeles	2-2		18		Chicago	3-1

Entry Draft Selections 1998-84

1998
Pick
39 John Erskine
57 Tyler Bouck
86 Gabriel Karlsson
153 Pavel Patera
173 Niko Kapanen
200 Scott Perry

1997
Pick
25 Brenden Morrow
52 Roman Lyashenko
77 Steve Gainey
105 Marc Kristoffersson
132 Teemu Elomo
160 Alexei Timkin
189 Jeff McKercher
216 Alexei Komarov
242 Brett McLean

1996
Pick
5 Richard Jackman
70 Jonathan Sim
90 Mike Hurley
112 Ryan Christie
113 Evgeny Tysbuk
166 Eoin McInerney
194 Joel Kwiatkowski
220 Nick Bootland

1995
Pick
11 Jarome Iginla
37 Patrick Cote
63 Petr Buzek
69 Sergey Gusev
115 Wade Strand
141 Dominic Marleau
173 Jeff Dewar
193 Anatoli Kovesnikov
202 Sergei Luchinkin
219 Stephen Lowe

1994
Pick
20 Jason Botterill
46 Lee Jinman
98 Jamie Wright
124 Marty Turco
150 Yevgeny Petrochinin
228 Marty Flichel
254 Jimmy Roy
280 Chris Szysky

1993
Pick
9 Todd Harvey
35 Jamie Langenbrunner
87 Chad Lang
136 Rick Mrozik
139 Per Svartvadet
165 Jeremy Stasiuk
191 Rob Lurtsema
243 Jordan Willis
249 Bill Lang
269 Cory Peterson

1992
Pick
34 Jarkko Varvio
58 Jeff Bes
88 Jere Lehtinen
130 Michael Johnson
154 Kyle Peterson
178 Juha Lind
202 Lars Edstrom
226 Jeff Romfo
250 Jeffrey Moen

1991
Pick
8 Richard Matvichuk
74 Mike Torchia
97 Mike Kennedy
118 Mark Lawrence
137 Geoff Finch
174 MichaelBurkett
184 Derek Herlofsky
206 Tom Nemeth
228 Shayne Green
250 Jukka Suomalainen

1990
Pick
8 Derian Hatcher
50 Laurie Billeck
70 Cal McGowan
71 Frank Kovacs
92 Enrico Ciccone
113 Roman Turek
134 Jeff Levy
155 Doug Barrault
176 Joe Biondi
197 Troy Binnie
218 Ole-Eskild Dahlstrom
239 John McKersie

1989
Pick
7 Doug Zmolek
28 Mike Craig
60 Murray Garbutt
75 Jean-François Quintin
87 Pat MacLeod
91 Bryan Schoen
97 Rhys Hollyman
112 Scott Cashman
154 Jonathan Pratt
175 Kenneth Blum
196 Arturs Irbe
217 Tom Pederson
238 Helmut Balderis

1988
Pick
1 Mike Modano
40 Link Gaetz
43 Shaun Kane
64 Jeffrey Stop
148 Ken MacArthur
169 Travis Richards
190 Ari Matilainen
211 Grant Bischoff
232 Trent Andison

1987
Pick
6 David Archibald
35 Scott McCrady
48 Kevin Kaminski
73 John Weisbrod
88 Teppo Kivela
109 Darcy Norton
130 Timo Kulonen
151 Don Schmidt
172 Jarmo Myllys
193 Larry Olimb
214 Mark Felicio
235 Dave hields

1986
Pick
12 Warren Babe
30 Neil Wilkinson
33 Dean Kolstad
54 Eric Bennett
55 Rob Zettler
58 Brad Turner
75 Kirk Tomlinson
96 Jari Gronstrand
159 Scott Mathias
180 Lance Pitlick
201 Dan Keczmer
222 Garth Joy
243 Kurt Stahura

1985
Pick
51 Stephane Roy
69 Mike Berger
90 Dwight Mullins
111 MikeMullowney
132 Mike Kelfer
153 Ross Johnson
174 Tim Helmer
195 Gordon Ernst
216 Ladislav Lubina
237 Tommy Sjodin

1984
Pick
13 David Quinn
46 Ken Hodge
76 Miroslav Maly
89 Jiri Poner
97 Kari Takko
118 Gary McColgan
139 Vladimir Kyhos
160 Darin MacInnis
181 Duane Wahlin
201 Mike Orn
222 Tom Terwilliger
242 Mike Nightenale

General Manager

GAINEY, BOB
Vice President of Hockey Operations/General Manager, Dallas Stars.
Born in Peterborough, Ont., December 13, 1953.

Bob Gainey enters his third season as the full-time general manager for the Dallas Stars after relinquishing his head coaching duties on January 8, 1996. Named general manager of the team on June 8, 1992, he held the dual role of coach and g.m. for over four seasons. Having been appointed head coach for the Stars on June 19, 1990, his five-plus consecutive seasons behind the bench was the longest tenure of any head coach in franchise history. He is the Stars' sixth general manager and was the team's 16th head coach.

Under Gainey's tutelage, the Stars improved their regular-season record in each of Gainey's first four seasons as coach, going from 27 wins and 68 points in his first year to 42 wins and 97 points in 1993-94. In his first season, 1990-91, Gainey led the Stars through to the Stanley Cup finals, surprising Chicago and St. Louis and eliminating defending champion Edmonton before bowing in six games to Pittsburgh. He finished his reign behind the Stars bench with a 165-190-60 regular season record.

Elected to the Hockey Hall of Fame in 1992, Gainey was Montreal's first choice (eighth overall) in the 1973 Amateur Draft. During his 16-year career with the Canadiens, Gainey was a member of five Stanley Cup-winning teams and was named the Conn Smythe Trophy winner in 1979. He was a four-time recipient of the Frank Selke Trophy (1978-81), awarded to the League's top defensive forward, and participated in four NHL All-Star Games (1977, 1978, 1980 and 1981). He served as team captain for eight seasons (1981-89). During his career, he played in 1,160 regular-season games, registering 239 goals and 262 assists for 501 points. In addition, he tallied 73 points (25-48-73) in 182 post-season games.

NHL Coaching Record

		Regular Season					Playoffs			
Season	**Team**	**Games**	**W**	**L**	**T**	**%**	**Games**	**W**	**L**	**%**
1990-91	Minnesota	80	27	39	14	.425	23	14	9	.643
1991-92	Minnesota	80	32	42	6	.438	7	3	4	.429
1992-93	Minnesota	84	36	38	10	.488	....	....	....	....
1993-94	Dallas	84	42	29	13	.577	9	5	4	.556
1994-95	Dallas	48	17	23	8	.438	5	1	4	.200
1995-96	Dallas	39	11	19	9	.397	....	....	....	....
	NHL Totals	**415**	**165**	**190**	**60**	**.470**	**44**	**23**	**21**	**.523**

Club Directory

Reunion Arena

Dallas Stars Hockey Club, Inc.
Dr Pepper StarCenter
211 Cowboys Parkway
Irving, TX 75063
Phone **972/868-2890**
FAX 972/868-2860
Ticket Information 214/GO STARS
Capacity: 16,928

Chairman of the Board & Owner	Thomas O. Hicks
President/Alternate Governor	James R. Lites
V.P. of Hockey Operations	Bob Gainey
V.P. of Marketing and Broadcasting	Bill Strong
V.P. of Marketing and Promotion	Jeff Cogen
V.P. and Chief Financial Officer	Rick McLaughlin
General Manager	Bob Gainey
Assistant to the General Manager	Doug Armstrong
Head Coach	Ken Hitchcock
Assistant Coaches	Doug Jarvis, Rick Wilson
Head Athletic Trainer	Dave Surprenant
Equipment Managers	Dave Smith, Rich Matthews
Strength and Conditioning Coach	J.J. McQueen
Director of Public Relations	Larry Kelly (972) 868-2807
Public Relations Manager	Kurt Daniels (972) 868-2818
P.R. Fax	(972) 868-2860
Radio Station	WBAP, 820 AM
TV Stations	KDFW, Ch. 4; KDFI, Ch. 27; Fox Sports Southwest
Web site	www.dallasstars.com

Mike Modano led the Dallas Stars with a plus/minus rating of +25.

Detroit Red Wings

1997-98 Results: 44W-23L-15T 103PTS. Second, Central Division

Nicklas Lidstrom earned a nomination for the Norris Trophy after leading all NHL defenseman with 57 points in 1997-98. He added 19 points in 22 playoff games when the Red Wings repeated as Stanley Cup champions.

1998-99 Schedule

Oct.	Sat.	10	at Toronto		Thu.	14	Nashville
	Tue.	13	at Washington		Sat.	16	at Vancouver
	Fri.	16	St. Louis		Sun.	17	at Edmonton
	Sun.	18	Calgary*		Tue.	19	at Calgary
	Wed.	21	Nashville		Thu.	21	Carolina
	Fri.	23	Toronto		Tue.	26	at Nashville
	Sat.	24	at Montreal		Sat.	30	NY Rangers
	Wed.	28	at Florida	Feb.	Mon.	1	at New Jersey
	Thu.	29	at St. Louis		Wed.	3	NY Islanders
	Sat.	31	at Dallas		Fri.	5	Colorado
Nov.	Tue.	3	Calgary		Sun.	7	at Pittsburgh*
	Fri.	6	at Phoenix		Tue.	9	at Nashville
	Sun.	8	at Anaheim		Thu.	11	Edmonton
	Wed.	11	St. Louis		Fri.	12	at Chicago
	Fri.	13	Dallas		Sun.	14	at NY Rangers*
	Mon.	16	at Calgary		Wed.	17	San Jose
	Wed.	18	at Edmonton		Fri.	19	New Jersey
	Sat.	21	at Vancouver		Sun.	21	at Buffalo*
	Wed.	25	Anaheim		Wed.	24	Los Angeles
	Fri.	27	Vancouver		Fri.	26	Florida
	Sun.	29	San Jose*		Sat.	27	at NY Islanders
Dec.	Wed.	2	at Colorado	Mar.	Fri.	5	at Phoenix
	Fri.	4	at San Jose		Sun.	7	at Anaheim
	Sat.	5	at Los Angeles		Tue.	9	at Los Angeles
	Tue.	8	Chicago		Fri.	12	at San Jose
	Fri.	11	Edmonton		Sun.	14	at Colorado*
	Sat.	12	at Carolina		Wed.	17	Phoenix
	Wed.	16	Boston		Fri.	19	at Tampa Bay
	Fri.	18	Dallas		Sun.	21	at Philadelphia*
	Sat.	19	at Boston		Wed.	24	Buffalo
	Tue.	22	Phoenix		Fri.	26	Tampa Bay
	Wed.	23	at Nashville		Sun.	28	Philadelphia*
	Sat.	26	at St. Louis		Wed.	31	Los Angeles
	Mon.	28	St. Louis	Apr.	Fri.	2	Chicago
	Thu.	31	Toronto		Sun.	4	at Dallas*
Jan.	Sat.	2	Chicago		Mon.	5	Anaheim
	Sun.	3	at Chicago		Wed.	7	Vancouver
	Wed.	6	Ottawa		Fri.	9	at St. Louis
	Sat.	9	Colorado*		Sun.	11	Pittsburgh*
	Sun.	10	at Ottawa*		Wed.	14	Nashville
	Tue.	12	Montreal		Sat.	17	at Chicago

* Denotes afternoon game.

Franchise date: September 25, 1926

CENTRAL DIVISION

73rd NHL Season

Year-by-Year Record

		Home			Road			Overall							
Season	**GP**	**W**	**L**	**T**	**W**	**L**	**T**	**W**	**L**	**T**	**GF**	**GA**	**Pts.**	**Finished**	**Playoff Result**
1997-98	**82**	**25**	**8**	**8**	**19**	**15**	**7**	**44**	**23**	**15**	**250**	**196**	**103**	**2nd, Central Div.**	**Won Stanley Cup**
1996-97	**82**	**20**	**12**	**9**	**18**	**14**	**9**	**38**	**26**	**18**	**253**	**197**	**94**	**2nd, Central Div.**	**Won Stanley Cup**
1995-96	82	36	3	2	26	10	5	62	13	7	325	181	131	1st, Central Div.	Lost Conf. Championship
1994-95	48	17	4	3	16	7	1	33	11	4	180	117	70	1st, Central Div.	Lost Final
1993-94	84	23	13	6	23	17	2	46	30	8	356	275	100	1st, Central Div.	Lost Conf. Quarter-Final
1992-93	84	25	14	3	22	14	6	47	28	9	369	280	103	2nd, Norris Div.	Lost Div. Semi-Final
1991-92	80	24	12	4	19	13	8	43	25	12	320	256	98	1st, Norris Div.	Lost Div. Final
1990-91	80	26	14	0	8	24	8	34	38	8	273	298	76	3rd, Norris Div.	Lost Div. Semi-Final
1989-90	80	20	14	6	8	24	8	28	38	14	288	323	70	5th, Norris Div.	Out of Playoffs
1988-89	80	20	14	6	14	20	6	34	34	12	313	316	80	1st, Norris Div.	Lost Div. Semi-Final
1987-88	80	24	10	6	17	18	5	41	28	11	322	269	93	1st, Norris Div.	Lost Conf. Championship
1986-87	80	20	14	6	14	22	4	34	36	10	260	274	78	2nd, Norris Div.	Lost Conf. Championship
1985-86	80	10	26	4	7	31	2	17	57	6	266	415	40	5th, Norris Div.	Out of Playoffs
1984-85	80	19	14	7	8	27	5	27	41	12	313	357	66	3rd, Norris Div.	Lost Div. Semi-Final
1983-84	80	18	20	2	13	22	5	31	42	7	298	323	69	3rd, Norris Div.	Lost Div. Semi-Final
1982-83	80	14	19	7	7	25	8	21	44	15	263	344	57	5th, Norris Div.	Out of Playoffs
1981-82	80	15	19	6	6	28	6	21	47	12	270	351	54	6th, Norris Div.	Out of Playoffs
1980-81	80	16	15	9	3	28	9	19	43	18	252	339	56	5th, Norris Div.	Out of Playoffs
1979-80	80	14	21	5	12	22	6	26	43	11	268	306	63	5th, Norris Div.	Out of Playoffs
1978-79	80	15	17	8	8	24	8	23	41	16	252	295	62	5th, Norris Div.	Out of Playoffs
1977-78	80	22	11	7	10	23	7	32	34	14	252	266	78	2nd, Norris Div.	Lost Quarter-Final
1976-77	80	12	22	6	4	33	3	16	55	9	183	309	41	5th, Norris Div.	Out of Playoffs
1975-76	80	17	15	8	9	29	2	26	44	10	226	300	62	4th, Norris Div.	Out of Playoffs
1974-75	80	17	17	6	6	28	6	23	45	12	259	335	58	4th, Norris Div.	Out of Playoffs
1973-74	78	21	12	6	8	27	4	29	39	10	255	319	68	6th, East Div.	Out of Playoffs
1972-73	78	22	12	5	15	17	7	37	29	12	265	243	86	5th, East Div.	Out of Playoffs
1971-72	78	25	11	3	8	24	7	33	35	10	261	262	76	5th, East Div.	Out of Playoffs
1970-71	78	17	15	7	5	30	4	22	45	11	209	308	55	7th, East Div.	Out of Playoffs
1969-70	76	20	11	7	20	10	8	40	21	15	246	199	95	3rd, East Div.	Lost Quarter-Final
1968-69	76	23	8	7	10	23	5	33	31	12	239	221	78	5th, East Div.	Out of Playoffs
1967-68	74	18	15	4	9	20	8	27	35	12	245	257	66	6th, East Div.	Out of Playoffs
1966-67	70	21	11	3	6	28	1	27	39	4	212	241	58	5th,	Out of Playoffs
1965-66	70	20	8	7	11	19	5	31	27	12	221	194	74	4th,	Lost Final
1964-65	70	25	7	3	15	16	4	40	23	7	224	175	87	1st,	Lost Semi-Final
1963-64	70	23	9	3	7	20	8	30	29	11	191	204	71	4th,	Lost Final
1962-63	70	19	10	6	13	15	7	32	25	13	200	194	77	4th,	Lost Final
1961-62	70	17	11	7	6	22	7	23	33	14	184	219	60	5th,	Out of Playoffs
1960-61	70	15	13	7	10	16	9	25	29	16	195	215	66	4th,	Lost Final
1959-60	70	18	14	3	8	15	12	26	29	15	186	197	67	4th,	Lost Semi-Final
1958-59	70	13	17	5	12	20	3	25	37	8	167	218	58	6th,	Out of Playoffs
1957-58	70	16	11	8	13	18	4	29	29	12	176	207	70	3rd,	Lost Semi-Final
1956-57	70	23	7	5	15	13	7	38	20	12	198	157	88	1st,	Lost Semi-Final
1955-56	70	21	6	8	9	18	8	30	24	16	183	148	76	2nd,	Lost Final
1954-55	**70**	**25**	**5**	**5**	**17**	**12**	**6**	**42**	**17**	**11**	**204**	**134**	**95**	**1st,**	**Won Stanley Cup**
1953-54	**70**	**24**	**4**	**7**	**13**	**15**	**7**	**37**	**19**	**14**	**191**	**132**	**88**	**1st,**	**Won Stanley Cup**
1952-53	70	20	5	10	16	11	8	36	16	18	222	133	90	1st,	Lost Semi-Final
1951-52	**70**	**24**	**7**	**4**	**20**	**7**	**8**	**44**	**14**	**12**	**215**	**133**	**100**	**1st,**	**Won Stanley Cup**
1950-51	70	25	3	7	19	10	6	44	13	13	236	139	101	1st,	Lost Semi-Final
1949-50	**70**	**19**	**9**	**7**	**18**	**10**	**7**	**37**	**19**	**14**	**229**	**164**	**88**	**1st,**	**Won Stanley Cup**
1948-49	60	21	6	3	13	13	4	34	19	7	195	145	75	1st,	Lost Final
1947-48	60	16	9	5	14	9	7	30	18	12	187	148	72	2nd,	Lost Final
1946-47	60	14	10	6	8	17	5	22	27	11	190	193	55	4th,	Lost Semi-Final
1945-46	50	16	5	4	4	15	6	20	20	10	146	159	50	4th,	Lost Semi-Final
1944-45	50	19	5	1	12	9	4	31	14	5	218	161	67	2nd,	Lost Final
1943-44	50	18	5	2	8	13	4	26	18	6	214	177	58	2nd,	Lost Semi-Final
1942-43	**50**	**16**	**4**	**5**	**9**	**10**	**6**	**25**	**14**	**11**	**169**	**124**	**61**	**1st,**	**Won Stanley Cup**
1941-42	48	14	7	3	5	18	1	19	25	4	140	147	42	5th,	Lost Final
1940-41	48	14	5	5	7	11	6	21	16	11	112	102	53	3rd,	Lost Final
1939-40	48	11	10	3	5	16	3	16	26	6	90	126	38	5th,	Lost Semi-Final
1938-39	48	14	8	2	4	16	4	18	24	6	107	128	42	5th,	Lost Semi-Final
1937-38	48	8	10	6	4	15	5	12	25	11	99	133	35	4th, Amn. Div.	Out of Playoffs
1936-37	**48**	**14**	**5**	**5**	**11**	**9**	**4**	**25**	**14**	**9**	**128**	**102**	**59**	**1st, Amn. Div.**	**Won Stanley Cup**
1935-36	**48**	**14**	**5**	**5**	**10**	**11**	**3**	**24**	**16**	**8**	**124**	**103**	**56**	**1st, Amn. Div.**	**Won Stanley Cup**
1934-35	48	11	8	5	8	14	2	19	22	7	127	114	45	4th, Amn. Div.	Out of Playoffs
1933-34	48	15	5	4	9	9	6	24	14	10	113	98	58	1st, Amn. Div.	Lost Final
1932-33*	48	17	3	4	8	12	4	25	15	8	111	93	58	2nd, Amn. Div.	Lost Semi-Final
1931-32	48	15	3	6	3	17	4	18	20	10	95	108	46	3rd, Amn. Div.	Lost Quarter-Final
1930-31**	44	10	7	5	6	14	2	16	21	7	102	105	39	4th, Amn. Div.	Out of Playoffs
1929-30	44	9	10	3	5	14	3	14	24	6	117	133	34	4th, Amn. Div.	Out of Playoffs
1928-29	44	11	6	5	8	10	4	19	16	9	72	63	47	3rd, Amn. Div.	Lost Quarter-Final
1927-28	44	9	10	3	10	9	3	19	19	6	88	79	44	4th, Amn. Div.	Out of Playoffs
1926-27***	44	5	16	0	7	12	4	12	28	4	76	105	28	5th, Amn. Div.	Out of Playoffs

* Team name changed to Red Wings. ** Team name changed to Falcons. *** Team named Cougars.

1998-99 Player Personnel

FORWARDS	HT	WT	S	Place of Birth	Date	1997-98 Club
AUDET, Philippe	6-2	175	L	Ottawa, Ont.	6/4/77	Adirondack
BROWN, Doug	5-10	185	R	Southborough, MA	6/12/64	Detroit
DANDENAULT, Mathieu	6-0	174	R	Sherbrooke, Que.	2/3/76	Detroit
DRAPER, Kris	5-11	185	L	Toronto, Ont.	5/24/71	Detroit
FEDOROV, Sergei	6-1	200	L	Pskov, USSR	12/13/69	Detroit-Russia
GILCHRIST, Brent	5-11	180	L	Moose Jaw, Sask.	4/3/67	Detroit
HOLMSTROM, Tomas	6-0	200	L	Pitea, Sweden	1/23/73	Detroit
KNUBLE, Michael	6-3	208	R	Toronto, Ont.	7/4/72	Detroit
KOCUR, Joe	6-0	205	R	Calgary, Alta.	12/21/64	Detroit
KOZLOV, Vyacheslav	5-10	180	L	Voskresensk, USSR	5/3/72	Detroit
LAPLANTE, Darryl	6-1	185	L	Calgary, Alta.	3/28/77	Detroit-Adirondack
LAPOINTE, Martin	5-11	200	R	Ville Ste. Pierre, Que.	9/12/73	Detroit
LARIONOV, Igor	5-9	170	L	Voskresensk, USSR	12/3/60	Detroit
MALTBY, Kirk	6-0	180	R	Guelph, Ont.	12/22/72	Detroit
McCARTY, Darren	6-1	210	R	Burnaby, B.C.	4/1/72	Detroit
ROEST, Stacy	5-9	192	R	Lethbridge, Alta.	3/15/74	Adirondack
SHANAHAN, Brendan	6-3	218	R	Mimico, Ont.	1/23/69	Detroit-Canada
YZERMAN, Steve	5-11	185	R	Cranbrook, B.C.	5/9/65	Detroit-Canada
DEFENSEMEN						
ERIKSSON, Anders	6-3	218	L	Bollnas, Sweden	1/9/75	Detroit
GILLAM, Sean	6-2	187	R	Lethbridge, Alta.	5/7/76	Adirondack
GOLUBOVSKY, Yan	6-3	183	R	Novosibirsk, USSR	3/9/76	Detroit-Adirondack
KRUPP, Uwe	6-6	235	R	Cologne, West Germany	6/24/65	Colorado-Germany
KUZNETSOV, Maxim	6-5	198	L	Pavlodar, USSR	3/24/77	Adirondack
LIDSTROM, Nicklas	6-2	185	L	Vasteras, Sweden	4/28/70	Detroit
MACOUN, Jamie	6-2	200	L	Newmarket, Ont.	8/17/61	Toronto-Detroit
MURPHY, Larry	6-2	210	R	Scarborough, Ont.	3/8/61	Detroit
WALLIN, Jesse	6-2	190	L	Saskatoon, Sask.	3/10/78	Red Deer-Canada
WARD, Aaron	6-2	200	R	Windsor, Ont.	1/17/73	Detroit
GOALTENDERS	**HT**	**WT**	**C**	**Place of Birth**	**Date**	**1997-98 Club**
HODSON, Kevin	6-0	182	L	Winnipeg, Man.	3/27/72	Detroit
MARACLE, Norm	5-9	175	L	Belleville, Ont.	10/2/74	Detroit-Adirondack
OSGOOD, Chris	5-10	160	L	Peace River, Alta.	11/26/72	Detroit

1997-98 Scoring

* – rookie

Regular Season

Pos	#	Player	Team	GP	G	A	Pts	+/–	PIM	PP	SH	GW	GT	S	%
C	19	Steve Yzerman	DET	75	24	45	69	3	46	6	2	0	2	188	12.8
D	5	Nicklas Lidstrom	DET	80	17	42	59	22	18	7	1	1	1	205	8.3
L	14	Brendan Shanahan	DET	75	28	29	57	6	154	15	1	9	1	266	10.5
L	13	Vyacheslav Kozlov	DET	80	25	27	52	14	46	6	0	1	0	221	11.3
D	55	Larry Murphy	DET	82	11	41	52	35	37	2	1	2	0	129	8.5
C	8	Igor Larionov	DET	69	8	39	47	14	40	3	0	2	1	93	8.6
D	15	Dmitri Mironov	ANA	66	6	30	36	-7	115	2	0	1	0	142	4.2
			DET	11	2	5	7	0	4	1	0	0	0	28	7.1
			TOTAL	77	8	35	43	-7	119	3	0	1	0	170	4.7
R	17	Doug Brown	DET	80	19	23	42	17	12	6	1	5	0	145	13.1
R	25	Darren McCarty	DET	71	15	22	37	0	157	5	1	2	0	166	9.0
R	20	Martin Lapointe	DET	79	15	19	34	0	106	4	0	3	2	154	9.7
C	41	Brent Gilchrist	DET	61	13	14	27	4	40	5	0	3	1	124	10.5
L	18	Kirk Maltby	DET	65	14	9	23	11	89	2	1	3	0	106	13.2
C	33	Kris Draper	DET	64	13	10	23	5	45	1	0	4	0	96	13.5
L	96	Tomas Holmstrom	DET	57	5	17	22	6	44	1	0	1	0	48	10.4
D	44 *	Anders Eriksson	DET	66	7	14	21	21	32	1	0	2	0	91	7.7
C	91	Sergei Fedorov	DET	21	6	11	17	10	25	2	0	2	0	68	8.8
R	11	Mathieu Dandenault	DET	68	5	12	17	5	43	0	0	0	0	75	6.7
D	2	Viacheslav Fetisov	DET	58	2	12	14	4	72	0	0	1	0	55	3.6
R	22 *	Michael Knuble	DET	53	7	6	13	2	16	0	0	0	0	54	13.0
D	3	Bob Rouse	DET	71	1	11	12	-9	57	0	0	0	0	54	1.9
R	26	Joey Kocur	DET	63	6	5	11	7	92	0	0	2	0	53	11.3
D	27	Aaron Ward	DET	52	5	5	10	-1	47	0	0	1	0	47	10.6
D	34	Jamie Macoun	TOR	67	0	7	7	-17	63	0	0	0	0	67	0.0
			DET	7	0	0	0	0	2	0	0	0	0	11	0.0
			TOTAL	74	0	7	7	-17	65	0	0	0	0	78	0.0
D	28 *	Yan Golubovsky	DET	12	0	2	2	1	6	0	0	0	0	9	0.0
C	21 *	Darryl Laplante	DET	2	0	0	0	0	0	0	0	0	0	2	0.0
G	34 *	Norm Maracle	DET	4	0	0	0	0	0	0	0	0	0	0	0.0
G	31 *	Kevin Hodson	DET	21	0	0	0	0	2	0	0	0	0	0	0.0
G	30	Chris Osgood	DET	64	0	0	0	0	31	0	0	0	0	0	0.0

Goaltending

No.	Goaltender	GPI	Mins	Avg	W	L	T	EN	SO	GA	SA	S%
34	* Norm Maracle	4	178	2.02	2	0	1	0	0	6	63	.905
30	Chris Osgood	64	3807	2.21	33	20	11	5	6	140	1605	.913
31	* Kevin Hodson	21	988	2.67	9	3	3	1	2	44	444	.901
	Totals	**82**	**4995**	**2.35**	**44**	**23**	**15**	**6**	**9**	**196**	**2118**	**.907**

Playoffs

Pos	#	Player	Team	GP	G	A	Pts	+/–	PIM	PP	SH	GW	OT	S	%
C	19	Steve Yzerman	DET	22	6	18	24	10	22	3	1	0	0	65	9.2
C	91	Sergei Fedorov	DET	22	10	10	20	0	12	2	1	1	0	86	11.6
L	96	Tomas Holmstrom	DET	22	7	12	19	9	16	2	0	0	0	27	25.9
D	5	Nicklas Lidstrom	DET	22	6	13	19	12	8	2	0	2	0	59	10.2
R	20	Martin Lapointe	DET	21	9	6	15	6	20	2	1	1	0	55	16.4
D	55	Larry Murphy	DET	22	3	12	15	12	2	1	2	1	0	36	8.3
L	13	Vyacheslav Kozlov	DET	22	6	8	14	4	10	1	0	4	0	47	12.8
C	8	Igor Larionov	DET	22	3	10	13	5	12	0	0	0	0	27	11.1
R	25	Darren McCarty	DET	22	3	8	11	9	34	0	0	1	0	46	6.5
L	14	Brendan Shanahan	DET	20	5	4	9	5	22	3	0	2	1	60	8.3
R	17	Doug Brown	DET	9	4	2	6	-1	0	3	0	1	0	19	21.1
D	44 *	Anders Eriksson	DET	18	0	5	5	7	16	0	0	0	0	17	0.0
R	26	Joey Kocur	DET	18	4	0	4	-3	30	0	0	0	0	13	30.8
L	18	Kirk Maltby	DET	22	3	1	4	2	30	0	1	0	0	31	9.7
D	34	Jamie Macoun	DET	22	2	2	4	3	18	0	0	2	0	21	9.5
C	33	Kris Draper	DET	19	1	3	4	4	12	0	0	1	1	20	5.0
C	41	Brent Gilchrist	DET	15	2	1	3	2	12	0	0	0	0	17	11.8
D	15	Dmitri Mironov	DET	7	0	3	3	1	14	0	0	0	0	15	0.0
D	2	Viacheslav Fetisov	DET	21	0	3	3	4	10	0	0	0	0	14	0.0
D	3	Bob Rouse	DET	22	0	3	3	2	16	0	0	0	0	22	0.0
R	11	Mathieu Dandenault	DET	3	1	0	1	-2	0	1	0	0	0	4	25.0
R	22 *	Michael Knuble	DET	3	0	1	1	0	0	0	0	0	0	1	0.0
G	30	Chris Osgood	DET	22	0	1	1	0	12	0	0	0	0	0	0.0
G	31 *	Kevin Hodson	DET	1	0	0	0	0	0	0	0	0	0	0	0.0

Goaltending

No.	Goaltender	GPI	Mins	Avg	W	L	EN	SO	GA	SA	S%
31	* Kevin Hodson	1	0	0.00	0	0	0	0	0	0	.000
30	Chris Osgood	22	1361	2.12	16	6	1	2	48	588	.918
	Totals	**22**	**1367**	**2.15**	**16**	**6**	**1**	**2**	**49**	**589**	**.917**

Director of Player Personnel/Coach

BOWMAN, WILLIAM SCOTT (SCOTTY)
Director of Player Personnel/Coach, Detroit Red Wings.
Born in Montreal, Que. September 18, 1933.

Scotty Bowman equalled Toe Blake's record for coaches in 1998 when he guided the Detroit Red Wings to a second consecutive Stanley Cup championship. The victory gave Bowman his eighth title as a coach and the ninth of his career including his victory as director of player development with the Pittsburgh Penguins in 1991. Bowman, who is also the all-time coaching leader in both regular-season and playoff victories, is the first coach to win the Stanley Cup with three different teams. Entering his sixth season in Detroit, Bowman's Red Wings will be aiming to become the first team to win the Stanley Cup three years in a row since the New York Islanders won four straight titles from 1980 to 1983.

Bowman began his NHL coaching career with the St. Louis Blues and led the team to the Stanley Cup finals three years in a row from 1968 to 1970. He was then appointed head coach of the Montreal Canadiens and led the team to five Stanley Cup titles in eight years.

Following an eight-season term as the general manager of the Buffalo Sabres, and a brief stint as a commentator for CBC Television, Bowman joined the Pittsburgh Penguins as director of player development, but returned to coaching when head coach Bob Johnson became ill in September, 1991. Bowman was elected to the Hockey Hall of Fame as a builder in 1991.

NHL Coaching Record

		Regular Season					Playoffs			
Season	Team	Games	W	L	T	%	Games	W	L	%
1967-68	St. Louis	58	23	21	14	.517	18	8	10	.444
1968-69	St. Louis	76	37	25	14	.579	12	8	4	.667
1969-70	St. Louis	76	37	27	12	.566	16	8	8	.500
1970-71	St. Louis	28	13	10	5	.554	6	2	4	.333
1971-72	Montreal	78	46	16	16	.692	6	2	4	.333
1972-73	Montreal	78	52	10	16	.769	17	12	5	.706*
1973-74	Montreal	78	45	24	9	.635	6	2	4	.333
1974-75	Montreal	80	47	14	19	.706	11	6	5	.545
1975-76	Montreal	80	58	11	11	.794	13	12	1	.923*
1976-77	Montreal	80	60	8	12	.825	14	12	2	.857*
1977-78	Montreal	80	59	10	11	.806	15	12	3	.800*
1978-79	Montreal	80	52	17	11	.719	16	12	4	.750*
1979-80	Buffalo	80	47	17	16	.688	14	9	5	.643
1981-82	Buffalo	35	18	10	7	.614	4	1	3	.250
1982-83	Buffalo	80	38	29	13	.556	10	6	4	.600
1983-84	Buffalo	80	48	25	7	.644	3	0	3	.000
1984-85	Buffalo	80	38	28	14	.563	5	2	3	.400
1985-86	Buffalo	37	18	18	1	.500	....	....	....	....
1986-87	Buffalo	12	3	7	2	.333	....	....	....	....
1991-92	Pittsburgh	80	39	32	9	.544	21	16	5	.762*
1992-93	Pittsburgh	84	56	21	7	.708	12	7	5	.583
1993-94	Detroit	84	46	30	8	.595	7	3	4	.429
1994-95	Detroit	48	33	11	4	.729	18	12	6	.667
1995-96	Detroit	82	62	13	7	.799	19	10	9	.526
1996-97	Detroit	82	38	26	18	.573	20	16	4	.800*
1997-98	Detroit	82	44	23	15	.628	22	16	6	.727*
	NHL Totals	**1818**	**1057**	**483**	**278**	**.658**	**305**	**194**	**111**	**.636**

* Stanley Cup win.

Club Records

Team

(Figures in brackets for season records are games played; records for fewest points, wins, ties, losses, goals, goals against are for 70 or more games)

Most Points	131	1995-96 (82)
Most Wins	*62	1995-96 (82)
Most Ties	18	1952-53 (70), 1980-81 (80), 1996-97 (82)
Most Losses	57	1985-86 (80)
Most Goals	369	1992-93 (84)
Most Goals Against	415	1985-86 (80)
Fewest Points	40	1985-86 (80)
Fewest Wins	16	1976-77 (80)
Fewest Ties	4	1966-67 (70)
Fewest Losses	13	1950-51 (70), 1995-96 (82)
Fewest Goals	167	1958-59 (70)
Fewest Goals Against	132	1953-54 (70)
Longest Winning Streak		
Overall	9	Mar. 3-21/51, Feb. 27-Mar. 20/55, Dec. 12-31/95, Mar. 3-22/96
Home	14	Jan. 21-Mar. 25/65
Away	7	Mar. 25-Apr. 14/95, Feb. 18-Mar. 20/96
Longest Undefeated Streak		
Overall	15	Nov. 27-Dec. 28/52 (8 wins, 7 ties)
Home	18	Nov. 19/31-Feb.28/32 (13 wins, 5 ties), Dec. 26/54-Mar. 20/55 (13 wins, 5 ties)
Away	15	Oct. 18-Dec. 20/51 (10 wins, 5 ties)
Longest Losing Streak		
Overall	14	Feb. 24-Mar. 25/82
Home	7	Feb. 20-Mar. 25/82
Away	14	Oct. 19-Dec. 21/66
Longest Winless Streak		
Overall	19	Feb. 26-Apr. 3/77 (18 losses, 1 tie)
Home	10	Dec. 11/85-Jan. 18/86 (9 losses, 1 tie)
Away	26	Dec. 15/76-Apr. 3/77 (23 losses, 3 ties)
Most Shutouts, Season	13	1953-54 (70)
Most. PIM, Season	2,393	1985-86 (80)
Most Goals, Game	15	Jan. 23/44 (NYR 0 at Det. 15)

Individual

Most Seasons	25	Gordie Howe
Most Games	1,687	Gordie Howe
Most Goals, Career	786	Gordie Howe
Most Assists, Career	1,023	Gordie Howe
Most Points, Career	1,809	Gordie Howe (786G, 1,023A)
Most PIM, Career	2,090	Bob Probert
Most Shutouts, Career	85	Terry Sawchuk
Longest Consecutive Games Streak	548	Alex Delvecchio (Dec. 13/56-Nov. 11/64)
Most Goals, Season	65	Steve Yzerman (1988-89)
Most Assists, Season	90	Steve Yzerman (1988-89)
Most Points, Season	155	Steve Yzerman (1988-89; 65G, 90A)
Most PIM, Season	398	Bob Probert (1987-88)
Most Points, Defenseman, Season	77	Paul Coffey (1993-94; 14G, 63A)
Most Points, Center, Season	155	Steve Yzerman (1988-89; 65G, 90A)
Most Points, Right Wing, Season	103	Gordie Howe (1968-69; 44G, 59A)
Most Points, Left Wing, Season	105	John Ogrodnick (1984-85; 55G, 50A)
Most Points, Rookie, Season	87	Steve Yzerman (1983-84; 39G, 48A)
Most Shutouts, Season	12	Terry Sawchuk (1951-52, 1953-54, 1954-55), Glenn Hall (1955-56)
Most Goals, Game	6	Syd Howe (Feb. 3/44)
Most Assists, Game	*7	Billy Taylor (Mar. 16/47)
Most Points, Game	7	Carl Liscombe (Nov. 5/42; 3G, 4A), Don Grosso (Feb. 3/44; 1G, 6A), Billy Taylor (Mar. 16/47; 7A)

* NHL Record.

Retired Numbers

1	Terry Sawchuk	1949-55, 57-64, 68-69
6	Larry Aurie	1927-1939
7	Ted Lindsay	1944-57, 64-65
9	Gordie Howe	1946-1971
10	Alex Delvecchio	1951-1973
12	Sid Abel	1938-43, 45-52

All-time Record vs. Other Clubs

Regular Season

	At Home							On Road							Total						
	GP	W	L	T	GF	GA	PTS	GP	W	L	T	GF	GA	PTS	GP	W	L	T	GF	GA	PTS
Anaheim	10	6	1	3	39	26	15	10	6	2	2	38	21	14	20	12	3	5	77	47	29
Boston	281	152	77	52	941	708	356	282	88	151	43	751	994	219	563	240	228	95	1692	1702	575
Buffalo	50	27	18	5	186	150	59	48	9	32	7	134	213	25	98	36	50	12	320	363	84
Calgary	47	24	14	9	181	147	57	48	16	26	6	153	193	38	95	40	40	15	334	340	95
Carolina	26	13	7	6	100	73	32	25	9	15	1	69	91	19	51	22	22	7	169	164	51
Chicago	319	196	93	30	1093	782	422	321	123	147	51	895	968	297	640	319	240	81	1988	1750	719
Colorado	28	16	11	1	107	90	33	29	9	16	4	101	115	22	57	25	27	5	208	205	55
Dallas	94	49	31	14	377	306	112	94	30	49	15	281	344	75	188	79	80	29	658	650	187
Edmonton	32	15	14	3	122	119	33	32	12	15	5	130	141	29	64	27	29	8	252	260	62
Florida	4	3	1	0	16	10	6	4	2	1	1	10	9	5	8	5	2	1	26	19	11
Los Angeles	67	28	28	11	267	246	67	68	19	36	13	213	282	51	135	47	64	24	480	528	118
Montreal	277	128	96	53	792	708	309	277	64	170	43	625	985	171	554	192	266	96	1417	1693	480
New Jersey	35	20	13	2	146	121	42	36	10	18	8	101	128	28	71	30	31	10	247	249	70
NY Islanders	40	21	17	2	142	129	44	41	16	22	3	123	152	35	81	37	39	5	265	281	79
NY Rangers	281	161	75	45	988	691	367	279	88	133	58	716	860	234	560	249	208	103	1704	1551	601
Ottawa	5	3	2	0	20	11	6	5	3	1	1	17	13	7	10	6	3	1	37	24	13
Philadelphia	54	26	18	10	192	173	62	55	13	31	11	162	221	37	109	39	49	21	354	394	99
Phoenix	39	21	13	5	163	133	47	37	12	14	11	117	120	35	76	33	27	16	280	253	82
Pittsburgh	61	38	11	12	240	166	88	60	15	41	4	179	268	34	121	53	52	16	419	434	122
St. Louis	93	39	38	16	336	296	94	94	27	52	15	262	340	69	187	66	90	31	598	636	163
San Jose	13	12	1	0	63	23	24	14	9	4	1	68	47	19	27	21	5	1	131	70	43
Tampa Bay	7	6	1	0	29	15	12	9	7	1	1	50	30	15	16	13	2	1	79	45	27
Toronto	313	164	103	46	937	764	374	311	104	162	45	837	1033	253	624	268	265	91	1774	1797	627
Vancouver	54	32	15	7	227	161	71	53	20	25	8	173	202	48	107	52	40	15	400	363	119
Washington	43	19	13	11	153	125	49	41	17	20	4	130	156	38	84	36	33	15	283	281	87
Defunct Clubs	141	76	40	25	430	307	177	141	49	63	29	364	375	127	282	125	103	54	794	682	304
Totals	**2414**	**1295**	**751**	**368**	**8287**	**6480**	**2958**	**2414**	**777**	**1247**	**390**	**6699**	**8301**	**1944**	**4828**	**2072**	**1998**	**758**	**14986**	**14781**	**4902**

Playoffs

	Series	W	L	GP	W	L	T	GF	GA	Last Mtg.	Round	Result
Anaheim	1	1	0	4	4	0	0	13	8	1997	CSF	W 4-0
Boston	7	3	4	33	14	19	0	98	96	1957	SF	L 1-4
Calgary	1	1	0	2	2	0	0	8	5	1978	PR	W 2-0
Chicago	14	6	8	69	31	38	0	190	210	1995	CF	W 4-1
Colorado	2	1	1	12	6	6	0	32	32	1997	CF	W 4-2
Dallas	3	3	0	18	12	6	0	55	40	1998	CF	W 4-2
Edmonton	2	0	2	10	2	8	0	26	39	1988	CF	L 1-4
Montreal	12	7	5	62	29	33	0	149	161	1978	QF	L 1-4
New Jersey	1	0	1	4	0	4	0	7	16	1995	F	L 0-4
NY Rangers	5	4	1	23	13	10	0	57	49	1950	F	W 4-3
Philadelphia	1	1	0	4	4	0	0	16	6	1997	F	W 4-0
Phoenix	2	2	0	12	8	4	0	44	28	1998	CQF	W 4-2
St. Louis	6	4	2	35	20	15	0	111	92	1998	CSF	W 4-2
San Jose	2	1	1	11	7	4	0	51	27	1995	CSF	W 4-0
Toronto	23	11	12	117	59	58	0	321	311	1993	DSF	L 3-4
Washington	1	1	0	4	4	0	0	13	7	1998	F	W 4-0
Defunct Clubs	4	3	1	10	7	2	1	21	13			
Totals	**87**	**49**	**38**	**430**	**222**	**207**	**1**	**1212**	**1140**			

Playoff Results 1998-94

Year	Round	Opponent	Result	GF	GA
1998	**F**	**Washington**	**W 4-0**	**13**	**7**
	CF	Dallas	W 4-2	15	11
	CSF	St. Louis	W 4-2	23	13
	CQF	Phoenix	W 4-2	24	18
1997	**F**	**Philadelphia**	**W 4-0**	**16**	**6**
	CF	Colorado	W 4-2	16	12
	CSF	Anaheim	W 4-0	13	8
	CQF	St. Louis	W 4-2	13	12
1996	CF	Colorado	L 2-4	16	20
	CSF	St. Louis	W 4-3	22	16
	CQF	Winnipeg	W 4-2	20	10
1995	F	New Jersey	L 0-4	7	16
	CF	Chicago	W 4-1	13	12
	CSF	San Jose	W 4-0	24	6
	CQF	Dallas	W 4-1	17	10
1994	CQF	San Jose	L 3-4	27	21

Abbreviations: Round: F – Final; **CF** – conference final; **CQF** – conference quarter-final; **CSF** – conference semi-final; **DSF** – division semi-final; **SF** – semi-final; **QF** – quarter-final; **PR** – preliminary round.

Calgary totals include Atlanta, 1972-73 to 1979-80. Carolina totals include Hartford, 1979-80 to 1996-97.
Colorado totals include Quebec, 1979-80 to 1994-95. Dallas totals include Minnesota, 1967-68 to 1992-93.
New Jersey totals include Kansas City, 1974-75 to 1975-76, and Colorado Rockies, 1976-77 to 1981-82.
Phoenix totals include Winnipeg, 1979-80 to 1995-96.

1997-98 Results

Oct.	1	at	Calgary	3-1		31		St. Louis	5-2
	3	at	Edmonton	8-2	**Jan.**	2		San Jose	1-4
	8		Dallas	3-1		4	at	Chicago	1-3
	10		Tampa Bay	3-0		6		Phoenix	2-0
	12		Calgary	4-4		9	at	Dallas	3-3
	14	at	Toronto	3-2		11		Washington	2-0
	15		Toronto	3-4		12	at	NY Islanders	1-1
	18		Carolina	4-2		14		Vancouver	4-0
	20		St. Louis	3-3		20	at	New Jersey	1-3
	22	at	Anaheim	4-1		21		Toronto	0-3
	23	at	Los Angeles	4-1		24		Philadelphia	1-0
	26	at	Vancouver	5-1		28		Phoenix	4-4
	29		San Jose	4-3		31	at	Pittsburgh	2-4
	31		Los Angeles	1-5	**Feb.**	1	at	Washington	4-2
Nov.	2		Anaheim	4-3		3	at	Florida	1-1
	5	at	Carolina	1-3		5	at	Tampa Bay	5-4
	7		Pittsburgh	1-1		7	at	St. Louis	1-4
	9		Calgary	6-3		25		Los Angeles	1-1
	11		Colorado	0-2		27		Florida	3-1
	13	at	Ottawa	4-2	**Mar.**	2	at	Phoenix	3-1
	15	at	St. Louis	2-5		4	at	Anaheim	2-0
	16	at	Chicago	3-3		5	at	San Jose	4-5
	19		NY Islanders	2-3		7	at	Los Angeles	1-2
	21		Dallas	4-2		10		Boston	3-6
	22	at	Montreal	5-2		12		Chicago	3-0
	26		Ottawa	4-1		14	at	Philadelphia	1-6
	28		Montreal	2-0		17		Edmonton	4-3
Dec.	1	at	Vancouver	3-3		18	at	Toronto	5-2
	3	at	Calgary	4-3		21	at	NY Rangers	4-3
	5	at	Edmonton	1-3		23		Chicago	5-5
	9		Vancouver	7-5		26		Anaheim	3-3
	12		Edmonton	2-3		28	at	St. Louis	2-3
	14	at	Phoenix	3-3		29		Buffalo	4-2
	16	at	San Jose	1-5	**Apr.**	1		Colorado	2-0
	17	at	Colorado	2-2		4	at	Chicago	3-2
	19		New Jersey	5-4		7		St. Louis	5-3
	22	at	Boston	4-2		9		Phoenix	5-1
	23	at	Buffalo	3-1		11		NY Rangers	5-2
	26		Toronto	4-1		14	at	Phoenix	1-2
	27	at	Toronto	8-1		15	at	Dallas	1-3
	29		Dallas	2-2		18	at	Colorado	3-4

Entry Draft Selections 1998-84

1998

Pick	
25	Jiri Fischer
55	Ryan Barnes
56	Tomek Valtonen
84	Jake McCracken
111	Brent Hobday
142	Calle Steen
151	Adam DeLeeuw
171	Pavel Datsyuk
198	Jeremy Goetzinger
226	David Petrasek
256	Petja Pietilainen

1997

Pick	
49	Yuri Butsayev
76	Petr Sykora
102	Quintin Laing
129	John Wikstrom
157	B.J. Young
186	Mike Laceby
213	Steve Wilejto
239	Greg Willers

1996

Pick	
26	Jesse Wallin
52	Aren Miller
108	Johan Forsander
135	Michal Podolka
144	Magnus Nilsson
162	Alexandre Jacques
189	Colin Beardsmore
215	Craig Stahl
241	Evgeniy Afanasiev

1995

Pick	
26	Maxim Kuznetsov
52	Philippe Audet
58	Darryl Laplante
104	Anatoly Ustugov
125	Chad Wilchynski
126	David Arsenault
156	Tyler Perry
182	Per Eklund
208	Andrei Samokvalov
234	David Engblom

1994

Pick	
23	Yan Golubovsky
49	Mathieu Dandenault
75	Sean Gillam
114	Frederic Deschenes
127	Doug Battaglia
153	Pavel Agarkov
205	Jason Elliot
231	Jeff Mikesch
257	Tomas Holmstrom
283	Toivo Suursoo

1993

Pick	
22	Anders Eriksson
48	Jonathan Coleman
74	Kevin Hilton
97	John Jakopin
100	Benoit Larose
126	Norm Maracle
152	Tim Spitzig
178	Yuri Yeresko
204	Vitezslav Skuta
230	Ryan Shanahan
256	James Kosecki
282	Gordon Hunt

1992

Pick	
22	Curtis Bowen
46	Darren McCarty
70	Sylvain Cloutier
118	Mike Sullivan
142	Jason MacDonald
166	Greg Scott
183	Justin Krall
189	C.J. Denomme
214	Jeff Walker
238	Daniel McGillis
262	Ryan Bach

1991

Pick	
10	Martin Lapointe
32	Jamie Pushor
54	Chris Osgood
76	Michael Knuble
98	Dmitri Motkov
142	Igor Malykhin
186	Jim Bermingham
208	Jason Firth
230	Bart Turner
252	Andrew Miller

1990

Pick	
3	Keith Primeau
45	Vyacheslav Kozlov
66	Stewart Malgunas
87	Tony Burns
108	Claude Barthe
129	Jason York
150	Wes McCauley
171	Anthony Gruba
192	Travis Tucker
213	Brett Larson
234	John Hendry

1989

Pick	
11	Mike Sillinger
32	Bob Boughner
53	Nicklas Lidstrom
74	Sergei Fedorov
95	Shawn McCosh
116	Dallas Drake
137	Scott Zygulski
158	Andy Suhy
179	Bob Jones
200	Greg Bignell
204	Rick Judson
221	Vladimir Konstantinov
242	Joseph Frederick
246	Jason Glickman

1988

Pick	
17	Kory Kocur
38	Serge Anglehart
47	Guy Dupuis
59	Petr Hrbek
80	Sheldon Kennedy
143	Kelly Hurd
164	Brian McCormack
185	Jody Praznik
206	Glen Goodall
227	Darren Colbourne
248	Donald Stone

1987

Pick	
11	Yves Racine
32	Gordon Kruppke
41	Bob Wilkie
52	Dennis Holland
74	Mark Reimer
95	Radomir Brazda
116	Sean Clifford
137	Mike Gober
158	Kevin Scott
179	Mikko Haapakoski
200	Darin Bannister
221	Craig Quinlan
242	Tomas Jansson

1986

Pick	
1	Joe Murphy
22	Adam Graves
43	Derek Mayer
64	Tim Cheveldae
85	Johan Garpenlov
106	Jay Stark
127	Per Djoos
148	Dean Morton
169	Marc Potvin
190	Scott King
211	Tom Bissett
232	Peter Ekroth

1985

Pick	
8	Brent Fedyk
29	Jeff Sharples
50	Steve Chiasson
71	Mark Gowans
92	Chris Luongo
113	Randy McKay
134	Thomas Bjur
155	Mike Luckraft
176	Rob Schenna
197	Erik Hamalainen
218	Bo Svanberg
239	Mikael Lindman

1984

Pick	
7	Shawn Burr
28	Doug Houda
49	Milan Chalupa
91	Mats Lundstrom
112	Randy Hansch
133	Stefan Larsson
152	Lars Karlsson
154	Urban Nordin
175	Bill Shibicky
195	Jay Rose
216	Tim Kaiser
236	Tom Nickolau

General Manager

HOLLAND, KEN

General Manager, Detroit Red Wings. Born in Vernon, B.C., Nov. 10, 1955.

Entering his 15th year with the Detroit Red Wings, Ken Holland began his tenure as the club's general manager after serving as assistant general manager for the previous three seasons. Holland was elevated to his present position July 18, 1997.

In his new and expanded role, he oversees all aspects of hockey operations including all matters relating to player personnel, development, contract negotiations and player movements. Holland also continues to be Detroit's point person at the NHL Entry Draft, as he has for the past eight years. In that capacity, he was instrumental in selecting some of Detroit's best young talent, including Vyacheslav Kozlov, Darren McCarty, Chris Osgood and Martin Lapointe, along with several other top prospects.

Holland has deftly handled several different front-office duties for the club over the past 14 years. At the conclusion of his playing days as a goaltender, spending most of his pro career at the American Hockey League level, Holland began his off-ice career in 1985 as a western Canada scout followed by five years as amateur scouting director before promotions leading to his current position as general manager.

A native of Vernon, BC, Holland played in the junior ranks for Medicine Hat (WHL) in 1974-75. He was Toronto's 13th pick (188th overall) in the 1975 draft but never saw action with the Maple Leafs. Holland twice signed with NHL teams as a free agent — in 1980 with Hartford and 1983 with Detroit. He spent most of his pro career with AHL clubs in Binghamton and Springfield, along with Adirondack, but did appear in four NHL games, making his debut with Hartford in 1980-81 and playing three contests for Detroit in 1983-84.

Ken and wife Cindy have four children, Brad, Julie, Rachel and Greg, and reside in suburban Detroit.

Club Directory

Joe Louis Arena
600 Civic Center Drive
Detroit, Michigan 48226
Phone **(313) 396-7544**
FAX PR: (313) 567-0296
Capacity: 19,983

Owner	Mike Ilitch
Owner/Secretary-Treasurer	Marian Ilitch
Vice Presidents	Atanas Ilitch, Christopher Ilitch
Senior Vice-President	Jim Devellano
General Manager	Ken Holland
Assistant General Manager	Jim Nill
Head Coach	Scotty Bowman
Associate Coaches	Barry Smith, Dave Lewis
NHL Scout	Dan Belisle
Pro Scout/Minor League Player Development	Mark Howe
Eastern Scout	Joe McDonnell
Western Scout	Bruce Haralson
USA, High School and College Scout	Mark Leach
Director of European Scouting	Hakan Andersson
Czech and Slovak Republic Scout	Vladimir Havluj
Russian Scout	Ruslan Shabanov
Scout	Paul Crowley
Scout	Marty Stein
Director of Finance	Paul McDonald
General Manger - Joe Louis Arena/ V.P. of Operations	John Pettit
General Sales Manager	Bill Ley
Senior Director of Marketing/ V.P. of Communications	Ted Speers
Box Office Manager	Bob Kerlin
Season Ticket Sales Director	Brad Ebben
Executive Assistant	Nancy Beard
Senior Account Executives	Jeffrey Ajluni, Dan Frank, Scott Miller
Advertising Sales Coordinator	Andy Loughnane
Marketing Manager	Kevin Vaughn
Marketing Coordinator	Lori Shiels
Director of Media Relations	John Hahn
Community Relations Manager	Karen Davis
Public Relations Coordinator	Michael Kuta
Season Ticket Coordinator	Chuck Smith
Hockey Group Sales Coordinator	Mary Greener
Accounting Assistant	Kristin Armstrong
Athletic Trainer	John Wharton
Equipment Manager	Paul Boyer
Assistant Equipment Manager	Tim Abbott
Team Masseur	Bob Huddleston
Team Physicians	John Finley, D.O., Daivd Collon, M.D.
Team Dentist	C.J. Regula, D.M.D.

General Managers' History

Art Duncan and Duke Keats, 1926-27; Jack Adams, 1927-28 to 1961-62; Sid Abel, 1962-63 to 1969-70; Sid Abel and Ned Harkness, 1970-71; Ned Harkness, 1971-72 to 1973-74; Alex Delvecchio, 1974-75, 1975-76; Alex Delvecchio and Ted Lindsay, 1976-77; Ted Lindsay, 1977-78 to 1979-80; Jimmy Skinner, 1980-81, 1981-82; Jim Devellano, 1982-83 to 1989-90; Bryan Murray, 1990-91 to 1993-94; Jim Devellano (Senior Vice President), 1994-95 to 1996-97; Ken Holland, 1997-98 to date.

Coaching History

Art Duncan, 1926-27; Jack Adams, 1927-28 to 1946-47; Tommy Ivan, 1947-48 to 1953-54; Jimmy Skinner, 1954-55 to 1956-57; Jimmy Skinner and Sid Abel, 1957-58; Sid Abel, 1958-59 to 1967-68; Bill Gadsby, 1968-69; Bill Gadsby and Sid Abel, 1969-70; Ned Harkness and Doug Barkley, 1970-71; Doug Barkley and John Wilson, 1971-72; John Wilson, 1972-73; Ted Garvin and Alex Delvecchio, 1973-74; Alex Delvecchio, 1974-75; Doug Barkley and Alex Delvecchio, 1975-76; Alex Delvecchio and Larry Wilson, 1976-77; Bobby Kromm, 1977-78, 1978-79; Bobby Kromm and Ted Lindsay, 1979-80; Ted Lindsay and Wayne Maxner, 1980-81; Wayne Maxner and Billy Dea, 1981-82; Nick Polano, 1982-83 to 1984-85; Harry Neale and Brad Park, 1985-86; Jacques Demers, 1986-87 to 1989-90; Bryan Murray, 1990-91 to 1992-93; Scotty Bowman, 1993-94 to date.

Captains' History

Art Duncan, 1926-27; Reg Noble, 1927-28 to 1929-30; George Hay, 1930-31; Carson Cooper, 1931-32; Larry Aurie, 1932-33; Herbie Lewis, 1933-34; Ebbie Goodfellow, 1934-35; Doug Young, 1935-36 to 1937-38; Ebbie Goodfellow, 1938-39 to 1940-41; Ebbie Goodfellow and Syd Howe, 1941-42; Sid Abel, 1942-43; Mud Bruneteau, Bill Hollett (co-captains), 1943-44; Bill Hollett, 1944-45; Bill Hollett and Sid Abel, 1945-46; Sid Abel, 1946-47 to 1951-52; Ted Lindsay, 1952-53 to 1955-56; Red Kelly, 1956-57, 1957-58; Gordie Howe, 1958-59 to 1961-62; Alex Delvecchio, 1962-63 to 1972-73; Alex Delvecchio, Nick Libett, Red Berenson, Gary Bergman, Ted Harris, Mickey Redmond and Larry Johnston, 1973-74; Marcel Dionne, 1974-75; Danny Grant and Terry Harper, 1975-76; Danny Grant and Dennis Polonich, 1976-77; Dan Maloney and Dennis Hextall, 1977-78; Dennis Hextall, Nick Libett and Paul Woods, 1978-79; Dale McCourt, 1979-80; Errol Thompson and Reed Larson, 1980-81; Reed Larson, 1981-82; Danny Gare, 1982-83 to 1985-86; Steve Yzerman, 1986-87 to date.

Edmonton Oilers

1997-98 Results: 35W-37L-10T 80PTS. Third, Pacific Division

1998-99 Schedule

Month	Day	Date	Opponent
Oct.	Sat.	10	Los Angeles
	Tue.	13	Toronto
	Wed.	14	at Vancouver
	Sat.	17	at New Jersey
	Tue.	20	at NY Rangers
	Wed.	21	at NY Islanders
	Sat.	24	at Colorado
	Wed.	28	Washington
	Sat.	31	Pittsburgh
Nov.	Mon.	2	Vancouver
	Wed.	4	Nashville
	Fri.	6	Colorado
	Sun.	8	at Chicago
	Wed.	11	at Toronto
	Thu.	12	at Ottawa
	Sat.	14	at Montreal
	Wed.	18	Detroit
	Fri.	20	at Anaheim
	Sat.	21	at Phoenix
	Wed.	25	Colorado
	Fri.	27	at Calgary
	Sun.	29	Chicago
Dec.	Wed.	2	Phoenix
	Fri.	4	Tampa Bay
	Sun.	6	Dallas
	Tue.	8	at Nashville
	Wed.	9	at Chicago
	Fri.	11	at Detroit
	Sun.	13	at Philadelphia
	Tue.	15	at Carolina
	Fri.	18	at Tampa Bay
	Sat.	19	at Florida
	Wed.	23	San Jose
	Sun.	27	Vancouver
	Tue.	29	Montreal
Jan.	Sun.	3	Philadelphia*
	Tue.	5	Los Angeles
	Thu.	7	at Phoenix
	Sat.	9	at Los Angeles
	Sun.	10	at Anaheim
	Tue.	12	Dallas
	Thu.	14	at Vancouver
	Sun.	17	Detroit
	Thu.	21	at San Jose
	Wed.	27	Chicago
	Sat.	30	Anaheim
Feb.	Mon.	1	St. Louis
	Wed.	3	Ottawa
	Fri.	5	Nashville
	Mon.	8	at Calgary
	Tue.	9	Boston
	Thu.	11	at Detroit
	Sat.	13	at St. Louis
	Mon.	15	at Dallas
	Wed.	17	at Anaheim
	Thu.	18	at Los Angeles
	Sun.	21	NY Rangers
	Wed.	24	Anaheim
	Fri.	26	Buffalo
	Sat.	27	Carolina
Mar.	Mon.	1	at Colorado
	Wed.	3	at Buffalo
	Fri.	5	at Pittsburgh
	Sat.	6	at Washington
	Wed.	10	at Dallas
	Sat.	13	at St. Louis*
	Sun.	14	at Nashville*
	Wed.	17	New Jersey
	Sat.	20	Vancouver
	Mon.	22	Calgary
	Wed.	24	Montreal
	Fri.	26	St. Louis
	Sun.	28	San Jose*
	Tue.	30	Phoenix
Apr.	Thu.	1	Toronto
	Sat.	3	at Colorado
	Wed.	7	Calgary
	Fri.	9	at Calgary
	Sat.	10	at Vancouver
	Mon.	12	at San Jose
	Fri.	16	Colorado
	Sat.	17	Calgary

* Denotes afternoon game.

Year-by-Year Record

Season	GP	Home W	Home L	Home T	Road W	Road L	Road T	Overall W	Overall L	Overall T	GF	GA	Pts.	Finished		Playoff Result
1997-98	82	20	16	5	15	21	5	35	37	10	215	224	80	3rd,	Pacific Div.	Lost Conf. Semi-Final
1996-97	82	21	16	4	15	21	5	36	37	9	252	247	81	3rd,	Pacific Div.	Lost Conf. Semi-Final
1995-96	82	15	21	5	15	23	3	30	44	8	240	304	68	5th,	Pacific Div.	Out of Playoffs
1994-95	48	11	12	1	6	15	3	17	27	4	136	183	38	5th,	Pacific Div.	Out of Playoffs
1993-94	84	17	22	3	8	23	11	25	45	14	261	305	64	6th,	Pacific Div.	Out of Playoffs
1992-93	84	16	21	5	10	29	3	26	50	8	242	337	60	5th,	Smythe Div.	Out of Playoffs
1991-92	80	22	13	5	14	21	5	36	34	10	295	297	82	3rd,	Smythe Div.	Lost Conf. Championship
1990-91	80	22	15	3	15	22	3	37	37	6	272	272	80	3rd,	Smythe Div.	Lost Conf. Championship
1989-90	**80**	**23**	**11**	**6**	**15**	**17**	**8**	**38**	**28**	**14**	**315**	**283**	**90**	**2nd,**	**Smythe Div.**	**Won Stanley Cup**
1988-89	80	21	16	3	17	18	5	38	34	8	325	306	84	3rd,	Smythe Div.	Lost Div. Semi-Final
1987-88	**80**	**28**	**8**	**4**	**16**	**17**	**7**	**44**	**25**	**11**	**363**	**288**	**99**	**2nd,**	**Smythe Div.**	**Won Stanley Cup**
1986-87	**80**	**29**	**6**	**5**	**21**	**18**	**1**	**50**	**24**	**6**	**372**	**284**	**106**	**1st,**	**Smythe Div.**	**Won Stanley Cup**
1985-86	80	32	6	2	24	11	5	56	17	7	426	310	119	1st,	Smythe Div.	Lost Div. Final
1984-85	**80**	**26**	**7**	**7**	**23**	**13**	**4**	**49**	**20**	**11**	**401**	**298**	**109**	**1st,**	**Smythe Div.**	**Won Stanley Cup**
1983-84	**80**	**31**	**5**	**4**	**26**	**13**	**1**	**57**	**18**	**5**	**446**	**314**	**119**	**1st,**	**Smythe Div.**	**Won Stanley Cup**
1982-83	80	25	9	6	22	12	6	47	21	12	424	315	106	1st,	Smythe Div.	Lost Final
1981-82	80	31	5	4	17	12	11	48	17	15	417	295	111	1st,	Smythe Div.	Lost Div. Semi-Final
1980-81	80	17	13	10	12	22	6	29	35	16	328	327	74	4th,	Smythe Div.	Lost Quarter-Final
1979-80	80	17	14	9	11	25	4	28	39	13	301	322	69	4th,	Smythe Div.	Lost Prelim. Round

Only Wayne Gretzky has finished as the Oilers' top scorer more often than Doug Weight, who led the club for the fifth straight season with 70 points (26 goals, 44 assists) in 1997-98.

Franchise date: June 22, 1979

NORTHWEST
DIVISION

**20th
NHL
Season**

1998-99 Player Personnel

FORWARDS	HT	WT	S	Place of Birth	Date	1997-98 Club
BERANEK, Josef	6-2	195	L	Litvinov, Czechoslovakia	10/25/69	Petra Vsetin-Czech.
BONVIE, Dennis	5-11	205	R	Antigonish, N.S.	7/23/73	Edmonton-Hamilton
BOWEN, Jason	6-4	220	L	Port Alice, B.C.	11/9/73	Phi (AHL)-Edm-Hamilton-Canada
BROWN, Kevin	6-1	212	R	Birmingham, England	5/11/74	Carolina-New Haven
BUCHBERGER, Kelly	6-2	210	L	Langenburg, Sask.	12/2/66	Edmonton
CHIMERA, Jason	6-0	180	L	Edmonton, Alta.	5/2/79	Medicine Hat-Hamilton
COPELAND, Adam	6-1	215	R	St. Catharines, Ont.	6/5/76	Miami-Ohio
DAW, Jeff	6-3	190	R	Carlisle, Ont.	2/28/72	Hamilton
DEVEREAUX, Boyd	6-2	195	L	Seaforth, Ont.	4/16/78	Edmonton-Hamilton
FALLOON, Pat	5-11	190	R	Foxwarren, Man.	9/22/72	Philadelphia-Ottawa
FERRARO, Chris	5-10	185	R	Port Jefferson, NY	1/24/73	Pittsburgh
GRIER, Michael	6-1	227	R	Detroit, MI	1/5/75	Edmonton
GUERIN, Bill	6-2	210	R	Wilbraham, MA	11/9/70	N.J.-Edm-United States
HENRICH, Michael	6-2	206	R	Thornhill, Ont.	3/3/80	Barrie
HINZ, Chad	5-10	185	R	Saskatoon, Sask.	3/21/79	Moose Jaw
HUARD, Bill	6-1	215	L	Welland, Ont.	6/24/67	Edmonton
HULBIG, Joe	6-3	215	L	Norwood, MA	9/29/73	Edmonton-Hamilton
KOVALENKO, Andrei	5-10	215	L	Balakovo, USSR	6/7/70	Edmonton-Russia
LACOUTURE, Dan	6-3	210	L	Hyannis, MA	4/18/77	Hamilton
LARAQUE, Georges	6-3	230	R	Montreal, Que.	12/7/76	Edmonton-Hamilton
LINDGREN, Mats	6-2	202	L	Skelleftea, Sweden	10/1/74	Edmonton-Sweden
LINDQUIST, Fredrik	6-0	190	L	Sodertalje, Sweden	6/21/73	Djurgarden
MARCHANT, Todd	5-10	178	L	Buffalo, NY	8/12/73	Edmonton
McAMMOND, Dean	5-11	200	L	Grand Cache, Alta.	6/15/73	Edmonton
MOORE, Barrie	5-11	175	L	London, Ont.	5/22/75	Hamilton
MURRAY, Rem	6-2	195	L	Stratford, Ont.	10/9/72	Edmonton
PETERSON, Kyle	6-4	220	L	Calgary, Alta.	4/17/74	New Orleans
RIESEN, Michel	6-2	190	R	Oberbalm, Switzerland	4/11/79	HC Davos-Switzerland
SARNO, Peter	5-11	185	L	Toronto, Ont.	7/26/79	Windsor-Hamilton
SMYTH, Ryan	6-1	195	L	Banff, Alta.	2/21/76	Edmonton
WEIGHT, Doug	5-11	200	L	Warren, MI	1/21/71	Edmonton-United States
ZELEPUKIN, Valeri	6-1	200	L	Voskresensk, USSR	9/17/68	New Jersey-Edmonton-Russia
DEFENSEMEN						
BEREHOWSKY, Drake	6-2	212	R	Toronto, Ont.	1/3/72	Edmonton-Hamilton
BOLIBRUCK, Kevin	6-1	200	L	Peterborough, Ont.	2/8/77	Canada
BROWN, Sean	6-3	205	L	Oshawa, Ont.	11/5/76	Edmonton-Hamilton
DESCOTEAUX, Matthieu	6-3	220	L	Pierreville, Que.	9/23/77	Hamilton
ELLIOTT, Paul	6-0	202	L	White Rock, B.C.	6/2/80	Lethbridge-Medicine Hat
ETTINGER, Trevor	6-5	240	L	Truro, N.S.	7/13/80	Cape Breton
HAJT, Chris	6-3	206	L	Saskatoon, Sask.	7/5/78	Guelph-United States
HAMRLIK, Roman	6-2	215	L	Gottwaldov, Czech.	4/12/74	Tampa Bay-Edmonton-Czech.
HAUER, Brett	6-2	200	R	Richfield, MN	7/11/71	Manitoba
HENRY, Alex	6-5	216	L	Elliot Lake, Ont.	10/18/79	London
LEFEBVRE, Christian	6-5	212	L	Montreal, Que.	3/3/78	Baie-Comeau
MILLAR, Craig	6-2	205	L	Winnipeg, Man.	7/12/76	Edmonton-Hamilton
MIRONOV, Boris	6-3	223	R	Moscow, USSR	3/21/72	Edmonton-Russia
MUSIL, Frantisek	6-3	215	L	Pardubice, Czech.	12/17/64	Indianapolis-Detroit (IHL)-Edm
NIINIMAA, Janne	6-2	220	L	Raahe, Finland	5/22/75	Philadelphia-Finland-Edmonton
NORTON, Brad	6-4	225	L	Cambridge, MA	2/13/75	U. Mass.-Amherst-Detroit (IHL)
POTI, Tom	6-3	215	L	Worcester, MA	3/22/77	Boston U.
SYMES, Brad	6-2	210	L	Edmonton, Alta.	4/26/76	New Orleans
YERKOVICH, Sergei	6-3	210	L	Minsk, USSR	9/3/74	Las Vegas-Belarus
ZHURIK, Alexander	6-3	195	L	Minsk, USSR	5/29/75	Hamilton-Belarus
de VRIES, Greg	6-3	215	L	Sundridge, Ont.	1/4/73	Edmonton

GOALTENDERS	HT	WT	C	Place of Birth	Date	1997-98 Club
ANTILA, Kristian	6-3	207	L	Vammala, Finland	1/10/80	Ilves Tampere
DOVIGI, Patrick	6-0	180	L	Sault Ste. Marie, Ont.	7/2/79	Erie (OHL)
ESSENSA, Bob	6-0	188	L	Toronto, Ont.	1/14/65	Edmonton
FICHAUD, Eric	5-11	171	L	Anjou, Que.	11/4/75	NY Islanders-Utica
MINARD, Mike	6-3	205	L	Owen Sound, Ont.	11/1/76	Brantford-Ham-New Orleans-Milw
PASSMORE, Steve	5-9	165	L	Thunder Bay, Ont.	1/29/73	San Antonio-Hamilton
THOMAS, Tim	5-11	180	L	Flint, MI	4/15/74	U.S.A.-Helsinki-Bir-Houston
WICKENHEISER, Chris	6-1	185	L	Lethbridge, Alta.	1/20/76	Huntington-Hamilton

Coach

LOW, RONALD ALBERT (RON)
Head Coach, Edmonton Oilers. Born in Birtie, Man., June 21, 1950.

The 1998-99 season sees Ron Low enter his fifth season as head coach of the Edmonton Oilers. After serving as an assistant coach with the Edmonton Oilers for six seasons, Ron Low became the team's fifth head coach when he was named to the position on April 6, 1995. Low has become known around the League as a coach who successfully develops talented, young prospects into solid NHL performers.

On August 3, 1989, Low was appointed to the Edmonton Oilers' coaching staff as an assistant coach. He also played parts of four seasons with Edmonton from 1979-80 to 1982-83. The Oilers were one of six teams Low played for in an 11-year NHL career that saw him tend goal for Toronto, Washington, Detroit, Quebec, Edmonton and New Jersey. From 1972-73 to 1984-85, he played 382 NHL games and registered a 4.28 goals-against average with four shutouts and a 102-203-38 record.

In 1985-86 he was named assistant playing coach with the Nova Scotia Oilers, Edmonton's American Hockey League affiliate. Following two years as an assistant coach he was named Nova Scotia's head coach in 1987-88 and kept that position when the team became the Cape Breton Oilers in 1988-89. Low compiled a 62-83-15 record as an AHL head coach before joining the NHL coaching ranks.

Coaching Record

		Regular Season					Playoffs			
Season	Team	Games	W	L	T	%	Games	W	L	%
1987-88	Nova Scotia (AHL)	80	35	36	9	.506	5	1	4	.200
1988-89	Cape Breton (AHL)	80	27	47	6	.375	....	....	....	....
1994-95	**Edmonton (NHL)**	**13**	**5**	**7**	**1**	**.423**	....	....	....	....
1995-96	**Edmonton (NHL)**	**82**	**30**	**44**	**8**	**.415**	....	....	....	....
1996-97	**Edmonton (NHL)**	**82**	**36**	**37**	**9**	**.494**	**12**	**5**	**7**	**.417**
1997-98	**Edmonton (NHL)**	**82**	**35**	**37**	**10**	**.488**	**12**	**5**	**7**	**.417**
	NHL Totals	**259**	**106**	**125**	**28**	**.463**	**24**	**10**	**14**	**.417**

1997-98 Scoring

* – rookie

Regular Season

Pos	#	Player	Team	GP	G	A	Pts	+/–	PIM	PP	SH	GW	GT	S	%
C	39	Doug Weight	EDM	79	26	44	70	1	69	9	0	4	0	205	12.7
L	37	Dean McAmmond	EDM	77	19	31	50	9	46	8	0	3	0	128	14.8
D	2	Boris Mironov	EDM	81	16	30	46	-8	100	10	1	1	1	203	7.9
D	24	Janne Niinimaa	PHI	66	3	31	34	6	56	2	0	1	0	115	2.6
			EDM	11	1	8	9	7	6	1	0	0	0	19	5.3
			TOTAL	77	4	39	43	13	62	3	0	1	0	134	3.0
D	22	Roman Hamrlik	T.B.	37	3	12	15	-18	22	1	0	0	0	86	3.5
			EDM	41	6	20	26	3	48	4	1	3	0	112	5.4
			TOTAL	78	9	32	41	-15	70	5	1	3	0	198	4.5
R	9	Bill Guerin	N.J.	19	5	5	10	0	13	1	0	2	0	48	10.4
			EDM	40	13	16	29	1	80	8	0	2	0	130	10.0
			TOTAL	59	18	21	39	1	93	9	0	4	0	178	10.1
L	26	Todd Marchant	EDM	76	14	21	35	9	71	2	1	3	0	194	7.2
L	94	Ryan Smyth	EDM	65	20	13	33	-24	44	10	0	2	2	205	9.8
C	20	Tony Hrkac	DAL	13	5	3	8	0	0	3	0	0	0	14	35.7
			EDM	36	8	11	19	3	10	4	0	1	0	43	18.6
			TOTAL	49	13	14	27	3	10	7	0	1	0	57	22.8
C	14	Mats Lindgren	EDM	82	13	13	26	0	42	1	3	3	0	131	9.9
C	18 *	Scott Fraser	EDM	29	12	11	23	6	6	6	0	2	0	61	19.7
L	51	Andrei Kovalenko	EDM	59	6	17	23	-14	28	1	0	2	1	89	6.7
R	16	Kelly Buchberger	EDM	82	6	17	23	-10	122	1	1	1	0	86	7.0
L	21	Valeri Zelepukin	N.J.	35	2	8	10	0	32	0	0	0	0	54	3.7
			EDM	33	2	10	12	-2	57	0	0	0	0	47	4.3
			TOTAL	68	4	18	22	-2	89	0	0	0	0	101	4.0
L	17	Rem Murray	EDM	61	9	9	18	-9	39	2	2	0	0	59	15.3
R	25	Mike Grier	EDM	66	9	6	15	-3	73	1	0	1	0	90	10.0
D	5	Greg De Vries	EDM	65	7	4	11	-17	80	1	0	0	0	53	13.2
D	6	Bobby Dollas	ANA	22	0	1	1	-12	27	0	0	0	0	11	0.0
			EDM	30	2	5	7	6	22	0	0	0	0	27	7.4
			TOTAL	52	2	6	8	-6	49	0	0	0	0	38	5.3
D	15	Drake Berehowsky	EDM	67	1	6	7	1	169	1	0	1	0	58	1.7
C	19 *	Boyd Devereaux	EDM	38	1	4	5	-5	6	0	0	0	0	27	3.7
D	32 *	Craig Millar	EDM	11	4	0	4	-3	8	1	0	0	0	10	40.0
L	12 *	Joe Hulbig	EDM	17	2	2	4	-1	2	0	0	1	0	8	25.0
C	9 *	Mike Watt	EDM	14	1	2	3	-4	4	0	0	1	0	14	7.1
D	8	Frank Musil	EDM	17	1	2	3	1	8	0	1	1	0	8	12.5
G	31	Curtis Joseph	EDM	71	0	2	2	0	4	0	0	0	0	0	0.0
D	23 *	Sean Brown	EDM	18	0	1	1	-1	43	0	0	0	0	9	0.0
L	28	Bill Huard	EDM	30	0	1	1	-5	72	0	0	0	0	12	0.0
D	40 *	Scott Ferguson	EDM	1	0	0	0	1	0	0	0	0	0	0	0.0
D	21 *	Ladislav Benysek	EDM	2	0	0	0	-2	0	0	0	0	0	0	0.0
D	29	Jason Bowen	EDM	4	0	0	0	0	10	0	0	0	0	3	0.0
R	36 *	Dennis Bonvie	EDM	4	0	0	0	0	27	0	0	0	0	0	0.0
D	4	Kevin Lowe	EDM	7	0	0	0	-3	22	0	0	0	0	5	0.0
D	6 *	Bryan Muir	EDM	7	0	0	0	0	17	0	0	0	0	6	0.0
D	38 *	Terran Sandwith	EDM	8	0	0	0	-4	6	0	0	0	0	4	0.0
R	27 *	Georges Laraque	EDM	11	0	0	0	-4	59	0	0	0	0	4	0.0
G	30	Bob Essensa	EDM	16	0	0	0	0	0	0	0	0	0	0	0.0
L	8	Doug Friedman	EDM	16	0	0	0	0	20	0	0	0	0	8	0.0

Goaltending

No.	Goaltender	GPI	Mins	Avg	W	L	T	EN	SO	GA	SA	S%
30	Bob Essensa	16	825	2.55	6	6	1	2	0	35	404	.913
31	Curtis Joseph	71	4132	2.63	29	31	9	6	8	181	1901	.905
	Totals	**82**	**4980**	**2.70**	**35**	**37**	**10**	**8**	**8**	**224**	**2313**	**.903**

Playoffs

Pos	#	Player	Team	GP	G	A	Pts	+/–	PIM	PP	SH	GW	OT	S	%
C	39	Doug Weight	EDM	12	2	7	9	-4	14	2	0	1	0	26	7.7
R	9	Bill Guerin	EDM	12	7	1	8	-6	17	4	0	0	0	47	14.9
D	2	Boris Mironov	EDM	12	3	3	6	-3	27	1	0	1	0	26	11.5
D	22	Roman Hamrlik	EDM	12	0	6	6	-4	12	0	0	0	0	19	0.0
L	17	Rem Murray	EDM	11	1	4	5	-1	2	0	0	0	0	15	6.7
L	37	Dean McAmmond	EDM	12	1	4	5	0	12	0	0	0	0	22	4.5
R	25	Mike Grier	EDM	12	2	2	4	4	13	0	0	1	0	14	14.3
L	94	Ryan Smyth	EDM	12	1	3	4	-2	16	1	0	0	0	24	4.2
L	21	Valeri Zelepukin	EDM	8	1	2	3	3	2	0	0	0	0	8	12.5
D	15	Drake Berehowsky	EDM	12	1	2	3	1	14	0	0	1	0	4	25.0
R	16	Kelly Buchberger	EDM	12	1	2	3	0	25	0	0	0	0	13	7.7
C	20	Tony Hrkac	EDM	12	0	3	3	2	2	0	0	0	0	11	0.0
C	18 *	Scott Fraser	EDM	11	1	1	2	0	0	0	0	0	0	17	5.9
D	24	Janne Niinimaa	EDM	11	1	1	2	3	12	0	0	1	0	20	5.0
C	14	Mats Lindgren	EDM	12	1	1	2	0	10	0	0	0	0	16	6.3
L	26	Todd Marchant	EDM	12	1	1	2	0	10	0	0	0	0	17	5.9
G	30	Bob Essensa	EDM	1	0	0	0	0	0	0	0	0	0	0	0.0
D	4	Kevin Lowe	EDM	1	0	0	0	0	4	0	0	0	0	0	0.0
L	51	Andrei Kovalenko	EDM	1	0	0	0	0	2	0	0	0	0	2	0.0
L	28	Bill Huard	EDM	4	0	0	0	0	2	0	0	0	0	3	0.0
D	8	Frank Musil	EDM	7	0	0	0	1	6	0	0	0	0	0	0.0
D	5	Greg De Vries	EDM	7	0	0	0	-4	21	0	0	0	0	2	0.0
D	6	Bobby Dollas	EDM	11	0	0	0	2	16	0	0	0	0	10	0.0
G	31	Curtis Joseph	EDM	12	0	0	0	0	2	0	0	0	0	0	0.0

Goaltending

No.	Goaltender	GPI	Mins	Avg	W	L	EN	SO	GA	SA	S%
31	Curtis Joseph	12	716	1.93	5	7	1	3	23	319	.928
30	Bob Essensa	1	27	2.22	0	0	0	0	1	11	.909
	Totals	**12**	**749**	**2.00**	**5**	**7**	**1**	**3**	**25**	**331**	**.924**

General Managers' History

Larry Gordon, 1979-80; Glen Sather, 1980-81 to date.

Club Records

Team

(Figures in brackets for season records are games played; records for fewest points, wins, ties, losses, goals, goals against are for 70 or more games)

Most Points	119	1983-84 (80), 1985-86 (80)
Most Wins	57	1983-84 (80)
Most Ties	16	1980-81 (80)
Most Losses	50	1992-93 (84)
Most Goals	*446	1983-84 (80)
Most Goals Against	327	1980-81 (80)
Fewest Points	60	1992-93 (84)
Fewest Wins	25	1993-94 (84)
Fewest Ties	5	1983-84 (80)
Fewest Losses	17	1981-82 (80), 1985-86 (80)
Fewest Goals	215	1997-98 (82)
Fewest Goals Against	224	1997-98 (82)
Longest Winning Streak		
Overall	8	Five times
Home	8	Jan. 19-Feb. 22/85, Feb. 24-Apr. 2/86
Away	8	Dec. 9/86-Jan. 17/87
Longest Undefeated Streak		
Overall	15	Oct. 11-Nov. 9/84 (12 wins, 3 ties)
Home	14	Nov. 15/89-Jan. 6/90 (11 wins, 3 ties)
Away	9	Jan. 17-Mar. 2/82 (6 wins, 3 ties), Nov. 23/82-Jan. 18/83 (7 wins, 2 ties)
Longest Losing Streak		
Overall	11	Oct. 16-Nov. 7/93
Home	9	Oct. 16-Nov. 24/93
Away	9	Nov. 25-Dec. 30/80
Longest Winless Streak		
Overall	14	Oct. 11-Nov. 7/93 (13 losses, 1 tie)
Home	9	Oct. 16-Nov. 24/93 (9 losses)
Away	9	Three times
Most Shutouts, Season	8	1997-98 (82)
Most PIM, Season	2,173	1987-88 (80)
Most Goals, Game	13	Nov. 19/83 (N.J. 4 at Edm. 13), Nov. 8/85 (Van. 0 at Edm. 13)

Individual

Most Seasons	15	Kevin Lowe
Most Games	1,037	Kevin Lowe
Most Goals, Career	583	Wayne Gretzky
Most Assists, Career	1,086	Wayne Gretzky
Most Points, Career	1,669	Wayne Gretzky (583G, 1,086A)
Most PIM, Career	1,679	Kelly Buchberger
Most Shutouts, Career	14	Curtis Joseph
Longest Consecutive Games Streak	521	Craig MacTavish (Oct. 11/86-Jan. 2/93)
Most Goals, Season	*92	Wayne Gretzky (1981-82)
Most Assists, Season	*163	Wayne Gretzky (1985-86)
Most Points, Season	*215	Wayne Gretzky (1985-86; 52G, 163A)
Most PIM, Season	286	Steve Smith (1987-88)
Most Points, Defenseman, Season	138	Paul Coffey (1985-86; 48G, 90A)
Most Points, Center, Season	*215	Wayne Gretzky (1985-86; 52G, 163A)
Most Points, Right Wing, Season	135	Jari Kurri (1984-85; 71G, 64A)
Most Points, Left Wing, Season	106	Mark Messier (1982-83; 48G, 58A)
Most Points, Rookie, Season	75	Jari Kurri (1980-81; 32G, 43A)
Most Shutouts, Season	8	Curtis Joseph (1997-98)
Most Goals, Game	5	Wayne Gretzky (Feb. 18/81, Dec. 30/81, Dec. 15/84, Dec. 6/87), Jari Kurri (Nov. 19/83), Pat Hughes (Feb. 3/84)
Most Assists, Game	*7	Wayne Gretzky (Feb. 15/80, Dec. 11/85, Feb. 14/86)
Most Points, Game	8	Wayne Gretzky (Nov. 19/83; 3G, 5A), (Jan. 4/84; 4G, 4A), Paul Coffey (Mar. 14/86; 2G, 6A)

* NHL Record.

Captains' History

Ron Chipperfield, 1979-80; Blair MacDonald and Lee Fogolin, 1980-81; Lee Fogolin, 1981-82, 1982-83; Wayne Gretzky, 1983-84 to 1987-88; Mark Messier, 1988-89 to 1990-91; Kevin Lowe, 1991-92; Craig MacTavish, 1992-93, 1993-94; Shayne Corson, 1994-95; Kelly Buchberger, 1995-96 to date.

Retired Numbers

3	Al Hamilton	1972-1980

Coaching History

Glen Sather, 1979-80; Bryan Watson and Glen Sather, 1980-81; Glen Sather, 1981-82 to 1988-89; John Muckler, 1989-90, 1990-91; Ted Green, 1991-92, 1992-93; Ted Green and Glen Sather, 1993-94; George Burnett and Ron Low, 1994-95; Ron Low, 1995-96 to date.

All-time Record vs. Other Clubs

Regular Season

	At Home							On Road							Total						
	GP	W	L	T	GF	GA	PTS	GP	W	L	T	GF	GA	PTS	GP	W	L	T	GF	GA	PTS
Anaheim	13	6	7	0	26	33	12	13	3	9	1	31	40	7	26	9	16	1	57	73	19
Boston	25	9	13	3	85	88	21	26	6	18	2	74	113	14	51	15	31	5	159	201	35
Buffalo	25	18	5	2	106	67	38	26	10	10	6	98	104	26	51	28	15	8	204	171	64
Calgary	65	34	22	9	266	231	77	64	22	36	6	234	291	50	129	56	58	15	500	522	127
Carolina	26	18	5	3	109	79	39	25	10	10	5	92	104	25	51	28	15	8	201	183	64
Chicago	33	15	14	4	127	122	34	32	10	17	5	118	132	25	65	25	31	9	245	254	59
Colorado	30	17	11	2	141	99	36	30	15	13	2	128	125	32	60	32	24	4	269	224	68
Dallas	32	17	9	6	141	107	40	33	13	14	6	106	121	32	65	30	23	12	247	228	72
Detroit	32	15	12	5	141	130	35	32	14	15	3	119	122	31	64	29	27	8	260	252	66
Florida	4	2	2	0	12	10	4	4	1	2	1	12	12	3	8	3	4	1	24	22	7
Los Angeles	65	34	17	14	312	243	82	65	28	24	13	282	267	69	130	62	41	27	594	510	151
Montreal	26	13	13	0	90	85	26	25	7	14	4	78	90	18	51	20	27	4	168	175	44
New Jersey	28	14	8	6	129	102	34	28	13	13	2	94	99	28	56	27	21	8	223	201	62
NY Islanders	26	16	6	4	99	74	36	26	5	12	9	97	113	19	52	21	18	13	196	187	55
NY Rangers	25	11	12	2	95	90	24	25	13	6	6	100	94	32	50	24	18	8	195	184	56
Ottawa	5	4	1	0	23	14	8	5	3	2	0	13	9	6	10	7	3	0	36	23	14
Philadelphia	25	14	7	4	91	74	32	26	6	19	1	74	120	13	51	20	26	5	165	194	45
Phoenix	60	38	18	4	271	200	80	59	32	23	4	268	243	68	119	70	41	8	539	443	148
Pittsburgh	26	20	5	1	138	90	41	26	12	13	1	118	104	25	52	32	18	2	256	194	66
St. Louis	32	17	12	3	127	118	37	32	15	13	4	129	118	34	64	32	25	7	256	236	71
San Jose	21	15	3	3	83	45	33	20	8	11	1	63	71	17	41	23	14	4	146	116	50
Tampa Bay	6	5	1	0	16	14	10	6	2	2	2	14	18	6	12	7	3	2	30	32	16
Toronto	32	19	7	6	155	109	44	32	14	16	2	141	134	30	64	33	23	8	296	243	74
Vancouver	64	42	16	6	306	202	90	66	31	27	8	274	253	70	130	73	43	14	580	455	160
Washington	25	11	10	4	97	83	26	25	9	14	2	88	105	20	50	20	24	6	185	188	46
Totals	**751**	**424**	**236**	**91**	**3186**	**2509**	**939**	**751**	**302**	**353**	**96**	**2845**	**3002**	**700**	**1502**	**726**	**589**	**187**	**6031**	**5511**	**1639**

Playoffs

	Series	W	L	GP	W	L	T	GF	GA	Last Mtg.	Round	Result
Boston	2	2	0	9	8	1	0	41	20	1990	F	W 4-1
Calgary	5	4	1	30	19	11	0	132	96	1991	DSF	W 4-3
Chicago	4	3	1	20	12	8	0	102	77	1992	CF	L 0-4
Colorado	2	1	1	12	5	7	0	30	35	1998	CQF	W 4-3
Dallas	4	2	2	21	10	11	0	62	57	1998	CSF	L 1-4
Detroit	2	2	0	10	8	2	0	39	26	1988	CF	W 4-1
Los Angeles	7	5	2	36	24	12	0	154	127	1992	DSF	W 4-2
Montreal	1	1	0	3	3	0	0	15	6	1981	PR	W 3-0
NY Islanders	3	1	2	15	6	9	0	47	58	1984	F	W 4-1
Philadelphia	3	2	1	15	8	7	0	49	44	1987	F	W 4-3
Vancouver	2	2	0	9	7	2	0	35	20	1992	DF	W 4-2
Winnipeg	6	6	0	26	22	4	0	120	75	1990	DSF	W 4-3
Totals	**41**	**31**	**10**	**206**	**132**	**74**	**0**	**826**	**641**			

Calgary totals include Atlanta, 1979-80.
Colorado totals include Quebec, 1979-80 to 1994-95.
New Jersey totals include Colorado Rockies, 1979-80 to 1981-82.

Playoff Results 1998-94

Year	Round	Opponent	Result	GF	GA
1998	CSF	Dallas	L 1-4	5	9
	CQF	Colorado	W 4-3	19	16
1997	CSF	Colorado	L 1-4	11	19
	CQF	Dallas	W 4-3	21	18

Abbreviations: Round: F – Final; **CF** – conference final; **CQF** – conference quarter-final; **CSF** – conference semi-final; **DF** – division final; **DSF** – division semi-final; **PR** – preliminary round.

Carolina totals include Hartford, 1979-80 to 1996-97.
Dallas totals include Minnesota, 1979-80 to 1992-93.
Phoenix totals include Winnipeg, 1979-80 to 1995-96.

1997-98 Results

Oct.	1	at	San Jose	5-3		4		Los Angeles	2-3
	3		Detroit	2-8		7		Florida	3-2
	5		Colorado	0-3		9	at	Anaheim	5-1
	8		NY Rangers	3-3		10	at	Los Angeles	4-3
	11		Toronto	2-1		12		St. Louis	2-1
	13	at	Vancouver	0-3		14		Calgary	5-2
	15		Colorado	2-6		20		Phoenix	6-2
	17	at	Anaheim	1-2		23	at	San Jose	2-3
	19	at	Los Angeles	3-2		24	at	Phoenix	5-2
	21		Boston	1-2		26	at	Colorado	1-2
	24		Pittsburgh	4-3		28		New Jersey	1-1
	29		Phoenix	3-2		31		Vancouver	3-6
Nov.	1	at	Boston	1-3	**Feb.**	2		Los Angeles	1-0
	3	at	NY Rangers	2-2		4		San Jose	0-3
	5	at	NY Islanders	4-4		6	at	Vancouver	4-5
	6	at	Philadelphia	2-6		7	at	Calgary	2-4
	8	at	Washington	1-2		25		Ottawa	5-2
	10	at	Buffalo	4-4		27		Anaheim	0-4
	12		Carolina	4-6		28		San Jose	4-1
	15		Calgary	2-2	**Mar.**	2	at	Colorado	5-4
	17	at	Phoenix	3-6		4		Tampa Bay	4-2
	19	at	Dallas	2-3		7	at	Toronto	1-4
	20	at	St. Louis	3-0		9	at	Chicago	4-3
	22	at	Ottawa	1-0		11	at	Tampa Bay	2-0
	25		Chicago	2-2		13	at	Florida	4-0
	28		Anaheim	1-3		15	at	Carolina	1-4
	30		San Jose	6-1		17	at	Detroit	3-4
Dec.	2	at	Colorado	2-4		18	at	Pittsburgh	2-4
	3	at	Dallas	1-4		21		St. Louis	2-0
	5		Detroit	3-1		22		NY Islanders	1-3
	7	at	Chicago	3-3		25		Washington	4-2
	10	at	New Jersey	2-4		27		Buffalo	0-1
	12	at	Detroit	3-2		30		Calgary	3-1
	13	at	St. Louis	4-1	**Apr.**	1	at	Vancouver	2-4
	17		Chicago	0-0		3		Dallas	4-1
	20		Dallas	1-2		6		Vancouver	3-2
	22	at	Montreal	3-3		8	at	Anaheim	2-4
	23	at	Toronto	4-5		9	at	Los Angeles	4-0
	27		Colorado	1-5		11	at	Calgary	5-4
	30		Philadelphia	1-3		15		Anaheim	5-3
Jan.	2		Montreal	3-5		18		Toronto	4-3

Entry Draft Selections 1998-84

1998
Pick
13 Michael Henrich
67 Alex Henry
99 Shawn Horcoff
113 Kristian Antila
128 Paul Elliott
144 Oleg Smirnov
159 Trevor Ettinger
186 Michael Morrison
213 Christian Lefebvre
241 Maxim Spiridonov

1997
Pick
14 Michel Riesen
41 Patrick Dovigi
68 Sergei Yerkovich
94 Jonas Elofsson
121 Jason Chimera
141 Peter Sarno
176 Kevin Bolibruck
187 Chad Hinz
205 Chris Kerr
231 Alexandre Fomitchev

1996
Pick
6 Boyd Devereaux
19 Matthieu Descoteaux
32 Chris Hajt
59 Tom Poti
114 Brian Urick
141 Bryan Randall
168 David Bernier
170 Brandon Lafrance
195 Fernando Pisani
221 John Hultberg

1995
Pick
6 Steve Kelly
31 Georges Laraque
57 Lukas Zib
83 Mike Minard
109 Jan Snopek
161 Martin Cerven
187 Stephen Douglas
213 Jiri Antonin

1994
Pick
4 Jason Bonsignore
6 Ryan Smyth
32 Mike Watt
53 Corey Neilson
60 Brad Symes
79 Adam Copeland
95 Jussi Tarvainen
110 Jon Gaskins
136 Terry Marchant
160 Curtis Sheptak
162 Dmitri Shulga
179 Chris Wickenheiser
185 Rob Guinn
188 Jason Reid
214 Jeremy Jablonski
266 Ladislav Benysek

1993
Pick
7 Jason Arnott
16 Nick Stajduhar
33 David Vyborny
59 Kevin Paden
60 Alexander Kerch
111 Miroslav Satan
163 Alexander Zhurik
189 Martin Bakula
215 Brad Norton
241 Oleg Maltsev
267 Ilja Byakin

1992
Pick
13 Joe Hulbig
37 Martin Reichel
61 Simon Roy
65 Kirk Maltby
96 Ralph Intranuovo
109 Joaquin Gage
157 Steve Gibson
181 Kyuin Shim
190 Colin Schmidt
205 Marko Tuomainen
253 Bryan Rasmussen

1991
Pick
12 Tyler Wright
20 Martin Rucinsky
34 Andrew Verner
56 George Breen
78 Mario Nobili
93 Ryan Haggerty
144 David Oliver
166 Gary Kitching
210 Vegar Barlie
232 Evgeny Belosheikin
254 Juha Riihijarvi

1990
Pick
17 Scott Allison
38 Alexandre Legault
59 Joe Crowley
67 Joel Blain
101 Greg Louder
122 Keijo Sailynoja
143 Mike Power
164 Roman Mejzlik
185 Richard Zemlicka
206 Petr Korinek
227 invalid claim
248 Sami Nuutinen

1989
Pick
15 Jason Soules
36 Richard Borgo
78 Josef Beranek
92 Peter White
120 Anatoli Semenov
140 Davis Payne
141 Sergei Yashin
162 Darcy Martini
225 Roman Bozek

1988
Pick
19 Francois Leroux
39 Petro Koivunen
53 Trevor Sim
61 Collin Bauer
82 Cam Brauer
103 Don Martin
124 Len Barrie
145 Mike Glover
166 Shjon Podein
187 Tom Cole
208 Vladimir Zubkov
229 Darin MacDonald
250 Tim Tisdale

1987
Pick
21 Peter Soberlak
42 Brad Werenka
63 Geoff Smith
64 Peter Eriksson
105 Shaun Van Allen
126 Radek Toupal
147 Tomas Srsen
168 Age Ellingsen
189 Gavin Armstrong
210 Mike Tinkham
231 Jeff Pauletti
241 Jesper Duus
252 Igor Vyazmikin

1986
Pick
21 Kim Issel
42 Jamie Nichols
63 Ron Shudra
84 Dan Currie
105 David Haas
126 Jim Ennis
147 Ivan Matulik
168 Nicolas Beaulieu
189 Mike Greenlay
210 Matt Lanza
231 Mojmir Bozik
252 Tony Hand

1985
Pick
20 Scott Metcalfe
41 Todd Carnelley
62 Mike Ware
104 Tomas Kapusta
125 Brian Tessier
146 Shawn Tyers
167 Tony Fairfield
188 Kelly Buchberger
209 Mario Barbe
230 Peter Headon
251 John Haley

1984
Pick
21 Selmar Odelein
42 Daryl Reaugh
63 Todd Norman
84 Rich Novak
105 Richard Lambert
106 Emanuel Viveiros
126 Ivan Dornic
147 Heikki Riihijarvi
168 Todd Ewen
209 Joel Curtis
229 Simon Wheeldon
250 Darren Gani

President and General Manager

SATHER, GLEN CAMERON
President and General Manager, Edmonton Oilers.
Born in High River, Alta., Sept. 2, 1943.

The architect of the Edmonton Oilers' five Stanley Cup championships, Glen Sather is one of the most respected administrators in the NHL. The 1998-99 season is his 18th as general manager of the NHL Oilers and his 23rd with Edmonton since joining the organization in August of 1976.

Named coach and vice president of hockey operation for the Oilers when the franchise joined the NHL on June 15, 1979, Sather became coach, general manager and club president in May of 1980. He coached through the 1988-89 season and also returned for 60 games behind the bench in 1993-94. His .616 winning percentage in 842 regular-season games ranked seventh on the NHL's all-time coaching list. His playoff winning percentage of .706 ranks first.

Sather-coached teams won the Stanley Cup four times in the 1980s. As general manager, Sather was instrumental in the Oilers' fifth Cup triumph in 1990.

He has extensive international hockey experience, most recently as g.m. and coach of Team Canada at the 1996 World Cup of Hockey. He has also coached or managed tournament-winning teams at the Canada Cup and the IIHF World Championships.

Sather played for six different teams during a nine-year NHL career. He scored 80 goals in 658 games.

NHL Coaching Record

		Regular Season					Playoffs			
Season	Team	Games	W	L	T	%	Games	W	L	%
1979-80	Edmonton	80	28	39	13	.431	3	0	3	.000
1980-81	Edmonton	62	25	26	11	.492	9	5	4	.555
1981-82	Edmonton	80	48	17	15	.694	5	2	3	.400
1982-83	Edmonton	80	47	21	12	.663	16	11	5	.687
1983-84	Edmonton	80	57	18	5	.744	19	15	4	.789*
1984-85	Edmonton	80	49	20	11	.681	18	15	3	.833*
1985-86	Edmonton	80	56	17	7	.744	10	6	4	.600
1986-87	Edmonton	80	50	24	6	.663	21	16	5	.762*
1987-88	Edmonton	80	44	25	11	.619	18	16	2	.889*
1988-89	Edmonton	80	38	34	8	.538	7	3	4	.429
1993-94	Edmonton	60	22	27	11	.458	....	....	....	....
	NHL Totals	**842**	**464**	**268**	**110**	**.616**	**126**	**89**	**37**	**.706**

* Stanley Cup win.

Club Directory

Edmonton Oilers
11230 – 110 Street
Edmonton, Alberta T5G 3G8
Phone **403/414-4000**
Ticketing 403/414-4400
FAX 403/414-4659
Capacity: 17,099

Owner	Edmonton Investors Group Ltd.
Governor	Jim Hole
President/General Manager	Glen Sather
Executive Vice-President/Asst General Manager	Bruce MacGregor
Vice-President, Hockey Operations	Doug Risebrough
Coach	Ron Low
Assistant Coaches	Ted Green, Kevin Lowe
Chief Scout	Barry Fraser
Director of Player Personnel/Hockey Operations	Kevin Prendergast
Director of Hockey Administration	Peter Stephan
Video Coordinator	Brian Ross
Scouting Staff	Ed Chadwick, Brad Davis, Lorne Davis, Harry Howell, Gilles Leger, Chris McCarthy, Kent Nilsson, Dave Semenko, Tom Thompson
Executive Assistant to the President	Betsy Freedman
Executive Assistant to the Vice-President	Yvonne Ewaskow
Receptionist/Secretary	Cheryl Zaruk
Medical and Training Staff	
Athletic Trainer/Therapist	Ken Lowe
Equipment Manager	Barrie Stafford
Assistant Equipment Manager	Lyle Kulchisky
Massage Therapist	Stewart Poirier
Team Medical Chief of Staff/Director of Glen Sather Sports Medicine Clinic	Dr. David C. Reid
Team Physician	Dr. Boris Boyko
Team Dermatologist	Dr. Don Groot
Team Dentists	Dr. Tony Sneazwell, Dr. Brian Nord
Fitness Consultant	Dr. Art Quinney
Physical Therapy Consultant	Dr. Dave Magee
Team Acupuncturist	Dr. Steven Aung
Team Optometrist	Dr. Brent Saik
Fitness Consultant	Daryl Duke
Finance	
Vice President, Finance	Richard Hughes
Director of Fiance	Darryl Boessenkool
Manager of Human Resources	Pat Stanic
Financial Analysis	Colleen Stewart
Systems Administrator	Terry Rhoades, Kevin Miller
Finance Staff	Donna Chizen, Sahar Saloor, Lynn Schmidl
Public Relations	
Vice President, Public Relations	Bill Tuele
Information Coordinator	Steve Knowles
Public Relations Manager	Bryn Griffiths
Public & Community Relations Coordinator	Fiona Liew
Public Relations & Special Events Assistant	Warren Suitor
Business Operations	
Executive VP of Business Operations	Doug Piper
Vice President, Sponsorships, Sales & Services	Allan Watt
Vice President, Corporate Communications & Marketing	Trish Kerr
Manager, Corporate Sponsorships	Brad MacGregor
Manager, Corporate Sponsorships	Greg McDannold
Coordinator, Sponsorships, Sales & Services	Nicole Wiens
Sponsorships, Sales & Services Representative	Sean Price
Communications & Marketing Coordinator	Melanie Harysh
Director of Broadcast	Don Metz
Game Night Operations	Glenn Wiun
Coordinator of Publications	Amanda Ross
New Media Coordinator	Andreas Schwabe
Properties Department	
Director of Properties	Darrell Holowaychuk
Product Coordinator	Brent Gibbs
Properties Manager	Linda Malito
Administration/Staffing Coordinator	Heather Allen
Systems Coordinator	Lena Gilje
Mailorder Coordinator	Doug Allen
Warehouse Supervisor	Doug Wadlow
Ticketing Operations	
Director of Ticketing Operations	John Yeomans
Box Office Manager	Bob Haromy
Ticket Client Services	Sheila McCaskill, Marcella Kinsman, Sandy Langley, Sherry Smith
Suite Manager	Debra Rose
Ticketing Sales	
Director of Ticket Sales	Michael Lake
Sales & Marketing Assistant	Melanie Dudek
Group Sales Representatives	Greg Hope, Dean Skoubis
Corporate Sales Representatives	D'Arcy Evans, David Grout, Darren Simmons, Robbin Tylor, Mark Wollen
Edmonton Coliseum	
Opened	November 10, 1974
Location of Press Box	East Side at top (Radio/TV) West Side at top (Media)
Ends of Rink	Herculite extends above boards around rink
Team Information	
Training Camp Site	Edmonton Coliseum; Edmonton, Alberta
Television Outlets	A-Channel, CBXT TV (Channel 5, Cable 4), CTV Sports Net
Radio Station	630 CHED (AM), Rod Phillips (play-by-play), Morley Scott (colour)

Florida Panthers

1997-98 Results: 24W-43L-15T 63PTS. Sixth, Atlantic Division

Year-by-Year Record

		Home			Road			Overall							
Season	GP	W	L	T	W	L	T	W	L	T	GF	GA	Pts.	Finished	Playoff Result
1997-98	82	11	24	6	13	19	9	24	43	15	203	256	63	6th, Atlantic Div.	Out of Playoffs
1996-97	82	21	12	8	14	16	11	35	28	19	221	201	89	3rd, Atlantic Div.	Lost Conf. Quarter-Final
1995-96	82	25	12	4	16	19	6	41	31	10	254	234	92	3rd, Atlantic Div.	Lost Final
1994-95	48	9	12	3	11	10	3	20	22	6	115	127	46	5th, Atlantic Div.	Out of Playoffs
1993-94	84	15	18	9	18	16	8	33	34	17	233	233	83	5th, Atlantic Div.	Out of Playoffs

1998-99 Schedule

Oct.	Fri.	9	Tampa Bay
	Sat.	10	at Nashville
	Fri.	16	at Buffalo
	Wed.	21	Los Angeles
	Fri.	23	Vancouver
	Sat.	24	at Washington
	Wed.	28	Detroit
	Fri.	30	at Chicago
	Sat.	31	at New Jersey
Nov.	Mon.	2	at NY Islanders
	Wed.	4	Chicago
	Sat.	7	New Jersey*
	Wed.	11	NY Rangers
	Thu.	12	at Philadelphia
	Sat.	14	at Pittsburgh
	Thu.	19	at Boston
	Sat.	21	at New Jersey*
	Sun.	22	Philadelphia
	Wed.	25	Boston
	Fri.	27	at Tampa Bay
	Sat.	28	Buffalo
Dec.	Tue.	1	at NY Rangers
	Wed.	2	at Buffalo
	Sat.	5	Carolina
	Wed.	9	Ottawa
	Sat.	12	Calgary
	Wed.	16	Pittsburgh
	Sat.	19	Edmonton
	Wed.	23	Washington
	Sat.	26	at Tampa Bay
	Mon.	28	NY Islanders
	Wed.	30	at Pittsburgh
Jan.	Fri.	1	Carolina*
	Sat.	2	Pittsburgh
	Tue.	5	at Phoenix
	Wed.	6	at Colorado
	Fri.	8	at Vancouver
	Sun.	10	at Calgary*
	Wed.	13	Toronto
	Thu.	14	at Carolina
	Sat.	16	NY Islanders
	Mon.	18	Buffalo
	Wed.	20	at NY Islanders
	Thu.	21	at NY Rangers
	Tue.	26	at Philadelphia
	Wed.	27	Montreal
	Sat.	30	Dallas
Feb.	Wed.	3	Toronto
	Fri.	5	at Pittsburgh
	Sat.	6	at Carolina
	Mon.	8	St. Louis
	Thu.	11	at Ottawa
	Sat.	13	at Montreal
	Mon.	15	San Jose
	Wed.	17	at Dallas
	Thu.	18	at St. Louis
	Sat.	20	Phoenix
	Wed.	24	Philadelphia
	Fri.	26	at Detroit
	Sat.	27	at Toronto
Mar.	Wed.	3	Colorado
	Sat.	6	Carolina
	Mon.	8	at Montreal
	Tue.	9	at Boston
	Thu.	11	at Washington
	Sat.	13	Tampa Bay
	Wed.	17	at San Jose
	Sat.	20	at Los Angeles
	Sun.	21	at Anaheim
	Wed.	24	NY Rangers
	Fri.	26	Nashville
	Sun.	28	New Jersey
	Wed.	31	NY Islanders
Apr.	Thu.	1	at Washington
	Sat.	3	Ottawa
	Mon.	5	Washington
	Wed.	7	Boston
	Fri.	9	at Buffalo
	Sat.	10	at Toronto
	Mon.	12	at Ottawa
	Wed.	14	Montreal
	Sat.	17	Tampa Bay

* Denotes afternoon game.

Robert Svehla was the top-scoring defenseman in Florida for the third straight season with 43 points in 1997-98. He also led the club in assists (34) for the third year in a row.

Franchise date: June 14, 1993

EASTERN CONFERENCE
SOUTHEAST DIVISION

6th NHL Season

1998-99 Player Personnel

FORWARDS	HT	WT	S	Place of Birth	Date	1997-98 Club
BROWN, Mike	6-5	185	L	Surrey, B.C.	4/27/79	Kamloops
BUTSAYEV, Viacheslav	6-2	200	L	Togliatti, USSR	6/13/70	Fort Wayne
CABANA, Chad	6-1	200	L	Bonnyville, Alta.	10/1/74	New Haven-Fort Wayne
CICCARELLI, Dino	5-10	185	R	Sarnia, Ont.	2/8/60	Tampa Bay-Florida
DUERDEN, Dave	6-2	200	L	Oshawa, Ont.	4/11/77	P. Huron-New Haven-Fort Wayne
DVORAK, Radek	6-1	194	R	Tabor, Czech.	3/9/77	Florida
FERGUSON, Craig	5-11	190	L	Castro Valley, CA	4/8/70	New Haven
GAGNER, Dave	5-10	188	L	Chatham, Ont.	12/11/64	Florida
GARPENLOV, Johan	5-11	185	L	Stockholm, Sweden	3/21/68	Florida
HAY, Dwayne	6-1	183	L	London, Ont.	2/11/77	Wsh-Portland (AHL)-New Haven
JOHNSON, Ryan	6-2	185	L	Thunder Bay, Ont.	6/14/76	Florida-New Haven
KOZLOV, Viktor	6-5	232	R	Togliatti, USSR	2/14/75	San Jose-Florida-Russia
KVASHA, Oleg	6-5	205	R	Moscow, USSR	7/26/78	New Haven-Russia
LINDSAY, Bill	6-	195	L	Big Fork, MT	5/17/71	Florida
MELLANBY, Scott	6-1	205	R	Montreal, Que.	6/11/66	Florida
MULLER, Kirk	6-0	205	L	Kingston, Ont.	2/8/66	Florida
NEMIROVSKY, David	6-1	192	R	Toronto, Ont.	8/1/76	Florida-New Haven
NIEDERMAYER, Rob	6-2	204	L	Cassiar, B.C.	12/28/74	Florida
NILSON, Marcus	6-1	183	R	Stockholm, Sweden	3/1/78	Djurgarden
PARRISH, Mark	6-0	185	R	Edina, MN	2/2/77	United States-Seattle
POIRIER, Gaetan	6-2	200	L	Moncton, N.B.	12/28/76	Port Huron-Fort Wayne
VASILJEVS, Herbert	5-11	170	R	Riga, USSR	5/27/76	New Haven
WASHBURN, Steve	6-2	198	L	Ottawa, Ont.	4/10/75	Florida-New Haven
WELLS, Chris	6-6	223	L	Calgary, Alta.	11/12/75	Florida
WHITNEY, Ray	5-10	175	R	Fort Saskatchewan, Alta.	5/8/72	Edmonton-Florida-Canada
WORRELL, Peter	6-6	225	L	Pierre Fonds, Que.	8/18/77	Florida-New Haven
DEFENSEMEN						
ALLEN, Chris	6-2	193	R	Chatham, Ont.	5/8/78	Kingston-Florida
CARKNER, Terry	6-3	210	L	Smiths Falls, Ont.	3/7/66	Florida
JAKOPIN, John	6-5	220	R	Toronto, Ont.	5/16/75	Florida-New Haven
JOVANOVSKI, Ed	6-2	210	L	Windsor, Ont.	6/26/76	Florida-Canada
KUBA, Filip	6-3	202	L	Ostrava, Czech.	12/29/76	New Haven
LAUS, Paul	6-1	212	R	Beamsville, Ont.	9/26/70	Florida
MURPHY, Gord	6-2	195	R	Willowdale, Ont.	3/23/67	Florida-Canada
NORTON, Jeff	6-2	200	L	Acton, MA	11/25/65	Tampa Bay-Florida
SPACEK, Jaroslav	5-11	198	L	Rokycany, Czechoslovakia	2/11/74	Farjestad
SVEHLA, Robert	6-1	210	R	Martin, Czech.	1/2/69	Florida-Slovakia
WARRENER, Rhett	6-1	209	L	Shaunavon, Sask.	1/27/76	Florida
GOALTENDERS	**HT**	**WT**	**C**	**Place of Birth**	**Date**	**1997-98 Club**
LEMANOWICZ, David	6-2	190	L	Edmonton, Alta.	3/8/76	Tallahasee-New Haven
MacDONALD, Todd	6-0	167	L	Charlottetown, P.E.I.	7/5/75	Bir-Cin (IHL)-New Haven
McLEAN, Kirk	6-0	180	L	Willowdale, Ont.	6/26/66	Vancouver-Carolina-Florida
WEEKES, Kevin	6-0	195	L	Toronto, Ont.	4/4/75	Florida-Fort Wayne

1997-98 Scoring

* – rookie

Regular Season

Pos	#	Player	Team	GP	G	A	Pts	+/–	PIM	PP	SH	GW	GT	S	%
L	14	Ray Whitney	EDM	9	1	3	4	-1	0	0	0	0	0	19	5.3
			FLA	68	32	29	61	10	28	12	0	2	0	156	20.5
			TOTAL	77	33	32	65	9	28	12	0	2	0	175	18.9
C	15	Dave Gagner	FLA	78	20	28	48	-21	55	5	1	1	0	165	12.1
D	24	Robert Svehla	FLA	79	9	34	43	-3	113	3	0	0	0	144	6.3
R	27	Scott Mellanby	FLA	79	15	24	39	-14	127	6	0	1	0	188	8.0
R	19	Radek Dvorak	FLA	64	12	24	36	-1	33	2	3	0	1	112	10.7
R	22	Dino Ciccarelli	T.B.	34	11	6	17	-14	42	3	0	3	1	104	10.6
			FLA	28	5	11	16	-2	28	2	0	1	1	57	8.8
			TOTAL	62	16	17	33	-16	70	5	0	4	2	161	9.9
C	25	Viktor Kozlov	S.J.	18	5	2	7	-2	2	2	0	0	0	51	9.8
			FLA	46	12	11	23	-1	14	3	2	0	0	114	10.5
			TOTAL	64	17	13	30	-3	16	5	2	0	0	165	10.3
C	9	Kirk Muller	FLA	70	8	21	29	-14	54	1	0	3	1	115	7.0
L	11	Bill Lindsay	FLA	82	12	16	28	-2	80	0	2	5	0	150	8.0
D	55	Ed Jovanovski	FLA	81	9	14	23	-12	158	2	1	3	1	142	6.3
R	51	David Nemirovsky	FLA	41	9	12	21	-3	8	2	0	1	0	62	14.5
C	17 *	Steve Washburn	FLA	58	11	8	19	-6	32	4	0	2	0	61	18.0
D	5	Gord Murphy	FLA	79	6	11	17	-3	46	3	0	0	0	123	4.9
D	6	Jeff Norton	T.B.	37	4	6	10	-25	26	4	0	0	1	41	9.8
			FLA	19	0	7	7	-7	18	0	0	0	0	20	0.0
			TOTAL	56	4	13	17	-32	44	4	0	0	1	61	6.6
C	44	Rob Niedermayer	FLA	33	8	7	15	-9	41	5	0	2	0	64	12.5
C	23	Chris Wells	FLA	61	5	10	15	4	47	0	1	0	0	57	8.8
D	3	Paul Laus	FLA	77	0	11	11	-5	293	0	0	0	0	64	0.0
D	2	Terry Carkner	FLA	74	1	7	8	6	63	0	0	1	0	34	2.9
L	29	Johan Garpenlov	FLA	39	2	3	5	-6	8	0	0	0	0	43	4.7
D	7	Rhett Warrener	FLA	79	0	4	4	-16	99	0	0	0	0	66	0.0
G	34	J. Vanbiesbrouck	FLA	60	0	3	3	0	6	0	0	0	0	0	0.0
C	16 *	Ryan Johnson	FLA	10	0	2	2	-4	0	0	0	0	0	6	0.0
D	8	Dallas Eakins	FLA	23	0	1	1	1	44	0	0	0	0	16	0.0
G	1	Kirk McLean	VAN	29	0	0	0	0	0	0	0	0	0	0	0.0
			CAR	8	0	1	1	0	0	0	0	0	0	0	0.0
			FLA	7	0	0	0	0	0	0	0	0	0	0	0.0
			TOTAL	44	0	1	1	0	0	0	0	0	0	0	0.0
D	12 *	Chris Allen	FLA	1	0	0	0	0	2	0	0	0	0	1	0.0
D	4 *	John Jakopin	FLA	2	0	0	0	-3	4	0	0	0	0	1	0.0
G	1 *	Kevin Weekes	FLA	11	0	0	0	0	0	0	0	0	0	0	0.0
L	28 *	Peter Worrell	FLA	19	0	0	0	-4	153	0	0	0	0	15	0.0

Goaltending

No.	Goaltender	GPI	Mins	Avg	W	L	T	EN	SO	GA	SA	S%
34	J. Vanbiesbrouck	60	3451	2.87	18	29	11	4	4	165	1638	.899
30	Mark Fitzpatrick	12	640	3.00	2	7	2	0	1	32	265	.879
1	Kirk McLean	7	406	3.25	4	2	1	0	0	22	207	.894
1	* Kevin Weekes	11	485	3.96	0	5	1	1	0	32	247	.870
	Totals	**82**	**5009**	**3.07**	**24**	**43**	**15**	**5**	**5**	**256**	**2362**	**.892**

Ray Whitney established career highs in goals, assists and points during his first season with Florida in 1997-98. He led the club with 32 goals and 61 points and was second on the team with 29 assists.

General Manager

MURRAY, BRYAN CLARENCE
Vice President and General Manager, Florida Panthers.
Born in Shawville, Que., December 5, 1942.

Bryan, 55, is entering his fifth season as vice president and general manager of the Panthers.

Before joining the Panthers, he served as coach and general manager of the Detroit Red Wings from 1990-93 and as general manager during the 1993-94 campaign. In 328 games under Murray's control, the Wings won a total of 170 games, while losing 121 and tying 37, an average of 43 wins and 94 points a season. Bryan left his mark in the NHL record book as a coach with a career record of 484-368-123 (.559 winning pct.) in 975 regular-season games, placing him seventh on the all-time victory list.

Murray broke into the NHL coaching ranks with the Washington Capitals on November 11, 1981. He spent the next 8½ seasons with the Caps and earned the Jack Adams Award as the NHL's coach of the year in 1983-84. In 1988-89, he led the Capitals to the Patrick Division title, the only first-place finish in team history. On January 15, 1990, Bryan was replaced by his brother, Terry.

Born in Shawville, Quebec on Dec. 5, 1942, Bryan is a graduate of McGill University in Montreal. He spent four years as athletic director and hockey coach at the school before leaving to coach the Regina Pats to a WHL title in 1979-80. Bryan moved up to the Hershey Bears (AHL) the following season and was named *The Hockey News'* minor league coach of the year after guiding that team to its best record in 40 years.

Bryan and his wife, Geri, have two daughters, Heide, 27 and Brittany 13.

Captains' History

Brian Skrudland, 1993-94 to 1996-97; Scott Mellanby, 1997-98 to date.

General Managers' History

Bob Clarke, 1993-94; Bryan Murray, 1994-95 to date.

NHL Coaching Record

		Regular Season					Playoffs			
Season	Team	Games	W	L	T	%	Games	W	L	%
1981-82	Washington	76	25	28	13	.477	....	....	....	....
1982-83	Washington	80	39	25	16	.588	4	1	3	.250
1983-84	Washington	80	48	27	5	.631	8	4	4	.500
1984-85	Washington	80	46	25	9	.631	5	2	3	.400
1985-86	Washington	80	50	23	7	.669	9	5	4	.556
1986-87	Washington	80	38	32	10	.538	7	3	4	.429
1987-88	Washington	80	38	33	9	.531	14	7	7	.500
1988-89	Washington	80	41	29	10	.575	6	2	4	.333
1989-90	Washington	46	18	24	4	.435	....	....	....	....
1990-91	Detroit	80	34	38	8	.475	7	3	4	.429
1991-92	Detroit	80	43	25	12	.613	11	4	7	.364
1992-93	Detroit	84	47	28	9	.613	7	3	4	.429
1997-98	Florida	59	17	31	11	.381	....	....	....	....
	NHL Totals	**975**	**484**	**368**	**123**	**.559**	**78**	**34**	**44**	**.436**

Club Records

Team

(Figures in brackets for season records are games played; records for fewest points, wins, ties, losses, goals, goals against are for 70 or more games)

Most Points	**92**	1995-96 (82)
Most Wins	**41**	1995-96 (82)
Most Ties	**19**	1996-97 (82)
Most Losses	**43**	1997-98 (82)
Most Goals	**254**	1995-96 (82)
Most Goals Against	**256**	1997-98 (82)
Fewest Points	**63**	1997-98 (82)
Fewest Wins	**24**	1997-98 (82)
Fewest Ties	**10**	1995-96 (82)
Fewest Losses	**28**	1996-97 (82)
Fewest Goals	**203**	1997-98 (82)
Fewest Goals Against	**201**	1996-97 (82)
Longest Winning Streak		
Overall	**7**	Nov. 2-14/95
Home	**5**	Nov. 5-14/95
Away	**4**	Dec. 2-12/95, Nov. 13-Dec 1/96, Oct. 25-Nov. 22/97
Longest Undefeated Streak		
Overall	**12**	Oct. 5-30/96 (8 wins, 4 ties)
Home	**8**	Nov. 5-26/95 (7 wins, 1 tie)
Away	**7**	Twice
Longest Losing Streak		
Overall	**13**	Feb. 7-Mar. 23/98
Home	**6**	Feb. 25-Mar. 23/98
Away	**7**	Feb. 7-Mar. 21/98
Longest Winless Streak		
Overall	**15**	Feb. 1-Mar. 23/98 (14 losses, 1 tie)
Home	**8**	Feb. 1-Mar. 23/98 (7 losses, 1 tie)
Away	**16**	Jan. 2-Mar. 21/98 (12 losses, 4 ties)
Most Shutouts, Season	**6**	1994-95 (48)
Most PIM, Season	**1,676**	1997-98 (82)
Most Goals, Game	**10**	Nov. 26/97 (Bos. 5 at Fla. 10)

Individual

Most Seasons	**5**	Several Players
Most Games	**368**	Scott Mellanby
Most Goals, Career	**117**	Scott Mellanby
Most Assists, Career	**133**	Scott Mellanby
Most Points, Career	**250**	Scott Mellanby (117G, 133A)
Most PIM, Career	**1,089**	Paul Laus
Most Shutouts, Career	**13**	John Vanbiesbrouck
Longest Consecutive Games Streak	**221**	Robert Svehla
Most Goals, Season	**32**	Scott Mellanby (1995-96); Ray Whitney (1997-98)
Most Assists, Season	**49**	Robert Svehla (1995-96)
Most Points, Season	**70**	Scott Mellanby (1995-96; 32G, 38A)
Most PIM, Season	**313**	Paul Laus (1996-97)
Most Shutouts, Season	**4**	John Vanbiesbrouck (1994-95, 1997-98)
Most Points, Defenseman, Season	**57**	Robert Svehla (1995-96; 8G, 49A)
Most Points, Center, Season	**61**	Rob Niedermayer (1995-96; 26G, 35A)
Most Points, Right Wing, Season	**70**	Scott Mellanby (1995-96; 32G, 38A)
Most Points, Left Wing, Season	**61**	Ray Whitney (1997-98; 32G, 29A)
Most Points, Rookie, Season	**50**	Jesse Belanger (1993-94; 17G, 33A)
Most Goals, Game	**3**	Seven times
Most Assists, Game	**4**	Scott Mellanby (Nov. 26/97)
Most Points, Game	**4**	Jesse Belanger (Jan. 19/94; 2G, 2A); Scott Mellanby (Jan. 4/97; 1G, 3A), (Nov. 26/97; 4A); Ray Whitney (Nov. 26/97; 2G, 2A)

All-time Record vs. Other Clubs

Regular Season

	At Home							On Road							Total						
	GP	W	L	T	GF	GA	PTS	GP	W	L	T	GF	GA	PTS	GP	W	L	T	GF	GA	PTS
Anaheim	4	1	1	2	10	11	4	4	2	2	0	12	16	4	8	3	3	2	22	27	8
Boston	9	4	5	0	28	27	8	10	5	3	2	28	25	12	19	9	8	2	56	52	20
Buffalo	9	5	4	0	27	28	10	10	2	7	1	14	38	5	19	7	11	1	41	66	15
Calgary	4	2	2	0	8	9	4	4	1	2	1	9	10	3	8	3	4	1	17	19	7
Carolina	10	5	3	2	29	19	12	10	6	4	0	30	30	12	20	11	7	2	59	49	24
Chicago	4	1	3	0	12	19	2	4	2	1	1	15	13	5	8	3	4	1	27	32	7
Colorado	7	1	6	0	17	28	2	6	2	2	2	17	17	6	13	3	8	2	34	45	8
Dallas	4	2	1	1	14	12	5	4	1	1	2	12	15	4	8	3	2	3	26	27	9
Detroit	4	1	2	1	9	10	3	4	1	3	0	10	16	2	8	2	5	1	19	26	5
Edmonton	4	2	1	1	12	12	5	4	2	2	0	10	12	4	8	4	3	1	22	24	9
Los Angeles	4	2	0	2	13	6	6	4	2	2	0	14	11	4	8	4	2	2	27	17	10
Montreal	10	4	4	2	36	30	10	9	4	4	1	22	28	9	19	8	8	3	58	58	19
New Jersey	13	6	4	3	31	28	15	12	4	6	2	23	32	10	25	10	10	5	54	60	25
NY Islanders	12	6	3	3	37	32	15	13	7	4	2	32	28	16	25	13	7	5	69	60	31
NY Rangers	13	5	7	1	32	41	11	12	4	4	4	30	32	12	25	9	11	5	62	73	23
Ottawa	10	6	3	1	34	25	13	10	5	3	2	33	25	12	20	11	6	3	67	50	25
Philadelphia	12	3	9	0	32	43	6	13	5	5	3	32	29	13	25	8	14	3	64	72	19
Phoenix	4	1	3	0	10	12	2	5	2	2	1	14	13	5	9	3	5	1	24	25	7
Pittsburgh	10	5	5	0	27	25	10	10	2	6	2	29	36	6	20	7	11	2	56	61	16
St. Louis	4	1	2	1	8	10	3	4	1	3	0	9	13	2	8	2	5	1	17	23	5
San Jose	4	1	0	3	11	8	5	4	1	1	2	10	8	4	8	2	1	5	21	16	9
Tampa Bay	12	8	2	2	32	18	18	13	5	4	4	34	29	14	25	13	6	6	66	47	32
Toronto	5	1	2	2	13	13	4	4	1	3	0	12	13	2	9	2	5	2	25	26	6
Vancouver	4	2	1	1	11	11	5	4	1	1	2	10	14	4	8	3	2	3	21	25	9
Washington	13	6	5	2	40	36	14	12	4	5	3	32	35	11	25	10	10	5	72	71	25
Totals	**189**	**81**	**78**	**30**	**533**	**513**	**192**	**189**	**72**	**80**	**37**	**493**	**538**	**181**	**378**	**153**	**158**	**67**	**1026**	**1051**	**373**

Playoffs

	Series	W	L	GP	W	L	T	GF	GA	Last Mtg.	Round	Result
Boston	1	1	0	5	4	1	0	22	16	1996	CQF	W 4-1
Colorado	1	0	1	4	0	4	0	4	15	1996	F	L 0-4
NY Rangers	1	0	1	5	1	4	0	10	13	1997	CQF	L 1-4
Philadelphia	1	1	0	6	4	2	0	15	11	1996	CSF	W 4-2
Pittsburgh	1	1	0	7	4	3	0	20	15	1996	CF	W 4-3
Totals	**5**	**3**	**2**	**27**	**13**	**14**	**0**	**71**	**70**			

Playoff Results 1998-94

Year	Round	Opponent	Result	GF	GA
1997	CQF	NY Rangers	L 1-4	10	13
1996	F	Colorado	L 0-4	4	15
	CF	Pittsburgh	W 4-3	20	15
	CSF	Philadelphia	W 4-2	15	11
	CQF	Boston	W 4-1	22	16

Abbreviations: Round: F – Final; **CF** – conference final; **CQF** – conference quarter-final; **CSF** – conference semi-final.

Colorado totals include Quebec, 1993-94 to 1994-95. Carolina totals include Hartford, 1993-94 to 1996-97.
Phoenix totals include Winnipeg, 1993-94 to 1995-96.

1997-98 Results

Oct.	1	at	Philadelphia	1-3		2	at	Tampa Bay	2-2
	4	at	Pittsburgh	5-3		4		Anaheim	3-3
	11	at	St. Louis	3-5		7	at	Edmonton	2-3
	13		NY Islanders	2-2		9	at	Calgary	3-3
	15		Tampa Bay	2-1		10	at	Vancouver	2-2
	16	at	Dallas	0-4		12	at	Colorado	1-3
	19		Pittsburgh	1-4		14	at	Phoenix	2-3
	22	at	Montreal	0-3		21	at	Anaheim	3-8
	23	at	Ottawa	2-2		22	at	Los Angeles	1-3
	25	at	Boston	5-4		24	at	San Jose	1-1
	28		Los Angeles	2-2		27		Carolina	3-0
	30		Ottawa	2-5		29		Dallas	3-2
Nov.	1		Buffalo	3-4		31		Tampa Bay	2-0
	5		New Jersey	2-4	**Feb.**	1		Buffalo	2-5
	6	at	Buffalo	4-2		3		Detroit	1-1
	9		Washington	3-2		7	at	Toronto	2-3
	12		NY Islanders	2-2		25		New Jersey	2-3
	14		Philadelphia	2-5		27	at	Detroit	1-3
	15	at	NY Islanders	1-0	**Mar.**	4		NY Rangers	3-4
	18		NY Rangers	1-3		7	at	Washington	3-6
	20		Calgary	1-2		9	at	Montreal	1-6
	22	at	New Jersey	2-1		11	at	Ottawa	3-5
	23		Washington	2-5		13		Edmonton	0-4
	26		Boston	10-5		15		Chicago	4-8
	28		Colorado	2-3		17		Vancouver	2-4
	30	at	NY Rangers	1-1		19	at	Buffalo	1-6
Dec.	1		Phoenix	2-3		21	at	Tampa Bay	1-5
	5	at	Washington	2-3		23		Carolina	3-5
	7		Washington	5-4		26		Montreal	5-4
	10	at	Carolina	5-2		28	at	Boston	3-2
	12	at	NY Rangers	4-3		29	at	Chicago	4-0
	13	at	NY Islanders	1-4	**Apr.**	1		Montreal	3-4
	15		Boston	2-6		4	at	Philadelphia	4-1
	17		NY Rangers	2-4		5		Pittsburgh	3-1
	18	at	Washington	4-0		7		Toronto	1-3
	20	at	Philadelphia	0-2		9		Philadelphia	3-2
	23		St. Louis	2-3		11	at	Pittsburgh	3-3
	26	at	Carolina	5-2		12	at	New Jersey	5-5
	27	at	NY Islanders	6-2		14		Ottawa	2-3
	30		San Jose	2-2		16		Philadelphia	3-7
Jan.	1		New Jersey	2-1		18	at	Tampa Bay	2-2

Entry Draft Selections 1998-93

1998

Pick	
30	Kyle Rossiter
61	Joe DiPenta
63	Lance Ward
89	Ryan Jardine
117	Jaroslav Spacek
148	Chris Ovington
176	B.J. Ketcheson
203	Ian Jacobs
231	Adrian Wischer

1997

Pick	
20	Mike Brown
47	Kristian Huselius
56	Vratislav Cech
74	Nick Smith
95	Ivan Novoseltsev
127	Pat Parthenais
155	Keith Delaney
183	Tyler Palmer
211	Doug Schueller
237	Benoit Cote

1996

Pick	
20	Marcus Nilson
60	Chris Allen
65	Oleg Kvasha
82	Joey Tetarenko
129	Andrew Long
156	Gaetan Poirier
183	Alexandre Couture
209	Denis Khloptonov
235	Russell Smith

1995

Pick	
10	Radek Dvorak
36	Aaron MacDonald
62	Mike O'Grady
80	Dave Duerden
88	Daniel Tjarnqvist
114	Francois Cloutier
166	Peter Worrell
192	Filip Kuba
218	David Lemanowicz

1994

Pick	
1	Ed Jovanovski
27	Rhett Warrener
31	Jason Podollan
36	Ryan Johnson
84	David Nemirovsky
105	Dave Geris
157	Matt O'Dette
183	Jasson Boudrias
235	Tero Lehtera
261	Per Gustafsson

1993

Pick	
5	Rob Niedermayer
41	Kevin Weekes
57	Chris Armstrong
67	Mikael Tjallden
78	Steve Washburn
83	Bill McCauley
109	Todd MacDonald
135	Alain Nasreddine
161	Trevor Doyle
187	Briane Thompson
213	Chad Cabana
239	John Demarco
265	Eric Montreuil

Coaching History

Roger Neilson, 1993-94, 1994-95; Doug MacLean, 1995-96, 1996-97; Doug MacLean and Bryan Murray, 1997-98; Terry Murray, 1998-99.

Coach

MURRAY, TERRY RODNEY
Coach, Florida Panthers. Born in Shawville, Que., July 20, 1950.

Florida vice president and general manager Bryan Murray appointed his brother Terry Murray to the Panthers coaching position on June 21, 1998. Terry becomes the fourth coach in franchise history, taking over from his brother who served on an interim basis after taking over from Doug MacLean during the 1997-98 season. Terry previously took over the coaching reigns from Bryan when he replaced him as bench boss with the Washington Capitals during the 1989-90 campaign.

Terry Murray, 48, has spent eight seasons as an NHL head coach and has a career coaching record of 281-198-58 for a .577 winning percentage. He has posted winning records in seven of his eight NHL seasons. His teams have never missed the playoffs and have never finished below third place in their division.

Murray was named head coach of the Philadelphia Flyers on June 23, 1994 and coached the team for three seasons. He compiled a record of 118-64-30 and won two Atlantic Division titles. Murray was a finalist for the Jack Adams Award as coach of the year following the 1994-95 season and guided the Flyers to the Stanley Cup finals in 1997. His playoff winning percentage of .609 in Philadelphia is better than Fred Shero (.578), Pat Quinn (.564) or Mike Keenan (.561).

Terry replaced Bryan as coach of the Capitals back on January 15, 1990. In his first full season behind the bench in 1990-91, he led Washington to the Wales Conference finals for the first time in club history. During his tenure with the Capitals, Murray had a record of 163-134-28. In between his coaching stints in Washington and Philadelphia, he served briefly as coach of the Panthers' International Hockey League affiliate in Cincinnati. Murray had a record of 17-7-4 in 28 games with the Cyclones to close out the 1993-94 season and guide them to a second-place finish in the IHL's Central Division.

Over a 12-year professional playing career, Terry Murray appeared in 302 NHL regular-season games with the California Golden Seals, Philadelphia Flyers, Detroit Red Wings and Washington Capitals. He had four goals and 76 assists for 80 points and had 199 penalty minutes. Terry and his wife Linda have two daughters, Megan and Lindsey.

Coaching Record

		Regular Season					Playoffs			
Season	**Team**	**Games**	**W**	**L**	**T**	**%**	**Games**	**W**	**L**	**%**
1988-89	Baltimore (AHL)	80	30	46	4	.400	....	....	....	....
1989-90	Baltimore (AHL)	44	26	17	1	.603	....	....	....	....
1989-90	**Washington (NHL)**	**34**	**18**	**14**	**2**	**.559**	**15**	**8**	**7**	**.533**
1990-91	**Washington (NHL)**	**80**	**37**	**36**	**7**	**.506**	**11**	**5**	**6**	**.455**
1991-92	**Washington (NHL)**	**80**	**45**	**27**	**8**	**.613**	**7**	**3**	**4**	**.429**
1992-93	**Washington (NHL)**	**84**	**43**	**34**	**7**	**.554**	**6**	**2**	**4**	**.333**
1993-94	**Washington (NHL)**	**47**	**20**	**23**	**4**	**.468**	....	....	....	....
	Cincinnati (IHL)	28	17	7	4	.679	11	6	5	.545
1994-95	**Philadelphia (NHL)**	**48**	**28**	**16**	**4**	**.625**	**15**	**10**	**5**	**.667**
1995-96	**Philadelphia (NHL)**	**82**	**45**	**24**	**13**	**.628**	**12**	**6**	**6**	**.500**
1996-97	**Philadelphia (NHL)**	**82**	**45**	**24**	**13**	**.628**	**19**	**12**	**7**	**.632**
	NHL Totals	**537**	**281**	**198**	**58**	**.577**	**85**	**46**	**39**	**.541**

Club Directory

National Car Rental Center
One Panthers Parkway
Sunrise, FL 33323
Phone **954/835-7000**
FAX 954/835-7600
Website: www.flpanthers.com
Capacity: 19,200

Chairman and CEO	H. Wayne Huizenga
President & Governor	William A. Torrey
Special Consultant	Richard C. Rochon
Executive Assistants to President	Deanna Cocozzelli, Cathy Stevenson
Hockey Operations	
Vice President and General Manager	Bryan Murray
Assistant General Manager	Chuck Fletcher
Head Coach	Terry Murray
Assistant Coaches	Bill Smith, Slavomir Lener
Pro Scouts	Micheal Abbamont, Duane Sutter
Director of Amateur Scouting	Tim Murray
Director of Player Development	Paul Henry
Amateur Scouts	Ron Harris, Matti Vaisanen, Wayne Meier, Billy Dea
Executive Assistant to Vice President and General Manager	Vanessa Rey
Head Medical Trainer	David Smith
Equipment Manager	Mark Brennan
Associate Equipment Managers	Tim LeRoy, Scott Tinkler
Team Services Coordinator	Marni Share
Equipment Staff Assistant	Andre Szucko
Internist	Charles Posternack, M.D.
Orthopedic Surgeon	David E. Attarian, M.D.
Assistant Physicians	Stephen R. Southworth, M.D., James Guerra, M.D.
Team Cardiologist	Howard Bush, M.D.
Plastic Surgeon	Harry K. Moon
Team Dentist	Marty Robins, D.D.S.
Minor League Affiliates	New Haven (AHL), Fort Wayne (IHL), Miami (ECHL) & Port Huron (UHL)
Marketing Department	
Vice President of Marketing	Declan J. Bolger
Director of Season & Group Sales	Chris Trinceri
Director of Game Day Presentation	Scott Cunningham
Senior Manager of Promotions	Ed Krajewski
Promotions Coordinator	Tim Dieter
Mascot Coordinator	Phil Crowhurst
Account Executives	Christopher Brown, Brent Flahr, Leo Sarmiento, Valerie Stephens
Executive Assistant to Vice President of Marketing	Janine Shea
Admin. Assistant, Promotions and Sales	TBA
Corporate Sales Department	
Vice President of Corporate Sales & Sponsorship	Kimberly Terranova
Manager of Corporate Sales & Sponsorship	Scott Baynes
Corporate Account Manager	Brette Sadler
Corporate Sales Account Executive	Craig Petrus
Corporate Sales Coordinator	Shelly Londer
Administrative Assistant to Vice President of Corporate Sales & Sponsorship	Susan Ferro
Ticket/Event Operations	
Vice President of Operations	Steve Dangerfield
Director of Ticket Operations	Scott Wampold
Director of Merchandising	Ron Dennis
Manager of Ticket Operations	Matt Coyne
Ticket Operations Coordinator	Lauri Carr
Retail Manager	Maria Medina
Buyer	Jennifer Borell
Inventory Operations Supervisor	Beatrice Cutter
Executive Assistant to Vice President of Operations	Mary Lou Poag
Admin. Assistant to Director of Merchandising	Alex Rodriguez
Communications Department	
Director of Communications	Mike Hanson
Communications Manager	Tom Ziermann
Publications Manager	Jon Kramer
Youth & Amateur Hockey Programs Manager	Liz Ridley
Assistant to the Director of Communications	Stephanie Cuzzacrea
Archives Manager	Jonas Kalkstein
Finance & Administration	
Director of Finance/Controller	Evelyn Lopez
Manager of Information Systems	Kelly Connor
Manager of Payroll/Human Resources	Mary Santimaw
Office Manager	Laura Barrera
Accounting Manager	Kelley Donado
Staff Accountant, Accounts Receivable	Ana Carrasquilla
Staff Accountant, Accounts Payable	Tammy Gasiorek
Office Services Analyst	Kerri Gustin
Systems Analyst	Jon Paul Hernandez
Human Resources Administrator	Rachel Levine
Payroll Coordinator	Gloria Julienne
Receptionist	Marilyn Klees
Office Services Coordinator	Anthony Vandaley
Office Services Assistant	Lee Bancroft
Administrative Assistant to Director of Finance/Controller	Cathy Cuffe
General Information	
Press Box Phone	(954) 835-7801
Dimensions of Rink	200 feet by 85 feet
Team Colors	Red, Navy Blue, Yellow, Gold
Television	SportsChannel
Television Announcers	Jeff Rimer, Denis Potvin, Randy Moller
Radio Flagship	WQAM 560 AM
Radio Announcers	Chris Moore, Randy Moller, Steve Goldstein
Spanish Radio Announcers	Felix DeJesus, Omar Salazar

Los Angeles Kings

1997-98 Results: 38W-33L-11T 87PTS. Second, Pacific Division

1998-99 Schedule

Oct.	Sat.	10	at Edmonton
	Mon.	12	at Vancouver*
	Fri.	16	Boston
	Sun.	18	Colorado
	Wed.	21	at Florida
	Fri.	23	at Tampa Bay
	Sun.	25	at Carolina
	Tue.	27	at NY Islanders
	Wed.	28	at New Jersey
	Fri.	30	Tampa Bay
Nov.	Sun.	1	Phoenix
	Thu.	5	St. Louis
	Sat.	7	Dallas
	Mon.	9	at Vancouver
	Tue.	10	at Calgary
	Thu.	12	Nashville
	Sat.	14	Carolina
	Mon.	16	at Anaheim
	Wed.	18	at San Jose
	Thu.	19	NY Rangers
	Sat.	21	Chicago
	Sat.	28	Phoenix
	Mon.	30	at Montreal
Dec.	Wed.	2	at Toronto
	Thu.	3	at Ottawa
	Sat.	5	Detroit
	Wed.	9	Washington
	Sat.	12	Vancouver
	Sun.	13	at Anaheim
	Thu.	17	NY Islanders
	Sat.	19	at St. Louis
	Sun.	20	at Chicago
	Tue.	22	at Pittsburgh
	Sat.	26	Phoenix
	Mon.	28	at Phoenix
	Wed.	30	San Jose
Jan.	Sat.	2	Colorado
	Tue.	5	at Edmonton
	Thu.	7	Buffalo
	Sat.	9	Edmonton
	Mon.	11	at San Jose
	Thu.	14	Calgary
	Sat.	16	Pittsburgh
	Tue.	19	Colorado
	Thu.	21	New Jersey
	Wed.	27	at Dallas
	Fri.	29	at Washington
	Sat.	30	at Buffalo
Feb.	Mon.	1	at Philadelphia
	Thu.	4	Chicago
	Sat.	6	San Jose
	Wed.	10	at Phoenix
	Thu.	11	Philadelphia
	Sat.	13	Dallas
	Mon.	15	Anaheim
	Thu.	18	Edmonton
	Sat.	20	at Calgary
	Mon.	22	at St. Louis
	Wed.	24	at Detroit
	Fri.	26	at Chicago
	Sun.	28	at Dallas*
Mar.	Wed.	3	at Anaheim
	Thu.	4	Nashville
	Sat.	6	Calgary
	Tue.	9	Detroit
	Sat.	13	Vancouver
	Mon.	15	Ottawa
	Thu.	18	Anaheim
	Sat.	20	Florida
	Sun.	21	at Phoenix
	Thu.	25	Dallas
	Sun.	28	at Colorado*
	Tue.	30	at Boston
	Wed.	31	at Detroit
Apr.	Sat.	3	at Nashville
	Mon.	5	at Colorado
	Thu.	8	San Jose
	Sun.	11	at Dallas*
	Mon.	12	at Nashville
	Thu.	15	Anaheim
	Fri.	16	at San Jose
	Sun.	18	St. Louis*

* Denotes afternoon game.

Rob Blake led all NHL defensemen with a career-high 23 goals in 1997-98. He earned the Norris Trophy and helped the Kings make the playoffs for the first time since reaching the Stanley Cup finals in 1993. He also represented Canada at the Nagano Olympics, where he was named the tournament's top defenseman.

Franchise date: June 5, 1967

PACIFIC DIVISION

32nd NHL Season

Year-by-Year Record

		Home			Road			Overall							
Season	GP	W	L	T	W	L	T	W	L	T	GF	GA	Pts.	Finished	Playoff Result
1997-98	82	22	16	3	16	17	8	38	33	11	227	225	87	2nd, Pacific Div.	Lost Conf. Quater-Final
1996-97	82	18	16	7	10	27	4	28	43	11	214	268	67	6th, Pacific Div.	Out of Playoffs
1995-96	82	16	16	9	8	24	9	24	40	18	256	302	66	6th, Pacific Div.	Out of Playoffs
1994-95	48	7	11	6	9	12	3	16	23	9	142	174	41	4th, Pacific Div.	Out of Playoffs
1993-94	84	18	19	5	9	26	7	27	45	12	294	322	66	5th, Pacific Div.	Out of Playoffs
1992-93	84	22	15	5	17	20	5	39	35	10	338	340	88	3rd, Smythe Div.	Lost Final
1991-92	80	20	11	9	15	20	5	35	31	14	287	296	84	2nd, Smythe Div.	Lost Div. Semi-Final
1990-91	80	26	9	5	20	15	5	46	24	10	340	254	102	1st, Smythe Div.	Lost Div. Final
1989-90	80	21	16	3	13	23	4	34	39	7	338	337	75	4th, Smythe Div.	Lost Div. Final
1988-89	80	25	12	3	17	19	4	42	31	7	376	335	91	2nd, Smythe Div.	Lost Div. Final
1987-88	80	19	18	3	11	24	5	30	42	8	318	359	68	4th, Smythe Div.	Lost Div. Semi-Final
1986-87	80	20	17	3	11	24	5	31	41	8	318	341	70	4th, Smythe Div.	Lost Div. Semi-Final
1985-86	80	9	27	4	14	22	4	23	49	8	284	389	54	5th, Smythe Div.	Out of Playoffs
1984-85	80	20	14	6	14	18	8	34	32	14	339	326	82	4th, Smythe Div.	Lost Div. Semi-Final
1983-84	80	13	19	8	10	25	5	23	44	13	309	376	59	5th, Smythe Div.	Out of Playoffs
1982-83	80	20	13	7	7	28	5	27	41	12	308	365	66	5th, Smythe Div.	Out of Playoffs
1981-82	80	19	15	6	5	26	9	24	41	15	314	369	63	4th, Smythe Div.	Lost Div. Final
1980-81	80	22	11	7	21	13	6	43	24	13	337	290	99	2nd, Norris Div.	Lost Prelim. Round
1979-80	80	18	13	9	12	23	5	30	36	14	290	313	74	2nd, Norris Div.	Lost Prelim. Round
1978-79	80	20	13	7	14	21	5	34	34	12	292	286	80	3rd, Norris Div.	Lost Prelim. Round
1977-78	80	18	16	6	13	18	9	31	34	15	243	245	77	3rd, Norris Div.	Lost Prelim. Round
1976-77	80	20	13	7	14	18	8	34	31	15	271	241	83	2nd, Norris Div.	Lost Quarter-Final
1975-76	80	22	13	5	16	20	4	38	33	9	263	265	85	2nd, Norris Div.	Lost Quarter-Final
1974-75	80	22	7	11	20	10	10	42	17	21	269	185	105	2nd, Norris Div.	Lost Prelim. Round
1973-74	78	22	13	4	11	20	8	33	33	12	233	231	78	3rd, West Div.	Lost Quarter-Final
1972-73	78	21	11	7	10	25	4	31	36	11	232	245	73	6th, West Div.	Out of Playoffs
1971-72	78	14	23	2	6	26	7	20	49	9	206	305	49	7th, West Div.	Out of Playoffs
1970-71	78	17	14	8	8	26	5	25	40	13	239	303	63	5th, West Div.	Out of Playoffs
1969-70	76	12	22	4	2	30	6	14	52	10	168	290	38	6th, West Div.	Out of Playoffs
1968-69	76	19	14	5	5	28	5	24	42	10	185	260	58	4th, West Div.	Lost Semi-Final
1967-68	74	20	13	4	11	20	6	31	33	10	200	224	72	2nd, West Div.	Lost Quarter-Final

1998-99 Player Personnel

FORWARDS	HT	WT	S	Place of Birth	Date	1997-98 Club
BARNEY, Scott	6-4	198	R	Oshawa, Ont.	3/27/79	Peterborough
BYLSMA, Dan	6-2	209	L	Grand Haven, MI	9/19/70	Los Angeles-Long Beach
COURTNALL, Russ	5-11	185	R	Duncan, B.C.	6/2/65	Los Angeles
FERRARO, Ray	5-9	193	L	Trail, B.C.	8/23/64	Los Angeles
GREEN, Josh	6-4	212	L	Camrose, Alta.	11/16/77	Swft-Port (WHL)-Fred
JOHNSON, Craig	6-2	197	L	St. Paul, MN	3/8/72	Los Angeles
JOHNSON, Matt	6-5	232	L	Welland, Ont.	11/23/75	Los Angeles
JOKINEN, Olli	6-3	208	L	Kuopio, Finland	12/5/78	L.A.-Helsinki-Finland
LaFAYETTE, Nathan	6-1	200	R	New Westminster, B.C.	2/17/73	Los Angeles-Fredericton
LAPERRIERE, Ian	6-1	197	R	Montreal, Que.	1/19/74	Los Angeles
MacLEAN, Donald	6-2	199	L	Sydney, N.S.	1/14/77	Los Angeles-Fredericton
McKENNA, Steve	6-8	247	L	Toronto, Ont.	8/21/73	Los Angeles-Fredericton
MOGER, Sandy	6-4	220	R	100 Mile House, B.C.	3/21/69	Los Angeles
MORGAN, Jason	6-1	200	L	St. John's, Nfld.	10/9/76	Los Angeles-Springfield
MURRAY, Glen	6-3	222	R	Halifax, N.S.	11/1/72	Los Angeles-Canada
PERREAULT, Yanic	5-11	188	L	Sherbrooke, Que.	4/4/71	Los Angeles
ROBITAILLE, Luc	6-1	205	L	Montreal, Que.	2/17/66	Los Angeles
STUMPEL, Jozef	6-3	216	R	Nitra, Czech.	7/20/72	Los Angeles-Slovakia
TSYPLAKOV, Vladimir	6-1	197	L	Moscow, USSR	4/18/69	Los Angeles-Belarus
VOPAT, Roman	6-3	223	L	Litvinov, Czech.	4/21/76	Los Angeles-Fredericton
DEFENSEMEN						
BERG, Aki-Petteri	6-3	203	L	Turku, Finland	2/28/77	Los Angeles-Finland
BLAKE, Rob	6-4	220	R	Simcoe, Ont.	12/10/69	Los Angeles-Canada
BODGER, Doug	6-2	210	L	Chemainus, B.C.	6/18/66	San Jose-New Jersey
BOUCHER, Philippe	6-2	214	R	St. Apollinaire, Que.	3/24/73	Los Angeles-Long Beach
DUCHESNE, Steve	5-11	195	L	Sept-Iles, Que.	6/30/65	St. Louis
GALLEY, Garry	6-0	207	L	Montreal, Que.	4/16/63	Los Angeles
NORSTROM, Mattias	6-2	201	L	Stockholm, Sweden	1/2/72	Los Angeles-Sweden
O'DONNELL, Sean	6-3	230	L	Ottawa, Ont.	10/13/71	Los Angeles

GOALTENDERS	HT	WT	C	Place of Birth	Date	1997-98 Club
CHABOT, Frederic	5-11	187	L	Hebertville-Station, Que.	2/12/68	Los Angeles-Houston
FISET, Stephane	6-1	198	L	Montreal, Que.	6/17/70	Los Angeles
LEGACE, Manny	5-9	162	L	Toronto, Ont.	2/4/73	Springfield-Las Vegas
STORR, Jamie	6-2	198	L	Brampton, Ont.	12/28/75	Los Angeles-Long Beach

General Managers' History

Larry Regan, 1967-68 to 1972-73; Larry Regan and Jake Milford, 1973-74; Jake Milford, 1974-75 to 1976-77; George Maguire, 1977-78 to 1982-83; George Maguire and Rogie Vachon, 1983-84; Rogie Vachon, 1984-85 to 1991-92; Nick Beverley, 1992-93, 1993-94; Sam McMaster, 1994-95 to 1996-97; Dave Taylor, 1997-98 to date.

General Manager

TAYLOR, DAVE

General Manager, Los Angeles Kings. Born in Levack, Ont., December 4, 1955.

No player in the history of the Kings ever wore the uniform with more distinction and class than Dave Taylor. For 17 seasons, Taylor gave his all, both on and off the ice, receiving All-Star status for his outstanding play.

Fittingly, after finishing his illustrious career during the 1993-94 season, Taylor remains a key part of the Kings organization, now serving as vice president and general manager for the NHL club. Taylor, 42, assumed his current responsibilities on April 22, 1997, becoming the seventh GM in team history. He joined the Kings front office three years ago as an assistant to his predecessor, Sam McMaster.

An All-American hockey player while at Clarkson University, Taylor was relatively unknown when the Kings' picked him in the 15th round of the 1975 draft. His grit and work ethic kept him around long enough to hook up with a center named Marcel Dionne, who virtually ignited Taylor's career. As a member of the renowned Triple Crown line with Dionne and left winger Charlie Simmer, Taylor became a prolific scorer who also packed a fearsome check. Taylor's NHL career stats include a Kings-record 1,111 games, 431 goals, 638 assists and 1,069 points.

A five-time NHL All-Star Game selection, Taylor served as the Kings captain for four seasons (1985-89). After posting career highs in goals (47) and points (112) during the 1980-81 season, Taylor earned a spot on the NHL Second All-Star Team. On April 3, 1995, Taylor's jersey No. 18 was retired, joining Rogie Vachon (No. 30) and Marcel Dionne (No. 16) on the wall of the Great Western Forum. For all his individual accomplishments in hockey, his crowing glory was reaching the Stanley Cup Finals with the 1992-93 Kings.

Away from the ice, Taylor has worked tirelessly for numerous charities throughout the years. Each year he hosts the Dave Taylor Golf Classic benefiting the Cystic Fibrosis Foundation, which annually raises more than $125,000. In 1991, the NHL honored Taylor's contributions to hockey and the community by awarding him both the Bill Masterton and King Clancy trophies.

Dave and his wife, Beth, live in Tarzana, CA with their daughters Jamie, 14, and Katie, 11.

1997-98 Scoring

* – rookie

Regular Season

Pos	#	Player	Team	GP	G	A	Pts	+/–	PIM	PP	SH	GW	GT	S	%
C	15	Jozef Stumpel	L.A.	77	21	58	79	17	53	4	0	2	1	162	13.0
R	27	Glen Murray	L.A.	81	29	31	60	6	54	7	3	7	0	193	15.0
L	9	Vladimir Tsyplakov	L.A.	73	18	34	52	15	18	2	0	1	0	113	15.9
D	4	Rob Blake	L.A.	81	23	27	50	-3	94	11	0	4	0	261	8.8
C	44	Yanic Perreault	L.A.	79	28	20	48	6	32	3	2	3	0	206	13.6
L	20	Luc Robitaille	L.A.	57	16	24	40	5	66	5	0	7	0	130	12.3
L	23	Craig Johnson	L.A.	74	17	21	38	9	42	6	0	2	0	125	13.6
D	3	Garry Galley	L.A.	74	9	28	37	-5	63	7	0	0	0	128	7.0
R	45	Sandy Moger	L.A.	62	11	13	24	4	70	1	0	2	0	89	12.4
C	22	Ian Laperriere	L.A.	77	6	15	21	0	131	0	1	1	0	74	8.1
R	19	Russ Courtnall	L.A.	58	12	6	18	-2	27	1	4	4	0	97	12.4
D	6	Sean O'Donnell	L.A.	80	2	15	17	7	179	0	0	1	0	71	2.8
D	28	Philippe Boucher	L.A.	45	6	10	16	6	49	1	0	0	0	80	7.5
C	26	Ray Ferraro	L.A.	40	6	9	15	-10	42	0	0	2	0	45	13.3
D	14	Mattias Norstrom	L.A.	73	1	12	13	14	90	0	0	0	0	61	1.6
L	42	Dan Bylsma	L.A.	65	3	9	12	9	33	0	0	0	1	57	5.3
C	24	Nathan Lafayette	L.A.	34	5	3	8	2	32	1	0	1	0	60	8.3
L	7 *	Steve McKenna	L.A.	62	4	4	8	-9	150	1	0	0	1	42	9.5
D	2	Doug Zmolek	L.A.	46	0	8	8	0	111	0	0	0	0	23	0.0
D	5	Aki Berg	L.A.	72	0	8	8	3	61	0	0	0	0	58	0.0
C	10 *	Donald MacLean	L.A.	22	5	2	7	-1	4	2	0	0	0	25	20.0
L	17	Matt Johnson	L.A.	66	2	4	6	-8	249	0	0	0	0	18	11.1
D	33	Jan Vopat	L.A.	21	1	5	6	8	10	0	0	1	0	13	7.7
C	12	Roman Vopat	L.A.	25	0	3	3	-7	55	0	0	0	0	36	0.0
C	52 *	Jason Morgan	L.A.	11	1	0	1	-7	4	0	0	0	0	5	20.0
R	43	Vitali Yachmenev	L.A.	4	0	1	1	1	4	0	0	0	0	4	0.0
G	35	Stephane Fiset	L.A.	60	0	1	1	0	8	0	0	0	0	0	0.0
C	21 *	Olli Jokinen	L.A.	8	0	0	0	-5	6	0	0	0	0	12	0.0
G	31	Frederic Chabot	L.A.	12	0	0	0	0	0	0	0	0	0	0	0.0
G	1 *	Jamie Storr	L.A.	17	0	0	0	0	0	0	0	0	0	0	0.0

Goaltending

No.	Goaltender	GPI	Mins	Avg	W	L	T	EN	SO	GA	SA	S%
1	* Jamie Storr	17	920	2.22	9	5	1	0	2	34	482	.929
35	Stephane Fiset	60	3497	2.71	26	25	8	4	2	158	1728	.909
31	Frederic Chabot	12	554	3.14	3	3	2	0	0	29	267	.891
	Totals	**82**	**4990**	**2.71**	**38**	**33**	**11**	**4**	**4**	**225**	**2481**	**.909**

Playoffs

Pos	#	Player	Team	GP	G	A	Pts	+/–	PIM	PP	SH	GW	OT	S	%
L	20	Luc Robitaille	L.A.	4	1	2	3	1	6	0	0	0	0	13	7.7
C	15	Jozef Stumpel	L.A.	4	1	2	3	2	2	0	0	0	0	7	14.3
C	44	Yanic Perreault	L.A.	4	1	2	3	-1	6	1	0	0	0	7	14.3
D	5	Aki Berg	L.A.	4	0	3	3	3	0	0	0	0	0	7	0.0
R	27	Glen Murray	L.A.	4	2	0	2	2	6	0	0	0	0	13	15.4
L	23	Craig Johnson	L.A.	4	1	0	1	0	4	0	0	0	0	3	33.3
D	6	Sean O'Donnell	L.A.	4	1	0	1	1	36	0	0	0	0	7	14.3
C	22	Ian Laperriere	L.A.	4	1	0	1	0	6	0	0	0	0	6	16.7
D	33	Jan Vopat	L.A.	2	0	1	1	1	2	0	0	0	0	1	0.0
C	26	Ray Ferraro	L.A.	3	0	1	1	1	2	0	0	0	0	5	0.0
L	7 *	Steve McKenna	L.A.	3	0	1	1	1	8	0	0	0	0	3	0.0
D	3	Garry Galley	L.A.	4	0	1	1	-2	2	0	0	0	0	6	0.0
L	9	Vladimir Tsyplakov	L.A.	4	0	1	1	-1	8	0	0	0	0	4	0.0
G	35	Stephane Fiset	L.A.	2	0	0	0	0	0	0	0	0	0	0	0.0
L	42	Dan Bylsma	L.A.	2	0	0	0	-3	0	0	0	0	0	1	0.0
D	2	Doug Zmolek	L.A.	2	0	0	0	0	2	0	0	0	0	0	0.0
G	1 *	Jamie Storr	L.A.	3	0	0	0	0	0	0	0	0	0	0	0.0
D	4	Rob Blake	L.A.	4	0	0	0	-4	6	0	0	0	0	15	0.0
R	19	Russ Courtnall	L.A.	4	0	0	0	-2	2	0	0	0	0	7	0.0
C	24	Nathan Lafayette	L.A.	4	0	0	0	-2	2	0	0	0	0	4	0.0
D	14	Mattias Norstrom	L.A.	4	0	0	0	-1	2	0	0	0	0	3	0.0
L	17	Matt Johnson	L.A.	4	0	0	0	-1	6	0	0	0	0	0	0.0

Goaltending

No.	Goaltender	GPI	Mins	Avg	W	L	EN	SO	GA	SA	S%
1	* Jamie Storr	3	145	3.72	0	2	0	0	9	77	.883
35	Stephane Fiset	2	93	4.52	0	2	0	0	7	61	.885
	Totals	**4**	**240**	**4.00**	**0**	**4**	**0**	**0**	**16**	**138**	**.884**

Coaching History

Red Kelly, 1967-68, 1968-69; Hal Laycoe and John Wilson, 1969-70; Larry Regan, 1970-71; Larry Regan and Fred Glover, 1971-72; Bob Pulford, 1972-73 to 1976-77; Ron Stewart, 1977-78; Bob Berry, 1978-79 to 1980-81; Parker MacDonald and Don Perry, 1981-82; Don Perry, 1982-83; Don Perry, Rogie Vachon and Roger Neilson, 1983-84; Pat Quinn, 1984-85, 1985-86; Pat Quinn and Mike Murphy 1986-87; Mike Murphy, Rogie Vachon and Robbie Ftorek, 1987-88; Robbie Ftorek, 1988-89; Tom Webster, 1989-90 to 1991-92; Barry Melrose, 1992-93, 1993-94; Barry Melrose and Rogie Vachon, 1994-95; Larry Robinson, 1995-96 to date.

Captains' History

Bob Wall, 1967-68, 1968-69; Larry Cahan, 1969-70, 1970-71; Bob Pulford, 1971-72, 1972-73; Terry Harper, 1973-74, 1974-75; Mike Murphy, 1975-76 to 1980-81; Dave Lewis, 1981-82, 1982-83; Terry Ruskowski, 1983-84, 1984-85; Dave Taylor, 1985-86 to 1988-89; Wayne Gretzky, 1989-90 to 1991-92; Wayne Gretzky and Luc Robitaille, 1992-93; Wayne Gretzky, 1993-94, 1994-95; Wayne Gretzky and Rob Blake, 1995-96; Rob Blake, 1996-97 to date.

Club Records

Team

(Figures in brackets for season records are games played; records for fewest points, wins, ties, losses, goals, goals against are for 70 or more games)

Most Points	**105**	1974-75 (80)
Most Wins	**46**	1990-91 (80)
Most Ties	**21**	1974-75 (80)
Most Losses	**52**	1969-70 (76)
Most Goals	**376**	1988-89 (80)
Most Goals Against	**389**	1985-86 (80)
Fewest Points	**38**	1969-70 (76)
Fewest Wins	**14**	1969-70 (76)
Fewest Ties	**7**	1988-89 (80), 1989-90 (80)
Fewest Losses	**17**	1974-75 (80)
Fewest Goals	**168**	1969-70 (76)
Fewest Goals Against	**185**	1974-75 (80)
Longest Winning Streak		
Overall	**8**	Oct. 21-Nov. 7/72
Home	**12**	Oct. 10-Dec. 5/92
Away	**8**	Dec. 18/74-Jan. 16/75
Longest Undefeated Streak		
Overall	**11**	Feb. 28-Mar. 24/74 (9 wins, 2 ties)
Home	**13**	Oct. 10-Dec. 8/92 (12 wins, 1 tie)
Away	**11**	Oct. 10-Dec. 11/74 (6 wins, 5 ties)
Longest Losing Streak		
Overall	**10**	Feb. 22-Mar. 9/84
Home	**9**	Feb. 8-Mar. 12/86
Away	**12**	Jan. 11-Feb. 15/70
Longest Winless Streak		
Overall	**17**	Jan. 29-Mar. 5/70 (13 losses, 4 ties)
Home	**9**	Jan. 29-Mar. 5/70 (8 losses, 1 tie), Feb. 8-Mar. 12/86 (9 losses)
Away	**21**	Jan. 11-Apr. 3/70 (17 losses, 4 ties)
Most Shutouts, Season	**9**	1974-75 (80)
Most PIM, Season	**2,228**	1990-91 (80)
Most Goals, Game	**12**	Nov. 28/84 (Van. 1 at L.A. 12)

Individual

Most Seasons	**17**	Dave Taylor
Most Games	**1,111**	Dave Taylor
Most Goals, Career	**550**	Marcel Dionne
Most Assists, Career	**757**	Marcel Dionne
Most Points Career	**1,307**	Marcel Dionne
Most PIM, Career	**1,846**	Marty McSorley
Most Shutouts, Career	**32**	Rogie Vachon
Longest Consecutive Games Streak	**324**	Marcel Dionne (Jan. 7/78-Jan. 9/82)
Most Goals, Season	**70**	Bernie Nicholls (1988-89)
Most Assists, Season	**122**	Wayne Gretzky (1990-91)
Most Points, Season	**168**	Wayne Gretzky (1988-89; 54G, 114A)
Most PIM, Season	**399**	Marty McSorley (1992-93)
Most Points, Defenseman, Season	**76**	Larry Murphy (1980-81; 16G, 60A)
Most Points, Center, Season	**168**	Wayne Gretzky (1988-89; 54G, 114A)
Most Points, Right Wing, Season	**112**	Dave Taylor (1980-81; 47G, 65A)
Most Points, Left Wing, Season	***125**	Luc Robitaille (1992-93; 63G, 62A)
Most Points, Rookie, Season	**84**	Luc Robitaille (1986-87; 45G, 39A)
Most Shutouts, Season	**8**	Rogie Vachon (1976-77)
Most Goals, Game	**4**	Sixteen times
Most Assists, Game	**6**	Bernie Nicholls (Dec. 1/88), Tomas Sandstrom (Oct. 9/93)
Most Points, Game	**8**	Bernie Nicholls (Dec. 1/88; 2G, 6A)

* NHL Record.

Retired Numbers

16	Marcel Dionne	1975-1987
18	Dave Taylor	1977-1994
30	Rogie Vachon	1971-1978

All-time Record vs. Other Clubs

Regular Season

	At Home							On Road							Total						
	GP	W	L	T	GF	GA	PTS	GP	W	L	T	GF	GA	PTS	GP	W	L	T	GF	GA	PTS
Anaheim	14	8	4	2	42	33	18	13	4	6	3	37	47	11	27	12	10	5	79	80	29
Boston	56	19	31	6	195	213	44	57	10	43	4	159	273	24	113	29	74	10	354	486	68
Buffalo	49	18	22	9	168	173	45	48	15	24	9	145	195	39	97	33	46	18	313	368	84
Calgary	79	40	30	9	309	290	89	82	23	50	9	272	380	55	161	63	80	18	581	670	144
Carolina	25	14	8	3	110	98	31	26	9	13	4	102	103	22	51	23	21	7	212	201	53
Chicago	62	27	29	6	212	218	60	63	24	31	8	192	237	56	125	51	60	14	404	455	116
Colorado	30	18	10	2	128	99	38	30	13	14	3	112	122	29	60	31	24	5	240	221	67
Dallas	66	27	21	18	230	200	72	67	16	39	12	186	274	44	133	43	60	30	416	474	116
Detroit	68	36	19	13	282	213	85	67	28	28	11	246	267	67	135	64	47	24	528	480	152
Edmonton	65	24	28	13	267	282	61	65	17	34	14	243	312	48	130	41	62	27	510	594	109
Florida	4	2	2	0	11	14	4	4	0	2	2	6	13	2	8	2	4	2	17	27	6
Montreal	61	17	35	9	188	243	43	60	7	42	11	153	279	25	121	24	77	20	341	522	68
New Jersey	38	27	5	6	196	116	60	38	16	17	5	136	129	37	76	43	22	11	332	245	97
NY Islanders	40	19	14	7	145	129	45	40	13	23	4	115	153	30	80	32	37	11	260	282	75
NY Rangers	55	22	24	9	184	197	53	54	15	33	6	153	216	36	109	37	57	15	337	413	89
Ottawa	5	5	0	0	31	13	10	5	1	3	1	13	17	3	10	6	3	1	44	30	13
Philadelphia	61	19	34	8	180	208	46	59	15	37	7	151	230	37	120	34	71	15	331	438	83
Phoenix	57	22	25	10	242	236	54	60	22	29	9	214	253	53	117	44	54	19	456	489	107
Pittsburgh	65	41	16	8	252	170	90	67	20	38	9	210	252	49	132	61	54	17	462	422	139
St. Louis	66	33	24	9	236	194	75	66	15	42	9	171	249	39	132	48	66	18	407	443	114
San Jose	20	13	6	1	76	58	27	21	8	10	3	70	77	19	41	21	16	4	146	135	46
Tampa Bay	6	1	5	0	16	23	2	5	3	2	0	12	11	6	11	4	7	0	28	34	8
Toronto	64	34	21	9	230	187	77	63	20	32	11	212	254	51	127	54	53	20	442	441	128
Vancouver	87	45	29	13	363	285	103	85	27	44	14	274	334	68	172	72	73	27	637	619	171
Washington	42	24	12	6	168	131	54	41	17	18	6	153	176	40	83	41	30	12	321	307	94
Defunct Clubs	35	27	6	2	141	76	56	34	11	14	9	91	109	31	69	38	20	11	232	185	87
Totals	**1220**	**582**	**460**	**178**	**4602**	**4099**	**1342**	**1220**	**369**	**668**	**183**	**3828**	**4962**	**921**	**2440**	**951**	**1128**	**361**	**8430**	**9061**	**2263**

Playoffs

	Series	W	L	GP	W	L	T	GF	GA	Last Mtg.	Round	Result
Boston	2	0	2	13	5	8	0	38	56	1977	QF	L 2-4
Calgary	6	4	2	26	13	13	0	105	112	1993	DSF	W 4-2
Chicago	1	0	1	5	1	4	0	7	10	1974	QF	L 1-4
Dallas	1	0	1	7	3	4	0	21	26	1968	QF	L 3-4
Edmonton	7	2	5	36	12	24	0	124	150	1992	DSF	L 2-4
Montreal	1	0	1	5	1	4	0	12	15	1993	F	L 1-4
NY Islanders	1	0	1	4	1	3	0	10	21	1980	PR	L 1-3
NY Rangers	2	0	2	6	1	5	0	14	32	1981	PR	L 1-3
St. Louis	2	0	2	8	0	8	0	13	32	1998	CQF	L 0-4
Toronto	3	1	2	12	5	7	0	31	41	1993	CF	W 4-3
Vancouver	3	2	1	17	9	8	0	66	60	1993	DF	W 4-2
Defunct Clubs	1	1	0	7	4	3	0	23	25			
Totals	**30**	**10**	**20**	**146**	**55**	**91**	**0**	**467**	**584**			

Calgary totals include Atlanta, 1972-73 to 1979-80. Carolina totals include Hartford, 1979-80 to 1996-97. Colorado totals include Quebec, 1979-80 to 1994-95. Dallas totals include Minnesota, 1967-68 to 1992-93. New Jersey totals include Kansas City, 1974-75 to 1975-76, and Colorado Rockies, 1976-77 to 1981-82. Phoenix totals include Winnipeg, 1979-80 to 1995-96.

Playoff Results 1998-94

Year	Round	Opponent	Result	GF	GA
1998	CQF	St. Louis	L 0-4	8	16

Abbreviations: Round: F – Final; **CF** – conference final; **CQF** – conference quarter-final; **DF** – division final; **DSF** – division semi-final; **QF** – quarter-final; **PR** – preliminary round.

1997-98 Results

Oct.	1	at	Pittsburgh	3-3		5	at	Vancouver	2-3
	2	at	Boston	5-6		8		Buffalo	2-2
	5	at	NY Rangers	2-2		10		Edmonton	3-4
	7	at	Carolina	3-3		12		Anaheim	3-2
	9	at	St. Louis	2-3		14	at	San Jose	4-2
	12		Ottawa	7-4		20		Calgary	4-3
	15		Boston	3-5		22		Florida	3-1
	17		Philadelphia	5-1		24	at	Anaheim	3-3
	19		Edmonton	2-3		29		Calgary	5-3
	21		NY Islanders	3-2		31		Chicago	3-0
	23		Detroit	1-4	**Feb.**	2	at	Edmonton	0-1
	26	at	Tampa Bay	3-1		3	at	Calgary	6-3
	28	at	Florida	2-2		5		NY Rangers	3-1
	31	at	Detroit	5-1		7	at	Anaheim	5-2
Nov.	1	at	NY Islanders	2-4		25	at	Detroit	1-1
	4	at	New Jersey	3-0		26	at	Chicago	7-4
	6		Tampa Bay	5-2		28		St. Louis	2-5
	8		Montreal	1-4	**Mar.**	2		Vancouver	2-2
	11		Vancouver	8-2		5		Carolina	1-2
	13		San Jose	6-3		7		Detroit	2-1
	15		Dallas	1-5		9		Anaheim	4-3
	20		Chicago	4-3		10	at	Phoenix	4-3
	23	at	Colorado	2-1		12		Toronto	1-2
	26	at	Dallas	1-4		14		Colorado	5-2
	27	at	St. Louis	2-2		16	at	San Jose	1-2
	29		New Jersey	4-1		17		Dallas	3-4
Dec.	3	at	Montreal	0-2		21		Phoenix	3-2
	4	at	Ottawa	2-3		24	at	San Jose	4-3
	6	at	Toronto	2-7		26		San Jose	2-5
	9		Pittsburgh	1-2		28	at	Calgary	2-5
	13		Washington	2-2		30	at	Toronto	3-2
	15	at	Vancouver	0-7	**Apr.**	1	at	Buffalo	0-4
	18		Toronto	5-2		2	at	Philadelphia	0-3
	20	at	Calgary	4-1		4	at	Washington	2-3
	22	at	Chicago	1-0		6	at	Colorado	3-1
	23	at	Colorado	1-5		9		Edmonton	0-4
	27		Phoenix	2-4		11		Colorado	4-3
	29		Vancouver	5-2		13		Calgary	4-2
	31	at	Dallas	2-2		15	at	Vancouver	2-0
Jan.	1	at	Phoenix	0-4		16		St. Louis	3-7
	4	at	Edmonton	3-2		18		Anaheim	1-4

Entry Draft Selections 1998-84

1998
Pick
21 Mathieu Biron
46 Justin Papineau
76 Alexei Volkov
103 Kip Brennan
133 Joe Rullier
163 Tomas Zizka
190 Tommi Hannus
217 Jim Henkel
248 Matthew Yeats

1997
Pick
3 Olli Jokinen
15 Matt Zultek
29 Scott Barney
83 Joseph Corvo
99 Sean Blanchard
137 Richard Seeley
150 Jeff Katcher
193 Jay Kopischke
220 Konrad Brand

1996
Pick
30 Josh Green
37 Marian Cisar
57 Greg Phillips
84 Mikael Simons
96 Eric Belanger
120 Jesse Black
123 Peter Hogan
190 Stephen Valiquette
193 Kai Nurminen
219 Sebastien Simard

1995
Pick
3 Aki-Petteri Berg
33 Donald MacLean
50 Pavel Rosa
59 Vladimir Tsyplakov
118 Jason Morgan
137 Igor Melyakov
157 Benoit Larose
163 Juha Vuorivirta
215 Brian Stewart

1994
Pick
7 Jamie Storr
33 Matt Johnson
59 Vitali Yachmenev
111 Chris Schmidt
163 Luc Gagne
189 Andrew Dale
215 Jan Nemecek
241 Sergei Shalomai

1993
Pick
42 Shayne Toporowski
68 Jeffrey Mitchell
94 Bob Wren
105 Frederick Beaubien
117 Jason Saal
120 Tomas Vlasak
146 Jere Karalahti
172 Justin Martin
198 John-Tra Dillabough
224 Martin Strbak
250 Kimmo Timonen
276 Patrick Howald

1992
Pick
39 Justin Hocking
63 Sandy Allan
87 Kevin Brown
111 Jeff Shevalier
135 Raymond Murray
207 Magnus Wernblom
231 Ryan Pisiak
255 Jukka Tiilikainen

1991
Pick
42 Guy Leveque
79 Keith Redmond
81 Alexei Zhitnik
108 Pauli Jaks
130 Brett Seguin
152 Kelly Fairchild
196 Craig Brown
218 Mattias Olsson
240 Andre Bouliane
262 Michael Gaul

1990
Pick
7 Darryl Sydor
28 Brandy Semchuk
49 Bob Berg
91 David Goverde
112 Erik Andersson
133 Robert Lang
154 Dean Hulett
175 Denis LeBlanc
196 Patrik Ross
217 K.J. (Kevin) White
238 Troy Mohns

1989
Pick
39 Brent Thompson
81 Jim Maher
102 Eric Ricard
103 Thomas Newman
123 Daniel Rydmark
144 Ted Kramer
165 Sean Whyte
182 Jim Giacin
186 Martin Maskarinec
207 Jim Hiller
228 Steve Jaques
249 Kevin Sneddon

1988
Pick
7 Martin Gelinas
28 Paul Holden
49 John Van Kessel
70 Rob Blake
91 Jeff Robison
109 Micah Aivazoff
112 Robert Larsson
133 Jeff Kruesel
154 Timo Peltomaa
175 Jim Larkin
196 Brad Hyatt
217 Doug Laprade
238 Joe Flanagan

1987
Pick
4 Wayne McBean
27 Mark Fitzpatrick
43 Ross Wilson
90 Mike Vukonich
111 Greg Batters
132 Kyosti Karjalainen
174 Jeff Gawlicki
195 John Preston
216 Rostislav Vlach
237 Mikael Lindholm

1986
Pick
2 Jimmy Carson
44 Denis Larocque
65 Sylvain Couturier
86 Dave Guden
107 Robb Stauber
128 Sean Krakiwsky
149 Rene Chapdelaine
170 Trevor Pochipinski
191 Paul Kelly
212 Russ Mann
233 Brian Hayton

1985
Pick
9 Craig Duncanson
10 Dan Gratton
30 Par Edlund
72 Perry Florio
93 Petr Prajsler
135 Tim Flannigan
156 John Hyduke
177 Steve Horner
219 Trent Ciprick
240 Marian Horwath

1984
Pick
6 Craig Redmond
24 Brian Wilks
48 John English
69 Tom Glavine
87 Dave Grannis
108 Greg Strome
129 Tim Hanley
150 Shannon Deegan
171 Luc Robitaille
191 Jeff Crossman
212 Paul Kenny
232 Brian Martin

Coach

ROBINSON, LARRY
Coach, Los Angeles Kings. Born in Winchester, Ont., June 2, 1951.

Larry Robinson enters his fourth season as head coach in 1998-99. Robinson became the 18th head coach of the Los Angeles Kings on July 26, 1995, replacing Barry Melrose (Rogie Vachon served as interim coach for the final seven games of the 1994-95 season). He also served as an assistant coach with the New Jersey Devils for two seasons, helping them win the Stanley Cup in 1995. One of the great defensemen in NHL history, Robinson enjoyed a stellar 20-year playing career with the Montreal Canadiens and the Kings (1972-73–1991-92). In his 17 seasons with Montreal, the Habs won five Stanley Cup championships including four straight titles (1975-76–1978-79). Robinson played in 1,384 career games (9th all-time), scoring 208 goals, 750 assists (3rd all-time defenseman) and 958 points (4th all-time defenseman). In playoff action, he holds NHL records for most career games played (227) and most consecutive years in playoffs (20). Robinson's individual honors include two Norris Trophies as the NHL's top defenseman, a Conn Smythe Trophy as playoff MVP, three seasons each as a First Team All-Star and Second Team All-Star, and 10 appearances in the NHL All-Star Game.

Coaching Record

		Regular Season					Playoffs			
Season	**Team**	**Games**	**W**	**L**	**T**	**%**	**Games**	**W**	**L**	**%**
1995-96	**Los Angeles (NHL)**	**82**	**24**	**40**	**18**	**.402**	....	....	....	....
1996-97	**Los Angeles (NHL)**	**82**	**28**	**43**	**11**	**.409**	....	....	....	....
1997-98	**Los Angeles (NHL)**	**82**	**38**	**33**	**11**	**.530**	**4**	**0**	**4**	**.000**
	NHL Totals	**246**	**90**	**116**	**40**	**.447**	**4**	**0**	**4**	**.000**

Club Directory

The Great Western Forum
P.O. Box 17013
3900 West Manchester Blvd.
Inglewood, CA 90308
Phone **310/419-3160**
GM FAX 310/672-1490
PR FAX 310/673-8927
Website: www.lakings.com
Capacity: 16,005

Executive
Owner . . . . . Philip F. Anschutz
Owner . . . . . Edward P. Roski
Governor . . . . . Robert Sanderman
President/Alt. Govenor . . . . . Tim Leiweke
Vice President, New Business Development . . . . . Mitch Huberman
Vice President, Chief Financial Officer . . . . . Dan Beckerman
Vice President, General Counsel . . . . . Ted Fikre
Vice President, Marketing and Communications . . . John Cimperman
Vice President, Client Services . . . . . Sheila Gonzaga
Vice President, Special Projects . . . . . Rogie Vachon
Legal Counsel . . . . . Kristine Braun
Executive Assistant to the President . . . . . Lisa Tran
Executive Assistant to V.P., New Business Development . . . . . Carrie Abramson
Executive Assistant to V.P., Chief Financial Officer . . Kely Lyon
Executive Assistant to V.P., General Counsel . . . . . Tiffany Collins
Executive Assistant to V.P., Marketing and Communications . . . . . Jackie C. Howard

Hockey Operations
Vice President, General Manager . . . . . Dave Taylor
Director, Player Personnel . . . . . Bill O'Flaherty
Assistant to General Manager . . . . . John Wolf
Executive Assistant to General Manager . . . . . Marcia Galloway
Head Coach . . . . . Larry Robinson
Assistant Coaches . . . . . Rick Green, Jay Leach, Don Edwards
Director, Amateur Scouting . . . . . Al Murray
Director, Pro Scouting . . . . . Ace Bailey
Scouting Staff . . . . . Serge Aubry, Greg Dreschel, Rob Laird, Vaclav Nedomansky, John Stanton, Ari Vuori
Video Coordinator . . . . . Bill Gurney

Medical Staff
Trainer . . . . . Pete Demers
Equipment Manager . . . . . Peter Millar
Assistant Equipment Manager . . . . . Rick Garcia
Equipment Assistant . . . . . Greg Brohamer
Rehabilitation Trainer/Strength and Conditioning Coach . . . . . Robert Zolg
Massage Therapist . . . . . Dan Garcia
Fitness Consultant . . . . . Guy LeMasurier
Team Physicians . . . . . Dr. Ronald Kvitne, Jobe Orthopaedic Clinic
Internist . . . . . Dr. Michael Mellman
Dentist . . . . . Dr. Jeffrey Hoy
Opthamologist . . . . . Dr. Howard Lazerson

Communications
Director, Media Relations and Team Services . . . . . Mike Altieri
Director, Community Development . . . . . Kelly Malcomb Davis
Manager, Media Relations and Team Services . . . . . Jeff Moeller
Manager, Fan Development . . . . . Steve Bogoyevac
Community Relations Coordinator . . . . . Kris Nakamura
Media Relations Assistant . . . . . Jason Pommier
Fan Development Assistant . . . . . Annie Cumins
Team Photographer . . . . . Andrew D. Bernstein
Receptionist . . . . . Lara Frandzel

Marketing/Corporate Sales
Director, Marketing and Promotions . . . . . Kurt Schwartzkopf
Director, Corporate Sales . . . . . Karen Marumoto
Account Executives, Client Services . . . . . Annie Goshert, Susan Long, Mike Muraska
Account Coordinator . . . . . Jason Bednar
Executive Assistant/Account Coordinator . . . . . Courtney Coffland
Graphics Coordinator . . . . . Terry Dennis

Ticket Operations/Sales
Director, Sales . . . . . Steve Delay
Director, Ticket Operations . . . . . Bill Chapin
Director, Group Events . . . . . Lynn Wittenburg
Director, Management Information Systems . . . . . Ali Reza Shama
Manager, Ticket Operations . . . . . Chris Cockrell
Ticket Coordinator/Web Site Maintenance . . . . . Nell Nicolas
Ticket Coordinators . . . . . Robert Anderson, Ian McDonald
Account Executives . . . . . Myrna Powell, Eric Ogawa, Vince Cimmarrusti
Group Events Coordinators . . . . . Tony Barnachea, Marne Orsillo
Hockey Group Events Coordinator . . . . . Jason Webb
Corporate Account Executives . . . . . Chris Maier, Jeff Olsen, Shawn Jeffers, Tim Sullivan, Marcos Rodriguez, Mark McMahon
Sales Coordinator . . . . . Shelby Russell

Personnel/Accounting
Director, Finance . . . . . Peter Mazur
Accounts Payable . . . . . Emma Harris
Accounts Receivable . . . . . Heather O'Conner
Benefits Manager . . . . . Margaret Castaneda

Entertainment and Events/Merchandise
Director, Entertainment and Events . . . . . Marianne Herman
Director, Merchandise . . . . . Mark Mochlenkamp
Public Address Announcer . . . . . David Courtney
Supervisor, Off-Ice Officials . . . . . Bill Meuris

Broadcasting
Play-by-Play Announcer, Television . . . . . Bob Miller
Play-by-Play Announcer, Radio . . . . . Nick Nickson
Color Commentator, Television . . . . . Jim Fox
Color Commentator, Radio . . . . .
Television Network . . . . . Fox Sports West
Radio Station . . . . . KRLA (1110 AM)

Montreal Canadiens

1997-98 Results: 37W-32L-13T 87PTS. Fourth, Northeast Division

Vladimir Malakhov (38), Saku Koivu (11) and Shayne Corson (27) celebrate another goal by les bleu, blanc et rouge at the Molson Centre.

1998-99 Schedule

Oct.	Sat.	10	NY Rangers		Tue.	12	at Detroit
	Tue.	13	Anaheim		Fri.	15	at Washington
	Fri.	16	at Washington		Sat.	16	NY Rangers
	Sat.	17	Buffalo		Mon.	18	Washington
	Mon.	19	Chicago		Thu.	21	at Chicago
	Wed.	21	Ottawa		Tue.	26	at Tampa Bay
	Sat.	24	Detroit		Wed.	27	at Florida
	Wed.	28	Boston		Sat.	30	Carolina*
	Thu.	29	at Boston		Sun.	31	Pittsburgh*
	Sat.	31	at Ottawa	Feb.	Wed.	3	Vancouver
Nov.	Wed.	4	at NY Rangers		Thu.	4	at Philadelphia
	Sat.	7	NY Islanders		Sat.	6	Buffalo
	Mon.	9	Philadelphia		Tue.	9	at Pittsburgh
	Wed.	11	at New Jersey		Thu.	11	at Buffalo
	Thu.	12	at NY Islanders		Sat.	13	Florida
	Sat.	14	Edmonton		Wed.	17	at NY Rangers
	Tue.	17	at Carolina		Thu.	18	at Philadelphia
	Thu.	19	Calgary		Sat.	20	at Toronto
	Sat.	21	Colorado		Thu.	25	at Ottawa
	Fri.	27	at Boston*		Sat.	27	Ottawa
	Sat.	28	Pittsburgh	Mar.	Tue.	2	Philadelphia
	Mon.	30	Los Angeles		Wed.	3	at Pittsburgh
Dec.	Wed.	2	at Carolina		Sat.	6	Tampa Bay
	Fri.	4	at New Jersey		Mon.	8	Florida
	Sat.	5	Toronto		Thu.	11	at St. Louis
	Wed.	9	at Phoenix		Sat.	13	Toronto
	Fri.	11	at Dallas		Thu.	18	Nashville
	Sat.	12	at Nashville		Sat.	20	Washington
	Mon.	14	Phoenix		Mon.	22	San Jose
	Fri.	18	at Buffalo		Wed.	24	at Edmonton
	Sat.	19	New Jersey		Thu.	25	at Calgary
	Mon.	21	Dallas		Sat.	27	at Vancouver*
	Wed.	23	at Ottawa	Apr.	Thu.	1	Boston
	Sat.	26	at Toronto		Sat.	3	Buffalo
	Tue.	29	at Edmonton		Mon.	5	at Boston
	Thu.	31	at Calgary		Wed.	7	Carolina
Jan.	Sat.	2	at Vancouver		Thu.	8	at NY Islanders
	Mon.	4	at Colorado		Sat.	10	New Jersey
	Thu.	7	Tampa Bay		Tue.	13	at Tampa Bay
	Sat.	9	NY Islanders		Wed.	14	at Florida
	Mon.	11	St. Louis		Sat.	17	Toronto

* Denotes afternoon game.

Year-by-Year Record

		Home			Road			Overall							
Season	GP	W	L	T	W	L	T	W	L	T	GF	GA	Pts.	Finished	Playoff Result
1997-98	82	15	17	9	22	15	4	37	32	13	235	208	87	4th, Northeast Div.	Lost Conf. Semi-Final
1996-97	82	17	17	7	14	19	8	31	36	15	249	276	77	4th, Northeast Div.	Lost Conf. Quarter-Final
1995-96	82	23	12	6	17	20	4	40	32	10	265	248	90	3rd, Northeast Div.	Lost Conf. Quarter-Final
1994-95	48	15	5	4	3	18	3	18	23	7	125	148	43	6th, Northeast Div.	Out of Playoffs
1993-94	84	26	12	4	15	17	10	41	29	14	283	248	96	3rd, Northeast Div.	Lost Conf. Quarter-Final
1992-93	**84**	**27**	**13**	**2**	**21**	**17**	**4**	**48**	**30**	**6**	**326**	**280**	**102**	**3rd, Adams Div.**	**Won Stanley Cup**
1991-92	80	27	8	5	14	20	6	41	28	11	267	207	93	1st, Adams Div.	Lost Div. Final
1990-91	80	23	12	5	16	18	6	39	30	11	273	249	89	2nd, Adams Div.	Lost Div. Final
1989-90	80	26	8	6	15	20	5	41	28	11	288	234	93	3rd, Adams Div.	Lost Div. Final
1988-89	80	30	6	4	23	12	5	53	18	9	315	218	115	1st, Adams Div.	Lost Final
1987-88	80	26	8	6	19	14	7	45	22	13	298	238	103	1st, Adams Div.	Lost Div. Final
1986-87	80	27	9	4	14	20	6	41	29	10	277	241	92	2nd, Adams Div.	Lost Conf. Championship
1985-86	**80**	**25**	**11**	**4**	**15**	**22**	**3**	**40**	**33**	**7**	**330**	**280**	**87**	**2nd, Adams Div.**	**Won Stanley Cup**
1984-85	80	24	10	6	17	17	6	41	27	12	309	262	94	1st, Adams Div.	Lost Div. Final
1983-84	80	19	19	2	16	21	3	35	40	5	286	295	75	4th, Adams Div.	Lost Conf. Championship
1982-83	80	25	6	9	17	18	5	42	24	14	350	286	98	2nd, Adams Div.	Lost Div. Semi-Final
1981-82	80	25	6	9	21	11	8	46	17	17	360	223	109	1st, Adams Div.	Lost Div. Semi-Final
1980-81	80	31	7	2	14	15	11	45	22	13	332	232	103	1st, Norris Div.	Lost Prelim. Round
1979-80	80	30	7	3	17	13	10	47	20	13	328	240	107	1st, Norris Div.	Lost Quarter-Final
1978-79	**80**	**29**	**6**	**5**	**23**	**11**	**6**	**52**	**17**	**11**	**337**	**204**	**115**	**1st, Norris Div.**	**Won Stanley Cup**
1977-78	**80**	**32**	**4**	**4**	**27**	**6**	**7**	**59**	**10**	**11**	**359**	**183**	**129**	**1st, Norris Div.**	**Won Stanley Cup**
1976-77	**80**	**33**	**1**	**6**	**27**	**7**	**6**	**60**	**8**	**12**	**387**	**171**	**132**	**1st, Norris Div.**	**Won Stanley Cup**
1975-76	**80**	**32**	**3**	**5**	**26**	**8**	**6**	**58**	**11**	**11**	**337**	**174**	**127**	**1st, Norris Div.**	**Won Stanley Cup**
1974-75	80	27	8	5	20	6	14	47	14	19	374	225	113	1st, Norris Div.	Lost Semi-Final
1973-74	78	24	12	3	21	12	6	45	24	9	293	240	99	2nd, East Div.	Lost Quarter-inal
1972-73	**78**	**29**	**4**	**6**	**23**	**6**	**10**	**52**	**10**	**16**	**329**	**184**	**120**	**1st, East Div.**	**Won Stanley Cup**
1971-72	78	29	3	7	17	13	9	46	16	16	307	205	108	3rd, East Div.	Lost Quarter-Final
1970-71	**78**	**29**	**7**	**3**	**13**	**16**	**10**	**42**	**23**	**13**	**291**	**216**	**97**	**3rd, East Div.**	**Won Stanley Cup**
1969-70	76	21	9	8	17	13	8	38	22	16	244	201	92	5th, East Div.	Out of Playoffs
1968-69	**76**	**26**	**7**	**5**	**20**	**12**	**6**	**46**	**19**	**11**	**271**	**202**	**103**	**1st, East Div.**	**Won Stanley Cup**
1967-68	**74**	**26**	**5**	**6**	**16**	**17**	**4**	**42**	**22**	**10**	**236**	**167**	**94**	**1st, East Div.**	**Won Stanley Cup**
1966-67	70	19	9	7	13	16	6	32	25	13	202	188	77	2nd,	Lost Final
1965-66	**70**	**23**	**11**	**1**	**18**	**10**	**7**	**41**	**21**	**8**	**239**	**173**	**90**	**1st,**	**Won Stanley Cup**
1964-65	**70**	**20**	**8**	**7**	**16**	**15**	**4**	**36**	**23**	**11**	**211**	**185**	**83**	**2nd,**	**Won Stanley Cup**
1963-64	70	22	7	6	14	14	7	36	21	13	209	167	85	1st,	Lost Semi-Final
1962-63	70	15	10	10	13	9	13	28	19	23	225	183	79	3rd,	Lost Semi-Final
1961-62	70	26	2	7	16	12	7	42	14	14	259	166	98	1st,	Lost Semi-Final
1960-61	70	24	6	5	17	13	5	41	19	10	254	188	92	1st,	Lost Semi-Final
1959-60	**70**	**23**	**4**	**8**	**17**	**14**	**4**	**40**	**18**	**12**	**255**	**178**	**92**	**1st,**	**Won Stanley Cup**
1958-59	**70**	**21**	**8**	**6**	**18**	**10**	**7**	**39**	**18**	**13**	**258**	**158**	**91**	**1st,**	**Won Stanley Cup**
1957-58	**70**	**23**	**8**	**4**	**20**	**9**	**6**	**43**	**17**	**10**	**250**	**158**	**96**	**1st,**	**Won Stanley Cup**
1956-57	**70**	**23**	**6**	**6**	**12**	**17**	**6**	**35**	**23**	**12**	**210**	**155**	**82**	**2nd,**	**Won Stanley Cup**
1955-56	**70**	**29**	**5**	**1**	**16**	**10**	**9**	**45**	**15**	**10**	**222**	**131**	**100**	**1st,**	**Won Stanley Cup**
1954-55	70	26	5	4	15	13	7	41	18	11	228	157	93	2nd,	Lost Final
1953-54	70	27	5	3	8	19	8	35	24	11	195	141	81	2nd,	Lost Final
1952-53	**70**	**18**	**12**	**5**	**10**	**11**	**14**	**28**	**23**	**19**	**155**	**148**	**75**	**2nd,**	**Won Stanley Cup**
1951-52	70	22	8	5	12	18	5	34	26	10	195	164	78	2nd,	Lost Final
1950-51	70	17	10	8	8	20	7	25	30	15	173	184	65	3rd,	Lost Final
1949-50	70	17	8	10	12	14	9	29	22	19	172	150	77	2nd,	Lost Semi-Final
1948-49	60	19	8	3	9	15	6	28	23	9	152	126	65	3rd,	Lost Semi-Final
1947-48	60	13	13	4	7	16	7	20	29	11	147	169	51	5th,	Out of Playoffs
1946-47	60	19	6	5	15	10	5	34	16	10	189	138	78	1st,	Lost Final
1945-46	**50**	**16**	**6**	**3**	**12**	**11**	**2**	**28**	**17**	**5**	**172**	**134**	**61**	**1st,**	**Won Stanley Cup**
1944-45	50	21	2	2	17	6	2	38	8	4	228	121	80	1st,	Lost Semi-Final
1943-44	**50**	**22**	**0**	**3**	**16**	**5**	**4**	**38**	**5**	**7**	**234**	**109**	**83**	**1st,**	**Won Stanley Cup**
1942-43	50	14	4	7	5	15	5	19	19	12	181	191	50	4th,	Lost Semi-Final
1941-42	48	12	10	2	6	17	1	18	27	3	134	173	39	6th,	Lost Quarter-Final
1940-41	48	11	9	4	5	17	2	16	26	6	121	147	38	6th,	Lost Quarter-Final
1939-40	48	5	14	5	5	19	0	10	33	5	90	167	25	7th,	Out of Playoffs
1938-39	48	8	11	5	7	13	4	15	24	9	115	146	39	6th,	Lost Quarter-Final
1937-38	48	13	4	7	5	13	6	18	17	13	123	128	49	3rd, Cdn. Div.	Lost Quarter-Final
1936-37	48	16	8	0	8	10	6	24	18	6	115	111	54	1st, Cdn. Div.	Lost Semi-Final
1935-36	48	5	11	8	6	15	3	11	26	11	82	123	33	4th, Cdn. Div.	Out of Playoffs
1934-35	48	11	11	2	8	12	4	19	23	6	110	145	44	3rd, Cdn. Div.	Lost Quarter-Final
1933-34	48	16	6	2	6	14	4	22	20	6	99	101	50	2nd, Cdn. Div.	Lost Quarter-Final
1932-33	48	15	5	4	3	20	1	18	25	5	92	115	41	3rd, Cdn. Div.	Lost Quarter-Final
1931-32	48	18	3	3	7	13	4	25	16	7	128	111	57	1st, Cdn. Div.	Lost Semi-Final
1930-31	**44**	**15**	**3**	**4**	**11**	**7**	**4**	**26**	**10**	**8**	**129**	**89**	**60**	**1st, Cdn. Div.**	**Won Stanley Cup**
1929-30	**44**	**13**	**5**	**4**	**8**	**9**	**5**	**21**	**14**	**9**	**142**	**114**	**51**	**2nd, Cdn. Div.**	**Won Stanley Cup**
1928-29	44	12	4	6	10	3	9	22	7	15	71	43	59	1st, Cdn. Div.	Lost Semi-Final
1927-28	44	12	7	3	14	4	4	26	11	7	116	48	59	1st, Cdn. Div.	Lost Semi-Final
1926-27	44	15	5	2	13	9	0	28	14	2	99	67	58	2nd, Cdn. Div.	Lost Semi-Final
1925-26	36	5	12	1	6	12	0	11	24	1	79	108	23	7th,	Out of Playoffs
1924-25	30	10	5	0	7	6	2	17	11	2	93	56	36	3rd,	Lost Final
1923-24	**24**	**10**	**2**	**0**	**3**	**9**	**0**	**13**	**11**	**0**	**59**	**48**	**26**	**2nd,**	**Won Stanley Cup**
1922-23	24	10	2	0	3	7	2	13	9	2	73	61	28	2nd,	Lost NHL Final
1921-22	24	8	3	1	4	8	0	12	11	1	88	94	25	3rd,	Out of Playoffs
1920-21	24	9	3	0	4	8	0	13	11	0	112	99	26	3rd and 2nd*	Out of Playoffs
1919-20	24	8	4	0	5	7	0	13	11	0	129	113	26	2nd and 3rd*	Out of Playoffs
1918-19	18	7	2	0	3	6	0	10	8	0	88	78	20	1st and 2nd*	Cup Final but no Decision
1917-18	22	8	3	0	5	6	0	13	9	0	115	84	26	1st and 3rd*	Lost NHL Final

* Season played in two halves with no combined standing at end.
From 1917-18 through 1925-26, NHL champions played against PCHA champions for Stanley Cup.

Franchise date: November 22, 1917

NORTHEAST DIVISION

82nd NHL Season

1998-99 Player Personnel

FORWARDS	HT	WT	S	Place of Birth	Date	1997-98 Club
BASHKIROV, Andrei	6-0	198	L	Shelekhov, USSR	6/22/70	Las Vegas-Fort Wayne
BLOUIN, Sylvain	6-2	207	L	Montreal, Que.	5/21/74	NY Rangers-Hartford
BRUNET, Benoit	6-	195	L	Ste-Anne-de-Bellevue, Que.	8/24/68	Montreal
CHOUINARD, Eric	6-2	195	L	Atlanta, GA	7/8/80	Quebec (QMJHL)
CORSON, Shayne	6-1	200	L	Barrie, Ont.	8/13/66	Montreal-Canada
DAMPHOUSSE, Vincent	6-1	191	L	Montreal, Que.	12/17/67	Montreal
DELISLE, Jonathan	5-10	193	R	Ste-Anne-des-Plaines, Que.	6/30/77	Fredericton
GENDRON, Martin	5-9	190	R	Valleyfield, Que.	2/15/74	Chi-Ind-Milw-Fred
HIGGINS, Matt	6-2	182	L	Calgary, Alta.	10/29/77	Montreal-Fredericton
HOGLUND, Jonas	6-3	215	R	Hammaro, Swe.	8/29/72	Calgary-Montreal
HOUDE, Eric	5-11	191	L	Montreal, Que.	12/19/76	Montreal-Fredericton
HOULE, Jean-Francois	5-9	185	L	Charlesbourg, Que.	1/14/75	Fredericton-New Orleans
KOIVU, Saku	5-10	183	L	Turku, Finland	11/23/74	Montreal-Finland
LOJKIN, Alexei	5-9	176	L	Minsk, USSR	2/21/74	Fredericton
MORIN, Olivier	6-	176	R	Montreal, Que.	4/2/78	Val D'Or
MORISSETTE, Dave	6-1	220	L	Baie Comeau, Que.	12/24/71	Houston
OLSON, Boyd	6-1	187	L	Edmonton, Alta.	4/4/76	Fredericton
POULIN, Patrick	6-1	210	L	Vanier, Que.	4/23/73	Tampa Bay-Montreal
RECCHI, Mark	5-10	185	L	Kamloops, B.C.	2/1/68	Montreal-Canada
RUCINSKY, Martin	6-1	205	L	Most, Czech.	3/11/71	Montreal-Czech.
RYAN, Terry	6-1	201	L	St. John's, Nfld.	1/14/77	Montreal-Fredericton
SAVAGE, Brian	6-2	192	L	Sudbury, Ont.	2/24/71	Montreal
STEVENSON, Turner	6-3	220	R	Prince George, B.C.	5/18/72	Montreal
THORNTON, Scott	6-3	219	L	London, Ont.	1/9/71	Montreal
WARD, Jason	6-2	184	R	Chapleau, Ont.	1/16/79	Erie (OHL)-Wndsr-Fred-Canada
DEFENSEMEN						
BRISEBOIS, Patrice	6-2	209	R	Montreal, Que.	1/27/71	Montreal
BROWN, Brad	6-4	218	R	Baie Verte, Nfld.	12/27/75	Fredericton
CHEREDARYK, Steve	6-3	213	L	Calgary, Alta.	11/20/75	Fredericton-New Orleans
CLARK, Brett	6-0	182	L	Moosomin, Sask.	12/23/76	Montreal-Fredericton
DROLET, Jimmy	6-0	190	L	Vanier, Que.	2/19/76	Fredericton-New Orleans
GUREN, Miloslav	6-2	210	L	Uherske. Hradiste, Czech.	9/24/76	Fredericton
MALAKHOV, Vladimir	6-4	229	L	Ekaterinburg, USSR	8/30/68	Montreal
MANSON, Dave	6-2	219	L	Prince Albert, Sask.	1/27/67	Montreal
QUINTAL, Stephane	6-3	230	R	Boucherville, Que.	10/22/68	Montreal
RAZIN, Gennady	6-3	175	L	Kharkov, USSR	2/3/78	Kamloops
RIVET, Craig	6-2	195	R	North Bay, Ont.	9/13/74	Montreal
ROBIDAS, Stephane	5-11	195	R	Sherbrooke, Que.	3/3/77	Fredericton
ULANOV, Igor	6-2	205	L	Krasnokamsk, USSR	10/1/69	Tampa Bay-Montreal

GOALTENDERS	HT	WT	C	Place of Birth	Date	1997-98 Club
GARON, Mathieu	6-1	187	R	Chandler, Que.	1/9/78	Victoriaville-Canada
THEODORE, Jose	5-8	177	R	Laval, Que.	9/13/76	Fredericton-Montreal
THIBAULT, Jocelyn	5-11	170	L	Montreal, Que.	1/12/75	Montreal

General Managers' History

Jack Laviolette and Joseph Cattarinich, 1909-1910; George Kennedy, 1910-11 to 1920-21; Leo Dandurand, 1921-22 to 1934-35; Ernest Savard, 1935-36; Cecil Hart, 1936-37 to 1938-39; Jules Dugal, 1939-40; Tom P. Gorman, 1940-41 to 1945-46; Frank J. Selke, 1946-47 to 1963-64; Sam Pollock, 1964-65 to 1977-78; Irving Grundman, 1978-79 to 1982-83; Serge Savard, 1983-84 to 1994-95; Serge Savard and Réjean Houle, 1995-96; Réjean Houle, 1996-97 to date.

Coaching History

Jack Laviolette, 1909-10; Adolphe Lecours, 1910-11; Napoleon Dorval, 1911-12, 1912-13; Jimmy Gardner, 1913-14, 1914-15; Newsy Lalonde, 1915-16 to 1920-21; Newsy Lalonde and Léo Dandurand, 1921-22; Léo Dandurand, 1922-23 to 1925-26; Cecil Hart, 1926-27 to 1931-32; Newsy Lalonde, 1932-33, 1933-34; Newsy Lalonde and Léo Dandurand, 1934-35; Sylvio Mantha, 1935-36; Cecil Hart, 1936-37, 1937-38; Cecil Hart and Jules Dugal, 1938-39; Babe Siebert, 1939*; Pit Lepine, 1939-40; Dick Irvin 1940-41 to 1954-55; Toe Blake, 1955-56 to 1967-68; Claude Ruel, 1968-69, 1969-70; Claude Ruel and Al MacNeil, 1970-71; Scotty Bowman, 1971-72 to 1978-79; Bernie Geoffrion and Claude Ruel, 1979-80; Claude Ruel, 1980-81; Bob Berry, 1981-82, 1982-83; Bob Berry and Jacques Lemaire, 1983-84; Jacques Lemaire, 1984-85; Jean Perron, 1985-86 to 1987-88; Pat Burns, 1988-89 to 1991-92; Jacques Demers, 1992-93 to 1994-95; Jacques Demers and Mario Tremblay, 1995-96; Mario Tremblay, 1996-97; Alain Vigneault, 1997-98 to date.

* Named coach in summer but died before 1939-40 season began.

Coach

VIGNEAULT, ALAIN

Coach, Montreal Canadiens. Born in Quebec, Que., May 14, 1961.

Alain Vigneault was named the 24th head coach in the history of the Montreal Canadiens on May 26, 1997. At age 36, he became the second youngest coach in team history.

Vigneault, who guided the Canadiens to the Eastern Conference semi-finals during his first season, possesses more than ten years of coaching experience. He coached the QMJHL Beauport Harfangs for two seasons (1995-96 and 1996-97), following more than three years as an assistant coach with the NHL Ottawa Senators.

Vigneault was the head coach of the Hull Olympiques for five seasons (1987 to 1992), leading his team to the Memorial Cup Tournament in his first season. His coaching career began in 1986-87 with the Trois-Rivières Draveurs of the QMJHL. As head coach at the junior hockey level, Vigneault had a record of 257 victories, 213 losses and 35 ties. In 505 games, he posted a .544 winning percentage.

Vigneault was assistant coach on Canada's National Junior Team in 1989 and 1991, winning the gold medal at the 1991 World Junior Championships in Saskatoon. He was honored once as CHL coach of the year (1987-88), and twice as head coach of the QMJHL Second All-Star Team.

Alain Vigneault played a total of 42 games in the NHL from 1981 to 1983 with the St. Louis Blues. He resides in Montreal with his spouse, Josée Doucet, and their two daughters, Andréanne, 9, and Janie, 5.

1997-98 Scoring

* – rookie

Regular Season

Pos	#	Player	Team	GP	G	A	Pts	+/–	PIM	PP	SH	GW	GT	S	%
R	8	Mark Recchi	MTL	82	32	42	74	11	51	9	1	6	0	216	14.8
C	25	Vincent Damphousse	MTL	76	18	41	59	14	58	2	1	5	0	164	11.0
C	11	Saku Koivu	MTL	69	14	43	57	8	48	2	2	3	0	145	9.7
L	27	Shayne Corson	MTL	62	21	34	55	2	108	14	1	1	0	142	14.8
L	26	Martin Rucinsky	MTL	78	21	32	53	13	84	5	3	3	0	192	10.9
D	38	Vladimir Malakhov	MTL	74	13	31	44	16	70	8	0	2	0	166	7.8
L	49	Brian Savage	MTL	64	26	17	43	11	36	8	0	7	2	152	17.1
D	43	Patrice Brisebois	MTL	79	10	27	37	16	67	5	0	1	0	125	8.0
D	22	Dave Manson	MTL	81	4	30	34	22	122	2	0	0	0	148	2.7
L	17	Benoit Brunet	MTL	68	12	20	32	11	61	1	2	2	1	87	13.8
L	44	Jonas Hoglund	CGY	50	6	8	14	-9	16	0	0	0	0	124	4.8
			MTL	28	6	5	11	2	6	4	0	0	0	62	9.7
			TOTAL	78	12	13	25	-7	22	4	0	0	0	186	6.5
C	28	Marc Bureau	MTL	74	13	6	19	0	12	0	0	2	0	82	15.9
L	37	Patrick Poulin	T.B.	44	2	7	9	-3	19	0	0	0	0	49	4.1
			MTL	34	4	6	10	-1	8	0	1	1	0	39	10.3
			TOTAL	78	6	13	19	-4	27	0	1	1	0	88	6.8
D	5	Stephane Quintal	MTL	71	6	10	16	13	97	0	0	0	0	88	6.8
C	24	Scott Thornton	MTL	67	6	9	15	0	158	1	0	1	2	51	11.8
D	3	Zarley Zalapski	CGY	35	2	7	9	-12	41	2	0	1	0	46	4.3
			MTL	28	1	5	6	-1	22	0	1	0	0	27	3.7
			TOTAL	63	3	12	15	-13	63	2	1	1	0	73	4.1
C	71	Sebastien Bordeleau	MTL	53	6	8	14	5	36	2	1	0	1	55	10.9
R	23	Turner Stevenson	MTL	63	4	6	10	-8	110	1	0	0	0	43	9.3
D	55	Igor Ulanov	T.B.	45	2	7	9	-5	85	1	0	0	0	32	6.3
			MTL	4	0	1	1	-2	12	0	0	0	0	4	0.0
			TOTAL	49	2	8	10	-7	97	1	0	0	0	36	5.6
D	34	Peter Popovic	MTL	69	2	6	8	-6	38	0	0	0	0	40	5.0
G	41	Jocelyn Thibault	MTL	47	0	2	2	0	0	0	0	0	0	0	0.0
D	52	Craig Rivet	MTL	61	0	2	2	-3	93	0	0	0	0	26	0.0
C	15 *	Eric Houde	MTL	9	1	0	1	-3	0	0	0	1	0	4	25.0
D	29 *	Brett Clark	MTL	41	1	0	1	-3	20	0	0	0	0	26	3.8
R	21	Mick Vukota	T.B.	42	1	0	1	0	116	0	0	0	0	15	6.7
			MTL	22	0	0	0	-4	76	0	0	0	0	8	0.0
			TOTAL	64	1	0	1	-4	192	0	0	0	0	23	4.3
D	48 *	Francois Groleau	MTL	1	0	0	0	1	0	0	0	0	0	3	0.0
R	51 *	David Ling	MTL	1	0	0	0	-1	0	0	0	0	0	1	0.0
C	46 *	Matt Higgins	MTL	1	0	0	0	-1	0	0	0	0	0	1	0.0
L	14 *	Terry Ryan	MTL	4	0	0	0	0	31	0	0	0	0	0	0.0
G	35	Andy Moog	MTL	42	0	0	0	0	4	0	0	0	0	0	0.0

Goaltending

No.	Goaltender	GPI	Mins	Avg	W	L	T	EN	SO	GA	SA	S%
41	Jocelyn Thibault	47	2652	2.47	19	15	8	1	2	109	1109	.902
35	Andy Moog	42	2337	2.49	18	17	5	1	3	97	1024	.905
	Totals	**82**	**5009**	**2.49**	**37**	**32**	**13**	**2**	**5**	**208**	**2135**	**.903**

Playoffs

Pos	#	Player	Team	GP	G	A	Pts	+/–	PIM	PP	SH	GW	GT	S	%
R	8	Mark Recchi	MTL	10	4	8	12	2	6	0	0	2	0	22	18.2
L	27	Shayne Corson	MTL	10	3	6	9	3	26	1	0	1	0	33	9.1
C	25	Vincent Damphousse	MTL	10	3	6	9	-4	22	1	0	0	0	42	7.1
D	38	Vladimir Malakhov	MTL	9	3	4	7	-3	10	2	0	0	0	19	15.8
R	23	Turner Stevenson	MTL	10	3	4	7	1	12	0	0	0	0	21	14.3
C	11	Saku Koivu	MTL	6	2	3	5	4	2	1	0	0	0	14	14.3
D	55	Igor Ulanov	MTL	10	1	4	5	3	12	0	0	0	0	6	16.7
L	26	Martin Rucinsky	MTL	10	3	0	3	-2	4	1	0	0	0	35	8.6
C	28	Marc Bureau	MTL	10	1	2	3	-1	6	0	0	0	0	16	6.3
L	44	Jonas Hoglund	MTL	10	2	0	2	-1	0	0	0	0	0	7	28.6
D	34	Peter Popovic	MTL	10	1	1	2	2	2	0	0	0	0	3	33.3
D	5	Stephane Quintal	MTL	9	0	2	2	2	4	0	0	0	0	12	0.0
C	24	Scott Thornton	MTL	9	0	2	2	0	10	0	0	0	0	13	0.0
L	49	Brian Savage	MTL	9	0	2	2	-2	6	0	0	0	0	24	0.0
L	17	Benoit Brunet	MTL	8	1	0	1	1	4	0	0	1	1	5	20.0
D	43	Patrice Brisebois	MTL	10	1	0	1	-5	0	0	0	0	0	26	3.8
G	41	Jocelyn Thibault	MTL	2	0	1	1	0	0	0	0	0	0	0	0.0
D	3	Zarley Zalapski	MTL	6	0	1	1	-3	4	0	0	0	0	0	0.0
D	22	Dave Manson	MTL	10	0	1	1	0	14	0	0	0	0	25	0.0
R	21	Mick Vukota	MTL	1	0	0	0	0	0	0	0	0	0	0	0.0
L	37	Patrick Poulin	MTL	3	0	0	0	-1	0	0	0	0	0	1	0.0
G	60 *	Jose Theodore	MTL	3	0	0	0	0	0	0	0	0	0	0	0.0
D	52	Craig Rivet	MTL	5	0	0	0	-2	2	0	0	0	0	5	0.0
C	71	Sebastien Bordeleau	MTL	5	0	0	0	-1	2	0	0	0	0	1	0.0
G	35	Andy Moog	MTL	9	0	0	0	0	0	0	0	0	0	0	0.0

Goaltending

No.	Goaltender	GPI	Mins	Avg	W	L	EN	SO	GA	SA	S%
60	* Jose Theodore	3	120	0.50	0	1	1	0	1	35	.971
35	Andy Moog	9	474	3.04	4	5	1	1	24	204	.882
41	Jocelyn Thibault	2	43	5.58	0	0	1	0	4	16	.750
	Totals	**10**	**643**	**2.99**	**4**	**6**	**3**	**1**	**32**	**258**	**.876**

Coaching Record

		Regular Season					Playoffs			
Season	Team	Games	W	L	T	%	Games	W	L	%
1986-87	Trois-Rivières (QMJHL)	65	26	37	2	.415	....	....	....	....
1987-88	Hull (QMJHL)	70	43	23	4	.643	....	....	....	....
1988-89	Hull (QMJHL)	66	36	25	5	.583	....	....	....	....
1989-90	Hull (QMJHL)	70	36	29	5	.550	....	....	....	....
1990-91	Hull (QMJHL)	65	33	25	7	.562	....	....	....	....
1991-92	Hull (QMJHL)	68	40	23	5	.625	....	....	....	....
1995-96	Beauport (QMJHL)	31	19	7	5	.694	....	....	....	....
1996-97	Beauport (QMJHL)	70	24	44	2	.357	....	....	....	....
1997-98	**Montreal (NHL)**	**82**	**37**	**32**	**13**	**.530**	**10**	**4**	**6**	**.400**
	NHL Totals	**82**	**37**	**32**	**13**	**.530**	**10**	**4**	**6**	**.400**

Club Records

Team

(Figures in brackets for season records are games played; records for fewest points, wins, ties, losses, goals, goals against are for 70 or more games)

Most Points	*132	1976-77 (80)
Most Wins	60	1976-77 (80)
Most Ties	23	1962-63 (70)
Most Losses	40	1983-84 (80)
Most Goals	387	1976-77 (80)
Most Goals Against	295	1983-84 (80)
Fewest Points	65	1950-51 (70)
Fewest Wins	25	1950-51 (70)
Fewest Ties	5	1983-84 (80)
Fewest Losses	*8	1976-77 (80)
Fewest Goals	155	1952-53 (70)
Fewest Goals Against	*131	1955-56 (70)
Longest Winning Streak		
Overall	12	Jan. 6-Feb. 3/68
Home	13	Nov. 2/43-Jan. 8/44, Jan. 30-Mar. 26/77
Away	8	Dec. 18/77-Jan. 18/78, Jan. 21-Feb. 21/82
Longest Undefeated Streak		
Overall	28	Dec. 18/77-Feb. 23/78 (23 wins, 5 ties)
Home	*34	Nov. 1/76-Apr. 2/77 (28 wins, 6 ties)
Away	*23	Nov. 27/74-Mar. 12/75 (14 wins, 9 ties)
Longest Losing Streak		
Overall	12	Feb. 13-Mar. 13/26
Home	7	Dec. 16/39-Jan. 18/40
Away	10	Jan. 16-Mar. 13/26
Longest Winless Streak		
Overall	12	Feb. 13-Mar. 13/26 (12 losses), Nov. 28-Dec. 29/35 (8 losses, 4 ties)
Home	15	Dec. 16/39-Mar. 7/40 (12 losses, 3 ties)
Away	12	Nov. 26/33-Jan. 28/34 (8 losses, 4 ties), Oct. 20/50-Dec. 13/51 (8 losses, 4 ties)
Most Shutouts, Season	*22	1928-29 (44)
Most PIM, Season	1,847	1995-96 (82)
Most Goals, Game	*16	Mar. 3/20 (Mtl. 16 at Que. 3)

Individual

Most Seasons	20	Henri Richard, Jean Beliveau
Most Games	1,256	Henri Richard
Most Goals, Career	544	Maurice Richard
Most Assists, Career	728	Guy Lafleur
Most Points, Career	1,246	Guy Lafleur (518G, 728A)
Most PIM, Career	2,248	Chris Nilan
Most Shutouts, Career	75	George Hainsworth
Longest Consecutive Games Streak	560	Doug Jarvis (Oct. 8/75-Apr. 4/82)
Most Goals, Season	60	Steve Shutt (1976-77), Guy Lafleur (1977-78)
Most Assists, Season	82	Peter Mahovlich (1974-75)
Most Points, Season	136	Guy Lafleur (1976-77; 56G, 80A)
Most PIM, Season	358	Chris Nilan (1984-85)
Most Points, Defenseman, Season	85	Larry Robinson (1976-77; 19G, 66A)
Most Points, Center, Season	117	Peter Mahovlich (1974-75; 35G, 82A)
Most Points, Right Wing, Season	136	Guy Lafleur (1976-77; 56G, 80A)
Most Points, Left Wing, Season	110	Mats Naslund (1985-86; 43G, 67A)
Most Points, Rookie, Season	71	Mats Naslund (1982-83; 26G, 45A), Kjell Dahlin (1985-86; 32G, 39A)
Most Shutouts, Season	*22	George Hainsworth (1928-29)
Most Goals, Game	6	Newsy Lalonde (Jan. 10/20)
Most Assists, Game	6	Elmer Lach (Feb. 6/43)
Most Points, Game	8	Maurice Richard (Dec. 28/44; 5G, 3A), Bert Olmstead (Jan. 9/54; 4G, 4A)

* NHL Record.

Retired Numbers

1	Jacques Plante	1952-1963
2	Doug Harvey	1947-1961
4	Jean Béliveau	1950-1971
7	Howie Morenz	1923-1937
9	Maurice Richard	1942-1960
10	Guy Lafleur	1971-1984
16	Henri Richard	1955-1975

All-time Record vs. Other Clubs

Regular Season

	At Home							On Road							Total						
	GP	W	L	T	GF	GA	PTS	GP	W	L	T	GF	GA	PTS	GP	W	L	T	GF	GA	PTS
Anaheim	4	1	2	1	16	15	3	4	3	1	0	17	15	6	8	4	3	1	33	30	9
Boston	319	184	90	45	1085	747	413	319	119	146	54	869	943	292	638	303	236	99	1954	1690	705
Buffalo	87	49	26	12	351	264	110	87	25	43	19	239	271	69	174	74	69	31	590	535	179
Calgary	41	23	11	7	147	100	53	40	23	12	5	144	125	51	81	46	23	12	291	225	104
Carolina	63	42	14	7	275	186	91	66	32	25	9	238	200	73	129	74	39	16	513	386	164
Chicago	270	171	51	48	1049	636	390	270	123	92	55	754	725	301	540	294	143	103	1803	1361	691
Colorado	59	37	13	9	251	187	83	60	26	29	5	212	201	57	119	63	42	14	463	388	140
Dallas	54	37	10	7	241	132	81	55	30	14	11	199	142	71	109	67	24	18	440	274	152
Detroit	277	170	64	43	985	625	383	277	96	128	53	708	792	245	554	266	192	96	1693	1417	628
Edmonton	25	14	7	4	90	78	32	26	13	13	0	85	90	26	51	27	20	4	175	168	58
Florida	9	4	4	1	28	22	9	10	4	4	2	30	36	10	19	8	8	3	58	58	19
Los Angeles	60	42	7	11	279	153	95	61	35	17	9	243	188	79	121	77	24	20	522	341	174
New Jersey	42	28	9	5	163	109	61	42	24	16	2	175	124	50	84	52	25	7	338	233	111
NY Islanders	48	27	12	9	181	146	63	48	22	21	5	147	153	49	96	49	33	14	328	299	112
NY Rangers	278	186	56	36	1094	639	408	278	111	113	54	810	812	276	556	297	169	90	1904	1451	684
Ottawa	18	10	5	3	57	50	23	15	11	4	0	53	39	22	33	21	9	3	110	89	45
Philadelphia	62	30	19	13	226	196	73	61	22	25	14	185	188	58	123	52	44	27	411	384	131
Phoenix	25	22	3	0	131	59	44	25	11	8	6	99	82	28	50	33	11	6	230	141	72
Pittsburgh	70	54	8	8	341	175	116	70	34	24	12	249	211	80	140	88	32	20	590	386	196
St. Louis	55	39	9	7	243	148	85	54	27	12	15	189	140	69	109	66	21	22	432	288	154
San Jose	7	6	0	1	30	11	13	7	3	2	2	19	20	8	14	9	2	3	49	31	21
Tampa Bay	10	6	3	1	31	23	13	11	3	6	2	26	30	8	21	9	9	3	57	53	21
Toronto	317	193	84	40	1129	782	426	318	113	161	44	832	962	270	635	306	245	84	1961	1744	696
Vancouver	48	36	8	4	236	125	76	46	31	7	8	184	113	70	94	67	15	12	420	238	146
Washington	48	30	12	6	198	100	66	47	19	20	8	150	131	46	95	49	32	14	348	231	112
Defunct Clubs	231	148	58	25	779	469	321	230	98	97	35	586	606	231	461	246	155	60	1365	1075	552
Totals	**2527**	**1589**	**585**	**353**	**9636**	**6177**	**3531**	**2527**	**1058**	**1040**	**429**	**7442**	**7339**	**2545**	**5054**	**2647**	**1625**	**782**	**17078**	**13516**	**6076**

Playoffs

	Series	W	L	GP	W	L	T	GF	GA	Last Mtg.	Round	Result
Boston	28	21	7	139	87	52	0	430	339	1994	CQF	L 3-4
Buffalo	7	4	3	35	18	17	0	124	111	1998	CSF	L 0-4
Calgary	2	1	1	11	6	5	0	31	32	1989	F	L 2-4
Chicago	17	12	5	81	50	29	2	261	185	1976	QF	W 4-0
Colorado	5	3	2	31	17	14	0	105	85	1993	DSF	W 4-2
Dallas	2	1	1	13	7	6	0	48	37	1980	QF	L 3-4
Detroit	12	5	7	62	33	29	0	161	149	1978	QF	W 4-1
Edmonton	1	0	1	3	0	3	0	6	15	1981	PR	L 0-3
Hartford	5	5	0	27	19	8	0	96	70	1992	DSF	W 4-3
Los Angeles	1	1	0	5	4	1	0	15	12	1993	F	W 4-1
NY Islanders	4	3	1	22	14	8	0	64	55	1993	CF	W 4-1
NY Rangers	14	7	7	61	34	25	2	188	158	1996	CQF	L 2-4
New Jersey	1	0	1	5	1	4	0	11	22	1997	CQF	L 1-4
Philadelphia	4	3	1	21	14	7	0	72	52	1989	CF	W 4-2
Pittsburgh	1	1	0	6	4	2	0	18	15	1998	CQF	W 4-2
St. Louis	3	3	0	12	12	0	0	42	14	1977	QF	W 4-0
Toronto	15	8	7	71	42	29	0	215	160	1979	QF	W 4-0
Vancouver	1	1	0	5	4	1	0	20	9	1975	QF	W 4-1
Defunct Clubs	11*	6	4	28	15	9	4	70	71			
Totals	**134***	**85**	**48**	**638**	**381**	**249**	**8**	**1977**	**1591**			

* 1919 Final incomplete due to influenza epidemic.

Calgary totals include Atlanta, 1972-73 to 1979-80. Carolina totals include Hartford, 1979-80 to 1996-97.
Colorado totals include Quebec, 1979-80 to 1994-95. Dallas totals include Minnesota, 1967-68 to 1992-93.
New Jersey totals include Kansas City, 1974-75 to 1975-76, and Colorado Rockies, 1976-77 to 1981-82.
Phoenix totals include Winnipeg, 1979-80 to 1995-96.

Playoff Results 1998-94

Year	Round	Opponent	Result	GF	GA
1998	CSF	Buffalo	L 0-4	10	17
	CQF	Pittsburgh	W 4-2	18	15
1997	CQF	New Jersey	L 1-4	11	22
1996	CQF	NY Rangers	L 2-4	17	19
1994	CQF	Boston	L 3-4	20	22

Abbreviations: Round: F – Final; **CF** – conference final; **CQF** – conference quarter-final; **CSF** – conference semi-final; **DSF** – division semi-final; **QF** – quarter-final; **PR** – preliminary round.

1997-98 Results

Oct.	1		Ottawa	2-2		31	at	Calgary	3-2
	4	at	Boston	4-1	**Jan.**	2	at	Edmonton	5-3
	8	at	Pittsburgh	3-0		3	at	Vancouver	4-2
	11		Philadelphia	2-6		7		Boston	1-2
	15		Pittsburgh	1-1		8	at	NY Islanders	8-2
	17	at	Buffalo	5-1		10		NY Rangers	4-1
	18		Washington	2-3		12	at	Tampa Bay	6-3
	22		Florida	3-0		14	at	Philadelphia	3-3
	23	at	New Jersey	1-2		21		Boston	4-2
	25	at	Ottawa	4-2		24		Carolina	3-4
	27		Chicago	4-2		25		New Jersey	1-3
	29		NY Islanders	2-5		29	at	Philadelphia	3-2
Nov.	1		Toronto	5-1		31		Ottawa	3-4
	3		Dallas	6-4	**Feb.**	1	at	Carolina	6-3
	5		Phoenix	4-2		4	at	NY Islanders	2-4
	7	at	San Jose	4-3		7		Buffalo	1-4
	8	at	Los Angeles	4-1		25		Pittsburgh	2-6
	12	at	Anaheim	4-3		28	at	Toronto	0-4
	13	at	Phoenix	5-2	**Mar.**	4	at	Dallas	3-1
	15		Washington	2-3		5	at	St. Louis	0-4
	17		Tampa Bay	4-1		7		Buffalo	1-2
	19	at	Carolina	1-2		9		Florida	6-1
	22		Detroit	2-5		11		Vancouver	2-2
	24		San Jose	2-2		14		New Jersey	4-2
	26	at	Washington	6-5		16		Calgary	3-3
	28	at	Detroit	0-2		18	at	NY Rangers	1-2
	29	at	Pittsburgh	3-6		19	at	Chicago	0-1
Dec.	1		Pittsburgh	0-1		21		Anaheim	4-5
	3		Los Angeles	2-0		25	at	Tampa Bay	2-1
	6		NY Rangers	3-3		26	at	Florida	4-5
	8		Colorado	4-2		28		Tampa Bay	8-2
	10		St. Louis	4-3		31	at	Carolina	3-3
	12	at	New Jersey	2-5	**Apr.**	1	at	Florida	4-3
	13	at	Boston	2-4		4		Carolina	0-1
	15		Philadelphia	1-3		6	at	Washington	2-2
	19	at	Buffalo	0-1		7	at	NY Rangers	3-2
	20		Ottawa	4-1		10	at	Buffalo	1-2
	22		Edmonton	3-3		11		NY Islanders	3-3
	23	at	Ottawa	3-4		15		Boston	2-6
	27	at	Pittsburgh	1-0		16	at	Ottawa	2-0
	29	at	Colorado	1-1		18		Buffalo	3-3

Entry Draft Selections 1998-84

1998

Pick	
16	Eric Chouinard
45	Mike Ribeiro
75	Francois Beauchemin
132	Andrei Bashkirov
152	Gordie Dwyer
162	Andrei Markov
189	Andrei Kruchinin
201	Craig Murray
216	Michael Ryder
247	Darcy Harris

1997

Pick	
11	Jason Ward
37	Gregor Baumgartner
65	Ilkka Mikkola
91	Daniel Tetrault
118	Konstantin Sidulov
122	Gennady Razin
145	Jonathan Desroches
172	Ben Guite
197	Petr Kubos
202	Andrei Sidyakin
228	Jarl-Espen Ygranes

1996

Pick	
18	Matt Higgins
44	Mathieu Garon
71	Arron Asham
92	Kim Staal
99	Etienne Drapeau
127	Daniel Archambault
154	Brett Clark
181	Timo Vertala
207	Mattia Baldi
233	Michel Tremblay

1995

Pick	
8	Terry Ryan
60	Miroslav Guren
74	Martin Hohenberger
86	Jonathan Delisle
112	Niklas Anger
138	Boyd Olson
164	Stephane Robidas
190	Greg Hart
216	Eric Houde

1994

Pick	
18	Brad Brown
44	Jose Theodore
54	Chris Murray
70	Marko Kiprusoff
74	Martin Belanger
96	Arto Kuki
122	Jimmy Drolet
148	Joel Irving
174	Jessie Rezansoff
200	Peter Strom
226	Tomas Vokoun
252	Chris Aldous
278	Ross Parsons

1993

Pick	
21	Saku Koivu
47	Rory Fitzpatrick
73	Sebastien Bordeleau
85	Adam Wiesel
99	Jean-Francois Houle
113	Jeff Lank
125	Dion Darling
151	Darcy Tucker
177	David Ruhly
203	Alan Letang
229	Alexandre Duchesne
255	Brian Larochelle
281	Russell Guzior

1992

Pick	
20	David Wilkie
33	Valeri Bure
44	Keli Corpse
68	Craig Rivet
82	Louis Bernard
92	Marc Lamothe
116	Don Chase
140	Martin Sychra
164	Christian Proulx
188	Michael Burman
212	Earl Cronan
236	Trent Cavicchi
260	Hiroyuki Miura

1991

Pick	
17	Brent Bilodeau
28	Jim Campbll
43	Craig Darby
61	Yves Sarault
73	Vladimir Vujtek
83	Sylvain Lapointe
100	Brad Layzell
105	Tony Prpic
127	Oleg Petrov
149	Brady Kramer
171	Brian Savage
193	Scott Fraser
215	Greg MacEachern
237	Paul Lepler
259	Dale Hooper

1990

Pick	
12	Turner Stevenson
39	Ryan Kuwabara
58	Charles Poulin
60	Robert Guillet
81	Gilbert Dionne
102	Paul DiPietro
123	Craig Conroy
144	Stephen Rohr
165	Brent Fleetwood
186	Derek Maguire
207	Mark Kettelhut
228	John Uniac
249	Sergei Martynyuk

1989

Pick	
13	Lindsay Vallis
30	Patrice Brisebois
41	Steve Larouche
51	Pierre Sevigny
83	Andre Racicot
104	Marc Deschamps
146	Craig Ferguson
167	Patrick Lebeu
188	Roy Mitchell
209	Ed Henrich
230	Justin Duberman
251	Steve Cadieux

1988

Pick	
20	Eric Charron
34	Martin St. Amour
46	Neil Carnes
83	Patrik Kjellberg
93	Peter Popovic
104	Jean-Claude Bergeron
125	Patrik Carnback
146	Tim Chase
167	Sean Hill
188	Harijs Vitolinsh
209	Yuri Krivokhizha
230	Kevin Dahl
251	Dave Kunda

1987

Pick	
17	Andrew Cassels
33	John LeClair
38	Eric Desjardins
44	Mathieu Schneider
58	Francois Gravel
80	Kris Miller
101	Steve McCool
122	Les Kuntar
143	Rob Kelley
164	Will Geist
185	Eric Tremblay
206	Barry McKinlay
227	Ed Ronan
248	Bryan Herring

1986

Pick	
15	Mark Pederson
27	Benoit Brunet
57	Jyrki Lumme
78	Brent Bobyck
94	Eric Aubertin
99	Mario Milani
120	Steve Bisson
141	Lyle Odelein
162	Rick Hayward
183	Antonin Routa
204	Eric Bohemier
225	Charlie Moore
246	Karel Svoboda

1985

Pick	
12	Jose Charbonneau
16	Tom Chorske
33	Todd Richards
47	Rocky Dundas
75	Martin Desjardins
79	Brent Gilchrist
96	Tom Sagissor
117	Donald Dufresne
142	Ed Cristofoli
163	Mike Claringbull
184	Roger Beedon
198	Maurice Mansi
205	Chad Arthur
226	Mike Bishop
247	John Ferguson Jr.

1984

Pick	
5	Petr Svoboda
8	Shayne Corson
29	Stephane Richer
51	Patrick Roy
54	Graeme Bonar
65	Lee Brodeur
95	Gerald Johannson
116	Jim Nesich
137	Scott MacTavish
158	Brad McCughey
179	Eric Demers
199	Ron Annear
220	Dave Tanner
240	Troy Crosby

General Manager

HOULE, RÉJEAN
Vice President, Hockey and General Manager, Montreal Canadiens.
Born in Rouyn-Noranda, Que., October 25, 1949.

Réjean Houle was appointed general manager of the Montreal Canadiens on October 21, 1995. Houle played for the Canadiens from 1969 to 1983, with the exception of a three-year stint with the Quebec Nordiques (WHA), and was a member of five Stanley Cup-winning teams with Montreal. Houle played in 635 NHL regular season games, posting totals of 161 goals and 247 assists. Prior to becoming general manager of the Canadiens, and following his playing career, Houle was an executive with Molson-O'Keefe Breweries.

Captains' History

Jack Laviolette, 1909-10; Newsy Lalonde, 1910-11; Jack Laviolette, 1911-12; Newsy Lalonde, 1912-13; Jimmy Gardner, 1913-14, 1914-15; Howard McNamara, 1915-16; Newsy Lalonde, 1916-17 to 1921-22; Sprague Cleghorn, 1922-23 to 1924-25; Bill Coutu, 1925-26; Sylvio Mantha, 1926-27 to 1931-32; George Hainsworth, 1932-33; Sylvio Mantha, 1933-34 to 1935-36; Babe Siebert, 1936-37 to 1938-39; Walter Buswell, 1939-40; Toe Blake, 1940-41 to 1946-47; Toe Blake and Bill Durnan, 1947-48; Emile Bouchard, 1948-49 to 1955-56; Maurice Richard, 1956-57 to 1959-60; Doug Harvey, 1960-61; Jean Beliveau, 1961-62 to 1970-71; Henri Richard, 1971-72 to 1974-75; Yvan Cournoyer, 1975-76 to 1978-79; Serge Savard, 1979-80, 1980-81; Bob Gainey, 1981-82 to 1988-89, Guy Carbonneau and Chris Chelios (co-captains), 1989-90; Guy Carbonneau, 1990-91 to 1993-94; Kirk Muller and Mike Keane, 1994-95; Mike Keane and Pierre Turgeon, 1995-96; Pierre Turgeon and Vincent Damphousse, 1996-97; Vincent Damphousse, 1997-98 to date.

Club Directory

Centre Molson
1260 de La Gauchetière St. W.
Montréal, QC H3B 5E8
Phone **514/932-2582**
FAX (Hockey) 514/932-8736
Team Services 514/989-2717
P.R. 514/932-9296
Media 514/932-8285
Web site: www.canadiens.com
Capacity: 21,273

Owner: The Molson Companies Limited

Chairman of the Board, President and Governor	Ronald Corey
Vice-President Hockey, General Manager and Alternate Governor	Réjean Houle
Vice-President, Finance and Administration and Alternate Governor	Fred Steer
Vice-President and General Manager, Centre Molson	Aldo Giampaolo
Vice-President, Communications and Marketing Services	Bernard Brisset
Administrative Assistant to the General Manager	Phil Scheuer
Head Coach	Alain Vigneault
Assistant Coaches	Dave King, Clément Jodoin, Roland Melanson
Chief Scout	Pierre Dorion
Director of Player Development and Scout	Claude Ruel
Pro Scouts	Pierre Mondou, Mario Tremblay
Director of Team Services	Michèle Lapointe
Chief Scout	Doug Robinson
Scouting Staff	Neil Armstrong, Fred E. Bandel, Elmer Benning, Mats Naslund, Gerry O'Flaherty, Doug Robinson, Antonin Routa, Richard Scammell
AHL Affiliation	Fredericton Canadiens
Governor	Phil Scheuer
Head Coach	Michel Therrien
Assistant Coach	Gerry Fleming
Director of Operations	Wayne Gamble
Medical and Training Staff	
Sports Psychologist	Wayne Halliwell
Club Physician	Dr. D.G. Kinnear
Chief Surgeon	Dr. David Mulder
Orthopedist	Dr. Eric Lenczner
Opthamologist	Dr. John Little
McGill Sport Medicine Clinic	Dr. Vincent Lacroix
Athletic Trainer	Gaétan Lefebvre
Assistant to the Athletic Trainer	Graham Rynbend
Strength & Conditioning Coach	Stéphane Dubé
Supervisor of Purchasing, Hockey	Eddy Palchak
Equipment Manager	Pierre Gervais
Assistants to the Equipment Manager	Robert Boulanger, Pierre Ouellette
Video Supervisor	Mario Leblanc
Advertising and Sponsorship	
EFFIX Inc.	François-Xavier Seigneur
Communications	
Director of Communications	Donald Beauchamp
Assistant to the Director of Communications	Dominick Saillant
Secretary, Communications Department	Sylvie Lambert
Coordinator, Photos and Archives	Claude Rompré
Production Supervisor (Broadcast)	Frédérique Cardinal
Supervisor, Production Room (Jumbotron)	Paul Shubin
Game Presentation	Michel Quidoz
Finance	
Director of Finance	Jacques Aubé
Controller	Dennis McKinley
Administrative Supervisor	Dave Poulton
Controller – Financial Reporting	Françoise Brault
Supervisor – Accounting, Centre Molson Operations	Linda Guertin
Accounting Supervisors	Paule Jolicoeur, Pascal Pepin
M.I.S. Director	Sylvain Roy
Centre Molson	
Director, Building and Operations	Alain Gauthier
Director, Concessions, Food & Beverage	Michel T. Tremblay
Director, Box Office and Customer Service	Richard Primeau
Director, Events	Louise Laliberté
Director, Boutiques Souvenirs	Yves Renaud
Assistant Director, Building and Operations	Jean-François Garneau
Supervisor, Box Office	Cathy D'Ascoli

Executive Assistants
President, Lise Beaudry; General Manager, Donna Stuart; V.P. Communications, Normande Herget; V.P. Finance, Susan Cryans; V.P. and General Manager (Centre Molson), Vicki Mercuri; Hockey, Claudine Crépin

Location of Press Box	Suspended above ice – East side
Location of Radio and TV booth	Suspended above ice – West side
Dimensions of rink	200 feet by 85 feet
Club colors	Red, White and Blue
Club trains at	Centre Molson
Play-by-Play – Radio/TV	Claude Quenneville, Pierre Houde, André Côté, Pierre Rinfret (French) Dino Sisto, Paul Romanuk (English)
TV Channels	CBFT (2), TQS (35) (French)
Cable TV	RDS (33) (French), TSN (28) (English)
Radio Stations	CKAC (730) (French), CJAD (800) (English)

Nashville Predators

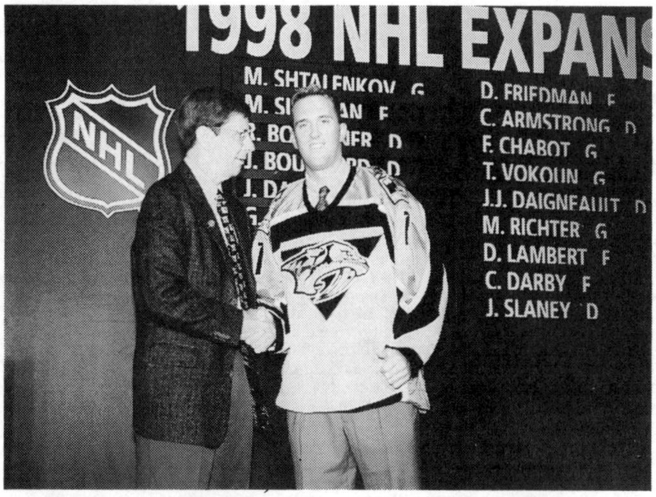

After getting only limited playing time as a backup to Martin Brodeur in New Jersey for two seasons, U.S. national team graduate Mike Dunham should see plenty of action with the Predators in 1998-99.

1998-99 Schedule

Oct.	Sat.	10	Florida		Fri.	15	Phoenix
	Tue.	13	Carolina		Mon.	18	at Boston*
	Sat.	17	at Ottawa		Tue.	19	Vancouver
	Mon.	19	at Toronto		Thu.	21	Tampa Bay
	Wed.	21	at Detroit		Tue.	26	Detroit
	Fri.	23	Calgary		Thu.	28	at Buffalo
	Sat.	24	at Chicago		Sat.	30	at New Jersey*
	Tue.	27	Vancouver		Sun.	31	Phoenix*
	Sat.	31	Colorado	**Feb.**	Thu.	4	at Calgary
Nov.	Wed.	4	at Edmonton		Fri.	5	at Edmonton
	Fri.	6	at Calgary		Tue.	9	Detroit
	Sat.	7	at Vancouver		Fri.	12	at NY Islanders
	Tue.	10	at San Jose		Sat.	13	Pittsburgh
	Thu.	12	at Los Angeles		Mon.	15	NY Rangers
	Sat.	14	at St. Louis		Fri.	19	Colorado
	Tue.	17	Chicago		Sat.	20	at St. Louis
	Thu.	19	St. Louis		Tue.	23	Dallas
	Sat.	21	NY Islanders		Wed.	24	at Dallas
	Tue.	24	at St. Louis		Sat.	27	at Colorado
	Wed.	25	Calgary	**Mar.**	Tue.	2	St. Louis
	Fri.	27	Anaheim		Thu.	4	at Los Angeles
	Sun.	29	at NY Rangers*		Fri.	5	at Anaheim
Dec.	Tue.	1	Ottawa		Sun.	7	at Phoenix
	Sat.	5	Buffalo		Wed.	10	at Chicago
	Tue.	8	Edmonton		Fri.	12	Chicago
	Thu.	10	San Jose		Sun.	14	Edmonton*
	Sat.	12	Montreal		Tue.	16	Calgary
	Wed.	16	at Anaheim		Thu.	18	at Montreal
	Thu.	17	at San Jose		Sat.	20	at Pittsburgh*
	Sat.	19	at Vancouver		Wed.	24	at Tampa Bay
	Wed.	23	Detroit		Fri.	26	at Florida
	Sat.	26	Washington		Sun.	28	Dallas*
	Mon.	28	at Dallas		Tue.	30	at Washington
	Wed.	30	Boston	**Apr.**	Thu.	1	Philadelphia
Jan.	Fri.	1	St. Louis*		Sat.	3	Los Angeles
	Sat.	2	at Carolina*		Wed.	7	at Colorado
	Mon.	4	Anaheim		Fri.	9	at Phoenix
	Thu.	7	San Jose		Mon.	12	Los Angeles
	Sat.	9	Chicago		Wed.	14	at Detroit
	Mon.	11	at Philadelphia		Thu.	15	at Chicago
	Thu.	14	at Detroit		Sat.	17	New Jersey

* Denotes afternoon game.

Franchise date: June 25, 1997

CENTRAL DIVISION

1st NHL Season

1998-99 Player Personnel

FORWARDS	HT	WT	S	Place of Birth	Date	1997-98 Club
ARKHIPOV, Denis	6-3	196	L	Kazan, USSR	5/19/79	Ak Bars Kazan
ATCHEYNUM, Blair	6-2	210	R	Estevan, Sask.	4/20/69	St. Louis
BORDELEAU, Sebastien	5-11	187	R	Vancouver, B.C.	2/15/75	Montreal
BROUSSEAU, Paul	6-2	203	R	Pierrefonds, Que.	9/18/73	Tampa Bay-Adirondack
BRUNEL, Craig	6-0	201	R	Winnipeg, Man.	11/12/79	Prince Albert
BRUNETTE, Andrew	6-0	212	L	Sudbury, Ont.	8/24/73	Washington-Portland (AHL)
CISAR, Marian	6-0	176	R	Bratislava, Czech.	2/25/78	Spokane-Slovakia
COTE, Patrick	6-3	199	L	Lasalle, Que.	1/24/75	Dallas-Michigan
DANIELS, Jeff	6-1	200	L	Oshawa, Ont.	6/24/68	Carolina-New Haven
DARBY, Craig	6-3	200	R	Oneida, NY	9/26/72	Phi-Philadelphia (AHL)
DOWD, Jim	6-1	190	R	Brick, NJ	12/25/68	Calgary-Saint John
FITZGERALD, Tom	6-1	191	R	Melrose, MA	8/28/68	Florida-Colorado
FRIEDMAN, Doug	6-1	195	L	Cape Elizabeth, ME	9/1/71	Edmonton-Hamilton
GOSSELIN, David	6-0	175	R	Levis, Que.	6/22/77	Chicoutimi
HENDERSON, Matt	6-1	200	L	White Bear Lake, MN	6/22/74	North Dakota
JOHNSON, Greg	5-10	185	L	Thunder Bay, Ont.	3/16/71	Pittsburgh-Chicago
KJELLBERG, Patrik	6-2	196	L	Falun, Sweden	6/17/69	Djurgarden
KOCH, Geoff	6-1	190	L	Virginia	6/27/79	U. of Michigan
KRIVOKRASOV, Sergei	5-11	185	L	Angarsk, USSR	4/15/74	Chicago-Russia
LAMBERT, Denny	5-11	200	L	Wawa, Ont.	1/7/70	Ottawa
LEGWAND, David	6-1	175	L	Detroit, MI	8/17/80	Plymouth
MOWERS, Mark	5-11	188	R	Whitesboro, NY	1/6/74	New Hampshire
NELSON, Jeff	6-0	190	L	Prince Albert, Sask.	12/18/72	Milwaukee
PELTONEN, Ville	5-11	180	L	Vantaa, Finland	5/24/73	V. Frolunda-Finland
SMYTH, Brad	6-0	200	R	Ottawa, Ont.	3/13/73	Los Angeles-NY Rangers-Hartford
SYKORA, Petr	6-2	180	R	Pardubice, Czech.	12/21/78	Pardubice
TURCOTTE, Darren	6-0	178	L	Boston, MA	3/2/68	St. Louis
VALICEVIC, Robert	6-2	197	R	Detroit, MI	1/6/71	Houston
WALKER, Scott	5-10	189	R	Montreal, Que.	7/19/73	Vancouver
YACHMENEV, Vitali	5-9	180	L	Chelyabinsk, USSR	1/8/75	Los Angeles-Long Beach
DEFENSEMEN						
ARMSTRONG, Chris	6-0	198	L	Regina, Sask.	6/26/75	Fort Wayne
BEAUCHESNE, Martin	6-0	200	L	Cap-de-la-madaleine, Que.	7/8/80	Sherbrooke
BOUCHARD, Joel	6-0	190	L	Montreal, Que.	1/23/74	Calgary-Saint John
BOUGHNER, Bob	6-0	206	R	Windsor, Ont.	3/8/71	Buffalo
DAIGNEAULT, J.J.	5-10	186	L	Montreal, Que.	10/12/65	Anaheim-NY Islanders
HEWARD, Jamie	6-2	207	R	Regina, Sask.	3/30/71	Philadelphia (AHL)
LINNA, Kaj	6-2	209	L	Helsinki, Finland	1/24/71	TPS Turku
MORE, Jayson	6-1	210	R	Souris, Man.	1/12/69	Phoenix-Chicago
SAUER, Kent	6-2	226	R	St. Cloud, MN	5/10/79	North Iowa
SKRASTINSH, Karlis	6-1	196	L	Riga, USSR	7/9/74	TPS Turku
SLANEY, John	6-0	185	L	St. John's, Nfld.	2/7/72	Phoenix-Las Vegas
STAPLES, Jeff	6-2	207	L	Kitimat, B.C.	3/4/75	Philadelphia (AHL)
TIMONEN, Kimmo	5-9	180	L	Kuopio, Finland	3/18/75	Helsinki-Finland
VOPAT, Jan	6-0	205	L	Most, Czech.	3/22/73	Los Angeles-Utah
ZETTLER, Rob	6-3	200	L	Sept Iles, Que.	3/8/68	Toronto
GOALTENDERS	**HT**	**WT**	**C**	**Place of Birth**	**Date**	**1997-98 Club**
DUNHAM, Michael	6-3	200	L	Johnson City, NY	6/1/72	New Jersey-United States
ROUSSEL, Dominic	6-1	191	L	Hull, Que.	2/22/70	Canada-Rosenheim
SHTALENKOV, Mikhail	6-2	185	L	Moscow, USSR	10/20/65	Anaheim-Russia
VOKOUN, Tomas	5-11	208	R	Karlovy Vary, Czech.	7/2/76	Fredericton

Entry Draft Selections 1998

1998
Pick

Pick	Player
2	David Legwand
60	Denis Arkhipov
85	Geoff Koch
88	Kent Sauer
138	Martin Beauchesne
147	Craig Brunel
202	Martin Bartek
230	Karlis Skrastins

General Managers' History

David Poile, 1998-99.

Coaching History

Barry Trotz, 1998-99.

Captains' History

Tom Fitzgerald, 1998-99.

General Manager

POILE, DAVID
General Manager, Nashville Predators.
Born in Toronto, Ont., February 14, 1949.

On July 9, 1997, David Poile was named executive vice president of hockey operations/general manager of the Nashville Predators.

Poile came to Nashville from the Washington Capitals where in 1982 he was named vice president/general manager. While in Washington, the team began a string of fourteen straight entries into the postseason, winning their first Patrick Division crown in 1989 and advancing to the conference finals in 1990. During Poile's fifteen years in Washington, the Capitals compiled a record of 594-454-124, finished first or second in the Atlantic Division eight seasons and scored 90+ points seven different seasons. Poile's Capitals were ranked in the NHL's top five in winning percentage during his fifteen years with a .559 mark. Over those fifteen years, Poile became known for his outstanding draft picks and strong trades. Some of the top draft picks were 50-goal scorer Peter Bondra and 1996 Vezina Trophy (best NHL goaltender) winner Jim Carey. Poile acquired players via trades such as two-time Norris Trophy winner Rod Langway and potential Hall-of-Famers Dale Hunter, Larry Murphy and Dino Ciccarelli.

Poile started his professional hockey career as an administrative assistant for the Atlanta Flames in 1972, shortly after he graduated from Northeastern University in Boston. At Northeastern, he was hockey team captain, leading scorer and most valuable player for two years. In 1977, he was named assistant general manager of the Atlanta Flames (moved to Calgary in 1980), serving as the manager and coordinator of the Calgary farm club.

Poile is a member of the NHL's general managers committee and was instrumental in the NHL's adoption of the instant replay rule in 1991. He was awarded *Inside Hockey's* man of the year for his leadership on the issue. He was also twice honored as *The Sporting News* NHL executive of the year following the 1982-83 and 1983-84 seasons.

Professional hockey has always been a part of David Poile's life. As a child, Poile was introduced to hockey by watching his father Bud Poile play seven seasons in the NHL and become general manager for the Philadelphia Flyers (1967) and the Vancouver Canucks (1970), both NHL expansion franchises at the time. In 1989, Bud was a co-winner of the Lester Patrick Award (outstanding service to hockey in the United States), and was inducted into the Hockey Hall of Fame a year later.

David, 49, and his wife, Elizabeth, reside in Nashville and have two children, Brian and Lauren.

Coach

TROTZ, BARRY
Coach, Nashville Predators. Born in Winnipeg, Man., July 15, 1962.

On August 6, 1997, Barry Trotz was named the first head coach of the Nashville Predators after serving the same position with the Portland Pirates the previous four seasons. This is the first NHL coaching position for Trotz, who spent the 1997-98 season preparing for Nashville's first season by scouting NHL teams and players extensively.

In 1993, Trotz became head coach and director of hockey operations for the American Hockey League's Portland Pirates. While in Portland, Trotz guided the Pirates to two AHL Calder Cup Final appearances in the team's first four years. In January of 1995, Trotz was chosen to coach the U.S. team at the American Hockey League All-Star Game in Providence, Rhode Island. Trotz's 1994-95 campaign ended with him being named American Hockey League coach of the year after his team posted a 43-27-10 record, won the Northern Conference Playoffs and defeated Moncton, 4-2, to win the Calder Cup. Overall, Trotz is 191-166-59 as a professional head coach.

Trotz began his professional career as the chief western scout for the Washington Capitals in 1988 where he was responsible for evaluating and reporting on all available hockey talent in North America. In 1991, he was appointed assistant coach of the Baltimore Skipjacks, a development club for the Washington Capitals in the American Hockey League and in 1992 was appointed head coach for the Skipjacks until 1993 when he made the move to Portland.

Trotz played junior hockey for the Western Hockey League's Regina Pats from 1979-83. During that time, he recorded 39 goals, 121 assists (150 total points) and 490 penalty minutes in 204 games. Following Regina, Trotz moved to the University of Manitoba where he was an assistant coach for one season. He then moved over to the Western Hockey League's Dauphin Kings as a head coach and general manager before making his move to the Capitals organization.

Barry and his wife Kim reside in Brentwood along with their three children, Shalan, Tyson and Tiana.

Coaching Record

		Regular Season					Playoffs			
Season	Team	Games	W	L	T	%	Games	W	L	%
1992-93	Baltimore (AHL)	80	28	40	12	.425	7	3	4	.429
1993-94	Portland (AHL)	80	43	27	10	.600	8	6	2	.750
1994-95	Portland (AHL)	80	46	22	12	.650	7	3	4	.429
1995-96	Portland (AHL)	80	32	38	10	.463	24	14	10	.583
1996-97	Portland (AHL)	80	37	33	10	.525	5	2	3	.400

Club Directory

Nashville Arena
501 Broadway
Nashville, TN 37203
Phone **615/770-2300**
FAX 615/770-2309
Website:
www.nashvillepredators.com
Capacity: 17,500

Owner, Chairman and Governor	Craig Leipold
General Partner	Nashville Predators, LLC
Limited Partner	Gaylord Entertainment
Alternate Governor	Terry London
President, COO and Alternate Governor	Jack Diller
Executive Vice President/General Manager and Alternate Governor	David Poile
Executive Vice President/Business Operations	Tom Ward
Vice President/Chief Financial Officer	Ed Lang
Vice President/Communications & Development	Gerry Helper
Hockey Operations	
Head Coach	Barry Trotz
Assistant Coaches	Paul Gardner, Brent Peterson
Strength and Conditioning Coach	Mark Nemish
Goaltending Coach	Mitch Korn
Director of Player Personnel	Paul Fenton
Chief Amateur Scout	Craig Channell
Administrator of Hockey Operations	Angela Gorgone
Scouting Coordinator	Stu Judge
Professional Scout	Fred Devereaux
European Scout	Alexei Dementiev
Quebec Scout	Luc Gauthier
Eastern Canada Scout	Alan Hepple
Western Canada Scout	Rick Knickle
Ontario Scout	Greg Royce
Maritimes Scout	Darrell Young
Saskatchewan Scout	Glen Zacharias
Amateur Scouts	Milan Tichy, Stefan Soderholm, Lucas Bergman
Head Athletic Trainer	Dan Redmond
Equipment Manager	Pete Rogers
Assistant Equipment Manager	Chris Scoppetto
Equipment Assistant	Ryan McLean
Massage Therapist	Anthony Garrett
Nutritonist	Donna Gurchiek
Manager of Team Services	Robert Bouchard
Executive Assistant	Laura Hallahan
Team Doctors	
Team Physician	Dr. Michael J. Pagnani, MD
Team Dentist	Dr. James W. McPherson Jr., DDS
Team Ophthalmologist	Dr. Daniel Weikert, MD
Team Plastic Surgeon	Dr. Bryan D. Oslin, MD, Dr. Donald Griffin, MD
Team Neurosurgeon	Dr. Carl Hampf, MD
Team Internist	Dr. Richard W. Garman MD
Comunications/Development	
Manager of Media Relations	Frank Buonomo
Communications Coordinator	Judd Hancock
Communications Assistant	Greg Harvey
Director of Community Relations	Jenny Hannon
Community Relations Assistant	Alexis Herbster
Amateur Hockey Coordinator	David Large
Team Photographer	John Russell
Business/Marketing/Corporate Sales	
Director of Premium Seating/Sponsor Services	Susie Masotti
Director of Marketing	Randy Campbell
Premium Seating Manager	Britt Kincheloe, Evelyn Finch
Managing Director, Corporate Sponsorship	Paul D'Aiuto
National Sales Manager	Bill McKay
Local Sales Manager	David Nivison, Kennon Dennis
Manager Promotions/Game Day Operations	Jim Hennessey
Promotions & Presentations Coordinator	Candace Price
Promotions Assistant	Bryan Shaffer
Entertainment Coordinator	Mark Irason, Brett Rhinehardt
Special Events Manager	Jamie Evans
Sponsor Service Account Manager	Holly Conner, Jennie Wise
Administrative Assistants	Linda Adams, Kelly Preuett
Finance/Human Resources	
Director of Finance	Julie Carpenter
Accountant	Virginia Blount
Accounting Clerk	Connie Dale
Accounting Assistant	Susan Charnley
Director of Human Resources	Kim Marrone
Administrative Assistant	Elaine Lewis
Project Coordinator	Scott Pilkinton
Office Coordinator	Robin Krokker
Office Assistant	Mike Corbett
Television/Radio Broadcast Department	
Director of Broadcasting	John Guagliano
Manager of Technical Services	Jimmy Corn
Feature Producer	Erik Barnhart
Traffic Manager	Susan Morgan
Production Assistant	Peggy Bartishell
Ticket Operations	
Director of Ticket Sales	Scott Loft
Club/Suite Sales Executive	Tom Phillips
Group Sales Manager	Allison Gay
Account Executives	Sid Chambless, Geoff Dunnuck, Slayton Gorman, Tom Lynch, Jonathan Tuschl, Bill Walker
Fan Relations Manager	Lisa Hays
Fan Relations Account Service Representatives	Gene Connelly, Josh Gravot, Nat Harden
Minor League Affiliate	Milwaukee Admirals (IHL), Hampton Roads Admirals (ECHL)
Radio Flagship	WTN-FM (99.7 FM)
TV Flagship	WNAB-TV & FOX Sports South

New Jersey Devils

1997-98 Results: 48W-23L-11T 107PTS. First, Atlantic Division

Year-by-Year Record

Season	GP	Home W	Home L	Home T	Road W	Road L	Road T	Overall W	Overall L	Overall T	GF	GA	Pts.	Finished		Playoff Result
1997-98	82	29	10	2	19	13	9	48	23	11	225	166	107	1st,	Atlantic Div.	Lost Conf. Quarter-Final
1996-97	82	23	9	9	22	14	5	45	23	14	231	182	104	1st,	Atlantic Div.	Lost Conf. Semi-Final
1995-96	82	22	17	2	15	16	10	37	33	12	215	202	86	6th,	Atlantic Div.	Out of Playoffs
1994-95	**48**	**14**	**4**	**6**	**8**	**14**	**2**	**22**	**18**	**8**	**136**	**121**	**52**	**2nd,**	**Atlantic Div.**	**Won Stanley Cup**
1993-94	84	29	11	2	18	14	10	47	25	12	306	220	106	2nd,	Atlantic Div.	Lost Conf. Championship
1992-93	84	24	14	4	16	23	3	40	37	7	308	299	87	4th,	Patrick Div.	Lost Div. Semi-Final
1991-92	80	24	12	4	14	19	3	38	31	11	289	259	87	4th,	Patrick Div.	Lost Div. Semi-Final
1990-91	80	23	10	7	9	23	8	32	33	15	272	264	79	4th,	Patrick Div.	Lost Div. Semi-Final
1989-90	80	22	15	3	15	19	6	37	34	9	295	288	83	2nd,	Patrick Div.	Lost Div. Semi-Final
1988-89	80	17	18	5	10	23	7	27	41	12	281	325	66	5th,	Patrick Div.	Out of Playoffs
1987-88	80	23	16	1	15	20	5	38	36	6	295	296	82	4th,	Patrick Div.	Lost Conf. Championship
1986-87	80	20	17	3	9	28	3	29	45	6	293	368	64	6th,	Patrick Div.	Out of Playoffs
1985-86	80	17	21	2	11	28	1	28	49	3	300	374	59	6th,	Patrick Div.	Out of Playoffs
1984-85	80	13	21	6	9	27	4	22	48	10	264	346	54	5th,	Patrick Div.	Out of Playoffs
1983-84	80	10	28	2	7	28	5	17	56	7	231	350	41	5th,	Patrick Div.	Out of Playoffs
1982-83	80	11	20	9	6	29	5	17	49	14	230	338	48	5th,	Patrick Div.	Out of Playoffs
1981-82**	80	14	21	5	4	28	8	18	49	13	241	362	49	5th,	Smythe Div.	Out of Playoffs
1980-81**	80	15	16	9	7	29	4	22	45	13	258	344	57	5th,	Smythe Div.	Out of Playoffs
1979-80**	80	12	20	8	7	28	5	19	48	13	234	308	51	6th,	Smythe Div.	Out of Playoffs
1978-79**	80	8	24	8	7	29	4	15	53	12	210	331	42	4th,	Smythe Div.	Out of Playoffs
1977-78**	80	17	14	9	2	26	12	19	40	21	257	305	59	2nd,	Smythe Div.	Lost Prelim. Round
1976-77**	80	12	20	8	8	26	6	20	46	14	226	307	54	5th,	Smythe Div.	Out of Playoffs
1975-76*	80	8	24	8	4	32	4	12	56	12	190	351	36	5th,	Smythe Div.	Out of Playoffs
1974-75*	80	12	20	8	3	34	3	15	54	11	184	328	41	5th,	Smythe Div.	Out of Playoffs

* Kansas City Scouts. ** Colorado Rockies.

1998-99 Schedule

Oct.	Sat.	10	at Chicago
	Wed.	14	Pittsburgh
	Fri.	16	at NY Rangers
	Sat.	17	Edmonton
	Thu.	22	at Philadelphia
	Sat.	24	Boston
	Wed.	28	Los Angeles
	Thu.	29	at NY Islanders
	Sat.	31	Florida
Nov.	Tue.	3	NY Rangers
	Sat.	7	at Florida*
	Sun.	8	at Tampa Bay*
	Wed.	11	Montreal
	Fri.	13	Pittsburgh
	Sat.	14	at Philadelphia
	Thu.	19	Carolina
	Sat.	21	Florida*
	Sun.	22	at Carolina*
	Wed.	25	at Dallas
	Thu.	26	at Phoenix
	Sat.	28	at Colorado
Dec.	Tue.	1	at Washington
	Fri.	4	Montreal
	Sat.	5	at NY Islanders
	Tue.	8	Philadelphia
	Thu.	10	at Philadelphia
	Sat.	12	Colorado*
	Wed.	16	NY Rangers
	Fri.	18	Calgary
	Sat.	19	at Montreal
	Wed.	23	St. Louis
	Sat.	26	Buffalo
	Mon.	28	at Buffalo
	Wed.	30	at Washington
Jan.	Sat.	2	at Ottawa
	Tue.	5	San Jose
	Wed.	6	at NY Rangers
	Sat.	9	Washington
	Mon.	11	Ottawa
	Thu.	14	at Ottawa
	Fri.	15	Tampa Bay
	Mon.	18	at San Jose
	Wed.	20	at Anaheim
	Thu.	21	at Los Angeles
	Tue.	26	Ottawa
	Thu.	28	at Boston
	Sat.	30	Nashville*
Feb.	Mon.	1	Detroit
	Wed.	3	at Carolina
	Thu.	4	at St. Louis
	Sat.	6	Toronto
	Tue.	9	Vancouver
	Fri.	12	Washington
	Sat.	13	Carolina
	Mon.	15	Toronto
	Wed.	17	Tampa Bay
	Fri.	19	at Detroit
	Sat.	20	NY Islanders
	Mon.	22	at Tampa Bay
	Thu.	25	at Boston
	Sun.	28	Phoenix*
Mar.	Wed.	3	at Toronto
	Fri.	5	Boston
	Sun.	7	at NY Islanders*
	Tue.	9	at Pittsburgh
	Mon.	15	at Vancouver
	Wed.	17	at Edmonton
	Sat.	20	at Toronto
	Tue.	23	Buffalo
	Thu.	25	Pittsburgh
	Sat.	27	Chicago*
	Sun.	28	at Florida
	Wed.	31	Anaheim
Apr.	Sat.	3	at Pittsburgh*
	Sun.	4	NY Rangers*
	Tue.	6	at Carolina
	Thu.	8	Washington
	Sat.	10	at Montreal
	Mon.	12	NY Islanders
	Wed.	14	at Buffalo
	Fri.	16	Philadelphia
	Sat.	17	at Nashville

* Denotes afternoon game.

Captain Scott Stevens and goaltender Martin Brodeur are two reasons for New Jersey's defensive excellence. The Devils surrendered a league-low 166 goals in 1997-98 as Brodeur won the William M. Jennings Trophy for the second year in a row.

Franchise date: June 11, 1974
Transferred from Denver to New Jersey, June 30, 1982.
Previously transferred from Kansas City to Denver, Colorado.

ATLANTIC DIVISION

25th NHL Season

1998-99 Player Personnel

FORWARDS	HT	WT	S	Place of Birth	Date	1997-98 Club
ANDREYCHUK, Dave	6-4	220	R	Hamilton, Ont.	9/29/63	New Jersey
ARNOTT, Jason	6-3	220	R	Collingwood, Ont.	10/11/74	Edmonton-New Jersey
BENOIT, Mathieu	5-11	200	R	St. Clec, Que.	7/12/79	Chicoutimi
BERTRAND, Eric	6-0	205	L	St. Ephrem, Que.	4/16/75	Albany
BICEK, Jiri	5-11	185	L	Kosice, Czech.	12/3/78	Albany
BRULE, Steve	6-0	195	R	Montreal, Que.	1/15/75	Albany
BRYLIN, Sergei	5-10	190	L	Moscow, USSR	1/13/74	New Jersey-Albany
CARPENTER, Bob	6-0	200	L	Beverly, MA	7/13/63	New Jersey
CUNNIFF, David	5-10	185	L	South Boston, MA	10/9/73	Raleigh-Albany
DAGENAIS, Pierre	6-4	200	L	Blainville, Que.	3/4/78	Rouyn-Noranda
DANIELS, Scott	6-3	215	L	Prince Albert, Sask.	9/19/69	New Jersey
DUCE, Bryan	6-0	190	R	Thunder Bay, Ont.	1/15/78	Kitchener-S.S. Marie
ELIAS, Patrik	6-0	195	L	Trebic, Czech.	4/13/76	New Jersey-Albany-Czech.
FLINN, Ryan	6-4	210	L	Halifax, N.S.	4/20/80	Laval
GOMEZ, Scott	5-11	180	L	Anchorage, Alaska	12/23/79	Tri-City
GRON, Stanislav	6-1	190	L	Bratislava, Czech.	10/28/78	Seattle-Slovakia
HELD, Ryan	6-1	175	L	London, Ont.	1/30/80	Kitchener
HOLIK, Bobby	6-3	225	R	Jihlava, Czech.	1/1/71	New Jersey
HOUSE, Bobby	6-1	205	R	Whitehorse, Yukon	1/7/73	Alb-Her-Que (IHL)-Syr
LAKOVIC, Sasha	6-0	205	L	Vancouver, B.C.	9/7/71	New Jersey-Albany
LARIVIERE, Jacques	6-1	210	L	Sorel, Que.	12/18/79	Moncton
MADDEN, John	5-11	185	L	Barrie, Ont.	5/4/75	Albany
McKAY, Randy	6-2	210	R	Montreal, Que.	1/25/67	New Jersey
MORRISON, Brendan	5-11	180	L	N. Vancouver, B.C.	8/12/75	New Jersey-Albany
OLIWA, Krzysztof	6-5	235	L	Tychy, Poland	4/12/73	New Jersey
PANDOLFO, Jay	6-1	200	L	Winchester, MA	12/27/74	New Jersey-Albany
PEDERSON, Denis	6-2	205	R	Prince Albert, Sask.	9/10/75	New Jersey
ROCHEFORT, Richard	5-10	185	R	North Bay, Ont.	1/7/77	Albany
ROLSTON, Brian	6-2	200	L	Flint, MI	2/21/73	New Jersey
SHARIFIJANOV, Vadim	6-0	205	L	Ufa, USSR	12/23/75	Albany
SKOREPA, Zdenek	6-0	185	L	Duchcov, Czech.	8/10/76	Detroit (IHL)-Albany
SKRLAC, Rob	6-5	250	L	Campbell, B.C.	6/10/76	Albany
SYKORA, Petr	5-11	185	L	Plzen, Czech.	11/19/76	New Jersey-Albany
THOMPSON, Chris	6-0	180	L	Prince Albert, Sask.	4/10/78	Seattle
WILLIAMS, Jeff	6-0	195	L	Pointe-Claire, Que.	2/11/76	Albany
DEFENSEMEN						
BOMBARDIR, Brad	6-1	205	L	Powell River, B.C.	5/5/72	New Jersey-Albany
DANEYKO, Ken	6-0	215	L	Windsor, Ont.	4/17/64	New Jersey
DEAN, Kevin	6-3	205	L	Madison, WI	4/1/69	New Jersey-Albany-United States
DEWOLF, Josh	6-2	190	L	Bloomington, MN	7/25/77	St. Cloud State-Albany
GOC, Sascha	6-2	196	R	Calw, Germany	4/17/79	Schwenningen-Germany
JOHNSTONE, Alex	6-1	170	L	Halifax, N.S.	12/28/79	Halifax
KINNEAR, Geordie	6-1	195	L	Simcoe, Ont.	7/9/73	Albany
KROUPA, Vlastimil	6-3	210	L	Most, Czech.	4/27/75	New Jersey-Albany
MUIR, Bryan	6-4	220	L	Winnipeg, Man.	6/8/73	Edmonton-Hamilton-Albany
NEHRLING, Lucas	6-4	195	R	Peterborough, Ont.	8/14/79	Sarnia-Kingston
NIEDERMAYER, Scott	6-0	205	L	Edmonton, Alta.	8/31/73	New Jersey
ODELEIN, Lyle	5-11	210	R	Quill Lake, Sask.	7/21/68	New Jersey
REHNBERG, Henrik	6-2	195	L	Grava, Sweden	7/20/77	Farjestad
SOURAY, Sheldon	6-4	235	L	Elk Point, Alta.	7/13/76	New Jersey-Albany
STEVENS, Scott	6-1	215	L	Kitchener, Ont.	4/1/64	New Jersey-Canada
SUTTON, Ken	6-0	205	L	Edmonton, Alta.	11/5/69	New Jersey-Albany-San Jose
VYSHEDKEVICH, Sergei	6-0	195	L	Dedovsk, USSR	1/3/75	Albany
WHITE, Colin	6-3	215	L	New Glasgow, N.S.	12/12/77	Albany

GOALTENDERS	HT	WT	C	Place of Birth	Date	1997-98 Club
BRODEUR, Martin	6-1	205	L	Montreal, Que.	5/6/72	New Jersey-Canada
BUZAK, Mike	6-3	215	L	Edson, Alta.	2/10/73	Long Beach
DAMPHOUSSE, Jean-Francois	6-0	175	L	St-Alexis-des-Monts, Que.	7/21/79	Moncton
HENRY, Frederic	5-11	170	L	Cap-Rouge, Que.	8/9/77	Raleigh-Albany
LAMBERT, Judd	6-1	175	L	Richmond, B.C.	6/3/74	Dayton-Albany-Fort Wayne
SHULMISTRA, Richard	6-2	185	R	Sudbury, Ont.	4/1/71	Fort Wayne-New Jersey-Albany
TERRERI, Chris	5-8	160	L	Providence, RI	11/15/64	Chicago-Indianapolis

General Managers' History

Sid Abel, 1974-75, 1975-76; Ray Miron, 1976-77 to 1980-81; Billy MacMillan, 1981-82, 1982-83; Billy MacMillan and Max McNab, 1983-84; Max McNab 1984-85 to 1986-87; Lou Lamoriello, 1987-88 to date.

General Manager

LAMORIELLO, LOU
President and General Manager, New Jersey Devils.
Born in Providence, Rhode Island, October 21, 1942.

Lou Lamoriello's life-long dedication to the game of hockey was rewarded in 1992 when he was named a recipient of the Lester Patrick Trophy for outstanding service to hockey in the United States. Lamoriello is entering his twelfth season as president and general manager of the Devils following more than 20 years with Providence College as a player, coach and administrator. His trades, signings and draft choices helped lead the Devils to their first Stanley Cup championship in 1995. A member of the varsity hockey Friars during his undergraduate days, he became an assistant coach with the college club after graduating in 1963. Lamoriello was later named head coach and in the ensuing 15 years, led his teams to a 248-179-13 record, a .578 winning percentage and appearances in 10 post-season tournaments, including the 1983 NCAA Final Four. Lamoriello also served a five-year term as athletic director at Providence and was a co-founder of Hockey East, one of the strongest collegiate hockey conferences in the U.S. He remained as athletic director until he was hired as president of the Devils on April 30, 1987. He assumed the dual responsibility of general manager on September 10, 1987. He was g.m. of Team USA for the first World Cup of Hockey in 1996 as the U.S. captured the championship. He was also the g.m. for the 1998 U.S. Olympic Team.

1997-98 Scoring

* – rookie

Regular Season

Pos	#	Player	Team	GP	G	A	Pts	+/–	PIM	PP	SH	GW	GT	S	%
C	16	Bobby Holik	N.J.	82	29	36	65	23	100	8	0	8	1	238	12.2
D	27	Scott Niedermayer	N.J.	81	14	43	57	5	27	11	0	1	0	175	8.0
C	93	Doug Gilmour	N.J.	63	13	40	53	10	68	3	0	5	0	94	13.8
R	21	Randy McKay	N.J.	74	24	24	48	30	86	8	0	5	0	141	17.0
L	23	Dave Andreychuk	N.J.	75	14	34	48	19	26	4	0	2	0	180	7.8
R	26 *	Patrik Elias	N.J.	74	18	19	37	18	28	5	0	6	1	147	12.2
C	17	Petr Sykora	N.J.	58	16	20	36	0	22	3	1	4	0	130	12.3
C	25	Jason Arnott	EDM	35	5	13	18	-16	78	1	0	0	0	100	5.0
			N.J.	35	5	10	15	-8	21	3	0	2	0	99	5.1
			TOTAL	70	10	23	33	-24	99	4	0	2	0	199	5.0
L	14	Brian Rolston	N.J.	76	16	14	30	7	16	0	2	1	0	185	8.6
C	10	Denis Pederson	N.J.	80	15	13	28	-6	97	7	0	1	1	135	11.1
D	4	Scott Stevens	N.J.	80	4	22	26	19	80	1	0	1	0	94	4.3
R	32	Steve Thomas	N.J.	55	14	10	24	4	32	3	0	4	1	111	12.6
D	24	Lyle Odelein	N.J.	79	4	19	23	11	171	1	0	0	0	76	5.3
D	5	Doug Bodger	S.J.	28	4	6	10	0	32	0	0	1	0	41	9.8
			N.J.	49	5	5	10	-1	25	3	0	0	0	55	9.1
			TOTAL	77	9	11	20	-1	57	3	0	1	0	96	9.4
C	19	Bob Carpenter	N.J.	66	9	9	18	-4	22	0	1	1	0	81	11.1
D	2 *	Sheldon Souray	N.J.	60	3	7	10	18	85	0	0	1	0	74	4.1
C	9 *	Brendan Morrison	N.J.	11	5	4	9	3	0	0	0	1	1	19	26.3
D	28	Kevin Dean	N.J.	50	1	8	9	12	12	1	0	0	0	28	3.6
D	6 *	Brad Bombardir	N.J.	43	1	5	6	11	8	0	0	0	0	16	6.3
C	18	Sergei Brylin	N.J.	18	2	3	5	4	0	0	0	0	1	20	10.0
L	29 *	Krzysztof Oliwa	N.J.	73	2	3	5	3	295	0	0	2	0	53	3.8
L	20	Jay Pandolfo	N.J.	23	1	3	4	-4	4	0	0	0	0	23	4.3
L	22	Scott Daniels	N.J.	26	0	3	3	1	102	0	0	0	0	17	0.0
G	30	Martin Brodeur	N.J.	70	0	3	3	0	10	0	0	0	0	0	0.0
D	5	Vlastimil Kroupa	N.J.	2	0	1	1	1	0	0	0	0	0	1	0.0
G	1	Mike Dunham	N.J.	15	0	1	1	0	0	0	0	0	0	0	0.0
D	3	Ken Daneyko	N.J.	37	0	1	1	3	57	0	0	0	0	18	0.0
G	31	Peter Sidorkiewicz	N.J.	1	0	0	0	0	0	0	0	0	0	0	0.0
G	35	Rich Shulmistra	N.J.	1	0	0	0	0	0	0	0	0	0	0	0.0
L	8	Sasha Lakovic	N.J.	2	0	0	0	0	5	0	0	0	0	2	0.0

Goaltending

No.	Goaltender	GPI	Mins	Avg	W	L	T	EN	SO	GA	SA	S%
30	Martin Brodeur	70	4128	1.89	43	17	8	4	10	130	1569	.917
35	Rich Shulmistra	1	62	1.94	0	1	0	0	0	2	30	.933
1	Mike Dunham	15	773	2.25	5	5	3	0	1	29	332	.913
31	Peter Sidorkiewicz	1	20	3.00	0	0	0	0	0	1	8	.875
	Totals	**82**	**4991**	**2.00**	**48**	**23**	**11**	**4**	**11**	**166**	**1943**	**.915**

Playoffs

Pos	#	Player	Team	GP	G	A	Pts	+/–	PIM	PP	SH	GW	OT	S	%
C	93	Doug Gilmour	N.J.	6	5	2	7	4	4	1	0	1	0	12	41.7
R	32	Steve Thomas	N.J.	6	0	3	3	1	2	0	0	0	0	12	0.0
D	24	Lyle Odelein	N.J.	6	1	1	2	2	21	1	0	1	0	7	14.3
C	10	Denis Pederson	N.J.	6	1	1	2	0	2	0	1	0	0	8	12.5
L	20	Jay Pandolfo	N.J.	3	0	2	2	0	0	0	0	0	0	1	0.0
C	25	Jason Arnott	N.J.	5	0	2	2	1	0	0	0	0	0	6	0.0
D	27	Scott Niedermayer	N.J.	6	0	2	2	0	4	0	0	0	0	15	0.0
D	28	Kevin Dean	N.J.	5	1	0	1	-1	2	0	0	0	0	4	25.0
L	23	Dave Andreychuk	N.J.	6	1	0	1	-2	4	1	0	0	0	17	5.9
C	19	Bob Carpenter	N.J.	6	1	0	1	0	0	0	0	0	0	3	33.3
D	4	Scott Stevens	N.J.	6	1	0	1	4	8	0	0	0	0	11	9.1
L	14	Brian Rolston	N.J.	6	1	0	1	2	2	0	1	0	0	14	7.1
C	9 *	Brendan Morrison	N.J.	3	0	1	1	-1	0	0	0	0	0	4	0.0
D	2 *	Sheldon Souray	N.J.	3	0	1	1	0	2	0	0	0	0	1	0.0
L	26 *	Patrik Elias	N.J.	4	0	1	1	-2	0	0	0	0	0	9	0.0
D	3	Ken Daneyko	N.J.	6	0	1	1	0	10	0	0	0	0	7	0.0
R	21	Randy McKay	N.J.	6	0	1	1	-1	0	0	0	0	0	7	0.0
G	30	Martin Brodeur	N.J.	6	0	1	1	0	0	0	0	0	0	0	0.0
L	22	Scott Daniels	N.J.	1	0	0	0	0	0	0	0	0	0	0	0.0
C	17	Petr Sykora	N.J.	2	0	0	0	0	0	0	0	0	0	5	0.0
D	5	Doug Bodger	N.J.	5	0	0	0	-5	0	0	0	0	0	8	0.0
C	16	Bobby Holik	N.J.	5	0	0	0	-4	8	0	0	0	0	18	0.0
L	29 *	Krzysztof Oliwa	N.J.	6	0	0	0	0	23	0	0	0	0	5	0.0

Goaltending

No.	Goaltender	GPI	Mins	Avg	W	L	EN	SO	GA	SA	S%
30	Martin Brodeur	6	366	1.97	2	4	1	0	12	164	.927
	Totals	**6**	**369**	**2.11**	**2**	**4**	**1**	**0**	**13**	**165**	**.921**

Coaching History

Bep Guidolin, 1974-75; Bep Guidolin, Sid Abel and Eddie Bush, 1975-76; John Wilson, 1976-77; Pat Kelly, 1977-78; Pat Kelly and Aldo Guidolin, 1978-79; Don Cherry, 1979-80; Bill MacMillan, 1980-81; Bert Marshall and Marshall Johnston, 1981-82; Bill MacMillan, 1982-83; Bill MacMillan and Tom McVie, 1983-84; Doug Carpenter, 1984-85 to 1986-87; Doug Carpenter and Jim Schoenfeld, 1987-88; Jim Schoenfeld, 1988-89; Jim Schoenfeld and John Cunniff, 1989-90; John Cunniff and Tom McVie, 1990-91; Tom McVie, 1991-92; Herb Brooks, 1992-93; Jacques Lemaire, 1993-94 to 1997-98; Robbie Ftorek, 1998-99.

Captains' History

Simon Nolet, 1974-75 to 1976-77; Wilf Paiement, 1977-78; Gary Croteau, 1978-79; Mike Christie, Rene Robert and Lanny McDonald, 1979-80; Lanny McDonald, 1980-81, Lanny McDonald and Rob Ramage, 1981-82; Don Lever, 1982-83; Don Lever and Mel Bridgman, 1983-84; Mel Bridgman, 1984-85 to 1986-87; Kirk Muller, 1987-88 to 1990-91; Bruce Driver, 1991-92; Scott Stevens, 1992-93 to date.

Club Records

Team

(Figures in brackets for season records are games played; records for fewest points, wins, ties, losses, goals, goals against are for 70 or more games)

Most Points	**107**	1997-98 (82)
Most Wins	**48**	1997-98 (82)
Most Ties	**21**	1977-78 (80)
Most Losses	**56**	1983-84 (80), 1975-76 (80)
Most Goals	**308**	1992-93 (84)
Most Goals Against	**374**	1985-86 (80)
Fewest Points	***36**	1975-76 (80)
	41	1983-84 (80)
Fewest Wins	***12**	1975-76 (80)
	17	1982-83 (80), 1983-84 (80)
Fewest Ties	**3**	1985-86 (80)
Fewest Losses	**23**	1996-97 (82); 1997-98 (82)
Fewest Goals	***184**	1974-75 (80)
	225	1997-98 (82)
Fewest Goals Against	**166**	1997-98 (82)
Longest Winning Streak		
Overall	**8**	Oct. 27-Nov. 15/97
Home	**8**	Oct. 9-Nov. 7/87
Away	**5**	Dec. 10-20/96, Oct. 27-Nov. 15/97
Longest Undefeated Streak		
Overall	**13**	Jan. 24-Feb. 20/97 (6 wins, 7 ties), Jan. 31-Mar. 12/98 (9 wins, 4 ties)
Home	**15**	Jan. 8-Mar. 15/97 (9 wins, 6 tie)
Away	**8**	Nov. 5-Dec. 2/93 (5 wins, 3 ties), Jan. 31-Mar. 12/98 (5 wins, 3 ties)
Longest Losing Streak		
Overall	***14**	Dec. 30/75-Jan. 29/76
	10	Oct. 14-Nov. 4/83
Home	**9**	Dec. 22/85-Feb. 6/86
Away	**12**	Oct. 19-Dec. 1/83
Longest Winless Streak		
Overall	***27**	Feb. 12-Apr. 4/76 (21 losses, 6 ties)
	18	Oct. 20-Nov. 26/82 (14 losses 4 ties)
Home	***14**	Feb. 12-Mar. 30/76 (10 losses, 4 ties), Feb. 4-Mar. 31/79 (12 losses, 2 ties)
	9	Dec. 22/85-Feb. 6/86 (9 losses)
Away	***32**	Nov. 12/77-Mar. 15/78 (22 losses, 10 ties)
	14	Dec. 26/82-Mar. 5/83 (13 losses, 1 tie)
Most Shutouts, Season	**13**	1996-97 (82)
Most PIM, Season	**2,494**	1988-89 (80)
Most Goals, Game	**9**	Seven times

Individual

Most Seasons	**15**	Ken Daneyko, John MacLean
Most Games	**934**	John MacLean
Most Goals, Career	**347**	John MacLean
Most Assists, Career	**354**	John MacLean
Most Points, Career	**701**	John MacLean (347G, 354A)
Most PIM, Career	**2,178**	Ken Daneyko
Most Shutouts, Career	**32**	Martin Brodeur
Longest Consecutive Games Streak	**388**	Ken Daneyko (Nov. 4/89-Mar. 29/94)
Most Goals, Season	**46**	Pat Verbeek (1987-88)
Most Assists, Season	**60**	Scott Stevens (1993-94)
Most Points, Season	**94**	Kirk Muller (1987-88; 37G, 57A)
Most PIM, Season	**295**	Krzysztof Oliwa (1997-98)
Most Points, Defenseman, Season	**78**	Scott Stevens (1993-94; 18G, 60A)
Most Points, Center, Season	**94**	Kirk Muller (1987-88; 37G, 57A)
Most Points, Right Wing, Season	***87**	Wilf Paiement (1977-78; 31G, 56A)
	87	John MacLean (1988-89; 42G, 45A)
Most Points, Left Wing, Season	**86**	Kirk Muller (1989-90; 30G, 56A)
Most Points, Rookie, Season	**63**	Kevin Todd (1991-92; 21G, 42A)
Most Shutouts, Season	**10**	Martin Brodeur (1996-97, 1997-98)
Most Goals, Game	**4**	Bob MacMillan (Jan. 8/82), Pat Verbeek (Feb. 28/88)
Most Assists, Game	**5**	Greg Adams (Oct. 10/85), Kirk Muller (Mar. 25/87), Tom Kurvers (Feb. 13/89)
Most Points, Game	**6**	Kirk Muller (Nov. 29/86; 3G, 3A)

* Records include Kansas City Scouts and Colorado Rockies, 1974-75 through 1981-82.

All-time Record vs. Other Clubs

Regular Season

	At Home							On Road							Total						
	GP	W	L	T	GF	GA	PTS	GP	W	L	T	GF	GA	PTS	GP	W	L	T	GF	GA	PTS
Anaheim	4	3	1	0	14	7	6	4	1	3	0	8	14	2	8	4	4	0	22	21	8
Boston	41	10	22	9	108	139	29	44	12	27	5	137	187	29	85	22	49	14	245	326	58
Buffalo	42	12	22	8	130	154	32	42	10	27	5	131	181	25	84	22	49	13	261	335	57
Calgary	40	13	24	3	114	148	29	39	5	27	7	101	175	17	79	18	51	10	215	323	46
Carolina	33	18	12	3	118	108	39	31	10	14	7	95	109	27	64	28	26	10	213	217	66
Chicago	41	15	16	10	121	128	40	42	10	23	9	117	171	29	83	25	39	19	238	299	69
Colorado	31	16	12	3	127	107	35	29	11	15	3	87	108	25	60	27	27	6	214	215	60
Dallas	40	19	18	3	135	125	41	40	10	24	6	104	157	26	80	29	42	9	239	282	67
Detroit	36	18	10	8	128	101	44	35	13	20	2	121	146	28	71	31	30	10	249	247	72
Edmonton	28	13	13	2	99	94	28	28	8	14	6	102	129	22	56	21	27	8	201	223	50
Florida	12	6	4	2	32	23	14	13	4	6	3	28	31	11	25	10	10	5	60	54	25
Los Angeles	38	17	16	5	129	136	39	38	5	27	6	116	196	16	76	22	43	11	245	332	55
Montreal	42	16	24	2	124	175	34	42	9	28	5	109	163	23	84	25	52	7	233	338	57
NY Islanders	69	27	32	10	235	259	64	69	10	50	9	191	315	29	138	37	82	19	426	574	93
NY Rangers	70	33	32	5	239	250	71	69	17	39	13	208	289	47	139	50	71	18	447	539	118
Ottawa	11	7	2	2	37	23	16	12	9	2	1	35	19	19	23	16	4	3	72	42	35
Philadelphia	68	35	29	4	248	254	74	69	16	45	8	172	281	40	137	51	74	12	420	535	114
Phoenix	24	8	10	6	76	77	22	26	5	18	3	70	101	13	50	13	28	9	146	178	35
Pittsburgh	65	31	22	12	248	223	74	64	23	37	4	221	259	50	129	54	59	16	469	482	124
St. Louis	42	18	17	7	136	124	43	41	9	25	7	128	180	25	83	27	42	14	264	304	68
San Jose	7	4	3	0	27	14	8	6	4	1	1	20	11	9	13	8	4	1	47	25	17
Tampa Bay	14	12	1	1	54	20	25	13	7	3	3	39	31	17	27	19	4	4	93	51	42
Toronto	35	14	11	10	128	110	38	36	8	24	4	117	155	20	71	22	35	14	245	265	58
Vancouver	44	19	19	6	140	145	44	44	8	25	11	124	166	27	88	27	44	17	264	311	71
Washington	66	31	28	7	209	201	69	67	19	43	5	190	271	43	133	50	71	12	399	472	112
Defunct Clubs	8	4	2	2	25	19	10	8	2	3	3	19	27	7	16	6	5	5	44	46	17
Totals	**951**	**419**	**402**	**130**	**3181**	**3164**	**968**	**951**	**245**	**570**	**136**	**2790**	**3872**	**626**	**1902**	**664**	**972**	**266**	**5971**	**7036**	**1594**

Playoffs

	Series	W	L	GP	W	L	T	GF	GA	Last Mtg.	Round	Result
Boston	3	2	1	18	11	7	0	55	52	1995	CQF	W 4-1
Buffalo	1	1	0	7	4	3	0	14	14	1994	CQF	W 4-3
Detroit	1	1	0	4	4	0	0	16	7	1995	F	W 4-0
Montreal	1	1	0	5	4	1	0	22	11	1997	CQF	W 4-1
NY Islanders	1	1	0	6	4	2	0	23	18	1988	DSF	W 4-2
NY Rangers	3	0	3	19	7	12	0	46	56	1997	CSF	L 1-4
Ottawa	1	0	1	6	2	4	0	12	13	1998	CQF	L 2-4
Philadelphia	2	1	1	8	4	4	0	23	20	1995	CF	W 4-2
Pittsburgh	3	1	2	17	8	9	0	47	56	1995	CSF	W 4-1
Washington	2	1	1	13	6	7	0	43	44	1990	DSF	L 2-4
Totals	**18**	**9**	**9**	**103**	**54**	**49**	**0**	**301**	**291**			

Playoff Results 1998-94

Year	Round	Opponent	Result	GF	GA
1998	CQF	Ottawa	L 2-4	12	13
1997	CSF	NY Rangers	L 1-4	5	10
	CQF	Montreal	W 4-1	22	11
1995	**F**	**Detroit**	**W 4-0**	**16**	**7**
	CF	Philadelphia	W 4-2	20	14
	CSF	Pittsburgh	W 4-1	17	8
	CQF	Boston	W 4-1	14	5
1994	CF	NY Rangers	L 3-4	16	18
	CSF	Boston	W 4-2	22	17
	CQF	Buffalo	W 4-3	14	14

Abbreviations: Round: F – Final; **CF** – conference final; **CQF** – conference quarter-final; **CSF** – conference semi-final; **DSF** – division semi-final.

Calgary totals include Atlanta, 1974-75 to 1979-80. Carolina totals include Hartford, 1979-80 to 1996-97.
Colorado totals include Quebec, 1979-80 to 1994-95. Dallas totals include Minnesota, 1974-75 to 1992-93.
New Jersey totals include Kansas City, 1974-75 to 1975-76, and Colorado Rockies, 1976-77 to 1981-82.
Phoenix totals include Winnipeg, 1979-80 to 1995-96.

1997-98 Results

Oct.	3	at	Tampa Bay	4-3		7		Pittsburgh	3-1
	4	at	Washington	1-4		9		Tampa Bay	4-1
	8		Philadelphia	4-1		10	at	Pittsburgh	1-4
	10	at	Carolina	1-2		12	at	Boston	1-1
	11		Buffalo	3-2		14		NY Rangers	4-1
	17	at	Ottawa	2-4		20		Detroit	3-1
	18		Tampa Bay	5-0		22		Pittsburgh	2-3
	23		Montreal	2-1		24	at	NY Rangers	3-3
	25		San Jose	3-4		25	at	Montreal	3-1
	27	at	Philadelphia	5-0		28	at	Edmonton	1-1
	30		Vancouver	8-1		30	at	Vancouver	1-3
Nov.	1		Washington	3-1		31	at	Calgary	2-2
	4		Los Angeles	0-3	**Feb.**	2	at	Ottawa	1-0
	5	at	Florida	4-2		4		Ottawa	2-0
	8		Boston	2-0		7	at	NY Islanders	3-2
	10	at	NY Islanders	3-1		25	at	Florida	3-2
	12	at	NY Rangers	3-2		26	at	Tampa Bay	4-1
	14		Colorado	4-1		28		Carolina	4-3
	15	at	Buffalo	3-2	**Mar.**	2		Philadelphia	4-3
	18		Calgary	2-1		5		Boston	1-1
	20		NY Islanders	5-1		7		NY Rangers	6-3
	22		Florida	1-2		9	at	NY Rangers	2-2
	26	at	Anaheim	0-2		10	at	Philadelphia	2-2
	28	at	San Jose	4-2		12	at	Carolina	2-0
	29	at	Los Angeles	1-4		14	at	Montreal	2-4
Dec.	2		St. Louis	1-3		18		Anaheim	3-0
	4	at	Pittsburgh	4-0		20	at	Washington	0-2
	6		Tampa Bay	4-2		21		Washington	3-2
	10		Edmonton	4-2		24		Philadelphia	3-2
	12		Montreal	5-2		26	at	Colorado	2-0
	13	at	Toronto	3-0		28	at	Phoenix	3-0
	16		NY Rangers	4-3		29	at	Dallas	1-3
	18	at	St. Louis	4-4	**Apr.**	1		Carolina	0-4
	19	at	Detroit	4-5		3		Ottawa	2-3
	23	at	Washington	1-1		5		Phoenix	3-2
	26		NY Islanders	4-3		8	at	NY Islanders	2-3
	29	at	Buffalo	3-1		11	at	Boston	3-2
	30		Chicago	2-6		12		Florida	5-5
Jan.	1	at	Florida	1-2		15		Buffalo	5-4
	3		Toronto	4-2		16	at	Chicago	1-1
	5		Dallas	3-4		18		NY Islanders	1-2

Entry Draft Selections 1998-84

1998
Pick
26 Mike Van Ryn
27 Scott Gomez
37 Christian Berglund
82 Brian Gionta
96 Mikko Jokela
105 Pierre Dagenais
119 Anton But
143 Ryan Flinn
172 Jacques Lariviere
199 Erik Jensen
227 Marko Ahosilta
257 Ryan Held

1997
Pick
24 J-F Damphousse
38 Stanislav Gron
104 Lucas Nehrling
131 Jiri Bicek
159 Sascha Goc
188 Mathieu Benoit
215 Scott Clemmensen
241 Jan Sorinko

1996
Pick
10 Lance Ward
38 Wesley Mason
41 Joshua Dewolf
47 Pierre Dagenais
49 Colin White
63 Scott Parker
91 Josef Boumedienne
101 Josh MacNevin
118 Glenn Crawford
145 Sean Ritchlin
173 Daryl Andrews
199 Willie Mitchell
205 Jay Bertsch
225 Pasi Petrilainen

1995
Pick
18 Petr Sykora
44 Nathan Perrott
70 Sergei Vyshedkevich
78 David Gosselin
79 Alyn McCauley
96 Henrik Rehnberg
122 Chris Mason
148 Adam Young
174 Richard Rochefort
200 Frederic Henry
226 Colin O'Hara

1994
Pick
25 Vadim Sharifijanov
51 Patrik Elias
71 Sheldon Souray
103 Zdenek Skorepa
129 Christian Gosselin
134 Ryan Smart
155 Luciano Caravaggio
181 Jeff Williams
207 Eric Bertrand
233 Steve Sullivan
259 Scott Swanjord
269 Mike Hanson

1993
Pick
13 Denis Pederson
32 Jay Pandolfo
39 Brendan Morrison
65 Krzysztof Oliwa
110 John Guirestante
143 Steve Brule
169 Nikolai Zavarukhin
195 Thomas Cullen
221 Judd Lambert
247 Jimmy Provencher
273 Michael Legg

1992
Pick
18 Jason Smith
42 Sergei Brylin
66 Cale Hulse
90 Vitali Tomilin
94 Scott McCabe
114 Ryan Black
138 Daniel Trebil
162 Geordie Kinnear
186 Stephane Yelle
210 Jeff Toms
234 Heath Weenk
258 Vladislav Yakovenko

1991
Pick
3 Scott Niedermayer
11 Brian Rolston
33 Donevan Hextall
55 Fredrik Lindqvist
77 Bradley Willner
121 Curt Regnier
143 David Craievich
165 Paul Wolanski
187 Daniel Reimann
231 Kevin Riehl
253 Jason Hehr

1990
Pick
20 Martin Brodeur
24 David Harlock
29 Chris Gotziaman
53 Michael Dunham
56 Brad Bombardir
64 Mike Bodnarchuk
95 Dean Malkoc
104 Petr Kuchyna
116 Lubomir Kolnik
137 Chris McAlpine
179 Jaroslav Modry
200 Corey Schwab
221 Valeri Zelepukin
242 Todd Reirden

1989
Pick
5 Bill Guerin
18 Jason Miller
26 Jarrod Skalde
47 Scott Pellerin
89 Mike Heinke
110 David Emma
152 Sergei Starikov
173 Andre Faust
215 Jason Simon
236 Peter Larsson

1988
Pick
12 Corey Foster
23 Jeff Christian
54 Zdeno Ciger
65 Matt Ruchty
75 Scott Luik
96 Chris Nelson
117 Chad Johnson
138 Chad Erickson
159 Bryan Lafort
180 Sergei Svetlov
201 Bob Woods
207 Alexander Semak
222 Charles Hughes
243 Michael Pohl

1987
Pick
2 Brendan Shanahan
23 Rickard Persson
65 Brian Sullivan
86 Kevin Dean
107 Ben Hankinson
128 Tom Neziol
149 Jim Dowd
170 John Blessman
191 Peter Fry
212 Alain Charland

1986
Pick
3 Neil Brady
24 Todd Copeland
45 Janne Ojanen
62 Marc Laniel
66 Anders Carlsson
108 Troy Crowder
129 Kevin Todd
150 Ryan Pardoski
171 Scott McCormack
192 Frederic Chabot
213 John Andersen
236 Doug Kirton

1985
Pick
3 Craig Wolanin
24 Sean Burke
32 Eric Weinrich
45 Myles O'Connor
66 Gregg Polak
108 Bill McMillan
129 Kevin Schrader
150 Ed Krayer
171 Jamie Huscroft
192 Terry Shold
213 Jamie McKinley
234 David Williams

1984
Pick
2 Kirk Muller
23 Craig Billington
44 Neil Davey
74 Paul Ysebaert
86 Jon Morris
107 Kirk McLean
128 Ian Ferguson
149 Vladimir Kames
170 Mike Roth
190 Mike Peluso
211 Jarkko Piiparinen
231 Chris Kiene

Coach

FTOREK, ROBBIE
Coach, New Jersey Devils. Born in Needham, MA, January 2, 1952.

The New Jersey Devils promoted Robbie Ftorek to the position of head coach on May 21, 1998. Ftorek, 46, will be entering his eighth season with the organization, having joined the Devils on July 9, 1991. He spent the past two seasons as an assistant coach, having also served the organization in that capacity during the 1991-92 season. Ftorek was head coach of the Devils' top minor-league development club for four seasons, 1992-93 through 1995-96, and led the Albany River Rats to the 1995 American Hockey League's Calder Cup championship.

Prior to joining the Devils, Ftorek spent two seasons in the Quebec Nordiques organization. He was named head coach of the Halifax Citadels (AHL) prior to 1989-90 and assumed the post as Nordiques' assistant coach during that season. Ftorek began his coaching career upon his retirement as a player when he was named to guide the New Haven Nighthawks (AHL) in 1985. On December 9, 1987, Ftorek was named head coach of the Los Angeles Kings, where he guided the team to a 65-56-11 (.534) mark over one and a half seasons.

Coaching Record

		Regular Season					Playoffs			
Season	**Team**	**Games**	**W**	**L**	**T**	**%**	**Games**	**W**	**L**	**%**
1985-86	New Haven (AHL)	80	36	37	7	.494	5	1	4	.200
1986-87	New Haven (AHL)	80	44	25	11	.619	7	3	4	.429
1987-88	New Haven (AHL)	27	16	8	3	.667	....	....	....	....
	Los Angeles (NHL)	**52**	**23**	**25**	**4**	**.481**	**5**	**1**	**4**	**.200**
1988-89	**Los Angeles (NHL)**	**80**	**42**	**31**	**7**	**.569**	**11**	**4**	**7**	**.364**
1989-90	Halifax (AHL)	48	25	19	4	.563	....	....	....	....
1992-93	Utica (AHL)	80	33	36	11	.481	5	1	4	.200
1993-94	Albany (AHL)	80	38	34	8	.525	5	1	4	.200
1994-95	Albany (AHL)	80	46	17	17	.681	14	12	2	.857
1995-96	Albany (AHL)	80	54	19	17	.719	4	1	3	.250
	NHL Totals	**132**	**65**	**56**	**11**	**.534**	**16**	**5**	**11**	**.313**

Club Directory

Continental Airlines Arena
50 Route 120 North
P.O. Box 504
East Rutherford, NJ 07073
Phone **201/935-6050**
FAX 201/935-2127
Website:
www.newjerseydevils.com
Capacity: 19,040

Chairman	Dr. John J. McMullen
President/General Manager	Louis A. Lamoriello
Executive Vice President	Peter S. McMullen
Executive Vice President	Chris Modrzynski
Vice President, General Counsel	Joseph C. Benedetti
Vice President, Ticket Operations	Terry Farmer
Vice President, Corporate Partnerships	Kenneth F. Ferriter
Vice President, Communications/Broadcasting	Rick Minch
Vice President, Finance	Scott Struble

Hockey Club Personnel

Head Coach	Robbie Ftorek
Assistant Coach	Viacheslav Fetisov
Goaltending Coach	Jacques Caron
Director of Scouting	David Conte
Scouting Staff	Claude Carrier, Glen Dirk, Milt Fisher, Ferny Flaman, Dan Labraaten, Chris Lamoriello, Joe Mahoney, Larry Perris, Marcel Pronovost, Lou Reycroft, Vaclav Slansky, Geoff Stevens, Ed Thomlinson, Les Widdifield
Pro Scouting Staff	Andre Boudrias, Bob Hoffmeyer, Jan Ludvig
Special Assignment Scout	Jacques Lemaire
Hockey Operations Video Coordinator	Taran Singleton
Scouting Staff Assistant	Callie A. Smith
Strength/Conditioning Coordinator	Michael Vasalani
Medical Trainer	Bill Murray
Equipment Manager	Dave Nichols
Assistant Equipment Managers	Alex Abasto, Lou Centanni
Massage Therapist	Juergen Merz
Team Cardiologist	Dr. Joseph Niznik
Team Dentist	Dr. H. Hugh Gardy
Team Optometrist	Dr. Paul Berman
Team Orthopedists	Dr. Barry Fisher, Dr. Len Jaffe
Exercise Physiologist	Dr. Garret Caffrey
Physical Therapist	David M. Feniger
Video Consultant	Mitch Kaufman
Head Coach, Albany	John Cunniff
Assistant Coach, Albany	Dennis Gendron
Athletic Trainer, Albany	Chris Scarlata
Equipment Manager, Albany	Dana McGuane

Administration Dept.

Hockey Operations Executive Assistant to the President/General Manager	Marie Carnevale
Corporate Executive Assistant to the President/General Manager	Mary K. Morrison
Receptionists	Jelsa Belotta, Pat Maione
Corporate Staff Assistant	Mary Montemurro
Operations Staff Assistant	David Biunno

Ticket Department

Director, Ticket Operations	Tom Bates
Director, Customer Service/Gold Circle	Gail DeRisi
Director, Customer Service/ Season Ticket Accounts	Dave Beck
Customer Service Representative	Andrea Marchesani
Director, Group Sales	Neil Desormeaux
Group Account Manager	Rich Davis

Marketing Department

Senior Director, Ticket Sales	Paul Solby
Director, Season Ticket Sales	Kevin Morgan
Account Managers	Joanne Byrne, Joel De Castro, Carmine D'Urso, Nick Mike-Mayer, Frank Vella, Mike Yencik
Account Managers, Corporate Partnerships	Mike Kozak, Michael DeMartino
Coordinator, Corporate Partnerships/ Publication Sales	Eileen Begg
Director, Community Development	Jackie Dooley
Assistant Director, Community Development	Paul Viola
Coordinator, Game Entertainment	Joe Schilp
Sales Receptionist	Stephanie Haggan

Communications Department

Director, Public Relations	Kevin Dessart
Director, Information/Publications	Mike Levine
Coordinator, Communications	Jana Spaulding
Communications Assistant	Jeff Altstadter
Team Photographer	Bruce Bennett Studios

Finance Department

Staff Accountants	Suzanne Folkerts, Michael Merolla
Administrative Assistant	Eileen Musikant

Merchandising Department

Merchandising Manager	David Perricone
Customer Service Representative	Stephanie Toskos

Computer Operations

Director, Programming/Computer Operations	Jack Skelley
Systems Administrator	Mike Tukes
Director, Internet Operations	Susan Amerian

Television/Radio

Television Outlet	Fox Sports New York
Broadcasters	Mike Emrick, Play-by-Play; Glenn Resch, Color
Radio Outlet	WABC 77AM
Broadcasters	Mike Miller, Play-by-Play; Randy Velischek, Color
Dimensions of Rink	200 feet × 85 feet
Club Colors	Red, Black & White

New York Islanders

1997-98 Results: 30W-41L-11T 71PTS. Fourth, Atlantic Division

1998-99 Schedule

Oct.	Sat.	10	Pittsburgh
	Mon.	12	at Boston*
	Wed.	14	at Tampa Bay
	Sat.	17	at St. Louis
	Wed.	21	Edmonton
	Thu.	22	at NY Rangers
	Sat.	24	Buffalo
	Tue.	27	Los Angeles
	Thu.	29	New Jersey
	Sat.	31	Philadelphia
Nov.	Mon.	2	Florida
	Thu.	5	Carolina
	Sat.	7	at Montreal
	Mon.	9	at Toronto
	Tue.	10	at Pittsburgh
	Thu.	12	Montreal
	Sat.	14	Washington
	Tue.	17	at Colorado
	Fri.	20	at Dallas
	Sat.	21	at Nashville
	Wed.	25	Philadelphia
	Thu.	26	at Ottawa
	Sat.	28	Carolina*
Dec.	Wed.	2	NY Rangers
	Fri.	4	at Washington
	Sat.	5	New Jersey
	Tue.	8	Colorado
	Sat.	12	Tampa Bay
	Tue.	15	at San Jose
	Thu.	17	at Los Angeles
	Fri.	18	at Anaheim
	Sun.	20	at Phoenix*
	Tue.	22	St. Louis
	Sat.	26	Boston
	Mon.	28	at Florida
	Tue.	29	at Tampa Bay
	Thu.	31	at Chicago
Jan.	Sat.	2	San Jose*
	Tue.	5	Chicago
	Thu.	7	at Philadelphia
	Sat.	9	at Montreal
	Mon.	11	at Washington
	Wed.	13	at NY Rangers
	Sat.	16	at Florida
	Wed.	20	Florida
	Thu.	21	at Pittsburgh
	Tue.	26	Boston
	Fri.	29	Phoenix
	Sat.	30	at Ottawa
Feb.	Wed.	3	at Detroit
	Thu.	4	at Boston
	Sun.	7	Vancouver*
	Tue.	9	Washington
	Fri.	12	Nashville
	Sat.	13	at Buffalo
	Mon.	15	Tampa Bay*
	Wed.	17	Pittsburgh
	Sat.	20	at New Jersey
	Sun.	21	at Carolina
	Thu.	25	Toronto
	Sat.	27	Detroit
Mar.	Tue.	2	Ottawa
	Thu.	4	Dallas
	Sat.	6	at Philadelphia*
	Sun.	7	New Jersey*
	Tue.	9	Philadelphia
	Thu.	11	Toronto
	Sun.	14	NY Rangers*
	Mon.	15	at Buffalo
	Fri.	19	at Vancouver
	Sun.	21	at Calgary*
	Wed.	24	at Carolina
	Sat.	27	Ottawa
	Mon.	29	at NY Rangers
	Wed.	31	at Florida
Apr.	Sat.	3	Anaheim
	Tue.	6	Buffalo
	Thu.	8	Montreal
	Sat.	10	Carolina
	Mon.	12	at New Jersey
	Wed.	14	at Toronto
	Sat.	17	at Pittsburgh*

* Denotes afternoon game.

After spending his entire career in Vancouver, Trevor Linden (trailed by Mike Hough) was traded by the Canucks on February 6, 1998. He had 10 goals in just 25 games with the Islanders in 1997-98.

Franchise date: June 6, 1972

ATLANTIC DIVISION

27th NHL Season

Year-by-Year Record

		Home			Road			Overall							
Season	**GP**	**W**	**L**	**T**	**W**	**L**	**T**	**W**	**L**	**T**	**GF**	**GA**	**Pts.**	**Finished**	**Playoff Result**
1997-98	82	17	20	4	13	21	7	30	41	11	212	225	71	4th, Atlantic Div.	Out of Playoffs
1996-97	82	19	18	4	10	23	8	29	41	12	240	250	70	7th, Atlantic Div.	Out of Playoffs
1995-96	82	14	21	6	8	29	4	22	50	10	229	315	54	7th, Atlantic Div.	Out of Playoffs
1994-95	48	10	11	3	5	17	2	15	28	5	126	158	35	7th, Atlantic Div.	Out of Playoffs
1993-94	84	23	15	4	13	21	8	36	36	12	282	264	84	4th, Atlantic Div.	Lost Conf. Quarter-Final
1992-93	84	20	19	3	20	18	4	40	37	7	335	297	87	3rd, Patrick Div.	Lost Conf. Championship
1991-92	80	20	15	5	14	20	6	34	35	11	291	299	79	5th, Patrick Div.	Out of Playoffs
1990-91	80	15	19	6	10	26	4	25	45	10	223	290	60	6th, Patrick Div.	Out of Playoffs
1989-90	80	15	17	8	16	21	3	31	38	11	281	288	73	4th, Patrick Div.	Lost Div. Semi-Final
1988-89	80	19	18	3	9	29	2	28	47	5	265	325	61	6th, Patrick Div.	Out of Playoffs
1987-88	80	24	10	6	15	21	4	39	31	10	308	267	88	1st, Patrick Div.	Lost Div. Semi-Final
1986-87	80	20	15	5	15	18	7	35	33	12	279	281	82	3rd, Patrick Div.	Lost Div. Final
1985-86	80	22	11	7	17	18	5	39	29	12	327	284	90	3rd, Patrick Div.	Lost Div. Semi-Final
1984-85	80	26	11	3	14	23	3	40	34	6	345	312	86	3rd, Patrick Div.	Lost Div. Final
1983-84	80	28	11	1	22	15	3	50	26	4	357	269	104	1st, Patrick Div.	Lost Final
1982-83	**80**	**26**	**11**	**3**	**16**	**15**	**9**	**42**	**26**	**12**	**302**	**226**	**96**	**2nd, Patrick Div.**	**Won Stanley Cup**
1981-82	**80**	**33**	**3**	**4**	**21**	**13**	**6**	**54**	**16**	**10**	**385**	**250**	**118**	**1st, Patrick Div.**	**Won Stanley Cup**
1980-81	**80**	**23**	**6**	**11**	**25**	**12**	**3**	**48**	**18**	**14**	**355**	**260**	**110**	**1st, Patrick Div.**	**Won Stanley Cup**
1979-80	**80**	**26**	**9**	**5**	**13**	**19**	**8**	**39**	**28**	**13**	**281**	**247**	**91**	**2nd, Patrick Div.**	**Won Stanley Cup**
1978-79	80	31	3	6	20	12	8	51	15	14	358	214	116	1st, Patrick Div.	Lost Semi-Final
1977-78	80	29	3	8	19	14	7	48	17	15	334	210	111	1st, Patrick Div.	Lost Quarter-Final
1976-77	80	24	11	5	23	10	7	47	21	12	288	193	106	2nd, Patrick Div.	Lost Semi-Final
1975-76	80	24	8	8	18	13	9	42	21	17	297	190	101	2nd, Patrick Div.	Lost Semi-Final
1974-75	80	22	6	12	11	19	10	33	25	22	264	221	88	3rd, Patrick Div.	Lost Semi-Final
1973-74	78	13	17	9	6	24	9	19	41	18	182	247	56	8th, East Div.	Out of Playoffs
1972-73	78	10	25	4	2	35	2	12	60	6	170	347	30	8th, East Div.	Out of Playoffs

1998-99 Player Personnel

FORWARDS	HT	WT	S	Place of Birth	Date	1997-98 Club
BELANGER, Ken	6-4	225	L	Sault Ste. Marie, Ont.	5/14/74	NY Islanders
CHORSKE, Tom	6-1	212	R	Minneapolis, MN	9/18/66	NY Islanders-United States
CZERKAWSKI, Mariusz	6-0	195	L	Radomsko, Poland	4/13/72	NY Islanders
DAWE, Jason	5-10	189	L	North York, Ont.	5/29/73	Buffalo-NY Islanders
HAGGERTY, Sean	6-1	186	L	Rye, NY	2/11/76	NY Islanders-Kentucky
HOUGH, Mike	6-1	197	L	Montreal, Que.	2/6/63	NY Islanders
JACKSON, Dane	6-1	200	R	Castlegar, B.C.	5/17/70	NY Islanders-Rochester
LAPOINTE, Claude	5-9	181	L	Lachine, Que.	10/11/68	NY Islanders
LAWRENCE, Mark	6-4	215	R	Burlington, Ont.	1/27/72	NY Islanders-Utah
LINDEN, Trevor	6-4	210	R	Medicine Hat, Alta.	4/11/70	Van-NYI-Canada
NABOKOV, Dmitri	6-2	216	R	Novosibirsk, USSR	1/4/77	Chicago-Indianapolis
NEMCHINOV, Sergei	6-0	200	L	Moscow, USSR	1/14/64	NY Islanders-Russia
ODJICK, Gino	6-3	210	L	Maniwaki, Que.	9/7/70	Vancouver-NY Islanders
ORSZAGH, Vladimir	5-11	173	L	Banska Bystrica, Czech.	5/24/77	NY Islanders-Utah
PALFFY, Zigmund	5-10	183	L	Skalica, Czech.	5/5/72	NY Islanders
REICHEL, Robert	5-10	185	L	Litvinov, Czech.	6/25/71	NY Islanders-Czech.
RUPP, Michael	6-5	218	L	Cleveland, OH	1/13/80	Windsor-Erie (OHL)
SACCO, Joe	6-1	195	L	Medford, MA	2/4/69	Anaheim-NY Islanders
SMOLINSKI, Bryan	6-1	202	R	Toledo, OH	12/27/71	NY Islanders-United States
WATT, Mike	6-2	212	L	Seaforth, Ont.	3/31/76	Edmonton-Hamilton
WEBB, Steve	6-0	195	R	Peterborough, Ont.	4/20/75	NY Islanders-Kentucky
DEFENSEMEN						
BERARD, Bryan	6-1	190	L	Woonsocket, RI	3/5/77	NY Islanders-United States
BREWER, Eric	6-3	195	L	Vernon, B.C.	4/17/79	Prince George-Canada
CHARA, Zdeno	6-9	255	L	Trencin, Czech.	3/18/77	NY Islanders-Kentucky
CHEBATURKIN, Vladimir	6-2	213	L	Tyumen, USSR	4/23/75	NY Islanders-Kentucky
GAUL, Michael	6-1	200	R	Lachine, Que.	4/22/73	Hershey
HARLOCK, David	6-2	205	L	Toronto, Ont.	3/16/71	Washington-Portland (AHL)
JONSSON, Kenny	6-3	195	L	Angelholm, Sweden	10/6/74	NY Islanders
LACHANCE, Scott	6-1	196	L	Charlottesville, VA	10/22/72	NY Islanders
MALKOC, Dean	6-3	215	L	Vancouver, B.C.	1/26/70	Boston
PILON, Richard	6-0	205	L	Saskatoon, Sask.	4/30/68	NY Islanders
RICHTER, Barry	6-2	200	L	Madison, WI	9/11/70	Providence (AHL)
SCHULTZ, Ray	6-2	200	L	Red Deer, Alta.	11/14/76	NY Islanders-Kentucky

GOALTENDERS	HT	WT	C	Place of Birth	Date	1997-98 Club
COUSINEAU, Marcel	5-9	180	L	Delson, Que.	4/30/73	Toronto-St. John's
FLAHERTY, Wade	6-0	170	L	Terrace, B.C.	1/11/68	NY Islanders-Utah
McARTHUR, Mark	5-10	175	L	East York, Ont.	11/16/75	Utah
SALO, Tommy	5-11	173	L	Surahammar, Sweden	2/1/71	NY Islanders-Sweden

1997-98 Scoring

* – rookie

Regular Season

Pos	#	Player	Team	GP	G	A	Pts	+/–	PIM	PP	SH	GW	GT	S	%
R	16	Zigmund Palffy	NYI	82	45	42	87	-2	34	17	2	5	1	277	16.2
C	21	Robert Reichel	NYI	82	25	40	65	-11	32	8	0	2	2	201	12.4
D	34	Bryan Berard	NYI	75	14	32	46	-32	59	8	1	2	1	192	7.3
C	20	Bryan Smolinski	NYI	81	13	30	43	-16	34	3	0	4	0	203	6.4
D	29	Kenny Jonsson	NYI	81	14	26	40	-2	58	6	0	2	0	108	13.0
R	44	Jason Dawe	BUF	68	19	17	36	10	36	4	1	3	1	115	16.5
			NYI	13	1	2	3	-2	6	0	0	0	0	19	5.3
			TOTAL	81	20	19	39	8	42	4	1	3	1	134	14.9
C	32	Trevor Linden	VAN	42	7	14	21	-13	49	2	0	1	0	74	9.5
			NYI	25	10	7	17	-1	33	3	2	1	0	59	16.9
			TOTAL	67	17	21	38	-14	82	5	2	2	0	133	12.8
L	14	Tom Chorske	NYI	82	12	23	35	7	39	1	4	2	0	132	9.1
C	17	Sergei Nemchinov	NYI	74	10	19	29	3	24	2	1	1	0	94	10.6
R	25	Mariusz Czerkawski	NYI	68	12	13	25	11	23	2	0	1	0	136	8.8
R	10	Joe Sacco	ANA	55	8	11	19	-1	24	0	2	2	0	90	8.9
			NYI	25	3	3	6	1	10	0	0	0	0	32	9.4
			TOTAL	80	11	14	25	0	34	0	2	2	0	122	9.0
D	36	J.J. Daigneault	ANA	53	2	15	17	-10	28	1	0	1	0	74	2.7
			NYI	18	0	6	6	1	21	0	0	0	0	18	0.0
			TOTAL	71	2	21	23	-9	49	1	0	1	0	92	2.2
C	13	Claude Lapointe	NYI	78	10	10	20	-9	47	0	1	3	0	82	12.2
D	7	Scott Lachance	NYI	63	2	11	13	-11	45	1	0	0	0	62	3.2
L	18	Mike Hough	NYI	74	5	7	12	-4	27	0	0	0	0	44	11.4
D	2	Richard Pilon	NYI	76	0	7	7	1	291	0	0	0	0	37	0.0
L	24	Gino Odjick	VAN	35	3	2	5	-3	181	0	0	1	0	36	8.3
			NYI	13	0	0	0	1	31	0	0	0	0	16	0.0
			TOTAL	48	3	2	5	-2	212	0	0	1	0	52	5.8
L	33	Ken Belanger	NYI	37	3	1	4	1	101	0	0	1	0	10	30.0
C	54	Kip Miller	NYI	9	1	3	4	-2	2	0	0	0	0	11	9.1
D	28	Dennis Vaske	NYI	19	0	3	3	2	12	0	0	0	0	16	0.0
R	36	Dane Jackson	NYI	8	1	1	2	1	4	0	0	1	0	5	20.0
D	55	* Vladimir Chebaturkin	NYI	2	0	2	2	-1	0	0	0	0	0	0	0.0
D	58	Yevgeny Namestnikov	NYI	6	0	1	1	-1	4	0	0	0	0	2	0.0
R	42	Dan Plante	NYI	7	0	1	1	-1	6	0	0	0	0	7	0.0
R	49	* Vladimir Orsagh	NYI	11	0	1	1	-3	2	0	0	0	0	9	0.0
D	60	* Ray Schultz	NYI	13	0	1	1	3	45	0	0	0	0	4	0.0
G	30	Wade Flaherty	NYI	16	0	1	1	0	0	0	0	0	0	0	0.0
D	3	* Zdeno Chara	NYI	25	0	1	1	1	50	0	0	0	0	10	0.0
G	35	Tommy Salo	NYI	62	0	1	1	0	31	0	0	0	0	0	0.0
D	37	* Jeff Libby	NYI	1	0	0	0	0	0	0	0	0	0	0	0.0
R	52	* Mark Lawrence	NYI	2	0	0	0	0	2	0	0	0	0	4	0.0
L	11	* Sean Haggerty	NYI	5	0	0	0	-3	0	0	0	0	0	2	0.0
R	48	* Warren Luhning	NYI	8	0	0	0	-4	0	0	0	0	0	6	0.0
D	46	* Jason Holland	NYI	8	0	0	0	-4	4	0	0	0	0	6	0.0
G	1	Eric Fichaud	NYI	17	0	0	0	0	0	0	0	0	0	0	0.0
R	8	Steve Webb	NYI	20	0	0	0	-2	35	0	0	0	0	6	0.0

Goaltending

No.	Goaltender	GPI	Mins	Avg	W	L	T	EN	SO	GA	SA	S%
30	Wade Flaherty	16	694	1.99	4	4	3	0	3	23	309	.926
35	Tommy Salo	62	3461	2.64	23	29	5	9	4	152	1617	.906
1	Eric Fichaud	17	807	2.97	3	8	3	1	0	40	422	.905
	Totals	**82**	**4982**	**2.71**	**30**	**41**	**11**	**10**	**8**	**225**	**2358**	**.905**

General Manager and Coach

MILBURY, MIKE
General Manager and Coach, New York Islanders.
Born in Walpole, MA, June 17, 1952.

Milbury, 46, came to the Islanders with 20 years of professional hockey experience with the Boston Bruins — as a player, assistant coach, assistant general manager, general manager and coach on both the NHL and AHL levels. Milbury took over as general manager from Don Maloney on December 12, 1995.

Milbury joined the Boston organization after graduating from Colgate University with a degree in urban sociology and enjoyed a nine-year playing career with the team. He retired May 6, 1985 and took over as assistant coach. He returned to the ice late in the 1985-86 season when injuries decimated the Bruins defense.

Milbury's playing career concluded after the 1986-87 season and on July 16, 1987 he took over as coach of the Maine Mariners, Boston's top AHL affiliate. In his first year with the team he guided the Mariners to the AHL's Northern Division title and was named both AHL coach of the year and *The Hockey News* minor league coach of the year.

He was named the assistant general manager and coach of the Boston Bruins May 16, 1989. He guided the Bruins to consecutive 100-point seasons and Adams Division titles, the 1990 Presidents' Trophy and Wales Conference championship, and an appearance in the Stanley Cup finals in 1990. He earned coach of the year honors from both *The Hockey News* and *The Sporting News* for this effort.

Milbury and his wife, Debbie, have two sons, Owen and Luke, and two daughters, Alison and Caitlin.

NHL Coaching Record

		Regular Season					Playoffs			
Season	Team	Games	W	L	T	%	Games	W	L	%
1989-90	Boston	80	46	25	9	.631	21	13	8	.619
1990-91	Boston	80	44	24	12	.606	19	10	9	.526
1995-96	NY Islanders	82	22	50	10	.329	....	....	....	....
1996-97	NY Islanders	45	13	23	9	.389	....	....	....	....
1997-98	NY Islanders	19	8	9	2	.474	....	....	....	....
	NHL Totals	**306**	**133**	**131**	**42**	**.503**	**40**	**23**	**17**	**.575**

General Managers' History

Bill Torrey, 1972-73 to 1991-92; Don Maloney, 1992-93 to 1994-95; Don Maloney and Mike Milbury, 1995-96; Mike Milbury, 1996-97 to date.

Coaching History

Phil Goyette and Earl Ingarfield, 1972-73; Al Arbour, 1973-74 to 1985-86; Terry Simpson, 1986-87, 1987-88; Terry Simpson and Al Arbour, 1988-89; Al Arbour, 1989-90 to 1993-94; Lorne Henning, 1994-95; Mike Milbury, 1995-96; Mike Milbury and Rick Bowness, 1996-97; Rick Bowness and Mike Milbury, 1997-98; Mike Milbury, 1998-99.

Captains' History

Ed Westfall, 1972-73 to 1975-76; Ed Westfall and Clark Gillies, 1976-77; Clark Gillies, 1977-78, 1978-79; Denis Potvin, 1979-80 to 1986-87; Brent Sutter, 1987-88 to 1990-91; Brent Sutter and Pat Flatley, 1991-92; Pat Flatley, 1992-93 to 1995-96; no captain, 1996-97; Bryan McCabe and Trevor Linden, 1997-98; Trevor Linden, 1998-99.

Club Records

Team

(Figures in brackets for season records are games played; records for fewest points, wins, ties, losses, goals, goals against are for 70 or more games)

Most Points	**118**	1981-82 (80)
Most Wins	**54**	1981-82 (80)
Most Ties	**22**	1974-75 (80)
Most Losses	**60**	1972-73 (78)
Most Goals	**385**	1981-82 (80)
Most Goals Against	**347**	1972-73 (78)
Fewest Points	**30**	1972-73 (78)
Fewest Wins	**12**	1972-73 (78)
Fewest Ties	**4**	1983-84 (80)
Fewest Losses	**15**	1978-79 (80)
Fewest Goals	**170**	1972-73 (78)
Fewest Goals Against	**190**	1975-76 (80)
Longest Winning Streak		
Overall	**15**	Jan. 21-Feb. 20/82
Home	**14**	Jan. 2-Feb. 27/82
Away	**8**	Feb. 27-Mar. 31/81
Longest Undefeated Streak		
Overall	**15**	Jan. 21-Feb. 20/82 (15 wins), Nov. 4-Dec. 4/80 (13 wins, 2 ties)
Home	**23**	Oct. 17/78-Jan. 27/79 (19 wins, 4 ties), Jan. 2-Apr. 3/82 (21 wins, 2 ties)
Away	**8**	Four times
Longest Losing Streak		
Overall	**12**	Dec. 27/72-Jan. 16/73, Nov. 22-Dec. 15/88
Home	**5**	Four times
Away	**15**	Jan. 20-Mar. 31/73
Longest Winless Streak		
Overall	**15**	Nov. 22-Dec. 21/72 (12 losses, 3 ties)
Home	**7**	Oct. 14-Nov. 21/72 (6 losses, 1 tie), Nov. 28-Dec. 23/72 (5 losses, 2 ties), Feb. 13-Mar. 13/90 (4 losses, 3 ties)
Away	**20**	Nov. 3/72-Jan. 13/73 (19 losses, 1 tie)
Most Shutouts, Season	**10**	1975-76 (80)
Most PIM, Season	**1,857**	1986-87 (80)
Most Goals, Game	**11**	Dec. 20/83 (Pit. 3 at NYI 11), Mar. 3/84 (NYI 11 at Tor. 6)

Individual

Most Seasons	**17**	Billy Smith
Most Games	**1,123**	Bryan Trottier
Most Goals, Career	**573**	Mike Bossy
Most Assists, Career	**853**	Bryan Trottier
Most Points, Career	**1,353**	Bryan Trottier (500G, 853A)
Most PIM, Career	**1,879**	Mick Vukota
Most Shutouts, Career	**25**	Glenn Resch
Longest Consecutive Games Streak	**576**	Bill Harris (Oct. 7/72-Nov. 30/79)
Most Goals, Season	**69**	Mike Bossy (1978-79)
Most Assists, Season	**87**	Bryan Trottier (1978-79)
Most Points, Season	**147**	Mike Bossy (1981-82; 64G, 83A)
Most PIM, Season	**356**	Brian Curran (1986-87)
Most Points, Defenseman, Season	**101**	Denis Potvin (1978-79; 31G, 70A)
Most Points, Center, Season	**134**	Bryan Trottier (1978-79; 47G, 87A)
Most Points, Right Wing, Season	**147**	Mike Bossy (1981-82; 64G, 83A)
Most Points, Left Wing, Season	**100**	John Tonelli (1984-85; 42G, 58A)
Most Points, Rookie, Season	**95**	Bryan Trottier (1975-76; 32G, 63A)
Most Shutouts, Season	**7**	Glenn Resch (1975-76)
Most Goals, Game	**5**	Bryan Trottier (Dec. 23/78, Feb. 13/82), John Tonelli (Jan. 6/81)
Most Assists, Game	**6**	Mike Bossy (Jan. 6/81)
Most Points, Game	**8**	Bryan Trottier (Dec. 23/78; 5G, 3A)

Retired Numbers

5	Denis Potvin	1973-1988
9	Clark Gillies	1974-1986
22	Mike Bossy	1977-1987
23	Bob Nystrom	1972-1986
31	Billy Smith	1972-1989

All-time Record vs. Other Clubs

Regular Season

	At Home							On Road							Total						
	GP	W	L	T	GF	GA	PTS	GP	W	L	T	GF	GA	PTS	GP	W	L	T	GF	GA	PTS
Anaheim	4	2	2	0	10	13	4	4	2	1	1	12	9	5	8	4	3	1	22	22	9
Boston	49	19	24	6	163	165	44	47	11	26	10	135	184	32	96	30	50	16	298	349	76
Buffalo	49	21	20	8	142	136	50	49	16	26	7	141	174	39	98	37	46	15	283	310	89
Calgary	46	25	12	9	185	124	59	46	13	22	11	139	166	37	92	38	34	20	324	290	96
Carolina	31	17	10	4	112	82	38	33	13	15	5	120	122	31	64	30	25	9	232	204	69
Chicago	42	17	12	13	150	127	47	44	16	23	5	150	150	37	86	33	35	18	300	277	84
Colorado	28	15	12	1	115	100	31	29	10	17	2	90	110	22	57	25	29	3	205	210	53
Dallas	42	23	11	8	162	121	54	42	19	16	7	156	124	45	84	42	27	15	318	245	99
Detroit	41	22	16	3	152	123	47	40	17	21	2	129	142	36	81	39	37	5	281	265	83
Edmonton	26	12	5	9	113	97	33	26	6	16	4	74	99	16	52	18	21	13	187	196	49
Florida	13	4	7	2	28	32	10	12	3	6	3	32	37	9	25	7	13	5	60	69	19
Los Angeles	40	23	13	4	153	115	50	40	14	19	7	129	145	35	80	37	32	11	282	260	85
Montreal	48	21	22	5	153	147	47	48	12	27	9	146	181	33	96	33	49	14	299	328	80
New Jersey	69	50	10	9	315	191	109	69	32	27	10	259	235	74	138	82	37	19	574	426	183
NY Rangers	81	52	22	7	333	246	111	80	24	47	9	243	314	57	161	76	69	16	576	560	168
Ottawa	12	3	6	3	41	44	9	11	3	5	3	39	34	9	23	6	11	6	80	78	18
Philadelphia	82	45	24	13	322	237	103	80	23	49	8	238	305	54	162	68	73	21	560	542	157
Phoenix	26	13	7	6	104	80	32	25	14	8	3	95	77	31	51	27	15	9	199	157	63
Pittsburgh	71	37	26	8	291	237	82	72	27	34	11	251	276	65	143	64	60	19	542	513	147
St. Louis	44	24	10	10	170	110	58	43	17	17	9	143	158	43	87	41	27	19	313	268	101
San Jose	7	5	1	1	34	21	11	6	3	2	1	24	15	7	13	8	3	2	58	36	18
Tampa Bay	13	5	8	0	36	41	10	14	7	6	1	47	36	15	27	12	14	1	83	77	25
Toronto	41	24	14	3	176	125	51	43	20	20	3	155	148	43	84	44	34	6	331	273	94
Vancouver	42	23	11	8	159	117	54	44	20	21	3	145	147	43	86	43	32	11	304	264	97
Washington	69	40	28	1	270	215	81	69	29	30	10	225	221	68	138	69	58	11	495	436	149
Defunct Clubs	13	11	0	2	75	33	24	13	4	5	4	35	41	12	26	15	5	6	110	74	36
Totals	**1029**	**553**	**333**	**143**	**3964**	**3079**	**1249**	**1029**	**375**	**506**	**148**	**3352**	**3650**	**898**	**2058**	**928**	**839**	**291**	**7316**	**6729**	**2147**

Playoffs

	Series	W	L	GP	W	L	T	GF	GA	Last Mtg.	Round	Result
Boston	2	2	0	11	8	3	0	49	35	1983	CF	W 4-2
Buffalo	3	3	0	16	12		0	59	45	1980	SF	W 4-2
Chicago	2	2	0	6	6	0	0	21	6	1979	QF	W 4-0
Colorado	1	1	0	4	4	0	0	18	9	1982	CF	W 4-0
Dallas	1	1	0	5	4	1	0	26	16	1981	F	W 4-1
Edmonton	3	2	1	15	9	6	0	58	47	1984	F	L 1-4
Los Angeles	1	1	0	4	3	1	0	21	10	1980	PR	W 3-1
Montreal	4	1	3	22	8	14	0	55	64	1993	CF	L 1-4
New Jersey	1	0	1	6	2	4	0	18	23	1988	DSF	L 2-4
NY Rangers	8	5	3	39	20	19	0	129	132	1994	CQF	L 0-4
Philadelphia	4	1	3	25	11	14	0	69	83	1987	DF	L 3-4
Pittsburgh	3	3	0	19	11	8	0	67	58	1993	DF	W 4-3
Toronto	2	1	1	10	6	4	0	33	20	1981	PR	W 3-0
Vancouver	2	2	0	6	6	0	0	26	14	1982	F	W 4-0
Washington	6	5	1	30	18	12	0	99	88	1993	DSF	W 4-2
Totals	**43**	**30**	**13**	**218**	**128**	**90**	**0**	**748**	**650**			

Calgary totals include Atlanta, 1972-73 to 1979-80. Carolina totals include Hartford, 1979-80 to 1996-97.
Colorado totals include Quebec, 1979-80 to 1994-95. Dallas totals include Minnesota, 1972-73 to 1992-93.
New Jersey totals include Kansas City, 1974-75 to 1975-76, and Colorado Rockies, 1976-77 to 1981-82.
Phoenix totals include Winnipeg, 1979-80 to 1995-96.

Playoff Results 1998-94

Year	Round	Opponent	Result	GF	GA
1994	CQF	NY Rangers	L 0-4	3	22

Abbreviations: Round: F – Final; **CF** – conference final; **CQF** – conference quarter-final; **DF** – division final; **DSF** – division semi-final; **SF** – semi-final; **QF** – quarter-final; **PR** – preliminary round.

1997-98 Results

Oct.	3	at	NY Rangers	2-2
	4		Toronto	3-0
	8		Washington	3-6
	11	at	Washington	1-3
	13	at	Florida	2-2
	16	at	San Jose	5-2
	19	at	Anaheim	5-2
	21	at	Los Angeles	2-3
	25		Anaheim	2-4
	27		San Jose	1-2
	29	at	Montreal	5-2
	30		NY Rangers	5-3
Nov.	1		Los Angeles	4-2
	5		Edmonton	4-4
	7	at	Carolina	3-2
	8		Chicago	2-4
	10		New Jersey	1-3
	12	at	Florida	2-2
	14	at	Tampa Bay	4-1
	15		Florida	0-1
	19	at	Detroit	3-2
	20	at	New Jersey	1-5
	22	at	Buffalo	1-6
	26		NY Rangers	4-1
	28	at	Philadelphia	1-4
	29		St. Louis	4-2
Dec.	2		Ottawa	2-4
	3	at	Carolina	3-5
	6		Phoenix	4-0
	9		Calgary	1-3
	11	at	Philadelphia	3-4
	13		Florida	4-1
	16	at	Washington	2-2
	17		Buffalo	4-0
	20	at	Boston	4-3
	22		Ottawa	1-4
	26	at	New Jersey	3-4
	27		Florida	2-6
	29	at	Pittsburgh	1-5
	31	at	Colorado	1-3
Jan.	2	at	Dallas	1-2
	3	at	Phoenix	1-2
	6		Pittsburgh	2-4
	8		Montreal	2-8
	10		Carolina	1-2
	12		Detroit	1-1
	14	at	Tampa Bay	7-1
	20	at	Chicago	2-5
	22	at	St. Louis	3-3
	24	at	Ottawa	2-3
	26	at	Philadelphia	1-3
	28		Philadelphia	6-1
	30		Carolina	2-0
Feb.	1		Boston	2-2
	2	at	Pittsburgh	4-2
	4		Montreal	4-2
	7		New Jersey	2-3
	25		Dallas	1-4
Mar.	1		Boston	4-5
	3		Philadelphia	3-1
	6	at	Buffalo	4-2
	7		Colorado	2-4
	10		Buffalo	2-2
	12		Washington	1-2
	14		Vancouver	2-6
	18	at	Ottawa	4-4
	20	at	Calgary	1-4
	22	at	Edmonton	3-1
	24	at	Vancouver	3-4
	26		Pittsburgh	4-3
	28	at	Toronto	3-4
	31	at	Washington	2-5
Apr.	1		Tampa Bay	4-0
	4		NY Rangers	3-0
	6	at	Tampa Bay	3-0
	8		New Jersey	3-2
	9	at	Boston	1-4
	11	at	Montreal	3-3
	13		Washington	0-2
	15	at	NY Rangers	2-4
	16		Tampa Bay	4-0
	18	at	New Jersey	2-1

Entry Draft Selections 1998-84

1998

Pick	
9	Michael Rupp
36	Chris Neilson
95	Andy Burnham
123	Jiri Dopita
155	Kevin Clauson
182	Evgeny Korolev
209	Frederik Brindamour
237	Ben Blais
242	Jason Doyle
250	Radek Matejovsky

1997

Pick	
4	Roberto Luongo
5	Eric Brewer
31	Jeff Zehr
59	Jarrett Smith
79	Robert Schnabel
85	Petr Mika
115	Adam Edinger
139	Bobby Leavins
166	Kris Knoblauch
196	Jeremy Symington
222	Ryan Clark

1996

Pick	
3	Jean-Pierre Dumont
29	Dan Lacouture
56	Zdeno Chara
83	Tyrone Garner
109	Andy Berenzweig
128	Petr Sachl
138	Todd Miller
165	Joe Prestifilippo
192	Evgeny Korolev
218	Mike Muzechka

1995

Pick	
2	Wade Redden
28	Jan Hlavac
41	Denis Smith
106	Vladimir Orszagh
158	Andrew Taylor
210	David MacDonald
211	Mike Broda

1994

Pick	
9	Brett Lindros
38	Jason Holland
63	Jason Strudwick
90	Brad Lukowich
112	Mark McArthur
116	Albert O'Connell
142	Jason Stewart
194	Mike Loach
203	Peter Hogardh
220	Gord Walsh
246	Kirk Dewaele
272	Dick Tarnstrom

1993

Pick	
23	Todd Bertuzzi
40	Bryan McCabe
66	Vladim Chebaturkin
92	Warren Luhning
118	Tommy Salo
144	Peter Leboutillier
170	Darren Van Impe
196	Rod Hinks
222	Daniel Johansson
248	Stephane Larocque
274	Carl Charland

1992

Pick	
5	Darius Kasparaitis
56	Jarrett Deuling
104	Tomas Klimt
105	Ryan Duthie
128	Derek Armstrong
152	Vladimir Grachev
159	Steve O'Rourke
176	Jason Widmer
200	Daniel Paradis
224	David Wainwright
248	Andrei Vasiljev

1991

Pick	
4	Scott Lachance
26	Zigmund Palffy
48	Jamie McLennan
70	Milan Hnilicka
92	Steve Junker
114	Robert Valicevic
136	Andreas Johansson
158	Todd Sparks
180	John Johnson
202	Robert Canavan
224	Marcus Thuresson
246	Marty Schriner

1990

Pick	
6	Scott Scissons
27	Chris Taylor
48	Dan Plante
90	Chris Marinucci
111	Joni Lehto
132	Michael Guilbert
153	Sylvain Fleury
174	John Joyce
195	Richard Enga
216	Martin Lacroix
237	Andy Shirr

1989

Pick	
2	Dave Chyzowski
23	Travis Green
44	Jason Zent
65	Brent Grieve
86	Jace Reed
90	Steve Young
99	Kevin O'Sullivan
128	Jon Larson
133	Brett Harkins
149	Phil Huber
170	Matthew Robbins
191	Vladimir Malakhov
212	Kelly Ens
233	Iain Fraser

1988

Pick	
16	Kevin Cheveldayoff
29	Wayne Doucet
37	Sean LeBrun
58	Danny Lorenz
79	Andre Brassard
100	Paul Rutherford
111	Pavel Gross
121	Jason Rathbone
142	Yves Gaucher
163	Marty McInnis
184	Jeff Blumer
205	Jeff Kampersal
226	Phillip Neururer
247	Joe Capprini

1987

Pick	
13	Dean Chynoweth
34	Jeff Hackett
55	Dean Ewen
76	George Maneluk
97	Petr Vlk
118	Rob DiMaio
139	Knut Walbye
160	Jeff Saterdalen
181	Shawn Howard
202	John Herlihy
223	Michael Erickson
244	Will Averill

1986

Pick	
17	Tom Fitzgerald
38	Dennis Vaske
59	Bill Berg
80	Shawn Byram
101	Dean Sexsmith
104	Todd McLellan
122	Tony Schmalzbauer
138	Will Anderson
143	Richard Pilon
164	Peter Harris
185	Jeff Jablonski
206	Kerry Clark
227	Dan Beaudette
248	Paul Thompson

1985

Pick	
6	Brad Dalgarno
13	Derek King
34	Brad Lauer
55	Jeff Finley
76	Kevin Herom
89	Tommy Hedlund
97	Jeff Sveen
118	Rod Dallman
139	Kurt Lackten
160	Hank Lammens
181	Rich Wiest
202	Real Arsenault
223	Mike Volpe
244	Tony Grenier

1984

Pick	
20	Duncan MacPherson
41	Bruce Melanson
62	Jeff Norton
70	Doug Wieck
83	Ari Haanpaa
104	Mike Murray
125	Jim Wilharm
146	Kelly Murphy
167	Franco Desantis
187	Tom Warden
208	David Volek
228	Russ Becker
249	Allister Brown

For the third year in a row, Zigmund Palffy led the Islanders in goals and points and also ranked among the lead leaders. His totals for 1997-98 were 45 goals and 42 assists for 87 points.

Club Directory

Nassau Veterans' Memorial Coliseum
Uniondale, NY 11553
Phone **516/794-4100**
FAX 516/542-9348
www.xice.com
Capacity: 16,297

Owner	John O. Pickett Jr.
Governor and General Counsel	William Skehan
Senior Vice President, CFO and Alternate Governor	Arthur McCarthy
Alternate Governors	John Krumpe, Barrett N. Pickett
Hockey Operations	
General Manager	Mike Milbury
Director of Player Personnel	Gordie Clark
Consultant to the General Manager	Al Arbour
Head Coach	Mike Milbury
Assistant Coaches	Wayne Fleming, Brad McCrimmon
Strength and Conditioning Coach	Steig Theander
Assistants to the General Manager	Joanne Holewa, Mike Santos
Head Amateur Scout	Tony Feltrin
Western Scout	Earl Ingarfield
Director of Pro Scouting	Ken Morrow
Assistant Director of Pro Scouting	Kevin Maxwell
Director of Player Development	Chris Pryor
Scouting Staff	Jim Madigan, Jim McMahon, Mario Saraceno
Video Coordinator	Bob Smith
Administrative Assistant	Pam Genzardi
Medical Staff	
Director of Medical Services	Dr. Elliot Pellman
Internist	Dr. Clifford Cooper
Team Orthopedists	Dr. Elliott Hershman, Dr. Stephen Nicholas, Dr. Kenneth Montgomery
Team Dentists	Dr. Bruce Michnik, Dr. Jan Sherman
Training Staff	
Head Trainer	Rich Campbell
Assistant Trainer	Sean Donellan
Equipment Staff	
Head Equipment Manager	Joe McMahon
Assistant Equipment Manager	Eric Miklich
Lockerroom Attendants	Tom Severance, Charles E. Nass
Communications Staff	
Vice President/Communications	Patrick Calabria
Director of Game Events	Tim Beach
Director of Media and Public Relations	Ginger Killian
Director of Publishing/Public Relations Associate	Chris Botta
Director of Game Events	Tim Beach
Director of Special Events	Maureen Brady
Media Relations Assistant	Jason Lagnese
Public Relations Assistant/Manager of Amateur Hockey Development	Tom Bigliani
Administrative Assistant	Giselle Marinello
Office Attendant	Todd Aronovich
Sales and Administration	
Vice President/Media Sales	Arthur Adler
Controller	Ralph Sellitti
Assistant Controller	Ginna Cotton
Director of Administration	Joseph Dreyer
Director of Corporate Relations	Bob Nystrom
Director of Corporate Sales	Bill Kain
Director of Executive Suites	Tracy F. Matthews
Director of Marketing and Ticket Sales	Brian Edwards
Director of Merchandising	Gary DiSimone
Director of Suite Operations	Sam Buonogura
Office Manager/Group Administrator	Kathleen Maloney
Accountants	Christine Bowler, Lois Odermatt
Ticket Manager	Vincent DiOrio
Assistant Ticket Managers	Joy Rusciano, Kerry Cornils
Premier Seat Coordinator	Margaret Barrett
Sales Managers	Tom Engel, Brian Rabinowitz, Richard Gaudet, Andrew Smith
Account Executives	Rich Davis, Joseph Graves, Scott Lindquist, Matthew Manfredi, Eric Schiebe, Rob Zampolin
Corporate Sales Representative	Ted Van Zelst
Account Representatives	Larry Fitzpatrick, Brian Reynolds, Frank Gulotta
Marketing Manager	Dierdre Hannett
Team Store Managers	Chris DiPierri, Maryanne Steves
Receptionists	Colleen Touhey-Ramirez, Margaret Petrocelli
Promotional Assistants	Howard Hutton, Brian Huhl, Randy Risorto
Team Information	
Colors	Orange, blue, white, silver, Atlantic green
Television Coverage	SportsChannel
Announcers	Howie Rose, Ed Westfall, Stan Fischler
Radio	WLIR – 92.7 & 98.5
Announcers	Jim Cerny, Chris Botta

New York Rangers

1997-98 Results: 25W-39L-18T 68PTS. Fifth, Atlantic Division

Wayne Gretzky tied Jaromir Jagr for the NHL lead with 67 assists in 1997-98, marking the 16th time he has led or shared the NHL lead in assists. Twice previously Gretzky had tied Jagr's former teammate Mario Lemieux.

1998-99 Schedule

Oct.	Fri.	9	Philadelphia		Fri.	15	Chicago
	Sat.	10	at Montreal		Sat.	16	at Montreal
	Mon.	12	St. Louis		Tue.	19	Ottawa
	Fri.	16	New Jersey		Thu.	21	Florida
	Sat.	17	at Pittsburgh		Tue.	26	at Washington
	Tue.	20	Edmonton		Thu.	28	at Carolina
	Thu.	22	NY Islanders		Sat.	30	at Detroit
	Sat.	24	at Philadelphia*	**Feb.**	Mon.	1	Washington
	Tue.	27	Buffalo		Thu.	4	Vancouver
	Fri.	30	Carolina		Sun.	7	at Boston*
Nov.	Tue.	3	at New Jersey		Fri.	12	Carolina
	Wed.	4	Montreal		Sun.	14	Detroit*
	Sat.	7	at Toronto		Mon.	15	at Nashville
	Tue.	10	at Tampa Bay		Wed.	17	Montreal
	Wed.	11	at Florida		Fri.	19	Pittsburgh
	Fri.	13	Boston		Sun.	21	at Edmonton
	Wed.	18	at Anaheim		Mon.	22	at Calgary
	Thu.	19	at Los Angeles		Fri.	26	Phoenix
	Sat.	21	at San Jose		Sun.	28	Philadelphia*
	Wed.	25	at Buffalo	**Mar.**	Tue.	2	Dallas
	Fri.	27	at Pittsburgh		Thu.	4	at Washington
	Sun.	29	Nashville*		Sun.	7	at Boston*
Dec.	Tue.	1	Florida		Mon.	8	Toronto
	Wed.	2	at NY Islanders		Wed.	10	Ottawa
	Sat.	5	at Ottawa		Fri.	12	Boston
	Mon.	7	Toronto		Sun.	14	at NY Islanders*
	Wed.	9	Colorado		Mon.	15	Washington
	Fri.	11	at Buffalo		Fri.	19	Buffalo
	Mon.	14	Calgary		Sun.	21	Pittsburgh*
	Wed.	16	at New Jersey		Mon.	22	at Tampa Bay
	Sat.	19	at Toronto		Wed.	24	at Florida
	Wed.	23	Carolina		Sat.	27	at Philadelphia*
	Sat.	26	at Carolina		Mon.	29	NY Islanders
	Wed.	30	at Phoenix	**Apr.**	Fri.	2	Anaheim
	Thu.	31	at Colorado		Sun.	4	at New Jersey*
Jan.	Sat.	2	at St. Louis		Mon.	5	at Philadelphia
	Mon.	4	San Jose		Thu.	8	at Chicago
	Wed.	6	New Jersey		Fri.	9	at Dallas
	Thu.	7	at Washington		Mon.	12	Tampa Bay
	Sun.	10	Tampa Bay*		Thu.	15	at Ottawa
	Wed.	13	NY Islanders		Sun.	18	Pittsburgh*

* Denotes afternoon game.

Franchise date: May 15, 1926

ATLANTIC DIVISION

73rd NHL Season

Year-by-Year Record

		Home			Road			Overall							
Season	GP	W	L	T	W	L	T	W	L	T	GF	GA	Pts.	Finished	Playoff Result
1997-98	82	14	18	9	11	21	9	25	39	18	197	231	68	5th, Atlantic Div.	Out of Playoffs
1996-97	82	21	14	6	17	20	4	38	34	10	258	231	86	4th, Atlantic Div.	Lost Conf. Final
1995-96	82	22	10	9	19	17	5	41	27	14	272	237	96	2nd, Atlantic Div.	Lost Conf. Semi-Final
1994-95	48	11	10	3	11	13	0	22	23	3	139	134	47	4th, Atlantic Div.	Lost Conf. Semi-Final
1993-94	**84**	**28**	**8**	**6**	**24**	**16**	**2**	**52**	**24**	**8**	**299**	**231**	**112**	**1st, Atlantic Div.**	**Won Stanley Cup**
1992-93	84	20	17	5	14	22	6	34	39	11	304	308	79	6th, Patrick Div.	Out of Playoffs
1991-92	80	28	8	4	22	17	1	50	25	5	321	246	105	1st, Patrick Div.	Lost Div. Final
1990-91	80	22	11	7	14	20	6	36	31	13	297	265	85	2nd, Patrick Div.	Lost Div. Semi-Final
1989-90	80	20	11	9	16	20	4	36	31	13	279	267	85	1st, Patrick Div.	Lost Div. Final
1988-89	80	21	17	2	16	18	6	37	35	8	310	307	82	3rd, Patrick Div.	Lost Div. Semi-Final
1987-88	80	22	13	5	14	21	5	36	34	10	300	283	82	5th, Patrick Div.	Out of Playoffs
1986-87	80	18	18	4	16	20	4	34	38	8	307	323	76	4th, Patrick Div.	Lost Div. Semi-Final
1985-86	80	20	18	2	16	20	4	36	38	6	280	276	78	4th, Patick Div.	Lost Conf. Championship
1984-85	80	16	18	6	10	26	4	26	44	10	295	345	62	4th, Patrick Div.	Lost Div. Semi-Final
1983-84	80	27	12	1	15	17	8	42	29	9	314	304	93	4th, Patrick Div.	Lost Div. Semi-Final
1982-83	80	24	13	3	11	22	7	35	35	10	306	287	80	4th, Patrick Div.	Lost Div. Final
1981-82	80	19	15	6	20	12	8	39	27	14	316	306	92	2nd, Patrick Div.	Lost Div. Final
1980-81	80	17	13	10	13	23	4	30	36	14	312	317	74	4th, Patrick Div.	Lost Semi-Final
1979-80	80	22	10	8	16	22	2	38	32	10	308	284	86	3rd, Patrick Div.	Lost Quarter-Final
1978-79	80	19	13	8	21	16	3	40	29	11	316	292	91	3rd, Patrick Div.	Lost Final
1977-78	80	18	15	7	12	22	6	30	37	13	279	280	73	4th, Patrick Div.	Lost Prelim. Round
1976-77	80	17	18	5	12	19	9	29	37	14	272	310	72	4th, Patrick Div.	Out of Playoffs
1975-76	80	16	16	8	13	26	1	29	42	9	262	333	67	4th, Patrick Div.	Out of Playoffs
1974-75	80	21	11	8	16	18	6	37	29	14	319	276	88	2nd, Patrick Div.	Lost Prelim. Round
1973-74	78	26	7	6	14	17	8	40	24	14	300	251	94	3rd, East Div.	Lost Semi-Final
1972-73	78	26	8	5	21	15	3	47	23	8	297	208	102	3rd, East Div.	Lost Semi-Final
1971-72	78	26	6	7	22	11	6	48	17	13	317	192	109	2nd, East Div.	Lost Final
1970-71	78	30	2	7	19	16	4	49	18	11	259	177	109	2nd, East Div.	Lost Semi-Final
1969-70	76	22	8	8	16	14	8	38	22	16	246	189	92	4th, East Div.	Lost Quarter-Final
1968-69	76	27	7	4	14	19	5	41	26	9	231	196	91	3rd, East Div.	Lost Quarter-Final
1967-68	74	22	8	7	17	15	5	39	23	12	226	183	90	2nd, East Div.	Lost Quarter-Final
1966-67	70	18	12	5	12	16	7	30	28	12	188	189	72	4th,	Lost Semi-Final
1965-66	70	12	16	7	6	25	4	18	41	11	195	261	47	6th,	Out of Playoffs
1964-65	70	8	19	8	12	19	4	20	38	12	179	246	52	5th,	Out of Playoffs
1963-64	70	14	13	8	8	25	2	22	38	10	186	242	54	5th,	Out of Playoffs
1962-63	70	12	17	6	10	19	6	22	36	12	211	233	56	5th,	Out of Playoffs
1961-62	70	16	11	8	10	21	4	26	32	12	195	207	64	4th,	Lost Semi-Final
1960-61	70	15	15	5	7	23	5	22	38	10	204	248	54	5th,	Out of Playoffs
1959-60	70	10	15	10	7	23	5	17	38	15	187	247	49	6th,	Out of Playoffs
1958-59	70	14	16	5	12	16	7	26	32	12	201	217	64	5th,	Out of Playoffs
1957-58	70	14	15	6	18	10	7	32	25	13	195	188	77	2nd,	Lost Semi-Final
1956-57	70	15	12	8	11	18	6	26	30	14	184	227	66	4th,	Lost Semi-Final
1955-56	70	20	7	8	12	21	2	32	28	10	204	203	74	3rd,	Lost Semi-Final
1954-55	70	10	12	13	7	23	5	17	35	18	150	210	52	5th,	Out of Playoffs
1953-54	70	18	12	5	11	19	5	29	31	10	161	182	68	5th,	Out of Playoffs
1952-53	70	11	14	10	6	23	6	17	37	16	152	211	50	6th,	Out of Playoffs
1951-52	70	16	13	6	7	21	7	23	34	13	192	219	59	5th,	Out of Playoffs
1950-51	70	14	11	10	6	18	11	20	29	21	169	201	61	5th,	Out of Playoffs
1949-50	70	19	12	4	9	19	7	28	31	11	170	189	67	4th,	Lost Final
1948-49	60	13	12	5	5	19	6	18	31	11	133	172	47	6th,	Out of Playoffs
1947-48	60	11	12	7	10	14	6	21	26	13	176	201	55	4th,	Lost Semi-Final
1946-47	60	11	14	5	11	18	1	22	32	6	167	186	50	5th,	Out of Playoffs
1945-46	50	8	12	5	5	16	4	13	28	9	144	191	35	6th,	Out of Playoffs
1944-45	50	7	11	7	4	18	3	11	29	10	154	247	32	6th,	Out of Playoffs
1943-44	50	4	17	4	2	22	1	6	39	5	162	310	17	6th,	Out of Playoffs
1942-43	50	7	13	5	4	18	3	11	31	8	161	253	30	6th,	Out of Playoffs
1941-42	48	15	8	1	14	9	1	29	17	2	177	143	60	1st,	Lost Semi-Final
1940-41	48	13	7	4	8	12	4	21	19	8	143	125	50	4th,	Lost Quarter-Final
1939-40	**48**	**17**	**4**	**3**	**10**	**7**	**7**	**27**	**11**	**10**	**136**	**77**	**64**	**2nd,**	**Won Stanley Cup**
1938-39	48	13	8	3	13	8	3	26	16	6	149	105	58	2nd,	Lost Semi-Final
1937-38	48	15	5	4	12	10	2	27	15	6	149	96	60	2nd, Amn. Div.	Lost Quarter-Final
1936-37	48	9	7	8	10	13	1	19	20	9	117	106	47	3rd, Amn. Div.	Lost Final
1935-36	48	11	6	7	8	11	5	19	17	12	91	96	50	4th, Amn. Div.	Out of Playoffs
1934-35	48	11	8	5	11	12	1	22	20	6	137	139	50	3rd, Amn. Div.	Lost Semi-Final
1933-34	48	11	7	6	10	12	2	21	19	8	120	113	50	3rd, Amn. Div.	Lost Quarter-Final
1932-33	**48**	**12**	**7**	**5**	**11**	**10**	**3**	**23**	**17**	**8**	**135**	**107**	**54**	**3rd, Amn. Div.**	**Won Stanley Cup**
1931-32	48	13	7	4	10	10	4	23	17	8	134	112	54	1st, Amn. Div.	Lost Final
1930-31	44	10	9	3	9	7	6	19	16	9	106	87	47	3rd, Amn. Div.	Lost Semi-Final
1929-30	44	11	5	6	6	12	4	17	17	10	136	143	44	3rd, Amn. Div.	Lost Semi-Final
1928-29	44	12	6	4	9	7	6	21	13	10	72	65	52	2nd, Amn. Div.	Lost Final
1927-28	**44**	**10**	**8**	**4**	**9**	**8**	**5**	**19**	**16**	**9**	**94**	**79**	**47**	**2nd, Amn. Div.**	**Won Stanley Cup**
1926-27	44	13	5	4	12	8	2	25	13	6	95	72	56	1st, Amn. Div.	Lost Quarter-Final

1998-99 Player Personnel

FORWARDS	HT	WT	S	Place of Birth	Date	1997-98 Club
ARMSTRONG, Derek	5-11	188	R	Ottawa, Ont.	4/23/73	Ottawa-Detroit (IHL)-Hartford
BERG, Bill	6-1	205	L	St. Catharines, Ont.	10/21/67	NY Rangers
CHERNESKI, Stefan	6-0	195	L	Winnipeg, Man.	9/19/78	Brandon
DUBE, Christian	5-11	170	R	Sherbrooke, Que.	4/25/77	Hartford
ERREY, Bob	5-10	185	L	Montreal, Que.	9/21/64	Dallas-NY Rangers
FEDYK, Brent	6-0	194	R	Yorkton, Sask.	3/8/67	Detroit (IHL)-Cincinnati (IHL)
FRASER, Scott	6-1	178	R	Moncton, N.B.	5/3/72	Edmonton-Hamilton
GERNANDER, Ken	5-10	180	L	Coleraine, MN	6/30/69	Hartford
GONEAU, Daniel	6-0	194	L	Montreal, Que.	1/16/76	NY Rangers-Hartford
GRAVES, Adam	6-0	210	L	Toronto, Ont.	4/12/68	NY Rangers
GRETZKY, Wayne	6-0	185	L	Brantford, Ont.	1/26/61	NY Rangers-Canada
HALL, Todd	6-1	212	L	Hamden, CT	1/22/73	Hartford
HARVEY, Todd	6-0	195	R	Hamilton, Ont.	2/17/75	Dallas
KANE, Boyd	6-1	207	L	Swift Current, Sask.	4/18/78	Regina
KOVALEV, Alexei	6-0	210	L	Togliatti, USSR	2/24/73	NY Rangers-Russia
LANGDON, Darren	6-1	200	L	Deer Lake, Nfld.	1/8/71	NY Rangers
MacLEAN, John	6-0	210	R	Oshawa, Ont.	11/20/64	New Jersey-San Jose
MALHOTRA, Manny	6-1	210	L	Mississauga, Ont.	5/18/80	Guelph
PROSKURNICKI, Andrew	6-3	201	L	Hamilton, Ont.	7/24/78	Sarnia-Hartford
SAVARD, Marc	5-10	174	L	Ottawa, Ont.	7/17/77	NY Rangers-Hartford
STEVENS, Kevin	6-3	217	L	Brockton, MA	4/15/65	NY Rangers
STOCK, P.J.	5-10	190	L	Victoriaville, Que.	5/26/75	Hartford-NY Rangers
SUNDSTROM, Niklas	6-0	185	L	Ornskoldsvik, Sweden	6/6/75	NY Rangers-Sweden
VOROBIEV, Vladimir	6-0	185	R	Cherepovets, USSR	10/2/72	NY Rangers-Hartford
WINNES, Chris	6-0	201	R	Ridgefield, CT	2/12/68	San Antonio-Hartford
WITEHALL, Johan	6-1	198	L	Kungsbacka, Sweden	1/7/72	Leksand
YORK, Harry	6-2	215	L	Ponoka, Alta.	4/16/74	St. Louis-NY Rangers
DEFENSEMEN						
BEUKEBOOM, Jeff	6-5	230	R	Ajax, Ont.	3/28/65	NY Rangers
BRENNAN, Rich	6-2	200	R	Schenectady, NY	11/26/72	San Jose-Kentucky-Hartford
BROWN, Jeff	6-1	217	R	Mississauga, Ont.	4/24/78	London
CAIRNS, Eric	6-5	230	L	Oakville, Ont.	6/27/74	NY Rangers-Hartford
CAMPBELL, Ed	6-2	212	L	Worcester, MA	11/26/74	Hartford-Fort Wayne
FINLEY, Jeff	6-2	205	L	Edmonton, Alta.	4/14/67	NY Rangers
GALANOV, Maxim	6-1	195	L	Krasnoyarsk, USSR	3/13/74	NY Rangers-Hartford
HENRY, Burke	6-2	190	L	Ste. Rose, Man.	1/21/79	Brandon
JARVIS, Wes	6-4	203	L	Toronto, Ont.	4/16/79	Kitchener
KARPOVTSEV, Alexander	6-1	205	R	Moscow, USSR	4/7/70	NY Rangers
LEETCH, Brian	5-11	190	L	Corpus Christi, TX	3/3/68	NY Rangers-United States
MARTIN, Mike	6-2	204	R	Stratford, Ont.	10/27/76	Hartford
MERTZIG, Jan	6-4	218	L	Huddinge, Sweden	7/18/70	Lulea
POPOVIC, Peter	6-6	235	L	Koping, Sweden	2/10/68	Montreal
PURINTON, Dale	6-2	190	L	Fort Wayne, IN	10/11/76	Hartford-Charlotte
RISIDORE, Ryan	6-4	195	L	Hamilton, Ont.	4/4/76	Indianapolis
SAMUELSSON, Ulf	6-1	205	L	Fagersta, Sweden	3/26/64	NY Rangers-Sweden
SMITH, Adam	6-0	190	L	Digby, N.S.	5/24/76	Hartford
SMITH, Geoff	6-3	194	L	Edmonton, Alta.	3/7/69	NY Rangers-Hartford
SOROCHAN, Lee	5-11	210	L	Edmonton, Alta.	9/9/75	Hartford
THOMPSON, Brent	6-2	200	L	Calgary, Alta.	1/9/71	Hartford
VASILIEV, Alexei	6-1	190	L	Yaroslavl, USSR	9/1/77	
ZALAPSKI, Zarley	6-1	215	L	Edmonton, Alta.	4/22/68	Calgary-Montreal

GOALTENDERS	HT	WT	C	Place of Birth	Date	1997-98 Club
CLOUTIER, Dan	6-1	182	L	Mont-Laurier, Que.	4/22/76	NY Rangers-Hartford
HOLMQVIST, Johan	6-1	200	L	Tolfta, Sweden	5/24/78	Brynas Gavle
LABBE, Jean-Francois	5-9	170	L	Sherbrooke, Que.	6/15/72	Hamilton
RICHTER, Mike	5-11	187	L	Abington, PA	9/22/66	NY Rangers-United States
WHITMORE, Kay	5-11	175	L	Sudbury, Ont.	4/10/67	Long Beach

General Manager

SMITH, NEIL

General Manager, New York Rangers. Born in Toronto, Ont., January 9, 1954.

As he enters his tenth season with the club, Neil Smith joins the legendary Lester Patrick and Emile Francis among the longest-serving leaders in club history. Since taking over the reigns as general manager on July 17, 1989, Smith has seen the team win three division titles, two Presidents' Trophy honors and a Stanley Cup championship. The championship in 1993-94 was the culmination of a season in which the Rangers set club records with 52 wins and 112 points and ended a 54-year run of Stanley Cup frustration. Following the season, Neil was rewarded as *The Hockey News* executive of the year.

In his first three seasons as Rangers general manager, the club finished in first place twice and enjoyed the best three consecutive finishes in team history. After the 1991-92 season, Smith was named NHL executive of the year by the *Sporting News*.

On June 19, 1992, he was promoted to the position of president and general manager, becoming the ninth president in Rangers' history and the first president to also hold the title of general manager.

A native of Toronto, Ontario, Smith played junior hockey at Brockville, Ontario, before entering Western Michigan University where he became an All-American defenseman as a freshman and team captain in his second year.

After being selected by the New York Islanders in the NHL Amateur Draft and playing two seasons in the International Hockey League, Neil joined the Islanders scouting department during the 1980-81 season. Following two seasons in that capacity, he joined the Detroit Red Wings in 1982 as director of professional scouting and soon after became director of their farm system.

Smith was then named director of scouting, and general manager/governor of the Adirondack Red Wings of the AHL, where he won two Calder Cup championships.

1997-98 Scoring

* – rookie

Regular Season

Pos	#	Player	Team	GP	G	A	Pts	+/–	PIM	PP	SH	GW	GT	S	%
C	99	Wayne Gretzky	NYR	82	23	67	90	-11	28	6	0	4	2	201	11.4
C	16	Pat LaFontaine	NYR	67	23	39	62	-16	36	11	0	2	3	160	14.4
R	27	Alexei Kovalev	NYR	73	23	30	53	-22	44	8	0	3	1	173	13.3
D	2	Brian Leetch	NYR	76	17	33	50	-36	32	11	0	2	2	230	7.4
R	24	Niklas Sundstrom	NYR	70	19	28	47	0	24	4	0	1	0	115	16.5
L	17	Kevin Stevens	NYR	80	14	27	41	-7	130	5	0	3	1	144	9.7
L	9	Adam Graves	NYR	72	23	12	35	-30	41	10	0	2	1	226	10.2
R	37	Tim Sweeney	NYR	56	11	18	29	7	26	2	0	1	1	75	14.7
D	33	Bruce Driver	NYR	75	5	15	20	-3	46	1	0	0	0	116	4.3
D	5	Ulf Samuelsson	NYR	73	3	9	12	1	122	0	0	2	0	59	5.1
L	12	Bob Errey	DAL	59	2	9	11	7	46	0	0	0	0	34	5.9
			NYR	12	0	0	0	-5	7	0	0	0	0	11	0.0
			TOTAL	71	2	9	11	2	53	0	0	0	0	45	4.4
C	32	Harry York	STL	58	4	6	10	0	31	0	0	0	0	42	9.5
			NYR	2	0	0	0	-1	0	0	0	0	0	2	0.0
			TOTAL	60	4	6	10	-1	31	0	0	0	0	44	9.1
D	25	Alexander Karpovtsev	NYR	47	3	7	10	-1	38	1	0	1	0	46	6.5
L	18	Bill Berg	NYR	67	1	9	10	-15	55	0	0	0	0	74	1.4
R	14 *	Peter Ferraro	PIT	29	3	4	7	-2	12	0	0	0	0	34	8.8
			NYR	1	0	0	0	-2	2	0	0	0	0	3	0.0
			TOTAL	30	3	4	7	-4	14	0	0	0	0	37	8.1
D	26	Jeff Finley	NYR	63	1	6	7	-3	55	0	0	0	0	32	3.1
L	15	Darren Langdon	NYR	70	3	3	6	0	197	0	0	0	0	15	20.0
C	10 *	Marc Savard	NYR	28	1	5	6	-4	4	0	0	0	0	32	3.1
C	28 *	P.J. Stock	NYR	38	2	3	5	4	114	0	0	1	0	9	22.2
D	23	Jeff Beukeboom	NYR	63	0	5	5	-25	195	0	0	0	0	23	0.0
R	39 *	Vladimir Vorobiev	NYR	15	2	2	4	-10	6	0	0	1	0	27	7.4
R	8	Brad Smyth	L.A.	9	1	3	4	-1	4	0	0	0	0	12	8.3
			NYR	1	0	0	0	0	0	0	0	0	0	1	0.0
			TOTAL	10	1	3	4	-1	4	0	0	0	0	13	7.7
L	21	Johan Lindbom	NYR	38	1	3	4	4	28	0	0	0	0	38	2.6
D	6	Doug Lidster	NYR	36	0	4	4	2	24	0	0	0	0	25	0.0
D	29	Eric Cairns	NYR	39	0	3	3	-3	92	0	0	0	0	17	0.0
L	36	Daniel Goneau	NYR	11	2	0	2	-4	4	0	0	1	0	13	15.4
D	14	Geoff Smith	NYR	15	1	1	2	-4	6	1	0	0	0	11	9.1
D	4 *	Maxim Galanov	NYR	6	0	1	1	1	2	0	0	0	0	5	0.0
G	35	Mike Richter	NYR	72	0	1	1	0	2	0	0	0	0	0	0.0
D	30 *	Sylvain Blouin	NYR	1	0	0	0	0	5	0	0	0	0	0	0.0
D	38	Ronnie Sundin	NYR	1	0	0	0	0	0	0	0	0	0	0	0.0
L	36	Pierre Sevigny	NYR	3	0	0	0	0	2	0	0	0	0	1	0.0
G	34 *	Dan Cloutier	NYR	12	0	0	0	0	19	0	0	0	0	0	0.0

Goaltending

No.	Goaltender	GPI	Mins	Avg	W	L	T	EN	SO	GA	SA	S%
34	* Dan Cloutier	12	551	2.50	4	5	1	0	0	23	248	.907
35	Mike Richter	72	4143	2.66	21	31	15	6	0	184	1888	.903
30	Jason Muzzatti	6	313	3.26	0	3	2	1	0	17	156	.891
	Totals	**82**	**5028**	**2.76**	**25**	**39**	**18**	**7**	**0**	**231**	**2299**	**.900**

Captains' History

Bill Cook, 1926-27 to 1936-37; Art Coulter, 1937-38 to 1941-42; Ott Heller, 1942-43 to 1944-45; Neil Colville 1945-46 to 1948-49; Buddy O'Connor, 1949-50; Frank Eddolls, 1950-51; Frank Eddolls and Allan Stanley, 1951-52; Allan Stanley, 1952-53; Allan Stanley and Don Raleigh, 1953-54; Don Raleigh, 1954-55; Harry Howell, 1955-56, 1956-57; Red Sullivan, 1957-58 to 1960-61; Andy Bathgate, 1961-62, 1962-63; Andy Bathgate and Camille Henry, 1963-64; Camille Henry and Bob Nevin, 1964-65; Bob Nevin 1965-66 to 1970-71; Vic Hadfield, 1971-72 to 1973-74; Brad Park, 1974-75; Brad Park and Phil Esposito, 1975-76; Phil Esposito, 1976-77, 1977-78; Dave Maloney, 1978-79, 1979-80; Dave Maloney, Walt Tkaczuk and Barry Beck, 1980-81; Barry Beck, 1981-82 to 1985-86; Ron Greschner, 1986-87; Ron Greschner and Kelly Kisio, 1987-88; Kelly Kisio, 1988-89 to 1990-91; Mark Messier, 1991-92 to 1996-97; Brian Leetch, 1997-98 to date.

General Managers' History

Lester Patrick, 1927-28 to 1945-46; Frank Boucher, 1946-47 to 1954-55; Muzz Patrick, 1955-56 to 1963-64; Emile Francis, 1964-65 to 1974-75; Emile Francis and John Ferguson, 1975-76; John Ferguson, 1976-77, 1977-78; John Ferguson and Fred Shero, 1978-79; Fred Shero, 1979-80; Fred Shero and Craig Patrick, 1980-81; Craig Patrick, 1981-82 to 1985-86; Phil Esposito, 1986-87 to 1988-89; Neil Smith, 1989-90 to date.

Club Records

Team

(Figures in brackets for season records are games played; records for fewest points, wins, ties, losses, goals, goals against are for 70 or more games)

Most Points	**112**	1993-94 (84)
Most Wins	**52**	1993-94 (84)
Most Ties	**21**	1950-51 (70)
Most Losses	**44**	1984-85 (80)
Most Goals	**371**	1991-92 (80)
Most Goals Against	**345**	1984-85 (80)
Fewest Points	**47**	1965-66 (70)
Fewest Wins	**17**	1952-53, 1954-55, 1959-60 (70)
Fewest Ties	**5**	1991-92 (80)
Fewest Losses	**17**	1971-72 (78)
Fewest Goals	**150**	1954-55 (70)
Fewest Goals Against	**177**	1970-71 (78)
Longest Winning Streak		
Overall	**10**	Dec. 19/39-Jan. 13/40, Jan. 19-Feb. 10/73
Home	**14**	Dec. 19/39-Feb. 25/40
Away	**7**	Jan. 12-Feb. 12/35, Oct. 28-Nov. 29/78
Longest Undefeated Streak		
Overall	**19**	Nov. 23/39-Jan. 13/40 (14 wins, 5 ties)
Home	**26**	Mar. 29/70-Jan. 31/71 (19 wins, 7 ties)
Away	**11**	Nov. 5/39-Jan. 13/40 (6 wins, 5 ties)
Longest Losing Streak		
Overall	**11**	Oct. 30-Nov. 27/43
Home	**7**	Oct. 20-Nov. 14/76, Mar. 24-Apr. 14/93
Away	**10**	Oct. 30-Dec. 23/43
Longest Winless Streak		
Overall	**21**	Jan. 23-Mar. 19/44 (17 losses, 4 ties)
Home	**10**	Jan. 30-Mar. 19/44 (7 losses, 3 ties)
Away	**16**	Oct. 9-Dec. 20/52 (12 losses, 4 ties)
Most Shutouts, Season	**13**	1928-29 (44)
Most PIM, Season	**2,018**	1989-90 (80)
Most Goals, Game	**12**	Nov. 21/71 (Cal. 1 at NYR 12)

Individual

Most Seasons	**17**	Harry Howell
Most Games	**1,160**	Harry Howell
Most Goals, Career	**406**	Rod Gilbert
Most Assists, Career	**615**	Rod Gilbert
Most Points, Career	**1,021**	Rod Gilbert (406G, 615A)
Most PIM, Career	**1,226**	Ron Greschner
Most Shutouts, Career	**49**	Ed Giacomin
Longest Consecutive Games Streak	**560**	Andy Hebenton (Oct. 7/55-Mar. 24/63)
Most Goals, Season	**52**	Adam Graves (1993-94)
Most Assists, Season	**80**	Brian Leetch (1991-92)
Most Points, Season	**109**	Jean Ratelle (1971-72; 46G, 63A)
Most PIM, Season	**305**	Troy Mallette (1989-90)
Most Points, Defenseman, Season	**102**	Brian Leetch (1991-92; 22G, 80A)
Most Points, Center, Season	**109**	Jean Ratelle (1971-72; 46G, 63A)
Most Points, Right Wing, Season	**97**	Rod Gilbert (1971-72; 43G, 54A), (1974-75; 36G, 61A)
Most Points, Left Wing, Season	**106**	Vic Hadfield (1971-72; 50G, 56A)
Most Points, Rookie, Season	**76**	Mark Pavelich (1981-82; 33G, 43A)
Most Shutouts, Season	**13**	John Ross Roach (1928-29)
Most Goals, Game	**5**	Don Murdoch (Oct. 12/76), Mark Pavelich (Feb. 23/83)
Most Assists, Game	**5**	Walt Tkaczuk (Feb. 12/72), Rod Gilbert (Mar. 2/75, Mar. 30/75, Oct. 8/76), Don Maloney (Jan. 3/87), Brian Leetch (Apr. 18/95)
Most Points, Game	**7**	Steve Vickers (Feb. 18/76; 3G, 4A)

Retired Numbers

1	Ed Giacomin	1965-1976
7	Rod Gilbert	1960-1978

All-time Record vs. Other Clubs

Regular Season

	At Home							On Road							Total						
	GP	W	L	T	GF	GA	PTS	GP	W	L	T	GF	GA	PTS	GP	W	L	T	GF	GA	PTS
Anaheim	4	2	1	1	13	10	5	4	0	4	0	10	18	0	8	2	5	1	23	28	5
Boston	290	126	110	54	881	816	306	286	92	153	41	803	1038	225	576	218	263	95	1684	1854	531
Buffalo	54	24	17	13	183	146	61	56	16	33	7	180	243	39	110	40	50	20	363	389	100
Calgary	47	21	21	5	166	170	47	46	10	26	10	139	205	30	93	31	47	15	305	375	77
Carolina	32	20	9	3	139	93	43	31	11	17	3	103	115	25	63	31	26	6	242	208	68
Chicago	282	116	111	55	833	798	287	281	113	126	42	780	854	268	563	229	237	97	1613	1652	555
Colorado	28	18	6	4	118	77	40	30	12	15	3	117	125	27	58	30	21	7	235	202	67
Dallas	57	34	13	10	200	155	78	56	30	16	10	211	167	70	113	64	29	20	411	322	148
Detroit	279	133	88	58	860	716	324	281	75	161	45	691	988	195	560	208	249	103	1551	1704	519
Edmonton	25	6	13	6	94	100	18	25	12	11	2	90	95	26	50	18	24	8	184	195	44
Florida	12	4	4	4	32	30	12	13	7	5	1	41	32	15	25	11	9	5	73	62	27
Los Angeles	54	33	15	6	216	153	72	55	24	22	9	197	184	57	109	57	37	15	413	337	129
Montreal	278	113	111	54	812	810	280	278	56	186	36	639	1094	148	556	169	297	90	1451	1904	428
New Jersey	69	39	17	13	289	208	91	70	32	33	5	250	239	69	139	71	50	18	539	447	160
NY Islanders	80	47	24	9	314	243	103	81	22	52	7	246	333	51	161	69	76	16	560	576	154
Ottawa	11	8	3	0	49	33	16	11	8	2	1	36	29	17	22	16	5	1	85	62	33
Philadelphia	95	42	30	23	313	274	107	93	35	45	13	271	313	83	188	77	75	36	584	587	190
Phoenix	25	15	8	2	118	96	32	26	13	10	3	94	92	29	51	28	18	5	212	188	61
Pittsburgh	85	45	33	7	347	291	97	85	39	34	12	324	308	90	170	84	67	19	671	599	187
St. Louis	56	44	6	6	236	125	94	58	26	23	9	188	173	61	114	70	29	15	424	298	155
San Jose	6	5	0	1	32	18	11	7	7	0	0	32	15	14	13	12	0	1	64	33	25
Tampa Bay	15	7	7	1	53	56	15	13	5	6	2	38	44	12	28	12	13	3	91	100	27
Toronto	271	114	101	56	833	794	284	270	81	151	38	703	922	200	541	195	252	94	1536	1716	484
Vancouver	50	36	9	5	224	126	77	48	33	12	3	199	154	69	98	69	21	8	423	280	146
Washington	70	34	29	7	275	249	75	71	27	35	9	236	266	63	141	61	64	16	511	515	138
Defunct Clubs	139	87	30	22	460	290	196	139	82	34	23	441	291	187	278	169	64	45	901	581	383
Totals	**2414**	**1173**	**816**	**425**	**8090**	**6877**	**2771**	**2414**	**868**	**1212**	**334**	**7059**	**8337**	**2070**	**4828**	**2041**	**2028**	**759**	**15149**	**15214**	**4841**

Playoffs

	Series	W	L	GP	W	L	T	GF	GA	Last Mtg.	Round	Result
Boston	9	3	6	42	18	22	2	104	114	1973	QF	W 4-1
Buffalo	1	0	1	3	1	2	0	6	11	1978	PR	L 1-2
Calgary	1	1	0	4	3	1	0	14	8	1980	PR	W 3-1
Chicago	5	1	4	24	10	14	0	54	66	1973	SF	L 1-4
Colorado	1	1	0	6	4	2	0	25	19	1995	CQF	W 4-2
Detroit	5	1	4	23	10	13	0	49	57	1950	F	L 3-4
Florida	1	1	0	5	4	1	0	13	10	1997	CQF	W 4-1
Los Angeles	2	2	0	6	5	1	0	32	14	1981	PR	W 3-1
Montreal	14	7	7	61	25	34	2	158	188	1996	CQF	W 4-2
New Jersey	3	3	0	19	12	7	0	56	46	1997	CSF	W 4-1
NY Islanders	8	3	5	39	19	20	0	132	129	1994	CQF	W 4-0
Philadelphia	10	4	6	47	20	27	0	153	157	1997	CF	L 1-4
Pittsburgh	3	0	3	15	3	12	0	45	65	1996	CSF	L 1-4
St. Louis	1	1	0	6	4	2	0	29	22	1981	QF	W 4-2
Toronto	8	5	3	35	19	16	0	86	86	1971	QF	W 4-2
Vancouver	1	1	0	7	4	3	0	21	19	1994	F	W 4-3
Washington	4	2	2	22	11	11	0	71	75	1994	CSF	W 4-1
Defunct	9	6	3	22	11	7	4	43	29			
Totals	**86**	**42**	**44**	**386**	**183**	**195**	**8**	**1091**	**1114**			

Calgary totals include Atlanta, 1972-73 to 1979-80. Carolina totals include Hartford, 1979-80 to 1996-97.
Colorado totals include Quebec, 1979-80 to 1994-95. Dallas totals include Minnesota, 1967-68 to 1992-93.
New Jersey totals include Kansas City, 1974-75 to 1975-76, and Colorado Rockies, 1976-77 to 1981-82.
Phoenix totals include Winnipeg, 1979-80 to 1995-96.

Playoff Results 1998-94

Year	Round	Opponent	Result	GF	GA
1997	CF	Philadelphia	L 1-4	13	20
	CSF	New Jersey	W 4-1	10	5
	CQF	Florida	W 4-1	13	10
1996	CSF	Pittsburgh	L 1-4	15	21
	CQF	Montreal	W 4-2	19	17
1995	CSF	Philadelphia	L 0-4	10	18
	CQF	Quebec	W 4-2	25	19
1994	F	Vancouver	W 4-3	21	19
	CF	New Jersey	W 4-3	18	16
	CSF	Washington	W 4-1	20	12
	CQF	NY Islanders	W 4-0	22	3

Abbreviations: Round: F – Final; **CF** – conference final; **CQF** – conference quarter-final; **CSF** – conference semi-final; **SF** – semi-final; **QF** – quarter-final; **PR** – preliminary round.

1997-98 Results

Oct.	3		NY Islanders	2-2		31	at	Tampa Bay	0-2
	5		Los Angeles	2-2	**Jan.**	3	at	Washington	3-2
	8	at	Edmonton	3-3		6		Carolina	4-2
	9	at	Calgary	1-1		8		Washington	3-5
	11	at	Vancouver	6-3		10	at	Montreal	1-4
	14		Pittsburgh	0-1		12		Toronto	3-2
	15	at	Ottawa	1-5		14	at	New Jersey	1-4
	18	at	St. Louis	3-5		20		St. Louis	3-1
	20		Carolina	4-2		22		Philadelphia	3-4
	22		Chicago	0-1		24		New Jersey	3-3
	24		Tampa Bay	4-3		26		Washington	2-2
	26		Anaheim	3-3		29	at	Ottawa	2-2
	28		Dallas	2-3		31	at	Boston	2-4
	30	at	NY Islanders	3-5	**Feb.**	2	at	San Jose	3-2
Nov.	3		Edmonton	2-2		4	at	Anaheim	2-3
	5	at	Colorado	4-2		5	at	Los Angeles	1-3
	7	at	Dallas	2-2		7	at	Phoenix	1-1
	12		New Jersey	2-3		26	at	Toronto	5-2
	14		Pittsburgh	3-1		28		Philadelphia	1-3
	16		Colorado	4-1	**Mar.**	2		Buffalo	0-1
	18	at	Florida	3-1		4	at	Florida	4-3
	19	at	Tampa Bay	3-6		7	at	New Jersey	3-6
	21	at	Carolina	4-3		9		New Jersey	2-2
	22	at	Pittsburgh	3-4		11		San Jose	5-3
	25		Vancouver	2-4		14	at	Boston	1-5
	26	at	NY Islanders	1-4		16		Ottawa	5-4
	28	at	Buffalo	3-3		18		Montreal	2-1
	30		Florida	1-1		21		Detroit	3-4
Dec.	2		Washington	2-3		22	at	Philadelphia	4-5
	5		Philadelphia	4-4		25		Ottawa	2-3
	6	at	Montreal	3-3		26	at	Carolina	1-4
	8		Phoenix	3-1		28	at	Pittsburgh	2-2
	10		Calgary	1-4		30		Tampa Bay	1-3
	12		Florida	3-4	**Apr.**	1		Boston	2-4
	16	at	New Jersey	3-4		4	at	NY Islanders	0-3
	17	at	Florida	4-2		5	at	Chicago	2-1
	20	at	Tampa Bay	2-2		7		Montreal	2-3
	21		Buffalo	0-2		11	at	Detroit	2-5
	23		Tampa Bay	4-1		14	at	Washington	1-3
	26	at	Buffalo	0-3		15		NY Islanders	4-2
	28		Boston	4-3		18	at	Philadelphia	2-1

Entry Draft Selections 1998-84

1998

Pick	
7	Manny Malhotra
40	Randy Copley
66	Jason Labarbera
114	Boyd Kane
122	Patrick Leahy
131	Tomas Kloucek
180	Stefan Lundqvist
207	Johan Witehall
235	Jan Mertzig

1997

Pick	
19	Stefan Cherneski
46	Wes Jarvis
73	Burke Henry
93	Tomi Kallarsson
126	Jason McLean
134	Johan Lindbom
136	Michael York
154	Shawn Degagne
175	Johan Holmqvist
182	Mike Mottau
210	Andrew Proskurnicki
236	Richard Miller

1996

Pick	
22	Jeff Brown
48	Daniel Goneau
76	Dmitri Subbotin
131	Colin Pepperall
158	Ola Sandberg
185	Jeff Dessner
211	Ryan McKie
237	Ronnie Sundin

1995

Pick	
39	Christian Dube
65	Mike Martin
91	Marc Savard
110	Alexei Vasiliev
117	Dale Purinton
143	Peter Slamiar
169	Jeff Heil
195	Ilja Gorohov
221	Bob Maudie

1994

Pick	
26	Dan Cloutier
52	Rudolf Vercik
78	Adam Smith
100	Alexander Korobolin
104	Sylvain Blouin
130	Martin Ethier
135	Yuri Litvinov
156	David Brosseau
182	Alexei Lazarenko
208	Craig Anderson
209	Vitali Yeremeyev
234	Eric Boulton
260	Radoslav Kropac
267	Jamie Butt
286	Kim Johnsson

1993

Pick	
8	Niklas Sundstrom
34	Lee Sorochan
61	Maxim Galanov
86	Sergei Olimpiyev
112	Gary Roach
138	Dave Trofimenkoff
162	Sergei Kondrashkin
164	Todd Marchant
190	Eddy Campbell
216	Ken Shepard
242	Andrei Kudinov
261	Pavel Komarov
268	Maxim Smelnitsky

1992

Pick	
24	Peter Ferraro
48	Mattias Norstrom
72	Eric Cairns
85	Chris Ferraro
120	Dmitri Starostenko
144	David Dal Grande
168	Matt Oates
192	Mickey Elick
216	Dan Brierley
240	Vladimir Vorobjev

1991

Pick	
15	Alexei Kovalev
37	Darcy Werenka
96	Corey Machanic
125	Fredrik Jax
128	Barry Young
147	John Rushin
169	Corey Hirsch
191	Viacheslav Uvayev
213	Jamie Ram
235	Vitali Chinakhov
257	Brian Wiseman

1990

Pick	
13	Michael Stewart
34	Doug Weight
55	John Vary
69	Jeff Nielsen
76	Rick Willis
85	Sergei Zubov
99	Lubos Rob
118	Jason Weinrich
139	Bryan Lonsinger
160	Todd Hedlund
181	Andrew Silverman
202	Jon Hillebrandt
223	Brett Lievers
244	Sergei Nemchinov

1989

Pick	
20	Steven Rice
40	Jason Prosofsky
45	Rob Zamuner
49	Louie DeBrusk
67	Jim Cummins
88	Aaron Miller
118	Joby Messier
139	Greg Leahy
160	Greg Spenrath
181	Mark Bavis
202	Roman Oksyuta
223	Steve Locke
244	Ken MacDermid

1988

Pick	
22	Troy Mallette
26	Murray Duval
68	Tony Amonte
99	Martin Bergeron
110	Dennis Vial
131	Mike Rosati
152	Eric Couvrette
173	Shorty Forrest
194	Paul Cain
202	Eric Fenton
215	Peter Fiorentino
236	Keith Slifstien

1987

Pick	
10	Jayson More
31	Daniel Lacroix
46	Simon Gagne
69	Michael Sullivan
94	Eric O'Borsky
115	Ludek Cajka
136	Clint Thomas
157	Charles Wiegand
178	Eric Burrill
199	David Porter
205	Brett Barnett
220	Lance Marciano

1986

Pick	
9	Brian Leetch
51	Bret Walter
53	Shawn Clouston
72	Mark Janssens
93	Jeff Bloemberg
114	Darren Turcotte
135	Robb Graham
156	Barry Chyzowski
177	Pat Scanlon
198	Joe Ranger
219	Russell Parent
240	Soren True

1985

Pick	
7	Ulf Dahlen
28	Mike Richter
49	Sam Lindstahl
70	Pat Janostin
91	Brad Stephan
112	Brian McReynolds
133	Neil Pilon
154	Larry Bernard
175	Stephane Brochu
196	Steve Nemeth
217	Robert Burakowsky
238	Rudy Poeschek

1984

Pick	
14	Terry Carkner
35	Raimo Helminen
77	Paul Broten
98	Clark Donatelli
119	Kjell Samuelsson
140	Thomas Hussey
161	Brian Nelson
182	Ville Kentala
188	Heinz Ehlers
202	Kevin Miller
223	Tom Lorentz
243	Scott Brower

Coach

MUCKLER, JOHN
Coach, New York Rangers. Born in Midland, Ont., April 3, 1934.

John Muckler begins his first full season behind the New York Rangers bench in 1998-99, having taken over as coach of the club on February 19, 1998. Muckler is the 28th head coach in the history of the Rangers and has been involved with professional hockey since the 1959-60 season. He has served in various capacities in the National Hockey League, including eight years as a head coach.

Muckler spent the 1966-67 season as the director of player personnel for the Rangers before joining the Minnesota North Stars organization for the following six seasons. He coached the team briefly during the 1968-69 campaign. Muckler rejoined the Rangers organization in 1973 and spent four seasons as head coach of their minor-league affiliate in Providence.

Muckler's head coaching experience includes serving with the Buffalo Sabres from 1991-92 to 1994-95, posting a 125-109-34 record and ranking second on the team's all-time list for games coached with 268. Prior to joining Buffalo, he was head coach of the Edmonton Oilers from 1989-90 to 1990-91, posting a 75-65-20 record. Muckler guided the Oilers to a Stanley Cup title in 1990 and was an associate coach with Edmonton's four Stanley Cup championship teams of the 1980s.

NHL Coaching Record

		Regular Season					Playoffs			
Season	Team	Games	W	L	T	%	Games	W	L	%
1968-69	Minnesota	35	6	23	6	.257	....	....	....	....
1989-90	Edmonton	80	38	28	14	.563	22	16	6	.727*
1990-91	Edmonton	80	37	37	6	.500	18	9	9	.500
1991-92	Buffalo	52	22	22	8	.500	7	3	4	.429
1992-93	Buffalo	84	38	36	10	.512	8	4	4	.500
1993-94	Buffalo	84	43	32	9	.565	7	3	4	.429
1994-95	Buffalo	48	22	19	7	.531	5	1	4	.200
1997-98	NY Rangers	25	8	15	2	.360	....	....	....	....
	NHL Totals	**488**	**214**	**212**	**62**	**.502**	**67**	**36**	**31**	**.537**

* Won Stanley Cup.

Club Directory

Madison Square Garden
14th Floor
2 Pennsylvania Plaza
New York, New York 10121
Phone **212/465-6000**
PR FAX 212/465-6494
Capacity: 18,200

Executive Management	
Chief Executive Officer/Governor	David W. Checketts
President and General Manager/Alternate Governor	Neil Smith
Executive Vice President and General Counsel	Kenneth W. Munoz
Vice President and Business Manager	Francis P. Murphy
Vice President, Legal and Business Affairs	Marc Schoenfeld
Vice President, Controller	John Cudmore
Alternate Governors	Marc Lustgarten, Kenneth W. Munoz
Hockey Club Personnel	
Assistant General Manager	Don Maloney
Head Coach	John Muckler
Assistant Coaches	Keith Acton, Charlie Huddy, Craig MacTavish
Development Coach	E.J. McGuire
Assistant Development Coach	Mike Busniuk
Goaltending Analyst	Sam St. Laurent
Director of Scouting	Martin Madden
Director of Professional Scouting	John Paddock
Scouting Staff	Darwin Bennett, Ray Clearwater, Herb Hammond, Martin Madden Jr., Kevin McDonald, Christer Rockstom, Dick Todd
Scouting Manager	Bill Short
Video Assistant	Jerry Dineen
Business Operations Department	
Vice President of Operations	Mark Piazza
Manager of Business Administration	Barbara Cahill
Manager of Team Operations	Darren Blake
Operations Assistant	Victor Saljanen
Public Relations Department	
Director of Public Relations	John Rosasco
Assistant Director of Public Relations	Rob Koch
Public Relations Assistant	Jeff Schwartzenberg
Administrative Assistant	Ann Marie Gilmartin
Marketing Department	
Vice President of Marketing	John Hall
Director of Marketing	Jeanie Baumgartner
Director of Community Relations	Rod Gilbert
Marketing Assistant	John Commiskey
Medical\Training Staff	
Team Physician and Orthopedic Surgeon	Dr. Barton Nisonson
Assistant Team Physician	Dr. Anthony Maddalo
Medical Consultants	Drs. Howard Chester, Frank Gardner, Ronald Weissman
Team Dentists	Drs. Irwin Miller and Don Soloman
Sports Physiologist	Howie Wenger
Medical Trainer	Jim Ramsay
Equipment Manager	Mike Folga
Massage Therapist	Bruce Lifrieri
Assistant Equipment Manager	Acacio Marques
Coaching Staff Assistant	Damian Echevarrieta
Additional Information	
Executive Offices	Madison Square Garden
Home Ice	Madison Square Garden
Seating Capacity	18,200
Largest Crowd	18,200
Press Facilities	33rd Street
Television Facilities	31st Street
Radio Facilities	33rd Street
Rink Dimensions	200 feet x 85 feet
Ends and Sides of Rink	Plexiglass (8 feet)
Club Colors	Blue, Red, White
Uniforms	Home- Base color white, trimmed with blue and red Road- Base color blue, trimmed with red and white Third- Base color white, trimmed with silver, red and navy blue
Practice Facility	Rye, New York

Coaching History

Lester Patrick, 1926-27 to 1938-39; Frank Boucher, 1939-40 to 1947-48; Frank Boucher and Lynn Patrick, 1948-49; Lynn Patrick, 1949-50; Neil Colville, 1950-51; Neil Colville and Bill Cook, 1951-52; Bill Cook, 1952-53; Frank Boucher and Muzz Patrick, 1953-54; Muzz Patrick, 1954-55; Phil Watson, 1955-56 to 1958-59; Phil Watson and Alf Pike, 1959-60; Alf Pike, 1960-61; Doug Harvey, 1961-62; Muzz Patrick and Red Sullivan, 1962-63; Red Sullivan, 1963-64, 1964-65; Red Sullivan and Emile Francis, 1965-66; Emile Francis, 1966-67, 1967-68; Bernie Geoffrion and Emile Francis, 1968-69; Emile Francis, 1969-70 to 1972-73; Larry Popein and Emile Francis, 1973-74; Emile Francis, 1974-75; Ron Stewart and John Ferguson, 1975-76; John Ferguson, 1976-77; Jean-Guy Talbot, 1977-78; Fred Shero, 1978-79, 1979-80; Fred Shero and Craig Patrick, 1980-81; Herb Brooks, 1981-82 to 1983-84; Herb Brooks and Craig Patrick, 1984-85; Ted Sator, 1985-86; Ted Sator, Tom Webster and Phil Esposito, 1986-87; Michel Bergeron, 1987-88; Michel Bergeron and Phil Esposito, 1988-89; Roger Neilson, 1989-90 to 1991-92; Roger Neilson and Ron Smith, 1992-93; Mike Keenan, 1993-94; Colin Campbell, 1994-95 to 1996-97; Colin Campbell and John Muckler, 1997-98; John Muckler, 1998-99.

Ottawa Senators

1997-98 Results: 34W-33L-15T 83PTS. Fifth, Northeast Division

Year-by-Year Record

		Home			Road			Overall							
Season	GP	W	L	T	W	L	T	W	L	T	GF	GA	Pts.	Finished	Playoff Result
1997-98	82	18	16	7	16	17	8	34	33	15	193	200	83	5th, Northeast Div.	Lost Conf. Semi-Final
1996-97	82	16	17	8	15	19	7	31	36	15	226	234	77	3rd, Northeast Div.	Lost Conf. Quarter-Final
1995-96	82	8	28	5	10	31	0	18	59	5	191	291	41	6th, Northeast Div.	Out of Playoffs
1994-95	48	5	16	3	4	18	2	9	34	5	117	174	23	7th, Northeast Div.	Out of Playoffs
1993-94	84	8	30	4	6	31	5	14	61	9	201	397	37	7th, Northeast Div.	Out of Playoffs
1992-93	84	9	29	4	1	41	0	10	70	4	202	395	24	6th, Adams Div.	Out of Playoffs

1998-99 Schedule

Oct.	Sat.	10	at Colorado
	Sun.	11	at Phoenix
	Sat.	17	Nashville
	Wed.	21	at Montreal
	Thu.	22	St. Louis
	Sat.	24	Carolina
	Thu.	29	Philadelphia
	Sat.	31	Montreal
Nov.	Sun.	1	at Philadelphia
	Thu.	5	Pittsburgh
	Sat.	7	Washington
	Tue.	10	at Buffalo
	Thu.	12	Edmonton
	Sat.	14	at Toronto
	Sun.	15	at Chicago
	Fri.	20	at Washington
	Sat.	21	Calgary
	Mon.	23	Vancouver
	Thu.	26	NY Islanders
	Sat.	28	at Toronto
Dec.	Tue.	1	at Nashville
	Thu.	3	Los Angeles
	Sat.	5	NY Rangers
	Tue.	8	at Tampa Bay
	Wed.	9	at Florida
	Sat.	12	Phoenix
	Thu.	17	at Boston
	Fri.	18	Carolina
	Sun.	20	Dallas*
	Wed.	23	Montreal
	Sat.	26	at Pittsburgh
	Mon.	28	Anaheim
	Wed.	30	at Buffalo
Jan.	Fri.	1	at Washington*
	Sat.	2	New Jersey
	Mon.	4	at Carolina
	Wed.	6	at Detroit
	Fri.	8	Tampa Bay
	Sun.	10	Detroit*
	Mon.	11	at New Jersey
	Thu.	14	New Jersey
	Sat.	16	Buffalo
	Mon.	18	Philadelphia
	Tue.	19	at NY Rangers
	Thu.	21	at Boston
	Tue.	26	at New Jersey
	Sat.	30	NY Islanders
Feb.	Mon.	1	at Vancouver
	Wed.	3	at Edmonton
	Sat.	6	at Calgary
	Tue.	9	Buffalo
	Thu.	11	Florida
	Sat.	13	Washington
	Mon.	15	Chicago
	Thu.	18	Boston
	Sat.	20	Philadelphia
	Tue.	23	at Boston
	Thu.	25	Montreal
	Sat.	27	at Montreal
Mar.	Tue.	2	at NY Islanders
	Thu.	4	at Philadelphia
	Sat.	6	Toronto
	Mon.	8	Tampa Bay
	Wed.	10	at NY Rangers
	Sat.	13	at San Jose
	Mon.	15	at Los Angeles
	Wed.	17	at Anaheim
	Fri.	19	at Dallas
	Sat.	20	at St. Louis
	Wed.	24	Boston
	Fri.	26	San Jose
	Sat.	27	at NY Islanders
	Tue.	30	at Pittsburgh
Apr.	Thu.	1	Pittsburgh
	Sat.	3	at Florida
	Mon.	5	at Tampa Bay
	Wed.	7	at Toronto
	Thu.	8	Toronto
	Sat.	10	Buffalo
	Mon.	12	Florida
	Thu.	15	NY Rangers
	Sat.	17	at Carolina

* Denotes afternoon game.

Damien Rhodes, sporting the Senators' "third jersey," posted a career-high 19 wins and a career-low 2.34 goals-against average in 1997-98.

Franchise date: December 16, 1991

NORTHEAST DIVISION

7th NHL Season

1998-99 Player Personnel

FORWARDS	HT	WT	S	Place of Birth	Date	1997-98 Club
ALFREDSSON, Daniel	5-11	194	R	Goteborg, Sweden	12/11/72	Ottawa-Sweden
ARVEDSON, Magnus	6-2	198	L	Karlstad, Swe.	11/25/71	Ottawa
BONK, Radek	6-3	210	L	Krnov, Czech.	1/9/76	Ottawa
CIERNIK, Ivan	6-1	198	L	Levice, Czech.	10/30/77	Ottawa-Worcester
CROWE, Philip	6-2	215	L	Nanton, Alta.	4/14/70	Ottawa-Detroit (IHL)
DACKELL, Andreas	5-11	191	R	Gavle, Sweden	12/29/72	Ottawa
EMMONS, John	6-2	205	L	San Jose, CA	8/17/74	Michigan
FELSNER, Brian	5-11	189	L	Mt. Clemens, MI	11/11/72	Chicago-Indianapolis-Milwaukee
GARDINER, Bruce	6-1	193	R	Barrie, Ont.	2/11/72	Ottawa
HOSSA, Marian	6-1	194	L	Stara Lubovna, Czech.	1/12/79	Portland (WHL)-Slovakia-Ottawa
MARTINS, Steve	5-9	175	L	Gatineau, Que.	4/13/72	Carolina-Chicago (IHL)
McEACHERN, Shawn	5-11	195	L	Waltham, MA	2/28/69	Ottawa
MURRAY, Chris	6-2	209	R	Port Hardy, B.C.	10/25/74	Carolina-Ottawa
OLIVER, David	6-0	190	R	Sechelt, B.C.	4/17/71	Houston
PROKOPEC, Mike	6-2	190	R	Toronto, Ont.	5/17/74	Worcester
PROSPAL, Vaclav	6-2	185	L	Ceske-Budejovice, Czech.	2/17/75	Philadelphia-Ottawa
SARAULT, Yves	6-1	185	L	Valleyfield, Que.	12/23/72	Colorado-Hershey
VAN ALLEN, Shaun	6-1	200	L	Calgary, Alta.	8/29/67	Ottawa
YASHIN, Alexei	6-3	225	R	Sverdlovsk, USSR	11/5/73	Ottawa-Russia
DEFENSEMEN						
BICANEK, Radim	6-1	195	L	Uherske Hradiste, Czech.	1/18/75	Ottawa-Detroit (IHL)-Manitoba
GRUDEN, John	6-0	190	L	Virginia, MN	6/4/70	Detroit (IHL)
KRAVCHUK, Igor	6-1	200	L	Ufa, USSR	9/13/66	Ottawa-Russia
LAUKKANEN, Janne	6-0	180	L	Lahti, Finland	3/19/70	Ottawa-Finland
NECKAR, Stanislav	6-1	212	L	Ceske Budejovice, Czech.	12/22/75	Ottawa
PHILLIPS, Chris	6-2	200	L	Fort McMurray, Alta.	3/9/78	Ottawa
PITLICK, Lance	6-0	203	R	Minneapolis, MN	11/5/67	Ottawa
REDDEN, Wade	6-2	193	L	Lloydminster, Sask.	6/12/77	Ottawa
SALO, Sami	6-3	190	R	Turku, Finland	9/2/74	Jokerit
TRAVERSE, Patrick	6-3	190	L	Montreal, Que.	3/14/74	Hershey
YORK, Jason	6-2	198	R	Nepean, Ont.	5/20/70	Ottawa

GOALTENDERS	HT	WT	C	Place of Birth	Date	1997-98 Club
HURME, Jani	6-0	187	L	Turku, Finland	1/7/75	Detroit (IHL)-Indianapolis
RHODES, Damian	6-0	180	L	St. Paul, MN	5/28/69	Ottawa
TUGNUTT, Ron	5-11	155	L	Scarborough, Ont.	10/22/67	Ottawa

1997-98 Scoring

* – rookie

Regular Season

Pos	#	Player	Team	GP	G	A	Pts	+/–	PIM	PP	SH	GW	GT	S	%
C	19	Alexei Yashin	OTT	82	33	39	72	6	24	5	0	6	0	291	11.3
L	15	Shawn McEachern	OTT	81	24	24	48	1	42	8	2	4	2	229	10.5
R	11	Daniel Alfredsson	OTT	55	17	28	45	7	18	7	0	7	0	149	11.4
D	29	Igor Kravchuk	OTT	81	8	27	35	-19	8	3	1	1	1	191	4.2
R	10	Andreas Dackell	OTT	82	15	18	33	-11	24	3	2	2	1	130	11.5
L	20 *	Magnus Arvedson	OTT	61	11	15	26	2	36	0	1	0	1	90	12.2
C	13 *	Vaclav Prospal	PHI	41	5	13	18	-10	17	4	0	0	0	60	8.3
			OTT	15	1	6	7	-1	4	0	0	0	0	28	3.6
			TOTAL	56	6	19	25	-11	21	4	0	0	0	88	6.8
C	16	Sergei Zholtok	OTT	78	10	13	23	-7	16	7	0	1	1	127	7.9
D	6	Wade Redden	OTT	80	8	14	22	17	27	3	0	2	0	103	7.8
D	27	Janne Laukkanen	OTT	60	4	17	21	-15	64	2	0	2	0	69	5.8
L	28	Denny Lambert	OTT	72	9	10	19	4	250	0	0	1	1	76	11.8
C	22	Shaun Van Allen	OTT	80	4	15	19	4	48	0	0	0	0	104	3.8
R	12	Pat Falloon	PHI	30	5	7	12	3	8	1	0	0	0	63	7.9
			OTT	28	3	3	6	-11	8	2	0	0	0	73	4.1
			TOTAL	58	8	10	18	-8	16	3	0	0	0	136	5.9
C	25	Bruce Gardiner	OTT	55	7	11	18	2	50	0	0	0	0	64	10.9
C	14	Radek Bonk	OTT	65	7	9	16	-13	16	1	0	0	0	93	7.5
D	4 *	Chris Phillips	OTT	72	5	11	16	2	38	2	0	2	0	107	4.7
D	33	Jason York	OTT	73	3	13	16	8	62	0	0	0	0	109	2.8
L	7	Randy Cunneyworth	OTT	71	2	11	13	-14	63	1	0	0	0	81	2.5
R	17	Chris Murray	CAR	7	0	1	1	2	22	0	0	0	0	3	0.0
			OTT	46	5	3	8	1	96	0	0	2	0	48	10.4
			TOTAL	53	5	4	9	3	118	0	0	2	0	51	9.8
D	2	Lance Pitlick	OTT	69	2	7	9	8	50	0	0	0	0	66	3.0
D	3	Per Gustafsson	TOR	22	1	4	5	-5	10	0	0	0	0	24	4.2
			OTT	9	0	1	1	3	6	0	0	0	0	12	0.0
			TOTAL	31	1	5	6	-2	16	0	0	0	0	36	2.8
D	24	Stanislav Neckar	OTT	60	2	2	4	-14	31	0	0	0	0	43	4.7
R	26	Philip Crowe	OTT	9	3	0	3	3	24	0	0	1	0	6	50.0
C	42	Derek Armstrong	OTT	9	2	0	2	1	9	0	0	1	0	8	25.0
L	18 *	Marian Hossa	OTT	7	0	1	1	-1	0	0	0	0	0	10	0.0
G	1	Damian Rhodes	OTT	50	0	1	1	0	0	0	0	0	0	0	0.0
D	23	Radim Bicanek	OTT	1	0	0	0	0	0	0	0	0	0	0	0.0
R	48 *	Ivan Ciernik	OTT	2	0	0	0	0	0	0	0	0	0	0	0.0
L	38	Jason Zent	OTT	3	0	0	0	0	4	0	0	0	0	1	0.0
L	21	Dennis Vial	OTT	19	0	0	0	0	45	0	0	0	0	9	0.0
G	31	Ron Tugnutt	OTT	42	0	0	0	0	0	0	0	0	0	0	0.0

Goaltending

No.	Goaltender	GPI	Mins	Avg	W	L	T	EN	SO	GA	SA	S%
31	Ron Tugnutt	42	2236	2.25	15	14	8	6	3	84	882	.905
1	Damian Rhodes	50	2743	2.34	19	19	7	3	5	107	1148	.907
	Totals	**82**	**5002**	**2.40**	**34**	**33**	**15**	**9**	**8**	**200**	**2039**	**.902**

Playoffs

Pos	#	Player	Team	GP	G	A	Pts	+/–	PIM	PP	SH	GW	OT	S	%
R	11	Daniel Alfredsson	OTT	11	7	2	9	-4	20	2	1	1	0	36	19.4
C	19	Alexei Yashin	OTT	11	5	3	8	-6	8	3	0	2	1	42	11.9
D	29	Igor Kravchuk	OTT	11	2	3	5	-2	4	0	0	0	0	24	8.3
D	27	Janne Laukkanen	OTT	11	2	2	4	-3	8	1	0	1	0	14	14.3
C	25	Bruce Gardiner	OTT	11	1	3	4	-2	2	0	0	1	1	21	4.8
L	15	Shawn McEachern	OTT	11	0	4	4	-6	8	0	0	0	0	27	0.0
D	33	Jason York	OTT	7	1	1	2	-2	7	1	0	0	0	13	7.7
R	10	Andreas Dackell	OTT	11	1	1	2	-4	2	1	0	0	0	14	7.1
D	6	Wade Redden	OTT	9	0	2	2	-5	2	0	0	0	0	11	0.0
C	16	Sergei Zholtok	OTT	11	0	2	2	-1	0	0	0	0	0	23	0.0
D	4 *	Chris Phillips	OTT	11	0	2	2	-2	2	0	0	0	0	24	0.0
R	17	Chris Murray	OTT	11	1	0	1	-2	8	0	0	0	0	12	8.3
L	7	Randy Cunneyworth	OTT	6	0	1	1	0	6	0	0	0	0	2	0.0
C	22	Shaun Van Allen	OTT	11	0	1	1	-3	10	0	0	0	0	16	0.0
D	2	Lance Pitlick	OTT	11	0	1	1	-3	17	0	0	0	0	6	0.0
L	20 *	Magnus Arvedson	OTT	11	0	1	1	-6	6	0	0	0	0	21	0.0
R	12	Pat Falloon	OTT	1	0	0	0	0	0	0	0	0	0	2	0.0
D	3	Per Gustafsson	OTT	1	0	0	0	-2	0	0	0	0	0	3	0.0
G	31	Ron Tugnutt	OTT	2	0	0	0	0	0	0	0	0	0	0	0.0
C	14	Radek Bonk	OTT	5	0	0	0	-3	2	0	0	0	0	6	0.0
C	13 *	Vaclav Prospal	OTT	6	0	0	0	-2	0	0	0	0	0	7	0.0
D	24	Stanislav Neckar	OTT	9	0	0	0	-4	2	0	0	0	0	4	0.0
G	1	Damian Rhodes	OTT	10	0	0	0	0	0	0	0	0	0	0	0.0
L	28	Denny Lambert	OTT	11	0	0	0	2	19	0	0	0	0	5	0.0

Goaltending

No.	Goaltender	GPI	Mins	Avg	W	L	EN	SO	GA	SA	S%
1	Damian Rhodes	10	590	2.14	5	5	3	0	21	236	.911
31	Ron Tugnutt	2	74	4.86	0	1	0	0	6	25	.760
	Totals	**11**	**669**	**2.69**	**5**	**6**	**3**	**0**	**30**	**264**	**.886**

General Managers' History

Mel Bridgman, 1992-93; Randy Sexton, 1993-94 to 1994-95; Randy Sexton and Pierre Gauthier, 1995-96; Pierre Gauthier, 1996-97, 1997-98; Rick Dudley, 1998-99.

General Manager

DUDLEY, RICK

General Manager, Ottawa Senators. Born in Toronto, Ont., January 31, 1949.

On June 30, 1998, the Ottawa Senators announced the appointment of Rick Dudley as the club's fourth general manager. The 49-year-old Dudley joined the Senators from the Detroit Vipers of the International Hockey League where he had served as coach and general manager in the club's inaugural season in 1994-95. For the 1996-97 season, he promoted assistant head coach Steve Ludzik to bench boss in order to focus on the general manager duties. The Vipers won the Turner Cup (IHL championship) in 1996-97 and reached the finals again in 1998.

Dudley has been to the finals eight times in 10 years as a g.m. in three different leagues (International Hockey League; American Hockey League and East Coast Hockey League). He has won four championships as a g.m., including the 1996-97 Turner Cup (Detroit) and ECHL championships with Carolina in 1984, 1985 and 1986. He has never missed the playoffs since starting as a g.m. and head coach in 1980 and has posted a career record of 476-196-51 as a g.m. and a career playoff record of 100-59.

Prior to joining the Vipers, Dudley served as the director of pro scouting and minor league operations with the Los Angeles Kings in 1993 and coached the Kings' IHL affiliate in Phoenix. As head coach of San Diego (IHL) in 1992-93, Dudley led the Gulls to the most victories in a single season in professional hockey history (62), earning 132 points and a berth in the IHL finals.

In 1989, Dudley was named the head coach of the Buffalo Sabres, the team with whom he had broken into the NHL as a player back in 1972. During his two-and-a-half seasons behind the Sabres' bench, Dudley recorded an 85-72-31 overall mark. His most successful season was his first campaign (1989-90) as the team posted a 45-27-8 record, securing third-place overall in the NHL with 98 points — the club's third-best finish ever. Dudley finished third in balloting for the Jack Adams Award for NHL coach of the year that year.

NHL Coaching Record

		Regular Season					Playoffs			
Season	Team	Games	W	L	T	%	Games	W	L	%
1989-90	Buffalo	80	45	27	8	.613	6	2	4	.333
1990-91	Buffalo	80	31	30	9	.506	6	2	4	.333
1991-92	Buffalo	28	9	15	4	.393	....	....	....	....
	NHL Totals	**188**	**85**	**72**	**31**	**.535**	**12**	**4**	**8**	**.333**

Club Records

Team

(Figures in brackets for season records are games played; records for fewest points, wins, ties, losses, goals, goals against are for 70 or more games)

Most Points	83	1997-98 (82)
Most Wins	34	1997-98 (82)
Most Ties	15	1996-97 (82), 1997-98 (82)
Most Losses	70	1992-93 (84)
Most Goals	226	1996-97 (82)
Most Goals Against	397	1993-94 (84)
Fewest Points	24	1992-93 (84)
Fewest Wins	10	1992-93 (84)
Fewest Ties	4	1992-93 (84)
Fewest Losses	36	1996-97 (82)
Fewest Goals	191	1995-96 (82)
Fewest Goals Against	200	1997-98 (82)
Longest Winning Streak		
Overall	4	Three times
Home	4	Three times
Away	5	Apr. 3-19/98
Longest Undefeated Streak		
Overall	5	Oct. 15-23/97 (4 wins, 1 tie)
Home	8	Feb. 5-Mar. 20/98 (5 wins, 3 ties)
Away	6	Mar. 29-Apr. 19/98 (5 wins, 1 tie)
Longest Losing Streak		
Overall	14	Mar. 2-Apr. 7/93
Home	*11	Oct. 27-Dec. 8/93
Away	*38	Oct. 10/92-Apr. 3/93**
Longest Winless Streak		
Overall	21	Oct. 10-Nov. 23/92 (20 losses, 1 tie)
Home	*17	Oct. 28/95-Jan. 27/96 (15 losses, 2 ties)
Away	*38	Oct. 10/92-Apr. 3/93 (38 losses)
Most Shutouts, Season	8	1997-98 (82)
Most PIM, Season	1,716	1992-93 (84)
Most Goals, Game	7	Four times

** NHL records do not include neutral site games

Individual

Most Seasons	5	Alexei Yashin, Dennis Vial, Alexandre Daigle
Most Games, Career	340	Alexei Yashin
Most Goals, Career	134	Alexei Yashin
Most Assists, Career	175	Alexei Yashin
Most Points, Career	309	Alexei Yashin (134G, 175A)
Most PIM, Career	600	Dennis Vial
Most Shutouts, Career	8	Damian Rhodes
Longest Consecutive Games Streak	210	Alexei Yashin (Feb. 23/95-date)
Most Goals, Season	35	Alexei Yashin (1996-97)
Most Assists, Season	49	Alexei Yashin (1993-94)
Most Points, Season	79	Alexei Yashin (1993-94; 30G, 49A)
Most PIM, Season	318	Mike Peluso (1992-93)
Most Points, Defenseman, Season	63	Norm Maciver (1992-93; 17G, 46A)
Most Points, Center, Season	79	Alexei Yashin (1993-94; 30G, 49A)
Most Points, Right Wing, Season	71	Daniel Alfredsson (1996-97; 24G, 47A)
Most Points, Left Wing, Season	48	Shawn McEachern (1997-98; 24G, 24A)
Most Points, Rookie, Season	79	Alexei Yashin (1993-94; 30G, 49A)
Most Shutouts, Season	5	Damian Rhodes (1997-98)
Most Goals, Game	3	Thirteen times
Most Assists, Game	4	Alexei Yashin (Nov. 5/93)
Most Points, Game	6	Dan Quinn (Oct. 15/95; 3G, 3A)

* NHL Record.

Retired Numbers

8	Frank Finnigan	1924-1934

Coaching History

Rick Bowness, 1992-93 to 1994-95; Rick Bowness, Dave Allison and Jacques Martin, 1995-96; Jacques Martin, 1996-97 to date.

Captains' History

Laurie Boschman, 1992-93; Brad Shaw, Mark Lamb and Gord Dineen, 1993-94; Randy Cunneyworth, 1994-95 to 1997-98.

All-time Record vs. Other Clubs

Regular Season

	At Home							On Road							Total						
	GP	W	L	T	GF	GA	PTS	GP	W	L	T	GF	GA	PTS	GP	W	L	T	GF	GA	PTS
Anaheim	4	1	3	0	11	13	2	4	0	3	1	5	14	1	8	1	6	1	16	27	3
Boston	16	1	13	2	30	60	4	17	3	12	2	46	74	8	33	4	25	4	76	134	12
Buffalo	17	4	10	3	37	56	11	16	4	12	0	22	62	8	33	8	22	3	59	118	19
Calgary	5	2	1	2	10	12	6	5	0	4	1	11	28	1	10	2	5	3	21	40	7
Carolina	17	5	9	3	42	55	13	15	1	14	0	29	54	2	32	6	23	3	71	109	15
Chicago	5	1	4	0	11	18	2	5	1	3	1	11	13	3	10	2	7	1	22	31	5
Colorado	13	4	7	2	40	60	10	11	0	10	1	29	58	1	24	4	17	3	69	118	11
Dallas	5	2	3	0	13	15	4	6	2	4	0	13	25	4	11	4	7	0	26	40	8
Detroit	5	1	3	1	13	17	3	5	2	3	0	11	20	4	10	3	6	1	24	37	7
Edmonton	5	2	3	0	9	13	4	5	1	4	0	14	23	2	10	3	7	0	23	36	6
Florida	10	3	5	2	25	33	8	10	3	6	1	25	34	7	20	6	11	3	50	67	15
Los Angeles	5	3	1	1	17	13	7	5	0	5	0	13	31	0	10	3	6	1	30	44	7
Montreal	15	4	11	0	39	53	8	18	5	10	3	50	57	13	33	9	21	3	89	110	21
New Jersey	12	2	9	1	19	35	5	11	2	7	2	23	37	6	23	4	16	3	42	72	11
NY Islanders	11	5	3	3	34	39	13	12	6	3	3	44	41	15	23	11	6	6	78	80	28
NY Rangers	11	2	8	1	29	36	5	11	3	8	0	33	49	6	22	5	16	1	62	85	11
Philadelphia	11	2	8	1	29	43	5	11	1	10	0	22	51	2	22	3	18	1	51	94	7
Phoenix	7	1	5	1	16	29	3	5	2	2	1	20	23	5	12	3	7	2	36	52	8
Pittsburgh	15	3	10	2	32	54	8	15	0	12	3	28	65	3	30	3	22	5	60	119	11
St. Louis	5	1	4	0	9	24	2	5	2	2	1	17	15	5	10	3	6	1	26	39	7
San Jose	5	2	0	3	17	14	7	5	2	3	0	6	8	4	10	4	3	3	23	22	11
Tampa Bay	11	4	7	0	28	30	8	11	6	5	0	31	32	12	22	10	12	0	59	62	20
Toronto	5	2	2	1	13	13	5	6	2	4	0	16	23	4	11	4	6	1	29	36	9
Vancouver	5	2	2	1	11	15	5	5	1	3	1	11	18	3	10	3	5	2	22	33	8
Washington	11	5	5	1	41	36	11	12	3	8	1	25	50	7	23	8	13	2	66	86	18
Totals	**231**	**64**	**136**	**31**	**575**	**786**	**159**	**231**	**52**	**157**	**22**	**555**	**905**	**126**	**462**	**116**	**293**	**53**	**1130**	**1691**	**285**

Playoffs

	Series	W	L	GP	W	L	T	GF	GA	Last Mtg.	Round	Result
Buffalo	1	0	1	7	3	4	0	13	14	1997	CQF	L 3-4
New Jersey	1	1	0	6	4	2	0	13	12	1998	CQF	W 4-2
Washington	1	0	1	5	1	4	0	7	18	1998	CSF	L 1-4
Totals	**3**	**1**	**2**	**18**	**8**	**10**	**0**	**33**	**44**			

Playoff Results 1998-94

Year	Round	Opponent	Result	GF	GA
1998	CSF	Washington	L 1-4	7	18
	CQF	New Jersey	W 4-2	13	12
1997	CQF	Buffalo	L 3-4	13	14

Abbreviations: Round: CQF – conference quarter-final; **CSF** – conference semi-final.

Colorado totals include Quebec, 1992-93 to 1994-95.
Dallas totals include Minnesota, 1992-93.
Carolina totals include Hartford, 1992-93 to 1996-97.
Phoenix totals include Winnipeg, 1992-93 to 1995-96.

1997-98 Results

Oct.	1	at	Montreal	2-2		3		Philadelphia	2-7
	3	at	Philadelphia	3-5		5	at	Carolina	1-4
	4		Carolina	3-2		7	at	Dallas	2-0
	7	at	San Jose	1-0		10	at	Colorado	3-3
	10	at	Anaheim	1-1		11	at	Phoenix	4-4
	12	at	Los Angeles	4-7		13	at	Washington	0-4
	15		NY Rangers	5-1		20	at	Pittsburgh	0-0
	17		New Jersey	4-2		22		Carolina	2-4
	19		Dallas	3-1		24		NY Islanders	3-2
	22	at	Toronto	6-2		26		Tampa Bay	2-1
	23		Florida	2-2		27	at	Boston	1-6
	25		Montreal	2-4		29		NY Rangers	2-2
	29	at	Tampa Bay	5-2		31	at	Montreal	4-3
	30	at	Florida	5-2	**Feb.**	2		New Jersey	0-1
Nov.	2		Boston	1-3		4	at	New Jersey	0-2
	6		Phoenix	4-1		5		Toronto	3-2
	8		Philadelphia	3-4		7		Pittsburgh	2-2
	9	at	Carolina	1-4		25	at	Edmonton	2-5
	11	at	Philadelphia	0-1		28	at	Vancouver	4-6
	13		Detroit	2-4	**Mar.**	1	at	Calgary	1-2
	15	at	Boston	3-3		5		Colorado	4-2
	17		Boston	2-4		7		Calgary	2-1
	20		Pittsburgh	0-2		11		Florida	5-3
	22		Edmonton	0-1		14		Washington	4-0
	26	at	Detroit	1-4		16	at	NY Rangers	4-5
	27		Washington	3-1		18		NY Islanders	4-4
	29		Chicago	2-3		20		Vancouver	1-1
Dec.	2	at	NY Islanders	4-2		22		Anaheim	2-5
	4		Los Angeles	3-2		25	at	NY Rangers	3-2
	6		Buffalo	3-0		27	at	Chicago	1-2
	11		St. Louis	1-2		29	at	Pittsburgh	1-1
	13		Tampa Bay	1-3	**Apr.**	2		San Jose	3-3
	15	at	St. Louis	3-1		3	at	New Jersey	3-2
	16	at	Carolina	1-2		5	at	Buffalo	1-0
	18		Carolina	3-2		7		Boston	2-4
	20	at	Montreal	1-4		9		Pittsburgh	4-1
	22	at	NY Islanders	4-1		11		Buffalo	4-4
	23		Montreal	4-3		13	at	Tampa Bay	3-2
	27	at	Washington	3-0		14	at	Florida	3-2
	31	at	Buffalo	0-3		16		Montreal	0-2
Jan.	1	at	Boston	0-0		19	at	Buffalo	2-1

Entry Draft Selections 1998-92

1998

Pick	
15	Mathieu Chouinard
44	Mike Fisher
58	Chris Bala
74	Julien Vauclair
101	Petr Schastlivy
130	Gavin McLeod
161	Christopher Neil
188	Michael Periard
223	Sergei Verenikin
246	Rastisla Pavlikovsky

1997

Pick	
12	Marian Hossa
58	Jani Hurme
66	Josh Langfeld
119	Magnus Arvedsson
146	Jeff Sullivan
173	Robin Bacul
203	Nick Gillis
229	Karel Rachunek

1996

Pick	
1	Chris Phillips
81	Antti-Jussi Niemi
136	Andreas Dackell
163	Francois Hardy
212	Erich Goldmann
216	Ivan Ciernik
239	Sami Salo

1995

Pick	
1	Bryan Berard
27	Marc Moro
53	Brad Larsen
89	Kevin Bolibruck
103	Kevin Boyd
131	David Hruska
183	Kaj Linna
184	Ray Schultz
231	Erik Kaminski

1994

Pick	
3	Radek Bonk
29	Stanislav Neckar
81	Bryan Masotta
131	Mike Gaffney
133	Daniel Alfredsson
159	Doug Sproule
210	Frederic Cassivi
211	Danny Dupont
237	Stephen MacKinnon
274	Antti Tormanen

1993

Pick	
1	Alexandre Daigle
27	Radim Bicanek
53	Patrick Charbonneau
91	Cosmo Dupaul
131	Rick Bodkin
157	Sergei Poleschuk
183	Jason Disher
209	Toby Kvalevog
227	Pavol Demitra
235	Rick Schuwerk

1992

Pick	
2	Alexei Yashin
25	Chad Penney
50	Patrick Traverse
73	Radek Hamr
98	Daniel Guerard
121	Al Sinclair
146	Jaroslav Miklenda
169	Jay Kenney
194	Claude Savoie
217	Jake Grimes
242	Tomas Jelinek
264	Petter Ronnqvist

Club Directory

Corel Centre

Corel Centre
1000 Palladium Drive
Kanata, Ontario
K2V 1A5
Phone **613/599-0250**
FAX 613/599-5562
Website:
www.ottawasenators.com
Capacity: 18,500

Chairman and Governor	Rod Bryden
President and CEO	Roy Mlakar
General Manager	Rick Dudley
Assistant General Manager	Ray Shero
Director, Player Personnel	Marshall Johnston
Head Coach	Jacques Martin
Assistant Coaches	Perry Pearn, TBA
Strength & Conditioning & Video Coach	Randy Lee
Chief Scout	Andre Savard
Scouting Coordinator	Trevor Timmins
VP, Communications	Phil Legault
Director, Media Relations	Morgan Quarry
Manager, Media Relations	Steve Keogh
Head Athletic Trainer	Kevin Wagner
Head Equipment Manager	Ed Georgica
Assistant Equipment Manager	John Gervais
Massage Therapist	Brad Joyal
Arena (Capacity)	Corel Centre (18,500)
General Office Phone	(613) 599-0250
Media Relations Phone	(613) 599-0327 / 599-0306 / 599-0326
Press Box Phone	(613) 599-4801
Media Relations Fax	(613) 599-5562
Team Colors	Red, Gold & Black
Radio	OSR 1200 (English), CJRC (French)
Commercial TV	CHRO
Cable TV	CTV SportsNet

Daniel Alfredsson tied with Sergei Zholtok for the Senators' lead in power-play goals with seven in 1997-98.

Coach

MARTIN, JACQUES
Coach, Ottawa Senators. Born in St. Pascal, Ont., October 1, 1952.

In 1997-98, Jacques Martin led the Ottawa Senators to their best season in team history.

When appointed the Senators' third head coach on January 24, 1996, Martin brought ten years of NHL coaching experience, including five with the Quebec Nordiques, an organization often compared with the Senators, in that both teams were built around young, talented players requiring patience and teaching.

Martin's coaching career began at the collegiate level in 1976. He was appointed head coach of the Guelph Platers (now Storm) in 1985, winning the OHL title, the Memorial Cup and being named the OHL coach of the year. That summer, Martin became head coach of the St. Louis Blues. In his NHL rookie year, he lead the Blues to the Norris Division championship and, in two seasons with the Blues, posted a 66-71-23 record. He then spent two seasons as an assistant to Chicago's head coach Mike Keenan, before joining the Nordiques in 1990. With Quebec, he worked four years as assistant coach and one year (1993-94) as both head coach and general manager of the AHL Cornwall Aces.

Coaching Record

		Regular Season					Playoffs			
Season	Team	Games	W	L	T	%	Games	W	L	%
1983-84	Peterborough (OHL)	70	43	23	4	.643	....	....	....	....
1984-85	Peterborough (OHL)	66	42	20	4	.667	....	....	....	....
1985-86	Guelph (OHL)	66	41	23	2	.636	....	....	....	....
1986-87	**St. Louis (NHL)**	**80**	**32**	**33**	**15**	**.494**	**6**	**2**	**4**	**.333**
1987-88	**St. Louis (NHL)**	**80**	**34**	**38**	**8**	**.475**	**10**	**5**	**5**	**.500**
1993-94	Cornwall (AHL)	80	33	36	11	.481	13	8	5	.615
1995-96	**Ottawa (NHL)**	**38**	**10**	**24**	**4**	**.316**	....	....	....	....
1996-97	**Ottawa (NHL)**	**82**	**31**	**36**	**15**	**.470**	**7**	**3**	**4**	**.429**
1997-98	**Ottawa (NHL)**	**82**	**34**	**33**	**15**	**.506**	**11**	**5**	**6**	**.455**
	NHL Totals	**362**	**141**	**164**	**57**	**.468**	**34**	**15**	**19**	**.441**

Philadelphia Flyers

1997-98 Results: 42W-29L-11T 95PTS. Second, Atlantic Division

Rod Brind'Amour enjoyed another solid season in 1997-98. His 36 goals and 74 points trailed only John LeClair (51, 87) in Philadelphia and ranked him among the league leaders. It was the fourth time in his career that Brind'Amour topped 30 goals.

1998-99 Schedule

Oct.	Fri.	9	at NY Rangers
	Sun.	11	Anaheim
	Fri.	16	at Tampa Bay
	Sat.	17	at Carolina
	Tue.	20	San Jose
	Thu.	22	New Jersey
	Sat.	24	NY Rangers*
	Tue.	27	St. Louis
	Thu.	29	at Ottawa
	Sat.	31	at NY Islanders
Nov.	Sun.	1	Ottawa
	Tue.	3	at Pittsburgh
	Sat.	7	Buffalo*
	Mon.	9	at Montreal
	Thu.	12	Florida
	Sat.	14	New Jersey
	Tue.	17	at Pittsburgh
	Fri.	20	at Carolina
	Sun.	22	at Florida
	Wed.	25	at NY Islanders
	Fri.	27	Toronto*
	Sun.	29	Vancouver
Dec.	Fri.	4	at Buffalo
	Sat.	5	Washington
	Tue.	8	at New Jersey
	Thu.	10	New Jersey
	Sat.	12	at Toronto
	Sun.	13	Edmonton
	Thu.	17	Calgary
	Sat.	19	Chicago*
	Sun.	20	Tampa Bay
	Wed.	23	at Boston
	Sat.	26	at Chicago
	Mon.	28	at San Jose
	Tue.	29	at Calgary
	Thu.	31	at Vancouver
Jan.	Sun.	3	at Edmonton*
	Thu.	7	NY Islanders
	Sat.	9	Carolina
	Mon.	11	Nashville
	Wed.	13	at Washington
	Sat.	16	Toronto
	Mon.	18	at Ottawa
	Thu.	21	Washington
	Tue.	26	Florida
	Thu.	28	Phoenix
	Sat.	30	Tampa Bay
Feb.	Mon.	1	Los Angeles
	Thu.	4	Montreal
	Sat.	6	Boston*
	Wed.	10	at Anaheim
	Thu.	11	at Los Angeles
	Sun.	14	at Colorado*
	Tue.	16	at Phoenix
	Thu.	18	Montreal
	Sat.	20	at Ottawa
	Sun.	21	Pittsburgh
	Wed.	24	at Florida
	Fri.	26	at Tampa Bay
	Sun.	28	at NY Rangers*
Mar.	Tue.	2	at Montreal
	Thu.	4	Ottawa
	Sat.	6	NY Islanders*
	Sun.	7	at Buffalo
	Tue.	9	at NY Islanders
	Thu.	11	Colorado
	Sat.	13	at Pittsburgh*
	Sun.	14	Dallas
	Tue.	16	at St. Louis
	Sun.	21	Detroit*
	Mon.	22	at Toronto
	Sat.	27	NY Rangers*
	Sun.	28	at Detroit*
	Tue.	30	Carolina
Apr.	Thu.	1	at Nashville
	Sat.	3	at Boston*
	Mon.	5	NY Rangers
	Thu.	8	Pittsburgh
	Sat.	10	at Washington
	Tue.	13	Buffalo
	Fri.	16	at New Jersey
	Sun.	18	Boston*

* Denotes afternoon game.

Franchise date: June 5, 1967

ATLANTIC DIVISION

32nd NHL Season

Year-by-Year Record

		Home			Road			Overall							
Season	**GP**	**W**	**L**	**T**	**W**	**L**	**T**	**W**	**L**	**T**	**GF**	**GA**	**Pts.**	**Finished**	**Playoff Result**
1997-98	82	24	11	6	18	18	5	42	29	11	242	193	95	2nd, Atlantic Div.	Lost Conf. Quarter-Final
1996-97	82	23	12	6	22	12	7	45	24	13	274	217	103	2nd, Atlantic Div.	Lost Final
1995-96	82	27	9	5	18	15	8	45	24	13	282	208	103	1st, Atlantic Div.	Lost Conf. Semi-Final
1994-95	48	16	7	1	12	9	3	28	16	4	150	132	60	1st, Atlantic Div.	Lost Conf. Championship
1993-94	84	19	20	3	16	19	7	35	39	10	294	314	80	6th, Atlantic Div.	Out of Playoffs
1992-93	84	23	14	5	13	23	6	36	37	11	319	319	83	5th, Patrick Div.	Out of Playoffs
1991-92	80	22	11	7	10	26	4	32	37	11	252	273	75	6th, Patrick Div.	Out of Playoffs
1990-91	80	18	16	6	15	21	4	33	37	10	252	267	76	5th, Patrick Div.	Out of Playoffs
1989-90	80	17	19	4	13	20	7	30	39	11	290	297	71	6th, Patrick Div.	Out of Playoffs
1988-89	80	22	15	3	14	21	5	36	36	8	307	285	80	4th, Patrick Div.	Lost Conf. Championship
1987-88	80	20	14	6	18	19	3	38	33	9	292	292	85	3rd, Patrick Div.	Lost Div. Semi-Final
1986-87	80	29	9	2	17	17	6	46	26	8	310	245	100	1st, Patrick Div.	Lost Final
1985-86	80	33	6	1	20	17	3	53	23	4	335	241	110	1st, Patrick Div.	Lost Div. Semi-Final
1984-85	80	32	4	4	21	16	3	53	20	7	348	241	113	1st, Patrick Div.	Lost Final
1983-84	80	25	10	5	19	16	5	44	26	10	350	290	98	3rd, Patrick Div.	Lost Div. Semi-Final
1982-83	80	29	8	3	20	15	5	49	23	8	326	240	106	1st, Patrick Div.	Lost Div. Semi-Final
1981-82	80	25	10	5	13	21	6	38	31	11	325	313	87	3rd. Patrick Div.	Lost Div. Semi-Final
1980-81	80	23	9	8	18	15	7	41	24	15	313	249	97	2nd, Patrick Div.	Lost Quarter-Final
1979-80	80	27	5	8	21	7	12	48	12	20	327	254	116	1st, Patrick Div.	Lost Final
1978-79	80	26	10	4	14	15	11	40	25	15	281	248	95	2nd, Patrick Div.	Lost Quarter-Final
1977-78	80	29	6	5	16	14	10	45	20	15	296	200	105	2nd, Patrick Div.	Lost Semi-Final
1976-77	80	33	6	1	15	10	15	48	16	16	323	213	112	1st, Patrick Div.	Lost Semi-Final
1975-76	80	36	2	2	15	11	14	51	13	16	348	209	118	1st, Patrick Div.	Lost Final
1974-75	**80**	**32**	**6**	**2**	**19**	**12**	**9**	**51**	**18**	**11**	**293**	**181**	**113**	**1st, Patrick Div.**	**Won Stanley Cup**
1973-74	**78**	**28**	**6**	**5**	**22**	**10**	**7**	**50**	**16**	**12**	**273**	**164**	**112**	**1st, West Div.**	**Won Stanley Cup**
1972-73	78	27	8	4	10	22	7	37	30	11	296	256	85	2nd, West Div.	Lost Semi-Final
1971-72	78	19	13	7	7	25	7	26	38	14	200	236	66	5th, West Div.	Out of Playoffs
1970-71	78	20	10	9	8	23	8	28	33	17	207	225	73	3rd, West Div.	Lost Quarter-Final
1969-70	76	11	14	13	6	21	11	17	35	24	197	225	58	5th, West Div.	Out of Playoffs
1968-69	76	14	16	8	6	19	13	20	35	21	174	225	61	3rd, West Div.	Lost Quarter-Final
1967-68	74	17	13	7	14	19	4	31	32	11	173	179	73	1st, West Div.	Lost Quarter-Final

1998-99 Player Personnel

FORWARDS	HT	WT	S	Place of Birth	Date	1997-98 Club
BELANGER, Francis	6-2	216	L	Bellefeuille, Que.	1/15/78	Hull-Rimouski
BIALOWAS, Frank	5-11	220	L	Winnipeg, Man.	9/25/69	Philadelphia (AHL)
BOISVENUE, Martin	6-0	192	L	Cornwall, Ont.	4/24/77	Baie-Comeau
BOULERICE, Jesse	6-1	214	R	Plattsburgh, NY	8/10/78	Plymouth-United States
BRIND'AMOUR, Rod	6-1	202	L	Ottawa, Ont.	8/9/70	Philadelphia-Canada
BUREAU, Marc	6-1	198	R	Trois-Rivières, Que.	5/19/66	Montreal
CERVEN, Martin	6-4	200	L	Trencin, Czech.	3/7/77	Philadelphia (AHL)
DAIGLE, Alexandre	6-0	195	L	Montreal, Que.	2/7/75	Ottawa-Philadelphia
FEDORUK, Todd	6-1	205	L	Redwater, Alta.	2/13/79	Kelowna-Regina
FORBES, Colin	6-3	205	L	New Westminster, B.C.	2/16/76	Phi-Philadelphia (AHL)
GAGNE, Simon	6-0	165	L	Ste. Foy, Que.	2/29/80	Quebec (QMJHL)
GRATTON, Chris	6-4	218	L	Brantford, Ont.	7/5/75	Philadelphia-Canada
GREIG, Mark	5-11	190	R	High River, Alta.	1/25/70	Grand Rapids
HEALEY, Paul	6-2	196	R	Edmonton, Alta.	3/20/75	Phi-Philadelphia (AHL)
KAVANAGH, Pat	6-3	192	R	Ottawa, Ont.	3/14/79	Peterborough
KLATT, Trent	6-1	205	R	Robbinsdale, MN	1/30/71	Philadelphia
KORDIC, Dan	6-5	234	L	Edmonton, Alta.	4/18/71	Philadelphia
LACROIX, Daniel	6-2	205	L	Montreal, Que.	3/11/69	Philadelphia
LeCLAIR, John	6-3	226	L	St. Albans, VT	7/5/69	Philadelphia-United States
LINDROS, Eric	6-4	236	R	London, Ont.	2/28/73	Philadelphia-Canada
MANELUK, Mike	5-11	188	R	Winnipeg, Man.	10/1/73	Worcester-Philadelphia (AHL)
McCOSH, Shawn	6-0	197	R	Oshawa, Ont.	6/5/69	Philadelphia (AHL)
MONTGOMERY, Jim	5-10	185	R	Montreal, Que.	6/30/69	Philadelphia (AHL)
PARK, Richard	5-11	190	R	Seoul, S. Korea	5/27/76	Anaheim-Cincinatti (AHL)
PAYETTE, Andre	6-2	205	L	Cornwall, Ont.	7/29/76	Philadelphia (AHL)
PODEIN, Shjon	6-2	200	L	Rochester, MN	3/5/68	Philadelphia-United States
SILLINGER, Mike	5-10	190	R	Regina, Sask.	6/29/71	Vancouver-Philadelphia
WESENBERG, Brian	6-3	187	R	Peterborough, Ont.	5/9/77	Philadelphia (AHL)
WHITE, Peter	5-11	200	L	Montreal, Que.	3/15/69	Philadelphia (AHL)
ZENT, Jason	5-11	204	L	Buffalo, NY	4/15/71	Ottawa-Detroit (IHL)-Worcester
ZUBRUS, Dainius	6-3	215	L	Elektrenai, USSR	6/16/78	Philadelphia
DEFENSEMEN						
BABYCH, Dave	6-2	215	L	Edmonton, Alta.	5/23/61	Vancouver-Philadelphia
CHERNOV, Mikhail	6-2	196	R	Prokopjevsk, USSR	11/11/78	Yaroslavl
DELMORE, Andy	6-1	192	R	LaSalle, Ont.	12/26/76	Philadelphia (AHL)
DESJARDINS, Eric	6-1	200	R	Rouyn, Que.	6/14/69	Philadelphia-Canada
EATON, Mark	6-3	195	L	Wilmington, DE	5/6/77	Notre Dame
FLODELL, Jordon	6-2	198	R	Melfort, Sask.	4/28/79	Moose Jaw
JOSEPH, Chris	6-2	202	R	Burnaby, B.C.	9/10/69	Phi-Philadelphia (AHL)
KLIMENTJEV, Sergei	5-11	200	L	Kiev, USSR	4/5/75	Rochester
LANK, Jeff	6-3	205	L	Indian Head, Sask.	3/1/75	Philadelphia (AHL)
MacISAAC, Dave	6-2	225	L	Arlington, MA	4/23/72	Philadelphia (AHL)-Italy
MALLETTE, Kris	6-3	220	R	North Bay, Ont.	1/19/79	Kelowna
McGILLIS, Daniel	6-2	225	L	Hawkesbury, Ont.	7/1/72	Edmonton-Philadelphia
McLAREN, Steve	6-0	194	L	Owen Sound, Ont.	2/3/75	Indianapolis
RICHARDSON, Luke	6-4	210	L	Ottawa, Ont.	3/26/69	Philadelphia
STEVENS, John	6-1	195	L	Campbellton, N.B.	5/4/66	Philadelphia (AHL)
SVOBODA, Petr	6-1	195	L	Most, Czech.	2/14/66	Philadelphia-Czech.
TERTYSHNY, Dimitri	6-1	176	L	Chelyabinsk, USSR	12/26/76	Chelyabinsk
THERIEN, Chris	6-5	230	L	Ottawa, Ont.	12/14/71	Philadelphia

GOALTENDERS	HT	WT	C	Place of Birth	Date	1997-98 Club
BOUCHER, Brian	6-1	190	L	Woonsocket, RI	1/2/77	Philadelphia (AHL)
HEXTALL, Ron	6-3	192	L	Brandon, Man.	5/3/64	Philadelphia
LITTLE, Neil	6-1	193	L	Medicine Hat, Alta.	12/18/71	Philadelphia (AHL)
PELLETIER, Jean-Marc	6-3	200	L	Atlanta, GA	3/4/78	Rimouski-United States
VANBIESBROUCK, John	5-8	176	L	Detroit, MI	9/4/63	Florida-United States

Captains' History

Lou Angotti, 1967-68; Ed Van Impe, 1968-69 to 1971-72; Ed Van Impe and Bobby Clarke, 1972-73; Bobby Clarke, 1973-74 to 1978-79; Mel Bridgman, 1979-80, 1980-81; Bill Barber, 1981-82; Bill Barber and Bobby Clarke, 1982-83; Bobby Clarke, 1983-84; Dave Poulin, 1984-85 to 1988-89; Dave Poulin and Ron Sutter, 1989-90; Ron Sutter, 1990-91; Rick Tocchet, 1991-92; no captain, 1992-93; Kevin Dineen, 1993-94; Eric Lindros, 1994-95 to date.

President and General Manager

CLARKE, ROBERT EARLE (BOB)
President/General Manager, Philadelphia Flyers.
Born in Flin Flon, Man., August 13, 1949.

Bob Clarke was named president and general manager of the Philadelphia Flyers on June 15, 1994. Clarke's appointment marks the second time he has served as the Flyers' general manager. The Flin Flon native was the Flyers' vice president and general manager from 1984-90. During his ten years as the team's general manager, the Flyers have won five divisional titles, three conference championships, reached the Stanley Cup semifinals five times and the Finals three times.

Prior to re-joining the Flyers' family in 1994, Clarke served as vice president and general manager of the Florida Panthers. In 1993-94, their first season in the NHL, the Panthers established NHL records for wins (33) and points (83) by an expansion franchise. Clarke also served as the vice president and general manager of the Minnesota North Stars from 1990-92, guiding the team to the Stanley Cup Finals in 1991.

As a player, the former Philadelphia captain led his club to Stanley Cup championships in 1974 and 1975 and captured numerous individual awards, including the Hart Trophy as the League's most valuable player in 1973, 1975 and 1976. The four-time All-Star also received the Bill Masterton Memorial Trophy (perseverance and dedication) in 1972 and the Frank J. Selke Trophy (top defensive forward) in 1983. He appeared in eight All-Star Games and was elected to the Hockey Hall of Fame in 1987. He was awarded the Lester Patrick Trophy in 1979-80 in recognition of his contribution to hockey in the United States. Clarke appeared in 1,144 regular season games, recording 358 goals and 852 assists for 1,210 points. He also added 119 points in 136 playoff games.

1997-98 Scoring

* – rookie

Regular Season

Pos	#	Player	Team	GP	G	A	Pts	+/–	PIM	PP	SH	GW	GT	S	%
L	10	John LeClair	PHI	82	51	36	87	30	32	16	0	9	1	303	16.8
L	17	Rod Brind'Amour	PHI	82	36	38	74	-2	54	10	2	8	0	205	17.6
C	88	Eric Lindros	PHI	63	30	41	71	14	134	10	1	4	0	202	14.9
C	55	Chris Gratton	PHI	82	22	40	62	11	159	5	0	2	0	182	12.1
R	19	Alexandre Daigle	OTT	38	7	9	16	-7	8	4	0	2	0	68	10.3
			PHI	37	9	17	26	-1	6	4	0	3	1	78	11.5
			TOTAL	75	16	26	42	-8	14	8	0	5	1	146	11.0
R	20	Trent Klatt	PHI	82	14	28	42	2	16	5	0	3	0	143	9.8
C	11	Mike Sillinger	VAN	48	10	9	19	-14	34	1	2	1	0	56	17.9
			PHI	27	11	11	22	3	16	1	2	0	0	40	27.5
			TOTAL	75	21	20	41	-11	50	2	4	1	0	96	21.9
R	9	Dainius Zubrus	PHI	69	8	25	33	29	42	1	0	5	0	101	7.9
D	37	Eric Desjardins	PHI	77	6	27	33	11	36	2	1	0	0	150	4.0
D	3	Daniel McGillis	EDM	67	10	15	25	-17	74	5	0	3	1	119	8.4
			PHI	13	1	5	6	-4	35	1	0	0	0	18	5.6
			TOTAL	80	11	20	31	-21	109	6	0	3	1	137	8.0
D	77	Paul Coffey	PHI	57	2	27	29	3	30	1	0	1	0	107	1.9
L	25	Shjon Podein	PHI	82	11	13	24	8	53	1	1	2	0	126	8.7
L	12 *	Colin Forbes	PHI	63	12	7	19	2	59	2	0	2	0	93	12.9
D	6	Chris Therien	PHI	78	3	16	19	5	80	1	0	1	0	102	2.9
D	23	Petr Svoboda	PHI	56	3	15	18	19	83	2	0	0	0	44	6.8
D	44	Dave Babych	VAN	47	0	9	9	-11	37	0	0	0	0	40	0.0
			PHI	6	0	0	0	2	12	0	0	0	0	6	0.0
			TOTAL	53	0	9	9	-9	49	0	0	0	0	46	0.0
C	29	Joel Otto	PHI	68	3	4	7	-2	78	0	0	0	1	53	5.7
D	22	Luke Richardson	PHI	81	2	3	5	7	139	2	0	0	0	57	3.5
C	32	Daniel Lacroix	PHI	56	1	4	5	0	135	0	0	0	0	28	3.6
R	26	John Druce	PHI	23	1	2	3	0	2	0	0	0	0	18	5.6
D	28	Kjell Samuelsson	PHI	49	0	3	3	9	28	0	0	0	0	23	0.0
L	21	Dan Kordic	PHI	61	1	1	2	-4	210	0	0	0	0	12	8.3
G	33	Sean Burke	CAR	25	0	1	1	0	6	0	0	0	0	0	0.0
			VAN	16	0	1	1	0	14	0	0	0	0	0	0.0
			PHI	11	0	0	0	0	0	0	0	0	0	0	0.0
			TOTAL	52	0	2	2	0	20	0	0	0	0	0	0.0
C	14	Craig Darby	PHI	3	1	0	1	0	0	0	0	0	0	3	33.3
D	24	Chris Joseph	PHI	15	1	0	1	1	19	0	0	1	0	20	5.0
R	38 *	Paul Healey	PHI	4	0	0	0	0	12	0	0	0	0	0	0.0
R	18	Brantt Myhres	PHI	23	0	0	0	-1	169	0	0	0	0	0	0.0
G	27	Ron Hextall	PHI	46	0	0	0	0	10	0	0	0	0	0	0.0

Goaltending

No.	Goaltender	GPI	Mins	Avg	W	L	T	EN	SO	GA	SA	S%
27	Ron Hextall	46	2688	2.17	21	17	7	2	4	97	1089	.911
30	Garth Snow	29	1651	2.43	14	9	4	0	1	67	682	.902
33	Sean Burke	11	632	2.56	7	3	0	0	1	27	311	.913
	Totals	**82**	**4988**	**2.32**	**42**	**29**	**11**	**2**	**6**	**193**	**2084**	**.907**

Playoffs

Pos	#	Player	Team	GP	G	A	Pts	+/–	PIM	PP	SH	GW	OT	S	%
L	17	Rod Brind'Amour	PHI	5	2	2	4	2	7	0	0	0	0	15	13.3
C	88	Eric Lindros	PHI	5	1	2	3	-3	17	0	0	0	0	13	7.7
D	3	Daniel McGillis	PHI	5	1	2	3	0	10	1	0	0	0	14	7.1
C	55	Chris Gratton	PHI	5	2	0	2	-1	10	0	0	0	0	16	12.5
L	10	John LeClair	PHI	5	1	1	2	-4	8	1	0	1	0	19	5.3
R	19	Alexandre Daigle	PHI	5	0	2	2	0	0	0	0	0	0	6	0.0
C	11	Mike Sillinger	PHI	3	1	0	1	1	0	0	0	0	0	7	14.3
D	44	Dave Babych	PHI	5	1	0	1	2	4	1	0	0	0	12	8.3
D	23	Petr Svoboda	PHI	3	0	1	1	-1	4	0	0	0	0	1	0.0
D	37	Eric Desjardins	PHI	5	0	1	1	-3	0	0	0	0	0	17	0.0
D	6	Chris Therien	PHI	5	0	1	1	-1	4	0	0	0	0	15	0.0
R	9	Dainius Zubrus	PHI	5	0	1	1	2	2	0	0	0	0	6	0.0
G	27	Ron Hextall	PHI	1	0	0	0	0	0	0	0	0	0	0	0.0
D	24	Chris Joseph	PHI	1	0	0	0	0	2	0	0	0	0	2	0.0
D	28	Kjell Samuelsson	PHI	1	0	0	0	1	0	0	0	0	0	0	0.0
R	26	John Druce	PHI	2	0	0	0	-1	2	0	0	0	0	3	0.0
C	32	Daniel Lacroix	PHI	4	0	0	0	0	4	0	0	0	0	0	0.0
G	33	Sean Burke	PHI	5	0	0	0	0	0	0	0	0	0	0	0.0
C	29	Joel Otto	PHI	5	0	0	0	-1	0	0	0	0	0	8	0.0
D	22	Luke Richardson	PHI	5	0	0	0	-3	0	0	0	0	0	2	0.0
R	20	Trent Klatt	PHI	5	0	0	0	-6	0	0	0	0	0	6	0.0
L	25	Shjon Podein	PHI	5	0	0	0	-1	10	0	0	0	0	5	0.0
L	12 *	Colin Forbes	PHI	5	0	0	0	2	2	0	0	0	0	9	0.0

Goaltending

No.	Goaltender	GPI	Mins	Avg	W	L	EN	SO	GA	SA	S%
27	Ron Hextall	1	20	3.00	0	0	0	0	1	8	.875
33	Sean Burke	5	283	3.60	1	4	0	0	17	121	.860
	Totals	**5**	**306**	**3.53**	**1**	**4**	**0**	**0**	**18**	**129**	**.860**

General Managers' History

Bud Poile, 1967-68, 1968-69; Bud Poile and Keith Allen, 1969-70; Keith Allen, 1970-71 to 1982-83; Bob McCammon, 1983-84; Bob Clarke, 1984-85 to 1989-90; Russ Farwell, 1990-91 to 1993-94; Bob Clarke, 1994-95 to date.

Coaching History

Keith Allen, 1967-68, 1968-69; Vic Stasiuk, 1969-70, 1970-71; Fred Shero, 1971-72 to 1977-78; Bob McCammon and Pat Quinn, 1978-79; Pat Quinn, 1979-80, 1980-81; Pat Quinn and Bob McCammon, 1981-82; Bob McCammon, 1982-83, 1983-84; Mike Keenan, 1984-85 to 1987-88; Paul Holmgren, 1988-89 to 1990-91; Paul Holmgren and Bill Dineen, 1991-92; Bill Dineen, 1992-93; Terry Simpson, 1993-94; Terry Murray, 1994-95 to 1996-97; Wayne Cashman and Roger Neilson, 1997-98; Roger Neilson, 1998-99.

Club Records

Team

(Figures in brackets for season records are games played; records for fewest points, wins, ties, losses, goals, goals against are for 70 or more games)

Most Points	118	1975-76 (80)
Most Wins	53	1984-85 (80), 1985-86 (80)
Most Ties	*24	1969-70 (76)
Most Losses	39	1993-94 (84)
Most Goals	350	1983-84 (80)
Most Goals Against	319	1992-93 (84)
Fewest Points	58	1969-70 (76)
Fewest Wins	17	1969-70 (76)
Fewest Ties	4	1985-86 (80)
Fewest Losses	12	1979-80 (80)
Fewest Goals	173	1967-68 (74)
Fewest Goals Against	164	1973-74 (78)
Longest Winning Streak		
Overall	13	Oct. 19-Nov. 17/85
Home	*20	Jan. 4-Apr. 3/76
Away	8	Dec. 22/82-Jan. 16/83
Longest Undefeated Streak		
Overall	*35	Oct. 14/79-Jan. 6/80 (25 wins, 10 ties)
Home	26	Oct. 11/79-Feb. 3/80 (19 wins, 7 ties)
Away	16	Oct. 20/79-Jan. 6/80 (11 wins, 5 ties)
Longest Losing Streak		
Overall	6	Mar. 25-Apr. 4/70, Dec. 5-Dec. 17/92, Jan. 25-Feb. 5/94
Home	5	Jan. 30-Feb. 15/69
Away	8	Oct. 25-Nov. 26/72
Longest Winless Streak		
Overall	11	Nov. 21-Dec. 14/68 (9 losses, 2 ties), Dec. 10/70-Jan. 3/71 (9 losses, 2 ties)
Home	8	Dec. 19/68-Jan. 18/69 (4 losses, 4 ties)
Away	19	Oct. 23/71-Jan. 27/72 (15 losses, 4 ties)
Most Shutouts, Season	13	1974-75 (80)
Most PIM, Season	2,621	1980-81 (80)
Most Goals, Game	13	Mar. 22/84 (Pit. 4 at Phi. 13), Oct. 18/84 (Van. 2 at Phi. 13)

Individual

Most Seasons	15	Bobby Clarke
Most Games	1,144	Bobby Clarke
Most Goals, Career	420	Bill Barber
Most Assists, Career	852	Bobby Clarke
Most Points, Career	1,210	Bobby Clarke (358G, 852A)
Most PIM, Career	1,683	Rick Tocchet
Most Shutouts, Career	50	Bernie Parent
Longest Consecutive Game Streak	402	Rod Brind'Amour (Feb. 24/93-date)
Most Goals, Season	61	Reggie Leach (1975-76)
Most Assists, Season	89	Bobby Clarke (1974-75, 1975-76)
Most Points, Season	123	Mark Recchi (1992-93; 53G, 70A)
Most PIM, Season	*472	Dave Schultz (1974-75)
Most Points, Defenseman, Season	82	Mark Howe (1985-86; 24G, 58A)
Most Points, Center, Season	119	Bobby Clarke (1975-76; 30G, 89A)
Most Points, Right Wing, Season	123	Mark Recchi (1992-93; 53G, 70A)
Most Points, Left Wing, Season	112	Bill Barber (1975-76; 50G, 62A)
Most Points, Rookie, Season	82	Mikael Renberg (1993-94; 38G, 44A)
Most Shutouts, Season	12	Bernie Parent (1973-74, 1974-75)
Most Goals, Game	4	Thirteen times
Most Assists, Game	6	Eric Lindros (Feb. 26/97)
Most Points, Game	8	Tom Bladon (Dec. 11/77; 4G, 4A)

* NHL Record.

Retired Numbers

1	Bernie Parent	1967-1971, 1973-1979
4	Barry Ashbee	1970-1974
7	Bill Barber	1972-1985
16	Bobby Clarke	1969-1984

All-time Record vs. Other Clubs

Regular Season

	At Home							On Road							Total						
	GP	W	L	T	GF	GA	PTS	GP	W	L	T	GF	GA	PTS	GP	W	L	T	GF	GA	PTS
Anaheim	4	1	1	2	10	8	4	4	2	1	1	13	13	5	8	3	2	3	23	21	9
Boston	61	27	27	7	206	180	61	64	14	42	8	183	260	36	125	41	69	15	389	440	97
Buffalo	55	32	13	10	200	145	74	51	20	25	6	157	179	46	106	52	38	16	357	324	120
Calgary	47	32	13	2	187	125	66	48	15	24	9	157	197	39	95	47	37	11	344	322	105
Carolina	31	21	8	2	124	84	44	32	16	10	6	132	116	38	63	37	18	8	256	200	82
Chicago	57	30	16	11	185	153	71	56	12	25	19	159	200	43	113	42	41	30	344	353	114
Colorado	30	21	7	2	112	78	44	29	9	10	10	105	108	28	59	30	17	12	217	186	72
Dallas	62	41	9	12	247	143	94	62	23	25	14	206	205	60	124	64	34	26	453	348	154
Detroit	55	31	13	11	221	162	73	54	18	26	10	173	192	46	109	49	39	21	394	354	119
Edmonton	26	19	6	1	120	74	39	25	7	14	4	74	91	18	51	26	20	5	194	165	57
Florida	13	5	5	3	29	32	13	12	9	3	0	43	32	18	25	14	8	3	72	64	31
Los Angeles	59	37	15	7	230	151	81	61	34	19	8	208	180	76	120	71	34	15	438	331	157
Montreal	61	25	22	14	188	185	64	62	19	30	13	196	226	51	123	44	52	27	384	411	115
New Jersey	69	45	16	8	281	172	98	68	29	35	4	254	248	62	137	74	51	12	535	420	160
NY Islanders	80	49	23	8	305	238	106	82	24	45	13	237	322	61	162	73	68	21	542	560	167
NY Rangers	93	45	35	13	313	271	103	95	30	42	23	274	313	83	188	75	77	36	587	584	186
Ottawa	11	10	1	0	51	22	20	11	8	2	1	43	29	17	22	18	3	1	94	51	37
Phoenix	26	19	7	0	115	72	38	25	13	10	2	88	79	28	51	32	17	2	203	151	66
Pittsburgh	91	69	15	7	399	233	145	90	32	41	17	293	318	81	181	101	56	24	692	551	226
St. Louis	62	41	11	10	247	142	92	62	31	24	7	197	180	69	124	72	35	17	444	322	161
San Jose	6	3	2	1	22	14	7	7	6	1	0	24	13	12	13	9	3	1	46	27	19
Tampa Bay	13	8	1	4	44	23	20	14	9	4	1	46	38	19	27	17	5	5	90	61	39
Toronto	55	36	11	8	221	127	80	55	22	20	13	188	186	57	110	58	31	21	409	313	137
Vancouver	48	33	14	1	212	142	67	48	26	10	12	192	139	64	96	59	24	13	404	281	131
Washington	71	42	24	5	268	202	89	68	29	26	13	231	233	71	139	71	50	18	499	435	160
Defunct Clubs	34	24	4	6	137	67	54	35	13	14	8	102	89	34	69	37	18	14	239	156	88
Totals	**1220**	**746**	**319**	**155**	**4674**	**3245**	**1647**	**1220**	**470**	**528**	**222**	**3975**	**4186**	**1162**	**2440**	**1216**	**847**	**377**	**8649**	**7431**	**2809**

Playoffs

	Series	W	L	GP	W	L	T	GF	GA	Last Mtg.	Round	Result
Boston	4	2	2	20	9	11	0	57	60	1978	QF	L 1-4
Buffalo	5	4	1	26	17	9	0	83	67	1998	CQF	W 1-4
Calgary	2	1	1	11	7	4	0	43	28	1981	QF	L 3-4
Chicago	1	0	1	4	0	4	0	8	20	1971	QF	L 0-4
Colorado	2	2	0	11	7	4	0	39	29	1985	CF	W 4-2
Dallas	2	2	0	11	8	3	0	41	26	1980	SF	W 4-1
Detroit	1	0	1	4	0	4	0	6	16	1997	F	L 0-4
Edmonton	3	1	2	15	7	8	0	44	49	1987	F	L 3-4
Florida	1	0	1	6	2	4	0	11	15	1996	CSF	L 2-4
Montreal	4	1	3	21	6	15	0	52	72	1989	CF	L 2-4
New Jersey	2	1	1	8	4	4	0	20	23	1995	CF	L 2-4
NY Islanders	4	3	1	25	14	11	0	83	69	1987	DF	W 4-3
NY Rangers	10	6	4	47	27	20	0	157	153	1997	CF	W 4-1
Pittsburgh	2	2	0	12	8	4	0	51	37	1997	CQF	W 4-1
St. Louis	2	0	2	11	3	8	0	20	34	1969	QF	L 0-4
Tampa Bay	1	1	0	6	4	2	0	26	13	1996	CQF	W 4-2
Toronto	3	3	0	17	12	5	0	67	47	1977	QF	W 4-2
Vancouver	1	1	0	3	2	1	0	15	9	1979	PR	W 2-1
Washington	3	1	2	16	7	9	0	55	65	1989	DSF	W 4-2
Totals	**53**	**31**	**22**	**274**	**145**	**129**	**0**	**878**	**832**			

Calgary totals include Atlanta, 1972-73 to 1979-80. Carolina totals include Hartford, 1979-80 to 1996-97.
Colorado totals include Quebec, 1979-80 to 1994-95. Dallas totals include Minnesota, 1967-68 to 1992-93.
New Jersey totals include Kansas City, 1974-75 to 1975-76, and Colorado Rockies, 1976-77 to 1981-82.
Phoenix totals include Winnipeg, 1979-80 to 1995-96.

Playoff Results 1998-94

Year	Round	Opponent	Result	GF	GA
1998	CQF	Buffalo	L 1-4	9	18
1997	F	Detroit	L 0-4	6	16
	CF	NY Rangers	W 4-1	20	13
	CSF	Buffalo	W 4-1	21	13
	CQF	Pittsburgh	W 4-1	20	13
1996	CSF	Florida	L 2-4	11	15
	CQF	Tampa Bay	W 4-2	26	13
1995	CF	New Jersey	L 2-4	14	20
	CSF	NY Rangers	W 4-0	18	10
	CQF	Buffalo	W 4-1	18	13

Abbreviations: Round: F – Final; **CF** – conference final; **CQF** – conference quarter-final; **CSF** – conference semi-final; **DF** – division final; **DSF** – division semi-final; **SF** – semi-final; **QF** – quarter-final; **PR** – preliminary round.

1997-98 Results

Oct.	1		Florida	3-1		8	at	Carolina	3-3
	3		Ottawa	5-3		9	at	Washington	1-4
	5		Phoenix	1-2		11	at	Tampa Bay	5-2
	8	at	New Jersey	1-4		14		Montreal	3-3
	9		Pittsburgh	3-1		20		Buffalo	3-0
	11	at	Montreal	6-2		22	at	NY Rangers	4-3
	13	at	San Jose	3-2		24	at	Detroit	0-1
	15	at	Anaheim	2-2		26		NY Islanders	3-1
	17	at	Los Angeles	1-5		28	at	NY Islanders	1-6
	21		Tampa Bay	7-1		29		Montreal	2-3
	23		Calgary	4-3		31		Washington	2-3
	27		New Jersey	0-5	**Feb.**	4	at	Dallas	0-1
	29		St. Louis	2-3		5	at	Phoenix	6-2
	31	at	Washington	2-2		7	at	Colorado	2-3
Nov.	2		Dallas	3-3		28	at	NY Rangers	3-1
	3	at	St. Louis	5-1	**Mar.**	2	at	New Jersey	3-4
	6		Edmonton	6-2		3	at	NY Islanders	1-3
	8	at	Ottawa	4-3		5		Washington	3-2
	11		Ottawa	1-0		7	at	Pittsburgh	4-6
	13		Colorado	1-2		8		Pittsburgh	4-3
	14	at	Florida	5-2		10		New Jersey	2-2
	16		Tampa Bay	3-2		12		Vancouver	3-2
	19	at	Toronto	1-3		14		Detroit	6-1
	20		San Jose	0-3		16		Toronto	4-1
	26	at	Buffalo	3-1		19		Anaheim	3-3
	28		NY Islanders	4-1		21	at	Pittsburgh	3-4
	29	at	Tampa Bay	3-3		22		NY Rangers	5-4
Dec.	1		Buffalo	1-1		24	at	New Jersey	2-3
	3		Boston	0-3		26	at	Boston	2-4
	5	at	NY Rangers	4-4		28		Carolina	2-4
	11		NY Islanders	4-3		29	at	Carolina	3-1
	12	at	Chicago	3-2		31		Chicago	3-2
	14		Tampa Bay	3-0	**Apr.**	2		Los Angeles	3-0
	15	at	Montreal	3-1		4		Florida	1-4
	18		Boston	2-2		8	at	Tampa Bay	6-1
	20		Florida	2-0		9	at	Florida	2-3
	23		Carolina	4-2		11		Washington	4-3
	27	at	Calgary	2-5		13	at	Buffalo	1-2
	30	at	Edmonton	3-1		16	at	Florida	7-3
	31	at	Vancouver	8-0		18		NY Rangers	1-2
Jan.	3	at	Ottawa	7-2		19	at	Boston	1-2

Entry Draft Selections 1998-84

1998
Pick
22 Simon Gagne
42 Jason Beckett
51 Ian Forbes
109 Jean-Philippe Morin
124 Francis Belanger
139 Garrett Prosofsky
168 Antero Niittymaki
175 Cam Ondrik
195 Tomas Divisek
222 Lubomir Pistek
243 Petr Hubacek
253 Bruno St. Jacques
258 Sergei Skrobat

1997
Pick
30 Jean-Marc Pelletier
50 Pat Kavanagh
62 Kris Mallette
103 Mihail Chernov
158 Jordon Flodell
164 Todd Fedoruk
214 Marko Kauppinen
240 Par Styf

1996
Pick
15 Dainius Zubrus
64 Chester Gallant
124 Per-Ragna Bergqvist
133 Jesse Boulerice
187 Roman Malov
213 Jeff Milleker

1995
Pick
22 Brian Boucher
48 Shane Kenny
100 Radovan Somik
132 Dimitri Tertyshny
135 Jamie Sokolsky
152 Martin Spanhel
178 Martin Streit
204 Ruslan Shafikov
230 Jeff Lank

1994
Pick
62 Artem Anisimov
88 Adam Magarrell
101 Sebastien Vallee
140 Alexander Selivanov
166 Colin Forbes
192 Derek Diener
202 Raymond Giroux
218 Johan Hedberg
244 Andre Payette
270 Jan Lipiansky

1993
Pick
36 Janne Niinimaa
71 Vaclav Prospal
77 Milos Holan
114 Vladimir Krechin
140 Mike Crowley
166 Aaron Israel
192 Paul Healey
218 Tripp Tracy
226 E.J. Bradley
244 Jeffrey Staples
270 Kenneth Hemmenway

1992
Pick
7 Ryan Sittler
15 Jason Bowen
31 Denis Metlyuk
103 Vladislav Buljin
127 Roman Zolotov
151 Kirk Daubenspeck
175 Claude Jutras Jr.
199 Jonas Hakansson
223 Chris Herperger
247 Patrice Paquin

1991
Pick
6 Peter Forsberg
50 Yanick Dupre
86 Aris Brimanis
94 Yanick Degrace
116 Clayton Norris
122 Dmitri Yushkevich
138 Andrei Lomakin
182 James Bode
204 Josh Bartell
226 Neil Little
248 John Porco

1990
Pick
4 Mike Ricci
25 Chris Simon
40 Mikael Renberg
42 Terran Sandwith
44 Kimbi Daniels
46 Bill Armstrong
47 Chris Therien
52 Al Kinisky
88 Dan Kordic
109 Viacheslav Butsayev
151 Patrik Englund
172 Toni Porkka
193 Greg Hanson
214 Tommy Soderstrom
235 William Lund

1989
Pick
33 Greg Johnson
34 Patrik Juhlin
72 Reid Simpson
117 Niklas Eriksson
138 John Callahan Jr.
159 Sverre Sears
180 Glen Wisser
201 Al Kummu
222 Matt Brait
243 James Pollio

1988
Pick
14 Claude Boivin
35 Pat Murray
56 Craig Fisher
63 Dominic Roussel
77 Scott Lagrand
98 Edward O'Brien
119 Gordie Frantti
140 Jamie Cooke
161 Johan Salle
182 Brian Arthur
203 Jeff Dandreta
224 Scott Billey
245 Drahomir Kadlec

1987
Pick
20 Darren Rumble
30 Jeff Harding
62 Martin Hostak
83 Tomaz Eriksson
104 Bill Gall
125 Tony Link
146 Mark Strapon
167 Darryl Ingham
188 Bruce McDonald
209 Steve Morrow
230 Darius Rusnak
251 Dale Roehl

1986
Pick
20 Kerry Huffman
23 Jukka Seppo
28 Kent Hawley
83 Mark Bar
125 Steve Scheifele
146 Sami Wahlsten
167 Murray Baron
188 Blaine Rude
209 Shawn Sabol
230 Brett Lawrence
251 Daniel Stephano

1985
Pick
21 Glen Seabrooke
42 Bruce Rendall
48 Darryl Gilmour
63 Shane Whelan
84 Paul Marshall
105 Daril Holmes
126 Ken Alexander
147 Tony Horacek
168 Mike Cusack
189 Gordon Murphy
231 Rod Williams
252 Paul Maurice

1984
Pick
22 Greg Smyth
27 Scott Mellanby
37 Jeff Chychrun
43 Dave McLay
47 John Stevens
79 Dave Hanson
100 Brian Dobbin
121 John Dzikowski
142 Tom Allen
163 Luke Vitale
184 Bill Powers
204 Daryn Fersovitch
245 Juraj Bakos

Coach

NEILSON, ROGER PAUL
Coach, Philadelphia Flyers. Born in Toronto, Ont., June 16, 1934.

On March 9, 1998, Roger Neilson took over from Wayne Cashman behind the Flyers bench. The Philadelphia job is Neilson's seventh head coaching assignment in the NHL. He had been serving as an assistant coach in St. Louis until he was hired by the Flyers. Neilson guided Philadelphia to a 10-9-2 record over the final 21 games of the 1997-98 season.

His previous NHL head coaching jobs have been with the Toronto Maple Leafs, Buffalo Sabres, Vancouver Canucks, Los Angeles Kings, New York Rangers and Florida Panthers. Neilson's Rangers posted the NHL's best record in 1991-92.

Neilson began his coaching career in 1966-67 and spent 10 seasons with the Peterborough Petes.

NHL Coaching Record

		Regular Season					Playoffs			
Season	Team	Games	W	L	T	%	Games	W	L	%
1977-78	Toronto	80	41	29	10	.575	13	6	7	.462
1978-79	Toronto	80	34	33	13	.506	6	2	4	.333
1980-81	Buffalo	80	39	20	21	.619	8	4	4	.500
1981-82	Vancouver	5	4	0	1	.900	17	11	6	.647
1982-83	Vancouver	80	30	35	15	.469	4	1	3	.250
1983-84	Vancouver	48	17	26	5	.406	....	....	....	....
1983-84	Los Angeles	28	8	17	3	.339	....	....	....	....
1989-90	NY Rangers	80	36	31	13	.531	10	5	5	.500
1990-91	NY Rangers	80	36	31	13	.531	6	2	4	.333
1991-92	NY Rangers	80	50	25	5	.656	13	6	7	.462
1992-93	NY Rangers	40	19	17	4	.525	....	....	....	....
1993-94	Florida	84	33	34	17	.494	....	....	....	....
1994-95	Florida	48	20	22	6	.479	....	....	....	....
1997-98	Philadelphia	21	10	9	2	.524	5	1	4	.200
	NHL Totals	**834**	**377**	**329**	**128**	**.529**	**82**	**38**	**44**	**.463**

Club Directory

First Union Center
3601 South Broad Street
Philadelphia, PA 19148
Phone **215/465-4500**
PR FAX 215/389-9403
Capacity: 19,519

Executive Management	
Chairman	Ed Snider
Limited Partners	Pat Croce, Jay Snider, Sylvan and Fran Tobin
President and General Manager	Bob Clarke
Chairman of the Board, Emeritus	Joe Scott
Chief Operating Officer	Ron Ryan
Executive Vice President	Keith Allen
Governor	Ed Snider
Alternate Governors	Bob Clarke, Ron Ryan, Phil Weinberg
Executive Assistant	Kathy Nasevich
Receptionist	Carol Poole
Hockey Club Personnel	
Head Coach	Roger Neilson
Assistant General Manager	John Blackwell
Assistant Coach	Wayne Cashman
Assistant Coach	Craig Ramsay
Goaltending Coach	Rejean Lemelin
Video Coach	Rob Cookson
Director of Player Personnel	Paul Holmgren
Chief Scout	Dennis Patterson
Scouting Staff	Serge Boudreault, John Chapman, Inge Hammarstrom, Simon Nolet, Blair Reid, Vaclav Slansky, Evgeny Zimin
Pro Scout	Al Hill
Director of Team Services	Barry Hanrahan
Computer Analyst	David Gelberg
Executive Assistant	Dianna Taylor
Receptionist	Judy DiCinti
Medical/Training Staff	
Team Physicians	Arthur Bartolozzi, M.D.; Jeff Hartzell, M.D.; Gary Dorshimer, M.D.; Mike Weinik, M.D.; Guy Lanzi, D.D.S.
Athletic Trainer	John Worley
Strength and Conditioning Instructor	Jim McCrossin
Head Equipment Manager	Jim Evers
Equipment Managers	Rusty Pearl, Anthony Oratorio, Casey Taylor
Public Relations Department	
Director of Public Relations	Zack Hill
Director of Publications	Joe Klueg
Director of Community Relations	Linda Panasci
Director of Youth Hockey and Fan Development	Eric Turner
Director of Fan Services	Joe Kadlec
Assistant Director of Public Relations	Jody White
Assistant Director of Publications	Linda Held
Assistant Director of Youth Hockey and Fan Development	Melissa Wilson
Public Relations Assistants	Lisa Hanrahan, Jill Lipson
Archivist	Kerrianne Farrelly
Sales/Marketing Department	
Vice President, Marketing	Bob Schwartz
Vice President, Sales	Jack Betson
Ticket Manager	Cecilia Baker
Marketing Managers	Michael Dunphy, Christina Ruskey
Assistant Marketing Manager	Elyse Moreno
Assistant Ticket Manager	Chelsie Snyder
Ticket Office Assistants	Pat Piazza, Lisa Albertson, Linda DiTommaso, Micki Golkow
Finance Department	
Vice President, Finance	Dan Clemmens
Director of Finance	Dave Jablonski
Controller	Lisa Cataldo
Payroll Accountant	Susann Schaffer
Accounts Payable Manager	Patrick Montgomery
Advertising Sales Department	
Vice President, Advertising Sales	Joe Croce
Executive Assistant	Donna Schroeder
Director, Advertising Sales	Jeffrey Kirk
General Sales Manager	John McGuinness
National Sales Manager	Bill Drolet
Manager, Advertising Services	Carol Roosevelt
Senior Account Executives	Ivan Shlichtman, Joe Watson
Account Executives	Lisa Fusco, Mike Garrity, Chris Heck, Ray Lyons, Ciara Perrotti, Steve Rex, Ron Skotarczak
Sponsorship Manager	Carolyn Wollman
Contracts Coordinator	Colleen Molloy
Sales Associate	David Siegel
Sales Assistants	Megan Bossuyt, Thea Crum, Rita Kradzinski, Kevin Morley
Broadcast Department	
TV Play-by-Play, Color Commentary	Jim Jackson, Gary Dornhoefer
Radio Play-by-Play, Color Commentary	Tim Saunders, Steve Coates
Director, Broadcasting	Bryan Cooper
Broadcast Advisor	Gene Hart
Public Address Announcer	Lou Nolan
Flyers Wives Charities	
Executive Director	Fran Tobin
Director of Marketing	Rita Johanson
Event Coordinator	Diane Smith

Phoenix Coyotes

1997-98 Results: 35W-35L-12T 82PTS. Fourth, Central Division

Few goalies in the NHL were busier than Nikolai Khabibulin in 1997-98. Only Dominik Hasek, Curtis Joseph and Mike Richter played more than his 70 games and only Richter and Felix Potvin faced more than his 1,835 shots.

1998-99 Schedule

Oct.	Sun.	11	Ottawa
	Thu.	15	Colorado
	Mon.	19	Boston
	Thu.	22	at Dallas
	Sun.	25	at Anaheim
	Mon.	26	at Colorado
	Wed.	28	at San Jose
Nov.	Sun.	1	at Los Angeles
	Fri.	6	Detroit
	Tue.	10	Colorado
	Wed.	11	at Dallas
	Sat.	14	Tampa Bay
	Wed.	18	Vancouver
	Fri.	20	at San Jose
	Sat.	21	Edmonton
	Tue.	24	Chicago
	Thu.	26	New Jersey
	Sat.	28	at Los Angeles
Dec.	Wed.	2	at Edmonton
	Sat.	5	at Calgary
	Sun.	6	at Vancouver
	Wed.	9	Montreal
	Sat.	12	at Ottawa
	Mon.	14	at Montreal
	Wed.	16	at Toronto
	Thu.	17	at St. Louis
	Sun.	20	NY Islanders*
	Tue.	22	at Detroit
	Wed.	23	at Chicago
	Sat.	26	at Los Angeles
	Mon.	28	Los Angeles
	Wed.	30	NY Rangers
Jan.	Fri.	1	Dallas
	Tue.	5	Florida
	Thu.	7	Edmonton
	Fri.	8	at Anaheim
	Mon.	11	Buffalo
	Wed.	13	Pittsburgh
	Fri.	15	at Nashville
	Sun.	17	at Chicago
	Tue.	19	St. Louis
	Thu.	21	Anaheim
	Tue.	26	at Buffalo
	Thu.	28	at Philadelphia
	Fri.	29	at NY Islanders
	Sun.	31	at Nashville*
Feb.	Tue.	2	Calgary
	Thu.	4	San Jose
	Sat.	6	Chicago*
	Mon.	8	San Jose
	Wed.	10	Los Angeles
	Sat.	13	at Colorado*
	Sun.	14	Anaheim
	Tue.	16	Philadelphia
	Fri.	19	at Tampa Bay
	Sat.	20	at Florida
	Mon.	22	at Pittsburgh
	Wed.	24	at Washington
	Fri.	26	at NY Rangers
	Sun.	28	at New Jersey*
Mar.	Tue.	2	at Boston
	Fri.	5	Detroit
	Sun.	7	Nashville
	Tue.	9	at San Jose
	Thu.	11	Vancouver
	Sat.	13	Anaheim
	Mon.	15	Carolina
	Wed.	17	at Detroit
	Thu.	18	at St. Louis
	Sun.	21	Los Angeles
	Tue.	23	Dallas
	Thu.	25	Washington
	Sat.	27	Calgary
	Mon.	29	at Vancouver
	Tue.	30	at Edmonton
Apr.	Thu.	1	at Calgary
	Tue.	6	San Jose
	Fri.	9	Nashville
	Sun.	11	at Anaheim
	Wed.	14	at Dallas
	Thu.	15	St. Louis
	Sat.	17	Dallas*

* Denotes afternoon game.

Franchise date: June 22, 1979
Transferred from Winnipeg to Phoenix, July 1, 1996

PACIFIC DIVISION

20th NHL Season

Year-by-Year Record

		Home			Road			Overall							
Season	**GP**	**W**	**L**	**T**	**W**	**L**	**T**	**W**	**L**	**T**	**GF**	**GA**	**Pts.**	**Finished**	**Playoff Result**
1997-98	82	19	16	6	16	19	6	35	35	12	224	227	82	4th, Central Div.	Lost Conf. Quarter-Final
1996-97	82	15	19	7	23	18	0	38	37	7	240	243	83	3rd, Central Div.	Lost Conf. Quarter-Final
1995-96*	82	22	16	3	14	24	3	36	40	6	275	291	78	5th, Central Div.	Lost Conf. Quarter-Final
1994-95*	48	10	10	4	6	15	3	16	25	7	157	177	39	6th, Central Div.	Out of Playoffs
1993-94*	84	15	23	4	9	28	5	24	51	9	245	344	57	6th, Central Div.	Out of Playoffs
1992-93*	84	23	16	3	17	21	4	40	37	7	322	320	87	4th, Smythe Div.	Lost Div. Semi-Final
1991-92*	80	20	14	6	13	18	9	33	32	15	251	244	81	4th, Smythe Div.	Lost Div. Semi-Final
1990-91*	80	17	18	5	9	25	6	26	43	11	260	288	63	5th, Smythe Div.	Out of Playoffs
1989-90*	80	22	13	5	15	19	6	37	32	11	298	290	85	3rd, Smythe Div.	Lost Div. Semi-Final
1988-89*	80	17	18	5	9	24	7	26	42	12	300	355	64	5th, Smythe Div.	Out of Playoffs
1987-88*	80	20	14	6	13	22	5	33	36	11	292	310	77	3rd, Smythe Div.	Lost Div. Semi-Final
1986-87*	80	25	12	3	15	20	5	40	32	8	279	271	88	3rd, Smythe Div.	Lost Div. Final
1985-86*	80	18	19	3	8	28	4	26	47	7	295	372	59	3rd, Smythe Div.	Lost Div. Semi-Final
1984-85*	80	21	13	6	22	14	4	43	27	10	358	332	96	2nd, Smythe Div.	Lost Div. Final
1983-84*	80	17	15	8	14	23	3	31	38	11	340	374	73	4th, Smythe Div.	Lost Div. Semi-Final
1982-83*	80	22	16	2	11	23	6	33	39	8	311	333	74	4th, Smythe Div.	Lost Div. Semi-Final
1981-82*	80	18	13	9	15	20	5	33	33	14	319	332	80	2nd, Norris Div.	Lost Div. Semi-Final
1980-81*	80	7	25	8	2	32	6	9	57	14	246	400	32	6th, Smythe Div.	Out of Playoffs
1979-80*	80	13	19	8	7	30	3	20	49	11	214	314	51	5th, Smythe Div.	Out of Playoffs

* Winnipeg Jets

1998-99 Player Personnel

FORWARDS	HT	WT	S	Place of Birth	Date	1997-98 Club
ADAMS, Greg A.	6-3	195	L	Nelson, B.C.	8/15/63	Dallas
BRIERE, Daniel	5-9	170	L	Gatineau, Que.	10/6/77	Phoenix-Springfield
CORKUM, Bob	6-	222	R	Salisbury, MA	12/18/67	Phoenix
CUMMINS, Jim	6-2	219	R	Dearborn, MI	5/17/70	Chicago-Phoenix
DeBRUSK, Louie	6-2	215	L	Cambridge, Ont.	3/19/71	Tampa Bay-San Antonio
DOAN, Shane	6-2	217	R	Halkirk, Alta.	10/10/76	Phoenix-Springfield
DRAKE, Dallas	6-0	185	L	Trail, B.C.	2/4/69	Phoenix
DZIEDZIC, Joe	6-3	227	L	Minneapolis, MN	12/18/71	Cleveland
HANSEN, Tavis	6-1	180	R	Prince Albert, Sask.	6/17/75	Springfield
ISBISTER, Brad	6-3	222	R	Edmonton, Alta.	5/7/77	Phoenix-Springfield
JOMPHE, Jean-Francois	6-1	195	L	Harve' St. Pierre, Que.	12/28/72	Ana-Cin (AHL)-Que (IHL)
LEMIEUX, Jocelyn	5-11	220	L	Mont-Laurier, Que.	11/18/67	Phoenix-Long Beach-Springfield
LETOWSKI, Trevor	5-10	170	R	Thunder Bay, Ont.	4/5/77	Springfield
MURRAY, Rob	6-1	180	R	Toronto, Ont.	4/4/67	Springfield
NIECKAR, Barry	6-3	205	L	Rama, Sask.	12/16/67	Anaheim-Cincinatti (AHL)
ROENICK, Jeremy	6-0	192	R	Boston, MA	1/17/70	Phoenix-United States
RONNING, Cliff	5-8	167	L	Burnaby, B.C.	10/1/65	Phoenix
STAPLETON, Mike	5-10	183	R	Sarnia, Ont.	5/5/66	Phoenix
SULLIVAN, Mike	6-2	190	L	Marshfield, MA	2/27/68	Boston
TKACHUK, Keith	6-2	220	L	Melrose, MA	3/28/72	Phoenix-United States
TOCCHET, Rick	6-0	214	R	Scarborough, Ont.	4/9/64	Phoenix
VASILYEV, Andrei	5-9	180	R	Voskresensk, USSR	3/30/72	Long Beach
YLONEN, Yuha	6-0	180	L	Helsinki, Finland	2/13/72	Phoenix-Finland
DEFENSEMEN						
CARNEY, Keith	6-2	205	L	Providence, RI	2/3/70	Chicago-United States-Phoenix
DIDUCK, Gerald	6-2	217	R	Edmonton, Alta.	4/6/65	Phoenix
DOIG, Jason	6-3	220	R	Montreal, Que.	1/29/77	Phoenix-Springfield
FOCHT, Dan	6-6	226	L	Regina, Sask.	12/31/77	Springfield
GAGNON, Sean	6-2	210	L	Sault Ste. Marie, Ont.	9/11/73	Phoenix-Springfield
HELMER, Bryan	6-1	200	R	Sault Ste. Marie, Ont.	7/15/72	Albany
LINTNER, Richard	6-3	194	R	Trencin, Czech.	11/15/77	Springfield
LUMME, Jyrki	6-1	205	L	Tampere, Finland	7/16/66	Vancouver-Finland
MARTONE, Mike	6-2	200	R	Sault Ste. Marie, Ont.	9/26/77	Peterborough
NUMMINEN, Teppo	6-1	190	R	Tampere, Finland	7/3/68	Phoenix-Finland
PETIT, Michel	6-1	205	R	St. Malo, Que.	2/12/64	Detroit (IHL)-Phoenix
QUINT, Deron	6-2	201	L	Durham, NH	3/12/76	Phoenix-Springfield
SUCHY, Radoslav	6-1	185	L	Poprad, Czechoslovakia	7/4/76	Las Vegas-Springfield
TILEY, Brad	6-1	185	L	Markdale, Ont.	7/5/71	Phoenix-Springfield
TVERDOVSKY, Oleg	6-0	195	L	Donetsk, USSR	5/18/76	Hamilton-Phoenix

GOALTENDERS	HT	WT	C	Place of Birth	Date	1997-98 Club
DAIGLE, Sylvain	5-8	185	R	St-Hyacinthe, Que.	10/20/76	Springfield
ESCHE, Robert	6-0	188	L	Utica, NY	1/22/78	Plymouth-United States
KHABIBULIN, Nikolai	6-1	176	L	Sverdlovsk, USSR	1/13/73	Phoenix
LANGKOW, Scott	5-11	190	L	Sherwood Park, Alta.	4/21/75	Phoenix-Springfield
WAITE, Jimmy	6-1	180	L	Sherbrooke, Que.	4/15/69	Phoenix

Coach

SCHOENFELD, JAMES GRANT (JIM)
Coach, Phoenix Coyotes. Born in Galt, Ont., September 4, 1952.

The 46-year-old native of Galt, Ontario began his coaching career as head coach of the Rochester Americans in the American Hockey League, a position he held for one season before rejoining the Buffalo Sabres as a player. Schoenfeld resumed his career behind the bench during the 1985-86 season, when he compiled a 19-19-5 record with the Sabres until g.m. Scotty Bowman opted to return as head coach. In 1988, Schoenfeld joined the New Jersey Devils, and in his first season led the Devils to within one game of the Stanley Cup Finals. The Devils lost to the Boston Bruins in the Wales Conference Finals. Schoenfeld then served as head coach of the Washington Capitals for four successful seasons (1993-1997) before being hired as the head coach of the Phoenix Coyotes in 1997.

Schoenfeld's playing career spanned 13 years and three teams (Buffalo, Detroit and Boston). The majority of his career was spent with Buffalo, where Schoenfeld was considered one of the most popular defensemen in Sabres team history. He was best known for his durability and outstanding defensive play.

Schoenfeld was drafted by Buffalo in the first round (fifth overall) in the 1972 NHL Entry Draft. Two years later, he was named the Sabres captain, becoming the youngest team captain in League history at that time. In 1974-75, Schoenfeld played in 20 NHL playoff games, leading the Sabres to the club's first berth in the Stanley Cup Finals against Philadelphia. He was named to the NHL's Second All-Star Team in 1979-80 and finished third in Norris Trophy voting that season after setting a current single-season Sabres club record for plus-minus rating with a plus-60. Schoenfeld was also voted the NHL's top rookie defenseman for the 1972 season, and played in the 1977 and 1980 NHL All-Star games, before ending his career in 1985.

Schoenfeld played in 719 career NHL games, scoring 51 goals and adding 204 assists for 255 points. In addition, he racked up 1,132 penalty minutes. His most productive playing season came during the 1979-80 campaign, when he reached career highs in games played (77), goals (9), assists (27) and points (36). Schoenfeld also appeared in 75 NHL playoff games, all with Buffalo, scoring 3 goals and adding 13 assists for 16 points and 151 PIM.

Jim and his wife Theresa have four children; Justin, Katie, Adam and Nathan.

1997-98 Scoring

* – rookie

Regular Season

Pos	#	Player	Team	GP	G	A	Pts	+/–	PIM	PP	SH	GW	GT	S	%
L	7	Keith Tkachuk	PHX	69	40	26	66	9	147	11	0	8	1	232	17.2
C	97	Jeremy Roenick	PHX	79	24	32	56	5	103	6	1	3	1	182	13.2
C	77	Cliff Ronning	PHX	80	11	44	55	5	36	3	0	0	1	197	5.6
C	15	Craig Janney	PHX	68	10	43	53	5	12	4	0	0	0	72	13.9
D	27	Teppo Numminen	PHX	82	11	40	51	25	30	6	0	2	0	126	8.7
R	92	Rick Tocchet	PHX	68	26	19	45	1	157	8	0	6	0	161	16.1
R	11	Dallas Drake	PHX	60	11	29	40	17	71	3	0	2	0	112	9.8
R	22	Mike Gartner	PHX	60	12	15	27	-4	24	4	0	2	1	145	8.3
D	3	Keith Carney	CHI	60	2	13	15	-7	73	0	1	0	0	53	3.8
			PHX	20	1	6	7	5	18	1	0	0	0	18	5.6
			TOTAL	80	3	19	22	-2	91	1	1	0	0	71	4.2
C	21	Bob Corkum	PHX	76	12	9	21	-7	28	0	5	0	0	105	11.4
D	10	Oleg Tverdovsky	PHX	46	7	12	19	1	12	4	0	1	1	83	8.4
D	4	Gerald Diduck	PHX	78	8	10	18	14	118	1	0	4	0	104	7.7
R	16	* Brad Isbister	PHX	66	9	8	17	4	102	1	0	1	0	115	7.8
D	26	John Slaney	PHX	55	3	14	17	-3	24	1	0	1	0	74	4.1
L	34	Darrin Shannon	PHX	58	2	12	14	4	26	0	0	0	0	57	3.5
C	18	Mark Janssens	ANA	55	4	5	9	-22	116	0	0	1	0	43	9.3
			NYI	12	0	0	0	-3	34	0	0	0	0	4	0.0
			PHX	7	1	2	3	4	4	0	0	0	0	6	16.7
			TOTAL	74	5	7	12	-21	154	0	0	1	0	53	9.4
C	36	* Juha Ylonen	PHX	55	1	11	12	-3	10	0	1	0	0	60	1.7
R	19	Shane Doan	PHX	33	5	6	11	-3	35	0	0	3	0	42	11.9
D	5	Deron Quint	PHX	32	4	7	11	-6	16	1	0	1	0	61	6.6
C	14	Mike Stapleton	PHX	64	5	5	10	-4	36	1	1	1	0	69	7.2
D	44	Norm Maciver	PHX	41	2	6	8	-11	38	0	1	0	0	37	5.4
L	33	Jim McKenzie	PHX	64	3	4	7	-7	146	0	0	0	0	35	8.6
D	24	Michel Petit	PHX	32	4	2	6	-4	77	1	0	0	0	34	11.8
R	32	Jocelyn Lemieux	PHX	30	3	3	6	0	27	1	0	0	0	32	9.4
D	2	Murray Baron	PHX	45	1	5	6	-10	106	0	0	0	0	23	4.3
D	8	Jim Johnson	PHX	16	2	1	3	0	18	0	0	0	0	17	11.8
G	35	N. Khabibulin	PHX	70	0	2	2	0	22	0	0	0	0	0	0.0
R	20	Jim Cummins	CHI	55	0	2	2	-9	178	0	0	0	0	33	0.0
			PHX	20	0	0	0	-7	47	0	0	0	0	10	0.0
			TOTAL	75	0	2	2	-16	225	0	0	0	0	43	0.0
C	54	* Daniel Briere	PHX	5	1	0	1	1	2	0	0	0	0	4	25.0
D	55	* Jason Doig	PHX	4	0	1	1	-4	12	0	0	0	0	1	0.0
D	48	* Sean Gagnon	PHX	5	0	1	1	1	14	0	0	0	0	3	0.0
L	72	Jeff Christian	PHX	1	0	0	0	-1	0	0	0	0	0	0	0.0
D	39	Brad Tiley	PHX	1	0	0	0	1	0	0	0	0	0	0	0.0
R	29	Scott Levins	PHX	2	0	0	0	-1	5	0	0	0	0	2	0.0
G	31	* Scott Langkow	PHX	3	0	0	0	0	0	0	0	0	0	0	0.0
G	28	Jim Waite	PHX	17	0	0	0	0	2	0	0	0	0	0	0.0

Goaltending

No.	Goaltender	GPI	Mins	Avg	W	L	T	EN	SO	GA	SA	S%
28	Jim Waite	17	793	2.12	5	6	1	1	1	28	322	.913
35	N. Khabibulin	70	4026	2.74	30	28	10	4	4	184	1835	.900
31	* Scott Langkow	3	137	4.38	0	1	1	0	0	10	60	.833
	Totals	**82**	**4985**	**2.73**	**35**	**35**	**12**	**5**	**5**	**227**	**2222**	**.898**

Playoffs

Pos	#	Player	Team	GP	G	A	Pts	+/–	PIM	PP	SH	GW	OT	S	%
R	92	Rick Tocchet	PHX	6	6	2	8	0	25	3	0	0	0	12	50.0
C	97	Jeremy Roenick	PHX	6	5	3	8	-1	4	2	2	2	0	20	25.0
D	10	Oleg Tverdovsky	PHX	6	0	7	7	-2	0	0	0	0	0	7	0.0
L	7	Keith Tkachuk	PHX	6	3	3	6	-1	10	0	0	0	0	24	12.5
C	77	Cliff Ronning	PHX	6	1	3	4	-1	4	0	0	0	0	17	5.9
C	15	Craig Janney	PHX	6	0	3	3	-2	0	0	0	0	0	6	0.0
D	2	Murray Baron	PHX	6	0	2	2	2	6	0	0	0	0	4	0.0
D	4	Gerald Diduck	PHX	6	0	2	2	-4	20	0	0	0	0	14	0.0
R	22	Mike Gartner	PHX	5	1	0	1	-2	18	1	0	0	0	11	9.1
C	21	Bob Corkum	PHX	6	1	0	1	-3	4	0	0	0	0	3	33.3
R	19	Shane Doan	PHX	6	1	0	1	-2	6	0	0	0	0	7	14.3
R	11	Dallas Drake	PHX	4	0	1	1	-4	2	0	0	0	0	4	0.0
G	35	N. Khabibulin	PHX	4	0	1	1	0	0	0	0	0	0	0	0.0
L	34	Darrin Shannon	PHX	5	0	1	1	-1	4	0	0	0	0	2	0.0
D	44	Norm Maciver	PHX	6	0	1	1	0	2	0	0	0	0	6	0.0
C	18	Mark Janssens	PHX	1	0	0	0	0	2	0	0	0	0	0	0.0
L	33	Jim McKenzie	PHX	1	0	0	0	0	0	0	0	0	0	0	0.0
D	27	Teppo Numminen	PHX	1	0	0	0	0	0	0	0	0	0	0	0.0
R	20	Jim Cummins	PHX	3	0	0	0	0	4	0	0	0	0	2	0.0
G	28	Jim Waite	PHX	4	0	0	0	0	0	0	0	0	0	0	0.0
D	24	Michel Petit	PHX	5	0	0	0	-1	8	0	0	0	0	4	0.0
R	16	* Brad Isbister	PHX	5	0	0	0	-1	2	0	0	0	0	6	0.0
C	14	Mike Stapleton	PHX	6	0	0	0	0	2	0	0	0	0	5	0.0
D	3	Keith Carney	PHX	6	0	0	0	-3	4	0	0	0	0	2	0.0

Goaltending

No.	Goaltender	GPI	Mins	Avg	W	L	EN	SO	GA	SA	S%
28	Jim Waite	4	171	3.86	0	3	0	0	11	97	.887
35	N. Khabibulin	4	185	4.22	2	1	0	0	13	106	.877
	Totals	**6**	**360**	**4.00**	**2**	**4**	**0**	**0**	**24**	**203**	**.882**

Coaching Record

		Regular Season					Playoffs			
Season	Team	Games	W	L	T	%	Games	W	L	%
1984-85	Rochester (AHL)	25	17	6	2	.720	....	....	....	....
1985-86	**Buffalo (NHL)**	**43**	**19**	**19**	**5**	**.500**	....	....	....	....
1987-88	**New Jersey (NHL)**	**30**	**17**	**12**	**1**	**.583**	**20**	**11**	**9**	**.550**
1988-89	**New Jersey (NHL)**	**80**	**27**	**41**	**12**	**.413**	....	....	....	....
1989-90	**New Jersey (NHL)**	**14**	**6**	**6**	**2**	**.500**	....	....	....	....
1993-94	**Washington (NHL)**	**37**	**19**	**12**	**6**	**.595**	**11**	**5**	**6**	**.455**
1994-95	**Washington (NHL)**	**48**	**22**	**18**	**8**	**.542**	**7**	**3**	**4**	**.429**
1995-96	**Washington (NHL)**	**82**	**39**	**32**	**11**	**.543**	**6**	**2**	**4**	**.333**
1996-97	**Washington (NHL)**	**82**	**33**	**40**	**9**	**.457**	....	....	....	....
1997-98	**Phoenix (NHL)**	**82**	**35**	**35**	**12**	**.500**	**6**	**2**	**4**	**.333**
	NHL Totals	**498**	**217**	**215**	**66**	**.502**	**50**	**23**	**27**	**.460**

Club Records

Team

(Figures in brackets for season records are games played; records for fewest points, wins, ties, losses, goals, goals against are for 70 or more games)

Most Points	96	1984-85 (80)
Most Wins	43	1984-85 (80)
Most Ties	15	1991-92 (80)
Most Losses	57	1980-81 (80)
Most Goals	358	1984-85 (80)
Most Goals Against	400	1980-81 (80)
Fewest Points	32	1980-81 (80)
Fewest Wins	9	1980-81 (80)
Fewest Ties	7	1985-86 (80), 1992-93 (84), 1996-97 (82)
Fewest Losses	27	1984-85 (80)
Fewest Goals	214	1979-80 (80)
Fewest Goals Against	227	1997-98 (82)
Longest Winning Streak		
Overall	9	Mar. 8-27/85
Home	9	Dec. 27/92-Jan. 23/93
Away	8	Feb. 25-Apr. 6/85
Longest Undefeated Streak		
Overall	13	Mar. 8-Apr. 7/85 (10 wins, 3 ties)
Home	11	Dec. 23/83-Feb. 5/84 (6 wins, 5 ties)
Away	9	Feb. 25-Apr. 7/85 (8 wins, 1 tie)
Longest Losing Streak		
Overall	10	Nov. 30-Dec. 20/80, Feb. 6-25/94
Home	5	Oct. 29-Nov. 13/93
Away	13	Jan. 26-Apr. 14/94
Longest Winless Streak		
Overall	*30	Oct. 19-Dec. 20/80 (23 losses, 7 ties)
Home	14	Oct. 19-Dec. 14/80 (9 losses, 5 ties)
Away	18	Oct. 10-Dec. 20/80 (16 losses, 2 ties)
Most Shutouts, Season	8	1996-97 (82)
Most PIM, Season	2,278	1987-88 (80)
Most Goals, Game	12	Feb. 25/85 (Wpg. 12 at NYR 5)

Individual

Most Seasons	14	Thomas Steen
Most Games	950	Thomas Steen
Most Goals, Career	379	Dale Hawerchuk
Most Assists, Career	553	Thomas Steen
Most Points, Career	929	Dale Hawerchuk (379G, 550A)
Most PIM, Career	1,338	Laurie Boschman
Most Shutouts, Career	14	Bob Essensa
Longest Consecutive Games Streak	475	Dale Hawerchuk (Dec. 19/82-Dec. 10/88)
Most Goals, Season	76	Teemu Selanne (1992-93)
Most Assists, Season	79	Phil Housley (1992-93)
Most Points, Season	132	Teemu Selanne (1992-93; 76G, 56A)
Most PIM, Season	347	Tie Domi (1993-94)
Most Points, Defenseman, Season	97	Phil Housley (1992-93; 18G, 79A)
Most Points, Center, Season	130	Dale Hawerchuk (1984-85; 53G, 77A)
Most Points, Right Wing, Season	132	Teemu Selanne (1992-93; 76G, 56A)
Most Points, Left Wing, Season	98	Keith Tkachuk (1995-96; 50G, 48A)
Most Points, Rookie, Season	*132	Teemu Selanne (1992-93; 76G, 56A)
Most Shutouts, Season	7	Nikolai Khabibulin (1996-97)
Most Goals, Game	5	Willy Lindstrom (Mar. 2/82), Alexei Zhamnov (Apr. 1/95)
Most Assists, Game	5	Dale Hawerchuk (Mar. 6/84, Mar. 18/89, Mar. 4/90), Phil Housley (Jan. 18/93)
Most Points, Game	6	Willy Lindstrom (Mar. 2/82; 5G, 1A), Dale Hawerchuk (Dec. 14/83; 3G, 3A, Mar. 5/88; 2G, 4A, Mar. 18/89; 1G, 5A), Thomas Steen (Oct. 24/84; 2G, 4A), Ed Olczyk (Dec. 21/91; 2G, 4A)

* NHL Record.

Records include Winnipeg Jets, 1979-80 through 1995-96.

Coaching History

Tom McVie and Bill Sutherland, 1979-80; Tom McVie, Bill Sutherland and Mike Smith, 1980-81; Tom Watt, 1981-82, 1982-83; Tom Watt and Barry Long, 1983-84; Barry Long, 1984-85; Barry Long and John Ferguson, 1985-86; Dan Maloney, 1986-87, 1987-88; Dan Maloney and Rick Bowness, 1988-89; Bob Murdoch, 1989-90, 1990-91; John Paddock, 1991-92 to 1993-94; John Paddock and Terry Simpson, 1994-95; Terry Simpson, 1995-96; Don Hay, 1996-97; Jim Schoenfeld, 1997-98 to date.

Captains' History

Lars-Erik Sjoberg, 1979-80; Morris Lukowich, 1980-81; Dave Christian, 1981-82; Dave Christian and Lucien DeBlois, 1982-83; Lucien DeBlois, 1983-84; Dale Hawerchuk, 1984-85 to 1988-89; Randy Carlyle, Dale Hawerchuk and Thomas Steen (tri-captains), 1989-90; Randy Carlyle and Thomas Steen (co-captains), 1990-91; Troy Murray, 1991-92; Troy Murray and Dean Kennedy, 1992-93; Dean Kennedy and Keith Tkachuk, 1993-94; Keith Tkachuk, 1994-95; Kris King, 1995-96; Keith Tkachuk, 1996-97 to date.

Winnipeg Jets Retired Numbers

9	Bobby Hull	1972-1980
25	Thomas Steen	1981-1995

All-time Record vs. Other Clubs

Regular Season

	At Home							On Road							Total						
	GP	W	L	T	GF	GA	PTS	GP	W	L	T	GF	GA	PTS	GP	W	L	T	GF	GA	PTS
Anaheim	10	5	5	0	40	36	10	10	3	7	0	25	33	6	20	8	12	0	65	69	16
Boston	26	10	14	2	93	98	22	25	4	18	3	81	117	11	51	14	32	5	174	215	33
Buffalo	25	11	12	2	83	87	24	25	2	20	3	61	115	7	50	13	32	5	144	202	31
Calgary	58	27	21	10	232	206	64	59	16	36	7	193	273	39	117	43	57	17	425	479	103
Carolina	27	12	14	1	93	98	25	25	7	12	6	78	97	20	52	19	26	7	171	195	45
Chicago	38	21	13	4	140	125	46	37	10	23	4	107	159	24	75	31	36	8	247	284	70
Colorado	28	10	13	5	106	112	25	29	11	14	4	106	114	26	57	21	27	9	212	226	51
Dallas	37	18	17	2	130	131	38	39	13	21	5	124	160	31	76	31	38	7	254	291	69
Detroit	37	14	12	11	120	117	39	39	13	21	5	133	163	31	76	27	33	16	253	280	70
Edmonton	59	23	32	4	243	268	50	60	18	38	4	200	271	40	119	41	70	8	443	539	90
Florida	5	2	2	1	13	14	5	4	3	1	0	12	10	6	9	5	3	1	25	24	11
Los Angeles	60	29	22	9	253	214	67	57	25	22	10	236	242	60	117	54	44	19	489	456	127
Montreal	25	8	11	6	82	99	22	25	3	22	0	59	131	6	50	11	33	6	141	230	28
New Jersey	26	18	5	3	101	70	39	24	10	8	6	77	76	26	50	28	13	9	178	146	65
NY Islanders	25	8	14	3	77	95	19	26	7	13	6	80	104	20	51	15	27	9	157	199	39
NY Rangers	26	10	13	3	92	94	23	25	8	15	2	96	118	18	51	18	28	5	188	212	41
Ottawa	5	2	2	1	23	20	5	7	5	1	1	29	16	11	12	7	3	2	52	36	16
Philadelphia	25	10	13	2	79	88	22	26	7	19	0	72	115	14	51	17	32	2	151	203	36
Pittsburgh	25	9	13	3	90	91	21	26	8	18	0	76	110	16	51	17	31	3	166	201	37
St. Louis	39	19	14	6	129	120	44	38	11	18	9	113	142	31	77	30	32	15	242	262	75
San Jose	18	11	4	3	68	51	25	16	7	7	2	64	60	16	34	18	11	5	132	111	41
Tampa Bay	6	3	3	0	18	15	6	6	4	2	0	23	18	8	12	7	5	0	41	33	14
Toronto	38	20	12	6	157	137	46	38	21	15	2	148	133	44	76	41	27	8	305	270	90
Vancouver	57	28	21	8	223	215	64	60	17	35	8	178	234	42	117	45	56	16	401	449	106
Washington	26	13	7	6	98	95	32	25	5	17	3	72	110	13	51	18	24	9	170	205	45
Totals	**751**	**341**	**309**	**101**	**2783**	**2696**	**783**	**751**	**238**	**423**	**90**	**2443**	**3121**	**566**	**1502**	**579**	**732**	**191**	**5226**	**5817**	**1349**

Playoffs

	Series	W	L	GP	W	L	T	GF	GA	Last Mtg.	Round	Result
Anaheim	1	0	1	7	3	4	0	17	17	1997	CQF	L 3-4
Calgary	3	2	1	13	7	6	0	45	43	1987	DSF	W 4-2
Detroit	2	0	2	12	4	8	0	28	44	1998	CQF	L 2-4
Edmonton	6	0	6	26	4	22	0	75	120	1990	DSF	L 3-4
St. Louis	1	0	1	4	1	3	0	13	20	1982	DSF	L 1-3
Vancouver	2	0	2	13	5	8	0	34	50	1993	DSF	L 2-4
Totals	**15**	**2**	**13**	**75**	**24**	**51**	**0**	**212**	**294**			

Playoff Results 1998-94

Year	Round	Opponent	Result	GF	GA
1998	CQF	Detroit	L 2-4	18	24
1997	CQF	Anaheim	L 3-4	17	17
1996	CQF	Detroit	L 2-4	10	20
1993	DSF	Vancouver	L 2-4	17	21

Abbreviations: Round: CQF – conference quarter-final; **DSF** – division semi-final.

Calgary totals include Atlanta, 1979-80.
Carolina totals include Hartford, 1979-80 to 1996-97.
Colorado totals include Quebec, 1979-80 to 1994-95.
Dallas totals include Minnesota, 1979-80 to 1992-93.
New Jersey totals include Colorado Rockies, 1979-80 to 1981-82.

1997-98 Results

Oct.	1		Chicago	6-2		3		NY Islanders	2-1
	3	at	St. Louis	2-7		6	at	Detroit	0-2
	5	at	Philadelphia	2-1		8	at	Boston	2-5
	8		Boston	2-3		9	at	Chicago	4-2
	11	at	Colorado	3-3		11		Ottawa	4-4
	13		Chicago	2-1		14		Florida	3-2
	19		San Jose	5-3		20	at	Edmonton	2-6
	21		Anaheim	3-4		21	at	Vancouver	6-1
	23		Washington	3-3		24		Edmonton	2-5
	26		Buffalo	6-1		26		Vancouver	4-2
	29	at	Edmonton	2-3		28	at	Detroit	4-4
	30	at	Calgary	2-4		30	at	Buffalo	3-3
Nov.	2		Calgary	3-1		31	at	Toronto	5-2
	5	at	Montreal	2-4	**Feb.**	3		Chicago	2-4
	6	at	Ottawa	1-4		5		Philadelphia	2-6
	8	at	Toronto	3-0		7		NY Rangers	1-1
	11		Tampa Bay	5-2		25		Colorado	2-4
	13		Montreal	2-5		26	at	Colorado	0-3
	15	at	San Jose	3-2		28	at	Dallas	0-4
	17		Edmonton	6-3	**Mar.**	2		Detroit	1-3
	20	at	Vancouver	2-4		6		Carolina	4-5
	22		Toronto	2-0		8	at	Dallas	1-1
	25		St. Louis	3-2		10		Los Angeles	3-4
	27		Dallas	1-4		12		Dallas	5-4
	29	at	Dallas	2-5		14	at	St. Louis	2-0
Dec.	1	at	Florida	3-2		16	at	Washington	1-2
	3	at	Tampa Bay	1-2		19		Colorado	3-4
	5	at	Carolina	2-2		21	at	Los Angeles	2-3
	6	at	NY Islanders	0-4		22		San Jose	3-1
	8	at	NY Rangers	1-3		24		Toronto	4-2
	10	at	Chicago	3-3		28		New Jersey	0-3
	12		Pittsburgh	2-2	**Apr.**	1	at	Anaheim	5-1
	14		Detroit	3-3		3		Anaheim	6-3
	17		Vancouver	1-5		5	at	New Jersey	2-3
	19	at	Anaheim	6-2		7	at	Pittsburgh	2-1
	20		Toronto	2-3		9	at	Detroit	1-5
	23		Calgary	2-2		11	at	St. Louis	4-3
	26	at	San Jose	4-0		12	at	Chicago	2-1
	27	at	Los Angeles	4-2		14		Detroit	2-1
	29	at	Calgary	5-3		16		Dallas	3-2
Jan.	1		Los Angeles	4-0		18		St. Louis	4-5

Entry Draft Selections 1998-84

1998
Pick
14 Patrick DesRochers
43 Ossi Vaananen
73 Pat O'Leary
100 Ryan Vanbuskirk
115 Jay Leach
116 Josh Blackburn
129 Robert Schnabel
160 Rickard Wallin
187 Erik Westrum
214 Justin Hanson

1997
Pick
43 Juha Gustafsson
96 Scott McCallum
123 Curtis Suter
151 Robert Francz
207 Alex Andreyev
233 Wyatt Smith

1996
Pick
11 Dan Focht
24 Daniel Briere
62 Per-Anton Lundstrom
119 Richard Lintner
139 Robert Esche
174 Trevor Letowski
200 Nicholas Lent
226 Marc-Etienne Hubert

1995
Pick
7 Shane Doan
32 Marc Chouinard
34 Jason Doig
67 Brad Isbister
84 Justin Kurtz
121 Brian Elder
136 Sylvain Daigle
162 Paul Traynor
188 Jaroslav Obsut
189 Frederik Loven
214 Rob Deciantis

1994
Pick
30 Deron Quint
56 Dorian Anneck
58 Tavis Hansen
82 Steve Cheredaryk
108 Craig Mills
143 Steve Vezina
146 Chris Kibermanis
186 Ramil Saifullin
212 Henrik Smangs
238 Mike Mader
264 Jason Issel

1993
Pick
15 Mats Lindgren
31 Scott Langkow
43 Alexei Budayev
79 Ruslan Batyrshin
93 Ravil Gusmanov
119 Larry Courville
145 Michal Grosek
171 Martin Woods
197 Adrian Murray
217 Vladimir Potapov
223 Ilja Stashenkov
228 Harijs Vitolinsh
285 Russell Hewson

1992
Pick
17 Sergei Bautin
27 Boris Mironov
60 Jeremy Stevenson
84 Mark Visheau
132 Alexander Alexeyev
155 Artur Oktyabrev
156 Andrei Raisky
204 Nikolai Khaibulin
228 Yevgeny Garanin
229 Teemu Numminen
252 Andrei Karpovtsev
254 Ivan Vologzhaninov

1991
Pick
5 Aaron Ward
49 Dmitri Filimonov
91 Juha Ylonen
99 Yan Kaminsky
115 Jeff Sebastian
159 Jeff Ricciardi
181 Sean Gauthier
203 Igor Ulanov
225 Jason Jennings
247 Sergei Sorokin

1990
Pick
19 Keith Tkachuk
35 Mike Muller
74 Roman Meluzin
75 Scott Levins
77 Alexei Zhamnov
98 Craig Martin
119 Daniel Jardemyr
140 John Lilley
161 Henrik Andersson
182 Rauli Raitanen
203 Mika Alatalo
224 Sergei Selyanin
245 Keith Morris

1989
Pick
4 Stu Barnes
25 Dan Ratushny
46 Jason Cirone
62 Kris Draper
64 Mark Brownschidle
69 Alain Roy
109 Dan Bylsma
130 Pekka Peltola
131 Doug Evans
151 Jim Solly
172 Stephane Gauvin
193 Joe Larson
214 Bradley Podiak
235 Evgeny Davydov
240 Sergei Kharin

1988
Pick
10 Teemu Selanne
31 Russell Romaniuk
52 Stephane Beauregard
73 Brian Hunt
94 Anthony Joseph
101 Benoit Lebeau
115 Ronald Jones
127 Markus Akerblom
136 Jukka Marttila
157 Mark Smith
178 Mike Helber
199 Pavel Kostichkin
220 Kevin Heise
241 Kyle Galloway

1987
Pick
16 Bryan Marchment
37 Patrik Erickson
79 Don McLennan
96 Ken Gernander
100 Darrin Amundson
121 Joe Harwell
142 Tod Hartje
163 Markku Kyllonen
184 Jim Fernholz
226 Roger Rougelot
247 Hans Goran Elo

1986
Pick
8 Pat Elynuik
29 Teppo Numminen
50 Esa Palosaari
71 Hannu Jarvenpaa
92 Craig Endean
113 Robertson Bateman
155 Frank Furlan
176 Mark Green
197 John Blue
218 Matt Cote
239 Arto Blomsten

1985
Pick
18 Ryan Stewart
39 Roger Ohman
60 Daniel Berthiaume
81 Fredrik Olausson
102 John Borrell
123 Danton Cole
144 Brent Mowery
165 Tom Draper
186 Nevin Kardum
207 Dave Quigley
228 Chris Norton
249 Anssi Melametsa

1984
Pick
30 Peter Douris
68 Chris Mills
72 Sean Clement
93 Scott Schneider
99 Brent Severyn
114 Gary Lorden
135 Luciano Borsato
156 Brad Jones
177 Gord Whitaker
197 Rick Forst
218 Mike Warus
238 Jim Edmonds

General Managers' History

John Ferguson, 1979-80 to 1987-88; John Ferguson and Mike Smith, 1988-89; Mike Smith, 1989-90 to 1992-93; Mike Smith and John Paddock, 1993-94; John Paddock, 1994-95, 1995-96; John Paddock and Bobby Smith, 1996-97; Bobby Smith, 1997-98 to date.

General Manager

SMITH, BOBBY
General Manager, Phoenix Coyotes.
Born in North Sydney, N.S., February 12, 1958.

After 15 outstanding seasons as a National Hockey League player and eight years as the vice president of the NHL Players' Association, Bobby Smith became the Phoenix Coyotes first executive vice president of hockey operations on May 21, 1996.

A product of Ottawa's minor hockey system, in 1978 Smith was named Canadian Major Junior player of the year and was drafted by the Minnesota North Stars first overall in the NHL Entry Draft. A year later, he was named the Calder Trophy winner as the NHL's top rookie after scoring 30 goals and 74 points in his first season. Smith went on to have a remarkable NHL career with Minnesota and Montreal. Smith played in 1,077 games with the North Stars and Canadiens recording (357-679) 1,036 points. He led the North Stars in scoring four of his first five years with the club. His finest season with Minnesota came during the 1981-82 campaign when Smith achieved career highs in games played (80), goals (43), assists (71) and points (114). He was one of three players who played on both of Minnesota's Stanley Cup Finalist teams in 1981 and 1991. Following a trade to Montreal in 1983, Smith played seven seasons with the Canadiens, recording 70-plus points in five of those years. In 1986, he helped guide the Canadiens to a Stanley Cup victory over the Calgary Flames. Smith scored the Stanley Cup game-winning goal in a 4-3 win over Calgary. After 13 playoff seasons and 184 games with Minnesota and Montreal, Smith retired with 64 goals and 96 assists for 160 points, ranking him 12th on the NHL all-time playoff point leaders list. Smith also played in four NHL All-Star Games (1981, 1982, 1989, 1990) during his career.

After retiring from hockey, Smith focused his energy on education and completed two degrees at the Curt Carlson School of Management at the University of Minnesota; a Bachelor of Science (in business) and a Masters of Business Administration.

Bobby and his wife Elizabeth along with their three children Ryan, Megan and Daniel reside in Scottsdale, AZ.

Club Directory

Cellular One Ice Den
9375 E. Bell Road
Scottsdale, AZ 85260
Phone **602/473-5600**
FAX 602/473-5640
Website:
www.phoenixcoyotes.com
Capacity: 16,210

CEO & Governor .... Richard Burke
President & Chief Operating Officer .... Shawn Hunter
General Manager & Alternate Governor .... Bobby Smith
President, Coyotes Ice, LLC .... Mike O'Hearn
Administrative Assistant to the President .... Lisa Mardeusz
Executive Assistant, Hockey Operations .... Lesa Guth

Hockey Operations
Assistant General Manager .... Taylor Burke
Director of Hockey Operations .... Laurence Gilman
Director of Amateur Scouting .... Bill Lesuk
Director of Player Personnel .... Sean Coady
Director of Hockey Information .... Igor Kuperman
Head Coach .... Jim Schoenfeld
Assistant Coach .... John Tortorella
Assistant Coach/Dir. of Player Development .... Gordie Roberts
Goaltending Coach .... Benoit Allaire
Professional Scout .... Tom Kurvers
Amateur Scouts .... Vaughn Karpan, Terry Doran, Connie Broden, Larry Hornung, Blair Mackasey, Glen Sonmor, Paul Coady, Evzen Slansky, Claes Wallin, Boris Yemeljanov
Athletic Therapist .... Gord Hart
Equipment Manager .... Stan Wilson
Massage Therapist .... Jukka Nieminen
Equipment Manager .... Tony DaCosta
Assistant Equipment Manager .... Tony Silva
Strength & Conditioning Coach .... Stieg Theander
Video Coordinator .... Steve Peters
Sports Physiologist .... Dr. Dan Halvorsen
Director of Strength & Conditioning .... Kevin Ziegler
Team Physicians .... Matt Maddox, D.O., Dana Seltzer, M.D.
Team Dentists .... Dr. Rick Lawson, Dr. Lawrence Emmott
Springfield Falcons (AHL) Head Coach .... Dave Farrish
Springfield Falcons (AHL) Assistant Coach .... Ron Wilson

Communications
Director of Media & Player Relations .... Richard Nairn
Assistant Director of Media Relations .... Jeffrey Hecht
Manager of Media Relations & Publications .... Rick Braunstein

Broadcasting
Vice President of Broadcasting .... Mark Hulsey
Broadcasting Manager .... Craig Amazeen
Broadcasting Intern .... Tom Hanny
TV Play-by-Play .... Doug McLeod
TV Color Commentator .... Charlie Simmer
Radio Play-by-Play .... Curt Keilback
Radio Color Commentator .... Jim Johnson

Business Development
Vice President of Business Operations .... Joe Levy
Director of Suite Sales .... Renee Tauer
Suite Sales Coordinator .... Kelly Joyce
Website Coordinator .... John Mellor

Information & Technology
Director of Information & Technology .... Ken Oates

Community Relations
Director of Community Relations/Exec. Dir - Phx. Coyotes Goals For Kids Foundation .... Lori Summers
Event & Program Manager - Phoenix Coyotes Goals For Kids Foundation .... Aimee Zeff
Administrative Assistant .... Marcy Fileccia
Community Relations Intern .... Courtney Gallipo

Corporate Sales & Service
Vice President of Corporate Sales .... Tim Weil
Director of Corporate Sales .... Rip Reynolds
Senior Corporate Account Executive .... Kelly Staley
Corporate Account Executives .... Tara Pisciotta, Jeff Pilcher

Finance & Administration
Chief Financial Officer/VP Administration .... Mark Peterson
Controller .... Joe Leibfried
Assistant Controller .... Larry Silver
Payroll Administrator .... Cheri Sedor
Accounting Assistant .... Julie deWit

Marketing
Senior Vice President of Marketing & Sales .... Brenda Tinnen
Director of Marketing .... Tim McBride
Manager of Fan Development .... Staci Grevillius
Marketing Assistant .... Brett Rogers

Ticket Sales & Service
Director of Ticket Operations .... Bruce Bielenberg
Director of Ticket Sales .... Dave Smrek
Manager of Ticket Operations .... Steve Kunsey
Senior Account Executives .... Brian Tollefson, Jim Willits
Account Executives .... Adam Link, Ann Marie Montaldi, Scott Newhouse, Amy Sun, Brian Wilkinson
Customer Service Representative .... Scott Epp
Receptionist .... Liz Scott

Cellular One Ice Den
Executive Director .... Justin Maloof
Director of Facility Operations .... Don Moffatt
Director of Amateur Hockey .... Harry Mahood
Director of Programming/Skating .... Julie Patterson
Director of Administration .... Mica Berroteran
Coyotes Ice Sports Manager .... Ken Fleger
Coyotes Ice Sports Supervisor .... Paul Warriner

Cable Television Station .... FOX Sports Arizona
Broadcast Television Stations .... KTVK (Ch. 3), KASW (WB-61)
Radio Stations .... KDKB 93.3 FM, KDUS 1060 AM

Pittsburgh Penguins

1997-98 Results: 40W-24L-18T 98PTS. First, Northeast Division

1998-99 Schedule

Month	Day	Date	Opponent
Oct.	Sat.	10	at NY Islanders
	Wed.	14	at New Jersey
	Sat.	17	NY Rangers
	Wed.	21	at Tampa Bay
	Sat.	24	Toronto
	Mon.	26	at Toronto
	Wed.	28	at Calgary
	Fri.	30	at Vancouver
	Sat.	31	at Edmonton
Nov.	Tue.	3	Philadelphia
	Thu.	5	at Ottawa
	Sat.	7	Boston*
	Tue.	10	NY Islanders
	Fri.	13	at New Jersey
	Sat.	14	Florida
	Tue.	17	Philadelphia
	Thu.	19	at Tampa Bay
	Sat.	21	Tampa Bay
	Wed.	25	at Washington
	Fri.	27	NY Rangers
	Sat.	28	at Montreal
Dec.	Tue.	1	Anaheim
	Fri.	4	at Carolina
	Sat.	5	at Boston
	Sat.	12	at St. Louis
	Tue.	15	Tampa Bay
	Wed.	16	at Florida
	Sat.	19	Washington
	Mon.	21	at Toronto
	Tue.	22	Los Angeles
	Sat.	26	Ottawa
	Wed.	30	Florida
Jan.	Sat.	2	at Florida
	Tue.	5	Calgary
	Thu.	7	Carolina
	Sat.	9	St. Louis
	Wed.	13	at Phoenix
	Fri.	15	at San Jose
	Sat.	16	at Los Angeles
	Mon.	18	at Anaheim
	Thu.	21	NY Islanders
	Tue.	26	Carolina
	Thu.	28	Toronto
	Sat.	30	Boston*
	Sun.	31	at Montreal*
Feb.	Tue.	2	Buffalo
	Fri.	5	Florida
	Sun.	7	Detroit*
	Tue.	9	Montreal
	Thu.	11	Vancouver
	Sat.	13	at Nashville
	Mon.	15	Washington
	Wed.	17	at NY Islanders
	Fri.	19	at NY Rangers
	Sun.	21	at Philadelphia
	Mon.	22	Phoenix
	Thu.	25	at Colorado
	Fri.	26	at Dallas
	Sun.	28	at Washington*
Mar.	Wed.	3	Montreal
	Fri.	5	Edmonton
	Sun.	7	Colorado*
	Tue.	9	New Jersey
	Wed.	10	at Carolina
	Sat.	13	Philadelphia*
	Tue.	16	Dallas
	Wed.	17	at Tampa Bay
	Sat.	20	Nashville*
	Sun.	21	at NY Rangers*
	Tue.	23	Chicago
	Thu.	25	at New Jersey
	Sat.	27	Buffalo*
	Sun.	28	at Buffalo*
	Tue.	30	Ottawa
Apr.	Thu.	1	at Ottawa
	Sat.	3	New Jersey*
	Mon.	5	at Buffalo
	Thu.	8	at Philadelphia
	Sun.	11	at Detroit*
	Thu.	15	at Boston
	Sat.	17	NY Islanders*
	Sun.	18	at NY Rangers*

* Denotes afternoon game.

Year-by-Year Record

		Home			Road			Overall							
Season	GP	W	L	T	W	L	T	W	L	T	GF	GA	Pts.	Finished	Playoff Result
1997-98	82	21	10	10	19	14	8	40	24	18	228	188	98	1st, Northeast Div.	Lost Conf. Quarter-Final
1996-97	82	25	11	5	13	25	3	38	36	8	285	280	84	2nd, Northeast Div.	Lost Conf. Quarter-Final
1995-96	82	32	9	0	17	20	4	49	29	4	362	284	102	1st, Northeast Div.	Lost Conf. Championship
1994-95	48	18	5	1	11	11	2	29	16	3	181	158	61	2nd, Northeast Div.	Lost Conf. Semi-Final
1993-94	84	25	9	8	19	18	5	44	27	13	299	285	101	1st, Northeast Div.	Lost Conf. Quarter-Final
1992-93	84	32	6	4	24	15	3	56	21	7	367	268	119	1st, Patrick Div.	Lost Div. Final
1991-92	**80**	**21**	**13**	**6**	**18**	**19**	**3**	**39**	**32**	**9**	**343**	**308**	**87**	**3rd, Patrick Div.**	**Won Stanley Cup**
1990-91	**80**	**25**	**12**	**3**	**16**	**21**	**3**	**41**	**33**	**6**	**342**	**305**	**88**	**1st, Patrick Div.**	**Won Stanley Cup**
1989-90	80	22	15	3	10	25	5	32	40	8	318	359	72	5th, Patrick Div.	Out of Playoffs
1988-89	80	24	13	3	16	20	4	40	33	7	347	349	87	2nd, Patrick Div.	Lost Div. Final
1987-88	80	22	12	6	14	23	3	36	35	9	319	316	81	6th, Patrick Div.	Out of Playoffs
1986-87	80	19	15	6	11	23	6	30	38	12	297	290	72	5th, Patrick Div.	Out of Playoffs
1985-86	80	20	15	5	14	23	3	34	38	8	313	305	76	5th, Patrick Div.	Out of Playoffs
1984-85	80	17	20	3	7	31	2	24	51	5	276	385	53	6th, Patrick Div.	Out of Playoffs
1983-84	80	7	29	4	9	29	2	16	58	6	254	390	38	6th, Patrick Div.	Out of Playoffs
1982-83	80	14	22	4	4	31	5	18	53	9	257	394	45	6th, Patrick Div.	Out of Playoffs
1981-82	80	21	11	8	10	25	5	31	36	13	310	337	75	4th, Patrick Div.	Lost Div. Semi-Final
1980-81	80	21	16	3	9	21	10	30	37	13	302	345	73	3rd, Norris Div.	Lost Prelim. Round
1979-80	80	20	13	7	10	24	6	30	37	13	251	303	73	3rd, Norris Div.	Lost Prelim. Round
1978-79	80	23	12	5	13	19	8	36	31	13	281	279	85	2nd, Norris Div.	Lost Quarter-Final
1977-78	80	16	15	9	9	22	9	25	37	18	254	321	68	4th, Norris Div.	Out of Playoffs
1976-77	80	22	12	6	12	21	7	34	33	13	240	252	81	3rd, Norris Div.	Lost Prelim. Round
1975-76	80	23	11	6	12	22	6	35	33	12	339	303	82	3rd, Norris Div.	Lost Prelim. Round
1974-75	80	25	5	10	12	23	5	37	28	15	326	289	89	3rd, Norris Div.	Lost Quarter-Final
1973-74	78	15	18	6	13	23	3	28	41	9	242	273	65	5th, West Div.	Out of Playoffs
1972-73	78	24	11	4	8	26	5	32	37	9	257	265	73	5th, West Div.	Out of Playoffs
1971-72	78	18	15	6	8	23	8	26	38	14	220	258	66	4th, West Div.	Lost Quarter-Final
1970-71	78	18	12	9	3	25	11	21	37	20	221	240	62	6th, West Div.	Out of Playoffs
1969-70	76	17	13	8	9	25	4	26	38	12	182	238	64	2nd, West Div.	Lost Semi-Final
1968-69	76	12	20	6	8	25	5	20	45	11	189	252	51	5th, West Div.	Out of Playoffs
1967-68	74	15	12	10	12	22	3	27	34	13	195	216	67	5th, West Div.	Out of Playoffs

Teammate Jaromir Jagr led the NHL with 102 points, but Stu Barnes was another key contributor to the Penguins' success in 1997-98. Barnes was tied for third in the NHL with 15 power-play goals and had 30 goals and 65 points overall.

Franchise date: June 5, 1967

EASTERN CONFERENCE

ATLANTIC DIVISION

32nd NHL Season

1998-99 Player Personnel

FORWARDS	HT	WT	S	Place of Birth	Date	1997-98 Club
BARNES, Stu	5-11	174	R	Spruce Grove, Alta.	12/25/70	Pittsburgh
BONIN, Brian	5-10	185	L	St. Paul, MN	11/28/73	Syracuse
BROWN, Rob	5-10	183	L	Kingston, Ont.	4/10/68	Pittsburgh
DOME, Robert	6-	205	L	Skalica, Czech.	1/29/79	Pittsburgh-Syracuse
HLUSHKO, Todd	5-11	185	L	Toronto, Ont.	2/7/70	Calgary-Saint John
HRDINA, Jan	6-0	197	R	Hradec Kralove, Czech.	2/5/76	Syracuse
JAGR, Jaromir	6-2	228	L	Kladno, Czech.	2/15/72	Pittsburgh-Czech.
KESA, Dan	6-0	198	R	Vancouver, B.C.	11/23/71	Detroit (IHL)
KOLKUNOV, Alexei	6-2	185	R	Belgorod, USSR	2/3/77	Soviet Wings
LANG, Robert	6-2	216	R	Teplice, Czech.	12/19/70	Bos-Czech Republic-Pit-Houston
MATHIEU, Alexandre	6-1	176	L	Repentigny, Que.	2/12/79	Halifax
MORAN, Ian	6-0	206	R	Cleveland, OH	8/24/72	Pittsburgh
MOROZOV, Alexei	6-1	180	L	Moscow, USSR	2/16/77	Soviet Wings-Pit-Russia
MOROZOV, Valentin	5-11	176	L	Moscow, USSR	6/1/75	Soviet Wings
NEDVED, Petr	6-3	195	L	Liberec, Czech.	12/9/71	Sparta Praha-Las Vegas
O'BRIEN, Sean	6-1	200	L	Belmont, MA	2/9/72	Fayetteville-Phi (AHL)-Utah
PRONGER, Sean	6-2	205	L	Dryden, Ont.	11/30/72	Anaheim-Pittsburgh
PROTSENKO, Boris	5-11	194	R	Kiev, USSR	8/21/78	Calgary (WHL)
SAVOIA, Ryan	6-1	204	R	Thorold, Ont.	5/6/73	Helsinki-Syracuse-Johnstown
STRAKA, Martin	5-10	175	L	Plzen, Czech.	9/3/72	Pittsburgh-Czech.
TITOV, German	6-1	190	L	Moscow, USSR	10/16/65	Calgary-Russia
WRIGHT, Tyler	5-11	185	R	Canora, Sask.	4/6/73	Pittsburgh
DEFENSEMEN						
BERGKVIST, Stefan	6-2	224	L	Leksand, Sweden	3/10/75	Cleveland
BUTENSCHON, Sven	6-4	215	L	Itzehoe, West Germany	3/22/76	Pittsburgh-Syracuse
DOLLAS, Bobby	6-2	212	L	Montreal, Que.	1/31/65	Anaheim-Edmonton
FERENCE, Andrew	5-10	187	L	Edmonton, Alta.	3/17/79	Portland (WHL)
GRONMAN, Tuomas	6-3	219	R	Viitasaari, Finland	3/22/74	Ind-Pit-Syr-Finland
HATCHER, Kevin	6-3	232	R	Detroit, MI	9/9/66	Pittsburgh-United States
IGNATJEV, Victor	6-4	215	L	Riga, USSR	4/26/70	Long Beach
KASPARAITIS, Darius	5-11	209	L	Elektrenai, USSR	10/16/72	Pittsburgh-Russia
KELLEHER, Chris	6-1	215	L	Cambridge, MA	3/23/75	Boston U.
MELICHAR, Josef	6-3	198	L	Budejovice, Czech.	1/20/79	Tri-City
O'CONNOR, Tom	6-2	190	L	Springfield, MA	1/9/76	U. Mass-Amherst
PRATT, Harlan	6-2	191	R	Fort McMurray, Alta.	12/10/78	Prince Albert-Regina
ROZSIVAL, Michal	6-1	194	R	Vlasim, Czech.	9/3/78	Swift Current
SKRBEK, Pavel	6-3	191	L	Kladno, Czech.	8/9/78	Poldi Kladno-Czech.
SLEGR, Jiri	6-0	207	L	Jihlava, Czech.	5/30/71	Pittsburgh-Czech.
TAMER, Chris	6-1	207	L	Dearborn, MI	11/17/70	Pittsburgh
WERENKA, Brad	6-1	221	L	Two Hills, Alta.	2/12/69	Pittsburgh
WILKINSON, Neil	6-3	194	R	Selkirk, Man.	8/15/67	Pittsburgh
GOALTENDERS	**HT**	**WT**	**C**	**Place of Birth**	**Date**	**1997-98 Club**
AUBIN, Jean-Sebastien	5-11	179	R	Montreal, Que.	7/19/77	Syracuse-Dayton
BARRASSO, Tom	6-3	211	R	Boston, MA	3/31/65	Pittsburgh
HILLIER, Craig	6-1	176	L	Cole Harbour, N.S.	2/28/78	Ottawa (OHL)
SKUDRA, Peter	6-1	182	L	Riga, USSR	4/24/73	Pittsburgh-Houston-Kansas City

Coach

CONSTANTINE, KEVIN
Head Coach, Pittsburgh Penguins.
Born in International Falls, MN, December 27, 1958.

Recognized as one of the bright young coaches in the game, the 39-year-old Constantine was named head coach of the Penguins on June 12, 1997.

The former college goaltender now has three-plus seasons of NHL coaching experience on his resume, including 157 games as head coach of the San Jose Sharks from 1993-95. Constantine led the young Sharks to two playoff appearances during his tenure, and oversaw a much-publicized playoff upset of Detroit in 1994.

Constantine played three seasons as a goaltender at Rensselaer Polytechnic Institute (RPI) from 1978-80 and was a ninth-round draft choice of the Montreal Canadiens in 1978. He had a brief tryout with the Canadiens in 1980.

He began to attract notice as a young coach when he led Rochester to the USHL title in 1987-88. He landed his first professional head coaching job at age 32 in 1991-92 and rewarded his bosses by leading Kansas City to the International Hockey League championship. In two seasons with the Blades, Constantine compiled a record of 102-48-14, prompting a promotion to the NHL and San Jose in 1993-94. He was 55-78-24 in two-plus seasons with the Sharks.

Coaching Record

		Regular Season					Playoffs			
Season	Team	Games	W	L	T	%	Games	W	L	%
1985-86	North Iowa (USHL)	48	17	31	0	.354	....	....	....	....
1987-88	Rochester (USHL)	48	39	7	2	.833	15	9	4	.692*
1991-92	Kansas City (IHL)	82	56	22	4	.707	15	12	3	.800
1992-93	Kansas City (IHL)	82	46	26	10	.622	12	6	6	.500
1993-94	**San Jose (NHL)**	**84**	**33**	**35**	**16**	**.488**	**14**	**7**	**7**	**.500**
1994-95	**San Jose (NHL)**	**48**	**19**	**25**	**4**	**.438**	**11**	**4**	**7**	**.364**
1995-96	**San Jose (NHL)**	**25**	**3**	**18**	**4**	**.250**	....	....	....	....
1997-98	**Pittsburgh (NHL)**	**82**	**40**	**24**	**18**	**.598**	**6**	**2**	**4**	**.333**
	NHL Totals	**239**	**95**	**102**	**42**	**.485**	**31**	**13**	**18**	**.419**

* includes 2 ties.

1997-98 Scoring

* – rookie

Regular Season

Pos	#	Player	Team	GP	G	A	Pts	+/–	PIM	PP	SH	GW	GT	S	%
R	68	Jaromir Jagr	PIT	77	35	67	102	17	64	7	0	8	2	262	13.4
C	10	Ron Francis	PIT	81	25	62	87	12	20	7	0	5	2	189	13.2
C	14	Stu Barnes	PIT	78	30	35	65	15	30	15	1	5	0	196	15.3
D	4	Kevin Hatcher	PIT	74	19	29	48	-3	66	13	1	3	1	169	11.2
C	82	Martin Straka	PIT	75	19	23	42	-1	28	4	3	4	1	117	16.2
R	44	Rob Brown	PIT	82	15	25	40	-1	59	4	0	4	0	172	8.7
D	23	Fredrik Olausson	PIT	76	6	27	33	13	42	2	0	1	0	89	6.7
R	95	* Alexei Morozov	PIT	76	13	13	26	-4	8	2	0	3	0	80	16.3
R	16	Ed Olczyk	PIT	56	11	11	22	-9	35	5	1	1	0	123	8.9
C	20	Robert Lang	BOS	3	0	0	0	1	2	0	0	0	0	2	0.0
			PIT	51	9	13	22	6	14	1	1	2	0	64	14.1
			TOTAL	54	9	13	22	7	16	1	1	2	0	66	13.6
C	12	Sean Pronger	ANA	62	5	15	20	-9	30	1	0	2	0	68	7.4
			PIT	5	1	0	1	-1	2	0	0	1	0	5	20.0
			TOTAL	67	6	15	21	-10	32	1	0	3	0	73	8.2
L	33	Alex Hicks	PIT	58	7	13	20	4	54	0	0	1	1	78	9.0
D	5	Brad Werenka	PIT	71	3	15	18	15	46	2	0	0	0	50	6.0
D	71	Jiri Slegr	PIT	73	5	12	17	10	109	1	1	0	0	131	3.8
C	38	Andreas Johansson	PIT	50	5	10	15	4	20	0	1	0	0	49	10.2
D	11	Darius Kasparaitis	PIT	81	4	8	12	3	127	0	2	0	0	71	5.6
C	15	* Robert Dome	PIT	30	5	2	7	-1	12	1	0	0	0	29	17.2
R	57	* Chris Ferraro	PIT	46	3	4	7	-2	43	0	0	0	0	42	7.1
C	29	Tyler Wright	PIT	82	3	4	7	-3	112	1	0	0	0	46	6.5
R	24	Ian Moran	PIT	37	1	6	7	0	19	0	0	1	0	33	3.0
D	2	Chris Tamer	PIT	79	0	7	7	4	181	0	0	0	0	55	0.0
D	6	Neil Wilkinson	PIT	34	2	4	6	0	24	1	0	0	0	19	10.5
L	18	Garry Valk	PIT	39	2	1	3	-3	33	0	0	0	1	32	6.3
D	42	* Tuomas Gronman	PIT	22	1	2	3	3	25	1	0	1	0	33	3.0
G	35	Tom Barrasso	PIT	63	0	2	2	0	14	0	0	0	0	0	0.0
G	1	* Peter Skudra	PIT	17	0	1	1	0	2	0	0	0	0	0	0.0
D	22	* Sven Butenschon	PIT	8	0	0	0	-1	6	0	0	0	0	4	0.0
G	31	Ken Wregget	PIT	15	0	0	0	0	6	0	0	0	0	0	0.0

Goaltending

No.	Goaltender	GPI	Mins	Avg	W	L	T	EN	SO	GA	SA	S%
1	* Peter Skudra	17	851	1.83	6	4	3	2	0	26	341	.924
35	Tom Barrasso	63	3542	2.07	31	14	13	8	7	122	1556	.922
31	Ken Wregget	15	611	2.75	3	6	2	2	0	28	293	.904
	Totals	**82**	**5022**	**2.25**	**40**	**24**	**18**	**12**	**7**	**188**	**2202**	**.915**

Playoffs

Pos	#	Player	Team	GP	G	A	Pts	+/–	PIM	PP	SH	GW	OT	S	%
R	68	Jaromir Jagr	PIT	6	4	5	9	5	2	1	0	0	0	23	17.4
C	14	Stu Barnes	PIT	6	3	3	6	2	2	0	0	1	0	12	25.0
C	10	Ron Francis	PIT	6	1	5	6	5	2	0	0	0	0	19	5.3
D	71	Jiri Slegr	PIT	6	0	4	4	3	2	0	0	0	0	10	0.0
D	23	Fredrik Olausson	PIT	6	0	3	3	0	2	0	0	0	0	17	0.0
C	20	Robert Lang	PIT	6	0	3	3	-4	2	0	0	0	0	6	0.0
R	16	Ed Olczyk	PIT	6	2	0	2	-3	4	1	1	1	0	6	33.3
C	82	Martin Straka	PIT	6	2	0	2	-3	2	0	1	0	0	10	20.0
R	44	Rob Brown	PIT	6	1	0	1	-4	4	1	0	0	0	10	10.0
D	4	Kevin Hatcher	PIT	6	1	0	1	1	12	1	0	0	0	15	6.7
D	5	Brad Werenka	PIT	6	1	0	1	-3	8	0	1	0	0	3	33.3
D	2	Chris Tamer	PIT	6	0	1	1	-1	4	0	0	0	0	2	0.0
C	29	Tyler Wright	PIT	6	0	1	1	0	4	0	0	0	0	3	0.0
R	95	* Alexei Morozov	PIT	6	0	1	1	-3	2	0	0	0	0	10	0.0
C	38	Andreas Johansson	PIT	1	0	0	0	0	0	0	0	0	0	0	0.0
D	42	* Tuomas Gronman	PIT	1	0	0	0	0	0	0	0	0	0	0	0.0
C	12	Sean Pronger	PIT	5	0	0	0	-1	4	0	0	0	0	4	0.0
D	11	Darius Kasparaitis	PIT	5	0	0	0	-2	8	0	0	0	0	3	0.0
G	35	Tom Barrasso	PIT	6	0	0	0	0	2	0	0	0	0	0	0.0
R	24	Ian Moran	PIT	6	0	0	0	-1	2	0	0	0	0	0	0.0
L	33	Alex Hicks	PIT	6	0	0	0	-5	2	0	0	0	0	6	0.0

Goaltending

No.	Goaltender	GPI	Mins	Avg	W	L	EN	SO	GA	SA	S%
35	Tom Barrasso	6	376	2.71	2	4	1	0	17	171	.901
	Totals	**6**	**379**	**2.85**	**2**	**4**	**1**	**0**	**18**	**172**	**.895**

Club Records

Team

(Figures in brackets for season records are games played; records for fewest points, wins, ties, losses, goals, goals against are for 70 or more games)

Most Points	119	1992-93 (84)
Most Wins	56	1992-93 (84)
Most Ties	20	1970-71 (78)
Most Losses	58	1983-84 (80)
Most Goals	367	1992-93 (84)
Most Goals Against	394	1982-83 (80)
Fewest Points	38	1983-84 (80)
Fewest Wins	16	1983-84 (80)
Fewest Ties	4	1995-96 (82)
Fewest Losses	21	1992-93 (84)
Fewest Goals	182	1969-70 (76)
Fewest Goals Against	188	1997-98 (82)
Longest Winning Streak		
Overall	*17	Mar. 9-Apr. 10/93
Home	11	Jan. 5-Mar. 7/91
Away	7	Mar. 14-Apr. 9/93
Longest Undefeated Streak		
Overall	18	Mar. 9-Apr. 14/93 (17 wins, 1 tie)
Home	20	Nov. 30/74-Feb. 22/75 (12 wins, 8 ties)
Away	8	Mar. 14-Apr. 14/93 (7 wins, 1 tie)
Longest Losing Streak		
Overall	11	Jan. 22-Feb. 10/83
Home	7	Oct. 8-29/83
Away	18	Dec. 23/82-Mar. 4/83
Longest Winless Streak		
Overall	18	Jan. 2-Feb. 10/83 (17 losses, 1 tie)
Home	11	Oct. 8-Nov. 19/83 (9 losses, 2 ties)
Away	18	Oct. 25/70-Jan. 14/71 (11 losses, 7 ties), Dec. 23/82-Mar. 4/83 (18 losses)
Most Shutouts, Season	7	1997-98 (82)
Most PIM, Season	*2,670	1988-89 (80)
Most Goals, Game	12	Mar. 15/75 (Wsh. 1 at Pit. 12), Dec. 26/91 (Tor. 1 at Pit. 12)

Individual

Most Seasons	12	Mario Lemieux
Most Games	753	Jean Pronovost
Most Goals, Career	613	Mario Lemieux
Most Assists, Career	881	Mario Lemieux
Most Points, Career	1,494	Mario Lemieux (613G, 881A)
Most PIM, Career	980	Troy Loney
Most Shutouts, Career	17	Tom Barrasso
Longest Consecutive Games Streak	320	Ron Schock (Oct. 24/73-Apr. 3/77)
Most Goals, Season	85	Mario Lemieux (1988-89)
Most Assists, Season	114	Mario Lemieux (1988-89)
Most Points, Season	199	Mario Lemieux (1988-89; 85G, 114A)
Most PIM, Season	409	Paul Baxter (1981-82)
Most Points, Defenseman, Season	113	Paul Coffey (1988-89; 30G, 83A)
Most Points, Center, Season	199	Mario Lemieux (1988-89; 85G, 114A)
Most Points, Right Wing, Season	*149	Jaromir Jagr (1995-96; 62G, 87A)
Most Points, Left Wing, Season	123	Kevin Stevens (1991-92; 54G, 69A)
Most Points, Rookie, Season	100	Mario Lemieux (1984-85; 43G, 57A)
Most Shutouts, Season	7	Tom Barrasso (1997-98)
Most Goals, Game	5	Mario Lemieux (Three times)
Most Assists, Game	6	Ron Stackhouse (Mar. 8/75), Greg Malone (Nov. 28/79), Mario Lemieux (Three times)
Most Points, Game	8	Mario Lemieux (Oct. 15/88; 3G, 5A, Dec. 31/88; 5G, 3A)

* NHL Record.

Retired Numbers

21	Michel Brière	1969-1970
66	Mario Lemieux	1984-1997

Coaching History

Red Sullivan, 1967-68, 1968-69; Red Kelly, 1969-70 to 1971-72; Red Kelly and Ken Schinkel, 1972-73; Ken Schinkel and Marc Boileau, 1973-74; Marc Boileau, 1974-75; Marc Boileau and Ken Schinkel, 1975-76; Ken Schinkel, 1976-77; John Wilson, 1977-78 to 1979-80; Eddie Johnston, 1980-81 to 1982-83; Lou Angotti, 1983-84; Bob Berry, 1984-85 to 1986-87; Pierre Creamer, 1987-88; Gene Ubriaco, 1988-89; Gene Ubriaco and Craig Patrick, 1989-90; Bob Johnson, 1990-91 to 1991-92; Scotty Bowman, 1991-92, 1992-93; Eddie Johnston, 1993-94 to 1995-96; Eddie Johnston and Craig Patrick, 1996-97; Kevin Constantine, 1997-98 to date.

Captains' History

Ab McDonald, 1967-68; no captain, 1968-69 to 1972-73; Ron Schock, 1973-74 to 1976-77; Jean Pronovost, 1977-78; Orest Kindrachuk, 1978-79 to 1980-81; Randy Carlyle, 1981-82 to 1983-84; Mike Bullard, 1984-85, 1985-86; Mike Bullard and Terry Ruskowski, 1986-87; Dan Frawley and Mario Lemieux, 1987-88; Mario Lemieux, 1988-89 to 1993-94; Ron Francis, 1994-95; Mario Lemieux, 1995-96, 1996-97; Ron Francis, 1997-98.

All-time Record vs. Other Clubs

Regular Season

	At Home							On Road							Total						
	GP	W	L	T	GF	GA	PTS	GP	W	L	T	GF	GA	PTS	GP	W	L	T	GF	GA	PTS
Anaheim	4	3	0	1	17	9	7	4	3	1	0	18	13	6	8	6	1	1	35	22	13
Boston	68	29	27	12	245	253	70	66	13	47	6	195	305	32	134	42	74	18	440	558	102
Buffalo	59	29	16	14	229	194	72	59	13	30	16	159	247	42	118	42	46	30	388	441	114
Calgary	41	21	10	10	154	129	52	41	9	25	7	125	183	25	82	30	35	17	279	312	77
Carolina	34	19	10	5	161	132	43	36	17	17	2	140	142	36	70	36	27	7	301	274	79
Chicago	54	25	23	6	191	180	56	55	8	38	9	147	231	25	109	33	61	15	338	411	81
Colorado	31	15	12	4	134	128	34	28	12	14	2	113	129	26	59	27	26	6	247	257	60
Dallas	59	36	18	5	225	166	77	60	21	33	6	199	225	48	119	57	51	11	424	391	125
Detroit	60	41	15	4	268	179	86	61	11	38	12	166	240	34	121	52	53	16	434	419	120
Edmonton	26	13	12	1	104	118	27	26	5	20	1	90	138	11	52	18	32	2	194	256	38
Florida	10	6	2	2	36	29	14	10	5	5	0	25	27	10	20	11	7	2	61	56	24
Los Angeles	67	38	20	9	252	210	85	65	16	41	8	170	252	40	132	54	61	17	422	462	125
Montreal	70	24	34	12	211	249	60	70	8	54	8	175	341	24	140	32	88	20	386	590	84
New Jersey	64	37	23	4	259	221	78	65	22	31	12	223	248	56	129	59	54	16	482	469	134
NY Islanders	72	34	27	11	276	251	79	71	26	37	8	237	291	60	143	60	64	19	513	542	139
NY Rangers	85	34	39	12	308	324	80	85	33	45	7	291	347	73	170	67	84	19	599	671	153
Ottawa	15	12	0	3	65	28	27	15	10	3	2	54	32	22	30	22	3	5	119	60	49
Philadelphia	90	41	32	17	318	293	99	91	15	69	7	233	399	37	181	56	101	24	551	692	136
Phoenix	26	18	8	0	110	76	36	25	13	9	3	91	90	29	51	31	17	3	201	166	65
St. Louis	59	28	19	12	225	180	68	60	14	40	6	161	235	34	119	42	59	18	386	415	102
San Jose	6	3	2	1	32	20	7	7	6	0	1	45	13	13	13	9	2	2	77	33	20
Tampa Bay	11	7	2	2	49	24	16	10	6	3	1	40	32	13	21	13	5	3	89	56	29
Toronto	57	31	20	6	240	183	68	56	19	26	11	190	229	49	113	50	46	17	430	412	117
Vancouver	46	31	8	7	215	159	69	46	22	21	3	176	167	47	92	53	29	10	391	326	116
Washington	71	37	27	7	278	235	81	74	30	37	7	276	315	67	145	67	64	14	554	550	148
Defunct Clubs	35	22	6	7	148	93	51	34	13	10	11	108	101	37	69	35	16	18	256	194	88
Totals	**1220**	**634**	**412**	**174**	**4750**	**4063**	**1442**	**1220**	**370**	**694**	**156**	**3847**	**4972**	**896**	**2440**	**1004**	**1106**	**330**	**8597**	**9035**	**2338**

Playoffs

	Series	W	L	GP	W	L	T	GF	GA	Last Mtg.	Round	Result
Boston	4	2	2	19	10	9	0	67	62	1992	CF	W 4-0
Buffalo	1	1	0	3	2	1	0	9	9	1979	PR	W 2-1
Chicago	2	1	1	8	4	4	0	23	24	1992	F	W 4-0
Dallas	1	1	0	6	4	2	0	28	16	1991	F	W 4-2
Florida	1	0	1	7	3	4	0	15	20	1996	CF	L 3-4
Montreal	1	0	1	6	2	4	0	15	18	1998	CQF	L 2-4
New Jersey	3	2	1	17	9	8	0	56	47	1995	CSF	L 1-4
NY Islanders	3	0	3	19	8	11	0	58	67	1993	DF	L 3-4
NY Rangers	3	3	0	15	12	3	0	65	45	1996	CSF	W 4-1
Philadelphia	2	0	2	12	4	8	0	37	51	1997	CQF	L 1-4
St. Louis	3	1	2	13	6	7	0	40	45	1981	PR	L 2-3
Toronto	2	0	2	6	2	4	0	13	21	1977	PR	L 1-2
Washington	5	4	1	31	18	13	0	106	103	1996	CQF	W 4-2
Defunct Clubs	1	1	0	4	4	0	0	13	6			
Totals	**32**	**16**	**16**	**166**	**88**	**78**	**0**	**544**	**534**			

Playoff Results 1998-94

Year	Round	Opponent	Result	GF	GA
1998	CQF	Montreal	L 2-4	15	18
1997	CQF	Philadelphia	L 1-4	13	20
1996	CF	Florida	L 3-4	15	20
	CSF	NY Rangers	W 4-1	21	15
	CQF	Washington	W 4-2	21	17
1995	CSF	New Jersey	L 1-4	8	17
	CQF	Washington	W 4-3	29	26
1994	CQF	Washington	L 2-4	12	20

Abbreviations: Round: F – Final; **CF** – conference final; **CQF** – conference quarter-final; **CSF** – conference semi-final; **DF** – division final; **PR** – preliminary round.

Calgary totals include Atlanta, 1972-73 to 1979-80. Carolina totals include Hartford, 1979-80 to 1996-97. Colorado totals include Quebec, 1979-80 to 1994-95. Dallas totals include Minnesota, 1967-68 to 1992-93. New Jersey totals include Kansas City, 1974-75 to 1975-76, and Colorado Rockies, 1976-77 to 1981-82. Phoenix totals include Winnipeg, 1979-80 to 1995-96.

1997-98 Results

Oct.	1		Los Angeles	3-3	Jan.	3		Colorado	4-5
	3	at	Carolina	4-3		6	at	NY Islanders	4-2
	4		Florida	3-5		7	at	New Jersey	1-3
	8		Montreal	0-3		10		New Jersey	4-1
	9	at	Philadelphia	1-3		12	at	Carolina	4-1
	11		Carolina	4-1		14	at	Boston	2-5
	14	at	NY Rangers	1-0		20		Ottawa	0-0
	15	at	Montreal	1-1		22	at	New Jersey	3-2
	17	at	Tampa Bay	4-1		24		Boston	4-2
	19	at	Florida	4-1		26		St. Louis	4-2
	22	at	San Jose	5-2		28	at	Washington	2-2
	24	at	Edmonton	3-4		29	at	Boston	4-2
	25	at	Vancouver	3-2		31		Detroit	4-2
	28	at	Calgary	3-6	Feb.	2		NY Islanders	2-4
Nov.	1		Vancouver	7-6		4		Washington	2-2
	2	at	Chicago	1-3		6	at	Buffalo	2-2
	5		Dallas	2-5		7	at	Ottawa	2-2
	7	at	Detroit	1-1		25	at	Montreal	6-2
	8		Buffalo	2-2		28	at	Boston	2-6
	12		Washington	1-4	Mar.	2		Toronto	3-1
	14	at	NY Rangers	1-3		5		Chicago	2-2
	15	at	Toronto	5-0		7		Philadelphia	6-4
	19		Boston	3-3		8	at	Philadelphia	3-4
	20	at	Ottawa	2-0		11		Calgary	4-1
	22		NY Rangers	4-3		14		Buffalo	2-1
	24		Buffalo	5-1		15	at	Buffalo	0-3
	26		Carolina	3-2		18		Edmonton	4-2
	29		Montreal	6-3		21		Philadelphia	4-3
Dec.	1	at	Montreal	1-0		22	at	Dallas	0-0
	4		New Jersey	0-4		26	at	NY Islanders	3-4
	6		Anaheim	5-2		28		NY Rangers	2-2
	9	at	Los Angeles	2-1		29		Ottawa	1-1
	10	at	Anaheim	3-0	Apr.	1		San Jose	2-3
	12	at	Phoenix	2-2		4	at	Tampa Bay	4-1
	16		Tampa Bay	1-1		5	at	Florida	1-3
	19	at	Colorado	3-3		7		Phoenix	1-2
	20	at	St. Louis	1-4		9	at	Ottawa	1-4
	26	at	Washington	4-1		11		Florida	3-3
	27		Montreal	0-1		15		Tampa Bay	5-1
	29		NY Islanders	5-1		16	at	Carolina	4-1
	31		Carolina	3-2		18		Boston	5-2

Entry Draft Selections 1998-84

1998
Pick
23 Milan Kraft
54 Alexander Zevakhin
80 David Cameron
110 Scott Myers
134 Robert Scuderi
169 Jan Fadmy
196 Joel Scherban
224 Mika Lehto
244 Toby Peterson
254 Matt Hussey

1997
Pick
17 Robert Dome
44 Brian Gaffaney
71 Josef Melichar
97 Alexandre Mathieu
124 Harlan Pratt
152 Petr Havelka
179 Mark Moore
208 Andrew Ference
234 Eric Lind

1996
Pick
23 Craig Hillier
28 Pavel Skrbek
72 Boyd Kane
77 Boris Protsenko
105 Michal Rozsival
150 Peter Bergman
186 Eric Meloche
238 Timo Seikkula

1995
Pick
24 Alexei Morozov
76 J-Sebastien Aubin
102 Oleg Belov
128 Jan Hrdina
154 Alexei Kolkunov
180 Derrick Pyke
206 Sergei Voronov
232 Frank Ivankovic

1994
Pick
24 Chris Wells
50 Richard Park
57 Sven Butenschon
73 Greg Crozier
76 Alexei Krivchenkov
102 Thomas O'Connor
128 Clint Johnson
154 Valentin Morozov
161 Serge Aubin
180 Drew Palmer
206 Boris Zelenko
232 Jason Godbout
258 Mikhail Kazakevich
284 Brian Leitza

1993
Pick
26 Stefan Bergkvist
52 Domenic Pittis
62 Dave Roche
104 Jonas Andersson-Junkka
130 Chris Kelleher
156 Patrick Lalime
182 Sean Selmser
208 Larry McMorran
234 Timothy Harberts
260 Leonid Toropchenko
286 Hans Jonsson

1992
Pick
19 Martin Straka
43 Marc Hussey
67 Travis Thiessen
91 Todd Klassen
115 Philipp De Rouville
139 Artem Kopot
163 Jan Alinc
187 Fran Bussey
211 Brian Bonin
235 Brian Callahan

1991
Pick
16 Markus Naslund
38 Rusty Fitzgerald
60 Shane Peacock
82 Joe Tamminen
104 Robert Melanson
126 Brian Clifford
148 Ed Patterson
170 Peter McLaughlin
192 Jeff Lembke
214 Chris Tok
236 Paul Dyck
258 Pasi Huura

1990
Pick
5 Jaromir Jagr
61 Joe Dziedzic
68 Chris Tamer
89 Brian Farrell
107 Ian Moran
110 Denis Casey
130 Mika Valila
131 Ken Plaquin
145 Pat Neaton
152 Petteri Koskimaki
173 Ladislav Karabin
194 Timothy Fingerhut
215 Michael Thompson
236 Brian Bruininks

1989
Pick
16 Jamie Heward
37 Paul Laus
58 John Brill
79 Todd Nelson
100 Tom Nevers
121 Mike Markovich
126 Mike Needham
142 Patrick Schafhauser
163 Dave Shute
184 Andrew Wolf
205 Greg Hagen
226 Scott Farrell
247 Jason Smart

1988
Pick
4 Darrin Shannon
25 Mark Major
62 Daniel Gauthier
67 Mark Recchi
88 Greg Andrusak
130 Troy Mick
151 Jeff Blaeser
172 Rob Gaudreau
193 Donald Pancoe
214 Cory Laylin
235 Darren Stolk

1987
Pick
5 Chris Joseph
26 Richard Tabaracci
47 Jamie Leach
68 Risto Kurkinen
89 Jeff Waver
110 Shawn McEachern
131 Jim Bodden
152 Jiri Kucera
173 Jack MacDougall
194 Daryn McBride
215 Mark Carlson
236 Ake Lilljebjorn

1986
Pick
4 Zarley Zalapski
25 Dave Capuano
46 Brad Aitken
67 Rob Brown
88 Sandy Smith
109 Jeff Daniels
130 Doug Hobson
151 Steve Rohlik
172 Dave McLlwain
193 Kelly Cain
214 Stan Drulia
235 Rob Wilson

1985
Pick
2 Craig Simpson
23 Lee Giffin
58 Bruce Racine
86 Steve Gotaas
107 Kevin Clemens
114 Stuart Marston
128 Steve Titus
149 Paul Stanton
170 Jim Paek
191 Steve Shaunessy
212 Doug Greschuk
233 Gregory Choules

1984
Pick
1 Mario Lemieux
9 Doug Bodger
16 Roger Belanger
64 Mark Teevens
85 Arto Javanainen
127 Tom Ryan
169 John Del Col
189 Steve Hurt
210 Jim Steen
230 Mark Ziliotto

General Manager

PATRICK, CRAIG
General Manager, Pittsburgh Penguins. Born in Detroit, MI, May 20, 1946.

Known for his calm and patient management style, Patrick has led the Penguins to two Stanley Cup championships, one Presidents' Trophy title and five division championships since taking over as g.m. on Dec. 5, 1989.

Patrick also has served two stints as interim coach of the Penguins, most recently over the final 20 games of the 1996-97 season.

A member of one of hockey's most famous families — including grandfather Lester, father Lynn and uncle Muzz — Patrick played collegiate hockey at the University of Denver and captained the Pioneers to the NCAA championship in 1969. He played eight NHL seasons with five different teams, registering 72 goals and 163 points in 401 games before retiring in 1979. He made the transition to management and coaching when he landed the dual role of assistant coach and assistant g.m. of the 1980 U.S. Olympic Team that won the gold medal at Lake Placid.

Patrick joined the New York Rangers organization as director of operations in 1980 and became the youngest general manager in club history on June 14, 1981. He served in that capacity through the 1985-86 season, leading his team to the playoffs every year.

Prior to joining the Penguins, Patrick spent two years as director of athletics and recreation at the University of Denver.

NHL Coaching Record

		Regular Season					Playoffs			
Season	Team	Games	W	L	T	%	Games	W	L	%
1980-81	NY Rangers	60	26	23	11	.525	14	7	7	.500
1984-85	NY Rangers	35	11	22	2	.343	3	0	3	.000
1989-90	Pittsburgh	54	22	26	6	.463	....	....	....	....
1996-97	Pittsburgh	20	7	10	3	.425	5	1	4	.200
	NHL Totals	**169**	**66**	**81**	**22**	**.456**	**22**	**8**	**14**	**.364**

Club Directory

Civic Arena
66 Mario Lemieux Place
Pittsburgh, PA 15219
Phone **412/642-1300**
FAX 412/642-1859
Media Relations FAX
412/642-1322
Capacity: 16,958

Ownership	Roger M. Marino, Howard L. Baldwin
Administration	
Vice President, General Counsel	Greg Cribbs
Director of Planning and Design	Scott Baldwin
Director of Development	William R. Craig
Executive Assistants	Elaine Heufelder, Amy Hirsh, Pam Douglas
Hockey Operations	
Executive VP/General Manager	Craig Patrick
Assistant General Manager	Ed Johnston
Head Coach	Kevin Constantine
Assistant Coaches	Mike Eaves, Don Jackson, Troy Ward
Goaltending Coach & Scout	Gilles Meloche
Pro Scout	Rick Kehoe
Head Scout	Greg Malone
Scouts	Les Binkley, Herb Brooks, Charlie Hodge, Mark Kelley, Ralph Cox
Strength & Conditioning Coach	John Welday
Equipment Manager	Steve Latin
Trainer	TBA
Executive Assistant	Tracey Botsford
Assistant Equipment Manager	Paul Flati
Minor League Coach	Glenn Patrick
Communications	
Vice President, Communications	Tom McMillan
Director of Media Relations	Steve Bovino
Assistant Director, Media Relations	Brian Coe
Director of Public Relations	Cindy Himes
Director of Entertainment	Paul Barto
Manager, Community Relations	Renee Petrichevich
Finance	
Vice President, Finance & Administration	Bob Vogel
Controller	Kevin Hart
Accounting Staff	Tawni Love, Troy Ussack
Ticketing	
Director of Ticketing	Mark Anderson
Director, Premium Seating	Rich Hixon
Manager, Premium Services	Terri Smith
Group Sales	Mike Guiffre, Scott Bollheimer
Box Office Manager	Carol Coulson
Manager, Ticketing Operations	Allison Quigley
Senior Ticket Sales Manager	James Santilli
Manager, Inside Ticket Sales	Chad Slencak
Manager, Customer Services	Laura Bryer
Ticketing Staff	Heather Abramovitz, Daneen Napolitano
Assistant Manager, Premium Services	Michelle Follen
Premium Seating Account Executive	Doug Smoyer
Account Executives	Bonnie Golinski, Brennan Mault, Ted Miller, Chuck Pukansky
Advertising	
Vice President, Marketing	David Soltesz
Managers, Corporate Sponsorships	Arden Robbins, Taylor Baldwin, Kimberly Bogesdorfer, Mimi York
Director of Event Marketing	Kevin Saundry
Marketing Manager	Marie Mays
Assistant Marketing Manager	Amy Gillespie
Marketing and Sales Administrator	Barb Pilarski
Iceoplex at Southpointe	
Director	Harry Sanders
Director of Skating	Igor Novodran
Director of Hockey Programs	Joanne DeFazio
Director of Operations	Paul McKean
Director of Off-Ice Events	Bobby Dyer
Assistant Director of Off-Ice Events	Ryan Mance
Administrative Assistants	Tersea Kauffman, Becky Krynock
Operations Staff	Robert Arquillo
General Information	
Home Ice	Civic Arena
Dimensions of Rink	200 feet by 85 feet
Team Colors	Black, gold and white
TV Station	Fox Sports Pittsburgh
TV Announcers	Mike Lange, Paul Steigerwald
Flagship Radio Station	WDVE 102.5 FM
Radio Announcers	Matt McConnell, Peter Taglianetti
Minor League Affiliates	Syracuse Crunch (AHL), Wilkes-Barre/Scranton (AHL-1999), Wheeling Nailers (ECHL)

General Managers' History

Jack Riley, 1967-68 to 1969-70; Red Kelly, 1970-71; Red Kelly and Jack Riley, 1971-72; Jack Riley, 1972-73; Jack Riley and Jack Button, 1973-74; Jack Button, 1974-75; Wren Blair, 1975-76; Wren Blair and Baz Bastien, 1976-77; Baz Bastien, 1977-78 to 1982-83; Ed Johnston, 1983-84 to 1987-88; Tony Esposito, 1988-89; Tony Esposito and Craig Patrick, 1989-90; Craig Patrick, 1990-91 to date.

St. Louis Blues

1997-98 Results: 45W-29L-8T 98PTS. Third, Central Division

Year-by-Year Record

		Home			Road			Overall							
Season	GP	W	L	T	W	L	T	W	L	T	GF	GA	Pts.	Finished	Playoff Result
1997-98	82	26	10	5	19	19	3	45	29	8	256	204	98	3rd, Central Div.	Lost Conf. Semi-Final
1996-97	82	17	20	4	19	15	7	36	35	11	236	239	83	4th, Central Div.	Lost Conf. Quarter-Final
1995-96	82	15	17	9	17	17	7	32	34	16	219	248	80	4th, Central Div.	Lost Conf. Semi-Final
1994-95	48	16	6	2	12	9	3	28	15	5	178	135	61	2nd, Central Div.	Lost Conf. Quarter-Final
1993-94	84	23	11	8	17	22	3	40	33	11	270	283	91	4th, Central Div.	Lost Conf. Quarter-Final
1992-93	84	22	13	7	15	23	4	37	36	11	282	278	85	4th, Norris Div.	Lost Div. Final
1991-92	80	25	12	3	11	21	8	36	33	11	279	266	83	3rd, Norris Div.	Lost Div. Semi-Final
1990-91	80	24	9	7	23	13	4	47	22	11	310	250	105	2nd, Norris Div.	Lost Div. Final
1989-90	80	20	15	5	17	19	4	37	34	9	295	279	83	2nd, Norris Div.	Lost Div. Final
1988-89	80	22	11	7	11	24	5	33	35	12	275	285	78	2nd, Norris Div.	Lost Div. Final
1987-88	80	18	17	5	16	21	3	34	38	8	278	294	76	2nd, Norris Div.	Lost Div. Final
1986-87	80	21	12	7	11	21	8	32	33	15	281	293	79	1st, Norris Div.	Lost Div. Semi-Final
1985-86	80	23	11	6	14	23	3	37	34	9	302	291	83	3rd, Norris Div.	Lost Conf. Championship
1984-85	80	21	12	7	16	19	5	37	31	12	299	288	86	1st, Norris Div.	Lost Div. Semi-Final
1983-84	80	23	14	3	9	27	4	32	41	7	293	316	71	2nd, Norris Div.	Lost Div. Final
1982-83	80	16	16	8	9	24	7	25	40	15	285	316	65	4th, Norris Div.	Lost Div. Semi-Final
1981-82	80	22	14	4	10	26	4	32	40	8	315	349	72	3rd Norris Div.	Lost Div. Final
1980-81	80	29	7	4	16	11	13	45	18	17	352	281	107	1st, Smythe Div.	Lost Quarter-Final
1979-80	80	20	13	7	14	21	5	34	34	12	266	278	80	2nd, Smythe Div.	Lost Prelim. Round
1978-79	80	14	20	6	4	30	6	18	50	12	249	348	48	3rd, Smythe Div.	Out of Playoffs
1977-78	80	12	20	8	8	27	5	20	47	13	195	304	53	4th, Smythe Div.	Out of Playoffs
1976-77	80	22	13	5	10	26	4	32	39	9	239	276	73	1st, Smythe Div.	Lost Quarter-Final
1975-76	80	20	12	8	9	25	6	29	37	14	249	290	72	3rd, Smythe Div.	Lost Prelim. Round
1974-75	80	23	13	4	12	18	10	35	31	14	269	267	84	2nd, Smythe Div.	Lost Prelim. Round
1973-74	78	16	16	7	10	24	5	26	40	12	206	248	64	6th, West Div.	Out of Playoffs
1972-73	78	21	11	7	11	23	5	32	34	12	233	251	76	4th, West Div.	Lost Quarter-Final
1971-72	78	17	17	5	11	22	6	28	39	11	208	247	67	3rd, West Div.	Lost Semi-Final
1970-71	78	23	7	9	11	18	10	34	25	19	223	208	87	2nd, West Div.	Lost Quarter-Final
1969-70	76	24	9	5	13	18	7	37	27	12	224	179	86	1st, West Div.	Lost Final
1968-69	76	21	8	9	16	17	5	37	25	14	204	157	88	1st, West Div.	Lost Final
1967-68	74	18	12	7	9	19	9	27	31	16	177	191	70	3rd, West Div.	Lost Final

1998-99 Schedule

Oct.	Sat.	10	at Boston		Thu.	21	Toronto
	Mon.	12	at NY Rangers		Tue.	26	at San Jose
	Fri.	16	at Detroit		Thu.	28	at Vancouver
	Sat.	17	NY Islanders		Sat.	30	at Calgary
	Thu.	22	at Ottawa	**Feb.**	Mon.	1	at Edmonton
	Sat.	24	Calgary		Thu.	4	New Jersey
	Tue.	27	at Philadelphia		Sat.	6	Anaheim
	Thu.	29	Detroit		Mon.	8	at Florida
	Sat.	31	Anaheim		Wed.	10	at Tampa Bay
Nov.	Wed.	4	at Anaheim		Thu.	11	San Jose
	Thu.	5	at Los Angeles		Sat.	13	Edmonton
	Sat.	7	at San Jose		Mon.	15	Vancouver*
	Tue.	10	Chicago		Thu.	18	Florida
	Wed.	11	at Detroit		Sat.	20	Nashville
	Sat.	14	Nashville		Mon.	22	Los Angeles
	Thu.	19	at Nashville		Wed.	24	Chicago
	Sat.	21	Dallas		Fri.	26	at Calgary
	Tue.	24	Nashville		Sun.	28	at Chicago
	Fri.	27	San Jose*	**Mar.**	Tue.	2	at Nashville
	Sat.	28	Washington		Thu.	4	Toronto
Dec.	Fri.	4	at Colorado		Sun.	7	at Dallas*
	Sat.	5	Colorado		Tue.	9	Calgary
	Tue.	8	Buffalo		Thu.	11	Montreal
	Sat.	12	Pittsburgh		Sat.	13	Edmonton*
	Mon.	14	at Colorado		Sun.	14	at Chicago*
	Tue.	15	at Dallas		Tue.	16	Philadelphia
	Thu.	17	Phoenix		Thu.	18	Phoenix
	Sat.	19	Los Angeles		Sat.	20	Ottawa
	Tue.	22	at NY Islanders		Mon.	22	Carolina
	Wed.	23	at New Jersey		Thu.	25	at Vancouver
	Sat.	26	Detroit		Fri.	26	at Edmonton
	Mon.	28	at Detroit		Sun.	28	at Chicago*
Jan.	Fri.	1	at Nashville*	**Apr.**	Thu.	1	Tampa Bay
	Sat.	2	NY Rangers		Sat.	3	Dallas*
	Mon.	4	Vancouver		Mon.	5	at Toronto
	Thu.	7	Chicago		Wed.	7	at Washington
	Sat.	9	at Pittsburgh		Fri.	9	Detroit
	Mon.	11	at Montreal		Sun.	11	Colorado*
	Wed.	13	at Buffalo		Wed.	14	at Anaheim
	Sat.	16	at Colorado*		Thu.	15	at Phoenix
	Tue.	19	at Phoenix		Sun.	18	at Los Angeles*

* Denotes afternoon game.

Franchise date: June 5, 1967

CENTRAL DIVISION

32nd NHL Season

Named captain of the Blues prior to the 1997-98 campaign, Chris Pronger went on to establish himself as one of the best defensemen in the game. He led the league with a plus/minus rating of +47 and was nominated for the Norris Trophy.

1998-99 Player Personnel

FORWARDS	HT	WT	S	Place of Birth	Date	1997-98 Club
BARTECKO, Lubos	6-1	200	L	Kezmarok, Czechoslovakia	7/14/76	Worcester
CAMPBELL, Jim	6-2	185	R	Worcester, MA	4/3/73	St. Louis
CHASE, Kelly	5-11	193	R	Porcupine Plain, Sask.	10/25/67	St. Louis
CONROY, Craig	6-2	198	R	Potsdam, NY	9/4/71	St. Louis
CORSO, Daniel	5-9	155	L	Montreal, Que.	4/3/78	Victoriaville-Canada
COURTNALL, Geoff	6-1	195	L	Duncan, B.C.	8/18/62	St. Louis
DEMITRA, Pavol	6-0	189	L	Dubnica, Czech.	11/29/74	St. Louis
EASTWOOD, Mike	6-3	205	R	Ottawa, Ont.	7/1/67	NY Rangers-St. Louis
HANDZUS, Michal	6-3	191	L	Banska Bystrica, Czech.	3/11/77	Worcester
HECHT, Jochen	6-1	180	L	Mannheim, Germany	6/21/77	Mannheim-Germany
KENADY, Chris	6-2	195	R	Mound, MN	4/10/73	St. Louis-Worcester
LOW, Reed	6-4	220	R	Moose Jaw, Sask.	6/21/76	Worcester-Baton Rouge
MAYERS, Jamal	6-0	190	R	Toronto, Ont.	10/24/74	Worcester
NAGY, Ladislav	5-11	183	L	Saca, Czechoslovakia	6/1/79	HC Kosice
NASH, Tyson	6-0	185	L	Edmonton, Alta.	3/11/75	Syracuse
PELLERIN, Scott	5-11	180	L	Shediac, N.B.	1/9/70	St. Louis
PICARD, Michel	5-11	190	L	Beauport, Que.	11/7/69	Grand Rapids-St. Louis
PODKONICKY, Andrej	6-0	174	L	Zvolen, Czech.	5/9/78	Portland (WHL)-Slovakia
POESCHEK, Rudy	6-2	218	R	Kamloops, B.C.	9/29/66	St. Louis
REASONER, Marty	6-1	185	L	Rochester, NY	2/26/77	Boston College
RHEAUME, Pascal	6-1	200	L	Quebec, Que.	6/21/73	St. Louis
ROY, Stephane	5-10	173	L	Ste-Martine, Que.	1/26/76	Worcester
TURGEON, Pierre	6-1	195	L	Rouyn, Que.	8/28/69	St. Louis
TWIST, Tony	6-1	220	L	Sherwood Park, Alta.	5/9/68	St. Louis
YAKE, Terry	5-11	190	R	New Westminster, B.C.	10/22/68	St. Louis
YOUNG, Scott	6-0	190	R	Clinton, MA	10/1/67	Anaheim
DEFENSEMEN						
BERGEVIN, Marc	6-1	197	L	Montreal, Que.	8/11/65	St. Louis
DIENER, Derek	6-5	197	L	Burnaby, B.C.	7/13/76	Worcester
FITZPATRICK, Rory	6-1	205	R	Rochester, NY	1/11/75	Worcester
GILL, Todd	6-0	180	L	Cardinal, Ont.	11/9/65	San Jose-St. Louis
HARLTON, Tyler	6-3	201	L	Pense, Sask.	1/11/76	Michigan State
HORACEK, Jan	6-3	198	R	Benesov, Czech.	5/22/79	Moncton
MacINNIS, Al	6-2	196	R	Inverness, N.S.	7/11/63	St. Louis-Canada
McALPINE, Chris	6-0	210	R	Roseville, MN	12/1/71	St. Louis
PERSSON, Ricard	6-2	205	L	Ostersund, Sweden	8/24/69	St. Louis-Worcester
PRONGER, Chris	6-5	220	L	Dryden, Ont.	10/10/74	St. Louis-Canada
RIVERS, Jamie	6-0	190	L	Ottawa, Ont.	3/16/75	St. Louis
SALVADOR, Bryce	6-2	194	L	Brandon, Man.	2/11/76	Worcester
SMITH, Matt	6-6	215	R	Kent, England	12/23/76	U-Mass.-Amherst-Worcester
WIDMER, Jason	6-0	200	L	Calgary, Alta.	8/1/73	Kentucky
ZABRANSKY, Libor	6-3	196	L	Brno, Czech.	11/25/73	St. Louis-Worcester

GOALTENDERS	HT	WT	C	Place of Birth	Date	1997-98 Club
FUHR, Grant	5-9	190	R	Spruce Grove, Alta.	9/28/62	St. Louis
JOHNSON, Brent	6-1	175	L	Farmington, MI	3/12/77	Worcester
McLENNAN, Jamie	6-0	190	L	Edmonton, Alta.	6/30/71	St. Louis
PARENT, Rich	6-3	195	L	Montreal, Que.	1/12/73	StL-Manitoba-Detroit (IHL)

Coaching History

Lynn Patrick and Scotty Bowman, 1967-68; Scotty Bowman, 1968-69, 1969-70; Al Arbour and Scotty Bowman, 1970-71; Sid Abel, Bill McCreary and Al Arbour, 1971-72; Al Arbour and Jean-Guy Talbot, 1972-73; Jean-Guy Talbot and Lou Angotti, 1973-74; Lou Angotti, Lynn Patrick and Garry Young, 1974-75; Garry Young, Lynn Patrick and Leo Boivin, 1975-76; Emile Francis, 1976-77; Leo Boivin and Barclay Plager, 1977-78; Barclay Plager, 1978-79; Barclay Plager and Red Berenson, 1979-80; Red Berenson, 1980-81; Red Berenson and Emile Francis, 1981-82; Emile Francis and Barclay Plager, 1982-83; Jacques Demers, 1983-84 to 1985-86; Jacques Martin, 1986-87, 1987-88; Brian Sutter, 1988-89 to 1991-92; Bob Plager and Bob Berry, 1992-93; Bob Berry, 1993-94; Mike Keenan, 1994-95, 1995-96; Mike Keenan, Jim Roberts and Joel Quenneville, 1996-97; Joel Quenneville, 1997-98 to date.

Coach

QUENNEVILLE, JOEL
Head Coach, St. Louis Blues.
Born in Windsor, Ont., September 15, 1958.

Joel Quenneville was named head coach on January 6, 1997, becoming the 19th head coach in Blues history. His first game in St. Louis was on January 7, 1997. In his first full season behind the bench in 1997-98, coach "Q" guided the Blues to the league's fourth-best record (45-29-8) and to the second round of the Stanley Cup Playoffs.

Prior to joining the Blues the former NHL defenseman spent three seasons with the Colorado Avalanche organization as an assistant coach. He was instrumental in the Avalanche's drive for their first Stanley Cup championship during the 1995-96 season.

Prior to joining the Avalanche he was head coach for the Springfield Indians of the American Hockey League during the 1993-94 season. He retired from hockey after the 1991-92 season after serving the St. John's Maple Leafs (AHL) as a player/coach. Quenneville played 13 NHL seasons and finished with 803 career games played, 54 goals, 136 assists and 705 penalty minutes. His best years on the ice were spent with Hartford where he earned most valuable defenseman honors in 1985 and 1986. He played an integral part in helping Hartford win a divisional championship in 1986-87.

Quenneville and his wife Elizabeth have three children: Dylan, Lily and Anna.

Coaching Record

		Regular Season					Playoffs			
Season	**Team**	**Games**	**W**	**L**	**T**	**%**	**Games**	**W**	**L**	**%**
1996-97	**St. Louis (NHL)**	**40**	**18**	**15**	**7**	**.538**	**6**	**2**	**4**	**.333**
1997-98	**St. Louis (NHL)**	**82**	**45**	**29**	**8**	**.598**	**10**	**6**	**4**	**.600**
	NHL Totals	**122**	**63**	**44**	**15**	**.578**	**16**	**8**	**8**	**.500**

1997-98 Scoring

* – rookie

Regular Season

Pos	#	Player	Team	GP	G	A	Pts	+/–	PIM	PP	SH	GW	GT	S	%
R	16	Brett Hull	STL	66	27	45	72	-1	26	10	0	6	0	211	12.8
C	77	Pierre Turgeon	STL	60	22	46	68	13	24	6	0	4	0	140	15.7
L	14	Geoff Courtnall	STL	79	31	31	62	12	94	6	0	5	0	189	16.4
D	28	Steve Duchesne	STL	80	14	42	56	9	32	5	1	1	0	153	9.2
L	38	Pavol Demitra	STL	61	22	30	52	11	22	4	4	6	1	147	15.0
D	2	Al MacInnis	STL	71	19	30	49	6	80	9	1	2	0	227	8.4
C	22	Craig Conroy	STL	81	14	29	43	20	46	0	3	1	0	118	11.9
R	10	Jim Campbell	STL	76	22	19	41	0	55	7	0	6	1	147	15.0
D	44	Chris Pronger	STL	81	9	27	36	47	180	1	0	2	0	145	6.2
D	5	Todd Gill	S.J.	64	8	13	21	-13	31	4	0	1	0	100	8.0
			STL	11	5	4	9	2	10	3	0	1	0	22	22.7
			TOTAL	75	13	17	30	-11	41	7	0	2	0	122	10.7
L	33	Scott Pellerin	STL	80	8	21	29	14	62	1	1	0	0	96	8.3
R	23	Blair Atcheynum	STL	61	11	15	26	5	10	0	1	3	0	103	10.7
R	27	Terry Yake	STL	65	10	15	25	1	38	3	1	4	0	60	16.7
C	9	Darren Turcotte	STL	62	12	6	18	6	26	3	0	1	0	75	16.0
L	25 *	Pascal Rheaume	STL	48	6	9	15	4	35	1	0	0	0	45	13.3
C	32	Mike Eastwood	NYR	48	5	5	10	-2	16	0	0	0	0	34	14.7
			STL	10	1	0	1	0	6	0	0	1	0	4	25.0
			TOTAL	58	6	5	11	-2	22	0	0	1	0	38	15.8
D	19	Chris McAlpine	STL	54	3	7	10	14	36	0	0	0	0	35	8.6
D	4	Marc Bergevin	STL	81	3	7	10	-2	90	0	0	0	0	40	7.5
L	34	Michel Picard	STL	16	1	8	9	3	29	0	0	0	0	19	5.3
D	20	Rudy Poeschek	STL	50	1	7	8	-5	64	0	0	0	0	29	3.4
R	39	Kelly Chase	STL	67	4	3	7	10	231	0	0	1	0	29	13.8
D	6 *	Jamie Rivers	STL	59	2	4	6	5	36	1	0	1	0	53	3.8
L	18	Tony Twist	STL	60	1	1	2	-4	105	0	0	0	0	17	5.9
R	12 *	Christopher Kenady	STL	5	0	2	2	1	0	0	0	0	0	3	0.0
G	31	Grant Fuhr	STL	58	0	2	2	0	6	0	0	0	0	0	0.0
D	43	Libor Zabransky	STL	6	0	1	1	-3	6	0	0	0	0	2	0.0
D	7	Ricard Persson	STL	1	0	0	0	0	0	0	0	0	0	0	0.0
G	30 *	Rich Parent	STL	1	0	0	0	0	0	0	0	0	0	0	0.0
G	29	Jamie McLennan	STL	30	0	0	0	0	4	0	0	0	0	0	0.0

Goaltending

No.	Goaltender	GPI	Mins	Avg	W	L	T	EN	SO	GA	SA	S%
30	* Rich Parent	1	12	0.00	0	0	0	0	0	0	1	.000
29	Jamie McLennan	30	1658	2.17	16	8	2	1	2	60	618	.903
31	Grant Fuhr	58	3274	2.53	29	21	6	5	3	138	1354	.898
	Totals	**82**	**4970**	**2.46**	**45**	**29**	**8**	**6**	**5**	**204**	**1979**	**.897**

Playoffs

Pos	#	Player	Team	GP	G	A	Pts	+/–	PIM	PP	SH	GW	OT	S	%
R	10	Jim Campbell	STL	10	7	3	10	-1	12	4	0	2	0	23	30.4
L	14	Geoff Courtnall	STL	10	2	8	10	-2	18	1	0	0	0	24	8.3
D	44	Chris Pronger	STL	10	1	9	10	-2	26	0	0	0	0	24	4.2
C	77	Pierre Turgeon	STL	10	4	4	8	-5	2	2	0	0	0	27	14.8
D	2	Al MacInnis	STL	8	2	6	8	1	12	1	0	0	0	27	7.4
R	16	Brett Hull	STL	10	3	3	6	-3	2	1	0	1	0	32	9.4
L	38	Pavol Demitra	STL	10	3	3	6	-3	2	0	0	0	0	32	9.4
D	5	Todd Gill	STL	10	2	2	4	-3	10	1	1	0	0	16	12.5
L	25 *	Pascal Rheaume	STL	10	1	3	4	0	8	1	0	0	0	10	10.0
D	28	Steve Duchesne	STL	10	0	4	4	-8	6	0	0	0	0	28	0.0
R	27	Terry Yake	STL	10	2	1	3	-3	6	2	0	1	0	6	33.3
C	22	Craig Conroy	STL	10	1	2	3	-1	8	0	0	1	0	17	5.9
L	33	Scott Pellerin	STL	10	0	2	2	1	10	0	0	0	0	10	0.0
C	32	Mike Eastwood	STL	3	1	0	1	-1	0	0	0	1	0	4	25.0
D	4	Marc Bergevin	STL	10	0	1	1	-1	8	0	0	0	0	6	0.0
G	31	Grant Fuhr	STL	10	0	1	1	0	2	0	0	0	0	0	0.0
G	29	Jamie McLennan	STL	1	0	0	0	0	0	0	0	0	0	0	0.0
D	20	Rudy Poeschek	STL	2	0	0	0	-2	6	0	0	0	0	0	0.0
R	39	Kelly Chase	STL	7	0	0	0	-2	23	0	0	0	0	0	0.0
C	9	Darren Turcotte	STL	10	0	0	0	-4	2	0	0	0	0	5	0.0
R	23	Blair Atcheynum	STL	10	0	0	0	-2	2	0	0	0	0	13	0.0
D	19	Chris McAlpine	STL	10	0	0	0	-1	16	0	0	0	0	5	0.0

Goaltending

No.	Goaltender	GPI	Mins	Avg	W	L	EN	SO	GA	SA	S%
31	Grant Fuhr	10	616	2.73	6	4	2	0	28	297	.906
29	Jamie McLennan	1	14	4.29	0	0	0	0	1	4	.750
	Totals	**10**	**631**	**2.95**	**6**	**4**	**2**	**0**	**31**	**303**	**.898**

Captains' History

Al Arbour, 1967-68 to 1969-70; Red Berenson and Barclay Plager, 1970-71; Barclay Plager, 1971-72 to 1975-76; no captain, 1976-77; Red Berenson, 1977-78; Barry Gibbs, 1978-79; Brian Sutter, 1979-80 to 1987-88; Bernie Federko, 1988-89; Rick Meagher, 1989-90; Scott Stevens, 1990-91; Garth Butcher, 1991-92; Brett Hull, 1992-93 to 1994-95; Brett Hull, Shayne Corson and Wayne Gretzky, 1995-96; no captain, 1996-97; Chris Pronger, 1997-98 to date.

Club Records

Team

(Figures in brackets for season records are games played; records for fewest points, wins, ties, losses, goals, goals against are for 70 or more games)

Most Points	**107**	1980-81 (80)
Most Wins	**47**	1990-91 (80)
Most Ties	**19**	1970-71 (78)
Most Losses	**50**	1978-79 (80)
Most Goals	**352**	1980-81 (80)
Most Goals Against	**349**	1981-82 (80)
Fewest Points	**48**	1978-79 (80)
Fewest Wins	**18**	1978-79 (80)
Fewest Ties	**7**	1983-84 (80)
Fewest Losses	**18**	1980-81 (80)
Fewest Goals	**177**	1967-68 (74)
Fewest Goals Against	**157**	1968-69 (76)
Longest Winning Streak		
Overall	**7**	Jan. 21-Feb. 3/88, Mar. 19-31/91, Oct. 3-18/97
Home	**9**	Jan. 26-Feb. 26/91
Away	**4**	Four times
Longest Undefeated Streak		
Overall	**12**	Nov. 10-Dec. 8/68 (5 wins, 7 ties)
Home	**11**	Feb. 12-Mar. 19/69 (5 wins, 6 ties), Feb. 7-Mar. 29/75 (9 wins, 2 ties), Oct. 7-Nov. 26/93 (7 wins, 4 ties)
Away	**7**	Dec. 9-26/87 (4 wins, 3 ties)
Longest Losing Streak		
Overall	**7**	Nov. 12-26/67, Feb. 12-25/89
Home	**5**	Nov. 19-Dec. 6/77
Away	**10**	Jan. 20-Mar. 8/82
Longest Winless Streak		
Overall	**12**	Jan. 17-Feb. 15/78 (10 losses, 2 ties)
Home	**7**	Dec. 28/82-Jan. 25/83 (5 losses, 2 ties)
Away	**17**	Jan. 23-Oct. 9/74 (13 losses, 4 ties)
Most Shutouts, Season	**13**	1968-69 (76)
Most PIM, Season	**2,041**	1990-91 (80)
Most Goals, Game	**11**	Feb. 26/94 (St.L. 11 at Ott. 1)

Individual

Most Seasons	**13**	Bernie Federko
Most Games	**927**	Bernie Federko
Most Goals, Career	**527**	Brett Hull
Most Assists, Career	**721**	Bernie Federko
Most Points, Career	**1,073**	Bernie Federko (352G, 721A)
Most PIM, Career	**1,786**	Brian Sutter
Most Shutouts, Career	**16**	Glenn Hall
Longest Consecutive Games Streak	**662**	Garry Unger (Feb. 7/71-Apr. 8/79)
Most Goals, Season	**86**	Brett Hull (1990-91)
Most Assists, Season	**90**	Adam Oates (1990-91)
Most Points, Season	**131**	Brett Hull (1990-91) (86G, 45A)
Most PIM, Season	**306**	Bob Gassoff (1975-76)
Most Points, Defenseman, Season	**78**	Jeff Brown (1992-93; 25G, 53A)
Most Points, Center, Season	**115**	Adam Oates (1990-91; 25G, 90A)
Most Points, Right Wing, Season	**131**	Brett Hull (1990-91; 86G, 45A)
Most Points, Left Wing, Season	**102**	Brendan Shanahan (1993-94; 52G, 50A)
Most Points, Rookie, Season	**73**	Jorgen Pettersson (1980-81; 37G, 36A)
Most Shutouts, Season	**8**	Glenn Hall (1968-69)
Most Goals, Game	**6**	Red Berenson (Nov. 7/68)
Most Assists, Game	**5**	Brian Sutter (Nov. 22/88), Bernie Federko (Feb. 27/88), Adam Oates (Jan. 26/91)
Most Points, Game	**7**	Red Berenson (Nov. 7/68; 6G, 1A), Garry Unger (Mar. 13/71; 3G, 4A)

Retired Numbers

3	Bob Gassoff	1973-1977
8	Barclay Plager	1967-1977
11	Brian Sutter	1976-1988
24	Bernie Federko	1976-1989

All-time Record vs. Other Clubs

Regular Season

	At Home							On Road							Total						
	GP	W	L	T	GF	GA	PTS	GP	W	L	T	GF	GA	PTS	GP	W	L	T	GF	GA	PTS
Anaheim	10	5	4	1	35	32	11	10	6	3	1	32	28	13	20	11	7	2	67	60	24
Boston	55	23	23	9	175	192	55	54	12	34	8	146	234	32	109	35	57	17	321	426	87
Buffalo	46	26	14	6	168	120	58	47	12	29	6	145	193	30	93	38	43	12	313	313	88
Calgary	51	23	20	8	179	159	54	50	21	25	4	149	175	46	101	44	45	12	328	334	100
Carolina	26	16	8	2	104	82	34	27	14	11	2	86	85	30	53	30	19	4	190	167	64
Chicago	98	47	34	17	326	307	111	102	30	58	14	310	396	74	200	77	92	31	636	703	185
Colorado	28	19	6	3	123	88	41	28	11	14	3	91	103	25	56	30	20	6	214	191	66
Dallas	106	58	29	19	388	300	135	103	38	46	19	311	349	95	209	96	75	38	699	649	230
Detroit	94	52	27	15	340	262	119	93	38	39	16	296	336	92	187	90	66	31	636	598	211
Edmonton	32	13	15	4	118	129	30	32	12	17	3	118	127	27	64	25	32	7	236	256	57
Florida	4	3	1	0	13	9	6	4	2	1	1	10	8	5	8	5	2	1	23	17	11
Los Angeles	66	42	15	9	249	171	93	66	24	33	9	194	236	57	132	66	48	18	443	407	150
Montreal	54	12	27	15	140	189	39	55	9	39	7	148	243	25	109	21	66	22	288	432	64
New Jersey	41	25	9	7	180	128	57	42	17	18	7	124	136	41	83	42	27	14	304	264	98
NY Islanders	43	17	17	9	158	143	43	44	10	24	10	110	170	30	87	27	41	19	268	313	73
NY Rangers	58	23	26	9	173	188	55	56	6	44	6	125	236	18	114	29	70	15	298	424	73
Ottawa	5	2	2	1	15	17	5	5	4	1	0	24	9	8	10	6	3	1	39	26	13
Philadelphia	62	24	31	7	180	197	55	62	11	41	10	142	247	32	124	35	72	17	322	444	87
Phoenix	38	18	11	9	142	113	45	39	14	19	6	120	129	34	77	32	30	15	262	242	79
Pittsburgh	60	40	14	6	235	161	86	59	19	28	12	180	225	50	119	59	42	18	415	386	136
San Jose	15	12	3	0	58	31	24	12	10	2	0	44	30	20	27	22	5	0	102	61	44
Tampa Bay	7	6	1	0	28	19	12	8	3	3	2	25	24	8	15	9	4	2	53	43	20
Toronto	94	55	26	13	329	262	123	94	26	58	10	273	356	62	188	81	84	23	602	618	185
Vancouver	59	33	18	8	220	177	74	60	28	25	7	190	182	63	119	61	43	15	410	359	137
Washington	36	15	13	8	149	122	38	35	12	20	3	103	129	27	71	27	33	11	252	251	65
Defunct Clubs	32	25	4	3	131	55	53	33	11	10	12	95	100	34	65	36	14	15	226	155	87
Totals	**1220**	**634**	**398**	**188**	**4356**	**3653**	**1456**	**1220**	**400**	**642**	**178**	**3591**	**4486**	**978**	**2440**	**1034**	**1040**	**366**	**7947**	**8139**	**2434**

Playoffs

	Series	W	L	GP	W	L	T	GF	GA	Last Mtg.	Round	Result
Boston	2	0	2	8	0	8	0	15	48	1972	SF	L 0-4
Buffalo	1	0	1	3	1	2	0	8	7	1976	PR	L 1-2
Calgary	1	0	1	7	3	4	0	22	28	1986	CF	L 3-4
Chicago	9	2	7	45	18	27	0	129	166	1993	DSF	W 4-0
Dallas	10	5	5	56	26	30	0	162	174	1994	CQF	L 0-4
Detroit	6	2	4	35	15	20	0	92	111	1998	CQF	L 2-4
Los Angeles	2	2	0	8	8	0	0	32	13	1998	CSF	W 4-0
Montreal	3	0	3	12	0	12	0	14	42	1977	QF	L 0-4
NY Rangers	1	0	1	6	2	4	0	22	29	1981	QF	L 2-4
Philadelphia	2	2	0	11	8	3	0	34	20	1969	QF	W 4-0
Pittsburgh	3	2	1	13	7	6	0	45	40	1981	PR	W 3-2
Toronto	5	3	2	31	17	14	0	88	90	1996	CQF	W 4-2
Vancouver	1	0	1	7	3	4	0	27	27	1995	CQF	L 3-4
Winnipeg	1	1	0	4	3	1	0	20	13	1982	DSF	W 3-1
Totals	**47**	**19**	**28**	**246**	**111**	**135**	**0**	**710**	**808**			

Playoff Results 1998-94

Year	Round	Opponent	Result	GF	GA
1998	CSF	Detroit	L 2-4	13	23
	CQF	Los Angeles	W 4-0	16	8
1997	CQF	Detroit	L 2-4	12	13
1996	CSF	Detroit	L 3-4	16	22
	CQF	Toronto	W 4-2	21	15
1995	CQF	Vancouver	L 3-4	27	27
1994	CQF	Dallas	L 0-4	10	16

Abbreviations: Round: CF – conference final; **CQF** – conference quarter-final; **CSF** – conference semi-final; **DSF** – division semi-final; **SF** – semi-final; **QF** – quarter-final; **PR** – preliminary round.

Calgary totals include Atlanta, 1972-73 to 1979-80. Carolina totals include Hartford, 1979-80 to 1996-97.
Colorado totals include Quebec, 1979-80 to 1994-95. Dallas totals include Minnesota, 1967-68 to 1992-93.
New Jersey totals include Kansas City, 1974-75 to 1975-76, and Colorado Rockies, 1976-77 to 1981-82.
Phoenix totals include Winnipeg, 1979-80 to 1995-96.

1997-98 Results

Oct.	1		Buffalo	1-3		29	at	Washington	2-4
	3		Phoenix	7-2		31	at	Detroit	2-5
	4	at	Dallas	2-1	**Jan.**	3		Calgary	4-3
	9		Los Angeles	3-2		6	at	San Jose	5-1
	11		Florida	5-3		7	at	Vancouver	3-2
	13		Carolina	3-1		10	at	Calgary	5-1
	17	at	Chicago	2-0		12	at	Edmonton	1-2
	18		NY Rangers	5-3		14		Dallas	1-2
	20	at	Detroit	3-3		20	at	NY Rangers	1-3
	22	at	Carolina	3-4		22		NY Islanders	3-3
	23		Vancouver	4-1		24	at	Chicago	4-5
	25		Washington	5-2		26	at	Pittsburgh	2-4
	29	at	Philadelphia	3-2		27	at	Buffalo	3-3
	30		Colorado	2-2		29		Toronto	2-0
Nov.	1		San Jose	2-0		31		Dallas	6-3
	3		Philadelphia	1-5	**Feb.**	4	at	Toronto	2-3
	6	at	Chicago	1-2		5	at	Boston	3-1
	8	at	Colorado	1-4		7		Detroit	4-1
	10	at	Dallas	7-1		26	at	San Jose	1-3
	13		Boston	4-2		28	at	Los Angeles	5-2
	15		Detroit	5-2	**Mar.**	1	at	Anaheim	6-2
	17	at	Toronto	3-2		3		Chicago	5-3
	20		Edmonton	0-3		5		Montreal	4-0
	22		Anaheim	0-2		7		Dallas	2-1
	25	at	Phoenix	2-3		9	at	Vancouver	4-0
	27		Los Angeles	2-2		11	at	Colorado	2-3
	29	at	NY Islanders	2-4		14		Phoenix	0-2
Dec.	2	at	New Jersey	3-1		21	at	Edmonton	0-2
	4		Toronto	4-3		22	at	Calgary	3-5
	6		Calgary	4-3		26		Tampa Bay	3-2
	8		Vancouver	5-1		28		Detroit	3-2
	10	at	Montreal	3-4		30		San Jose	6-2
	11	at	Ottawa	2-1	**Apr.**	1	at	Toronto	6-4
	13		Edmonton	1-4		4		Colorado	4-1
	15		Ottawa	1-3		7	at	Detroit	3-5
	18		New Jersey	4-4		9		Chicago	3-2
	20		Pittsburgh	4-1		11		Phoenix	3-4
	22	at	Tampa Bay	2-2		12	at	Dallas	3-4
	23	at	Florida	3-2		16	at	Los Angeles	7-3
	26		Chicago	1-4		18	at	Phoenix	5-4
	27		Anaheim	5-5		19	at	Anaheim	5-3

Entry Draft Selections 1998-84

1998
Pick
24 Christian Backman
41 Maxim Linnik
83 Matt Walker
157 Brad Voth
170 Andrei Trochinsky
197 Brad Twordik
225 Yevgeny Pastukh
255 John Pohl

1997
Pick
40 Tyler Rennette
86 Didier Tremblay
98 Jan Horacek
106 Jame Pollock
149 Nicholas Bilotto
177 Ladislav Nagy
206 Bobby Haglund
232 Dmitri Plekhanov
244 Marek Ivan

1996
Pick
14 Marty Reasoner
67 Gordie Dwyer
95 Jonathan Zukiwsky
97 Andrei Petrakov
159 Stephen Wagner
169 Daniel Corso
177 Reed Low
196 Andrei Podkonicky
203 Anthony Hutchins
229 Konstantin Shafranov

1995
Pick
49 Jochen Hecht
75 Scott Roche
101 Michal Handzus
127 Jeff Ambrosio
153 Denis Hamel
179 J-Luc Grand-Pierre
205 Derek Bekar
209 Libor Zabransky

1994
Pick
68 Stephane Roy
94 Tyler Harlton
120 Edvin Frylen
172 Roman Vopat
198 Steve Noble
224 Marc Stephan
250 Kevin Harper
276 Scott Fankhouser

1993
Pick
37 Maxim Bets
63 Jamie Rivers
89 Jamal Mayers
141 Todd Kelman
167 Mike Buzak
193 Eric Boguniecki
219 Michael Grier
245 Libor Prochazka
271 Alexander Vasilevsky
275 Christer Olsson

1992
Pick
38 Igor Korolev
62 Vitali Karamnov
64 Vitali Prokhorov
86 Lee J. Leslie
134 Bob Lachance
158 Ian LaPerriere
160 Lance Burns
180 Igor Boldin
182 Nicholas Naumenko
206 Todd Harris
230 Yuri Gunko
259 Wade Salzman

1991
Pick
27 Steve Staios
64 Kyle Reeves
65 Nathan Lafayette
87 Grayden Reid
109 Jeff Callinan
131 Bruce Gardiner
153 Terry Hollinger
175 Christopher Kenady
197 Jed Fiebelkorn
219 Chris MacKenzie
241 Kevin Rappana
263 Mike Veisor

1990
Pick
33 Craig Johnson
54 Patrice Tardif
96 Jason Ruff
117 Kurtis Miller
138 Wayne Conlan
180 Parris Duffus
201 Steve Widmeyer
222 Joe Hawley
243 Joe Fleming

1989
Pick
9 Jason Marshall
31 Rick Corriveau
55 Denny Felsner
93 Daniel Laperriere
114 David Roberts
124 Derek Frenette
135 Jeff Batters
156 Kevin Plager
177 John Roderick
198 John Valo
219 Brian Lukowski

1988
Pick
9 Rod Brind' Amour
30 Adrien Plavsic
51 Rob Fournier
72 Jaan Luik
105 Dave Lacouture
114 Dan Fowler
135 Matt Hayes
156 John McCoy
177 Tony Twist
198 Bret Hedican
219 Heath DeBoer
240 Michael Francis

1987
Pick
12 Keith Osborne
54 Kevin Miehm
59 Robert Nordmark
75 Darin Smith
82 Andy Rymsha
117 Rob Robinson
138 Todd Crabtree
159 Guy Hebert
180 Robert Dumas
201 David Marvin
207 Andy Cesarski
222 Dan Rolfe
243 Ray Savard

1986
Pick
10 Jocelyn Lemieux
31 Mike Posma
52 Tony Hejna
73 Glen Featherstone
87 Michael Wolak
115 Mike O'Toole
136 Andy May
157 Randy Skarda
178 Martyn Ball
199 Rod Thacker
220 Terry MacLean
234 Bill Butler
241 David O'Brien

1985
Pick
37 Herb Raglan
44 Nelson Emerson
54 Ned Desmond
100 Dan Brooks
121 Rich Burchill
138 Pat Jablonski
159 Scott Brickey
180 Jeff Urban
201 Vince Guidotti
222 Ron Saatzer
243 Dave Jecha

1984
Pick
26 Brian Benning
32 Tony Hrkac
50 Toby Ducolon
53 Robert Dirk
56 Alan Perry
71 Graham Herring
92 Scott Paluch
113 Steve Tuttle
134 Cliff Ronning
148 Don Porter
155 Jim Vesey
176 Daniel Jomphe
196 Tom Tilley
217 Mark Cupolo
237 Mark Lanigan

General Managers' History

Lynn Patrick, 1967-68; Scotty Bowman, 1968-69 to 1970-71; Lynn Patrick, 1971-72; Sid Abel, 1972-73; Charles Catto, 1973-74; Gerry Ehman, 1974-75; Dennis Ball, 1975-76; Emile Francis, 1976-77 to 1982-83; Ron Caron, 1983-84 to 1993-94; Mike Keenan, 1994-95, 1995-96; Mike Keenan and Ron Caron, 1996-97; Larry Pleau, 1997-98 to date.

General Manager

PLEAU, LARRY
General Manager, St. Louis Blues. Born in Lynn, MA, June 29, 1947.

Larry Pleau was named general manager on June 9, 1997, becoming the tenth person to hold that position in team history.

Pleau joined the Blues after spending eight seasons with the New York Rangers organization, most recently as vice president of player personnel. He joined the Rangers in 1989 as assistant general manager of player development. During Pleau's tenure in New York, the Rangers drafted NHL stars Sergei Zubov, Doug Weight, Alexei Kovalev, Niklas Sundstrom, Todd Marchant and Sergei Nemchinov, along with Corey Hirsch, Daniel Goneau and Mattias Norstrom. Prior to joining the Rangers, Pleau spent 17 seasons with the Hartford Whalers organization as a player, assistant coach, head coach, general manager and minor league general manager and head coach. He was also instrumental in drafting Ray Ferraro, Ron Francis, Kevin Dineen and Ulf Samuelsson while a member of the Whalers organization.

Pleau played three seasons with the Montreal Canadiens (1969-1972) in the National Hockey League before being the first player signed by the Hartford Whalers of the World Hockey Association. He was a center/left wing for the Whalers from 1972 until his retirement in 1979. He played in 468 regular season games for Hartford, accumulating 157 goals and 215 assists for 372 points. He also played for the 1968 United States Olympic Team, the 1969 U.S. National Team and for Team USA in the 1976 Canada Cup tournament.

Pleau and his wife, Wendy, have a son, Steve, and a daughter, Shannon.

Club Directory

Kiel Center
1401 Clark Avenue
St. Louis, MO 63103-2709
Phone **314/622-2500**
FAX 314/622-2582
Website: www.stlouisblues.com
Capacity: 19,260

Owner	Clark Enterprises
Chairman of the Board	Jerry Ritter
President & CEO	Mark Sauer
Senior Vice President & General Manager	Larry Pleau
Senior Vice President, Marketing & Communications	Jim Woodcock
Senior Vice President, Kiel Center	Roger Dixon
Vice President, Sales	Bruce Affleck
Vice President, Operations	Fred Corsi
Vice President, Human Resources	David Coverstone
Vice President, Food & Merchandise	Dennis Petrullo
Vice President, Finance & Hockey Administration	Jarry Jasiek
Vice President, Marketing	JoAnn Miles
Advisor to the President	Ron Caron
Hockey Operations	
General Manager	Larry Pleau
Assistant General Manager	John Ferguson Jr.
Head Coach	Joel Quenneville
Assistant Coaches	Mike Kitchen, Jim Roberts
Golatending Coordinator	Keith Allain
Director of Pro Scouting	Bob Plager
Pro Scouts	Rick Meagher, Bill Dineen
Director of Amateur Scouting	Teddy Hampson
Special Assignment	Jack Evans, Peter Stastny
Amateur Scouts	Don Boyd, Anders Steen, Bill Terry
Part-time Scouts	Jim Bzdel, Dick Cherry, Wayne Mundey, Miroslav Termer, Ken Williamson, Georgi Zhuravlev, Paul Guay
Director of Team Services	Michael Caruso
Video Coordinator	Jamie Kompon
Executive Assistant to the General Manager	Donna Lembke
Head Coach, Worcester IceCats	Greg Gilbert
Associate Coach, Worcester IceCats	Steve Pleau
Medical Staff	
Athletic Trainer	Ray Barile
Massage Therapist	Jeff Cope
Strength & Conditioning Coordinator	Robb Rogers
Equipment Manager	Bert Godin
Assistant Equipment Manager	Eric Bechtol
Equipment Assistant	Greg Cable
Orthopedic Surgeon	Dr. Jerome Gilden, Dr. Rick Wright, Dr. Matt Matava
Internist	Dr. Aaron Birenbaum, Dr. William Birenbaum
General Surgery	Dr. Michael Brunt
Dentist	Dr. Glenn Edwards
Optometrist	Dr. N. Rex Ghormley
Communications/Marketing	
Director of Communications	Jeff Trammel
Assistant Director of Communications	Tony Ommen
Communications Assistant	Joe Campbell
Manager of Publications	Renee St. John
Director of Corporate Sponsorships	Chris Arger
Manager of Corporate Sales & Promotions	Rob Rixford
Manager of Community Relations/ Fan Development	Yvette Horwitz
Manager of Amateur Hockey & Community Programs	Dan Kelly
Marketing/Public Relations Assistant	Donna Quirk
Receptionists	Leslie Simon, Marian Brooks
Finance/Sales	
Director of Finance	Jeff Horstmann
Sales Representatives	Wes Edwards, Jill Mann, Jennifer Foppe, Paula Barnes, Jill Serve, Kari Palmer, Jennifer Gruner
Accounting Staff	Jim Bergman, Craig Bryant, Fred Giles, Phil Siddle
Radio Stations	KMOX 1120 am
TV Stations	Fox Sports Midwest, KPLR-TV, WBII

NHL Coaching Record

		Regular Season					Playoffs			
Season	Team	Games	W	L	T	%	Games	W	L	%
1980-81	Hartford	20	6	12	2	.350	....	....	....	....
1981-82	Hartford	80	21	41	18	.375	....	....	....	....
1982-83	Hartford	18	4	13	1	.250	....	....	....	....
1987-88	Hartford	26	13	13	0	.500	6	2	4	.333
1988-89	Hartford	80	37	38	5	.494	4	0	4	.000
	NHL Totals	**224**	**81**	**117**	**26**	**.420**	**10**	**2**	**8**	**.200**

San Jose Sharks

1997-98 Results: 34W-38L-10T 78PTS. Fourth, Pacific Division

Year-by-Year Record

		Home			Road			Overall							
Season	GP	W	L	T	W	L	T	W	L	T	GF	GA	Pts.	Finished	Playoff Result
1997-98	82	17	19	5	17	19	5	34	38	10	210	216	78	4th, Pacific Div.	Lost Conf. Quarter-Final
1996-97	82	14	23	4	13	24	4	27	47	8	211	278	62	7th, Pacific Div.	Out of Playoffs
1995-96	82	12	26	3	8	29	4	20	55	7	252	357	47	7th, Pacific Div.	Out of Playoffs
1994-95	48	10	13	1	9	12	3	19	25	4	129	161	42	3rd, Pacific Div.	Lost Conf. Semi-Final
1993-94	84	19	13	10	14	22	6	33	35	16	252	265	82	3rd, Pacific Div.	Lost Conf. Semi-Final
1992-93	84	8	33	1	3	38	1	11	71	2	218	414	24	6th, Smythe Div.	Out of Playoffs
1991-92	80	14	23	3	3	35	2	17	58	5	219	359	39	6th, Smythe Div.	Out of Playoffs

1998-99 Schedule

Oct.	Fri.	9	at Calgary
	Sat.	10	Calgary
	Sun.	18	Boston
	Tue.	20	at Philadelphia
	Thu.	22	at Chicago
	Sat.	24	at Dallas
	Wed.	28	Phoenix
	Thu.	29	at Colorado
	Sat.	31	Tampa Bay
Nov.	Wed.	4	Dallas
	Fri.	6	at Anaheim
	Sat.	7	St. Louis
	Tue.	10	Nashville
	Thu.	12	Carolina
	Wed.	18	Los Angeles
	Fri.	20	Phoenix
	Sat.	21	NY Rangers
	Mon.	23	at Dallas
	Wed.	25	at Carolina
	Fri.	27	at St. Louis*
	Sun.	29	at Detroit*
Dec.	Wed.	2	Dallas
	Fri.	4	Detroit
	Sun.	6	Anaheim
	Wed.	9	at Dallas
	Thu.	10	at Nashville
	Sat.	12	Washington
	Tue.	15	NY Islanders
	Thu.	17	Nashville
	Sat.	19	Colorado
	Wed.	23	at Edmonton
	Sat.	26	Vancouver
	Mon.	28	Philadelphia
	Wed.	30	at Los Angeles
Jan.	Sat.	2	at NY Islanders*
	Mon.	4	at NY Rangers
	Tue.	5	at New Jersey
	Thu.	7	at Nashville
	Sat.	9	Buffalo
	Mon.	11	Los Angeles
	Wed.	13	Dallas
	Fri.	15	Pittsburgh
	Sat.	16	Calgary
	Mon.	18	New Jersey
	Thu.	21	Edmonton
	Tue.	26	St. Louis
	Sat.	30	at Colorado
Feb.	Mon.	1	Chicago
	Thu.	4	at Phoenix
	Sat.	6	at Los Angeles
	Mon.	8	at Phoenix
	Wed.	10	at Chicago
	Thu.	11	at St. Louis
	Sat.	13	at Tampa Bay
	Mon.	15	at Florida
	Wed.	17	at Detroit
	Fri.	19	at Buffalo
	Sat.	20	at Washington
	Wed.	24	Vancouver
	Fri.	26	at Anaheim
	Sat.	27	Anaheim
Mar.	Mon.	1	at Calgary
	Wed.	3	at Vancouver
	Sat.	6	Chicago*
	Tue.	9	Phoenix
	Fri.	12	Detroit
	Sat.	13	Ottawa
	Wed.	17	Florida
	Sat.	20	at Boston*
	Mon.	22	at Montreal
	Wed.	24	at Toronto
	Fri.	26	at Ottawa
	Sun.	28	at Edmonton*
	Wed.	31	Colorado
Apr.	Fri.	2	at Vancouver
	Sat.	3	Vancouver
	Tue.	6	at Phoenix
	Thu.	8	at Los Angeles
	Fri.	9	at Anaheim
	Mon.	12	Edmonton
	Fri.	16	Los Angeles
	Sat.	17	Anaheim

* Denotes afternoon game.

The first German-born player ever selected in the first round of the NHL Entry Draft (21st overall in 1996), Marco Strum had 10 goals and 20 assists in 74 games as a rookie in 1997-98. His 30 points ranked him among the top-scoring freshmen in the league.

Franchise date: May 9, 1990

PACIFIC DIVISION

8th NHL Season

1998-99 Player Personnel

FORWARDS	HT	WT	S	Place of Birth	Date	1997-98 Club
BRADLEY, Matt	6-2	195	R	Stittsville, Ont.	6/13/78	Kingston-Canada
BURR, Shawn	6-1	205	L	Sarnia, Ont.	7/1/66	San Jose
CRAIG, Mike	6-1	180	R	St. Mary's, Ont.	6/6/71	San Antonio-Kansas City
CRAVEN, Murray	6-2	185	L	Medicine Hat, Alta.	7/20/64	San Jose
DEULING, Jarrett	6-0	202	L	Vernon, B.C.	3/4/74	Milwaukee
FRIESEN, Jeff	6-1	200	L	Meadow Lake, Sask.	8/5/76	San Jose
GRANATO, Tony	5-10	185	R	Downers Grove, IL	6/25/64	San Jose
GUOLLA, Stephen	6-0	190	L	Scarborough, Ont.	3/15/73	San Jose-Kentucky
KOROLYUK, Alexander	5-9	190	L	Moscow, USSR	1/15/76	San Jose-Kentucky
MARLEAU, Patrick	6-2	200	L	Swift Current, Sask.	9/15/79	San Jose
MATTEAU, Stephane	6-4	220	L	Rouyn-Noranda, Que.	9/2/69	San Jose
MURPHY, Joe	6-	190	L	London, Ont.	10/16/67	St. Louis-San Jose
MYHRES, Brantt	6-4	222	R	Edmonton, Alta.	3/18/74	Phi-Philadelphia (AHL)
NICHOLLS, Bernie	6-	185	R	Haliburton, Ont.	6/24/61	San Jose
NOLAN, Owen	6-1	205	R	Belfast, Ireland	2/12/72	San Jose
ODUYA, Fredrik	6-3	220	L	Stockholm, Sweden	5/31/75	Kentucky
RICCI, Mike	6-0	190	L	Scarborough, Ont.	10/27/71	Colorado-San Jose
ROED, Peter	5-11	190	L	St. Paul, MN	11/15/76	Kentucky-Louisville
SKALDE, Jarrod	6-0	175	L	Niagara Falls, Ont.	2/26/71	S.J.-Kentucky-Chi-Ind-Dal
SMITH, Mark	5-10	190	L	Edmonton, Alta.	10/24/77	Lethbridge
STERN, Ron	6-0	195	R	Ste. Agathe, Que.	1/11/67	Calgary
STURM, Marco	6-	190	L	Dingolfing, Germany	9/8/78	San Jose-Germany
SUTTER, Ron	6-0	180	R	Viking, Alta.	12/2/63	San Jose
YEGOROV, Alexei	5-11	185	L	St. Petersburg, USSR	5/21/75	Kentucky
DEFENSEMEN						
ALLEN, Peter	6-2	200	R	Calgary, Alta.	3/6/70	Kentucky
BOIKOV, Alexander	6-0	195	L	Chelyabinsk, USSR	2/7/75	Soviet Wings-Kentucky
BURNETT, Garrett	6-3	225	L	Coquitlam, B.C.	9/23/75	Johnstown-Philadelphia (AHL)
GOSSELIN, Christian	6-5	225	R	Laval, Que.	8/21/76	Pensacola-Fredericton
HANNAN, Scott	6-2	210	L	Richmond, B.C.	1/23/79	Kelowna
HEINS, Shawn	6-4	215	L	Eganville, Ont.	12/24/73	Kansas City
HOULDER, Bill	6-2	210	L	Thunder Bay, Ont.	3/11/67	San Jose
LINGREN, Steve	6-0	193	L	Lake Cowachin, B.C.	7/23/73	Hershey
MARCHMENT, Bryan	6-1	205	L	Scarborough, Ont.	5/1/69	Edmonton-Tampa Bay-San Jose
PIETROPAULO, Didier	6-1	204	L	Laval, Que.	2/9/79	Rouyn-Noranda
RAGNARSSON, Marcus	6-1	215	L	Ostervala, Sweden	8/13/71	San Jose-Sweden
RATHJE, Mike	6-5	230	L	Mannville, Alta.	5/11/74	San Jose
ROHLOFF, Jon	5-11	221	R	Mankato, MN	10/3/69	Providence (AHL)
ROUSE, Bob	6-2	220	R	Surrey, B.C.	6/18/64	Detroit
SHAW, David	6-2	205	R	St. Thomas, Ont.	5/25/64	Tampa Bay-Las Vegas
STUART, Brad	6-2	215	L	Rocky Mountain House, AB	11/6/79	Regina
SUTER, Gary	6-0	205	L	Madison, WI	6/24/64	Chicago-United States
SUTTON, Andy	5-10	192	L	Edmonton, Alta.	10/24/77	Michigan Tech-Kentucky
ZYUZIN, Andrei	6-1	195	L	Ufa, USSR	1/21/78	San Jose-Kentucky

GOALTENDERS	HT	WT	C	Place of Birth	Date	1997-98 Club
FORSBERG, Jonas	5-10	160	L	Stockholm, Sweden	6/15/75	Sodertalje
FRIESEN, Terry	5-11	190	L	Winkler, Man.	10/29/77	Swift Current
GAUTHIER, Sean	5-11	195	L	Sudbury, Ont.	3/28/71	Pensacola
HEDBERG, Johan	5-11	180	L	Leksand, Sweden	5/5/73	Baton Rouge-Det (IHL)-Man-Swe
NABOKOV, Yevgeni	6-0	180	L	Ust-Kamenogorsk, USSR	7/25/75	Kentucky
SHIELDS, Steve	6-3	210	L	Toronto, Ont.	7/19/72	Buffalo-Rochester
VERNON, Mike	5-9	170	L	Calgary, Alta.	2/24/63	San Jose

Coach

SUTTER, DARRYL JOHN
Coach, San Jose Sharks. Born in Viking, Alta., August 19, 1958.

Darryl Sutter, 40, became the Sharks' fifth head coach on June 9, 1997. Sutter played eight NHL seasons, all with the Chicago Blackhawks (1979-87). He began his coaching career as an assistant in Chicago in 1987-88 before taking over as head coach of the Blackhawks' IHL affiliate that played in Saginaw (1988-89) and in Indianapolis (1989-90). His club won an IHL Turner Cup championship in 1990 and Sutter was named coach of the year.

He later served as an associate coach under Mike Keenan in Chicago in 1990-91 and 1991-92 and began a three-year tenure as head coach of the Blackhawks in 1992-93. As coach of Chicago, Sutter's teams reached the playoffs in all three seasons. His career winning percentage of .569 ranks second among Chicago coaches. He resigned as head coach following the 1994-95 season to spend more time with his family and worked as a consultant to the Blackhawks for special assignments in 1995-96 and 1996-97.

In 16 years of hockey as a player and coach, Sutter has never failed to qualify for post-season play. During his eight-year playing career, he scored 161 goals and added 118 assists in 406 regular-season games. He added 24 goals and 19 assists in 51 playoff games. Drafted 179th overall by Chicago in the 1978 NHL Entry Draft, he scored a remarkable 40 goals during his rookie season. The left winger served as team captain from 1982-83 until injuries forced his retirement after the 1986-87 season.

He is one of six brothers to play in the NHL. The others are Brian, Brent, Duane, Rich and Ron. All are involved in the Sutter Foundation which raises raises money for non-profit organizations in their home province of Alberta.

Coaching Record

		Regular Season					Playoffs			
Season	Team	Games	W	L	T	%	Games	W	L	%
1988-89	Saginaw (IHL)	82	46	26	10	.560	6	2	4	.333
1989-90	Indianapolis (IHL)	82	53	21	8	.646	14	12	2	.857
1992-93	**Chicago (NHL)**	**84**	**47**	**25**	**12**	**.631**	**4**	**0**	**4**	**.000**
1993-94	**Chicago (NHL)**	**84**	**39**	**36**	**9**	**.518**	**6**	**2**	**4**	**.333**
1994-95	**Chicago (NHL)**	**48**	**24**	**19**	**5**	**.552**	**16**	**9**	**7**	**.563**
1997-98	**San Jose (NHL)**	**82**	**34**	**38**	**10**	**.476**	**6**	**2**	**4**	**.333**
	NHL Totals	**298**	**144**	**118**	**36**	**.544**	**32**	**13**	**19**	**.406**

1997-98 Scoring

* – rookie

Regular Season

Pos	#	Player	Team	GP	G	A	Pts	+/–	PIM	PP	SH	GW	GT	S	%
L	39	Jeff Friesen	S.J.	79	31	32	63	8	40	7	6	7	0	186	16.7
R	15	John MacLean	N.J.	26	3	8	11	-6	14	1	0	1	0	74	4.1
			S.J.	51	13	19	32	0	28	5	0	2	1	139	9.4
			TOTAL	77	16	27	43	-6	42	6	0	3	1	213	7.5
R	11	Owen Nolan	S.J.	75	14	27	41	-2	144	3	1	1	0	192	7.3
C	14 *	Patrick Marleau	S.J.	74	13	19	32	5	14	1	0	2	0	90	14.4
D	2	Bill Houlder	S.J.	82	7	25	32	13	48	4	0	2	0	102	6.9
C	19 *	Marco Sturm	S.J.	74	10	20	30	-2	40	2	0	3	0	118	8.5
L	37	Stephane Matteau	S.J.	73	15	14	29	4	60	1	0	2	2	79	19.0
L	22	Murray Craven	S.J.	67	12	17	29	4	25	2	3	3	0	107	11.2
C	9	Bernie Nicholls	S.J.	60	6	22	28	-4	26	3	0	0	0	81	7.4
C	18	Mike Ricci	COL	6	0	4	4	0	2	0	0	0	0	5	0.0
			S.J.	59	9	14	23	-4	30	5	0	2	0	86	10.5
			TOTAL	65	9	18	27	-4	32	5	0	2	0	91	9.9
L	21	Tony Granato	S.J.	59	16	9	25	3	70	3	0	2	0	119	13.4
D	10	Marcus Ragnarsson	S.J.	79	5	20	25	-11	65	3	0	2	0	91	5.5
R	17	Joe Murphy	STL	27	4	9	13	8	22	2	0	0	0	52	7.7
			S.J.	10	5	4	9	1	14	2	0	0	0	29	17.2
			TOTAL	37	9	13	22	9	36	4	0	0	0	81	11.1
D	40	Mike Rathje	S.J.	81	3	12	15	-4	59	1	0	0	0	61	4.9
D	20 *	Andrei Zyuzin	S.J.	56	6	7	13	8	66	2	0	2	0	72	8.3
D	27	Bryan Marchment	EDM	27	0	4	4	-2	58	0	0	0	0	23	0.0
			T.B.	22	2	4	6	-3	43	0	0	0	0	20	10.0
			S.J.	12	0	3	3	2	43	0	0	0	0	13	0.0
			TOTAL	61	2	11	13	-3	144	0	0	0	0	56	3.6
L	28	Shawn Burr	S.J.	42	6	6	12	2	50	0	0	0	0	63	9.5
D	33	Marty McSorley	S.J.	56	2	10	12	10	140	0	0	0	0	46	4.3
D	43	Al Iafrate	S.J.	21	2	7	9	-1	28	2	0	0	0	37	5.4
C	12	Ron Sutter	S.J.	57	2	7	9	-2	22	0	0	1	0	57	3.5
L	26	Dave Lowry	FLA	7	0	0	0	-1	2	0	0	0	0	4	0.0
			S.J.	50	4	4	8	0	51	0	0	1	0	47	8.5
			TOTAL	57	4	4	8	-1	53	0	0	1	0	51	7.8
C	27 *	Alexander Korolyuk	S.J.	19	2	3	5	-5	6	1	0	0	0	23	8.7
D	7 *	Richard Brennan	S.J.	11	1	2	3	-4	2	1	0	0	0	24	4.2
L	17	Stephen Guolla	S.J.	7	1	1	2	-2	0	0	0	0	0	9	11.1
G	29	Mike Vernon	S.J.	62	0	2	2	0	24	0	0	0	0	0	0.0
L	24	Barry Potomski	S.J.	9	0	1	1	1	30	0	0	0	0	4	0.0
L	34	Niklas Andersson	S.J.	5	0	0	0	-1	2	0	0	0	0	6	0.0
G	30	Jason Muzzatti	NYR	6	0	0	0	0	10	0	0	0	0	0	0.0
			S.J.	1	0	0	0	0	0	0	0	0	0	0	0.0
			TOTAL	7	0	0	0	0	10	0	0	0	0	0	0.0
C	16	Dody Wood	S.J.	8	0	0	0	-3	40	0	0	0	0	4	0.0
D	5	Ken Sutton	N.J.	13	0	0	0	1	6	0	0	0	0	5	0.0
			S.J.	8	0	0	0	-4	15	0	0	0	0	7	0.0
			TOTAL	21	0	0	0	-3	21	0	0	0	0	12	0.0
G	32	Kelly Hrudey	S.J.	28	0	0	0	0	2	0	0	0	0	0	0.0

Goaltending

No.	Goaltender	GPI	Mins	Avg	W	L	T	EN	SO	GA	SA	S%
29	Mike Vernon	62	3564	2.46	30	22	8	2	5	146	1401	.896
32	Kelly Hrudey	28	1360	2.74	4	16	2	4	1	62	600	.897
30	Jason Muzzatti	1	27	4.44	0	0	0	0	0	2	13	.846
	Totals	**82**	**4973**	**2.61**	**34**	**38**	**10**	**6**	**7**	**216**	**2020**	**.893**

Playoffs

Pos	#	Player	Team	GP	G	A	Pts	+/–	PIM	PP	SH	GW	OT	S	%
R	15	John MacLean	S.J.	6	2	3	5	1	4	1	0	0	0	18	11.1
C	9	Bernie Nicholls	S.J.	6	0	5	5	-2	8	0	0	0	0	6	0.0
R	11	Owen Nolan	S.J.	6	2	2	4	-1	26	2	0	1	0	16	12.5
C	18	Mike Ricci	S.J.	6	1	3	4	0	6	0	0	0	0	8	12.5
D	2	Bill Houlder	S.J.	6	1	2	3	0	2	0	0	0	0	8	12.5
L	22	Murray Craven	S.J.	6	1	1	2	-2	0	0	0	0	0	6	16.7
R	17	Joe Murphy	S.J.	6	1	1	2	-1	20	1	0	0	0	10	10.0
D	43	Al Iafrate	S.J.	6	1	0	1	-4	10	1	0	0	0	10	10.0
C	12	Ron Sutter	S.J.	6	1	0	1	-1	14	0	0	0	0	7	14.3
D	40	Mike Rathje	S.J.	6	1	0	1	-3	6	1	0	0	0	2	50.0
D	20 *	Andrei Zyuzin	S.J.	6	1	0	1	-2	14	0	0	1	1	6	16.7
L	37	Stephane Matteau	S.J.	4	0	1	1	1	0	0	0	0	0	2	0.0
C	14 *	Patrick Marleau	S.J.	5	0	1	1	-1	0	0	0	0	0	2	0.0
L	39	Jeff Friesen	S.J.	6	0	1	1	-1	2	0	0	0	0	9	0.0
L	21	Tony Granato	S.J.	1	0	0	0	0	0	0	0	0	0	2	0.0
G	32	Kelly Hrudey	S.J.	1	0	0	0	0	0	0	0	0	0	0	0.0
C	19 *	Marco Sturm	S.J.	2	0	0	0	-2	0	0	0	0	0	3	0.0
L	28	Shawn Burr	S.J.	6	0	0	0	-1	8	0	0	0	0	4	0.0
L	26	Dave Lowry	S.J.	6	0	0	0	0	18	0	0	0	0	3	0.0
D	27	Bryan Marchment	S.J.	6	0	0	0	1	10	0	0	0	0	5	0.0
G	29	Mike Vernon	S.J.	6	0	0	0	0	0	0	0	0	0	0	0.0
D	10	Marcus Ragnarsson	S.J.	6	0	0	0	2	4	0	0	0	0	4	0.0

Goaltending

No.	Goaltender	GPI	Mins	Avg	W	L	EN	SO	GA	SA	S%
29	Mike Vernon	6	348	2.41	2	4	1	1	14	138	.899
32	Kelly Hrudey	1	20	3.00	0	0	0	0	1	6	.833
	Totals	**6**	**370**	**2.59**	**2**	**4**	**1**	**1**	**16**	**145**	**.890**

Captains' History

Doug Wilson, 1991-92, 1992-93; Bob Errey, 1993-94; Bob Errey and Jeff Odgers, 1994-95; Jeff Odgers, 1995-96; Todd Gill, 1996-97, 1997-98.

Coaching History

George Kingston, 1991-92, 1992-93; Kevin Constantine, 1993-94, 1994-95; Kevin Constantine and Jim Wiley, 1995-96; Al Sims, 1996-97; Darryl Sutter, 1997-98 to date.

Club Records

Team

(Figures in brackets for season records are games played; records for fewest points, wins, ties, losses, goals, goals against are for 70 or more games)

Most Points	**82**	1993-94 (84)
Most Wins	**34**	1997-98 (82)
Most Ties	**16**	1993-94 (84)
Most Losses	***71**	1992-93 (84)
Most Goals	**252**	1993-94 (84), 1995-96 (82)
Most Goals Against	**414**	1992-93 (84)
Fewest Points	**24**	1992-93 (84)
Fewest Wins	**11**	1992-93 (84)
Fewest Ties	***2**	1992-93 (84)
Fewest Losses	**35**	1993-94 (84)
Fewest Goals	**210**	1997-98 (82)
Fewest Goals Against	**216**	1997-98 (82)
Longest Winning Streak		
Overall	**7**	Mar. 24-Apr. 5/94
Home	**5**	Jan. 21-Feb. 15/95
Away	**4**	Mar. 24-Apr. 5/94, Dec. 4-21/97
Longest Undefeated Streak		
Overall	**9**	Mar. 20-Apr. 5/94 (7 wins, 2 ties)
Home	**6**	Mar. 20-Apr. 13/94 (4 wins, 2 ties)
Away	**5**	Two times
Longest Losing Streak		
Overall	***17**	Jan. 4-Feb. 12/93
Home	**9**	Nov. 19-Dec. 19/92
Away	**19**	Nov. 27/92-Feb. 12/93
Longest Winless Streak		
Overall	**20**	Dec. 29/92-Feb. 12/93 (19 losses, 1 tie)
Home	**9**	Nov. 19-Dec. 19/92 (9 losses)
Away	**19**	Nov. 27/92-Feb. 12/93 (19 losses)
Most Shutouts, Season	**7**	1997-98 (82)
Most PIM, Season	**2134**	1992-93 (84)
Most Goals, Game	**10**	Jan. 13/96 (S.J. 10 at Pit. 8)

Individual

Most Seasons	**5**	Four players
Most Games, Career	**334**	Jeff Odgers
Most Goals, Career	**89**	Jeff Friesen
Most Assists, Career	**107**	Jeff Friesen
Most Points, Career	**196**	Jeff Friesen (89G, 107A)
Most PIM, Career	**1,001**	Jeff Odgers
Most Shutouts, Career	**8**	Arturs Irbe
Longest Consecutive Games Streak	**131**	Viktor Kozlov (Dec. 2/95-Mar. 26/97)
Most Goals, Season	**31**	Owen Nolan (1996-97); Jeff Friesen (1997-98)
Most Assists, Season	**52**	Kelly Kisio (1992-93)
Most Points, Season	**78**	Kelly Kisio (1992-93; 26G, 52A)
Most PIM, Season	**326**	Link Gaetz (1991-92)
Most Shutouts, Season	**5**	Mike Vernon (1997-98)
Most Points, Defenseman, Season	**64**	Sandis Ozolnish (1993-94; 26G, 38A)
Most Points, Center, Season	**78**	Kelly Kisio (1992-93; 26G, 52A)
Most Points, Right Wing, Season	**68**	Sergei Makarov (1993-94; 30G, 38A)
Most Points, Left Wing, Season	**66**	Johan Garpenlov (1992-93; 22G, 44A)
Most Points, Rookie, Season	**59**	Pat Falloon (1991-92; 25G, 34A)
Most Goals, Game	**4**	Owen Nolan (Dec. 19/95)
Most Assists, Game	**4**	Three times
Most Points, Game	**5**	Owen Nolan (Dec. 19/95; 4G, 1A)

* NHL Record.

General Manager

LOMBARDI, DEAN
Executive Vice President and General Manager, San Jose Sharks.
Born in Holyoke, Massachusetts, March 5, 1958.

Dean Lombardi, 40, is an 11-year veteran of NHL front office duties. A charter member of the Sharks' management team, Lombardi joined the club in 1990 as assistant general manager after having served in a similar capacity with the Minnesota North Stars. He was named San Jose's director of hockey operations on June 26, 1992 and became the club's general manager on March 6, 1996. As the team's top hockey executive, he oversees player personnel decisions, negotiates player contracts and coordinates the efforts of the Sharks' scouting and player evaluation departments.

Lombardi oversaw the acquisition of key veterans for the Sharks: forwards Owen Nolan, Bernie Nicholls, Tony Granato and Darren Turcotte; goaltender Kelly Hrudey and defensemen Doug Bodger, Marty McSorley, Todd Gill and Al Iafrate. He is also firmly committed to building through the Entry Draft. San Jose draft picks making important contributions to the club include forwards Jeff Friesen, Patrick Marleau and Marco Sturm along with defensemen Marcus Ragnarsson and Mike Rathje.

After the 1993-94 season that saw the Sharks post an NHL record single-season improvement of 58 points, Lombardi finished third in *The Hockey News* award voting for executive of the year.

General Managers' History

Jack Ferreira, 1991-92; Office of the General Manager: Chuck Grillo (V.P. Director of Player Personnel) and Dean Lombardi (V.P. Director of Hockey Operations), 1992-93 to 1995-96; Dean Lombardi, 1996-97 to date.

All-time Record vs. Other Clubs

Regular Season

	At Home							On Road							Total						
	GP	W	L	T	GF	GA	PTS	GP	W	L	T	GF	GA	PTS	GP	W	L	T	GF	GA	PTS
Anaheim	13	6	6	1	43	42	13	14	9	5	0	52	39	18	27	15	11	1	95	81	31
Boston	6	1	3	2	18	26	4	6	0	5	1	15	24	1	12	1	8	3	33	50	5
Buffalo	6	3	1	2	24	23	8	7	0	7	0	21	37	0	13	3	8	2	45	60	8
Calgary	22	6	15	1	61	74	13	20	6	13	1	55	90	13	42	12	28	2	116	164	26
Carolina	6	3	3	0	31	23	6	7	4	3	0	18	23	8	13	7	6	0	49	46	14
Chicago	14	7	7	0	34	41	14	13	4	8	1	35	47	9	27	11	15	1	69	88	23
Colorado	12	5	7	0	42	53	10	11	2	8	1	26	53	5	23	7	15	1	68	106	15
Dallas	13	5	8	0	32	43	10	13	6	6	1	35	41	13	26	11	14	1	67	84	23
Detroit	14	4	9	1	47	68	9	13	1	12	0	23	63	2	27	5	21	1	70	131	11
Edmonton	20	11	8	1	71	63	23	21	3	15	3	45	83	9	41	14	23	4	116	146	32
Florida	4	1	1	2	8	10	4	4	0	1	3	8	11	3	8	1	2	5	16	21	7
Los Angeles	21	10	8	3	77	70	23	20	6	13	1	58	76	13	41	16	21	4	135	146	36
Montreal	7	2	3	2	20	19	6	7	0	6	1	11	30	1	14	2	9	3	31	49	7
New Jersey	6	1	4	1	11	20	3	7	3	4	0	14	27	6	13	4	8	1	25	47	9
NY Islanders	6	2	3	1	15	24	5	7	1	5	1	21	34	3	13	3	8	2	36	58	8
NY Rangers	7	0	7	0	15	32	0	6	0	5	1	18	32	1	13	0	12	1	33	64	1
Ottawa	5	3	2	0	8	6	6	5	0	2	3	14	17	3	10	3	4	3	22	23	9
Philadelphia	7	1	6	0	13	24	2	6	2	3	1	14	22	5	13	3	9	1	27	46	7
Phoenix	16	7	7	2	60	64	16	18	4	11	3	51	68	11	34	11	18	5	111	132	27
Pittsburgh	7	0	6	1	13	45	1	6	2	3	1	20	32	5	13	2	9	2	33	77	6
St. Louis	12	2	10	0	30	44	4	15	3	12	0	31	58	6	27	5	22	0	61	102	10
Tampa Bay	6	1	5	0	18	25	2	6	2	4	0	13	19	4	12	3	9	0	31	44	6
Toronto	14	5	7	2	30	38	12	13	3	9	1	30	51	7	27	8	16	3	60	89	19
Vancouver	21	6	11	4	64	72	16	20	4	15	1	44	84	9	41	10	26	5	108	156	25
Washington	6	2	3	1	18	20	5	6	2	4	0	16	20	4	12	4	7	1	34	40	9
Totals	**271**	**94**	**150**	**27**	**803**	**969**	**215**	**271**	**67**	**179**	**25**	**688**	**1081**	**159**	**542**	**161**	**329**	**52**	**1491**	**2050**	**374**

Playoffs

	Series	W	L	GP	W	L	T	GF	GA	Last Mtg.	Round	Result
Calgary	1	1	0	7	4	3	0	26	35	1995	CQF	W 4-3
Dallas	1	0	1	6	2	4	0	12	16	1998	CQF	W 2-4
Detroit	2	1	1	11	4	7	0	27	51	1995	CSF	L 0-4
Toronto	1	0	1	7	3	4	0	21	26	1994	CSF	L 3-4
Totals	**5**	**2**	**3**	**31**	**13**	**18**	**0**	**86**	**128**			

Playoff Results 1998-94

Year	Round	Opponent	Result	GF	GA
1998	CQF	Dallas	L 2-4	12	16
1995	CSF	Detroit	L 0-4	6	24
	CQF	Calgary	W 4-3	26	35
1994	CSF	Toronto	L 3-4	21	26
	CQF	Detroit	W 4-3	21	27

Abbreviations: Round: CQF – conference quarter-final; **CSF** – conference semi-final.

Carolina totals include Hartford, 1991-92 to 1996-97.
Dallas totals include Minnesota, 1991-92 to 1992-93.
Colorado totals include Quebec, 1991-92 to 1994-95.
Phoenix totals include Winnipeg, 1991-92 to 1995-96.

1997-98 Results

Oct.	1		Edmonton	3-5		6		St. Louis	1-5
	4		Chicago	3-2		10		Buffalo	5-2
	7		Ottawa	0-1		12		Dallas	1-3
	9	at	Colorado	2-3		14		Los Angeles	2-4
	11		Boston	5-2		15	at	Colorado	2-2
	13		Philadelphia	2-3		21		Calgary	7-1
	16		NY Islanders	2-5		23		Edmonton	3-2
	19	at	Phoenix	3-5		24		Florida	1-1
	22		Pittsburgh	2-5		27		Anaheim	4-2
	25	at	New Jersey	4-3		29		Chicago	0-3
	27	at	NY Islanders	2-1		31		Colorado	5-2
	29	at	Detroit	3-4	**Feb.**	2		NY Rangers	2-3
	31	at	Chicago	3-5		4	at	Edmonton	3-0
Nov.	1	at	St. Louis	0-2		5	at	Calgary	2-4
	4		Toronto	0-0		7	at	Vancouver	3-6
	7		Montreal	3-4		26		St. Louis	3-1
	8		Tampa Bay	3-1		28	at	Edmonton	1-4
	10	at	Anaheim	6-4	**Mar.**	2		Carolina	1-3
	12		Vancouver	2-5		5		Detroit	5-4
	13	at	Los Angeles	3-6		6	at	Anaheim	3-0
	15		Phoenix	2-3		9		Toronto	3-2
	18		Anaheim	4-2		11	at	NY Rangers	3-5
	20	at	Philadelphia	3-0		12	at	Buffalo	1-3
	22	at	Washington	5-2		14	at	Carolina	2-1
	24	at	Montreal	2-2		16		Los Angeles	2-1
	25	at	Toronto	1-3		18		Dallas	1-3
	28		New Jersey	2-4		21		Colorado	0-2
	30	at	Edmonton	1-6		22	at	Phoenix	1-3
Dec.	1	at	Calgary	2-3		24		Los Angeles	3-4
	4	at	Vancouver	3-2		26	at	Los Angeles	5-2
	10		Washington	3-3		28	at	Dallas	4-1
	12	at	Dallas	1-0		30	at	St. Louis	2-6
	14	at	Chicago	2-1	**Apr.**	1	at	Pittsburgh	3-2
	16		Detroit	5-1		2	at	Ottawa	3-3
	18		Vancouver	0-0		4	at	Toronto	5-3
	21	at	Anaheim	4-2		7		Calgary	6-0
	26		Phoenix	0-4		9		Anaheim	5-2
	29	at	Tampa Bay	1-2		11		Vancouver	1-1
	30	at	Florida	2-2		15	at	Calgary	3-3
Jan.	2	at	Detroit	4-1		16	at	Colorado	1-4
	3	at	Boston	0-3		18		Calgary	4-1

Entry Draft Selections 1998-91

1998

Pick	
3	Brad Stuart
29	Jonathon Cheechoo
65	Eric LaPlante
98	Rob Davison
104	Miroslav Zalesak
127	Brandon Coalter
145	Mikael Samuelsson
185	Robert Mulick
212	Jim Fahey

1997

Pick	
2	Patrick Marleau
23	Scott Hannan
82	Adam Colagiacomo
107	Adam Nittel
163	Joe Dusbabek
192	Cam Severson
219	Mark Smith

1996

Pick	
2	Andrei Zyuzin
21	Marco Sturm
55	Terry Friesen
102	Matt Bradley
137	Michel Larocque
164	Jake Deadmarsh
191	Cory Cyrenne
217	David Thibeault

1995

Pick	
12	Teemu Riihijarvi
38	Peter Roed
64	Marko Makinen
90	Vesa Toskala
116	Miikka Kiprusoff
130	Michal Bros
140	Timo Hakanen
142	Jaroslav Kudrna
167	Brad Mehalko
168	Robert Jindrich
194	Ryan Kraft
220	Miiko Markkanen

1994

Pick	
11	Jeff Friesen
37	Angel Nikolov
66	Alexei Yegorov
89	Vaclav Varada
115	Brian Swanson
141	Alexander Korolyuk
167	Sergei Gorbachev
193	Eric Landry
219	Yevgeny Nabokov
240	Tomas Pisa
245	Aniket Dhadphale
271	David Beauregard

1993

Pick	
6	Viktor Kozlov
28	Shean Donovan
45	Vlastimil Kroupa
58	Ville Peltonen
80	Alexander Osadchy
106	Andrei Buschan
132	Petri Varis
154	Fredrik Oduya
158	Anatoli Filatov
184	Todd Holt
210	Jonas Forsberg
236	Jeff Salajko
262	Jamie Matthews

1992

Pick	
3	Mike Rathje
10	Andrei Nazarov
51	Alexander Cherbajev
75	Jan Caloun
99	Marcus Ragnarsson
123	Michal Sykora
147	Eric Bellerose
171	Ryan Smith
195	Chris Burns
219	A. Kholomeyev
243	Victor Ignatjev

1991

Pick	
2	Pat Falloon
23	Ray Whitney
30	Sandis Ozolinsh
45	Dody Wood
67	Kerry Toporowski
89	Dan Ryder
111	Fredrik Nilsson
133	Jaroslav Otevrel
155	Dean Grillo
177	Corwin Saurdiff
199	Dale Craigwell
221	Aaron Kriss
243	Mikhail Kravets

Club Directory

San Jose Arena
525 West Santa Clara Street
San Jose, CA 95113
Phone **408/287-7070**
FAX 408/999-5797
Internet http://www.sj-sharks.com
Capacity: 17,483

Executive Staff

Owner & Chairman	George Gund III
Co-Owner	Gordon Gund
President & Chief Executive Officer	Greg Jamison
Senior Executive Vice President & Chief Operating Officer	Frank Jirik
Executive Vice President of Business Operations	Malcolm Bordelon
Executive Vice President of Development	Matt Levine
Executive Vice President & General Manager	Dean Lombardi
Executive Vice President & Chief Financial Officer	Gregg Olson
Vice Chairman	Tom McEnery
Vice President & General Manager (San Jose Arena)	Jim Goddard
Vice President & General Counsel	Don Gralnek
Vice President of Marketing	Elaine Sullivan-Digre
Executive Assistant	Michelle Simmons

Hockey

Assistant General Manager	Wayne Thomas
Head Coach	Darryl Sutter
Assistant Coach	Paul Baxter
Assistant Coach	Bob Berry
Senior Professional Scout	John Ferguson
Professional Scout	Barry Long
Professional Scout	Cap Raeder
Director of Pro Development	Doug Wilson
Director of Amateur Scouting	Tim Burke
Chief Scout	Ray Payne
Assistant to the General Manager	Joe Will
Scouts	Gilles Cote, Pat Funk, Rob Grillo, Brian Gross, Karel Masopust, Ilkka Sinisalo
Executive Assistant	Brenda Will
Video Scouting Coordinator	Bob Friedlander
Goaltender Consultant	Warren Strelow
Development Coach	Vasily Tikhonov
Head Athletic Trainer	Ray Tufts, ATC
Athletic Trainer	Tom Woodcock
Strength & Conditioning Coordinator	Mac Read
Massage Therapist	Wes Howard
Equipment Manager	Mike Aldrich
Assistant Equipment Manager	Kurt Harvey
Equipment Assistant & Equipment Transportation	Jason Rudee
Team Services Coordinator	Aaron Abrams
Dir. of Hockey Operations, Kentucky Thoroughblades	Jim Wiley
Head Coach, Kentucky Thoroughblades	Roy Sommer
Assistant Coach, Kentucky Thoroughblades	Nick Fotiu
Head Trainer, Kentucky Thoroughblades	Jerry Iannarelli
Team Physician	Arthur J. Ting, M.D.
Team Dentist	Robert Bonahoom, D.D.S.
Team Vision Specialist	Vincent S. Zuccaro, O.D., F.A.A.O.
Medical Staff	Warren King, M.D., Mark Sontag, M.D., Will Straw, M.D.

Business Operations

Director of Broadcasting	Frank Albin
Director of Media Relations	Ken Arnold
Director of Sponsorship Sales	Greg Elliott
Director of Community Development	Eric Stanion
Director of Event Services	Jason Minsky
Sponsorship Sales Manager	Kirk Berridge, Mark Foxton, Jennifer Birmingham
Educational Programs & Arena Tours Manager	Dianna Carthew
Youth and Amateur Hockey Manager	Derek Eisler
Mascot Operations Manager	Tim Patnode
Media Relations Manager	Roger Ross
Community Development Coordinator	Julie Vennewitz
The Sharks Foundation Coordinator	Jackie Fuce
Advertising Sales Manager	Chris Parker
Sponsorship, Promotion and Traffic Coordinator	Anna Saalfield
Sponsorship Services Coordinator	Valerie Bigelow
Executive Assistant	Dawn Beres
Media Relations Assistant	Chris Kelleher
Event Services Assistant	Steve Maroni

Marketing

Director of Advertising & Publicity	Beth Brigino
Director of Suite Hospitality	Coleen Duncan
Director of Ticket Sales & Promotions	Kent Russell
Tennis Tournament Manager, Sybase Open	Kristi Breisch
Account Sales Managers	Michael Dunnett, Jeff Goda, Mike Hollywood
Ticket Operations Manager	Mary Enriquez
Account Sales Manager, Sybase Open	Bill Rapp
Corporate Sales Account Manager, Sybase Open	Cam Severson
Suite Hospitality Manager	Jay O'Sullivan
Account Service Manager	Sharon Holman, Kristin Lyon, Kathy Payne
Marketing Manager	Jim Sparaco
Ticket Operations Coordinator	John Castro
Administrative Assistant	Steward Diner

Development

Development Coordinator	Kimberly Brown

Finance

Director of Finance	Ken Caveney
Finance Manager	Steve Calamia
Human Resources Manager	Carol Ross
Information Systems Manager	James Struckle
Staff Accountant	Jim Boyle, Tina Park
Payroll Accounting Associate	Sue Feachen
Accounts Payable Accounting Associate	Catherine Layman
Accounts Receivable Accounting Associate	Diane Rubino
Network Administrator	John Huh
System Support Specialist	Josh Schlieff
Executive Assistant	Tricia Nordquist

Building Operations

Director of Ticket Operations	Daniel DeBoer
Director of Guest Services	Rick Mears
Director of Building Operations	Rich Sotelo
Facilities Technical Director	Greg Carrolan
Chief Engineer	Jay Farr
Asst. Chief Engineer	Ted Ludwick
Security Supervisor	Geoff Pepe
Telephone Systems Manager	Bob Davis
Booking & Event Manager	Bob Herrfeldt, Steve Kirsner
Building Services Manager	Bruce Tharaldson
Ticket Operations Manager	Judy Jones
Ushering Guest Services Manager	Kellie Elliott
Parking Guest Services Manager	Kimberly Gutierrez
Building Services Coordinator	George Gund IV, Greg Gund
Ticket Operations Coordinator	Rossanna Lira
Mailroom Coordinator	Richard Perez
Guest Services Coordinator	Julie Radford, Vikki Klass, Andrea Teed, Darcy Teed
Executive Assistant	Christine de la Cruz
Administrative Assistant	Beth Ganeff, Maureen Miller
Receptionist	Jessica Gould

ARAMARK Leisure Services

General Manager	Dale Haynes
Human Resources Director	Valerie Davison
Executive Chef	Dennis Glafkides
Executive Sous Chef	Victor Lopez
Financial Controller	TBA
Director of Suite Catering	Wendy Riggs
Merchandise Manager	Eric Pearson
Restaurant Manager	Tracy Ingram
Concessions Manager	David Cesarez
Assistant Concessions Manager	Gretchen La Due

Miscellaneous

Team Colors	Deep Pacific Teal, Shimmering Gray, Burnt Orange & Black
Dimensions of Rink	200' × 85'
Television Stations	KICU-TV 36, Fox Sports Bay Area
Radio Network Flagship	KARA (105.7 FM)
Television Play-By-Play Broadcaster	Randy Hahn
Television Color Analyst	Steve Konroyd
Radio Play-By-Play Broadcaster	Dan Rusanowsky
Radio Color Analyst	Drew Remenda
Team Photographers	Don Smith, Rocky Widner
P.A. Announcer	Joe Ike
Anthem Singer	Dennis Leach
Organist	Jim Sealy
Mascot	S.J. Sharkie

Tampa Bay Lightning

1997-98 Results: 17W-55L-10T 44PTS. Seventh, Atlantic Division

Year-by-Year Record

		Home			Road			Overall							
Season	GP	W	L	T	W	L	T	W	L	T	GF	GA	Pts.	Finished	Playoff Result
1997-98	82	11	23	7	6	32	3	17	55	10	151	269	44	7th, Atlantic Div.	Out of Playoffs
1996-97	82	15	18	8	17	22	2	32	40	10	217	247	74	6th, Atlantic Div.	Out of Playoffs
1995-96	82	22	14	5	16	18	7	38	32	12	238	248	88	5th, Atlantic Div.	Lost Conf. Quarter-Final
1994-95	48	10	14	0	7	14	3	17	28	3	120	144	37	6th, Atlantic Div.	Out of Playoffs
1993-94	84	14	22	6	16	21	5	30	43	11	224	251	71	7th, Atlantic Div.	Out of Playoffs
1992-93	84	12	27	3	11	27	4	23	54	7	245	332	53	6th, Norris Div.	Out of Playoffs

1998-99 Schedule

Oct.	Fri.	9	at Florida
	Sat.	10	at Carolina
	Wed.	14	NY Islanders
	Fri.	16	Philadelphia
	Sun.	18	Washington
	Wed.	21	Pittsburgh
	Fri.	23	Los Angeles
	Sun.	25	Vancouver
	Wed.	28	at Anaheim
	Fri.	30	at Los Angeles
	Sat.	31	at San Jose
Nov.	Wed.	4	at Washington
	Fri.	6	Chicago
	Sun.	8	New Jersey*
	Tue.	10	NY Rangers
	Fri.	13	at Colorado
	Sat.	14	at Phoenix
	Thu.	19	Pittsburgh
	Sat.	21	at Pittsburgh
	Tue.	24	Boston
	Fri.	27	Florida
	Sun.	29	Buffalo
Dec.	Thu.	3	at Calgary
	Fri.	4	at Edmonton
	Sun.	6	at Chicago
	Tue.	8	Ottawa
	Fri.	11	Calgary
	Sat.	12	at NY Islanders
	Tue.	15	at Pittsburgh
	Fri.	18	Edmonton
	Sun.	20	at Philadelphia
	Mon.	21	at Boston
	Wed.	23	at Buffalo
	Sat.	26	Florida
	Tue.	29	NY Islanders
	Wed.	30	at Carolina
Jan.	Mon.	4	at Toronto
	Thu.	7	at Montreal
	Fri.	8	at Ottawa
	Sun.	10	at NY Rangers*
	Tue.	12	Toronto
	Fri.	15	at New Jersey
	Sat.	16	at Boston
	Tue.	19	Buffalo
	Thu.	21	at Nashville
	Tue.	26	Montreal
	Fri.	29	Dallas
	Sat.	30	at Philadelphia
Feb.	Tue.	2	Toronto
	Wed.	3	at Washington
	Fri.	5	Anaheim
	Wed.	10	St. Louis
	Sat.	13	San Jose
	Mon.	15	at NY Islanders*
	Wed.	17	at New Jersey
	Fri.	19	Phoenix
	Sat.	20	Carolina
	Mon.	22	New Jersey
	Fri.	26	Philadelphia
Mar.	Tue.	2	Washington
	Thu.	4	Colorado
	Sat.	6	at Montreal
	Mon.	8	at Ottawa
	Tue.	9	at Toronto
	Thu.	11	at Buffalo
	Sat.	13	at Florida
	Wed.	17	Pittsburgh
	Fri.	19	Detroit
	Mon.	22	NY Rangers
	Wed.	24	Nashville
	Fri.	26	at Detroit
	Sun.	28	at Carolina*
	Wed.	31	at Dallas
Apr.	Thu.	1	at St. Louis
	Sat.	3	Washington
	Mon.	5	Ottawa
	Thu.	8	Boston
	Sat.	10	at Boston*
	Mon.	12	at NY Rangers
	Tue.	13	Montreal
	Fri.	16	Carolina
	Sat.	17	at Florida

* Denotes afternoon game.

Former Flyer Mikael Renberg, named captain during his first season in Tampa Bay, tied Alexander Selivanov for the Lightning lead with 16 goals in 1997-98.

Franchise date: December 16, 1991

SOUTHEAST DIVISION

7th NHL Season

1998-99 Player Personnel

FORWARDS	HT	WT	S	Place of Birth	Date	1997-98 Club
ANDERSSON, Mikael	5-11	181	L	Malmo, Sweden	5/10/66	Tampa Bay-Sweden
BELANGER, Jesse	6-1	190	R	St. Georges de Beauce, Que	6/15/69	SC Herisau-Las Vegas
BONSIGNORE, Jason	6-4	220	R	Rochester, NY	4/15/76	Hamilton-S.Antonio-T.B.-Clev
BRADLEY, Brian	5-10	180	R	Kitchener, Ont.	1/21/65	Tampa Bay
CLARK, Wendel	5-11	194	L	Kelvington, Sask.	10/25/66	Toronto
HOGUE, Benoit	5-10	194	L	Repentigny, Que.	10/28/66	Dallas
JANNEY, Craig	6-1	190	L	Hartford, CT	9/26/67	Phoenix
KELLY, Steve	6-1	190	L	Vancouver, B.C.	10/26/76	Edm-Hamilton-T.B.-Milw-Clev
LANGKOW, Daymond	5-11	175	L	Edmonton, Alta	9/27/76	Tampa Bay
LECAVALIER, Vincent	6-4	180	L	Ile Bizard, Que.	4/21/80	Rimouski
McCARTHY, Sandy	6-3	225	R	Toronto, Ont.	6/15/72	Calgary-Tampa Bay
NAZAROV, Andrei	6-5	230	R	Chelyabinsk, USSR	5/22/74	San Jose-Tampa Bay-Russia
PETERSON, Brent	6-3	200	L	Calgary, Alta.	7/20/72	Tampa Bay-Milwaukee
RENBERG, Mikael	6-2	218	L	Pitea, Sweden	5/5/72	Tampa Bay-Sweden
RICHER, Stephane	6-2	215	R	Ripon, Que.	6/7/66	Montreal-Tampa Bay
SELIVANOV, Alex	6-	206	L	Moscow, USSR	3/23/71	Tampa Bay
TUCKER, Darcy	5-10	179	L	Castor, Alta.	3/15/75	Montreal-Tampa Bay
YSEBAERT, Paul	6-1	194	L	Sarnia, Ont.	5/15/66	Tampa Bay
ZAMUNER, Rob	6-2	206	L	Oakville, Ont.	9/17/69	Tampa Bay-Canada
DEFENSEMEN						
CICCONE, Enrico	6-5	220	L	Montreal, Que.	4/10/70	Carolina-Vancouver-Tampa Bay
CROSS, Cory	6-5	219	L	Lloydminster, Alta.	1/3/71	Tampa Bay-Canada
CULLIMORE, Jassen	6-5	225	L	Simcoe, Ont.	12/4/72	Montreal-Fredericton-Tampa Bay
DYKHUIS, Karl	6-3	214	L	Sept-Iles, Que.	7/8/72	Tampa Bay
KUBINA, Pavel	6-3	213	R	Celadna, Czech.	4/15/77	Tampa Bay-Adirondack
LAROCQUE, Mario	6-2	182	L	Montreal, Que.	4/24/78	Sherbrooke
MARA, Paul	6-4	202	L	Ridgewood, NJ	9/7/79	Sudbury-Plymouth-United States
McBAIN, Mike	6-2	195	L	Kimberley, B.C.	1/12/77	Tampa Bay-Adirondack
SKOPINTSEV, Andrei	6-0	185	R	Elekrostal, USSR	9/28/71	TPS Turku-Russia
SYKORA, Michal	6-5	225	L	Pardubice, Czech.	7/5/73	Chicago-Indianapolis-Pardubice
WILKIE, David	6-2	210	R	Ellensburgh, WA	5/30/74	Montreal-Tampa Bay

GOALTENDERS	HT	WT	C	Place of Birth	Date	1997-98 Club
PUPPA, Daren	6-4	205	R	Kirkland Lake, Ont.	3/23/65	Tampa Bay
RANFORD, Bill	5-11	185	L	Brandon, Man.	12/14/66	Washington
SCHWAB, Corey	6-0	180	L	North Battleford, Sask.	11/4/70	Tampa Bay
WILKINSON, Derek	6-0	170	L	Lasalle, Ont.	7/29/74	Tampa Bay-Cleveland

Coach

DEMERS, JACQUES
Coach, Tampa Bay Lightning. Born in Montreal, Que., August 25, 1944.

Jacques Demers begins his first full season behind the bench with the Tampa Bay Lightning in 1998-99, having succeeded Terry Crisp as just the second full-time bench boss in club history when he was hired on November 12, 1997.

Demers, 54, who has coached in the NHL previously with the Quebec Nordiques (1979-80), St. Louis Blues (1983 to 1986), Detroit Red Wings (1986 to 1990) and Montreal Canadiens (1992 to 1995), captured the Stanley Cup with the Canadiens in 1992-93. Demers has guided teams to the Stanley Cup Playoffs in eight of his 11 seasons.

A native of Montreal, Demers began coaching in the junior ranks during the 1960s. He joined the pros in 1972-73 with Chicago of the World Hockey Association, and also coached Indianapolis and Cincinnati of the WHA before taking his first NHL job with Quebec in 1979-80. Demers remained in the Quebec organization as coach of their AHL affiliate in Fredericton from 1981-83, and was named AHL coach of the year following the 1982-83 campaign.

Demers took over the helm for the St. Louis Blues prior to the 1983-84 season, and remained there until 1986, when he led the Blues to the Campbell Conference finals. The following season he was named head coach of the Detroit Red Wings, and he remained in Detroit four seasons, becoming the only coach to win the Jack Adams Award as the NHL's coach of the year in back-to-back years (1987 and 1988).

Demers was named head coach of his hometown team — the Canadiens — in 1992-93 and promptly led Montreal to a 48-30-6 regular-season mark and a 16-4 playoff mark en route to the Stanley Cup championship. Demers remained as coach of the Canadiens until early in the 1995-96 season, when he was relieved of his duties and named a professional scout.

Coaching Record

		Regular Season					Playoffs			
Season	Team	Games	W	L	T	%	Games	W	L	%
1975-76	Indianapolis (WHA)	80	35	39	6	.475	7	3	4	.429
1976-77	Indianapolis (WHA)	81	36	37	8	.494	9	5	4	.556
1977-78	Cincinnati (WHA)	80	35	42	3	.456	....	....	....	....
1978-79	Quebec (WHA)	80	41	34	5	.544	4	0	4	.000
1979-80	**Quebec (NHL)**	**80**	**25**	**44**	**11**	**.381**	....	....	....	....
1981-82	Fredericton (AHL)	80	20	55	5	.281	....	....	....	....
1982-83	Fredericton (AHL)	80	45	27	8	.544	12	6	6	.500
1983-84	**St. Louis (NHL)**	**80**	**32**	**41**	**7**	**.444**	**11**	**6**	**5**	**.545**
1984-85	**St. Louis (NHL)**	**80**	**37**	**31**	**12**	**.538**	**3**	**0**	**3**	**.000**
1985-86	**St. Louis (NHL)**	**80**	**37**	**34**	**9**	**.519**	**19**	**10**	**9**	**.526**
1986-87	**Detroit (NHL)**	**80**	**34**	**36**	**10**	**.488**	**16**	**9**	**7**	**.563**
1987-88	**Detroit (NHL)**	**80**	**41**	**28**	**11**	**.581**	**16**	**9**	**7**	**.563**
1988-89	**Detroit (NHL)**	**80**	**34**	**34**	**12**	**.500**	**6**	**2**	**4**	**.333**
1989-90	**Detroit (NHL)**	**80**	**28**	**38**	**14**	**.437**	....	....	....	....
1992-93	**Montreal (NHL)**	**84**	**48**	**30**	**6**	**.607**	**20**	**16**	**4**	**.800***
1993-94	**Montreal (NHL)**	**84**	**41**	**29**	**14**	**.571**	**7**	**3**	**4**	**.429**
1994-95	**Montreal (NHL)**	**48**	**18**	**23**	**7**	**.448**	....	....	....	....
1995-96	**Montreal (NHL)**	**5**	**0**	**5**	**0**	**.000**	....	....	....	....
1997-98	**Tampa Bay (NHL)**	**63**	**15**	**40**	**8**	**.302**	....	....	....	....
	NHL Totals	**924**	**390**	**413**	**121**	**.488**	**98**	**55**	**43**	**.561**

* Stanley Cup win.

1997-98 Scoring

* – rookie

Regular Season

Pos	#	Player	Team	GP	G	A	Pts	+/–	PIM	PP	SH	GW	GT	S	%
L	15	Paul Ysebaert	T.B.	82	13	27	40	-43	32	2	1	0	0	145	9.0
R	20	Mikael Renberg	T.B.	68	16	22	38	-37	34	6	3	0	1	175	9.1
R	29	Alexander Selivanov	T.B.	70	16	19	35	-38	85	4	0	3	1	206	7.8
L	44	Stephane Richer	MTL	14	5	4	9	1	5	2	0	0	0	24	20.8
			T.B.	26	9	11	20	-7	36	3	0	2	0	71	12.7
			TOTAL	40	14	15	29	-6	41	5	0	2	0	95	14.7
L	7	Rob Zamuner	T.B.	77	14	12	26	-31	41	0	3	4	1	126	11.1
C	18	Daymond Langkow	T.B.	68	8	14	22	-9	62	2	0	1	0	156	5.1
C	16	Darcy Tucker	MTL	39	1	5	6	-6	57	0	0	0	0	19	5.3
			T.B.	35	6	8	14	-8	89	1	1	0	0	44	13.6
			TOTAL	74	7	13	20	-14	146	1	1	0	0	63	11.1
R	10	Sandy McCarthy	CGY	52	8	5	13	-18	170	1	0	1	0	68	11.8
			T.B.	14	0	5	5	-1	71	0	0	0	0	26	0.0
			TOTAL	66	8	10	18	-19	241	1	0	1	0	94	8.5
R	34	Mikael Andersson	T.B.	72	6	11	17	-4	29	0	1	1	0	105	5.7
D	14	Karl Dykhuis	T.B.	78	5	9	14	-8	110	0	1	0	0	91	5.5
C	64 *	Jason Bonsignore	T.B.	35	2	8	10	-11	22	0	0	0	0	29	6.9
D	4	Cory Cross	T.B.	74	3	6	9	-24	77	0	1	0	0	72	4.2
R	21	Jody Hull	FLA	21	2	0	2	1	4	0	1	0	0	23	8.7
			T.B.	28	2	4	6	2	4	0	0	2	0	28	7.1
			TOTAL	49	4	4	8	3	8	0	1	2	0	51	7.8
D	33	Yves Racine	T.B.	60	0	8	8	-23	41	0	0	0	0	76	0.0
C	19	Brian Bradley	T.B.	14	2	5	7	-9	6	2	0	0	0	24	8.3
D	6	David Wilkie	MTL	5	1	0	1	-1	4	0	0	1	0	2	50.0
			T.B.	29	1	5	6	-21	17	0	0	0	0	46	2.2
			TOTAL	34	2	5	7	-22	21	0	0	1	0	48	4.2
C	79	Vladimir Vujtek	T.B.	30	2	4	6	-2	16	0	0	1	0	44	4.5
L	17 *	Brent Peterson	T.B.	19	5	0	5	-2	2	0	0	0	0	15	33.3
C	11 *	Steve Kelly	EDM	19	0	2	2	-4	8	0	0	0	0	5	0.0
			T.B.	24	2	1	3	-9	15	1	0	0	0	17	11.8
			TOTAL	43	2	3	5	-13	23	1	0	0	0	22	9.1
R	62	Andrei Nazarov	S.J.	40	1	1	2	-4	112	0	0	0	0	31	3.2
			T.B.	14	1	1	2	-9	58	0	0	0	0	19	5.3
			TOTAL	54	2	2	4	-13	170	0	0	0	0	50	4.0
D	39	Enrico Ciccone	CAR	14	0	3	3	3	83	0	0	0	0	8	0.0
			VAN	13	0	1	1	-2	47	0	0	0	0	7	0.0
			T.B.	12	0	0	0	-3	45	0	0	0	0	7	0.0
			TOTAL	39	0	4	4	-2	175	0	0	0	0	22	0.0
D	3 *	Pavel Kubina	T.B.	10	1	2	3	-1	22	0	0	0	0	8	12.5
D	5	Jassen Cullimore	MTL	3	0	0	0	0	4	0	0	0	0	1	0.0
			T.B.	25	1	2	3	-4	22	1	0	0	0	17	5.9
			TOTAL	28	1	2	3	-4	26	1	0	0	0	18	5.6
L	36	Louie Debrusk	T.B.	54	1	2	3	-2	166	0	0	0	0	14	7.1
R	10	Paul Brousseau	T.B.	11	0	2	2	0	27	0	0	0	0	6	0.0
D	27	David Shaw	T.B.	14	0	2	2	-2	12	0	0	0	0	12	0.0
C	28	Corey Spring	T.B.	8	1	0	1	-1	10	0	0	0	0	12	8.3
D	2 *	Mike McBain	T.B.	27	0	1	1	-10	8	0	0	0	0	17	0.0
G	30	Mark Fitzpatrick	FLA	12	0	0	0	0	2	0	0	0	0	0	0.0
			T.B.	34	0	1	1	0	14	0	0	0	0	0	0.0
			TOTAL	46	0	1	1	0	16	0	0	0	0	0	0.0
L	16	Troy Mallette	T.B.	3	0	0	0	0	7	0	0	0	0	0	0.0
G	35 *	Derek Wilkinson	T.B.	8	0	0	0	0	0	0	0	0	0	0	0.0
C	25	Alan Egeland	T.B.	8	0	0	0	0	9	0	0	0	0	4	0.0
G	1 *	Zac Bierk	T.B.	13	0	0	0	0	0	0	0	0	0	0	0.0
G	32	Corey Schwab	T.B.	16	0	0	0	0	2	0	0	0	0	0	0.0
G	93	Daren Puppa	T.B.	26	0	0	0	0	6	0	0	0	0	0	0.0

Goaltending

No.	Goaltender	GPI	Mins	Avg	W	L	T	EN	SO	GA	SA	S%
93	Daren Puppa	26	1456	2.72	5	14	6	6	0	66	660	.900
32	Corey Schwab	16	821	2.92	2	9	1	2	1	40	370	.892
30	Mark Fitzpatrick	34	1938	3.16	7	24	1	5	1	102	975	.895
35	* Derek Wilkinson	8	311	3.28	2	4	1	1	0	17	148	.885
1	* Zac Bierk	13	433	4.16	1	4	1	0	0	30	210	.857
	Totals	**82**	**4978**	**3.24**	**17**	**55**	**10**	**14**	**3**	**269**	**2377**	**.887**

Coaching History

Terry Crisp, 1992-93 to 1996-97; Terry Crisp, Rick Paterson and Jacques Demers, 1997-98; Jacques Demers, 1998-99.

Karl Dykhuis was acquired by Tampa Bay from the Philadelphia Flyers along with Mikael Renberg. His five goals for the Lightning in 1997-98 tied a career high.

Club Records

Team

(Figures in brackets for season records are games played; records for fewest points, wins, ties, losses, goals, goals against are for 70 or more games)

Most Points	**88**	1995-96 (82)
Most Wins	**38**	1995-96 (82)
Most Ties	**12**	1995-96 (82)
Most Losses	**55**	1997-98 (82)
Most Goals	**245**	1992-93 (84)
Most Goals Against	**332**	1992-93 (84)
Fewest Points	**44**	1997-98 (82)
Fewest Wins	**23**	1992-93 (84)
Fewest Ties	**7**	1992-93 (84)
Fewest Losses	**32**	1995-96 (82)
Fewest Goals	**151**	1997-98 (82)
Fewest Goals Against	**247**	1996-97 (82)
Longest Winning Streak		
Overall	**5**	Twice
Home	**6**	Feb. 15-Mar. 10/96
Away	**4**	Jan. 6-13/97
Longest Undefeated Streak		
Overall	**7**	Feb. 28-Mar. 13/96 (5 wins, 2 ties)
Home	**8**	Feb. 15-Mar. 23/96 (6 wins, 2 ties)
Away	**6**	Dec. 28/93-Jan. 12/94 (5 wins, 1 tie)
Longest Losing Streak		
Overall	**13**	Jan. 3-Feb. 2/98
Home	**8**	Jan. 3-Feb. 2/98
Away	**7**	Oct. 24-Nov. 17/97
Longest Winless Streak		
Overall	**16**	Twice
Home	**10**	Jan. 2-Feb. 5/98 (9 losses, 1 tie)
Away	**12**	Oct. 10-Nov. 17/97 (11 losses, 1 ties)
Most Shutouts, Season	**6**	1996-97 (82)
Most PIM, Season	**1,823**	1997-98 (82)
Most Goals, Game	**7**	Five times

Individual

Most Seasons	**6**	Several players
Most Games, Career	**417**	Rob Zamuner
Most Goals, Career	**111**	Brian Bradley
Most Assists, Career	**189**	Brian Bradley
Most Points, Career	**300**	Brian Bradley (111G, 189A)
Most PIM, Career	**580**	Enrico Ciccone
Most Shutouts, Career	**10**	Daren Puppa
Longest Consecutive Games Streak	**226**	Rob Zamuner
Most Goals, Season	**42**	Brian Bradley (1992-93)
Most Assists, Season	**56**	Brian Bradley (1995-96)
Most Points, Season	**86**	Brian Bradley (1992-93; 42G, 44A)
Most PIM, Season	**258**	Enrico Ciccone (1995-96)
Most Shutouts, Season	**5**	Daren Puppa (1995-96)
Most Points, Defenseman, Season	**65**	Roman Hamrlik (1995-96; 16G, 49A)
Most Points, Center, Season	**86**	Brian Bradley (1992-93; 42G, 44A)
Most Points, Right Wing, Season	**60**	Dino Ciccarelli (1996-97; 35G, 25A)
Most Points, Left Wing, Season	**51**	Chris Kontos (1992-93; 27G, 24A)
Most Points, Rookie, Season	**43**	Rob Zamuner (1992-93; 15G, 28A)
Most Goals, Game	**4**	Chris Kontos (Oct. 7/92)
Most Assists, Game	**4**	Joe Reekie (Oct. 7/92), Marc Bureau (Feb. 1/93)
Most Points, Game	**6**	Doug Crossman (Nov. 7/92; 3G, 3A)

Captains' History

No captain, 1992-93 to 1994-95; Paul Ysebaert, 1995-96, 1996-97; Paul Ysebaert and Mikael Renberg, 1997-98.

All-time Record vs. Other Clubs

Regular Season

	At Home							On Road							Total						
	GP	W	L	T	GF	GA	PTS	GP	W	L	T	GF	GA	PTS	GP	W	L	T	GF	GA	PTS
Anaheim	4	2	2	0	7	11	4	4	1	2	1	9	12	3	8	3	4	1	16	23	7
Boston	11	4	5	2	29	31	10	10	1	7	2	23	37	4	21	5	12	4	52	68	14
Buffalo	11	1	9	1	20	38	3	11	5	5	1	36	29	11	22	6	14	2	56	67	14
Calgary	6	3	2	1	22	23	7	5	2	3	0	11	18	4	11	5	5	1	33	41	11
Carolina	11	6	4	1	34	30	13	11	2	8	1	26	37	5	22	8	12	2	60	67	18
Chicago	7	4	2	1	19	17	9	8	3	3	2	19	18	8	15	7	5	3	38	35	17
Colorado	8	6	1	1	29	21	13	8	2	5	1	20	34	5	16	8	6	2	49	55	18
Dallas	8	1	5	2	13	22	4	7	1	5	1	15	25	3	15	2	10	3	28	47	7
Detroit	9	1	7	1	30	50	3	7	1	6	0	15	29	2	16	2	13	1	45	79	5
Edmonton	6	2	2	2	18	14	6	6	1	5	0	14	16	2	12	3	7	2	32	30	8
Florida	13	4	5	4	29	34	12	12	2	8	2	18	32	6	25	6	13	6	47	66	18
Los Angeles	5	2	3	0	11	12	4	6	5	1	0	23	16	10	11	7	4	0	34	28	14
Montreal	11	6	3	2	30	26	14	10	3	6	1	23	31	7	21	9	9	3	53	57	21
New Jersey	13	3	7	3	31	39	9	14	1	12	1	20	54	3	27	4	19	4	51	93	12
NY Islanders	14	6	7	1	36	47	13	13	8	5	0	41	36	16	27	14	12	1	77	83	29
NY Rangers	13	6	5	2	44	38	14	15	7	7	1	56	53	15	28	13	12	3	100	91	29
Ottawa	11	5	6	0	32	31	10	11	7	4	0	30	28	14	22	12	10	0	62	59	24
Philadelphia	14	4	9	1	38	46	9	13	1	8	4	23	44	6	27	5	17	5	61	90	15
Phoenix	6	2	4	0	18	23	4	6	3	3	0	15	18	6	12	5	7	0	33	41	10
Pittsburgh	10	3	6	1	32	40	7	11	2	7	2	24	49	6	21	5	13	3	56	89	13
St. Louis	8	3	3	2	24	25	8	7	1	6	0	19	28	2	15	4	9	2	43	53	10
San Jose	6	4	2	0	19	13	8	6	5	1	0	25	18	10	12	9	3	0	44	31	18
Toronto	8	1	7	0	15	31	2	10	5	5	0	26	35	10	18	6	12	0	41	66	12
Vancouver	5	2	3	0	16	19	4	6	0	6	0	9	31	0	11	2	9	0	25	50	4
Washington	13	3	9	1	25	37	7	14	4	6	4	34	45	12	27	7	15	5	59	82	19
Totals	**231**	**84**	**118**	**29**	**621**	**718**	**197**	**231**	**73**	**134**	**24**	**574**	**773**	**170**	**462**	**157**	**252**	**53**	**1195**	**1491**	**367**

Playoffs

	Series	W	L	GP	W	L	T	GF	GA	Last Mtg.	Round	Result
Philadelphia	1	0	1	6	2	4	0	13	26	1996	CQF	L 2-4
Totals	**1**	**0**	**1**	**6**	**2**	**4**	**0**	**13**	**26**			

Playoff Results 1998-94

Year	Round	Opponent	Result	GF	GA
1996	CQF	Philadelphia	L 2-4	13	26

Abbreviations: Round: CQF – conference quarter-final.

Carolina totals include Hartford, 1992-93 to 1996-97. Dallas totals include Minnesota, 1992-93.

Colorado totals include Quebec, 1992-93 to 1994-95. Phoenix totals include Winnipeg, 1992-93 to 1995-96.

1997-98 Results

Oct.	1		Carolina	4-2
	3		New Jersey	3-4
	5		Buffalo	1-1
	9	at	Chicago	4-1
	10	at	Detroit	0-3
	15	at	Florida	1-2
	17		Pittsburgh	1-4
	18	at	New Jersey	0-5
	21	at	Philadelphia	1-7
	23	at	Boston	2-2
	24	at	NY Rangers	3-4
	26		Los Angeles	1-3
	29		Ottawa	2-5
Nov.	5	at	Anaheim	2-5
	6	at	Los Angeles	2-5
	8	at	San Jose	1-3
	11	at	Phoenix	2-5
	14		NY Islanders	1-4
	16	at	Philadelphia	2-3
	17	at	Montreal	1-4
	19		NY Rangers	6-3
	22		Calgary	4-3
	26		Colorado	3-3
	28	at	Carolina	0-2
	29		Philadelphia	3-3
Dec.	3		Phoenix	2-1
	5	at	Buffalo	0-4
	6	at	New Jersey	2-4
	10	at	Dallas	0-3
	13	at	Ottawa	3-1
	14	at	Philadelphia	0-3
	16	at	Pittsburgh	1-1
	17		Boston	2-0
	20		NY Rangers	2-2
	22		St. Louis	2-2
	23	at	NY Rangers	1-4
	27		Boston	1-3
	29		San Jose	2-1
	31		NY Rangers	2-0
Jan.	2		Florida	2-2
	3		Anaheim	1-4
	7		Toronto	2-5
	9	at	New Jersey	1-4
	11		Philadelphia	2-5
	12		Montreal	3-6
	14		NY Islanders	1-7
	21		Washington	2-3
	23	at	Buffalo	1-4
	24	at	Toronto	2-5
	26	at	Ottawa	1-2
	28		Carolina	2-3
	31	at	Florida	0-2
Feb.	2		Buffalo	3-7
	4	at	Carolina	3-3
	5		Detroit	4-5
	7	at	Washington	4-3
	25	at	Washington	4-3
	26		New Jersey	1-4
	28		Washington	5-2
Mar.	3	at	Calgary	1-2
	4	at	Edmonton	2-4
	7	at	Vancouver	2-5
	9	at	Colorado	2-1
	11		Edmonton	0-2
	14		Chicago	1-0
	16	at	Boston	3-4
	18		Vancouver	4-2
	21		Florida	5-1
	25		Montreal	1-2
	26	at	St. Louis	2-3
	28	at	Montreal	2-8
	30	at	NY Rangers	3-1
Apr.	1	at	NY Islanders	0-4
	2	at	Washington	1-4
	4		Pittsburgh	1-4
	6		NY Islanders	0-3
	8		Philadelphia	1-6
	11		Dallas	1-5
	13		Ottawa	2-3
	15	at	Pittsburgh	1-5
	16	at	NY Islanders	0-4
	18		Florida	2-2

Entry Draft Selections 1998-92

1998

Pick	
1	Vincent Lecavalier
64	Brad Richards
72	Dimitry Afanasenkov
92	Eric Beaudoin
121	Curtis Rich
146	Sergei Kuznetsov
174	Brett Allan
194	Oak Hewer
221	Daniel Hulak
229	Chris Lyness
252	Martin Cibak

1997

Pick	
7	Paul Mara
33	Kyle Kos
61	Matt Elich
108	Mark Thompson
109	Jan Sulc
112	Karel Betik
153	Andrei Skopintsev
168	Justin Jack
170	Eero Somervuori
185	Samuel St-Pierre
198	Shawn Skolney
224	Paul Comrie

1996

Pick	
16	Mario Larocque
69	Curtis Tipler
125	Jason Robinson
152	Nikolai Ignatov
157	Xavier Delisle
179	Pavel Kubina

1995

Pick	
5	Daymond Langkow
30	Mike McBain
56	Shane Willis
108	Konsta Golokhvastov
134	Eduard Pershin
160	Cory Murphy
186	Joe Cardarelli
212	Zac Bierk

1994

Pick	
8	Jason Wiemer
34	Colin Cloutier
55	Vadim Epachintsev
86	Dmitri Klevakin
137	Daniel Juden
138	Bryce Salvador
164	Chris Maillet
190	Alexei Baranov
216	Yuri Smirnov
242	Shawn Gervais
268	Brian White

1993

Pick	
3	Chris Gratton
29	Tyler Moss
55	Allan Egeland
81	Marian Kacir
107	Ryan Brown
133	Kiley Hill
159	Mathieu Raby
185	Ryan Nauss
211	Alexandre Laporte
237	Brett Duncan
263	Mark Szoke

1992

Pick	
1	Roman Hamrlik
26	Drew Bannister
49	Brent Gretzky
74	Aaron Gavey
97	Brantt Myhres
122	Martin Tanguay
145	Derek Wilkinson
170	Dennis Maxwell
193	Andrew Kemper
218	Marc Tardif
241	Tom MacDonald

General Managers' History

Phil Esposito, 1992-93 to date.

General Manager

ESPOSITO, PHIL
General Manager, Tampa Bay Lightning.
Born in Sault Ste. Marie, Ont., February 20, 1942.

No one deserves more credit for the creation of the Tampa Bay Lightning than general manager Phil Esposito. While many words can describe Phil — including dynamic, charismatic and creative — perhaps when speaking of the Lightning and Phil's association, none is more appropriate than determined.

It was Phil Esposito's determination and persistence that led to the awarding of an expansion franchise in 1990. Despite predictions that the franchise might not perform well, Phil's determination brought the Lightning a highly competitive — and respected — team in 1992-93 when the Lightning first hit the ice. And it was Phil's determination that continued the building process and led the team to the playoffs for the first time after only four seasons.

One of hockey's greatest performers — he ranks fourth on the NHL all-time goal-scoring list and is a member of the Hockey Hall of Fame — Phil has distinguished himself in his role with the Lightning as the person in charge of all aspects of hockey operations. Phil has utilized every avenue available to build the Lightning — be it through the Expansion Draft, Entry Draft, free agent signings, waiver draft selections and trade.

Esposito's spectacular 18-year playing career was highlighted by two Stanley Cup championships as a member of the Boston Bruins in 1970 and 1972. Originally a member of the Chicago Blackhawks (1963-67), Esposito was the central figure in one of hockey's biggest trades when he was sent to Boston in 1967. Over the next eight seasons, he virtually rewrote the NHL record books. He became the first player in NHL history to score 100 points in a season (1969-70) and, two seasons later, set single season standards of 76 goals and 152 points, which stood until Wayne Gretzky eclipsed those marks a decade later. Over a five-year period (1970-71 to 1974-75), Phil scored 55 or more goals and totalled 127 points or more in each season with combined totals of 326 goals and 687 points. Once again part of one of hockey's biggest trades in 1975, Esposito was dealt to the New York Rangers where he led the Rangers in scoring for four years and helped them to the Stanley Cup Finals in 1979.

His 717 goals place him fourth on the all-time list behind Gretzky (862), Gordie Howe (801) and Marcel Dionne (731) and his 1,590 points are fifth all-time behind Gretzky, Howe, Dionne and Mark Messier.

Phil was also an integral member of several international teams, including Team Canada's memorable come-from-behind effort in the historic first Summit Series in 1972 against Russia.

Prior to his efforts with the Lightning, Esposito, now 56, was vice president and general manager of the New York Rangers from 1986-88.

Phil resides in Tampa. He has three daughters, Laurie, Carrie and Cherise and two grandsons, Dylan and Dakoda.

NHL Coaching Record

		Regular Season					Playoffs			
Season	Team	Games	W	L	T	%	Games	W	L	%
1986-87	NY Rangers	43	24	19	0	.558	6	2	4	.333
1988-89	NY Rangers	2	0	2	0	.000	4	0	4	.000
	NHL Totals	**45**	**24**	**21**	**0**	**.533**	**10**	**2**	**8**	**.200**

Club Directory

Ice Palace

Ice Palace
401 Channelside Drive
Tampa, FL 33602
Admin. Office **813/229-2658**
FAX 813/229-3350
Ticket Info. 813/229-8800
www.tampabaylightning.com
Capacity: 19,758

Executive Staff

Owner	Arthur L. Williams
President, CEO & Governor	Billy McGehee
Executive Vice President	Jeffrey C. Gaines
Chief Financial Officer	Steve Noble
Director of Business Relations	Donna Ferris
Executive Assistant	Connie Troy
Executive Assistant	Evelyn Hicks

Hockey Operations

General Manager & Alt. Governor	Phil Esposito
Head Coach/Dir. Player Personnel	Jacques Demers
Assistant General Manager	Tony Esposito
Counsel	Henry Lee Paul – Lazzara & Paul, P.A.
Assistant Coaches	Rick Paterson, Paulin Bordeleau
Head Scout	Don Murdoch
Pro Scout	Peter Mahovlich
Scouting Staff	Angelo Bumbacco, Jake Goertzen, Doug Macauley, Richard Rose, Luke Williams, Stephen Baker, Robert Murdoch
Medical Trainers	Curtis Bell, John Shipman
Equipment Manager	Jacques (Jocko) Cayer
Assistant Equipment Managers	James Pickard, Michael Wall
Hockey Operations Assistant	Kathy Skelton
Director of Team Services	Phil Thibodeau
Video Coordinator	Nigel Kirwan
Receptionists	Patsy Rodenbostel, Mary Sharpe
Minor League Affiliate	Cleveland Lumberjaks (IHL)

Media Relations

Director of Media Relations	Jay Preble
Media Information Manager	John R. Sternal
Publications Manager	Brian Potter

Community Relations

Director of Community Relations	David Tagliarino
Community Relations Coordinator	Stephanie Hanchey
Youth Hockey Coordinator	David Walkowiak

Executive Suites & Premium Seating

Director of Suite Sales & Service	Debbie Cagle
Suite Sales Manager	Theresa Huffman
Suite Service Managers	Mike Vargo, Pam Goniwiecha

Finance

Director of Finance	Eddie Diliberto
Accounting Manager	Vincent Ascanio
Staff Accountant	Robin Hughes
Accounts Payable Clerk	Alina Simonds
Administrative Assistant	Kelly McElveen
Human Resources	TBD

Marketing

Director of Marketing	April Melquist
Creative Services/Game Operations Manager	Killeen Mullen
Marketing Assistant	TBD
Promotions Coordinator	Jason Gulledge

Corporate Sales

VP of Corporate Sales & Service	Kevin Kline
Corporate Sales Manager	Fred Doremus
Corporate Sales Account Executive	Sonya Michael
Sponsorship Coordinator	Parrish Lamb
Administrative Assistant	TBD

Ticket Operations

Director of Ticket Sales	Jim Van Stone
Ticket Sales Manager	Brendan Cunningham
Group Sales Manager	Cliff Gault
Ticket Office Manager	Marylin Brace
Season Ticket Service Manager	Dan Pekarek
Sales Representatives	Mike Centanni, Missy Davis

Medical Staff

Team Physician	Dr. David Leffers

Broadcast Information

Television	Sunshine Network, WTTA TV38
Television Broadcasters	Rick Peckham, Bobby Taylor
Radio	WDAE AM1250
Radio Broadcaster	Larry Hirsch

Toronto Maple Leafs

1997-98 Results: 30W-43L-9T 69PTS. Sixth, Central Division

Mike Johnson's 15 goals and 32 assists in 1997-98 tied him with Boston's Sergei Samsonov for the rookie scoring lead with 47 points. Johnson's point total trailed only Mat Sundin (74) among Leafs scorers.

TORONTO MAPLE LEAFS ®

1998-99 Schedule

Oct.	Sat.	10	Detroit
	Tue.	13	at Edmonton
	Fri.	16	at Calgary
	Sat.	17	at Vancouver
	Mon.	19	Nashville
	Fri.	23	at Detroit
	Sat.	24	at Pittsburgh
	Mon.	26	Pittsburgh
	Fri.	30	at Buffalo
	Sat.	31	Buffalo
Nov.	Wed.	4	Colorado
	Thu.	5	at Boston
	Sat.	7	NY Rangers
	Mon.	9	NY Islanders
	Wed.	11	Edmonton
	Thu.	12	at Chicago
	Sat.	14	Ottawa
	Wed.	18	at Washington
	Fri.	20	at Buffalo
	Sat.	21	Buffalo
	Mon.	23	Calgary
	Wed.	25	Vancouver
	Fri.	27	at Philadelphia*
	Sat.	28	Ottawa
Dec.	Wed.	2	Los Angeles
	Sat.	5	at Montreal
	Mon.	7	at NY Rangers
	Fri.	11	at Chicago
	Sat.	12	Philadelphia
	Wed.	16	Phoenix
	Sat.	19	NY Rangers
	Mon.	21	Pittsburgh
	Wed.	23	Dallas
	Sat.	26	Montreal
	Wed.	30	Anaheim
	Thu.	31	at Detroit
Jan.	Sat.	2	Washington
	Mon.	4	Tampa Bay
	Thu.	7	at Boston
	Sat.	9	Boston
	Tue.	12	at Tampa Bay
	Wed.	13	at Florida
	Sat.	16	at Philadelphia
	Mon.	18	at Carolina
	Wed.	20	at Dallas
	Thu.	21	at St. Louis
	Thu.	28	at Pittsburgh
	Sat.	30	Washington
Feb.	Tue.	2	at Tampa Bay
	Wed.	3	at Florida
	Sat.	6	at New Jersey
	Wed.	10	Carolina
	Sat.	13	Chicago
	Mon.	15	at New Jersey
	Wed.	17	at Buffalo
	Sat.	20	Montreal
	Mon.	22	at Washington
	Wed.	24	Carolina
	Thu.	25	at NY Islanders
	Sat.	27	Florida
Mar.	Wed.	3	New Jersey
	Thu.	4	at St. Louis
	Sat.	6	at Ottawa
	Mon.	8	at NY Rangers
	Tue.	9	Tampa Bay
	Thu.	11	at NY Islanders
	Sat.	13	at Montreal
	Wed.	17	Boston
	Sat.	20	New Jersey
	Mon.	22	Philadelphia
	Wed.	24	San Jose
	Fri.	26	at Carolina
	Sat.	27	Boston
	Wed.	31	at Vancouver
Apr.	Thu.	1	at Edmonton
	Sat.	3	at Calgary
	Mon.	5	St. Louis
	Wed.	7	Ottawa
	Thu.	8	at Ottawa
	Sat.	10	Florida
	Wed.	14	NY Islanders
	Sat.	17	at Montreal

* Denotes afternoon game.

Year-by-Year Record

		Home			Road			Overall							
Season	GP	W	L	T	W	L	T	W	L	T	GF	GA	Pts.	Finished	Playoff Result
1997-98	82	16	20	5	14	23	4	30	43	9	194	237	69	6th, Central Div.	Out of Playoffs
1996-97	82	18	20	3	12	24	5	30	44	8	230	273	68	6th, Central Div.	Out of Playoffs
1995-96	82	19	15	7	15	21	5	34	36	12	247	252	80	3rd, Central Div.	Lost Conf. Quarter-Final
1994-95	48	15	7	2	6	12	6	21	19	8	135	146	50	4th, Central Div.	Lost Conf. Quarter-Final
1993-94	84	23	15	4	20	14	8	43	29	12	280	243	98	2nd, Central Div.	Lost Conf. Championship
1992-93	84	25	11	6	19	18	5	44	29	11	288	241	99	3rd, Norris Div.	Lost Conf. Championship
1991-92	80	21	16	3	9	27	4	30	43	7	234	294	67	5th, Norris Div.	Out of Playoffs
1990-91	80	15	21	4	8	25	7	23	46	11	241	318	57	5th, Norris Div.	Out of Playoffs
1989-90	80	24	14	2	14	24	2	38	38	4	337	358	80	3rd, Norris Div.	Lost Div. Semi-Final
1988-89	80	15	20	5	13	26	1	28	46	6	259	342	62	5th, Norris Div.	Out of Playoffs
1987-88	80	14	20	6	7	29	4	21	49	10	273	345	52	4th, Norris Div.	Lost Div. Semi-Final
1986-87	80	22	14	4	10	28	2	32	42	6	286	319	70	4th, Norris Div.	Lost Div. Final
1985-86	80	16	21	3	9	27	4	25	48	7	311	386	57	4th, Norris Div.	Lost Div. Final
1984-85	80	10	28	2	10	24	6	20	52	8	253	358	48	5th, Norris Div.	Out of Playoffs
1983-84	80	17	16	7	9	29	2	26	45	9	303	387	61	5th, Norris Div.	Out of Playoffs
1982-83	80	20	15	5	8	25	7	28	40	12	293	330	68	3rd, Norris Div.	Lost Div. Semi-Final
1981-82	80	12	20	8	8	24	8	20	44	16	298	380	56	5th, Norris Div.	Out of Playoffs
1980-81	80	14	21	5	14	16	10	28	37	15	322	367	71	5th, Adams Div.	Lost Prelim. Round
1979-80	80	17	19	4	18	21	1	35	40	5	304	327	75	4th, Adams Div.	Lost Prelim. Round
1978-79	80	20	12	8	14	21	5	34	33	13	267	252	81	3rd, Adams Div.	Lost Quarter-Final
1977-78	80	21	13	6	20	16	4	41	29	10	271	237	92	3rd, Adams Div.	Lost Semi-Final
1976-77	80	18	13	9	15	19	6	33	32	15	301	285	81	3rd, Adams Div.	Lost Quarter-Final
1975-76	80	23	12	5	11	19	10	34	31	15	294	276	83	3rd, Adams Div.	Lost Quarter-Final
1974-75	80	19	12	9	12	21	7	31	33	16	280	309	78	3rd, Adams Div.	Lost Quarter-Final
1973-74	78	21	11	7	14	16	9	35	27	16	274	230	86	4th, East Div.	Lost Quarter-Final
1972-73	78	20	12	7	7	29	3	27	41	10	247	279	64	6th, East Div.	Out of Playoffs
1971-72	78	21	11	7	12	20	7	33	31	14	209	208	80	4th, East Div.	Lost Quarter-Final
1970-71	78	24	9	6	13	24	2	37	33	8	248	211	82	4th, East Div.	Lost Quarter-Final
1969-70	76	18	13	7	11	21	6	29	34	13	222	242	71	6th, East Div.	Out of Playoffs
1968-69	76	20	8	10	15	18	5	35	26	15	234	217	85	4th, East Div.	Lost Quarter-Final
1967-68	74	24	9	4	9	22	6	33	31	10	209	176	76	5th, East Div.	Out of Playoffs
1966-67	**70**	**21**	**8**	**6**	**11**	**19**	**5**	**32**	**27**	**11**	**204**	**211**	**75**	**3rd,**	**Won Stanley Cup**
1965-66	70	22	9	4	12	16	7	34	25	11	208	187	79	3rd,	Lost Semi-Final
1964-65	70	17	15	3	13	11	11	30	26	14	204	173	74	4th,	Lost Semi-Final
1963-64	**70**	**22**	**7**	**6**	**11**	**18**	**6**	**33**	**25**	**12**	**192**	**172**	**78**	**3rd,**	**Won Stanley Cup**
1962-63	**70**	**21**	**8**	**6**	**14**	**15**	**6**	**35**	**23**	**12**	**221**	**180**	**82**	**1st,**	**Won Stanley Cup**
1961-62	**70**	**25**	**5**	**5**	**12**	**17**	**6**	**37**	**22**	**11**	**232**	**180**	**85**	**2nd,**	**Won Stanley Cup**
1960-61	70	21	6	8	18	13	4	39	19	12	234	176	90	2nd,	Lost Semi-Final
1959-60	70	20	9	6	15	17	3	35	26	9	199	195	79	2nd,	Lost Final
1958-59	70	17	13	5	10	19	6	27	32	11	189	201	65	4th,	Lost Final
1957-58	70	12	16	7	9	22	4	21	38	11	192	226	53	6th,	Out of Playoffs
1956-57	70	12	16	7	9	18	8	21	34	15	174	192	57	5th,	Out of Playoffs
1955-56	70	19	10	6	5	23	7	24	33	13	153	181	61	4th,	Lost Semi-Final
1954-55	70	14	10	11	10	14	11	24	24	22	147	135	70	3rd,	Lost Semi-Final
1953-54	70	22	6	7	10	18	7	32	24	14	152	131	78	3rd,	Lost Semi-Final
1952-53	70	17	12	6	10	18	7	27	30	13	156	167	67	5th,	Out of Playoffs
1951-52	70	17	10	8	12	15	8	29	25	16	168	157	74	3rd,	Lost Semi-Final
1950-51	**70**	**22**	**8**	**5**	**19**	**8**	**8**	**41**	**16**	**13**	**212**	**138**	**95**	**2nd,**	**Won Stanley Cup**
1949-50	70	18	9	8	13	18	4	31	27	12	176	173	74	3rd,	Lost Semi-Final
1948-49	**60**	**12**	**8**	**10**	**10**	**17**	**3**	**22**	**25**	**13**	**147**	**161**	**57**	**4th,**	**Won Stanley Cup**
1947-48	**60**	**22**	**3**	**5**	**10**	**12**	**8**	**32**	**15**	**13**	**182**	**143**	**77**	**1st,**	**Won Stanley Cup**
1946-47	**60**	**20**	**8**	**2**	**11**	**11**	**8**	**31**	**19**	**10**	**209**	**172**	**72**	**2nd,**	**Won Stanley Cup**
1945-46	50	10	13	2	9	11	5	19	24	7	174	185	45	5th,	Out of Playoffs
1944-45	**50**	**13**	**9**	**3**	**11**	**13**	**1**	**24**	**22**	**4**	**183**	**161**	**52**	**3rd,**	**Won Stanley Cup**
1943-44	50	13	11	1	10	12	3	23	23	4	214	174	50	3rd,	Lost Semi-Final
1942-43	50	17	6	2	5	13	7	22	19	9	198	159	53	3rd,	Lost Semi-Final
1941-42	**48**	**18**	**6**	**0**	**9**	**12**	**3**	**27**	**18**	**3**	**158**	**136**	**57**	**2nd,**	**Won Stanley Cup**
1940-41	48	16	5	3	12	9	3	28	14	6	145	99	62	2nd,	Lost Semi-Final
1939-40	48	15	3	6	10	14	0	25	17	6	134	110	56	3rd,	Lost Final
1938-39	48	13	8	3	6	12	6	19	20	9	114	107	47	3rd,	Lost Final
1937-38	48	13	6	5	11	9	4	24	15	9	151	127	57	1st, Cdn. Div.	Lost Final
1936-37	48	14	9	1	8	12	4	22	21	5	119	115	49	3rd, Cdn. Div.	Lost Quarter-Final
1935-36	48	15	4	5	8	15	1	23	19	6	126	106	52	2nd, Cdn. Div.	Lost Final
1934-35	48	16	6	2	14	8	2	30	14	4	157	111	64	1st, Cdn. Div.	Lost Final
1933-34	48	19	2	3	7	11	6	26	13	9	174	119	61	1st, Cdn. Div.	Lost Semi-Final
1932-33	48	16	4	4	8	14	2	24	18	6	119	111	54	1st, Cdn. Div.	Lost Final
1931-32	**48**	**17**	**4**	**3**	**6**	**14**	**4**	**23**	**18**	**7**	**155**	**127**	**53**	**2nd, Cdn. Div.**	**Won Stanley Cup**
1930-31	44	15	4	3	7	9	6	22	13	9	118	99	53	2nd, Cdn. Div.	Lost Quarter-Final
1929-30	44	10	8	4	7	13	2	17	21	6	116	124	40	4th, Cdn. Div.	Out of Playoffs
1928-29	44	15	5	2	6	13	3	21	18	5	85	69	47	3rd, Cdn. Div.	Lost Semi-Final
1927-28	44	9	8	5	9	10	3	18	18	8	89	88	44	4th, Cdn. Div.	Out of Playoffs
1926-27*	44	10	10	2	5	14	3	15	24	5	79	94	35	5th, Cdn. Div.	Out of Playoffs
1925-26	36	11	5	2	1	16	1	12	21	3	92	114	27	6th,	Out of Playoffs
1924-25	30	10	5	0	9	6	0	19	11	0	90	84	38	2nd,	Lost NHL S-Final
1923-24	24	7	5	0	3	9	0	10	14	0	59	85	20	3rd,	Out of Playoffs
1922-23	24	10	1	1	3	9	0	13	10	1	82	88	27	3rd,	Out of Playoffs
1921-22	**24**	**8**	**4**	**0**	**5**	**6**	**1**	**13**	**10**	**1**	**98**	**97**	**27**	**2nd,**	**Won Stanley Cup**
1920-21	24	9	3	0	6	6	0	15	9	0	105	100	30	2nd and 1st***	Lost NHL Final
1919-20**	24	8	4	0	4	8	0	12	12	0	119	106	24	3rd and 2nd***	Out of Playoffs
1918-19	18	5	4	0	0	9	0	5	13	0	64	92	10	3rd and 3rd***	Out of Playoffs
1917-18	**22**	**10**	**1**	**0**	**3**	**8**	**0**	**13**	**9**	**0**	**108**	**109**	**26**	**2nd and 1st*** **	**Won Stanley Cup**

* Name changed from St. Patricks to Maple Leafs. ** Name changed from Arenas to St. Patricks.
*** Season played in two halves with no combined standing at end.

Franchise date: November 22, 1917

EASTERN NHL CONFERENCE

NORTHEAST DIVISION

82nd NHL Season

1998-99 Player Personnel

FORWARDS	HT	WT	S	Place of Birth	Date	1997-98 Club
ADAMS, Kevyn	6-1	195	R	Washington, D.C.	10/8/74	Toronto-St. John's
BEREZIN, Sergei	5-10	197	R	Voskresensk, USSR	11/5/71	Toronto-Russia
BOHONOS, Lonny	5-11	190	R	Winnipeg, Man.	5/20/73	Van-Syracuse-Tor-St. John's
DOMI, Tie	5-10	200	R	Windsor, Ont.	11/1/69	Toronto
HENDRICKSON, Darby	6-0	185	L	Richfield, MN	8/28/72	Toronto
JOHNSON, Mike	6-2	190	R	Scarborough, Ont.	10/3/74	Toronto
KING, Derek	6-0	212	L	Hamilton, Ont.	2/11/67	Toronto
KING, Kris	5-11	208	L	Bracebridge, Ont.	2/18/66	Toronto
KOHN, Ladislav	5-10	180	L	Uherske Hradiste, Czech.	3/4/75	Calgary-Saint John
KOROLEV, Igor	6-1	187	L	Moscow, USSR	9/6/70	Toronto
McCAULEY, Alyn	5-11	185	L	Brockville, Ont.	5/29/77	Toronto
MODIN, Fredrik	6-3	222	L	Sundsvall, Sweden	10/8/74	Toronto-Sweden
PEARSON, Scott	6-1	205	L	Cornwall, Ont.	12/19/69	Chicago (IHL)
PODOLLAN, Jason	6-1	192	R	Vernon, B.C.	2/18/76	St. John's
SULLIVAN, Steve	5-9	155	R	Timmins, Ont.	7/6/74	Toronto
SUNDIN, Mats	6-4	228	R	Bromma, Sweden	2/13/71	Toronto-Sweden
THOMAS, Steve	5-11	190	L	Stockport, England	7/15/63	New Jersey
THORNTON, Shawn	6-1	196	R	Oshawa, Ont.	7/23/79	St. John's
WARRINER, Todd	6-1	188	L	Blenheim, Ont.	1/3/74	Toronto
DEFENSEMEN						
COTE, Sylvain	6-0	190	R	Quebec City, Que.	1/19/66	Washington-Toronto
EAKINS, Dallas	6-2	195	L	Dade City, FL	2/27/67	Florida-New Haven
MARKOV, Daniil	6-1	196	L	Moscow, USSR	7/11/76	Toronto-St. John's-Russia
SCHNEIDER, Mathieu	5-10	192	L	New York, NY	6/12/69	Toronto-United States
SMITH, D.J.	6-1	200	L	Windsor, Ont.	5/13/77	St. John's
SMITH, Jason	6-3	205	R	Calgary, Alta.	11/2/73	Toronto
TREMBLAY, Yannick	6-2	185	R	Pointe-aux-Trembles, Que.	11/15/75	Toronto-St. John's
WARE, Jeff	6-4	220	L	Toronto, Ont.	5/19/77	Toronto-St. John's
YUSHKEVICH, Dimitri	5-11	208	R	Yaroslavl, USSR	11/19/71	Toronto

GOALTENDERS	HT	WT	C	Place of Birth	Date	1997-98 Club
HEALY, Glenn	5-10	185	L	Pickering, Ont.	8/23/62	Toronto
JOSEPH, Curtis	5-10	185	L	Keswick, Ont.	4/29/67	Edmonton-Canada
LARIVEE, Francis	6-2	198	L	Montreal, Que.	11/8/77	St. John's
POTVIN, Felix	6-1	190	L	Anjou, Que.	6/23/71	Toronto-Canada
ROBITAILLE, Marc	5-10	185	L	Gloucester, Ont.	6/7/76	Northeastern

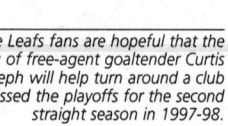

Maple Leafs fans are hopeful that the signing of free-agent goaltender Curtis Joseph will help turn around a club that missed the playoffs for the second straight season in 1997-98.

General Managers' History

Conn Smythe, 1927-28 to 1956-57; Hap Day, 1957-58; Punch Imlach, 1958-59 to 1968-69; Jim Gregory, 1969-70 to 1978-79; Punch Imlach, 1979-80, 1980-81; Punch Imlach and Gerry McNamara, 1981-82; Gerry McNamara, 1982-83 to 1987-88; Gord Stellick, 1988-89; Floyd Smith, 1989-90, 1990-91; Cliff Fletcher, 1991-92 to 1996-97; Ken Dryden, 1997-98 to date.

President and General Manager

DRYDEN, KEN
President and General Manager, Toronto Maple Leafs.
Born in Hamilton, Ont., August 8, 1947.

Ken Dryden, 51, was named president of Toronto Maple Leafs on May 30, 1997. He added the duties of the general manager on August 20, 1997.

As a goaltender, Dryden backstopped the Montreal Canadiens to six Stanley Cup championships after joining the team late in 1971. He was instrumental in the Canadiens winning the 1971 Stanley Cup after having been promoted from the minors and playing just six games down the stretch. While playing all 20 games in the playoffs, Dryden won the Conn Smythe Trophy as playoff MVP. He added the Calder Trophy as the NHL's top rookie the following season and went on to win or share the Vezina Trophy on five occasions. A six-time NHL All-Star, Dryden was inducted into the Hockey Hall of Fame in 1983. He also participated in the historic series between Team Canada and the Soviet National team in 1972.

He played from 1966 to 1969 at Cornell University and was a three-time NCAA East All-American. While playing for the Canadiens, he successfully completed law school at McGill University. Upon retiring after the 1978-79 season, he wrote two best-selling books about hockey, *The Game* and *Home Game*. He also wrote *The Moved and the Shaken: The Story of One Man's Life* and *In School*. He also authored a report for the University of Moncton pertaining to the attack on a referee and the future of hockey at the university.

Dryden initiated the "Ken Dryden Scholarships" to students from foster homes or group homes for study at a university or college. He also coordinated youth employment programs for the governments of the Yukon and Ontario.

Dryden also possesses a background in hockey broadcasting. He was a color commentator for ABC TV at the 1980, 1984 and 1988 Olympic Winter Games.

Ken and his wife Lynda live in Toronto with their two children, Sarah and Michael.

1997-98 Scoring

* – rookie

Regular Season

Pos	#	Player	Team	GP	G	A	Pts	+/–	PIM	PP	SH	GW	GT	S	%
C	13	Mats Sundin	TOR	82	33	41	74	-3	49	9	1	5	1	219	15.1
R	20	* Mike Johnson	TOR	82	15	32	47	-4	24	5	0	0	1	143	10.5
L	7	Derek King	TOR	77	21	25	46	-7	43	4	0	3	0	166	12.7
C	22	Igor Korolev	TOR	78	17	22	39	-18	22	6	3	5	0	97	17.5
D	72	Mathieu Schneider	TOR	76	11	26	37	-12	44	4	1	1	0	181	6.1
L	19	Fredrik Modin	TOR	74	16	16	32	-5	32	1	0	4	0	137	11.7
R	94	Sergei Berezin	TOR	68	16	15	31	-3	10	3	0	3	1	167	9.6
C	11	Steve Sullivan	TOR	63	10	18	28	-8	40	1	0	1	0	112	8.9
D	3	Sylvain Cote	WSH	59	1	15	16	-5	36	0	0	0	0	83	1.2
			TOR	12	3	6	9	2	6	1	0	1	0	20	15.0
			TOTAL	71	4	21	25	-3	42	1	0	1	0	103	3.9
L	17	Wendel Clark	TOR	47	12	7	19	-21	80	4	0	3	0	140	8.6
C	18	* Alyn McCauley	TOR	60	6	10	16	-7	6	0	0	1	0	77	7.8
D	25	Jason Smith	TOR	81	3	13	16	-5	100	0	0	0	0	97	3.1
R	28	Tie Domi	TOR	80	4	10	14	-5	365	0	0	0	1	72	5.6
L	8	Todd Warriner	TOR	45	5	8	13	5	20	0	0	1	0	73	6.8
C	14	Darby Hendrickson	TOR	80	8	4	12	-20	67	0	0	0	0	115	7.0
D	36	Dimitri Yushkevich	TOR	72	0	12	12	-13	78	0	0	0	0	92	0.0
R	16	Lonny Bohonos	VAN	31	2	1	3	-9	4	0	0	0	0	37	5.4
			TOR	6	3	3	6	1	4	0	0	0	0	13	23.1
			TOTAL	37	5	4	9	-8	8	0	0	0	0	50	10.0
D	55	* Daniil Markov	TOR	25	2	5	7	0	28	1	0	0	0	15	13.3
D	2	Rob Zettler	TOR	59	0	7	7	-8	108	0	0	0	0	28	0.0
L	12	Kris King	TOR	82	3	3	6	-13	199	0	0	2	0	53	5.7
L	21	* Martin Prochazka	TOR	29	2	4	6	-1	8	0	0	0	0	40	5.0
D	38	* Yannick Tremblay	TOR	38	2	4	6	-6	6	1	0	0	0	45	4.4
C	16	Jamie Baker	TOR	13	0	5	5	1	10	0	0	0	0	16	0.0
D	33	* David Cooper	TOR	9	0	4	4	2	8	0	0	0	0	13	0.0
G	31	* Marcel Cousineau	TOR	2	0	0	0	0	0	0	0	0	0	0	0.0
D	23	* Jeff Ware	TOR	2	0	0	0	1	0	0	0	0	0	0	0.0
C	42	* Kevyn Adams	TOR	5	0	0	0	0	7	0	0	0	0	3	0.0
D	26	Craig Wolanin	TOR	10	0	0	0	-9	6	0	0	0	0	5	0.0
G	30	Glenn Healy	TOR	21	0	0	0	0	0	0	0	0	0	0	0.0
G	29	Felix Potvin	TOR	67	0	0	0	0	8	0	0	0	0	0	0.0

Goaltending

No.	Goaltender	GPI	Mins	Avg	W	L	T	EN	SO	GA	SA	S%
31	* Marcel Cousineau	2	17	0.00	0	0	0	0	0	0	9	.000
29	Felix Potvin	67	3864	2.73	26	33	7	4	5	176	1882	.906
30	Glenn Healy	21	1068	2.98	4	10	2	4	0	53	453	.883
	Totals	**82**	**4970**	**2.86**	**30**	**43**	**9**	**8**	**6**	**237**	**2352**	**.899**

Coaching History

Conn Smythe, 1927-28 to 1929-30; Conn Smythe and Art Duncan, 1930-31; Art Duncan and Dick Irvin, 1931-32; Dick Irvin, 1932-33 to 1939-40; Hap Day, 1940-41 to 1949-50; Joe Primeau, 1950-51 to 1952-53; King Clancy, 1953-54 to 1955-56; Howie Meeker, 1956-57; Billy Reay, 1957-58; Billy Reay and Punch Imlach, 1958-59; Punch Imlach, 1959-60 to 1968-69; John McLellan, 1969-70, 1970-71; John McLellan and King Clancy, 1971-72; John McLellan, 1972-73; Red Kelly, 1973-74 to 1976-77; Roger Neilson, 1977-78, 1978-79; Floyd Smith, Dick Duff and Punch Imlach, 1979-80; Punch Imlach, Joe Crozier and Mike Nykoluk, 1980-81; Mike Nykoluk, 1981-82 to 1983-84; Dan Maloney, 1984-85, 1985-86; John Brophy, 1986-87, 1987-88; John Brophy and George Armstrong, 1988-89; Doug Carpenter, 1989-90; Doug Carpenter and Tom Watt, 1990-91; Tom Watt, 1991-92; Pat Burns, 1992-93 to 1994-95; Pat Burns and Nick Beverley, 1995-96; Mike Murphy, 1996-97, 1997-98; Pat Quinn, 1998-99.

Coach

QUINN, PAT
Coach, Toronto Maple Leafs. Born in Hamilton, Ont., January 29, 1943.

On June 26, 1998, the Toronto Maple Leafs introduced Pat Quinn as the 25th head coach in club history. Quinn, 55, spent the past 11 seasons at the helm of the Vancouver Canucks hockey operation. When he joined the Canucks as president and general manager in 1987, he inherited a club that had endured 11 consecutive losing seasons. He took over the Vancouver coaching reins on January 31, 1991 and he eventually led the team to single-season records for wins (46), and points (101) in 1992-93. Pat's coaching portfolio includes the Jack Adams Award as the NHL's coach of the year in 1991-92 with Vancouver and 1979-80 with the Philadelphia Flyers, as well as Stanley Cup appearances in 1980 and 1994. Quinn also coached in Los Angeles from 1984 to 1987. He has a career coaching record of 357-285-102 for a winning percentage of .548.

Quinn spent the 1968-69 and 1969-70 seasons in a Maple Leafs uniform. In 99 games in the blue and white, the defenceman scored two goals and added 12 assists for 14 points with 183 penalty minutes. He holds a law degree from Widener University, Delaware School of Law.

NHL Coaching Record

		Regular Season					Playoffs			
Season	Team	Games	W	L	T	%	Games	W	L	%
1978-79	Philadelphia	30	18	8	4	.667	8	3	5	.375
1979-80	Philadelphia	80	48	12	20	.725	19	13	6	.684
1980-81	Philadelphia	80	41	24	15	.606	12	6	6	.500
1981-82	Philadelphia	72	34	29	9	.535	....	....	....	....
1984-85	Los Angeles	80	34	32	14	.513	3	0	3	.000
1985-86	Los Angeles	80	23	49	8	.338	....	....	....	....
1986-87	Los Angeles	42	18	20	4	.476	....	....	....	....
1990-91	Vancouver	26	9	13	4	.423	6	2	4	.333
1991-92	Vancouver	80	42	26	12	.600	13	6	7	.462
1992-93	Vancouver	84	46	29	9	.601	12	6	6	.500
1993-94	Vancouver	84	41	40	3	.506	24	15	9	.625
1995-96	Vancouver	6	3	3	0	.500	6	2	4	.333
	Totals	**744**	**357**	**285**	**102**	**.548**	**103**	**53**	**50**	**.515**

Club Records

Team

(Figures in brackets for season records are games played; records for fewest points, wins, ties, losses, goals, goals against are for 70 or more games)

Most Points	**99**	1992-93 (84)
Most Wins	**44**	1992-93 (84)
Most Ties	**22**	1954-55 (70)
Most Losses	**52**	1984-85 (80)
Most Goals	**337**	1989-90 (80)
Most Goals Against	**387**	1983-84 (80)
Fewest Points	**48**	1984-85 (80)
Fewest Wins	**20**	1981-82, 1984-85 (80)
Fewest Ties	**4**	1989-90 (80)
Fewest Losses	**16**	1950-51 (70)
Fewest Goals	**147**	1954-55 (70)
Fewest Goals Against	***131**	1953-54 (70)
Longest Winning Streak		
Overall	**10**	Oct. 7-28/93
Home	**9**	Nov. 11-Dec. 26/53
Away	**7**	Nov. 14-Dec. 15/40, Dec. 4/60-Jan. 5/61
Longest Undefeated Streak		
Overall	**11**	Oct. 15-Nov. 8/50 (8 wins, 3 ties), Jan. 6-Feb. 1/94 (7 wins, 4 ties)
Home	**18**	Nov. 28/33-Mar. 10/34 (15 wins, 3 ties), Oct. 31/53-Jan. 23/54 (16 wins, 2 ties)
Away	**9**	Nov. 30/47-Jan. 11/48 (4 wins, 5 ties)
Longest Losing Streak		
Overall	**10**	Jan. 15-Feb. 8/67
Home	**7**	Nov. 11-Dec. 5/84
Away	**11**	Feb. 20-Apr. 1/88
Longest Winless Streak		
Overall	**15**	Dec. 26/87-Jan. 25/88 (11 losses, 4 ties)
Home	**11**	Dec. 19/87-Jan. 25/88 (7 losses, 4 ties)
Away	**18**	Oct. 6/82-Jan. 5/83 (13 losses, 5 ties)
Most Shutouts, Season	**13**	1953-54 (70)
Most PIM, Season	**2,419**	1989-90 (80)
Most Goals, Game	**14**	Mar. 16/57 (NYR 1 at Tor. 14)

Individual

Most Seasons	**21**	George Armstrong
Most Games	**1,187**	George Armstrong
Most Goals, Career	**389**	Darryl Sittler
Most Assists, Career	**620**	Borje Salming
Most Points, Career	**916**	Darryl Sittler (389G, 527A)
Most PIM, Career	**1,670**	Dave Williams
Most Shutouts, Career	**62**	Turk Broda
Longest Consecutive Games Streak	**486**	Tim Horton (Feb. 11/61-Feb. 4/68)
Most Goals, Season	**54**	Rick Vaive (1981-82)
Most Assists, Season	**95**	Doug Gilmour (1992-93)
Most Points, Season	**127**	Doug Gilmour (1992-93; 32G, 95A)
Most PIM, Season	**365**	Tie Domi (1997-98)
Most Points, Defenseman, Season	**79**	Ian Turnbull (1976-77; 22G, 57A)
Most Points, Center, Season	**127**	Doug Gilmour (1992-93; 32G, 95A)
Most Points, Right Wing, Season	**97**	Wilf Paiement (1980-81; 40G, 57A)
Most Points, Left Wing, Season	**99**	Dave Andreychuk (1993-94; 53G, 46A)
Most Points, Rookie, Season	**66**	Peter Ihnacak (1982-83; 28G, 38A)
Most Shutouts, Season	**13**	Harry Lumley (1953-54)
Most Goals, Game	**6**	Corb Denneny (Jan. 26/21), Darryl Sittler (Feb. 7/76)
Most Assists, Game	**6**	Babe Pratt (Jan. 8/44), Doug Gilmour (Feb. 13/93)
Most Points, Game	***10**	Darryl Sittler (Feb. 7/76; 6G, 4A)

* NHL Record.

Retired Numbers

5	Bill Barilko	1946-1951
6	Ace Bailey	1926-1934

Honored Numbers

1	Turk Broda	1936-43, 45-52
	Johnny Bower	1958-1970
7	King Clancy	1930-1937
	Tim Horton	1949-50, 51-70
9	Charlie Conacher	1929-1938
	Ted Kennedy	1942-55, 56-57
10	Syl Apps	1936-43, 45-48
	George Armstrong	1949-50, 51-71

All-time Record vs. Other Clubs

Regular Season

	At Home							On Road							Total						
	GP	W	L	T	GF	GA	PTS	GP	W	L	T	GF	GA	PTS	GP	W	L	T	GF	GA	PTS
Anaheim	10	5	1	4	32	22	14	10	5	4	1	27	29	11	20	10	5	5	59	51	25
Boston	283	148	86	49	963	736	345	283	84	152	47	754	930	215	566	232	238	96	1717	1666	560
Buffalo	52	19	24	9	159	192	47	53	16	33	4	151	223	36	105	35	57	13	310	415	83
Calgary	48	24	17	7	185	177	55	50	15	30	5	156	212	35	98	39	47	12	341	389	90
Carolina	25	9	13	3	88	96	21	25	6	15	4	81	117	16	50	15	28	7	169	213	37
Chicago	310	163	94	53	1059	802	379	310	114	154	42	806	950	270	620	277	248	95	1865	1752	649
Colorado	29	12	14	3	99	121	27	29	7	17	5	87	111	19	58	19	31	8	186	232	46
Dallas	97	48	33	16	345	306	112	94	34	49	11	296	358	79	191	82	82	27	641	664	191
Detroit	311	162	104	45	1033	837	369	313	103	164	46	764	937	252	624	265	268	91	1797	1774	621
Edmonton	32	16	14	2	134	141	34	32	7	19	6	109	155	20	64	23	33	8	243	296	54
Florida	4	3	1	0	13	12	6	5	2	1	2	13	13	6	9	5	2	2	26	25	12
Los Angeles	63	32	20	11	254	212	75	64	21	34	9	187	230	51	127	53	54	20	441	442	126
Montreal	318	161	113	44	962	832	366	317	84	193	40	782	1129	208	635	245	306	84	1744	1961	574
New Jersey	36	24	8	4	155	117	52	35	11	14	10	110	128	32	71	35	22	14	265	245	84
NY Islanders	43	20	20	3	148	155	43	41	14	24	3	125	176	31	84	34	44	6	273	331	74
NY Rangers	270	151	81	38	922	703	340	271	101	114	56	794	833	258	541	252	195	94	1716	1536	598
Ottawa	6	4	2	0	23	16	8	5	2	2	1	13	13	5	11	6	4	1	36	29	13
Philadelphia	55	20	22	13	186	188	53	55	11	36	8	127	221	30	110	31	58	21	313	409	83
Phoenix	38	15	21	2	133	148	32	38	12	20	6	137	157	30	76	27	41	8	270	305	62
Pittsburgh	56	26	19	11	229	190	63	57	20	31	6	183	240	46	113	46	50	17	412	430	109
St. Louis	94	58	26	10	356	273	126	94	26	55	13	262	329	65	188	84	81	23	618	602	191
San Jose	13	9	3	1	51	30	19	14	7	5	2	38	30	16	27	16	8	3	89	60	35
Tampa Bay	10	5	5	0	35	26	10	8	7	1	0	31	15	14	18	12	6	0	66	41	24
Vancouver	55	25	20	10	204	185	60	53	17	26	10	175	182	44	108	42	46	20	379	367	104
Washington	37	20	13	4	172	130	44	38	12	24	2	105	147	26	75	32	37	6	277	277	70
Defunct Clubs	232	158	53	21	860	515	337	233	84	120	29	607	745	197	465	242	173	50	1467	1260	534
Totals	**2527**	**1337**	**827**	**363**	**8800**	**7162**	**3037**	**2527**	**822**	**1337**	**368**	**6920**	**8610**	**2012**	**5054**	**2159**	**2164**	**731**	**15720**	**15772**	**5049**

Playoffs

	Series	W	L	GP	W	L	T	GF	GA	Last Mtg.	Round	Result
Boston	13	8	5	62	31	30	1	150	153	1974	QF	L 0-4
Calgary	1	1	0	2	2	0	0	9	5	1979	PR	W 2-0
Chicago	9	6	3	38	22	15	1	111	89	1995	CQF	L 3-4
Dallas	2	0	2	7	1	6	0	26	35	1983	DSF	L 1-3
Detroit	23	12	11	117	58	59	0	311	321	1993	DSF	W 4-3
Los Angeles	3	2	1	12	7	5	0	41	31	1993	CF	L 3-4
Montreal	15	7	8	71	29	42	0	160	215	1979	QF	L 0-4
NY Islanders	2	1	1	10	4	6	0	20	33	1981	PR	L 0-3
NY Rangers	8	3	5	35	16	19	0	86	86	1971	QF	L 2-4
Philadelphia	3	0	3	17	5	12	0	47	67	1977	QF	L 2-4
Pittsburgh	2	2	0	6	4	2	0	21	13	1977	PR	W 2-1
St. Louis	5	2	3	31	14	17	0	90	88	1996	CQF	L 2-4
San Jose	1	1	0	7	4	3	0	26	21	1994	CSF	W 4-3
Vancouver	1	0	1	5	1	4	0	9	16	1994	CF	L 1-4
Defunct	8	6	2	24	12	10	2	59	57			
Totals	**96**	**51**	**45**	**444**	**210**	**230**	**4**	**1166**	**1246**			

Calgary totals include Atlanta, 1972-73 to 1979-80. Carolina totals include Hartford, 1979-80 to 1996-97.
Colorado totals include Quebec, 1979-80 to 1994-95. Dallas totals include Minnesota, 1967-68 to 1992-93.
New Jersey totals include Kansas City, 1974-75 to 1975-76, and Colorado Rockies, 1976-77 to 1981-82.
Phoenix totals include Winnipeg, 1979-80 to 1995-96.

Playoff Results 1998-94

Year	Round	Opponent	Result	GF	GA
1996	CQF	St. Louis	L 2-4	15	21
1995	CQF	Chicago	L 3-4	20	22
1994	CF	Vancouver	L 1-4	9	16
	CSF	San Jose	W 4-3	26	21
	CQF	Chicago	W 4-2	15	10

Abbreviations: Round: CF – conference final; **CQF** – conference quarter-final; **CSF** – conference semi-final; **DSF** – division semi-final; **QF** – quarter-final; **PR** – preliminary round.

1997-98 Results

Oct.	1		Washington	1-4
	4	at	NY Islanders	0-3
	7	at	Calgary	2-1
	9	at	Vancouver	2-2
	11	at	Edmonton	1-2
	14		Detroit	2-3
	15	at	Detroit	4-3
	18		Dallas	4-5
	22		Ottawa	2-6
	25		Calgary	4-3
	28		Anaheim	2-2
Nov.	1	at	Montreal	1-5
	4	at	San Jose	0-0
	5	at	Calgary	4-3
	8		Phoenix	0-3
	11		Chicago	5-2
	13	at	Chicago	2-1
	15		Pittsburgh	0-5
	17		St. Louis	2-3
	19		Philadelphia	3-1
	21	at	Colorado	1-3
	22	at	Phoenix	0-2
	25		San Jose	3-1
	29		Vancouver	2-4
Dec.	2		Anaheim	3-3
	4	at	St. Louis	3-4
	6		Los Angeles	7-2
	8		Dallas	3-0
	10		Colorado	2-2
	13		New Jersey	0-3
	15	at	Colorado	2-3
	17	at	Anaheim	6-2
	18	at	Los Angeles	2-5
	20	at	Phoenix	3-2
	23		Edmonton	5-4
	26	at	Detroit	1-4
	27		Detroit	1-8
	31		Boston	2-2
Jan.	1	at	Chicago	3-3
	3	at	New Jersey	2-4
	6	at	Washington	3-5
	7	at	Tampa Bay	5-2
	10		Chicago	3-4
	12	at	NY Rangers	2-3
	14		Buffalo	1-4
	21	at	Detroit	3-0
	22	at	Chicago	3-0
	24		Tampa Bay	5-2
	26	at	Dallas	1-5
	29	at	St. Louis	0-2
	31		Phoenix	2-5
Feb.	2		Dallas	1-5
	4		St. Louis	3-2
	5	at	Ottawa	2-3
	7		Florida	3-2
	25	at	Buffalo	2-2
	26		NY Rangers	2-5
	28		Montreal	4-0
Mar.	2	at	Pittsburgh	1-3
	4		Colorado	3-5
	7		Edmonton	4-1
	9	at	San Jose	2-3
	11	at	Anaheim	3-1
	12	at	Los Angeles	2-1
	14		Calgary	2-1
	16	at	Philadelphia	1-4
	18		Detroit	2-5
	19	at	Boston	0-4
	21		Vancouver	1-1
	24	at	Phoenix	2-4
	26	at	Dallas	1-0
	28		NY Islanders	4-3
	30		Los Angeles	2-3
Apr.	1		St. Louis	4-6
	4		San Jose	3-5
	6	at	Dallas	2-4
	7	at	Florida	3-1
	9	at	Carolina	2-5
	11		Carolina	5-1
	15		Chicago	3-2
	18	at	Edmonton	3-4
	19	at	Vancouver	2-1

Entry Draft Selections 1998-84

1998
Pick
10 Nikolai Antropov
35 Petr Svoboda
69 Jamie Hodson
87 Alexei Ponikarovsky
126 Morgan Warren
154 Allan Rourke
181 Jonathan Gagnon
215 Dwight Wolfe
228 Mihail Travnicek
236 Sergei Rostov

1997
Pick
57 Jeff Farkas
84 Adam Mair
111 Frantisek Mrazek
138 Eric Gooldy
165 Hugo Marchand
190 Shawn Thornton
194 Russ Bartlett
221 Jonathan Hedstrom

1996
Pick
36 Marek Posmyk
50 Francis Larivee
66 Mike Lankshear
68 Konstantin Kalmikov
86 Jason Sessa
103 Vladimir Antipov
110 Peter Cava
111 Brandon Sugden
140 Dmitriy Yakushin
148 Chris Bogas
151 Lucio DeMartinis
178 Reggie Berg
204 Tomas Kaberle
230 Jared Hope

1995
Pick
15 Jeff Ware
54 Ryan Pepperall
139 Doug Bonner
145 Yannick Tremblay
171 Marek Melenovsky
197 Mark Murphy
223 Daniil Markov

1994
Pick
16 Eric Fichaud
48 Sean Haggerty
64 Fredrik Modin
126 Mark Deyell
152 Kam White
178 Tommi Rajamaki
204 Rob Butler
256 Sergei Berezin
282 Doug Nolan

1993
Pick
12 Kenny Jonsson
19 Landon Wilson
123 Zdenek Nedved
149 Paul Vincent
175 Jeff Andrews
201 David Brumby
253 Kyle Ferguson
279 Mikhail Lapin

1992
Pick
8 Brandon Convery
23 Grant Marshall
77 Nikolai Borschevsky
95 Mark Raiter
101 Janne Gronvall
106 Chris Deruiter
125 Mikael Hakansson
149 Patrik Augusta
173 Ryan Vandenbussche
197 Wayne Clarke
221 Sergei Simonov
245 Nathan Dempsey

1991
Pick
47 Yanic Perreault
69 Terry Chitaroni
102 Alexei Kudashov
113 Jeff Perry
120 Alexander Kuzminsky
135 Martin Prochazka
160 Dmitri Mironov
164 Robb McIntyre
167 Tomas Kucharcik
179 Guy Lehoux
201 Gary Miller
223 Jonathan Kelley
245 Chris O'Rourke

1990
Pick
10 Drake Berehowsky
31 Felix Potvin
73 Darby Hendrickson
80 Greg Walters
115 Alexander Godynyuk
136 Eric Lacroix
157 Dan Stiver
178 Robert Horyna
199 Rob Chebator
220 Scott Malone
241 Nick Vachon

1989
Pick
3 Scott Thornton
12 Rob Pearson
21 Steve Bancroft
66 Matt Martin
96 Keith Carney
108 David Burke
125 Michael Doers
129 Keith Merkler
150 Derek Langille
171 Jeffrey St. Laurent
192 Justin Tomberlin
213 Mike Jackson
234 Steve Chartrand

1988
Pick
6 Scott Pearson
27 Tie Domi
48 Peter Ing
69 Ted Crowley
88 Leonard Esau
132 Matt Mallgrave
153 Roger Elvenas
174 Mike Delay
195 David Sacco
216 Mike Gregorio
237 Peter DeBoer

1987
Pick
7 Luke Richardson
28 Daniel Marois
49 John McIntyre
71 Joe Sacco
91 Mike Eastwood
112 Damian Rhodes
133 Trevor Jobe
154 Chris Jensen
175 Brian Blad
196 Ron Bernacci
217 Ken Alexander
238 Alex Weinrich

1986
Pick
6 Vincent Damphousse
36 Darryl Shannon
48 Sean Boland
69 Kent Hulst
90 Scott Taylor
111 Stephane Giguere
132 Danny Hie
153 Stephen Brennan
174 Brian Bellefeuille
195 Sean Davidson
216 Mark Holick
237 Brian Hoard

1985
Pick
1 Wendel Clark
22 Ken Spangler
43 Dave Thomlinson
64 Greg Vey
85 Jeff Serowik
106 Jiri Latal
127 Tim Bean
148 Andy Donahue
169 Todd Whittemore
190 Bob Reynolds
211 Tim Armstrong
232 Mitch Murphy

1984
Pick
4 Al Iafrate
25 Todd Gill
67 Jeff Reese
88 Jack Capuano
109 Fabian Joseph
130 Joe McInnis
151 Derek Laxdal
172 Dan Turner
192 David Buckley
213 Mikael Wurst
233 Peter Slanina

Captains' History

Hap Day, 1927-28 to 1936-37; Charlie Conacher, 1937-38; Red Horner, 1938-39, 1939-40; Syl Apps, 1940-41 to 1942-43; Bob Davidson, 1943-44, 1944-45; Syl Apps, 1945-46 to 1947-48; Ted Kennedy, 1948-49 to 1954-55; Sid Smith, 1955-56; Jim Thomson, Ted Kennedy, 1956-57; George Armstrong, 1957-58 to 1968-69; Dave Keon, 1969-70 to 1974-75; Darryl Sittler, 1975-76 to 1980-81; Rick Vaive, 1981-82 to 1985-86; no captain, 1986-87 to 1988-89; Rob Ramage, 1989-90, 1990-91; Wendel Clark, 1991-92 to 1993-94; Doug Gilmour, 1994-95 to 1996-97; Mats Sundin, 1997-98 to date.

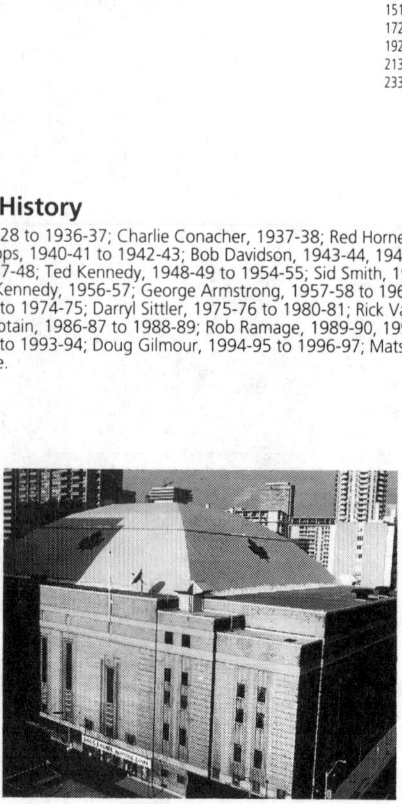

Maple Leaf Gardens

Club Directory

Air Canada Centre

Maple Leaf Gardens
60 Carlton Street
Toronto, Ontario M5B 1L1
Phone **416/977-1641**
FAX 416/977-5364
Website:
www.torontomapleleafs.com
Capacity: 15,746 (standing 100)
After Feb. 1, 1998
Air Canada Centre
40 Bay St., Suite 300
Toronto, Ontario M5J 2X2

Board of Directors
Brian P. Bellmore, Robert G. Bertram, John MacIntyre, Dean Metcalf, Steve A. Stavro, Larry Tanenbaum

Advisory Board
J. Donald Crump, Chris Dundas, Terence V. Kelly, Ted Nikolaou, W. Ron Pringle, George E. Whyte

Management

President and General Manager	Ken Dryden
Associate General Manager	Mike Smith
Assistant to the President	Bill Watters
Assistant General Manager and Director of Player Development	Anders Hedberg
Marketing/Community Consultant	Darryl Sittler
Director of Pro Scouting	Nick Beverley
Director of Player Evaluation	Joe Yannetti
Head Coach	Pat Quinn
Assistant Coach	Rick Ley
Assistant Coach	Alpo Suhonen
Scouts	George Armstrong, Jack Gardiner, Mark Hillier, Bob Johnson, Peter Johnson, Floyd Smith
European Scouts	Jan Kovac, Thommie Bergman
Video Coordinator	Paul Dennis
Manager, Hockey Operations	Casey Vanden Heuvel
Prospect Developer	Chris MacDonald

Hockey Communications

Vice-President, Sports Communications and Community Development	John Lashway
Manager, Media Relations	Pat Park
Manager, Community Relations	Kristy Fletcher
Manager, Community Development	Angela McManus
Travel Coordinator	Mary Speck
Game Operations and Promotions Coordinator	Nancy Gilks
Game Operations and Promotions Coordinator	Mike Ferriman
Media Relations Coordinator	Anthony Alfred
Administrative Assistant	Christine Buchanan
Executive Assistant to President and General Manager	Ann Clark
Executive Assistant to Associate General Manager	Maria Tomasevic

Medical and Training Staff

Head Athletic Therapist	Chris Broadhurst
Athletic Therapist	Brent Smith
Strength and Conditioning Coach	Phil Walker
Equipment Manager	Brian Papineau
Assistant Equipment Manager	Dave Aleo
Trainer	Scott McKay
Team Doctors	Dr. Michael Clarfield, Dr. Darrell Ogilvie-Harris, Dr. Leith Douglas, Dr. Rob Devenyi, Dr. Simon McGrail
Team Dentist	Dr. Ernie Lewis
Team Psychologist	Robert Offenberger, Ph.D.

St. John's Maple Leafs

Head Coach	Al MacAdam
Assistant Coach	Rich Brown
Athletic Therapist	Nick Addey-Jibb
Equipment Manager	Don Alcock
Director of Hockey and Business Operations	Glen Stanford
Media/Team Services Coordinator	Chris Schwartz

Maple Leaf Sports & Entertainment Ltd.

Chairman of the Board	Steve A. Stavro
Alternate Governor	Brian P. Bellmore
President and Chief Executive Officer	Richard Peddie
Executive Vice President	Ken Dryden
Vice President and General Manager, Air Canada Centre	Bob Hunter
Vice President, Business Development	Brian Cooper
Vice President, Construction	Kent Harvey
Vice President, Finance and Administration	Ian Clarke
Vice President, Project Director	Tom Anselmi
Vice President, Sales and Marketing	Michael Downey
Vice President, Sports Communications and Community Development	John Lashway
Vice President, People	Mardi Walker
Vice President, General Counsel	Robin Brudner
Corporate Secretary	Paul Perantinos
Executive Assistant to President and Chief Executive Officer	Alda Byers

Vancouver Canucks

1997-98 Results: 25W-43L-14T 64PTS. Seventh, Pacific Division

1998-99 Schedule

Oct.	Mon.	12	Los Angeles*
	Wed.	14	Edmonton
	Sat.	17	Toronto
	Tue.	20	at Carolina
	Wed.	21	at Washington
	Fri.	23	at Florida
	Sun.	25	at Tampa Bay
	Tue.	27	at Nashville
	Fri.	30	Pittsburgh
Nov.	Sun.	1	Washington
	Mon.	2	at Edmonton
	Sat.	7	Nashville
	Mon.	9	Los Angeles
	Thu.	12	at Calgary
	Fri.	13	Anaheim
	Sun.	15	Colorado
	Wed.	18	at Phoenix
	Thu.	19	at Colorado
	Sat.	21	Detroit
	Mon.	23	at Ottawa
	Wed.	25	at Toronto
	Fri.	27	at Detroit
	Sun.	29	at Philadelphia
Dec.	Tue.	1	at Boston
	Fri.	4	Dallas
	Sun.	6	Phoenix
	Wed.	9	at Anaheim
	Sat.	12	at Los Angeles
	Thu.	17	Colorado
	Sat.	19	Nashville
	Tue.	22	at Calgary
	Wed.	23	Calgary
	Sat.	26	at San Jose
	Sun.	27	at Edmonton
	Tue.	29	Colorado
	Thu.	31	Philadelphia
Jan.	Sat.	2	Montreal
	Mon.	4	at St. Louis
	Wed.	6	at Dallas
	Fri.	8	Florida
	Sun.	10	Dallas
	Thu.	14	Edmonton
	Sat.	16	Detroit
	Mon.	18	at Dallas
	Tue.	19	at Nashville
	Thu.	28	St. Louis
	Sat.	30	Chicago
Feb.	Mon.	1	Ottawa
	Wed.	3	at Montreal
	Thu.	4	at NY Rangers
	Sun.	7	at NY Islanders*
	Tue.	9	at New Jersey
	Thu.	11	at Pittsburgh
	Sat.	13	Boston
	Mon.	15	at St. Louis*
	Wed.	17	at Chicago
	Sat.	20	Anaheim
	Tue.	23	at Colorado
	Wed.	24	at San Jose
	Fri.	26	Carolina
	Sun.	28	Buffalo
Mar.	Wed.	3	San Jose
	Fri.	5	Calgary
	Sun.	7	Chicago
	Wed.	10	at Anaheim
	Thu.	11	at Phoenix
	Sat.	13	at Los Angeles
	Mon.	15	New Jersey
	Fri.	19	NY Islanders
	Sat.	20	at Edmonton
	Wed.	24	at Colorado
	Thu.	25	St. Louis
	Sat.	27	Montreal*
	Mon.	29	Phoenix
	Wed.	31	Toronto
Apr.	Fri.	2	San Jose
	Sat.	3	at San Jose
	Mon.	5	at Chicago
	Wed.	7	at Detroit
	Sat.	10	Edmonton
	Mon.	12	at Calgary
	Wed.	14	Calgary

* Denotes afternoon game.

Year-by-Year Record

		Home			Road			Overall							
Season	GP	W	L	T	W	L	T	W	L	T	GF	GA	Pts.	Finished	Playoff Result
1997-98	82	15	22	4	10	21	10	25	43	14	224	273	64	7th, Pacific Div.	Out of Playoffs
1996-97	82	20	17	4	15	23	3	35	40	7	257	273	77	4th, Pacific Div.	Out of Playoffs
1995-96	82	15	19	7	17	16	8	32	35	15	278	278	79	3rd, Pacific Div.	Lost Conf. Quarter-Final
1994-95	48	10	8	6	8	10	6	18	18	12	153	148	48	2nd, Pacific Div.	Lost Conf. Semi-Final
1993-94	84	20	19	3	21	21	0	41	40	3	279	276	85	2nd, Pacific Div.	Lost Final
1992-93	84	27	11	4	19	18	5	46	29	9	346	278	101	1st, Smythe Div.	Lost Div. Final
1991-92	80	23	10	7	19	16	5	42	26	12	285	250	96	1st, Smythe Div.	Lost Div. Final
1990-91	80	18	17	5	10	26	4	28	43	9	243	315	65	4th, Smythe Div.	Lost Div. Semi-Final
1989-90	80	13	16	11	12	25	3	25	41	14	245	306	64	5th, Smythe Div.	Out of Playoffs
1988-89	80	19	15	6	14	24	2	33	39	8	251	253	74	4th, Smythe Div.	Lost Div. Semi-Final
1987-88	80	15	20	5	10	26	4	25	46	9	272	320	59	5th, Smythe Div.	Out of Playoffs
1986-87	80	17	19	4	12	24	4	29	43	8	282	314	66	5th, Smythe Div.	Out of Playoffs
1985-86	80	17	18	5	6	26	8	23	44	13	282	333	59	4th, Smythe Div.	Lost Div. Semi-Final
1984-85	80	15	21	4	10	25	5	25	46	9	284	401	59	5th, Smythe Div.	Out of Playoffs
1983-84	80	20	16	4	12	23	5	32	39	9	306	328	73	3rd, Smythe Div.	Lost Div. Semi-Final
1982-83	80	20	12	8	10	23	7	30	35	15	303	309	75	3rd, Smythe Div.	Lost Div. Semi-Final
1981-82	80	20	8	12	10	25	5	30	33	17	290	286	77	2nd, Smythe Div.	Lost Final
1980-81	80	17	12	11	11	20	9	28	32	20	289	301	76	3rd, Smythe Div.	Lost Prelim. Round
1979-80	80	14	17	9	13	20	7	27	37	16	256	281	70	3rd, Smythe Div.	Lost Prelim. Round
1978-79	80	15	18	7	10	24	6	25	42	13	217	291	63	2nd, Smythe Div.	Lost Prelim. Round
1977-78	80	13	15	12	7	28	5	20	43	17	239	320	57	3rd, Smythe Div.	Out of Playoffs
1976-77	80	13	21	6	12	21	7	25	42	13	235	294	63	4th, Smythe Div.	Out of Playoffs
1975-76	80	22	11	7	11	21	8	33	32	15	271	272	81	2nd, Smythe Div.	Lost Prelim. Round
1974-75	80	23	12	5	15	20	5	38	32	10	271	254	86	1st, Smythe Div.	Lost Quarter-Final
1973-74	78	14	18	7	10	25	4	24	43	11	224	296	59	7th, East Div.	Out of Playoffs
1972-73	78	17	18	4	5	29	5	22	47	9	233	339	53	7th, East Div.	Out of Playoffs
1971-72	78	14	20	5	6	30	3	20	50	8	203	297	48	7th, East Div.	Out of Playoffs
1970-71	78	17	18	4	7	28	4	24	46	8	229	296	56	6th, East Div.	Out of Playoffs

Vancouver's first choice (13th overall) in the 1994 Entry Draft, Mattias Ohlund was the highest-scoring rookie defenseman in the NHL with 30 points in 1997-98. He was nominated for the Calder Trophy.

Franchise date: May 22, 1970

NORTHWEST DIVISION

29th NHL Season

1998-99 Player Personnel

FORWARDS	HT	WT	S	Place of Birth	Date	1997-98 Club
BERTUZZI, Todd	6-3	224	L	Sudbury, Ont.	2/2/75	NY Islanders-Vancouver-Canada
BODTKER, Stewart	6-1	190	R	Vancouver, B.C.	9/15/76	Colorado (WCHA)
BRASHEAR, Donald	6-2	225	L	Bedford, IN	1/7/72	Vancouver-United States
BURE, Pavel	5-10	189	L	Moscow, USSR	3/31/71	Vancouver-Russia
CABANA, Paul	6-1	185	R	Calgary, Alta.	9/28/78	Fort McMurray
CHUBAROV, Artem	6-1	189	L	Gorky, USSR	12/13/79	Moscow D'amo
CONVERY, Brandon	6-1	195	R	Kingston, Ont.	2/4/74	St. John's-Vancouver-Syracuse
COOKE, Matt	5-11	200	L	Belleville, Ont.	9/7/78	Windsor-Canada-Kingston
COURVILLE, Larry	6-1	195	L	Timmins, Ont.	4/2/75	Vancouver-Syracuse
DRUKEN, Harold	6-	205	L	St. John's, Nfld.	1/26/79	Plymouth
FERONE, Paul	5-11	180	R	Vancouver, B.C.	4/2/76	Syracuse-Raleigh
GORDON, Robb	5-11	190	R	Murrayville, B.C.	1/13/76	Syracuse-Raleigh
HOLDEN, Josh	6-0	190	L	Calgary, Alta.	1/18/78	Regina-Canada
IRWIN, Richard	6-3	219	L	Toronto, Ont.	8/31/77	Raleigh-Syracuse
MARTYNYUK, Denis	6-3	190	L	Kapfenberg, Austria	7/26/79	Spartak-2
MAY, Brad	6-1	210	L	Toronto, Ont.	11/29/71	Buffalo-Vancouver
MESSIER, Mark	6-1	205	L	Edmonton, Alta.	1/18/61	Vancouver
MOGILNY, Alexander	5-11	200	L	Khabarovsk, USSR	2/18/69	Vancouver
MORRISON, Justin	6-3	205	R	Los Angeles, CA	9/10/79	Colorado College
MUCKALT, Bill	6-0	190	R	Surrey, B.C.	7/15/74	U. of Michigan
NASLUND, Markus	6-0	186	L	Ornskoldsvik, Sweden	7/30/73	Vancouver
RUUTU, Jarkko	6-2	194	L	Vantaa, Finland	8/23/75	HIFK Helsinki
SCATCHARD, Dave	6-2	220	R	Hinton, Alta.	2/20/76	Vancouver
SCHAEFER, Peter	5-11	190	L	Yellow Grass, Sask.	7/12/77	Syracuse
SCISSONS, Jeff	6-1	190	L	Saskatoon, Sask.	11/24/76	U. Minn-Duluth
SINCLAIR, Darren	6-0	200	L	Brooks, Alta.	8/24/76	Syracuse-Raleigh
STAIOS, Steve	6-0	200	R	Hamilton, Ont.	7/28/73	Vancouver
VAIC, Lubomir	5-9	178	L	Spisska Nova Ves, Czech.	3/6/77	Vancouver-Syracuse
ZEZEL, Peter	5-11	220	L	Toronto, Ont.	4/22/65	New Jersey-Albany-Vancouver
DEFENSEMEN						
ALLAN, Chad	6-1	200	L	Saskatoon, Sask.	7/12/76	Syracuse
ALLEN, Bryan	6-4	210	L	Kingston, Ont.	8/21/80	Oshawa
AUCOIN, Adrian	6-2	210	R	Ottawa, Ont.	7/3/73	Vancouver
BARON, Murray	6-3	215	L	Prince George, B.C.	6/1/67	Phoenix
BERTRAN, Rick	6-3	190	L	Niagara Falls, Ont.	3/12/80	Kitchener
BONNI, Ryan	6-4	190	L	Winnipeg, Man.	2/18/79	Saskatoon
CABANA, Clint	6-2	195	R	Bonnyville, Alta.	4/28/78	Edmonton (WHL)-Regina
DARBY, Regan	6-2	200	L	Estevan, Sask.	7/17/80	Spokane-Tri-City
FERENCE, Brad	6-3	196	R	Calgary, Alta.	4/2/79	Canada-Spokane
HEDICAN, Bret	6-2	205	L	St. Paul, MN	8/10/70	Vancouver
HUSCROFT, Jamie	6-2	210	R	Creston, B.C.	1/9/67	Tampa Bay-Vancouver
KOMARNISKI, Zenith	6-0	200	L	Edmonton, Alta.	8/13/78	Tri-City-Spokane-Canada
LEROUX, Rod	6-4	204	L	Calgary, Alta.	8/21/79	Seattle
McALLISTER, Chris	6-7	235	L	Saskatoon, Sask.	6/16/75	Vancouver-Syracuse
McCABE, Bryan	6-1	210	L	St. Catharines, Ont.	6/8/75	NY Islanders-Vancouver-Canada
MURZYN, Dana	6-2	200	L	Calgary, Alta.	12/9/66	Vancouver
OHLUND, Mattias	6-3	209	L	Pitea, Sweden	9/9/76	Vancouver-Sweden
ROBERTSSON, Bert	6-3	205	L	Sodertalje, Sweden	6/30/74	Vancouver-Syracuse
ROHLIN, Leif	6-1	198	L	Vasteras, Sweden	2/26/68	Ambri
SOPEL, Brent	6-1	190	R	Calgary, Alta.	1/7/77	Syracuse
STRUDWICK, Jason	6-3	215	L	Edmonton, Alta.	7/17/75	NYI-Kentucky-Van-Syracuse
WOTTON, Mark	6-0	190	L	Foxwarren, Man.	11/16/73	Vancouver-Syracuse
YTFELDT, David	6-0	187	L	Ornskoldsvik, Sweden	9/29/79	Leksand-Leksand

GOALTENDERS	HT	WT	C	Place of Birth	Date	1997-98 Club
BRADY, Peter	6-1	175	L	Cap-Rouge, Que.	10/25/77	Alaska-Anch.
HIRSCH, Corey	5-10	175	L	Medicine Hat, Alta.	7/1/72	Vancouver-Syracuse
HITCHEN, Allan	6-1	195	L	North York, Ont.	3/6/78	London-North Bay
KEYES, Tim	5-11	185	L	Ganonoque, Ont.	5/28/76	Syracuse-Raleigh-Dayton
SNOW, Garth	6-3	200	L	Wrentham, MA	7/28/69	Phi-Van-United States
VALLEY, Mike	6-0	190	L	Delta, B.C.	9/3/76	U. of Wisconsin

Coach

KEENAN, MICHAEL (MIKE)
Coach, Vancouver Canucks. Born in Whitby, Ontario, October 21, 1949.

Mike Keenan was hired on November 13, 1997 becoming the 14th head coach in Canucks history. Heading into the 1998-99 season he is seventh on the NHL's all-time regular season coaching list with 951 games coached and is fifth in all-time wins with 491. Keenan won the Stanley Cup in 1994 with the New York Rangers, coached the Chicago Blackhawks to the finals in 1992 and took Philadelphia to the Stanley Cup finals in 1985 and in 1987. He also won the Jack Adams Award as NHL coach of the year in 1985.

Keenan has coached his teams to the Presidents' Trophy three times (1985, 1991 and 1994) and has led his teams to six first-place divisional titles. He has coached in three All-Star Games (1986-87, 1988-89 and 1993-94). In addition to his coaching duties, Keenan also served as general manager with Chicago from 1990 to 1992 and in St. Louis from 1995 to 1997.

As a national team head coach, Keenan led Team Canada to Canada Cup victories in 1987 and 1991. His international career also includes head coaching jobs with Team Canada at the 1980 World Junior Championships and the World Championships in 1993. Keenan guided the Peterborough Petes of the Ontario Hockey League to the Memorial Cup finals in 1980, took the Rochester Americans of the American Hockey League to the Calder Cup finals in 1983 and won a CIAU championship with the University of Toronto in 1984.

1997-98 Scoring

* – rookie

Regular Season

Pos	#	Player	Team	GP	G	A	Pts	+/–	PIM	PP	SH	GW	GT	S	%
R	10	Pavel Bure	VAN	82	51	39	90	5	48	13	6	4	1	329	15.5
C	11	Mark Messier	VAN	82	22	38	60	-10	58	8	2	2	0	139	15.8
R	89	Alexander Mogilny	VAN	51	18	27	45	-6	36	5	4	1	1	118	15.3
L	19	Markus Naslund	VAN	76	14	20	34	5	56	2	1	0	0	106	13.2
L	27	Todd Bertuzzi	NYI	52	7	11	18	-19	58	1	0	1	0	63	11.1
			VAN	22	6	9	15	2	63	1	1	1	0	39	15.4
			TOTAL	74	13	20	33	-17	121	2	1	2	0	102	12.7
D	21	Jyrki Lumme	VAN	74	9	21	30	-25	34	4	0	1	1	117	7.7
D	2 *	Mattias Ohlund	VAN	77	7	23	30	3	76	1	0	0	0	172	4.1
D	3	Bret Hedican	VAN	71	3	24	27	3	79	1	0	0	1	84	3.6
R	28	Brian Noonan	VAN	82	10	15	25	-19	62	1	0	2	2	87	11.5
C	20 *	Dave Scatchard	VAN	76	13	11	24	-4	165	0	0	1	1	85	15.3
D	23	Bryan McCabe	NYI	56	3	9	12	9	145	1	0	0	0	81	3.7
			VAN	26	1	11	12	10	64	0	1	0	0	42	2.4
			TOTAL	82	4	20	24	19	209	1	1	0	0	123	3.3
L	9	Brad May	BUF	36	4	7	11	2	113	0	0	0	0	41	9.8
			VAN	27	9	3	12	0	41	4	0	2	0	56	16.1
			TOTAL	63	13	10	23	2	154	4	0	2	0	97	13.4
C	22	Peter Zezel	N.J.	5	0	3	3	2	0	0	0	0	0	3	0.0
			VAN	25	5	12	17	13	2	2	0	1	0	37	13.5
			TOTAL	30	5	15	20	15	2	2	0	1	0	40	12.5
L	8	Donald Brashear	VAN	77	9	9	18	-9	372	0	0	1	1	64	14.1
R	24	Scott Walker	VAN	59	3	10	13	-8	164	0	1	1	0	40	7.5
D	5	Dana Murzyn	VAN	31	5	2	7	-3	42	0	0	2	0	29	17.2
R	25	Steve Staios	VAN	77	3	4	7	-3	134	0	0	1	0	45	6.7
D	6	Adrian Aucoin	VAN	35	3	3	6	-4	21	1	0	1	0	44	6.8
D	48 *	Bert Robertsson	VAN	30	2	4	6	2	24	0	0	0	0	19	10.5
D	7	Jamie Huscroft	T.B.	44	0	3	3	-4	122	0	0	0	0	21	0.0
			VAN	7	0	1	1	2	55	0	0	0	0	5	0.0
			TOTAL	51	0	4	4	-2	177	0	0	0	0	26	0.0
D	36 *	Chris McAllister	VAN	36	1	2	3	-12	106	0	0	0	0	15	6.7
C	9 *	Lubomir Vaic	VAN	5	1	1	2	-2	2	0	0	0	0	8	12.5
L	7	David Roberts	VAN	13	1	1	2	-1	4	0	0	0	0	14	7.1
C	26	Brandon Convery	VAN	7	0	2	2	0	0	0	0	0	0	2	0.0
D	34 *	Jason Strudwick	NYI	17	0	1	1	1	36	0	0	0	0	3	0.0
			VAN	11	0	1	1	-3	29	0	0	0	0	5	0.0
			TOTAL	28	0	2	2	-2	65	0	0	0	0	8	0.0
G	31	Corey Hirsch	VAN	1	0	0	0	0	0	0	0	0	0	0	0.0
D	27	Mark Wotton	VAN	5	0	0	0	-2	6	0	0	0	0	3	0.0
L	22 *	Larry Courville	VAN	11	0	0	0	-7	5	0	0	0	0	3	0.0
G	32	Arturs Irbe	VAN	41	0	0	0	0	2	0	0	0	0	0	0.0
G	30	Garth Snow	PHI	29	0	0	0	0	18	0	0	0	0	0	0.0
			VAN	12	0	0	0	0	4	0	0	0	0	0	0.0
			TOTAL	41	0	0	0	0	22	0	0	0	0	0	0.0

Goaltending

No.	Goaltender	GPI	Mins	Avg	W	L	T	EN	SO	GA	SA	S%
32	Arturs Irbe	41	1999	2.73	14	11	6	3	2	91	982	.907
30	Garth Snow	12	504	3.10	3	6	0	0	0	26	262	.901
33	Sean Burke	16	838	3.51	2	9	4	1	0	49	396	.876
1	Kirk McLean	29	1583	3.68	6	17	4	1	1	97	800	.879
31	Corey Hirsch	1	50	6.00	0	0	0	0	0	5	34	.853
	Totals	**82**	**4996**	**3.28**	**25**	**43**	**14**	**5**	**3**	**273**	**2479**	**.890**

Coaching History

Hal Laycoe, 1970-71, 1971-72; Vic Stasiuk, 1972-73; Bill McCreary and Phil Maloney, 1973-74; Phil Maloney, 1974-75, 1975-76; Phil Maloney and Orland Kurtenbach, 1976-77; Orland Kurtenbach, 1977-78; Harry Neale, 1978-79 to 1980-81; Harry Neale and Roger Neilson, 1981-82; Roger Neilson, 1982-83; Roger Neilson and Harry Neale, 1983-84; Harry Neale and Bill Laforge, 1984-85; Tom Watt, 1985-86, 1986-87; Bob McCammon, 1987-88 to 1989-90; Bob McCammon and Pat Quinn, 1990-91; Pat Quinn, 1991-92 to 1993-94; Rick Ley, 1994-95; Rick Ley and Pat Quinn, 1995-96; Tom Renney, 1996-97; Tom Renney and Mike Keenan, 1997-98; Mike Keenan, 1998-99.

Coaching Record

		Regular Season					Playoffs			
Season	Team	Games	W	L	T	%	Games	W	L	%
1979-80	Peterborough (OHL)	68	47	20	1	.699	18	15	3	.833
1980-81	Rochester (AHL)	80	30	42	8	.425	....	....	....	....
1981-82	Rochester (AHL)	80	40	31	9	.556	9	4	5	.444
1982-83	Rochester (AHL)	80	46	25	9	.631	16	12	4	.750
1983-84	U. of Toronto (CIAU)	49	41	5	3	.867	....	....	....	....
1984-85	**Philadelphia (NHL)**	**80**	**53**	**20**	**7**	**.706**	**19**	**12**	**7**	**.632**
1985-86	**Philadelphia (NHL)**	**80**	**53**	**23**	**4**	**.688**	**5**	**2**	**3**	**.400**
1986-87	**Philadelphia (NHL)**	**80**	**46**	**26**	**8**	**.625**	**26**	**15**	**11**	**.577**
1987-88	**Philadelphia (NHL)**	**80**	**38**	**33**	**9**	**.531**	**7**	**3**	**4**	**.429**
1988-89	**Chicago (NHL)**	**80**	**27**	**41**	**12**	**.413**	**16**	**9**	**7**	**.563**
1989-90	**Chicago (NHL)**	**80**	**41**	**33**	**6**	**.550**	**20**	**10**	**10**	**.500**
1990-91	**Chicago (NHL)**	**80**	**49**	**23**	**8**	**.663**	**6**	**2**	**4**	**.333**
1991-92	**Chicago (NHL)**	**80**	**36**	**29**	**15**	**.544**	**18**	**12**	**6**	**.667**
1993-94	**NY Rangers (NHL)**	**84**	**52**	**24**	**8**	**.667**	**23**	**16**	**7**	**.696***
1994-95	**St. Louis (NHL)**	**48**	**28**	**15**	**5**	**.635**	**7**	**3**	**4**	**.429**
1995-96	**St. Louis (NHL)**	**82**	**32**	**34**	**16**	**.488**	**13**	**7**	**6**	**.538**
1996-97	**St. Louis (NHL)**	**33**	**15**	**17**	**1**	**.470**	....	....	....	....
1997-98	**Vancouver (NHL)**	**63**	**21**	**30**	**12**	**.421**	....	....	....	....
	NHL Totals	**950**	**491**	**348**	**111**	**.575**	**160**	**91**	**69**	**.569**

* Stanley Cup win.

Club Records

Team

(Figures in brackets for season records are games played; records for fewest points, wins, ties, losses, goals, goals against are for 70 or more games)

Most Points	101	1992-93 (84)
Most Wins	46	1992-93 (84)
Most Ties	20	1980-81 (80)
Most Losses	50	1971-72 (78)
Most Goals	346	1992-93 (84)
Most Goals Against	401	1984-85 (80)
Fewest Points	48	1971-72 (78)
Fewest Wins	20	1971-72 (78), 1977-78 (80)
Fewest Ties	3	1993-94 (84)
Fewest Losses	26	1991-92 (80)
Fewest Goals	203	1971-72 (78)
Fewest Goals Against	250	1991-92 (80)
Longest Winning Streak		
Overall	7	Feb. 10-23/89
Home	9	Nov. 6-Dec. 9/92
Away	5	Jan. 14-25/92, Oct. 6-Nov. 2/93
Longest Undefeated Streak		
Overall	10	Mar. 5-25/77 (5 wins, 5 ties)
Home	18	Nov. 4/92-Jan. 16/93 (16 wins, 2 ties)
Away	5	Six times
Longest Losing Streak		
Overall	10	Oct. 23-Nov. 11/97
Home	6	Dec. 18/70-Jan. 20/71
Away	12	Nov. 28/81-Feb. 6/82
Longest Winless Streak		
Overall	13	Nov. 9-Dec. 7/73 (10 losses, 3 ties)
Home	11	Dec. 18/70-Feb. 6/71 (10 losses, 1 tie)
Away	20	Jan. 2-Apr. 2/86 (14 losses, 6 ties)
Most Shutouts, Season	8	1974-75 (80)
Most PIM, Season	2,326	1992-93 (84)
Most Goals, Game	11	Mar. 28/71 (Cal. 5 at Van. 11), Nov. 25/86 (L.A. 5 at Van. 11), Mar. 1/92 (Cgy. 0 at Van. 11)

Individual

Most Seasons	13	Stan Smyl
Most Games	896	Stan Smyl
Most Goals, Career	262	Stan Smyl
Most Assists, Career	411	Stan Smyl
Most Points, Career	673	Stan Smyl (262G, 411A)
Most PIM, Career	2,127	Gino Odjick
Most Shutouts, Career	20	Kirk McLean
Longest Consecutive Games Streak	482	Trevor Linden (Oct. 4/90-Dec. 3/96)
Most Goals, Season	60	Pavel Bure (1992-93, 1993-94)
Most Assists, Season	62	André Boudrias (1974-75)
Most Points, Season	110	Pavel Bure (1992-93; 60G, 50A)
Most PIM, Season	371	Gino Odjick (1996-97)
Most Points, Defenseman, Season	63	Doug Lidster (1986-87; 12G, 51A)
Most Points, Center, Season	91	Patrik Sundstrom (1983-84; 38G, 53A)
Most Points, Right Wing, Season	110	Pavel Bure (1992-93; 60G, 50A)
Most Points, Left Wing, Season	81	Darcy Rota (1982-83; 42G, 39A)
Most Points, Rookie, Season	60	Ivan Hlinka (1981-82; 23G, 37A), Pavel Bure (1991-92; 34G, 26A)
Most Shutouts, Season	6	Gary Smith (1974-75)
Most Goals, Game	4	Several times
Most Assists, Game	6	Patrik Sundstrom (Feb. 29/84)
Most Points, Game	7	Patrik Sundstrom (Feb. 29/84; 1G, 6A)

Retired Numbers

12	Stan Smyl	1978-1991

Captains' History

Orland Kurtenbach, 1970-71 to 1973-74; no captain, 1974-75; Andre Boudrias, 1975-76; Chris Oddleifson, 1976-77; Don Lever, 1977-78; Don Lever and Kevin McCarthy, 1978-79; Kevin McCarthy, 1979-80 to 1981-82; Stan Smyl, 1982-83 to 1989-90; Dan Quinn, Doug Lidster and Trevor Linden, 1990-91; Trevor Linden, 1991-92 to 1996-97; Mark Messier, 1997-98 to date.

General Managers' History

Bud Poile, 1970-71 to 1972-73; Hal Laycoe, 1973-74; Phil Maloney, 1974-75 to 1976-77; Jake Milford, 1977-78 to 1981-82; Harry Neale, 1982-83 to 1984-85; Jack Gordon, 1985-86, 1986-87; Pat Quinn, 1987-88 to 1997-98; Brian Burke, 1998-99.

All-time Record vs. Other Clubs

Regular Season

	At Home							On Road							Total						
	GP	W	L	T	GF	GA	PTS	GP	W	L	T	GF	GA	PTS	GP	W	L	T	GF	GA	PTS
Anaheim	14	9	5	0	50	35	18	13	7	4	2	40	30	16	27	16	9	2	90	65	34
Boston	47	14	25	8	154	198	36	46	6	36	4	110	203	16	93	20	61	12	264	401	52
Buffalo	47	22	15	10	176	155	54	48	16	24	8	142	176	40	95	38	39	18	318	331	94
Calgary	82	30	35	17	288	278	77	82	16	54	12	235	358	44	164	46	89	29	523	636	121
Carolina	26	11	9	6	94	75	28	25	10	11	4	88	83	24	51	21	20	10	182	158	52
Chicago	60	27	19	14	181	176	68	59	14	39	6	137	226	34	119	41	58	20	318	402	102
Colorado	30	11	14	5	114	128	27	31	11	14	6	88	105	28	61	22	28	11	202	233	55
Dallas	59	27	22	10	223	183	64	59	16	32	11	176	227	43	118	43	54	21	399	410	107
Detroit	53	25	20	8	202	173	58	54	15	32	7	161	227	37	107	40	52	15	363	400	95
Edmonton	66	27	31	8	253	274	62	64	16	42	6	202	306	38	130	43	73	14	455	580	100
Florida	4	1	1	2	14	10	4	4	1	2	1	11	11	3	8	2	3	3	25	21	7
Los Angeles	85	44	27	14	334	274	102	87	29	45	13	285	363	71	172	73	72	27	619	637	173
Montreal	46	7	31	8	113	184	22	48	8	36	4	125	236	20	94	15	67	12	238	420	42
New Jersey	44	25	8	11	166	124	61	44	19	19	6	145	140	44	88	44	27	17	311	264	105
NY Islanders	44	21	20	3	147	145	45	42	11	23	8	117	159	30	86	32	43	11	264	304	75
NY Rangers	48	12	33	3	154	199	27	50	9	36	5	126	224	23	98	21	69	8	280	423	50
Ottawa	5	3	1	1	18	11	7	5	2	2	1	15	11	5	10	5	3	2	33	22	12
Philadelphia	48	10	26	12	139	192	32	48	14	33	1	142	212	29	96	24	59	13	281	404	61
Phoenix	60	35	17	8	234	178	78	57	21	28	8	215	223	50	117	56	45	16	449	401	128
Pittsburgh	46	21	22	3	167	176	45	46	8	31	7	159	215	23	92	29	53	10	326	391	68
St. Louis	60	25	28	7	182	190	57	59	18	33	8	177	220	44	119	43	61	15	359	410	101
San Jose	20	15	4	1	84	44	31	21	11	6	4	72	64	26	41	26	10	5	156	108	57
Tampa Bay	6	6	0	0	31	9	12	5	3	2	0	19	16	6	11	9	2	0	50	25	18
Toronto	53	26	17	10	182	175	62	55	20	25	10	185	204	50	108	46	42	20	367	379	112
Washington	35	15	15	5	117	115	35	36	11	21	4	105	126	26	71	26	36	9	222	241	61
Defunct Clubs	19	14	3	2	82	48	30	19	10	8	1	71	68	21	38	24	11	3	153	116	51
Totals	**1107**	**483**	**448**	**176**	**3899**	**3749**	**1142**	**1107**	**322**	**638**	**147**	**3348**	**4433**	**791**	**2214**	**805**	**1086**	**323**	**7247**	**8182**	**1933**

Playoffs

	Series	W	L	GP	W	L	T	GF	GA	Last Mtg.	Round	Result
Buffalo	2	0	2	7	1	6	0	14	28	1981	PR	L 0-3
Calgary	5	2	3	25	12	13	0	80	82	1994	CQF	W 4-3
Chicago	2	1	1	9	4	5	0	24	24	1995	CSF	L 0-4
Colorado	1	0	1	6	2	4	0	17	24	1996	CQF	L 2-4
Dallas	1	1	0	5	4	1	0	18	11	1994	CSF	W 4-1
Edmonton	2	0	2	9	2	7	0	20	35	1992	DF	L 2-4
Los Angeles	3	1	2	17	8	9	0	60	66	1993	DF	L 2-4
Montreal	1	0	1	5	1	4	0	9	20	1975	QF	L 1-4
NY Islanders	2	0	2	6	0	6	0	14	26	1982	F	L 0-4
NY Rangers	1	0	1	7	3	4	0	19	21	1994	F	L 3-4
Philadelphia	1	0	1	3	1	2	0	9	15	1979	PR	L 1-2
St. Louis	1	1	0	7	4	3	0	27	27	1995	CQF	W 4-3
Toronto	1	1	0	5	4	1	0	16	9	1994	CF	W 4-1
Winnipeg	2	2	0	13	8	5	0	50	34	1993	DSF	W 4-2
Totals	**25**	**9**	**16**	**124**	**54**	**70**	**0**	**377**	**422**			

Playoff Results 1998-94

Year	Round	Opponent	Result	GF	GA
1996	CQF	Colorado	L 2-4	17	24
1995	CSF	Chicago	L 0-4	6	11
	CQF	St. Louis	W 4-3	27	27
1994	F	NY Rangers	L 3-4	19	21
	CF	Toronto	W 4-1	16	9
	CSF	Dallas	W 4-1	18	11
	CQF	Calgary	W 4-3	23	20

Abbreviations: Round: F – Final; **CF** – conference final; **CQF** – conference quarter-final; **CSF** – conference semi-final; **DF** – division final; **DSF** – division semi-final; **QF** – quarter-final; **PR** – preliminary round.

Calgary totals include Atlanta, 1972-73 to 1979-80. Carolina totals include Hartford, 1979-80 to 1996-97.
Colorado totals include Quebec, 1979-80 to 1994-95. Dallas totals include Minnesota, 1970-71 to 1992-93.
New Jersey totals include Kansas City, 1974-75 to 1975-76, and Colorado Rockies, 1976-77 to 1981-82.
Phoenix totals include Winnipeg, 1979-80 to 1995-96.

1997-98 Results

Oct.	3		Anaheim	3-2		5		Los Angeles	3-2
	4	at	Anaheim	2-3		7		St. Louis	2-3
	9		Toronto	2-2		8	at	Colorado	4-4
	11		NY Rangers	3-6		10		Florida	2-2
	13		Edmonton	3-0		12	at	Chicago	2-3
	17		Boston	0-2		14	at	Detroit	0-4
	19		Colorado	4-4		15	at	Buffalo	2-6
	21	at	Dallas	5-1		21		Phoenix	1-6
	23	at	St. Louis	1-4		24	at	Calgary	2-5
	25		Pittsburgh	2-3		26	at	Phoenix	2-4
	26		Detroit	1-5		28	at	Colorado	1-6
	29	at	Chicago	0-3		30		New Jersey	3-1
	30	at	New Jersey	1-8		31	at	Edmonton	6-3
Nov.	1	at	Pittsburgh	6-7	**Feb.**	2		Colorado	1-2
	3	at	Carolina	3-5		6		Edmonton	5-4
	4	at	Washington	1-2		7		San Jose	6-3
	8		Anaheim	2-3		25		Anaheim	5-2
	11	at	Los Angeles	2-8		27	at	Calgary	4-4
	12	at	San Jose	5-2		28		Ottawa	6-4
	14	at	Anaheim	3-3	**Mar.**	2	at	Los Angeles	2-2
	16		Carolina	4-1		5		Calgary	2-6
	20		Phoenix	4-2		7		Tampa Bay	5-2
	22		Chicago	4-5		9		St. Louis	0-4
	25	at	NY Rangers	4-2		11	at	Montreal	2-2
	28	at	Boston	5-2		12	at	Philadelphia	2-3
	29	at	Toronto	4-2		14	at	NY Islanders	6-2
Dec.	1		Detroit	3-3		17	at	Florida	4-2
	4		San Jose	2-3		18	at	Tampa Bay	2-4
	6	at	Colorado	4-6		20	at	Ottawa	1-1
	8	at	St. Louis	1-5		21	at	Toronto	1-1
	9	at	Detroit	5-7		24		NY Islanders	4-3
	13		Colorado	2-5		26		Buffalo	2-5
	15		Los Angeles	7-0		28		Washington	2-3
	17	at	Phoenix	5-1	**Apr.**	1		Edmonton	4-2
	18	at	San Jose	0-0		4		Dallas	5-3
	20		Chicago	0-5		6	at	Edmonton	2-3
	23		Dallas	1-3		9	at	Calgary	6-3
	27	at	Dallas	3-3		11	at	San Jose	1-1
	29	at	Los Angeles	2-5		15		Los Angeles	0-2
	31		Philadelphia	0-8		17		Calgary	2-4
Jan.	3		Montreal	2-4		19		Toronto	1-2

Entry Draft Selections 1998-84

1998

Pick	
4	Bryan Allen
31	Artem Chubarov
68	Jarkko Ruutu
81	Justin Morrison
90	Regan Darby
136	David Jonsson
140	Rick Bertran
149	Paul Cabana
177	Vincent Malts
204	Graig Mischler
219	Curtis Valentine
232	Jason Metcalfe

1997

Pick	
10	Brad Ference
34	Ryan Bonni
36	Harold Druken
64	Kyle Freadrich
90	Chris Stanley
114	David Darguzas
117	Matt Cockell
144	Matt Cooke
148	Larry Shapley
171	Rod Leroux
201	Denis Martynyuk
227	Peter Brady

1996

Pick	
12	Josh Holden
75	Zenith Komarniski
93	Jonas Soling
121	Tyler Prosofsky
147	Nolan McDonald
175	Clint Cabana
201	Jeff Scissons
227	Lubomir Vaic

1995

Pick	
40	Chris McAllister
61	Larry Courville
66	Peter Schaefer
92	Lloyd Shaw
120	Todd Norman
144	Brent Sopel
170	Stewart Bodtker
196	Tyler Willis
222	Jason Cugnet

1994

Pick	
13	Mattias Ohlund
39	Robb Gordon
42	Dave Scatchard
65	Chad Allan
92	Mike Dubinsky
117	Yanick Dube
169	Yuri Kuznetsov
195	Rob Trumbley
221	Bill Muckalt
247	Tyson Nash
273	Robert Longpre

1993

Pick	
20	Mike Wilson
46	Rick Girard
98	Dieter Kochan
124	Scott Walker
150	Troy Creurer
176	Yevgeny Babariko
202	Sean Tallaire
254	Bert Robertsson
280	Sergei Tkachenko

1992

Pick	
21	Libor Polasek
40	Mike Peca
45	Michael Fountain
69	Jeff Connolly
93	Brent Tully
110	Brian Loney
117	Adrian Aucoin
141	Jason Clark
165	Scott Hollis
213	Sonny Mignacca
237	Mark Wotton
261	Aaron Boh

1991

Pick	
7	Alex Stojanov
29	Jassen Cullimore
51	Sean Pronger
95	Danny Kesa
117	Evgeny Namestnikov
139	Brent Thurston
161	Eric Johnson
183	David Neilson
205	Brad Barton
227	Jason Fitzsimmons
249	Xavier Majic

1990

Pick	
2	Petr Nedved
18	Shawn Antoski
23	Jiri Slegr
65	Darin Bader
86	Gino Odjick
128	Daryl Filipek
149	Paul O'Hagan
170	Mark Cipriano
191	Troy Neumier
212	Tyler Ertel
233	Karri Kivi

1989

Pick	
8	Jason Herter
29	Robert Woodward
71	Brett Hauer
113	Pavel Bure
134	James Revenberg
155	Rob Sangster
176	Sandy Moger
197	Gus Morschauser
218	Hayden O'Rear
239	Darcy Cahill
248	Jan Bergman

1988

Pick	
2	Trevor Linden
33	Leif Rohlin
44	Dane Jackson
107	Corrie D'Alessio
122	Phil Von Stefenelli
128	Dixon Ward
149	Greg Geldart
170	Roger Akerstrom
191	Paul Constantin
212	Chris Wolanin
233	Stefan Nilsson

1987

Pick	
24	Rob Murphy
45	Steve Veilleux
66	Doug Torrel
87	Sean Fabian
108	Garry Valk
129	Todd Fanning
150	Viktor Tumenev
171	Craig Daly
192	John Fletcher
213	Roger Hansson
233	Neil Eisenhut
234	Matt Evo

1986

Pick	
7	Dan Woodley
49	Don Gibson
70	Ronnie Stern
91	Eric Murano
112	Steve Herniman
133	Jon Helgeson
154	Jeff Noble
175	Matt Merton
196	Marc Lyons
217	Todd Hawkins
238	Vladimir Krutov

1985

Pick	
4	Jim Sandlak
25	Troy Gamble
46	Shane Doyle
67	Randy Siska
88	Robert Kron
109	Martin Hrstka
130	Brian McFarlane
151	Hakan Ahlund
172	Curtis Hunt
193	Carl Valimont
214	Igor Larionov
235	Darren Taylor

1984

Pick	
10	J.J. Daigneault
31	Jeff Rohlicek
52	Dave Saunders
55	Landis Chaulk
58	Mike Stevens
73	Brian Bertuzzi
94	Brett MacDonald
115	Jeff Korchinski
136	Blaine Chrest
157	Jim Agnew
178	Rex Grant
198	Ed Lowney
219	Doug Clarke
239	Ed Kister

President and General Manager

BURKE, BRIAN
President and General Manager, Vancouver Canucks.
Born in Providence, RI, June 30, 1955.

The Vancouver Canucks announced the appointment of Brian Burke to the position of president and general manager on June 22, 1998. Burke became the eighth general manager in Canucks history after serving as the National Hockey League's senior vice president and director of hockey operations for the past five years.

Burke joins the Canucks with experience in every area of the hockey business. He is a strong negotiator with valuable time spent as a general manager, an NHL senior vice president and player agent. He has a keen eye for hockey talent and has an appreciation for the challenges of operating an NHL franchise in Canada.

In five years as NHL senior vice president, Burke was most visible in his role as the league's chief disciplinarian. He spent much of his time overseeing the league's on-ice officials and was responsible for many disciplinary decisions handed down by the NHL based on his interpretation of league rules. Brian worked closely with NHL commissioner Gary Bettman on the direction of the league and was a key member of the group that introduced NHL excitement to Japan last October when the Vancouver Canucks and Mighty Ducks of Anaheim opened the 1997-98 regular season in Tokyo.

Brian Burke was appointed general manager of the Hartford Whalers on May 26, 1992. In his only season in Hartford, Brian made a number of player moves, changed the team's uniform and completed a major draft-day trade in 1993. After acquiring a second overall selection from San Jose, Burke selected Chris Pronger who has developed into one of the NHL's premier defenceman as is evidenced by his nomination for the 1998 Norris Trophy.

Burke's prior experience with the Canucks began when he was named vice president and director of hockey operations on June 2, 1987. Burke worked with former Canucks president and general manager Pat Quinn for five seasons and assisted in rebuilding Vancouver's team through his contract negotiation skills and his overseeing of the club's scouting systems and its minor league affiliates. Burke helped reshape the Canucks from a 59 point team in 1987-88, to a 96 point team in his final season of 1991-92. It was the first time since the 1974-75 regular season that the Canucks finished first in the Smythe Division.

Brian has four children who reside in the Boston area. Kathleen, 17, Patrick, 15, Brendan, 9, and Molly, 7.

Club Directory

General Motors Place
800 Griffiths Way
Vancouver, B.C. V6B 6G1
Phone **604/899-4600**
FAX 604/899-4640
Website: www.orcabay.com
Capacity: 18,422

Orca Bay Sports & Entertainment Executive Directory

Chairman, OBSE; Governor, NBA and NHL	John E. McCaw, Jr.
Deputy Chairman, OBSE; Alternate Governor, NBA and NHL	Stanley B. McCammon
President and Chief Executive Officer, Alternate Governor, NBA and NHL	Stephen T. Bellringer
President & General Manager, Vancouver Canucks, Alternate Governor, NHL	Brian Burke
President & General Manager, Vancouver Grizzlies, Alternate Governor, NBA	Stu Jackson
Executive Vice President, Business	David Cobb
Vice President, Finance & Chief Financial Officer	Victor de Bonis
Vice President, Communications & Community Investment	Kevin Gass
Vice President & General Manager, Operations	Harvey Jones

Hockey Operations

President & General Manager	Brian Burke
Senior Vice-President, Hockey Operations	David Nonis
Vice President, Player Personnel	Steve Tambellini
Vice President, Amateur Scouting	Mike Penny
Vice-President, Finance, Hockey Operations	Carlos Mascarenhas
Executive Assistant	Patti Timms
Executive Assistant	Kalli Quinn
Scouting Information Coordinator	Jonathan Wall
Media Relations	Chris Brumwell
Manager, Community Relations	Veronica Varhaug
Coordinator, Education Programs & Community Relations	Lisa Ryan
Office Assistant	Brenda Eascott
Head Coach	Mike Keenan
Assistant Coaches	Stan Smyl, Glen Hanlon
Strength & Conditioning Coach	Peter Twist
Video Coordinator	Doug Cole
Medical Trainer	Mike Burnstein
Massage Therapist	Dave Schima
Equipment Manager	Pat O'Neill
Assistant Equipment Manager	Darren Granger
Dressing Room Attendant	Tim Gross
Team Doctors	Dr. Ross Davidson, Dr. Doug Clement
Team Dentist	Dr. David Lawson
Team Optometrist	Dr. Alan R. Boyco
Head Coach, Syracuse Crunch	Jack McIlhargey
Medical Trainer, Syracuse Crunch	Ralph Krugler
Equipment Trainer, Syracuse Crunch	Rodney Blachford
Scouts	Shawn Dineen, Jack Birch, Ken Slater, Ron Delorme, Sergei Chibisov, Thomas Gradin, Jack McCartan, Jim Eagle

Communications & Community Investment

Vice President, Communications & Community Investment	Kevin Gass
Executive Asst. to the Vice President Communications/Community Investment	Marie Graf
Director, Corporate Communications	Nancy McHarg
Creative Services	Anna-Lea Dahl, Jackie Boucher

Broadcasting & Game Presentation

Vice President, Broadcasting	Chris Hebb
Executive Assistant & Promotions Coordinator	Shannon Baker
Manager and Director of In-house Productions	Paul Brettell
Producer, Canucks	Mike Hall
Associate Producer	Al Klein
Manager, Game Presentation & Special Events	Stephanie Willox
Coordinator, Game Presentation	Karen Brydon
Assistant Coordinator, Game Presentation	Ryan Halkett

Business Development

Vice President, Business Development	Leila Bell-Irving
Corporate Counsel	James Conrad
Director, Business Development	Dave Doroghy
Director, Business Development	David Altman
Director, Business Development	Ric Thomsen
Manager, Corporate Sales & Services	Dave Cannon
Manager, Corporate Services	Beth Robertson
Account Executives	Simone Lehmann, Bonnie Blair, Darren Moscovitch, Chris Coughlan
Executive Assistant to the Vice President, Business Development	Cathy Binstead

Customer Sales and Service

Vice President, Customer Sales and Service	John Rizzardini
Executive Asst. to the Vice President Customer Sales and Service	Annabelle Kroes
Managing Director, Customer Sales & Service	John Rocha
Assistant, Customer Sales and Service	Michelle Carriere
Executive Manager, Customer Sales and Service	Caley Denton
Manager, Promotions/Media	Paul Dal Monte
Manager, Asian Promotions/Media	Dora Sun
Manager, Promotions and Advertising	Rick Ramsbottom
Manager, Group Sales	Teddy Kim
Account Managers	Karla Ewachniuk, Avril Shepard, Mark Roxborough, Teri Gayton, Bruce Foreman, Al Bryant
Managers, Customer Sales	Jordan Thorsteinson, Reid Mitchell, Travis Tinning, Sharon Butler, Richard Cameron, Graham Wall
Ticketing Coordinator	Wendy Johnston
Manager, Executive Suite Services	Valerie Lewis
Manager, Executive Suite Sales	Chris Bradley

Miscellaneous

Radio Affiliation	CKNW 98 (AM 980)
Television Affilation	VTV (channel 9), CTV Sportsnet

Washington Capitals

1997-98 Results: 40W-30L-12T 92PTS. Third, Atlantic Division

1998-99 Schedule

Oct.	Sat.	10	Anaheim
	Tue.	13	Detroit
	Fri.	16	Montreal
	Sun.	18	at Tampa Bay
	Wed.	21	Vancouver
	Fri.	23	at Buffalo
	Sat.	24	Florida
	Wed.	28	at Edmonton
	Fri.	30	at Calgary
Nov.	Sun.	1	at Vancouver
	Wed.	4	Tampa Bay
	Fri.	6	Carolina
	Sat.	7	at Ottawa
	Thu.	12	Buffalo
	Sat.	14	at NY Islanders
	Wed.	18	Toronto
	Fri.	20	Ottawa
	Sat.	21	at Boston
	Wed.	25	Pittsburgh
	Fri.	27	at Dallas
	Sat.	28	at St. Louis
Dec.	Tue.	1	New Jersey
	Fri.	4	NY Islanders
	Sat.	5	at Philadelphia
	Wed.	9	at Los Angeles
	Fri.	11	at Anaheim
	Sat.	12	at San Jose
	Thu.	17	at Chicago
	Sat.	19	at Pittsburgh
	Wed.	23	at Florida
	Sat.	26	at Nashville
	Mon.	28	Boston
	Wed.	30	New Jersey
Jan.	Fri.	1	Ottawa*
	Sat.	2	at Toronto
	Thu.	7	NY Rangers
	Sat.	9	at New Jersey
	Mon.	11	NY Islanders
	Wed.	13	Philadelphia
	Fri.	15	Montreal
	Sat.	16	at Carolina
	Mon.	18	at Montreal
	Thu.	21	at Philadelphia
	Tue.	26	NY Rangers
	Fri.	29	Los Angeles
	Sat.	30	at Toronto
Feb.	Mon.	1	at NY Rangers
	Wed.	3	Tampa Bay
	Fri.	5	Carolina
	Sun.	7	Buffalo
	Tue.	9	at NY Islanders
	Fri.	12	at New Jersey
	Sat.	13	at Ottawa
	Mon.	15	at Pittsburgh
	Thu.	18	at Carolina
	Sat.	20	San Jose
	Mon.	22	Toronto
	Wed.	24	Phoenix
	Sat.	27	at Boston*
	Sun.	28	Pittsburgh*
Mar.	Tue.	2	at Tampa Bay
	Thu.	4	NY Rangers
	Sat.	6	Edmonton
	Tue.	9	Colorado
	Thu.	11	Florida
	Sat.	13	Calgary
	Mon.	15	at NY Rangers
	Wed.	17	Dallas
	Sat.	20	at Montreal
	Sun.	21	Boston
	Thu.	25	at Phoenix
	Fri.	26	at Colorado
	Tue.	30	Nashville
Apr.	Thu.	1	Florida
	Sat.	3	at Tampa Bay
	Mon.	5	at Florida
	Wed.	7	St. Louis
	Thu.	8	at New Jersey
	Sat.	10	Philadelphia
	Mon.	12	Chicago
	Wed.	14	at Carolina
	Sun.	18	at Buffalo*

* Denotes afternoon game.

Olaf Kolzig was 33-18-10 with a 2.20 goals-against average during the 1997-98 regular season, then outperformed Dominik Hasek in the Eastern Conference championship to lead the Capitals to the Stanley Cup finals for the first time.

Franchise date: June 11, 1974

SOUTHEAST DIVISION

25th NHL Season

Year-by-Year Record

		Home			Road			Overall							
Season	GP	W	L	T	W	L	T	W	L	T	GF	GA	Pts.	Finished	Playoff Result
1997-98	82	23	12	6	17	18	6	40	30	12	219	202	92	3rd, Atlantic Div.	Lost Final
1996-97	82	19	17	5	14	23	4	33	40	9	214	231	75	5th, Atlantic Div.	Out of Playoffs
1995-96	82	21	15	5	18	17	6	39	32	11	234	204	89	4th, Atlantic Div.	Lost Conf. Quarter-Final
1994-95	48	15	6	3	7	12	5	22	18	8	136	120	52	3rd, Atlantic Div.	Lost Conf. Quarter-Final
1993-94	84	17	16	9	22	19	1	39	35	10	277	263	88	3rd, Atlantic Div.	Lost Conf. Semi-Final
1992-93	84	21	15	6	22	19	1	43	34	7	325	286	93	2nd, Patrick Div.	Lost Div. Semi-Final
1991-92	80	25	12	3	20	15	5	45	27	8	330	275	98	2nd, Patrick Div.	Lost Div. Semi-Final
1990-91	80	21	14	5	16	22	2	37	36	7	258	258	81	3rd, Patrick Div.	Lost Div. Final
1989-90	80	19	18	3	17	20	3	36	38	6	284	275	78	3rd, Patrick Div.	Lost Conf. Championship
1988-89	80	25	12	3	16	17	7	41	29	10	305	259	92	1st, Patrick Div.	Lost Div. Semi-Final
1987-88	80	22	14	4	16	19	5	38	33	9	281	249	85	2nd, Patrick Div.	Lost Div. Final
1986-87	80	22	15	3	16	17	7	38	32	10	285	278	86	2nd, Patrick Div.	Lost Div. Semi-Final
1985-86	80	30	8	2	20	15	5	50	23	7	315	272	107	2nd, Patrick Div.	Lost Div. Final
1984-85	80	27	11	2	19	14	7	46	25	9	322	240	101	2nd, Patrick Div.	Lost Div. Semi-Final
1983-84	80	26	11	3	22	16	2	48	27	5	308	226	101	2nd, Patrick Div.	Lost Div. Final
1982-83	80	22	12	6	17	13	10	39	25	16	306	283	94	3rd, Patrick Div.	Lost Div. Semi-Final
1981-82	80	16	16	8	10	25	5	26	41	13	319	338	65	5th, Patrick Div.	Out of Playoffs
1980-81	80	16	17	7	10	19	11	26	36	18	286	317	70	5th, Patrick Div.	Out of Playoffs
1979-80	80	20	14	6	7	26	7	27	40	13	261	293	67	5th, Patrick Div.	Out of Playoffs
1978-79	80	15	19	6	9	22	9	24	41	15	273	338	63	4th, Norris Div.	Out of Playoffs
1977-78	80	10	23	7	7	26	7	17	49	14	195	321	48	5th, Norris Div.	Out of Playoffs
1976-77	80	17	15	8	7	27	6	24	42	14	221	307	62	4th, Norris Div.	Out of Playoffs
1975-76	80	6	26	8	5	33	2	11	59	10	224	394	32	5th, Norris Div.	Out of Playoffs
1974-75	80	7	28	5	1	39	0	8	67	5	181	446	21	5th, Norris Div.	Out of Playoffs

1998-99 Player Personnel

FORWARDS	HT	WT	S	Place of Birth	Date	1997-98 Club
BELLOWS, Brian	5-11	210	R	St. Catharines, Ont.	9/1/64	Berlin-Washington
BERUBE, Craig	6-1	205	L	Calahoo, Alta.	12/17/65	Washington
BONDRA, Peter	6-1	200	L	Luck, USSR	2/7/68	Washington
BULIS, Jan	6-0	194	L	Pardubice, Czech.	3/18/78	Kingston-Wsh-Portland (AHL)
EAGLES, Mike	5-10	190	L	Sussex, N.B.	3/7/63	Washington
HERR, Matt	6-1	180	L	Hackensack, NJ	5/26/76	U. of Michigan
HORNUNG, Todd	6-0	200	L	Swift Current, Sask.	9/3/80	Portland (WHL)
HUNTER, Dale	5-10	198	L	Petrolia, Ont.	7/31/60	Washington
JUNEAU, Joe	6-0	195	L	Pont-Rouge, Que.	1/5/68	Washington
KLEE, Ken	6-1	205	R	Indianapolis, IN	4/24/71	Washington
KONOWALCHUK, Steve	6-1	195	L	Salt Lake City, UT	11/11/72	Washington
MAJOR, Mark	6-3	223	L	Toronto, Ont.	3/20/70	Portland (AHL)
MILLER, Kelly	5-11	197	L	Lansing, MI	3/3/63	Washington
NIKOLISHIN, Andrei	5-11	200	L	Vorkuta, USSR	3/25/73	Washington-Portland (AHL)
OATES, Adam	5-11	185	R	Weston, Ont.	8/27/62	Washington
PIVONKA, Michal	6-2	195	L	Kladno, Czech.	1/28/66	Washington
SIMON, Chris	6-3	225	L	Wawa, Ont.	1/30/72	Washington
SVEJKOVSKY, Jaroslav	5-11	185	R	Plzen, Czech.	10/1/76	Washington-Portland (AHL)
TOMS, Jeff	6-5	200	L	Swift Current, Sask.	6/4/74	Tampa Bay-Washington
USTORF, Stefan	6-0	185	L	Kaufbeuren, Germany	1/3/74	Berlin-Germany
VOLCHKOV, Alexander	6-1	205	L	Moscow, USSR	9/25/77	Portland (AHL)
ZEDNIK, Richard	5-11	190	L	Bystrica, Czech.	1/6/76	Washington
DEFENSEMEN						
BAUMGARTNER, Nolan	6-1	200	R	Calgary, Alta.	3/23/76	Washington-Portland (AHL)
BOILEAU, Patrick	6-0	190	R	Montreal, Que.	2/22/75	Portland (AHL)
GONCHAR, Sergei	6-2	212	L	Chelyabinsk, USSR	4/13/74	Lada-Washington-Russia
JOHANSSON, Calle	5-11	200	L	Goteborg, Sweden	2/14/67	Washington-Sweden
MALGUNAS, Stewart	6-0	200	L	Prince George, B.C.	4/21/70	Washington-Portland (AHL)
MIRONOV, Dmitri	6-3	215	R	Moscow, USSR	12/25/65	Anaheim-Russia-Detroit
MROZIK, Rick	6-2	185	L	Duluth, MN	1/2/75	Portland (AHL)
REEKIE, Joe	6-3	220	L	Victoria, B.C.	2/22/65	Washington
TINORDI, Mark	6-4	213	L	Red Deer, Alta.	5/9/66	Washington
WITT, Brendan	6-1	205	L	Humbolt, Sask.	2/20/75	Washington

GOALTENDERS	HT	WT	C	Place of Birth	Date	1997-98 Club
BROCHU, Martin	5-10	200	L	Anjou, Que.	3/10/73	Portland (AHL)
KOLZIG, Olaf	6-3	225	L	Johannesburg, South Africa	4/9/70	Washington-Germany
ROSATI, Mike	5-10	170	L	Toronto, Ont.	1/7/68	Mannheim
TABARACCI, Rick	6-1	180	L	Toronto, Ont.	1/2/69	Calgary

Coach

WILSON, RON
Coach, Washington Capitals. Born in Windsor, Ont., May 28, 1955.

In his first season as head coach of the Washington Capitals, Ron Wilson proved why he has been considered one of the top coaches in the National Hockey League in recent years and why on June 9, 1997 Abe Polin chose him to lead the Caps in the quest for the Stanley Cup. Wilson's team came within reach of the Cup when, after posting a 40-30-12 regular season record, the Caps advanced to the Stanley Cup finals for the first time in the franchise's 24-year history.

Prior to joining the Capitals, Wilson served as head coach of the Mighty Ducks of Anaheim for four years. In his last season with the Ducks (1996-97) he led the team to its first playoff appearance. Wilson posted a 120-145-31 (.458) overall record in Anaheim. He also spent three years in Vancouver as an assistant coach to Pat Quinn from 1990-93.

Wilson, 43, also served as the head coach for Team USA at the 1996 World Cup of Hockey. Team USA won the championship series, two games to one, over Canada.

Wilson has significant playing experience in professional, amateur and international hockey. He played four years at Providence College where he was a two-time All-American and two-time ECAC First Team All-Star. Wilson was ECAC player of the year in 1975 when he led the nation in scoring with 26-61-87 points in 27 games. He remains Providence's all-time leading scorer and ranks as the NCAA all-time leading scorer among defensemen with 250 points. Wilson received a Bachelor of Arts degree in economics from Providence College.

Drafted by the Toronto Maple Leafs (132nd overall) in 1975, Wilson began his professional hockey career in 1976-77 with the Dallas Blackhawks in the Central Hockey League. He joined the Toronto Maple Leafs in 1977-78, playing in 64 NHL contests over three seasons. Wilson then moved to Switzerland in 1980 and competed for the Swiss teams Kloten and Davos for six seasons. The former defenseman/winger signed with the Minnesota North Stars as a free agent in 1985 where he played through 1988. Ron enjoyed his finest offensive season in 1986-87 when he recorded 12 goals and 29 assists in 65 games with the North Stars.

Although born in Canada, Wilson was raised in the United States and remains a U.S. citizen. He was a four-time player for U.S. National Teams (1975, 1981, 1983, 1987) and coached the 1994 squad at the World Championships in Italy, leading Team USA to a 4-4-0 record with a fourth-place finish. Wilson also coached the 1996 squad, earning a bronze medal for Team USA.

Coaching Record

		Regular Season					Playoffs			
Season	**Team**	**Games**	**W**	**L**	**T**	**%**	**Games**	**W**	**L**	**%**
1993-94	**Anaheim (NHL)**	**84**	**33**	**46**	**5**	**.423**	....	....	....	....
1994-95	**Anaheim (NHL)**	**48**	**16**	**27**	**5**	**.385**	....	....	....	....
1995-96	**Anaheim (NHL)**	**82**	**35**	**39**	**8**	**.476**	....	....	....	....
1996-97	**Anaheim (NHL)**	**82**	**36**	**33**	**13**	**.518**	**11**	**4**	**7**	**.364**
1997-98	**Washington (NHL)**	**82**	**40**	**30**	**12**	**.561**	**21**	**12**	**9**	**.571**
	NHL Totals	**378**	**160**	**175**	**43**	**.480**	**32**	**16**	**16**	**.500**

1997-98 Scoring

* – rookie

Regular Season

Pos	#	Player	Team	GP	G	A	Pts	+/–	PIM	PP	SH	GW	GT	S	%
R	12	Peter Bondra	WSH	76	52	26	78	14	44	11	5	13	2	284	18.3
C	77	Adam Oates	WSH	82	18	58	76	6	36	3	2	3	0	121	14.9
D	6	Calle Johansson	WSH	73	15	20	35	-11	30	10	1	1	2	163	9.2
L	22	Steve Konowalchuk	WSH	80	10	24	34	9	80	2	0	2	0	131	7.6
C	90	Joe Juneau	WSH	56	9	22	31	-8	26	4	1	1	0	87	10.3
D	96	Phil Housley	WSH	64	6	25	31	-10	24	4	1	0	0	116	5.2
D	28	Jeff Brown	CAR	32	3	10	13	-1	16	3	0	0	0	57	5.3
			TOR	19	1	8	9	2	10	1	0	0	0	30	3.3
			WSH	9	0	6	6	4	6	0	0	0	0	15	0.0
			TOTAL	60	4	24	28	5	32	4	0	0	0	102	3.9
L	44	* Richard Zednik	WSH	65	17	9	26	-2	28	2	0	2	0	148	11.5
C	32	Dale Hunter	WSH	82	8	18	26	1	103	0	0	1	0	82	9.8
L	18	Andrew Brunette	WSH	28	11	12	23	2	12	4	0	2	2	42	26.2
D	55	Sergei Gonchar	WSH	72	5	16	21	2	66	2	0	0	0	134	3.7
L	11	Esa Tikkanen	FLA	28	1	8	9	-7	16	0	0	0	0	34	2.9
			WSH	20	2	10	12	-4	2	1	0	2	0	33	6.1
			TOTAL	48	3	18	21	-11	18	1	0	2	0	67	4.5
D	24	Mark Tinordi	WSH	47	8	9	17	9	39	0	1	0	0	57	14.0
L	17	Chris Simon	WSH	28	7	10	17	-1	38	4	0	1	0	71	9.9
C	13	Andrei Nikolishin	WSH	38	6	10	16	1	14	1	0	1	0	40	15.0
C	8	* Jan Bulis	WSH	48	5	11	16	-5	18	0	0	0	1	37	13.5
L	27	Craig Berube	WSH	74	6	9	15	-3	189	0	0	0	0	68	8.8
L	10	Kelly Miller	WSH	76	7	7	14	-2	41	0	3	3	1	68	10.3
L	9	Todd Krygier	WSH	45	2	12	14	-3	30	0	0	1	0	71	2.8
L	21	Jeff Toms	T.B.	13	1	2	3	-6	7	0	0	0	0	14	7.1
			WSH	33	3	4	7	-11	8	0	0	1	0	55	5.5
			TOTAL	46	4	6	10	-17	15	0	0	1	0	69	5.8
D	29	Joe Reekie	WSH	68	2	8	10	15	70	0	0	1	0	59	3.4
L	23	Brian Bellows	WSH	11	6	3	9	-3	6	5	0	2	0	26	23.1
C	20	Michal Pivonka	WSH	33	3	6	9	5	20	0	0	1	0	38	7.9
D	19	Brendan Witt	WSH	64	1	7	8	-11	112	0	0	0	0	68	1.5
D	2	Ken Klee	WSH	51	4	2	6	-3	46	0	0	1	0	44	9.1
L	34	* Jaroslav Svejkovsky	WSH	17	4	1	5	-5	10	2	0	1	0	29	13.8
L	36	Mike Eagles	WSH	36	1	3	4	-2	16	0	0	0	0	25	4.0
C	28	* Jan Benda	WSH	9	0	3	3	1	6	0	0	0	0	8	0.0
D	38	* Nolan Baumgartner	WSH	4	0	1	1	0	0	0	0	0	0	4	0.0
C	48	* Benoit Gratton	WSH	6	0	1	1	1	6	0	0	0	0	5	0.0
G	30	Bill Ranford	WSH	22	0	1	1	0	0	0	0	0	0	0	0.0
G	37	Olaf Kolzig	WSH	64	0	1	1	0	12	0	0	0	0	0	0.0
C	14	Pat Peake	WSH	1	0	0	0	0	4	0	0	0	0	0	0.0
L	25	* Brad Church	WSH	2	0	0	0	0	0	0	0	0	0	4	0.0
L	42	* Dwayne Hay	WSH	2	0	0	0	0	2	0	0	0	0	1	0.0
C	26	* Ryan Mulhern	WSH	3	0	0	0	0	0	0	0	0	0	1	0.0
D	43	David Harlock	WSH	6	0	0	0	2	4	0	0	0	0	2	0.0
D	4	Stewart Malgunas	WSH	8	0	0	0	1	12	0	0	0	0	5	0.0

Goaltending

No.	Goaltender	GPI	Mins	Avg	W	L	T	EN	SO	GA	SA	S%
37	Olaf Kolzig	64	3788	2.20	33	18	10	5	5	139	1729	.920
30	Bill Ranford	22	1183	2.79	7	12	2	3	0	55	555	.901
	Totals	**82**	**4997**	**2.43**	**40**	**30**	**12**	**8**	**5**	**202**	**2292**	**.912**

Playoffs

Pos	#	Player	Team	GP	G	A	Pts	+/–	PIM	PP	SH	GW	OT	S	%
C	90	Joe Juneau	WSH	21	7	10	17	6	8	1	1	4	2	54	13.0
C	77	Adam Oates	WSH	21	6	11	17	8	8	1	1	1	0	31	19.4
C	13	Andrei Nikolishin	WSH	21	1	13	14	4	12	1	0	0	0	29	3.4
L	23	Brian Bellows	WSH	21	6	7	13	6	6	2	0	1	1	62	9.7
R	12	Peter Bondra	WSH	17	7	5	12	4	12	3	0	2	1	48	14.6
D	55	Sergei Gonchar	WSH	21	7	4	11	2	30	3	1	2	0	37	18.9
L	44	* Richard Zednik	WSH	17	7	3	10	0	16	2	0	0	0	40	17.5
D	6	Calle Johansson	WSH	21	2	8	10	9	16	0	0	0	0	42	4.8
L	11	Esa Tikkanen	WSH	21	3	3	6	-2	20	1	0	0	0	23	13.0
D	96	Phil Housley	WSH	18	0	4	4	-2	4	0	0	0	0	27	0.0
C	32	Dale Hunter	WSH	21	0	4	4	-1	30	0	0	0	0	14	0.0
L	9	Todd Krygier	WSH	13	1	2	3	-2	6	0	0	1	1	12	8.3
D	29	Joe Reekie	WSH	21	1	2	3	4	20	0	0	0	0	16	6.3
D	24	Mark Tinordi	WSH	21	1	2	3	6	42	0	0	0	0	14	7.1
C	20	Michal Pivonka	WSH	13	0	3	3	5	0	0	0	0	0	16	0.0
D	28	Jeff Brown	WSH	2	0	2	2	1	0	0	0	0	0	2	0.0
L	36	Mike Eagles	WSH	12	0	2	2	1	2	0	0	0	0	7	0.0
D	2	Ken Klee	WSH	9	1	0	1	2	10	0	0	0	0	6	16.7
D	19	Brendan Witt	WSH	16	1	0	1	-1	14	0	0	0	0	9	11.1
L	17	Chris Simon	WSH	18	1	0	1	-3	26	0	0	0	0	17	5.9
L	27	Craig Berube	WSH	21	1	0	1	0	21	0	0	1	0	15	6.7
L	10	Kelly Miller	WSH	10	0	1	1	2	4	0	0	0	0	8	0.0
L	21	Jeff Toms	WSH	1	0	0	0	-1	0	0	0	0	0	0	0.0
L	34	* Jaroslav Svejkovsky	WSH	1	0	0	0	0	2	0	0	0	0	0	0.0
G	37	Olaf Kolzig	WSH	21	0	0	0	0	4	0	0	0	0	0	0.0

Goaltending

No.	Goaltender	GPI	Mins	Avg	W	L	EN	SO	GA	SA	S%
37	Olaf Kolzig	21	1351	1.95	12	9	0	4	44	740	.941
	Totals	**21**	**1357**	**1.95**	**12**	**9**	**0**	**4**	**44**	**740**	**.941**

Coaching History

Jim Anderson, Red Sullivan and Milt Schmidt, 1974-75; Milt Schmidt and Tom McVie, 1975-76; Tom McVie, 1976-77, 1977-78; Danny Belisle, 1978-79; Danny Belisle and Gary Green, 1979-80; Gary Green, 1980-81; Gary Green, Roger Crozier and Bryan Murray, 1981-82; Bryan Murray, 1982-83 to 1988-89; Bryan Murray and Terry Murray, 1989-90; Terry Murray, 1990-91 to 1992-93; Terry Murray and Jim Schoenfeld, 1993-94; Jim Schoenfeld, 1994-95 to 1996-97; Ron Wilson, 1997-98 to date.

Club Records

Team

(Figures in brackets for season records are games played; records for fewest points, wins, ties, losses, goals, goals against are for 70 or more games)

Most Points	107	1985-86 (80)
Most Wins	50	1985-86 (80)
Most Ties	18	1980-81 (80)
Most Losses	67	1974-75 (80)
Most Goals	330	1991-92 (80)
Most Goals Against	*446	1974-75 (80)
Fewest Points	*21	1974-75 (80)
Fewest Wins	*8	1974-75 (80)
Fewest Ties	5	1974-75 (80), 1983-84 (80)
Fewest Losses	23	1985-86 (80)
Fewest Goals	181	1974-75 (80)
Fewest Goals Against	202	1997-98 (82)
Longest Winning Streak		
Overall	10	Jan. 27-Feb. 18/84
Home	9	Mar. 3-Oct. 6/89
Away	6	Feb. 26-Apr. 1/84
Longest Undefeated Streak		
Overall	14	Nov. 24-Dec. 23/82 (9 wins, 5 ties), Jan. 17-Feb. 18/84 (13 wins, 1 tie)
Home	13	Nov. 25/92-Jan. 31/93 (9 wins, 4 ties)
Away	10	Nov. 24/82-Jan. 8/83 (6 wins, 4 ties)
Longest Losing Streak		
Overall	*17	Feb. 18-Mar. 26/75
Home	*11	Feb. 18-Mar. 30/75
Away	37	Oct. 9/74-Mar. 26/75
Longest Winless Streak		
Overall	25	Nov. 29/75-Jan. 21/76 (22 losses, 3 ties)
Home	14	Dec. 3/75-Jan. 21/76 (11 losses, 3 ties)
Away	37	Oct. 9/74-Mar. 26/75 (37 losses)
Most Shutouts, Season	9	1995-96 (82)
Most PIM, Season	2,204	1989-90 (80)
Most Goals, Game	12	Feb. 6/90 (Que. 2 at Wsh. 12)

Individual

Most Seasons	12	Michal Pivonka, Kelly Miller
Most Games	878	Kelly Miller
Most Goals, Career	397	Mike Gartner
Most Assists, Career	412	Michal Pivonka
Most Points, Career	789	Mike Gartner (397G, 392A)
Most PIM, Career	1,901	Dale Hunter
Most Shutouts, Career	14	Jim Carey
Longest Consecutive Games Streak	422	Bob Carpenter
Most Goals, Season	60	Dennis Maruk (1981-82)
Most Assists, Season	76	Dennis Maruk (1981-82)
Most Points, Season	136	Dennis Maruk (1981-82; 60G, 76A)
Most PIM, Season	339	Alan May (1989-90)
Most Points, Defenseman, Season	81	Larry Murphy (1986-87; 23G, 58A)
Most Points, Center, Season	136	Dennis Maruk (1981-82; 60G, 76A)
Most Points, Right Wing, Season	102	Mike Gartner (1984-85; 50G, 52A)
Most Points, Left Wing, Season	87	Ryan Walter (1981-82; 38G, 49A)
Most Points, Rookie, Season	67	Bobby Carpenter (1981-82; 32G, 35A), Chris Valentine (1981-82; 30G, 37A)
Most Shutouts, Season	9	Jim Carey (1995-96)
Most Goals, Game	5	Bengt Gustafsson (Jan. 8/84), Peter Bondra (Feb. 5/94)
Most Assists, Game	6	Mike Ridley (Jan. 7/89)
Most Points, Game	7	Dino Ciccarelli (Mar. 18/89; 4G, 3A)

* NHL Record.

Retired Numbers

5	Rod Langway	1982-1993
7	Yvon Labre	1974-1981

Captains' History

Doug Mohns, 1974-75; Bill Clement and Yvon Labre, 1975-76; Yvon Labre, 1976-77, 1977-78; Guy Charron, 1978-79; Ryan Walter, 1979-80 to 1981-82; Rod Langway, 1982-83 to 1991-92; Rod Langway and Kevin Hatcher, 1992-93; Kevin Hatcher, 1993-94; Dale Hunter, 1994-95 to date.

All-time Record vs. Other Clubs

Regular Season

	At Home							On Road							Total						
	GP	W	L	T	GF	GA	PTS	GP	W	L	T	GF	GA	PTS	GP	W	L	T	GF	GA	PTS
Anaheim	4	2	2	0	8	8	4	4	1	2	1	15	15	3	8	3	4	1	23	23	7
Boston	43	11	22	10	126	159	32	44	13	25	6	120	169	32	87	24	47	16	246	328	64
Buffalo	44	11	26	7	118	164	29	44	9	29	6	121	182	24	88	20	55	13	239	346	53
Calgary	36	18	13	5	137	126	41	35	6	24	5	85	152	17	71	24	37	10	222	278	58
Carolina	32	20	10	2	109	88	42	33	17	11	5	113	92	39	65	37	21	7	222	180	81
Chicago	36	20	12	4	133	113	44	35	9	21	5	105	141	23	71	29	33	9	238	254	67
Colorado	29	16	9	4	122	96	36	29	12	13	4	106	95	28	58	28	22	8	228	191	64
Dallas	36	14	15	7	113	115	35	35	11	16	8	102	132	30	71	25	31	15	215	247	65
Detroit	41	20	17	4	156	130	44	43	13	19	11	125	153	37	84	33	36	15	281	283	81
Edmonton	25	14	9	2	105	88	30	25	10	11	4	83	97	24	50	24	20	6	188	185	54
Florida	12	5	4	3	35	32	13	13	5	6	2	36	40	12	25	10	10	5	71	72	25
Los Angeles	41	18	17	6	176	153	42	42	12	24	6	131	168	30	83	30	41	12	307	321	72
Montreal	47	20	19	8	131	150	48	48	12	30	6	100	198	30	95	32	49	14	231	348	78
New Jersey	67	43	19	5	271	190	91	66	28	31	7	201	209	63	133	71	50	12	472	399	154
NY Islanders	69	30	29	10	221	225	70	69	28	40	1	215	270	57	138	58	69	11	436	495	127
NY Rangers	71	35	27	9	266	236	79	70	29	34	7	249	275	65	141	64	61	16	515	511	144
Ottawa	12	8	3	1	50	25	17	11	5	5	1	36	41	11	23	13	8	2	86	66	28
Philadelphia	68	26	29	13	233	231	65	71	24	42	5	202	268	53	139	50	71	18	435	499	118
Phoenix	25	17	5	3	110	72	37	26	7	13	6	95	98	20	51	24	18	9	205	170	57
Pittsburgh	74	37	30	7	315	276	81	71	27	37	7	235	278	61	145	64	67	14	550	554	142
St. Louis	35	20	12	3	129	103	43	36	13	15	8	122	149	34	71	33	27	11	251	252	77
San Jose	6	4	2	0	20	16	8	6	3	2	1	20	18	7	12	7	4	1	40	34	15
Tampa Bay	14	6	4	4	45	34	16	13	9	3	1	37	25	19	27	15	7	5	82	59	35
Toronto	38	24	12	2	147	105	50	37	13	20	4	130	172	30	75	37	32	6	277	277	80
Vancouver	36	21	11	4	126	105	46	35	15	15	5	115	117	35	71	36	26	9	241	222	81
Defunct Clubs	10	2	8	0	28	42	4	10	4	5	1	30	39	9	20	6	13	1	58	81	13
Totals	**951**	**462**	**366**	**123**	**3430**	**3082**	**1047**	**951**	**335**	**493**	**123**	**2929**	**3593**	**793**	**1902**	**797**	**859**	**246**	**6359**	**6675**	**1840**

Playoffs

	Series	W	L	GP	W	L	T	GF	GA	Last Mtg.	Round	Result
Boston	2	1	1	10	4	6	0	15	13	1998	CQF	W 4-2
Buffalo	1	1	0	6	4	2	0	13	11	1998	CF	W 4-2
Detroit	1	0	1	4	0	4	0	7	13	1998	F	L 0-4
New Jersey	2	1	1	13	7	6	0	44	43	1990	DSF	W 4-2
NY Islanders	6	1	5	30	12	18	0	88	89	1993	DSF	L 2-4
NY Rangers	4	2	2	22	11	11	0	75	71	1994	CSF	L 1-4
Ottawa	1	1	0	5	4	1	0	18	7	1998	CSF	W 4-1
Philadelphia	3	2	1	16	9	7	0	65	55	1989	DSF	L 2-4
Pittsburgh	5	1	4	31	13	18	0	103	106	1996	CQF	L 2-4
Totals	**25**	**10**	**15**	**137**	**64**	**73**	**0**	**434**	**433**			

Playoff Results 1998-94

Year	Round	Opponent	Result	GF	GA
1998	F	Detroit	L 0-4	7	13
	CF	Buffalo	W 4-2	13	11
	CSF	Ottawa	W 4-1	18	7
	CQF	Boston	W 4-2	15	13
1996	CQF	Pittsburgh	L 2-4	17	21
1995	CQF	Pittsburgh	L 3-4	26	29
1994	CSF	NY Rangers	L 1-4	12	20
	CQF	Pittsburgh	W 4-2	20	12

Abbreviations: Round: F – Final; **CF** – conference final; **CQF** – conference quarter-final; **CSF** – conference semi-final; **DSF** – division semi-final.

Calgary totals include Atlanta, 1974-75 to 1979-80. Carolina totals include Hartford, 1979-80 to 1996-97. Colorado totals include Quebec, 1979-80 to 1994-95. Dallas totals include Minnesota, 1974-75 to 1992-93. New Jersey totals include Kansas City, 1974-75 to 1975-76, and Colorado Rockies, 1976-77 to 1981-82. Phoenix totals include Winnipeg, 1979-80, 1995-96.

1997-98 Results

Oct.	1	at	Toronto	4-1		3		NY Rangers	2-3
	3		Buffalo	6-2		6		Toronto	5-3
	4		New Jersey	4-1		8	at	NY Rangers	5-3
	8	at	NY Islanders	6-3		9		Philadelphia	4-1
	9	at	Buffalo	2-5		11	at	Detroit	0-2
	11		NY Islanders	3-1		13		Ottawa	4-0
	15	at	Chicago	2-0		15		Chicago	3-2
	18	at	Montreal	3-2		21	at	Tampa Bay	3-2
	22	at	Colorado	3-4		25		Boston	4-1
	23	at	Phoenix	3-3		26	at	NY Rangers	2-2
	25	at	St. Louis	2-5		28		Pittsburgh	2-2
	29		Dallas	3-4		31	at	Philadelphia	3-2
	31		Philadelphia	2-2	**Feb.**	1		Detroit	2-4
Nov.	1	at	New Jersey	1-3		4	at	Pittsburgh	2-2
	4		Vancouver	2-1		7		Tampa Bay	3-4
	6	at	Boston	0-2		25		Tampa Bay	3-4
	8		Edmonton	2-1		28	at	Tampa Bay	2-5
	9	at	Florida	2-3	**Mar.**	1		Buffalo	0-3
	12	at	Pittsburgh	4-1		3		Boston	0-3
	13	at	Buffalo	3-2		5	at	Philadelphia	2-3
	15	at	Montreal	3-2		7		Florida	6-3
	18		Colorado	6-6		9		Calgary	5-2
	22		San Jose	2-5		12	at	NY Islanders	2-1
	23	at	Florida	5-2		14	at	Ottawa	0-4
	26		Montreal	5-6		16		Phoenix	2-1
	27	at	Ottawa	1-3		18		Carolina	1-0
	29	at	Boston	1-1		20		New Jersey	2-0
Dec.	2	at	NY Rangers	3-2		21	at	New Jersey	2-3
	5		Florida	3-2		25	at	Edmonton	2-4
	7	at	Florida	4-5		26	at	Calgary	2-3
	10	at	San Jose	3-3		28	at	Vancouver	3-2
	12	at	Anaheim	4-6		31		NY Islanders	5-2
	13	at	Los Angeles	2-2	**Apr.**	2		Tampa Bay	4-1
	16		NY Islanders	2-2		4		Los Angeles	3-2
	18		Florida	0-4		6		Montreal	2-2
	20	at	Carolina	2-1		8	at	Dallas	1-2
	23		New Jersey	1-1		11	at	Philadelphia	3-4
	26		Pittsburgh	1-4		13	at	NY Islanders	2-0
	27		Ottawa	0-3		14		NY Rangers	3-1
	29		St. Louis	4-2		18	at	Carolina	4-3
Jan.	1		Anaheim	3-2		19		Carolina	2-1

Entry Draft Selections 1998-84

1998

Pick	
49	Jomar Cruz
59	Todd Hornung
106	Krys Barch
107	Chris Corrinet
118	Mike Siklenka
125	Erik Wendell
179	Nathan Forster
193	Ratislav Stana
220	Michael Farrell
251	Blake Evans

1997

Pick	
9	Nicholas Boynton
35	J-F Fortin
89	Curtis Cruickshank
116	Kevin Caulfield
143	Henrik Petre
200	Pierre-Luc Therrien
226	Matt Oikawa

1996

Pick	
4	Alexander Volchkov
17	Jaroslav Svejkovsky
43	Jan Bulis
58	Sergei Zimakov
74	Dave Weninger
78	Shawn McNeil
85	Justin Davis
126	Matthew Lahey
153	Andrew Van Bruggen
180	Michael Anderson
206	Oleg Orekhovsky
232	Chad Cavanagh

1995

Pick	
17	Brad Church
23	Miikka Elomo
43	Dwayne Hay
93	Sebasti Charpentier
95	Joel Theriault
105	Benoit Gratton
124	Joel Cort
147	Frederick Jobin
199	Vasili Turkovsky
225	Scott Swanson

1994

Pick	
10	Nolan Baumgartner
15	Alexander Kharlamov
41	Scott Cherrey
93	Matthew Herr
119	Yanick Jean
145	Dmitri Mekeshkin
171	Daniel Reja
197	Chris Patrick
223	John Tuohy
249	Richard Zednik
275	Sergei Tertyshny

1993

Pick	
11	Brendan Witt
17	Jason Allison
69	Patrick Boileau
147	Frank Banham
173	Daniel Hendrickson
174	Andrew Brunette
199	Joel Poirier
225	Jason Gladney
251	Mark Seliger
277	Dany Bousquet

1992

Pick	
14	Sergei Gonchar
32	Jim Carey
53	Stefan Ustorf
71	Martin Gendron
119	John Varga
167	Mark Matier
191	Mike Mathers
215	Brian Stagg
239	Gregory Callahan
263	Billy Jo MacPherson

1991

Pick	
14	Pat Peake
21	Trevor Halverson
25	Eric Lavigne
36	Jeff Nelson
58	Steve Konowalchuk
80	Justin Morrison
146	Dave Morissette
168	Rick Corriveau
190	Trevor Duhaime
209	Rob Leask
212	Carl LeBlanc
234	Rob Puchniak
256	Bill Kovacs

1990

Pick	
9	John Slaney
30	Rod Pasma
51	Chris Longo
72	Randy Pearce
93	Brian Sakic
94	Mark Ouimet
114	Andrei Kovalev
135	Roman Kontsek
156	Peter Bondra
159	Steve Martell
177	Ken Klee
198	Michael Boback
219	Alan Brown
240	Todd Hlushko

1989

Pick	
19	Olaf Kolzig
35	Byron Dafoe
59	Jim Mathieson
61	Jason Woolley
82	Trent Klatt
145	Dave Lorentz
166	Dean Holoien
187	Victor Gervais
208	Jiri Vykoukal
229	Andrei Sidorov
250	Ken House

1988

Pick	
15	Reginald Savage
36	Tim Taylor
41	Wade Bartley
57	Duane Derksen
78	Rob Krauss
120	Dmitri Khristich
141	Keith Jones
144	Brad Schlegel
162	Todd Hilditch
183	Petr Pavlas
192	Mark Sorensen
204	Claudio Scremin
225	Chris Venkus
246	Ron Pascucci

1987

Pick	
36	Jeff Ballantyne
57	Steve Maltais
78	Tyler Larter
99	Pat Beauchesne
120	Rich Defreitas
141	Devon Oleniuk
162	Thomas Sjogren
204	Chris Clarke
225	Milos Vanik
240	Dan Brettschneider
246	Ryan Kummu

1986

Pick	
19	Jeff Greenlaw
40	Steve Seftel
60	Shawn Simpson
61	Jimmy Hrivnak
82	Erin Ginnell
103	John Purves
124	Stefan Nilsson
145	Peter Choma
166	Lee Davidson
187	Tero Toivola
208	Bobby Bobcock
229	John Schratz
250	Scott McCrory

1985

Pick	
19	Yvon Corriveau
40	John Druce
61	Rob Murray
82	Bill Houlder
83	Larry Shaw
103	Claude Dumas
124	Doug Stromback
145	Jamie Nadjiwan
166	Mark Haarmann
187	Steve Hollett
208	Dallas Eakins
229	Steve Hrynewich
250	Frank DiMuzio

1984

Pick	
17	Kevin Hatcher
34	Steve Leach
59	Michal Pivonka
80	Kris King
122	Vito Cramarossa
143	Timo Iljina
164	Frank Joo
185	Jim Thomson
205	Paul Cavallini
225	Mikhail Tatarinov
246	Per Schedrin

General Managers' History

Milt Schmidt, 1974-75; Milt Schmidt and Max McNab, 1975-76; Max McNab, 1976-77 to 1980-81; Max McNab and Roger Crozier, 1981-82; David Poile, 1982-83 to 1996-97; George McPhee, 1997-98 to date.

General Manager

McPHEE, GEORGE
General Manager, Washington Capitals. Born in Guelph, Ont., July 2, 1958.

In his first season as general manager of the Washington Capitals, George McPhee led the Caps to their first Stanley Cup Finals appearance. Now back for his second year, McPhee and the team hope that last season was just a warm-up for things to come.

Last season, McPhee and head coach Ron Wilson joined forces to make several end-of-the-season deals that contributed to Washington's storied season. En route to the playoffs, he was responsible for bringing left wing Esa Tikkanen (from the Florida Panthers), defenseman Jeff Brown (from Toronto) and left wing Brian Bellows (from the Berlin Capitals of the German professional league) to Washington.

With degrees in law and business, McPhee joined the Capitals after many years of playing on the ice and then several years working in the business side of hockey. The fifth general manager in Washington Capitals history, he came to Washington from Vancouver where he served as vice president of hockey operations for the Canucks.

A back injury forced McPhee to retire as an active player at the conclusion of the 1988-89 season, after a seven year playing career with the New York Rangers and New Jersey Devils. McPhee originally signed as a free agent with the Rangers in July, 1982, after graduating from Bowling Green State University with a business degree. McPhee did not waste any time in college, tallying 40 goals and 48 assists in his freshman season and easily winning CCHA rookie of the year honors. His outstanding collegiate hockey career was capped off when he was named the recipient of the Hobey Baker Award as the top U.S. collegiate player in his senior season. McPhee also earned All-America honors as a senior and finished his career at Bowling Green as the CCHA's all-time leading scorer with 114-153-267. He was the first player in CCHA history to make the Conference's all-academic team three straight seasons.

Club Directory

MCI Center

MCI Center
601 F Street, NW
Washington, DC 20004
Phone **202/661-5000**
PR FAX 202/661-5113
www.washingtoncaps.com
Capacity: 19,740

Washington Sports & Entertainment

Chairman	Abe Pollin
President	Susan O'Malley
Executive Vice President	Wes Unseld

Washington Capitals

Board of Directors	David P. Bindeman, Stuart L. Bindeman, James A. Cafritz, A. James Clark, Albert Cohen, J. Martin Irving, R. Robert Linowes, Arthur K. Mason, Dr. Jack Meshel, David M. Osnos, Richard M. Patrick
President and Governor	Richard M. Patrick
Vice President and General Manager	George McPhee
Head Coach	Ron Wilson
Assistant Coaches	Tim Army, Tim Hunter
Goaltending Coach	Dave Prior
Equipment Manager	Doug Shearer
Assistant Equipment Manager	Craig Leydig
Equipment Assistant	Brian Metzger
Trainer	Stan Wong
Strength and Conditioning Coach	Frank Costello
Massage Therapist	Curt Millar
Senior Vice President of Communications	Matt Williams
Director of Public Relations	Doug Hicks
Asst. Director of PR	Jesse Price
PR Assistant	Amy Keller
Communications Coordinator	Kristen Peifer

MCI Center

Press room phone	202-628-3200 x7500
Press room fax	202-661-5011
Press box phone	202-628-3200 x7600
Press entrance	202-628-3200 x7599
Radio	TBA
TV	HTS Cable, WBDC-50

Peter Bondra's three-season total of 150 goals from 1995-96 to 1997-98 led all NHL scorers.

NHL Expansion Franchises

THREE ADDITIONAL FRANCHISES will join the National Hockey League in 1999-2000 and 2000-2001. The addition of the Atlanta Thrashers, Columbus Blue Jackets and Minnesota Wild will result in a 30-team NHL made up of two 15-team conferences, each of which is comprised of three five-team divisions. Divisional alignment and scheduling are described on the inside front cover of this book.

Atlanta Thrashers

First NHL season: 1999–2000

Southeast Division, Eastern Conference

One CNN Center
13th South Tower
Box 105366
Atlanta, GA 30303
Tel: 404/827-5300
Fax: 404/827-5212

www.atlantahockey.com

CLUB OFFICERS AND EXECUTIVES

Governor and President	Dr. Harvey Schiller
Executive Vice President	Dave Maggard
Vice President and General Manager	Don Waddell
Vice President Sales and Marketing	Derek Schiller
Vice President Public Relations	Greg Hughes
Director of Player Evaluation and Development	Bob Owen
Director of Ticket Sales	Dan Froelich
Director of Marketing	Jim Pfeifer

MEDIA RELATIONS INFORMATION

Vice President, Public Relations	Greg Hughes
Director, Public Relations	Tom Hughes
Public Relations phone:	404/827-3394
Public Relations fax:	404/827-5212

Columbus Blue Jackets

First NHL season: 2000–2001

Central Division, Western Conference

150 E. Wilson Bridge Road
Suite 235
Worthington, OH 43085
Tel: 614/540-GOAL
Fax: 614/540-1189

www.columbusbluejackets.com

MEDIA CONTACT

Cathy Mayne Lyttle	614/540-4625

Minnesota Wild

First NHL season: 2000–2001

Northwest Division, Western Conference

Piper Jaffrey Plaza
444 Cedar Street, Suite 2000
St. Paul, MN 55101
Tel: 651/333-PUCK (7825)
Fax: 651/222-1055

http://www.wild.com

Note: Area codes in the Twin Cities will change as of January, 1999. St. Paul area codes will become (651). Minneapolis area codes will remain (612).

CLUB OFFICERS AND EXECUTIVES

Chairman	Bob Naegele, Jr.
Chief Executive Officer	Jac K. Sperling
Chief Financial Officer	Martha Larson
New Saint Paul Arena Project Director	Ray Chandler
General Manager of New Saint Paul Arena	Chris Hansen
Director of Marketing	Carin Anderson
Director of Retail Operations	Matt Majka

MEDIA RELATIONS INFORMATION

Vice President of Communications	Bill Robertson
Public Relations fax:	651/293-9574

NHL League and Team Websites

National Hockey League	**www.nhl.com**
Anaheim	www.mightyducks.com
Atlanta	www.atlantathrashers.com
Boston	www.bostonbruins.com
Buffalo	www.sabres.com
Calgary	www.calgaryflames.com
Carolina	www.caneshockey.com
Chicago	www.chicagoblackhawks.com
Colorado	www.coloradoavalanche.com
Columbus	www.columbusbluejackets.com
Dallas	www.dallasstars.com
Detroit	www.detroitredwings.com
Edmonton	www.edmontonoilers.com
Florida	www.flpanthers.com
Los Angeles	www.lakings.com
Minnesota	www.wild.com
Montreal	www.canadiens.com
Nashville	www.nashvillepredators.com
New Jersey	www.newjerseydevils.com
NY Islanders	www.xice.com
NY Rangers	www.newyorkrangers.com
Ottawa	www.ottawasenators.com
Philadelphia	www.philadelphiaflyers.com
Phoenix	www.phoenixcoyotes.com
Pittsburgh	www.pittsburghpenguins.com
St. Louis	www.stlouisblues.com
San Jose	www.sj-sharks.com
Tampa Bay	www.tampabaylightning.com
Toronto	www.torontomapleleafs.com
Vancouver	www.orcabay.com/canucks
Washington	www.washingtoncaps.com

1997-98 Final Statistics

Standings

Abbreviations: GA – goals against; **GF** – goals for; **GP** – games played; **L** – losses; **PTS** – points; **T** – ties; **W** – wins; **%** – percentage of games won.

EASTERN CONFERENCE

Northeast Division

	GP	W	L	T	GF	GA	PTS	%
Pittsburgh	82	40	24	18	228	188	98	.598
Boston	82	39	30	13	221	194	91	.555
Buffalo	82	36	29	17	211	187	89	.543
Montreal	82	37	32	13	235	208	87	.530
Ottawa	82	34	33	15	193	200	83	.506
Carolina	82	33	41	8	200	219	74	.451

Atlantic Division

	GP	W	L	T	GF	GA	PTS	%
New Jersey	82	48	23	11	225	166	107	.652
Philadelphia	82	42	29	11	242	193	95	.579
Washington	82	40	30	12	219	202	92	.561
NY Islanders	82	30	41	11	212	225	71	.433
NY Rangers	82	25	39	18	197	231	68	.415
Florida	82	24	43	15	203	256	63	.384
Tampa Bay	82	17	55	10	151	269	44	.268

WESTERN CONFERENCE

Central Division

	GP	W	L	T	GF	GA	PTS	%
Dallas	82	49	22	11	242	167	109	.665
Detroit	82	44	23	15	250	196	103	.628
St. Louis	82	45	29	8	256	204	98	.598
Phoenix	82	35	35	12	224	227	82	.500
Chicago	82	30	39	13	192	199	73	.445
Toronto	82	30	43	9	194	237	69	.421

Pacific Division

	GP	W	L	T	GF	GA	PTS	%
Colorado	82	39	26	17	231	205	95	.579
Los Angeles	82	38	33	11	227	225	87	.530
Edmonton	82	35	37	10	215	224	80	.488
San Jose	82	34	38	10	210	216	78	.476
Calgary	82	26	41	15	217	252	67	.409
Anaheim	82	26	43	13	205	261	65	.396
Vancouver	82	25	43	14	224	273	64	.390

Peter Forsberg continued his outstanding play during the 1997-98 campaign, compiling 91 points, the second-highest total in the NHL. The slick-skating Swede led all Avalanche skaters in assists (60), points (91), shorthanded goals (3) and game-winning goals (7)

INDIVIDUAL LEADERS

Goal Scoring

Player	Team	GP	G
Teemu Selanne	Anaheim	73	52
Peter Bondra	Washington	76	52
John LeClair	Philadelphia	82	51
Pavel Bure	Vancouver	82	51
Zigmund Palffy	NY Islanders	82	45
Keith Tkachuk	Phoenix	69	40
Joe Nieuwendyk	Dallas	73	39
Rod Brind'Amour	Philadelphia	82	36
Jaromir Jagr	Pittsburgh	77	35

Assists

Player	Team	GP	A
Jaromir Jagr	Pittsburgh	77	67
Wayne Gretzky	NY Rangers	82	67
Peter Forsberg	Colorado	72	66
Ron Francis	Pittsburgh	81	62
Jozef Stumpel	Los Angeles	77	58
Adam Oates	Washington	82	58
Theoren Fleury	Calgary	82	51
Jason Allison	Boston	81	50
Sergei Zubov	Dallas	73	47
Pierre Turgeon	St. Louis	60	46

Power-play Goals

Player	Team	GP	PP
Zigmund Palffy	NY Islanders	82	17
John LeClair	Philadelphia	82	16
Brendan Shanahan	Detroit	75	15
Stu Barnes	Pittsburgh	78	15
Shayne Corson	Montreal	62	14
Joe Nieuwendyk	Dallas	73	14
Kevin Hatcher	Pittsburgh	74	13
Dmitri Khristich	Boston	82	13
Pavel Bure	Vancouver	82	13

Short-handed Goals

Player	Team	GP	SH
Jeff Friesen	San Jose	79	6
Pavel Bure	Vancouver	82	6
Mike Modano	Dallas	52	5
Michael Peca	Buffalo	61	5
Peter Bondra	Washington	76	5
Bob Corkum	Phoenix	76	5

Game-winning Goals

Player	Team	GP	GW
Peter Bondra	Washington	76	13
Joe Nieuwendyk	Dallas	73	11
Teemu Selanne	Anaheim	73	10
Brendan Shanahan	Detroit	75	9
John LeClair	Philadelphia	82	9

Game-tying Goals

Player	Team	GP	GT
Pat LaFontaine	NY Rangers	67	3
Teemu Selanne	Anaheim	73	3
Adam Deadmarsh	Colorado	73	3

Shots

Player	Team	GP	S
Pavel Bure	Vancouver	82	329
John LeClair	Philadelphia	82	303
Tony Amonte	Chicago	82	296
Alexei Yashin	Ottawa	82	291
Peter Bondra	Washington	76	284

Shooting Percentage

(minimum 82 shots)

Player	Team	GP	G	S	%
Mike Sillinger	Van.-Phi.	75	21	96	21.9
Jason Allison	Boston	81	33	158	20.9
Dmitri Khristich	Boston	82	29	144	20.1
Teemu Selanne	Anaheim	73	52	268	19.4
Joe Nieuwendyk	Dallas	73	39	203	19.2

Penalty Minutes

Player	Team	GP	PIM
Donald Brashear	Vancouver	77	372
Tie Domi	Toronto	80	365
Krzysztof Oliwa	New Jersey	73	295
Paul Laus	Florida	77	293
Richard Pilon	NY Islanders	76	291

Plus/Minus

Player	Team	GP	+/–
Chris Pronger	St. Louis	81	47
Larry Murphy	Detroit	82	35
Jason Allison	Boston	81	33
Randy McKay	New Jersey	74	30
John LeClair	Philadelphia	82	30
Dainius Zubrus	Philadelphia	69	29

Individual Leaders

Abbreviations: * – rookie eligible for Calder Trophy; **A** – assists; **G** – goals; **GP** – games played; **GT** – game-tying goals; **GW** – game-winning goals; **PIM** – penalties in minutes; **PP** – power play goals; **Pts** – points; **S** – shots on goal; **SH** – short-handed goals; **%** – percentage of shots on goal resulting in goals; **+/–** – difference between Goals For (**GF**) scored when a player is on the ice with his team at even strength or short-handed and Goals Against (**GA**) scored when the same player is on the ice with his team at even strength or on a power play.

Individual Scoring Leaders for Art Ross Trophy

Player	Team	GP	G	A	Pts	+/–	PIM	PP	SH	GW	GT	S	%
Jaromir Jagr	Pittsburgh	77	35	67	102	17	64	7	0	8	2	262	13.4
Peter Forsberg	Colorado	72	25	66	91	6	94	7	3	7	1	202	12.4
Pavel Bure	Vancouver	82	51	39	90	5	48	13	6	4	1	329	15.5
Wayne Gretzky	NY Rangers	82	23	67	90	–11	28	6	0	4	2	201	11.4
John LeClair	Philadelphia	82	51	36	87	30	32	16	0	9	1	303	16.8
Zigmund Palffy	NY Islanders	82	45	42	87	–2	34	17	2	5	1	277	16.2
Ron Francis	Pittsburgh	81	25	62	87	12	20	7	0	5	2	189	13.2
Teemu Selanne	Anaheim	73	52	34	86	12	30	10	1	10	3	268	19.4
Jason Allison	Boston	81	33	50	83	33	60	5	0	8	2	158	20.9
Jozef Stumpel	Los Angeles	77	21	58	79	17	53	4	0	2	1	162	13.0
Peter Bondra	Washington	76	52	26	78	14	44	11	5	13	2	284	18.3
Theoren Fleury	Calgary	82	27	51	78	0	197	3	2	4	1	282	9.6
Adam Oates	Washington	82	18	58	76	6	36	3	2	3	0	121	14.9
Rod Brind'Amour	Philadelphia	82	36	38	74	–2	54	10	2	8	0	205	17.6
Mats Sundin	Toronto	82	33	41	74	–3	49	9	1	5	1	219	15.1
Mark Recchi	Montreal	82	32	42	74	11	51	9	1	6	0	216	14.8
Tony Amonte	Chicago	82	31	42	73	21	66	7	3	5	0	296	10.5
Alexei Yashin	Ottawa	82	33	39	72	6	24	5	0	6	0	291	11.3
Brett Hull	St. Louis	66	27	45	72	–1	26	10	0	6	0	211	12.8
Eric Lindros	Philadelphia	63	30	41	71	14	134	10	1	4	0	202	14.9
Doug Weight	Edmonton	79	26	44	70	1	69	9	0	4	0	205	12.7
Joe Nieuwendyk	Dallas	73	39	30	69	16	30	14	0	11	0	203	19.2
Steve Yzerman	Detroit	75	24	45	69	3	46	6	2	0	2	188	12.8
Pierre Turgeon	St. Louis	60	22	46	68	13	24	6	0	4	0	140	15.7
Keith Tkachuk	Phoenix	69	40	26	66	9	147	11	0	8	1	232	17.2
Dmitri Khristich	Boston	82	29	37	66	25	42	13	2	1	0	144	20.1

Defensemen Scoring Leaders

Player	Team	GP	G	A	Pts	+/–	PIM	PP	SH	GW	GT	S	%
Nicklas Lidstrom	Detroit	80	17	42	59	22	18	7	1	1	1	205	8.3
Scott Niedermayer	New Jersey	81	14	43	57	5	27	11	0	1	0	175	8.0
Sergei Zubov	Dallas	73	10	47	57	16	16	5	1	2	1	148	6.8
Steve Duchesne	St. Louis	80	14	42	56	9	32	5	1	1	0	153	9.2
Larry Murphy	Detroit	82	11	41	52	35	37	2	1	2	0	129	8.5
Sandis Ozolinsh	Colorado	66	13	38	51	–12	65	9	0	2	1	135	9.6
Teppo Numminen	Phoenix	82	11	40	51	25	30	6	0	2	0	126	8.7
Rob Blake	Los Angeles	81	23	27	50	–3	94	11	0	4	0	261	8.8
Brian Leetch	NY Rangers	76	17	33	50	–36	32	11	0	2	2	230	7.4
Al MacInnis	St. Louis	71	19	30	49	6	80	9	1	2	0	227	8.4
Kevin Hatcher	Pittsburgh	74	19	29	48	–3	66	13	1	3	1	169	11.2
Ray Bourque	Boston	82	13	35	48	2	80	9	0	3	1	264	4.9
Boris Mironov	Edmonton	81	16	30	46	–8	100	10	1	1	1	203	7.9
Bryan Berard	NY Islanders	75	14	32	46	–32	59	8	1	2	1	192	7.3
Darryl Sydor	Dallas	79	11	35	46	17	51	4	1	1	0	166	6.6
Alexei Zhitnik	Buffalo	78	15	30	45	19	102	2	3	3	2	191	7.9
Vladimir Malakhov	Montreal	74	13	31	44	16	70	8	0	2	0	166	7.8
Robert Svehla	Florida	79	9	34	43	–3	113	3	0	0	0	144	6.3
Dmitri Mironov	Ana.-Det.	77	8	35	43	–7	119	3	0	1	0	170	4.7
Janne Niinimaa	Phi.-Edm.	77	4	39	43	13	62	3	0	1	0	134	3.0
Gary Suter	Chicago	73	14	28	42	1	74	5	2	0	0	199	7.0
Chris Chelios	Chicago	81	3	39	42	–7	151	1	0	0	0	205	1.5
Roman Hamrlik	T.B.-Edm.	78	9	32	41	–15	70	5	1	3	0	198	4.5
Kenny Jonsson	NY Islanders	81	14	26	40	–2	58	6	0	2	0	108	13.0
Mathieu Schneider	Toronto	76	11	26	37	–12	44	4	1	1	0	181	6.1
Patrice Brisebois	Montreal	79	10	27	37	16	67	5	0	1	0	125	8.0

Larry Murphy returned to the ranks of the NHL's premier offensive defensemen in 1997-98. His 52 points (11 goals, 41 assists) placed him fifth among blueliners while his plus/minus rating of +35 trailed only Chris Pronger's league-leading +47.

CONSECUTIVE SCORING STREAKS

Goals

Games	Player	Team	G
11	Teemu Selanne	Anaheim	17
7	Joe Sakic	Colorado	7
6	John LeClair	Philadelphia	8
6	John LeClair	Philadelphia	7
6	Peter Forsberg	Colorado	7
6	Ed Olczyk	Pittsburgh	6
6	Keith Primeau	Carolina	6
6	Andrew Brunette	Washington	6
5	Peter Bondra	Washington	7
5	John LeClair	Philadelphia	7
5	Pavel Bure	Vancouver	7
5	Peter Bondra	Washington	6
5	Randy McKay	New Jersey	6
5	Valeri Kamensky	Colorado	6
5	Keith Tkachuk	Phoenix	6
5	Derek King	Toronto	5
5	John MacLean	N.J.-S.J.	5
5	Pavel Bure	Vancouver	5
5	Steve Heinze	Boston	5
5	Alexei Zhamnov	Chicago	5
5	Scott Fraser	Edmonton	5

Assists

Games	Player	Team	A
8	Adam Oates	Washington	10
8	Wayne Gretzky	NY Rangers	9
7	Shayne Corson	Montreal	9
7	Robert Reichel	NY Islanders	8
7	Joe Sakic	Colorado	8
7	Valeri Kamensky	Colorado	8
7	Mike Modano	Dallas	7
7	Keith Primeau	Carolina	7
6	Wayne Gretzky	NY Rangers	11
6	Jaromir Jagr	Pittsburgh	11
6	Brett Hull	St. Louis	9
6	Andrew Brunette	Washington	9
6	Brett Hull	St. Louis	8
6	Anson Carter	Boston	8
6	Greg Johnson	Pit.-Chi.	7
6	Craig Janney	Phoenix	6
6	Claude Lemieux	Colorado	6
6	Dallas Drake	Phoenix	6

Points

Games	Player	Team	G	A	PTS
13	Zigmund Palffy	NY Islanders	10	8	18
12	Pierre Turgeon	St. Louis	7	11	18
11	Teemu Selanne	Anaheim	17	2	19
11	Peter Bondra	Washington	12	6	18
10	Pavel Bure	Vancouver	8	8	16
10	Andrew Brunette	Washington	5	10	15
10	Mark Messier	Vancouver	5	9	14
9	Zigmund Palffy	NY Islanders	6	7	13
9	Claude Lemieux	Colorado	4	7	11
9	German Titov	Calgary	6	3	9
8	Teemu Selanne	Anaheim	8	11	19
8	Jaromir Jagr	Pittsburgh	7	8	15
8	Joe Sakic	Colorado	7	8	15
8	Shayne Corson	Montreal	5	9	14
8	Adam Oates	Washington	3	10	13
8	Jozef Stumpel	Los Angeles	5	8	13
8	Keith Primeau	Carolina	5	7	12
8	Jozef Stumpel	Los Angeles	2	10	12
8	Wayne Gretzky	NY Rangers	3	8	11
8	Wayne Gretzky	NY Rangers	1	9	10

Sergei Samsonov joined Sergei Makarov and Pavel Bure as the only Russian-trained players to win the Calder Trophy after leading all first-year players with 22 goals. His 25 assists was second to Toronto's Mike Johnson (32), as the two led all rookies with 47 points apiece.

Individual Rookie Scoring Leaders

Rookie	Team	GP	G	A	Pts	+/–	PIM	PP	SH	GW	GT	S	%
Sergei Samsonov	Boston	81	22	25	47	9	8	7	0	3	0	159	13.8
Mike Johnson	Toronto	82	15	32	47	–4	24	5	0	0	1	143	10.5
Patrik Elias	New Jersey	74	18	19	37	18	28	5	0	6	1	147	12.2
Patrick Marleau	San Jose	74	13	19	32	5	14	1	0	2	0	90	14.4
Marco Sturm	San Jose	74	10	20	30	–2	40	2	0	3	0	118	8.5
Mattias Ohlund	Vancouver	77	7	23	30	3	76	1	0	0	0	172	4.1
Derek Morris	Calgary	82	9	20	29	1	88	5	1	1	1	120	7.5
Per Axelsson	Boston	82	8	19	27	–14	38	2	0	1	0	144	5.6
Matt Cullen	Anaheim	61	6	21	27	–4	23	2	0	0	0	75	8.0
Richard Zednik	Washington	65	17	9	26	–2	28	2	0	2	0	148	11.5
Alexei Morozov	Pittsburgh	76	13	13	26	–4	8	2	0	3	0	80	16.3
Magnus Arvedson	Ottawa	61	11	15	26	2	36	0	1	0	1	90	12.2
Vaclav Prospal	Phi.-Ott.	56	6	19	25	–11	21	4	0	0	0	88	6.8
Dave Scatchard	Vancouver	76	13	11	24	–4	165	0	0	1	1	85	15.3
Scott Fraser	Edmonton	29	12	11	23	6	6	6	0	2	0	61	19.7
Anders Eriksson	Detroit	66	7	14	21	21	32	1	0	2	0	91	7.7
Colin Forbes	Philadelphia	63	12	7	19	2	59	2	0	2	0	93	12.9
Steve Washburn	Florida	58	11	8	19	–6	32	4	0	2	0	61	18.0
Josef Marha	Col.-Ana.	23	9	9	18	4	4	3	0	0	0	31	29.0
Brad Isbister	Phoenix	66	9	8	17	4	102	1	0	1	0	115	7.8
Hnat Domenichelli	Calgary	31	9	7	16	4	6	1	0	1	2	70	12.9
Alyn McCauley	Toronto	60	6	10	16	–7	6	0	0	1	0	77	7.8
Jan Bulis	Washington	48	5	11	16	–5	18	0	0	0	1	37	13.5
Chris Phillips	Ottawa	72	5	11	16	2	38	2	0	2	0	107	4.7
Eric Messier	Colorado	62	4	12	16	4	20	0	0	0	0	66	6.1
Pascal Rheaume	St. Louis	48	6	9	15	4	35	1	0	0	0	45	13.3

Goal Scoring

Name	Team	GP	G
Sergei Samsonov	Boston	81	22
Patrik Elias	New Jersey	74	18
Richard Zednik	Washington	65	17
Mike Johnson	Toronto	82	15
Patrick Marleau	San Jose	74	13
Dave Scatchard	Vancouver	76	13
Alexei Morozov	Pittsburgh	76	13
Scott Fraser	Edmonton	29	12
Colin Forbes	Philadelphia	63	12
Steve Washburn	Florida	58	11
Magnus Arvedson	Ottawa	61	11
Marco Sturm	San Jose	74	10

Assists

Name	Team	GP	A
Mike Johnson	Toronto	82	32
Sergei Samsonov	Boston	81	25
Mattias Ohlund	Vancouver	77	23
Matt Cullen	Anaheim	61	21
Marco Sturm	San Jose	74	20
Derek Morris	Calgary	82	20
Vaclav Prospal	Phi.-Ott.	56	19
Patrik Elias	New Jersey	74	19
Patrick Marleau	San Jose	74	19
Per Axelsson	Boston	82	19

Power-play Goals

Name	Team	GP	PP
Sergei Samsonov	Boston	81	7
Scott Fraser	Edmonton	29	6
Patrik Elias	New Jersey	74	5
Derek Morris	Calgary	82	5
Mike Johnson	Toronto	82	5
Vaclav Prospal	Phi.-Ott.	56	4
Steve Washburn	Florida	58	4
Josef Marha	Col.-Ana.	23	3
Dmitri Nabokov	Chicago	25	3

Short-handed Goals

Name	Team	GP	SH
Juha Ylonen	Phoenix	55	1
Magnus Arvedson	Ottawa	61	1
Derek Morris	Calgary	82	1

Game-winning Goals

Name	Team	GP	GW
Patrik Elias	New Jersey	74	6
Marco Sturm	San Jose	74	3
Alexei Morozov	Pittsburgh	76	3
Sergei Samsonov	Boston	81	3
Jamie Wright	Dallas	21	2
Dmitri Nabokov	Chicago	25	2
Scott Fraser	Edmonton	29	2
Andrei Zyuzin	San Jose	56	2
Steve Washburn	Florida	58	2
Colin Forbes	Philadelphia	63	2
Richard Zednik	Washington	65	2
Anders Eriksson	Detroit	66	2
Chris Phillips	Ottawa	72	2
Krzysztof Oliwa	New Jersey	73	2
Patrick Marleau	San Jose	74	2

Game-tying Goals

Name	Team	GP	GT
Frank Banham	Anaheim	21	2
Hnat Domenichelli	Calgary	31	2
Brendan Morrison	New Jersey	11	1
Espen Knutsen	Anaheim	19	1
Vaclav Varada	Buffalo	27	1
Pavel Trnka	Anaheim	48	1
Jan Bulis	Washington	48	1
Magnus Arvedson	Ottawa	61	1
Steve McKenna	Los Angeles	62	1
Patrik Elias	New Jersey	74	1
Dave Scatchard	Vancouver	76	1
Derek Morris	Calgary	82	1
Mike Johnson	Toronto	82	1

Shots

Name	Team	GP	S
Mattias Ohlund	Vancouver	77	172
Sergei Samsonov	Boston	81	159
Richard Zednik	Washington	65	148
Patrik Elias	New Jersey	74	147
Per Axelsson	Boston	82	144
Mike Johnson	Toronto	82	143
Derek Morris	Calgary	82	120
Marco Sturm	San Jose	74	118
Brad Isbister	Phoenix	66	115
Chris Phillips	Ottawa	72	107

Shooting Percentage

(minimum 82 shots)

Name	Team	GP	G	S	%
Dave Scatchard	Vancouver	76	13	85	15.3
Patrick Marleau	San Jose	74	13	90	14.4
Sergei Samsonov	Boston	81	22	159	13.8
Colin Forbes	Philadelphia	63	12	93	12.9
Patrik Elias	New Jersey	74	18	147	12.2
Magnus Arvedson	Ottawa	61	11	90	12.2
Richard Zednik	Washington	65	17	148	11.5
Mike Johnson	Toronto	82	15	143	10.5
Marco Sturm	San Jose	74	10	118	8.5
Brad Isbister	Phoenix	66	9	115	7.8

Penalty Minutes

Name	Team	GP	PIM
Krzysztof Oliwa	New Jersey	73	295
Dave Scatchard	Vancouver	76	165
Peter Worrell	Florida	19	153
Steve McKenna	Los Angeles	62	150
Chris Dingman	Calgary	70	149

Plus/Minus

Name	Team	GP	+/–
Anders Eriksson	Detroit	66	21
Sheldon Souray	New Jersey	60	18
Patrik Elias	New Jersey	74	18
Christian Laflamme	Chicago	72	14
Brad Bombardir	New Jersey	43	11

Three-or-More-Goal Games

Player	Team	Date	Final Score	G
Jason Allison	Boston	Jan. 08	Pho. 2 Bos. 5	3
Jason Allison	Boston	Mar. 14	NYR 1 Bos. 5	3
Stu Barnes	Pittsburgh	Jan. 10	N.J. 1 Pit. 4	3
Peter Bondra	Washington	Jan. 08	Wsh. 5 NYR 3	3
Doug Brown	Detroit	Dec. 19	N.J. 4 Det. 5	3
Pavel Bure	Vancouver	Oct. 21	Van. 5 Dal. 1	3
Pavel Bure	Vancouver	Dec. 06	Van. 4 Col. 6	3
Pavel Bure	Vancouver	Dec. 15	L.A. 0 Van. 7	3
Valeri Bure	Calgary	Feb. 07	Edm. 2 Cgy. 4	3
Geoff Courtnall	St. Louis	Mar. 22	St.L. 3 Cgy. 5	3
Alexandre Daigle	Philadelphia	Mar. 14	Det. 1 Phi. 6	3
Vincent Damphousse	Montreal	Nov. 08	Mtl. 4 L.A. 1	3
Vincent Damphousse	Montreal	Mar. 28	T.B. 2 Mtl. 8	3
Jason Dawe	Buffalo	Nov. 10	Edm. 4 Buf. 4	3
Eric Daze	Chicago	Mar. 15	Chi. 8 Fla. 4	**4**
Ron Francis	Pittsburgh	Dec. 29	NYI 1 Pit. 5	3
Dave Gagner	Florida	Oct. 04	Fla. 5 Pit. 3	3
Wayne Gretzky	NY Rangers	Oct. 11	NYR 6 Van. 3	3
Steve Heinze	Boston	Dec. 06	Car. 1 Bos. 4	3
Steve Heinze	Boston	Apr. 07	Bos. 4 Ott. 2	3
Brett Hull	St. Louis	Oct. 09	L.A. 2 St.L. 3	3
Valeri Kamensky	Colorado	Jan. 03	Col. 5 Pit. 4	3
Sami Kapanen	Carolina	Nov. 12	Car. 6 Edm. 4	3
Sami Kapanen	Carolina	Mar. 15	Edm. 1 Car. 4	3
Paul Kariya	Anaheim	Jan. 21	Fla. 3 Ana. 8	3
Derek King	Toronto	Dec. 04	Tor. 3 St.L. 4	3
John LeClair	Philadelphia	Oct. 11	Phi. 6 Mtl. 2	3
Claude Lemieux	Colorado	Nov. 18	Col. 6 Wsh. 6	3
Eric Lindros	Philadelphia	Dec. 11	NYI 3 Phi. 4	3
Vladimir Malakhov	Montreal	Feb. 01	Mtl. 6 Car. 3	3
Kirk Maltby	Detroit	Dec. 27	Det. 8 Tor. 1	3
Shawn McEachern	Ottawa	Oct. 22	Ott. 6 Tor. 2	3
Marty McInnis	Calgary	Jan. 24	Van. 2 Cgy. 5	3
Randy McKay	New Jersey	Mar. 24	Phi. 2 N.J. 3	3
Mike Modano	Dallas	Oct. 10	Chi. 0 Dal. 7	3
Glen Murray	Los Angeles	Apr. 13	Cgy. 2 L.A. 4	3
Joe Nieuwendyk	Dallas	Nov. 05	Dal. 5 Pit. 2	3
Joe Nieuwendyk	Dallas	Mar. 13	Ana. 3 Dal. 6	**4**
Adam Oates	Washington	Oct. 08	Wsh. 6 NYI 3	3
Zigmund Palffy	NY Islanders	Oct. 16	NYI 5 S.J. 2	3
Zigmund Palffy	NY Islanders	Jan. 28	Phi. 1 NYI 6	3
Yanic Perreault	Los Angeles	Oct. 31	L.A. 5 Det. 1	3
Yanic Perreault	Los Angeles	Nov. 11	Van. 2 L.A. 8	3
Mark Recchi	Montreal	Oct. 04	Mtl. 4 Bos. 1	3
Robert Reichel	NY Islanders	Nov. 26	NYR 1 NYI 4	3
Mikael Renberg	Tampa Bay	Mar. 21	Fla. 1 T.B. 5	3
Gary Roberts	Carolina	Apr. 09	Tor. 2 Car. 5	3
*Sergei Samsonov	Boston	Apr. 09	NYI 1 Bos. 4	3
Miroslav Satan	Buffalo	Mar. 01	Buf. 3 Wsh. 0	3
Brian Savage	Montreal	Jan. 08	Mtl. 8 NYI 2	**4**
Teemu Selanne	Anaheim	Oct. 26	Ana. 3 NYR 3	3
Teemu Selanne	Anaheim	Nov. 10	S.J. 6 Ana. 4	3
Teemu Selanne	Anaheim	Mar. 22	Ana. 5 Ott. 2	3
Ray Sheppard	Florida	Nov. 26	Bos. 5 Fla. 10	3
Cory Stillman	Calgary	Oct. 12	Cgy. 4 Det. 4	3
Martin Straka	Pittsburgh	Apr. 18	Bos. 2 Pit. 5	3
Jozef Stumpel	Los Angeles	Feb. 03	L.A. 6 Cgy. 3	3
Darryl Sydor	Dallas	Jan. 03	Dal. 6 Car. 1	3
Keith Tkachuk	Phoenix	Dec. 01	Pho. 3 Fla. 2	3
Keith Tkachuk	Phoenix	Dec. 26	Pho. 4 S.J. 0	3
Keith Tkachuk	Phoenix	Apr. 03	Ana. 3 Pho. 6	3
Pat Verbeek	Dallas	Mar. 20	Car. 1 Dal. 6	3
Alexei Yashin	Ottawa	Jan. 10	Ott. 3 Col. 3	3
Rob Zamuner	Tampa Bay	Nov. 19	NYR 3 T.B. 6	3

NOTE: *64* Three-or-more-goal games recorded in 1997-98.

Left: Joe Nieuwendyk, Eric Daze and Brian Savage were the only players in the NHL to score four goals in a game in 1997-98. Nieuwendyk also ranked second in the league with 11 game-winning goals. Below: Tom Barrasso was third in the league with a 2.07 average and ranked sixth with seven shutouts.

Goaltending Leaders

Minimum 26 games

Goals Against Average

Goaltender	Team	GPI	Mins	GA	Avg
Ed Belfour	Dallas	61	3581	112	1.88
Martin Brodeur	New Jersey	70	4128	130	1.89
Tom Barrasso	Pittsburgh	63	3542	122	2.07
Dominik Hasek	Buffalo	72	4220	147	2.09
Ron Hextall	Philadelphia	46	2688	97	2.17
Trevor Kidd	Carolina	47	2685	97	2.17
Jamie McLennan	St. Louis	30	1658	60	2.17

Wins

Goaltender	Team	GPI	MINS	W	L	T
Martin Brodeur	New Jersey	70	4128	43	17	8
Ed Belfour	Dallas	61	3581	37	12	10
Olaf Kolzig	Washington	64	3788	33	18	10
Chris Osgood	Detroit	64	3807	33	20	11
Dominik Hasek	Buffalo	72	4220	33	23	13
Tom Barrasso	Pittsburgh	63	3542	31	14	13
Patrick Roy	Colorado	65	3835	31	19	13

Save Percentage

Goaltender	Team	GPI	MINS	GA	SA	S%	W	L	T
Dominik Hasek	Buffalo	72	4220	147	2149	.932	33	23	13
Tom Barrasso	Pittsburgh	63	3542	122	1556	.922	31	14	13
Trevor Kidd	Carolina	47	2685	97	1237	.922	21	21	3
Olaf Kolzig	Washington	64	3788	139	1729	.920	33	18	10
Martin Brodeur	New Jersey	70	4128	130	1569	.917	43	17	8
Jeff Hackett	Chicago	58	3441	126	1520	.917	21	25	11
Patrick Roy	Colorado	65	3835	153	1825	.916	31	19	13
Ed Belfour	Dallas	61	3581	112	1335	.916	37	12	10
Byron Dafoe	Boston	65	3693	138	1602	.914	30	25	9
Chris Osgood	Detroit	64	3807	140	1605	.913	33	20	11

Shutouts

Goaltender	Team	GPI	MINS	SO	W	L	T
Dominik Hasek	Buffalo	72	4220	13	33	23	13
Martin Brodeur	New Jersey	70	4128	10	43	17	8
Ed Belfour	Dallas	61	3581	9	37	12	10
Jeff Hackett	Chicago	58	3441	8	21	25	11
Curtis Joseph	Edmonton	71	4132	8	29	31	9

Team-by-Team Point Totals

1993-94 to 1997-98

(Ranked by five-year winning %)

	97-98	96-97	95-96	94-95	93-94	W%
Detroit	103	94	131	70	100	.659
New Jersey	107	104	86	52	106	.602
Que./Col.	95	107	104	65	76	.591
Pittsburgh	98	84	102	61	101	.590
Philadelphia	95	103	103	60	80	.583
Dallas	109	104	66	42	97	.553
St. Louis	98	83	80	61	91	.546
NY Rangers	68	86	96	47	112	.541
Buffalo	89	92	73	51	95	.529
Boston	91	61	91	57	97	.525
Washington	92	75	89	52	88	.524
Montreal	87	77	90	43	96	.520
Chicago	73	81	94	53	87	.513
Florida	63	89	92	46	83	.493
Calgary	67	73	79	55	97	.491
Toronto	69	68	80	50	98	.483
Vancouver	64	77	79	48	85	.467
Wpg./Pho.	82	83	78	39	57	.448
Anaheim	65	85	78	37	71	.444
Hfd./Car.	74	75	77	43	63	.439
Edmonton	80	81	68	38	64	.438
Los Angeles	87	67	66	41	66	.433
NY Islanders	71	70	54	35	84	.415
Tampa Bay	44	74	88	37	71	.415
San Jose	78	62	47	42	82	.411
Ottawa	83	77	41	23	37	.345

Team Record When Scoring First Goal of a Game

Team	GP	FG	W	L	T
Dallas	82	58	42	8	8
St. Louis	82	47	33	7	7
New Jersey	82	46	33	8	5
Detroit	82	43	33	7	3
Boston	82	43	31	6	6
Philadelphia	82	44	31	8	5
Colorado	82	47	29	9	9
Los Angeles	82	38	31	5	2
Montreal	82	41	27	7	7
Buffalo	82	39	27	7	5
Pittsburgh	82	40	26	8	6
Edmonton	82	41	24	11	6
NY Islanders	82	46	23	15	8
Phoenix	82	46	23	15	8
Ottawa	82	34	23	5	6
Chicago	82	44	22	14	8
Washington	82	40	22	11	7
Carolina	82	41	22	13	6
San Jose	82	35	22	11	2
Toronto	82	33	20	9	4
Vancouver	82	40	19	16	5
Anaheim	82	36	19	13	4
Florida	82	37	14	12	11
Calgary	82	33	15	10	8
NY Rangers	82	34	15	12	7
Tampa Bay	82	34	11	17	6

Team Plus/Minus Differential

Team	GF	PPGF	Net GF	GA	PPGA	Net GA	Goal Differential
Dallas	242	77	**165**	167	42	**125**	+ 40
St. Louis	256	62	**194**	204	49	**155**	+ 39
Detroit	250	67	**183**	196	51	**145**	+ 38
Buffalo	211	51	**160**	187	65	**122**	+ 38
New Jersey	225	63	**162**	166	41	**125**	+ 37
Philadelphia	242	71	**171**	193	51	**142**	+ 29
Montreal	235	68	**167**	208	62	**146**	+ 21
Pittsburgh	228	67	**161**	188	46	**142**	+ 19
Los Angeles	227	52	**175**	225	63	**162**	+ 13
Boston	221	62	**159**	194	44	**150**	+ 9
Phoenix	224	57	**167**	227	66	**161**	+ 6
Colorado	231	74	**157**	205	53	**152**	+ 5
Chicago	192	47	**145**	199	58	**141**	+ 4
Washington	219	55	**164**	202	39	**163**	+ 1
San Jose	210	54	**156**	216	59	**157**	– 1
Ottawa	193	48	**145**	200	47	**153**	– 8
Calgary	217	43	**174**	252	69	**183**	– 9
Carolina	200	50	**150**	219	58	**161**	– 11
Vancouver	224	48	**176**	273	77	**196**	– 20
NY Islanders	212	77	**138**	224	66	**158**	– 20
Edmonton	215	77	**138**	224	54	**171**	– 20
Florida	203	55	**148**	256	82	**174**	– 26
Anaheim	205	46	**159**	261	72	**189**	– 30
Toronto	194	41	**153**	237	50	**187**	– 34
NY Rangers	197	62	**135**	231	55	**176**	– 41
Tampa Bay	151	33	**118**	269	72	**197**	– 79

Team Record when Leading, Trailing, Tied

Team	Leading after 1 period			Leading after 2 periods			Trailing after 1 period			Trailing after 2 periods			Tied after 1 period			Tied after 2 periods		
	W	L	T	W	L	T	W	L	T	W	L	T	W	L	T	W	L	T
Anaheim	15	8	0	19	3	1	5	26	4	1	35	7	6	9	9	6	5	5
Boston	22	1	1	31	1	4	4	17	2	2	27	5	13	12	10	6	2	4
Buffalo	18	2	5	27	2	4	4	19	8	3	24	7	14	8	4	6	3	6
Calgary	10	5	5	17	3	5	10	27	4	4	30	4	6	9	6	5	8	6
Carolina	14	5	2	24	1	1	6	22	2	3	33	3	13	14	4	6	7	4
Chicago	15	7	7	26	2	6	1	16	2	0	28	1	14	16	4	4	9	6
Colorado	22	6	6	29	5	4	8	11	5	4	17	6	9	9	6	6	4	7
Dallas	32	2	6	39	4	4	5	12	1	3	15	0	12	8	4	7	3	7
Detroit	22	3	1	36	2	3	2	12	9	2	16	6	20	8	5	6	5	6
Edmonton	14	6	4	23	4	1	5	23	3	3	26	2	16	8	3	9	7	7
Florida	10	5	5	18	1	7	1	26	2	0	33	5	13	12	8	6	9	3
Los Angeles	22	1	3	28	0	5	4	23	4	3	26	3	12	9	4	7	7	3
Montreal	23	3	5	30	3	2	6	15	3	2	21	4	8	14	5	5	8	7
New Jersey	27	3	2	41	3	3	11	11	1	1	15	4	10	9	8	6	5	4
NY Islanders	18	9	5	25	1	6	4	20	2	1	33	2	8	12	4	4	7	3
NY Rangers	10	7	4	15	3	6	4	21	8	2	30	6	11	11	6	8	6	6
Ottawa	18	2	4	26	1	5	6	18	4	2	31	4	10	13	7	6	1	6
Philadelphia	20	5	3	30	1	3	4	14	0	3	21	2	18	10	8	9	7	6
Phoenix	16	8	5	25	1	1	6	19	2	3	28	4	13	8	5	7	6	7
Pittsburgh	22	5	1	31	0	4	7	10	5	3	16	4	11	9	12	6	8	10
San Jose	19	7	0	28	0	4	6	19	1	3	27	3	9	12	9	3	11	3
St. Louis	28	5	6	36	3	4	7	14	1	0	24	3	10	10	1	9	2	1
Tampa Bay	8	12	2	13	4	2	4	27	4	0	42	4	5	16	4	4	9	4
Toronto	15	3	1	24	0	3	6	21	3	3	36	3	9	19	5	3	7	3
Vancouver	17	8	4	21	5	5	3	23	6	2	32	4	5	12	4	2	6	5
Washington	19	7	3	26	3	5	6	10	4	3	22	2	15	13	5	11	5	5

Team Statistics

TEAMS' HOME-AND-ROAD RECORD

Northeast Division

	Home GP	W	L	T	GF	GA	PTS	%	Road GP	W	L	T	GF	GA	PTS	%
PIT	41	21	10	10	125	98	52	.634	41	19	14	8	103	90	46	.561
BOS	41	19	16	6	108	94	44	.537	41	20	14	7	113	100	47	.573
BUF	41	20	13	8	113	82	48	.585	41	16	16	9	98	105	41	.500
MTL	41	15	17	9	117	109	39	.476	41	22	15	4	118	99	48	.585
OTT	41	18	16	7	102	98	43	.524	41	16	17	8	91	102	40	.488
CAR	41	16	18	7	106	109	39	.476	41	17	23	1	94	110	35	.427
Total	**246**	**109**	**90**	**47**	**671**	**590**	**265**	**.539**	**246**	**110**	**99**	**37**	**617**	**606**	**257**	**.522**

Atlantic Division

	Home GP	W	L	T	GF	GA	PTS	%	Road GP	W	L	T	GF	GA	PTS	%
N.J.	41	29	10	2	131	86	60	.732	41	19	13	9	94	80	47	.573
PHI	41	24	11	6	116	86	54	.659	41	18	18	5	126	107	41	.500
WSH	41	23	12	6	116	94	52	.634	41	17	18	6	103	108	40	.488
NYI	41	17	20	4	106	104	38	.463	41	13	21	7	106	121	33	.402
NYR	41	14	18	9	102	103	37	.451	41	11	21	9	95	128	31	.378
FLA	41	11	24	6	102	135	28	.341	41	13	19	9	101	121	35	.427
T.B.	41	11	23	7	88	127	29	.354	41	6	32	3	63	142	15	.183
Total	**287**	**129**	**118**	**40**	**761**	**735**	**298**	**.519**	**287**	**97**	**142**	**48**	**688**	**807**	**242**	**.422**

Central Division

	Home GP	W	L	T	GF	GA	PTS	%	Road GP	W	L	T	GF	GA	PTS	%
DAL	41	26	8	7	123	73	59	.720	41	23	14	4	119	94	50	.610
DET	41	25	8	8	130	92	58	.707	41	19	15	7	120	104	45	.549
ST.L.	41	26	10	5	131	94	57	.695	41	19	19	3	125	110	41	.500
PHO	41	19	16	6	123	115	44	.537	41	16	19	6	101	112	38	.463
CHI	41	14	19	8	82	90	36	.439	41	16	20	5	110	109	37	.451
TOR	41	16	20	5	110	128	37	.451	41	14	23	4	84	109	32	.390
Total	**246**	**126**	**81**	**39**	**699**	**592**	**291**	**.591**	**246**	**107**	**110**	**29**	**659**	**638**	**243**	**.494**

Pacific Division

	Home GP	W	L	T	GF	GA	PTS	%	Road GP	W	L	T	GF	GA	PTS	%
COL	41	21	10	10	119	95	52	.634	41	18	16	7	112	110	43	.524
L.A.	41	22	16	3	128	115	47	.573	41	16	17	8	99	110	40	.488
EDM	41	20	16	5	103	103	45	.549	41	15	21	5	112	121	35	.427
S.J.	41	17	19	5	106	102	39	.476	41	17	19	5	104	114	39	.476
CGY	41	18	17	6	118	118	42	.512	41	8	24	9	99	134	25	.305
ANA	41	12	23	6	94	134	30	.366	41	14	20	7	111	127	35	.427
VAN	41	15	22	4	110	131	34	.415	41	10	21	10	114	142	30	.366
Total	**287**	**125**	**123**	**39**	**778**	**798**	**289**	**.503**	**287**	**98**	**138**	**51**	**751**	**858**	**247**	**.430**
	1066	**489**	**412**	**165**	**2909**	**2715**	**1143**	**.536**	**1066**	**412**	**489**	**165**	**2715**	**2909**	**989**	**.464**

TEAMS' DIVISIONAL RECORD

Northeast Division

	Against Own Division GP	W	L	T	GF	GA	PTS	%	Against Other Division GP	W	L	T	GF	GA	PTS	%
PIT	28	15	6	7	73	56	37	.661	54	25	18	11	155	132	61	.565
BOS	28	13	10	5	75	69	31	.554	54	26	20	8	146	125	60	.556
BUF	28	12	9	7	60	56	31	.554	54	24	20	10	151	131	58	.537
MTL	28	9	15	4	65	68	22	.393	54	28	17	9	170	140	65	.602
OTT	28	8	13	7	50	70	23	.411	54	26	20	8	143	130	60	.556
CAR	28	11	15	2	66	70	24	.429	54	22	26	6	134	149	50	.463
Total	**168**	**68**	**68**	**32**	**389**	**389**	**168**	**.500**	**324**	**151**	**121**	**52**	**899**	**807**	**354**	**.546**

Atlantic Division

	Against Own Division GP	W	L	T	GF	GA	PTS	%	Against Other Division GP	W	L	T	GF	GA	PTS	%
N.J.	32	21	6	5	101	64	47	.734	50	27	17	6	124	102	60	.600
PHI	32	17	11	4	97	82	38	.594	50	25	18	7	145	111	57	.570
WSH	32	17	11	4	94	75	38	.594	50	23	19	8	125	127	54	.540
NYI	32	13	15	4	83	75	30	.469	50	17	26	7	129	150	41	.410
NYR	32	8	17	7	78	98	23	.359	50	17	22	11	119	133	45	.450
FLA	32	12	14	6	77	89	30	.469	50	12	29	9	126	167	33	.330
T.B.	32	7	21	4	61	108	18	.281	50	10	34	6	90	161	26	.260
Total	**224**	**95**	**95**	**34**	**591**	**591**	**224**	**.500**	**350**	**131**	**165**	**54**	**858**	**951**	**316**	**.451**

Central Division

	Against Own Division GP	W	L	T	GF	GA	PTS	%	Against Other Division GP	W	L	T	GF	GA	PTS	%
DAL	28	14	10	4	79	62	32	.571	54	35	12	7	163	105	77	.713
DET	28	13	8	7	87	68	33	.589	54	31	15	8	163	128	70	.648
ST.L.	28	16	11	1	91	73	33	.589	54	29	18	7	165	131	65	.602
PHO	28	14	10	4	73	75	32	.571	54	21	25	8	151	152	50	.463
CHI	28	6	17	5	58	86	17	.304	54	24	22	8	134	113	56	.519
TOR	28	10	17	1	63	87	21	.375	54	20	26	8	131	150	48	.444
Total	**168**	**73**	**73**	**22**	**451**	**451**	**168**	**.500**	**324**	**160**	**118**	**46**	**907**	**779**	**366**	**.565**

Pacific Division

	Against Own Division GP	W	L	T	GF	GA	PTS	%	Against Other Division GP	W	L	T	GF	GA	PTS	%
COL	32	16	11	5	105	82	37	.578	50	23	15	12	126	123	58	.580
L.A.	32	19	11	2	100	88	40	.625	50	19	22	9	127	137	47	.470
EDM	32	14	17	1	85	93	29	.453	50	21	20	9	130	131	51	.510
S.J.	32	15	13	4	95	85	34	.531	50	19	25	6	115	131	44	.440
CGY	32	12	15	5	95	112	29	.453	50	14	26	10	122	140	38	.380
ANA	32	11	17	4	86	101	26	.406	50	15	26	9	119	160	39	.390
VAN	32	11	14	7	97	102	29	.453	50	14	29	7	127	171	35	.350
Total	**224**	**98**	**98**	**28**	**663**	**663**	**224**	**.500**	**350**	**125**	**163**	**62**	**866**	**993**	**312**	**.446**

TEAM STREAKS

Consecutive Wins

Games	Team	From	To
8	New Jersey	Nov. 5	Nov. 20
7	St. Louis	Oct. 3	Oct. 18
7	Montreal	Nov. 1	Nov. 13
7	Dallas	Nov. 22	Dec. 5
7	New Jersey	Feb. 2	Mar. 2
6	Pittsburgh	Nov. 20	Dec. 1
6	New Jersey	Dec. 4	Dec. 16
6	Edmonton	Jan. 7	Jan. 20
6	St. Louis	Feb. 28	Mar. 9
6	Detroit	Mar. 29	Apr. 11
5	Boston	Oct. 13	Oct. 21
5	Chicago	Oct. 29	Nov. 8
5	Colorado	Nov. 28	Dec. 6
5	Boston	Dec. 3	Dec. 15
5	Detroit	Dec. 19	Dec. 27
5	Phoenix	Dec. 26	Jan. 3
5	Dallas	Jan. 12	Jan. 26
5	Colorado	Feb. 2	Feb. 26
5	Dallas	Feb. 2	Feb. 28
5	St. Louis	Mar. 26	Apr. 4
5	Dallas	Apr. 6	Apr. 15

Consecutive Home Wins

Games	Team	From	To
8	Washington	Mar. 7	Apr. 4
7	St. Louis	Oct. 3	Oct. 25
7	Dallas	Nov. 19	Dec. 10
6	Los Angeles	Jan. 12	Feb. 5
6	St. Louis	Jan. 29	Mar. 7
6	Dallas	Mar. 29	Apr. 18
5	New Jersey	Dec. 6	Dec. 26
5	Washington	Jan. 6	Jan. 25
5	Dallas	Jan. 21	Feb. 28
5	Colorado	Jan. 26	Feb. 26
5	Pittsburgh	Mar. 7	Mar. 21
5	St. Louis	Mar. 26	Apr. 9
5	Detroit	Mar. 29	Apr. 11
5	Edmonton	Mar. 30	Apr. 18

Consecutive Road Wins

Games	Team	From	To
6	Detroit	Oct. 1	Oct. 26
6	Boston	Oct. 13	Nov. 2
5	Montreal	Oct. 25	Nov. 13
5	New Jersey	Oct. 27	Nov. 15
5	Pittsburgh	Nov. 15	Dec. 10
5	Chicago	Dec. 20	Jan. 14
5	Montreal	Dec. 31	Jan. 12
5	Carolina	Mar. 23	Apr. 6
5	Ottawa	Apr. 3	Apr. 19
4	Florida	Oct. 25	Nov. 22
4	Washington	Nov. 12	Nov. 23
4	San Jose	Dec. 4	Dec. 21
4	Phoenix	Dec. 19	Dec. 29
4	New Jersey	Feb. 2	Feb. 26
4	Carolina	Mar. 2	Mar. 8

Consecutive Undefeated

Games	Team	W	T	From	To
13	Buffalo	7	6	Jan. 21	Mar. 2
13	New Jersey	9	4	Jan. 31	Mar. 12
10	Colorado	6	4	Dec. 13	Jan. 3
10	Dallas	7	3	Dec. 15	Jan. 5
8	St. Louis	7	1	Oct. 3	Oct. 20
8	New Jersey	8	0	Nov. 5	Nov. 20
8	Pittsburgh	7	1	Nov. 15	Dec. 1
8	Philadelphia	6	2	Dec. 5	Dec. 23
8	Detroit	6	2	Dec. 17	Dec. 31
7	Colorado	5	2	Oct. 1	Oct. 15
7	Montreal	7	0	Nov. 1	Nov. 13
7	Dallas	7	0	Nov. 22	Dec. 5
7	New Jersey	6	1	Dec. 4	Dec. 18
7	San Jose	5	2	Dec. 4	Dec. 21
7	Boston	4	3	Dec. 31	Jan. 14
7	Los Angeles	6	1	Jan. 12	Jan. 31
7	Washington	5	2	Jan. 13	Jan. 31
7	Pittsburgh	5	2	Jan. 20	Jan. 31
7	San Jose	4	3	Apr. 1	Apr. 15

Consecutive Home Undefeated

Games	Team	W	T	From	To
11	Washington	10	1	Mar. 7	Apr. 19
10	Buffalo	4	6	Dec. 31	Feb. 25
10	Pittsburgh	6	4	Feb. 4	Mar. 29
9	St. Louis	8	1	Oct. 3	Nov. 1
9	Detroit	7	2	Mar. 12	Apr. 11
8	Colorado	4	4	Oct. 1	Nov. 1
8	Dallas	7	1	Nov. 12	Dec. 10
8	Tampa Bay	4	4	Nov. 19	Dec. 22
8	Colorado	5	3	Dec. 2	Dec. 31
8	Philadelphia	6	2	Dec. 11	Jan. 26
8	New Jersey	7	1	Feb. 4	Mar. 24
8	Ottawa	5	3	Feb. 5	Mar. 20
8	Philadelphia	6	2	Mar. 5	Mar. 22
7	St. Louis	6	1	Jan. 22	Mar. 7
7	Calgary	6	1	Feb. 5	Mar. 22
6	Florida	4	2	Dec. 30	Jan. 31
6	Boston	4	2	Jan. 1	Jan. 27
6	Washington	5	1	Jan. 6	Jan. 28
6	Dallas	5	1	Jan. 9	Feb. 28
6	Los Angeles	6	0	Jan. 12	Feb. 5
6	Dallas	6	0	Mar. 29	Apr. 18

Consecutive Road Undefeated

Games	Team	W	T	From	To
10	Montreal	8	2	Dec. 27	Feb. 1
8	New Jersey	5	3	Jan. 31	Mar. 12
8	Buffalo	6	2	Feb. 1	Mar. 10
7	Pittsburgh	5	2	Nov. 15	Dec. 19
7	Boston	4	3	Feb. 1	Mar. 21
6	Detroit	6	0	Oct. 1	Oct. 26
6	Boston	6	0	Oct. 13	Nov. 2
6	Florida	4	2	Oct. 23	Nov. 30
6	Chicago	5	1	Dec. 17	Jan. 14
6	Dallas	5	1	Dec. 18	Jan. 5
6	Pittsburgh	3	3	Jan. 22	Feb. 25
6	Florida	3	3	Mar. 28	Apr. 18
6	Ottawa	5	1	Mar. 29	Apr. 19

TEAM PENALTIES

Abbreviations: GP – games played; **PEN** – total penalty minutes including bench minutes; **BMI** – total bench minor minutes; **AVG** – average penalty minutes/game calculated by dividing total penalty minutes by games played

Team	GP	PEN	BMI	AVG
OTT	82	1091	14	13.3
BOS	82	1117	12	13.6
WSH	82	1198	2	14.6
PIT	82	1225	10	14.9
DAL	82	1301	14	15.9
DET	82	1346	12	16.4
ST.L.	82	1414	8	17.2
S.J.	82	1417	20	17.3
CAR	82	1455	12	17.7
N.J.	82	1488	8	18.1
TOR	82	1481	6	18.1
CHI	82	1546	12	18.9
MTL	82	1547	16	18.9
NYR	82	1548	12	18.9
PHO	82	1602	20	19.5
NYI	82	1646	10	20.1
FLA	82	1676	20	20.4
EDM	82	1690	10	20.6
COL	82	1729	24	21.1
L.A.	82	1763	22	21.5
PHI	82	1766	18	21.5
BUF	82	1768	16	21.6
T.B.	82	1823	12	22.2
ANA	82	1843	10	22.5
CGY	82	1859	10	22.7
VAN	82	2166	18	26.4
Total	**1066**	**40505**	**348**	**38.0**

Michael Peca, right, and Detroit's Nicklas Lidstrom battle for position during a game between the Sabres and Red Wings. Peca, who finished a close second to Dallas Stars forward Jere Lehtinen in the Selke Trophy race, led all Buffalo penalty killers with five shorthanded goals and nine shorthanded points.

TEAMS' POWER-PLAY RECORD

Abbreviations: ADV – total advantages; **PPGF** – power-play goals for; **%** – calculated by dividing number of power-play goals by total advantages.

	Home					Road					Overall				
	Team	GP	ADV	PPGF	%	Team	GP	ADV	PPGF	%	Team	GP	ADV	PPGF	%
1	N.J.	41	158	38	24.1	DAL	41	185	40	21.6	DAL	82	385	77	20.0
2	NYI	41	198	38	19.2	PHI	41	190	38	20.0	N.J.	82	333	63	18.9
3	ST.L.	41	201	38	18.9	MTL	41	186	37	19.9	MTL	82	372	68	18.3
4	NYR	41	175	33	18.9	BOS	41	162	31	19.1	PHI	82	399	71	17.8
5	DAL	41	200	37	18.5	COL	41	207	38	18.4	NYR	82	351	62	17.7
6	DET	41	195	35	17.9	EDM	41	237	43	18.1	DET	82	381	67	17.6
7	WSH	41	174	31	17.8	DET	41	186	32	17.2	COL	82	426	74	17.4
8	PIT	41	209	37	17.7	NYR	41	176	29	16.5	BOS	82	359	62	17.3
9	MTL	41	186	31	16.7	CHI	41	174	27	15.5	ST.L.	82	368	62	16.8
10	COL	41	219	36	16.4	PHO	41	187	29	15.5	NYI	82	365	61	16.7
11	PHI	41	209	33	15.8	S.J.	41	181	28	15.5	PIT	82	407	67	16.5
12	BOS	41	197	31	15.7	VAN	41	175	27	15.4	EDM	82	483	77	15.9
13	BUF	41	197	30	15.2	PIT	41	198	30	15.2	WSH	82	350	55	15.7
14	OTT	41	199	30	15.1	L.A.	41	156	23	14.7	PHO	82	384	57	14.8
15	TOR	41	186	27	14.5	ST.L.	41	167	24	14.4	L.A.	82	366	52	14.2
16	PHO	41	197	28	14.2	N.J.	41	175	25	14.3	S.J.	82	400	54	13.5
17	EDM	41	246	34	13.8	ANA	41	202	28	13.9	FLA	82	409	55	13.4
18	L.A.	41	210	29	13.8	NYI	41	167	23	13.8	CAR	82	378	50	13.2
19	FLA	41	207	28	13.5	WSH	41	176	24	13.6	BUF	82	396	51	12.9
20	CAR	41	195	26	13.3	FLA	41	202	27	13.4	CHI	82	363	47	12.9
21	CGY	41	180	22	12.2	CAR	41	183	24	13.1	OTT	82	375	48	12.8
22	S.J.	41	219	26	11.9	CGY	41	176	21	11.9	VAN	82	374	48	12.8
23	VAN	41	199	21	10.6	BUF	41	199	21	10.6	CGY	82	356	43	12.1
24	CHI	41	189	20	10.6	OTT	41	176	18	10.2	ANA	82	392	46	11.7
25	T.B.	41	182	19	10.4	T.B.	41	171	14	8.2	TOR	82	359	41	11.4
26	ANA	41	190	18	9.5	TOR	41	173	14	8.1	T.B.	82	353	33	9.3
Total		**1066**	**5117**	**776**	**15.2**		**1066**	**4767**	**715**	**15.0**		**1066**	**9884**	**1491**	**15.1**

SHORT-HANDED GOALS FOR

	Home			Road			Overall		
	Team	GP	SHGF	Team	GP	SHGF	Team	GP	SHGF
1	CGY	41	11	VAN	41	13	VAN	82	19
2	MTL	41	10	CHI	41	10	CGY	82	18
3	BUF	41	9	FLA	41	9	BUF	82	15
4	EDM	41	8	DAL	41	9	WSH	82	14
5	T.B.	41	7	WSH	41	7	MTL	82	13
6	COL	41	7	ST.L.	41	7	CHI	82	13
7	WSH	41	7	CGY	41	7	FLA	82	12
8	NYI	41	7	BUF	41	6	ST.L.	82	12
9	L.A.	41	7	PHO	41	6	PIT	82	11
10	PIT	41	6	ANA	41	6	T.B.	82	11
11	VAN	41	6	PIT	41	5	DAL	82	11
12	ST.L.	41	5	S.J.	41	5	NYI	82	11
13	S.J.	41	5	OTT	41	4	L.A.	82	10
14	DET	41	5	CAR	41	4	PHO	82	10
15	PHI	41	4	NYI	41	4	S.J.	82	10
16	TOR	41	4	T.B.	41	4	EDM	82	10
17	PHO	41	4	L.A.	41	3	ANA	82	9
18	BOS	41	4	DET	41	3	CAR	82	8
19	CAR	41	4	MTL	41	3	COL	82	8
20	ANA	41	3	PHI	41	3	DET	82	8
21	CHI	41	3	EDM	41	2	PHI	82	7
22	FLA	41	3	N.J.	41	2	OTT	82	6
23	OTT	41	2	COL	41	1	TOR	82	5
24	DAL	41	2	TOR	41	1	BOS	82	5
25	N.J.	41	2	BOS	41	1	N.J.	82	4
26	NYR	41	0	NYR	41	0	NYR	82	0
Total		**1066**	**135**		**1066**	**125**		**1066**	**260**

TEAMS' PENALTY KILLING RECORD

Abbreviations: TSH – total times short-handed; **PPGA** – power-play goals against; **%** – calculated by dividing times short minus power-play goals against by times short.

	Home					Road					Overall				
	Team	GP	TSH	PPGA	%	Team	GP	TSH	PPGA	%	Team	GP	TSH	PPGA	%
1	PHI	41	171	15	91.2	WSH	41	193	21	89.1	WSH	82	362	39	89.2
2	WSH	41	169	18	89.3	TOR	41	191	21	89.0	DAL	82	351	42	88.0
3	DET	41	194	21	89.2	PIT	41	173	21	87.9	COL	82	409	53	87.0
4	BUF	41	187	21	88.8	COL	41	209	26	87.6	N.J.	82	309	41	86.7
5	DAL	41	175	20	88.6	DAL	41	176	22	87.5	PHI	82	382	51	86.6
6	MTL	41	194	25	87.1	S.J.	41	207	27	87.0	TOR	82	372	50	86.6
7	NYI	41	186	24	87.1	N.J.	41	167	22	86.8	ST.L.	82	367	49	86.6
8	ST.L.	41	189	25	86.8	ST.L.	41	178	24	86.5	PIT	82	338	46	86.4
9	N.J.	41	142	19	86.6	BOS	41	147	20	86.4	DET	82	376	51	86.4
10	COL	41	200	27	86.5	CHI	41	198	28	85.9	NYI	82	384	54	85.9
11	CGY	41	201	28	86.1	T.B.	41	198	29	85.4	NYR	82	377	55	85.4
12	NYR	41	170	24	85.9	CAR	41	197	29	85.3	CAR	82	391	58	85.2
13	CAR	41	194	29	85.1	L.A.	41	193	29	85.0	S.J.	82	398	59	85.2
14	OTT	41	141	21	85.1	NYR	41	207	31	85.0	CHI	82	382	58	84.8
15	PIT	41	165	25	84.8	NYI	41	198	30	84.8	BOS	82	285	44	84.6
16	TOR	41	181	29	84.0	PHO	41	209	33	84.2	MTL	82	401	62	84.5
17	CHI	41	184	30	83.7	EDM	41	201	32	84.1	OTT	82	303	47	84.5
18	L.A.	41	206	34	83.5	OTT	41	162	26	84.0	BUF	82	413	65	84.3
19	PHO	41	199	33	83.4	DET	41	182	30	83.5	L.A.	82	399	63	84.2
20	EDM	41	205	34	83.4	VAN	41	216	37	82.9	CGY	82	430	69	84.0
21	S.J.	41	191	32	83.2	PHI	41	211	36	82.9	PHO	82	408	66	83.8
22	BOS	41	138	24	82.6	ANA	41	220	39	82.3	EDM	82	406	66	83.7
23	VAN	41	216	40	81.5	MTL	41	207	37	82.1	T.B.	82	410	72	82.4
24	ANA	41	176	33	81.3	CGY	41	229	41	82.1	VAN	82	432	77	82.2
25	T.B.	41	212	43	79.7	FLA	41	222	41	81.5	ANA	82	396	72	81.8
26	FLA	41	181	41	77.3	BUF	41	226	44	80.5	FLA	82	403	82	79.7
Total		**1066**	**4767**	**715**	**85.0**		**1066**	**5117**	**776**	**84.8**		**1066**	**9884**	**1491**	**84.9**

SHORT-HANDED GOALS AGAINST

	Home			Road			Overall		
	Team	GP	SHGA	Team	GP	SHGA	Team	GP	SHGA
1	ST.L.	41	1	L.A.	41	1	BOS	82	3
2	WSH	41	1	BOS	41	1	WSH	82	4
3	CHI	41	1	PHO	41	2	ST.L.	82	4
4	PHI	41	2	MTL	41	2	CHI	82	5
5	COL	41	2	S.J.	41	2	S.J.	82	5
6	BOS	41	2	WSH	41	3	PHO	82	6
7	S.J.	41	3	ST.L.	41	3	DET	82	7
8	OTT	41	3	CHI	41	4	MTL	82	8
9	DAL	41	3	DET	41	4	OTT	82	9
10	DET	41	3	N.J.	41	4	PHI	82	9
11	PHO	41	4	ANA	41	4	DAL	82	9
12	CAR	41	4	CGY	41	4	N.J.	82	9
13	NYR	41	4	EDM	41	5	CAR	82	10
14	T.B.	41	5	PIT	41	5	ANA	82	10
15	BUF	41	5	TOR	41	5	EDM	82	11
16	N.J.	41	5	OTT	41	6	L.A.	82	12
17	FLA	41	5	CAR	41	6	BUF	82	12
18	MTL	41	6	DAL	41	6	COL	82	12
19	EDM	41	6	VAN	41	6	VAN	82	12
20	VAN	41	6	BUF	41	7	TOR	82	13
21	ANA	41	6	NYI	41	7	CGY	82	13
22	TOR	41	8	PHI	41	7	NYR	82	13
23	CGY	41	9	NYR	41	9	PIT	82	16
24	NYI	41	9	COL	41	10	FLA	82	16
25	PIT	41	11	FLA	41	11	T.B.	82	16
26	L.A.	41	11	T.B.	41	11	NYI	82	16
Total		**1066**	**125**		**1066**	**135**		**1066**	**260**

Overtime Results

1988-89 to 1997-98

Team	1997-98 GP	W	L	T	1996-97 GP	W	L	T	1995-96 GP	W	L	T	1994-95 GP	W	L	T	1993-94 GP	W	L	T
ANA	20	3	4	13	16	3	0	13	16	6	2	8	7	2	0	5	12	2	5	5
BOS	17	3	1	13	15	3	3	9	19	2	6	11	8	2	3	3	17	2	2	13
BUF	21	3	1	17	21	5	4	12	15	2	6	7	9	1	1	7	13	0	4	9
CGY	22	4	3	15	16	3	4	9	16	2	3	11	9	1	1	7	18	3	2	13
HFD/CAR	12	2	2	8	18	3	4	11	14	2	3	9	9	4	0	5	14	4	1	9
CHI	18	1	4	13	19	1	5	13	19	1	4	14	7	2	0	5	16	2	5	9
QUE/COL	22	2	3	17	15	2	3	10	6	1	0	5	8	0	0	8	15	3	3	9
MIN/DAL	17	5	1	11	15	4	3	8	15	1	0	14	9	0	1	8	22	6	3	13
DET	15	0	0	15	27	7	2	18	11	3	1	7	4	0	0	4	15	5	2	8
EDM	15	3	2	10	16	1	6	9	14	4	2	8	7	1	2	4	21	1	6	14
FLA	20	3	2	15	26	3	4	19	13	0	3	10	9	0	3	6	24	2	5	17
L.A.	16	3	2	11	14	0	3	11	23	3	2	18	9	0	0	9	18	3	3	12
MTL	20	3	4	13	21	2	4	15	15	2	3	10	10	1	2	7	19	3	2	14
N.J.	16	2	3	11	17	1	2	14	19	7	0	12	11	1	2	8	14	1	1	12
NYI	13	0	2	11	17	3	2	12	17	2	5	10	7	1	1	5	19	5	2	12
NYR	24	2	4	18	13	3	0	10	17	2	1	14	3	0	0	3	12	3	1	8
OTT	17	2	0	15	17	0	2	15	8	0	3	5	7	1	1	5	17	4	4	9
PHI	15	3	1	11	18	3	2	13	20	4	3	13	8	3	1	4	18	3	5	10
WPG/PHX	14	0	2	12	16	5	4	7	8	2	0	6	9	0	2	7	15	1	5	9
PIT	23	3	2	18	13	1	4	8	9	3	2	4	5	1	1	3	19	4	2	13
ST.L.	12	2	2	8	13	1	1	11	18	1	1	16	7	1	1	5	17	4	2	11
S.J.	12	0	2	10	12	3	1	8	9	1	1	7	5	1	0	4	19	2	1	16
T.B.	13	0	3	10	16	4	2	10	18	3	3	12	7	2	2	3	18	3	4	11
TOR	10	1	0	9	10	1	1	8	18	4	2	12	8	0	0	8	17	4	1	12
VAN	17	0	3	14	14	5	2	7	20	1	4	15	13	0	1	12	12	5	4	3
WSH	17	4	1	12	13	2	2	9	16	4	1	11	9	0	1	8	14	2	2	10
Totals	**219**	**54**		**165**	**214**	**70**		**144**	**201**	**64**		**137**	**101**	**26**		**75**	**214**	**74**		**140**

Team	1992-93 GP	W	L	T	1991-92 GP	W	L	T	1990-91 GP	W	L	T	1989-90 GP	W	L	T	1988-89 GP	W	L	T
ANA																				
BOS	15	5	3	7	20	6	2	12	17	5	0	12	14	3	2	9	19	3	2	14
BUF	18	4	4	10	16	2	2	12	24	3	2	19	15	4	3	8	13	2	4	7
CGY	19	4	4	11	19	2	5	12	15	3	4	8	21	3	3	15	17	5	3	9
HFD/CAR	18	3	9	6	18	2	3	13	18	2	5	11	9	0	0	9	10	1	4	5
CHI	16	1	3	12	19	2	2	15	12	3	1	8	10	2	2	6	17	2	3	12
QUE/COL	15	4	1	10	17	0	5	12	18	1	3	14	8	0	1	7	10	2	1	7
MIN/DAL	10	0	0	10	8	0	2	6	17	0	3	14	11	3	4	4	17	0	1	16
DET	11	2	0	9	16	3	1	12	14	2	4	8	17	2	1	14	16	3	1	12
EDM	17	5	4	8	12	0	2	10	15	4	5	6	20	5	1	14	15	4	3	8
FLA																				
L.A.	13	2	1	10	16	1	1	14	16	4	2	10	12	3	2	7	14	6	1	7
MTL	14	5	3	6	20	6	3	11	17	3	3	11	17	4	2	11	11	2	0	9
N.J.	11	4	0	7	17	2	4	11	17	1	1	15	16	3	4	9	17	1	4	12
NYI	13	3	3	7	16	3	2	11	15	2	3	10	16	3	2	11	11	3	3	5
NYR	17	2	4	11	11	5	1	5	16	1	2	13	17	2	2	13	10	1	1	8
OTT	10	0	6	4																
PHI	17	4	2	11	17	2	4	11	11	1	0	10	18	2	5	11	14	1	5	8
WPG/PHX	11	2	2	7	20	1	4	15	14	1	2	11	19	4	4	11	20	6	2	12
PIT	10	3	0	7	12	2	1	9	12	4	2	6	14	3	3	8	10	2	1	7
ST.L.	17	2	4	11	15	2	2	11	18	3	4	11	15	2	4	9	16	3	1	12
S.J.	10	3	5	2	9	1	3	5												
T.B.	14	3	4	7																
TOR	13	1	1	11	11	4	0	7	17	4	2	11	11	3	4	4	11	1	4	6
VAN	10	1	0	9	17	4	1	12	15	3	3	9	21	2	5	14	14	2	4	8
WSH	11	2	2	7	12	2	2	8	14	4	3	7	9	2	1	6	16	2	4	10
Totals	**165**	**65**		**100**	**169**	**52**		**117**	**166**	**54**		**112**	**155**	**55**		**100**	**149**	**52**		**97**

1997-98
Home Team Wins: 27
Visiting Team Wins: 27

The first American-born player to lead the NHL in goals, Keith Tkachuk missed adding another tally to his impressive count when he was robbed by Edmonton's Bob Essensa on a penalty shot during the Oilers' 5-2 win over Phoenix on January 24, 1998.

1997-98 Penalty Shots

Scored

Jere Lehtinen (Dallas) scored against Dominik Hasek (Buffalo), October 7. Final score: Dallas 4 at Buffalo 2.

Doug Weight (Edmonton) scored against Mike Richter (NY Rangers), October 8. Final score: NY Rangers 3 at Edmonton 3.

Mike Keane (NY Rangers) scored against Corey Schwab (Tampa Bay), October 24. Final score: Tampa Bay 3 at NY Rangers 4.

Joe Sakic (Colorado) scored against Tyler Moss (Calgary), November 1. Final score: Calgary 3 at Colorado 3.

Pavel Bure (Vancouver) scored against Mike Vernon (San Jose), November 12. Final score: Vancouver 5 at San Jose 2.

Joe Sacco (Anaheim) scored against Jocelyn Thibault (Montreal), November 12. Final score: Montreal 4 at Anaheim 3.

Alexander Mogilny (Vancouver) scored against Chris Osgood (Detroit), December 1. Final score: Detroit 3 at Vancouver 3.

Robert Reichel (NY Islanders) scored against Zac Bierk (Tampa Bay), January 14. Final score: NY Islanders 7 at Tampa Bay 1.

Paul Kariya (Anaheim) scored against Kevin Weekes (Florida), January 21. Final score: Florida 3 at Anaheim 8.

Pavel Bure (Vancouver) scored against Nikolai Khabibulin (Phoenix), January 26. Final score: Vancouver 2 at Phoenix 4.

Derek King (Toronto) scored against John Vanbiesbrouck (Florida), February 7. Final score: Florida 2 at Toronto 3.

Hnat Domenichelli (Calgary) scored against Arturs Irbe (Vancouver), February 27. Final score: Vancouver 4 at Calgary 4.

Pavel Bure (Vancouver) scored against Damian Rhodes (Ottawa), February 28. Final score: Ottawa 4 at Vancouver 6.

Tom Chorske (NY Islanders) scored against Patrick Roy (Colorado), March 7. Final score: Colorado 4 at NY Islanders 2.

Dixon Ward (Buffalo) scored against Damian Rhodes (Ottawa), April 11. Final score: Buffalo 4 at Ottawa 4.

Tim Taylor (Boston) scored against Jocelyn Thibault (Montreal), April 15. Final score: Boston 6 at Montreal 2.

Stopped

John Vanbiesbrouck (Florida) stopped Trent Klatt (Philadelphia), October 1. Final score: Florida 1 at Philadelphia 3.

Andy Moog (Montreal) stopped Rob Dimaio (Boston), October 4. Final score: Montreal 4 at Boston 1.

Chris Terreri (Chicago) stopped Rob Zamuner (Tampa Bay), October 9. Final score: Tampa Bay 4 at Chicago 1.

Trevor Kidd (Carolina) stopped Brendan Shanahan (Detroit), November 5. Final score: Detroit 1 at Carolina 3.

Nikolai Khabibulin (Phoenix) stopped Dino Ciccarelli (Tampa Bay), December 3. Final score: Phoenix 1 at Tampa Bay 2.

Corey Schwab (Tampa Bay) stopped Steve Heinze (Boston), December 17. Final score: Boston 0 at Tampa Bay 2.

Andrei Trefilov (Chicago) stopped Mats Sundin (Toronto), January 10. Final score: Chicago 4 at Toronto 3.

Bob Essensa (Edmonton) stopped Keith Tkachuk (Phoenix), January 24. Final score: Edmonton 5 at Phoenix 2.

Mark Fitzpatrick (Tampa Bay) stopped Tom Fitzgerald (Florida), January 31. Final score: Tampa Bay 0 at Florida 2.

Guy Hebert (Anaheim) stopped Tony Amonte (Chicago), February 1. Final score: Chicago 3 at Anaheim 4.

Guy Hebert (Anaheim) stopped Glen Murray (Los Angeles), February 7. Final score: Los Angeles 5 at Anaheim 2.

Ron Hextall (Philadelphia) stopped Stu Barnes (Pittsburgh), March 8. Final score: Pittsburgh 3 at Philadelphia 4.

Mike Richter (NY Rangers) stopped Marc Bureau (Montreal), March 12. Final score: NY Rangers 1 at Montreal 4.

Sean Burke (Philadelphia) stopped Kevin Stevens (NY Rangers), March 22. Final score: NY Rangers 4 at Philadelphia 5.

Rick Tabaracci (Calgary) stopped Darren Turcotte (St. Louis), March 22. Final score: St. Louis 3 at Calgary 5.

Stephane Fiset (Los Angeles) stopped Peter Bondra (Washington), April 4. Final score: Los Angeles 2 at Washington 3.

Dwayne Roloson (Calgary) stopped Rob Blake (Los Angeles), April 13. Final score: Calgary 2 at Los Angeles 4.

Curtis Joseph (Edmonton) stopped Jean-Francois Jomphe (Anaheim), April 15. Final score: Anaheim 3 at Edmonton 5.

Summary

34 penalty shots resulted in 16 goals.

CZECH REPUBLIC WINS MEN'S HOCKEY GOLD AT THE 1998 WINTER OLYMPICS

THE 1998 WINTER OLYMPICS in Nagano, Japan featured superb hockey and a balanced field of teams built around many of the NHL's finest players. Dominik Hasek, the NHL's most valuable player and top goaltender in each of the past two seasons, played superbly, leading the Czech Republic to the gold medal, defeating three of the tournament's top-rated teams, the USA, Canada and Russia. Hasek's heroics were matched by the inspired play of his teammates who minimized their opponents' scoring chances particularly in the medal round and gold medal games.

Hasek was named the tournament's top goaltender. Pavel Bure of Russia was named top forward and Rob Blake of Canada was the top defenseman.

In addition to fine perfomances by players well known to NHL fans, skaters and goaltenders from emerging hockey nations also impressed. Five of the tournament's top ten scorers played for teams that participated in the preliminary round of the tournament.

1998 Men's Hockey
18th Olympic Tournament
Nagano (Japan), February 7- 22, 1998

1998 Olympic Final Standings, Men

Preliminary Round

Group A

Team	GP	W	L	T	GF	GA	PTS
Kazakhstan	3	2	0	1	14	11	5
Slovakia	3	1	1	1	9	9	3
Italy	3	1	2	0	11	11	2
Austria	3	0	1	2	9	12	2

Group B

Team	GP	W	L	T	GF	GA	PTS
Belarus	3	2	0	1	14	4	5
Germany	3	2	1	0	7	9	4
France	3	1	2	0	5	8	2
Japan	3	0	2	1	5	10	1

Final Round

Group A

Team	GP	W	L	T	GF	GA	PTS
Canada	3	3	0	0	12	3	6
Sweden	3	2	1	0	11	7	4
USA	3	1	2	0	8	10	2
Belarus	3	0	3	0	4	15	0

Group A

Team	GP	W	L	T	GF	GA	PTS
Russia	3	3	0	0	15	6	6
Czech Republic	3	2	1	0	12	4	4
Finland	3	1	2	0	11	9	2
Kazakhstan	3	0	3	0	6	25	0

Quarterfinals

Canada	4	Kazakhstan	1
Czech Republic	4	USA	1
Finland	2	Sweden	1
Russia	4	Belarus	1

Semifinals

Czech Republic	2	Canada	1
Russia	7	Finland	4

Bronze medal game

Finland	3	Canada	2

Gold medal game

Czech Republic	1	Russia	0

1998 Final Rankings, Men

1.	Czech Republic	Gold
2.	Russia	Silver
3.	Finland	Bronze
4.	Canada	
5-8.	USA	
5-8.	Sweden	
5-8.	Belarus	
5-8.	Kazakhstan	
9.	Germany	
10.	Slovakia	
11.	France	
12.	Italy	
13.	Japan	
14.	Austria	

1998 Olympic Scoring Leaders, Men

Name	Team	GP	G	A	PTS	PIM
Teemu Selanne	Finland	5	4	6	10	8
Saku Koivu	Finland	6	2	8	10	4
Pavel Bure	Russia	6	9	0	9	2
Alexander Koreshkov	Kazakhstan	7	3	6	9	2
Phillipe Bozon	France	4	5	2	7	4
Konstantin Shafranov	Kazakhstan	7	4	3	7	6
Dominik Lavoie	Austria	4	5	1	6	8
Jere Lehtinen	Finland	6	4	2	6	2
Alexei Yashin	Russia	6	3	3	6	0
Serge Poudrier	France	6	2	4	6	4
Sergei Fedorov	Russia	6	1	5	6	8

1998 Olympic Indiviual Scoring, Men

Austria

Pos.	Name	GP	G	A	TP	PIM
D	Dominik Lavoie	4	5	1	6	8
C	Andreas Puschnig	4	2	2	4	6
D	Martin Ulrich	4	0	3	3	0
L	Gerald Ressmann	4	2	0	2	4
R	Christian Perthaler	4	1	1	2	2
D	Thomas Searle	4	0	2	2	2
R	Wolfgang Kromp	4	1	0	1	4
L	Gerhard Puschnik	4	1	0	1	18
L	Dieter Kalt	4	0	1	1	2
L	Richard Nasheim	4	0	1	1	4
R	Mario Schaden	4	0	1	1	2
R	Simon Wheeldon	4	0	1	1	8
C	Christoph Brandner	4	0	0	0	2
D	Herbert Hohenberger	4	0	0	0	4
F	Martin Hohenberger	4	0	0	0	2
C	Normand Krumpschmid	4	0	0	0	2
D	Michael Lampert	4	0	0	0	8
C	Patrick Pilloni	4	0	0	0	2
D	Gerhard Unterluggauer	4	0	0	0	4
D	Engelbert Linder	2	0	0	0	0
G	Michael Puschacher	Did Not Play				
G	Reinhard Divis	2	0	0	0	0
G	Claus Dalpiaz	3	0	0	0	0

Belarus

Pos.	Name	GP	G	A	TP	PIM
C	Vadim Bekbulatov	5	2	2	4	4
R	Andrei Skabelka	7	2	2	4	0
D	Oleg Romanov	7	1	3	4	4
R	Andrei Kovalev	7	1	3	4	2
C	Viktor Karachun	7	2	1	3	8
C	Alexander Galchenyuk	7	1	2	3	0
D	Igor Matushkin	7	1	2	3	4
L	Alexander Andriyevsky	6	1	2	3	8
D	Sergei Yerkovich	6	2	0	2	16
L	Vladimir Tsyplakov	5	1	1	2	2
D	Alexander Alekseyev	7	1	1	2	0
D	Oleg Khmyl	7	0	2	2	4
R	Alexei Lozhkin	7	0	2	2	0
C	Yevgeny Roschin	6	0	2	2	0
C	Alexei Kalyuzhny	7	1	0	1	6
D	Ruslan Salei	7	1	0	1	4
C	Vasili Pankov	7	1	0	1	6
D	Sergei Stas	7	0	1	1	8
	Eduard Zankovets	4	0	0	0	2
D	Alexander Zhurik	4	0	0	0	10
G	Leonid Grishukevich	Did Not Play				
G	Alexander Shumidub	2	0	0	0	0
G	Andrei Mezin	6	0	0	0	0

Canada

Pos.	Name	GP	G	A	TP	PIM
R	Eric Lindros	6	2	3	5	2
C	Joe Niewendyk	6	2	3	5	2
R	Theoren Fleury	6	1	3	4	2
C	Wayne Gretzky	6	0	4	4	2
L	Keith Primeau	6	2	1	3	4
D	Ray Bourque	6	1	2	3	4
C	Joe Sakic	4	1	2	3	4
L	Rod Brind'Amour	6	1	2	3	0
L	Brendan Shanahan	6	2	0	2	0
D	Al MacInnis	6	2	0	2	2
D	Rob Blake	6	1	1	2	2
L	Shayne Corson	6	1	1	2	2
C	Steve Yzerman	6	1	1	2	10
F	Mark Recchi	5	0	2	2	0
L	Rob Zamuner	6	1	0	1	8
R	Trevor Linden	6	1	0	1	10
D	Adam Foote	6	0	1	1	4
D	Eric Desjardins	6	0	0	0	2
D	Chris Pronger	6	0	0	0	4
D	Scott Stevens	6	0	0	0	2
G	Martin Brodeur	Did Not Play				
G	Curtis Joseph	Did Not Play				
G	Patrick Roy	6	0	0	0	0

Czech Republic

Pos.	Name	GP	G	A	TP	PIM
C	Pavel Patera	6	2	3	5	0
R	Jaromir Jagr	6	1	4	5	2
L	Martin Rucinsky	6	3	1	4	4
C	Robert Reichel	6	3	0	3	0
C	Vladimir Ruzicka	6	3	0	3	0
R	Martin Straka	6	1	2	3	0
C	Jiri Dopita	6	1	2	3	0
C	Robert Lang	6	0	3	3	0
L	Martin Prochazka	6	1	1	2	0
D	Petr Svoboda	6	1	1	2	39
L	Josef Beranek	6	1	0	1	4
D	Roman Hamrlik	6	1	0	1	2
D	Jiri Slegr	6	1	0	1	8
L	David Moravec	6	0	1	1	2
D	Richard Smehlik	6	0	1	1	4
D	Frantisek Kucera	6	0	0	0	0
D	Jaroslav Spacek	6	0	0	0	4
R	Milan Hejduk	4	0	0	0	2
R	Jan Caloun	3	0	0	0	6
D	Libor Prochazka	1	0	0	0	0
G	Milan Hnilicka	Did Not Play				
G	Roman Cechmanek	Did Not Play				
G	Dominik Hasek	6	0	0	0	0

Best-on-best in the gold medal game: Tournament top forward Pavel Bure, who recorded nine goals in Nagano, is turned away by top goaltender Dominik Hasek who finished with a goals-against average of 0.97.

Finland

Pos.	Name	GP	G	A	TP	PIM
R	Teemu Selanne	5	4	6	10	8
C	Saku Koivu	6	2	8	10	4
R	Jere Lehtinen	6	4	2	6	2
R	Jari Kurri	6	1	4	5	2
L	Ville Peltonen	6	2	1	3	6
L	Mika Nieminen	5	1	2	3	2
D	Janne Niinimaa	6	0	3	3	8
C	Raimo Helminen	6	2	0	2	2
D	Teppo Numminen	6	1	1	2	2
L	Esa Tikkanen	6	1	1	2	0
D	Jyrki Lumme	6	1	0	1	16
L	Kimmo Rintanen	6	1	0	1	0
L	Sami Kapanen	6	0	1	1	0
L	Juha Lind	6	0	1	1	6
D	Kimmo Timonen	6	0	1	1	2
D	Aki-Petteri Berg	6	0	0	0	6
D	Janne Laukkanen	6	0	0	0	4
C	Juha Ylonen	6	0	0	0	8
R	Antti Tormanen	5	0	0	0	0
D	Tuomas Gronman	4	0	0	0	2
G	Jukka Tammi	Did Not Play				
G	Ari Sulander	2	0	0	0	0
G	Jarmo Myllys	4	0	0	0	0

France

Pos.	Name	GP	G	A	TP	PIM
R	Philippe Bozon	4	5	2	7	4
D	Serge Poudrier	6	2	4	6	4
L	Christian Pouget	4	1	2	3	8
R	Stephane Barin	4	1	0	1	2
C	Arnaud Briand	4	1	0	1	4
D	Gregory Dubois	4	0	1	1	2
D	Jean-Philippe Lemoine	4	0	1	1	10
C	Anthony Mortas	4	0	1	1	0
C	Robert Ouellet	4	0	1	1	2
L	Richard Aimonetto	4	0	0	0	0
R	Pierre Allard	4	0	0	0	6
D	Serge Djelloul	4	0	0	0	2
D	Karl DeWolf	3	0	0	0	4
D	Jean-Christophe Filippin	4	0	0	0	4
R	Laurent Gras	4	0	0	0	2
D	Denis Perez	4	0	0	0	0
L	Maurice Rozenthal	4	0	0	0	6
C	Jonathan Zwinkel	4	0	0	0	0
R	Roger Dube	3	0	0	0	29
R	Francois Rozenthal	2	0	0	0	0
G	Fabrice Lhenry	Did Not Play				
G	Francois Gravel	2	0	0	0	0
G	Christopher Huet	2	0	0	0	0

Germany

Pos.	Name	GP	G	A	TP	PIM
C	Peter Draizaitl	4	2	2	4	0
C	Mark MacKay	4	1	3	4	6
R	Jan Benda	4	3	0	3	8
D	Mirko Ludermann	4	1	1	2	0
D	Brad Bergen	3	1	1	2	0
D	Uwe Krupp	2	0	2	2	4
D	Markus Wieland	4	0	2	2	6
L	Dieter Hegen	3	1	0	1	0
D	Daniel Kunce	3	1	0	1	2
C	Jochen Hecht	4	1	0	1	6
C	Thomas Brandl	4	0	1	1	8
D	Lars Bruggermann	4	0	1	1	0
D	Erich Goldmann	4	0	1	1	27
C	Benoit Doucet	4	0	0	0	6
L	Andreas Lupzig	4	0	0	0	4
D	Jochen Molling	4	0	0	0	4
R	Reemt Pyka	4	0	0	0	0
R	Jurgen Rumrich	4	0	0	0	0
C	Stefan Ustorf	4	0	0	0	0
R	Marco Sturm	2	0	0	0	0
G	Olaf Kolzig	2	0	0	0	0
G	Josef Heiss	1	0	0	0	0
G	Klaus Merk	1	0	0	0	0

Italy

Pos.	Name	GP	G	A	TP	PIM
C	Stefan Figliuzzi	4	3	2	5	2
L	Bruno Zarrillo	4	3	0	3	6
C	Gates Orlando	4	1	2	3	4
R	Mario Chitarroni	4	2	0	2	12
R	Dino Felicetti	4	2	0	2	2
D	Mike De Angelis	4	0	2	2	4
D	Bob Nardella	4	0	2	2	6
R	Lucio Topatigh	4	0	2	2	6
R	Roland Ramoser	4	1	1	2	2
D	Leo Insam	3	0	1	1	0
D	Chris Bartolone	4	0	1	1	2
D	Chad Biafore	4	0	1	1	6
R	Giuseppe Busillo	4	0	1	1	4
L	Maurizio Mansi	4	0	1	1	2
L	Patrick Brugnoli	4	0	0	0	0
C	Markus Brunner	4	0	0	0	4
D	Martin Pavlu	4	0	0	0	0
D	Larry Rucchin	4	0	0	0	4
D	Robert Oberrauch	3	0	0	0	4
L	Stefano Margoni	2	0	0	0	0
G	Mike Rosati	4	0	0	0	0
G	Mario Brunetta	1	0	0	0	0
G	David Delfino	Did Not Play				

Japan

Pos.	Name	GP	G	A	TP	PIM
C	Shin Yahata	4	2	3	5	4
L	Akihito Sugisawa	4	2	2	4	4
R	Ryan Kuwabara	4	2	0	2	4
C	Kiyoshi Fujita	4	1	1	2	2
C	Tsutsumi Otomo	4	1	1	2	12
C	Toshiyuki Sakai	4	0	2	2	6
D	Takeshi Yamanaka	4	0	2	2	6
C	Mattew Kabayama	4	1	0	1	0
D	Atsuo Kudoh	4	0	1	1	0
C	Yuji Iga	4	0	0	0	2
D	Tatsuki Katayama	4	0	0	0	4
D	Yutaka Kawaguchi	4	0	0	0	0
R	Makoto Kawahira	4	0	0	0	2
D	Takayuki Kobori	4	0	0	0	6
D	Hiroyki Miura	4	0	0	0	4
D	Takayuki Miura	4	0	0	0	2
L	Kanihiko Sakurai	4	0	0	0	4
C	Steven Tsujura	4	0	0	0	6
R	Chris Yute	4	0	0	0	0
R	Hiroshi Matsuura	1	0	0	0	0
G	Jiro Nihei	Did Not Play				
G	Dusly Imoo	3	0	0	0	0
G	Shinichi Iwasaki	1	0	0	0	0

Kazakhstan

Pos.	Name	GP	G	A	TP	PIM
L	Alexander Koreshkov	7	3	6	9	2
R	Konstantin Shafranov	7	4	3	7	6
R	Mikhail Borodulin	7	3	0	3	10
C	Yevgeny Koreshkov	7	2	1	3	8
L	Andrei Pchelyakov	7	1	2	3	4
C	Vladimir Zavyalov	7	0	3	3	4
D	Igor Zemlyanoj	7	0	3	3	8
C	Pavel Kamentsev	7	2	0	2	4
D	Vladimir Antipin	7	1	1	2	4
R	Dmitri Dudarev	7	1	1	2	0
D	Andrei Sokolov	7	1	1	2	4
D	Vadim Glovatsky	7	0	2	2	6
D	Igor Nikitin	7	1	0	1	6
R	Erlan Sagimbayev	7	1	0	1	4
D	Vitali Tregubov	7	1	0	1	4
D	Alexei Troschinsky	7	0	1	1	32
D	Andrei Savenkov	7	0	1	1	4
R	Petr Devyatkin	7	0	0	0	27
C	Igor Dorokhin	7	0	0	0	4
L	Oleg Kryazhev	7	0	0	0	0
G	Vitali Yeremeyev	7	0	0	0	0
G	Alexander Shimin	5	0	0	0	0

Russia

Pos.	Name	GP	G	A	TP	PIM
R	Pavel Bure	6	9	0	9	2
C	Alexei Yashin	6	3	3	6	0
C	Sergei Fedorov	6	1	5	6	8
R	Andrei Kovalenko	6	4	1	5	14
R	Alexei Morozov	6	2	2	4	0
C	Alexei Zhamnov	6	2	1	3	2
L	Valeri Kamensky	6	1	2	3	0
L	Valeri Zelepukin	6	1	2	3	0
D	Dmitri Mironov	6	0	3	3	0
D	Sergei Gonchar	6	0	2	2	0
D	Darius Kasparaitis	6	0	2	2	6
D	Igor Kravchuk	6	0	2	2	2
D	Boris Mironov	6	0	2	2	2
D	Alexei Zhitnik	6	0	2	2	2
L	Valeri Bure	6	1	0	1	0
C	Sergei Nemchinov	6	1	0	1	0
C	German Titov	6	1	0	1	6
D	Alexei Gusarov	6	0	1	1	8
R	Sergei Krivokrasov	6	0	0	0	4
D	Dmitri Yushkevich	6	0	0	0	2
G	Oleg Shevtsov	Did Not Play				
G	Mikhail Shtalenkov	5	0	0	0	0
G	Andrei Trefilov	2	0	0	0	0

Cumulative Men's Olympic Hockey Medal Standings, 1924-1998

		Gold	Silver	Bronze	Total	Last Medal
1.	Russia/USSR	8	2	1	11	Silver 98
2.	Canada	5	4	2	11	Silver 94
3.	USA	2	5	1	8	Gold 80
4.	Czechoslovakia/ Czech Republic	1	4	3	8	Gold 98
5.	Sweden	1	2	4	7	Gold 94
6.	Finland	0	1	2	3	Bronze 98
7.	Great Britain	1	0	1	2	Gold 36
8.	W. Germany	0	0	2	2	Bronze 76
9.	Switzerland	0	0	2	2	Bronze 48

Slovakia

Pos.	Name	GP	G	A	TP	PIM
R	Vlastimil Plavukha	4	4	0	4	2
D	Lubomir Sekeras	4	0	4	4	2
C	Robert Petrovicky	4	2	1	3	0
L	Josef Dano	4	1	2	3	4
L	Zdeno Ciger	4	1	1	2	4
R	Petr Bondra	2	1	0	1	25
L	Bronislav Janos	4	1	0	1	2
R	Jan Pardavy	4	1	0	1	0
D	Robert Svehla	2	0	1	1	0
R	Roman Konstek	4	0	1	1	0
D	Ivan Droppa	4	0	0	0	0
L	Lubomir Kolnik	4	0	0	0	2
D	Stanislav Jasecko	4	0	0	0	4
C	Karol Rusznyak	4	0	0	0	0
D	Jan Varholik	4	0	0	0	14
D	Miroslav Mosnar	3	0	0	0	6
C	Roman Stantien	3	0	0	0	0
D	Lubomir Visnovsky	3	0	0	0	2
C	Oto Hascak	2	0	0	0	4
R	Petr Pucher	2	0	0	0	0
G	Pavot Rybar	Did Not Play				
G	Miroslav Simanovic	Did Not Play				
G	Igor Murin	4	0	0	0	0

Sweden

Pos.	Name	GP	G	A	TP	PIM
R	Daniel Alfredsson	4	2	3	5	2
C	Peter Forsberg	4	1	4	5	6
R	Mats Sundin	4	3	0	3	4
R	Mikael Renberg	4	1	2	3	4
L	Mikael Andersson	4	1	1	2	0
D	Nicklas Lindstrom	4	1	1	2	2
L	Niklas Sundstrom	4	1	1	2	2
L	Ulf Dahlen	4	1	0	1	2
L	Patric Kjellberg	4	1	0	1	0
D	Marcus Ragnarsson	3	0	1	1	0
D	Ulf Samuelsson	3	0	1	1	4
D	Mattias Norstrom	4	0	1	1	2
D	Mattias Ohlund	4	0	1	1	4
R	Tomas Sandstrom	4	0	1	1	0
C	Mats Lindgren	4	0	0	0	2
D	Calle Johansson	4	0	0	0	2
C	Michael Nylander	4	0	0	0	6
D	Tommy Albelin	3	0	0	0	4
L	Andreas Johansson	3	0	0	0	2
C	Jorgen Jonsson	1	0	0	0	0
G	Johan Hedberg	Did Not Play				
G	Tommy Soderstrom	Did Not Play				
G	Tommy Salo	4	0	0	0	0

USA

Pos.	Name	GP	G	A	TP	PIM
L	Brett Hull	4	2	1	3	0
R	Bill Guerin	4	0	3	3	2
D	Chris Chelios	4	2	0	2	2
C	Mike Modano	4	2	0	2	0
R	Pat LaFontaine	4	1	1	2	0
D	Brian Leetch	4	1	1	2	0
D	Kevin Hatcher	3	0	2	2	0
L	Keith Tkachuk	4	0	2	2	6
C	Doug Weight	4	0	2	2	2
L	Adam Deadmarsh	4	1	0	1	2
R	Tony Amonte	4	0	1	1	4
L	John LeClair	4	0	1	1	0
R	Jeremy Roenick	4	0	1	1	6
D	Keith Carney	4	0	0	0	2
D	Derian Hatcher	4	0	0	0	0
C	Joel Otto	4	0	0	0	0
D	Mathieu Schneider	4	0	0	0	6
D	Gary Suter	4	0	0	0	2
L	Jamie Langenbrunner	3	0	0	0	4
D	Bryan Berard	2	0	0	0	0
G	Guy Hebert	Did Not Play				
G	John Vanbiesbrouck	1	0	0	0	0
G	Mike Richter	4	0	0	0	0

Teemu Selanne four goals and six assists left him tied him for the Olympic point scoring lead with Finnish teammate Saku Koivu. Nagano was Selanne's second Olympic competition. He finished with 11 points in Albertville in 1992. Finland won the bronze medal in both of Selanne's Olympic appearances.

1998 Olympic Goaltending, Men

Austria

Name	GP	Mins	GA	SO	Avg	SA	S%
Claus Dalpiaz	3	147	10	0	4.06	85	.882
Reinhard Divis	2	102	6	0	3.52	40	.850
Michael Puschacher	Did Not Play						

Belarus

Name	GP	Mins	GA	SO	Avg	SA	S%
Leonid Grishukevich	Did Not Play						
Andrei Mezin	6	356	21	1	3.54	176	.881
Alexander Shumidub	2	64	2	0	1.87	24	.917

Canada

Name	GP	Mins	GA	SO	Avg	SA	S%
Martin Brodeur	Did Not Play						
Curtis Joseph	Did Not Play						
Patrick Roy	6	369	9	1	1.46	139	.935

Czech Republic

Name	GP	Mins	GA	SO	Avg	SA	S%
Roman Cechmanek	Did Not Play						
Dominik Hasek	6	369	6	2	0.97	155	.961
Milan Hnilicka	Did Not Play						

Finland

Name	GP	Mins	GA	SO	Avg	SA	S%
Jarmo Myllys	4	237	14	0	3.54	94	.851
Ari Sulander	2	120	4	0	2.00	49	.918
Jukka Tammi	Did Not Play						

France

Name	GP	Mins	GA	SO	Avg	SA	S%
Francois Gravel	2	119	4	0	2.01	52	.923
Christopher Huet	2	120	5	0	2.50	67	.925
Fabrice Lhenry	Did Not Play						

Germany

Name	GP	Mins	GA	SO	Avg	SA	S%
Josef Heiss	1	60	1	0	1.00	22	.955
Olaf Kolzig	2	120	2	1	1.00	58	.966
Klaus Merk	1	60	8	0	8.00	31	.742

Italy

Name	GP	Mins	GA	SO	Avg	SA	S%
Mario Brunetta	1	23	4	0	10.17	8	.500
David Delfino	Did Not Play						
Mike Rosati	4	215	12	0	3.35	79	.848

Japan

Name	GP	Mins	GA	SO	Avg	SA	S%
Dusly Imoo	3	189	8	0	2.54	107	.925
Shinichi Iwasaki	1	60	3	0	3.00	33	.909
Jiro Nihei	Did Not Play						

Kazakhstan

Name	GP	Mins	GA	SO	Avg	SA	S%
Alexander Shimin	5	128	12	0	5.61	55	.782
Vitali Yeremeyev	7	292	28	0	5.76	170	.835

Russia

Name	GP	Mins	GA	SO	Avg	SA	S%
Oleg Shevtsov	Did Not Play						
Mikhail Shtalenkov	5	290	8	0	1.65	115	.930
Andrei Trefilov	2	69	4	0	3.45	38	.895

Slovakia

Name	GP	Mins	GA	SO	Avg	SA	S%
Igor Murin	4	240	13	0	3.25	84	.845
Pavot Rybar	Did Not Play						
Miroslav Simanovic	Did Not Play						

Sweden

Name	GP	Mins	GA	SO	Avg	SA	S%
Johan Hedberg	Did Not Play						
Tommy Salo	4	238	9	0	2.27	103	.913
Tommy Soderstrom	Did Not Play						

USA

Name	GP	Mins	GA	SO	Avg	SA	S%
Guy Hebert	Did Not Play						
Mike Richter	4	237	14	0	3.55	93	.849
John Vanbiesbrouck	1	1	0	0	0.00	1	1.000

TEAM USA WINS FIRST GOLD MEDAL IN WOMEN'S OLYMPIC HOCKEY

WOMEN'S HOCKEY made its debut at the 1998 Winter Olympics in Nagano, Japan. Women's world championship tournaments have been played since the late 1980s. In these events Canada and the USA have always vied for first place with Canada finishing on top in each championship.

The U.S. women's team, coached by Ben Smith, focussed on the Olympics and built a system of attack and defense designed to counteract Canada's. The American approach proved sound, as Team USA bested Canada 7-4 in round-robin play and 3-1 in the gold medal game.

Finland was a deserving bronze medal winner. Chinese goaltender Hong Guo was one of the tournament's top players.

Women's Hockey 1st Olympic Tournament Nagano (Japan), February 8 - 17, 1998

1998 Olympic Final Standings, Women

Team	GP	W	L	T	GF	GA	PTS
USA	5	5	0	0	33	7	10
Canada	5	4	1	0	28	12	8
Finland	5	3	2	0	27	10	6
China	5	2	3	0	10	15	4
Sweden	5	1	4	0	10	21	2
Japan	5	0	5	0	2	45	0

Bronze medal game

Finland 4 China 1

Gold medal game

USA 3 Canada 1

1998 Olympic Final Rankings, Women

1. USA — Gold
2. Canada — Silver
3. Finland — Bronze
4. China
5. Sweden
6. Japan

Karen Bye was one of four Team USA forwards to finish with eight points at Nagano.

1998 Olympic Scoring Leaders, Women

Name	Team	GP	G	A	PTS	PIM
Rikka Nieminen	Finland	6	7	5	12	4
Danielle Goyette	Canada	6	8	1	9	10
Karyn Bye	USA	6	5	3	8	4
Cammi Granato	USA	6	4	4	8	0
Katie King	USA	6	4	4	8	2
Gretchen Ulion	USA	6	3	5	8	4
Hayley Wickenheiser	Canada	6	2	6	8	4
Therese Brisson	Canada	6	5	2	7	6
Kirsi Hanninen	Finland	6	4	3	7	6
Laurie Baker	USA	6	4	3	7	6

1998 Olympic Indiviual Scoring, Women

Canada

Pos.	Name	GP	G	A	TP	PIM
G	Leslie Reddon	3	0	0	0	0
G	Manon Rheaume	4	0	0	0	0
D	Therese Brisson	6	5	2	7	6
D	Cassie Campbell	6	1	2	3	8
D	Judy Diduck	6	1	2	3	10
D	Geraldine Heaney	6	2	4	6	2
D	Becky Kellar	6	1	2	3	2
D	Fiona Smith	5	1	1	2	2
F	Jennifer Botterill	6	0	0	0	0
F	Nancy Drolet	6	1	2	3	10
F	Lori Dupuis	6	2	1	3	6
F	Danielle Goyette	6	8	1	9	10
F	Jayna Hefford	6	1	0	1	6
F	Kathy McCormack	6	0	0	0	0
F	Karen Nystrom	5	1	0	1	2
F	Laura Schuler	6	0	0	0	4
F	France St-Louis	6	1	2	3	0
F	Vicky Sunohara	6	1	3	4	0
F	Hayley Wickenheiser	6	2	6	8	4
F	Stacey Wilson	6	1	5	6	0

China

Pos.	Name	GP	G	A	TP	PIM
G	Hong Guo	6	0	0	0	0
G	Lina Huo	1	0	0	0	0
D	Jing Chen	6	0	0	0	2
D	Ming Gong	6	0	1	1	10
D	Xuan Li	6	0	1	1	6
D	Yan Lu	6	0	1	1	2
D	Wang Wei	6	0	2	2	2
D	Jing Zhang	6	0	0	0	2
F	Hong Dang	6	0	0	0	0
F	Ying Diao	3	0	0	0	0
F	Lili Guo	1	0	0	0	0
F	Wei Guo	6	3	1	4	6
F	Hongmei Liu	6	2	3	5	4
F	Jinping Ma	6	0	0	0	6
F	Xiaojun Ma	1	0	0	0	0
F	Hong Sang	6	1	0	1	4
F	Lei Xu	6	0	1	1	4
F	Xiuqing Yang	6	3	2	5	12
F	Chunhua Liu	5	0	0	0	2
F	Lan Zhang	6	2	1	3	0

Finland

Pos.	Name	GP	G	A	TP	PIM
G	Lisa-Maria Sneck	2	0	0	0	0
G	Tuula Puputti	5	0	0	0	0
D	Emma Laaksonen	4	0	0	0	2
D	Katja Lehto	6	1	3	4	0
D	Satu Huotari	6	0	1	1	4
D	Johanna Ikonen	6	4	1	5	6
D	Kirsi Hanninen	6	4	3	7	6
D	Maria-Helena Palvila	6	0	0	0	0
D	Paivi Salo	6	0	0	0	4
F	Marianne Ihalainen	5	0	0	0	0
F	Sari Fisk	6	2	4	6	4
F	Riikka Nieminen	6	7	5	12	4
F	Maria Selin	5	0	1	1	2
F	Tiia Reima	4	2	1	3	0
F	Sari Krooks	6	2	2	4	12
F	Petra Vaarakallio	6	2	2	4	2
F	Sanna Lankosaari	5	2	1	3	6
F	Marika Lehtimaki	5	2	3	5	0
F	Katja Riipi	6	1	2	3	4
F	Karolina Rantamaki	6	2	1	3	0

Japan

Pos.	Name	GP	G	A	TP	PIM
G	Yka Oda	5	0	0	0	0
G	Haruka Watanabe	3	0	0	0	0
D	Yoko Kondo	5	0	0	0	0
D	Rie Sato	5	0	0	0	2
D	Akiko Hatanaka	5	1	0	1	4
D	Chie Sakuma	5	0	0	0	6
D	Maiko Obikawa	5	0	1	1	4
D	Naho Yoshimi	5	0	1	1	2
D	Yuiko Satomi	5	0	0	0	0
F	Satomi Ono	5	0	0	0	10
F	Yuki Togawa	5	0	0	0	16
F	Miharu Araki	5	0	0	0	0
F	Ayumi Sato	5	0	0	0	0
F	Mitsuko Igarashi	5	0	0	0	2
F	Yukari Ohno	5	0	0	0	6
F	Masako Sato	5	1	0	1	6
F	Aki Sudo	5	0	0	0	20
F	Shiho Fujiwara	5	0	1	1	4
F	Aki Tsuchida	5	0	0	0	6
F	Akiko Naka	5	0	0	0	0

Sweden

Pos.	Name	GP	G	A	TP	PIM
G	Lotta Gothesson	2	0	0	0	0
G	Annika Ahlen	3	0	0	0	0
D	Gunilla Andersson	5	1	1	2	20
D	Pernilla Burholm	4	1	0	1	4
D	Linda Gustafsson	4	0	0	0	2
D	Asa Lidstrom	5	0	0	0	2
D	Yiva Lindberg	4	0	0	0	2
D	Pia Morelius	4	0	0	0	14
D	Therese Sjolander	5	1	2	3	6
F	Lotta Almblad	5	0	2	2	4
F	Kristina Bergstrand	4	0	0	0	2
F	Susanne Ceder	4	0	0	0	3
F	Ann-Louise Edstrand	5	0	0	0	2
F	Joa Elfsberg	5	0	1	1	10
F	Asa Elfving	4	0	1	1	2
F	Anne Ferm	5	0	0	0	0
F	Malin Gustafsson	4	2	0	2	8
F	Erika Holst	5	2	3	5	8
F	Tina Mansson	5	1	0	1	2
F	Maria Rooth	5	2	0	2	0

USA

Pos.	Name	GP	G	A	TP	PIM
G	Sara DeCosta	6	0	0	0	0
G	Sarah Tueting	6	0	0	0	0
D	Chris Bailey	6	0	1	1	4
D	Colleen Coyne	6	0	0	0	4
D	Sue Merz	6	1	5	6	6
D	Tara Mounsey	6	2	4	6	12
D	Vicki Movsessian	6	1	0	1	10
D	Angela Ruggiero	6	0	0	0	18
F	Laurie Baker	6	4	3	7	6
F	Alana Blahoski	6	0	2	2	0
F	Lisa Brown-Miller	6	1	2	3	2
F	Karyn Bye	6	5	3	8	4
F	Tricia Dunn	6	1	0	1	6
F	Cammi Granato	6	4	4	8	0
F	Katie King	6	4	4	8	2
F	Shelley Looney	6	4	1	5	0
F	A.J. Mleczko	6	2	2	4	4
F	Jenny Schmidgall	6	2	3	5	4
F	Gretchen Ulion	6	3	5	8	4
F	Sandra Whyte	6	2	2	4	0

1998 Olympic Goaltending, Women

Canada

Name	GP	Mins	GA	SO	Avg	SA	S%
Leslie Reddon	3	150	9	1	3.58	41	.780
Manon Rheaume	4	207	4	1	1.15	54	.926

China

Name	GP	Mins	GA	SO	Avg	SA	S%
Hong Guo	6	349	16	0	2.75	150	.893
Lina Huo	1	9	2	0	12.08	6	.667

Finland

Name	GP	Mins	GA	SO	Avg	SA	S%
Tuula Puputti	5	270	7	1	1.55	67	.896
Lisa Snek	2	88	4	0	2.70	20	.800

Japan

Name	GP	Mins	GA	SO	Avg	SA	S%
Yuka Oda	5	225	30	0	7.98	176	.830
Haruka Watanabe	3	74	15	0	12.14	67	.776

Sweden

Name	GP	Mins	GA	SO	Avg	SA	S%
Annica Ahlen	3	179	16	0	5.36	98	.837
Lotta Goethesson	1	120	5	1	2.50	53	.906

USA

Name	GP	Mins	GA	SO	Avg	SA	S%
Sara Decosta	3	150	4	1	1.59	32	.875
Sarah Tueting	4	209	4	1	1.15	64	.938

Cumulative Women's Olympic Hockey Medal Standings, 1998

	Gold	Silver	Bronze	Total	Last Medal
1. USA	1	0	0	1	Gold 98
2. Canada	0	1	0	1	Silver 98
3. Finland	0	0	1	1	Bronze 98

NHL Record Book

Year-By-Year Final Standings & Leading Scorers

*Stanley Cup winner

1917-18

First Half

Team	GP	W	L	T	GF	GA	PTS
Montreal	14	10	4	0	81	47	20
Toronto	14	8	6	0	71	75	16
Ottawa	14	5	9	0	67	79	10
**Mtl. Wanderers	6	1	5	0	17	35	2

**Montreal Arena burned down and Wanderers forced to withdraw from League. Montreal Canadiens and Toronto each counted a win for defaulted games with Wanderers.

Second Half

Team	GP	W	L	T	GF	GA	PTS
*Toronto	8	5	3	0	37	34	10
Ottawa	8	4	4	0	35	35	8
Montreal	8	3	5	0	34	37	6

Leading Scorers

Player	Club	GP	G	A	PTS	PIM
Malone, Joe	Montreal	20	44	4	48	30
Denneny, Cy	Ottawa	20	36	10	46	80
Noble, Reg	Toronto	20	30	10	40	35
Lalonde, Newsy	Montreal	14	23	7	30	51
Denneny, Corb	Toronto	21	20	9	29	14
Cameron, Harry	Toronto	21	17	10	27	28
Pitre, Didier	Montreal	20	17	6	23	29
Gerard, Eddie	Ottawa	20	13	7	20	26
Darragh, Jack	Ottawa	18	14	5	19	26
Nighbor, Frank	Ottawa	10	11	8	19	6
Meeking, Harry	Toronto	21	10	9	19	28

1918-19

First Half

Team	GP	W	L	T	GF	GA	PTS
Montreal	10	7	3	0	57	50	14
Ottawa	10	5	5	0	39	39	10
Toronto	10	3	7	0	42	49	6

Second Half

Team	GP	W	L	T	GF	GA	PTS
Ottawa	8	7	1	0	32	14	14
Montreal	8	3	5	0	31	28	6
Toronto	8	2	6	0	22	43	4

Leading Scorers

Player	Club	GP	G	A	PTS	PIM
Lalonde, Newsy	Montreal	17	23	10	33	42
Cleghorn, Odie	Montreal	18	21	6	27	33
Nighbor, Frank	Ottawa	18	18	9	27	27
Denneny, Cy	Ottawa	18	18	6	24	55
Pitre, Didier	Montreal	17	14	4	18	15
Skinner, Alf	Toronto	16	12	5	17	26
Cleghorn, Sprague	Ottawa	18	7	9	16	27
Cameron, Harry	Tor., Ott.	14	11	4	15	35
Darragh, Jack	Ottawa	14	11	4	15	30
Randall, Ken	Toronto	15	9	6	15	26

All-Time Standings of NHL Teams

(ranked by percentage)

Active Clubs

Team	Games	Wins	Losses	Ties	Goals For	Goals Against	Points	%	First Season
Montreal	5054	2647	1625	782	17078	13516	6076	.601	1917-18
Philadelphia	2440	1216	847	377	8649	7431	2809	.576	1967-68
Boston	4894	2345	1830	719	16112	14585	5409	.553	1924-25
Buffalo	2214	1040	826	348	7815	7049	2428	.548	1970-71
Edmonton	1502	726	589	187	6031	5511	1639	.546	1979-80
Calgary	2058	951	797	310	7585	6961	2212	.537	1972-73
NY Islanders	2058	928	839	291	7316	6729	2147	.522	1972-73
Detroit	4828	2072	1998	758	14986	14781	4902	.508	1926-27
NY Rangers	4828	2041	2028	759	15149	15214	4841	.501	1926-27
Toronto	5054	2159	2164	731	15720	15772	5049	.500	1917-18
St. Louis	2440	1034	1040	366	7947	8139	2434	.499	1967-68
Florida	378	153	158	67	1026	1051	373	.493	1993-94
Chicago	4828	1994	2087	747	14578	14704	4735	.490	1926-27
Colorado	1502	632	674	196	5459	5533	1460	.486	1979-80
Washington	1902	797	859	246	6359	6675	1840	.484	1974-75
Pittsburgh	2440	1004	1106	330	8597	9035	2338	.479	1967-68
Dallas	2440	940	1112	388	7833	8418	2268	.465	1967-68
Los Angeles	2440	951	1128	361	8430	9061	2263	.464	1967-68
Phoenix	1502	579	732	191	5226	5817	1349	.449	1979-80
Anaheim	378	146	188	44	1038	1156	336	.444	1993-94
Carolina	1502	567	750	185	4904	5564	1319	.439	1979-80
Vancouver	2214	805	1086	323	7247	8182	1933	.437	1970-71
New Jersey	1902	664	972	266	5971	7036	1594	.419	1974-75
Tampa Bay	462	157	252	53	1195	1491	367	.397	1992-93
San Jose	542	161	329	52	1491	2050	374	.345	1991-92
Ottawa	462	116	293	53	1130	1691	285	.308	1992-93

Defunct Clubs

Team	Games	Wins	Losses	Ties	Goals For	Goals Against	Points	%	First Season	Last Season
Ottawa Senators	542	258	221	63	1458	1333	579	.534	1917-18	1933-34
Montreal Maroons	622	271	260	91	1474	1405	633	.509	1924-25	1937-38
NY/Brooklyn Americans	784	255	402	127	1643	2182	637	.406	1925-26	1941-42
Hamilton Tigers	126	47	78	1	414	475	95	.377	1920-21	1924-25
Cleveland Barons	160	47	87	26	470	617	120	.375	1976-77	1977-78
Pittsburgh Pirates	212	67	122	23	376	519	157	.370	1925-26	1929-30
Calif./Oakland Seals	698	182	401	115	1826	2580	479	.343	1967-68	1975-76
St. Louis Eagles	48	11	31	6	86	144	28	.292	1934-35	1934-35
Quebec Bulldogs	24	4	20	0	91	177	8	.167	1919-20	1919-20
Montreal Wanderers	6	1	5	0	17	35	2	.167	1917-18	1917-18
Philadelphia Quakers	44	4	36	4	76	184	12	.136	1930-31	1930-31

Calgary totals include Atlanta, 1972-73 to 1979-80.
Carolina totals include Hartford, 1979-80 to 1996-97.
Colorado totals include Quebec, 1979-80 to 1994-95.
Dallas totals include Minnesota, 1967-68 to 1992-93.
Detroit totals include Cougars, 1926-27 to 1929-30, and Falcons, 1930-31 to 1931-32.
New Jersey totals include Kansas City, 1974-75 to 1975-76, and Colorado Rockies, 1976-77 to 1981-82.
Phoenix totals include Winnipeg, 1979-80 to 1995-96.
Toronto totals include Arenas, 1917-18 to 1918-19, and St. Patricks, 1919-20 to 1925-56.

1919-20

First Half

Team	GP	W	L	T	GF	GA	PTS
Ottawa	12	9	3	0	59	23	18
Montreal	12	8	4	0	62	51	16
Toronto	12	5	7	0	52	62	10
Quebec	12	2	10	0	44	81	4

Second Half

Team	GP	W	L	T	GF	GA	PTS
*Ottawa	12	10	2	0	62	41	20
Montreal	12	5	7	0	67	62	10
Toronto	12	7	5	0	67	44	14
Quebec	12	2	10	0	47	96	4

Leading Scorers

Player	Club	GP	G	A	PTS	PIM
Malone, Joe	Quebec	24	39	10	49	12
Lalonde, Newsy	Montreal	23	37	9	46	34
Nighbor, Frank	Ottawa	23	26	15	41	18
Denneny, Corb	Toronto	24	24	12	36	20
Darragh, Jack	Ottawa	23	22	14	36	22
Noble, Reg	Toronto	24	24	9	33	51
Arbour, Amos	Montreal	22	21	5	26	13
Wilson, Cully	Toronto	23	20	6	26	86
Pitre, Didier	Montreal	22	14	12	26	6
Broadbent, Punch	Ottawa	21	19	6	25	40

1920-21

First Half

Team	GP	W	L	T	GF	GA	PTS
*Ottawa	10	8	2	0	49	23	16
Toronto	10	5	5	0	39	47	10
Montreal	10	4	6	0	37	51	8
Hamilton	10	3	7	0	34	38	6

Second Half

Team	GP	W	L	T	GF	GA	PTS
Toronto	14	10	4	0	66	53	20
Montreal	14	9	5	0	75	48	18
Ottawa	14	6	8	0	48	52	12
Hamilton	14	3	11	0	58	94	6

Leading Scorers

Player	Club	GP	G	A	PTS	PIM
Lalonde, Newsy	Montreal	24	32	11	43	36
Dye, Babe	Ham., Tor.	24	35	5	40	32
Denneny, Cy	Ottawa	24	34	5	39	10
Malone, Joe	Hamilton	20	28	9	37	6
Nighbor, Frank	Ottawa	24	19	10	29	10
Noble, Reg	Toronto	24	19	8	27	54
Cameron, Harry	Toronto	24	18	9	27	35
Prodgers, Goldie	Hamilton	24	18	9	27	8
Denneny, Corb	Toronto	20	19	7	26	29
Darragh, Jack	Ottawa	24	11	15	26	20

1921-22

Team	GP	W	L	T	GF	GA	PTS
Ottawa	24	14	8	2	106	84	30
*Toronto	24	13	10	1	98	97	27
Montreal	24	12	11	1	88	94	25
Hamilton	24	7	17	0	88	105	14

Leading Scorers

Player	Club	GP	G	A	PTS	PIM
Broadbent, Punch	Ottawa	24	32	14	46	24
Denneny, Cy	Ottawa	22	27	12	39	18
Dye, Babe	Toronto	24	30	7	37	18
Malone, Joe	Hamilton	24	25	7	32	4
Cameron, Harry	Toronto	24	19	8	27	18
Denneny, Corb	Toronto	24	19	7	26	28
Noble, Reg	Toronto	24	17	8	25	10
Cleghorn, Odie	Montreal	23	21	3	24	26
Cleghorn, Sprague	Montreal	24	17	7	24	63
Reise, Leo	Hamilton	24	9	14	23	8

1922-23

Team	GP	W	L	T	GF	GA	PTS
*Ottawa	24	14	9	1	77	54	29
Montreal	24	13	9	2	73	61	28
Toronto	24	13	10	1	82	88	27
Hamilton	24	6	18	0	81	110	12

Leading Scorers

Player	Club	GP	G	A	PTS	PIM
Dye, Babe	Toronto	22	26	11	37	19
Denneny, Cy	Ottawa	24	21	10	31	20
Adams, Jack	Toronto	23	19	9	28	42
Boucher, Billy	Montreal	24	23	4	27	52
Cleghorn, Odie	Montreal	24	19	7	26	14
Roach, Mickey	Hamilton	23	17	8	25	8
Boucher, George	Ottawa	23	15	9	24	44
Joliat, Aurel	Montreal	24	13	9	22	31
Noble, Reg	Toronto	24	12	10	22	41
Wilson, Cully	Hamilton	23	16	3	19	46

1923-24

Team	GP	W	L	T	GF	GA	PTS
Ottawa	24	16	8	0	74	54	32
*Montreal	24	13	11	0	59	48	26
Toronto	24	10	14	0	59	85	20
Hamilton	24	9	15	0	63	68	18

Leading Scorers

Player	Club	GP	G	A	PTS	PIM
Denneny, Cy	Ottawa	21	22	1	23	10
Boucher, Billy	Montreal	23	16	6	22	33
Joliat, Aurel	Montreal	24	15	5	20	19
Dye, Babe	Toronto	19	17	2	19	23
Boucher, George	Ottawa	21	14	5	19	28
Burch, Billy	Hamilton	24	16	2	18	4
Clancy, King	Ottawa	24	9	8	17	18
Adams, Jack	Toronto	22	13	3	16	49
Morenz, Howie	Montreal	24	13	3	16	20
Noble, Reg	Toronto	23	12	3	15	23

1924-25

Team	GP	W	L	T	GF	GA	PTS
Hamilton	30	19	10	1	90	60	39
Toronto	30	19	11	0	90	84	38
Montreal	30	17	11	2	93	56	36
Ottawa	30	17	12	1	83	66	35
Mtl. Maroons	30	9	19	2	45	65	20
Boston	30	6	24	0	49	119	12

Leading Scorers

Player	Club	GP	G	A	PTS	PIM
Dye, Babe	Toronto	29	38	6	44	41
Denneny, Cy	Ottawa	28	27	15	42	16
Joliat, Aurel	Montreal	24	29	11	40	85
Morenz, Howie	Montreal	30	27	7	34	31
Boucher, Billy	Montreal	30	18	13	31	92
Adams, Jack	Toronto	27	21	8	29	66
Burch, Billy	Hamilton	27	20	4	24	10
Green, Red	Hamilton	30	19	4	23	63
Herberts, Jimmy	Boston	30	17	5	22	50
Day, Hap	Toronto	26	10	12	22	27

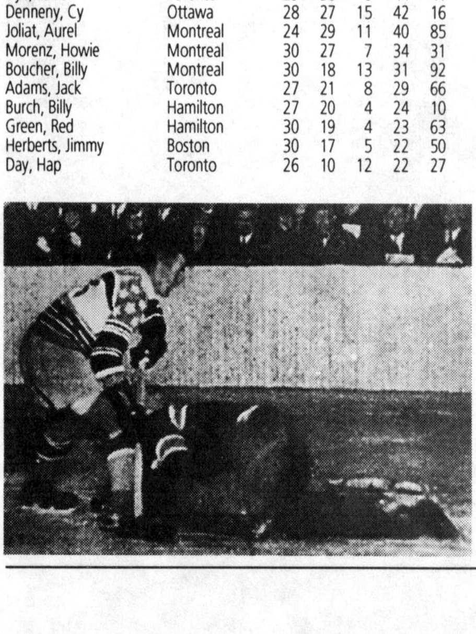

Red Green slips the puck past netminder Harry Rheaume in this December 15, 1925 match between the NY Americans and Montreal Canadiens. Green and teammate Billy Burch both finished among the top ten scorers in the 1924-25 season.

1925-26

Team	GP	W	L	T	GF	GA	PTS
Ottawa	36	24	8	4	77	42	52
*Mtl. Maroons	36	20	11	5	91	73	45
Pittsburgh	36	19	16	1	82	70	39
Boston	36	17	15	4	92	85	38
NY Americans	36	12	20	4	68	89	28
Toronto	36	12	21	3	92	114	27
Montreal	36	11	24	1	79	108	23

Leading Scorers

Player	Club	GP	G	A	PTS	PIM
Stewart, Nels	Mtl. Maroons	36	34	8	42	119
Denneny, Cy	Ottawa	36	24	12	36	18
Cooper, Carson	Boston	36	28	3	31	10
Herberts, Jimmy	Boston	36	26	5	31	47
Morenz, Howie	Montreal	31	23	3	26	39
Adams, Jack	Toronto	36	21	5	26	52
Joliat, Aurel	Montreal	35	17	9	26	52
Burch, Billy	NY Americans	36	22	3	25	33
Smith, Hooley	Ottawa	28	16	9	25	53
Nighbor, Frank	Ottawa	35	12	13	25	40

1926-27

Canadian Division

Team	GP	W	L	T	GF	GA	PTS
*Ottawa	44	30	10	4	86	69	64
Montreal	44	28	14	2	99	67	58
Mtl. Maroons	44	20	20	4	71	68	44
NY Americans	44	17	25	2	82	91	36
Toronto	44	15	24	5	79	94	35

American Division

Team	GP	W	L	T	GF	GA	PTS
New York	44	25	13	6	95	72	56
Boston	44	21	20	3	97	89	45
Chicago	44	19	22	3	115	116	41
Pittsburgh	44	15	26	3	79	108	33
Detroit	44	12	28	4	76	105	28

Leading Scorers

Player	Club	GP	G	A	PTS	PIM
Cook, Bill	New York	44	33	4	37	58
Irvin, Dick	Chicago	43	18	18	36	34
Morenz, Howie	Montreal	44	25	7	32	49
Fredrickson, Frank	Det., Bos.	41	18	13	31	46
Dye, Babe	Chicago	41	25	5	30	14
Bailey, Ace	Toronto	42	15	13	28	82
Boucher, Frank	New York	44	13	15	28	17
Burch, Billy	NY Americans	43	19	8	27	40
Oliver, Harry	Boston	42	18	6	24	17
Keats, Duke	Bos., Det.	42	16	8	24	52

1927-28

Canadian Division

Team	GP	W	L	T	GF	GA	PTS
Montreal	44	26	11	7	116	48	59
Mtl. Maroons	44	24	14	6	96	77	54
Ottawa	44	20	14	10	78	57	50
Toronto	44	18	18	8	89	88	44
NY Americans	44	11	27	6	63	128	28

American Division

Team	GP	W	L	T	GF	GA	PTS
Boston	44	20	13	11	77	70	51
*New York	44	19	16	9	94	79	47
Pittsburgh	44	19	17	8	67	76	46
Detroit	44	19	19	6	88	79	44
Chicago	44	7	34	3	68	134	17

Leading Scorers

Player	Club	GP	G	A	PTS	PIM
Morenz, Howie	Montreal	43	33	18	51	66
Joliat, Aurel	Montreal	44	28	11	39	105
Boucher, Frank	New York	44	23	12	35	15
Hay, George	Detroit	42	22	13	35	20
Stewart, Nels	Mtl. Maroons	41	27	7	34	104
Gagne, Art	Montreal	44	20	10	30	75
Cook, Bun	New York	44	14	14	28	45
Carson, Bill	Toronto	32	20	6	26	36
Finnigan, Frank	Ottawa	38	20	5	25	34
Cook, Bill	New York	43	18	6	24	42
Keats, Duke	Det., Chi.	38	14	10	24	60

1928-29

Canadian Division

Team	GP	W	L	T	GF	GA	PTS
Montreal	44	22	7	15	71	43	59
NY Americans	44	19	13	12	53	53	50
Toronto	44	21	18	5	85	69	47
Ottawa	44	14	17	13	54	67	41
Mtl. Maroons	44	15	20	9	67	65	39

American Division

Team	GP	W	L	T	GF	GA	PTS
*Boston	44	26	13	5	89	52	57
New York	44	21	13	10	72	65	52
Detroit	44	19	16	9	72	63	47
Pittsburgh	44	9	27	8	46	80	26
Chicago	44	7	29	8	33	85	22

Leading Scorers

Player	Club	GP	G	A	PTS	PIM
Bailey, Ace	Toronto	44	22	10	32	78
Stewart, Nels	Mtl. Maroons	44	21	8	29	74
Cooper, Carson	Detroit	43	18	9	27	14
Morenz, Howie	Montreal	42	17	10	27	47
Blair, Andy	Toronto	44	12	15	27	41
Boucher, Frank	New York	44	10	16	26	8
Oliver, Harry	Boston	43	17	6	23	24
Cook, Bill	New York	43	15	8	23	41
Ward, Jimmy	Mtl. Maroons	43	14	8	22	46

Seven players tied with 19 points

1929-30

Canadian Division

Team	GP	W	L	T	GF	GA	PTS
Mtl. Maroons	44	23	16	5	141	114	51
*Montreal	44	21	14	9	142	114	51
Ottawa	44	21	15	8	138	118	50
Toronto	44	17	21	6	116	124	40
NY Americans	44	14	25	5	113	161	33

American Division

Team	GP	W	L	T	GF	GA	PTS
Boston	44	38	5	1	179	98	77
Chicago	44	21	18	5	117	111	47
New York	44	17	17	10	136	143	44
Detroit	44	14	24	6	117	133	34
Pittsburgh	44	5	36	3	102	185	13

Leading Scorers

Player	Club	GP	G	A	PTS	PIM
Weiland, Cooney	Boston	44	43	30	73	27
Boucher, Frank	New York	42	26	36	62	16
Clapper, Dit	Boston	44	41	20	61	48
Cook, Bill	New York	44	29	30	59	56
Kilrea, Hec	Ottawa	44	36	22	58	72
Stewart, Nels	Mtl. Maroons	44	39	16	55	81
Morenz, Howie	Montreal	44	40	10	50	72
Himes, Normie	NY Americans	44	28	22	50	15
Lamb, Joe	Ottawa	44	29	20	49	119
Gainor, Norm	Boston	42	18	31	49	39

1930-31

Canadian Division

Team	GP	W	L	T	GF	GA	PTS
*Montreal	44	26	10	8	129	89	60
Toronto	44	22	13	9	118	99	53
Mtl. Maroons	44	20	18	6	105	106	46
NY Americans	44	18	16	10	76	74	46
Ottawa	44	10	30	4	91	142	24

American Division

Team	GP	W	L	T	GF	GA	PTS
Boston	44	28	10	6	143	90	62
Chicago	44	24	17	3	108	78	51
New York	44	19	16	9	106	87	47
Detroit	44	16	21	7	102	105	39
Philadelphia	44	4	36	4	76	184	12

Leading Scorers

Player	Club	GP	G	A	PTS	PIM
Morenz, Howie	Montreal	39	28	23	51	49
Goodfellow, Ebbie	Detroit	44	25	23	48	32
Conacher, Charlie	Toronto	37	31	12	43	78
Cook, Bill	New York	43	30	12	42	39
Bailey, Ace	Toronto	40	23	19	42	46
Primeau, Joe	Toronto	38	9	32	41	18
Stewart, Nels	Mtl. Maroons	42	25	14	39	75
Boucher, Frank	New York	44	12	27	39	20
Weiland, Cooney	Boston	44	25	13	38	14
Cook, Bun	New York	44	18	17	35	72
Joliat, Aurel	Montreal	43	13	22	35	73

1931-32

Canadian Division

Team	GP	W	L	T	GF	GA	PTS
Montreal	48	25	16	7	128	111	57
*Toronto	48	23	18	7	155	127	53
Mtl. Maroons	48	19	22	7	142	139	45
NY Americans	48	16	24	8	95	142	40

American Division

Team	GP	W	L	T	GF	GA	PTS
New York	48	23	17	8	134	112	54
Chicago	48	18	19	11	86	101	47
Detroit	48	18	20	10	95	108	46
Boston	48	15	21	12	122	117	42

Leading Scorers

Player	Club	GP	G	A	PTS	PIM
Jackson, Harvey	Toronto	48	28	25	53	63
Primeau, Joe	Toronto	46	13	37	50	25
Morenz, Howie	Montreal	48	24	25	49	46
Conacher, Charlie	Toronto	44	34	14	48	66
Cook, Bill	New York	48	34	14	48	33
Trottier, Dave	Mtl. Maroons	48	26	18	44	94
Smith, Reg	Mtl. Maroons	43	11	33	44	49
Siebert, Babe	Mtl. Maroons	48	21	18	39	64
Clapper, Dit	Boston	48	17	22	39	21
Joliat, Aurel	Montreal	48	15	24	39	46

1932-33

Canadian Division

Team	GP	W	L	T	GF	GA	PTS
Toronto	48	24	18	6	119	111	54
Mtl. Maroons	48	22	20	6	135	119	50
Montreal	48	18	25	5	92	115	41
NY Americans	48	15	22	11	91	118	41
Ottawa	48	11	27	10	88	131	32

American Division

Team	GP	W	L	T	GF	GA	PTS
Boston	48	25	15	8	124	88	58
Detroit	48	25	15	8	111	93	58
*New York	48	23	17	8	135	107	54
Chicago	48	16	20	12	88	101	44

Leading Scorers

Player	Club	GP	G	A	PTS	PIM
Cook, Bill	New York	48	28	22	50	51
Jackson, Harvey	Toronto	48	27	17	44	43
Northcott, Baldy	Mtl. Maroons	48	22	21	43	30
Smith, Reg	Mtl. Maroons	48	20	21	41	66
Haynes, Paul	Mtl. Maroons	48	16	25	41	18
Joliat, Aurel	Montreal	48	18	21	39	53
Barry, Marty	Boston	48	24	13	37	40
Cook, Bun	New York	48	22	15	37	35
Stewart, Nels	Boston	47	18	18	36	62
Morenz, Howie	Montreal	46	14	21	35	32
Gagnon, Johnny	Montreal	48	12	23	35	64
Shore, Eddie	Boston	48	8	27	35	102
Boucher, Frank	New York	47	7	28	35	4

1933-34

Canadian Division

Team	GP	W	L	T	GF	GA	PTS
Toronto	48	26	13	9	174	119	61
Montreal	48	22	20	6	99	101	50
Mtl. Maroons	48	19	18	11	117	122	49
NY Americans	48	15	23	10	104	132	40
Ottawa	48	13	29	6	115	143	32

American Division

Team	GP	W	L	T	GF	GA	PTS
Detroit	48	24	14	10	113	98	58
*Chicago	48	20	17	11	88	83	51
New York	48	21	19	8	120	113	50
Boston	48	18	25	5	111	130	41

Leading Scorers

Player	Club	GP	G	A	PTS	PIM
Conacher, Charlie	Toronto	42	32	20	52	38
Primeau, Joe	Toronto	45	14	32	46	8
Boucher, Frank	New York	48	14	30	44	4
Barry, Marty	Boston	48	27	12	39	12
Dillon, Cecil	New York	48	13	26	39	10
Stewart, Nels	Boston	48	21	17	38	68
Jackson, Harvey	Toronto	38	20	18	38	38
Joliat, Aurel	Montreal	48	22	15	37	27
Smith, Reg	Mtl. Maroons	47	18	19	37	58
Thompson, Paul	Chicago	48	20	16	36	17

1934-35

Canadian Division

Team	GP	W	L	T	GF	GA	PTS
Toronto	48	30	14	4	157	111	64
*Mtl. Maroons	48	24	19	5	123	92	53
Montreal	48	19	23	6	110	145	44
NY Americans	48	12	27	9	100	142	33
St. Louis	48	11	31	6	86	144	28

American Division

Team	GP	W	L	T	GF	GA	PTS
Boston	48	26	16	6	129	112	58
Chicago	48	26	17	5	118	88	57
New York	48	22	20	6	137	139	50
Detroit	48	19	22	7	127	114	45

Leading Scorers

Player	Club	GP	G	A	PTS	PIM
Conacher, Charlie	Toronto	47	36	21	57	24
Howe, Syd	St.L., Det.	50	22	25	47	34
Aurie, Larry	Detroit	48	17	29	46	24
Boucher, Frank	New York	48	13	32	45	2
Jackson, Harvey	Toronto	42	22	22	44	27
Lewis, Herb	Detroit	47	16	27	43	26
Chapman, Art	NY Americans	47	9	34	43	4
Barry, Marty	Boston	48	20	20	40	33
Schriner, Sweeney	NY Americans	48	18	22	40	6
Stewart, Nels	Boston	47	21	18	39	45
Thompson, Paul	Chicago	48	16	23	39	20

1935-36

Canadian Division

Team	GP	W	L	T	GF	GA	PTS
Mtl. Maroons	48	22	16	10	114	106	54
Toronto	48	23	19	6	126	106	52
NY Americans	48	16	25	7	109	122	39
Montreal	48	11	26	11	82	123	33

American Division

Team	GP	W	L	T	GF	GA	PTS
*Detroit	48	24	16	8	124	103	56
Boston	48	22	20	6	92	83	50
Chicago	48	21	19	8	93	92	50
New York	48	19	17	12	91	96	50

Leading Scorers

Player	Club	GP	G	A	PTS	PIM
Schriner, Sweeney	NY Americans	48	19	26	45	8
Barry, Marty	Detroit	48	21	19	40	16
Thompson, Paul	Chicago	45	17	23	40	19
Thoms, Bill	Toronto	48	23	15	38	29
Conacher, Charlie	Toronto	44	23	15	38	74
Smith, Reg	Mtl. Maroons	47	19	19	38	75
Romnes, Doc	Chicago	48	13	25	38	6
Chapman, Art	NY Americans	47	10	28	38	14
Lewis, Herb	Detroit	45	14	23	37	25
Northcott, Baldy	Mtl. Maroons	48	15	21	36	41

1936-37

Canadian Division

Team	GP	W	L	T	GF	GA	PTS
Montreal	48	24	18	6	115	111	54
Mtl. Maroons	48	22	17	9	126	110	53
Toronto	48	22	21	5	119	115	49
NY Americans	48	15	29	4	122	161	34

American Division

Team	GP	W	L	T	GF	GA	PTS
*Detroit	48	25	14	9	128	102	59
Boston	48	23	18	7	120	110	53
New York	48	19	20	9	117	106	47
Chicago	48	14	27	7	99	131	35

Leading Scorers

Player	Club	GP	G	A	PTS	PIM
Schriner, Sweeney	NY Americans	48	21	25	46	17
Apps, Syl	Toronto	48	16	29	45	10
Barry, Marty	Detroit	48	17	27	44	6
Aurie, Larry	Detroit	45	23	20	43	20
Jackson, Harvey	Toronto	46	21	19	40	12
Gagnon, Johnny	Montreal	48	20	16	36	38
Gracie, Bob	Mtl. Maroons	47	11	25	36	18
Stewart, Nels	Bos., NYA	43	23	12	35	37
Thompson, Paul	Chicago	47	17	18	35	28
Cowley, Bill	Boston	46	13	22	35	4

1937-38

Canadian Division

Team	GP	W	L	T	GF	GA	PTS
Toronto	48	24	15	9	151	127	57
NY Americans	48	19	18	11	110	111	49
Montreal	48	18	17	13	123	128	49
Mtl. Maroons	48	12	30	6	101	149	30

American Division

Team	GP	W	L	T	GF	GA	PTS
Boston	48	30	11	7	142	89	67
New York	48	27	15	6	149	96	60
*Chicago	48	14	25	9	97	139	37
Detroit	48	12	25	11	99	133	35

Leading Scorers

Player	Club	GP	G	A	PTS	PIM
Drillon, Gordie	Toronto	48	26	26	52	4
Apps Sr., Syl	Toronto	47	21	29	50	9
Thompson, Paul	Chicago	48	22	22	44	14
Mantha, Georges	Montreal	47	23	19	42	12
Dillon, Cecil	New York	48	21	18	39	6
Cowley, Bill	Boston	48	17	22	39	8
Schriner, Sweeney	NY Americans	49	21	17	38	22
Thoms, Bill	Toronto	48	14	24	38	14
Smith, Clint	New York	48	14	23	37	0
Stewart, Nels	NY Americans	48	19	17	36	29
Colville, Neil	New York	45	17	19	36	11

1938-39

Team	GP	W	L	T	GF	GA	PTS
*Boston	48	36	10	2	156	76	74
New York	48	26	16	6	149	105	58
Toronto	48	19	20	9	114	107	47
NY Americans	48	17	21	10	119	157	44
Detroit	48	18	24	6	107	128	42
Montreal	48	15	24	9	115	146	39
Chicago	48	12	28	8	91	132	32

Leading Scorers

Player	Club	GP	G	A	PTS	PIM
Blake, Toe	Montreal	48	24	23	47	10
Schriner, Sweeney	NY Americans	48	13	31	44	20
Cowley, Bill	Boston	34	8	34	42	2
Smith, Clint	New York	48	21	20	41	2
Barry, Marty	Detroit	48	13	28	41	4
Apps Sr., Syl	Toronto	44	15	25	40	4
Anderson, Tom	NY Americans	48	13	27	40	14
Gottselig, Johnny	Chicago	48	16	23	39	15
Haynes, Paul	Montreal	47	5	33	38	27
Conacher, Roy	Boston	47	26	11	37	12
Carr, Lorne	NY Americans	46	19	18	37	16
Colville, Neil	New York	48	18	19	37	12
Watson, Phil	New York	48	15	22	37	42

1939-40

Team	GP	W	L	T	GF	GA	PTS
Boston	48	31	12	5	170	98	67
*New York	48	27	11	10	136	77	64
Toronto	48	25	17	6	134	110	56
Chicago	48	23	19	6	112	120	52
Detroit	48	16	26	6	90	126	38
NY Americans	48	15	29	4	106	140	34
Montreal	48	10	33	5	90	167	25

Leading Scorers

Player	Club	GP	G	A	PTS	PIM
Schmidt, Milt	Boston	48	22	30	52	37
Dumart, Woody	Boston	48	22	21	43	16
Bauer, Bobby	Boston	48	17	26	43	2
Drillon, Gordie	Toronto	43	21	19	40	13
Cowley, Bill	Boston	48	13	27	40	24
Hextall Sr., Bryan	New York	48	24	15	39	52
Colville, Neil	New York	48	19	19	38	22
Howe, Syd	Detroit	46	14	23	37	17
Blake, Toe	Montreal	48	17	19	36	48
Armstrong, Murray	NY Americans	48	16	20	36	12

For a brief 10-month period between February 1952 and December 1953, Elmer Lach was the NHL's all-time leading scorer. Lach overtook Boston's Bill Cowley with a second-period goal that helped the Canadiens blank the Bruins 7-0 on February 23, 1952.

1940-41

Team	GP	W	L	T	GF	GA	PTS
*Boston	48	27	8	13	168	102	67
Toronto	48	28	14	6	145	99	62
Detroit	48	21	16	11	112	102	53
New York	48	21	19	8	143	125	50
Chicago	48	16	25	7	112	139	39
Montreal	48	16	26	6	121	147	38
NY Americans	48	8	29	11	99	186	27

Leading Scorers

Player	Club	GP	G	A	PTS	PIM
Cowley, Bill	Boston	46	17	45	62	16
Hextall Sr., Bryan	New York	48	26	18	44	16
Drillon, Gordie	Toronto	42	23	21	44	2
Apps Sr., Syl	Toronto	41	20	24	44	6
Patrick, Lynn	New York	48	20	24	44	12
Howe, Syd	Detroit	48	20	24	44	8
Colville, Neil	New York	48	14	28	42	28
Wiseman, Eddie	Boston	48	16	24	40	10
Bauer, Bobby	Boston	48	17	22	39	2
Schriner, Sweeney	Toronto	48	24	14	38	6
Conacher, Roy	Boston	40	24	14	38	7
Schmidt, Milt	Boston	44	13	25	38	23

1941-42

Team	GP	W	L	T	GF	GA	PTS
New York	48	29	17	2	177	143	60
*Toronto	48	27	18	3	158	136	57
Boston	48	25	17	6	160	118	56
Chicago	48	22	23	3	145	155	47
Detroit	48	19	25	4	140	147	42
Montreal	48	18	27	3	134	173	39
Brooklyn	48	16	29	3	133	175	35

Leading Scorers

Player	Club	GP	G	A	PTS	PIM
Hextall Sr., Bryan	New York	48	24	32	56	30
Patrick, Lynn	New York	47	32	22	54	18
Grosso, Don	Detroit	48	23	30	53	13
Watson, Phil	New York	48	15	37	52	48
Abel, Sid	Detroit	48	18	31	49	45
Blake, Toe	Montreal	47	17	28	45	19
Thoms, Bill	Chicago	47	15	30	45	8
Drillon, Gordie	Toronto	48	23	18	41	6
Apps Sr., Syl	Toronto	38	18	23	41	0
Anderson, Tom	Brooklyn	48	12	29	41	54

1942-43

Team	GP	W	L	T	GF	GA	PTS
*Detroit	50	25	14	11	169	124	61
Boston	50	24	17	9	195	176	57
Toronto	50	22	19	9	198	159	53
Montreal	50	19	19	12	181	191	50
Chicago	50	17	18	15	179	180	49
New York	50	11	31	8	161	253	30

Leading Scorers

Player	Club	GP	G	A	PTS	PIM
Bentley, Doug	Chicago	50	33	40	73	18
Cowley, Bill	Boston	48	27	45	72	10
Bentley, Max	Chicago	47	26	44	70	2
Patrick, Lynn	New York	50	22	39	61	28
Carr, Lorne	Toronto	50	27	33	60	15
Taylor, Billy	Toronto	50	18	42	60	2
Hextall Sr., Bryan	New York	50	27	32	59	28
Blake, Toe	Montreal	48	23	36	59	28
Lach, Elmer	Montreal	45	18	40	58	14
O'Connor, Buddy	Montreal	50	15	43	58	2

1943-44

Team	GP	W	L	T	GF	GA	PTS
*Montreal	50	38	5	7	234	109	83
Detroit	50	26	18	6	214	177	58
Toronto	50	23	23	4	214	174	50
Chicago	50	22	23	5	178	187	49
Boston	50	19	26	5	223	268	43
New York	50	6	39	5	162	310	17

Leading Scorers

Player	Club	GP	G	A	PTS	PIM
Cain, Herb	Boston	48	36	46	82	4
Bentley, Doug	Chicago	50	38	39	77	22
Carr, Lorne	Toronto	50	36	38	74	9
Liscombe, Carl	Detroit	50	36	37	73	17
Lach, Elmer	Montreal	48	24	48	72	23
Smith, Clint	Chicago	50	23	49	72	4
Cowley, Bill	Boston	36	30	41	71	12
Mosienko, Bill	Chicago	50	32	38	70	10
Jackson, Art	Boston	49	28	41	69	8
Bodnar, Gus	Toronto	50	22	40	62	18

1944-45

Team	GP	W	L	T	GF	GA	PTS
Montreal	50	38	8	4	228	121	80
Detroit	50	31	14	5	218	161	67
*Toronto	50	24	22	4	183	161	52
Boston	50	16	30	4	179	219	36
Chicago	50	13	30	7	141	194	33
New York	50	11	29	10	154	247	32

Leading Scorers

Player	Club	GP	G	A	PTS	PIM
Lach, Elmer	Montreal	50	26	54	80	37
Richard, Maurice	Montreal	50	50	23	73	36
Blake, Toe	Montreal	49	29	38	67	15
Cowley, Bill	Boston	49	25	40	65	2
Kennedy, Ted	Toronto	49	29	25	54	14
Mosienko, Bill	Chicago	50	28	26	54	0
Carveth, Joe	Detroit	50	26	28	54	6
DeMarco Sr., Ab	New York	50	24	30	54	10
Smith, Clint	Chicago	50	23	31	54	0
Howe, Syd	Detroit	46	17	36	53	6

1945-46

Team	GP	W	L	T	GF	GA	PTS
*Montreal	50	28	17	5	172	134	61
Boston	50	24	18	8	167	156	56
Chicago	50	23	20	7	200	178	53
Detroit	50	20	20	10	146	159	50
Toronto	50	19	24	7	174	185	45
New York	50	13	28	9	144	191	35

Leading Scorers

Player	Club	GP	G	A	PTS	PIM
Bentley, Max	Chicago	47	31	30	61	6
Stewart, Gaye	Toronto	50	37	15	52	8
Blake, Toe	Montreal	50	29	21	50	2
Smith, Clint	Chicago	50	26	24	50	2
Richard, Maurice	Montreal	50	27	21	48	50
Mosienko, Bill	Chicago	40	18	30	48	12
DeMarco Sr., Ab	New York	50	20	27	47	20
Lach, Elmer	Montreal	50	13	34	47	34
Kaleta, Alex	Chicago	49	19	27	46	17
Taylor, Billy	Toronto	48	23	18	41	14
Horeck, Pete	Chicago	50	20	21	41	34

1946-47

Team	GP	W	L	T	GF	GA	PTS
Montreal	60	34	16	10	189	138	78
*Toronto	60	31	19	10	209	172	72
Boston	60	26	23	11	190	175	63
Detroit	60	22	27	11	190	193	55
New York	60	22	32	6	167	186	50
Chicago	60	19	37	4	193	274	42

Leading Scorers

Player	Club	GP	G	A	PTS	PIM
Bentley, Max	Chicago	60	29	43	72	12
Richard, Maurice	Montreal	60	45	26	71	69
Taylor, Billy	Detroit	60	17	46	63	35
Schmidt, Milt	Boston	59	27	35	62	40
Kennedy, Ted	Toronto	60	28	32	60	27
Bentley, Doug	Chicago	52	21	34	55	18
Bauer, Bobby	Boston	58	30	24	54	4
Conacher, Roy	Detroit	60	30	24	54	6
Mosienko, Bill	Chicago	59	25	27	52	2
Dumart, Woody	Boston	60	24	28	52	12

1947-48

Team	GP	W	L	T	GF	GA	PTS
*Toronto	60	32	15	13	182	143	77
Detroit	60	30	18	12	187	148	72
Boston	60	23	24	13	167	168	59
New York	60	21	26	13	176	201	55
Montreal	60	20	29	11	147	169	51
Chicago	60	20	34	6	195	225	46

Leading Scorers

Player	Club	GP	G	A	PTS	PIM
Lach, Elmer	Montreal	60	30	31	61	72
O'Connor, Buddy	New York	60	24	36	60	8
Bentley, Doug	Chicago	60	20	37	57	16
Stewart, Gaye	Tor., Chi.	61	27	29	56	83
Bentley, Max	Chi., Tor.	59	26	28	54	14
Poile, Bud	Tor., Chi.	58	25	29	54	17
Richard, Maurice	Montreal	53	28	25	53	89
Apps Sr., Syl	Toronto	55	26	27	53	12
Lindsay, Ted	Detroit	60	33	19	52	95
Conacher, Roy	Chicago	52	22	27	49	4

1948-49

Team	GP	W	L	T	GF	GA	PTS
Detroit	60	34	19	7	195	145	75
Boston	60	29	23	8	178	163	66
Montreal	60	28	23	9	152	126	65
*Toronto	60	22	25	13	147	161	57
Chicago	60	21	31	8	173	211	50
New York	60	18	31	11	133	172	47

Leading Scorers

Player	Club	GP	G	A	PTS	PIM
Conacher, Roy	Chicago	60	26	42	68	8
Bentley, Doug	Chicago	58	23	43	66	38
Abel, Sid	Detroit	60	28	26	54	49
Lindsay, Ted	Detroit	50	26	28	54	97
Conacher, Jim	Det., Chi.	59	26	23	49	43
Ronty, Paul	Boston	60	20	29	49	11
Watson, Harry	Toronto	60	26	19	45	0
Reay, Billy	Montreal	60	22	23	45	33
Bodnar, Gus	Chicago	59	19	26	45	14
Peirson, Johnny	Boston	59	22	21	43	45

1949-50

Team	GP	W	L	T	GF	GA	PTS
*Detroit	70	37	19	14	229	164	88
Montreal	70	29	22	19	172	150	77
Toronto	70	31	27	12	176	173	74
New York	70	28	31	11	170	189	67
Boston	70	22	32	16	198	228	60
Chicago	70	22	38	10	203	244	54

Leading Scorers

Player	Club	GP	G	A	PTS	PIM
Lindsay, Ted	Detroit	69	23	55	78	141
Abel, Sid	Detroit	69	34	35	69	46
Howe, Gordie	Detroit	70	35	33	68	69
Richard, Maurice	Montreal	70	43	22	65	114
Ronty, Paul	Boston	70	23	36	59	8
Conacher, Roy	Chicago	70	25	31	56	16
Bentley, Doug	Chicago	64	20	33	53	28
Peirson, Johnny	Boston	57	27	25	52	49
Prystai, Metro	Chicago	65	29	22	51	31
Guidolin, Bep	Chicago	70	17	34	51	42

Leonard Kelly, Detroit's redheaded rearguard, was the only defenseman to finish among the top-ten scorers three times during the 1950s. Kelly was ninth in 1950-51, eighth in 1952-53 and sixth in 1953-54.

1950-51

Team	GP	W	L	T	GF	GA	PTS
Detroit	70	44	13	13	236	139	101
*Toronto	70	41	16	13	212	138	95
Montreal	70	25	30	15	173	184	65
Boston	70	22	30	18	178	197	62
New York	70	20	29	21	169	201	61
Chicago	70	13	47	10	171	280	36

Leading Scorers

Player	Club	GP	G	A	PTS	PIM
Howe, Gordie	Detroit	70	43	43	86	74
Richard, Maurice	Montreal	65	42	24	66	97
Bentley, Max	Toronto	67	21	41	62	34
Abel, Sid	Detroit	69	23	38	61	30
Schmidt, Milt	Boston	62	22	39	61	33
Kennedy, Ted	Toronto	63	18	43	61	32
Lindsay, Ted	Detroit	67	24	35	59	110
Sloan, Tod	Toronto	70	31	25	56	105
Kelly, Red	Detroit	70	17	37	54	24
Smith, Sid	Toronto	70	30	21	51	10
Gardner, Cal	Toronto	66	23	28	51	42

1951-52

Team	GP	W	L	T	GF	GA	PTS
*Detroit	70	44	14	12	215	133	100
Montreal	70	34	26	10	195	164	78
Toronto	70	29	25	16	168	157	74
Boston	70	25	29	16	162	176	66
New York	70	23	34	13	192	219	59
Chicago	70	17	44	9	158	241	43

Leading Scorers

Player	Club	GP	G	A	PTS	PIM
Howe, Gordie	Detroit	70	47	39	86	78
Lindsay, Ted	Detroit	70	30	39	69	123
Lach, Elmer	Montreal	70	15	50	65	36
Raleigh, Don	New York	70	19	42	61	14
Smith, Sid	Toronto	70	27	30	57	6
Geoffrion, Bernie	Montreal	67	30	24	54	66
Mosienko, Bill	Chicago	70	31	22	53	10
Abel, Sid	Detroit	62	17	36	53	32
Kennedy, Ted	Toronto	70	19	33	52	33
Schmidt, Milt	Boston	69	21	29	50	57
Peirson, Johnny	Boston	68	20	30	50	30

1952-53

Team	GP	W	L	T	GF	GA	PTS
Detroit	70	36	16	18	222	133	90
*Montreal	70	28	23	19	155	148	75
Boston	70	28	29	13	152	172	69
Chicago	70	27	28	15	169	175	69
Toronto	70	27	30	13	156	167	67
New York	70	17	37	16	152	211	50

Leading Scorers

Player	Club	GP	G	A	PTS	PIM
Howe, Gordie	Detroit	70	49	46	95	57
Lindsay, Ted	Detroit	70	32	39	71	111
Richard, Maurice	Montreal	70	28	33	61	112
Hergesheimer, Wally	New York	70	30	29	59	10
Delvecchio, Alex	Detroit	70	16	43	59	28
Ronty, Paul	New York	70	16	38	54	20
Prystai, Metro	Detroit	70	16	34	50	12
Kelly, Red	Detroit	70	19	27	46	8
Olmstead, Bert	Montreal	69	17	28	45	83
Mackell, Fleming	Boston	65	27	17	44	63
McFadden, Jim	Chicago	70	23	21	44	29

1953-54

Team	GP	W	L	T	GF	GA	PTS
*Detroit	70	37	19	14	191	132	88
Montreal	70	35	24	11	195	141	81
Toronto	70	32	24	14	152	131	78
Boston	70	32	28	10	177	181	74
New York	70	29	31	10	161	182	68
Chicago	70	12	51	7	133	242	31

Leading Scorers

Player	Club	GP	G	A	PTS	PIM
Howe, Gordie	Detroit	70	33	48	81	109
Richard, Maurice	Montreal	70	37	30	67	112
Lindsay, Ted	Detroit	70	26	36	62	110
Geoffrion, Bernie	Montreal	54	29	25	54	87
Olmstead, Bert	Montreal	70	15	37	52	85
Kelly, Red	Detroit	62	16	33	49	18
Reibel, Earl	Detroit	69	15	33	48	18
Sandford, Ed	Boston	70	16	31	47	42
Mackell, Fleming	Boston	67	15	32	47	60
Mosdell, Kenny	Montreal	67	22	24	46	64
Ronty, Paul	New York	70	13	33	46	18

1954-55

Team	GP	W	L	T	GF	GA	PTS
*Detroit	70	42	17	11	204	134	95
Montreal	70	41	18	11	228	157	93
Toronto	70	24	24	22	147	135	70
Boston	70	23	26	21	169	188	67
New York	70	17	35	18	150	210	52
Chicago	70	13	40	17	161	235	43

Leading Scorers

Player	Club	GP	G	A	PTS	PIM
Geoffrion, Bernie	Montreal	70	38	37	75	57
Richard, Maurice	Montreal	67	38	36	74	125
Beliveau, Jean	Montreal	70	37	36	73	58
Reibel, Earl	Detroit	70	25	41	66	15
Howe, Gordie	Detroit	64	29	33	62	68
Sullivan, Red	Chicago	69	19	42	61	51
Olmstead, Bert	Montreal	70	10	48	58	103
Smith, Sid	Toronto	70	33	21	54	14
Mosdell, Kenny	Montreal	70	22	32	54	82
Lewicki, Danny	New York	70	29	24	53	8

1955-56

Team	GP	W	L	T	GF	GA	PTS
*Montreal	70	45	15	10	222	131	100
Detroit	70	30	24	16	183	148	76
New York	70	32	28	10	204	203	74
Toronto	70	24	33	13	153	181	61
Boston	70	23	34	13	147	185	59
Chicago	70	19	39	12	155	216	50

Leading Scorers

Player	Club	GP	G	A	PTS	PIM
Beliveau, Jean	Montreal	70	47	41	88	143
Howe, Gordie	Detroit	70	38	41	79	100
Richard, Maurice	Montreal	70	38	33	71	89
Olmstead, Bert	Montreal	70	14	56	70	94
Sloan, Tod	Toronto	70	37	29	66	100
Bathgate, Andy	New York	70	19	47	66	59
Geoffrion, Bernie	Montreal	59	29	33	62	66
Reibel, Earl	Detroit	68	17	39	56	10
Delvecchio, Alex	Detroit	70	25	26	51	24
Creighton, Dave	New York	70	20	31	51	43
Gadsby, Bill	New York	70	9	42	51	84

1956-57

Team	GP	W	L	T	GF	GA	PTS
Detroit	70	38	20	12	198	157	88
*Montreal	70	35	23	12	210	155	82
Boston	70	34	24	12	195	174	80
New York	70	26	30	14	184	227	66
Toronto	70	21	34	15	174	192	57
Chicago	70	16	39	15	169	225	47

Leading Scorers

Player	Club	GP	G	A	PTS	PIM
Howe, Gordie	Detroit	70	44	45	89	72
Lindsay, Ted	Detroit	70	30	55	85	103
Beliveau, Jean	Montreal	69	33	51	84	105
Bathgate, Andy	New York	70	27	50	77	60
Litzenberger, Ed	Chicago	70	32	32	64	48
Richard, Maurice	Montreal	63	33	29	62	74
McKenney, Don	Boston	69	21	39	60	31
Moore, Dickie	Montreal	70	29	29	58	56
Richard, Henri	Montreal	63	18	36	54	71
Ullman, Norm	Detroit	64	16	36	52	47

1957-58

Team	GP	W	L	T	GF	GA	PTS
*Montreal	70	43	17	10	250	158	96
New York	70	32	25	13	195	188	77
Detroit	70	29	29	12	176	207	70
Boston	70	27	28	15	199	194	69
Chicago	70	24	39	7	163	202	55
Toronto	70	21	38	11	192	226	53

Leading Scorers

Player	Club	GP	G	A	PTS	PIM
Moore, Dickie	Montreal	70	36	48	84	65
Richard, Henri	Montreal	67	28	52	80	56
Bathgate, Andy	New York	65	30	48	78	42
Howe, Gordie	Detroit	64	33	44	77	40
Horvath, Bronco	Boston	67	30	36	66	71
Litzenberger, Ed	Chicago	70	32	30	62	63
Mackell, Fleming	Boston	70	20	40	60	72
Beliveau, Jean	Montreal	55	27	32	59	93
Delvecchio, Alex	Detroit	70	21	38	59	22
McKenney, Don	Boston	70	28	30	58	22

1958-59

Team	GP	W	L	T	GF	GA	PTS
*Montreal	70	39	18	13	258	158	91
Boston	70	32	29	9	205	215	73
Chicago	70	28	29	13	197	208	69
Toronto	70	27	32	11	189	201	65
New York	70	26	32	12	201	217	64
Detroit	70	25	37	8	167	218	58

Leading Scorers

Player	Club	GP	G	A	PTS	PIM
Moore, Dickie	Montreal	70	41	55	96	61
Beliveau, Jean	Montreal	64	45	46	91	67
Bathgate, Andy	New York	70	40	48	88	48
Howe, Gordie	Detroit	70	32	46	78	57
Litzenberger, Ed	Chicago	70	33	44	77	37
Geoffrion, Bernie	Montreal	59	22	44	66	30
Sullivan, Red	New York	70	21	42	63	56
Hebenton, Andy	New York	70	33	29	62	8
McKenney, Don	Boston	70	32	30	62	20
Sloan, Tod	Chicago	59	27	35	62	79

1959-60

Team	GP	W	L	T	GF	GA	PTS
*Montreal	70	40	18	12	255	178	92
Toronto	70	35	26	9	199	195	79
Chicago	70	28	29	13	191	180	69
Detroit	70	26	29	15	186	197	67
Boston	70	28	34	8	220	241	64
New York	70	17	38	15	187	247	49

Leading Scorers

Player	Club	GP	G	A	PTS	PIM
Hull, Bobby	Chicago	70	39	42	81	68
Horvath, Bronco	Boston	68	39	41	80	60
Beliveau, Jean	Montreal	60	34	40	74	57
Bathgate, Andy	New York	70	26	48	74	28
Richard, Henri	Montreal	70	30	43	73	66
Howe, Gordie	Detroit	70	28	45	73	46
Geoffrion, Bernie	Montreal	59	30	41	71	36
McKenney, Don	Boston	70	20	49	69	28
Stasiuk, Vic	Boston	69	29	39	68	121
Prentice, Dean	New York	70	32	34	66	43

1960-61

Team	GP	W	L	T	GF	GA	PTS
Montreal	70	41	19	10	254	188	92
Toronto	70	39	19	12	234	176	90
*Chicago	70	29	24	17	198	180	75
Detroit	70	25	29	16	195	215	66
New York	70	22	38	10	204	248	54
Boston	70	15	42	13	176	254	43

Leading Scorers

Player	Club	GP	G	A	PTS	PIM
Geoffrion, Bernie	Montreal	64	50	45	95	29
Béliveau, Jean	Montreal	69	32	58	90	57
Mahovlich, Frank	Toronto	70	48	36	84	131
Bathgate, Andy	New York	70	29	48	77	22
Howe, Gordie	Detroit	64	23	49	72	30
Ullman, Norm	Detroit	70	28	42	70	34
Kelly, Red	Toronto	64	20	50	70	12
Moore, Dickie	Montreal	57	35	34	69	62
Richard, Henri	Montreal	70	24	44	68	91
Delvecchio, Alex	Detroit	70	27	35	62	26

1961-62

Team	GP	W	L	T	GF	GA	PTS
Montreal	70	42	14	14	259	166	98
*Toronto	70	37	22	11	232	180	85
Chicago	70	31	26	13	217	186	75
New York	70	26	32	12	195	207	64
Detroit	70	23	33	14	184	219	60
Boston	70	15	47	8	177	306	38

Leading Scorers

Player	Club	GP	G	A	PTS	PIM
Hull, Bobby	Chicago	70	50	34	84	35
Bathgate, Andy	New York	70	28	56	84	44
Howe, Gordie	Detroit	70	33	44	77	54
Mikita, Stan	Chicago	70	25	52	77	97
Mahovlich, Frank	Toronto	70	33	38	71	87
Delvecchio, Alex	Detroit	70	26	43	69	18
Backstrom, Ralph	Montreal	66	27	38	65	29
Ullman, Norm	Detroit	70	26	38	64	54
Hay, Bill	Chicago	60	11	52	63	34
Provost, Claude	Montreal	70	33	29	62	22

Although Johnny Bower was able to snag this hot shot, Gordie Howe was able to find the odd hole in the China Wall's armor, slipping over 40 shots past the venerable Leaf netminder during his career.

Bernie "Boom Boom" Geoffrion puts the finishing touches on his Stanley Cup-winning goal that lifted the Habs over Boston in the 1958 Stanley Cup finals. The Boomer captured his second Art Ross Trophy title in 1960-61, leading all NHL sharpshooters with 50 goals and 95 points.

1962-63

Team	GP	W	L	T	GF	GA	PTS
*Toronto	70	35	23	12	221	180	82
Chicago	70	32	21	17	194	178	81
Montreal	70	28	19	23	225	183	79
Detroit	70	32	25	13	200	194	77
New York	70	22	36	12	211	233	56
Boston	70	14	39	17	198	281	45

Leading Scorers

Player	Club	GP	G	A	PTS	PIM
Howe, Gordie	Detroit	70	38	48	86	100
Bathgate, Andy	New York	70	35	46	81	54
Mikita, Stan	Chicago	65	31	45	76	69
Mahovlich, Frank	Toronto	67	36	37	73	56
Richard, Henri	Montreal	67	23	50	73	57
Beliveau, Jean	Montreal	69	18	49	67	68
Bucyk, John	Boston	69	27	39	66	36
Delvecchio, Alex	Detroit	70	20	44	64	8
Hull, Bobby	Chicago	65	31	31	62	27
Oliver, Murray	Boston	65	22	40	62	38

1963-64

Team	GP	W	L	T	GF	GA	PTS
Montreal	70	36	21	13	209	167	85
Chicago	70	36	22	12	218	169	84
*Toronto	70	33	25	12	192	172	78
Detroit	70	30	29	11	191	204	71
New York	70	22	38	10	186	242	54
Boston	70	18	40	12	170	212	48

Leading Scorers

Player	Club	GP	G	A	PTS	PIM
Mikita, Stan	Chicago	70	39	50	89	146
Hull, Bobby	Chicago	70	43	44	87	50
Beliveau, Jean	Montreal	68	28	50	78	42
Bathgate, Andy	NYR, Tor.	71	19	58	77	34
Howe, Gordie	Detroit	69	26	47	73	70
Wharram, Kenny	Chicago	70	39	32	71	18
Oliver, Murray	Boston	70	24	44	68	41
Goyette, Phil	New York	67	24	41	65	15
Gilbert, Rod	New York	70	24	40	64	62
Keon, Dave	Toronto	70	23	37	60	6

1964-65

Team	GP	W	L	T	GF	GA	PTS
Detroit	70	40	23	7	224	175	87
*Montreal	70	36	23	11	211	185	83
Chicago	70	34	28	8	224	176	76
Toronto	70	30	26	14	204	173	74
New York	70	20	38	12	179	246	52
Boston	70	21	43	6	166	253	48

Leading Scorers

Player	Club	GP	G	A	PTS	PIM
Mikita, Stan	Chicago	70	28	59	87	154
Ullman, Norm	Detroit	70	42	41	83	70
Howe, Gordie	Detroit	70	29	47	76	104
Hull, Bobby	Chicago	61	39	32	71	32
Delvecchio, Alex	Detroit	68	25	42	67	16
Provost, Claude	Montreal	70	27	37	64	28
Gilbert, Rod	New York	70	25	36	61	52
Pilote, Pierre	Chicago	68	14	45	59	162
Bucyk, John	Boston	68	26	29	55	24
Backstrom, Ralph	Montreal	70	25	30	55	41
Esposito, Phil	Chicago	70	23	32	55	44

1965-66

Team	GP	W	L	T	GF	GA	PTS
*Montreal	70	41	21	8	239	173	90
Chicago	70	37	25	8	240	187	82
Toronto	70	34	25	11	208	187	79
Detroit	70	31	27	12	221	194	74
Boston	70	21	43	6	174	275	48
New York	70	18	41	11	195	261	47

Leading Scorers

Player	Club	GP	G	A	PTS	PIM
Hull, Bobby	Chicago	65	54	43	97	70
Mikita, Stan	Chicago	68	30	48	78	58
Rousseau, Bobby	Montreal	70	30	48	78	20
Beliveau, Jean	Montreal	67	29	48	77	50
Howe, Gordie	Detroit	70	29	46	75	83
Ullman, Norm	Detroit	70	31	41	72	35
Delvecchio, Alex	Detroit	70	31	38	69	16
Nevin, Bob	New York	69	29	33	62	10
Richard, Henri	Montreal	62	22	39	61	47
Oliver, Murray	Boston	70	18	42	60	30

1966-67

Team	GP	W	L	T	GF	GA	PTS
Chicago	70	41	17	12	264	170	94
Montreal	70	32	25	13	202	188	77
*Toronto	70	32	27	11	204	211	75
New York	70	30	28	12	188	189	72
Detroit	70	27	39	4	212	241	58
Boston	70	17	43	10	182	253	44

Leading Scorers

Player	Club	GP	G	A	PTS	PIM
Mikita, Stan	Chicago	70	35	62	97	12
Hull, Bobby	Chicago	66	52	28	80	52
Ullman, Norm	Detroit	68	26	44	70	26
Wharram, Kenny	Chicago	70	31	34	65	21
Howe, Gordie	Detroit	69	25	40	65	53
Rousseau, Bobby	Montreal	68	19	44	63	58
Esposito, Phil	Chicago	69	21	40	61	40
Goyette, Phil	New York	70	12	49	61	6
Mohns, Doug	Chicago	61	25	35	60	58
Richard, Henri	Montreal	65	21	34	55	28
Delvecchio, Alex	Detroit	70	17	38	55	10

Lanky left winger Frank Mahovlich attempts to bunt this bouncing puck past a prone Terry Sawchuk while Detroit defender Marcel Pronovost gives the Big M one of his patented midriff chops. Mahovlich led the Leafs in goals for six straight seasons from 1960-61 to 1964-65.

1967-68

East Division

Team	GP	W	L	T	GF	GA	PTS
*Montreal	74	42	22	10	236	167	94
New York	74	39	23	12	226	183	90
Boston	74	37	27	10	259	216	84
Chicago	74	32	26	16	212	222	80
Toronto	74	33	31	10	209	176	76
Detroit	74	27	35	12	245	257	66

West Division

Team	GP	W	L	T	GF	GA	PTS
Philadelphia	74	31	32	11	173	179	73
Los Angeles	74	31	33	10	200	224	72
St. Louis	74	27	31	16	177	191	70
Minnesota	74	27	32	15	191	226	69
Pittsburgh	74	27	34	13	195	216	67
Oakland	74	15	42	17	153	219	47

Leading Scorers

Player	Club	GP	G	A	PTS	PIM
Mikita, Stan	Chicago	72	40	47	87	14
Esposito, Phil	Boston	74	35	49	84	21
Howe, Gordie	Detroit	74	39	43	82	53
Ratelle, Jean	New York	74	32	46	78	18
Gilbert, Rod	New York	73	29	48	77	12
Hull, Bobby	Chicago	71	44	31	75	39
Ullman, Norm	Det., Tor.	71	35	37	72	28
Delvecchio, Alex	Detroit	74	22	48	70	14
Bucyk, John	Boston	72	30	39	69	8
Wharram, Kenny	Chicago	74	27	42	69	18

1968-69

East Division

Team	GP	W	L	T	GF	GA	PTS
*Montreal	76	46	19	11	271	202	103
Boston	76	42	18	16	303	221	100
New York	76	41	26	9	231	196	91
Toronto	76	35	26	15	234	217	85
Detroit	76	33	31	12	239	221	78
Chicago	76	34	33	9	280	246	77

West Division

Team	GP	W	L	T	GF	GA	PTS
St. Louis	76	37	25	14	204	157	88
Oakland	76	29	36	11	219	251	69
Philadelphia	76	20	35	21	174	225	61
Los Angeles	76	24	42	10	185	260	58
Pittsburgh	76	20	45	11	189	252	51
Minnesota	76	18	43	5	189	270	51

Leading Scorers

Player	Club	GP	G	A	PTS	PIM
Esposito, Phil	Boston	74	49	77	126	79
Hull, Bobby	Chicago	74	58	49	107	48
Howe, Gordie	Detroit	76	44	59	103	58
Mikita, Stan	Chicago	74	30	67	97	52
Hodge, Ken	Boston	75	45	45	90	75
Cournoyer, Yvan	Montreal	76	43	44	87	31
Delvecchio, Alex	Detroit	72	25	58	83	8
Berenson, Red	St. Louis	76	35	47	82	43
Beliveau, Jean	Montreal	69	33	49	82	55
Mahovlich, Frank	Detroit	76	49	29	78	38
Ratelle, Jean	New York	75	32	46	78	26

1969-70

East Division

Team	GP	W	L	T	GF	GA	PTS
Chicago	76	45	22	9	250	170	99
*Boston	76	40	17	19	277	216	99
Detroit	76	40	21	15	246	199	95
New York	76	38	22	16	246	189	92
Montreal	76	38	22	16	244	201	92
Toronto	76	29	34	13	222	242	71

West Division

Team	GP	W	L	T	GF	GA	PTS
St. Louis	76	37	27	12	224	179	86
Pittsburgh	76	26	38	12	182	238	64
Minnesota	76	19	35	22	224	257	60
Oakland	76	22	40	14	169	243	58
Philadelphia	76	17	35	24	197	225	58
Los Angeles	76	14	52	10	168	290	38

Leading Scorers

Player	Club	GP	G	A	PTS	PIM
Orr, Bobby	Boston	76	33	87	120	125
Esposito, Phil	Boston	76	43	56	99	50
Mikita, Stan	Chicago	76	39	47	86	50
Goyette, Phil	St. Louis	72	29	49	78	16
Tkaczuk, Walt	New York	76	27	50	77	38
Ratelle, Jean	New York	75	32	42	74	28
Berenson, Red	St. Louis	67	33	39	72	38
Parise, Jean-Paul	Minnesota	74	24	48	72	72
Howe, Gordie	Detroit	76	31	40	71	58
Mahovlich, Frank	Detroit	74	38	32	70	59
Balon, Dave	New York	76	33	37	70	100
McKenzie, John	Boston	72	29	41	70	114

1970-71

East Division

Team	GP	W	L	T	GF	GA	PTS
Boston	78	57	14	7	399	207	121
New York	78	49	18	11	259	177	109
*Montreal	78	42	23	13	291	216	97
Toronto	78	37	33	8	248	211	82
Buffalo	78	24	39	15	217	291	63
Vancouver	78	24	46	8	229	296	56
Detroit	78	22	45	11	209	308	55

West Division

Team	GP	W	L	T	GF	GA	PTS
Chicago	78	49	20	9	277	184	107
St. Louis	78	34	25	19	223	208	87
Philadelphia	78	28	33	17	207	225	73
Minnesota	78	28	34	16	191	223	72
Los Angeles	78	25	40	13	239	303	63
Pittsburgh	78	21	37	20	221	240	62
California	78	20	53	5	199	320	45

Leading Scorers

Player	Club	GP	G	A	PTS	PIM
Esposito, Phil	Boston	78	76	76	152	71
Orr, Bobby	Boston	78	37	102	139	91
Bucyk, John	Boston	78	51	65	116	8
Hodge, Ken	Boston	78	43	62	105	113
Hull, Bobby	Chicago	78	44	52	96	32
Ullman, Norm	Toronto	73	34	51	85	24
Cashman, Wayne	Boston	77	21	58	79	100
McKenzie, John	Boston	65	31	46	77	120
Keon, Dave	Toronto	76	38	38	76	4
Beliveau, Jean	Montreal	70	25	51	76	40
Stanfield, Fred	Boston	75	24	52	76	12

1971-72

East Division

Team	GP	W	L	T	GF	GA	PTS
*Boston	78	54	13	11	330	204	119
New York	78	48	17	13	317	192	109
Montreal	78	46	16	16	307	205	108
Toronto	78	33	31	14	209	208	80
Detroit	78	33	35	10	261	262	76
Buffalo	78	16	43	19	203	289	51
Vancouver	78	20	50	8	203	297	48

West Division

Team	GP	W	L	T	GF	GA	PTS
Chicago	78	46	17	15	256	166	107
Minnesota	78	37	29	12	212	191	86
St. Louis	78	28	39	11	208	247	67
Pittsburgh	78	26	38	14	220	258	66
Philadelphia	78	26	38	14	200	236	66
California	78	21	39	18	216	288	60
Los Angeles	78	20	49	9	206	305	49

Leading Scorers

Player	Club	GP	G	A	PTS	PIM
Esposito, Phil	Boston	76	66	67	133	76
Orr, Bobby	Boston	76	37	80	117	106
Ratelle, Jean	New York	63	46	63	109	4
Hadfield, Vic	New York	78	50	56	106	142
Gilbert, Rod	New York	73	43	54	97	64
Mahovlich, Frank	Montreal	76	43	53	96	36
Hull, Bobby	Chicago	78	50	43	93	24
Cournoyer, Yvan	Montreal	73	47	36	83	15
Bucyk, John	Boston	78	32	51	83	4
Clarke, Bobby	Philadelphia	78	35	46	81	87
Lemaire, Jacques	Montreal	77	32	49	81	26

1972-73

East Division

Team	GP	W	L	T	GF	GA	PTS
*Montreal	78	52	10	16	329	184	120
Boston	78	51	22	5	330	235	107
NY Rangers	78	47	23	8	297	208	102
Buffalo	78	37	27	14	257	219	88
Detroit	78	37	29	12	265	243	86
Toronto	78	27	41	10	247	279	64
Vancouver	78	22	47	9	233	339	53
NY Islanders	78	12	60	6	170	347	30

West Division

Team	GP	W	L	T	GF	GA	PTS
Chicago	78	42	27	9	284	225	93
Philadelphia	78	37	30	11	296	256	85
Minnesota	78	37	30	11	254	230	85
St. Louis	78	32	34	12	233	251	76
Pittsburgh	78	32	37	9	257	265	73
Los Angeles	78	31	36	11	232	245	73
Atlanta	78	25	38	15	191	239	65
California	78	16	46	16	213	323	48

Leading Scorers

Player	Club	GP	G	A	PTS	PIM
Esposito, Phil	Boston	78	55	75	130	87
Clarke, Bobby	Philadelphia	78	37	67	104	80
Orr, Bobby	Boston	63	29	72	101	99
MacLeish, Rick	Philadelphia	78	50	50	100	69
Lemaire, Jacques	Montreal	77	44	51	95	16
Ratelle, Jean	NY Rangers	78	41	53	94	12
Redmond, Mickey	Detroit	76	52	41	93	24
Bucyk, John	Boston	78	40	53	93	12
Mahovlich, Frank	Montreal	78	38	55	93	51
Pappin, Jim	Chicago	76	41	51	92	82

1973-74

East Division

Team	GP	W	L	T	GF	GA	PTS
Boston	78	52	17	9	349	221	113
Montreal	78	45	24	9	293	240	99
NY Rangers	78	40	24	14	300	251	94
Toronto	78	35	27	16	274	230	86
Buffalo	78	32	34	12	242	250	76
Detroit	78	29	39	10	255	319	68
Vancouver	78	24	43	11	224	296	59
NY Islanders	78	19	41	18	182	247	56

West Division

Team	GP	W	L	T	GF	GA	PTS
*Philadelphia	78	50	16	12	273	164	112
Chicago	78	41	14	23	272	164	105
Los Angeles	78	33	33	12	233	231	78
Atlanta	78	30	34	14	214	238	74
Pittsburgh	78	28	41	9	242	273	65
St. Louis	78	26	40	12	206	248	64
Minnesota	78	23	38	17	235	275	63
California	78	13	55	10	195	342	36

Leading Scorers

Player	Club	GP	G	A	PTS	PIM
Esposito, Phil	Boston	78	68	77	145	58
Orr, Bobby	Boston	74	32	90	122	82
Hodge, Ken	Boston	76	50	55	105	43
Cashman, Wayne	Boston	78	30	59	89	111
Clarke, Bobby	Philadelphia	77	35	52	87	113
Martin, Rick	Buffalo	78	52	34	86	38
Apps Jr., Syl	Pittsburgh	75	24	61	85	37
Sittler, Darryl	Toronto	78	38	46	84	55
MacDonald, Lowell	Pittsburgh	78	43	39	82	14
Park, Brad	NY Rangers	78	25	57	82	148
Hextall, Dennis	Minnesota	78	20	62	82	138

The first player from a post-1967 expansion team to win the Hart Trophy, Bobby Clarke finished among the NHL's top ten scorers seven times during the 1970s.

1974-75

PRINCE OF WALES CONFERENCE

Norris Division

Team	GP	W	L	T	GF	GA	PTS
Montreal	80	47	14	19	374	225	113
Los Angeles	80	42	17	21	269	185	105
Pittsburgh	80	37	28	15	326	289	89
Detroit	80	23	45	12	259	335	58
Washington	80	8	67	5	181	446	21

Adams Division

Team	GP	W	L	T	GF	GA	PTS
Buffalo	80	49	16	15	354	240	113
Boston	80	40	26	14	345	245	94
Toronto	80	31	33	16	280	309	78
California	80	19	48	13	212	316	51

CLARENCE CAMPBELL CONFERENCE

Patrick Division

Team	GP	W	L	T	GF	GA	PTS
*Philadelphia	80	51	18	11	293	181	113
NY Rangers	80	37	29	14	319	276	88
NY Islanders	80	33	25	22	264	221	88
Atlanta	80	34	31	15	243	233	83

Smythe Division

Team	GP	W	L	T	GF	GA	PTS
Vancouver	80	38	32	10	271	254	86
St. Louis	80	35	31	14	269	267	84
Chicago	80	37	35	8	268	241	82
Minnesota	80	23	50	7	221	341	53
Kansas City	80	15	54	11	184	328	41

Leading Scorers

Player	Club	GP	G	A	PTS	PIM
Orr, Bobby	Boston	80	46	89	135	101
Esposito, Phil	Boston	79	61	66	127	62
Dionne, Marcel	Detroit	80	47	74	121	14
Lafleur, Guy	Montreal	70	53	66	119	37
Mahovlich, Pete	Montreal	80	35	82	117	64
Clarke, Bobby	Philadelphia	80	27	89	116	125
Robert, Rene	Buffalo	74	40	60	100	75
Gilbert, Rod	NY Rangers	76	36	61	97	22
Perreault, Gilbert	Buffalo	68	39	57	96	36
Martin, Rick	Buffalo	68	52	43	95	72

1975-76

PRINCE OF WALES CONFERENCE

Norris Division

Team	GP	W	L	T	GF	GA	PTS
*Montreal	80	58	11	11	337	174	127
Los Angeles	80	38	33	9	263	265	85
Pittsburgh	80	35	33	12	339	303	82
Detroit	80	26	44	10	226	300	62
Washington	80	11	59	10	224	394	32

Adams Division

Team	GP	W	L	T	GF	GA	PTS
Boston	80	48	15	17	313	237	113
Buffalo	80	46	21	13	339	240	105
Toronto	80	34	31	15	294	276	83
California	80	27	42	11	250	278	65

CLARENCE CAMPBELL CONFERENCE

Patrick Division

Team	GP	W	L	T	GF	GA	PTS
Philadelphia	80	51	13	16	348	209	118
NY Islanders	80	42	21	17	297	190	101
Atlanta	80	35	33	12	262	237	82
NY Rangers	80	29	42	9	262	333	67

Smythe Division

Team	GP	W	L	T	GF	GA	PTS
Chicago	80	32	30	18	254	261	82
Vancouver	80	33	32	15	271	272	81
St. Louis	80	29	37	14	249	290	72
Minnesota	80	20	53	7	195	303	47
Kansas City	80	12	56	12	190	351	36

Leading Scorers

Player	Club	GP	G	A	PTS	PIM
Lafleur, Guy	Montreal	80	56	69	125	36
Clarke, Bobby	Philadelphia	76	30	89	119	13
Perreault, Gilbert	Buffalo	80	44	69	113	36
Barber, Bill	Philadelphia	80	50	62	112	104
Larouche, Pierre	Pittsburgh	76	53	58	111	33
Ratelle, Jean	Bos., NYR	80	36	69	105	18
Mahovlich, Pete	Montreal	80	34	71	105	76
Pronovost, Jean	Pittsburgh	80	52	52	104	24
Sittler, Darryl	Toronto	79	41	59	100	90
Apps Jr., Syl	Pittsburgh	80	32	67	99	24

1976-77

PRINCE OF WALES CONFERENCE

Norris Division

Team	GP	W	L	T	GF	GA	PTS
*Montreal	80	60	8	12	387	171	132
Los Angeles	80	34	31	15	271	241	83
Pittsburgh	80	34	33	13	240	252	81
Washington	80	24	42	14	221	307	62
Detroit	80	16	55	9	183	309	41

Adams Division

Team	GP	W	L	T	GF	GA	PTS
Boston	80	49	23	8	312	240	106
Buffalo	80	48	24	8	301	220	104
Toronto	80	33	32	15	301	285	81
Cleveland	80	25	42	13	240	292	63

CLARENCE CAMPBELL CONFERENCE

Patrick Division

Team	GP	W	L	T	GF	GA	PTS
Philadelphia	80	48	16	16	323	213	112
NY Islanders	80	47	21	12	288	193	106
Atlanta	80	34	34	12	264	265	80
NY Rangers	80	29	37	14	272	310	72

Smythe Division

Team	GP	W	L	T	GF	GA	PTS
St. Louis	80	32	39	9	239	276	73
Minnesota	80	23	39	18	240	310	64
Chicago	80	26	43	11	240	298	63
Vancouver	80	25	42	13	235	294	63
Colorado	80	20	46	14	226	307	54

Leading Scorers

Player	Club	GP	G	A	PTS	PIM
Lafleur, Guy	Montreal	80	56	80	136	20
Dionne, Marcel	Los Angeles	80	53	69	122	12
Shutt, Steve	Montreal	80	60	45	105	28
MacLeish, Rick	Philadelphia	79	49	48	97	42
Perreault, Gilbert	Buffalo	80	39	56	95	30
Young, Tim	Minnesota	80	29	66	95	58
Ratelle, Jean	Boston	78	33	61	94	22
McDonald, Lanny	Toronto	80	46	44	90	77
Sittler, Darryl	Toronto	73	38	52	90	89
Clarke, Bobby	Philadelphia	80	27	63	90	71

1977-78

PRINCE OF WALES CONFERENCE

Norris Division

Team	GP	W	L	T	GF	GA	PTS
*Montreal	80	59	10	11	359	183	129
Detroit	80	32	34	14	252	266	78
Los Angeles	80	31	34	15	243	245	77
Pittsburgh	80	25	37	18	254	321	68
Washington	80	17	49	14	195	321	48

Adams Division

Team	GP	W	L	T	GF	GA	PTS
Boston	80	51	18	11	333	218	113
Buffalo	80	44	19	17	288	215	105
Toronto	80	41	29	10	271	237	92
Cleveland	80	22	45	13	230	325	57

CLARENCE CAMPBELL CONFERENCE

Patrick Division

Team	GP	W	L	T	GF	GA	PTS
NY Islanders	80	48	17	15	334	210	111
Philadelphia	80	45	20	15	296	200	105
Atlanta	80	34	27	19	274	252	87
NY Rangers	80	30	37	13	279	280	73

Smythe Division

Team	GP	W	L	T	GF	GA	PTS
Chicago	80	32	29	19	230	220	83
Colorado	80	19	40	21	257	305	59
Vancouver	80	20	43	17	239	320	57
St. Louis	80	20	47	13	195	304	53
Minnesota	80	18	53	9	218	325	45

Leading Scorers

Player	Club	GP	G	A	PTS	PIM
Lafleur, Guy	Montreal	79	60	72	132	26
Trottier, Bryan	NY Islanders	77	46	77	123	46
Sittler, Darryl	Toronto	80	45	72	117	100
Lemaire, Jacques	Montreal	76	36	61	97	14
Potvin, Denis	NY Islanders	80	30	64	94	81
Bossy, Mike	NY Islanders	73	53	38	91	6
O'Reilly, Terry	Boston	77	29	61	90	211
Perreault, Gilbert	Buffalo	79	41	48	89	20
Clarke, Bobby	Philadelphia	71	21	68	89	83
McDonald, Lanny	Toronto	74	47	40	87	54
Paiement, Wilf	Colorado	80	31	56	87	114

1978-79

PRINCE OF WALES CONFERENCE

Norris Division

Team	GP	W	L	T	GF	GA	PTS
*Montreal	80	52	17	11	337	204	115
Pittsburgh	80	36	31	13	281	279	85
Los Angeles	80	34	34	12	292	286	80
Washington	80	24	41	15	273	338	63
Detroit	80	23	41	16	252	295	62

Adams Division

Team	GP	W	L	T	GF	GA	PTS
Boston	80	43	23	14	316	270	100
Buffalo	80	36	28	16	280	263	88
Toronto	80	34	33	13	267	252	81
Minnesota	80	28	40	12	257	289	68

CLARENCE CAMPBELL CONFERENCE

Patrick Division

Team	GP	W	L	T	GF	GA	PTS
NY Islanders	80	51	15	14	358	214	116
Philadelphia	80	40	25	15	281	248	95
NY Rangers	80	40	29	11	316	292	91
Atlanta	80	41	31	8	327	280	90

Smythe Division

Team	GP	W	L	T	GF	GA	PTS
Chicago	80	29	36	15	244	277	73
Vancouver	80	25	42	13	217	291	63
St. Louis	80	18	50	12	249	348	48
Colorado	80	15	53	12	210	331	42

Leading Scorers

Player	Club	GP	G	A	PTS	PIM
Trottier, Bryan	NY Islanders	76	47	87	134	50
Dionne, Marcel	Los Angeles	80	59	71	130	30
Lafleur, Guy	Montreal	80	52	77	129	28
Bossy, Mike	NY Islanders	80	69	57	126	25
MacMillan, Bob	Atlanta	79	37	71	108	14
Chouinard, Guy	Atlanta	80	50	57	107	14
Potvin, Denis	NY Islanders	73	31	70	101	58
Federko, Bernie	St. Louis	74	31	64	95	14
Taylor, Dave	Los Angeles	78	43	48	91	124
Gillies, Clark	NY Islanders	75	35	56	91	68

1979-80

PRINCE OF WALES CONFERENCE

Norris Division

Team	GP	W	L	T	GF	GA	PTS
Montreal	80	47	20	13	328	240	107
Los Angeles	80	30	36	14	290	313	74
Pittsburgh	80	30	37	13	251	303	73
Hartford	80	27	34	19	303	312	73
Detroit	80	26	43	11	268	306	63

Adams Division

Team	GP	W	L	T	GF	GA	PTS
Buffalo	80	47	17	16	318	201	110
Boston	80	46	21	13	310	234	105
Minnesota	80	36	28	16	311	253	88
Toronto	80	35	40	5	304	327	75
Quebec	80	25	44	11	248	313	61

CLARENCE CAMPBELL CONFERENCE

Patrick Division

Team	GP	W	L	T	GF	GA	PTS
Philadelphia	80	48	12	20	327	254	116
*NY Islanders	80	39	28	13	281	247	91
NY Rangers	80	38	32	10	308	284	86
Atlanta	80	35	32	13	282	269	83
Washington	80	27	40	13	261	293	67

Smythe Division

Team	GP	W	L	T	GF	GA	PTS
Chicago	80	34	27	19	241	250	87
St. Louis	80	34	34	12	266	278	80
Vancouver	80	27	37	16	256	281	70
Edmonton	80	28	39	13	301	322	69
Winnipeg	80	20	49	11	214	314	51
Colorado	80	19	48	13	234	308	51

Leading Scorers

Player	Club	GP	G	A	PTS	PIM
Dionne, Marcel	Los Angeles	80	53	84	137	32
Gretzky, Wayne	Edmonton	79	51	86	137	21
Lafleur, Guy	Montreal	74	50	75	125	12
Perreault, Gilbert	Buffalo	80	40	66	106	57
Rogers, Mike	Hartford	80	44	61	105	10
Trottier, Bryan	NY Islanders	78	42	62	104	68
Simmer, Charlie	Los Angeles	64	56	45	101	65
Stoughton, Blaine	Hartford	80	56	44	100	16
Sittler, Darryl	Toronto	73	40	57	97	62
MacDonald, Blair	Edmonton	80	46	48	94	6
Federko, Bernie	St. Louis	79	38	56	94	24

1980-81

PRINCE OF WALES CONFERENCE

Norris Division

Team	GP	W	L	T	GF	GA	PTS
Montreal	80	45	22	13	332	232	103
Los Angeles	80	43	24	13	337	290	99
Pittsburgh	80	30	37	13	302	345	73
Hartford	80	21	41	18	292	372	60
Detroit	80	19	43	18	252	339	56

Adams Division

Team	GP	W	L	T	GF	GA	PTS
Buffalo	80	39	20	21	327	250	99
Boston	80	37	30	13	316	272	87
Minnesota	80	35	28	17	291	263	87
Quebec	80	30	32	18	314	318	78
Toronto	80	28	37	15	322	367	71

CLARENCE CAMPBELL CONFERENCE

Patrick Division

Team	GP	W	L	T	GF	GA	PTS
*NY Islanders	80	48	18	14	355	260	110
Philadelphia	80	41	24	15	313	249	97
Calgary	80	39	27	14	329	298	92
NY Rangers	80	30	36	14	312	317	74
Washington	80	26	36	18	286	317	70

Smythe Division

Team	GP	W	L	T	GF	GA	PTS
St. Louis	80	45	18	17	352	281	107
Chicago	80	31	33	16	304	315	78
Vancouver	80	28	32	20	289	301	76
Edmonton	80	29	35	16	328	327	74
Colorado	80	22	45	13	258	344	57
Winnipeg	80	9	57	14	246	400	32

Leading Scorers

Player	Club	GP	G	A	PTS	PIM
Gretzky, Wayne	Edmonton	80	55	109	164	28
Dionne, Marcel	Los Angeles	80	58	77	135	70
Nilsson, Kent	Calgary	80	49	82	131	26
Bossy, Mike	NY Islanders	79	68	51	119	32
Taylor, Dave	Los Angeles	72	47	65	112	130
Stastny, Peter	Quebec	77	39	70	109	37
Simmer, Charlie	Los Angeles	65	56	49	105	62
Rogers, Mike	Hartford	80	40	65	105	32
Federko, Bernie	St. Louis	78	31	73	104	47
Richard, Jacques	Quebec	78	52	51	103	39
Middleton, Rick	Boston	80	44	59	103	16
Trottier, Bryan	NY Islanders	73	31	72	103	74

1981-82

CLARENCE CAMPBELL CONFERENCE

Norris Division

Team	GP	W	L	T	GF	GA	PTS
Minnesota	80	37	23	20	346	288	94
Winnipeg	80	33	33	14	319	332	80
St. Louis	80	32	40	8	315	349	72
Chicago	80	30	38	12	332	363	72
Toronto	80	20	44	16	298	380	56
Detroit	80	21	47	12	270	351	54

Smythe Division

Team	GP	W	L	T	GF	GA	PTS
Edmonton	80	48	17	15	417	295	111
Vancouver	80	30	33	17	290	286	77
Calgary	80	29	34	17	334	345	75
Los Angeles	80	24	41	15	314	369	63
Colorado	80	18	49	13	241	362	49

PRINCE OF WALES CONFERENCE

Adams Division

Team	GP	W	L	T	GF	GA	PTS
Montreal	80	46	17	17	360	223	109
Boston	80	43	27	10	323	285	96
Buffalo	80	39	26	15	307	273	93
Quebec	80	33	31	16	356	345	82
Hartford	80	21	41	18	264	351	60

Patrick Division

Team	GP	W	L	T	GF	GA	PTS
*NY Islanders	80	54	16	10	385	250	118
NY Rangers	80	39	27	14	316	306	92
Philadelphia	80	38	31	11	325	313	87
Pittsburgh	80	31	36	13	310	337	75
Washington	80	26	41	13	319	338	65

Leading Scorers

Player	Club	GP	G	A	PTS	PIM
Gretzky, Wayne	Edmonton	80	92	120	212	26
Bossy, Mike	NY Islanders	80	64	83	147	22
Stastny, Peter	Quebec	80	46	93	139	91
Maruk, Dennis	Washington	80	60	76	136	128
Trottier, Bryan	NY Islanders	80	50	79	129	88
Savard, Denis	Chicago	80	32	87	119	82
Dionne, Marcel	Los Angeles	78	50	67	117	50
Smith, Bobby	Minnesota	80	43	71	114	82
Ciccarelli, Dino	Minnesota	76	55	51	106	138
Taylor, Dave	Los Angeles	78	39	67	106	130

1982-83

CLARENCE CAMPBELL CONFERENCE

Norris Division

Team	GP	W	L	T	GF	GA	PTS
Chicago	80	47	23	10	338	268	104
Minnesota	80	40	24	16	321	290	96
Toronto	80	28	40	12	293	330	68
St. Louis	80	25	40	15	285	316	65
Detroit	80	21	44	15	263	344	57

Smythe Division

Team	GP	W	L	T	GF	GA	PTS
Edmonton	80	47	21	12	424	315	106
Calgary	80	32	34	14	321	317	78
Vancouver	80	30	35	15	303	309	75
Winnipeg	80	33	39	8	311	333	74
Los Angeles	80	27	41	12	308	365	66

PRINCE OF WALES CONFERENCE

Adams Division

Team	GP	W	L	T	GF	GA	PTS
Boston	80	50	20	10	327	228	110
Montreal	80	42	24	14	350	286	98
Buffalo	80	38	29	13	318	285	89
Quebec	80	34	34	12	343	336	80
Hartford	80	19	54	7	261	403	45

Patrick Division

Team	GP	W	L	T	GF	GA	PTS
Philadelphia	80	49	23	8	326	240	106
*NY Islanders	80	42	26	12	302	226	96
Washington	80	39	25	16	306	283	94
NY Rangers	80	35	35	10	306	287	80
New Jersey	80	17	49	14	230	338	48
Pittsburgh	80	18	53	9	257	394	45

Leading Scorers

Player	Club	GP	G	A	PTS	PIM
Gretzky, Wayne	Edmonton	80	71	125	196	59
Stastny, Peter	Quebec	75	47	77	124	78
Savard, Denis	Chicago	78	35	86	121	99
Bossy, Mike	NY Islanders	79	60	58	118	20
Dionne, Marcel	Los Angeles	80	56	51	107	22
Pederson, Barry	Boston	77	46	61	107	47
Messier, Mark	Edmonton	77	48	58	106	72
Goulet, Michel	Quebec	80	57	48	105	51
Anderson, Glenn	Edmonton	72	48	56	104	70
Nilsson, Kent	Calgary	80	46	58	104	10
Kurri, Jari	Edmonton	80	45	59	104	22

1983-84

CLARENCE CAMPBELL CONFERENCE

Norris Division

Team	GP	W	L	T	GF	GA	PTS
Minnesota	80	39	31	10	345	344	88
St. Louis	80	32	41	7	293	316	71
Detroit	80	31	42	7	298	323	69
Chicago	80	30	42	8	277	311	68
Toronto	80	26	45	9	303	387	61

Smythe Division

Team	GP	W	L	T	GF	GA	PTS
*Edmonton	80	57	18	5	446	314	119
Calgary	80	34	32	14	311	314	82
Vancouver	80	32	39	9	306	328	73
Winnipeg	80	31	38	11	340	374	73
Los Angeles	80	23	44	13	309	376	59

PRINCE OF WALES CONFERENCE

Adams Division

Team	GP	W	L	T	GF	GA	PTS
Boston	80	49	25	6	336	261	104
Buffalo	80	48	25	7	315	257	103
Quebec	80	42	28	10	360	278	94
Montreal	80	35	40	5	286	295	75
Hartford	80	28	42	10	288	320	66

Patrick Division

Team	GP	W	L	T	GF	GA	PTS
NY Islanders	80	50	26	4	357	269	104
Washington	80	48	27	5	308	226	101
Philadelphia	80	44	26	10	350	290	98
NY Rangers	80	42	29	9	314	304	93
New Jersey	80	17	56	7	231	350	41
Pittsburgh	80	16	58	6	254	390	38

Leading Scorers

Player	Club	GP	G	A	PTS	PIM
Gretzky, Wayne	Edmonton	74	87	118	205	39
Coffey, Paul	Edmonton	80	40	86	126	104
Goulet, Michel	Quebec	75	56	65	121	76
Stastny, Peter	Quebec	80	46	73	119	73
Bossy, Mike	NY Islanders	67	51	67	118	8
Pederson, Barry	Boston	80	39	77	116	64
Kurri, Jari	Edmonton	64	52	61	113	14
Trottier, Bryan	NY Islanders	68	40	71	111	59
Federko, Bernie	St. Louis	79	41	66	107	43
Middleton, Rick	Boston	80	47	58	105	14

1984-85

CLARENCE CAMPBELL CONFERENCE

Norris Division

Team	GP	W	L	T	GF	GA	PTS
St. Louis	80	37	31	12	299	288	86
Chicago	80	38	35	7	309	299	83
Detroit	80	27	41	12	313	357	66
Minnesota	80	25	43	12	268	321	62
Toronto	80	20	52	8	253	358	48

Smythe Division

Team	GP	W	L	T	GF	GA	PTS
*Edmonton	80	49	20	11	401	298	109
Winnipeg	80	43	27	10	358	332	96
Calgary	80	41	27	12	363	302	94
Los Angeles	80	34	32	14	339	326	82
Vancouver	80	25	46	9	284	401	59

PRINCE OF WALES CONFERENCE

Adams Division

Team	GP	W	L	T	GF	GA	PTS
Montreal	80	41	27	12	309	262	94
Quebec	80	41	30	9	323	275	91
Buffalo	80	38	28	14	290	237	90
Boston	80	36	34	10	303	287	82
Hartford	80	30	41	9	268	318	69

Patrick Division

Team	GP	W	L	T	GF	GA	PTS
Philadelphia	80	53	20	7	348	241	113
Washington	80	46	25	9	322	240	101
NY Islanders	80	40	34	6	345	312	86
NY Rangers	80	26	44	10	295	345	62
New Jersey	80	22	48	10	264	346	54
Pittsburgh	80	24	51	5	276	385	53

Leading Scorers

Player	Club	GP	G	A	PTS	PIM
Gretzky, Wayne	Edmonton	80	73	135	208	52
Kurri, Jari	Edmonton	73	71	64	135	30
Hawerchuk, Dale	Winnipeg	80	53	77	130	74
Dionne, Marcel	Los Angeles	80	46	80	126	46
Coffey, Paul	Edmonton	80	37	84	121	97
Bossy, Mike	NY Islanders	76	58	59	117	38
Ogrodnick, John	Detroit	79	55	50	105	30
Savard, Denis	Chicago	79	38	67	105	56
Federko, Bernie	St. Louis	76	30	73	103	27
Gartner, Mike	Washington	80	50	52	102	71

1985-86

CLARENCE CAMPBELL CONFERENCE

Norris Division

Team	GP	W	L	T	GF	GA	PTS
Chicago	80	39	33	8	351	349	86
Minnesota	80	38	33	9	327	305	85
St. Louis	80	37	34	9	302	291	83
Toronto	80	25	48	7	311	386	57
Detroit	80	17	57	6	266	415	40

Smythe Division

Team	GP	W	L	T	GF	GA	PTS
Edmonton	80	56	17	7	426	310	119
Calgary	80	40	31	9	354	315	89
Winnipeg	80	26	47	7	295	372	59
Vancouver	80	23	44	13	282	333	59
Los Angeles	80	23	49	8	284	389	54

PRINCE OF WALES CONFERENCE

Adams Division

Team	GP	W	L	T	GF	GA	PTS
Quebec	80	43	31	6	330	289	92
*Montreal	80	40	33	7	330	280	87
Boston	80	37	31	12	311	288	86
Hartford	80	40	36	4	332	302	84
Buffalo	80	37	37	6	296	291	80

Patrick Division

Team	GP	W	L	T	GF	GA	PTS
Philadelphia	80	53	23	4	335	241	110
Washington	80	50	23	7	315	272	107
NY Islanders	80	39	29	12	327	284	90
NY Rangers	80	36	38	6	280	276	78
Pittsburgh	80	34	38	8	313	305	76
New Jersey	80	28	49	3	300	374	59

Leading Scorers

Player	Club	GP	G	A	PTS	PIM
Gretzky, Wayne	Edmonton	80	52	163	215	52
Lemieux, Mario	Pittsburgh	79	48	93	141	43
Coffey, Paul	Edmonton	79	48	90	138	120
Kurri, Jari	Edmonton	78	68	63	131	22
Bossy, Mike	NY Islanders	80	61	62	123	14
Stastny, Peter	Quebec	76	41	81	122	60
Savard, Denis	Chicago	80	47	69	116	111
Naslund, Mats	Montreal	80	43	67	110	16
Hawerchuk, Dale	Winnipeg	80	46	59	105	44
Broten, Neal	Minnesota	80	29	76	105	47

Bryan Trottier is one of only four players to win two-or-more Stanley Cup titles with two-or-more teams. "Trotts" won his only NHL scoring title with 47 goals and 134 points in 1978-79.

1986-87

CLARENCE CAMPBELL CONFERENCE

Norris Division

Team	GP	W	L	T	GF	GA	PTS
St. Louis	80	32	33	15	281	293	79
Detroit	80	34	36	10	260	274	78
Chicago	80	29	37	14	290	310	72
Toronto	80	32	42	6	286	319	70
Minnesota	80	30	40	10	296	314	70

Smythe Division

Team	GP	W	L	T	GF	GA	PTS
*Edmonton	80	50	24	6	372	284	106
Calgary	80	46	31	3	318	289	95
Winnipeg	80	40	32	8	279	271	88
Los Angeles	80	31	41	8	318	341	70
Vancouver	80	29	43	8	282	314	66

PRINCE OF WALES CONFERENCE

Adams Division

Team	GP	W	L	T	GF	GA	PTS
Hartford	80	43	30	7	287	270	93
Montreal	80	41	29	10	277	241	92
Boston	80	39	34	7	301	276	85
Quebec	80	31	39	10	267	276	72
Buffalo	80	28	44	8	280	308	64

Patrick Division

Team	GP	W	L	T	GF	GA	PTS
Philadelphia	80	46	26	8	310	245	100
Washington	80	38	32	10	285	278	86
NY Islanders	80	35	33	12	279	281	82
NY Rangers	80	34	38	8	307	323	76
Pittsburgh	80	30	38	12	297	290	72
New Jersey	80	29	45	6	293	368	64

Leading Scorers

Player	Club	GP	G	A	PTS	PIM
Gretzky, Wayne	Edmonton	79	62	121	183	28
Kurri, Jari	Edmonton	79	54	54	108	41
Lemieux, Mario	Pittsburgh	63	54	53	107	57
Messier, Mark	Edmonton	77	37	70	107	73
Gilmour, Doug	St. Louis	80	42	63	105	58
Ciccarelli, Dino	Minnesota	80	52	51	103	92
Hawerchuk, Dale	Winnipeg	80	47	53	100	54
Goulet, Michel	Quebec	75	49	47	96	61
Kerr, Tim	Philadelphia	75	58	37	95	57
Bourque, Ray	Boston	78	23	72	95	36

1987-88

CLARENCE CAMPBELL CONFERENCE

Norris Division

Team	GP	W	L	T	GF	GA	PTS
Detroit	80	41	28	11	322	269	93
St. Louis	80	34	38	8	278	294	76
Chicago	80	30	41	9	284	328	69
Toronto	80	21	49	10	273	345	52
Minnesota	80	19	48	13	242	349	51

Smythe Division

Team	GP	W	L	T	GF	GA	PTS
Calgary	80	48	23	9	397	305	105
*Edmonton	80	44	25	11	363	288	99
Winnipeg	80	33	36	11	292	310	77
Los Angeles	80	30	42	8	318	359	68
Vancouver	80	25	46	9	272	320	59

PRINCE OF WALES CONFERENCE

Adams Division

Team	GP	W	L	T	GF	GA	PTS
Montreal	80	45	22	13	298	238	103
Boston	80	44	30	6	300	251	94
Buffalo	80	37	32	11	283	305	85
Hartford	80	35	38	7	249	267	77
Quebec	80	32	43	5	271	306	69

Patrick Division

Team	GP	W	L	T	GF	GA	PTS
NY Islanders	80	39	31	10	308	267	88
Washington	80	38	33	9	281	249	85
Philadelphia	80	38	33	9	292	292	85
New Jersey	80	38	36	6	295	296	82
NY Rangers	80	36	34	10	300	283	82
Pittsburgh	80	36	35	9	319	316	81

Leading Scorers

Player	Club	GP	G	A	PTS	PIM
Lemieux, Mario	Pittsburgh	76	70	98	168	92
Gretzky, Wayne	Edmonton	64	40	109	149	24
Savard, Denis	Chicago	80	44	87	131	95
Hawerchuk, Dale	Winnipeg	80	44	77	121	59
Robitaille, Luc	Los Angeles	80	53	58	111	82
Stastny, Peter	Quebec	76	46	65	111	69
Messier, Mark	Edmonton	77	37	74	111	103
Carson, Jimmy	Los Angeles	80	55	52	107	45
Loob, Hakan	Calgary	80	50	56	106	47
Goulet, Michel	Quebec	80	48	58	106	56

1988-89

CLARENCE CAMPBELL CONFERENCE

Norris Division

Team	GP	W	L	T	GF	GA	PTS
Detroit	80	34	34	12	313	316	80
St. Louis	80	33	35	12	275	285	78
Minnesota	80	27	37	16	258	278	70
Chicago	80	27	41	12	297	335	66
Toronto	80	28	46	6	259	342	62

Smythe Division

Team	GP	W	L	T	GF	GA	PTS
*Calgary	80	54	17	9	354	226	117
Los Angeles	80	42	31	7	376	335	91
Edmonton	80	38	34	8	325	306	84
Vancouver	80	33	39	8	251	253	74
Winnipeg	80	26	42	12	300	355	64

PRINCE OF WALES CONFERENCE

Adams Division

Team	GP	W	L	T	GF	GA	PTS
Montreal	80	53	18	9	315	218	115
Boston	80	37	29	14	289	256	88
Buffalo	80	38	35	7	291	299	83
Hartford	80	37	38	5	299	290	79
Quebec	80	27	46	7	269	342	61

Patrick Division

Team	GP	W	L	T	GF	GA	PTS
Washington	80	41	29	10	305	259	92
Pittsburgh	80	40	33	7	347	349	87
NY Rangers	80	37	35	8	310	307	82
Philadelphia	80	36	36	8	307	285	80
New Jersey	80	27	41	12	281	325	66
NY Islanders	80	28	47	5	265	325	61

Leading Scorers

Player	Club	GP	G	A	PTS	PIM
Lemieux, Mario	Pittsburgh	76	85	114	199	100
Gretzky, Wayne	Los Angeles	78	54	114	168	26
Yzerman, Steve	Detroit	80	65	90	155	61
Nicholls, Bernie	Los Angeles	79	70	80	150	96
Brown, Rob	Pittsburgh	68	49	66	115	118
Coffey, Paul	Pittsburgh	75	30	83	113	193
Mullen, Joe	Calgary	79	51	59	110	16
Kurri, Jari	Edmonton	76	44	58	102	69
Carson, Jimmy	Edmonton	80	49	51	100	36
Robitaille, Luc	Los Angeles	78	46	52	98	65

1989-90

CLARENCE CAMPBELL CONFERENCE

Norris Division

Team	GP	W	L	T	GF	GA	PTS
Chicago	80	41	33	6	316	294	88
St. Louis	80	37	34	9	295	279	83
Toronto	80	38	38	4	337	358	80
Minnesota	80	36	40	4	284	291	76
Detroit	80	28	38	14	288	323	70

Smythe Division

Team	GP	W	L	T	GF	GA	PTS
Calgary	80	42	23	15	348	265	99
*Edmonton	80	38	28	14	315	283	90
Winnipeg	80	37	32	11	298	290	85
Los Angeles	80	34	39	7	338	337	75
Vancouver	80	25	41	14	245	306	64

PRINCE OF WALES CONFERENCE

Adams Division

Team	GP	W	L	T	GF	GA	PTS
Boston	80	46	25	9	289	232	101
Buffalo	80	45	27	8	286	248	98
Montreal	80	41	28	11	288	234	93
Hartford	80	38	33	9	275	268	85
Quebec	80	12	61	7	240	407	31

Patrick Division

Team	GP	W	L	T	GF	GA	PTS
NY Rangers	80	36	31	13	279	267	85
New Jersey	80	37	34	9	295	288	83
Washington	80	36	38	6	284	275	78
NY Islanders	80	31	38	11	281	288	73
Pittsburgh	80	32	40	8	318	359	72
Philadelphia	80	30	39	11	290	297	71

Leading Scorers

Player	Club	GP	G	A	PTS	PIM
Gretzky, Wayne	Los Angeles	73	40	102	142	42
Messier, Mark	Edmonton	79	45	84	129	79
Yzerman, Steve	Detroit	79	62	65	127	79
Lemieux, Mario	Pittsburgh	59	45	78	123	78
Hull, Brett	St. Louis	80	72	41	113	24
Nicholls, Bernie	L.A., NYR	79	39	73	112	86
Turgeon, Pierre	Buffalo	80	40	66	106	29
LaFontaine, Pat	NY Islanders	74	54	51	105	38
Coffey, Paul	Pittsburgh	80	29	74	103	95
Sakic, Joe	Quebec	80	39	63	102	27
Oates, Adam	St. Louis	80	23	79	102	30

1990-91

CLARENCE CAMPBELL CONFERENCE

Norris Division

Team	GP	W	L	T	GF	GA	PTS
Chicago	80	49	23	8	284	211	106
St. Louis	80	47	22	11	310	250	105
Detroit	80	34	38	8	273	298	76
Minnesota	80	27	39	14	256	266	68
Toronto	80	23	46	11	241	318	57

Smythe Division

Team	GP	W	L	T	GF	GA	PTS
Los Angeles	80	46	24	10	340	254	102
Calgary	80	46	26	8	344	263	100
Edmonton	80	37	37	6	272	272	80
Vancouver	80	28	43	9	243	315	65
Winnipeg	80	26	43	11	260	288	63

PRINCE OF WALES CONFERENCE

Adams Division

Team	GP	W	L	T	GF	GA	PTS
Boston	80	44	24	12	299	264	100
Montreal	80	39	30	11	273	249	89
Buffalo	80	31	30	19	292	278	81
Hartford	80	31	38	11	238	276	73
Quebec	80	16	50	14	236	354	46

Patrick Division

Team	GP	W	L	T	GF	GA	PTS
*Pittsburgh	80	41	33	6	342	305	88
NY Rangers	80	36	31	13	297	265	85
Washington	80	37	36	7	258	258	81
New Jersey	80	32	33	15	272	264	79
Philadelphia	80	33	37	10	252	267	76
NY Islanders	80	25	45	10	223	290	60

Leading Scorers

Player	Club	GP	G	A	PTS	PIM
Gretzky, Wayne	Los Angeles	78	41	122	163	16
Hull, Brett	St. Louis	78	86	45	131	22
Oates, Adam	St. Louis	61	25	90	115	29
Recchi, Mark	Pittsburgh	78	40	73	113	48
Cullen, John	Pit., Hfd.	78	39	71	110	101
Sakic, Joe	Quebec	80	48	61	109	24
Yzerman, Steve	Detroit	80	51	57	108	34
Fleury, Theoren	Calgary	79	51	53	104	136
MacInnis, Al	Calgary	78	28	75	103	90
Larmer, Steve	Chicago	80	44	57	101	79

1991-92

CLARENCE CAMPBELL CONFERENCE

Norris Division

Team	GP	W	L	T	GF	GA	PTS
Detroit	80	43	25	12	320	256	98
Chicago	80	36	29	15	257	236	87
St. Louis	80	36	33	11	279	266	83
Minnesota	80	32	42	6	246	278	70
Toronto	80	30	43	7	234	294	67

Smythe Division

Team	GP	W	L	T	GF	GA	PTS
Vancouver	80	42	26	12	285	250	96
Los Angeles	80	35	31	14	287	296	84
Edmonton	80	36	34	10	295	297	82
Winnipeg	80	33	32	15	251	244	81
Calgary	80	31	37	12	296	305	74
San Jose	80	17	58	5	219	359	39

PRINCE OF WALES CONFERENCE

Adams Division

Team	GP	W	L	T	GF	GA	PTS
Montreal	80	41	28	11	267	207	93
Boston	80	36	32	12	270	275	84
Buffalo	80	31	37	12	289	299	74
Hartford	80	26	41	13	247	283	65
Quebec	80	20	48	12	255	318	52

Patrick Division

Team	GP	W	L	T	GF	GA	PTS
NY Rangers	80	50	25	5	321	246	105
Washington	80	45	27	8	330	275	98
*Pittsburgh	80	39	32	9	343	308	87
New Jersey	80	38	31	11	289	259	87
NY Islanders	80	34	35	11	291	299	79
Philadelphia	80	32	37	11	252	273	75

Leading Scorers

Player	Club	GP	G	A	PTS	PIM
Lemieux, Mario	Pittsburgh	64	44	87	131	94
Stevens, Kevin	Pittsburgh	80	54	69	123	254
Gretzky, Wayne	Los Angeles	74	31	90	121	34
Hull, Brett	St. Louis	73	70	39	109	48
Robitaille, Luc	Los Angeles	80	44	63	107	95
Messier, Mark	NY Rangers	79	35	72	107	76
Roenick, Jeremy	Chicago	80	53	50	103	23
Yzerman, Steve	Detroit	79	45	58	103	64
Leetch, Brian	NY Rangers	80	22	80	102	26
Oates, Adam	St. L., Bos.	80	20	79	99	22

1992-93

CLARENCE CAMPBELL CONFERENCE

Norris Division

Team	GP	W	L	T	GF	GA	PTS
Chicago	84	47	25	12	279	230	106
Detroit	84	47	28	9	369	280	103
Toronto	84	44	29	11	288	241	99
St. Louis	84	37	36	11	282	278	85
Minnesota	84	36	38	10	272	293	82
Tampa Bay	84	23	54	7	245	332	53

Smythe Division

Team	GP	W	L	T	GF	GA	PTS
Vancouver	84	46	29	9	346	278	101
Calgary	84	43	30	11	322	282	97
Los Angeles	84	39	35	10	338	340	88
Winnipeg	84	40	37	7	322	320	87
Edmonton	84	26	50	8	242	337	60
San Jose	84	11	71	2	218	414	24

PRINCE OF WALES CONFERENCE

Adams Division

Team	GP	W	L	T	GF	GA	PTS
Boston	84	51	26	7	332	268	109
Quebec	84	47	27	10	351	300	104
*Montreal	84	48	30	6	326	280	102
Buffalo	84	38	36	10	335	297	86
Hartford	84	26	52	6	284	369	58
Ottawa	84	10	70	4	202	395	24

Patrick Division

Team	GP	W	L	T	GF	GA	PTS
Pittsburgh	84	56	21	7	367	268	119
Washington	84	43	34	7	325	286	93
NY Islanders	84	40	37	7	335	297	87
New Jersey	84	40	37	7	308	299	87
Philadelphia	84	36	37	11	319	319	83
NY Rangers	84	34	39	11	304	308	79

Leading Scorers

Player	Club	GP	G	A	PTS	PIM
Lemieux, Mario	Pittsburgh	60	69	91	160	38
LaFontaine, Pat	Buffalo	84	53	95	148	63
Oates, Adam	Boston	84	45	97	142	32
Yzerman, Steve	Detroit	84	58	79	137	44
Selanne, Teemu	Winnipeg	84	76	56	132	45
Turgeon, Pierre	NY Islanders	83	58	74	132	26
Mogilny, Alexander	Buffalo	77	76	51	127	40
Gilmour, Doug	Toronto	83	32	95	127	100
Robitaille, Luc	Los Angeles	84	63	62	125	100
Recchi, Mark	Philadelphia	84	53	70	123	95

1993-94

EASTERN CONFERENCE

Northeast Division

Team	GP	W	L	T	GF	GA	PTS
Pittsburgh	84	44	27	13	299	285	101
Boston	84	42	29	13	289	252	97
Montreal	84	41	29	14	283	248	96
Buffalo	84	43	32	9	282	218	95
Quebec	84	34	42	8	277	292	76
Hartford	84	27	48	9	227	288	63
Ottawa	84	14	61	9	201	397	37

Atlantic Division

Team	GP	W	L	T	GF	GA	PTS
*NY Rangers	84	52	24	8	299	231	112
New Jersey	84	47	25	12	306	220	106
Washington	84	39	35	10	277	263	88
NY Islanders	84	36	36	12	282	264	84
Florida	84	33	34	17	233	233	83
Philadelphia	84	35	39	10	294	314	80
Tampa Bay	84	30	43	11	224	251	71

WESTERN CONFERENCE

Central Division

Team	GP	W	L	T	GF	GA	PTS
Detroit	84	46	30	8	356	275	100
Toronto	84	43	29	12	280	243	98
Dallas	84	42	29	13	286	265	97
St. Louis	84	40	33	11	270	283	91
Chicago	84	39	36	9	254	240	87
Winnipeg	84	24	51	9	245	344	57

Pacific Division

Team	GP	W	L	T	GF	GA	PTS
Calgary	84	42	29	13	302	256	97
Vancouver	84	41	40	3	279	276	85
San Jose	84	33	35	16	252	265	82
Anaheim	84	33	46	5	229	251	71
Los Angeles	84	27	45	12	294	322	66
Edmonton	84	25	45	14	261	305	64

Leading Scorers

Player	Club	GP	G	A	PTS	PIM
Gretzky, Wayne	Los Angeles	81	38	92	130	20
Fedorov, Sergei	Detroit	82	56	64	120	34
Oates, Adam	Boston	77	32	80	112	45
Gilmour, Doug	Toronto	83	27	84	111	105
Bure, Pavel	Vancouver	76	60	47	107	86
Roenick, Jeremy	Chicago	84	46	61	107	125
Recchi, Mark	Philadelphia	84	40	67	107	46
Shanahan, Brendan	St. Louis	81	52	50	102	211
Andreychuk, Dave	Toronto	83	53	46	99	98
Jagr, Jaromir	Pittsburgh	80	32	67	99	61

1994-95

EASTERN CONFERENCE

Northeast Division

Team	GP	W	L	T	GF	GA	PTS
Quebec	48	30	13	5	185	134	65
Pittsburgh	48	29	16	3	181	158	61
Boston	48	27	18	3	150	127	57
Buffalo	48	22	19	7	130	119	51
Hartford	48	19	24	5	127	141	43
Montreal	48	18	23	7	125	148	43
Ottawa	48	9	34	5	117	174	23

Atlantic Division

Team	GP	W	L	T	GF	GA	PTS
Philadelphia	48	28	16	4	150	132	60
*New Jersey	48	22	18	8	136	121	52
Washington	48	22	18	8	136	120	52
NY Rangers	48	22	23	3	139	134	47
Florida	48	20	22	6	115	127	46
Tampa Bay	48	17	28	3	120	144	37
NY Islanders	48	15	28	5	126	158	35

WESTERN CONFERENCE

Central Division

Team	GP	W	L	T	GF	GA	PTS
Detroit	48	33	11	4	180	117	70
St. Louis	48	28	15	5	178	135	61
Chicago	48	24	19	5	156	115	53
Toronto	48	21	19	8	135	146	50
Dallas	48	17	23	8	136	135	42
Winnipeg	48	16	25	7	157	177	39

Pacific Division

Team	GP	W	L	T	GF	GA	PTS
Calgary	48	24	17	7	163	135	55
Vancouver	48	18	18	12	153	148	48
San Jose	48	19	25	4	129	161	42
Los Angeles	48	16	23	9	142	174	41
Edmonton	48	17	27	4	136	183	38
Anaheim	48	16	27	5	125	164	37

Leading Scorers

Player	Club	GP	G	A	PTS	PIM
Jagr, Jaromir	Pittsburgh	48	32	38	70	37
Lindros, Eric	Philadelphia	46	29	41	70	60
Zhamnov, Alexei	Winnipeg	48	30	35	65	20
Sakic, Joe	Quebec	47	19	43	62	30
Francis, Ron	Pittsburgh	44	11	48	59	18
Fleury, Theoren	Calgary	47	29	29	58	112
Coffey, Paul	Detroit	45	14	44	58	72
Renberg, Mikael	Philadelphia	47	26	31	57	20
LeClair, John	Mtl., Phi.	46	26	28	54	30
Messier, Mark	NY Rangers	46	14	39	53	40
Oates, Adam	Boston	48	12	41	53	8

1995-96

EASTERN CONFERENCE

Northeast Division

Team	GP	W	L	T	GF	GA	PTS
Pittsburgh	82	49	29	4	362	284	102
Boston	82	40	31	11	282	269	91
Montreal	82	40	32	10	265	248	90
Hartford	82	34	39	9	237	259	77
Buffalo	82	33	42	7	247	262	73
Ottawa	82	18	59	5	191	291	41

Atlantic Division

Team	GP	W	L	T	GF	GA	PTS
Philadelphia	82	45	24	13	282	208	103
NY Rangers	82	41	27	14	272	237	96
Florida	82	41	31	10	254	234	92
Washington	82	39	32	11	234	204	89
Tampa Bay	82	38	32	12	238	248	88
New Jersey	82	37	33	12	215	202	86
NY Islanders	82	22	50	10	229	315	54

WESTERN CONFERENCE

Central Division

Team	GP	W	L	T	GF	GA	PTS
Detroit	82	62	13	7	325	181	131
Chicago	82	40	28	14	273	220	94
Toronto	82	34	36	12	247	252	80
St. Louis	82	32	34	16	219	248	80
Winnipeg	82	36	40	6	275	291	78
Dallas	82	26	42	14	227	280	66

Pacific Division

Team	GP	W	L	T	GF	GA	PTS
*Colorado	82	47	25	10	326	240	104
Calgary	82	34	37	11	241	240	79
Vancouver	82	32	35	15	278	278	79
Anaheim	82	35	39	8	234	247	78
Edmonton	82	30	44	8	240	304	68
Los Angeles	82	24	40	18	256	302	66
San Jose	82	20	55	7	252	357	47

Leading Scorers

Player	Club	GP	G	A	PTS	PIM
Lemieux, Mario	Pittsburgh	70	69	92	161	54
Jagr, Jaromir	Pittsburgh	82	62	87	149	96
Sakic, Joe	Colorado	82	51	69	120	44
Francis, Ron	Pittsburgh	77	27	92	119	56
Forsberg, Peter	Colorado	82	30	86	116	47
Lindros, Eric	Philadelphia	73	47	68	115	163
Kariya, Paul	Anaheim	82	50	58	108	20
Selanne, Teemu	Wpg., Ana.	79	40	68	108	22
Mogilny, Alexander	Vancouver	79	55	52	107	16
Fedorov, Sergei	Detroit	78	39	68	107	48

1996-97

EASTERN CONFERENCE

Northeast Division

Team	GP	W	L	T	GF	GA	PTS
Buffalo	82	40	30	12	237	208	92
Pittsburgh	82	38	36	8	285	280	84
Ottawa	82	31	36	15	226	234	77
Montreal	82	31	36	15	249	276	77
Hartford	82	32	39	11	226	256	75
Boston	82	26	47	9	234	300	61

Atlantic Division

Team	GP	W	L	T	GF	GA	PTS
New Jersey	82	45	23	14	231	182	104
Philadelphia	82	45	24	13	274	217	103
Florida	82	35	28	19	221	201	89
NY Rangers	82	38	34	10	258	231	86
Washington	82	33	40	9	214	231	75
Tampa Bay	82	32	40	10	217	247	74
NY Islanders	82	29	41	12	240	250	70

WESTERN CONFERENCE

Central Division

Team	GP	W	L	T	GF	GA	PTS
Dallas	82	48	26	8	252	198	104
*Detroit	82	38	26	18	253	197	94
Phoenix	82	38	37	7	240	243	83
St. Louis	82	36	35	11	236	239	83
Chicago	82	34	35	13	223	210	81
Toronto	82	30	44	8	230	273	68

Pacific Division

Team	GP	W	L	T	GF	GA	PTS
Colorado	82	49	24	9	277	205	107
Anaheim	82	36	33	13	245	233	85
Edmonton	82	36	37	9	252	247	81
Vancouver	82	35	40	7	257	273	77
Calgary	82	32	41	9	214	239	73
Los Angeles	82	28	43	11	214	268	67
San Jose	82	27	47	8	211	278	62

Leading Scorers

Player	Club	GP	G	A	PTS	PIM
Lemieux, Mario	Pittsburgh	76	50	72	122	65
Selanne, Teemu	Anaheim	78	51	58	109	34
Kariya, Paul	Anaheim	69	44	55	99	6
LeClair, John	Philadelphia	82	50	47	97	58
Gretzky, Wayne	NY Rangers	82	25	72	97	28
Jagr, Jaromir	Pittsburgh	63	47	48	95	40
Sundin, Mats	Toronto	82	41	53	94	59
Palffy, Zigmund	NY Islanders	80	48	42	90	43
Francis, Ron	Pittsburgh	81	27	63	90	20
Shanahan, Brendan	Hfd., Det.	81	47	41	88	131

1997-98

EASTERN CONFERENCE

Northeast Division

Team	GP	W	L	T	GF	GA	PTS
Pittsburgh	82	40	24	18	228	188	98
Boston	82	39	30	13	221	194	91
Buffalo	82	36	29	17	211	187	89
Montreal	82	37	32	13	235	208	87
Ottawa	82	34	33	15	193	200	83
Carolina	82	33	41	8	200	219	74

Atlantic Division

Team	GP	W	L	T	GF	GA	PTS
New Jersey	82	48	23	11	225	166	107
Philadelphia	82	42	29	11	242	193	95
Washington	82	40	30	12	219	202	92
NY Islanders	82	30	41	11	212	225	71
NY Rangers	82	25	39	18	197	231	68
Florida	82	24	43	15	203	256	63
Tampa Bay	82	17	55	10	151	269	44

WESTERN CONFERENCE

Central Division

Team	GP	W	L	T	GF	GA	PTS
Dallas	82	49	22	11	242	167	109
*Detroit	82	44	23	15	250	196	103
St. Louis	82	45	29	8	256	204	98
Phoenix	82	35	35	12	224	227	82
Chicago	82	30	39	13	192	199	73
Toronto	82	30	43	9	194	237	69

Pacific Division

Team	GP	W	L	T	GF	GA	PTS
Colorado	82	39	26	17	231	205	95
Los Angeles	82	38	33	11	227	225	87
Edmonton	82	35	37	10	215	224	80
San Jose	82	34	38	10	210	216	78
Calgary	82	26	41	15	217	252	67
Anaheim	82	26	43	13	205	261	65
Vancouver	82	25	43	14	224	273	64

Leading Scorers

Player	Club	GP	G	A	PTS	PIM
Jagr, Jaromir	Pittsburgh	77	35	67	102	64
Forsberg, Peter	Colorado	72	25	66	91	94
Bure, Pavel	Vancouver	82	51	39	90	48
Gretzky, Wayne	NY Rangers	82	23	67	90	28
LeClair, John	Philadelphia	82	51	36	87	32
Palffy, Zigmund	NY Islanders	82	45	42	87	34
Francis, Ron	Pittsburgh	81	25	62	87	20
Selanne, Teemu	Anaheim	73	52	34	86	30
Allison, Jason	Boston	81	33	50	83	60
Stumpel, Jozef	Los Angeles	77	21	58	79	53

Note: Detailed statistics for 1997-98 are listed in the Final Statistics, 1997-98 section of the **NHL Guide & Record Book.** **See page 121.**

"Lucky" Luc Robitaille, seen here testing Winnipeg's Stephane Beauregard, was the NHL's dominant left winger from 1987 to 1993, earning six consecutive All-Star berths and collecting a career-high 125 points in 1992-93.

Team Records

Regular Season

FINAL STANDINGS

MOST POINTS, ONE SEASON:
132 —Montreal Canadiens, 1976-77. 60W-8L-12T. 80GP
131 —Detroit Red Wings, 1995-96. 62W-13L-7T. 82GP
129 —Montreal Canadiens, 1977-78. 59W-10L-11T. 80GP

BEST WINNING PERCENTAGE, ONE SEASON:
.875 —Boston Bruins, 1929-30. 38W-5L-1T. 77PTS in 44GP
.830 —Montreal Canadiens, 1943-44. 38W-5L-7T. 83PTS in 50GP
.825 —Montreal Canadiens, 1976-77. 60W-8L-12T. 132PTS in 80GP
.806 —Montreal Canadiens, 1977-78. 59W-10L-11T. 129PTS in 80GP
.800 —Montreal Canadiens, 1944-45. 38W-8L-4T. 80PTS in 50GP

FEWEST POINTS, ONE SEASON:
8 —Quebec Bulldogs, 1919-20. 4W-20L-0T. 24GP
10 —Toronto Arenas, 1918-19. 5W-13L-0T. 18GP
12 —Hamilton Tigers, 1920-21. 6W-18L-0T. 24GP
—Hamilton Tigers, 1922-23. 6W-18L-0T. 24GP
—Boston Bruins, 1924-25. 6W-24L-0T. 30GP
—Philadelphia Quakers, 1930-31. 4W-36L-4T. 44GP

FEWEST POINTS, ONE SEASON (MINIMUM 70-GAME SCHEDULE):
21 —Washington Capitals, 1974-75. 8W-67L-5T. 80GP
24 —Ottawa Senators, 1992-93. 10W-70L-4T. 84GP
—San Jose Sharks, 1992-93. 11W-71L-2T. 84GP
30 —NY Islanders, 1972-73. 12W-60L-6T. 78GP

WORST WINNING PERCENTAGE, ONE SEASON:
.131 —Washington Capitals, 1974-75. 8W-67L-5T. 21PTS in 80GP
.136 —Philadelphia Quakers, 1930-31. 4W-36L-4T. 12PTS in 44GP
.143 —Ottawa Senators, 1992-93. 10W-70L-4T. 24PTS in 84GP
.143 —San Jose Sharks, 1992-93. 11W-71L-2T. 24PTS in 84GP
.148 —Pittsburgh Pirates, 1929-30. 5W-36L-3T. 13PTS in 44GP

TEAM WINS

Most Wins

MOST WINS, ONE SEASON:
62 —Detroit Red Wings, 1995-96. 82GP
60 —Montreal Canadiens, 1976-77. 80GP
59 —Montreal Canadiens, 1977-78. 80GP

MOST HOME WINS, ONE SEASON:
36 —Philadelphia Flyers, 1975-76. 40GP
—Detroit Red Wings, 1995-96. 41GP
33 —Boston Bruins, 1970-71. 39GP
—Boston Bruins, 1973-74. 39GP
—Montreal Canadiens, 1976-77. 40GP
—Philadelphia Flyers, 1976-77. 40GP
—NY Islanders, 1981-82. 40GP
—Philadelphia Flyers, 1985-86. 40GP

MOST ROAD WINS, ONE SEASON:
27 —Montreal Canadiens, 1976-77. 40GP
—Montreal Canadiens, 1977-78. 40GP
26 —Boston Bruins, 1971-72. 39GP
—Montreal Canadiens, 1975-76. 40GP
—Edmonton Oilers, 1983-84. 40GP
—Detroit Red Wings, 1995-96. 41GP

Fewest Wins

FEWEST WINS, ONE SEASON:
4 —Quebec Bulldogs, 1919-20. 24GP
—Philadelphia Quakers, 1930-31. 44GP
5 —Toronto Arenas, 1918-19. 18GP
—Pittsburgh Pirates, 1929-30. 44GP

FEWEST WINS, ONE SEASON (MINIMUM 70-GAME SCHEDULE):
8 —Washington Capitals, 1974-75. 80GP
9 —Winnipeg Jets, 1980-81. 80GP
10 —Ottawa Senators, 1992-93. 84GP

FEWEST HOME WINS, ONE SEASON:
2 —Chicago Blackhawks, 1927-28. 22GP
3 —Boston Bruins, 1924-25. 15GP
—Chicago Blackhawks, 1928-29. 22GP
—Philadelphia Quakers, 1930-31. 22GP

FEWEST HOME WINS, ONE SEASON (MINIMUM 70-GAME SCHEDULE):
6 —Chicago Blackhawks, 1954-55. 35GP
—Washington Capitals, 1975-76. 40GP
7 —Boston Bruins, 1962-63. 35GP
—Washington Capitals, 1974-75. 40GP
—Winnipeg Jets, 1980-81. 40GP
—Pittsburgh Penguins, 1983-84. 40GP

FEWEST ROAD WINS, ONE SEASON:
0 —Toronto Arenas, 1918-19. 9GP
—Quebec Bulldogs, 1919-20. 12GP
—Pittsburgh Pirates, 1929-30. 22GP
1 —Hamilton Tigers, 1921-22. 12GP
—Toronto St. Patricks, 1925-26. 18GP
—Philadelphia Quakers, 1930-31. 22GP
—NY Americans, 1940-41. 24GP
—Washington Capitals, 1974-75. 40GP
* —Ottawa Senators, 1992-93. 41GP

FEWEST ROAD WINS, ONE SEASON (MINIMUM 70-GAME SCHEDULE):
1 —Washington Capitals, 1974-75. 40GP
*** —Ottawa Senators,** 1992-93. 41GP
2 —Boston Bruins, 1960-61. 35GP
—Los Angeles Kings, 1969-70. 38GP
—NY Islanders, 1972-73. 39GP
—California Seals, 1973-74. 39GP
—Colorado Rockies, 1977-78. 40GP
—Winnipeg Jets, 1980-81. 40GP
—Quebec Nordiques, 1991-92. 40GP

TEAM LOSSES

Fewest Losses

FEWEST LOSSES, ONE SEASON:
5 —Ottawa Senators, 1919-20. 24GP
—Boston Bruins, 1929-30. 44GP
—Montreal Canadiens, 1943-44. 50GP

FEWEST HOME LOSSES, ONE SEASON:
0 —Ottawa Senators, 1922-23. 12GP
—Montreal Canadiens, 1943-44. 25GP
1 —Toronto Arenas, 1917-18. 11GP
—Ottawa Senators, 1918-19. 9GP
—Ottawa Senators, 1919-20. 12GP
—Toronto St. Patricks, 1922-23. 12GP
—Boston Bruins, 1929-30. 22GP
—Boston Bruins, 1930-31. 22GP
—Montreal Canadiens, 1976-77. 40GP
—Quebec Nordiques, 1994-95. 24GP

FEWEST ROAD LOSSES, ONE SEASON:
3 —Montreal Canadiens, 1928-29. 22GP
4 —Ottawa Senators, 1919-20. 12GP
—Montreal Canadiens, 1927-28. 22GP
—Boston Bruins, 1929-30. 20GP
—Boston Bruins, 1940-41. 24GP

FEWEST LOSSES, ONE SEASON (MINIMUM 70-GAME SCHEDULE):
8 —Montreal Canadiens, 1976-77. 80GP
10 —Montreal Canadiens, 1972-73. 78GP
—Montreal Canadiens, 1977-78. 80GP
11 —Montreal Canadiens, 1975-76. 80GP

FEWEST HOME LOSSES, ONE SEASON (MINIMUM 70-GAME SCHEDULE):
1 —Montreal Canadiens, 1976-77. 40GP
2 —Montreal Canadiens, 1961-62. 35GP
—NY Rangers, 1970-71. 39GP
—Philadelphia Flyers, 1975-76. 40GP

FEWEST ROAD LOSSES, ONE SEASON (MINIMUM 70-GAME SCHEDULE):
6 —Montreal Canadiens, 1972-73. 39GP
—Montreal Canadiens, 1974-75. 40GP
—Montreal Canadiens, 1977-78. 40GP
7 —Detroit Red Wings, 1951-52. 35GP
—Montreal Canadiens, 1976-77. 40GP
—Philadelphia Flyers, 1979-80. 40GP

Most Losses

MOST LOSSES, ONE SEASON:
71 —San Jose Sharks, 1992-93. 84GP
70 —Ottawa Senators, 1992-93. 84GP
67 —Washington Capitals, 1974-75. 80GP
61 —Quebec Nordiques, 1989-90. 80GP
—Ottawa Senators, 1993-94. 84GP

MOST HOME LOSSES, ONE SEASON:
***32 —San Jose Sharks,** 1992-93. 41GP
29 —Pittsburgh Penguins, 1983-84. 40GP
* —Ottawa Senators, 1993-94. 41GP

MOST ROAD LOSSES, ONE SEASON:
***40 —Ottawa Senators,** 1992-93. 41GP
39 —Washington Capitals, 1974-75. 40GP
37 —California Seals, 1973-74. 39GP
* —San Jose Sharks, 1992-93. 41GP

* – Does not include neutral site games.

TEAM TIES

Most Ties

MOST TIES, ONE SEASON:
24 —Philadelphia Flyers, 1969-70. 76GP
23 —Montreal Canadiens, 1962-63. 70GP
—Chicago Blackhawks, 1973-74. 78GP

MOST HOME TIES, ONE SEASON:
13 —NY Rangers, 1954-55. 35GP
—Philadelphia Flyers, 1969-70. 38GP
—California Seals, 1971-72. 39GP
—California Seals, 1972-73. 39GP
—Chicago Blackhawks, 1973-74. 39GP

MOST ROAD TIES, ONE SEASON:
15 —Philadelphia Flyers, 1976-77. 40GP
14 —Montreal Canadiens, 1952-53. 35GP
—Montreal Canadiens, 1974-75. 40GP
—Philadelphia Flyers, 1975-76. 40GP

Fewest Ties

FEWEST TIES, ONE SEASON (Since 1926-27):
1 —Boston Bruins, 1929-30. 44GP
2 —NY Americans, 1926-27. 44GP
—Montreal Canadiens, 1926-27. 44GP
—Boston Bruins, 1938-39. 48GP
—NY Rangers, 1941-42. 48GP
—San Jose Sharks, 1992-93. 84GP

FEWEST TIES, ONE SEASON (MINIMUM 70-GAME SCHEDULE):
2 —San Jose Sharks, 1992-93. 84GP
3 —New Jersey Devils, 1985-86. 80GP
—Calgary Flames, 1986-87. 80GP
—Vancouver Canucks, 1993-94. 84GP

WINNING STREAKS

LONGEST WINNING STREAK, ONE SEASON:
17 Games —Pittsburgh Penguins, Mar. 9 - Apr. 10, 1993.
15 Games —NY Islanders, Jan. 21 - Feb. 20, 1982.
14 Games —Boston Bruins, Dec. 3, 1929 - Jan. 9, 1930.

LONGEST HOME WINNING STREAK, ONE SEASON:
20 Games —Boston Bruins, Dec. 3, 1929 - Mar. 18, 1930.
—Philadelphia Flyers, Jan. 4 - Apr. 3, 1976.

LONGEST ROAD WINNING STREAK, ONE SEASON:
10 Games —Buffalo Sabres, Dec. 10, 1983 - Jan. 23, 1984.
8 Games —Boston Bruins, Feb. 17 - Mar. 8, 1972.
—Los Angeles Kings, Dec. 18, 1974 - Jan. 16, 1975.
—Montreal Canadiens, Dec. 18, 1977 - Jan. 18, 1978.
—NY Islanders, Feb. 27 - Mar. 29, 1981.
—Montreal Canadiens, Jan. 21 - Feb. 21, 1982.
—Philadelphia Flyers, Dec. 22, 1982 - Jan. 16, 1983.
—Winnipeg Jets, Feb. 25 - Apr. 6, 1985.
—Edmonton Oilers, Dec. 9, 1986 - Jan. 17, 1987.
—Boston Bruins, Mar. 15 - Apr. 14, 1993.

LONGEST WINNING STREAK FROM START OF SEASON:
10 Games —Toronto Maple Leafs, 1993-94.
8 Games —Toronto Maple Leafs, 1934-35.
—Buffalo Sabres, 1975-76.
7 Games —Edmonton Oilers, 1983-84.
—Quebec Nordiques, 1985-86.
—Pittsburgh Penguins, 1986-87.
—Pittsburgh Penguins, 1994-95.

LONGEST HOME WINNING STREAK FROM START OF SEASON:
11 Games —Chicago Blackhawks, 1963-64.
10 Games —Ottawa Senators, 1925-26.
9 Games —Montreal Canadiens, 1953-54.
—Chicago Blackhawks, 1971-72.

LONGEST ROAD WINNING STREAK FROM START OF SEASON:
7 Games —Toronto Maple Leafs, Nov. 14 - Dec. 15, 1940.

LONGEST WINNING STREAK, INCLUDING PLAYOFFS:
15 Games —Detroit Red Wings, Feb. 27 - Apr. 5, 1955. Nine regular-season games, six playoff games.

LONGEST HOME WINNING STREAK, INCLUDING PLAYOFFS:
24 Games —Philadelphia Flyers, Jan. 4 - Apr. 25, 1976. Twenty regular-season games, four playoff games.

LONGEST ROAD WINNING STREAK, INCLUDING PLAYOFFS:
8 Games —NY Islanders, Apr. 4 - May 1, 1980. One regular season game, seven playoff games.

UNDEFEATED STREAKS

LONGEST UNDEFEATED STREAK, ONE SEASON:
35 Games —Philadelphia Flyers, Oct. 14, 1979 - Jan. 6, 1980. 25W-10T.
28 Games —Montreal Canadiens, Dec. 18, 1977 - Feb. 23, 1978. 23W-5T.
23 Games —Boston Bruins, Dec. 22, 1940 - Feb. 23, 1941. 15W-8T.
—Philadelphia Flyers, Jan. 29 - Mar. 18, 1976. 17W-6T.

LONGEST HOME UNDEFEATED STREAK, ONE SEASON:
34 Games —Montreal Canadiens, Nov. 1, 1976 - Apr. 2, 1977. 28W-6T.
27 Games —Boston Bruins, Nov. 22, 1970 - Mar. 20, 1971. 26W-1T.

LONGEST ROAD UNDEFEATED STREAK, ONE SEASON:
23 Games —Montreal Canadiens, Nov. 27, 1974 - Mar. 12, 1975. 14W-9T.
17 Games —Montreal Canadiens, Dec. 18, 1977 - Mar. 1, 1978. 14W-3T.
16 Games —Philadelphia Flyers, Oct. 20, 1979 - Jan. 6, 1980. 11W-5T.

LONGEST UNDEFEATED STREAK FROM START OF SEASON:
15 Games —Edmonton Oilers, 1984-85. 12W-3T.
14 Games —Montreal Canadiens, 1943-44. 11W-3T.
13 Games —Montreal Canadiens, 1972-73. 9W-4T.
—Pittsburgh Penguins, 1994-95. 12W-1T.

LONGEST HOME UNDEFEATED STREAK FROM START OF SEASON:
25 Games —Montreal Canadiens, Oct. 30, 1943 - Mar. 18, 1944. 22W-3T.

LONGEST ROAD UNDEFEATED STREAK FROM START OF SEASON:
15 Games —Detroit Red Wings, Oct. 18 - Dec. 20, 1951. 10W-5T.

LONGEST UNDEFEATED STREAK, INCLUDING PLAYOFFS:
21 Games —Pittsburgh Penguins, Mar. 9 - Apr. 22, 1993. 17W-1T in regular season and 3W in playoffs.

LONGEST HOME UNDEFEATED STREAK, INCLUDING PLAYOFFS:
38 Games —Montreal Canadiens, Nov. 1, 1976 - Apr. 26, 1977. 28W-6T in regular season and 4W in playoff.

LONGEST ROAD UNDEFEATED STREAK, INCLUDING PLAYOFFS:
13 Games —Montreal Canadiens, Feb. 26 - Apr. 20, 1980. 6W-4T in regular season and 3W in playoffs.
—NY Islanders, Mar. 16 - May 1, 1980. 3W-3T in regular season and 7W in playoffs.

LOSING STREAKS

LONGEST LOSING STREAK, ONE SEASON:
17 Games —Washington Capitals, Feb. 18 - Mar. 26, 1975.
—San Jose Sharks, Jan. 4 - Feb. 12, 1993.
15 Games —Philadelphia Quakers, Nov. 29, 1930 - Jan. 8, 1931.

LONGEST HOME LOSING STREAK, ONE SEASON:
11 Games —Boston Bruins, Dec. 8, 1924 - Feb. 17, 1925.
—Washington Capitals, Feb. 18 - Mar. 30, 1975.
—Ottawa Senators, Oct. 27 - Dec. 8, 1993.

LONGEST ROAD LOSING STREAK, ONE SEASON:
***38 Games —Ottawa Senators,** Oct. 10, 1992 - Apr. 3, 1993.
37 Games —Washington Capitals, Oct. 9, 1974 - Mar. 26, 1975.

LONGEST LOSING STREAK FROM START OF SEASON:
11 Games —NY Rangers, 1943-44.
7 Games —Montreal Canadiens, 1938-39.
—Chicago Blackhawks, 1947-48.
—Washington Capitals, 1983-84.
—Chicago Blackhawks, 1997-88.

LONGEST HOME LOSING STREAK FROM START OF SEASON:
8 Games —Los Angeles Kings, Oct. 13 - Nov. 6, 1971.

LONGEST ROAD LOSING STREAK FROM START OF SEASON:
***38 Games —Ottawa Senators,** Oct. 10, 1992 - Apr. 3, 1993.

WINLESS STREAKS

LONGEST WINLESS STREAK, ONE SEASON:
30 Games —Winnipeg Jets, Oct. 19 - Dec. 20, 1980. 23L-7T.
27 Games —Kansas City Scouts, Feb. 12 - Apr. 4, 1976. 21L-6T.
25 Games —Washington Capitals, Nov. 29, 1975 - Jan. 21, 1976. 22L-3T.

LONGEST HOME WINLESS STREAK, ONE SEASON:
17 Games —Ottawa Senators, Oct. 28, 1995 - Jan. 27, 1996. 15L-2T.
15 Games —Chicago Blackhawks, Dec. 16, 1928 - Feb. 28, 1929. 11L-4T.
—Montreal Canadiens, Dec. 16, 1939 - Mar. 7, 1940. 12L-3T.

LONGEST ROAD WINLESS STREAK, ONE SEASON:
***38 Games —Ottawa Senators,** Oct. 10, 1992 - Apr. 3, 1993. 38L-0T.
37 Games —Washington Capitals, Oct. 9, 1974 - Mar. 26, 1975. 37L-0T.

LONGEST WINLESS STREAK FROM START OF SEASON:
15 Games —NY Rangers, 1943-44. 14L-1T.
11 Games —Pittsburgh Pirates, 1927-28. 8L-3T.
—Minnesota North Stars, 1973-74. 5L-6T.
—San Jose Sharks, 1995-96. 7L-4T.

LONGEST HOME WINLESS STREAK FROM START OF SEASON:
11 Games —Pittsburgh Penguins, Oct. 8 - Nov. 19, 1983. 9L-2T.

LONGEST ROAD WINLESS STREAK FROM START OF SEASON:
***38 Games —Ottawa Senators,** Oct. 10, 1992 - Apr. 3, 1993. 38L-0T.

* – Does not include neutral site games.

NON-SHUTOUT STREAKS

LONGEST NON-SHUTOUT STREAK:
264 Games — Calgary Flames, Nov. 12, 1981 - Jan. 9, 1985.
262 Games — Los Angeles Kings, Mar. 15, 1986 - Oct. 25, 1989.
244 Games — Washington Capitals, Oct. 31, 1989 - Nov. 11, 1993.
230 Games — Quebec Nordiques, Feb. 10, 1980 - Jan. 13, 1983.
229 Games — Edmonton Oilers, Mar. 15, 1981 - Feb. 11, 1984.

LONGEST NON-SHUTOUT STREAK INCLUDING PLAYOFFS:
264 Games — Los Angeles Kings, Mar. 15, 1986 - Apr. 6, 1989. (5 playoff games in 1987; 5 in 1988; 2 in 1989).
262 Games — Chicago Blackhawks, Mar. 14, 1970 - Feb. 21, 1973. (8 playoff games in 1970; 18 in 1971; 8 in 1972).
251 Games — Quebec Nordiques, Feb. 10, 1980 - Jan. 13, 1983. (5 playoff games in 1981; 16 in 1982).
245 Games — Pittsburgh Penguins, Jan. 7, 1989 - Oct. 26, 1991. (11 playoff games in 1989; 23 in 1991).

TEAM GOALS

Most Goals

MOST GOALS, ONE SEASON:
446 — Edmonton Oilers, 1983-84. 80GP
426 — Edmonton Oilers, 1985-86. 80GP
424 — Edmonton Oilers, 1982-83. 80GP
417 — Edmonton Oilers, 1981-82. 80GP
401 — Edmonton Oilers, 1984-85. 80GP

MOST GOALS, ONE TEAM, ONE GAME:
16 — Montreal Canadiens, Mar. 3, 1920, at Quebec. Defeated Que. Bulldogs 16-3.

MOST GOALS, BOTH TEAMS, ONE GAME:
21 — Montreal Canadiens, Toronto St. Patricks, at Montreal, Jan. 10, 1920. Montreal won 14-7.
— Edmonton Oilers, Chicago Blackhawks, at Chicago, Dec. 11, 1985. Edmonton won 12-9.
20 — Edmonton Oilers, Minnesota North Stars, at Edmonton, Jan. 4, 1984. Edmonton won 12-8.
— Toronto Maple Leafs, Edmonton Oilers, at Toronto, Jan. 8, 1986. Toronto won 11-9.
19 — Montreal Wanderers, Toronto Arenas, at Montreal, Dec. 19, 1917. Montreal won 10-9.
— Montreal Canadiens, Quebec Bulldogs, at Quebec, Mar. 3, 1920. Montreal won 16-3.
— Montreal Canadiens, Hamilton Tigers, at Montreal, Feb. 26, 1921. Montreal won 13-6.
— Boston Bruins, NY Rangers, at Boston, Mar. 4, 1944. Boston won 10-9.
— Boston Bruins, Detroit Red Wings, at Detroit, Mar. 16, 1944. Detroit won 10-9.
— Vancouver Canucks, Minnesota North Stars, at Vancouver, Oct. 7, 1983. Vancouver won 10-9.

MOST GOALS, ONE TEAM, ONE PERIOD:
9 — Buffalo Sabres, Mar. 19, 1981, at Buffalo, second period during 14-4 win over Toronto.
8 — Detroit Red Wings, Jan. 23, 1944, at Detroit, third period during 15-0 win over NY Rangers.
— Boston Bruins, Mar. 16, 1969, at Boston, second period during 11-3 win over Toronto.
— NY Rangers, Nov. 21, 1971, at New York, third period during 12-1 win over California.
— Philadelphia Flyers, Mar. 31, 1973, at Philadelphia, second period during 10-2 win over NY Islanders.
— Buffalo Sabres, Dec. 21, 1975, at Buffalo, third period during 14-2 win over Washington.
— Minnesota North Stars, Nov. 11, 1981, at Minnesota, second period during 15-2 win over Winnipeg.
— Pittsburgh Penguins, Dec. 17, 1991, at Pittsburgh, second period during 10-2 win over San Jose.

MOST GOALS, BOTH TEAMS, ONE PERIOD:
12 — Buffalo Sabres, Toronto Maple Leafs, at Buffalo, March 19, 1981, second period. Buffalo scored 9 goals, Toronto 3. Buffalo won 14-4.
— Edmonton Oilers, Chicago Blackhawks, at Chicago, Dec. 11, 1985, second period. Edmonton scored 6 goals, Chicago 6. Edmonton won 12-9.
10 — NY Rangers, NY Americans, at NY Americans, March 16, 1939, third period. NY Rangers scored 7 goals, NY Americans 3. NY Rangers won 11-5.
— Toronto Maple Leafs, Detroit Red Wings, at Detroit, March 17, 1946, third period. Toronto scored 6 goals, Detroit 4. Toronto won 11-7.
— Vancouver Canucks, Buffalo Sabres, at Buffalo, Jan. 8, 1976, third period. Buffalo scored 6 goals, Vancouver 4. Buffalo won 8-5.
— Buffalo Sabres, Montreal Canadiens, at Montreal, Oct. 26, 1982, first period. Montreal scored 5 goals, Buffalo 5. 7-7 tie.
— Boston Bruins, Quebec Nordiques, at Quebec, Dec. 7, 1982, second period. Quebec scored 6 goals, Boston 4. Quebec won 10-5.
— Calgary Flames, Vancouver Canucks, at Vancouver, Jan. 16, 1987, first period. Vancouver scored 6 goals, Calgary 4. Vancouver won 9-5.
— Winnipeg Jets, Detroit Red Wings, at Detroit, Nov. 25, 1987, third period. Detroit scored 7 goals, Winnipeg 3. Detroit won 10-8.
— Chicago Blackhawks, St. Louis Blues, at St. Louis, March 15, 1988, third period. Chicago scored 5 goals, St. Louis 5. 7-7 tie.

MOST CONSECUTIVE GOALS, ONE TEAM, ONE GAME:
15 — Detroit Red Wings, Jan. 23, 1944, at Detroit. Defeated NY Rangers 15-0.

Fewest Goals

FEWEST GOALS, ONE SEASON:
33 — Chicago Blackhawks, 1928-29. 44GP
45 — Montreal Maroons, 1924-25. 30GP
46 — Pittsburgh Pirates, 1928-29. 44GP

FEWEST GOALS, ONE SEASON (MINIMUM 70-GAME SCHEDULE):
133 — Chicago Blackhawks, 1953-54. 70GP
147 — Toronto Maple Leafs, 1954-55. 70GP
— Boston Bruins, 1955-56. 70GP
150 — NY Rangers, 1954-55. 70GP

TEAM POWER-PLAY GOALS

MOST POWER-PLAY GOALS, ONE SEASON:
119 — Pittsburgh Penguins, 1988-89. 80GP
113 — Detroit Red Wings, 1992-93. 84GP
111 — NY Rangers, 1987-88. 80GP
110 — Pittsburgh Penguins, 1987-88. 80GP
— Winnipeg Jets, 1987-88, 80GP

TEAM SHORTHAND GOALS

MOST SHORTHAND GOALS, ONE SEASON:
36 — Edmonton Oilers, 1983-84. 80GP
28 — Edmonton Oilers, 1986-87. 80GP
27 — Edmonton Oilers, 1985-86. 80GP
— Edmonton Oilers, 1988-89. 80GP

TEAM GOALS-PER-GAME

HIGHEST GOALS-PER-GAME AVERAGE, ONE SEASON:
5.58 — Edmonton Oilers, 1983-84. 446G in 80GP
5.38 — Montreal Canadiens, 1919-20. 129G in 24GP
5.33 — Edmonton Oilers, 1985-86. 426G in 80GP
5.30 — Edmonton Oilers, 1982-83. 424G in 80GP
5.23 — Montreal Canadiens, 1917-18. 115G in 22GP

LOWEST GOALS-PER-GAME AVERAGE, ONE SEASON:
.75 — Chicago Blackhawks, 1928-29, 33G in 44GP
1.05 — Pittsburgh Pirates, 1928-29. 46G in 44GP
1.20 — NY Americans, 1928-29. 53G in 44GP

TEAM ASSISTS

MOST ASSISTS, ONE SEASON:
737 — Edmonton Oilers, 1985-86. 80GP
736 — Edmonton Oilers, 1983-84. 80GP
706 — Edmonton Oilers, 1981-82. 80GP

FEWEST ASSISTS, ONE SEASON:
45 — NY Rangers, 1926-27. 44GP

FEWEST ASSISTS, ONE SEASON (MINIMUM 70-GAME SCHEDULE):
206 — Chicago Blackhawks, 1953-54. 70GP

TEAM TOTAL POINTS

MOST SCORING POINTS, ONE SEASON:
1,182 — Edmonton Oilers, 1983-84. 80GP
1,163 — Edmonton Oilers, 1985-86. 80GP
1,123 — Edmonton Oilers, 1981-82. 80GP

MOST SCORING POINTS, ONE TEAM, ONE GAME:
40 — Buffalo Sabres, Dec. 21, 1975, at Buffalo. Buffalo defeated Washington 14-2, receiving 26A.
39 — Minnesota North Stars, Nov. 11, 1981, at Minnesota. Minnesota defeated Winnipeg 15-2, receiving 24A.
37 — Detroit Red Wings, Jan. 23, 1944, at Detroit. Detroit defeated NY Rangers 15-0, receiving 22A.
— Toronto Maple Leafs, Mar. 16, 1957, at Toronto. Toronto defeated NY Rangers 14-1, receiving 23A.
— Buffalo Sabres, Feb. 25, 1978, at Cleveland. Buffalo defeated Cleveland 13-3, receiving 24A.
— Calgary Flames, Feb. 10, 1993, at Calgary. Calgary defeated San Jose 13-1, receiving 24A.

MOST SCORING POINTS, BOTH TEAMS, ONE GAME:
62 — Edmonton Oilers, Chicago Blackhawks, at Chicago, Dec. 11, 1985. Edmonton won 12-9. Edmonton had 24A, Chicago, 17.
53 — Quebec Nordiques, Washington Capitals, at Washington, Feb. 22, 1981. Quebec won 11-7. Quebec had 22A, Washington, 13.
— Edmonton Oilers, Minnesota North Stars, at Edmonton, Jan. 4, 1984. Edmonton won 12-8. Edmonton had 20A, Minnesota 13.
— Minnesota North Stars, St. Louis Blues, at St. Louis, Jan. 27, 1984. Minnesota won 10-8. Minnesota had 19A, St. Louis 16.
— Toronto Maple Leafs, Edmonton Oilers, at Toronto, Jan. 8, 1986. Toronto won 11-9. Toronto had 17A, Edmonton 16.
52 — Mtl. Maroons, NY Americans, at New York, Feb. 18, 1936. 8-8 tie. New York had 20A, Montreal 16. (3A allowed for each goal.)
— Vancouver Canucks, Minnesota North Stars, at Vancouver, Oct. 7, 1983. Vancouver won 10-9. Vancouver had 16A, Minnesota 17.

MOST SCORING POINTS, ONE TEAM, ONE PERIOD:
23 —NY Rangers, Nov. 21, 1971, at New York, third period during 12-1 win over California. NY Rangers scored 8G and 15A.
—Buffalo Sabres, Dec. 21, 1975, at Buffalo, third period during 14-2 win over Washington. Buffalo scored 8G and 15A.
—Buffalo Sabres, March 19, 1981, at Buffalo, second period, during 14-4 win over Toronto. Buffalo scored 9G and 14A.
22 —Detroit Red Wings, Jan. 23, 1944, at Detroit, third period during 15-0 win over NY Rangers. Detroit scored 8G and 14A.
—Boston Bruins, March 16, 1969, at Boston, second period during 11-3 win over Toronto Maple Leafs. Boston scored 8G and 14A.
—Minnesota North Stars, Nov. 11, 1981, at Minnesota, second period during 15-2 win over Winnipeg. Minnesota scored 8G and 14A.
—Pittsburgh Penguins, Dec. 17, 1991, at Pittsburgh, second period during 10-2 win over San Jose. Pittsburgh scored 8G and 14A.

MOST SCORING POINTS, BOTH TEAMS, ONE PERIOD:
35 —Edmonton, Oilers, Chicago Blackhawks, at Chicago, Dec. 11, 1985, second period. Edmonton had 6G, 12A; Chicago, 6G, 11A. Edmonton won 12-9.
31 —Buffalo Sabres, Toronto Maple Leafs, at Buffalo, March 19, 1981, second period. Buffalo had 9G, 14A; Toronto, 3G, 5A. Buffalo won 14-4.
29 —Winnipeg Jets, Detroit Red Wings, at Detroit, Nov. 25, 1987, third period. Detroit had 7G, 13A; Winnipeg had 3G, 6A. Detroit won 10-8.
—Chicago Blackhawks, St. Louis Blues, at St. Louis, March 15, 1988, third period. St. Louis had 5G, 10A; Chicago had 5G, 9A. 7-7 tie.

FASTEST GOALS

FASTEST SIX GOALS, BOTH TEAMS
3 Minutes, 15 Seconds — Montreal Canadiens, Toronto Maple Leafs, at Montreal, Jan. 4, 1944, first period. Montreal scored 4G, Toronto 2. Montreal won 6-3.

FASTEST FIVE GOALS, BOTH TEAMS:
1 Minute, 24 Seconds — Chicago Blackhawks, Toronto Maple Leafs, at Toronto, Oct. 15, 1983, second period. Scorers: Gaston Gingras, Toronto, 16:49; Denis Savard, Chicago, 17:12; Steve Larmer, Chicago, 17:27; Savard, 17:42; John Anderson, Toronto, 18:13. Toronto won 10-8.
1 Minute, 39 Seconds — Detroit Red Wings, Toronto Maple Leafs, at Toronto, Nov. 15, 1944, third period. Scorers: Ted Kennedy, Toronto, 10:36 and 10:55; Hal Jackson, Detroit, 11:48; Steve Wochy, Detroit, 12:02; Don Grosso, Detroit, 12:15. Detroit won 8-4.

FASTEST FIVE GOALS, ONE TEAM:
2 Minutes, 7 Seconds — Pittsburgh Penguins, at Pittsburgh, Nov. 22, 1972, third period. Scorers: Bryan Hextall, 12:00; Jean Pronovost, 12:18; Al McDonough, 13:40; Ken Schinkel, 13:49; Ron Schock, 14:07. Pittsburgh defeated St. Louis 10-4.
2 Minutes, 37 Seconds — NY Islanders, at New York, Jan. 26, 1982, first period. Scorers: Duane Sutter, 1:31; John Tonelli, 2:30; Bryan Trottier, 2:46; Bryan Trottier, 3:31; Duane Sutter, 4:08. NY Islanders defeated Pittsburgh 9-2.
2 Minutes, 55 Seconds — Boston Bruins, at Boston, Dec. 19, 1974. Scorers: Bobby Schmautz, 19:13 (first period); Ken Hodge, 0:18; Phil Esposito, 0:43; Don Marcotte, 0:58; John Bucyk, 2:08 (second period). Boston defeated NY Rangers 11-3.

FASTEST FOUR GOALS, BOTH TEAMS:
53 Seconds — Chicago Blackhawks, Toronto Maple Leafs, at Toronto, Oct. 15, 1983, second period. Scorers: Gaston Gingras, Toronto, 16:49; Denis Savard, Chicago, 17:12; Steve Larmer, Chicago, 17:27; and Savard, 17:42. Toronto won 10-8.
57 Seconds — Quebec Nordiques, Detroit Red Wings, at Quebec, Jan. 27, 1990, first period. Scorers: Paul Gillis, Quebec, 18:01; Claude Loiselle, Quebec, 18:12; Joe Sakic, Quebec, 18:27; and Jimmy Carson, Detroit, 18:58. Detroit won 8-6.
1 Minute, 1 Second — Colorado Rockies, NY Rangers, at New York, Jan. 15, 1980, first period. Scorers: Doug Sulliman, NY Rangers, 7:52; Ed Johnstone, NY Rangers, 7:57; Warren Miller, NY Rangers, 8:20; Rob Ramage, Colorado, 8:53. 6-6 tie.
— Chicago Blackhawks, Toronto Maple Leafs, at Toronto, Oct. 15, 1983, second period. Scorers: Denis Savard, Chicago, 17:12; Steve Larmer, Chicago, 17:27; Savard, 17:42; John Anderson, Toronto, 18:13. Toronto won 10-8.

FASTEST FOUR GOALS, ONE TEAM:
1 Minute, 20 Seconds — Boston Bruins, at Boston, Jan. 21, 1945, second period. Scorers: Bill Thoms, 6:34; Frank Mario, 7:08 and 7:27; and Ken Smith, 7:54. Boston defeated NY Rangers 14-3.

FASTEST THREE GOALS, BOTH TEAMS:
15 Seconds — Minnesota North Stars, NY Rangers, at Minnesota, Feb. 10, 1983, second period. Scorers: Mark Pavelich, NY Rangers, 19:18; Ron Greschner, NY Rangers, 19:27; Willi Plett, Minnesota, 19:33. Minnesota won 7-5.
18 Seconds — Montreal Canadiens, NY Rangers, at Montreal, Dec. 12, 1963, first period. Scorers: Dave Balon, Montreal, 0:58; Gilles Tremblay, Montreal, 1:04; Camille Henry, NY Rangers, 1:16. Montreal won 6-4.
— California Golden Seals, Buffalo Sabres, at California, Feb. 1, 1976, third period. Scorers: Jim Moxey, California, 19:38; Wayne Merrick, California, 19:45; Danny Gare, Buffalo, 19:56. Buffalo won 9-5.

FASTEST THREE GOALS, ONE TEAM:
20 Seconds — Boston Bruins, at Boston, Feb. 25, 1971, third period. Scorers: John Bucyk, 4:50; Ed Westfall, 5:02; Ted Green, 5:10. Boston defeated Vancouver 8-3.
21 Seconds — Chicago Blackhawks, at New York, Mar. 23, 1952, third period. Bill Mosienko scored all three goals, at 6:09, 6:20 and 6:30. Chicago defeated NY Rangers 7-6.
— Washington Capitals, at Washington, Nov. 23, 1990, first period. Scorers: Michal Pivonka, 16:18; Stephen Leach, 16:29 and 16:39. Washington defeated Pittsburgh 7-3.

FASTEST THREE GOALS FROM START OF PERIOD, BOTH TEAMS:
1 Minute, 5 Seconds — Hartford Whalers, Montreal Canadiens, at Montreal, March 11, 1989, second period. Scorers: Kevin Dineen, Hartford, 0:11; Guy Carbonneau, Montreal, 0:36; Petr Svoboda, Montreal, 1:05. Montreal won 5-3.

FASTEST THREE GOALS FROM START OF PERIOD, ONE TEAM:
53 Seconds — Calgary Flames, at Calgary, Feb. 10, 1993, third period. Scorers: Gary Suter, 0:17; Chris Lindbergh, 0:40; Ron Stern, 0:53. Calgary defeated San Jose 13-1.

FASTEST TWO GOALS, BOTH TEAMS:
2 Seconds — St. Louis Blues, Boston Bruins, at Boston, Dec. 19, 1987, third period. Scorers: Ken Linseman, Boston, 19:50; Doug Gilmour, St. Louis, 19:52. St. Louis won 7-5.
3 Seconds — Chicago Blackhawks, Minnesota North Stars, at Minnesota, Nov. 5, 1988, third period. Scorers: Steve Thomas, Chicago, 6:03; Dave Gagner, Minnesota, 6:06. 5-5 tie.

FASTEST TWO GOALS, ONE TEAM:
4 Seconds — Montreal Maroons, at Montreal, Jan. 3, 1931, third period. Nels Stewart scored both goals, at 8:24 and 8:28. Mtl. Maroons defeated Boston 5-3.
— Buffalo Sabres, at Buffalo, Oct. 17, 1974, third period. Scorers: Lee Fogolin, 14:55; Don Luce, 14:59. Buffalo defeated California 6-1.
— Toronto Maple Leafs, at Quebec, Dec. 29, 1988, third period. Scorers: Ed Olczyk, 5:24; Gary Leeman, 5:28. Toronto defeated Quebec 6-5.
— Calgary Flames, at Quebec, Oct. 17, 1989, third period. Scorers: Doug Gilmour, 19:45; Paul Ranheim, 19:49. Calgary and Quebec tied 8-8.
— Winnipeg Jets, at Winnipeg, Dec. 15, 1995, second period. Deron Quint scored both goals, at 7:51 and 7:55. Winnipeg defeated Edmonton 9-4.

FASTEST TWO GOALS FROM START OF GAME, ONE TEAM:
24 Seconds — Edmonton Oilers, Mar. 28, 1982, at Los Angeles. Scorers: Mark Messier, 0:14; Dave Lumley, 0:24. Edmonton defeated Los Angeles 6-2.
29 Seconds — Pittsburgh Penguins, Dec. 6, 1980, at Pittsburgh. Scorers: George Ferguson, 0:17; Greg Malone, 0:29. Pittsburgh defeated Chicago 6-4.
32 Seconds — Calgary Flames, Mar. 11, 1987, at Hartford. Scorers: Doug Risebrough 0:09; Colin Patterson, 0:32. Calgary defeated Hartford 6-1.

FASTEST TWO GOALS FROM START OF PERIOD, BOTH TEAMS:
14 Seconds — NY Rangers, Quebec Nordiques, at Quebec, Nov. 5, 1983, third period. Scorers: Andre Savard, Quebec, 0:08; Pierre Larouche, NY Rangers, 0:14. 4-4 tie.
26 Seconds — Buffalo Sabres, St. Louis Blues, at Buffalo, Jan. 3, 1993, third period. Scorers: Alexander Mogilny, Buffalo, 0:08; Phillippe Bozon, St. Louis, 0:26. Buffalo won 6-5.
28 Seconds — Boston Bruins, Montreal Canadiens, at Montreal, Oct. 11, 1989, third period. Scorers: Jim Wiemer, Boston 0:10; Tom Chorske, Montreal 0:28. Montreal won 4-2.

FASTEST TWO GOALS FROM START OF PERIOD, ONE TEAM:
21 Seconds — Chicago Blackhawks, Nov. 5, 1983, at Minnesota, second period. Scorers: Ken Yaremchuk, 0:12; Darryl Sutter, 0:21. Minnesota defeated Chicago 10-5.
30 Seconds — Washington Capitals, Jan. 27, 1980, at Washington, second period. Scorers: Mike Gartner, 0:08; Bengt Gustafsson, 0:30. Washington defeated NY Islanders 7-1.
31 Seconds —Buffalo Sabres, Jan. 10, 1974, at Buffalo, third period. Scorers: Rene Robert, 0:21; Rick Martin, 0:31. Buffalo defeated NY Rangers 7-2.
— NY Islanders, Feb. 22, 1986, at New York, third period. Scorers: Roger Kortko, 0:10; Bob Bourne, 0:31. NY Islanders defeated Detroit 5-2.

After a less than inspiring effort in the first period of their March 11, 1989 tilt against Hartford, the Montreal Canadiens scored three goals in 65 seconds, including one by Guy Carbonneau (below), to set a new mark for the quickest three goals from the start of a period.

50, 40, 30, 20-GOAL SCORERS

MOST 50-OR-MORE-GOAL SCORERS, ONE SEASON:

3 — Edmonton Oilers, 1983-84. Wayne Gretzky, 87; Glenn Anderson, 54; Jari Kurri, 52. 80GP
— Edmonton Oilers, 1985-86. Jari Kurri, 68; Glenn Anderson, 54; Wayne Gretzky, 52. 80GP
2 — Boston Bruins, 1970-71. Phil Esposito, 76; John Bucyk, 51. 78GP
— Boston Bruins, 1973-74. Phil Esposito, 68; Ken Hodge, 50. 78GP
— Philadelphia Flyers, 1975-76. Reggie Leach, 61; Bill Barber, 50. 80GP
— Pittsburgh Penguins, 1975-76. Pierre Larouche, 53; Jean Pronovost, 52. 80GP
— Montreal Canadiens, 1976-77. Steve Shutt, 60; Guy Lafleur, 56. 80GP
— Los Angeles Kings, 1979-80. Charlie Simmer, 56; Marcel Dionne, 53. 80GP
— Montreal Canadiens, 1979-80. Pierre Larouche, 50; Guy Lafleur, 50. 80GP
— Los Angeles Kings, 1980-81. Marcel Dionne, 58; Charlie Simmer, 56. 80GP
— Edmonton Oilers, 1981-82. Wayne Gretzky, 92; Mark Messier, 50. 80GP
— NY Islanders, 1981-82. Mike Bossy, 64; Bryan Trottier, 50. 80GP
— Edmonton Oilers, 1984-85. Wayne Gretzky, 73; Jari Kurri, 71. 80GP
— Washington Capitals, 1984-85. Bob Carpenter, 53; Mike Gartner, 50. 80GP
— Edmonton Oilers, 1986-87. Wayne Gretzky, 62; Jari Kurri, 54. 80GP
— Calgary Flames, 1987-88. Joe Nieuwendyk, 51; Hakan Loob, 50. 80GP
— Los Angeles Kings, 1987-88. Jimmy Carson, 55; Luc Robitaille, 53. 80GP
— Los Angeles Kings, 1988-89. Bernie Nicholls, 70; Wayne Gretzky, 54. 80GP
— Calgary Flames, 1988-89. Joe Nieuwendyk, 51; Joe Mullen, 51. 80GP
— Buffalo Sabres, 1992-93. Alexander Mogilny, 76; Pat LaFontaine, 53. 84GP
— Pittsburgh Penguins, 1992-93. Mario Lemieux, 69; Kevin Stevens, 55. 84GP
— St. Louis Blues, 1992-93. Brett Hull, 54; Brendan Shanahan, 51. 84GP
— St. Louis Blues, 1993-94. Brett Hull, 57; Brendan Shanahan, 52. 84GP
— Detroit Red Wings, 1993-94. Sergei Fedorov, 56; Ray Sheppard, 52. 84GP
— Pittsburgh Penguins, 1995-96. Mario Lemieux, 69; Jaromir Jagr, 62. 82GP

MOST 40-OR-MORE-GOAL SCORERS, ONE SEASON:

4 — Edmonton Oilers, 1982-83. Wayne Gretzky, 71; Glenn Anderson, 48; Mark Messier, 48; Jari Kurri, 45. 80GP
— Edmonton Oilers, 1983-84. Wayne Gretzky, 87; Glenn Anderson, 54; Jari Kurri, 52; Paul Coffey, 40. 80GP
— Edmonton Oilers, 1984-85. Wayne Gretzky, 73; Jari Kurri, 71; Mike Krushelnyski, 43; Glenn Anderson, 42. 80GP
— Edmonton Oilers, 1985-86. Jari Kurri, 68; Glenn Anderson, 54; Wayne Gretzky, 52; Paul Coffey, 48. 80GP
— Calgary Flames, 1987-88. Joe Nieuwendyk, 51; Hakan Loob, 50; Mike Bullard, 48; Joe Mullen, 40. 80GP
3 — Boston Bruins, 1970-71. Phil Esposito, 76; John Bucyk, 51; Ken Hodge, 43. 78GP
— NY Rangers, 1971-72. Vic Hadfield, 50; Jean Ratelle, 46; Rod Gilbert, 43. 78GP
— Buffalo Sabres, 1975-76. Danny Gare, 50; Rick Martin, 49; Gilbert Perreault, 44. 80GP
— Montreal Canadiens, 1979-80. Guy Lafleur, 50; Pierre Larouche, 50; Steve Shutt, 47. 80GP
— Buffalo Sabres, 1979-80. Danny Gare, 56; Rick Martin, 45; Gilbert Perreault, 40. 80GP
— Los Angeles Kings, 1980-81. Marcel Dionne, 58; Charlie Simmer, 56; Dave Taylor, 47. 80GP
— Los Angeles Kings, 1984-85. Marcel Dionne, 46; Bernie Nicholls, 46; Dave Taylor, 41. 80GP
— NY Islanders, 1984-85. Mike Bossy, 58; Brent Sutter, 42; John Tonelli; 42. 80GP
— Chicago Blackhawks, 1985-86. Denis Savard, 47; Troy Murray, 45; Al Secord, 40. 80GP
— Chicago Blackhawks, 1987-88. Denis Savard, 44; Rick Vaive, 43; Steve Larmer, 41. 80GP
— Edmonton Oilers, 1987-88. Craig Simpson, 43; Jari Kurri, 43; Wayne Gretzky, 40. 80GP
— Los Angeles Kings, 1988-89. Bernie Nicholls, 70; Wayne Gretzky, 54; Luc Robitaille, 46. 80GP
— Los Angeles Kings, 1990-91. Luc Robitaille, 45; Tomas Sandstrom, 45; Wayne Gretzky 41. 80GP
— Pittsburgh Penguins, 1991-92. Kevin Stevens, 54; Mario Lemieux, 44; Joe Mullen, 42. 80GP
— Pittsburgh Penguins, 1992-93. Mario Lemieux, 69; Kevin Stevens, 55; Rick Tocchet, 48. 84GP
— Calgary Flames, 1993-94. Gary Roberts, 41; Robert Reichel, 40; Theoren Fleury, 40. 84GP
— Pittsburgh Penguins, 1995-96. Mario Lemieux, 69; Jaromir Jagr, 62; Petr Nedved, 45. 82GP

MOST 30-OR-MORE GOAL SCORERS, ONE SEASON:

6 — Buffalo Sabres, 1974-75. Rick Martin, 52; Rene Robert, 40; Gilbert Perreault, 39; Don Luce, 33; Rick Dudley, Danny Gare, 31 each. 80GP
— NY Islanders, 1977-78, Mike Bossy, 53; Bryan Trottier, 46; Clark Gillies, 35; Denis Potvin, Bob Nystrom, Bob Bourne, 30 each. 80GP
— Winnipeg Jets, 1984-85. Dale Hawerchuk, 53; Paul MacLean, 41; Laurie Boschman, Brian Mullen, 32 each; Doug Smail, 31; Thomas Steen, 30. 80GP
5 — Chicago Blackhawks, 1968-69. 76GP
— Boston Bruins, 1970-71. 78GP
— Montreal Canadiens, 1971-72. 78GP
— Philadelphia Flyers, 1972-73. 78GP
— Boston Bruins, 1973-74. 78GP
— Montreal Canadiens, 1974-75. 80GP
— Montreal Canadiens, 1975-76. 80GP
— Pittsburgh Penguins, 1975-76. 80GP
— NY Islanders, 1978-79. 80GP
— Detroit Red Wings, 1979-80. 80GP
— Philadelphia Flyers, 1979-80. 80GP
— NY Islanders, 1980-81. 80GP
— St. Louis Blues, 1980-81. 80GP
— Chicago Blackhawks, 1981-82. 80GP
— Edmonton Oilers, 1981-82. 80GP
— Montreal Canadiens, 1981-82. 80GP
— Quebec Nordiques, 1981-82. 80GP
— Washington Capitals, 1981-82. 80GP
— Edmonton Oilers, 1982-83. 80GP
— Edmonton Oilers, 1983-84. 80GP
— Edmonton Oilers, 1984-85. 80GP
— Los Angeles Kings, 1984-85. 80GP
— Edmonton Oilers, 1985-86. 80GP
— Edmonton Oilers, 1986-87. 80GP
— Edmonton Oilers, 1987-88. 80GP
— Edmonton Oilers, 1988-89. 80GP
— Detroit Red Wings, 1991-92. 80GP
— NY Rangers, 1991-92. 80GP
— Pittsburgh Penguins, 1991-92. 80GP
— Detroit Red Wings, 1992-93. 84GP
— Pittsburgh Penguins, 1992-93. 84GP

MOST 20-OR-MORE GOAL SCORERS, ONE SEASON:

11 — Boston Bruins, 1977-78; Peter McNab, 41; Terry O'Reilly, 29; Bobby Schmautz, Stan Jonathan, 27 each; Jean Ratelle, Rick Middleton, 25 each; Wayne Cashman, 24; Gregg Sheppard, 23; Brad Park, 22; Don Marcotte, Bob Miller, 20 each. 80GP
10 — Boston Bruins, 1970-71. 78GP
— Montreal Canadiens, 1974-75. 80GP
— St. Louis Blues, 1980-81. 80GP

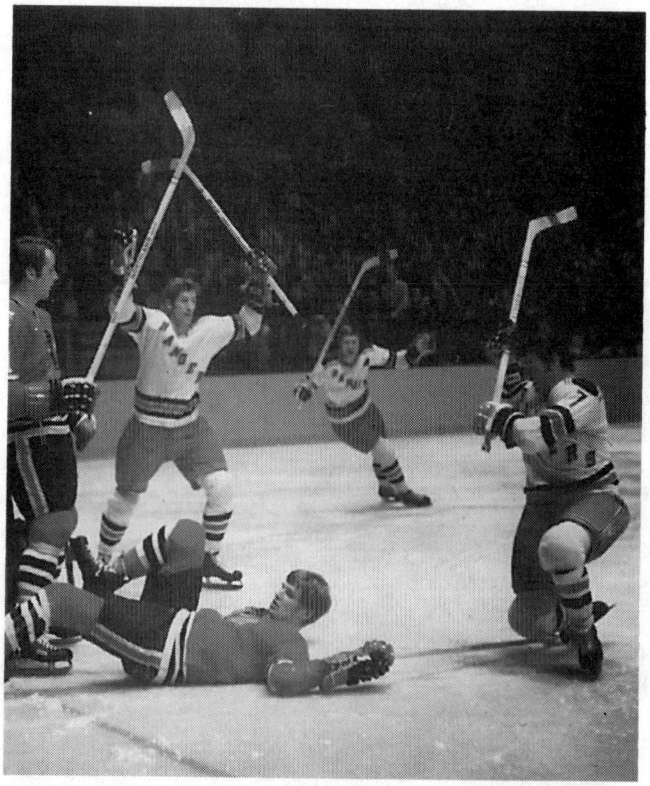

For many of his 18 seasons with the New York Rangers, Rod Gilbert, right, was the toast of the town. During the 1971-72 season, however, he had to share the spotlight with teammates Vic Hadfield and Jean Ratelle, left,. All three forwards scored over forty goals, the only time in club history that three members of the Broadway Blueshirts reached the 40-goal plateau.

100-POINT SCORERS

MOST 100 OR-MORE-POINT SCORERS, ONE SEASON:

4 —Boston Bruins, 1970-71, Phil Esposito, 76G-76A-152PTS; Bobby Orr, 37G-102A-139PTS; John Bucyk, 51G-65A-116PTS; Ken Hodge, 43G-62A-105PTS. 78GP
—Edmonton Oilers, 1982-83, Wayne Gretzky, 71G-125A-196PTS; Mark Messier, 48G-58A-106PTS; Glenn Anderson, 48G-56A-104PTS; Jari Kurri, 45G-59A-104PTS. 80GP
—Edmonton Oilers, 1983-84, Wayne Gretzky, 87G-118A-205PTS; Paul Coffey, 40G-86A-126PTS; Jari Kurri, 52G-61A-113PTS; Mark Messier, 37G-64A-101PTS. 80GP
—Edmonton Oilers,1985-86, Wayne Gretzky, 52G-163A-215PTS; Paul Coffey, 48G-90A-138PTS; Jari Kurri, 68G-63A-131PTS; Glenn Anderson, 54G-48A-102PTS. 80GP
—Pittsburgh Penguins,1992-93, Mario Lemieux, 69G-91A-160PTS; Kevin Stevens, 55G-56A-111PTS; Rick Tocchet, 48G-61A-109PTS; Ron Francis, 24G-76A-100PTS. 84GP
3 —Boston Bruins, 1973-74, Phil Esposito, 68G-77A-145PTS; Bobby Orr, 32G-90A-122PTS; Ken Hodge, 50G-55A-105PTS. 78GP
—NY Islanders, 1978-79, Bryan Trottier, 47G-87A-134PTS; Mike Bossy, 69G-57A-126PTS; Denis Potvin, 31G-70A-101PTS. 80GP
—Los Angeles Kings, 1980-81, Marcel Dionne, 58G-77A-135PTS; Dave Taylor, 47 G-65A-112PTS; Charlie Simmer, 56G-49A-105PTS. 80GP
—Edmonton Oilers, 1984-85, Wayne Gretzky, 73G-135A-208PTS; Jari Kurri, 71G-64A-135PTS; Paul Coffey, 37G-84A-121PTS. 80GP
—NY Islanders, 1984-85. Mike Bossy, 58G-59A-117PTS; Brent Sutter, 42G-60A-102PTS; John Tonelli, 42G-58A-100PTS. 80GP
—Edmonton Oilers, 1986-87, Wayne Gretzky, 62G-121A-183PTS; Jari Kurri, 54G-54A-108PTS; Mark Messier, 37G-70A-107PTS. 80GP
—Pittsburgh Penguins, 1988-89, Mario Lemieux, 85G-114A-199PTS; Rob Brown, 49G-66A-115PTS; Paul Coffey, 30G-83A-113PTS. 80GP
—Pittsburgh Penguins, 1995-96, Mario Lemieux, 69G-92A-161PTS; Jaromir Jagr, 62G-87A-149PTS; Ron Francis, 27G-92A-119PTS. 82GP

SHOTS ON GOAL

MOST SHOTS, BOTH TEAMS, ONE GAME:

141 —NY Americans, Pittsburgh Pirates, Dec. 26, 1925, at New York. NY Americans, who won game 3-1, had 73 shots; Pit. Pirates, 68 shots.

MOST SHOTS, ONE TEAM, ONE GAME:

83 —Boston Bruins, March 4, 1941, at Boston. Boston defeated Chicago 3-2.
73 —NY Americans, Dec. 26, 1925, at New York. NY Americans defeated Pit. Pirates 3-1.
—Boston Bruins, March 21, 1991, at Boston. Boston tied Quebec 3-3.
72 —Boston Bruins, Dec. 10, 1970, at Boston. Boston defeated Buffalo 8-2.

MOST SHOTS, ONE TEAM, ONE PERIOD:

33 —Boston Bruins, March 4, 1941, at Boston, second period. Boston defeated Chicago 3-2.

TEAM GOALS-AGAINST

Fewest Goals-Against

FEWEST GOALS AGAINST, ONE SEASON:

42 —Ottawa Senators, 1925-26. 36GP
43 —Montreal Canadiens, 1928-29. 44GP
48 —Montreal Canadiens, 1923-24. 24GP
—Montreal Canadiens, 1927-28. 44GP

FEWEST GOALS AGAINST, ONE SEASON (MINIMUM 70-GAME SCHEDULE):

131 —Toronto Maple Leafs, 1953-54. 70GP
—Montreal Canadiens, 1955-56. 70GP
132 —Detroit Red Wings, 1953-54. 70GP
133 —Detroit Red Wings, 1951-52. 70GP
—Detroit Red Wings, 1952-53. 70GP

LOWEST GOALS-AGAINST-PER-GAME AVERAGE, ONE SEASON:

.98 —Montreal Canadiens, 1928-29. 43GA in 44GP.
1.09 —Montreal Canadiens, 1927-28. 48GA in 44GP.
1.17 —Ottawa Senators, 1925-26. 42GA in 36GP.

Most Goals-Against

MOST GOALS AGAINST, ONE SEASON:

446 —Washington Capitals, 1974-75. 80GP
415 —Detroit Red Wings, 1985-86. 80GP
414 —San Jose Sharks, 1992-93. 84GP
407 —Quebec Nordiques, 1989-90. 80GP
403 —Hartford Whalers, 1982-83. 80GP

HIGHEST GOALS-AGAINST-PER-GAME AVERAGE, ONE SEASON:

7.38 —Quebec Bulldogs, 1919-20, 177GA in 24GP.
6.20 —NY Rangers, 1943-44, 310GA in 50GP.
5.58 —Washington Capitals, 1974-75, 446GA in 80GP.

MOST POWER-PLAY GOALS AGAINST, ONE SEASON:

122 —Chicago Blackhawks, 1988-89. 80GP
120 —Pittsburgh Penguins, 1987-88. 80GP
115 —New Jersey Devils, 1988-89. 80GP
—Ottawa Senators, 1992-93. 84GP
114 —Los Angeles Kings, 1992-93. 84GP

MOST SHORTHAND GOALS AGAINST, ONE SEASON:

22 —Pittsburgh Penguins, 1984-85. 80GP
—Minnesota North Stars, 1991-92. 80GP
—Colorado Avalanche, 1995-96. 82GP
21 —Calgary Flames, 1984-85. 80GP
—Pittsburgh Penguins, 1989-90. 80GP

SHUTOUTS

MOST SHUTOUTS, ONE SEASON:

22 —Montreal Canadiens, 1928-29. All by George Hainsworth. 44GP
16 —NY Americans, 1928-29. Roy Worters had 13; Flat Walsh 3. 44GP
15 —Ottawa Senators, 1925-26. All by Alex Connell. 36GP
—Ottawa Senators, 1927-28. All by Alex Connell. 44GP
—Boston Bruins, 1927-28. All by Hal Winkler. 44GP
—Chicago Blackhawks, 1969-70. All by Tony Esposito. 76GP

MOST CONSECUTIVE SHUTOUTS, ONE SEASON:

6 —Ottawa Senators, Jan. 31 - Feb. 18, 1928.

MOST CONSECUTIVE SHUTOUTS TO START SEASON:

5 —Toronto Maple Leafs, Nov. 13 - 22, 1930.

MOST GAMES SHUTOUT, ONE SEASON:

20 —Chicago Blackhawks, 1928-29. 44GP

MOST CONSECUTIVE GAMES SHUTOUT:

8 —Chicago Blackhawks, Feb. 7 - 28, 1929.

MOST CONSECUTIVE GAMES SHUTOUT TO START SEASON:

3 —Montreal Maroons, Nov. 11 - 18, 1930.

TEAM PENALTIES

MOST PENALTY MINUTES, ONE SEASON:

2,713 —Buffalo Sabres, 1991-92. 80GP
2,670 —Pittsburgh Penguins, 1988-89. 80GP
2,663 —Chicago Blackhawks, 1991-92. 80GP
2,643 —Calgary Flames, 1991-92. 80GP
2,621 —Philadelphia Flyers, 1980-81. 80GP

MOST PENALTIES, BOTH TEAMS, ONE GAME:

85 Penalties — Edmonton Oilers (44), Los Angeles Kings (41) at Los Angeles, Feb. 28, 1990. Edmonton received 26 minors, 7 majors, 6 10-minute misconducts, 4 game misconducts and 1 match penalty; Los Angeles received 26 minors, 9 majors, 3 10-minute misconducts and 3 game misconducts.

MOST PENALTY MINUTES, BOTH TEAMS, ONE GAME:

406 Minutes — Minnesota North Stars, Boston Bruins at Boston, Feb. 26, 1981. Minnesota received 18 minors, 13 majors, 4 10-minute misconducts and 7 game misconducts; a total of 211PIM. Boston received 20 minors, 13 majors, 3 10-minute misconducts and six game misconducts; a total of 195PIM.

MOST PENALTIES, ONE TEAM, ONE GAME:

44 —Edmonton Oilers, Feb. 28, 1990, at Los Angeles. Edmonton received 26 minors, 7 majors, 6 10-minute misconducts, 4 game misconducts and 1 match penalty.
42 —Minnesota North Stars, Feb. 26, 1981, at Boston. Minnesota received 18 minors, 13 majors, 4 10-minute misconducts and 7 game misconducts.
—Boston Bruins, Feb. 26, 1981, at Boston vs. Minnesota. Boston received 20 minors, 13 majors, 3 10-minute misconducts and 6 game misconducts.

MOST PENALTY MINUTES, ONE TEAM, ONE GAME:

211 —Minnesota North Stars, Feb. 26, 1981, at Boston. Minnesota received 18 minors, 13 majors, 4 10-minute misconducts and 7 game misconducts.

MOST PENALTIES, BOTH TEAMS, ONE PERIOD:

67 —Minnesota North Stars, Boston Bruins, at Boston, Feb. 26, 1981, first period. Minnesota received 15 minors, 8 majors, 4 10-minute misconducts and 7 game misconducts, a total of 34 penalties. Boston had 16 minors, 8 majors, 3 10-minute misconducts and 6 game misconducts, a total of 33 penalties.

MOST PENALTY MINUTES, BOTH TEAMS, ONE PERIOD:

372 —Los Angeles Kings, Philadelphia Flyers at Philadelphia, March 11, 1979, first period. Philadelphia received 4 minors, 8 majors, 6 10-minute misconducts and 8 game misconducts for 188 minutes. Los Angeles received 2 minors, 8 majors, 6 10-minute misconducts and 8 game misconducts for 184 minutes.

MOST PENALTIES, ONE TEAM, ONE PERIOD:

34 —Minnesota North Stars, Feb. 26, 1981, at Boston, first period. 15 minors, 8 majors, 4 10-minute misconducts, 7 game misconducts.

MOST PENALTY MINUTES, ONE TEAM, ONE PERIOD:

188 —Philadelphia Flyers, March 11, 1979, at Philadelphia vs. Los Angeles, first period. Flyers received 4 minors, 8 majors, 6 10-minute misconducts and 8 game misconducts.

NHL Individual Scoring Records – History

SIX INDIVIDUAL SCORING RECORDS stand as benchmarks in the history of the game: most goals, single-season and career; most assists, single-season and career; and most points, single-season and career. The evolution of these six records is traced here, beginning with 1917-18, the NHL's first season. New research has resulted in changes to scoring records in the NHL's first four seasons.

MOST GOALS, ONE SEASON

44 – Joe Malone, Montreal, 1917-18.
Scored goal #44 against Toronto's Harry Holmes on March 2, 1918 and finished season with 44 goals.
50 – Maurice Richard, Montreal, 1944-45.
Scored goal #45 against Toronto's Frank McCool on February 25, 1945 and finished the season with 50 goals.
50 – Bernie Geoffrion, Montreal, 1960-61.
Scored goal #50 against Toronto's Cesare Maniago on March 16, 1961 and finished the season with 50 goals.
50 – Bobby Hull, Chicago, 1961-62.
Scored goal #50 against NY Rangers' Gump Worsley on March 25, 1962 and finished the season with 50 goals.
54 – Bobby Hull, Chicago, 1965-66.
Scored goal #51 against NY Rangers' Cesare Maniago on March 12, 1966 and finished the season with 54 goals.
58 – Bobby Hull, Chicago, 1968-69.
Scored goal #55 against Boston's Gerry Cheevers on March 20, 1969 and finished the season with 58 goals.
76 – Phil Esposito, Boston, 1970-71.
Scored goal #59 against Los Angeles' Denis DeJordy on March 11, 1971 and finished the season with 76 goals.
92 – Wayne Gretzky, Edmonton, 1981-82.
Scored goal #77 against Buffalo's Don Edwards on February 24, 1982 and finished the season with 92 goals.

MOST ASSISTS, ONE SEASON

10 – Cy Denneny, Ottawa, 1917-18.
– Reg Noble, Toronto, 1917-18.
– Harry Cameron, Toronto, 1917-18.
15 – Frank Nighbor, Ottawa, 1919-20.
18 – Dick Irvin, Chicago, 1926-27.
18 – Howie Morenz, Montreal, 1927-28.
36 – Frank Boucher, NY Rangers, 1929-30.
37 – Joe Primeau, Toronto, 1931-32.
45 – Bill Cowley, Boston, 1940-41.
45 – Bill Cowley, Boston, 1942-43.
49 – Clint Smith, Chicago, 1943-44.
54 – Elmer Lach, Montreal, 1944-45.
55 – Ted Lindsay, Detroit, 1949-50.
56 – Bert Olmstead, Montreal, 1955-56.
58 – Jean Beliveau, Montreal, 1960-61.
58 – Andy Bathgate, NY Rangers/Toronto, 1963-64.
59 – Stan Mikita, Chicago, 1964-65.
62 – Stan Mikita, Chicago, 1966-67.
77 – Phil Esposito, Boston, 1968-69.
87 – Bobby Orr, Boston, 1969-70.
102 – Bobby Orr, Boston, 1970-71.
109 – Wayne Gretzky, Edmonton, 1980-81.
120 – Wayne Gretzky, Edmonton, 1981-82.
125 – Wayne Gretzky, Edmonton, 1982-83.
135 – Wayne Gretzky, Edmonton, 1984-85.
163 – Wayne Gretzky, Edmonton, 1985-86.

MOST POINTS, ONE SEASON

48 – Joe Malone, Montreal, 1917-18.
49 – Joe Malone, Montreal, 1919-20.
51 – Howie Morenz, Montreal, 1927-28.
73 – Cooney Weiland, Boston, 1929-30.
73 – Doug Bentley, Chicago, 1942-43.
82 – Herb Cain, Boston, 1943-44.
86 – Gordie Howe, Detroit, 1950-51.
95 – Gordie Howe, Detroit, 1952-53.
96 – Dickie Moore, Montreal, 1958-59.
97 – Bobby Hull, Chicago, 1965-66.
97 – Stan Mikita, Chicago, 1966-67.
126 – Phil Esposito, Boston, 1968-69.
152 – Phil Esposito, Boston, 1970-71.
164 – Wayne Gretzky, Edmonton, 1980-81.
212 – Wayne Gretzky, Edmonton, 1981-82.
215 – Wayne Gretzky, Edmonton, 1985-86.

When the legendary Maurice Richard retired shortly before the start of the 1960-61 season, he was the NHL's all-time leading scorer with 544 goals and 421 assists. This is the penultimate goal of his career, a wicked wrister that escaped the grasp of Johnny Bower on March 9, 1960.

MOST REGULAR-SEASON GOALS, CAREER

44 – Joe Malone, 1917-18, Montreal.
Malone led the NHL in goals in the league's first season and finished with 44 goals in 22 games in 1917-18.
54 – Cy Denneny, 1918-19, Ottawa.
Denneny passed Malone during the 1918-19 season, finishing the year with a two-year total of 54 goals. He held the career goal-scoring mark until 1919-20.
146 – Joe Malone, Montreal, Quebec Bulldogs, Hamilton.
Malone passed Denneny in 1919-20 and remained the NHL's career goal-scoring leader until his retirement. He finished with a career total of 146 goals.
246 – Cy Denneny, Ottawa, Boston.
Denneny passed Malone with goal #147 in 1922-23 and remained the NHL's career goal-scoring leader until his retirement. He finished with a career total of 246 goals.
270 – Howie Morenz, Montreal, NY Rangers, Chicago.
Morenz passed Denneny with goal #247 in 1933-34 and finished his career with 270 goals.
324 – Nels Stewart, Montreal Maroons, Boston, NY Americans.
Stewart passed Morenz with goal #271 in 1936-37 and remained the NHL's career goal-scoring leader until his retirement. He finished his career with 324 goals.
544 – Maurice Richard, Montreal.
Richard passed Nels Stewart with goal #325 on Nov. 8, 1952 and remained the NHL's career goal-scoring leader until his retirement. He finished his career with 544 goals.
801 – Gordie Howe, Detroit, Hartford.
Howe passed Richard with goal #545 on Nov. 10, 1963 and remained the NHL's career goal-scoring leader until his retirement. He finished his career with 801 goals.
885 – Wayne Gretzky, Edmonton, Los Angeles, St. Louis, NY Rangers.
Gretzky passed Gordie Howe with goal #802 on March 23, 1994. He is the current career goal-scoring leader with 885.

"The Golden Jet" Bobby Hull scored at least 30 goals in 13 straight seasons before signing with the Winnipeg Jets of the World Hockey Association in June 1972. He went on to collect 303 goals in the WHA before finally returning to the NHL with Winnipeg and Hartford in 1979-80.

MOST REGULAR-SEASON ASSISTS, CAREER (minimum 100 assists)

100 – Frank Boucher, Ottawa, NY Rangers.
In 1930-31, Boucher became the first NHL player to reach the 100-assist milestone.

262 – Frank Boucher, Ottawa, NY Rangers.
Boucher retired as the NHL's career assist leader in 1938 with 252. He returned to the NHL in 1943-44 and remained the NHL's career assist leader until he was overtaken by Bill Cowley in 1943-44. He finished his career with 262 assists.

353 – Bill Cowley, St. Louis Eagles, Boston.
Cowley passed Boucher with assist #263 in 1943-44. He retired as the NHL's career assist leader in 1947 with 353.

408 – Elmer Lach, Montreal.
Lach passed Cowley with assist #354 in 1951-52. He retired as the NHL's career assist leader in 1954 with 408.

1,049 – Gordie Howe, Detroit, Hartford.
Howe passed Lach with assist #409 in 1957-58. He retired as the NHL's career assist leader in 1980 with 1,049.

1,910 – Wayne Gretzky, Edmonton, Los Angeles, St. Louis, NY Rangers.
Gretzky passed Howe with assist #1,050 in 1988-89. He is the current career assist leader with 1,910.

MOST REGULAR-SEASON POINTS, CAREER (minimum 100 points)

100 – Joe Malone, Montreal, Quebec Bulldogs, Hamilton.
In 1919-20, Malone became the first player in NHL history to record 100 points.

200 – Cy Denneny, Ottawa.
In 1923-24, Denneny became the first player in NHL history to record 200 points.

300 – Cy Denneny, Ottawa.
In 1926-27, Denneny became the first player in NHL history to record 300 points.

315 – Cy Denneny, Ottawa, Boston.
Denneny retired as the NHL's career point-scoring leader in 1929 with 315 points.

467 – Howie Morenz, Montreal, Chicago, NY Rangers.
Morenz passed Cy Denneny with point #316 in 1931-32. At the time his career ended in 1937, he was the NHL's career point-scoring leader with 467 points.

515 – Nels Stewart, Montreal Maroons, Boston, NY Americans.
Stewart passed Morenz with point #468 in 1938-39. He retired as the NHL's career point-scoring leader in 1940 with 515 points.

528 – Syd Howe, Ottawa, Philadelphia Quakers, Toronto, St. Louis Eagles, Detroit.
Howe passed Nels Stewart with point #516 on March 8, 1945. He retired as the NHL's career point-scoring leader in 1946 with 528 points.

548 – Bill Cowley, St. Louis Eagles, Boston.
Cowley passed Syd Howe with point #529 on Feb. 12, 1947. He retired as the NHL's career point-scoring leader in 1947 with 548 points.

610 – Elmer Lach, Montreal.
Lach passed Bill Cowley with point #549 on Feb. 23, 1952. He remained the NHL's career point-scoring leader until he was overtaken by Maurice Richard in 1953-54. He finished his career with 623 points.

946 – Maurice Richard, Montreal.
Richard passed teammate Elmer Lach with point #611 on Dec. 12, 1953. He remained the NHL's career point-scoring leader until he was overtaken by Gordie Howe in 1959-60. He finished his career with 965 points.

1,850 – Gordie Howe, Detroit, Hartford.
Howe passed Richard with point #947 on Jan. 16, 1960. He retired as the NHL's career point-scoring leader in 1980 with 1,850 points.

2,795 – Wayne Gretzky, Edmonton, Los Angeles, St. Louis, NY Rangers.
Gretzky passed Howe with point #1,851 on Oct. 15, 1989. He is the current career point-scoring leader with 2,795.

Individual Records

Regular Season

SEASONS

MOST SEASONS:
26 —Gordie Howe, Detroit, 1946-47 – 1970-71; Hartford, 1979-80.
24 —Alex Delvecchio, Detroit, 1950-51 – 1973-74.
—Tim Horton, Toronto, NY Rangers, Pittsburgh, Buffalo, 1949-50, 1951-52 – 1973-74.
23 —John Bucyk, Detroit, Boston, 1955-56 – 1977-78.
22 —Dean Prentice, NY Rangers, Boston, Detroit, Pittsburgh, Minnesota, 1952-53 – 1973-74.
—Doug Mohns, Boston, Chicago, Minnesota, Atlanta, Washington, 1953-54 – 1974-75.
—Stan Mikita, Chicago, 1958-59 – 1979-80.

GAMES

MOST GAMES:
1,767 —Gordie Howe, Detroit, 1946-47 – 1970-71; Hartford, 1979-80.
1,549 —Alex Delvecchio, Detroit, 1950-51 – 1973-74.
1,540 —John Bucyk, Detroit, Boston, 1955-56 – 1977-78.

MOST GAMES, INCLUDING PLAYOFFS:
1,924 —Gordie Howe, Detroit, Hartford, 1,767 regular-season and 157 playoff games.
1,670 —Alex Delvecchio, Detroit, 1,549 regular-season and 121 playoff games.
1,664 —John Bucyk, Detroit, Boston, 1,540 regular-season and 124 playoff games.

MOST CONSECUTIVE GAMES:
964 —Doug Jarvis, Montreal, Washington, Hartford, from Oct. 8, 1975 – Oct. 10, 1987.
914 —Garry Unger, Toronto, Detroit, St. Louis, Atlanta from Feb. 24, 1968 – Dec. 21, 1979.
884 —Steve Larmer, Chicago, from Oct. 6, 1982 – Apr. 16, 1993.
776 —Craig Ramsay, Buffalo, from Mar. 27, 1973 – Feb. 10, 1983.
630 —Andy Hebenton, NY Rangers, Boston, Oct. 6, 1956 – Mar. 22, 1964.

GOALS

MOST GOALS:
885 —Wayne Gretzky, Edmonton, Los Angeles, St. Louis, NY Rangers, in 19 seasons, 1,417GP.
801 —Gordie Howe, Detroit, Hartford, in 26 seasons, 1,767GP.
731 —Marcel Dionne, Detroit, Los Angeles, NY Rangers, in 18 seasons, 1,348GP.
717 —Phil Esposito, Chicago, Boston, NY Rangers, in 18 seasons, 1,282GP.
708 —Mike Gartner, Washington, Minnesota, NY Rangers, Toronto, Phoenix, in 19 seasons, 1,432GP.

MOST GOALS, INCLUDING PLAYOFFS:
1,007 —Wayne Gretzky, Edmonton, Los Angeles, St. Louis, NY Rangers, 885 regular-season and 122 playoff goals.
869 —Gordie Howe, Detroit, Hartford, 801 regular-season and 68 playoff goals.
778 —Phil Esposito, Chicago, Boston, NY Rangers, 717 regular-season and 61 playoff goals.
752 —Marcel Dionne, Detroit, Los Angeles, NY Rangers, 731 regular-season and 21 playoff goals.

MOST GOALS, ONE SEASON:
92 —Wayne Gretzky, Edmonton, 1981-82. 80 game schedule.
87 —Wayne Gretzky, Edmonton, 1983-84. 80 game schedule.
86 —Brett Hull, St. Louis, 1990-91. 80 game schedule.
85 —Mario Lemieux, Pittsburgh, 1988-89. 80 game schedule.
76 —Phil Esposito, Boston, 1970-71. 78 game schedule.
—Alexander Mogilny, Buffalo, 1992-93. 84 game schedule.
—Teemu Selanne, Winnipeg, 1992-93. 84 game schedule.
73 —Wayne Gretzky, Edmonton, 1984-85. 80 game schedule.
72 —Brett Hull, St. Louis, 1989-90. 80 game schedule.
71 —Jari Kurri, Edmonton, 1984-85. 80 game schedule.
—Wayne Gretzky, Edmonton, 1982-83. 80 game schedule.
70 —Mario Lemieux, Pittsburgh, 1987-1988. 80 game schedule.
—Bernie Nicholls, Los Angeles, 1988-89. 80 game schedule.
—Brett Hull, St. Louis, 1991-92. 80 game schedule.

MOST GOALS, ONE SEASON, INCLUDING PLAYOFFS:
100 —Wayne Gretzky, Edmonton, 1983-84, 87G in 74 regular-season games and 13G in 19 playoff games.
97 —Wayne Gretzky, Edmonton, 1981-82, 92G in 80 regular-season games and 5G in 5 playoff games.
—Mario Lemieux, Pittsburgh, 1988-89, 85G in 76 regular-season games and 12G in 11 playoff games.
—Brett Hull, St. Louis, 1990-91, 86G in 78 regular-season games and 11G in 13 playoff games.
90 —Wayne Gretzky, Edmonton, 1984-85, 73G in 80 regular-season games and 17G in 18 playoff games.
—Jari Kurri, Edmonton, 1984-85, 71G in 80 regular-season games and 19G in 18 playoff games.
85 —Mike Bossy, NY Islanders, 1980-81, 68G in 79 regular-season games and 17G in 18 playoff games.
—Brett Hull, St. Louis, 1989-90, 72G in 80 regular-season games and 13G in 12 playoff games.
83 —Wayne Gretzky, Edmonton, 1982-83, 71G in 73 regular-season games and 12G in 16 playoff games.
—Alexander Mogilny, Buffalo, 1992-93, 76G in 77 regular-season games and 7G in 7 playoff games.

MOST GOALS, 50 GAMES FROM START OF SEASON:
61 —Wayne Gretzky, Edmonton, 1981-82. Oct. 7, 1981 - Jan. 22, 1982. (80-game schedule)
—Wayne Gretzky, Edmonton, 1983-84. Oct. 5, 1983 - Jan. 25, 1984. (80-game schedule)
54 —Mario Lemieux, Pittsburgh, 1988-89. Oct. 7, 1988 - Jan. 31, 1989. (80-game schedule)
53 —Wayne Gretzky, Edmonton, 1984-85. Oct. 11, 1984 - Jan. 28, 1985. (80-game schedule).
52 —Brett Hull, St. Louis, 1990-91. Oct. 4, 1990 - Jan. 26, 1991. (80-game schedule).
50 —Maurice Richard, Montreal, 1944-45. Oct. 28, 1944 - March 18, 1945. (50-game schedule)
—Mike Bossy, NY Islanders, 1980-81. Oct. 11, 1980 - Jan. 24, 1981. (80-game schedule)
—Brett Hull, St. Louis, 1991-92. Oct. 5, 1991 – Jan 28, 1992. (80 game schedule)

MOST GOALS, ONE GAME:
7 —Joe Malone, Que. Bulldogs, Jan. 31, 1920, at Quebec. Quebec 10, Toronto 6.
6 —Newsy Lalonde, Montreal, Jan. 10, 1920, at Montreal. Montreal 14, Toronto 7.
—Joe Malone, Que. Bulldogs, March 10, 1920, at Quebec. Quebec 10, Ottawa 4.
—Corb Denneny, Toronto, Jan. 26, 1921, at Toronto. Toronto 10, Hamilton 3.
—Cy Denneny, Ottawa, Mar. 7, 1921, at Ottawa. Ottawa 12, Hamilton 5.
—Syd Howe, Detroit, Feb. 3, 1944, at Detroit. Detroit 12, NY Rangers 2.
—Red Berenson, St. Louis, Nov. 7, 1968, at Philadelphia. St. Louis 8, Philadelphia 0.
—Darryl Sittler, Toronto, Feb. 7, 1976, at Toronto. Toronto 11, Boston 4.

One of the NHL's classiest careers came to end during the summer of 1998 when Mike Gartner hung up the skates after 19 years and 708 goals. Gartner is the only player in league history to score at least 30 goals for five different teams.

Ray Bourque, one of only two defensemen to record 1000 career assists, is the only player to earn a spot on the post-season All-Star Team in each of his first 17 seasons in the league.

MOST GOALS, ONE ROAD GAME:
6 —Red Berenson, St. Louis, Nov. 7, 1968, at Philadelphia. St. Louis 8, Philadelphia 0.
5 —Joe Malone, Montreal, Dec. 19, 1917, at Ottawa. Montreal 9, Ottawa 4.
—Red Green, Hamilton, Dec. 5, 1924, at Toronto. Hamilton 10, Toronto 3.
—Babe Dye, Toronto, Dec. 22, 1924, at Boston. Toronto 10, Boston 2.
—Harry Broadbent, Mtl. Maroons, Jan. 7, 1925, at Hamilton. Mtl. Maroons 6, Hamilton 2.
—Don Murdoch, NY Rangers, Oct. 12, 1976, at Minnesota. NY Rangers 10, Minnesota 4.
—Tim Young, Minnesota, Jan. 15, 1979, at NY Rangers. Minnesota 8, NY Rangers 1.
—Willy Lindstrom, Winnipeg, Mar. 2, 1982, at Philadelphia. Winnipeg 7, Philadelphia 6.
—Bengt Gustafsson, Washington, Jan. 8, 1984, at Philadelphia. Washington 7, Philadelphia 1.
—Wayne Gretzky, Edmonton, Dec. 15, 1984, at St. Louis. Edmonton 8, St. Louis 2.
—Dave Andreychuk, Buffalo, Feb. 6, 1986, at Boston. Buffalo 8, Boston 6.
—Mats Sundin, Quebec, Mar. 5, 1992, at Hartford. Quebec 10, Hartford 4.
—Mario Lemieux, Pittsburgh, Apr. 9, 1993, at New York. Pittsburgh 10, NY Rangers 4.
—Mike Ricci, Quebec, Feb. 17, 1994, at San Jose. Quebec 8, San Jose 2.
—Alexei Zhamnov, Winnipeg, Apr. 1, 1995, at Los Angeles. Winnipeg 7, Los Angeles 7.

MOST GOALS, ONE PERIOD:
4 —Harvey Jackson, Toronto, Nov. 20, 1934, at St. Louis, third period. Toronto 5, St. Louis Eagles 2.
—Max Bentley, Chicago, Jan. 28, 1943, at Chicago, third period. Chicago 10, NY Rangers 1.
—Clint Smith, Chicago, Mar. 4, 1945, at Chicago, third period. Chicago 6, Montreal 4.
—Red Berenson, St. Louis, Nov. 7, 1968, at Philadelphia, second period. St. Louis 8, Philadelphia 0.
—Wayne Gretzky, Edmonton, Feb. 18, 1981, at Edmonton, third period. Edmonton 9, St. Louis 2.
—Grant Mulvey, Chicago, Feb. 3, 1982, at Chicago, first period. Chicago 9, St. Louis 5.
—Bryan Trottier, NY Islanders, Feb. 13, 1982, at New York, second period. NY Islanders 8, Philadelphia 2.
—Al Secord, Chicago, Jan. 7, 1987, at Chicago, second period. Chicago 6, Toronto 4.
—Joe Nieuwendyk, Calgary, Jan. 11, 1989, at Calgary, second period. Calgary 8, Winnipeg 3.
—Peter Bondra, Washington, Feb. 5, 1994, at Washington, first period. Washington 6, Tampa Bay 3.
—Mario Lemieux, Pittsburgh, Jan. 26, 1997, at Montreal, third period. Pittsburgh 5, Montreal 2.

ASSISTS

MOST ASSISTS:
1,910 —Wayne Gretzky, Edmonton, Los Angeles, St. Louis, NY Rangers, in 19 seasons, 1,417GP.
1,090 —Paul Coffey, Edmonton, Pittsburgh, Los Angeles, Detroit, Hartford, Philadelphia, in 18 seasons, 1,268GP.
1,049 —Gordie Howe, Detroit, Hartford in 26 seasons, 1,767GP.
1,040 —Marcel Dionne, Detroit, Los Angeles, NY Rangers in 18 seasons, 1,348GP.
1,036 —Ray Bourque, Boston in 19 seasons, 1,372GP.

MOST ASSISTS, INCLUDING PLAYOFFS:
2,170 —Wayne Gretzky, Edmonton, Los Angeles, St. Louis, NY Rangers, 1,910 regular-season and 260 playoff assists.
1,226 —Paul Coffey, Edmonton, Pittsburgh, Los Angeles, Detroit, Hartford, Philadelphia, 1,090 regular-season and 136 playoff assists.
1,201 —Mark Messier, Edmonton, NY Rangers, 1,015 regular-season and 186 playoff assists.
1,141 —Gordie Howe, Detroit, Hartford, 1,049 regular-season and 92 playoff assists.
1,064 —Marcel Dionne, Detroit, Los Angeles, NY Rangers, 1,040 regular-season and 24 playoff assists.

MOST ASSISTS, ONE SEASON:
163 —Wayne Gretzky, Edmonton, 1985-86. 80 game schedule.
135 —Wayne Gretzky, Edmonton, 1984-85. 80 game schedule.
125 —Wayne Gretzky, Edmonton, 1982-83. 80 game schedule.
122 —Wayne Gretzky, Los Angeles, 1990-91. 80 game schedule.
121 —Wayne Gretzky, Edmonton, 1986-87. 80 game schedule.
120 —Wayne Gretzky, Edmonton, 1981-82. 80 game schedule.
118 —Wayne Gretzky, Edmonton, 1983-84. 80 game schedule.
114 —Wayne Gretzky, Los Angeles, 1988-89. 80 game schedule.
—Mario Lemieux, Pittsburgh, 1988-89. 80 game schedule.
109 —Wayne Gretzky, Edmonton, 1980-81. 80 game schedule.
—Wayne Gretzky, Edmonton, 1987-88. 80 game schedule.
102 —Bobby Orr, Boston, 1970-71. 78 game schedule.
—Wayne Gretzky, Los Angeles, 1989-90. 80 game schedule.

MOST ASSISTS, ONE SEASON, INCLUDING PLAYOFFS:
174 —Wayne Gretzky, Edmonton, 1985-86, 163A in 80 regular-season games and 11A in 10 playoff games.
165 —Wayne Gretzky, Edmonton, 1984-85, 135A in 80 regular-season games and 30A in 18 playoff games.
151 —Wayne Gretzky, Edmonton, 1982-83, 125A in 80 regular-season games and 26A in 16 playoff games.
150 —Wayne Gretzky, Edmonton, 1986-87, 121A in 79 regular-season games and 29A in 21 playoff games.
140 —Wayne Gretzky, Edmonton, 1983-84, 118A in 74 regular-season games and 22A in 19 playoff games.
—Wayne Gretzky, Edmonton, 1987-88, 109A in 64 regular-season games and 31A in 19 playoff games.
133 —Wayne Gretzky, Los Angeles, 1990-91, 122A in 78 regular-season games and 11A in 12 playoff games.
131 —Wayne Gretzky, Los Angeles, 1988-89, 114A in 78 regular-season games and 17A in 11 playoff games.
127 —Wayne Gretzky, Edmonton, 1981-82, 120A in 80 regular-season games and 7A in 5 playoff games.
123 —Wayne Gretzky, Edmonton, 1980-81, 109A in 80 regular-season games and 14A in 9 playoff games.
121 —Mario Lemieux, Pittsburgh, 1988-89, 114A in 76 regular-season games and 7A in 11 playoff games.

MOST ASSISTS, ONE GAME:
7 —Billy Taylor, Detroit, Mar. 16, 1947, at Chicago. Detroit 10, Chicago 6.
—Wayne Gretzky, Edmonton, Feb. 15, 1980, at Edmonton. Edmonton 8, Washington 2.
—Wayne Gretzky, Edmonton, Dec. 11, 1985, at Chicago. Edmonton 12, Chicago 9.
—Wayne Gretzky, Edmonton, Feb. 14, 1986, at Edmonton. Edmonton 8, Quebec 2.
6 —Elmer Lach, Montreal, Feb. 6, 1943.
—Babe Pratt, Toronto, Jan. 8, 1944.
—Don Grosso, Detroit, Feb. 3, 1944.
—Pat Stapleton, Chicago, Mar. 30, 1969.
—Ken Hodge, Boston, Feb. 9, 1971.
—Bobby Orr, Boston, Jan. 1, 1973.
—Ron Stackhouse, Pittsburgh, Mar. 8, 1975.
—Greg Malone, Pittsburgh, Nov. 28, 1979.
—Mike Bossy, NY Islanders, Jan. 6, 1981.
—Guy Chouinard, Calgary, Feb. 25, 1981.
—Mark Messier, Edmonton, Jan. 4, 1984.
—Patrik Sundstrom, Vancouver, Feb 29, 1984.
—Wayne Gretzky, Edmonton, Dec. 20, 1985.
—Paul Coffey, Edmonton, Mar. 14, 1986.
—Gary Suter, Calgary, Apr. 4, 1986.
—Ron Francis, Hartford, Mar. 5, 1987.
—Mario Lemieux, Pittsburgh, Oct. 15, 1988.
—Bernie Nicholls, Los Angeles, Dec. 1, 1988.
—Mario Lemieux, Pittsburgh, Dec. 31, 1988.
—Mario Lemieux, Pittsburgh, Dec. 5, 1992.
—Doug Gilmour, Toronto, Feb. 13, 1993.
—Tomas Sandstrom, Los Angeles, Oct. 9, 1993.
—Eric Lindros, Philadelphia, Feb. 26, 1997.

MOST ASSISTS, ONE ROAD GAME:
7 —Billy Taylor, Detroit, Mar. 16, 1947, at Chicago. Detroit 10, Chicago 6.
—Wayne Gretzky, Edmonton, Dec. 11, 1985, at Chicago. Edmonton 12, Chicago 9.
6 —Bobby Orr, Boston, Jan. 1, 1973, at Vancouver. Boston 8, Vancouver 2.
—Patrik Sundstrom, Vancouver, Feb. 29, 1984, at Pittsburgh. Vancouver 9, Pittsburgh 5.
—Mario Lemieux, Pittsburgh, Dec. 5, 1992, at San Jose. Pittsburgh 9, San Jose 4.
—Eric Lindros, Philadelphia, Feb. 26, 1997, at Ottawa. Philadelphia 8, Ottawa 5.

MOST ASSISTS, ONE PERIOD:
5 —Dale Hawerchuk, Winnipeg, Mar. 6, 1984, at Los Angeles, second period. Winnipeg 7, Los Angeles 3.
4 —Four assists have been recorded in one period on 51 occasions since Buddy O'Connor of Montreal first accomplished the feat vs. NY Rangers on Nov. 8, 1942. Most recent player, Rob Blake of Los Angeles Kings, (Jan. 29, 1998 vs Calgary).

POINTS

MOST POINTS:
2,795 —Wayne Gretzky, Edmonton, Los Angeles, St. Louis, NY Rangers, in 19 seasons, 1,417GP (885G-1910A).
1,850 —Gordie Howe, Detroit, Hartford, in 26 seasons, 1,767GP (801G-1049A).
1,771 —Marcel Dionne, Detroit, Los Angeles, NY Rangers, in 18 seasons, 1,348GP (731G-1,040A).
1,612 —Mark Messier, Edmonton, NY Rangers, Vancouver, in 19 seasons, 1,354GP (597G-1015A).
1,590 —Phil Esposito, Chicago, Boston, NY Rangers in 18 seasons, 1,282GP (717G-873A).

MOST POINTS, INCLUDING PLAYOFFS:
3,177 —Wayne Gretzky, Edmonton, Los Angeles, St. Louis, NY Rangers, 2,795 regular-season and 382 playoff points.
2,010 —Gordie Howe, Detroit, Hartford, 1,850 regular-season and 160 playoff assists.
1,907 —Mark Messier, Edmonton, NY Rangers, Vancouver, 1,612 regular-season and 295 playoff points.
1,816 —Marcel Dionne, Detroit, Los Angeles, NY Rangers, 1,771 regular-season and 45 playoff points.
1,727 —Phil Esposito, Chicago, Boston, NY Rangers, 1,590 regular-season and 137 playoff points.

MOST POINTS, ONE SEASON:
215 —Wayne Gretzky, Edmonton, 1985-86. 80 game schedule.
212 —Wayne Gretzky, Edmonton, 1981-82. 80 game schedule.
208 —Wayne Gretzky, Edmonton, 1984-85. 80 game schedule.
205 —Wayne Gretzky, Edmonton, 1983-84. 80 game schedule.
199 —Mario Lemieux, Pittsburgh, 1988-89. 80 game schedule.
196 —Wayne Gretzky, Edmonton, 1982-83. 80 game schedule.
183 —Wayne Gretzky, Edmonton, 1986-87. 80 game schedule.
168 —Mario Lemieux, Pittsburgh, 1987-88, 80 game schedule.
—Wayne Gretzky, Los Angeles, 1988-89. 80 game schedule.
164 —Wayne Gretzky, Edmonton, 1980-81. 80 game schedule.
163 —Wayne Gretzky, Los Angeles, 1990-91. 80 game schedule.
161 —Mario Lemieux, Pittsburgh, 1995-96. 82 game schedule.
160 —Mario Lemieux, Pittsburgh, 1992-93. 84 game schedule.

MOST POINTS, ONE SEASON, INCLUDING PLAYOFFS:
255 —Wayne Gretzky, Edmonton, 1984-85, 208PTS in 80 regular-season games and 47PTS in 18 playoff games.
240 —Wayne Gretzky, Edmonton, 1983-84, 205PTS in 74 regular-season games and 35PTS in 19 playoff games.
234 —Wayne Gretzky, Edmonton, 1982-83, 196PTS in 80 regular-season games and 38PTS in 16 playoff games.
—Wayne Gretzky, Edmonton, 1985-86, 215PTS in 80 regular-season games and 19PTS in 10 playoff games.
224 —Wayne Gretzky, Edmonton, 1981-82, 212PTS in 80 regular-season games and 12PTS in 5 playoff games.
218 —Mario Lemieux, Pittsburgh, 1988-89, 199PTS in 76 regular-season games and 19PTS in 11 playoff games.
217 —Wayne Gretzky, Edmonton, 1986-87, 183PTS in 79 regular-season games and 34PTS in 21 playoff games.
192 —Wayne Gretzky, Edmonton, 1987-88, 149PTS in 64 regular-season games and 43PTS in 19 playoff games.
190 —Wayne Gretzky, Los Angeles, 1988-89, 168PTS in 78 regular-season games and 22PTS in 11 playoff games.
188 —Mario Lemieux, Pittsburgh, 1995-96, 161PTS in 70 regular-season games and 27PTS in 18 playoff games.
185 —Wayne Gretzky, Edmonton, 1980-81, 164PTS in 80 regular-season games and 21PTS in 9 playoff games.

Eric Lindros, who tied Bobby Clarke's club record with five assists against Ottawa in 1994, established a new team high when he set up a career-high six goals in an 8-5 win over the Senators on February 26, 1997.

MOST POINTS, ONE GAME:

10 —Darryl Sittler, Toronto, Feb. 7, 1976, at Toronto, 6G-4A. Toronto 11, Boston 4.
8 —Maurice Richard, Montreal, Dec. 28, 1944, at Montreal, 5G-3A. Montreal 9, Detroit 1.
—Bert Olmstead, Montreal, Jan. 9, 1954, at Montreal, 4G-4A. Montreal 12, Chicago 1.
—Tom Bladon, Philadelphia, Dec. 11, 1977, at Philadelphia, 4G-4A. Philadelphia 11, Cleveland 1.
—Bryan Trottier, NY Islanders, Dec. 23, 1978, at New York, 5G-3A. NY Islanders 9, NY Rangers 4.
—Peter Stastny, Quebec, Feb. 22, 1981, at Washington, 4G-4A. Quebec 11, Washington 7.
—Anton Stastny, Quebec, Feb. 22, 1981, at Washington, 3G-5A. Quebec 11, Washington 7.
—Wayne Gretzky, Edmonton, Nov. 19, 1983, at Edmonton, 3G-5A. Edmonton 13, New Jersey 4.
—Wayne Gretzky, Edmonton, Jan. 4, 1984, at Edmonton, 4G-4A. Edmonton 12, Minnesota 8.
—Paul Coffey, Edmonton, Mar. 14, 1986, at Edmonton, 2G-6A. Edmonton 12, Detroit 3.
—Mario Lemieux, Pittsburgh, Oct. 15, 1988, at Pittsburgh, 2G-6A. Pittsburgh 9, St. Louis 2.
—Bernie Nicholls, Los Angeles, Dec. 1, 1988, at Los Angeles, 2G-6A. Los Angeles 9, Toronto 3.
—Mario Lemieux, Pittsburgh, Dec. 31, 1988, at Pittsburgh, 5G-3A. Pittsburgh 8, New Jersey 6.

MOST POINTS, ONE ROAD GAME:

8 —Peter Stastny, Quebec, Feb. 22, 1981, at Washington, 4G-4A. Quebec 11, Washington 7.
—Anton Stastny, Quebec, Feb. 22, 1981, at Washington, 3G-5A. Quebec 11, Washington 7.
7 —Billy Taylor, Detroit, Mar. 16, 1947, at Chicago, 7A. Detroit 10, Chicago 6.
—Red Berenson, St. Louis, Nov. 7, 1968, at Philadelphia, 6G-1A. St. Louis 8, Philadelphia 0.
—Gilbert Perreault, Buffalo, Feb. 1, 1976, at California, 2G-5A. Buffalo 9, California 5.
—Peter Stastny, Quebec, Apr. 1, 1982, at Boston, 3G-4A. Quebec 8, Boston 5.
—Wayne Gretzky, Edmonton, Nov. 6, 1983, at Winnipeg, 4G-3A. Edmonton 8, Winnipeg 5.
—Patrik Sundstrom, Vancouver, Feb. 29, 1984, at Pittsburgh, 1G-6A. Vancouver 9, Pittsburgh 5.
—Wayne Gretzky, Edmonton, Dec. 11, 1985, at Chicago. 7A, Edmonton 12, Chicago 9.
—Cam Neely, Boston, Oct. 16, 1988, at Chicago, 3G-4A. Boston 10, Chicago 3.
—Mario Lemieux, Pittsburgh, Jan. 21, 1989, at Edmonton, 2G-5A. Pittsburgh 7, Edmonton 4.
—Dino Ciccarelli, Washington, Mar. 18, 1989, at Hartford, 4G-3A. Washington 8, Hartford 2.
—Mats Sundin, Quebec, Mar. 5, 1992, at Hartford, 5G-2A. Quebec 10, Hartford 4.
—Mario Lemieux, Pittsburgh, Dec. 5, 1992, at San Jose, 1G-6A. Pittsburgh 9, San Jose 4.
—Eric Lindros, Philadelphia, Feb. 26, 1997, at Ottawa, 1G-6A. Philadelphia 8, Ottawa 5.

MOST POINTS, ONE PERIOD:

6 —Bryan Trottier, NY Islanders, Dec. 23, 1978, at NY Islanders, second period. 3G-3A. NY Islanders 9, NY Rangers 4.
5 —Les Cunningham, Chicago, Jan. 28, 1940, at Chicago, third period. 2G- 3A. Chicago 8, Montreal 1.
—Max Bentley, Chicago, Jan. 28, 1943, at Chicago, third period. 4G-1A, Chicago 10, NY Rangers 1.
—Leo Labine, Boston, Nov. 28, 1954, at Boston, second period, 3G-2A. Boston 6, Detroit 2.
—Darryl Sittler, Toronto, Feb. 7, 1976, at Toronto, second period. 3G-2A. Toronto 11, Boston 4.
—Grant Mulvey, Chicago, Feb. 3, 1982, at Chicago, first period. 4G-1A. Chicago 9, St. Louis 5.
—Dale Hawerchuk, Winnipeg, Mar. 6, 1984, at Los Angeles, second period. 5A. Winnipeg 7, Los Angeles 3.
—Jari Kurri, Edmonton, Oct. 26, 1984 at Edmonton, second period. 2G-3A. Edmonton 8, Los Angeles 2.
—Pat Elynuik, Winnipeg, Jan. 20, 1989, at Winnipeg, second period. 2G- 3A. Winnipeg 7, Pittsburgh 3.
—Ray Ferraro, Hartford, Dec. 9, 1989, at Hartford, first period. 3G-2A. Hartford 7, New Jersey 3.
—Stephane Richer, Montreal, Feb. 14, 1990, at Montreal, first period. 2G- 3A. Montreal 10, Vancouver 1.
—Cliff Ronning, Vancouver, Apr. 15, 1993, at Los Angeles, third period. 3G- 2A. Vancouver 8, Los Angeles 6.

POWER-PLAY and SHORTHAND GOALS

MOST POWER-PLAY GOALS, ONE SEASON:

34 —Tim Kerr, Philadelphia, 1985-86. 80 game schedule.
32 —Dave Andreychuk, Buffalo, Toronto, 1992-93. 84 game schedule.
31 —Joe Nieuwendyk, Calgary, 1987-88. 80 game schedule.
—Mario Lemieux, Pittsburgh, 1988-89. 80 game schedule.
—Mario Lemieux, Pittsburgh, 1995-96. 82 game schedule.
29 —Michel Goulet, Quebec, 1987-88. 80 game schedule.
—Brett Hull, St. Louis, 1990-91. 80 game schedule.
—Brett Hull, St. Louis, 1992-93. 84 game schedule.

MOST SHORTHAND GOALS, ONE SEASON:

13 —Mario Lemieux, Pittsburgh, 1988-89. 80 game schedule.
12 —Wayne Gretzky, Edmonton, 1983-84. 80 game schedule.
11 —Wayne Gretzky, Edmonton, 1984-85. 80 game schedule.
10 —Marcel Dionne, Detroit, 1974-75. 80 game schedule.
—Mario Lemieux, Pittsburgh, 1987-88. 80 game schedule.
—Dirk Graham, Chicago, 1988-89. 80 game schedule.

MOST SHORTHAND GOALS, ONE GAME:

3 —Theoren Fleury, Calgary, Mar. 9, 1991, at St. Louis. Calgary 8, St. Louis 4.

OVERTIME SCORING

MOST OVERTIME GOALS, CAREER:

9 —Mario Lemieux, Pittsburgh.
8 —Bob Sweeney, Boston, Buffalo, Calgary.
—Steve Thomas, Toronto, Chicago, NY Islanders, New Jersey.
—Tomas Sandstrom, NY Rangers, Los Angeles, Pittsburgh, Detroit, Anaheim.
7 —Geoff Courtnall, Boston, Edmonton, Washington, Vancouver, St. Louis.
—Jari Kurri, Edmonton, Los Angeles, NY Rangers, Anaheim, Colorado.
—Stephane Richer, Montreal, New Jersey, Tampa Bay.
—Mike Gartner, Washington, Minnesota, NY Rangers, Toronto, Phoenix.

MOST OVERTIME ASSISTS, CAREER:

14 —Wayne Gretzky, Edmonton, Los Angeles, St. Louis, NY Rangers.
12 —Doug Gilmour, St. Louis, Calgary, Toronto, New Jersey.
11 —Mark Messier, Edmonton, NY Rangers, Vancouver.
—Paul Coffey, Edmonton, Pittsburgh, Los Angeles, Detroit, Hartford, Philadelphia.
—Adam Oates, Detroit, St. Louis, Boston, Washington.
10 —Mario Lemieux, Pittsburgh.

MOST OVERTIME POINTS, CAREER:

19 —Mario Lemieux, Pittsburgh, 9G-10A
17 —Mark Messier, Edmonton, NY Rangers, Vancouver. 6G-11A
16 —Wayne Gretzky, Edmonton, Los Angeles, St. Louis, NY Rangers. 2G-14A
14 —Tomas Sandstrom, NY Rangers, Los Angeles, Pittsburgh, Detroit, Anaheim. 8G-6A
13 —Ray Bourque, Boston. 5G-8A
—Doug Gilmour, St. Louis, Calgary, Toronto, New Jersey. 1G-12A
—Jari Kurri, Edmonton, Los Angeles, NY Rangers, Anaheim, Colorado. 7G-6A
—Paul MacLean, Winnipeg, Detroit, St. Louis. 6G-7A
—Dale Hawerchuk, Winnipeg, Buffalo, St. Louis, Philadelphia. 4G-9A
—Steve Thomas, Toronto, Chicago, NY Islanders, New Jersey. 8G-5A
—Adam Oates, Detroit, St. Louis, Boston, Washington, 2G-11A.

SCORING BY A CENTER

MOST GOALS BY A CENTER, CAREER

885 —Wayne Gretzky, Edmonton, Los Angeles, St. Louis, NY Rangers, in 19 seasons.
731 —Marcel Dionne, Detroit, Los Angeles, NY Rangers, in 18 seasons.
717 —Phil Esposito, Chicago, Boston, NY Rangers, in 18 seasons.
613 —Mario Lemieux, Pittsburgh, in 12 seasons.
597 —Mark Messier, Edmonton, NY Rangers, Vancouver, in 19 seasons.

MOST GOALS BY A CENTER, ONE SEASON:

92 —Wayne Gretzky, Edmonton, 1981-82. 80 game schedule.
87 —Wayne Gretzky, Edmonton, 1983-84. 80 game schedule.
85 —Mario Lemieux, Pittsburgh, 1988-89. 80 game schedule.
76 —Phil Esposito, Boston, 1970-71. 78 game schedule.
73 —Wayne Gretzky, Edmonton, 1984-85. 80 game schedule.

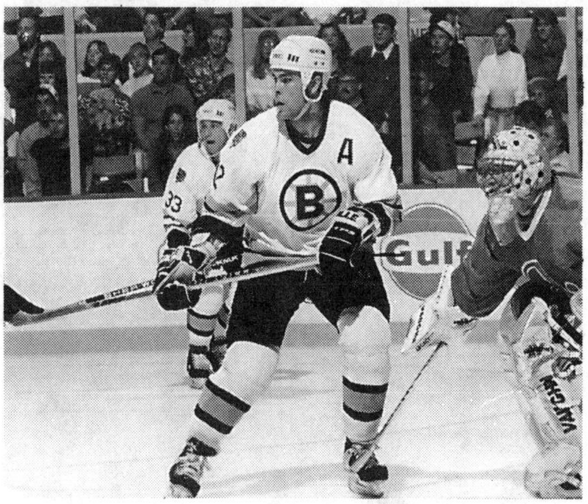

A clever stickhandler and a nifty passer, Adam Oates has recorded at least 50 assists in nine of his 13 NHL seasons. The potent playmaker ranks third all-time with 11 regular-season overtime assists.

MOST ASSISTS BY A CENTER, CAREER:
1,910 —Wayne Gretzky, Edmonton, Los Angeles, St. Louis, NY Rangers, in 19 seasons.
1,040 —Marcel Dionne, Detroit, Los Angeles, NY Rangers, in 18 seasons.
1,015 —Mark Messier, Edmonton, NY Rangers, Vancouver, in 19 seasons.
1,006 —Ron Francis, Hartford, Pittsburgh, in 17 seasons.
926 —Stan Mikita, Chicago, in 22 seasons.

MOST ASSISTS BY A CENTER, ONE SEASON:
163 —Wayne Gretzky, Edmonton, 1985-86. 80 game schedule.
135 —Wayne Gretzky, Edmonton, 1984-85. 80 game schedule.
125 —Wayne Gretzky, Edmonton, 1982-83. 80 game schedule.
122 —Wayne Gretzky, Los Angeles, 1990-91. 80 game schedule.
121 —Wayne Gretzky, Edmonton, 1986-87. 80 game schedule.

MOST POINTS BY A CENTER, CAREER:
2,795 —Wayne Gretzky, Edmonton, Los Angeles, St. Louis, NY Rangers, in 19 seasons.
1,771 —Marcel Dionne, Detroit, Los Angeles, NY Rangers, in 18 seasons.
1,612 —Mark Messier, Edmonton, NY Rangers, Vancouver in 19 seasons.
1,590 —Phil Esposito, Chicago, Boston, NY Rangers, in 18 seasons.
1,467 —Stan Mikita, Chicago, in 22 seasons.

MOST POINTS BY A CENTER, ONE SEASON:
215 —Wayne Gretzky, Edmonton, 1985-86. 80 game schedule.
212 —Wayne Gretzky, Edmonton, 1981-82. 80 game schedule.
208 —Wayne Gretzky, Edmonton, 1984-85. 80 game schedule.
205 —Wayne Gretzky, Edmonton, 1983-84. 80 game schedule.
199 —Mario Lemieux, Pittsburgh, 1988-89. 80 game schedule.

SCORING BY A LEFT WING

MOST GOALS BY A LEFT WING, CAREER:
610 —Bobby Hull, Chicago, Winnipeg, Hartford, in 16 seasons.
556 —John Bucyk, Detroit, Boston, in 23 seasons.
548 —Michel Goulet, Quebec, Chicago, in 15 seasons.
533 —Frank Mahovlich, Toronto, Detroit, Montreal, in 18 seasons.
517 —Dave Andreychuk, Buffalo, Toronto, New Jersey, in 16 seasons.

MOST GOALS BY A LEFT WING, ONE SEASON:
63 —Luc Robitaille, Los Angeles, 1992-93. 84 game schedule.
60 —Steve Shutt, Montreal, 1976-77. 80 game schedule.
58 —Bobby Hull, Chicago, 1968-69. 76 game schedule.
57 —Michel Goulet, Quebec, 1982-83. 80 game schedule.
56 —Charlie Simmer, Los Angeles, 1979-80. 80 game schedule.
—Charlie Simmer, Los Angeles, 1980-81. 80 game schedule.
—Michel Goulet, Quebec, 1983-84. 80 game schedule.

MOST ASSISTS BY A LEFT WING, CAREER:
813 —John Bucyk, Detroit, Boston, in 23 seasons.
604 —Michel Goulet, Quebec, Chicago, in 15 seasons.
595 —Dave Andreychuk, Buffalo, Toronto, New Jersey, in 16 seasons.
579 —Brian Propp, Philadelphia, Boston, Minnesota, Hartford, in 15 seasons.
570 —Frank Mahovlich, Toronto, Detroit, Montreal, in 18 seasons.

MOST ASSISTS BY A LEFT WING, ONE SEASON:
70 —Joe Juneau, Boston, 1992-93. 84 game schedule.
69 —Kevin Stevens, Pittsburgh, 1991-92. 80 game schedule.
67 —Mats Naslund, Montreal, 1985-86. 80 game schedule.
65 —John Bucyk, Boston, 1970-71. 78 game schedule.
—Michel Goulet, Quebec, 1983-84. 80 game schedule.
64 —Mark Messier, Edmonton, 1983-84. 80 game schedule.

MOST POINTS BY A LEFT WING, CAREER:
1,369 —John Bucyk, Detroit, Boston, in 23 seasons.
1,170 —Bobby Hull, Chicago, Winnipeg, Hartford, in 16 seasons.
1,152 —Michel Goulet, Quebec, Chicago, in 15 seasons.
1,112 —Dave Andreychuk, Buffalo, Toronto, New Jersey, in 16 seasons.
1,103 —Frank Mahovlich, Toronto, Detroit, Montreal, in 18 seasons.

MOST POINTS BY A LEFT WING, ONE SEASON:
125 —Luc Robitaille, Los Angeles, 1992-93. 84 game schedule.
123 —Kevin Stevens, Pittsburgh, 1991-92. 80 game schedule.
121 —Michel Goulet, Quebec, 1983-84. 80 game schedule.
116 —John Bucyk, Boston, 1970-71. 78 game schedule.
112 —Bill Barber, Philadelphia, 1975-76. 80 game schedule.

SCORING BY A RIGHT WING

MOST GOALS BY A RIGHT WING, CAREER:
801 —Gordie Howe, Detroit, Hartford, in 26 seasons.
708 —Mike Gartner, Washington, Minnesota, NY Rangers, Toronto, Phoenix, in 19 seasons.
602 —Dino Ciccarelli, Minnesota, Washington, Detroit, Tampa Bay, Florida, in 18 seasons.
601 —Jari Kurri, Edmonton, Los Angeles, NY Rangers, Anaheim, Colorado in 17 seasons.
573 —Mike Bossy, NY Islanders, in 10 seasons.

MOST GOALS BY A RIGHT WING, ONE SEASON:
86 —Brett Hull, St. Louis, 1990-91. 80 game schedule.
76 —Alexander Mogilny, Buffalo, 1992-93. 84 game schedule.
—Teemu Selanne, Winnipeg, 1992-93. 84 game schedule.
72 —Brett Hull, St. Louis, 1989-90. 80 game schedule.
71 —Jari Kurri, Edmonton, 1984-85. 80 game schedule.
70 —Brett Hull, St. Louis, 1991-92. 80 game schedule.

MOST ASSISTS BY A RIGHT WING, CAREER:
1,049 —Gordie Howe, Detroit, Hartford, in 26 seasons.
797 —Jari Kurri, Edmonton, Los Angeles, NY Rangers, Anaheim, Colorado in 17 seasons.
793 —Guy Lafleur, Montreal, NY Rangers, Quebec, in 17 seasons.
638 —Dave Taylor, Los Angeles, in 17 seasons.
627 —Mike Gartner, Washington, Minnesota, NY Rangers, Toronto, Phoenix, in 19 seasons.

MOST ASSISTS BY A RIGHT WING, ONE SEASON:
87 —Jaromir Jagr, Pittsburgh, 1995-96. 82 game schedule.
83 —Mike Bossy, NY Islanders, 1981-82. 80 game schedule.
80 —Guy Lafleur, Montreal, 1976-77. 80 game schedule.
77 —Guy Lafleur, Montreal, 1978-79. 80 game schedule.

No goaltender in NHL history can match Grant Fuhr's offensive output. While he hasn't been able to score a goal, he has collected an NHL record 46 assists. In 1983-84, he set up 14 goals and collected more points than 13 of his teammates.

Dave Taylor surprised many hockey experts by molding himself into one of the NHL's top right wingers. Selected 210th overall in the 1975 Amateur Draft, Taylor toyed with the idea of signing with the WHA's Houston Aeros before deciding to return to Clarkson College.

MOST POINTS BY A RIGHT WING, CAREER:
1,850 —Gordie Howe, Detroit, Hartford, in 26 seasons.
1,398 —Jari Kurri, Edmonton, Los Angeles, NY Rangers, Anaheim, Colorado in 17 seasons.
1,353 —Guy Lafleur, Montreal, NY Rangers, Quebec, in 17 seasons.
1,335 —Mike Gartner, Washington, Minnesota, NY Rangers, Toronto, Phoenix, in 19 seasons.

MOST POINTS BY A RIGHT WING, ONE SEASON:
149 —Jaromir Jagr, Pittsburgh, 1995-96. 82 game schedule.
147 —Mike Bossy, NY Islanders, 1981-82. 80 game schedule.
136 —Guy Lafleur, Montreal, 1976-77. 80 game schedule.
135 —Jari Kurri, Edmonton, 1984-85. 80 game schedule.
132 —Guy Lafleur, Montreal, 1977-78. 80 game schedule.
—Teemu Selanne, Winnipeg, 1992-93. 84 game schedule.

SCORING BY A DEFENSEMAN

MOST GOALS BY A DEFENSEMAN, CAREER:
383 —Paul Coffey, Edmonton, Pittsburgh, Los Angeles, Detroit, Hartford, Philadelphia, in 18 seasons.
375 —Ray Bourque, Boston, in 19 seasons.
310 —Denis Potvin, NY Islanders, in 15 seasons.
291 —Phil Housley, Buffalo, Winnipeg, St. Louis, Calgary, New Jersey, Washington, in 16 seasons.
270 —Bobby Orr, Boston, Chicago, in 12 seasons.
—Al MacInnis, Calgary, St. Louis, in 17 seasons.

MOST GOALS BY A DEFENSEMAN, ONE SEASON:
48 —Paul Coffey, Edmonton, 1985-86. 80 game schedule.
46 —Bobby Orr, Boston, 1974-75. 80 game schedule.
40 —Paul Coffey, Edmonton, 1983-84. 80 game schedule.
39 —Doug Wilson, Chicago, 1981-82. 80 game schedule.
37 —Bobby Orr, Boston, 1970-71. 78 game schedule.
—Bobby Orr, Boston, 1971-72. 78 game schedule.
—Paul Coffey, Edmonton, 1984-85. 80 game schedule.

MOST GOALS BY A DEFENSEMAN, ONE GAME:
5 —Ian Turnbull, Toronto, Feb. 2, 1977, at Toronto. Toronto 9, Detroit 1.
4 —Harry Cameron, Toronto, Dec. 26, 1917, at Toronto. Toronto 7, Montreal 5.
—Harry Cameron, Montreal, Mar. 3, 1920, at Quebec City. Montreal 16, Que. Bulldogs 3.
—Sprague Cleghorn, Montreal, Jan. 14, 1922, at Montreal. Montreal 10, Hamilton 6.
—Johnny McKinnon, Pit. Pirates, Nov. 19, 1929, at Pittsburgh. Pit. Pirates 10, Toronto 5.
—Hap Day, Toronto, Nov. 19, 1929, at Pittsburgh. Pit. Pirates 10, Toronto 5.
—Tom Bladon, Philadelphia, Dec. 11, 1977, at Philadelphia. Philadelphia 11, Cleveland 1.
—Ian Turnbull, Los Angeles, Dec. 12, 1981, at Los Angeles. Los Angeles 7, Vancouver 5.
—Paul Coffey, Edmonton, Oct. 26, 1984, at Calgary. Edmonton 6, Calgary 5.

MOST ASSISTS BY A DEFENSEMAN, CAREER:
1,090 —Paul Coffey, Edmonton, Pittsburgh, Los Angeles, Detroit, Hartford, Philadelphia, in 18 seasons.
1,036 —Ray Bourque, Boston, in 19 seasons.
838 —Larry Murphy, Los Angeles, Washington, Minnesota, Pittsburgh, Toronto, Detroit, in 18 seasons.
750 —Larry Robinson, Montreal, Los Angeles, in 20 seasons.
742 —Denis Potvin, NY Islanders, in 15 seasons.

MOST ASSISTS BY A DEFENSEMAN, ONE SEASON:
102 —Bobby Orr, Boston, 1970-71. 78 game schedule.
90 —Paul Coffey, Edmonton, 1985-86. 80 game schedule.
90 —Bobby Orr, Boston, 1973-74. 78 game schedule.
89 —Bobby Orr, Boston, 1974-75. 80 game schedule.

MOST ASSISTS BY A DEFENSEMAN, ONE GAME:
6 —Babe Pratt, Toronto, Jan. 8, 1944, at Toronto. Toronto 12, Boston 3.
—Pat Stapleton, Chicago, Mar. 30, 1969, at Chicago. Chicago 9, Detroit 5.
—Bobby Orr, Boston, Jan. 1, 1973, at Vancouver, Boston 8, Vancouver 2.
—Ron Stackhouse, Pittsburgh, Mar. 8, 1975, at Pittsburgh. Pittsburgh 8, Philadelphia 2.
—Paul Coffey, Edmonton, Mar. 14, 1986, at Edmonton. Edmonton 12, Detroit 3.
—Gary Suter, Calgary, Apr. 4, 1986, at Calgary. Calgary 9, Edmonton 3.

MOST POINTS BY A DEFENSEMAN, CAREER:
1,473 —Paul Coffey, Edmonton, Pittsburgh, Los Angeles, Detroit, Hartford, Philadelphia in 18 seasons.
1,411 —Ray Bourque, Boston, in 19 seasons.
1,103 —Larry Murphy, Los Angeles, Washington, Minnesota, Pittsburgh, Toronto, Detroit, in 18 seasons.
1,052 —Denis Potvin, NY Islanders, in 15 seasons.
1,021 —Phil Housley, Buffalo, Winnipeg, St. Louis, Calgary, New Jersey, Washington, in 16 seasons.

MOST POINTS BY A DEFENSEMAN, ONE SEASON:
139 —Bobby Orr, Boston, 1970-71. 78 game schedule.
138 —Paul Coffey, Edmonton, 1985-86. 80 game schedule.
135 —Bobby Orr, Boston, 1974-75. 80 game schedule.
126 —Paul Coffey, Edmonton, 1983-84. 80 game schedule.
122 —Bobby Orr, Boston, 1973-74. 78 game schedule.

MOST POINTS BY A DEFENSEMAN, ONE GAME:
8 —Tom Bladon, Philadelphia, Dec. 11, 1977, at Philadelphia. 4G-4A. Philadelphia 11, Cleveland 1.
—Paul Coffey, Edmonton, Mar. 14, 1986, at Edmonton. 2G-6A. Edmonton 12, Detroit 3.
7 —Bobby Orr, Boston, Nov. 15, 1973, at Boston, 3G-4A. Boston 10, NY Rangers 2.

SCORING BY A GOALTENDER

MOST POINTS BY A GOALTENDER, CAREER:
46 —Grant Fuhr, Edmonton, Toronto, Buffalo, Los Angeles, St. Louis, in 17 seasons. (46A)
45 —Tom Barrasso, Buffalo, Pittsburgh, in 15 seasons. (45A)

MOST POINTS BY A GOALTENDER, ONE SEASON:
14 —Grant Fuhr, Edmonton, 1983-84. (14A)
9 —Curtis Joseph, St. Louis, 1991-92. (9A)
8 —Mike Palmateer, Washington, 1980-81. (8A)
—Grant Fuhr, Edmonton, 1987-88. (8A)
—Ron Hextall, Philadelphia, 1988-89. (8A)
—Tom Barrasso, Pittsburgh, 1992-93. (8A)
7 —Ron Hextall, Philadelphia, 1987-88. (1G-6A)
—Mike Vernon, Calgary, 1987-88. (7A)

MOST POINTS BY A GOALTENDER, ONE GAME:
3 —Jeff Reese, Calgary, Feb. 10, 1993, at Calgary. Calgary 13, San Jose 1. (3A)

SCORING BY A ROOKIE

MOST GOALS BY A ROOKIE, ONE SEASON:
- **76 —Teemu Selanne,** Winnipeg, 1992-93. 84 game schedule.
- 53 —Mike Bossy, NY Islanders, 1977-78. 80 game schedule.
- 51 —Joe Nieuwendyk, Calgary, 1987-88. 80 game schedule.
- 45 —Dale Hawerchuk, Winnipeg, 1981-82. 80 game schedule.
- —Luc Robitaille, Los Angeles, 1986-87. 80 game schedule.

MOST GOALS BY A PLAYER IN HIS FIRST NHL SEASON, ONE GAME:
- **5 —Howie Meeker,** Toronto, Jan. 8, 1947, at Toronto. Toronto 10, Chicago 4.
- **—Don Murdoch,** NY Rangers, Oct. 12, 1976, at Minnesota. NY Rangers 10, Minnesota 4.

MOST GOALS BY A PLAYER IN HIS FIRST NHL GAME:
- **3 —Alex Smart,** Montreal, Jan. 14, 1943, at Montreal. Montreal 5, Chicago 1.
- **—Real Cloutier,** Quebec, Oct. 10, 1979, at Quebec. Atlanta 5, Quebec 3.

MOST ASSISTS BY A ROOKIE, ONE SEASON:
- **70 —Peter Stastny,** Quebec, 1980-81. 80 game schedule.
- **—Joe Juneau,** Boston, 1992-93. 84 game schedule.
- 63 —Bryan Trottier, NY Islanders, 1975-76. 80 game schedule.
- 62 —Sergei Makarov, Calgary, 1989-90. 80 game schedule.
- 60 —Larry Murphy, Los Angeles, 1980-81. 80 game schedule.

MOST ASSISTS BY A PLAYER IN HIS FIRST NHL SEASON, ONE GAME:
- **7 —Wayne Gretzky,** Edmonton, Feb. 15, 1980, at Edmonton. Edmonton 8, Washington 2.
- 6 —Gary Suter, Calgary, Apr. 4, 1986, at Calgary. Calgary 9, Edmonton 3.

MOST ASSISTS BY A PLAYER IN HIS FIRST NHL GAME:
- **4 —Earl Reibel,** Detroit, Oct. 8, 1953, at Detroit. Detroit 4, NY Rangers 1.
- **—Roland Eriksson,** Minnesota, Oct. 6, 1976, at New York. NY Rangers 6, Minnesota 5.
- 3 —Al Hill, Philadelphia, Feb. 14, 1977, at Philadelphia. Philadelphia 6, St. Louis 4.

MOST POINTS BY A ROOKIE, ONE SEASON:
- **132 —Teemu Selanne,** Winnipeg, 1992-93, 84 game schedule.
- 109 —Peter Stastny, Quebec, 1980-81. 80 game schedule.
- 103 —Dale Hawerchuk, Winnipeg, 1981-82. 80 game schedule.
- 102 —Joe Juneau, Boston, 1992-93. 84 game schedule.
- 100 —Mario Lemieux, Pittsburgh, 1984-85. 80 game schedule.

MOST POINTS BY A PLAYER IN HIS FIRST NHL SEASON, ONE GAME:
- **8 —Peter Stastny,** Quebec, Feb. 22, 1981, at Washington. 4G-4A. Quebec 11, Washington 7.
- **—Anton Stastny,** Quebec, Feb. 22, 1981, at Washington. 3G-5A. Quebec 11, Washington 7.
- 7 —Wayne Gretzky, Edmonton, Feb. 15, 1980, at Edmonton. 7A. Edmonton 8, Washington 2.
- —Sergei Makarov, Calgary, Feb. 25, 1990, at Calgary. 2G-5A. Calgary 10, Edmonton 4.
- 6 —Wayne Gretzky, Edmonton, Mar. 29, 1980, at Toronto. 2G-4A. Edmonton 8, Toronto 5.
- —Gary Suter, Calgary, Apr. 4, 1986, at Calgary. 6A. Calgary 9, Edmonton 3.

MOST POINTS BY A PLAYER IN HIS FIRST NHL GAME:
- **5 —Al Hill,** Philadelphia, Feb. 14, 1977, at Philadelphia. 2G-3A. Philadelphia 6, St. Louis 4.
- 4 —Alex Smart, Montreal, Jan. 14, 1943, at Montreal. 3G-1A. Montreal 5, Chicago 1.
- —Earl Reibel, Detroit, Oct. 8, 1953, at Detroit. 4A. Detroit 4, NY Rangers 1.
- —Roland Eriksson, Minnesota, Oct. 6, 1976 at New York. 4A. NY Rangers 6, Minnesota 5.

SCORING BY A ROOKIE DEFENSEMAN

MOST GOALS BY A ROOKIE DEFENSEMAN, ONE SEASON:
- **23 —Brian Leetch,** NY Rangers, 1988-89. 80 game schedule.
- 22 —Barry Beck, Colorado, 1977-78. 80 game schedule.
- 19 —Reed Larson, Detroit, 1977-78. 80 game schedule.
- —Phil Housley, Buffalo, 1982-83. 80 game schedule.

MOST ASSISTS BY A ROOKIE DEFENSEMAN, ONE SEASON:
- **60 —Larry Murphy,** Los Angeles, 1980-81. 80 game schedule.
- 55 —Chris Chelios, Montreal, 1984-85. 80 game schedule.
- 50 —Stefan Persson, NY Islanders, 1977-78. 80 game schedule.
- —Gary Suter, Calgary, 1985-86. 80 game schedule.
- 49 —Nicklas Lidstrom, Detroit, 1991-92. 80 game schedule.

MOST POINTS BY A ROOKIE DEFENSEMAN, ONE SEASON:
- **76 —Larry Murphy,** Los Angeles, 1980-81. 80 game schedule.
- 71 —Brian Leetch, NY Rangers, 1988-89. 80 game schedule.
- 68 —Gary Suter, Calgary, 1985-86. 80 game schedule.
- 66 —Phil Housley, Buffalo, 1982-83. 80 game schedule.
- 65 —Ray Bourque, Boston, 1979-80. 80 game schedule.

Left: In a game against Washington on February 22, 1981, Peter Stastny, shown here, and his brother Anton each recorded a rookie-record eight points as the Nordiques downed the Capitals 11-7. The record-breaking point came when Anton set up brother Peter with only five seconds remaining in the game. Below: A late offensive charge by Calgary defenseman Gary Suter enabled him to outpace Toronto's Wendel Clark and capture the Calder Trophy as the league's top rookie in 1985-86. Suter recorded 68 points in his freshman campaign, the third-highest total among rookie rearguards.

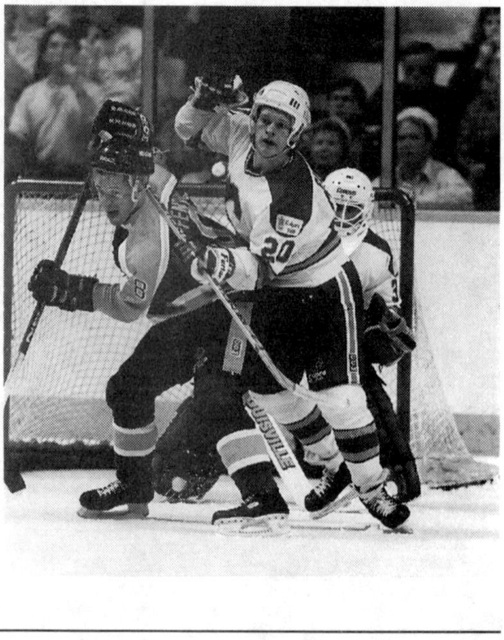

PER-GAME SCORING AVERAGES

HIGHEST GOALS-PER-GAME AVERAGE, CAREER (AMONG PLAYERS WITH 200 OR MORE GOALS):

.823 —Mario Lemieux, Pittsburgh, 613G, 745GP, from 1984-85 – 1996-97.
.762 —Mike Bossy, NY Islanders, 573G, 752GP, from 1977-78 – 1986-87.
.754 —Cy Denneny, Ottawa, Boston, 246G, 326GP, from 1917-18 – 1928-29.
.692 —Brett Hull, Calgary, St. Louis, 554G, 801GP, from 1986-87 – 1997-98.
.649 —Teemu Selanne, Winnipeg, Anaheim, 266G, 410GP, from 1992-93 – 1997-98.
.625 —Wayne Gretzky, Edmonton, Los Angeles, St. Louis, NY Rangers, 885G, 1,417GP, from 1979-80 – 1997-98.
.619 —Eric Lindros, Philadelphia, 223G, 360GP, from 1992-93 – 1997-98.

HIGHEST GOALS-PER-GAME AVERAGE, ONE SEASON (AMONG PLAYERS WITH 20-OR-MORE GOALS):

2.20 —Joe Malone, Montreal, 1917-18, with 44G in 20GP.
1.80 —Cy Denneny, Ottawa, 1917-18, with 36G in 20GP.
1.64 —Newsy Lalonde, Montreal, 1917-18, with 23G in 14GP.
1.63 —Joe Malone, Quebec, 1919-20, with 39G in 24GP.
1.61 —Newsy Lalonde, Montreal, 1919-20, with 37G in 23GP.

HIGHEST GOALS-PER-GAME AVERAGE, ONE SEASON (AMONG PLAYERS WITH 50-OR-MORE GOALS):

1.18 —Wayne Gretzky, Edmonton, 1983-84, with 87G in 74GP.
1.15 —Wayne Gretzky, Edmonton, 1981-82, with 92G in 80GP.
—Mario Lemieux, Pittsburgh, 1992-93, with 69G in 60GP.
1.12 —Mario Lemieux, Pittsburgh, 1988-89, with 85G in 76GP.
1.10 —Brett Hull, St. Louis, 1990-91, with 86G in 78GP.
1.02 —Cam Neely, Boston, 1993-94, with 50G in 49GP.
1.00 —Maurice Richard, Montreal, 1944-45, with 50G in 50GP.

HIGHEST ASSISTS-PER-GAME AVERAGE, CAREER (AMONG PLAYERS WITH 300 OR MORE ASSISTS):

1.348 —Wayne Gretzky, Edmonton, Los Angeles, St. Louis, NY Rangers, 1,910A, 1,417GP from 1979-80 – 1997-98.
1.183 —Mario Lemieux, Pittsburgh, 881A, 745GP from 1984-85 – 1996-97.
.982 —Bobby Orr, Boston, Chicago, 645A, 657GP from 1966-67 – 1978-79.
.877 —Adam Oates, Detroit, St. Louis, Boston, Washington, 796A, 908GP from 1984-85 – 1997-98.
.860 —Paul Coffey, Edmonton, Pittsburgh, Los Angeles, Detroit, Hartford, Philadelphia, 1,090A, 1,268GP from 1980-81 – 1997-98.

HIGHEST ASSISTS-PER-GAME AVERAGE, ONE SEASON (AMONG PLAYERS WITH 35-OR-MORE ASSISTS):

2.04 —Wayne Gretzky, Edmonton, 1985-86, with 163A in 80GP.
1.70 —Wayne Gretzky, Edmonton, 1987-88, with 109A in 64GP.
1.69 —Wayne Gretzky, Edmonton, 1984-85, with 135A in 80GP.
1.59 —Wayne Gretzky, Edmonton, 1983-84, with 118A in 74GP.
1.56 —Wayne Gretzky, Edmonton, 1982-83, with 125A in 80GP.
1.56 —Wayne Gretzky, Los Angeles, 1990-91, with 122A in 78GP.
1.53 —Wayne Gretzky, Edmonton, 1986-87, with 121A in 79GP.
1.52 —Mario Lemieux, Pittsburgh, 1992-93, with 91A in 60GP.
1.50 —Wayne Gretzky, Edmonton, 1981-82, with 120A in 80GP.
1.50 —Mario Lemieux, Pittsburgh, 1988-89, with 114A in 76GP.

HIGHEST POINTS-PER-GAME AVERAGE, CAREER: (AMONG PLAYERS WITH 500 OR MORE POINTS):

2.005 —Mario Lemieux, Pittsburgh, 1,494PTS (613G-881A), 745GP from 1984-85 – 1996-97.
1.972 —Wayne Gretzky, Edmonton, Los Angeles, St. Louis, NY Rangers, 2,795PTS (885G-1,910A), 1,417GP from 1979-80 – 1997-98.
1.497 —Mike Bossy, NY Islanders, 1,126PTS (573G-553A), 752GP from 1978-79 – 1986-87.
1.393 —Bobby Orr, Boston, Chicago, 915PTS (270G-645A), 657GP from 1966-67 – 1978-79.
1.310 —Teemu Selanne, Winnipeg, Anaheim, 537PTS (266G-271A), 410GP from 1992-93 – 1997-98.
1.283 —Steve Yzerman, Detroit, 1,409PTS (563G-846A), 1,098GP from 1983-84 – 1997-98.

HIGHEST POINTS-PER-GAME AVERAGE, ONE SEASON (AMONG PLAYERS WITH 50-OR-MORE POINTS):

2.77 —Wayne Gretzky, Edmonton, 1983-84, with 205PTS in 74GP.
2.69 —Wayne Gretzky, Edmonton, 1985-86, with 215PTS in 80GP.
2.67 —Mario Lemieux, Pittsburgh, 1992-93, with 160PTS in 60GP.
2.65 —Wayne Gretzky, Edmonton, 1981-82, with 212PTS in 80GP.
2.62 —Mario Lemieux, Pittsburgh, 1988-89, with 199PTS in 78GP.
2.60 —Wayne Gretzky, Edmonton, 1984-85, with 208PTS in 80GP.
2.45 —Wayne Gretzky, Edmonton, 1982-83, with 196PTS in 80GP.
2.33 —Wayne Gretzky, Edmonton, 1987-88, with 149PTS in 64GP.
2.32 —Wayne Gretzky, Edmonton, 1986-87, with 183PTS in 79GP.
2.30 —Mario Lemieux, Pittsburgh, 1995-96 with 161PTS in 70GP.
2.18 —Mario Lemieux, Pittsburgh, 1987-88 with 168PTS in 77GP.
2.15 —Wayne Gretzky, Los Angeles, 1988-89, with 168PTS in 78GP.
2.09 —Wayne Gretzky, Los Angeles, 1990-91, with 163 PTS in 78GP.
2.08 —Mario Lemieux, Pittsburgh, 1989-90, with 123 PTS in 59GP.
2.05 —Wayne Gretzky, Edmonton, 1980-81, with 164PTS in 80GP.

SCORING PLATEAUS

MOST 20-OR-MORE GOAL SEASONS:

22 —Gordie Howe, Detroit, Hartford in 26 seasons.
17 —Marcel Dionne, Detroit, Los Angeles, NY Rangers, in 18 seasons.
—Mike Gartner, Washington, Minnesota, NY Rangers, Toronto, Phoenix, in 19 seasons.
—Wayne Gretzky, Edmonton, Los Angeles, St. Louis, NY Rangers, in 19 seasons.
16 —Phil Esposito, Chicago, Boston, NY Rangers, in 18 seasons.
—Norm Ullman, Detroit, Toronto, in 20 seasons.
—John Bucyk, Detroit, Boston, in 23 seasons.
—Mark Messier, Edmonton, NY Ranagers, Vancouver, in 19 seasons.
—Ron Francis, Hartford, Pittsburgh, in 17 seasons.

MOST CONSECUTIVE 20-OR-MORE GOAL SEASONS:

22 —Gordie Howe, Detroit, 1949-50 – 1970-71.
17 —Marcel Dionne, Detroit, Los Angeles, NY Rangers, 1971-72 – 1987-88.
16 —Phil Esposito, Chicago, Boston, NY Rangers, 1964-65 – 1979-80.
15 —Mike Gartner, Washington, Minnesota, NY Rangers, Toronto, 1979-80 – 1993-94.
14 —Maurice Richard, Montreal, 1943-44 – 1956-57.
—Stan Mikita, Chicago, 1961-62 – 1974-75.
—Michel Goulet, Quebec, Chicago, 1979-80 – 1992-93.

MOST 30-OR-MORE GOAL SEASONS:

17 —Mike Gartner, Washington, Minnesota, NY Rangers, Toronto, Phoenix, in 19 seasons.
14 —Gordie Howe, Detroit, Hartford, in 26 seasons.
—Marcel Dionne, Detroit, Los Angeles, NY Rangers, in 18 seasons.
—Wayne Gretzky, Edmonton, Los Angeles, St. Louis, NY Rangers, in 19 seasons.
13 —Bobby Hull, Chicago, Winnipeg, Hartford, in 16 seasons.
—Phil Esposito, Chicago, Boston, NY Rangers, in 18 seasons.

Born Stanislaus Gvoth in Sokolce, Czechoslovakia, Stan Mikita was a young boy when his parents sent him to Canada to live with an uncle. Mikita adopted his uncle's name and went on to record 14 consecutive 20-goal seasons with the Chicago Black Hawks.

MOST CONSECUTIVE 30-OR-MORE GOAL SEASONS:
15 —Mike Gartner, Washington, Minnesota, NY Rangers, Toronto, 1979-80 – 1993-94.
13 —Bobby Hull, Chicago, 1959-60 – 1971-72.
—Phil Esposito, Boston, NY Rangers, 1967-68 – 1979-80.
—Wayne Gretzky, Edmonton, Los Angeles, 1979-80 – 1991-92.
12 —Marcel Dionne, Detroit, Los Angeles,1974-75 – 1985-86.
10 —Darryl Sittler, Toronto, Philadelphia, 1973-74 – 1982-83.
—Mike Bossy, NY Islanders, 1977-78 – 1986-87.
—Jari Kurri, Edmonton, 1980-81 – 1989-90.

MOST 40-OR-MORE GOAL SEASONS:
12 —Wayne Gretzky, Edmonton, Los Angeles, St. Louis, NY Rangers, in 19 seasons.
10 —Marcel Dionne, Detroit, Los Angeles, NY Rangers, in 18 seasons.
—Mario Lemieux, Pittsburgh, in 12 seasons.
9 —Mike Bossy, NY Islanders, in 10 seasons.
—Mike Gartner, Washington, Minnesota, NY Rangers, Toronto, Phoenix, in 19 seasons.

MOST CONSECUTIVE 40-OR-MORE GOAL SEASONS:
12 —Wayne Gretzky, Edmonton, Los Angeles, 1979-80 – 1990-91.
9 —Mike Bossy, NY Islanders, 1977-78 – 1985-86.
8 —Luc Robitaille, Los Angeles, 1986-87 – 1993-94.
7 —Phil Esposito, Boston, 1968-69 – 1974-75.
—Michel Goulet, Quebec, 1981-82 – 1987-88.
—Jari Kurri, Edmonton, 1982-83 – 1988-89.

MOST 50-OR-MORE GOAL SEASONS:
9 —Mike Bossy, NY Islanders, in 10 seasons.
—Wayne Gretzky, Edmonton, Los Angeles, St. Louis, NY Rangers, in 18 seasons.
6 —Guy Lafleur, Montreal, NY Rangers, Quebec, in 17 seasons.
—Marcel Dionne, Detroit, Los Angeles, NY Rangers, in 18 seasons.
—Mario Lemieux, Pittsburgh, in 12 seasons.
5 —Bobby Hull, Chicago, Winnipeg, Hartford, in 16 seasons.
—Phil Esposito, Chicago, Boston, NY Rangers, in 18 seasons.
—Brett Hull, Calgary, St. Louis, in 12 seasons.
—Steve Yzerman, Detroit, in 15 seasons.

MOST CONSECUTIVE 50-OR-MORE GOAL SEASONS:
9 —Mike Bossy, NY Islanders, 1977-78 – 1985-86.
8 —Wayne Gretzky, Edmonton, 1979-80 – 1986-87.
6 —Guy Lafleur, Montreal, 1974-75 – 1979-80.
5 —Phil Esposito, Boston, 1970-71 – 1974-75.
—Marcel Dionne, Los Angeles, 1978-79 – 1982-83.
—Brett Hull, St. Louis, 1989-90 – 1993-94.

MOST 60-OR-MORE GOAL SEASONS:
5 —Mike Bossy, NY Islanders, in 10 seasons.
—Wayne Gretzky, Edmonton, Los Angeles, St. Louis, NY Rangers, in 19 seasons.
4 —Phil Esposito, Chicago, Boston, NY Rangers, in 18 seasons.
—Mario Lemieux, Pittsburgh, in 12 seasons.

MOST CONSECUTIVE 60-OR-MORE GOAL SEASONS:
4 —Wayne Gretzky, Edmonton, 1981-82 – 1984-85.
3 —Mike Bossy, NY Islanders, 1980-81 – 1982-83.
—Brett Hull, St. Louis, 1989-90 – 1991-92.
2 —Phil Esposito, Boston, 1970-71 – 1971-72, 1973-74 – 1974-75.
—Jari Kurri, Edmonton, 1984-85 – 1985-86.
—Mario Lemieux, Pittsburgh, 1987-88 – 1988-89.
—Steve Yzerman, Detroit, 1988-89 – 1989-90.
—Pavel Bure, Vancouver, 1992-93 – 1993-94.

MOST 100-OR-MORE POINT SEASONS:
15 —Wayne Gretzky, Edmonton, Los Angeles, St. Louis, NY Rangers, in 19 seasons.
10 —Mario Lemieux, Pittsburgh, in 12 seasons.
8 —Marcel Dionne, Detroit, Los Angeles, NY Rangers, in 18 seasons.
7 —Mike Bossy, NY Islanders, in 10 seasons.
—Peter Stastny, Quebec, New Jersey, St. Louis, in 15 seasons.

MOST CONSECUTIVE 100-OR-MORE POINT SEASONS:
13 —Wayne Gretzky, Edmonton, Los Angeles, 1979-80 – 1991-92.
6 —Bobby Orr, Boston, 1969-70 – 1974-75.
—Guy Lafleur, Montreal, 1974-75 – 1979-80.
—Mike Bossy, NY Islanders,1980-81 – 1985-86.
—Peter Stastny, Quebec, 1980-81 – 1985-86.
—Mario Lemieux, Pittsburgh, 1984-85 – 1989-90.
—Steve Yzerman, Detroit, 1987-88 – 1992-93.

THREE-OR-MORE-GOAL GAMES

MOST THREE-OR-MORE GOAL GAMES, CAREER:
50 —Wayne Gretzky, Edmonton, Los Angeles, St. Louis, NY Rangers, in 19 seasons, 37 three-goal games, 9 four-goal games, 4 five-goal games.
39 —Mike Bossy, NY Islanders, in 10 seasons, 30 three-goal games, 9 four-goal games.
—Mario Lemieux, Pittsburgh, in 12 seasons, 26 three-goal games, 10 four-goal games and 3 five-goal games.
32 —Phil Esposito, Chicago, Boston, NY Rangers, in 18 seasons, 27 three-goal games, 5 four-goal games.
28 —Bobby Hull, Chicago, Winnipeg, Hartford, in 16 seasons, 24 three-goal games, 4 four-goal games.
—Marcel Dionne, Detroit, Los Angeles, NY Rangers, in 18 seasons, 25 three-goal games, 3 four-goal games.
— Brett Hull, Calgary, St. Louis, in 12 seasons, 26 three-goal games, 2 four-goal games.
26 —Cy Denneny, Ottawa in 12 seasons. 20 three-goal games, 5 four-goal games, 1 six-goal game.
—Maurice Richard, Montreal, in 18 seasons, 23 three-goal games, 2 four-goal games, 1 five-goal game.

MOST THREE-OR-MORE GOAL GAMES, ONE SEASON:
10 —Wayne Gretzky, Edmonton, 1981-82. 6 three-goal games, 3 four-goal games, 1 five-goal game.
—Wayne Gretzky, Edmonton, 1983-84. 6 three-goal games, 4 four-goal games.
9 —Mike Bossy, NY Islanders, 1980-81. 6 three-goal games, 3 four-goal games.
—Mario Lemieux, Pittsburgh, 1988-89. 7 three-goal games, 1 four-goal game, 1 five-goal game.
8 —Brett Hull, St. Louis, 1991-92. 8 three-goal games.
7 —Joe Malone, Montreal, 1917-18. 2 three-goal games, 2 four-goal games, 3 five-goal games.
—Phil Esposito, Boston, 1970-71. 7 three-goal games.
—Rick Martin, Buffalo, 1975-76. 6 three-goal games, 1 four-goal game.
—Alexander Mogilny, Buffalo, 1992-93. 5 three-goal games, 2 four-goal games.

Dave "Tiger" Williams claws his way towards the Buffalo net with fellow tough-guy Jerry Korab in pursuit. Williams remains the NHL's all-time penalty leader, spending 3,966 minutes in the sin-bin. Korab was well acquainted with the penalty box as well, racking up 1,629 minutes of atonement time in the off-ice confessional.

SCORING STREAKS

LONGEST CONSECUTIVE GOAL-SCORING STREAK:
16 Games —Harry Broadbent, Ottawa, 1921-22. 25 goals during streak.
14 Games —Joe Malone, Montreal, 1917-18. 35 goals during streak.
13 Games —Newsy Lalonde, Montreal, 1920-21. 24 goals during streak.
—Charlie Simmer, Los Angeles, 1979-80. 17 goals during streak.
12 Games —Cy Denneny, Ottawa, 1917-18. 23 goals during streak.
—Dave Lumley, Edmonton, 1981-82. 15 goals during streak.
—Mario Lemieux, Pittsburgh, 1992-93. 18 goals during streak.

LONGEST CONSECUTIVE ASSIST-SCORING STREAK:
23 Games —Wayne Gretzky, Los Angeles, 1990-91. 48A during streak.
18 Games —Adam Oates, Boston, 1992-93. 28A during streak.
17 Games —Wayne Gretzky, Edmonton, 1983-84. 38A during streak.
—Paul Coffey, Edmonton, 1985-86. 27A during streak.
—Wayne Gretzky, Los Angeles, 1989-90. 35A during streak.
15 Games —Jari Kurri, Edmonton, 1983-84. 21A during streak.
—Brian Leetch, NY Rangers, 1991-92. 23A during streak.

LONGEST CONSECUTIVE POINT SCORING STREAK:
51 Games —Wayne Gretzky, Edmonton, 1983-84. 61G-92A-153PTS during streak.
46 Games —Mario Lemieux, Pittsburgh, 1989-90. 39G-64A-103PTS during streak.
39 Games —Wayne Gretzky, Edmonton, 1985-86. 33G-75A-108PTS during streak.
30 Games —Wayne Gretzky, Edmonton, 1982-83. 24G52A-76PTS during streak.
—Mats Sundin, Quebec, 1992-93. 21G-25A-46PTS during streak.
28 Games —Guy Lafleur, Montreal, 1976-77. 19G-42A-61PTS during streak.
—Wayne Gretzky, Edmonton, 1984-85. 20G-43A-63PTS during streak.
—Mario Lemieux, Pittsburgh, 1985-86. 21G-38A-59PTS during streak.
—Paul Coffey, Edmonton, 1985-86. 16G-39A-55PTS during streak.
—Steve Yzerman, Detroit, 1988-89. 29G-36A-65PTS during streak.

LONGEST CONSECUTIVE POINT-SCORING STREAK FROM START OF SEASON:
51 Games —Wayne Gretzky, Edmonton, 1983-84. 61G-92A-153PTS during streak which was stopped by goaltender Markus Mattsson and Los Angeles on Jan. 28, 1984.

LONGEST CONSECUTIVE POINT-SCORING STREAK BY A DEFENSEMAN:
28 Games —Paul Coffey, Edmonton, 1985-86. 16G-39A-55PTS during streak.
19 Games —Ray Bourque, Boston, 1987-88. 6G-21A-27PTS during streak.
17 Games —Ray Bourque, Boston, 1984-85. 4G-24A-28PTS during streak.
—Brian Leetch, NY Rangers, 1991-92. 5G-24A-29PTS during streak.
16 Games —Gary Suter, Calgary, 1987-88. 8G-17A-25PTS during streak.
15 Games —Bobby Orr, Boston, 1970-71. 10G-23A-33PTS during streak.
—Bobby Orr, Boston, 1973-74. 8G-15A-23PTS during streak.
—Steve Duchesne, Quebec, 1992-93. 4G-17A-21PTS during streak.
—Chris Chelios, Chicago, 1995-96. 4G-16A-20PTS during streak.

FASTEST GOALS AND ASSISTS

FASTEST GOAL FROM START OF A GAME:
5 Seconds — Doug Smail, Winnipeg, Dec. 20, 1981, at Winnipeg. Winnipeg 5, St. Louis 4.
— **Bryan Trottier,** NY Islanders, Mar. 22, 1984, at Boston. NY Islanders 3, Boston 3.
— **Alexander Mogilny,** Buffalo, Dec. 21, 1991, at Toronto. Buffalo 4, Toronto 1.
6 Seconds — Henry Boucha, Detroit, Jan. 28, 1973, at Montreal. Detroit 4, Montreal 2.
— Jean Pronovost, Pittsburgh, Mar. 25, 1976, at St. Louis. St. Louis 5, Pittsburgh 2.
7 Seconds — Charlie Conacher, Toronto, Feb. 6, 1932, at Toronto. Toronto 6, Boston 0.
— Danny Gare, Buffalo, Dec. 17, 1978, at Buffalo. Buffalo 6, Vancouver 3.
— Dave Williams, Los Angeles, Feb. 14, 1987 at Los Angeles. Los Angeles 5, Harford 2.
8 Seconds — Ron Martin, NY Americans, Dec. 4, 1932, at New York. NY Americans 4, Montreal 2.
— Chuck Arnason, Colorado, Jan. 28, 1977, at Atlanta. Colorado 3, Atlanta 3.
— Wayne Gretzky, Edmonton, Dec. 14, 1983, at New York. Edmonton 9, NY Rangers 4.
— Gaetan Duchesne, Washington, Mar. 14, 1987, at St. Louis. Washington 3, St. Louis 3.
— Tim Kerr, Philadelphia, Mar. 7, 1989, at Philadelphia. Philadelphia 4, Edmonton 4.
— Grant Ledyard, Buffalo, Dec. 4, 1991, at Winnipeg. Buffalo 4, Winnipeg 4.
— Brent Sutter, Chicago, Feb. 5, 1995, at Vancouver. Chicago 9, Vancouver 4.
— Paul Kariya, Anaheim, Mar. 9, 1997, at Colorado. Anaheim 2, Colorado 2.

FASTEST GOAL FROM START OF A PERIOD:
4 Seconds — Claude Provost, Montreal, Nov. 9, 1957, at Montreal, second period. Montreal 4, Boston 2.
— **Denis Savard,** Chicago, Jan. 12, 1986, at Chicago, third period. Chicago 4, Hartford 2.

FASTEST GOAL BY A PLAYER IN HIS FIRST NHL GAME:
15 Seconds — Gus Bodnar, Toronto, Oct. 30, 1943. Toronto 5, NY Rangers 2.
18 Seconds — Danny Gare, Buffalo, Oct. 10, 1974. Buffalo 9, Boston 5.
20 Seconds — Alexander Mogilny, Buffalo, Oct. 5, 1989. Buffalo 4, Quebec 3.

FASTEST TWO GOALS:
4 Seconds — Nels Stewart, Mtl. Maroons, Jan. 3, 1931, at Montreal at 8:24 and 8:28, third period. Mtl. Maroons 5, Boston 3.
— **Deron Quint,** Winnipeg, Dec. 15, 1995, at Winnipeg at 7:51 and 7:55, second period. Winnipeg 9, Edmonton 4.
5 Seconds — Pete Mahovlich, Montreal, Feb. 20, 1971, at Montreal at 12:16 and 12:21, third period. Montreal 7, Chicago 1.
6 Seconds — Jim Pappin, Chicago, Feb. 16, 1972, at Chicago at 2:57 and 3:03, third period. Chicago 3, Philadelphia 3.
— Ralph Backstrom, Los Angeles, Nov. 2, 1972, at Los Angeles at 8:30 and 8:36, third period. Los Angeles 5, Boston 2.
— Lanny McDonald, Calgary, Mar. 22, 1984, at Calgary at 16:23 and 16:29, first period. Detroit 6, Calgary 4.
— Sylvain Turgeon, Hartford, Mar. 28, 1987, at Hartford at 13:59 and 14:05, second period. Hartford 5, Pittsburgh 4.

FASTEST THREE GOALS:
21 Seconds — Bill Mosienko, Chicago, Mar. 23, 1952, at New York, against goaltender Lorne Anderson. Mosienko scored at 6:09, 6:20 and 6:30 of third period, all with both teams at full strength. Chicago 7, NY Rangers 6.
44 Seconds — Jean Béliveau, Montreal, Nov. 5, 1955, at Montreal, against goaltender Terry Sawchuk. Béliveau scored at :42, 1:08 and 1:26 of second period, all with Montreal holding a 6-4 man advantage. Montreal 4, Boston 2.

FASTEST THREE ASSISTS:
21 Seconds — Gus Bodnar, Chicago, Mar. 23, 1952, at New York, Bodnar assisted on Bill Mosienko's three goals at 6:09, 6:20, 6:30 of third period. Chicago 7, NY Rangers 6.
44 Seconds — Bert Olmstead, Montreal, Nov. 5, 1955, at Montreal against Boston. Olmstead assisted on Jean Béliveau's three goals at :42, 1:08 and 1:26 of second period. Montreal 4, Boston 2.

SHOTS ON GOAL

MOST SHOTS ON GOAL, ONE SEASON:
550 —Phil Esposito, Boston, 1970-71. 78 game schedule.
426 —Phil Esposito, Boston, 1971-72. 78 game schedule.
414 —Bobby Hull, Chicago, 1968-69. 76 game schedule.

PENALTIES

MOST PENALTY MINUTES, CAREER:
3,966 —Dave Williams, Toronto, Vancouver, Detroit, Los Angeles, Hartford, in 14 seasons, 962GP.
3,446 —Dale Hunter, Quebec, Washington, in 18 seasons, 1,345GP.
3,146 —Tim Hunter, Calgary, Quebec, Vancouver, San Jose, in 16 seasons, 815GP.
3,218 —Marty McSorley, Pittsburgh, Edmonton, Los Angeles, NY Rangers, San Jose, in 15 seasons, 888GP.
3,043 —Chris Nilan, Montreal, NY Rangers, Boston, in 13 seasons, 688GP.

MOST PENALTY MINUTES, CAREER, INCLUDING PLAYOFFS:
4,421 —Dave Williams, Toronto, Vancouver, Detroit, Los Angeles, Hartford, 3,966 in regular-season; 455 in playoffs.
4,137 —Dale Hunter, Quebec, Washington, 3,446 in regular-season; 691 in playoffs.
3,584 —Chris Nilan, Montreal, NY Rangers, Boston, 3,043 in regular-season; 541 in playoffs.
3,437 —Tim Hunter, Calgary, Quebec, Vancouver, 3,011 regular-season; 426 in playoffs.
3,590 —Marty McSorley, Pittsburgh, Edmonton, Los Angeles, NY Rangers, San Jose, 3,218 in regular-season; 372 in playoffs.

MOST PENALTY MINUTES, ONE SEASON:
472 —Dave Schultz, Philadelphia, 1974-75.
409 —Paul Baxter, Pittsburgh, 1981-82.
408 —Mike Peluso, Chicago, 1991-92.
405 —Dave Schultz, Los Angeles, Pittsburgh, 1977-78.

MOST PENALTIES, ONE GAME:
10 — Chris Nilan, Boston, Mar. 31, 1991, at Boston against Hartford. 6 minors, 2 majors, 1 10-minute misconduct, 1 game misconduct.
9 — Jim Dorey, Toronto, Oct. 16, 1968, at Toronto against Pittsburgh. 4 minors, 2 majors, 2 10-minute misconducts, 1 game misconduct.
— Dave Schultz, Pittsburgh, Apr. 6, 1978, at Detroit. 5 minors, 2 majors, 2 10-minute misconducts.
— Randy Holt, Los Angeles, Mar. 11, 1979, at Philadelphia. 1 minor, 3 majors, 2 10-minute misconducts, 3 game misconducts.
— Russ Anderson, Pittsburgh, Jan. 19, 1980, at Pittsburgh. 3 minors, 3 majors, 3 game misconducts.
— Kim Clackson, Quebec, Mar. 8, 1981, at Quebec. 4 minors, 3 majors, 2 game misconducts.
— Terry O'Reilly, Boston, Dec. 19, 1984 at Hartford. 5 minors, 3 majors, 1 game misconduct.
— Larry Playfair, Los Angeles, Dec. 9, 1986, at NY Islanders. 6 minors, 2 majors, 1 10-minute misconduct.
— Marty McSorley, Los Angeles, Apr. 14, 1992, at Vancouver. 5 minors, 2 majors, 1 10-minute misconduct, 1 game misconduct.

MOST PENALTY MINUTES, ONE GAME:
67 — Randy Holt, Los Angeles, Mar. 11, 1979, at Philadelphia. 1 minor, 3 majors, 2 10-minute misconducts, 3 game misconducts.
55 — Frank Bathe, Philadelphia, Mar. 11, 1979, at Philadelphia. 3 majors, 2 10-minute misconducts, 2 game misconducts.
51 — Russ Anderson, Pittsburgh, Jan. 19, 1980, at Pittsburgh. 3 minors, 3 majors, 3 game misconducts.

MOST PENALTIES, ONE PERIOD:
9 — Randy Holt, Los Angeles, Mar. 11, 1979, at Philadelphia, first period. 1 minor, 3 majors, 2 10-minute misconducts, 3 game misconducts.

MOST PENALTY MINUTES, ONE PERIOD:
67 — Randy Holt, Los Angeles, Mar. 11, 1979, at Philadelphia, first period. 1 minor, 3 majors, 2 10-minute misconducts, 3 game misconducts.

GOALTENDING

MOST GAMES APPEARED IN BY A GOALTENDER, CAREER:
971 — Terry Sawchuk, Detroit, Boston, Toronto, Los Angeles, NY Rangers from 1949-50 – 1969-70.
906 — Glenn Hall, Detroit, Chicago, St. Louis from 1952-53 – 1970-71.
886 — Tony Esposito, Montreal, Chicago from 1968-69 – 1983-84.
861 — Gump Worsley, NY Rangers, Montreal, Minnesota from 1952-53 – 1973-74.

MOST CONSECUTIVE COMPLETE GAMES BY A GOALTENDER:
502 — Glenn Hall, Detroit, Chicago. Played 502 games from beginning of 1955-56 season - first 12 games of 1962-63. In his 503rd straight game, Nov. 7, 1962, at Chicago, Hall was removed from the game against Boston with a back injury in the first period.

MOST GAMES APPEARED IN BY A GOALTENDER, ONE SEASON:
79 — Grant Fuhr, St. Louis, 1995-96.
77 — Martin Brodeur, New Jersey, 1995-96.
75 — Grant Fuhr, Edmonton, 1987-88.
74 — Ed Belfour, Chicago, 1990-91.
— Arturs Irbe, San Jose, 1993-94.
— Felix Potvin, Toronto, 1996-97.

MOST MINUTES PLAYED BY A GOALTENDER, CAREER:
57,228 — Terry Sawchuk, Detroit, Boston, Toronto, Los Angeles, NY Rangers, from 1949-50 – 1969-70.

MOST MINUTES PLAYED BY A GOALTENDER, ONE SEASON:
4,433 — Martin Brodeur, New Jersey, 1995-96.

MOST SHUTOUTS, CAREER:
103 — Terry Sawchuk, Detroit, Boston, Toronto, Los Angeles, NY Rangers in 21 seasons.
94 — George Hainsworth, Montreal Canadiens, Toronto in 10 seasons.
84 — Glenn Hall, Detroit, Chicago, St. Louis in 16 seasons.

MOST SHUTOUTS, ONE SEASON:
22 — George Hainsworth, Montreal, 1928-29. 44GP
15 — Alex Connell, Ottawa, 1925-26. 36GP
— Alex Connell, Ottawa, 1927-28. 44GP
— Hal Winkler, Boston, 1927-28. 44GP
— Tony Esposito, Chicago, 1969-70. 63GP
14 — George Hainsworth, Montreal, 1926-27. 44GP

LONGEST SHUTOUT SEQUENCE BY A GOALTENDER:
461 Minutes, 29 Seconds — Alex Connell, Ottawa, 1927-28, six consecutive shutouts. (Forward passing not permitted in attacking zones in 1927-1928.)
343 Minutes, 5 Seconds — George Hainsworth, Montreal, 1928-29, four consecutive shutouts.
324 Minutes, 40 Seconds — Roy Worters, NY Americans, 1930-31, four consecutive shutouts.
309 Minutes, 21 Seconds — Bill Durnan, Montreal, 1948-49, four consecutive shutouts.

MOST WINS BY A GOALTENDER, CAREER:
447 — Terry Sawchuk, Detroit, Boston, Toronto, Los Angeles, NY Rangaers, in 21 seasons. 971GP
434 — Jacques Plante, Montreal, NY Rangers, St. Louis, Toronto, Boston, in 18 seasons. 837GP
423 — Tony Esposito, Montreal, Chicago, in 16 seasons. 886GP

MOST WINS BY A GOALTENDER, ONE SEASON:
47 — Bernie Parent, Philadelphia, 1973-74. 73GP
44 — Bernie Parent, Philadelphia, 1974-75. 68GP
— Terry Sawchuk, Detroit, 1950-51. 70GP
— Terry Sawchuk, Detroit, 1951-52. 70GP

LONGEST WINNING STREAK BY A GOALTENDER, ONE SEASON:
17 — Gilles Gilbert, Boston, 1975-76.
14 — Don Beaupre, Minnesota, 1985-86.
— Ross Brooks, Boston, 1973-74.
— Tiny Thompson, Boston, 1929-30.
— Tom Barrasso, Pittsburgh, 1992-93.

LONGEST UNDEFEATED STREAK BY A GOALTENDER, ONE SEASON:
32 Games — Gerry Cheevers, Boston, 1971-72. 24W-8T
31 Games — Pete Peeters, Boston, 1982-83. 26W-5T
27 Games — Pete Peeters, Philadelphia, 1979-80. 22W-5T
23 Games — Frank Brimsek, Boston, 1940-41. 15W-8T
— Glenn Resch, NY Islanders, 1978-79. 15W-8T
— Grant Fuhr, Edmonton, 1981-82. 15W-8T

LONGEST UNDEFEATED STREAK BY A GOALTENDER IN HIS FIRST NHL SEASON:
23 Games — Grant Fuhr, 1981-82. 15W-8T.

LONGEST UNDEFEATED STREAK BY A GOALTENDER FROM START OF CAREER:
16 Games — Patrick Lalime, Pittsburgh, 1996-97. 14W-2T.

MOST 40-OR-MORE WIN SEASONS BY A GOALTENDER:
3 — Jacques Plante, Montreal, NY Rangers, St. Louis, Toronto, Boston in 18 seasons.
— Terry Sawchuk, Detroit, Boston, Toronto, Los Angeles, NY Rangers in 21 seasons.
2 — Bernie Parent, Boston, Philadelphia, Toronto in 13 seasons.
— Ken Dryden, Montreal in 8 seasons.
— Ed Belfour, Chicago, San Jose in 9 seasons.

MOST CONSECUTIVE 40-OR-MORE WIN SEASONS BY A GOALTENDER:
2 — Terry Sawchuk, Detroit, 1950-51 – 1951-52.
— Bernie Parent, Philadelphia, 1973-74 – 1974-75.
— Ken Dryden, Montreal, 1975-76 – 1976-77.

MOST 30-OR-MORE WIN SEASONS BY A GOALTENDER:
8 — Patrick Roy, Montreal, Colorado in 14 seasons.
— Tony Esposito, Montreal, Chicago in 16 seasons.
7 — Jacques Plante, Montreal, NY Rangers, St. Louis, Toronto, Boston in 18 seasons.
— Ken Dryden, Montreal, in 8 seasons.
6 — Glenn Hall, Detroit, Chicago, St. Louis in 18 seasons.

MOST CONSECUTIVE 30-OR-MORE WIN SEASONS BY A GOALTENDER:
7 — Tony Esposito, Chicago, 1969-70 – 1975-76.
6 — Jacques Plante, Montreal, 1954-55 – 1959-60.
5 — Ken Dryden, Montreal, 1974-75 – 1978-79.
— Terry Sawchuk, Detroit, 1950-51 – 1954-55.
4 — Ed Giacomin, NY Rangers, 1966-67 – 1969-70.

MOST LOSSES BY A GOALTENDER, CAREER:
352 — Gump Worsley, NY Rangers, Montreal, Minnesota, in 21 seasons. 861GP
351 — Gilles Meloche, Chicago, California, Cleveland, Minnesota, Pittsburgh, in 18 seasons. 788GP
330 — Terry Sawchuk, Detroit, Boston, Toronto, Los Angeles, NY Rangers, in 21 seasons. 971GP

MOST LOSSES BY A GOALTENDER, ONE SEASON:
48 — Gary Smith, California, 1970-71.
47 — Al Rollins, Chicago, 1953-54.

Boston fans growled their displeasure when the Bruins replaced crowd favorite Tiny Thompson with rookie goaltender Frank Brimsek early in the 1938-39 season. Four weeks later, those same fans were calling the Eveleth, Minnesota native "Mr. Zero" after he recorded six shutouts in his first month as a pro. Brimsek, who had a 23-game unbeaten streak in 1940-41, went on to have a Hall-of-Fame career, winning two Stanley Cup championships.

Active NHL Players' Three-or-More-Goal Games

Regular Season

Teams named are the ones the players were with at the time of their multiple-scoring games. Players listed alphabetically.

Miroslav Satan notched the second hat trick of his career when he provided all the offense in a 3-0 Buffalo blanking of the Washington Capitals on March 1, 1998.

Player	Team	3-Goals	4-Goals	5-Goals
Adams, Greg	Vancouver	1	1	—
Alfredsson, Daniel	Ottawa	1	—	—
Allison, Jason	Boston	2	—	—
Amonte, Tony	NYR, Chi	4	—	—
Andersson, Mikael	Tampa Bay	1	—	—
Andersson, Niklas	NY Islanders	1	—	—
Andreychuk, Dave	Buf., Tor.	7	2	1
Arnott, Jason	Edmonton	2	—	—
Audette, Donald	Buffalo	2	—	—
Babych, Dave	Vancouver	1	—	—
Barnes, Stu	Wpg., Pit.	2	—	—
Bellows, Brian	Min., Mtl., T.B.	6	3	—
Beranek, Josef	Philadelphia	1	—	—
Bondra, Peter	Washington	6	3	1
Bourque, Ray	Boston	1	—	—
Bradley, Brian	Tampa Bay	1	—	—
Brind'Amour, Rod	Philadelphia	1	—	—
Brown, Doug	Detroit	1	—	—
Brown, Rob	Pittsburgh	7	—	—
Buchberger, Kelly	Edmonton	1	—	—
Bure, Pavel	Vancouver	8	1	—
Bure, Valeri	Calgary	1	—	—
Burr, Shawn	Detroit	3	—	—
Burridge, Randy	Bos., Wsh.	4	—	—
Butsayev, Viacheslav	Philadelphia	1	—	—
Carbonneau, Guy	Montreal	1	1	—
Carpenter, Bob	Wsh, Bos.	2	1	—
Carson, Jimmy	L.A., Edm., Det.	9	1	—
Ciccarelli, Dino	Min., Wsh., Det., T.B.	15	4	—
Clark, Wendel	Tor., Que.	7	2	—
Coffey, Paul	Edmonton	4	1	—
Corson, Shayne	Mtl., Edm.	3	—	—
Courtnall, Geoff	Bos., Wsh., St.L.	4	—	—
Courtnall, Russ	Tor., Mtl., Min., Van.	5	—	—
Craven, Murray	Philadelphia	3	—	—
Cullen, John	Pit., Hfd.	3	—	—
Cunneyworth, R.	Pittsburgh	1	1	—
Czerkawski, Mariusz	Edmonton	2	—	—
Dahlen, Ulf	NYR, Min., S.J.	4	—	—
Daigle, Alexandre	Ott., Phi.	2	—	—
Damphousse, V.	Tor., Edm., Mtl.	10	1	—
Dawe, Jason	Buffalo	2	—	—
Daze, Eric	Chicago	1	1	—
Dineen, Kevin	Hfd., Phi.	9	1	—
Dionne, Gilbert	Montreal	1	—	—
Druce, John	Wsh., L.A.	2	—	—
Duchesne, Steve	L.A., Phi., St.L.	3	—	—
Emerson, Nelson	Winnipeg	1	—	—
Errey, Bob	Pittsburgh	1	—	—
Fedorov, Sergei	Detroit	1	1	1
Ferraro, Ray	Hfd., NYI, NYR	7	1	—
Fleury, Theo	Calgary	11	—	—
Forsberg, Peter	Colorado	3	—	—
Francis, Ron	Hfd., Pit.	10	1	—
Friesen, Jeff	San Jose	1	—	—
Gagner, Dave	Min., Dal., Fla.	4	1	—
Garpenlov, Johan	Det., S.J., Fla.	2	1	—
Gaudreau, Rob	San Jose	3	—	—
Gelinas, Martin	Edm., Van.	2	1	—
Gilchrist, Brent	Montreal	1	—	—
Gilmour, Doug	St.L., Tor.	3	—	—
Granato, Tony	NYR, L.A., S.J.	6	1	—
Gratton, Chris	Tampa Bay	1	—	—
Graves, Adam	Edm., NYR	6	—	—
Green, Travis	NY Islanders	1	—	—
Gretzky, Wayne	Edm., L.A., NYR	37	9	4
Grosek, Michal	Buffalo	1	—	—
Guerin, Bill	New Jersey	1	—	—
Harvey, Todd	Dallas	1	—	—
Hatcher, Kevin	Wsh., Dal.	2	—	—
Heinze, Steve	Boston	4	—	—
Hogue, Benoit	NY Islanders	1	—	—
Holik, Bobby	New Jersey	2	—	—
Housley, Phil	Buffalo	2	—	—
Hull, Brett	Cgy., St.L.	26	2	—
Hull, Jody	Hartford	1	—	—
Hunter, Dale	Que., Wsh.	4	—	—
Jagr, Jaromir	Pittsburgh	4	—	—
Janney, Craig	Bos., St.L.	3	—	—
Juneau, Joe	Bos., Wsh.	2	—	—
Kamensky, Valeri	Colorado	4	—	—
Kapanen, Sami	Carolina	2	—	—
Kariya, Paul	Anaheim	3	—	—
Khristich, Dimitri	Washington	2	—	—
King, Derek	NYI, Tor.	6	1	—
Klatt, Trent	Philadelphia	1	—	—
Klima, Petr	Det., Edm.	6	—	—
Konowalchuk, Steve	Washington	2	—	—
Korolev, Igor	Winnipeg	1	—	—
Kovalenko, Andrei	Quebec	1	—	—
Kovalev, Alexei	NY Rangers	2	—	—
Kozlov, Vyacheslav	Detroit	1	1	—
Krupp, Uwe	Quebec	1	—	—
Krygier, Todd	Washington	1	—	—
Lacroix, Eric	Colorado	1	—	—
Larionov, Igor	Van., S.J.	4	—	—
Larouche, Steve	Ottawa	1	—	—
LeClair, John	Philadelphia	6	1	—
Lemieux, Claude	Mtl., N.J., Col.	7	—	—
Lemieux, Jocelyn	Chicago	2	—	—
Linden, Trevor	Vancouver	4	—	—
Lindros, Eric	Philadelphia	9	1	—
MacInnis, Al	Cgy., St. L.	2	—	—
MacLean, John	New Jersey	6	—	—
Malakhov, Vladimir	Montreal	1	—	—
Maltby, Kirk	Detroit	1	—	—
Manderville, Kent	Hartford	1	—	—
McEachern, Shawn	Ottawa	1	—	—
McInnis, Marty	Calgary	1	—	—
McKay, Randy	New Jersey	1	—	—
McKenzie, Jim	Phoenix	1	—	—
Messier, Mark	Edm., NYR	15	4	—
Miller, Kevin	Det., St.L., S.J.	4	—	—
Modano, Mike	Min., Dal.	3	1	—
Mogilny, Alexander	Buf., Van.	12	2	—
Momesso, Sergio	Montreal	1	—	—
Muller, Kirk	N.J., Mtl., Tor.	7	—	—
Murray, Glen	Los Angeles	1	—	—
Murray, Rem	Edmonton	1	—	—
Murzyn, Dana	Calgary	1	—	—
Naslund, Markus	Pit., Van.	2	—	—
Nedved, Petr	Pittsburgh	—	1	—
Nemchinov, Sergei	NY Rangers	1	—	—
Nicholls, Bernie	L.A., N.J., Chi.	14	4	—
Nieuwendyk, Joe	Cgy., Dal.	8	3	1
Nolan, Owen	Que., S.J.	8	1	—
Noonan, Brian	Chi., NYR	3	1	—
Nylander, Michael	Hartford	1	—	—
Oates, Adam	Bos., Wsh.	6	1	—
Odelein, Lyle	Montreal	1	—	—
Olczyk, Ed	Tor., NYR, Wpg., L.A.	5	—	—
Oliver, David	Edmonton	1	—	—
O'Neill, Jeff	Hartford	1	—	—
Otto, Joel	Calgary	2	—	—
Palffy, Zigmund	NY Islanders	5	—	—
Perreault, Yanic	Los Angeles	2	—	—
Pivonka, Michal	Washington	1	—	—
Plante, Derek	Buffalo	1	—	—
Probert, Bob	Detroit	1	—	—
Ranheim, Paul	Calgary	1	—	—
Recchi, Mark	Pit., Mtl.	3	—	—
Reichel, Robert	Cgy., NYI	5	—	—
Reid, Dave	Bos., Dal.	2	—	—
Renberg, Mikael	Phi., T.B.	2	—	—
Ricci, Mike	Quebec	—	—	1
Rice, Steven	Hartford	1	—	—
Richer, Stephane	Mtl., N.J.	8	1	—
Roberts, Gary	Cgy., Car.	10	1	—
Robitaille, Luc	L.A., Pit.	9	3	—
Roenick, Jeremy	Chicago	4	2	—
Rolston, Brian	New Jersey	1	—	—
Ronning, Cliff	St.L., Van.	3	—	—
Rucinsky, Martin	Montreal	2	—	—
Sakic, Joe	Que., Col.	5	1	—
Samsonov, Sergei	Boston	1	—	—
Sanderson, Geoff	Hartford	5	—	—
Sandstrom, Tomas	NYR, L.A.	7	1	—
Satan, Miroslav	Buffalo	2	—	—
Savage, Brian	Montreal	2	1	—
Selanne, Teemu	Wpg., Ana.	12	2	—
Semak, Alexander	New Jersey	1	—	—
Shanahan, Brendan	N.J., St.L., Hfd., Det.	10	—	—
Sheppard, Ray	Buf., Det., S.J., Fla.	12	—	—
Smolinski, Bryan	Boston	1	—	—
Smyth, Ryan	Edmonton	1	—	—
Stern, Ronnie	Calgary	3	—	—
Stevens, Kevin	Pittsburgh	8	2	—
Stillman, Cory	Calgary	1	—	—
Straka, Martin	Pittsburgh	2	—	—
Stumpel, Jozef	Bos., L.A.	2	—	—
Sundin, Mats	Que., Tor.	4	—	1
Svejkovsky, Jaroslav	Washington	—	1	—
Sydor, Darryl	Dallas	1	—	—
Thomas, Steve	Chi., NYI	4	2	—
Tikkanen, Esa	Edmonton	3	—	—
Titov, German	Calgary	2	—	—
Tkachuk, Keith	Wpg., Phx.	5	2	—
Tocchet, Rick	Phi., Pit., L.A., Bos.	12	2	—
Turcotte, Darren	NY Rangers	4	—	—
Turgeon, Pierre	Buf., NYI, Mtl.	12	—	—
Valk, Garry	Anaheim	1	—	—
Verbeek, Pat	N.J., Hfd., NYR, Dal.	11	1	—
Vukota, Mick	NY Islanders	1	—	—
Weight, Doug	Edmonton	1	—	—
Wesley, Glen	Boston	1	—	—
Wiemer, Jason	Tampa Bay	1	—	—
Yachmenev, Vitali	Los Angeles	1	—	—
Yake, Terry	Anaheim	1	—	—
Yashin, Alexei	Ottawa	4	—	—
Yegorov, Alexei	San Jose	1	—	—
Young, Scott	Que., Col.	4	—	—
Yzerman, Steve	Detroit	17	1	—
Ysebaert, Paul	Detroit	1	—	—
Zamuner, Rob	Tampa Bay	1	—	—
Zezel, Peter	Philadelphia	1	—	—
Zhamnov, Alexei	Wpg., Chi.	5	—	1

Top 100 All-Time Goal-Scoring Leaders

	Player	Seasons	Games	Goals	Goals per game
* 1.	**Wayne Gretzky**, Edm., L.A., St.L., NYR	19	1417	**885**	.625
2.	**Gordie Howe**, Det., Hfd.	26	1767	**801**	.453
3.	**Marcel Dionne**, Det., L.A., NYR	18	1348	**731**	.542
4.	**Phil Esposito**, Chi., Bos., NYR	18	1282	**717**	.559
5.	**Mike Gartner**, Wsh., Min., NYR, Tor., Phx.	19	1432	**708**	.494
6.	**Mario Lemieux**, Pit.	12	745	**613**	.823
7.	**Bobby Hull**, Chi., Wpg., Hfd.	16	1063	**610**	.574
* 8.	**Dino Ciccarelli**, Min., Wsh., Det., T.B., Fla.	18	1218	**602**	.494
9.	**Jari Kurri**, Edm., L.A., NYR, Ana., Col.	17	1251	**601**	.480
* 10.	**Mark Messier**, Edm., NYR, Van.	19	1354	**597**	.441
11.	**Mike Bossy**, NYI	10	752	**573**	.762
* 12.	**Steve Yzerman**, Det.	15	1098	**563**	.513
13.	**Guy Lafleur**, Mtl., NYR, Que.	17	1126	**560**	.497
14.	**John Bucyk**, Det., Bos.,	23	1540	**556**	.361
* 15.	**Brett Hull**, Cgy., St.L.	13	801	**554**	.692
16.	**Michel Goulet**, Que., Chi.	15	1089	**548**	.503
17.	**Maurice Richard**, Mtl.	18	978	**544**	.556
18.	**Stan Mikita**, Chi.	22	1394	**541**	.388
19.	**Frank Mahovlich**, Tor., Det., Mtl.	18	1181	**533**	.451
20.	**Bryan Trottier**, NYI, Pit.	18	1279	**524**	.410
21.	**Dale Hawerchuk**, Wpg., Buf., St.L., Phi.	16	1188	**518**	.436
* 22.	**Dave Andreychuk**, Buf., Tor., N.J.	16	1158	**517**	.446
23.	**Gilbert Perreault**, Buf.	17	1191	**512**	.430
24.	**Jean Beliveau**, Mtl.	20	1125	**507**	.451
25.	**Joe Mullen**, St.L., Cgy., Pit., Bos.	17	1062	**502**	.473
26.	**Lanny McDonald**, Tor., Col., Cgy.	16	1111	**500**	.450
27.	**Glenn Anderson**, Edm., Tor., NYR, St.L.	16	1129	**498**	.441
28.	**Jean Ratelle**, NYR, Bos.	21	1281	**491**	.383
29.	**Norm Ullman**, Det., Tor.	20	1410	**490**	.348
30.	**Darryl Sittler**, Tor., Phi., Det.	15	1096	**484**	.442
* 31.	**Luc Robitaille**, L.A., Pit., NYR	12	889	**478**	.538
* 32.	**Bernie Nicholls**, L.A., NYR, Edm., N.J., Chi., S.J.	17	1117	**475**	.425
33.	**Denis Savard**, Chi., Mtl., T.B.	17	1196	**473**	.395
34.	**Pat LaFontaine**, NYI, Buf., NYR	15	865	**468**	.541
* 35.	**Brian Bellows**, Min., Mtl., T.B., Ana., Wsh.	16	1112	**468**	.421
* 36.	**Pat Verbeek**, N.J., Hfd., NYR, Dal.	16	1147	**461**	.402
37.	**Alex Delvecchio**, Det.	24	1549	**456**	.294
38.	**Peter Stastny**, Que., N.J., St.L.	15	977	**450**	.461
39.	**Rick Middleton**, NYR, Bos.	14	1005	**448**	.446
40.	**Rick Vaive**, Van., Tor., Chi., Buf.	13	876	**441**	.503
41.	**Steve Larmer**, Chi., NYR	15	1006	**441**	.438
42.	**Dave Taylor**, L.A.	17	1111	**431**	.388
43.	**Yvan Cournoyer**, Mtl.	16	968	**428**	.442
* 44.	**Ron Francis**, Hfd., Pit.	17	1247	**428**	.343
45.	**Brian Propp**, Phi., Bos., Min., Hfd.	15	1016	**425**	.418
46.	**Steve Shutt**, Mtl., L.A.	13	930	**424**	.456
47.	**Bill Barber**, Phi.	12	903	**420**	.465
48.	**Garry Unger**, Tor., Det., St.L., Atl., L.A., Edm.	16	1105	**413**	.374
49.	**Rod Gilbert**, NYR	18	1065	**406**	.381
50.	**John Ogrodnick**, Det., Que., NYR	14	928	**402**	.433
* 51.	**Joe Nieuwendyk**, Cgy., Dal.	12	768	**397**	.517
52.	**Dave Keon**, Tor., Hfd.	18	1296	**396**	.306
53.	**Cam Neely**, Van., Bos.	13	726	**395**	.544
54.	**Pierre Larouche**, Pit., Mtl., Hfd., NYR.	14	812	**395**	.486
55.	**Bernie Geoffrion**, Mtl., NYR	16	883	**393**	.445
56.	**Jean Pronovost**, Wsh., Pit., Atl.	14	998	**391**	.392
57.	**Dean Prentice**, Pit., Min., Det., NYR, Bos.	22	1378	**391**	.284
* 58.	**Rick Tocchet**, Phi., Pit., L.A., Bos., Wsh., Phx.	14	909	**385**	.424
59.	**Rick Martin**, Buf., L.A.	11	685	**384**	.561
* 60.	**Paul Coffey**, Edm., Pit., L.A., Det., Hfd., Phi.	18	1268	**383**	.302
61.	**Reggie Leach**, Bos., Cal., Phi., Det.	13	934	**381**	.408
* 62.	**Doug Gilmour**, St.L., Cgy., Tor., N.J.	15	1125	**381**	.339
* 63.	**Stephane Richer**, Mtl., N.J., T.B.	14	866	**380**	.439
* 64.	**Tomas Sandstrom**, NYR, L.A., Pit., Det., Ana.	14	925	**379**	.410
65.	**Ted Lindsay**, Det., Chi.	17	1068	**379**	.355
66.	**Butch Goring**, L.A., NYI, Bos.	16	1107	**375**	.339
* 67.	**Ray Bourque**, Bos.	19	1372	**375**	.273
68.	**Rick Kehoe**, Tor., Pit.	14	906	**371**	.409
69.	**Tim Kerr**, Phi., NYR, Hfd.	13	655	**370**	.565
70.	**Bernie Federko**, St.L., Det.	14	1000	**369**	.369
* 71.	**Pierre Turgeon**, Buf., NYI, Mtl., St.L.	11	810	**366**	.452
72.	**Jacques Lemaire**, Mtl.	12	853	**366**	.429
* 73.	**Brendan Shanahan**, N.J., St.L., Hfd., Det.	11	788	**363**	.461
74.	**Peter McNab**, Buf., Bos., Van., N.J.	14	954	**363**	.381
75.	**Brent Sutter**, NYI, Chi.	18	1111	**363**	.327
76.	**Ivan Boldirev**, Bos., Cal., Chi., Atl., Van., Det.	15	1052	**361**	.343
* 77.	**John MacLean**, N.J., S.J.	14	985	**360**	.365

* - Active

Rick Vaive made a career of standing in the slot, surviving the whacking and hacking long enough to pile 441 pucks behind enemy goaltenders during his 13-year career.

	Player	Seasons	Games	Goals	Goals per game
* 78.	**Geoff Courtnall**, Bos., Edm., Wsh., St.L., Van.	15	1018	**360**	.354
79.	**Bobby Clarke**, Phi.	15	1144	**358**	.313
80.	**Henri Richard**, Mtl.	20	1256	**358**	.285
81.	**Bobby Smith**, Min., Mtl.	15	1077	**357**	.331
82.	**Dennis Maruk**, Cal., Clev., Min., Wsh.	14	888	**356**	.401
83.	**Wilf Paiement**, K.C. Col., Tor., Que., NYR, Buf., Pit.	14	946	**356**	.376
84.	**Mike Foligno**, Det., Buf., Tor., Fla.	15	1018	**355**	.349
85.	**Danny Gare**, Buf., Det., Edm.	13	827	**354**	.428
86.	**Rick MacLeish**, Phi., Hfd., Pit., Det.	14	846	**349**	.413
87.	**Andy Bathgate**, NYR, Tor., Det., Pit.	17	1069	**349**	.326
88.	**Charlie Simmer**, Cal., Cle., L.A., Bos., Pit.	14	712	**342**	.480
89.	**Dave Christian**, Wpg., Wsh., Bos., St.L., Chi.	15	1009	**340**	.337
* 90.	**Joe Sakic**, Que., Col.	10	719	**334**	.465
* 91.	**Theoren Fleury**, Cgy.	10	731	**334**	.457
* 92.	**Kirk Muller**, N.J., Mtl., NYI, Tor., Fla.	14	1032	**334**	.324
* 93.	**Ray Ferraro**, Hfd., NYI, NYR, L.A.	14	955	**333**	.349
94.	**Ron Ellis**, Tor.	16	1034	**332**	.321
* 95.	**Kevin Dineen**, Hfd., Phi., Car.	14	925	**330**	.357
* 96.	**Ed Olczyk**, Chi., Tor., Wpg., NYR, L.A., Pit.	14	937	**330**	.352
97.	**Mike Bullard**, Pit., Cgy., St.L., Phi., Tor.	11	727	**329**	.453
98.	**Ken Hodge**, Chi., Bos., NYR	14	881	**328**	.372
* 99.	**Vincent Damphousse**, Tor., Edm., Mtl.	12	928	**328**	.353
100.	**John Tonelli**, NYI, Cgy., L.A., Chi., Que.	14	1028	**325**	.316

Top 100 Active Goal-Scoring Leaders

	Player	Games	Goals	Goals per game
1.	**Wayne Gretzky**, Edm., L.A., St.L., NYR	1417	**885**	.625
2.	**Dino Ciccarelli**, Min., Wsh., Det., T.B., Fla.	1218	**602**	.494
3.	**Mark Messier**, Edm., NYR, Van.	1354	**597**	.441
4.	**Steve Yzerman**, Det.	1098	**563**	.513
5.	**Brett Hull**, Cgy., St.L.	801	**554**	.692
6.	**Dave Andreychuk**, Buf., Tor., N.J.	1158	**517**	.446
7.	**Luc Robitaille**, L.A., Pit., NYR	889	**478**	.538
8.	**Bernie Nicholls**, L.A., NYR, Edm., N.J., Chi., S.J.	1117	**475**	.425
9.	**Brian Bellows**, Min., Mtl., T.B., Ana., Wsh.	1112	**468**	.421
10.	**Pat Verbeek**, N.J., Hfd., NYR, Dal.	1147	**461**	.402
11.	**Ron Francis**, Hfd., Pit.	1247	**428**	.343
12.	**Joe Nieuwendyk**, Cgy., Dal.	768	**397**	.517
13.	**Rick Tocchet**, Phi., Pit., L.A., Bos., Wsh., Phx.	909	**385**	.424
14.	**Paul Coffey**, Edm., Pit., L.A., Det., Hfd., Phi.	1268	**383**	.302
15.	**Doug Gilmour**, St.L., Cgy., Tor., N.J.	1125	**381**	.339
16.	**Stephane Richer**, Mtl., N.J., T.B.	866	**380**	.439
17.	**Tomas Sandstrom**, NYR, L.A., Pit., Det., Ana.	925	**379**	.410
18.	**Ray Bourque**, Bos.	1372	**375**	.273
19.	**Pierre Turgeon**, Buf., NYI, Mtl., St.L.	810	**366**	.452
20.	**Brendan Shanahan**, N.J., St.L., Hfd., Det.	788	**363**	.461
21.	**John MacLean**, N.J., S.J.	985	**360**	.365
22.	**Geoff Courtnall**, Bos., Edm., Wsh., St.L., Van.	1018	**360**	.354
23.	**Joe Sakic**, Que., Col.	719	**334**	.465
24.	**Theoren Fleury**, Cgy.	731	**334**	.457
25.	**Kirk Muller**, N.J., Mtl., NYI, Tor., Fla.	1032	**334**	.324
26.	**Ray Ferraro**, Hfd., NYI, NYR, L.A.	955	**333**	.349
27.	**Kevin Dineen**, Hfd., Phi., Car.	925	**330**	.357
28.	**Ed Olczyk**, Chi., Tor., Wpg., NYR, L.A., Pit.	937	**330**	.352
29.	**Vincent Damphousse**, Tor., Edm., Mtl.	928	**328**	.353
30.	**Steve Thomas**, Tor., Chi., NYI, N.J.	860	**324**	.377
31.	**Ray Sheppard**, Buf., NYR, Det., S.J., Fla., Car.	696	**322**	.463
32.	**Dale Hunter**, Que., Wsh.	1345	**321**	.239
33.	**Jeremy Roenick**, Chi., Phx.	675	**320**	.474
34.	**Bob Carpenter**, Wsh., NYR, L.A., Bos., N.J.	1122	**318**	.283
35.	**Mark Recchi**, Pit., Phi., Mtl.	710	**317**	.446
36.	**Alexander Mogilny**, Buf., Van.	587	**315**	.537
37.	**Dave Gagner**, NYR, Min., Dal., Tor., Cgy., Fla.	877	**312**	.356
38.	**Greg A. Adams**, N.J., Van., Dal.	852	**306**	.359
39.	**Jaromir Jagr**, Pit.	581	**301**	.518
40.	**Claude Lemieux**, Mtl., N.J., Colorado	836	**298**	.356
41.	**Wendel Clark**, Tor., Que., NYI	683	**294**	.430
42.	**Kevin Stevens**, Pit., Bos., L.A., NYR	668	**292**	.437
43.	**Russ Courtnall**, Tor., Mtl., Min., Dal., Van., NYR, L.A.	972	**291**	.299
44.	**Phil Housley**, Buf., Wpg., St.L., Cgy., N.J., Wsh.	1131	**291**	.257
45.	**Peter Bondra**, Wsh.	544	**285**	.524
46.	**Mike Modano**, Min., Dal.	633	**277**	.438
47.	**Gary Roberts**, Cgy., Car.	646	**277**	.429
48.	**Adam Oates**, Det., St.L., Bos., Wsh.	908	**276**	.304
49.	**Jimmy Carson**, L.A., Edm., Det., Van., Hfd.	626	**275**	.439
50.	**Al MacInnis**, Cgy., St.L.	1060	**270**	.255
51.	**Teemu Selanne**, Wpg., Ana.	410	**266**	.649
52.	**Mats Sundin**, Que., Tor.	611	**265**	.434
53.	**Larry Murphy**, L.A., Wsh., Min., Pit., Tor., Det.	1397	**265**	.190
54.	**Murray Craven**, Det., Phi., Hfd., Van., Chi., S.J.	1009	**262**	.260
55.	**Trevor Linden**, Van., NYI	727	**257**	.354
56.	**Pavel Bure**, Van.	428	**254**	.593
57.	**Rod Brind'Amour**, St.L., Phi.	696	**249**	.358
58.	**Sergei Fedorov**, Det.	527	**248**	.471
59.	**Guy Carbonneau**, Mtl., St.L., Dal.	1175	**246**	.209
60.	**Esa Tikkanen**, Edm., NYR, St.L., N.J., Van., Fla., Wsh.	845	**244**	.289
61.	**Scott Mellanby**, Phi., Edm., Fla.	872	**238**	.273
62.	**Keith Tkachuk**, Wpg., Phx.	458	**236**	.515
63.	**Derek King**, NYI, Hfd., Tor.	727	**235**	.323
64.	**Tony Granato**, NYR, L.A., S.J.	630	**232**	.368
65.	**Adam Graves**, Det., Edm., NYR	748	**232**	.310
66.	**Ulf Dahlen**, NYR, Min., Dal., S.J., Chi.	686	**231**	.337
67.	**John LeClair**, Mtl., Phi.	507	**226**	.446
68.	**Eric Lindros**, Phi.	360	**223**	.619
69.	**Shayne Corson**, Mtl., Edm., St.L.	809	**221**	.273
70.	**Peter Zezel**, Phi., St.L., Wsh., Tor., Dal., N.J., Van.	832	**213**	.256
71.	**Kevin Hatcher**, Wsh., Dal., Pit.	960	**208**	.217
72.	**Tony Amonte**, NYR, Chi.	533	**203**	.381
73.	**Steve Duchesne**, L.A., Phi., Que., St.L., Ott.	845	**202**	.239
74.	**Geoff Sanderson**, Hfd., Car., Van., Buf.	514	**200**	.389
75.	**Randy Burridge**, Bos., Wsh., L.A., Buf.	706	**199**	.282
76.	**Benoit Hogue**, Buf., NYI, Tor., Dal.	670	**197**	.294
77.	**Dimitri Khristich**, Wsh., L.A., Bos.	548	**196**	.358
78.	**Cliff Ronning**, St.L., Van., Phx.	695	**196**	.282
79.	**Ron Sutter**, Phi., St.L., Que., NYI, Bos., S.J.	935	**196**	.210
80.	**Joe Murphy**, Det., Edm., Chi., St.L., S.J.	634	**195**	.308
81.	**Joel Otto**, Cgy., Phi.	943	**195**	.207
82.	**Owen Nolan**, Que., Colorado, S.J.	487	**191**	.392
83.	**Darren Turcotte**, NYR, Hfd., Wpg., S.J., St.L.	586	**191**	.326
84.	**John Cullen**, Pit., Hfd., Tor., T.B.	617	**187**	.303
85.	**Randy Cunneyworth**, Buf., Pit., Wpg., Hfd., Chi., Ott.	852	**187**	.219
86.	**Scott Young**, Hfd., Pit., Que., Colorado, Ana.	672	**186**	.277
87.	**Robert Reichel**, Cgy., NYI	519	**183**	.353
88.	**Craig Janney**, Bos., St.L., S.J., Wpg., Phx.	704	**183**	.260
89.	**Brian Bradley**, Cgy., Van., Tor., T.B.	651	**182**	.280
90.	**Shawn Burr**, Det., T.B., S.J.	856	**181**	.211
91.	**Gary Suter**, Cgy., Chi.	918	**181**	.197
92.	**Kelly Miller**, NYR, Wsh.	995	**179**	.180
93.	**Michal Pivonka**, Wsh.	789	**176**	.223
94.	**Bob Errey**, Pit., Buf., S.J., Det., Dal., NYR	895	**170**	.190
95.	**Martin Gelinas**, Edm., Que., Van., Car.	587	**168**	.286
96.	**Rob Brown**, Pit., Hfd., Chi., Dal., L.A.	435	**167**	.384
97.	**Scott Stevens**, Wsh., St.L., N.J.	1200	**166**	.138
98.	**Donald Audette**, Buf.	409	**164**	.401
99.	**Brian Leetch**, NYR	725	**164**	.226
100.	**Petr Nedved**, Van., St.L., NYR, Pit.	441	**158**	.358

A consistent 20-goal scorer throughout his career, Ray Ferraro has "lit the lamp" 333 times during his 14-seasons in the NHL. Ferraro, who had a career-high 41 goals for Hartford in 1988-89, scored an amazing 108 goals for the WHL's Brandon Wheat Kings in his last year of junior hockey in 1983-84.

Top 100 All-Time Assist Leaders

	Player	Seasons	Games	Assists	Assist per game
* 1.	**Wayne Gretzky**, Edm., L.A., St.L., NYR	19	1417	**1910**	1.348
* 2.	**Paul Coffey**, Edm., Pit., L.A., Det., Hfd., Phi.	18	1268	**1090**	.860
3.	**Gordie Howe**, Det., Hfd.	26	1767	**1049**	.594
4.	**Marcel Dionne**, Det., L.A., NYR	18	1348	**1040**	.772
* 5.	**Ray Bourque**, Bos.	19	1372	**1036**	.755
* 6.	**Mark Messier**, Edm., NYR, Van.	19	1354	**1015**	.750
* 7.	**Ron Francis**, Hfd., Pit.	17	1247	**1006**	.807
8.	**Stan Mikita**, Chi.	22	1394	**926**	.664
9.	**Bryan Trottier**, NYI, Pit.	18	1279	**901**	.704
10.	**Dale Hawerchuk**, Wpg., Buf., St.L., Phi.	16	1188	**891**	.750
11.	**Mario Lemieux**, Pit.	12	745	**881**	1.18
12.	**Phil Esposito**, Chi., Bos., NYR	18	1282	**873**	.681
13.	**Denis Savard**, Chi., Mtl., T.B.	17	1196	**865**	.723
14.	**Bobby Clarke**, Phi.	15	1144	**852**	.745
* 15.	**Steve Yzerman**, Det.	15	1098	**846**	.770
* 16.	**Larry Murphy**, L.A., Wsh., Min., Pit., Tor., Det.	18	1397	**838**	.600
17.	**Alex Delvecchio**, Det.	24	1549	**825**	.533
18.	**Gilbert Perreault**, Buf.	17	1191	**814**	.683
19.	**John Bucyk**, Det., Bos.	23	1540	**813**	.528
20.	**Jari Kurri**, Edm., L.A., NYR, Ana., Col.	17	1251	**797**	.637
* 21.	**Adam Oates**, Det., St.L., Bos., Wsh.	13	908	**796**	.877
* 22.	**Doug Gilmour**, St.L., Cgy., Tor., N.J.	15	1125	**795**	.707
23.	**Guy Lafleur**, Mtl., NYR, Que.	17	1126	**793**	.704
24.	**Peter Stastny**, Que., N.J., St.L.	15	977	**789**	.808
25.	**Jean Ratelle**, NYR, Bos.	21	1281	**776**	.606
26.	**Bernie Federko**, St.L., Det.	14	1000	**761**	.761
27.	**Larry Robinson**, Mtl., L.A.	20	1384	**750**	.542
28.	**Denis Potvin**, NYI	15	1060	**742**	.700
29.	**Norm Ullman**, Det., Tor.	20	1410	**739**	.524
* 30.	**Al MacInnis**, Cgy., St.L.	17	1060	**733**	.692
* 31.	**Bernie Nicholls**, L.A., NYR, Edm., N.J., Chi., S.J.	17	1117	**732**	.655
* 32.	**Phil Housley**, Buf., Wpg., St.L., Cgy., N.J., Wsh.	16	1131	**730**	.645
33.	**Jean Beliveau**, Mtl.	20	1125	**712**	.633
34.	**Henri Richard**, Mtl.	20	1256	**688**	.548
* 35.	**Dale Hunter**, Que., Wsh.	18	1345	**688**	.512
36.	**Brad Park**, NYR, Bos., Det.	17	1113	**683**	.614
37.	**Bobby Smith**, Min., Mtl.	15	1077	**679**	.630
38.	**Bobby Orr**, Bos., Chi.	12	657	**645**	.982
39.	**Dave Taylor**, L.A.	17	1111	**638**	.574
40.	**Darryl Sittler**, Tor., Phi., Det.	15	1096	**637**	.581
41.	**Borje Salming**, Tor., Det.	17	1148	**637**	.555
42.	**Neal Broten**, Min., Dal., N.J., L.A.	17	1099	**634**	.577
43.	**Mike Gartner**, Wsh., Min., NYR, Tor., Phx.	19	1432	**627**	.438
44.	**Andy Bathgate**, NYR, Tor., Det., Pit.	17	1069	**624**	.584
45.	**Rod Gilbert**, NYR	18	1065	**615**	.577
* 46.	**Chris Chelios**, Mtl., Chi.	15	1001	**606**	.605
* 47.	**Scott Stevens**, Wsh., St.L., N.J.	16	1200	**606**	.505
48.	**Michel Goulet**, Que., Chi.	15	1089	**604**	.555
49.	**Glenn Anderson**, Edm., Tor., NYR, St.L.	16	1129	**601**	.532
* 50.	**Dave Andreychuk**, Buf., Tor., N.J.	16	1158	**595**	.514
* 51.	**Dino Ciccarelli**, Min., Wsh., Det., T.B., Fla.	18	1218	**591**	.485
52.	**Doug Wilson**, Chi., S.J.	16	1024	**590**	.576
53.	**Dave Keon**, Tor., Hfd.	18	1296	**590**	.455
54.	**Brian Propp**, Phi., Bos., Min., Hfd.	15	1016	**579**	.570
* 55.	**Dave Babych**, Wpg., Hfd., Van., Phi.	18	1154	**575**	.498
56.	**Steve Larmer**, Chi., NYR	15	1006	**571**	.568
57.	**Frank Mahovlich**, Tor., Det., Mtl.	18	1181	**570**	.483
* 58.	**Pierre Turgeon**, Buf., NYI, Mtl., St.L.	11	810	**566**	.699
* 59.	**Gary Suter**, Cgy., Chi.	13	918	**563**	.613
60.	**Joe Mullen**, St.L., Cgy., Pit., Bos.	17	1062	**561**	.528
61.	**Bobby Hull**, Chi., Wpg., Hfd.	16	1063	**560**	.527
62.	**Mike Bossy**, NYI	10	752	**553**	.735
63.	**Thomas Steen**, Wpg.	14	950	**553**	.582
* 64.	**Vincent Damphousse**, Tor., Edm., Mtl.	12	928	**552**	.595
65.	**Ken Linseman**, Phi., Edm., Bos., Tor.	14	860	**551**	.641
66.	**Tom Lysiak**, Atl., Chi.	13	919	**551**	.600
* 67.	**Joe Sakic**, Que., Colorado	10	719	**549**	.764
68.	**Pat LaFontaine**, NYI, Buf., NYR	15	865	**545**	.630
69.	**Mark Howe**, Hfd., Phi., Det.	16	929	**545**	.587
* 70.	**Kirk Muller**, N.J., Mtl., NYI, Tor., Fla.	14	1032	**542**	.525
71.	**Red Kelly**, Det., Tor.	20	1316	**542**	.412
* 72.	**Craig Janney**, Bos., St.L., S.J., Wpg., Phx.	11	704	**541**	.768
73.	**Rick Middleton**, NYR, Bos.	14	1005	**540**	.537
* 74.	**Brian Leetch**, NYR	11	725	**536**	.739
* 75.	**Luc Robitaille**, L.A., Pit., NYR	12	889	**524**	.589
76.	**Dennis Maruk**, Cal., Clev., Min., Wsh.	14	888	**522**	.588
* 77.	**Brian Bellows**, Min., Mtl., T.B., Ana., Wsh.	16	1112	**518**	.466
78.	**Wayne Cashman**, Bos.	17	1027	**516**	.502
79.	**Butch Goring**, L.A., NYI, Bos.	16	1107	**513**	.463
80.	**John Tonelli**, NYI, Cgy., L.A., Chi., Que.	14	1028	**511**	.497
81.	**Lanny McDonald**, Tor., Col., Cgy.	16	1111	**506**	.455

* - Active

One of the game's top two-way performers, Dave Keon was a persistent thorn in the side to countless NHL forwards during his Hall-of-Fame career. The dapper Noranda, Quebec native was also a playmaking specialist, delivering the goods to his teammates 590 times.

	Player	Seasons	Games	Assists	Assist per game
82.	**Ivan Boldirev**, Bos., Cal., Chi., Atl., Van., Det.	15	1052	**505**	.480
83.	**Randy Carlyle**, Tor., Pit., Wpg.	17	1055	**499**	.473
84.	**Pete Mahovlich**, Det., Mtl., Pit.	16	884	**485**	.549
85.	**Pit Martin**, Det., Bos., Chi., Van.	17	1101	**485**	.441
* 86.	**Murray Craven**, Det., Phi., Hfd., Van., Chi., S.J.	16	1009	**481**	.477
* 87.	**Mark Recchi**, Pit., Phi., Mtl.	10	710	**472**	.665
88.	**Ken Hodge**, Chi., Bos., NYR	14	881	**472**	.536
89.	**Ted Lindsay**, Det., Chi.	17	1068	**472**	.442
* 90.	**Pat Verbeek**, N.J., Hfd., NYR, Dal.	16	1147	**470**	.410
91.	**Jacques Lemaire**, Mtl.	12	853	**469**	.550
92.	**Dean Prentice**, Pit., Min., Det., NYR, Bos.	22	1378	**469**	.340
93.	**Phil Goyette**, Mtl., NYR, St.L., Buf.	16	941	**467**	.496
94.	**Mike Ridley**, NYR, Wsh., Tor., Van.	12	866	**466**	.538
95.	**Brent Sutter**, NYI, Chi.	18	1111	**466**	.419
96.	**Bill Barber**, Phi.	12	903	**463**	.513
97.	**Reed Larson**, Det., Bos., Edm., NYI, Min., Buf.	14	904	**463**	.512
98.	**Doug Mohns**, Bos., Chi., Min., Atl., Wsh.	22	1390	**462**	.332
99.	**Bobby Rousseau**, Mtl., Min., NYR	15	942	**458**	.486
100.	**Wilf Paiement**, K.C. Col., Tor., Que., NYR, Buf., Pit.	14	946	**458**	.484

Top 100 Active Assist Leaders

	Player	Games	Assists	Assists per game
1.	**Wayne Gretzky**, Edm., L.A., St.L., NYR	1417	**1910**	1.348
2.	**Paul Coffey**, Edm., Pit., L.A., Det., Hfd., Phi.	1268	**1090**	.860
3.	**Ray Bourque**, Bos.	1372	**1036**	.755
4.	**Mark Messier**, Edm., NYR, Van.	1354	**1015**	.750
5.	**Ron Francis**, Hfd., Pit.	1247	**1006**	.807
6.	**Steve Yzerman**, Det.	1098	**846**	.770
7.	**Larry Murphy**, L.A., Wsh., Min., Pit., Tor., Det.	1397	**838**	.600
8.	**Adam Oates**, Det., St.L., Bos., Wsh.	908	**796**	.877
9.	**Doug Gilmour**, St.L., Cgy., Tor., N.J.	1125	**795**	.707
10.	**Al MacInnis**, Cgy., St.L.	1060	**733**	.692
11.	**Bernie Nicholls**, L.A., NYR, Edm., N.J., Chi., S.J.	1117	**732**	.655
12.	**Phil Housley**, Buf., Wpg., St.L., Cgy., N.J., Wsh.	1131	**730**	.645
13.	**Dale Hunter**, Que., Wsh.	1345	**688**	.512
14.	**Chris Chelios**, Mtl., Chi.	1001	**606**	.605
15.	**Scott Stevens**, Wsh., St.L., N.J.	1200	**606**	.505
16.	**Dave Andreychuk**, Buf., Tor., N.J.	1158	**595**	.514
17.	**Dino Ciccarelli**, Min., Wsh., Det., T.B., Fla.	1218	**591**	.485
18.	**Dave Babych**, Wpg., Hfd., Van., Phi.	1154	**575**	.498
19.	**Pierre Turgeon**, Buf., NYI, Mtl., St.L.	810	**566**	.699
20.	**Gary Suter**, Cgy., Chi.	918	**563**	.613
21.	**Vincent Damphousse**, Tor., Edm., Mtl.	928	**552**	.595
22.	**Joe Sakic**, Que., Colorado	719	**549**	.764
23.	**Kirk Muller**, N.J., Mtl., NYI, Tor., Fla.	1032	**542**	.525
24.	**Craig Janney**, Bos., St.L., S.J., Wpg., Phx.	704	**541**	.768
25.	**Brian Leetch**, NYR	725	**536**	.739
26.	**Luc Robitaille**, L.A., Pit., NYR	889	**524**	.589
27.	**Brian Bellows**, Min., Mtl., T.B., Ana., Wsh.	1112	**518**	.466
28.	**Murray Craven**, Det., Phi., Hfd., Van., Chi., S.J.	1009	**481**	.477
29.	**Mark Recchi**, Pit., Phi., Mtl.	710	**472**	.665
30.	**Pat Verbeek**, N.J., Hfd., NYR, Dal.	1147	**470**	.410
31.	**Tomas Sandstrom**, NYR, L.A., Pit., Det., Ana.	925	**445**	.481
32.	**James Patrick**, NYR, Hfd., Cgy.	935	**439**	.470
33.	**Steve Duchesne**, L.A., Phi., Que., St.L., Ott.	845	**436**	.516
34.	**Rick Tocchet**, Phi., Pit., L.A., Bos., Wsh., Phx.	909	**436**	.480
35.	**Ed Olczyk**, Chi., Tor., Wpg., NYR, L.A., Pit.	937	**435**	.464
36.	**Jaromir Jagr**, Pit.	581	**434**	.747
37.	**Russ Courtnall**, Tor., Mtl., Min., Dal., Van., NYR, L.A.	972	**434**	.447
38.	**Brett Hull**, Cgy., St.L.	801	**433**	.541
39.	**Jeff Brown**, Que., St.L., Van., Hfd., Car., Tor., Wsh.	747	**430**	.576
40.	**Garry Galley**, L.A., Wsh., Bos., Phi., Buf.	963	**428**	.444
41.	**Theoren Fleury**, Cgy.	731	**427**	.584
42.	**Geoff Courtnall**, Bos., Edm., Wsh., St.L., Van.	1018	**423**	.416
43.	**Michal Pivonka**, Wsh.	789	**412**	.522
44.	**Doug Bodger**, Pit., Buf., S.J., N.J.	993	**410**	.413
45.	**Jeremy Roenick**, Chi., Phx.	675	**401**	.594
46.	**Dave Ellett**, Wpg., Tor., N.J., Bos.	1023	**401**	.392
47.	**Bob Carpenter**, Wsh., NYR, L.A., Bos., N.J.	1122	**400**	.357
48.	**Bruce Driver**, N.J., NYR	922	**390**	.423
49.	**Kevin Hatcher**, Wsh., Dal., Pit.	960	**390**	.406
50.	**Guy Carbonneau**, Mtl., St.L., Dal.	1175	**385**	.328
51.	**Esa Tikkanen**, Edm., NYR, St.L., N.J., Van., Fla., Wsh.	845	**383**	.453
52.	**Peter Zezel**, Phi., St.L., Wsh., Tor., Dal., N.J., Van.	832	**381**	.458
53.	**Rod Brind'Amour**, St.L., Phi.	696	**380**	.546
54.	**Brendan Shanahan**, N.J., St.L., Hfd., Det.	788	**380**	.482
55.	**Dave Gagner**, NYR, Min., Dal., Tor., Cgy., Fla.	877	**379**	.432
56.	**Mike Modano**, Min., Dal.	633	**377**	.596
57.	**Ray Ferraro**, Hfd., NYI, NYR, L.A.	955	**377**	.395
58.	**John MacLean**, N.J., S.J.	985	**373**	.379
59.	**Steve Thomas**, Tor., Chi., NYI, N.J.	860	**372**	.433
60.	**Kevin Dineen**, Hfd., Phi., Car.	925	**372**	.402
61.	**Joe Nieuwendyk**, Cgy., Dal.	768	**371**	.483
62.	**Mats Sundin**, Que., Tor.	611	**367**	.601
63.	**John Cullen**, Pit., Hfd., Tor., T.B.	617	**363**	.588
64.	**Cliff Ronning**, St.L., Van., Phx.	695	**363**	.522
65.	**Sergei Fedorov**, Det.	527	**361**	.685
66.	**Fredrik Olausson**, Wpg., Edm., Ana., Pit.	787	**356**	.452
67.	**Alexander Mogilny**, Buf., Van.	587	**354**	.603
68.	**Kevin Lowe**, Edm., NYR	1254	**347**	.277
69.	**Kevin Stevens**, Pit., Bos., L.A., NYR	668	**346**	.518
70.	**Stephane Richer**, Mtl., N.J., T.B.	866	**341**	.394
71.	**Trevor Linden**, Van., NYI	727	**329**	.453
72.	**Shayne Corson**, Mtl., Edm., St.L.	809	**328**	.405
73.	**Greg A. Adams**, N.J., Van., Dal.	852	**325**	.381
74.	**Calle Johansson**, Buf., Wsh.	783	**323**	.413
75.	**Brian Bradley**, Cgy., Van., Tor., T.B.	651	**321**	.493
76.	**Doug Weight**, NYR, Edm.	504	**320**	.635
77.	**Derek King**, NYI, Hfd., Tor.	727	**316**	.435
78.	**Ron Sutter**, Phi., St.L., Que., NYI, Bos., S.J.	935	**314**	.336
79.	**Joel Otto**, Cgy., Phi.	943	**313**	.332
80.	**Glen Wesley**, Bos., Hfd., Car.	803	**305**	.380
81.	**Claude Lemieux**, Mtl., N.J., Colorado	836	**302**	.361

Quiet and effective are two adjectives often used to describe the quality of Murray Craven's play. Detroit's first choice in the 1982 Entry Draft, Craven has been able to adapt to any on-ice situation, using his keen eye to set up 481 goals during his career.

	Player	Games	Assists	Assists per game
82.	**Andrew Cassels**, Mtl., Hfd., Cgy.	579	**299**	.516
83.	**Steve Chiasson**, Det., Cgy., Hfd., Car.	723	**297**	.411
84.	**Petr Svoboda**, Mtl., Buf., Phi.	880	**297**	.338
85.	**Scott Mellanby**, Phi., Edm., Fla.	872	**291**	.334
86.	**Joe Juneau**, Bos., Wsh.	410	**287**	.700
87.	**Jimmy Carson**, L.A., Edm., Det., Van., Hfd.	626	**286**	.457
88.	**Eric Lindros**, Phi.	360	**284**	.789
89.	**Zarley Zalapski**, Pit., Hfd., Cgy., Mtl.	625	**283**	.453
90.	**Steve Smith**, Edm., Chi.	702	**283**	.403
91.	**Igor Larionov**, Van., S.J., Det.	509	**282**	.554
92.	**Nicklas Lidstrom**, Det.	531	**279**	.525
93.	**Benoit Hogue**, Buf., NYI, Tor., Dal.	670	**279**	.416
94.	**Jeff Norton**, NYI, S.J., St.L., Edm., T.B., Fla.	591	**278**	.470
95.	**Gary Roberts**, Cgy., Car.	646	**277**	.429
96.	**Teppo Numminen**, Wpg., Pho.	711	**277**	.390
97.	**Kelly Miller**, NYR, Wsh.	995	**277**	.278
98.	**Jamie Macoun**, Cgy., Tor., Det.	1059	**272**	.257
99.	**Teemu Selanne**, Wpg., Ana.	410	**271**	.661
100.	**Doug Lidster**, Van., NYR, St.L.	880	**268**	.305

Top 100 All-Time Point Leaders

Player	Seasons	Games	Goals	Assists	Points	Points per game
* 1. **Wayne Gretzky**, Edm., L.A., St.L., NYR	19	1417	885	1910	**2795**	1.97
2. **Gordie Howe**, Det., Hfd.	26	1767	801	1049	**1850**	1.05
3. **Marcel Dionne**, Det., L.A., NYR	18	1348	731	1040	**1771**	1.31
* 4. **Mark Messier**, Edm., NYR, Van.	19	1354	597	1015	**1612**	1.19
5. **Phil Esposito**, Chi., Bos., NYR	18	1282	717	873	**1590**	1.24
6. **Mario Lemieux**, Pit.	12	745	613	881	**1494**	2.01
* 7. **Paul Coffey**, Edm., Pit., L.A., Det., Hfd., Phi.	18	1268	383	1090	**1473**	1.16
8. **Stan Mikita**, Chi.	22	1394	541	926	**1467**	1.05
* 9. **Ron Francis**, Hfd., Pit.	17	1247	428	1006	**1434**	1.15
10. **Bryan Trottier**, NYI, Pit.	18	1279	524	901	**1425**	1.11
* 11. **Ray Bourque**, Bos.	19	1372	375	1036	**1411**	1.03
* 12. **Steve Yzerman**, Det.	15	1098	563	846	**1409**	1.28
13. **Dale Hawerchuk**, Wpg., Buf., St.L., Phi.	16	1188	518	891	**1409**	1.19
14. **Jari Kurri**, Edm., L.A., NYR, Ana., Colorado	17	1251	601	797	**1398**	1.12
15. **John Bucyk**, Det., Bos.,	23	1540	556	813	**1369**	.889
16. **Guy Lafleur**, Mtl., NYR, Que.	17	1126	560	793	**1353**	1.20
17. **Denis Savard**, Chi., Mtl., T.B.	17	1196	473	865	**1338**	1.12
18. **Mike Gartner**, Wsh., Min., NYR, Tor., Phx.	19	1432	708	627	**1335**	.932
19. **Gilbert Perreault**, Buf.	17	1191	512	814	**1326**	1.11
20. **Alex Delvecchio**, Det.	24	1549	456	825	**1281**	.827
21. **Jean Ratelle**, NYR, Bos.	21	1281	491	776	**1267**	.989
22. **Peter Stastny**, Que., N.J., St.L.	15	977	450	789	**1239**	1.27
23. **Norm Ullman**, Det., Tor.	20	1410	490	739	**1229**	.872
24. **Jean Beliveau**, Mtl.	20	1125	507	712	**1219**	1.08
25. **Bobby Clarke**, Phi.	15	1144	358	852	**1210**	1.06
* 26. **Bernie Nicholls**, L.A., NYR, Edm., N.J., Chi., S.J.	17	1117	475	732	**1207**	1.08
* 27. **Dino Ciccarelli**, Min., Wsh., Det., T.B., Fla.	18	1218	602	591	**1193**	.979
* 28. **Doug Gilmour**, St.L., Cgy., Tor., N.J.	15	1125	381	795	**1176**	1.05
29. **Bobby Hull**, Chi., Wpg., Hfd.	16	1063	610	560	**1170**	1.10
30. **Michel Goulet**, Que., Chi.	15	1089	548	604	**1152**	1.06
31. **Bernie Federko**, St.L., Det.	14	1000	369	761	**1130**	1.13
32. **Mike Bossy**, NYI.	10	752	573	553	**1126**	1.50
33. **Darryl Sittler**, Tor., Phi., Det.	15	1096	484	637	**1121**	1.02
* 34. **Dave Andreychuk**, Buf., Tor., N.J.	16	1158	517	595	**1112**	.960
35. **Frank Mahovlich**, Tor., Det., Mtl.	18	1181	533	570	**1103**	.934
* 36. **Larry Murphy**, L.A., Wsh., Min., Pit., Tor., Det.	18	1397	265	838	**1103**	.790
37. **Glenn Anderson**, Edm., Tor., NYR, St.L.	16	1129	498	601	**1099**	.973
* 38. **Adam Oates**, Det., St.L., Bos., Wsh.	13	908	276	796	**1072**	1.18
39. **Dave Taylor**, L.A.	17	1111	431	638	**1069**	.962
40. **Joe Mullen**, St.L., Cgy., Pit., Bos.	17	1062	502	561	**1063**	1.00
41. **Denis Potvin**, NYI	15	1060	310	742	**1052**	.992
42. **Henri Richard**, Mtl.	20	1256	358	688	**1046**	.833
43. **Bobby Smith**, Min., Mtl.	15	1077	357	679	**1036**	.962
44. **Rod Gilbert**, NYR	18	1065	406	615	**1021**	.959
* 45. **Phil Housley**, Buf., Wpg., St.L., Cgy., N.J., Wsh.	16	1131	291	730	**1021**	.903
46. **Pat LaFontaine**, NYI, Buf., NYR	15	865	468	545	**1013**	1.17
47. **Steve Larmer**, Chi., NYR	15	1006	441	571	**1012**	1.01
* 48. **Dale Hunter**, Que., Wsh.	18	1345	321	688	**1009**	.750
49. **Lanny McDonald**, Tor., Col., Cgy.	16	1111	500	506	**1006**	.905
50. **Brian Propp**, Phi., Bos., Min., Hfd.	15	1016	425	579	**1004**	.988
* 51. **Al MacInnis**, Cgy., St.L.	17	1060	270	733	**1003**	.946
* 52. **Luc Robitaille**, L.A., Pit., NYR.	12	889	478	524	**1002**	1.13
53. **Rick Middleton**, NYR, Bos.	14	1005	448	540	**988**	.983
* 54. **Brett Hull**, Cgy., St.L.	13	801	554	433	**987**	1.23
* 55. **Brian Bellows**, Min., Mtl., T.B., Ana., Wsh.	16	1112	468	518	**986**	.887
56. **Dave Keon**, Tor., Hfd.	18	1296	396	590	**986**	.761
57. **Andy Bathgate**, NYR, Tor., Det., Pit.	17	1069	349	624	**973**	.910
58. **Maurice Richard**, Mtl.	18	978	544	421	**965**	.987
59. **Larry Robinson**, Mtl., L.A.	20	1384	208	750	**958**	.692
* 60. **Pierre Turgeon**, Buf., NYI, Mtl., St.L.	11	810	366	566	**932**	1.15
* 61. **Pat Verbeek**, N.J., Hfd., NYR, Dal.	16	1147	461	470	**931**	.812
62. **Neal Broten**, Min., Dal., N.J., L.A.	17	1099	289	634	**923**	.840
63. **Bobby Orr**, Bos., Chi.	12	657	270	645	**915**	1.39
64. **Brad Park**, NYR, Bos., Det.	17	1113	213	683	**896**	.805
65. **Butch Goring**, L.A., NYI, Bos.	16	1107	375	513	**888**	.802
* 66. **Joe Sakic**, Que., Col.	10	719	334	549	**883**	1.23
67. **Bill Barber**, Phi.	12	903	420	463	**883**	.978
* 68. **Vincent Damphousse**, Tor., Edm., Mtl.	12	928	328	552	**880**	.948
69. **Dennis Maruk**, Cal., Clev., Min., Wsh.	14	888	356	522	**878**	.989
* 70. **Kirk Muller**, N.J., Mtl., NYI, Tor., Fla.	14	1032	334	542	**876**	.849
71. **Ivan Boldirev**, Bos., Cal., Chi., Atl., Van., Det.	15	1052	361	505	**866**	.823
72. **Yvan Cournoyer**, Mtl.	16	968	428	435	**863**	.892
73. **Dean Prentice**, Pit., Min., Det., NYR, Bos.	22	1378	391	469	**860**	.624
74. **Ted Lindsay**, Det., Chi.	17	1068	379	472	**851**	.797
75. **Tom Lysiak**, Atl., Chi.	13	919	292	551	**843**	.917
76. **John Tonelli**, NYI, Cgy., L.A., Chi., Que.	14	1028	325	511	**836**	.813
77. **Jacques Lemaire**, Mtl.	12	853	366	469	**835**	.979
78. **Brent Sutter**, NYI, Chi.	18	1111	363	466	**829**	.746
79. **John Ogrodnick**, Det., Que., NYR	14	928	402	425	**827**	.891
80. **Doug Wilson**, Chi., S.J.	16	1024	237	590	**827**	.808
* 81. **Tomas Sandstrom**, NYR, L.A., Pit., Det., Ana.	14	925	379	445	**824**	.891
82. **Red Kelly**, Det., Tor.	20	1316	281	542	**823**	.625
83. **Pierre Larouche**, Pit., Mtl., Hfd., NYR.	14	812	395	427	**822**	1.01
84. **Bernie Geoffrion**, Mtl., NYR.	16	883	393	429	**822**	.931
* 85. **Rick Tocchet**, Phi., Pit., L.A., Bos., Wsh., Phx.	14	909	385	436	**821**	.903
86. **Steve Shutt**, Mtl., L.A.	13	930	424	393	**817**	.878
87. **Thomas Steen**, Wpg.	14	950	264	553	**817**	.860
88. **Wilf Paiement**, K.C. Col., Tor., Que., NYR, Buf., Pit.	14	946	356	458	**814**	.860
89. **Peter McNab**, Buf., Bos., Van., N.J.	14	954	363	450	**813**	.852
90. **Pit Martin**, Det., Bos., Chi., Van.	17	1101	324	485	**809**	.735
91. **Ken Linseman**, Phi., Edm., Bos., Tor.	14	860	256	551	**807**	.938
92. **Garry Unger**, Tor., Det., St.L., Atl., L.A., Edm.	16	1105	413	391	**804**	.728
93. **Ken Hodge**, Chi., Bos., NYR	14	881	328	472	**800**	.908
94. **Wayne Cashman**, Bos.	17	1027	277	516	**793**	.772
* 95. **Mark Recchi**, Pit., Phi., Mtl.	10	710	317	472	**789**	1.11
96. **Rick Vaive**, Van., Tor., Chi., Buf.	13	876	441	347	**788**	.900
97. **Borje Salming**, Tor., Det.	17	1148	150	637	**787**	.686
* 98. **Geoff Courtnall**, Bos., Edm., Wsh., St.L., Van.	15	1018	360	423	**783**	.769
99. **Jean Pronovost**, Wsh., Pit., Atl.	14	998	391	383	**774**	.776
100. **Pete Mahovlich**, Det., Mtl., Pit.	16	884	288	485	**773**	.874

When Mario Lemieux retired following the 1996-97 season, he became the only player more than two points per game during his career. As staggering as that statistic may seem, the Magnificent Mario was even more proficient as a junior, averaging 2.8 points-per-game during his three seasons with the Laval Titan of the Quebec Major Junior League.

* - Active

Top 100 Active Points Leaders

	Player	Games	Goals	Assists	Points	Points per game
1.	**Wayne Gretzky**, Edm., L.A., St.L., NYR	1417	885	1910	**2795**	1.972
2.	**Mark Messier**, Edm., NYR, Van.	1354	597	1015	**1612**	1.191
3.	**Paul Coffey**, Edm., Pit., L.A., Det., Hfd., Phi.	1268	383	1090	**1473**	1.162
4.	**Ron Francis**, Hfd., Pit.	1247	428	1006	**1434**	1.150
5.	**Ray Bourque**, Bos.	1372	375	1036	**1411**	1.028
6.	**Steve Yzerman**, Det.	1098	563	846	**1409**	1.283
7.	**Bernie Nicholls**, L.A., NYR, Edm., N.J., Chi., S.J.	1117	475	732	**1207**	1.081
8.	**Dino Ciccarelli**, Min., Wsh., Det., T.B., Fla.	1218	602	591	**1193**	.979
9.	**Doug Gilmour**, St.L., Cgy., Tor., N.J.	1125	381	795	**1176**	1.045
10.	**Dave Andreychuk**, Buf., Tor., N.J.	1158	517	595	**1112**	.960
11.	**Larry Murphy**, L.A., Wsh., Min., Pit., Tor., Det.	1397	265	838	**1103**	.790
12.	**Adam Oates**, Det., St.L., Bos., Wsh.	908	276	796	**1072**	1.181
13.	**Phil Housley**, Buf., Wpg., St.L., Cgy., N.J., Wsh.	1131	291	730	**1021**	.903
14.	**Dale Hunter**, Que., Wsh.	1345	321	688	**1009**	.750
15.	**Al MacInnis**, Cgy., St.L.	1060	270	733	**1003**	.946
16.	**Luc Robitaille**, L.A., Pit., NYR	889	478	524	**1002**	1.127
17.	**Brett Hull**, Cgy., St.L.	801	554	433	**987**	1.232
18.	**Brian Bellows**, Min., Mtl., T.B., Ana., Wsh.	1112	468	518	**986**	.887
19.	**Pierre Turgeon**, Buf., NYI, Mtl., St.L.	810	366	566	**932**	1.151
20.	**Pat Verbeek**, N.J., Hfd., NYR, Dal.	1147	461	470	**931**	.812
21.	**Joe Sakic**, Que., Col.	719	334	549	**883**	1.228
22.	**Vincent Damphousse**, Tor., Edm., Mtl.	928	328	552	**880**	.948
23.	**Kirk Muller**, N.J., Mtl., NYI, Tor., Fla.	1032	334	542	**876**	.849
24.	**Tomas Sandstrom**, NYR, L.A., Pit., Det., Ana.	925	379	445	**824**	.891
25.	**Rick Tocchet**, Phi., Pit., L.A., Bos., Wsh., Phx.	909	385	436	**821**	.903
26.	**Mark Recchi**, Pit., Phi., Mtl.	710	317	472	**789**	1.111
27.	**Geoff Courtnall**, Bos., Edm., Wsh., St.L., Van.	1018	360	423	**783**	.769
28.	**Scott Stevens**, Wsh., St.L., N.J.	1200	166	606	**772**	.643
29.	**Joe Nieuwendyk**, Cgy., Dal.	768	397	371	**768**	1.000
30.	**Ed Olczyk**, Chi., Tor., Wpg., NYR, L.A., Pit.	937	330	435	**765**	.816
31.	**Chris Chelios**, Mtl., Chi.	1001	156	606	**762**	.761
32.	**Theoren Fleury**, Cgy.	731	334	427	**761**	1.041
33.	**Gary Suter**, Cgy., Chi.	918	181	563	**744**	.810
34.	**Brendan Shanahan**, N.J., St.L., Hfd., Det.	788	363	380	**743**	.943
35.	**Murray Craven**, Det., Phi., Hfd., Van., Chi., S.J.	1009	262	481	**743**	.736
36.	**Jaromir Jagr**, Pit.	581	301	434	**735**	1.265
37.	**John MacLean**, N.J., S.J.	985	360	373	**733**	.744
38.	**Russ Courtnall**, Tor., Mtl., Min., Dal., Van., NYR, L.A.	972	291	434	**725**	.746
39.	**Craig Janney**, Bos., St.L., S.J., Wpg., Phx.	704	183	541	**724**	1.028
40.	**Jeremy Roenick**, Chi., Phx.	675	320	401	**721**	1.068
41.	**Stephane Richer**, Mtl., N.J., T.B.	866	380	341	**721**	.833
42.	**Bob Carpenter**, Wsh., NYR, L.A., Bos., N.J.	1122	318	400	**718**	.640
43.	**Dave Babych**, Wpg., Hfd., Van., Phi.	1154	140	575	**715**	.620
44.	**Ray Ferraro**, Hfd., NYI, NYR, L.A.	955	333	377	**710**	.743
45.	**Kevin Dineen**, Hfd., Phi., Car.	925	330	372	**702**	.759
46.	**Brian Leetch**, NYR	725	164	536	**700**	.966
47.	**Steve Thomas**, Tor., Chi., NYI, N.J.	860	324	372	**696**	.809
48.	**Dave Gagner**, NYR, Min., Dal., Tor., Cgy., Fla.	877	312	379	**691**	.788
49.	**Alexander Mogilny**, Buf., Van.	587	315	354	**669**	1.140
50.	**Mike Modano**, Min., Dal.	633	277	377	**654**	1.033
51.	**Kevin Stevens**, Pit., Bos., L.A., NYR	668	292	346	**638**	.955
52.	**Steve Duchesne**, L.A., Phi., Que., St.L., Ott.	845	202	436	**638**	.755
53.	**Mats Sundin**, Que., Tor.	611	265	367	**632**	1.034
54.	**Greg A. Adams**, N.J., Van., Dal.	852	306	325	**631**	.741
55.	**Guy Carbonneau**, Mtl., St.L., Dal.	1175	246	385	**631**	.537
56.	**Rod Brind'Amour**, St.L., Phi.	696	249	380	**629**	.904
57.	**Esa Tikkanen**, Edm., NYR, St.L., N.J., Van., Fla., Wsh.	845	244	383	**627**	.742
58.	**Sergei Fedorov**, Det.	527	248	361	**609**	1.156
59.	**Claude Lemieux**, Mtl., N.J., Col.	836	298	302	**600**	.718
60.	**Kevin Hatcher**, Wsh., Dal., Pit.	960	208	390	**598**	.623
61.	**Peter Zezel**, Phi., St.L., Wsh., Tor., Dal., N.J., Van.	832	213	381	**594**	.714
62.	**Michal Pivonka**, Wsh.	789	176	412	**588**	.745
63.	**Trevor Linden**, Van., NYI	727	257	329	**586**	.806
64.	**Jeff Brown**, Que., St.L., Van., Hfd., Car., Tor., Wsh.	747	154	430	**584**	.782
65.	**Ray Sheppard**, Buf., NYR, Det., S.J., Fla., Car.	696	322	257	**579**	.832
66.	**James Patrick**, NYR, Hfd., Cgy.	935	126	439	**565**	.604
67.	**Jimmy Carson**, L.A., Edm., Det., Van., Hfd.	626	275	286	**561**	.896
68.	**Cliff Ronning**, St.L., Van., Phx.	695	196	363	**559**	.804
69.	**Gary Roberts**, Cgy., Car.	646	277	277	**554**	.858
70.	**Dave Ellett**, Wpg., Tor., N.J., Bos.	1023	151	401	**552**	.540
71.	**Derek King**, NYI, Hfd., Tor.	727	235	316	**551**	.758
72.	**John Cullen**, Pit., Hfd., Tor., T.B.	617	187	363	**550**	.891
73.	**Shayne Corson**, Mtl., Edm., St.L.	809	221	328	**549**	.679
74.	**Teemu Selanne**, Wpg., Ana.	410	266	271	**537**	1.310
75.	**Garry Galley**, L.A., Wsh., Bos., Phi., Buf.	963	106	428	**534**	.555
76.	**Scott Mellanby**, Phi., Edm., Fla.	872	238	291	**529**	.607
77.	**Doug Bodger**, Pit., Buf., S.J., N.J.	993	103	410	**513**	.517
78.	**Wendel Clark**, Tor., Que., NYI.	683	294	216	**510**	.747
79.	**Ron Sutter**, Phi., St.L., Que., NYI, Bos., S.J.	935	196	314	**510**	.545
80.	**Joel Otto**, Cgy., Phi.	943	195	313	**508**	.539
81.	**Eric Lindros**, Phi.	360	223	284	**507**	1.408
82.	**Brian Bradley**, Cgy., Van., Tor., T.B.	651	182	321	**503**	.773
83.	**Peter Bondra**, Wsh.	544	285	205	**490**	.901
84.	**Bruce Driver**, N.J., NYR	922	96	390	**486**	.527
85.	**Ulf Dahlen**, NYR, Min., Dal., S.J., Chi.	686	231	249	**480**	.700
86.	**Pavel Bure**, Van.	428	254	224	**478**	1.117
87.	**Benoit Hogue**, Buf., NYI, Tor., Dal.	670	197	279	**476**	.710
88.	**Fredrik Olausson**, Wpg., Edm., Ana., Pit.	787	112	356	**468**	.595
89.	**Tony Granato**, NYR, L.A., S.J.	630	232	226	**458**	.727
90.	**Kelly Miller**, NYR, Wsh.	995	179	277	**456**	.458
91.	**Randy Burridge**, Bos., Wsh., L.A., Buf.	706	199	251	**450**	.637
92.	**Doug Weight**, NYR, Edm.	504	128	320	**448**	.889
93.	**John LeClair**, Mtl., Phi.	507	226	222	**448**	.884
94.	**Adam Graves**, Det., Edm., NYR.	748	232	216	**448**	.599
95.	**Joe Murphy**, Det., Edm., Chi., St.L., S.J.	634	195	252	**447**	.705
96.	**Scott Young**, Hfd., Pit., Que., Col., Ana.	672	186	259	**445**	.662
97.	**Keith Tkachuk**, Wpg., Phx.	458	236	205	**441**	.963
98.	**Robert Reichel**, Cgy., NYI	519	183	255	**438**	.844
99.	**Shawn Burr**, Det., T.B., S.J.	856	181	256	**437**	.511
100.	**Dimitri Khristich**, Wsh., L.A., Bos.	548	196	240	**436**	.796

When Chris Chelios was 16 years old, he was cut from two midget teams because his coaches felt he didn't have the skill to compete at that level. It obviously takes the best to bring out the best because Chelios has been a six-time All-Star and a three-time winner of the Norris Trophy as the NHL's top defenseman.

All-Time Games Played Leaders

Regular Season

* active player

	Player	Team	Seasons	GP
1.	Gordie Howe	Detroit	25	1,687
		Hartford	1	80
		Total	**26**	**1,767**
2.	Alex Delvecchio	**Detroit**	**24**	**1,549**
3.	John Bucyk	Detroit	2	104
		Boston	21	1,436
		Total	**23**	**1,540**
4.	Tim Horton	Toronto	19¾	1,185
		NY Rangers	1¼	93
		Pittsburgh	1	44
		Buffalo	2	124
		Total	**24**	**1,446**
5.	Mike Gartner	Washington	9¾	758
		Minnesota	1	80
		NY Rangers	4	322
		Toronto	2¼	120
		Phoenix	2	142
		Total	**19**	**1,432**
* 6.	Wayne Gretzky	Edmonton	9	696
		Los Angeles	7¾	539
		St. Louis	¼	18
		NY Rangers	2	164
		Total	**19**	**1,417**
7.	Harry Howell	NY Rangers	17	1,160
		California	1½	83
		Los Angeles	2½	168
		Total	**21**	**1,411**
8.	Norm Ullman	Detroit	12½	875
		Toronto	7½	535
		Total	**20**	**1,410**
* 9.	Larry Murphy	Los Angeles	3¼	242
		Washington	5½	453
		Minnesota	1¾	121
		Pittsburgh	4½	336
		Toronto	1¾	151
		Detroit	1¼	94
		Total	**18**	**1,397**
10.	Stan Mikita	**Chicago**	**22**	**1,394**
11.	Doug Mohns	Boston	11	710
		Chicago	6½	415
		Minnesota	2½	162
		Atlanta	1	28
		Washington	1	75
		Total	**22**	**1,390**
12.	Larry Robinson	Montreal	17	1,202
		Los Angeles	3	182
		Total	**20**	**1,384**
13.	Dean Prentice	NY Rangers	10½	666
		Boston	3	170
		Detroit	3½	230
		Pittsburgh	2	144
		Minnesota	3	168
		Total	**22**	**1,378**
* 14.	Ray Bourque	**Boston**	**19**	**1,372**
* 15.	Mark Messier	Edmonton	12	851
		NY Rangers	6	421
		Vancouver	1	82
		Total	**19**	**1,354**
16.	Ron Stewart	Toronto	13	838
		Boston	2	126
		St. Louis	½	19
		NY Rangers	4	306
		Vancouver	1	42
		NY Islanders	½	22
		Total	**21**	**1,353**
17.	Marcel Dionne	Detroit	4	309
		Los Angeles	11¾	921
		NY Rangers	2¼	118
		Total	**18**	**1,348**
* 18.	Dale Hunter	Quebec	7	523
		Washington	11	822
		Total	**18**	**1,345**
19.	Red Kelly	Detroit	12½	846
		Toronto	7½	470
		Total	**20**	**1,316**
20.	Dave Keon	Toronto	15	1,062
		Hartford	3	234
		Total	**18**	**1,296**
21.	Phil Esposito	Chicago	4	235
		Boston	8¼	625
		NY Rangers	5¾	422
		Total	**18**	**1,282**
22.	Jean Ratelle	NY Rangers	15¼	862
		Boston	5¾	419
		Total	**21**	**1,281**
23.	Bryan Trottier	NY Islanders	15	1,123
		Pittsburgh	3	156
		Total	**18**	**1,279**
* 24.	Paul Coffey	Edmonton	7	532
		Pittsburgh	4¾	331
		Los Angeles	¾	60
		Detroit	3½	231
		Hartford	¼	20
		Philadelphia	1¾	94
		Total	**18**	**1,268**
25.	Henri Richard	**Montreal**	**20**	**1,256**
26.	Kevin Lowe	Edmonton	15	1,037
		NY Rangers	4	217
		Total	**19**	**1,254**
27.	Jari Kurri	Edmonton	10	754
		Los Angeles	4¾	331
		NY Rangers	¼	14
		Anaheim	1	82
		Colorado	1	70
		Total	**17**	**1,251**
28.	Bill Gadsby	Chicago	8½	468
		NY Rangers	6½	457
		Detroit	5	323
		Total	**20**	**1,248**
* 29.	Ron Francis	Hartford	9¾	714
		Pittsburgh	7¼	533
		Total	**17**	**1,247**
30.	Allan Stanley	NY Rangers	6¼	307
		Chicago	1¾	111
		Boston	2	129
		Toronto	9	633
		Philadelphia	1	64
		Total	**21**	**1,244**
31.	Eddie Westfall	Boston	11	734
		NY Islanders	7	493
		Total	**18**	**1,227**
32.	Brad McCrimmon	Boston	3	228
		Philadelphia	5	367
		Calgary	3	231
		Detroit	3	203
		Hartford	3	156
		Phoenix	1	37
		Total	**18**	**1,222**
33.	Eric Nesterenko	Toronto	5	206
		Chicago	16	1,013
		Total	**21**	**1,219**
* 34.	Dino Ciccarelli	Minnesota	8¾	602
		Washington	3¼	223
		Detroit	4	254
		Tampa Bay	1½	111
		Florida	½	28
		Total	**18**	**1,218**
35.	Marcel Pronovost	Detroit	16	983
		Toronto	5	223
		Total	**21**	**1,206**
36.	Denis Savard	Chicago	12¼	881
		Montreal	3	210
		Tampa Bay	1¾	105
		Total	**17**	**1,196**
* 37.	Scott Stevens	Washington	8	601
		St. Louis	1	78
		New Jersey	7	521
		Total	**16**	**1,200**
38.	Gilbert Perreault	**Buffalo**	**17**	**1,191**
39.	Dale Hawerchuk	Winnipeg	9	713
		Buffalo	5	342
		St. Louis	¾	66
		Philadelphia	1¼	67
		Total	**16**	**1,188**
40.	George Armstrong	**Toronto**	**21**	**1,187**
41.	Frank Mahovlich	Toronto	11¾	720
		Detroit	2¾	198
		Montreal	3½	263
		Total	**18**	**1,181**
42.	Don Marshall	Montreal	10	585
		NY Rangers	7	479
		Buffalo	1	62
		Toronto	1	50
		Total	**19**	**1,176**
* 43.	Craig Ludwig	Montreal	8	597
		NY Islanders	1	75
		Minnesota	2	151
		Dallas	5	353
		Total	**16**	**1,176**
* 44.	Guy Carbonneau	Montreal	13	912
		St. Louis	1	42
		Dallas	3	221
		Total	**17**	**1,175**
45.	Bob Gainey	**Montreal**	**16**	**1,160**
* 46.	Dave Andreychuk	Buffalo	10½	763
		Toronto	3¼	223
		New Jersey	2¼	172
		Total	**16**	**1,158**
* 47.	Dave Babych	Winnipeg	5¼	390
		Hartford	5¾	349
		Vancouver	6¾	409
		Philadelphia	¼	6
		Total	**18**	**1,154**
48.	Leo Boivin	Toronto	3¼	137
		Boston	11½	717
		Detroit	1¼	85
		Pittsburgh	1½	114
		Minnesota	1½	97
		Total	**19**	**1,150**
49.	Borje Salming	Toronto	16	1,099
		Detroit	1	49
		Total	**17**	**1,148**
* 50.	Pat Verbeek	New Jersey	7	463
		Hartford	5¾	433
		NY Rangers	1¼	88
		Dallas	2	163
		Total	**16**	**1,147**
51.	Bobby Clarke	**Philadelphia**	**15**	**1,144**
* 52.	Phil Housley	Buffalo	8	608
		Winnipeg	3	232
		St. Louis	1	26
		Calgary	1¾	102
		New Jersey	¼	22
		Washington	2	141
		Total	**16**	**1,131**
53.	Glenn Anderson	Edmonton	11½	845
		Toronto	2¾	221
		NY Rangers	¼	12
		St. Louis	1½	51
		Total	**16**	**1,129**
54.	Bob Nevin	Toronto	5¾	250
		NY Rangers	7¼	505
		Minnesota	2	138
		Los Angeles	3	235
		Total	**18**	**1,128**
55.	Murray Oliver	Detroit	2½	101
		Boston	6½	429
		Toronto	3	226
		Minnesota	5	371
		Total	**17**	**1,127**
56.	Guy Lafleur	Montreal	14	961
		NY Rangers	1	67
		Quebec	2	98
		Total	**17**	**1,126**
57.	Jean Beliveau	**Montreal**	**20**	**1,125**
* 58.	Doug Gilmour	St. Louis	5	384
		Calgary	3½	266
		Toronto	5¼	392
		New Jersey	1¼	83
		Total	**15**	**1,125**
* 59.	Bob Carpenter	Washington	6¼	490
		NY Rangers	½	28
		Los Angeles	1¾	120
		Boston	3½	187
		New Jersey	5	297
		Total	**17**	**1,122**
* 60.	Bernie Nicholls	Los Angeles	8½	602
		NY Rangers	1¾	104
		Edmonton	1¼	95
		New Jersey	1½	84
		Chicago	2	107
		San Jose	2	125
		Total	**17**	**1,117**
61.	Doug Harvey	Montreal	14	890
		NY Rangers	3	151
		Detroit	1	2
		St. Louis	1	70
		Total	**19**	**1,113**
62.	Brad Park	NY Rangers	7½	465
		Boston	7½	501
		Detroit	2	147
		Total	**17**	**1,113**
* 63.	Brian Bellows	Minnesota	10	753
		Montreal	3	200
		Tampa Bay	1¼	86
		Anaheim	¾	62
		Washington	1	11
		Total	**16**	**1,112**
64.	Lanny McDonald	Toronto	6½	477
		Colorado	1¾	142
		Calgary	7¾	441
		Total	**16**	**1,111**
65.	Dave Taylor	**Los Angeles**	**17**	**1,111**
66.	Brent Sutter	NY Islanders	11¼	694
		Chicago	6¾	417
		Total	**18**	**1,111**
67.	Butch Goring	Los Angeles	10¾	736
		NY Islanders	4¾	332
		Boston	½	39
		Total	**16**	**1,107**
68.	Garry Unger	Toronto	½	15
		Detroit	3	216
		St. Louis	8½	662
		Atlanta	1	79
		Los Angeles	¾	58
		Edmonton	2¼	75
		Total	**16**	**1,105**
69.	Pit Martin	Detroit	3¼	119
		Boston	1¾	111
		Chicago	10¼	740
		Vancouver	1¾	131
		Total	**17**	**1,101**

	Player	Team	Seasons	GP
70.	**Neal Broten**	Minnesota	13	876
		Dallas	2	116
		New Jersey	1¾	88
		Los Angeles	¼	19
		Total	**17**	**1,099**
71.	**Jay Wells**	Los Angeles	9	604
		Philadelphia	1¾	126
		Buffalo	2	85
		NY Rangers	3¼	186
		St. Louis	1	76
		Tampa Bay	1	21
		Total	**18**	**1,098**
* 72.	**Steve Yzerman**	**Detroit**	**15**	**1,098**
73.	**Gordie Roberts**	Hartford	1½	107
		Minnesota	7	555
		Philadelphia	¼	11
		St. Louis	2½	166
		Pittsburgh	1¾	134
		Boston	2	124
		Total	**15**	**1,097**
74.	**Darryl Sittler**	Toronto	11½	844
		Philadelphia	2½	191
		Detroit	1	61
		Total	**15**	**1,096**
75.	**Craig MacTavish**	Boston	5	217
		Edmonton	8¾	701
		NY Rangers	¼	12
		Philadelphia	1¾	100
		St. Louis	1¼	63
		Total	**17**	**1,093**
76.	**Michel Goulet**	Quebec	10¾	813
		Chicago	4¼	276
		Total	**15**	**1,089**
77.	**Carol Vadnais**	Montreal	2	42
		Oakland	2	152
		California	1¾	94
		Boston	3½	263
		NY Rangers	6¾	485
		New Jersey	1	51
		Total	**17**	**1,087**
78.	**Brad Marsh**	Atlanta	2	160
		Calgary	1¼	97
		Philadelphia	6¾	514
		Toronto	2¾	181
		Detroit	1¼	75
		Ottawa	1	59
		Total	**15**	**1,086**
79.	**Bob Pulford**	Toronto	14	947
		Los Angeles	2	132
		Total	**16**	**1,079**
80.	**Bobby Smith**	Minnesota	8¼	572
		Montreal	6¾	505
		Total	**15**	**1,077**
81.	**Craig Ramsay**	**Buffalo**	**14**	**1,070**
82.	**Mike Ramsey**	Buffalo	13¾	911
		Pittsburgh	1¼	77
		Detroit	3	82
		Total	**18**	**1,070**
83.	**Andy Bathgate**	NY Rangers	11¾	719
		Toronto	1¼	70
		Detroit	2	130
		Pittsburgh	2	150
		Total	**17**	**1,069**
84.	**Ted Lindsay**	Detroit	14	862
		Chicago	3	206
		Total	**17**	**1,068**
85.	**Terry Harper**	Montreal	10	554
		Los Angeles	3	234
		Detroit	4	252
		St. Louis	1	11
		Colorado	1	15
		Total	**19**	**1,066**
86.	**Rod Gilbert**	**NY Rangers**	**18**	**1,065**
87.	**Bobby Hull**	Chicago	15	1,036
		Winnipeg	⅔	18
		Hartford	⅓	9
		Total	**16**	**1,063**
88.	**Joe Mullen**	St. Louis	4½	301
		Calgary	4½	345
		Pittsburgh	6	379
		Boston	1	37
		Total	**16**	**1,062**
89.	**Denis Potvin**	**NY Islanders**	**15**	**1,060**
* 90.	**Al MacInnis**	Calgary	13	803
		St. Louis	4	257
		Total	**17**	**1,060**
* 91.	**Jamie Macoun**	Calgary	8½	586
		Toronto	6¼	466
		Detroit	¼	7
		Total	**15**	**1,059**
92.	**Jean Guy Talbot**	Montreal	13	791
		Minnesota	¼	4
		Detroit	½	32
		St. Louis	2½	172
		Buffalo	¾	57
		Total	**17**	**1,056**
93.	**Randy Carlyle**	Toronto	2	94
		Pittsburgh	5¾	397
		Winnipeg	9¼	564
		Total	**17**	**1,055**
94.	**Ivan Boldirev**	Boston	1¼	13
		California	2¾	191
		Chicago	4¾	384
		Atlanta	1	65
		Vancouver	2¾	216
		Detroit	2½	183
		Total	**15**	**1,052**
95.	**Eddie Shack**	NY Rangers	2¼	141
		Toronto	8¾	504
		Boston	2	120
		Los Angeles	1¼	84
		Buffalo	1½	111
		Pittsburgh	1¼	87
		Total	**17**	**1,047**
96.	**Rob Ramage**	Colorado	3	234
		St. Louis	5¾	441
		Calgary	1¼	80
		Toronto	2	160
		Minnesota	1	34
		Tampa Bay	¾	66
		Montreal	½	14
		Philadelphia	¾	15
		Total	**15**	**1,044**
97.	**Serge Savard**	Montreal	15	917
		Winnipeg	2	123
		Total	**17**	**1,040**
98.	**Ron Ellis**	**Toronto**	**16**	**1,034**
99.	**Harold Snepsts**	Vancouver	11¾	781
		Minnesota	1	71
		Detroit	3	120
		St. Louis	1¼	61
		Total	**17**	**1,033**
100.	**Ralph Backstrom**	Montreal	14½	844
		Los Angeles	2¼	172
		Chicago	¼	16
		Total	**17**	**1,032**
* 101.	**Kirk Muller**	New Jersey	7	556
		Montreal	3¾	267
		NY Islanders	¾	27
		Toronto	1¼	102
		Florida	1¼	80
		Total	**14**	**1,032**
102.	**Dick Duff**	Toronto	9¾	582
		NY Rangers	¾	43
		Montreal	5	305
		Los Angeles	¾	39
		Buffalo	1¾	61
		Total	**18**	**1,030**
103.	**John Tonelli**	NY Islanders	7¾	584
		Calgary	2¼	161
		Los Angeles	3	231
		Chicago	¾	33
		Quebec	¼	19
		Total	**14**	**1,028**
104.	**Gaetan Duchesne**	Washington	6	451
		Quebec	2	150
		Minnesota	4	297
		San Jose	1¾	117
		Florida	¼	13
		Total	**14**	**1,028**
105.	**Wayne Cashman**	**Boston**	**17**	**1,027**
106.	**Doug Wilson**	Chicago	14	938
		San Jose	2	86
		Total	**16**	**1,024**
107.	**Jim Neilson**	NY Rangers	12	810
		California	2	98
		Cleveland	2	115
		Total	**16**	**1,023**
108.	**Keith Acton**	Montreal	4¼	228
		Minnesota	4¼	343
		Edmonton	1	72
		Philadelphia	4½	303
		Washington	¼	6
		NY Islanders	¾	71
		Total	**15**	**1,023**
* 109.	**Dave Ellett**	Winnipeg	6¼	475
		Toronto	6½	446
		New Jersey	¼	20
		Boston	1	82
		Total	**14**	**1,023**
110.	**Don Lever**	Vancouver	7⅔	593
		Atlanta	⅓	28
		Calgary	1¼	85
		Colorado	¾	59
		New Jersey	3	216
		Buffalo	2	39
		Total	**15**	**1,020**
111.	**Mike Foligno**	Detroit	2½	186
		Buffalo	9	664
		Toronto	2¾	129
		Florida	¾	39
		Total	**15**	**1,018**
* 112.	**Geoff Courtnall**	Boston	4¾	259
		Edmonton	¼	12
		Washington	2	159
		St. Louis	3¾	296
		Vancouver	4¼	292
		Total	**15**	**1,018**
113.	**Charlie Huddy**	Edmonton	11	694
		Los Angeles	3¼	226
		Buffalo	2½	85
		St. Louis	¼	12
		Total	**17**	**1,017**
114.	**Phil Russell**	Chicago	6¾	504
		Atlanta	1¼	93
		Calgary	3	229
		New Jersey	2¾	172
		Buffalo	1¼	18
		Total	**15**	**1,016**
115.	**Brian Propp**	Philadelphia	10¾	790
		Boston	¼	14
		Minnesota	3	147
		Hartford	1	65
		Total	**15**	**1,016**
116.	**Laurie Boschman**	Toronto	2¾	187
		Edmonton	1	73
		Winnipeg	7¼	526
		New Jersey	2	153
		Ottawa	1	70
		Total	**14**	**1,009**
117.	**Dave Christian**	Winnipeg	4	230
		Washington	6½	504
		Boston	1½	128
		St. Louis	1	78
		Chicago	2	69
		Total	**15**	**1,009**
* 118.	**Murray Craven**	Detroit	2	46
		Philadelphia	7¼	523
		Hartford	1½	128
		Vancouver	1¼	88
		Chicago	3	157
		San Jose	1	67
		Total	**16**	**1,009**
119.	**Dave Lewis**	NY Islanders	6¾	514
		Los Angeles	3¼	221
		New Jersey	3	209
		Detroit	2	64
		Total	**15**	**1,008**
120.	**Bob Murray**	**Chicago**	**15**	**1,008**
121.	**Jim Roberts**	Montreal	9⅔	611
		St. Louis	5⅓	395
		Total	**15**	**1,006**
122.	**Steve Larmer**	Chicago	13	891
		NY Rangers	2	115
		Total	**15**	**1,006**
123.	**Claude Provost**	**Montreal**	**15**	**1,005**
124.	**Rick Middleton**	NY Rangers	2	124
		Boston	12	881
		Total	**14**	**1,005**
125.	**Ryan Walter**	Washington	4	307
		Montreal	9	604
		Vancouver	2	92
		Total	**15**	**1,003**
126.	**Vic Hadfield**	NY Rangers	13	839
		Pittsburgh	3	163
		Total	**16**	**1,002**
* 127.	**Chris Chelios**	Montreal	7	402
		Chicago	8	599
		Total	**15**	**1,001**
128.	**Bernie Federko**	St. Louis	14	927
		Detroit	1	73
		Total	**15**	**1,000**

Goaltending Records

All-Time Shutout Leaders

Goaltender	Team	Seasons	Games	Shutouts
Terry Sawchuk	Detroit	14	734	85
(1949-1970)	Boston	2	102	11
	Toronto	3	91	4
	Los Angeles	1	36	2
	NY Rangers	1	8	1
	Total	21	971	**103**
George Hainsworth	Montreal	7½	318	75
(1926-1937)	Toronto	3½	147	19
	Total	11	465	**94**
Glenn Hall	Detroit	4	148	17
(1952-1971)	Chicago	10	618	51
	St. Louis	4	140	16
	Total	18	906	**84**
Jacques Plante	Montreal	11	556	58
(1952-1973)	NY Rangers	2	98	5
	St. Louis	2	69	10
	Toronto	2¾	106	7
	Boston	¼	8	2
	Total	18	837	**82**
Tiny Thompson	Boston	10¼	468	74
(1928-1940)	Detroit	1¾	85	7
	Total	12	553	**81**
Alex Connell	Ottawa	8	293	64
(1924-1937)	Detroit	1	48	6
	NY Americans	1	1	0
	Mtl. Maroons	2	75	11
	Total	12	417	**81**
Tony Esposito	Montreal	1	13	2
(1968-1984)	Chicago	15	873	74
	Total	16	886	**76**
Lorne Chabot	NY Rangers	2	80	21
(1926-1937)	Toronto	5	214	33
	Montreal	1	47	8
	Chicago	1	48	8
	Mtl. Maroons	1	16	2
	NY Americans	1	6	1
	Total	11	411	**73**
Harry Lumley	Detroit	6½	324	26
(1943-1960)	NY Rangers	½	1	0
	Chicago	2	134	5
	Toronto	4	267	34
	Boston	3	78	6
	Total	16	804	**71**
Roy Worters	Pittsburgh Pirates	3	123	21
(1925-1937)	NY Americans	9	360	45
	* Montreal		1	0
	Total	12	484	**66**
Turk Broda	Toronto	14	629	**62**
(1936-1952)				
John Ross Roach	Toronto	7	222	13
(1921-1935)	NY Rangers	4	89	30
	Detroit	3	180	15
	Total	14	491	**58**
Clint Benedict	Ottawa	7	158	19
(1917-1930)	Mtl. Maroons	6	204	38
	Total	13	362	**57**
Bernie Parent	Boston	2	57	1
(1965-1979)	Philadelphia	9½	486	50
	Toronto	1½	65	3
	Total	13	608	**54**
Ed Giacomin	NY Rangers	10¼	539	49
(1965-1978)	Detroit	2¾	71	5
	Total	13	610	**54**
David Kerr	Mtl. Maroons	3	101	11
(1930-1941)	NY Americans	1	1	0
	NY Rangers	7	324	40
	Total	11	426	**51**
Rogie Vachon	Montreal	5¼	206	13
(1966-1982)	Los Angeles	6¾	389	32
	Detroit	2	109	4
	Boston	2	91	2
	Total	16	795	**51**
Ken Dryden	Montreal	8	397	**46**
(1970-1979)				
Gump Worsley	NY Rangers	10	582	24
(1952-1974)	Montreal	6½	172	16
	Minnesota	4½	107	3
	Total	21	861	**43**
Charlie Gardiner	Chicago	7	316	**42**
(1927-1934)				
Patrick Roy	Montreal	11½	551	29
(1984-1998)	Colorado	2½	166	12
	Total	14	717	**41**
Ed Belfour	Chicago	7⅔	415	30
(1988-1998)	San Jose	⅓	13	1
	Dallas	1	61	9
	Total	9	489	**40**
Frank Brimsek	Boston	9	444	35
(1938-1950)	Chicago	1	70	5
	Total	10	514	**40**
Johnny Bower	NY Rangers	3	77	5
(1953-1970)	Toronto	12	475	32
	Total	15	552	**37**
Bill Durnan	Montreal	7	383	**34**
(1943-1950)				
Dominik Hasek	Chicago	2	25	1
(1990-1998)	Buffalo	6	325	32
	Total	8	350	**33**
Martin Brodeur	New Jersey	6	305	**32**
(1991-1998)				
Eddie Johnston	Boston	11	444	27
(1962-1978)	Toronto	1	26	1
	St. Louis	3⅔	118	4
	Chicago	⅓	4	0
	Total	16	592	**32**

*Played 1 game for Canadiens in 1929-30.

Ten or More Shutouts, One Season

Number of Shutouts	Goaltender	Team	Season	Length of Schedule
22	George Hainsworth	Montreal	1928-29	44
15	Alex Connell	Ottawa	1925-26	36
	Alex Connell	Ottawa	1927-28	44
	Hal Winkler	Boston	1927-28	44
	Tony Esposito	Chicago	1969-70	76
14	George Hainsworth	Montreal	1926-27	44
13	Clint Benedict	Mtl. Maroons	1926-27	44
	Alex Connell	Ottawa	1926-27	44
	George Hainsworth	Montreal	1927-28	44
	John Roach	NY Rangers	1928-29	44
	Roy Worters	NY Americans	1928-29	44
	Harry Lumley	Toronto	1953-54	70
	Dominik Hasek	**Buffalo**	**1997-98**	**82**
12	Tiny Thompson	Boston	1928-29	44
	Lorne Chabot	Toronto	1928-29	44
	Chuck Gardiner	Chicago	1930-31	44
	Terry Sawchuk	Detroit	1951-52	70
	Terry Sawchuk	Detroit	1953-54	70
	Terry Sawchuk	Detroit	1954-55	70
	Glenn Hall	Detroit	1955-56	70
	Bernie Parent	Philadelphia	1973-74	78
	Bernie Parent	Philadelphia	1974-75	80
11	Lorne Chabot	NY Rangers	1927-28	44
	Harry Holmes	Detroit	1927-28	44
	Clint Benedict	Mtl. Maroons	1928-29	44
	Joe Miller	Pittsburgh Pirates	1928-29	44
	Tiny Thompson	Boston	1932-33	48
	Terry Sawchuk	Detroit	1950-51	70
10	Lorne Chabot	NY Rangers	1926-27	44
	Roy Worters	Pittsburgh Pirates	1927-28	44
	Clarence Dolson	Detroit	1928-29	44
	John Roach	Detroit	1932-33	48
	Chuck Gardiner	Chicago	1933-34	48
	Tiny Thompson	Boston	1935-36	48
	Frank Brimsek	Boston	1938-39	48
	Bill Durnan	Montreal	1948-49	60
	Gerry McNeil	Montreal	1952-53	70
	Harry Lumley	Toronto	1952-53	70
	Tony Esposito	Chicago	1973-74	78
	Ken Dryden	Montreal	1976-77	80
	Martin Brodeur	New Jersey	1996-97	82
	Martin Brodeur	**New Jersey**	**1997-98**	**82**

All-Time Win Leaders

(Minimum 200 Wins)

Wins	Goaltender	GP	Dec.	Losses	Ties	%
447	Terry Sawchuk	971	949	330	172	.562
434	Jacques Plante	837	827	247	146	.614
423	Tony Esposito	886	881	306	152	.566
407	Glenn Hall	906	896	326	163	.545
382	* Grant Fuhr	806	757	271	104	.573
380	* Patrick Roy	717	691	224	87	.613
372	Andy Moog	713	669	209	88	.622
355	Rogie Vachon	795	773	291	127	.541
335	Gump Worsley	861	837	352	150	.490
331	* Mike Vernon	624	605	201	73	.607
330	Harry Lumley	804	802	329	143	.501
326	* Tom Barrasso	665	634	232	76	.574
306	* John Vanbiesbrouck	717	681	285	90	.515
305	Billy Smith	680	643	233	105	.556
302	Turk Broda	629	627	224	101	.562
294	Mike Liut	663	639	271	74	.518
289	Ed Giacomin	610	594	208	97	.568
286	* Ron Hextall	585	558	207	65	.571
286	Dan Bouchard	655	631	232	113	.543
284	Tiny Thompson	553	553	194	75	.581
271	Bernie Parent	608	590	198	121	.562
271	Kelly Hrudey	677	624	265	88	.505
270	Gilles Meloche	788	752	351	131	.446
268	Don Beaupre	667	620	277	75	.493
258	Ken Dryden	397	389	57	74	.758
252	Frank Brimsek	514	514	182	80	.568
250	Johnny Bower	552	535	195	90	.551
246	George Hainsworth	465	465	145	74	.609
246	Pete Peeters	489	452	155	51	.601
241	* Ed Belfour	489	466	159	66	.588
236	Reggie Lemelin	507	461	162	63	.580
234	Eddie Johnston	592	572	257	81	.480
231	Glenn Resch	571	537	224	82	.507
230	Gerry Cheevers	418	406	102	74	.658
230	* Bill Ranford	595	554	255	69	.477
221	* Kirk McLean	537	518	234	63	.487
219	John Ross Roach	492	491	204	68	.515
215	Greg Millen	604	588	284	89	.441
213	* Curtis Joseph	457	439	172	54	.547
208	Bill Durnan	383	382	112	62	.626
208	Don Edwards	459	437	155	74	.561
206	Roger Crozier	518	473	197	70	.510
204	Rick Wamsley	407	381	131	46	.596
203	* Mike Richter	424	396	144	49	.574
203	Dave Kerr	427	426	148	75	.565
201	Lorne Chabot	411	411	148	62	.564
201	* Ken Wregget	519	474	226	47	.474

* active player

Active Shutout Leaders

(Minimum 15 Shutouts)

Goaltender	Teams	Seasons	Games	Shutouts
Patrick Roy	Montreal, Colorado	14	717	**41**
Ed Belfour	Chi., S.J., Dal.	9	489	**40**
Dominik Hasek	Chicago, Buffalo	8	350	**33**
Martin Brodeur	New Jersey	6	305	**32**
Tom Barrasso	Buffalo, Pittsburgh	15	665	**30**
John Vanbiesbrouck	NY Rangers, Florida	16	717	**29**
Ron Hextall	Phi., Que., NYI	12	585	**23**
Grant Fuhr	Edm., Tor., Buf., L.A., St.L.	17	806	**23**
Chris Osgood	Detroit	5	221	**20**
Kirk McLean	N.J., Van., Car., Fla.	13	537	**20**
Curtis Joseph	St. Louis, Edmonton	9	457	**19**
Mike Richter	NY Rangers	9	424	**18**
Mike Vernon	Cgy., Det., S.J.	15	624	**18**
Daren Puppa	Buf., Tor., T.B.	13	411	**17**
Jim Carey	Washington, Boston	4	168	**16**
Guy Hebert	St. Louis, Anaheim	7	300	**16**
Bob Essensa	Wpg., Det., Edm.	8	329	**16**
Jon Casey	Min., Bos., St.L.	12	425	**16**
Sean Burke	N.J., Hfd., Car., Van., Phi	10	470	**16**

Active Goaltending Leaders

(Ranked by winning percentage; minimum 250 games played)

Goaltender	Teams	Seasons	GP	Deci-sions	W	L	T	Winning %
Martin Brodeur	New Jersey	6	305	293	162	84	47	**.633**
Patrick Roy	Montreal, Colorado	14	717	691	380	224	87	**.613**
Mike Vernon	Cgy., Det., S.J.	15	624	605	331	201	73	**.607**
Ed Belfour	Chi., S.J., Dal.	9	489	466	241	159	66	**.588**
Mike Richter	NY Rangers	9	424	396	203	144	49	**.574**
Tom Barrasso	Buffalo, Pittsburgh	15	665	634	326	232	76	**.574**
Grant Fuhr	Edm., Tor., Buf., L.A., St.L.	17	806	757	382	271	104	**.573**
Ron Hextall	Phi., Que., NYI	12	585	558	286	207	65	**.571**
Dominik Hasek	Chicago, Buffalo	8	350	334	165	121	48	**.566**
Curtis Joseph	St. Louis, Edmonton	9	457	439	213	172	54	**.547**
Daren Puppa	Buf., Tor., T.B.	13	411	379	173	153	53	**.526**
Tim Cheveldae	Det., Wpg., Bos.	9	340	322	149	136	37	**.520**
Jon Casey	Min., Bos., St.L.	12	425	382	170	157	55	**.517**
John Vanbiesbrouck	NY Rangers, Florida	16	717	681	306	285	90	**.515**
Felix Potvin	Toronto	7	364	353	157	147	49	**.514**

Goals Against Average Leaders

(minimum 13 games played, 1994-95; minimum 27 games played, 1992-93 to 1993-94, 1995-96 to 1997-98; 25 games played, 1926-27 to 1991-92; 15 games played, 1917-18 to 1925-26.)

Season	Goaltender and Club	GP	Mins.	GA	SO	AVG.
1997-98	Ed Belfour, Dallas	61	3,581	112	9	1.88
1996-97	Martin Brodeur, New Jersey	67	3,838	120	10	1.88
1995-96	Ron Hextall, Philadelphia	53	3,102	112	4	2.17
1994-95	Dominik Hasek, Buffalo	41	2,416	85	5	2.11
1993-94	Dominik Hasek, Buffalo	58	3,358	109	7	1.95
1992-93	Felix Potvin, Toronto	48	2,781	116	2	2.50
1991-92	Patrick Roy, Montreal	67	3,935	155	5	2.36
1990-91	Ed Belfour, Chicago	74	4,127	170	4	2.47
1989-90	Mike Liut, Hartford, Washington	37	2,161	91	4	2.53
1988-89	Patrick Roy, Montreal	48	2,744	113	4	2.47
1987-88	Pete Peeters, Washington	35	1,896	88	2	2.78
1986-87	Brian Hayward, Montreal	37	2,178	102	1	2.81
1985-86	Bob Froese, Philadelphia	51	2,728	116	5	2.55
1984-85	Tom Barrasso, Buffalo	54	3,248	144	5	2.66
1983-84	Pat Riggin, Washington	41	2,299	102	4	2.66
1982-83	Pete Peeters, Boston	62	3,611	142	8	2.36
1981-82	Denis Herron, Montreal	27	1,547	68	3	2.64
1980-81	Richard Sevigny, Montreal	33	1,777	71	2	2.40
1979-80	Bob Sauve, Buffalo	32	1,880	74	4	2.36
1978-79	Ken Dryden, Montreal	47	2,814	108	5	2.30
1977-78	Ken Dryden, Montreal	52	3,071	105	5	2.05
1976-77	Michel Larocque, Montreal	26	1,525	53	4	2.09
1975-76	Ken Dryden, Montreal	62	3,580	121	8	2.03
1974-75	Bernie Parent, Philadelphia	68	4,041	137	12	2.03
1973-74	Bernie Parent, Philadelphia	73	4,314	136	12	1.89
1972-73	Ken Dryden, Montreal	54	3,165	119	6	2.26
1971-72	Tony Esposito, Chicago	48	2,780	82	9	1.77
1970-71	Jacques Plante, Toronto	40	2,329	73	4	1.88
1969-70	Ernie Wakely, St. Louis	30	1,651	58	4	2.11
1968-69	Jacques Plante, St. Louis	37	2,139	70	5	1.96
1967-68	Gump Worsley, Montreal	40	2,213	73	6	1.98
1966-67	Glenn Hall, Chicago	32	1,664	66	2	2.38
1965-66	Johnny Bower, Toronto	35	1,998	75	3	2.25
1964-65	Johnny Bower, Toronto	34	2,040	81	3	2.38
1963-64	Johnny Bower, Toronto	51	3,009	106	5	2.11
1962-63	Jacques Plante, Montreal	56	3,320	138	5	2.49
1961-62	Jacques Plante, Montreal	70	4,200	166	4	2.37
1960-61	Johnny Bower, Toronto	58	3,480	145	2	2.50
1959-60	Jacques Plante, Montreal	69	4,140	175	3	2.54
1958-59	Jacques Plante, Montreal	67	4,000	144	9	2.16
1957-58	Jacques Plante, Montreal	57	3,386	119	9	2.11
1956-57	Jacques Plante, Montreal	61	3,660	123	9	2.02
1955-56	Jacques Plante, Montreal	64	3,840	119	7	1.86
1954-55	Terry Sawchuk, Detroit	68	4,080	132	12	1.94
1953-54	Harry Lumley, Toronto	69	4,140	128	13	1.86
1952-53	Terry Sawchuk, Detroit	63	3,780	120	9	1.90
1951-52	Terry Sawchuk, Detroit	70	4,200	133	12	1.90
1950-51	Al Rollins, Toronto	40	2,367	70	5	1.77
1949-50	Bill Durnan, Montreal	64	3,840	141	8	2.20
1948-49	Bill Durnan, Montreal	60	3,600	126	10	2.10
1947-48	Turk Broda, Toronto	60	3,600	143	5	2.38
1946-47	Bill Durnan, Montreal	60	3,600	138	4	2.30
1945-46	Bill Durnan, Montreal	40	2,400	104	4	2.60
1944-45	Bill Durnan, Montreal	50	3,000	121	1	2.42
1943-44	Bill Durnan, Montreal	50	3,000	109	2	2.18
1942-43	Johnny Mowers, Detroit	50	3,010	124	6	2.47
1941-42	Frank Brimsek, Boston	47	2,930	115	3	2.35
1940-41	Turk Broda, Toronto	48	2,970	99	5	2.00
1939-40	Dave Kerr, NY Rangers	48	3,000	77	8	1.54
1938-39	Frank Brimsek, Boston	43	2,610	68	10	1.56
1937-38	Tiny Thompson, Boston	48	2,970	89	7	1.80
1936-37	Norman Smith, Detroit	48	2,980	102	6	2.05
1935-36	Tiny Thompson, Boston	48	2,930	82	10	1.68
1934-35	Lorne Chabot, Chicago	48	2,940	88	8	1.80
1933-34	Wilf Cude, Detroit, Montreal	30	1,920	47	5	1.47
1932-33	Tiny Thompson, Boston	48	3,000	88	11	1.76
1931-32	Chuck Gardiner, Chicago	48	2,989	92	4	1.85
1930-31	Roy Worters, NY Americans	44	2,760	74	8	1.61
1929-30	Tiny Thompson, Boston	44	2,680	98	3	2.19
1928-29	George Hainsworth, Montreal	44	2,800	43	22	0.92
1927-28	George Hainsworth, Montreal	44	2,730	48	13	1.05
1926-27	Clint Benedict, Mtl. Maroons	43	2,748	65	13	1.42
1925-26	Alex Connell, Ottawa	36	2,251	42	15	1.12
1924-25	Georges Vezina, Montreal	30	1,860	56	5	1.81
1923-24	Georges Vezina, Montreal	24	1,459	48	3	1.97
1922-23	Clint Benedict, Ottawa	24	1,478	54	4	2.18
1921-22	Clint Benedict, Ottawa	24	1,508	84	2	3.34
1920-21	Clint Benedict, Ottawa	24	1,457	75	2	3.09
1919-20	Clint Benedict, Ottawa	24	1,444	64	5	2.66
1918-19	Clint Benedict, Ottawa	18	1,113	53	2	2.86
1917-18	Georges Vezina, Montreal	21	1,282	84	1	3.93

All-Time Regular Season NHL Coaching Register

Regular Season, 1917-98

Coach	Team	Games Coached	Wins	Losses	Ties	%Wins	Years	Cup Wins	Career
Abel, Sid	Chicago	140	39	79	22	.357	2		
	Detroit	811	340	339	132	.501	12		
	St. Louis	10	3	6	1	.350	1		
	Kansas City	3	0	3	0	.000	1		
	Total	964	382	427	155	.477	16		1952-76
Adams, Jack	Toronto	18	10	7	1	.583	1		
	Detroit	964	413	390	161	.512	20	3	
	Total	982	423	397	162	.513	21	3	1922-47
Allen, Keith	Philadelphia	150	51	67	32	.447	2		1967-69
Allison, Dave	Ottawa	25	2	22	1	.100	1		1995-96
Anderson, Jim	Washington	54	4	45	5	.120	1		1974-75
Angotti, Lou	St. Louis	32	6	20	6	.281	2		
	Pittsburgh	80	16	58	6	.238	1		
	Total	112	22	78	12	.250	3		1973-84
Arbour, Al	St. Louis	107	42	40	25	.509	3		
	NY Islanders	1499	739	537	223	.567	19	4	
	Total	1606	781	577	248	.564	22	4	1970-94
Armstrong, George	Toronto	47	17	26	4	.404	1		1988-89
Barkley, Doug	Detroit	77	20	46	11	.331	3		1970-76
Beaulieu, Andre	Minnesota	32	6	23	3	.234	1		1977-78
Belisle, Danny	Washington	96	28	51	17	.380	2		1978-80
Berenson, Red	St. Louis	204	100	72	32	.569	3		1979-82
Bergeron, Michel	Quebec	634	265	283	86	.486	8		
	NY Rangers	158	73	67	18	.519	2		
	Total	792	338	350	104	.492	10		1980-90
Berry, Bob	Los Angeles	240	107	94	39	.527	3		
	Montreal	223	116	71	36	.601	3		
	Pittsburgh	240	88	127	25	.419	3		
	St. Louis	157	73	63	21	.532	2		
	Total	860	384	355	121	.517	11		1978-94
Beverley, Nick	Toronto	17	9	6	2	.588	1		1995-96
Blackburn, Don	Hartford	140	42	63	35	.425	2		1979-81
Blair, Wren	Minnesota	147	48	65	34	.442	3		1967-70
Blake, Toe	Montreal	914	500	255	159	.634	13	8	1955-68
Boileau, Marc	Pittsburgh	151	66	61	24	.517	3		1973-76
Boivin, Leo	St. Louis	97	28	53	16	.371	2		1975-78
Boucher, Frank	NY Rangers	527	181	263	83	.422	11	1	1939-54
Boucher, George	Mtl. Maroons	12	6	5	1	.542	1		
	Ottawa	48	13	29	6	.333	1		
	St. Louis	35	9	20	6	.343	1		
	Boston	70	22	32	16	.429	1		
	Total	165	50	86	29	.391	4		1930-50
Bowman, Scotty	St. Louis	238	110	83	45	.557	4		
	Montreal	634	419	110	105	.744	8	5	
	Buffalo	404	210	134	60	.594	7		
	Pittsburgh	164	95	53	16	.628	2	1	
	Detroit	378	223	103	52	.659	5	2	
	Total	1818	1057	483	278	.658	26	8	1967-98
Bowness, Rick	Winnipeg	28	8	17	3	.339	1		
	Boston	80	36	32	12	.525	1		
	Ottawa	235	39	178	18	.204	4		
	NY Islanders	100	38	50	12	.440	2		
	Total	443	121	277	45	.324	8		1988-98
Brooks, Herb	NY Rangers	285	131	113	41	.532	4		
	Minnesota	80	19	48	13	.319	1		
	New Jersey	84	40	37	7	.518	1		
	Total	449	190	198	61	.491	6		1981-93
Brophy, John	Toronto	193	64	111	18	.378	3		1986-89
Burnett, George	Edmonton	35	12	20	3	.386	1		1994-95
Burns, Charlie	Minnesota	86	22	50	14	.337	2		1969-75
Burns, Pat	Montreal	320	174	104	42	.609	4		
	Toronto	281	133	107	41	.546	4		
	Boston	82	39	30	13	.555	1		
	Total	683	346	241	96	.577	9		1988-98
Bush, Eddie	Kansas City	32	1	23	8	.156	1		1975-76
Campbell, Colin	NY Rangers	269	118	108	43	.519	4		1994-98
Caroll, Dick	Toronto	64	33	31	0	.516	3	1	1917-21
Carpenter, Doug	New Jersey	290	100	166	24	.386	4		
	Toronto	91	39	47	5	.456	2		
	Total	381	139	213	29	.403	6		1984-91
Cashman, Wayne	Philadelphia	61	32	20	9	.598	1		1997-98
Chambers, Dave	Quebec	98	19	64	15	.270	2		1990-92
Charron, Guy	Calgary	16	6	7	3	.469	1		1991-92
Cheevers, Gerry	Boston	376	204	126	46	.604	5		1980-85
Cherry, Don	Boston	400	231	105	64	.658	5		
	Colorado	80	19	48	13	.319	1		
	Total	480	250	153	77	.601	6		1974-80
Clancy, King	Mtl. Maroons	18	6	11	1	.361	1		
	Toronto	225	89	84	52	.511	4		
	Total	243	95	95	53	.500	5		1937-72
Clapper, Dit	Boston	230	102	88	40	.530	4		1945-49
Cleghorn, Odie	Pittsburgh	168	62	86	20	.429	4		1925-29
Cleghorn, Sprague	Mtl. Maroons	48	19	22	7	.469	1		1931-32
Colville, Neil	NY Rangers	93	26	41	26	.419	2		1950-52
Conacher, Charlie	Chicago	162	56	84	22	.414	3		1947-50
Conacher, Lionel	NY Americans	44	14	25	5	.375	1		1929-30
Constantine, Kevin	San Jose	157	55	78	24	.427	3		
	Pittsburgh	82	40	24	18	.598	1		
	Total	239	95	102	42	.485	4		1993-98
Cook, Bill	NY Rangers	117	34	59	24	.393	2		1951-53
Crawford, Marc	Quebec	48	30	13	5	.677	1		
	Colorado	246	135	75	36	.622	3	1	
	Total	294	165	88	41	.631	4	1	1994-98
Creamer, Pierre	Pittsburgh	80	36	35	9	.506	1		1987-88
Creighton, Fred	Atlanta	348	156	136	56	.529	5		
	Boston	73	40	20	13	.637	1		
	Total	421	196	156	69	.548	6		1974-80
Crisp, Terry	Calgary	240	144	63	33	.669	3	1	
	Tampa Bay	391	142	204	45	.421	6		
	Total	631	286	267	78	.515	9	1	1987-98
Crozier, Joe	Buffalo	192	77	80	35	.492	3		
	Toronto	40	13	22	5	.388	1		
	Total	232	90	102	40	.474	4		1971-81
Crozier, Roger	Washington	1	0	1	0	.000	1		1981-82
Cunniff, John	Hartford	13	3	9	1	.269	1		
	New Jersey	133	59	56	18	.511	2		
	Total	146	62	65	19	.490	3		1982-91
Dandurand, Leo	Montreal	163	78	76	9	.506	6	1	1921-35
Day, Hap	Toronto	546	259	206	81	.549	10	5	1940-50
Dea, Billy	Detroit	11	3	8	0	.273	1		1981-82
Delvecchio, Alex	Detroit	245	82	131	32	.400	4		1973-77
Demers, Jacques	Quebec	80	25	44	11	.381	1		
	St. Louis	240	106	106	28	.500	3		
	Detroit	320	137	136	47	.502	4		
	Montreal	221	107	87	27	.545	4	1	
	Tampa Bay	63	15	40	8	.302	1		
	Total	924	390	413	121	.488	13	1	1979-98
Denneny, Cy	Boston	44	26	13	5	.648	1	1	
	Ottawa	48	11	27	10	.333	1		
	Total	92	37	40	15	.484	2	1	1928-33
Dineen, Bill	Philadelphia	140	60	60	20	.500	2		1991-93
Dudley, Rick	Buffalo	188	85	72	31	.535	3		1989-92
Duff, Dick	Toronto	2	0	2	0	.000	1		1979-80
Dugal, Jules	Montreal	18	9	6	3	.583	1		1938-39
Duncan, Art	Detroit	33	10	21	2	.333	1		
	Toronto	47	21	16	10	.553	2	1	
	Total	80	31	37	12	.463	3	1	1926-32
Dutton, Red	NY Americans	288	90	151	47	.394	6		
	Brooklyn	48	16	29	3	.365	1		
	Total	336	106	180	50	.390	7		1935-42
Eddolls, Frank	Chicago	70	13	40	17	.307	1		1954-55
Esposito, Phil	NY Rangers	45	24	21	0	.533	2		1986-89
Evans, Jack	California	80	27	42	11	.406	1		
	Cleveland	160	47	87	26	.375	2		
	Hartford	374	163	174	37	.485	5		
	Total	614	237	303	74	.446	8		1975-88
Fashoway, Gordie	Oakland	10	4	5	1	.450	1		1967-68
Ferguson, John	NY Rangers	121	43	59	19	.434	2		
	Winnipeg	14	7	6	1	.536	1		
	Total	135	50	65	20	.444	3		1975-86
Filion, Maurice	Quebec	6	1	3	2	.333	1		1980-81
Francis, Emile	NY Rangers	654	342	209	103	.602	10		
	St. Louis	124	46	64	14	.427	3		
	Total	778	388	273	117	.574	13		1965-83

As Woody Dumart, left, and Milt Schmidt, right, watch the "on-ice" action in what is probably a posed publicity still, coach Lynn Patrick offers some strategic advice. Patrick, like his father Lester, son Craig and brother Muzz, began his NHL coaching career with the New York Rangers. He was also the first coach of the St. Louis Blues, eventually doing three tours of duty behind the Blues bench.

Coach	Team	Games Coached	Wins	Losses	Ties	%Wins	Years	Cup Wins	Career
Fredrickson, Frank	Pittsburgh	44	5	36	3	.148	1		1929-30
Ftorek, Robbie	Los Angeles	132	65	56	11	.534	2		1987-89
Gadsby, Bill	Detroit	78	35	31	12	.526	2		1968-70
Gainey, Bob	Minnesota	244	95	119	30	.451	3		
	Dallas	171	70	71	30	.497	3		
	Total	415	165	190	60	.470	6		1990-96
Gardiner, Herb	Chicago	44	7	29	8	.250	1		1928-29
Gardner, Jimmy	Hamilton	30	19	10	1	.650	1		1924-25
Garvin, Ted	Detroit	11	2	8	1	.227	1		1973-74
Geoffrion, Bernie	NY Rangers	43	22	18	3	.547	1		
	Atlanta	208	77	92	39	.464	3		
	Montreal	30	15	9	6	.600	1		
	Total	281	114	119	48	.491	5		1968-80
Gerard, Eddie	Ottawa	22	9	13	0	.409	1		
	Mtl. Maroons	294	129	122	43	.512	7	1	
	NY Americans	92	34	40	18	.467	2		
	St. Louis	13	2	11	0	.154	1		
	Total	421	174	186	61	.486	11	1	1917-35
Gill, David	Ottawa	132	64	41	27	.587	3	1	1926-29
Glover, Fred	Oakland	152	51	76	25	.418	2		
	California	204	45	131	28	.289	4		
	Los Angeles	68	18	42	8	.324	1		
	Total	424	114	249	61	.341	7		1968-74
Goodfellow, Ebbie	Chicago	140	30	91	19	.282	2		1950-52
Gordon, Jackie	Minnesota	289	116	123	50	.488	5		1970-75
Goring, Butch	Boston	93	44	36	13	.543	2		1985-87
Gorman, Tommy	NY Americans	80	31	33	16	.488	2		
	Chicago	73	28	28	17	.500	2	1	
	Mtl. Maroons	174	74	71	29	.509	4	1	
	Total	327	133	132	62	.502	8	2	1925-38
Gottselig, Johnny	Chicago	187	62	105	20	.385	4		1944-48
Goyette, Phil	NY Islanders	48	6	38	4	.167	1		1972-73
Green, Gary	Washington	157	50	78	29	.411	3		1979-82
Green, Pete	Ottawa	186	118	60	8	.656	7	3	1919-26
Green, Shorty	NY Americans	44	11	27	6	.318	1		1927-28
Green, Ted	Edmonton	188	65	102	21	.402	3		1991-94
Guidolin, Aldo	Colorado	59	12	39	8	.271	1		1978-79
Guidolin, Bep	Boston	104	72	23	9	.736	2		
	Kansas City	125	26	84	15	.268	2		
	Total	229	98	107	24	.480	4		1972-76
Harkness, Ned	Detroit	38	12	22	4	.368	1		1970-71
Harris, Ted	Minnesota	179	48	104	27	.344	3		1975-78
Hart, Cecil	Montreal	394	196	125	73	.590	9	2	1926-39
Hartsburg, Craig	Chicago	246	104	102	40	.504	3		1995-98
Harvey, Doug	NY Rangers	70	26	32	12	.457	1		1961-62
Hay, Don	Phoenix	82	38	37	7	.506	1		1996-97
Heffernan, Frank	Toronto	12	5	7	0	.417	1		1919-20
Henning, Lorne	Minnesota	158	68	72	18	.487	2		
	NY Islanders	48	15	28	5	.365	1		
	Total	206	83	100	23	.459	3		1985-95
Hitchcock, Ken	Dallas	207	112	71	24	.599	3		1995-98
Holmgren, Paul	Philadelphia	264	107	126	31	.464	4		
	Hartford	161	54	93	14	.379	4		
	Total	425	161	219	45	.432	8		1988-96
Howell, Harry	Minnesota	11	3	6	2	.364	1		1978-79
Imlach, Punch	Toronto	770	370	275	125	.562	12	4	
	Buffalo	119	32	62	25	.374	2		
	Total	889	402	337	150	.537	14	4	1958-80
Ingarfield, Earl	NY Islanders	30	6	22	2	.233	1		1972-73
Inglis, Bill	Buffalo	56	28	18	10	.589	1		1978-79
Irvin, Dick	Chicago	119	46	57	16	.454	3		
	Toronto	427	216	152	59	.575	9	1	
	Montreal	896	431	313	152	.566	15	3	
	Total	1442	693	522	227	.559	27	4	1930-56
Ivan, Tommy	Detroit	470	262	118	90	.653	7	3	
	Chicago	103	26	56	21	.354	2		
	Total	573	288	174	111	.599	9	3	1947-58
Iverson, Emil	Chicago	21	8	7	6	.524	1		1932-33
Johnson, Bob	Calgary	400	193	155	52	.548	5		
	Pittsburgh	80	41	33	6	.550	1	1	
	Total	480	234	188	58	.548	6	1	1982-91
Johnson, Marshall	Colorado	56	15	32	9	.348	1		1981-82
Johnson, Tom	Boston	208	142	43	23	.738	3	1	1970-73
Johnston, Eddie	Chicago	80	34	27	19	.544	1		
	Pittsburgh	516	232	224	60	.508	7		
	Total	596	266	251	79	.513	8		1979-97
Johnston, Marshall	California	69	13	45	11	.268	2		1973-75
Kasper, Steve	Boston	164	66	78	20	.463	2		1995-97
Keats, Duke	Detroit	11	2	7	2	.273	1		1926-27
Keenan, Mike	Philadelphia	320	190	102	28	.638	4		
	Chicago	320	153	126	41	.542	4		
	NY Rangers	84	52	24	8	.667	1	1	
	St. Louis	163	75	66	22	.528	3		
	Vancouver	63	21	30	12	.429	1		
	Total	950	491	348	111	.575	13	1	1984-98
Kelly, Pat	Colorado	101	22	54	25	.342	2		1977-79
Kelly, Red	Los Angeles	150	55	75	20	.433	2		
	Pittsburgh	274	90	132	52	.423	4		
	Toronto	318	133	123	62	.516	4		
	Total	742	278	330	134	.465	10		1967-77
King, Dave	Calgary	216	109	76	31	.576	3		1992-95
Kingston, George	San Jose	164	28	129	7	.192	2		1991-93
Kish, Larry	Hartford	49	12	32	5	.296	1		1982-83
Kromm, Bobby	Detroit	231	79	111	41	.431	3		1977-80
Kurtenbach, Orland	Vancouver	125	36	62	27	.396	2		1976-78
LaForge, Bill	Vancouver	20	4	14	2	.250	1		1984-85
Lalonde, Newsy	Montreal	207	96	97	14	.498	8		
	NY Americans	44	17	25	2	.409	1		
	Ottawa	88	31	45	12	.420	2		
	Total	339	144	167	28	.466	11		1917-35
Lapointe, Ron	Quebec	89	33	50	6	.404	2		1987-89
Laycoe, Hal	Los Angeles	24	5	18	1	.229	1		
	Vancouver	156	44	96	16	.333	2		
	Total	180	49	114	17	.319	3		1969-72
Lehman, Hugh	Chicago	21	3	17	1	.167	1		1927-28
Lemaire, Jacques	Montreal	97	48	37	12	.557	2		
	New Jersey	378	199	122	57	.602	5	1	
	Total	475	247	159	69	.593	7	1	1983-98
Lepine, Pit	Montreal	48	10	33	5	.260	1		1939-40
LeSueur, Percy	Hamilton	10	3	7	0	.300	1		1923-24
Ley, Rick	Hartford	160	69	71	20	.494	2		
	Vancouver	124	47	50	27	.488	2		
	Total	284	116	121	47	.491	4		1989-96
Lindsay, Ted	Detroit	29	5	21	3	.224	2		1979-81
Long, Barry	Winnipeg	205	87	93	25	.485	3		1983-86
Loughlin, Clem	Chicago	144	61	63	20	.493	3		1934-37
Low, Ron	Edmonton	259	106	125	28	.463	4		1994-98
MacDonald, Parker	Minnesota	61	20	30	11	.418	1		
	Los Angeles	42	13	24	5	.369	1		
	Total	103	33	54	16	.398	2		1973-82
MacLean, Doug	Florida	187	83	71	33	.532	3		1995-98
MacMillan, Bill	Colorado	80	22	45	13	.356	1		
	New Jersey	100	19	67	14	.260	2		
	Total	180	41	112	27	.303	3		1980-84
MacNeil, Al	Montreal	55	31	15	9	.645	1	1	
	Atlanta	80	35	32	13	.519	1		
	Calgary	160	68	61	31	.522	2		
	Total	295	134	108	53	.544	4	1	1970-82
Magnuson, Keith	Chicago	132	49	57	26	.470	2		1980-82
Maguire, Pierre	Hartford	67	23	37	7	.396	1		1993-94
Mahoney, Bill	Minnesota	93	42	39	12	.516	2		1983-85
Maloney, Dan	Toronto	160	45	100	15	.328	2		
	Winnipeg	212	91	93	28	.495	3		
	Total	372	136	193	43	.423	5		1984-89
Maloney, Phil	Vancouver	232	95	105	32	.478	4		1973-77
Mantha, Sylvio	Montreal	48	11	26	11	.344	1		1935-36
Marshall, Bert	Colorado	24	3	17	4	.208	1		1981-82
Martin, Jacques	St. Louis	160	66	71	23	.484	2		
	Ottawa	202	75	93	34	.455	3		
	Total	362	141	164	57	.468	5		1986-98
Matheson, Godfrey	Chicago	2	0	2	0	.000	1		1932-33
Maurice, Paul	Hartford	152	61	72	19	.464	2		
	Carolina	82	33	41	8	.451	1		
	Total	234	94	113	27	.459	3		1995-98
Maxner, Wayne	Detroit	129	34	68	27	.368	2		1980-82
McCammon, Bob	Philadelphia	218	119	68	31	.617	4		
	Vancouver	294	102	156	36	.408	4		
	Total	512	221	224	67	.497	8		1978-91
McCreary, Bill	St. Louis	24	6	14	4	.333	1		
	Vancouver	41	9	25	7	.305	1		
	California	32	8	20	4	.313	1		
	Total	97	23	59	15	.314	3		1971-75
McLellan, John	Toronto	295	117	136	42	.468	4		1969-73
McVie, Tom	Washington	204	49	122	33	.321	3		
	Winnipeg	105	20	67	18	.276	2		
	New Jersey	153	57	74	22	.444	3		
	Total	462	126	263	73	.352	8		1975-92
Meeker, Howie	Toronto	70	21	34	15	.407	1		1956-57
Melrose, Barry	Los Angeles	209	79	101	29	.447	3		1992-95
Milbury, Mike	Boston	160	90	49	21	.628	2		
	NY Islanders	146	43	82	21	.366	3		
	Total	306	133	131	42	.503	5		1989-98
Muckler, John	Minnesota	35	6	23	6	.257	1		
	Edmonton	160	75	65	20	.531	2	1	
	Buffalo	268	125	109	34	.530	4		
	NY Rangers	25	8	15	2	.360	1		
	Total	488	214	212	62	.502	8	1	1968-98
Muldoon, Pete	Chicago	44	19	22	3	.466	1		1926-27
Munro, Dunc	Mtl. Maroons	76	37	29	10	.553	2		1929-31
Murdoch, Bob	Winnipeg	160	63	75	22	.463	2		1989-91
Murphy, Mike	Los Angeles	65	20	37	8	.369	2		
	Toronto	164	60	87	17	.418	2		
	Total	229	80	124	25	.404	4		1986-98
Murray, Bryan	Washington	672	343	246	83	.572	9		
	Detroit	244	124	91	29	.568	3		
	Florida	59	17	31	11	.381	1		
	Total	975	484	368	123	.559	13		1981-98
Murray, Terry	Washington	325	163	134	28	.545	5		
	Philadelphia	212	118	64	30	.627	3		
	Total	537	281	198	58	.577	8		1989-97
Nanne, Lou	Minnesota	29	7	18	4	.310	1		1977-78
Neale, Harry	Vancouver	407	142	189	76	.442	6		
	Detroit	35	8	23	4	.286	1		
	Total	442	150	212	80	.430	7		1978-86
Neilson, Roger	Toronto	160	75	62	23	.541	2		
	Buffalo	80	39	20	21	.619	1		
	Vancouver	133	51	61	21	.462	3		
	Los Angeles	28	8	17	3	.339	1		
	NY Rangers	280	141	104	35	.566	4		
	Florida	132	53	56	23	.489	2		
	Philadelphia	21	10	9	2	.524	1		
	Total	834	377	329	128	.529	14		1977-98
Nolan, Ted	Buffalo	164	73	72	19	.503	2		1995-97
Nykoluk, Mike	Toronto	280	89	144	47	.402	4		1980-84
O'Reilly, Terry	Boston	227	113	88	26	.555	3		1986-89

Coach	Team	Games Coached	Wins	Losses	Ties	%Wins	Years	Cup Wins	Career
Oliver, Murray	Minnesota	41	21	12	8	.610	2		1981-83
Olmstead, Bert	Oakland	64	11	37	16	.297	1		1967-68
Paddock, John	Winnipeg	281	106	138	37	.443	4		1991-95
Page, Pierre	Minnesota	160	63	77	20	.456	2		
	Quebec	230	98	103	29	.489	3		
	Calgary	164	66	78	20	.463	2		
	Anaheim	82	26	43	13	.396	1		
	Total	636	253	301	82	.462	8		1988-98
Park, Brad	Detroit	45	9	34	2	.222	1		1985-86
Paterson, Rick	Tampa Bay	8	0	8	0	.000	1		1997-98
Patrick, Craig	NY Rangers	95	37	45	13	.458	2		
	Pittsburgh	74	29	36	9	.453	2		
	Total	169	66	81	22	.456	4		1980-97
Patrick, Frank	Boston	96	48	36	12	.563	2		1934-36
Patrick, Lester	NY Rangers	604	281	216	107	.554	13	2	1926-39
Patrick, Lynn	NY Rangers	107	40	51	16	.449	2		
	Boston	310	117	130	63	.479	5		
	St. Louis	26	8	15	3	.365	3		
	Total	443	165	196	82	.465	10		1948-76
Patrick, Muzz	NY Rangers	136	43	66	27	.415	4		1953-63
Perron, Jean	Montreal	240	126	84	30	.588	3	1	
	Quebec	47	16	26	5	.394	1		
	Total	287	142	110	35	.556	4	1	1985-89
Perry, Don	Los Angeles	168	52	85	31	.402	3		1981-84
Pike, Alf	NY Rangers	123	36	66	21	.378	2		1959-61
Pilous, Rudy	Chicago	387	162	151	74	.514	6	1	1957-63
Plager, Barclay	St. Louis	178	49	96	33	.368	4		1977-83
Plager, Bob	St. Louis	11	4	6	1	.409	1		1992-93
Pleau, Larry	Hartford	224	81	117	26	.420	5		1980-89
Polano, Nick	Detroit	240	79	127	34	.400	3		1982-85
Popein, Larry	NY Rangers	41	18	14	9	.549	1		1973-74
Powers, Eddie	Toronto	114	54	56	4	.491	4	1	1921-26
Primeau, Joe	Toronto	210	97	71	42	.562	3	1	1950-53
Pronovost, Marcel	Buffalo	104	52	29	23	.611	2		1977-79
Pulford, Bob	Los Angeles	396	178	150	68	.535	5		
	Chicago	455	187	197	71	.489	7		
	Total	851	365	347	139	.511	12		1972-88
Quenneville, Joel	St. Louis	122	63	44	15	.578	2		1996-98
Querrie, Charles	Toronto	6	3	3	0	.500	1		1922-23
Quinn, Mike	Quebec	24	4	20	0	.167	1		1919-20
Quinn, Pat	Philadelphia	262	141	73	48	.630	4		
	Los Angeles	202	75	101	26	.436	3		
	Vancouver	280	141	111	28	.554	5		
	Total	744	357	285	102	.548	12		1978-96
Ramsay, Craig	Buffalo	21	4	15	2	.238	1		1986-87
Randall, Ken	Hamilton	14	6	8	0	.429	1		1923-24
Reay, Billy	Toronto	90	26	50	14	.367	2		
	Chicago	1012	516	335	161	.589	14		
	Total	1102	542	385	175	.571	16		1957-77
Regan, Larry	Los Angeles	88	27	47	14	.386	2		1970-72
Renney, Tom	Vancouver	101	39	53	9	.431	2		1996-98
Risebrough, Doug	Calgary	144	71	56	17	.552	2		1990-92
Roberts, Jim	Buffalo	45	21	16	8	.556	1		
	Hartford	80	26	41	13	.406	1		
	St. Louis	9	3	3	3	.500	1		
	Total	134	50	60	24	.463	3		1981-97
Robinson, Larry	Los Angeles	246	90	116	40	.447	3		1995-98
Rodden, Mike	Toronto	30	8	18	4	.333	1		1926-27
Romeril, Alex	Toronto	14	7	6	1	.536	1		1926-27
Ross, Art	Mtl. Wanderers	6	1	5	0	.167	1		
	Hamilton	24	6	18	0	.250	1		
	Boston	728	361	277	90	.558	16	1	
	Total	758	368	300	90	.545	18	1	1917-45
Ruel, Claude	Montreal	305	172	82	51	.648	5	2	1968-81
Ruff, Lindy	Buffalo	82	36	29	17	.543	1		1997-98
Sather, Glen	Edmonton	842	464	268	110	.616	11	4	1979-94
Sator, Ted	NY Rangers	99	41	48	10	.465	2		
	Buffalo	207	96	89	22	.517	3		
	Total	306	137	137	32	.500	5		1985-89
Savard, Andre	Quebec	24	10	13	1	.438	1		1987-88
Schinkel, Ken	Pittsburgh	203	83	92	28	.478	4		1972-77
Schmidt, Milt	Boston	726	245	360	121	.421	11		
	Washington	44	5	34	5	.170	2		
	Total	770	250	394	126	.406	13		1954-76
Schoenfeld, Jim	Buffalo	43	19	19	5	.500	1		
	New Jersey	124	50	59	15	.464	3		
	Washington	249	113	102	34	.522	4		
	Phoenix	82	35	35	12	.500	1		
	Total	498	217	215	66	.502	9		1985-98
Shaughnessy, Tom	Chicago	21	10	8	3	.548	1		1929-30
Shero, Fred	Philadelphia	554	308	151	95	.642	7	2	
	NY Rangers	180	82	74	24	.522	3		
	Total	734	390	225	119	.612	10	2	1971-81
Simpson, Joe	NY Americans	144	42	72	30	.396	3		1932-35
Simpson, Terry	NY Islanders	187	81	82	24	.497	3		
	Philadelphia	84	35	39	10	.476	1		
	Winnipeg	97	43	47	7	.479	2		
	Total	368	159	168	41	.488	6		1986-96
Sims, Al	San Jose	82	27	47	8	.378	1		1996-97
Sinden, Harry	Boston	327	153	116	58	.557	6	1	1966-85
Skinner, Jimmy	Detroit	247	123	78	46	.591	4	1	1954-58
Smeaton, Cooper	Philadelphia	44	4	36	4	.136	1		1930-31
Smith, Alf	Ottawa	18	12	6	0	.667	1		1918-19
Smith, Floyd	Buffalo	241	143	62	36	.668	4		
	Toronto	68	30	33	5	.478	1		
	Total	309	173	95	41	.626	5		1971-80
Smith, Mike	Winnipeg	23	2	17	4	.174	1		1980-81
Smith, Ron	NY Rangers	44	15	22	7	.420	1		1992-93
Smythe, Conn	Toronto	134	57	57	20	.500	4		1927-31

Coach	Team	Games Coached	Wins	Losses	Ties	%Wins	Years	Cup Wins	Career
Sonmor, Glen	Minnesota	417	174	161	82	.516	7		1978-87
Sproule, Harry	Toronto	12	7	5	0	.583	1		1919-20
Stanley, Barney	Chicago	23	4	17	2	.217	1		1927-28
Stasiuk, Vic	Philadelphia	154	45	68	41	.425	2		
	California	75	21	38	16	.387	1		
	Vancouver	78	22	47	9	.340	1		
	Total	307	88	153	66	.394	4		1969-73
Stewart, Bill	Chicago	69	22	35	12	.406	2	1	1937-39
Stewart, Ron	NY Rangers	39	15	20	4	.436	1		
	Los Angeles	80	31	34	15	.481	1		
	Total	119	46	54	19	.466	2		1975-78
Sullivan, Red	NY Rangers	196	58	103	35	.385	4		
	Pittsburgh	150	47	79	24	.393	2		
	Washington	18	2	16	0	.111	1		
	Total	364	107	198	59	.375	7		1962-75
Sutherland, Bill	Winnipeg	32	7	22	3	.266	2		1979-81
Sutter, Brian	St. Louis	320	153	124	43	.545	4		
	Boston	216	120	73	23	.609	3		
	Calgary	82	26	41	15	.409	1		
	Total	618	299	238	81	.549	8		1988-98
Sutter, Darryl	Chicago	216	110	80	26	.569	3		
	San Jose	82	34	38	10	.476	1		
	Total	298	144	118	36	.544	4		1992-98
Talbot, Jean-Guy	St. Louis	120	52	53	15	.496	2		
	NY Rangers	80	30	37	13	.456	1		
	Total	200	82	90	28	.480	3		1972-78
Tessier, Orval	Chicago	213	99	93	21	.514	3		1982-85
Thompson, Paul	Chicago	272	104	127	41	.458	7		1938-45
Thompson, Percy	Hamilton	48	13	35	0	.271	2		1920-22
Tobin, Bill	Chicago	66	26	28	12	.485	2		1929-32
Tremblay, Mario	Montreal	159	71	63	25	.525	2		1995-97
Ubriaco, Gene	Pittsburgh	106	50	47	9	.514	2		1988-90
Vachon, Rogie	Los Angeles	10	4	3	3	.550	3		1983-95
Vigneault, Alain	Montreal	82	37	32	13	.530	1		1997-98
Watson, Bryan	Edmonton	18	4	9	5	.361	1		1980-81
Watson, Phil	NY Rangers	295	119	124	52	.492	5		
	Boston	84	16	55	13	.268	2		
	Total	379	135	179	65	.442	7		1955-63
Watt, Tom	Winnipeg	181	72	85	24	.464	3		
	Vancouver	160	52	87	21	.391	2		
	Toronto	149	52	80	17	.406	2		
	Total	490	176	252	62	.422	7		1981-92
Webster, Tom	NY Rangers	18	5	9	4	.389	1		
	Los Angeles	240	115	94	31	.544	3		
	Total	258	120	103	35	.533	4		1986-92
Weiland, Cooney	Boston	96	58	20	18	.698	2	1	1939-41
White, Bill	Chicago	46	16	24	6	.413	1		1976-77
Wiley, Jim	San Jose	57	17	37	3	.325	1		1995-96
Wilson, Johnny	Los Angeles	52	9	34	9	.260	1		
	Detroit	145	67	56	22	.538	2		
	Colorado	80	20	46	14	.338	1		
	Pittsburgh	240	91	105	44	.471	3		
	Total	517	187	241	89	.448	7		1969-80
Wilson, Larry	Detroit	36	3	29	4	.139	1		1976-77
Wilson, Ron	Anaheim	296	120	145	31	.458	4		
	Washington	82	40	30	12	.561	1		
	Total	378	160	175	43	.480	5		1993-98
Young, Garry	California	12	2	7	3	.292	1		
	St. Louis	98	41	41	16	.500	2		
	Total	110	43	48	19	.477	3		1972-76

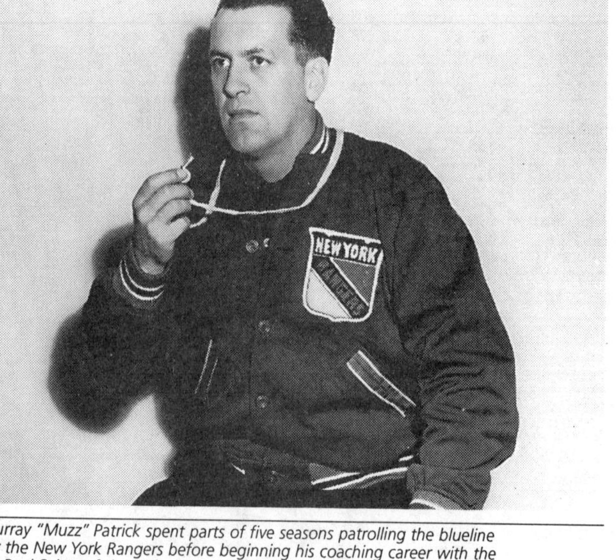

Murray "Muzz" Patrick spent parts of five seasons patrolling the blueline for the New York Rangers before beginning his coaching career with the St. Paul Saints of the United States Hockey League in 1946. He coached the Rangers for the first time midway through the 1953-54 season, resigning in 1955 to become the club's general manager.

All-Time Penalty-Minute Leaders

* active player

(Regular season. Minimum 1,500 minutes)

	Player	Teams	Seasons	Games	Penalty Minutes	Mins. per game
1.	**Dave Williams**	Tor., Van., Det., L.A., Hfd.	14	962	**3966**	4.12
* 2.	**Dale Hunter**	Que., Wsh.	18	1345	**3446**	2.56
* 3.	**Marty McSorley**	Pit., Edm., L.A., NYR, S.J.	15	888	**3218**	3.62
4.	**Tim Hunter**	Cgy., Que., Van., S.J.	16	815	**3146**	3.86
5.	**Chris Nilan**	Mtl., NYR, Bos.	13	688	**3043**	4.42
* 6.	**Bob Probert**	Det., Chi.	12	648	**2701**	4.17
* 7.	**Rick Tocchet**	Phi., Pit., L.A., Bos., Wsh., Phx.	14	909	**2626**	2.89
8.	**Willi Plett**	Atl., Cgy., Min., Bos.	13	834	**2572**	3.08
* 9.	**Pat Verbeek**	N.J., Hfd., NYR, Dal.	16	1147	**2532**	2.21
* 10.	**Craig Berube**	Phi., Tor., Cgy., Wsh.	12	719	**2457**	3.42
11.	**Basil McRae**	Que., Tor., Det., Min., T.B., St.L., Chi.	16	576	**2457**	4.27
* 12.	**Dave Manson**	Chi., Edm., Wpg., Phx., Mtl.	12	844	**2449**	2.90
* 13.	**Scott Stevens**	Wsh., St.L., N.J.	16	1200	**2440**	2.03
* 14.	**Joe Kocur**	Det., NYR, Van.	14	781	**2432**	3.11
15.	**Jay Wells**	L.A., Phi., Buf., NYR, St.L., T.B.	18	1098	**2359**	2.15
16.	**Garth Butcher**	Van., St.L., Que., Tor.	14	897	**2302**	2.57
* 17.	**Shane Churla**	Hfd., Cgy., Min., Dal., L.A., NYR	11	488	**2301**	4.72
* 18.	**Ulf Samuelsson**	Hfd., Pit., NYR.	14	960	**2296**	2.39
19.	**Dave Schultz**	Phi., L.A., Pit., Buf.	9	535	**2294**	4.29
* 20.	**Rob Ray**	Buf.	9	569	**2268**	3.99
21.	**Laurie Boschman**	Tor., Edm., Wpg., N.J., Ott.	14	1009	**2265**	2.25
* 22.	**Tie Domi**	Tor., NYR, Wpg.	9	486	**2260**	4.65
23.	**Rob Ramage**	Col., St.L., Cgy., Tor., Min., T.B., Mtl., Phi.	15	1044	**2226**	2.13
24.	**Bryan Watson**	Mtl., Oak., Pit., Det., St.L., Wsh.	16	878	**2212**	2.52
* 25.	**Chris Chelios**	Mtl., Chi.	15	1001	**2189**	2.19
* 26.	**Ken Daneyko**	N.J.	15	910	**2178**	2.39
* 27.	**Gino Odjick**	Van., NYI	8	457	**2158**	4.72
* 28.	**Ken Baumgartner**	L.A., NYI, Tor., Ana., Bos.	11	627	**2125**	3.39
29.	**Terry O'Reilly**	Bos.	14	891	**2095**	2.35
30.	**Al Secord**	Bos., Chi., Tor, Phi.	12	766	**2093**	2.73
* 31.	**Mick Vukota**	NYI, T.B., Mtl.	11	574	**2071**	3.61
32.	**Gord Donnelly**	Que., Wpg., Buf., Dal.	12	554	**2069**	3.74
33.	**Mike Foligno**	Det., Buf., Tor., Fla.	15	1018	**2049**	2.01
34.	**Phil Russell**	Chi., Atl., Cgy., N.J., Buf.	15	1016	**2038**	2.01
35.	**Harold Snepsts**	Van., Min., Det., St.L.	17	1033	**2009**	1.95
* 36.	**Steve Smith**	Edm., Chi.	13	702	**2000**	2.85
37.	**Andre Dupont**	NYR, St.L., Phi., Que.	13	800	**1986**	2.48
38.	**Mike Peluso**	Chi., Ott., N.J., St.L., Cgy.	9	458	**1951**	4.26
* 39.	**Joel Otto**	Cgy., Phi.	14	943	**1934**	2.05
* 40.	**Todd Ewen**	St.L., Mtl., Ana., S.J.	11	518	**1911**	3.69
* 41.	**Kevin Dineen**	Hfd., Phi., Car.	14	925	**1875**	2.03
* 41.	**Kris King**	Det., NYR, Wpg., Phx., Tor.	11	730	**1862**	2.55
* 42.	**Michel Petit**	Van., NYR, Que., Tor., Cgy., L.A., T.B., Edm., Phi., Phx.	16	827	**1839**	2.22
* 43.	**Gary Roberts**	Cgy., Car.	11	646	**1839**	2.85
44.	**Garry Howatt**	NYI, Hfd., N.J.	12	720	**1836**	2.55
* 45.	**Jeff Beukeboom**	Edm., NYR	13	759	**1830**	2.41
46.	**Carol Vadnais**	Mtl., Oak., Cal., Bos., NYR, N.J.	17	1087	**1813**	1.67
47.	**Larry Playfair**	Buf., L.A.	12	688	**1812**	2.63
48.	**Ted Lindsay**	Det., Chi.	17	1068	**1808**	1.69
49.	**Jim Korn**	Det., Tor., Buf., N.J., Cgy.	10	597	**1801**	3.02
50.	**David Brown**	Phi., Edm., S.J.	14	729	**1789**	2.45
51.	**Brian Sutter**	St.L.	12	779	**1786**	2.29
* 52.	**Ron Stern**	Van., Cgy.	10	493	**1768**	3.59
53.	**Bob McGill**	Tor., Chi., S.J., Det., NYI, Hfd.	13	705	**1766**	2.51
54.	**Wilf Paiement**	K.C. Col., Tor., Que., NYR, Buf., Pit.	14	946	**1757**	1.86
* 55.	**Kelly Chase**	St.L., Hfd., Tor.	9	388	**1756**	4.53
56.	**Torrie Robertson**	Wsh., Hfd., Det.	10	442	**1751**	3.96
57.	**Mario Marois**	NYR, Van., Que., Wpg., St.L.	15	955	**1746**	1.83
* 58.	**Scott Mellanby**	Phi., Edm., Fla.	13	872	**1734**	1.99
59.	**Ken Linseman**	Phi., Edm., Bos., Tor.	14	860	**1727**	2.01
* 60.	**Steven Finn**	Que., T.B., L.A.	12	725	**1724**	2.38
61.	**Jay Miller**	Bos., L.A.	7	446	**1723**	3.86
* 62.	**Shayne Corson**	Mtl., Edm., St.L.	13	809	**1708**	2.11
* 63.	**Paul Coffey**	Edm., Pit., L.A., Det., Hfd., Phi.	18	1268	**1704**	1.34
64.	**Randy Moller**	Que., NYR, Buf., Fla.	14	815	**1692**	2.08
65.	**Gordie Howe**	Det., Hfd.	26	1767	**1685**	.954
66.	**Paul Holmgren**	Phi., Min.	10	527	**1684**	3.20
* 67.	**Kelly Buchberger**	Edm.	12	743	**1679**	2.26
68.	**Gerard Gallant**	Det., T.B.	11	615	**1674**	2.72
69.	**Kevin McClelland**	Pit., Edm., Det., Tor., Wpg.	12	588	**1672**	2.84
* 70.	**Mark Messier**	Edm., NYR, Van.	19	1354	**1654**	1.22
* 71.	**Lyle Odelein**	Mtl., N.J.	9	578	**1648**	2.85
72.	**Jerry Korab**	Chi., Van., Buf., L.A.	15	975	**1629**	1.67
* 73.	**Brendan Shanahan**	N.J., St.L., Hfd., Det.	11	788	**1626**	2.06
74.	**Mel Bridgman**	Phi., Cgy., N.J., Det., Van.	14	977	**1625**	1.66
* 75.	**Wendel Clark**	Tor., Que., NYI	13	683	**1619**	2.37
76.	**Tim Horton**	Tor., NYR, Buf., Pit.	24	1446	**1611**	1.11
77.	**Dave Taylor**	L.A.	17	1111	**1589**	1.43
78.	**Gordie Roberts**	Hfd., Min., Phi., St.L., Pit., Bos.	15	1097	**1582**	1.44
79.	**Paul Baxter**	Que., Pit., Cgy.	8	472	**1564**	3.31
* 80.	**Sergio Momesso**	Mtl., St.L., Van., Tor., NYR	13	710	**1557**	2.19
81.	**Glen Cochrane**	Phi., Van., Chi., Edm.	10	411	**1556**	3.79
82.	**Stan Smyl**	Van.	13	896	**1556**	1.74
83.	**Mike Milbury**	Bos.	12	754	**1552**	2.06
* 84.	**Dana Murzyn**	Hfd., Cgy., Van.	13	826	**1550**	1.88
85.	**Dave Hutchison**	L.A., Tor., Chi., N.J.	10	584	**1550**	2.65
86.	**Doug Risebrough**	Mtl., Cgy.	13	740	**1542**	2.08
87.	**Bill Gadsby**	Chi., NYR, Det.	20	1248	**1539**	1.23
* 88.	**Terry Carkner**	NYR, Que., Phi., Det., Fla.	12	796	**1534**	1.93
* 89.	**Stu Grimson**	Cgy., Chi., Ana., Det., Hfd., Car.	10	504	**1528**	3.03

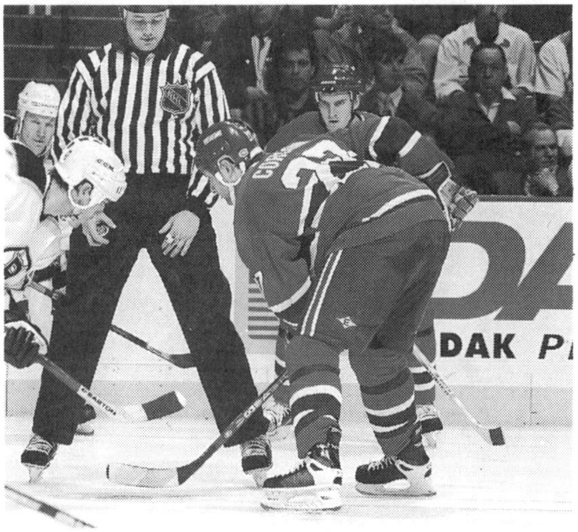

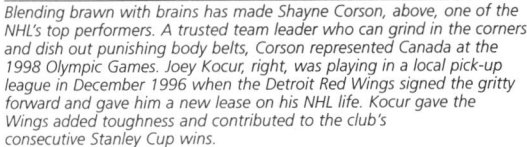

Blending brawn with brains has made Shayne Corson, above, one of the NHL's top performers. A trusted team leader who can grind in the corners and dish out punishing body belts, Corson represented Canada at the 1998 Olympic Games. Joey Kocur, right, was playing in a local pick-up league in December 1996 when the Detroit Red Wings signed the gritty forward and gave him a new lease on his NHL life. Kocur gave the Wings added toughness and contributed to the club's consecutive Stanley Cup wins.

Year-by-Year Individual Regular-Season Leaders

Season	Goals	G	Assists	A	Points	Pts.	Penalty Minutes	PIM
1917-18	Joe Malone	44	Cy Denneny	10	Joe Malone	48	Joe Hall	100
			Reg Noble	10				
			Harry Cameron	10				
1918-19	Newsy Lalonde	23	Newsy Lalonde	10	Newsy Lalonde	33	Joe Hall	135
			Eddie Gerard	10				
1919-20	Joe Malone	39	Frank Nighbor	15	Joe Malone	49	Cully Wilson	86
1920-21	Babe Dye	35	Jack Darragh	15	Newsy Lalonde	43	Bert Corbeau	86
1921-22	Punch Broadbent	32	Harry Broadbent	14	Punch Broadbent	46	Sprague Cleghorn	63
			Leo Reise	14				
1922-23	Babe Dye	26	Edmond Bouchard	12	Babe Dye	37	Billy Boucher	52
1923-24	Cy Denneny	22	King Clancy	8	Cy Denneny	23	Bert Corbeau	55
1924-25	Babe Dye	38	Cy Denneny	15	Babe Dye	44	Billy Boucher	92
1925-26	Nels Stewart	34	Frank Nighbor	13	Nels Stewart	42	Bert Corbeau	121
1926-27	Bill Cook	33	Dick Irvin	18	Bill Cook	37	Nels Stewart	133
1927-28	Howie Morenz	33	Howie Morenz	18	Howie Morenz	51	Eddie Shore	165
1928-29	Ace Bailey	22	Frank Boucher	16	Ace Bailey	32	Red Dutton	139
1929-30	Cooney Weiland	43	Frank Boucher	36	Cooney Weiland	73	Joe Lamb	119
1930-31	Charlie Conacher	31	Joe Primeau	32	Howie Morenz	51	Harvey Rockburn	118
1931-32	Charlie Conacher	34	Joe Primeau	37	Harvey Jackson	53	Red Dutton	107
	Bill Cook	34						
1932-33	Bill Cook	28	Frank Boucher	28	Bill Cook	50	Red Horner	144
1933-34	Charlie Conacher	32	Joe Primeau	32	Charlie Conacher	52	Red Horner	126 *
1934-35	Charlie Conacher	36	Art Chapman	34	Charlie Conacher	57	Red Horner	125
1935-36	Charlie Conacher	23	Art Chapman	28	Sweeney Schriner	45	Red Horner	167
	Bill Thoms	23						
1936-37	Larry Aurie	23	Syl Apps Sr.	29	Sweeney Schriner	46	Red Horner	124
	Nels Stewart	23						
1937-38	Gordie Drillon	26	Syl Apps Sr.	29	Gordie Drillon	52	Red Horner	82 *
1938-39	Roy Conacher	26	Bill Cowley	34	Toe Blake	47	Red Horner	85
1939-40	Bryan Hextall	24	Milt Schmidt	30	Milt Schmidt	52	Red Horner	87
1940-41	Bryan Hextall	26	Bill Cowley	45	Bill Cowley	62	Jimmy Orlando	99
1941-42	Lynn Patrick	32	Phil Watson	37	Bryan Hextall Sr.	56	Jimmy Orlando	81 **
1942-43	Doug Bentley	33	Bill Cowley	45	Doug Bentley	73	Jimmy Orlando	89 *
1943-44	Doug Bentley	38	Clint Smith	49	Herb Cain	82	Mike McMahon Sr.	98
1944-45	Maurice Richard	50	Elmer Lach	54	Elmer Lach	80	Pat Egan	86
1945-46	Gaye Stewart	37	Elmer Lach	34	Max Bentley	61	Jack Stewart	73
1946-47	Maurice Richard	45	Billy Taylor	46	Max Bentley	72	Gus Mortson	133
1947-48	Ted Lindsay	33	Doug Bentley	37	Elmer Lach	61	Bill Barilko	147
1948-49	Sid Abel	28	Doug Bentley	43	Roy Conacher	68	Bill Ezinicki	145
1949-50	Maurice Richard	43	Ted Lindsay	55	Ted Lindsay	78	Bill Ezinicki	144
1950-51	Gordie Howe	43	Gordie Howe	43	Gordie Howe	86	Gus Mortson	142
1951-52	Gordie Howe	47	Elmer Lach	50	Gordie Howe	86	Gus Kyle	127
1952-53	Gordie Howe	49	Gordie Howe	46	Gordie Howe	95	Maurice Richard	112
1953-54	Maurice Richard	37	Gordie Howe	48	Gordie Howe	81	Gus Mortson	132
1954-55	Maurice Richard	38	Bert Olmstead	48	Bernie Geoffrion	75	Fernie Flaman	150
	Bernie Geoffrion	38						
1955-56	Jean Beliveau	47	Bert Olmstead	56	Jean Beliveau	88	Lou Fontinato	202
1956-57	Gordie Howe	44	Ted Lindsay	55	Gordie Howe	89	Gus Mortson	147
1957-58	Dickie Moore	36	Henri Richard	52	Dickie Moore	84	Lou Fontinato	152
1958-59	Jean Beliveau	45	Dickie Moore	55	Dickie Moore	96	Ted Lindsay	184
1959-60	Bobby Hull	39	Don McKenney	49	Bobby Hull	81	Carl Brewer	150
1960-61	Bernie Geoffrion	50	Jean Beliveau	58	Bernie Geoffrion	95	Pierre Pilote	165
1961-62	Bobby Hull	50	Andy Bathgate	56	Bobby Hull	84	Lou Fontinato	167
					Andy Bathgate	84		
1962-63	Gordie Howe	38	Henri Richard	50	Gordie Howe	86	Howie Young	273
1963-64	Bobby Hull	43	Andy Bathgate	58	Stan Mikita	89	Vic Hadfield	151
1964-65	Norm Ullman	42	Stan Mikita	59	Stan Mikita	87	Carl Brewer	177
1965-66	Bobby Hull	54	Stan Mikita	48	Bobby Hull	97	Reggie Fleming	166
			Bobby Rousseau	48				
			Jean Beliveau	48				
1966-67	Bobby Hull	52	Stan Mikita	62	Stan Mikita	97	John Ferguson	177
1967-68	Bobby Hull	44	Phil Esposito	49	Stan Mikita	87	Barclay Plager	153
1968-69	Bobby Hull	58	Phil Esposito	77	Phil Esposito	126	Forbes Kennedy	219
1969-70	Phil Esposito	43	Bobby Orr	87	Bobby Orr	120	Keith Magnuson	213
1970-71	Phil Esposito	76	Bobby Orr	102	Phil Esposito	152	Keith Magnuson	291
1971-72	Phil Esposito	66	Bobby Orr	80	Phil Esposito	133	Bryan Watson	212
1972-73	Phil Esposito	55	Phil Esposito	75	Phil Esposito	130	Dave Schultz	259
1973-74	Phil Esposito	68	Bobby Orr	90	Phil Esposito	145	Dave Schultz	348
1974-75	Phil Esposito	61	Bobby Orr	89	Bobby Orr	135	Dave Schultz	472
			Bobby Clarke	89				
1975-76	Reggie Leach	61	Bobby Clarke	89	Guy Lafleur	125	Steve Durbano	370
1976-77	Steve Shutt	60	Guy Lafleur	80	Guy Lafleur	136	Dave Williams	338
1977-78	Guy Lafleur	60	Bryan Trottier	77	Guy Lafleur	132	Dave Schultz	405
1978-79	Mike Bossy	69	Bryan Trottier	87	Bryan Trottier	134	Dave Williams	298
1979-80	Charlie Simmer	56	Wayne Gretzky	86	Marcel Dionne	137	Jimmy Mann	287
	Danny Gare	56			Wayne Gretzky	137		
	Blaine Stoughton	56						
1980-81	Mike Bossy	68	Wayne Gretzky	109	Wayne Gretzky	164	Dave Williams	343
1981-82	Wayne Gretzky	92	Wayne Gretzky	120	Wayne Gretzky	212	Paul Baxter	409
1982-83	Wayne Gretzky	71	Wayne Gretzky	125	Wayne Gretzky	196	Randy Holt	275
1983-84	Wayne Gretzky	87	Wayne Gretzky	118	Wayne Gretzky	205	Chris Nilan	338
1984-85	Wayne Gretzky	73	Wayne Gretzky	135	Wayne Gretzky	208	Chris Nilan	358
1985-86	Jari Kurri	68	Wayne Gretzky	163	Wayne Gretzky	215	Joey Kocur	377
1986-87	Wayne Gretzky	62	Wayne Gretzky	121	Wayne Gretzky	183	Tim Hunter	361
1987-88	Mario Lemieux	70	Wayne Gretzky	109	Mario Lemieux	168	Bob Probert	398
1988-89	Mario Lemieux	85	Mario Lemieux	114	Mario Lemieux	199	Tim Hunter	375
			Wayne Gretzky	114				
1989-90	Brett Hull	72	Wayne Gretzky	102	Wayne Gretzky	142	Basil McRae	351
1990-91	Brett Hull	86	Wayne Gretzky	122	Wayne Gretzky	163	Rob Ray	350
1991-92	Brett Hull	70	Wayne Gretzky	90	Mario Lemieux	131	Mike Peluso	408
1992-93	Teemu Selanne	76	Adam Oates	97	Mario Lemieux	160	Marty McSorley	399
	Alexander Mogilny	76						
1993-94	Pavel Bure	60	Wayne Gretzky	92	Wayne Gretzky	130	Tie Domi	347
1994-95	Peter Bondra	34	Ron Francis	48	Jaromir Jagr	70	Enrico Ciccone	225
					Eric Lindros	70		
1995-96	Mario Lemieux	69	Mario Lemieux	92	Mario Lemieux	161	Matthew Barnaby	335
			Ron Francis	92				
1996-97	Keith Tkachuk	52	Mario Lemieux	72	Mario Lemieux	122	Gino Odjick	371
			Wayne Gretzky	72				
1997-98	Teemu Selanne	52	Jaromir Jagr	67	Jaromir Jagr	102	Donald Brashear	372
	Peter Bondra	52	Wayne Gretzky	67				

* Match Misconduct penalty not included in total penalty minutes. ** Three Match Misconduct penalties not included in total penalty minutes.
1946-47 was the first season that a Match penalty was automaticaly written into the player's total penalty minutes as 20 minutes.
Beginning in 1947-48 all penalties, Match, Game Misconduct, and Misconduct, are written as 10 minutes.

One Season Scoring Records

Goals-Per-Game Leaders, One Season

(Among players with 20 goals or more in one season)

Player	Team	Season	Games	Goals	Average
Joe Malone	Montreal	1917-18	20	44	2.20
Cy Denneny	Ottawa	1917-18	20	36	1.80
Newsy Lalonde	Montreal	1917-18	14	23	1.64
Joe Malone	Quebec	1919-20	24	39	1.63
Newsy Lalonde	Montreal	1919-20	23	37	1.61
Reg Noble	Toronto	1917-18	20	30	1.50
Babe Dye	Ham., Tor.	1920-21	24	35	1.46
Cy Denneny	Ottawa	1920-21	24	34	1.42
Joe Malone	Hamilton	1920-21	20	28	1.40
Newsy Lalonde	Montreal	1918-19	17	23	1.35
Newsy Lalonde	Montreal	1920-21	24	32	1.33
Punch Broadbent	Ottawa	1921-22	24	32	1.33
Babe Dye	Toronto	1924-25	29	38	1.31
Babe Dye	Toronto	1921-22	24	30	1.25
Cy Denneny	Ottawa	1921-22	22	27	1.23
Aurel Joliat	Montreal	1924-25	24	29	1.21
Wayne Gretzky	Edmonton	1983-84	74	87	1.18
Babe Dye	Toronto	1922-23	22	26	1.18
Odie Cleghorn	Montreal	1918-19	18	21	1.17
Wayne Gretzky	Edmonton	1981-82	80	92	1.15
Mario Lemieux	Pittsburgh	1992-93	60	69	1.15
Frank Nighbor	Ottawa	1919-20	23	26	1.13
Mario Lemieux	Pittsburgh	1988-89	76	85	1.12
Brett Hull	St. Louis	1990-91	78	86	1.10
Cy Denneny	Ottawa	1923-24	21	22	1.05
Joe Malone	Hamilton	1921-22	24	25	1.04
Billy Boucher	Montreal	1922-23	24	25	1.04
Cam Neely	Boston	1993-94	49	50	1.02
Maurice Richard	Montreal	1944-45	50	50	1.00
Howie Morenz	Montreal	1924-25	30	30	1.00
Reg Noble	Toronto	1919-20	24	24	1.00
Corb Denneny	Toronto	1919-20	24	24	1.00
Alexander Mogilny	Buffalo	1992-93	77	76	0.99
Mario Lemieux	Pittsburgh	1995-96	70	69	0.99
Cooney Weiland	Boston	1929-30	44	43	0.98
Phil Esposito	Boston	1970-71	78	76	0.97
Jari Kurri	Edmonton	1984-85	73	71	0.97

The all-time leading scorer in the history of the Hartford Whalers, Ron Francis recorded his 1,000th career assist on March 21, 1998. Francis has recorded at least 40 assists in each of his 17 NHL seasons.

Assists-Per-Game Leaders, One Season

(Among players with 35 assists or more in one season)

Player	Team	Season	Games	Assists	Average
Wayne Gretzky	Edmonton	1985-86	80	163	2.04
Wayne Gretzky	Edmonton	1987-88	64	109	1.70
Wayne Gretzky	Edmonton	1984-85	80	135	1.69
Wayne Gretzky	Edmonton	1983-84	74	118	1.59
Wayne Gretzky	Edmonton	1982-83	80	125	1.56
Wayne Gretzky	Los Angeles	1990-91	78	122	1.56
Wayne Gretzky	Edmonton	1986-87	79	121	1.53
Mario Lemieux	Pittsburgh	1992-93	60	91	1.52
Wayne Gretzky	Edmonton	1981-82	80	120	1.50
Mario Lemieux	Pittsburgh	1988-89	76	114	1.50
Adam Oates	St. Louis	1990-91	61	90	1.48
Wayne Gretzky	Los Angeles	1988-89	78	114	1.46
Wayne Gretzky	Los Angeles	1989-90	73	102	1.40
Wayne Gretzky	Edmonton	1980-81	80	109	1.36
Mario Lemieux	Pittsburgh	1991-92	64	87	1.36
Mario Lemieux	Pittsburgh	1989-90	59	78	1.32
Bobby Orr	Boston	1970-71	78	102	1.31
Mario Lemieux	Pittsburgh	1995-96	70	92	1.31
Mario Lemieux	Pittsburgh	1987-88	77	98	1.27
Bobby Orr	Boston	1973-74	74	90	1.22
Wayne Gretzky	Los Angeles	1991-92	74	90	1.22
Ron Francis	Pittsburgh	1995-96	77	92	1.19
Mario Lemieux	Pittsburgh	1985-86	79	93	1.18
Bobby Clarke	Philadelphia	1975-76	76	89	1.17
Peter Stastny	Quebec	1981-82	80	93	1.16
Adam Oates	Boston	1992-93	84	97	1.15
Doug Gilmour	Toronto	1992-93	83	95	1.14
Wayne Gretzky	Los Angeles	1993-94	81	92	1.14
Paul Coffey	Edmonton	1985-86	79	90	1.14
Bobby Orr	Boston	1969-70	76	87	1.14
Bryan Trottier	NY Islanders	1978-79	76	87	1.14
Bobby Orr	Boston	1972-73	63	72	1.14
Bill Cowley	Boston	1943-44	36	41	1.14
Pat LaFontaine	Buffalo	1992-93	84	95	1.13
Steve Yzerman	Detroit	1988-89	80	90	1.13
Paul Coffey	Pittsburgh	1987-88	46	52	1.13
Bobby Orr	Boston	1974-75	80	89	1.11
Bobby Clarke	Philadelphia	1974-75	80	89	1.11
Paul Coffey	Pittsburgh	1988-89	75	83	1.11
Wayne Gretzky	Los Angeles	1992-93	45	49	1.11
Denis Savard	Chicago	1982-83	78	86	1.10
Ron Francis	Pittsburgh	1994-95	44	48	1.09
Denis Savard	Chicago	1981-82	80	87	1.09
Denis Savard	Chicago	1987-88	80	87	1.09
Wayne Gretzky	Edmonton	1979-80	79	86	1.09
Paul Coffey	Edmonton	1983-84	80	86	1.08
Elmer Lach	Montreal	1944-45	50	54	1.08
Peter Stastny	Quebec	1985-86	76	81	1.07
Jaromir Jagr	Pittsburgh	1995-96	82	87	1.06
Mark Messier	Edmonton	1989-90	79	84	1.06
Peter Forsberg	Colorado	1995-96	82	86	1.05
Paul Coffey	Edmonton	1984-85	80	84	1.05
Marcel Dionne	Los Angeles	1979-80	80	84	1.05
Bobby Orr	Boston	1971-72	76	80	1.05
Mike Bossy	NY Islanders	1981-82	80	83	1.04
Adam Oates	Boston	1993-94	77	80	1.04
Phil Esposito	Boston	1968-69	74	77	1.04
Bryan Trottier	NY Islanders	1983-84	68	71	1.04
Pete Mahovlich	Montreal	1974-75	80	82	1.03
Kent Nilsson	Calgary	1980-81	80	82	1.03
Peter Stastny	Quebec	1982-83	75	77	1.03
Doug Gilmour	Toronto	1993-94	83	84	1.01
Bernie Nicholls	Los Angeles	1988-89	79	80	1.01
Guy Lafleur	Montreal	1979-80	74	75	1.01
Guy Lafleur	Montreal	1976-77	80	80	1.00
Marcel Dionne	Los Angeles	1984-85	80	80	1.00
Brian Leetch	NY Rangers	1991-92	80	80	1.00
Bryan Trottier	NY Islanders	1977-78	77	77	1.00
Mike Bossy	NY Islanders	1983-84	67	67	1.00
Jean Ratelle	NY Rangers	1971-72	63	63	1.00
Steve Yzerman	Detroit	1993-94	58	58	1.00
Ron Francis	Hartford	1985-86	53	53	1.00
Guy Chouinard	Calgary	1980-81	52	52	1.00
Elmer Lach	Montreal	1943-44	48	48	1.00

Points-Per-Game Leaders, One Season

(Among players with 50 points or more in one season)

Player	Team	Season	Games	Points	Average
Wayne Gretzky	Edmonton	1983-84	74	205	2.77
Wayne Gretzky	Edmonton	1985-86	80	215	2.69
Mario Lemieux	Pittsburgh	1992-93	60	160	2.67
Wayne Gretzky	Edmonton	1981-82	80	212	2.65
Mario Lemieux	Pittsburgh	1988-89	76	199	2.62
Wayne Gretzky	Edmonton	1984-85	80	208	2.60
Wayne Gretzky	Edmonton	1982-83	80	196	2.45
Wayne Gretzky	Edmonton	1987-88	64	149	2.33
Wayne Gretzky	Edmonton	1986-87	79	183	2.32
Mario Lemieux	Pittsburgh	1995-96	70	161	2.30
Mario Lemieux	Pittsburgh	1987-88	77	168	2.18
Wayne Gretzky	Los Angeles	1988-89	78	168	2.15
Wayne Gretzky	Los Angeles	1990-91	78	163	2.09
Mario Lemieux	Pittsburgh	1989-90	59	123	2.08
Wayne Gretzky	Edmonton	1980-81	80	164	2.05
Mario Lemieux	Pittsburgh	1991-92	64	131	2.05
Bill Cowley	Boston	1943-44	36	71	1.97
Phil Esposito	Boston	1970-71	78	152	1.95
Wayne Gretzky	Los Angeles	1989-90	73	142	1.95
Steve Yzerman	Detroit	1988-89	80	155	1.94
Bernie Nicholls	Los Angeles	1988-89	79	150	1.90
Adam Oates	St. Louis	1990-91	61	115	1.89
Phil Esposito	Boston	1973-74	78	145	1.86
Jari Kurri	Edmonton	1984-85	73	135	1.85
Mike Bossy	NY Islanders	1981-82	80	147	1.84
Jaromir Jagr	Pittsburgh	1995-96	82	149	1.82
Mario Lemieux	Pittsburgh	1985-86	79	141	1.78
Bobby Orr	Boston	1970-71	78	139	1.78
Jari Kurri	Edmonton	1983-84	64	113	1.77
Pat LaFontaine	Buffalo	1992-93	84	148	1.76
Bryan Trottier	NY Islanders	1978-79	76	134	1.76
Mike Bossy	NY Islanders	1983-84	67	118	1.76
Paul Coffey	Edmonton	1985-86	79	138	1.75
Phil Esposito	Boston	1971-72	76	133	1.75
Peter Stastny	Quebec	1981-82	80	139	1.74
Wayne Gretzky	Edmonton	1979-80	79	137	1.73
Jean Ratelle	NY Rangers	1971-72	63	109	1.73
Marcel Dionne	Los Angeles	1979-80	80	137	1.71
Herb Cain	Boston	1943-44	48	82	1.71
Guy Lafleur	Montreal	1976-77	80	136	1.70
Dennis Maruk	Washington	1981-82	80	136	1.70
Phil Esposito	Boston	1968-69	74	126	1.70
Guy Lafleur	Montreal	1974-75	70	119	1.70
Mario Lemieux	Pittsburgh	1986-87	63	107	1.70
Adam Oates	Boston	1992-93	84	142	1.69
Bobby Orr	Boston	1974-75	80	135	1.69
Marcel Dionne	Los Angeles	1980-81	80	135	1.69
Guy Lafleur	Montreal	1977-78	78	132	1.69
Guy Lafleur	Montreal	1979-80	74	125	1.69
Rob Brown	Pittsburgh	1988-89	68	115	1.69
Jari Kurri	Edmonton	1985-86	78	131	1.68
Brett Hull	St. Louis	1990-91	78	131	1.68
Phil Esposito	Boston	1972-73	78	130	1.67
Cooney Weiland	Boston	1929-30	44	73	1.66
Alexander Mogilny	Buffalo	1992-93	77	127	1.65
Peter Stastny	Quebec	1982-83	75	124	1.65
Bobby Orr	Boston	1973-74	74	122	1.65
Kent Nilsson	Calgary	1980-81	80	131	1.64
Wayne Gretzky	Los Angeles	1991-92	74	121	1.64
Denis Savard	Chicago	1987-88	80	131	1.64
Steve Yzerman	Detroit	1992-93	84	137	1.63
Marcel Dionne	Los Angeles	1978-79	80	130	1.63
Dale Hawerchuk	Winnipeg	1984-85	80	130	1.63
Mark Messier	Edmonton	1989-90	79	129	1.63
Bryan Trottier	NY Islanders	1983-84	68	111	1.63
Pat LaFontaine	Buffalo	1991-92	57	93	1.63
Charlie Simmer	Los Angeles	1980-81	65	105	1.62
Guy Lafleur	Montreal	1978-79	80	129	1.61
Bryan Trottier	NY Islanders	1981-82	80	129	1.61
Phil Esposito	Boston	1974-75	79	127	1.61
Steve Yzerman	Detroit	1989-90	79	127	1.61
Peter Stastny	Quebec	1985-86	76	122	1.61
Mario Lemieux	Pittsburgh	1996-97	76	122	1.61
Michel Goulet	Quebec	1983-84	75	121	1.61
Wayne Gretzky	Los Angeles	1993-94	81	130	1.60
Bryan Trottier	NY Islanders	1977-78	77	123	1.60
Bobby Orr	Boston	1972-73	63	101	1.60
Guy Chouinard	Calgary	1980-81	52	83	1.60
Elmer Lach	Montreal	1944-45	50	80	1.60
Pierre Turgeon	NY Islanders	1992-93	83	132	1.59
Steve Yzerman	Detroit	1987-88	64	102	1.59
Mike Bossy	NY Islanders	1978-79	80	126	1.58
Paul Coffey	Edmonton	1983-84	80	126	1.58
Marcel Dionne	Los Angeles	1984-85	80	126	1.58
Bobby Orr	Boston	1969-70	76	120	1.58
Eric Lindros	Philadelphia	1995-96	73	115	1.58
Charlie Simmer	Los Angeles	1979-80	64	101	1.58
Teemu Selanne	Winnipeg	1992-93	84	132	1.57
Bobby Clarke	Philadelphia	1975-76	76	119	1.57
Guy Lafleur	Montreal	1975-76	80	125	1.56
Dave Taylor	Los Angeles	1980-81	72	112	1.56
Denis Savard	Chicago	1982-83	78	121	1.55
Ron Francis	Pittsburgh	1995-96	77	119	1.55
Mike Bossy	NY Islanders	1985-86	80	123	1.54
Bobby Orr	Boston	1971-72	76	117	1.54
Kevin Stevens	Pittsburgh	1991-92	80	123	1.54
Mike Bossy	NY Islanders	1984-85	76	117	1.54
Kevin Stevens	Pittsburgh	1992-93	72	111	1.54
Doug Bentley	Chicago	1943-44	50	77	1.54
Doug Gilmour	Toronto	1992-93	83	127	1.53
Marcel Dionne	Los Angeles	1976-77	80	122	1.53
Eric Lindros	Philadelphia	1996-97	52	79	1.52
Eric Lindros	Philadelphia	1994-95	46	70	1.52
Marcel Dionne	Detroit	1974-75	80	121	1.51
Dale Hawerchuk	Winnipeg	1987-88	80	121	1.51
Paul Coffey	Pittsburgh	1988-89	75	113	1.51
Jaromir Jagr	Pittsburgh	1996-97	63	95	1.51
Cam Neely	Boston	1993-94	49	74	1.51

The diminutive Doug "Killer" Gilmour electrified Toronto Maple Leaf fans with his exhaustive never-say-die performance during the 1992-93 season. Gilmour became the first Leaf player since Dave Keon to win a major NHL award when he captured the Selke Trophy as the league's top defensive forward.

Left: The first European-trained player to make an impression with the Montreal Canadiens, Mats Naslund set a team rookie record by racking up 71 points during his freshman season of 1982-83. Below: Although he was an All-Star defenseman in junior, Wendel Clark was shifted to forward when he joined the Toronto Maple Leafs in 1985-86. The former Notre Dame Hound made an immediate impact on opposing players, many of whom went home nursing numerous bumps and bruises after an on-ice collision with the Kelvington Kid.

Rookie Scoring Records

All-Time Top 50 Goal-Scoring Rookies

	Rookie	Team	Position	Season	GP	G	A	PTS
1	* Teemu Selanne	Winnipeg	Right wing	1992-93	84	**76**	56	132
2.	* Mike Bossy	NY Islanders	Right wing	1977-78	73	**53**	38	91
3.	* Joe Nieuwendyk	Calgary	Center	1987-88	75	**51**	41	92
4	* Dale Hawerchuk	Winnipeg	Center	1981-82	80	**45**	58	103
	* Luc Robitaille	Los Angeles	Left wing	1986-87	79	**45**	39	84
6.	Rick Martin	Buffalo	Left wing	1971-72	73	**44**	30	74
	Barry Pederson	Boston	Center	1981-82	80	**44**	48	92
8.	* Steve Larmer	Chicago	Right wing	1982-83	80	**43**	47	90
	* Mario Lemieux	Pittsburgh	Center	1984-85	73	**43**	57	100
10.	Eric Lindros	Philadelphia	Center	1992-93	61	**41**	34	75
11.	Darryl Sutter	Chicago	Left wing	1980-81	76	**40**	22	62
	Sylvain Turgeon	Hartford	Left wing	1983-84	76	**40**	32	72
	Warren Young	Pittsburgh	Left wing	1984-85	80	**40**	32	72
14.	* Eric Vail	Atlanta	Left wing	1974-75	72	**39**	21	60
	Anton Stastny	Quebec	Left wing	1980-81	80	**39**	46	85
	* Peter Stastny	Quebec	Center	1980-81	77	**39**	70	109
	Steve Yzerman	Detroit	Center	1983-84	80	**39**	48	87
18.	* Gilbert Perreault	Buffalo	Center	1970-71	78	**38**	34	72
	Neal Broten	Minnesota	Center	1981-82	73	**38**	60	98
	Ray Sheppard	Buffalo	Right wing	1987-88	74	**38**	27	65
	Mikael Renberg	Philadelphia	Left wing	1993-94	83	**38**	44	82
22	Jorgen Pettersson	St. Louis	Left wing	1980-81	62	**37**	36	73
	Jimmy Carson	Los Angeles	Centre	1986-87	80	**37**	42	79
24.	Mike Foligno	Detroit	Right wing	1979-80	80	**36**	35	71
	Mike Bullard	Pittsburgh	Center	1981-82	75	**36**	27	63
	Paul MacLean	Winnipeg	Right wing	1981-82	74	**36**	25	61
	Tony Granato	NY Rangers	Right wing	1988-89	78	**36**	27	63
28.	Marian Stastny	Quebec	Right wing	1981-82	74	**35**	54	89
	Brian Bellows	Minnesota	Right wing	1982-83	78	**35**	30	65
	Tony Amonte	NY Rangers	Right wing	1991-92	79	**35**	34	69
31	Nels Stewart	Mtl. Maroons	Center	1925-26	36	**34**	8	42
	* Danny Grant	Minnesota	Left wing	1968-69	75	**34**	31	65
	Norm Ferguson	Oakland	Right wing	1968-69	76	**34**	20	54
	Brian Propp	Philadelphia	Left wing	1979-80	80	**34**	41	75
	Wendel Clark	Toronto	Left wing	1985-86	66	**34**	11	45
	* Pavel Bure	Vancouver	Right wing	1991-92	65	**34**	26	60
37	* Willi Plett	Atlanta	Right wing	1976-77	64	**33**	23	56
	Dale McCourt	Detroit	Center	1977-78	76	**33**	39	72
	Mark Pavelich	NY Rangers	Center	1981-82	79	**33**	43	76
	Ron Flockhart	Philadelphia	Center	1981-82	72	**33**	39	72
	Steve Bozek	Los Angeles	Center	1981-82	71	**33**	23	56
	Jason Arnott	Edmonton	Center	1993-94	78	**33**	35	68
43.	Bill Mosienko	Chicago	Right wing	1943-44	50	**32**	38	70
	Michel Bergeron	Detroit	Right wing	1975-76	72	**32**	27	59
	* Bryan Trottier	NY Islanders	Center	1975-76	80	**32**	63	95
	Don Murdoch	NY Rangers	Right wing	1976-77	59	**32**	24	56
	Jari Kurri	Edmonton	Left wing	1980-81	75	**32**	43	75
	Bobby Carpenter	Washington	Center	1981-82	80	**32**	35	67
	Kjell Dahlin	Montreal	Right wing	1985-86	77	**32**	39	71
	Petr Klima	Detroit	Left wing	1985-86	74	**32**	24	56
	Darren Turcotte	NY Rangers	Right wing	1989-90	76	**32**	34	66
	Joe Juneau	Boston	Center	1992-93	84	**32**	70	102

* Calder Trophy Winner

All-Time Top 50 Point-Scoring Rookies

	Rookie	Team	Position	Season	GP	G	A	PTS
1.	* Teemu Selanne	Winnipeg	Right wing	1992-93	84	76	56	**132**
2.	* Peter Stastny	Quebec	Center	1980-81	77	39	70	**109**
3.	* Dale Hawerchuk	Winnipeg	Center	1981-82	80	45	58	**103**
4.	Joe Juneau	Boston	Center	1992-93	84	32	70	**102**
5.	* Mario Lemieux	Pittsburgh	Center	1984-85	73	43	57	**100**
6.	Neal Broten	Minnesota	Center	1981-82	73	38	60	**98**
7.	* Bryan Trottier	NY Islanders	Center	1975-76	80	32	63	**95**
8.	Barry Pederson	Boston	Center	1981-82	80	44	48	**92**
	* Joe Nieuwendyk	Calgary	Center	1987-88	75	51	41	**92**
10.	* Mike Bossy	NY Islanders	Right wing	1977-78	73	53	38	**91**
11.	* Steve Larmer	Chicago	Right wing	1982-83	80	43	47	**90**
12.	Marian Stastny	Quebec	Right wing	1981-82	74	35	54	**89**
13.	Steve Yzerman	Detroit	Center	1983-84	80	39	48	**87**
14.	* Sergei Makarov	Calgary	Right wing	1989-90	80	24	62	**86**
15.	Anton Stastny	Quebec	Left wing	1980-81	80	39	46	**85**
16.	* Luc Robitaille	Los Angeles	Left wing	1986-87	79	45	39	**84**
17.	Mikael Renberg	Philadelphia	Left wing	1993-94	83	38	44	**82**
18.	Jimmy Carson	Los Angeles	Center	1986-87	80	37	42	**79**
	Sergei Fedorov	Detroit	Center	1990-91	77	31	48	**79**
	Alexei Yashin	Ottawa	Center	1993-94	83	30	49	**79**
21.	Marcel Dionne	Detroit	Center	1971-72	78	28	49	**77**
22.	Larry Murphy	Los Angeles	Defense	1980-81	80	16	60	**76**
	Mark Pavelich	NY Rangers	Center	1981-82	79	33	43	**76**
	Dave Poulin	Philadelphia	Center	1983-84	73	31	45	**76**
25.	Brian Propp	Philadelphia	Left wing	1979-80	80	34	41	**75**
	Jari Kurri	Edmonton	Left wing	1980-81	75	32	43	**75**
	Denis Savard	Chicago	Center	1980-81	76	28	47	**75**
	Mike Modano	Minnesota	Center	1989-90	80	29	46	**75**
	Eric Lindros	Philadelphia	Center	1992-93	61	41	34	**75**
30.	Rick Martin	Buffalo	Left wing	1971-72	73	44	30	**74**
	* Bobby Smith	Minnesota	Center	1978-79	80	30	44	**74**
32.	Jorgen Pettersson	St. Louis	Left wing	1980-81	62	37	36	**73**
33.	* Gilbert Perreault	Buffalo	Center	1970-71	78	38	34	**72**
	Dale McCourt	Detroit	Center	1977-78	76	33	39	**72**
	Ron Flockhart	Philadelphia	Center	1981-82	72	33	39	**72**
	Sylvain Turgeon	Hartford	Left wing	1983-84	76	40	32	**72**
	Warren Young	Pittsburgh	Left wing	1984-85	80	40	32	**72**
	Carey Wilson	Calgary	Center	1984-85	74	24	48	**72**
	Alexei Zhamnov	Winnipeg	Center	1992-93	68	25	47	**72**
40.	Mike Foligno	Detroit	Right wing	1979-80	80	36	35	**71**
	Dave Christian	Winnipeg	Center	1980-81	80	28	43	**71**
	Mats Naslund	Montreal	Left wing	1982-83	74	26	45	**71**
	Kjell Dahlin	Montreal	Right wing	1985-86	77	32	39	**71**
	* Brian Leetch	NY Rangers	Defense	1988-89	68	23	48	**71**
45.	Bill Mosienko	Chicago	Right wing	1943-44	50	32	38	**70**
46.	Roland Eriksson	Minnesota	Center	1976-77	80	25	44	**69**
	Tony Amonte	NY Rangers	Right wing	1991-92	79	35	34	**69**
48.	Jude Drouin	Minnesota	Center	1970-71	75	16	52	**68**
	Pierre Larouche	Pittsburgh	Center	1974-75	79	31	37	**68**
	Ron Francis	Hartford	Center	1981-82	59	25	43	**68**
	* Gary Suter	Calgary	Defense	1985-86	80	18	50	**68**
	Jason Arnott	Edmonton	Center	1993-94	84	33	35	**68**

* Calder Trophy Winner

50-Goal Seasons

Bernie Geoffrion

Bobby Hull

Charlie Simmer

Player	Team	Date of 50th Goal	Score		Goaltender	Player's Game No.	Team Game No.	Total Goals	Total Games	Age When First 50th Scored (Yrs. & Mos.)
Maurice Richard	Mtl.	18-3-45	Mtl. 4	at Bos. 2	Harvey Bennett	50	50	50	50	23.7
Bernie Geoffrion	Mtl.	16-3-61	Tor. 2	at Mtl. 5	Cesare Maniago	62	68	50	64	30.1
Bobby Hull	Chi.	25-3-62	Chi. 1	at NYR 4	Gump Worsley	70	70	50	70	23.2
Bobby Hull	Chi.	2-3-66	Det. 4	at Chi. 5	Hank Bassen	52	57	54	65	
Bobby Hull	Chi.	18-3-67	Chi. 5	at Tor. 9	Bruce Gamble	63	66	52	66	
Bobby Hull	Chi.	5-3-69	NYR 4	at Chi. 4	Ed Giacomin	64	66	58	74	
Phil Esposito	Bos.	20-2-71	Bos. 4	at L.A. 5	Denis DeJordy	58	58	76	78	29.0
John Bucyk	Bos.	16-3-71	Bos. 11	at Det. 4	Roy Edwards	69	69	51	78	35.10
Phil Esposito	Bos.	20-2-72	Bos. 3	at Chi. 1	Tony Esposito	60	60	66	76	
Bobby Hull	Chi.	2-4-72	Det. 1	at Chi. 6	Andy Brown	78	78	50	78	
Vic Hadfield	NYR	2-4-72	Mtl. 6	at NYR 5	Denis DeJordy	78	78	50	78	31.6
Phil Esposito	Bos.	25-3-73	Buf. 1	at Bos. 6	Roger Crozier	75	75	55	78	
Mickey Redmond	Det.	27-3-73	Det. 8	at Tor. 1	Ron Low	73	75	52	76	25.3
Rick MacLeish	Phi.	1-4-73	Phi. 4	at Pit. 5	Cam Newton	78	78	50	78	23.2
Phil Esposito	Bos.	20-2-74	Bos. 5	at Min. 5	Cesare Maniago	56	56	68	78	
Mickey Redmond	Det.	23-3-74	NYR 3	at Det 5	Ed Giacomin	69	71	51	76	
Ken Hodge	Bos.	6-4-74	Bos. 2	at Mtl. 6	Michel Larocque	75	77	50	76	29.10
Rick Martin	Buf.	7-4-74	St. L. 2	at Buf. 5	Wayne Stephenson	78	78	52	78	22.9
Phil Esposito	Bos.	8-2-75	Bos. 8	at Det. 5	Jim Rutherford	54	54	61	79	
Guy Lafleur	Mtl.	29-3-75	K.C. 1	at Mtl. 4	Denis Herron	66	76	53	70	23.6
Danny Grant	Det.	2-4-75	Wsh. 3	at Det. 8	John Adams	78	78	50	80	29.2
Rick Martin	Buf.	3-4-75	Bos. 2	at Buf. 4	Ken Broderick	67	79	52	68	
Reggie Leach	Phi.	14-3-76	Atl. 1	at Phi. 6	Dan Bouchard	69	69	61	80	25.11
Jean Pronovost	Pit.	24-3-76	Bos. 5	at Pit. 5	Gilles Gilbert	74	74	52	80	30.3
Guy Lafleur	Mtl.	27-3-76	K.C. 2	at Mtl. 8	Denis Herron	76	76	56	80	
Bill Barber	Phi.	3-4-76	Buf. 2	at Phi. 5	Al Smith	79	79	50	80	23.9
Pierre Larouche	Pit.	3-4-76	Wsh. 5	at Pit. 4	Ron Low	75	79	53	76	20.5
Danny Gare	Buf.	4-4-76	Tor. 2	at Buf. 5	Gord McRae	79	80	50	79	21.11
Steve Shutt	Mtl.	1-3-77	Mtl. 5	at NYI 4	Glenn Resch	65	65	60	80	24.8
Guy Lafleur	Mtl.	6-3-77	Mtl. 1	at Buf. 4	Don Edwards	68	68	56	80	
Marcel Dionne	L.A.	2-4-77	Min. 2	at L.A. 7	Pete LoPresti	79	79	53	80	25.8
Guy Lafleur	Mtl.	8-3-78	Wsh. 3	at Mtl. 4	Jim Bedard	63	65	60	78	
Mike Bossy	NYI	1-4-78	Wsh. 2	at NYI 3	Bernie Wolfe	69	76	53	73	21.2
Mike Bossy	NYI	24-2-79	Det. 1	at NYI 3	Rogie Vachon	58	58	69	80	
Marcel Dionne	L.A.	11-3-79	L.A. 3	at Phi. 6	Wayne Stephenson	68	68	59	80	
Guy Lafleur	Mtl.	31-3-79	Pit. 3	at Mtl. 5	Denis Herron	76	76	52	80	
Guy Chouinard	Atl.	6-4-79	NYR 2	at Atl. 9	John Davidson	79	79	50	80	22.5
Marcel Dionne	L.A.	12-3-80	L.A. 2	at Pit. 4	Nick Ricci	70	70	53	80	
Mike Bossy	NYI	16-3-80	NYI 6	at Chi. 1	Tony Esposito	68	71	51	75	
Charlie Simmer	L.A.	19-3-80	Det. 3	at L.A. 4	Jim Rutherford	57	73	56	64	26.0
Pierre Larouche	Mtl.	25-3-80	Chi. 4	at Mtl. 8	Tony Esposito	72	75	50	73	
Danny Gare	Buf.	27-3-80	Det. 1	at Buf. 10	Jim Rutherford	71	75	56	76	
Blaine Stoughton	Hfd.	28-3-80	Hfd. 4	at Van. 4	Glen Hanlon	75	75	56	80	27.0
Guy Lafleur	Mtl.	2-4-80	Mtl. 7	at Det. 2	Rogie Vachon	72	78	50	74	
Wayne Gretzky	Edm.	2-4-80	Min. 1	at Edm. 1	Gary Edwards	78	79	51	79	19.2
Reggie Leach	Phi.	3-4-80	Wsh. 2	at Phi. 4	empty net	75	79	50	76	
Mike Bossy	NYI	24-1-81	Que. 3	at NYI 7	Ron Grahame	50	50	68	79	
Charlie Simmer	L.A.	26-1-81	L.A. 7	at Que. 5	Michel Dion	51	51	56	65	
Marcel Dionne	L.A.	8-3-81	L.A. 4	at Wpg. 1	Markus Mattsson	68	68	58	80	
Wayne Babych	St. L.	12-3-81	St. L. 3	at Mtl. 4	Richard Sevigny	70	68	54	78	22.9
Wayne Gretzky	Edm.	15-3-81	Edm. 3	at Cgy. 3	Pat Riggin	69	69	55	80	
Rick Kehoe	Pit.	16-3-81	Pit. 7	at Edm. 6	Eddie Mio	70	70	55	80	29.7
Jacques Richard	Que.	29-3-81	Mtl. 0	at Que. 4	Richard Sevigny	76	75	52	78	28.6
Dennis Maruk	Wsh.	5-4-81	Det. 2	at Wsh. 7	Larry Lozinski	80	80	50	80	25.3
Wayne Gretzky	Edm.	30-12-81	Phi. 5	at Edm. 7	empty net	39	39	92	80	
Dennis Maruk	Wsh.	21-2-82	Wpg. 3	at Wsh. 6	Doug Soetaert	61	61	60	80	
Mike Bossy	NYI	4-3-82	Tor. 1	at NYI 10	Michel Larocque	66	66	64	80	
Dino Ciccarelli	Min.	8-3-82	St. L. 1	at Min. 8	Mike Liut	67	68	55	76	21.7
Rick Vaive	Tor.	24-3-82	St. L. 3	at Tor. 4	Mike Liut	72	75	54	77	22.10
Blaine Stoughton	Hfd.	28-3-82	Min. 5	at Hfd. 2	Gilles Meloche	76	76	52	80	
Rick Middleton	Bos.	28-3-82	Bos. 5	at Buf. 9	Paul Harrison	72	77	51	75	28.11
Marcel Dionne	L.A.	30-3-82	Cgy. 7	at L.A. 5	Pat Riggin	75	77	50	78	
Mark Messier	Edm.	31-3-82	L.A. 3	at Edm. 7	Mario Lessard	78	79	50	78	21.3
Bryan Trottier	NYI	3-4-82	Phi. 3	at NYI 6	Pete Peeters	79	79	50	80	25.9
Lanny McDonald	Cgy.	18-2-83	Cgy. 1	at Buf. 5	Bob Sauve	60	60	66	80	30.0
Wayne Gretzky	Edm.	19-2-83	Edm. 10	at Pit. 7	Nick Ricci	60	60	71	80	
Michel Goulet	Que.	5-3-83	Hfd. 3	at Que. 10	Mike Veisor	67	67	57	80	22.11
Mike Bossy	NYI	12-3-83	Wsh. 2	at NYI 6	Al Jensen	70	71	60	79	
Marcel Dionne	L.A.	17-3-83	Que. 3	at L.A. 4	Dan Bouchard	71	71	56	80	
Al Secord	Chi.	20-3-83	Tor. 3	at Chi. 7	Mike Palmateer	73	73	54	80	25.0
Rick Vaive	Tor.	30-3-83	Tor. 4	at Det. 2	Gilles Gilbert	76	78	51	78	
Wayne Gretzky	Edm.	7-1-84	Hfd. 3	at Edm. 5	Greg Millen	42	42	87	74	
Michel Goulet	Que.	8-3-84	Que. 8	at Pit. 6	Denis Herron	63	69	56	75	
Rick Vaive	Tor.	14-3-84	Min. 3	at Tor. 3	Gilles Meloche	69	72	52	76	
Mike Bullard	Pit.	14-3-84	Pit. 6	at L.A. 7	Markus Mattsson	71	72	51	76	23.0
Jari Kurri	Edm.	15-3-84	Edm. 2	at Mtl. 3	Rick Wamsley	57	73	52	64	23.10
Glenn Anderson	Edm.	21-3-84	Hfd. 3	at Edm. 5	Greg Millen	76	76	54	80	23.6
Tim Kerr	Phi.	22-3-84	Pit. 4	at Phi. 13	Denis Herron	74	75	54	79	24.3
Mike Bossy	NYI	31-3-84	NYI 3	at Wsh. 1	Pat Riggin	67	79	51	67	

Player	Team	Date of 50th Goal	Score		Goaltender	Player's Game No.	Team Game No.	Total Goals	Total Games	Age When First 50th Scored (Yrs. & Mos.)
Wayne Gretzky	Edm.	26-1-85	Pit. 3	at Edm. 6	Denis Herron	49	49	73	80	
Jari Kurri	Edm.	3-2-85	Hfd. 3	at Edm. 6	Greg Millen	50	53	71	73	
Mike Bossy	NYI	5-3-85	Phi. 5	at NYI 4	Bob Froese	61	65	58	76	
Michel Goulet	Que.	6-3-85	Buf. 3	at Que. 4	Tom Barrasso	62	73	55	69	
Tim Kerr	Phi.	7-3-85	Wsh. 6	at Phi. 9	Pat Riggin	63	65	54	74	
John Ogrodnick	Det.	13-3-85	Det. 6	at Edm. 7	Grant Fuhr	69	69	55	79	25.9
Bob Carpenter	Wsh.	21-3-85	Wsh. 2	at Mtl. 3	Steve Penney	72	72	53	80	21.9
Dale Hawerchuk	Wpg.	29-3-85	Chi. 5	at Wpg. 5	W. Skorodenski	77	77	53	80	21.11
Mike Gartner	Wsh.	7-4-85	Pit. 3	at Wsh. 7	Brian Ford	80	80	50	80	25.5
Jari Kurri	Edm.	4-3-86	Edm. 6	at Van. 2	Richard Brodeur	63	65	68	78	
Mike Bossy	NYI	11-3-86	Cgy. 4	at NYI 8	Rejean Lemelin	67	67	61	80	
Glenn Anderson	Edm.	14-3-86	Det. 3	at Edm. 12	Greg Stefan	63	71	54	72	
Michel Goulet	Que.	17-3-86	Que. 8	at Mtl. 6	Patrick Roy	67	72	53	75	
Wayne Gretzky	Edm.	18-3-86	Wpg. 2	at Edm. 6	Brian Hayward	72	72	52	80	
Tim Kerr	Phi.	20-3-86	Pit. 1	at Phi. 5	Roberto Romano	68	72	58	76	
Wayne Gretzky	Edm.	4-2-87	Edm. 6	at Min. 5	Don Beaupre	55	55	62	79	
Dino Ciccarelli	Min.	7-3-87	Pit. 7	at Min. 3	Gilles Meloche	66	66	52	80	
Mario Lemieux	Pit.	12-3-87	Que. 3	at Pit. 6	Mario Gosselin	53	70	54	63	21.5
Tim Kerr	Phi.	17-3-87	NYR 1	at Phi. 4	J. Vanbiesbrouck	67	71	58	75	
Jari Kurri	Edm.	17-3-87	N.J. 4	at Edm. 7	Craig Billington	69	70	54	79	
Mario Lemieux	Pit.	2-2-88	Wsh. 2	at Pit. 3	Pete Peeters	51	54	70	77	
Steve Yzerman	Det.	1-3-88	Buf. 0	at Det. 4	Tom Barrasso	64	64	50	64	22.10
Joe Nieuwendyk	Cgy.	12-3-88	Buf. 4	at Cgy. 10	Tom Barrasso	66	70	51	75	21.5
Craig Simpson	Edm.	15-3-88	Buf. 4	at Edm. 6	Jacques Cloutier	71	71	56	80	21.1
Jimmy Carson	L.A.	26-3-88	Chi. 5	at L.A. 9	Darren Pang	77	77	55	88	19.8
Luc Robitaille	L.A.	1-4-88	L.A. 6	at Cgy. 3	Mike Vernon	79	79	53	80	21.10
Hakan Loob	Cgy.	3-4-88	Min. 1	at Cgy. 4	Don Beaupre	80	80	50	80	27.9
Stephane Richer	Mtl.	3-4-88	Mtl. 4	at Buf. 4	Tom Barrasso	72	80	50	72	21.10
Mario Lemieux	Pit.	20-1-89	Pit. 3	at Wpg. 7	Pokey Reddick	44	46	85	76	
Bernie Nicholls	L.A.	28-1-89	Edm. 7	at L.A. 6	Grant Fuhr	51	51	70	79	27.7
Steve Yzerman	Det.	5-2-89	Det. 6	at Wpg. 2	Pokey Reddick	55	55	65	80	
Wayne Gretzky	L.A.	4-3-89	Phi. 2	at L.A. 6	Ron Hextall	66	67	54	78	
Joe Nieuwendyk	Cgy.	21-3-89	NYI 1	at Cgy. 4	Mark Fitzpatrick	72	74	51	77	
Joe Mullen	Cgy.	31-3-89	Wpg. 1	at Cgy. 4	Bob Essensa	78	79	51	79	32.1
Brett Hull	St. L.	6-2-90	Tor. 4	at St. L. 6	Jeff Reese	54	54	72	80	25.6
Steve Yzerman	Det.	24-2-90	Det. 3	at NYI 3	Glenn Healy	63	63	62	79	
Cam Neely	Bos.	10-3-90	Bos. 3	at NYI 3	Mark Fitzpatrick	69	71	55	76	24.9
Luc Robitaille	L.A.	21-3-90	L.A. 3	at Van. 6	Kirk McLean	79	79	52	80	
Brian Bellows	Min.	22-3-90	Min. 5	at Det. 1	Tim Cheveldae	75	75	55	80	25.6
Pat LaFontaine	NYI	24-3-90	NYI 5	at Edm. 5	Bill Ranford	71	77	54	74	25.1
Stephane Richer	Mtl.	24-3-90	Mtl. 4	at Hfd. 7	Peter Sidorkiewicz	75	77	51	75	
Gary Leeman	Tor.	28-3-90	NYI 6	at Tor. 3	Mark Fitzpatrick	78	78	51	80	26.1
Brett Hull	St. L.	25-1-91	St. L. 9	at Det. 4	David Gagnon	49	49	86	78	
Cam Neely	Bos.	26-3-91	Bos. 7	at Que. 4	empty net	67	78	51	69	
Theoren Fleury	Cgy.	26-3-91	Van. 2	at Cgy. 7	Bob Mason	77	77	51	79	22.9
Steve Yzerman	Det.	30-3-91	NYR 5	at Det. 6	Mike Richter	79	79	51	80	
Brett Hull	St. L.	28-1-92	St. L. 3	at L.A. 3	Kelly Hrudey	50	50	70	73	
Jeremy Roenick	Chi.	7-3-92	Chi. 2	at Bos. 1	Daniel Berthiaume	67	67	53	80	22.2
Kevin Stevens	Pit.	24-3-92	Pit. 3	at Det. 4	Tim Cheveldae	74	74	54	80	26.11
Gary Roberts	Cgy.	31-3-92	Edm. 2	at Cgy. 5	Bill Ranford	73	77	53	76	25.10
Alexander Mogilny	Buf.	3-2-93	Hfd. 2	at Buf. 3	Sean Burke	46	53	76	77	23.11
Teemu Selanne	Wpg.	28-2-93	Min. 6	at Wpg. 7	Darcy Wakaluk	63	63	76	84	22.6
Pavel Bure	Van.	1-3-93	Van. 5	at Buf. 2*	Grant Fuhr	63	63	60	83	21.11
Steve Yzerman	Det.	10-3-93	Det. 6	at Edm. 3	Bill Ranford	70	70	58	84	
Luc Robitaille	L.A.	15-3-93	L.A. 4	at Buf. 2	Grant Fuhr	69	69	63	84	
Brett Hull	St. L.	20-3-93	St. L. 2	at L.A. 3	Robb Stauber	73	73	54	80	
Mario Lemieux	Pit.	21-3-93	Pit. 6	at Edm. 4**	Ron Tugnutt	48	72	69	60	
Kevin Stevens	Pit.	21-3-93	Pit. 6	at Edm. 4**	Ron Tugnutt	62	72	55	72	
Dave Andreychuk	Tor.	23-3-93	Tor. 5	at Wpg. 4	Bob Essensa	72	73	54	83	29.6
Pat LaFontaine	Buf.	28-3-93	Ott. 1	at Buf. 3	Peter Sidorkiewicz	75	75	53	84	
Pierre Turgeon	NYI	2-4-93	NYI 3	at NYR 2	Mike Richter	75	76	58	83	23.8
Mark Recchi	Phi.	3-4-93	T.B. 2	at Phi. 6	J-C Bergeron	77	77	53	84	25.2
Jeremy Roenick	Chi.	15-4-93	Tor. 2	at Chi. 3	Felix Potvin	84	84	50	84	
Brendan Shanahan	St. L.	15-4-93	T.B. 5	at St. L. 6	Pat Jablonski	71	84	51	71	24.3
Cam Neely	Bos.	7-3-94	Wsh. 3	at Bos. 6	Don Beaupre	44	66	50	49	
Sergei Fedorov	Det.	15-3-94	Van. 2	at Det. 5	Kirk McLean	67	69	56	82	24.3
Pavel Bure	Van.	23-3-94	Van. 6	at L.A. 3	empty net	65	73	60	76	
Adam Graves	NYR	23-3-94	NYR 5	at Edm. 3	Bill Ranford	74	74	51	84	25.11
Dave Andreychuk	Tor	24-3-94	S.J. 2	at Tor. 1	Arturs Irbe	73	74	53	83	
Brett Hull	St.L.	25-3-94	Dal. 3	at St.L. 5	Andy Moog	71	74	52	81	
Ray Sheppard	Det.	29-3-94	Hfd. 2	at Det. 6	Sean Burke	74	76	52	82	27.10
Brendan Shanahan	St.L.	12-4-94	St.L. 5	at Dal. 9	Andy Moog	80	83	52	81	
Mike Modano	Dal.	12-4-94	St.L. 5	at Dal. 9	Curtis Joseph	75	83	50	76	23.11
Mario Lemieux	Pit.	23-2-96	Hfd. 4	at Pit. 5	Sean Burke	50	59	69	70	
Jaromir Jagr	Pit.	23-2-96	Hfd. 4	at Pit. 5	Sean Burke	59	59	62	82	24.0
Alexander Mogilny	Van.	29-2-96	St.L. 2	at Van. 2	Grant Fuhr	60	63	55	79	
Peter Bondra	Wsh.	3-4-96	Wsh. 5	at Buf. 1	Andrei Trefilov	62	77	52	67	28.1
Joe Sakic	Col.	7-4-96	Col. 4	at Dal. 1	empty net	79	79	51	82	26.7
John LeClair	Phi.	10-4-96	Phi. 5	at N.J. 1	Corey Schwab	80	80	51	82	26.7
Keith Tkachuk	Wpg.	12-4-96	L.A. 3	at Wpg. 5	empty net	75	81	50	76	24.0
Paul Kariya	Ana.	14-4-96	Wpg. 2	at Ana. 5	N. Khabibulin	82	82	50	82	21.5
Keith Tkachuk	Phx.	6-4-97	Phx. 1	at Col. 2	Patrick Roy	78	79	52	81	
Teemu Selanne	Ana.	9-4-97	L.A. 1	at Ana. 4	empty net	77	81	51	78	
Mario Lemieux	Pit.	11-4-97	Pit. 2	at Fla. 4	J. Vanbiesbrouck	75	81	50	76	
John LeClair	Phi.	13-4-97	N.J. 4	at Phi. 5	Mike Dunham	82	82	50	82	
Teemu Selanne	Ana.	25-3-98	Ana. 3	at Chi. 2	Jeff Hackett	66	71	52	73	
John LeClair	Phi.	13-4-98	Phi. 1	at Buf. 2	Dominik Hasek	79	79	51	82	
Pavel Bure	Van.	17-4-98	Cgy. 4	at Van. 2	Dwayne Roloson	81	81	51	82	
Peter Bondra	Wsh.	18-4-98	Wsh. 4	at Car. 3	Mike Fountain	75	80	52	76	

Tim Kerr

Mario Lemieux

Gary Leeman

Gordie Howe

Steve Shutt

Wayne Gretzky

100-Point Seasons

Player	Team	Date of 100th Point	G or A	Score	Player's Game No.	Team Game No.	Points G - A PTS	Total Games	Age when first 100th point scored (Yrs. & Mos.)
Phil Esposito	Bos.	2-3-69	(G)	Pit. 0 at Bos. 4	60	62	49-77 — 126	74	27.1
Bobby Hull	Chi.	20-3-69	(G)	Chi. 5 at Bos. 5	71	71	58-49 — 107	76	30.2
Gordie Howe	Det.	30-3-69	(G)	Det. 5 at Chi. 9	76	76	44-59 — 103	76	41.0
Bobby Orr	Bos.	15-3-70	(G)	Det. 5 at Bos. 5	67	67	33-87 — 120	76	22.11
Phil Esposito	Bos.	6-2-71	(A)	Buf. 3 at Bos. 4	51	51	76-76 — 152	78	
Bobby Orr	Bos.	22-2-71	(A)	Bos. 4 at L.A. 5	58	58	37-102 — 139	78	
John Bucyk	Bos.	13-3-71	(G)	Bos. 6 at Van. 3	68	68	51-65 — 116	78	35.10
Ken Hodge	Bos.	21-3-71	(A)	Buf. 7 at Bos. 5	72	72	43-62 — 105	78	26.9
Jean Ratelle	NYR	18-2-72	(A)	NYR 2 at Cal. 2	58	58	46-63 — 109	63	31.4
Phil Esposito	Bos.	19-2-72	(A)	Bos. 6 at Min. 4	59	59	66-67 — 133	76	
Bobby Orr	Bos.	2-3-72	(A)	Van. 3 at Bos. 7	64	64	37-80 — 117	76	
Vic Hadfield	NYR	25-3-72	(A)	NYR 3 at Mtl. 3	74	74	50-56 — 106	78	31.5
Phil Esposito	Bos.	3-3-73	(A)	Bos. 1 at Mtl. 5	64	64	55-75 — 130	78	
Bobby Clarke	Phi.	29-3-73	(G)	Atl. 2 at Phi. 4	76	76	37-67 — 104	78	23.7
Bobby Orr	Bos.	31-3-73	(G)	Bos. 3 at Tor. 7	62	77	29-72 — 101	63	
Rick MacLeish	Phi.	1-4-73	(G)	Phi. 4 at Pit. 5	78	78	50-50 — 100	78	23.3
Phil Esposito	Bos.	13-2-74	(A)	Bos. 9 at Cal. 6	53	53	68-77 — 145	78	
Bobby Orr	Bos.	12-3-74	(A)	Buf. 0 at Bos. 4	62	66	32-90 — 122	74	
Ken Hodge	Bos.	24-3-74	(A)	Mtl. 3 at Bos. 6	72	72	50-55 — 105	76	
Phil Esposito	Bos.	8-2-75	(A)	Bos. 8 at Det. 5	54	54	61-66 — 127	79	
Bobby Orr	Bos.	13-2-75	(A)	Bos. 1 at Buf. 3	57	57	46-89 — 135	80	
Guy Lafleur	Mtl.	7-3-75	(G)	Wsh. 4 at Mtl. 8	56	66	53-66 — 119	70	24.6
Pete Mahovlich	Mtl.	9-3-75	(G)	Mtl. 5 at NYR 3	67	67	35-82 — 117	80	29.5
Marcel Dionne	Det.	9-3-75	(A)	Det. 5 at Phi. 8	67	67	47-74 — 121	80	23.7
Bobby Clarke	Phi.	22-3-75	(A)	Min. 0 at Phi. 4	72	72	27-89 — 116	80	
Rene Robert	Buf.	5-4-75	(A)	Buf. 4 at Tor. 2	74	80	40-60 — 100	74	26.4
Guy Lafleur	Mtl.	10-3-76	(G)	Mtl. 5 at Chi. 1	69	69	56-69 — 125	80	
Bobby Clarke	Phi.	11-3-76	(A)	Buf. 1 at Phi. 6	64	68	30-89 — 119	76	
Bill Barber	Phi.	18-3-76	(A)	Van. 2 at Phi. 3	71	71	50-62 — 112	80	23.8
Gilbert Perreault	Buf.	21-3-76	(A)	K.C. 1 at Buf. 3	73	73	44-69 — 113	80	25.4
Pierre Larouche	Pit.	24-3-76	(G)	Bos. 5 at Pit. 5	70	74	53-58 — 111	76	20.4
Pete Mahovlich	Mtl.	28-3-76	(A)	Mtl. 2 at Bos. 2	77	77	34-71 — 105	80	
Jean Ratelle	Bos.	30-3-76	(G)	Buf. 4 at Bos. 4	77	77	36-69 — 105	80	
Jean Pronovost	Pit.	3-4-76	(A)	Wsh. 5 at Pit. 4	79	79	52-52 — 104	80	30.4
Darryl Sittler	Tor.	3-4-76	(A)	Bos. 4 at Tor. 2	78	79	41-59 — 100	79	26.7
Guy Lafleur	Mtl.	26-2-77	(A)	Clev. 3 at Mtl. 5	63	63	56-80 — 136	80	
Marcel Dionne	L.A.	5-3-77	(G)	Pit. 3 at L.A. 3	67	67	53-69 — 122	80	
Steve Shutt	Mtl.	27-3-77	(A)	Mtl. 6 at Det. 0	77	77	60-45 — 105	80	24.9
Bryan Trottier	NYI	25-2-78	(A)	Chi. 1 at NYI 7	59	60	46-77 — 123	77	21.7
Guy Lafleur	Mtl.	28-2-78	(G)	Det. 3 at Mtl. 9	69	61	60-72 — 132	78	
Darryl Sittler	Tor.	12-3-78	(A)	Tor. 7 at Pit. 1	67	67	45-72 — 117	80	
Guy Lafleur	Mtl.	27-2-79	(A)	Mtl. 3 at NYI 7	61	61	52-77 — 129	80	
Bryan Trottier	NYI	6-3-79	(A)	Buf. 3 at NYI 2	59	63	47-87 — 134	76	
Marcel Dionne	L.A.	8-3-79	(G)	L.A. 4 at Buf. 6	66	66	59-71 — 130	80	
Mike Bossy	NYI	11-3-79	(G)	NYI 4 at Bos. 4	66	66	69-57 — 126	80	22.2
Bob MacMillan	Atl.	15-3-79	(A)	Atl. 4 at Phi. 5	68	69	37-71 — 108	79	26.6
Guy Chouinard	Atl.	30-3-79	(G)	L.A. 3 at Atl. 5	75	75	50-57 — 107	80	22.5
Denis Potvin	NYI	8-4-79	(A)	NYI 5 at NYR 2	73	80	31-70 — 101	73	25.5
Marcel Dionne	L.A.	6-2-80	(A)	L.A. 3 at Hfd. 7	53	53	53-84 — 137	80	
Guy Lafleur	Mtl.	10-2-80	(A)	Mtl. 3 at Bos. 2	55	55	50-75 — 125	74	
Wayne Gretzky	Edm.	24-2-80	(A)	Bos. 4 at Edm. 2	61	62	51-86 — 137	79	19.2
Bryan Trottier	NYI	30-3-80	(A)	NYI 9 at Que. 6	75	77	42-62 — 104	78	
Gilbert Perreault	Buf.	1-4-80	(A)	Buf. 5 at Atl. 2	77	77	40-66 — 106	80	
Mike Rogers	Hfd.	4-4-80	(A)	Que. 2 at Hfd. 9	79	79	44-61 — 105	80	25.5
Charlie Simmer	L.A.	5-4-80	(G)	Van. 5 at L.A. 3	64	80	56-45 — 101	64	26.0
Blaine Stoughton	Hfd.	6-4-80	(A)	Det. 3 at Hfd. 5	80	80	56-44 — 100	80	27.0
Wayne Gretzky	Edm.	6-2-81	(G)	Wpg. 4 at Edm. 10	53	53	55-109 — 164	80	
Marcel Dionne	L.A.	12-2-81	(A)	L.A. 5 at Chi. 5	58	58	58-77 — 135	80	
Charlie Simmer	L.A.	14-2-81	(A)	Bos. 5 at L.A. 4	59	59	56-49 — 105	65	
Kent Nilsson	Cgy.	27-2-81	(G)	Hfd. 1 at Cgy. 5	64	64	49-82 — 131	80	24.6
Mike Bossy	NYI	3-3-81	(G)	Edm. 8 at NYI 8	65	66	68-51 — 119	79	
Dave Taylor	L.A.	14-3-81	(G)	Min. 4 at L.A. 10	63	70	47-65 — 112	72	25.3
Mike Rogers	Hfd.	22-3-81	(G)	Tor. 3 at Hfd. 3	74	74	40-65 — 105	80	
Bernie Federko	St. L.	28-3-81	(A)	Buf. 4 at St. L. 7	74	76	31-73 — 104	78	24.10
Rick Middleton	Bos.	28-3-81	(A)	Chi. 2 at Bos. 5	76	76	44-59 — 103	80	27.4
Jacques Richard	Que.	29-3-81	(G)	Mtl. 0 at Que. 4	75	76	52-51 — 103	78	28.6
Bryan Trottier	NYI	29-3-81	(G)	NYI 5 at Wsh. 4	69	76	31-72 — 103	73	
Peter Stastny	Que.	29-3-81	(A)	Mtl. 0 at Que. 4	73	76	39-70 — 109	77	24.6
Wayne Gretzky	Edm.	27-12-81	(G)	L.A. 3 at Edm. 10	38	38	92-120 — 212	80	
Mike Bossy	NYI	13-2-82	(A)	Phi. 2 at NYI 8	55	55	64-83 — 147	80	
Peter Stastny	Que.	16-2-82	(A)	Wpg. 3 at Que. 7	60	60	46-93 — 139	80	
Dennis Maruk	Wsh.	20-2-82	(G)	Wsh. 3 at Min. 7	60	60	60-76 — 136	80	26.3
Bryan Trottier	NYI	23-2-82	(G)	Chi. 1 at NYI 5	61	61	50-79 — 129	80	
Denis Savard	Chi.	27-2-82	(A)	Chi. 5 at L.A. 3	64	64	32-87 — 119	80	21.1
Bobby Smith	Min.	3-3-82	(A)	Det. 4 at Min. 6	66	66	43-71 — 114	80	24.1
Marcel Dionne	L.A.	6-3-82	(G)	L.A. 6 at Hfd. 7	64	66	50-67 — 117	78	
Dave Taylor	L.A.	20-3-82	(A)	Pit. 5 at L.A. 7	71	72	39-67 — 106	78	
Dale Hawerchuk	Wpg.	24-3-82	(G)	L.A. 3 at Wpg.	74	74	45-58 — 103	80	18.11
Dino Ciccarelli	Min.	27-3-82	(A)	Min. 6 at Bos. 5	72	76	55-52 — 107	76	21.8
Glenn Anderson	Edm.	28-3-82	(G)	Edm. 6 at L.A. 2	78	78	38-67 — 105	80	21.7
Mike Rogers	NYR	2-4-82	(G)	Pit. 7 at NYR 5	79	79	38-65 — 103	80	

Player	Team	Date of 100th Point	G or A	Score	Player's Game No.	Team Game No.	Points G - A PTS	Total Games	Age when first 100th point scored (Yrs. & Mos.)
Wayne Gretzky	Edm.	5-1-83	(A)	Edm. 8 at Wpg. 3	42	42	71-125 — 196	80	
Mike Bossy	NYI	3-3-83	(A)	Tor. 1 at NYI. 5	66	67	60-58 — 118	79	
Peter Stastny	Que.	5-3-83	(A)	Hfd. 3 at Que. 10	62	67	47-77 — 124	75	
Denis Savard	Chi.	6-3-83	(G)	Mtl. 4 at Chi. 5	65	67	35-86 — 121	78	
Mark Messier	Edm.	23-3-83	(G)	Edm. 4 at Wpg. 7	73	76	48-58 — 106	77	22.2
Barry Pederson	Bos.	26-3-83	(A)	Hfd. 4 at Bos. 7	73	76	46-61 — 107	77	22.0
Marcel Dionne	L.A.	26-3-83	(A)	Edm. 9 at L.A. 3	75	75	56-51 — 107	80	
Michel Goulet	Que.	27-3-83	(A)	Que. 6 at Buf. 6	77	77	57-48 — 105	80	22.11
Glenn Anderson	Edm.	29-3-83	(A)	Edm. 7 at Van. 4	70	78	48-56 — 104	72	
Jari Kurri	Edm.	29-3-83	(A)	Edm. 7 at Van. 4	78	78	45-59 — 104	80	22.10
Kent Nilsson	Cgy.	29-3-83	(G)	L.A. 3 at Cgy. 5	78	78	46-58 — 104	80	
Wayne Gretzky	Edm.	18-12-83	(G)	Edm. 7 at Wpg. 5	34	34	87-118 — 205	74	
Paul Coffey	Edm.	4-3-84	(A)	Mtl. 1 at Edm. 6	68	68	40-86 — 126	80	22.9
Michel Goulet	Que.	4-3-84	(A)	Que. 1 at Buf. 1	62	67	56-65 — 121	75	
Jari Kurri	Edm.	7-3-84	(G)	Chi. 4 at Edm. 7	53	69	52-61 — 113	64	
Peter Stastny	Que.	8-3-84	(A)	Que. 8 at Pit. 6	69	69	46-73 — 119	80	
Mike Bossy	NYI	8-3-84	(G)	Tor. 5 at NYI 9	56	68	51-67 — 118	67	
Barry Pederson	Bos.	14-3-84	(A)	Bos. 4 at Det. 2	71	71	39-77 — 116	80	
Bryan Trottier	NYI	18-3-84	(G)	NYI 4 at Hfd. 5	62	73	40-71 — 111	68	
Bernie Federko	St. L.	20-3-84	(A)	Wpg. 3 at St. L. 9	75	76	41-66 — 107	79	
Rick Middleton	Bos.	27-3-84	(G)	Bos. 6 at Que. 4	77	77	47-58 — 105	80	
Dale Hawerchuk	Wpg.	27-3-84	(G)	Wpg. 3 at L.A. 3	77	77	37-65 — 102	80	
Mark Messier	Edm.	27-3-84	(G)	Edm. 9 at Cgy. 2	72	79	37-64 — 101	73	
Wayne Gretzky	Edm.	29-12-84	(A)	Det. 3 at Edm. 6	35	35	73-135 — 208	80	
Jari Kurri	Edm.	29-1-85	(G)	Edm. 4 at Cgy. 2	48	51	71-64 — 135	73	
Mike Bossy	NYI	23-2-85	(G)	Bos. 1 at NYI 7	56	60	58-59 — 117	76	
Dale Hawerchuk	Wpg.	25-2-85	(A)	Wpg. 12 at NYR 5	64	64	53-77 — 130	80	
Marcel Dionne	L.A.	5-3-85	(A)	Pit. 0 at L.A. 6	66	66	46-80 — 126	80	
Brent Sutter	NYI	12-3-85	(A)	NYI 6 at St. L. 5	68	68	42-60 — 102	72	22.10
John Ogrodnick	Det.	22-3-85	(A)	NYR 3 at Det. 5	73	73	55-50 — 105	79	25.9
Paul Coffey	Edm.	26-3-85	(G)	Edm. 7 at NYI 5	74	74	37-84 — 121	80	
Denis Savard	Chi.	29-3-85	(A)	Chi. 5 at Wpg. 5	75	76	38-67 — 105	79	
Peter Stastny	Que.	2-4-85	(A)	Bos. 4 at Que. 6	74	77	32-68 — 100	75	
Bernie Federko	St. L.	4-4-85	(A)	NYR 5 at St. L. 4	74	78	30-73 — 103	76	
John Tonelli	NYI	6-4-85	(G)	NJ 5 at NYI 5	80	80	42-58 — 100	80	28.1
Paul MacLean	Wpg.	6-4-85	(A)	Wpg. 6 at Edm. 5	78	79	41-60 — 101	79	27.1
Bernie Nicholls	L.A.	6-4-85	(A)	Van. 4 at L.A. 4	80	80	46-54 — 100	80	22.9
Mike Gartner	Wsh.	7-4-85	(G)	Pit. 3 at Wsh. 7	80	80	50-52 — 102	80	25.6
Mario Lemieux	Pit.	7-4-85	(G)	Pit. 3 at Wsh. 7	73	80	43-57 — 100	73	19.6
Wayne Gretzky	Edm.	4-1-86	(A)	Hfd. 3 at Edm. 4	39	39	52-163 — 215	80	
Mario Lemieux	Pit.	15-2-86	(G)	Van. 4 at Pit. 9	55	56	48-93 — 141	79	
Paul Coffey	Edm.	19-2-86	(A)	Tor. 5 at Edm. 9	59	60	48-90 — 138	79	
Peter Stastny	Que.	1-3-86	(A)	Buf. 8 at Que. 4	66	68	41-81 — 122	76	
Jari Kurri	Edm.	2-3-86	(G)	Phi. 1 at Edm. 2	62	64	68-63 — 131	78	
Mike Bossy	NYI	8-3-86	(G)	Wsh. 6 at NYI 2	65	65	61-62 — 123	80	
Denis Savard	Chi.	12-3-86	(A)	Buf. 7 at Chi. 6	69	69	47-69 — 116	80	
Mats Naslund	Mtl.	13-3-86	(A)	Mtl. 2 at Bos. 3	70	70	43-67 — 110	80	26.4
Michel Goulet	Que.	24-3-86	(A)	Que. 1 at Min. 0	70	75	53-50 — 103	75	
Glenn Anderson	Edm.	25-3-86	(G)	Edm. 7 at Det. 2	66	74	54-48 — 102	72	
Neal Broten	Min.	26-3-86	(A)	Min. 6 at Tor. 1	76	76	29-76 — 105	80	26.4
Dale Hawerchuk	Wpg	31-3-86	(A)	Wpg. 5 at L.A. 2	78	78	46-59 — 105	80	
Bernie Federko	St. L.	5-4-86	(G)	Chi. 5 at St. L. 7	79	79	34-68 — 102	80	
Wayne Gretzky	Edm.	11-1-87	(A)	Cgy. 3 at Edm. 5	42	42	62-121 — 183	79	
Jari Kurri	Edm.	14-3-87	(A)	Buf. 3 at Edm. 5	67	68	54-54 — 108	79	
Mario Lemieux	Pit.	18-3-87	(A)	St. L. 4 at Pit. 5	55	72	54-53 — 107	63	
Mark Messier	Edm.	19-3-87	(A)	Edm. 4 at Cgy. 5	71	71	37-70 — 107	77	
Dino Ciccarelli	Min.	30-3-87	(A)	NYR 6 at Min. 5	78	78	52-51 — 103	80	
Doug Gilmour	St. L.	2-4-87	(A)	Buf. 3 at St. L. 5	78	78	42-63 — 105	80	23.10
Dale Hawerchuk	Wpg.	5-4-87	(A)	Wpg. 3 at Cgy. 1	80	80	47-53 — 100	80	
Mario Lemieux	Pit.	20-1-88	(G)	Pit. 8 at Chi. 3	45	48	70-98 — 168	77	
Wayne Gretzky	Edm.	11-2-88	(A)	Edm. 7 at Van. 2	43	56	40-109 — 149	64	
Denis Savard	Chi.	12-2-88	(A)	St. L. 3 at Chi. 4	57	57	44-87 — 131	80	
Dale Hawerchuk	Wpg.	23-2-88	(G)	Wpg. 4 at Pit. 3	61	61	44-77 — 121	80	
Steve Yzerman	Det.	27-2-88	(A)	Det. 4 at Que. 5	63	63	50-52 — 102	64	22.10
Peter Stastny	Que.	8-3-88	(A)	Hfd. 4 at Que. 6	63	67	46-65 — 111	76	
Mark Messier	Edm.	15-3-88	(A)	Buf. 4 at Edm. 6	68	71	37-74 — 111	77	
Jimmy Carson	L.A.	26-3-88	(A)	Chi. 5 at L.A. 9	77	77	55-52 — 107	80	19.8
Hakan Loob	Cgy.	26-3-88	(A)	Van. 1 at Cgy. 6	76	76	50-56 — 106	80	27.9
Mike Bullard	Cgy.	26-3-88	(A)	Van. 1 at Cgy. 6	76	76	48-55 — 103	79	27.1
Michel Goulet	Que.	27-3-88	(A)	Pit. 6 at Que. 3	76	76	48-58 — 106	80	
Luc Robitaille	L.A.	30-3-88	(G)	Cgy. 7 at L.A. 9	78	78	53-58 — 111	80	22.1
Mario Lemieux	Pit.	31-12-88	(A)	N.J. 6 at Pit. 8	36	38	85-114 — 199	76	
Wayne Gretzky	L.A.	21-1-89	(A)	L.A. 4 at Hfd. 5	47	48	54-114 — 168	78	
Bernie Nicholls	L.A.	21-1-89	(A)	L.A. 4 at Hfd. 5	48	48	70-80 — 150	79	
Steve Yzerman	Det.	27-1-89	(G)	Tor. 1 at Det. 8	50	50	65-90 — 155	80	
Rob Brown	Pit.	16-3-89	(A)	Pit. 2 at N.J. 1	60	72	49-66 — 115	68	20.11
Paul Coffey	Pit.	20-3-89	(A)	Pit. 2 at Min. 7	69	74	30-83 — 113	75	
Joe Mullen	Cgy.	23-3-89	(A)	L.A. 2 at Cgy. 4	74	75	51-59 — 110	79	32.1
Jari Kurri	Edm.	29-3-89	(A)	Edm. 5 at Van. 2	75	79	44-58 — 102	76	
Jimmy Carson	Edm.	2-4-89	(A)	Edm. 2 at Cgy. 4	80	80	49-51 — 100	80	
Mario Lemieux	Pit.	28-1-90	(G)	Pit. 2 at Buf. 7	50	50	45-78 — 123	59	
Wayne Gretzky	L.A.	30-1-90	(A)	N.J. 2 at L.A. 5	51	51	40-102 — 142	73	
Steve Yzerman	Det.	19-2-90	(A)	Mtl. 5 at Det. 5	61	61	62-65 — 127	79	
Mark Messier	Edm.	20-2-90	(A)	Edm. 4 at Van. 2	62	62	45-84 — 129	79	
Brett Hull	St. L.	3-3-90	(A)	NYI 4 at St. L. 5	67	67	72-41 — 113	80	25.7
Bernie Nicholls	NYR	12-3-90	(A)	L.A. 6 at NYR 2	70	71	39-73 — 112	79	
Pierre Turgeon	Buf.	25-3-90	(G)	N.J. 4 at Buf. 3	76	76	40-66 — 106	80	20.7
Paul Coffey	Pit.	25-3-90	(A)	Pit. 2 at Hfd. 4	77	77	29-74 — 103	80	
Pat LaFontaine	NYI	27-3-90	(G)	Cgy. 4 at NYI 2	72	78	54-51 — 105	74	25.1

Peter Stastny

Bobby Smith

Paul Coffey

John Ogrodnick

Brian Leetch

Jaromir Jagr

Player	Team	Date of 100th Point	G or A	Score	Player's Game No.	Team Game No.	Points G - A PTS	Total Games	Age when first 100th point scored (Yrs. & Mos.)
Adam Oates	St. L.	29-3-90	(G)	Pit 4 at St. L. 5	79	79	23-79 — 102	80	27.7
Joe Sakic	Que.	31-3-90	(G)	Hfd. 3 at Que. 2	79	79	39-63 — 102	80	20.8
Ron Francis	Hfd.	31-3-90	(G)	Hfd. 3 at Que. 2	79	79	32-69 — 101	80	27.0
Luc Robitaille	L.A.	1-4-90	(A)	L.A. 4 at Cgy. 8	80	80	52-49 — 101	80	
Wayne Gretzky	L.A.	30-1-91	(A)	N.J. 4 at L.A. 2	50	51	41-122 — 163	78	
Brett Hull	St. L.	23-2-91	(G)	Bos. 2 at St. L. 9	60	62	86-45 — 131	78	
Mark Recchi	Pit.	5-3-91	(G)	Van. 1 at Pit. 4	66	67	40-73 — 113	78	23.1
Steve Yzerman	Det.	10-3-91	(G)	Det. 4 at St. L. 1	72	72	51-57 — 108	80	
John Cullen	Hfd.	16-3-91	(G)	N.J. 2 at Hfd. 6	71	71	39-71 — 110	78	26.7
Adam Oates	St. L.	17-3-91	(A)	St. L. 4 at Chi. 6	54	73	25-90 — 115	61	
Joe Sakic	Que.	19-3-91	(G)	Edm. 7 at Que. 6	74	74	48-61 — 109	80	
Steve Larmer	Chi.	24-3-91	(A)	Min. 4 at Chi. 5	76	76	44-57 — 101	80	29.9
Theoren Fleury	Cgy.	26-3-91	(G)	Van. 2 at Cgy. 7	77	77	51-53 — 104	79	22.9
Al MacInnis	Cgy.	28-3-91	(A)	Edm. 4 at Cgy. 4	78	78	28-75 — 103	78	27.8
Brett Hull	St. L.	2-3-92	(G)	St. L. 5 at Van. 3	66	66	70-39 — 109	73	
Wayne Gretzky	L.A.	3-3-92	(A)	Phi. 1 at L.A. 4	60	66	31-90 — 121	74	
Kevin Stevens	Pit.	7-3-92	(A)	Pit. 3 at L.A. 5	66	66	54-69 — 123	80	26.11
Mario Lemieux	Pit.	10-3-92	(A)	Cgy. 2 at Pit. 5	53	67	44-87 — 131	64	
Luc Robitaille	L.A.	17-3-92	(A)	Wpg. 4 at L.A. 5	73	73	44-63 — 107	80	
Mark Messier	NYR	22-3-92	(G)	N.J. 3 at NYR 6	74	75	35-72 — 107	79	
Jeremy Roenick	Chi.	29-3-92	(A)	Tor. 1 at Chi. 5	77	77	53-50 — 103	80	22.2
Steve Yzerman	Det.	14-4-92	(G)	Det. 7 at Min. 4	79	80	45-58 — 103	79	
Brian Leetch	NYR	16-4-92	(G)	Pit. 1 at NYR 7	80	80	22-80 — 102	80	24.1
Mario Lemieux	Pit.	31-12-92	(G)	Tor. 3 at Pit. 3	38	39	69-91 — 160	60	
Pat LaFontaine	Buf.	10-2-93	(A)	Buf. 6 at Wpg. 2	55	55	53-95 — 148	84	
Adam Oates	Bos.	14-2-93	(A)	Bos. 3 at T.B. 3	58	58	45-97 — 142	84	
Steve Yzerman	Det.	24-2-93	(A)	Det. 7 at Buf. 10	64	64	58-79 — 137	84	
Pierre Turgeon	NYI	28-2-93	(G)	NYI 7 at Hfd. 6	62	63	58-74 — 132	83	
Doug Gilmour	Tor.	3-3-93	(A)	Min. 1 at Tor. 3	64	64	32-95 — 127	83	
Alexander Mogilny	Buf.	5-3-93	(A)	Hfd. 4 at Buf. 2	58	65	76-51 — 127	77	24.1
Mark Recchi	Phi.	7-3-93	(G)	Phi. 3 at N.J. 7	66	66	53-70 — 123	84	
Teemu Selanne	Wpg.	9-3-93	(G)	Wpg. 4 at T.B. 2	68	68	76-56 — 132	84	22.7
Luc Robitaille	L.A.	15-3-93	(A)	L.A. 4 at Buf. 2	69	69	63-62 — 125	84	
Kevin Stevens	Pit.	23-3-93	(A)	S.J. 2 at Pit. 7	63	73	55-56 — 111	72	
Mats Sundin	Que.	27-3-93	(G)	Phi. 3 at Que. 8	71	75	47-67 — 114	80	22.1
Pavel Bure	Van.	1-4-93	(G)	Van. 5 at T.B. 3	77	77	60-50 — 110	83	22.0
Jeremy Roenick	Chi.	4-4-93	(G)	St. L. 4 at Chi. 5	79	79	50-57 — 107	84	
Craig Janney	St. L.	4-4-93	(G)	St. L. 4 at Chi. 5	79	79	24-82 — 106	84	25.7
Rick Tocchet	Pit.	7-4-93	(G)	Mtl. 3 at Pit. 4	77	81	48-61 — 109	80	28.11
Joe Sakic	Que.	8-4-93	(A)	Que. 2 at Bos. 6	75	81	48-57 — 105	78	
Ron Francis	Pit.	9-4-93	(A)	Pit. 10 at NYR 4	82	82	24-76 — 100	84	
Brett Hull	St. L.	11-4-93	(G)	Min. 1 at St. L. 5	78	82	54-47 — 101	80	
Theoren Fleury	Cgy.	11-4-93	(G)	Cgy. 3 at Van. 6	82	82	34-66 — 100	83	
Joe Juneau	Bos.	14-4-93	(A)	Bos. 4 at Ott. 2	84	84	32-70 — 102	84	25.3
Wayne Gretzky	L.A.	14-2-94	(A)	Bos. 3 at L.A. 2	56	56	38-92 — 130	81	
Sergei Fedorov	Det.	1-3-94	(A)	Cgy. 2 at Det. 5	63	63	56-64 — 120	82	24.2
Doug Gilmour	Tor.	23-3-94	(G)	Tor. 1 at Fla. 1	74	74	27-84 — 111	83	
Adam Oates	Bos.	26-3-94	(A)	Mtl. 3 at Bos. 6	68	75	32-80 — 112	77	
Mark Recchi	Phi.	27-3-94	(A)	Ana. 3 at Phi. 2	76	76	40-67 — 107	84	
Pavel Bure	Van.	28-3-94	(A)	Tor. 2 at Van. 3	68	76	60-47 — 107	76	
Jeremy Roenick	Chi.	31-3-94	(G)	Chi. 3 at Wsh. 6	78	78	46-61 — 107	84	
Brendan Shanahan	St.L.	12-4-94	(G)	St.L. 5 at Dal. 9	80	83	52-50 — 102	81	25.2
Mario Lemieux	Pit.	16-1-96	(G)	Col. 5 at Pit. 2	38	44	69-92 — 161	70	
Jaromir Jagr	Pit.	6-2-96	(G)	Bos. 5 at Pit. 6	52	52	62-87 — 149	82	23.12
Ron Francis	Pit.	9-3-96	(A)	N.J. 4 at Pit. 3	61	66	27-92 — 119	77	
Peter Forsberg	Col.	9-3-96	(A)	Col. 7 at Van. 5	68	68	30-86 — 116	82	22.7
Joe Sakic	Col.	17-3-96	(A)	Edm. 1 at Col. 8	70	70	51-69 — 120	82	
Teemu Selanne	Ana.	25-3-96	(A)	Ana. 1 at Det. 5	70	73	40-68 — 108	79	
Alexander Mogilny	Van.	25-3-96	(A)	L.A. 1 at Van. 4	72	75	55-52 — 107	79	
Eric Lindros	Phi.	25-3-96	(A)	Hfd. 0 at Phi. 3	65	73	47-68 — 115	73	23.0
Wayne Gretzky	St.L.	28-3-96	(A)	N.J. 4 at St.L. 4	76	75	23-79 — 102	80	
Doug Weight	Edm.	30-3-96	(G)	Tor. 4 at Edm. 3	76	76	25-79 — 104	82	25.3
Sergei Fedorov	Det.	2-4-96	(A)	Det. 3 at S.J. 6	72	76	39-68 — 107	78	
Paul Kariya	Ana.	7-4-96	(G)	Ana. 5 at S.J. 3	78	78	50-58 — 108	82	21.5
Mario Lemieux	Pit.	8-3-97	(A)	Phi. 2 at Pit. 3	61	65	50-72 — 122	76	
Teemu Selanne	Ana.	1-4-97	(A)	Chi. 3 at Ana. 3	74	78	51-58 — 109	78	
Jaromir Jagr	Pit.	15-4-98	(G)	T.B. 1 at Pit. 5	76	80	35-67 — 102	77	

Darryl Sittler, seen here battling the Los Angles Kings during the 1975 playoffs, is the last NHL player to score six goals in a single game. The Toronto captain victimized Boston rookie netminder Dave Reece for a league record six goals and four assists in an 11-4 Leaf win on February 7, 1976.

Five-or-more-Goal Games

Player	Team	Date	Score		Opposing Goaltender
SEVEN GOALS					
Joe Malone	Quebec Bulldogs	Jan. 31/20	Tor. 6	at Que. 10	Ivan Mitchell
SIX GOALS					
Newsy Lalonde	Montreal	Jan. 10/20	Tor. 7	at Mtl. 14	Ivan Mitchell
Joe Malone	Quebec Bulldogs	Mar. 10/20	Ott. 4	at Que. 10	Clint Benedict
Corb Denneny	Toronto St. Pats	Jan. 26/21	Ham. 3	at Tor. 10	Howard Lockhart
Cy Denneny	Ottawa Senators	Mar. 7/21	Ham. 5	at Ott. 12	Howard Lockhart
Syd Howe	Detroit	Feb. 3/44	NYR 2	at Det. 12	Ken McAuley
Red Berenson	St. Louis	Nov. 7/68	St. L. 8	at Phil 0	Doug Favell
Darryl Sittler	Toronto	Feb. 7/76	Bos. 4	at Tor. 11	Dave Reece
FIVE GOALS					
Joe Malone	Montreal	Dec. 19/17	Mtl. 7	at Ott. 4	Clint Benedict
Harry Hyland	Mtl. Wanderers	Dec. 19/17	Tor. 9	at Mtl. W. 10	Arthur Brooks
Joe Malone	Montreal	Jan. 12/18	Ott. 4	at Mtl. 9	Clint Benedict
Joe Malone	Montreal	Feb. 2/18	Tor. 2	at Mtl. 11	Harry Holmes
Mickey Roach	Toronto St. Pats	Mar. 6/20	Que. 2	at Tor. 11	Frank Brophy
Newsy Lalonde	Montreal	Feb. 16/21	Ham. 5	at Mtl. 10	Howard Lockhart
Babe Dye	Toronto St. Pats	Dec. 16/22	Mtl. 2	at Tor. 7	Georges Vezina
Red Green	Hamilton Tigers	Dec. 5/24	Ham. 10	at Tor. 3	John Ross Roach
Babe Dye	Toronto St. Pats	Dec. 22/24	Tor. 10	at Bos. 1	Charles Stewart
Harry Broadbent	Mtl. Maroons	Jan. 7/25	Mtl. 6	at Ham. 2	Jake Forbes
Pit Lepine	Montreal	Dec. 14/29	Ott. 4	at Mtl. 6	Alex Connell
Howie Morenz	Montreal	Mar. 18/30	NYA 3	at Mtl. 8	Roy Worters
Charlie Conacher	Toronto	Jan. 19/32	NYA 3	at Tor. 11	Roy Worters
Ray Getliffe	Montreal	Feb. 6/43	Bos. 3	at Mtl. 8	Frank Brimsek
Maurice Richard	Montreal	Dec. 28/44	Det. 1	at Mtl. 9	Harry Lumley
Howie Meeker	Toronto	Jan. 8/47	Chi. 4	at Tor. 10	Paul Bibeault
Bernie Geoffrion	Montreal	Feb. 19/55	NYR 2	at Mtl. 10	Gump Worsley
Bobby Rousseau	Montreal	Feb. 1/64	Det. 3	at Mtl. 9	Roger Crozier
Yvan Cournoyer	Montreal	Feb. 15/75	Chi. 3	at Mtl. 12	Mike Veisor
Don Murdoch	NY Rangers	Oct. 12/76	NYR 10	at Min. 4	Gary Smith
Ian Turnbull	Toronto	Feb. 2/77	Det. 1	at Tor. 9	Ed Giacomin (2) Jim Rutherford (3)
Bryan Trottier	NY Islanders	Dec. 23/78	NYR 4	at NYI 9	Wayne Thomas (4) John Davidson (1)
Tim Young	Minnesota	Jan. 15/79	Min. 8	at NYR 1	Doug Soetaert (3) Wayne Thomas (2)
John Tonelli	NY Islanders	Jan. 6/81	Tor. 3	at NYI 6	Jiri Crha (4) empty net (1)
Wayne Gretzky	Edmonton	Feb. 18/81	St. L. 2	at Edm. 9	Mike Liut (3) Ed Staniowski (2)
Wayne Gretzky	Edmonton	Dec. 30/81	Phi. 5	at Edm. 7	Pete Peeters (4) empty net (1)
Grant Mulvey	Chicago	Feb. 3/82	St. L. 5	at Chi. 9	Mike Liut (4) Gary Edwards (1)
Bryan Trottier	NY Islanders	Feb. 13/82	Phi. 2	at NYI 8	Pete Peeters
Willy Lindstrom	Winnipeg	Mar. 2/82	Wpg. 7	at Phi. 6	Pete Peeters
Mark Pavelich	NY Rangers	Feb. 23/83	Hfd. 3	at NYR 11	Greg Millen
Jari Kurri	Edmonton	Nov. 19/83	NJ. 4	at Edm. 13	Glenn Resch (3) Ron Low (2)
Bengt Gustafsson	Washington	Jan. 8/84	Wsh. 7	at Phi. 1	Pelle Lindbergh
Pat Hughes	Edmonton	Feb. 3/84	Cgy. 5	at Edm. 10	Don Edwards (3) Rejean Lemelin (2)
Wayne Gretzky	Edmonton	Dec. 15/84	Edm. 8	at St. L. 2	Rick Wamsley (4) Mike Liut(1)
Dave Andreychuk	Buffalo	Feb. 6/86	Buf. 8	at Bos. 6	Pat Riggin (1) Doug Keans (4)
Wayne Gretzky	Edmonton	Dec. 6/87	Min. 4	at Edm. 10	Don Beaupre (4) Kari Takko (1)
Mario Lemieux	Pittsburgh	Dec. 31/88	N.J. 6	at Pit. 8	Bob Sauve (3) Chris Terreri (2)
Joe Nieuwendyk	Calgary	Jan. 11/89	Wpg. 3	at Cgy. 8	Daniel Berthiaume
Mats Sundin	Quebec	Mar. 5/92	Que. 10	at Hfd. 4	Peter Sidorkiewicz (3) Kay Whitmore (2)
Mario Lemieux	Pittsburgh	Apr. 9/93	Pit. 10	at NYR 4	Corey Hirsch (3) Mike Richter (2)
Peter Bondra	Washington	Feb. 5/94	T.B. 3	at Wsh. 6	Darren Puppa (4) Pat Jablonski (1)
Mike Ricci	Quebec	Feb. 17/94	Que. 8	at S.J. 2	Arturs Irbe (3) Jimmy Waite (2)
Alexei Zhamnov	Winnipeg	Apr. 1/95	Wpg. 7	at L.A. 7	Kelly Hrudey (3) Grant Fuhr (2)
Mario Lemieux	Pittsburgh	Mar. 26/96	St. L. 4	at Pit. 8	Grant Fuhr (1) Jon Casey (4)
Sergei Fedorov	Detroit	Dec. 26/96	Wsh. 4	at Det. 5	Jim Carey

Players' 500th Goals

Regular Season

Player	Team	Date	Game No.	Score		Opposing Goaltender	Total Goals	Total Games
Maurice Richard	Montreal	Oct. 19/57	863	Chi. 1	at Mtl. 3	Glenn Hall	544	978
Gordie Howe	Detroit	Mar. 14/62	1,045	Det. 2	at NYR 3	Gump Worsley	801	1,767
Bobby Hull	Chicago	Feb. 21/70	861	NYR. 2	at Chi. 4	Ed Giacomin	610	1,063
Jean Béliveau	Montreal	Feb. 11/71	1,101	Min. 2	at Mtl. 6	Gilles Gilbert	507	1,125
Frank Mahovlich	Montreal	Mar. 21/73	1,105	Van. 2	at Mtl. 3	Dunc Wilson	533	1,181
Phil Esposito	Boston	Dec. 22/74	803	Det. 4	at Bos. 5	Jim Rutherford	717	1,282
John Bucyk	Boston	Oct. 30/75	1,370	St. L. 2	at Bos. 3	Yves Bélanger	556	1,540
Stan Mikita	Chicago	Feb. 27/77	1,221	Van. 4	at Chi. 3	Cesare Maniago	541	1,394
Marcel Dionne	Los Angeles	Dec. 14/82	887	L.A. 2	at Wsh. 7	Al Jensen	731	1,348
Guy Lafleur	Montreal	Dec. 20/83	918	Mtl. 6	at N.J. 0	Glenn Resch	560	1,126
Mike Bossy	NY Islanders	Jan. 2/86	647	Bos. 5	at NYI 7	empty net	573	752
Gilbert Perreault	Buffalo	Mar. 9/86	1,159	NJ 3	at Buf. 4	Alain Chevrier	512	1,191
*Wayne Gretzky	Edmonton	Nov. 22/86	575	Van. 2	at Edm. 5	empty net	885	1,417
Lanny McDonald	Calgary	Mar. 21/89	1,107	NYI 1	at Cgy. 4	Mark Fitzpatrick	500	1,111
Bryan Trottier	NY Islanders	Feb. 13/90	1,104	Cgy. 4	at NYI 2	Rick Wamsley	524	1,279
Mike Gartner	NY Rangers	Oct. 14/91	936	Wsh. 5	at NYR 3	Mike Liut	708	1,432
Michel Goulet	Chicago	Feb. 16/92	951	Cgy. 5	at Chi. 5	Jeff Reese	548	1,089
Jari Kurri	Los Angeles	Oct. 17/92	833	Bos. 6	at L.A. 8	empty net	601	1,251
*Dino Ciccarelli	Detroit	Jan. 8/94	946	Det. 6	at L.A. 3	Kelly Hrudey	602	1,218
Mario Lemieux	Pittsburgh	Oct. 26/95	605	Pit. 7	at NYI 5	Tommy Soderstrom	613	745
*Mark Messier	NY Rangers	Nov. 6/95	1,141	Cgy. 2	at NYR 4	Rick Tabaracci	597	1,354
*Steve Yzerman	Detroit	Jan. 17/96	906	Col. 2	at Det. 3	Patrick Roy	563	1,098
Dale Hawerchuk	St. Louis	Jan. 31/96	1,103	St. L. 4	at Tor. 0	Felix Potvin	518	1,188
*Brett Hull	St. Louis	Dec. 22/96	693	L.A. 4	at St. L. 7	Stephane Fiset	554	801
Joe Mullen	Pittsburgh	Mar. 14/97	1,052	Pit. 3	at Col. 6	Patrick Roy	502	1,062
*Dave Andreychuk	New Jersey	Mar. 15/97	1,070	Wsh. 2	at N.J. 3	Bill Ranford	517	1,158

*Active

Above: Long-time Capitals captain Dale Hunter became the third Washington player to reach the 1000-point milestone during the 1997-98 season when he rammed home the insurance marker in the Capitals' 5-3 win over the New York Rangers on January 8, 1998. Hunter, who has spent 11 years in the Capitals' organization, joined well-travelled veterans Phil Housley and Adam Oates, below, as the newest members of the NHL's exclusive 1000-point club.

Players' 1,000th Points

Regular Season

Player	Team	Date	Game No.	G or A	Score		Total Points G A PTS	Total Games
Gordie Howe	Detroit	Nov. 27/60	938	(A)	Tor. 0	at Det. 2	801-1,049–1,850	1,767
Jean Béliveau	Montreal	Mar. 3/68	911	(G)	Mtl. 2	at Det. 5	507-712–1,219	1,125
Alex Delvecchio	Detroit	Feb. 16/69	1,143	(A)	LA 3	at Det. 6	456-825–1,281	1,549
Bobby Hull	Chicago	Dec. 12/70	909	(A)	Minn. 3	at Chi. 5	610-560–1,170	1,063
Norm Ullman	Toronto	Oct. 16/71	1,113	(A)	NYR 5	at Tor. 3	490-739–1,229	1,410
Stan Mikita	Chicago	Oct. 15/72	924	(A)	St.L. 3	at Chi. 1	541-926–1,467	1,394
John Bucyk	Boston	Nov. 9/72	1,144	(G)	Det. 3	at Bos. 8	556-813–1,369	1,540
Frank Mahovlich	Montreal	Feb. 17/73	1,090	(A)	Phi. 7	at Mtl. 6	533-570–1,103	1,181
Henri Richard	Montreal	Dec. 20/73	1,194	(A)	Mtl. 2	at Buf. 2	358-688–1,046	1,256
Phil Esposito	Boston	Feb. 15/74	745	(A)	Bos. 4	at Van. 2	717-873–1,590	1,282
Rod Gilbert	NY Rangers	Feb. 19/77	1,027	(G)	NYR 2	at NYI 5	406-615–1,021	1,065
Jean Ratelle	Boston	Apr. 3/77	1,007	(A)	Tor. 4	at Bos. 7	491-776–1,267	1,281
Marcel Dionne	Los Angeles	Jan. 7/81	740	(G)	L.A. 5	at Hfd. 3	731-1,040–1,771	1,348
Guy Lafleur	Montreal	Mar. 4/81	720	(G)	Mtl. 9	at Wpg. 3	560-793–1,353	1,126
Bobby Clarke	Philadelphia	Mar. 19/81	922	(G)	Bos. 3	at Phi. 5	358-852–1,210	1,144
Gilbert Perreault	Buffalo	Apr. 3/82	871	(A)	Buf. 5	at Mtl.4	512-814–1,326	1,191
Darryl Sittler	Philadelphia	Jan. 20/83	927	(G)	Cgy 2	at Phi. 5	484-637–1,121	1,096
*Wayne Gretzky	Edmonton	Dec. 19/84	424	(A)	L.A. 3	at Edm. 7	885-1,910–2,795	1,417
Bryan Trottier	NY Islanders	Jan. 29/85	726	(G)	Min. 4	at NYI 4	524-901–1,425	1,279
Mike Bossy	NY Islanders	Jan. 24/86	656	(A)	NYI 7	at Wsh. 5	573-553–1,126	752
Denis Potvin	NY Islanders	Apr. 4/87	987	(G)	Buf. 6	at NYI 6	310-742–1,052	1,060
Bernie Federko	St. Louis	Mar 19/88	855	(A)	Hfd. 5	at St.L. 3	369-761–1,130	1,000
Lanny McDonald	Calgary	Mar. 7/89	1,101	(G)	Wpg. 5	at Cgy. 9	500-506–1,006	1,111
Peter Stastny	Quebec	Oct. 19/89	682	(G)	Que. 5	at Chi. 3	450-789–1,239	977
Jari Kurri	Edmonton	Jan. 2/90	716	(A)	Edm. 6	at St.L. 4	601-797–1,398	1,251
Denis Savard	Chicago	Mar. 11/90	727	(A)	St.L. 6	at Chi. 4	473-865–1,338	1,196
*Paul Coffey	Pittsburgh	Dec. 22/90	770	(A)	Pit. 4	at NYI 3	383-1,090–1,473	1,268
*Mark Messier	Edmonton	Jan. 13/91	822	(A)	Edm. 5	at Phi. 3	597-1,015–1,612	1,354
Dave Taylor	Los Angeles	Feb. 5/91	930	(A)	L.A. 3	at Phi. 2	431-638–1,069	1,111
Michel Goulet	Chicago	Feb. 23/91	878	(G)	Chi. 3	at Min. 3	548-604–1,152	1,089
Dale Hawerchuk	Buffalo	Mar. 8/91	781	(G)	Chi. 5	at Buf. 3	518-891–1,409	1,188
Bobby Smith	Minnesota	Nov. 30/91	986	(A)	Min. 4	at Tor. 3	357-679–1,036	1,077
Mike Gartner	NY Rangers	Jan. 4/92	971	(G)	NYR 4	at N.J. 6	708-627–1,335	1,432
*Ray Bourque	Boston	Feb. 29/92	933	(A)	Wsh. 5	at Bos. 5	375-1,036–1,411	1,372
Mario Lemieux	Pittsburgh	Mar. 24/92	513	(A)	Pit. 3	at Det. 4	613-881–1,494	745
Glenn Anderson	Toronto	Feb. 22/93	954	(G)	Tor. 8	at Van. 1	498-601–1,099	1,129
*Steve Yzerman	Detroit	Feb. 24/93	737	(A)	Det. 7	at Buf. 10	563-846–1,409	1,098
*Ron Francis	Pittsburgh	Oct. 28/93	893	(G)	Que. 7	at Pit. 3	428-1,006–1,434	1,247
*Bernie Nicholls	New Jersey	Feb. 13/94	858	(G)	N.J. 3	at T.B. 3	475-732–1,207	1,117
*Dino Ciccarelli	Detroit	Mar. 9/94	957	(G)	Det. 5	at Cgy. 1	602-591–1,193	1,218
Brian Propp	Hartford	Mar. 19/94	1,008	(G)	Hfd. 5	at Phi. 3	425-579–1,004	1,016
Joe Mullen	Pittsburgh	Feb. 7/95	935	(A)	Fla. 3	at Pit. 7	502-561–1,063	1,062
Steve Larmer	NY Rangers	Mar. 8/95	983	(A)	N.J. 4	at NYR 6	441-571–1,012	1,006
*Doug Gilmour	Toronto	Dec. 23/95	935	(A)	Edm. 1	at Tor. 6	381-795–1,176	1,125
*Larry Murphy	Toronto	Mar. 27/96	1,228	(G)	Tor. 6	at Van. 2	265-838–1,103	1,397
*Dave Andreychuk	New Jersey	Apr. 7/96	998	(G)	NYR 2	at N.J. 4	517-595–1,112	1,158
*Adam Oates	Washington	Oct. 8/97	830	(G)	Wsh. 6	at NYI 3	276-796–1,072	908
*Phil Housley	Washington	Nov. 8/97	1,081	(A)	Edm. 1	at Wsh. 2	291-730–1,021	1,131
*Dale Hunter	Washington	Jan. 9/98	1,308	(A)	Phi. 1	at Wsh. 4	321-688–1,009	1,345
Pat Lafontaine	NY Rangers	Jan. 22/98	847	(G)	Phi. 4	at NYR 3	468-545–1,013	865
*Luc Robitaille	Los Angeles	Jan. 29/98	882	(A)	Cgy. 3	at L.A. 5	478-524–1,002	889
*Al MacInnis	St. Louis	Apr. 7/98	1,056	(A)	St. L. 3	at Det. 5	270-733–1,003	1,060

*Active

Individual Awards

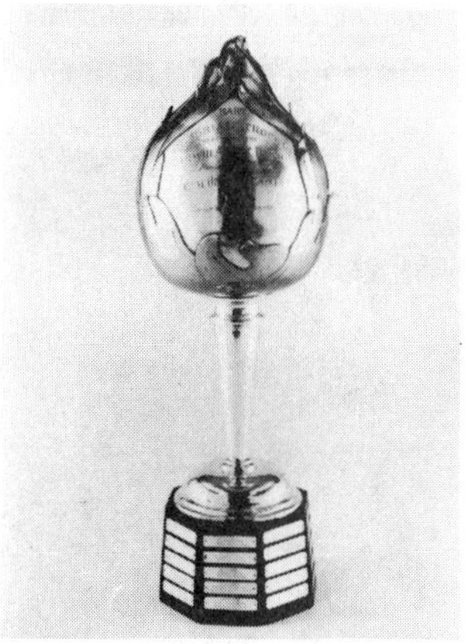

Hart Memorial Trophy

Art Ross Trophy

Calder Memorial Trophy

James Norris Memorial Trophy

HART MEMORIAL TROPHY

An annual award "to the player adjudged to be the most valuable to his team." Winner selected in poll by the Professional Hockey Writers' Association in the 26 NHL cities at the end of the regular schedule. The winner receives $10,000 and the runners-up $6,000 and $4,000.

History: The Hart Memorial Trophy was presented by the National Hockey League in 1960 after the original Hart Trophy was retired to the Hockey Hall of Fame. The original Hart Trophy was donated to the NHL in 1923 by Dr. David A. Hart, father of Cecil Hart, former manager-coach of the Montreal Canadiens.

1997-98 Winner: **Dominik Hasek, Buffalo Sabres**
Runners-up: **Jaromir Jagr, Pittsburgh Penguins**
Teemu Selanne, Mighty Ducks of Anaheim

Dominik Hasek of the Buffalo Sabres captured the Hart Memorial Trophy for the second straight year. Hasek was a top-five selection on all 54 ballots, attracting 43 first-place votes and 499 total points. He becomes the first goaltender in NHL history to win the Hart Trophy more than once and is the only multiple trophy winner of 1997-98, having captured the Vezina Trophy.

Hasek led NHL goaltenders with 13 shutouts, the most in a single season since Tony Esposito had 15 in 1969-70 with Chicago. He posted the league's top save percentage for the fifth consecutive year, stopping 93.2% of the shots he faced. He finished third in wins (with a 33-23-13 record in 72 games) and fourth in goals-against average (2.09).

CALDER MEMORIAL TROPHY

An annual award "to the player selected as the most proficient in his first year of competition in the National Hockey League." Winner selected in poll by the Professional Hockey Writers' Association at the end of the regular schedule. The winner receives $10,000 and the runners-up $6,000 and $4,000.

History: From 1936-37 until his death in 1943, Frank Calder, NHL President, bought a trophy each year to be given permanently to the outstanding rookie. After Calder's death, the NHL presented the Calder Memorial Trophy in his memory and the trophy is to be kept in perpetuity. To be eligible for the award, a player cannot have played more than 25 games in any single preceding season nor in six or more games in each of any two preceding seasons in any major professional league. Beginning in 1990-91, to be eligible for this award a player must not have attained his twenty-sixth birthday by September 15th of the season in which he is eligible.

1997-98 Winner: **Sergei Samsonov, Boston Bruins**
Runners-up: **Mattias Ohlund, Vancouver Canucks**
Patrick Elias, New Jersey Devils

Left winger Sergei Samsonov of the Boston Bruins was selected as the winner of the Calder Memorial Trophy. He was a top-five selection on all 54 ballots and polled 503 points, well ahead of Vancouver Canucks defenseman Mattias Ohlund who was second with 308 points.

Samsonov appeared in 81 of Boston's 82 games and led all rookie scorers with 22 goals. He is the third Russian winner of the award, following Sergei Makarov in 1990 and Pavel Bure in 1992. Selected as the International Hockey League's rookie of the year in 1997, Samsonov is the first player to capture the IHL and NHL awards as top rookie in consecutive years.

ART ROSS TROPHY

An annual award "to the player who leads the league in scoring points at the end of the regular season." The winner receives $10,000 and the runners-up $6,000 and $4,000.

History: Arthur Howie Ross, former manager-coach of Boston Bruins, presented the trophy to the National Hockey League in 1947. If two players finish the schedule with the same number of points, the trophy is awarded in the following manner: 1. Player with most goals. 2. Player with fewer games played. 3. Player scoring first goal of the season.

1997-98 Winner: **Jaromir Jagr, Pittsburgh Penguins**
Runners-up: **Peter Forsberg, Colorado Avalanche**
Pavel Bure, Vancouver Canucks

Right winger Jaromir Jagr of the Pittsburgh Penguins received the Art Ross Trophy for the second time after tallying 102 points (35 goals, 67 assists) in 77 games in 1997-98. The season marked the second time in Jagr's career that he reached the 100-point mark. His total of 67 assists tied him for the league lead with Wayne Gretzky of the New York Rangers. The Klano, Czech Republic native made history by winning the Art Ross Trophy for the first time in 1995, becoming the first European-trained player to capture the award.

JAMES NORRIS MEMORIAL TROPHY

An annual award "to the defense player who demonstrates throughout the season the greatest all-round ability in the position." Winner selected in poll by the Professional Hockey Writers' Association at the end of the regular schedule. The winner receives $10,000 and the runners-up $6,000 and $4,000.

History: The James Norris Memorial Trophy was presented in 1953 by the four children of the late James Norris in memory of the former owner-president of the Detroit Red Wings.

1997-98 Winner: **Rob Blake, Los Angeles Kings**
Runners-up: **Nicklas Lidstrom, Detroit Red Wings**
Chris Pronger, St. Louis Blues

Rob Blake of the Los Angeles Kings won the Norris Trophy for the first time in his career. He was named on 50 of 54 ballots, including 27 first-place votes, and earned 401 points in finishing ahead of second-place Nicklas Lidstrom of the Detroit Red Wings. Lidstrom was named on 52 of the 54 ballots and polled 369 points, while third-place finisher Chris Pronger of the St. Louis Blues received 316 points.

Blake played in 81 of 82 games for the Kings, leading all defensemen in goal scoring with a career-high 23 goals and finishing eighth in points with 50. The Kings finished the regular season with a 20-point improvement over 1996-97, the second-largest gain in the NHL.

Vezina Trophy

Lady Byng Memorial Trophy

Frank J. Selke Trophy

Conn Smythe Trophy

VEZINA TROPHY

An annual award "to the goalkeeper adjudged to be the best at his position" as voted by the general managers of each of the 26 clubs. Over-all winner receives $10,000, runners-up $6,000 and $4,000.

History: Leo Dandurand, Louis Letourneau and Joe Cattarinich, former owners of the Montreal Canadiens, presented the trophy to the National Hockey League in 1926-27 in memory of Georges Vezina, outstanding goalkeeper of the Canadiens who collapsed during an NHL game on November 28, 1925, and died of tuberculosis a few months later. Until the 1981-82 season, the goalkeeper(s) of the team allowing the fewest number of goals during the regular season were awarded the Vezina Trophy.

1997-98 Winner: **Dominik Hasek, Buffalo Sabres**
Runners-up: **Martin Brodeur, New Jersey Devils**
Tom Barrasso, Pittsburgh Penguins

Dominik Hasek of the Buffalo Sabres captured the Vezina Trophy for the second year in a row and the fourth time in his career. Hasek was a runaway winner in this year's balloting, having been named on all 26 ballots and receiving 24 of 26 first-place votes for a total of 126 points. Martin Brodeur of the New Jersey Devils finished as the runner-up. Brodeur earned votes on 21 of 26 ballots, including two first-place votes, and finished with 57 points, ahead of third-place finisher Tom Barrasso of the Pittsburgh Penguins (26 points).

Hasek becomes the first four-time winner of the Vezina Trophy since the current criteria for the award were established in 1981-82.

CONN SMYTHE TROPHY

An annual award "to the most valuable player for his team in the playoffs." Winner selected by the Professional Hockey Writers' Association at the conclusion of the final game in the Stanley Cup Finals. The winner receives $10,000.

History: Presented by Maple Leaf Gardens Limited in 1964 to honor Conn Smythe, the former coach, manager, president and owner-governor of the Toronto Maple Leafs.

1997-98 Winner: **Steve Yzerman, Detroit Red Wings**

Steve Yzerman captured his first major NHL award when he was presented with the Conn Smythe Trophy following Detroit's second consecutive Stanley Cup victory in 1997. The popular Red Wings captain led all playoff performers with 18 assists and 24 points.

LADY BYNG MEMORIAL TROPHY

An annual award "to the player adjudged to have exhibited the best type of sportsmanship and gentlemanly conduct combined with a high standard of playing ability." Winner selected in poll by the Professional Hockey Writers' Association at the end of the regular schedule. The winner receives $10,000 and the runners-up $6,000 and $4,000.

History: Lady Byng, wife of Canada's Governor-General at the time, presented the Lady Byng Trophy in 1925. After Frank Boucher of the New York Rangers won the award seven times in eight seasons, he was given the trophy to keep and Lady Byng donated another trophy in 1936. After Lady Byng's death in 1949, the National Hockey League presented a new trophy, changing the name to Lady Byng Memorial Trophy.

1997-98 Winner: **Ron Francis, Pittsburgh Penguins**
Runners-up: **Teemu Selanne, Mighty Ducks of Anaheim**
Craig Conroy, St. Louis Blues

Center Ron Francis of the Pittsburgh Penguins (now with the Carolina Hurricanes) won the Lady Byng Memorial Trophy for the second time in his career. He was named on 48 of the 54 ballots and received 352 points to edge Anaheim winger Teemu Selanne, runner-up for the second consecutive year with 288 points. Francis again finished among the NHL's scoring leaders in 1997-98 by posting 87 points (25 goals, 62 assists) in 81 games and received just 20 minutes in penalties. He became the seventh player in NHL history to reach 1,000 career assists on March 21 vs. Philadelphia and the 11th player to record 1,400 career points on January 29 at Boston.

FRANK J. SELKE TROPHY

An annual award "to the forward who best excels in the defensive aspects of the game." Winner selected in poll by the Professional Hockey Writers' Association at the end of the regular schedule. The winner receives $10,000 and the runners-up $6,000 and $4,000.

History: Presented to the National Hockey League in 1977 by the Board of Governors of the NHL in honor of Frank J. Selke, one of the great architects of NHL championship teams.

1997-98 Winner: **Jere Lehtinen, Dallas Stars**
Runners-up: **Michael Peca, Buffalo Sabres**
Craig Conroy, St. Louis Blues

Right winger Jere Lehtinen of the Dallas Stars was awarded the 1997-98 Frank J. Selke Trophy. He received votes on 46 of 54 ballots for 328 points, edging last year's Selke Trophy winner Michael Peca of the Buffalo Sabres (297) in the closest trophy race of the year. Lehtinen had finished third in Selke balloting in 1996-97, his first year as an NHL Trophy finalist.

Playing in his third NHL season, Lehtinen finished third among Dallas forwards in plus-minus at +19, helping the Stars allow the second fewest goals in the league (167). Other Stars personnel to have won the Selke Trophy include general manager Bob Gainey, assistant coach Doug Jarvis and center Guy Carbonneau.

WILLIAM M. JENNINGS TROPHY

An annual award "to the goalkeeper(s) having played a minimum of 25 games for the team with the fewest goals scored against it." Winners selected on regular-season play. Overall winner receives $10,000, runners-up $6,000 and $4,000.

History: The Jennings Trophy was presented in 1981-82 by the National Hockey League's Board of Governors to honor the late William M. Jennings, longtime governor and president of the New York Rangers and one of the great builders of hockey in the United States.

1997-98 Winner: **Martin Brodeur, New Jersey Devils**
Runners-up: **Ed Belfour, Dallas Stars**
Dominik Hasek, Buffalo Sabres

Goaltender Martin Brodeur of the New Jersey Devils was presented with the William M. Jennings Trophy for the second year in a row, having shared the award with former teammate Mike Dunham in 1996-97. Brodeur appeared in 70 of New Jersey's 82 games in 1997-98 and helped the Devils post the league's best defensive record, allowing only 166 goals. He led all netminders with 43 wins as New Jersey captured its second straight Eastern Conference regular-season title. Brodeur finished second in the NHL behind Ed Belfour with a 1.89 goals-against average, second in shutouts behind Dominik Hasek with 10, and fifth in save percentage (.917).

LESTER B. PEARSON AWARD

An annual award presented to the NHL's outstanding player as selected by the members of the National Hockey League Players' Association. The winner receives $10,000.

History: The award was presented in 1970-71 by the NHLPA in honor of the late Lester B. Pearson, former Prime Minister of Canada.

1997-98 Winner: **Dominik Hasek, Buffalo Sabres**

Dominik Hasek captured the Lester B. Pearson Award for the second year in a row, becoming the first repeat winner since Wayne Gretzky won the award four years in a row from 1982 to 1986. Mike Liut, who took the honor in 1981, is the only other goaltender to win the award.

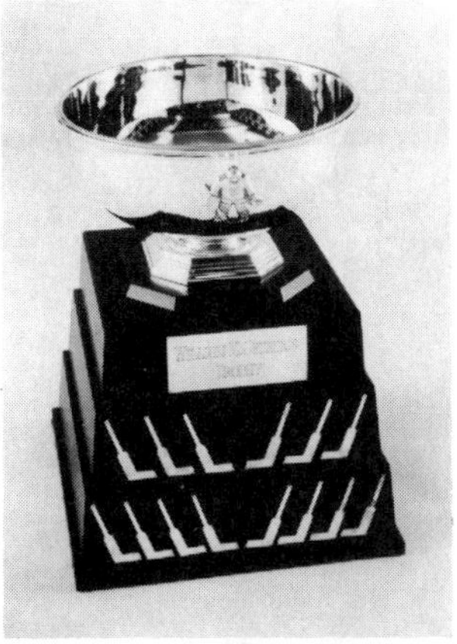

William M. Jennings Trophy

Jack Adams Award

Bill Masterton Trophy

Lester Patrick Trophy

Lester B. Pearson Award

JACK ADAMS AWARD

An annual award presented by the National Hockey League Broadcasters' Association to "the NHL coach adjudged to have contributed the most to his team's success." Winner selected by a poll among members of the NHL Broadcasters' Association at the end of the regular season. The winner receives $1,000 from the NHLBA.

History: The award was presented by the NHL Broadcasters' Association in 1974 to commemorate the late Jack Adams, coach and general manager of the Detroit Red Wings, whose lifetime dedication to hockey serves as an inspiration to all who aspire to further the game.

1997-98 Winner: Pat Burns, Boston Bruins
Runners-up: Larry Robinson, Los Angeles Kings
Ken Hitchcock, Dallas Stars

Boston Bruins head coach Pat Burns captured the 1997-98 Jack Adams Award, polling 48 of a possible 87 first-place votes and 306 points overall. Burns finished well ahead of Los Angeles Kings head coach Larry Robinson, who had 149 points including 10 first-place votes. Ken Hitchcock of Dallas, last year's runner-up, finished third in the balloting with 123 points, including 17 first-place votes.

In his first season behind the Boston bench, Burns led the Bruins back to the Stanley Cup Playoffs after a one-year absence with a 39-30-13 record for 91 points and second place in the Northeast Division. The Bruins posted a 30-point improvement over 1996-97, the largest gain in the NHL.

Burns becomes the first three-time Jack Adams Award winner since the trophy's inception in 1974, winning with three different clubs—Montreal (1989), Toronto (1993) and Boston (1998). Burns is the first Bruins coach to capture the award since Don Cherry in 1976.

BILL MASTERTON MEMORIAL TROPHY

An annual award under the trusteeship of the Professional Hockey Writers' Association to "the National Hockey League player who best exemplifies the qualities of perseverance, sportsmanship and dedication to hockey." Winner selected by a poll among the 26 chapters of the PHWA at the end of the regular season. A $2,500 grant from the PHWA is awarded annually to the Bill Masterton Scholarship Fund, based in Bloomington, MN, in the name of the Masterton Trophy winner.

History: The trophy was presented by the NHL Writers' Association in 1968 to commemorate the late William Masterton, a player of the Minnesota North Stars, who exhibited to a high degree the qualities of perseverance, sportsmanship and dedication to hockey, and who died January 15, 1968.

1997-98 Winner: Jamie McLennan, St. Louis Blues
Runners-up; Viacheslav Fetisov, Detroit Red Wings
Rob Blake, Los Angeles Kings

Goaltender Jamie McLennan of the St. Louis Blues overcame a life-threatening bout of bacterial meningitis to make it back to the NHL in 1997-98. On May 6, 1996, he contracted the illness while visiting friends in Lethbridge, Alberta. McLennan spent five days in intensive care and three more weeks in the hospital, losing 30 pounds and so much of his muscle mass and energy that he had to teach himself how to walk again. In 1997-98, McLennan earned the backup role to Grant Fuhr in St. Louis and compiled a 16-8-2 record with a 2.17 goals-against average in 30 games.

LESTER PATRICK TROPHY

An annual award "for outstanding service to hockey in the United States." Eligible recipients are players, officials, coaches, executives and referees. Winner selected by an award committee consisting of the president of the NHL, an NHL governor, a representative of the New York Rangers, a member of the Hockey Hall of Fame builder's section, a member of the Hockey Hall of Fame player's section, a member of the U.S. Hockey Hall of Fame, a member of the NHL Broadcasters' Association and a member of the Professional Hockey Writers' Association. Each except the League President is rotated annually. The winner receives a miniature of the trophy.

History: Presented by the New York Rangers in 1966 to honor the late Lester Patrick, longtime general manager and coach of the New York Rangers, whose teams finished out of the playoffs only once in his first 16 years with the club.

1997-98 Winners: Peter Karmanos
Neal Broten
John Mayasich
Max McNab

Peter Karmanos, Corporate Chairman and Chief Executive Officer of Compuware, a leading computer software company, has been a huge sponsor of amateur hockey in the Detroit area for 22 years, developing one of the premier youth hockey programs in the world. The Karmanos-sponsored Plymouth Junior Whalers were the first United States-based team to play in the Ontario Hockey League, producing top NHL prospects over the years.

Mr. Karmanos is the Chief Executive Officer and Governor of the Carolina Hurricanes. He and his associates had acquired the franchise in Hartford on June 28, 1994.

Neal Broten, who retired in 1997 after 17 seasons and 1,099 games in the NHL, was the first United States-born player to score more than 100 points in an NHL season (105 with the Minnesota North Stars in 1985-86). Broten won the Stanley Cup as a member of the New Jersey Devils in 1995.

Prior to his NHL career, Broten was a member of the 1980 United States Olympic Team that won the gold medal at Lake Placid, NY. He later captured the Hobey Baker Award as the outstanding United States college player in 1981, and was an All-American selection in his senior year at the University of Minnesota.

John Mayasich, considered one of the finest amateur players ever produced in the United States, was a member of the 1960 United States Olympic Team that won the gold medal at Squaw Valley, California. Mayasich was a three-time All-American at the University of Minnesota and remains the school's all-time leading scorer. He captured the Western Collegiate Hockey Association scoring championship in 1954 and 1955. He is a member of the United States Hockey Hall of Fame.

Max McNab has spent a lifetime in hockey, more than 50 years, in virtually every capacity—player, coach, general manager, team and league executive. Prior to his executive career, he played for the Detroit Red Wings for four seasons, winning the Stanley Cup in 1950.

McNab had a long coaching and managerial career in the Western Hockey League, from 1953 to 1971. He helped build the Washington Capitals as general manager, beginning in 1975, and was the first general manager and later executive vice president of the New Jersey Devils, beginning in 1984.

NEW AWARD...

Beginning in 1998-99, the National Hockey League will acknowledge the League's top regular-season goal scorer with a new trophy. This award will be named after Maurice "Rocket" Richard of the Montreal Canadiens. Richard was the first NHL player to score 50 goals in a season, reaching this mark in 1944-45. He retired in 1960, having scored 544 goals in the regular season and 82 more in the playoffs.

King Clancy Memorial Trophy

Bud Ice Plus-Minus Award

KING CLANCY MEMORIAL TROPHY

An annual award "to the player who best exemplifies leadership qualities on and off the ice and has made a noteworthy humanitarian contribution in his community."

History: The King Clancy Memorial Trophy was presented to the National Hockey League by the Board of Governors in 1988 to honor the late Frank "King" Clancy.

1997-98 Winner: Kelly Chase, St. Louis Blues

St. Louis Blues right winger Kelly Chase is the 1997-98 recipient of the King Clancy Trophy. He is one of the most popular Blues players and a consistent supporter of community functions in St. Louis. Chase's signature charitable effort is his very own—the Gateway Special Hockey Program, allowing children and young adults born with developmental disabilities such as Downs Syndrome and autism to participate in organized ice hockey.

Chase began the program in St. Louis five years ago, and with the help and involvement of friends and teammates throughout the NHL, it has grown across North America. Gateway Special Hockey programs have been developed in Denver, Hartford, Ottawa, Westchester (New York), Mississauga and Durham (Ontario), with plans for teams to begin play next year in California, Alberta and Long Island, New York.

In recognition of his hard work and success in bringing hockey to young lives touched with disabilities, the NHL Foundation—the charitable arm of the National Hockey League—recently awarded its first annual player grant of $25,000 to Chase on behalf of his work with Gateway Special Hockey.

BUD ICE PLUS-MINUS AWARD

An annual award "to the player, having played a minimum of 60 games, who leads the League in plus/minus statistics" at the end of the regular season. Bud Ice will contribute $5,000 on behalf of the winner to the charity of his choice.

History: The award was presented to the NHL in 1996-97 by Bud Ice to recognize the League leader in plus-minus statistics. Plus-minus statistics are calculated by giving a player a "plus" when on-ice for an even-strength or shorthand goal scored by his team. He receives a "minus" when on-ice for an even-strength or shorthand goal scored by the opposing team. A plus-minus award has been presented since the 1982-83 season.

1997-98 Winner: Chris Pronger, St. Louis Blues

In his first year as captain of the St. Louis Blues, defenseman Chris Pronger led the NHL in +/- with a rating of +47 in 81 games played. Pronger, who received a nomination for the Norris Trophy in 1997-98, finished well ahead of Detroit's Larry Murphy who was +35. Jason Allison of Boston was third at +33.

Team Award

PRESIDENTS' TROPHY

An annual award to the club finishing the regular-season with the best overall record. The winner receives $350,000, to be split between the team and its players.

History: Presented to the National Hockey League in 1985-86 by the NHL Board of Governors to recognize the team compiling the top regular-season record.

1997-98 Winner: Dallas Stars
Runners-up: New Jersey Devils
Detroit Red Wings

The Dallas Stars won the Presidents' Trophy for the first time in 1997-98, compiling the NHL's best regular-season record of 49-22-11 for 109 points.

The New Jersey Devils finished second in a close race with 107 points after a record of 48-23-11. The Detroit Red Wings had the third-best regular-season mark with a record of 44-23-15 for 103 points.

PRESIDENTS' TROPHY

	Winner	Runner-up
1998	Dallas Stars	New Jersey Devils
1997	Colorado Avalanche	Dallas Stars
1996	Detroit Red Wings	Colorado Avalanche
1995	Detroit Red Wings	Quebec Nordiques
1994	New York Rangers	New Jersey Devils
1993	Pittsburgh Penguins	Boston Bruins
1992	New York Rangers	Washington Capitals
1991	Chicago Blackhawks	St. Louis Blues
1990	Boston Bruins	Calgary Flames
1989	Calgary Flames	Montreal Canadiens
1988	Calgary Flames	Montreal Canadiens
1987	Edmonton Oilers	Philadelphia Flyers
1986	Edmonton Oilers	Philadelphia Flyers

Presidents' Trophy

MasterCard Cutting Edge Play of the Year

Duracell/NHL PowerPlay Award

MASTERCARD CUTTING EDGE PLAY OF THE YEAR

An acrobatic "spread eagle on the ice" goal by Shjon Podein of the Philadelphia Flyers was named the MasterCard Cutting Edge Play of the Year. The award was chosen by NHL fans. In recognition of Podein's remarkable performance, MasterCard donated $100,000 to Big Brothers Big Sisters of America.

1997-98 Winner: Goal by Shjon Podein, Philadelphia Flyers

In the winning play, Podein swiped the puck into a gaping net from a sharp angle while sliding in a spread eagle position on the ice, having been knocked over by Los Angeles Kings goaltender Jamie Storr. Podein's goal took place during the Flyers' 3-0 win over Los Angeles on April 4, 1998.

Norelco Face-off Award

NORELCO FACE-OFF AWARD

A monthly and annual award to the player and team with the best face-off winning percentage. To be eligible, a player must take a minimum of 15% of his club's total face-offs. Norelco made charitable donations on behalf of the month and yearly winners totalling $24,000.

The 1997-98 Norelco/NHL Face-Off Award winners are as follows:

Month	Team Award	Player Award
October	Dallas Stars	Steve Dubinsky, Chicago Blackhawks
November	Philadelphia Flyers	Eric Lindros, Philadelphia Flyers
December	Mighty Ducks of Anaheim	Guy Carbonneau, Dallas Stars
January	Philadelphia Flyers	Eric Lindros, Philadelphia Flyers
February	Vancouver Canucks	Doug Gilmour, New Jersey Devils
March	Dallas Stars	Tim Taylor, Boston Bruins
April	Boston Bruins	Bernie Nicholls, San Jose Sharks
Year-End	Dallas Stars	Eric Lindros, Philadelphia Flyers

DURACELL/NHL POWERPLAY AWARD

A monthly and annual award "to the NHL team with the best monthly and yearly power-play percentage." From October 1997 to April 1998, the Duracell PowerPlay Award recognized the team that displayed League-wide superiority on the power-play, as calculated by dividing the number of power-play goals a club scored by the number of power-play opportunities it had. In addition to a monthly on-ice trophy presentation, Duracell contributed $1,000 to the winning team's charity of choice. The Dallas Stars recorded the best power-play percentage in the regular season. The Stars tallied 77 power-play goals in 385 opportunities for a 20.0% success rate. Duracell made a $3,000 contribution to the Stars' charity of choice, bringing the Award's total yearly charitable contribution to $10,000.

The 1997-98 Duracell/NHL PowerPlay Award winners are as follows:

Month	Winning Team	Power Play %
October	New Jersey Devils	27.1%
November	Dallas Stars	25.4%
December	New Jersey Devils	22.7%
January	New York Rangers	33.3%
February	New York Islanders	37.5%
March	Detroit Red Wings	25.3%
April	Boston Bruins	27.9%
Year-End	Dallas Stars	20.0%

NHL AWARD MONEY BREAKDOWN — 1997-98

(Players on each club determine how team award money is divided. All award monies are in U.S. funds.)

TEAM AWARDS

Stanley Cup Playoffs	Number of Clubs	Share Per Club	Total
Conference Quarter-Final Losers	8	$ 237,500	$1,900,000
Conference Semi-Final Losers	4	412,500	1,650,000
Conference Championship Losers	2	737,500	1,475,000
Stanley Cup Loser	1	1,137,500	1,137,500
Stanley Cup Winners	1	1,812,500	1,812,500
TOTAL PLAYOFF AWARD MONEY			$7,975,000

Final Standings, Regular Season	Number of Clubs	Share Per Club	Total
Presidents' Trophy			
Club's Share	1	$ 100,000	$ 100,000
Players' Share	1	250,000	250,000
Division Winners	4	425,000	1,700,000
Division Second Place	4	200,000	800,000
TOTAL REGULAR-SEASON AWARD MONEY			$2,850,000

INDIVIDUAL AWARDS	Winner	First Runner-up	Second Runner-up
Hart, Calder, Norris, Ross, Vezina, Byng, Selke, Jennings, Masterton Trophies	$10,000	$6,000	$4,000
King Clancy Trophy	$ 3,000	$1,000	
Conn Smythe Trophy	$10,000		
TOTAL INDIVIDUAL AWARD MONEY			$194,000

ALL-STARS	Number of winners	Per Player	Total
First Team All-Stars	6	$10,000	$ 60,000
Second Team All-Stars	6	5,000	$ 30,000
All-Star Game Winners			$250,000
TOTAL ALL-STAR AWARD MONEY			$340,000
TOTAL ALL AWARDS			**$11,359,000**

1997-98 NHL Player of the Week Award Winners

Player of the Week

Week Ending	Player	Team
October 6	**Patrick Roy**	Colorado
October 13	**Brett Hull**	St. Louis
October 20	**Jim Carey/Byron Dafoe**	Boston
October 27	**Teemu Selanne**	Anaheim
November 3	**Patrick Elias**	New Jersey
November 10	**John LeClair**	Philadelphia
November 17	**Brett Hull**	St. Louis
November 24	**Claude Lemieux**	Colorado
December 1	**Ed Belfour**	Dallas
December 8	**Dominik Hasek**	Buffalo
December 15	**Mike Gartner**	Phoenix
December 22	**Mike Vernon**	San Jose
December 29	**Chris Osgood**	Detroit
January 5	**Mark Recchi**	Montreal
January 12	**Al MacInnis**	St. Louis
January 19	**Teemu Selanne**	Anaheim
January 26	**Paul Kariya**	Anaheim
February 2	**Tom Barrasso**	Pittsburgh
February 9	**Martin Brodeur**	New Jersey
February 16	**WINTER BREAK/OLYMPICS**	
February 23	**WINTER BREAK/OLYMPICS**	
March 2	**Jason Allison**	Boston
March 9	**Trevor Kidd**	Carolina
March 16	**Felix Potvin**	Toronto
March 23	**Olaf Kolzig**	Washington
March 30	**Keith Primeau**	Carolina
April 6	**Peter Bondra**	Washington
April 13	**Joe Nieuwendyk**	Dallas
April 20	**Olaf Kolzig**	Washington

1997-98 Player of the Month

Month	Player	Team
October	**Mike Modano**	Dallas
November	**Martin Brodeur**	New Jersey
December	**Dominik Hasek**	Buffalo
January	**Paul Kariya**	Anaheim
February	**Dominik Hasek**	Buffalo
March	**Jaromir Jagr**	Pittsburgh
April	**Joe Nieuwendyk**	Dallas

1997-98 Rookie of the Month

Month	Player	Team
October	**Eric Messier**	Colorado
November	**Marco Sturm**	San Jose
December	**Mike Johnson**	Toronto
January	**Sergei Samsonov**	Boston
March	**Scott Fraser**	Edmonton
April	**Scott Fraser**	Edmonton

NATIONAL HOCKEY LEAGUE INDIVIDUAL AWARD WINNERS

ART ROSS TROPHY

	Winner	Runner-up
1998	Jaromir Jagr, Pit.	Peter Forsberg, Col.
1997	Mario Lemieux, Pit.	Teemu Selanne, Ana.
1996	Mario Lemieux, Pit.	Jaromir Jagr, Pit.
1995	Jaromir Jagr, Pit.	Eric Lindros, Phi.
1994	Wayne Gretzky, L.A.	Sergei Fedorov, Det.
1993	Mario Lemieux, Pit.	Pat LaFontaine, Buf.
1992	Mario Lemieux, Pit.	Kevin Stevens, Pit.
1991	Wayne Gretzky, L.A.	Brett Hull, St.L.
1990	Wayne Gretzky, L.A.	Mark Messier, Edm.
1989	Mario Lemieux, Pit.	Wayne Gretzky, L.A.
1988	Mario Lemieux, Pit.	Wayne Gretzky, Edm.
1987	Wayne Gretzky, Edm.	Jari Kurri, Edm.
1986	Wayne Gretzky, Edm.	Mario Lemieux, Pit.
1985	Wayne Gretzky, Edm.	Jari Kurri, Edm.
1984	Wayne Gretzky, Edm.	Paul Coffey, Edm.
1983	Wayne Gretzky, Edm.	Peter Stastny, Que.
1982	Wayne Gretzky, Edm.	Mike Bossy, NYI
1981	Wayne Gretzky, Edm.	Marcel Dionne, L.A.
1980	Marcel Dionne, L.A.	Wayne Gretzky, Edm.
1979	Bryan Trottier, NYI	Marcel Dionne, L.A.
1978	Guy Lafleur, Mtl.	Bryan Trottier, NYI
1977	Guy Lafleur, Mtl.	Marcel Dionne, L.A.
1976	Guy Lafleur, Mtl.	Bobby Clarke, Phi.
1975	Bobby Orr, Bos.	Phil Esposito, Bos.
1974	Phil Esposito, Bos.	Bobby Orr, Bos.
1973	Phil Esposito, Bos.	Bobby Clarke, Phi.
1972	Phil Esposito, Bos.	Bobby Orr, Bos.
1971	Phil Esposito, Bos.	Bobby Orr, Bos.
1970	Bobby Orr, Bos.	Phil Esposito, Bos.
1969	Phil Esposito, Bos.	Bobby Hull, Chi.
1968	Stan Mikita, Chi.	Phil Esposito, Bos.
1967	Stan Mikita, Chi.	Bobby Hull, Chi.
1966	Bobby Hull, Chi.	Stan Mikita, Chi.
1965	Stan Mikita, Chi.	Norm Ullman, Det.
1964	Stan Mikita, Chi.	Bobby Hull, Chi.
1963	Gordie Howe, Det.	Andy Bathgate, NYR
1962	Bobby Hull, Chi.	Andy Bathgate, NYR
1961	Bernie Geoffrion, Mtl.	Jean Beliveau, Mtl.
1960	Bobby Hull, Chi.	Bronco Horvath, Bos.
1959	Dickie Moore, Mtl.	Jean Beliveau, Mtl.
1958	Dickie Moore, Mtl.	Henri Richard, Mtl.
1957	Gordie Howe, Det.	Ted Lindsay, Det.
1956	Jean Beliveau, Mtl.	Gordie Howe, Det.
1955	Bernie Geoffrion, Mtl.	Maurice Richard, Mtl.
1954	Gordie Howe, Det.	Maurice Richard, Mtl.
1953	Gordie Howe, Det.	Ted Lindsay, Det.
1952	Gordie Howe, Det.	Ted Lindsay, Det.
1951	Gordie Howe, Det.	Maurice Richard, Mtl.
1950	Ted Lindsay, Det.	Sid Abel, Det.
1949	Roy Conacher, Chi.	Doug Bentley, Chi.
1948*	Elmer Lach, Mtl.	Buddy O'Connor, NYR
1947	Max Bentley, Chi.	Maurice Richard, Mtl.
1946	Max Bentley, Chi.	Gaye Stewart, Tor.
1945	Elmer Lach, Mtl.	Maurice Richard, Mtl.
1944	Herb Cain, Bos.	Doug Bentley, Chi.
1943	Doug Bentley, Chi.	Bill Cowley, Bos.
1942	Bryan Hextall, NYR	Lynn Patrick, NYR
1941	Bill Cowley, Bos.	Bryan Hextall, NYR
1940	Milt Schmidt, Bos.	Woody Dumart, Bos.
1939	Toe Blake, Mtl.	Dave Schriner, NYA
1938	Gordie Drillon, Tor.	Syl Apps, Tor.
1937	Dave Schriner, NYA	Syl Apps, Tor.
1936	Dave Schriner, NYA	Marty Barry, Det.
1935	Charlie Conacher, Tor.	Syd Howe, St.L-Det.
1934	Charlie Conacher, Tor.	Joe Primeau, Tor
1933	Bill Cook, NYR	Harvey Jackson, Tor.
1932	Harvey Jackson, Tor.	Joe Primeau, Tor.
1931	Howie Morenz, Mtl.	Ebbie Goodfellow, Det.
1930	Cooney Weiland, Bos.	Frank Boucher, NYR
1929	Ace Bailey, Tor.	Nels Stewart, Mtl.M
1928	Howie Morenz, Mtl.	Aurel Joliat, Mtl.
1927	Bill Cook, NYR	Dick Irvin, Chi.
1926	Nels Stewart, Mtl.M.	Cy Denneny, Ott.
1925	Babe Dye, Tor.	Cy Denneny, Ott.
1924	Cy Denneny, Ott.	Billy Boucher, Mtl.
1923	Babe Dye, Tor.	Cy Denneny, Ott.
1922	Punch Broadbent, Ott.	Cy Denneny, Ott.
1921	Newsy Lalonde, Mtl.	Cy Denneny, Ott.
1920	Joe Malone, Que.	Newsy Lalonde, Mtl.
1919	Newsy Lalonde, Mtl.	Odie Cleghorn, Mtl.
1918	Joe Malone, Mtl.	Cy Denneny, Ott.

* Trophy first awarded in 1948.
Scoring leaders listed from 1918 to 1947.

KING CLANCY MEMORIAL TROPHY WINNERS

1998	Kelly Chase	St. Louis Blues
1997	Trevor Linden	Vancouver
1996	Kris King	Winnipeg
1995	Joe Nieuwendyk	Calgary
1994	Adam Graves	NY Rangers
1993	Dave Poulin	Boston
1992	Ray Bourque	Boston
1991	Dave Taylor	Los Angeles
1990	Kevin Lowe	Edmonton
1989	Bryan Trottier	NY Islanders
1988	Lanny McDonald	Calgary

HART TROPHY

	Winner	Runner-up
1998	Dominik Hasek, Buf.	Jaromir Jagr, Pit.
1997	Dominik Hasek, Buf.	Paul Kariya, Ana.
1996	Mario Lemieux, Pit.	Mark Messier, NYR
1995	Eric Lindros, Phi.	Jaromir Jagr, Pit.
1994	Sergei Fedorov, Det.	Dominik Hasek, Buf.
1993	Mario Lemieux, Pit.	Doug Gilmour, Tor.
1992	Mark Messier, NYR	Patrick Roy, Mtl.
1991	Brett Hull, St.L.	Wayne Gretzky, L.A.
1990	Mark Messier, Edm.	Ray Bourque, Bos.
1989	Wayne Gretzky, L.A.	Mario Lemieux, Pit.
1988	Mario Lemieux, Pit.	Grant Fuhr, Edm.
1987	Wayne Gretzky, Edm.	Ray Bourque, Bos.
1986	Wayne Gretzky, Edm.	Mario Lemieux, Pit.
1985	Wayne Gretzky, Edm.	Dale Hawerchuk, Wpg.
1984	Wayne Gretzky, Edm.	Rod Langway, Wsh.
1983	Wayne Gretzky, Edm.	Pete Peeters, Bos.
1982	Wayne Gretzky, Edm.	Bryan Trottier, NYI
1981	Wayne Gretzky, Edm.	Mike Liut, St.L.
1980	Wayne Gretzky, Edm.	Marcel Dionne, L.A.
1979	Bryan Trottier, NYI	Guy Lafleur, Mtl
1978	Guy Lafleur, Mtl.	Bryan Trottier, NYI
1977	Guy Lafleur, Mtl.	Bobby Clarke, Phi.
1976	Bobby Clarke, Phi.	Denis Potvin, NYI
1975	Bobby Clarke, Phi.	Rogatien Vachon, L.A.
1974	Phil Esposito, Bos.	Bernie Parent, Phi.
1973	Bobby Clarke, Phi.	Phil Esposito, Bos.
1972	Bobby Orr, Bos.	Ken Dryden, Mtl.
1971	Bobby Orr, Bos.	Phil Esposito, Bos.
1970	Bobby Orr, Bos.	Tony Esposito, Chi.
1969	Phil Esposito, Bos.	Jean Beliveau, Mtl.
1968	Stan Mikita, Chi.	Jean Beliveau, Mtl.
1967	Stan Mikita, Chi.	Ed Giacomin, NYR
1966	Bobby Hull, Chi.	Jean Beliveau, Mtl.
1965	Bobby Hull, Chi.	Norm Ullman, Det.
1964	Jean Beliveau, Mtl.	Bobby Hull, Chi.
1963	Gordie Howe, Det.	Stan Mikita, Chi.
1962	Jacques Plante, Mtl.	Doug Harvey, NYR
1961	Bernie Geoffrion, Mtl.	Johnny Bower, Tor.
1960	Gordie Howe, Det.	Bobby Hull, Chi.
1959	Andy Bathgate, NYR	Gordie Howe, Det.
1958	Gordie Howe, Det.	Andy Bathgate, NYR
1957	Gordie Howe, Det.	Jean Beliveau, Mtl.
1956	Jean Beliveau, Mtl.	Tod Sloan, Tor.
1955	Ted Kennedy, Tor.	Harry Lumley, Tor.
1954	Al Rollins, Chi.	Red Kelly, Det.
1953	Gordie Howe, Det.	Al Rollins, Chi.
1952	Gordie Howe, Det.	Elmer Lach, Mtl.
1951	Milt Schmidt, Bos.	Maurice Richard, Mtl.
1950	Chuck Rayner, NYR	Ted Kennedy, Tor.
1949	Sid Abel, Det.	Bill Durnan, Mtl.
1948	Buddy O'Connor, NYR	Frank Brimsek, Bos.
1947	Maurice Richard, Mtl.	Milt Schmidt, Bos.
1946	Max Bentley, Chi.	Gaye Stewart, Tor.
1945	Elmer Lach, Mtl.	Maurice Richard, Mtl.
1944	Babe Pratt, Tor.	Bill Cowley, Bos.
1943	Bill Cowley, Bos.	Doug Bentley, Chi.
1942	Tom Anderson, Bro.	Syl Apps, Tor.
1941	Bill Cowley, Bos.	Dit Clapper, Bos.
1940	Ebbie Goodfellow, Det.	Syl Apps, Tor.
1939	Toe Blake, Mtl.	Syl Apps, Tor.
1938	Eddie Shore, Bos.	Paul Thompson, Chi.
1937	Babe Siebert, Mtl.	Lionel Conacher, Mtl.M
1936	Eddie Shore, Bos.	Hooley Smith, Mtl.M
1935	Eddie Shore, Bos.	Charlie Conacher, Tor.
1934	Aurel Joliat, Mtl.	Lionel Conacher, Chi.
1933	Eddie Shore, Bos.	Bill Cook, NYR
1932	Howie Morenz, Mtl.	Ching Johnson, NYR
1931	Howie Morenz, Mtl.	Eddie Shore, Bos.
1930	Nels Stewart, Mtl.M.	Lionel Hitchman, Bos.
1929	Roy Worters, NYA	Ace Bailey, Tor.
1928	Howie Morenz, Mtl.	Roy Worters, Pit.
1927	Herb Gardiner, Mtl.	Bill Cook, NYR
1926	Nels Stewart, Mtl.M.	Sprague Cleghorn, Bos.
1925	Billy Burch, Ham.	Howie Morenz, Mtl.

LADY BYNG TROPHY

	Winner	Runner-up
1998	Ron Francis, Pit.	Teemu Selanne, Ana.
1997	Paul Kariya, Ana.	Teemu Selanne, Ana.
1996	Paul Kariya, Ana.	Adam Oates, Bos.
1995	Ron Francis, Pit.	Adam Oates, Bos.
1994	Wayne Gretzky, L.A.	Adam Oates, Bos.
1993	Pierre Turgeon, NYI	Adam Oates, Bos.
1992	Wayne Gretzky, L.A.	Joe Sakic, Que.
1991	Wayne Gretzky, L.A.	Brett Hull, St.L.
1990	Brett Hull, St.L.	Wayne Gretzky, L.A.
1989	Joe Mullen, Cgy.	Wayne Gretzky, L.A.
1988	Mats Naslund, Mtl.	Wayne Gretzky, Edm.
1987	Joe Mullen, Cgy.	Wayne Gretzky, Edm.
1986	Mike Bossy, NYI	Jari Kurri, Edm.
1985	Jari Kurri, Edm.	Joe Mullen, St.L.
1984	Mike Bossy, NYI	Rick Middleton, Bos.
1983	Mike Bossy, NYI	Rick Middleton, Bos.
1982	Rick Middleton, Bos.	Mike Bossy, NYI
1981	Rick Kehoe, Pit.	Wayne Gretzky, Edm.
1980	Wayne Gretzky, Edm.	Marcel Dionne, L.A.
1979	Bob MacMillan, Atl.	Marcel Dionne, L.A.
1978	Butch Goring, L.A.	Peter McNab, Bos.
1977	Marcel Dionne, L.A.	Jean Ratelle, Bos.
1976	Jean Ratelle, NYR-Bos.	Jean Pronovost, Pit.
1975	Marcel Dionne, Det.	John Bucyk, Bos.
1974	John Bucyk, Bos.	Lowell MacDonald, Pit.
1973	Gilbert Perreault, Buf.	Jean Ratelle, NYR
1972	Jean Ratelle, NYR	John Bucyk, Bos.
1971	John Bucyk, Bos.	Dave Keon, Tor.
1970	Phil Goyette, St.L.	John Bucyk, Bos.
1969	Alex Delvecchio, Det.	Ted Hampson, Oak.
1968	Stan Mikita, Chi.	John Bucyk, Bos.
1967	Stan Mikita, Chi.	Dave Keon, Tor.
1966	Alex Delvecchio, Det.	Bobby Rousseau, Mtl.
1965	Bobby Hull, Chi.	Alex Delvecchio, Det.
1964	Ken Wharram, Chi.	Dave Keon, Tor.
1963	Dave Keon, Tor.	Camille Henry, NYR
1962	Dave Keon, Tor.	Claude Provost, Mtl.
1961	Red Kelly, Tor.	Norm Ullman, Det.
1960	Don McKenney, Bos.	Andy Hebenton, NYR
1959	Alex Delvecchio, Det.	Andy Hebenton, NYR
1958	Camille Henry, NYR	Don Marshall, Mtl.
1957	Andy Hebenton, NYR	Earl Reibel, Det.
1956	Earl Reibel, Det.	Floyd Curry, Mtl.
1955	Sid Smith, Tor.	Danny Lewicki, NYR
1954	Red Kelly, Det.	Don Raleigh, NYR
1953	Red Kelly, Det.	Wally Hergesheimer, NYR
1952	Sid Smith, Tor.	Red Kelly, Det.
1951	Red Kelly, Det.	Woody Dumart, Bos.
1950	Edgar Laprade, NYR	Red Kelly, Det.
1949	Bill Quackenbush, Det.	Harry Watson, Tor.
1948	Buddy O'Connor, NYR	Syl Apps, Tor.
1947	Bobby Bauer, Bos.	Syl Apps, Tor.
1946	Toe Blake, Mtl.	Clint Smith, Chi.
1945	Bill Mosienko, Chi.	Syd Howe, Det.
1944	Clint Smith, Chi.	Herb Cain, Bos.
1943	Max Bentley, Chi.	Buddy O'Connor, Mtl.
1942	Syl Apps, Tor.	Gordie Drillon, Tor.
1941	Bobby Bauer, Bos.	Gordie Drillon, Tor.
1940	Bobby Bauer, Bos.	Clint Smith, NYR
1939	Clint Smith, NYR	Marty Barry, Det.
1938	Gordie Drillon, Tor.	Clint Smith, NYR
1937	Marty Barry, Det.	Gordie Drillon, Tor.
1936	Doc Romnes, Chi.	Dave Schriner, NYA
1935	Frank Boucher, NYR	Russ Blinco, Mtl.M
1934	Frank Boucher, NYR	Joe Primeau, Tor.
1933	Frank Boucher, NYR	Joe Primeau, Tor.
1932	Joe Primeau, Tor.	Frank Boucher, NYR
1931	Frank Boucher, NYR	Normie Himes, NYA
1930	Frank Boucher, NYR	Normie Himes, NYA
1929	Frank Boucher, NYR	Harry Darragh, Pit.
1928	Frank Boucher, NYR	George Hay, Det.
1927	Billy Burch, NYA	Dick Irvin, Chi.
1926	Frank Nighbor, Ott.	Billy Burch, NYA
1925	Frank Nighbor, Ott.	none

FRANK J. SELKE TROPHY WINNERS

	Winner	Runner-up
1998	Jere Lehtinen, Dal.	Michael Peca, Buf.
1997	Michael Peca, Buf.	Peter Forsberg, Col.
1996	Sergei Fedorov, Det.	Ron Francis, Pit.
1995	Ron Francis, Pit.	Esa Tikkanen, St.L.
1994	Sergei Fedorov, Det.	Doug Gilmour, Tor.
1993	Doug Gilmour, Tor.	Dave Poulin, Bos.
1992	Guy Carbonneau, Mtl.	Sergei Fedorov, Det.
1991	Dirk Graham, Chi.	Esa Tikkanen, Edm.
1990	Rick Meagher, St.L.	Guy Carbonneau, Mtl.
1989	Guy Carbonneau, Mtl.	Esa Tikkanen, Edm.
1988	Guy Carbonneau, Mtl.	Steve Kasper, Bos.
1987	Dave Poulin, Phi.	Guy Carbonneau, Mtl.
1986	Troy Murray, Chi.	Ron Sutter, Phi.
1985	Craig Ramsay, Buf.	Doug Jarvis, Wsh.
1984	Doug Jarvis, Wsh.	Bryan Trottier, NYI
1983	Bobby Clarke, Phi.	Jari Kurri, Edm.
1982	Steve Kasper, Bos.	Bob Gainey, Mtl.
1981	Bob Gainey, Mtl.	Craig Ramsay, Buf.
1980	Bob Gainey, Mtl.	Craig Ramsay, Buf.
1979	Bob Gainey, Mtl.	Don Marcotte, Bos.
1978	Bob Gainey, Mtl.	Craig Ramsay, Buf.

VEZINA TROPHY

	Winner	Runner-up
1998	Dominik Hasek, Buf.	Martin Brodeur, N.J.
1997	Dominik Hasek, Buf.	Martin Brodeur, N.J.
1996	Jim Carey, Wsh.	Chris Osgood, Det.
1995	Dominik Hasek, Buf.	Ed Belfour, Chi.
1994	Dominik Hasek, Buf.	John Vanbiesbrouck, Fla.
1993	Ed Belfour, Chi.	Tom Barrasso, Pit.
1992	Patrick Roy, Mtl.	Kirk McLean, Van.
1991	Ed Belfour, Chi.	Patrick Roy, Mtl.
1990	Patrick Roy, Mtl.	Daren Puppa, Buf.
1989	Patrick Roy, Mtl.	Mike Vernon, Cgy.
1988	Grant Fuhr, Edm.	Tom Barrasso, Buf.
1987	Ron Hextall, Phi.	Mike Liut, Hfd.
1986	John Vanbiesbrouck, NYR	Bob Froese, Phi.
1985	Pelle Lindbergh, Phi.	Tom Barrasso, Buf.
1984	Tom Barrasso, Buf.	Rejean Lemelin, Cgy.
1983	Pete Peeters, Bos.	Roland Melanson, NYI
1982	Billy Smith, NYI	Grant Fuhr, Edm.
1981	Richard Sevigny, Mtl.	Pete Peeters, Phi.
	Denis Herron, Mtl.	Rick St. Croix, Phi.
	Michel Larocque, Mtl.	
1980	Bob Sauve, Buf.	Gerry Cheevers, Bos.
	Don Edwards, Buf.	Gilles Gilbert, Bos.
1979	Ken Dryden, Mtl.	Glenn Resch, NYI
	Michel Larocque, Mtl.	Billy Smith, NYI
1978	Ken Dryden, Mtl.	Bernie Parent, Phi.
	Michel Larocque	Wayne Stephenson, Phi.
1977	Ken Dryden, Mtl.	Glenn Resch, NYI
	Michel Larocque, Mtl.	Billy Smith, NYI
1976	Ken Dryden, Mtl.	Glenn Resch, NYI
		Billy Smith, NYI
1975	Bernie Parent, Phi.	Rogie Vachon, L.A.
		Gary Edwards, L.A.
1974	Bernie Parent, Phi. (tie)	Gilles Gilbert, Bos.
	Tony Esposito, Chi. (tie)	
1973	Ken Dryden, Mtl.	Ed Giacomin, NYR
		Gilles Villemure, NYR
1972	Tony Esposito, Chi.	Cesare Maniago, Min.
	Gary Smith, Chi.	Gump Worsley, Min.
1971	Ed Giacomin, NYR	Tony Esposito, Chi.
	Gilles Villemure, NYR	
1970	Tony Esposito, Chi.	Jacques Plante, St.L.
		Ernie Wakely, St.L.
1969	Jacques Plante, St.L.	Ed Giacomin, NYR
	Glenn Hall, St.L.	
1968	Gump Worsley, Mtl.	Johnny Bower, Tor.
	Rogie Vachon, Mtl.	Bruce Gamble, Tor.
1967	Glenn Hall, Chi.	Charlie Hodge, Mtl.
	Denis Dejordy, Chi.	
1966	Gump Worsley, Mtl.	Glenn Hall, Chi.
	Charlie Hodge, Mtl.	
1965	Terry Sawchuk, Tor.	Roger Crozier, Det.
	Johnny Bower, Tor.	
1964	Charlie Hodge, Mtl.	Glenn Hall, Chi.
1963	Glenn Hall, Chi.	Johnny Bower, Tor.
		Don Simmons, Tor.
1962	Jacques Plante, Mtl.	Johnny Bower, Tor.
1961	Johnny Bower, Tor.	Glenn Hall, Chi.
1960	Jacques Plante, Mtl.	Glenn Hall, Chi.
1959	Jacques Plante, Mtl.	Johnny Bower, Tor.
		Ed Chadwick, Tor.
1958	Jacques Plante, Mtl.	Gump Worsley, NYR
		Marcel Paille, NYR
1957	Jacques Plante, Mtl.	Glenn Hall, Det.
1956	Jacques Plante, Mtl.	Glenn Hall, Det.
1955	Terry Sawchuk, Det.	Harry Lumley, Tor.
1954	Harry Lumley, Tor.	Terry Sawchuk, Det.
1953	Terry Sawchuk, Det.	Gerry McNeil, Mtl.
1952	Terry Sawchuk, Det.	Al Rollins, Tor.
1951	Al Rollins, Tor.	Terry Sawchuk, Det.
1950	Bill Durnan, Mtl.	Harry Lumley, Det.
1949	Bill Durnan, Mtl.	Harry Lumley, Det.
1948	Turk Broda, Tor.	Harry Lumley, Det.
1947	Bill Durnan, Mtl.	Turk Broda, Tor.
1946	Bill Durnan, Mtl.	Frank Brimsek, Bos.
1945	Bill Durnan, Mtl.	Frank McCool, Tor. (tie)
		Harry Lumley, Det. (tie)
1944	Bill Durnan, Mtl.	Paul Bibeault, Tor.
1943	Johnny Mowers, Det.	Turk Broda, Tor.
1942	Frank Brimsek, Bos.	Turk Broda, Tor.
1941	Turk Broda, Tor.	Frank Brimsek, Bos. (tie)
		Johnny Mowers, Det. (tie)
1940	Dave Kerr, NYR	Frank Brimsek, Bos.
1939	Frank Brimsek, Bos.	Dave Kerr, NYR
1938	Tiny Thompson, Bos.	Dave Kerr, NYR
1937	Normie Smith, Det.	Dave Kerr, NYR
1936	Tiny Thompson, Bos.	Mike Karakas, Chi.
1935	Lorne Chabot, Chi.	Alex Connell, Mtl.M
1934	Charlie Gardiner, Chi.	Wilf Cude, Det.
1933	Tiny Thompson, Bos.	John Roach, Det.
1932	Charlie Gardiner, Chi.	Alex Connell, Det.
1931	Roy Worters, NYA	Charlie Gardiner, Chi.
1930	Tiny Thompson, Bos.	Charlie Gardiner, Chi.
1929	George Hainsworth, Mtl.	Tiny Thompson, Bos.
1928	George Hainsworth, Mtl.	Alex Connell, Ott.
1927	George Hainsworth, Mtl.	Clint Benedict, Mtl.M

BILL MASTERTON TROPHY WINNERS

1998	Jamie McLennan	St. Louis
1997	Tony Granato	San Jose
1996	Gary Roberts	Calgary
1995	Pat LaFontaine	Buffalo
1994	Cam Neely	Boston
1993	Mario Lemieux	Pittsburgh
1992	Mark Fitzpatrick	NY Islanders
1991	Dave Taylor	Los Angeles
1990	Gord Kluzak	Boston
1989	Tim Kerr	Philadelphia
1988	Bob Bourne	Los Angeles
1987	Doug Jarvis	Hartford
1986	Charlie Simmer	Boston
1985	Anders Hedberg	NY Rangers
1984	Brad Park	Detroit
1983	Lanny McDonald	Calgary
1982	Glenn Resch	Colorado
1981	Blake Dunlop	St. Louis
1980	Al MacAdam	Minnesota
1979	Serge Savard	Montreal
1978	Butch Goring	Los Angeles
1977	Ed Westfall	NY Islanders
1976	Rod Gilbert	NY Rangers
1975	Don Luce	Buffalo
1974	Henri Richard	Montreal
1973	Lowell MacDonald	Pittsburgh
1972	Bobby Clarke	Philadelphia
1971	Jean Ratelle	NY Rangers
1970	Pit Martin	Chicago
1969	Ted Hampson	Oakland
1968	Claude Provost	Montreal

CALDER MEMORIAL TROPHY WINNERS

	Winner	Runner-up
1998	Sergei Samsonov, Bos.	Mattias Ohlund, Van.
1997	Bryan Berard, NYI	Jarome Iginla, Cgy.
1996	Daniel Alfredsson, Ott.	Eric Daze, Chi.
1995	Peter Forsberg, Que.	Jim Carey, Wsh.
1994	Martin Brodeur, N.J.	Jason Arnott, Edm.
1993	Teemu Selanne, Wpg.	Joe Juneau, Bos.
1992	Pavel Bure, Van.	Nicklas Lidstrom, Det
1991	Ed Belfour, Chi.	Sergei Fedorov, Det.
1990	Sergei Makarov, Cgy.	Mike Modano, Min.
1989	Brian Leetch, NYR	Trevor Linden, Van.
1988	Joe Nieuwendyk, Cgy.	Ray Sheppard, Buf.
1987	Luc Robitaille, L.A.	Ron Hextall, Phi.
1986	Gary Suter, Cgy.	Wendel Clark, Tor.
1985	Mario Lemieux, Pit.	Chris Chelios, Mtl.
1984	Tom Barrasso, Buf.	Steve Yzerman, Det.
1983	Steve Larmer, Chi.	Phil Housley, Buf.
1982	Dale Hawerchuk, Wpg.	Barry Pederson, Bos.
1981	Peter Stastny, Que.	Larry Murphy, L.A.
1980	Ray Bourque, Bos.	Mike Foligno, Det.
1979	Bobby Smith, Min	Ryan Walter, Wsh.
1978	Mike Bossy, NYI	Barry Beck, Col.
1977	Willi Plett, Atl.	Don Murdoch, NYR
1976	Bryan Trottier, NYI	Glenn Resch, NYI
1975	Eric Vail, Atl.	Pierre Larouche, Pit.
1974	Denis Potvin, NYI	Tom Lysiak, Atl.
1973	Steve Vickers, NYR	Bill Barber, Phi.
1972	Ken Dryden, Mtl.	Rick Martin, Buf.
1971	Gilbert Perreault, Buf.	Jude Drouin, Min.
1970	Tony Esposito, Chi.	Bill Fairbairn, NYR
1969	Danny Grant, Min.	Norm Ferguson, Oak.
1968	Derek Sanderson, Bos.	Jacques Lemaire, Mtl.
1967	Bobby Orr, Bos.	Ed Van Impe, Chi.
1966	Brit Selby, Tor.	Bert Marshall, Det.
1965	Roger Crozier, Det.	Ron Ellis, Tor.
1964	Jacques Laperriere, Mtl.	John Ferguson, Mtl.
1963	Kent Douglas, Tor.	Doug Barkley, Det.
1962	Bobby Rousseau, Mtl.	Cliff Pennington, Bos.
1961	Dave Keon, Tor.	Bob Nevin, Tor.
1960	Bill Hay, Chi.	Murray Oliver, Det.
1959	Ralph Backstrom, Mtl.	Carl Brewer, Tor.
1958	Frank Mahovlich, Tor.	Bobby Hull, Chi.
1957	Larry Regan, Bos.	Ed Chadwick, Tor.
1956	Glenn Hall, Det.	Andy Hebenton, NYR
1955	Ed Litzenberger, Chi.	Don McKenney, Bos.
1954	Camille Henry, NYR	Earl Reibel, Det.
1953	Gump Worsley, NYR	Gordie Hannigan, Tor.
1952	Bernie Geoffrion, Mtl.	Hy Buller, NYR
1951	Terry Sawchuk, Det.	Al Rollins, Tor.
1950	Jack Gelineau, Bos.	Phil Maloney, Bos.
1949	Pentti Lund, NYR	Allan Stanley, NYR
1948	Jim McFadden, Det.	Pete Babando, Bos.
1947	Howie Meeker, Tor.	Jimmy Conacher, Det.
1946	Edgar Laprade, NYR	George Gee, Chi.
1945	Frank McCool, Tor.	Ken Smith, Bos.
1944	Gus Bodnar, Tor.	Bill Durnan, Mtl.
1943	Gaye Stewart, Tor.	Glen Harmon, Mtl.
1942	Grant Warwick, NYR	Buddy O'Connor, Mtl.
1941	Johnny Quilty, Mtl.	Johnny Mowers, Det.
1940	Kilby MacDonald, NYR	Wally Stanowski, Tor.
1939	Frank Brimsek, Bos.	Roy Conacher, Bos.
1938	Cully Dahlstrom, Chi.	Murph Chamberlain, Tor.
1937	Syl Apps, Tor.	Gordie Drillon, Tor.
1936	Mike Karakas, Chi.	Bucko McDonald, Det.
1935	Dave Schriner, NYA	Bert Connolly, NYR
1934	Russ Blinko, Mtl.M.	
1933	Carl Voss, Det.	

CONN SMYTHE TROPHY WINNERS

1998	Steve Yzerman	Detroit
1997	Mike Vernon	Detroit
1996	Joe Sakic	Colorado
1995	Claude Lemieux	New Jersey
1994	Brian Leetch	NY Rangers
1993	Patrick Roy	Montreal
1992	Mario Lemieux	Pittsburgh
1991	Mario Lemieux	Pittsburgh
1990	Bill Ranford	Edmonton
1989	Al MacInnis	Calgary
1988	Wayne Gretzky	Edmonton
1987	Ron Hextall	Philadelphia
1986	Patrick Roy	Montreal
1985	Wayne Gretzky	Edmonton
1984	Mark Messier	Edmonton
1983	Billy Smith	NY Islanders
1982	Mike Bossy	NY Islanders
1981	Butch Goring	NY Islanders
1980	Bryan Trottier	NY Islanders
1979	Bob Gainey	Montreal
1978	Larry Robinson	Montreal
1977	Guy Lafleur	Montreal
1976	Reggie Leach	Philadelphia
1975	Bernie Parent	Philadelphia
1974	Bernie Parent	Philadelphia
1973	Yvan Cournoyer	Montreal
1972	Bobby Orr	Boston
1971	Ken Dryden	Montreal
1970	Bobby Orr	Boston
1969	Serge Savard	Montreal
1968	Glenn Hall	St. Louis
1967	Dave Keon	Toronto
1966	Roger Crozier	Detroit
1965	Jean Béliveau	Montreal

JAMES NORRIS TROPHY WINNERS

	Winner	Runner-up
1998	Rob Blake, L.A.	Nicklas Lidstrom, Det.
1997	Brian Leetch, NYR	V. Konstantinov, Det.
1996	Chris Chelios, Chi.	Ray Bourque, Bos.
1995	Paul Coffey, Det.	Chris Chelios, Chi.
1994	Ray Bourque, Bos.	Scott Stevens, N.J.
1993	Chris Chelios, Chi.	Ray Bourque, Bos.
1992	Brian Leetch, NYR	Ray Bourque, Bos.
1991	Ray Bourque, Bos.	Al MacInnis, Cgy.
1990	Ray Bourque, Bos.	Al MacInnis, Cgy.
1989	Chris Chelios, Mtl	Paul Coffey, Pit.
1988	Ray Bourque, Bos.	Scott Stevens, Wsh.
1987	Ray Bourque, Bos.	Mark Howe, Phi.
1986	Paul Coffey, Edm.	Mark Howe, Phi.
1985	Paul Coffey, Edm.	Ray Bourque, Bos.
1984	Rod Langway, Wsh.	Paul Coffey, Edm.
1983	Rod Langway, Wsh.	Mark Howe, Phi.
1982	Doug Wilson, Chi.	Ray Bourque, Bos.
1981	Randy Carlyle, Pit.	Denis Potvin, NYI
1980	Larry Robinson, Mtl.	Borje Salming, Tor.
1979	Denis Potvin, NYI	Larry Robinson, Mtl.
1978	Denis Potvin, NYI	Brad Park, Bos.
1977	Larry Robinson, Mtl.	Borje Salming, Tor.
1976	Denis Potvin, NYI	Brad Park, NYR-Bos.
1975	Bobby Orr, Bos.	Denis Potvin, NYI
1974	Bobby Orr, Bos.	Brad Park, NYR
1973	Bobby Orr, Bos.	Guy Lapointe, Mtl.
1972	Bobby Orr, Bos.	Brad Park, NYR
1971	Bobby Orr, Bos.	Brad Park, NYR
1970	Bobby Orr, Bos.	Brad Park, NYR
1969	Bobby Orr, Bos.	Tim Horton, Tor.
1968	Bobby Orr, Bos.	J.C. Tremblay, Mtl
1967	Harry Howell, NYR	Pierre Pilote, Chi.
1966	Jacques Laperriere, Mtl.	Pierre Pilote, Chi.
1965	Pierre Pilote, Chi.	Jacques Laperriere, Mtl.
1964	Pierre Pilote, Chi.	Tim Horton, Tor.
1963	Pierre Pilote, Chi.	Carl Brewer, Tor.
1962	Doug Harvey, NYR	Pierre Pilote, Chi.
1961	Doug Harvey, Mtl.	Marcel Pronovost, Det.
1960	Doug Harvey, Mtl.	Allan Stanley, Tor.
1959	Tom Johnson, Mtl.	Bill Gadsby, NYR
1958	Doug Harvey, Mtl.	Bill Gadsby, NYR
1957	Doug Harvey, Mtl.	Red Kelly, Det.
1956	Doug Harvey, Mtl.	Bill Gadsby, NYR
1955	Doug Harvey, Mtl.	Red Kelly, Det.
1954	Red Kelly, Det.	Doug Harvey, Mtl.

MASTERCARD CUTTING EDGE PLAY OF THE YEAR WINNER

1998	Shjon Podein	Philadelphia
1997	Valeri Kamensky	Colorado

LESTER PATRICK TROPHY WINNERS

1998 Peter Karmanos
Neal Broten
John Mayasich
Max McNab
1997 Seymour H. Knox III
Bill Cleary
Pat LaFontaine
1996 George Gund
Ken Morrow
Milt Schmidt
1995 Joe Mullen
Brian Mullen
Bob Fleming
1994 Wayne Gretzky
Robert Ridder
1993 *Frank Boucher
*Mervyn (Red) Dutton
Bruce McNall
Gil Stein
1992 Al Arbour
Art Berglund
Lou Lamoriello
1991 Rod Gilbert
Mike Ilitch
1990 Len Ceglarski
1989 Dan Kelly
Lou Nanne
*Lynn Patrick
Bud Poile
1988 Keith Allen
Fred Cusick
Bob Johnson
1987 *Hobey Baker
Frank Mathers
1986 John MacInnes
Jack Riley
1985 Jack Butterfield
Arthur M. Wirtz
1984 John A. Ziegler Jr.
*Arthur Howie Ross
1983 Bill Torrey
1982 Emile P. Francis
1981 Charles M. Schulz
1980 Bobby Clarke
Edward M. Snider
Frederick A. Shero
1980 U.S. Olympic Hockey Team
1979 Bobby Orr
1978 Phil Esposito
Tom Fitzgerald
William T. Tutt
William W. Wirtz
1977 John P. Bucyk
Murray A. Armstrong
John Mariucci
1976 Stanley Mikita
George A. Leader
Bruce A. Norris
1975 Donald M. Clark
William L. Chadwick
Thomas N. Ivan
1974 Alex Delvecchio
Murray Murdoch
*Weston W. Adams, Sr.
*Charles L. Crovat
1973 Walter L. Bush, Jr.
1972 Clarence S. Campbell
John A. "Snooks" Kelly
Ralph "Cooney" Weiland
*James D. Norris
1971 William M. Jennings
*John B. Sollenberger
*Terrance G. Sawchuk
1970 Edward W. Shore
*James C. V. Hendy
1969 Robert M. Hull
*Edward J. Jeremiah
1968 Thomas F. Lockhart
*Walter A. Brown
*Gen. John R. Kilpatrick
1967 Gordon Howe
*Charles F. Adams
*James Norris, Sr.
1966 J.J. "Jack" Adams

* awarded posthumously

BUD ICE PLUS-MINUS AWARD WINNER

1998	Chris Pronger	St. Louis
1997	John LeClair	Philadelphia

WILLIAM M. JENNINGS TROPHY WINNERS

	Winner	Runner-up
1998	Martin Brodeur, N.J.	Ed Belfour, Dal.
1997	Martin Brodeur, N.J. Mike Dunham	Chris Osgood, Det. Mike Vernon
1996	Chris Osgood, Det. Mike Vernon	Martin Brodeur, N.J.
1995	Ed Belfour, Chi.	Mike Vernon, Det. Chris Osgood
1994	Dominik Hasek, Buf. Grant Fuhr	Martin Brodeur, N.J. Chris Terreri
1993	Ed Belfour, Chi.	Felix Potvin, Tor. Grant Fuhr
1992	Patrick Roy, Mtl.	Ed Belfour, Chi.
1991	Ed Belfour, Chi.	Patrick Roy, Mtl.
1990	Andy Moog, Bos. Rejean Lemelin	Patrick Roy, Mtl. Brian Hayward
1989	Patrick Roy, Mtl. Brian Hayward	Mike Vernon, Cgy. Rick Wamsley
1988	Patrick Roy, Mtl. Brian Hayward	Clint Malarchuk, Wsh. Pete Peeters
1987	Patrick Roy, Mtl. Brian Hayward	Ron Hextall, Phi.
1986	Bob Froese, Phi. Darren Jensen	Al Jensen, Wsh. Pete Peeters
1985	Tom Barrasso, Buf. Bob Sauve	Pat Riggin, Wsh.
1984	Al Jensen, Wsh. Pat Riggin	Tom Barrasso, Buf. Bob Sauve
1983	Roland Melanson, NYI Billy Smith	Pete Peeters, Bos.
1982	Rick Wamsley, Mtl. Denis Herron	Billy Smith, NYI Roland Melanson

LESTER B. PEARSON AWARD WINNERS

1998	Dominik Hasek	Buffalo
1997	Dominik Hasek	Buffalo
1996	Mario Lemieux	Pittsburgh
1995	Eric Lindros	Philadelphia
1994	Sergei Fedorov	Detroit
1993	Mario Lemieux	Pittsburgh
1992	Mark Messier	NY Rangers
1991	Brett Hull	St. Louis
1990	Mark Messier	Edmonton
1989	Steve Yzerman	Detroit
1988	Mario Lemieux	Pittsburgh
1987	Wayne Gretzky	Edmonton
1986	Mario Lemieux	Pittsburgh
1985	Wayne Gretzky	Edmonton
1984	Wayne Gretzky	Edmonton
1983	Wayne Gretzky	Edmonton
1982	Wayne Gretzky	Edmonton
1981	Mike Liut	St. Louis
1980	Marcel Dionne	Los Angeles
1979	Marcel Dionne	Los Angeles
1978	Guy Lafleur	Montreal
1977	Guy Lafleur	Montreal
1976	Guy Lafleur	Montreal
1975	Bobby Orr	Boston
1974	Phil Esposito	Boston
1973	Bobby Clarke	Philadelphia
1972	Jean Ratelle	NY Rangers
1971	Phil Esposito	Boston

JACK ADAMS AWARD WINNERS

	Winner	Runner-up
1998	Pat Burns, Bos.	Larry Robinson, L.A.
1997	Ted Nolan, Buf.	Ken Hitchcock, Dal.
1996	Scotty Bowman, Det.	Doug MacLean, Fla.
1995	Marc Crawford, Que.	Scotty Bowman, Det.
1994	Jacques Lemaire, N.J.	Kevin Constantine, S.J.
1993	Pat Burns, Tor.	Brian Sutter, Bos.
1992	Pat Quinn, Van.	Roger Neilson, NYR
1991	Brian Sutter, St.L.	Tom Webster, L.A.
1990	Bob Murdoch, Wpg.	Mike Milbury, Bos.
1989	Pat Burns, Mtl.	Bob McCammon, Van.
1988	Jacques Demers, Det.	Terry Crisp, Cgy.
1987	Jacques Demers, Det.	Jack Evans, Hfd.
1986	Glen Sather, Edm.	Jacques Demers, St.L.
1985	Mike Keenan, Phi.	Barry Long, Wpg.
1984	Bryan Murray, Wsh.	Scotty Bowman, Buf.
1983	Orval Tessier, Chi.	
1982	Tom Watt, Wpg.	
1981	Red Berenson, St.L.	Bob Berry, L.A.
1980	Pat Quinn, Phi.	
1979	Al Arbour, NYI	Fred Shero, NYR
1978	Bobby Kromm, Det.	Don Cherry, Bos.
1977	Scotty Bowman, Mtl.	Tom McVie, Wsh.
1976	Don Cherry, Bos.	
1975	Bob Pulford, L.A.	
1974	Fred Shero, Phi.	

NHL Amateur and Entry Draft

History

Year	Site	Date	Total Players Drafted
1963	Queen Elizabeth Hotel	June 5	21
1964	Queen Elizabeth Hotel	June 11	24
1965	Queen Elizabeth Hotel	April 27	11
1966	Mount Royal Hotel	April 25	24
1967	Queen Elizabeth Hotel	June 7	18
1968	Queen Elizabeth Hotel	June 13	24
1969	Queen Elizabeth Hotel	June 12	84
1970	Queen Elizabeth Hotel	June 11	115
1971	Queen Elizabeth Hotel	June 10	117
1972	Queen Elizabeth Hotel	June 8	152
1973	Mount Royal Hotel	May 15	168
1974	NHL Montreal Office	May 28	247
1975	NHL Montreal Office	June 3	217
1976	NHL Montreal Office	June 1	135
1977	NHL Montreal Office	June 14	185
1978	Queen Elizabeth Hotel	June 15	234
1979	Queen Elizabeth Hotel	August 9	126
1980	Montreal Forum	June 11	210
1981	Montreal Forum	June 10	211
1982	Montreal Forum	June 9	252
1983	Montreal Forum	June 8	242
1984	Montreal Forum	June 9	250
1985	Toronto Convention Centre	June 15	252
1986	Montreal Forum	June 21	252
1987	Joe Louis Sports Arena	June 13	252
1988	Montreal Forum	June 11	252
1989	Metropolitan Sports Center	June 17	252
1990	B. C. Place	June 16	250
1991	Memorial Auditorium	June 9	264
1992	Montreal Forum	June 20	264
1993	Colisée de Québec	June 26	286
1994	Hartford Civic Center	June 28-29	286
1995	Edmonton Coliseum	July 8	234
1996	Kiel Center	June 22	241
1997	Civic Arena	June 21	246
1998	Marine Midland Arena	June 27	258

* The NHL Amateur Draft became the NHL Entry Draft in 1979

With the top pick in the 1998 NHL Entry Draft the Tampa Bay Lightning went with consensus number-one prospect Vincent Lecavalier of the Rimouski Oceanic of the Quebec Major Junior Hockey League. A strong skater with excellent puck control, the 6'4" Lecavalier plays with poise and confidence. Profiles of all 27 first-round selections are found on page 204.

First Selections

Year	Player	Pos	Drafted By	Drafted From	Age
1969	Rejean Houle	LW	Montreal	Montreal Jr. Canadiens	19.8
1970	Gilbert Perreault	C	Buffalo	Montreal Jr. Canadiens	19.7
1971	Guy Lafleur	RW	Montreal	Quebec Remparts	19.9
1972	Billy Harris	RW	NY Islanders	Toronto Marlboros	20.4
1973	Denis Potvin	D	NY Islanders	Ottawa 67's	19.7
1974	Greg Joly	D	Washington	Regina Pats	20.0
1975	Mel Bridgman	C	Philadelphia	Victoria Cougars	20.1
1976	Rick Green	D	Washington	London Knights	20.3
1977	Dale McCourt	C	Detroit	St. Catharines Fincups	20.4
1978	Bobby Smith	C	Minnesota	Ottawa 67's	20.4
1979	Rob Ramage	D	Colorado	London Knights	20.5
1980	Doug Wickenheiser	C	Montreal	Regina Pats	19.2
1981	Dale Hawerchuk	C	Winnipeg	Cornwall Royals	18.2
1982	Gord Kluzak	D	Boston	Nanaimo Islanders	18.3
1983	Brian Lawton	C	Minnesota	Mount St. Charles HS	18.11
1984	Mario Lemieux	C	Pittsburgh	Laval Voisins	18.8
1985	Wendel Clark	LW/D	Toronto	Saskatoon Blades	18.7
1986	Joe Murphy	C	Detroit	Michigan State	18.8
1987	Pierre Turgeon	C	Buffalo	Granby Bisons	17.10
1988	Mike Modano	C	Minnesota	Prince Albert Raiders	18.0
1989	Mats Sundin	RW	Quebec	Nacka (Sweden)	18.4
1990	Owen Nolan	RW	Quebec	Cornwall Royals	18.4
1991	Eric Lindros	C	Quebec	Oshawa Generals	18.3
1992	Roman Hamrlik	D	Tampa Bay	ZPS Zlin (Czech.)	18.2
1993	Alexandre Daigle	C	Ottawa	Victoriaville Tigres	18.5
1994	Ed Jovanovski	D	Florida	Windsor Spitfires	18.0
1995	Bryan Berard	D	Ottawa	Detroit Jr. Red Wings	18.4
1996	Chris Phillips	D	Ottawa	Prince Albert Raiders	18.3
1997	Joe Thornton	C	Boston	Sault Ste. Marie	17.11
1998	Vincent Lecavalier	C	Tampa Bay	Rimouski Oceanic	18.2

Draft Summary

Following is a summary of the number of players drafted from the Ontario Hockey League (OHL), Western Hockey League (WHL), Quebec Major Junior Hockey League (QMJHL), United States Colleges, United States High Schools, European Leagues and other Leagues throughout North America since 1969:

	OHL	WHL	QMJHL	US Colleges	US HS	International	Other
1969	36	20	11	7	0	1	9
1970	51	22	13	16	0	0	13
1971	41	28	13	22	0	0	13
1972	46	44	30	21	0	0	11
1973	56	49	24	25	0	0	14
1974	69	66	40	41	0	6	25
1975	55	57	28	59	0	6	12
1976	47	33	18	26	0	8	3
1977	42	44	40	49	0	5	5
1978	59	48	22	73	0	16	16
1979	48	37	19	15	0	6	1
1980	73	41	24	42	7	13	10
1981	59	37	28	21	17	32	17
1982	60	55	17	20	47	35	18
1983	57	41	24	14	35	34	37
1984	55	38	16	22	44	40	36
1985	59	47	15	20	48	31	31
1986	66	32	22	22	40	28	42
1987	32	36	17	40	69	38	20
1988	32	30	22	48	56	39	25
1989	39	44	16	48	47	38	20
1990	39	33	14	38	57	53	16
1991	43	40	25	43	37	55	21
1992	57	45	22	9	25	84	22
1993	60	44	23	17	33	78	31
1994	45	66	28	6	28	80	33
1995	54	55	35	5	2	69	14
1996	51	54	31	25	6	58	16
1997	52	63	19	26	4	63	19
1998	50	44	41	27	7	75	14
Total	**1533**	**1293**	**697**	**847**	**609**	**991**	**564**

Total Drafted, 1969-1998: 6,534

Ontario Hockey League

Club	'69	'70	'71	'72	'73	'74	'75	'76	'77	'78	'79	'80	'81	'82	'83	'84	'85	'86	'87	'88	'89	'90	'91	'92	'93	'94	'95	'96	'97	'98	Total
Peterborough	5	5	4	5	9	4	8	1	4	6	9	10	3	5	7	3	9	2	5	2	2	4	3	4	4	2	5	4	5	1	140
Oshawa	5	4	3	5	5	7	6	6	1	3	3	2	9	5	5	6	6	6	3	2	4	2	4	4	4	1	10	1	3	4	129
Kitchener	1	6	2	8	4	13	3	1	3	4	4	4	5	5	8	4	6	3	2	1	7	5	3	1	4	2	4	2	3	5	123
London	4	9	1	5	6	6	3	5	4	3	6	2	5	5	3	7	1	3	2	6	3	3	1	3	4	1	1	4	1	8	115
Ottawa	2	4	3	4	6	5	6	5	5	5	3	8	4	9	2	2	3	3	2	1	–	5	5	6	4	1	1	2	5	2	113
S.S. Marie	–	–	–	–	4	5	2	5	1	5	3	3	8	1	6	4	5	7	1	2	3	1	2	7	3	4	3	4	1	4	94
Sudbury	–	–	–	–	6	6	4	5	4	4	3	7	2	4	–	2	5	3	1	–	1	2	8	2	10	2	2	1	3	5	92
Kingston	–	–	–	–	–	4	4	6	4	9	2	8	5	2	1	3	3	4	1	1	–	2	2	3	5	2	3	4	4	1	83
Niagara Falls	4	2	1	4	–	–	–	–	2	3	5	8	6	6	–	–	–	–	–	–	4	4	4	4	4	3	2	6	–	–	72
Windsor	–	–	–	–	–	–	–	2	1	4	2	3	5	3	2	2	3	7	–	5	2	1	–	3	–	3	4	1	5	1	59
Guelph	–	–	–	–	–	–	–	–	–	–	–	–	–	–	1	5	3	8	2	–	4	–	–	2	2	7	5	6	1	5	51
North Bay	–	–	–	–	–	–	–	–	–	–	–	–	–	–	4	4	3	3	3	3	1	4	2	5	2	7	2	1	1	2	47
Belleville	–	–	–	–	–	–	–	–	–	–	–	–	–	–	3	4	4	5	2	–	4	2	1	4	–	3	3	–	5	2	42
Det./Plymouth	–	–	–	–	–	–	–	–	–	–	–	–	–	–	–	–	–	–	–	–	–	–	2	2	7	2	6	3	4	2	28
Owen Sound	–	–	–	–	–	–	–	–	–	–	–	–	–	–	–	–	–	–	–	–	–	1	1	2	4	3	2	3	2	1	19
Sarnia	–	–	–	–	–	–	–	–	–	–	–	–	–	–	–	–	–	–	–	–	–	–	–	–	–	–	1	7	2	3	13
Barrie	–	–	–	–	–	–	–	–	–	–	–	–	–	–	–	–	–	–	–	–	–	–	–	–	–	–	–	2	4	3	9
Erie	–	–	–	–	–	–	–	–	–	–	–	–	–	–	–	–	–	–	–	–	–	–	–	–	–	–	–	–	3	1	4
Teams no longer operating																															
Toronto	3	7	6	5	6	8	4	4	7	5	4	10	2	6	4	4	3	4	1	2	2	–	–	–	–	–	–	–	–	–	97
Hamilton	2	3	5	4	6	4	7	3	–	8	1	–	–	–	–	–	3	6	4	4	–	–	2	–	–	–	–	–	–	–	62
St. Catharines	5	5	8	5	4	7	8	4	6	–	–	–	–	–	–	–	–	–	–	–	–	–	–	–	–	–	–	–	–	–	52
Cornwall	–	–	–	–	–	–	–	–	–	–	–	–	–	7	4	3	2	2	3	3	2	3	3	5	–	–	–	–	–	–	37
Brantford	–	–	–	–	–	–	–	–	–	–	3	8	5	2	7	2	–	–	–	–	–	–	–	–	–	–	–	–	–	–	27
Montreal	5	6	8	1	–	–	–	–	–	–	–	–	–	–	–	–	–	–	–	–	–	–	–	–	–	–	–	–	–	–	20
Newmarket	–	–	–	–	–	–	–	–	–	–	–	–	–	–	–	–	–	–	–	–	–	–	–	–	3	2	–	–	–	–	5

Year	Total Ontario Drafted	Total Players Drafted	Ontario %
1969	36	84	42.9
1970	51	115	44.3
1971	41	117	35.0
1972	46	152	30.3
1973	56	168	33.3
1974	69	247	27.9
1975	55	217	25.3
1976	47	135	34.8
1977	42	185	22.7
1978	59	234	25.2
1979	48	126	38.1
1980	73	210	34.8
1981	59	211	28.0
1982	60	252	23.8
1983	57	242	23.6
1984	55	250	22.0
1985	59	252	23.4
1986	66	252	26.2
1987	32	252	12.7
1988	32	252	12.7
1989	39	252	15.5
1990	39	250	15.6
1991	43	264	16.3
1992	57	264	21.6
1993	60	286	21.0
1994	45	286	15.7
1995	54	234	23.1
1996	51	241	21.1
1997	52	246	21.1
1998	50	258	19.4
Total	**1533**	**6534**	**23.5**

Western Hockey League

Club	'69	'70	'71	'72	'73	'74	'75	'76	'77	'78	'79	'80	'81	'82	'83	'84	'85	'86	'87	'88	'89	'90	'91	'92	'93	'94	'95	'96	'97	'98	Total
Regina	–	–	5	5	1	8	5	3	1	4	1	3	5	6	8	4	4	3	2	–	5	1	–	4	–	3	2	4	3	2	92
Saskatoon	1	–	1	3	8	4	5	3	4	1	2	2	3	5	5	3	1	5	4	4	3	2	2	3	2	4	2	2	2	2	88
Portland	–	–	–	–	–	–	–	–	4	8	7	8	6	7	7	5	2	4	3	1	4	1	1	4	4	3	2	1	3	3	88
Medicine Hat	–	–	–	4	6	4	5	3	5	4	–	4	2	1	2	1	6	2	5	1	4	1	3	3	1	6	2	7	2	3	87
Brandon	–	3	1	5	2	7	4	–	3	1	10	5	2	2	1	3	2	1	3	3	–	1	1	1	2	5	6	2	5	4	85
Kamloops	–	–	–	–	–	4	4	4	4	–	–	–	–	2	4	4	4	4	3	1	5	4	6	3	2	9	5	4	3	1	80
Lethbridge	–	–	–	–	–	–	3	2	3	5	4	1	4	7	2	1	5	1	–	3	3	4	7	3	4	3	3	1	5	1	75
Seattle	–	–	–	–	–	–	–	–	–	4	2	3	–	6	–	1	3	1	2	4	2	6	3	2	4	5	5	1	8	2	64
Prince Albert	–	–	–	–	–	–	–	–	–	–	–	–	–	4	2	2	6	6	1	3	3	4	6	2	5	3	4	3	5	3	62
Spokane	–	–	–	–	–	–	–	–	–	–	–	–	1	–	–	–	–	–	1	3	2	1	5	7	4	4	4	5	4	1	42
Swift Current	1	–	1	–	3	6	–	–	–	–	–	–	–	–	–	–	–	–	5	2	2	2	1	1	5	4	4	1	2	2	42
Moose Jaw	–	–	–	–	–	–	–	–	–	–	–	–	–	–	–	–	4	1	3	–	3	1	2	3	2	3	4	4	4	2	36
Tri-City	–	–	–	–	–	–	–	–	–	–	–	–	–	–	–	–	–	–	–	–	4	3	3	5	2	2	6	6	1	4	36
Red Deer	–	–	–	–	–	–	–	–	–	–	–	–	–	–	–	–	–	–	–	–	–	–	–	–	3	5	2	4	3	5	22
Kelowna	–	–	–	–	–	–	–	–	–	–	–	–	–	–	–	–	–	–	–	–	–	–	–	–	–	–	–	4	7	2	13
Prince George	–	–	–	–	–	–	–	–	–	–	–	–	–	–	–	–	–	–	–	–	–	–	–	–	–	–	2	2	2	4	10
Calgary	–	–	–	–	–	–	–	–	–	–	–	–	–	–	–	–	–	–	–	–	–	–	–	–	–	–	–	3	–	3	6
Edmonton	–	–	–	–	–	–	–	–	–	–	–	–	–	–	–	–	–	–	–	–	–	–	–	–	–	–	–	–	4	–	4
Teams no longer operating																															
Victoria	–	–	–	2	2	5	7	4	3	3	1	8	6	2	3	4	2	1	2	4	4	2	–	1	2	2	–	–	–	–	70
Calgary	3	5	2	7	4	8	4	4	4	3	–	2	5	4	3	3	3	2	–	–	–	–	–	–	–	–	–	–	–	–	66
New Westm'r	–	–	–	6	8	7	9	5	8	6	5	1	–	–	–	2	1	1	2	1	–	–	–	–	–	–	–	–	–	–	62
Flin Flon	4	4	5	2	4	7	4	3	1	5	–	–	–	–	–	–	–	–	–	–	–	–	–	–	–	–	–	–	–	–	39
Winnipeg	3	2	4	2	5	4	4	–	4	–	–	–	1	4	1	–	–	–	–	–	–	–	–	–	–	–	–	–	–	–	34
Edmonton	4	4	5	6	6	2	3	2	–	–	2	–	–	–	–	–	–	–	–	–	–	–	–	–	–	–	–	–	–	–	34
Billings	–	–	–	–	–	–	–	–	–	4	3	4	2	–	–	–	–	–	–	–	–	–	–	–	–	–	–	–	–	–	13
Estevan	4	4	4	–	–	–	–	–	–	–	–	–	–	–	–	–	–	–	–	–	–	–	–	–	–	–	–	–	–	–	12
Tacoma	–	–	–	–	–	–	–	–	–	–	–	–	–	–	–	–	–	–	–	–	–	–	–	3	2	5	2	–	–	–	12
Kelowna	–	–	–	–	–	–	–	–	–	–	–	–	–	–	2	4	5	–	–	–	–	–	–	–	–	–	–	–	–	–	11
Nanaimo	–	–	–	–	–	–	–	–	–	–	–	–	–	5	1	–	–	–	–	–	–	–	–	–	–	–	–	–	–	–	6
Vancouver	–	–	–	2	–	–	–	–	–	–	–	–	–	–	–	–	–	–	–	–	–	–	–	–	–	–	–	–	–	–	2

Year	Total Western Drafted	Total Players Drafted	Western %
1969	20	84	23.8
1970	22	115	19.1
1971	28	117	23.9
1972	44	152	28.9
1973	49	168	29.2
1974	66	247	26.7
1975	57	217	26.3
1976	33	135	24.4
1977	44	185	23.8
1978	48	234	20.5
1979	37	126	29.4
1980	41	210	19.5
1981	37	211	17.5
1982	55	252	21.8
1983	41	242	16.9
1984	37	250	14.8
1985	48	252	19.0
1986	32	252	12.7
1987	36	252	14.3
1988	30	252	11.9
1989	44	252	17.5
1990	33	250	13.2
1991	40	264	15.2
1992	45	264	17.0
1993	44	286	15.4
1994	66	286	23.0
1995	55	234	23.5
1996	54	241	22.4
1997	63	246	25.6
1998	44	258	17.0
Total	**1293**	**6534**	**19.8**

The only goalie to go directly from high school to the NHL, Tom Barrasso was selected 5th overall by the Buffalo Sabres in 1983. After an injury-plagued 1996-97 season, Barrasso returned to top form in 1997-98, recording a GAA of 2.07 and a career-high seven shutouts.

Quebec Major Junior Hockey League

Club	'69	'70	'71	'72	'73	'74	'75	'76	'77	'78	'79	'80	'81	'82	'83	'84	'85	'86	'87	'88	'89	'90	'91	'92	'93	'94	'95	'96	'97	'98	Total
Shawinigan	3	2	1	6	1	5	3	–	3	–	–	2	2	5	5	2	–	2	1	–	2	–	2	3	1	1	2	4	1	3	62
Sherbrooke	–	–	2	2	4	3	7	5	6	3	4	1	5	2	–	–	–	–	–	–	–	–	–	–	3	2	4	–	1	5	59
Laval	–	–	–	1	–	2	1	1	4	2	1	–	–	2	1	2	–	5	3	1	3	3	4	1	2	5	4	2	1	3	54
Hull	–	–	–	–	–	–	3	2	2	3	–	3	1	–	3	1	–	4	3	2	2	3	3	3	3	1	3	3	–	3	51
Drummondville	2	4	1	4	2	1	–	–	–	–	–	–	–	–	–	1	2	2	2	4	1	–	4	2	2	1	4	3	2	2	46
Chicoutimi	–	–	–	–	–	1	–	–	5	1	1	3	6	1	3	–	3	1	2	2	1	1	–	1	1	3	2	–	2	1	41
Granby	–	–	–	–	–	–	–	–	–	–	–	–	–	2	1	3	2	2	4	–	2	–	2	–	1	5	2	3	1	–	30
Beauport	–	–	–	–	–	–	–	–	–	–	–	–	–	–	–	–	–	–	–	–	–	–	1	3	1	3	7	3	3	–	21
Victoriaville	–	–	–	–	–	–	–	–	–	–	–	–	–	–	–	–	–	–	–	4	–	1	–	2	6	1	1	3	2	1	21
St. Hyacinthe	–	–	–	–	–	–	–	–	–	–	–	–	–	–	–	–	–	–	–	–	–	3	1	2	1	4	–	4	–	–	15
Halifax	–	–	–	–	–	–	–	–	–	–	–	–	–	–	–	–	–	–	–	–	–	–	–	–	–	–	3	1	3	3	10
Val D'Or	–	–	–	–	–	–	–	–	–	–	–	–	–	–	–	–	–	–	–	–	–	–	–	–	–	1	2	4	2	–	9
Rimouski	–	–	–	–	–	–	–	–	–	–	–	–	–	–	–	–	–	–	–	–	–	–	–	–	–	–	–	–	–	5	5
Moncton	–	–	–	–	–	–	–	–	–	–	–	–	–	–	–	–	–	–	–	–	–	–	–	–	–	–	–	1	1	2	4
Quebec	–	–	–	–	–	–	–	–	–	–	–	–	–	–	–	–	–	–	–	–	–	–	–	–	–	–	–	–	–	4	4
Rouyn-Noranda	–	–	–	–	–	–	–	–	–	–	–	–	–	–	–	–	–	–	–	–	–	–	–	–	–	–	–	–	–	3	3
Cape Breton	–	–	–	–	–	–	–	–	–	–	–	–	–	–	–	–	–	–	–	–	–	–	–	–	–	–	–	–	–	3	3
Baie-Comeau	–	–	–	–	–	–	–	–	–	–	–	–	–	–	–	–	–	–	–	–	–	–	–	–	–	–	–	–	–	3	3
Teams no longer operating																															
Quebec	1	1	2	4	6	6	1	3	7	1	3	2	2	1	2	2	3	–	–	–	–	–	–	–	–	–	–	–	–	–	47
Trois Rivieres	–	1	2	2	2	2	3	2	6	3	2	2	2	1	3	–	3	–	1	3	3	1	2	1	–	–	–	–	–	–	47
Cornwall	2	1	2	6	4	8	1	3	1	6	1	5	5	–	–	–	–	–	–	–	–	–	–	–	–	–	–	–	–	–	45
Montreal	–	–	–	–	4	4	8	1	3	2	4	3	–	3	–	–	–	–	–	–	–	–	–	–	–	–	–	–	–	–	32
Sorel	2	3	1	3	1	8	1	1	3	–	–	–	5	–	–	–	–	–	–	–	–	–	–	–	–	–	–	–	–	–	28
Verdun	–	1	1	2	–	–	–	–	–	1	3	3	–	–	3	3	–	3	0	3	1	–	–	3	–	–	–	–	–	–	27
St. Jean	–	–	–	–	–	–	–	–	–	–	–	–	–	–	2	–	1	1	0	3	1	–	3	1	2	1	1	–	–	–	16
Longueuil	–	–	–	–	–	–	–	–	–	–	–	–	–	–	1	2	1	2	1	–	–	2	3	–	–	–	–	–	–	–	12
St. Jerome	1	–	1	–	–	–	–	–	–	–	–	–	–	–	–	–	–	–	–	–	–	–	–	–	–	–	–	–	–	–	2

Year	Total Quebec Drafted	Total Players Drafted	Quebec %
1969	11	84	13.1
1970	13	115	11.3
1971	13	117	11.1
1972	30	152	19.7
1973	24	168	14.3
1974	40	247	16.2
1975	28	217	12.9
1976	18	135	13.3
1977	40	185	21.6
1978	22	234	9.4
1979	19	126	15.1
1980	24	210	11.4
1981	28	211	13.3
1982	17	252	6.7
1983	24	242	9.9
1984	16	250	6.4
1985	15	252	5.9
1986	22	252	8.7
1987	17	252	6.7
1988	22	252	8.7
1989	16	252	6.3
1990	14	250	5.6
1991	25	264	9.5
1992	22	264	8.3
1993	23	286	8.0
1994	28	286	9.7
1995	35	234	14.9
1996	31	241	12.8
1997	19	246	7.7
1998	41	258	15.9
Total	**697**	**6534**	**10.7**

United States Colleges

Club	'69	'70	'71	'72	'73	'74	'75	'76	'77	'78	'79	'80	'81	'82	'83	'84	'85	'86	'87	'88	'89	'90	'91	'92	'93	'94	'95	'96	'97	'98	Total
Minnesota	1	3	2	–	–	9	4	4	5	5	2	3	1	1	1	–	–	2	1	1	1	–	–	–	–	–	2	3	2	1	54
Michigan	1	–	–	–	2	2	3	3	1	6	–	4	–	–	–	1	1	–	1	2	3	5	4	2	1	1	–	3	1	3	50
Michigan Tech	–	–	3	1	2	5	4	4	1	2	1	4	–	1	–	2	2	2	1	1	2	1	2	–	1	2	–	1	–	–	45
Boston U.	–	4	–	–	1	1	1	1	4	5	1	–	1	–	–	1	1	2	2	3	1	2	2	1	1	–	1	1	1	2	40
Denver	1	3	2	4	2	3	1	2	2	2	2	1	–	1	–	–	1	2	4	1	1	–	–	–	–	–	–	–	3	–	38
Wisconsin	–	1	2	4	5	4	4	2	3	–	1	–	3	2	–	1	1	–	1	–	1	–	1	–	–	–	–	–	–	–	36
Michigan State	–	–	1	–	1	1	1	1	–	–	–	2	–	2	–	2	–	1	1	4	4	5	4	1	1	1	–	1	1	1	36
North Dakota	2	3	3	1	4	2	1	–	1	2	3	3	1	–	–	1	–	–	–	–	2	1	1	–	–	–	–	–	2	–	33
Providence	–	–	–	–	–	–	3	2	3	4	–	5	4	1	2	–	1	1	–	–	–	1	–	–	–	–	–	–	1	2	30
Clarkson	–	–	2	2	1	–	2	–	2	2	1	1	1	1	1	1	–	–	1	1	1	3	2	1	1	–	–	–	–	3	30
New Hampshire	–	–	–	1	1	3	6	–	4	1	1	2	1	1	1	2	–	–	–	1	–	–	–	–	–	–	–	–	1	–	26
Harvard	–	–	2	–	–	–	2	–	2	2	–	–	–	1	1	–	2	–	1	1	2	–	–	–	2	1	–	3	1	2	25
Boston College	–	1	–	–	–	–	1	1	–	5	–	2	1	1	–	–	–	1	2	–	2	–	–	–	–	–	–	2	3	3	25
Cornell	–	–	–	2	1	1	–	1	1	1	–	1	1	1	–	1	2	–	1	2	5	2	–	–	–	–	–	–	1	–	24
Colorado	2	1	–	–	–	1	3	1	2	2	–	1	–	–	–	3	–	1	–	1	–	2	–	–	–	–	1	–	–	3	24
Bowling Green	–	–	–	–	–	1	3	2	1	1	1	1	–	–	1	–	–	–	–	3	2	1	3	1	–	–	–	–	1	1	23
Lake Superior	–	–	–	–	1	1	1	–	–	3	–	–	–	–	–	1	–	3	–	3	2	3	1	–	1	–	–	1	1	–	22
Notre Dame	–	–	2	3	–	–	7	2	–	3	1	1	–	–	–	–	–	–	–	–	–	–	–	–	–	–	–	1	2	–	22
W. Michigan	–	–	–	–	–	–	–	–	2	–	–	2	–	–	2	2	–	2	1	1	1	1	4	–	2	–	–	–	1	1	22
St. Lawrence	–	–	–	–	–	–	1	–	1	4	–	–	–	3	–	1	1	1	1	1	1	1	2	–	1	–	–	1	1	–	21
RPI	–	–	–	–	1	–	–	–	1	3	–	1	2	1	1	–	1	–	2	2	–	–	3	1	–	–	–	–	1	–	20
Northern Mich.	–	–	–	–	–	–	–	–	–	4	–	1	2	1	–	–	–	–	4	1	2	–	1	–	–	–	–	1	–	–	17
Vermont	–	–	–	–	1	–	4	–	1	1	–	1	1	–	1	1	2	–	–	1	–	–	1	–	–	1	–	1	–	–	17
Miami of Ohio	–	–	–	–	–	–	–	–	–	–	–	–	–	–	–	–	1	–	2	4	2	–	2	1	1	–	–	–	–	1	14
Ohio State	–	–	–	–	–	–	–	–	2	1	–	–	–	–	–	1	–	–	2	2	–	1	1	1	1	–	–	1	1	–	14
Maine	–	–	–	–	–	–	–	–	–	–	–	–	–	1	1	–	–	1	–	3	2	1	–	–	1	–	–	1	1	1	13
Minn.-Duluth	–	–	2	1	–	–	–	–	1	1	–	–	1	–	–	–	–	–	–	2	1	2	1	–	–	–	–	–	–	1	13
Brown	–	–	–	–	1	2	1	–	3	2	–	–	–	1	–	–	–	–	–	–	–	–	1	–	–	–	–	–	–	–	11
Colgate	–	–	–	–	–	1	–	–	–	2	1	–	–	–	–	–	–	–	–	1	1	2	2	–	–	–	–	–	–	–	10
Yale	–	–	–	1	–	–	1	–	–	2	–	1	–	–	–	–	–	1	2	–	1	–	–	–	1	–	–	–	–	–	10

Colleges with fewer than 10 players drafted:

9 - Northeastern, Princeton; **7** - Ferris State; **6** - Illinois-Chicago, St. Louis; **5** - Dartmouth, Merrimack, Pennsylvania; **4** - Alaska-Anchorage, Lowell, Union College; **3** - Babson College, St. Cloud State; **2** - Alaska-Fairbanks; **1** - American International College, Army, Bemidji State, Greenway, Hamilton, St. Anselen College, St. Thomas, Salem State, San Diego U., Wisconsin-River Falls.

Year	Total College Drafted	Total Players Drafted	College %
1969	7	84	8.3
1970	16	115	13.9
1971	22	117	18.8
1972	21	152	13.8
1973	25	168	14.9
1974	41	247	16.6
1975	59	217	26.7
1976	26	135	19.3
1977	49	185	26.5
1978	73	234	31.2
1979	15	126	11.9
1980	42	210	20.0
1981	21	211	10.0
1982	20	252	7.9
1983	14	242	5.8
1984	22	250	8.8
1985	20	252	7.9
1986	22	252	8.7
1987	40	252	15.9
1988	48	252	19.0
1989	48	252	19.0
1990	38	250	15.2
1991	43	264	16.3
1992	9	264	3.4
1993	17	286	5.9
1994	6	286	2.1
1995	5	234	2.1
1996	25	241	10.4
1997	26	246	10.5
1998	27	258	10.4
Total	**847**	**6534**	**12.9**

United States High Schools (10 or more players drafted)

Club	'80	'81	'82	'83	'84	'85	'86	'87	'88	'89	'90	'91	'92	'93	'94	'95	'96	'97	'98	Total
Northwood Prep (NY)	–	–	2	1	–	2	2	4	1	1	3	1	–	1	1	–	–	–	–	19
Belmont Hill (MA)	–	–	–	1	–	2	1	2	1	3	2	1	2	–	1	–	–	–	–	16
Cushing Acad. (MA)	–	–	–	–	1	–	–	–	3	2	3	1	–	2	2	–	1	1	–	16
Edina (MN)	–	1	4	2	2	–	–	1	2	2	1	–	1	–	–	–	–	–	–	16
Hill-Murray (MN)	–	–	–	–	3	–	3	3	–	2	3	–	–	–	1	–	–	–	–	15
Mount St. Charles (RI)	–	1	–	3	1	–	2	1	2	1	1	–	–	–	–	–	–	–	–	12
Culver Mil. Acad. (IN)	–	–	–	–	–	–	–	2	1	2	2	1	2	2	–	–	–	–	–	12
Catholic Memorial (MA)	–	–	–	–	–	2	–	1	1	2	–	–	2	1	2	–	–	–	1	12
Canterbury (CT)	–	–	–	–	–	–	2	–	3	–	2	–	2	1	–	–	–	–	–	10
Matignon (MA)	1	1	1	–	3	–	–	3	–	–	–	1	–	–	–	–	–	–	–	10
Roseau (MN)	1	–	1	1	1	–	1	–	–	1	3	1	–	–	–	–	–	–	–	10

Year	Total USHS Drafted	Total Players Drafted	USHS %
1980	7	210	3.3
1981	17	211	8.1
1982	47	252	18.6
1983	35	242	14.5
1984	44	250	17.6
1985	48	252	19.1
1986	40	252	15.9
1987	69	252	27.4
1988	56	252	22.2
1989	47	252	18.7
1990	57	250	22.8
1991	37	264	14.0
1992	25	264	9.5
1993	33	286	11.5
1994	28	286	9.7
1995	2	234	0.9
1996	6	241	2.4
1997	4	246	1.6
1998	7	258	2.7
Total	**609**	**6534**	**9.3**

International

Country	'69	'70	'71	'72	'73	'74	'75	'76	'77	'78	'79	'80	'81	'82	'83	'84	'85	'86	'87	'88	'89	'90	'91	'92	'93	'94	'95	'96	'97	'98	Total
USSR/CIS	–	–	–	–	–	–	1	–	–	2	–	–	–	3	5	1	2	1	2	11	18	14	25	45	31	35	27	17	16	22	278
Sweden	–	–	–	–	–	5	2	5	2	8	5	9	14	14	10	14	16	9	15	14	9	7	11	11	18	17	8	16	14	19	272
Czech Republic and Slovakia	–	–	–	–	–	–	–	–	–	–	–	2	1	–	4	13	8	6	11	5	8	21	9	17	15	18	21	14	17	20	232
Finland	1	–	–	–	–	1	3	2	3	2	–	4	12	5	9	10	4	10	6	7	3	9	6	8	9	8	12	7	11	12	164
Germany	–	–	–	–	–	–	–	–	–	2	–	–	2	–	1	2	1	–	1	2	–	–	1	1	3	1	1	3	1	–	23
Switzerland	–	–	–	–	–	–	–	1	–	–	–	–	–	–	–	–	–	–	–	–	–	–	1	–	2	1	–	1	3	2	11
Norway	–	–	–	–	–	–	–	–	–	–	–	–	–	–	–	–	–	–	2	–	–	2	1	–	–	–	–	–	1	–	6
Denmark	–	–	–	–	–	–	–	–	–	–	–	–	–	–	–	–	–	1	1	–	–	–	–	–	–	–	–	–	–	–	2
Scotland	–	–	–	–	–	–	–	–	–	–	–	–	–	–	–	–	–	1	–	–	–	–	–	–	–	–	–	–	–	–	1
Poland	–	–	–	–	–	–	–	–	–	–	–	–	–	–	–	–	–	–	–	–	–	–	1	–	–	–	–	–	–	–	1
Japan	–	–	–	–	–	–	–	–	–	–	–	–	–	–	–	–	–	–	–	–	–	–	–	1	–	–	–	–	–	–	1

Year	Total International Drafted	Total Players Drafted	International %
1969	1	84	1.2
1970	0	115	0
1971	0	117	0
1972	0	152	0
1973	0	168	0
1974	6	247	2.4
1975	6	217	2.8
1976	8	135	5.9
1977	5	185	2.7
1978	16	234	6.8
1979	6	126	4.8
1980	13	210	6.2
1981	32	211	15.2
1982	35	252	13.9
1983	34	242	14.0
1984	40	250	17.6
1985	31	252	12.3
1986	28	252	11.1
1987	38	252	15.1
1988	39	252	15.5
1989	38	252	15.1
1990	53	250	21.2
1991	55	264	20.8
1992	84	264	31.4
1993	78	286	27.3
1994	80	286	27.9
1995	69	234	29.5
1996	58	241	24.0
1997	63	246	25.6
1998	75	258	29.0
Total	**991**	**6534**	**15.1**

Note: Players drafted in the international category played outside North America in their draft year. European-born players drafted from the OHL, QMJHL, WHL or U.S. Colleges are not counted as International players. See Country of Origin, below.

Sweden

Club	'74	'75	'76	'77	'78	'79	'80	'81	'82	'83	'84	'85	'86	'87	'88	'89	'90	'91	'92	'93	'94	'95	'96	'97	'98	Total
Farjestad Karlstad	–	–	–	2	2	–	1	2	1	1	1	2	–	–	–	1	–	1	2	1	–	2	–	3	6	28
Djurgarden Stockholm	1	1	1	–	–	1	2	–	1	2	1	–	1	2	–	1	1	2	1	1	–	3	2	2	–	26
MoDo Hockey Ornskoldsvik	–	–	1	–	–	1	–	–	1	–	2	–	–	1	–	–	–	2	2	5	–	–	3	3	–	21
Leksand	1	–	–	–	–	1	–	–	1	–	2	2	1	1	2	1	–	2	–	2	2	–	1	–	2	21
AIK Solna	–	–	1	–	1	1	–	2	3	1	–	4	–	–	–	–	1	1	1	–	1	–	–	1	1	19
Brynas Gavle	1	–	–	–	1	1	1	1	–	1	2	–	–	4	–	–	–	–	–	1	–	–	1	1	2	17
Sodertalje	–	–	–	–	1	–	–	1	1	1	2	2	2	–	–	2	–	–	–	1	–	–	–	–	1	14
Vastra Frolunda Goteborg	–	–	–	–	–	–	–	–	–	–	2	1	–	1	1	1	–	–	1	–	3	1	1	–	1	13
HV 71 Jonkoping	–	–	–	–	–	–	–	1	–	–	–	–	–	1	1	–	1	–	–	–	2	–	2	1	4	13
Skelleftea	–	1	1	–	–	–	–	1	1	2	1	–	–	–	1	–	–	–	–	1	–	–	–	1	–	10
Vasteras	–	–	–	–	–	–	–	–	–	–	–	–	–	–	2	2	1	1	–	1	1	–	–	–	–	8
Rogle Angelholm	–	–	–	–	–	–	–	–	–	–	–	–	–	1	2	–	–	–	–	2	2	1	–	–	–	8
Lulea	–	–	–	–	–	–	1	1	–	–	–	–	1	1	1	–	–	–	1	–	–	–	–	1	1	8
Sundsvall Timra[1]	–	–	–	–	–	–	1	2	–	–	–	1	1	–	–	–	–	–	–	–	1	–	–	–	–	6
Malmo	–	–	–	–	–	–	–	–	–	–	–	–	–	–	1	–	–	–	1	1	1	–	2	–	–	6
Bjorkloven Umea	–	–	–	–	–	–	2	1	–	–	–	1	–	–	1	–	–	–	–	–	–	–	–	–	–	5
Orebro	–	–	1	–	1	–	–	–	–	1	–	1	–	1	–	–	–	–	–	–	–	–	–	–	–	5
Hammarby Stockholm	–	–	–	–	–	–	1	1	–	–	–	–	–	–	–	–	–	–	–	1	1	–	–	–	1	5
Nacka	–	–	–	–	–	–	–	–	–	–	–	–	1	–	–	1	–	–	2	–	–	–	–	–	–	4
Mora	–	–	–	–	–	–	–	–	–	1	–	–	1	–	–	–	–	–	–	–	–	–	1	1	–	4
Falun	–	–	–	–	–	–	–	1	–	–	–	–	–	–	1	–	–	1	–	–	–	–	–	–	–	3
Team Kiruna	–	–	–	–	1	–	–	–	1	–	–	–	–	–	–	–	–	–	–	1	–	–	–	–	–	3
Boden	1	–	–	–	–	–	–	–	–	–	–	–	1	–	–	–	–	–	–	–	1	–	–	–	–	3
Pitea	–	–	–	–	–	–	–	–	1	–	–	–	–	–	–	–	1	–	–	–	1	–	–	–	–	3
Huddinge	–	–	–	–	–	–	–	–	–	–	–	–	–	–	–	–	–	1	–	–	–	–	2	–	–	3
Troja	–	–	–	–	–	–	–	–	–	–	–	1	–	–	1	–	–	–	–	–	–	–	–	–	–	2
Ostersund	–	–	–	–	–	–	–	–	–	–	–	1	–	1	–	–	–	–	–	–	–	–	–	–	–	2
Almtuna	–	–	–	–	–	–	–	–	1	–	–	–	–	–	–	–	–	–	–	–	–	–	–	–	–	1
Danderyd Hockey	–	–	–	–	–	–	–	–	–	–	–	–	–	–	–	–	1	–	–	–	–	–	–	–	–	1
Fagersta	–	–	–	–	–	–	–	–	1	–	–	–	–	–	–	–	–	–	–	–	–	–	–	–	–	1
Karskoga	–	–	–	–	1	–	–	–	–	–	–	–	–	–	–	–	–	–	–	–	–	–	–	–	–	1
Stocksund	–	–	–	–	–	–	–	–	1	–	–	–	–	–	–	–	–	–	–	–	–	–	–	–	–	1
S/G Hockey 83 Gavle	–	–	–	–	–	–	–	–	–	–	1	–	–	–	–	–	–	–	–	–	–	–	–	–	–	1
Talje	–	–	–	–	–	–	–	–	–	–	–	–	–	1	–	–	–	–	–	–	–	–	–	–	–	1
Tunabro	1	–	–	–	–	–	–	–	–	–	–	–	–	–	–	–	–	–	–	–	–	–	–	–	–	1
Uppsala	–	–	–	–	–	–	–	–	–	–	–	–	–	–	–	–	1	–	–	–	–	–	–	–	–	1
Grums	–	–	–	–	–	–	–	–	–	–	–	–	–	–	–	–	–	–	–	–	1	–	–	–	–	1
Vallentuna	–	–	–	–	–	–	–	–	–	–	–	–	–	–	–	–	–	–	–	–	–	1	–	–	–	1
Vita Hasten	–	–	–	–	–	–	–	–	–	–	–	–	–	–	–	–	–	–	–	–	–	–	1	–	–	1

Former club names: [1]–Timra

Russia/C.I.S.

Club	'74	'75	'76	'77	'78	'79	'80	'81	'82	'83	'84	'85	'86	'87	'88	'89	'90	'91	'92	'93	'94	'95	'96	'97	'98	Total
CSKA Moscow	–	–	–	–	1	–	–	–	1	4	–	1	1	1	5	8	3	4	7	3	5	2	3	–	1	50
Dynamo Moscow	–	–	–	–	–	–	–	–	–	–	–	–	–	–	2	3	4	7	10	2	1	7	1	1	1	39
Krylja Sovetov Moscow	–	–	–	–	–	–	–	–	–	–	–	–	–	–	1	1	2	4	3	1	5	3	2	1	1	24
Spartak Moscow	–	–	–	–	–	–	–	–	1	–	–	1	–	1	–	–	–	1	4	–	6	1	–	–	–	15
Traktor Chelyabinsk	–	–	–	–	–	–	–	–	–	–	–	–	–	–	–	2	–	–	2	7	1	1	–	1	1	15
Torpedo Yaroslavl	–	–	–	–	–	–	–	–	–	–	–	–	–	–	–	–	1	2	–	–	1	5	1	1	3	14
Sokol Kiev	–	–	–	–	–	–	–	–	–	–	1	–	–	–	1	–	1	2	3	1	–	2	–	–	–	11
Khimik Voskresensk	–	–	–	–	–	–	–	–	–	1	–	–	–	–	–	1	3	1	2	–	1	–	–	–	2	11
Dynamo-2 Moscow	–	–	–	–	–	–	–	–	–	–	–	–	–	–	–	–	–	–	2	1	2	–	–	3	3	11
Pardaugava Riga[1]	–	1	–	–	–	–	–	–	–	–	–	–	–	–	1	2	–	1	4	1	–	–	–	–	–	10
Torpedo-2 Yaroslavl	–	–	–	–	–	–	–	–	–	–	–	–	–	–	–	–	–	–	–	–	–	1	2	2	4	9
Lada Togliatti	–	–	–	–	–	–	–	–	–	–	–	–	–	–	–	–	–	–	1	2	–	–	1	3	1	8
Salavat Yulayev Ufa	–	–	–	–	–	–	–	–	–	–	–	–	–	–	–	–	–	–	–	2	2	1	1	1	–	7
Torpedo Ust Kamenogorsk	–	–	–	–	–	–	–	–	–	–	–	–	–	–	–	–	–	–	1	1	2	1	–	–	2	7
SKA St. Peterburg[2]	–	–	–	–	1	–	–	–	1	–	–	–	–	–	–	–	–	2	1	–	1	–	–	–	–	6
CSKA-2 Moscow	–	–	–	–	–	–	–	–	–	–	–	–	–	–	–	–	–	–	–	–	1	–	2	2	–	5
Tivali Minsk[3]	–	–	–	–	–	–	–	–	–	–	–	–	–	–	1	–	–	–	–	2	1	–	–	–	–	4
Avangard Omsk	–	–	–	–	–	–	–	–	–	–	–	–	–	–	–	–	–	–	–	–	3	–	1	–	–	4
Severstal Cherepovets[5]	–	–	–	–	–	–	–	–	–	–	–	–	–	–	–	–	–	–	1	1	–	1	1	–	–	4
Kristall Elektrostal	–	–	–	–	–	–	–	–	–	–	–	–	–	–	–	–	–	–	–	3	–	–	–	–	1	4
Torpedo Nizhny Novgorod[4]	–	–	–	–	–	–	–	–	–	–	–	–	–	–	–	–	–	1	–	2	–	–	–	–	–	3
Molot Perm	–	–	–	–	–	–	–	–	–	–	–	–	–	–	–	–	–	–	–	–	1	1	–	–	–	2
Itil Kazan	–	–	–	–	–	–	–	–	–	–	–	–	–	–	–	–	–	–	–	–	1	–	–	–	1	2
Avtomobilist Yekaterinburg	–	–	–	–	–	–	–	–	–	–	–	–	–	–	–	–	–	–	–	–	–	–	1	–	1	2
Argus Moscow	–	–	–	–	–	–	–	–	–	–	–	–	–	–	–	–	–	–	1	–	–	–	–	–	–	1
Dizelist Penza	–	–	–	–	–	–	–	–	–	–	–	–	–	–	–	–	–	–	1	–	–	–	–	–	–	1
Dynamo Kharkov	–	–	–	–	–	–	–	–	–	–	–	–	–	–	–	1	–	–	–	–	–	–	–	–	–	1
Izhorets St. Peterburg	–	–	–	–	–	–	–	–	–	–	–	–	–	–	–	–	–	–	1	–	–	–	–	–	–	1
Khimik Novopolotsk	–	–	–	–	–	–	–	–	–	–	–	–	–	–	–	–	–	–	–	1	–	–	–	–	–	1
Kristall Saratov	–	–	–	–	–	–	–	–	–	–	–	–	–	–	–	–	–	–	1	–	–	–	–	–	–	1
Krylja Sovetov-2 Moscow	–	–	–	–	–	–	–	–	–	–	–	–	–	–	–	–	–	–	–	1	–	–	–	–	–	1
Mechel Chelyabinsk	–	–	–	–	–	–	–	–	–	–	–	–	–	–	–	–	–	–	–	–	1	–	–	–	–	1
CSK VVS Samara	–	–	–	–	–	–	–	–	–	–	–	–	–	–	–	–	–	–	–	–	–	1	–	–	–	1
Salavat Novoil Ufa	–	–	–	–	–	–	–	–	–	–	–	–	–	–	–	–	–	–	–	–	–	–	1	–	–	1
Neftekhimik Nizhnekamsk	–	–	–	–	–	–	–	–	–	–	–	–	–	–	–	–	–	–	–	–	–	–	–	1	–	1

Former club names: [1]–Dynamo Riga, HC Riga, [2]–SKA Leningrad, [3]–Dynamo Minsk, [4]–Torpedo Gorky, [5]–Metallurg Cherepovets

1998 Entry Draft Analysis

Country of Origin

Country	Players Drafted
Canada	129
USA	40
Russia	25
Czech Republic	21
Sweden	17
Finland	12
Slovakia	6
Switzerland	2
Kazakhstan	2
Ukraine	1
Latvia	1
Austria	1
Slovenia	1

Position

Position	Players Drafted
Defense	84
Center	66
Right Wing	46
Left Wing	39
Goaltender	23

Birth Year

Year	Players Drafted
1980	138
1979	64
1978	39
1977	2
1976	3
1975	2
1974	4
1973	1
1972	1
1971	1
1970	2
1968	1

Czech Republic and Slovakia

Club	'69	'70	'71	'72	'73	'74	'75	'76	'77	'78	'79	'80	'81	'82	'83	'84	'85	'86	'87	'88	'89	'90	'91	'92	'93	'94	'95	'96	'97	'98	Total
Dukla Jihlava	–	–	–	–	–	–	–	–	–	–	–	–	–	2	4	3	1	–	3	1	1	3	2	1	1	1	2	2	–	–	27
Chemopetrol Litvinov[1]	–	–	–	–	–	–	–	–	–	–	–	–	–	3	1	2	–	–	–	–	2	2	1	3	2	4	2	2	2	1	27
HC Ceske Budejovice[6]	–	–	–	–	–	–	–	–	–	–	–	–	–	2	1	1	–	–	1	–	1	2	–	–	1	2	3	1	2	1	18
Sparta Praha	–	–	–	–	–	–	–	–	–	–	–	–	–	1	–	2	1	1	1	2	1	2	–	1	1	–	1	–	1	1	16
Slovan Bratislava	–	–	–	–	–	–	–	–	–	1	1	–	–	2	–	–	1	1	1	–	–	1	–	–	–	3	–	1	1	1	14
ZPS Zlin[2]	–	–	–	–	–	–	–	–	–	–	–	–	–	–	1	–	1	1	1	–	–	–	2	2	1	–	2	–	1	2	14
HC Kladno[7]	–	–	–	–	–	–	–	–	–	–	–	–	2	1	–	1	–	1	–	–	–	1	2	–	1	2	–	2	–	–	13
Dukla Trencin	–	–	–	–	–	–	–	–	–	–	–	–	–	–	–	1	–	–	–	1	1	2	–	2	2	–	1	2	1	–	13
HC Vitkovice[8]	–	–	–	–	–	–	–	–	–	1	–	–	1	–	–	–	–	–	–	–	–	1	–	1	3	1	1	1–	–	1	11
HC Kosice[3]	–	–	–	–	–	–	–	–	–	–	–	–	1	2	–	2	–	1	–	–	–	2	–	–	–	–	–	1	1	1	11
Slavia Praha	–	–	–	–	–	–	–	–	–	–	–	–	–	–	–	1	–	–	–	–	–	–	–	–	1	–	–	–	4	5	11
HC Pardubice[4]	–	–	–	–	–	–	–	–	–	–	–	–	–	–	2	–	2	–	1	–	–	–	–	–	–	2	1	–	1	–	9
Interconex Plzen[9]	–	–	–	–	–	–	–	–	–	–	–	–	–	–	–	–	–	1	–	–	1	1	–	3	–	1	1	–	–	1	9
Zetor Brno	–	–	–	–	–	–	–	–	–	–	–	–	–	–	–	–	1	–	3	–	–	2	–	1	–	–	–	–	–	1	8
HC Olomouc[5]	–	–	–	–	–	–	–	–	–	–	–	–	–	–	–	–	–	–	–	–	1	–	–	2	–	1	2	–	–	1	7
AC Nitra	–	–	–	–	–	–	–	–	–	–	–	–	–	–	–	–	–	–	–	–	–	–	2	–	1	–	–	1	–	1	5
ZTS Martin	–	–	–	–	–	–	–	–	–	–	–	–	–	–	–	–	–	–	–	1	–	–	–	–	–	–	2	–	–	–	3
ZTK Zvolen	–	–	–	–	–	–	–	–	–	–	–	–	–	–	–	–	–	–	–	–	–	–	–	1	–	–	1	1	–	–	3
Petra Vsetin	–	–	–	–	–	–	–	–	–	–	–	–	–	–	–	–	–	–	–	–	–	–	–	–	–	–	–	–	2	1	3
IS Banska Bystrica	–	–	–	–	–	–	–	–	–	–	–	–	–	–	–	–	–	–	–	–	–	–	–	–	–	1	1	–	–	–	2
ZPA Presov	–	–	–	–	–	–	–	–	–	–	–	–	–	–	–	–	–	–	–	–	–	–	–	–	1	–	–	–	1	–	2
Partizan Liptovsky Mikulas	–	–	–	–	–	–	–	–	–	–	–	–	–	–	–	–	–	–	–	–	–	1	–	–	–	–	–	–	–	1	2
Ingstav Brno	–	–	–	–	–	–	–	–	–	–	–	–	–	–	–	–	1	–	–	–	–	–	–	–	–	–	–	–	–	–	1
VTJ Pisek	–	–	–	–	–	–	–	–	–	–	–	–	–	–	–	–	–	–	–	–	–	1	–	–	–	–	–	–	–	–	1
Banik Sokolov	–	–	–	–	–	–	–	–	–	–	–	–	–	–	–	–	–	–	–	–	–	–	–	–	–	–	1	–	–	–	1
Havlickuv Brod	–	–	–	–	–	–	–	–	–	–	–	–	–	–	–	–	–	–	–	–	–	–	–	–	–	–	–	–	–	1	1

Former club names: [1]–CHZ Litvinov, [2]–TJ Gottwaldov, TJ Zlin, [3]–VSZ Kosice, [4]–Tesla Pardubice, [5]–DS Olomouc, [6]–Motor Ceske Budejovice, [7]–Poldi Kladno, [8]–TJ Vitkovice, [9]–Skoda Plzen

Finland

Club	'69	'70	'71	'72	'73	'74	'75	'76	'77	'78	'79	'80	'81	'82	'83	'84	'85	'86	'87	'88	'89	'90	'91	'92	'93	'94	'95	'96	'97	'98	Total
TPS Turku	–	–	–	–	–	–	–	–	–	–	–	1	6	–	–	–	1	1	–	–	–	–	–	–	3	2	3	1	3	3	24
HIFK Helsinki	1	–	–	–	–	–	1	–	1	–	–	–	1	1	2	2	1	–	–	2	1	–	–	–	2	–	1	–	1	2	19
Ilves Tampere	–	–	–	–	–	–	–	–	1	2	–	–	2	–	2	2	–	1	–	1	–	1	1	–	–	–	2	–	–	2	17
Jokerit Helsinki	–	–	–	–	–	–	–	–	–	–	–	2	1	–	–	1	–	–	1	1	–	2	–	3	–	1	–	1	1	1	15
Tappara Tampere	–	–	–	–	–	1	–	–	–	–	–	–	–	2	–	–	–	4	–	1	–	1	–	–	–	–	1	1	2	–	13
Assat Pori	–	–	–	–	–	–	2	–	–	–	–	–	1	–	2	2	–	–	–	1	–	1	–	–	1	1	1	–	–	1	13
Karpat Oulu	–	–	–	–	–	–	–	–	–	–	–	1	–	1	–	1	–	2	2	–	–	–	1	–	1	–	–	–	1	1	11
Lukko Rauma	–	–	–	–	–	–	–	2	1	–	–	–	–	–	2	–	1	–	1	–	–	1	–	1	–	–	–	–	–	–	9
Kiekko-Espoo	–	–	–	–	–	–	–	–	–	–	–	–	–	–	–	–	–	–	–	1	–	1	1	2	–	2	1	–	1	–	9
Reipas Lahti	–	–	–	–	–	–	–	–	–	–	–	–	–	1	1	1	–	–	–	–	–	–	2	–	1	–	–	1	–	–	7
KalPa Kuopio	–	–	–	–	–	–	–	–	–	–	–	–	–	–	–	–	–	–	1	–	–	–	–	–	1	2	–	–	–	1	5
HPK Hameenlinna	–	–	–	–	–	–	–	–	–	–	–	–	–	–	–	–	–	–	–	–	1	–	–	2	–	–	–	–	1	1	5
JyP HT Jyvaskyla	–	–	–	–	–	–	–	–	–	–	–	–	–	–	–	–	–	–	1	–	–	–	–	–	–	–	–	2	1	–	4
Kiekoo-67 Turku	–	–	–	–	–	–	–	–	–	–	–	–	–	–	–	–	–	–	–	–	–	–	–	–	–	–	3	–	–	–	3
SaiPa Lappeenranta	–	–	–	–	–	–	–	–	–	–	–	–	1	–	–	–	–	–	–	–	–	1	–	–	–	–	–	–	–	–	2
Sapko Savonlinna	–	–	–	–	–	–	–	–	–	–	–	–	–	–	–	–	1	1	–	–	–	–	–	–	–	–	–	–	–	–	2
Sport Vaasa	–	–	–	–	–	–	–	–	–	–	–	–	–	–	–	–	–	1	–	–	1	–	–	–	–	–	–	–	–	–	2
GrIFK Kauniainen	–	–	–	–	–	–	–	–	–	–	–	–	–	–	–	–	–	–	–	–	–	–	1	–	–	–	–	–	–	–	1
Koo Koo Kouvola	–	–	–	–	–	–	–	–	–	–	–	–	–	–	–	–	–	–	–	–	–	1	–	–	–	–	–	–	–	–	1
S-Kiekko Seinajoki	–	–	–	–	–	–	–	–	–	–	–	–	–	–	–	–	1	–	–	–	–	–	–	–	–	–	–	–	–	–	1
Junkkarit Kalajoki	–	–	–	–	–	–	–	–	–	–	–	–	–	–	–	–	–	–	–	–	–	–	–	–	–	–	–	1	–	–	1

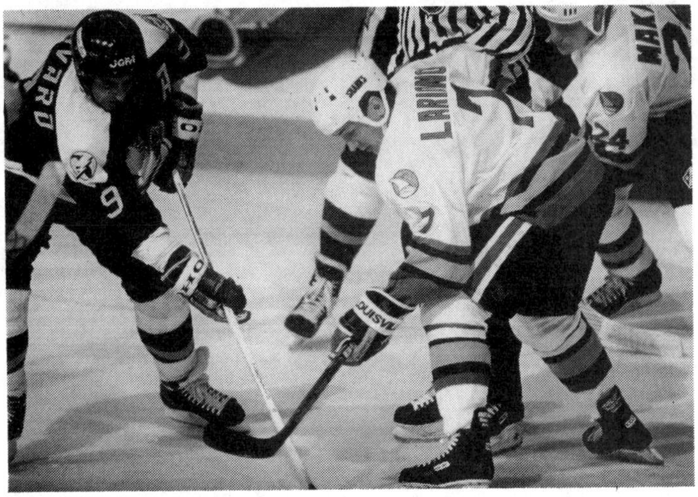

International superstar Igor Larionov, shown here with San Jose in a face-off with Denis Savard, was drafted as a 25-year-old by the Vancouver Canucks in 1985. The notion of top players from the Soviet Union being allowed to emigrate to play for pay in the NHL was a remote one in the mid-1980s, a fact that accounts for Larionov's being selected 214th overall in the Entry Draft. He and Slava Fetisov are the only players to win Olympic gold, IIHF World senior and junior championships, a Canada/World Cup title and the Stanley Cup.

First Round Draft Selections, 1998

1. TAMPA BAY • **VINCENT LECAVALIER** • C • An excellent skater with great balance and agility, Vincent Lecavalier also possesses a mean streak that makes him tough as well as talented. At 6'4" he has excellent size and reach. He handles the puck extremely well and plays with poise and confidence. He was both the QMJHL and CHL rookie of the year in 1996-97 and was named to the QMJHL First All-Star Team in 1997-98. Lecavalier played for Team Canada at the World Junior Championships in 1998.

2. NASHVILLE • **DAVID LEGWAND** • C • Only the second U.S.-born player to win MVP honors in the OHL (Pat Peake, 1993) and the first rookie MVP since Jack Valiquette in 1973-74, David Legwand burst upon the scene with the Plymouth Whalers in 1997-98. He led all rookies in scoring with 105 points and ranked third in the league to garner rookie of the year and First All-Star Team honors in addition to his MVP award. Legwand is a strong skater with a hard shot. He has excellent vision and is a good passer.

3. SAN JOSE • **BRAD STUART** • D • A powerful skater with excellent mobility, Brad Stuart stands 6'2 1/2" and weighs 215 pounds. He plays an aggressive, physical game, but also has solid puck-handling skills and can lead the offensive attack. Stuart recorded the hardest shot (95.5 mph) and the fastest 60' sprint time at the CHL Top Prospects skills competition in 1997-98. He was a nominee for WHL honors as the best defenseman and was an Eastern Conference Second Team All-Star.

4. VANCOUVER • **BRYAN ALLEN** • D • At 6'4 1/2" and 208 pounds, Bryan Allen has exceptional size and plays a physical game. He is strong in the corners and can easily clear out the area in front of the net. Allen has a powerful shot and though he does not play an offensive game he has the skating skill to carry the puck out of his own end. He played in the Memorial Cup tournament in 1997 and was an assistant captain with the Oshawa Generals in 1997-98.

5. ANAHEIM • **VITALY VISHNEVSKY** • D • A fierce competitor with an aggressive style, Vitaly Vishnevsky is also a good skater with excellent speed. He's effective in front of his own net and is a creative playmaker with strong puckhandling skills who could become an effective "quarterback" on the power-play. At age 17 Vishnevsky was the youngest member of the Russian team at the World Junior Championships in 1998.

6. CALGARY • **RICO FATA** • C • Blinding speed and exceptional acceleration are the key aspects of Rico Fata's game. He was the fastest skater in the CHL Top Prospects skills competition in 1997-98 and also has good puckhandling skills. Fata played the wing on a line with Joe Thornton in his first junior season at Sault Ste. Marie. He has spent two years as a center with the London Knights, but may wind up as a winger in the NHL.

7. NY RANGERS • **MANNY MALHOTRA** • C • An excellent two-way player with more offensive potential than his numbers indicate, Manny Malhotra is effective on special teams and very reliable in crucial situations. A good skater with a powerful stride and good speed, Malhotra plays with drive and determination and never backs down from a challenge. He possesses strong leadership qualities.

8. CHICAGO • **MARK BELL** • C • A good skater who can use his speed to pass defensemen on the outside, Mark Bell has good puckhandling skills and is a smart passer. He has a tremendous wrist shot and a hard slapshot and is skilled at deflecting drives from the blue line. Bell is a solid competitor who, at 6'3" and 185 pounds, has excellent size and strength. He has played center with the Ottawa 67's, but could wind up as a left winger in the NHL.

9. NY ISLANDERS • **MICHAEL RUPP** • LW • A diamond in the rough at 6'5" and 218 pounds, Michael Rupp is big and strong with a hard, heavy shot, but he has not played much competitive hockey and needs to better develop his hockey sense. He plays a physical game and battles to the net where he works for his scoring opportunities. Rupp can dominate one-on-one situations and has the potential to develop into a good power forward.

10. TORONTO • **NIKOLAI ANTROPOV** • C • A surprising choice by the Maple Leafs, Nikolai Antropov was not heavily scouted but has the potential to emerge as an NHL star. At 6'3" and 191 pounds, Antropov has excellent size and possesses strong offensive skills, but will need to improve his skating. He has played in the Russian minor leagues and has represented his native Kazakhstan at the World Junior Championships in 1997 and 1998. He starred at the D Pool European Championships in 1998.

11. CAROLINA • **JEFF HEEREMA** • C • With excellent speed and quickness combined with balance and agility, Jeff Heerema finished fourth in scoring among OHL rookies in 1997-98. He is an exceptional puckhandler and playmaker with a good touch around the net. Heerema works well in traffic and has shown his willingness to take a hit in order to make the play or score a goal.

12. COLORADO • **ALEX TANGUAY** • C • A competitive spirit and a solid hockey sense make Alex Tanguay a top NHL prospect. A well-balanced skater, he lacks true breakaway speed, but is a clever playmaker with a natural scoring touch. Tanguay's 47 goals were three more than Vincent Lecavalier scored in the QMJHL in 1997-98 and he also outperformed the number-one draft choice at the 1998 World Junior Championships, but Tanguay lacks Lecavalier's size.

13. EDMONTON • **MICHAEL HENRICH** • RW • At 6'2" and 206 pounds, Michael Henrich has size and strength, though he is not considered a power forward. He has great speed on the attack and a long reach and is an excellent goal scorer. Henrich has a hard shot with a quick, accurate release and is very effective on the power-play. He was named one of the Players of the Game at the 1997-98 Top Prospects Game.

14. PHOENIX • **PATRICK DESROCHERS** • G • As expected, Patrick DesRochers was the top goaltender selected in the 1998 draft. Though he actually performed better in 1996-97 than in 1997-98, DesRochers was still the top-rated goaltender available. He has good mobility, quick reflexes and excellent reaction time. DesRochers can play a standup style, but relies mostly on the butterfly. He has a quick glove hand and handles the puck well.

15. OTTAWA • **MATHIEU CHOUINARD** • G • The winningest goalie in the QMJHL with 32 victories in 1997-98, Mathieu Chouinard plays an unorthodox butterfly style that sees him go down on virtually every shot. He has excellent reflexes and a good glove hand, but prefers to use his body to stop most shots. He is physically strong and a fierce competitor with excellent focus and concentration.

16. MONTREAL • **ERIC CHOUINARD** • C • The son of former NHL player Guy Chouinard, who coached him with the Quebec Remparts in 1997-98, Eric Chouinard possesses many of the attributes that made his father a star. He has a long, fluid skating stride with excellent outside speed and good hands around the net. At 6'2" and 195 pounds, Chouinard is big and strong, but is a finesse player who is excellent at maneuvering through traffic.

17. COLORADO • **MARTIN SKOULA** • D • Skoula was not considered a top prospect while playing in his native Czech Republic, but made a smooth transition to the North American game while playing with the OHL's Barrie Colts in 1997-98. He is an extremely mobile defenseman who reacts quickly to the developing play and is very quick to the puck. He has size and strength at 6'2" and 195 pounds, but is not an overly physical player. Skoula has a good, accurate shot. He was named to the OHL All-Rookie Team.

18. BUFFALO • **DMITRI KALININ** • D • He has failed to score a goal in 66 league games in Russia over the last three years, but Dmitri Kalinin is considered one of the top defensive prospects in Europe. An excellent skater with very good mobility and lateral movement, Kalinin has the ability to rush the puck out of the defensive zone. He has strong passing skills and a good shot and is very effective on special teams. Kalinin has a solid understanding of the game and an excellent work ethic.

19. COLORADO • **ROBYN REGEHR** • D • Though not projected to be a star, Robyn Regehr is seen as a solid defensive defenseman who could enjoy a long career in the NHL. An intelligent player with excellent decision-making abilities, Regehr also has size and strength at 6'2 1/2" and 211 pounds. Though he is very defense oriented, he is a powerful skater with quick acceleration and can move the puck up ice.

20. COLORADO • **SCOTT PARKER** • RW • Drafted in the third round by the New Jersey Devils in 1996, Scott Parker chose to re-enter the draft and was selected as the Avalanche's fourth pick in the first round of the 1998 draft. At 6'4" and 220 pounds, Parker is both big and strong and led the WHL with 330 penalty minutes for the Kelowna Rockets in 1996-97. He moves well for a big man and had 122 points and 123 penalty minutes in 1997-98.

21. LOS ANGELES • **MATHIEU BIRON** • D • Towering at 6'6 1/2"and 212 pounds, Mathieu Biron was the biggest player selected in the first round of the draft. Biron was named to the QMJHL's 1997-98 All-Rookie Team after demonstrating surprising speed and mobility. He has a long, smooth skating stride with excellent speed and acceleration and is difficult to knock off his feet. Biron has demonstrated a good attitude and the desire to improve his game.

22. PHILADELPHIA • **SIMON GAGNE** • C • Simon Gagne's strength is skating, with an effortless stride, good acceleration and a quick change of pace. He's also a creative puckhandler who creates opportunities for his teammate and possesses natural scoring instincts. Though not considered a physical player, he is an effective checker. Had he not missed 15 games due to a broken finger, his 1997-98 numbers would have been more impressive.

23. PITTSBURGH • **MILAN KRAFT** • C • Milan Kraft is a gifted playmaker and scorer who has the ability to dominate a game, though he needs to improve his consistency. He starred at the European Junior Championships in 1997-98 and also excelled at the Viking Cup in Camrose, Alberta where he seemed to thrive on the smaller North American ice surface.

24. ST. LOUIS • **CHRISTIAN BACKMAN** • D • A strong skater with good agility and lateral movement, Christian Backman is an offensive defenseman who can carry the puck from end to end. He anticipates the play well and is quick to the puck in the defensive end. Backman has a powerful shot and is effective on the power-play. He is also a good passer. Backman starred for the Swedish team that won the European junior championship in 1998.

25. DETROIT • **JIRI FISCHLER** • D • A strong skater with quick acceleration, Jiri Fischler also has soft hands and is a strong, accurate passer. He stands 6'5 1/2" and weighs 210 pounds, giving him both size and strength, but he is not a punishing checker and does not always use his size to his advantage though he is difficult to beat one-on-one. Fischler has great anticipation and a booming shot.

26. NEW JERSEY • **MIKE VAN RYN** • D • Mike Van Ryn was a year older than most players available in the 1998 draft after choosing to spend the 1997-98 season at the University of Michigan. He was the only collegiate player on Canada's team at the 1998 World Junior Championships. Van Ryn has a low, accurate shot from the point and is also a good skater with strong passing skills. He plays an aggressive style and can effectively clear the area in front of the net

27. NEW JERSEY • **SCOTT GOMEZ** • C • Born to Mexican-American parents living in Anchorage, Alaska, Scott Gomez was a member of the U.S. team that played at the 1998 World Junior Championships. He had been the rookie of the year in the British Columbia Junior Hockey League in 1996-97 before moving up to the Tri-City Americans of the WHL. A deceptively fast skater with strong hockey instincts, Gomez was named to the WHL All-Rookie Team for the 1997-98 season.

1998 Entry Draft

Transferred draft choice notation:

Example: Col.-Ana. represents a draft choice transferred **from** Colorado **to** Anaheim.

Pick	Player	Claimed By	Amateur Club	Position
ROUND #1				
1	LECAVALIER, Vincent	Fla.-S.J.-T.B.	Rimouski	C
2	LEGWAND, David	T.B.-S.J.-Nsh.	Plymouth	C
3	STUART, Brad	Nsh.-S.J.	Regina	D
4	ALLEN, Bryan	Van.	Oshawa	D
5	VISHNEVSKY, Vitaly	Ana.	Torpedo-2 Yaroslavl	D
6	FATA, Rico	Cgy.	London	C
7	MALHOTRA, Manny	NYR	Guelph	C
8	BELL, Mark	Tor.-Chi.	Ottawa	LW
9	RUPP, Michael	NYI	Erie	LW
10	ANTROPOV, Nikolai	Chi.-Tor.	Torpedo Ust-Kamenogorsk	C
11	HEEREMA, Jeff	Car.	Sarnia	RW
12	TANGUAY, Alex	S.J.-Col.	Halifax	C
13	HENRICH, Michael	Edm.	Barrie	RW
14	DESROCHERS, Patrick	Phx.	Sarnia	G
15	CHOUINARD, Mathieu	Ott.	Shawinigan	G
16	CHOUINARD, Eric	Mtl.	Quebec	C
17	SKOULA, Martin	L.A.-Col.	Barrie	D
18	KALININ, Dimitri	Buf.	Traktor Chelyabinsk	D
19	REGEHER, Robyn	Bos.-Col.	Kamloops	D
20	PARKER, Scott	Wsh.-Col.	Kelowna	D
21	BIRON, Mathieu	Col.-L.A.	Shawinigan	D
22	GAGNE, Simon	Phi.-T.B.-Phi.	Quebec	C
23	KRAFT, Milan	T.B.	Keramika Plzen Jr.	C
24	BACKMAN, Christian	St.L.	Vastra Frolunda Jr.	D
25	FISCHER, Jiri	Det.	Hull	D
26	VAN RYN, Mike	N.J.	U. of Michigan	D
27	GOMEZ, Scott	Dal.-N.J.	Tri-City	C
ROUND #2				
28	ABID, Ramzi	T.B.-Col.	Chicoutimi	LW
29	CHEECHOO, Jonathon	Nsh.-S.J.	Belleville	RW
30	ROSSITER, Kyle	Fla.	Spokane	D
31	CHUBAROV, Artem	Van.	Dynamo Moscow	C
32	PEAT, Stephen	Ana.	Red Deer	D
33	BETTS, Blair	Cgy.	Prince George	C
34	PETERS, Andrew	NYR-Buf.	Oshawa	LW
35	SVOBODA, Petr	Tor.	Havlickuv Brod	D
36	NEILSON, Chris	NYI	Calgary	C
37	BERGLUND, Christian	N.J.	Farjestad Karlstad Jr.	C
38	SAUVE, Philippe	Chi-Col.	Rimouski	G
39	ERSKINE, John	Car.-N.J.-Dal.	London	D
40	COPLEY, Randy	NYR	Cape Breton	RW
41	LINNIK, Maxim	S.J.-Det.-St.L.	St. Thomas Jr. B	D
42	BECKETT, Jason	Edm.-Phi.	Seattle	D
43	VAANANEN, Ossi	Phx.	Jokerit Helsinki Jr.	D
44	FISHER, Mike	Ott.	Sudbury	C
45	RIBEIRO, Mike	Mtl.	Rouyn-Noranda	C
46	PAPINEAU, Justin	L.A.	Belleville	C
47	MILLEY, Norman	Buf.	Sudbury	RW
48	GIRARD, Jonathon	Bos.	Laval	D
49	CRUZ, Jomar	Wsh.	Brandon	G
50	KRISTEK, Jaroslav	Col.-S.J.-Buf.	ZPS Zlin	RW
51	FORBES, Ian	Phi.	Guelph	D
52	ALLEN, Bobby	Bos.	Boston College	D
53	MOORE, Steve	Col.	Harvard	C
54	ZEVAKHIN, Alexander	Pit.	CSKA Moscow	RW
55	BARNES, Ryan	St.L-Det.	Sudbury	LW
56	VALTONEN, Tomek	Det.	Ilves Tampere Jr.	LW
57	BOUCK, Tyler	N.J.-Dal.	Prince George	RW
58	BALA, Chris	Dal.-Phi.-Ott.	Harvard	LW
ROUND #3				
59	HORNUNG, Todd	Wsh.	Portland	C
60	ARKHIPOV, Denis	Nsh.	Ak Bars Kazan	LW
61	DIPENTA, Joe	Fla.	Boston U.	D
62	MANNING, Paul	Van.-Car.-Cgy.	Colorado College	D
63	WARD, Lance	Ana.-Col.-Fla.	Red Deer	D
64	RICHARDS, Brad	Cgy.-T.B.	Rimouski	LW
65	LAPLANTE, Eric	S.J.	Halifax	LW
66	LABARBERA, Jason	NYR	Portland	G
67	HENRY, Alex	Tor.-T.B.-Edm.	London	D
68	RUUTU, Jarkko	NYI-Van.	HIFK Helsinki	LW
69	HODSON, Jamie	Chi.-Tor.	Brandon	G
70	HOLDRIDGE, Kevin	Car.	Plymouth	D
71	COLE, Erik	S.J.-Car.	Clarkson	LW
72	AFANASENKOV, Dimitry	Edm.-T.B.	Torpedo-2 Yaroslavl	LW
73	O'LEARY, Pat	Phx.	Robbinsdale-Armstrong H.S.	C
74	VAUCLAIR, Julien	Ott.	Lugano	D
75	BEAUCHEMIN, Francois	Mtl.	Laval	D
76	VOLKOV, Alexei	L.A.	Krylja Sovetov-2	G
77	PANDOLFO, Mike	Buf.	St. Sebastians H.S.	LW
78	NORDSTROM, Peter	Bos.	Farjestad Karl. Jr.	LW
79	LAZAREV, Yevgeny	Wsh.-Col.	Kitchener Jr. B	LW
80	CAMERON, David	Col.-Pit.	Prince Albert	C
81	MORRISON, Justin	Phi-Van.	Colorado College	RW
82	GIONTA, Brian	Pit.-Edm.-N.J.	Boston College	RW
83	WALKER, Matt	St.L.	Portland	D
84	MCCRACKEN, Jake	Det.	Sault Ste. Marie	G
85	KOCH, Geoff	N.J.-S.J.-Nsh.	U. of Michigan	LW
86	KARLSSON, Gabriel	DAL	HV 71 Jonkoping Jr.	C

Players selected first through tenth in the 1998 NHL Entry Draft: (All rows left to right)
Top row: 1. Vincent Lecavalier, C, Tampa Bay; 2. David Legwand, C, Nashville
Second row: 3. Brad Stuart, D, San Jose; 4. Bryan Allan, D, Vancouver
Third row: 5. Vitaly Vishnevski, D, Anaheim; 6. Rico Fata, D, Calgary
Fourth row: 7. Manny Malhotra, C, NY Rangers; 8. Mark Bell, LW, Chicago
Bottom: 9. Michael Rupp, LW, NY Islanders; 10. Nikolai Antropov, C, Toronoto.

ROUND #4

87	PONIKAROVSKY, Alexei	T.B.-Det.-Tor.	Dynamo-2 Moscow	LW
88	SAUER, Kent	Nsh.	North Iowa Jr. A	D
89	JARDINE, Ryan	Fla.	Sault Ste. Marie	LW
90	DARBY, Regan	Van.	Tri-City	D
91	VASICEK, Josef	Ana-Car.	Slavia Praha Jr.	C
92	BEAUDOIN, Eric	Cgy.-T.B.	Guelph	LW
93	WESTLUND, Tommy	NYR-Car.	Brynas Gavle	RW
94	TRATTNIG, Matthias	Tor.-Chi.	U. of Maine	C
95	BURNHAM, Andy	NYI	Windsor	RW
96	JOKELA, Mikko	Chi-N.J.	HIFK Helsinki	D
97	MADDEN, Chris	Car.	Guelph	G
98	DAVISON, Rob	S.J.	North Bay	D
99	HORCOFF, Shawn	Edm.	Michigan State	C
100	VANBUSKIRK, Ryan	Phx.	Sarnia	D
101	SCHASTLIVY, Petr	Ott.	Torpedo Yaroslavl	LW
102	SUTTER, Shaun	Mtl.-Cgy.	Lethbridge	C
103	BRENNAN, Kip	L.A.	Sudbury	D
104	ZALESAK, Miroslav	Buf.-S.J.	Plastika Nitra	RW
105	DAGENAIS, Pierre	Bos.-L.A.-N.J.	Rouyn-Noranda	LW
106	BARCH, Krys	Wsh.-Col.-Wsh.	London	LW
107	CORRINET, Chris	Wsh.-Col.	Princeton	RW
108	SABOURIN, Dany	Cgy.	Sherbrooke	G
109	MORIN, Jean-Philippe	Phi.	Drummondville	D
110	MYERS, Scott	Pit.	Prince George	G
111	HOBDAY, Brent	St.L-Det.	Moose Jaw	C
112	WALLIN, Viktor	Det.-Ana.	HV 71 Jonkoping Jr.	LW
113	ANTILA, Kristian	N.J.-Tor.-N.J.-Edm.	Ilves Tampere	G
114	KANE, Boyd	Dal.-NYR	Regina	LW

ROUND #5

115	LEACH, Jay	T.B.-Phx.	Providence College	D
116	BLACKBURN, Josh	Nsh.-S.J.-Phx.	Lincoln Jr. A	G
117	SPACEK, Jaroslav	Fla.-S.J.-Fla.	Farjestad Karlstad	D
118	SIKLENKA, Mike	Wsh.	Lloydminster	D
119	BUT, Anton	Van.-N.J.	Torpedo Yaroslavl 2	RW
120	GAUVREAU, Brent	Ana.-Cgy.	Oshawa	RW
121	RICH, Curtis	T.B.	Calgary	D
122	LEAHY, Patrick	NYR	Miami of Ohio	RW
123	DOPITA, Jiri	Tor.-NYI	Petra Vsetin	C
124	BELANGER, Francis	NYI-Chi.-Phi.	Rimouski	LW
125	WENDELL, Erik	Chi-Wsh.	Maple Grove H.S.	C
126	WARREN, Morgan	Car.-Chi-Tor.	Moncton	RW
127	COALTER, Brandon	S.J.	Oshawa	LW
128	ELLIOTT, Paul	Edm.	Medicine Hat	D
129	SCHNABEL, Robert	Phx.	Red Deer	D
130	MCLEOD, Gavin	Ott.	Kelowna	D
131	KLOUCEK, Tomas	NYR	Slavia Praha Jr.	D
132	BASHKIROV, Andrei	Mtl.	Fort Wayne/Las Vegas	LW
133	RULLIER, Joe	L.A.	Rimouski	D
134	SCUDERI, Robert	Buf.-Pit.	Boston College	D
135	RAYCROFT, Andrew	Bos.	Sudbury	G
136	JONSSON, David	Wsh.-Van.	Leksand	D
137	GOLDADE, Aaron	Buf.	Brandon	C
138	BEAUCHESNE, Martin	Col.-Nsh.	Sherbrooke	D
139	PROSOFSKY, Garrett	Phi.-Van.-Phi.	Saskatoon	C
140	BERTRAN, Rick	Pit.-Van.	Kitchener	D
141	TIMMONS, Kristinn	St.L.-Col.	Tri-City	LW
142	STEEN, Calle	Det.	Hammarby	LW
143	FLINN, Ryan	N.J.	Laval	LW
144	SMIRNOV, Oleg	N.J.-Edm.	Kristall Elektrostal	RW
145	SAMUELSSON, Mikael	Dal.-S.J.	Sodertalje	LW

ROUND #6

146	KUZNETSOV, Sergei	T.B.	Torpedo Yaroslavl 2	C
147	BRUNEL, Craig	Nsh.	Prince Albert	RW
148	OVINGTON, Chris	Fla.	Red Deer	D
149	CABANA, Paul	Van.	Fort McMurray	RW
150	HUNTER, Trent	Ana.	Prince George	RW
151	DELEEUW, Adam	Det.	Barrie	LW
152	DWYER, Gordie	Cgy.-Mtl.	Quebec	LW
153	PATERA, Pavel	NYR-Dal.	AIK Solna	LW
154	ROURKE, Allan	Tor.	Kitchener	D
155	CLAUSON, Kevin	NYI	Western Michigan	D
156	HUSKINS, Kent	Chi.	Clarkson	D
157	VOTH, Brad	Car.-St.L.	Medicine Hat	D
158	VIUHKOLA, Jari	S.J.-Chi.	Karpat Oulu	C
159	ETTINGER, Trevor	Edm.	Cape Breton	D
160	WALLIN, Rickard	Phx.	Farjestad Karl. Jr.	C
161	NEIL, Christopher	Ott.-Chi.-Ott.	North Bay	RW
162	MARKOV, Andrei	Mtl.	Khimik Voskresensk	D
163	ZIZKA, Tomas	L.A.	ZPS Zlin	D
164	KOTALIK, Ales	Buf.	Ceske Budejovice Jr.	RW
165	MILANOVIC, Ryan	Bos.	Kitchener	LW
166	PELLETIER, Jonathan	Chi.	Drummondville	G
167	RYAZANTSEV, Alexander	Col.	Victoriaville	D
168	NIITTYMAKI, Antero	Phi.	TPS Turku Jr.	G
169	FADMY, Jan	Pit.	Slavia Praha	C
170	TROCHINSKY, Andrei	St.L.	Torpedo Ust-Kamenogorsk	C
171	DATSYUK, Pavel	Det.	Dynamo-E. Yeka'burg	C
172	LARIVIERE, Jacques	N.J.	Moncton	LW
173	KAPANEN, Niko	DAL	HPK Hameenlinna	C

ROUND #7

174	ALLAN, Brett	T.B.	Swift Current	C
175	ONDRIK, Cam	Phi.	Medicine Hat	G
176	KETCHESON, B.J.	Fla.	Peterborough	D
177	MALTS, Vincent	Van.	Hull	RW
178	FIBIGER, Jesse	Ana.	U. of Minnesota-Duluth	D
179	FORSTER, Nathan	Cgy.-Wsh.	Seattle	D
180	LUNDQVIST, Stefan	NYR	Brynas Gavle	LW
181	GAGNON, Jonathan	Tor.	Cape Breton	C
182	KOROLEV, Evgeny	NYI	London	D
183	ARNASON, Tyler	Chi.	Fargo-Moorehead Jr. A	C
184	SMITH, Donald	Car.	Clarkson	C
185	MULICK, Robert	S.J.	Sault Ste. Marie	D
186	MORRISON, Michael	Edm.	Exeter H.S.	G
187	WESTRUM, Erik	Phx.	U. of Minnesota	C
188	PERIARD, Michael	Ott.	Shawinigan	D
189	KRUCHININ, Andrei	Mtl.	Lada Togliatti	D
190	HANNUS, Tommi	L.A.	TPS Turku Jr.	C
191	MORAN, Brad	Buf.	Calgary	C
192	DUDA, Radek	Bos.-Cgy.	Sparta Praha	RW
193	STANA, Ratislav	Wsh.	HC Kosice	G
194	HEWER, Oak	Col.-T.B.	Sault Ste. Marie	C
195	DIVISEK, Tomas	Phi.	Slavia Praha	LW
196	SCHERBAN, Joel	Pit.	London	C
197	TWORDIK, Brad	St.L.	Brandon	C
198	GOETZINGER, Jeremy	Det.	Prince Albert	D
199	JENSEN, Erik	N.J.	Des Moines Jr. A	RW
200	PERRY, Scott	DAL	Boston University	C

ROUND #8

201	MURRAY, Craig	T.B.-Mtl.	Penticton	C
202	BARTEK, Martin	Nsh.	Sherbrooke	LW
203	JACOBS, Ian	Fla.	Ottawa	RW
204	MISCHLER, Graig	Van.	Northeastern	C
205	BERNIER, David	Ana.	Quebec	RW
206	FROGREN, Jonas	Cgy.	Farjestad Karlstad Jr.	D
207	WITEHALL, Johan	NYR	Leksand	LW
208	SVOBODA, Jaroslav	Tor.-Car.	HC Olomouc	LW
209	BRINDAMOUR, Frederik	NYI	Sherbrooke	G
210	GRIFFIN, Sean	Chi.	Kingston	D
211	KOSICK, Mark	Car.	U. of Michigan	C
212	FAHEY, Jim	S.J.	Catholic Memorial H.S.	D
213	LEFEBVRE, Christian	Edm.	Baie-Comeau	D
214	HANSON, Justin	Phx.	Moose Jaw	RW
215	WOLFE, Dwight	Ott.-Tor.	Halifax	D
216	RYDER, Michael	Mtl.	Hull	C
217	HENKEL, Jim	L.A.	New England	C
218	MORAVEC, David	Buf.	HC Vitkovice	RW
219	VALENTINE, Curtis	Bos.-Van.	Bowling Green	LW
220	FARRELL, Michael	Wsh.	Providence College	D
221	HULAK, Daniel	Col.-T.B.	Swift Current	D
222	PISTEK, Lubomir	Phi.	Slovan Bratislava Jr.	RW
223	VERENIKIN, Sergei	S.J.-Ott.	Torpedo Yaroslavl	LW
224	LEHTO, Mika	Pit.	Assat Pori Jr.	G
225	PASTUKH, Vevgeny	St.L.	Torpedo Yaroslavl	LW
226	PETRASEK, David	Det.	HV 71 Jonkoping	D
227	AHOSILTA, Marko	N.J.	KalPa Kuopio Jr.	C
228	TRAVNICEK, Mihail	Dal.-Tor.	Chemopetrol Litvinov Jr.	RW

ROUND #9

229	LYNESS, Chris	T.B.	Rouyn-Noranda	D
230	SKRASTINS, Karlis	Nsh.	TPS Turku	D
231	WISCHER, Adrian	Fla.	EHC Kloten	C
232	METCALFE, Jason	Van.	London	D
233	PRESTBERG, Pelle	Ana.	Farjestad Karlstad	LW
234	MITCHELL, Kevin	Cgy.	Guelph	D
235	MERTZIG, Jan	NYR	Lulea	D
236	ROSTOV, Sergei	Tor.	Dynamo-2 Moscow	D
237	BLAIS, Ben	NYI	Walpole H.S.	D
238	COUTURE, Alexandre	Chi.	Sherbrooke	LW
239	MCDONALD, Brent	Car.	Red Deer	C
240	YERSHOV, Andrei	S.J.-Chi.	Khimik Voskresensk	D
241	SPIRIDONOV, Maxim	Edm.	London	RW
242	DOYLE, Jason	Phx.-NYI.	Owen Sound	RW
243	HUBACEK, Petr	Phi.	Kometa Brno	C
244	PETERSON, Toby	Pit.	Colorado College	C
245	ANDERSSON, Andreas	Ana.	HV 71 Jonkoping	G
246	PAVLIKOVSKY, Rastisla	Ott.	Utah	C
247	HARRIS, Darcy	Mtl.	Kitchener	RW
248	YEATS, Matthew	L.A.	Olds	G
249	TERGLAV, Edo	Buf.	Baie-Comeau	RW
250	MATEJOVSKY, Radek	Bos.-NYI	Slavia Praha	RW
251	EVANS, Blake	Wsh.	Tri-City	C
252	CIBAK, Martin	Col.-T.B.	HK 32 Liptovsky Mikulas	C
253	ST. JACQUES, Bruno	Phi.	Baie-Comeau	D
254	HUSSEY, Matt	Pit.	Avon Old Farms H.S.	C
255	POHL, John	St.L.	Red Wing H.S.	C
256	PIETILAINEN, Petja	Det.	Saskatoon	LW
257	HELD, Ryan	N.J.	Kitchener	C
258	SKROBAT, Sergei	Dal.-Phi.	Dynamo-2 Moscow	D

Draft Choices, 1997-69

1997

FIRST ROUND

Selection	Claimed By	Amateur Club	
1 THORNTON, Joe	Bos.	Sault Ste. Marie	C
2 MARLEAU, Patrick	S.J.	Seattle	C
3 JOKINEN, Olli	L.A.	HIFK Helsinki	C
4 LUONGO, Roberto	Tor.-NYI	Val D'Or	G
5 BREWER, Eric	NYI	Prince George	D
6 TKACZUK, Daniel	Cgy.	Barrie	C
7 MARA, Paul	T.B.	Sudbury	D
8 SAMSONOV, Sergei	Car.-Bos.	Detroit	LW
9 BOYNTON, Nicholas	Wsh.	Ottawa	D
10 FERENCE, Brad	Van.	Spokane	D
11 WARD, Jason	Mtl.	Erie	C
12 HOSSA, Marian	Ott.	Dukla Trencin	RW
13 CLEARY, Daniel	Chi.	Belleville	LW
14 RIESEN, Michel	Edm.	Biel-Bienne	LW
15 ZULTEK, Matt	St.L-Edm.-St.L.-L.A.	Ottawa	LW
16 JONES, Ty	Pho.-Chi.	Spokane	RW
17 DOME, Robert	Pit.	Long Beach/ Las Vegas	RW
18 HOLMQVIST, Mikael	Ana.	Djurgarden	C
19 CHERNESKI, Stefan	NYR	Brandon	RW
20 BROWN, Mike	Fla.	Red Deer	C
21 NORONEN, Mika	Buf.	Tappara Tampere	G
22 TSELIOS, Nikos	Det.-Car.	Belleville	D
23 HANNAN, Scott	Phi.-Car.-S.J.	Kelowna	D
24 DAMPHOUSSE, J-F	N.J.	Moncton	G
25 MORROW, Brenden	Dal.	Portland	LW
26 GRIMES, Kevin	Col.	Kingston	D

SECOND ROUND

Selection	Claimed By	Amateur Club	
27 CLYMER, Ben	Bos.	U. of Minnesota	D
28 DEFAUW, Brad	S.J.-Car.	U. of North Dakota	LW
29 BARNEY, Scott	L.A.	Peterborough	C
30 PELLETIER, Jean-Marc	Tor.-Phi.	Cornell U.	G
31 ZEHR, Jeff	NYI	Windsor	LW
32 LINDSAY, Evan	Cgy.	Prince Albert	G
33 KOS, Kyle	T.B.	Red Deer	D
34 BONNI, Ryan	Car.-Van.	Saskatoon	D
35 FORTIN, J-F	Wsh.	Sherbrooke	D
36 DRUKEN, Harold	Van.	Detroit	LW
37 BAUMGARTNER, Gregor	Mtl.	Laval	C
38 GRON, Stanislav	Ott.-N.J.	Slovan Bratislava Jr.	C
39 REICH, Jeremy	Chi.	Seattle	C
40 RENNETTE, Tyler	St.L.	North Bay	C
41 DOVIGI, Patrick	Edm.	Erie	G
42 TRIPP, John	St.L.-Cgy.	Oshawa	RW
43 GUSTAFSSON, Juha	Pho.	Kiekko-Espoo Jr.	D
44 GAFFANEY, Brian	Pit.	North Iowa Jr. A	D
45 BALMOCHNYKH, Maxim	Ana.	Lada Togliatti	LW
46 JARVIS, Wes	NYR	Kitchener	D
47 HUSELIUS, Kristian	Fla.	Farjestad Karlstad	LW
48 TALLINDER, Henrik	Buf.	AIK Solna	D
49 BUTSAYEV, Yuri	Det.	Lada Togliatti	C
50 KAVANAGH, Pat	Phi.	Peterborough	RW
51 KOKOREV, Dmitri	N.J.-Car.-Cgy.	Dynamo-2 Moscow	D
52 LYASHENKO, Roman	Dal.	Torpedo Yaroslavl	C
53 BELAK, Graham	Col.	Edmonton	D

1996

FIRST ROUND

Selection	Claimed By	Amateur Club	
1 PHILLIPS, Chris	Ott.	Prince Albert	D
2 ZYUZIN, Andrei	S.J.	Salavat Yulayev Ufa	D
3 DUMONT, Jean-Pierre	NYI	Val d'Or	RW
4 VOLCHKOV, Alexander	L.A.-Wsh.	Barrie	C
5 JACKMAN, Richard	Dal.	Sault Ste. Marie	D
6 DEVEREAUX, Boyd	Edm.	Kitchener	C
7 RASMUSSEN, Erik	Buf.	U. of Minnesota	C
8 AITKEN, Johnathan	Hfd.-Bos.	Medicine Hat	D
9 SALEI, Ruslan	Ana.	Las Vegas	D
10 WARD, Lance	N.J.	Red Deer	D
11 FOCHT, Dan	Pho.	Tri-City	D
12 HOLDEN, Josh	Van.	Regina	C
13 MORRIS, Derek	Cgy.	Regina	D
14 REASONER, Marty	St.L.-Edm.-St.L.	Boston College	C
15 ZUBRUS, Dainius	Tor.-Phi.	Pembroke	RW
16 LAROCQUE, Mario	T.B.	Hull	D
17 SVEJKOVSKY, Jaroslav	Wsh.	Tri-City	RW
18 HIGGINS, Matt	Mtl.	Moose Jaw	C
19 DESCOTEAUX, Matthieu	Bos.-Edm.	Shawinigan	D
20 NILSON, Marcus	Fla.	Djurgarden Stockholm	C
21 STURM, Marco	Chi.-S.J.	Landshut	C
22 BROWN, Jeff	NYR	Sarnia	D
23 HILLIER, Craig	Pit.	Ottawa	G
24 BRIERE, Daniel	Phi.-Pho.	Drummondville	C
25 RATCHUK, Peter	Col.	Shattuck St. Mary's	D
26 WALLIN, Jesse	Det.	Red Deer	D

SECOND ROUND

Selection	Claimed By	Amateur Club	
27 SARICH, Cory	Ott.-St.L.-Buf.	Saskatoon	D
28 SKRBEK, Pavel	S.J.-N.J.-Pit.	HC Kladno	D
29 LACOUTURE, Dan	NYI	Jr. Whalers	LW
30 GREEN, Josh	L.A.	Medicine Hat	LW
31 ROYER, Remi	Dal.-Pho.-S.J.-Chi.	St-Hyacinthe	D
32 HAJT, Chris	Edm.	Guelph	D
33 VAN OENE, Darren	Buf.	Brandon	LW
34 WASYLUK, Trevor	Hfd.	Medicine Hat	LW
35 CULLEN, Matt	Ana.	St. Cloud State	C
36 POSMYK, Marek	N.J.-Tor.	Dukla Jihlava	D
37 CISAR, Marian	Pho.-L.A.	Slovan Bratislava	W
38 MASON, Wesley	Van.-N.J.	Sarnia	LW
39 BRIGLEY, Travis	Cgy.	Lethbridge	LW
40 BEGIN, Steve	St.L.-Cgy.	Val d'Or	C
41 DEWOLF, Joshua	Tor.-Pit.-N.J.	Twin Cities	D
42 PAUL, Jeff	T.B.-Chi.	Niagara Falls	D
43 BULIS, Jan	Wsh.	Barrie	C
44 GARON, Mathieu	Mtl.	Victoriaville	G
45 KUSTER, Henry	Bos.	Medicine Hat	RW
46 PETERS, Geoff	Fla.-S.J.-Chi.	Niagara Falls	C
47 DAGENAIS, Pierre	Chi.-T.B.-N.J.	Moncton	LW
48 GONEAU, Daniel	NYR	Granby	LW
49 WHITE, Colin	Pit.-N.J.	Hull	D
50 LARIVEE, Francis	Phi.-Tor.	Laval	G
51 BABENKO, Yuri	Col.	Krylja Sovetov	C
52 MILLER, Aren	Det.	Spokane	G

1995

FIRST ROUND

Selection	Claimed By	Amateur Club	
1. BERARD, Bryan	Ott.	Detroit	D
2. REDDEN, Wade	NYI	Brandon	D
3. BERG, Aki-Petteri	L.A.	Kiekko-67 Turku	D
4. KILGER, Chad	Ana.	Kingston	C
5. LANGKOW, Daymond	T.B.	Tri-City	C
6. KELLY, Steve	Edm.	Prince Albert	C
7. DOAN, Shane	Wpg.	Kamloops	RW
8. RYAN, Terry	Mtl.	Tri-City	LW
9. McLAREN, Kyle	Hfd.-Bos.	Tacoma	D
10. DVORAK, Radek	Fla.	HC Ceske Budejovice	W
11. IGINLA, Jarome	Dal.	Kamloops	C
12. RIIHIJARVI, Teemu	S.J.	Kiekko-Espoo Jr.	LW
13. GIGUERE, J-Sebastien	NYR-Hfd.	Halifax	G
14. McKEE, Jay	Van.-Buf.	Niagara Falls	D
15. WARE, Jeff	Tor.	Oshawa	D
16. BIRON, Martin	Buf.	Beauport	G
17. CHURCH, Brad	Wsh.	Prince Albert	LW
18. SYKORA, Petr	N.J.	Detroit	C
19. NABOKOV, Dmitri	Chi.	Krylja Sovetov	C
20. GAUTHIER, Denis Jr.	Cgy.	Drummondville	D
21. BROWN, Sean	Bos.	Belleville	D
22. BOUCHER, Brian	Phi.	Tri-City	G
23. ELOMO, Miika	St.L.-Wsh.	Kiekko-67 Turku	LW
24. MOROZOV, Alexei	Pit.	Krylja Sovetov	RW
25. DENIS, Marc	Col.	Chicoutimi	G
26. KUZNETSOV, Maxim	Det.	Dynamo Moscow	D

SECOND ROUND

Selection	Claimed By	Amateur Club	
27. MORO, Marc	Ott.	Kingston	D
28. HLAVAC, Jan	NYI	Sparta Praha	LW
29. WESENBERG, Brian	Ana.	Guelph	RW
30. McBAIN, Mike	T.B.	Red Deer	D
31. LARAQUE, Georges	Edm.	St-Jean	RW
32. CHOUINARD, Marc	Wpg.	Beauport	C
33. MacLEAN, Donald	L.A.	Beauport	C
34. DOIG, Jason	Mtl.-Wpg.	Laval	D
35. FEDOTOV, Sergei	Hfd.	Dynamo Moscow	D
36. MacDONALD, Aaron	Fla.	Swift Current	G
37. COTE, Patrick	Dal.	Beauport	LW
38. ROED, Peter	S.J.	White Bear Lake	C
39. DUBE, Christian	NYR	Sherbrooke	C
40. McALLISTER, Chris	Van.	Saskatoon	D
41. SMITH, Denis (D.J.)	Tor.-NYI	Windsor	D
42. DUTIAUME, Mark	Buf.	Brandon	LW
43. HAY, Dwayne	Wsh.	Guelph	LW
44. PERROTT, Nathan	N.J.	Oshawa	RW
45. LAFLAMME, Christian	Chi.	Beauport	D
46. SMIRNOV, Pavel	Cgy.	Molot Perm	RW/C
47. SCHAFER, Paxton	Bos.	Medicine Hat	G
48. KENNY, Shane	Phi.	Owen Sound	D
49. HECHT, Jochen	St.L.	Mannheim	C
50. ROSA, Pavel	Pit.-L.A.	Litvinov Jr.	RW
51. BEAUDOIN, Nic	Col.	Detroit	LW
52. AUDET, Philippe	Det.	Granby	LW

The NY Islanders' second round selection in the 1993 draft, Bryan McCabe, pictured here after being traded to the Vancouver Canucks in the deal that sent Trevor Linden to Long Island, has never missed a game in his three seasons in the league.

1994

FIRST ROUND

Selection	Claimed By	Amateur Club	
1. JOVANOVSKI, Ed	Fla.	Windsor	D
2. TVERDOVSKY, Oleg	Ana.	Soviet Wings	D
3. BONK, Radek	Ott.	Las Vegas	C
4. BONSIGNORE, Jason	Wpg.-Edm.	Niagara Falls	C
5. O'NEILL, Jeff	Hfd.	Guelph	C
6. SMYTH, Ryan	Edm.	Moose Jaw	LW
7. STORR, Jamie	L.A.	Owen Sound	G
8. WIEMER, Jason	T.B.	Portland	LW
9. LINDROS, Brett	Que.-NYI	Kingston	RW
10. BAUMGARTNER, Nolan	Phi.-Que.-Tor.-Wsh.	Kamloops	D
11. FRIESEN, Jeff	S.J.	Regina	LW
12. BELAK, Wade	NYI-Que.	Saskatoon	D
13. OHLUND, Mattias	Van.	Pitea	D
14. MOREAU, Ethan	Chi.	Niagara Falls	LW
15. KHARLAMOV, Alexander	Wsh.	CSKA Moscow	C
16. FICHAUD, Eric	St.L.-Wsh.-Tor.	Chicoutimi	G
17. PRIMEAU, Wayne	Buf.	Owen Sound	C
18. BROWN, Brad	Mtl.	North Bay	C
19. DINGMAN, Chris	Cgy.	Brandon	LW
20. BOTTERILL, Jason	Dal.	U. of Michigan	LW
21. RYABCHIKOV, Evgeni	Bos.	Molot Perm	G
22. KEALTY, Jeffrey	Tor.-Que.	Catholic Memorial	D
23. GOLUBOVSKY, Yan	Det.	CSKA Jr. Moscow	D
24. WELLS, Chris	Pit.	Seattle	G
25. SHARIFIJANOV, Vadim	N.J.	Salavat Yulayev ufa	RW
26. CLOUTIER, Dan	NYR	Sault Ste. Marie	G

SECOND ROUND

Selection	Claimed By	Amateur Club	
27. WARRENER, Rhett	Fla.	Saskatoon	D
28. DAVIDSSON, Johan	Ana.	HV 71	C
29. NECKAR, Stanislav	Ott.	Ceske Budejovice	D
30. QUINT, Deron	Wpg.	Seattle	D
31. PODOLLAN, Jason	Hfd.-Fla.	Spokane	C
32. WATT, Mike	Edm.	Stratford Jr. B	LW
33. JOHNSON, Matt	L.A.	Peterborough	LW
34. CLOUTIER, Colin	T.B.	Brandon	C
35. MARHA, Josef	Que.	Dukla Jihlava	C
36. JOHNSON, Ryan	Phi.-Fla.	Thunder Bay Jr. A	C
37. NIKOLOV, Angel	S.J.	Litvinov	D
38. HOLLAND, Jason	NYI	Kamloops	D
39. GORDON, Robb	Van.	Powell River Jr. A	C
40. LEROUX, Jean-Yves	Chi.	Beauport	LW
41. CHERREY, Scott	Wsh.	North Bay	LW
42. SCATCHARD, Dave	St.L.-Van.	Portland	C
43. BROWN, Curtis	Buf.	Moose Jaw	C
44. THEODORE, Jose	Mtl.	St-Jean	G
45. RYABYKIN, Dmitri	Cgy.	Dynamo-2	D
46. JINMAN, Lee	Dal.	North Bay	C
47. GONEAU, Daniel	Bos.	Laval	LW
48. HAGGERTY, Sean	Tor.	Detroit	LW
49. DANDENAULT, Mathieu	Det.	Sherbrooke	RW
50. PARK, Richard	Pit.	Belleville	C
51. ELIAS, Patrik	N.J.	Kladno	LW
52. VERCIK, Rudolf	NYR	Slovan Bratislava	LW

1993

FIRST ROUND

Selection	Claimed By	Amateur Club	
1. DAIGLE, Alexandre	Ott.	Victoriaville	C
2. PRONGER, Chris	S.J.-Hfd.	Peterborough	D
3. GRATTON, Chris	T.B.	Kingston	C
4. KARIYA, Paul	Ana.	University of Maine	LW
5. NIEDERMAYER, Rob	Fla.	Medicine Hat	C
6. KOZLOV, Viktor	Hfd.-S.J.	Dynamo Moscow	LW
7. ARNOTT, Jason	Edm.	Oshawa	C
8. SUNDSTROM, Niklas	NYR	MoDo	LW
9. HARVEY, Todd	Dal.	Detroit	C
10. THIBAULT, Jocelyn	Phi.-Que.	Sherbrooke	G
11. WITT, Brendan	St. L.-Wsh.	Seattle	D
12. JONSSON, Kenny	Buf.-Tor.	Rogle Angelholm	D
13. PEDERSON, Denis	N.J.	Prince Albert	C
14. DEADMARSH, Adam	NYI-Que.	Portland	C
15. LINDGREN, Mats	Wpg.	Skelleftea	C
16. STAJDUHAR, Nick	L.A.-Edm.	London	D
17. ALLISON, Jason	Wsh.	London	C
18. MATTSSON, Jesper	Cgy.	Malmo	C
19. WILSON, Landon	Tor.	Dubuque Jr. A	RW
20. WILSON, Mike	Van.	Sudbury	D
21. KOIVU, Saku	Mtl.	TPS Turku	C
22. ERIKSSON, Anders	Det.	MoDo	D
23. BERTUZZI, Todd	Que.-NYI	Guelph	C
24. LECOMPTE, Eric	Chi.	Hull	LW
25. ADAMS, Kevyn	Bos.	Miami-Ohio	C
26. BERGQVIST, Stefan	Pit.	Leksand	D

SECOND ROUND

Selection	Claimed By	Amateur Club	
27. BICANEK, Radim	Ott.	Dukla Jihlava	D
28. DONOVAN, Shean	S.J.	Ottawa	RW
29. MOSS, Tyler	T.B.	Kingston	G
30. TSULYGIN, Nikolai	Ana.	Salavat Yulalev Ufa	D
31. LANGKOW, Scott	Fla.-Wpg.	Portland	G
32. PANDOLFO, Jay	Hfd.-N.J.	Boston University	LW
33. VYBORNY, David	Edm.	Sparta Praha	C
34. SOROCHAN, Lee	NYR	Lethbridge	D
35. LANGENBRUNNER, Jamie	Dal.	Cloquet	C
36. NIINIMAA, Janne	Phi.	Karpat Oulu	D
37. BETS, Maxim	St. L.	Spokane	LW
38. TSYGUROV, Denis	Buf.	Lada Togliatti	D
39. MORRISON, Brendan	N.J.	Penticton T-II Jr. A	C
40. McCABE, Bryan	NYI	Spokane	D
41. WEEKES, Kevin	Wpg.-Fla.	Owen Sound	G
42. TOPOROWSKI, Shayne	L.A.	Prince Albert	RW
43. BUDAYEV, Alexei	Wsh.-Wpg.	Kristall Elektrostal	C
44. ALLISON, Jamie	Cgy.	Detroit	D
45. KROUPA, Vlastimil	Tor.-Hfd.-S.J.	Chemopetrol Litvinov	D
46. GIRARD, Rick	Van.	Swift Current	C
47. FITZPATRICK, Rory	Mtl.	Sudbury	D
48. COLEMAN, Jonathan	Det.	Andover Academy	D
49. BUCKBERGER, Ashley	Que.	Swift Current	RW
50. MANLOW, Eric	Chi.	Kitchener	C
51. ALVEY, Matt	Bos.	Springfield Jr. B	RW
52. PITTIS, Domenic	Pit.	Lethbridge	C

1992

FIRST ROUND

Selection	Claimed By	Amateur Club	
1. HAMRLIK, Roman	T.B.	ZPS Zlin (Czech.)	D
2. YASHIN, Alexei	Ott.	Dynamo Moscow (CIS)	C
3. RATHJE, Mike	S.J.	Medicine Hat	D
4. WARRINER, Todd	Que.	Windsor	LW
5. KASPARAITIS, Darius	Tor.-NYI	Dynamo Moscow (CIS)	D
6. STILLMAN, Cory	Cgy.	Windsor	C
7. SITTLER, Ryan	Phi.	Nichols	LW
8. CONVERY, Brandon	NYI-Tor.	Sudbury	C
9. PETROVICKY, Robert	Hfd.	Dukla Trencin (Czech.)	C
10. NAZAROV, Andrei	Min.-S.J.	Dynamo Moscow	LW
11. COOPER, David	Buf.	Medicine Hat	D
12. KRIVOKRASOV, Sergei	Wpg.-Chi.	CSKA Moscow (CIS)	RW
13. HULBIG, Joe	Edm.	St. Sebastian's	LW
14. GONCHAR, Sergei	St.L.-Wsh.	Chelybinsk (CIS)	D
15. BOWEN, Jason	L.A.-Pit.-Phi.	Tri-City	LW
16. KVARTALNOV, Dmitri	Bos.	San Diego	LW
17. BAUTIN, Sergei	Chi.-Wpg.	Dynamo Moscow (CIS)	D
18. SMITH, Jason	N.J.	Regina	D
19. STRAKA, Martin	Pit.	Skoda Plzen (Czech.)	C
20. WILKIE, David	Mtl.	Kamloops	D
21. POLASEK, Libor	Van.	TJ Vitkovice (Czech.)	C
22. BOWEN, Curtis	Det.	Ottawa	LW
23. MARSHALL, Grant	Wsh.-Tor.	Ottawa	RW
24. FERRARO, Peter	NYR	Waterloo Jr. A	C

SECOND ROUND

Selection	Claimed By	Amateur Club	
25. PENNEY, Chad	Ott.	North Bay	LW
26. BANNISTER, Drew	T.B.	Sault-Ste-Marie	D
27. MIRONOV, Boris	S.J.-Chi.-Wpg.	CSKA Moscow (CIS)	D
28. BROUSSEAU, Paul	Que.	Hull	RW
29. GRONMAN, Toumas	Tor.-Que.	Tacoma	D
30. O'SULLIVAN, Chris	Cgy.	Catholic Memorial	D
31. METLYUK, Denis	Phi.	Lada Togliatti (CIS)	C
32. CAREY, Jim	NYI-Tor.-Wsh.	Catholic Memorial	G
33. BURE, Valeri	Hfd.-Mtl.	Spokane	LW
34. VARVIO, Jarkko	Min.	HPK (Finland)	RW
35. CIERNY, Jozef	Buf.	ZTK Zvolen (Czech.)	LW
36. SHANTZ, Jeff	Wpg.-Chi.	Regina	C
37. REICHEL, Martin	Edm.	Freiburg (Germany)	RW
38. KOROLEV, Igor	St.L.	Dynamo Moscow	RW
39. HOCKING, Justin	L.A.	Spokane	D
40. PECA, Mike	Bos.-Van.	Ottawa	C
41. KLIMOVICH, Sergei	Chi.	Dynamo Moscow	C
42. BRYLIN, Sergei	N.J.	CSKA Moscow (CIS)	C
43. HUSSEY, Marc	Pit.	Moose Jaw	D
44. CORPSE, Keli	Mtl.	Kingston	C
45. FOUNTAIN, Michael	Van.	Oshawa	G
46. McCARTY, Darren	Det.	Belleville	RW
47. NIKOLISHIN, Andrei	Wsh.-Hfd.	Dynamo Moscow	LW
48. NORSTROM, Mattias	NYR	AIK (Sweden)	D

1991

FIRST ROUND

Selection	Claimed By	Amateur Club	
1. LINDROS, Eric	Que.	Oshawa	C
2. FALLOON, Pat	S.J.	Spokane	RW
3. NIEDERMAYER, Scott	Tor.-N.J.	Kamloops	D
4. LACHANCE, Scott	NYI	Boston University	D
5. WARD, Aaron	Wpg.	U. of Michigan	D
6. FORSBERG, Peter	Phi.	MoDo (Sweden)	C
7. STOJANOV, Alex	Van.	Hamilton	RW
8. MATVICHUK, Richard	Min.	Saskatoon	D
9. POULIN, Patrick	Hfd.	St.-Hyacinthe	LW
10. LAPOINTE, Martin	Det.	Laval	RW
11. ROLSTON, Brian	N.J.	Detroit Comp. Jr. A	C
12. WRIGHT, Tyler	Edm.	Swift Current	C
13. BOUCHER, Phillipe	Buf.	Granby	D
14. PEAKE, Pat	Wsh.	Detroit	C
15. KOVALEV, Alexei	NYR	D'amo Moscow	RW
16. NASLUND, Markus	Pit.	MoDo	RW
17. BILODEAU, Brent	Mtl.	Seattle	D
18. MURRAY, Glen	Bos.	Sudbury	RW
19. SUNDBLAD, Niklas	Cgy.	AIK (Sweden)	RW
20. RUCINSKY, Martin	L.A.-Edm.	CHZ Litvinov (Czech.)	LW
21. HALVERSON, Trevor	St.L.-Wsh.	North Bay	LW
22. McAMMOND, Dean	Chi.	Prince Albert	C

SECOND ROUND

Selection	Claimed By	Amateur Club	
23. WHITNEY, Ray	S.J.	Spokane	C
24. CORBET, Rene	Que.	Drummondville	LW
25. LAVIGNE, Eric	Tor.-Que.-Wsh.	Hull	D
26. PALFFY, Zigmund	NYI	AC Nitra (Czech.)	LW
27. STAIOS, Steve	Wpg.-St.L.	Niagara Falls	D
28. CAMPBELL, Jim	Phi.-Mtl.	Northwood Prep	C
29. CULLIMORE, Jassen	Van.	Peterborough	D
30. OZOLINSH, Sandis	Min.-S.J.	Dynamo Riga (USSR)	D
31. HAMRLIK, Martin	Hfd.	TJ Zin (Czech.)	D
32. PUSHOR, Jamie	Det.	Lethbridge	D
33. HEXTALL, Donevan	N.J.	Prince Albert	LW
34. VERNER, Andrew	Edm.	Peterborough	G
35. DAWE, Jason	Buf.	Peterborough	LW
36. NELSON, Jeff	Wsh.	Prince Albert	C
37. WERENKA, Darcy	NYR	Lethbridge	D
38. FITZGERALD, Rusty	Pit.	Duluth East HS	C
39. POMICHTER, Michael	Mtl.-Chi.	Springfield Jr. B	C
40. STUMPEL, Jozef	Bos.	AC Nitra (Czech.)	RW
41. GROLEAU, Francois	Cgy.	Shawinigan	D
42. LEVEQUE, Guy	L.A.	Cornwall	C
43. DARBY, Craig	St.L.-Mtl.	Albany Academy	C
44. MATTHEWS, Jamie	Chi.	Sudbury	C

1990

FIRST ROUND

Selection	Claimed By	Amateur Club	
1. NOLAN, Owen	Que.	Cornwall	RW
2. NEDVED, Petr	Van.	Seattle	C
3. PRIMEAU, Keith	Det.	Niagara Falls	C
4. RICCI, Mike	Phi.	Peterborough	C
5. JAGR, Jaromir	Pit.	Poldi Kladno (Czech.)	LW
6. SCISSONS, Scott	NYI	Saskatoon	C
7. SYDOR, Darryl	L.A.	Kamloops	D
8. HATCHER, Derian	Min.	North Bay	D
9. SLANEY, John	Wsh.	Cornwall	D
10. BEREHOWSKY, Drake	Tor.	Kingston	D
11. KIDD, Trevor	N.J.-Cgy.	Brandon	G
12. STEVENSON, Turner	St.L.-Mtl.	Seattle	RW
13. STEWART, Michael	NYR	Michigan State	D
14. MAY, Brad	Wpg.-Buf.	Niagara Falls	LW
15. GREIG, Mark	Hfd.	Lethbridge	RW
16. DYKHUIS, Karl	Chi.	Hull	D
17. ALLISON, Scott	Edm.	Prince Albert	C
18. ANTOSKI, Shawn	Mtl.-St.L.-Van.	North Bay	LW
19. TKACHUK, Keith	Buf.-Wpg.	Malden Catholic	LW
20. BRODEUR, Martin	Cgy.-N.J.	St. Hyacinthe	G
21. SMOLINSKI, Bryan	Bos.	Michigan State	C

SECOND ROUND

Selection	Claimed By	Amateur Club	
22. HUGHES, Ryan	Que.	Cornell	C
23. SLEGR, Jiri	Van.	CHZ Litvinov (Czech.)	D
24. HARLOCK, David	Det.-Cgy.-N.J.	U. of Michigan	D
25. SIMON, Chris	Phi.	Ottawa	LW
26. PERREAULT, Nicolas P.	Pit.-Cgy.	Hawkesbury Jr. A	D
27. TAYLOR, Chris	NYI	London	C
28. SEMCHUK, Brandy	L.A.	Canadian National	RW
29. GOTZIAMAN, Chris	Min.-Cgy.-N.J.	Roseau	RW
30. PASMA, Rod	Wsh.	Cornwall	D
31. POTVIN, Felix	Tor.	Chicoutimi	G
32. VIITAKOSKI, Vesa	N.J.-Cgy.	SaiPa (Finland)	LW
33. JOHNSON, Craig	St.L.	Hill-Murray HS	C
34. WEIGHT, Doug	NYR	Lake Superior	C
35. MULLER, Mike	Wpg.	Wayzata	D
36. SANDERSON, Geoff	Hfd.	Swift Current	C
37. DROPPA, Ivan	Chi.	Partizan (Czech.)	D
38. LEGAULT, Alexandre	Edm.	Boston University	RW
39. KUWABARA, Ryan	Mtl.	Ottawa	RW
40. RENBERG, Mikael	Buf.-Phi.	Pitea (Sweden)	LW
41. BELZILE, Etienne	Cgy.	Cornell	D
42. SANDWITH, Terran	Bos.-Phi.	Tri-Cities	D

1989

FIRST ROUND

Selection	Claimed By	Amateur Club	
1. SUNDIN, Mats	Que.	Nacka (Sweden)	RW
2. CHYZOWSKI, Dave	NYI	Kamloops	LW
3. THORNTON, Scott	Tor.	Belleville	C
4. BARNES, Stu	Wpg.	Tri-Cities	C
5. GUERIN, Bill	N.J.	Springfield Jr. B	RW
6. BENNETT, Adam	Chi.	Sudbury	D
7. ZMOLEK, Doug	Min.	John Marshall	D
8. HERTER, Jason	Van.	U. of North Dakota	D
9. MARSHALL, Jason	St.L.	Vernon Jr. A	D
10. HOLIK, Robert	Hfd.	Dukla Jihlava (Czech.)	C
11. SILLINGER, Mike	Det.	Regina	C
12. PEARSON, Rob	Phi.-Tor.	Belleville	RW
13. VALLIS, Lindsay	NYR-Mtl.	Seattle	RW
14. HALLER, Kevin	Buf.	Regina	D
15. SOULES, Jason	Edm.	Niagara Falls	D
16. HEWARD, Jamie	Pit.	Regina	RW
17. STEVENSON, Shayne	Bos.	Kitchener	RW
18. MILLER, Jason	L.A.-Edm.-N.J.	Medicine Hat	C
19. KOLZIG, Olaf	Wsh.	Tri-Cities	G
20. RICE, Steven	Mtl.-NYR	Kitchener	RW
21. BANCROFT, Steve	Cgy.-Tor.	Belleville	D

SECOND ROUND

Selection	Claimed By	Amateur Club	
22. FOOTE, Adam	Que.	Sault Ste. Marie	D
23. GREEN, Travis	NYI	Spokane	C
24. MANDERVILLE, Kent	Tor.-Cgy.	Notre Dame Jr. A	LW
25. RATUSHNY, Dan	Wpg.	Cornell	D
26. SKALDE, Jarrod	N.J.	Oshawa	C
27. SPEER, Michael	Chi.	Guelph	D
28. CRAIG, Mike	Min.	Oshawa	RW
29. WOODWARD, Robert	Van.	Deerfield	LW
30. BRISEBOIS, Patrice	St.L.-Mtl.	Laval	D
31. CORRIVEAU, Rick	Hfd.-St.L.	London	D
32. BOUGHNER, Bob	Det.	Sault-Ste. Marie	D
33. JOHNSON, Greg	Phi.	Thunder Bay Jr. A	C
34. JUHLIN, Patrik	NYR-Phi.	Vasteras (Sweden)	LW
35. DAFOE, Byron	Buf.-Wsh.	Portland	D
36. BORGO, Richard	Edm.	Kitchener	G
37. LAUS, Paul	Pit.	Niagara Falls	D
38. PARSON, Mike	Bos.	Guelph	G
39. THOMPSON, Brent	L.A.	Medicine Hat	D
40. PROSOFSKY, Jason	Wsh.-NYR	Medicine Hat	RW
41. LAROUCHE, Steve	Mtl.	Trois-Rivieres	C
42. DRURY, Ted	Cgy.	Fairfield Prep	C

1988

FIRST ROUND

Selection	Claimed By	Amateur Club	
1. MODANO, Mike	Min.	Prince Albert	C
2. LINDEN, Trevor	Van.	Medicine Hat	RW
3. LESCHYSHYN, Curtis	Que.	Saskatoon	D
4. SHANNON, Darrin	Pit.	Windsor	LW
5. DORE, Daniel	NYR-Que.	Drummondville	RW
6. PEARSON, Scott	Tor.	Kingston	LW
7. GELINAS, Martin	L.A.	Hull	LW
8. ROENICK, Jeremy	Chi.	Thayer Academy	C
9. BRIND'AMOUR, Rod	St.L.	Notre Dame Jr. A	C
10. SELANNE, Teemu	Wpg.	Jokerit (Finland)	RW
11. GOVEDARIS, Chris	Hfd.	Toronto	LW
12. FOSTER, Corey	N.J.	Peterborough	D
13. SAVAGE, Joel	Buf.	Victoria	RW
14. BOIVIN, Claude	Phi.	Drummondville	LW
15. SAVAGE, Reginald	Wsh.	Victoriaville	C
16. CHEVELDAYOFF, Kevin	NYI	Brandon	D
17. KOCUR, Kory	Det.	Saskatoon	RW
18. CIMETTA, Robert	Bos.	Toronto	LW
19. LEROUX, Francois	Edm.	St. Jean	D
20. CHARRON, Eric	Mtl.	Trois-Rivieres	D
21. MUZZATTI, Jason	Cgy.	Michigan State	G

SECOND ROUND

Selection	Claimed By	Amateur Club	
22. MALLETTE, Troy	Min.-NYR	Sault Ste. Marie	C
23. CHRISTIAN, Jeff	Van.-N.J.	London	LW
24. FISET, Stephane	Que.	Victoriaville	G
25. MAJOR, Mark	Pit.	North Bay	D
26. DUVAL, Murray	NYR	Spokane	RW
27. DOMI, Tie	Tor.	Peterborough	RW
28. HOLDEN, Paul	L.A.	London	D
29. DOUCET, Wayne	Chi.-NYI	Hamilton	LW
30. PLAVSIC, Adrien	St.L.	U. of New Hampshire	D
31. ROMANIUK, Russell	Wpg.	St. Boniface Jr. A	LW
32. RICHTER, Barry	Hfd.	Culver Academy	D
33. ROHLIN, Leif	N.J.-Van.	Vasteras (Sweden)	D
34. ST. AMOUR, Martin	Buf.-Mtl.	Verdun	LW
35. MURRAY, Pat	Phi.	Michigan State	LW
36. TAYLOR, Tim	Wsh.	London	C
37. LEBRUN, Sean	NYI	New Westminster	LW
38. ANGLEHART, Serge	Det.	Drummondville	D
39. KOIVUNEN, Petro	Bos.-Edm.	Espoo (Finland)	C
40. GAETZ, Link	Edm.-Min.	Spokane	D
41. BARTLEY, Wade	Mtl.-St.L.-Wsh.	Dauphin Jr. A	D
42. HARKINS, Todd	Cgy.	Miami-Ohio	RW

1987

FIRST ROUND

Selection	Claimed By	Amateur Club	
1. TURGEON, Pierre	Buf.	Granby	C
2. SHANAHAN, Brendan	N.J.	London	C
3. WESLEY, Glen	Van.-Bos.	Portland	D
4. McBEAN, Wayne	Min.-L.A.	Medicine Hat	D
5. JOSEPH, Chris	Pit.	Seattle	D
6. ARCHIBALD, David	L.A.-Min.	Portland	C/LW
7. RICHARDSON, Luke	Tor.	Peterborough	D
8. WAITE, Jimmy	Chi.	Chicoutimi	G
9. FOGARTY, Bryan	Que.	Kingston	D
10. MORE, Jayson	NYR	New Westminster	D
11. RACINE, Yves	Det.	Longueuil	D
12. OSBORNE, Keith	St.L.	North Bay	RW
13. CHYNOWETH, Dean	NYI	Medicine Hat	D
14. QUINTAL, Stephane	Bos.	Granby	D
15. SAKIC, Joe	Wsh.-Que.	Swift Current	C
16. MARCHMENT, Bryan	Wpg.	Belleville	D
17. CASSELS, Andrew	Mtl.	Ottawa	C
18. HULL, Jody	Hfd.	Peterborough	RW
19. DEASLEY, Bryan	Cgy.	U. of Michigan	LW
20. RUMBLE, Darren	Phi.	Kitchener	D
21. SOBERLAK, Peter	Edm.	Swift Current	LW

SECOND ROUND

Selection	Claimed By	Amateur Club	
22. MILLER, Brad	Buf.	Regina	D
23. PERSSON, Rickard	N.J.	Ostersund (Sweden)	D
24. MURPHY, Rob	Van.	Laval	C
25. MATTEAU, Stephane	Min.-Cgy.	Hull	LW
26. TABARACCI, Richard	Pit.	Cornwall	G
27. FITZPATRICK, Mark	L.A.	Medicine Hat	G
28. MAROIS, Daniel	Tor.	Chicoutimi	RW
29. McGILL, Ryan	Chi.	Swift Current	D
30. HARDING, Jeff	Que.-Phi.	St. Michael's Jr. B	LW
31. LACROIX, Daniel	NYR	Granby	LW
32. KRUPPKE, Gordon	Det.	Prince Albert	D
33. LECLAIR, John	St.L.-Mtl.	Bellows Academy	D
34. HACKETT, Jeff	NYI	Oshawa	G
35. McCRADY, Scott	Bos.-Min.	Medicine Hat	D
36. BALLANTYNE, Jeff	Wsh.	Ottawa	D
37. ERICKSSON, Patrik	Wpg.	Brynas (Sweden)	C
38. DESJARDINS, Eric	Mtl.	Granby	D
39. BURT, Adam	Hfd.	North Bay	D
40. GRANT, Kevin	Cgy.	Kitchener	D
41. WILKIE, Bob	Phi.-Det.	Swift Current	D
42. WERENKA, Brad	Edm.	N. Michigan	D

1986

FIRST ROUND

Selection	Claimed By	Amateur Club	
1. MURPHY, Joe	Det.	Michigan State	C
2. CARSON, Jimmy	L.A.	Verdun	C
3. BRADY, Neil	N.J.	Medicine Hat	C
4. ZALAPSKI, Zarley	Pit.	Canadian National	D
5. ANDERSON, Shawn	Buf.	Canadian National	D
6. DAMPHOUSSE, Vincent	Tor.	Laval	LW
7. WOODLEY, Dan	Van.	Portland	C
8. ELYNUIK, Pat	Wpg.	Prince Albert	RW
9. LEETCH, Brian	NYR	Avon Old Farms HS	D
10. LEMIEUX, Jocelyn	St.L.	Laval	RW
11. YOUNG, Scott	Hfd.	Boston University	RW
12. BABE, Warren	Min.	Lethbridge	LW
13. JANNEY, Craig	Bos.	Boston College	C
14. SANIPASS, Everett	Chi.	Verdun	LW
15. PEDERSON, Mark	Mtl.	Medicine Hat	LW
16. PELAWA, George	Cgy.	Bemidji HS	RW
17. FITZGERALD, Tom	NYI	Austin Prep	C
18. McRAE, Ken	Que.	Sudbury	C
19. GREENLAW, Jeff	Wsh.	Canadian National	LW
20. HUFFMAN, Kerry	Phi.	Guelph	D
21. ISSEL, Kim	Edm.	Prince Albert	RW

SECOND ROUND

Selection	Claimed By	Amateur Club	
22. GRAVES, Adam	Det.	Windsor	C
23. SEPPO, Jukka	L.A.-Phi.	Sport (Finland)	LW
24. COPELAND, Todd	N.J.	Belmont Hill HS	D
25. CAPUANO, Dave	Pit.	Mt. St. Charles HS	C
26. BROWN, Greg	Buf.	St. Mark's	D
27. BRUNET, Benoit	Tor.-Mtl.	Hull	LW
28. HAWLEY, Kent	Van.-Phi.	Ottawa	C
29. NUMMINEN, Teppo	Wpg.	Tappara (Finland)	D
30. WILKINSON, Neil	NYR-Min.	Selkirk	D
31. POSMA, Mike	St.L.	Buffalo Jr. A	D
32. LaFORGE, Marc	Hfd.	Kingston	D
33. KOLSTAD, Dean	Min.	Prince Albert	D
34. TIRKKONEN, Pekka	Bos.	SaPKo (Finland)	C
35. KURZAWSKI, Mark	Chi.	Windsor	D
36. SHANNON, Darryl	Mtl.-Tor.	Windsor	D
37. GLYNN, Brian	Cgy.	Saskatoon	D
38. VASKE, Dennis	NYI	Armstrong HS	D
39. ROUTHIER, Jean-Marc	Que.	Hull	RW
40. SEFTEL, Steve	Wsh.	Kingston	LW
41. GUERARD, Stephane	Phi.-Que.	Shawinigan	D
42. NICHOLS, Jamie	Edm.	Portland	LW

1985

FIRST ROUND

Selection	Claimed By	Amateur Club	
1. CLARK, Wendel	Tor.	Saskatoon	D
2. SIMPSON, Craig	Pit.	Michigan State	C
3. WOLANIN, Craig	N.J.	Kitchener	D
4. SANDLAK, Jim	Van.	London	RW
5. MURZYN, Dana	Hfd.	Calgary	D
6. DALGARNO, Brad	Min.-NYI	Hamilton	RW
7. DAHLEN, Ulf	NYR	Ostersund (Sweden)	C
8. FEDYK, Brent	Det.	Regina	RW
9. DUNCANSON, Craig	L.A.	Sudbury	LW
10. GRATTON, Dan	Bos.-L.A.	Oshawa	C
11. MANSON, David	Chi.	Prince Albert	D
12. CHARBONNEAU, Jose	St.L.-Mtl.	Drummondville	RW
13. KING, Derek	NYI	Sault Ste. Marie	LW
14. JOHANSSON, Calle	Buf.	V. Frolunda (Sweden)	D
15. LATTA, Dave	Que.	Kitchener	LW
16. CHORSKE, Tom	Mtl.	Minneapolis SW HS	LW
17. BIOTTI, Chris	Cgy.	Belmont Hill HS	D
18. STEWART, Ryan	Wpg.	Kamloops	C
19. CORRIVEAU, Yvon	Wsh.	Toronto	LW
20. METCALFE, Scott	Edm.	Kingston	LW
21. SEABROOKE, Glen	Phi.	Peterborough	C

SECOND ROUND

Selection	Claimed By	Amateur Club	
22. SPANGLER, Ken	Tor.	Calgary	D
23. GIFFIN, Lee	Pit.	Oshawa	RW
24. BURKE, Sean	N.J.	Toronto	G
25. GAMBLE, Troy	Van.	Medicine Hat	G
26. WHITMORE, Kay	Hfd.	Peterborough	G
27. NIEUWENDYK, Joe	Min.-Cgy.	Cornell	C
28. RICHTER, Mike	NYR	Northwood Prep.	G
29. SHARPLES, Jeff	Det.	Kelowna	D
30. EDLUND, Par	L.A.	Bjorkloven (Sweden)	RW
31. COTE, Alain	Bos.	Quebec	D
32. WEINRICH, Eric	Chi.-N.J.	North Yarmouth	D
33. RICHARD, Todd	Mtl.	Armstrong HS	D
34. LAUER, Brad	NYI	Regina	RW
35. HOGUE, Benoit	Buf.	St-Jean	C
36. LAFRENIERE, Jason	Que.	Hamilton	C
37. RAGLAN, Herb	Mtl.-St.L.	Kingston	RW
38. WENAAS, Jeff	Cgy.	Medicine Hat	C
39. OHMAN, Roger	Wpg.	Leksand (Sweden)	D
40. DRUCE, John	Wsh.	Peterborough	RW
41. CARNELLEY, Todd	Edm.	Kamloops	D
42. RENDALL, Bruce	Phi.	Chatham	LW

1984

FIRST ROUND

Selection	Claimed By	Amateur Club	
1. LEMIEUX, Mario	Pit.	Laval	C
2. MULLER, Kirk	N.J.	Cdn-Nat.-Guelph	C
3. OLCZYK, Ed	L.A.-Chi.	U.S. National	RW
4. IAFRATE, Al	Tor.	U.S. National-Belleville	D
5. SVOBODA, Petr	Hfd.-Mtl.	CHZ (Czech.)	D
6. REDMOND, Craig	Chi.-L.A.	Canadian National	D
7. BURR, Shawn	Det.	Kitchener	C
8. CORSON, Shayne	St.L.-Mtl.	Brantford	C
9. BODGER, Doug	Wpg.-Pit.	Kamloops Jr. A	D
10. DAIGNEAULT, J.J.	Van.	Cdn. Nat.-Longueuil	D
11. COTE, Sylvain	Mtl.-Hfd.	Quebec	D
12. ROBERTS, Gary	Cgy.	Ottawa	LW
13. QUINN, David	Min.	Kent HS	D
14. CARKNER, Terry	NYR	Peterborough	D
15. STIENBURG, Trevor	Que.	Guelph	C
16. BELANGER, Roger	Phi.-Pit.	Kingston	D
17. HATCHER, Kevin	Wsh.	North Bay	D
18. ANDERSSON, Mikael	Buf.	V. Frolunda (Sweden)	C
19. PASIN, Dave	Bos.	Prince Albert	RW
20. MacPHERSON, Duncan	NYI	Saskatoon	D
21. ODELEIN, Selmar	Edm.	Regina	D

SECOND ROUND

Selection	Claimed By	Amateur Club	
22. SMYTH, Greg	Phi.	London	D
23. BILLINGTON, Craig	N.J.	Belleville	G
24. WILKS, Brian	L.A.	Kitchener	C
25. GILL, Todd	Tor.	Windsor	D
26. BENNING, Brian	Hfd.-St.L.	Portland	D
27. MELLANBY, Scott	Chi.-Phi.	Henry Carr Jr. B	RW
28. HOUDA, Doug	Det.	Calgary	D
29. RICHER, Stephane	St.L.-Mtl.	Granby	C
30. DOURIS, Peter	Wpg.	U. of New Hampshire	C
31. ROHLICEK, Jeff	Van.	Portland	LW
32. HRKAC, Anthony	Mtl.-St.L.	Orillia Jr. A	C
33. SABOURIN, Ken	Cgy.	Sault Ste. Marie	D
34. LEACH, Stephen	Min.-Wsh.	Matignon HS	RW
35. HELMINEN, Raimo	NYR	Ilves (Finland)	C
36. BROWN, Jeff	Que.	Sudbury	D
37. CHYCHRUN, Jeff	Phi.	Kingston	D
38. RANHEIM, Paul	Wsh.-Cgy.	Edina Hornets HS	C
39. TRAPP, Doug	Buf.	Regina	LW
40. PODLOSKI, Ray	Bos.	Portland	C
41. MELANSON, Bruce	NYI	Oshawa	RW
42. REAUGH, Daryl	Edm.	Kamloops Jr. A	G

1983

FIRST ROUND

Selection	Claimed By	Amateur Club	
1. LAWTON, Brian	Pit.-Min.	Mount St. Charles HS	C
2. TURGEON, Sylvain	Hfd.	Hull	C
3. LaFONTAINE, Pat	N.J.-NYI	Verdun	C
4. YZERMAN, Steve	Det.	Peterborough	C
5. BARRASSO, Tom	St.L.-L.A.-Buf.	Acton-Boxboro HS	G
6. MacLEAN, John	L.A.-N.J.	Oshawa	RW
7. COURTNALL, Russ	Tor.	Victoria	C
8. McBAIN, Andrew	Wpg.	North Bay	RW
9. NEELY, Cam	Van.	Portland	RW
10. LACOMBE, Normand	Cgy.-Buf.	U. of New Hampshire	RW
11. CREIGHTON, Adam	Que.-Buf.	Ottawa	C
12. GAGNER, Dave	NYR	Brantford	C
13. QUINN, Dan	Buf.-Cgy.	Belleville	C
14. DOLLAS, Bobby	Wsh.-Wpg.	Laval	D
15. ERREY, Bob	Min.-Pit.	Peterborough	LW
16. DIDUCK, Gerald	NYI	Lethbridge	D
17. TURCOTTE, Alfie	Mtl.	Portland	C
18. CASSIDY, Bruce	Chi.	Ottawa	D
19. BEUKEBOOM, Jeff	Edm.	Sault Ste. Marie	D
20. JENSEN, David	Phi.-Hfd.	Lawrence	C
21. MARKWART, Nevin	Bos.	Regina	LW

SECOND ROUND

Selection	Claimed By	Amateur Club	
22. CHARLESWORTH, Todd	Pit.	Oshawa	D
23. SIREN, Ville	Hfd.	Ilves (Finland)	D
24. EVANS, Shawn	N.J.	Peterborough	D
25. LAMBERT, Lane	Det.	Saskatoon	RW
26. LEMIEUX, Claude	St.L.-Mtl.	Trois-Rivières	RW
27. MOMESSO, Sergio	L.A.-Mtl.	Shawinigan	C
28. JACKSON, Jeff	Tor.	Brantford	LW
29. BERRY, Brad	Wpg.	St. Albert	D
30. BRUCE, Dave	Van.	Kitchener	RW
31. TUCKER, John	Cgy.-Buf.	Kitchener	C
32. HEROUX, Yves	Que.	Chicoutimi	RW
33. HEATH, Randy	NYR	Portland	LW
34. HAJDU, Richard	Wsh.-Buf.	Kamloops Jr. A	LW
35. FRANCIS, Todd	Mtl.	Brantford	RW
36. PARKS, Malcolm	Min.	St. Albert	C
37. McKECHNEY, Garnet	NYI	Kitchener	RW
38. MUSIL, Frantisek	Mtl.-Min.	Tesla (Czech.)	D
39. PRESLEY, Wayne	Chi.	Kitchener	RW
40. GOLDEN, Mike	Edm.	Reading HS	C
41. ZEZEL, Peter	Phi.	Toronto	C
42. JOHNSTON, Greg	Bos.	Toronto	RW

1982

FIRST ROUND

Selection	Claimed By	Amateur Club	
1. KLUZAK, Gord	Col.-Bos.	Nanaimo	D
2. BELLOWS, Brian	Det.-Min.	Kitchener	RW
3. NYLUND, Gary	Tor.	Portland	D
4. SUTTER, Ron	Hfd.-Phi.	Lethbridge	C
5. STEVENS, Scott	L.A.-Wsh.	Kitchener	D
6. HOUSLEY, Phil	Wsh.-Buf.	S. St. Paul HS	D
7. YAREMCHUK, Ken	Chi.	Portland	C
8. TROTTIER, Rocky	St.L.-N.J.	Nanaimo	RW
9. CYR, Paul	Cgy.-Buf.	Victoria	LW
10. SUTTER, Rich	Pit.	Lethbridge	RW
11. PETIT, Michel	Van.	Sherbrooke	D
12. KYTE, Jim	Wpg.	Cornwall	D
13. SHAW, David	Que.	Kitchener	D
14. LAWLESS, Paul	Phi.-Hfd.	Windsor	LW
15. KONTOS, Chris	NYR	Toronto	C
16. ANDREYCHUK, Dave	Buf.	Oshawa	LW
17. CRAVEN, Murray	Min.-Det.	Medicine Hat	C
18. DANEYKO, Ken	Bos.-N.J.	Seattle	D
19. HEROUX, Alain	Mtl.	Chicoutimi	LW
20. PLAYFAIR, Jim	Edm.	Portland	D
21. FLATLEY, Pat	NYI	U. of Wisconsin	RW

SECOND ROUND

Selection	Claimed By	Amateur Club	
22. CURRAN, Brian	Col.-Bos.	Portland	D
23. COURTEAU, Yves	Det.	Laval	RW
24. LEEMAN, Gary	Tor.	Regina	D
25. IHNACAK, Peter	Hfd.-Tor.	Sparta (Czech.)	C
26. ANDERSON, Mike	L.A.-Buf.	N. St. Paul HS	C
27. HEIDT, Mike	Wsh.-L.A.	Calgary	D
28. BADEAU, Rene	St.L.-Chi.	Quebec	D
29. REIERSON, Dave	Cgy.	Prince Albert	D
30. JOHANSSON, Jens	Buf.	Pitea (Sweden)	D
31. GAUVREAU, Jocelyn	Pit.-Mtl.	Granby	D
32. CARLSON, Kent	Van.-Mtl.	St. Lawrence University	D
33. MALEY, David	Wpg.-Mtl.	Edina HS	C
34. GILLIS, Paul	Que.	Niagara Falls	C
35. PATERSON, Mark	Phi.-Hfd.	Ottawa	D
36. SANDSTROM, Tomas	NYR	Farjestads (Sweden)	RW
37. KROMM, Richard	Buf.-Cgy.	Portland	LW
38. HRYNEWICH, Tim	Min.-Pit.	Sudbury	LW
39. BYERS, Lyndon	Bos.	Regina	RW
40. SANDELIN, Scott	Mtl.	Hibbing HS	D
41. GRAVES, Steve	Edm.	Sault Ste. Marie	C
42. SMITH, Vern	NYI	Lethbridge	D

1981

FIRST ROUND

Selection	Claimed By	Amateur Club	
1. HAWERCHUK, Dale	Wpg.	Cornwall	C
2. SMITH, Doug	Det.-L.A.	Ottawa	C
3. CARPENTER, Bobby	Col.-Wsh.	St. John's HS	C
4. FRANCIS, Ron	Hfd.	Sault Ste. Marie	C
5. CIRELLA, Joe	Wsh.-Col.	Oshawa	D
6. BENNING, Jim	Tor.	Portland	D
7. HUNTER, Mark	Pit.-Mtl.	Brantford	RW
8. FUHR, Grant	Edm.	Victoria	G
9. PATRICK, James	NYR	Prince Albert	D
10. BUTCHER, Garth	Van.	Regina	D
11. MOLLER, Randy	Que.	Lethbridge	D
12. TANTI, Tony	Chi.	Oshawa	RW
13. MEIGHAN, Ron	Min.	Niagara Falls	D
14. LEVEILLE, Normand	Bos.	Chicoutimi	LW
15. MacINNIS, Allan	Cgy.	Kitchener	D
16. SMITH, Steve	Phi.	Sault Ste. Marie	D
17. DUDACEK, Jiri	Buf.	Poldi Kladno (Czech.)	RW
18. DELORME, Gilbert	L.A.-Mtl.	Chicoutimi	D
19. INGMAN, Jan	Mtl.	Farjestad (Sweden)	LW
20. RUFF, Marty	St.L.	Lethbridge	D
21. BOUTILIER, Paul	NYI	Sherbrooke	D

SECOND ROUND

Selection	Claimed By	Amateur Club	
22. ARNIEL, Scott	Wpg.	Cornwall	LW
23. LOISELLE, Claude	Det.	Windsor	C
24. YAREMCHUK, Gary	Col.-Tor.	Portland	C
25. GRIFFIN, Kevin	Hfd.-Chi.	Portland	LW
26. CHERNOMAZ, Rich	Wsh.-Col.	Victoria	C
27. DONNELLY, Dave	Tor.-Min.	St. Albert	C
28. GATZOS, Steve	Pit.	Sault Ste. Marie	RW
29. STRUEBY, Todd	Edm.	Regina	LW
30. ERIXON, Jan	NYR	Skelleftea (Sweden)	RW
31. SANDS, Mike	Van.-Min.	Sudbury	G
32. ERIKSSON, Lars	Que.-Mtl.	Brynas (Sweden)	G
33. HIRSCH, Tom	Chi.-Min.	Patrick Henry HS	D
34. PREUSS, Dave	Min.	St. Thomas Academy	RW
35. DUFOUR, Luc	Bos.	Chicoutimi	RW
36. NORDIN, Hakan	Cgy.-St.L.	Farjestad (Sweden)	D
37. COSTELLO, Rich	Phi.	Natick HS	C
38. VIRTA, Hannu	Buf.	TPS (Finland)	D
39. KENNEDY, Dean	L.A.	Brandon	D
40. CHELIOS, Chris	Mtl.	Moose Jaw	D
41. WAHLSTEN, Jali	St.L.-Min.	TPS (Finland)	C
42. DINEEN, Gord	NYI	Sault Ste. Marie	D

1980

FIRST ROUND

Selection	Claimed By	Amateur Club	
1. WICKENHEISER, Doug	Col.-Mtl.	Regina	C
2. BABYCH, Dave	Wpg.	Portland	D
3. SAVARD, Denis	Que.-Chi.	Montreal	C
4. MURPHY, Larry	Det.-L.A.	Peterborough	D
5. VEITCH, Darren	Wsh.	Regina	D
6. COFFEY, Paul	Edm.	Kitchener	D
7. LANZ, Rick	Van.	Oshawa	D
8. ARTHUR, Fred	Hfd.	Cornwall	D
9. BULLARD, Mike	Pit.	Brantford	C
10. FOX, Jimmy	L.A.	Ottawa	RW
11. BLAISDELL, Mike	Tor.-Det.	Regina	RW
12. WILSON, Rik	St.L.	Kingston	D
13. CYR, Denis	Cgy.	Montreal	RW
14. MALONE, Jim	NYR	Toronto	C
15. DUPONT, Jerome	Chi.	Toronto	D
16. PALMER, Brad	Min.	Victoria	LW
17. SUTTER, Brent	NYI	Red Deer	C
18. PEDERSON, Barry	Bos.	Victoria	C
19. GAGNE, Paul	Mtl.-Col.	Windsor	LW
20. PATRICK, Steve	Buf.	Brandon	RW
21. STOTHERS, Mike	Phi.	Kingston	D

SECOND ROUND

Selection	Claimed By	Amateur Club	
22. WARD, Joe	Col.	Seattle	C
23. MANTHA, Moe	Wpg.	Toronto	D
24. ROCHEFORT, Normand	Que.	Quebec	D
25. MUNI, Craig	Det.-Tor.	Kingston	D
26. McGILL, Bob	Wsh.-Tor.	Victoria	D
27. NATTRESS, Ric	Edm.-Mtl.	Brantford	D
28. LUDZIK, Steve	Van.-Chi.	Niagara Falls	C
29. GALARNEAU, Michel	Hfd.	Hull	C
30. SOLHEIM, Ken	Pit.-Chi.	Medicine Hat	LW
31. CURTALE, Tony	L.A.-Cgy.	Brantford	D
32. LaVALLEE, Kevin	Tor.-Cgy.	Brantford	LW
33. TERRION, Greg	St.L.-L.A.	Brantford	LW
34. MORRISON, Dave	Cgy.-L.A.	Peterborough	RW
35. ALLISON, Mike	NYR	Sudbury	LW
36. DAWES, Len	Chi.	Victoria	D
37. BEAUPRE, Don	Min.	Sudbury	G
38. HRUDEY, Kelly	NYI	Medicine Hat	G
39. KONROYD, Steve	Cgy.	Oshawa	D
40. CHABOT, John	Mtl.	Hull	C
41. MOLLER, Mike	Buf.	Lethbridge	RW
42. FRASER, Jay	Phi.	Ottawa	LW

1979

FIRST ROUND

Selection	Claimed By	Amateur Club	
1. RAMAGE, Rob	Col.	London	D
2. TURNBULL, Perry	St.L.	Portland	C
3. FOLIGNO, Mike	Det.	Sudbury	RW
4. GARTNER, Mike	Wsh.	Niagara Falls	RW
5. VAIVE, Rick	Van.	Sherbrooke	RW
6. HARTSBURG, Craig	Min.	Sault St. Marie	D
7. BROWN, Keith	Chi.	Portland	D
8. BOURQUE, Raymond	L.A.-Bos.	Verdun	D
9. BOSCHMAN, Laurie	Tor.	Brandon	C
10. McCARTHY, Tom	Wsh.-Min.	Oshawa	LW
11. RAMSEY, Mike	Buf.	U. of Minnesota	D
12. REINHART, Paul	Atl.	Kitchener	D
13. SULLIMAN, Doug	NYR	Kitchener	RW
14. PROPP, Brian	Phi.	Brandon	LW
15. McCRIMMON, Brad	Bos.	Brandon	D
16. WELLS, Jay	Mtl.-L.A.	Kingston	D
17. SUTTER, Duane	NYI	Lethbridge	RW
18. ALLISON, Ray	Hfd.	Brandon	RW
19. MANN, Jimmy	Wpg.	Sherbrooke	RW
20. GOULET, Michel	Que.	Quebec	LW
21. LOWE, Kevin	Edm.	Quebec	D

SECOND ROUND

Selection	Claimed By	Amateur Club	
22. WESLEY, Blake	Col.-Phi.	Portland	D
23. PEROVICH, Mike	St.L.-Atl.	Brandon	D
24. RAUSSE, Errol	Det.-Wsh.	Seattle	LW
25. JONSSON, Tomas	Wsh.-NYI	MoDo AIK (Sweden)	D
26. ASHTON, Brent	Van.	Saskatoon	LW
27. GINGRAS, Gaston	Min.-Mtl.	Hamilton	D
28. TRIMPER, Tim	Chi.	Peterborough	LW
29. HOPKINS, Dean	L.A.	London	RW
30. HARDY, Mark	Tor.-L.A.	Montreal	D
31. MARSHALL, Paul	Wsh.-Pit.	Brantford	LW
32. RUFF, Lindy	Buf.	Lethbridge	D
33. RIGGIN, Pat	Atl.	London	G
34. HOSPODAR, Ed	NYR	Ottawa	D
35. LINDBERGH, Pelle	Phi.	AIK Solna (Sweden)	G
36. MORRISON, Doug	Bos.	Lethbridge	RW
37. NASLUND, Mats	Mtl.	Brynas IFK (Sweden)	LW
38. CARROLL, Billy	NYI	London	C
39. SMITH, Stuart	Hfd.	Peterborough	D
40. CHRISTIAN, Dave	Wpg.	U. of North Dakota	C
41. HUNTER, Dale	Que.	Sudbury	C
42. BROTEN, Neal	Min.	U. of Minnesota	C

1978

FIRST ROUND

Selection	Claimed By	Amateur Club	
1. SMITH, Bobby	Min.	Ottawa	C
2. WALTER, Ryan	Wsh.	Seattle	LW
3. BABYCH, Wayne	St.L.	Portland	RW
4. DERLAGO, Bill	Van.	Brandon	C
5. GILLIS, Mike	Col.	Kingston	LW
6. WILSON, Behn	Pit.-Phi.	Kingston	D
7. LINSEMAN, Ken	NYR-Phi.	Kingston	C
8. GEOFFRION, Danny	L.A.-Mtl.	Cornwall	RW
9. HUBER, Willie	Det.	Hamilton	D
10. HIGGINS, Tim	Chi.	Ottawa	RW
11. MARSH, Brad	Atl.	London	D
12. PETERSON, Brent	Tor.-Det.	Portland	C
13. PLAYFAIR, Larry	Buf.	Portland	D
14. LUCAS, Danny	Phi.	Sault Ste. Marie	RW
15. TAMBELLINI, Steve	NYI	Lethbridge	C
16. SECORD, Al	Bos.	Hamilton	LW
17. HUNTER, Dave	Mtl.	Sudbury	LW
18. COULIS, Tim	Wsh.	Hamilton	LW

SECOND ROUND

Selection	Claimed By	Amateur Club	
19. PAYNE, Steve	Min.	Ottawa	LW
20. MULVEY, Paul	Wsh.	Portland	RW
21. QUENNEVILLE, Joel	Tor.	Windsor	D
22. FRASER, Curt	Van.	Victoria	LW
23. MacKINNON, Paul	Wsh.	Peterborough	D
24. CHRISTOFF, Steve	Min.	U. of Minnesota	C
25. MEEKER, Mike	Pit.	Peterborough	RW
26. MALONEY, Don	NYR	Kitchener	LW
27. MALINOWSKI, Merlin	Col.	Medicine Hat	C
28. HICKS, Glenn	Det.	Flin Flon	LW
29. LECUYER, Doug	Chi.	Portland	LW
30. YAKIWCHUK, Dale	Mtl.	Portland	C
31. JENSEN, Al	Det.	Hamilton	G
32. McKEGNEY, Tony	Buf.	Kingston	LW
33. SIMURDA, Mike	Phi.	Kingston	RW
34. JOHNSTON, Randy	NYI	Peterborough	D
35. NICOLSON, Graeme	Bos.	Cornwall	D
36. CARTER, Ron	Mtl.	Sherbrooke	RW

1977

FIRST ROUND

Selection	Claimed By	Amateur Club	
1. McCOURT, Dale	Det.	St. Catharines	C
2. BECK, Barry	Col.	New Westminster	D
3. PICARD, Robert	Wsh.	Montreal	D
4. GILLIS, Jere	Van.	Sherbrooke	LW
5. CROMBEEN, Mike	Cle.	Kingston	RW
6. WILSON, Doug	Chi.	Ottawa	D
7. MAXWELL, Brad	Min.	New Westminster	D
8. DEBLOIS, Lucien	NYR	Sorel	C
9. CAMPBELL, Scott	St.L.	London	D
10. NAPIER, Mark	Atl.-Mtl.	Toronto	RW
11. ANDERSON, John	Tor.	Toronto	RW
12. JOHANSEN, Trevor	Pit.-Tor.	Toronto	D
13. DUGUAY, Ron	L.A.-NYR	Sudbury	C
14. SEILING, Ric	Buf.	St. Catharines	RW
15. BOSSY, Mike	NYI	Laval	RW
16. FOSTER, Dwight	Bos.	Kitchener	C/RW
17. McCARTHY, Kevin	Phi.	Winnipeg	D
18. DUPONT, Norm	Mtl.	Montreal	C

SECOND ROUND

Selection	Claimed By	Amateur Club	
19. SAVARD, Jean	Det.-Chi.	Quebec	C
20. ZAHARKO, Miles	Col.-Atl.	New Westminister	D
21. LOFTHOUSE, Mark	Wsh.	New Westminster	RW
22. BANDURA, Jeff	Van.	Portland	D
23. CHICOINE, Daniel	Cle.	Sherbrooke	RW
24. GLADNEY, Bob	Chi.-Tor.	Oshawa	D
25. SEMENKO, Dave	Min.	Brandon	LW
26. KEATING, Mike	NYR	St. Catherines	LW
27. LABATTE, Neil	St.L.	Toronto	D
28. LAURENCE, Don	Atl.	Kitchener	C
29. SAGANIUK, Rocky	Tor.	Lethbridge	RW
30. HAMILTON, Jim	Pit.	London	RW
31. HILL, Brian	L.A.-Atl.	Medicine Hat	RW
32. ARESHENKOFF, Ron	Buf.	Medicine Hat	C
33. TONELLI, John	NYI	Toronto	LW
34. PARRO, Dave	Bos.	Saskatoon	G
35. GORENCE, Tom	Phi.	U. of Minnesota	RW
36. LANGWAY, Rod	Mtl.	U. of New Hampshire	D

1976

FIRST ROUND

Selection	Claimed By	Amateur Club	
1. GREEN, Rick	K.C.-Wsh.	London	D
2. CHAPMAN, Blair	Pit.	Saskatoon	RW
3. SHARPLEY, Glen	Min.	Hull	C
4. WILLIAMS, Fred	Det.	Saskatoon	C
5. JOHANSSON, Bjorn	Cal.	Sweden	D
6. MURDOCH, Don	NYR	Medicine Hat	RW
7. FEDERKO, Bernie	St.L.	Saskatoon	C
8. SHAND, Dave	Van.-Atl.	Peterborough	D
9. CLOUTIER, Real	Chi.	Quebec	RW
10. PHILLIPOFF, Harold	Atl.	New Westminster	LW
11. GARDNER, Paul	Pit.-K.C.	Oshawa	C
12. LEE, Peter	Tor.-Mtl.	Ottawa	RW
13. SCHUTT, Rod	L.A.-Mtl.	Sudbury	LW
14. McKENDRY, Alex	NYI	Sudbury	LW
15. CARROLL, Greg	Buf.-Wsh.	Medicine Hat	C
16. PACHAL, Clayton	Bos.	New Westminster	C
17. SUZOR, Mark	Phi.	Kingston	D
18. BAKER, Bruce	Mtl.	Ottawa	RW

SECOND ROUND

Selection	Claimed By	Amateur Club	
19. MALONE, Greg	Wsh.-Pit.	Oshawa	C
20. SUTTER, Brian	K.C.-St.L.	Lethbridge	LW
21. CLIPPINGDALE, Steve	Min.-L.A.	New Westminster	LW
22. LARSON, Reed	Det.	U. of Minnesota	D
23. STENLUND, Vern	Cal.	London	C
24. FARRISH, Dave	NYR	Sudbury	D
25. SMRKE, John	St.L.	Toronto	LW
26. MANNO, Bob	Van.	St. Catharines	D
27. McDILL, Jeff	Chi.	Victoria	RW
28. SIMPSON, Bobby	Atl.	Sherbrooke	LW
29. MARSH, Peter	Pit.	Sherbrooke	RW
30. CARLYLE, Randy	Tor.	Sudbury	D
31. ROBERTS, Jim	L.A.-Min.	Ottawa	LW
32. KASZYCKI, Mike	NYI	Sault Ste. Marie	C
33. KOWAL, Joe	Buf.	Hamilton	LW
34. GLOECKNER, Larry	Bos.	Victoria	D
35. CALLANDER, Drew	Phi.	Regina	C
36. MELROSE, Barry	Mtl.	Kamloops	D

1975

FIRST ROUND

Selection	Claimed By	Amateur Club	
1. BRIDGMAN, Mel	Wsh.-Phi.	Victoria	C
2. DEAN, Barry	K.C.	Medicine Hat	LW
3. KLASSEN, Ralph	Cal.	Saskatoon	C
4. MAXWELL, Brian	Min.	Medicine Hat	D
5. LAPOINTE, Rick	Det.	Victoria	D
6. ASHBY, Don	Tor.	Calgary	C
7. VAYDIK, Greg	Chi.	Medicine Hat	C
8. MULHERN, Richard	Atl.	Sherbrooke	D
9. SADLER, Robin	St.L.-Mtl.	Edmonton	D
10. BLIGHT, Rick	Van.	Brandon	RW
11. PRICE, Pat	NYI	Saskatoon	D
12. DILLON, Wayne	NYR	Toronto	C
13. LAXTON, Gord	Pit.	New Westminster	G
14. HALWARD, Doug	Bos.	Peterborough	D
15. MONDOU, Pierre	L.A.-Mtl.	Montreal	C
16. YOUNG, Tim	Mtl.-L.A.	Ottawa	C
17. SAUVE, Bob	Buf.	Laval	G
18. FORSYTH, Alex	Phi.-Wsh.	Kingston	C

SECOND ROUND

Selection	Claimed By	Amateur Club	
19. SCAMURRA, Peter	Wsh.	Peterborough	D
20. CAIRNS, Don	K.C.	Victoria	LW
21. MARUK, Dennis	Cal.	London	C
22. ENGBLOM, Brian	Min.-Mtl.	U. of Wisconsin	D
23. ROLLINS, Jerry	Det.	Winnipeg	D
24. JARVIS, Doug	Tor.	Peterborough	C
25. ARNDT, Daniel	Chi.	Saskatoon	LW
26. BOWNESS, Rick	Atl.	Montreal	RW
27. STANIOWSKI, Ed	St.L.	Regina	G
28. GASSOFF, Brad	Van.	Kamloops	D
29. SALVIAN, David	NYI	St. Catharines	RW
30. SOETAERT, Doug	NYR	Edmonton	G
31. ANDERSON, Russ	Pit.	U. of Minnesota	D
32. SMITH, Barry	Bos.	New Westminster	C
33. BUCYK, Terry	L.A.	Lethbridge	RW
34. GREENBANK, Kelvin	Mtl.	Winnipeg	RW
35. BREITENBACH, Ken	Buf.	St. Catharines	D
36. MASTERS, Jamie	Phi.-St.L.	Ottawa	D

1974

FIRST ROUND

Selection	Claimed By	Amateur Club	
1. JOLY, Greg	Wsh.	Regina	D
2. PAIEMENT, Wilfred	K.C.	St. Catharines	RW
3. HAMPTON, Rick	Cal.	St. Catharines	D
4. GILLIES, Clark	NYI	Regina	LW
5. CONNOR, Cam	Van.-Mtl.	Flin Flon	RW
6. HICKS, Doug	Min.	Flin Flon	D
7. RISEBROUGH, Doug	St.L.-Mtl.	Kitchener	C
8. LAROUCHE, Pierre	Pit.	Sorel	C
9. LOCHEAD, Bill	Det.	Oshawa	LW
10. CHARTRAW, Rick	Atl.-Mtl.	Kitchener	D
11. FOGOLIN, Lee	Buf.	Oshawa	D
12. TREMBLAY, Mario	L.A.-Mtl.	Montreal	RW
13. VALIQUETTE, Jack	Tor.	Sault Ste. Marie	C
14. MALONEY, Dave	NYR	Kitchener	D
15. McTAVISH, Gord	Mtl.	Sudbury	C
16. MULVEY, Grant	Chi.	Calgary	RW
17. CHIPPERFIELD, Ron	Phi.-Cal.	Brandon	C
18. LARWAY, Don	Bos.	Swift Current	RW

SECOND ROUND

Selection	Claimed By	Amateur Club	
19. MARSON, Mike	Wsh.	Sudbury	LW
20. BURDON, Glen	K.C.	Regina	C
21. AFFLECK, Bruce	Cal.	U. of Denver	D
22. TROTTIER, Bryan	NYI	Swift Current	C
23. SEDLBAUER, Ron	Van.	Kitchener	LW
24. NANTAIS, Rick	Min.	Quebec	LW
25. HOWE, Mark	St.L.-Bos.	Toronto	D
26. HESS, Bob	Pit.-St.L.	New Westminster	D
27. COSSETTE, Jacques	Det.-Pit.	Sorel	RW
28. CHOUINARD, Guy	Atl.	Quebec	C
29. GARE, Danny	Buf.	Calgary	RW
30. MacGREGOR, Gary	L.A.-Mtl.	Cornwall	C
31. WILLIAMS, Dave	Tor.	Swift Current	LW
32. GRESCHNER, Ron	NYR	New Westminster	D
33. LUPIEN, Gilles	Mtl.	Montreal	D
34. DAIGLE, Alain	Chi.	Trois-Rivières	RW
35. McLEAN, Don	Phi.	Sudbury	D
36. STURGEON, Peter	Bos.	Kitchener	LW

1973

FIRST ROUND

Selection	Claimed By	Amateur Club	
1. POTVIN, Denis	NYI	Ottawa	D
2. LYSIAK, Tom	Cal.-Mtl.-Atl.	Medicine Hat	C
3. VERVERGAERT, Dennis	Van.	London	RW
4. McDONALD, Lanny	Tor.	Medicine Hat	RW
5. DAVIDSON, John	Atl.-Mtl.-St.L.	Calgary	G
6. SAVARD, Andre	L.A.-Bos.	Quebec	C
7. STOUGHTON, Blaine	Pit.	Flin Flon	RW
8. GAINEY, Bob	St.L.-Mtl.	Peterborough	LW
9. DAILEY, Bob	Min.-Mtl.-Van.	Toronto	D
10. NEELY, Bob	Phi.-Tor.	Peterborough	LW
11. RICHARDSON, Terry	Det.	New Westminster	G
12. TITANIC, Morris	Buf.	Sudbury	LW
13. ROTA, Darcy	Chi.	Edmonton	LW
14. MIDDLETON, Rick	NYR	Oshawa	RW
15. TURNBULL, Ian	Bos.-Tor.	Ottawa	D
16. MERCREDI, Vic	Mtl.-Atl.	New Westminster	C

SECOND ROUND

Selection	Claimed By	Amateur Club	
17. GOLDUP, Glen	NYI-Mtl.	Toronto	RW
18. DUNLOP, Blake	Cal.-Min.	Ottawa	C
19. BORDELEAU, Paulin	Van.	Toronto	RW
20. GOODENOUGH, Larry	Tor.-Phi.	London	D
21. VAIL, Eric	Atl.	Sudbury	LW
22. MARRIN, Peter	L.A.-Mtl.	Toronto	C
23. BIANCHIN, Wayne	Pit.	Flin Flon	LW
24. PESUT, George	St.L.	Saskatoon	D
25. ROGERS, John	Min.	Edmonton	RW
26. LEVINS, Brent	Phi.	Swift Current	
27. CAMPBELL, Colin	Det.-Pit.	Peterborough	D
28. LANDRY, Jean	Buf.	Quebec	D
29. THOMAS, Reg	Chi.	London	LW
30. HICKEY, Pat	NYR	Hamilton	LW
31. JONES, Jim	Bos.	Peterborough	RW
32. ANDRUFF, Ron	Mtl.	Flin Flon	C

1972

FIRST ROUND

Selection	Claimed By	Amateur Club	
1. HARRIS, Billy	NYI	Toronto	RW
2. RICHARD, Jacques	Atl.	Quebec	LW
3. LEVER, Don	Van.	Niagara Falls	C
4. SHUTT, Steve	L.A.-Mtl.	Toronto	LW
5. SCHOENFELD, Jim	Buf.	Niagara Falls	D
6. LAROCQUE, Michel	Cal.-Mtl.	Ottawa	G
7. BARBER, Bill	Phi.	Kitchener	LW
8. GARDNER, Dave	Pit.-Min.-Mtl.	Toronto	C
9. MERRICK, Wayne	St.L.	Ottawa	C
10. BLANCHARD, Albert	Det.-NYR	Kitchener	LW
11. FERGUSON, George	Tor.	Toronto	C
12. BYERS, Jerry	Min.	Kitchener	LW
13. RUSSELL, Phil	Chi.	Edmonton	D
14. VAN BOXMEER, John	Mtl.	Guelph	D
15. MacMILLAN, Bobby	NYR	St. Catharines	RW
16. BLOOM, Mike	Bos.	St. Catharines	LW

SECOND ROUND

Selection	Claimed By	Amateur Club	
17. HENNING Lorne	NYI	New Westminster	C
18. BIALOWAS, Dwight	Atl.	Regina	D
19. McSHEFFREY, Brian	Van.	Ottawa	RW
20. KOZAK, Don	L.A.	Edmonton	RW
21. SACHARUK, Larry	Buf.-NYR	Saskatoon	D
22. CASSIDY, Tom	Cal.	Kitchener	C
23. BLADON, Tom	Phi.	Edmonton	D
24. LYNCH, Jack	Pit.	Oshawa	D
25. CARRIERE, Larry	St.L.-Buf.	Loyola College	D
26. GUITE, Pierre	Det.	St. Catharines	LW
27. OSBURN, Randy	Tor.	London	LW
28. WEIR, Stan	Min.-Cal.	Medicine Hat	C
29. OGILVIE, Brian	Chi.	Edmonton	C
30. LUKOWICH, Bernie	Mtl.-Pit.	New Westminster	RW
31. VILLEMURE, Rene	NYR	Shawinigan	LW
32. ELDER, Wayne	Bos.	London	D

1971

FIRST ROUND

Selection	Claimed By	Amateur Club	
1. LAFLEUR, Guy	Cal.-Mtl.	Quebec	RW
2. DIONNE, Marcel	Det.	St. Catharines	C
3. GUEVREMONT, Jocelyn	Van.	Montreal	D
4. CARR, Gene	Pit.-St.L.	Flin Flon	C
5. MARTIN, Rick	Buf.	Montreal	LW
6. JONES, Ron	L.A.-Bos.	Edmonton	D
7. ARNASON, Chuck	Min.-Mtl.	Flin Flon	RW
8. WRIGHT, Larry	Phi.	Regina	C
9. PLANTE, Pierre	Tor.-Phi.	Drummondville	RW
10. VICKERS, Steve	St.L.-NYR	Toronto	LW
11. WILSON, Murray	Mtl.	Ottawa	LW
12. SPRING, Dan	Chi.	Edmonton	C
13. DURBANO, Steve	NYR	Toronto	D
14. O'REILLY, Terry	Bos.	Oshawa	RW

SECOND ROUND

Selection	Claimed By	Amateur Club	
15. BAIRD, Ken	Cal.	Flin Flon	D
16. BOUCHA, Henry	Det.	U.S. Nationals	C
17. LALONDE, Bobby	Van.	Montreal	C
18. McKENZIE, Brian	Pit.	St. Catharines	LW
19. RAMSAY, Craig	Buf.	Peterborough	LW
20. ROBINSON, Larry	L.A.-Mtl.	Kitchener	D
21. NORRISH, Rod	Min.	Regina	LW
22. KEHOE, Rick	Phi.-Tor.	Hamilton	RW
23. FORTIER, Dave	Tor.	St. Catharines	D
24. DEGUISE, Michel	St.L.-Mtl.	Sorel	G
25. FRENCH, Terry	Mtl.	Ottawa	C
26. KRYSKOW, Dave	Chi.	Edmonton	LW
27. WILLIAMS, Tom	NYR	Hamilton	LW
28. RIDLEY, Curt	Bos.	Portage	G

1970

FIRST ROUND

Selection	Claimed By	Amateur Club	
1. PERREAULT, Gilbert	Buf.	Montreal	C
2. TALLON, Dale	Van.	Toronto	D
3. LEACH, Reg	L.A.-Bos.	Flin Flon	LW
4. MacLEISH, Rick	Phi.-Bos.	Peterborough	C
5. MARTINIUK, Ray	Oak.-Mtl.	Flin Flon	G
6. LEFLEY, Chuck	Min.-Mtl.	Canadian Nationals	C
7. POLIS, Greg	Pit.	Estevan	LW
8. SITTLER, Darryl	Tor.	London	C
9. PLUMB, Ron	Bos.	Peterborough	D
10. ODDLEIFSON, Chris	St.L.-Oak.	Winnipeg	C
11. GRATTON, Norm	Mtl.-NYR	Montreal	LW
12. LAJEUNESSE, Serge	Det.	Montreal	RW
13. STEWART, Bob	Bos.	Oshawa	D
14. MALONEY, Dan	Chi.	London	LW

SECOND ROUND

Selection	Claimed By	Amateur Club	
15. DEADMARSH, Butch	Buf.	Brandon	LW
16. HARGREAVES, Jim	Van.	Winnipeg	D
17. HARVEY, Fred	L.A.-Min.	Hamilton	RW
18. CLEMENT, Bill	Phi.	Ottawa	C
19. LAFRAMBOISE, Pete	Oak.	Ottawa	C
20. BARRETT, Fred	Min.	Toronto	D
21. STEWART, John	Pit.	Flin Flon	LW
22 THOMPSON, Errol	Tor.	Charlottetown	LW
23. KEOGH, Murray	St.L.	U. of Minnesota	C
24. McDONOUGH, Al	Mtl.-L.A.	St. Catharines	RW
25. MURPHY, Mike	NYR	Toronto	RW
26. GUINDON, Bobby	Det.	Montreal	LW
27. BOUCHARD, Dan	Bos.	London	G
28. ARCHAMBAULT, Mike	Chi.	Drummondville	LW

1969

FIRST ROUND

Selection	Claimed By	Amateur Club	
1. HOULE, Rejean	Mtl.	Montreal	LW
2. TARDIF, Marc	Mtl.	Montreal	LW
3. TANNAHILL, Don	Min.-Bos.	Niagara Falls	LW
4. SPRING, Frank	Pit.-Bos.	Edmonton	RW
5. REDMOND, Dick	L.A.-Mtl.-Min.	St. Catharines	D
6. CURRIER, Bob	Phi.	Cornwall	C
7. FEATHERSTONE, Tony	Oak.	Peterborough	RW
8. DUPONT, André	St.L.-NYR	Montreal	D
9. MOSER, Ernie	Det.-Tor.	Estevan	RW
10. RUTHERFORD, Jim	Det.	Hamilton	G
11. BOLDIREV, Ivan	Bos.	Oshawa	C
12. JARRY, Pierre	NYR	Ottawa	LW
13. BORDELEAU, J.-P.	Chi.	Montreal	RW
14. O'BRIEN, Dennis	Min.	St. Catharines	D

SECOND ROUND

Selection	Claimed By	Amateur Club	
15. KESSELL, Rick	Pit.	Oshawa	C
16. HOGANSON, Dale	L.A.	Estevan	D
17. CLARKE, Bobby	Phi.	Flin Flon	C
18. STACKHOUSE, Ron	Oak.	Peterborough	D
19. LOWE, Mike	St.L.	Loyola College	
20. BRINDLEY, Doug	Tor.	Niagara Falls	C
21. GARWASIUK, Ron	Det.	Regina	LW
22. QUOQUOCHI, Art	Bos.	Montreal	
23. WILSON, Bert	NYR	London	LW
24. ROMANCHYCH, Larry	Chi.	Flin Flon	RW
25. GILBERT, Gilles	Min.	London	G
26. BRIERE, Michel	Pit.	Shawinigan Falls	C
27. BODDY, Greg	L.A.	Edmonton	D
28. BROSSART, Bill	Phi.	Estevan	D

Gil Perreault provided the foundation that supported the Buffalo Sabres during their first 17 seasons in the NHL. The first player selected in the 1972 Amateur Draft, Perreault played his entire career with the Sabres and still holds the club record for seasons (17), games (1191), goals (512), assists (814) and points (1326).

NHL All-Stars

Active Players' All-Star Selection Records

	First Team Selections	Second Team Selections	Total
GOALTENDERS			
Patrick Roy	(3) 1988-89; 1989-90; 1991-92.	(2) 1987-88; 1990-91.	5
Dominik Hasek	(4) 1993-94; 1994-95; 1996-97; 1997-98.	(0)	4
Ed Belfour	(2) 1990-91; 1992-93.	(1) 1994-95.	3
Tom Barrasso	(1) 1983-84.	(2) 1984-85; 1992-93.	3
Grant Fuhr	(1) 1987-88.	(1) 1981-82.	2
J.Vanbiesbrouck	(1) 1985-86.	(1) 1993-94.	2
Martin Brodeur	(0)	(2) 1996-97.	2
Ron Hextall	(1) 1986-87.	(0)	1
Jim Carey	(1) 1995-96.	(0)	1
Mike Vernon	(0)	(1) 1988-89.	1
Daren Puppa	(0)	(1) 1989-90.	1
Kirk McLean	(0)	(1) 1991-92.	1
Chris Osgood	(0)	(1) 1995-96.	1
DEFENSEMEN			
Ray Bourque	(12) 1979-80; 1981-82; 1983-84; 1984-85; 1986-87; 1987-88; 1989-90; 1990-91; 1991-92; 1992-93; 1993-94; 1995-96.	(5) 1980-81; 1982-83; 1985-86; 1988-89; 1994-95.	17
Paul Coffey	(4) 1984-85; 1985-86; 1988-89; 1994-95.	(4) 1981-82; 1982-83; 1983-84; 1989-90.	8
Chris Chelios	(4) 1988-89; 1992-93; 1994-95; 1995-96.	(2) 1990-91; 1996-97.	6
Al MacInnis	(2) 1989-90; 1990-91.	(3) 1986-87; 1988-89; 1993-94.	5
Brian Leetch	(2) 1991-92; 1996-97.	(3) 1990-91; 1993-94; 1995-96.	5
Scott Stevens	(2) 1987-88; 1993-94.	(2) 1991-92; 1996-97.	4
Larry Murphy	(0)	(3) 1986-87; 1992-93; 1994-95.	3
Sandis Ozolinsh	(1) 1996-97.	(0)	1
Nicklas Lidstrom	(1) 1997-98.	(0)	1
Rob Blake	(1) 1997-98.	(0)	1
Gary Suter	(0)	(1) 1987-88.	1
Phil Housley	(0)	(1) 1991-92.	1
V. Konstantinov	(0)	(1) 1995-96.	1
Chris Pronger	(0)	(1) 1997-98.	1
Scott Niedermayer	(0)	(1) 1997-98.	1
CENTERS			
Wayne Gretzky	(8) 1980-81; 1981-82; 1982-83; 1983-84; 1984-85; 1985-86; 1986-87; 1990-91.	(7) 1979-80; 1987-88; 1988-89; 1989-90; 1993-94; 1996-97; 1997-98.	15
Mark Messier	(2) 1989-90; 1991-92.	(0)	2
Eric Lindros	(1) 1994-95.	(1) 1995-96.	2
Sergei Fedorov	(1) 1993-94.	(0)	1
Peter Forsberg	(1) 1997-98.	(0)	1
Adam Oates	(0)	(1) 1990-91.	1
Alexei Zhamnov	(0)	(1) 1994-95.	1
RIGHT WINGERS			
Jaromir Jagr	(3) 1994-95; 1995-96; 1997-98.	(1) 1996-97.	4
Brett Hull	(3) 1989-90; 1990-91; 1991-92.	(0)	3
Teemu Selanne	(2) 1992-93; 1996-97.	(1) 1997-98.	3
Alexander Mogilny	(0)	(2) 1992-93; 1995-96.	2
Pavel Bure	(1) 1993-94.	(0)	1
Mark Recchi	(0)	(1) 1991-92.	1
Theoren Fleury	(0)	(1) 1994-95.	1
LEFT WINGERS			
Luc Robitaille	(5) 1987-88; 1988-89; 1989-90; 1990-91; 1992-93.	(2) 1986-87; 1991-92.	7
John LeClair	(2) 1994-95, 1997-98.	(2) 1995-96; 1996-97.	4
Mark Messier	(2) 1981-82; 1982-83.	(1) 1983-84.	3
Kevin Stevens	(1) 1991-92.	(2) 1990-91; 1992-93.	3
Paul Kariya	(2) 1995-96; 1996-97.	(0)	2
Keith Tkachuk	(0)	(2) 1994-95; 1997-98.	2
Brendan Shanahan	(1) 1993-94.	(0)	1
Brian Bellows	(0)	(1) 1989-90.	1
Adam Graves	(0)	(1) 1993-94.	1

Leading NHL All-Stars 1930-98

Player	Pos	Team	NHL Seasons	First Team Selections	Second Team Selections	Total Selections
Howe, Gordie	RW	Detroit	26	12	9	21
* Bourque, Ray	D	Boston	19	12	5	17
* Gretzky, Wayne	C	Edm., L.A., NYR	19	8	7	15
Richard, Maurice	RW	Montreal	18	8	6	14
Hull, Bobby	LW	Chicago	16	10	2	12
Harvey, Doug	D	Mtl., NYR	19	10	1	11
Hall, Glenn	G	Det., Chi., St.L.	18	7	4	11
Beliveau, Jean	C	Montreal	20	6	4	10
Seibert, Earl	D	NYR., Chi	15	4	6	10
Orr, Bobby	D	Boston	12	8	1	9
Lindsay, Ted	LW	Detroit	17	8	1	9
Mahovlich, Frank	LW	Tor., Det., Mtl.	18	3	6	9
Shore, Eddie	D	Boston	14	7	1	8
Mikita, Stan	C	Chicago	22	6	2	8
Kelly, Red	D	Detroit	20	6	2	8
Esposito, Phil	C	Boston	18	6	2	8
Pilote, Pierre	D	Chicago	14	5	3	8
Lemieux, Mario	C	Pittsburgh	12	5	3	8
* Coffey, Paul	D	Edm., Pit., Det.	17	4	4	8
Brimsek, Frank	G	Boston	10	2	6	8
Bossy, Mike	RW	NY Islanders	10	5	3	8
* Robitaille, Luc	LW	Los Angeles	11	5	2	7
Potvin, Denis	D	NY Islanders	15	5	2	7
Park, Brad	D	NYR, Bos.	17	5	2	7
Plante, Jacques	G	Mtl., Tor.	18	3	4	7
Gadsby, Bill	D	Chi., NYR, Det.	20	3	4	7
Sawchuk, Terry	G	Detroit	21	3	4	7
Durnan, Bill	G	Montreal	7	6	0	6
Lafleur, Guy	RW	Montreal	16	6	0	6
Dryden, Ken	G	Montreal	8	5	1	6
* Chelios, Chris	D	Mtl., Chi.	14	4	2	6
Clapper, Dit	RW/D	Boston	20	3	3	6
Robinson, Larry	D	Montreal	20	3	3	6
Horton, Tim	D	Toronto	24	3	3	6
Salming, Borje	D	Toronto	17	1	5	6
Cowley, Bill	C	Boston	13	4	1	5
* Messier, Mark	LW/C	Edm., NYR	18	4	1	5
Jackson, Harvey	LW	Toronto	15	4	1	5
Goulet, Michel	LW	Quebec	15	3	2	5
Conacher, Charlie	RW	Toronto	12	3	2	5
Stewart, Jack	D	Detroit	12	3	2	5
Lach, Elmer	C	Montreal	14	3	2	5
Quackenbush, Bill	D	Det., Bos.	14	3	2	5
Blake, Toe	LW	Montreal	15	3	2	5
Esposito, Tony	G	Chicago	16	3	2	5
* Roy, Patrick	G	Montreal	13	2	3	5
Reardon, Ken	D	Montreal	7	2	3	5
Kurri, Jari	RW	Edmonton	16	2	3	5
Apps, Syl	C	Toronto	10	2	3	5
Giacomin, Ed	G	NY Rangers	13	2	3	5
* MacInnis, Al	D	Calgary	16	2	3	5
Leetch, Brian	D	NY Rangers	10	2	3	5

* Active

Position Leaders in All-Star Selections

Position	Player	First Team	Second Team	Total
GOAL	Glenn Hall	7	4	11
	Frank Brimsek	2	6	8
	Jacques Plante	3	4	7
	Terry Sawchuk	3	4	7
	Bill Durnan	6	0	6
	Ken Dryden	5	1	6
DEFENSE	* Ray Bourque	12	5	17
	Doug Harvey	10	1	11
	Earl Seibert	4	6	10
	Bobby Orr	8	1	9
	Eddie Shore	7	1	8
	Red Kelly	6	2	8
	Pierre Pilote	5	3	8
	* Paul Coffey	4	4	8

Position	Player	First Team	Second Team	Total
LEFT WING	Bobby Hull	10	2	12
	Ted Lindsay	8	1	9
	Frank Mahovlich	3	6	9
	* Luc Robitaille	5	2	7
	Harvey Jackson	4	1	5
	Michel Goulet	3	2	5
	Toe Blake	3	2	5
RIGHT WING	Gordie Howe	12	9	21
	Maurice Richard	8	6	14
	Mike Bossy	5	3	8
	Guy Lafleur	6	0	6
	Charlie Conacher	3	2	5
	Jari Kurri	2	3	5
CENTER	* Wayne Gretzky	8	7	15
	Jean Beliveau	6	4	10
	Stan Mikita	6	2	8
	Phil Esposito	6	2	8
	Mario Lemieux	5	3	8

* active player

All-Star Teams
1930-98

Voting for the NHL All-Star Team is conducted among the representatives of the Professional Hockey Writers' Association at the end of the season.

Following is a list of the First and Second All-Star Teams since their inception in 1930-31.

1997-98

First Team		Second Team
Hasek, Dominik, Buf.	G	Brodeur, Martin, N.J.
Lidstrom, Nicklas, Det.	D	Pronger, Chris, St.L.
Blake, Rob, L.A.	D	Niedermayer, Scott, N.J.
Forsberg, Peter, Col.	C	Gretzky, Wayne, NYR
Jagr, Jaromir, Pit.	RW	Selanne, Teemu, Ana.
LeClair, John, Phi.	LW	Tkachuk, Keith, Phx.

1996-97

First Team		Second Team
Hasek, Dominik, Buf.	G	Brodeur, Martin, N.J.
Leetch, Brian, NYR	D	Chelios, Chris, Chi.
Ozolinsh, Sandis, Col.	D	Stevens, Scott, N.J.
Lemieux, Mario, Pit.	C	Gretzky, Wayne, NYR
Selanne, Teemu, Ana.	RW	Jagr, Jaromir, Pit.
Kariya, Paul, Ana.	LW	LeClair, John, Phi.

1995-96

First Team		Second Team
Carey, Jim, Wsh.	G	Osgood, Chris, Det.
Chelios, Chris, Chi.	D	Konstantinov, V., Det.
Bourque, Ray, Bos.	D	Leetch, Brian, NYR.
Lemieux, Mario, Pit.	C	Lindros, Eric, Phi.
Jagr, Jaromir, Pit.	RW	Mogilny, Alexander, Van.
Kariya, Paul, Ana.	LW	LeClair, John, Phi.

1994-95

First Team		Second Team
Hasek, Dominik, Buf.	G	Belfour, Ed, Chi.
Coffey, Paul, Det.	D	Bourque, Ray, Bos.
Chelios, Chris, Chi.	D	Murphy, Larry, Pit.
Lindros, Eric, Phi.	C	Zhamnov, Alexei, Wpg.
Jagr, Jaromir, Pit.	RW	Fleury, Theoren, Cgy.
LeClair, John, Mtl., Phi.	LW	Tkachuk, Keith, Wpg.

1993-94

First Team		Second Team
Hasek, Dominik, Buf.	G	Vanbiesbrouck, John, Fla.
Bourque, Ray, Bos.	D	MacInnis, Al, Cgy.
Stevens, Scott, N.J.	D	Leetch, Brian, NYR
Fedorov, Sergei, Det.	C	Gretzky, Wayne, L.A.
Bure, Pavel, Van.	RW	Neely, Cam, Bos.
Shanahan, Brendan, St. L.	LW	Graves, Adam, NYR

1992-93

First Team		Second Team
Belfour, Ed, Chi.	G	Barrasso, Tom, Pit.
Chelios, Chris, Chi.	D	Murphy, Larry, Pit.
Bourque, Ray, Bos.	D	Iafrate, Al, Wsh.
Lemieux, Mario, Pit.	C	LaFontaine, Pat, Buf.
Selanne, Teemu, Wpg.	RW	Mogilny, Alexander, Buf.
Robitaille, Luc, L.A.	LW	Stevens, Kevin, Pit.

1991-92

First Team		Second Team
Roy, Patrick, Mtl.	G	McLean, Kirk, Van.
Leetch, Brian, NYR	D	Housley, Phil, Wpg.
Bourque, Ray, Bos.	D	Stevens, Scott, N.J.
Messier, Mark, NYR	C	Lemieux, Mario, Pit.
Hull, Brett, St. L.	RW	Recchi, Mark, Pit., Phi.
Stevens, Kevin, Pit.	LW	Robitaille, Luc, L.A.

1990-91

First Team		Second Team
Belfour, Ed, Chi.	G	Roy, Patrick, Mtl.
Bourque, Ray, Bos.	D	Chelios, Chris, Chi.
MacInnis, Al, Cgy.	D	Leetch, Brian, NYR
Gretzky, Wayne, L.A.	C	Oates, Adam, St. L.
Hull, Brett, St. L.	RW	Neely, Cam, Bos.
Robitaille, Luc, L.A.	LW	Stevens, Kevin, Pit.

1989-90

First Team		Second Team
Roy, Patrick, Mtl.	G	Puppa, Daren, Buf.
Bourque, Ray, Bos.	D	Coffey, Paul, Pit.
MacInnis, Al, Cgy.	D	Wilson, Doug, Chi.
Messier, Mark, Edm.	C	Gretzky, Wayne, L.A.
Hull, Brett, St. L.	RW	Neely, Cam, Bos.
Robitaille, Luc, L.A.	LW	Bellows, Brian, Min.

1988-89

First Team		Second Team
Roy, Patrick, Mtl.	G	Vernon, Mike, Cgy.
Chelios, Chris, Mtl.	D	MacInnis, Al, Cgy.
Coffey, Paul, Pit.	D	Bourque, Ray, Bos.
Lemieux, Mario, Pit.	C	Gretzky, Wayne, L.A.
Mullen, Joe, Cgy.	RW	Kurri, Jari, Edm.
Robitaille, Luc, L.A.	LW	Gallant, Gerard, Det.

1987-88

First Team		Second Team
Fuhr, Grant, Edm.	G	Roy, Patrick, Mtl.
Bourque, Ray, Bos.	D	Suter, Gary, Cgy.
Stevens, Scott, Wsh.	D	McCrimmon, Brad, Cgy.
Lemieux, Mario, Pit.	C	Gretzky, Wayne, Edm.
Loob, Hakan, Cgy.	RW	Neely, Cam, Bos.
Robitaille, Luc, L.A.	LW	Goulet, Michel, Que.

1986-87

First Team		Second Team
Hextall, Ron, Phi.	G	Liut, Mike, Hfd.
Bourque, Ray, Bos.	D	Murphy, Larry, Wsh.
Howe, Mark, Phi.	D	MacInnis, Al, Cgy.
Gretzky, Wayne, Edm.	C	Lemieux, Mario, Pit.
Kurri, Jari, Edm.	RW	Kerr, Tim, Phi.
Goulet, Michel, Que.	LW	Robitaille, Luc, L.A.

1985-86

First Team		Second Team
Vanbiesbrouck, J., NYR	G	Froese, Bob, Phi.
Coffey, Paul, Edm.	D	Robinson, Larry, Mtl.
Howe, Mark, Phi.	D	Bourque, Ray, Bos.
Gretzky, Wayne, Edm.	C	Lemieux, Mario, Pit.
Bossy, Mike, NYI	RW	Kurri, Jari, Edm.
Goulet, Michel, Que.	LW	Naslund, Mats, Mtl.

1984-85

First Team		Second Team
Lindbergh, Pelle, Phi.	G	Barrasso, Tom, Buf.
Coffey, Paul, Edm.	D	Langway, Rod, Wsh.
Bourque, Ray, Bos.	D	Wilson, Doug, Chi.
Gretzky, Wayne, Edm.	C	Hawerchuk, Dale, Wpg.
Kurri, Jari, Edm.	RW	Bossy, Mike, NYI
Ogrodnick, John, Det.	LW	Tonelli, John, NYI

Despite becoming the first goaltender since Bernie Parent to record back-to-back seasons with 10 or more shutouts, Martin Brodeur was relegated to a spot on the NHL's Second All-Star Team because of the brilliant play of Buffalo netminder Dominik Hasek.

1983-84

First Team		Second Team
Barrasso, Tom, Buf.	G	Riggin, Pat, Wsh.
Langway, Rod, Wsh.	D	Coffey, Paul, Edm.
Bourque, Ray, Bos.	D	Potvin, Denis, NYI
Gretzky, Wayne, Edm.	C	Trottier, Bryan, NYI
Bossy, Mike, NYI	RW	Kurri, Jari, Edm.
Goulet, Michel, Que.	LW	Messier, Mark, Edm.

1982-83

First Team		Second Team
Peeters, Pete, Bos.	G	Melanson, Rollie, NYI
Howe, Mark, Phi.	D	Bourque, Ray, Bos.
Langway, Rod, Wsh.	D	Coffey, Paul, Edm.
Gretzky, Wayne, Edm.	C	Savard, Denis, Chi.
Bossy, Mike, NYI	RW	McDonald, Lanny, Cgy.
Messier, Mark, Edm.	LW	Goulet, Michel, Que.

1981-82

First Team		Second Team
Smith, Billy, NYI	G	Fuhr, Grant, Edm.
Wilson, Doug, Chi.	D	Coffey, Paul, Edm.
Bourque, Ray, Bos.	D	Engblom, Brian, Mtl.
Gretzky, Wayne, Edm.	C	Trottier, Bryan, NYI
Bossy, Mike, NYI	RW	Middleton, Rick, Bos.
Messier, Mark, Edm.	LW	Tonelli, John, NYI

1980-81

First Team		Second Team
Liut, Mike, St.L.	G	Lessard, Mario, L.A.
Potvin, Denis, NYI	D	Robinson, Larry, Mtl.
Carlyle, Randy, Pit.	D	Bourque, Ray, Bos.
Gretzky, Wayne, Edm.	C	Dionne, Marcel, L.A.
Bossy, Mike, NYI	RW	Taylor, Dave, L.A.
Simmer, Charlie, L.A.	LW	Barber, Bill, Phi.

1979-80

First Team		Second Team
Esposito, Tony, Chi.	G	Edwards, Don, Buf.
Robinson, Larry, Mtl.	D	Salming, Borje, Tor.
Bourque, Ray, Bos.	D	Schoenfeld, Jim, Buf.
Dionne, Marcel, L.A.	C	Gretzky, Wayne, Edm.
Lafleur, Guy, Mtl.	RW	Gare, Danny, Buf.
Simmer, Charlie, L.A.	LW	Shutt, Steve, Mtl.

1978-79

First Team		Second Team
Dryden, Ken, Mtl.	G	Resch, Glenn, NYI
Potvin, Denis, NYI	D	Salming, Borje, Tor.
Robinson, Larry, Mtl.	D	Savard, Serge, Mtl.
Trottier, Bryan, NYI	C	Dionne, Marcel, L.A.
Lafleur, Guy, Mtl.	RW	Bossy, Mike, NYI
Gillies, Clark, NYI	LW	Barber, Bill, Phi.

1977-78

First Team		Second Team
Dryden, Ken, Mtl.	G	Edwards, Don, Buf.
Potvin, Denis, NYI	D	Robinson, Larry, Mtl.
Park, Brad, Bos.	D	Salming, Borje, Tor.
Trottier, Bryan, NYI	C	Sittler, Darryl, Tor.
Lafleur, Guy, Mtl.	RW	Bossy, Mike, NYI
Gillies, Clark, NYI	LW	Shutt, Steve, Mtl.

1976-77

First Team		Second Team
Dryden, Ken, Mtl.	G	Vachon, Rogie, L.A.
Robinson, Larry, Mtl.	D	Potvin, Denis, NYI
Salming, Borje, Tor.	D	Lapointe, Guy, Mtl.
Dionne, Marcel, L.A.	C	Perreault, Gilbert, Buf.
Lafleur, Guy, Mtl.	RW	McDonald, Lanny, Tor.
Shutt, Steve, Mtl.	LW	Martin, Rick, Buf.

1975-76

First Team		Second Team
Dryden, Ken, Mtl.	G	Resch, Glenn, NYI
Potvin, Denis, NYI	D	Salming, Borje, Tor.
Park, Brad, Bos.	D	Lapointe, Guy, Mtl.
Clarke, Bobby, Phi.	C	Perreault, Gilbert, Buf.
Lafleur, Guy, Mtl.	RW	Leach, Reggie, Phi.
Barber, Bill, Phi.	LW	Martin, Rick, Buf.

1974-75

First Team		Second Team
Parent, Bernie, Phi.	G	Vachon, Rogie, L.A.
Orr, Bobby, Bos.	D	Lapointe, Guy, Mtl.
Potvin, Denis, NYI	D	Salming, Borje, Tor.
Clarke, Bobby, Phi.	C	Esposito, Phil, Bos.
Lafleur, Guy, Mtl.	RW	Robert, René, Buf.
Martin, Rick, Buf.	LW	Vickers, Steve, NYR

1973-74

First Team		Second Team
Parent, Bernie, Phi.	G	Esposito, Tony, Chi.
Orr, Bobby, Bos.	D	White, Bill, Chi.
Park, Brad, NYR	D	Ashbee, Barry, Phi.
Esposito, Phil, Bos.	C	Clarke, Bobby, Phi.
Hodge, Ken, Bos.	RW	Redmond, Mickey, Det.
Martin, Rick, Buf.	LW	Cashman, Wayne, Bos.

1972-73

First Team		Second Team
Dryden, Ken, Mtl.	G	Esposito, Tony, Chi.
Orr, Bobby, Bos.	D	Park, Brad, NYR
Lapointe, Guy, Mtl.	D	White, Bill, Chi.
Esposito, Phil, Bos.	C	Clarke, Bobby, Phi.
Redmond, Mickey, Det.	RW	Cournoyer, Yvan, Mtl.
Mahovlich, Frank, Mtl.	LW	Hull, Dennis, Chi.

1971-72

First Team		Second Team
Esposito, Tony, Chi.	G	Dryden, Ken, Mtl.
Orr, Bobby, Bos.	D	White, Bill, Chi.
Park, Brad, NYR	D	Stapleton, Pat, Chi.
Esposito, Phil, Bos.	C	Ratelle, Jean, NYR
Gilbert, Rod, NYR	RW	Cournoyer, Yvan, Mtl.
Hull, Bobby, Chi.	LW	Hadfield, Vic, NYR

1970-71

First Team		Second Team
Giacomin, Ed, NYR	G	Plante, Jacques, Tor.
Orr, Bobby, Bos.	D	Park, Brad, NYR
Tremblay, J.C., Mtl.	D	Stapleton, Pat, Chi.
Esposito, Phil, Bos.	C	Keon, Dave, Tor.
Hodge, Ken, Bos.	RW	Cournoyer, Yvan, Mtl.
Bucyk, John, Bos.	LW	Hull, Bobby, Chi.

1969-70

First Team		Second Team
Esposito, Tony, Chi.	G	Giacomin, Ed, NYR
Orr, Bobby, Bos.	D	Brewer, Carl, Det.
Park, Brad, NYR	D	Laperriere, Jacques, Mtl.
Esposito, Phil, Bos.	C	Mikita, Stan, Chi.
Howe, Gordie, Det.	RW	McKenzie, John, Bos.
Hull, Bobby, Chi.	LW	Mahovlich, Frank, Det.

1968-69

First Team		Second Team
Hall, Glenn, St.L.	G	Giacomin, Ed, NYR
Orr, Bobby, Bos.	D	Green, Ted, Bos.
Horton, Tim, Tor.	D	Harris, Ted, Mtl.
Esposito, Phil, Bos.	C	Béliveau, Jean, Mtl.
Howe, Gordie, Det.	RW	Cournoyer, Yvan, Mtl.
Hull, Bobby, Chi.	LW	Mahovlich, Frank, Det.

1967-68

First Team		Second Team
Worsley, Gump, Mtl.	G	Giacomin, Ed, NYR
Orr, Bobby, Bos.	D	Tremblay, J.C., Mtl.
Horton, Tim, Tor.	D	Neilson, Jim, NYR
Mikita, Stan, Chi.	C	Esposito, Phil, Bos.
Howe, Gordie, Det.	RW	Gilbert, Rod, NYR
Hull, Bobby, Chi.	LW	Bucyk, John, Bos.

1966-67

First Team		Second Team
Giacomin, Ed, NYR	G	Hall, Glenn, Chi.
Pilote, Pierre, Chi.	D	Horton, Tim, Tor.
Howell, Harry, NYR	D	Orr, Bobby, Bos.
Mikita, Stan, Chi.	C	Ullman, Norm, Det.
Wharram, Kenny, Chi.	RW	Howe, Gordie, Det.
Hull, Bobby, Chi.	LW	Marshall, Don, NYR

1965-66

First Team		Second Team
Hall, Glenn, Chi.	G	Worsley, Gump, Mtl.
Laperriere, Jacques, Mtl.	D	Stanley, Allan, Tor.
Pilote, Pierre, Chi.	D	Stapleton, Pat, Chi.
Mikita, Stan, Chi.	C	Béliveau, Jean, Mtl.
Howe, Gordie, Det.	RW	Rousseau, Bobby, Mtl.
Hull, Bobby, Chi.	LW	Mahovlich, Frank, Tor.

1964-65

First Team		Second Team
Crozier, Roger, Det.	G	Hodge, Charlie, Mtl.
Pilote, Pierre, Chi.	D	Gadsby, Bill, Det.
Laperriere, Jacques, Mtl.	D	Brewer, Carl, Tor.
Ullman, Norm, Det.	C	Mikita, Stan, Chi.
Provost, Claude, Mtl.	RW	Howe, Gordie, Det.
Hull, Bobby, Chi.	LW	Mahovlich, Frank, Tor.

1963-64

First Team		Second Team
Hall, Glenn, Chi.	G	Hodge, Charlie, Mtl.
Pilote, Pierre, Chi.	D	Vasko, Elmer, Chi.
Horton, Tim, Tor.	D	Laperriere, Jacques, Mtl.
Mikita, Stan, Chi.	C	Béliveau, Jean, Mtl.
Wharram, Kenny, Chi.	RW	Howe, Gordie, Det.
Hull, Bobby, Chi.	LW	Mahovlich, Frank, Tor.

1962-63

First Team		Second Team
Hall, Glenn, Chi.	G	Sawchuk, Terry, Det.
Pilote, Pierre, Chi.	D	Horton, Tim, Tor.
Brewer, Carl, Tor.	D	Vasko, Elmer, Chi.
Mikita, Stan, Chi.	C	Richard, Henri, Mtl.
Howe, Gordie, Det.	RW	Bathgate, Andy, NYR
Mahovlich, Frank, Tor.	LW	Hull, Bobby, Chi.

1961-62

First Team		Second Team
Plante, Jacques, Mtl.	G	Hall, Glenn, Chi.
Harvey, Doug, NYR	D	Brewer, Carl, Tor.
Talbot, Jean-Guy, Mtl.	D	Pilote, Pierre, Chi.
Mikita, Stan, Chi.	C	Keon, Dave, Tor.
Bathgate, Andy, NYR	RW	Howe, Gordie, Det.
Hull, Bobby, Chi.	LW	Mahovlich, Frank, Tor.

1960-61

First Team		Second Team
Bower, Johnny, Tor.	G	Hall, Glenn, Chi.
Harvey, Doug, Mtl.	D	Stanley, Allan, Tor.
Pronovost, Marcel, Det.	D	Pilote, Pierre, Chi.
Béliveau, Jean, Mtl.	C	Richard, Henri, Mtl.
Geoffrion, Bernie, Mtl.	RW	Howe, Gordie, Det.
Mahovlich, Frank, Tor.	LW	Moore, Dickie, Mtl.

1959-60

First Team		Second Team
Hall, Glenn, Chi.	G	Plante, Jacques, Mtl.
Harvey, Doug, Mtl.	D	Stanley, Allan, Tor.
Pronovost, Marcel, Det.	D	Pilote, Pierre, Chi.
Béliveau, Jean, Mtl.	C	Horvath, Bronco, Bos.
Howe, Gordie, Det.	RW	Geoffrion, Bernie, Mtl.
Hull, Bobby, Chi.	LW	Prentice, Dean, NYR

1958-59

First Team		Second Team
Plante, Jacques, Mtl.	G	Sawchuk, Terry, Det.
Johnson, Tom, Mtl.	D	Pronovost, Marcel, Det.
Gadsby, Bill, NYR	D	Harvey, Doug, Mtl.
Béliveau, Jean, Mtl.	C	Richard, Henri, Mtl.
Bathgate, Andy, NYR	RW	Howe, Gordie, Det.
Moore, Dickie, Mtl.	LW	Delvecchio, Alex, Det.

1957-58

First Team		Second Team
Hall, Glenn, Chi.	G	Plante, Jacques, Mtl.
Harvey, Doug, Mtl.	D	Flaman, Fern, Bos.
Gadsby, Bill, NYR	D	Pronovost, Marcel, Det.
Richard, Henri, Mtl.	C	Béliveau, Jean, Mtl.
Howe, Gordie, Det.	RW	Bathgate, Andy, NYR
Moore, Dickie, Mtl.	LW	Henry, Camille, NYR

1956-57

First Team		Second Team
Hall, Glenn, Det.	G	Plante, Jacques, Mtl.
Harvey, Doug, Mtl.	D	Flaman, Fern, Bos.
Kelly, Red, Det.	D	Gadsby, Bill, NYR
Béliveau, Jean, Mtl.	C	Litzenberger, Ed, Chi.
Howe, Gordie, Det.	RW	Richard, Maurice, Mtl.
Lindsay, Ted, Det.	LW	Chevrefils, Real, Bos.

1955-56

First Team		Second Team
Plante, Jacques, Mtl.	G	Hall, Glenn, Det.
Harvey, Doug, Mtl.	D	Kelly, Red, Det.
Gadsby, Bill, NYR	D	Johnson, Tom, Mtl.
Béliveau, Jean, Mtl.	C	Sloan, Tod, Tor.
Richard, Maurice, Mtl.	RW	Howe, Gordie, Det.
Lindsay, Ted, Det.	LW	Olmstead, Bert, Mtl.

1954-55

First Team		Second Team
Lumley, Harry, Tor.	G	Sawchuk, Terry, Det.
Harvey, Doug, Mtl.	D	Goldham, Bob, Det.
Kelly, Red, Det.	D	Flaman, Fern, Bos.
Béliveau, Jean, Mtl.	C	Mosdell, Ken, Mtl.
Richard, Maurice, Mtl.	RW	Geoffrion, Bernie, Mtl.
Smith, Sid, Tor.	LW	Lewicki, Danny, NYR

1953-54

First Team		Second Team
Lumley, Harry, Tor.	G	Sawchuk, Terry, Det.
Kelly, Red, Det.	D	Gadsby, Bill, Chi.
Harvey, Doug, Mtl.	D	Horton, Tim, Tor.
Mosdell, Kenny, Mtl.	C	Kennedy, Ted, Tor.
Howe, Gordie, Det.	RW	Richard, Maurice, Mtl.
Lindsay, Ted, Det.	LW	Sandford, Ed, Bos.

1952-53

First Team		Second Team
Sawchuk, Terry, Det.	G	McNeil, Gerry, Mtl.
Kelly, Red, Det.	D	Quackenbush, Bill, Bos.
Harvey, Doug, Mtl.	D	Gadsby, Bill, Chi.
Mackell, Fleming, Bos.	C	Delvecchio, Alex, Det.
Howe, Gordie, Det.	RW	Richard, Maurice, Mtl.
Lindsay, Ted, Det.	LW	Olmstead, Bert, Mtl.

1951-52

First Team		Second Team
Sawchuk, Terry, Det.	G	Henry, Jim, Bos.
Kelly, Red, Det.	D	Buller, Hy, NYR
Harvey, Doug, Mtl.	D	Thomson, Jimmy, Tor.
Lach, Elmer, Mtl.	C	Schmidt, Milt, Bos.
Howe, Gordie, Det.	RW	Richard, Maurice, Mtl.
Lindsay, Ted, Det.	LW	Smith, Sid, Tor.

1950-51

First Team		Second Team
Sawchuk, Terry, Det.	G	Rayner, Chuck, NYR
Kelly, Red, Det.	D	Thomson, Jim, Tor.
Quackenbush, Bill, Bos.	D	Reise Jr., Leo, Det.
Schmidt, Milt, Bos.	C	Abel, Sid, Det.
	(tied)	Kennedy, Ted, Tor.
Howe, Gordie, Det.	RW	Richard, Maurice, Mtl.
Lindsay, Ted, Det.	LW	Smith, Sid, Tor.

1949-50

First Team		Second Team
Durnan, Bill, Mtl.	G	Rayner, Chuck, NYR
Mortson, Gus, Tor.	D	Reise Jr., Leo, Det.
Reardon, Ken, Mtl.	D	Kelly, Red, Det.
Abel, Sid, Det.	C	Kennedy, Ted, Tor.
Richard, Maurice, Mtl.	RW	Howe, Gordie, Det.
Lindsay, Ted, Det.	LW	Leswick, Tony, NYR

1948-49

First Team		Second Team
Durnan, Bill, Mtl.	G	Rayner, Chuck, NYR
Quackenbush, Bill, Det.	D	Harmon, Glen, Mtl.
Stewart, Jack, Det.	D	Reardon, Ken, Mtl.
Abel, Sid, Det.	C	Bentley, Doug, Chi.
Richard, Maurice, Mtl.	RW	Howe, Gordie, Det.
Conacher, Roy, Chi.	LW	Lindsay, Ted, Det.

1947-48

First Team		Second Team
Broda, Turk, Tor.	G	Brimsek, Frank, Bos.
Quackenbush, Bill, Det.	D	Reardon, Ken, Mtl.
Stewart, Jack, Det.	D	Colville, Neil, NYR
Lach, Elmer, Mtl.	C	O'Connor, Buddy, NYR
Richard, Maurice, Mtl.	RW	Poile, Bud, Chi.
Lindsay, Ted, Det.	LW	Stewart, Gaye, Chi.

1946-47

First Team		Second Team
Durnan, Bill, Mtl.	G	Brimsek, Frank, Bos.
Reardon, Ken, Mtl.	D	Stewart, Jack, Det.
Bouchard, Butch, Mtl.	D	Quackenbush, Bill, Det.
Schmidt, Milt, Bos.	C	Bentley, Max, Chi.
Richard, Maurice, Mtl.	RW	Bauer, Bobby, Bos.
Bentley, Doug, Chi.	LW	Dumart, Woody, Bos.

1945-46

First Team		Second Team
Durnan, Bill, Mtl.	G	Brimsek, Frank, Bos.
Crawford, Jack, Bos.	D	Reardon, Ken, Mtl.
Bouchard, Butch, Mtl.	D	Stewart, Jack, Det.
Bentley, Max, Chi.	C	Lach, Elmer, Mtl.
Richard, Maurice, Mtl.	RW	Mosienko, Bill, Chi.
Stewart, Gaye, Tor.	LW	Blake, Toe, Mtl.
Irvin, Dick, Mtl.	Coach	Gottselig, Johnny, Chi.

1944-45

First Team		Second Team
Durnan, Bill, Mtl.	G	Karakas, Mike, Chi.
Bouchard, Butch, Mtl.	D	Harmon, Glen, Mtl.
Hollett, Flash, Det.	D	Pratt, Babe, Tor.
Lach, Elmer, Mtl.	C	Cowley, Bill, Bos.
Richard, Maurice, Mtl.	RW	Mosienko, Bill, Chi.
Blake, Toe, Mtl.	LW	Howe, Syd, Det.
Irvin, Dick, Mtl.	Coach	Adams, Jack, Det.

1943-44

First Team		Second Team
Durnan, Bill, Mtl.	G	Bibeault, Paul, Tor.
Seibert, Earl, Chi.	D	Bouchard, Butch, Mtl.
Pratt, Babe, Tor.	D	Clapper, Dit, Bos.
Cowley, Bill, Bos.	C	Lach, Elmer, Mtl.
Carr, Lorne, Tor.	RW	Richard, Maurice, Mtl.
Bentley, Doug, Chi.	LW	Cain, Herb, Bos.
Irvin, Dick, Mtl.	Coach	Day, Hap, Tor.

1942-43

First Team		Second Team
Mowers, Johnny, Det.	G	Brimsek, Frank, Bos.
Seibert, Earl, Chi.	D	Crawford, Jack, Bos.
Stewart, Jack, Det.	D	Hollett, Flash, Bos.
Cowley, Bill, Bos.	C	Apps Sr., Syl, Tor.
Carr, Lorne, Tor.	RW	Hextall Sr., Bryan, NYR
Bentley, Doug, Chi.	LW	Patrick, Lynn, NYR
Adams, Jack, Det.	Coach	Ross, Art, Bos.

1941-42

First Team		Second Team
Brimsek, Frank, Bos.	G	Broda, Turk, Tor.
Seibert, Earl, Chi.	D	Egan, Pat, Bro.
Anderson, Tom, Bro.	D	McDonald, Bucko, Tor.
Apps Sr., Syl, Tor.	C	Watson, Phil, NYR
Hextall, Bryan, NYR	RW	Drillon, Gordie, Tor.
Patrick, Lynn, NYR	LW	Abel, Sid, Det.
Boucher, Frank, NYR	Coach	Thompson, Paul, Chi.

1940-41

First Team		Second Team
Broda, Turk, Tor.	G	Brimsek, Frank, Bos.
Clapper, Dit, Bos.	D	Seibert, Earl, Chi.
Stanowski, Wally, Tor.	D	Heller, Ott, NYR
Cowley, Bill, Bos.	C	Apps Sr., Syl, Tor.
Hextall Sr., Bryan, NYR	RW	Bauer, Bobby, Bos.
Schriner, Sweeney, Tor.	LW	Dumart, Woody, Bos.
Weiland, Cooney, Bos.	Coach	Irvin, Dick, Mtl.

1939-40

First Team		Second Team
Kerr, Dave, NYR	G	Brimsek, Frank, Bos.
Clapper, Dit, Bos.	D	Coulter, Art, NYR
Goodfellow, Ebbie, Det.	D	Seibert, Earl, Chi.
Schmidt, Milt, Bos.	C	Colville, Neil, NYR
Hextall Sr., Bryan, NYR	RW	Bauer, Bobby, Bos.
Blake, Toe, Mtl.	LW	Dumart, Woody, Bos.
Thompson, Paul, Chi.	Coach	Boucher, Frank, NYR

1938-39

First Team		Second Team
Brimsek, Frank, Bos.	G	Robertson, Earl, NYA
Shore, Eddie, Bos.	D	Seibert, Earl, Chi.
Clapper, Dit, Bos.	D	Coulter, Art, NYR
Apps Sr., Syl, Tor.	C	Colville, Neil, NYR
Drillon, Gordie, Tor.	RW	Bauer, Bobby, Bos.
Blake, Toe, Mtl.	LW	Gottselig, Johnny, Chi.
Ross, Art, Bos.	Coach	Dutton, Red, NYA

1937-38

First Team		Second Team
Thompson, Tiny, Bos.	G	Kerr, Dave, NYR
Shore, Eddie, Bos.	D	Coulter, Art, NYR
Siebert, Babe, Mtl.	D	Seibert, Earl, Chi.
Cowley, Bill, Bos.	C	Apps Sr., Syl, Tor.
Dillon, Cecil, NYR	RW	
Drillon, Gordie, Tor.	(tied)	
Thompson, Paul, Chi.	LW	Blake, Toe, Mtl.
Patrick, Lester, NYR	Coach	Ross, Art, Bos.

1936-37

First Team		Second Team
Smith, Norman, Det.	G	Cude, Wilf, Mtl.
Siebert, Babe, Mtl.	D	Seibert, Earl, Chi.
Goodfellow, Ebbie, Det.	D	Conacher, Lionel, Mtl. M.
Barry, Marty, Det.	C	Chapman, Art, NYA
Aurie, Larry, Det.	RW	Dillon, Cecil, NYR
Jackson, Harvey, Tor.	LW	Schriner, Sweeney, NYA
Adams, Jack, Det.	Coach	Hart, Cecil, Mtl.

1935-36

First Team		Second Team
Thompson, Tiny, Bos.	G	Cude, Wilf, Mtl.
Shore, Eddie, Bos.	D	Seibert, Earl, Chi.
Siebert, Babe, Bos.	D	Goodfellow, Ebbie, Det.
Smith, Hooley, Mtl. M.	C	Thoms, Bill, Tor.
Conacher, Charlie, Tor.	RW	Dillon, Cecil, NYR
Schriner, Sweeney, NYA	LW	Thompson, Paul, Chi.
Patrick, Lester, NYR	Coach	Gorman, Tommy, Mtl. M.

1934-35

First Team		Second Team
Chabot, Lorne, Chi.	G	Thompson, Tiny, Bos.
Shore, Eddie, Bos.	D	Wentworth, Cy, Mtl. M.
Seibert, Earl, NYR	D	Coulter, Art, Chi.
Boucher, Frank, NYR	C	Weiland, Cooney, Det.
Conacher, Charlie, Tor.	RW	Clapper, Dit, Bos.
Jackson, Harvey, Tor.	LW	Joliat, Aurel, Mtl.
Patrick, Lester, NYR	Coach	Irvin, Dick, Tor.

1933-34

First Team		Second Team
Gardiner, Chuck, Chi.	G	Worters, Roy, NYA
Clancy, King, Tor.	D	Shore, Eddie, Bos.
Conacher, Lionel, Chi.	D	Johnson, Ivan, NYR
Boucher, Frank, NYR	C	Primeau, Joe, Tor.
Conacher, Charlie, Tor.	RW	Cook, Bill, NYR
Jackson, Harvey, Tor.	LW	Joliat, Aurel, Mtl.
Patrick, Lester, NYR	Coach	Irvin, Dick, Tor.

1932-33

First Team		Second Team
Roach, John Ross, Det.	G	Gardiner, Chuck, Chi.
Shore, Eddie, Bos.	D	Clancy, King, Tor.
Johnson, Ivan, NYR	D	Conacher, Lionel, Mtl. M.
Boucher, Frank, NYR	C	Morenz, Howie, Mtl.
Cook, Bill, NYR	RW	Conacher, Charlie, Tor.
Northcott, Baldy, Mtl M.	LW	Jackson, Harvey, Tor.
Patrick, Lester, NYR	Coach	Irvin, Dick, Tor.

1931-32

First Team		Second Team
Gardiner, Chuck, Chi.	G	Worters, Roy, NYA
Shore, Eddie, Bos.	D	Mantha, Sylvio, Mtl.
Johnson, Ivan, NYR	D	Clancy, King, Tor.
Morenz, Howie, Mtl.	C	Smith, Hooley, Mtl. M.
Cook, Bill, NYR	RW	Conacher, Charlie, Tor.
Jackson, Harvey, Tor.	LW	Joliat, Aurel, Mtl.
Patrick, Lester, NYR	Coach	Irvin, Dick, Tor.

1930-31

First Team		Second Team
Gardiner, Chuck, Chi.	G	Thompson, Tiny, Bos.
Shore, Eddie, Bos.	D	Mantha, Sylvio, Mtl.
Clancy, King, Tor.	D	Johnson, Ivan, NYR
Morenz, Howie, Mtl.	C	Boucher, Frank, NYR
Cook, Bill, NYR	RW	Clapper, Dit, Bos.
Joliat, Aurel, Mtl.	LW	Cook, Bun, NYR
Patrick, Lester, NYR	Coach	Irvin, Dick, Chi.

All-Star Game Results

Year	Venue	Score	Coaches	Attendance
1998	Vancouver	North America 8, World 7	Jacques Lemaire, Ken Hitchcock	18,422
1997	San Jose	Eastern 11, Western 7	Doug MacLean, Ken Hitchcock	17,422
1996	Boston	Eastern 5, Western 4	Doug MacLean, Scotty Bowman	17,565
1994	NY Rangers	Eastern 9, Western 8	Jacques Demers, Barry Melrose	18,200
1993	Montreal	Wales 16, Campbell 6	Scotty Bowman, Mike Keenan	17,137
1992	Philadelphia	Campbell 10, Wales 6	Bob Gainey, Scotty Bowman	17,380
1991	Chicago	Campbell 11, Wales 5	John Muckler, Mike Milbury	18,472
1990	Pittsburgh	Wales 12, Campbell 7	Pat Burns, Terry Crisp	16,236
1989	Edmonton	Campbell 9, Wales 5	Glen Sather, Terry O'Reilly	17,503
1988	St. Louis	Wales 6, Campbell 5 OT	Mike Keenan, Glen Sather	17,878
1986	Hartford	Wales 4, Campbell 3 OT	Mike Keenan, Glen Sather	15,100
1985	Calgary	Wales 6, Campbell 4	Al Arbour, Glen Sather	16,825
1984	New Jersey	Wales 7, Campbell 6	Al Arbour, Glen Sather	18,939
1983	NY Islanders	Campbell 9, Wales 3	Roger Neilson, Al Arbour	15,230
1982	Washington	Wales 4, Campbell 2	Al Arbour, Glen Sonmor	18,130
1981	Los Angeles	Campbell 4, Wales 1	Pat Quinn, Scotty Bowman	15,761
1980	Detroit	Wales 6, Campbell 3	Scotty Bowman, Al Arbour	21,002
1978	Buffalo	Wales 3, Campbell 2 OT	Scotty Bowman, Fred Shero	16,433
1977	Vancouver	Wales 4, Campbell 3	Scotty Bowman, Fred Shero	15,607
1976	Philadelphia	Wales 7, Campbell 5	Floyd Smith, Fred Shero	16,436
1975	Montreal	Wales 7, Campbell 1	Bep Guidolin, Fred Shero	16,080
1974	Chicago	West 6, East 4	Billy Reay, Scotty Bowman	16,426
1973	New York	East 5, West 4	Tom Johnson, Billy Reay	16,986
1972	Minnesota	East 3, West 2	Al MacNeil, Billy Reay	15,423
1971	Boston	West 2, East 1	Scotty Bowman, Harry Sinden	14,790
1970	St. Louis	East 4, West 1	Claude Ruel, Scotty Bowman	16,587
1969	Montreal	East 3, West 3	Toe Blake, Scotty Bowman	16,260
1968	Toronto	Toronto 4, All-Stars 3	Punch Imlach, Toe Blake	15,753
1967	Montreal	Montreal 3, All-Stars 0	Toe Blake, Sid Abel	14,284
1965	Montreal	All-Stars 5, Montreal 2	Billy Reay, Toe Blake	13,529
1964	Toronto	All-Stars 3, Toronto 2	Sid Abel, Punch Imlach	14,232
1963	Toronto	All-Stars 3, Toronto 3	Sid Abel, Punch Imlach	14,034
1962	Toronto	Toronto 4, All-Stars 1	Punch Imlach, Rudy Pilous	14,236
1961	Chicago	All-Stars 3, Chicago 1	Sid Abel, Rudy Pilous	14,534
1960	Montreal	All-Stars 2, Montreal 1	Punch Imlach, Toe Blake	13,949
1959	Montreal	Montreal 6, All-Stars 1	Toe Blake, Punch Imlach	13,818
1958	Montreal	Montreal 6, All-Stars 3	Toe Blake, Milt Schmidt	13,989
1957	Montreal	All-Stars 5, Montreal 3	Milt Schmidt, Toe Blake	13,003
1956	Montreal	All-Stars 1, Montreal 1	Jim Skinner, Toe Blake	13,095
1955	Detroit	Detroit 3, All-Stars 1	Jim Skinner, Dick Irvin	10,111
1954	Detroit	All-Stars 2, Detroit 2	King Clancy, Jim Skinner	10,689
1953	Montreal	All-Stars 3, Montreal 1	Lynn Patrick, Dick Irvin	14,153
1952	Detroit	1st team 1, 2nd team 1	Tommy Ivan, Dick Irvin	10,680
1951	Toronto	1st team 2, 2nd team 2	Joe Primeau, Hap Day	11,469
1950	Detroit	Detroit 7, All-Stars 1	Tommy Ivan, Lynn Patrick	9,166
1949	Toronto	All-Stars 3, Toronto 1	Tommy Ivan, Hap Day	13,541
1948	Chicago	All-Stars 3, Toronto 1	Tommy Ivan, Hap Day	12,794
1947	Toronto	All-Stars 4, Toronto 3	Dick Irvin, Hap Day	14,169

There was no All-Star contest during the calendar year of 1966 because the game was moved from the start of season to mid-season. In 1979, the Challenge Cup series between the Soviet Union and Team NHL replaced the All-Star Game. In 1987, Rendez-Vous '87, two games between the Soviet Union and Team NHL replaced the All-Star Game. Rendez-Vous '87 scores: game one, NHL All-Stars 4, Soviet Union 3; game two, Soviet Union 5, NHL All-Stars 3. There was no All-Star Game in 1995 due to a labor disruption.

1997-98 All-Star Game Summary

January 18, 1998 at Vancouver North America 8, World 7

PLAYERS ON ICE: **North America** — Belfour, Brodeur, Roy, Leetch, Stevens, Sydor, Chelios, Recchi, Modano, LeClair, Messier, Amonte, Shanahan, Tkachuk, Sakic, MacInnis, Corson, Niedermayer, Weight, Fleury, Bourque, Lindros, Gretzky

The World — Khabibulin, Kolzig, Hasek, Fetisov, Lidstrom, Ozolinsh, Larionov, Selanne, Koivu, Bure, Alfredsson, Bondra, Sundin, Mironov, Holik, Kurri, Kamensky, Forsberg, Palffy, Lehtinen, Kravchuk, Zubov, Jagr

SUMMARY

First Period

1. World	Selanne 1	(Koivu)	0:53
2. World	Jagr 1	(Bondra, Mironov)	2:15
3. World	Selanne 2	(Lehtinen, Fetisov)	4:00
4. North America	LeClair 1	(Gretzky, Chelios)	4:13
5. North America	Tkachuk 1	(Fleury, Chelios)	10:50
6. North America	Niedermayer 1	(Sakic, Recchi)	18:25

PENALTIES: Fetisov World (cross-checking) 10:04

Second Period

7. North America	Fleury 1	(Modano, Tkachuk)	1:53
8. World	Selanne 3	(Lehtinen, Koivu)	7:11
9. World	Kurri 1	(Koivu, Lehtinen)	12:36
10. North America	Lindros 1	(Chelios, Messier)	14:46
11. North America	Amonte 1	(Sakic, Bourque)	16:19

Penalties: Fleury North America (tripping — obstruction) 18:48

Third Period

12. North America	Tkachuk 2	(Modano, Fleury)	1:36
13. North America	Messier 1	(Gretzky)	4:00
14. World	Kravchuk 1	(Sundin, Forsberg)	7:03
15. World	Larionov 1	(Bure)	9:41

Penalties: Weight North America (tripping) 16:32

SHOTS ON GOAL BY:

North America	13	17	13	**43**
World	7	11	11	**29**

	Goaltenders:	Time	SA	GA	ENG	Dec
N. America	Roy	20:00	7	3	0	
N. America	Belfour	20:00	11	2	0	
N. America	Brodeur	20:00	11	2	0	W
World	Hasek	20:00	13	3	0	
World	Kolzig	19:59	17	3	0	
World	Khabibulin	19:57	13	2	0	L

PP Conversions: North America 1/1; World 0/2.

Referee: Paul Stewart Linesmen: Michael Cvik, Shane Heyer.
Attendance: 18,422.

NHL ALL-ROOKIE TEAM

Voting for the NHL All-Rookie Team is conducted among the representatives of the Professional Hockey Writers' Association at the end of the season. The rookie all-star team was first selected for the 1982-83 season.

1997-98		1996-97
Jamie Storr, Los Angeles	*Goal*	Patrick Lalime, Pittsburgh
Mattias Ohlund, Vancouver	*Defense*	Bryan Berard, NY Islanders
Derek Morris, Calgary	*Defense*	Janne Niinimaa, Philadelphia
Sergei Samsonov, Boston	*Forward*	Jarome Iginla, Calgary
Patrick Elias, New Jersey	*Forward*	Jim Campbell, St. Louis
Mike Johnson, Toronto	*Forward*	Sergei Berezin, Toronto

1995-96		1994-95
Corey Hirsch, Vancouver	*Goal*	Jim Carey, Washington
Ed Jovanovski, Florida	*Defense*	Chris Therien, Philadelphia
Kyle McLaren, Boston	*Defense*	Kenny Jonsson, Toronto
Daniel Alfredsson, Ottawa	*Forward*	Peter Forsberg, Quebec
Eric Daze, Chicago	*Forward*	Jeff Friesen, San Jose
Petr Sykora, New Jersey	*Forward*	Paul Kariya, Anaheim

1993-94		1992-93
Martin Brodeur, New Jersey	*Goal*	Felix Potvin, Toronto
Chris Pronger, Hartford	*Defense*	Vladimir Malakhov, NY Islanders
Boris Mironov, Wpg., Edm.	*Defense*	Scott Niedermayer, New Jersey
Jason Arnott, Edmonton	*Center*	Eric Lindros, Philadelphia
Mikael Renberg, Philadelphia	*Wing*	Teemu Selanne, Winnipeg
Oleg Petrov, Montreal	*Wing*	Joe Juneau, Boston

1991-92		1990-91
Dominik Hasek, Chicago	*Goal*	Ed Belfour, Chicago
Nicklas Lidstrom, Detroit	*Defense*	Eric Weinrich, New Jersey
Vladimir Konstantinov, Detroit	*Defense*	Rob Blake, Los Angeles
Kevin Todd, New Jersey	*Center*	Sergei Fedorov, Detroit
Tony Amonte, NY Rangers	*Right Wing*	Ken Hodge, Boston
Gilbert Dionne, Montreal	*Left Wing*	Jaromir Jagr, Pittsburgh

1989-90		1988-89
Bob Essensa, Winnipeg	*Goal*	Peter Sidorkiewicz, Hartford
Brad Shaw, Hartford	*Defense*	Brian Leetch, NY Rangers
Geoff Smith, Edmonton	*Defense*	Zarley Zalapski, Pittsburgh
Mike Modano, Minnesota	*Center*	Trevor Linden, Vancouver
Sergei Makarov, Calgary	*Right Wing*	Tony Granato, NY Rangers
Rod Brind'Amour, St. Louis	*Left Wing*	David Volek, NY Islanders

1987-88		1986-87
Darren Pang, Chicago	*Goal*	Ron Hextall, Philadelphia
Glen Wesley, Boston	*Defense*	Steve Duchesne, Los Angeles
Calle Johansson, Buffalo	*Defense*	Brian Benning, St. Louis
Joe Nieuwendyk, Calgary	*Center*	Jimmy Carson, Los Angeles
Ray Sheppard, Buffalo	*Right Wing*	Jim Sandlak, Vancouver
Iain Duncan, Winnipeg	*Left Wing*	Luc Robitaille, Los Angeles

1985-86		1984-85
Patrick Roy, Montreal	*Goal*	Steve Penney, Montreal
Gary Suter, Calgary	*Defense*	Chris Chelios, Montreal
Dana Murzyn, Hartford	*Defense*	Bruce Bell, Quebec
Mike Ridley, NY Rangers	*Center*	Mario Lemieux, Pittsburgh
Kjell Dahlin, Montreal	*Right Wing*	Tomas Sandstrom, NY Rangers
Wendel Clark, Toronto	*Left Wing*	Warren Young, Pittsburgh

1983-84		1982-83
Tom Barrasso, Buffalo	*Goal*	Pelle Lindbergh, Philadelphia
Thomas Eriksson, Philadelphia	*Defense*	Scott Stevens, Washington
Jamie Macoun, Calgary	*Defense*	Phil Housley, Buffalo
Steve Yzerman, Detroit	*Center*	Dan Daoust, Montreal/Toronto
Hakan Loob, Calgary	*Right Wing*	Steve Larmer, Chicago
Sylvain Turgeon, Hartford	*Left Wing*	Mats Naslund, Montreal

All-Star Game Records 1947 through 1998

TEAM RECORDS

MOST GOALS, BOTH TEAMS, ONE GAME:
22 — Wales 16, Campbell 6, 1993 at Montreal
19 — Wales 12, Campbell 7, 1990 at Pittsburgh
18 — East 11, West 7, 1997 at San Jose
17 — East 9, West 8, 1994 at NY Rangers
16 — Campbell 11, Wales 5, 1991 at Chicago
— Campbell 10, Wales 6, 1992 at Philadelphia
15 — North America 8, World 7, 1998 at Vancouver
14 — Campbell 9, Wales 5, 1989 at Edmonton
13 — Wales 7, Campbell 6, 1984 at New Jersey

FEWEST GOALS, BOTH TEAMS, ONE GAME:
2 — NHL All-Stars 1, Montreal Canadiens 1, 1956 at Montreal
— First Team All-Stars 1, Second Team All-Stars 1, 1952 at Detroit
3 — West 2, East 1, 1971 at Boston
— Montreal Canadiens 3, NHL All-Stars 0, 1967 at Montreal
— NHL All-Stars 2, Montreal Canadiens 1, 1960 at Montreal

MOST GOALS, ONE TEAM, ONE GAME:
16 — Wales 16, Campbell 6, 1993 at Montreal
12 — Wales 12, Campbell 7, 1990 at Pittsburgh
11 — Campbell 11, Wales 5, 1991 at Chicago
— East 11, West 7, 1997 at San Jose
10 — Campbell 10, Wales 6, 1992 at Philadelphia

FEWEST GOALS, ONE TEAM, ONE GAME:
0 — NHL All-Stars 0, Montreal Canadiens 3, 1967 at Montreal
1 — 17 times (1981, 1975, 1971, 1970, 1962, 1961, 1960, 1959, both teams 1956, 1955, 1953, both teams 1952, 1950, 1949, 1948)

MOST SHOTS, BOTH TEAMS, ONE GAME (SINCE 1955):
102 — 1994 at NY Rangers — East 9 (56 shots), West 8 (46 shots)
90 — 1993 at Montreal — Wales 16 (49 shots), Campbell 6 (41 shots)
87 — 1990 at Pittsburgh — Wales 12 (45 shots), Campbell 7 (42 shots)
— 1997 at San Jose — East 11 (41 shots), West 7 (46 shots)
83 — 1992 at Philadelphia — Campbell 10 (42 shots), Wales 6 (41 shots)

FEWEST SHOTS, BOTH TEAMS, ONE GAME (SINCE 1955):
52 — 1978 at Buffalo — Campbell 2 (12 shots) Wales 3 (40 shots)
53 — 1960 at Montreal — NHL All-Stars 2 (27 shots) Montreal Canadiens 1 (26 shots)
55 — 1956 at Montreal — NHL All-Stars 1 (28 shots) Montreal Canadiens 1 (27 shots)
— 1971 at Boston — West 2 (28 shots) East 1 (27 shots)

MOST SHOTS, ONE TEAM, ONE GAME (SINCE 1955):
56 — 1994 at NY Rangers — East (9-8 vs. West)
49 — 1993 at Montreal — Wales (16-6 vs. Campbell)
46 — 1994 at NY Rangers — West (8-9 vs. East)
— 1997 at San Jose — West (7-11 vs. East)
45 — 1990 at Pittsburgh — Wales (12-7 vs. Campbell)

FEWEST SHOTS, ONE TEAM, ONE GAME (SINCE 1955):
12 — 1978 at Buffalo — Campbell (2-3 vs. Wales)
17 — 1970 at St. Louis — West (1-4 vs. East)
23 — 1961 at Chicago — Chicago Black Hawks (1-3 vs. NHL All-Stars)
24 — 1976 at Philadelphia — Campbell (5-7 vs. Wales)

MOST POWER-PLAY GOALS, BOTH TEAMS, ONE GAME (SINCE 1950):
3 — 1953 at Montreal — NHL All-Stars 3 (2 power-play goals), Montreal Canadiens 1 (1 power-play goal)
— 1954 at Detroit — NHL All-Stars 2 (1 power-play goal) Detroit Red Wings 2 (2 power-play goals)
— 1958 at Montreal — NHL All-Stars 3 (1 power-play goal) Montreal Canadiens 6 (2 power-play goals)

FEWEST POWER-PLAY GOALS, BOTH TEAMS, ONE GAME (SINCE 1950):
0 — 15 times (1952, 1959, 1960, 1967, 1968, 1969, 1972, 1973, 1976, 1980, 1981, 1984, 1985, 1992, 1994, 1996)

FASTEST TWO GOALS, BOTH TEAMS, FROM START OF GAME:
37 seconds — 1970 at St. Louis — Jacques Laperriere of East scored at 20 seconds and Dean Prentice of West scored at 37 seconds. Final score: East 4, West 1.

2:15 — 1998 at Vancouver — Teemu Selanee scored at 0:53 and Jaromir Jagr scored at 2:15 for World. Final score: North America 8, World 7.

3:37 — 1993 at Montreal — Mike Gartner scored at 3:15 and at 3:37 for Wales. Final score: Wales 16, Campbell 6.

FASTEST TWO GOALS, BOTH TEAMS:
8 seconds — 1997 at San Jose — Owen Nolan scored at 18:54 and 19:02 of second period for West. Final Score: East 11, West 7.

10 seconds — 1976 at Philadelphia — Dennis Ververgaert scored at 4:33 and at 4:43 of third period for Campbell. Final score: Wales 7, Campbell 5.

13 seconds — 1998 at Vancouver — Teemu Selanne scored at 4:00 of first period for World and John LeClair scored at 4:13 for North America. Final score: North America 8, World 7.

FASTEST THREE GOALS, BOTH TEAMS:
1:08 — 1993 at Montreal — all by Wales — Mike Gartner scored at 3:15 and at 3:37 of first period; Peter Bondra scored at 4:23. Final score: Wales 16, Campbell 6.

1:14 — 1994 at NY Rangers — Bob Kudelski scored at 9:46 of first period for East; Sergei Fedorov scored at 10:20 for West; Eric Lindros scored at 11:00 for East. Final score: East 9, West 8.

1:25 — 1992 at Philadelphia — Bryan Trottier scored at 4:03 of third period for Wales; Brian Bellows scored at 4:50 for Campbell; Alexander Mogilny scored at 5:28 for Wales. Final score: Campbell 10, Wales 6.

FASTEST FOUR GOALS, BOTH TEAMS:
2:24 — 1997 at San Jose — Brendan Shanahan scored at 16:38 of second period for West; Dale Hawerchuk scored at 17:28 for East; Owen Nolan scored at 18:54 and 19:02 for West. Final score: East 11, West 7.

3:04 — 1997 at San Jose — Mark Recchi scored at 15:32 of first period for East; Dale Hawerchuk scored at 16:19 for East; Pavel Bure scored at 17:36 for West; Paul Kariya scored at 18:36 for West. Final score: East 11, West 7.

3:29 — 1994 at NY Rangers — Jeremy Roenick scored at 7:31 of first period for West; Bob Kudelski scored at 9:46 for East; Sergei Fedorov scored at 10:20 for West; Eric Lindros scored at 11:00 for East. Final score: East 9, West 8.

FASTEST TWO GOALS, ONE TEAM, FROM START OF GAME:
2:15 — 1998 at Vancouver — World — Teemu Selanee scored at 0:53 and Jaromir Jagr scored at 2:15. Final score: North America 8, World 7.

3:37 — 1993 at Montreal — Wales — Mike Gartner scored at 3:15 and at 3:37. Final score: Wales 16, Campbell 6.

4:19 — 1980 at Detroit — Wales — Larry Robinson scored at 3:58 and Steve Payne scored at 4:19. Final score: Wales 6, Campbell 3.

FASTEST TWO GOALS, ONE TEAM:
8 seconds — 1997 at San Jose — West — Owen Nolan scored at 18:54 and at 19:02 of second period. Final score: East 11, West 7.

10 seconds — 1976 at Philadelphia — Campbell — Dennis Ververgaert scored at 4:33 and at 4:43 of third period. Final score: Wales 7, Campbell 5.

14 seconds — 1989 at Edmonton — Campbell — Steve Yzerman and Gary Leeman scored at 17:21 and 17:35 of second period. Final score: Campbell 9, Wales 5.

FASTEST THREE GOALS, ONE TEAM:
1:08 — 1993 at Montreal — Wales — Mike Gartner scored at 3:15 and 3:37 of first period; Peter Bondra scored at 4:23. Final score: Wales 16, Campbell 6.

1:32 — 1980 at Detroit — Wales — Ron Stackhouse scored at 11:40 of third period; Craig Hartsburg scored at 12:40; Reed Larson scored at 13:12. Final score: Wales 6, Campbell 3.

1:42 — 1993 at Montreal — Wales — Alexander Mogilny scored at 11:40 of first period; Pierre Turgeon scored at 13:05; Mike Gartner scored at 13:22. Final score: Wales 16, Campbell 6.

FASTEST FOUR GOALS, ONE TEAM:
4:19 — 1992 at Philadelphia — Campbell — Brian Bellows scored at 7:40 of second period; Jeremy Roenick scored at 8:13; Theoren Fleury scored at 11:06, Brett Hull scored at 11:59. Final score: Campbell 10, Wales 6.

4:26 — 1980 at Detroit — Wales — Ron Stackhouse scored at 11:40 of third period; Craig Hartsburg scored at 12:40; Reed Larson scored at 13:12; Real Cloutier scored at 16:06. Final score: Wales 6, Campbell 3.

5:34 — 1993 at Montreal — Campbell — Doug Gilmour scored at 13:57 of third period; Teemu Selanne scored at 17:03; Pavel Bure scored at 18:44 and 19:31. Final score: Wales 16, Campbell 6.

MOST GOALS, BOTH TEAMS, ONE PERIOD:
10 — 1997 at San Jose — Second period — East (6), West (4). Final score: East 11, West 7.

9 — 1990 at Pittsburgh — First period — Wales (7), Campbell (2). Final score: Wales 12, Campbell 7.

8 — 1992 at Philadelphia — Second period — Campbell (6), Wales (2). Final Score: Campbell 10, Wales 6.

— 1993 at Montreal — Second period — Wales (6), Campbell (2). Final score: Wales 16, Campbell 6.

— 1993 at Montreal — Third period — Wales (4), Campbell (4). Final score: Wales 16, Campbell 6.

MOST GOALS, ONE TEAM, ONE PERIOD:
7 — 1990 at Pittsburgh — First period — Wales. Final score: Wales 12, Campbell 7.
6 — 1983 at NY Islanders — Third period — Campbell.
Final score: Campbell 9, Wales 3.
— 1992 at Philadelphia — Second Period — Campbell.
Final score: Campbell 10, Wales 6.
— 1993 at Montreal — First period — Wales.
Final score: Wales 16, Campbell 6.
— 1993 at Montreal — Second period — Wales.
Final score: Wales 16, Campbell 6.
— 1997 at San Jose — Second period — East.
Final score: East 11, West 7.

MOST SHOTS, BOTH TEAMS, ONE PERIOD:
39 — 1994 at NY Rangers — Second period — West (21) East (18).
Final score: East 9, West 8.
36 — 1990 at Pittsburgh — Third period — Campbell (22), Wales (14).
Final score: Wales 12, Campbell 7.
— 1994 at NY Rangers — First period — East (19), West (17).
Final score: East 9, West 8.

MOST SHOTS, ONE TEAM, ONE PERIOD:
22 — 1990 at Pittsburgh — Third period — Campbell.
Final score: Wales 12, Campbell 7.
— 1991 at Chicago — Third Period — Wales.
Final score: Campbell 11, Wales 5.
— 1993 at Montreal — First period — Wales.
Final score: Wales 16, Campbell 6.

FEWEST SHOTS, BOTH TEAMS, ONE PERIOD:
9 — 1971 at Boston — Third period — East (2), West (7).
Final score: West 2, East 1.
— 1980 at Detroit — Second period — Campbell (4), Wales (5).
Final score: Wales 6, Campbell 3.
13 — 1982 at Washington — Third period — Campbell (6), Wales (7).
Final score: Wales 4, Campbell 2.
14 — 1978 at Buffalo — First period — Campbell (7), Wales (7).
Final score: Wales 3, Campbell 2.
— 1986 at Hartford — First period — Campbell (6), Wales (8).
Final score: Wales 4, Campbell 3.

FEWEST SHOTS, ONE TEAM, ONE PERIOD:
2 — 1971 at Boston — Third period — East.
Final score: West 2, East 1.
— 1978 at Buffalo — Second period — Campbell.
Final score: Wales 3, Campbell 2.
3 — 1978 at Buffalo — Third period — Campbell.
Final score: Wales 3, Campbell 2.
4 — 1955 at Detroit — First period — NHL All-Stars.
Final score: Detroit Red Wings 3, NHL All-Stars 1.
4 — 1980 at Detroit — Second period — Campbell.
Final score: Wales 6, Campbell 3.

Campbell Conference All-Stars Denis Savard, right, and Glenn Anderson, center, surround Wales All-Star Brian Propp during the 1986 midseason classic. The Wales team overcame a last-second goal by Dale Hawerchuk to win the match 4-3 in overtime.

INDIVIDUAL RECORDS

Games

MOST GAMES PLAYED:
23 — Gordie Howe from 1948 through 1980
17 — Wayne Gretzky from 1980 through 1998
16 — Ray Bourque from 1981 through 1998
15 — Frank Mahovlich from 1959 through 1974
14 — Paul Coffey from 1982 through 1997

Goals

MOST GOALS (CAREER):
12 — Wayne Gretzky in 16GP
11 — Mario Lemieux in 8GP
10 — Gordie Howe in 23GP
8 — Frank Mahovlich in 15GP
7 — Maurice Richard in 13GP

MOST GOALS, ONE GAME:
4 — Wayne Gretzky, Campbell, 1983
— Mario Lemieux, Wales, 1990
— Vince Damphousse, Campbell, 1991
— Mike Gartner, Wales, 1993
3 — Ted Lindsay, Detroit Red Wings, 1950
— Mario Lemieux, Wales, 1988
— Pierre Turgeon, Wales, 1993
— Mark Recchi, East, 1997
— Owen Nolan, West, 1997
— Teemu Selanne, World, 1998

MOST GOALS, ONE PERIOD:
4 — Wayne Gretzky, Campbell, Third period, 1983
3 — Mario Lemieux, Wales, First period, 1990
— Vince Damphousse, Campbell, Third period, 1991
— Mike Gartner, Wales, First period, 1993
2 — Ted Lindsay, Detroit, First period, 1950
— Wally Hergesheimer, NHL All-Stars, First period, 1953
— Andy Bathgate, NHL All-Stars, Third period, 1958
— Frank Mahovlich, Toronto, First period, 1963
— Dennis Ververgaert, Campbell, Third period, 1976
— Richard Martin, Wales, Third period, 1977
— Pierre Turgeon, Wales, First period, 1990
— Luc Robitaille, Campbell, Third period, 1990
— Theoren Fleury, Campbell, Second period, 1992
— Brett Hull, Campbell, Second period, 1992
— Rick Tocchet, Wales, Second period, 1993
— Pavel Bure, Campbell, Third period, 1993
— Mark Recchi, East, Second period, 1997
— Owen Nolan, West, Second period, 1997
— Teemu Selanne, World, First period, 1998

Assists

MOST ASSISTS (CAREER):
12 — Adam Oates in 5GP
— Mark Messier in 13GP
— Joe Sakic in 7GP
— Ray Bourque in 16GP
10 — Paul Coffey in 14GP
— Wayne Gretzky in 17GP

MOST ASSISTS, ONE GAME:
5 — Mats Naslund, Wales, 1988
4 — Ray Bourque, Wales, 1985
— Adam Oates, Campbell, 1991
— Adam Oates, Wales, 1993
— Mark Recchi, Wales, 1993
— Pierre Turgeon, East All-Stars, 1994
3 — Dickie Moore, Montreal, 1958
— Doug Harvey, Montreal, 1959
— Guy Lafleur, Wales, 1975
— Pete Mahovlich, Wales, 1976
— Mark Messier, Campbell, 1983
— Rick Vaive, Campbell, 1984
— Mark Johnson, Wales, 1984
— Don Maloney, Wales, 1984
— Mike Krushelnyski, Campbell, 1985
— Mario Lemieux, Wales, 1988
— Brett Hull, Campbell, 1990
— Luc Robitaille, Campbell, 1992
— Joe Sakic, Wales, 1993
— Sandis Ozolinsh, West, 1997
— Chris Chelios, North America, 1998
— Saku Koivu, World, 1998
— Jere Lehtinen, World, 1998

MOST ASSISTS, ONE PERIOD:
4 — Adam Oates, Wales, First period, 1993
3 — Mark Messier, Campbell, Third period, 1983

Points

MOST POINTS, CAREER:
22 — Wayne Gretzky (12G-10A in 17GP)
20 — **Mario Lemieux** (11G-9A in 8GP)
19 — Gordie Howe (10G-9A in 23GP)
17 — Mark Messier (5G-12A in 13GP)
15 — Ray Bourque (3G-12A in 16GP)

MOST POINTS, ONE GAME:
6 — Mario Lemieux, Wales, 1988 (3G-3A)
5 — Mats Naslund, Wales, 1988 (5A)
— Adam Oates, Campbell, 1991 (1G-4A)
— Mike Gartner, Wales, 1993 (4G-1A)
— Mark Recchi, Wales, 1993 (1G-4A)
— Pierre Turgeon, Wales, 1993 (3G-2A)

MOST POINTS, ONE PERIOD:
4 — Wayne Gretzky, Campbell, Third period, 1983 (4G)
— Mike Gartner, Wales, First period, 1993 (3G-1A)
— Adam Oates, Wales, First period, 1993 (4A)
3 — Gordie Howe, NHL All-Stars, Second period, 1965 (1G-2A)
— Pete Mahovlich, Wales, First period, 1976 (1G-2A)
— Mark Messier, Campbell, Third period, 1983 (3A)
— Mario Lemieux, Wales, Second period, 1988 (1G-2A)
— Mario Lemieux, Wales, First period, 1990 (3G)
— Vince Damphousse, Campbell, Third period, 1991 (3G)
— Mark Recchi, Wales, Second period, 1993 (1G-2A)

Power-Play Goals

MOST POWER-PLAY GOALS, CAREER:
6 — Gordie Howe in 23GP
3 — Bobby Hull in 12GP
2 — Maurice Richard in 13GP

Fastest Goals

FASTEST GOAL FROM START OF GAME:
19 seconds — Ted Lindsay, Detroit, 1950
20 seconds — Jacques Laperriere, East All-Stars, 1970
21 seconds — Mario Lemieux, Wales, 1990
36 seconds — Chico Maki, West All-Stars, 1971
37 seconds — Dean Prentice, West All-Stars, 1970

FASTEST GOAL FROM START OF A PERIOD:
19 seconds — Ted Lindsay, Detroit, 1950 (first period)
— Rick Tocchet, Wales, 1993 (second period)
20 seconds — Jacques Laperriere, East, 1970 (first period)
21 seconds — Mario Lemieux, Wales, 1990 (first period)
26 seconds — Wayne Gretzky, Campbell, 1982 (second period)
28 seconds — Maurice Richard, NHL All-Stars, 1947 (third period)

FASTEST TWO GOALS (ONE PLAYER) FROM START OF GAME:
3:37 — Mike Gartner, Wales, 1993, at 3:15 and 3:37.
4:00 — Teemu Selanne, World, 1998, at 0:53 and 4:00
5:25 — Wally Hergesheimer, NHL All-Stars, 1953, at 4:06 and 5:25.

FASTEST TWO GOALS (ONE PLAYER) FROM START OF A PERIOD:
3:37 — Mike Gartner, Wales, 1993, at 3:15 and 3:37 of first period.
4:43 — Dennis Ververgaert, Campbell, 1976, at 4:33 and 4:43 of third period.
4:57 — Rick Tocchet, Wales, 1993, at :19 and 4:57 of second period.

FASTEST TWO GOALS (ONE PLAYER):
8 seconds — Owen Nolan, West, 1997. Scored at 18:54 and 19:02 of second period.
10 seconds — Dennis Ververgaert, Campbell, 1976. Scored at 4:33 and 4:43 of third period.
22 seconds — Mike Gartner, Wales, 1993. Scored at 3:15 and 3:37 of first period.

Penalties

MOST PENALTY MINUTES:
27 — Gordie Howe in 23GP
21 — Gus Mortson in 9GP
16 — Harry Howell in 7GP

Goaltenders

MOST GAMES PLAYED:
13 — Glenn Hall from 1955-1969
11 — Terry Sawchuk from 1950-1968
8 — Jacques Plante from 1956-1970
— Patrick Roy from 1988-1998
6 — Tony Esposito from 1970-1980
— Ed Giacomin from 1967-1973
— Grant Fuhr from 1982-1989

MOST MINUTES PLAYED:
467 — Terry Sawchuk in 11GP
421 — Glenn Hall in 13GP
370 — Jacques Plante in 8GP
209 — Turk Broda in 4GP
190 — Patrick Roy in 8GP
182 — Ed Giacomin in 6GP
177 — Grant Fuhr in 6GP

MOST GOALS AGAINST:
24 — Patrick Roy in 8GP
22 — Glenn Hall in 13GP
21 — Mike Vernon in 5GP
19 — Terry Sawchuk in 11GP
18 — Jacques Plante in 8GP
— Andy Moog in 4GP

BEST GOALS-AGAINST-AVERAGE AMONG THOSE WITH AT LEAST TWO GAMES PLAYED:
0.68 — Gilles Villemure in 3GP
1.02 — Frank Brimsek in 2GP
1.59 — Johnny Bower in 4GP
1.64 — Gump Worsley in 4GP
1.98 — Gerry McNeil in 3GP
2.03 — Don Edwards in 2GP
2.44 — Terry Sawchuk in 11GP

The 1991-92 All-Rookie team included future superstar netminder Dominik Hasek (bottom); forwards Gilbert Dionne (top row, left), Kevin Todd (middle row, left) and Tony Amonte (middle row, right); and the Detroit blueline tandem of Vladimir Konstantinov (center) and Nicklas Lidstrom (top row, right).

Hockey Hall of Fame

(Year of induction is listed after each Honored Members name)

The traditional three-year waiting period was waived for Mario Lemieux, allowing him to enter the Hockey Hall of Fame just a few months after retiring in 1997.

Location: BCE Place, at the corner of Front and Yonge Streets in the heart of downtown Toronto. Easy access from all major highways running into Toronto. Close to TTC and Union Station.

Telephone: administration (416) 360-7735; information (416) 360-7765.

Summer and Christmas/March break hours: Monday to Saturday 9:30 a.m. to 6 p.m.; Sunday 10:00 a.m. to 6 p.m.

Fall/Winter/Spring hours (except Christmas/March break): Monday to Friday 10 a.m. to 5 p.m.; Saturday 9:30 a.m. to 6 p.m.; Sunday 10:30 a.m. to 5 p.m.

The Hockey Hall of Fame can be booked for private functions after hours.

Website address: www.hhof.com

History: The Hockey Hall of Fame was established in 1943. Members were first honored in 1945. On August 26, 1961, the Hockey Hall of Fame opened its doors to the public in a building located on the grounds of the Canadian National Exhibition in Toronto. The Hockey Hall of Fame relocated to its new site at BCE Place and welcomed the hockey world on June 18, 1993.

Honor Roll: There are 309 Honored Members in the Hockey Hall of Fame. 212 have been inducted as players, 84 as builders and 13 as Referees/Linesmen. In addition, there are 56 media honorees.

Sponsors: Special thanks to Blockbuster Video, Bell Canada, Coca-Cola Canada, Household Finance, Ford of Canada, IBM Canada, Imperial Oil, International Ice Hockey Federation, Kodak Canada, Molson Breweries, National Hockey League, London Life, TSN/RDS and The Toronto Sun.

PLAYERS

Abel, Sidney Gerald 1969
* Adams, John James "Jack" 1959
Apps, Charles Joseph Sylvanus "Syl" 1961
Armstrong, George Edward 1975
* Bailey, Irvine Wallace "Ace" 1975
* Bain, Donald H. "Dan" 1945
* Baker, Hobart "Hobey" 1945
Barber, William Charles "Bill" 1990
* Barry, Martin J. "Marty" 1965
Bathgate, Andrew James "Andy" 1978
* Bauer, Robert Theodore "Bobby" 1996
Béliveau, Jean Arthur 1972
* Benedict, Clinton S. 1965
* Bentley, Douglas Wagner 1964
* Bentley, Maxwell H. L. 1966
* Blake, Hector Toe 1966
Boivin, Leo Joseph 1986
* Boon, Richard R. "Dickie" 1952
Bossy, Michael 1991
Bouchard, Butch Joseph "Butch" 1966
* Boucher, Frank 1958
* Boucher, George "Buck" 1960
Bower, John William 1976
* Bowie, Russell 1945
Brimsek, Francis Charles 1966
* Broadbent, Harry L. "Punch" 1962
* Broda, Walter Edward "Turk" 1967
Bucyk, John Paul 1981
* Burch, Billy 1974
* Cameron, Harold Hugh "Harry" 1962
Cheevers, Gerald Michael "Gerry" 1985
* Clancy, Francis Michael "King" 1958
* Clapper, Aubrey "Dit" 1947
Clarke, Robert "Bobby" 1987
* Cleghorn, Sprague 1958
* Colville, Neil MacNeil 1967
* Conacher, Charles W. 1961
* Conacher, Lionel Pretoria 1994
* Connell, Alex 1958
* Cook, Fred "Bun" 1995
* Cook, William Osser 1952
Coulter, Arthur Edmund 1974
Cournoyer, Yvan Serge 1982
* Cowley, William Mailes 1968
* Crawford, Samuel Russell "Rusty" 1962
* Darragh, John Proctor "Jack" 1962
* Davidson, Allan M. "Scotty" 1950
* Day, Clarence Henry Hap 1961
Delvecchio, Alex 1977
* Denneny, Cyril "Cy" 1959
Dionne, Marcel 1992
* Drillon, Gordon Arthur 1975
* Drinkwater, Charles Graham 1950
Dryden, Kenneth Wayne 1983
Dumart, Woodrow "Woody" 1992
* Dunderdale, Thomas 1974
* Durnan, William Ronald 1964
* Dutton, Mervyn A. "Red" 1958
* Dye, Cecil Henry "Babe" 1970
Esposito, Anthony James "Tony" 1988
Esposito, Philip Anthony 1984
* Farrell, Arthur F. 1965
Flaman, Ferdinand Charles "Fern" 1990
* Foyston, Frank 1958
* Frederickson, Frank 1958
Gadsby, William Alexander 1970
Gainey, Bob 1992
* Gardiner, Charles Robert "Chuck" 1945
* Gardiner, Herbert Martin "Herb" 1958
* Gardner, James Henry "Jimmy" 1962
Geoffrion, Jos. A. Bernard "Boom Boom" 1972
* Gerard, Eddie 1945
Giacomin, Edward "Eddie" 1987
Gilbert, Rodrigue Gabriel "Rod" 1982
* Gilmour, Hamilton Livingstone "Billy" 1962
* Goheen, Frank Xavier "Moose" 1952
* Goodfellow, Ebenezer R. "Ebbie" 1963
* Grant, Michael "Mike" 1950
* Green, Wilfred "Shorty" 1962
* Griffis, Silas Seth "Si" 1950
* Hainsworth, George 1961
Hall, Glenn Henry 1975
* Hall, Joseph Henry 1961
* Harvey, Douglas Norman 1973
* Hay, George 1958
* Hern, William Milton "Riley" 1962
* Hextall, Bryan Aldwyn 1969
* Holmes, Harry Hap 1972
* Hooper, Charles Thomas "Tom" 1962
Horner, George Reginald "Red" 1965
* Horton, Miles Gilbert "Tim" 1977
Howe, Gordon 1972
* Howe, Sydney Harris 1965
Howell, Henry Vernon "Harry" 1979
Hull, Robert Marvin 1983
* Hutton, John Bower "Bouse" 1962
* Hyland, Harry M. 1962
* Irvin, James Dickenson "Dick" 1958
* Jackson, Harvey "Busher" 1971
* Johnson, Ernest "Moose" 1952
* Johnson, Ivan "Ching" 1958
Johnson, Thomas Christian 1970
* Joliat, Aurel 1947
* Keats, Gordon "Duke" 1958
Kelly, Leonard Patrick "Red" 1969
Kennedy, Theodore Samuel "Teeder" 1966
Keon, David Michael 1986
Lach, Elmer James 1966
Lafleur, Guy Damien 1988
* Lalonde, Edouard Charles "Newsy" 1950
Laperriere, Jacques 1987
Lapointe, Guy 1993
Laprade, Edgar 1993
* Laviolette, Jean Baptiste "Jack" 1962
* Lehman, Hugh 1958
Lemaire, Jacques Gerard 1984
Lemieux, Mario 1997
* LeSueur, Percy 1961
* Lewis, Herbert A. 1989
Lindsay, Robert Blake Theodore "Ted" 1966
Lumley, Harry 1980
* MacKay, Duncan "Mickey" 1952
Mahovlich, Frank William 1981
* Malone, Joseph "Joe" 1950
* Mantha, Sylvio 1960
* Marshall, John "Jack" 1965
* Maxwell, Fred G. "Steamer" 1962
McDonald, Lanny 1992
* McGee, Frank 1945
* McGimsie, William George "Billy" 1962
* McNamara, George 1958
Mikita, Stanley 1983
Moore, Richard Winston 1974
* Moran, Patrick Joseph "Paddy" 1958
* Morenz, Howie 1945
* Mosienko, William "Billy" 1965
* Nighbor, Frank 1947
* Noble, Edward Reginald "Reg" 1962
* O'Connor, Herbert William "Buddy" 1988
* Oliver, Harry 1967
Olmstead, Murray Bert "Bert" 1985
Orr, Robert Gordon 1979
Parent, Bernard Marcel 1984
Park, Douglas Bradford "Brad" 1988
* Patrick, Joseph Lynn 1980
* Patrick, Lester 1947
Perreault, Gilbert 1990
* Phillips, Tommy 1945
Pilote, Joseph Albert Pierre Paul 1975
* Pitre, Didier "Pit" 1962
* Plante, Joseph Jacques Omer 1978
Potvin, Denis 1991
* Pratt, Walter "Babe" 1966
* Primeau, A. Joseph 1963
Pronovost, Joseph René Marcel 1978
Pulford, Bob 1991
* Pulford, Harvey 1945
Quackenbush, Hubert George "Bill" 1976
* Rankin, Frank 1961

Ratelle, Joseph Gilbert Yvan Jean "Jean" 1985
Rayner, Claude Earl "Chuck" 1973
Reardon, Kenneth Joseph 1966
Richard, Joseph Henri 1979
Richard, Joseph Henri Maurice "Rocket" 1961
* Richardson, George Taylor 1950
* Roberts, Gordon 1971
Robinson, Larry 1995
* Ross, Arthur Howie 1945
* Russel, Blair 1965
* Russell, Ernest 1965
* Ruttan, J.D. "Jack" 1962
Salming, Borje Anders 1996
Savard, Serge A. 1986
* Sawchuk, Terrance Gordon "Terry" 1971
* Scanlan, Fred 1965
Schmidt, Milton Conrad "Milt" 1961
* Schriner, David "Sweeney" 1962
* Seibert, Earl Walter 1963
* Seibert, Oliver Levi 1961
* Shore, Edward W. "Eddie" 1947
Shutt, Stephen 1993
* Siebert, Albert C. "Babe" 1964
* Simpson, Harold Edward "Bullet Joe" 1962
Sittler, Darryl Glen 1989
* Smith, Alfred E. 1962
Smith, Clint 1991
* Smith, Reginald "Hooley" 1972
* Smith, Thomas James 1973
Smith, William John "Billy" 1993
Stanley, Allan Herbert 1981
* Stanley, Russell "Barney" 1962
* Stewart, John Sherratt "Black Jack" 1964
* Stewart, Nelson "Nels" 1962
* Stuart, Bruce 1961
* Stuart, Hod 1945
* Taylor, Frederic "Cyclone" (O.B.E.) 1947
* Thompson, Cecil R. "Tiny" 1959
Tretiak, Vladislav 1989
* Trihey, Col. Harry J. 1950
Trottier, Bryan 1997
Ullman, Norman V. Alexander "Norm" 1982
* Vezina, Georges 1945
* Walker, John Phillip "Jack" 1960
* Walsh, Martin "Marty" 1962
* Watson, Harry E. 1962
Watson, Harry 1994
* Weiland, Ralph "Cooney" 1971
* Westwick, Harry 1962
* Whitcroft, Fred 1962
* Wilson, Gordon Allan "Phat" 1962
Worsley, Lorne John "Gump" 1980
* Worters, Roy 1969

BUILDERS

Adams, Charles 1960
* Adams, Weston W. 1972
* Aheam, Thomas Franklin "Frank" 1962
* Ahearne, John Francis "Bunny" 1977
* Allan, Sir Montagu (C.V.O.) 1945
Allen, Keith 1992
Arbour, Alger Joseph "Al" 1996
* Ballard, Harold Edwin 1977
* Bauer, Father David 1989
* Bickell, John Paris 1978
Bowman, Scott 1991
* Brown, George V. 1961
* Brown, Walter A. 1962
* Buckland, Frank 1975
Butterfield, Jack Arlington 1980
* Calder, Frank 1947
* Campbell, Angus D. 1964
* Campbell, Clarence Sutherland 1966
* Cattarinich, Joseph 1977
* Dandurand, Joseph Viateur "Leo" 1963
* Dilio, Francis Paul 1964
* Dudley, George S. 1958
* Dunn, James A. 1968
Francis, Emile 1982
* Gibson, Dr. John L. "Jack" 1976
* Gorman, Thomas Patrick "Tommy" 1963
* Griffiths, Frank A. 1993
* Hanley, William 1986
* Hay, Charles 1974
* Hendy, James C. 1968
* Hewitt, Foster 1965
* Hewitt, William Abraham 1947
* Hume, Fred J. 1962
* Imlach, George "Punch" 1984
Ivan, Thomas N. 1974
* Jennings, William M. 1975
* Johnson, Bob 1992
* Juckes, Gordon W. 1979
* Kilpatrick, Gen. John Reed 1960
* Knox, Seymour H. III 1993
* Leader, George Alfred 1969
LeBel, Robert 1970
* Lockhart, Thomas F. 1965
* Loicq, Paul 1961
* Mariucci, John 1985
Mathers, Frank 1992
* McLaughlin, Major Frederic 1963
* Milford, John "Jake" 1984
Molson, Hon. Hartland de Montarville 1973
* Nelson, Francis 1947
* Norris, Bruce A. 1969
* Norris, Sr., James 1958
* Norris, James Dougan 1962
* Northey, William M. 1947
* O'Brien, John Ambrose 1962
O'Neill, Brian 1994
* Page, Fred 1993
* Patrick, Frank 1958
* Pickard, Allan W. 1958
* Pilous, Rudy 1985
Poile, Norman "Bud" 1990
Pollock, Samuel Patterson Smyth 1978
* Raymond, Sen. Donat 1958
* Robertson, John Ross 1947
* Robinson, Claude C. 1947
* Ross, Philip D. 1976
Sabetzki, Dr. Gunther 1995
Sather, Glen 1997
* Selke, Frank J. 1960
Sinden, Harry James 1983
* Smith, Frank D. 1962
* Smythe, Conn 1958
Snider, Edward M. 1988
* Stanley of Preston, Lord (G.C.B.) 1945
* Sutherland, Cap. James T. 1947
* Tarasov, Anatoli V. 1974
Torrey, Bill 1995
* Turner, Lloyd 1958
* Tutt, William Thayer 1978
* Voss, Carl Potter 1974
* Waghorn, Fred C. 1961
* Wirtz, Arthur Michael 1971
Wirtz, William W. "Bill" 1976
Ziegler, John A. Jr. 1987

REFEREES/LINESMEN

Armstrong, Neil 1991
Ashley, John George 1981
Chadwick, William L. 1964
D'Amico, John 1993
* Elliott, Chaucer 1961
* Hayes, George William 1988
* Hewitson, Robert W. 1963
* Ion, Fred J. "Mickey" 1961
Pavelich, Matt 1987
* Rodden, Michael J. "Mike" 1962
* Smeaton, J. Cooper 1961
Storey, Roy Alvin "Red" 1967
Udvari, Frank Joseph 1973

Elmer Ferguson Memorial Award Winners

In recognition of distinguished members of the newspaper profession whose words have brought honor to journalism and to hockey. Selected by the Professional Hockey Writers' Association.

* Barton, Charlie, Buffalo-Courier Express 1985
* Beauchamp, Jacques, Montreal Matin/Journal de Montréal 1984
* Brennan, Bill, Detroit News 1987
* Burchard, Jim, New York World Telegram 1984
* Burnett, Red, Toronto Star 1984
* Carroll, Dink, Montreal Gazette 1984
Coleman, Jim, Southam Newspapers 1984
* Damata, Ted, Chicago Tribune 1984
Delano, Hugh, New York Post 1991
Desjardins, Marcel, Montréal La Presse 1984
* Dulmage, Jack, Windsor Star 1984
Dunnell, Milt, Toronto Star 1984
* Ferguson, Elmer, Montreal Herald/Star 1984
Fisher, Red, Montreal Star/Gazette 1985
* Fitzgerald, Tom, Boston Globe 1984
Frayne, Trent, Toronto Telegram/Globe and Mail/Sun 1984
Gatecliff, Jack, St. Catherines Standard 1995
Gross, George, Toronto Telegram/Sun 1985
Johnston, Dick, Buffalo News 1986
* Laney, Al, New York Herald-Tribune 1984
Larochelle, Claude, Le Soleil 1989
L'Esperance, Zotique, Journal de Montréal/le Petit Journal 1985
* Mayer, Charles, le Journal de Montréal/la Patrie 1985
MacLeod, Rex, Toronto Globe and Mail/Star 1987
McKenzie, Ken, The Hockey News 1997
Monahan, Leo, Boston Daily Record/Record-American/Herald American 1986
Moriarty, Tim, UPI/Newsday 1986
* Nichols, Joe, New York Times 1984
* O'Brien, Andy, Weekend Magazine 1985
Orr, Frank, Toronto Star 1989
Olan, Ben, New York Associated Press 1987
* O'Meara, Basil, Montreal Star 1984
Proudfoot, Jim, Toronto Star 1988
Raymond, Bertrand, le Journal de Montréal 1990
Rosa, Fran, Boston Globe 1987
Strachan, Al, Globe and Mail/Toronto Sun 1993
* Vipond, Jim, Toronto Globe and Mail 1984
Walter, Lewis, Detroit Times 1984
Young, Scott, Toronto Globe and Mail/Telegram 1988

Foster Hewitt Memorial Award Winners

In recognition of members of the radio and television industry who made outstanding contributions to their profession and the game during their career in hockey broadcasting. Selected by the NHL Broadcasters' Association.

Cole, Bob, Hockey Night in Canada 1996
Cusick, Fred, Boston 1984
* Darling, Ted, Buffalo 1994
* Gallivan, Danny, Montreal 1984
Hart, Gene, Philadelphia 1997
* Hewitt, Foster, Toronto 1984
Irvin, Dick, Montreal 1988
* Kelly, Dan, St. Louis 1989
Lecavelier, René, Montreal 1984
Lynch, Budd, Detroit 1985
Martyn, Bruce, Detroit 1991
McDonald, Jiggs, Los Angeles, Atlanta, NY Islanders 1990
McFarlane, Brian, Hockey Night in Canada 1995
* McKnight, Wes, Toronto 1986
Pettit, Lloyd, Chicago 1986
Robson, Jim, Vancouver 1992
Shaver, Al, Minnesota 1993
* Smith, Doug, Montreal 1985
Wilson, Bob, Boston 1987

United States Hockey Hall of Fame

The United States Hockey Hall of Fame is located in Eveleth, Minnesota, 60 miles north of Duluth, on Highway 53. The facility is open Monday to Saturday 9 a.m. to 5 p.m. and Sundays 11 a.m to 5 p.m.; Individual Admission $4.00; Family rate $7.00. Call for any further information: 1-800-443-7825. Website address: www.ushockeyhall.com

The Hall was dedicated and opened on June 21, 1973, largely as the result of the work of D. Kelly Campbell, Chairman of the Eveleth Civic Association's Project H Committee. There are now 96 enshrinees consisting of 57 players, 22 coaches, 16 administrators, and one referee. New members are inducted annually in October and must have made a significant contribution toward hockey in the United States through the vehicle of their careers. Support for the Hall comes from sponsorship and membership programs, grants from the hockey community, and government agencies.

PLAYERS

* Abel, Clarence "Taffy"
* Baker, Hobart "Hobey"
Bartholome, Earl
* Bessone, Peter
Blake, Robert
Boucha, Henry
Brimsek, Frank
Cavanagh, Joe
* Chaisson, Ray
* Chase, John P.
Christian, Roger
Christian, William "Bill"
Cleary, Robert
Cleary, William
* Conroy, Anthony
Dahlstrom, Carl "Cully"
* Desjardins, Victor
* Desmond, Richard
* Dill, Robert
Everett, Doug
Ftorek, Robbie
* Garrison, John B.
Garrity, Jack
* Goheen, Frank "Moose"
Grant, Wally
* Harding, Austin "Austie"
* Iglehart, Stewart
* Johnson, Virgil
* Karakas, Mike
Kirrane, Jack
* Lane, Myles J.
Langevin, David R.
Larson, Reed
* Linder, Joseph
* LoPresti, Sam L.
* Mariucci, John
Matchefts, John
Mayasich, John
McCartan, Jack
Moe, William
Morrow, Ken
* Moseley, Fred
* Murray, Hugh "Muzz" Sr.
* Nelson, Hubert "Hub"
* Nyrop, William D.
Olson , Eddie
* Owen, Jr., George
* Palmer, Winthrop
Paradise, Robert
Purpur, Clifford "Fido"
Riley, William
* Romnes, Elwin "Doc"
Rondeau, Richard
Sheehy, Timothy K.
* Williams, Thomas
* Winters, Frank "Coddy"
* Yackel, Ken

COACHES

* Almquist, Oscar
Bessone, Amo
Brooks, Herbert
Ceglarski, Len
* Fullerton, James
Gambucci, Sergio
* Gordon, Malcolm K.
Harkness, Nevin D. "Ned"
Heyliger, Victor
Holt, Charles E.
Ikola, Willard
* Jeremiah, Edward J.
* Johnson, Bob
* Kelley, John "Snooks"
Kelley, John H. "Jack"
Patrick, Craig
Pleban, John "Connie"
Riley, Jack
* Ross, Larry
* Thompson, Clifford, R.
* Stewart, William
* Winsor, Alfred "Ralph"

ADMINISTRATORS

* Brown, George V.
* Brown, Walter A.
Bush, Walter
Clark, Donald
Claypool, James
* Gibson, J.C. "Doc"
* Jennings, William M.
* Kahler, Nick
* Lockhart, Thomas F.
Marvin, Cal
Ridder, Robert
Schulz, Charles M.
Trumble, Harold
* Tutt, William Thayer
Wirtz, William W. "Bill"
* Wright, Lyle Z.

REFEREE

Chadwick, William

*Deceased

Dave Langevin learned the game of hockey on the playgrounds of St. Paul, Minnesota. After earning all-American honors at the University of Minnesota-Duluth in 1974, he turned pro with the Edmonton Oilers of the WHA before joining the New York Islanders for the 1979-80 season. Langevin played on four consecutive Stanley Cup championship teams with the Islanders.

1998 Stanley Cup Playoffs

Results

CONFERENCE QUARTER-FINALS
(Best-of-seven series)

Eastern Conference

Series 'A'

Wed. Apr. 22	Ottawa 2	at	New Jersey 1 OT
Fri. Apr. 24	Ottawa 1	at	New Jersey 3
Sun. Apr. 26	New Jersey 1	at	Ottawa 2 OT
Tue. Apr. 28	New Jersey 3	at	Ottawa 4
Thu. Apr. 30	Ottawa 1	at	New Jersey 3
Sat. May 2	New Jersey 1	at	Ottawa 3

Ottawa Won Series 4-2

Series 'B'

Thu. Apr. 23	Montreal 3	at	Pittsburgh 2 OT
Sat. Apr. 25	Montreal 1	at	Pittsburgh 4
Mon. Apr. 27	Pittsburgh 1	at	Montreal 3
Wed. Apr. 29	Pittsburgh 6	at	Montreal 3
Fri. May 1	Montreal 5	at	Pittsburgh 2
Sun. May 3	Pittsburgh 0	at	Montreal 3

Montreal Won Series 4-2

Series 'C'

Wed. Apr. 22	Buffalo 3	at	Philadelphia 2
Fri. Apr. 24	Buffalo 2	at	Philadelphia 3
Mon. Apr. 27	Philadelphia 1	at	Buffalo 6
Wed. Apr. 29	Philadelphia 1	at	Buffalo 4
Fri. May 1	Buffalo 3	at	Philadelphia 2 OT

Buffalo Won Series 4-1

Series 'D'

Wed. Apr. 22	Boston 1	at	Washington 3
Fri. Apr. 24	Boston 4	at	Washington 3 OT
Sun. Apr. 26	Washington 3	at	Boston 2 OT
Tue. Apr. 28	Washington 3	at	Boston 0
Fri. May 1	Boston 4	at	Washington 0
Sun. May 3	Washington 3	at	Boston 2 OT

Washington Won Series 4-2

Western Conference

Series 'E'

Wed. Apr. 22	San Jose 1	at	Dallas 4
Fri. Apr. 24	San Jose 2	at	Dallas 5
Sun. Apr. 26	Dallas 1	at	San Jose 4
Tue. Apr. 28	Dallas 0	at	San Jose 1 OT
Thu. Apr. 30	San Jose 2	at	Dallas 3
Sat. May 2	Dallas 3	at	San Jose 2 OT

Dallas Won Series 4-2

Series 'F'

Wed. Apr. 22	Edmonton 3	at	Colorado 2
Fri. Apr. 24	Edmonton 2	at	Colorado 5
Sun. Apr. 26	Colorado 5	at	Edmonton 4 OT
Tue. Apr. 28	Colorado 3	at	Edmonton 1
Thu. Apr. 30	Edmonton 3	at	Colorado 1
Sat. May 2	Colorado 0	at	Edmonton 2
Mon. May 4	Edmonton 4	at	Colorado 0

Edmonton Won Series 4-3

Series 'G'

Wed. Apr. 22	Phoenix 3	at	Detroit 6
Fri. Apr. 24	Phoenix 7	at	Detroit 4
Sun. Apr. 26	Detroit 2	at	Phoenix 3
Tue. Apr. 28	Detroit 4	at	Phoenix 2
Thu. Apr. 30	Phoenix 1	at	Detroit 3
Sun. May 3	Detroit 5	at	Phoenix 2

Detroit Won Series 4-2

Series 'H'

Thu. Apr. 23	Los Angeles 3	at	St. Louis 8
Sat. Apr. 25	Los Angeles 1	at	St. Louis 2
Mon. Apr. 27	St. Louis 4	at	Los Angeles 3
Wed. Apr. 29	St. Louis 2	at	Los Angeles 1

St. Louis Won Series 4-0

CONFERENCE SEMI-FINALS
(Best-of-seven series)

Eastern Conference

Series 'I'

Thu. May 7	Ottawa 2	at	Washington 4
Sat. May 9	Ottawa 1	at	Washington 6
Mon. May 11	Washington 3	at	Ottawa 4
Wed. May 13	Washington 2	at	Ottawa 0
Fri. May 15	Ottawa 0	at	Washington 3

Washington Won Series 4-1

Series 'J'

Fri. May 8	Montreal 2	at	Buffalo 3 OT
Sun. May 10	Montreal 3	at	Buffalo 6
Tue. May 12	Buffalo 5	at	Montreal 4 OT
Thu. May 14	Buffalo 3	at	Montreal 1

Buffalo Won Series 4-0

Western Conference

Series 'K'

Thu. May 7	Edmonton 1	at	Dallas 3
Sat. May 9	Edmonton 2	at	Dallas 0
Mon. May 11	Dallas 1	at	Edmonton 0 OT
Wed. May 13	Dallas 3	at	Edmonton 1
Sat. May 16	Edmonton 1	at	Dallas 2

Dallas Won Series 4-1

Series 'L'

Fri. May 8	St. Louis 4	at	Detroit 2
Sun. May 10	St. Louis 1	at	Detroit 6
Tue. May 12	Detroit 3	at	St. Louis 2 OT
Thu. May 14	Detroit 5	at	St. Louis 2
Sun. May 17	St. Louis 3	at	Detroit 1
Tue. May 19	Detroit 6	at	St. Louis 1

Detroit Won Series 4-2

CONFERENCE FINALS
(Best-of-seven series)

Eastern Conference

Series 'M'

Sat. May 23	Buffalo 2	at	Washington 0
Mon. May 25	Buffalo 2	at	Washington 3 OT
Thu. May 28	Washington 4	at	Buffalo 3 OT
Sat. May 30	Washington 2	at	Buffalo 0
Tue. Jun. 2	Buffalo 2	at	Washington 1
Thu. Jun. 4	Washington 3	at	Buffalo 2 OT

Washington Won Series 4-2

Western Conference

Series 'N'

Sun. May 24	Detroit 2	at	Dallas 0
Tue. May 26	Detroit 1	at	Dallas 3
Fri. May 29	Dallas 3	at	Detroit 5
Sun. May 31	Dallas 2	at	Detroit 3
Wed. Jun. 3	Detroit 2	at	Dallas 3 OT
Fri. Jun. 5	Dallas 0	at	Detroit 2

Detroit Won Series 4-2

STANLEY CUP CHAMPIONSHIP
(Best-of-seven series)

Series 'O'

Tue. Jun. 9	Washington 1	at	Detroit 2
Thu. Jun. 11	Washington 4	at	Detroit 5 OT
Sat. Jun. 13	Detroit 2	at	Washington 1
Tue. Jun. 16	Detroit 4	at	Washington 1

Detroit Won Series 4-0

Team Playoff Records

	GP	W	L	GF	GA	%
Detroit	22	16	6	75	49	.727
Washington	21	12	9	53	44	.571
Buffalo	15	10	5	46	32	.667
Dallas	17	10	7	36	32	.588
St. Louis	10	6	4	29	31	.600
Ottawa	11	5	6	20	30	.455
Edmonton	12	5	7	24	25	.417
Montreal	10	4	6	28	32	.400
Colorado	7	3	4	16	19	.429
New Jersey	6	2	4	12	13	.333
Boston	6	2	4	13	15	.333
Pittsburgh	6	2	4	15	18	.333
San Jose	6	2	4	12	16	.333
Phoenix	6	2	4	18	24	.333
Philadelphia	5	1	4	9	18	.200
Los Angeles	4	0	4	8	16	.000

Individual Leaders

Abbreviations: * – rookie eligible for Calder Trophy; **A** – assists; **G** – goals; **GP** – Games Played; **OT** – overtime goals; **GW** – game-winning goals; **PIM** – penalties in minutes; **PP** – power play goals; **Pts** – points; **S** – shots on goal; **SH** – short-handed goals; **%** – percentage shots resulting in goals; **+/–** – difference between Goals For (**GF**) scored when a player is on the ice with his team at even strength or short-handed and Goals Against (**GA**) scored when the same player is on the ice with his team at even strength or on a power play.

Playoff Scoring Leaders

Player	Team	GP	G	A	Pts	+/–	PIM	PP	SH	GW	OT	S	%
Steve Yzerman	Detroit	22	6	18	24	10	22	3	1	0	0	65	9.2
Sergei Fedorov	Detroit	22	10	10	20	0	12	2	1	1	0	86	11.6
Tomas Holmstrom	Detroit	22	7	12	19	9	16	2	0	0	0	27	25.9
Nicklas Lidstrom	Detroit	22	6	13	19	12	8	2	0	2	0	59	10.2
Joe Juneau	Washington	21	7	10	17	6	8	1	1	4	2	54	13.0
Adam Oates	Washington	21	6	11	17	8	8	1	1	1	0	31	19.4
Martin Lapointe	Detroit	21	9	6	15	6	20	2	1	1	0	55	16.4
Larry Murphy	Detroit	22	3	12	15	12	2	1	2	1	0	36	8.3
Vyacheslav Kozlov	Detroit	22	6	8	14	4	10	1	0	4	0	47	12.8
Mike Modano	Dallas	17	4	10	14	4	12	1	0	1	0	49	8.2
Andrei Nikolishin	Washington	21	1	13	14	4	12	1	0	0	0	29	3.4
Matthew Barnaby	Buffalo	15	7	6	13	6	22	3	0	1	0	25	28.0
Brian Bellows	Washington	21	6	7	13	6	6	2	0	1	1	62	9.7
Donald Audette	Buffalo	15	5	8	13	–4	10	3	0	2	0	31	16.1
Igor Larionov	Detroit	22	3	10	13	5	12	0	0	0	0	27	11.1
Peter Bondra	Washington	17	7	5	12	4	12	3	0	2	1	48	14.6
Mark Recchi	Montreal	10	4	8	12	2	6	0	0	2	0	22	18.2
Sergei Gonchar	Washington	21	7	4	11	2	30	3	1	2	0	37	18.9
Peter Forsberg	Colorado	7	6	5	11	3	12	2	0	0	0	18	33.3
Brian Holzinger	Buffalo	15	4	7	11	–2	18	1	1	0	0	24	16.7
Dixon Ward	Buffalo	15	3	8	11	8	6	0	0	0	0	29	10.3
Darren McCarty	Detroit	22	3	8	11	9	34	0	0	1	0	46	6.5
Jason Woolley	Buffalo	15	2	9	11	8	12	1	0	1	0	32	6.3

Playoff Defensemen Scoring Leaders

Player	Team	GP	G	A	Pts	+/–	PIM	PP	SH	GW	OT	S	%
Nicklas Lidstrom	Detroit	22	6	13	19	12	8	2	0	2	0	59	10.2
Larry Murphy	Detroit	22	3	12	15	12	2	1	2	1	0	36	8.3
Sergei Gonchar	Washington	21	7	4	11	2	30	3	1	2	0	37	18.9
Jason Woolley	Buffalo	15	2	9	11	8	12	1	0	1	0	32	6.3
Calle Johansson	Washington	21	2	8	10	9	16	0	0	0	0	42	4.8
Chris Pronger	St. Louis	10	1	9	10	–2	26	0	0	0	0	24	4.2
Sergei Zubov	Dallas	17	4	5	9	3	2	3	0	1	0	34	11.8
Al MacInnis	St. Louis	8	2	6	8	1	12	1	0	0	0	27	7.4
Vladimir Malakhov	Montreal	9	3	4	7	–3	10	2	0	0	0	19	15.8
Oleg Tverdovsky	Phoenix	6	0	7	7	–2	0	0	0	0	0	7	.0
Sandis Ozolinsh	Colorado	7	0	7	7	–3	14	0	0	0	0	19	.0

GOALTENDING LEADERS

Goals Against Average

Goaltender	Team	GPI	Mins.	GA	Avg.
Ed Belfour	Dallas	17	1039	31	1.79
Curtis Joseph	Edmonton	12	716	23	1.93
Olaf Kolzig	Washington	21	1351	44	1.95
Dominik Hasek	Buffalo	15	948	32	2.03
Chris Osgood	Detroit	22	1361	48	2.12

Wins

Goaltender	Team	GPI	Mins.	W	L
Chris Osgood	Detroit	22	1361	16	6
Olaf Kolzig	Washington	21	1351	12	9
Dominik Hasek	Buffalo	15	948	10	5
Ed Belfour	Dallas	17	1039	10	7
Grant Fuhr	St. Louis	10	616	6	4

Save Percentage

Goaltender	Team	GPI	Mins.	GA	SA	S%	W	L
Olaf Kolzig	Washington	21	1351	44	740	.941	12	9
Dominik Hasek	Buffalo	15	948	32	514	.938	10	5
Curtis Joseph	Edmonton	12	716	23	319	.928	5	7
Ed Belfour	Dallas	17	1039	31	399	.922	10	7
Chris Osgood	Detroit	22	1361	48	588	.918	16	6

Shutouts

Goaltender	Team	GPI	Mins.	SO
Olaf Kolzig	Washington	21	1351	4
Curtis Joseph	Edmonton	12	716	3
Chris Osgood	Detroit	22	1361	2
Mike Vernon	San Jose	6	348	1
Byron Dafoe	Boston	6	422	1
Andy Moog	Montreal	9	474	1
Dominik Hasek	Buffalo	15	948	1
Ed Belfour	Dallas	17	1039	1

Goal Scoring

Name	Team	GP	G
Sergei Fedorov	Detroit	22	10
Martin Lapointe	Detroit	21	9
Jim Campbell	St. Louis	10	7
Daniel Alfredsson	Ottawa	11	7
Bill Guerin	Edmonton	12	7
Matthew Barnaby	Buffalo	15	7
Peter Bondra	Washington	17	7
*Richard Zednik	Washington	17	7
Joe Juneau	Washington	21	7
Sergei Gonchar	Washington	21	7
Tomas Holmstrom	Detroit	22	7

Assists

Name	Team	GP	A
Steve Yzerman	Detroit	22	18
Andrei Nikolishin	Washington	21	13
Nicklas Lidstrom	Detroit	22	13
Larry Murphy	Detroit	22	12
Tomas Holmstrom	Detroit	22	12
Adam Oates	Washington	21	11

Power-play Goals

Name	Team	GP	PP
Jim Campbell	St. Louis	10	4
Bill Guerin	Edmonton	12	4
Miroslav Satan	Buffalo	14	4
Rick Tocchet	Phoenix	6	3
Doug Brown	Detroit	9	3
Alexei Yashin	Ottawa	11	3
Donald Audette	Buffalo	15	3
Matthew Barnaby	Buffalo	15	3
Peter Bondra	Washington	17	3
Sergei Zubov	Dallas	17	3
Brendan Shanahan	Detroit	20	3
Sergei Gonchar	Washington	21	3
Steve Yzerman	Detroit	22	3

Game-winning Goals

Name	Team	GP	GW
Joe Juneau	Washington	21	4
Vyacheslav Kozlov	Detroit	22	4
Michal Grosek	Buffalo	15	3
Jeremy Roenick	Phoenix	6	2
Joe Sakic	Colorado	6	2
Mark Recchi	Montreal	10	2
Jim Campbell	St. Louis	10	2

Short-handed Goals

Name	Team	GP	SH
Jeremy Roenick	Phoenix	6	2
Larry Murphy	Detroit	22	2

Overtime Goals

Name	Team	GP	OT
Joe Juneau	Washington	21	2
Joe Sakic	Colorado	6	1
Darren Van Impe	Boston	6	1
*Andrei Zyuzin	San Jose	6	1
Benoit Brunet	Montreal	8	1
Bruce Gardiner	Ottawa	11	1
Alexei Yashin	Ottawa	11	1
Todd Krygier	Washington	13	1
Michael Peca	Buffalo	13	1
Geoff Sanderson	Buffalo	14	1
Michal Grosek	Buffalo	15	1
Jamie Langenbrunner	Dallas	16	1
Benoit Hogue	Dallas	17	1
Peter Bondra	Washington	17	1
Mike Keane	Dallas	17	1
Kris Draper	Detroit	19	1
Brendan Shanahan	Detroit	20	1
Brian Bellows	Washington	21	1

Shots

Name	Team	GP	S
Sergei Fedorov	Detroit	22	86
Steve Yzerman	Detroit	22	65
Brian Bellows	Washington	21	62
Brendan Shanahan	Detroit	20	60
Nicklas Lidstrom	Detroit	22	59

Plus/Minus

Name	Team	GP	+/–
Larry Murphy	Detroit	22	12
Nicklas Lidstrom	Detroit	22	12
Steve Yzerman	Detroit	22	10

TEAMS' HOME-AND-ROAD RECORD

	Home						Road					
	GP	W	L	GF	GA	%	GP	W	L	GF	GA	%
DET	11	8	3	39	29	.727	11	8	3	36	20	.727
WSH	11	5	6	25	24	.455	10	7	3	28	20	.700
BUF	7	4	3	24	16	.571	8	6	2	22	16	.750
DAL	9	7	2	23	14	.778	8	3	5	13	18	.375
ST.L.	5	2	3	15	18	.400	5	4	1	14	13	.800
OTT	5	4	1	13	10	.800	6	1	5	7	20	.167
EDM	5	1	4	8	12	.200	7	4	3	16	13	.571
MTL	5	2	3	14	15	.400	5	2	3	14	17	.400
COL	4	1	3	8	12	.250	3	2	1	8	7	.667
N.J.	3	2	1	7	4	.667	3	0	3	5	9	.000
BOS	3	0	3	4	9	.000	3	2	1	9	6	.667
PIT	3	1	2	8	9	.333	3	1	2	7	9	.333
S.J.	3	2	1	7	4	.667	3	0	3	5	12	.000
PHO	3	1	2	7	11	.333	3	1	2	11	13	.333
PHI	3	1	2	7	8	.333	2	0	2	2	10	.000
L.A.	2	0	2	4	6	.000	2	0	2	4	10	.000
Total	**82**	**41**	**41**	**213**	**201**	**.500**	**82**	**41**	**41**	**201**	**213**	**.500**

TEAM PENALTIES

Abbreviations: GP – games played; **PEN** – total penalty minutes, including bench penalties; **BMI** – total bench penalty minutes; **AVG** – average penalty minutes per game.

Team	GP	PEN	BMI	AVG
PIT	6	70	0	11.7
OTT	11	135	2	12.3
BOS	6	75	0	12.5
MTL	10	148	0	14.8
DET	22	334	6	15.2
WSH	21	319	6	15.2
N.J.	6	92	0	15.3
DAL	17	300	4	17.6
BUF	15	268	2	17.9
PHI	5	90	4	18.0
ST.L.	10	185	4	18.5
EDM	12	245	4	20.4
PHO	6	127	0	21.2
S.J.	6	152	0	25.3
L.A.	4	108	0	27.0
COL	7	209	0	29.9
Total	**82**	**2857**	**32**	**34.8**

TEAMS' POWER-PLAY RECORD

Abbreviations: Adv-total advantages; **PPGF**-power play goals for; **%** arrived by dividing number of power-play goals by total advantages.

Home						Road					Overall				
	Team	GP	ADV	PPGF	%	Team	GP	ADV	PPGF	%	Team	GP	ADV	PPGF	%
1	OTT	5	22	7	31.8	BOS	3	17	4	23.5	PHO	6	33	6	18.2
2	PHO	3	18	4	22.2	DET	11	60	13	21.7	BUF	15	89	16	18.0
3	S.J.	3	20	4	20.0	WSH	10	40	8	20.0	ST.L.	10	75	13	17.3
4	BUF	7	44	8	18.2	BUF	8	45	8	17.8	S.J.	6	36	6	16.7
5	ST.L.	5	35	6	17.1	ST.L.	5	40	7	17.5	WSH	21	84	14	16.7
6	N.J.	3	12	2	16.7	PIT	3	21	3	14.3	OTT	11	51	8	15.7
7	COL	4	21	3	14.3	COL	3	14	2	14.3	DET	22	129	20	15.5
8	WSH	11	44	6	13.6	PHO	3	15	2	13.3	BOS	6	40	6	15.0
9	MTL	5	24	3	12.5	S.J.	3	16	2	12.5	COL	7	35	5	14.3
10	DAL	9	65	8	12.3	EDM	7	43	5	11.6	N.J.	6	23	3	13.0
11	EDM	5	29	3	10.3	MTL	5	26	3	11.5	PIT	6	33	4	12.1
12	DET	11	69	7	10.1	N.J.	3	11	1	9.1	MTL	10	50	6	12.0
13	BOS	3	23	2	8.7	PHI	2	12	1	8.3	EDM	12	72	8	11.1
14	PIT	3	12	1	8.3	DAL	8	35	2	5.7	DAL	17	100	10	10.0
15	PHI	3	24	2	8.3	OTT	6	29	1	3.4	PHI	5	36	3	8.3
16	L.A.	2	13	1	7.7	L.A.	2	16	0	.0	L.A.	4	29	1	3.4
Total		**82**	**475**	**67**	**14.1**		**82**	**440**	**62**	**14.1**		**82**	**915**	**129**	**14.1**

TEAMS' PENALTY KILLING RECORD

Abbreviations: TSH – Total times short-handed; **PPGA** – power-play goals against; **%** arrived by dividing times short minus power-play goals against by times short.

Home						Road					Overall				
	Team	GP	TSH	PPGA	%	Team	GP	TSH	PPGA	%	Team	GP	TSH	PPGA	%
1	N.J.	3	13	0	100.0	BUF	8	51	4	92.2	BUF	15	90	9	90.0
2	EDM	5	24	2	91.7	ST.L.	5	37	3	91.9	ST.L.	10	69	7	89.9
3	DAL	9	46	5	89.1	WSH	10	58	6	89.7	EDM	12	67	7	89.6
4	DET	11	62	7	88.7	BOS	3	9	1	88.9	DAL	17	93	11	88.2
5	S.J.	3	8	1	87.5	EDM	7	43	5	88.4	DET	22	119	14	88.2
6	ST.L.	5	32	4	87.5	MTL	5	25	3	88.0	WSH	21	115	15	87.0
7	BUF	7	39	5	87.2	DET	11	57	7	87.7	BOS	6	20	3	85.0
8	COL	4	28	4	85.7	DAL	8	47	6	87.2	COL	7	46	7	84.8
9	PIT	3	13	2	84.6	PHO	3	22	3	86.4	MTL	10	58	9	84.5
10	WSH	11	57	9	84.2	COL	3	18	3	83.3	N.J.	6	25	4	84.0
11	OTT	5	18	3	83.3	OTT	6	21	4	81.0	PHO	6	42	7	83.3
12	BOS	3	11	2	81.8	S.J.	3	30	6	80.0	OTT	11	39	7	82.1
13	MTL	5	33	6	81.8	PIT	3	14	3	78.6	S.J.	6	38	7	81.6
14	PHO	3	20	4	80.0	L.A.	2	18	4	77.8	PIT	6	27	5	81.5
15	L.A.	2	18	4	77.8	N.J.	3	12	4	66.7	L.A.	4	36	8	77.8
16	PHI	3	18	4	77.8	PHI	2	13	5	61.5	PHI	5	31	9	71.0
Total		**82**	**440**	**62**	**85.9**		**82**	**475**	**67**	**85.9**		**82**	**915**	**129**	**85.9**

SHORT-HANDED GOALS

For			Against		
Team	Games	Goals	Team	Games	Goals
DET	22	6	COL	7	0
PIT	6	3	N.J.	6	0
WSH	21	3	PIT	6	0
N.J.	6	2	BOS	6	0
PHO	6	2	PHO	6	0
BUF	15	2	L.A.	4	0
COL	7	1	BUF	15	1
ST.L.	10	1	EDM	12	1
OTT	11	1	S.J.	6	1
DAL	17	1	WSH	21	2
L.A.	4	0	DAL	17	2
PHI	5	0	PHI	5	2
BOS	6	0	DET	22	3
S.J.	6	0	MTL	10	3
MTL	10	0	ST.L.	10	3
EDM	12	0	OTT	11	4
Total	**82**	**22**	**Total**	**82**	**22**

Chris Osgood overcame his own shaky play to lead the Detroit Red Wings back into the Stanley Cup winners' circle with a command playoff performance in 1998.

Stanley Cup Record Book

History: The Stanley Cup, the oldest trophy competed for by professional athletes in North America, was donated by Frederick Arthur, Lord Stanley of Preston and son of the Earl of Derby, in 1893. Lord Stanley purchased the trophy for 10 guineas ($50 at that time) for presentation to the amateur hockey champions of Canada. Since 1910, when the National Hockey Association took possession of the Stanley Cup, the trophy has been the symbol of professional hockey supremacy. It has been competed for only by NHL teams since 1926 and has been under the exclusive control of the NHL since 1946.

Stanley Cup Standings

1918-98

(ranked by Cup wins)

Teams	Cup Wins	Yrs.	Series	Wins	Losses	Games	Wins	Losses	Ties	Goals For	Goals Against	Winning %
Montreal	23[1]	72	134[2]	85	48	638	381	249	8	1977	1591	.603
Toronto	13	58	96	51	45	444	210	230	4	1166	1246	.477
Detroit	9	47	87	49	38	430	222	207	1	1212	1140	.517
Boston	5	58	99	46	53	482	230	246	6	1418	1437	.483
Edmonton	5	15	41	31	10	206	132	74	0	826	641	.641
NY Rangers	4	48	86	42	44	386	183	195	8	1091	1114	.484
NY Islanders	4	17	43	30	13	218	128	90	0	748	650	.587
Chicago	3	52	89	40	49	406	187	214	5	1171	1298	.467
Philadelphia	2	24	53	31	22	274	145	129	0	878	832	.529
Pittsburgh	2	18	32	16	16	166	88	78	0	544	534	.530
Calgary[3]	1	21	32	12	20	156	69	87	0	529	573	.442
Colorado[4]	1	12	23	12	11	126	64	62	0	402	397	.508
New Jersey[5]	1	10	18	9	9	103	54	49	0	301	291	.524
St. Louis	0	28	47	19	28	246	111	135	0	710	808	.451
Buffalo	0	22	35	13	22	170	77	93	0	521	546	.453
Dallas[6]	0	21	38	17	21	204	99	105	0	644	677	.485
Los Angeles	0	20	30	10	20	146	55	91	0	467	584	.377
Vancouver	0	16	25	9	16	124	54	70	0	377	422	.435
Washington	0	15	25	10	15	137	64	73	0	434	433	.467
Phoenix[7]	0	13	15	2	13	75	24	51	0	212	294	.320
Carolina[8]	0	8	9	1	8	49	18	31	0	143	177	.367
Florida	0	2	5	3	2	27	13	14	0	71	70	.481
San Jose	0	3	5	2	3	31	13	18	0	86	128	.419
Anaheim	0	1	2	1	1	11	4	7	0	25	30	.364
Ottawa	0	2	3	1	2	18	8	10	0	33	44	.444
Tampa Bay	0	1	1	0	1	6	2	4	0	13	26	.333

1 Montreal also won the Stanley Cup in 1916.
2 1919 final incomplete due to influenza epidemic.
3 Includes totals of Atlanta 1972-80.
4 Includes totals of Quebec 1979-95.
5 Includes totals of Colorado Rockies 1976-82.
6 Includes totals of Minnesota 1967-93.
7 Includes totals of Winnipeg 1979-96.
8 Includes totals of Hartford 1979-97.

Stanley Cup Winners Prior to Formation of NHL in 1917

Season	Champions	Manager	Coach
1916-17	Seattle Metropolitans	Pete Muldoon	Pete Muldoon
1915-16	Montreal Canadiens	George Kennedy	George Kennedy
1914-15	Vancouver Millionaires	Frank Patrick	Frank Patrick
1913-14	Toronto Blueshirts	Jack Marshall	Scotty Davidson*
1912-13**	Quebec Bulldogs	M.J. Quinn	Joe Malone*
1911-12	Quebec Bulldogs	M.J. Quinn	C. Nolan
1910-11	Ottawa Senators		Bruce Stuart*
1909-10	Montreal Wanderers	R. R. Boon	Pud Glass*
1908-09	Ottawa Senators		Bruce Stuart*
1907-08	Montreal Wanderers	R. R. Boon	Cecil Blachford
1906-07	Montreal Wanderers (March)	R. R. Boon	Cecil Blachford
1906-07	Kenora Thistles (January)	F.A. Hudson	Tommy Phillips*
1905-06	Montreal Wanderers		Cecil Blachford*
1904-05	Ottawa Silver Seven		A. T. Smith
1903-04	Ottawa Silver Seven		A. T. Smith
1902-03	Ottawa Silver Seven		A. T. Smith
1901-02	Montreal A.A.A.		C. McKerrow
1900-01	Winnipeg Victorias		D. H. Bain
1899-1900	Montreal Shamrocks		H.J. Trihey*
1898-99	Montreal Shamrocks		H.J. Trihey*
1897-98	Montreal Victorias		F. Richardson
1896-97	Montreal Victorias		Mike Grant*
1895-96	Montreal Victorias (December, 1896)		Mike Grant*
1895-96	Winnipeg Victorias (February)		J.C. G. Armytage
1894-95	Montreal Victorias		Mike Grant*
1893-94	Montreal A.A.A.		
1892-93	Montreal A.A.A.		

** Victoria defeated Quebec in challenge series. No official recognition.
* In the early years the teams were frequently run by the Captain. *Indicates Captain

Stanley Cup Winners

Year	W&L in Finals	Winner	Coach	Finalist	Coach
1998	4-0	Detroit	Scotty Bowman	Washington	Ron Wilson
1997	4-0	Detroit	Scotty Bowman	Philadelphia	Terry Murray
1996	4-0	Colorado	Marc Crawford	Florida	Doug MacLean
1995	4-0	New Jersey	Jacques Lemaire	Detroit	Scotty Bowman
1994	4-3	NY Rangers	Mike Keenan	Vancouver	Pat Quinn
1993	4-1	Montreal	Jacques Demers	Los Angeles	Barry Melrose
1992	4-0	Pittsburgh	Scotty Bowman	Chicago	Mike Keenan
1991	4-2	Pittsburgh	Bob Johnson	Minnesota	Bob Gainey
1990	4-1	Edmonton	John Muckler	Boston	Mike Milbury
1989	4-2	Calgary	Terry Crisp	Montreal	Pat Burns
1988	4-0	Edmonton	Glen Sather	Boston	Terry O'Reilly
1987	4-3	Edmonton	Glen Sather	Philadelphia	Mike Keenan
1986	4-1	Montreal	Jean Perron	Calgary	Bob Johnson
1985	4-1	Edmonton	Glen Sather	Philadelphia	Mike Keenan
1984	4-1	Edmonton	Glen Sather	NY Islanders	Al Arbour
1983	4-0	NY Islanders	Al Arbour	Edmonton	Glen Sather
1982	4-0	NY Islanders	Al Arbour	Vancouver	Roger Neilson
1981	4-1	NY Islanders	Al Arbour	Minnesota	Glen Sonmor
1980	4-2	NY Islanders	Al Arbour	Philadelphia	Pat Quinn
1979	4-1	Montreal	Scotty Bowman	NY Rangers	Fred Shero
1978	4-2	Montreal	Scotty Bowman	Boston	Don Cherry
1977	4-0	Montreal	Scotty Bowman	Boston	Don Cherry
1976	4-0	Montreal	Scotty Bowman	Philadelphia	Fred Shero
1975	4-2	Philadelphia	Fred Shero	Buffalo	Floyd Smith
1974	4-2	Philadelphia	Fred Shero	Boston	Bep Guidolin
1973	4-2	Montreal	Scotty Bowman	Chicago	Billy Reay
1972	4-2	Boston	Tom Johnson	NY Rangers	Emile Francis
1971	4-3	Montreal	Al MacNeil	Chicago	Billy Reay
1970	4-0	Boston	Harry Sinden	St. Louis	Scotty Bowman
1969	4-0	Montreal	Claude Ruel	St. Louis	Scotty Bowman
1968	4-0	Montreal	Toe Blake	St. Louis	Scotty Bowman
1967	4-2	Toronto	Punch Imlach	Montreal	Toe Blake
1966	4-2	Montreal	Toe Blake	Detroit	Sid Abel
1965	4-3	Montreal	Toe Blake	Chicago	Billy Reay
1964	4-3	Toronto	Punch Imlach	Detroit	Sid Abel
1963	4-1	Toronto	Punch Imlach	Detroit	Sid Abel
1962	4-2	Toronto	Punch Imlach	Chicago	Rudy Pilous
1961	4-2	Chicago	Rudy Pilous	Detroit	Sid Abel
1960	4-0	Montreal	Toe Blake	Toronto	Punch Imlach
1959	4-1	Montreal	Toe Blake	Toronto	Punch Imlach
1958	4-2	Montreal	Toe Blake	Boston	Milt Schmidt
1957	4-1	Montreal	Toe Blake	Boston	Milt Schmidt
1956	4-1	Montreal	Toe Blake	Detroit	Jimmy Skinner
1955	4-3	Detroit	Jimmy Skinner	Montreal	Dick Irvin
1954	4-3	Detroit	Tommy Ivan	Montreal	Dick Irvin
1953	4-1	Montreal	Dick Irvin	Boston	Lynn Patrick
1952	4-0	Detroit	Tommy Ivan	Montreal	Dick Irvin
1951	4-1	Toronto	Joe Primeau	Montreal	Dick Irvin
1950	4-3	Detroit	Tommy Ivan	NY Rangers	Lynn Patrick
1949	4-0	Toronto	Hap Day	Detroit	Tommy Ivan
1948	4-0	Toronto	Hap Day	Detroit	Tommy Ivan
1947	4-2	Toronto	Hap Day	Montreal	Dick Irvin
1946	4-1	Montreal	Dick Irvin	Boston	Dit Clapper
1945	4-3	Toronto	Hap Day	Detroit	Jack Adams
1944	4-0	Montreal	Dick Irvin	Chicago	Paul Thompson
1943	4-0	Detroit	Jack Adams	Boston	Art Ross
1942	4-3	Toronto	Hap Day	Detroit	Jack Adams
1941	4-0	Boston	Cooney Weiland	Detroit	Ebbie Goodfellow
1940	4-2	NY Rangers	Frank Boucher	Toronto	Dick Irvin
1939	4-1	Boston	Art Ross	Toronto	Dick Irvin
1938	3-1	Chicago	Bill Stewart	Toronto	Dick Irvin
1937	3-2	Detroit	Jack Adams	NY Rangers	Lester Patrick
1936	3-1	Detroit	Jack Adams	Toronto	Dick Irvin
1935	3-0	Mtl. Maroons	Tommy Gorman	Toronto	Dick Irvin
1934	3-1	Chicago	Tommy Gorman	Detroit	Herbie Lewis
1933	3-1	NY Rangers	Lester Patrick	Toronto	Dick Irvin
1932	3-0	Toronto	Dick Irvin	NY Rangers	Lester Patrick
1931	3-2	Montreal	Cecil Hart	Chicago	Dick Irvin
1930	2-0	Montreal	Cecil Hart	Boston	Art Ross
1929	2-0	Boston	Cy Denneny	NY Rangers	Lester Patrick
1928	3-2	NY Rangers	Lester Patrick	Mtl. Maroons	Eddie Gerard
1927	2-0-2	Ottawa	Dave Gill	Boston	Art Ross
		The National Hockey League assumed control of Stanley Cup competition after 1926			
1926	3-1	Mtl. Maroons	Eddie Gerard	Victoria	Lester Patrick
1925	3-1	Victoria	Lester Patrick	Montreal	Leo Dandurand
1924	2-0	Montreal	Leo Dandurand	Cgy. Tigers	—
	2-0			Van. Maroons	—
1923	2-0	Ottawa	Pete Green	Edm. Eskimos	—
	3-1			Van. Maroons	—
1922	3-2	Tor. St. Pats	Eddie Powers	Van. Millionaires	Frank Patrick
1921	3-2	Ottawa	Pete Green	Van. Millionaires	Frank Patrick
1920	3-2	Ottawa	Pete Green	Seattle	—
1919	2-2-1	No decision - series between Montreal and Seattle cancelled due to influenza epidemic			
1918	3-2	Tor. Arenas	Dick Carroll	Van. Millionaires	Frank Patrick

Championship Trophies

PRINCE OF WALES TROPHY

Beginning with the 1993-94 season, the club which advances to the Stanley Cup Finals as the winner of the Eastern Conference Championship is presented with the Prince of Wales Trophy.

History: His Royal Highness, the Prince of Wales, donated the trophy to the National Hockey League in 1924. From 1927-28 through 1937-38, the award was presented to the team finishing first in the American Division of the NHL. From 1938-39, when the NHL reverted to one section, to 1966-67, it was presented to the team winning the NHL regular season championship. With expansion in 1967-68, it again became a divisional trophy, awarded to the regular season champions of the East Division through to the end of the 1973-74 season. Beginning in 1974-75, it was awarded to the regular-season winner of the conference bearing the name of the trophy. From 1981-82 to 1992-93 the trophy was presented to the playoff champion in the Wales Conference. Since 1993-94, the trophy has been presented to the playoff champion in the Eastern Conference.

1997-98 Winner: Washington Capitals

The Washington Capitals won the Prince of Wales Trophy for the first time in franchise history on June 4, 1998 when Joe Juneau scored in overtime for a 3-2 win over Buffalo in game six of the Eastern Conference Championship series. Before defeating the Sabres, the Capitals had series wins over the Boston Bruins and Ottawa Senators.

PRINCE OF WALES TROPHY WINNERS

1997-98	**Washington Capitals**	1959-60	Montreal Canadiens
1996-97	Philadelphia Flyers	1958-59	Montreal Canadiens
1995-96	Florida Panthers	1957-58	Montreal Canadiens
1994-95	New Jersey Devils	1956-57	Detroit Red Wings
1993-94	New York Rangers	1955-56	Montreal Canadiens
1992-93	Montreal Canadiens	1954-55	Detroit Red Wings
1991-92	Pittsburgh Penguins	1953-54	Detroit Red Wings
1990-91	Pittsburgh Penguins	1952-53	Detroit Red Wings
1989-90	Boston Bruins	1951-52	Detroit Red Wings
1988-89	Montreal Canadiens	1950-51	Detroit Red Wings
1987-88	Boston Bruins	1949-50	Detroit Red Wings
1986-87	Philadelphia Flyers	1948-49	Detroit Red Wings
1985-86	Montreal Canadiens	1947-48	Toronto Maple Leafs
1984-85	Philadelphia Flyers	1946-47	Montreal Canadiens
1983-84	New York Islanders	1945-46	Montreal Canadiens
1982-83	New York Islanders	1944-45	Montreal Canadiens
1981-82	New York Islanders	1943-44	Montreal Canadiens
1980-81	Montreal Canadiens	1942-43	Detroit Red Wings
1979-80	Buffalo Sabres	1941-42	New York Rangers
1978-79	Montreal Canadiens	1940-41	Boston Bruins
1977-78	Montreal Canadiens	1939-40	Boston Bruins
1976-77	Montreal Canadiens	1938-39	Boston Bruins
1975-76	Montreal Canadiens	1937-38	Boston Bruins
1974-75	Buffalo Sabres	1936-37	Detroit Red Wings
1973-74	Boston Bruins	1935-36	Detroit Red Wings
1972-73	Montreal Canadiens	1934-35	Boston Bruins
1971-72	Boston Bruins	1933-34	Detroit Red Wings
1970-71	Boston Bruins	1932-33	Boston Bruins
1969-70	Chicago Blackhawks	1931-32	New York Rangers
1968-69	Montreal Canadiens	1930-31	Boston Bruins
1967-68	Montreal Canadiens	1929-30	Boston Bruins
1966-67	Chicago Blackhawks	1928-29	Boston Bruins
1965-66	Montreal Canadiens	1927-28	Boston Bruins
1964-65	Detroit Red Wings	1926-27	Ottawa Senators
1963-64	Montreal Canadiens	1925-26	Montreal Maroons
1962-63	Toronto Maple Leafs	1924-25	Montreal Canadiens
1961-62	Montreal Canadiens	1923-24	Montreal Canadiens
1960-61	Montreal Canadiens		

CLARENCE S. CAMPBELL BOWL

Beginning with the 1993-94 season, the club which advances to the Stanley Cup Finals as the winner of the Western Conference Championship is presented with the Clarence S. Campbell Bowl.

History: Presented by the member clubs in 1968 for perpetual competition by the National Hockey League in recognition of the services of Clarence S. Campbell, President of the NHL from 1946 to 1977. From 1967-68 through 1973-74, the trophy was awarded to the regular season champions of the West Division. Beginning in 1974-75, it was awarded to the regular-season winner of the conference bearing the name of the trophy. From 1981-82 to 1992-93 the trophy was presented to the playoff champion in the Campbell Conference. Since 1993-94, the trophy has been presented to the playoff champion in the Western Conference. The trophy itself is a hallmark piece made of sterling silver and was crafted by a British silversmith in 1878.

1997-98 Winner: Detroit Red Wings

The Detroit Red Wings won the Clarence Campbell Bowl for the second year in a row and third time in four seasons with a 2-0 win over the Dallas Stars in game six of the Western Conference Championship series on June 5, 1998. Previous series wins for the Red Wings had come over the Phoenix Coyotes and St. Louis Blues.

CLARENCE S. CAMPBELL BOWL WINNERS

1997-98	**Detroit Red Wings**	1981-82	Vancouver Canucks
1996-97	Detroit Red Wings	1980-81	New York Islanders
1995-96	Colorado Avalanche	1979-80	Philadelphia Flyers
1994-95	Detroit Red Wings	1978-79	New York Islanders
1993-94	Vancouver Canucks	1977-78	New York Islanders
1992-93	Los Angeles Kings	1976-77	Philadelphia Flyers
1991-92	Chicago Blackhawks	1975-76	Philadelphia Flyers
1990-91	Minnesota North Stars	1974-75	Philadelphia Flyers
1989-90	Edmonton Oilers	1973-74	Philadelphia Flyers
1988-89	Calgary Flames	1972-73	Chicago Blackhawks
1987-88	Edmonton Oilers	1971-72	Chicago Blackhawks
1986-87	Edmonton Oilers	1970-71	Chicago Blackhawks
1985-86	Calgary Flames	1969-70	St. Louis Blues
1984-85	Edmonton Oilers	1968-69	St. Louis Blues
1983-84	Edmonton Oilers	1967-68	Philadelphia Flyers
1982-83	Edmonton Oilers		

Prince of Wales Trophy

Clarence S. Campbell Bowl

Stanley Cup

Stanley Cup Winners:

Rosters and Final Series Scores

1997-98 — Detroit Red Wings — Steve Yzerman (Captain), Doug Brown, Mathieu Dandenault, Kris Draper, Anders Eriksson, Sergei Fedorov, Viacheslav Fetisov, Brent Gilchrist, Kevin Hodson, Tomas Holmstrom, Michael Knuble, Joey Kocur, Vladimir Konstantinov, Vyacheslav Kozlov, Martin Lapointe, Igor Larionov, Nicklas Lidstrom, Jamie Macoun, Kirk Maltby, Darren McCarty, Dmitri Mironov, Larry Murphy, Chris Osgood, Bob Rouse, Brendan Shanahan, Aaron Ward, Mike Ilitch, (Owner/Chairman), Marian Ilitch (Owner), Atanas Ilitch (Vice President), Christopher Ilitch (Vice President), Denise Ilitch, Ronald Ilitch, Michael Ilitch Jr., Lisa Ilitch Murray, Carole Ilitch Trepeck, Jim Devellano (Senior Vice President), Scotty Bowman (Head Coach), Ken Holland (General Manager), Don Waddell (Assistant General Manager), Barry Smith (Associate Coach), Dave Lewis (Associate Coach), Jim Bedard (Goaltending Consultant), Jim Nill (Director of Player Development), Dan Belisle (Pro Scout), Mark Howe (Pro Scout), Hakan Andersson (Director of European Scouting), Mark Leach (USA Scout), Moe McDonnell (Eastern Scout), Bruce Haralson (Western Scout), John Wharton (Athletic Trainer), Paul Boyer (Equipment Manager) Tim Abbott (Assistant Equipment Manager), Bob Huddleston (Masseur), Sergei Mnatsakonov (Masseur), Wally Crossman (Dressing Room Assistant).
Scores: June 9 at Detroit — Detroit 2, Washington 1; June 11 at Detroit — Detroit 5, Washington 4; June 13 at Washington — Detroit 2, Washington 1; June 16 at Washington — Detroit 4, Washington 1.

1996-97 — Detroit Red Wings — Steve Yzerman (Captain), Doug Brown, Mathieu Dandenault, Kris Draper, Sergei Fedorov, Viacheslav Fetisov, Kevin Hodson, Tomas Holmstrom, Joe Kocur, Vladimir Konstantinov, Vyacheslav Kozlov, Martin Lapointe, Igor Larionov, Nicklas Lidstrom, Kirk Maltby, Darren McCarty, Larry Murphy, Chris Osgood, Jamie Pushor, Bob Rouse, Tomas Sandstrom, Brendan Shanahan, Tim Taylor, Mike Vernon, Aaron Ward, Mike Ilitch (Owner/Chairman), Marian Ilitch (Owner), Atanas Ilitch (Vice President), Christopher Ilitch (Vice President), Denise Ilitch Lites, Ronald Ilitch, Michael Ilitch, Jr., Lisa Ilitch Murray, Carole Ilitch Trepeck, Jim Devellano (Senior Vice President), Scotty Bowman (Head Coach/Director of Player Personnel), Ken Holland (Assistant General Manager), Barry Smith (Associate Coach), Dave Lewis (Associate Coach), Mike Krushelnyski (Assistant Coach). Jim Nill (Director of Player Development), Dan Belisle (Pro Scout), Mark Howe (Pro Scout), Hakan Andersson (Director of European Scouting), John Wharton (Athletic Trainer), Paul Boyer (Equipment Manager) Tim Abbott (Assistant Equipment Manager), Sergei Mnatsakanov (Masseur).
Scores: May 31 at Philadelphia — Detroit 4, Philadelphia 2; June 3 at Philadelphia — Detroit 4, Philadelphia 2; June 5 at Detroit — Detroit 6, Philadelphia 1; June 7 at Detroit — Detroit 2, Philadelphia 1.

1995-96 — Colorado Avalanche — Joe Sakic (Captain), Rene Corbet, Adam Deadmarsh, Stephane Fiset, Adam Foote, Peter Forsberg, Alexei Gusarov, Dave Hannan, Valeri Kamensky, Mike Keane, Jon Klemm, Uwe Krupp, Sylvain Lefebvre, Claude Lemieux, Curtis Leschyshyn, Troy Murray, Sandis Ozolinsh, Mike Ricci, Patrick Roy, Warren Rychel, Chris Simon, Craig Wolanin, Stephane Yelle, Scott Young, Charlie Lyons (Chairman, CEO), Pierre Lacroix (Exec. V.P., G.M.), Marc Crawford (Head Coach), Joel Quenneville (Assistant Coach), Jacques Cloutier (Assistant Coach), Francois Giguere (Assistant General Manager), Michel Goulet (Director of Player Personnel), Dave Draper (Chief Scout), Jean Martineau (Director of Public Relations), Pat Karns (Trainer), Matthew Sokolowski (Assistant Trainer), Rob McLean (Equipment Manager), Mike Kramer (Assistant Equipment Manager), Brock Gibbins (Assistant Equipment Manager), Skip Allen (Strength and Conditioning Coach), Paul Fixter (Video Coordinator), Leo Vyssokov (Massage Therapist).
Scores: June 4 at Colorado — Colorado 3, Florida 1; June 6 at Colorado — Colorado 8, Florida 1; June 8 at Florida — Colorado 3, Florida 2; June 10 at Florida — Colorado 1, Florida 0.

1994-95 — New Jersey Devils — Scott Stevens (Captain), Tommy Albelin, Martin Brodeur, Neil Broten, Sergei Brylin, Bob Carpenter, Shawn Chambers, Tom Chorske, Danton Cole, Ken Daneyko, Kevin Dean, Jim Dowd, Bruce Driver (Alternate Captain), Bill Guerin, Bobby Holik, Claude Lemieux, John MacLean (Alternate Captain), Chris McAlpine, Randy McKay, Scott Niedermayer, Mike Peluso, Stephane J.J. Richer, Brian Rolston, Chris Terreri, Valeri Zelepukin, Dr. John J. McMullen (Owner/Chairman), Peter S. McMullen (Owner), Lou Lamoriello (President/General Manager), Jacques Lemaire (Head Coach), Jacques Caron (Goaltender Coach), Dennis Gendron (Assistant Coach), Larry Robinson (Assistant Coach), Robbie Ftorek (AHL Coach), Alex Abasto (Assistant Equipment Manager), Bob Huddleston (Massage Therapist), David Nichols (Equipment Manager), Ted Schuch (Medical Trainer), Mike Vasalani (Strength Coach), David Conte (Director of Scouting) Claude Carrier (Scout), Milt Fisher (Scout), Dan Labraaten (Scout), Marcel Pronovost (Scout).
Scores: June 17 at Detroit — New Jersey 2, Detroit 1; June 20 at Detroit — New Jersey 4, Detroit 2; June 22 at New Jersey — New Jersey 5, Detroit 2; June 24 at New Jersey — New Jersey 5, Detroit 2.

1993-94 — New York Rangers — Mark Messier (Captain), Brian Leetch, Kevin Lowe, Adam Graves, Steve Larmer, Glenn Anderson, Jeff Beukeboom, Greg Gilbert, Mike Hartman, Glenn Healy, Mike Hudson, Alexander Karpovtsev, Joe Kocur, Alexei Kovalev, Nick Kypreos, Doug Lidster, Stephane Matteau, Craig MacTavish, Sergei Nemchinov, Brian Noonan, Ed Olczyk, Mike Richter, Esa Tikkanen, Jay Wells, Sergei Zubov, Neil Smith (President, General Manager and Governor), Robert Gutkowski, Stanley Jaffe, Kenneth Munoz (Governors), Larry Pleau (Assistant General Manager), Mike Keenan (Head Coach), Colin Campbell (Associate Coach), Dick Todd (Assistant Coach), Matthew Loughren (Manager, Team Operations), Barry Watkins (Director, Communications), Christer Rockstrom, Tony Feltrin, Martin Madden, Herb Hammond, Darwin Bennett (Scouts), Dave Smith, Joe Murphy, Mike Folga, Bruce Lifrieri (Trainers).
Scores: May 31 at New York — Vancouver 3, NY Rangers 2; June 2 at New York — NY Rangers 3, Vancouver 1; June 4 at Vancouver — NY Rangers 5, Vancouver 1; June 7 at Vancouver — NY Rangers 4, Vancouver 2; June 9 at New York — Vancouver 6 at NY Rangers 3; June 11 at Vancouver — Vancouver 4, NY Rangers 1; June 14 at New York — NY Rangers 3, Vancouver 2.

1992-93 — Montreal Canadiens — Guy Carbonneau (Captain), Patrick Roy, Mike Keane, Eric Desjardins, Stephan Lebeau, Mathieu Schneider, Jean-Jacques Daigneault, Denis Savard, Lyle Odelein, Todd Ewen, Kirk Muller, John LeClair, Gilbert Dionne, Benoit Brunet, Patrice Brisebois, Paul Di Pietro, Andre Racicot, Donald Dufresne, Mario Roberge, Sean Hill, Ed Ronan, Kevin Haller, Vincent Damphousse, Brian Bellows, Gary Leeman, Rob Ramage, Ronald Corey (President), Serge Savard (Managing Director & Vice-President Hockey), Jacques Demers (Head Coach), Jacques Laperriere (Assistant Coach), Charles Thiffault (Assistant Coach), Francois Allaire (Goaltending Instructor), Jean Béliveau (Senior Vice-President, Corporate Affairs), Fred Steer (Vice-President, Finance & Adminstration), Aldo Giampaolo (Vice-President, Operations), Bernard Brisset (Vice-President, Marketing & Communications), André Boudrias (Assistant to the Managing Director & Director of Scouting), Jacques Lemaire (Assistant to the Managing Director), Gaeten Lefebvre (Athletic Trainer), John Shipman (Assistant to the Athletic Trainer), Eddy Palchak (Equipment Manager), Pierre Gervais (Assistant to the Equipment Manager), Robert Boulanger (Assistant to the Equipment Manager), Pierre Ouellete (Assistant to the Equipment Manager).
Scores: June 1 at Montreal — Los Angeles 4, Montreal 1; June 2 at Montreal — Montreal 3, Los Angeles 2; June 5 at Los Angeles — Montreal 4, Los Angeles 3; June 7 at Los Angeles — Montreal 3, Los Angeles 2; June 9 at Montreal — Montreal 4, Los Angeles 1.

1991-92 — Pittsburgh Penguins — Mario Lemieux (Captain), Ron Francis, Bryan Trottier, Kevin Stevens, Bob Errey, Phil Bourque, Troy Loney, Rick Tocchet, Joe Mullen, Jaromir Jagr, Jiri Hrdina, Shawn McEachern, Ulf Samuelsson, Kjell Samuelsson, Larry Murphy, Gord Roberts, Jim Paek, Paul Stanton, Tom Barrasso, Ken Wregget, Jay Caufield, Jamie Leach, Wendell Young, Grant Jennings, Peter Taglianetti, Jock Callander, Dave Michayluk, Mike Needham, Jeff Chychrun, Ken Priestlay, Jeff Daniels, Howard Baldwin (Owner and President), Morris Belzberg (Owner), Thomas Ruta (Owner), Donn Patton (Executive Vice President and Chief Financial Officer), Paul Martha (Executive Vice President and General Counsel), Craig Patrick (Executive Vice President and General Manager), Bob Johnson (Coach), Scotty Bowman (Director of Player Development and Coach), Barry Smith, Rick Kehoe, Pierre McGuire, Gilles Meloche, Rick Paterson (Assistant Coaches), Steve Latin (Equipment Manager), Skip Thayer (Trainer), John Welday (Strength and Conditioning Coach), Greg Malone, Les Binkley, Charlie Hodge, John Gill, Ralph Cox (Scouts).
Scores: May 26 at Pittsburgh — Pittsburgh 5, Chicago 4; May 28 at Pittsburgh — Pittsburgh 3, Chicago 1; May 30 at Chicago — Pittsburgh 1, Chicago 0; June 1 at Chicago — Pittsburgh 6, Chicago 5.

Three proud Canadiens veterans, Larry Robinson, left, Mats Naslund, center, and Bob Gainey, right, share a victory celebration after the Habs downed the Calgary Flames to win the 1986 Stanley Cup title.

1990-91 — Pittsburgh Penguins — Mario Lemieux (Captain), Paul Coffey, Randy Hillier, Bob Errey, Tom Barrasso, Phil Bourque, Jay Caufield, Ron Francis, Randy Gilhen, Jiri Hrdina, Jaromir Jagr, Grant Jennings, Troy Loney, Joe Mullen, Larry Murphy, Jim Paek, Frank Pietrangelo, Barry Pederson, Mark Recchi, Gordie Roberts, Ulf Samuelsson, Paul Stanton, Kevin Stevens, Peter Taglianetti, Bryan Trottier, Scott Young, Wendell Young, Edward J. DeBartolo, Sr. (Owner), Marie D. DeBartolo York (President), Paul Martha (Vice-President & General Counsel), Craig Patrick (General Manager), Scotty Bowman (Director of Player Development & Recruitment), Bob Johnson (Coach), Rick Kehoe (Assistant Coach), Gilles Meloche (Goaltending Coach & Scout), Rick Paterson (Assistant Coach), Barry Smith (Assistant Coach), Steve Latin (Equipment Manager), Skip Thayer (Trainer), John Welday (Strength & Conditioning Coach), Greg Malone (Scout).
Scores: May 15 at Pittsburgh — Minnesota 5, Pittsburgh 4; May 17 at Pittsburgh — Pittsburgh 4, Minnesota 1; May 19 at Minnesota — Minnesota 3, Pittsburgh 1; May 21 at Minnesota — Pittsburgh 5, Minnesota 3; May 23 at Pittsburgh — Pittsburgh 6, Minnesota 4; May 25 at Minnesota — Pittsburgh 8, Minnesota 0.

1989-90 — Edmonton Oilers — Kevin Lowe, Steve Smith, Jeff Beukeboom, Mark Lamb, Joe Murphy, Glenn Anderson, Mark Messier, Adam Graves, Craig MacTavish, Kelly Buchberger, Jari Kurri, Craig Simpson, Martin Gelinas, Randy Gregg, Charlie Huddy, Geoff Smith, Reijo Ruotsalainen, Craig Muni, Bill Ranford, Dave Brown, Pokey Reddick, Petr Klima, Esa Tikkanen, Grant Fuhr, Peter Pocklington (Owner), Glen Sather (President/General Manager), John Muckler (Coach), Ted Green (Co-Coach), Ron Low (Ass't Coach), Bruce MacGregor (Ass't General Manager), Barry Fraser (Director of Player Personnel), John Blackwell (Director of Operations, AHL), Ace Bailey, Ed Chadwick, Lorne Davis, Harry Howell, Matti Vaisanen and Albert Reeves (Scouts), Bill Tuele (Director of Public Relations), Werner Baum (Controller), Dr. Gordon Cameron (Medical Chief of Staff), Dr. David Reid (Team Physician), Barrie Stafford (Athletic Trainer), Ken Lowe (Athletic Therapist), Stuart Poirier (Massage Therapist), Lyle Kulchisky (Ass't Trainer).
Scores: May 15 at Boston — Edmonton 3, Boston 2; May 18 at Boston — Edmonton 7, Boston 2; May 20 at Edmonton — Boston 2, Edmonton 1; May 22 at Edmonton — Edmonton 5, Boston 1; May 24 at Boston — Edmonton 4, Boston 1.

1988-89 — Calgary Flames — Mike Vernon, Rick Wamsley, Al MacInnis, Brad McCrimmon, Dana Murzyn, Ric Nattress, Joe Mullen, Lanny McDonald (Co-captain), Gary Roberts, Colin Patterson, Hakan Loob, Theoren Fleury, Jiri Hrdina, Tim Hunter (Ass't. captain), Gary Suter, Mark Hunter, Jim Peplinski (Co-captain), Joe Nieuwendyk, Brian MacLellan, Joel Otto, Jamie Macoun, Doug Gilmour, Rob Ramage. Norman Green, Harley Hotchkiss, Norman Kwong, Sonia Scurfield, B.J. Seaman, D.K. Seaman (Owners), Cliff Fletcher (President and General Manager), Al MacNeil (Ass't General Manager), Al Coates (Ass't to the President), Terry Crisp (Head Coach), Doug Risebrough, Tom Watt (Ass't Coaches), Glenn Hall (Goaltending Consultant), Jim Murray (Trainer), Bob Stewart (Equipment Manager), Al Murray (Ass't Trainer).
Scores: May 14 at Calgary — Calgary 3, Montreal 2; May 17 at Calgary— Montreal 4, Calgary 2; May 19 at Montreal — Montreal 4, Calgary 3; May 21 at Montreal — Calgary 4, Montreal 2; May 23 at Calgary — Calgary 3, Montreal 2; May 25 at Montreal — Calgary 4, Montreal 2.

1987-88 — Edmonton Oilers — Keith Acton, Glenn Anderson, Jeff Beukeboom, Geoff Courtnall, Grant Fuhr, Randy Gregg, Wayne Gretzky, Dave Hannan, Charlie Huddy, Mike Krushelnyski, Jari Kurri, Normand Lacombe, Kevin Lowe, Craig MacTavish, Kevin McClelland, Marty McSorley, Mark Messier, Craig Muni, Bill Ranford, Craig Simpson, Steve Smith, Esa Tikkanen, Peter Pocklington (Owner), Glen Sather (General Manager/Coach), John Muckler (Co-Coach), Ted Green (Ass't Coach), Bruce MacGregor (Ass't General Manager), Barry Fraser (Director of Player Personnel), Bill Tuele (Director of Public Relations), Dr. Gordon Cameron (Team Physician), Peter Millar (Athletic Therapist), Barrie Stafford (Trainer), Juergen Mers (Massage Therapist), Lyle Kulchisky (Ass't Trainer).
Scores: May 18 at Edmonton — Edmonton 2, Boston 1; May 20 at Edmonton — Edmonton 4, Boston 2; May 22 at Boston — Edmonton 6, Boston 3; May 24 at Boston — Boston 3, Edmonton 3 (suspended due to power failure); May 26 at Edmonton — Edmonton 6, Boston 3.

1986-87 — Edmonton Oilers — Glenn Anderson, Jeff Beukeboom, Kelly Buchberger, Paul Coffey, Grant Fuhr, Randy Gregg, Wayne Gretzky, Charlie Huddy, Dave Hunter, Mike Krushelnyski, Jari Kurri, Moe Lemay, Kevin Lowe, Craig MacTavish, Kevin McClelland, Marty McSorley, Mark Messier, Andy Moog, Craig Muni, Kent Nilsson, Jaroslav Pouzar, Reijo Ruotsalainen, Steve Smith, Esa Tikkanen, Peter Pocklington (Owner), Glen Sather (General Manager/Coach), John Muckler (Co-Coach), Ted Green (Ass't. Coach), Ron Low (Ass't. Coach), Bruce MacGregor (Ass't. General Manager), Barry Fraser (Director of Player Personnel), Peter Millar (Athletic Therapist), Barrie Stafford (Trainer), Lyle Kulchisky (Ass't Trainer).
Scores: May 17 at Edmonton — Edmonton 4, Philadelphia 2; May 20 at Edmonton — Edmonton 3, Philadelphia 2; May 22 at Philadelphia — Philadelphia 5, Edmonton 3; May 24 at Philadelphia — Edmonton 4, Philadelphia 1; May 26 at Edmonton — Philadelphia 4, Edmonton 3; May 28 at Philadelphia — Philadelphia 3, Edmonton 2; May 31 at Edmonton — Edmonton 3, Philadelphia 1.

1985-86 — Montreal Canadiens — Bob Gainey, Doug Soetaert, Patrick Roy, Rick Green, David Maley, Ryan Walter, Serge Boisvert, Mario Tremblay, Bobby Smith, Craig Ludwig, Tom Kurvers, Kjell Dahlin, Larry Robinson, Guy Carbonneau, Chris Chelios, Petr Svoboda, Mats Naslund, Lucien DeBlois, Steve Rooney, Gaston Gingras, Mike Lalor, Chris Nilan, John Kordic, Claude Lemieux, Mike McPhee, Brian Skrudland, Stephane Richer, Ronald Corey (President), Serge Savard (General Manager), Jean Perron (Coach), Jacques Laperrière (Ass't. Coach), Jean Béliveau (Vice President), Francois-Xavier Seigneur (Vice President), Fred Steer (Vice President), Jacques Lemaire (Ass't. General Manager), André Boudrias (Ass't. General Manager), Claude Ruel, Yves Belanger (Athletic Therapist), Gaetan Lefebvre (Ass't. Athletic Therapist), Eddy Palchek (Trainer), Sylvain Toupin (Ass't. Trainer).
Scores: May 16 at Calgary — Calgary 5, Montreal 2; May 18 at Calgary — Montreal 3, Calgary 2; May 20 at Montreal — Montreal 5, Calgary 3; May 22 at Montreal — Montreal 1, Calgary 0; May 24 at Calgary — Montreal 4, Calgary 3.

1984-85 — Edmonton Oilers — Glenn Anderson, Bill Carroll, Paul Coffey, Lee Fogolin, Grant Fuhr, Randy Gregg, Wayne Gretzky, Charlie Huddy, Pat Hughes, Dave Hunter, Don Jackson, Mike Krushelnyski, Jari Kurri, Willy Lindstrom, Kevin Lowe, Dave Lumley, Kevin McClelland, Larry Melnyk, Mark Messier, Andy Moog, Mark Napier, Jaroslav Pouzar, Dave Semenko, Esa Tikkanen, Peter Pocklington (Owner), Glen Sather (General Manager/Coach), John Muckler (Ass't. Coach), Ted Green (Ass't. Coach), Bruce MacGregor (Ass't. General Manager), Barry Fraser (Director of Player Personnel/Chief Scout), Peter Millar (Athletic Therapist), Barrie Stafford, Lyle Kulchisky (Trainers)
Scores: May 21 at Philadelphia — Philadelphia 4, Edmonton 1; May 23 at Philadelphia — Edmonton 3, Philadelphia 1; May 25 at Edmonton — Edmonton 4, Philadelphia 3; May 28 at Edmonton — Edmonton 5, Philadelphia 3; May 30 at Edmonton — Edmonton 8, Philadelphia 3.

1983-84 — Edmonton Oilers — Glenn Anderson, Paul Coffey, Pat Conacher, Lee Fogolin, Grant Fuhr, Randy Gregg, Wayne Gretzky, Charlie Huddy, Pat Hughes, Dave Hunter, Don Jackson, Jari Kurri, Willy Lindstrom, Ken Linseman, Kevin Lowe, Dave Lumley, Kevin McClelland, Mark Messier, Andy Moog, Jaroslav Pouzar, Dave Semenko, Peter Pocklington (Owner), Glen Sather (General Manager/Coach), John Muckler (Ass't. Coach), Ted Green (Ass't. Coach), Bruce MacGregor (Ass't. General Manager), Barry Fraser (Director of Player Personnel/Chief Scout), Peter Millar (Athletic Therapist), Barrie Stafford (Trainer)
Scores: May 10 at New York — Edmonton 1, NY Islanders 0; May 12 at New York — NY Islanders 6, Edmonton 1; May 15 at Edmonton — Edmonton 7, NY Islanders 2; May 17 at Edmonton — Edmonton 7, NY Islanders 2; May 19 at Edmonton — Edmonton 5, NY Islanders 2.

1982-83 — New York Islanders — Mike Bossy, Bob Bourne, Paul Boutilier, Billy Carroll, Greg Gilbert, Clark Gillies, Butch Goring, Mats Hallin, Tomas Jonsson, Anders Kallur, Gord Lane, Dave Langevin, Mike McEwen, Rollie Melanson, Wayne Merrick, Ken Morrow, Bob Nystrom, Stefan Persson, Denis Potvin, Billy Smith, Brent Sutter, Duane Sutter, John Tonelli, Bryan Trottier, Al Arbour (coach), Lorne Henning (ass't coach), Bill Torrey (general manager), Ron Waske, Jim Pickard (trainers)
Scores: May 10 at Edmonton — NY Islanders 2, Edmonton 0; May 12 at Edmonton — NY Islanders 6, Edmonton 3; May 14 at New York — NY Islanders 5, Edmonton 1; May 17 at New York — NY Islanders 4, Edmonton 2

1981-82 — New York Islanders — Mike Bossy, Bob Bourne, Billy Carroll, Butch Goring, Greg Gilbert, Clark Gillies, Tomas Jonsson, Anders Kallur, Gord Lane, Dave Langevin, Hector Marini, Mike McEwen, Rollie Melanson, Wayne Merrick, Ken Morrow, Bob Nystrom, Stefan Persson, Denis Potvin, Billy Smith, Brent Sutter, Duane Sutter, John Tonelli, Bryan Trottier, Al Arbour (coach), Lorne Henning (ass't coach), Bill Torrey (general manager), Ron Waske, Jim Pickard (trainers)
Scores: May 8 at New York — NY Islanders 6, Vancouver 5; May 11 at New York — NY Islanders 6, Vancouver 4; May 13 at Vancouver — NY Islanders 3, Vancouver 0; May 16 at Vancouver — NY Islanders 3, Vancouver 1

1980-81 — New York Islanders — Denis Potvin, Mike McEwen, Ken Morrow, Gord Lane, Bob Lorimer, Stefan Persson, Dave Langevin, Mike Bossy, Bryan Trottier, Butch Goring, Wayne Merrick, Clark Gillies, John Tonelli, Bob Nystrom, Bill Carroll, Bob Bourne, Hector Marini, Anders Kallur, Duane Sutter, Garry Howatt, Lorne Henning, Billy Smith, Rollie Melanson, Al Arbour (coach), Bill Torrey (general manager), Ron Waske, Jim Pickard (trainers).
Scores: May 12 at New York — NY Islanders 6, Minnesota 3; May 14 at New York — NY Islanders 6, Minnesota 3; May 17 at Minnesota — NY Islanders 7, Minnesota 5; May 19 at Minnesota— Minnesota 4, NY Islanders 2; May 21 at New York — NY Islanders 5, Minnesota 1.

1979-80 — New York Islanders — Gord Lane, Jean Potvin, Bob Lorimer, Denis Potvin, Stefan Persson, Ken Morrow, Dave Langevin, Duane Sutter, Garry Howatt, Clark Gillies, Lorne Henning, Wayne Merrick, Bob Bourne, Steve Tambellini, Bryan Trottier, Mike Bossy, Bob Nystrom, John Tonelli, Anders Kallur, Butch Goring, Alex McKendry, Glenn Resch, Billy Smith, Al Arbour (coach), Bill Torrey (general manager), Ron Waske, Jim Pickard (trainers).
Scores: May 13 at Philadelphia — NY Islanders 4, Philadelphia 3; May 15 at Philadelphia — Philadelphia 8, NY Islanders 3; May 17 at New York — NY Islanders 6, Philadelphia 2; May 19 at New York — NY Islanders 5, Philadelphia 2; May 22 at Philadelphia — Philadelphia 6, NY Islanders 3; May 24 at New York — NY Islanders 5, Philadelphia 4.

1978-79 — Montreal Canadiens — Ken Dryden, Larry Robinson, Serge Savard, Guy Lapointe, Brian Engblom, Gilles Lupien, Rick Chartraw, Guy Lafleur, Steve Shutt, Jacques Lemaire, Yvan Cournoyer, Réjean Houle, Pierre Mondou, Bob Gainey, Doug Jarvis, Yvon Lambert, Doug Risebrough, Pierre Larouche, Mario Tremblay, Cam Connor, Pat Hughes, Rod Langway, Mark Napier, Michel Larocque, Richard Sévigny, Scotty Bowman (coach), Irving Grundman (managing director), Eddy Palchak, Pierre Meilleur (trainers).
Scores: May 13 at Montreal — NY Rangers 4, Montreal 1; May 15 at Montreal — Montreal 6, NY Rangers 2; May 17 at New York — Montreal 4, NY Rangers 1; May 19 at New York — Montreal 4, NY Rangers 3; May 21 at Montreal — Montreal 4, NY Rangers 1.

1977-78 — Montreal Canadiens — Ken Dryden, Larry Robinson, Serge Savard, Guy Lapointe, Bill Nyrop, Pierre Bouchard, Brian Engblom, Gilles Lupien, Rick Chartraw, Guy Lafleur, Steve Shutt, Jacques Lemaire, Yvan Cournoyer, Réjean Houle, Pierre Mondou, Bob Gainey, Doug Jarvis, Yvon Lambert, Doug Risebrough, Pierre Larouche, Mario Tremblay, Michel Larocque, Murray Wilson, Scotty Bowman (coach), Sam Pollock (general manager), Eddy Palchak, Pierre Meilleur (trainers).
Scores: May 13 at Montreal — Montreal 4, Boston 1; May 16 at Montreal — Montreal 3, Boston 2; May 18 at Boston — Boston 4, Montreal 0; May 21 at Boston — Boston 4, Montreal 3; May 23 at Montreal — Montreal 4, Boston 1; May 25 at Boston — Montreal 4, Boston 1.

1976-77 — Montreal Canadiens — Ken Dryden, Guy Lapointe, Larry Robinson, Serge Savard, Jimmy Roberts, Rick Chartraw, Bill Nyrop, Pierre Bouchard, Brian Engblom, Yvan Cournoyer, Guy Lafleur, Jacques Lemaire, Steve Shutt, Pete Mahovlich, Murray Wilson, Doug Jarvis, Yvon Lambert, Bob Gainey, Doug Risebrough, Mario Tremblay, Rejean Houle, Pierre Mondou, Mike Polich, Michel Larocque, Scotty Bowman (coach), Sam Pollock (general manager), Eddy Palchak, Pierre Meilleur (trainers).
Scores: May 7 at Montreal — Montreal 7, Boston 3; May 10 at Montreal — Montreal 3, Boston 0; May 12 at Boston — Montreal 4, Boston 2; May 14 at Boston — Montreal 2, Boston 1.

1975-76 — Montreal Canadiens — Ken Dryden, Serge Savard, Guy Lapointe, Larry Robinson, Bill Nyrop, Pierre Bouchard, Jimmy Roberts, Guy Lafleur, Steve Shutt, Pete Mahovlich, Yvan Cournoyer, Jacques Lemaire, Yvon Lambert, Bob Gainey, Doug Jarvis, Doug Risebrough, Murray Wilson, Mario Tremblay, Rick Chartraw, Michel Larocque, Scotty Bowman (coach), Sam Pollock (general manager), Eddy Palchak, Pierre Meilleur (trainers).
Scores: May 9 at Montreal — Montreal 4, Philadelphia 3; May 11 at Montreal — Montreal 2, Philadelphia 1; May 13 at Philadelphia — Montreal 3, Philadelphia 2; May 16 at Philadelphia — Montreal 5, Philadelphia 3.

1974-75 — Philadelphia Flyers — Bernie Parent, Wayne Stephenson, Ed Van Impe, Tom Bladon, André Dupont, Joe Watson, Jimmy Watson, Ted Harris, Larry Goodenough, Rick MacLeish, Bobby Clarke, Bill Barber, Reggie Leach, Gary Dornhoefer, Ross Lonsberry, Bob Kelly, Terry Crisp, Don Saleski, Dave Schultz, Orest Kindrachuk, Bill Clement, Fred Shero (coach), Keith Allen (general manager), Frank Lewis, Jim McKenzie (trainers).
Scores: May 15 at Philadelphia — Philadelphia 4, Buffalo 1; May 18 at Philadelphia — Philadelphia 2, Buffalo 1; May 20 at Buffalo — Buffalo 5, Philadelphia 4; May 22 at Buffalo — Buffalo 4, Philadelphia 2; May 25 at Philadelphia — Philadelphia 5, Buffalo 1; May 27 at Buffalo — Philadelphia 2, Buffalo 0.

1973-74 — Philadelphia Flyers — Bernie Parent, Ed Van Impe, Tom Bladon, André Dupont, Joe Watson, Jimmy Watson, Barry Ashbee, Bill Barber, Dave Schultz, Don Saleski, Gary Dornhoefer, Terry Crisp, Bobby Clarke, Simon Nolet, Ross Lonsberry, Rick MacLeish, Bill Flett, Orest Kindrachuk, Bill Clement, Bob Kelly, Bruce Cowick, Al MacAdam, Bobby Taylor, Fred Shero (coach), Keith Allen (general manager), Frank Lewis, Jim McKenzie (trainers).
Scores: May 7 at Boston — Boston 3, Philadelphia 2; May 9 at Boston — Philadelphia 3, Boston 2; May 12 at Philadelphia — Philadelphia 4, Boston 1; May 14 at Philadelphia — Philadelphia 4, Boston 2; May 16 at Boston — Boston 5, Philadelphia 1; May 19 at Philadelphia — Philadelphia 1, Boston 0.

1972-73 — Montreal Canadiens — Ken Dryden, Guy Lapointe, Serge Savard, Larry Robinson, Jacques Laperrière, Bob Murdoch, Pierre Bouchard, Jimmy Roberts, Yvan Cournoyer, Frank Mahovlich, Jacques Lemaire, Pete Mahovlich, Marc Tardif, Henri Richard, Réjean Houle, Guy Lafleur, Chuck Lefley, Claude Larose, Murray Wilson, Steve Shutt, Michel Plasse, Scotty Bowman (coach), Sam Pollock (general manager), Ed Palchak, Bob Williams (trainers).
Scores: April 29 at Montreal — Montreal 8, Chicago 3; May 1 at Montreal — Montreal 4, Chicago 1; May 3 at Chicago — Chicago 7, Montreal 4; May 6 at Chicago — Montreal 4, Chicago 0; May 8 at Montreal — Chicago 8, Montreal 7; May 10 at Chicago — Montreal 6, Chicago 4.

1971-72 — Boston Bruins — Gerry Cheevers, Eddie Johnston, Bobby Orr, Ted Green, Carol Vadnais, Dallas Smith, Don Awrey, Phil Esposito, Ken Hodge, John Bucyk, Mike Walton, Wayne Cashman, Garnet Bailey, Derek Sanderson, Fred Stanfield, Ed Westfall, John McKenzie, Don Marcotte, Garry Peters, Chris Hayes, Tom Johnson (coach), Milt Schmidt (general manager), Dan Canney, John Forristall (trainers).
Scores: April 30 at Boston — Boston 6, NY Rangers 5; May 2 at Boston — Boston 2, NY Rangers 1; May 4 at New York — NY Rangers 5, Boston 2; May 7 at New York — Boston 3, NY Rangers 2; May 9 at Boston — NY Rangers 3, Boston 2; May 11 at New York — Boston 3, NY Rangers 0.

1970-71 — Montreal Canadiens — Ken Dryden, Rogie Vachon, Jacques Laperrière, J.C. Tremblay, Guy Lapointe, Terry Harper, Pierre Bouchard, Jean Béliveau, Marc Tardif, Yvan Cournoyer, Réjean Houle, Claude Larose, Henri Richard, Phil Roberto, Pete Mahovlich, Leon Rochefort, John Ferguson, Bobby Sheehan, Jacques Lemaire, Frank Mahovlich, Bob Murdoch, Chuck Lefley, Al MacNeil (coach), Sam Pollock (general manager), Yvon Belanger, Ed Palchak (trainers).
Scores: May 4 at Chicago — Chicago 2, Montreal 1; May 6 at Chicago — Chicago 5, Montreal 3; May 9 at Montreal — Montreal 4, Chicago 2; May 11 at Montreal — Montreal 5, Chicago 2; May 13 at Chicago — Chicago 2, Montreal 0; May 16 at Montreal — Montreal 4, Chicago 3; May 18 at Chicago — Montreal 3, Chicago 2.

1969-70 — Boston Bruins — Gerry Cheevers, Eddie Johnston, Bobby Orr, Rick Smith, Dallas Smith, Bill Speer, Gary Doak, Don Awrey, Phil Esposito, Ken Hodge, John Bucyk, Wayne Carleton, Wayne Cashman, Derek Sanderson, Fred Stanfield, Ed Westfall, John McKenzie, Jim Lorentz, Don Marcotte, Bill Lesuk, Dan Schock, Harry Sinden (coach), Milt Schmidt (general manager), Dan Canney, John Forristall (trainers).
Scores: May 3 at St. Louis — Boston 6, St. Louis 1; May 5 at St. Louis — Boston 6, St. Louis 2; May 7 at Boston — Boston 4, St. Louis 1; May 10 at Boston — Boston 4, St. Louis 3.

1968-69 — Montreal Canadiens — Gump Worsley, Rogie Vachon, Jacques Laperrière, J.C. Tremblay, Ted Harris, Serge Savard, Terry Harper, Larry Hillman, Jean Béliveau, Ralph Backstrom, Dick Duff, Yvan Cournoyer, Claude Provost, Bobby Rousseau, Henri Richard, John Ferguson, Christian Bordeleau, Mickey Redmond, Jacques Lemaire, Lucien Grenier, Tony Esposito, Claude Ruel (coach), Sam Pollock (general manager), Larry Aubut, Eddy Palchak (trainers).
Scores: April 27 at Montreal — Montreal 3, St. Louis 1; April 29 at Montreal — Montreal 3, St. Louis 1; May 1 at St. Louis — Montreal 4, St. Louis 0; May 4 at St. Louis — Montreal 2, St. Louis 1.

1967-68 — Montreal Canadiens — Gump Worsley, Rogie Vachon, Jacques Laperrière, J.C. Tremblay, Ted Harris, Serge Savard, Terry Harper, Carol Vadnais, Jean Béliveau, Gilles Tremblay, Ralph Backstrom, Dick Duff, Claude Larose, Yvan Cournoyer, Claude Provost, Bobby Rousseau, Henri Richard, John Ferguson, Danny Grant, Jacques Lemaire, Mickey Redmond, Toe Blake (coach), Sam Pollock (general manager), Larry Aubut, Eddy Palchak (trainers).
Scores: May 5 at St. Louis — Montreal 3, St. Louis 2; May 7 at St. Louis — Montreal 1, St. Louis 0; May 9 at Montreal — Montreal 4, St. Louis 3; May 11 at Montreal — Montreal 3, St. Louis 2.

1966-67 — Toronto Maple Leafs — Johnny Bower, Terry Sawchuk, Larry Hillman, Marcel Pronovost, Tim Horton, Bob Baun, Aut Erickson, Allan Stanley, Red Kelly, Ron Ellis, George Armstrong, Pete Stemkowski, Dave Keon, Mike Walton, Jim Pappin, Bob Pulford, Brian Conacher, Eddie Shack, Frank Mahovlich, Milan Marcetta, Larry Jeffrey, Bruce Gamble, Punch Imlach (manager-coach), Bob Haggart (trainer).
Scores: April 20 at Montreal — Toronto 2, Montreal 6; April 22 at Montreal — Toronto 3, Montreal 0; April 25 at Toronto — Toronto 3, Montreal 2; April 27 at Toronto — Toronto 2, Montreal 6; April 29 at Montreal — Toronto 4, Montreal 1; May 2 at Toronto — Toronto 3, Montreal 1.

1965-66 — Montreal Canadiens — Gump Worsley, Charlie Hodge, Jean-Claude Tremblay, Ted Harris, Jean-Guy Talbot, Terry Harper, Jacques Laperrière, Noel Price, Jean Béliveau, Ralph Backstrom, Dick Duff, Gilles Tremblay, Claude Larose, Yvan Cournoyer, Claude Provost, Bobby Rousseau, Henri Richard, Dave Balon, John Ferguson, Leon Rochefort, Jim Roberts, Toe Blake (coch), Sam Pollock (general manager), Larry Aubut, Andy Galley (trainers).
Scores: April 24 at Montreal — Detroit 3, Montreal 2; April 26 at Montreal — Detroit 5, Montreal 2; April 28 at Detroit — Montreal 4, Detroit 2; May 1 at Detroit — Montreal 2, Detroit 1; May 3 at Montreal — Montreal 5, Detroit 1; May 5 at Detroit — Montreal 3, Detroit 2.

1964-65 — Montreal Canadiens — Gump Worsley, Charlie Hodge, Jean-Claude Tremblay, Ted Harris, Jean-Guy Talbot, Terry Harper, Jacques Laperrière, Jean Gauthier, Noel Picard, Jean Béliveau, Ralph Backstrom, Dick Duff, Claude Larose, Yvan Cournoyer, Claude Provost, Bobby Rousseau, Henri Richard, Dave Balon, John Ferguson, Red Berenson, Jim Roberts, Toe Blake (coach), Sam Pollock (general manager), Larry Aubut, Andy Galley (trainers).
Scores: April 17 at Montreal — Montreal 3, Chicago 2; April 20 at Montreal — Montreal 2, Chicago 0; April 22 at Chicago — Montreal 1, Chicago 3; April 25 at Chicago — Montreal 1, Chicago 5; April 7 at Montreal — Montreal 6, Chicago 0; April 29 at Chicago — Montreal 1, Chicago 2; May 1 at Montreal — Montreal 4, Chicago 0.

1963-64 — Toronto Maple Leafs — Johnny Bower, Carl Brewer, Tim Horton, Bob Baun, Allan Stanley, Larry Hillman, Al Arbour, Red Kelly, Gerry Ehman, Andy Bathgate, George Armstrong, Ron Stewart, Dave Keon, Billy Harris, Don McKenney, Jim Pappin, Bob Pulford, Eddie Shack, Frank Mahovlich, Ed Litzenberger, Punch Imlach (manager-coach), Bob Haggert (trainer).
Scores April 11 at Toronto — Toronto 3, Detroit 2; April 14 at Toronto — Toronto 3, Detroit 4; April 16 at Detroit — Toronto 3, Detroit 4; April 18 at Detroit — Toronto 4, Detroit 2; April 21 at Toronto — Toronto 1, Detroit 2; April 23 at Detroit — Toronto 4, Detroit 3; April 25 at Toronto — Toronto 4, Detroit 0.

1962-63 — Toronto Maple Leafs — Johnny Bower, Don Simmons, Carl Brewer, Tim Horton, Kent Douglas, Allan Stanley, Bob Baun, Larry Hillman, Red Kelly, Dick Duff, George Armstrong, Bob Nevin, Ron Stewart, Dave Keon, Billy Harris, Bob Pulford, Eddie Shack, Ed Litzenberger, Frank Mahovlich, John MacMillan, Punch Imlach (manager-coach), Bob Haggert (trainer).
Scores: April 9 at Toronto — Toronto 4, Detroit 2; April 11 at Toronto — Toronto 4, Detroit 2; April 14 at Detroit — Toronto 2, Detroit 3; April 16 at Detroit — Toronto 4, Detroit 2; April 18 at Toronto — Toronto 3, Detroit 1.

1961-62 — Toronto Maple Leafs — Johnny Bower, Don Simmons, Carl Brewer, Tim Horton, Bob Baun, Allan Stanley, Al Arbour, Larry Hillman, Red Kelly, Dick Duff, George Armstrong, Frank Mahovlich, Bob Nevin, Ron Stewart, Billy Harris, Bert Olmstead, Bob Pulford, Eddie Shack, Dave Keon, Ed Litzenberger, John MacMillan, Punch Imlach (manager-coach), Bob Haggert (trainer).
Scores: April 10 at Toronto — Toronto 4, Chicago 1; April 12 at Toronto — Toronto 3, Chicago 2; April 15 at Chicago — Toronto 0, Chicago 3; April 17 at Chicago — Toronto 1, Chicago 4; April 19 at Toronto —Toronto 8, Chicago 4; April 22 at Chicago — Toronto 2, Chicago 1.

1960-61 — Chicago Black Hawks — Glenn Hall, Al Arbour, Pierre Pilote, Elmer Vasko, Jack Evans, Dollard St. Laurent, Reggie Fleming, Tod Sloan, Ron Murphy, Ed Litzenberger, Bill Hay, Bobby Hull, Ab McDonald, Eric Nesterenko, Kenny Wharram, Earl Balfour, Stan Mikita, Murray Balfour, Chico Maki, Wayne Hicks, Tommy Ivan (manager), Rudy Pilous (coach), Nick Garen (trainer).
Scores: April 6 at Chicago — Chicago 3, Detroit 2; April 8 at Detroit — Detroit 3, Chicago 1; April 10 at Chicago — Chicago 3, Detroit 1; April 12 at Detroit — Detroit 2, Chicago 1; April 14 at Chicago — Chicago 6, Detroit 3; April 16 at Detroit — Chicago 5, Detroit 1.

1959-60 — Montreal Canadiens — Jacques Plante, Charlie Hodge, Doug Harvey, Tom Johnson, Bob Turner, Jean-Guy Talbot, Albert Langlois, Ralph Backstrom, Jean Béliveau, Marcel Bonin, Bernie Geoffrion, Phil Goyette, Bill Hicke, Don Marshall, Ab McDonald, Dickie Moore, André Pronovost, Claude Provost, Henri Richard, Maurice Richard, Frank Selke (manager), Toe Blake (coach), Hector Dubois, Larry Aubut (trainers).
Scores: April 7 at Montreal — Montreal 4, Toronto 2; April 9 at Montreal — Montreal 2, Toronto 1; April 12 at Toronto — Montreal 5, Toronto 2; April 14 at Toronto — Montreal 4, Toronto 0.

1958-59 — Montreal Canadiens — Jacques Plante, Charlie Hodge, Doug Harvey, Tom Johnson, Bob Turner, Jean-Guy Talbot, Albert Langlois, Bernie Geoffrion, Ralph Backstrom, Bill Hicke, Maurice Richard, Dickie Moore, Claude Provost, Ab McDonald, Henri Richard, Marcel Bonin, Phil Goyette, Don Marshall, André Pronovost, Jean Béliveau, Frank Selke (manager), Toe Blake (coach), Hector Dubois, Larry Aubut (trainers).
Scores: April 9 at Montreal — Montreal 5, Toronto 3; April 11 at Montreal — Montreal 3, Toronto 1; April 14 at Toronto — Toronto 3, Montreal 2; April 16 at Toronto — Montreal 3, Toronto 2; April 18 at Montreal — Montreal 5, Toronto 3.

1957-58 — Montreal Canadiens — Jacques Plante, Gerry McNeil, Doug Harvey, Tom Johnson, Bob Turner, Dollard St-Laurent, Jean-Guy Talbot, Albert Langlois, Jean Béliveau, Bernie Geoffrion, Maurice Richard, Dickie Moore, Claude Provost, Floyd Curry, Bert Olmstead, Henri Richard, Marcel Bonin, Phil Goyette, Don Marshall, André Pronovost, Connie Broden, Frank Selke (manager), Toe Blake (coach), Hector Dubois, Larry Aubut (trainers).
Scores: April 8 at Montreal —Montreal 2, Boston 1; April 10 at Montreal — Boston 5, Montreal 2; April 13 at Boston — Montreal 3, Boston 0; April 15 at Boston — Boston 3, Montreal 1; April 17 at Montreal — Montreal 3, Boston 2; April 20 at Boston — Montreal 5, Boston 3.

May 10, 1970: Coach Harry Sinden is hoisted into the air by a gleeful group of Boston players after the Bruins swept the St. Louis Blues to win their first Stanley Cup crown in 29 years.

1956-57 — Montreal Canadiens — Jacques Plante, Gerry McNeil, Doug Harvey, Tom Johnson, Bob Turner, Dollard St. Laurent, Jean-Guy Talbot, Jean Béliveau, Bernie Geoffrion, Floyd Curry, Dickie Moore, Maurice Richard, Claude Provost, Bert Olmstead, Henri Richard, Phil Goyette, Don Marshall, André Pronovost, Connie Broden, Frank Selke (manager), Toe Blake (coach), Hector Dubois, Larry Aubut (trainers).
Scores: April 6, at Montreal — Montreal 5, Boston 1; April 9, at Montreal — Montreal 1, Boston 0; April 11, at Boston — Montreal 4, Boston 2; April 14, at Boston — Boston 2, Montreal 0; April 16, at Montreal — Montreal 5, Boston 1.

1955-56 — Montreal Canadiens — Jacques Plante, Doug Harvey, Butch Bouchard, Bob Turner, Tom Johnson, Jean-Guy Talbot, Dollard St. Laurent, Jean Béliveau, Bernie Geoffrion, Bert Olmstead, Floyd Curry, Jackie Leclair, Maurice Richard, Dickie Moore, Henri Richard, Kenny Mosdell, Don Marshall, Claude Provost, Frank Selke (manager), Toe Blake (coach), Hector Dubois (trainer).
Scores: March 31, at Montreal — Montreal 6, Detroit 4; April 3, at Montreal — Montreal 5, Detroit 1; April 5, at Detroit — Detroit 3, Montreal 1; April 8, at Detroit — Montreal 3, Detroit 0; April 10, at Montreal — Montreal 3, Detroit 1.

1954-55 — Detroit Red Wings — Terry Sawchuk, Red Kelly, Bob Goldham, Marcel Pronovost, Benny Woit, Jim Hay, Larry Hillman, Ted Lindsay, Tony Leswick, Gordie Howe, Alex Delvecchio, Marty Pavelich, Glen Skov, Earl Reibel, John Wilson, Bill Dineen, Vic Stasiuk, Marcel Bonin, Jack Adams (manager), Jimmy Skinner (coach), Carl Mattson (trainer).
Scores: April 3, at Detroit — Detroit 4, Montreal 2; April 5, at Detroit — Detroit 7, Montreal 1, April 7 at Montreal — Montreal 4, Detroit 2; April 9, at Montreal — Montreal 5, Detroit 3; April 10, at Detroit — Detroit 5, Montreal 1; April 12, at Montreal — Montreal 6, Detroit 3; April 14, at Detroit — Detroit 3, Montreal 1

1953-54 — Detroit Red Wings — Terry Sawchuk, Red Kelly, Bob Goldham, Benny Woit, Marcel Pronovost, Al Arbour, Keith Allen, Ted Lindsay, Tony Leswick, Gordie Howe, Marty Pavelich, Alex Delvecchio, Metro Prystai, Glen Skov, Johnny Wilson, Bill Dineen, Jim Peters, Earl Reibel, Vic Stasiuk, Jack Adams (manager), Tommy Ivan (coach), Carl Mattson (trainer).
Scores: April 4, at Detroit — Detroit 3, Montreal 1; April 6, at Detroit — Montreal 3, Detroit 1; April 8, at Montreal — Detroit 5, Montreal 2; April 10, at Montreal — Detroit 2, Montreal 0; April 11, at Detroit — Montreal 1, Detroit 0; April 13, at Montreal — Montreal 4, Detroit 1; April 16, at Detroit — Detroit 2, Montreal 1.

1952-53 — Montreal Canadiens — Gerry McNeil, Jacques Plante, Doug Harvey, Butch Bouchard, Tom Johnson, Dollard St. Laurent, Bud MacPherson, Maurice Richard, Elmer Lach, Bert Olmstead, Bernie Geoffrion, Floyd Curry, Paul Masnick, Billy Reay, Dickie Moore, Kenny Mosdell, Dick Gamble, Johnny McCormack, Lorne Davis, Calum MacKay, Eddie Mazur, Frank Selke (manager), Dick Irvin (coach), Hector Dubois (trainer).
Scores: April 9, at Montreal — Montreal 4, Boston 2; April 11, at Montreal — Boston 4, Montreal 1; April 12, at Boston — Montreal 3, Boston 0; April 14, at Boston — Montreal 7, Boston 3; April 16, at Montreal — Montreal 1, Boston 0.

1951-52 — Detroit Red Wings — Terry Sawchuk, Bob Goldham, Benny Woit, Red Kelly, Leo Reise Jr., Marcel Pronovost, Ted Lindsay, Tony Leswick, Gordie Howe, Metro Prystai, Marty Pavelich, Sid Abel, Glen Skov, Alex Delvecchio, John Wilson, Vic Stasiuk, Larry Zeidel, Jack Adams (manager) Tommy Ivan (coach), Carl Mattson (trainer).
Scores: April 10, at Montreal — Detroit 3, Montreal 1; April 12 at Montreal — Detroit 2, Montreal 1; April 13, at Detroit — Detroit 3, Montreal 0; April 15, at Detroit — Detroit 3, Montreal 0.

1950-51 — Toronto Maple Leafs — Turk Broda, Al Rollins, Jim Thomson, Gus Mortson, Bill Barilko, Bill Juzda, Fern Flaman, Hugh Bolton, Ted Kennedy, Sid Smith, Tod Sloan, Cal Gardner, Howie Meeker, Harry Watson, Max Bentley, Joe Klukay, Danny Lewicki, Ray Timgren, Fleming Mackell, Johnny McCormack, Bob Hassard, Conn Smythe (manager), Joe Primeau (coach), Tim Daly (trainer).
Scores: April 11, at Toronto — Toronto 3, Montreal 2; April 14, at Toronto — Montreal 3, Toronto 2; April 17, at Montreal — Toronto 2, Montreal 1; April 19, at Montreal — Toronto 3, Montreal 2; April 21, at Toronto — Toronto 3, Montreal 2.

1949-50 — Detroit Red Wings — Harry Lumley, Jack Stewart, Leo Reise Jr., Clare Martin, Al Dewsbury, Lee Fogolin, Marcel Pronovost, Red Kelly, Ted Lindsay, Sid Abel, Gordie Howe, George Gee, Jimmy Peters, Marty Pavelich, Jim McFadden, Pete Babando, Max McNab, Gerry Couture, Joe Carveth, Steve Black, John Wilson, Larry Wilson, Jack Adams (manager), Tommy Ivan (coach), Carl Mattson (trainer).
Scores: April 11, at Detroit — Detroit 4, NY Rangers 1; April 13, at Toronto* — NY Rangers 3, Detroit 1; April 15, at Toronto — Detroit 4, NY Rangers 0; April 18, at Detroit — NY Rangers 4, Detroit 3; April 20, at Detroit — NY Rangers 2, Detroit 1; April 22, at Detroit — Detroit 5, NY Rangers 4; April 23, at Detroit — Detroit 4, NY Rangers 3.

* Ice was unavailable in Madison Square Garden and Rangers elected to play second and third games on Toronto ice.

1948-49 — Toronto Maple Leafs — Turk Broda, Jim Thomson, Gus Mortson, Bill Barilko, Garth Boesch, Bill Juzda, Ted Kennedy, Howie Meeker, Vic Lynn, Harry Watson, Bill Ezinicki, Cal Gardner, Max Bentley, Joe Klukay, Sid Smith, Don Metz, Ray Timgren, Fleming Mackell, Harry Taylor, Bob Dawes, Tod Sloan, Conn Smythe (manager), Hap Day (coach), Tim Daly (trainer).
Scores: April 8, at Detroit — Toronto 3, Detroit 2; April 10, at Detroit — Toronto 3, Detroit 1; April 13, at Toronto — Toronto 3, Detroit 1; April 16, at Toronto — Toronto 3, Detroit 1.

1947-48 — Toronto Maple Leafs — Turk Broda, Jim Thomson, Wally Stanowski, Garth Boesch, Bill Barilko, Gus Mortson, Phil Samis, Syl Apps, Bill Ezinicki, Harry Watson, Ted Kennedy, Howie Meeker, Vic Lynn, Nick Metz, Max Bentley, Joe Klukay, Les Costello, Don Metz, Sid Smith, Conn Smythe (manager), Hap Day (coach), Tim Daly (trainer).
Scores: April 7, at Toronto — Toronto 5, Detroit 3; April 10, at Toronto — Toronto 4, Detroit 2; April 11, at Detroit — Toronto 2, Detroit 0; April 14, at Detroit — Toronto 7, Detroit 2.

The smiles on the faces of, left to right, Harris, Stewart, Bower, Stanley, Bathgate, Armstrong, Pulford, Shack, Baun and Horton say it all. The Toronto Maple Leafs were the NHL's best in 1964.

1946-47 — Toronto Maple Leafs — Turk Broda, Garth Boesch, Gus Mortson, Jim Thomson, Wally Stanowski, Bill Barilko, Harry Watson, Bud Poile, Ted Kennedy, Syl Apps, Don Metz, Nick Metz, Bill Ezinicki, Vic Lynn, Howie Meeker, Gaye Stewart, Joe Klukay, Gus Bodnar, Bob Goldham, Conn Smythe (manager), Hap Day (coach), Tim Daly (trainer).
Scores: April 8, at Montreal — Montreal 6, Toronto 0; April 10, at Montreal — Toronto 4, Montreal 0; April 12, at Toronto — Toronto 4, Montreal 2; April 15, at Toronto — Toronto 2, Montreal 1; April 17, at Montreal — Montreal 3, Toronto 1; April 19, at Toronto — Toronto 2, Montreal 1.

1945-46 — Montreal Canadiens — Elmer Lach, Toe Blake, Maurice Richard, Bob Fillion, Dutch Hiller, Murph Chamberlain, Ken Mosdell, Buddy O'Connor, Glen Harmon, Jimmy Peters Sr., Butch Bouchard, Billy Reay, Ken Reardon, Leo Lamoureux, Frank Eddolls, Gerry Plamondon, Bill Durnan, Tommy Gorman (manager), Dick Irvin (coach), Ernie Cook (trainer).
Scores: March 30, at Montreal — Montreal 4, Boston 3; April 2, at Montreal — Montreal 3, Boston 2; April 4, at Boston — Montreal 4, Boston 2; April 7, at Boston — Boston 3, Montreal 2; April 9, at Montreal — Montreal 6, Boston 3.

1944-45 — Toronto Maple Leafs — Don Metz, Frank McCool, Wally Stanowski, Reg Hamilton, Elwyn Morris, Johnny McCreedy, Tommy O'Neill, Ted Kennedy, Babe Pratt, Gus Bodnar, Art Jackson, Jack McLean, Mel Hill, Nick Metz, Bob Davidson, Sweeney Schriner, Lorne Carr, Conn Smythe (manager), Frank Selke (business manager), Hap Day (coach), Tim Daly (trainer).
Scores: April 6, at Detroit — Toronto 1, Detroit 0; April 8, at Detroit — Toronto 2, Detroit 0; April 12, at Toronto — Toronto 1, Detroit 0; April 14, at Toronto — Detroit 5, Toronto 3; April 19, at Detroit — Detroit 2, Toronto 0; April 21, at Toronto — Detroit 1, Toronto 0; April 22, at Detroit — Toronto 2, Detroit 1.

1943-44 — Montreal Canadiens — Toe Blake, Maurice Richard, Elmer Lach, Ray Getliffe, Murph Chamberlain, Phil Watson, Butch Bouchard, Glen Harmon, Buddy O'Connor, Jerry Heffernan, Mike McMahon Sr., Leo Lamoureux, Fernand Majeau, Bob Fillion, Bill Durnan, Tommy Gorman (manager), Dick Irvin (coach), Ernie Cook (trainer).
Scores: April 4, at Montreal — Montreal 5, Chicago 1; April 6, at Chicago — Montreal 3, Chicago 1; April 9, at Chicago — Montreal 3, Chicago 2; April 13, at Montreal — Montreal 5, Chicago 4.

1942-43 — Detroit Red Wings — Jack Stewart, Jimmy Orlando, Sid Abel, Alex Motter, Harry Watson, Joe Carveth, Mud Bruneteau, Eddie Wares, Johnny Mowers, Cully Simon, Don Grosso, Carl Liscombe, Connie Brown, Syd Howe, Les Douglas, Hal Jackson, Joe Fisher, Jack Adams (manager), Ebbie Goodfellow (playing-coach), Honey Walker (trainer).
Scores: April 1, at Detroit — Detroit 6, Boston 2; April 4, at Detroit — Detroit 4, Boston 3; April 7, at Boston — Detroit 4, Boston 0; April 8, at Boston — Detroit 2, Boston 0.

1941-42 — Toronto Maple Leafs — Wally Stanowski, Syl Apps Sr., Bob Goldham, Gordie Drillon, Hank Goldup, Ernie Dickens, Dave Schriner, Bucko McDonald, Bob Davidson, Nick Metz, Bingo Kampman, Don Metz, Gaye Stewart, Turk Broda, Johnny McCreedy, Lorne Carr, Pete Langelle, Billy Taylor, Conn Smythe (manager), Hap Day (coach), Frank Selke (business manager), Tim Daly (trainer).
Scores: April 4, at Toronto — Detroit 3, Toronto 2; April 7, at Toronto — Detroit 4, Toronto 2; April 9, at Detroit — Detroit 5, Toronto 2; April 12, at Detroit — Toronto 4, Detroit 3; April 14, at Toronto — Toronto 9, Detroit 3; April 16, at Detroit — Toronto 3, Detroit 0; April 18, at Toronto — Toronto 3, Detroit 1.

1940-41 — Boston Bruins — Bill Cowley, Des Smith, Dit Clapper, Frank Brimsek, Flash Hollett, John Crawford, Bobby Bauer, Pat McReavy, Herb Cain, Mel Hill, Milt Schmidt, Woody Dumart, Roy Conacher, Terry Reardon, Art Jackson, Eddie Wiseman, Art Ross (manager), Cooney Weiland (coach), Win Green (trainer).
Scores: April 6, at Boston — Detroit 2, Boston 3; April 8, at Boston — Detroit 1, Boston 2; April 10, at Detroit — Boston 4, Detroit 2; April 12, at Detroit — Boston 3, Detroit 1.

1939-40 — New York Rangers — Dave Kerr, Art Coulter, Ott Heller, Alex Shibicky, Mac Colville, Neil Colville, Phil Watson, Lynn Patrick, Clint Smith, Muzz Patrick, Babe Pratt, Bryan Hextall Sr., Kilby Macdonald, Dutch Hiller, Alf Pike, Sanford Smith, Lester Patrick (manager), Frank Boucher (coach), Harry Westerby (trainer).
Scores: April 2, at New York — NY Rangers 2, Toronto 1; April 3, at New York — NY Rangers 6, Toronto 2; April 6, at Toronto — NY Rangers 1, Toronto 2; April 9, at Toronto — NY Rangers 0, Toronto 3; April 11, at Toronto — NY Rangers 2, Toronto 1; April 13, at Toronto — NY Rangers 3, Toronto 2.

1938-39 — Boston Bruins — Bobby Bauer, Mel Hill, Flash Hollett, Roy Conacher, Gord Pettinger, Milt Schmidt, Woody Dumart, Jack Crawford, Ray Getliffe, Frank Brimsek, Eddie Shore, Dit Clapper, Bill Cowley, Jack Portland, Red Hamill, Cooney Weiland, Art Ross (manager-coach), Win Green (trainer).
Scores: April 6, at Boston — Toronto 1, Boston 2; April 9, at Boston — Toronto 3, Boston 2; April 11, at Toronto — Toronto 1, Boston 3; April 13 at Toronto — Toronto 0, Boston 2; April 16, at Boston — Toronto 1, Boston 3.

1937-38 — Chicago Black Hawks — Art Wiebe, Carl Voss, Hal Jackson, Mike Karakas, Mush March, Jack Shill, Earl Seibert, Cully Dahlstrom, Alex Levinsky, Johnny Gottselig, Lou Trudel, Pete Palangio, Bill MacKenzie, Doc Romnes, Paul Thompson, Roger Jenkins, Alf Moore, Bert Connolly, Virgil Johnson, Paul Goodman, Bill Stewart (manager-coach), Eddie Froelich (trainer).
Scores: April 5, at Toronto — Chicago 3, Toronto 1; April 7, at Toronto — Chicago 1, Toronto 5; April 10 at Chicago — Chicago 2, Toronto 1; April 12, at Chicago — Chicago 4, Toronto 1.

1936-37 — Detroit Red Wings — Norman Smith, Pete Kelly, Larry Aurie, Herbie Lewis, Hec Kilrea, Mud Bruneteau, Syd Howe, Wally Kilrea, Jimmy Franks, Bucko McDonald, Gord Pettinger, Ebbie Goodfellow, John Gallagher, Ralph Bowman, John Sorrell, Marty Barry, Earl Robertson, John Sherf, Howard Mackie, Jack Adams (manager-coach), Honey Walker (trainer).
Scores: April 6, at New York — Detroit 1, NY Rangers 5; April 8, at Detroit — Detroit 4, NY Rangers 2; April 11, at Detroit — Detroit 0, NY Rangers 1; April 13, at Detroit — Detroit 1, NY Rangers 0; April 15, at Detroit — Detroit 3, NY Rangers 0.

1935-36 — Detroit Red Wings — John Sorrell, Syd Howe, Marty Barry, Herbie Lewis, Mud Bruneteau, Wally Kilrea, Hec Kilrea, Gord Pettinger, Bucko McDonald, Ralph Bowman, Pete Kelly, Doug Young, Ebbie Goodfellow, Norman Smith, Jack Adams (manager-coach), Honey Walker (trainer).
Scores: April 5, at Detroit — Detroit 3, Toronto 1; April 7, at Detroit — Detroit 9, Toronto 4; April 9, at Toronto — Detroit 3, Toronto 4; April 11, at Toronto — Detroit 3, Toronto 2.

1934-35 — Montreal Maroons — Cy Wentworth, Alex Connell, Toe Blake, Stewart Evans, Earl Robinson, Bill Miller, Dave Trottier, Jimmy Ward, Larry Northcott, Hooley Smith, Russ Blinco, Allan Shields, Sammy McManus, Gus Marker, Bob Gracie, Herb Cain, Tommy Gorman (manager), Lionel Conacher (coach), Bill O'Brien (trainer).
Scores: April 4, at Toronto — Mtl. Maroons 3, Toronto 2; April 6, at Toronto — Mtl. Maroons 3, Toronto 1; April 9, at Montreal — Mtl. Maroons 4, Toronto 1.

1933-34 — Chicago Black Hawks — Clarence Abel, Rosie Couture, Lou Trudel, Lionel Conacher, Paul Thompson, Leroy Goldsworthy, Art Coulter, Roger Jenkins, Don McFayden, Tom Cook, Doc Romnes, Johnny Gottselig, Mush March, Johnny Sheppard, Chuck Gardiner (captain), Bill Kendall, Tommy Gorman (manager-coach), Eddie Froelich (trainer).
Scores: April 3, at Detroit — Chicago 2, Detroit 1; April 5, at Detroit — Chicago 4, Detroit 1; April 8, at Chicago — Detroit 5, Chicago 2; April 10, at Chicago — Chicago 1, Detroit 0.

1932-33 — New York Rangers — Ching Johnson, Butch Keeling, Frank Boucher, Art Somers, Babe Siebert, Bun Cook, Andy Aikenhead, Ott Heller, Oscar Asmundson, Gord Pettinger, Doug Brennan, Cecil Dillon, Bill Cook (captain), Murray Murdoch, Earl Seibert, Lester Patrick (manager-coach), Harry Westerby (trainer).
Scores: April 4, at New York — NY Rangers 5, Toronto 1; April 8, at Toronto — NY Rangers 3, Toronto 1; April 11, at Toronto — Toronto 3, NY Rangers 2; April 13, at Toronto — NY Rangers 1, Toronto 0.

1931-32 — Toronto Maple Leafs — Charlie Conacher, Harvey Jackson, King Clancy, Andy Blair, Red Horner, Lorne Chabot, Alex Levinsky, Joe Primeau, Hal Darragh, Hal Cotton, Frank Finnigan, Hap Day, Ace Bailey, Bob Gracie, Fred Robertson, Earl Miller, Conn Smythe (manager), Dick Irvin (coach), Tim Daly (trainer).
Scores: April 5 at New York — Toronto 6, NY Rangers 4; April 7, at Boston* — Toronto 6, NY Rangers 2; April 9, at Toronto — Toronto 6, NY Rangers 4.

* Ice was unavailable in Madison Square Garden and Rangers elected to play the second game on neutral ice.

1930-31 — Montreal Canadiens — George Hainsworth, Wildor Larochelle, Marty Burke, Sylvio Mantha, Howie Morenz, Johnny Gagnon, Aurel Joliat, Armand Mondou, Pit Lepine, Albert Leduc, Georges Mantha, Art Lesieur, Nick Wasnie, Bert McCaffrey, Gus Rivers, Jean Pusie, Léo Dandurand (manager), Cecil Hart (coach), Ed Dufour (trainer).
Scores: April 3, at Chicago — Montreal 2, Chicago 1; April 5, at Chicago — Chicago 2, Montreal 1; April 9, at Montreal — Chicago 3, Montreal 2; April 11, at Montreal — Montreal 4, Chicago 2; April 14, at Montreal — Montreal 2, Chicago 0.

1929-30 — Montreal Canadiens — George Hainsworth, Marty Burke, Sylvio Mantha, Howie Morenz, Bert McCaffrey, Aurel Joliat, Albert Leduc, Pit Lepine, Wildor Larochelle, Nick Wasnie, Gerald Carson, Armand Mondou, Georges Mantha, Gus Rivers, Léo Dandurand (manager), Cecil Hart (coach), Ed Dufour (trainer).
Scores: April 1 at Boston — Montreal 3, Boston 0; April 3 at Montreal — Montreal 4, Boston 3.

1928-29 — Boston Bruins — Tiny Thompson, Eddie Shore, Lionel Hitchman, Perk Galbraith, Eric Pettinger, Frank Fredrickson, Mickey Mackay, Red Green, Dutch Gainor, Harry Oliver, Eddie Rodden, Dit Clapper, Cooney Weiland, Lloyd Klein, Cy Denneny, Bill Carson, George Owen, Myles Lane, Art Ross (manager-coach), Win Green (trainer).
Scores: March 28 at Boston — Boston 2, NY Rangers 0; March 29 at New York — Boston 2, NY Rangers 1.

1927-28 — New York Rangers — Lorne Chabot, Clarence Abel, Leon Bourgault, Ching Johnson, Bill Cook, Bun Cook, Frank Boucher, Bill Boyd, Murray Murdoch, Paul Thompson, Alex Gray, Joe Miller, Patsy Callighen, Lester Patrick (manager-coach), Harry Westerby (trainer).
Scores: April 5 at Montreal — Mtl. Maroons 2, NY Rangers 0; April 7 at Montreal — NY Rangers 2, Mtl. Maroons 1; April 10 at Montreal — Mtl. Maroons 2, NY Rangers 0; April 12 at Montreal — NY Rangers 1, Mtl. Maroons 0; April 14 at Montreal — NY Rangers 2, Mtl. Maroons 1.

1926-27 — Ottawa Senators — Alex Connell, King Clancy, George Boucher, Ed Gorman, Frank Finnigan, Alex Smith, Hec Kilrea, Hooley Smith, Cy Denneny, Frank Nighbor, Jack Adams, Milt Halliday, Dave Gill (manager-coach).
Scores: April 7 at Boston — Ottawa 0, Boston 0; April 9 at Boston — Ottawa 3, Boston 1; April 11 at Ottawa — Boston 1, Ottawa 1; April 13 at Ottawa — Ottawa 3, Boston 1.

1925-26 — Montreal Maroons — Clint Benedict, Reg Noble, Frank Carson, Dunc Munro, Nels Stewart, Harry Broadbent, Babe Siebert, Chuck Dinsmore, Bill Phillips, Hobie Kitchen, Sam Rothschield, Albert Holway, George Horne, Bernie Brophy, Eddie Gerard (manager-coach), Bill O'Brien (trainer).
Scores: March 30 at Montreal — Mtl. Maroons 3, Victoria 0; April 1 at Montreal — Mtl. Maroons 3, Victoria 0; April 3 at Montreal — Victoria 3, Mtl. Maroons 2; April 6 at Montreal — Mtl. Maroons 2, Victoria 0.

The series in the spring of 1926 ended the annual playoffs between the champions of the East and the champions of the West. Since 1926-27 the annual playoffs in the National Hockey League have decided the Stanley Cup champions.

1924-25 — Victoria Cougars — Harry Holmes, Clem Loughlin, Gord Fraser, Frank Fredrickson, Jack Walker, Wilf Hart, Harold Halderson, Frank Foyston, Wally Elmer, Harry Meeking, Jocko Anderson, Lester Patrick (manager-coach).
Scores: March 21 at Victoria — Victoria 5, Montreal 2; March 23 at Vancouver — Victoria 3, Montreal 1; March 27 at Victoria — Montreal 4, Victoria 2; March 30 at Victoria — Victoria 6, Montreal 1.

1923-24 — Montreal Canadiens — Georges Vezina, Sprague Cleghorn, Billy Couture, Howie Morenz, Aurel Joliat, Billy Boucher, Odie Cleghorn, Sylvio Mantha, Bobby Boucher, Billy Bell, Billy Cameron, Joe Malone, Charles Fortier, Leo Dandurand (manager-coach).
Scores: March 18 at Montreal — Montreal 3, Van. Maroons 2; March 20 at Montreal — Montreal 2, Van. Maroons 1. March 22 at Montreal — Montreal 6, Cgy. Tigers 1; March 25 at Ottawa* — Montreal 3, Cgy. Tigers 0.

* Game transferred to Ottawa to benefit from artificial ice surface.

1922-23 — Ottawa Senators — George Boucher, Lionel Hitchman, Frank Nighbor, King Clancy, Harry Helman, Clint Benedict, Jack Darragh, Eddie Gerard, Cy Denneny, Harry Broadbent, Tommy Gorman (manager), Pete Green (coach), F. Dolan (trainer).
Scores: March 16 at Vancouver — Ottawa 1, Van. Maroons 0; March 19 at Vancouver — Van. Maroons 4, Ottawa 1; March 23 at Vancouver — Ottawa 3, Van. Maroons 2; March 26 at Vancouver — Ottawa 5, Van. Maroons 1; March 29 at Vancouver — Ottawa 2, Edm. Eskimos 1; March 31 at Vancouver — Ottawa 1, Edm. Eskimos 0.

The 1939-40 New York Rangers needed three overtime wins to upset the Toronto Maple Leafs and capture the 1940 Stanley Cup championship in a six-game nailbiter. The Broadway Blues were forced to play four games in Toronto after the circus invaded Madison Square Garden.

1921-22 — Toronto St. Pats — Ted Stackhouse, Corb Denneny, Rod Smylie, Lloyd Andrews, John Ross Roach, Harry Cameron, Billy Stuart, Babe Dye, Ken Randall, Reg Noble, Eddie Gerard (borrowed for one game from Ottawa), Stan Jackson, Nolan Mitchell, Charlie Querrie (manager), Eddie Powers (coach).
Scores: March 17 at Toronto — Van. Millionaires 4, Toronto 3; March 20 at Toronto — Toronto 2, Van. Millionaires 1; March 23 at Toronto — Van. Millionaires 3, Toronto 0; March 25 at Toronto — Toronto 6, Van. Millionaires 0; March 28 at Toronto — Toronto 5, Van. Millionaires 1.

1920-21 — Ottawa Senators — Jack McKell, Jack Darragh, Morley Bruce, George Boucher, Eddie Gerard, Clint Benedict, Sprague Cleghorn, Frank Nighbor, Harry Broadbent, Cy Denneny, Leth Graham, Tommy Gorman (manager),Pete Green (coach), F. Dolan (trainer).
Scores: March 21 at Vancouver — Van. Millionaires 2, Ottawa 1; March 24 at Vancouver — Ottawa 4, Van. Millionaires 3; March 28 at Vancouver — Ottawa 3, Van. Millionaires 2; March 31 at Vancouver — Van. Millionaires 3, Ottawa 2; April 4 at Vancouver — Ottawa 2, Van. Millionaires 1

1919-20 — Ottawa Senators — Jack McKell, Jack Darragh, Morley Bruce, Horrace Merrill, George Boucher, Eddie Gerard, Clint Benedict, Sprague Cleghorn, Frank Nighbor, Harry Broadbent, Cy Denneny, Price, Tommy Gorman (manager), Pete Green (coach).
Scores: March 22 at Ottawa — Ottawa 3, Seattle 2; March 24 at Ottawa — Ottawa 3, Seattle 0; March 27 at Ottawa — Seattle 3, Ottawa 1; March 30 at Toronto* — Seattle 5, Ottawa 2; April 1 at Toronto* — Ottawa 6, Seattle 1.
* Games transferred to Toronto to benefit from artificial ice surface.

1918-19 — No decision, Series halted by Spanish influenza epidemic, illness of several players and death of Joe Hall of Montreal Canadiens from flu. Five games had been played when the series was halted, each team having won two and tied one. The results are shown:
Scores: March 19 at Seattle — Seattle 7, Montreal 0; March 22 at Seattle — Montreal 4, Seattle 2; March 24 at Seattle — Seattle 7, Montreal 2; March 26 at Seattle — Montreal 0, Seattle 0; March 30 at Seattle — Montreal 4, Seattle 3.

1917-18 — Toronto Arenas — Rusty Crawford, Harry Meeking, Ken Randall, Corb Denneny, Harry Cameron, Jack Adams, Alf Skinner, Harry Mummery, Harry Holmes, Reg Noble, Sammy Hebert, Jack Marks, Jack Coughlin, Charlie Querrie (manager), Dick Carroll (coach), Frank Carroll (trainer).
Scores: March 20 at Toronto — Toronto 5, Van. Millionaires 3; March 23 at Toronto — Van. Millionaires 6, Toronto 4; March 26 at Toronto — Toronto 6, Van. Millionaires 3; March 28 at Toronto — Van. Millionaires 8, Toronto 1; March 30 at Toronto — Toronto 2, Van. Millionaires 1.

1916-17 — Seattle Metropolitans — Harry Holmes, Ed Carpenter, Cully Wilson, Jack Walker, Bernie Morris, Frank Foyston, Roy Rickey, Jim Riley, Bobby Rowe (captain), Peter Muldoon (manager).
Scores: March 17 at Seattle — Montreal 8, Seattle 4; March 20 at Seattle — Seattle 6, Montreal 1; March 23 at Seattle — Seattle 4, Montreal 1; March 25 at Seattle — Seattle 9, Montreal 1.

1915-16 — Montreal Canadiens — Georges Vezina, Bert Corbeau, Jack Laviolette, Newsy Lalonde, Louis Berlinguette, Goldie Prodgers, Howard McNamara, Didier Pitre, Skene Ronan, Amos Arbour, Georges Poulin, Jacques Fournier, George Kennedy (manager).
Scores: March 20 at Montreal — Portland 2, Montreal 0; March 22 at Montreal — Montreal 2, Portland 1; March 25 at Montreal — Montreal 6, Portland 3; March 28 at Montreal — Portland 6, Montreal 5; March 30 at Montreal — Montreal 2, Portland 1.

1914-15 — Vancouver Millionaires — Kenny Mallen, Frank Nighbor, Fred (Cyclone) Taylor, Hughie Lehman, Lloyd Cook, Mickey MacKay, Barney Stanley, Jim Seaborn, Si Griffis (captain), Jean Matz, Frank Patrick (playing manager).
Scores: March 22 at Vancouver — Van. Millionaires 6, Ottawa 2; March 24 at Vancouver — Van. Millionaires 8, Ottawa 3; March 26 at Vancouver — Van. Millionaires 12, Ottawa 3.

1913-14 — Toronto Blueshirts — Con Corbeau, F. Roy McGiffen, Jack Walker, George McNamara, Cully Wilson, Frank Foyston, Harry Cameron, Harry Holmes, Alan M. Davidson (captain), Harriston, Jack Marshall (playing-manager), Frank and Dick Carroll (trainers).
Scores: March 14 at Toronto — Toronto 5, Victoria 2; March 17 at Toronto — Toronto 6, Victoria 5; March 19 at Toronto — Toronto 2, Victoria 1.

1912-13 — Quebec Bulldogs — Joe Malone, Joe Hall, Paddy Moran, Harry Mummery, Tommy Smith, Jack Marks, Russell Crawford, Billy Creighton, Jeff Malone, Rocket Power, M.J. Quinn (manager), D. Beland (trainer).
Scores: March 8 at Quebec — Que. Bulldogs 14, Sydney 3; March 10 at Quebec — Que. Bulldogs 6, Sydney 2.

Victoria challenged Quebec but the Bulldogs refused to put the Stanley Cup in competition so the two teams played an exhibition series with Victoria winning two games to one by scores of 7-5, 3-6, 6-1. It was the first meeting between the Eastern champions and the Western champions. The following year, and until the Western Hockey League disbanded after the 1926 playoffs, the Cup went to the winner of the series between East and West.

1911-12 — Quebec Bulldogs — Goldie Prodgers, Joe Hall, Walter Rooney, Paddy Moran, Jack Marks, Jack McDonald, Eddie Oatman, George Leonard, Joe Malone (captain), C. Nolan (coach), M.J. Quinn (manager), D. Beland (trainer).
Scores: March 11 at Quebec — Que. Bulldogs 9, Moncton 3; March 13 at Quebec — Que. Bulldogs 8, Moncton 0.

Prior to 1912, teams could challenge the Stanley Cup champions for the title, thus there was more than one Championship Series played in most of the seasons between 1894 and 1911.

1910-11 — Ottawa Senators — Hamby Shore, Percy LeSueur, Jack Darragh, Bruce Stuart, Marty Walsh, Bruce Ridpath, Fred Lake, Albert (Dubby) Kerr, Alex Currie, Horace Gaul.
Scores: March 13 at Ottawa — Ottawa 7, Galt 4; March 16 at Ottawa — Ottawa 13, Port Arthur 4.

1909-10 — Montreal Wanderers — Cecil W. Blachford, Ernie (Moose) Johnson, Ernie Russell, Riley Hern, Harry Hyland, Jack Marshall, Frank (Pud) Glass (captain), Jimmy Gardner, R. R. Boon (manager).
Scores: March 12 at Montreal — Mtl. Wanderers 7, Berlin (Kitchener) 3.

1908-09 — Ottawa Senators — Fred Lake, Percy LeSueur, Fred (Cyclone) Taylor, H.L. (Billy) Gilmour, Albert Kerr, Edgar Dey, Marty Walsh, Bruce Stuart (captain).
Scores: Ottawa, as champions of the Eastern Canada Hockey Association took over the Stanley Cup in 1909 and, although a challenge was accepted by the Cup trustees from Winnipeg Shamrocks, games could not be arranged because of the lateness of the season. No other challenges were made in 1909. The following season — 1909-10 — however, the Senators accepted two challenges as defending Cup Champions. The first was against Galt in a two-game, total-goals series, and the second against Edmonton, also a two-game, total-goals series. Results: January 5 at Ottawa —Ottawa 12, Galt 3; January 7 at Ottawa — Ottawa 3, Galt 1. January 18 at Ottawa — Ottawa 8, Edm. Eskimos 4; January 20 at Ottawa — Ottawa 13, Edm. Eskimos 7.

1907-08 — Montreal Wanderers — Riley Hern, Art Ross, Walter Smaill, Frank (Pud) Glass, Bruce Stuart, Ernie Russell, Ernie (Moose) Johnson, Cecil Blachford (captain), Tom Hooper, Larry Gilmour, Ernie Liffiton, R.R. Boon (manager).
Scores: Wanderers accepted four challenges for the Cup: January 9 at Montreal — Mtl. Wanderers 9, Ott. Victorias 3; January 13 at Montreal — Mtl. Wanderers 13, Ott. Victorias 1; March 10 at Montreal — Mtl. Wanderers 11, Wpg. Maple Leafs 5; March 12 at Montreal — Mtl. Wanderers 9, Wpg. Maple Leafs 3; March 14 at Montreal — Mtl. Wanderers 6, Toronto (OPHL) 4. At start of following season, 1908-09, Wanderers were challenged by Edmonton. Results: December 28 at Montreal — Mtl. Wanderers 7, Edm. Eskimos 3; December 30 at Montreal — Edm. Eskimos 7, Mtl. Wanderers 6. Total goals: Mtl. Wanderers 13, Edm. Eskimos 10.

1906-07 — (March) — **Montreal Wanderers** — W. S. (Billy) Strachan, Riley Hern, Lester Patrick, Hod Stuart, Frank (Pud) Glass, Ernie Russell, Cecil Blachford (captain), Ernie (Moose) Johnson, Rod Kennedy, Jack Marshall, R.R. Boon (manager).
Scores: March 23 at Winnipeg — Mtl. Wanderers 7, Kenora 2; March 25 at Winnipeg — Kenora 6, Mtl. Wanderers 5. Total goals: Mtl. Wanderers 12, Kenora 8.

1906-07 — (January) — **Kenora Thistles** — Eddie Geroux, Art Ross, Si Griffis, Tom Hooper, Billy McGimsie, Roxy Beaudro, Tom Phillips.
Scores: January 17 at Montreal — Kenora 4, Mtl. Wanderers 2; Jan. 21 at Montreal — Kenora 8, Mtl. Wanderers 6.

1905-06 — (March) — **Montreal Wanderers** — Henri Menard, Billy Strachan, Rod Kennedy, Lester Patrick, Frank (Pud) Glass, Ernie Russell, Ernie (Moose) Johnson, Cecil Blachford (captain), Josh Arnold, R.R. Boon (manager).
Scores: March 14 at Montreal — Mtl. Wanderers 9, Ottawa 1; March 17 at Ottawa — Ottawa 9, Mtl. Wanderers 3. Total goals: Mtl. Wanderers 12, Ottawa 10. Wanderers accepted a challenge from New Glasgow, N.S., prior to the start of the 1906-07 season. Results: December 27 at Montreal — Mtl. Wanderers 10, New Glasgow 3; December 29 at Montreal — Mtl. Wanderers 7, New Glasgow 2.

1905-06 — (February) — **Ottawa Silver Seven** — Harvey Pulford (captain), Arthur Moore, Harry Westwick, Frank McGee, Alf Smith (playing coach), Billy Gilmour, Billy Hague, Percy LeSueur, Harry Smith, Tommy Smith, Dion, Ebbs.
Scores: February 27 at Ottawa — Ottawa 16, Queen's University 7; February 28 at Ottawa — Ottawa 12, Queen's University 7; March 6 at Ottawa — Ottawa 6, Smiths Falls 5; March 8 at Ottawa — Ottawa 8, Smiths Falls 2.

1904-05 — Ottawa Silver Seven — Dave Finnie, Harvey Pulford (captain), Arthur Moore, Harry Westwick, Frank McGee, Alf Smith (playing coach), Billy Gilmour, Frank White, Horace Gaul, Hamby Shore, Bones Allen.
Scores: January 13 at Ottawa — Ottawa 9, Dawson City 2; January 16 at Ottawa — Ottawa 23, Dawson City 2; March 7 at Ottawa — Rat Portage 9, Ottawa 3; March 9 at Ottawa — Ottawa 4, Rat Portage 2; March 11 at Ottawa — Ottawa 5, Rat Portage 4.

1903-04 — Ottawa Silver Seven — S.C. (Suddy) Gilmour, Arthur Moore, Frank McGee, J.B. (Bouse) Hutton, H.L. (Billy) Gilmour, Jim McGee, Harry Westwick, E. H. (Harvey) Pulford (captain), Scott, Alf Smith (playing coach).
Scores: December 30 at Ottawa — Ottawa 9, Wpg. Rowing Club 1; January 1 at Ottawa — Wpg. Rowing Club 6, Ottawa 2; January 4 at Ottawa — Ottawa 2, Wpg. Rowing Club 0. February 23 at Ottawa — Ottawa 6, Tor. Marlboros 3; February 25 at Ottawa — Ottawa 11, Tor. Marlboros 2; March 2 at Montreal — Ottawa 5, Mtl. Wanderers 5. Following the tie game, a new two-game series was ordered to be played in Ottawa but the Wanderers refused unless the tie game was replayed in Montreal. When no settlement could be reached, the series was abandoned and Ottawa retained the Cup and accepted a two-game challenge from Brandon. Results: (both games at Ottawa), March 9, Ottawa 6, Brandon 3; March 11, Ottawa 9, Brandon 3.

1902-03 — (March) — **Ottawa Silver Seven** — S.C. (Suddy) Gilmour, P.T. (Percy) Sims, J.B. (Bouse) Hutton, D.J. (Dave) Gilmour, H.L. (Billy) Gilmour, Harry Westwick, Frank McGee, F.H. Wood, A.A. Fraser, Charles D. Spittal, E.H. (Harvey) Pulford (captain), Arthur Moore, Alf Smith (coach.)
Scores: March 7 at Montreal — Ottawa 1, Mtl. Victorias 1; March 10 at Ottawa — Ottawa 8, Mtl. Victorias 0. Total goals: Ottawa 9, Mtl. Victorias 1; March 12 at Ottawa — Ottawa 6, Rat Portage 2; March 14 at Ottawa — Ottawa 4, Rat Portage 2.

1902-03 — (February) — **Montreal AAA** — Tom Hodge, R.R. (Dickie) Boon, W.C. (Billy) Nicholson, Tom Phillips, Art Hooper, W.J. (Billy) Bellingham, Charles A. Liffiton, Jack Marshall, Jim Gardner, Cecil Blachford, George Smith.
Scores: January 29 at Montreal — Mtl. AAA 8, Wpg. Victorias 1; January 31 at Montreal — Wpg. Victorias 2, Mtl. AAA 2; February 2 at Montreal — Wpg. Victorias 4, Mtl. AAA 2; February 4 at Montreal — Mtl. AAA 5, Wpg. Victorias 1.

1901-02 — (March) — **Montreal AAA** — Tom Hodge, R.R. (Dickie) Boon, William C. (Billy) Nicholson, Archie Hooper, W.J. (Billy) Bellingham, Charles A. Liffiton, Jack Marshall, Roland Elliott, Jim Gardner.
Scores: March 13 at Winnipeg — Wpg. Victorias 1, Mtl. AAA 0; March 15 at Winnipeg — Mtl. AAA 5, Wpg. Victorias 0; March 17 at Winnipeg — Mtl. AAA 2, Wpg. Victorias 1.

1901-02 — (January) — **Winnipeg Victorias** — Burke Wood, A.B. (Tony) Gingras, Charles W. Johnstone, R.M. (Rod) Flett, Magnus L. Flett, Dan Bain (captain), Fred Scanlon, F. Cadham, G. Brown.
Scores: January 21 at Winnipeg — Wpg. Victorias 5, Tor Wellingtons 3; January 23 at Winnipeg — Wpg. Victorias 5, Tor. Wellingtons 3.

1900-01 — Winnipeg Victorias — Burke Wood, Jack Marshall, A.B. (Tony) Gingras, Charles W. Johnstone, R.M. (Rod) Flett, Magnus L. Flett, Dan Bain (captain), G. Brown.
Scores: January 29 at Montreal — Wpg. Victorias 4, Mtl. Shamrocks 3; January 31 at Montreal — Wpg. Victorias 2, Mtl. Shamrocks 1.

1899-1900 — Montreal Shamrocks — Joe McKenna, Frank Tansey, Frank Wall, Art Farrell, Fred Scanlon, Harry Trihey (captain), Jack Brannen.
Scores: February 12 at Montreal — Mtl. Shamrocks 4, Wpg. Victorias 3; February 14 at Montreal — Wpg. Victorias 3, Mtl. Shamrocks 2; February 16 at Montreal — Mtl. Shamrocks 5, Wpg. Victorias 4; March 5 at Montreal — Mtl. Shamrocks 10, Halifax 2; March 7 at Montreal — Mtl. Shamrocks 11, Halifax 0.

1898-99 — (March) — **Montreal Shamrocks** — Jim McKenna, Frank Tansey, Frank Wall, Harry Trihey (captain), Art Farrell, Fred Scanlon, Jack Brannen, John Dobby, Charles Hoerner.
Scores: March 14 at Montreal — Mtl. Shamrocks 6, Queen's University 2.

1898-99 — (February) — **Montreal Victorias** — Gordon Lewis, Mike Grant, Graham Drinkwater, Cam Davidson, Bob McDougall, Ernie McLea, Frank Richardson, Jack Ewing, Russell Bowie, Douglas Acer, Fred McRobie.
Scores: February 15 at Montreal — Mtl. Victorias 2, Wpg. Victorias 1; February 18 at Montreal — Mtl. Victorias 3, Wpg. Victorias 2.

1897-98 — Montreal Victorias — Gordon Lewis, Hartland McDougall, Mike Grant, Graham Drinkwater, Cam Davidson, Bob McDougall, Ernie McLea, Frank Richardson (captain), Jack Ewing. The Victorias as champions of the Amateur Hockey Association, retained the Cup and were not called upon to defend it.

1896-97 — Montreal Victorias — Gordon Lewis, Harold Henderson, Mike Grant (captain), Cam Davidson, Graham Drinkwater, Robert McDougall, Ernie McLea, Shirley Davidson, Hartland McDougall, Jack Ewing, Percy Molson, David Gillilan, McLellan.
Scores: December 27 at Montreal — Mtl. Victorias 15, Ott. Capitals 2.

1895-96 — (December) — **Montreal Victorias** — Harold Henderson, Mike Grant (captain), Robert McDougall, Graham Drinkwater, Shirley Davidson, Ernie McLea, Robert Jones, Cam Davidson, David Gillilan, Stanley Willett.
Scores: December 30 at Winnipeg — Mtl. Victorias 6, Wpg. Victorias 5.

1895-96 — (February) — **Winnipeg Victorias** — G.H. Merritt, Rod Flett, Fred Higginbotham, Jack Armitage (captain), C.J. (Tote) Campbell, Dan Bain, Charles Johnstone, H. Howard.
Scores: February 14 at Montreal — Wpg. Victorias 2, Mtl. Victorias 0.

1894-95 — Montreal Victorias — Robert Jones, Harold Henderson, Mike Grant (captain), Shirley Davidson, Bob McDougall, Norman Rankin, Graham Drinkwater, Roland Elliot, William Pullan, Hartland McDougall, Jim Fenwick, A. McDougall. Montreal Victorias, as champions of the Amateur Hockey Association, were prepared to defend the Stanley Cup. However, the Stanley Cup trustees had already accepted a challenge match between the 1894 champion Montreal AAA and Queen's University. It was declared that if Montreal AAA defeated Queen's University, Montreal Victorias would be declared Stanley Cup champions. If Queen's University won, the Cup would go to the university club. In a game played March 9, 1895, Montreal AAA defeated Queen's University 5-1. As a result, Montreal Victorias were awarded the Stanley Cup.

1893-94 — Montreal AAA — Herbert Collins, Allan Cameron, George James, Billy Barlow, Clare Mussen, Archie Hodgson, Haviland Routh, Alex Irving, James Stewart, A.C. (Toad) Wand, A. Kingan.
Scores: March 17 at Mtl. Victorias — Mtl. AAA 3, Mtl. Victorias 2; March 22 at Montreal — Mtl. AAA 3, Ott. Capitals 1.

1892-93 — Montreal AAA — Tom Paton, James Stewart, Allan Cameron, Haviland Routh, Archie Hodgson, Billy Barlow, A.B. Kingan, G.S. Lowe.
In accordance with the terms governing the presentation of the Stanley Cup, it was awarded for the first time to the Montreal AAA as champions of the Amateur Hockey Association in 1893. Once Montreal AAA had been declared holders of the Stanley Cup, any Canadian hockey team could challenge for the trophy.

All-Time NHL Playoff Formats

1917-18 — The regular-season was split into two halves. The winners of both halves faced each other in a two-game, total-goals series for the NHL championship and the right to meet the PCHA champion in the best-of-five Stanley Cup Finals.

1918-19 — Same as 1917-18, except that the Stanley Cup Finals was extended to a best-of-seven series.

1919-20 — Same as 1917-1918, except that Ottawa won both halves of the split regular-season schedule to earn an automatic berth into the best-of-five Stanley Cup Finals against the PCHA champions.

1921-22 — The top two teams at the conclusion of the regular-season faced each other in a two-game, total-goals series for the NHL championship. The NHL champion then moved on to play the winner of the PCHA-WCHL playoff series in the best-of-five Stanley Cup Finals.

1922-23 — The top two teams at the conclusion of the regular-season faced each other in a two-game, total-goals series for the NHL championship. The NHL champion then moved on to play the PCHA champion in the best-of-three Stanley Cup Semi-Finals, and the winner of the Semi-Finals played the WCHL champion, which had been given a bye, in the best-of-three Stanley Cup Finals.

1923-24 — The top two teams at the conclusion of the regular-season faced each other in a two-game, total-goals series for the NHL championship. The NHL champion then moved to play the loser of the PCHA-WCHL playoff (the winner of the PCHA-WCHL playoff earned a bye into the Stanley Cup Finals) in the best-of-three Stanley Cup Semi-Finals. The winner of this series met the PCHA-WCHL playoff winner in the best-of-three Stanley Cup Finals.

1924-25 — The first place team (Hamilton) at the conclusion of the regular-season was supposed to play the winner of a two-game, total goals series between the second (Toronto) and third (Montreal) place clubs. However, Hamilton refused to abide by this new format, demanding greater compensation than offered by the League. Thus, Toronto and Montreal played their two-game, total-goals series, and the winner (Montreal) earned the NHL title and then played the WCHL champion (Victoria) in the best-of-five Stanley Cup Finals.

1925-26 — The format which was intended for 1924-25 went into effect. The winner of the two-game, total-goals series between the second and third place teams squared off against the first place team in the two-game, total-goals NHL championship series. The NHL champion then moved on to play the WHL champion in the best-of-five Stanley Cup Finals.

After the 1925-26 season, the NHL was the only major professional hockey league still in existence and consequently took over sole control of the Stanley Cup competition.

1926-27 — The 10-team league was divided into two divisions — Canadian and American — of five teams apiece. In each division, the winner of the two-game, total-goals series between the second and third place teams faced the first place team in a two-game, total-goals series for the division title. The two division title winners then met in the best-of-five Stanley Cup Finals.

1928-29 — Both first place teams in the two divisions played each other in a best-of-five series. Both second place teams in the two divisions played each other in a two-game, total-goals series as did the two third place teams. The winners of these latter two series then played each other in a best-of-three series for the right to meet the winner of the series between the two first place clubs. This Stanley Cup Final was a best-of-three.

Series A: First in Canadian Division versus first in American (best-of-five)
Series B: Second in Canadian Division versus second in American (two-game, total-goals)
Series C: Third in Canadian Division versus third in American (two-game, total-goals)
Series D: Winner of Series B versus winner of Series C (best-of-three)
Series E: Winner of Series A versus winner of Series D (best of three) for Stanley Cup

1931-32 — Same as 1928-29, except that Series D was changed to a two-game, total-goals format and Series E was changed to best of five.

1936-37 — Same as 1931-32, except that Series B, C, and D were each best-of-three.

1938-39 — With the NHL reduced to seven teams, the two-division system was replaced by one seven-team league. Based on final regular-season standings, the following playoff format was adopted:

Series A: First versus Second (best-of-seven)
Series B: Third versus Fourth (best-of-three)
Series C: Fifth versus Sixth (best-of-three)
Series D: Winner of Series B versus winner of Series C (best-of-three)
Series E: Winner of Series A versus winner of Series D (best-of-seven)

1942-43 — With the NHL reduced to six teams (the "original six"), only the top four finishers qualified for playoff action. The best-of-seven Semi-Finals pitted Team #1 vs Team #3 and Team #2 vs Team #4. The winners of each Semi-Final series met in the best-of-seven Stanley Cup Finals.

1967-68 — When it doubled in size from 6 to 12 teams, the NHL once again was divided into two divisions — East and West — of six teams apiece. The top four clubs in each division qualified for the playoffs (all series were best-of-seven):

Series A; Team #1 (East) vs Team #3 (East)
Series B: Team #2 (East) vs Team #4 (East)
Series C: Team #1 (West) vs Team #3 (West)
Series D: Team #2 (West) vs Team #4 (West)
Series E: Winner of Series A vs winner of Series B
Series F: Winner of Series C vs winner of Series D
Series G: Winner of Series E vs Winner of Series F

1970-71 — Same as 1967-68 except that Series E matched the winners of Series A and D, and Series F matched the winners of Series B and C.

1971-72 — Same as 1970-71, except that Series A and C matched Team #1 vs Team #4, and Series B and D matched Team #2 vs Team #3.

1974-75 — With the League now expanded to 18 teams in four divisions, a completely new playoff format was introduced. First, the #2 and #3 teams in each of the four divisions were pooled together in the Preliminary round. These eight (#2 and #3) clubs were ranked #1 to #8 based on regular-season record:

Series A: Team #1 vs Team #8 (best-of-three)
Series B: Team #2 vs Team #7 (best-of-three)
Series C: Team #3 vs Team #6 (best-of-three)
Series D: Team #4 vs Team #5 (best-of-three)
The winners of this Preliminary round then pooled together with the four division winners, which had received byes into this Quarter-Final round. These eight teams were again ranked #1 to #8 based on regular-season record:
Series E: Team #1 vs Team #8 (best-of-seven)
Series F: Team #2 vs Team #7 (best-of-seven)
Series G: Team #3 vs Team #6 (best-of-seven)
Series H: Team #4 vs Team #5 (best-of-seven)
The four Quarter-Finals winners, which moved on to the Semi-Finals, were then ranked #1 to #4 based on regular season record:
Series I: Team #1 vs Team #4 (best-of-seven)
Series J: Team #2 vs Team #3 (best-of-seven)
Series K: Winner of Series I vs winner of Series J (best-of-seven)

1977-78 — Same as 1974-75, except that the Preliminary round consisted of the #2 teams in the four divisions and the next four teams based on regular-season record (not their standings within their divisions).

1979-80 — With the addition of four WHA franchises, the League expanded its playoff structure to include 16 of its 21 teams. The four first place teams in the four divisions automatically earned playoff berths. Among the 17 other clubs, the top 12, according to regular-season record, also earned berths. All 16 teams were then pooled together and ranked #1 to #16 based on regular-season record:

Series A: Team #1 vs Team #16 (best-of-five)
Series B: Team #2 vs Team #15 (best-of-five)
Series C: Team #3 vs Team #14 (best-of-five)
Series D: Team #4 vs Team #13 (best-of-five)
Series E: Team #5 vs Team #12 (best-of-five)
Series F: Team #6 vs Team #11 (best-of-five)
Series G: Team #7 vs Team #10 (best-of-five)
Series H: Team #8 vs Team # 9 (best-of-five)
The eight Preliminary round winners, ranked #1 to #8 based on regular-season record, moved on to the Quarter-Finals:
Series I: Team #1 vs Team #8 (best-of-seven)
Series J: Team #2 vs Team #7 (best-of-seven)
Series K: Team #3 vs Team #6 (best-of-seven)
Series L: Team #4 vs Team #5 (best-of-seven)
The eight Quarter-Finals winners, ranked #1 to #4 based on regular-season record, moved on to the semi-finals:
Series M: Team #1 vs Team #4 (best-of-seven)
Series N: Team #2 vs Team #3 (best-of-seven)
Series O: Winner of Series M vs winner of Series N (best-of-seven)

1981-82 — The first four teams in each division earned playoff berths. In each division, the first-place team opposed the fourth-place team and the second-place team opposed the third-place team in a best-of-five Division Semi-Final series (DSF). In each division, the two winners of the DSF met in a best-of-seven Division Final series (DF). The two winners in each conference met in a best-of-seven Conference Final series (CF). In the Prince of Wales Conference, the Adams Division winner opposed the Patrick Division winner; in the Clarence Campbell Conference, the Smythe Division winner opposed the Norris Division winner. The two CF winners met in a best-of-seven Stanley Cup Final (F) series.

1986-87 — Division Semi-Final series changed from best-of-five to best-of-seven.

1993-94 — The NHL's playoff draw conference-based rather than division-based. At the conclusion of the regular season, the top eight teams in each of the Eastern and Western Conferences qualify for the playoffs. The teams that finish in first place in each of the League's divisions are seeded first and second in each conference's playoff draw and are assured of home ice advantage in the first two playoff rounds. The remaining teams are seeded based on their regular-season point totals. In each conference, the team seeded #1 plays #8; #2 vs. #7; #3 vs. #6; and #4 vs. #5. All series are best-of-seven with home ice rotating on a 2-2-1-1-1 basis, with the exception of matchups between Central and Pacific Division teams. These matchups will be played on a 2-3-2 basis to reduce travel. In a 2-3-2 series, the team with the most points will have its choice to start the series at home or on the road. The Eastern Conference champion will face the Western Conference champion in the Stanley Cup Final.

1994-95 — Same as 1993-94, except that in first, second or third-round playoff series involving Central and Pacific Division teams, the team with the better record has the choice of using either a 2-3-2 or a 2-2-1-1-1 format. When a 2-3-2 format is selected, the higher-ranked team also has the choice of playing games 1, 2, 6 and 7 at home or playing games 3, 4 and 5 at home. The format for the Stanley Cup Final remains 2-2-1-1-1.

1998-99 — The NHL's 27 clubs are re-aligned into two conferences each consisting of three divisions. The number of teams qualifying for the 1999 Stanley Cup Playoffs remains unchanged at 16.

First-round playoff berths will be awarded to the first-place team in each division as well as to the next five best teams based on regular-season point totals in each conference. The three division winners in each conference will be seeded first though third for the playoffs and the next five best teams, in order of points, will be seeded fourth through eighth. In each conference, the team seeded #1 will play #8; #2 vs. #7; #3 vs. #6; and #4 vs. #5 in the quarterfinal round.

Teams will be re-seeded based on regular-season point totals at the start of the Conference Semifinals and Conference Finals. Home-ice advantage for the Stanley Cup Finals will be determined by points.

All series remain best-of-seven.

Denis Potvin made sure that the New York Islanders' first foray into the Stanley Cup was a successful one by potting the overtime winner in game one of the finals against Philadelphia. Potvin rallied for five goals and nine points in the six-game final as the Islanders won their first championship.

Team Records

1918-1998

GAMES PLAYED

MOST GAMES PLAYED BY ALL TEAMS, ONE PLAYOFF YEAR:
92 — 1991. There were 51 DSF, 24 DF, 11 CF and 6 F games.
90 — 1994. There were 48 CQF, 23 CSF, 12 CF and 7 F games.
87 — 1987. There were 44 DSF, 25 DF, 11 CF and 7 F games.

MOST GAMES PLAYED, ONE TEAM, ONE PLAYOFF YEAR:
26 — Philadelphia Flyers, 1987. Won DSF 4-2 against NY Rangers, DF 4-3 against NY Islanders, CF 4-2 against Montreal, and lost F 4-3 against Edmonton.
24 — Pittsburgh Penguins,1991. Won DSF 4-3 against New Jersey, DF 4-1 against Washington, CF 4-2 against Boston, and F 4-2 against Minnesota.
— Los Angeles Kings, 1993. Won DSF 4-2 against Calgary, DF 4-2 against Vancouver, CF 4-3 against Toronto, and lost F 4-1 against Montreal.
— Vancouver Canucks, 1994. Won CQF 4-3 against Calgary, CSF 4-1 against Dallas, CF 4-1 against Toronto, and lost F 4-3 against NY Rangers.

PLAYOFF APPEARANCES

MOST STANLEY CUP CHAMPIONSHIPS:
23 — Montreal Canadiens 1924-30-31-44-46-53-56-57-58-59-60-65-66-68-69-71-73-76-77-78-79-86-93
13 — Toronto Maple Leafs 1918-22-32-42-45-47-48-49-51-62-63-64-67
9 — Detroit Red Wings 1936-37-43-50-52-54-55-97-98

MOST CONSECUTIVE STANLEY CUP CHAMPIONSHIPS:
5 — Montreal Canadiens (1956-57-58-59-60)
4 — Montreal Canadiens (1976-77-78-79)
— NY Islanders (1980-81-82-83)

MOST FINAL SERIES APPEARANCES:
32 — Montreal Canadiens in 81-year history.
21 — Toronto Maple Leafs in 81-year history.
— Detroit Red Wings in 72-year history.

MOST CONSECUTIVE FINAL SERIES APPEARANCES:
10 — Montreal Canadiens (1951-60, inclusive)
5 — Montreal Canadiens, (1965-69, inclusive)
— NY Islanders, (1980-84, inclusive)

MOST YEARS IN PLAYOFFS:
72 — Montreal Canadiens in 81-year history.
58 — Toronto Maple Leafs in 81-year history.
— Boston Bruins in 74-year history.

MOST CONSECUTIVE PLAYOFF APPEARANCES:
29 — Boston Bruins (1968-96, inclusive)
28 — Chicago Blackhawks (1970-97, inclusive)
24 — Montreal Canadiens (1971-94, inclusive)
21 — Montreal Canadiens (1949-69, inclusive)
20 — Detroit Red Wings (1939-58, inclusive)

TEAM WINS

MOST HOME WINS, ONE TEAM, ONE PLAYOFF YEAR:
11 — Edmonton Oilers, 1988 in 11 home-ice games.
10 — Edmonton Oilers, 1985 in 10 home-ice games.
— Montreal Canadiens, 1986 in 11 home-ice games.
— Montreal Canadiens, 1993 in 11 home-ice games.

MOST ROAD WINS, ONE TEAM, ONE PLAYOFF YEAR:
10 — New Jersey Devils, 1995. Won three at Boston in CQF; two at Pittsburgh in CSF; three at Philadelphia in CF; and two at Detroit in F series.
8 — NY Islanders, 1980. Won two at Los Angeles in PR; three at Boston in QF; two at Buffalo in SF; and one at Philadelphia in F series.
— Philadelphia Flyers, 1987. Won two at NY Rangers in DSF; two at NY Islanders in DF; three at Montreal in CF; and one at Edmonton in F series.
— Edmonton Oilers, 1990. Won one at Winnipeg in DSF; two at Los Angeles in DF; two at Chicago in CF and three at Boston in F series.
— Pittsburgh Penguins, 1992. Won two at Washington in DSF; two at NY Rangers in DF; two at Boston in CF; and two at Chicago in F series.
— Vancouver Canucks, 1994. Won three at Calgary in CQF; two at Dallas in CSF; one at Toronto in CF; and two at NY Rangers in F series.
— Colorado Avalanche, 1996. Won two at Vancouver in CQF; two at Chicago in CSF; two at Detroit in CF; and two at Florida in F series.
— Detroit Red Wings, 1998. Won two at Phoenix in CQF; three at St. Louis in CSF; one at Dallas in CF; and two at Washington in F series.

MOST ROAD WINS, ALL TEAMS, ONE PLAYOFF YEAR:
46 — 1987. Of 87 games played, road teams won 46 (22 DSF, 14 DF, 8 CF and 2 Stanley Cup final).

MOST OVERTIME WINS, ONE TEAM, ONE PLAYOFF YEAR:
10 — Montreal Canadiens, 1993. Two against Quebec in DSF; three against Buffalo in DF; two against NY Islanders in CF; and three against Los Angeles in F. Montreal played 20 games.
6 — NY Islanders, 1980. One against Los Angeles in PR; two against Boston in QF; one against Buffalo in SF; and two against Philadelphia in F. Islanders played 21 games.
— Vancouver Canucks, 1994. Three against Calgary in CQF; one against Dallas in CSF; one against Toronto in CF; and one against NY Rangers in F. Vancouver played 24 games.

MOST OVERTIME WINS AT HOME, ONE TEAM, ONE PLAYOFF YEAR:
4 — St. Louis Blues, 1968. Won one vs. Philadelphia in QF and three vs. Minnesota in SF.
— Montreal Canadiens, 1993. Won one vs. Quebec in DSF, one vs. Buffalo in DF, one vs. NY Islanders in CF and one vs. Los Angeles in F series.

MOST OVERTIME WINS ON THE ROAD, ONE TEAM, ONE PLAYOFF YEAR:
6 — Montreal Canadiens, 1993. Won one vs. Quebec in DSF, two vs. Buffalo in DF, one vs. NY Islanders in CF and two vs. Los Angeles in F series.

TEAM LOSSES

MOST LOSSES, ONE TEAM, ONE PLAYOFF YEAR:
11 — Philadelphia Flyers, 1987. Lost two vs. NY Rangers in DSF; three vs. NY Islanders in DF; two vs. Montreal in CF; and four vs. Edmonton in F series.

MOST HOME LOSSES, ONE TEAM, ONE PLAYOFF YEAR:
6 — Philadelphia Flyers, 1987. Lost one vs. NY Rangers in DSF; two vs. NY Islanders in DF; two vs. Montreal in CF; and one vs. Edmonton in F series.
Washington Capitals, 1998. Lost two vs. Boston in CQF; two vs. Buffalo in CF; and two vs. Detroit in F series.

MOST ROAD LOSSES, ONE TEAM, ONE PLAYOFF YEAR:
6 — St. Louis Blues, 1968. Lost two at Philadelphia in QF; two at Minnesota in SF; and two at Montreal in F series.
— **St. Louis Blues, 1970.** Lost two at Minnesota in QF; two at Pittsburgh in SF; and two at Boston in F series.
— **NY Islanders, 1984.** Lost one at NY Rangers in DSF; two at Montreal in CF; and three at Edmonton in F series.
— **Los Angeles Kings, 1993.** Lost one at Calgary in DSF; one at Vancouver in DF; two at Toronto in CF; and two at Montreal in F series.

MOST OVERTIME LOSSES, ONE TEAM, ONE PLAYOFF YEAR:
4 — Montreal Canadiens, 1951. Lost four vs. Toronto in F series.
— **St. Louis Blues, 1968.** Lost one vs. Philadelphia in QF; one vs. Minnesota in SF; and two vs. Montreal in F series.
— **Los Angeles Kings, 1991.** Lost one vs. Vancouver in DSF; and three vs. Edmonton in DF series.
— **Los Angeles Kings, 1993.** Lost one vs. Toronto in CF; and three vs. Montreal in F series.
— **Philadelphia Flyers, 1996**. Lost two vs. Tampa Bay in CQF; and two vs. Florida in CSF series.

MOST OVERTIME LOSSES AT HOME, ONE TEAM, ONE PLAYOFF YEAR:
2 — Two overtime losses at home by one team in one playoff year has occurred 36 times. The Buffalo Sabres are the most recent team to equal this mark when they lost twice in overtime at home to the Washington Capitals in the 1998 Stanley Cup CF series.

MOST OVERTIME LOSSES ON THE ROAD, ONE TEAM, ONE PLAYOFF YEAR:
3 — Los Angeles Kings, 1991. Lost one at Vancouver in DSF; and two at Edmonton in DF series.
— St. Louis Blues, 1996. Lost two at Toronto in CQF; and one at Detroit in CSF series.

PLAYOFF WINNING STREAKS

LONGEST PLAYOFF WINNING STREAK:
14 — Pittsburgh Penguins. Streak started May 9, 1992, at Pittsburgh with a 5-4 win in fourth game of DF series against NY Rangers, won by Pittsburgh 4-2. Continued with a four-game win over Boston in 1992 CF and a four-game sweep of Chicago in 1992 F. Pittsburgh then won the first three games of 1993 DSF versus New Jersey. New Jersey ended the streak April 25, 1993, at New Jersey with a 4-1 win.
12 — Edmonton Oilers. Streak started May 15, 1984 at Edmonton with a 7-2 win in third game of F series against NY Islanders won by Edmonton 4-1. Continued with a three-game sweep of Winnipeg in 1985 DF, Edmonton then won the first two games of 1985 CF versus Chicago Chicago ended the streak May 9, 1985, at Chicago with a 5-2 win.

MOST CONSECUTIVE WINS, ONE TEAM, ONE PLAYOFF YEAR:
11 — Chicago Blackhawks in 1992. Chicago won last three games of DSF against St. Louis to win series 4-2 and then defeated Detroit 4-0 in DF and Edmonton 4-0 in CF.
— **Pittsburgh Penguins** in 1992. Pittsburgh won last three games of DF against NY Rangers to win series 4-2 and then defeated Boston 4-0 in CF and Chicago 4-0 in F.
— **Montreal Canadiens** in 1993. Montreal won last four games of DSF against Quebec to win series 4-2, defeated Buffalo 4-0 in DF and won first three games of CF against NY Islanders.

PLAYOFF LOSING STREAKS

LONGEST PLAYOFF LOSING STREAK:
16 Games — Chicago Blackhawks. Streak started in 1975 QF against Buffalo when Chicago lost last two games. Then Chicago lost four games to Montreal in 1976 QF; two games to NY Islanders in 1977 PR; four games to Boston in 1978 QF and four games to NY Islanders in 1979 QF. Streak ended on April 8, 1980 when Chicago defeated St. Louis 3-2 in the opening game of their 1980 PR series.
12 Games — Toronto Maple Leafs. Streak started on April 16, 1979 as Toronto lost four straight games in a QF series against Montreal. Continued with three-game PR defeats versus Philadelphia and NY Islanders in 1980 and 1981 respectively. Toronto failed to qualify for the 1982 playoffs and lost the first two games of a 1983 DSF against Minnesota. Toronto ended the streak with a 6-3 win against the North Stars on April 9, 1983.

Maurice Richard addresses the Montreal faithful with Jacques Plante and NHL president Clarence Campbell at his side after the Habs swept the Leafs in the 1960 finals. It would be the last time the Canadiens' fans would see the Rocket's red glare. The rambunctious right winger retired in September 1960.

MOST GOALS IN A SERIES, ONE TEAM

MOST GOALS, ONE TEAM, ONE PLAYOFF SERIES:
44 — Edmonton Oilers in 1985 CF. Edmonton won best-of-seven series 4-2, outscoring Chicago 44-25.
35 — Edmonton Oilers in 1983 DF. Edmonton won best-of-seven series 4-1, outscoring Calgary 35-13.
— Calgary Flames in 1995 CQF. Calgary lost best-of-seven series 3-4, outscoring San Jose 35-26.

MOST GOALS, ONE TEAM, TWO-GAME SERIES:
11 — Buffalo Sabres in 1977 PR. Buffalo won best-of-three series 2-0, outscoring Minnesota 11-3.
— Toronto Maple Leafs in 1978 PR. Toronto won best-of-three series 2-0, outscoring Los Angeles 11-3.
10 — Boston Bruins in 1927 QF. Boston won two-game total goal series 10-5.

MOST GOALS, ONE TEAM, THREE-GAME SERIES:
23 — Chicago Blackhawks in 1985 DSF. Chicago won best-of-five series 3-0, outscoring Detroit 23-8.
20 — Minnesota North Stars in 1981 PR. Minnesota won best-of-five series 3-0, outscoring Boston 20-13.
— NY Islanders in 1981 PR. New York won best-of-five series 3-0, outscoring Toronto 20-4.

MOST GOALS, ONE TEAM, FOUR-GAME SERIES:
28 — Boston Bruins in 1972 SF. Boston won best-of-seven series 4-0, outscoring St. Louis 28-8.

MOST GOALS, ONE TEAM, FIVE-GAME SERIES:
35 — Edmonton Oilers in 1983 DF. Edmonton won best-of-seven series 4-1, outscoring Calgary 35-13.
32 — Edmonton Oilers in 1987 DSF. Edmonton won best-of-seven series 4-1, outscoring Los Angeles 32-20.
28 — NY Rangers in 1979 QF. NY Rangers won best-of-seven series 4-1, outscoring Philadelphia 28-8.
27 — Philadelphia Flyers in 1980 SF. Philadelphia won best-of-seven series 4-1, outscoring Minnesota 27-14.
— Los Angeles Kings, in 1982 DSF. Los Angeles won best-of-five series 3-2, outscoring Edmonton 27-23.

MOST GOALS, ONE TEAM, SIX-GAME SERIES:
44 — Edmonton Oilers in 1985 CF. Edmonton won best-of-seven series 4-2, outscoring Chicago 44-25.
33 — Chicago Blackhawks in 1985 DF. Chicago won best-of-seven series 4-2, outscoring Minnesota 33-29.
— Montreal Canadiens in 1973 F. Montreal won best-of-seven series 4-2, outscoring Chicago 33-23.
— Los Angeles Kings in 1993 DSF. Los Angeles won best-of-seven series 4-2, outscoring Calgary 33-28.

MOST GOALS, ONE TEAM, SEVEN-GAME SERIES:
35 — Calgary Flames in 1995 CQF. Calgary lost best-of-seven series 3-4, outscoring San Jose 35-26.
33 — Philadelphia Flyers in 1976 QF. Philadelphia won best-of-seven series 4-3, outscoring Toronto 33-23.
— Boston Bruins in 1983 DF. Boston won best-of-seven series 4-3, outscoring Buffalo 33-23.
— Edmonton Oilers in 1984 DF. Edmonton won best-of-seven series 4-3, outscoring Calgary 33-27.

FEWEST GOALS IN A SERIES, ONE TEAM

FEWEST GOALS, ONE TEAM, TWO-GAME SERIES:
0 — NY Americans in 1929 SF. Lost two-game total-goal series 1-0 against NY Rangers.
— **Chicago Blackhawks** in 1935 SF. Lost two-game total-goal series 1-0 against Mtl. Maroons.
— **Mtl. Maroons** in 1937 SF. Lost best-of-three series 2-0 to NY Rangers while being outscored 5-0.
— **NY Americans** in 1939 QF. Lost best-of-three series 2-0 to Toronto while being outscored 6-0.

FEWEST GOALS, ONE TEAM, THREE-GAME SERIES:
1 — Mtl. Maroons in 1936 SF. Lost best-of-five series 3-0 to Detroit and were outscored 6-1.

FEWEST GOALS, ONE TEAM, FOUR-GAME SERIES:
2 — Boston Bruins in 1935 SF. Toronto won best-of-five series 3-1, outscoring Boston 7-2.
— **Montreal Canadiens** in 1952 F. Detroit won best-of-seven series 4-0, outscoring Montreal 11-2.

FEWEST GOALS, ONE TEAM, FIVE-GAME SERIES:
5 — NY Rangers in 1928 F. NY Rangers won best-of-five series 3-2, while being outscored by Mtl. Maroons 6-5.
— **Boston Bruins** in 1995 CQF. New Jersey won best-of-seven series 4-1, while outscoring Boston 14-5.
— **New Jersey Devils** in 1997 CSF. NY Rangers won best-of-seven series 4-1, while outscoring New Jersey 10-5.

FEWEST GOALS, ONE TEAM, SIX-GAME SERIES:
5 — Boston Bruins in 1951 SF. Toronto won best-of-seven series 4-1 with 1 tie, outscoring Boston 17-5.

FEWEST GOALS, ONE TEAM, SEVEN-GAME SERIES:
9 — Toronto Maple Leafs, in 1945 F. Toronto won best-of- seven series 4-3; teams tied in scoring 9-9.
— **Detroit Red Wings,** in 1945 F. Toronto won best-of-seven series 4-3; teams tied in scoring 9-9.

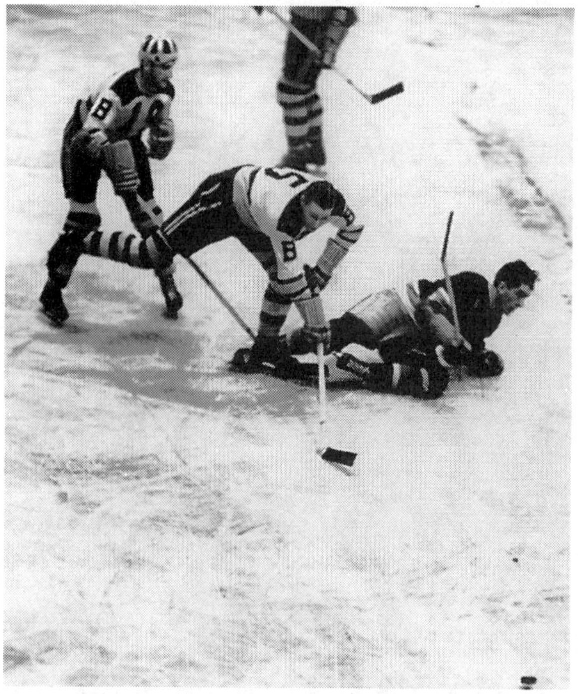

Late in his career, classy Boston captain Dit Clapper (#5) was shifted to defense, where he was best known for preventing goals. In the 1935 semi-finals, the Bruins could have used some of the offense he showed when he was an All-Star right winger. The Toronto Maple Leafs smothered the Bruins, allowing only two goals in the best-of-five series.

MOST GOALS IN A SERIES, BOTH TEAMS

MOST GOALS, BOTH TEAMS, ONE PLAYOFF SERIES:
69 — Edmonton Oilers, Chicago Blackhawks in 1985 CF. Edmonton won best-of-seven series 4-2, outscoring Chicago 44-25.
62 — Chicago Blackhawks, Minnesota North Stars in 1985 DF. Chicago won best-of-seven series 4-2, outscoring Minnesota 33-29.
61 — Los Angeles Kings, Calgary Flames in 1993 DSF. Los Angeles won best-of-seven series 4-2, outscoring Calgary 33-28.
— San Jose Sharks, Calgary Flames in 1995 CQF. San Jose won best-of-seven series 4-3, while being outscored 35-26.

MOST GOALS, BOTH TEAMS, TWO-GAME SERIES:
17 — Toronto St. Patricks, Montreal Canadiens in 1918 NHL F. Toronto won two-game total goal series 10-7.
15 — Boston Bruins, Chicago Blackhawks in 1927 QF. Boston won two-game total goal series 10-5.
— Pittsburgh Penguins, St. Louis Blues in 1975 PR. Pittsburgh won best-of-three series 2-0, outscoring St. Louis 9-6.

MOST GOALS, BOTH TEAMS, THREE-GAME SERIES:
33 — Minnesota North Stars, Boston Bruins in 1981 PR. Minnesota won best-of-five series 3-0, outscoring Boston 20-13.
31 — Chicago Blackhawks, Detroit Red Wings in 1985 DSF. Chicago won best-of-five series 3-0, outscoring Detroit 23-8.
28 — Toronto Maple Leafs, NY Rangers in 1932 F. Toronto won best-of-five series 3-0, outscoring New York 18-10.

MOST GOALS, BOTH TEAMS, FOUR-GAME SERIES:
36 — Boston Bruins, St. Louis Blues in 1972 SF. Boston won best-of-seven series 4-0, outscoring St. Louis 28-8.
— **Edmonton Oilers, Chicago Blackhawks** in 1983 CF. Edmonton won best-of-seven series 4-0, outscoring Chicago 25-11.
— **Minnesota North Stars, Toronto Maple Leafs** in 1983 DSF. Minnesota won best-of-five series 3-1; teams tied in scoring 18-18.
35 — NY Rangers, Los Angeles Kings in 1981 PR. NY Rangers won best-of-five series 3-1, outscoring Los Angeles 23-12.

MOST GOALS, BOTH TEAMS, FIVE-GAME SERIES:
52 — Edmonton Oilers, Los Angeles Kings in 1987 DSF. Edmonton won best-of-seven series 4-1, outscoring Los Angeles 32-20.
50 — Los Angeles Kings, Edmonton Oilers in 1982 DSF. Los Angeles won best-of-five series 3-2, outscoring Edmonton 27-23.
48 — Edmonton Oilers, Calgary Flames in 1983 DF. Edmonton won best-of-seven series 4-1, outscoring Calgary 35-13.
— Calgary Flames, Los Angeles Kings in 1988 DSF. Calgary won best-of-seven series 4-1, outscoring Los Angeles 30-18.

MOST GOALS, BOTH TEAMS, SIX-GAME SERIES:
69 — Edmonton Oilers, Chicago Blackhawks in 1985 CF. Edmonton won best-of-seven series 4-2, outscoring Chicago 44-25.
62 — Chicago Blackhawks, Minnesota North Stars in 1985 DF. Chicago won best-of-seven series 4-2, outscoring Minnesota 33-29.
61 — Los Angeles Kings, Calgary Flames in 1993 DSF. Los Angeles won best-of-seven series 4-2, outscoring Calgary 33-28.

MOST GOALS, BOTH TEAMS, SEVEN-GAME SERIES:
61 — San Jose Sharks, Calgary Flames in 1995 CQF. San Jose won best-of-seven series 4-3, while being outscored 35-26.
60 — Edmonton Oilers, Calgary Flames in 1984 DF. Edmonton won best-of-seven series 4-3, outscoring Calgary 33-27.

FEWEST GOALS IN A SERIES, BOTH TEAMS

FEWEST GOALS, BOTH TEAMS, TWO-GAME SERIES:
1 — NY Rangers, NY Americans, in 1929 SF. NY Rangers defeated NY Americans 1-0 in two-game, total-goal series.
— Mtl. Maroons, Chicago Blackhawks in 1935 SF. Mtl. Maroons defeated Chicago 1-0 in two-game, total-goal series.

FEWEST GOALS, BOTH TEAMS, THREE-GAME SERIES:
7 — Boston Bruins, Montreal Canadiens in 1929 SF. Boston won best-of-five series 3-0, outscoring Montreal 5-2.
— Detroit Red Wings, Mtl. Maroons in 1936 SF. Detroit won best-of-five series 3-0, outscoring Mtl. Maroons 6-1.

FEWEST GOALS, BOTH TEAMS, FOUR-GAME SERIES:
9 — Toronto Maple Leafs, Boston Bruins in 1935 SF. Toronto won best-of-five series 3-1, outscoring Boston 7-2.

FEWEST GOALS, BOTH TEAMS, FIVE-GAME SERIES:
11 — NY Rangers, Mtl. Maroons in 1928 F. NY Rangers won best-of-five series 3-2, while being outscored by Mtl. Maroons 6-5.

FEWEST GOALS, BOTH TEAMS, SIX-GAME SERIES:
22 — Toronto Maple Leafs, Boston Bruins in 1951 SF. Toronto won best-of-seven series 4-1 with 1 tie, outscoring Boston 17-5.

FEWEST GOALS, BOTH TEAMS, SEVEN-GAME SERIES:
18 — Toronto Maple Leafs, Detroit Red Wings in 1945 F. Toronto won best-of-seven series 4-3; teams tied in scoring 9-9.

MOST GOALS IN A GAME OR PERIOD

MOST GOALS, ONE TEAM, ONE GAME:
13 — Edmonton Oilers at Edmonton, April 9, 1987. Edmonton 13, Los Angeles 3. Edmonton won best-of-seven DSF 4-1.
12 — Los Angeles Kings at Los Angeles, April 10, 1990. Los Angeles 12, Calgary 4. Los Angeles won best-of-seven DSF 4-2.
11 — Montreal Canadiens at Montreal, March 30, 1944. Montreal 11, Toronto 0. Canadiens won best-of-seven SF 4-1.
— Edmonton Oilers at Edmonton, May 4, 1985. Edmonton 11, Chicago 2. Edmonton won best-of-seven CF 4-2.

Although he had his finest seasons as a member of the Philadelphia Flyers, Brian Propp saved one his finest playoff performances for his first taste of post-season play with the Minnesota North Stars. The Stars set an NHL record with 35 power-play goals during the 1991 playoffs and Propp was their main weapon. All eight goals the shifty left winger scored during the North Stars' improbable run to the Stanley Cup finals were scored while Minnesota enjoyed the man advantage.

MOST GOALS, ONE TEAM, ONE PERIOD:
7 — Montreal Canadiens, March 30, 1944, at Montreal in third period, during 11-0 win against Toronto.

MOST GOALS, BOTH TEAMS, ONE GAME:
18 — Los Angeles Kings, Edmonton Oilers at Edmonton, April 7, 1982. Los Angeles 10, Edmonton 8. Los Angeles won best-of-five DSF 3-2.
17 — Pittsburgh Penguins, Philadelphia Flyers at Pittsburgh, April 25, 1989. Pittsburgh 10, Philadelphia 7. Philadelphia won best-of-seven DF 4-3.
16 — Edmonton Oilers, Los Angeles Kings at Edmonton, April 9, 1987. Edmonton 13, Los Angeles 3. Edmonton won best-of-seven DSF 4-1.
— Los Angeles Kings, Calgary Flames at Los Angeles, April 10, 1990. Los Angeles 12, Calgary 4. Los Angeles won best-of-seven DF 4-2.

MOST GOALS, BOTH TEAMS, ONE PERIOD:
9 — NY Rangers, Philadelphia Flyers, April 24, 1979, at Philadelphia, third period. NY Rangers won 8-3, scoring six of nine third-period goals.
— Los Angeles Kings, Calgary Flames, at Los Angeles, April 10, 1990, second period. Los Angeles won game 12-4, scoring five of nine second-period goals.
8 — Chicago Blackhawks, Montreal Canadiens, at Montreal, May 8, 1973, second period. Chicago won 8-7, scoring five of eight second-period goals.
— Chicago Blackhawks, Edmonton Oilers, at Chicago, May 12, 1985, first period. Chicago won 8-6, scoring five of eight first-period goals.
— Edmonton Oilers, Winnipeg Jets, at Edmonton, April 6, 1988, third period. Edmonton won 7-4, scoring six of eight third period goals.
— Hartford Whalers, Montreal Canadiens, at Hartford, April 10, 1988, third period. Hartford won 7-5, scoring five of eight third period goals.
— Vancouver Canucks, NY Rangers, at New York, June 9, 1994, third period. Vancouver won 6-3, scoring five of eight third period goals.

TEAM POWER-PLAY GOALS

MOST POWER-PLAY GOALS BY ALL TEAMS, ONE PLAYOFF YEAR:
199 — 1988 in 83 games.

MOST POWER-PLAY GOALS, ONE TEAM, ONE PLAYOFF YEAR:
35 — Minnesota North Stars, 1991 in 23 games.
32 — Edmonton Oilers, 1988 in 18 games.
31 — NY Islanders, 1981, in 18 games.

MOST POWER-PLAY GOALS, ONE TEAM, ONE SERIES:
15 — NY Islanders in 1980 F against Philadelphia. NY Islanders won series 4-2.
— Minnesota North Stars in 1991 DSF against Chicago. Minnesota won series 4-2.
13 — NY Islanders in 1981 QF against Edmonton. NY Islanders won series 4-2.
— Calgary Flames in 1986 CF against St. Louis. Calgary won series 4-3.
12 — Toronto Maple Leafs in 1976 QF series won by Philadelphia 4-3.

MOST POWER-PLAY GOALS, BOTH TEAMS, ONE SERIES:
21 — NY Islanders, Philadelphia Flyers in 1980 F, won by NY Islanders 4-2. NY Islanders had 15 and Flyers 6.
— NY Islanders, Edmonton Oilers in 1981 QF, won by NY Islanders 4-2. NY Islanders had 13 and Edmonton 8.
— Philadelphia Flyers, Pittsburgh Penguins in 1989 DF, won by Philadelphia 4-3. Philadelphia had 11 and Pittsburgh 10.
— Minnesota North Stars, Chicago Blackhawks in 1991 DSF, won by Minnesota 4-2. Minnesota had 15 and Chicago 6.
20 — Toronto Maple Leafs, Philadelphia Flyers in 1976 QF series won by Philadelphia 4-3. Toronto had 12 and Philadelphia 8.

MOST POWER-PLAY GOALS, ONE TEAM, ONE GAME:
6 — Boston Bruins, April 2, 1969, at Boston against Toronto. Boston won 10-0.

MOST POWER-PLAY GOALS, BOTH TEAMS, ONE GAME:
8 — Minnesota North Stars, St. Louis Blues, April 24, 1991 at Minnesota. Minnesota had 4, St. Louis 4. Minnesota won 8-4.
7 — Minnesota North Stars, Edmonton Oilers, April 28, 1984 at Minnesota. Minnesota had 4, Edmonton 3. Edmonton won 8-5.
— Philadelphia Flyers, NY Rangers, April 13, 1985 at New York. Philadelphia had 4, NY Rangers 3. Philadelphia won 6-5.
— Edmonton Oilers, Chicago Blackhawks, May 14, 1985 at Edmonton. Chicago had 5, Edmonton 2. Edmonton won 10-5.
— Edmonton Oilers, Los Angeles Kings, April 9, 1987 at Edmonton. Edmonton had 5, Los Angeles 2. Edmonton won 13-3.
— Vancouver Canucks, Calgary Flames, April 9, 1989 at Vancouver. Vancouver had 4, Calgary 3. Vancouver won 5-3.

MOST POWER-PLAY GOALS, ONE TEAM, ONE PERIOD:
4 — Toronto Maple Leafs, March 26, 1936, second period against Boston at Toronto. Toronto won 8-3.
— Minnesota North Stars, April 28, 1984, second period against Edmonton at Minnesota. Edmonton won 8-5.
— Boston Bruins, April 11, 1991, third period against Hartford at Boston. Boston won 6-1.
— Minnesota North Stars, April 24, 1991, second period against St. Louis at Minnesota. Minnesota won 8-4.
— St. Louis Blues, April 27, 1998, third period at Los Angeles. St. Louis won 4-3.

MOST POWER-PLAY GOALS, BOTH TEAMS, ONE PERIOD:
5 — Minnesota North Stars, Edmonton Oilers, April 28, 1984, second period, at Minnesota. Minnesota had 4 and Edmonton 1. Edmonton won 8-5.
— Vancouver Canucks, Calgary Flames, April 9, 1989, third period at Vancouver. Vancouver had 3 and Calgary 2. Vancouver won 5-3.
— Minnesota North Stars, St. Louis Blues, April 24, 1991, second period, at Minnesota. Minnesota had 4 and St. Louis 1. Minnesota won 8-4.

TEAM SHORTHAND GOALS

MOST SHORTHAND GOALS BY ALL TEAMS, ONE PLAYOFF YEAR:
33 — 1988, in 83 games.

MOST SHORTHAND GOALS, ONE TEAM, ONE PLAYOFF YEAR:
10 — Edmonton Oilers, 1983, in 16 games.
9 — NY Islanders, 1981, in 19 games.
8 — Philadelphia Flyers, 1989, in 19 games.

MOST SHORTHAND GOALS, ONE TEAM, ONE SERIES:
6 — Calgary Flames in 1995 against San Jose in best-of-seven CQF won by San Jose 4-3.
— **Vancouver Canucks** in 1995 against St. Louis in best-of-seven CQF won by Vancouver 4-3.
5 — Edmonton Oilers in 1983 against Calgary in best-of-seven DF won by Edmonton 4-1.
— NY Rangers in 1979 against Philadelphia in best-of-seven QF, won by NY Rangers 4-1.

MOST SHORTHAND GOALS, BOTH TEAMS, ONE SERIES:
7 — Boston Bruins (4), NY Rangers (3), in 1958 SF won by Boston 4-2.
— **Edmonton Oilers (5), Calgary Flames (2),** in 1983 DF won by Edmonton 4-1.
— **Vancouver Canucks (6), St. Louis Blues (1),** in 1995 CQF won by Vancouver 4-3.

MOST SHORTHAND GOALS, ONE TEAM, ONE GAME:
3 — Boston Bruins, April 11, 1981, at Minnesota. Minnesota won 6-3.
— **NY Islanders,** April 17, 1983, at NY Rangers. NY Rangers won 7-6.
— **Toronto Maple Leafs,** May 8, 1994, at San Jose. Toronto won 8-3.

MOST SHORTHAND GOALS, BOTH TEAMS, ONE GAME:
4 — NY Islanders, NY Rangers, April 17, 1983, at NY Rangers. NY Islanders had 3 shorthand goals, NY Rangers 1. NY Rangers won 7-6.
— **Boston Bruins, Minnesota North Stars,** April 11, 1981, at Minnesota. Boston had 3 shorthand goals, Minnesota 1. Minnesota won 6-3.
— **San Jose Sharks, Toronto Maple Leafs,** May 8, 1994, at San Jose. Toronto had 3 shorthand goals, San Jose 1. Toronto won 8-3.
3 — Toronto Maple Leafs, Detroit Red Wings, April 5, 1947, at Toronto. Toronto had 2 shorthand goals, Detroit 1. Toronto won 6-1.
— NY Rangers, Boston Bruins, April 1, 1958, at Boston. NY Rangers had 2 shorthand goals, Boston 1. NY Rangers won 5-2.
— Minnesota North Stars, Philadelphia Flyers, May 4, 1980, at Minnesota. Minnesota had 2 shorthand goals, Philadelphia 1. Philadelphia won 5-3.
— Edmonton Oilers, Winnipeg Jets, April 9, 1988, at Winnipeg. Winnipeg had 2 shorthand goals, Edmonton 1. Winnipeg won 6-4.
— New Jersey Devils, NY Islanders, April 14, 1988, at New Jersey. NY Islanders had 2 shorthand goals, New Jersey 1. New Jersey won 6-5.
— Montreal Canadiens, New Jersey Devils, April 17, 1997, at New Jersey. Montreal had 2 shorthand goals, New Jersey 1. New Jersey won 5-2

MOST SHORTHAND GOALS, ONE TEAM, ONE PERIOD:
2 — Toronto Maple Leafs, April 5, 1947, at Toronto against Detroit, first period. Toronto won 6-1.
— **Toronto Maple Leafs,** April 13, 1965, at Toronto against Montreal, first period. Montreal won 4-3.
— **Boston Bruins,** April 20, 1969, at Boston against Montreal, first period. Boston won 3-2.
— **Boston Bruins,** April 8, 1970, at Boston against NY Rangers, second period. Boston won 8-2.
— **Boston Bruins,** April 30, 1972, at Boston against NY Rangers, first period. Boston won 6-5.
— **Chicago Blackhawks,** May 3, 1973, at Chicago against Montreal, first period. Chicago won 7-4.
— **Montreal Canadiens,** April 23, 1978, at Detroit, first period. Montreal won 8-0.
— **NY Islanders,** April 8, 1980, at New York against Los Angeles, second period. NY Islanders won 8-1.
— **Los Angeles Kings,** April 9, 1980, at NY Islanders, first period. Los Angeles won 6-3.
— **Boston Bruins,** April 13, 1980, at Pittsburgh, second period. Boston won 8-3.
— **Minnesota North Stars,** May 4, 1980, at Minnesota against Philadelphia, second period. Philadelphia won 5-3.
— **Boston Bruins,** April 11, 1981, at Minnesota, third period. Minnesota won 6-3.
— **NY Islanders,** May 12, 1981, at New York against Minnesota, first period. NY Islanders won 6-3.
— **Montreal Canadiens,** April 7, 1982, at Montreal against Quebec, third period. Montreal won 5-1.
— **Edmonton Oilers,** April 24, 1983, at Edmonton against Chicago, third period. Edmonton won 8-4.
— **Winnipeg Jets,** April 14, 1985, at Calgary, second period. Winnipeg won 5-3.
— **Boston Bruins,** April 6, 1988, at Boston against Buffalo, first period. Boston won 7-3.
— **NY Islanders,** April 14, 1988, at New Jersey, third period. New Jersey won 6-5.
— **Detroit Red Wings,** April 29, 1993, at Toronto, second period. Detroit won 7-3.
— **Toronto Maple Leafs,** May 8, 1994, at San Jose, third period. Toronto won 8-3.
— **Calgary Flames,** May 11, 1995, at San Jose, first period. Calgary won 9-2.
— **Vancouver Canucks,** May 15, 1995 at St. Louis, second period. Vancouver won 6-5.
— **Montreal Canadiens,** April 17, 1997, at New Jersey, second period. New Jersey won 5-2.
— **Philadelphia Flyers,** April 26, 1997, at Philadelphia against Pittsburgh, first period. Philadelphia won 6-3.
— **Phoenix Coyotes,** April 24, 1998, at Detroit, second period. Phoenix won 7-4.
— **Buffalo Sabres,** April 27, 1998, at Buffalo against Philadelphia, second period. Buffalo won 6-1.

MOST SHORTHAND GOALS, BOTH TEAMS, ONE PERIOD:
3 — Toronto Maple Leafs, Detroit Red Wings, April 5, 1947, at Toronto, first period. Toronto had 2 shorthand goals, Detroit 1. Toronto won 6-1.
— **Toronto Maple Leafs, San Jose Sharks,** May 8, 1994, at San Jose, third period. Toronto had 2 shorthand goals, San Jose 1. Toronto won 8-3.

FASTEST GOALS

FASTEST FIVE GOALS, BOTH TEAMS:
3 Minutes, 6 Seconds — Chicago Blackhawks, Minnesota North Stars, at Chicago April 21, 1985. Keith Brown scored for Chicago at 1:12, second period; Ken Yaremchuk, Chicago, 1:27; Dino Ciccarelli, Minnesota, 2:48; Tony McKegney, Minnesota, 4:07; and Curt Fraser, Chicago, 4:18. Chicago won 6-2 and best-of-seven DF 4-2.
3 Minutes, 20 Seconds — Minnesota North Stars, Philadelphia Flyers, at Philadelphia, April 29, 1980. Paul Shmyr scored for Minnesota at 13:20, first period; Steve Christoff, Minnesota, 13:59; Ken Linseman, Philadelphia, 14:54; Tom Gorence, Philadelphia, 15:36; and Linseman, 16:40. Minnesota won 6-5. Philadelphia won best-of-seven SF 4-1.
4 Minutes, 19 Seconds — Toronto Maple Leafs, NY Rangers at Toronto, April 9, 1932. Ace Bailey scored for Toronto at 15:07, third period; Fred Cook, NY Rangers, 16:32; Bob Gracie, Toronto, 17:36; Frank Boucher, NY Rangers, 18:26 and again at 19:26. Toronto won 6-4 and best-of-five F 3-0.

FASTEST FIVE GOALS, ONE TEAM:
3 Minutes, 36 Seconds — Montreal Canadiens at Montreal, March 30, 1944, against Toronto. Toe Blake scored at 7:58 of third period and again at 8:37; Maurice Richard, 9:17; Ray Getliffe, 10:33; and Buddy O'Connor, 11:34. Canadiens won 11-0 and best-of-seven SF 4-1.

FASTEST FOUR GOALS, BOTH TEAMS:
1 Minute, 33 Seconds — Philadelphia Flyers, Toronto Maple Leafs at Philadelphia, April 20, 1976. Don Saleski of Philadelphia scored at 10:04 of second period; Bob Neely, Toronto, 10:42; Gary Dornhoefer, Philadelphia, 11:24; and Don Saleski, 11:37. Philadelphia won 7-1 and best-of-seven QF series 4-3.
1 minute, 34 seconds — Montreal Canadiens, Calgary Flames at Montreal, May 20, 1986. Joel Otto of Calgary scored at 17:59 of first period; Bobby Smith, Montreal, 18:25; Mats Naslund, Montreal, 19:17; and Bob Gainey, Montreal, 19:33. Montreal won 5-3 and best-of-seven F series 4-1.
1 Minute, 38 Seconds — Boston Bruins, Philadelphia Flyers at Philadelphia, April 26, 1977. Gregg Sheppard of Boston scored at 14:01 of second period; Mike Milbury, Boston, 15:01; Gary Dornhoefer, Philadelphia, 15:16; and Jean Ratelle, Boston, 15:39. Boston won 5-4 and best-of-seven SF series 4-0.

FASTEST FOUR GOALS, ONE TEAM:
2 Minutes, 35 Seconds — Montreal Canadiens at Montreal, March 30, 1944, against Toronto. Toe Blake scored at 7:58 of third period and again at 8:37; Maurice Richard, 9:17; Ray Getliffe, 10:33. Montreal won 11-0 and best-of-seven SF 4-1.

FASTEST THREE GOALS, BOTH TEAMS:
21 Seconds — Edmonton Oilers, Chicago Blackhawks at Edmonton, May 7, 1985. Behn Wilson scored for Chicago at 19:22 of third period, Jari Kurri at 19:36 and Glenn Anderson at 19:43 for Edmonton. Edmonton won 7-3 and best-of-seven CF 4-2.
27 Seconds — Phoenix Coyotes, Detroit Red Wings at Detroit, April 24, 1998. Jeremy Roenick scored for Phoenix at 13:24 of the second period. Mathieu Dandenault scored for Detroit at 13:32, and Keith Tkachuk scored for Phoenix at 13:51. Phoenix won 7-4, Detroit won the best-of-seven CQF 4-2.
30 Seconds — Chicago Blackhawks, Pittsburgh Penguins at Chicago, June 1, 1992. Dirk Graham scored for Chicago at 6:21 of first period, Kevin Stevens for Pittsburgh at 6:33 and Graham for Chicago at 6:51. Pittsburgh won 6-5 and best-of-seven F 4-0.

FASTEST THREE GOALS, ONE TEAM:
23 Seconds — Toronto Maple Leafs at Toronto, April 12, 1979, against Atlanta. Darryl Sittler scored at 4:04 of first period and again at 4:16 and Ron Ellis at 4:27. Leafs won 7-4 and best-of-three PR 2-0.
38 Seconds — NY Rangers at New York, April 12, 1986 against Philadelphia. Jim Wiemer scored at 12:29 of third period, Bob Brooke at 12:43 and Ron Greschner at 13:07. NY Rangers won 5-2 and best-of-five DSF 3-2.
56 Seconds — Montreal Canadiens at Detroit, April 6, 1954. Dickie Moore scored at 15:03 of first period, Maurice Richard at 15:28 and again at 15:59. Montreal won 3-1. Detroit won best-of-seven F 4-3.

FASTEST TWO GOALS, BOTH TEAMS:
5 Seconds — Pittsburgh Penguins, Buffalo Sabres at Buffalo, April 14, 1979. Gilbert Perreault scored for Buffalo at 12:59 and Jim Hamilton for Pittsburgh at 13:04 of first period. Pittsburgh won 4-3 and best-of-three PR 2-1.
8 Seconds — Minnesota North Stars, St. Louis Blues at Minnesota, April 9, 1989. Bernie Federko scored for St. Louis at 2:28 of third period and Perry Berezan at 2:36 for Minnesota. Minnesota won 5-4. St. Louis won best-of-seven DSF 4-1.
— Phoenix Coyotes, Detroit Red Wings, at Detroit, April 24, 1998. Jeremy Roenick scored for Phoenix at 13:24 of the second period and Mathieu Dandenault scored for Detroit at 13:32. Phoenix won 7-4, Detroit won the best-of-seven CQF 4-2.
9 Seconds — NY Islanders, Washington Capitals at Washington, April 10, 1986. Bryan Trottier scored for New York at 18:26 of second period and Scott Stevens at 18:35 for Washington. Washington won 5-2, and best-of-five DSF 3-0.

FASTEST TWO GOALS, ONE TEAM:
5 Seconds — Detroit Red Wings at Detroit, April 11, 1965, against Chicago. Norm Ullman scored at 17:35 and 17:40, second period. Detroit won 4-2. Chicago won best-of-seven SF 4-3.

Pete Stemkowski lit up Broadway when he banged this shot past Tony Esposito early in the third overtime period to give the New York Rangers a heart-wrenching 3-2 win over the Chicago Black Hawks in game six of the 1971 semifinals.

OVERTIME

SHORTEST OVERTIME:
9 Seconds — Montreal Canadiens, Calgary Flames, at Calgary, May 18, 1986. Montreal won 3-2 on Brian Skrudland's goal and captured the best-of-seven F 4-1.
11 Seconds — NY Islanders, NY Rangers, at NY Rangers, April 11, 1975. NY Islanders won 4-3 on Jean-Paul Parise's goal and captured the best-of-three PR 2-1.

LONGEST OVERTIME:
116 Minutes, 30 Seconds — Detroit Red Wings, Mtl. Maroons at Montreal, March 24, 25, 1936. Detroit 1, Mtl. Maroons 0. Mud Bruneteau scored, assisted by Hec Kilrea, at 16:30 of sixth overtime period, or after 176 minutes, 30 seconds from start of game, which ended at 2:25 a.m. Detroit won best-of-five SF 3-0.

MOST OVERTIME GAMES, ONE PLAYOFF YEAR:
28 — 1993. Of 85 games played, 28 went into overtime.
19 — 1996. Of 86 games played, 19 went into overtime.
— 1998. Of 82 games played, 19 went into overtime.
18 — 1994. Of 90 games played, 18 went into overtime.
— 1995. Of 81 games played, 18 went into overtime.

FEWEST OVERTIME GAMES, ONE PLAYOFF YEAR:
0 — 1963. None of the 16 games went into overtime, the only year since 1926 that no overtime was required in any playoff series.

MOST OVERTIME GAMES, ONE SERIES:
5 — Toronto Maple Leafs, Montreal Canadiens in 1951. Toronto won best-of-seven F 4-1.
4 — Toronto Maple Leafs, Boston Bruins in 1933. Toronto won best-of-five SF 3-2.
— Boston Bruins, NY Rangers in 1939. Boston won best-of-seven SF 4-3.
— St. Louis Blues, Minnesota North Stars in 1968. St. Louis won best-of-seven SF 4-3.

THREE-OR-MORE GOAL GAMES

MOST THREE-OR-MORE GOAL GAMES BY ALL TEAMS, ONE PLAYOFF YEAR:
12 — **1983** in 66 games.
— **1988** in 83 games.
11 — 1985 in 70 games.
— 1992 in 86 games.

MOST THREE-OR-MORE GOAL GAMES, ONE TEAM, ONE PLAYOFF YEAR:
6 — Edmonton Oilers in 16 games, 1983.
— Edmonton Oilers in 18 games, 1985.

SHUTOUTS

MOST SHUTOUTS, ONE PLAYOFF YEAR, ALL TEAMS:
18 — 1997. Of 82 games played, Colorado and NY Rangers had 3 each, Edmonton, New Jersey, and St. Louis had 2 each, while Anaheim, Buffalo, Detroit, Florida, Ottawa and Phoenix had 1 each.
16 — 1994. Of 90 games played, NY Rangers and Vancouver had 4 each, Toronto had 3, Buffalo had 2, while Washington, Detroit and New Jersey had 1 each.

FEWEST SHUTOUTS, ONE PLAYOFF YEAR, ALL TEAMS:
0 — 1959. 18 games played.

MOST SHUTOUTS, BOTH TEAMS, ONE SERIES:
5 — 1945 F, Toronto Maple Leafs, Detroit Red Wings. Toronto had 3 shutouts, Detroit 2. Toronto won best-of-seven series 4-3.
— 1950 SF, Toronto Maple Leafs, Detroit Red Wings. Toronto had 3 shutouts, Detroit 2. Detroit won best-of-seven series 4-3.

TEAM PENALTIES

FEWEST PENALTIES, BOTH TEAMS, BEST-OF-SEVEN SERIES:
19 — Detroit Red Wings, Toronto Maple Leafs in 1945 F, won by Toronto 4-3. Detroit received 10 minors, Toronto had 9 minors.

FEWEST PENALTIES, ONE TEAM, BEST-OF-SEVEN SERIES:
9 — Toronto Maple Leafs in 1945 F, won by Toronto 4-3 against Detroit.

MOST PENALTIES, BOTH TEAMS, ONE SERIES:
219 — New Jersey Devils, Washington Capitals in 1988 DF won by New Jersey 4-3. New Jersey received 98 minors, 11 majors, 9 misconducts and 1 match penalty. Washington received 80 minors, 11 majors, 8 misconducts and 1 match penalty.

MOST PENALTY MINUTES, BOTH TEAMS, ONE SERIES:
656 — New Jersey Devils, Washington Capitals in 1988 DF won by New Jersey 4-3. New Jersey had 351 minutes; Washington 305.

MOST PENALTIES, ONE TEAM, ONE SERIES:
119 — New Jersey Devils in 1988 DF versus Washington. New Jersey received 98 minors, 11 majors, 9 misconducts and 1 match penalty.

MOST PENALTY MINUTES, ONE TEAM, ONE SERIES:
351 — New Jersey Devils in 1988 DF versus Washington. Series won by New Jersey 4-3.

MOST PENALTIES, BOTH TEAMS, ONE GAME:
66 — Detroit Red Wings, St. Louis Blues, at St. Louis, April 12, 1991. Detroit received 33 penalties; St. Louis 33. St. Louis won 6-1.
62 — New Jersey Devils, Washington Capitals, at New Jersey, April 22, 1988. New Jersey received 32 penalties; Washington 30. New Jersey won 10-4.

MOST PENALTY MINUTES, BOTH TEAMS, ONE GAME:
298 Minutes — Detroit Red Wings, St. Louis Blues, at St. Louis, April 12, 1991. Detroit received 33 penalties for 152 minutes; St. Louis 33 penalties for 146 minutes. St. Louis won 6-1.
267 Minutes — NY Rangers, Los Angeles Kings, at Los Angeles, April 9, 1981. NY Rangers received 31 penalties for 142 minutes; Los Angeles 28 penalties for 125 minutes. Los Angeles won 5-4.

MOST PENALTIES, ONE TEAM, ONE GAME:
33 — Detroit Red Wings, at St. Louis, April 12,1991. St. Louis won 6-1.
— St. Louis Blues, at St. Louis, April 12, 1991. St. Louis won 6-1.
32 — New Jersey Devils, at Washington, April 22,1988. New Jersey won 10-4.
31 — NY Rangers, at Los Angeles, April 9, 1981. Los Angeles won 5-4.
30 — Philadelphia Flyers, at Toronto, April 15, 1976. Toronto won 5-4.

MOST PENALTY MINUTES, ONE TEAM, ONE GAME:
152 — Detroit Red Wings, at St. Louis, April 12, 1991. St. Louis won 6-1.
146 — St. Louis Blues, at St. Louis, April 12, 1991. St. Louis won 6-1.
142 — NY Rangers, at Los Angeles, April 9, 1981. Los Angeles won 5-4.

MOST PENALTIES, BOTH TEAMS, ONE PERIOD:
43 — NY Rangers, Los Angeles Kings, April 9, 1981, at Los Angeles, first period. NY Rangers had 24 penalties; Los Angeles 19. Los Angeles won 5-4.

MOST PENALTY MINUTES, BOTH TEAMS, ONE PERIOD:
248 — NY Islanders, Boston Bruins, April 17, 1980, first period, at Boston. Each team received 124 minutes. Islanders won 5-4.

MOST PENALTIES, ONE TEAM, ONE PERIOD: (AND) MOST PENALTY MINUTES, ONE TEAM, ONE PERIOD:
24 Penalties; 125 Minutes — NY Rangers, April 9, 1981, at Los Angeles, first period. Los Angeles won 5-4.

Individual Records

GAMES PLAYED

MOST YEARS IN PLAYOFFS:
20 — Gordie Howe, Detroit, Hartford (1947-58 incl.; 60-61; 63-66 incl.; 70 & 80)
— Larry Robinson, Montreal, Los Angeles (1973-92 incl.)
19 — Red Kelly, Detroit, Toronto
18 — Stan Mikita, Chicago
— Henri Richard, Montreal
— Ray Bourque, Boston
— Kevin Lowe, Edmonton, NY Rangers

MOST CONSECUTIVE YEARS IN PLAYOFFS:
20 — Larry Robinson, Montreal, Los Angeles (1973-1992, inclusive).
17 — Brad Park, NY Rangers, Boston, Detroit (1969-1985, inclusive).
— Ray Bourque, Boston (1980-96, inclusive).
16 — Jean Beliveau, Montreal (1954-69, inclusive).
— Bob Gainey, Montreal (1974-89, inclusive).
— Dale Hunter, Quebec, Washington (1981-96, inclusive)

MOST PLAYOFF GAMES:
236 — Mark Messier, Edmonton, NY Rangers
227 — Larry Robinson, Montreal, Los Angeles
225 — Glenn Anderson, Edmonton, Toronto, NY Rangers, St. Louis
221 — Bryan Trottier, NY Islanders, Pittsburgh
214 — Kevin Lowe, Edmonton, NY Rangers

GOALS

MOST GOALS IN PLAYOFFS (CAREER):
122 — Wayne Gretzky, Edmonton, Los Angeles, St. Louis, NY Rangers
109 — Mark Messier, Edmonton, NY Rangers
106 — Jari Kurri, Edmonton, Los Angeles, NY Rangers, Anaheim
93 — Glenn Anderson, Edmonton, Toronto, NY Rangers, St. Louis
85 — Mike Bossy, NY Islanders

MOST GOALS, ONE PLAYOFF YEAR:
19 — Reggie Leach, Philadelphia, 1976. 16 games.
— Jari Kurri, Edmonton, 1985. 18 games.
18 — Joe Sakic, Colorado, 1996. 22 games.
17 — Newsy Lalonde, Montreal, 1919. 10 games.
— Mike Bossy, NY Islanders, 1981. 18 games.
— Steve Payne, Minnesota, 1981. 19 games.
— Mike Bossy, NY Islanders, 1982. 19 games.
— Mike Bossy, NY Islanders, 1983. 19 games
— Wayne Gretzky, Edmonton, 1985. 18 games.
— Kevin Stevens, Pittsburgh, 1991. 24 games.

MOST GOALS IN ONE SERIES (OTHER THAN FINAL):
12 — Jari Kurri, Edmonton, in 1985 CF, 6 games vs. Chicago.
11 — Newsy Lalonde, Montreal, in 1919 NHL F, 5 games vs. Ottawa.
10 — Tim Kerr, Philadelphia, in 1989 DF, 7 games vs. Pittsburgh.
9 — Reggie Leach, Philadelphia, in 1976 SF, 5 games vs. Boston.
— Bill Barber, Philadelphia, in 1980 SF, 5 games vs. Minnesota.
— Mike Bossy, NY Islanders, in 1983 CF, 6 games vs. Boston.
— Mario Lemieux, Pittsburgh, in 1989 DF, 7 games vs. Philadelphia.

MOST GOALS IN FINAL SERIES:
9 — Babe Dye, Toronto, in 1922, 5 games vs. Van. Millionaires.
8 — Alf Skinner, Toronto, in 1918, 5 games vs. Van. Millionaires.
7 — Jean Beliveau, Montreal, in 1956, 5 games vs. Detroit.
— Mike Bossy, NY Islanders, in 1982, 4 games vs. Vancouver.
— Wayne Gretzky, Edmonton, in 1985, 5 games vs. Philadelphia.

MOST GOALS, ONE GAME:
5 — Newsy Lalonde, Montreal, March 1, 1919, at Montreal. Final score: Montreal 6, Ottawa 3.
— Maurice Richard, Montreal, March 23, 1944, at Montreal. Final score: Montreal 5, Toronto 1.
— Darryl Sittler, Toronto, April 22, 1976, at Toronto. Final score: Toronto 8, Philadelphia 5.
— Reggie Leach, Philadelphia, May 6, 1976, at Philadelphia. Final score: Philadelphia 6, Boston 3.
— Mario Lemieux, Pittsburgh, April 25, 1989, at Pittsburgh. Final score: Pittsburgh 10, Philadelphia 7.

MOST GOALS, ONE PERIOD:
4 — Tim Kerr, Philadelphia, April 13, 1985, at New York vs. NY Rangers, second period. Final score: Philadelphia 6, NY Rangers 5.
— Mario Lemieux, Pittsburgh, April 25, 1989, at Pittsburgh vs. Philadelphia, first period. Final score: Pittsburgh 10, Philadelphia 7.

ASSISTS

MOST ASSISTS IN PLAYOFFS (CAREER):
260 — Wayne Gretzky, Edmonton, Los Angeles, St. Louis, NY Rangers
186 — Mark Messier, Edmonton, NY Rangers
136 — Paul Coffey, Edmonton, Pittsburgh, Los Angeles, Detroit, Philadelphia
127 — Jari Kurri, Edmonton, Los Angeles, NY Rangers, Anaheim
121 — Glenn Anderson, Edmonton, Toronto, NY Rangers, St. Louis

MOST ASSISTS, ONE PLAYOFF YEAR:
31 — Wayne Gretzky, Edmonton, 1988. 19 games.
30 — Wayne Gretzky, Edmonton, 1985. 18 games.
29 — Wayne Gretzky, Edmonton, 1987. 21 games.
28 — Mario Lemieux, Pittsburgh, 1991. 23 games.
26 — Wayne Gretzky, Edmonton, 1983. 16 games.

MOST ASSISTS IN ONE SERIES (OTHER THAN FINAL):
14 — Rick Middleton, Boston, in 1983 DF, 7 games vs. Buffalo.
— Wayne Gretzky, Edmonton, in 1985 CF, 6 games vs. Chicago.
13 — Wayne Gretzky, Edmonton, in 1987 DSF, 5 games vs. Los Angeles.
— Doug Gilmour, Toronto, in 1994 CSF, 7 games vs. San Jose.
11 — Mark Messier, Edmonton, in 1989 DSF, 7 games vs. Los Angeles.
— Al MacInnis, Calgary, in 1984 DF, 7 games vs. Edmonton.
— Mike Ridley, Washington, in 1992 DSF, 7 games vs. Pittsburgh.
— Ron Francis, Pittsburgh, in 1995 CQF, 7 games vs. Washington.
10 — Fleming Mackell, Boston, in 1958 SF, 6 games vs. NY Rangers.
— Stan Mikita, Chicago, in 1962 SF, 6 games vs. Montreal.
— Bob Bourne, NY Islanders, in 1983 DF, 6 games vs. NY Rangers.
— Wayne Gretzky, Edmonton, in 1988 DSF, 5 games vs. Winnipeg.
— Mario Lemieux, Pittsburgh, in 1992 DSF, 6 games vs. Washington.

MOST ASSISTS IN FINAL SERIES:
10 — Wayne Gretzky, Edmonton, in 1988, 4 games plus suspended game vs. Boston.
9 — Jacques Lemaire, Montreal, in 1973, 6 games vs. Chicago.
— Wayne Gretzky, Edmonton, in 1987, 7 games vs. Philadelphia.
— Larry Murphy, Pittsburgh, in 1991, 6 games vs. Minnesota.

MOST ASSISTS, ONE GAME:
6 — Mikko Leinonen, NY Rangers, April 8, 1982, at New York. Final score: NY Rangers 7, Philadelphia 3.
— Wayne Gretzky, Edmonton, April 9, 1987, at Edmonton. Final score: Edmonton 13, Los Angeles 3.
5 — Toe Blake, Montreal, March 23, 1944, at Montreal. Final score: Montreal 5, Toronto 1.
— Maurice Richard, Montreal, March 27, 1956, at Montreal. Final score: Montreal 7, NY Rangers 0.
— Bert Olmstead, Montreal, March 30, 1957, at Montreal. Final score: Montreal 8, NY Rangers 3.
— Don McKenney, Boston, April 5, 1958, at Boston. Final score: Boston 8, NY Rangers 2.
— Stan Mikita, Chicago, April 4, 1973, at Chicago. Final score: Chicago 7, St. Louis 1.
— Wayne Gretzky, Edmonton, April 8, 1981, at Montreal. Final score: Edmonton 6, Montreal 3.
— Paul Coffey, Edmonton, May 14, 1985, at Edmonton. Final score: Edmonton 10, Chicago 5.
— Doug Gilmour, St. Louis, April 15, 1986, at Minnesota. Final score: St. Louis 6, Minnesota 3.
— Risto Siltanen, Quebec, April 14, 1987, at Hartford. Final score: Quebec 7, Hartford 5.
— Patrik Sundstrom, New Jersey, April 22, 1988, at New Jersey. Final score: New Jersey 10, Washington 4.
— Geoff Courtnall, St. Louis Blues, April 23, 1998, at St. Louis. Final score: St. Louis 8, Los Angeles 3.

MOST ASSISTS, ONE PERIOD:
3 — Three assists by one player in one period of a playoff game has been recorded on 70 occasions. Al MacInnis and Chris Pronger of the St. Louis Blues are the most recent to equal this mark with 3 assists each in the third period at Los Angeles, April 27, 1998. Final score: St. Louis 4, Los Angeles 3.
— Wayne Gretzky has had 3 assists in one period 5 times; Ray Bourque, 3 times; Toe Blake, Jean Beliveau, Doug Harvey and Bobby Orr, twice. Nick Metz of Toronto was the first player to be credited with 3 assists in one period of a playoff game Mar. 21, 1941 at Toronto vs. Boston.

POINTS

MOST POINTS IN PLAYOFFS (CAREER):
382 — Wayne Gretzky, Edmonton, Los Angeles, St. Louis, NY Rangers, 122G, 260A
295 — Mark Messier, Edmonton, NY Rangers, 109G, 186A
233 — Jari Kurri, Edmonton, Los Angeles, NY Rangers, Anaheim, 106G, 127A
214 — Glenn Anderson, Edmonton, Toronto, NY Rangers, St. Louis, 93G, 121A
195 — Paul Coffey, Edmonton, Pittsburgh, Los Angeles, Detroit, Philadelphia, 59G, 136A

MOST POINTS, ONE PLAYOFF YEAR:
47 — Wayne Gretzky, Edmonton, in 1985. 17 goals, 30 assists in 18 games.
44 — Mario Lemieux, Pittsburgh, in 1991. 16 goals, 28 assists in 23 games.
43 — Wayne Gretzky, Edmonton, in 1988. 12 goals, 31 assists in 19 games.
40 — Wayne Gretzky, Los Angeles, in 1993. 15 goals, 25 assists in 24 games.
38 — Wayne Gretzky, Edmonton, in 1983. 12 goals, 26 assists in 16 games.

MOST POINTS IN ONE SERIES (OTHER THAN FINAL):

19 — Rick Middleton, Boston, in 1983 DF, 7 games vs. Buffalo. 5 goals, 14 assists.
18 — Wayne Gretzky, Edmonton, in 1985 CF, 6 games vs. Chicago. 4 goals, 14 assists.
17 — Mario Lemieux, Pittsburgh, in 1992 DSF, 6 games vs. Washington. 7 goals, 10 assists.
16 — Barry Pederson, Boston, in 1983 DF, 7 games vs. Buffalo. 7 goals, 9 assists.
— Doug Gilmour, Toronto, in 1994 CSF, 7 games vs. San Jose. 3 goals, 13 assists.
15 — Jari Kurri, Edmonton, in 1985 CF, 6 games vs. Chicago. 12 goals, 3 assists.
— Wayne Gretzky, Edmonton, in 1987 DSF, 5 games vs. Los Angeles. 2 goals, 13 assists.
— Tim Kerr, Philadelphia, in 1989 DF, 7 games vs. Pittsburgh. 10 goals, 5 assists.
— Mario Lemieux, Pittsburgh, in 1991 CF, 6 games vs. Boston. 6 goals, 9 assists.

MOST POINTS IN FINAL SERIES:

13 — Wayne Gretzky, Edmonton, in 1988, 4 games plus suspended game vs. Boston. 3 goals, 10 assists.
12 — Gordie Howe, Detroit, in 1955, 7 games vs. Montreal. 5 goals, 7 assists.
— Yvan Cournoyer, Montreal, in 1973, 6 games vs. Chicago. 6 goals, 6 assists.
— Jacques Lemaire, Montreal, in 1973, 6 games vs. Chicago. 3 goals, 9 assists.
— Mario Lemieux, Pittsburgh, in 1991, 5 games vs. Minnesota. 5 goals, 7 assists.

MOST POINTS, ONE GAME:

8 — Patrik Sundstrom, New Jersey, April 22, 1988 at New Jersey during 10-4 win over Washington. Sundstrom had 3 goals, 5 assists.
— Mario Lemieux, Pittsburgh, April 25, 1989 at Pittsburgh during 10-7 win over Philadelphia. Lemieux had 5 goals, 3 assists.
7 — Wayne Gretzky, Edmonton, April 17, 1983 at Calgary during 10-2 win. Gretzky had 4 goals, 3 assists.
— Wayne Gretzky, Edmonton, April 25,1985 at Winnipeg during 8-3 win. Gretzky had 3 goals, 4 assists.
— Wayne Gretzky, Edmonton, April 9, 1987, at Edmonton during 13-3 win over Los Angeles. Gretzky had 1 goal, 6 assists.
6 — Dickie Moore, Montreal, March 25, 1954, at Montreal during 8-1 win over Boston. Moore had 2 goals, 4 assists.
— Phil Esposito, Boston, April 2, 1969, at Boston during 10-0 win over Toronto. Esposito had 4 goals, 2 assists.
— Darryl Sittler, Toronto, April 22, 1976, at Toronto during 8-5 win over Philadelphia. Sittler had 5 goals, 1 assist.
— Guy Lafleur, Montreal, April 11, 1977, at Montreal during 7-2 win over St. Louis. Lafleur had 3 goals, 3 assists.
— Mikko Leinonen, NY Rangers, April 8, 1982, at New York during 7-3 win over Philadelphia. Leinonen had 6 assists.
— Paul Coffey, Edmonton, May 14, 1985 at Edmonton during 10-5 win over Chicago. Coffey had 1 goal, 5 assists.
— John Anderson, Hartford, April 12, 1986 at Hartford during 9-4 win over Quebec. Anderson had 2 goals, 4 assists.
— Mario Lemieux, Pittsburgh, April 23, 1992 at Pittsburgh during 6-4 win over Washington. Lemieux had 3 goals, 3 assists.
— Geoff Courtnall, St. Louis Blues, April 23, 1998 at St. Louis during 8-3 win over Los Angeles. Courtnall had 1 goal, 5 assists.

MOST POINTS, ONE PERIOD:

4 — Maurice Richard, Montreal, March 29, 1945, at Montreal vs. Toronto. Third period, 3 goals, 1 assist. Final score: Montreal 10, Toronto 3.
— Dickie Moore, Montreal, March 25, 1954, at Montreal vs. Boston. First period, 2 goals, 2 assists. Final score: Montreal 8, Boston 1.
— Barry Pederson, Boston, April 8, 1982, at Boston vs. Buffalo. Second period, 3 goals, 1 assist. Final score: Boston 7, Buffalo 3.
— Peter McNab, Boston, April 11, 1982, at Buffalo. Second period, 1 goal, 3 assists. Final score: Boston 5, Buffalo 2.
— Tim Kerr, Philadelphia, April 13, 1985 at New York. Second period, 4 goals. Final score: Philadelphia 6, Rangers 5.
— Ken Linseman, Boston, April 14, 1985 at Boston vs. Montreal. Second period, 2 goals, 2 assists. Final score: Boston 7, Montreal 6.
— Wayne Gretzky, Edmonton, April 12, 1987, at Los Angeles. Third period, 1 goal, 3 assists. Final score: Edmonton 6, Los Angeles 3.
— Glenn Anderson, Edmonton, April 6, 1988, at Edmonton vs. Winnipeg. Third period, 3 goals, 1 assist. Final score: Edmonton 7, Winnipeg 4.
— Mario Lemieux, Pittsburgh, April 25, 1989, at Pittsburgh vs. Philadelphia. First period, 4 goals. Final score: Pittsburgh 10, Philadelphia 7.
— Dave Gagner, Minnesota, April 8, 1991, at Minnesota vs. Chicago. First period, 2 goals, 2 assists. Final score: Chicago 6, Minnesota 5.
— Mario Lemieux, Pittsburgh, April 23, 1992, at Pittsburgh vs. Washington. Second period, 2 goals, 2 assists. Final score: Pittsburgh 6, Washington 4.

POWER-PLAY GOALS

MOST POWER-PLAY GOALS IN PLAYOFFS (CAREER):

35 — Mike Bossy, NY Islanders
34 — Dino Ciccarelli, Minnesota, Washington, Detroit
— Wayne Gretzky, Edmonton, Los Angeles, St. Louis, NY Rangers
28 — Mario Lemieux, Pittsburgh
27 — Denis Potvin, NY Islanders

MOST POWER-PLAY GOALS, ONE PLAYOFF YEAR:

9 — Mike Bossy, NY Islanders, 1981. 18 games against Toronto, Edmonton, NY Rangers and Minnesota.
— Cam Neely, Boston, 1991. 19 games against Hartford, Montreal, Pittsburgh.
8 — Tim Kerr, Philadelphia, 1989. 19 games.
— John Druce, Washington, 1990. 15 games.
— Brian Propp, Minnesota, 1991. 23 games.
— Mario Lemieux, Pittsburgh, 1992. 15 games.

MOST POWER-PLAY GOALS, ONE PLAYOFF SERIES:

6 — Chris Kontos, Los Angeles, 1989, DSF vs. Edmonton, won by Los Angeles 4-3.
5 — Andy Bathgate, Detroit, 1966, SF vs. Chicago, won by Detroit 4-2.
— Denis Potvin, NY Islanders, 1981, QF vs. Edmonton, won by NY Islanders 4-2.
— Ken Houston, Calgary, 1981, QF vs. Philadelphia, won by Calgary 4-3.
— Rick Vaive, Chicago, 1988, DSF vs. St. Louis, won by St. Louis 4-1.
— Tim Kerr, Philadelphia, 1989, DF vs. Pittsburgh, won by Philadelphia 4-3.
— Mario Lemieux, Pittsburgh, 1989, DF vs. Philadelphia won by Philadelphia 4-3.
— John Druce, Washington, 1990, DF vs. NY Rangers won by Washington 4-1.
— Pat LaFontaine, Buffalo, 1992, DSF vs. Boston won by Boston 4-3.
— Adam Graves, NY Rangers, 1996, CQF vs Montreal, won by NY Rangers 4-2.

MOST POWER-PLAY GOALS, ONE GAME:

3 — Syd Howe, Detroit, March 23, 1939, at Detroit vs. Montreal. Detroit won 7-3.
— Sid Smith, Toronto, April 10, 1949, at Detroit. Toronto won 3-1.
— Phil Esposito, Boston, April 2, 1969, at Boston vs. Toronto. Boston won 10-0.
— John Bucyk, Boston, April 21, 1974, at Boston vs. Chicago. Boston won 8-6.
— Denis Potvin, NY Islanders, April 17, 1981, at New York vs. Edmonton. NY Islanders won 6-3.
— Tim Kerr, Philadelphia, April 13, 1985, at NY Rangers. Philadelphia won 6-5.
— Jari Kurri, Edmonton, April 9, 1987, at Edmonton vs. Los Angeles. Edmonton won 13-3.
— Mark Johnson, New Jersey, April 22, 1988, at New Jersey vs. Washington. New Jersey won 10-4.
— Dino Ciccarelli, Detroit, April 29, 1993, at Toronto. Detroit won 7-3.
— Dino Ciccarelli, Detroit, May 11, 1995, at Dallas. Detroit won 5-1.
— Valeri Kamensky, Colorado, April 24, 1997, at Colorado vs. Chicago. Colorado won 7-0.

MOST POWER-PLAY GOALS, ONE PERIOD:

3 — Tim Kerr, Philadelphia, April 13, 1985 at New York, second period in 6-5 win vs. NY Rangers.
2 — Two power-play goals have been scored by one player in one period on 53 occasions. Charlie Conacher of Toronto was the first to score two power-play goals in one period, setting the mark on March 26, 1936. Brendan Shanahan of the Detroit Red Wings is the most recent to equal this mark with two power-play goals in the first period at Phoenix, May 3, 1998. Final score: Detroit 5, Phoenix 2.

SHORTHAND GOALS

MOST SHORTHAND GOALS IN PLAYOFFS (CAREER):

14 — Mark Messier, Edmonton, NY Rangers
11 — Wayne Gretzky, Edmonton, Los Angeles, St. Louis
10 — Jari Kurri, Edmonton, Los Angeles, NY Rangers
8 — Ed Westfall, Boston, NY Islanders
— Hakan Loob, Calgary

MOST SHORTHAND GOALS, ONE PLAYOFF YEAR:

3 — Derek Sanderson, Boston, 1969. 1 against Toronto in QF, won by Boston 4-0; 2 against Montreal in SF, won by Montreal, 4-2.
— Bill Barber, Philadelphia, 1980. All against Minnesota in SF, won by Philadelphia 4-1.
— Lorne Henning, NY Islanders, 1980. 1 against Boston in QF won by NY Islanders 4-1; 1 against Buffalo in SF, won by NY Islanders 4-2, 1 against Philadelphia in F, won by NY Islanders 4-2.
— Wayne Gretzky, Edmonton, 1983. 2 against Winnipeg in DSF won by Edmonton 3-0; 1 against Calgary in DF, won by Edmonton 4-1.
— Wayne Presley, Chicago, 1989. All against Detroit in DSF won by Chicago 4-2.
— Todd Marchant, Edmonton, 1997. 1 against Dallas in CQF won by Edmonton 4-3; 2 against Colorado in CSF won by Colorado 4-1.

MOST SHORTHAND GOALS, ONE PLAYOFF SERIES:

3 — Bill Barber, Philadelphia, 1980, SF vs. Minnesota, won by Philadelphia 4-1.
— Wayne Presley, Chicago, 1989, DSF vs. Detroit, won by Chicago 4-2.
2 — Mac Colville, NY Rangers, 1940, SF vs. Boston, won by NY Rangers 4-2.
— Jerry Toppazzini, Boston, 1958, SF vs. NY Rangers, won by Boston 4-2.
— Dave Keon, Toronto, 1963, F vs. Detroit, won by Toronto 4-1.
— Bob Pulford, Toronto, 1964, F vs. Detroit, won by Toronto 4-3.
— Serge Savard, Montreal, 1968, F vs. St. Louis, won by Montreal 4-0.
— Derek Sanderson, Boston, 1969, SF vs. Montreal, won by Montreal 4-2.
— Bryan Trottier, NY Islanders, 1980, PR vs. Los Angeles, won by NY Islanders 3-1.
— Bobby Lalonde, Boston, 1981, PR vs. Minnesota, won by Minnesota 3-0.
— Butch Goring, NY Islanders, 1981, SF vs. NY Rangers, won by NY Islanders 4-0.
— Wayne Gretzky, Edmonton, 1983, DSF vs. Winnipeg, won by Edmonton 3-0.
— Mark Messier, Edmonton, 1983, DF vs. Calgary, won by Edmonton 4-1.
— Jari Kurri, Edmonton, 1983, CF vs. Chicago, won by Edmonton 4-0.
— Wayne Gretzky, Edmonton, 1985, DF vs. Winnipeg, won by Edmonton 4-0.
— Kevin Lowe, Edmonton, 1987, F vs. Philadelphia, won by Edmonton 4-3.
— Bob Gould, Washington, 1988, DSF vs. Philadelphia, won by Washington 4-3.
— Dave Poulin, Philadelphia, 1989, DF vs. Pittsburgh, won by Philadelphia 4-3.
— Russ Courtnall, Montreal, 1991, DF vs. Boston, won by Boston 4-3.
— Sergei Fedorov, Detroit, 1992 DSF vs. Minnesota, won by Detroit 4-3.
— Mark Messier, NY Rangers, 1992, DSF vs. New Jersey, won by NY Rangers 4-3.
— Tom Fitzgerald, NY Islanders, 1993, DF vs. Pittsburgh, won by NY Islanders 4-3.
— Mark Osborne, Toronto, 1994, CSF vs. San Jose, won by Toronto 4-3.
— Tony Amonte, Chicago, 1997, CQF vs. Colorado, won by Colorado 4-2.
— Brian Rolston, New Jersey, 1997, CQF vs. Montreal, won by New Jersey 4-1.
— Rod Brind'Amour, Philadelphia, 1997, CQF vs. Pittsburgh, won by Philadelphia 4-1.
— Todd Marchant, Edmonton, 1997, CSF vs. Colorado, won by Colorado 4-1.
— Jeremy Roenick, Phoenix, 1998, CQF vs. Detroit, won by Detroit 4-2.

MOST SHORTHAND GOALS, ONE GAME:

2 — Dave Keon, Toronto, April 18, 1963, at Toronto, in 3-1 win vs. Detroit.
— Bryan Trottier, NY Islanders, April 8, 1980 at New York, in 8-1 win vs. Los Angeles.
— Bobby Lalonde, Boston, April 11, 1981 at Minnesota, in 6-3 win by Minnesota.
— Wayne Gretzky, Edmonton, April 6, 1983 at Edmonton, in 6-3 win vs. Winnipeg.
— Jari Kurri, Edmonton, April 24, 1983, at Edmonton, in 8-3 win vs. Chicago.
— Mark Messier, NY Rangers, April 21, 1992, at New York, in 7-3 loss vs. New Jersey.
— Tom Fitzgerald, NY Islanders, May 8, 1993, at Long Island, in 6-5 win vs. Pittsburgh.
— Rod Brind'Amour, Philadelphia, April 26, 1997, at Philadelphia, in 6-3 win vs. Pittsburgh.
— Jeremy Roenick, Phoenix, April 24, 1998, at Detroit, in 7-4 win by Phoenix.

MOST SHORTHAND GOALS, ONE PERIOD:

2 — Bryan Trottier, NY Islanders, April 8, 1980, second period at New York in 8-1 win vs. Los Angeles.
— Bobby Lalonde, Boston, April 11, 1981, third period at Minnesota in 6-3 win by Minnesota.
— Jari Kurri, Edmonton, April 24, 1983, third period at Edmonton in 8-4 win vs. Chicago.
— Rod Brind'Amour, Philadelphia, April 26, 1997, first period at Philadelphia in 6-3 win vs. Pittsburgh.
— Jeremy Roenick, Phoenix, April 24, 1998, second period at Detroit in 7-4 win by Phoenix.

GAME-WINNING GOALS

MOST GAME-WINNING GOALS IN PLAYOFFS (CAREER):

24 — Wayne Gretzky, Edmonton, Los Angeles, St. Louis, NY Rangers
19 — Claude Lemieux, Montreal, New Jersey, Colorado
18 — Maurice Richard, Montreal
17 — Mike Bossy, NY Islanders
— Glenn Anderson, Edmonton, Toronto, NY Rangers, St. Louis

MOST GAME-WINNING GOALS, ONE PLAYOFF YEAR:

6 — Joe Sakic, Colorado, 1996. 22 games.
5 — Mike Bossy, NY Islanders, 1983. 19 games.
— Jari Kurri, Edmonton, 1987. 21 games.
— Bobby Smith, Minnesota, 1991. 23 games.
— Mario Lemieux, Pittsburgh, 1992. 15 games.

MOST GAME-WINNING GOALS, ONE PLAYOFF SERIES:

4 — Mike Bossy, NY Islanders, 1983, CF vs. Boston, won by NY Islanders 4-2.

OVERTIME GOALS

MOST OVERTIME GOALS IN PLAYOFFS (CAREER):

6 — Maurice Richard, Montreal (1 in 1946; 3 in 1951; 1 in 1957; 1 in 1958.)
5 — Glenn Anderson, Edmonton, Toronto, NY Rangers, St. Louis
4 — Bob Nystrom, NY Islanders
— Dale Hunter, Quebec, Washington
— Wayne Gretzky, Edmonton, Los Angeles
— Stephane Richer, Montreal, New Jersey
— Joe Murphy, Edmonton, Chicago
— Esa Tikkanen, Edmonton, NY Rangers
3 — Mel Hill, Boston
— Rene Robert, Buffalo
— Danny Gare, Buffalo
— Jacques Lemaire, Montreal
— Bobby Clarke, Philadelphia
— Terry O'Reilly, Boston
— Mike Bossy, NY Islanders
— Steve Payne, Minnesota
— Ken Morrow, NY Islanders
— Lanny McDonald, Toronto, Calgary
— Peter Stastny, Quebec
— Dino Ciccarelli, Minnesota, Washington
— Russ Courtnall, Montreal
— Kirk Muller, Montreal
— Doug Gilmour, St. Louis, Calgary, Toronto
— Greg Adams, Vancouver
— Claude Lemieux, Montreal, Colorado
— Mike Gartner, Washington, Toronto
— Jeremy Roenick, Chicago, Phoenix

MOST OVERTIME GOALS, ONE PLAYOFF YEAR:

3 — Mel Hill, Boston, 1939. All against NY Rangers in best-of-seven SF, won by Boston 4-3.
— Maurice Richard, Montreal, 1951. 2 against Detroit in best-of-seven SF, won by Montreal 4-2; 1 against Toronto best-of-seven F, won by Toronto 4-1.

MOST OVERTIME GOALS, ONE PLAYOFF SERIES:

3 — Mel Hill, Boston, 1939, SF vs. NY Rangers, won by Boston 4-3. Hill scored at 59:25 of overtime March 21 for a 2-1 win; at 8:24, March 23 for a 3-2 win; and at 48:00, April 2 for a 2-1 win.

Bobby Orr, left, became the first defenseman in NHL history to score a hat trick in the playoffs when he tallied a trio of goals in Boston's 5-2 win over Montreal in the fourth game of the 1971 quarterfinals.One of the greatest clutch performers to strap on the blades, Claude Lemieux, below, always plays best in the big games. The Conn Smythe Trophy winner in 1995, Lemieux scored his 19th playoff game-winning goal in Colorado's opening round loss to Edmonton in the 1998 playoffs.

SCORING BY A DEFENSEMAN

MOST GOALS BY A DEFENSEMAN, ONE PLAYOFF YEAR:
12 — Paul Coffey, Edmonton, 1985. 18 games.
11 — Brian Leetch, NY Rangers, 1994. 23 games.
9 — Bobby Orr, Boston, 1970. 14 games.
— Brad Park, Boston, 1978. 15 games.
8 — Denis Potvin, NY Islanders, 1981. 18 games.
— Ray Bourque, Boston, 1983. 17 games.
— Denis Potvin, NY Islanders, 1983. 20 games.
— Paul Coffey, Edmonton, 1984. 19 games.

MOST GOALS BY A DEFENSEMAN, ONE GAME:
3 — Bobby Orr, Boston, April 11, 1971 at Montreal. Final score: Boston 5, Montreal 2.
— Dick Redmond, Chicago, April 4, 1973 at Chicago. Final score: Chicago 7, St. Louis 1.
— Denis Potvin, NY Islanders, April 17, 1981 at New York. Final score: NY Islanders 6, Edmonton 3.
— Paul Reinhart, Calgary, April 14, 1983 at Edmonton. Final score: Edmonton 6, Calgary 3.
— Doug Halward, Vancouver, April 7, 1984 at Vancouver. Final score: Vancouver 7, Calgary 0.
— Paul Reinhart, Calgary, April 8, 1984 at Vancouver. Final score: Calgary 5, Vancouver 1.
— Al Iafrate, Washington, April 26, 1993 at Washington. Final score: Washington 6, NY Islanders 4.
— Eric Desjardins, Montreal, June 3, 1993 at Montreal. Final score: Montreal 3, Los Angeles 2.
— Gary Suter, Chicago, April 24, 1994, at Chicago. Final score: Chicago 4, Toronto 3.
— Brian Leetch, NY Rangers, May 22, 1995 at Philadelphia. Final score: Philadelphia 4, NY Rangers 3.

MOST ASSISTS BY A DEFENSEMAN, ONE PLAYOFF YEAR:
25 — Paul Coffey, Edmonton, 1985. 18 games.
24 — Al MacInnis, Calgary, 1989. 22 games.
23 — Brian Leetch, NY Rangers, 1994. 23 games.
19 — Bobby Orr, Boston, 1972. 15 games.
18 — Ray Bourque, Boston, 1988. 23 games.
— Ray Bourque, Boston, 1991. 19 games.
— Larry Murphy, Pittsburgh, 1991. 23 games.

MOST ASSISTS BY A DEFENSEMAN, ONE GAME:
5 — Paul Coffey, Edmonton, May 14, 1985 at Edmonton vs. Chicago. Edmonton won 10-5.
— Risto Siltanen, Quebec, April 14, 1987 at Hartford. Quebec won 7-5.

MOST POINTS BY A DEFENSEMAN, ONE PLAYOFF YEAR:
37 — Paul Coffey, Edmonton, in 1985. 12 goals, 25 assists in 18 games.
34 — Brian Leetch, NY Rangers, in 1994. 11 goals, 23 assists in 23 games.
31 — Al MacInnis, Calgary, in 1989. 7 goals, 24 assists in 22 games.
25 — Denis Potvin, NY Islanders, in 1981. 8 goals, 17 assists in 18 games.
— Ray Bourque, Boston, in 1991. 7 goals, 18 assists in 19 games.

MOST POINTS BY A DEFENSEMAN, ONE GAME:
6 — Paul Coffey, Edmonton, May 14, 1985 at Edmonton vs. Chicago. 1 goal, 5 assists. Edmonton won 10-5.
5 — Eddie Bush, Detroit, April 9, 1942, at Detroit vs. Toronto. 1 goal, 4 assists. Detroit won 5-2.
— Bob Dailey, Philadelphia, May 1, 1980, at Philadelphia vs. Minnesota. 1 goal, 4 assists. Philadelphia won 7-0.
— Denis Potvin, NY Islanders, April 17, 1981, at New York vs. Edmonton. 3 goals, 2 assists. NY Islanders won 6-3.
— Risto Siltanen, Quebec, April 14, 1987 at Hartford. 5 assists. Quebec won 7-5.

SCORING BY A ROOKIE

MOST GOALS BY A ROOKIE, ONE PLAYOFF YEAR:
14 — Dino Ciccarelli, Minnesota, 1981. 19 games.
11 — Jeremy Roenick, Chicago, 1990. 20 games.
10 — Claude Lemieux, Montreal, 1986. 20 games.
9 — Pat Flatley, NY Islanders, 1984. 21 games
8 — Steve Christoff, Minnesota, 1980. 14 games.
— Brad Palmer, Minnesota, 1981. 19 games.
— Mike Krushelnyski, Boston, 1983. 17 games.
— Bob Joyce, Boston, 1988. 23 games.

MOST POINTS BY A ROOKIE, ONE PLAYOFF YEAR:
21 — Dino Ciccarelli, Minnesota, in 1981. 14 goals, 7 assists in 19 games.
20 — Don Maloney, NY Rangers, in 1979. 7 goals, 13 assists in 18 games.

THREE-OR-MORE-GOAL GAMES

MOST THREE-OR-MORE-GOAL GAMES IN PLAYOFFS (CAREER):
10 — Wayne Gretzky, Edmonton, Los Angeles, St. Louis, NY Rangers. Eight three-goal games; two four-goal games.
7 — Maurice Richard, Montreal. Four three-goal games; two four-goal games; one five-goal game.
— Jari Kurri, Edmonton, Los Angeles, NY Rangers. Six three-goal games; one four-goal game.
6 — Dino Ciccarelli, Minnesota, Washington, Detroit. Five three-goal games; one four-goal game.
5 — Mike Bossy, NY Islanders. Four three-goal games; one four-goal game.

MOST THREE-OR-MORE-GOAL GAMES, ONE PLAYOFF YEAR:
4 — Jari Kurri, Edmonton, 1985. 1 four-goal game, 3 three-goal games.
3 — Mark Messier, Edmonton, 1983. 3 three-goal games.
— Mike Bossy, NY Islanders, 1983. 1 four-goal game, 2 three-goal games
2 — Newsy Lalonde, Montreal, 1919. 1 five-goal game, 1 four-goal game.
— Maurice Richard, Montreal, 1944. 1 five-goal game; 1 three-goal game.
— Doug Bentley, Chicago, 1944. 2 three-goal games.
— Norm Ullman, Detroit, 1964. 2 three-goal games.
— Phil Esposito, Boston, 1970. 2 three-goal games.
— Pit Martin, Chicago, 1973. 2 three-goal games.
— Rick MacLeish, Philadelphia, 1975. 2 three-goal games.
— Lanny McDonald, Toronto, 1977. 1 three-goal game; 1 four-goal game.
— Wayne Gretzky, Edmonton, 1981. 2 three-goal games.
— Wayne Gretzky, Edmonton, 1983. 2 four-goal games.
— Wayne Gretzky, Edmonton, 1985. 2 three-goal games.
— Petr Klima, Detroit, 1988. 2 three-goal games.
— Cam Neely, Boston, 1991. 2 three-goal games.
— Wayne Gretzky, NY Rangers, 1997. 2 three-goal games.
— Daniel Alfredsson, Ottawa, 1998. 2 three-goal games.

MOST THREE-OR-MORE-GOAL GAMES, ONE PLAYOFF SERIES:
3 — Jari Kurri, Edmonton 1985, CF vs. Chicago won by Edmonton 4-2. Kurri scored 3 G May 7 at Edmonton in 7-3 win, 3 G May 14 in 10-5 win and 4 G May 16 at Chicago in 8-2 win.
2 — Doug Bentley, Chicago, 1944, SF vs. Detroit, won by Chicago 4-1. Bentley scored 3 G Mar. 28 at Chicago in 7-1 win and 3 G Mar. 30 at Detroit in 5-2 win.
— Norm Ullman, Detroit, 1964, SF vs. Chicago, won by Detroit 4-3. Ullman scored 3 G Mar. 29 at Chicago in 7-1 win and 3 G April 7 at Detroit in 7-2 win.
— Mark Messier, Edmonton, 1983, DF vs. Calgary won by Edmonton 4-1. Messier scored 4 G April 14 at Edmonton in 6-3 win and 3 G April 17 at Calgary in 10-2 win.
— Mike Bossy, NY Islanders, 1983, CF vs. Boston won by NY Islanders 4-2. Bossy scored 3 G May 3 at New York in 8-3 win and 4 G on May 7 at New York in 8-4 win.

SCORING STREAKS

LONGEST CONSECUTIVE GOAL-SCORING STREAK, ONE PLAYOFF YEAR:
10 Games — Reggie Leach, Philadelphia, 1976. Streak started April 17 at Toronto and ended May 9 at Montreal. He scored one goal in each of eight games; two in one game; and five in another; a total of 14 goals.

LONGEST CONSECUTIVE POINT-SCORING STREAK, ONE PLAYOFF YEAR:
18 games — Bryan Trottier, NY Islanders, 1981. 11 goals, 18 assists, 29 points.
17 games — Wayne Gretzky, Edmonton, 1988. 12 goals, 29 assists, 41 points.
— Al MacInnis, Calgary, 1989. 7 goals, 19 assists, 24 points.

LONGEST CONSECUTIVE POINT-SCORING STREAK, MORE THAN ONE PLAYOFF YEAR:
27 games — Bryan Trottier, NY Islanders, 1980, 1981 and 1982. 7 games in 1980 (3 G, 5 A, 8 PTS), 18 games in 1981 (11 G, 18 A, 29 PTS), and two games in 1982 (2 G, 3 A, 5 PTS). Total points, 42.
19 games — Wayne Gretzky, Edmonton, Los Angeles, 1988 and 1989. 17 games in 1988 (12 G, 29 A, 41 PTS with Edmonton), 2 games in 1989 (1 G, 2 A, 3 PTS with Los Angeles). Total points, 44.
18 games — Phil Esposito, Boston, 1970 and 1971. 13 G, 20 A, 33 PTS.

FASTEST GOALS

FASTEST GOAL FROM START OF GAME:
6 Seconds — Don Kozak, Los Angeles, April 17, 1977, at Los Angeles vs. Boston and goaltender Gerry Cheevers. Los Angeles won 7-4.
7 Seconds — Bob Gainey, Montreal, May 5, 1977, at New York vs. NY Islanders and goaltender Glenn Resch. Montreal won 2-1.
— Terry Murray, Philadelphia, April 12, 1981, at Quebec vs. goaltender Dan Bouchard. Quebec won 4-3 in overtime.
8 Seconds — Stan Smyl, Vancouver, April 7, 1982, at Vancouver vs. Calgary and goaltender Pat Riggin. Vancouver won 5-3.

FASTEST GOAL FROM START OF PERIOD (OTHER THAN FIRST):
6 Seconds — Pelle Eklund, Philadelphia, April 25, 1989, at Pittsburgh vs. goaltender Tom Barrasso, second period. Pittsburgh won 10-7.
9 Seconds — Bill Collins, Minnesota, April 9, 1968, at Minnesota vs. Los Angeles and goaltender Wayne Rutledge, third period. Minnesota won 7-5.
— Dave Balon, Minnesota, April 25, 1968, at St. Louis vs. goaltender Glenn Hall, third period. Minnesota won 5-1.
— Murray Oliver, Minnesota, April 8, 1971, at St. Louis vs. goaltender Ernie Wakely, third period. St. Louis won 4-2.
— Clark Gillies, NY Islanders, April 15, 1977, at Buffalo vs. goaltender Don Edwards, third period. NY Islanders won 4-3.
— Eric Vail, Atlanta, April 11, 1978, at Atlanta vs. Detroit and goaltender Ron Low, third period. Detroit won 5-3.
— Stan Smyl, Vancouver, April 10, 1979, at Philadelphia vs. goaltender Wayne Stephenson, third period. Vancouver won 3-2.
— Wayne Gretzky, Edmonton, April 6, 1983, at Edmonton vs. Winnipeg and goaltender Brian Hayward, second period. Edmonton won 6-3.
— Mark Messier, Edmonton, April 16, 1984, at Calgary vs. goaltender Don Edwards, third period. Edmonton won 5-3.
— Brian Skrudland, Montreal, May 18, 1986 at Calgary and goaltender Mike Vernon, overtime. Montreal won 3-2.

FASTEST TWO GOALS:
5 Seconds — Norm Ullman, Detroit, at Detroit, April 11, 1965, vs. Chicago and goaltender Glenn Hall. Ullman scored at 17:35 and 17:40 of second period. Detroit won 4-2.

FASTEST TWO GOALS FROM START OF A GAME:
1 Minute, 8 Seconds — Dick Duff, Toronto, April 9, 1963 at Toronto vs. Detroit and goaltender Terry Sawchuk. Duff scored at 49 seconds and 1:08. Final score: Toronto 4, Detroit 2.

FASTEST TWO GOALS FROM START OF A PERIOD:
35 Seconds — Pat LaFontaine, NY Islanders, May 19, 1984 at Edmonton vs. goaltender Andy Moog. LaFontaine scored at 13 and 35 seconds of third period. Final score: Edmonton 5, NY Islanders 2.

PENALTIES

MOST PENALTY MINUTES IN PLAYOFFS (CAREER):
691 — Dale Hunter, Quebec, Washington
541 — Chris Nilan, Montreal, NY Rangers, Boston
466 — Willi Plett, Atlanta, Calgary, Minnesota, Boston
463 — Claude Lemieux, Montreal, New Jersey, Colorado
455 — Dave Williams, Toronto, Vancouver, Los Angeles
442 — Glenn Anderson, Edmonton, Toronto, NY Rangers, St. Louis

MOST PENALTIES, ONE GAME:
8 — Forbes Kennedy, Toronto, April 2, 1969, at Boston. Four minors, 2 majors, 1 10-minute misconduct, 1 game misconduct. Final score: Boston 10, Toronto 0.
— Kim Clackson, Pittsburgh, April 14, 1980, at Boston. Five minors, 2 majors, 1 10-minute misconduct. Final score: Boston 6, Pittsburgh 2

MOST PENALTY MINUTES, ONE GAME:
42 — Dave Schultz, Philadelphia, April 22, 1976, at Toronto. One minor, 2 majors, 1 10-minute misconduct and 2 game-misconducts. Final score: Toronto 8, Philadelphia 5.

MOST PENALTIES, ONE PERIOD AND MOST PENALTY MINUTES, ONE PERIOD:
6 Penalties; 39 Minutes — Ed Hospodar, NY Rangers, April 9, 1981, at Los Angeles, first period. Two minors, 1 major, 1 10-minute misconduct, 2 game misconducts. Final score: Los Angeles 5, NY Rangers 4.

GOALTENDING

MOST PLAYOFF GAMES APPEARED IN BY A GOALTENDER (CAREER):
160 — Patrick Roy, Montreal, Colorado
137 — Grant Fuhr, Edmonton, Toronto, Buffalo, Los Angeles, St. Louis
132 — Bill Smith, Los Angeles, NY Islanders
— Andy Moog, Edmonton, Boston, Dallas, Montreal
129 — Mike Vernon, Calgary, Detroit

MOST MINUTES PLAYED BY A GOALTENDER (CAREER):
9,882 — Patrick Roy, Montreal, Colorado
8,044 — Grant Fuhr, Edmonton, Toronto, Buffalo, Los Angeles, St. Louis
7,656 — Mike Vernon, Calgary, Detroit, San Jose
7,645 — Bill Smith, Los Angeles, NY Islanders
7,452 — Andy Moog, Edmonton, Boston, Dallas, Montreal

MOST MINUTES PLAYED BY A GOALTENDER, ONE PLAYOFF YEAR:
1,544 — Kirk McLean, Vancouver, 1994. 24 games.
1,540 — Ron Hextall, Philadelphia, 1987. 26 games.
1,477 — Mike Richter, NY Rangers, 1994. 23 games.
1,454 — Patrick Roy, Colorado, 1996. 22 games.
1,401 — Bill Ranford, Edmonton, 1990. 22 games.

MOST SHUTOUTS IN PLAYOFFS (CAREER):
15 — Clint Benedict, Ottawa, Mtl. Maroons
14 — Jacques Plante, Montreal, St. Louis
13 — Turk Broda, Toronto
12 — Terry Sawchuk, Detroit, Toronto, Los Angeles

MOST SHUTOUTS, ONE PLAYOFF YEAR:
4 — Clint Benedict, Mtl. Maroons, 1926. 8 games.
— Clint Benedict, Mtl. Maroons, 1928. 9 games.
— Dave Kerr, NY Rangers, 1937. 9 games.
— Frank McCool, Toronto, 1945. 13 games.
— Terry Sawchuk, Detroit, 1952. 8 games.
— Bernie Parent, Philadelphia, 1975. 17 games.
— Ken Dryden, Montreal, 1977. 14 games.
— Mike Richter, NY Rangers, 1994. 23 games.
— Kirk McLean, Vancouver, 1994. 24 games.
— Olaf Kolzig, Washington, 1998. 21 games.

MOST WINS BY A GOALTENDER, (CAREER):
99 — Patrick Roy, Montreal, Colorado
88 — Bill Smith, Los Angeles, NY Islanders
86 — Grant Fuhr, Edmonton, Buffalo, St. Louis
80 — Ken Dryden, Montreal

MOST WINS BY A GOALTENDER, ONE PLAYOFF YEAR:
16 — Grant Fuhr, Edmonton, 1988. 19 games.
— Mike Vernon, Calgary, 1989. 22 games.
— Bill Ranford, Edmonton, 1990. 22 games
— Tom Barrasso, Pittsburgh, 1992. 21 games.
— Patrick Roy, Montreal, 1993. 20 games.
— Mike Richter, NY Rangers, 1994. 23 games.
— Martin Brodeur, New Jersey, 1995. 20 games.
— Patrick Roy, Colorado, 1996. 22 games.
— Mike Vernon, Detroit, 1997. 20 games.
— Chris Osgood, Detroit, 1998. 22 games.

MOST CONSECUTIVE WINS BY A GOALTENDER, ONE PLAYOFF YEAR:
11 — Ed Belfour, Chicago, 1992. 3 wins against St. Louis in DSF, won by Chicago 4-2; 4 wins against Detroit in DF, won by Chicago 4-0; and 4 wins against Edmonton in CF, won by Chicago 4-0.
— Tom Barrasso, Pittsburgh, 1992. 3 wins against NY Rangers in DF, won by Pittsburgh 4-2; 4 wins against Boston in CF, won by Pittsburgh 4-0; and 4 wins against Chicago in F, won by Pittsburgh 4-0.
— Patrick Roy, Montreal, 1993. 4 wins against Quebec in DSF, won by Montreal 4-2; 4 wins against Buffalo in DF, won by Montreal 4-0; and 3 wins against NY Islanders in CF, won by Montreal 4-1.

LONGEST SHUTOUT SEQUENCE:
248 Minutes, 32 Seconds — Norm Smith, Detroit, 1936. In best-of-five SF, Smith shut out Mtl. Maroons 1-0, March 24, in 116:30 overtime; shut out Maroons 3-0 in second game, March 26; and was scored against at 12:02 of first period, March 29, by Gus Marker. Detroit won SF 3-0.

MOST CONSECUTIVE SHUTOUTS:
3 — Clint Benedict, Mtl. Maroons, 1926. Benedict shut out Ottawa 1-0, Mar. 27; he then shut out Victoria twice, 3-0, Mar. 30; 3-0, Apr. 1. Mtl. Maroons won NHL F vs. Ottawa 2 goals to 1 and won the best-of-five F vs. Victoria 3-1.
— John Roach, NY Rangers, 1929. Roach shut out NY Americans twice, 0-0, Mar. 19; 1-0, Mar. 21; he then shut out Toronto 1-0, Mar. 24. NY Rangers won QF vs. NY Americans 1 goal to 0 and won the best-of-three SF vs. Toronto 2-0.
— Frank McCool, Toronto, 1945. McCool shut out Detroit 1-0, April 6; 2-0, April 8; 1-0, April 12. Toronto won the best-of-seven F 4-3.

Early Playoff Records

1893-1918

Team Records

MOST GOALS, BOTH TEAMS, ONE GAME:
25 — Ottawa Silver Seven, Dawson City at Ottawa, Jan. 16, 1905. Ottawa 23, Dawson City 2. Ottawa won best-of-three series 2-0.

MOST GOALS, ONE TEAM, ONE GAME:
23 — Ottawa Silver Seven at Ottawa, Jan. 16, 1905. Ottawa defeated Dawson City 23-2.

MOST GOALS, BOTH TEAMS, BEST-OF-THREE SERIES:
42 — Ottawa Silver Seven, Queen's University at Ottawa, 1906. Ottawa defeated Queen's 16-7, Feb. 27, and 12-7, Feb. 28.

MOST GOALS, ONE TEAM, BEST-OF-THREE SERIES:
32 — Ottawa Silver Seven in 1905 at Ottawa. Defeated Dawson City 9-2, Jan. 13, and 23-2, Jan. 16.

MOST GOALS, BOTH TEAMS, BEST-OF-FIVE SERIES:
39 — Toronto Arenas, Vancouver Millionaires at Toronto, 1918. Toronto won 5-3, Mar. 20; 6-3, Mar. 26; 2-1, Mar. 30. Vancouver won 6-4, Mar. 23, and 8-1, Mar. 28. Toronto scored 18 goals; Vancouver 21.

MOST GOALS, ONE TEAM, BEST-OF-FIVE SERIES:
26 — Vancouver Millionaires in 1915 at Vancouver. Defeated Ottawa Senators 6-2, Mar. 22; 8-3, Mar. 24; and 12-3 Mar. 26.

Individual Records

MOST GOALS IN PLAYOFFS:
63 — Frank McGee, Ottawa Silver Seven, in 22 playoff games. Seven goals in four games, 1903; 21 goals in eight games, 1904; 18 goals in four games, 1905; 17 goals in six games, 1906.

MOST GOALS, ONE PLAYOFF SERIES:
15 — Frank McGee, Ottawa Silver Seven, in two games in 1905 at Ottawa. Scored one goal, Jan. 13, in 9-2 victory over Dawson City and 14 goals, Jan. 16, in 23-2 victory.

MOST GOALS, ONE PLAYOFF GAME:
14 — Frank McGee, Ottawa Silver Seven, Jan. 16, 1905 at Ottawa in 23-2 victory over Dawson City.

FASTEST THREE GOALS:
40 Seconds — Marty Walsh, Ottawa Senators, at Ottawa, March 16, 1911, at 3:00, 3:10, and 3:40 of third period. Ottawa defeated Port Arthur 13-4.

Henri Richard, seen here causing havoc for Glenn Hall, Tim Ecclestone and Al Arbour, pocketed his eighth Stanley Cup ring in 1968 after the Habs outlasted the overachieving but outclassed St. Louis Blues during the Stanley Cup finals.

* - Active

All-Time Playoff Goal Leaders since 1918

(40 or more goals)

Player	Teams	Yrs.	GP	G
* Wayne Gretzky	Edm., L.A., St.L. NYR	16	208	122
* Mark Messier	Edm., NYR	17	236	109
Jari Kurri	Edm., L.A., NYR, Ana., Col.	14	200	106
Glenn Anderson	Edm., Tor., NYR, St.L.	15	225	93
Mike Bossy	NYI	10	129	85
Maurice Richard	Mtl.	15	133	82
Jean Beliveau	Mtl.	17	162	79
* Claude Lemieux	Mtl., N.J., Col.	13	179	73
* Dino Ciccarelli	Min., Wsh., Det.	14	141	73
* Esa Tikkanen	Edm., NYR, St.L., Van., Wsh.	13	186	72
Bryan Trottier	NYI, Pit.	17	221	71
Mario Lemieux	Pit.	7	89	70
* Brett Hull	Cgy., St.L.	13	108	69
Gordie Howe	Det., Hfd.	20	157	68
Denis Savard	Chi., Mtl., T.B.	16	169	66
Yvan Cournoyer	Mtl.	12	147	64
Bobby Smith	Min., Mtl.	13	184	64
Brian Propp	Phi., Bos., Min., Hfd.	13	160	64
Bobby Hull	Chi., Wpg., Hfd.	14	119	62
Jacques Lemaire	Mtl.	11	145	61
Phil Esposito	Chi., Bos., NYR	15	130	61
Joe Mullen	St.L., Cgy., Pit., Bos.	15	143	60
Stan Mikita	Chi.	18	155	59
* Paul Coffey	Edm., Pit., L.A., Det., Phi.	15	189	59
Guy Lafleur	Mtl., NYR, Que.	14	128	58
Bernie Geoffrion	Mtl., NYR	16	132	58
Cam Neely	Van., Bos.	9	93	57
Denis Potvin	NYI	14	185	56
Steve Larmer	Chi., NYR	13	140	56
Rick MacLeish	Phi., Hfd., Pit., Det.	11	114	54
* Doug Gilmour	St.L., Cgy., Tor., N.J.	14	152	54
Bill Barber	Phi.	11	129	53
* Steve Yzerman	Det.	13	135	52
* Stephane Richer	Mtl., N.J.	11	128	52
Frank Mahovlich	Tor., Det., Mtl	14	137	51
* Brian Bellows	Min., Mtl., T.B., Ana., Wsh.	13	143	51
Steve Shutt	Mtl., L.A.	12	99	50
* Jaromir Jagr	Pit.	9	104	50
Henri Richard	Mtl.	18	180	49
Ted Lindsay	Det., Chi.	16	133	47
Reggie Leach	Bos., Cal., Phi., Det.	8	94	47
Clark Gillies	NYI, Buf.	13	164	47
* Rick Tocchet	Phi., Pit., L.A., Bos., Phx.	10	114	47
* Luc Robitaille	L.A., Pit., NYR	11	115	47
Dickie Moore	Mtl., Tor., St.L.	14	135	46
Rick Middleton	NYR, Bos.	12	114	45
Lanny McDonald	Tor., Col., Cgy.	13	117	44
* Kevin Stevens	Pit.	6	86	43
Ken Linseman	Phi., Edm., Bos., Tor.	11	113	43
Mike Gartner	Wsh., Min., NYR, Tor., Phx.	15	122	43
Bobby Clarke	Phi.	13	136	42
* Jeremy Roenick	Chi., Phx.	10	94	42
* Bernie Nicholls	L.A., NYR, Edm., N.J., Chi., S.J.	13	118	42
John Bucyk	Det., Bos.	14	124	41
* Dale Hunter	Que., Wsh.	17	167	41
Peter McNab	Buf., Bos., Van., N.J.	10	107	40
Bob Bourne	NYI, L.A.	13	139	40
John Tonelli	NYI, Cgy., L.A., Chi., Que.	13	172	40
Tim Kerr	Phi., NYR, Hfd.	10	81	40
* Ron Francis	Hfd., Pit.	13	130	40

All-Time Playoff Assist Leaders since 1918

(60 or more assists)

Player	Teams	Yrs.	GP	A
* Wayne Gretzky	Edm., L.A., St.L. NYR	16	208	260
* Mark Messier	Edm., NYR	17	236	186
* Paul Coffey	Edm., Pit., L.A., Det., Phi.	15	189	136
Jari Kurri	Edm., L.A., NYR, Ana., Col.	14	200	127
Glenn Anderson	Edm., Tor., NYR, St.L.	15	225	121
* Doug Gilmour	St.L., Cgy., Tor., N.J.	14	152	117
Larry Robinson	Mtl., L.A.	20	227	116
* Ray Bourque	Bos.	18	168	116
Bryan Trottier	NYI, Pit.	17	221	113
Denis Savard	Chi., Mtl., T.B.	16	169	109
* Larry Murphy	L.A., Wsh., Min., Pit., Tor., Det.	17	190	109
Denis Potvin	NYI	14	185	108
* Adam Oates	Det., St.L., Bos., Wsh.	11	126	100
Jean Beliveau	Mtl.	17	162	97
Bobby Smith	Min., Mtl.	13	184	96
* Al MacInnis	Cgy., St.L.	14	129	94
Gordie Howe	Det., Hfd.	20	157	92
Stan Mikita	Chi.	18	155	91
Brad Park	NYR, Bos., Det.	17	161	90
* Chris Chelios	Mtl., Chi.	14	163	88
* Craig Janney	Bos., St.L., S.J., Wpg., Phx.	11	120	86
Mario Lemieux	Pit.	7	89	85
Brian Propp	Phi., Bos., Min., Hfd.	13	160	84
* Steve Yzerman	Det.	13	135	83
* Ron Francis	Hfd., Pit.	13	130	82
Henri Richard	Mtl.	18	180	80
* Sergei Fedorov	Det.	8	110	80
Jacques Lemaire	Mtl.	11	145	78
Bobby Clarke	Phi.	13	136	77
Ken Linseman	Phi., Edm., Bos., Tor.	11	113	77
Guy Lafleur	Mtl., NYR, Que.	14	128	76
Phil Esposito	Chi., Bos., NYR	15	130	76
Mike Bossy	NYI	10	129	75
John Tonelli	NYI, Cgy., L.A., Chi., Que.	13	172	75
Steve Larmer	Chi., NYR	13	140	75
* Dale Hunter	Que., Wsh.	17	167	73
Peter Stastny	Que., N.J., St.L.	12	93	72
* Bernie Nicholls	L.A., NYR, Edm., N.J., Chi., S.J.	13	118	72
* Brian Bellows	Min., Mtl., T.B., Ana., Wsh.	13	143	71
Gilbert Perreault	Buf.	11	90	70
* Scott Stevens	Wsh., St.L., N.J.	15	148	70
Alex Delvecchio	Det.	14	121	69
Dale Hawerchuk	Wpg., Buf., St.L., Phi.	15	97	69
Frank Mahovlich	Tor., Det., Mtl.	14	137	67
Bobby Hull	Chi., Wpg., Hfd.	14	119	67
Jean Ratelle	NYR, Bos.	15	123	66
Bobby Orr	Bos., Chi.	8	74	66
Bernie Federko	St.L., Det.	11	91	66
Charlie Huddy	Edm., L.A., Buf., St.L.	14	183	66
* Geoff Courtnall	Bos., Edm., Wsh., Van., St.L.	14	143	66
Dickie Moore	Mtl., Tor., St.L.	14	135	64
Doug Harvey	Mtl., NYR, Det., St.L.	15	137	64
Yvan Cournoyer	Mtl.	12	147	63
Neal Broten	Min., Dal., N.J., L.A.	13	135	63
John Bucyk	Det., Bos.,	14	124	62
Doug Wilson	Chi., S.J.	12	95	61
* Brian Leetch	NYR	7	82	61
Bernie Geoffrion	Mtl., NYR	16	132	60
* Esa Tikkanen	Edm., NYR, St.L., Van., Wsh.	13	186	60
* Claude Lemieux	Mtl., N.J., Col.	13	179	60

All-Time Playoff Point Leaders since 1918

(100 or more points)

Player	Teams	Yrs.	GP	G	A	Pts.
* Wayne Gretzky	Edm., L.A., St.L. NYR	16	208	122	260	382
* Mark Messier	Edm., NYR	17	236	109	186	295
Jari Kurri	Edm., L.A., NYR, Ana.,Col.	14	200	106	127	233
Glenn Anderson	Edm., Tor., NYR, St.L.	15	225	93	121	214
* Paul Coffey	Edm., Pit., L.A., Det.,Phi.	15	189	59	136	195
Bryan Trottier	NYI, Pit.	17	221	71	113	184
Jean Beliveau	Mtl.	17	162	79	97	176
Denis Savard	Chi., Mtl., T.B.	16	169	66	109	175
* Doug Gilmour	St.L., Cgy., Tor., N.J.	14	152	54	117	171
Denis Potvin	NYI	14	185	56	108	164
Gordie Howe	Det., Hfd.	20	157	68	92	160
Mike Bossy	NYI	10	129	85	75	160
Bobby Smith	Min., Mtl.	13	184	64	96	160
Mario Lemieux	Pit.	7	89	70	85	155
* Ray Bourque	Bos.	18	168	35	116	151
Stan Mikita	Chi.	18	155	59	91	150
Brian Propp	Phi., Bos., Min., Hfd.	13	160	64	84	148
Larry Robinson	Mtl., L.A.	20	227	28	116	144
* Larry Murphy	L.A., Wsh., Min., Pit.,Tor., Det.	17	190	35	109	144
Jacques Lemaire	Mtl.	11	145	61	78	139
* Adam Oates	Det., St.L., Bos., Wsh.	11	126	38	100	138
Phil Esposito	Chi., Bos., NYR	15	130	61	76	137
* Steve Yzerman	Det.	13	135	52	83	135
Guy Lafleur	Mtl., NYR, Que.	14	128	58	76	134
* Claude Lemieux	Mtl., N.J., Col.	13	179	73	60	133
* Esa Tikkanen	Edm., NYR, St.L., Van.,Wsh.	13	186	72	60	132
Steve Larmer	Chi., NYR	13	140	56	75	131
Henri Richard	Mtl.	18	180	49	80	129
Bobby Hull	Chi., Wpg., Hfd.	14	119	62	67	129
Yvan Cournoyer	Mtl.	12	147	64	63	127
Maurice Richard	Mtl.	15	133	82	44	126
* Al MacInnis	Cgy., St.L.	14	129	32	94	126
Brad Park	NYR, Bos., Det.	17	161	35	90	125
* Ron Francis	Hfd., Pit.	13	130	40	82	122
* Brian Bellows	Min., Mtl., T.B. Ana., Wsh.	13	143	51	71	122
Ken Linseman	Phi., Edm., Bos., Tor.	11	113	43	77	120
* Brett Hull	Cgy., St.L.	13	108	69	51	120
Bobby Clarke	Phi.	13	136	42	77	119
Frank Mahovlich	Tor., Det., Mtl.	14	137	51	67	118
Bernie Geoffrion	Mtl., NYR	16	132	58	60	118
* Dino Ciccarelli	Min., Wsh., Det.	14	141	73	45	118
* Sergei Fedorov	Det.	8	110	37	80	117
* Chris Chelios	Mtl., Chi.	14	163	28	88	116
John Tonelli	NYI, Cgy., L.A., Chi., Que.	13	172	40	75	115
* Bernie Nicholls	L.A., NYR, Edm., N.J., Chi., S.J.	13	118	42	72	114
* Dale Hunter	Que., Wsh.	17	167	41	73	114
Dickie Moore	Mtl., Tor., St.L.	14	135	46	64	110
* Craig Janney	Bos., St.L., S.J., Wpg., Phx.	11	120	24	86	110
Bill Barber	Phi.	11	129	53	55	108
Rick MacLeish	Phi., Hfd., Pit., Det.	11	114	54	53	107
* Jaromir Jagr	Pit.	9	104	50	57	107
* Luc Robitaille	L.A., Pit., NYR	11	115	47	59	106
Joe Mullen	St.L., Cgy., Pit., Bos.	15	143	60	46	106
Peter Stastny	Que., N.J., St.L.	12	93	33	72	105
Alex Delvecchio	Det.	14	121	35	69	104
Gilbert Perreault	Buf.	11	90	33	70	103
John Bucyk	Det., Bos.,	14	124	41	62	103
* Geoff Courtnall	Bos., Edm., Wsh., Van., St.L.	14	143	37	66	103
Bernie Federko	St.L., Det.	11	91	35	66	101
Rick Middleton	NYR, Bos.	12	114	45	55	100
* Kevin Stevens	Pit.	6	86	43	57	100

Three-or-more-Goal Games, Playoffs 1918 – 1998

Player	Team	Date	City	Total Goals	Opposing Goaltender	Score	
Wayne Gretzky (10)	Edm.	Apr. 11/81	Edm.	3	Richard Sevigny	Edm. 6	Mtl. 2
		Apr. 19/81	Edm.	3	Billy Smith	Edm. 5	NYI 2
		Apr. 6/83	Edm.	4	Brian Hayward	Edm. 6	Wpg. 3
		Apr. 17/83	Cgy.	4	Rejean Lemelin	Edm. 10	Cgy. 2
		Apr. 25/85	Wpg.	3	Bryan Hayward (2)		
					Marc Behrend (1)	Edm. 8	Wpg. 3
		May 25/85	Edm.	3	Pelle Lindbergh	Edm. 4	Phi. 3
		Apr. 24/86	Cgy.	3	Mike Vernon	Edm. 7	Cgy. 4
	L.A.	May 29/93	Tor.	3	Felix Potvin	L.A. 5	Tor. 4
	NYR	Apr. 23/97	NYR	3	John Vanbiesbrouck	NYR 3	Fla. 2
		May 18/97	Phi.	3	Garth Snow	NYR 5	Phi. 4
Maurice Richard (7)	Mtl.	Mar. 23/44	Mtl.	5	Paul Bibeault	Mtl. 5	Tor. 1
		Apr. 7/44	Chi.	3	Mike Karakas	Mtl. 3	Chi. 1
		Mar. 29/45	Mtl.	4	Frank McCool	Mtl. 10	Tor. 3
		Apr. 14/53	Bos.	3	Gord Henry	Mtl. 7	Bos. 3
		Mar. 20/56	Mtl.	3	Gump Worsley	Mtl. 7	NYR 1
		Apr. 6/57	Mtl.	4	Don Simmons	Mtl. 5	Bos. 1
		Apr. 1/58	Det.	3	Terry Sawchuk	Mtl. 4	Det. 3
Jari Kurri (7)	Edm.	Apr. 4/84	Edm.	3	Doug Soetaert (1)		
					Mike Veisor (2)	Edm. 9	Wpg. 2
		Apr. 25/85	Wpg.	3	Bryan Hayward (2)		
					Marc Behrend (1)	Edm. 8	Wpg. 3
		May 7/85	Edm.	3	Murray Bannerman	Edm. 7	Chi. 3
		May 14/85	Edm.	3	Murray Bannerman	Edm. 10	Chi. 5
		May 16/85	Chi.	4	Murray Bannerman	Edm. 8	Chi. 2
		Apr. 9/87	Edm.	4	Rollie Melanson (2)		
					Daren Eliot (2)	Edm. 13	L.A. 3
		May 18/90	Bos.	3	Andy Moog (2)		
					Rejean Lemelin (1)	Edm. 7	Bos. 2
Dino Ciccarelli (6)	Min.	May 5/81	Min.	3	Pat Riggin	Min. 7	Cgy. 4
		Apr. 10/82	Min.	3	Murray Bannerman	Min. 7	Chi. 1
	Wsh.	Apr. 5/90	N.J.	3	Sean Burke	Wsh. 5	N.J. 4
		Apr. 25/92	Pit.	4	Tom Barrasso (1)		
					Ken Wregget (3)	Wsh. 7	Pit. 2
	Det.	Apr. 29/93	Tor.	3	Felix Potvin (2)		
					Daren Puppa (1)	Det. 7	Tor. 3
		May 11/95	Dal.	3	Andy Moog (2)		
					Darcy Wakaluk (1)	Det. 5	Dal. 1
Mike Bossy (5)	NYI	Apr. 16/79	NYI	3	Tony Esposito	NYI 6	Chi. 2
		May 8/82	NYI	3	Richard Brodeur	NYI 6	Van. 5
		Apr. 10/83	Wsh.	3	Al Jensen	NYI 6	Wsh. 3
		May 3/83	NYI	3	Pete Peeters	NYI 8	Bos. 3
		May 7/83	NYI	4	Pete Peeters	NYI 8	Bos. 4
Phil Esposito (4)	Bos.	Apr. 2/69	Bos.	4	Bruce Gamble	Bos. 10	Tor. 0
		Apr. 8/70	Bos.	3	Ed Giacomin	Bos. 8	NYR 2
		Apr. 19/70	Chi.	3	Tony Esposito	Bos. 6	Chi. 3
		Apr. 8/75	Bos.	3	Tony Esposito (2)		
					Michel Dumas (1)	Bos. 8	Chi. 2
Mark Messier (4)	Edm.	Apr. 14/83	Edm.	4	Rejean Lemelin	Edm. 6	Cgy. 3
		Apr. 17/83	Cgy.	3	Rejean Lemelin (1)	Edm. 10	Cgy. 2
					Don Edwards (2)		
		Apr. 26/83	Edm.	3	Murray Bannerman	Edm. 8	Chi. 2
	NYR	May 25/94	N.J.	3	Martin Brodeur (2)	NYR 4	N.J. 2
					ENG (1)		
Bernie Geoffrion (3)	Mtl.	Mar. 27/52	Mtl.	3	Jim Henry	Mtl. 4	Bos. 0
		Apr. 7/55	Mtl.	3	Terry Sawchuk	Mtl. 4	Det. 2
		Mar. 30/57	Mtl.	3	Gump Worsley	Mtl. 8	NYR 3
Norm Ullman (3)	Det.	Mar. 29/64	Chi.	3	Glenn Hall	Det. 5	Chi. 4
		Apr. 7/64	Det.	3	Glenn Hall (2)		
					Denis DeJordy (1)	Det. 7	Chi. 2
		Apr. 11/65	Det.	3	Glenn Hall	Det. 4	Chi. 2
John Bucyk (3)	Bos.	May 3/70	St. L.	3	Jacques Plante (1)		
					Ernie Wakely (2)	Bos. 6	St. L. 1
		Apr. 20/72	Bos.	3	Jacques Caron (1)		
					Ernie Wakely (2)	Bos. 10	St. L. 2
		Apr. 21/74	Bos.	3	Tony Esposito	Bos. 8	Chi. 6
Rick MacLeish (3)	Phi.	Apr. 11/74	Phi.	3	Phil Myre	Phi. 5	Atl. 1
		Apr. 13/75	Phi.	3	Gord McRae	Phi. 6	Tor. 3
		May 13/75	Phi.	3	Glenn Resch	Phi. 4	NYI 1
Denis Savard (3)	Chi.	Apr. 19/82	Chi.	3	Mike Liut	Chi. 7	StL. 4
		Apr. 10/86	Chi.	4	Ken Wregget	Tor. 6	Chi. 4
		Apr. 9/88	St. L.	3	Greg Millen	Chi. 6	St. L. 3
Tim Kerr (3)	Phi.	Apr. 13/85	NYR	4	Glen Hanlon	Phi. 6	NYR 5
		Apr. 20/87	Phi.	3	Kelly Hrudey	Phi. 4	NYI 2
		Apr. 19/89	Pit.	3	Tom Barrasso	Phi. 4	Pit. 2
Cam Neely (3)	Bos.	Apr. 9/87	Mtl.	3	Patrick Roy	Mtl. 4	Bos. 3
		Apr. 5/91	Bos.	3	Peter Sidorkiewicz	Bos. 4	Hfd. 3
		Apr. 25/91	Bos.	3	Patrick Roy	Bos. 4	Mtl. 1
Petr Klima (3)	Det.	Apr. 7/88	Tor.	3	Alan Bester (2)		
					Ken Wregett (1)	Det. 6	Tor. 2
		Apr. 21/88	St. L.	3	Greg Millen	Det. 6	St. L. 0
	Edm.	May 4/91	Edm.	3	Jon Casey	Edm. 7	Min. 2
Esa Tikkanen (3)	Edm.	May 22/88	Edm.	3	Rejean Lemelin	Edm. 6	Bos. 3
		Apr. 16/91	Cgy.	3	Mike Vernon	Edm. 5	Cgy. 4
		Apr. 26/92	L.A.	3	Kelly Hrudey	Edm. 5	L.A. 2
Steve Yzerman (3)	Det.	Apr. 6/89	Det.	3	Alain Chevrier	Chi. 5	Det. 4
		Apr. 4/91	St. L.	3	Vincent Riendeau (2)	Det. 6	St. L. 3
					Pat Jablonski (1)		
		May 8/96	St.L.	3	Jon Casey	St.L. 5	Det. 4
Mario Lemieux (3)	Pit.	Apr. 25/89	Pit.	5	Ron Hextall	Pit. 10	Phi. 7
		Apr. 23/92	Pit.	3	Don Beaupre	Pit. 6	Wsh. 4
		May 11/96	Pit.	3	Mike Richter	Pit. 7	NYR 3

Player	Team	Date	City	Total Goals	Opposing Goaltender	Score	
Mike Gartner (3)	NYR	Apr. 13/90	NYR	3	Mark Fitzpatrick (2)		
					Glenn Healy (1)	NYR 6	NYI 5
		Apr. 27/92	NYR	3	Chris Terreri	NYR 8	N.J. 5
	Tor.	Apr. 25/96	Tor.	3	Jon Casey	Tor. 5	St.L. 4
Newsy Lalonde (2)	Mtl.	Mar. 1/19	Mtl.	5	Clint Benedict	Mtl. 6	Ott. 3
		Mar. 22/19	Sea.	4	Harry Holmes	Mtl. 4	Sea. 2
Howie Morenz (2)	Mtl.	Mar. 22/24	Mtl.	3	Charles Reid	Mtl. 6	Cgy.T. 1
		Mar. 27/25	Mtl.	3	Harry Holmes	Mtl. 4	Vic. 2
Toe Blake (2)	Mtl.	Mar. 22/38	Mtl.	3	Mike Karakas	Mtl. 6	Chi. 4
		Mar. 26/46	Chi.	3	Mike Karakas	Mtl. 7	Chi. 2
Doug Bentley (2)	Chi.	Mar. 28/44	Chi.	3	Connie Dion	Chi. 7	Det. 1
		Mar. 30/44	Det.	3	Connie Dion	Chi. 5	Det. 2
Ted Kennedy (2)	Tor.	Apr. 14/45	Tor.	3	Harry Lumley	Det. 5	Tor. 3
		Mar. 27/48	Tor.	4	Frank Brimsek	Tor. 5	Bos. 3
Bobby Hull (2)	Chi.	Apr. 7/63	Det.	3	Terry Sawchuk	Det. 7	Chi. 4
		Apr. 9/72	Pit.	3	Jim Rutherford	Chi. 6	Pit. 5
F. St. Marseille (2)	St. L.	Apr. 28/70	St. L.	3	Al Smith	St. L. 5	Pit. 0
		Apr. 6/72	Min.	3	Cesare Maniago	Min. 6	St. L. 5
Pit Martin (2)	Chi.	Apr. 4/73	Chi.	3	Wayne Stephenson	Chi. 7	St. L. 1
		May 10/73	Chi.	3	Ken Dryden	Mtl. 6	Chi. 4
Yvan Cournoyer (2)	Mtl.	Apr. 5/73	Mtl.	3	Dave Dryden	Mtl. 7	Buf. 3
		Apr. 11/74	Mtl.	3	Ed Giacomin	Mtl. 4	NYR 1
Guy Lafleur (2)	Mtl.	May 1/75	Mtl.	3	Roger Crozier (1)		
					Gerry Desjardins (2)	Mtl. 7	Buf. 0
		Apr. 11/77	Mtl.	3	Ed Staniowski	Mtl. 7	St. L. 2
Lanny McDonald (2)	Tor.	Apr. 9/77	Pit.	3	Denis Herron	Tor. 5	Pit. 2
		Apr. 17/77	Tor.	4	Wayne Stephenson	Phi. 6	Tor. 5
Butch Goring (2)	L.A.	Apr. 9/77	L.A.	3	Phil Myre	L.A. 4	Atl. 2
	NYI	May 17/81	Min.	3	Gilles Meloche	NYI 7	Min. 5
Bryan Trottier (2)	NYI	Apr. 8/80	NYI	3	Doug Keans	NYI 8	L.A. 1
		Apr. 9/81	NYI	3	Michel Larocque	NYI 5	Tor. 1
Bill Barber (2)	Phi.	May 4/80	Min.	4	Gilles Meloche	Phi. 5	Min. 3
		Apr. 9/81	Phi.	3	Dan Bouchard	Phi. 8	Que. 5
Brian Propp (2)	Phi.	Apr. 22/81	Phi.	3	Pat Riggin	Phi. 9	Cgy. 4
		Apr. 21/85	Phi.	3	Billy Smith	Phi. 5	NYI 2
Paul Reinhart (2)	Cgy	Apr. 14/83	Edm.	3	Andy Moog	Edm. 6	Cgy. 3
		Apr. 8/84	Van	3	Richard Brodeur	Cgy. 5	Van. 1
Peter Stastny (2)	Que.	Apr. 5/83	Bos.	3	Pete Peeters	Bos. 4	Que. 3
		Apr. 11/87	Que.	3	Mike Liut (2)		
					Steve Weeks (1)	Que. 5	Hfd. 1
Glenn Anderson (2)	Edm.	Apr. 26/83	Edm.	4	Murray Bannerman	Edm. 8	Chi. 2
		Apr. 6/88	Wpg.	3	Daniel Berthiaume	Edm. 7	Wpg. 4
Michel Goulet (2)	Que.	Apr. 23/85	Que.	3	Steve Penney	Que. 7	Mtl. 6
		Apr. 12/87	Que.	3	Mike Liut	Que. 4	Hfd. 1
Peter Zezel (2)	Phi.	Apr. 13/86	NYR	3	John Vanbiesbrouck	Phi. 7	NYR 1
	St. L.	Apr. 11/89	St. L.	3	Jon Casey (2)		
					Kari Takko (1)	St. L. 6	Min. 1
Geoff Courtnall (2)	Van.	Apr. 4/91	L.A.	3	Kelly Hrudey	Van. 6	L.A. 5
		Apr. 30/92	Van.	3	Rick Tabaracci	Van. 5	Win. 0
Joe Sakic (2)	Que.	May 6/95	Que.	3	Mike Richter	Que. 5	NYR 4
	Col.	Apr. 25/96	Col.	3	Corey Hirsch	Col. 5	Van. 4
Daniel Alfredsson (2)	Ott.	Apr. 28/98	Ott.	3	Martin Brodeur	N.J. 3	Ott. 4
		May 11/98	Ott.	3	Olaf Kolzig	Wsh. 3	Ott. 4
Harry Meeking	Tor.	Mar. 11/18	Tor.	3	Georges Vezina	Tor. 7	Mtl. 3
Alf Skinner	Tor.	Mar. 23/18	Tor.	3	Hugh Lehman	Van.M. 6	Tor. 4
Joe Malone	Mtl.	Feb. 23/19	Mtl.	3	Clint Benedict	Mtl. 8	Ott. 4
Odie Cleghorn	Mtl.	Feb. 27/19	Ott.	3	Clint Benedict	Mtl. 5	Ott. 3
Jack Darragh	Ott.	Apr. 1/20	Tor.	3	Harry Holmes	Ott. 6	Sea. 1
George Boucher	Ott.	Mar. 10/21	Ott.	3	Jake Forbes	Ott. 5	Tor. 0
Babe Dye	Tor.	Mar. 28/22	Tor.	4	Hugh Lehman	Tor. 5	Van.M. 1
Percy Galbraith	Bos.	Mar. 31/27	Bos.	3	Hugh Lehman	Bos. 4	Chi. 4
Harvey Jackson	Tor.	Apr. 5/32	NYR	3	John Ross Roach	Tor. 6	NYR 4
Frank Boucher	NYR	Apr. 9/32	Tor.	3	Lorne Chabot	Tor. 6	NYR 4
Charlie Conacher	Tor.	Mar. 26/36	Tor.	3	Tiny Thompson	Tor. 8	Bos. 3
Syd Howe	Det.	Mar. 23/39	Det.	3	Claude Bourque	Det. 7	Mtl. 3
Bryan Hextall Sr.	NYR	Apr. 3/40	NYR	3	Turk Broda	NYR 6	Tor. 2
Joe Benoit	Mtl.	Mar. 22/41	Mtl.	3	Sam LoPresti	Mtl. 4	Chi. 3
Syl Apps Sr.	Tor.	Mar. 25/41	Tor.	3	Frank Brimsek	Tor. 7	Bos. 2
Jack McGill	Bos.	Mar. 29/42	Bos.	3	Johnny Mowers	Det. 6	Bos. 4
Don Metz	Tor.	Apr. 14/42	Tor.	3	Johnny Mowers	Tor. 9	Det. 3
Mud Bruneteau	Det.	Apr. 1/43	Det.	3	Frank Brimsek	Det. 6	Bos. 2
Don Grosso	Det.	Apr. 7/43	Bos.	3	Frank Brimsek	Det. 4	Bos. 0
Carl Liscombe	Det.	Apr. 3/45	Bos.	4	Paul Bibeault	Det. 5	Bos. 3
Billy Reay	Mtl.	Apr. 1/47	Bos.	4	Frank Brimsek	Mtl. 5	Bos. 1
Gerry Plamondon	Mtl.	Mar. 24/49	Det.	3	Harry Lumley	Mtl. 4	Det. 3
Sid Smith	Tor.	Apr. 10/49	Det.	3	Harry Lumley	Tor. 3	Det. 1
Pentti Lund	NYR	Apr. 2/50	NYR	3	Bill Durnan	NYR 4	Mtl. 1
Ted Lindsay	Det.	Apr. 5/55	Det.	4	Charlie Hodge (1)		
					Jacques Plante (3)	Det. 7	Mtl. 1
Gordie Howe	Det.	Apr. 10/55	Det.	3	Jacques Plante	Det. 5	Mtl. 1
Phil Goyette	Mtl.	Mar. 25/58	Mtl.	3	Terry Sawchuk	Mtl. 8	Det. 1
Jerry Toppazzini	Bos.	Apr. 5/58	Bos.	3	Gump Worsley	Bos. 8	NYR 2
Bob Pulford	Tor.	Apr. 19/62	Tor.	3	Glenn Hall	Tor. 8	Chi. 4
Dave Keon	Tor.	Apr. 9/64	Mtl.	3	Charlie Hodge	Tor. 3	Mtl. 1
Henri Richard	Mtl.	Apr. 20/67	Mtl.	3	Terry Sawchuk (2)		
					Johnny Bower (1)	Mtl. 6	Tor. 2
Rosaire Paiement	Phi.	Apr. 13/68	Phi.	3	Glenn Hall (1)		
					Seth Martin (2)	Phi. 6	St. L. 1
Jean Beliveau	Mtl.	Apr. 20/68	Mtl.	3	Denis DeJordy	Mtl. 4	Chi. 1
Red Berenson	St. L.	Apr. 15/69	St. L.	3	Gerry Desjardins	St. L. 4	L.A. 0
Ken Schinkel	Pit.	Apr. 11/70	Oak.	3	Gary Smith	Pit. 5	Oak. 2
Jim Pappin	Chi.	Apr. 11/71	Phi.	3	Bruce Gamble	Chi. 6	Phi. 2

Player	Team	Date	City	Total Goals	Opposing Goaltender	Score	
Bobby Orr	Bos.	Apr. 11/71	Mtl.	3	Ken Dryden	Bos. 5	Mtl. 2
Jacques Lemaire	Mtl.	Apr. 20/71	Mtl.	3	Gump Worsley	Mtl. 7	Min. 2
Vic Hadfield	NYR	Apr. 22/71	NYR	3	Tony Esposito	NYR 4	Chi. 1
Fred Stanfield	Bos.	Apr. 18/72	Bos.	3	Jacques Caron	Bos. 6	St. L. 1
Ken Hodge	Bos.	Apr. 30/72	Bos.	3	Eddie Giacomin	Bos. 6	NYR 5
Steve Vickers	NYR	Apr. 10/73	Bos.	3	Ross Brooks (2)		
					Eddie Johnston (1)	NYR 6	Bos. 3
Dick Redmond	Chi.	Apr. 4/73	Chi.	3	Wayne Stephenson	Chi. 7	St. L. 1
Tom Williams	L.A.	Apr. 14/74	L.A.	3	Mike Veisor	L.A. 5	Chi. 1
Marcel Dionne	L.A.	Apr. 15/76	L.A.	3	Gilles Gilbert	L.A. 6	Bos. 4
Don Saleski	Phi.	Apr. 20/76	Phi.	3	Wayne Thomas	Phi. 7	Tor. 1
Darryl Sittler	Tor.	Apr. 22/76	Tor.	5	Bernie Parent	Tor. 8	Phi. 5
Reggie Leach	Phi.	May 6/76	Phi.	5	Gilles Gilbert	Phi. 6	Bos. 3
Jim Lorentz	Buf.	Apr. 7/77	Min.	3	Pete LoPresti (2)		
					Gary Smith (1)	Buf. 7	Min. 1
Bobby Schmautz	Bos.	Apr. 11/77	Bos.	3	Rogie Vachon	Bos. 8	L.A. 3
Billy Harris	NYI	Apr. 23/77	Mtl.	3	Ken Dryden	Mtl. 4	NYI 3
George Ferguson	Tor.	Apr. 11/78	Tor.	3	Rogie Vachon	Tor. 7	L.A. 3
Jean Ratelle	Bos.	May 3/79	Bos.	3	Ken Dryden	Bos. 4	Mtl. 3
Stan Jonathan	Bos.	May 8/79	Bos.	3	Ken Dryden	Bos. 5	Mtl. 2
Ron Duguay	NYR	Apr. 20/80	NYR	3	Pete Peeters	NYR 4	Phi. 2
Steve Shutt	Mtl.	Apr. 22/80	Mtl.	3	Gilles Meloche	Mtl. 6	Min. 2
Gilbert Perreault	Buf.	May 6/80	NYI	3	Billy Smith (2)		
					ENG (1)	Buf. 7	NYI 4
Paul Holmgren	Phi.	May 15/80	Phil	3	Billy Smith	Phi. 8	NYI 3
Steve Payne	Min.	Apr. 8/81	Bos.	3	Rogie Vachon	Min. 5	Bos. 4
Denis Potvin	NYI	Apr. 17/81	NYI	3	Andy Moog	NYI 6	Edm. 3
Barry Pederson	Bos.	Apr. 8/82	Bos.	3	Don Edwards	Bos. 7	Buf. 3
Duane Sutter	NYI	Apr. 15/83	NYI	3	Glen Hanlon	NYI 5	NYR 0
Doug Halward	Van.	Apr. 7/84	Van.	3	Rejean Lemelin (2)		
					Don Edwards (1)	Van. 7	Cgy. 0
Jorgen Pettersson	St. L.	Apr. 8/84	Det.	3	Eddie Mio	St. L. 3	Det. 2
Clark Gillies	NYI	May 12/84	NYI	3	Grant Fuhr	NYI 6	Edm. 1
Ken Linseman	Bos.	Apr. 14/85	Bos.	3	Steve Penney	Bos. 7	Mtl. 6
Dave Andreychuk	Buf.	Apr. 14/85	Buf.	3	Dan Bouchard	Que. 4	Buf. 7
Greg Paslawski	St. L.	Apr. 15/86	Min.	3	Don Beaupre	St. L. 6	Min. 3
Doug Risebrough	Cgy.	May 4/86	Cgy.	3	Rick Wamsley	Cgy. 8	St. L. 2
Mike McPhee	Mtl.	Apr. 11/87	Bos.	3	Doug Keans	Mtl. 5	Bos. 4
John Ogrodnick	Que.	Apr. 14/87	Hfd.	3	Mike Liut	Que. 7	Hfd. 5
Pelle Eklund	Phi.	May 10/87	Mtl.	3	Patrick Roy (1)		
					Bryan Hayward (2)	Phi. 6	Mtl. 3
John Tucker	Buf.	Apr. 9/88	Bos.	4	Andy Moog	Buf. 6	Bos. 2
Tony Hrkac	St. L.	Apr. 10/88	St. L.	4	Darren Pang	St. L. 6	Chi. 5
Hakan Loob	Cgy.	Apr. 10/88	Cgy.	3	Glenn Healy	Cgy. 7	L.A. 3
Ed Olczyk	Tor.	Apr. 12/88	Tor.	3	Greg Stefan (2)		
					Glen Hanlon (1)	Tor. 6	Det. 5
Aaron Broten	N.J.	Apr. 20/88	N.J.	3	Pete Peeters	N.J. 5	Wsh. 2
Mark Johnson	N.J.	Apr. 22/88	Wsh.	4	Pete Peeters	N.J. 10	Wsh. 4
Patrik Sundstrom	N.J.	Apr. 22/88	Wsh.	3	Pete Peeters (2)		
					Clint Malarchuk (1)	N.J. 10	Wsh. 4
Bob Brooke	Min.	Apr. 5/89	St. L.	3	Greg Millen	St. L. 4	Min. 3
Chris Kontos	L.A.	Apr. 6/89	L.A.	3	Grant Fuhr	L.A. 5	Edm. 2
Wayne Presley	Chi.	Apr. 13/89	Chi.	3	Greg Stefan (1)		
					Glen Hanlon (2)	Chi. 7	Det. 1
Tony Granato	L.A.	Apr. 10/90	L.A.	3	Mike Vernon (1)		
					Rick Wamsley (2)	L.A. 12	Cgy. 4
Tomas Sandstrom	L.A.	Apr. 10/90	L.A.	3	Mike Vernon (1)		
					Rick Wamsley (2)	L.A. 12	Cgy. 4
Dave Taylor	L.A.	Apr. 10/90	L.A.	3	Mike Vernon (1)		
					Rick Wamsley (2)	L.A. 12	Cgy. 4
Bernie Nicholls	NYR	Apr. 19/90	NYR	3	Mike Liut	NYR 7	Wsh. 3
John Druce	Wsh.	Apr. 21/90	NYR	3	John Vanbiesbrouck	Wsh. 6	NYR 3
Adam Oates	St. L.	Apr. 12/91	St. L.	3	Tim Chevaldae	St. L. 6	Det. 1
Luc Robitaille	L.A.	Apr. 26/91	L.A.	3	Grant Fuhr	L.A. 5	Edm. 2
Ron Francis	Pit.	May 9/92	Pit.	3	Mike Richter (2)		
					John V'brouck (1)	Pit. 5	NYR. 4
Dirk Graham	Chi.	June 1/92	Chi.	3	Tom Barrasso	Pit. 5	Chi. 2
Joe Murphy	Edm.	May 6/92	Edm.	3	Kirk McLean	Edm. 5	Van. 2
Ray Sheppard	Det.	Apr. 24/92	Min.	3	Jon Casey	Min. 5	Det. 2
Kevin Stevens	Pit.	May 21/92	Bos.	4	Andy Moog	Pit. 5	Bos. 2
Pavel Bure	Van.	Apr. 28/92	Wpg.	3	Rick Tabaracci	Van. 8	Wpg. 3
Brian Noonan	Chi.	Apr. 18/93	Chi.	3	Curtis Joseph	St. L. 4	Chi. 3
Dale Hunter	Wsh.	Apr. 20/93	Wsh.	3	Glenn Healy	NYI 5	Wsh. 4
Teemu Selanne	Wpg.	Apr. 23/93	Wpg.	3	Kirk McLean	Wpg. 5	Van. 4
Ray Ferraro	NYI	Apr. 26/93	Wsh.	4	Don Beaupre	Wsh. 6	NYI 4
Al Iafrate	Wsh.	Apr. 26/93	Wsh.	3	Glenn Healy (2)		
					Mark Fitzpatrick (1)	Wsh. 6	NYI 4
Paul Di Pietro	Mtl.	Apr. 28/93	Mtl.	3	Ron Hextall	Mtl. 6	Que. 2
Wendel Clark	Tor.	May 27/93	L.A.	3	Kelly Hrudey	L.A. 5	Tor. 4
Eric Desjardins	Mtl.	Jun. 3/93	Mtl.	3	Kelly Hrudey	Mtl. 3	L.A. 2
Tony Amonte	Chi.	Apr. 23/94	Chi.	4	Felix Potvin	Chi. 5	Tor. 4
Gary Suter	Chi.	Apr. 24/94	Chi.	3	Felix Potvin	Chi. 4	Tor. 3
Ulf Dahlen	S.J.	May 6/94	S.J.	3	Felix Potvin	S.J. 5	Tor. 2
Mike Sullivan	Cgy.	May 11/95	S.J.	3	Arturs Irbe (2)		
					Wade Flaherty (1)	Cgy. 9	S.J. 2
Theoren Fleury	Cgy.	May 13/95	S.J.	4	Arturs Irbe (3)		
					ENG (1)	Cgy. 6	S.J. 4
Brendan Shanahan	St. L.	May 13/95	Van.	3	Kirk McLean	St. L. 5	Van. 2
John LeClair	Phi.	May 21/95	Phi.	3	Mike Richter	Phi. 5	NYR 4
Brian Leetch	NYR	May 22/95	Phi.	3	Ron Hextall	Phi. 4	NYR 3
Trevor Linden	Van.	Apr. 25/96	Col.	3	Patrick Roy	Col. 5	Van. 4
Jaromir Jagr	Pit.	May 11/96	Pit.	3	Mike Richter	Pit. 7	NYR 3
Peter Forsberg	Col.	Jun. 6/96	Col.	3	John Vanbiesbrouck	Col. 8	Fla. 1
Valeri Zelepukin	N.J.	Apr. 22/97	Mtl.	3	Jocelyn Thibault	N.J. 6	Mtl. 4
Valeri Kamensky	Col.	Apr. 24/97	Col.	3	Jeff Hackett (2)		
					Chris Terreri (1)	Col. 7	Chi. 0
Eric Lindros	Phi.	May 20/97	NYR	3	Mike Richter	Phi. 6	NYR 3
Matthew Barnaby	Buf.	May 10/98	Buf.	3	Andy Moog (2)	Mtl. 3	Buf. 6
					ENG (1)		

Leading Playoff Scorers, 1918–1998

Season	Player and Club	Games Played	Goals	Assists	Points
1997-98	Steve Yzerman, Detroit	22	6	18	24
1996-97	Eric Lindros, Philadelphia	19	12	14	26
1995-96	Joe Sakic, Colorado	22	18	16	34
1994-95	Sergei Fedorov, Detroit	17	7	17	24
1993-94	Brian Leetch, NY Rangers	23	11	23	34
1992-93	Wayne Gretzky, Los Angeles	24	15	25	40
1991-92	Mario Lemieux, Pittsburgh	15	16	18	34
1990-91	Mario Lemieux, Pittsburgh	23	16	28	44
1989-90	Craig Simpson, Edmonton	22	16	15	31
	Mark Messier, Edmonton	22	9	22	31
1988-89	Al MacInnis, Calgary	22	7	24	31
1987-88	Wayne Gretzky, Edmonton	19	12	31	43
1986-87	Wayne Gretzky, Edmonton	21	5	29	34
1985-86	Doug Gilmour, St. Louis	19	9	12	21
	Bernie Federko, St. Louis	19	7	14	21
1984-85	Wayne Gretzky, Edmonton	18	17	30	47
1983-84	Wayne Gretzky, Edmonton	19	13	22	35
1982-83	Wayne Gretzky, Edmonton	16	12	26	38
1981-82	Bryan Trottier, NY Islanders	19	6	23	29
1980-81	Mike Bossy, NY Islanders	18	17	18	35
1979-80	Bryan Trottier, NY Islanders	21	12	17	29
1978-79	Jacques Lemaire, Montreal	16	11	12	23
	Guy Lafleur, Montreal	16	10	13	23
1977-78	Guy Lafleur, Montreal	15	10	11	21
	Larry Robinson, Montreal	15	4	17	21
1976-77	Guy Lafleur, Montreal	14	9	17	26
1975-76	Reggie Leach, Philadelphia	16	19	5	24
1974-75	Rick MacLeish, Philadelphia	17	11	9	20
1973-74	Rick MacLeish, Philadelphia	17	13	9	22
1972-73	Yvan Cournoyer, Montreal	17	15	10	25
1971-72	Phil Esposito, Boston	15	9	15	24
	Bobby Orr, Boston	15	5	19	24
1970-71	Frank Mahovlich, Montreal	20	14	13	27
1969-70	Phil Esposito, Boston	14	13	14	27
1968-69	Phil Esposito, Boston	10	8	10	18
1967-68	Bill Goldsworthy, Minnesota	14	8	7	15
1966-67	Jim Pappin, Toronto	12	7	8	15
1965-66	Norm Ullman, Detroit	12	6	9	15
1964-65	Bobby Hull, Chicago	14	10	7	17
1963-64	Gordie Howe, Detroit	14	9	10	19
1962-63	Gordie Howe, Detroit	11	7	9	16
	Norm Ullman, Detroit	11	4	12	16
1961-62	Stan Mikita, Chicago	12	6	15	21
1960-61	Gordie Howe, Detroit	11	4	11	15
	Pierre Pilote, Chicago	12	3	12	15
1959-60	Henri Richard, Montreal	8	3	9	12
	Bernie Geoffrion, Montreal	8	2	10	12
1958-59	Dickie Moore, Montreal	11	5	12	17
1957-58	Fleming Mackell, Boston	12	5	14	19
1956-57	Bernie Geoffrion, Montreal	11	11	7	18
1955-56	Jean Béliveau, Montreal	10	12	7	19
1954-55	Gordie Howe, Detroit	11	9	11	20
1953-54	Dickie Moore, Montreal	11	5	8	13
1952-53	Ed Sanford, Boston	11	8	3	11
1951-52	Ted Lindsay, Detroit	8	5	2	7
	Floyd Curry, Montreal	11	4	3	7
	Metro Prystai, Detroit	8	2	5	7
	Gordie Howe, Detroit	8	2	5	7
1950-51	Maurice Richard, Montreal	11	9	4	13
	Max Bentley, Toronto	11	2	11	13
1949-50	Pentti Lund, NY Rangers	12	6	5	11
1948-49	Gordie Howe, Detroit	11	8	3	11
1947-48	Ted Kennedy, Toronto	9	8	6	14
1946-47	Maurice Richard, Montreal	10	6	5	11
1945-46	Elmer Lach, Montreal	9	5	12	17
1944-45	Joe Carveth, Detroit	14	5	6	11
1943-44	Toe Blake, Montreal	9	7	11	18
1942-43	Carl Liscombe, Detroit	10	6	8	14
1941-42	Don Grosso, Detroit	12	8	6	14
1940-41	Milt Schmidt, Boston	11	5	6	11
1939-40	Phil Watson, NY Rangers	12	3	6	9
	Neil Colville, NY Rangers	12	2	7	9
1938-39	Bill Cowley, Boston	12	3	11	14
1937-38	Johnny Gottselig, Chicago	10	5	3	8
1936-37	Marty Barry, Detroit	10	4	7	11
1935-36	Frank Boll, Toronto	9	7	3	10
1934-35	Baldy Northcott, Mtl. Maroons	7	4	1	5
	Harvey Jackson, Toronto	7	3	2	5
	Cy Wentworth, Mtl. Maroons	7	3	2	5
1933-34	Larry Aurie, Detroit	9	3	7	10
1932-33	Cecil Dillon, NY Rangers	8	8	2	10
1931-32	Frank Boucher, NY Rangers	7	3	6	9
1930-31	Cooney Weiland, Boston	5	6	3	9
1929-30	Marty Barry, Boston	6	3	3	6
	Cooney Weiland, Boston	6	1	5	6
1928-29	Andy Blair, Toronto	4	3	0	3
	Butch Keeling, NY Rangers	6	3	0	3
	Ace Bailey, Toronto	4	1	2	3
1927-28	Frank Boucher, NY Rangers	9	7	3	10
1926-27	Harry Oliver, Boston	8	4	2	6
	Percy Galbraith, Boston	8	3	3	6
	Frank Fredrickson, Boston	8	2	4	6
1925-26	Nels Stewart, Mtl. Maroons	8	6	3	9
1924-25	Howie Morenz, Montreal	6	7	1	8
1923-24	Howie Morenz, Montreal	6	7	2	9
1922-23	Punch Broadbent, Ottawa	8	6	1	7
1921-22	Babe Dye, Toronto	7	11	2	13
1920-21	Cy Denneny, Ottawa	7	4	2	6
1919-20	Frank Nighbor, Ottawa	5	6	1	7
	Jack Darragh, Ottawa	5	5	2	7
1918-19	Newsy Lalonde, Montreal	10	17	1	18
1917-18	Alf Skinner, Toronto	7	8	1	9

Overtime Games since 1918

Abbreviations: Teams/Cities: — **Ana.** - Anaheim; **Atl.** - Atlanta; **Bos.** - Boston; **Buf.** - Buffalo; **Cgy.** - Calgary; **Cgy. T.** - Calgary Tigers (Western Canada Hockey League); **Chi.** - Chicago; **Col.** - Colorado; **Dal.** - Dallas; **Det.** - Detroit; **Edm.** - Edmonton; **Edm. E.** - Edmonton Eskimos (WCHL); **Fla.** - Florida; **Hfd.** - Hartford; **K.C.** - Kansas City; **L.A.** - Los Angeles; **Min.** - Minnesota; **Mtl.** - Montreal; **Mtl.M.** - Montreal Maroons; **N.J.** - New Jersey; **NYA** - NY Americans; **NYI** - New York Islanders; **NYR** - New York Rangers; **Oak.** - Oakland; **Ott.** - Ottawa; **Phi.** - Philadelphia; **Phx.** - Phoenix; **Pit.** - Pittsburgh; **Que.** - Quebec; **St. L.** - St. Louis; **Sea.** - Seattle Metropolitans (Pacific Coast Hockey Association); **S.J.** - San Jose; **T.B.** - Tampa Bay; **Tor.** - Toronto; **Van.** - Vancouver; **Van. M** - Vancouver Millionaires (PCHA); **Vic.** - Victoria Cougars (WCHL); **Wpg.** - Winnipeg; **Wsh.** - Washington.

SERIES — **CF** - conference final; **CSF** - conference semi-final; **CQF** - conference quarter-final; **DF** - division final; **DSF** - division semi-final; **F** - final; **PR** - preliminary round; **QF** - quarter final; **SF** - semi-final.

Date	City	Series	Score		Scorer	Overtime	Series Winner
Mar. 26/19	Sea.	F	Mtl. 0	Sea. 0	no scorer	20:00	
Mar. 30/19	Sea.	F	Mtl. 4	Sea. 3	Odie Cleghorn	15:57	
Mar. 20/22	Tor.	F	Tor 2	Van.M. 1	Babe Dye	4:50	Tor.
Mar. 29/23	Van.	F	Ott. 2	Edm.E. 1	Cy Denneny	2:08	Ott.
Mar. 31/27	Mtl.	QF	Mtl. 1	Mtl. M. 0	Howie Morenz	12:05	Mtl.
Apr. 7/27	Bos.	F	Ott. 0	Bos. 0	no scorer	20:00	Ott.
Apr. 11/27	Ott.	F	Bos. 1	Ott. 1	no scorer	20:00	Ott.
Apr. 3/28	Mtl.	QF	Mtl. M. 1	Mtl. 0	Russ Oatman	8:20	Mtl. M.
Apr. 7/28	Mtl.	F	NYR 2	Mtl. M. 1	Frank Boucher	7:05	NYR
Mar. 21/29	NY	QF	NYR 1	NYA 0	Butch Keeling	29:50	NYR
Mar. 26/29	Tor.	SF	NYR 2	Tor. 1	Frank Boucher	2:03	NYR
Mar. 20/30	Mtl.	SF	Bos. 2	Mtl. M. 1	Harry Oliver	45:35	Bos.
Mar. 25/30	Bos.	SF	Mtl. M. 1	Bos. 0	Archie Wilcox	26:27	Bos.
Mar. 26/30	Mtl.	QF	Chi. 2	Mtl. 2	Howie Morenz (Mtl.)	51:43	Mtl.
Mar. 28/30	Mtl.	SF	Mtl. 2	NYR 1	Gus Rivers	68:52	Mtl.
Mar. 24/31	Bos.	SF	Bos. 5	Mtl. 4	Cooney Weiland	18:56	Mtl.
Mar. 26/31	Chi.	QF	Chi. 2	Tor. 1	Stew Adams	19:20	Chi.
Mar. 28/31	Mtl.	SF	Mtl. 4	Bos. 3	Georges Mantha	5:10	Mtl.
Apr. 1/31	Mtl.	SF	Mtl. 3	Bos. 2	Wildor Larochelle	19:00	Mtl.
Apr. 5/31	Chi.	F	Chi. 2	Mtl. 1	Johnny Gottselig	24:50	Mtl.
Apr. 9/31	Mtl.	F	Chi. 3	Mtl. 2	Cy Wentworth	53:50	Mtl.
Mar. 26/32	Mtl.	SF	NYR 4	Mtl. 3	Fred Cook	59:32	NYR
Apr. 2/32	Tor.	SF	Tor. 3	Mtl. M. 2	Bob Gracie	17:59	Tor.
Mar. 25/33	Bos.	SF	Bos. 2	Tor. 1	Marty Barry	14:14	Tor.
Mar. 28/33	Bos.	SF	Tor. 1	Bos. 0	Busher Jackson	15:03	Tor.
Mar. 30/33	Tor.	SF	Bos. 2	Tor. 1	Eddie Shore	4:23	Tor.
Apr. 3/33	Tor.	SF	Tor. 1	Bos. 0	Ken Doraty	104:46	Tor.
Apr. 13/33	Tor.	F	NYR 1	Tor. 0	Bill Cook	7:33	NYR
Mar. 22/34	Tor.	SF	Det. 2	Tor. 1	Herbie Lewis	1:33	Det.
Mar. 25/34	Chi.	QF	Chi. 1	Mtl. 1	Mush March (Chi)	11:05	Chi.
Apr. 3/34	Det.	F	Chi. 2	Det. 1	Paul Thompson	21:10	Chi.
Apr. 10/34	Chi.	F	Chi. 1	Det. 0	Mush March	30:05	Chi.
Mar. 23/35	Bos.	SF	Bos. 1	Tor. 0	Dit Clapper	33:26	Tor.
Mar. 26/35	Chi.	QF	Mtl. M. 1	Chi. 0	Baldy Northcott	4:02	Mtl. M.
Mar. 30/35	Tor.	SF	Tor. 2	Bos. 1	Pep Kelly	1:36	Tor.
Apr. 4/35	Tor.	F	Mtl. M. 3	Tor. 2	Dave Trottier	5:28	Mtl. M.
Mar. 24/36	Mtl.	SF	Det. 1	Mtl. M. 0	Mud Bruneteau	116:30	Det.
Apr. 9/36	Tor.	F	Tor. 4	Det. 3	Buzz Boll	0:31	Det.
Mar. 25/37	NY	QF	NYR 2	Tor. 1	Babe Pratt	13:05	NYR
Apr. 1/37	Mtl.	SF	Det. 2	Mtl. 1	Hec Kilrea	51:49	Det.
Mar. 22/38	NY	QF	NYA 2	NYR 1	Johnny Sorrell	21:25	NYA
Mar. 24/38	Tor.	SF	Tor. 1	Bos. 0	George Parsons	21:31	Tor.
Mar. 26/38	Mtl.	QF	Chi. 3	Mtl. 2	Paul Thompson	11:49	Chi.
Mar. 27/38	NY	QF	NYA 3	NYR 2	Lorne Carr	60:40	NYA
Mar. 29/38	Bos.	SF	Tor. 3	Bos. 2	Gordie Drillon	10:04	Tor.
Mar. 31/38	Chi.	SF	Chi. 1	NYA 0	Cully Dahlstrom	33:01	Chi.
Mar. 21/39	NY	SF	Bos. 2	NYR 1	Mel Hill	59:25	Bos.
Mar. 23/39	Bos.	SF	Bos. 3	NYR 2	Mel Hill	8:24	Bos.
Mar. 26/39	Det.	QF	Det. 1	Mtl. 0	Marty Barry	7:47	Det.
Mar. 30/39	Bos.	SF	NYR 2	Bos. 1	Clint Smith	17:19	Bos.
Apr. 1/39	Tor.	SF	Tor. 5	Det. 4	Gordie Drillon	5:42	Tor.
Apr. 2/39	Bos.	SF	Bos. 2	NYR 1	Mel Hill	48:00	Bos.
Apr. 9/39	Bos.	F	Tor. 3	Bos. 2	Doc Romnes	10:38	Bos.
Mar. 19/40	Det.	QF	Det. 2	NYA 1	Syd Howe	0:25	Det.
Mar. 19/40	Tor.	QF	Tor. 3	Chi. 2	Syl Apps Sr.	6:35	Tor.
Apr. 2/40	NY	F	NYR 2	Tor. 1	Alf Pike	15:30	NYR
Apr. 11/40	Tor.	F	NYR 2	Tor. 1	Muzz Patrick	31:43	NYR
Apr. 13/40	Tor.	F	NYR 3	Tor. 2	Bryan Hextall Sr.	2:07	NYR
Mar. 20/41	Det.	QF	Det. 2	NYR 1	Gus Giesebrecht	12:01	Det.
Mar. 22/41	Mtl.	QF	Mtl. 4	Chi. 3	Charlie Sands	34:04	Chi.
Mar. 29/41	Bos.	SF	Tor. 2	Bos. 1	Pete Langelle	17:31	Bos.
Mar. 30/41	Chi.	SF	Det. 2	Chi. 1	Gus Giesebrecht	9:15	Det.
Mar. 22/42	Chi.	QF	Bos. 2	Chi. 1	Des Smith	6:51	Bos.
Mar. 21/43	Bos.	SF	Bos. 5	Mtl. 4	Don Gallinger	12:30	Bos.
Mar. 23/43	Det.	SF	Tor. 3	Det. 2	Jack McLean	70:18	Det.
Mar. 25/43	Mtl.	SF	Bos. 3	Mtl. 2	Harvey Jackson	3:20	Bos.
Mar. 30/43	Tor.	SF	Det. 3	Tor. 2	Adam Brown	9:21	Det.
Mar. 30/43	Bos.	SF	Bos. 5	Mtl. 4	Ab DeMarco	3:41	Bos.
Apr. 13/44	Mtl.	F	Mtl. 5	Chi. 4	Toe Blake	9:12	Mtl.
Mar. 27/45	Tor.	SF	Tor. 4	Mtl. 3	Gus Bodnar	12:36	Tor.
Mar. 29/45	Det.	SF	Det. 3	Bos. 2	Mud Bruneteau	17:12	Det.
Apr. 21/45	Tor.	F	Det. 1	Tor. 0	Ed Bruneteau	14:16	Tor.
Mar. 28/46	Bos.	SF	Bos. 4	Det. 3	Don Gallinger	9:51	Bos.
Mar. 30/46	Mtl.	F	Mtl. 4	Bos. 3	Maurice Richard	9:08	Mtl.
Apr. 2/46	Mtl.	F	Mtl. 3	Bos. 2	Jim Peters	16:55	Mtl.
Apr. 7/46	Bos.	F	Bos. 3	Mtl. 2	Terry Reardon	15:13	Mtl.
Mar. 26/47	Tor.	SF	Tor. 3	Det. 2	Howie Meeker	3:05	Tor.
Mar. 27/47	Mtl.	SF	Mtl. 2	Bos. 1	Kenny Mosdell	5:38	Mtl.
Apr. 3/47	Mtl.	SF	Mtl. 4	Bos. 3	John Quilty	36:40	Mtl.
Apr. 15/47	Tor.	F	Tor. 2	Mtl. 1	Syl Apps Sr.	16:36	Tor.
Mar. 24/48	Tor.	SF	Tor. 5	Bos. 4	Nick Metz	17:03	Tor.
Mar. 22/49	Det.	SF	Det. 2	Mtl. 1	Max McNab	44:52	Det.
Mar. 24/49	Det.	SF	Mtl. 4	Det. 3	Gerry Plamondon	2:59	Det.
Mar. 26/49	Tor.	SF	Bos. 5	Tor. 4	Woody Dumart	16:14	Tor.
Apr. 8/49	Det.	F	Tor. 3	Det. 2	Joe Klukay	17:31	Tor.
Apr. 4/50	Tor.	SF	Det. 2	Tor. 1	Leo Reise Sr.	20:38	Det.
Apr. 4/50	Mtl.	SF	Mtl. 3	NYR 2	Elmer Lach	15:19	NYR
Apr. 9/50	Det.	SF	Det. 1	Tor. 0	Leo Reise	8:39	Det.
Apr. 18/50	Det.	F	NYR 4	Det. 3	Don Raleigh	8:34	Det.
Apr. 20/50	Det.	F	NYR 2	Det. 1	Don Raleigh	1:38	Det.
Apr. 23/50	Det.	F	Det. 4	NYR 3	Pete Babando	28:31	Det.
Mar. 27/51	Det.	SF	Mtl. 3	Det. 2	Maurice Richard	61:09	Mtl.
Mar. 29/51	Det.	SF	Mtl. 1	Det. 0	Maurice Richard	42:20	Mtl.
Mar. 31/51	Tor.	SF	Bos. 1	Tor. 1	no scorer	20:00	Tor.
Apr. 11/51	Tor.	F	Tor. 3	Mtl. 2	Sid Smith	5:51	Tor.
Apr. 14/51	Tor.	F	Mtl. 3	Tor. 2	Maurice Richard	2:55	Tor.
Apr. 17/51	Mtl.	F	Tor. 2	Mtl. 1	Ted Kennedy	4:47	Tor.
Apr. 19/51	Mtl.	F	Tor. 3	Mtl. 2	Harry Watson	5:15	Tor.
Apr. 21/51	Tor.	F	Tor. 3	Mtl. 2	Bill Barilko	2:53	Tor.
Apr. 6/52	Bos.	SF	Mtl. 3	Bos. 2	Paul Masnick	27:49	Mtl.
Mar. 29/53	Bos.	SF	Bos. 2	Det. 1	Jack McIntyre	12:29	Bos.
Mar. 29/53	Chi.	SF	Chi. 2	Mtl. 1	Al Dewsbury	5:18	Mtl.
Apr. 16/53	Mtl.	F	Mtl. 1	Bos. 0	Elmer Lach	1:22	Mtl.
Apr. 1/54	Det.	SF	Det. 4	Tor. 3	Ted Lindsay	21:01	Det.
Apr. 11/54	Det.	F	Mtl. 1	Det. 0	Kenny Mosdell	5:45	Det.
Apr. 16/54	Det.	F	Det. 2	Mtl. 1	Tony Leswick	4:29	Det.
Mar. 29/55	Bos.	SF	Mtl. 4	Bos. 3	Don Marshall	3:05	Mtl.
Mar. 24/56	Tor.	SF	Det. 5	Tor. 4	Ted Lindsay	4:22	Det.
Mar. 28/57	NY	SF	NYR 4	Mtl. 3	Andy Hebenton	13:38	Mtl.
Apr. 4/57	Mtl.	SF	Mtl. 4	NYR 3	Maurice Richard	1:11	Mtl.
Mar. 27/58	NY	SF	Bos. 4	NYR 3	Jerry Toppazzini	4:46	Bos.
Mar. 30/58	Det.	SF	Mtl. 2	Det. 1	André Pronovost	11:52	Mtl.
Apr. 17/58	Mtl.	F	Mtl. 3	Bos. 2	Maurice Richard	5:45	Mtl.
Mar. 28/59	Tor.	SF	Tor. 3	Bos. 2	Gerry Ehman	5:02	Tor.
Mar. 31/59	Tor.	SF	Tor. 3	Bos. 2	Frank Mahovlich	11:21	Tor.
Apr. 14/59	Tor.	F	Tor. 3	Mtl. 2	Dick Duff	10:06	Mtl.
Mar. 26/60	Mtl.	SF	Mtl. 4	Chi. 3	Doug Harvey	8:38	Mtl.
Mar. 27/60	Det.	SF	Tor. 5	Det. 4	Frank Mahovlich	43:00	Tor.
Mar. 29/60	Det.	SF	Det. 2	Tor. 1	Gerry Melnyk	1:54	Tor.
Mar. 22/61	Tor.	SF	Tor. 3	Det. 2	George Armstrong	24:51	Det.
Mar. 26/61	Chi.	SF	Chi. 2	Mtl. 1	Murray Balfour	52:12	Chi.
Apr. 5/62	Tor.	SF	Tor. 3	NYR 2	Red Kelly	24:23	Tor.
Apr. 2/64	Det.	SF	Chi. 3	Det. 2	Murray Balfour	8:21	Det.
Apr. 14/64	Tor.	F	Det. 4	Tor. 3	Larry Jeffrey	7:52	Tor.
Apr. 23/64	Det.	F	Tor. 4	Det. 3	Bob Baun	1:43	Tor.
Apr. 6/65	Tor.	SF	Tor. 3	Mtl. 2	Dave Keon	4:17	Mtl.
Apr. 13/65	Tor.	SF	Mtl. 4	Tor. 3	Claude Provost	16:33	Mtl.
May 5/66	Det.	F	Mtl. 3	Det. 2	Henri Richard	2:20	Mtl.
Apr. 13/67	NY	SF	Mtl. 2	NYR 1	John Ferguson	6:28	Mtl.
Apr. 25/67	Tor.	F	Tor. 3	Mtl. 2	Bob Pulford	28:26	Tor.
Apr. 10/68	St. L.	QF	St. L. 3	Phi. 2	Larry Keenan	24:10	St. L.
Apr. 16/68	St. L.	QF	Phi. 2	St. L. 1	Don Blackburn	31:18	St. L.
Apr. 16/68	Min.	QF	Min. 4	L.A. 3	Milan Marcetta	9:11	Min.
Apr. 22/68	Min.	SF	Min. 3	St. L. 2	Parker MacDonald	3:41	St. L.
Apr. 27/68	St. L.	SF	St. L. 4	Min. 3	Gary Sabourin	1:32	St. L.
Apr. 28/68	Mtl.	SF	Mtl. 4	Chi. 3	Jacques Lemaire	2:14	Mtl.
Apr. 29/68	St. L.	SF	St. L. 3	Min. 2	Bill McCreary	17:27	St. L.
May 3/68	St. L.	SF	St. L. 2	Min. 1	Ron Schock	22:50	St. L.
May 5/68	St. L.	F	Mtl. 3	St. L. 2	Jacques Lemaire	1:41	Mtl.
May 9/68	Mtl.	F	Mtl. 4	St. L. 3	Bobby Rousseau	1:13	Mtl.
Apr. 2/69	Oak.	QF	L.A. 5	Oak. 4	Ted Irvine	0:19	L.A.
Apr. 10/69	Mtl.	SF	Mtl. 3	Bos. 2	Ralph Backstrom	0:42	Mtl.
Apr. 13/69	Mtl.	SF	Mtl. 4	Bos. 3	Mickey Redmond	4:55	Mtl.
Apr. 24/69	Bos.	SF	Mtl. 2	Bos. 1	Jean Béliveau	31:28	Mtl.
Apr. 12/70	Oak.	QF	Pit. 3	Oak. 2	Michel Briere	8:28	Pit.
May 10/70	Bos.	F	Bos. 4	St. L. 3	Bobby Orr	0:40	Bos.
Apr. 15/71	Tor.	QF	NYR 2	Tor. 1	Bob Nevin	9:07	NYR
Apr. 18/71	Chi.	SF	NYR 2	Chi. 1	Pete Stemkowski	1:37	Chi.
Apr. 27/71	Chi.	SF	Chi. 3	NYR 2	Bobby Hull	6:35	Chi.
Apr. 29/71	NY	SF	NYR 3	Chi. 2	Pete Stemkowski	41:29	Chi.
May 4/71	Chi.	F	Chi. 2	Mtl. 1	Jim Pappin	21:11	Mtl.
Apr. 6/72	Bos.	QF	Tor. 4	Bos. 3	Jim Harrison	2:58	Bos.
Apr. 6/72	Min.	QF	Min. 6	St. L. 5	Bill Goldsworthy	1:36	St. L.
Apr. 9/72	Pit.	QF	Chi. 6	Pit. 5	Pit Martin	0:12	Chi.
Apr. 16/72	Min.	QF	St. L. 2	Min. 1	Kevin O'Shea	10:07	St. L.
Apr. 1/73	Mtl.	QF	Buf. 3	Mtl. 2	René Robert	9:18	Mtl.
Apr. 10/73	Phi.	QF	Phi. 3	Min. 2	Gary Dornhoefer	8:35	Phi.
Apr. 14/73	Mtl.	SF	Phi. 5	Mtl. 4	Rick MacLeish	2:56	Mtl.
Apr. 17/73	Mtl.	SF	Mtl. 4	Phi. 3	Larry Robinson	6:45	Mtl.
Apr. 14/74	Tor.	QF	Bos. 4	Tor. 3	Ken Hodge	1:27	Bos.
Apr. 14/74	Atl.	QF	Phi. 4	Atl. 3	Dave Schultz	5:40	Phi.
Apr. 16/74	Mtl.	QF	NYR 3	Mtl. 2	Ron Harris	4:07	NYR
Apr. 23/74	Chi.	SF	Chi. 4	Bos. 3	Jim Pappin	3:48	Bos.
Apr. 28/74	NY	SF	NYR 2	Phi. 1	Rod Gilbert	4:20	Phi.
May 9/74	Bos.	F	Phi. 3	Bos. 2	Bobby Clarke	12:01	Phi.
Apr. 8/75	L.A.	PR	L.A. 3	Tor. 2	Mike Murphy	8:53	Tor.
Apr. 10/75	Tor.	PR	Tor. 3	L.A. 2	Blaine Stoughton	10:19	Tor.
Apr. 10/75	Chi.	PR	Chi. 4	Bos. 3	Ivan Boldirev	7:33	Chi.
Apr. 11/75	NY	PR	NYI 4	NYR 3	Jean-Paul Parise	0:11	NYI
Apr. 19/75	Tor.	QF	Phi. 4	Tor. 3	André Dupont	1:45	Phi.
Apr. 17/75	Chi.	QF	Chi. 5	Buf. 4	Stan Mikita	2:31	Buf.
Apr. 22/75	Mtl.	QF	Mtl. 5	Van. 4	Guy Lafleur	17:06	Mtl.
May 1/75	Phi.	SF	Phi. 5	NYI 4	Bobby Clarke	2:56	Phi.
May 7/75	NYI	SF	NYI 4	Phi. 3	Jude Drouin	1:53	Phi.
Apr. 27/75	Buf.	SF	Buf. 6	Mtl. 5	Danny Gare	4:42	Buf.
May 6/75	Buf.	SF	Buf. 5	Mtl. 4	René Robert	5:56	Buf.
May 20/75	Buf.	F	Buf. 5	Phi. 4	René Robert	18:29	Phi.
Apr. 8/76	Buf.	PR	Buf. 3	St. L. 2	Danny Gare	11:43	Buf.
Apr. 9/76	Buf.	PR	Buf. 2	St. L. 1	Don Luce	14:27	Buf.
Apr. 13/76	Bos.	QF	L.A. 3	Bos. 2	Butch Goring	0:27	Bos.
Apr. 13/76	Buf.	QF	Buf. 3	NYI 2	Danny Gare	14:04	NYI
Apr. 22/76	L.A.	QF	L.A. 4	Bos. 3	Butch Goring	18:28	Bos.
Apr. 29/76	Phi.	SF	Phi. 2	Bos. 1	Reggie Leach	13:38	Phi.
Apr. 15/77	Tor.	QF	Phi. 4	Tor. 3	Rick MacLeish	2:55	Phi.
Apr. 17/77	Tor.	QF	Phi. 6	Tor. 5	Reggie Leach	19:10	Phi.
Apr. 24/77	Phi.	SF	Bos. 4	Phi. 3	Rick Middleton	2:57	Bos.
Apr. 26/77	Phi.	SF	Bos. 5	Phi. 4	Terry O'Reilly	30:07	Bos.
May 3/77	Mtl.	SF	NYI 4	Mtl. 3	Billy Harris	3:58	Mtl.
May 14/77	Bos.	F	Mtl. 2	Bos. 1	Jacques Lemaire	4:32	Mtl.

Date	City	Series	Score		Scorer	Overtime	Series Winner
Apr. 11/78	Phi.	PR	Phi. 3	Col. 2	Mel Bridgman	0:23	Phi.
Apr. 13/78	NY	PR	NYR 4	Buf. 3	Don Murdoch	1:37	Buf.
Apr. 19/78	Bos.	QF	Bos. 4	Chi. 3	Terry O'Reilly	1:50	Bos.
Apr. 19/78	NYI	QF	NYI 3	Tor. 2	Mike Bossy	2:50	Tor.
Apr. 21/78	Chi.	QF	Bos. 4	Chi. 3	Peter McNab	10:17	Bos.
Apr. 25/78	NYI	QF	NYI 2	Tor. 1	Bob Nystrom	8:02	Tor.
Apr. 29/78	NYI	QF	Tor. 2	NYI 1	Lanny McDonald	4:13	Tor.
May 2/78	Bos.	SF	Bos. 3	Phi. 2	Rick Middleton	1:43	Bos.
May 16/78	Mtl.	F	Mtl. 3	Bos. 2	Guy Lafleur	13:09	Mtl.
May 21/78	Bos.	F	Bos. 4	Mtl. 3	Bobby Schmautz	6:22	Mtl.
Apr. 12/79	L.A.	PR	NYR 2	L.A. 1	Phil Esposito	6:11	NYR
Apr. 14/79	Buf.	PR	Pit. 4	Buf. 3	George Ferguson	0:47	Pit.
Apr. 16/79	Phi.	QF	Phi. 3	NYR 2	Ken Linseman	0:44	NYR
Apr. 18/79	NYI	QF	NYI 1	Chi. 0	Mike Bossy	2:31	NYI
Apr. 21/79	Tor.	QF	Mtl. 4	Tor. 3	Cam Connor	25:25	Mtl.
Apr. 22/79	Tor.	QF	Mtl. 5	Tor. 4	Larry Robinson	4:14	Mtl.
Apr. 28/79	NYI	SF	NYI 4	NYR 3	Denis Potvin	8:02	NYR
May 3/79	NY	SF	NYI 3	NYR 2	Bob Nystrom	3:40	NYR
May 3/79	Bos.	SF	Bos. 4	Mtl. 3	Jean Ratelle	3:46	Mtl.
May 10/79	Mtl.	SF	Mtl. 5	Bos. 4	Yvon Lambert	9:33	Mtl.
May 19/79	NY	F	Mtl. 4	NYR 3	Serge Savard	7:25	Mtl.
Apr. 8/80	NY	PR	NYR 2	Atl. 1	Steve Vickers	0:33	NYR
Apr. 8/80	Phi.	PR	Phi. 4	Edm. 3	Bobby Clarke	8:06	Phi.
Apr. 8/80	Chi.	PR	Chi. 3	St. L. 2	Doug Lecuyer	12:34	Chi.
Apr. 11/80	Hfd.	PR	Mtl. 4	Hfd. 3	Yvon Lambert	0:29	Mtl.
Apr. 11/80	Tor.	PR	Min. 4	Tor. 3	Al MacAdam	0:32	Min.
Apr. 11/80	L.A.	PR	NYI 4	L.A. 3	Ken Morrow	6:55	NYI
Apr. 11/80	Edm.	PR	Phi. 3	Edm. 2	Ken Linseman	23:56	Phi.
Apr. 16/80	Bos.	QF	NYI 2	Bos. 1	Clark Gillies	1:02	NYI
Apr. 17/80	Bos.	QF	NYI 5	Bos. 4	Bob Bourne	1:24	NYI
Apr. 21/80	NYI	QF	Bos. 4	NYI 3	Terry O'Reilly	17:13	NYI
May 1/80	Buf.	SF	NYI 2	Buf. 1	Bob Nystrom	21:20	NYI
May 13/80	Phi.	F	NYI 4	Phi. 3	Denis Potvin	4:07	NYI
May 24/80	NYI	F	NYI 5	Phi. 4	Bob Nystrom	7:11	NYI
Apr. 8/81	Buf.	PR	Buf. 3	Van. 2	Alan Haworth	5:00	Buf.
Apr. 8/81	Bos.	PR	Min. 5	Bos. 4	Steve Payne	3:34	Min.
Apr. 11/81	Chi.	PR	Cgy. 5	Chi. 4	Willi Plett	35:17	Cgy.
Apr. 12/81	Que.	PR	Que. 4	Phi. 3	Dale Hunter	0:37	Phi.
Apr. 14/81	St. L.	PR	St. L. 4	Pit. 3	Mike Crombeen	25:16	St. L.
Apr. 16/81	Buf.	QF	Min. 4	Buf. 3	Steve Payne	0:22	Min.
Apr. 20/81	Min.	QF	Buf. 5	Min. 4	Craig Ramsay	16:32	Min.
Apr. 20/81	Edm.	QF	NYI 5	Edm. 4	Ken Morrow	5:41	NYI
Apr. 7/82	Min.	DSF	Chi. 3	Min. 2	Greg Fox	3:34	Chi.
Apr. 8/82	Edm.	DSF	Edm. 3	L.A. 2	Wayne Gretzky	6:20	L.A.
Apr. 8/82	Van.	DSF	Van. 2	Cgy. 1	Dave Williams	14:20	Van.
Apr. 10/82	Pit.	DSF	Pit. 2	NYI 1	Rick Kehoe	4:14	NYI
Apr. 10/82	L.A.	DSF	L.A. 6	Edm. 5	Daryl Evans	2:35	L.A.
Apr. 13/82	Mtl.	DSF	Que. 3	Mtl. 2	Dale Hunter	0:22	Que.
Apr. 13/82	NYI	DSF	NYI 4	Pit. 3	John Tonelli	6:19	NYI
Apr. 16/82	Van.	DF	L.A. 3	Van. 2	Steve Bozek	4:33	Van.
Apr. 18/82	Que.	DF	Que. 3	Bos. 2	Wilf Paiement	11:44	Que.
Apr. 18/82	NY	DF	NYI 4	NYR 3	Bryan Trottier	3:00	NYI
Apr. 18/82	L.A.	DF	Van. 4	L.A. 3	Colin Campbell	1:23	Van.
Apr. 21/82	St. L.	DF	St. L. 3	Chi. 2	Bernie Federko	3:28	Chi.
Apr. 23/82	Que.	DF	Bos. 6	Que. 5	Peter McNab	10:54	Que.
Apr. 27/82	Chi.	CF	Van. 2	Chi. 1	Jim Nill	28:58	Van.
May 1/82	Que.	CF	NYI 5	Que. 4	Wayne Merrick	16:52	NYI
May 8/82	NYI	F	NYI 6	Van. 5	Mike Bossy	19:58	NYI
Apr. 5/83	Bos.	DSF	Bos. 4	Que. 3	Barry Pederson	1:46	Bos.
Apr. 6/83	Cgy.	DSF	Cgy. 4	Van. 3	Eddy Beers	12:27	Cgy.
Apr. 7/83	Min.	DSF	Min. 5	Tor. 4	Bobby Smith	5:03	Min.
Apr. 10/83	Tor.	DSF	Min. 5	Tor. 4	Dino Ciccarelli	8:05	Min.
Apr. 10/83	Van.	DSF	Cgy. 4	Van. 3	Greg Meredith	1:06	Cgy.
Apr. 18/83	Min.	DF	Chi. 4	Min. 3	Rich Preston	10:34	Chi.
Apr. 24/83	Bos.	DF	Bos. 3	Buf. 2	Brad Park	1:52	Bos.
Apr. 5/84	Edm.	DSF	Edm. 5	Wpg. 4	Randy Gregg	0:21	Edm.
Apr. 7/84	Det.	DSF	St. L. 4	Det. 3	Mark Reeds	37:07	St. L.
Apr. 8/84	Det.	DSF	St. L. 3	Det. 2	Jorgen Pettersson	2:42	St. L.
Apr. 10/84	NYI	DSF	NYI 3	NYR 2	Ken Morrow	8:56	NYI
Apr. 13/84	Min.	DF	St. L. 4	Min. 3	Doug Gilmour	16:16	Min.
Apr. 13/84	Edm.	DF	Cgy. 6	Edm. 5	Carey Wilson	3:42	Edm.
Apr. 13/84	NYI	DF	NYI 5	Wsh. 4	Anders Kallur	7:35	NYI
Apr. 16/84	Mtl.	DF	Que. 4	Mtl. 3	Bo Berglund	3:00	Mtl.
Apr. 20/84	Cgy.	DF	Cgy. 5	Edm. 4	Lanny McDonald	1:04	Edm.
Apr. 22/84	Min.	DF	Min. 4	St. L. 3	Steve Payne	6:00	Min.
Apr. 10/85	Phi.	DSF	Phi. 5	NYR 4	Mark Howe	8:01	Phi.
Apr. 10/85	Wsh.	DSF	Wsh. 4	NYI 3	Alan Haworth	2:28	NYI
Apr. 10/85	Edm.	DSF	Edm. 3	L.A. 2	Lee Fogolin	3:01	Edm.
Apr. 10/85	Wpg.	DSF	Wpg. 5	Cgy. 4	Brian Mullen	7:56	Wpg.
Apr. 11/85	Wsh.	DSF	Wsh. 2	NYI 1	Mike Gartner	21:23	NYI
Apr. 13/85	L.A.	DSF	Edm. 4	L.A. 3	Glenn Anderson	0:46	Edm.
Apr. 18/85	Mtl.	DF	Que. 2	Mtl. 1	Mark Kumpel	12:23	Que.
Apr. 23/85	Que.	DF	Que. 7	Mtl. 6	Dale Hunter	18:36	Que.
May 2/85	Mtl.	DF	Que. 3	Mtl. 2	Peter Stastny	2:22	Que.
Apr. 25/85	Min.	DF	Chi. 7	Min. 6	Darryl Sutter	21:57	Chi.
Apr. 28/85	Chi.	DF	Min. 5	Chi. 4	Dennis Maruk	1:14	Chi.
Apr. 30/85	Min.	DF	Chi. 6	Min. 5	Darryl Sutter	15:41	Chi.
May 5/85	Que.	CF	Que. 2	Phi. 1	Peter Stastny	6:20	Phi.
Apr. 9/86	Que.	DSF	Hfd. 3	Que. 2	Sylvain Turgeon	2:36	Hfd.
Apr. 12/86	Wpg.	DSF	Cgy. 4	Wpg. 3	Lanny McDonald	8:25	Cgy.
Apr. 17/86	Wsh.	DF	NYR 4	Wsh. 3	Brian MacLellan	1:16	NYR
Apr. 20/86	Edm.	DF	Edm. 6	Cgy. 5	Glenn Anderson	1:04	Cgy.

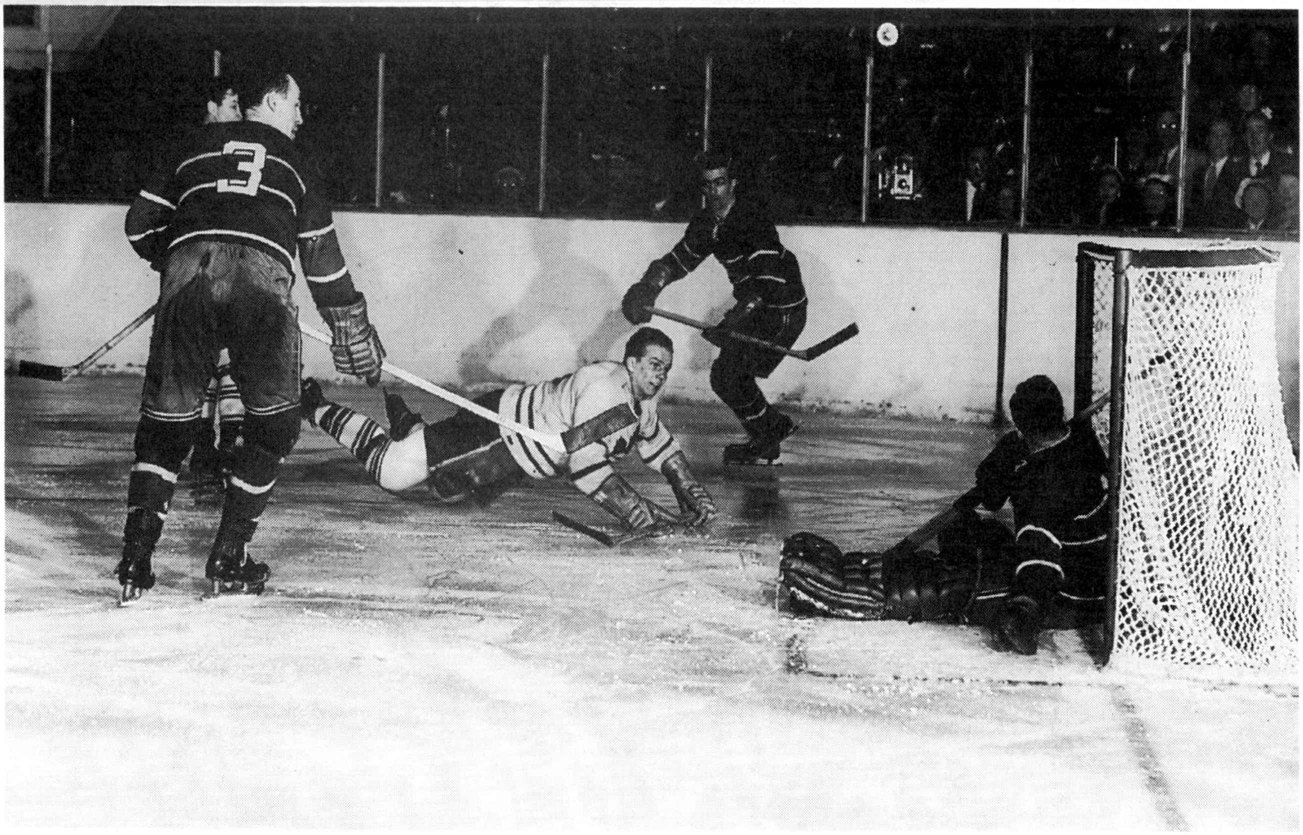

With Maple Leaf Gardens closing its doors to NHL hockey in February of 1999, this goal by Bill Barilko that ended the 1951 playoffs will remain the most famous image ever recorded in the Carlton Street Cathedral.

Date	City	Series	Score		Scorer	Overtime	Series Winner
Apr. 23/86	Hfd.	DF	Hfd. 2	Mtl. 1	Kevin Dineen	1:07	Mtl.
Apr. 23/86	NYR	DF	NYR 6	Wsh. 5	Bob Brooke	2:40	NYR
Apr. 26/86	St L.	DF	St L. 4	Tor. 3	Mark Reeds	7:11	St L.
Apr. 29/86	Mtl.	DF	Mtl. 2	Hfd. 1	Claude Lemieux	5:55	Mtl.
May 5/86	NYR	CF	Mtl. 4	NYR 3	Claude Lemieux	9:41	Mtl.
May 12/86	St L.	CF	St L. 6	Cgy. 5	Doug Wickenheiser	7:30	Cgy.
May 18/86	Cgy.	F	Mtl. 3	Cgy. 2	Brian Skrudland	0:09	Mtl.
Apr. 8/87	Hfd.	DSF	Hfd. 3	Que. 2	Paul MacDermid	2:20	Que.
Apr. 9/87	Mtl.	DSF	Mtl. 4	Bos. 3	Mats Naslund	2:38	Mtl.
Apr. 9/87	St. L.	DSF	Tor. 3	St. L. 2	Rick Lanz	10:17	Tor.
Apr. 11/87	Wpg.	DSF	Cgy. 3	Wpg. 2	Mike Bullard	3:53	Wpg.
Apr. 11/87	Chi.	DSF	Det. 4	Chi. 3	Shawn Burr	4:51	Det.
Apr. 16/87	Que.	DSF	Que. 5	Hfd. 4	Peter Stastny	6:05	Que.
Apr. 18/87	Wsh.	DSF	NYI 3	Wsh. 2	Pat LaFontaine	68:47	NYI
Apr. 21/87	Edm.	DF	Edm. 3	Wpg. 2	Glenn Anderson	0:36	Edm.
Apr. 26/87	Que.	DF	Mtl. 3	Que. 2	Mats Naslund	5:30	Mtl.
Apr. 27/87	Tor.	DF	Tor. 3	Det. 2	Mike Allison	9:31	Det.
May 4/87	Phi.	CF	Phi. 4	Mtl. 3	Ilkka Sinisalo	9:11	Phi.
May 20/87	Edm.	F	Edm. 3	Phi. 2	Jari Kurri	6:50	Edm.
Apr. 6/88	NYI	DSF	NYI 4	N.J. 3	Pat LaFontaine	6:11	N.J.
Apr. 10/88	Phi.	DSF	Phi. 5	Wsh. 4	Murray Craven	1:18	Wsh.
Apr. 10/88	N.J.	DSF	NYI 5	N.J. 4	Brent Sutter	15:07	N.J.
Apr. 10/88	Buf.	DSF	Buf. 6	Bos. 5	John Tucker	5:32	Bos.
Apr. 12/88	Det.	DSF	Tor. 6	Det. 5	Ed Olczyk	0:34	Det.
Apr. 16/88	Wsh.	DSF	Wsh. 5	Phi. 4	Dale Hunter	5:57	Wsh.
Apr. 21/88	Cgy.	DF	Edm. 5	Cgy. 4	Wayne Gretzky	7:54	Edm.
May 4/88	Bos.	CF	N.J. 3	Bos. 2	Doug Brown	17:46	Bos.
May 9/88	Det.	CF	Edm. 4	Det. 3	Jari Kurri	11:02	Edm.
Apr. 5/89	St. L.	DSF	St. L. 4	Min. 3	Brett Hull	11:55	St. L.
Apr. 5/89	Cgy.	DSF	Van. 4	Cgy. 3	Paul Reinhart	2:47	Cgy.
Apr. 6/89	St. L.	DSF	St. L. 4	Min. 3	Rick Meagher	5:30	St. L.
Apr. 6/89	Det.	DSF	Chi. 5	Det. 4	Duane Sutter	14:36	Chi.
Apr. 8/89	Hfd.	DSF	Mtl. 5	Hfd. 4	Stephane Richer	5:01	Mtl.
Apr. 8/89	Phi.	DSF	Wsh. 4	Phi. 3	Kelly Miller	0:51	Phi.
Apr. 9/89	Hfd.	DSF	Mtl. 4	Hfd. 3	Russ Courtnall	15:12	Mtl.
Apr. 15/89	Cgy.	DSF	Cgy. 4	Van. 3	Joel Otto	19:21	Cgy.
Apr. 18/89	Cgy.	DF	Cgy. 4	L.A. 3	Doug Gilmour	7:47	Cgy.
Apr. 19/89	Mtl.	DF	Mtl. 3	Bos. 2	Bobby Smith	12:24	Mtl.
Apr. 20/89	St. L.	DF	St. L. 5	Chi. 4	Tony Hrkac	33:49	Chi.
Apr. 21/89	Phi.	DF	Pit. 4	Phi. 3	Phil Bourque	12:08	Phi.
May 8/89	Chi.	CF	Cgy. 2	Chi. 1	Al MacInnis	15:05	Cgy.
May 9/89	Mtl.	CF	Phi. 2	Mtl. 1	Dave Poulin	5:02	Mtl.
May 19/89	Mtl.	F	Mtl. 4	Cgy. 3	Ryan Walter	38:08	Cgy.
Apr. 5/90	N.J.	DSF	Wsh. 5	N.J. 4	Dino Ciccarelli	5:34	Wsh.
Apr. 6/90	Edm.	DSF	Edm. 3	Wpg. 2	Mark Lamb	4:21	Edm.
Apr. 8/90	Tor.	DSF	St. L. 6	Tor. 5	Sergio Momesso	6:04	St. L.
Apr. 8/90	L.A.	DSF	L.A. 2	Cgy. 1	Tony Granato	8:37	L.A.
Apr. 9/90	Mtl.	DSF	Mtl. 2	Buf. 1	Brian Skrudland	12:35	Mtl.
Apr. 9/90	NYI	DSF	NYI 4	NYR 3	Brent Sutter	20:59	NYR
Apr. 10/90	Wpg.	DSF	Wpg. 4	Edm. 3	Dave Ellett	21:08	Edm.
Apr. 14/90	L.A.	DSF	L.A. 4	Cgy. 3	Mike Krushelnyski	23:14	L.A.
Apr. 15/90	Hfd.	DSF	Hfd. 3	Bos. 2	Kevin Dineen	12:30	Bos.
Apr. 21/90	Bos.	DF	Bos. 5	Mtl. 4	Garry Galley	3:42	Bos.
Apr. 24/90	L.A.	DF	Edm. 6	L.A. 5	Joe Murphy	4:42	Edm.
Apr. 25/90	Wsh.	DF	Wsh. 4	NYR 3	Rod Langway	0:34	Wsh.
Apr. 27/90	NYR	DF	Wsh. 2	NYR 1	John Druce	6:48	Wsh.
May 15/90	Bos.	F	Edm. 3	Bos. 2	Petr Klima	55:13	Edm.
Apr. 4/91	Chi.	DSF	Min. 4	Chi. 3	Brian Propp	4:14	Min.
Apr. 5/91	Pit.	DSF	Pit. 5	N.J. 4	Jaromir Jagr	8:52	Pit.
Apr. 6/91	L.A.	DSF	L.A. 3	Van. 2	Wayne Gretzky	11:08	L.A.
Apr. 8/91	Van.	DSF	Van. 2	L.A. 1	Cliff Ronning	3:12	L.A.
Apr. 11/91	NYR	DSF	Wsh. 5	NYR 4	Dino Ciccarelli	6:44	Wsh.
Apr. 11/91	Mtl.	DSF	Mtl. 4	Buf. 3	Russ Courtnall	5:56	Mtl.
Apr. 14/91	Edm.	DSF	Cgy. 2	Edm. 1	Theoren Fleury	4:40	Edm.
Apr. 16/91	Cgy.	DSF	Edm. 5	Cgy. 4	Esa Tikkanen	6:58	Edm.
Apr. 18/91	L.A.	DF	L.A. 4	Edm. 3	Luc Robitaille	2:13	Edm.
Apr. 19/91	Bos.	DF	Mtl. 4	Bos. 3	Stephane Richer	0:27	Bos.
Apr. 19/91	Pit.	DF	Pit. 7	Wsh. 6	Kevin Stevens	8:10	Pit.
Apr. 20/91	L.A.	DF	Edm. 4	L.A. 3	Petr Klima	24:48	Edm.
Apr. 22/91	Edm.	DF	Edm. 4	L.A. 3	Esa Tikkanen	20:48	Edm.
Apr. 27/91	Mtl.	DF	Mtl. 3	Bos. 2	Shayne Corson	17:47	Bos.
Apr. 28/91	Edm.	DF	Edm. 4	L.A. 3	Craig MacTavish	16:57	Edm.
May 3/91	Bos.	CF	Bos. 5	Pit. 4	Vladimir Ruzicka	8:14	Pit.
Apr. 21/92	Bos.	DSF	Bos. 3	Buf. 2	Adam Oates	11:14	Bos.
Apr. 22/92	Min.	DSF	Det. 5	Min. 4	Yves Racine	1:15	Det.
Apr. 22/92	St. L.	DSF	St. L. 5	Chi. 4	Brett Hull	23:33	Chi.
Apr. 25/92	Buf.	DSF	Bos. 5	Buf. 4	Ted Donato	2:08	Bos.
Apr. 28/92	Min.	DSF	Det. 1	Min. 0	Sergei Fedorov	16:13	Det.
Apr. 29/92	Hfd.	DSF	Hfd. 2	Mtl. 1	Yvon Corriveau	0:24	Mtl.
May 1/92	Mtl.	DSF	Mtl. 3	Hfd. 2	Russ Courtnall	25:26	Mtl.
May 3/92	Van.	DF	Edm. 4	Van. 3	Joe Murphy	8:36	Edm.
May 5/92	Mtl.	DF	Bos. 3	Mtl. 2	Peter Douris	3:12	Bos.
May 7/92	Pit.	DF	NYR 6	Pit. 5	Kris King	1:29	Pit.
May 9/92	Pit.	DF	Pit. 5	NYR 4	Ron Francis	2:47	Pit.
May 17/92	Pit.	CF	Pit. 4	Bos. 3	Jaromir Jagr	9:44	Pit.
May 20/92	Edm.	CF	Chi. 4	Edm. 3	Jeremy Roenick	2:45	Chi.
Apr. 18/93	Bos.	DSF	Buf. 5	Bos. 4	Bob Sweeney	11:03	Buf.
Apr. 18/93	Que.	DSF	Que. 3	Mtl. 2	Scott Young	16:49	Mtl.
Apr. 20/93	Wsh.	DSF	NYI 5	Wsh. 4	Brian Mullen	34:50	NYI
Apr. 22/93	Mtl.	DSF	Mtl. 2	Que. 1	Vincent Damphousse	10:30	Mtl.
Apr. 22/93	Buf.	DSF	Buf. 4	Bos. 3	Yuri Khmylev	1:05	Buf.
Apr. 22/93	NYI	DSF	NYI 4	Wsh. 3	Ray Ferraro	4:46	NYI
Apr. 24/93	Buf.	DSF	Buf. 6	Bos. 5	Brad May	4:48	Buf.
Apr. 24/93	NYI	DSF	NYI 4	Wsh. 3	Ray Ferraro	25:40	NYI
Apr. 25/93	St. L.	DSF	St. L. 4	Chi. 3	Craig Janney	10:43	St. L.
Apr. 26/93	Que.	DSF	Mtl. 5	Que. 4	Kirk Muller	8:17	Mtl.
Apr. 27/93	Det.	DSF	Tor. 5	Det. 4	Mike Foligno	2:05	Tor.
Apr. 27/93	Van.	DSF	Wpg. 4	Van. 3	Teemu Selanne	6:18	Van.
Apr. 29/93	Wpg.	DSF	Van. 4	Wpg. 3	Greg Adams	4:30	Van.
May 1/93	Det.	DSF	Tor. 4	Det. 3	Nikolai Borschevsky	2:35	Tor.
May 3/93	Tor.	DF	Tor. 2	St. L. 1	Doug Gilmour	23:16	Tor.
May 4/93	Mtl.	DF	Mtl. 4	Buf. 3	Guy Carbonneau	2:50	Mtl.

Date	City	Series	Score		Scorer	Overtime	Series Winner
May 5/93	Tor.	DF	St. L. 2	Tor. 1	Jeff Brown	23:03	Tor.
May 6/93	Buf.	DF	Mtl. 4	Buf. 3	Gilbert Dionne	8:28	Mtl.
May 8/93	Buf.	DF	Mtl. 4	Buf. 3	Kirk Muller	11:37	Mtl.
May 11/93	Van.	DF	L.A. 4	Van. 3	Gary Shuchuk	26:31	L.A.
May 14/93	Pit.	DF	NYI 4	Pit. 3	Dave Volek	5:16	NYI
May 18/93	Mtl.	CF	Mtl. 4	NYI 3	Stephan Lebeau	26:21	Mtl.
May 20/93	NYI	CF	Mtl. 2	NYI 1	Guy Carbonneau	12:34	Mtl.
May 25/93	Tor.	CF	Tor. 3	L.A. 2	Glenn Anderson	19:20	L.A.
May 27/93	L.A.	CF	L.A. 5	Tor. 4	Wayne Gretzky	1:41	L.A.
Jun. 3/93	Mtl.	F	Mtl. 3	L.A. 2	Eric Desjardins	0:51	Mtl.
Jun. 5/93	L.A.	F	Mtl. 4	L.A. 3	John LeClair	0:34	Mtl.
Jun. 7/93	L.A.	F	Mtl. 3	L.A. 2	John LeClair	14:37	Mtl.
Apr. 20/94	Tor.	CQF	Tor. 1	Chi. 0	Todd Gill	2:15	Tor.
Apr. 22/94	St. L.	CQF	Dal. 5	St. L. 4	Paul Cavallini	8:34	Dal.
Apr. 24/94	Chi.	CQF	Chi. 4	Tor. 3	Jeremy Roenick	1:23	Tor.
Apr. 25/94	Bos.	CQF	Mtl. 2	Bos. 1	Kirk Muller	17:18	Bos.
Apr. 26/94	Cgy.	CQF	Van. 2	Cgy. 1	Geoff Courtnall	7:15	Van.
Apr. 27/94	Buf.	CQF	Buf. 1	N.J. 0	Dave Hannan	65:43	N.J.
Apr. 28/94	Van.	CQF	Van. 3	Cgy. 2	Trevor Linden	16:43	Van.
Apr. 30/94	Cgy.	CQF	Van. 4	Cgy. 3	Pavel Bure	22:20	Van.
May 3/94	N.J.	CSF	Bos. 6	N.J. 5	Don Sweeney	9:08	N.J.
May 7/94	Bos.	CSF	N.J. 5	Bos. 4	Stephane Richer	14:19	N.J.
May 8/94	Van.	CSF	Van. 2	Dal. 1	Sergio Momesso	11:01	Van.
May 12/94	Tor.	CSF	Tor. 3	S.J. 2	Mike Gartner	8:53	Tor.
May 15/94	NYR	CF	N.J. 4	NYR 3	Stephane Richer	35:23	NYR
May 16/94	Tor.	CF	Tor. 3	Van. 2	Peter Zezel	16:55	Van.
May 19/94	N.J.	CF	NYR 3	N.J. 2	Stephane Matteau	26:13	NYR
May 24/94	Van.	CF	Van. 4	Tor. 3	Greg Adams	20:14	Van.
May 27/94	NYR	CF	NYR 2	N.J. 1	Stephane Matteau	24:24	NYR
May 31/94	NYR	F	Van. 3	NYR 2	Greg Adams	19:26	NYR
May 7/95	Phi.	CQF	Phi. 4	Buf. 3	Karl Dykhuis	10:06	Phi.
May 9/95	Cgy.	CQF	S.J. 5	Cgy. 4	Ulf Dahlen	12:21	S.J.
May 12/95	NYR	CQF	NYR 3	Que. 2	Steve Larmer	8:09	NYR
May 12/95	N.J.	CQF	N.J. 1	Bos. 0	Randy McKay	8:51	N.J.
May 14/95	Pit.	CQF	Pit. 6	Wsh. 5	Luc Robitaille	4:30	Pit.
May 15/95	St. L.	CQF	Van. 6	St. L. 5	Cliff Ronning	1:48	Van.
May 17/95	Tor.	CQF	Tor. 5	Chi. 4	Randy Wood	10:00	Chi.
May 19/95	Cgy.	CQF	S.J. 5	Cgy. 4	Ray Whitney	21:54	S.J.
May 21/95	Phi.	CSF	Phi. 5	NYR 4	Eric Desjardins	7:03	Phi.
May 21/95	Chi.	CSF	Chi. 2	Van. 1	Joe Murphy	9:04	Chi.
May 22/95	Phi.	CSF	Phi. 4	NYR 3	Kevin Haller	0:25	Phi.
May 25/95	Van.	CSF	Chi. 3	Van. 2	Chris Chelios	6:22	Chi.
May 26/95	N.J.	CSF	N.J. 2	Pit. 1	Neal Broten	18:36	N.J.
May 27/95	Van.	CSF	Chi. 4	Van. 3	Chris Chelios	5:35	Chi.
Jun. 1/95	Det.	CF	Det. 2	Chi. 1	Nicklas Lidstrom	1:01	Det.
Jun. 6/95	Chi.	CF	Det. 4	Chi. 3	Vladimir Konstantinov	29:25	Det.
Jun. 7/95	N.J.	CF	Phi. 3	N.J. 2	Eric Lindros	4:19	N.J.
Jun. 11/95	Det.	CF	Det. 2	Chi. 1	Vyacheslav Kozlov	22:25	Det.
Apr. 16/96	NYR	CQF	Mtl. 3	NYR 2	Vincent Damphousse	5:04	NYR
Apr. 18/96	Tor.	CQF	Tor. 5	St. L. 4	Mats Sundin	4:02	St. L.
Apr. 18/96	Phi.	CQF	T.B. 2	Phi. 1	Brian Bellows	9:05	Phi.
Apr. 21/96	St. L.	CQF	St. L. 3	Tor. 2	Glenn Anderson	1:24	St. L.
Apr. 21/96	T.B.	CQF	T.B. 5	Phi. 4	Alexander Selivanov	2:04	Phi.
Apr. 23/96	Cgy.	CQF	Chi. 2	Cgy. 1	Joe Murphy	50:02	Chi.
Apr. 24/96	Wsh.	CQF	Pit. 3	Wsh. 2	Petr Nedved	79:15	Pit.
Apr. 25/96	Col.	CQF	Col. 5	Van. 4	Joe Sakic	0:51	Col.
Apr. 25/96	Tor.	CQF	Tor. 5	St. L. 4	Mike Gartner	7:31	St. L.
May 2/96	Col.	CSF	Chi. 3	Col. 2	Jeremy Roenick	6:29	Col.
May 6/96	Chi.	CSF	Chi. 4	Col. 3	Sergei Krivokrasov	0:46	Col.
May 8/96	St. L.	CSF	St. L. 5	Det. 4	Igor Kravchuk	3:23	Det.
May 8/96	Chi.	CSF	Col. 3	Chi. 2	Joe Sakic	44:33	Col.
May 9/96	Fla.	CSF	Fla. 4	Phi. 3	Dave Lowry	4:06	Fla.
May 12/96	Phi.	CSF	Fla. 2	Phi. 1	Mike Hough	28:05	Fla.
May 13/96	Chi.	CSF	Col. 4	Chi. 3	Sandis Ozolinsh	25:18	Col.
May 16/96	Det.	CSF	Det. 1	St. L. 0	Steve Yzerman	21:15	Det.
May 19/96	Det.	CF	Col. 3	Det. 2	Mike Keane	17:31	Col.
Jun. 10/96	Fla.	F	Col. 1	Fla. 0	Uwe Krupp	44:31	Col.
Apr. 20/97	Chi.	CQF	Chi. 4	Col. 3	Sergei Krivokrasov	31:03	Col.
Apr. 20/97	Edm.	CQF	Edm. 4	Dal. 3	Kelly Buchberger	9:15	Edm.
Apr. 22/97	NYR	CQF	NYR 4	Fla. 3	Esa Tikkanen	16:29	NYR
Apr. 23/97	Ott.	CQF	Ott. 1	Buf. 0	Daniel Alfredsson	2:34	Buf.
Apr. 24/97	Mtl.	CQF	Mtl. 4	N.J. 3	Patrice Brisebois	47:37	N.J.
Apr. 25/97	Fla.	CQF	NYR 3	Fla. 2	Esa Tikkanen	12:02	NYR
Apr. 25/97	Dal.	CQF	Edm. 1	Dal. 0	Ryan Smyth	20:22	Edm.
Apr. 27/97	Phx.	CQF	Ana. 3	Phx. 2	Paul Kariya	7:29	Ana.
Apr. 29/97	Buf.	CQF	Buf. 3	Ott. 2	Derek Plante	5:24	Buf.
Apr. 29/97	Dal.	CQF	Edm. 4	Dal. 3	Todd Marchant	12:26	Edm.
May 2/97	Det.	CSF	Det. 2	Ana. 1	Martin Lapointe	0:59	Det.
May 4/97	Det.	CSF	Det. 3	Ana. 2	Vyacheslav Kozlov	41:31	Det.
May 8/97	Ana.	CSF	Det. 3	Ana. 2	Brendan Shanahan	37:03	Det.
May 9/97	Phi.	CSF	Buf. 5	Phi. 4	Ed Ronan	6:24	Phi.
May 9/97	Edm.	CSF	Col. 3	Edm. 2	Claude Lemieux	8:35	Col.
May 11/97	N.J.	CSF	NYR 2	N.J. 1	Adam Graves	14:08	NYR
Apr. 22/98	N.J.	CQF	OTT. 2	N.J. 1	Bruce Gardiner	5:58	Ott.
Apr. 23/98	Pit.	CQF	Mtl. 3	Pit. 2	Benoit Brunet	18:43	Mtl.
Apr. 24/98	Wsh.	CQF	Bos. 4	Wsh. 3	Darren Van Impe	20:54	Wsh.
Apr. 26/98	Ott.	CQF	Ott. 2	N.J. 1	Alexei Yashin	2:47	Ott.
Apr. 26/98	Bos.	CQF	Wsh. 3	Bos. 2	Joe Juneau	26:31	Wsh.
Apr. 26/98	Edm.	CQF	Col. 5	Edm. 4	Joe Sakic	15:25	Edm.
Apr. 28/98	S.J.	CQF	S.J. 1	Dal. 0	Andrei Zyuzin	6:31	Dal.
May 1/98	Phi.	CQF	Buf. 3	Phi. 2	Michal Grosek	5:40	Buf.
May 2/98	S.J.	CQF	Dal. 3	S.J. 2	Mike Keane	3:43	Dal.
May 3/98	Bos.	CQF	Wsh. 3	Bos. 2	Brian Bellows	15:24	Wsh.
May 3/98	Buf.	CSF	Buf. 3	Mtl. 2	Geoff Sanderson	2:37	Buf.
May 11/98	Edm.	CSF	Dal. 1	Edm. 0	Benoit Hogue	13:07	Dal.
May 12/98	Mtl.	CSF	Buf. 5	Mtl. 4	Michael Peca	21:24	Buf.
May 12/98	St.L.	CSF	Det. 3	St.L. 2	Brendan Shanahan	31:12	Det.
May 25/98	Wsh.	CF	Wsh. 3	Buf. 2	Todd Krygier	3:01	Wsh.
May 28/98	Buf.	CF	Wsh. 4	Buf. 3	Peter Bondra	9:37	Wsh.
Jun. 3/98	Dal.	CF	Dal. 3	Det. 2	Jamie Langenbrunner	0:46	Det.
Jun. 4/98	Buf.	CF	Wsh. 3	Buf. 2	Joe Juneau	6:24	Wsh.
Jun. 11/98	Det.	F	Det. 5	Wsh. 4	Kris Draper	15:24	Det.

NHL Playoff Coaching Records

Coach	Team	Games Coached	Wins	Losses	Ties	%Wins	Playoff Years	Cup Wins	Career
Abel, Sid	Chicago	7	3	4	0	.429	1		
	Detroit	69	29	40	0	.420	8		
	Total	**76**	**32**	**44**	**0**	**.421**	**9**		**1952-76**
Adams, Jack	**Detroit**	**105**	**52**	**52**	**1**	**.500**	**15**	**3**	**1922-47**
Allen, Keith	**Philadelphia**	**11**	**3**	**8**	**0**	**.273**	**2**		**1967-69**
Arbour, Al	St. Louis	11	4	7	0	.364	1		
	NY Islanders	198	119	79	0	.601	15	4	
	Total	**209**	**123**	**86**	**0**	**.589**	**16**	**4**	**1970-94**
Berenson, Red	**St. Louis**	**14**	**5**	**9**	**0**	**.357**	**2**		**1979-82**
Bergeron, Michel	**Quebec**	**68**	**31**	**37**	**0**	**.456**	**7**		**1980-90**
Berry, Bob	Los Angeles	10	2	8	0	.200	3		
	Montreal	8	2	6	0	.250	2		
	St. Louis	15	7	8	0	.467	2		
	Total	**33**	**11**	**22**	**0**	**.333**	**7**		**1978-94**
Beverley, Nick	**Toronto**	**6**	**2**	**4**	**0**	**.333**	**1**		**1995-96**
Blackburn, Don	**Hartford**	**3**	**0**	**3**	**0**	**.000**	**1**		**1979-81**
Blair, Wren	**Minnesota**	**14**	**7**	**7**	**0**	**.500**	**1**		**1967-70**
Blake, Toe	**Montreal**	**119**	**82**	**37**	**0**	**.689**	**13**	**8**	**1955-68**
Boileau, Marc	**Pittsburgh**	**9**	**5**	**4**	**0**	**.556**	**1**		**1973-76**
Boivin, Leo	**St. Louis**	**3**	**1**	**2**	**0**	**.333**	**1**		**1975-78**
Boucher, Frank	**NY Rangers**	**27**	**13**	**14**	**0**	**.481**	**4**	**1**	**1939-54**
Boucher, George	**Mtl. Maroons**	**2**	**0**	**2**	**0**	**.000**	**1**		**1930-50**
Bowman, Scotty	St. Louis	52	26	26	0	.500	4		
	Montreal	98	70	28	0	.714	8	5	
	Buffalo	36	18	18	0	.500	5		
	Pittsburgh	33	23	10	0	.697	2	1	
	Detroit	86	57	29	0	.663	5	2	
	Total	**305**	**194**	**111**	**0**	**.636**	**24**	**8**	**1967-98**
Bowness, Rick	**Boston**	**15**	**8**	**7**	**0**	**.533**	**1**		**1988-98**
Brooks, Herb	NY Rangers	24	12	12	0	.500	3		
	New Jersey	5	1	4	0	.200	1		
	Total	**29**	**13**	**16**	**0**	**.448**	**4**		**1981-93**
Brophy, John	**Toronto**	**19**	**9**	**10**	**0**	**.474**	**2**		**1986-89**
Burns, Charlie	**Minnesota**	**6**	**2**	**4**	**0**	**.333**	**1**		**1969-75**
Burns, Pat	Montreal	56	30	26	0	.536	4		
	Toronto	46	23	23	0	.500	3		
	Boston	6	2	4	0	.333	1		
	Total	**108**	**55**	**53**	**0**	**.509**	**8**		**1988-98**
Campbell, Colin	**NY Rangers**	**36**	**18**	**18**	**0**	**.500**	**3**		**1994-98**
Caroll, Dick	**Toronto**	**9**	**4**	**5**	**0**	**.444**	**2**	**1**	**1917-21**
Carpenter, Doug	**Toronto**	**5**	**1**	**4**	**0**	**.200**	**1**		**1984-91**
Cheevers, Gerry	**Boston**	**34**	**15**	**19**	**0**	**.441**	**4**		**1980-85**
Cherry, Don	**Boston**	**55**	**31**	**24**	**0**	**.564**	**5**		**1974-80**
Clancy, King	**Toronto**	**19**	**3**	**16**	**0**	**.158**	**4**		**1937-72**
Clapper, Dit	**Boston**	**25**	**8**	**17**	**0**	**.320**	**4**		**1945-49**
Cleghorn, Odie	**Pittsburgh**	**4**	**1**	**2**	**1**	**.375**	**2**		**1925-29**
Cleghorn, Sprague	**Mtl. Maroons**	**4**	**1**	**1**	**2**	**.500**	**1**		**1931-32**
Constantine, Kevin	San Jose	25	11	14	0	.440	2		
	Pittsburgh	6	2	4	0	.333	1		
	Total	**31**	**13**	**18**	**0**	**.419**	**3**		**1993-98**
Crawford, Marc	Quebec	6	2	4	0	.333	1		
	Colorado	46	29	17	0	.630	3	1	
	Total	**52**	**31**	**21**	**0**	**.596**	**4**	**1**	**1994-98**
Creighton, Fred	**Atlanta**	**9**	**2**	**7**	**0**	**.222**	**4**		**1974-80**
Crisp, Terry	Calgary	37	22	15	0	.595	3	1	
	Tampa Bay	6	2	4	0	.333	1		
	Total	**43**	**24**	**19**	**0**	**.558**	**4**	**1**	**1987-98**
Crozier, Joe	**Buffalo**	**6**	**2**	**4**	**0**	**.333**	**1**		**1971-81**
Cunniff, John	**New Jersey**	**6**	**2**	**4**	**0**	**.333**	**1**		**1982-91**
Dandurand, Leo	**Montreal**	**16**	**10**	**6**	**0**	**.625**	**4**	**1**	**1921-35**
Day, Hap	**Toronto**	**80**	**49**	**31**	**0**	**.613**	**9**	**5**	**1940-50**
Demers, Jacques	St. Louis	33	16	17	0	.485	3		
	Detroit	38	20	18	0	.526	3		
	Montreal	27	19	8	0	.704	2	1	
	Total	**98**	**55**	**43**	**0**	**.561**	**8**	**1**	**1979-98**
Denneny, Cy	**Boston**	**5**	**5**	**0**	**0**	**1.000**	**1**	**1**	**1928-33**
Dudley, Rick	**Buffalo**	**12**	**4**	**8**	**0**	**.333**	**2**		**1989-92**
Dugal, Jules	**Montreal**	**3**	**1**	**2**	**0**	**.333**	**1**		**1938-39**
Duncan, Art	**Toronto**	**2**	**0**	**1**	**1**	**.250**	**1**	**1**	**1926-32**
Dutton, Red	**NY Americans**	**16**	**6**	**10**	**0**	**.375**	**4**		**1935-42**
Esposito, Phil	**NY Rangers**	**10**	**2**	**8**	**0**	**.200**	**2**		**1986-89**
Evans, Jack	**Hartford**	**16**	**8**	**8**	**0**	**.500**	**2**		**1975-88**
Ferguson, John	**Winnipeg**	**3**	**0**	**3**	**0**	**.000**	**1**		**1975-86**
Francis, Emile	NY Rangers	75	34	41	0	.453	9		
	St. Louis	14	5	9	0	.357	2		
	Total	**89**	**39**	**50**	**0**	**.438**	**11**		**1965-83**
Ftorek, Robbie	**Los Angeles**	**16**	**5**	**11**	**0**	**.313**	**2**		**1987-89**
Gainey, Bob	Minnesota	30	17	13	0	.567	2		
	Dallas	14	6	8	0	.429	2		
	Total	**44**	**23**	**21**	**0**	**.523**	**4**		**1990-96**
Geoffrion, Bernie	**Atlanta**	**4**	**0**	**4**	**0**	**.000**	**1**		**1968-80**
Gerard, Eddie	**Mtl. Maroons**	**25**	**11**	**9**	**5**	**.540**	**5**	**1**	**1917-35**
Gill, David	**Ottawa**	**8**	**3**	**2**	**3**	**.563**	**2**	**1**	**1926-29**
Glover, Fred	**Oakland**	**11**	**3**	**8**	**0**	**.273**	**2**		**1968-74**
Gordon, Jackie	**Minnesota**	**25**	**11**	**14**	**0**	**.440**	**3**		**1970-75**
Goring, Butch	**Boston**	**3**	**0**	**3**	**0**	**.000**	**1**		**1985-87**
Gorman, Tommy	NY Americans	2	0	1	1	.250	1		
	Chicago	8	6	1	1	.813	1	1	
	Mtl. Maroons	15	7	6	2	.533	3	1	
	Total	**25**	**13**	**8**	**4**	**.600**	**5**	**2**	**1925-38**
Gottselig, Johnny	**Chicago**	**4**	**0**	**4**	**0**	**.000**	**1**		**1944-48**
Green, Pete	**Ottawa**	**26**	**14**	**9**	**3**	**.596**	**6**	**3**	**1919-26**
Green, Ted	**Edmonton**	**16**	**8**	**8**	**0**	**.500**	**1**		**1991-94**
Guidolin, Bep	**Boston**	**21**	**11**	**10**	**0**	**.524**	**2**		**1972-76**
Harris, Ted	**Minnesota**	**2**	**0**	**2**	**0**	**.000**	**1**		**1975-78**
Hart, Cecil	**Montreal**	**37**	**16**	**17**	**4**	**.486**	**8**	**2**	**1926-39**
Hartsburg, Craig	**Chicago**	**16**	**8**	**8**	**0**	**.500**	**2**		**1995-98**
Harvey, Doug	**NY Rangers**	**6**	**2**	**4**	**0**	**.333**	**1**		**1961-62**
Hay, Don	**Phoenix**	**7**	**3**	**4**	**0**	**.429**	**1**		**1996-97**
Henning, Lorne	**Minnesota**	**5**	**2**	**3**	**0**	**.400**	**1**		**1985-95**
Hitchcock, Ken	**Dallas**	**24**	**13**	**11**	**0**	**.542**	**2**		**1995-98**
Holmgren, Paul	**Philadelphia**	**19**	**10**	**9**	**0**	**.526**	**1**		**1988-96**
Imlach, Punch	**Toronto**	**92**	**44**	**48**	**0**	**.478**	**11**	**4**	**1958-80**
Inglis, Bill	**Buffalo**	**3**	**1**	**2**	**0**	**.333**	**1**		**1978-79**
Irvin, Dick	Chicago	9	5	3	1	.611	1		
	Toronto	66	33	32	1	.508	9	1	
	Montreal	115	62	53	0	.539	14	3	
	Total	**190**	**100**	**88**	**2**	**.532**	**24**	**4**	**1930-56**
Ivan, Tommy	**Detroit**	**67**	**36**	**31**	**0**	**.537**	**7**	**3**	**1947-58**
Johnson, Bob	Calgary	52	25	27	0	.481	5		
	Pittsburgh	24	16	8	0	.667	1	1	
	Total	**76**	**41**	**35**	**0**	**.539**	**6**	**1**	**1982-91**
Johnson, Tom	**Boston**	**22**	**15**	**7**	**0**	**.682**	**2**	**1**	**1970-73**
Johnston, Eddie	Chicago	7	3	4	0	.429	1		
	Pittsburgh	46	22	24	0	.478	5		
	Total	**53**	**25**	**28**	**0**	**.472**	**6**		**1979-97**
Kasper, Steve	**Boston**	**5**	**1**	**4**	**0**	**.200**	**1**		**1995-97**
Keenan, Mike	Philadelphia	57	32	25	0	.561	4		
	Chicago	60	33	27	0	.550	4		
	NY Rangers	23	16	7	0	.696	1	1	
	St. Louis	20	10	10	0	.500	2		
	Total	**160**	**91**	**69**	**0**	**.569**	**11**	**1**	**1984-98**
Kelly, Pat	**Colorado**	**2**	**0**	**2**	**0**	**.000**	**1**		**1977-79**
Kelly, Red	Los Angeles	18	7	11	0	.389	2		
	Pittsburgh	14	6	8	0	.429	2		
	Toronto	30	11	19	0	.367	4		
	Total	**62**	**24**	**38**	**0**	**.387**	**8**		**1967-77**
King, Dave	**Calgary**	**20**	**8**	**12**	**0**	**.400**	**3**		**1992-95**
Kromm, Bobby	**Detroit**	**7**	**3**	**4**	**0**	**.429**	**1**		**1977-80**
Lalonde, Newsy	Montreal	16	7	6	3	.531	4		
	Ottawa	2	0	1	1	.250	1		
	Total	**18**	**7**	**7**	**4**	**.500**	**5**		**1917-35**
Lemaire, Jacques	Montreal	27	15	12	0	.556	2		
	New Jersey	56	34	22	0	.607	4	1	
	Total	**83**	**49**	**34**	**0**	**.590**	**6**	**1**	**1983-98**
Ley, Rick	Hartford	13	5	8	0	.385	2		
	Vancouver	11	4	7	0	.364	1		
	Total	**24**	**9**	**15**	**0**	**.375**	**3**		**1989-96**
Long, Barry	**Winnipeg**	**11**	**3**	**8**	**0**	**.273**	**2**		**1983-86**
Loughlin, Clem	**Chicago**	**4**	**1**	**2**	**1**	**.375**	**2**		**1934-37**
Low, Ron	**Edmonton**	**24**	**10**	**14**	**0**	**.417**	**2**		**1994-98**
MacLean, Doug	**Florida**	**27**	**13**	**14**	**0**	**.481**	**2**		**1995-98**
MacNeil, Al	Montreal	20	12	8	0	.600	1	1	
	Atlanta	4	1	3	0	.250	1		
	Calgary	19	9	10	0	.474	2		
	Total	**43**	**22**	**21**	**0**	**.512**	**4**	**1**	**1970-82**
Magnuson, Keith	**Chicago**	**3**	**0**	**3**	**0**	**.000**	**1**		**1980-82**
Mahoney, Bill	**Minnesota**	**16**	**7**	**9**	**0**	**.438**	**1**		**1983-85**
Maloney, Dan	Toronto	10	6	4	0	.600	1		
	Winnipeg	15	5	10	0	.333	2		
	Total	**25**	**11**	**14**	**0**	**.440**	**3**		**1984-89**
Maloney, Phil	**Vancouver**	**7**	**1**	**6**	**0**	**.143**	**2**		**1973-77**
Martin, Jacques	St. Louis	16	7	9	0	.438	2		
	Ottawa	18	8	10	0	.444	2		
	Total	**34**	**15**	**19**	**0**	**.441**	**4**		**1986-98**
McCammon, Bob	Philadelphia	10	1	9	0	.100	3		
	Vancouver	7	3	4	0	.429	1		
	Total	**17**	**4**	**13**	**0**	**.235**	**4**		**1978-91**
McLellan, John	**Toronto**	**6**	**2**	**4**	**0**	**.333**	**1**		**1969-73**
McVie, Tom	**New Jersey**	**14**	**6**	**8**	**0**	**.429**	**2**		**1975-92**
Melrose, Barry	**Los Angeles**	**24**	**13**	**11**	**0**	**.542**	**1**		**1992-95**
Milbury, Mike	**Boston**	**40**	**23**	**17**	**0**	**.575**	**2**		**1989-98**
Muckler, John	Edmonton	40	25	15	0	.625	2	1	
	Buffalo	27	11	16	0	.407	4		
	Total	**67**	**36**	**31**	**0**	**.537**	**6**	**1**	**1968-98**
Muldoon, Pete	**Chicago**	**2**	**0**	**1**	**1**	**.250**	**1**		**1926-27**
Munro, Dunc	**Mtl. Maroons**	**4**	**1**	**3**	**0**	**.250**	**1**		**1929-31**
Murdoch, Bob	**Winnipeg**	**7**	**3**	**4**	**0**	**.429**	**1**		**1989-91**
Murphy, Mike	**Los Angeles**	**5**	**1**	**4**	**0**	**.200**	**1**		**1986-98**
Murray, Bryan	Washington	53	24	29	0	.453	7		
	Detroit	25	10	15	0	.400	3		
	Total	**78**	**34**	**44**	**0**	**.436**	**10**		**1981-98**
Murray, Terry	Washington	39	18	21	0	.462	4		
	Philadelphia	46	28	18	0	.609	3		
	Total	**85**	**46**	**39**	**0**	**.541**	**7**		**1989-97**
Neale, Harry	**Vancouver**	**14**	**3**	**11**	**0**	**.214**	**4**		**1978-86**
Neilson, Roger	Toronto	19	8	11	0	.421	2		
	Buffalo	8	4	4	0	.500	1		
	Vancouver	21	12	9	0	.571	2		
	NY Rangers	29	13	16	0	.448	3		
	Philadelphia	5	1	4	0	.200	1		
	Total	**82**	**38**	**44**	**0**	**.463**	**9**		**1977-98**
Nolan, Ted	**Buffalo**	**12**	**5**	**7**	**0**	**.417**	**1**		**1995-97**
Nykoluk, Mike	**Toronto**	**7**	**1**	**6**	**0**	**.143**	**2**		**1980-84**
O'Reilly, Terry	**Boston**	**37**	**17**	**19**	**1**	**.473**	**3**		**1986-89**
Oliver, Murray	**Minnesota**	**13**	**5**	**8**	**0**	**.385**	**2**		**1981-83**

Coach	Team	Games Coached	Wins	Losses	Ties	%Wins	Playoff Years	Cup Wins	Career
Paddock, John	Winnipeg	13	5	8	0	.385	2		1991-95
Page, Pierre	Minnesota	12	4	8	0	.333	2		
	Quebec	6	2	4	0	.333	1		
	Calgary	4	0	4	0	.000	1		
	Total	22	6	16	0	.273	4		1988-98
Patrick, Craig	NY Rangers	17	7	10	0	.412	2		
	Pittsburgh	5	1	4	0	.200	1		
	Total	22	8	14	0	.364	3		1980-97
Patrick, Frank	Boston	6	2	4	0	.333	2		1934-36
Patrick, Lester	NY Rangers	65	32	26	7	.546	12	2	1926-39
Patrick, Lynn	NY Rangers	12	7	5	0	.583	1		
	Boston	28	9	18	1	.339	4		
	Total	40	16	23	1	.413	5		1948-76
Perron, Jean	Montreal	48	30	18	0	.625	3	1	1985-89
Perry, Don	Los Angeles	10	4	6	0	.400	1		1981-84
Pilous, Rudy	Chicago	41	19	22	0	.463	5	1	1957-63
Plager, Barclay	St. Louis	4	1	3	0	.250	1		1977-83
Pleau, Larry	Hartford	10	2	8	0	.200	2		1980-89
Polano, Nick	Detroit	7	1	6	0	.143	2		1982-85
Powers, Eddie	Toronto	9	4	4	1	.500	2	1	1921-26
Primeau, Joe	Toronto	15	8	6	1	.567	2	1	1950-53
Pronovost, Marcel	Buffalo	8	3	5	0	.375	1		1977-79
Pulford, Bob	Los Angeles	26	10	16	0	.385	4		
	Chicago	50	18	32	0	.360	7		
	Total	76	28	48	0	.368	11		1972-88
Quenneville, Joel	St. Louis	16	8	8	0	.500	2		1996-98
Quinn, Pat	Philadelphia	39	22	17	0	.564	3		
	Los Angeles	3	0	3	0	.000	1		
	Vancouver	61	31	30	0	.508	5		
	Total	103	53	50	0	.515	9		1978-96
Reay, Billy	Chicago	116	56	60	0	.483	12		1957-77
Risebrough, Doug	Calgary	7	3	4	0	.429	1		1990-92
Roberts, Jim	Hartford	7	3	4	0	.429	1		1981-97
Robinson, Larry	Los Angeles	4	0	4	0	.000	1		1995-98
Ross, Art	Boston	65	27	33	5	.454	11	1	1917-45
Ruel, Claude	Montreal	27	18	9	0	.667	3	2	1968-81
Ruff, Lindy	Buffalo	15	10	5	0	.667	1		1997-98
Sather, Glen	Edmonton	127	89	37	1	.705	10	4	1979-94
Sator, Ted	NY Rangers	16	8	8	0	.500	1		
	Buffalo	11	3	8	0	.273	2		
	Total	27	11	16	0	.407	3		1985-89
Schinkel, Ken	Pittsburgh	6	2	4	0	.333	2		1972-77
Schmidt, Milt	Boston	34	15	19	0	.441	4		1954-76
Schoenfeld, Jim	New Jersey	20	11	9	0	.550	1		
	Washington	24	10	14	0	.417	3		
	Phoenix	6	2	4	0	.333	1		
	Total	50	23	27	0	.460	5		1985-98
Shero, Fred	Philadelphia	83	48	35	0	.578	6	2	
	NY Rangers	27	15	12	0	.556	2		
	Total	110	63	47	0	.573	8	2	1971-81
Simpson, Terry	NY Islanders	20	9	11	0	.450	2		
	Winnipeg	6	2	4	0	.333	1		
	Total	26	11	15	0	.423	3		1986-96
Sinden, Harry	Boston	43	24	19	0	.558	5	1	1966-85
Skinner, Jimmy	Detroit	26	14	12	0	.538	3	1	1954-58
Smith, Alf	Ottawa	5	1	4	0	.200	1		1918-19
Smith, Floyd	Buffalo	32	16	16	0	.500	3		1971-80
Smythe, Conn	Toronto	4	2	2	0	.500	1		1927-31
Sonmor, Glen	Minnesota	43	25	18	0	.581	3		1978-87
Stasiuk, Vic	Philadelphia	4	0	4	0	.000	1		1969-73
Stewart, Bill	Chicago	10	7	3	0	.700	1	1	1937-39
Stewart, Ron	Los Angeles	2	0	2	0	.000	1		1975-78
Sutter, Brian	St. Louis	41	20	21	0	.488	4		
	Boston	22	7	15	0	.318	3		
	Total	63	27	36	0	.429	7		1988-98
Sutter, Darryl	Chicago	26	11	15	0	.423	3		
	San Jose	6	2	4	0	.333	1		
	Total	32	13	19	0	.406	4		1992-98
Talbot, Jean-Guy	St. Louis	5	1	4	0	.200	1		
	NY Rangers	3	1	2	0	.333	1		
	Total	8	2	6	0	.250	2		1972-78
Tessier, Orval	Chicago	18	9	9	0	.500	2		1982-85
Thompson, Paul	Chicago	19	7	12	0	.368	4		1938-45
Tobin, Bill	Chicago	4	1	2	1	.375	2		1929-32
Tremblay, Mario	Montreal	11	3	8	0	.273	2		1995-97
Ubriaco, Gene	Pittsburgh	11	7	4	0	.636	1		1988-90
Vigneault, Alain	Montreal	10	4	6	0	.400	1		1997-98
Watson, Phil	NY Rangers	16	4	12	0	.250	3		1955-63
Watt, Tom	Winnipeg	7	1	6	0	.143	2		
	Vancouver	3	0	3	0	.000	1		
	Total	10	1	9	0	.100	3		1981-92
Webster, Tom	Los Angeles	28	12	16	0	.429	3		1986-92
Weiland, Cooney	Boston	17	10	7	0	.588	2	1	1939-41
White, Bill	Chicago	2	0	2	0	.000	1		1976-77
Wilson, Johnny	Pittsburgh	12	4	8	0	.333	2		1969-80
Wilson, Ron	Anaheim	11	4	7	0	.364	1		
	Washington	21	12	9	0	.571	1		
	Total	32	16	16	0	.500	2		1993-98
Young, Garry	St. Louis	2	0	2	0	.000	1		1972-76

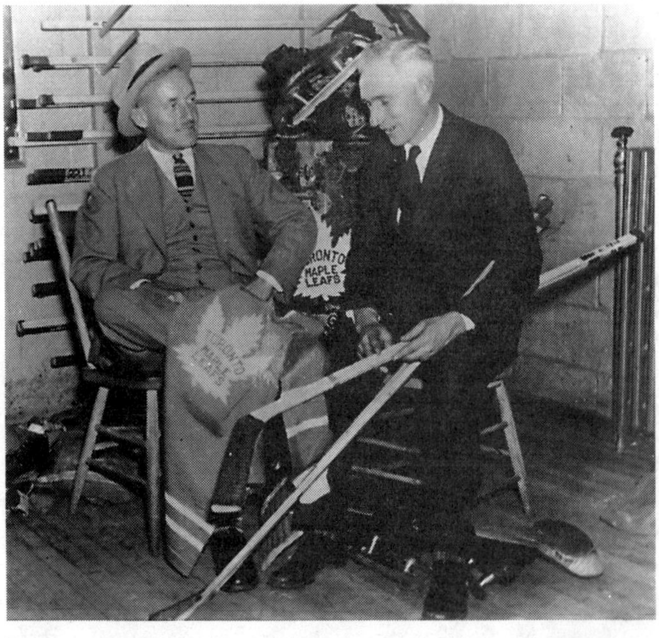

The "I" Formation: Dick Irvin Sr. (photo above, at right) chats with Conn Smythe, the manager/owner of the Maple Leafs. Irvin was the first coach to pilot three different teams (Chicago, Toronto and Montreal) into the Stanley Cup finals. Right: Coach Tommy Ivan won three Stanley Cup titles with the Detroit Red Wings before taking on the task of rebuilding the Chicago Black Hawks in the mid-1950s.

Penalty Shots in Stanley Cup Playoff Games

Date	Player	Goaltender	Scored	Final Score	Series
Mar. 25/37	Lionel Conacher, Mtl. Maroons	Tiny Thompson, Boston	No	Mtl. M. 0 at Bos. 4	QF
Apr. 15/37	Alex Shibicky, NY Rangers	Earl Robertson, Detroit	No	NYR 0 at Det. 3	F
Apr. 13/44	Virgil Johnson, Chicago	Bill Durnan, Montreal	No	Chi. 4 at Mtl. 5*	F
Apr. 9/68	Wayne Connelly, Minnesota	Terry Sawchuk, Los Angeles	Yes	L.A. 5 at Min. 7	QF
Apr. 27/68	Jim Roberts, St. Louis	Cesare Maniago, Minnesota	No	St. L. 4 at Min. 3	SF
May 16/71	Frank Mahovlich, Montreal	Tony Esposito, Chicago	No	Chi. 3 at Mtl. 4	F
May 7/75	Bill Barber, Philadelphia	Glenn Resch, NY Islanders	No	Phi. 3 at NYI 4*	SF
Apr. 20/79	Mike Walton, Chicago	Glenn Resch, NY Islanders	No	NYI 4 at Chi. 0	QF
Apr. 9/81	Peter McNab, Boston	Don Beaupre, Minnesota	No	Min. 5 at Bos. 4*	PR
Apr. 17/81	Anders Hedberg, NY Rangers	Mike Liut, St. Louis	Yes	NYR 6 at St. L. 4	QF
Apr. 9/83	Denis Potvin, NY Islanders	Pat Riggin, Washington	No	NYI 6 at Wsh. 2	DSF
Apr. 28/84	Wayne Gretzky, Edmonton	Don Beaupre, Minnesota	Yes	Edm. 8 at Min. 5	CF
May 1/84	Mats Naslund, Montreal	Billy Smith, NY Islanders	No	Mtl. 1 at NYI 3	CF
Apr. 14/85	Bob Carpenter, Washington	Billy Smith, NY Islanders	No	Wsh. 4 at NYI. 6	DF
May 28/85	Ron Sutter, Philadelphia	Grant Fuhr, Edmonton	No	Phi. 3 at Edm. 5	F
May 30/85	Dave Poulin, Philadelphia	Grant Fuhr, Edmonton	No	Phi. 3 at Edm. 8	F
Apr. 9/88	John Tucker, Buffalo	Andy Moog, Boston	Yes	Bos. 2 at Buf. 6	DSF
Apr. 9/88	Petr Klima, Detroit	Allan Bester, Toronto	Yes	Det. 6 at Tor. 3	DSF
Apr. 8/89	Neal Broten, Minnesota	Greg Millen, St. Louis	Yes	St. L. 5 at Min. 3	DSF
Apr. 4/90	Al MacInnis, Calgary	Kelly Hrudey, Los Angeles	Yes	L.A. 5 at Cgy. 3	DSF
Apr. 5/90	Randy Wood, NY Islanders	Mike Richter, NY Rangers	No	NYI 1 at NYR 2	DSF
May 3/90	Kelly Miller, Washington	Andy Moog, Boston	No	Wsh. 3 at Bos. 5	CF
May 18/90	Petr Klima, Edmonton	Rejean Lemelin, Boston	No	Edm. 7 at Bos. 2	F
Apr. 6/91	Basil McRae, Minnesota	Ed Belfour, Chicago	Yes	Min. 2 at Chi. 5	DSF
Apr. 10/91	Steve Duchesne, Los Angeles	Kirk McLean, Vancouver	Yes	L.A. 6 at Van. 1	DSF
May 11/92	Jaromir Jagr, Pittsburgh	John Vanbiesbrouck, NYR	Yes	Pit. 3 at NYR 2	DF
May 13/92	Shawn McEachern, Pittsburgh	John Vanbiesbrouck, NYR	No	NYR 1 at Pit. 5	DF
June 7/94	Pavel Bure, Vancouver	Mike Richter, NYR	No	NYR 4 at Van. 2	F
May 9/95	Patrick Poulin, Chicago	Felix Potvin, Toronto	No	Tor. 3 at Chi. 0	CQF
May 10/95	Michal Pivonka, Washington	Tom Barrasso, Pittsburgh	No	Pit. 2 at Wsh. 6	CQF
Apr. 24/96	Joe Juneau, Washington	Ken Wregget, Pittsburgh	No	Pit. 3 at Wsh. 2**	CQF
May 11/97	Eric Lindros, Philadelphia	Steve Shields, Buffalo	Yes	Phi. 6 at Buf. 3	CSF
Apr. 23/98	Alexei Morozov, Pittsburgh	Andy Moog, Montreal	No	Mtl. 3 at Pit. 2**	CQF

* Game was decided in overtime, but shot taken during regulation time.
** Shot taken in overtime.

John Vanbiesbrouck, above, was the second goaltender to face two penalty shots in the same playoff series. During the Rangers' 1992 post-season showdown with the Pittsburgh Penguins, the "Beezer" stopped Shawn McEachern but was beaten by Jaromir Jagr. Pittsburgh rookie Alexei Morozov, below, was the only player to be awarded a penalty shot in the 1998 playoffs. In the opening game of the Pittsburgh-Montreal series, Morozov was stopped by veteran goaltender Andy Moog who, despite having a year remaining on his contract, chose to annouce his retirement after the 1998 playoffs.

Ten Longest Overtime Games

Date	City	Series	Score		Scorer	Overtime	Series Winner
Mar. 24/36	Mtl.	SF	Det. 1	Mtl. M. 0	Mud Bruneteau	116:30	Det.
Apr. 3/33	Tor.	SF	Tor. 1	Bos. 0	Ken Doraty	104:46	Tor.
Apr. 24/96	Wsh.	CQF	Pit. 3	Wsh. 2	Petr Nedved	79:15	Pit.
Mar. 23/43	Det.	SF	Tor. 3	Det. 2	Jack McLean	70:18	Det.
Mar. 28/30	Mtl.	SF	Mtl. 2	NYR 1	Gus Rivers	68:52	Mtl.
Apr. 18/87	Wsh.	DSF	NYI 3	Wsh. 2	Pat LaFontaine	68:47	NYI
Apr. 27/94	Buf.	CQF	Buf. 1	N.J. 0	Dave Hannan	65:43	N.J.
Mar. 27/51	Det.	SF	Mtl. 3	Det. 2	Maurice Richard	61:09	Mtl.
Mar. 27/38	NY	QF	NYA 3	NYR 2	Lorne Carr	60:40	NYA
Mar. 26/32	Mtl.	SF	NYR 4	Mtl. 3	Fred Cook	59:32	NYR

Overtime Record of Current Teams

(Listed by number of OT games played)

	Overall				Home					Road				
Team	GP	W	L	T	GP	W	L	T	Last OT Game	GP	W	L	T	Last OT Game
Montreal	120	69	49	2	55	36	18	1	May 12/98	65	33	31	1	May 8/98
Boston	96	37	56	3	45	20	24	1	May 3/98	51	17	32	2	Apr. 24/98
Toronto	90	46	43	1	57	30	26	1	Apr. 25/96	33	16	17	0	Apr. 21/96
NY Rangers	63	30	33	0	27	12	15	0	Apr. 22/97	36	18	18	0	May 11/97
Chicago	62	30	30	2	30	16	13	1	Apr. 20/97	32	14	17	1	May 2/96
Detroit	63	31	32	0	38	16	22	0	Jun. 11/98	25	15	10	0	Jun. 3/98
Philadelphia	44	22	22	0	20	11	9	0	May 1/98	24	11	13	0	May 9/96
NY Islanders	38	29	9	0	17	14	3	0	May 20/93	21	15	6	0	May 18/93
St. Louis	39	21	18	0	20	15	5	0	May 12/98	19	6	13	0	May 16/96
Buffalo	37	19	18	0	21	13	8	0	Jun. 4/98	16	6	10	0	May 25/98
* Dallas	35	15	20	0	17	6	11	0	Jun. 3/98	18	9	9	0	May 11/98
Edmonton	33	20	13	0	18	10	8	0	May 11/98	15	10	5	0	Apr. 29/97
Los Angeles	30	12	18	0	16	8	8	0	Jun. 7/93	14	4	10	0	Jun. 3/93
** Calgary	30	11	19	0	14	4	10	0	Apr. 23/96	16	7	9	0	Apr. 28/94
Vancouver	29	13	16	0	12	5	7	0	May 27/95	17	8	9	0	Apr. 25/96
*** Colorado	29	17	12	0	13	7	6	0	May 2/96	16	10	6	0	Apr. 26/98
Washington	26	13	13	0	10	5	5	0	May 25/98	16	8	8	0	Jun. 11/98
Pittsburgh	18	10	8	0	10	6	4	0	Apr. 23/98	8	4	4	0	Apr. 24/96
**** New Jersey	19	5	14	0	9	2	7	0	Apr. 22/98	10	3	7	0	Apr. 26/98
***** Carolina	11	5	6	0	7	4	3	0	Apr. 29/92	4	1	3	0	May 1/92
Phoenix	10	4	6	0	6	2	4	0	Apr. 27/97	4	2	2	0	Apr. 27/93
Florida	5	2	3	0	3	1	2	0	Apr. 25/97	2	1	1	0	Apr. 22/97
Anaheim	4	1	3	0	1	0	1	0	May 8/97	3	1	2	0	May 4/97
San Jose	5	3	2	0	2	1	1	0	May 2/98	3	2	1	0	May 19/95
Tampa Bay	2	2	0	0	1	1	0	0	Apr. 21/96	1	1	0	0	Apr. 18/96
Ottawa	2	2	0	0	1	1	0	0	Apr. 26/98	1	1	0	0	Apr. 22/98

*Totals include those of Minnesota 1967-93.
**Totals include those of Atlanta 1972-80.
***Totals include those of Quebec 1979-95.
****Totals include those of Kansas City and Colorado 1974-82.
*****Totals include those of Hartford 1979-97.

Notes

Key to Player and Goaltender Registers

Demographics: Position, shooting side (catching hand for goaltenders), height, weight, place and date of birth are found on first line. Draft information, if any, is located on second line.

Major Junior, NCAA, minor pro, senior European and NHL clubs form a permanent part of each player's data panel. If a player sees action with more than one club in any of the above categories, a separate line is included for each one.

High school, prep school, Tier II junior, European junior and U.S. junior listings are deleted if a player accumulates two or more years of Major Junior or senior European experience.

Olympic Team statistics are also listed.

Some data is unavailable at press time. Readers are encouraged to contribute.

See page 5 for contact names and addresses.

Player's NHL organization as of September 5, 1998. This includes players under contract, unsigned draft choices and other players on reserve lists. Free agents as of September 5, 1998 show a blank here.

The complete career data panels of players with NHL experience who announced their retirement before the start of the 1998-99 season are included in the 1998-99 Player Register. These newly-retired players also show a blank here.

Each NHL club's minor-pro affiliates are listed at the bottom of this page.

All-star team selections and awards are listed below player's year-by-year data.

PLAYER, JOHN SAMPLE (PLAY-uhr) **PHX.**

Center. Shoots left. 6'1", 200 lbs. Born, Moncton, N.B., April 14, 1974.
(Pittsburgh's 3rd choice, 62nd overall in the 1992 Entry Draft).

			Regular Season					Playoffs				
Season	**Club**	**League**	**GP**	**G**	**A**	**TP**	**PIM**	**GP**	**G**	**A**	**TP**	**PIM**
1992-93	Brandon	WHL	66	15	13	28	17	4	3	1	4	6
1993-94	Brandon	WHL	72	36	30	66	72	12	4	5	9	12
1994-95	Brandon	WHL	70	47	59	106	83	16	*16	8	*24	14
1995-96	**Pittsburgh**	**NHL**	**10**	**1**	**2**	**3**	**6**	....	....	....	....	....
	Cleveland	IHL	64	31	22	53	71	5	3	2	5	8
1996-97	**Montreal**	**NHL**	**24**	**7**	**6**	**13**	**42**	**1**	**0**	**0**	**0**	**0**
	Fredericton	AHL	47	41	31	72	106	....	....	....	....	....
1997-98	**Detroit**	**NHL**	**68**	**27**	**35**	**62**	**88**	**14**	**4**	**6**	**10**	**12** ♦
	NHL Totals		**102**	**35**	**43**	**78**	**136**	**15**	**4**	**6**	**10**	**12**

WHL East Second All-Star Team (1995) • Won Stafford Smythe Trophy (Memorial Cup MVP) (1995)

Played in NHL All-Star Game (1998)

Traded to **Montreal** by **Pittsburgh** for Montreal's third round choice (Yuri Leftovski) in 1997 Entry Draft, June 14, 1996. Traded to **Detroit** by **Montreal** for Bill Winger, June 17, 1997. Signed as a free agent by **Phoenix**, August 23, 1998.

Asterisk (*) indicates league leader in this statistical category.

Member of Stanley Cup-winning team.

All trades, free agent signings and other transactions involving NHL clubs are listed in chronological order. First draft selection for players who re-enter the NHL Entry Draft is noted here. Other special notes are also listed here. These are highlighted with a bullet (•).

NHL All-Star Game appearances are listed above trade notes.

Free agent signing dates are based on when the player's contract is filed with NHL Central Registry. This date often differs from the date when the club announces that it has come to terms with a free agent.

NHL Clubs and Minor-League Affiliates 1998-99

NHL Club	Minor League Affiliate
Anaheim	Cincinnati Mighty Ducks (AHL) Huntington Blizzard (ECHL)
Boston	Providence Bruins (AHL) Greenville Grrrowl (ECHL)
Buffalo	Rochester Americans (AHL) South Carolina Stingrays (ECHL)
Calgary	Saint John Flames (AHL) Johnstown Chiefs (ECHL)
Carolina	The Beast of New Haven (AHL) Florida Everblades (ECHL)
Chicago	Indianapolis Ice (IHL)
Colorado	Hershey Bears (AHL)
Dallas	Michigan K-Wings (IHL)
Detroit	Adirondack Red Wings (AHL) Toledo Storm (ECHL)
Edmonton	Hamilton Bulldogs (AHL) New Orleans Brass (ECHL)
Florida	The Beast of New Haven (AHL) Fort Wayne Komets (IHL) Miami Matadors (ECHL) Port Huron Border Cats (UHL)
Los Angeles	Springfield Falcons (AHL) Long Beach Ice Dogs (IHL)
Montreal	Fredericton Canadiens (AHL) New Orleans Brass (ECHL)
Nashville	Milwaukee Admirals (IHL) Hampton Roads Admirals (ECHL)
New Jersey	Albany River Rats (AHL) Augusta Lynx (ECHL)
NY Islanders	Lowell Lock Monsters (AHL)
NY Rangers	Hartford Wolf Pack (AHL)
Ottawa	Detroit Vipers (IHL)
Philadelphia	Philadelphia Phantoms (AHL)
Phoenix	Springfield Falcons (AHL) Las Vegas Thunder (IHL) Mississippi Sea Wolves (ECHL)
Pittsburgh	Syracuse Crunch (AHL) Wheeling Nailers (ECHL)
St. Louis	Worcester IceCats (AHL) Peoria Rivermen (ECHL)
San Jose	Kentucky Thoroughblades (AHL) Richmond Renegades (ECHL)
Tampa Bay	Cleveland Lumberjacks (IHL) Chesapeake Icebreakers (ECHL)
Toronto	St. John's Maple Leafs (AHL)
Vancouver	Syracuse Crunch (AHL)
Washington	Portland Pirates (AHL) Hampton Roads Admirals (ECHL)

Pronunciation of Player Names

United Press International phonetic style.

AY	long A as in mate
A	short A as in cat
AI	nasal A as on air
AH	short A as in father
AW	broad A as in talk
EE	long E as in meat
EH	short E as in get
UH	hollow E as in "the"
AY	French long E with acute accent as in Pathe
IH	middle E as in pretty
EW	EW dipthong as in few
IGH	long I as in time
EE	French long I as in machine
IH	short I as in pity
OH	long O as in note
AH	short O as in hot
AW	broad O as in fought
OI	OI dipthong as in noise
OO	long double OO as in fool
UH	short double O as in ouch
OW	OW dipthong as in how
EW	long U as in mule
OO	long U as in rule
U	middle U as in put
UH	short U as in shut or hurt
K	hard C as in cat
S	soft C as in cease
SH	soft CH as in machine
CH	hard CH or TCH as in catch
Z	hard S as in bells
S	soft S as in sun
G	hard G as in gang
J	soft G as in general
ZH	soft J as in French version of Joliet
KH	gutteral CH as in Scottish version of Loch

Late Additions to Player and Goaltender Registers

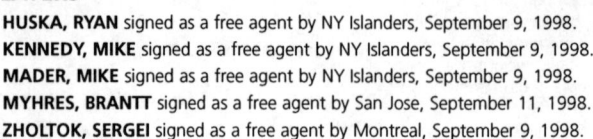

IRWIN, RICHARD — VAN.

Right wing. Shoots left. 6'3", 219 lbs. Born, Toronto, Ont., August 31, 1977.

			Regular Season					Playoffs				
Season	**Club**	**Lea**	**GP**	**G**	**A**	**TP**	**PIM**	**GP**	**G**	**A**	**TP**	**PIM**
1997-98	Raleigh	ECHL	54	5	4	9	225	....	....	....	....	....
	Syracuse	AHL	5	0	0	0	2	....	....	....	....	....

Signed as a free agent by **Vancouver**, April 8, 1998.

O'CONNOR, TOM — PIT.

Defense. Shoots left. 6'2", 190 lbs. Born, Springfield, MA, January 9, 1976.
(Pittsburgh's 6th choice, 102nd overall, in 1994 Entry Draft).

			Regular Season					Playoffs				
Season	**Club**	**Lea**	**GP**	**G**	**A**	**TP**	**PIM**	**GP**	**G**	**A**	**TP**	**PIM**
1993-94	Springfield	NEJHL	36	4	15	19	73	....	....	....	....	....
1994-95	U. Mass-Amherst	H.E.	34	1	2	3	44	....	....	....	....	....
1995-96	U. Mass-Amherst	H.E.	35	2	4	6	48	....	....	....	....	....
1996-97	U. Mass-Amherst	H.E.	30	3	8	11	42	....	....	....	....	....
1997-98	U. Mass-Amherst	H.E.	33	2	16	18	30	....	....	....	....	....

PANKEWICZ, GREG — (PAN-kuh-wihts) CGY.

Right wing. Shoots right. 6', 185 lbs. Born, Drayton Valley, Alta., November 6, 1970.

			Regular Season					Playoffs				
Season	**Club**	**Lea**	**GP**	**G**	**A**	**TP**	**PIM**	**GP**	**G**	**A**	**TP**	**PIM**
1989-90	Regina	WHL	63	14	24	38	136	10	1	3	4	19
1990-91	Regina	WHL	72	39	41	80	134	8	4	7	11	12
1991-92	Knoxville	ECHL	59	41	39	80	214	....	....	....	....	....
1992-93	New Haven	AHL	62	23	20	43	163	....	....	....	....	....
1993-94	**Ottawa**	**NHL**	**3**	**0**	**0**	**0**	**2**	....	....	....	....	....
	P.E.I.	AHL	69	33	29	62	241	....	....	....	....	....
1994-95	P.E.I.	AHL	75	37	30	67	161	6	1	1	2	24
1995-96	Portland	AHL	28	9	12	21	99	....	....	....	....	....
	Chicago	IHL	45	9	16	25	164	5	4	0	4	8
1996-97	Manitoba	IHL	79	32	34	66	222	....	....	....	....	....
1997-98	Manitoba	IHL	76	42	34	76	246	3	0	0	0	6
	NHL Totals		**3**	**0**	**0**	**0**	**2**	....	....	....	....	....

Signed as a free agent by **Ottawa**, May 27, 1993. Signed as a free agent by **Calgary**, September 1, 1998.

SHELLEY, JODY — CGY.

Left wing. Shoots left. 6'3", 228 lbs. Born, Yarmouth, N.S., February 7, 1976.

			Regular Season					Playoffs				
Season	**Club**	**Lea**	**GP**	**G**	**A**	**TP**	**PIM**	**GP**	**G**	**A**	**TP**	**PIM**
1994-95	Halifax	QMJHL	72	10	12	22	194	7	0	1	1	12
1995-96	Halifax	QMJHL	50	13	19	32	319	6	0	2	2	36
1996-97	Halifax	QMJHL	58	25	19	44	448	17	6	6	12	123
1997-98	Dalhousie	AUAA	19	6	11	17	145	....	....	....	....	....
	Saint John	AHL	18	1	1	2	50	....	....	....	....	....

Signed as a free agent by **Calgary**, September 1, 1998.

Free Agent Signings

PLAYERS

HUSKA, RYAN signed as a free agent by NY Islanders, September 9, 1998.

KENNEDY, MIKE signed as a free agent by NY Islanders, September 9, 1998.

MADER, MIKE signed as a free agent by NY Islanders, September 9, 1998.

MYHRES, BRANTT signed as a free agent by San Jose, September 11, 1998.

ZHOLTOK, SERGEI signed as a free agent by Montreal, September 9, 1998.

GOALTENDERS

RACINE, BRUCE signed as a free agent by San Jose, September 8, 1998.

VALIQUETTE, STEPHEN signed as a free agent by NY Islanders, September 9, 1998.

1998-99 Player Register

Note: The 1998-99 Player Register lists forwards and defensemen only. Goaltenders are listed separately. The Player Register lists every skater who appeared in an NHL game in the 1997-98 season, every skater drafted in the first six rounds of the 1998 Entry Draft, players on NHL Reserve Lists and other players. Trades and roster changes are current as of September 5, 1998.

Abbreviations: A – assists; **G** – goals; **GP** – games played; **Lea** – league; **PIM** – penalties in minutes; **TP** – total points; * – league-leading total; ♦ – member of Stanley Cup-winning team.

Pronunciations courtesy of the NHL Broadcasters' Association and Igor Kuperman, Phoenix Coyotes

Goaltender Register begins on page 449.

LEAGUES:

ACHL	Atlantic Coast Hockey League
AHL	American Hockey League
AJHL	Alberta Junior Hockey League
Alpen.	Alpenliga
AMHA	Alberta Minor Hockey Association
AUAA	Atlantic Universities Athletic Association
BCJHL	British Columbia Junior Hockey League
CCHA	Central Collegiate Hockey Association
CHL	Central Hockey League
CIAU	Canadian Interuniversity Athletic Union
CIS	Commonwealth of Independent States (former USSR)
COJHL	Central Ontario Junior Hockey League
ColHL	Colonial Hockey League
CWUAA	Canada West Universities Athletic Association
ECAC	Eastern Collegiate Athletic Conference
ECHL	East Coast Hockey League
EJHL	Eastern Junior Hockey League
EuroHL	European Hockey League
G.N.	Great Northern
GPAC	Great Plains Athletic Conference
H.E.	Hockey East
H.S.	High School
IHL	International Hockey League
Jr.	Junior
MJHA	(New York) Metropolitan Junior Hockey Association
MJHL	Manitoba Junior Hockey League
NAJHL	North American Junior Hockey League
Nat-Tm	National Team
NCAA	National Collegiate Athletic Association
NCHA	Northern Collegiate Hockey Association
NEJHL	New England Junior Hockey League
NHL	**National Hockey League**
OHA	Ontario Hockey Association
OHL	Ontario Hockey League
OJHL	Ontario Junior Hockey Leagues
OUAA	Ontario Universities Athletic Association
QAAA	Quebec Amateur Athletic Association
QJHL	Quebec Junior Hockey League
QMJHL	Quebec Major Junior Hockey League
RMJHL	Rocky Mountain Junior Hockey League
SJHL	Saskatchewan Junior Hockey League
SOHL	Southern Ontario Hockey League
UHL	United Hockey League
USHL	United States Hockey League (Junior A)
WCHA	Western Collegiate Hockey Association
WCHL	West Coast Hockey League
WPHL	Western Professional Hockey League
WHA	World Hockey Association
WHL	Western Hockey League

AALTO, ANTTI (AL-toh, AN-tee) ANA.

Center. Shoots left. 6'2", 195 lbs. Born, Lappeenranta, Finland, March 4, 1975.
(Anaheim's 6th choice, 134th overall, in 1993 Entry Draft).

			Regular Season					Playoffs				
Season	**Club**	**Lea**	**GP**	**G**	**A**	**TP**	**PIM**	**GP**	**G**	**A**	**TP**	**PIM**
1991-92	SaiPa	Finland-2	20	6	6	12	20	....	....	....	....	....
1992-93	SaiPa	Finland-2	23	6	8	14	14	....	....	....	....	....
	TPS Turku	Finland	1	0	0	0	0	....	....	....	....	....
1993-94	TPS Turku	Finland	33	5	9	14	16	10	1	1	2	4
1994-95	TPS Turku	Finland	44	11	7	18	18	5	0	1	1	2
1995-96	TPS Turku	Finland	40	15	16	31	22	11	3	5	8	14
	Kiekko	Finland-2	2	0	2	2	2	....	....	....	....	....
1996-97	TPS Turku	Finland	44	15	19	34	60	11	5	6	11	31
1997-98	**Anaheim**	**NHL**	**3**	**0**	**0**	**0**	**0**	....	....	....	....	....
	Cincinnati	AHL	29	4	9	13	30	....	....	....	....	....
	NHL Totals		**3**	**0**	**0**	**0**	**0**	....	....	....	....	....

ABID, RAMZI (a-BIHD, RAM-zee) COL.

Left wing. Shoots left. 6'2", 195 lbs. Born, Montreal, Que., March 24, 1980.
(Colorado's 5th choice, 28th overall, in 1998 Entry Draft).

			Regular Season					Playoffs				
Season	**Club**	**Lea**	**GP**	**G**	**A**	**TP**	**PIM**	**GP**	**G**	**A**	**TP**	**PIM**
1996-97	Chicoutimi	QMJHL	65	13	24	37	141	21	2	12	14	28
1997-98	Chicoutimi	QMJHL	68	50	*85	*135	266	6	3	4	7	10

QMJHL First All-Star Team (1998)

ABRAHAMSSON, ELIAS (AH-brah-ham-suhn, eh-LEE-ahs) BOS.

Defense. Shoots left. 6'3", 240 lbs. Born, Uppsala, Sweden, June 15, 1977.
(Boston's 6th choice, 132nd overall, in 1996 Entry Draft).

			Regular Season					Playoffs				
Season	**Club**	**Lea**	**GP**	**G**	**A**	**TP**	**PIM**	**GP**	**G**	**A**	**TP**	**PIM**
1994-95	Halifax	QMJHL	25	0	3	3	41	....	....	....	....	....
1995-96	Halifax	QMJHL	64	3	11	14	268	6	2	2	4	8
1996-97	Halifax	QMJHL	30	4	10	14	231	18	4	9	13	74
1997-98	Providence	AHL	29	0	1	1	47	....	....	....	....	....

ADAMS, CRAIG CAR.

Right wing. Shoots right. 6', 200 lbs. Born, Calgary, Alta., April 26, 1977.
(Hartford's 9th choice, 223rd overall, in 1996 Entry Draft).

			Regular Season					Playoffs				
Season	**Club**	**Lea**	**GP**	**G**	**A**	**TP**	**PIM**	**GP**	**G**	**A**	**TP**	**PIM**
1995-96	Harvard	ECAC	34	8	9	17	56	....	....	....	....	....
1996-97	Harvard	ECAC	32	6	4	10	36	....	....	....	....	....
1997-98	Harvard	ECAC	12	6	6	12	12	....	....	....	....	....

Rights transferred to **Carolina** after **Hartford** franchise relocated, June 25, 1997.

ADAMS, GREG A. PHX.

Left wing. Shoots left. 6'3", 195 lbs. Born, Nelson, B.C., August 15, 1963.

			Regular Season					Playoffs				
Season	**Club**	**Lea**	**GP**	**G**	**A**	**TP**	**PIM**	**GP**	**G**	**A**	**TP**	**PIM**
1981-82	Kelowna	BCJHL	45	31	42	73	24	....	....	....	....	....
1982-83	North Arizona	NCAA	29	14	21	35	19	....	....	....	....	....
1983-84	North Arizona	NCAA	26	44	29	73	34	....	....	....	....	....
1984-85	**New Jersey**	**NHL**	**36**	**12**	**9**	**21**	**14**	....	....	....	....	....
	Maine	AHL	41	15	20	35	12	11	3	4	7	0
1985-86	**New Jersey**	**NHL**	**78**	**35**	**42**	**77**	**30**	....	....	....	....	....
1986-87	**New Jersey**	**NHL**	**72**	**20**	**27**	**47**	**19**	....	....	....	....	....
1987-88	**Vancouver**	**NHL**	**80**	**36**	**40**	**76**	**30**	....	....	....	....	....
1988-89	**Vancouver**	**NHL**	**61**	**19**	**14**	**33**	**24**	**7**	**2**	**3**	**5**	**2**
1989-90	**Vancouver**	**NHL**	**65**	**30**	**20**	**50**	**18**	....	....	....	....	....
1990-91	**Vancouver**	**NHL**	**55**	**21**	**24**	**45**	**10**	**5**	**0**	**0**	**0**	**2**
1991-92	**Vancouver**	**NHL**	**76**	**30**	**27**	**57**	**26**	**6**	**0**	**2**	**2**	**4**
1992-93	**Vancouver**	**NHL**	**53**	**25**	**31**	**56**	**14**	**12**	**7**	**6**	**13**	**6**
1993-94	**Vancouver**	**NHL**	**68**	**13**	**24**	**37**	**20**	**23**	**6**	**8**	**14**	**2**
1994-95	**Vancouver**	**NHL**	**31**	**5**	**10**	**15**	**12**	....	....	....	....	....
	Dallas	**NHL**	**12**	**3**	**3**	**6**	**4**	**5**	**2**	**0**	**2**	**0**
1995-96	**Dallas**	**NHL**	**66**	**22**	**21**	**43**	**33**	....	....	....	....	....
1996-97	**Dallas**	**NHL**	**50**	**21**	**15**	**36**	**2**	**3**	**0**	**1**	**1**	**0**
1997-98	**Dallas**	**NHL**	**49**	**14**	**18**	**32**	**20**	**12**	**2**	**2**	**4**	**0**
	NHL Totals		**852**	**306**	**325**	**631**	**276**	**73**	**19**	**22**	**41**	**16**

Played in NHL All-Star Game (1988)

Signed as a free agent by **New Jersey**, June 25, 1984. Traded to **Vancouver** by **New Jersey** with Kirk McLean and New Jersey's 2nd round choice (Leif Rohlin) in 1988 Entry Draft for Patrik Sundstrom and Vancouver's 2nd (Jeff Christian) and 4th (Matt Ruchty) round choices in 1988 Entry Draft, September 10, 1987. Traded to **Dallas** by **Vancouver** with Dan Kesa and Vancouver's 5th round choice (later traded to LA Kings — LA Kings selected Jason Morgan) in 1995 Entry Draft for Russ Courtnall, April 7, 1995. Signed as a free agent by **Phoenix**, September 1, 1998.

ADAMS, KEVYN TOR.

Center. Shoots right. 6'1", 195 lbs. Born, Washington, D.C., October 8, 1974.
(Boston's 1st choice, 25th overall, in 1993 Entry Draft).

			Regular Season					Playoffs				
Season	**Club**	**Lea**	**GP**	**G**	**A**	**TP**	**PIM**	**GP**	**G**	**A**	**TP**	**PIM**
1991-92	Niagara Scenics	NAJHL	40	25	33	58	51	....	....	....	....	....
1992-93	Miami-Ohio	CCHA	40	17	15	32	18	....	....	....	....	....
1993-94	Miami-Ohio	CCHA	36	15	28	43	24	....	....	....	....	....
1994-95	Miami-Ohio	CCHA	38	20	29	49	30	....	....	....	....	....
1995-96	Miami-Ohio	CCHA	36	17	30	47	30	....	....	....	....	....
1996-97	Grand Rapids	IHL	82	22	25	47	47	5	1	1	2	4
1997-98	**Toronto**	**NHL**	**5**	**0**	**0**	**0**	**7**	....	....	....	....	....
	St. John's	AHL	59	17	20	37	99	4	0	0	0	4
	NHL Totals		**5**	**0**	**0**	**0**	**7**	....	....	....	....	....

CCHA Second All-Star Team (1995)

Signed as a free agent by **Toronto**, August 7, 1997.

ADDUONO, JEREMY BUF.

Right wing. Shoots right. 6', 182 lbs. Born, Thunder Bay, Ont., August 4, 1978.
(Buffalo's 8th choice, 184th overall, in 1997 Entry Draft).

			Regular Season					Playoffs				
Season	**Club**	**Lea**	**GP**	**G**	**A**	**TP**	**PIM**	**GP**	**G**	**A**	**TP**	**PIM**
1995-96	Sudbury	OHL	66	15	22	37	14	....	....	....	....	....
1996-97	Sudbury	OHL	66	29	40	69	24	....	....	....	....	....
1997-98	Sudbury	OHL	66	37	69	106	40	10	5	5	10	10

AFANASENKOV, DMITRI (ah-fahn-AH-sehn-kahv) T.B.

Left wing. Shoots right. 6'1", 180 lbs. Born, Arkhangelsk, USSR, May 12, 1980.
(Tampa Bay's 3rd choice, 72nd overall, in 1998 Entry Draft).

			Regular Season					Playoffs				
Season	Club	Lea	GP	G	A	TP	PIM	GP	G	A	TP	PIM
1995-96	Yaroslavl 2	Russia-2	25	10	5	15	10	....	....	....	....	....
	Yaroslavl	Rus-Jr.	35	28	16	44	8	....	....	....	....	....
1996-97	Yaroslavl 2	Russia-3	45	20	15	35	14	....	....	....	....	....
1997-98	Yaroslavl 2	Russia-2	48	14	7	21	20	....	....	....	....	....

AFINOGENOV, MAXIM (ah-fihn-ah-GEHN-ahf) BUF.

Right wing. Shoots left. 5'11", 176 lbs. Born, Moscow, USSR, September 4, 1979.
(Buffalo's 3rd choice, 69th overall, in 1997 Entry Draft).

			Regular Season					Playoffs				
Season	Club	Lea	GP	G	A	TP	PIM	GP	G	A	TP	PIM
1995-96	Moscow D'amo 2	Russia-2			STATISTICS NOT AVAILABLE							
	Moscow D'amo	CIS	1	0	0	0	0	....	....	....	....	....
1996-97	Moscow D'amo	Russia	29	6	5	11	10	4	0	2	2	0
1997-98	Moscow D'amo	Russia	35	10	5	15	53	....	....	....	....	....
	Moscow D'amo	EuroHL	6	3	1	4	27	....	....	....	....	....

AHMAOJA, TIMO (ahkh-mah-OH-yah) ANA.

Defense. Shoots right. 6'1", 180 lbs. Born, Jyvaskyla, Finland, August 8, 1978.
(Anaheim's 5th choice, 172nd overall, in 1996 Entry Draft).

			Regular Season					Playoffs				
Season	Club	Lea	GP	G	A	TP	PIM	GP	G	A	TP	PIM
1995-96	JyP HT	Finland	4	0	0	0	4	....	....	....	....	....
	JyP HT	Fin-Jr.	28	0	7	7	16	6	1	0	1	2
1996-97	JyP HT	Finland	35	0	4	4	8	....	....	....	....	....
	JyP HT	Fin-Jr.	19	4	5	9	24	....	....	....	....	....
1997-98	JyP HT	Finland	10	0	0	0	4	....	....	....	....	....
	Lukko Rauma	Finland	10	0	0	0	0	....	....	....	....	....
	Diskos.	Finland-2	23	1	2	3	14	....	....	....	....	....

AITKEN, JOHNATHAN BOS.

Defense. Shoots left. 6'4", 215 lbs. Born, Edmonton, Alta., May 24, 1978.
(Boston's 1st choice, 8th overall, in 1996 Entry Draft).

			Regular Season					Playoffs				
Season	Club	Lea	GP	G	A	TP	PIM	GP	G	A	TP	PIM
1994-95	Medicine Hat	WHL	53	0	5	5	71	5	0	0	0	0
1995-96	Medicine Hat	WHL	71	6	14	20	131	5	1	0	1	6
1996-97	Brandon	WHL	65	4	18	22	211	6	0	0	0	4
1997-98	Brandon	WHL	69	9	25	34	183	18	0	8	8	67

WHL East Second All-Star Team (1998)

AIVAZOFF, MICAH (A-vuh-zahf, MIGH-kuh)

Center. Shoots left. 6', 195 lbs. Born, Powell River, B.C., May 4, 1969.
(Los Angeles' 6th choice, 109th overall, in 1988 Entry Draft).

			Regular Season					Playoffs				
Season	Club	Lea	GP	G	A	TP	PIM	GP	G	A	TP	PIM
1986-87	Victoria	WHL	72	18	39	57	112	5	1	0	1	2
1987-88	Victoria	WHL	69	26	57	83	79	8	3	4	7	14
1988-89	Victoria	WHL	70	35	65	100	136	8	5	7	12	2
1989-90	New Haven	AHL	77	20	39	59	71	....	....	....	....	....
1990-91	New Haven	AHL	79	11	29	40	84	....	....	....	....	....
1991-92	Adirondack	AHL	61	9	20	29	50	19	2	8	10	25
1992-93	Adirondack	AHL	79	32	53	85	100	11	8	6	14	10
1993-94	**Detroit**	**NHL**	**59**	**4**	**4**	**8**	**38**	....	....	....	....	....
1994-95	**Edmonton**	**NHL**	**21**	**0**	**1**	**1**	**2**	....	....	....	....	....
1995-96	**NY Islanders**	**NHL**	**12**	**0**	**1**	**1**	**6**	....	....	....	....	....
	Utah	IHL	59	14	21	35	58	22	3	5	8	33
1996-97	Binghamton	AHL	75	12	36	48	70	4	1	1	2	0
1997-98	San Antonio	IHL	54	13	33	46	33	....	....	....	....	....
	NHL Totals		**92**	**4**	**6**	**10**	**46**	....	....	....	....	....

Signed as a free agent by **Detroit**, March 18, 1993. Claimed by **Pittsburgh** from **Detroit** in Waiver Draft, January 18, 1995. Claimed by **Edmonton** from **Pittsburgh** in Waiver Draft, January 18, 1995. Signed as a free agent by **NY Islanders**, August 23, 1995. Signed as a free agent by **NY Rangers**, August 23, 1996.

ALATALO, MIKA PHX.

Left wing. Shoots left. 5'11", 185 lbs. Born, Oulu, Finland, May 11, 1971.
(Winnipeg's 11th choice, 203rd overall, in 1990 Entry Draft).

			Regular Season					Playoffs				
Season	Club	Lea	GP	G	A	TP	PIM	GP	G	A	TP	PIM
1988-89	KooKoo	Finland	34	8	6	14	10	....	....	....	....	....
1989-90	KooKoo	Finland	41	3	5	8	22	....	....	....	....	....
1990-91	Lukko	Finland	39	10	1	11	10	....	....	....	....	....
1991-92	Lukko	Finland	43	20	17	37	32	2	0	0	0	0
1992-93	Lukko	Finland	48	16	19	35	38	3	0	0	0	0
1993-94	Lukko	Finland	45	19	15	34	77	9	2	2	4	4
1994-95	TPS Turku	Finland	44	23	13	36	79	13	2	5	7	8
1995-96	TPS Turku	Finland	49	19	18	37	44	11	3	4	7	8
1996-97	Lulea	Sweden	50	19	18	37	54	10	2	3	5	22
1997-98	Lulea	Sweden	45	14	10	24	22	2	0	0	0	0

Transferred to **Phoenix** after **Winnipeg** franchise relocated, July 1, 1996.

ALBELIN, TOMMY (AL-buh-LEEN) CGY.

Defense. Shoots left. 6'1", 200 lbs. Born, Stockholm, Sweden, May 21, 1964.
(Quebec's 7th choice, 158th overall, in 1983 Entry Draft).

			Regular Season					Playoffs				
Season	Club	Lea	GP	G	A	TP	PIM	GP	G	A	TP	PIM
1982-83	Djurgarden	Sweden	19	2	5	7	4	6	1	0	1	2
1983-84	Djurgarden	Sweden	30	9	5	14	26	4	0	1	1	2
1984-85	Djurgarden	Sweden	32	9	8	17	22	8	2	1	3	4
1985-86	Djurgarden	Sweden	35	4	8	12	26	....	....	....	....	....
1986-87	Djurgarden	Sweden	33	7	5	12	49	2	0	0	0	0
1987-88	**Quebec**	**NHL**	**60**	**3**	**23**	**26**	**47**	....	....	....	....	....
1988-89	**Quebec**	**NHL**	**14**	**2**	**4**	**6**	**27**	....	....	....	....	....
	Halifax	AHL	8	2	5	7	4	....	....	....	....	....
	New Jersey	**NHL**	**46**	**7**	**24**	**31**	**40**	....	....	....	....	....
1989-90	**New Jersey**	**NHL**	**68**	**6**	**23**	**29**	**63**	....	....	....	....	....
1990-91	**New Jersey**	**NHL**	**47**	**2**	**12**	**14**	**44**	**3**	**0**	**1**	**1**	**2**
	Utica	AHL	14	4	2	6	10	....	....	....	....	....
1991-92	**New Jersey**	**NHL**	**19**	**0**	**4**	**4**	**4**	**1**	**1**	**1**	**2**	**0**
	Utica	AHL	11	4	6	10	4	....	....	....	....	....
1992-93	**New Jersey**	**NHL**	**36**	**1**	**5**	**6**	**14**	**5**	**2**	**0**	**2**	**0**
1993-94	**New Jersey**	**NHL**	**62**	**2**	**17**	**19**	**36**	**20**	**2**	**5**	**7**	**14**
	Albany	AHL	4	0	2	2	17	....	....	....	....	....
1994-95	**New Jersey**	**NHL**	**48**	**5**	**10**	**15**	**20**	**20**	**1**	**7**	**8**	**2** ♦
1995-96	**New Jersey**	**NHL**	**53**	**1**	**12**	**13**	**14**	....	....	....	....	....
	Calgary	**NHL**	**20**	**0**	**1**	**1**	**4**	**4**	**0**	**0**	**0**	**0**
1996-97	**Calgary**	**NHL**	**72**	**4**	**11**	**15**	**14**	....	....	....	....	....
1997-98	**Calgary**	**NHL**	**69**	**2**	**17**	**19**	**32**	....	....	....	....	....
	Sweden	Olympics	3	0	0	0	4	....	....	....	....	....
	NHL Totals		**614**	**35**	**163**	**198**	**359**	**53**	**6**	**14**	**20**	**18**

Swedish World All-Star Team (1987, 1997)

Traded to **New Jersey** by **Quebec** for New Jersey's 4th round choice (Niclas Andersson) in 1989 Entry Draft, December 12, 1988. Traded to **Calgary** by **New Jersey** with Cale Hulse and Jocelyn Lemieux for Phil Housley and Dan Keczmer, February 26, 1996.

ALDOUS, CHRIS MTL.

Defense. Shoots left. 6'3", 181 lbs. Born, Massena, NY, November 19, 1975.
(Montreal's 12th choice, 252nd overall, in 1994 Entry Draft).

			Regular Season					Playoffs				
Season	Club	Lea	GP	G	A	TP	PIM	GP	G	A	TP	PIM
1993-94	Northwood Prep	H.S.	41	9	42	51	18	....	....	....	....	....
1994-95	RPI	ECAC	31	0	1	1	4	....	....	....	....	....
1995-96	RPI	ECAC	35	1	3	4	26	....	....	....	....	....
1996-97	RPI	ECAC	36	3	13	16	18	....	....	....	....	....
1997-98	RPI	ECAC	35	6	8	14	24	....	....	....	....	....

ALFREDSSON, DANIEL (AHL-frehd-suhn) OTT.

Right wing. Shoots right. 5'11", 194 lbs. Born, Goteborg, Sweden, December 11, 1972.
(Ottawa's 5th choice, 133rd overall, in 1994 Entry Draft).

			Regular Season					Playoffs				
Season	Club	Lea	GP	G	A	TP	PIM	GP	G	A	TP	PIM
1991-92	Molndal	Sweden-2	32	12	8	20	43	....	....	....	....	....
1992-93	V. Frolunda	Sweden	20	1	5	6	8	....	....	....	....	....
1993-94	V. Frolunda	Sweden	39	20	10	30	18	4	1	1	2	....
1994-95	V. Frolunda	Sweden	22	7	11	18	22	....	....	....	....	....
1995-96	**Ottawa**	**NHL**	**82**	**26**	**35**	**61**	**28**	....	....	....	....	....
1996-97	**Ottawa**	**NHL**	**76**	**24**	**47**	**71**	**30**	**7**	**5**	**2**	**7**	**6**
1997-98	**Ottawa**	**NHL**	**55**	**17**	**28**	**45**	**18**	**11**	**7**	**2**	**9**	**20**
	Sweden	Olympics	4	2	3	5	2	....	....	....	....	....
	NHL Totals		**213**	**67**	**110**	**177**	**76**	**18**	**12**	**4**	**16**	**26**

NHL All-Rookie Team (1996) • Won Calder Memorial Trophy (1996)

Played in NHL All-Star Game (1996, 1997, 1998)

ALINC, JAN (AH-lihnch, YAHN) PIT.

Center. Shoots left. 6'2", 190 lbs. Born, Most, Czech., May 27, 1972.
(Pittsburgh's 7th choice, 163rd overall, in 1992 Entry Draft).

			Regular Season					Playoffs				
Season	Club	Lea	GP	G	A	TP	PIM	GP	G	A	TP	PIM
1990-91	Litvinov	Czech.	7	1	1	2	....	....	....	....	....	....
1991-92	Litvinov	Czech.	45	21	16	37	24	....	....	....	....	....
1992-93	Litvinov	Czech.	36	16	13	29	....	....	....	....	....	....
1993-94	Litvinov	Cze-Rep.	36	16	25	41	....	4	1	4	5	....
	Czech Republic	Olympics	6	2	0	2	4	....	....	....	....	....
1994-95	Litvinov	Cze-Rep.	42	16	32	48	50	4	3	2	5	2
1995-96	Litvinov	Cze-Rep.	38	15	29	44	....	16	2	5	7	....
1996-97	Assat Pori	Finland	47	9	16	25	16	4	0	4	4	2
1997-98	Assat Pori	Finland	15	2	8	10	10	....	....	....	....	....
	Litvinov	Cze-Rep.	33	12	32	44	14	4	1	2	3	12

ALLAN, CHAD VAN.

Defense. Shoots left. 6'1", 200 lbs. Born, Saskatoon, Sask., July 12, 1976.
(Vancouver's 4th choice, 65th overall, in 1994 Entry Draft).

			Regular Season					Playoffs				
Season	Club	Lea	GP	G	A	TP	PIM	GP	G	A	TP	PIM
1991-92	Saskatoon	WHL	1	0	0	0	2	....	....	....	....	....
1992-93	Saskatoon	WHL	69	2	10	12	67	9	0	0	0	25
1993-94	Saskatoon	WHL	70	6	16	22	123	16	1	1	2	21
1994-95	Saskatoon	WHL	63	14	29	43	95	9	0	3	3	2
1995-96	Saskatoon	WHL	57	8	30	38	106	4	0	0	0	5
1996-97	Syracuse	AHL	73	3	10	13	83	3	0	1	1	0
1997-98	Syracuse	AHL	73	2	10	12	121	5	0	0	0	4

WHL East First All-Star Team (1995) • WHL East Second All-Star Team (1996)

ALLEN, BOBBY BOS.

Defense. Shoots left. 6'1", 198 lbs. Born, Braintree, MA, November 14, 1978.
(Boston's 2nd choice, 52nd overall, in 1998 Entry Draft).

			Regular Season					Playoffs				
Season	Club	Lea	GP	G	A	TP	PIM	GP	G	A	TP	PIM
1996-97	Cushing Academy	H.S.	36	11	33	44	28	....	....	....	....	....
1997-98	Boston College	H.E.	40	7	21	28	49	....	....	....	....	....

ALLEN, BRYAN VAN.

Defense. Shoots left. 6'4", 210 lbs. Born, Kingston, Ont., August 21, 1980.
(Vancouver's 1st choice, 4th overall, in 1998 Entry Draft).

			Regular Season					Playoffs				
Season	Club	Lea	GP	G	A	TP	PIM	GP	G	A	TP	PIM
1996-97	Oshawa	OHL	60	2	4	6	76	18	1	3	4	26
1997-98	Oshawa	OHL	48	6	13	19	126	5	0	5	5	18

ALLEN, CHRIS — FLA.

Defense. Shoots right. 6'2", 193 lbs. Born, Chatham, Ont., May 8, 1978.
(Florida's 2nd choice, 60th overall, in 1996 Entry Draft).

			Regular Season					Playoffs				
Season	Club	Lea	GP	G	A	TP	PIM	GP	G	A	TP	PIM
1994-95	Kingston	OHL	43	3	5	8	15	2	0	0	0	0
1995-96	Kingston	OHL	55	21	18	39	58	6	0	2	2	8
1996-97	Kingston	OHL	61	14	29	43	81	5	1	2	3	4
	Carolina	AHL	9	0	0	0	2	....	....	....	....	....
1997-98	Kingston	OHL	66	38	57	95	91	10	4	2	6	6
	Florida	**NHL**	**1**	**0**	**0**	**0**	**2**	....	....	....	....	....
	NHL Totals		**1**	**0**	**0**	**0**	**2**	....	....	....	....	....

OHL First All-Star Team (1998) • Canadian Major Junior First All-Star Team (1998)

ALLEN, PETER — S.J.

Defense. Shoots right. 6'2", 200 lbs. Born, Calgary, Alta., March 6, 1970.
(Boston's 1st choice, 24th overall, in 1991 Supplemental Draft).

			Regular Season					Playoffs				
Season	Club	Lea	GP	G	A	TP	PIM	GP	G	A	TP	PIM
1989-90	Yale	ECAC	26	2	4	6	16	....	....	....	....	....
1990-91	Yale	ECAC	17	0	6	6	14	....	....	....	....	....
1991-92	Yale	ECAC	26	5	13	18	26	....	....	....	....	....
1992-93	Yale	ECAC	30	3	15	18	32	....	....	....	....	....
1993-94	Richmond	ECHL	52	2	16	18	62	....	....	....	....	....
	P.E.I.	AHL	6	0	1	1	6	....	....	....	....	....
1994-95	Canada	Nat-Tm	52	5	15	20	36	....	....	....	....	....
1995-96	**Pittsburgh**	**NHL**	**8**	**0**	**0**	**0**	**8**	....	....	....	....	....
	Cleveland	IHL	65	3	45	48	55	3	0	0	0	2
1996-97	Cleveland	IHL	81	14	31	45	75	14	0	6	6	24
1997-98	Kentucky	AHL	72	0	18	18	73	3	0	1	1	4
	NHL Totals		**8**	**0**	**0**	**0**	**8**	....	....	....	....	....

Signed as a free agent by **Pittsburgh**, August 10, 1995. Signed as a free agent by **San Jose**, August 19, 1997.

ALLISON, JAMIE — CGY.

Defense. Shoots left. 6'1", 195 lbs. Born, Lindsay, Ont., May 13, 1975.
(Calgary's 2nd choice, 44th overall, in 1993 Entry Draft).

			Regular Season					Playoffs				
Season	Club	Lea	GP	G	A	TP	PIM	GP	G	A	TP	PIM
1991-92	Windsor	OHL	59	4	8	12	70	4	1	1	2	2
1992-93	Detroit	OHL	61	0	13	13	64	15	2	5	7	23
1993-94	Detroit	OHL	40	2	22	24	69	17	2	9	11	35
1994-95	Detroit	OHL	50	1	14	15	119	18	2	7	9	35
	Calgary	**NHL**	**1**	**0**	**0**	**0**	**0**	....	....	....	....	....
1995-96	Saint John	AHL	71	3	16	19	223	14	0	2	2	16
1996-97	**Calgary**	**NHL**	**20**	**0**	**0**	**0**	**35**	....	....	....	....	....
	Saint John	AHL	46	3	6	9	139	5	0	1	1	4
1997-98	**Calgary**	**NHL**	**43**	**3**	**8**	**11**	**104**	....	....	....	....	....
	Saint John	AHL	16	0	5	5	49	....	....	....	....	....
	NHL Totals		**64**	**3**	**8**	**11**	**139**	....	....	....	....	....

ALLISON, JASON — BOS.

Center. Shoots right. 6'3", 205 lbs. Born, North York, Ont., May 29, 1975.
(Washington's 2nd choice, 17th overall, in 1993 Entry Draft).

			Regular Season					Playoffs				
Season	Club	Lea	GP	G	A	TP	PIM	GP	G	A	TP	PIM
1991-92	London	OHL	65	11	19	30	15	7	0	0	0	0
1992-93	London	OHL	66	42	76	118	50	12	7	13	20	8
1993-94	London	OHL	56	55	87	*142	68	5	2	13	15	13
	Washington	**NHL**	**2**	**0**	**1**	**1**	**0**	....	....	....	....	....
	Portland	AHL	....	....	....	....	....	6	2	1	3	0
1994-95	London	OHL	15	15	21	36	43	....	....	....	....	....
	Washington	**NHL**	**12**	**2**	**1**	**3**	**6**	....	....	....	....	....
	Portland	AHL	8	5	4	9	2	7	3	8	11	2
1995-96	**Washington**	**NHL**	**19**	**0**	**3**	**3**	**2**	....	....	....	....	....
	Portland	AHL	57	28	41	69	42	6	1	6	7	9
1996-97	**Washington**	**NHL**	**53**	**5**	**17**	**22**	**25**	....	....	....	....	....
	Boston	**NHL**	**19**	**3**	**9**	**12**	**9**	....	....	....	....	....
1997-98	**Boston**	**NHL**	**81**	**33**	**50**	**83**	**60**	**6**	**2**	**6**	**8**	**4**
	NHL Totals		**186**	**43**	**81**	**124**	**102**	**6**	**2**	**6**	**8**	**4**

OHL First All-Star Team (1994) • Canadian Major Junior First All-Star Team (1994) • Canadian Major Junior Player of the Year (1994)

Traded to **Boston** by **Washington** with Jim Carey, Anson Carter and Washington's 3rd round choice (Lee Goren) in 1997 Entry Draft for Bill Ranford, Adam Oates and Rick Tocchet, March 1, 1997.

ALVEY, MATT — BOS.

Right wing. Shoots right. 6'5", 200 lbs. Born, Troy, NY, May 15, 1975.
(Boston's 2nd choice, 51st overall, in 1993 Entry Draft).

			Regular Season					Playoffs				
Season	Club	Lea	GP	G	A	TP	PIM	GP	G	A	TP	PIM
1992-93	Springfield	NEJHL	38	22	37	59	85	....	....	....	....	....
1993-94	Lake Superior	CCHA	41	6	8	14	16	....	....	....	....	....
1994-95	Lake Superior	CCHA	25	4	7	11	32	....	....	....	....	....
1995-96	Lake Superior	CCHA	39	14	8	22	40	....	....	....	....	....
1996-97	Lake Superior	CCHA	18	10	8	18	49	....	....	....	....	....
	Pensacola	ECHL	7	1	2	3	0	3	0	0	0	4
1997-98	Charlotte	ECHL	38	17	15	32	37	7	3	1	4	6

AMONTE, TONY — (eh-MAHN-tee) — CHI.

Right wing. Shoots left. 6', 195 lbs. Born, Hingham, MA, August 2, 1970.
(NY Rangers' 3rd choice, 68th overall, in 1988 Entry Draft).

			Regular Season					Playoffs				
Season	Club	Lea	GP	G	A	TP	PIM	GP	G	A	TP	PIM
1987-88	Thayer Academy	H.S.	Statistics Not Available									
1988-89	Thayer Academy	H.S.	25	35	38	73	....	....	....	....	....	....
1989-90	Boston University	H.E.	41	25	33	58	52	....	....	....	....	....
1990-91	Boston University	H.E.	38	31	37	68	82	....	....	....	....	....
	NY Rangers	**NHL**	....	....	....	....	....	**2**	**0**	**2**	**2**	**2**
1991-92	**NY Rangers**	**NHL**	**79**	**35**	**34**	**69**	**55**	**13**	**3**	**6**	**9**	**2**
1992-93	**NY Rangers**	**NHL**	**83**	**33**	**43**	**76**	**49**	....	....	....	....	....
1993-94	**NY Rangers**	**NHL**	**72**	**16**	**22**	**38**	**31**	....	....	....	....	....
	Chicago	**NHL**	**7**	**1**	**3**	**4**	**6**	**6**	**4**	**2**	**6**	**4**
1994-95	Fassa	Italy	14	22	16	38	10	....	....	....	....	....
	Chicago	**NHL**	**48**	**15**	**20**	**35**	**41**	**16**	**3**	**3**	**6**	**10**
1995-96	**Chicago**	**NHL**	**81**	**31**	**32**	**63**	**62**	**7**	**2**	**4**	**6**	**6**
1996-97	**Chicago**	**NHL**	**81**	**41**	**36**	**77**	**64**	**6**	**4**	**2**	**6**	**8**
1997-98	**Chicago**	**NHL**	**82**	**31**	**42**	**73**	**66**	....	....	....	....	....
	United States	Olympics	4	0	1	1	4	....	....	....	....	....
	NHL Totals		**533**	**203**	**232**	**435**	**374**	**50**	**16**	**19**	**35**	**32**

Hockey East Second All-Star Team (1991) • NCAA Championship All-Tournament Team (1991) • NHL/Upper Deck All-Rookie Team (1992)

Played in NHL All-Star Game (1997, 1998)

Traded to **Chicago** by **NY Rangers** with the rights to Matt Oates for Stephane Matteau and Brian Noonan, March 21, 1994.

ANDERSON, CRAIG — NYR

Defense. Shoots left. 6'1", 171 lbs. Born, Minneapolis, MN, January 6, 1976.
(NY Rangers' 10th choice, 208th overall, in 1994 Entry Draft).

			Regular Season					Playoffs				
Season	Club	Lea	GP	G	A	TP	PIM	GP	G	A	TP	PIM
1993-94	Park Center	H.S.	24	24	18	42	....	....	....	....	....	....
1994-95	U. of Wisconsin	WCHA	Did Not Play – Freshman									
1995-96	U. of Wisconsin	WCHA	16	1	3	4	2	....	....	....	....	....
1996-97	U. of Wisconsin	WCHA	34	3	8	11	22	....	....	....	....	....
1997-98	U. of Wisconsin	WCHA	41	12	30	42	24	....	....	....	....	....

WCHA First All-Star Team (1998)

ANDERSON, MICHAEL — WSH.

Right wing. Shoots right. 6'1", 186 lbs. Born, Edina, MN, December 24, 1976.
(Washington's 10th choice, 180th overall, in 1996 Entry Draft).

			Regular Season					Playoffs				
Season	Club	Lea	GP	G	A	TP	PIM	GP	G	A	TP	PIM
1995-96	U. of Minnesota	WCHA	28	3	6	9	51	....	....	....	....	....
1996-97	U. of Minnesota	WCHA	42	9	11	20	46	....	....	....	....	....
1997-98	U. of Minnesota	WCHA	31	12	13	25	62	....	....	....	....	....

ANDERSON, SHAWN

Defense. Shoots left. 6'1", 200 lbs. Born, Montreal, Que., February 7, 1968.
(Buffalo's 1st choice, 5th overall, in 1986 Entry Draft).

			Regular Season					Playoffs				
Season	Club	Lea	GP	G	A	TP	PIM	GP	G	A	TP	PIM
1984-85	Lac St-Louis	QAAA	42	23	42	65	10	....	....	....	....	....
1985-86	U. of Maine	H.E.	16	5	8	13	22	....	....	....	....	....
	Canada	Nat-Tm	33	2	6	8	16	....	....	....	....	....
1986-87	**Buffalo**	**NHL**	**41**	**2**	**11**	**13**	**23**	....	....	....	....	....
	Rochester	AHL	15	2	5	7	11	....	....	....	....	....
1987-88	**Buffalo**	**NHL**	**23**	**1**	**2**	**3**	**17**	....	....	....	....	....
	Rochester	AHL	22	5	16	21	19	6	0	0	0	0
1988-89	**Buffalo**	**NHL**	**33**	**2**	**10**	**12**	**18**	**5**	**0**	**1**	**1**	**4**
	Rochester	AHL	31	5	14	19	24	....	....	....	....	....
1989-90	**Buffalo**	**NHL**	**16**	**1**	**3**	**4**	**8**	....	....	....	....	....
	Rochester	AHL	39	2	16	18	41	9	1	0	1	4
1990-91	**Quebec**	**NHL**	**31**	**3**	**10**	**13**	**21**	....	....	....	....	....
	Halifax	AHL	4	0	1	1	2	....	....	....	....	....
1991-92	Weiswasser	Germany	38	7	15	22	83	....	....	....	....	....
1992-93	**Washington**	**NHL**	**60**	**2**	**6**	**8**	**18**	**6**	**0**	**0**	**0**	**0**
	Baltimore	AHL	10	1	5	6	8	....	....	....	....	....
1993-94	**Washington**	**NHL**	**50**	**0**	**9**	**9**	**12**	**8**	**1**	**0**	**1**	**12**
1994-95	**Philadelphia**	**NHL**	**1**	**0**	**0**	**0**	**0**	....	....	....	....	....
	Hershey	AHL	31	9	21	30	18	6	2	3	5	19
1995-96	Milwaukee	IHL	79	22	39	61	68	5	0	7	7	0
1996-97	Wedemark	Ger-2	8	1	0	1	4	....	....	....	....	....
	Utah	IHL	31	2	12	14	21	....	....	....	....	....
	Manitoba	IHL	17	2	7	9	5	....	....	....	....	....
1997-98	Revier Lowen	Germany	32	5	14	19	45	....	....	....	....	....
	NHL Totals		**255**	**11**	**51**	**62**	**117**	**19**	**1**	**1**	**2**	**16**

Traded to **Washington** by **Buffalo** for Bill Houlder, September 30, 1990. Claimed by **Quebec** from **Washington** in NHL Waiver Draft, October 1, 1990. Traded to **Winnipeg** by **Quebec** for Sergei Kharin, October 22, 1991. Traded to **Washington** by **Winnipeg** for future considerations, October 23, 1991. Signed as a free agent by **Philadelphia**, August 16, 1994.

ANDERSSON, ERIK — (AN-duhr-suhn) — CGY.

Center. Shoots left. 6'3", 210 lbs. Born, Stockholm, Sweden, August 19, 1971.
(Calgary's 6th choice, 70th overall, in 1997 Entry Draft).

			Regular Season					Playoffs				
Season	Club	Lea	GP	G	A	TP	PIM	GP	G	A	TP	PIM
1989-90	Danderyd	Sweden-2	30	14	5	19	16	....	....	....	....	....
1990-91	AIK Solna	Sweden	32	1	1	2	10	....	....	....	....	....
1991-92	AIK Solna	Sweden	3	0	0	0	0	....	....	....	....	....
1992-93			Did Not Play									
1993-94	U. of Denver	WCHA	38	10	20	30	26	....	....	....	....	....
1994-95	U. of Denver	WCHA	42	12	19	31	42	....	....	....	....	....
1995-96	U. of Denver	WCHA	39	12	35	47	40	....	....	....	....	....
1996-97	U. of Denver	WCHA	39	17	17	34	42	....	....	....	....	....
1997-98	**Calgary**	**NHL**	**12**	**2**	**1**	**3**	**8**	....	....	....	....	....
	Saint John	AHL	29	5	9	14	29	....	....	....	....	....
	NHL Totals		**12**	**2**	**1**	**3**	**8**	....	....	....	....	....

• Re-entered NHL draft. Originally LA Kings' 5th choice, 112th overall, in 1990 Entry Draft.

ANDERSSON, MIKAEL (AN-duhr-suhn) T.B.

Left wing. Shoots left. 5'11", 181 lbs. Born, Malmo, Sweden, May 10, 1966.
(Buffalo's 1st choice, 18th overall, in 1984 Entry Draft).

			Regular Season					Playoffs				
Season	Club	Lea	GP	G	A	TP	PIM	GP	G	A	TP	PIM
1982-83	V. Frolunda	Sweden	1	1	0	1	0	....	....	....	....	....
1983-84	V. Frolunda	Sweden	18	0	3	3	6	....	....	....	....	....
1984-85	V. Frolunda	Sweden	30	16	11	27	18	6	3	2	5	2
1985-86	**Buffalo**	**NHL**	**32**	**1**	**9**	**10**	**4**	....	....	....	....	....
	Rochester	AHL	20	10	4	14	6	....	....	....	....	....
1986-87	**Buffalo**	**NHL**	**16**	**0**	**3**	**3**	**0**	....	....	....	....	....
	Rochester	AHL	42	6	20	26	14	9	1	2	3	2
1987-88	**Buffalo**	**NHL**	**37**	**3**	**20**	**23**	**10**	**1**	**1**	**0**	**1**	**0**
	Rochester	AHL	35	12	24	36	16	....	....	....	....	....
1988-89	**Buffalo**	**NHL**	**14**	**0**	**1**	**1**	**4**	....	....	....	....	....
	Rochester	AHL	56	18	33	51	12	....	....	....	....	....
1989-90	**Hartford**	**NHL**	**50**	**13**	**24**	**37**	**6**	**5**	**0**	**3**	**3**	**2**
1990-91	**Hartford**	**NHL**	**41**	**4**	**7**	**11**	**8**	....	....	....	....	....
	Springfield	AHL	26	7	22	29	10	18	*10	8	18	12
1991-92	**Hartford**	**NHL**	**74**	**18**	**29**	**47**	**14**	**7**	**0**	**2**	**2**	**6**
1992-93	**Tampa Bay**	**NHL**	**77**	**16**	**11**	**27**	**14**	....	....	....	....	....
1993-94	**Tampa Bay**	**NHL**	**76**	**13**	**12**	**25**	**23**	....	....	....	....	....
1994-95	V. Frolunda	Sweden	7	1	0	1	31	....	....	....	....	....
	Tampa Bay	**NHL**	**36**	**4**	**7**	**11**	**4**	....	....	....	....	....
1995-96	**Tampa Bay**	**NHL**	**64**	**8**	**11**	**19**	**2**	**6**	**1**	**1**	**2**	**0**
1996-97	**Tampa Bay**	**NHL**	**70**	**5**	**14**	**19**	**8**	....	....	....	....	....
1997-98	**Tampa Bay**	**NHL**	**72**	**6**	**11**	**17**	**29**	....	....	....	....	....
	Sweden	Olympics	4	1	1	2	0	....	....	....	....	....
	NHL Totals		**659**	**91**	**159**	**250**	**126**	**19**	**2**	**6**	**8**	**8**

Claimed by **Hartford** from **Buffalo** in NHL Waiver Draft, October 2, 1989. Signed as a free agent by **Tampa Bay**, June 29, 1992.

ANDERSSON, NIKLAS (AN-duhr-suhn) TOR.

Left wing. Shoots left. 5'9", 175 lbs. Born, Kungalv, Sweden, May 20, 1971.
(Quebec's 5th choice, 68th overall, in 1989 Entry Draft).

			Regular Season					Playoffs				
Season	Club	Lea	GP	G	A	TP	PIM	GP	G	A	TP	PIM
1987-88	V. Frolunda	Sweden-2	15	5	5	10	6	8	6	4	10	4
1988-89	V. Frolunda	Sweden-2	30	13	24	37	24	....	....	....	....	....
1989-90	V. Frolunda	Sweden	38	10	21	31	14	....	....	....	....	....
1990-91	V. Frolunda	Sweden	22	6	10	16	16	....	....	....	....	....
1991-92	Halifax	AHL	57	8	26	34	41	....	....	....	....	....
1992-93	**Quebec**	**NHL**	**3**	**0**	**1**	**1**	**2**	....	....	....	....	....
	Halifax	AHL	76	32	50	82	42	....	....	....	....	....
1993-94	Cornwall	AHL	42	18	34	52	8	....	....	....	....	....
1994-95	Denver	IHL	66	22	39	61	28	15	8	13	21	10
1995-96	**NY Islanders**	**NHL**	**47**	**14**	**12**	**26**	**12**	....	....	....	....	....
	Utah	IHL	30	13	22	35	25	....	....	....	....	....
1996-97	**NY Islanders**	**NHL**	**74**	**12**	**31**	**43**	**57**	....	....	....	....	....
1997-98	**San Jose**	**NHL**	**5**	**0**	**0**	**0**	**2**	....	....	....	....	....
	Kentucky	AHL	37	10	28	38	54	....	....	....	....	....
	Utah	IHL	21	6	20	26	24	4	3	1	4	4
	NHL Totals		**129**	**26**	**44**	**70**	**73**	....	....	....	....	....

Signed as a free agent by **NY Islanders**, July 15, 1994. Signed as a free agent by **San Jose**, September 17, 1997. Signed as a free agent by **Toronto**, September 4, 1998.

ANDERSSON-JUNKKA, JONAS PIT.

Defense. Shoots right. 6'2", 170 lbs. Born, Kiruna, Sweden, May 4, 1975.
(Pittsburgh's 4th choice, 104th overall, in 1993 Entry Draft).

			Regular Season					Playoffs				
Season	Club	Lea	GP	G	A	TP	PIM	GP	G	A	TP	PIM
1991-92	Kiruna	Sweden-2	1	0	0	0	0	....	....	....	....	....
1992-93	Kiruna	Sweden-2	30	3	7	10	32	....	....	....	....	....
1993-94	Kiruna	Sweden-2	32	6	10	16	84	....	....	....	....	....
1994-95	V. Frolunda	Sweden	19	0	2	2	2	....	....	....	....	....
1995-96	V. Frolunda	Sweden	31	3	1	4	20	13	1	0	1	6
1996-97	MoDo	Sweden	12	1	3	4	10	....	....	....	....	....
1997-98	MoDo	Sweden	35	5	5	10	12	1	0	0	0	0

ANDREWS, DARYL N.J.

Defense. Shoots left. 6'2", 205 lbs. Born, Campbell River, B.C., April 27, 1977.
(New Jersey's 11th choice, 173rd overall, in 1996 Entry Draft).

			Regular Season					Playoffs				
Season	Club	Lea	GP	G	A	TP	PIM	GP	G	A	TP	PIM
1995-96	Melfort	SJHL	55	2	12	14	51	....	....	....	....	....
1996-97	Western Michigan	CCHA	37	6	20	26	86	....	....	....	....	....
1997-98	Western Michigan	CCHA	36	3	0	3	81	....	....	....	....	....

ANDREYCHUK, DAVE (AN-druh-chuhk) N.J.

Left wing. Shoots right. 6'4", 220 lbs. Born, Hamilton, Ont., September 29, 1963.
(Buffalo's 3rd choice, 16th overall, in 1982 Entry Draft).

			Regular Season					Playoffs				
Season	Club	Lea	GP	G	A	TP	PIM	GP	G	A	TP	PIM
1980-81	Oshawa	OHA	67	22	22	44	80	10	3	2	5	20
1981-82	Oshawa	OHL	67	57	43	100	71	3	1	4	5	16
1982-83	Oshawa	OHL	14	8	24	32	6	....	....	....	....	....
	Buffalo	**NHL**	**43**	**14**	**23**	**37**	**16**	**4**	**1**	**0**	**1**	**4**
1983-84	**Buffalo**	**NHL**	**78**	**38**	**42**	**80**	**42**	**2**	**0**	**1**	**1**	**2**
1984-85	**Buffalo**	**NHL**	**64**	**31**	**30**	**61**	**54**	**5**	**4**	**2**	**6**	**4**
1985-86	**Buffalo**	**NHL**	**80**	**36**	**51**	**87**	**61**	....	....	....	....	....
1986-87	**Buffalo**	**NHL**	**77**	**25**	**48**	**73**	**46**	....	....	....	....	....
1987-88	**Buffalo**	**NHL**	**80**	**30**	**48**	**78**	**112**	**6**	**2**	**4**	**6**	**0**
1988-89	**Buffalo**	**NHL**	**56**	**28**	**24**	**52**	**40**	**5**	**0**	**3**	**3**	**0**
1989-90	**Buffalo**	**NHL**	**73**	**40**	**42**	**82**	**42**	**6**	**2**	**5**	**7**	**2**
1990-91	**Buffalo**	**NHL**	**80**	**36**	**33**	**69**	**32**	**6**	**2**	**2**	**4**	**8**
1991-92	**Buffalo**	**NHL**	**80**	**41**	**50**	**91**	**71**	**7**	**1**	**3**	**4**	**12**
1992-93	**Buffalo**	**NHL**	**52**	**29**	**32**	**61**	**48**	....	....	....	....	....
	Toronto	**NHL**	**31**	**25**	**13**	**38**	**8**	**21**	**12**	**7**	**19**	**35**
1993-94	**Toronto**	**NHL**	**83**	**53**	**46**	**99**	**98**	**18**	**5**	**5**	**10**	**16**
1994-95	**Toronto**	**NHL**	**48**	**22**	**16**	**38**	**34**	**7**	**3**	**2**	**5**	**25**
1995-96	**Toronto**	**NHL**	**61**	**20**	**24**	**44**	**54**	....	....	....	....	....
	New Jersey	**NHL**	**15**	**8**	**5**	**13**	**10**	....	....	....	....	....
1996-97	**New Jersey**	**NHL**	**82**	**27**	**34**	**61**	**48**	**1**	**0**	**0**	**0**	**0**
1997-98	**New Jersey**	**NHL**	**75**	**14**	**34**	**48**	**26**	**6**	**1**	**0**	**1**	**4**
	NHL Totals		**1158**	**517**	**595**	**1112**	**842**	**94**	**33**	**34**	**67**	**112**

Played in NHL All-Star Game (1990, 1994)

Traded to **Toronto** by **Buffalo** with Daren Puppa and Buffalo's 1st round choice (Kenny Jonsson) in 1993 Entry Draft for Grant Fuhr and Toronto's 5th round choice (Kevin Popp) in 1995 Entry Draft, February 2, 1993. Traded to **New Jersey** by **Toronto** for New Jersey's 2nd round choice (Marek Posmyk) in 1996 Entry Draft and future considerations, March 13, 1996.

ANDREYEV, ALEXANDER (an-DRAY-ehv) PHX.

Defense. Shoots left. 6'4", 220 lbs. Born, Riga, Latvia, September 14, 1979.
(Phoenix's 5th choice, 207th overall, in 1997 Entry Draft).

			Regular Season					Playoffs				
Season	Club	Lea	GP	G	A	TP	PIM	GP	G	A	TP	PIM
1996-97	Essamika Riga	Latvia	5	0	0	0	6	....	....	....	....	....
	Weyburn	SJHL	13	0	1	1	81	....	....	....	....	....
1997-98	Prince George	WHL	23	0	1	1	30	....	....	....	....	....

ANGELSTAD, MEL (AN-gehl-stahd) DAL.

Defense. Shoots left. 6'2", 210 lbs. Born, Saskatoon, Sask., October 31, 1971.

			Regular Season					Playoffs				
Season	Club	Lea	GP	G	A	TP	PIM	GP	G	A	TP	PIM
1992-93	Thunder Bay	ColHL	42	2	5	7	256	....	....	....	....	....
	Nashville	ECHL	1	0	0	0	14	....	....	....	....	....
1993-94	Thunder Bay	ColHL	58	1	20	21	374	9	1	2	3	65
	P.E.I.	AHL	1	0	0	0	5	....	....	....	....	....
1994-95	Thunder Bay	ColHL	46	0	8	8	317	7	0	3	3	62
	P.E.I.	AHL	3	0	0	0	16	....	....	....	....	....
1995-96	Thunder Bay	ColHL	51	3	3	6	335	16	0	6	6	94
	Phoenix	IHL	5	0	0	0	43	....	....	....	....	....
1996-97	Thunder Bay	ColHL	66	10	21	31	422	7	0	1	1	21
1997-98	Fort Worth	WPHL	19	1	6	7	102	....	....	....	....	....
	Las Vegas	IHL	3	0	0	0	5	....	....	....	....	....
	Orlando	IHL	63	1	3	4	321	8	0	0	0	29

Signed as a free agent by **Dallas**, July 29, 1998.

ANGER, NIKLAS (AN-guhr) MTL.

Right wing. Shoots left. 6'1", 185 lbs. Born, Gavle, Sweden, July 31, 1977.
(Montreal's 5th choice, 112th overall, in 1995 Entry Draft).

			Regular Season					Playoffs				
Season	Club	Lea	GP	G	A	TP	PIM	GP	G	A	TP	PIM
1994-95	Djurgarden	Swe-Jr.	30	14	12	26	26	....	....	....	....	....
	Djurgarden	Sweden	1	0	0	0	0	....	....	....	....	....
1995-96	Djurgarden	Sweden	10	0	0	0	2	....	....	....	....	....
1996-97	Djurgarden	Sweden	4	0	0	0	0	....	....	....	....	....
	Arlanda	Sweden-2	16	5	9	14	6	....	....	....	....	....
	Lindsay	Sweden-2	7	2	1	3	10	....	....	....	....	....
1997-98	Djurgarden	Sweden	45	2	5	7	37	12	0	1	1	2

ANISIMOV, ARTEM (ah-NIH-sih-mohv) PHI.

Defense. Shoots left. 6'1", 187 lbs. Born, Kazan, USSR, July 27, 1976.
(Philadelphia's 1st choice, 62nd overall, in 1994 Entry Draft).

			Regular Season					Playoffs				
Season	Club	Lea	GP	G	A	TP	PIM	GP	G	A	TP	PIM
1993-94	Ak Bars Kazan	CIS	38	0	1	1	12	5	0	0	0	0
1994-95	Ak Bars Kazan	CIS	46	3	2	5	55	1	0	0	0	0
1995-96	Ak Bars Kazan	CIS	30	0	2	2	8	....	....	....	....	....
1996-97	Ak Bars Kazan	Russia	5	0	1	1	2	....	....	....	....	....
1997-98	Ak Bars Kazan	Russia	44	0	0	0	26	....	....	....	....	....

ANTONIN, JIRI (AHN-toh-nihn) EDM.

Defense. Shoots left. 6'3", 207 lbs. Born, Pardubice, Czech., November 15, 1975.
(Edmonton's 8th choice, 213th overall, in 1995 Entry Draft).

			Regular Season					Playoffs				
Season	Club	Lea	GP	G	A	TP	PIM	GP	G	A	TP	PIM
1995-96	Pardubice	Cze-Rep.	20	1	1	2	....	....	....	....	....	....
1996-97	Brno	Czech-2	26	0	3	3	....	....	....	....	....	....
1997-98	Trutnov	Czech-3	STATISTICS NOT AVAILABLE									

ANTOSKI, SHAWN (an-TAW-skee)

Left wing. Shoots left. 6'4", 235 lbs. Born, Brantford, Ont., March 25, 1970.
(Vancouver's 2nd choice, 18th overall, in 1990 Entry Draft).

			Regular Season					Playoffs				
Season	Club	Lea	GP	G	A	TP	PIM	GP	G	A	TP	PIM
1987-88	North Bay	OHL	52	3	4	7	163	....	....	....	....	....
1988-89	North Bay	OHL	57	6	21	27	201	9	5	3	8	24
1989-90	North Bay	OHL	59	25	31	56	201	5	1	2	3	17
1990-91	**Vancouver**	**NHL**	**2**	**0**	**0**	**0**	**0**	....	....	....	....	....
	Milwaukee	IHL	62	17	7	24	330	5	1	2	3	10
1991-92	**Vancouver**	**NHL**	**4**	**0**	**0**	**0**	**29**	....	....	....	....	....
	Milwaukee	IHL	52	17	16	33	346	5	2	0	2	20
1992-93	**Vancouver**	**NHL**	**2**	**0**	**0**	**0**	**0**	....	....	....	....	....
	Hamilton	AHL	41	3	4	7	172	....	....	....	....	....
1993-94	**Vancouver**	**NHL**	**55**	**1**	**2**	**3**	**190**	**16**	**0**	**1**	**1**	**36**
1994-95	**Vancouver**	**NHL**	**7**	**0**	**0**	**0**	**46**	....	....	....	....	....
	Philadelphia	**NHL**	**25**	**0**	**0**	**0**	**61**	**13**	**0**	**1**	**1**	**10**
1995-96	**Philadelphia**	**NHL**	**64**	**1**	**3**	**4**	**204**	**7**	**1**	**1**	**2**	**28**
1996-97	**Pittsburgh**	**NHL**	**13**	**0**	**0**	**0**	**49**	....	....	....	....	....
	Anaheim	**NHL**	**2**	**0**	**0**	**0**	**2**	....	....	....	....	....
1997-98	**Anaheim**	**NHL**	**9**	**1**	**0**	**1**	**18**	....	....	....	....	....
	NHL Totals		**183**	**3**	**5**	**8**	**599**	**36**	**1**	**3**	**4**	**74**

Traded to **Philadelphia** by **Vancouver** for Josef Beranek, February 15, 1995. Signed as a free agent by **Pittsburgh**, July 31, 1996. Traded to **Anaheim** by **Pittsburgh** with Dmitri Mironov for Alex Hicks and Fredrik Olausson, November 19, 1996.

ANTROPOV, NIKOLAI (an-TROH-pahv) TOR.

Center. Shoots left. 6'5", 191 lbs. Born, Ust-Kamenogorsk, USSR, February 18, 1980.
(Toronto's 1st choice, 10th overall, in 1998 Entry Draft).

			Regular Season					Playoffs				
Season	Club	Lea	GP	G	A	TP	PIM	GP	G	A	TP	PIM
1995-96	Kamenogorsk	Rus-Jr.	20	18	20	38	30	....	....	....	....	....
1996-97	Kamenogorsk	Russia-2	8	2	1	3	6	....	....	....	....	....
1997-98	Kamenogorsk	Russia-2	42	15	24	39	62	....	....	....	....	....

ARCHAMBAULT, DANIEL (ahr-sham-BOH)

Defense. Shoots left. 6', 200 lbs. Born, Ste-Agathe, Que., March 28, 1978.
(Montreal's 6th choice, 127th overall, in 1996 Entry Draft).

			Regular Season					Playoffs				
Season	Club	Lea	GP	G	A	TP	PIM	GP	G	A	TP	PIM
1994-95	Val d'Or	QMJHL	54	3	1	4	165	....	....	....	....	....
1995-96	Val d'Or	QMJHL	43	1	12	13	254	13	1	1	2	74
1996-97	Val d'Or	QMJHL	38	3	9	12	229	10	0	1	1	29
1997-98	Chicoutimi	QMJHL	66	11	34	45	318	5	1	1	2	28

ARCHIBALD, DAVE

Center/Left wing. Shoots left. 6'1", 210 lbs. Born, Chilliwack, B.C., April 14, 1969.
(Minnesota's 1st choice, 6th overall, in 1987 Entry Draft).

			Regular Season					Playoffs				
Season	Club	Lea	GP	G	A	TP	PIM	GP	G	A	TP	PIM
1984-85	Portland	WHL	47	7	11	18	10	3	0	2	2	0
1985-86	Portland	WHL	70	29	35	64	56	15	6	7	13	11
1986-87	Portland	WHL	65	50	57	107	40	20	10	18	28	11
1987-88	**Minnesota**	**NHL**	**78**	**13**	**20**	**33**	**26**	....	....	....	....	....
1988-89	**Minnesota**	**NHL**	**72**	**14**	**19**	**33**	**14**	**5**	**0**	**1**	**1**	**0**
1989-90	**Minnesota**	**NHL**	**12**	**1**	**5**	**6**	**6**	....	....	....	....	....
	NY Rangers	**NHL**	**19**	**2**	**3**	**5**	**6**	....	....	....	....	....
	Flint	IHL	41	14	38	52	16	4	3	2	5	0
1990-91	Canada	Nat-Tm	29	19	12	31	20	....	....	....	....	....
1991-92	Canada	Nat-Tm	58	20	43	63	64	....	....	....	....	....
	Canada	Olympics	8	7	1	8	18	....	....	....	....	....
	HC Bolzano	Italy	5	4	3	7	16	7	8	5	13	7
1992-93	Binghamton	AHL	8	6	3	9	10	....	....	....	....	....
	Ottawa	**NHL**	**44**	**9**	**6**	**15**	**32**	....	....	....	....	....
1993-94	**Ottawa**	**NHL**	**33**	**10**	**8**	**18**	**14**	....	....	....	....	....
1994-95	**Ottawa**	**NHL**	**14**	**2**	**2**	**4**	**19**	....	....	....	....	....
1995-96	**Ottawa**	**NHL**	**44**	**6**	**4**	**10**	**18**	....	....	....	....	....
	Utah	IHL	19	1	4	5	10	....	....	....	....	....
1996-97	**NY Islanders**	**NHL**	**7**	**0**	**0**	**0**	**4**	....	....	....	....	....
	Frankfurt	Germany	34	10	19	29	48	9	4	2	6	16
1997-98	San Antonio	IHL	55	11	21	32	10	....	....	....	....	....
	NHL Totals		**323**	**57**	**67**	**124**	**139**	**5**	**0**	**1**	**1**	**0**

Traded to **NY Rangers** by **Minnesota** for Jayson More, November 1, 1989. Traded to **Ottawa** by **NY Rangers** for Ottawa's 5th round choice (later traded to LA Kings — LA Kings selected Frederick Beaubien) in 1993 Entry Draft, November 5, 1992. Signed as a free agent by **NY Islanders**, October 10, 1996

ARKHIPOV, DENIS (ahr-KHEE-pahv) NSH.

Right wing. Shoots left. 6'3", 196 lbs. Born, Kazan, USSR, May 19, 1979.
(Nashville's 2nd choice, 60th overall, in 1998 Entry Draft).

			Regular Season					Playoffs				
Season	Club	Lea	GP	G	A	TP	PIM	GP	G	A	TP	PIM
1994-95	Ak Bars Kazan	Rus-Jr.	40	20	12	32	10	....	....	....	....	....
1995-96	Ak Bars Kazan	Rus-Jr.	40	15	8	23	30	....	....	....	....	....
	Ak Bars Kazan 2	Russia-2	15	10	8	18	10	....	....	....	....	....
1996-97	Ak Bars Kazan 2	Russia-3	50	17	23	40	20	....	....	....	....	....
	Ak Bars Kazan	Russia	1	1	0	1	0	....	....	....	....	....
1997-98	Ak Bars Kazan	Russia	29	2	2	4	2	....	....	....	....	....

ARMSTRONG, CHRIS NSH.

Defense. Shoots left. 6', 198 lbs. Born, Regina, Sask., June 26, 1975.
(Florida's 3rd choice, 57th overall, in 1993 Entry Draft).

			Regular Season					Playoffs				
Season	Club	Lea	GP	G	A	TP	PIM	GP	G	A	TP	PIM
1991-92	Moose Jaw	WHL	43	2	7	9	19	4	0	0	0	0
1992-93	Moose Jaw	WHL	67	9	35	44	104	....	....	....	....	....
1993-94	Moose Jaw	WHL	64	13	55	68	54	....	....	....	....	....
	Cincinnati	IHL	1	0	0	0	0	10	1	3	4	2
1994-95	Moose Jaw	WHL	66	17	54	71	61	10	2	12	14	22
	Cincinnati	IHL	....	....	....	....	....	9	1	3	4	10
1995-96	Carolina	AHL	78	9	33	42	65	....	....	....	....	....
1996-97	Carolina	AHL	66	9	23	32	38	....	....	....	....	....
1997-98	Fort Wayne	IHL	79	8	36	44	66	4	0	2	2	4

WHL East First All-Star Team (1994) • Canadian Major Junior Second All-Star Team (1994) • WHL East Second All-Star Team (1995)

Claimed by **Nashville** from **Florida** in Expansion Draft, June 26, 1998.

ARMSTRONG, DEREK NYR

Center. Shoots right. 5'11", 188 lbs. Born, Ottawa, Ont., April 23, 1973.
(NY Islanders' 5th choice, 128th overall, in 1992 Entry Draft).

			Regular Season					Playoffs				
Season	Club	Lea	GP	G	A	TP	PIM	GP	G	A	TP	PIM
1990-91	Hawkesbury	OJHL	54	27	45	75	49	....	....	....	....	....
	Sudbury	OHL	2	0	2	2	0	....	....	....	....	....
1991-92	Sudbury	OHL	66	31	54	85	22	9	2	2	4	2
1992-93	Sudbury	OHL	66	44	62	106	56	14	9	10	19	26
1993-94	**NY Islanders**	**NHL**	**1**	**0**	**0**	**0**	**0**	....	....	....	....	....
	Salt Lake	IHL	76	23	35	58	61	....	....	....	....	....
1994-95	Denver	IHL	59	13	18	31	65	6	0	2	2	0
1995-96	**NY Islanders**	**NHL**	**19**	**1**	**3**	**4**	**14**	....	....	....	....	....
	Worcester	AHL	51	11	15	26	33	4	2	1	3	0
1996-97	**NY Islanders**	**NHL**	**50**	**6**	**7**	**13**	**33**	....	....	....	....	....
	Utah	IHL	17	4	8	12	10	6	0	4	4	4
1997-98	**Ottawa**	**NHL**	**9**	**2**	**0**	**2**	**9**	....	....	....	....	....
	Detroit	IHL	10	0	1	1	2	....	....	....	....	....
	Hartford	AHL	54	16	30	46	40	15	2	6	8	22
	NHL Totals		**79**	**9**	**10**	**19**	**56**	....	....	....	....	....

Signed as a free agent by **Ottawa**, July 28, 1997. Signed as a free agent by **NY Rangers**, August 10, 1998.

ARNOTT, JASON (AHR-nawt) N.J.

Center. Shoots right. 6'3", 220 lbs. Born, Collingwood, Ont., October 11, 1974.
(Edmonton's 1st choice, 7th overall, in 1993 Entry Draft).

			Regular Season					Playoffs				
Season	Club	Lea	GP	G	A	TP	PIM	GP	G	A	TP	PIM
1990-91	Lindsay	OJHL	42	17	44	61	10	....	....	....	....	....
1991-92	Oshawa	OHL	57	9	15	24	12	....	....	....	....	....
1992-93	Oshawa	OHL	56	41	57	98	74	13	9	9	18	20
1993-94	**Edmonton**	**NHL**	**78**	**33**	**35**	**68**	**104**	....	....	....	....	....
1994-95	**Edmonton**	**NHL**	**42**	**15**	**22**	**37**	**128**	....	....	....	....	....
1995-96	**Edmonton**	**NHL**	**64**	**28**	**31**	**59**	**87**	....	....	....	....	....
1996-97	**Edmonton**	**NHL**	**67**	**19**	**38**	**57**	**92**	**12**	**3**	**6**	**9**	**18**
1997-98	**Edmonton**	**NHL**	**35**	**5**	**13**	**18**	**78**	....	....	....	....	....
	New Jersey	**NHL**	**35**	**5**	**10**	**15**	**21**	**5**	**0**	**2**	**2**	**0**
	NHL Totals		**321**	**105**	**149**	**254**	**510**	**17**	**3**	**8**	**11**	**18**

NHL/Upper Deck All-Rookie Team (1994)

Played in NHL All-Star Game (1997)

Traded to **New Jersey** by **Edmonton** with Bryan Muir for Valeri Zelepukin and Bill Guerin, January 4, 1998.

ARVEDSON, MAGNUS (AHR-vehd-suhn, MAGH-nuhs) OTT.

Center. Shoots left. 6'2", 198 lbs. Born, Karlstad, Swe., November 25, 1971.
(Ottawa's 4th choice, 119th overall, in 1997 Entry Draft).

			Regular Season					Playoffs				
Season	Club	Lea	GP	G	A	TP	PIM	GP	G	A	TP	PIM
1991-92	Orebro	Sweden-2	32	12	21	33	30	7	4	4	8	4
1992-93	Orebro	Sweden-2	36	11	18	29	34	6	2	1	3	0
1993-94	Farjestad	Sweden	16	1	7	8	10	....	....	....	....	....
1994-95	Farjestad	Sweden	36	1	6	7	45	4	0	0	0	6
1995-96	Farjestad	Sweden	40	10	14	24	40	8	0	3	3	10
1996-97	Farjestad	Sweden	48	13	11	24	36	14	4	7	11	8
1997-98	**Ottawa**	**NHL**	**61**	**11**	**15**	**26**	**36**	**11**	**0**	**1**	**1**	**6**
	NHL Totals		**61**	**11**	**15**	**26**	**36**	**11**	**0**	**1**	**1**	**6**

ASHAM, ARRON (ASH-uhm, AIR-uhn) MTL.

Right wing. Shoots right. 5'11", 176 lbs. Born, Portage La Prairie, Man., April 13, 1978.
(Montreal's 3rd choice, 71st overall, in 1996 Entry Draft).

			Regular Season					Playoffs				
Season	Club	Lea	GP	G	A	TP	PIM	GP	G	A	TP	PIM
1994-95	Red Deer	WHL	62	11	16	27	126	....	....	....	....	....
1995-96	Red Deer	WHL	70	32	45	77	174	10	6	3	9	20
1996-97	Red Deer	WHL	67	45	51	96	149	16	12	14	26	36
1997-98	Red Deer	WHL	67	43	49	92	153	5	0	2	2	8

ATCHEYNUM, BLAIR (ATCH-uh-num) NSH.

Right wing. Shoots right. 6'2", 210 lbs. Born, Estevan, Sask., April 20, 1969.
(Hartford's 2nd choice, 52nd overall, in 1989 Entry Draft).

			Regular Season					Playoffs				
Season	Club	Lea	GP	G	A	TP	PIM	GP	G	A	TP	PIM
1985-86	Saskatoon	WHL	19	1	4	5	22	....	....	....	....	....
	North Battleford	SJHL	33	16	14	30	41	6	2	0	2	6
1986-87	Saskatoon	WHL	21	0	4	4	4	....	....	....	....	....
	Swift Current	WHL	5	2	1	3	0	....	....	....	....	....
	Moose Jaw	WHL	12	3	0	3	2	....	....	....	....	....
1987-88	Moose Jaw	WHL	60	32	16	48	52	....	....	....	....	....
1988-89	Moose Jaw	WHL	71	70	68	138	70	7	2	5	7	13
1989-90	Binghamton	AHL	78	20	21	41	45	....	....	....	....	....
1990-91	Springfield	AHL	72	25	27	52	42	13	0	6	6	6
1991-92	Springfield	AHL	62	16	21	37	64	6	1	1	2	2
1992-93	**Ottawa**	**NHL**	**4**	**0**	**1**	**1**	**0**	....	....	....	....	....
	New Haven	AHL	51	16	18	34	47	....	....	....	....	....
1993-94	Columbus	ECHL	16	15	12	27	10	....	....	....	....	....
	Portland	AHL	2	0	0	0	0	....	....	....	....	....
	Springfield	AHL	40	18	22	40	13	6	0	2	2	0
1994-95	Minnesota	IHL	17	4	6	10	7	....	....	....	....	....
	Worcester	AHL	55	17	29	46	26	....	....	....	....	....
1995-96	Cape Breton	AHL	79	30	42	72	65	....	....	....	....	....
1996-97	Hershey	AHL	77	42	45	87	57	13	6	11	17	6
1997-98	**St. Louis**	**NHL**	**61**	**11**	**15**	**26**	**10**	**10**	**0**	**0**	**0**	**2**
	NHL Totals		**65**	**11**	**16**	**27**	**10**	**10**	**0**	**0**	**0**	**2**

WHL First All-Star Team (1989) • AHL First All-Star Team (1997)

Claimed by **Ottawa** from **Hartford** in Expansion Draft, June 18, 1992. Signed as a free agent by **St. Louis**, September 15, 1997. Claimed by **Nashville** from **St. Louis** in Expansion Draft, June 26, 1998.

AUCOIN, ADRIAN (oh-KWEHN) VAN.

Defense. Shoots right. 6'2", 210 lbs. Born, Ottawa, Ont., July 3, 1973.
(Vancouver's 7th choice, 117th overall, in 1992 Entry Draft).

			Regular Season					Playoffs				
Season	Club	Lea	GP	G	A	TP	PIM	GP	G	A	TP	PIM
1990-91	Nepean	OJHL	56	17	33	50	125	....	....	....	....	....
1991-92	Boston University	H.E.	32	2	10	12	60	....	....	....	....	....
1992-93	Canada	Nat-Tm	42	8	10	18	71	....	....	....	....	....
1993-94	Canada	Nat-Tm	59	5	12	17	80	....	....	....	....	....
	Canada	Olympics	4	0	0	0	2	....	....	....	....	....
	Hamilton	AHL	13	1	2	3	19	4	0	2	2	6
1994-95	**Vancouver**	**NHL**	**1**	**1**	**0**	**1**	**0**	**4**	**1**	**0**	**1**	**0**
	Syracuse	AHL	71	13	18	31	52	....	....	....	....	....
1995-96	**Vancouver**	**NHL**	**49**	**4**	**14**	**18**	**34**	**6**	**0**	**0**	**0**	**2**
	Syracuse	AHL	29	5	13	18	47	....	....	....	....	....
1996-97	**Vancouver**	**NHL**	**70**	**5**	**16**	**21**	**63**	....	....	....	....	....
1997-98	**Vancouver**	**NHL**	**35**	**3**	**3**	**6**	**21**	....	....	....	....	....
	NHL Totals		**155**	**13**	**33**	**46**	**118**	**10**	**1**	**0**	**1**	**2**

AUDET, PHILIPPE (aw-DEHT) DET.

Left wing. Shoots left. 6'2", 175 lbs. Born, Ottawa, Ont., June 4, 1977.
(Detroit's 2nd choice, 52nd overall, in 1995 Entry Draft).

			Regular Season					Playoffs				
Season	Club	Lea	GP	G	A	TP	PIM	GP	G	A	TP	PIM
1994-95	Granby	QMJHL	62	19	17	36	93	13	2	5	7	10
1995-96	Granby	QMJHL	67	40	43	83	162	21	12	18	30	32
1996-97	Granby	QMJHL	67	52	56	108	138	4	4	1	5	35
	Adirondack	AHL	3	1	1	2	0	1	1	0	1	0
1997-98	Adirondack	AHL	50	7	8	15	43	1	0	0	0	0

Memorial Cup All-Star Team (1996) • QMJHL First All-Star Team (1997)

AUDETTE, DONALD (aw-DEHT) BUF.

Right wing. Shoots right. 5'8", 184 lbs. Born, Laval, Que., September 23, 1969.
(Buffalo's 8th choice, 183rd overall, in 1989 Entry Draft).

			Regular Season					Playoffs				
Season	Club	Lea	GP	G	A	TP	PIM	GP	G	A	TP	PIM
1986-87	Laval	QMJHL	66	17	22	39	36	14	2	6	8	10
1987-88	Laval	QMJHL	63	48	61	109	56	14	7	12	19	20
1988-89	Laval	QMJHL	70	76	85	161	123	17	17	12	29	43
1989-90	Rochester	AHL	70	42	46	88	78	15	9	8	17	29
	Buffalo	**NHL**	....	....	....	....	....	**2**	**0**	**0**	**0**	**0**
1990-91	**Buffalo**	**NHL**	**8**	**4**	**3**	**7**	**4**	....	....	....	....	....
	Rochester	AHL	5	4	0	4	2	....	....	....	....	....
1991-92	**Buffalo**	**NHL**	**63**	**31**	**17**	**48**	**75**	....	....	....	....	....
1992-93	**Buffalo**	**NHL**	**44**	**12**	**7**	**19**	**51**	**8**	**2**	**2**	**4**	**6**
	Rochester	AHL	6	8	4	12	10	....	....	....	....	....
1993-94	**Buffalo**	**NHL**	**77**	**29**	**30**	**59**	**41**	**7**	**0**	**1**	**1**	**6**
1994-95	**Buffalo**	**NHL**	**46**	**24**	**13**	**37**	**27**	**5**	**1**	**1**	**2**	**4**
1995-96	**Buffalo**	**NHL**	**23**	**12**	**13**	**25**	**18**	....	....	....	....	....
1996-97	**Buffalo**	**NHL**	**73**	**28**	**22**	**50**	**48**	**11**	**4**	**5**	**9**	**6**
1997-98	**Buffalo**	**NHL**	**75**	**24**	**20**	**44**	**59**	**15**	**5**	**8**	**13**	**10**
	NHL Totals		**409**	**164**	**125**	**289**	**323**	**48**	**12**	**17**	**29**	**32**

QMJHL First All-Star Team (1989) • AHL First All-Star Team (1990) • Won Dudley "Red" Garret Memorial Trophy (Top Rookie - AHL) (1990)

AUGER, VINCENT (OH-zhay, VIHN-cehnt) COL.

Center. Shoots left. 5'10", 175 lbs. Born, Quebec, Que., March 7, 1975.
(Quebec's 11th choice, 231st overall, in 1993 Entry Draft).

			Regular Season					Playoffs				
Season	Club	Lea	GP	G	A	TP	PIM	GP	G	A	TP	PIM
1992-93	Hawkesbury	OJHL	52	41	36	77	104	....	....	....	....	....
1993-94	Cornell	ECAC	29	11	13	24	33	....	....	....	....	....
1994-95			DID NOT PLAY									
1995-96	Cornell	ECAC	23	5	15	20	22	....	....	....	....	....
1996-97	Cornell	ECAC	26	11	7	18	36	....	....	....	....	....
1997-98	Cornell	ECAC	4	2	5	7	4	....	....	....	....	....

Rights transferred to **Colorado** after **Quebec** franchise relocated, June 21, 1995.

AUGUSTA, PATRIK (ah-GOOS-tuh, pa-TREEK)

Right wing. Shoots left. 5'10", 170 lbs. Born, Jihlava, Czech., November 13, 1969.
(Toronto's 8th choice, 149th overall, in 1992 Entry Draft).

			Regular Season					Playoffs				
Season	Club	Lea	GP	G	A	TP	PIM	GP	G	A	TP	PIM
1988-89	Dukla Jihlava	Czech.	15	3	1	4	4	....	....	....	....	....
1989-90	Dukla Jihlava	Czech.	46	12	12	24	....	....	....	....	....	....
1990-91	Dukla Jihlava	Czech.	51	20	23	43	....	....	....	....	....	....
1991-92	Dukla Jihlava	Czech.	42	16	16	32	26	....	....	....	....	....
	Czech Republic	Olympics	8	3	2	5	0	....	....	....	....	....
1992-93	St. John's	AHL	75	32	45	77	74	8	3	3	6	23
1993-94	**Toronto**	**NHL**	**2**	**0**	**0**	**0**	**0**	....	....	....	....	....
	St. John's	AHL	77	*53	43	96	105	11	4	8	12	4
1994-95	St. John's	AHL	71	37	32	69	98	4	2	0	2	7
1995-96	Los Angeles	IHL	79	34	51	85	83	....	....	....	....	....
1996-97	Long Beach	IHL	82	45	42	87	96	18	4	4	8	33
1997-98	Long Beach	IHL	82	41	40	81	84	17	11	7	18	20
	NHL Totals		**2**	**0**	**0**	**0**	**0**	....	....	....	....	....

AHL Second All-Star Team (1994) • IHL Second All-Star Team (1997)

AXELSSON, PER-JOHAN (AHX-ehl-suhn, PAIR, YEW-hahn) BOS.

Left wing. Shoots left. 6'1", 174 lbs. Born, Kungalv, Sweden, February 26, 1975.
(Boston's 7th choice, 177th overall, in 1995 Entry Draft).

			Regular Season					Playoffs				
Season	Club	Lea	GP	G	A	TP	PIM	GP	G	A	TP	PIM
1993-94	V. Frolunda	Sweden	11	0	0	0	4	4	0	0	0	0
1994-95	V. Frolunda	Sweden	8	2	1	3	6	....	....	....	....	....
1995-96	V. Frolunda	Sweden	36	15	5	20	10	13	3	0	3	10
1996-97	V. Frolunda	Sweden	50	19	15	34	34	3	0	2	2	0
1997-98	**Boston**	**NHL**	**82**	**8**	**19**	**27**	**38**	**6**	**1**	**0**	**1**	**0**
	NHL Totals		**82**	**8**	**19**	**27**	**38**	**6**	**1**	**0**	**1**	**0**

BABENKO, YURI (bah-BEHN-koh) COL.

Center. Shoots left. 6', 185 lbs. Born, Penza, USSR, January 2, 1978.
(Colorado's 2nd choice, 51st overall, in 1996 Entry Draft).

			Regular Season					Playoffs				
Season	Club	Lea	GP	G	A	TP	PIM	GP	G	A	TP	PIM
1995-96	Soviet Wings	CIS	21	0	0	0	16	....	....	....	....	....
1996-97	Soviet Wings	Russia	4	1	0	1	4	....	....	....	....	....
	Soviet Wings 2	Russia-3	26	8	10	18	24	....	....	....	....	....
	CSKA Moscow	Russia-2	24	3	3	6	12	....	....	....	....	....
1997-98	Plymouth	OHL	59	22	34	56	22	15	3	7	10	24

BABYCH, DAVE (BAB-itch) PHI.

Defense. Shoots left. 6'2", 215 lbs. Born, Edmonton, Alta., May 23, 1961.
(Winnipeg's 1st choice, 2nd overall, in 1980 Entry Draft).

			Regular Season					Playoffs				
Season	Club	Lea	GP	G	A	TP	PIM	GP	G	A	TP	PIM
1977-78	Portland	WCJHL	6	1	3	4	4	....	....	....	....	....
1978-79	Portland	WHL	67	20	59	79	63	25	7	22	29	22
1979-80	Portland	WHL	50	22	60	82	71	8	1	10	11	2
1980-81	**Winnipeg**	**NHL**	**69**	**6**	**38**	**44**	**90**	....	....	....	....	....
1981-82	**Winnipeg**	**NHL**	**79**	**19**	**49**	**68**	**92**	**4**	**1**	**2**	**3**	**29**
1982-83	**Winnipeg**	**NHL**	**79**	**13**	**61**	**74**	**56**	**3**	**0**	**0**	**0**	**0**
1983-84	**Winnipeg**	**NHL**	**66**	**18**	**39**	**57**	**62**	**3**	**1**	**1**	**2**	**0**
1984-85	**Winnipeg**	**NHL**	**78**	**13**	**49**	**62**	**78**	**8**	**2**	**7**	**9**	**6**
1985-86	**Winnipeg**	**NHL**	**19**	**4**	**12**	**16**	**14**	....	....	....	....	....
	Hartford	**NHL**	**62**	**10**	**43**	**53**	**36**	**8**	**1**	**3**	**4**	**14**
1986-87	**Hartford**	**NHL**	**66**	**8**	**33**	**41**	**44**	**6**	**1**	**1**	**2**	**14**
1987-88	**Hartford**	**NHL**	**71**	**14**	**36**	**50**	**54**	**6**	**3**	**2**	**5**	**2**
1988-89	**Hartford**	**NHL**	**70**	**6**	**41**	**47**	**54**	**4**	**1**	**5**	**6**	**2**
1989-90	**Hartford**	**NHL**	**72**	**6**	**37**	**43**	**62**	**7**	**1**	**2**	**3**	**0**
1990-91	**Hartford**	**NHL**	**8**	**0**	**6**	**6**	**4**	....	....	....	....	....
1991-92	**Vancouver**	**NHL**	**75**	**5**	**24**	**29**	**63**	**13**	**2**	**6**	**8**	**10**
1992-93	**Vancouver**	**NHL**	**43**	**3**	**16**	**19**	**44**	**12**	**2**	**5**	**7**	**6**
1993-94	**Vancouver**	**NHL**	**73**	**4**	**28**	**32**	**52**	**24**	**3**	**5**	**8**	**12**
1994-95	**Vancouver**	**NHL**	**40**	**3**	**11**	**14**	**18**	**11**	**2**	**2**	**4**	**14**
1995-96	**Vancouver**	**NHL**	**53**	**3**	**21**	**24**	**38**	....	....	....	....	....
1996-97	**Vancouver**	**NHL**	**78**	**5**	**22**	**27**	**38**	....	....	....	....	....
1997-98	**Vancouver**	**NHL**	**47**	**0**	**9**	**9**	**37**	....	....	....	....	....
	Philadelphia	**NHL**	**6**	**0**	**0**	**0**	**12**	**5**	**1**	**0**	**1**	**4**
	NHL Totals		**1154**	**140**	**575**	**715**	**948**	**114**	**21**	**41**	**62**	**113**

WHL First All-Star Team (1980)

Played in NHL All-Star Game (1983, 1984)

Traded to **Hartford** by **Winnipeg** for Ray Neufeld, November 21, 1985. Claimed by **Minnesota** from **Hartford** in Expansion Draft, May 30, 1991. Traded to **Vancouver** by **Minnesota** for Tom Kurvers, June 22, 1991. Traded to **Philadelphia** by **Vancouver** with Philadelphia's 5th round choice (previously acquired, Philadelphia selected Garrett Prosofsky) in 1998 Entry Draft for Philadelphia's 3rd round choice (Justin Morrison) in 1998 Entry Draft, March 24, 1998.

BACKMAN, CHRISTIAN ST.L.

Defense. Shoots left. 6'2", 187 lbs. Born, Alingsas, Sweden, April 28, 1980.
(St. Louis' 1st choice, 24th overall, in 1998 Entry Draft).

			Regular Season					Playoffs				
Season	Club	Lea	GP	G	A	TP	PIM	GP	G	A	TP	PIM
1996-97	V. Frolunda	Swe-Jr.	26	2	5	7	16	....	....	....	....	....
1997-98	V. Frolunda	Swe-Jr.	28	5	14	19	12	2	0	1	1	4

BAKER, JAMIE

Center. Shoots left. 6', 195 lbs. Born, Ottawa, Ont., August 31, 1966.
(Quebec's 2nd choice, 8th overall, in 1988 Supplemental Draft).

			Regular Season					Playoffs				
Season	Club	Lea	GP	G	A	TP	PIM	GP	G	A	TP	PIM
1985-86	St. Lawrence	ECAC	31	9	16	25	52	....	....	....	....	....
1986-87	St. Lawrence	ECAC	32	8	24	32	59	....	....	....	....	....
1987-88	St. Lawrence	ECAC	34	26	24	50	38	....	....	....	....	....
1988-89	St. Lawrence	ECAC	13	11	16	27	16	....	....	....	....	....
1989-90	**Quebec**	**NHL**	**1**	**0**	**0**	**0**	**0**	....	....	....	....	....
	Halifax	AHL	74	17	43	60	47	6	0	0	0	7
1990-91	**Quebec**	**NHL**	**18**	**2**	**0**	**2**	**8**	....	....	....	....	....
	Halifax	AHL	50	14	22	36	85	....	....	....	....	....
1991-92	**Quebec**	**NHL**	**52**	**7**	**10**	**17**	**32**	....	....	....	....	....
	Halifax	AHL	9	5	0	5	12	....	....	....	....	....
1992-93	**Ottawa**	**NHL**	**76**	**19**	**29**	**48**	**54**	....	....	....	....	....
1993-94	**San Jose**	**NHL**	**65**	**12**	**5**	**17**	**38**	**14**	**3**	**2**	**5**	**30**
1994-95	**San Jose**	**NHL**	**43**	**7**	**4**	**11**	**22**	**11**	**2**	**2**	**4**	**12**
1995-96	**San Jose**	**NHL**	**77**	**16**	**17**	**33**	**79**	....	....	....	....	....
1996-97	**Toronto**	**NHL**	**58**	**8**	**8**	**16**	**28**	....	....	....	....	....
1997-98	**Toronto**	**NHL**	**13**	**0**	**5**	**5**	**10**	....	....	....	....	....
	Chicago	IHL	53	11	34	45	80	22	4	5	9	42
	NHL Totals		**403**	**71**	**78**	**149**	**271**	**25**	**5**	**4**	**9**	**42**

Signed as a free agent by **Ottawa**, September 2, 1992. Signed as a free agent by **San Jose**, September 11, 1993. Traded to **Toronto** by **San Jose** with San Jose's 5th round choice (Peter Cava) in 1996 Entry Draft for Todd Gill, June 14, 1996.

BALA, CHRIS OTT.

Left wing. Shoots left. 6'1", 180 lbs. Born, Virginia, September 24, 1978.
(Ottawa's 3rd choice, 58th overall, in 1998 Entry Draft).

			Regular Season					Playoffs				
Season	Club	Lea	GP	G	A	TP	PIM	GP	G	A	TP	PIM
1996-97	Hill High	H.S.	23	28	33	61	36	....	....	....	....	....
1997-98	Harvard	ECAC	33	16	14	30	23	....	....	....	....	....

BALMOCHNYKH, MAXIM (bahl-MAWCH-nihky, mahx-EEM) ANA.

Left wing. Shoots left. 6', 185 lbs. Born, Lipetsk, USSR, March 7, 1979.
(Anaheim's 2nd choice, 45th overall, in 1997 Entry Draft).

			Regular Season					Playoffs				
Season	Club	Lea	GP	G	A	TP	PIM	GP	G	A	TP	PIM
1994-95	Lipetsk	CIS-2	3	0	1	1	4	....	....	....	....	....
1995-96	Lipetsk	CIS-2	40	15	5	20	60	....	....	....	....	....
1996-97	Togliatti	Russia	18	6	1	7	22	....	....	....	....	....
1997-98	Togliatti	Russia	37	10	4	14	46	....	....	....	....	....
	Chelyabinsk	Russia	2	0	0	0	2	....	....	....	....	....

BANCROFT, STEVE

Defense. Shoots left. 6'1", 214 lbs. Born, Toronto, Ont., October 6, 1970.
(Toronto's 3rd choice, 21st overall, in 1989 Entry Draft).

			Regular Season					Playoffs				
Season	Club	Lea	GP	G	A	TP	PIM	GP	G	A	TP	PIM
1987-88	Belleville	OHL	56	1	8	9	42	....	....	....	....	....
1988-89	Belleville	OHL	66	7	30	37	99	5	0	2	2	10
1989-90	Belleville	OHL	53	10	33	43	135	11	3	9	12	38
1990-91	Newmarket	AHL	9	0	3	3	22	....	....	....	....	....
	Maine	AHL	53	2	12	14	46	2	0	0	0	2
1991-92	Maine	AHL	26	1	3	4	45	....	....	....	....	....
	Indianapolis	IHL	36	8	23	31	49	....	....	....	....	....
1992-93	**Chicago**	**NHL**	**1**	**0**	**0**	**0**	**0**	....	....	....	....	....
	Indianapolis	IHL	53	10	35	45	138	....	....	....	....	....
	Moncton	AHL	21	3	13	16	16	5	0	0	0	16
1993-94	Cleveland	IHL	33	2	12	14	58	....	....	....	....	....
1994-95	Detroit	IHL	6	1	3	4	0	....	....	....	....	....
	Fort Wayne	IHL	50	7	17	24	100	....	....	....	....	....
	St. John's	AHL	4	2	0	2	2	5	0	3	3	8
1995-96	Los Angeles	IHL	15	3	10	13	22	....	....	....	....	....
	Chicago	IHL	64	9	41	50	91	9	1	7	8	22
1996-97	Chicago	IHL	39	6	10	16	66	....	....	....	....	....
	Las Vegas	IHL	36	9	28	37	64	3	0	0	0	2
1997-98	Las Vegas	IHL	70	15	44	59	148	....	....	....	....	....
	Saint John	AHL	9	0	4	4	12	19	2	11	13	30
	NHL Totals		**1**	**0**	**0**	**0**	**0**	....	....	....	....	....

Traded to **Boston** by **Toronto** for Rob Cimetta, November 9, 1990. Traded to **Chicago** by **Boston** with Boston's 11th round choice (later traded to Winnipeg — Winnipeg selected Russel Hewson) in 1993 Entry Draft for Chicago's 11th round choice (Eugene Pavlov) in 1992 Entry Draft, January 9, 1992. Traded to **Winnipeg** by **Chicago** with future considerations for Troy Murray, February 21, 1993. Claimed by **Florida** from **Winnipeg** in Expansion Draft, June 24, 1993. Signed as a free agent by **Pittsburgh**, August 2, 1993.

BANHAM, FRANK ANA.

Right wing. Shoots right. 6', 190 lbs. Born, Calahoo, Alta., April 14, 1975.
(Washington's 4th choice, 147th overall, in 1993 Entry Draft).

			Regular Season					Playoffs				
Season	Club	Lea	GP	G	A	TP	PIM	GP	G	A	TP	PIM
1992-93	Saskatoon	WHL	71	29	33	62	55	9	2	7	9	8
1993-94	Saskatoon	WHL	65	28	39	67	99	16	8	11	19	36
1994-95	Saskatoon	WHL	70	50	39	89	63	8	2	6	8	12
1995-96	Saskatoon	WHL	72	*83	69	152	116	4	6	0	6	2
	Baltimore	AHL	9	1	4	5	0	7	1	1	2	2
1996-97	**Anaheim**	**NHL**	**3**	**0**	**0**	**0**	**0**	....	....	....	....	....
	Baltimore	AHL	21	11	13	24	4	....	....	....	....	....
1997-98	**Anaheim**	**NHL**	**21**	**9**	**2**	**11**	**12**	....	....	....	....	....
	Cincinnati	AHL	35	7	8	15	39	....	....	....	....	....
	NHL Totals		**24**	**9**	**2**	**11**	**12**	....	....	....	....	....

WHL East First All-Star Team (1996)

Signed as a free agent by **Anaheim**, January 27, 1996.

BANNISTER, DREW — ANA.

Defense. Shoots right. 6'2", 200 lbs. Born, Belleville, Ont., September 4, 1974.
(Tampa Bay's 2nd choice, 26th overall, in 1992 Entry Draft).

			Regular Season					Playoffs				
Season	Club	Lea	GP	G	A	TP	PIM	GP	G	A	TP	PIM
1990-91	S.S. Marie	OHL	41	2	8	10	51	4	0	0	0	0
1991-92	S.S. Marie	OHL	64	4	21	25	122	16	3	10	13	36
1992-93	S.S. Marie	OHL	59	5	28	33	114	18	2	7	9	12
1993-94	S.S. Marie	OHL	58	7	43	50	108	14	6	9	15	20
1994-95	Atlanta	IHL	72	5	7	12	74	5	0	2	2	22
1995-96	Tampa Bay	NHL	13	0	1	1	4	....	....	....	....	....
	Atlanta	IHL	61	3	13	16	105	3	0	0	0	4
1996-97	Tampa Bay	NHL	64	4	13	17	44	....	....	....	....	....
	Edmonton	NHL	1	0	1	1	0	12	0	0	0	30
1997-98	Edmonton	NHL	34	0	2	2	42	....	....	....	....	....
	Anaheim	NHL	27	0	6	6	47	....	....	....	....	....
	NHL Totals		139	4	23	27	137	12	0	0	0	30

Memorial Cup All-Star Team (1993) • OHL Second All-Star Team (1994)

Traded to **Edmonton** by **Tampa Bay** with Tampa Bay's 6th round choice (Peter Sarno) in 1997 Entry Draft for Jeff Norton, March 18, 1997. Traded to **Anaheim** by **Edmonton** for Bobby Dollas, January 9, 1998.

BARCH, KRYS — WSH.

Left wing. Shoots left. 6'1", 195 lbs. Born, Guelph, Ont., March 26, 1980.
(Washington's 3rd choice, 106th overall, in 1998 Entry Draft).

			Regular Season					Playoffs				
Season	Club	Lea	GP	G	A	TP	PIM	GP	G	A	TP	PIM
1996-97	Georgetown	OJHL	51	18	26	44	58	....	....	....	....	....
1997-98	London	OHL	65	9	27	36	62	16	4	3	7	16

BARNABY, MATTHEW — BUF.

Right wing. Shoots left. 6', 188 lbs. Born, Ottawa, Ont., May 4, 1973.
(Buffalo's 5th choice, 83rd overall, in 1992 Entry Draft).

			Regular Season					Playoffs				
Season	Club	Lea	GP	G	A	TP	PIM	GP	G	A	TP	PIM
1990-91	Beauport	QMJHL	52	9	5	14	262	....	....	....	....	....
1991-92	Beauport	QMJHL	63	29	37	66	*476	....	....	....	....	....
1992-93	Buffalo	NHL	2	1	0	1	10	1	0	1	1	4
	Victoriaville	QMJHL	65	44	67	111	*448	6	2	4	6	44
1993-94	Buffalo	NHL	35	2	4	6	106	3	0	0	0	17
	Rochester	AHL	42	10	32	42	153	....	....	....	....	....
1994-95	Buffalo	NHL	23	1	1	2	116	....	....	....	....	....
	Rochester	AHL	56	21	29	50	274	....	....	....	....	....
1995-96	Buffalo	NHL	73	15	16	31	*335	....	....	....	....	....
1996-97	Buffalo	NHL	68	19	24	43	249	8	0	4	4	36
1997-98	Buffalo	NHL	72	5	20	25	289	15	7	6	13	22
	NHL Totals		273	43	65	108	1105	27	7	11	18	79

BARNES, RYAN — DET.

Left wing. Shoots left. 6'1", 201 lbs. Born, Dunnville, Ont., January 30, 1980.
(Detroit's 2nd choice, 55th overall, in 1998 Entry Draft).

			Regular Season					Playoffs				
Season	Club	Lea	GP	G	A	TP	PIM	GP	G	A	TP	PIM
1997-98	Sudbury	OHL	46	13	18	31	111	10	0	2	2	24

BARNES, STU — PIT.

Center. Shoots right. 5'11", 174 lbs. Born, Spruce Grove, Alta., December 25, 1970.
(Winnipeg's 1st choice, 4th overall, in 1989 Entry Draft).

			Regular Season					Playoffs				
Season	Club	Lea	GP	G	A	TP	PIM	GP	G	A	TP	PIM
1987-88	New Westminster	WHL	71	37	64	101	88	5	2	3	5	6
1988-89	Tri-City	WHL	70	59	82	141	117	7	6	5	11	10
1989-90	Tri-City	WHL	63	52	92	144	165	7	1	5	6	26
1990-91	Canada	Nat-Tm	53	22	27	49	68	....	....	....	....	....
1991-92	Winnipeg	NHL	46	8	9	17	26	....	....	....	....	....
	Moncton	AHL	30	13	19	32	10	11	3	9	12	6
1992-93	Winnipeg	NHL	38	12	10	22	10	6	1	3	4	2
	Moncton	AHL	42	23	31	54	58	....	....	....	....	....
1993-94	Winnipeg	NHL	18	5	4	9	8	....	....	....	....	....
	Florida	NHL	59	18	20	38	30	....	....	....	....	....
1994-95	Florida	NHL	41	10	19	29	8	....	....	....	....	....
1995-96	Florida	NHL	72	19	25	44	46	22	6	10	16	4
1996-97	Florida	NHL	19	2	8	10	10	....	....	....	....	....
	Pittsburgh	NHL	62	17	22	39	16	5	0	1	1	0
1997-98	Pittsburgh	NHL	78	30	35	65	30	6	3	3	6	2
	NHL Totals		433	121	152	273	184	39	10	17	27	8

WHL West Second All-Star Team (1988, 1989)

Traded to **Florida** by **Winnipeg** with St. Louis' 6th round choice (previously acquired by Winnipeg — later traded to Edmonton — later traded to Winnipeg — Winnipeg selected Chris Kibermanis) in 1994 Entry Draft for Randy Gilhen, November 25, 1993. Traded to **Pittsburgh** by **Florida** with Jason Woolley for Chris Wells, November 19, 1996.

BARNEY, SCOTT — L.A.

Center. Shoots right. 6'4", 198 lbs. Born, Oshawa, Ont., March 27, 1979.
(Los Angeles' 3rd choice, 29th overall, in 1997 Entry Draft).

			Regular Season					Playoffs				
Season	Club	Lea	GP	G	A	TP	PIM	GP	G	A	TP	PIM
1995-96	Peterborough	OHL	60	22	24	46	52	24	6	8	14	38
1996-97	Peterborough	OHL	64	21	33	54	110	9	0	3	3	16
1997-98	Peterborough	OHL	62	44	32	76	60	4	1	0	1	6

BARON, MURRAY — VAN.

Defense. Shoots left. 6'3", 215 lbs. Born, Prince George, B.C., June 1, 1967.
(Philadelphia's 7th choice, 167th overall, in 1986 Entry Draft).

			Regular Season					Playoffs				
Season	Club	Lea	GP	G	A	TP	PIM	GP	G	A	TP	PIM
1985-86	Vernon	BCJHL	46	12	32	44	179	7	1	2	3	13
1986-87	North Dakota	WCHA	41	4	10	14	62	....	....	....	....	....
1987-88	North Dakota	WCHA	41	1	10	11	95	....	....	....	....	....
1988-89	North Dakota	WCHA	40	2	6	8	92	....	....	....	....	....
	Hershey	AHL	9	0	3	3	8	....	....	....	....	....
1989-90	Philadelphia	NHL	16	2	2	4	12	....	....	....	....	....
	Hershey	AHL	50	0	10	10	101	....	....	....	....	....
1990-91	Philadelphia	NHL	67	8	8	16	74	....	....	....	....	....
	Hershey	AHL	6	2	3	5	0	....	....	....	....	....
1991-92	St. Louis	NHL	67	3	8	11	94	2	0	0	0	2
1992-93	St. Louis	NHL	53	2	2	4	59	11	0	0	0	12
1993-94	St. Louis	NHL	77	5	9	14	123	4	0	0	0	10
1994-95	St. Louis	NHL	39	0	5	5	93	7	1	1	2	2
1995-96	St. Louis	NHL	82	2	9	11	190	13	1	0	1	20
1996-97	St. Louis	NHL	11	0	2	2	11	....	....	....	....	....
	Montreal	NHL	60	1	5	6	107	....	....	....	....	....
	Phoenix	NHL	8	0	0	0	4	1	0	0	0	0
1997-98	Phoenix	NHL	45	1	5	6	106	6	0	2	2	6
	NHL Totals		525	24	55	79	873	44	2	3	5	52

Traded to **St. Louis** by **Philadelphia** with Ron Sutter for Dan Quinn and Rod Brind'Amour, September 22, 1991. Traded to **Montreal** by **St. Louis** with Shayne Corson and St. Louis' 5th round choice (Gennady Razin) in 1997 Entry Draft for Pierre Turgeon, Rory Fitzpatrick and Craig Conroy, October 29, 1996. Traded to **Phoenix** by **Montreal** with Chris Murray for Dave Manson, March 18, 1997. Signed as a free agent by **Vancouver**, July 15, 1998.

BARRIE, LEN

Center. Shoots left. 6', 200 lbs. Born, Kimberley, B.C., June 4, 1969.
(Edmonton's 7th choice, 124th overall, in 1988 Entry Draft).

			Regular Season					Playoffs				
Season	Club	Lea	GP	G	A	TP	PIM	GP	G	A	TP	PIM
1985-86	Calgary	WHL	32	3	0	3	18	....	....	....	....	....
1986-87	Calgary	WHL	34	13	13	26	81	....	....	....	....	....
	Victoria	WHL	34	7	6	13	92	5	0	1	1	15
1987-88	Victoria	WHL	70	37	49	86	192	8	2	0	2	29
1988-89	Victoria	WHL	67	39	48	87	157	7	5	2	7	23
1989-90	Kamloops	WHL	70	*85	*100	*185	108	17	*14	23	*37	24
	Philadelphia	NHL	1	0	0	0	0	....	....	....	....	....
1990-91	Hershey	AHL	63	26	32	58	60	7	4	0	4	12
1991-92	Hershey	AHL	75	42	43	85	78	3	0	2	2	32
1992-93	Philadelphia	NHL	8	2	2	4	9	....	....	....	....	....
	Hershey	AHL	61	31	45	76	162	....	....	....	....	....
1993-94	Florida	NHL	2	0	0	0	0	....	....	....	....	....
	Cincinnati	IHL	77	45	71	116	246	11	8	13	21	60
1994-95	Cleveland	IHL	28	13	30	43	137	....	....	....	....	....
	Pittsburgh	NHL	48	3	11	14	66	4	1	0	1	8
1995-96	Pittsburgh	NHL	5	0	0	0	18	....	....	....	....	....
	Cleveland	IHL	55	29	43	72	178	3	2	3	5	6
1996-97	San Antonio	IHL	57	26	40	66	196	9	5	5	10	20
1997-98	San Antonio	IHL	32	7	13	20	90	....	....	....	....	....
	Frankfurt	Germany	25	11	19	30	32	6	2	3	5	35
	NHL Totals		64	5	13	18	93	4	1	0	1	8

WHL West First All-Star Team (1990) • IHL Second All-Star Team (1994)

Signed as a free agent by **Philadelphia**, February 28, 1990. Signed as a free agent by **Florida**, July 20, 1993. Signed as a free agent by **Pittsburgh**, August 15, 1994.

BARTECKO, LUBOS — ST.L.

Left wing. Shoots left. 6'1", 200 lbs. Born, Kezmarok, Czechoslovakia, July 14, 1976.

			Regular Season					Playoffs				
Season	Club	Lea	GP	G	A	TP	PIM	GP	G	A	TP	PIM
1995-96	Chicoutimi	QMJHL	70	32	41	73	50	17	8	15	23	10
1996-97	Drummondville	QMJHL	58	40	51	91	49	8	1	8	9	4
1997-98	Worcester	AHL	34	10	12	22	24	10	4	2	6	2

Signed as a free agent by **St. Louis**, October 3, 1997.

BASHKIROV, ANDREI (bahsh-KIHR-ahf) — MTL.

Left wing. Shoots left. 6', 198 lbs. Born, Shelekhov, USSR, June 22, 1970.
(Montreal's 4th choice, 132nd overall, in 1998 Entry Draft).

			Regular Season					Playoffs				
Season	Club	Lea	GP	G	A	TP	PIM	GP	G	A	TP	PIM
1990-91	Yermak Angarsk	USSR-3			STATISTICS NOT AVAILABLE							
1991-92	Khimik	CIS	11	2	0	2	4	....	....	....	....	....
1992-93	Yermak Angarsk	CIS-3			STATISTICS NOT AVAILABLE							
1993-94	Charlotte	ECHL	62	28	42	70	25	3	1	0	1	0
	Providence	AHL	1	0	0	0	2	....	....	....	....	....
1994-95	Charlotte	ECHL	61	19	27	46	20	3	0	0	0	0
1995-96	Huntington	ECHL	55	19	39	58	35	....	....	....	....	....
1996-97	Huntington	ECHL	47	29	41	70	12	....	....	....	....	....
	Detroit	IHL	2	0	0	0	0	....	....	....	....	....
	Las Vegas	IHL	27	10	12	22	0	2	0	0	0	0
1997-98	Las Vegas	IHL	15	2	3	5	5	....	....	....	....	....
	Fort Wayne	IHL	65	28	48	76	16	4	2	2	4	2

BASSEN, BOB — CGY.

Center. Shoots left. 5'10", 185 lbs. Born, Calgary, Alta., May 6, 1965.

			Regular Season					Playoffs				
Season	Club	Lea	GP	G	A	TP	PIM	GP	G	A	TP	PIM
1982-83	Medicine Hat	WHL	4	3	2	5	0	3	0	0	0	4
1983-84	Medicine Hat	WHL	72	29	29	58	93	14	5	11	16	12
1984-85	Medicine Hat	WHL	65	32	50	82	143	10	2	8	10	39
1985-86	**NY Islanders**	**NHL**	**11**	**2**	**1**	**3**	**6**	**3**	**0**	**1**	**1**	**0**
	Springfield	AHL	54	13	21	34	111	....	....	....	....	....
1986-87	**NY Islanders**	**NHL**	**77**	**7**	**10**	**17**	**89**	**14**	**1**	**2**	**3**	**21**
1987-88	**NY Islanders**	**NHL**	**77**	**6**	**16**	**22**	**99**	**6**	**0**	**1**	**1**	**23**
1988-89	**NY Islanders**	**NHL**	**19**	**1**	**4**	**5**	**21**	....	....	....	....	....
	Chicago	**NHL**	**49**	**4**	**12**	**16**	**62**	**10**	**1**	**1**	**2**	**34**
1989-90	**Chicago**	**NHL**	**6**	**1**	**1**	**2**	**8**	**1**	**0**	**0**	**0**	**2**
	Indianapolis	IHL	73	22	32	54	179	12	3	8	11	33
1990-91	**St. Louis**	**NHL**	**79**	**16**	**18**	**34**	**183**	**13**	**1**	**3**	**4**	**24**
1991-92	**St. Louis**	**NHL**	**79**	**7**	**25**	**32**	**167**	**6**	**0**	**2**	**2**	**4**
1992-93	**St. Louis**	**NHL**	**53**	**9**	**10**	**19**	**63**	**11**	**0**	**0**	**0**	**10**
1993-94	**St. Louis**	**NHL**	**46**	**2**	**7**	**9**	**44**	....	....	....	....	....
	Quebec	**NHL**	**37**	**11**	**8**	**19**	**55**	....	....	....	....	....
1994-95	**Quebec**	**NHL**	**47**	**12**	**15**	**27**	**33**	**5**	**2**	**4**	**6**	**0**
1995-96	**Dallas**	**NHL**	**13**	**0**	**1**	**1**	**15**	....	....	....	....	....
	Michigan	IHL	1	0	0	0	4	....	....	....	....	....
1996-97	**Dallas**	**NHL**	**46**	**5**	**7**	**12**	**41**	**7**	**3**	**1**	**4**	**4**
1997-98	**Dallas**	**NHL**	**58**	**3**	**4**	**7**	**57**	**17**	**1**	**0**	**1**	**12**
	NHL Totals		**697**	**86**	**139**	**225**	**943**	**93**	**9**	**15**	**24**	**134**

WHL First All-Star Team (1985) • IHL First All-Star Team (1990)

Signed as a free agent by **NY Islanders**, October 19, 1984. Traded to **Chicago** by **NY Islanders** with Steve Konroyd for Marc Bergevin and Gary Nylund, November 25, 1988. Claimed by **St. Louis** from **Chicago** in NHL Waiver Draft, October 1, 1990. Traded to **Quebec** by **St. Louis** with Garth Butcher and Ron Sutter for Steve Duchesne and Denis Chasse, January 23, 1994. Signed as a free agent by **Dallas**, August 10, 1995. Traded to **Calgary** by **Dallas** for Aaron Gavey, July 14, 1998.

BAST, RYAN — PHI.

Defense. Shoots left. 6'2", 190 lbs. Born, Spruce Grove, Alta., August 27, 1975.

			Regular Season					Playoffs				
Season	Club	Lea	GP	G	A	TP	PIM	GP	G	A	TP	PIM
1993-94	Portland	WHL	6	0	0	0	4	....	....	....	....	....
	Prince Albert	WHL	47	2	8	10	139	....	....	....	....	....
1994-95	Prince Albert	WHL	42	1	10	11	149	14	0	3	3	13
1995-96	Swift Current	WHL	72	9	18	27	203	6	1	0	1	21
1996-97	Saint John	AHL	12	0	0	0	21	5	0	0	0	4
	Las Vegas	IHL	49	2	3	5	266	....	....	....	....	....
1997-98	Saint John	AHL	77	3	8	11	187	21	0	1	1	55

Signed as a free agent by **Philadelphia**, May 18, 1998.

BATES, SHAWN — BOS.

Center. Shoots right. 5'11", 205 lbs. Born, Melrose, MA, April 3, 1975.
(Boston's 4th choice, 103rd overall, in 1993 Entry Draft).

			Regular Season					Playoffs				
Season	Club	Lea	GP	G	A	TP	PIM	GP	G	A	TP	PIM
1992-93	Medford High	H.S.	25	49	46	95	20	....	....	....	....	....
1993-94	Boston University	H.E.	41	10	19	29	24	....	....	....	....	....
1994-95	Boston University	H.E.	38	18	12	30	48	....	....	....	....	....
1995-96	Boston University	H.E.	40	28	22	50	54	....	....	....	....	....
1996-97	Boston University	H.E.	41	17	18	35	64	....	....	....	....	....
1997-98	**Boston**	**NHL**	**13**	**2**	**0**	**2**	**2**	....	....	....	....	....
	Providence	AHL	50	15	19	34	22	....	....	....	....	....
	NHL Totals		**13**	**2**	**0**	**2**	**2**	....	....	....	....	....

NCAA Championship All-Tournament Team (1995)

BATHERSON, NORM

Left wing. Shoots left. 6'1", 198 lbs. Born, North Sydney, N.S., March 27, 1969.

			Regular Season					Playoffs				
Season	Club	Lea	GP	G	A	TP	PIM	GP	G	A	TP	PIM
1992-93	Acadia	AUAA	20	16	21	37	44	....	....	....	....	....
1993-94	P.E.I.	AHL	67	14	23	37	85	....	....	....	....	....
1994-95	Portland	AHL	77	27	34	61	64	7	3	4	7	4
1995-96	Portland	AHL	45	6	21	27	72	24	11	8	19	16
1996-97	Portland	AHL	53	15	28	43	43	5	2	1	3	0
1997-98	Portland	AHL	17	3	5	8	4	....	....	....	....	....
	Fort Wayne	IHL	54	8	18	26	46	....	....	....	....	....

Signed as a free agent by **Washington**, August 21, 1995.

BATTAGLIA, BATES (buh-TAG-lee-ah) — CAR.

Left wing. Shoots left. 6'2", 185 lbs. Born, Chicago, IL, December 13, 1975.
(Anaheim's 6th choice, 132nd overall, in 1994 Entry Draft).

			Regular Season					Playoffs				
Season	Club	Lea	GP	G	A	TP	PIM	GP	G	A	TP	PIM
1993-94	Caledon	OJHL	47	35	39	74	212	....	....	....	....	....
1994-95	Lake Superior	CCHA	38	6	14	20	34	....	....	....	....	....
1995-96	Lake Superior	CCHA	40	13	22	35	48	....	....	....	....	....
1996-97	Lake Superior	CCHA	38	12	27	39	80	....	....	....	....	....
1997-98	**Carolina**	**NHL**	**33**	**2**	**4**	**6**	**10**	....	....	....	....	....
	New Haven	AHL	48	15	21	36	48	1	0	0	0	0
	NHL Totals		**33**	**2**	**4**	**6**	**10**	....	....	....	....	....

Traded to **Hartford** by **Anaheim** with Anaheim's 4th round choice (Josef Vasicek) in 1998 Entry Draft for Mark Janssens, March 18, 1997. Rights transferred to **Carolina** after **Hartford** franchise relocated, June 25, 1997.

BATTAGLIA, DOUG — DET.

Left wing. Shoots left. 6'1", 185 lbs. Born, Newmarket, Ont., October 26, 1975.
(Detroit's 5th choice, 127th overall, in 1994 Entry Draft).

			Regular Season					Playoffs				
Season	Club	Lea	GP	G	A	TP	PIM	GP	G	A	TP	PIM
1993-94	Brockville	OJHL	47	35	39	74	212	....	....	....	....	....
1994-95	RPI	ECAC	34	1	4	5	57	....	....	....	....	....
1995-96	RPI	ECAC	33	5	5	10	37	....	....	....	....	....
1996-97	RPI	ECAC	36	19	11	30	50	....	....	....	....	....
1997-98	RPI	ECAC	31	4	5	9	60	....	....	....	....	....

BAUMGARTNER, GREGOR — MTL.

Left wing. Shoots left. 6', 170 lbs. Born, Leoben, Austria, July 13, 1979.
(Montreal's 2nd choice, 37th overall, in 1997 Entry Draft).

			Regular Season					Playoffs				
Season	Club	Lea	GP	G	A	TP	PIM	GP	G	A	TP	PIM
1996-97	Laval	QMJHL	68	19	45	64	15	3	0	0	0	0
1997-98	Laval	QMJHL	68	31	51	82	10	16	5	12	17	6

BAUMGARTNER, KEN (BAWM-gahrt-nuhr) — BOS.

Left wing. Shoots left. 6'1", 205 lbs. Born, Flin Flon, Man., March 11, 1966.
(Buffalo's 12th choice, 245th overall, in 1985 Entry Draft).

			Regular Season					Playoffs				
Season	Club	Lea	GP	G	A	TP	PIM	GP	G	A	TP	PIM
1983-84	Prince Albert	WHL	57	1	6	7	203	4	0	0	0	23
1984-85	Prince Albert	WHL	60	3	9	12	252	13	1	3	4	89
1985-86	Prince Albert	WHL	70	4	23	27	277	20	3	9	12	112
1986-87	New Haven	AHL	13	0	3	3	99	6	0	0	0	60
1987-88	**Los Angeles**	**NHL**	**30**	**2**	**3**	**5**	**189**	**5**	**0**	**1**	**1**	**28**
	New Haven	AHL	48	1	5	6	181	....	....	....	....	....
1988-89	**Los Angeles**	**NHL**	**49**	**1**	**3**	**4**	**288**	**5**	**0**	**0**	**0**	**8**
	New Haven	AHL	10	1	3	4	26	....	....	....	....	....
1989-90	**Los Angeles**	**NHL**	**12**	**1**	**0**	**1**	**28**	....	....	....	....	....
	NY Islanders	**NHL**	**53**	**0**	**5**	**5**	**194**	**4**	**0**	**0**	**0**	**27**
1990-91	**NY Islanders**	**NHL**	**78**	**1**	**6**	**7**	**282**	....	....	....	....	....
1991-92	**NY Islanders**	**NHL**	**44**	**0**	**1**	**1**	**202**	....	....	....	....	....
	Toronto	**NHL**	**11**	**0**	**0**	**0**	**23**	....	....	....	....	....
1992-93	**Toronto**	**NHL**	**63**	**1**	**0**	**1**	**155**	**7**	**1**	**0**	**1**	**0**
1993-94	**Toronto**	**NHL**	**64**	**4**	**4**	**8**	**185**	**10**	**0**	**0**	**0**	**18**
1994-95	**Toronto**	**NHL**	**2**	**0**	**0**	**0**	**5**	....	....	....	....	....
1995-96	**Toronto**	**NHL**	**60**	**2**	**3**	**5**	**152**	....	....	....	....	....
	Anaheim	**NHL**	**12**	**0**	**1**	**1**	**41**	....	....	....	....	....
1996-97	**Anaheim**	**NHL**	**67**	**0**	**11**	**11**	**182**	**11**	**0**	**1**	**1**	**11**
1997-98	**Boston**	**NHL**	**82**	**0**	**1**	**1**	**199**	**6**	**0**	**0**	**0**	**14**
	NHL Totals		**627**	**12**	**38**	**50**	**2125**	**48**	**1**	**2**	**3**	**106**

Traded to **LA Kings** by **Buffalo** with Sean McKenna and Larry Playfair for Brian Engblom and Doug Smith, January 29, 1986. Traded to **NY Islanders** by **LA Kings** with Hubie McDonough for Mikko Makela, November 29, 1989. Traded to **Toronto** by **NY Islanders** with Dave McLlwain for Daniel Marois and Claude Loiselle, March 10, 1992. Traded to **Anaheim** by **Toronto** for Winnipeg's 4th round choice (previously acquired by Anaheim — later traded to Montreal — Montreal selected Kim Staal) in 1996 Entry Draft, March 20, 1996. Signed as a free agent by **Boston**, July 14, 1997.

BAUMGARTNER, NOLAN (BAWM-gahrt-nuhr) — WSH.

Defense. Shoots right. 6'1", 200 lbs. Born, Calgary, Alta., March 23, 1976.
(Washington's 1st choice, 10th overall, in 1994 Entry Draft).

			Regular Season					Playoffs				
Season	Club	Lea	GP	G	A	TP	PIM	GP	G	A	TP	PIM
1992-93	Kamloops	WHL	43	0	5	5	30	11	1	1	2	0
1993-94	Kamloops	WHL	69	13	42	55	109	19	3	14	17	33
1994-95	Kamloops	WHL	62	8	36	44	71	21	4	13	17	16
1995-96	Kamloops	WHL	28	13	15	28	45	16	1	9	10	26
	Washington	**NHL**	**1**	**0**	**0**	**0**	**0**	**1**	**0**	**0**	**0**	**10**
1996-97	Portland	AHL	8	2	2	4	4	....	....	....	....	....
1997-98	**Washington**	**NHL**	**4**	**0**	**1**	**1**	**0**	....	....	....	....	....
	Portland	AHL	70	2	24	26	70	10	1	4	5	10
	NHL Totals		**5**	**0**	**1**	**1**	**0**	**1**	**0**	**0**	**0**	**10**

Memorial Cup All-Star Team (1994, 1995) • WHL West First All-Star Team (1995, 1996) • Canadian Major Junior First All-Star Team (1995) • Canadian Major Junior Defenseman of the Year (1995)

BAXTER, JIM — BOS.

Defense. Shoots right. 6'2", 186 lbs. Born, Brantford, Ont., August 24, 1979.
(Boston's 9th choice, 180th overall, in 1997 Entry Draft).

			Regular Season					Playoffs				
Season	Club	Lea	GP	G	A	TP	PIM	GP	G	A	TP	PIM
1996-97	Oshawa	OHL	47	3	6	9	4	15	0	0	0	0
1997-98	Oshawa	OHL	65	4	28	32	18	7	3	4	7	0

BEARDSMORE, COLIN

Center. Shoots left. 6'1", 194 lbs. Born, Peterborough, Ont., February 7, 1978.
(Detroit's 7th choice, 189th overall, in 1996 Entry Draft).

			Regular Season					Playoffs				
Season	Club	Lea	GP	G	A	TP	PIM	GP	G	A	TP	PIM
1995-96	North Bay	OHL	65	12	12	24	27	....	....	....	....	....
1996-97	North Bay	OHL	40	21	21	42	19	....	....	....	....	....
	Owen Sound	OHL	30	7	13	20	29	4	0	2	2	8
1997-98	Owen Sound	OHL	65	24	46	70	51	11	3	4	7	4

BEAUCHEMIN, FRANCOIS — MTL.

Defense. Shoots left. 5'11", 190 lbs. Born, Sorel, Que., June 4, 1980.
(Montreal's 3rd choice, 75th overall, in 1998 Entry Draft).

			Regular Season					Playoffs				
Season	Club	Lea	GP	G	A	TP	PIM	GP	G	A	TP	PIM
1996-97	Laval	QMJHL	66	7	21	28	132	3	0	0	0	2
1997-98	Laval	QMJHL	70	12	35	47	132	16	1	3	4	23

BEAUCHESNE, MARTIN — NSH.

Defense. Shoots left. 6', 200 lbs. Born, Cap-de-la-madaleine, Que., July 8, 1980.
(Nashville's 5th choice, 138th overall, in 1998 Entry Draft).

			Regular Season					Playoffs				
Season	Club	Lea	GP	G	A	TP	PIM	GP	G	A	TP	PIM
1996-97	Sherbrooke	QMJHL	65	1	2	3	125	3	0	0	0	4
1997-98	Sherbrooke	QMJHL	37	1	3	4	105	....	....	....	....	....

BEAUDOIN, ERIC (boh-DWEH) — T.B.

Left wing. Shoots left. 6'3", 180 lbs. Born, Ottawa, Ont., May 3, 1980.
(Tampa Bay's 4th choice, 92nd overall, in 1998 Entry Draft).

			Regular Season					Playoffs				
Season	Club	Lea	GP	G	A	TP	PIM	GP	G	A	TP	PIM
1996-97	Ottawa	OJHL	54	12	19	31	55	....	....	....	....	....
1997-98	Guelph	OHL	62	9	13	22	43	12	3	2	5	4

BEAUFAIT, MARK

Center. Shoots right. 5'9", 170 lbs. Born, Livonia, MI, May 13, 1970.
(San Jose's 2nd choice, 7th overall, in 1991 Supplemental Draft).

			Regular Season					Playoffs				
Season	Club	Lea	GP	G	A	TP	PIM	GP	G	A	TP	PIM
1988-89	North. Michigan	WCHA	11	2	1	3	2	....	....	....	....	....
1989-90	North. Michigan	WCHA	34	10	14	24	12	....	....	....	....	....
1990-91	North. Michigan	WCHA	47	19	30	49	18	....	....	....	....	....
1991-92	North. Michigan	WCHA	39	31	44	75	43	....	....	....	....	....
1992-93	**San Jose**	**NHL**	**5**	**1**	**0**	**1**	**0**	....	....	....	....	....
	Kansas City	IHL	66	19	40	59	22	9	1	1	2	8
1993-94	United States	Nat-Tm	51	22	29	51	36	....	....	....	....	....
	United States	Olympics	8	1	4	5	2	....	....	....	....	....
	Kansas City	IHL	21	12	9	21	18	....	....	....	....	....
1994-95	San Diego	IHL	68	24	39	63	22	5	2	2	4	2
1995-96	Orlando	IHL	77	30	79	109	87	22	9	*19	*28	22
1996-97	Orlando	IHL	80	26	65	91	63	10	5	8	13	18
1997-98	Orlando	IHL	76	24	61	85	56	17	6	16	22	10
	NHL Totals		**5**	**1**	**0**	**1**	**0**	....	....	....	....	....

IHL Second All-Star Team (1997)

BECKETT, JASON — PHI.

Defense. Shoots right. 6'2", 203 lbs. Born, Lethbridge, Alta., July 23, 1980.
(Philadelphia's 2nd choice, 42nd overall, in 1998 Entry Draft).

			Regular Season					Playoffs				
Season	Club	Lea	GP	G	A	TP	PIM	GP	G	A	TP	PIM
1996-97	Lethbridge	AMHA	34	7	10	17	118	....	....	....	....	....
1997-98	Seattle	WHL	71	1	11	12	241	5	0	0	0	16

BEDDOES, CLAYTON

Center. Shoots left. 5'11", 190 lbs. Born, Bentley, Alta., November 10, 1970.

			Regular Season					Playoffs				
Season	Club	Lea	GP	G	A	TP	PIM	GP	G	A	TP	PIM
1990-91	Lake Superior	CCHA	45	14	28	42	26	....	....	....	....	....
1991-92	Lake Superior	CCHA	38	14	26	40	24	....	....	....	....	....
1992-93	Lake Superior	CCHA	43	18	40	58	30	....	....	....	....	....
1993-94	Lake Superior	CCHA	44	23	31	54	56	....	....	....	....	....
1994-95	Providence	AHL	65	16	20	36	39	13	3	1	4	18
1995-96	**Boston**	**NHL**	**39**	**1**	**6**	**7**	**44**	....	....	....	....	....
	Providence	AHL	32	10	15	25	24	4	2	3	5	0
1996-97	**Boston**	**NHL**	**21**	**1**	**2**	**3**	**13**	....	....	....	....	....
	Providence	AHL	36	11	23	34	60	7	2	0	2	4
1997-98	Detroit	IHL	65	22	24	46	63	22	5	10	15	16
	NHL Totals		**60**	**2**	**8**	**10**	**57**	....	....	....	....	....

CCHA Second All-Star Team (1994) • NCAA West Second All-American Team (1994) • NCAA Championship All-Tournament Team (1994)

Signed as a free agent by **Boston**, June 2, 1994. Signed as a free agent by **Ottawa**, July 28, 1997.

BEGIN, STEVE (bay-ZHIN) — CGY.

Center. Shoots left. 5'11", 185 lbs. Born, Trois-Rivieres, Que., June 14, 1978.
(Calgary's 3rd choice, 40th overall, in 1996 Entry Draft).

			Regular Season					Playoffs				
Season	Club	Lea	GP	G	A	TP	PIM	GP	G	A	TP	PIM
1995-96	Val d'Or	QMJHL	64	13	23	36	218	13	1	3	4	33
1996-97	Val d'Or	QMJHL	58	13	33	46	229	10	0	3	3	8
	Saint John	AHL	....	....	....	....	....	4	0	2	2	6
1997-98	Val d'Or	QMJHL	35	18	17	35	73	15	2	12	14	34
	Calgary	**NHL**	**5**	**0**	**0**	**0**	**23**	....	....	....	....	....
	NHL Totals		**5**	**0**	**0**	**0**	**23**	....	....	....	....	....

BEKAR, DEREK — ST.L.

Center. Shoots left. 6'3", 185 lbs. Born, Burnaby, B.C., September 15, 1975.
(St. Louis' 7th choice, 205th overall, in 1995 Entry Draft).

			Regular Season					Playoffs				
Season	Club	Lea	GP	G	A	TP	PIM	GP	G	A	TP	PIM
1994-95	Powell River	BCJHL	46	33	29	62	35	....	....	....	....	....
1995-96	New Hampshire	H.E.	34	15	18	33	4	....	....	....	....	....
1996-97	New Hampshire	H.E.	39	18	21	39	34	....	....	....	....	....
1997-98	New Hampshire	H.E.	35	32	28	60	46	....	....	....	....	....

Hockey East Second All-Star Team (1998)

BELAK, GRAHAM (BEE-lak) — COL.

Defense. Shoots left. 6'4", 210 lbs. Born, Battleford, Sask., August 1, 1979.
(Colorado's 2nd choice, 53rd overall, in 1997 Entry Draft).

			Regular Season					Playoffs				
Season	Club	Lea	GP	G	A	TP	PIM	GP	G	A	TP	PIM
1995-96	North Battleford	SJHL	55	3	14	17	110	....	....	....	....	....
1996-97	Edmonton	WHL	61	3	5	8	251	....	....	....	....	....
1997-98	Edmonton	WHL	47	5	5	10	168	....	....	....	....	....
	Hershey	AHL	1	0	0	0	15	....	....	....	....	....

BELAK, WADE (BEE-lak) — COL.

Defense. Shoots right. 6'4", 213 lbs. Born, Saskatoon, Sask., July 3, 1976.
(Quebec's 1st choice, 12th overall, in 1994 Entry Draft).

			Regular Season					Playoffs				
Season	Club	Lea	GP	G	A	TP	PIM	GP	G	A	TP	PIM
1992-93	North Battleford	SJHL	50	5	15	20	146	....	....	....	....	....
	Saskatoon	WHL	7	0	0	0	23	7	0	0	0	0
1993-94	Saskatoon	WHL	69	4	13	17	226	16	2	2	4	43
1994-95	Saskatoon	WHL	72	4	14	18	290	9	0	0	0	36
	Cornwall	AHL	....	....	....	....	....	11	1	2	3	40
1995-96	Saskatoon	WHL	63	3	15	18	207	4	0	0	0	9
	Cornwall	AHL	5	0	0	0	18	2	0	0	0	2
1996-97	**Colorado**	**NHL**	**5**	**0**	**0**	**0**	**11**	....	....	....	....	....
	Hershey	AHL	65	1	7	8	320	16	0	1	1	61
1997-98	**Colorado**	**NHL**	**8**	**1**	**1**	**2**	**27**	....	....	....	....	....
	Hershey	AHL	11	0	0	0	30	....	....	....	....	....
	NHL Totals		**13**	**1**	**1**	**2**	**38**	....	....	....	....	....

Rights transferred to **Colorado** after **Quebec** franchise relocated, June 21, 1995.

BELANGER, ERIC (buh-LAWN-zhay) — L.A.

Center. Shoots left. 6', 177 lbs. Born, Sherbrooke, Que., December 16, 1977.
(Los Angeles' 5th choice, 96th overall, in 1996 Entry Draft).

			Regular Season					Playoffs				
Season	Club	Lea	GP	G	A	TP	PIM	GP	G	A	TP	PIM
1994-95	Beauport	QMJHL	71	12	28	40	24	18	5	9	14	25
1995-96	Beauport	QMJHL	59	35	38	83	18	20	13	14	27	6
1996-97	Beauport	QMJHL	31	13	37	50	30	....	....	....	....	....
	Rimouski	QMJHL	31	26	41	67	36	4	2	3	5	10
1997-98	Fredericton	AHL	56	17	34	51	28	4	2	1	3	2

BELANGER, FRANCIS (buh-LAWN-zhay) — PHI.

Left wing. Shoots left. 6'2", 216 lbs. Born, Bellefeuille, Que., January 15, 1978.
(Philadelphia's 5th choice, 124th overall, in 1998 Entry Draft).

			Regular Season					Playoffs				
Season	Club	Lea	GP	G	A	TP	PIM	GP	G	A	TP	PIM
1996-97	Hull	QMJHL	53	13	13	26	134	8	2	2	4	57
1997-98	Hull	QMJHL	33	22	23	45	133	....	....	....	....	....
	Rimouski	QMJHL	30	18	10	28	248	17	14	8	22	61

BELANGER, JESSE (buh-LAWN-zhay) — T.B.

Center. Shoots right. 6'1", 190 lbs. Born, St. Georges de Beauce, Que., June 15, 1969.

			Regular Season					Playoffs				
Season	Club	Lea	GP	G	A	TP	PIM	GP	G	A	TP	PIM
1987-88	Granby	QMJHL	69	33	43	76	10	5	3	3	6	0
1988-89	Granby	QMJHL	67	40	63	103	26	4	0	5	5	0
1989-90	Granby	QMJHL	67	53	54	107	53	....	....	....	....	....
1990-91	Fredericton	AHL	75	40	58	98	30	6	2	4	6	0
1991-92	**Montreal**	**NHL**	**4**	**0**	**0**	**0**	**0**	....	....	....	....	....
	Fredericton	AHL	65	30	41	71	26	7	3	3	6	2
1992-93	**Montreal**	**NHL**	**19**	**4**	**2**	**6**	**4**	**9**	**0**	**1**	**1**	**0 ♦**
	Fredericton	AHL	39	19	32	51	24	....	....	....	....	....
1993-94	**Florida**	**NHL**	**70**	**17**	**33**	**50**	**16**	....	....	....	....	....
1994-95	**Florida**	**NHL**	**47**	**15**	**14**	**29**	**18**	....	....	....	....	....
1995-96	**Florida**	**NHL**	**63**	**17**	**21**	**38**	**10**	....	....	....	....	....
	Vancouver	**NHL**	**9**	**3**	**0**	**3**	**4**	**3**	**0**	**2**	**2**	**2**
1996-97	**Edmonton**	**NHL**	**6**	**0**	**0**	**0**	**0**	....	....	....	....	....
	Hamilton	AHL	6	4	3	7	0	....	....	....	....	....
	Quebec	IHL	47	34	28	62	18	9	3	5	8	13
1997-98	SC Herisau	Switz.	5	4	3	7	4	....	....	....	....	....
	Las Vegas	IHL	54	32	36	68	20	4	0	1	1	0
	NHL Totals		**218**	**56**	**70**	**126**	**52**	**12**	**0**	**3**	**3**	**2**

Signed as a free agent by **Montreal**, October 3, 1990. Claimed by **Florida** from **Montreal** in Expansion Draft, June 24, 1993. Traded to **Vancouver** by **Florida** for Vancouver's 3rd round choice (Oleg Kvasha) in 1996 Entry Draft and future considerations, March 20, 1996. Signed as a free agent by **Edmonton**, September 16, 1996. Signed as a free agent by **Tampa Bay**, August 18, 1998.

BELANGER, KEN (buh-LAWN-zhay) — NYI

Left wing. Shoots left. 6'4", 225 lbs. Born, Sault Ste. Marie, Ont., May 14, 1974.
(Hartford's 7th choice, 153rd overall, in 1992 Entry Draft).

			Regular Season					Playoffs				
Season	Club	Lea	GP	G	A	TP	PIM	GP	G	A	TP	PIM
1991-92	Ottawa	OHL	51	4	4	8	174	11	0	0	0	24
1992-93	Ottawa	OHL	34	6	12	18	139	....	....	....	....	....
	Guelph	OHL	29	10	14	24	86	5	2	1	3	14
1993-94	Guelph	OHL	55	11	22	33	185	9	2	3	5	30
1994-95	St. John's	AHL	47	5	5	10	246	4	0	0	0	30
	Toronto	**NHL**	**3**	**0**	**0**	**0**	**9**	....	....	....	....	....
1995-96	St. John's	AHL	40	16	14	30	222	....	....	....	....	....
	NY Islanders	**NHL**	**7**	**0**	**0**	**0**	**27**	....	....	....	....	....
1996-97	**NY Islanders**	**NHL**	**18**	**0**	**2**	**2**	**102**	....	....	....	....	....
	Kentucky	AHL	38	10	12	22	164	4	0	1	1	27
1997-98	**NY Islanders**	**NHL**	**37**	**3**	**1**	**4**	**101**	....	....	....	....	....
	NHL Totals		**65**	**3**	**3**	**6**	**239**	....	....	....	....	....

Traded to **Toronto** by **Hartford** for Toronto's 9th round choice (Matt Ball) in 1994 Entry Draft, March 18, 1994. Traded to **NY Islanders** by **Toronto** with Damian Rhodes for future considerations (Kirk Muller and Don Beaupre, January 23, 1996), January 23, 1996.

BELL, MARK — CHI.

Center. Shoots left. 6'3", 185 lbs. Born, St. Paul's, Ont., August 5, 1980.
(Chicago's 1st choice, 8th overall, in 1998 Entry Draft).

			Regular Season					Playoffs				
Season	Club	Lea	GP	G	A	TP	PIM	GP	G	A	TP	PIM
1996-97	Ottawa	OHL	65	8	12	20	40	24	4	7	11	13
1997-98	Ottawa	OHL	55	34	26	60	87	13	6	5	11	14

BELLOWS, BRIAN — WSH.

Left wing. Shoots right. 5'11", 210 lbs. Born, St. Catharines, Ont., September 1, 1964.
(Minnesota's 1st choice, 2nd overall, in 1982 Entry Draft).

			Regular Season					Playoffs				
Season	Club	Lea	GP	G	A	TP	PIM	GP	G	A	TP	PIM
1980-81	Kitchener	OHA	66	49	67	116	23	16	14	13	27	13
1981-82	Kitchener	OHL	47	45	52	97	23	15	16	13	29	11
1982-83	**Minnesota**	**NHL**	**78**	**35**	**30**	**65**	**27**	**9**	**5**	**4**	**9**	**18**
1983-84	**Minnesota**	**NHL**	**78**	**41**	**42**	**83**	**66**	**16**	**2**	**12**	**14**	**6**
1984-85	**Minnesota**	**NHL**	**78**	**26**	**36**	**62**	**72**	**9**	**2**	**4**	**6**	**9**
1985-86	**Minnesota**	**NHL**	**77**	**31**	**48**	**79**	**46**	**5**	**5**	**0**	**5**	**16**
1986-87	**Minnesota**	**NHL**	**65**	**26**	**27**	**53**	**34**	....	....	....	....	....
1987-88	**Minnesota**	**NHL**	**77**	**40**	**41**	**81**	**81**	....	....	....	....	....
1988-89	**Minnesota**	**NHL**	**60**	**23**	**27**	**50**	**55**	**5**	**2**	**3**	**5**	**8**
1989-90	**Minnesota**	**NHL**	**80**	**55**	**44**	**99**	**72**	**7**	**4**	**3**	**7**	**10**
1990-91	**Minnesota**	**NHL**	**80**	**35**	**40**	**75**	**43**	**23**	**10**	**19**	**29**	**30**
1991-92	**Minnesota**	**NHL**	**80**	**30**	**45**	**75**	**41**	**7**	**4**	**4**	**8**	**14**
1992-93	**Montreal**	**NHL**	**82**	**40**	**48**	**88**	**44**	**18**	**6**	**9**	**15**	**18 ♦**
1993-94	**Montreal**	**NHL**	**77**	**33**	**38**	**71**	**36**	**6**	**1**	**2**	**3**	**2**
1994-95	**Montreal**	**NHL**	**41**	**8**	**8**	**16**	**8**	....	....	....	....	....
1995-96	**Tampa Bay**	**NHL**	**79**	**23**	**26**	**49**	**39**	**6**	**2**	**0**	**2**	**4**
1996-97	**Tampa Bay**	**NHL**	**7**	**1**	**2**	**3**	**0**	....	....	....	....	....
	Anaheim	**NHL**	**62**	**15**	**13**	**28**	**22**	**11**	**2**	**4**	**6**	**2**
1997-98	Berlin	Germany	31	15	17	32	18	....	....	....	....	....
	Washington	**NHL**	**11**	**6**	**3**	**9**	**6**	**21**	**6**	**7**	**13**	**6**
	NHL Totals		**1112**	**468**	**518**	**986**	**692**	**143**	**51**	**71**	**122**	**143**

OHL First All-Star Team (1982) • Won George Parsons Trophy (Memorial Cup Tournament Most Sportsmanlike Player) (1982) • NHL Second All-Star Team (1990)

Played in NHL All-Star Game (1984, 1988, 1992)

Traded to **Montreal** by **Minnesota** for Russ Courtnall, August 31, 1992. Traded to **Tampa Bay** by **Montreal** for Marc Bureau, June 30, 1995. Traded to **Anaheim** by **Tampa Bay** for Anaheim's 6th round choice (Andrei Skopintsev) in 1997 Entry Draft, November 19, 1996. Signed as a free agent by **Washington**, March 21, 1998.

BELTER, SHANE — BOS.

Defense. Shoots right. 6'1", 205 lbs. Born, Swift Current, Sask., October 5, 1977.

			Regular Season					Playoffs				
Season	Club	Lea	GP	G	A	TP	PIM	GP	G	A	TP	PIM
1995-96	Seattle	WHL	63	9	22	31	133	5	0	0	0	11
1996-97	Seattle	WHL	13	1	4	5	29	....	....	....	....	....
	Lethbridge	WHL	34	4	24	28	30	17	2	9	11	18
1997-98	Lethbridge	WHL	8	1	4	5	14	....	....	....	....	....
	Kamloops	WHL	57	21	35	56	69	4	0	1	1	8

Signed as a free agent by **Boston**, April 20, 1998.

BENDA, JAN — (BEHN-duh, YAHN)

Center. Shoots right. 6'2", 208 lbs. Born, Reef, Belgium, March 28, 1972.

			Regular Season					Playoffs				
Season	Club	Lea	GP	G	A	TP	PIM	GP	G	A	TP	PIM
1990-91	Oshawa	OHL	51	4	11	15	64	16	2	4	6	19
1991-92	Oshawa	OHL	61	12	23	35	68	7	1	1	2	12
1992-93	Freiburg	Germany	41	6	11	17	49	9	3	3	6	12
1993-94	Munchen	Germany	43	16	11	27	67	10	3	2	5	21
1994-95	Binghamton	AHL	4	0	0	0	0	....	....	....	....	....
	Richmond	ECHL	62	21	39	60	187	17	8	5	13	50
1995-96	Slavia Praha	Cze-Rep.	28	8	11	19	....	7	1	5	6	....
1996-97	Sparta Praha	Cze-Rep.	49	7	21	28	61	10	1	1	2	12
1997-98	**Washington**	**NHL**	**9**	**0**	**3**	**3**	**6**	....	....	....	....	....
	Portland	AHL	62	25	29	54	90	8	0	7	7	6
	NHL Totals		**9**	**0**	**3**	**3**	**6**	....	....	....	....	....

Signed as a free agent by **Washington**, October 1, 1997.

BENOIT, MATHIEU — N.J.

Right wing. Shoots right. 5'11", 200 lbs. Born, St. Clec, Que., July 12, 1979.
(New Jersey's 6th choice, 188th overall, in 1997 Entry Draft).

			Regular Season					Playoffs				
Season	Club	Lea	GP	G	A	TP	PIM	GP	G	A	TP	PIM
1995-96	Chicoutimi	QMJHL	61	6	14	20	17	17	0	0	0	0
1996-97	Chicoutimi	QMJHL	64	35	36	71	22	9	2	2	4	0
1997-98	Chicoutimi	QMJHL	59	56	61	117	32	6	2	3	5	2

BENYSEK, LADISLAV — (BEHN-ih-sihk) EDM.

Defense. Shoots left. 6'2", 190 lbs. Born, Olomouc, Czech., March 24, 1975.
(Edmonton's 16th choice, 266th overall, in 1994 Entry Draft).

			Regular Season					Playoffs				
Season	Club	Lea	GP	G	A	TP	PIM	GP	G	A	TP	PIM
1993-94	HC Olomouc	Czech-Jr.			STATISTICS NOT AVAILABLE							
1994-95	Cape Breton	AHL	58	2	7	9	54	....	....	....	....	....
1995-96	HC Olomouc	Cze-Rep.	33	1	4	5	....	4	0	0	0	....
1996-97	Sparta Praha	Cze-Rep.	36	5	5	10	28	5	0	1	1	2
1997-98	**Edmonton**	**NHL**	**2**	**0**	**0**	**0**	**0**	....	....	....	....	....
	Hamilton	AHL	53	2	14	16	29	9	1	1	2	2
	NHL Totals		**2**	**0**	**0**	**0**	**0**	....	....	....	....	....

BERANEK, JOSEF — (buh-RAH-nehk, JOH-sehf) EDM.

Left wing. Shoots left. 6'2", 195 lbs. Born, Litvinov, Czechoslovakia, October 25, 1969.
(Edmonton's 3rd choice, 78th overall, in 1989 Entry Draft).

			Regular Season					Playoffs				
Season	Club	Lea	GP	G	A	TP	PIM	GP	G	A	TP	PIM
1987-88	Litvinov	Czech.	14	7	4	11	12	....	....	....	....	....
1988-89	Litvinov	Czech.	32	18	10	28	47	....	....	....	....	....
1989-90	Dukla Trencin	Czech.	49	19	23	42	....	....	....	....	....	....
1990-91	Litvinov	Czech.	58	29	31	60	98	....	....	....	....	....
1991-92	**Edmonton**	**NHL**	**58**	**12**	**16**	**28**	**18**	**12**	**2**	**1**	**3**	**0**
1992-93	**Edmonton**	**NHL**	**26**	**2**	**6**	**8**	**28**	....	....	....	....	....
	Cape Breton	AHL	6	1	2	3	8	....	....	....	....	....
	Philadelphia	**NHL**	**40**	**13**	**12**	**25**	**50**	....	....	....	....	....
1993-94	**Philadelphia**	**NHL**	**80**	**28**	**21**	**49**	**85**	....	....	....	....	....
1994-95	Petra Vsetin	Cze-Rep.	16	7	7	14	26	....	....	....	....	....
	Philadelphia	**NHL**	**14**	**5**	**5**	**10**	**2**	....	....	....	....	....
	Vancouver	**NHL**	**37**	**8**	**13**	**21**	**28**	**11**	**1**	**1**	**2**	**12**
1995-96	**Vancouver**	**NHL**	**61**	**6**	**14**	**20**	**60**	**3**	**2**	**1**	**3**	**0**
1996-97	Petra Vsetin	Cze-Rep.	39	19	24	43	115	3	3	2	5	4
	Pittsburgh	**NHL**	**8**	**3**	**1**	**4**	**4**	**5**	**0**	**0**	**0**	**2**
1997-98	Petra Vsetin	EuroHL	8	5	4	9	10	....	....	....	....	....
	Petra Vsetin	Cze-Rep.	45	24	27	51	92	10	2	8	10	14
	Czech Republic	Olympics	6	1	0	1	4	....	....	....	....	....
	NHL Totals		**324**	**77**	**88**	**165**	**275**	**31**	**5**	**3**	**8**	**14**

Traded to **Philadelphia** by **Edmonton** with Greg Hawgood for Brian Benning, January 16, 1993. Traded to **Vancouver** by **Philadelphia** for Shawn Antoski, February 15, 1995. Traded to **Pittsburgh** by **Vancouver** for future considerations, March 18, 1997. Traded to **Edmonton** by **Pittsburgh** for Bobby Dollas and Tony Hrkac, June 16, 1998.

BERARD, BRYAN — (buh-RAHRD) NYI

Defense. Shoots left. 6'1", 190 lbs. Born, Woonsocket, RI, March 5, 1977.
(Ottawa's 1st choice, 1st overall, in 1995 Entry Draft).

			Regular Season					Playoffs				
Season	Club	Lea	GP	G	A	TP	PIM	GP	G	A	TP	PIM
1993-94	Mt. St. Charles	H.S.	32	11	36	47	97	....	....	....	....	....
1994-95	Detroit	OHL	58	20	55	75	97	21	4	20	24	38
1995-96	Detroit	OHL	56	31	58	89	116	17	7	18	25	41
1996-97	**NY Islanders**	**NHL**	**82**	**8**	**40**	**48**	**86**	....	....	....	....	....
1997-98	**NY Islanders**	**NHL**	**75**	**14**	**32**	**46**	**59**	....	....	....	....	....
	United States	Olympics	2	0	0	0	0	....	....	....	....	....
	NHL Totals		**157**	**22**	**72**	**94**	**145**	....	....	....	....	....

OHL First All-Star Team (1995, 1996) • Canadian Major Junior First All-Star Team (1995, 1996) • Canadian Major Junior Rookie of the Year (1995) • Canadian Major Junior Defenseman of the Year (1996) • NHL All-Rookie Team (1997) • Won Calder Memorial Trophy (1997)

Traded to **NY Islanders** by **Ottawa** with Don Beaupre and Martin Straka for Damian Rhodes and Wade Redden, January 23, 1996.

BEREHOWSKY, DRAKE — (beh-reh-HOW-skee) EDM.

Defense. Shoots right. 6'2", 212 lbs. Born, Toronto, Ont., January 3, 1972.
(Toronto's 1st choice, 10th overall, in 1990 Entry Draft).

			Regular Season					Playoffs				
Season	Club	Lea	GP	G	A	TP	PIM	GP	G	A	TP	PIM
1988-89	Kingston	OHL	63	7	39	46	85	....	....	....	....	....
	Canada	Nat-Tm	1	0	0	0	0	....	....	....	....	....
1989-90	Kingston	OHL	9	3	11	14	28	....	....	....	....	....
1990-91	Kingston	OHL	13	5	13	18	38	....	....	....	....	....
	North Bay	OHL	26	7	23	30	51	10	2	7	9	21
	Toronto	**NHL**	**8**	**0**	**1**	**1**	**25**	....	....	....	....	....
1991-92	North Bay	OHL	62	19	63	82	147	21	7	24	31	22
	Toronto	**NHL**	**1**	**0**	**0**	**0**	**0**	....	....	....	....	....
	St. John's	AHL	....	....	....	....	....	6	0	5	5	21
1992-93	**Toronto**	**NHL**	**41**	**4**	**15**	**19**	**61**	....	....	....	....	....
	St. John's	AHL	28	10	17	27	38	....	....	....	....	....
1993-94	**Toronto**	**NHL**	**49**	**2**	**8**	**10**	**63**	....	....	....	....	....
	St. John's	AHL	18	3	12	15	40	....	....	....	....	....
1994-95	**Toronto**	**NHL**	**25**	**0**	**2**	**2**	**15**	....	....	....	....	....
	Pittsburgh	**NHL**	**4**	**0**	**0**	**0**	**13**	**1**	**0**	**0**	**0**	**0**
1995-96	**Pittsburgh**	**NHL**	**1**	**0**	**0**	**0**	**0**	....	....	....	....	....
	Cleveland	IHL	74	6	28	34	141	3	0	3	3	6
1996-97	Carolina	AHL	49	2	15	17	55	....	....	....	....	....
	San Antonio	IHL	16	3	4	7	36	....	....	....	....	....
1997-98	**Edmonton**	**NHL**	**67**	**1**	**6**	**7**	**169**	**12**	**1**	**2**	**3**	**14**
	Hamilton	AHL	8	2	0	2	21	....	....	....	....	....
	NHL Totals		**196**	**7**	**32**	**39**	**346**	**13**	**1**	**2**	**3**	**14**

Canadian Major Junior Defenseman of the Year (1992) • OHL First All-Star Team (1992)

Traded to **Pittsburgh** by **Toronto** for Grant Jennings, April 7, 1995. Signed as a free agent by **Edmonton**, September 30, 1997.

BERENZWEIG, ANDY — NYI

Defense. Shoots left. 6'2", 195 lbs. Born, Chicago, IL, August 8, 1977.
(NY Islanders' 5th choice, 109th overall, in 1996 Entry Draft).

			Regular Season					Playoffs				
Season	Club	Lea	GP	G	A	TP	PIM	GP	G	A	TP	PIM
1994-95	Loomis-Chaffee	H.S.	23	19	23	42	10	....	....	....	....	....
1995-96	U. of Michigan	CCHA	42	4	8	12	4	....	....	....	....	....
1996-97	U. of Michigan	CCHA	38	7	12	19	49	....	....	....	....	....
1997-98	U. of Michigan	CCHA	45	8	11	19	32	....	....	....	....	....

CCHA Second All-Star Team (1998) • NCAA Championship All-Tournament Team (1998)

BEREZIN, SERGEI — (BEH-reh-zihn) TOR.

Right wing. Shoots right. 5'10", 197 lbs. Born, Voskresensk, USSR, November 5, 1971.
(Toronto's 8th choice, 256th overall, in 1994 Entry Draft).

			Regular Season					Playoffs				
Season	Club	Lea	GP	G	A	TP	PIM	GP	G	A	TP	PIM
1990-91	Khimik	USSR	30	6	2	8	4	....	....	....	....	....
1991-92	Khimik	CIS	36	7	5	12	10	....	....	....	....	....
1992-93	Khimik	CIS	38	9	3	12	12	2	1	0	1	0
1993-94	Khimik	CIS	40	31	10	41	16	3	2	0	2	2
	Russia	Olympics	8	3	2	5	2	....	....	....	....	....
1994-95	Kolner Haie	Germany	43	38	19	57	8	18	17	8	25	14
1995-96	Kolner Haie	Germany	45	49	31	80	8	14	13	9	22	10
1996-97	**Toronto**	**NHL**	**73**	**25**	**16**	**41**	**2**	....	....	....	....	....
1997-98	**Toronto**	**NHL**	**68**	**16**	**15**	**31**	**10**	....	....	....	....	....
	NHL Totals		**141**	**41**	**31**	**72**	**12**	....	....	....	....	....

NHL All-Rookie Team (1997)

BERG, AKI-PETTERI — (BUHRG, AH-kee-PEHT-uhr-ee) L.A.

Defense. Shoots left. 6'3", 203 lbs. Born, Turku, Finland, February 28, 1977.
(Los Angeles' 1st choice, 3rd overall, in 1995 Entry Draft).

			Regular Season					Playoffs				
Season	Club	Lea	GP	G	A	TP	PIM	GP	G	A	TP	PIM
1993-94	TPS Turku	Finland	6	0	6	6	4	....	....	....	....	....
1994-95	Kiekko	Finland-2	28	3	9	12	34	....	....	....	....	....
	TPS Turku	Finland	5	0	0	0	4	....	....	....	....	....
1995-96	**Los Angeles**	**NHL**	**51**	**0**	**7**	**7**	**29**	....	....	....	....	....
	Phoenix	IHL	20	0	3	3	18	2	0	0	0	4
1996-97	**Los Angeles**	**NHL**	**41**	**2**	**6**	**8**	**24**	....	....	....	....	....
	Phoenix	IHL	23	1	3	4	21	....	....	....	....	....
1997-98	**Los Angeles**	**NHL**	**72**	**0**	**8**	**8**	**61**	**4**	**0**	**3**	**3**	**0**
	Finland	Olympics	6	0	0	0	6	....	....	....	....	....
	NHL Totals		**164**	**2**	**21**	**23**	**114**	**4**	**0**	**3**	**3**	**0**

BERG, BILL — NYR

Left wing. Shoots left. 6'1", 205 lbs. Born, St. Catharines, Ont., October 21, 1967.
(NY Islanders' 3rd choice, 59th overall, in 1986 Entry Draft).

			Regular Season					Playoffs				
Season	Club	Lea	GP	G	A	TP	PIM	GP	G	A	TP	PIM
1985-86	Toronto	OHL	64	3	35	38	143	4	0	0	0	19
	Springfield	AHL	4	1	1	2	4	....	....	....	....	....
1986-87	Toronto	OHL	57	3	15	18	138	....	....	....	....	....
1987-88	Springfield	AHL	76	6	26	32	148	....	....	....	....	....
	Peoria	IHL	5	0	1	1	8	7	0	3	3	31
1988-89	**NY Islanders**	**NHL**	**7**	**1**	**2**	**3**	**10**	....	....	....	....	....
	Springfield	AHL	69	17	32	49	122	....	....	....	....	....
1989-90	Springfield	AHL	74	12	42	54	74	15	5	12	17	35
1990-91	**NY Islanders**	**NHL**	**78**	**9**	**14**	**23**	**67**	....	....	....	....	....
1991-92	**NY Islanders**	**NHL**	**47**	**5**	**9**	**14**	**28**	....	....	....	....	....
	Capital District	AHL	3	0	2	2	16	....	....	....	....	....
1992-93	**NY Islanders**	**NHL**	**22**	**6**	**3**	**9**	**49**	....	....	....	....	....
	Toronto	**NHL**	**58**	**7**	**8**	**15**	**54**	**21**	**1**	**1**	**2**	**18**
1993-94	**Toronto**	**NHL**	**83**	**8**	**11**	**19**	**93**	**18**	**1**	**2**	**3**	**10**
1994-95	**Toronto**	**NHL**	**32**	**5**	**1**	**6**	**26**	**7**	**0**	**1**	**1**	**4**
1995-96	**Toronto**	**NHL**	**23**	**1**	**1**	**2**	**33**	....	....	....	....	....
	NY Rangers	**NHL**	**18**	**2**	**1**	**3**	**8**	**10**	**1**	**0**	**1**	**0**
1996-97	**NY Rangers**	**NHL**	**67**	**8**	**6**	**14**	**37**	**3**	**0**	**0**	**0**	**2**
1997-98	**NY Rangers**	**NHL**	**67**	**1**	**9**	**10**	**55**	....	....	....	....	....
	NHL Totals		**502**	**53**	**65**	**118**	**460**	**59**	**3**	**4**	**7**	**34**

Claimed on waivers by **Toronto** from **NY Islanders**, December 3, 1992. Traded to **NY Rangers** by **Toronto** for Nick Kypreos, February 29, 1996.

BERG, REGGIE

Center. Shoots left. 5'10", 180 lbs. Born, Coon Rapids, MN, September 18, 1976.
(Toronto's 12th choice, 178th overall, in 1996 Entry Draft).

			Regular Season					Playoffs				
Season	Club	Lea	GP	G	A	TP	PIM	GP	G	A	TP	PIM
1995-96	U. of Minnesota	WCHA	40	23	11	34	69	....	....	....	....	....
1996-97	U. of Minnesota	WCHA	38	11	26	37	48	....	....	....	....	....
1997-98	U. of Minnesota	WCHA	39	20	19	39	53	....	....	....	....	....

WCHA Second All-Star Team (1998)

BERGEVIN, MARC (BUHR-zheh-vihn) **ST.L.**

Defense. Shoots left. 6'1", 197 lbs. Born, Montreal, Que., August 11, 1965.
(Chicago's 3rd choice, 60th overall, in 1983 Entry Draft).

			Regular Season					Playoffs				
Season	Club	Lea	GP	G	A	TP	PIM	GP	G	A	TP	PIM
1982-83	Chicoutimi	QMJHL	64	3	27	30	113	....	....	....	....	....
1983-84	Chicoutimi	QMJHL	70	10	35	45	125	....	....	....	....	....
	Springfield	AHL	7	0	1	1	2	....	....	....	....	....
1984-85	**Chicago**	**NHL**	**60**	**0**	**6**	**6**	**54**	**6**	**0**	**3**	**3**	**2**
	Springfield	AHL	....	....	....	....	....	4	0	0	0	0
1985-86	**Chicago**	**NHL**	**71**	**7**	**7**	**14**	**60**	**3**	**0**	**0**	**0**	**0**
1986-87	**Chicago**	**NHL**	**66**	**4**	**10**	**14**	**66**	**3**	**1**	**0**	**1**	**2**
1987-88	**Chicago**	**NHL**	**58**	**1**	**6**	**7**	**85**	....	....	....	....	....
	Saginaw	IHL	10	2	7	9	20	....	....	....	....	....
1988-89	**Chicago**	**NHL**	**11**	**0**	**0**	**0**	**18**	....	....	....	....	....
	NY Islanders	**NHL**	**58**	**2**	**13**	**15**	**62**	....	....	....	....	....
1989-90	**NY Islanders**	**NHL**	**18**	**0**	**4**	**4**	**30**	....	....	....	....	....
	Springfield	AHL	47	7	16	23	66	17	2	11	13	16
1990-91	Capital District	AHL	7	0	5	5	6	....	....	....	....	....
	Hartford	**NHL**	**4**	**0**	**0**	**0**	**4**	....	....	....	....	....
	Springfield	AHL	58	4	23	27	85	18	0	7	7	26
1991-92	**Hartford**	**NHL**	**75**	**7**	**17**	**24**	**64**	**5**	**0**	**0**	**0**	**2**
1992-93	**Tampa Bay**	**NHL**	**78**	**2**	**12**	**14**	**66**	....	....	....	....	....
1993-94	**Tampa Bay**	**NHL**	**83**	**1**	**15**	**16**	**87**	....	....	....	....	....
1994-95	**Tampa Bay**	**NHL**	**44**	**2**	**4**	**6**	**51**	....	....	....	....	....
1995-96	**Detroit**	**NHL**	**70**	**1**	**9**	**10**	**33**	**17**	**1**	**0**	**1**	**14**
1996-97	**St. Louis**	**NHL**	**82**	**0**	**4**	**4**	**53**	**6**	**1**	**0**	**1**	**8**
1997-98	**St. Louis**	**NHL**	**81**	**3**	**7**	**10**	**90**	**10**	**0**	**1**	**1**	**8**
	NHL Totals		**859**	**30**	**114**	**144**	**823**	**50**	**3**	**4**	**7**	**36**

Traded to **NY Islanders** by **Chicago** with Gary Nylund for Steve Konroyd and Bob Bassen, November 25, 1988. Traded to **Hartford** by **NY Islanders** for Hartford's 5th round choice (Ryan Duthie) in 1992 Entry Draft, October 30, 1990. Signed as a free agent by **Tampa Bay**, July 9, 1992. Traded to **Detroit** by **Tampa Bay** with Ben Hankinson for Shawn Burr and Detroit's 3rd round choice (later traded to Boston — Boston selected Jason Doyle) in 1996 Entry Draft, August 17, 1995. Signed as a free agent by **St. Louis**, July 31, 1996.

BERGKVIST, STEFAN (BUHRG-kvihst, STEH-fan) **PIT.**

Defense. Shoots left. 6'2", 224 lbs. Born, Leksand, Sweden, March 10, 1975.
(Pittsburgh's 1st choice, 26th overall, in 1993 Entry Draft).

			Regular Season					Playoffs				
Season	Club	Lea	GP	G	A	TP	PIM	GP	G	A	TP	PIM
1992-93	Leksand IF	Sweden	15	0	0	0	6	....	....	....	....	....
1993-94	Leksand IF	Sweden	6	0	0	0	0	....	....	....	....	....
1994-95	London	OHL	64	3	17	20	93	4	0	0	0	5
1995-96	**Pittsburgh**	**NHL**	**2**	**0**	**0**	**0**	**2**	**4**	**0**	**0**	**0**	**2**
	Cleveland	IHL	61	2	8	10	58	3	0	0	0	14
1996-97	**Pittsburgh**	**NHL**	**5**	**0**	**0**	**0**	**7**	....	....	....	....	....
	Cleveland	IHL	33	0	1	1	54	4	0	0	0	0
1997-98	Cleveland	IHL	71	3	6	9	129	10	0	2	2	24
	NHL Totals		**7**	**0**	**0**	**0**	**9**	**4**	**0**	**0**	**0**	**2**

BERGLUND, CHRISTIAN **N.J.**

Right wing. Shoots left. 5'11", 183 lbs. Born, Orebro, Sweden, March 12, 1980.
(New Jersey's 3rd choice, 37th overall, in 1998 Entry Draft).

			Regular Season					Playoffs				
Season	Club	Lea	GP	G	A	TP	PIM	GP	G	A	TP	PIM
1994-95	Kariskoga	Sweden-4	20	14	13	27	....	....	....	....	....	....
1995-96	Kristinehamn	Sweden-3	23	8	8	16	12	....	....	....	....	....
1996-97	Farjestad	Swe-Jr.	21	2	3	5	24	....	....	....	....	....
1997-98	Farjestad	Swe-Jr.	29	23	19	42	88	2	0	0	0	0
	Farjestad	Sweden	1	0	0	0	0	....	....	....	....	....

BERGMAN, PETER

Center. Shoots left. 6'1", 195 lbs. Born, Regina, Sask., April 14, 1978.
(Pittsburgh's 6th choice, 150th overall, in 1996 Entry Draft).

			Regular Season					Playoffs				
Season	Club	Lea	GP	G	A	TP	PIM	GP	G	A	TP	PIM
1995-96	Kamloops	WHL	53	8	7	15	23	10	1	2	3	10
1996-97	Kamloops	WHL	3	0	1	1	4	....	....	....	....	....
	Calgary	WHL	61	10	17	27	57	....	....	....	....	....
1997-98	Calgary	WHL	71	16	21	37	94	17	5	4	9	32

BERNIER, DAVID **ANA.**

Right wing. Shoots right. 6'3", 205 lbs. Born, St-Hyacinthe, Que., January 9, 1978.
(Anaheim's 6th choice, 205th overall, in 1998 Entry Draft).

			Regular Season					Playoffs				
Season	Club	Lea	GP	G	A	TP	PIM	GP	G	A	TP	PIM
1994-95	St-Hyacinthe	QMJHL	66	15	16	31	40	1	0	1	1	0
1995-96	St-Hyacinthe	QMJHL	65	10	18	28	64	....	....	....	....	....
1996-97	Rouyn-Noranda	QMJHL	21	2	9	11	11	....	....	....	....	....
	Beauport	QMJHL	38	7	17	24	37	4	2	1	3	5
1997-98	Quebec	QMJHL	70	35	53	88	88	14	7	8	15	12

BERRY, BRAD

Defense. Shoots left. 6'2", 190 lbs. Born, Bashaw, Alta., April 1, 1965.
(Winnipeg's 3rd choice, 29th overall, in 1983 Entry Draft).

			Regular Season					Playoffs				
Season	Club	Lea	GP	G	A	TP	PIM	GP	G	A	TP	PIM
1982-83	St. Albert	AJHL	55	9	33	42	97	....	....	....	....	....
1983-84	North Dakota	WCHA	32	2	7	9	8	....	....	....	....	....
1984-85	North Dakota	WCHA	40	4	26	30	26	....	....	....	....	....
1985-86	North Dakota	WCHA	40	6	29	35	26	....	....	....	....	....
	Winnipeg	**NHL**	**13**	**1**	**0**	**1**	**10**	**3**	**0**	**0**	**0**	**0**
1986-87	**Winnipeg**	**NHL**	**52**	**2**	**8**	**10**	**60**	**7**	**0**	**1**	**1**	**14**
1987-88	**Winnipeg**	**NHL**	**48**	**0**	**6**	**6**	**75**	....	....	....	....	....
	Moncton	AHL	10	1	3	4	14	....	....	....	....	....
1988-89	**Winnipeg**	**NHL**	**38**	**0**	**9**	**9**	**45**	....	....	....	....	....
	Moncton	AHL	38	3	16	19	39	....	....	....	....	....
1989-90	**Winnipeg**	**NHL**	**12**	**1**	**2**	**3**	**6**	**1**	**0**	**0**	**0**	**0**
	Moncton	AHL	38	1	9	10	58	....	....	....	....	....
1990-91	Brynas IF	Sweden	38	3	1	4	38	....	....	....	....	....
	Canada	Nat-Tm	4	0	1	1	0	....	....	....	....	....
1991-92	**Minnesota**	**NHL**	**7**	**0**	**0**	**0**	**6**	**2**	**0**	**0**	**0**	**2**
	Kalamazoo	IHL	65	5	18	23	90	5	2	0	2	6
1992-93	**Minnesota**	**NHL**	**63**	**0**	**3**	**3**	**109**	....	....	....	....	....
1993-94	**Dallas**	**NHL**	**8**	**0**	**0**	**0**	**12**	....	....	....	....	....
	Kalamazoo	IHL	45	3	19	22	91	1	0	0	0	0
1994-95	Kalamazoo	IHL	65	4	11	15	146	1	0	0	0	0
1995-96	Michigan	IHL	80	4	13	17	73	10	0	5	5	12
1996-97	Michigan	IHL	77	4	7	11	68	4	0	0	0	4
1997-98	Michigan	IHL	67	3	8	11	60	....	....	....	....	....
	NHL Totals		**241**	**4**	**28**	**32**	**323**	**13**	**0**	**1**	**1**	**16**

Signed as a free agent by **Minnesota**, October 4, 1991. Transferred to **Dallas** after **Minnesota** franchise relocated, June 9, 1993.

BERRY, RICK **COL.**

Defense. Shoots left. 6'1", 192 lbs. Born, Brandon, Man., November 4, 1978.
(Colorado's 3rd choice, 55th overall, in 1997 Entry Draft).

			Regular Season					Playoffs				
Season	Club	Lea	GP	G	A	TP	PIM	GP	G	A	TP	PIM
1995-96	Seattle	WHL	59	4	9	13	103	1	0	0	0	0
1996-97	Seattle	WHL	72	12	21	33	125	15	3	7	10	23
1997-98	Seattle	WHL	37	5	12	17	100	....	....	....	....	....
	Spokane	WHL	22	4	9	13	31	17	1	4	5	26

BERTRAN, RICK **VAN.**

Defense. Shoots left. 6'3", 190 lbs. Born, Niagara Falls, Ont., March 12, 1980.
(Vancouver's 7th choice, 140th overall, in 1998 Entry Draft).

			Regular Season					Playoffs				
Season	Club	Lea	GP	G	A	TP	PIM	GP	G	A	TP	PIM
1997-98	Kitchener	OHL	56	0	9	9	149	6	0	0	0	11

BERTRAND, ERIC **N.J.**

Left wing. Shoots left. 6', 205 lbs. Born, St. Ephrem, Que., April 16, 1975.
(New Jersey's 9th choice, 207th overall, in 1994 Entry Draft).

			Regular Season					Playoffs				
Season	Club	Lea	GP	G	A	TP	PIM	GP	G	A	TP	PIM
1992-93	Granby	QMJHL	64	10	15	25	82	....	....	....	....	....
1993-94	Granby	QMJHL	60	11	15	26	151	6	1	0	1	18
1994-95	Granby	QMJHL	56	14	26	40	268	13	3	8	11	50
1995-96	Albany	AHL	70	16	13	29	199	4	0	0	0	6
1996-97	Albany	AHL	77	16	27	43	204	8	3	3	6	15
1997-98	Albany	AHL	76	20	29	49	256	13	5	5	10	4

BERTUZZI, TODD (buhr-TOO-zee) **VAN.**

Center. Shoots left. 6'3", 224 lbs. Born, Sudbury, Ont., February 2, 1975.
(NY Islanders' 1st choice, 23rd overall, in 1993 Entry Draft).

			Regular Season					Playoffs				
Season	Club	Lea	GP	G	A	TP	PIM	GP	G	A	TP	PIM
1991-92	Guelph	OHL	47	7	14	21	145	....	....	....	....	....
1992-93	Guelph	OHL	59	27	32	59	164	5	2	2	4	6
1993-94	Guelph	OHL	61	28	54	82	165	9	2	6	8	30
1994-95	Guelph	OHL	62	54	65	119	58	14	*15	18	33	41
1995-96	**NY Islanders**	**NHL**	**76**	**18**	**21**	**39**	**83**	....	....	....	....	....
1996-97	**NY Islanders**	**NHL**	**64**	**10**	**13**	**23**	**68**	....	....	....	....	....
	Utah	IHL	13	5	5	10	16	....	....	....	....	....
1997-98	**NY Islanders**	**NHL**	**52**	**7**	**11**	**18**	**58**	....	....	....	....	....
	Vancouver	**NHL**	**22**	**6**	**9**	**15**	**63**	....	....	....	....	....
	NHL Totals		**214**	**41**	**54**	**95**	**272**	....	....	....	....	....

OHL Second All-Star team (1995)

Traded to **Vancouver** by **NY Islanders** with Bryan McCabe and NY Islanders' 3rd round choice (Jarkko Ruutu) in 1998 Entry Draft for Trevor Linden, February 6, 1998.

BERUBE, CRAIG
(buh-ROO-bee) **WSH.**

Left wing. Shoots left. 6'1", 205 lbs. Born, Calahoo, Alta., December 17, 1965.

			Regular Season					Playoffs				
Season	Club	Lea	GP	G	A	TP	PIM	GP	G	A	TP	PIM
1982-83	Kamloops	WHL	4	0	0	0	0	....	....	....	....	....
1983-84	New Westminster	WHL	70	11	20	31	104	8	1	2	3	5
1984-85	New Westminster	WHL	70	25	44	69	191	10	3	2	5	4
1985-86	Kamloops	WHL	32	17	14	31	119	....	....	....	....	....
	Medicine Hat	WHL	34	14	16	30	95	25	7	8	15	102
1986-87	**Philadelphia**	**NHL**	**7**	**0**	**0**	**0**	**57**	**5**	**0**	**0**	**0**	**17**
	Hershey	AHL	63	7	17	24	325	....	....	....	....	....
1987-88	**Philadelphia**	**NHL**	**27**	**3**	**2**	**5**	**108**	....	....	....	....	....
	Hershey	AHL	31	5	9	14	119	....	....	....	....	....
1988-89	**Philadelphia**	**NHL**	**53**	**1**	**1**	**2**	**199**	**16**	**0**	**0**	**0**	**56**
	Hershey	AHL	7	0	2	2	19	....	....	....	....	....
1989-90	**Philadelphia**	**NHL**	**74**	**4**	**14**	**18**	**291**	....	....	....	....	....
1990-91	**Philadelphia**	**NHL**	**74**	**8**	**9**	**17**	**293**	....	....	....	....	....
1991-92	**Toronto**	**NHL**	**40**	**5**	**7**	**12**	**109**	....	....	....	....	....
	Calgary	**NHL**	**36**	**1**	**4**	**5**	**155**	....	....	....	....	....
1992-93	**Calgary**	**NHL**	**77**	**4**	**8**	**12**	**209**	**6**	**0**	**1**	**1**	**21**
1993-94	**Washington**	**NHL**	**84**	**7**	**7**	**14**	**305**	**8**	**0**	**0**	**0**	**21**
1994-95	**Washington**	**NHL**	**43**	**2**	**4**	**6**	**173**	**7**	**0**	**0**	**0**	**29**
1995-96	**Washington**	**NHL**	**50**	**2**	**10**	**12**	**151**	**2**	**0**	**0**	**0**	**19**
1996-97	**Washington**	**NHL**	**80**	**4**	**3**	**7**	**218**	....	....	....	....	....
1997-98	**Washington**	**NHL**	**74**	**6**	**9**	**15**	**189**	**21**	**1**	**0**	**1**	**21**
	NHL Totals		**719**	**47**	**78**	**125**	**2457**	**65**	**1**	**1**	**2**	**184**

Signed as a free agent by **Philadelphia**, March 19, 1986. Traded to **Edmonton** by **Philadelphia** with Craig Fisher and Scott Mellanby for Dave Brown, Corey Foster and Jari Kurri, May 30, 1991. Traded to **Toronto** by **Edmonton** with Grant Fuhr and Glenn Anderson for Vincent Damphousse, Peter Ing, Scott Thornton, Luke Richardson, future considerations and cash, September 19, 1991. Traded to **Calgary** by **Toronto** with Alexander Godynyuk, Gary Leeman, Michel Petit and Jeff Reese for Doug Gilmour, Jamie Macoun, Ric Nattress, Rick Wamsley and Kent Manderville, January 2, 1992. Traded to **Washington** by **Calgary** for Washington's 5th round choice (Darryl Lafrance) in 1993 Entry Draft, June 26, 1993.

BETIK, KAREL
(BEH-tihk, KAHR-ehl) **T.B.**

Defense. Shoots left. 6'2", 208 lbs. Born, Karvina, Czech., October 28, 1978.
(Tampa Bay's 6th choice, 112th overall, in 1997 Entry Draft).

			Regular Season					Playoffs				
Season	Club	Lea	GP	G	A	TP	PIM	GP	G	A	TP	PIM
1995-96	Vitkovice	Czech-Jr.	48	3	12	15	88	....	....	....	....	....
1996-97	Kelowna	WHL	56	3	10	13	76	6	1	1	2	2
1997-98	Kelowna	WHL	61	5	25	30	121	7	1	2	3	8

BETTS, BLAIR
CGY.

Center. Shoots left. 6'1", 183 lbs. Born, Edmonton, Alta., February 16, 1980.
(Calgary's 2nd choice, 33rd overall, in 1998 Entry Draft).

			Regular Season					Playoffs				
Season	Club	Lea	GP	G	A	TP	PIM	GP	G	A	TP	PIM
1996-97	Prince George	WHL	58	12	18	30	19	15	2	2	4	6
1997-98	Prince George	WHL	71	35	41	76	38	11	4	6	10	8

BEUKEBOOM, JEFF
(BOO-kuh-BOOM) **NYR**

Defense. Shoots right. 6'5", 230 lbs. Born, Ajax, Ont., March 28, 1965.
(Edmonton's 1st choice, 19th overall, in 1983 Entry Draft).

			Regular Season					Playoffs				
Season	Club	Lea	GP	G	A	TP	PIM	GP	G	A	TP	PIM
1982-83	S.S. Marie	OHL	70	0	25	25	143	16	1	4	5	46
1983-84	S.S. Marie	OHL	61	6	30	36	178	16	1	7	8	43
1984-85	S.S. Marie	OHL	37	4	20	24	85	16	4	6	10	47
1985-86	Nova Scotia	AHL	77	9	20	29	175	....	....	....	....	....
	Edmonton	**NHL**	....	....	....	....	....	**1**	**0**	**0**	**0**	**4**
1986-87	**Edmonton**	**NHL**	**44**	**3**	**8**	**11**	**124**	....	....	....	....	.... ♦
	Nova Scotia	AHL	14	1	7	8	35	....	....	....	....	....
1987-88	**Edmonton**	**NHL**	**73**	**5**	**20**	**25**	**201**	**7**	**0**	**0**	**0**	**16** ♦
1988-89	**Edmonton**	**NHL**	**36**	**0**	**5**	**5**	**94**	**1**	**0**	**0**	**0**	**2**
	Cape Breton	AHL	8	0	4	4	36	....	....	....	....	....
1989-90	**Edmonton**	**NHL**	**46**	**1**	**12**	**13**	**86**	**2**	**0**	**0**	**0**	**0** ♦
1990-91	**Edmonton**	**NHL**	**67**	**3**	**7**	**10**	**150**	**18**	**1**	**3**	**4**	**28**
1991-92	**Edmonton**	**NHL**	**18**	**0**	**5**	**5**	**78**	....	....	....	....	....
	NY Rangers	**NHL**	**56**	**1**	**10**	**11**	**122**	**13**	**2**	**3**	**5**	**47**
1992-93	**NY Rangers**	**NHL**	**82**	**2**	**17**	**19**	**153**	....	....	....	....	....
1993-94	**NY Rangers**	**NHL**	**68**	**8**	**8**	**16**	**170**	**22**	**0**	**6**	**6**	**50** ♦
1994-95	**NY Rangers**	**NHL**	**44**	**1**	**3**	**4**	**70**	**9**	**0**	**0**	**0**	**10**
1995-96	**NY Rangers**	**NHL**	**82**	**3**	**11**	**14**	**220**	**11**	**0**	**3**	**3**	**6**
1996-97	**NY Rangers**	**NHL**	**80**	**3**	**9**	**12**	**167**	**15**	**0**	**1**	**1**	**34**
1997-98	**NY Rangers**	**NHL**	**63**	**0**	**5**	**5**	**195**	....	....	....	....	....
	NHL Totals		**759**	**30**	**120**	**150**	**1830**	**99**	**3**	**16**	**19**	**197**

OHL First All-Star Team (1985)

Traded to **NY Rangers** by **Edmonton** for David Shaw, November 12, 1991.

BIALOWAS, FRANK
(bigh-uh-LOH-uhs) **PHI.**

Left wing. Shoots left. 5'11", 220 lbs. Born, Winnipeg, Man., September 25, 1969.

			Regular Season					Playoffs				
Season	Club	Lea	GP	G	A	TP	PIM	GP	G	A	TP	PIM
1991-92	Roanoke	ECHL	23	4	2	6	150	3	0	0	0	4
1992-93	Richmond	ECHL	60	3	18	21	261	1	0	0	0	2
	St. John's	AHL	7	1	0	1	28	1	0	0	0	0
1993-94	**Toronto**	**NHL**	**3**	**0**	**0**	**0**	**12**	....	....	....	....	....
	St. John's	AHL	69	2	8	10	352	7	0	3	3	25
1994-95	St. John's	AHL	51	2	3	5	277	4	0	0	0	12
1995-96	Portland	AHL	65	4	3	7	211	7	0	0	0	42
1996-97	Philadelphia	AHL	67	7	6	13	254	6	0	2	2	41
1997-98	Philadelphia	AHL	65	5	7	12	259	19	0	0	0	26
	NHL Totals		**3**	**0**	**0**	**0**	**12**	....	....	....	....	....

Signed as a free agent by **Toronto**, March 20, 1994. Signed as a free agent by **Washington**, September 8, 1995. Traded to **Philadelphia** by **Washington** for future considerations, July 18, 1996.

BICANEK, RADIM
(BEE-chah-nehk) **OTT.**

Defense. Shoots left. 6'1", 195 lbs. Born, Uherske Hradiste, Czech., January 18, 1975.
(Ottawa's 2nd choice, 27th overall, in 1993 Entry Draft).

			Regular Season					Playoffs				
Season	Club	Lea	GP	G	A	TP	PIM	GP	G	A	TP	PIM
1992-93	Dukla Jihlava	Czech.	43	2	3	5	....	....	....	....	....	....
1993-94	Belleville	OHL	63	16	27	43	49	12	2	8	10	21
1994-95	Belleville	OHL	49	13	26	39	61	16	6	5	11	30
	Ottawa	**NHL**	**6**	**0**	**0**	**0**	**0**	....	....	....	....	....
	P.E.I.	AHL	....	....	....	....	....	3	0	1	1	0
1995-96	P.E.I.	AHL	74	7	19	26	87	5	0	2	2	6
1996-97	**Ottawa**	**NHL**	**21**	**0**	**1**	**1**	**8**	**7**	**0**	**0**	**0**	**8**
	Worcester	AHL	44	1	15	16	22	....	....	....	....	....
1997-98	**Ottawa**	**NHL**	**1**	**0**	**0**	**0**	**0**	....	....	....	....	....
	Detroit	IHL	9	1	3	4	16	....	....	....	....	....
	Manitoba	IHL	42	1	7	8	52	....	....	....	....	....
	NHL Totals		**28**	**0**	**1**	**1**	**8**	**7**	**0**	**0**	**0**	**8**

BICEK, JIRI
(bee-CHEHK, YEH-ree) **N.J.**

Left wing. Shoots left. 5'11", 185 lbs. Born, Kosice, Czech., December 3, 1978.
(New Jersey's 4th choice, 131st overall, in 1997 Entry Draft).

			Regular Season					Playoffs				
Season	Club	Lea	GP	G	A	TP	PIM	GP	G	A	TP	PIM
1995-96	Kosice	Slovakia	30	10	15	25	16	9	2	4	6	0
1996-97	Kosice	Slovakia	44	11	14	25	20	7	1	3	4	....
1997-98	Albany	AHL	50	10	10	20	22	13	1	6	7	4

BIENVENUE, DANIEL
(bee-ehn-veh-nyoo) **BUF.**

Left wing. Shoots left. 6', 196 lbs. Born, Val d'Or, Que., June 10, 1977.
(Buffalo's 8th choice, 123rd overall, in 1995 Entry Draft).

			Regular Season					Playoffs				
Season	Club	Lea	GP	G	A	TP	PIM	GP	G	A	TP	PIM
1993-94	Chicoutimi	QMJHL	42	2	7	9	4	....	....	....	....	....
1994-95	Val d'Or	QMJHL	67	27	14	41	40	....	....	....	....	....
1995-96	Val d'Or	QMJHL	67	30	42	72	65	13	6	1	7	0
1996-97	Val d'Or	QMJHL	20	4	4	8	22	13	6	6	12	19
1997-98	Rochester	AHL	10	0	0	0	17	....	....	....	....	....
	South Carolina	ECHL	50	10	11	21	4	....	....	....	....	....

BILOTTO, NICHOLAS
(BIHL-awt-oh) **ST.L.**

Defense. Shoots right. 6'2", 198 lbs. Born, Montreal, Que., February 24, 1979.
(St. Louis' 5th choice, 149th overall, in 1997 Entry Draft).

			Regular Season					Playoffs				
Season	Club	Lea	GP	G	A	TP	PIM	GP	G	A	TP	PIM
1996-97	Beauport	QMJHL	29	3	2	5	28	4	0	1	1	2
1997-98	Quebec	QMJHL	64	7	25	32	124	14	3	6	9	20

BIRON, MATHIEU
(BEE-rawn, mat-yoo) **L.A.**

Defense. Shoots right. 6'6", 212 lbs. Born, Lac St. Charles, Que., April 29, 1980.
(Los Angeles' 1st choice, 21st overall, in 1998 Entry Draft).

			Regular Season					Playoffs				
Season	Club	Lea	GP	G	A	TP	PIM	GP	G	A	TP	PIM
1996-97	Ste-Foy	QAAA	40	4	22	26	49	....	....	....	....	....
1997-98	Shawinigan	QMJHL	59	8	28	36	60	....	....	....	....	....

BLACK, JAMES
CHI.

Center. Shoots left. 6', 202 lbs. Born, Regina, Sask., August 15, 1969.
(Hartford's 4th choice, 94th overall, in 1989 Entry Draft).

			Regular Season					Playoffs				
Season	Club	Lea	GP	G	A	TP	PIM	GP	G	A	TP	PIM
1987-88	Portland	WHL	72	30	50	80	50	....	....	....	....	....
1988-89	Portland	WHL	71	45	51	96	57	19	13	6	19	28
1989-90	**Hartford**	**NHL**	**1**	**0**	**0**	**0**	**0**	....	....	....	....	....
	Binghamton	AHL	80	37	35	72	34	....	....	....	....	....
1990-91	**Hartford**	**NHL**	**1**	**0**	**0**	**0**	**0**	....	....	....	....	....
	Springfield	AHL	79	35	61	96	34	18	9	9	18	6
1991-92	**Hartford**	**NHL**	**30**	**4**	**6**	**10**	**10**	....	....	....	....	....
	Springfield	AHL	47	15	25	40	33	10	3	2	5	18
1992-93	**Minnesota**	**NHL**	**10**	**2**	**1**	**3**	**4**	....	....	....	....	....
	Kalamazoo	IHL	63	25	45	70	40	....	....	....	....	....
1993-94	**Dallas**	**NHL**	**13**	**2**	**3**	**5**	**2**	....	....	....	....	....
	Buffalo	**NHL**	**2**	**0**	**0**	**0**	**0**	....	....	....	....	....
	Rochester	AHL	45	19	32	51	28	4	2	3	5	0
1994-95	Las Vegas	IHL	78	29	44	73	54	10	1	6	7	4
1995-96	**Chicago**	**NHL**	**13**	**3**	**3**	**6**	**16**	**8**	**1**	**0**	**1**	**2**
	Indianapolis	IHL	67	32	50	82	56	....	....	....	....	....
1996-97	**Chicago**	**NHL**	**64**	**12**	**11**	**23**	**20**	**5**	**1**	**1**	**2**	**2**
1997-98	**Chicago**	**NHL**	**52**	**10**	**5**	**15**	**8**	....	....	....	....	....
	NHL Totals		**186**	**33**	**29**	**62**	**60**	**13**	**2**	**1**	**3**	**4**

Traded to **Minnesota** by **Hartford** for Mark Janssens, September 3, 1992. Transferred to **Dallas** after **Minnesota** franchise relocated, June 9, 1993. Traded to **Buffalo** by **Dallas** with Dallas' 7th round choice (Steve Webb) in 1994 Entry Draft for Gord Donnelly, December 15, 1993. Signed as a free agent by **Chicago**, September 18, 1995.

BLACK, JESSE

Defense. Shoots right. 6'4", 197 lbs. Born, Thunder Bay, Ont., June 23, 1978.
(Los Angeles' 6th choice, 120th overall, in 1996 Entry Draft).

			Regular Season					Playoffs				
Season	Club	Lea	GP	G	A	TP	PIM	GP	G	A	TP	PIM
1995-96	Niagara Falls	OHL	59	1	3	4	27	10	0	2	2	0
1996-97	Erie	OHL	60	1	12	13	102	5	0	1	1	0
1997-98	Erie	OHL	61	7	14	21	57	7	1	0	1	0

BLAKE, ROB — L.A.

Defense. Shoots right. 6'4", 220 lbs. Born, Simcoe, Ont., December 10, 1969.
(Los Angeles' 4th choice, 70th overall, in 1988 Entry Draft).

			Regular Season					Playoffs				
Season	Club	Lea	GP	G	A	TP	PIM	GP	G	A	TP	PIM
1986-87	Stratford	OJHL	31	11	20	31	115	....	....	....	....	....
1987-88	Bowling Green	CCHA	43	5	8	13	88	....	....	....	....	....
1988-89	Bowling Green	CCHA	46	11	21	32	140	....	....	....	....	....
1989-90	Bowling Green	CCHA	42	23	36	59	140	....	....	....	....	....
	Los Angeles	**NHL**	**4**	**0**	**0**	**0**	**4**	**8**	**1**	**3**	**4**	**4**
1990-91	**Los Angeles**	**NHL**	**75**	**12**	**34**	**46**	**125**	**12**	**1**	**4**	**5**	**26**
1991-92	**Los Angeles**	**NHL**	**57**	**7**	**13**	**20**	**102**	**6**	**2**	**1**	**3**	**12**
1992-93	**Los Angeles**	**NHL**	**76**	**16**	**43**	**59**	**152**	**23**	**4**	**6**	**10**	**46**
1993-94	**Los Angeles**	**NHL**	**84**	**20**	**48**	**68**	**137**	....	....	....	....	....
1994-95	**Los Angeles**	**NHL**	**24**	**4**	**7**	**11**	**38**	....	....	....	....	....
1995-96	**Los Angeles**	**NHL**	**6**	**1**	**2**	**3**	**8**	....	....	....	....	....
1996-97	**Los Angeles**	**NHL**	**62**	**8**	**23**	**31**	**82**	....	....	....	....	....
1997-98	**Los Angeles**	**NHL**	**81**	**23**	**27**	**50**	**94**	**4**	**0**	**0**	**0**	**6**
	Canada	Olympics	6	1	1	2	2	....	....	....	....	....
	NHL Totals		**469**	**91**	**197**	**288**	**742**	**53**	**8**	**14**	**22**	**94**

CCHA Second All-Star Team (1989) • CCHA First All-Star Team (1990) • NCAA West First All-American Team (1990) • NHL/Upper Deck All-Rookie Team (1991) • NHL First All-Star Team (1998) • Won James Norris Memorial Trophy (1998)

Played in NHL All-Star Game (1994)

BLANCHARD, SEAN — L.A.

Defense. Shoots left. 5'11", 198 lbs. Born, Sudbury, Ont., March 29, 1978.
(Los Angeles' 5th choice, 99th overall, in 1997 Entry Draft).

			Regular Season					Playoffs				
Season	Club	Lea	GP	G	A	TP	PIM	GP	G	A	TP	PIM
1994-95	Ottawa	OHL	59	2	5	7	24	....	....	....	....	....
1995-96	Ottawa	OHL	64	7	29	36	49	4	1	3	4	7
1996-97	Ottawa	OHL	66	11	57	68	64	24	3	15	18	34
1997-98	Ottawa	OHL	57	13	51	64	43	13	0	5	5	27

OHL First All-Star Team (1997, 1998) • Canadian Major Junior First All-Star Team (1997) • Canadian Major Junior Defenseman of the Year (1997)

BLOEMBERG, JEFF — (BLOOM-buhrg)

Defense. Shoots right. 6'2", 205 lbs. Born, Listowel, Ont., January 31, 1968.
(NY Rangers' 5th choice, 93rd overall, in 1986 Entry Draft).

			Regular Season					Playoffs				
Season	Club	Lea	GP	G	A	TP	PIM	GP	G	A	TP	PIM
1984-85	Listowel	OJHL	31	7	14	21	....	....	....	....	....	....
1985-86	North Bay	OHL	60	2	11	13	76	8	1	2	3	9
1986-87	North Bay	OHL	60	5	13	18	91	21	1	6	7	13
1987-88	North Bay	OHL	46	9	26	35	60	4	1	4	5	2
	Colorado	IHL	5	0	0	0	0	11	1	0	1	8
1988-89	**NY Rangers**	**NHL**	**9**	**0**	**0**	**0**	**0**	....	....	....	....	....
	Denver	IHL	64	7	22	29	55	1	0	0	0	0
1989-90	**NY Rangers**	**NHL**	**28**	**3**	**3**	**6**	**25**	**7**	**0**	**3**	**3**	**5**
	Flint	IHL	41	7	14	21	24	....	....	....	....	....
1990-91	**NY Rangers**	**NHL**	**3**	**0**	**2**	**2**	**0**	....	....	....	....	....
	Binghamton	AHL	77	16	46	62	28	10	0	6	6	10
1991-92	**NY Rangers**	**NHL**	**3**	**0**	**1**	**1**	**0**	....	....	....	....	....
	Binghamton	AHL	66	6	41	47	22	11	1	10	11	10
1992-93	Cape Breton	AHL	76	6	45	51	34	16	5	10	15	10
1993-94	Springfield	AHL	78	8	28	36	36	6	0	3	3	8
1994-95	Adirondack	AHL	44	5	19	24	10	4	0	0	0	0
1995-96	Adirondack	AHL	72	10	28	38	32	3	0	1	1	4
1996-97	Adirondack	AHL	69	5	31	36	24	4	0	3	3	2
1997-98	Berlin	Germany	27	3	7	10	16	....	....	....	....	....
	NHL Totals		**43**	**3**	**6**	**9**	**25**	**7**	**0**	**3**	**3**	**5**

AHL Second All-Star Team (1991)

Claimed by **Tampa Bay** from **NY Rangers** in Expansion Draft, June 18, 1992. Traded to **Edmonton** by **Tampa Bay** for future considerations, September 25, 1992. Signed as a free agent by **Hartford**, August 9, 1993. Signed as a free agent by **Detroit**, May 9, 1995.

BLOUIN, SYLVAIN — (bluh-WEHN) MTL.

Left wing. Shoots left. 6'2", 207 lbs. Born, Montreal, Que., May 21, 1974.
(NY Rangers' 5th choice, 104th overall, in 1994 Entry Draft).

			Regular Season					Playoffs				
Season	Club	Lea	GP	G	A	TP	PIM	GP	G	A	TP	PIM
1991-92	Laval	QMJHL	28	0	0	0	23	9	0	0	0	35
1992-93	Laval	QMJHL	68	0	10	10	373	13	1	0	1	*66
1993-94	Laval	QMJHL	62	18	22	40	*492	21	4	13	17	*177
1994-95	Chicago	IHL	1	0	0	0	2	....	....	....	....	....
	Charlotte	ECHL	50	5	7	12	280	3	0	0	0	6
	Binghamton	AHL	10	1	0	1	46	2	0	0	0	24
1995-96	Binghamton	AHL	71	5	8	13	*352	4	0	3	3	4
1996-97	**NY Rangers**	**NHL**	**6**	**0**	**0**	**0**	**18**	....	....	....	....	....
	Binghamton	AHL	62	13	17	30	301	4	2	1	3	16
1997-98	**NY Rangers**	**NHL**	**1**	**0**	**0**	**0**	**5**	....	....	....	....	....
	Hartford	AHL	53	8	9	17	286	9	0	1	1	63
	NHL Totals		**7**	**0**	**0**	**0**	**23**	....	....	....	....	....

Traded to **Montreal** by **NY Rangers** with NY Rangers' 6th round choice in 1999 Entry Draft for Peter Popovic, June 30, 1998.

BODGER, DOUG — (BAW-juhr) L.A.

Defense. Shoots left. 6'2", 210 lbs. Born, Chemainus, B.C., June 18, 1966.
(Pittsburgh's 2nd choice, 9th overall, in 1984 Entry Draft).

			Regular Season					Playoffs				
Season	Club	Lea	GP	G	A	TP	PIM	GP	G	A	TP	PIM
1982-83	Kamloops	WHL	72	26	66	92	98	7	0	5	5	2
1983-84	Kamloops	WHL	70	21	77	98	90	17	2	15	17	12
1984-85	**Pittsburgh**	**NHL**	**65**	**5**	**26**	**31**	**67**	....	....	....	....	....
1985-86	**Pittsburgh**	**NHL**	**79**	**4**	**33**	**37**	**63**	....	....	....	....	....
1986-87	**Pittsburgh**	**NHL**	**76**	**11**	**38**	**49**	**52**	....	....	....	....	....
1987-88	**Pittsburgh**	**NHL**	**69**	**14**	**31**	**45**	**103**	....	....	....	....	....
1988-89	**Pittsburgh**	**NHL**	**10**	**1**	**4**	**5**	**7**	....	....	....	....	....
	Buffalo	**NHL**	**61**	**7**	**40**	**47**	**52**	**5**	**1**	**1**	**2**	**11**
1989-90	**Buffalo**	**NHL**	**71**	**12**	**36**	**48**	**64**	**6**	**1**	**5**	**6**	**6**
1990-91	**Buffalo**	**NHL**	**58**	**5**	**23**	**28**	**54**	**4**	**0**	**1**	**1**	**0**
1991-92	**Buffalo**	**NHL**	**73**	**11**	**35**	**46**	**108**	**7**	**2**	**1**	**3**	**2**
1992-93	**Buffalo**	**NHL**	**81**	**9**	**45**	**54**	**87**	**8**	**2**	**3**	**5**	**0**
1993-94	**Buffalo**	**NHL**	**75**	**7**	**32**	**39**	**76**	**7**	**0**	**3**	**3**	**6**
1994-95	**Buffalo**	**NHL**	**44**	**3**	**17**	**20**	**47**	**5**	**0**	**4**	**4**	**0**
1995-96	**Buffalo**	**NHL**	**16**	**0**	**5**	**5**	**18**	....	....	....	....	....
	San Jose	**NHL**	**57**	**4**	**19**	**23**	**50**	....	....	....	....	....
1996-97	**San Jose**	**NHL**	**81**	**1**	**15**	**16**	**64**	....	....	....	....	....
1997-98	**San Jose**	**NHL**	**28**	**4**	**6**	**10**	**32**	....	....	....	....	....
	New Jersey	**NHL**	**49**	**5**	**5**	**10**	**25**	**5**	**0**	**0**	**0**	**0**
	NHL Totals		**993**	**103**	**410**	**513**	**969**	**47**	**6**	**18**	**24**	**25**

WHL Second All-Star Team (1983)

Traded to **Buffalo** by **Pittsburgh** wih Darrin Shannon for Tom Barrasso and Buffalo's 3rd round choice (Joe Dziedzic) in 1990 Entry Draft, November 12, 1988. Traded to **San Jose** by **Buffalo** for Vaclav Varada, Martin Spanhel and Philadelphia's 1st (previously acquired by San Jose — later traded to Phoenix — Phoenix selected Daniel Briere) and 4th (previously acquired, Buffalo selected Mike Martone) round choices in 1996 Entry Draft, November 16, 1995. Traded to **New Jersey** by **San Jose** with Dody Wood for John MacLean and Ken Sutton, December 7, 1997. Traded to **LA Kings** by **New Jersey** for Boston's 4th round choice (previously acquired, New Jersey selected Pierre Dagenais) in 1998 Entry Draft, June 18, 1998.

BODTKER, STEWART — (BAWD-kuhr) VAN.

Center. Shoots right. 6'1", 190 lbs. Born, Vancouver, B.C., September 15, 1976.
(Vancouver's 7th choice, 170th overall, in 1995 Entry Draft).

			Regular Season					Playoffs				
Season	Club	Lea	GP	G	A	TP	PIM	GP	G	A	TP	PIM
1994-95	Colorado	WCHA	27	6	4	10	22	....	....	....	....	....
1995-96	Colorado	WCHA	42	6	7	13	40	....	....	....	....	....
1996-97	Colorado	WCHA	43	19	17	36	71	....	....	....	....	....
1997-98	Colorado	WCHA	30	11	15	26	50	....	....	....	....	....

BOGAS, CHRIS — (BOH-GUHS)

Defense. Shoots right. 6', 192 lbs. Born, Cleveland, OH, November 12, 1976.
(Toronto's 10th choice, 148th overall, in 1996 Entry Draft).

			Regular Season					Playoffs				
Season	Club	Lea	GP	G	A	TP	PIM	GP	G	A	TP	PIM
1995-96	Michigan State	CCHA	39	1	19	20	55	....	....	....	....	....
1996-97	Michigan State	CCHA	40	7	4	11	58	....	....	....	....	....
1997-98	Michigan State	CCHA	44	4	10	14	75	....	....	....	....	....

BOGUNIECKI, ERIC — (BOH-guhn-ih-kee)

Center. Shoots right. 5'8", 192 lbs. Born, New Haven, CT, May 6, 1975.
(St. Louis' 6th choice, 193rd overall, in 1993 Entry Draft).

			Regular Season					Playoffs				
Season	Club	Lea	GP	G	A	TP	PIM	GP	G	A	TP	PIM
1992-93	Westminster High	H.S.	24	30	24	54	55	....	....	....	....	....
1993-94	New Hampshire	H.E.	40	17	16	33	66	....	....	....	....	....
1994-95	New Hampshire	H.E.	34	12	16	28	62	....	....	....	....	....
1995-96	New Hampshire	H.E.	32	23	28	51	46	....	....	....	....	....
1996-97	New Hampshire	H.E.	36	26	31	57	58	....	....	....	....	....
1997-98	Dayton	ECHL	26	19	18	37	36	....	....	....	....	....
	Fort Wayne	IHL	35	4	8	12	29	4	1	2	3	10

Hockey East Second All-Star Team (1997)

BOHONOS, LONNY — (boh-HOH-nohz) TOR.

Right wing. Shoots right. 5'11", 190 lbs. Born, Winnipeg, Man., May 20, 1973.

			Regular Season					Playoffs				
Season	Club	Lea	GP	G	A	TP	PIM	GP	G	A	TP	PIM
1991-92	Moose Jaw	WHL	8	1	1	2	0	....	....	....	....	....
1992-93	Seattle	WHL	46	13	13	26	27	....	....	....	....	....
	Portland	WHL	27	20	17	37	16	15	8	13	21	19
1993-94	Portland	WHL	70	*62	*90	*152	80	10	8	11	19	13
1994-95	Syracuse	AHL	67	30	45	75	71	....	....	....	....	....
1995-96	**Vancouver**	**NHL**	**3**	**0**	**1**	**1**	**0**	....	....	....	....	....
	Syracuse	AHL	74	40	39	79	82	16	14	8	22	16
1996-97	**Vancouver**	**NHL**	**36**	**11**	**11**	**22**	**10**	....	....	....	....	....
	Syracuse	AHL	41	22	30	52	28	3	2	2	4	4
1997-98	**Vancouver**	**NHL**	**31**	**2**	**1**	**3**	**4**	....	....	....	....	....
	Syracuse	AHL	17	12	12	24	8	....	....	....	....	....
	Toronto	**NHL**	**6**	**3**	**3**	**6**	**4**	....	....	....	....	....
	St. John's	AHL	11	7	9	16	10	2	1	1	2	2
	NHL Totals		**76**	**16**	**16**	**32**	**18**	....	....	....	....	....

WHL West First All-Star Team (1994) • Canadian Major Junior First All-Star Team (1994)

Signed as a free agent by **Vancouver**, May 31, 1994. Traded to **Toronto** by **Vancouver** for Brandon Convery, March 7, 1998.

BOIKOV, ALEXANDER — (bohy-KAHV) S.J.

Defense. Shoots left. 6', 195 lbs. Born, Chelyabinsk, USSR, February 7, 1975.

			Regular Season					Playoffs				
Season	Club	Lea	GP	G	A	TP	PIM	GP	G	A	TP	PIM
1993-94	Victoria	WHL	70	4	31	35	250	....	....	....	....	....
1994-95	Prince George	WHL	46	5	23	28	115	....	....	....	....	....
	Tri-City	WHL	24	3	13	16	63	17	1	7	8	30
1995-96	Tri-City	WHL	71	3	49	52	230	11	2	4	6	28
1996-97	Kentucky	AHL	61	1	19	20	182	4	0	1	1	4
1997-98	Soviet Wings	Russia	43	7	8	15	10	....	....	....	....	....
	Kentucky	AHL	69	5	14	19	153	3	0	1	1	8

Signed as a free agent by **San Jose**, April 22, 1996.

BOILEAU, PATRICK — WSH.

Defense. Shoots right. 6', 190 lbs. Born, Montreal, Que., February 22, 1975.
(Washington's 3rd choice, 69th overall, in 1993 Entry Draft).

			Regular Season					Playoffs				
Season	Club	Lea	GP	G	A	TP	PIM	GP	G	A	TP	PIM
1992-93	Laval	QMJHL	69	4	19	23	73	13	1	2	3	10
1993-94	Laval	QMJHL	64	13	57	70	56	21	1	7	8	24
1994-95	Laval	QMJHL	38	8	25	33	46	20	4	16	20	24
1995-96	Portland	AHL	78	10	28	38	41	19	1	3	4	12
1996-97	**Washington**	**NHL**	**1**	**0**	**0**	**0**	**0**	....	....	....	....	....
	Portland	AHL	67	16	28	44	63	5	1	1	2	4
1997-98	Portland	AHL	47	6	21	27	53	10	0	1	1	8
	NHL Totals		**1**	**0**	**0**	**0**	**0**	....	....	....	....	....

BOISVENUE, MARTIN — PHI.

Center. Shoots left. 6', 192 lbs. Born, Cornwall, Ont., April 24, 1977.

			Regular Season					Playoffs				
Season	Club	Lea	GP	G	A	TP	PIM	GP	G	A	TP	PIM
1995-96	Val d'Or	QMJHL	37	9	13	22	24	13	2	8	10	4
1996-97	Val d'Or	QMJHL	28	7	12	19	54	....	....	....	....	....
1997-98	Baie-Comeau	QMJHL	11	3	5	8	0	....	....	....	....	....

Signed as a free agent by **Philadelphia**, October 2, 1996.

BOLIBRUCK, KEVIN — EDM.

Defense. Shoots left. 6'1", 200 lbs. Born, Peterborough, Ont., February 8, 1977.
(Edmonton's 7th choice, 176th overall, in 1997 Entry Draft).

			Regular Season					Playoffs				
Season	Club	Lea	GP	G	A	TP	PIM	GP	G	A	TP	PIM
1994-95	Peterborough	OHL	66	2	16	18	88	11	1	1	2	14
1995-96	Peterborough	OHL	57	6	21	27	105	24	3	6	9	46
1996-97	Peterborough	OHL	46	4	26	30	63	11	3	3	6	14
1997-98	Canada	Nat-Tm	49	2	5	7	65	....	....	....	....	....

OHL First All-Star Team (1996)

Rights traded to **Chicago** by **Ottawa** with Denis Chasse and Ottawa's 6th round choice in 1998 Entry Draft for Mike Prokopec, March 18, 1997. Re-entered NHL Entry Draft. Originally Ottawa's 4th choice, 89th overall, in 1995 Entry Draft.

BOMBARDIR, BRAD — (bawm-bahr-DEER) N.J.

Defense. Shoots left. 6'1", 205 lbs. Born, Powell River, B.C., May 5, 1972.
(New Jersey's 5th choice, 56th overall, in 1990 Entry Draft).

			Regular Season					Playoffs				
Season	Club	Lea	GP	G	A	TP	PIM	GP	G	A	TP	PIM
1989-90	Powell River	BCJHL	60	10	35	45	93	....	....	....	....	....
1990-91	North Dakota	WCHA	33	3	6	9	18	....	....	....	....	....
1991-92	North Dakota	WCHA	35	3	14	17	54	....	....	....	....	....
1992-93	North Dakota	WCHA	38	8	15	23	34	....	....	....	....	....
1993-94	North Dakota	WCHA	38	5	17	22	38	....	....	....	....	....
1994-95	Albany	AHL	77	5	22	27	22	14	0	3	3	6
1995-96	Albany	AHL	80	6	25	31	63	3	0	1	1	4
1996-97	Albany	AHL	32	0	8	8	6	16	1	3	4	8
1997-98	**New Jersey**	**NHL**	**43**	**1**	**5**	**6**	**8**	....	....	....	....	....
	Albany	AHL	5	0	0	0	0	....	....	....	....	....
	NHL Totals		**43**	**1**	**5**	**6**	**8**	....	....	....	....	....

AHL Second All-Star Team (1996)

BONDRA, PETER — WSH.

Right wing. Shoots left. 6'1", 200 lbs. Born, Luck, USSR, February 7, 1968.
(Washington's 9th choice, 156th overall, in 1990 Entry Draft).

			Regular Season					Playoffs				
Season	Club	Lea	GP	G	A	TP	PIM	GP	G	A	TP	PIM
1986-87	VSZ Kosice	Czech.	32	4	5	9	24	....	....	....	....	....
1987-88	VSZ Kosice	Czech.	45	27	11	38	20	....	....	....	....	....
1988-89	VSZ Kosice	Czech.	40	30	10	40	20	....	....	....	....	....
1989-90	VSZ Kosice	Czech.	49	36	19	55	....	....	....	....	....	....
1990-91	**Washington**	**NHL**	**54**	**12**	**16**	**28**	**47**	**4**	**0**	**1**	**1**	**2**
1991-92	**Washington**	**NHL**	**71**	**28**	**28**	**56**	**42**	**7**	**6**	**2**	**8**	**4**
1992-93	**Washington**	**NHL**	**83**	**37**	**48**	**85**	**70**	**6**	**0**	**6**	**6**	**0**
1993-94	**Washington**	**NHL**	**69**	**24**	**19**	**43**	**40**	**9**	**2**	**4**	**6**	**4**
1994-95	VSZ Kosice	Slovakia	2	1	0	1	0	....	....	....	....	....
	Washington	**NHL**	**47**	***34**	**9**	**43**	**24**	**7**	**5**	**3**	**8**	**10**
1995-96	Detroit	IHL	7	8	1	9	0	....	....	....	....	....
	Washington	**NHL**	**67**	**52**	**28**	**80**	**40**	**6**	**3**	**2**	**5**	**8**
1996-97	**Washington**	**NHL**	**77**	**46**	**31**	**77**	**72**	....	....	....	....	....
1997-98	**Washington**	**NHL**	**76**	***52**	**26**	**78**	**44**	**17**	**7**	**5**	**12**	**12**
	NHL Totals		**544**	**285**	**205**	**490**	**379**	**56**	**23**	**23**	**46**	**40**

Played in NHL All-Star Game (1993, 1996, 1997, 1998)

BONIN, BRIAN — PIT.

Center. Shoots left. 5'10", 185 lbs. Born, St. Paul, MN, November 28, 1973.
(Pittsburgh's 9th choice, 211th overall, in 1992 Entry Draft).

			Regular Season					Playoffs				
Season	Club	Lea	GP	G	A	TP	PIM	GP	G	A	TP	PIM
1991-92	White Bear Lake	H.S.	23	22	35	57	8	....	....	....	....	....
1992-93	U. of Minnesota	WCHA	38	10	18	28	10	....	....	....	....	....
1993-94	U. of Minnesota	WCHA	42	24	20	44	14	....	....	....	....	....
1994-95	U. of Minnesota	WCHA	44	32	31	*63	28	....	....	....	....	....
1995-96	U. of Minnesota	WCHA	42	34	*47	*81	30	....	....	....	....	....
1996-97	Cleveland	IHL	60	13	26	39	18	1	1	0	1	0
1997-98	Syracuse	AHL	67	31	38	69	46	5	1	3	4	6

WCHA First All-Star Team (1995, 1996) • NCAA West First All-American Team (1995, 1996) • Won Hobey Baker Memorial Award (Top U.S. Collegiate Player) (1996)

BONK, RADEK — (BOHNK) OTT.

Center. Shoots left. 6'3", 210 lbs. Born, Krnov, Czech., January 9, 1976.
(Ottawa's 1st choice, 3rd overall, in 1994 Entry Draft).

			Regular Season					Playoffs				
Season	Club	Lea	GP	G	A	TP	PIM	GP	G	A	TP	PIM
1992-93	ZPS Zlin	Czech.	30	5	5	10	10	....	....	....	....	....
1993-94	Las Vegas	IHL	76	42	45	87	208	5	1	2	3	10
1994-95	Las Vegas	IHL	33	7	13	20	62	....	....	....	....	....
	Ottawa	**NHL**	**42**	**3**	**8**	**11**	**28**	....	....	....	....	....
	P.E.I.	AHL	....	....	....	....	....	1	0	0	0	0
1995-96	**Ottawa**	**NHL**	**76**	**16**	**19**	**35**	**36**	....	....	....	....	....
1996-97	**Ottawa**	**NHL**	**53**	**5**	**13**	**18**	**14**	**7**	**0**	**1**	**1**	**4**
1997-98	**Ottawa**	**NHL**	**65**	**7**	**9**	**16**	**16**	**5**	**0**	**0**	**0**	**2**
	NHL Totals		**236**	**31**	**49**	**80**	**94**	**12**	**0**	**1**	**1**	**6**

Won Garry F. Longman Memorial Trophy (Top Rookie - IHL) (1994)

BONNI, RYAN — (baw-NEE) VAN.

Defense. Shoots left. 6'4", 190 lbs. Born, Winnipeg, Man., February 18, 1979.
(Vancouver's 2nd choice, 34th overall, in 1997 Entry Draft).

			Regular Season					Playoffs				
Season	Club	Lea	GP	G	A	TP	PIM	GP	G	A	TP	PIM
1995-96	Saskatoon	WHL	63	1	7	8	78	3	0	0	0	0
1996-97	Saskatoon	WHL	69	11	19	30	219	....	....	....	....	....
1997-98	Saskatoon	WHL	42	5	14	19	100	....	....	....	....	....

BONSIGNORE, JASON — (bohn-SEE-nohr) T.B.

Center. Shoots right. 6'4", 220 lbs. Born, Rochester, NY, April 15, 1976.
(Edmonton's 1st choice, 4th overall, in 1994 Entry Draft).

			Regular Season					Playoffs				
Season	Club	Lea	GP	G	A	TP	PIM	GP	G	A	TP	PIM
1992-93	Newmarket	OHL	66	22	20	42	6	7	0	3	3	0
1993-94	Newmarket	OHL	17	7	17	24	22	....	....	....	....	....
	United States	Nat-Tm	5	0	2	2	0	....	....	....	....	....
	Niagara Falls	OHL	41	15	47	62	41	....	....	....	....	....
1994-95	Niagara Falls	OHL	26	12	21	33	51	....	....	....	....	....
	Sudbury	OHL	23	15	14	29	45	17	13	10	23	12
	Edmonton	**NHL**	**1**	**1**	**0**	**1**	**0**	....	....	....	....	....
1995-96	Sudbury	OHL	18	10	16	26	37	....	....	....	....	....
	Edmonton	**NHL**	**20**	**0**	**2**	**2**	**4**	....	....	....	....	....
	Cape Breton	AHL	12	1	4	5	12	....	....	....	....	....
1996-97	Hamilton	AHL	78	21	33	54	78	7	0	0	0	4
1997-98	Hamilton	AHL	8	0	2	2	14	....	....	....	....	....
	San Antonio	IHL	22	3	8	11	34	....	....	....	....	....
	Tampa Bay	**NHL**	**35**	**2**	**8**	**10**	**22**	....	....	....	....	....
	Cleveland	IHL	6	4	0	4	32	8	1	1	2	20
	NHL Totals		**56**	**3**	**10**	**13**	**26**	....	....	....	....	....

Traded to **Tampa Bay** by **Edmonton** with Bryan Marchment and Steve Kelly for Roman Hamrlik and Paul Comrie, December 30, 1997.

BONVIE, DENNIS — (BOHN-vee) EDM.

Right wing/Defense. Shoots right. 5'11", 205 lbs. Born, Antigonish, N.S., July 23, 1973.

			Regular Season					Playoffs				
Season	Club	Lea	GP	G	A	TP	PIM	GP	G	A	TP	PIM
1991-92	Kitchener	OHL	7	1	1	2	23	....	....	....	....	....
	North Bay	OHL	49	0	12	12	261	21	0	1	1	91
1992-93	North Bay	OHL	64	3	21	24	*316	5	0	0	0	34
1993-94	Cape Breton	AHL	63	1	10	11	278	4	0	0	0	11
1994-95	**Edmonton**	**NHL**	**2**	**0**	**0**	**0**	**0**	....	....	....	....	....
	Cape Breton	AHL	74	5	15	20	422	....	....	....	....	....
1995-96	**Edmonton**	**NHL**	**8**	**0**	**0**	**0**	**47**	....	....	....	....	....
	Cape Breton	AHL	38	13	14	27	269	....	....	....	....	....
1996-97	Hamilton	AHL	73	9	20	29	*522	22	3	11	14	*91
1997-98	**Edmonton**	**NHL**	**4**	**0**	**0**	**0**	**27**	....	....	....	....	....
	Hamilton	AHL	57	11	19	30	295	9	0	5	5	18
	NHL Totals		**14**	**0**	**0**	**0**	**74**	....	....	....	....	....

Signed as a free agent by **Edmonton**, August 25, 1994.

BOOTLAND, NICK — COL.

Left wing. Shoots left. 6', 210 lbs. Born, Shelbourne, Ont., July 31, 1978.
(Dallas' 8th choice, 220th overall, in 1996 Entry Draft).

			Regular Season					Playoffs				
Season	Club	Lea	GP	G	A	TP	PIM	GP	G	A	TP	PIM
1995-96	Guelph	OHL	64	8	7	15	90	16	1	0	1	21
1996-97	Guelph	OHL	64	35	23	58	117	18	11	7	18	36
1997-98	Guelph	OHL	64	23	37	60	128	12	7	6	13	22

Signed as a free agent by **Colorado**, August 6, 1998.

BORDELEAU, SEBASTIEN — (BOHR-duh-loh) NSH.

Center. Shoots right. 5'11", 187 lbs. Born, Vancouver, B.C., February 15, 1975.
(Montreal's 3rd choice, 73rd overall, in 1993 Entry Draft).

			Regular Season					Playoffs				
Season	Club	Lea	GP	G	A	TP	PIM	GP	G	A	TP	PIM
1991-92	Hull	QMJHL	62	26	32	58	91	5	0	3	3	23
1992-93	Hull	QMJHL	60	18	39	57	95	10	3	8	11	20
1993-94	Hull	QMJHL	60	26	57	83	147	17	6	14	20	26
1994-95	Hull	QMJHL	68	52	76	128	142	18	*13	19	*32	25
	Fredericton	AHL	....	....	....	....	....	1	0	0	0	0
1995-96	**Montreal**	**NHL**	**4**	**0**	**0**	**0**	**0**	....	....	....	....	....
	Fredericton	AHL	43	17	29	46	68	7	0	2	2	8
1996-97	**Montreal**	**NHL**	**28**	**2**	**9**	**11**	**2**	....	....	....	....	....
	Fredericton	AHL	33	17	21	38	50	....	....	....	....	....
1997-98	**Montreal**	**NHL**	**53**	**6**	**8**	**14**	**36**	**5**	**0**	**0**	**0**	**2**
	NHL Totals		**85**	**8**	**17**	**25**	**38**	**5**	**0**	**0**	**0**	**2**

QMJHL First All-Star Team (1995)

Traded to **Nashville** by **Montreal** for future considerations, June 26, 1998.

BORSCHEVSKY, NIKOLAI — (bohr-SHEHV-skee)

Right wing. Shoots left. 5'9", 180 lbs. Born, Tomsk, USSR, January 12, 1965.
(Toronto's 3rd choice, 77th overall, in 1992 Entry Draft).

			Regular Season					Playoffs				
Season	Club	Lea	GP	G	A	TP	PIM	GP	G	A	TP	PIM
1983-84	Moscow D'amo	USSR	34	4	5	9	4	....	....	....	....	....
1984-85	Moscow D'amo	USSR	34	5	9	14	6	....	....	....	....	....
1985-86	Moscow D'amo	USSR	31	6	4	10	4	....	....	....	....	....
1986-87	Moscow D'amo	USSR	28	1	4	5	8	....	....	....	....	....
1987-88	Moscow D'amo	USSR	37	11	7	18	6	....	....	....	....	....
1988-89	Moscow D'amo	USSR	43	7	8	15	18	....	....	....	....	....
1989-90	Spartak	USSR	48	17	25	42	8	....	....	....	....	....
1990-91	Spartak	USSR	45	19	16	35	16	....	....	....	....	....
1991-92	Spartak	CIS	40	25	14	39	16	....	....	....	....	....
	Russia	Olympics	8	7	2	9	0	....	....	....	....	....
1992-93	**Toronto**	**NHL**	**78**	**34**	**40**	**74**	**28**	**16**	**2**	**7**	**9**	**0**
1993-94	**Toronto**	**NHL**	**45**	**14**	**20**	**34**	**10**	**15**	**2**	**2**	**4**	**4**
1994-95	Spartak	CIS	9	5	1	6	14	....	....	....	....	....
	Toronto	**NHL**	**19**	**0**	**5**	**5**	**0**	....	....	....	....	....
	Calgary	**NHL**	**8**	**0**	**5**	**5**	**0**	....	....	....	....	....
1995-96	**Dallas**	**NHL**	**12**	**1**	**3**	**4**	**6**	....	....	....	....	....
	Kolner Haie	Germany	8	0	4	4	27	8	2	2	4	4
1996-97	Spartak	Russia	42	15	*29	*44	52	....	....	....	....	....
1997-98	Spartak	Russia	46	10	17	27	30	....	....	....	....	....
	NHL Totals		**162**	**49**	**73**	**122**	**44**	**31**	**4**	**9**	**13**	**4**

Won Izvestia Trophy (Russian Top Scorer) (1997)

Traded to **Calgary** by **Toronto** for Calgary's 6th round choice (Chris Bogas) in 1996 Entry Draft, April 6, 1995. Signed as a free agent by **Dallas**, September 13, 1995.

BOTTERILL, JASON (BOH-tuhr-ihl) DAL.

Left wing. Shoots left. 6'3", 205 lbs. Born, Edmonton, Alta., May 19, 1976.
(Dallas' 1st choice, 20th overall, in 1994 Entry Draft).

			Regular Season					Playoffs				
Season	Club	Lea	GP	G	A	TP	PIM	GP	G	A	TP	PIM
1992-93	St. Paul's High	H.S.	22	22	26	48	....	....	....	....	....	....
1993-94	U. of Michigan	CCHA	36	20	19	39	94	....	....	....	....	....
1994-95	U. of Michigan	CCHA	34	14	14	28	117	....	....	....	....	....
1995-96	U. of Michigan	CCHA	37	*32	25	57	*143	....	....	....	....	....
1996-97	U. of Michigan	CCHA	42	*37	24	61	129	....	....	....	....	....
1997-98	**Dallas**	**NHL**	**4**	**0**	**0**	**0**	**19**	....	....	....	....	....
	Michigan	IHL	50	11	11	22	82	4	0	0	0	5
	NHL Totals		**4**	**0**	**0**	**0**	**19**	....	....	....	....	....

CCHA Second All-Star Team (1996) • NCAA West Second All-American Team (1997)

BOUCHARD, FREDERIC DAL.

Defense. Shoots right. 6', 181 lbs. Born, Beauport, Que., July 30, 1976.

			Regular Season					Playoffs				
Season	Club	Lea	GP	G	A	TP	PIM	GP	G	A	TP	PIM
1993-94	Granby	QMJHL	45	1	9	10	67	7	1	3	4	8
1994-95	Granby	QMJHL	70	17	49	66	190	13	3	6	9	20
1995-96	Granby	QMJHL	43	13	37	50	152	....	....	....	....	....
	St-Hyacinthe	QMJHL	23	7	10	17	48	12	3	8	11	38
1996-97	Rouyn-Noranda	QMJHL	6	1	5	6	6	....	....	....	....	....
	Chicoutimi	QMJHL	50	33	62	95	87	21	22	29	51	42
1997-98	Michigan	IHL	53	2	12	14	46	....	....	....	....	....
	Dayton	ECHL	3	1	2	3	0	5	1	5	6	2

QMJHL Second All-Star Team (1997)

Signed as a free agent by **Dallas**, August 28, 1997.

BOUCHARD, JOEL (BOO-shahrd) NSH.

Defense. Shoots left. 6', 190 lbs. Born, Montreal, Que., January 23, 1974.
(Calgary's 7th choice, 129th overall, in 1992 Entry Draft).

			Regular Season					Playoffs				
Season	Club	Lea	GP	G	A	TP	PIM	GP	G	A	TP	PIM
1990-91	Longueuil	QMJHL	53	3	19	22	34	8	1	0	1	11
1991-92	Verdun	QMJHL	70	9	20	29	55	19	1	7	8	20
1992-93	Verdun	QMJHL	60	10	49	59	126	4	0	2	2	4
1993-94	Verdun	QMJHL	60	15	55	70	62	4	1	0	1	6
	Saint John	AHL	1	0	0	0	0	2	0	0	0	0
1994-95	**Calgary**	**NHL**	**2**	**0**	**0**	**0**	**0**	....	....	....	....	....
	Saint John	AHL	77	6	25	31	63	5	1	0	1	4
1995-96	**Calgary**	**NHL**	**4**	**0**	**0**	**0**	**4**	....	....	....	....	....
	Saint John	AHL	74	8	25	33	104	16	1	4	5	10
1996-97	**Calgary**	**NHL**	**76**	**4**	**5**	**9**	**49**	....	....	....	....	....
1997-98	**Calgary**	**NHL**	**44**	**5**	**7**	**12**	**57**	....	....	....	....	....
	Saint John	AHL	3	2	1	3	6	....	....	....	....	....
	NHL Totals		**126**	**9**	**12**	**21**	**110**	....	....	....	....	....

QMJHL First All-Star Team (1994)

Claimed by **Nashville** from **Calgary** in Expansion Draft, June 26, 1998.

BOUCHER, PHILIPPE (boo-SHAY, fihl-EEP) L.A.

Defense. Shoots right. 6'2", 214 lbs. Born, St. Apollinaire, Que., March 24, 1973.
(Buffalo's 1st choice, 13th overall, in 1991 Entry Draft).

			Regular Season					Playoffs				
Season	Club	Lea	GP	G	A	TP	PIM	GP	G	A	TP	PIM
1990-91	Granby	QMJHL	69	21	46	67	92	....	....	....	....	....
1991-92	Granby	QMJHL	49	22	37	59	47	....	....	....	....	....
	Laval	QMJHL	16	7	11	18	36	10	5	6	11	8
1992-93	Laval	QMJHL	16	12	15	27	37	13	6	15	21	12
	Buffalo	**NHL**	**18**	**0**	**4**	**4**	**14**	....	....	....	....	....
	Rochester	AHL	5	4	3	7	8	3	0	1	1	2
1993-94	**Buffalo**	**NHL**	**38**	**6**	**8**	**14**	**29**	**7**	**1**	**1**	**2**	**2**
	Rochester	AHL	31	10	22	32	51	....	....	....	....	....
1994-95	**Buffalo**	**NHL**	**9**	**1**	**4**	**5**	**0**	....	....	....	....	....
	Rochester	AHL	43	14	27	41	26	....	....	....	....	....
	Los Angeles	**NHL**	**6**	**1**	**0**	**1**	**4**	....	....	....	....	....
1995-96	**Los Angeles**	**NHL**	**53**	**7**	**16**	**23**	**31**	....	....	....	....	....
	Phoenix	IHL	10	4	3	7	4	....	....	....	....	....
1996-97	**Los Angeles**	**NHL**	**60**	**7**	**18**	**25**	**25**	....	....	....	....	....
1997-98	**Los Angeles**	**NHL**	**45**	**6**	**10**	**16**	**49**	....	....	....	....	....
	Long Beach	IHL	2	0	1	1	4	....	....	....	....	....
	NHL Totals		**229**	**28**	**60**	**88**	**152**	**7**	**1**	**1**	**2**	**2**

Canadian Major Junior Rookie of the Year (1991) • QMJHL Second All-Star Team (1991, 1992)

Traded to **LA Kings** by **Buffalo** with Denis Tsygurov and Grant Fuhr for Alexei Zhitnik, Robb Stauber, Charlie Huddy and LA Kings' 5th round choice (Marian Menhart) in 1995 Entry Draft, February 14, 1995.

BOUCK, TYLER DAL.

Right wing. Shoots left. 6', 185 lbs. Born, Camrose, Alta., January 13, 1980.
(Dallas' 2nd choice, 57th overall, in 1998 Entry Draft).

			Regular Season					Playoffs				
Season	Club	Lea	GP	G	A	TP	PIM	GP	G	A	TP	PIM
1996-97	Prince George	WHL	12	0	2	2	11	....	....	....	....	....
1997-98	Prince George	WHL	65	11	26	37	90	11	1	0	1	21

BOUGHNER, BOB (BOOG-nuhr) NSH.

Defense. Shoots right. 6', 206 lbs. Born, Windsor, Ont., March 8, 1971.
(Detroit's 2nd choice, 32nd overall, in 1989 Entry Draft).

			Regular Season					Playoffs				
Season	Club	Lea	GP	G	A	TP	PIM	GP	G	A	TP	PIM
1988-89	S.S. Marie	OHL	64	6	15	21	182	....	....	....	....	....
1989-90	S.S. Marie	OHL	49	7	23	30	122	....	....	....	....	....
1990-91	S.S. Marie	OHL	64	13	33	46	156	14	2	9	11	35
1991-92	Toledo	ECHL	28	3	10	13	79	5	2	0	2	15
	Adirondack	AHL	1	0	0	0	7	....	....	....	....	....
1992-93	Adirondack	AHL	69	1	16	17	190	....	....	....	....	....
1993-94	Adirondack	AHL	72	8	14	22	292	10	1	1	2	18
1994-95	Cincinnati	IHL	81	2	14	16	192	10	0	0	0	18
1995-96	Carolina	AHL	46	2	15	17	127	....	....	....	....	....
	Buffalo	**NHL**	**31**	**0**	**1**	**1**	**104**	....	....	....	....	....
1996-97	**Buffalo**	**NHL**	**77**	**1**	**7**	**8**	**225**	**11**	**0**	**1**	**1**	**9**
1997-98	**Buffalo**	**NHL**	**69**	**1**	**3**	**4**	**165**	**14**	**0**	**4**	**4**	**15**
	NHL Totals		**177**	**2**	**11**	**13**	**494**	**25**	**0**	**5**	**5**	**24**

Signed as a free agent by **Florida**, July 25, 1994. Traded to **Buffalo** by **Florida** for Buffalo's 3rd round choice (Chris Allen) in 1996 Entry Draft, February 1, 1996. Claimed by **Nashville** from **Buffalo** in Expansion Draft, June 26, 1998.

BOULERICE, JESSE (BOO-luhr-ighs) PHI.

Right wing. Shoots right. 6'1", 214 lbs. Born, Plattsburgh, NY, August 10, 1978.
(Philadelphia's 4th choice, 133rd overall, in 1996 Entry Draft).

			Regular Season					Playoffs				
Season	Club	Lea	GP	G	A	TP	PIM	GP	G	A	TP	PIM
1995-96	Detroit	OHL	64	2	5	7	150	16	0	0	0	12
1996-97	Detroit	OHL	33	10	14	24	209	....	....	....	....	....
1997-98	Plymouth	OHL	53	20	23	43	170	13	2	4	6	35

BOUMEDIENNE, JOSEF (BOO-mih-dyehn) N.J.

Defense. Shoots left. 6'1", 190 lbs. Born, Stockholm, Sweden, January 12, 1978.
(New Jersey's 7th choice, 91st overall, in 1996 Entry Draft).

			Regular Season					Playoffs				
Season	Club	Lea	GP	G	A	TP	PIM	GP	G	A	TP	PIM
1995-96	Huddinge	Swe-Jr.	25	2	4	6	66	....	....	....	....	....
	Huddinge	Sweden-2	7	0	0	0	14	....	....	....	....	....
1996-97	Sodertalje	Sweden	32	1	1	2	32	....	....	....	....	....
1997-98	Sodertalje	Sweden	26	3	3	6	28	....	....	....	....	....

BOURQUE, RAY (BOHRK) BOS.

Defense. Shoots left. 5'11", 219 lbs. Born, Montreal, Que., December 28, 1960.
(Boston's 1st choice, 8th overall, in 1979 Entry Draft).

			Regular Season					Playoffs				
Season	Club	Lea	GP	G	A	TP	PIM	GP	G	A	TP	PIM
1976-77	Sorel	QMJHL	69	12	36	48	61	....	....	....	....	....
1977-78	Verdun	QMJHL	72	22	57	79	90	4	2	1	3	0
1978-79	Verdun	QMJHL	63	22	71	93	44	11	3	16	19	18
1979-80	**Boston**	**NHL**	**80**	**17**	**48**	**65**	**73**	**10**	**2**	**9**	**11**	**27**
1980-81	**Boston**	**NHL**	**67**	**27**	**29**	**56**	**96**	**3**	**0**	**1**	**1**	**2**
1981-82	**Boston**	**NHL**	**65**	**17**	**49**	**66**	**51**	**9**	**1**	**5**	**6**	**16**
1982-83	**Boston**	**NHL**	**65**	**22**	**51**	**73**	**20**	**17**	**8**	**15**	**23**	**10**
1983-84	**Boston**	**NHL**	**78**	**31**	**65**	**96**	**57**	**3**	**0**	**2**	**2**	**0**
1984-85	**Boston**	**NHL**	**73**	**20**	**66**	**86**	**53**	**5**	**0**	**3**	**3**	**4**
1985-86	**Boston**	**NHL**	**74**	**19**	**58**	**77**	**68**	**3**	**0**	**0**	**0**	**0**
1986-87	**Boston**	**NHL**	**78**	**23**	**72**	**95**	**36**	**4**	**1**	**2**	**3**	**0**
1987-88	**Boston**	**NHL**	**78**	**17**	**64**	**81**	**72**	**23**	**3**	**18**	**21**	**26**
1988-89	**Boston**	**NHL**	**60**	**18**	**43**	**61**	**52**	**10**	**0**	**4**	**4**	**6**
1989-90	**Boston**	**NHL**	**76**	**19**	**65**	**84**	**50**	**17**	**5**	**12**	**17**	**16**
1990-91	**Boston**	**NHL**	**76**	**21**	**73**	**94**	**75**	**19**	**7**	**18**	**25**	**12**
1991-92	**Boston**	**NHL**	**80**	**21**	**60**	**81**	**56**	**12**	**3**	**6**	**9**	**12**
1992-93	**Boston**	**NHL**	**78**	**19**	**63**	**82**	**40**	**4**	**1**	**0**	**1**	**2**
1993-94	**Boston**	**NHL**	**72**	**20**	**71**	**91**	**58**	**13**	**2**	**8**	**10**	**0**
1994-95	**Boston**	**NHL**	**46**	**12**	**31**	**43**	**20**	**5**	**0**	**3**	**3**	**0**
1995-96	**Boston**	**NHL**	**82**	**20**	**62**	**82**	**58**	**5**	**1**	**6**	**7**	**2**
1996-97	**Boston**	**NHL**	**62**	**19**	**31**	**50**	**18**	....	....	....	....	....
1997-98	**Boston**	**NHL**	**82**	**13**	**35**	**48**	**80**	**6**	**1**	**4**	**5**	**2**
	Canada	Olympics	6	1	2	3	4	....	....	....	....	....
	NHL Totals		**1372**	**375**	**1036**	**1411**	**1033**	**168**	**35**	**116**	**151**	**137**

QMJHL First All-Star Team (1978, 1979) • Won Calder Memorial Trophy (1980) • NHL First All-Star Team (1980, 1982, 1984, 1985, 1987, 1988, 1990, 1991, 1992, 1993, 1994, 1996) • NHL Second All-Star Team (1981, 1983, 1986, 1989, 1995) • Won James Norris Memorial Trophy (1987, 1988, 1990, 1991, 1994) • Won King Clancy Memorial Trophy (1992)

Played in NHL All-Star Game (1981, 1982, 1983, 1984, 1985, 1986, 1988, 1989, 1990, 1991, 1992, 1993, 1994, 1996, 1997, 1998)

BOWEN, CURTIS (BOW-ehn)

Left wing. Shoots left. 6'1", 195 lbs. Born, Kenora, Ont., March 24, 1974.
(Detroit's 1st choice, 22nd overall, in 1992 Entry Draft).

			Regular Season					Playoffs				
Season	Club	Lea	GP	G	A	TP	PIM	GP	G	A	TP	PIM
1990-91	Ottawa	OHL	42	12	14	26	31	....	....	....	....	....
1991-92	Ottawa	OHL	65	31	45	76	94	11	3	7	10	11
1992-93	Ottawa	OHL	21	9	19	28	51	....	....	....	....	....
1993-94	Ottawa	OHL	52	25	37	62	98	17	8	13	21	14
1994-95	Adirondack	AHL	64	6	11	17	71	4	0	2	2	4
1995-96	Canada	Nat-Tm	31	8	8	16	48	....	....	....	....	....
	Adirondack	AHL	3	0	0	0	0	....	....	....	....	....
1996-97	Adirondack	AHL	78	11	11	22	110	4	0	0	0	2
1997-98	Canada	Nat-Tm	46	8	22	30	73	....	....	....	....	....

BOWEN, JASON (BOW-ehn) EDM.

Left wing. Shoots left. 6'4", 220 lbs. Born, Port Alice, B.C., November 9, 1973.
(Philadelphia's 2nd choice, 15th overall, in 1992 Entry Draft).

			Regular Season					Playoffs				
Season	Club	Lea	GP	G	A	TP	PIM	GP	G	A	TP	PIM
1989-90	Tri-City	WHL	61	8	5	13	129	7	0	3	3	4
1990-91	Tri-City	WHL	60	7	13	20	252	6	2	2	4	18
1991-92	Tri-City	WHL	19	5	3	8	135	5	0	1	1	42
1992-93	Tri-City	WHL	62	10	12	22	219	3	1	1	2	18
	Philadelphia	**NHL**	**7**	**1**	**0**	**1**	**2**	....	....	....	....	....
1993-94	**Philadelphia**	**NHL**	**56**	**1**	**5**	**6**	**87**	....	....	....	....	....
1994-95	**Philadelphia**	**NHL**	**4**	**0**	**0**	**0**	**0**	....	....	....	....	....
	Hershey	AHL	55	5	5	10	116	6	0	0	0	46
1995-96	**Philadelphia**	**NHL**	**2**	**0**	**0**	**0**	**2**	....	....	....	....	....
	Hershey	AHL	72	6	7	13	128	4	2	0	2	13
1996-97	**Philadelphia**	**NHL**	**4**	**0**	**1**	**1**	**8**	....	....	....	....	....
	Philadelphia	AHL	61	10	12	22	160	6	0	1	1	10
1997-98	Philadelphia	AHL	3	0	0	0	19	....	....	....	....	....
	Edmonton	**NHL**	**4**	**0**	**0**	**0**	**10**	....	....	....	....	....
	Hamilton	AHL	51	5	14	19	108	7	1	1	2	22
	NHL Totals		**77**	**2**	**6**	**8**	**109**	....	....	....	....	....

Traded to **Edmonton** by **Philadelphia** for Brantt Myhres, October 15, 1997.

BOYLE, DAN FLA.

Defense. Shoots right. 5'11", 190 lbs. Born, Ottawa, Ont., July 12, 1976.

			Regular Season					Playoffs				
Season	Club	Lea	GP	G	A	TP	PIM	GP	G	A	TP	PIM
1994-95	Miami-Ohio	CCHA	35	8	18	26	24	....	....	....	....	....
1995-96	Miami-Ohio	CCHA	36	7	20	27	70	....	....	....	....	....
1996-97	Miami-Ohio	CCHA	40	11	43	54	52	....	....	....	....	....
1997-98	Miami-Ohio	CCHA	37	14	26	40	58	....	....	....	....	....

CCHA First All-Star Team (1997) • NCAA West First All-American Team (1997)

Signed as a free agent by **Florida**, March 30, 1998.

BOYNTON, NICHOLAS (BOHYN-tuhn) WSH.

Defense. Shoots right. 6'2", 210 lbs. Born, Etobicoke, Ont., January 14, 1979.
(Washington's 1st choice, 9th overall, in 1997 Entry Draft).

				Regular Season				Playoffs				
Season	Club	Lea	GP	G	A	TP	PIM	GP	G	A	TP	PIM
1995-96	Ottawa	OHL	64	10	14	24	90	4	0	3	3	10
1996-97	Ottawa	OHL	63	13	51	64	143	24	4	24	28	38
1997-98	Ottawa	OHL	40	7	31	38	94	13	0	4	4	24

BRADLEY, BRIAN T.B.

Center. Shoots right. 5'10", 180 lbs. Born, Kitchener, Ont., January 21, 1965.
(Calgary's 2nd choice, 52nd overall, in 1983 Entry Draft).

				Regular Season				Playoffs				
Season	Club	Lea	GP	G	A	TP	PIM	GP	G	A	TP	PIM
1982-83	London	OHL	67	37	82	119	37	3	1	0	1	0
1983-84	London	OHL	49	40	60	100	24	4	2	4	6	0
1984-85	London	OHL	32	27	49	76	22	8	5	10	15	4
1985-86	**Calgary**	**NHL**	**5**	**0**	**1**	**1**	**0**	**1**	**0**	**0**	**0**	**0**
	Moncton	AHL	59	23	42	65	40	10	6	9	15	4
1986-87	**Calgary**	**NHL**	**40**	**10**	**18**	**28**	**16**	....	....	....	....	....
	Moncton	AHL	20	12	16	28	8	....	....	....	....	....
1987-88	Canada	Nat-Tm	47	18	19	37	42	....	....	....	....	....
	Canada	Olympics	7	0	4	4	0	....	....	....	....	....
	Vancouver	**NHL**	**11**	**3**	**5**	**8**	**6**	....	....	....	....	....
1988-89	**Vancouver**	**NHL**	**71**	**18**	**27**	**45**	**42**	**7**	**3**	**4**	**7**	**10**
1989-90	**Vancouver**	**NHL**	**67**	**19**	**29**	**48**	**65**	....	....	....	....	....
1990-91	**Vancouver**	**NHL**	**44**	**11**	**20**	**31**	**42**	....	....	....	....	....
	Toronto	**NHL**	**26**	**0**	**11**	**11**	**20**	....	....	....	....	....
1991-92	**Toronto**	**NHL**	**59**	**10**	**21**	**31**	**48**	....	....	....	....	....
1992-93	**Tampa Bay**	**NHL**	**80**	**42**	**44**	**86**	**92**	....	....	....	....	....
1993-94	**Tampa Bay**	**NHL**	**78**	**24**	**40**	**64**	**56**	....	....	....	....	....
1994-95	**Tampa Bay**	**NHL**	**46**	**13**	**27**	**40**	**42**	....	....	....	....	....
1995-96	**Tampa Bay**	**NHL**	**75**	**23**	**56**	**79**	**77**	**5**	**0**	**3**	**3**	**6**
1996-97	**Tampa Bay**	**NHL**	**35**	**7**	**17**	**24**	**16**	....	....	....	....	....
1997-98	**Tampa Bay**	**NHL**	**14**	**2**	**5**	**7**	**6**	....	....	....	....	....
	NHL Totals		**651**	**182**	**321**	**503**	**528**	**13**	**3**	**7**	**10**	**16**

Played in NHL All-Star Game (1993, 1994)

Traded to **Vancouver** by **Calgary** with Peter Bakovic and Kevin Guy for Craig Coxe, March 6, 1988. Traded to **Toronto** by **Vancouver** for Tom Kurvers, January 12, 1991. Claimed by **Tampa Bay** from **Toronto** in Expansion Draft, June 18, 1992.

BRADLEY, MATT S.J.

Right wing. Shoots right. 6'2", 195 lbs. Born, Stittsville, Ont., June 13, 1978.
(San Jose's 4th choice, 102nd overall, in 1996 Entry Draft).

				Regular Season				Playoffs				
Season	Club	Lea	GP	G	A	TP	PIM	GP	G	A	TP	PIM
1995-96	Kingston	OHL	55	10	14	24	17	6	0	1	1	6
1996-97	Kingston	OHL	65	24	24	48	41	5	0	4	4	2
	Kentucky	AHL	1	0	1	1	0	....	....	....	....	....
1997-98	Kingston	OHL	55	33	50	83	24	8	3	4	7	7

BRADY, NEIL

Center. Shoots left. 6'2", 200 lbs. Born, Montreal, Que., April 12, 1968.
(New Jersey's 1st choice, 3rd overall, in 1986 Entry Draft).

				Regular Season				Playoffs				
Season	Club	Lea	GP	G	A	TP	PIM	GP	G	A	TP	PIM
1984-85	Calgary	AJHL	37	25	50	75	75	....	....	....	....	....
	Medicine Hat	WHL	....	....	....	....	....	3	0	0	0	2
1985-86	Medicine Hat	WHL	72	21	60	81	104	21	9	11	20	23
1986-87	Medicine Hat	WHL	57	19	64	83	126	18	1	4	5	25
1987-88	Medicine Hat	WHL	61	16	35	51	110	15	0	3	3	19
1988-89	Utica	AHL	75	16	21	37	56	4	0	3	3	0
1989-90	**New Jersey**	**NHL**	**19**	**1**	**4**	**5**	**13**	....	....	....	....	....
	Utica	AHL	38	10	13	23	21	5	0	1	1	10
1990-91	**New Jersey**	**NHL**	**3**	**0**	**0**	**0**	**0**	....	....	....	....	....
	Utica	AHL	77	33	63	96	91	....	....	....	....	....
1991-92	**New Jersey**	**NHL**	**7**	**1**	**0**	**1**	**4**	....	....	....	....	....
	Utica	AHL	33	12	30	42	28	....	....	....	....	....
1992-93	**Ottawa**	**NHL**	**55**	**7**	**17**	**24**	**57**	....	....	....	....	....
	New Haven	AHL	8	6	3	9	2	....	....	....	....	....
1993-94	**Dallas**	**NHL**	**5**	**0**	**1**	**1**	**21**	....	....	....	....	....
	Kalamazoo	IHL	43	10	16	26	188	5	1	1	2	10
1994-95	Kalamazoo	IHL	70	13	45	58	140	15	5	14	19	22
1995-96	Michigan	IHL	61	14	20	34	127	10	1	4	5	8
1996-97	Michigan	IHL	76	13	20	33	62	4	1	0	1	0
1997-98	Houston	IHL	65	9	26	35	56	4	2	0	2	34
	NHL Totals		**89**	**9**	**22**	**31**	**95**	....	....	....	....	....

Traded to **Ottawa** by **New Jersey** for future considerations, September 3, 1992. Signed as a free agent by **Dallas**, December 3, 1993.

BRAND, AARON TOR.

Center. Shoots left. 6', 190 lbs. Born, Toronto, Ont., June 14, 1975.

				Regular Season				Playoffs				
Season	Club	Lea	GP	G	A	TP	PIM	GP	G	A	TP	PIM
1993-94	Newmarket	OHL	65	19	45	64	55	....	....	....	....	....
1994-95	Sarnia	OHL	66	33	42	75	58	3	0	2	2	4
1995-96	Sarnia	OHL	66	46	*73	*119	110	10	7	11	18	18
	St. John's	AHL	1	0	1	1	0	4	0	0	0	4
1996-97	St. John's	AHL	75	15	25	40	80	11	3	2	5	2
1997-98	St. John's	AHL	79	10	20	30	107	4	2	2	4	6

OHL Second All-Star Team (1996)

Signed as a free agent by **Toronto**, March 21, 1996.

BRAND, KONRAD L.A.

Defense. Shoots left. 6'3", 200 lbs. Born, Saskatoon, Sask., July 14, 1979.
(Los Angeles' 9th choice, 220th overall, in 1997 Entry Draft).

				Regular Season				Playoffs				
Season	Club	Lea	GP	G	A	TP	PIM	GP	G	A	TP	PIM
1995-96	Kamloops	WHL	18	0	1	1	9	2	0	0	0	0
1996-97	Kamloops	WHL	40	1	4	5	50	....	....	....	....	....
	Medicine Hat	WHL	19	0	1	1	35	4	1	0	1	0
1997-98	Medicine Hat	WHL	71	1	7	8	121	....	....	....	....	....

BRASHEAR, DONALD (bra-SHEER) VAN.

Left wing. Shoots left. 6'2", 225 lbs. Born, Bedford, IN, January 7, 1972.

				Regular Season				Playoffs				
Season	Club	Lea	GP	G	A	TP	PIM	GP	G	A	TP	PIM
1989-90	Longueuil	QMJHL	64	12	14	26	169	7	0	0	0	11
1990-91	Longueuil	QMJHL	68	12	26	38	195	8	0	3	3	33
1991-92	Verdun	QMJHL	65	18	24	42	283	18	4	2	6	98
1992-93	Fredericton	AHL	76	11	3	14	261	5	0	0	0	8
1993-94	**Montreal**	**NHL**	**14**	**2**	**2**	**4**	**34**	**2**	**0**	**0**	**0**	**0**
	Fredericton	AHL	62	38	28	66	250	....	....	....	....	....
1994-95	Fredericton	AHL	29	10	9	19	182	17	7	5	12	77
	Montreal	**NHL**	**20**	**1**	**1**	**2**	**63**	....	....	....	....	....
1995-96	**Montreal**	**NHL**	**67**	**0**	**4**	**4**	**223**	**6**	**0**	**0**	**0**	**2**
1996-97	**Montreal**	**NHL**	**10**	**0**	**0**	**0**	**38**	....	....	....	....	....
	Vancouver	**NHL**	**59**	**8**	**5**	**13**	**207**	....	....	....	....	....
1997-98	**Vancouver**	**NHL**	**77**	**9**	**9**	**18**	***372**	....	....	....	....	....
	NHL Totals		**247**	**20**	**21**	**41**	**937**	**8**	**0**	**0**	**0**	**2**

Signed as a free agent by **Montreal**, July 28, 1992. Traded to **Vancouver** by **Montreal** for Jassen Cullimore, November 13, 1996.

BRENNAN, KIP L.A.

Defense. Shoots left. 6'4", 196 lbs. Born, Kingston, Ont., August 27, 1980.
(Los Angeles' 4th choice, 103rd overall, in 1998 Entry Draft).

				Regular Season				Playoffs				
Season	Club	Lea	GP	G	A	TP	PIM	GP	G	A	TP	PIM
1996-97	Windsor	OHL	42	0	10	10	156	5	0	1	1	16
1997-98	Windsor	OHL	24	0	7	7	103	....	....	....	....	....
	Sudbury	OHL	24	0	3	3	85	....	....	....	....	....

BRENNAN, RICH NYR

Defense. Shoots right. 6'2", 200 lbs. Born, Schenectady, NY, November 26, 1972.
(Quebec's 3rd choice, 46th overall, in 1991 Entry Draft).

				Regular Season				Playoffs				
Season	Club	Lea	GP	G	A	TP	PIM	GP	G	A	TP	PIM
1990-91	Tabor Academy	H.S.	34	13	37	50	91	....	....	....	....	....
1991-92	Boston University	H.E.	30	4	13	17	50	....	....	....	....	....
1992-93	Boston University	H.E.	40	9	11	20	68	....	....	....	....	....
1993-94	Boston University	H.E.	41	8	27	35	82	....	....	....	....	....
1994-95	Boston University	H.E.	31	5	22	27	56	....	....	....	....	....
1995-96	Brantford	ColHL	5	1	2	3	2	....	....	....	....	....
	Cornwall	AHL	36	4	8	12	61	7	0	0	0	6
1996-97	**Colorado**	**NHL**	**2**	**0**	**0**	**0**	**0**	....	....	....	....	....
	Hershey	AHL	74	11	45	56	88	23	2	16	18	22
1997-98	**San Jose**	**NHL**	**11**	**1**	**2**	**3**	**2**	....	....	....	....	....
	Kentucky	AHL	42	11	17	28	71	....	....	....	....	....
	Hartford	AHL	9	2	4	6	12	15	4	5	9	14
	NHL Totals		**13**	**1**	**2**	**3**	**2**	....	....	....	....	....

Hockey East First All-Star Team (1994) • NCAA East Second All-American Team (1994)

Rights transferred to **Colorado** after **Quebec** franchise relocated, June 21, 1995. Signed as a free agent by **San Jose**, July 9, 1997. Traded to **NY Rangers** by **San Jose** for Jason Muzzatti, March 24, 1998.

BREWER, ERIC NYI

Defense. Shoots left. 6'3", 195 lbs. Born, Vernon, B.C., April 17, 1979.
(NY Islanders' 2nd choice, 5th overall, in 1997 Entry Draft).

				Regular Season				Playoffs				
Season	Club	Lea	GP	G	A	TP	PIM	GP	G	A	TP	PIM
1994-95	Kamloops	BCJHL	40	19	19	38	62	....	....	....	....	....
1995-96	Prince George	WHL	63	4	10	14	25	....	....	....	....	....
1996-97	Prince George	WHL	71	5	24	29	81	15	2	4	6	16
1997-98	Prince George	WHL	34	5	28	33	45	11	4	2	6	19

WHL West Second All-Star Team (1998)

BRIERE, DANIEL (bree-AIR) PHX.

Center. Shoots left. 5'9", 170 lbs. Born, Gatineau, Que., October 6, 1977.
(Phoenix's 2nd choice, 24th overall, in 1996 Entry Draft).

				Regular Season				Playoffs				
Season	Club	Lea	GP	G	A	TP	PIM	GP	G	A	TP	PIM
1994-95	Drummondville	QMJHL	72	51	72	123	54	4	2	3	5	2
1995-96	Drummondville	QMJHL	67	*67	*96	*163	84	6	6	12	18	8
1996-97	Drummondville	QMJHL	59	52	78	130	94	8	7	7	14	14
1997-98	**Phoenix**	**NHL**	**5**	**1**	**0**	**1**	**2**	....	....	....	....	....
	Springfield	AHL	68	36	56	92	42	4	1	2	3	4
	NHL Totals		**5**	**1**	**0**	**1**	**2**	....	....	....	....	....

QMJHL Second All-Star Team (1996, 1997) • AHL First All-Star Team (1998) • Won Dudley "Red" Garrett Memorial Trophy (Top Rookie - AHL) (1998)

BRIGLEY, TRAVIS CGY.

Left wing. Shoots left. 6'1", 195 lbs. Born, Coronation, Alta., June 16, 1977.
(Calgary's 2nd choice, 39th overall, in 1996 Entry Draft).

				Regular Season				Playoffs				
Season	Club	Lea	GP	G	A	TP	PIM	GP	G	A	TP	PIM
1993-94	Lethbridge	WHL	1	0	0	0	0	....	....	....	....	....
1994-95	Lethbridge	WHL	64	14	18	32	14	....	....	....	....	....
1995-96	Lethbridge	WHL	69	34	43	77	94	4	2	3	5	8
1996-97	Lethbridge	WHL	71	43	47	90	56	19	9	9	18	31
1997-98	**Calgary**	**NHL**	**2**	**0**	**0**	**0**	**2**	....	....	....	....	....
	Saint John	AHL	79	17	15	32	28	8	0	0	0	0
	NHL Totals		**2**	**0**	**0**	**0**	**2**	....	....	....	....	....

BRIMANIS, ARIS (brih-MAN-ihs, AR-ihs)

Defense. Shoots right. 6'3", 210 lbs. Born, Cleveland, OH, March 14, 1972.
(Philadelphia's 3rd choice, 86th overall, in 1991 Entry Draft).

				Regular Season				Playoffs				
Season	Club	Lea	GP	G	A	TP	PIM	GP	G	A	TP	PIM
1990-91	Bowling Green	CCHA	38	3	6	9	42	....	....	....	....	....
1991-92	Bowling Green	CCHA	32	2	9	11	38	....	....	....	....	....
1992-93	Brandon	WHL	71	8	50	58	110	4	2	1	3	7
1993-94	**Philadelphia**	**NHL**	**1**	**0**	**0**	**0**	**0**	....	....	....	....	....
	Hershey	AHL	75	8	15	23	65	11	2	3	5	12
1994-95	Hershey	AHL	76	8	17	25	68	6	1	1	2	14
1995-96	**Philadelphia**	**NHL**	**17**	**0**	**2**	**2**	**12**	....	....	....	....	....
	Hershey	AHL	54	9	22	31	64	5	1	2	3	4
1996-97	**Philadelphia**	**NHL**	**3**	**0**	**1**	**1**	**0**	....	....	....	....	....
	Philadelphia	AHL	65	14	18	32	69	10	2	2	4	13
1997-98	Philadelphia	AHL	30	1	11	12	26	....	....	....	....	....
	Michigan	IHL	35	3	9	12	24	4	1	0	1	4
	NHL Totals		**21**	**0**	**3**	**3**	**12**	....	....	....	....	....

BRIND'AMOUR, ROD (BRIHND-uh-MOHR) PHI.

Center. Shoots left. 6'1", 202 lbs. Born, Ottawa, Ont., August 9, 1970.
(St. Louis' 1st choice, 9th overall, in 1988 Entry Draft).

			Regular Season					Playoffs				
Season	Club	Lea	GP	G	A	TP	PIM	GP	G	A	TP	PIM
1987-88	Notre Dame	SJHL	56	46	61	107	136	....	....	....	....	....
1988-89	Michigan State	CCHA	42	27	32	59	63	....	....	....	....	....
	St. Louis	NHL	....	....	....	....	....	5	2	0	2	4
1989-90	St. Louis	NHL	79	26	35	61	46	12	5	8	13	6
1990-91	St. Louis	NHL	78	17	32	49	93	13	2	5	7	10
1991-92	Philadelphia	NHL	80	33	44	77	100	....	....	....	....	....
1992-93	Philadelphia	NHL	81	37	49	86	89	....	....	....	....	....
1993-94	Philadelphia	NHL	84	35	62	97	85	....	....	....	....	....
1994-95	Philadelphia	NHL	48	12	27	39	33	15	6	9	15	8
1995-96	Philadelphia	NHL	82	26	61	87	110	12	2	5	7	6
1996-97	Philadelphia	NHL	82	27	32	59	41	19	*13	8	21	10
1997-98	Philadelphia	NHL	82	36	38	74	54	5	2	2	4	7
	Canada	Olympics	6	1	2	3	0	....	....	....	....	....
	NHL Totals		696	249	380	629	651	81	32	37	69	51

NHL All-Rookie Team (1990)

Played in NHL All-Star Game (1992)

Traded to **Philadelphia** by **St. Louis** with Dan Quinn for Ron Sutter and Murray Baron, September 22, 1991.

BRISEBOIS, PATRICE (BREES-bwah, pa-TREEZ) MTL.

Defense. Shoots right. 6'2", 209 lbs. Born, Montreal, Que., January 27, 1971.
(Montreal's 2nd choice, 30th overall, in 1989 Entry Draft).

			Regular Season					Playoffs				
Season	Club	Lea	GP	G	A	TP	PIM	GP	G	A	TP	PIM
1987-88	Laval	QMJHL	48	10	34	44	95	6	0	2	2	2
1988-89	Laval	QMJHL	50	20	45	65	95	17	8	14	22	45
1989-90	Laval	QMJHL	56	18	70	88	108	13	7	9	16	26
1990-91	Drummondville	QMJHL	54	17	44	61	72	14	6	18	24	49
	Montreal	NHL	10	0	2	2	4	....	....	....	....	....
1991-92	Montreal	NHL	26	2	8	10	20	11	2	4	6	6
	Fredericton	AHL	53	12	27	39	51	....	....	....	....	....
1992-93	Montreal	NHL	70	10	21	31	79	20	0	4	4	18 ♦
1993-94	Montreal	NHL	53	2	21	23	63	7	0	4	4	6
1994-95	Montreal	NHL	35	4	8	12	26	....	....	....	....	....
1995-96	Montreal	NHL	69	9	27	36	65	6	1	2	3	6
1996-97	Montreal	NHL	49	2	13	15	24	3	1	1	2	24
1997-98	Montreal	NHL	79	10	27	37	67	10	1	0	1	0
	NHL Totals		391	39	127	166	348	57	5	15	20	60

QMJHL Second All-Star Team (1990) • Canadian Major Junior Defenseman of the Year (1991) • QMJHL First All-Star Team (1991) • Memorial Cup All-Star Team (1991)

BRISKE, BYRON (BRIHS-kee) ANA.

Defense. Shoots right. 6'3", 200 lbs. Born, Humboldt, Sask., January 23, 1976.
(Anaheim's 4th choice, 80th overall, in 1994 Entry Draft).

			Regular Season					Playoffs				
Season	Club	Lea	GP	G	A	TP	PIM	GP	G	A	TP	PIM
1992-93	Victoria	WHL	66	1	10	11	110	....	....	....	....	....
1993-94	Red Deer	WHL	61	6	21	27	174	....	....	....	....	....
1994-95	Red Deer	WHL	48	4	17	21	116	....	....	....	....	....
	Tri-City	WHL	15	0	1	1	22	13	0	0	0	18
1995-96	Tri-City	WHL	72	15	38	53	189	11	0	5	5	36
1996-97	Baltimore	AHL	69	0	6	6	131	1	0	0	0	0
1997-98	Cincinnati	AHL	59	0	9	9	95	....	....	....	....	....

BROS, MICHAL (BROHSH, MEE-khahl) S.J.

Center. Shoots right. 6'1", 195 lbs. Born, Olomouc, Czech., January 25, 1976.
(San Jose's 6th choice, 130th overall, in 1995 Entry Draft).

			Regular Season					Playoffs				
Season	Club	Lea	GP	G	A	TP	PIM	GP	G	A	TP	PIM
1994-95	HC Olomouc	Czech-Jr.	34	29	32	61	....	....	....	....	....	....
1995-96	HC Olomouc	Cze-Rep.	35	8	11	19	....	4	2	0	2	....
1996-97	HC Olomouc	Cze-Rep.	50	13	14	27	28	....	....	....	....	....
1997-98	Vsetin	EuroHL	9	3	0	3	2	....	....	....	....	....
	Vsetin	Cze-Rep.	47	14	18	32	28	10	3	1	4	2

BROUSSEAU, PAUL NSH.

Right wing. Shoots right. 6'2", 203 lbs. Born, Pierrefonds, Que., September 18, 1973.
(Quebec's 2nd choice, 28th overall, in 1992 Entry Draft).

			Regular Season					Playoffs				
Season	Club	Lea	GP	G	A	TP	PIM	GP	G	A	TP	PIM
1989-90	Chicoutimi	QMJHL	57	17	24	41	32	7	0	3	3	0
1990-91	Trois-Rivieres	QMJHL	67	30	66	96	48	6	3	2	5	2
1991-92	Hull	QMJHL	57	35	61	96	54	6	3	5	8	10
1992-93	Hull	QMJHL	59	27	48	75	49	10	7	8	15	6
1993-94	Cornwall	AHL	69	18	26	44	35	1	0	0	0	0
1994-95	Cornwall	AHL	57	19	17	36	29	7	2	1	3	10
1995-96	Colorado	NHL	8	1	1	2	2	....	....	....	....	....
	Cornwall	AHL	63	21	22	43	60	8	4	0	4	2
1996-97	Tampa Bay	NHL	6	0	0	0	0	....	....	....	....	....
	Adirondack	AHL	66	35	31	66	25	4	1	2	3	0
1997-98	Tampa Bay	NHL	11	0	2	2	27	....	....	....	....	....
	Adirondack	AHL	67	45	20	65	18	3	1	1	2	0
	NHL Totals		25	1	3	4	29	....	....	....	....	....

AHL Second All-Star Team (1998)

Rights transferred to **Colorado** after **Quebec** franchise relocated, June 21, 1995. Signed as a free agent by **Tampa Bay**, September 10, 1996. Claimed by **Nashville** from **Tampa Bay** in Expansion Draft, June 26, 1998.

BROWN, BOBBY CGY.

Center. Shoots right. 6', 200 lbs. Born, Winnipeg, Man., September 26, 1975.

			Regular Season					Playoffs				
Season	Club	Lea	GP	G	A	TP	PIM	GP	G	A	TP	PIM
1992-93	Brandon	WHL	5	1	1	2	0	....	....	....	....	....
1993-94	Brandon	WHL	71	18	19	37	138	14	5	0	5	12
1994-95	Brandon	WHL	72	23	28	51	128	18	3	3	6	31
1995-96	Brandon	WHL	59	42	46	88	106	19	14	13	27	38
1996-97	Roanoke	ECHL	39	9	14	23	61	....	....	....	....	....
	Baton Rouge	ECHL	24	7	8	15	26	....	....	....	....	....
1997-98	Saint John	AHL	2	0	0	0	0	....	....	....	....	....
	Dayton	ECHL	65	25	28	53	117	5	3	2	5	6

Signed as a free agent by **Calgary**, August 6, 1996.

BROWN, BRAD MTL.

Defense. Shoots right. 6'4", 218 lbs. Born, Baie Verte, Nfld., December 27, 1975.
(Montreal's 1st choice, 18th overall, in 1994 Entry Draft).

			Regular Season					Playoffs				
Season	Club	Lea	GP	G	A	TP	PIM	GP	G	A	TP	PIM
1991-92	North Bay	OHL	49	2	9	11	170	18	0	6	6	43
1992-93	North Bay	OHL	61	4	9	13	228	2	0	2	2	13
1993-94	North Bay	OHL	66	8	24	32	196	18	3	12	15	33
1994-95	North Bay	OHL	64	8	38	46	172	6	1	4	5	8
1995-96	Barrie	OHL	27	3	13	16	82	....	....	....	....	....
	Fredericton	AHL	38	0	3	3	148	10	2	1	3	6
1996-97	Montreal	NHL	8	0	0	0	22	....	....	....	....	....
	Fredericton	AHL	64	3	7	10	368	....	....	....	....	....
1997-98	Fredericton	AHL	64	1	8	9	297	4	0	0	0	29
	NHL Totals		8	0	0	0	22	....	....	....	....	....

BROWN, CURTIS BUF.

Center. Shoots left. 6', 190 lbs. Born, Unity, Sask., February 12, 1976.
(Buffalo's 2nd choice, 43rd overall, in 1994 Entry Draft).

			Regular Season					Playoffs				
Season	Club	Lea	GP	G	A	TP	PIM	GP	G	A	TP	PIM
1992-93	Moose Jaw	WHL	71	13	16	29	30	....	....	....	....	....
1993-94	Moose Jaw	WHL	72	27	38	65	82	....	....	....	....	....
1994-95	Moose Jaw	WHL	70	51	53	104	63	10	8	7	15	20
	Buffalo	NHL	1	1	1	2	2	....	....	....	....	....
1995-96	Moose Jaw	WHL	25	20	18	38	30	....	....	....	....	....
	Prince Albert	WHL	19	12	21	33	8	18	10	15	25	18
	Buffalo	NHL	4	0	0	0	0	....	....	....	....	....
	Rochester	AHL	....	....	....	....	....	12	0	1	1	2
1996-97	Buffalo	NHL	28	4	3	7	18	....	....	....	....	....
	Rochester	AHL	51	22	21	43	30	10	4	6	10	4
1997-98	Buffalo	NHL	63	12	12	24	34	13	1	2	3	10
	NHL Totals		96	17	16	33	54	13	1	2	3	10

WHL East First All-Star Team (1995) • WHL East Second All-Star Team (1996)

BROWN, DOUG DET.

Right wing. Shoots right. 5'10", 185 lbs. Born, Southborough, MA, June 12, 1964.

			Regular Season					Playoffs				
Season	Club	Lea	GP	G	A	TP	PIM	GP	G	A	TP	PIM
1982-83	Boston College	ECAC	22	9	8	17	0	....	....	....	....	....
1983-84	Boston College	ECAC	38	11	10	21	6	....	....	....	....	....
1984-85	Boston College	H.E.	45	37	31	68	10	....	....	....	....	....
1985-86	Boston College	H.E.	38	16	40	56	16	....	....	....	....	....
1986-87	New Jersey	NHL	4	0	1	1	0	....	....	....	....	....
	Maine	AHL	73	24	34	58	15	....	....	....	....	....
1987-88	New Jersey	NHL	70	14	11	25	20	19	5	1	6	6
	Utica	AHL	2	0	2	2	2	....	....	....	....	....
1988-89	New Jersey	NHL	63	15	10	25	15	....	....	....	....	....
	Utica	AHL	4	1	4	5	0	....	....	....	....	....
1989-90	New Jersey	NHL	69	14	20	34	16	6	0	1	1	2
1990-91	New Jersey	NHL	58	14	16	30	4	7	2	2	4	2
1991-92	New Jersey	NHL	71	11	17	28	27	....	....	....	....	....
1992-93	New Jersey	NHL	15	0	5	5	2	....	....	....	....	....
	Utica	AHL	25	11	17	28	8	....	....	....	....	....
1993-94	Pittsburgh	NHL	77	18	37	55	18	6	0	0	0	2
1994-95	Detroit	NHL	45	9	12	21	16	18	4	8	12	2
1995-96	Detroit	NHL	62	12	15	27	4	13	3	3	6	4
1996-97	Detroit	NHL	49	6	7	13	8	14	3	3	6	2 ♦
1997-98	Detroit	NHL	80	19	23	42	12	9	4	2	6	0 ♦
	NHL Totals		663	132	174	306	142	92	21	20	41	20

Hockey East Second All-Star Team (1985, 1986)

Signed as a free agent by **New Jersey**, August 6, 1986. Signed as a free agent by **Pittsburgh**, September 28, 1993. Claimed by **Detroit** from **Pittsburgh** in NHL Waiver Draft, January 18, 1995. Claimed by **Nashville** from **Detroit** in Expansion Draft, June 26, 1998. Traded to **Detroit** by **Nashville** for Petr Sykora and Detroit's 3rd round choice in 1999 Entry Draft, July 14, 1998.

BROWN, JEFF

Defense. Shoots right. 6'1", 204 lbs. Born, Ottawa, Ont., April 30, 1966.
(Quebec's 2nd choice, 36th overall, in 1984 Entry Draft).

			Regular Season					Playoffs				
Season	Club	Lea	GP	G	A	TP	PIM	GP	G	A	TP	PIM
1982-83	Sudbury	OHL	65	9	37	46	39	....	....	....	....	....
1983-84	Sudbury	OHL	68	17	60	77	39	....	....	....	....	....
1984-85	Sudbury	OHL	56	16	48	64	26	....	....	....	....	....
1985-86	Sudbury	OHL	45	22	28	50	24	4	0	2	2	11
	Quebec	NHL	8	3	2	5	6	1	0	0	0	0
	Fredericton	AHL	....	....	....	....	....	1	0	1	1	0
1986-87	Quebec	NHL	44	7	22	29	16	13	3	3	6	2
	Fredericton	AHL	26	2	14	16	16	....	....	....	....	....
1987-88	Quebec	NHL	78	16	36	52	64	....	....	....	....	....
1988-89	Quebec	NHL	78	21	47	68	62	....	....	....	....	....
1989-90	Quebec	NHL	29	6	10	16	18	....	....	....	....	....
	St. Louis	NHL	48	10	28	38	37	12	2	10	12	4
1990-91	St. Louis	NHL	67	12	47	59	39	13	3	9	12	6
1991-92	St. Louis	NHL	80	20	39	59	38	6	2	1	3	2
1992-93	St. Louis	NHL	71	25	53	78	58	11	3	8	11	6
1993-94	St. Louis	NHL	63	13	47	60	46	....	....	....	....	....
	Vancouver	NHL	11	1	5	6	10	24	6	9	15	37
1994-95	Vancouver	NHL	33	8	23	31	16	5	1	3	4	2
1995-96	Vancouver	NHL	28	1	16	17	18	....	....	....	....	....
	Hartford	NHL	48	7	31	38	38	....	....	....	....	....
1996-97	Hartford	NHL	1	0	0	0	0	....	....	....	....	....
1997-98	Carolina	NHL	32	3	10	13	16	....	....	....	....	....
	Toronto	NHL	19	1	8	9	10	....	....	....	....	....
	Washington	NHL	9	0	6	6	6	2	0	2	2	0
	NHL Totals		747	154	430	584	498	87	20	45	65	59

OHL First All-Star Team (1986)

Traded to **St. Louis** by **Quebec** for Tony Hrkac and Greg Millen, December 13, 1989. Traded to **Vancouver** by **St. Louis** with Bret Hedican and Nathan Lafayette fro Craig Janney, March 21, 1994. Traded to **Hartford** by **Vancouver** with Vancouver's 3rd round choice (later traded to Calgary – Calgary selected Paul Manning) in 1998 Entry Draft for Jim Dowd, Frantisek Kucera and Hartford's 2nd round choice (Ryan Bonni) in 1997 Entry Draft, December 19, 1995. Transferred to **Carolina** after **Hartford** franchise relocated, June 25, 1997. Traded to **Toronto** by **Carolina** for future considerations, January 2, 1998. Traded to **Washington** by **Toronto** for Sylvain Cote, March 24, 1998.

BROWN, JEFF — NYR

Defense. Shoots right. 6'1", 217 lbs. Born, Mississauga, Ont., April 24, 1978.
(NY Rangers' 1st choice, 22nd overall, in 1996 Entry Draft).

			Regular Season					Playoffs				
Season	**Club**	**Lea**	**GP**	**G**	**A**	**TP**	**PIM**	**GP**	**G**	**A**	**TP**	**PIM**
1994-95	Sarnia	OHL	58	2	14	16	52	4	0	2	2	2
1995-96	Sarnia	OHL	65	8	20	28	111	10	1	2	3	12
1996-97	Sarnia	OHL	35	5	14	19	60	....	....	....	....	....
	London	OHL	28	1	17	18	32	....	....	....	....	....
1997-98	London	OHL	63	12	42	54	96	15	1	4	5	26

BROWN, KEVIN — EDM.

Right wing. Shoots right. 6'1", 212 lbs. Born, Birmingham, England, May 11, 1974.
(Los Angeles' 3rd choice, 87th overall, in 1992 Entry Draft).

			Regular Season					Playoffs				
Season	**Club**	**Lea**	**GP**	**G**	**A**	**TP**	**PIM**	**GP**	**G**	**A**	**TP**	**PIM**
1991-92	Belleville	OHL	66	24	24	48	52	5	1	4	5	8
1992-93	Belleville	OHL	6	2	5	7	4	....	....	....	....	....
	Detroit	OHL	56	48	86	134	76	15	10	18	28	18
1993-94	Detroit	OHL	57	54	81	135	85	17	14	*26	*40	28
1994-95	**Los Angeles**	**NHL**	**23**	**2**	**3**	**5**	**18**	....	....	....	....	....
	Phoenix	IHL	48	19	31	50	64	....	....	....	....	....
1995-96	**Los Angeles**	**NHL**	**7**	**1**	**0**	**1**	**4**	....	....	....	....	....
	Phoenix	IHL	45	10	16	26	39	....	....	....	....	....
	P.E.I.	AHL	8	3	6	9	2	3	1	3	4	0
1996-97	**Hartford**	**NHL**	**11**	**0**	**4**	**4**	**6**	....	....	....	....	....
	Springfield	AHL	48	32	16	48	45	17	*11	6	17	24
1997-98	**Carolina**	**NHL**	**4**	**0**	**0**	**0**	**0**	....	....	....	....	....
	New Haven	AHL	67	28	44	72	65	3	0	2	2	0
	NHL Totals		**45**	**3**	**7**	**10**	**28**	....	....	....	....	....

OHL Second All-Star Team (1993) • OHL First All-Star Team (1994) • Canadian Major Junior Second All-Star Team (1994)

Traded to **Ottawa** by **LA Kings** for Jaroslav Modry and Ottawa's 8th round choice (Stephen Valiquette) in 1996 Entry Draft, March 20, 1996. Traded to **Anaheim** by **Ottawa** for Mike Maneluk, July 1, 1996. Traded to **Hartford** by **Anaheim** for the rights to Espen Knutsen, October 1, 1996. Transferred to **Carolina** after **Hartford** franchise relocated, June 25, 1997. Signed as a free agent by **Edmonton**, August 14, 1998.

BROWN, MIKE — FLA.

Left wing. Shoots left. 6'5", 185 lbs. Born, Surrey, B.C., April 27, 1979.
(Florida's 1st choice, 20th overall, in 1997 Entry Draft).

			Regular Season					Playoffs				
Season	**Club**	**Lea**	**GP**	**G**	**A**	**TP**	**PIM**	**GP**	**G**	**A**	**TP**	**PIM**
1995-96	Red Deer	WHL	62	4	5	9	125	10	0	0	0	18
1996-97	Red Deer	WHL	70	19	13	32	243	16	1	2	3	47
1997-98	Kamloops	WHL	72	23	33	56	305	7	2	1	3	22

BROWN, ROB — PIT.

Right wing. Shoots left. 5'10", 183 lbs. Born, Kingston, Ont., April 10, 1968.
(Pittsburgh's 4th choice, 67th overall, in 1986 Entry Draft).

			Regular Season					Playoffs				
Season	**Club**	**Lea**	**GP**	**G**	**A**	**TP**	**PIM**	**GP**	**G**	**A**	**TP**	**PIM**
1984-85	Kamloops	WHL	60	29	50	79	95	15	8	8	26	28
1985-86	Kamloops	WHL	69	58	*115	*173	171	16	*18	*28	*46	14
1986-87	Kamloops	WHL	63	*76	*136	*212	101	5	6	5	11	6
1987-88	**Pittsburgh**	**NHL**	**51**	**24**	**20**	**44**	**56**	....	....	....	....	....
1988-89	**Pittsburgh**	**NHL**	**68**	**49**	**66**	**115**	**118**	**11**	**5**	**3**	**8**	**22**
1989-90	**Pittsburgh**	**NHL**	**80**	**33**	**47**	**80**	**102**	....	....	....	....	....
1990-91	**Pittsburgh**	**NHL**	**25**	**6**	**10**	**16**	**31**	....	....	....	....	....
	Hartford	**NHL**	**44**	**18**	**24**	**42**	**101**	**5**	**1**	**0**	**1**	**7**
1991-92	**Hartford**	**NHL**	**42**	**16**	**15**	**31**	**39**	....	....	....	....	....
	Chicago	**NHL**	**25**	**5**	**11**	**16**	**34**	**8**	**2**	**4**	**6**	**4**
1992-93	**Chicago**	**NHL**	**15**	**1**	**6**	**7**	**33**	....	....	....	....	....
	Indianapolis	IHL	19	14	19	33	32	2	0	1	1	2
1993-94	**Dallas**	**NHL**	**1**	**0**	**0**	**0**	**0**	....	....	....	....	....
	Kalamazoo	IHL	79	42	*113	*155	188	5	1	3	4	6
1994-95	Phoenix	IHL	69	34	73	107	135	9	4	12	16	0
	Los Angeles	**NHL**	**2**	**0**	**0**	**0**	**0**	....	....	....	....	....
1995-96	Chicago	IHL	79	52	*91	*143	100	9	4	11	15	6
1996-97	Chicago	IHL	76	37	*80	*117	98	4	2	4	6	16
1997-98	**Pittsburgh**	**NHL**	**82**	**15**	**25**	**40**	**59**	**6**	**1**	**0**	**1**	**4**
	NHL Totals		**435**	**167**	**224**	**391**	**573**	**30**	**9**	**7**	**16**	**37**

WHL First All-Star Team (1986, 1987) • Canadian Major Junior Player of the Year (1987) • IHL First All-Star Team (1994, 1996, 1997) • Won Leo P. Lamoureux Memorial Trophy (Top Scorer - IHL) (1994, 1996, 1997) • Won James Gatschene Memorial Trophy (MVP - IHL) (1994) • IHL Second All-Star Team (1995)

Played in NHL All-Star Game (1989)

Traded to **Hartford** by **Pittsburgh** for Scott Young, December 21, 1990. Traded to **Chicago** by **Hartford** for Steve Konroyd, January 24, 1992. Signed as a free agent by **Dallas**, August 12, 1993. Signed as a free agent by **LA Kings**, June 14, 1994. Signed as a free agent by **Pittsburgh**, October 1, 1997.

BROWN, SEAN — EDM.

Defense. Shoots left. 6'3", 205 lbs. Born, Oshawa, Ont., November 5, 1976.
(Boston's 2nd choice, 21st overall, in 1995 Entry Draft).

			Regular Season					Playoffs				
Season	**Club**	**Lea**	**GP**	**G**	**A**	**TP**	**PIM**	**GP**	**G**	**A**	**TP**	**PIM**
1993-94	Belleville	OHL	28	1	2	3	53	8	0	0	0	17
1994-95	Belleville	OHL	58	2	16	18	200	16	4	2	6	*67
1995-96	Belleville	OHL	37	10	23	33	150	....	....	....	....	....
	Sarnia	OHL	26	8	17	25	112	10	1	0	1	38
1996-97	**Edmonton**	**NHL**	**5**	**0**	**0**	**0**	**4**	....	....	....	....	....
	Hamilton	AHL	61	1	7	8	238	19	1	0	1	47
1997-98	**Edmonton**	**NHL**	**18**	**0**	**1**	**1**	**43**	....	....	....	....	....
	Hamilton	AHL	43	4	6	10	166	6	0	2	2	38
	NHL Totals		**23**	**0**	**1**	**1**	**47**	....	....	....	....	....

OHL Second All-Star Team (1996)

Rights traded to **Edmonton** by **Boston** with Mariusz Czerkawski and Boston's 1st round choice (Matthieu Descoteaux) in 1996 Entry Draft for Bill Ranford, January 11, 1996.

BRUCE, DAVID

Left wing. Shoots right. 5'11", 190 lbs. Born, Thunder Bay, Ont., October 7, 1964.
(Vancouver's 2nd choice, 30th overall, in 1983 Entry Draft).

			Regular Season					Playoffs				
Season	**Club**	**Lea**	**GP**	**G**	**A**	**TP**	**PIM**	**GP**	**G**	**A**	**TP**	**PIM**
1981-82	Thunder Bay	TBJHL	35	27	31	58	74	....	....	....	....	....
1982-83	Kitchener	OHL	67	36	35	71	199	12	7	9	16	27
1983-84	Kitchener	OHL	62	52	40	92	203	10	5	8	13	20
1984-85	Fredericton	AHL	56	14	11	25	104	5	0	0	0	37
1985-86	**Vancouver**	**NHL**	**12**	**0**	**1**	**1**	**14**	**1**	**0**	**0**	**0**	**0**
	Fredericton	AHL	66	25	16	41	151	2	0	1	1	12
1986-87	**Vancouver**	**NHL**	**50**	**9**	**7**	**16**	**109**	....	....	....	....	....
	Fredericton	AHL	17	7	6	13	73	....	....	....	....	....
1987-88	**Vancouver**	**NHL**	**28**	**7**	**3**	**10**	**57**	....	....	....	....	....
	Fredericton	AHL	30	27	18	45	115	....	....	....	....	....
1988-89	**Vancouver**	**NHL**	**53**	**7**	**7**	**14**	**65**	....	....	....	....	....
1989-90	Milwaukee	IHL	68	40	35	75	148	6	5	3	8	0
1990-91	**St. Louis**	**NHL**	**12**	**1**	**2**	**3**	**14**	**2**	**0**	**0**	**0**	**2**
	Peoria	IHL	60	*64	52	116	78	18	*18	11	*29	40
1991-92	**San Jose**	**NHL**	**60**	**22**	**16**	**38**	**46**	....	....	....	....	....
	Kansas City	IHL	7	5	5	10	6	....	....	....	....	....
1992-93	**San Jose**	**NHL**	**17**	**2**	**3**	**5**	**33**	....	....	....	....	....
1993-94	**San Jose**	**NHL**	**2**	**0**	**0**	**0**	**0**	....	....	....	....	....
	Kansas City	IHL	72	40	24	64	115	....	....	....	....	....
1994-95	Kansas City	IHL	63	33	25	58	80	....	....	....	....	....
1995-96	Kansas City	IHL	62	27	26	53	84	1	0	0	0	8
1996-97	Kansas City	IHL	79	45	24	69	90	3	0	0	0	2
1997-98	Kansas City	IHL	54	20	12	32	58	11	3	2	5	21
	NHL Totals		**234**	**48**	**39**	**87**	**338**	**3**	**0**	**0**	**0**	**2**

IHL First All-Star Team (1990, 1991) • Won James Gatschene Memorial Trophy (MVP - IHL) (1991)

Signed as a free agent by **St. Louis**, July 6, 1990. Claimed by **San Jose** from **St. Louis** in Expansion Draft, May 30, 1991.

BRUININKS, BRETT (broo-IHN-kihs)

Right wing. Shoots right. 6'4", 235 lbs. Born, Minneapolis, MN, March 10, 1972.

			Regular Season					Playoffs				
Season	**Club**	**Lea**	**GP**	**G**	**A**	**TP**	**PIM**	**GP**	**G**	**A**	**TP**	**PIM**
1992-93	Notre Dame	CCHA	36	9	7	16	98	....	....	....	....	....
1993-94	Notre Dame	CCHA	42	9	7	16	89	....	....	....	....	....
1994-95	Notre Dame	CCHA	42	10	3	13	103	....	....	....	....	....
1995-96	Notre Dame	CCHA	40	10	5	15	74	....	....	....	....	....
1996-97	Philadelphia	AHL	45	3	2	5	54	4	1	1	2	2
1997-98	Philadelphia	AHL	6	0	1	1	13	....	....	....	....	....
	Johnstown	ECHL	8	3	2	5	35	....	....	....	....	....
	Indianapolis	IHL	43	5	6	11	79	2	0	0	0	4

Signed as a free agent by **Philadelphia**, October 3, 1996.

BRULE, STEVE (broo-LAY) — N.J.

Center. Shoots right. 6', 195 lbs. Born, Montreal, Que., January 15, 1975.
(New Jersey's 6th choice, 143rd overall, in 1993 Entry Draft).

			Regular Season					Playoffs				
Season	**Club**	**Lea**	**GP**	**G**	**A**	**TP**	**PIM**	**GP**	**G**	**A**	**TP**	**PIM**
1992-93	St-Jean	QMJHL	70	33	47	80	46	4	0	0	0	9
1993-94	St-Jean	QMJHL	66	41	64	105	46	5	2	1	3	0
1994-95	St-Jean	QMJHL	69	44	64	108	42	7	3	4	7	8
	Albany	AHL	3	1	4	5	0	14	9	5	14	4
1995-96	Albany	AHL	80	30	21	51	37	4	0	0	0	17
1996-97	Albany	AHL	79	28	48	76	27	16	7	7	14	12
1997-98	Albany	AHL	80	34	43	77	34	13	8	3	11	4

QMJHL Second All-Star Team (1995)

BRUNEL, CRAIG — NSH.

Right wing. Shoots right. 6', 201 lbs. Born, Winnipeg, Man., November 12, 1979.
(Nashville's 6th choice, 147th overall, in 1998 Entry Draft).

			Regular Season					Playoffs				
Season	**Club**	**Lea**	**GP**	**G**	**A**	**TP**	**PIM**	**GP**	**G**	**A**	**TP**	**PIM**
1996-97	Prince Albert	WHL	57	5	2	7	208	4	0	0	0	13
1997-98	Prince Albert	WHL	58	6	12	18	247	....	....	....	....	....

BRUNET, BENOIT (broo-NAY, BEHN-wah) — MTL.

Left wing. Shoots left. 6', 195 lbs. Born, Ste-Anne-de-Bellevue, Que., August 24, 1968.
(Montreal's 2nd choice, 27th overall, in 1986 Entry Draft).

			Regular Season					Playoffs				
Season	**Club**	**Lea**	**GP**	**G**	**A**	**TP**	**PIM**	**GP**	**G**	**A**	**TP**	**PIM**
1985-86	Hull	QMJHL	71	33	37	70	81	....	....	....	....	....
1986-87	Hull	QMJHL	60	43	67	110	105	6	7	5	12	8
1987-88	Hull	QMJHL	62	54	89	143	131	10	3	10	13	11
1988-89	**Montreal**	**NHL**	**2**	**0**	**1**	**1**	**0**	....	....	....	....	....
	Sherbrooke	AHL	73	41	76	117	95	6	2	0	2	4
1989-90	Sherbrooke	AHL	72	32	35	67	82	12	8	7	15	20
1990-91	**Montreal**	**NHL**	**17**	**1**	**3**	**4**	**0**	....	....	....	....	....
	Fredericton	AHL	24	13	18	31	16	6	5	6	11	2
1991-92	**Montreal**	**NHL**	**18**	**4**	**6**	**10**	**14**	....	....	....	....	....
	Fredericton	AHL	6	7	9	16	27	....	....	....	....	....
1992-93	**Montreal**	**NHL**	**47**	**10**	**15**	**25**	**19**	**20**	**2**	**8**	**10**	**8** ♦
1993-94	**Montreal**	**NHL**	**71**	**10**	**20**	**30**	**20**	**7**	**1**	**4**	**5**	**16**
1994-95	**Montreal**	**NHL**	**45**	**7**	**18**	**25**	**16**	....	....	....	....	....
1995-96	**Montreal**	**NHL**	**26**	**7**	**8**	**15**	**17**	**3**	**0**	**2**	**2**	**0**
	Fredericton	AHL	3	2	1	3	6	....	....	....	....	....
1996-97	**Montreal**	**NHL**	**39**	**10**	**13**	**23**	**14**	**4**	**1**	**3**	**4**	**4**
1997-98	**Montreal**	**NHL**	**68**	**12**	**20**	**32**	**61**	**8**	**1**	**0**	**1**	**4**
	NHL Totals		**333**	**61**	**104**	**165**	**161**	**42**	**5**	**17**	**22**	**32**

QMJHL Second All-Star Team (1987) • AHL First All-Star Team (1989)

BRUNETTE, ANDREW (broo-NEHT) **NSH.**

Left wing. Shoots left. 6', 212 lbs. Born, Sudbury, Ont., August 24, 1973.
(Washington's 6th choice, 174th overall, in 1993 Entry Draft).

			Regular Season					Playoffs				
Season	Club	Lea	GP	G	A	TP	PIM	GP	G	A	TP	PIM
1990-91	Owen Sound	OHL	63	15	20	35	15	....	....	....	....	....
1991-92	Owen Sound	OHL	66	51	47	98	42	5	5	0	5	8
1992-93	Owen Sound	OHL	66	*62	*100	*162	91	8	8	6	14	16
1993-94	Portland	AHL	23	9	11	20	10	2	0	1	1	0
	Providence	AHL	3	0	0	0	0	....	....	....	....	....
	Hampton Roads	ECHL	20	12	18	30	32	7	7	6	13	18
1994-95	Portland	AHL	79	30	50	80	53	7	3	3	6	10
1995-96	**Washington**	**NHL**	**11**	**3**	**3**	**6**	**0**	**6**	**1**	**3**	**4**	**0**
	Portland	AHL	69	28	66	94	125	20	11	18	29	15
1996-97	**Washington**	**NHL**	**23**	**4**	**7**	**11**	**12**	....	....	....	....	....
	Portland	AHL	50	22	51	73	48	5	1	2	3	0
1997-98	**Washington**	**NHL**	**28**	**11**	**12**	**23**	**12**	....	....	....	....	....
	Portland	AHL	43	21	46	67	64	10	1	11	12	12
	NHL Totals		**62**	**18**	**22**	**40**	**24**	**6**	**1**	**3**	**4**	**0**

OHL First All-Star Team (1993) • Canadian Major Junior Second All-Star Team (1993) • AHL Second All-Star Team (1995)

Claimed by **Nashville** from **Washington** in Expansion Draft, June 26, 1998.

BRYLIN, SERGEI (BRIH-lin) **N.J.**

Center. Shoots left. 5'10", 190 lbs. Born, Moscow, USSR, January 13, 1974.
(New Jersey's 2nd choice, 42nd overall, in 1992 Entry Draft).

			Regular Season					Playoffs				
Season	Club	Lea	GP	G	A	TP	PIM	GP	G	A	TP	PIM
1991-92	CSKA Moscow	CIS	44	1	6	7	4	....	....	....	....	....
1992-93	CSKA Moscow	CIS	42	5	4	9	36	....	....	....	....	....
1993-94	CSKA Moscow	CIS	39	4	6	10	36	3	1	0	1	2
	Russian Penguins	IHL	13	4	5	9	18	....	....	....	....	....
1994-95	**New Jersey**	**NHL**	**26**	**6**	**8**	**14**	**8**	**12**	**1**	**2**	**3**	**4 ♦**
	Albany	AHL	63	19	35	54	78	....	....	....	....	....
1995-96	**New Jersey**	**NHL**	**50**	**4**	**5**	**9**	**26**	....	....	....	....	....
1996-97	**New Jersey**	**NHL**	**29**	**2**	**2**	**4**	**20**	....	....	....	....	....
	Albany	AHL	43	17	24	41	38	16	4	8	12	12
1997-98	**New Jersey**	**NHL**	**18**	**2**	**3**	**5**	**0**	....	....	....	....	....
	Albany	AHL	44	21	22	43	60	....	....	....	....	....
	NHL Totals		**123**	**14**	**18**	**32**	**54**	**12**	**1**	**2**	**3**	**4**

BUCHANAN, JEFF **COL.**

Defense. Shoots right. 6'2", 200 lbs. Born, Swift Current, Sask., May 23, 1971.

			Regular Season					Playoffs				
Season	Club	Lea	GP	G	A	TP	PIM	GP	G	A	TP	PIM
1989-90	Saskatoon	WHL	66	7	12	19	96	9	0	2	2	2
1990-91	Saskatoon	WHL	69	10	26	36	123	....	....	....	....	....
1991-92	Saskatoon	WHL	72	17	37	54	145	22	10	14	24	39
1992-93	Atlanta	IHL	68	4	18	22	282	9	0	0	0	26
1993-94	Atlanta	IHL	76	5	24	29	253	14	0	1	1	20
1994-95	Atlanta	IHL	4	0	1	1	9	....	....	....	....	....
	Indianapolis	IHL	25	3	9	12	63	....	....	....	....	....
1995-96	Indianapolis	IHL	77	4	14	18	277	5	0	1	1	9
1996-97	Orlando	IHL	81	11	27	38	246	....	....	....	....	....
1997-98	Orlando	IHL	61	5	20	25	131	....	....	....	....	....
	Kansas City	IHL	7	2	3	5	6	11	0	2	2	40

Signed as a free agent by **Tampa Bay**, July 13, 1992. Traded to **Chicago** by **Tampa Bay** with Jim Cummins and Tom Tilley for Paul Ysebaert and Rich Sutter, February 22, 1995. Signed as a free agent by **Colorado**, August 14, 1998.

BUCHBERGER, KELLY (BUK-buhr-guhr) **EDM.**

Right wing. Shoots left. 6'2", 210 lbs. Born, Langenburg, Sask., December 2, 1966.
(Edmonton's 8th choice, 188th overall, in 1985 Entry Draft).

			Regular Season					Playoffs				
Season	Club	Lea	GP	G	A	TP	PIM	GP	G	A	TP	PIM
1984-85	Moose Jaw	WHL	51	12	17	29	114	....	....	....	....	....
1985-86	Moose Jaw	WHL	72	14	22	36	206	13	11	4	15	37
1986-87	Nova Scotia	AHL	70	12	20	32	257	5	0	1	1	23
	Edmonton	**NHL**	....	....	....	....	....	**3**	**0**	**1**	**1**	**5 ♦**
1987-88	**Edmonton**	**NHL**	**19**	**1**	**0**	**1**	**81**	....	....	....	....	....
	Nova Scotia	AHL	49	21	23	44	206	2	0	0	0	11
1988-89	**Edmonton**	**NHL**	**66**	**5**	**9**	**14**	**234**	....	....	....	....	....
1989-90	**Edmonton**	**NHL**	**55**	**2**	**6**	**8**	**168**	**19**	**0**	**5**	**5**	**13 ♦**
1990-91	**Edmonton**	**NHL**	**64**	**3**	**1**	**4**	**160**	**12**	**2**	**1**	**3**	**25**
1991-92	**Edmonton**	**NHL**	**79**	**20**	**24**	**44**	**157**	**16**	**1**	**4**	**5**	**32**
1992-93	**Edmonton**	**NHL**	**83**	**12**	**18**	**30**	**133**	....	....	....	....	....
1993-94	**Edmonton**	**NHL**	**84**	**3**	**18**	**21**	**199**	....	....	....	....	....
1994-95	**Edmonton**	**NHL**	**48**	**7**	**17**	**24**	**82**	....	....	....	....	....
1995-96	**Edmonton**	**NHL**	**82**	**11**	**14**	**25**	**184**	....	....	....	....	....
1996-97	**Edmonton**	**NHL**	**81**	**8**	**30**	**38**	**159**	**12**	**5**	**2**	**7**	**16**
1997-98	**Edmonton**	**NHL**	**82**	**6**	**17**	**23**	**122**	**12**	**1**	**2**	**3**	**25**
	NHL Totals		**743**	**78**	**154**	**232**	**1679**	**74**	**9**	**15**	**24**	**116**

BUCKLEY, BRENDAN **ANA.**

Defense. Shoots right. 6'2", 196 lbs. Born, Boston, MA, February 26, 1977.
(Anaheim's 3rd choice, 113th overall, in 1996 Entry Draft).

			Regular Season					Playoffs				
Season	Club	Lea	GP	G	A	TP	PIM	GP	G	A	TP	PIM
1994-95	Boston Jr. Bruins	Jr. A	48	22	43	65	164	....	....	....	....	....
1995-96	Boston College	H.E.	34	0	4	4	72	....	....	....	....	....
1996-97	Boston College	H.E.	38	2	6	8	90	....	....	....	....	....
1997-98	Boston College	H.E.	41	1	12	13	69	....	....	....	....	....

BUCKLEY, TOM **CAR.**

Center. Shoots left. 6'1", 204 lbs. Born, Buffalo, NY, May 26, 1976.
(Hartford's 4th choice, 187th overall, in 1994 Entry Draft).

			Regular Season					Playoffs				
Season	Club	Lea	GP	G	A	TP	PIM	GP	G	A	TP	PIM
1994-95	Detroit	OHL	64	30	36	66	49	21	10	9	19	8
1995-96	Detroit	OHL	66	29	43	72	31	17	6	20	26	20
1996-97	Springfield	AHL	62	7	12	19	39	3	0	0	0	4
	Richmond	ECHL	3	0	0	0	14	....	....	....	....	....
1997-98	New Haven	AHL	14	1	0	1	4	....	....	....	....	....
	Richmond	ECHL	58	23	32	55	102	....	....	....	....	....

Rights transferred to **Carolina** after **Hartford** franchise relocated, June 25, 1997.

BULIS, JAN (BOO-lihs, YAHN) **WSH.**

Center. Shoots left. 6', 194 lbs. Born, Pardubice, Czech., March 18, 1978.
(Washington's 3rd choice, 43rd overall, in 1996 Entry Draft).

			Regular Season					Playoffs				
Season	Club	Lea	GP	G	A	TP	PIM	GP	G	A	TP	PIM
1995-96	Barrie	OHL	59	29	30	59	22	7	2	3	5	2
1996-97	Barrie	OHL	64	42	61	103	42	9	3	7	10	10
1997-98	Kingston	OHL	2	0	1	1	0	12	8	10	18	12
	Washington	**NHL**	**48**	**5**	**11**	**16**	**18**	....	....	....	....	....
	Portland	AHL	3	1	4	5	12	....	....	....	....	....
	NHL Totals		**48**	**5**	**11**	**16**	**18**	....	....	....	....	....

BURE, PAVEL (boo-RAY) **VAN.**

Right wing. Shoots left. 5'10", 189 lbs. Born, Moscow, USSR, March 31, 1971.
(Vancouver's 4th choice, 113th overall, in 1989 Entry Draft).

			Regular Season					Playoffs				
Season	Club	Lea	GP	G	A	TP	PIM	GP	G	A	TP	PIM
1987-88	CSKA Moscow	USSR	5	1	1	2	0	....	....	....	....	....
1988-89	CSKA Moscow	USSR	32	17	9	26	8	....	....	....	....	....
1989-90	CSKA Moscow	USSR	46	14	10	24	20	....	....	....	....	....
1990-91	CSKA Moscow	USSR	44	35	11	46	24	....	....	....	....	....
1991-92	**Vancouver**	**NHL**	**65**	**34**	**26**	**60**	**30**	**13**	**6**	**4**	**10**	**14**
1992-93	**Vancouver**	**NHL**	**83**	**60**	**50**	**110**	**69**	**12**	**5**	**7**	**12**	**8**
1993-94	**Vancouver**	**NHL**	**76**	***60**	**47**	**107**	**86**	**24**	***16**	**15**	**31**	**40**
1994-95	EV Landshut	Germany	1	3	0	3	2	....	....	....	....	....
	Spartak	CIS	1	2	0	2	2	....	....	....	....	....
	Vancouver	**NHL**	**44**	**20**	**23**	**43**	**47**	**11**	**7**	**6**	**13**	**10**
1995-96	**Vancouver**	**NHL**	**15**	**6**	**7**	**13**	**8**	....	....	....	....	....
1996-97	**Vancouver**	**NHL**	**63**	**23**	**32**	**55**	**40**	....	....	....	....	....
1997-98	**Vancouver**	**NHL**	**82**	**51**	**39**	**90**	**48**	....	....	....	....	....
	Russia	Olympics	6	*9	0	9	2	....	....	....	....	....
	NHL Totals		**428**	**254**	**224**	**478**	**328**	**60**	**34**	**32**	**66**	**72**

• Named Soviet National League Rookie-of-the-Year (1989) • Won Calder Memorial Trophy (1992)
• NHL First All-Star Team (1994)

Played in NHL All-Star Game (1993, 1994, 1997, 1998)

BURE, VALERI (boo-RAY) **CGY.**

Right wing. Shoots right. 5'11", 179 lbs. Born, Moscow, USSR, June 13, 1974.
(Montreal's 2nd choice, 33rd overall, in 1992 Entry Draft).

			Regular Season					Playoffs				
Season	Club	Lea	GP	G	A	TP	PIM	GP	G	A	TP	PIM
1990-91	CSKA Moscow	USSR	3	0	0	0	0	....	....	....	....	....
1991-92	Spokane	WHL	53	27	22	49	78	10	11	6	17	10
1992-93	Spokane	WHL	66	68	79	147	49	9	6	11	17	14
1993-94	Spokane	WHL	59	40	62	102	48	3	5	3	8	2
1994-95	**Montreal**	**NHL**	**24**	**3**	**1**	**4**	**6**	....	....	....	....	....
	Fredericton	AHL	45	23	25	48	32	....	....	....	....	....
1995-96	**Montreal**	**NHL**	**77**	**22**	**20**	**42**	**28**	**6**	**0**	**1**	**1**	**6**
1996-97	**Montreal**	**NHL**	**64**	**14**	**21**	**35**	**6**	**5**	**0**	**1**	**1**	**2**
1997-98	**Montreal**	**NHL**	**50**	**7**	**22**	**29**	**33**	....	....	....	....	....
	Calgary	**NHL**	**16**	**5**	**4**	**9**	**2**	....	....	....	....	....
	Russia	Olympics	6	1	0	1	0	....	....	....	....	....
	NHL Totals		**231**	**51**	**68**	**119**	**75**	**11**	**0**	**2**	**2**	**8**

WHL West First All-Star Team (1993) • WHL West Second All-Star Team (1994)

Traded to **Calgary** by **Montreal** with Montreal's 4th round choice (Shaun Sutter) in 1998 Entry Draft for Jonas Hoglund and Zarley Zalapski, February 1, 1998.

BUREAU, MARC (BEWR-oh) **PHI.**

Center. Shoots right. 6'1", 198 lbs. Born, Trois-Rivières, Que., May 19, 1966.

			Regular Season					Playoffs				
Season	Club	Lea	GP	G	A	TP	PIM	GP	G	A	TP	PIM
1983-84	Chicoutimi	QMJHL	56	6	16	22	14	....	....	....	....	....
1984-85	Chicoutimi	QMJHL	41	30	25	55	15	....	....	....	....	....
	Granby	QMJHL	27	20	45	65	14	....	....	....	....	....
1985-86	Granby	QMJHL	19	6	17	23	36	....	....	....	....	....
	Chicoutimi	QMJHL	44	30	45	75	33	9	3	7	10	10
1986-87	Longueuil	QMJHL	66	54	58	112	68	20	17	20	37	12
1987-88	Salt Lake	IHL	69	7	20	27	86	7	0	3	3	8
1988-89	Salt Lake	IHL	76	28	36	64	119	14	7	5	12	31
1989-90	**Calgary**	**NHL**	**5**	**0**	**0**	**0**	**4**	....	....	....	....	....
	Salt Lake	IHL	67	43	48	91	173	11	4	8	12	0
1990-91	**Calgary**	**NHL**	**5**	**0**	**0**	**0**	**2**	....	....	....	....	....
	Salt Lake	IHL	54	40	48	88	101	....	....	....	....	....
	Minnesota	**NHL**	**9**	**0**	**6**	**6**	**4**	**23**	**3**	**2**	**5**	**20**
1991-92	**Minnesota**	**NHL**	**46**	**6**	**4**	**10**	**50**	**5**	**0**	**0**	**0**	**14**
	Kalamazoo	IHL	7	2	8	10	2	....	....	....	....	....
1992-93	**Tampa Bay**	**NHL**	**63**	**10**	**21**	**31**	**111**	....	....	....	....	....
1993-94	**Tampa Bay**	**NHL**	**75**	**8**	**7**	**15**	**30**	....	....	....	....	....
1994-95	**Tampa Bay**	**NHL**	**48**	**2**	**12**	**14**	**30**	....	....	....	....	....
1995-96	**Montreal**	**NHL**	**65**	**3**	**7**	**10**	**46**	**6**	**1**	**1**	**2**	**4**
1996-97	**Montreal**	**NHL**	**43**	**6**	**9**	**15**	**16**	....	....	....	....	....
1997-98	**Montreal**	**NHL**	**74**	**13**	**6**	**19**	**12**	**10**	**1**	**2**	**3**	**6**
	NHL Totals		**433**	**48**	**72**	**120**	**305**	**44**	**5**	**5**	**10**	**44**

IHL Second All-Star Team (1990, 1991)

Signed as a free agent by **Calgary**, May 19, 1987. Traded to **Minnesota** by **Calgary** for Minnesota's 3rd round choice (Sandy McCarthy) in 1991 Entry Draft, March 5, 1991. Claimed on waivers by **Tampa Bay** from **Minnesota**, October 16, 1992. Traded to **Montreal** by **Tampa Bay** for Brian Bellows, June 30, 1995. Signed as a free agent by **Philadelphia**, July 20, 1998.

BURNETT, GARRETT **S.J.**

Defense. Shoots left. 6'3", 225 lbs. Born, Coquitlam, B.C., September 23, 1975.

			Regular Season					Playoffs				
Season	Club	Lea	GP	G	A	TP	PIM	GP	G	A	TP	PIM
1994-95	S.S. Marie	OHL	14	0	1	1	78	....	....	....	....	....
	Kitchener	OHL	22	0	1	1	74	....	....	....	....	....
1995-96	Utica	CoHL	15	0	1	1	78	....	....	....	....	....
	Oklahoma City	CHL	3	0	0	0	20	....	....	....	....	....
	Tulsa	CHL	6	1	0	1	94	....	....	....	....	....
	Nashville	ECHL	3	0	0	0	22	....	....	....	....	....
	Jacksonville	ECHL	3	0	1	1	38	....	....	....	....	....
1996-97	Knoxville	ECHL	50	5	11	16	321	....	....	....	....	....
1997-98	Johnstown	ECHL	34	1	1	2	331	....	....	....	....	....
	Philadelphia	AHL	14	1	2	3	129	....	....	....	....	....

Signed as a free agent by **San Jose**, July 22, 1998.

BURNHAM, ANDY — NYI

Right wing. Shoots right. 6'4", 201 lbs. Born, New Liskeard, Ont., July 2, 1980.
(NY Islanders' 3rd choice, 95th overall, in 1998 Entry Draft).

			Regular Season					Playoffs				
Season	Club	Lea	GP	G	A	TP	PIM	GP	G	A	TP	PIM
1997-98	Plymouth	OHL	28	1	3	4	55	....	....	....	....	....
	Windsor	OHL	10	1	1	2	23	....	....	....	....	....

BURR, SHAWN — S.J.

Left wing/Center. Shoots left. 6'1", 205 lbs. Born, Sarnia, Ont., July 1, 1966.
(Detroit's 1st choice, 7th overall, in 1984 Entry Draft).

			Regular Season					Playoffs				
Season	Club	Lea	GP	G	A	TP	PIM	GP	G	A	TP	PIM
1982-83	Sarnia	OJHL	52	50	85	135	125	....	....	....	....	....
1983-84	Kitchener	OHL	68	41	44	85	50	16	5	12	17	22
1984-85	Kitchener	OHL	48	24	42	66	50	4	3	3	6	2
	Detroit	NHL	9	0	0	0	2	....	....	....	....	....
	Adirondack	AHL	4	0	0	0	2	....	....	....	....	....
1985-86	Kitchener	OHL	59	60	67	127	104	5	2	3	5	8
	Detroit	NHL	5	1	0	1	4	....	....	....	....	....
	Adirondack	AHL	3	2	2	4	2	17	5	7	12	32
1986-87	Detroit	NHL	80	22	25	47	107	16	7	2	9	20
1987-88	Detroit	NHL	78	17	23	40	97	9	3	1	4	14
1988-89	Detroit	NHL	79	19	27	46	78	6	1	2	3	6
1989-90	Detroit	NHL	76	24	32	56	82	....	....	....	....	....
	Adirondack	AHL	3	4	2	6	2	....	....	....	....	....
1990-91	Detroit	NHL	80	20	30	50	112	7	0	4	4	15
1991-92	Detroit	NHL	79	19	32	51	118	11	1	5	6	10
1992-93	Detroit	NHL	80	10	25	35	74	7	2	1	3	2
1993-94	Detroit	NHL	51	10	12	22	31	7	2	0	2	6
1994-95	Detroit	NHL	42	6	8	14	60	16	0	2	2	6
1995-96	Tampa Bay	NHL	81	13	15	28	119	6	0	2	2	8
1996-97	Tampa Bay	NHL	74	14	21	35	106	....	....	....	....	....
1997-98	San Jose	NHL	42	6	6	12	50	6	0	0	0	8
	NHL Totals		856	181	256	437	1040	91	16	19	35	95

OHL Second All-Star Team (1986)

Traded to **Tampa Bay** by **Detroit** with Detroit's 3rd round choice (later traded to Boston — Boston selected Jason Doyle) in 1996 Entry Draft for Marc Bergevin and Ben Hankinson, August 17, 1995. Traded to **San Jose** by **Tampa Bay** for San Jose's 5th round choice (Mark Thompson) in 1997 Entry Draft, June 21, 1997.

BURRIDGE, RANDY

Left wing. Shoots left. 5'9", 188 lbs. Born, Fort Erie, Ont., January 7, 1966.
(Boston's 7th choice, 157th overall, in 1985 Entry Draft).

			Regular Season					Playoffs				
Season	Club	Lea	GP	G	A	TP	PIM	GP	G	A	TP	PIM
1982-83	Fort Erie	OJHL	42	32	56	88	32	....	....	....	....	....
1983-84	Peterborough	OHL	55	6	7	13	44	8	3	2	5	7
1984-85	Peterborough	OHL	66	49	57	106	88	17	9	16	25	18
1985-86	Peterborough	OHL	17	15	11	26	23	3	1	3	4	2
	Boston	NHL	52	17	25	42	28	3	0	4	4	12
	Moncton	AHL	....	....	....	....	....	3	0	2	2	2
1986-87	Boston	NHL	23	1	4	5	16	2	1	0	1	2
	Moncton	AHL	47	26	41	67	139	3	1	2	3	30
1987-88	Boston	NHL	79	27	28	55	105	23	2	10	12	16
1988-89	Boston	NHL	80	31	30	61	39	10	5	2	7	6
1989-90	Boston	NHL	63	17	15	32	47	21	4	11	15	14
1990-91	Boston	NHL	62	15	13	28	40	19	0	3	3	39
1991-92	Washington	NHL	66	23	44	67	50	2	0	1	1	0
1992-93	Washington	NHL	4	0	0	0	0	4	1	0	1	0
	Baltimore	AHL	2	0	1	1	2	....	....	....	....	....
1993-94	Washington	NHL	78	25	17	42	73	11	0	2	2	12
1994-95	Washington	NHL	2	0	0	0	2	....	....	....	....	....
	Los Angeles	NHL	38	4	15	19	8	....	....	....	....	....
1995-96	Buffalo	NHL	74	25	33	58	30	....	....	....	....	....
1996-97	Buffalo	NHL	55	10	21	31	20	12	5	1	6	2
1997-98	Buffalo	NHL	30	4	6	10	0	....	....	....	....	....
	Rochester	AHL	6	0	1	1	19	1	0	1	1	0
	NHL Totals		706	199	251	450	458	107	18	34	52	103

Played in NHL All-Star Game (1992)

Traded to **Washington** by **Boston** for Stephen Leach, June 21, 1991. Traded to **LA Kings** by **Washington** for Warren Rychel, February 10, 1995. Signed as a free agent by **Buffalo**, October 5, 1995.

BURT, ADAM — CAR.

Defense. Shoots left. 6'2", 207 lbs. Born, Detroit, MI, January 15, 1969.
(Hartford's 2nd choice, 39th overall, in 1987 Entry Draft).

			Regular Season					Playoffs				
Season	Club	Lea	GP	G	A	TP	PIM	GP	G	A	TP	PIM
1985-86	North Bay	OHL	49	0	11	11	81	10	0	0	0	24
1986-87	North Bay	OHL	57	4	27	31	138	24	1	6	7	68
1987-88	North Bay	OHL	66	17	53	70	176	2	0	3	3	6
	Binghamton	AHL	....	....	....	....	....	2	1	1	2	0
1988-89	North Bay	OHL	23	4	11	15	45	12	2	12	14	12
	Hartford	NHL	5	0	0	0	6	....	....	....	....	....
	Binghamton	AHL	5	0	2	2	13	....	....	....	....	....
1989-90	Hartford	NHL	63	4	8	12	105	2	0	0	0	0
1990-91	Hartford	NHL	42	2	7	9	63	....	....	....	....	....
	Springfield	AHL	9	1	3	4	22	....	....	....	....	....
1991-92	Hartford	NHL	66	9	15	24	93	2	0	0	0	0
1992-93	Hartford	NHL	65	6	14	20	116	....	....	....	....	....
1993-94	Hartford	NHL	63	1	17	18	75	....	....	....	....	....
1994-95	Hartford	NHL	46	7	11	18	65	....	....	....	....	....
1995-96	Hartford	NHL	78	4	9	13	121	....	....	....	....	....
1996-97	Hartford	NHL	71	2	11	13	79	....	....	....	....	....
1997-98	Carolina	NHL	76	1	11	12	106	....	....	....	....	....
	NHL Totals		575	36	103	139	829	4	0	0	0	0

OHL Second All-Star Team (1988)

Transferred to **Carolina** after **Hartford** franchise relocated, June 25, 1997.

BUT, ANTON — (BOOT) — N.J.

Left wing. Shoots left. 6'1", 187 lbs. Born, Kharkov, USSR, July 3, 1980.
(New Jersey's 7th choice, 119th overall, in 1998 Entry Draft).

			Regular Season					Playoffs				
Season	Club	Lea	GP	G	A	TP	PIM	GP	G	A	TP	PIM
1995-96	Yaroslavl 2	Russia-2	60	30	12	42	10	....	....	....	....	....
1996-97	Yaroslavl 2	Russia-3	70	30	20	50	20	....	....	....	....	....
1997-98	Yaroslavl 2	Russia-2	48	12	5	17	28	....	....	....	....	....

BUTENSCHON, SVEN — (BUH-tehn-shohn) — PIT.

Defense. Shoots left. 6'4", 215 lbs. Born, Itzehoe, West Germany, March 22, 1976.
(Pittsburgh's 3rd choice, 57th overall, in 1994 Entry Draft).

			Regular Season					Playoffs				
Season	Club	Lea	GP	G	A	TP	PIM	GP	G	A	TP	PIM
1993-94	Brandon	WHL	70	3	19	22	51	4	0	0	0	6
1994-95	Brandon	WHL	21	1	5	6	44	18	1	2	3	11
1995-96	Brandon	WHL	70	4	37	41	99	19	1	12	13	18
1996-97	Cleveland	IHL	75	3	12	15	68	10	0	1	1	4
1997-98	Pittsburgh	NHL	8	0	0	0	6	....	....	....	....	....
	Syracuse	AHL	65	14	23	37	66	5	1	2	3	0
	NHL Totals		8	0	0	0	6	....	....	....	....	....

BUTSAYEV, VIACHESLAV — (boot-SIGH-yehf) — FLA.

Center. Shoots left. 6'2", 200 lbs. Born, Togliatti, USSR, June 13, 1970.
(Philadelphia's 10th choice, 109th overall, in 1990 Entry Draft).

			Regular Season					Playoffs				
Season	Club	Lea	GP	G	A	TP	PIM	GP	G	A	TP	PIM
1989-90	CSKA Moscow	USSR	48	14	4	18	30	....	....	....	....	....
1990-91	CSKA Moscow	USSR	46	14	9	23	32	....	....	....	....	....
1991-92	CSKA Moscow	CIS	36	12	13	25	26	....	....	....	....	....
	Russia	Olympics	8	1	1	2	4	....	....	....	....	....
1992-93	CSKA Moscow	CIS	5	3	4	7	6	....	....	....	....	....
	Philadelphia	NHL	52	2	14	16	61	....	....	....	....	....
	Hershey	AHL	24	8	10	18	51	....	....	....	....	....
1993-94	Philadelphia	NHL	47	12	9	21	58	....	....	....	....	....
	San Jose	NHL	12	0	2	2	10	....	....	....	....	....
1994-95	Togliatti	CIS	9	2	6	8	6	....	....	....	....	....
	San Jose	NHL	6	2	0	2	0	....	....	....	....	....
	Kansas City	IHL	13	3	4	7	12	3	0	0	0	2
1995-96	Anaheim	NHL	7	1	0	1	0	....	....	....	....	....
	Baltimore	AHL	62	23	42	65	70	12	4	8	12	28
1996-97	Farjestad	Sweden	40	6	7	13	108	8	3	4	7	41
1997-98	Fort Wayne	IHL	76	36	51	87	128	4	2	2	4	4
	NHL Totals		124	17	25	42	129	....	....	....	....	....

IHL Second All-Star Team (1998)

Traded to **San Jose** by **Philadelphia** for Rob Zettler, February 1, 1994. Signed as a free agent by **Anaheim**, October 19, 1995. Signed as a free agent by **Florida**, August 12, 1998.

BUTSAYEV, YURI — (buht-SIGH-ehv, YOO-ree) — DET.

Center. Shoots left. 6'1", 183 lbs. Born, Togliatti, USSR, October 11, 1978.
(Detroit's 1st choice, 49th overall, in 1997 Entry Draft).

			Regular Season					Playoffs				
Season	Club	Lea	GP	G	A	TP	PIM	GP	G	A	TP	PIM
1995-96	Togliatti 2	CIS-2	STATISTICS NOT AVAILABLE									
	Togliatti	CIS	1	0	0	0	0	....	....	....	....	....
1996-97	Togliatti	Russia	42	13	11	24	38	11	2	2	4	8
1997-98	Togliatti	EuroHL	6	2	0	2	8	....	....	....	....	....
	Togliatti	Russia	44	8	9	17	63	....	....	....	....	....

BUZEK, PETR — (BOO-zehk) — DAL.

Defense. Shoots left. 6', 205 lbs. Born, Jihlava, Czech., April 26, 1977.
(Dallas' 3rd choice, 63rd overall, in 1995 Entry Draft).

			Regular Season					Playoffs				
Season	Club	Lea	GP	G	A	TP	PIM	GP	G	A	TP	PIM
1993-94	Dukla Jihlava	Cze-Rep.	3	0	0	0	....	....	....	....	....	....
1994-95	Dukla Jihlava	Cze-Rep.	43	2	5	7	47	2	0	0	0	2
1995-96			DID NOT PLAY – INJURED									
1996-97	Michigan	IHL	67	4	6	10	48	....	....	....	....	....
1997-98	Dallas	NHL	2	0	0	0	2	....	....	....	....	....
	Michigan	IHL	60	10	15	25	58	2	0	1	1	17
	NHL Totals		2	0	0	0	2	....	....	....	....	....

BYLSMA, DAN — (BEEL-smah) — L.A.

Right wing. Shoots left. 6'2", 209 lbs. Born, Grand Haven, MI, September 19, 1970.
(Winnipeg's 7th choice, 109th overall, in 1989 Entry Draft).

			Regular Season					Playoffs				
Season	Club	Lea	GP	G	A	TP	PIM	GP	G	A	TP	PIM
1987-88	St. Mary's	OJHL	40	30	39	69	33	....	....	....	....	....
1988-89	Bowling Green	CCHA	32	3	7	10	10	....	....	....	....	....
1989-90	Bowling Green	CCHA	44	13	17	30	30	....	....	....	....	....
1990-91	Bowling Green	CCHA	40	9	12	21	48	....	....	....	....	....
1991-92	Bowling Green	CCHA	34	11	14	25	24	....	....	....	....	....
1992-93	Greensboro	ECHL	60	25	35	60	66	1	0	1	1	10
	Rochester	AHL	2	0	1	1	0	....	....	....	....	....
1993-94	Greensboro	ECHL	25	14	16	30	52	....	....	....	....	....
	Albany	AHL	3	0	1	1	2	....	....	....	....	....
	Moncton	AHL	50	12	16	28	25	21	3	4	7	31
1994-95	Phoenix	IHL	81	19	23	42	41	9	4	4	8	4
1995-96	Los Angeles	NHL	4	0	0	0	0	....	....	....	....	....
	Phoenix	IHL	78	22	20	42	48	4	1	0	1	2
1996-97	Los Angeles	NHL	79	3	6	9	32	....	....	....	....	....
1997-98	Los Angeles	NHL	65	3	9	12	33	2	0	0	0	0
	Long Beach	IHL	8	2	3	5	0	....	....	....	....	....
	NHL Totals		148	6	15	21	65	2	0	0	0	0

Signed as a free agent by **LA Kings**, July 7, 1994.

CABANA, CHAD — FLA.

Left wing. Shoots left. 6'1", 200 lbs. Born, Bonnyville, Alta., October 1, 1974.
(Florida's 11th choice, 213th overall, in 1993 Entry Draft).

			Regular Season					Playoffs				
Season	Club	Lea	GP	G	A	TP	PIM	GP	G	A	TP	PIM
1991-92	Tri-City	WHL	57	5	8	13	145	4	0	1	1	21
1992-93	Tri-City	WHL	68	19	23	42	104	4	1	0	1	10
1993-94	Tri-City	WHL	67	27	33	60	201	4	2	0	2	24
1994-95	Tri-City	WHL	68	25	34	59	252	17	10	11	21	47
1995-96	Carolina	AHL	54	4	9	13	159	....	....	....	....	....
1996-97	Carolina	AHL	55	8	5	13	221	....	....	....	....	....
	Port Huron	ColHL	14	7	9	16	49	....	....	....	....	....
1997-98	New Haven	AHL	34	5	5	10	163	2	0	0	0	7
	Fort Wayne	IHL	6	0	0	0	22	....	....	....	....	....

CABANA, CLINT — VAN.

Defense. Shoots right. 6'2", 195 lbs. Born, Bonnyville, Alta., April 28, 1978.
(Vancouver's 6th choice, 175th overall, in 1996 Entry Draft).

			Regular Season					Playoffs				
Season	Club	Lea	GP	G	A	TP	PIM	GP	G	A	TP	PIM
1994-95	Medicine Hat	WHL	49	0	1	1	68	....	....	....	....	....
1995-96	Medicine Hat	WHL	71	1	11	12	156	5	0	1	1	35
1996-97	Medicine Hat	WHL	4	0	1	1	10	....	....	....	....	....
	Edmonton	WHL	67	3	12	15	302	....	....	....	....	....
	Syracuse	AHL	2	0	0	0	2	....	....	....	....	....
1997-98	Edmonton	WHL	17	1	5	6	60	....	....	....	....	....
	Regina	WHL	34	1	1	2	140	8	1	0	1	16

CABANA, PAUL — VAN.

Right wing. Shoots right. 6'1", 185 lbs. Born, Calgary, Alta., September 28, 1978.
(Vancouver's 8th choice, 149th overall, in 1998 Entry Draft).

			Regular Season					Playoffs				
Season	Club	Lea	GP	G	A	TP	PIM	GP	G	A	TP	PIM
1997-98	Fort McMurray	AJHL	52	48	32	80	111	....	....	....	....	....

CAIRNS, ERIC — NYR

Defense. Shoots left. 6'5", 230 lbs. Born, Oakville, Ont., June 27, 1974.
(NY Rangers' 3rd choice, 72nd overall, in 1992 Entry Draft).

			Regular Season					Playoffs				
Season	Club	Lea	GP	G	A	TP	PIM	GP	G	A	TP	PIM
1990-91	Burlington	OJHL	37	5	16	21	120	....	....	....	....	....
1991-92	Detroit	OHL	64	1	11	12	232	7	0	0	0	31
1992-93	Detroit	OHL	64	3	13	16	194	15	0	3	3	24
1993-94	Detroit	OHL	59	7	35	42	204	17	0	4	4	46
1994-95	Birmingham	ECHL	11	1	3	4	49	....	....	....	....	....
	Binghamton	AHL	27	0	3	3	134	9	1	1	2	28
1995-96	Binghamton	AHL	46	1	13	14	192	4	0	0	0	37
	Charlotte	ECHL	6	0	1	1	34	....	....	....	....	....
1996-97	**NY Rangers**	**NHL**	**40**	**0**	**1**	**1**	**147**	**3**	**0**	**0**	**0**	**0**
	Binghamton	AHL	10	1	1	2	96	....	....	....	....	....
1997-98	**NY Rangers**	**NHL**	**39**	**0**	**3**	**3**	**92**	....	....	....	....	....
	Hartford	AHL	7	1	2	3	43	....	....	....	....	....
	NHL Totals		**79**	**0**	**4**	**4**	**239**	**3**	**0**	**0**	**0**	**0**

CALDER, KYLE — CHI.

Center. Shoots left. 5'11", 180 lbs. Born, Mannville, Alta., January 5, 1979.
(Chicago's 7th choice, 130th overall, in 1997 Entry Draft).

			Regular Season					Playoffs				
Season	Club	Lea	GP	G	A	TP	PIM	GP	G	A	TP	PIM
1995-96	Regina	WHL	27	1	7	8	10	11	0	0	0	0
1996-97	Regina	WHL	62	25	34	59	17	5	3	0	3	6
1997-98	Regina	WHL	62	27	50	77	58	2	0	1	1	0

CALOUN, JAN — (CHAH-loon, YAHN) — S.J.

Right wing. Shoots right. 5'10", 190 lbs. Born, Usti-Nad-Labem, Czech., December 20, 1972.
(San Jose's 4th choice, 75th overall, in 1992 Entry Draft).

			Regular Season					Playoffs				
Season	Club	Lea	GP	G	A	TP	PIM	GP	G	A	TP	PIM
1990-91	Litvinov	Czech.	50	28	19	47	12	....	....	....	....	....
1991-92	Litvinov	Czech.	46	39	13	52	24	....	....	....	....	....
1992-93	Litvinov	Czech.	47	45	22	67	....	....	....	....	....	....
1993-94	Litvinov	Cze-Rep.	38	25	17	42	....	4	2	2	4	....
1994-95	Kansas City	IHL	76	34	39	73	50	21	13	10	23	18
1995-96	**San Jose**	**NHL**	**11**	**8**	**3**	**11**	**0**	....	....	....	....	....
	Kansas City	IHL	61	38	30	68	58	5	0	1	1	6
1996-97	**San Jose**	**NHL**	**2**	**0**	**0**	**0**	**0**	....	....	....	....	....
	Kentucky	AHL	66	43	43	86	68	4	0	1	1	4
1997-98	Helsinki	Finland	41	22	26	48	8	9	6	*11	*17	6
	Czech Republic	Olympics	3	0	0	0	6	....	....	....	....	....
	NHL Totals		**13**	**8**	**3**	**11**	**0**	....	....	....	....	....

AHL Second All-Star Team (1997)

CAMERON, DAVID — PIT.

Center. Shoots right. 6'1", 180 lbs. Born, Winnipeg, Man., April 27, 1980.
(Pittsburgh's 3rd choice, 80th overall, in 1998 Entry Draft).

			Regular Season					Playoffs				
Season	Club	Lea	GP	G	A	TP	PIM	GP	G	A	TP	PIM
1996-97	Lethbridge	WHL	38	3	3	6	5	....	....	....	....	....
	Prince Albert	WHL	18	3	4	7	11	3	0	2	2	0
1997-98	Prince Albert	WHL	69	20	36	56	42	....	....	....	....	....

CAMPBELL, BRIAN — BUF.

Defense. Shoots left. 5'11", 185 lbs. Born, Strathroy, Ont., May 23, 1979.
(Buffalo's 7th choice, 156th overall, in 1997 Entry Draft).

			Regular Season					Playoffs				
Season	Club	Lea	GP	G	A	TP	PIM	GP	G	A	TP	PIM
1995-96	Ottawa	OHL	66	5	22	27	23	4	0	1	1	2
1996-97	Ottawa	OHL	66	7	36	43	12	24	2	11	13	8
1997-98	Ottawa	OHL	66	14	39	53	31	13	1	14	15	0

CAMPBELL, ED — NYR

Defense. Shoots left. 6'2", 212 lbs. Born, Worcester, MA, November 26, 1974.
(NY Rangers' 9th choice, 190th overall, in 1993 Entry Draft).

			Regular Season					Playoffs				
Season	Club	Lea	GP	G	A	TP	PIM	GP	G	A	TP	PIM
1992-93	Omaha	USHL	42	9	19	28	160	....	....	....	....	....
1993-94	U. Mass-Lowell	H.E.	40	8	16	24	114	....	....	....	....	....
1994-95	U. Mass-Lowell	H.E.	34	6	24	30	105	....	....	....	....	....
1995-96	U. Mass-Lowell	H.E.	39	6	33	39	*107	....	....	....	....	....
1996-97	Binghamton	AHL	74	5	17	22	108	4	0	0	0	2
1997-98	Hartford	AHL	9	0	1	1	9	14	0	2	2	33
	Fort Wayne	IHL	50	10	5	15	147	....	....	....	....	....

CAMPBELL, JIM — ST.L.

Center. Shoots right. 6'2", 185 lbs. Born, Worcester, MA, April 3, 1973.
(Montreal's 2nd choice, 28th overall, in 1991 Entry Draft).

			Regular Season					Playoffs				
Season	Club	Lea	GP	G	A	TP	PIM	GP	G	A	TP	PIM
1990-91	Northwood Prep	H.S.	26	36	47	83	36	....	....	....	....	....
1991-92	Hull	QMJHL	64	41	44	85	51	6	7	3	10	8
1992-93	Hull	QMJHL	50	42	29	71	66	8	11	4	15	43
1993-94	United States	Nat-Tm	56	24	33	57	59	....	....	....	....	....
	United States	Olympics	8	0	0	0	6	....	....	....	....	....
	Fredericton	AHL	19	6	17	23	6	....	....	....	....	....
1994-95	Fredericton	AHL	77	27	24	51	103	12	0	7	7	8
1995-96	Fredericton	AHL	44	28	23	51	24	....	....	....	....	....
	Anaheim	**NHL**	**16**	**2**	**3**	**5**	**36**	....	....	....	....	....
	Baltimore	AHL	16	13	7	20	8	12	7	5	12	10
1996-97	**St. Louis**	**NHL**	**68**	**23**	**20**	**43**	**68**	**4**	**1**	**0**	**1**	**6**
1997-98	**St. Louis**	**NHL**	**76**	**22**	**19**	**41**	**55**	**10**	**7**	**3**	**10**	**12**
	NHL Totals		**160**	**47**	**42**	**89**	**159**	**14**	**8**	**3**	**11**	**18**

NHL All-Rookie Team (1997)

Traded to **Anaheim** by **Montreal** for Robert Dirk, January 21, 1996. Signed as a free agent by **St. Louis**, July 11, 1996.

CARBONNEAU, GUY — (KAR-buhn-oh, GEE) — DAL.

Center. Shoots right. 5'11", 186 lbs. Born, Sept-Iles, Que., March 18, 1960.
(Montreal's 4th choice, 44th overall, in 1979 Entry Draft).

			Regular Season					Playoffs				
Season	Club	Lea	GP	G	A	TP	PIM	GP	G	A	TP	PIM
1976-77	Chicoutimi	QMJHL	59	9	20	29	8	4	1	0	1	0
1977-78	Chicoutimi	QMJHL	70	28	55	83	60	....	....	....	....	....
1978-79	Chicoutimi	QMJHL	72	62	79	141	47	4	2	1	3	4
1979-80	Chicoutimi	QMJHL	72	72	110	182	66	12	9	15	24	28
	Nova Scotia	AHL	....	....	....	....	....	2	1	1	2	2
1980-81	**Montreal**	**NHL**	**2**	**0**	**1**	**1**	**0**	....	....	....	....	....
	Nova Scotia	AHL	78	35	53	88	87	6	1	3	4	9
1981-82	Nova Scotia	AHL	77	27	67	94	124	9	2	7	9	8
1982-83	**Montreal**	**NHL**	**77**	**18**	**29**	**47**	**68**	**3**	**0**	**0**	**0**	**2**
1983-84	**Montreal**	**NHL**	**78**	**24**	**30**	**54**	**75**	**15**	**4**	**3**	**7**	**12**
1984-85	**Montreal**	**NHL**	**79**	**23**	**34**	**57**	**43**	**12**	**4**	**3**	**7**	**8**
1985-86	**Montreal**	**NHL**	**80**	**20**	**36**	**56**	**57**	**20**	**7**	**5**	**12**	**35** ♦
1986-87	**Montreal**	**NHL**	**79**	**18**	**27**	**45**	**68**	**17**	**3**	**8**	**11**	**20**
1987-88	**Montreal**	**NHL**	**80**	**17**	**21**	**38**	**61**	**11**	**0**	**4**	**4**	**2**
1988-89	**Montreal**	**NHL**	**79**	**26**	**30**	**56**	**44**	**21**	**4**	**5**	**9**	**10**
1989-90	**Montreal**	**NHL**	**68**	**19**	**36**	**55**	**37**	**11**	**2**	**3**	**5**	**6**
1990-91	**Montreal**	**NHL**	**78**	**20**	**24**	**44**	**63**	**13**	**1**	**5**	**6**	**10**
1991-92	**Montreal**	**NHL**	**72**	**18**	**21**	**39**	**39**	**11**	**1**	**1**	**2**	**6**
1992-93	**Montreal**	**NHL**	**61**	**4**	**13**	**17**	**20**	**20**	**3**	**3**	**6**	**10** ♦
1993-94	**Montreal**	**NHL**	**79**	**14**	**24**	**38**	**48**	**7**	**1**	**3**	**4**	**4**
1994-95	**St. Louis**	**NHL**	**42**	**5**	**11**	**16**	**16**	**7**	**1**	**2**	**3**	**6**
1995-96	**Dallas**	**NHL**	**71**	**8**	**15**	**23**	**38**	....	....	....	....	....
1996-97	**Dallas**	**NHL**	**73**	**5**	**16**	**21**	**36**	**7**	**0**	**1**	**1**	**6**
1997-98	**Dallas**	**NHL**	**77**	**7**	**17**	**24**	**40**	**16**	**3**	**1**	**4**	**6**
	NHL Totals		**1175**	**246**	**385**	**631**	**753**	**191**	**34**	**47**	**81**	**143**

QMJHL Second All-Star Team (1980) • Won Frank J. Selke Trophy (1988, 1989, 1992)

Traded to **St. Louis** by **Montreal** for Jim Montgomery, August 19, 1994. Traded to **Dallas** by **St. Louis** for Paul Broten, October 2, 1995.

CARDARELLI, JOE — T.B.

Left wing. Shoots left. 6', 203 lbs. Born, Vancouver, B.C., June 13, 1977.
(Tampa Bay's 7th choice, 186th overall, in 1995 Entry Draft).

			Regular Season					Playoffs				
Season	Club	Lea	GP	G	A	TP	PIM	GP	G	A	TP	PIM
1993-94	Spokane	WHL	51	7	11	18	9	2	0	0	0	0
1994-95	Spokane	WHL	71	27	22	49	20	11	4	9	13	0
1995-96	Spokane	WHL	44	25	19	44	21	18	4	0	4	4
1996-97	Spokane	WHL	66	34	37	71	39	9	6	1	7	0
1997-98	Adirondack	AHL	30	0	3	3	2	....	....	....	....	....
	Chesapeake	ECHL	8	2	4	6	4	3	0	1	1	0

CARKNER, TERRY — FLA.

Defense. Shoots left. 6'3", 210 lbs. Born, Smiths Falls, Ont., March 7, 1966.
(NY Rangers' 1st choice, 14th overall, in 1984 Entry Draft).

			Regular Season					Playoffs				
Season	Club	Lea	GP	G	A	TP	PIM	GP	G	A	TP	PIM
1983-84	Peterborough	OHL	58	4	19	23	77	8	0	6	6	13
1984-85	Peterborough	OHL	64	14	47	61	125	17	2	10	12	11
1985-86	Peterborough	OHL	54	12	32	44	106	16	1	7	8	17
1986-87	**NY Rangers**	**NHL**	**52**	**2**	**13**	**15**	**118**	**1**	**0**	**0**	**0**	**0**
	New Haven	AHL	12	2	6	8	56	3	1	0	1	0
1987-88	**Quebec**	**NHL**	**63**	**3**	**24**	**27**	**159**	....	....	....	....	....
1988-89	**Philadelphia**	**NHL**	**78**	**11**	**32**	**43**	**149**	**19**	**1**	**5**	**6**	**28**
1989-90	**Philadelphia**	**NHL**	**63**	**4**	**18**	**22**	**169**	....	....	....	....	....
1990-91	**Philadelphia**	**NHL**	**79**	**7**	**25**	**32**	**204**	....	....	....	....	....
1991-92	**Philadelphia**	**NHL**	**73**	**4**	**12**	**16**	**195**	....	....	....	....	....
1992-93	**Philadelphia**	**NHL**	**83**	**3**	**16**	**19**	**150**	....	....	....	....	....
1993-94	**Detroit**	**NHL**	**68**	**1**	**6**	**7**	**130**	**7**	**0**	**0**	**0**	**4**
1994-95	**Detroit**	**NHL**	**20**	**1**	**2**	**3**	**21**	....	....	....	....	....
1995-96	**Florida**	**NHL**	**73**	**3**	**10**	**13**	**80**	**22**	**0**	**4**	**4**	**10**
1996-97	**Florida**	**NHL**	**70**	**0**	**14**	**14**	**96**	**5**	**0**	**0**	**0**	**6**
1997-98	**Florida**	**NHL**	**74**	**1**	**7**	**8**	**63**	....	....	....	....	....
	NHL Totals		**796**	**40**	**179**	**219**	**1534**	**54**	**1**	**9**	**10**	**48**

OHL Second All-Star Team (1985) • OHL First All-Star Team (1986)

Traded to **Quebec** by **NY Rangers** with Jeff Jackson for John Ogrodnick and David Shaw, September 30, 1987. Traded to **Philadelphia** by **Quebec** for Greg Smyth and Philadelphia's 3rd round choice (John Tanner) in the 1989 Entry Draft, July 25, 1988. Traded to **Detroit** by **Philadelphia** for Yves Racine and Detroit's 4th round choice (Sebastien Vallee) in 1994 Entry Draft, October 5, 1993. Signed as a free agent by **Florida**, August 8, 1995.

CARNEY, KEITH — PHX.

Defense. Shoots left. 6'2", 205 lbs. Born, Providence, RI, February 3, 1970.
(Buffalo's 3rd choice, 76th overall, in 1988 Entry Draft).

			Regular Season					Playoffs				
Season	Club	Lea	GP	G	A	TP	PIM	GP	G	A	TP	PIM
1987-88	Mt. St. Charles	H.S.	23	12	43	55	....	....	....	....	....	....
1988-89	U. of Maine	H.E.	40	4	22	26	24	....	....	....	....	....
1989-90	U. of Maine	H.E.	41	3	41	44	43	....	....	....	....	....
1990-91	U. of Maine	H.E.	40	7	49	56	38	....	....	....	....	....
1991-92	United States	Nat-Tm	49	2	17	19	16	....	....	....	....	....
	Buffalo	**NHL**	**14**	**1**	**2**	**3**	**18**	**7**	**0**	**3**	**3**	**0**
	Rochester	AHL	24	1	10	11	2	2	0	2	2	0
1992-93	**Buffalo**	**NHL**	**30**	**2**	**4**	**6**	**55**	**8**	**0**	**3**	**3**	**6**
	Rochester	AHL	41	5	21	26	32	....	....	....	....	....
1993-94	**Buffalo**	**NHL**	**7**	**1**	**3**	**4**	**4**	....	....	....	....	....
	Chicago	**NHL**	**30**	**3**	**5**	**8**	**35**	**6**	**0**	**1**	**1**	**4**
	Indianapolis	IHL	28	0	14	14	20	....	....	....	....	....
1994-95	**Chicago**	**NHL**	**18**	**1**	**0**	**1**	**11**	**4**	**0**	**1**	**1**	**0**
1995-96	**Chicago**	**NHL**	**82**	**5**	**14**	**19**	**94**	**10**	**0**	**3**	**3**	**4**
1996-97	**Chicago**	**NHL**	**81**	**3**	**15**	**18**	**62**	**6**	**1**	**1**	**2**	**2**
1997-98	**Chicago**	**NHL**	**60**	**2**	**13**	**15**	**73**	....	....	....	....	....
	United States	Olympics	4	0	0	0	2	....	....	....	....	....
	Phoenix	**NHL**	**20**	**1**	**6**	**7**	**18**	**6**	**0**	**0**	**0**	**4**
	NHL Totals		**342**	**19**	**62**	**81**	**370**	**47**	**1**	**12**	**13**	**20**

Hockey East Second All-Star Team (1990) • NCAA East Second All-American Team (1990) • Hockey East First All-Star Team (1991) • NCAA East First All-American Team (1991)

Traded to **Chicago** by **Buffalo** with Buffalo's 6th round choice (Marc Magliarditi) in 1995 Entry Draft for Craig Muni and Chicago's 5th round choice (Daniel Bienvenue) in 1995 Entry Draft, October 26, 1993. Traded to **Phoenix** by **Chicago** with Jim Cummins for Chad Kilger and Jayson More, March 4, 1998.

CARPENTER, BOB — N.J.

Center. Shoots left. 6', 200 lbs. Born, Beverly, MA, July 13, 1963.
(Washington's 1st choice, 3rd overall, in 1981 Entry Draft).

			Regular Season					Playoffs				
Season	Club	Lea	GP	G	A	TP	PIM	GP	G	A	TP	PIM
1980-81	St. John's Prep	H.S.	18	14	24	38	....	....	....	....	....	....
1981-82	**Washington**	**NHL**	**80**	**32**	**35**	**67**	**69**	....	....	....	....	....
1982-83	**Washington**	**NHL**	**80**	**32**	**37**	**69**	**64**	**4**	**1**	**0**	**1**	**2**
1983-84	**Washington**	**NHL**	**80**	**28**	**40**	**68**	**51**	**8**	**2**	**1**	**3**	**25**
1984-85	**Washington**	**NHL**	**80**	**53**	**42**	**95**	**87**	**5**	**1**	**4**	**5**	**8**
1985-86	**Washington**	**NHL**	**80**	**27**	**29**	**56**	**105**	**9**	**5**	**4**	**9**	**12**
1986-87	**Washington**	**NHL**	**22**	**5**	**7**	**12**	**21**	....	....	....	....	....
	NY Rangers	**NHL**	**28**	**2**	**8**	**10**	**20**	....	....	....	....	....
	Los Angeles	**NHL**	**10**	**2**	**3**	**5**	**6**	**5**	**1**	**2**	**3**	**2**
1987-88	**Los Angeles**	**NHL**	**71**	**19**	**33**	**52**	**84**	**5**	**1**	**1**	**2**	**0**
1988-89	**Los Angeles**	**NHL**	**39**	**11**	**15**	**26**	**16**	....	....	....	....	....
	Boston	**NHL**	**18**	**5**	**9**	**14**	**10**	**8**	**1**	**1**	**2**	**4**
1989-90	**Boston**	**NHL**	**80**	**25**	**31**	**56**	**97**	**21**	**4**	**6**	**10**	**39**
1990-91	**Boston**	**NHL**	**29**	**8**	**8**	**16**	**22**	**1**	**0**	**1**	**1**	**2**
1991-92	**Boston**	**NHL**	**60**	**25**	**23**	**48**	**46**	**8**	**0**	**1**	**1**	**6**
1992-93	**Washington**	**NHL**	**68**	**11**	**17**	**28**	**65**	**6**	**1**	**4**	**5**	**6**
1993-94	**New Jersey**	**NHL**	**76**	**10**	**23**	**33**	**51**	**20**	**1**	**7**	**8**	**20**
1994-95	**New Jersey**	**NHL**	**41**	**5**	**11**	**16**	**19**	**17**	**1**	**4**	**5**	**6** ♦
1995-96	**New Jersey**	**NHL**	**52**	**5**	**5**	**10**	**14**	....	....	....	....	....
1996-97	**New Jersey**	**NHL**	**62**	**4**	**15**	**19**	**14**	**10**	**1**	**2**	**3**	**2**
1997-98	**New Jersey**	**NHL**	**66**	**9**	**9**	**18**	**22**	**6**	**1**	**0**	**1**	**0**
	NHL Totals		**1122**	**318**	**400**	**718**	**883**	**133**	**21**	**38**	**59**	**134**

Played in NHL All-Star Game (1985)

Traded to **NY Rangers** by **Washington** with Washington's 2nd round choice (Jason Prosofsky) in 1989 Entry Draft for Bob Crawford, Kelly Miller and Mike Ridley, January 1, 1987. Traded to **LA Kings** by **NY Rangers** with Tom Laidlaw for Jeff Crossman, Marcel Dionne and LA Kings' 3rd round choice (later traded to Minnesota — Minnesota selected Murray Garbutt) in 1989 Entry Draft. Traded to **Boston** by **LA Kings** for Steve Kasper, January 23, 1989. Signed as a free agent by **Washington**, June 30, 1992. Signed as a free agent by **New Jersey**, September 30, 1993.

CARSON, JIMMY

Center. Shoots right. 6'1", 200 lbs. Born, Southfield, MI, July 20, 1968.
(Los Angeles' 1st choice, 2nd overall, in 1986 Entry Draft).

			Regular Season					Playoffs				
Season	Club	Lea	GP	G	A	TP	PIM	GP	G	A	TP	PIM
1984-85	Verdun	QMJHL	68	44	72	116	12	14	9	17	26	12
1985-86	Verdun	QMJHL	69	70	83	153	46	5	2	6	8	0
1986-87	**Los Angeles**	**NHL**	**80**	**37**	**42**	**79**	**22**	**5**	**1**	**2**	**3**	**6**
1987-88	**Los Angeles**	**NHL**	**80**	**55**	**52**	**107**	**45**	**5**	**5**	**3**	**8**	**4**
1988-89	**Edmonton**	**NHL**	**80**	**49**	**51**	**100**	**36**	**7**	**2**	**1**	**3**	**6**
1989-90	**Edmonton**	**NHL**	**4**	**1**	**2**	**3**	**0**	....	....	....	....	....
	Detroit	**NHL**	**44**	**20**	**16**	**36**	**8**	....	....	....	....	....
1990-91	**Detroit**	**NHL**	**64**	**21**	**25**	**46**	**28**	**7**	**2**	**1**	**3**	**4**
1991-92	**Detroit**	**NHL**	**80**	**34**	**35**	**69**	**30**	**11**	**2**	**3**	**5**	**0**
1992-93	**Detroit**	**NHL**	**52**	**25**	**26**	**51**	**18**	....	....	....	....	....
	Los Angeles	**NHL**	**34**	**12**	**10**	**22**	**14**	**18**	**5**	**4**	**9**	**2**
1993-94	**Los Angeles**	**NHL**	**25**	**4**	**7**	**11**	**2**	....	....	....	....	....
	Vancouver	**NHL**	**34**	**7**	**10**	**17**	**22**	**2**	**0**	**1**	**1**	**0**
1994-95	**Hartford**	**NHL**	**38**	**9**	**10**	**19**	**29**	....	....	....	....	....
1995-96	**Hartford**	**NHL**	**11**	**1**	**0**	**1**	**0**	....	....	....	....	....
	Lausanne	Switz.	13	3	4	7	14	....	....	....	....	....
1996-97	Detroit	IHL	18	7	16	23	4	13	4	6	10	12
1997-98	Detroit	IHL	49	10	28	38	34	9	3	4	7	6
	NHL Totals		**626**	**275**	**286**	**561**	**254**	**55**	**17**	**15**	**32**	**22**

QMJHL Second All-Star Team (1986) • Named to NHL All-Rookie Team (1987)

Played in NHL All-Star Game (1989)

Traded to **Edmonton** by **LA Kings** with Martin Gelinas, LA Kings' 1st round choices in 1989 (later traded to New Jersey — New Jersey selected Jason Miller), 1991 (Martin Rucinsky) and 1993 (Nick Stajduhar) Entry Drafts and cash for Wayne Gretzky, Mike Krushelnyski and Marty McSorley, August 9, 1988. Traded to **Detroit** by **Edmonton** with Kevin McClelland and Edmonton's 5th round choice (later traded to Montreal — Montreal selected Brad Layzell) in 1991 Entry Draft for Petr Klima, Joe Murphy, Adam Graves and Jeff Sharples, November 2, 1989. Traded to **LA Kings** by **Detroit** with Marc Potvin and Gary Shuchuk for Paul Coffey, Sylvain Couturier and Jim Hiller, January 29, 1993. Traded to **Vancouver** by **LA Kings** for Dixon Ward, January 8, 1994. Signed as a free agent by **Hartford**, July 15, 1994.

CARTER, ANSON — BOS.

Center. Shoots right. 6'1", 185 lbs. Born, Toronto, Ont., June 6, 1974.
(Quebec's 11th choice, 220th overall, in 1992 Entry Draft).

			Regular Season					Playoffs				
Season	Club	Lea	GP	G	A	TP	PIM	GP	G	A	TP	PIM
1991-92	Wexford	MJHL	42	18	22	40	24	....	....	....	....	....
1992-93	Michigan State	CCHA	34	15	7	22	20	....	....	....	....	....
1993-94	Michigan State	CCHA	39	30	24	54	36	....	....	....	....	....
1994-95	Michigan State	CCHA	39	34	17	51	40	....	....	....	....	....
1995-96	Michigan State	CCHA	42	23	20	43	36	....	....	....	....	....
1996-97	**Washington**	**NHL**	**19**	**3**	**2**	**5**	**7**	....	....	....	....	....
	Portland	AHL	27	19	19	38	11	....	....	....	....	....
	Boston	**NHL**	**19**	**8**	**5**	**13**	**2**	....	....	....	....	....
1997-98	**Boston**	**NHL**	**78**	**16**	**27**	**43**	**31**	**6**	**1**	**1**	**2**	**0**
	NHL Totals		**116**	**27**	**34**	**61**	**40**	**6**	**1**	**1**	**2**	**0**

CCHA First All-Star Team (1994, 1995) • NCAA West Second All-American Team (1995) • CCHA Second All-Star Team (1996)

Rights transferred to **Colorado** after **Quebec** franchise relocated, June 21, 1995. Traded to **Washington** by **Colorado** for Washington's 4th round choice (Ben Storey) in 1996 Entry Draft, April 3, 1996. Traded to **Boston** by **Washington** with Jim Carey, Jason Allison and Washington's 3rd round choice (Lee Goren) in 1997 Entry Draft for Bill Ranford, Adam Oates and Rick Tocchet, March 1, 1997.

CARTER, SHAWN

Center. Shoots left. 6'2", 210 lbs. Born, Eagle River, WI, April 16, 1973.

			Regular Season					Playoffs				
Season	Club	Lea	GP	G	A	TP	PIM	GP	G	A	TP	PIM
1992-93	U. of Wisconsin	WCHA	5	1	0	1	4	....	....	....	....	....
1993-94	U. of Wisconsin	WCHA	16	2	2	4	24	....	....	....	....	....
1994-95	U. of Wisconsin	WCHA	43	15	13	28	98	....	....	....	....	....
1995-96	U. of Wisconsin	WCHA	40	17	28	45	50	....	....	....	....	....
1996-97	Orlando	IHL	53	22	25	47	40	....	....	....	....	....
	St. John's	AHL	18	5	6	11	15	7	1	2	3	6
1997-98	St. John's	AHL	80	14	16	30	117	4	1	0	1	4

Signed as a free agent by **Toronto**, February 14, 1997.

CASSELMAN, MIKE

Center. Shoots left. 5'11", 190 lbs. Born, Morrisburg, Ont., August 23, 1968.
(Detroit's 1st choice, 3rd overall, in 1990 Supplemental Draft).

			Regular Season					Playoffs				
Season	Club	Lea	GP	G	A	TP	PIM	GP	G	A	TP	PIM
1987-88	Clarkson	ECAC	24	4	1	5	....	....	....	....	....	....
1988-89	Clarkson	ECAC	31	3	14	17	....	....	....	....	....	....
1989-90	Clarkson	ECAC	34	22	21	43	69	....	....	....	....	....
1990-91	Clarkson	ECAC	40	19	35	54	44	....	....	....	....	....
1991-92	Toledo	ECHL	61	39	60	99	83	5	0	1	1	6
	Adirondack	AHL	1	0	0	0	0	....	....	....	....	....
1992-93	Adirondack	AHL	60	12	19	31	27	8	3	3	6	0
	Toledo	ECHL	3	0	1	1	2	....	....	....	....	....
1993-94	Adirondack	AHL	77	17	38	55	34	12	2	4	6	10
1994-95	Adirondack	AHL	60	17	43	60	42	4	0	0	0	2
1995-96	**Florida**	**NHL**	**3**	**0**	**0**	**0**	**0**	....	....	....	....	....
	Carolina	AHL	70	34	68	102	46	....	....	....	....	....
1996-97	Cincinnati	IHL	68	30	34	64	54	3	1	0	1	2
1997-98	Cincinnati	IHL	55	19	28	47	44	....	....	....	....	....
	Rochester	AHL	25	8	7	15	14	4	1	1	2	2
	NHL Totals		**3**	**0**	**0**	**0**	**0**	....	....	....	....	....

ECHL Second All-Star Team (1992)

Signed as a free agent by **Florida**, October 31, 1995. Signed as a free agent by **San Jose**, September 24, 1997.

CASSELS, ANDREW — (KAS-uhls) — CGY.

Center. Shoots left. 6'1", 185 lbs. Born, Bramalea, Ont., July 23, 1969.
(Montreal's 1st choice, 17th overall, in 1987 Entry Draft).

			Regular Season					Playoffs				
Season	Club	Lea	GP	G	A	TP	PIM	GP	G	A	TP	PIM
1986-87	Ottawa	OHL	66	26	66	92	28	11	5	9	14	7
1987-88	Ottawa	OHL	61	48	*103	*151	39	16	8	*24	*32	13
1988-89	Ottawa	OHL	56	37	97	134	66	12	5	10	15	10
1989-90	**Montreal**	**NHL**	**6**	**2**	**0**	**2**	**2**	....	....	....	....	....
	Sherbrooke	AHL	55	22	45	67	25	12	2	11	13	6
1990-91	**Montreal**	**NHL**	**54**	**6**	**19**	**25**	**20**	**8**	**0**	**2**	**2**	**2**
1991-92	**Hartford**	**NHL**	**67**	**11**	**30**	**41**	**18**	**7**	**2**	**4**	**6**	**6**
1992-93	**Hartford**	**NHL**	**84**	**21**	**64**	**85**	**62**	....	....	....	....	....
1993-94	**Hartford**	**NHL**	**79**	**16**	**42**	**58**	**37**	....	....	....	....	....
1994-95	**Hartford**	**NHL**	**46**	**7**	**30**	**37**	**18**	....	....	....	....	....
1995-96	**Hartford**	**NHL**	**81**	**20**	**43**	**63**	**39**	....	....	....	....	....
1996-97	**Hartford**	**NHL**	**81**	**22**	**44**	**66**	**46**	....	....	....	....	....
1997-98	**Calgary**	**NHL**	**81**	**17**	**27**	**44**	**32**	....	....	....	....	....
	NHL Totals		**579**	**122**	**299**	**421**	**274**	**15**	**2**	**6**	**8**	**8**

OHL First All-Star Team (1988,1989)

Traded to **Hartford** by **Montreal** for Hartford's 2nd round choice (Valeri Bure) in 1992 Entry Draft, September 17, 1991. Transferred to **Carolina** after **Hartford** franchise relocated, June 25, 1997. Traded to **Calgary** by **Carolina** with Jean-Sebastien Giguere for Gary Roberts and Trevor Kidd, August 25, 1997.

CAULFIELD, KEVIN — WSH.

Right wing. Shoots right. 6'2", 210 lbs. Born, Boston, MA, January 7, 1978.
(Washington's 4th choice, 116th overall, in 1997 Entry Draft).

			Regular Season					Playoffs				
Season	Club	Lea	GP	G	A	TP	PIM	GP	G	A	TP	PIM
1995-96	Thayer Academy	H.S.	31	12	23	35	45	....	....	....	....	....
1996-97	Boston College	H.E.	38	5	10	15	90	....	....	....	....	....
1997-98	Boston College	H.E.	41	9	6	15	82	....	....	....	....	....

CAVA, PETER — (KAH-va)

Center. Shoots left. 5'11", 175 lbs. Born, Thunder Bay, Ont., February 14, 1978.
(Toronto's 7th choice, 110th overall, in 1996 Entry Draft).

			Regular Season					Playoffs				
Season	Club	Lea	GP	G	A	TP	PIM	GP	G	A	TP	PIM
1995-96	S.S. Marie	OHL	40	14	17	31	44	4	1	1	2	4
1996-97	S.S. Marie	OHL	55	14	36	50	64	11	5	4	9	27
1997-98	S.S. Marie	OHL	64	30	60	90	86	....	....	....	....	....
	St. John's	AHL	2	0	0	0	0	....	....	....	....	....
	Thunder Bay	UHL	....	....	....	....	....	5	2	4	6	4

CECH, VRATISLAV (CHEHKH) FLA.

Defense. Shoots left. 6'3", 196 lbs. Born, Tabor, Czech., January 28, 1979.
(Florida's 3rd choice, 56th overall, in 1997 Entry Draft).

			Regular Season					Playoffs				
Season	Club	Lea	GP	G	A	TP	PIM	GP	G	A	TP	PIM
1995-96	HC Brno	Czech-Jr.	37	10	13	23	....	....	....	....	....	....
1996-97	Kitchener	OHL	57	5	19	24	72	13	1	2	3	12
1997-98	Kitchener	OHL	63	9	33	42	66	6	2	2	4	13

CERVEN, MARTIN (CHEHR-vehn) PHI.

Center. Shoots left. 6'4", 200 lbs. Born, Trencin, Czech., March 7, 1977.
(Edmonton's 6th choice, 161st overall, in 1995 Entry Draft).

			Regular Season					Playoffs				
Season	Club	Lea	GP	G	A	TP	PIM	GP	G	A	TP	PIM
1994-95	Dukla Trencin	Slov-Jr.	22	8	3	11	....	....	....	....	....	....
1995-96	Spokane	WHL	40	9	9	18	42	....	....	....	....	....
	Seattle	WHL	27	6	14	20	10	5	1	2	3	0
1996-97	Seattle	WHL	72	27	25	52	64	15	2	6	8	14
1997-98	Philadelphia	AHL	50	7	11	18	27	8	1	2	3	2

Traded to **Philadelphia** by **Edmonton** for Philadelphia's 7th round choice (Chad Hinz) in 1997 Entry Draft, June 18, 1997.

CHAMBERS, SHAWN DAL.

Defense. Shoots left. 6'2", 200 lbs. Born, Sterling Hts., MI, October 11, 1966.
(Minnesota's 1st choice, 4th overall, in 1987 Supplemental Draft).

			Regular Season					Playoffs				
Season	Club	Lea	GP	G	A	TP	PIM	GP	G	A	TP	PIM
1985-86	Alaska-Fairbanks	G.N.	25	15	21	36	34	....	....	....	....	....
1986-87	Alaska-Fairbanks	G.N.	28	11	19	30	84	....	....	....	....	....
	Seattle	WHL	28	8	25	33	58	....	....	....	....	....
	Fort Wayne	IHL	12	2	6	8	0	10	1	4	5	5
1987-88	**Minnesota**	**NHL**	**19**	**1**	**7**	**8**	**21**	....	....	....	....	....
	Kalamazoo	IHL	19	1	6	7	22	....	....	....	....	....
1988-89	**Minnesota**	**NHL**	**72**	**5**	**19**	**24**	**80**	**3**	**0**	**2**	**2**	**0**
1989-90	**Minnesota**	**NHL**	**78**	**8**	**18**	**26**	**81**	**7**	**2**	**1**	**3**	**10**
1990-91	**Minnesota**	**NHL**	**29**	**1**	**3**	**4**	**24**	**23**	**0**	**7**	**7**	**16**
	Kalamazoo	IHL	3	1	1	2	0	....	....	....	....	....
1991-92	**Washington**	**NHL**	**2**	**0**	**0**	**0**	**2**	....	....	....	....	....
	Baltimore	AHL	5	2	3	5	9	....	....	....	....	....
1992-93	**Tampa Bay**	**NHL**	**55**	**10**	**29**	**39**	**36**	....	....	....	....	....
	Atlanta	IHL	6	0	2	2	18	....	....	....	....	....
1993-94	**Tampa Bay**	**NHL**	**66**	**11**	**23**	**34**	**23**	....	....	....	....	....
1994-95	**Tampa Bay**	**NHL**	**24**	**2**	**12**	**14**	**6**	....	....	....	....	....
	New Jersey	**NHL**	**21**	**2**	**5**	**7**	**6**	**20**	**4**	**5**	**9**	**2** ♦
1995-96	**New Jersey**	**NHL**	**64**	**2**	**21**	**23**	**18**	....	....	....	....	....
1996-97	**New Jersey**	**NHL**	**73**	**4**	**17**	**21**	**19**	**10**	**1**	**6**	**7**	**6**
1997-98	**Dallas**	**NHL**	**57**	**2**	**22**	**24**	**26**	**14**	**0**	**3**	**3**	**20**
	NHL Totals		**560**	**48**	**176**	**224**	**342**	**77**	**7**	**24**	**31**	**54**

Traded to **Washington** by **Minnesota** for Steve Maltais and Trent Klatt, June 21, 1991. Claimed by **Tampa Bay** from **Washington** in Expansion Draft, June 18, 1992. Traded to **New Jersey** by **Tampa Bay** with Danton Cole for Alexander Semak and Ben Hankinson, March 14, 1995. Signed as a free agent by **Dallas**, July 17, 1997.

CHARA, ZDENO (KHAH-rah, ZDEH-noh) NYI

Defense. Shoots left. 6'9", 255 lbs. Born, Trencin, Czech., March 18, 1977.
(NY Islanders' 3rd choice, 56th overall, in 1996 Entry Draft).

			Regular Season					Playoffs				
Season	Club	Lea	GP	G	A	TP	PIM	GP	G	A	TP	PIM
1994-95	Dukla Trencin	Slov-Jr.	2	0	0	0	0	....	....	....	....	....
	Dukla Trencin	Slov-Jr.	30	22	22	44	113	....	....	....	....	....
1995-96	Dukla Trencin	Slov-Jr.	22	1	13	14	80	....	....	....	....	....
	Piestany	Slov-2	10	1	3	4	10	....	....	....	....	....
	Sparta Praha	Czech-Jr.	15	1	2	3	42	....	....	....	....	....
	Sparta Praha	Cze-Rep.	1	0	0	0	0	....	....	....	....	....
1996-97	Prince George	WHL	49	3	19	22	120	15	1	7	8	45
1997-98	**NY Islanders**	**NHL**	**25**	**0**	**1**	**1**	**50**	....	....	....	....	....
	Kentucky	AHL	48	4	9	13	125	1	0	0	0	4
	NHL Totals		**25**	**0**	**1**	**1**	**50**	....	....	....	....	....

CHARRON, ERIC (shah-ROHN) CGY.

Defense. Shoots left. 6'3", 195 lbs. Born, Verdun, Que., January 14, 1970.
(Montreal's 1st choice, 20th overall, in 1988 Entry Draft).

			Regular Season					Playoffs				
Season	Club	Lea	GP	G	A	TP	PIM	GP	G	A	TP	PIM
1987-88	Trois-Rivieres	QMJHL	67	3	13	16	135	....	....	....	....	....
1988-89	Trois-Rivieres	QMJHL	38	2	16	18	111	....	....	....	....	....
	Verdun	QMJHL	28	2	15	17	66	....	....	....	....	....
	Sherbrooke	AHL	1	0	0	0	0	....	....	....	....	....
1989-90	St-Hyacinthe	QMJHL	68	13	38	51	152	11	3	4	7	67
	Sherbrooke	AHL	....	....	....	....	....	2	0	0	0	0
1990-91	Fredericton	AHL	71	1	11	12	108	2	1	0	1	29
1991-92	Fredericton	AHL	59	2	11	13	98	6	1	0	1	4
1992-93	**Montreal**	**NHL**	**3**	**0**	**0**	**0**	**2**	....	....	....	....	....
	Fredericton	AHL	54	3	13	16	93	....	....	....	....	....
	Atlanta	IHL	11	0	2	2	12	3	0	1	1	6
1993-94	**Tampa Bay**	**NHL**	**4**	**0**	**0**	**0**	**2**	....	....	....	....	....
	Atlanta	IHL	66	5	18	23	144	14	1	4	5	28
1994-95	**Tampa Bay**	**NHL**	**45**	**1**	**4**	**5**	**26**	....	....	....	....	....
1995-96	**Tampa Bay**	**NHL**	**14**	**0**	**0**	**0**	**18**	....	....	....	....	....
	Washington	**NHL**	**4**	**0**	**1**	**1**	**4**	**6**	**0**	**0**	**0**	**8**
	Portland	AHL	45	0	8	8	88	20	1	1	2	33
1996-97	**Washington**	**NHL**	**25**	**1**	**1**	**2**	**20**	....	....	....	....	....
	Portland	AHL	29	6	8	14	55	5	0	3	3	0
1997-98	**Calgary**	**NHL**	**2**	**0**	**0**	**0**	**4**	....	....	....	....	....
	Saint John	AHL	56	8	20	28	136	20	1	7	8	55
	NHL Totals		**97**	**2**	**6**	**8**	**76**	**6**	**0**	**0**	**0**	**8**

Traded to **Tampa Bay** by **Montreal** with Alain Cote and future considerations (Donald Dufresne, June 18, 1993) for Rob Ramage, March 20, 1993. Traded to **Washington** by **Tampa Bay** for Washington's 7th round choice (Eero Somervuori) in 1997 Entry Draft, November 16, 1995. Traded to **Calgary** by **Washington** for Calgary's 7th round choice (Nathan Forster) in 1998 Entry Draft, September 4, 1997.

CHASE, KELLY ST.L.

Right wing. Shoots right. 5'11", 193 lbs. Born, Porcupine Plain, Sask., October 25, 1967.

			Regular Season					Playoffs				
Season	Club	Lea	GP	G	A	TP	PIM	GP	G	A	TP	PIM
1985-86	Saskatoon	WHL	57	7	18	25	172	10	3	4	7	37
1986-87	Saskatoon	WHL	68	17	29	46	285	11	2	8	10	37
1987-88	Saskatoon	WHL	70	21	34	55	*343	9	3	5	8	32
1988-89	Peoria	IHL	38	14	7	21	278	....	....	....	....	....
1989-90	**St. Louis**	**NHL**	**43**	**1**	**3**	**4**	**244**	**9**	**1**	**0**	**1**	**46**
	Peoria	IHL	10	1	2	3	76	....	....	....	....	....
1990-91	**St. Louis**	**NHL**	**2**	**1**	**0**	**1**	**15**	**6**	**0**	**0**	**0**	**18**
	Peoria	IHL	61	20	34	54	406	10	4	3	7	61
1991-92	**St. Louis**	**NHL**	**46**	**1**	**2**	**3**	**264**	**1**	**0**	**0**	**0**	**7**
1992-93	**St. Louis**	**NHL**	**49**	**2**	**5**	**7**	**204**	....	....	....	....	....
1993-94	**St. Louis**	**NHL**	**68**	**2**	**5**	**7**	**278**	**4**	**0**	**1**	**1**	**6**
1994-95	**Hartford**	**NHL**	**28**	**0**	**4**	**4**	**141**	....	....	....	....	....
1995-96	**Hartford**	**NHL**	**55**	**2**	**4**	**6**	**230**	....	....	....	....	....
1996-97	**Hartford**	**NHL**	**28**	**1**	**2**	**3**	**122**	....	....	....	....	....
	Toronto	**NHL**	**2**	**0**	**0**	**0**	**27**	....	....	....	....	....
1997-98	**St. Louis**	**NHL**	**67**	**4**	**3**	**7**	**231**	**7**	**0**	**0**	**0**	**23**
	NHL Totals		**388**	**14**	**28**	**42**	**1756**	**27**	**1**	**1**	**2**	**100**

Won King Clancy Memorial Trophy (1998)

Signed as a free agent by **St. Louis**, February 23, 1988. Claimed by **Hartford** from **St. Louis** in NHL Waiver Draft, January 18, 1995. Traded to **Toronto** by **Hartford** for Toronto's 8th round choice (Hartford/Carolina selected Jaroslav Svoboda) in 1998 Entry Draft, March 18, 1997. Traded to **St. Louis** by **Toronto** for future considerations, September 30, 1997.

CHASSE, DENIS (shah-SAY)

Right wing. Shoots right. 6'2", 200 lbs. Born, Montreal, Que., February 7, 1970.

			Regular Season					Playoffs				
Season	Club	Lea	GP	G	A	TP	PIM	GP	G	A	TP	PIM
1987-88	St-Jean	QMJHL	13	0	1	1	2	1	0	0	0	0
1988-89	Verdun	QMJHL	38	12	12	24	61	....	....	....	....	....
	Drummondville	QMJHL	30	15	16	31	77	3	0	2	2	28
1989-90	Drummondville	QMJHL	34	14	29	43	85	....	....	....	....	....
	Chicoutimi	QMJHL	33	19	27	46	105	7	7	4	11	50
1990-91	Drummondville	QMJHL	62	47	54	101	246	13	9	11	20	56
1991-92	Halifax	AHL	73	26	35	61	254	....	....	....	....	....
1992-93	Halifax	AHL	75	35	41	76	242	....	....	....	....	....
1993-94	**St. Louis**	**NHL**	**3**	**0**	**1**	**1**	**15**	....	....	....	....	....
	Cornwall	AHL	48	27	39	66	194	....	....	....	....	....
1994-95	**St. Louis**	**NHL**	**47**	**7**	**9**	**16**	**133**	**7**	**1**	**7**	**8**	**23**
1995-96	**St. Louis**	**NHL**	**42**	**3**	**0**	**3**	**108**	....	....	....	....	....
	Worcester	AHL	3	0	0	0	6	....	....	....	....	....
	Washington	**NHL**	**3**	**0**	**0**	**0**	**5**	....	....	....	....	....
	Winnipeg	**NHL**	**15**	**0**	**0**	**0**	**12**	....	....	....	....	....
1996-97	**Ottawa**	**NHL**	**22**	**1**	**4**	**5**	**19**	....	....	....	....	....
	Detroit	IHL	9	2	1	3	33	....	....	....	....	....
	Indianapolis	IHL	3	0	0	0	10	4	1	1	2	23
1997-98	Mannheim	EuroHL	3	0	1	1	12	....	....	....	....	....
	Mannheim	Germany	15	2	5	7	72	....	....	....	....	....
	Augsburg	Germany	29	6	6	12	97	....	....	....	....	....
	NHL Totals		**132**	**11**	**14**	**25**	**292**	**7**	**1**	**7**	**8**	**23**

Signed as a free agent by **Quebec**, May 14, 1991. Traded to **St. Louis** by **Quebec** with Steve Duchesne for Garth Butcher, Ron Sutter and Bob Bassen, January 23, 1994. Traded to **Washington** by **St. Louis** for Rob Pearson, January 29, 1996. Traded to **Winnipeg** by **Washington** for Stewart Malgunas, February 15, 1996. Signed as a free agent by **Ottawa**, September 5, 1996. Traded to **Chicago** by **Ottawa** with the rights to Kevin Bolibruck and Ottawa's 6th round choice (traded back to Ottawa - Ottawa selected Christopher Neil) in 1998 Entry Draft for Mike Prokopec, March 18, 1997.

CHEBATURKIN, VLADIMIR (cheh-bah-TOOR-kihn) NYI

Defense. Shoots left. 6'2", 213 lbs. Born, Tyumen, USSR, April 23, 1975.
(NY Islanders' 3rd choice, 66th overall, in 1993 Entry Draft).

			Regular Season					Playoffs				
Season	Club	Lea	GP	G	A	TP	PIM	GP	G	A	TP	PIM
1993-94	Kristall	CIS-2	42	4	4	8	38	....	....	....	....	....
1994-95	Kristall	CIS	52	2	6	8	90	....	....	....	....	....
1995-96	Kristall	CIS	44	1	6	7	30	1	0	0	0	0
1996-97	Utah	IHL	68	0	4	4	34	....	....	....	....	....
1997-98	**NY Islanders**	**NHL**	**2**	**0**	**2**	**2**	**0**	....	....	....	....	....
	Kentucky	AHL	54	6	8	14	52	2	0	0	0	4
	NHL Totals		**2**	**0**	**2**	**2**	**0**	....	....	....	....	....

CHEECHOO, JONATHAN (CHEE-choo) S.J.

Right wing. Shoots right. 6', 205 lbs. Born, Moose Factory, Ont., July 15, 1980.
(San Jose's 2nd choice, 29th overall, in 1998 Entry Draft).

			Regular Season					Playoffs				
Season	Club	Lea	GP	G	A	TP	PIM	GP	G	A	TP	PIM
1996-97	Kitchener	OJHL	43	35	41	76	33	....	....	....	....	....
1997-98	Belleville	OHL	64	31	45	76	62	10	4	2	6	10

CHELIOS, CHRIS (CHELL-EE-ohs) CHI.

Defense. Shoots right. 6'1", 190 lbs. Born, Chicago, IL, January 25, 1962.
(Montreal's 5th choice, 40th overall, in 1981 Entry Draft).

			Regular Season					Playoffs				
Season	Club	Lea	GP	G	A	TP	PIM	GP	G	A	TP	PIM
1980-81	Moose Jaw	SJHL	54	23	64	87	175	....	....	....	....	....
1981-82	U. of Wisconsin	WCHA	43	6	43	49	50	....	....	....	....	....
1982-83	U. of Wisconsin	WCHA	26	9	17	26	50	....	....	....	....	....
1983-84	United States	Nat-Tm	60	14	35	49	58	....	....	....	....	....
	United States	Olympics	6	0	4	4	8	....	....	....	....	....
	Montreal	**NHL**	**12**	**0**	**2**	**2**	**12**	**15**	**1**	**9**	**10**	**17**
1984-85	**Montreal**	**NHL**	**74**	**9**	**55**	**64**	**87**	**9**	**2**	**8**	**10**	**17**
1985-86	**Montreal**	**NHL**	**41**	**8**	**26**	**34**	**67**	**20**	**2**	**9**	**11**	**49 ♦**
1986-87	**Montreal**	**NHL**	**71**	**11**	**33**	**44**	**124**	**17**	**4**	**9**	**13**	**38**
1987-88	**Montreal**	**NHL**	**71**	**20**	**41**	**61**	**172**	**11**	**3**	**1**	**4**	**29**
1988-89	**Montreal**	**NHL**	**80**	**15**	**58**	**73**	**185**	**21**	**4**	**15**	**19**	**28**
1989-90	**Montreal**	**NHL**	**53**	**9**	**22**	**31**	**136**	**5**	**0**	**1**	**1**	**8**
1990-91	**Chicago**	**NHL**	**77**	**12**	**52**	**64**	**192**	**6**	**1**	**7**	**8**	**46**
1991-92	**Chicago**	**NHL**	**80**	**9**	**47**	**56**	**245**	**18**	**6**	**15**	**21**	**37**
1992-93	**Chicago**	**NHL**	**84**	**15**	**58**	**73**	**282**	**4**	**0**	**2**	**2**	**14**
1993-94	**Chicago**	**NHL**	**76**	**16**	**44**	**60**	**212**	**6**	**1**	**1**	**2**	**8**
1994-95	EC Biel	Switz.	3	0	3	3	4	....	....	....	....	....
	Chicago	**NHL**	**48**	**5**	**33**	**38**	**72**	**16**	**4**	**7**	**11**	**12**
1995-96	**Chicago**	**NHL**	**81**	**14**	**58**	**72**	**140**	**9**	**0**	**3**	**3**	**8**
1996-97	**Chicago**	**NHL**	**72**	**10**	**38**	**48**	**112**	**6**	**0**	**1**	**1**	**8**
1997-98	**Chicago**	**NHL**	**81**	**3**	**39**	**42**	**151**	....	....	....	....	....
	United States	Olympics	2	0	2	2	2	....	....	....	....	....
	NHL Totals		**1001**	**156**	**606**	**762**	**2189**	**163**	**28**	**88**	**116**	**319**

WCHA Second All-Star Team (1983) • NCAA Championship All-Tournament Team (1983) • NHL All-Rookie Team (1985) • NHL First All-Star Team (1989, 1993, 1995, 1996) • Won James Norris Memorial Trophy (1989, 1993, 1996) • NHL Second All-Star Team (1991, 1997)

Played in NHL All-Star Game (1985, 1990, 1991, 1992, 1993, 1994, 1996, 1997, 1998)

Traded to **Chicago** by **Montreal** with Montreal's 2nd round choice (Michael Pomichter) in 1991 Entry Draft for Denis Savard, June 29, 1990.

CHEREDARYK, STEVE (shair-a-DAIR-ehk) MTL.

Defense. Shoots left. 6'3", 213 lbs. Born, Calgary, Alta., November 20, 1975.
(Winnipeg's 4th choice, 82nd overall, in 1994 Entry Draft).

			Regular Season					Playoffs				
Season	Club	Lea	GP	G	A	TP	PIM	GP	G	A	TP	PIM
1992-93	Medicine Hat	WHL	67	1	9	10	88	10	0	1	1	16
1993-94	Medicine Hat	WHL	72	3	35	38	151	3	0	1	1	9
1994-95	Medicine Hat	WHL	70	3	26	29	193	5	0	1	1	13
	Springfield	AHL	3	0	1	1	0	....	....	....	....	....
1995-96	Springfield	AHL	32	0	1	1	36	....	....	....	....	....
	Knoxville	ECHL	13	0	10	10	72	6	2	4	6	12
1996-97	Springfield	AHL	46	1	2	3	69	....	....	....	....	....
	Fredericton	AHL	14	0	1	1	24	....	....	....	....	....
	Mississippi	ECHL	9	0	1	1	33	....	....	....	....	....
1997-98	Fredericton	AHL	4	0	0	0	8	....	....	....	....	....
	New Orleans	ECHL	59	4	16	20	214	2	0	0	0	16

Rights transferred to **Phoenix** after **Winnipeg** franchise relocated, July 1, 1996. Traded to **Montreal** by **Phoenix** for Pat Jablonski, March 18, 1997.

CHERNESKI, STEFAN (chuhr-NEHS-kee) NYR

Right wing. Shoots left. 6', 195 lbs. Born, Winnipeg, Man., September 19, 1978.
(NY Rangers' 1st choice, 19th overall, in 1997 Entry Draft).

			Regular Season					Playoffs				
Season	Club	Lea	GP	G	A	TP	PIM	GP	G	A	TP	PIM
1995-96	Brandon	WHL	58	8	21	29	62	19	3	1	4	11
1996-97	Brandon	WHL	56	39	29	68	83	....	....	....	....	....
1997-98	Brandon	WHL	65	43	38	81	127	18	*15	8	23	21

CHERNOV, MIKHAIL (chair-NAHF) PHI.

Defense. Shoots right. 6'2", 196 lbs. Born, Prokopjevsk, USSR, November 11, 1978.
(Philadelphia's 4th choice, 103rd overall, in 1997 Entry Draft).

			Regular Season					Playoffs				
Season	Club	Lea	GP	G	A	TP	PIM	GP	G	A	TP	PIM
1996-97	Yaroslavl 2	Russia-3	33	4	2	6	40	....	....	....	....	....
	Yaroslavl	Russia	5	0	0	0	0	....	....	....	....	....
1997-98	Yaroslavl	Russia	7	0	0	0	4	....	....	....	....	....
	Yaroslavl 2	Russia-2	STATISTICS NOT AVAILABLE									

CHIASSON, STEVE (CHAY-sahn) CAR.

Defense. Shoots left. 6'1", 205 lbs. Born, Barrie, Ont., April 14, 1967.
(Detroit's 3rd choice, 50th overall, in 1985 Entry Draft).

			Regular Season					Playoffs				
Season	Club	Lea	GP	G	A	TP	PIM	GP	G	A	TP	PIM
1984-85	Guelph	OHL	61	8	22	30	139	....	....	....	....	....
1985-86	Guelph	OHL	54	12	30	42	126	18	10	10	20	37
1986-87	**Detroit**	**NHL**	**45**	**1**	**4**	**5**	**73**	**2**	**0**	**0**	**0**	**19**
1987-88	**Detroit**	**NHL**	**29**	**2**	**9**	**11**	**57**	**9**	**2**	**2**	**4**	**31**
	Adirondack	AHL	23	6	11	17	58	....	....	....	....	....
1988-89	**Detroit**	**NHL**	**65**	**12**	**35**	**47**	**149**	**5**	**2**	**1**	**3**	**6**
1989-90	**Detroit**	**NHL**	**67**	**14**	**28**	**42**	**114**	....	....	....	....	....
1990-91	**Detroit**	**NHL**	**42**	**3**	**17**	**20**	**80**	**5**	**3**	**1**	**4**	**19**
1991-92	**Detroit**	**NHL**	**62**	**10**	**24**	**34**	**136**	**11**	**1**	**5**	**6**	**12**
1992-93	**Detroit**	**NHL**	**79**	**12**	**50**	**62**	**155**	**7**	**2**	**2**	**4**	**19**
1993-94	**Detroit**	**NHL**	**82**	**13**	**33**	**46**	**122**	**7**	**2**	**3**	**5**	**2**
1994-95	**Calgary**	**NHL**	**45**	**2**	**23**	**25**	**39**	**7**	**1**	**2**	**3**	**9**
1995-96	**Calgary**	**NHL**	**76**	**8**	**25**	**33**	**62**	**4**	**2**	**1**	**3**	**0**
1996-97	**Calgary**	**NHL**	**47**	**5**	**11**	**16**	**32**	....	....	....	....	....
	Hartford	**NHL**	**18**	**3**	**11**	**14**	**7**	....	....	....	....	....
1997-98	**Carolina**	**NHL**	**66**	**7**	**27**	**34**	**65**	....	....	....	....	....
	NHL Totals		**723**	**92**	**297**	**389**	**1091**	**57**	**15**	**17**	**32**	**117**

Won Stafford Smythe Memorial Trophy (Memorial Cup Tournament MVP) (1986)

Played in NHL All-Star Game (1993)

Traded to **Calgary** by **Detroit** for Mike Vernon, June 29, 1994. Traded to **Hartford** by **Calgary** with Colorado's 3rd round choice (previously acquired, Hartford/Carolina selected Francis Lessard) in 1997 Entry Draft for Hnat Domenichelli, Glen Featherstone, New Jersey's 2nd round choice (previously acquired, Calgary selected Dimitri Kokorev) in 1997 Entry Draft and Vancouver's 3rd round choice (previously acquired, Calgary selected Paul Manning) in 1998 Entry Draft, March 5, 1997. Transferred to **Carolina** after **Hartford** franchise relocated, June 25, 1997.

CHIMERA, JASON (CHIHM-air-a) EDM.

Center. Shoots left. 6', 180 lbs. Born, Edmonton, Alta., May 2, 1979.
(Edmonton's 5th choice, 121st overall, in 1997 Entry Draft).

			Regular Season					Playoffs				
Season	Club	Lea	GP	G	A	TP	PIM	GP	G	A	TP	PIM
1996-97	Medicine Hat	WHL	71	16	23	39	64	4	0	1	1	4
1997-98	Medicine Hat	WHL	72	34	32	66	93	....	....	....	....	....
	Hamilton	AHL	4	0	0	0	8	....	....	....	....	....

CHORSKE, TOM (CHOHR-skee) NYI

Left wing. Shoots right. 6'1", 212 lbs. Born, Minneapolis, MN, September 18, 1966.
(Montreal's 2nd choice, 16th overall, in 1985 Entry Draft).

			Regular Season					Playoffs				
Season	Club	Lea	GP	G	A	TP	PIM	GP	G	A	TP	PIM
1984-85	Minn-Southwest	H.S.	23	44	26	70	....	....	....	....	....	....
1985-86	U. of Minnesota	WCHA	39	6	4	10	16	....	....	....	....	....
1986-87	U. of Minnesota	WCHA	47	20	22	42	20	....	....	....	....	....
1987-88	United States	Nat-Tm	36	9	16	25	24	....	....	....	....	....
1988-89	U. of Minnesota	WCHA	37	25	24	49	28	....	....	....	....	....
1989-90	**Montreal**	**NHL**	**14**	**3**	**1**	**4**	**2**	....	....	....	....	....
	Sherbrooke	AHL	59	22	24	46	54	12	4	4	8	8
1990-91	**Montreal**	**NHL**	**57**	**9**	**11**	**20**	**32**	....	....	....	....	....
1991-92	**New Jersey**	**NHL**	**76**	**19**	**17**	**36**	**32**	**7**	**0**	**3**	**3**	**4**
1992-93	**New Jersey**	**NHL**	**50**	**7**	**12**	**19**	**25**	**1**	**0**	**0**	**0**	**0**
	Utica	AHL	6	1	4	5	2	....	....	....	....	....
1993-94	**New Jersey**	**NHL**	**76**	**21**	**20**	**41**	**32**	**20**	**4**	**3**	**7**	**0**
1994-95	HC Milano	Italy	7	11	5	16	6	....	....	....	....	....
	New Jersey	**NHL**	**42**	**10**	**8**	**18**	**16**	**17**	**1**	**5**	**6**	**4 ♦**
1995-96	**Ottawa**	**NHL**	**72**	**15**	**14**	**29**	**21**	....	....	....	....	....
1996-97	**Ottawa**	**NHL**	**68**	**18**	**8**	**26**	**16**	**5**	**0**	**1**	**1**	**2**
1997-98	**NY Islanders**	**NHL**	**82**	**12**	**23**	**35**	**39**	....	....	....	....	....
	NHL Totals		**537**	**114**	**114**	**228**	**215**	**50**	**5**	**12**	**17**	**10**

WCHA First All-Star Team (1989)

Traded to **New Jersey** by **Montreal** with Stephane Richer for Kirk Muller and Roland Melanson, September 20, 1991. Claimed on waivers by **Ottawa** from **New Jersey**, October 5, 1995. Claimed by **NY Islanders** from **Ottawa** in NHL Waiver Draft, September 28, 1997.

CHOUINARD, ERIC (shwee-NAHR) MTL.

Center. Shoots left. 6'2", 195 lbs. Born, Atlanta, GA, July 8, 1980.
(Montreal's 1st choice, 16th overall, in 1998 Entry Draft).

			Regular Season					Playoffs				
Season	Club	Lea	GP	G	A	TP	PIM	GP	G	A	TP	PIM
1996-97	Ste-Foy	QAAA	40	29	41	70	40	....	....	....	....	....
1997-98	Quebec	QMJHL	68	41	42	83	18	14	7	10	17	6

CHOUINARD, MARC (shwee-NAHR) ANA.

Center. Shoots right. 6'5", 200 lbs. Born, Charlesbourg, Ont., May 5, 1977.
(Winnipeg's 2nd choice, 32nd overall, in 1995 Entry Draft).

			Regular Season					Playoffs				
Season	Club	Lea	GP	G	A	TP	PIM	GP	G	A	TP	PIM
1993-94	Beauport	QMJHL	62	11	19	30	23	13	2	5	7	2
1994-95	Beauport	QMJHL	68	24	40	64	32	18	1	6	7	4
1995-96	Beauport	QMJHL	30	14	21	35	19	....	....	....	....	....
	Halifax	QMJHL	24	6	12	18	17	6	2	1	3	2
1996-97	Halifax	QMJHL	63	24	49	73	74	18	9	16	25	12
1997-98	Cincinnati	AHL	8	1	2	3	4	....	....	....	....	....

Traded to **Anaheim** by **Winnipeg** with Teemu Selanne and Winnipeg's 4th round choice (later traded to Toronto — later traded to Montreal — Montreal selected Kim Staal) in 1996 Entry Draft for Chad Kilger, Oleg Tverdovsky and Anaheim's 3rd round choice (Per-Anton Ludstrom) in 1996 Entry Draft, February 7, 1996.

CHRISTIAN, JEFF

Left wing. Shoots left. 6'2", 210 lbs. Born, Burlington, Ont., July 30, 1970.
(New Jersey's 2nd choice, 23rd overall, in 1988 Entry Draft).

			Regular Season					Playoffs				
Season	Club	Lea	GP	G	A	TP	PIM	GP	G	A	TP	PIM
1987-88	London	OHL	64	15	29	44	154	9	1	5	6	27
1988-89	London	OHL	60	27	30	57	221	20	3	4	7	56
1989-90	London	OHL	18	14	7	21	64	....	....	....	....	....
	Owen Sound	OHL	37	19	26	45	145	10	6	7	13	43
1990-91	Utica	AHL	80	24	42	66	165	....	....	....	....	....
1991-92	**New Jersey**	**NHL**	**2**	**0**	**0**	**0**	**2**	....	....	....	....	....
	Utica	AHL	76	27	24	51	198	4	0	0	0	16
1992-93	Utica	AHL	22	4	6	10	39	....	....	....	....	....
	Hamilton	AHL	11	2	5	7	35	....	....	....	....	....
	Cincinnati	IHL	36	5	12	17	113	....	....	....	....	....
1993-94	Albany	AHL	76	34	43	77	227	5	1	2	3	19
1994-95	**Pittsburgh**	**NHL**	**1**	**0**	**0**	**0**	**0**	....	....	....	....	....
	Cleveland	IHL	56	13	24	37	126	2	0	1	1	8
1995-96	**Pittsburgh**	**NHL**	**3**	**0**	**0**	**0**	**2**	....	....	....	....	....
	Cleveland	IHL	66	23	32	55	131	3	0	1	1	8
1996-97	**Pittsburgh**	**NHL**	**11**	**2**	**2**	**4**	**13**	....	....	....	....	....
	Cleveland	IHL	69	40	40	80	262	12	6	8	14	44
1997-98	**Phoenix**	**NHL**	**1**	**0**	**0**	**0**	**0**	....	....	....	....	....
	Las Vegas	IHL	30	12	15	27	90	4	2	2	4	20
	NHL Totals		**18**	**2**	**2**	**4**	**17**	....	....	....	....	....

Signed as a free agent by **Pittsburgh**, August 2, 1994. Signed as a free agent by **Phoenix**, July 28, 1997.

CHRISTIE, RYAN DAL.

Left wing. Shoots left. 6'2", 175 lbs. Born, Beamsville, Ont., July 3, 1978.
(Dallas' 4th choice, 112th overall, in 1996 Entry Draft).

			Regular Season					Playoffs				
Season	Club	Lea	GP	G	A	TP	PIM	GP	G	A	TP	PIM
1995-96	Owen Sound	OHL	66	29	17	46	93	6	1	1	2	0
1996-97	Owen Sound	OHL	66	23	29	52	136	4	1	1	2	8
1997-98	Owen Sound	OHL	66	39	41	80	208	11	3	5	8	13

CHUBAROV, ARTEM (choo-BAH-rahf) VAN.

Center. Shoots left. 6'1", 189 lbs. Born, Gorky, USSR, December 13, 1979.
(Vancouver's 2nd choice, 31st overall, in 1998 Entry Draft).

			Regular Season					Playoffs				
Season	Club	Lea	GP	G	A	TP	PIM	GP	G	A	TP	PIM
1996-97	Nizhny Novogrod	Russia-3	40	24	5	29	16	....	....	....	....	....
	Nizhny Novgorod	Russia-2	15	1	1	2	8	....	....	....	....	....
1997-98	Moscow D'amo	Russia	30	1	4	5	4	....	....	....	....	....

CHURCH, BRAD — WSH.

Left wing. Shoots left. 6'1", 210 lbs. Born, Dauphin, Man., November 14, 1976.
(Washington's 1st choice, 17th overall, in 1995 Entry Draft).

			Regular Season					Playoffs				
Season	Club	Lea	GP	G	A	TP	PIM	GP	G	A	TP	PIM
1993-94	Prince Albert	WHL	71	33	20	53	197	....	....	....	....	....
1994-95	Prince Albert	WHL	62	26	24	50	184	15	6	9	15	32
1995-96	Prince Albert	WHL	69	42	46	88	123	18	15	*20	*35	74
1996-97	Portland	AHL	50	4	8	12	92	1	0	0	0	0
1997-98	**Washington**	**NHL**	**2**	**0**	**0**	**0**	**0**	....	....	....	....	....
	Portland	AHL	59	6	5	11	98	9	2	4	6	14
	NHL Totals		**2**	**0**	**0**	**0**	**0**	....	....	....	....	....

CHURLA, SHANE — (CHUHR-lah)

Right wing. Shoots right. 6'1", 200 lbs. Born, Fernie, B.C., June 24, 1965.
(Hartford's 4th choice, 110th overall, in 1985 Entry Draft).

			Regular Season					Playoffs				
Season	Club	Lea	GP	G	A	TP	PIM	GP	G	A	TP	PIM
1983-84	Medicine Hat	WHL	48	3	7	10	115	14	1	5	6	41
1984-85	Medicine Hat	WHL	70	14	20	34	370	9	1	0	1	55
1985-86	Binghamton	AHL	52	4	10	14	306	3	0	0	0	22
1986-87	**Hartford**	**NHL**	**20**	**0**	**1**	**1**	**78**	**2**	**0**	**0**	**0**	**42**
	Binghamton	AHL	24	1	5	6	249	....	....	....	....	....
1987-88	**Hartford**	**NHL**	**2**	**0**	**0**	**0**	**14**	....	....	....	....	....
	Binghamton	AHL	25	5	8	13	168	....	....	....	....	....
	Calgary	**NHL**	**29**	**1**	**5**	**6**	**132**	**7**	**0**	**1**	**1**	**17**
1988-89	**Calgary**	**NHL**	**5**	**0**	**0**	**0**	**25**	....	....	....	....	....
	Salt Lake	IHL	32	3	13	16	278	....	....	....	....	....
	Minnesota	**NHL**	**13**	**1**	**0**	**1**	**54**	....	....	....	....	....
1989-90	**Minnesota**	**NHL**	**53**	**2**	**3**	**5**	**292**	**7**	**0**	**0**	**0**	**44**
1990-91	**Minnesota**	**NHL**	**40**	**2**	**2**	**4**	**286**	**22**	**2**	**1**	**3**	**90**
1991-92	**Minnesota**	**NHL**	**57**	**4**	**1**	**5**	**278**	....	....	....	....	....
1992-93	**Minnesota**	**NHL**	**73**	**5**	**16**	**21**	**286**	....	....	....	....	....
1993-94	**Dallas**	**NHL**	**69**	**6**	**7**	**13**	**333**	**9**	**1**	**3**	**4**	**35**
1994-95	**Dallas**	**NHL**	**27**	**1**	**3**	**4**	**186**	**5**	**0**	**0**	**0**	**20**
1995-96	**Dallas**	**NHL**	**34**	**3**	**4**	**7**	**168**	....	....	....	....	....
	Los Angeles	**NHL**	**11**	**1**	**2**	**3**	**37**	....	....	....	....	....
	NY Rangers	**NHL**	**10**	**0**	**0**	**0**	**26**	**11**	**2**	**2**	**4**	**14**
1996-97	**NY Rangers**	**NHL**	**45**	**0**	**1**	**1**	**106**	**15**	**0**	**0**	**0**	**20**
1997-98	DID NOT PLAY – INJURED											
	NHL Totals		**488**	**26**	**45**	**71**	**2301**	**78**	**5**	**7**	**12**	**282**

Traded to **Calgary** by **Hartford** with Dana Murzyn for Neil Sheehy, Carey Wilson, and the rights to Lane MacDonald, January 3, 1988. Traded to **Minnesota** by **Calgary** with Perry Berezan for Brian MacLellan and Minnesota's 4th round choice (Robert Reichel) in 1989 Entry Draft, March 4, 1989. Claimed by **San Jose** from **Minnesota** in Dispersal Draft, May 30, 1991. Traded to **Minnesota** by **San Jose** for Kelly Kisio, June 3, 1991. Transferred to **Dallas** after **Minnesota** franchise relocated, June 9, 1993. Traded to **LA Kings** by **Dallas** with Doug Zmolek for Darryl Sydor and LA Kings' 5th round choice (Ryan Christie) in 1996 Entry Draft, February 17, 1996. Traded to **NY Rangers** by **LA Kings** with Marty McSorley and Jari Kurri for Ray Ferraro, Ian Laperriere, Mattias Norstrom, Nathan Lafayette and NY Rangers' 4th round choice (Sean Blanchard) in 1997 Entry Draft, March 14, 1996. • Missed entire 1997-98 season after undergoing off-season knee surgery.

CHYNOWETH, DEAN — (shih-NOWTH) BOS.

Defense. Shoots right. 6'1", 191 lbs. Born, Calgary, Alta., October 30, 1968.
(NY Islanders' 1st choice, 13th overall, in 1987 Entry Draft).

			Regular Season					Playoffs				
Season	Club	Lea	GP	G	A	TP	PIM	GP	G	A	TP	PIM
1985-86	Medicine Hat	WHL	69	3	12	15	208	17	3	2	5	52
1986-87	Medicine Hat	WHL	67	3	18	21	285	13	4	2	6	28
1987-88	Medicine Hat	WHL	64	1	21	22	274	16	0	6	6	*87
1988-89	**NY Islanders**	**NHL**	**6**	**0**	**0**	**0**	**48**	....	....	....	....	....
1989-90	**NY Islanders**	**NHL**	**20**	**0**	**2**	**2**	**39**	....	....	....	....	....
	Springfield	AHL	40	0	7	7	98	17	0	4	4	36
1990-91	**NY Islanders**	**NHL**	**25**	**1**	**1**	**2**	**59**	....	....	....	....	....
	Capital District	AHL	44	1	5	6	176	....	....	....	....	....
1991-92	**NY Islanders**	**NHL**	**11**	**1**	**0**	**1**	**23**	....	....	....	....	....
	Capital District	AHL	43	4	6	10	164	6	1	1	2	39
1992-93	Capital District	AHL	52	3	10	13	197	4	0	1	1	9
1993-94	**NY Islanders**	**NHL**	**39**	**0**	**4**	**4**	**122**	**2**	**0**	**0**	**0**	**2**
	Salt Lake	IHL	5	0	1	1	33	....	....	....	....	....
1994-95	**NY Islanders**	**NHL**	**32**	**0**	**2**	**2**	**77**	....	....	....	....	....
1995-96	**NY Islanders**	**NHL**	**14**	**0**	**1**	**1**	**40**	....	....	....	....	....
	Boston	**NHL**	**35**	**2**	**5**	**7**	**88**	**4**	**0**	**0**	**0**	**24**
1996-97	**Boston**	**NHL**	**57**	**0**	**3**	**3**	**171**	....	....	....	....	....
	Providence	AHL	2	0	0	0	13	....	....	....	....	....
1997-98	**Boston**	**NHL**	**2**	**0**	**0**	**0**	**0**	....	....	....	....	....
	Providence	AHL	28	2	2	4	123	....	....	....	....	....
	Quebec	IHL	15	2	2	4	39	....	....	....	....	....
	NHL Totals		**241**	**4**	**18**	**22**	**667**	**6**	**0**	**0**	**0**	**26**

Traded to **Boston** by **NY Islanders** for Boston's 5th round choice (Petr Sachl) in 1996 Entry Draft, December 9, 1995.

CHYZOWSKI, DAVE — (chih-ZOW-skee)

Left wing. Shoots left. 6'1", 190 lbs. Born, Edmonton, Alta., July 11, 1971.
(NY Islanders' 1st choice, 2nd overall, in 1989 Entry Draft).

			Regular Season					Playoffs				
Season	Club	Lea	GP	G	A	TP	PIM	GP	G	A	TP	PIM
1987-88	Kamloops	WHL	66	16	17	33	117	18	2	4	6	26
1988-89	Kamloops	WHL	68	56	48	104	139	16	15	13	28	32
1989-90	Kamloops	WHL	4	5	2	7	17	17	11	6	17	46
	NY Islanders	**NHL**	**34**	**8**	**6**	**14**	**45**	....	....	....	....	....
	Springfield	AHL	4	0	0	0	7	....	....	....	....	....
1990-91	**NY Islanders**	**NHL**	**56**	**5**	**9**	**14**	**61**	....	....	....	....	....
	Capital District	AHL	7	3	6	9	22	....	....	....	....	....
1991-92	**NY Islanders**	**NHL**	**12**	**1**	**1**	**2**	**17**	....	....	....	....	....
	Capital District	AHL	55	15	18	33	121	6	1	1	2	23
1992-93	Capital District	AHL	66	15	21	36	177	3	2	0	2	0
1993-94	**NY Islanders**	**NHL**	**3**	**1**	**0**	**1**	**4**	**2**	**0**	**0**	**0**	**0**
	Salt Lake	IHL	66	27	13	40	151	....	....	....	....	....
1994-95	**NY Islanders**	**NHL**	**13**	**0**	**0**	**0**	**11**	....	....	....	....	....
	Kalamazoo	IHL	4	0	4	4	8	16	9	5	14	27
1995-96	Adirondack	AHL	80	44	39	83	160	3	0	0	0	6
1996-97	**Chicago**	**NHL**	**8**	**0**	**0**	**0**	**6**	....	....	....	....	....
	Indianapolis	IHL	76	34	40	74	261	4	0	2	2	38
1997-98	Orlando	IHL	17	9	7	16	32	....	....	....	....	....
	San Antonio	IHL	10	1	5	6	39	....	....	....	....	....
	Kansas City	IHL	38	19	14	33	88	11	5	4	9	11
	NHL Totals		**126**	**15**	**16**	**31**	**144**	**2**	**0**	**0**	**0**	**0**

WHL West All-Star Team (1989)

Signed as a free agent by **Detroit**, August 29, 1995. Signed as a free agent by **Chicago**, September 26, 1996.

CIAVAGLIA, PETER — (see-a-VIHG-lee-a)

Center. Shoots left. 5'10", 173 lbs. Born, Albany, NY, July 15, 1969.
(Calgary's 8th choice, 145th overall, in 1987 Entry Draft).

			Regular Season					Playoffs				
Season	Club	Lea	GP	G	A	TP	PIM	GP	G	A	TP	PIM
1986-87	N. Wheatfield	NYJHL	23	53	84	137	....	....	....	....	....	....
1987-88	Harvard	ECAC	30	10	23	33	16	....	....	....	....	....
1988-89	Harvard	ECAC	34	15	48	63	36	....	....	....	....	....
1989-90	Harvard	ECAC	28	17	18	35	22	....	....	....	....	....
1990-91	Harvard	ECAC	27	24	*38	*62	2	....	....	....	....	....
1991-92	**Buffalo**	**NHL**	**2**	**0**	**0**	**0**	**0**	....	....	....	....	....
	Rochester	AHL	77	37	61	98	16	6	2	5	7	6
1992-93	**Buffalo**	**NHL**	**3**	**0**	**0**	**0**	**0**	....	....	....	....	....
	Rochester	AHL	64	35	67	102	32	17	9	16	25	12
1993-94	United States	Nat-Tm	18	2	9	11	6	....	....	....	....	....
	Leksand IF	Sweden	39	14	18	32	34	4	1	2	3	0
	United States	Olympics	8	2	4	6	0	....	....	....	....	....
1994-95	Detroit	IHL	73	22	59	81	83	5	1	1	2	6
1995-96	Detroit	IHL	75	22	56	78	38	12	6	11	17	12
1996-97	Detroit	IHL	72	21	51	72	54	21	*14	19	*33	32
1997-98	Detroit	IHL	35	11	30	41	10	23	8	11	19	12
	NHL Totals		**5**	**0**	**0**	**0**	**0**	....	....	....	....	....

ECAC Second All-Star Team (1989, 1991) • NCAA East Second All-American Team (1991) • Won "Bud" Poile Trophy (Playoff MVP - IHL) (1997)

Signed as a free agent by **Buffalo**, August 30, 1991.

CICCARELLI, DINO — (sih-sih-REHL-ee) FLA.

Right wing. Shoots right. 5'10", 185 lbs. Born, Sarnia, Ont., February 8, 1960.

			Regular Season					Playoffs				
Season	Club	Lea	GP	G	A	TP	PIM	GP	G	A	TP	PIM
1977-78	London	OHA	68	72	70	142	49	9	6	10	16	6
1978-79	London	OHA	30	8	11	19	35	7	3	5	8	0
1979-80	London	OHA	62	50	53	103	72	5	2	6	8	15
1980-81	**Minnesota**	**NHL**	**32**	**18**	**12**	**30**	**29**	**19**	**14**	**7**	**21**	**25**
	Oklahoma City	CHL	48	32	25	57	45	....	....	....	....	....
1981-82	**Minnesota**	**NHL**	**76**	**55**	**51**	**106**	**138**	**4**	**3**	**1**	**4**	**2**
1982-83	**Minnesota**	**NHL**	**77**	**37**	**38**	**75**	**94**	**9**	**4**	**6**	**10**	**11**
1983-84	**Minnesota**	**NHL**	**79**	**38**	**33**	**71**	**58**	**16**	**4**	**5**	**9**	**27**
1984-85	**Minnesota**	**NHL**	**51**	**15**	**17**	**32**	**41**	**9**	**3**	**3**	**6**	**8**
1985-86	**Minnesota**	**NHL**	**75**	**44**	**45**	**89**	**51**	**5**	**0**	**1**	**1**	**6**
1986-87	**Minnesota**	**NHL**	**80**	**52**	**51**	**103**	**88**	....	....	....	....	....
1987-88	**Minnesota**	**NHL**	**67**	**41**	**45**	**86**	**79**	....	....	....	....	....
1988-89	**Minnesota**	**NHL**	**65**	**32**	**27**	**59**	**64**	....	....	....	....	....
	Washington	**NHL**	**11**	**12**	**3**	**15**	**12**	**6**	**3**	**3**	**6**	**12**
1989-90	**Washington**	**NHL**	**80**	**41**	**38**	**79**	**122**	**8**	**8**	**3**	**11**	**6**
1990-91	**Washington**	**NHL**	**54**	**21**	**18**	**39**	**66**	**11**	**5**	**4**	**9**	**22**
1991-92	**Washington**	**NHL**	**78**	**38**	**38**	**76**	**78**	**7**	**5**	**4**	**9**	**14**
1992-93	**Detroit**	**NHL**	**82**	**41**	**56**	**97**	**81**	**7**	**4**	**2**	**6**	**16**
1993-94	**Detroit**	**NHL**	**66**	**28**	**29**	**57**	**73**	**7**	**5**	**2**	**7**	**14**
1994-95	**Detroit**	**NHL**	**42**	**16**	**27**	**43**	**39**	**16**	**9**	**2**	**11**	**22**
1995-96	**Detroit**	**NHL**	**64**	**22**	**21**	**43**	**99**	**17**	**6**	**2**	**8**	**26**
1996-97	**Tampa Bay**	**NHL**	**77**	**35**	**25**	**60**	**116**	....	....	....	....	....
1997-98	**Tampa Bay**	**NHL**	**34**	**11**	**6**	**17**	**42**	....	....	....	....	....
	Florida	**NHL**	**28**	**5**	**11**	**16**	**28**	....	....	....	....	....
	NHL Totals		**1218**	**602**	**591**	**1193**	**1398**	**141**	**73**	**45**	**118**	**211**

OHA Second All-Star Team (1978)

Played in NHL All-Star Game (1982, 1983, 1989, 1997)

Signed as a free agent by **Minnesota**, September 28, 1979. Traded to **Washington** by **Minnesota** with Bob Rouse for Mike Gartner and Larry Murphy, March 7, 1989. Traded to **Detroit** by **Washington** for Kevin Miller, June 20, 1992. Traded to **Tampa Bay** by **Detroit** for future considerations, August 27, 1996. Traded to **Florida** by **Tampa Bay** with Jeff Norton for Mark Fitzpatrick and Jody Hull, January 15, 1998.

CICCONE, ENRICO — (CHIH-koh-nee) T.B.

Defense. Shoots left. 6'5", 220 lbs. Born, Montreal, Que., April 10, 1970.
(Minnesota's 5th choice, 92nd overall, in 1990 Entry Draft).

			Regular Season					Playoffs				
Season	Club	Lea	GP	G	A	TP	PIM	GP	G	A	TP	PIM
1987-88	Shawinigan	QMJHL	61	2	12	14	324	....	....	....	....	....
1988-89	Shawinigan	QMJHL	34	7	11	18	132	....	....	....	....	....
	Trois-Rivieres	QMJHL	24	0	7	7	153	....	....	....	....	....
1989-90	Trois-Rivieres	QMJHL	40	4	24	28	227	3	0	0	0	15
1990-91	Kalamazoo	IHL	57	4	9	13	384	4	0	1	1	32
1991-92	**Minnesota**	**NHL**	**11**	**0**	**0**	**0**	**48**	....	....	....	....	....
	Kalamazoo	IHL	53	4	16	20	406	10	0	1	1	58
1992-93	**Minnesota**	**NHL**	**31**	**0**	**1**	**1**	**115**	....	....	....	....	....
	Kalamazoo	IHL	13	1	3	4	50	....	....	....	....	....
	Hamilton	AHL	6	1	3	4	44	....	....	....	....	....
1993-94	**Washington**	**NHL**	**46**	**1**	**1**	**2**	**174**	....	....	....	....	....
	Portland	AHL	6	0	0	0	27	....	....	....	....	....
	Tampa Bay	**NHL**	**11**	**0**	**1**	**1**	**52**	....	....	....	....	....
1994-95	**Tampa Bay**	**NHL**	**41**	**2**	**4**	**6**	***225**	....	....	....	....	....
1995-96	**Tampa Bay**	**NHL**	**55**	**2**	**3**	**5**	**258**	....	....	....	....	....
	Chicago	**NHL**	**11**	**0**	**1**	**1**	**48**	**9**	**1**	**0**	**1**	**30**
1996-97	**Chicago**	**NHL**	**67**	**2**	**2**	**4**	**233**	**4**	**0**	**0**	**0**	**18**
1997-98	**Carolina**	**NHL**	**14**	**0**	**3**	**3**	**83**	....	....	....	....	....
	Vancouver	**NHL**	**13**	**0**	**1**	**1**	**47**	....	....	....	....	....
	Tampa Bay	**NHL**	**12**	**0**	**0**	**0**	**45**	....	....	....	....	....
	NHL Totals		**312**	**7**	**17**	**24**	**1328**	**13**	**1**	**0**	**1**	**48**

Traded to **Washington** by **Dallas** to complete transaction that sent Paul Cavallini to Dallas (June 20, 1993), June 25, 1993. Traded to **Tampa Bay** by **Washington** with Washington's 3rd round choice (later traded to Anaheim — Anaheim selected Craig Reichert) in 1994 Entry Draft and the return of future draft choices transferred in the Pat Elynuik trade for Joe Reekie, March 21, 1994. Traded to **Chicago** by **Tampa Bay** with Tampa Bay's 2nd round choice (Jeff Paul) in 1996 Entry Draft for Patrick Poulin, Igor Ulanov and Chicago's 2nd round choice (later traded to New Jersey — New Jersey selected Pierre Dagenais) in 1996 Entry Draft, March 20, 1996. Traded to **Carolina** by **Chicago** for Ryan Risidore and Carolina's 5th round choice in 1998 Entry Draft, July 25, 1997. Traded to **Vancouver** by **Carolina** with Sean Burke and Geoff Sanderson for Kirk McLean and Martin Gelinas, January 3, 1998. Traded to **Tampa Bay** by **Vancouver** for Jamie Huscroft, March 14, 1998.

CIERNIK, IVAN (CHAIR-nihk, ee-VAHN) OTT.

Left wing. Shoots left. 6'1", 198 lbs. Born, Levice, Czech., October 30, 1977.
(Ottawa's 6th choice, 216th overall, in 1996 Entry Draft).

			Regular Season					Playoffs				
Season	Club	Lea	GP	G	A	TP	PIM	GP	G	A	TP	PIM
1994-95	MHC Nitra	Slov-Jr.	30	22	15	37	36	....	....	....	....	....
	MHC Nitra	Slovakia	7	1	0	1	2	....	....	....	....	....
1995-96	MHC Nitra	Slovakia	35	9	7	16	36	8	3	3	6	....
1996-97	MHC Nitra	Slovakia	41	11	19	30	....	....	....	....	....	....
1997-98	**Ottawa**	**NHL**	**2**	**0**	**0**	**0**	**0**	....	....	....	....	....
	Worcester	AHL	53	9	12	21	38	1	0	0	0	2
	NHL Totals		**2**	**0**	**0**	**0**	**0**	....	....	....	....	....

CIERNY, JOZEF (chee-ER-nee) EDM.

Left wing. Shoots left. 6'2", 185 lbs. Born, Zvolen, Czech., May 13, 1974.
(Buffalo's 2nd choice, 35th overall, in 1992 Entry Draft).

			Regular Season					Playoffs				
Season	Club	Lea	GP	G	A	TP	PIM	GP	G	A	TP	PIM
1991-92	ZTK Zvolen	Czech-2	26	10	3	13	8	....	....	....	....	....
1992-93	Rochester	AHL	54	27	27	54	36	....	....	....	....	....
1993-94	**Edmonton**	**NHL**	**1**	**0**	**0**	**0**	**0**	....	....	....	....	....
	Cape Breton	AHL	73	30	27	57	88	4	1	1	2	4
1994-95	Cape Breton	AHL	73	28	24	52	58	....	....	....	....	....
1995-96	Detroit	IHL	20	2	5	7	16	....	....	....	....	....
	Los Angeles	IHL	43	23	16	39	36	....	....	....	....	....
1996-97	Long Beach	IHL	68	27	27	54	106	16	8	5	13	7
1997-98	Nurnberg	Germany	45	20	22	42	61	....	....	....	....	....
	NHL Totals		**1**	**0**	**0**	**0**	**0**	....	....	....	....	....

Traded to **Edmonton** by **Buffalo** with Buffalo's 4th round choice (Jussi Tarvainen) in 1994 Entry Draft for Craig Simpson, September 1, 1993.

CIGER, ZDENO (SEE-gu, ZDEH-noh) EDM.

Left wing. Shoots left. 6'1", 190 lbs. Born, Martin, Czech., October 19, 1969.
(New Jersey's 3rd choice, 54th overall, in 1988 Entry Draft).

			Regular Season					Playoffs				
Season	Club	Lea	GP	G	A	TP	PIM	GP	G	A	TP	PIM
1987-88	Dukla Trencin	Czech.	8	3	4	7	2	....	....	....	....	....
1988-89	Dukla Trencin	Czech.	43	18	13	31	18	....	....	....	....	....
1989-90	Dukla Trencin	Czech.	53	18	28	46	....	....	....	....	....	....
1990-91	**New Jersey**	**NHL**	**45**	**8**	**17**	**25**	**8**	**6**	**0**	**2**	**2**	**4**
	Utica	AHL	8	5	4	9	2	....	....	....	....	....
1991-92	**New Jersey**	**NHL**	**20**	**6**	**5**	**11**	**10**	**7**	**2**	**4**	**6**	**0**
1992-93	**New Jersey**	**NHL**	**27**	**4**	**8**	**12**	**2**	....	....	....	....	....
	Edmonton	**NHL**	**37**	**9**	**15**	**24**	**6**	....	....	....	....	....
1993-94	**Edmonton**	**NHL**	**84**	**22**	**35**	**57**	**8**	....	....	....	....	....
1994-95	Dukla Trencin	Slovakia	34	23	25	48	8	9	2	9	11	2
	Edmonton	**NHL**	**5**	**2**	**2**	**4**	**0**	....	....	....	....	....
1995-96	**Edmonton**	**NHL**	**78**	**31**	**39**	**70**	**41**	....	....	....	....	....
1996-97	Bratislava	Slovakia	44	26	27	53	....	2	1	3	4	....
1997-98	Bratislava	EuroHL	8	1	5	6	6	....	....	....	....	....
	Bratislava	Slovakia	36	14	*31	45	2	11	6	*10	*16	4
	Slovakia	Olympics	4	1	1	2	4	....	....	....	....	....
	NHL Totals		**296**	**82**	**121**	**203**	**75**	**13**	**2**	**6**	**8**	**4**

Czechoslovakian Rookie of the Year (1989)

Traded to **Edmonton** by **New Jersey** with Kevin Todd for Bernie Nicholls, January 13, 1993.

CISAR, MARIAN (SIH-sahr) NSH.

Right wing. Shoots right. 6', 176 lbs. Born, Bratislava, Czech., February 25, 1978.
(Los Angeles' 2nd choice, 37th overall, in 1996 Entry Draft).

			Regular Season					Playoffs				
Season	Club	Lea	GP	G	A	TP	PIM	GP	G	A	TP	PIM
1994-95	Bratislava	Slov-Jr.	38	42	28	70	16	....	....	....	....	....
1995-96	Bratislava	Slov-Jr.	16	26	17	43	2	....	....	....	....	....
	Bratislava	Slovakia	13	3	3	6	0	6	3	0	3	0
1996-97	Spokane	WHL	70	31	35	66	52	9	6	2	8	4
1997-98	Spokane	WHL	52	33	40	73	34	18	8	5	13	8

Traded to **Nashville** by **LA Kings** for future considerations, May 29, 1998.

CLARK, BRETT MTL.

Defense. Shoots left. 6', 182 lbs. Born, Moosomin, Sask., December 23, 1976.
(Montreal's 7th choice, 154th overall, in 1996 Entry Draft).

			Regular Season					Playoffs				
Season	Club	Lea	GP	G	A	TP	PIM	GP	G	A	TP	PIM
1995-96	U. of Maine	H.E.	39	7	31	38	22	....	....	....	....	....
1996-97	Canada	Nat-Tm	57	6	21	27	52	....	....	....	....	....
1997-98	**Montreal**	**NHL**	**41**	**1**	**0**	**1**	**20**	....	....	....	....	....
	Fredericton	AHL	20	0	6	6	6	4	0	1	1	17
	NHL Totals		**41**	**1**	**0**	**1**	**20**	....	....	....	....	....

CLARK, CHRIS CGY.

Right wing. Shoots right. 6', 190 lbs. Born, Manchester, CT, March 8, 1976.
(Calgary's 3rd choice, 77th overall, in 1994 Entry Draft).

			Regular Season					Playoffs				
Season	Club	Lea	GP	G	A	TP	PIM	GP	G	A	TP	PIM
1993-94	Springfield	NAJHL	35	31	26	57	185	....	....	....	....	....
1994-95	Clarkson	ECAC	32	12	11	23	92	....	....	....	....	....
1995-96	Clarkson	ECAC	38	10	8	18	108	....	....	....	....	....
1996-97	Clarkson	ECAC	37	23	25	48	*86	....	....	....	....	....
1997-98	Clarkson	ECAC	35	18	21	39	*106	....	....	....	....	....

ECAC Second All-Star Team (1998)

CLARK, JUSTIN COL.

Right wing. Shoots right. 6'3", 220 lbs. Born, Madison, WI, January 29, 1977.
(Colorado's 13th choice, 240th overall, in 1996 Entry Draft).

			Regular Season					Playoffs				
Season	Club	Lea	GP	G	A	TP	PIM	GP	G	A	TP	PIM
1995-96	U. of Michigan	CCHA	11	1	2	3	2	....	....	....	....	....
1996-97	U. of Michigan	CCHA	30	3	4	7	38	....	....	....	....	....
1997-98	U. of Michigan	CCHA	41	3	4	7	27	....	....	....	....	....

CLARK, RYAN NYI

Defense. Shoots left. 6'3", 205 lbs. Born, Edmonton, Alta., October 30, 1977.
(NY Islanders' 11th choice, 222nd overall, in 1997 Entry Draft).

			Regular Season					Playoffs				
Season	Club	Lea	GP	G	A	TP	PIM	GP	G	A	TP	PIM
1996-97	Lincoln Stars	USHL	35	6	7	13	94	....	....	....	....	....
1997-98	Notre Dame	CCHA	38	0	6	6	22	....	....	....	....	....

CLARK, WENDEL T.B.

Left wing. Shoots left. 5'11", 194 lbs. Born, Kelvington, Sask., October 25, 1966.
(Toronto's 1st choice, 1st overall, in 1985 Entry Draft).

			Regular Season					Playoffs				
Season	Club	Lea	GP	G	A	TP	PIM	GP	G	A	TP	PIM
1983-84	Saskatoon	WHL	72	23	45	68	225	....	....	....	....	....
1984-85	Saskatoon	WHL	64	32	55	87	253	3	3	3	6	7
1985-86	**Toronto**	**NHL**	**66**	**34**	**11**	**45**	**227**	**10**	**5**	**1**	**6**	**47**
1986-87	**Toronto**	**NHL**	**80**	**37**	**23**	**60**	**271**	**13**	**6**	**5**	**11**	**38**
1987-88	**Toronto**	**NHL**	**28**	**12**	**11**	**23**	**80**	....	....	....	....	....
1988-89	**Toronto**	**NHL**	**15**	**7**	**4**	**11**	**66**	....	....	....	....	....
1989-90	**Toronto**	**NHL**	**38**	**18**	**8**	**26**	**116**	**5**	**1**	**1**	**2**	**19**
1990-91	**Toronto**	**NHL**	**63**	**18**	**16**	**34**	**152**	....	....	....	....	....
1991-92	**Toronto**	**NHL**	**43**	**19**	**21**	**40**	**123**	....	....	....	....	....
1992-93	**Toronto**	**NHL**	**66**	**17**	**22**	**39**	**193**	**21**	**10**	**10**	**20**	**51**
1993-94	**Toronto**	**NHL**	**64**	**46**	**30**	**76**	**115**	**18**	**9**	**7**	**16**	**24**
1994-95	**Quebec**	**NHL**	**37**	**12**	**18**	**30**	**45**	**6**	**1**	**2**	**3**	**6**
1995-96	**NY Islanders**	**NHL**	**58**	**24**	**19**	**43**	**60**	....	....	....	....	....
	Toronto	**NHL**	**13**	**8**	**7**	**15**	**16**	**6**	**2**	**2**	**4**	**2**
1996-97	**Toronto**	**NHL**	**65**	**30**	**19**	**49**	**75**	....	....	....	....	....
1997-98	**Toronto**	**NHL**	**47**	**12**	**7**	**19**	**80**	....	....	....	....	....
	NHL Totals		**683**	**294**	**216**	**510**	**1619**	**79**	**34**	**28**	**62**	**187**

WHL East First All-Star Team (1985) • NHL All-Rookie Team (1986)

Played in NHL All-Star Game (1986)

Traded to **Quebec** by **Toronto** with Sylvain Lefebvre, Landon Wilson and Toronto's 1st round choice (Jeffrey Kealty) in 1994 Entry Draft for Mats Sundin, Garth Butcher, Todd Warriner and Philadelphia's 1st round choice (previously acquired by Quebec — later traded to Washington — Washington selected Nolan Baumgartner) in 1994 Entry Draft, June 28, 1994. Transferred to **Colorado** after **Quebec** franchise relocated, June 21, 1995. Traded to **NY Islanders** by **Colorado** for Claude Lemieux, October 3, 1995. Traded to **Toronto** by **NY Islanders** with Mathieu Schneider and D.J. Smith for Darby Hendrickson, Sean Haggerty, Kenny Jonsson and Toronto's 1st round choice (Roberto Luongo) in 1997 Entry Draft, March 13, 1996. Signed as a free agent by **Tampa Bay**, July 31, 1998.

CLAUSON, KEVIN NYI

Defense. Shoots left. 6'5", 210 lbs. Born, Lebanon, NH, November 13, 1978.
(NY Islanders' 5th choice, 155th overall, in 1998 Entry Draft).

			Regular Season					Playoffs				
Season	Club	Lea	GP	G	A	TP	PIM	GP	G	A	TP	PIM
1997-98	Western Michigan	CCHA	36	1	1	2	56	....	....	....	....	....

CLEARY, DANIEL (KLIH-ree) CHI.

Left wing. Shoots left. 6', 203 lbs. Born, Carbonear, Nfld., December 18, 1978.
(Chicago's 1st choice, 13th overall, in 1997 Entry Draft).

			Regular Season					Playoffs				
Season	Club	Lea	GP	G	A	TP	PIM	GP	G	A	TP	PIM
1994-95	Belleville	OHL	62	26	55	81	62	16	7	10	17	23
1995-96	Belleville	OHL	64	53	62	115	74	14	10	17	27	40
1996-97	Belleville	OHL	64	32	48	80	88	6	3	4	7	6
1997-98	Belleville	OHL	30	16	31	47	14	10	6	*17	*23	10
	Chicago	**NHL**	**6**	**0**	**0**	**0**	**0**	....	....	....	....	....
	Indianapolis	IHL	4	2	1	3	6	....	....	....	....	....
	NHL Totals		**6**	**0**	**0**	**0**	**0**	....	....	....	....	....

OHL First All-Star Team (1996, 1997)

CLOUTIER, COLIN (klootz-YAY) T.B.

Center. Shoots left. 6'3", 224 lbs. Born, Winnipeg, Man., January 27, 1976.
(Tampa Bay's 2nd choice, 34th overall, in 1994 Entry Draft).

			Regular Season					Playoffs				
Season	Club	Lea	GP	G	A	TP	PIM	GP	G	A	TP	PIM
1992-93	Brandon	WHL	60	11	15	26	138	4	0	0	0	18
1993-94	Brandon	WHL	30	10	13	23	102	11	2	5	7	23
1994-95	Brandon	WHL	47	16	27	43	170	16	5	6	11	47
1995-96	Brandon	WHL	39	9	19	28	84	....	....	....	....	....
	Lethbridge	WHL	14	5	10	15	39	3	2	2	4	19
1996-97	Adirondack	AHL	52	5	15	20	127	2	0	0	0	0
1997-98	Adirondack	AHL	1	0	0	0	0	....	....	....	....	....
	Chesapeake	ECHL	31	7	10	17	215	....	....	....	....	....

CLOUTIER, SYLVAIN (klootz-YAY) CHI.

Center. Shoots left. 6', 195 lbs. Born, Mont-Laurier, Que., February 13, 1974.
(Detroit's 3rd choice, 70th overall, in 1992 Entry Draft).

			Regular Season					Playoffs				
Season	Club	Lea	GP	G	A	TP	PIM	GP	G	A	TP	PIM
1991-92	Guelph	OHL	62	35	31	66	74	....	....	....	....	....
1992-93	Guelph	OHL	44	26	29	55	78	5	0	5	5	14
1993-94	Guelph	OHL	66	45	71	116	127	9	7	9	16	32
	Adirondack	AHL	2	0	2	2	2	....	....	....	....	....
1994-95	Adirondack	AHL	71	7	26	33	144	....	....	....	....	....
1995-96	Adirondack	AHL	65	11	17	28	118	3	0	0	0	4
	Toledo	ECHL	6	4	2	6	4	....	....	....	....	....
1996-97	Adirondack	AHL	77	13	36	49	190	4	0	2	2	4
1997-98	Adirondack	AHL	72	14	22	36	155	....	....	....	....	....
	Detroit	IHL	8	0	1	1	18	21	7	5	12	31

Signed as a free agent by **Chicago**, August 17, 1998.

CLYMER, BEN BOS.

Defense. Shoots left. 6'1", 195 lbs. Born, Edina, MN, April 11, 1978.
(Boston's 3rd choice, 27th overall, in 1997 Entry Draft).

			Regular Season					Playoffs				
Season	Club	Lea	GP	G	A	TP	PIM	GP	G	A	TP	PIM
1995-96	Jefferson High	H.S.	23	12	34	46	34	....	....	....	....	....
1996-97	U. of Minnesota	WCHA	29	7	13	20	64	....	....	....	....	....
1997-98	U. of Minnesota	WCHA	1	0	0	0	2	....	....	....	....	....

COALTER, BRANDON S.J.

Left wing. Shoots left. 6'2", 201 lbs. Born, Richmond Hill, Ont., June 22, 1978.
(San Jose's 6th choice, 127th overall, in 1998 Entry Draft).

			Regular Season					Playoffs				
Season	Club	Lea	GP	G	A	TP	PIM	GP	G	A	TP	PIM
1995-96	Oshawa	OHL	37	1	5	6	40	5	0	0	0	0
1996-97	Oshawa	OHL	63	4	9	13	98	18	2	1	3	12
1997-98	Oshawa	OHL	64	8	13	21	143	7	3	3	6	6

COFFEY, PAUL — CHI.

Defense. Shoots left. 6', 190 lbs. Born, Weston, Ont., June 1, 1961.
(Edmonton's 1st choice, 6th overall, in 1980 Entry Draft).

			Regular Season					Playoffs				
Season	Club	Lea	GP	G	A	TP	PIM	GP	G	A	TP	PIM
1978-79	S.S. Marie	OHA	68	17	72	89	103	....	....	....	....	....
1979-80	S.S. Marie	OHA	23	10	21	31	63	....	....	....	....	....
	Kitchener	OHA	52	19	52	71	130	....	....	....	....	....
1980-81	**Edmonton**	**NHL**	**74**	**9**	**23**	**32**	**130**	**9**	**4**	**3**	**7**	**22**
1981-82	**Edmonton**	**NHL**	**80**	**29**	**60**	**89**	**106**	**5**	**1**	**1**	**2**	**6**
1982-83	**Edmonton**	**NHL**	**80**	**29**	**67**	**96**	**87**	**16**	**7**	**7**	**14**	**14**
1983-84	**Edmonton**	**NHL**	**80**	**40**	**86**	**126**	**104**	**19**	**8**	**14**	**22**	**21 ♦**
1984-85	**Edmonton**	**NHL**	**80**	**37**	**84**	**121**	**97**	**18**	**12**	**25**	**37**	**44 ♦**
1985-86	**Edmonton**	**NHL**	**79**	**48**	**90**	**138**	**120**	**10**	**1**	**9**	**10**	**30**
1986-87	**Edmonton**	**NHL**	**59**	**17**	**50**	**67**	**49**	**17**	**3**	**8**	**11**	**30 ♦**
1987-88	**Pittsburgh**	**NHL**	**46**	**15**	**52**	**67**	**93**	....	....	....	....	....
1988-89	**Pittsburgh**	**NHL**	**75**	**30**	**83**	**113**	**195**	**11**	**2**	**13**	**15**	**31**
1989-90	**Pittsburgh**	**NHL**	**80**	**29**	**74**	**103**	**95**	....	....	....	....	....
1990-91	**Pittsburgh**	**NHL**	**76**	**24**	**69**	**93**	**128**	**12**	**2**	**9**	**11**	**6 ♦**
1991-92	**Pittsburgh**	**NHL**	**54**	**10**	**54**	**64**	**62**	....	....	....	....	....
	Los Angeles	**NHL**	**10**	**1**	**4**	**5**	**25**	**6**	**4**	**3**	**7**	**2**
1992-93	**Los Angeles**	**NHL**	**50**	**8**	**49**	**57**	**50**	....	....	....	....	....
	Detroit	**NHL**	**30**	**4**	**26**	**30**	**27**	**7**	**2**	**9**	**11**	**2**
1993-94	**Detroit**	**NHL**	**80**	**14**	**63**	**77**	**106**	**7**	**1**	**6**	**7**	**8**
1994-95	**Detroit**	**NHL**	**45**	**14**	**44**	**58**	**72**	**18**	**6**	**12**	**18**	**10**
1995-96	**Detroit**	**NHL**	**76**	**14**	**60**	**74**	**90**	**17**	**5**	**9**	**14**	**30**
1996-97	**Hartford**	**NHL**	**20**	**3**	**5**	**8**	**18**	....	....	....	....	....
	Philadelphia	**NHL**	**37**	**6**	**20**	**26**	**20**	**17**	**1**	**8**	**9**	**6**
1997-98	**Philadelphia**	**NHL**	**57**	**2**	**27**	**29**	**30**	....	....	....	....	....
	NHL Totals		**1268**	**383**	**1090**	**1473**	**1704**	**189**	**59**	**136**	**195**	**262**

OHA Second All-Star Team (1980) • NHL Second All-Star Team (1982, 1983, 1984, 1990) • Won James Norris Memorial Trophy (1985, 1986, 1995) • NHL First All-Star Team (1985, 1986, 1989, 1995)

Played in NHL All-Star Game (1982, 1983, 1984, 1985, 1986, 1988, 1989, 1990, 1991, 1992, 1993, 1994, 1996, 1997)

Traded to **Pittsburgh** by **Edmonton** with Dave Hunter and Wayne Van Dorp for Craig Simpson, Dave Hannan, Moe Mantha and Chris Joseph, November 24, 1987. Traded to **LA Kings** by **Pittsburgh** for Brian Benning, Jeff Chychrun and LA Kings' 1st round choice (later traded to Philadelphia — Philadelphia selected Jason Bowen) in 1992 Entry Draft, February 19, 1992. Traded to **Detroit** by **LA Kings** with Sylvain Couturier and Jim Hiller for Jimmy Carson, Marc Potvin and Gary Shuchuk, January 29, 1993. Traded to **Hartford** by **Detroit** with Keith Primeau and Detroit's 1st round choice (Nikos Tselios) in 1997 Entry Draft for Brendan Shanahan and Brian Glynn, October 9, 1996. Traded to **Philadelphia** by **Hartford** with Hartford-Carolina's 3rd round choice (Kris Mallette) in 1997 Entry Draft for Kevin Haller, Philadelphia's 1st round choice (later traded to San Jose — San Jose selected Scott Hannan) in 1997 Entry Draft and Hartford's 7th round choice (previously acquired, Carolina selected Andrew Merrick) in 1997 Entry Draft, December 15, 1996. Traded to **Chicago** by **Philadelphia** for NY Islanders' 5th round choice (previously acquired, Philadelphia selected Francis Belanger) in 1998 Entry Draft, June 27, 1998.

COLAGIACOMO, ADAM (coh-lah-JAH-coh-moh) — S.J.

Right wing. Shoots right. 6'2", 205 lbs. Born, Toronto, Ont., March 17, 1979.
(San Jose's 3rd choice, 82nd overall, in 1997 Entry Draft).

			Regular Season					Playoffs				
Season	Club	Lea	GP	G	A	TP	PIM	GP	G	A	TP	PIM
1995-96	London	OHL	66	28	38	66	88	....	....	....	....	....
1996-97	London	OHL	26	11	11	22	37	....	....	....	....	....
	Oshawa	OHL	23	14	10	24	32	13	1	5	6	4
1997-98	Oshawa	OHL	58	25	31	56	80	7	1	0	1	2

COLE, DANTON

Center/Right wing. Shoots right. 5'11", 185 lbs. Born, Pontiac, MI, January 10, 1967.
(Winnipeg's 6th choice, 123rd overall, in 1985 Entry Draft).

			Regular Season					Playoffs				
Season	Club	Lea	GP	G	A	TP	PIM	GP	G	A	TP	PIM
1984-85	Aurora	OJHL	41	51	44	95	91	....	....	....	....	....
1985-86	Michigan State	CCHA	43	11	10	21	22	....	....	....	....	....
1986-87	Michigan State	CCHA	44	9	15	24	16	....	....	....	....	....
1987-88	Michigan State	CCHA	46	20	36	56	38	....	....	....	....	....
1988-89	Michigan State	CCHA	47	29	33	62	46	....	....	....	....	....
1989-90	**Winnipeg**	**NHL**	**2**	**1**	**1**	**2**	**0**	....	....	....	....	....
	Moncton	AHL	80	31	42	73	18	....	....	....	....	....
1990-91	**Winnipeg**	**NHL**	**66**	**13**	**11**	**24**	**24**	....	....	....	....	....
	Moncton	AHL	3	1	1	2	0	....	....	....	....	....
1991-92	**Winnipeg**	**NHL**	**52**	**7**	**5**	**12**	**32**	....	....	....	....	....
1992-93	**Tampa Bay**	**NHL**	**67**	**12**	**15**	**27**	**23**	....	....	....	....	....
	Atlanta	IHL	1	1	0	1	2	....	....	....	....	....
1993-94	**Tampa Bay**	**NHL**	**81**	**20**	**23**	**43**	**32**	....	....	....	....	....
1994-95	**Tampa Bay**	**NHL**	**26**	**3**	**3**	**6**	**6**	....	....	....	....	....
	New Jersey	**NHL**	**12**	**1**	**2**	**3**	**8**	**1**	**0**	**0**	**0**	**0 ♦**
1995-96	**NY Islanders**	**NHL**	**10**	**1**	**0**	**1**	**0**	....	....	....	....	....
	Utah	IHL	34	28	15	43	22	....	....	....	....	....
	Chicago	**NHL**	**2**	**0**	**0**	**0**	**0**	....	....	....	....	....
	Indianapolis	IHL	32	9	13	22	20	5	1	5	6	8
1996-97	Krefeld	Germany	28	7	12	19	14	....	....	....	....	....
	Grand Rapids	IHL	35	8	18	26	24	5	3	1	4	2
1997-98	Grand Rapids	IHL	81	13	13	26	36	3	1	1	2	0
	NHL Totals		**318**	**58**	**60**	**118**	**125**	**1**	**0**	**0**	**0**	**0**

Traded to **Tampa Bay** by **Winnipeg** for future considerations, June 19, 1992. Traded to **New Jersey** by **Tampa Bay** with Shawn Chambers for Alexander Semak and Ben Hankinson, March 14, 1995. Signed as a free agent by **NY Islanders**, August 26, 1995. Traded to **Chicago** by **NY Islanders** for Bob Halkidis, February 2, 1996.

COLE, ERIK — CAR.

Left wing. Shoots left. 6', 185 lbs. Born, Oswego, NY, November 6, 1978.
(Carolina's 3rd choice, 71st overall, in 1998 Entry Draft).

			Regular Season					Playoffs				
Season	Club	Lea	GP	G	A	TP	PIM	GP	G	A	TP	PIM
1996-97	Des Moines	USHL	48	30	34	64	140	....	....	....	....	....
1997-98	Clarkson	ECAC	34	11	20	31	55	....	....	....	....	....

COLEMAN, JON — DET.

Defense. Shoots right. 6'1", 190 lbs. Born, Boston, MA, March 9, 1975.
(Detroit's 2nd choice, 48th overall, in 1993 Entry Draft).

			Regular Season					Playoffs				
Season	Club	Lea	GP	G	A	TP	PIM	GP	G	A	TP	PIM
1992-93	Andover High	H.S.	23	14	20	34	10	....	....	....	....	....
1993-94	Boston University	H.E.	29	1	14	15	26	....	....	....	....	....
1994-95	Boston University	H.E.	40	5	23	28	42	....	....	....	....	....
1995-96	Boston University	H.E.	40	7	31	38	58	....	....	....	....	....
1996-97	Boston University	H.E.	39	5	27	32	20	....	....	....	....	....
1997-98	Detroit	IHL	1	0	0	0	0	....	....	....	....	....
	Adirondack	AHL	54	2	29	31	23	2	0	0	0	0

Hockey East Second All-Star Team (1996, 1997) • NCAA East Second All-American Team (1996) • NCAA East First All-American Team (1997)

CONROY, CRAIG — ST.L.

Center. Shoots right. 6'2", 198 lbs. Born, Potsdam, NY, September 4, 1971.
(Montreal's 7th choice, 123rd overall, in 1990 Entry Draft).

			Regular Season					Playoffs				
Season	Club	Lea	GP	G	A	TP	PIM	GP	G	A	TP	PIM
1989-90	Northwood Prep	H.S.	31	33	43	76	....	....	....	....	....	....
1990-91	Clarkson	ECAC	40	8	21	29	24	....	....	....	....	....
1991-92	Clarkson	ECAC	31	19	17	36	36	....	....	....	....	....
1992-93	Clarkson	ECAC	35	10	23	33	26	....	....	....	....	....
1993-94	Clarkson	ECAC	34	26	*40	*66	46	....	....	....	....	....
1994-95	**Montreal**	**NHL**	**6**	**1**	**0**	**1**	**0**	....	....	....	....	....
	Fredericton	AHL	55	26	18	44	29	11	7	3	10	6
1995-96	**Montreal**	**NHL**	**7**	**0**	**0**	**0**	**2**	....	....	....	....	....
	Fredericton	AHL	67	31	38	69	65	10	5	7	12	6
1996-97	Fredericton	AHL	9	10	6	16	10	....	....	....	....	....
	St. Louis	**NHL**	**61**	**6**	**11**	**17**	**43**	**6**	**0**	**0**	**0**	**8**
	Worcester	AHL	5	5	6	11	2	....	....	....	....	....
1997-98	**St. Louis**	**NHL**	**81**	**14**	**29**	**43**	**46**	**10**	**1**	**2**	**3**	**8**
	NHL Totals		**155**	**21**	**40**	**61**	**91**	**16**	**1**	**2**	**3**	**16**

ECAC First All-Star Team (1994) • NCAA East First All-American Team (1994) • NCAA Final Four All-Tournament Team (1994)

Traded to **St. Louis** by **Montreal** with Pierre Turgeon and Rory Fitzpatrick for Murray Baron, Shayne Corson and St. Louis' 5th round choice (Gennady Razin) in 1997 Entry Draft, October 29, 1996.

CONVERY, BRANDON — VAN.

Center. Shoots right. 6'1", 195 lbs. Born, Kingston, Ont., February 4, 1974.
(Toronto's 1st choice, 8th overall, in 1992 Entry Draft).

			Regular Season					Playoffs				
Season	Club	Lea	GP	G	A	TP	PIM	GP	G	A	TP	PIM
1990-91	Sudbury	OHL	56	26	22	48	18	5	1	1	2	2
1991-92	Sudbury	OHL	44	40	26	66	44	5	3	2	5	4
1992-93	Sudbury	OHL	7	7	9	16	6	....	....	....	....	....
	Niagara Falls	OHL	51	38	39	77	24	4	1	3	4	4
	St. John's	AHL	3	0	0	0	0	5	0	1	1	0
1993-94	Niagara Falls	OHL	29	24	29	53	30	....	....	....	....	....
	Belleville	OHL	23	16	19	35	22	12	4	10	14	13
	St. John's	AHL	....	....	....	....	....	1	0	0	0	0
1994-95	St. John's	AHL	76	34	37	71	43	5	2	2	4	4
1995-96	**Toronto**	**NHL**	**11**	**5**	**2**	**7**	**4**	**5**	**0**	**0**	**0**	**2**
	St. John's	AHL	57	22	23	45	28	....	....	....	....	....
1996-97	**Toronto**	**NHL**	**39**	**2**	**8**	**10**	**20**	....	....	....	....	....
	St. John's	AHL	25	14	14	28	15	....	....	....	....	....
1997-98	St. John's	AHL	49	27	36	63	35	....	....	....	....	....
	Vancouver	**NHL**	**7**	**0**	**2**	**2**	**0**	....	....	....	....	....
	Syracuse	AHL	2	1	2	3	5	....	....	....	....	....
	NHL Totals		**57**	**7**	**12**	**19**	**24**	**5**	**0**	**0**	**0**	**2**

Traded to **Vancouver** by **Toronto** for Lonny Bohonos, March 7, 1998.

COOKE, MATT — VAN.

Left wing. Shoots left. 5'11", 200 lbs. Born, Belleville, Ont., September 7, 1978.
(Vancouver's 8th choice, 144th overall, in 1997 Entry Draft).

			Regular Season					Playoffs				
Season	Club	Lea	GP	G	A	TP	PIM	GP	G	A	TP	PIM
1995-96	Windsor	OHL	61	8	11	19	102	7	1	3	4	6
1996-97	Windsor	OHL	65	45	50	95	146	5	5	5	10	10
1997-98	Windsor	OHL	23	14	19	33	50	....	....	....	....	....
	Kingston	OHL	25	8	13	21	49	12	8	8	16	20

COOPER, DAVID — CGY.

Defense. Shoots left. 6'2", 204 lbs. Born, Ottawa, Ont., November 2, 1973.
(Buffalo's 1st choice, 11th overall, in 1992 Entry Draft).

			Regular Season					Playoffs				
Season	Club	Lea	GP	G	A	TP	PIM	GP	G	A	TP	PIM
1989-90	Medicine Hat	WHL	61	4	11	15	65	3	0	2	2	2
1990-91	Medicine Hat	WHL	64	12	31	43	66	11	1	3	4	23
1991-92	Medicine Hat	WHL	72	17	47	64	176	4	1	4	5	8
1992-93	Medicine Hat	WHL	63	15	50	65	88	10	2	2	4	32
	Rochester	AHL	....	....	....	....	....	2	0	0	0	2
1993-94	Rochester	AHL	68	10	25	35	82	4	1	1	2	2
1994-95	Rochester	AHL	21	2	4	6	48	....	....	....	....	....
	South Carolina	ECHL	39	9	19	28	90	9	3	8	11	24
1995-96	Rochester	AHL	67	9	18	27	79	8	0	1	1	12
1996-97	**Toronto**	**NHL**	**19**	**3**	**3**	**6**	**16**	....	....	....	....	....
	St. John's	AHL	44	16	19	35	65	....	....	....	....	....
1997-98	**Toronto**	**NHL**	**9**	**0**	**4**	**4**	**8**	....	....	....	....	....
	St. John's	AHL	60	19	23	42	117	4	0	1	1	6
	NHL Totals		**28**	**3**	**7**	**10**	**24**	....	....	....	....	....

WHL East First All-Star Team (1992) • AHL Second All-Star Team (1998)

Signed as a free agent by **Toronto**, September 26, 1996. Traded to **Calgary** by **Toronto** for Ladislav Kohn, July 2, 1998.

COPELAND, ADAM — EDM.

Right wing. Shoots right. 6'1", 215 lbs. Born, St. Catharines, Ont., June 5, 1976.
(Edmonton's 6th choice, 79th overall, in 1994 Entry Draft).

			Regular Season					Playoffs				
Season	Club	Lea	GP	G	A	TP	PIM	GP	G	A	TP	PIM
1993-94	Burlington	OJHL	39	28	44	72	55	....	....	....	....	....
1994-95	Miami-Ohio	CCHA	39	6	4	10	28	....	....	....	....	....
1995-96	Miami-Ohio	CCHA	36	10	4	14	38	....	....	....	....	....
1996-97	Miami-Ohio	CCHA	40	18	22	40	62	....	....	....	....	....
1997-98	Miami-Ohio	CCHA	37	19	14	33	52	....	....	....	....	....

COPLEY, RANDY — NYR

Right wing. Shoots right. 6'1", 205 lbs. Born, Inverness, NS, October 4, 1979.
(NY Rangers' 2nd choice, 40th overall, in 1998 Entry Draft).

			Regular Season					Playoffs				
Season	Club	Lea	GP	G	A	TP	PIM	GP	G	A	TP	PIM
1996-97	Granby	QMJHL	70	7	14	21	114	5	0	0	0	5
1997-98	Cape Breton	QMJHL	69	34	42	76	194	4	0	0	0	16

CORBET, RENE (cohr-BAY, ruh-NAY) — COL.

Left wing. Shoots left. 6', 187 lbs. Born, St-Hyacinthe, Que., June 25, 1973.
(Quebec's 2nd choice, 24th overall, in 1991 Entry Draft).

			Regular Season					Playoffs				
Season	Club	Lea	GP	G	A	TP	PIM	GP	G	A	TP	PIM
1990-91	Drummondville	QMJHL	45	25	40	65	34	14	11	6	17	15
1991-92	Drummondville	QMJHL	56	46	50	96	90	4	1	2	3	17
1992-93	Drummondville	QMJHL	63	*79	69	*148	143	10	7	13	20	16
1993-94	**Quebec**	**NHL**	**9**	**1**	**1**	**2**	**0**	....	....	....	....	....
	Cornwall	AHL	68	37	40	77	56	13	7	2	9	18
1994-95	**Quebec**	**NHL**	**8**	**0**	**3**	**3**	**2**	**2**	**0**	**1**	**1**	**0**
	Cornwall	AHL	65	33	24	57	79	12	2	8	10	27
1995-96	**Colorado**	**NHL**	**33**	**3**	**6**	**9**	**33**	**8**	**3**	**2**	**5**	**2** ♦
	Cornwall	AHL	9	5	6	11	10	....	....	....	....	....
1996-97	**Colorado**	**NHL**	**76**	**12**	**15**	**27**	**67**	**17**	**2**	**2**	**4**	**27**
1997-98	**Colorado**	**NHL**	**68**	**16**	**12**	**28**	**133**	**2**	**0**	**0**	**0**	**2**
	NHL Totals		**194**	**32**	**37**	**69**	**235**	**29**	**5**	**5**	**10**	**31**

QMJHL First All-Star Team (1993) • Canadian Major Junior First All-Star Team (1993) • Won Dudley "Red" Garrett Memorial Trophy (Top Rookie - AHL) (1994)

Transferred to **Colorado** after **Quebec** franchise relocated, June 21, 1995.

CORKUM, BOB (KOHR-kuhm) — PHX.

Center. Shoots right. 6', 222 lbs. Born, Salisbury, MA, December 18, 1967.
(Buffalo's 3rd choice, 47th overall, in 1986 Entry Draft).

			Regular Season					Playoffs				
Season	Club	Lea	GP	G	A	TP	PIM	GP	G	A	TP	PIM
1984-85	Triton Regional	H.S.	18	35	36	71	....	....	....	....	....	....
1985-86	U. of Maine	H.E.	39	7	26	33	53	....	....	....	....	....
1986-87	U. of Maine	H.E.	35	18	11	29	24	....	....	....	....	....
1987-88	U. of Maine	H.E.	40	14	18	32	64	....	....	....	....	....
1988-89	U. of Maine	H.E.	45	17	31	48	64	....	....	....	....	....
1989-90	**Buffalo**	**NHL**	**8**	**2**	**0**	**2**	**4**	**5**	**1**	**0**	**1**	**4**
	Rochester	AHL	43	8	11	19	45	12	2	5	7	16
1990-91	Rochester	AHL	69	13	21	34	77	15	4	4	8	4
1991-92	**Buffalo**	**NHL**	**20**	**2**	**4**	**6**	**21**	**4**	**1**	**0**	**1**	**0**
	Rochester	AHL	52	16	12	28	47	8	0	6	6	8
1992-93	**Buffalo**	**NHL**	**68**	**6**	**4**	**10**	**38**	**5**	**0**	**0**	**0**	**2**
1993-94	**Anaheim**	**NHL**	**76**	**23**	**28**	**51**	**18**	....	....	....	....	....
1994-95	**Anaheim**	**NHL**	**44**	**10**	**9**	**19**	**25**	....	....	....	....	....
1995-96	**Anaheim**	**NHL**	**48**	**5**	**7**	**12**	**26**	....	....	....	....	....
	Philadelphia	**NHL**	**28**	**4**	**3**	**7**	**8**	**12**	**1**	**2**	**3**	**6**
1996-97	**Phoenix**	**NHL**	**80**	**9**	**11**	**20**	**40**	**7**	**2**	**2**	**4**	**4**
1997-98	**Phoenix**	**NHL**	**76**	**12**	**9**	**21**	**28**	**6**	**1**	**0**	**1**	**4**
	NHL Totals		**448**	**73**	**75**	**148**	**208**	**39**	**6**	**4**	**10**	**20**

Claimed by **Anaheim** from **Buffalo** in Expansion Draft, June 24, 1993. Traded to **Philadelphia** by **Anaheim** for Chris Herperger and Winnipeg's 7th round choice (previously acquired, Anaheim selected Tony Monahan) in 1997 Entry Draft, February 6, 1996. Claimed by **Phoenix** from **Philadelphia** in Waiver Draft, September 30, 1996.

CORNFORTH, MARK

Defense. Shoots left. 6'1", 193 lbs. Born, Montreal, Que., November 13, 1972.

			Regular Season					Playoffs				
Season	Club	Lea	GP	G	A	TP	PIM	GP	G	A	TP	PIM
1991-92	Merrimack	H.E.	23	1	9	10	40	....	....	....	....	....
1992-93	Merrimack	H.E.	36	3	18	21	75	....	....	....	....	....
1993-94	Merrimack	H.E.	37	5	13	18	58	....	....	....	....	....
1994-95	Merrimack	H.E.	30	8	20	28	93	....	....	....	....	....
	Syracuse	AHL	2	0	1	1	2	....	....	....	....	....
1995-96	**Boston**	**NHL**	**6**	**0**	**0**	**0**	**4**	....	....	....	....	....
	Providence	AHL	65	5	10	15	117	4	0	0	0	4
1996-97	Providence	AHL	61	8	12	20	47	....	....	....	....	....
	Cleveland	IHL	13	1	4	5	25	14	1	3	4	29
1997-98	Cleveland	IHL	68	5	15	20	146	....	....	....	....	....
	Grand Rapids	IHL	8	1	2	3	20	3	0	0	0	17
	NHL Totals		**6**	**0**	**0**	**0**	**4**	....	....	....	....	....

Signed as a free agent by **Boston**, October 6, 1995.

CORRINET, CHRIS — WSH.

Right wing. Shoots right. 6'3", 220 lbs. Born, Connecticut, October 29, 1978.
(Washington's 4th choice, 107th overall, in 1998 Entry Draft).

			Regular Season					Playoffs				
Season	Club	Lea	GP	G	A	TP	PIM	GP	G	A	TP	PIM
1996-97	Deerfield High	H.S.	16	6	15	21	10	....	....	....	....	....
1997-98	Princeton	ECAC	31	3	6	9	22	....	....	....	....	....

CORSO, DANIEL — ST.L.

Center. Shoots left. 5'9", 155 lbs. Born, Montreal, Que., April 3, 1978.
(St. Louis' 6th choice, 169th overall, in 1996 Entry Draft).

			Regular Season					Playoffs				
Season	Club	Lea	GP	G	A	TP	PIM	GP	G	A	TP	PIM
1994-95	Victoriaville	QMJHL	65	27	26	53	6	4	2	5	7	2
1995-96	Victoriaville	QMJHL	65	49	65	114	77	12	6	7	13	4
1996-97	Victoriaville	QMJHL	54	51	68	119	50	....	....	....	....	....
1997-98	Victoriaville	QMJHL	35	24	51	75	20	3	1	1	2	2

CORSON, SHAYNE — MTL.

Left wing. Shoots left. 6'1", 200 lbs. Born, Barrie, Ont., August 13, 1966.
(Montreal's 2nd choice, 8th overall, in 1984 Entry Draft).

			Regular Season					Playoffs				
Season	Club	Lea	GP	G	A	TP	PIM	GP	G	A	TP	PIM
1983-84	Brantford	OHL	66	25	46	71	165	6	4	1	5	26
1984-85	Hamilton	OHL	54	27	63	90	154	11	3	7	10	19
1985-86	Hamilton	OHL	47	41	57	98	153	....	....	....	....	....
	Montreal	**NHL**	**3**	**0**	**0**	**0**	**2**	....	....	....	....	....
1986-87	**Montreal**	**NHL**	**55**	**12**	**11**	**23**	**144**	**17**	**6**	**5**	**11**	**30**
1987-88	**Montreal**	**NHL**	**71**	**12**	**27**	**39**	**152**	**3**	**1**	**0**	**1**	**12**
1988-89	**Montreal**	**NHL**	**80**	**26**	**24**	**50**	**193**	**21**	**4**	**5**	**9**	**65**
1989-90	**Montreal**	**NHL**	**76**	**31**	**44**	**75**	**144**	**11**	**2**	**8**	**10**	**20**
1990-91	**Montreal**	**NHL**	**71**	**23**	**24**	**47**	**138**	**13**	**9**	**6**	**15**	**36**
1991-92	**Montreal**	**NHL**	**64**	**17**	**36**	**53**	**118**	**10**	**2**	**5**	**7**	**15**
1992-93	**Edmonton**	**NHL**	**80**	**16**	**31**	**47**	**209**	....	....	....	....	....
1993-94	**Edmonton**	**NHL**	**64**	**25**	**29**	**54**	**118**	....	....	....	....	....
1994-95	**Edmonton**	**NHL**	**48**	**12**	**24**	**36**	**86**	....	....	....	....	....
1995-96	**St. Louis**	**NHL**	**77**	**18**	**28**	**46**	**192**	**13**	**8**	**6**	**14**	**22**
1996-97	**St. Louis**	**NHL**	**11**	**2**	**1**	**3**	**24**	....	....	....	....	....
	Montreal	**NHL**	**47**	**6**	**15**	**21**	**80**	**5**	**1**	**0**	**1**	**4**
1997-98	**Montreal**	**NHL**	**62**	**21**	**34**	**55**	**108**	**10**	**3**	**6**	**9**	**26**
	Canada	Olympics	6	1	1	2	2					
	NHL Totals		**809**	**221**	**328**	**549**	**1708**	**103**	**36**	**41**	**77**	**230**

WJC-A All-Star Team (1986)

Played in NHL All-Star Game (1990, 1994, 1998)

Traded to **Edmonton** by **Montreal** with Brent Gilchrist and Vladimir Vujtek for Vincent Damphousse and Edmonton's 4th round choice (Adam Wiesel) in 1993 Entry Draft, August 27, 1992. Signed as a free agent by **St. Louis**, July 28, 1995. Traded to **Montreal** by **St. Louis** with Murray Baron and St. Louis' 5th round choice (Gennady Razin) in 1997 Entry Draft for Pierre Turgeon, Rory Fitzpatrick and Craig Conroy, October 29, 1996.

CORVO, JOSEPH — L.A.

Defense. Shoots right. 6', 205 lbs. Born, Oak Park, IL, June 20, 1977.
(Los Angeles' 4th choice, 83rd overall, in 1997 Entry Draft).

			Regular Season					Playoffs				
Season	Club	Lea	GP	G	A	TP	PIM	GP	G	A	TP	PIM
1995-96	Western Michigan	CCHA	41	5	25	30	38	....	....	....	....	....
1996-97	Western Michigan	CCHA	32	12	21	33	85	....	....	....	....	....
1997-98	Western Michigan	CCHA	32	5	12	17	93	....	....	....	....	....

COTE, PATRICK (KOH-tay) — NSH.

Left wing. Shoots left. 6'3", 199 lbs. Born, Lasalle, Que., January 24, 1975.
(Dallas' 2nd choice, 37th overall, in 1995 Entry Draft).

			Regular Season					Playoffs				
Season	Club	Lea	GP	G	A	TP	PIM	GP	G	A	TP	PIM
1993-94	Beauport	QMJHL	48	2	4	6	230	12	1	0	1	61
1994-95	Beauport	QMJHL	56	20	20	40	314	17	8	8	16	115
1995-96	**Dallas**	**NHL**	**2**	**0**	**0**	**0**	**5**	....	....	....	....	....
	Michigan	IHL	57	4	6	10	239	3	0	0	0	2
1996-97	**Dallas**	**NHL**	**3**	**0**	**0**	**0**	**27**	....	....	....	....	....
	Michigan	IHL	58	14	10	24	237	4	2	0	2	6
1997-98	**Dallas**	**NHL**	**3**	**0**	**0**	**0**	**15**	....	....	....	....	....
	Michigan	IHL	4	2	0	2	4	....	....	....	....	....
	NHL Totals		**8**	**0**	**0**	**0**	**47**	....	....	....	....	....

Claimed by **Nashville** from **Dallas** in Expansion Draft, June 26, 1998.

COTE, SYLVAIN (KOH-tay) — TOR.

Defense. Shoots right. 6', 190 lbs. Born, Quebec City, Que., January 19, 1966.
(Hartford's 1st choice, 11th overall, in 1984 Entry Draft).

			Regular Season					Playoffs				
Season	Club	Lea	GP	G	A	TP	PIM	GP	G	A	TP	PIM
1982-83	Quebec	QMJHL	66	10	24	34	50	....	....	....	....	....
1983-84	Quebec	QMJHL	66	15	50	65	89	5	1	1	2	0
1984-85	**Hartford**	**NHL**	**67**	**3**	**9**	**12**	**17**	....	....	....	....	....
1985-86	Hull	QMJHL	26	10	33	43	14	13	6	*28	34	22
	Hartford	**NHL**	**2**	**0**	**0**	**0**	**0**	....	....	....	....	....
	Binghamton	AHL	12	2	4	6	0	....	....	....	....	....
1986-87	**Hartford**	**NHL**	**67**	**2**	**8**	**10**	**20**	**2**	**0**	**2**	**2**	**2**
1987-88	**Hartford**	**NHL**	**67**	**7**	**21**	**28**	**30**	**6**	**1**	**1**	**2**	**4**
1988-89	**Hartford**	**NHL**	**78**	**8**	**9**	**17**	**49**	**3**	**0**	**1**	**1**	**4**
1989-90	**Hartford**	**NHL**	**28**	**4**	**2**	**6**	**14**	**5**	**0**	**0**	**0**	**2**
1990-91	**Hartford**	**NHL**	**73**	**7**	**12**	**19**	**17**	**6**	**0**	**2**	**2**	**2**
1991-92	**Washington**	**NHL**	**78**	**11**	**29**	**40**	**31**	**7**	**1**	**2**	**3**	**4**
1992-93	**Washington**	**NHL**	**77**	**21**	**29**	**50**	**34**	**6**	**1**	**1**	**2**	**4**
1993-94	**Washington**	**NHL**	**84**	**16**	**35**	**51**	**66**	**9**	**1**	**8**	**9**	**6**
1994-95	**Washington**	**NHL**	**47**	**5**	**14**	**19**	**53**	**7**	**1**	**3**	**4**	**2**
1995-96	**Washington**	**NHL**	**81**	**5**	**33**	**38**	**40**	**6**	**2**	**0**	**2**	**12**
1996-97	**Washington**	**NHL**	**57**	**6**	**18**	**24**	**28**	....	....	....	....	....
1997-98	**Washington**	**NHL**	**59**	**1**	**15**	**16**	**36**	....	....	....	....	....
	Toronto	**NHL**	**12**	**3**	**6**	**9**	**6**	....	....	....	....	....
	NHL Totals		**877**	**99**	**240**	**339**	**441**	**57**	**7**	**20**	**27**	**42**

QMJHL Second All-Star Team (1984) • QMJHL First All-Star Team (1986)

Traded to **Washington** by **Hartford** for Washington's 2nd round choice (Andrei Nikolishin) in 1992 Entry Draft, September 8, 1991. Traded to **Toronto** by **Washington** for Jeff Brown, March 24, 1998.

COURTNALL, GEOFF — ST.L.

Left wing. Shoots left. 6'1", 195 lbs. Born, Duncan, B.C., August 18, 1962.

			Regular Season					Playoffs				
Season	Club	Lea	GP	G	A	TP	PIM	GP	G	A	TP	PIM
1980-81	Victoria	WHL	11	3	4	7	6	15	2	1	3	7
1981-82	Victoria	WHL	72	35	57	92	100	4	1	0	1	2
1982-83	Victoria	WHL	71	41	73	114	186	12	6	7	13	42
1983-84	**Boston**	**NHL**	**4**	**0**	**0**	**0**	**0**	....	....	....	....	....
	Hershey	AHL	74	14	12	26	51	....	....	....	....	....
1984-85	**Boston**	**NHL**	**64**	**12**	**16**	**28**	**82**	**5**	**0**	**2**	**2**	**7**
	Hershey	AHL	9	8	4	12	4	....	....	....	....	....
1985-86	**Boston**	**NHL**	**64**	**21**	**16**	**37**	**61**	**3**	**0**	**0**	**0**	**2**
	Moncton	AHL	12	8	8	16	6	....	....	....	....	....
1986-87	**Boston**	**NHL**	**65**	**13**	**23**	**36**	**117**	**1**	**0**	**0**	**0**	**0**
1987-88	**Boston**	**NHL**	**62**	**32**	**26**	**58**	**108**	....	....	....	....	....
	Edmonton	**NHL**	**12**	**4**	**4**	**8**	**15**	**19**	**0**	**3**	**3**	**23 ♦**
1988-89	**Washington**	**NHL**	**79**	**42**	**38**	**80**	**112**	**6**	**2**	**5**	**7**	**12**
1989-90	**Washington**	**NHL**	**80**	**35**	**39**	**74**	**104**	**15**	**4**	**9**	**13**	**32**
1990-91	**St. Louis**	**NHL**	**66**	**27**	**30**	**57**	**56**	....	....	....	....	....
	Vancouver	**NHL**	**11**	**6**	**2**	**8**	**8**	**6**	**3**	**5**	**8**	**4**
1991-92	**Vancouver**	**NHL**	**70**	**23**	**34**	**57**	**116**	**12**	**6**	**8**	**14**	**20**
1992-93	**Vancouver**	**NHL**	**84**	**31**	**46**	**77**	**167**	**12**	**4**	**10**	**14**	**12**
1993-94	**Vancouver**	**NHL**	**82**	**26**	**44**	**70**	**123**	**24**	**9**	**10**	**19**	**51**
1994-95	**Vancouver**	**NHL**	**45**	**16**	**18**	**34**	**81**	**11**	**4**	**2**	**6**	**34**
1995-96	**St. Louis**	**NHL**	**69**	**24**	**16**	**40**	**101**	**13**	**0**	**3**	**3**	**14**
1996-97	**St. Louis**	**NHL**	**82**	**17**	**40**	**57**	**86**	**6**	**3**	**1**	**4**	**23**
1997-98	**St. Louis**	**NHL**	**79**	**31**	**31**	**62**	**94**	**10**	**2**	**8**	**10**	**18**
	NHL Totals		**1018**	**360**	**423**	**783**	**1431**	**143**	**37**	**66**	**103**	**252**

Signed as a free agent by **Boston**, July 6, 1983. Traded to **Edmonton** by **Boston** with Bill Ranford and future considerations for Andy Moog, March 8, 1988. Rights traded to **Washington** by **Edmonton** for Greg C. Adams, July 22, 1988. Traded to **St. Louis** by **Washington** for Peter Zezel and Mike Lalor, July 13, 1990. Traded to **Vancouver** by **St. Louis** with Robert Dirk, Sergio Momesso, Cliff Ronning and St. Louis' 5th round choice (Brian Loney) in 1992 Entry Draft for Dan Quinn and Garth Butcher, March 5, 1991. Signed as a free agent by **St. Louis**, July 14, 1995.

COURTNALL, RUSS — L.A.

Right wing. Shoots right. 5'11", 185 lbs. Born, Duncan, B.C., June 2, 1965.
(Toronto's 1st choice, 7th overall, in 1983 Entry Draft).

			Regular Season					Playoffs				
Season	Club	Lea	GP	G	A	TP	PIM	GP	G	A	TP	PIM
1982-83	Victoria	WHL	60	36	61	97	33	12	11	7	18	6
1983-84	Victoria	WHL	32	29	37	66	63	....	....	....	....	....
	Canada	Nat-Tm	16	4	7	11	10	....	....	....	....	....
	Canada	Olympics	7	1	3	4	2	....	....	....	....	....
	Toronto	**NHL**	**14**	**3**	**9**	**12**	**6**	....	....	....	....	....
1984-85	**Toronto**	**NHL**	**69**	**12**	**10**	**22**	**44**	....	....	....	....	....
1985-86	**Toronto**	**NHL**	**73**	**22**	**38**	**60**	**52**	**10**	**3**	**6**	**9**	**8**
1986-87	**Toronto**	**NHL**	**79**	**29**	**44**	**73**	**90**	**13**	**3**	**4**	**7**	**11**
1987-88	**Toronto**	**NHL**	**65**	**23**	**26**	**49**	**47**	**6**	**2**	**1**	**3**	**0**
1988-89	**Toronto**	**NHL**	**9**	**1**	**1**	**2**	**4**	....	....	....	....	....
	Montreal	**NHL**	**64**	**22**	**17**	**39**	**15**	**21**	**8**	**5**	**13**	**18**
1989-90	**Montreal**	**NHL**	**80**	**27**	**32**	**59**	**27**	**11**	**5**	**1**	**6**	**10**
1990-91	**Montreal**	**NHL**	**79**	**26**	**50**	**76**	**29**	**13**	**8**	**3**	**11**	**7**
1991-92	**Montreal**	**NHL**	**27**	**7**	**14**	**21**	**6**	**10**	**1**	**1**	**2**	**4**
1992-93	**Minnesota**	**NHL**	**84**	**36**	**43**	**79**	**49**	....	....	....	....	....
1993-94	**Dallas**	**NHL**	**84**	**23**	**57**	**80**	**59**	**9**	**1**	**8**	**9**	**0**
1994-95	**Dallas**	**NHL**	**32**	**7**	**10**	**17**	**13**	....	....	....	....	....
	Vancouver	**NHL**	**13**	**4**	**14**	**18**	**4**	**11**	**4**	**8**	**12**	**21**
1995-96	**Vancouver**	**NHL**	**81**	**26**	**39**	**65**	**40**	**6**	**1**	**3**	**4**	**2**
1996-97	**Vancouver**	**NHL**	**47**	**9**	**19**	**28**	**24**	....	....	....	....	....
	NY Rangers	**NHL**	**14**	**2**	**5**	**7**	**2**	**15**	**3**	**4**	**7**	**0**
1997-98	**Los Angeles**	**NHL**	**58**	**12**	**6**	**18**	**27**	**4**	**0**	**0**	**0**	**2**
	NHL Totals		**972**	**291**	**434**	**725**	**538**	**129**	**39**	**44**	**83**	**83**

Played in NHL All-Star Game (1994)

Traded to **Montreal** by **Toronto** for John Kordic and Montreal's 6th round choice (Michael Doers) in 1989 Entry Draft, November 7, 1988. Traded to **Minnesota** by **Montreal** for Brian Bellows, August 31, 1992. Transferred to **Dallas** after **Minnesota** franchise relocated, June 9, 1993. Traded to **Vancouver** by **Dallas** for Greg Adams, Dan Kesa and Vancouver's 5th round choice (later traded to LA Kings — LA Kings selected Jason Morgan) in 1995 Entry Draft, April 7, 1995. Traded to **NY Rangers** by **Vancouver** with Esa Tikkanen for Sergei Nemchinov and Brian Noonan, March 8, 1997. Signed as a free agent by **LA Kings**, November 7, 1997.

COURVILLE, LARRY (KOOR-vihl) — VAN.

Left wing. Shoots left. 6'1", 195 lbs. Born, Timmins, Ont., April 2, 1975.
(Vancouver's 2nd choice, 61st overall, in 1995 Entry Draft).

			Regular Season					Playoffs				
Season	Club	Lea	GP	G	A	TP	PIM	GP	G	A	TP	PIM
1991-92	Cornwall	OHL	60	8	12	20	80	6	0	0	0	8
1992-93	Newmarket	OHL	64	21	18	39	181	7	0	6	6	14
1993-94	Newmarket	OHL	39	20	19	39	134	....	....	....	....	....
	Moncton	AHL	8	2	0	2	37	10	2	2	4	27
1994-95	Sarnia	OHL	16	9	9	18	58	....	....	....	....	....
	Oshawa	OHL	28	25	30	55	72	7	4	10	14	10
1995-96	**Vancouver**	**NHL**	**3**	**1**	**0**	**1**	**0**	....	....	....	....	....
	Syracuse	AHL	71	17	32	49	127	14	5	3	8	10
1996-97	**Vancouver**	**NHL**	**19**	**0**	**2**	**2**	**11**	....	....	....	....	....
	Syracuse	AHL	54	20	24	44	103	3	0	1	1	20
1997-98	**Vancouver**	**NHL**	**11**	**0**	**0**	**0**	**5**	....	....	....	....	....
	Syracuse	AHL	29	6	12	18	84	....	....	....	....	....
	NHL Totals		**33**	**1**	**2**	**3**	**16**	....	....	....	....	....

OHL Second All-Star Team (1995)

• Re-entered NHL Entry Draft. Originally Winnipeg's 6th choice, 119th overall in 1993 Entry Draft.

COUTURE, ALEXANDRE (koo-TUHR)

Defense. Shoots right. 6'4", 197 lbs. Born, Hamnord, Que., December 18, 1977.
(Florida's 7th choice, 183rd overall, in 1996 Entry Draft).

			Regular Season					Playoffs				
Season	Club	Lea	GP	G	A	TP	PIM	GP	G	A	TP	PIM
1994-95	Victoriaville	QMJHL	24	4	7	11	4	4	1	2	3	2
1995-96	Victoriaville	QMJHL	67	3	10	13	121	11	0	0	0	10
1996-97	Victoriaville	QMJHL	47	2	12	14	113	5	0	1	1	4
1997-98	Victoriaville	QMJHL	6	0	0	0	13	....	....	....	....	....
	Halifax	QMJHL	36	7	18	25	59	5	3	0	3	12

COWAN, JEFF — CGY.

Left wing. Shoots left. 6'2", 185 lbs. Born, Scarborough, Ont., September 27, 1976.

			Regular Season					Playoffs				
Season	Club	Lea	GP	G	A	TP	PIM	GP	G	A	TP	PIM
1993-94	Guelph	OHL	17	1	0	1	5	....	....	....	....	....
1994-95	Guelph	OHL	51	10	7	17	14	14	1	1	2	0
1995-96	Barrie	OHL	66	38	14	52	29	5	1	2	3	6
1996-97	Saint John	AHL	22	5	5	10	8	....	....	....	....	....
	Roanoke	ECHL	47	21	13	34	42	....	....	....	....	....
1997-98	Saint John	AHL	69	15	13	28	23	13	4	1	5	14

Signed as a free agent by **Calgary**, October 2, 1995.

CRAIG, MIKE — S.J.

Right wing. Shoots right. 6'1", 180 lbs. Born, St. Mary's, Ont., June 6, 1971.
(Minnesota's 2nd choice, 28th overall, in 1989 Entry Draft).

			Regular Season					Playoffs				
Season	Club	Lea	GP	G	A	TP	PIM	GP	G	A	TP	PIM
1987-88	Oshawa	OHL	61	6	10	16	39	7	7	0	1	11
1988-89	Oshawa	OHL	63	36	36	72	34	6	3	1	4	6
1989-90	Oshawa	OHL	43	36	40	76	85	17	10	16	26	46
1990-91	**Minnesota**	**NHL**	**39**	**8**	**4**	**12**	**32**	**10**	**1**	**1**	**2**	**20**
1991-92	**Minnesota**	**NHL**	**67**	**15**	**16**	**31**	**155**	**4**	**1**	**0**	**1**	**7**
1992-93	**Minnesota**	**NHL**	**70**	**15**	**23**	**38**	**106**	....	....	....	....	....
1993-94	**Dallas**	**NHL**	**72**	**13**	**24**	**37**	**139**	**4**	**0**	**0**	**0**	**2**
1994-95	**Toronto**	**NHL**	**37**	**5**	**5**	**10**	**12**	**2**	**0**	**1**	**1**	**2**
1995-96	**Toronto**	**NHL**	**70**	**8**	**12**	**20**	**42**	**6**	**0**	**0**	**0**	**18**
1996-97	**Toronto**	**NHL**	**65**	**7**	**13**	**20**	**62**	....	....	....	....	....
1997-98	San Antonio	IHL	12	4	1	5	18	....	....	....	....	....
	Kansas City	IHL	59	14	33	47	68	11	5	5	10	28
	NHL Totals		**420**	**71**	**97**	**168**	**548**	**26**	**2**	**2**	**4**	**49**

Transferred to **Dallas** after **Minnesota** franchise relocated, June 9, 1993. Signed as a free agent by **Toronto**, July 29, 1994. Signed as a free agent by **San Jose**, August 1, 1998.

CRAIGHEAD, JOHN

Right wing. Shoots right. 6', 195 lbs. Born, Vancouver, B.C., November 23, 1971.

			Regular Season					Playoffs				
Season	Club	Lea	GP	G	A	TP	PIM	GP	G	A	TP	PIM
1991-92	West Palm Beach	SunHL	39	12	17	29	160	....	....	....	....	....
1992-93			STATISTICS NOT AVAILABLE									
1993-94	Huntington	ECHL	9	4	2	6	44	....	....	....	....	....
	Richmond	ECHL	28	18	12	30	89	....	....	....	....	....
1994-95	Detroit	IHL	44	5	7	12	285	3	0	1	1	4
1995-96	Detroit	IHL	63	7	9	16	368	10	2	3	5	28
1996-97	**Toronto**	**NHL**	**5**	**0**	**0**	**0**	**10**	....	....	....	....	....
	St. John's	AHL	53	9	10	19	318	7	1	1	2	22
1997-98	Cleveland	IHL	49	9	7	16	233	....	....	....	....	....
	Quebec	IHL	13	2	2	4	73	....	....	....	....	....
	NHL Totals		**5**	**0**	**0**	**0**	**10**	....	....	....	....	....

Signed as a free agent by **Toronto**, July 22, 1996.

CRAIGWELL, DALE

Center. Shoots left. 5'11", 180 lbs. Born, Toronto, Ont., April 24, 1971.
(San Jose's 11th choice, 199th overall, in 1991 Entry Draft).

			Regular Season					Playoffs				
Season	Club	Lea	GP	G	A	TP	PIM	GP	G	A	TP	PIM
1988-89	Oshawa	OHL	55	9	14	23	15	....	....	....	....	....
1989-90	Oshawa	OHL	64	22	41	63	39	17	7	7	14	11
1990-91	Oshawa	OHL	56	27	68	95	34	16	7	16	23	9
1991-92	**San Jose**	**NHL**	**32**	**5**	**11**	**16**	**8**	....	....	....	....	....
	Kansas City	IHL	48	6	19	25	29	12	4	7	11	4
1992-93	**San Jose**	**NHL**	**8**	**3**	**1**	**4**	**4**	....	....	....	....	....
	Kansas City	IHL	60	15	38	53	24	12	*7	5	12	2
1993-94	**San Jose**	**NHL**	**58**	**3**	**6**	**9**	**16**	....	....	....	....	....
	Kansas City	IHL	5	3	1	4	0	....	....	....	....	....
1994-95			DID NOT PLAY – INJURED									
1995-96	San Francisco	IHL	75	11	49	60	38	4	2	0	2	0
1996-97	Kansas City	IHL	82	17	51	68	34	3	1	0	1	0
1997-98	Kansas City	IHL	81	13	42	55	12	11	2	9	11	2
	NHL Totals		**98**	**11**	**18**	**29**	**28**	....	....	....	....	....

CRAVEN, MURRAY — S.J.

Left wing. Shoots left. 6'2", 185 lbs. Born, Medicine Hat, Alta., July 20, 1964.
(Detroit's 1st choice, 17th overall, in 1982 Entry Draft).

			Regular Season					Playoffs				
Season	Club	Lea	GP	G	A	TP	PIM	GP	G	A	TP	PIM
1980-81	Medicine Hat	WHL	69	5	10	15	18	5	0	0	0	2
1981-82	Medicine Hat	WHL	72	35	46	81	49	....	....	....	....	....
1982-83	Medicine Hat	WHL	28	17	29	46	35	....	....	....	....	....
	Detroit	**NHL**	**31**	**4**	**7**	**11**	**6**	....	....	....	....	....
1983-84	Medicine Hat	WHL	48	38	56	94	53	4	5	3	8	4
	Detroit	**NHL**	**15**	**0**	**4**	**4**	**6**	....	....	....	....	....
1984-85	**Philadelphia**	**NHL**	**80**	**26**	**35**	**61**	**30**	**19**	**4**	**6**	**10**	**11**
1985-86	**Philadelphia**	**NHL**	**78**	**21**	**33**	**54**	**34**	**5**	**0**	**3**	**3**	**4**
1986-87	**Philadelphia**	**NHL**	**77**	**19**	**30**	**49**	**38**	**12**	**3**	**1**	**4**	**9**
1987-88	**Philadelphia**	**NHL**	**72**	**30**	**46**	**76**	**58**	**7**	**2**	**5**	**7**	**4**
1988-89	**Philadelphia**	**NHL**	**51**	**9**	**28**	**37**	**52**	**1**	**0**	**0**	**0**	**0**
1989-90	**Philadelphia**	**NHL**	**76**	**25**	**50**	**75**	**42**	....	....	....	....	....
1990-91	**Philadelphia**	**NHL**	**77**	**19**	**47**	**66**	**53**	....	....	....	....	....
1991-92	**Philadelphia**	**NHL**	**12**	**3**	**3**	**6**	**8**	....	....	....	....	....
	Hartford	**NHL**	**61**	**24**	**30**	**54**	**38**	**7**	**3**	**3**	**6**	**6**
1992-93	**Hartford**	**NHL**	**67**	**25**	**42**	**67**	**20**	....	....	....	....	....
	Vancouver	**NHL**	**10**	**0**	**10**	**10**	**12**	**12**	**4**	**6**	**10**	**4**
1993-94	**Vancouver**	**NHL**	**78**	**15**	**40**	**55**	**30**	**22**	**4**	**9**	**13**	**18**
1994-95	**Chicago**	**NHL**	**16**	**4**	**3**	**7**	**2**	**16**	**5**	**5**	**10**	**4**
1995-96	**Chicago**	**NHL**	**66**	**18**	**29**	**47**	**36**	**9**	**1**	**4**	**5**	**2**
1996-97	**Chicago**	**NHL**	**75**	**8**	**27**	**35**	**12**	**2**	**0**	**0**	**0**	**2**
1997-98	**San Jose**	**NHL**	**67**	**12**	**17**	**29**	**25**	**6**	**1**	**1**	**2**	**0**
	NHL Totals		**1009**	**262**	**481**	**743**	**502**	**118**	**27**	**43**	**70**	**64**

Traded to **Philadelphia** by **Detroit** with Joe Paterson for Darryl Sittler, October 10, 1984. Traded to **Hartford** by **Philadelphia** with Philadelphia's 4th round choice (Kevin Smyth) in 1992 Entry Draft for Kevin Dineen, November 13, 1991. Traded to **Vancouver** by **Hartford** with Vancouver's 5th round choice (previously acquired, Vancouver selected Scott Walker) in 1993 Entry Draft for Robert Kron, Vancouver's 3rd round choice (Marek Malik) in 1993 Entry Draft and future considerations (Jim Sandlak, May 17, 1993), March 22, 1993. Traded to **Chicago** by **Vancouver** for Christian Ruutu, March 10, 1995. Traded to **San Jose** by **Chicago** for the rights to Petri Varis and San Jose's 6th round choice (Jari Viuhkola) in 1998 Entry Draft, July 25, 1997.

CROSS, CORY — T.B.

Defense. Shoots left. 6'5", 219 lbs. Born, Lloydminster, Alta., January 3, 1971.
(Tampa Bay's 1st choice, 1st overall, in 1992 Supplemental Draft).

			Regular Season					Playoffs				
Season	Club	Lea	GP	G	A	TP	PIM	GP	G	A	TP	PIM
1990-91	U. of Alberta	CWUAA	20	2	5	7	16	....	....	....	....	....
1991-92	U. of Alberta	CWUAA	41	4	11	15	82	....	....	....	....	....
1992-93	U. of Alberta	CWUAA	43	11	28	39	105	....	....	....	....	....
	Atlanta	IHL	7	0	1	1	2	4	0	0	0	6
1993-94	Tampa Bay	NHL	5	0	0	0	6	....	....	....	....	....
	Atlanta	IHL	70	4	14	18	72	9	1	2	3	14
1994-95	Tampa Bay	NHL	43	1	5	6	41	....	....	....	....	....
	Atlanta	IHL	41	5	10	15	67	....	....	....	....	....
1995-96	Tampa Bay	NHL	75	2	14	16	66	6	0	0	0	22
1996-97	Tampa Bay	NHL	72	4	5	9	95	....	....	....	....	....
1997-98	Tampa Bay	NHL	74	3	6	9	77	....	....	....	....	....
	NHL Totals		**269**	**10**	**30**	**40**	**285**	**6**	**0**	**0**	**0**	**22**

CROWE, PHILIP — (KROH) OTT.

Left wing. Shoots left. 6'2", 215 lbs. Born, Nanton, Alta., April 14, 1970.

			Regular Season					Playoffs				
Season	Club	Lea	GP	G	A	TP	PIM	GP	G	A	TP	PIM
1991-92	Adirondack	AHL	6	1	0	1	29	....	....	....	....	....
	Columbus	ECHL	32	4	7	11	145	....	....	....	....	....
	Toledo	ECHL	2	0	0	0	0	5	0	0	0	58
1992-93	Phoenix	IHL	53	3	3	6	190	....	....	....	....	....
1993-94	Fort Wayne	IHL	5	0	1	1	26	....	....	....	....	....
	Los Angeles	NHL	31	0	2	2	77	....	....	....	....	....
	Phoenix	IHL	2	0	0	0	0	....	....	....	....	....
1994-95	Hershey	AHL	46	11	6	17	132	6	0	1	1	19
1995-96	Philadelphia	NHL	16	1	1	2	28	....	....	....	....	....
	Hershey	AHL	39	6	8	14	105	5	1	2	3	19
1996-97	Ottawa	NHL	26	0	1	1	30	3	0	0	0	16
	Detroit	IHL	41	7	7	14	83	....	....	....	....	....
1997-98	Ottawa	NHL	9	3	0	3	24	....	....	....	....	....
	Detroit	IHL	55	6	13	19	160	20	5	2	7	48
	NHL Totals		**82**	**4**	**4**	**8**	**159**	**3**	**0**	**0**	**0**	**16**

Signed as a free agent by **LA Kings**, November 8, 1993. Signed as a free agent by **Philadelphia**, July 19, 1994. Signed as a free agent by **Ottawa**, July 29, 1996.

CROWLEY, MIKE — ANA.

Defense. Shoots left. 5'11", 190 lbs. Born, Bloomington, MN, July 4, 1975.
(Philadelphia's 5th choice, 140th overall, in 1993 Entry Draft).

			Regular Season					Playoffs				
Season	Club	Lea	GP	G	A	TP	PIM	GP	G	A	TP	PIM
1992-93	Bloomington	H.S.	22	10	32	42	18	....	....	....	....	....
1993-94	Bloomington	H.S.	28	23	54	77	26	....	....	....	....	....
1994-95	U. of Minnesota	WCHA	41	11	27	38	60	....	....	....	....	....
1995-96	U. of Minnesota	WCHA	42	17	46	63	28	....	....	....	....	....
1996-97	U. of Minnesota	WCHA	42	9	*47	*56	24	....	....	....	....	....
1997-98	Anaheim	NHL	8	2	2	4	8	....	....	....	....	....
	Cincinnati	AHL	76	12	26	38	91	....	....	....	....	....
	NHL Totals		**8**	**2**	**2**	**4**	**8**	....	....	....	....	....

WCHA First All-Star Team (1996, 1997) • NCAA West First All-American Team (1996, 1997)

Traded to **Anaheim** by **Philadelphia** with Anatoli Semenov for Brian Wesenberg, March 19, 1996.

CROWLEY, TED — COL.

Defense. Shoots right. 6'2", 188 lbs. Born, Concord, MA, May 3, 1970.
(Toronto's 4th choice, 69th overall, in 1988 Entry Draft).

			Regular Season					Playoffs				
Season	Club	Lea	GP	G	A	TP	PIM	GP	G	A	TP	PIM
1987-88	Lawrence Acad.	H.S.	23	11	23	34	....	....	....	....	....	....
1988-89	Lawrence Acad.	H.S.	23	12	24	36	....	....	....	....	....	....
1989-90	Boston College	H.E.	39	7	24	31	34	....	....	....	....	....
1990-91	Boston College	H.E.	39	12	24	36	61	....	....	....	....	....
1991-92	United States	Nat-Tm	42	6	7	13	65	....	....	....	....	....
	St. John's	AHL	29	5	4	9	33	10	3	1	4	11
1992-93	St. John's	AHL	79	19	38	57	41	9	2	2	4	4
1993-94	United States	Nat-Tm	48	9	13	22	80	....	....	....	....	....
	United States	Olympics	8	0	2	2	8	....	....	....	....	....
	Hartford	NHL	21	1	2	3	10	....	....	....	....	....
1994-95	Chicago	IHL	53	8	23	31	68	....	....	....	....	....
	Houston	IHL	23	4	9	13	35	3	0	1	1	0
1995-96	Providence	AHL	72	12	30	42	47	4	1	2	3	2
1996-97	Cincinnati	IHL	39	9	9	18	24	....	....	....	....	....
	Phoenix	IHL	30	5	8	13	21	....	....	....	....	....
1997-98	Springfield	AHL	78	14	35	49	55	4	1	1	2	2
	NHL Totals		**21**	**1**	**2**	**3**	**10**	....	....	....	....	....

Hockey East First All-Star Team (1991) • NCAA East Second All-American Team (1991)

Traded to **Hartford** by **Toronto** for Mark Greig and Hartford's 6th round choice (later traded to NY Rangers — NY Rangers selected Yuri Litvinov) in 1994 Entry Draft, January 25, 1994. Signed as a free agent by **Boston**, August 9, 1995. Signed as a free agent by **Phoenix**, June 27, 1997. Signed as a free agent by **Colorado**, August 14, 1998.

CROZIER, GREG — PIT.

Left wing. Shoots left. 6'4", 200 lbs. Born, Calgary, Alta., July 6, 1976.
(Pittsburgh's 4th choice, 73rd overall, in 1994 Entry Draft).

			Regular Season					Playoffs				
Season	Club	Lea	GP	G	A	TP	PIM	GP	G	A	TP	PIM
1993-94	Lawrence Acad.	H.S.	18	22	26	48	12	....	....	....	....	....
1994-95	Lawrence Acad.	H.S.	31	45	32	77	22	....	....	....	....	....
1995-96	U. of Michigan	CCHA	42	14	10	24	46	....	....	....	....	....
1996-97	U. of Michigan	CCHA	31	5	15	20	45	....	....	....	....	....
1997-98	U. of Michigan	CCHA	45	12	10	22	26	....	....	....	....	....

CULLEN, JOHN

Center. Shoots right. 5'10", 182 lbs. Born, Fort Erie, Ont., August 2, 1964.
(Buffalo's 2nd choice, 10th overall, in 1986 Supplemental Draft).

			Regular Season					Playoffs				
Season	Club	Lea	GP	G	A	TP	PIM	GP	G	A	TP	PIM
1983-84	Boston University	H.E.	40	23	33	56	28	....	....	....	....	....
1984-85	Boston University	H.E.	41	27	32	59	46	....	....	....	....	....
1985-86	Boston University	H.E.	43	25	49	74	54	....	....	....	....	....
1986-87	Boston University	H.E.	36	23	29	52	35	....	....	....	....	....
1987-88	Flint	IHL	81	48	*109	*157	113	16	11	*15	26	16
1988-89	Pittsburgh	NHL	79	12	37	49	112	11	3	6	9	28
1989-90	Pittsburgh	NHL	72	32	60	92	138	....	....	....	....	....
1990-91	Pittsburgh	NHL	65	31	63	94	83	....	....	....	....	....
	Hartford	NHL	13	8	8	16	18	6	2	7	9	10
1991-92	Hartford	NHL	77	26	51	77	141	7	2	1	3	12
1992-93	Hartford	NHL	19	5	4	9	58	....	....	....	....	....
	Toronto	NHL	47	13	28	41	53	12	2	3	5	0
1993-94	Toronto	NHL	53	13	17	30	67	3	0	0	0	0
1994-95	Pittsburgh	NHL	46	13	24	37	66	9	0	2	2	8
1995-96	Tampa Bay	NHL	76	16	34	50	65	5	3	3	6	0
1996-97	Tampa Bay	NHL	70	18	37	55	95	....	....	....	....	....
1997-98	Tampa Bay	NHL	DID NOT PLAY									
	NHL Totals		**617**	**187**	**363**	**550**	**896**	**53**	**12**	**22**	**34**	**58**

Hockey East First All-Star Team (1985, 1986) • NCAA East Second All-American Team (1986) • Hockey East Second All-Star Team (1987) • IHL First All-Star Team (1988) • Won James Gatschene Memorial Trophy (MVP - IHL) (1988) • Shared Garry F. Longman Memorial Trophy (Top Rookie - IHL) with Ed Belfour (1988) • Won Leo P. Lamoureux Memorial Trophy (Top Scorer - IHL) (1988)

Played in NHL All-Star Game (1991, 1992)

Signed as a free agent by **Pittsburgh**, June 21, 1988. Traded to **Hartford** by **Pittsburgh** with Jeff Parker and Zarley Zalapski for Ron Francis, Grant Jennings and Ulf Samuelsson, March 4, 1991. Traded to **Toronto** by **Hartford** for future considerations, November 24, 1992. Signed as a free agent by **Pittsburgh**, August 3, 1994. Signed as a free agent by **Tampa Bay**, September 11, 1995. • Missed entire 1997-98 season recovering from treatment and surgery for non-Hodgkins Lymphoma.

CULLEN, MATT — ANA.

Center. Shoots left. 6'1", 195 lbs. Born, Virginia, MN, November 2, 1976.
(Anaheim's 2nd choice, 35th overall, in 1996 Entry Draft).

			Regular Season					Playoffs				
Season	Club	Lea	GP	G	A	TP	PIM	GP	G	A	TP	PIM
1994-95	Moorehead High	H.S.	28	47	42	89	78	....	....	....	....	....
1995-96	St. Cloud State	WCHA	39	12	29	41	28	....	....	....	....	....
1996-97	St. Cloud State	WCHA	36	15	30	45	70	....	....	....	....	....
	Baltimore	AHL	6	3	3	6	7	3	0	2	2	0
1997-98	Anaheim	NHL	61	6	21	27	23	....	....	....	....	....
	Cincinnati	AHL	18	15	12	27	2	....	....	....	....	....
	NHL Totals		**61**	**6**	**21**	**27**	**23**	....	....	....	....	....

WCHA Second All-Star Team (1997)

CULLIMORE, JASSEN — (KUHL-ih-mohr) T.B.

Defense. Shoots left. 6'5", 225 lbs. Born, Simcoe, Ont., December 4, 1972.
(Vancouver's 2nd choice, 29th overall, in 1991 Entry Draft).

			Regular Season					Playoffs				
Season	Club	Lea	GP	G	A	TP	PIM	GP	G	A	TP	PIM
1989-90	Peterborough	OHL	59	2	6	8	61	11	0	2	2	8
1990-91	Peterborough	OHL	62	8	16	24	74	4	1	0	1	7
1991-92	Peterborough	OHL	54	9	37	46	65	10	3	6	9	8
1992-93	Hamilton	AHL	56	5	7	12	60	....	....	....	....	....
1993-94	Hamilton	AHL	71	8	20	28	86	3	0	1	1	2
1994-95	Vancouver	NHL	34	1	2	3	39	11	0	0	0	12
	Syracuse	AHL	33	2	7	9	66	....	....	....	....	....
1995-96	Vancouver	NHL	27	1	1	2	21	....	....	....	....	....
1996-97	Vancouver	NHL	3	0	0	0	2	....	....	....	....	....
	Montreal	NHL	49	2	6	8	42	2	0	0	0	2
1997-98	Montreal	NHL	3	0	0	0	4	....	....	....	....	....
	Fredericton	AHL	5	1	0	1	8	....	....	....	....	....
	Tampa Bay	NHL	25	1	2	3	22	....	....	....	....	....
	NHL Totals		**141**	**5**	**11**	**16**	**130**	**13**	**0**	**0**	**0**	**14**

OHL Second All-Star Team (1992)

Traded to **Montreal** by **Vancouver** for Donald Brashear, November 13, 1996. Claimed on waivers by **Tampa Bay** from **Montreal**, January 22, 1998.

CUMMINS, JIM — PHX.

Right wing. Shoots right. 6'2", 219 lbs. Born, Dearborn, MI, May 17, 1970.
(NY Rangers' 5th choice, 67th overall, in 1989 Entry Draft).

			Regular Season					Playoffs				
Season	Club	Lea	GP	G	A	TP	PIM	GP	G	A	TP	PIM
1988-89	Michigan State	CCHA	30	3	8	11	98	....	....	....	....	....
1989-90	Michigan State	CCHA	41	8	7	15	94	....	....	....	....	....
1990-91	Michigan State	CCHA	34	9	6	15	110	....	....	....	....	....
1991-92	Detroit	NHL	1	0	0	0	7	....	....	....	....	....
	Adirondack	AHL	65	7	13	20	338	5	0	0	0	19
1992-93	Detroit	NHL	7	1	1	2	58	....	....	....	....	....
	Adirondack	AHL	43	16	4	20	179	9	3	1	4	4
1993-94	Philadelphia	NHL	22	1	2	3	71	....	....	....	....	....
	Hershey	AHL	17	6	6	12	70	....	....	....	....	....
	Tampa Bay	NHL	4	0	0	0	13	....	....	....	....	....
	Atlanta	IHL	7	4	5	9	14	13	1	2	3	90
1994-95	Tampa Bay	NHL	10	1	0	1	41	....	....	....	....	....
	Chicago	NHL	27	3	1	4	117	14	1	1	2	4
1995-96	Chicago	NHL	52	2	4	6	180	10	0	0	0	2
1996-97	Chicago	NHL	65	6	6	12	199	6	0	0	0	24
1997-98	Chicago	NHL	55	0	2	2	178	....	....	....	....	....
	Phoenix	NHL	20	0	0	0	47	3	0	0	0	4
	NHL Totals		**263**	**14**	**16**	**30**	**911**	**33**	**1**	**1**	**2**	**34**

Traded to **Detroit** by **NY Rangers** with Kevin Miller and Dennis Vial for Joey Kocur and Per Djoos, March 5, 1991. Traded to **Philadelphia** by **Detroit** with Philadelphia's 4th round choice (previously acquired by Detroit — later traded to Boston — Boston selected Charles Paquette) in 1993 Entry Draft for Greg Johnson and Philadelphia's 5th round choice (Frederic Deschenes) in 1994 Entry Draft, June 20, 1993. Traded to **Tampa Bay** by **Philadelphia** with Philadelphia's 4th round choice (later traded back to Philadelphia — Philadelphia selected Radovan Somik) in 1995 Entry Draft for Rob DiMaio, March 18, 1994. Traded to **Chicago** by **Tampa Bay** with Tom Tilley and Jeff Buchanan for Paul Ysebaert and Rich Sutter, February 22, 1995. Traded to **Phoenix** by **Chicago** with Keith Carney for Chad Kilger and Jayson More, March 4, 1998.

CUNNEYWORTH, RANDY (KUH-nee-wuhrth) BUF.

Left wing. Shoots left. 6', 198 lbs. Born, Etobicoke, Ont., May 10, 1961.
(Buffalo's 9th choice, 167th overall, in 1980 Entry Draft).

			Regular Season					Playoffs				
Season	**Club**	**Lea**	**GP**	**G**	**A**	**TP**	**PIM**	**GP**	**G**	**A**	**TP**	**PIM**
1979-80	Ottawa	OHA	63	16	25	41	145	11	0	1	1	13
1980-81	Ottawa	OHA	67	54	74	128	240	15	5	8	13	35
	Buffalo	**NHL**	**1**	**0**	**0**	**0**	**2**	....	....	....	....	....
	Rochester	AHL	1	0	1	1	2	....	....	....	....	....
1981-82	**Buffalo**	**NHL**	**20**	**2**	**4**	**6**	**47**	....	....	....	....	....
	Rochester	AHL	57	12	15	27	86	9	4	0	4	30
1982-83	Rochester	AHL	78	23	33	56	111	16	4	4	8	35
1983-84	Rochester	AHL	54	18	17	35	85	17	5	5	10	55
1984-85	Rochester	AHL	72	30	38	68	148	5	2	1	3	16
1985-86	**Pittsburgh**	**NHL**	**75**	**15**	**30**	**45**	**74**	....	....	....	....	....
1986-87	**Pittsburgh**	**NHL**	**79**	**26**	**27**	**53**	**142**	....	....	....	....	....
1987-88	**Pittsburgh**	**NHL**	**71**	**35**	**39**	**74**	**141**	....	....	....	....	....
1988-89	**Pittsburgh**	**NHL**	**70**	**25**	**19**	**44**	**156**	**11**	**3**	**5**	**8**	**26**
1989-90	**Winnipeg**	**NHL**	**28**	**5**	**6**	**11**	**34**	....	....	....	....	....
	Hartford	**NHL**	**43**	**9**	**9**	**18**	**41**	**4**	**0**	**0**	**0**	**2**
1990-91	**Hartford**	**NHL**	**32**	**9**	**5**	**14**	**49**	**1**	**0**	**0**	**0**	**0**
	Springfield	AHL	2	0	0	0	5	....	....	....	....	....
1991-92	**Hartford**	**NHL**	**39**	**7**	**10**	**17**	**71**	**7**	**3**	**0**	**3**	**9**
1992-93	**Hartford**	**NHL**	**39**	**5**	**4**	**9**	**63**	....	....	....	....	....
1993-94	**Hartford**	**NHL**	**63**	**9**	**8**	**17**	**87**	....	....	....	....	....
	Chicago	**NHL**	**16**	**4**	**3**	**7**	**13**	**6**	**0**	**0**	**0**	**8**
1994-95	**Ottawa**	**NHL**	**48**	**5**	**5**	**10**	**68**	....	....	....	....	....
1995-96	**Ottawa**	**NHL**	**81**	**17**	**19**	**36**	**130**	....	....	....	....	....
1996-97	**Ottawa**	**NHL**	**76**	**12**	**24**	**36**	**99**	**7**	**1**	**1**	**2**	**10**
1997-98	**Ottawa**	**NHL**	**71**	**2**	**11**	**13**	**63**	**6**	**0**	**1**	**1**	**6**
	NHL Totals		**852**	**187**	**223**	**410**	**1280**	**42**	**7**	**7**	**14**	**61**

Traded to **Pittsburgh** by **Buffalo** with Mike Moller for Pat Hughes, October 4, 1985. Traded to **Winnipeg** by **Pittsburgh** with Rick Tabaracci and Dave McLlwain for Jim Kyte, Andrew McBain and Randy Gilhen, June 17, 1989. Traded to **Hartford** by **Winnipeg** for Paul MacDermid, December 13, 1989. Traded to **Chicago** by **Hartford** with Gary Suter and Hartford's 3rd round choice (later traded to Vancouver — Vancouver selected Larry Courville) in 1995 Entry Draft for Frantisek Kucera and Jocelyn Lemieux, March 11, 1994. Signed as a free agent by **Ottawa**, July 15, 1994. Signed as a free agent by **Buffalo**, August 27, 1998.

CUNNIFF, DAVID N.J.

Left wing. Shoots left. 5'10", 185 lbs. Born, South Boston, MA, October 9, 1973.

			Regular Season					Playoffs				
Season	**Club**	**Lea**	**GP**	**G**	**A**	**TP**	**PIM**	**GP**	**G**	**A**	**TP**	**PIM**
1995-96	Salem State	ECAC-2	27	12	17	29	62	....	....	....	....	....
1996-97	Jacksonville	ECHL	16	4	5	9	75	....	....	....	....	....
	Raleigh	ECHL	46	14	6	20	67	....	....	....	....	....
1997-98	Raleigh	ECHL	62	12	12	24	168	....	....	....	....	....
	Albany	AHL	4	0	0	0	13	....	....	....	....	....

Signed as a free agent by **New Jersey**, October 1, 1997.

CYRENNE, CORY (suh-REEN)

Center. Shoots left. 5'9", 170 lbs. Born, Winnipeg, Man., August 25, 1977.
(San Jose's 7th choice, 191st overall, in 1996 Entry Draft).

			Regular Season					Playoffs				
Season	**Club**	**Lea**	**GP**	**G**	**A**	**TP**	**PIM**	**GP**	**G**	**A**	**TP**	**PIM**
1995-96	Brandon	WHL	69	38	59	97	58	19	6	14	20	18
1996-97	Brandon	WHL	55	26	56	82	23	6	3	3	6	0
1997-98	Brandon	WHL	72	47	71	118	28	18	10	14	24	10

WHL East First All-Star Team (1998) • Canadian Major Junior Most Sportsmanlike Player of the Year (1998)

CZERKAWSKI, MARIUSZ (chehr-KAWV-skee) NYI

Right wing. Shoots left. 6', 195 lbs. Born, Radomsko, Poland, April 13, 1972.
(Boston's 5th choice, 106th overall, in 1991 Entry Draft).

			Regular Season					Playoffs				
Season	**Club**	**Lea**	**GP**	**G**	**A**	**TP**	**PIM**	**GP**	**G**	**A**	**TP**	**PIM**
1990-91	Tychy	Poland	24	25	15	40	....	....	....	....	....	....
1991-92	Djurgarden	Sweden	39	8	5	13	4	3	0	0	0	2
	Poland	Olympics	5	0	1	1	4	....	....	....	....	....
1992-93	Hammarby	Sweden-2	32	39	30	69	74	....	....	....	....	....
1993-94	Djurgarden	Sweden	39	13	21	34	20	6	3	1	4	2
	Boston	**NHL**	**4**	**2**	**1**	**3**	**0**	**13**	**3**	**3**	**6**	**4**
1994-95	Kiekko	Finland	7	9	3	12	10	....	....	....	....	....
	Boston	**NHL**	**47**	**12**	**14**	**26**	**31**	**5**	**1**	**0**	**1**	**0**
1995-96	**Boston**	**NHL**	**33**	**5**	**6**	**11**	**10**	....	....	....	....	....
	Edmonton	**NHL**	**37**	**12**	**17**	**29**	**8**	....	....	....	....	....
1996-97	**Edmonton**	**NHL**	**76**	**26**	**21**	**47**	**16**	**12**	**2**	**1**	**3**	**10**
1997-98	**NY Islanders**	**NHL**	**68**	**12**	**13**	**25**	**23**	....	....	....	....	....
	NHL Totals		**265**	**69**	**72**	**141**	**88**	**30**	**6**	**4**	**10**	**14**

Traded to **Edmonton** by **Boston** with Sean Brown and Boston's 1st round choice (Matthieu Descoteaux) in 1996 Entry Draft for Bill Ranford, January 11, 1996. Traded to **NY Islanders** by **Edmonton** for Dan Lacouture, August 25, 1997.

DACKELL, ANDREAS (DA-kuhl, an-DRAY-uhs) OTT.

Right wing. Shoots right. 5'11", 191 lbs. Born, Gavle, Sweden, December 29, 1972.
(Ottawa's 3rd choice, 136th overall, in 1996 Entry Draft).

			Regular Season					Playoffs				
Season	**Club**	**Lea**	**GP**	**G**	**A**	**TP**	**PIM**	**GP**	**G**	**A**	**TP**	**PIM**
1990-91	Brynas IF	Sweden	3	0	1	1	2	....	....	....	....	....
1991-92	Brynas IF	Sweden	4	0	0	0	2	2	0	1	1	4
1992-93	Brynas IF	Sweden	40	12	15	27	12	10	4	5	9	2
1993-94	Brynas IF	Sweden	38	12	17	29	47	7	2	2	4	8
	Sweden	Olympics	4	0	0	0	0	....	....	....	....	....
1994-95	Brynas IF	Sweden	39	17	16	33	34	14	3	3	6	14
1995-96	Brynas IF	Sweden	22	6	6	12	8	....	....	....	....	....
1996-97	**Ottawa**	**NHL**	**79**	**12**	**19**	**31**	**8**	**7**	**1**	**0**	**1**	**0**
1997-98	**Ottawa**	**NHL**	**82**	**15**	**18**	**33**	**24**	**11**	**1**	**1**	**2**	**2**
	NHL Totals		**161**	**27**	**37**	**64**	**32**	**18**	**2**	**1**	**3**	**2**

DAFOE, KYLE CAR.

Defense. Shoots right. 6'5", 195 lbs. Born, Charlottetown, P.E.I., January 11, 1979.
(Carolina's 5th choice, 142nd overall, in 1997 Entry Draft).

			Regular Season					Playoffs				
Season	**Club**	**Lea**	**GP**	**G**	**A**	**TP**	**PIM**	**GP**	**G**	**A**	**TP**	**PIM**
1996-97	Owen Sound	OHL	41	1	1	2	58	3	0	0	0	0
1997-98	Owen Sound	OHL	30	1	3	4	55	....	....	....	....	....
	Sudbury	OHL	21	0	3	3	112	10	0	0	0	29

DAGENAIS, PIERRE (da-ZHUH-nay) N.J.

Left wing. Shoots left. 6'4", 200 lbs. Born, Blainville, Que., March 4, 1978.
(New Jersey's 6th choice, 105th overall, in 1998 Entry Draft).

			Regular Season					Playoffs				
Season	**Club**	**Lea**	**GP**	**G**	**A**	**TP**	**PIM**	**GP**	**G**	**A**	**TP**	**PIM**
1995-96	Moncton	QMJHL	67	43	25	68	59	....	....	....	....	....
1996-97	Moncton	QMJHL	6	4	2	6	0	....	....	....	....	....
	Laval	QMJHL	37	16	14	30	40	....	....	....	....	....
	Rouyn-Noranda	QMJHL	27	21	8	29	22	....	....	....	....	....
1997-98	Rouyn-Noranda	QMJHL	60	*66	67	133	50	6	6	2	8	2

QMJHL Second All-Star Team (1998)

• Re-entered NHL draft. Originally New Jersey's 4th choice, 47th overall, in 1996 Entry Draft.

DAHL, KEVIN (DAHL)

Defense. Shoots right. 5'11", 190 lbs. Born, Regina, Sask., December 30, 1968.
(Montreal's 12th choice, 230th overall, in 1988 Entry Draft).

			Regular Season					Playoffs				
Season	**Club**	**Lea**	**GP**	**G**	**A**	**TP**	**PIM**	**GP**	**G**	**A**	**TP**	**PIM**
1986-87	Bowling Green	CCHA	32	2	6	8	54	....	....	....	....	....
1987-88	Bowling Green	CCHA	44	2	23	25	78	....	....	....	....	....
1988-89	Bowling Green	CCHA	46	9	26	35	51	....	....	....	....	....
1989-90	Bowling Green	CCHA	43	8	22	30	74	....	....	....	....	....
1990-91	Fredericton	AHL	32	1	15	16	45	9	0	1	1	11
	Winston-Salem	ECHL	36	7	17	24	58	....	....	....	....	....
1991-92	Canada	Nat-Tm	45	2	15	17	44	....	....	....	....	....
	Canada	Olympics	8	2	0	2	6	....	....	....	....	....
	Salt Lake	IHL	13	0	2	2	12	5	0	0	0	13
1992-93	**Calgary**	**NHL**	**61**	**2**	**9**	**11**	**56**	**6**	**0**	**2**	**2**	**8**
1993-94	**Calgary**	**NHL**	**33**	**0**	**3**	**3**	**23**	**6**	**0**	**0**	**0**	**4**
	Saint John	AHL	2	0	0	0	0	....	....	....	....	....
1994-95	**Calgary**	**NHL**	**34**	**4**	**8**	**12**	**38**	**3**	**0**	**0**	**0**	**0**
1995-96	**Calgary**	**NHL**	**32**	**1**	**1**	**2**	**26**	**1**	**0**	**0**	**0**	**0**
	Saint John	AHL	23	4	11	15	37	....	....	....	....	....
1996-97	**Phoenix**	**NHL**	**2**	**0**	**0**	**0**	**0**	....	....	....	....	....
	Las Vegas	IHL	73	10	21	31	101	3	0	0	0	2
1997-98	**Calgary**	**NHL**	**19**	**0**	**1**	**1**	**6**	....	....	....	....	....
	Chicago	IHL	45	8	9	17	61	20	1	8	9	32
	NHL Totals		**181**	**7**	**22**	**29**	**149**	**16**	**0**	**2**	**2**	**12**

Signed as a free agent by **Calgary**, July 27, 1991. Signed as a free agent by **Phoenix**, September 4, 1996. Signed as a free agent by **Calgary**, September 8, 1997.

DAHLEN, ULF (DAH-lehn)

Right wing. Shoots left. 6'2", 195 lbs. Born, Ostersund, Sweden, January 12, 1967.
(NY Rangers' 1st choice, 7th overall, in 1985 Entry Draft).

			Regular Season					Playoffs				
Season	**Club**	**Lea**	**GP**	**G**	**A**	**TP**	**PIM**	**GP**	**G**	**A**	**TP**	**PIM**
1983-84	Ostersund	Sweden-2	36	15	11	26	10	....	....	....	....	....
1984-85	Ostersund	Sweden-2	36	33	26	59	20	....	....	....	....	....
1985-86	Bjorkloven	Sweden	22	4	3	7	8	....	....	....	....	....
1986-87	Bjorkloven	Sweden	31	9	12	21	20	6	6	2	8	4
1987-88	**NY Rangers**	**NHL**	**70**	**29**	**23**	**52**	**26**	....	....	....	....	....
	Colorado	IHL	2	2	2	4	0	....	....	....	....	....
1988-89	**NY Rangers**	**NHL**	**56**	**24**	**19**	**43**	**50**	**4**	**0**	**0**	**0**	**0**
1989-90	**NY Rangers**	**NHL**	**63**	**18**	**18**	**36**	**30**	....	....	....	....	....
	Minnesota	**NHL**	**13**	**2**	**4**	**6**	**0**	**7**	**1**	**4**	**5**	**2**
1990-91	**Minnesota**	**NHL**	**66**	**21**	**18**	**39**	**6**	**15**	**2**	**6**	**8**	**4**
1991-92	**Minnesota**	**NHL**	**79**	**36**	**30**	**66**	**10**	**7**	**0**	**3**	**3**	**2**
1992-93	**Minnesota**	**NHL**	**83**	**35**	**39**	**74**	**6**	....	....	....	....	....
1993-94	**Dallas**	**NHL**	**65**	**19**	**38**	**57**	**10**	....	....	....	....	....
	San Jose	**NHL**	**13**	**6**	**6**	**12**	**0**	**14**	**6**	**2**	**8**	**0**
1994-95	**San Jose**	**NHL**	**46**	**11**	**23**	**34**	**11**	**11**	**5**	**4**	**9**	**0**
1995-96	**San Jose**	**NHL**	**59**	**16**	**12**	**28**	**27**	....	....	....	....	....
1996-97	**San Jose**	**NHL**	**43**	**8**	**11**	**19**	**8**	....	....	....	....	....
	Chicago	**NHL**	**30**	**6**	**8**	**14**	**10**	**5**	**0**	**1**	**1**	**0**
1997-98	HV 71 Jonkoping	Sweden	29	9	22	31	16	5	1	3	4	12
	Sweden	Olympics	4	1	0	1	2	....	....	....	....	....
	NHL Totals		**686**	**231**	**249**	**480**	**194**	**63**	**14**	**20**	**34**	**8**

Traded to **Minnesota** by **NY Rangers** with LA Kings' 4th round choice (previously acquired by NY Rangers — Minnesota selected Cal McGowan) in 1990 Entry Draft and future considerations for Mike Gartner, March 6, 1990. Transferred to **Dallas** after **Minnesota** franchise relocated, June 9, 1993. Traded to **San Jose** by **Dallas** with Dallas' 7th round choice (Brad Mehalko) in 1995 Entry Draft for Doug Zmolek, Mike Lalor and cash, March 19, 1994. Traded to **Chicago** by **San Jose** with Chris Terreri and Michal Sykora for Ed Belfour, January 25, 1997.

DAIGLE, ALEXANDRE (DAYG) PHI.

Center. Shoots left. 6', 195 lbs. Born, Montreal, Que., February 7, 1975.
(Ottawa's 1st choice, 1st overall, in 1993 Entry Draft).

			Regular Season					Playoffs				
Season	**Club**	**Lea**	**GP**	**G**	**A**	**TP**	**PIM**	**GP**	**G**	**A**	**TP**	**PIM**
1991-92	Victoriaville	QMJHL	66	35	75	110	63	....	....	....	....	....
1992-93	Victoriaville	QMJHL	53	45	92	137	85	6	5	6	11	4
1993-94	**Ottawa**	**NHL**	**84**	**20**	**31**	**51**	**40**	....	....	....	....	....
1994-95	Victoriaville	QMJHL	18	14	20	34	16	....	....	....	....	....
	Ottawa	**NHL**	**47**	**16**	**21**	**37**	**14**	....	....	....	....	....
1995-96	**Ottawa**	**NHL**	**50**	**5**	**12**	**17**	**24**	....	....	....	....	....
1996-97	**Ottawa**	**NHL**	**82**	**26**	**25**	**51**	**33**	**7**	**0**	**0**	**0**	**2**
1997-98	**Ottawa**	**NHL**	**38**	**7**	**9**	**16**	**8**	....	....	....	....	....
	Philadelphia	**NHL**	**37**	**9**	**17**	**26**	**6**	**5**	**0**	**2**	**2**	**0**
	NHL Totals		**338**	**83**	**115**	**198**	**125**	**12**	**0**	**2**	**2**	**2**

QMJHL Second All-Star Team (1992) • Canadian Major Junior Rookie of the Year (1992) • QMJHL First All-Star Team (1993)

Traded to **Philadelphia** by **Ottawa** for Vaclav Prospal, Pat Falloon and Dallas' 2nd round choice (previously acquired, Ottawa selected Chris Bala) in 1998 Entry Draft, January 17, 1998.

DAIGNEAULT, J.J. (DAYN-yoh) NSH.

Defense. Shoots left. 5'10", 186 lbs. Born, Montreal, Que., October 12, 1965.
(Vancouver's 1st choice, 10th overall, in 1984 Entry Draft).

			Regular Season					Playoffs				
Season	Club	Lea	GP	G	A	TP	PIM	GP	G	A	TP	PIM
1981-82	Laval	QMJHL	64	4	25	29	41	18	1	3	4	2
1982-83	Longueuil	QMJHL	70	26	58	84	58	15	4	11	15	35
1983-84	Longueuil	QMJHL	10	2	11	13	6	14	3	13	16	30
	Canada	Nat-Tm	55	5	14	19	40	....	....	....	....	....
	Canada	Olympics	7	1	1	2	0	....	....	....	....	....
1984-85	**Vancouver**	**NHL**	**67**	**4**	**23**	**27**	**69**	....	....	....	....	....
1985-86	**Vancouver**	**NHL**	**64**	**5**	**23**	**28**	**45**	**3**	**0**	**2**	**2**	**0**
1986-87	**Philadelphia**	**NHL**	**77**	**6**	**16**	**22**	**56**	**9**	**1**	**0**	**1**	**0**
1987-88	**Philadelphia**	**NHL**	**28**	**2**	**2**	**4**	**12**	....	....	....	....	....
	Hershey	AHL	10	1	5	6	8	....	....	....	....	....
1988-89	Hershey	AHL	12	0	10	10	13	....	....	....	....	....
	Sherbrooke	AHL	63	10	33	43	48	6	1	3	4	2
1989-90	**Montreal**	**NHL**	**36**	**2**	**10**	**12**	**14**	**9**	**0**	**0**	**0**	**2**
	Sherbrooke	AHL	28	8	19	27	18	....	....	....	....	....
1990-91	**Montreal**	**NHL**	**51**	**3**	**16**	**19**	**31**	**5**	**0**	**1**	**1**	**0**
1991-92	**Montreal**	**NHL**	**79**	**4**	**14**	**18**	**36**	**11**	**0**	**3**	**3**	**4**
1992-93	**Montreal**	**NHL**	**66**	**8**	**10**	**18**	**57**	**20**	**1**	**3**	**4**	**22** ♦
1993-94	**Montreal**	**NHL**	**68**	**2**	**12**	**14**	**73**	**7**	**0**	**1**	**1**	**12**
1994-95	**Montreal**	**NHL**	**45**	**3**	**5**	**8**	**40**	....	....	....	....	....
1995-96	**Montreal**	**NHL**	**7**	**0**	**1**	**1**	**6**	....	....	....	....	....
	St. Louis	**NHL**	**37**	**1**	**3**	**4**	**24**	....	....	....	....	....
	Worcester	AHL	9	1	10	11	10	....	....	....	....	....
	Pittsburgh	**NHL**	**13**	**3**	**3**	**6**	**23**	**17**	**1**	**9**	**10**	**36**
1996-97	**Pittsburgh**	**NHL**	**53**	**3**	**14**	**17**	**36**	....	....	....	....	....
	Anaheim	**NHL**	**13**	**2**	**9**	**11**	**22**	**11**	**2**	**7**	**9**	**16**
1997-98	**Anaheim**	**NHL**	**53**	**2**	**15**	**17**	**28**	....	....	....	....	....
	NY Islanders	**NHL**	**18**	**0**	**6**	**6**	**21**	....	....	....	....	....
	NHL Totals		**775**	**50**	**182**	**232**	**593**	**92**	**5**	**26**	**31**	**92**

QMJHL First All-Star Team (1983)

Traded to **Philadelphia** by **Vancouver** with Vancouver's 2nd round choice (Kent Hawley) in 1986 Entry Draft for Dave Richter, Rich Sutter and Vancouver's 3rd round choice (previously acquired, Vancouver selected Don Gibson) in 1986 Entry Draft, June 6, 1986. Traded to **Montreal** by **Philadelphia** for Scott Sandelin, November 7, 1988. Traded to **St. Louis** by **Montreal** for Pat Jablonski, November 7, 1995. Traded to **Pittsburgh** by **St. Louis** for Pittsburgh's 6th round choice (Stephen Wagner) in 1996 Entry Draft, March 20, 1996. Traded to **Anaheim** by **Pittsburgh** for Garry Valk, February 21, 1997. Traded to **NY Islanders** by **Anaheim** with Joe Sacco and Mark Janssens for Travis Green, Doug Houda and Tony Tuzzolino, February 6, 1998. Claimed by **Nashville** from **NY Islanders** in Expansion Draft, June 26, 1998.

DALE, ANDREW L.A.

Right wing. Shoots left. 6'1", 203 lbs. Born, Sudbury, Ont., February 16, 1976.
(Los Angeles' 6th choice, 189th overall, in 1994 Entry Draft).

			Regular Season					Playoffs				
Season	Club	Lea	GP	G	A	TP	PIM	GP	G	A	TP	PIM
1993-94	Sudbury	OHL	53	8	13	21	21	9	0	3	3	4
1994-95	Sudbury	OHL	65	21	30	51	99	18	2	9	11	37
1995-96	Sudbury	OHL	40	32	24	56	47	....	....	....	....	....
	Kitchener	OHL	24	12	21	33	28	12	5	5	10	25
1996-97	Mississippi	ECHL	19	6	9	15	16	2	0	1	1	0
	Phoenix	IHL	32	7	6	13	19	....	....	....	....	....
1997-98	Springfield	AHL	40	3	6	9	32	....	....	....	....	....
	Mississippi	ECHL	3	1	2	3	2	....	....	....	....	....

DAMPHOUSSE, VINCENT (DAHM-fooz) MTL.

Center. Shoots left. 6'1", 191 lbs. Born, Montreal, Que., December 17, 1967.
(Toronto's 1st choice, 6th overall, in 1986 Entry Draft).

			Regular Season					Playoffs				
Season	Club	Lea	GP	G	A	TP	PIM	GP	G	A	TP	PIM
1983-84	Laval	QMJHL	66	29	36	65	25	....	....	....	....	....
1984-85	Laval	QMJHL	68	35	68	103	62	....	....	....	....	....
1985-86	Laval	QMJHL	69	45	110	155	70	14	9	27	36	12
1986-87	**Toronto**	**NHL**	**80**	**21**	**25**	**46**	**26**	**12**	**1**	**5**	**6**	**8**
1987-88	**Toronto**	**NHL**	**75**	**12**	**36**	**48**	**40**	**6**	**0**	**1**	**1**	**10**
1988-89	**Toronto**	**NHL**	**80**	**26**	**42**	**68**	**75**	....	....	....	....	....
1989-90	**Toronto**	**NHL**	**80**	**33**	**61**	**94**	**56**	**5**	**0**	**2**	**2**	**2**
1990-91	**Toronto**	**NHL**	**79**	**26**	**47**	**73**	**65**	....	....	....	....	....
1991-92	**Edmonton**	**NHL**	**80**	**38**	**51**	**89**	**53**	**16**	**6**	**8**	**14**	**8**
1992-93	**Montreal**	**NHL**	**84**	**39**	**58**	**97**	**98**	**20**	**11**	**12**	**23**	**16** ♦
1993-94	**Montreal**	**NHL**	**84**	**40**	**51**	**91**	**75**	**7**	**1**	**2**	**3**	**8**
1994-95	Ratingen	Germany	11	5	7	12	24	....	....	....	....	....
	Montreal	**NHL**	**48**	**10**	**30**	**40**	**42**	....	....	....	....	....
1995-96	**Montreal**	**NHL**	**80**	**38**	**56**	**94**	**158**	**6**	**4**	**4**	**8**	**0**
1996-97	**Montreal**	**NHL**	**82**	**27**	**54**	**81**	**82**	**5**	**0**	**0**	**0**	**2**
1997-98	**Montreal**	**NHL**	**76**	**18**	**41**	**59**	**58**	**10**	**3**	**6**	**9**	**22**
	NHL Totals		**928**	**328**	**552**	**880**	**828**	**87**	**26**	**40**	**66**	**76**

QMJHL Second All-Star Team (1986)

Played in NHL All-Star Game (1991, 1992)

Traded to **Edmonton** by **Toronto** with Peter Ing, Scott Thornton, Luke Richardson, future considerations and cash for Grant Fuhr, Glenn Anderson and Craig Berube, September 19, 1991. Traded to **Montreal** by **Edmonton** with Edmonton's 4th round choice (Adam Wiesel) in 1993 Entry Draft for Shayne Corson, Brent Gilchrist and Vladimir Vujtek, August 27, 1992.

DANDENAULT, MATHIEU (DAHN-deh-noh) DET.

Right wing/defense. Shoots right. 6', 174 lbs. Born, Sherbrooke, Que., February 3, 1976.
(Detroit's 2nd choice, 49th overall, in 1994 Entry Draft).

			Regular Season					Playoffs				
Season	Club	Lea	GP	G	A	TP	PIM	GP	G	A	TP	PIM
1993-94	Sherbrooke	QMJHL	67	17	36	53	67	12	4	10	14	12
1994-95	Sherbrooke	QMJHL	67	37	70	107	76	7	1	7	8	10
1995-96	**Detroit**	**NHL**	**34**	**5**	**7**	**12**	**6**	....	....	....	....	....
	Adirondack	AHL	4	0	0	0	0	....	....	....	....	....
1996-97	**Detroit**	**NHL**	**65**	**3**	**9**	**12**	**28**	....	....	....	....	.... ♦
1997-98	**Detroit**	**NHL**	**68**	**5**	**12**	**17**	**43**	**3**	**1**	**0**	**1**	**0** ♦
	NHL Totals		**167**	**13**	**28**	**41**	**77**	**3**	**1**	**0**	**1**	**0**

DANEYKO, KEN (DAN-ee-KOH) N.J.

Defense. Shoots left. 6', 215 lbs. Born, Windsor, Ont., April 17, 1964.
(New Jersey's 2nd choice, 18th overall, in 1982 Entry Draft).

			Regular Season					Playoffs				
Season	Club	Lea	GP	G	A	TP	PIM	GP	G	A	TP	PIM
1980-81	Spokane	WHL	62	6	13	19	140	4	0	0	0	6
1981-82	Spokane	WHL	26	1	11	12	147	....	....	....	....	....
	Seattle	WHL	38	1	22	23	151	14	1	9	10	49
1982-83	Seattle	WHL	69	17	43	60	150	4	1	3	4	14
1983-84	Kamloops	WHL	19	6	28	34	52	17	4	9	13	28
	New Jersey	**NHL**	**11**	**1**	**4**	**5**	**17**	....	....	....	....	....
1984-85	**New Jersey**	**NHL**	**1**	**0**	**0**	**0**	**10**	....	....	....	....	....
	Maine	AHL	80	4	9	13	206	11	1	3	4	36
1985-86	**New Jersey**	**NHL**	**44**	**0**	**10**	**10**	**100**	....	....	....	....	....
	Maine	AHL	21	3	2	5	75	....	....	....	....	....
1986-87	**New Jersey**	**NHL**	**79**	**2**	**12**	**14**	**183**	....	....	....	....	....
1987-88	**New Jersey**	**NHL**	**80**	**5**	**7**	**12**	**239**	**20**	**1**	**6**	**7**	**83**
1988-89	**New Jersey**	**NHL**	**80**	**5**	**5**	**10**	**283**	....	....	....	....	....
1989-90	**New Jersey**	**NHL**	**74**	**6**	**15**	**21**	**219**	**6**	**2**	**0**	**2**	**21**
1990-91	**New Jersey**	**NHL**	**80**	**4**	**16**	**20**	**249**	**7**	**0**	**1**	**1**	**10**
1991-92	**New Jersey**	**NHL**	**80**	**1**	**7**	**8**	**170**	**7**	**0**	**3**	**3**	**16**
1992-93	**New Jersey**	**NHL**	**84**	**2**	**11**	**13**	**236**	**5**	**0**	**0**	**0**	**8**
1993-94	**New Jersey**	**NHL**	**78**	**1**	**9**	**10**	**176**	**20**	**0**	**1**	**1**	**45**
1994-95	**New Jersey**	**NHL**	**25**	**1**	**2**	**3**	**54**	**20**	**1**	**0**	**1**	**22** ♦
1995-96	**New Jersey**	**NHL**	**80**	**2**	**4**	**6**	**115**	....	....	....	....	....
1996-97	**New Jersey**	**NHL**	**77**	**2**	**7**	**9**	**70**	**10**	**0**	**0**	**0**	**28**
1997-98	**New Jersey**	**NHL**	**37**	**0**	**1**	**1**	**57**	**6**	**0**	**1**	**1**	**10**
	NHL Totals		**910**	**32**	**110**	**142**	**2178**	**101**	**4**	**12**	**16**	**243**

DANIELS, JEFF NSH.

Left wing. Shoots left. 6'1", 200 lbs. Born, Oshawa, Ont., June 24, 1968.
(Pittsburgh's 6th choice, 109th overall, in 1986 Entry Draft).

			Regular Season					Playoffs				
Season	Club	Lea	GP	G	A	TP	PIM	GP	G	A	TP	PIM
1984-85	Oshawa	OHL	59	7	11	18	16	....	....	....	....	....
1985-86	Oshawa	OHL	62	13	19	32	23	6	0	1	1	0
1986-87	Oshawa	OHL	54	14	9	23	22	15	3	2	5	5
1987-88	Oshawa	OHL	64	29	39	68	59	4	2	3	5	0
1988-89	Muskegon	IHL	58	21	21	42	58	11	3	5	8	11
1989-90	Muskegon	IHL	80	30	47	77	39	6	1	1	2	7
1990-91	**Pittsburgh**	**NHL**	**11**	**0**	**2**	**2**	**2**	....	....	....	....	....
	Muskegon	IHL	62	23	29	52	18	5	1	3	4	2
1991-92	**Pittsburgh**	**NHL**	**2**	**0**	**0**	**0**	**0**	....	....	....	....	....
	Muskegon	IHL	44	19	16	35	38	10	5	4	9	9
1992-93	**Pittsburgh**	**NHL**	**58**	**5**	**4**	**9**	**14**	**12**	**3**	**2**	**5**	**0**
	Cleveland	IHL	3	2	1	3	0	....	....	....	....	....
1993-94	**Pittsburgh**	**NHL**	**63**	**3**	**5**	**8**	**20**	....	....	....	....	....
	Florida	**NHL**	**7**	**0**	**0**	**0**	**0**	....	....	....	....	....
1994-95	**Florida**	**NHL**	**3**	**0**	**0**	**0**	**0**	....	....	....	....	....
	Detroit	IHL	25	8	12	20	6	5	1	0	1	0
1995-96	Springfield	AHL	72	22	20	42	32	10	3	0	3	2
1996-97	**Hartford**	**NHL**	**10**	**0**	**2**	**2**	**0**	....	....	....	....	....
	Springfield	AHL	38	18	14	32	19	16	7	3	10	4
1997-98	**Carolina**	**NHL**	**2**	**0**	**0**	**0**	**0**	....	....	....	....	....
	New Haven	AHL	71	24	27	51	34	3	0	1	1	0
	NHL Totals		**156**	**8**	**13**	**21**	**36**	**12**	**3**	**2**	**5**	**0**

Traded to **Florida** by **Pittsburgh** for Greg Hawgood, March 19, 1994. Signed as a free agent by **Hartford**, August 18, 1995. Transferred to **Carolina** after **Hartford** franchise relocated, June 25, 1997. Claimed by **Nashville** from **Carolina** in Expansion Draft, June 26, 1998.

DANIELS, SCOTT N.J.

Left wing. Shoots left. 6'3", 215 lbs. Born, Prince Albert, Sask., September 19, 1969.
(Hartford's 6th choice, 136th overall, in 1989 Entry Draft).

			Regular Season					Playoffs				
Season	Club	Lea	GP	G	A	TP	PIM	GP	G	A	TP	PIM
1986-87	Kamloops	WHL	43	6	4	10	68	....	....	....	....	....
	New Westminster	WHL	19	4	7	11	30	....	....	....	....	....
1987-88	New Westminster	WHL	37	6	11	17	157	....	....	....	....	....
	Regina	WHL	19	2	3	5	83	....	....	....	....	....
1988-89	Regina	WHL	64	21	26	47	241	....	....	....	....	....
1989-90	Regina	WHL	52	28	31	59	171	....	....	....	....	....
1990-91	Springfield	AHL	40	2	6	8	121	....	....	....	....	....
	Louisville	ECHL	9	5	3	8	34	1	0	2	2	0
1991-92	Springfield	AHL	54	7	15	22	213	10	0	0	0	32
1992-93	**Hartford**	**NHL**	**1**	**0**	**0**	**0**	**19**	....	....	....	....	....
	Springfield	AHL	60	11	12	23	181	12	2	7	9	12
1993-94	Springfield	AHL	52	9	11	20	185	6	0	1	1	53
1994-95	**Hartford**	**NHL**	**12**	**0**	**2**	**2**	**55**	....	....	....	....	....
	Springfield	AHL	48	9	5	14	277	....	....	....	....	....
1995-96	**Hartford**	**NHL**	**53**	**3**	**4**	**7**	**254**	....	....	....	....	....
	Springfield	AHL	6	4	1	5	17	....	....	....	....	....
1996-97	**Philadelphia**	**NHL**	**56**	**5**	**3**	**8**	**237**	....	....	....	....	....
1997-98	**New Jersey**	**NHL**	**26**	**0**	**3**	**3**	**102**	**1**	**0**	**0**	**0**	**0**
	NHL Totals		**148**	**8**	**12**	**20**	**667**	**1**	**0**	**0**	**0**	**0**

Signed as a free agent by **Philadelphia**, June 27, 1996. Claimed by **New Jersey** from **Philadelphia** in NHL Waiver Draft, September 28, 1997.

DARBY, CRAIG NSH.

Center. Shoots right. 6'3", 200 lbs. Born, Oneida, NY, September 26, 1972.
(Montreal's 3rd choice, 43rd overall, in 1991 Entry Draft).

			Regular Season					Playoffs				
Season	Club	Lea	GP	G	A	TP	PIM	GP	G	A	TP	PIM
1990-91	Albany Academy	H.S.	29	32	61	94	....	....	....	....	....	....
1991-92	Providence	H.E.	35	17	24	41	47	....	....	....	....	....
1992-93	Providence	H.E.	35	11	21	32	62	....	....	....	....	....
1993-94	Fredericton	AHL	66	23	33	56	51	....	....	....	....	....
1994-95	**Montreal**	**NHL**	**10**	**0**	**2**	**2**	**0**	....	....	....	....	....
	Fredericton	AHL	64	21	47	68	82	....	....	....	....	....
	NY Islanders	**NHL**	**3**	**0**	**0**	**0**	**0**	....	....	....	....	....
1995-96	**NY Islanders**	**NHL**	**10**	**0**	**2**	**2**	**0**	....	....	....	....	....
	Worcester	AHL	68	22	28	50	47	4	1	1	2	2
1996-97	**Philadelphia**	**NHL**	**9**	**1**	**4**	**5**	**2**	....	....	....	....	....
	Philadelphia	AHL	59	26	33	59	24	10	3	6	9	0
1997-98	**Philadelphia**	**NHL**	**3**	**1**	**0**	**1**	**0**	....	....	....	....	....
	Philadelphia	AHL	77	*42	45	87	34	20	5	9	14	4
	NHL Totals		**35**	**2**	**8**	**10**	**2**	....	....	....	....	....

AHL First All-Star Team (1998)

Traded to **NY Islanders** by **Montreal** with Kirk Muller and Mathieu Schneider for Pierre Turgeon and Vladimir Malakhov, April 5, 1995. Claimed on waivers by **Philadelphia** from **NY Islanders**, June 4, 1996. Claimed by **Nashville** from **Philadelphia** in Expansion Draft, June 26, 1998.

DARBY, REGAN — VAN.

Defense. Shoots left. 6'2", 200 lbs. Born, Estevan, Sask., July 17, 1980.
(Vancouver's 5th choice, 90th overall, in 1998 Entry Draft).

			Regular Season					Playoffs				
Season	Club	Lea	GP	G	A	TP	PIM	GP	G	A	TP	PIM
1997-98	Spokane	WHL	7	0	1	1	28	....	....	....	....	....
	Tri-City	WHL	32	1	2	3	125	....	....	....	....	....

DARGUZAS, DAVID — (DAHR-goo-suhs) — VAN.

Center. Shoots left. 6'2", 205 lbs. Born, Maple Ridge, Alta., January 20, 1979.
(Vancouver's 6th choice, 114th overall, in 1997 Entry Draft).

			Regular Season					Playoffs				
Season	Club	Lea	GP	G	A	TP	PIM	GP	G	A	TP	PIM
1995-96	Brandon	WHL	47	3	9	12	51	3	0	0	0	0
1996-97	Edmonton	WHL	71	23	32	55	124	....	....	....	....	....
1997-98	Edmonton	WHL	29	5	6	11	42	....	....	....	....	....
	Tri-City	WHL	19	2	2	4	20	....	....	....	....	....

DATSYUK, PAVEL — (daht-SOOK) — DET.

Center. Shoots left. 5'11", 180 lbs. Born, Sverdlovsk, USSR, July 20, 1978.
(Detroit's 8th choice, 171st overall, in 1998 Entry Draft).

			Regular Season					Playoffs				
Season	Club	Lea	GP	G	A	TP	PIM	GP	G	A	TP	PIM
1996-97	Yekaterinburg	Russia	18	2	2	4	4	....	....	....	....	....
	Yekaterinburg	Russia-2	36	12	10	22	12	....	....	....	....	....
1997-98	Yekaterinburg	Russia	24	3	5	8	4	....	....	....	....	....
	Yekaterinburg	Russia-2	22	7	8	15	4	....	....	....	....	....

DAVIDSON, MATT — BUF.

Right wing. Shoots right. 6'2", 190 lbs. Born, Flin Flon, Man., August 9, 1977.
(Buffalo's 5th choice, 94th overall, in 1995 Entry Draft).

			Regular Season					Playoffs				
Season	Club	Lea	GP	G	A	TP	PIM	GP	G	A	TP	PIM
1993-94	Portland	WHL	59	4	12	16	18	10	0	0	0	4
1994-95	Portland	WHL	72	17	20	37	51	9	1	3	4	0
1995-96	Portland	WHL	70	24	26	50	96	7	2	2	4	2
1996-97	Portland	WHL	72	44	27	71	47	6	0	1	1	2
1997-98	Rochester	AHL	72	15	12	27	12	3	1	0	1	2

DAVIDSSON, JOHAN — (DAH-vihd-suhn) — ANA.

Center. Shoots right. 6'1", 190 lbs. Born, Jonkoping, Sweden, January 6, 1976.
(Anaheim's 2nd choice, 28th overall, in 1994 Entry Draft).

			Regular Season					Playoffs				
Season	Club	Lea	GP	G	A	TP	PIM	GP	G	A	TP	PIM
1992-93	HV 71 Jonkoping	Sweden	8	1	0	1	0	....	....	....	....	....
1993-94	HV 71 Jonkoping	Sweden	38	2	5	7	4	....	....	....	....	....
1994-95	HV 71 Jonkoping	Sweden	37	4	7	11	20	13	3	2	5	0
1995-96	HV 71 Jonkoping	Sweden	39	7	11	18	20	4	0	2	2	0
1996-97	HV 71 Jonkoping	Sweden	50	18	21	39	18	5	0	3	3	2
1997-98	Helsinki	Finland	43	10	30	40	8	9	3	10	13	0

DAVIS, JUSTIN

Right wing. Shoots right. 6'2", 175 lbs. Born, Burlington, Ont., March 1, 1978.
(Washington's 7th choice, 85th overall, in 1996 Entry Draft).

			Regular Season					Playoffs				
Season	Club	Lea	GP	G	A	TP	PIM	GP	G	A	TP	PIM
1995-96	Kingston	OHL	64	30	18	48	20	6	2	3	5	0
1996-97	Kingston	OHL	35	8	17	25	17	....	....	....	....	....
	S.S. Marie	OHL	20	1	5	6	2	3	0	1	1	0
1997-98	S.S. Marie	OHL	2	0	0	0	0	....	....	....	....	....
	Ottawa	OHL	58	32	23	55	14	9	5	5	10	0

DAVISON, ROB — S.J.

Right wing. Shoots left. 6'2", 210 lbs. Born, St. Catharines, Ont., May 1, 1980.
(San Jose's 4th choice, 98th overall, in 1998 Entry Draft).

			Regular Season					Playoffs				
Season	Club	Lea	GP	G	A	TP	PIM	GP	G	A	TP	PIM
1997-98	North Bay	OHL	59	0	11	11	200	....	....	....	....	....

DAW, JEFF — EDM.

Center. Shoots right. 6'3", 190 lbs. Born, Carlisle, Ont., February 28, 1972.

			Regular Season					Playoffs				
Season	Club	Lea	GP	G	A	TP	PIM	GP	G	A	TP	PIM
1992-93	U. Mass-Lowell	H.E.	37	12	18	30	14	....	....	....	....	....
1993-94	U. Mass-Lowell	H.E.	40	6	12	18	12	....	....	....	....	....
1994-95	U. Mass-Lowell	H.E.	40	27	15	42	24	....	....	....	....	....
1995-96	U. Mass-Lowell	H.E.	40	23	28	51	10	....	....	....	....	....
1996-97	Wheeling	ECHL	13	3	8	11	26	....	....	....	....	....
	Hamilton	AHL	56	11	8	19	39	19	4	5	9	0
1997-98	Hamilton	AHL	79	28	35	63	20	9	6	3	9	0

Signed as a free agent by **Edmonton**, August 1, 1996.

DAWE, JASON — (DAW) — NYI

Right wing. Shoots left. 5'10", 189 lbs. Born, North York, Ont., May 29, 1973.
(Buffalo's 2nd choice, 35th overall, in 1991 Entry Draft).

			Regular Season					Playoffs				
Season	Club	Lea	GP	G	A	TP	PIM	GP	G	A	TP	PIM
1989-90	Peterborough	OHL	50	15	18	33	19	12	4	7	11	4
1990-91	Peterborough	OHL	66	43	27	70	43	4	3	1	4	0
1991-92	Peterborough	OHL	66	53	55	108	55	4	5	0	5	0
1992-93	Peterborough	OHL	59	58	68	126	80	21	18	33	51	18
	Rochester	AHL	....	....	....	....	....	3	1	0	1	0
1993-94	**Buffalo**	**NHL**	**32**	**6**	**7**	**13**	**12**	**6**	**0**	**1**	**1**	**6**
	Rochester	AHL	48	22	14	36	44	....	....	....	....	....
1994-95	Rochester	AHL	44	27	19	46	24	....	....	....	....	....
	Buffalo	**NHL**	**42**	**7**	**4**	**11**	**19**	**5**	**2**	**1**	**3**	**6**
1995-96	**Buffalo**	**NHL**	**67**	**25**	**25**	**50**	**33**	....	....	....	....	....
	Rochester	AHL	7	5	4	9	2	....	....	....	....	....
1996-97	**Buffalo**	**NHL**	**81**	**22**	**26**	**48**	**32**	**11**	**2**	**1**	**3**	**6**
1997-98	**Buffalo**	**NHL**	**68**	**19**	**17**	**36**	**36**	....	....	....	....	....
	NY Islanders	**NHL**	**13**	**1**	**2**	**3**	**6**	....	....	....	....	....
	NHL Totals		**303**	**80**	**81**	**161**	**138**	**22**	**4**	**3**	**7**	**18**

OHL First All-Star Team (1993) • Canadian Major Junior Second All-Star Team (1993) • Won George Parsons Trophy (Memorial Cup Tournament Most Sportsmanlike Player) (1993)

Traded to **NY Islanders** by **Buffalo** for Jason Holland and Paul Kruse, March 24, 1998.

DAZE, ERIC — (dah-ZAY) — CHI.

Left wing. Shoots left. 6'6", 220 lbs. Born, Montreal, Que., July 2, 1975.
(Chicago's 5th choice, 90th overall, in 1993 Entry Draft).

			Regular Season					Playoffs				
Season	Club	Lea	GP	G	A	TP	PIM	GP	G	A	TP	PIM
1992-93	Beauport	QMJHL	68	19	36	55	24	....	....	....	....	....
1993-94	Beauport	QMJHL	66	59	48	107	31	15	16	8	24	2
1994-95	Beauport	QMJHL	57	54	45	99	20	16	9	12	21	23
	Chicago	**NHL**	**4**	**1**	**1**	**2**	**2**	**16**	**0**	**1**	**1**	**4**
1995-96	**Chicago**	**NHL**	**80**	**30**	**23**	**53**	**18**	**10**	**3**	**5**	**8**	**0**
1996-97	**Chicago**	**NHL**	**71**	**22**	**19**	**41**	**16**	**6**	**2**	**1**	**3**	**2**
1997-98	**Chicago**	**NHL**	**80**	**31**	**11**	**42**	**22**	....	....	....	....	....
	NHL Totals		**235**	**84**	**54**	**138**	**58**	**32**	**5**	**7**	**12**	**6**

QMJHL First All-Star Team (1994, 1995) • Canadian Major Junior Most Sportsmanlike Player of the Year (1995) • NHL All-Rookie Team (1996)

DEADMARSH, ADAM — COL.

Center. Shoots right. 6', 195 lbs. Born, Trail, B.C., May 10, 1975.
(Quebec's 2nd choice, 14th overall, in 1993 Entry Draft).

			Regular Season					Playoffs				
Season	Club	Lea	GP	G	A	TP	PIM	GP	G	A	TP	PIM
1991-92	Portland	WHL	68	30	30	60	81	6	3	3	6	13
1992-93	Portland	WHL	58	33	36	69	126	16	7	8	15	29
1993-94	Portland	WHL	65	43	56	99	212	10	9	8	17	33
1994-95	Portland	WHL	29	28	20	48	129	....	....	....	....	....
	Quebec	**NHL**	**48**	**9**	**8**	**17**	**56**	**6**	**0**	**1**	**1**	**0**
1995-96	**Colorado**	**NHL**	**78**	**21**	**27**	**48**	**142**	**22**	**5**	**12**	**17**	**25** ♦
1996-97	**Colorado**	**NHL**	**78**	**33**	**27**	**60**	**136**	**17**	**3**	**6**	**9**	**24**
1997-98	**Colorado**	**NHL**	**73**	**22**	**21**	**43**	**125**	**7**	**2**	**0**	**2**	**4**
	United States	Olympics	4	1	0	1	2	....	....	....	....	....
	NHL Totals		**277**	**85**	**83**	**168**	**459**	**52**	**10**	**19**	**29**	**53**

Transferred to **Colorado** after **Quebec** franchise relocated, June 21, 1995.

DEAN, KEVIN — N.J.

Defense. Shoots left. 6'3", 205 lbs. Born, Madison, WI, April 1, 1969.
(New Jersey's 4th choice, 86th overall, in 1987 Entry Draft).

			Regular Season					Playoffs				
Season	Club	Lea	GP	G	A	TP	PIM	GP	G	A	TP	PIM
1986-87	Culver Academy	H.S.	25	19	25	44	30	....	....	....	....	....
1987-88	New Hampshire	H.E.	27	1	6	7	34	....	....	....	....	....
1988-89	New Hampshire	H.E.	34	1	12	13	28	....	....	....	....	....
1989-90	New Hampshire	H.E.	39	2	6	8	42	....	....	....	....	....
1990-91	New Hampshire	H.E.	31	10	12	22	22	....	....	....	....	....
	Utica	AHL	7	0	1	1	2	....	....	....	....	....
1991-92	Utica	AHL	23	0	3	3	6	....	....	....	....	....
	Cincinnati	ECHL	30	3	22	25	43	9	1	6	7	8
1992-93	Cincinnati	IHL	13	2	1	3	15	....	....	....	....	....
	Utica	AHL	57	2	16	18	76	5	1	0	1	8
1993-94	Albany	AHL	70	9	33	42	92	5	0	2	2	7
1994-95	**New Jersey**	**NHL**	**17**	**0**	**1**	**1**	**4**	**3**	**0**	**2**	**2**	**0** ♦
	Albany	AHL	68	5	37	42	66	8	0	4	4	4
1995-96	**New Jersey**	**NHL**	**41**	**0**	**6**	**6**	**28**	....	....	....	....	....
	Albany	AHL	1	1	0	1	2	....	....	....	....	....
1996-97	**New Jersey**	**NHL**	**28**	**2**	**4**	**6**	**6**	**1**	**1**	**0**	**1**	**0**
	Albany	AHL	2	0	1	1	4	....	....	....	....	....
1997-98	**New Jersey**	**NHL**	**50**	**1**	**8**	**9**	**12**	**5**	**1**	**0**	**1**	**2**
	Albany	AHL	2	0	1	1	2	....	....	....	....	....
	NHL Totals		**136**	**3**	**19**	**22**	**50**	**9**	**2**	**2**	**4**	**2**

AHL First All-Star Team (1995)

DEBRUSK, LOUIE — (dah-BRUHSK) — PHX.

Left wing. Shoots left. 6'2", 215 lbs. Born, Cambridge, Ont., March 19, 1971.
(NY Rangers' 4th choice, 49th overall, in 1989 Entry Draft).

			Regular Season					Playoffs				
Season	Club	Lea	GP	G	A	TP	PIM	GP	G	A	TP	PIM
1988-89	London	OHL	59	11	11	22	149	19	1	1	2	43
1989-90	London	OHL	61	21	19	40	198	6	2	2	4	24
1990-91	London	OHL	61	31	33	64	*223	7	2	2	4	14
	Binghamton	AHL	2	0	0	0	7	2	0	0	0	9
1991-92	**Edmonton**	**NHL**	**25**	**2**	**1**	**3**	**124**	....	....	....	....	....
	Cape Breton	AHL	28	2	2	4	73	....	....	....	....	....
1992-93	**Edmonton**	**NHL**	**51**	**8**	**2**	**10**	**205**	....	....	....	....	....
1993-94	**Edmonton**	**NHL**	**48**	**4**	**6**	**10**	**185**	....	....	....	....	....
	Cape Breton	AHL	5	3	1	4	58	....	....	....	....	....
1994-95	**Edmonton**	**NHL**	**34**	**2**	**0**	**2**	**93**	....	....	....	....	....
1995-96	**Edmonton**	**NHL**	**38**	**1**	**3**	**4**	**96**	....	....	....	....	....
1996-97	**Edmonton**	**NHL**	**32**	**2**	**0**	**2**	**94**	**6**	**0**	**0**	**0**	**4**
1997-98	**Tampa Bay**	**NHL**	**54**	**1**	**2**	**3**	**166**	....	....	....	....	....
	San Antonio	IHL	17	7	4	11	130	....	....	....	....	....
	NHL Totals		**282**	**20**	**14**	**34**	**963**	**6**	**0**	**0**	**0**	**4**

Traded to **Edmonton** by **NY Rangers** with Bernie Nicholls and Steven Rice for Mark Messier and future considerations, October 4, 1991. Signed as a free agent by **Tampa Bay**, September 23, 1997. Traded to **Phoenix** by **Tampa Bay** with Tampa Bay's 5th round choice (Jay Leach) in 1998 Entry Draft for Craig Janney, June 11, 1998.

DEFAUW, BRAD — CAR.

Left wing. Shoots left. 6'2", 210 lbs. Born, Edina, MN, November 10, 1977.
(Carolina's 2nd choice, 28th overall, in 1997 Entry Draft).

			Regular Season					Playoffs				
Season	Club	Lea	GP	G	A	TP	PIM	GP	G	A	TP	PIM
1995-96	Apple Valley	H.S.	28	21	34	55	14	....	....	....	....	....
1996-97	North Dakota	WCHA	37	7	6	13	39	....	....	....	....	....
1997-98	North Dakota	WCHA	36	9	11	20	34	....	....	....	....	....

DEGERMAN, TOMMI — (DAI-guhr-mahn) — ANA.

Left wing. Shoots left. 6'2", 185 lbs. Born, Espoo, Finland, February 23, 1976.
(Anaheim's 8th choice, 235th overall, in 1997 Entry Draft).

			Regular Season					Playoffs				
Season	Club	Lea	GP	G	A	TP	PIM	GP	G	A	TP	PIM
1994-95	Kiekko-Espoo	Fin-Jr.	26	4	7	11	14	5	1	0	1	4
1995-96	Kiekko-Espoo	Fin-Jr.	36	11	15	26	14	....	....	....	....	....
1996-97	Kiekko-Espoo	Fin-Jr.	3	3	0	3	0	....	....	....	....	....
	Pelicans Lahti	Finland-2	4	0	4	4	0	....	....	....	....	....
	Kiekko-Espoo	Finland	23	2	0	2	2	....	....	....	....	....
	Boston University	H.E.	17	6	10	16	19	....	....	....	....	....
1997-98	Boston University	H.E.	35	12	20	32	37	....	....	....	....	....

DELANEY, KEITH — FLA.

Center. Shoots left. 6'1", 196 lbs. Born, Labrador City, Nfld., May 7, 1979.
(Florida's 7th choice, 155th overall, in 1997 Entry Draft).

			Regular Season					Playoffs				
Season	Club	Lea	GP	G	A	TP	PIM	GP	G	A	TP	PIM
1996-97	Barrie	OHL	64	5	5	10	19	9	0	1	1	0
1997-98	Barrie	OHL	66	24	30	54	28	6	4	1	5	2

DELEEUW, ADAM — DET.

Left wing. Shoots left. 6', 206 lbs. Born, Brampton, Ont., February 29, 1980.
(Detroit's 7th choice, 151st overall, in 1998 Entry Draft).

			Regular Season					Playoffs				
Season	Club	Lea	GP	G	A	TP	PIM	GP	G	A	TP	PIM
1996-97	Brampton	OJHL	45	11	17	28	97	....	....	....	....	....
1997-98	Barrie	OHL	56	10	6	16	224	....	....	....	....	....

DELISLE, JONATHAN (duh-LIGHL) — MTL.

Right wing. Shoots right. 5'10", 193 lbs. Born, Ste-Anne-des-Plaines, Que., June 30, 1977.
(Montreal's 4th choice, 86th overall, in 1995 Entry Draft).

			Regular Season					Playoffs				
Season	Club	Lea	GP	G	A	TP	PIM	GP	G	A	TP	PIM
1993-94	Verdun	QMJHL	61	16	17	33	130	4	0	1	1	14
1994-95	Hull	QMJHL	60	21	38	59	218	19	11	8	19	43
1995-96	Hull	QMJHL	62	31	57	88	193	18	6	13	19	64
1996-97	Hull	QMJHL	61	35	54	89	228	14	11	13	24	46
1997-98	Fredericton	AHL	78	15	21	36	138	4	0	1	1	7

DELISLE, XAVIER (duh-LIGHL) — T.B.

Center. Shoots right. 5'11", 182 lbs. Born, Quebec City, Que., May 24, 1977.
(Tampa Bay's 5th choice, 157th overall, in 1996 Entry Draft).

			Regular Season					Playoffs				
Season	Club	Lea	GP	G	A	TP	PIM	GP	G	A	TP	PIM
1993-94	Granby	QMJHL	46	11	22	33	25	7	2	0	2	0
1994-95	Granby	QMJHL	72	18	36	54	48	13	2	6	8	4
1995-96	Granby	QMJHL	67	45	75	120	45	20	13	*27	*40	12
1996-97	Granby	QMJHL	59	36	56	92	20	5	1	4	5	6
1997-98	Adirondack	AHL	76	10	19	29	47	3	0	0	0	0

QMJHL Second All-Star Team (1996) • Memorial Cup All-Star Team (1996)

DELMORE, ANDY — PHI.

Defense. Shoots right. 6'1", 192 lbs. Born, LaSalle, Ont., December 26, 1976.

			Regular Season					Playoffs				
Season	Club	Lea	GP	G	A	TP	PIM	GP	G	A	TP	PIM
1993-94	North Bay	OHL	45	2	7	9	33	17	0	0	0	2
1994-95	North Bay	OHL	40	2	14	16	21	....	....	....	....	....
	Sarnia	OHL	27	5	13	18	27	3	0	0	0	2
1995-96	Sarnia	OHL	64	21	38	59	45	10	3	7	10	2
1996-97	Sarnia	OHL	64	18	60	78	39	12	2	10	12	10
	Fredericton	AHL	4	0	1	1	0	....	....	....	....	....
1997-98	Philadelphia	AHL	73	9	30	39	46	18	4	4	8	21

OHL First All-Star Team (1997)

Signed as a free agent by **Philadelphia**, June 9, 1997.

DEMIDOV, ILJA (deh-MEE-dahf, ihl-YA) — CGY.

Defense. Shoots left. 6'3", 185 lbs. Born, Moscow, USSR, April 14, 1979.
(Calgary's 10th choice, 140th overall, in 1997 Entry Draft).

			Regular Season					Playoffs				
Season	Club	Lea	GP	G	A	TP	PIM	GP	G	A	TP	PIM
1995-96	Moscow D'amo 2	CIS-2	10	0	14	14	....	....	....	....	....	....
1996-97	Moscow D'amo 2	Russia-3	32	1	0	1	60	....	....	....	....	....
1997-98	Oshawa	OHL	61	4	16	20	67	7	0	1	1	2

DEMITRA, PAVOL (deh-MIHT-rah) — ST.L.

Left wing. Shoots left. 6', 189 lbs. Born, Dubnica, Czech., November 29, 1974.
(Ottawa's 8th choice, 227th overall, in 1993 Entry Draft).

			Regular Season					Playoffs				
Season	Club	Lea	GP	G	A	TP	PIM	GP	G	A	TP	PIM
1991-92	Dubnica	Czech-2	28	13	10	23	12	....	....	....	....	....
1992-93	Dubnica	Czech-2	4	3	0	3	....	....	....	....	....	....
	Dukla Trencin	Czech.	46	10	18	28	....	....	....	....	....	....
1993-94	**Ottawa**	**NHL**	**12**	**1**	**1**	**2**	**4**	....	....	....	....	....
	P.E.I.	AHL	41	18	23	41	8	....	....	....	....	....
1994-95	P.E.I.	AHL	61	26	48	74	23	5	0	7	7	0
	Ottawa	**NHL**	**16**	**4**	**3**	**7**	**0**	....	....	....	....	....
1995-96	**Ottawa**	**NHL**	**31**	**7**	**10**	**17**	**6**	....	....	....	....	....
	P.E.I.	AHL	48	28	53	81	44	....	....	....	....	....
1996-97	Dukla Trencin	Slovakia	1	1	1	2	....	....	....	....	....	....
	St. Louis	**NHL**	**8**	**3**	**0**	**3**	**2**	**6**	**1**	**3**	**4**	**6**
	Las Vegas	IHL	22	8	13	21	10	....	....	....	....	....
	Grand Rapids	IHL	42	20	30	50	24	....	....	....	....	....
1997-98	**St. Louis**	**NHL**	**61**	**22**	**30**	**52**	**22**	**10**	**3**	**3**	**6**	**2**
	NHL Totals		**128**	**37**	**44**	**81**	**34**	**16**	**4**	**6**	**10**	**8**

Traded to **St. Louis** by **Ottawa** for Christer Olsson, November 27, 1996.

DEMPSEY, NATHAN — TOR.

Left wing. Shoots left. 6', 170 lbs. Born, Spruce Grove, Alta., July 14, 1974.
(Toronto's 12th choice, 245th overall, in 1992 Entry Draft).

			Regular Season					Playoffs				
Season	Club	Lea	GP	G	A	TP	PIM	GP	G	A	TP	PIM
1991-92	Regina	WHL	70	4	22	26	72	....	....	....	....	....
1992-93	Regina	WHL	72	12	29	41	95	13	3	8	11	14
	St. John's	AHL	....	....	....	....	....	2	0	0	0	0
1993-94	Regina	WHL	56	14	36	50	100	4	0	0	0	4
1994-95	St. John's	AHL	74	7	30	37	91	5	1	0	1	11
1995-96	St. John's	AHL	73	5	15	20	103	4	1	0	1	9
1996-97	**Toronto**	**NHL**	**14**	**1**	**1**	**2**	**2**	....	....	....	....	....
	St. John's	AHL	52	8	18	26	108	6	1	0	1	4
1997-98	St. John's	AHL	68	12	16	28	85	4	0	0	0	0
	NHL Totals		**14**	**1**	**1**	**2**	**2**	....	....	....	....	....

WHL East Second All-Star Team (1994)

DESCOTEAUX, MATTHIEU (DAY-koh-toh) — EDM.

Defense. Shoots left. 6'3", 220 lbs. Born, Pierreville, Que., September 23, 1977.
(Edmonton's 2nd choice, 19th overall, in 1996 Entry Draft).

			Regular Season					Playoffs				
Season	Club	Lea	GP	G	A	TP	PIM	GP	G	A	TP	PIM
1994-95	Shawinigan	QMJHL	50	3	2	5	28	15	1	1	2	19
1995-96	Shawinigan	QMJHL	69	2	13	15	129	6	0	0	0	6
1996-97	Shawinigan	QMJHL	38	6	18	24	121	....	....	....	....	....
	Hull	QMJHL	32	6	19	25	34	14	1	8	9	29
1997-98	Hamilton	AHL	67	2	8	10	70	2	0	0	0	0

DESJARDINS, ERIC (deh-ZHAHR-dai) — PHI.

Defense. Shoots right. 6'1", 200 lbs. Born, Rouyn, Que., June 14, 1969.
(Montreal's 3rd choice, 38th overall, in 1987 Entry Draft).

			Regular Season					Playoffs				
Season	Club	Lea	GP	G	A	TP	PIM	GP	G	A	TP	PIM
1986-87	Granby	QMJHL	66	14	24	38	178	8	3	2	5	10
1987-88	Granby	QMJHL	62	18	49	67	138	5	0	3	3	10
	Sherbrooke	AHL	3	0	0	0	6	4	0	2	2	2
1988-89	**Montreal**	**NHL**	**36**	**2**	**12**	**14**	**26**	**14**	**1**	**1**	**2**	**6**
1989-90	**Montreal**	**NHL**	**55**	**3**	**13**	**16**	**51**	**6**	**0**	**0**	**0**	**10**
1990-91	**Montreal**	**NHL**	**62**	**7**	**18**	**25**	**27**	**13**	**1**	**4**	**5**	**8**
1991-92	**Montreal**	**NHL**	**77**	**6**	**32**	**38**	**50**	**11**	**3**	**3**	**6**	**4**
1992-93	**Montreal**	**NHL**	**82**	**13**	**32**	**45**	**98**	**20**	**4**	**10**	**14**	**23** ♦
1993-94	**Montreal**	**NHL**	**84**	**12**	**23**	**35**	**97**	**7**	**0**	**2**	**2**	**4**
1994-95	**Montreal**	**NHL**	**9**	**0**	**6**	**6**	**2**	....	....	....	....	....
	Philadelphia	**NHL**	**34**	**5**	**18**	**23**	**12**	**15**	**4**	**4**	**8**	**10**
1995-96	**Philadelphia**	**NHL**	**80**	**7**	**40**	**47**	**45**	**12**	**0**	**6**	**6**	**2**
1996-97	**Philadelphia**	**NHL**	**82**	**12**	**34**	**46**	**50**	**19**	**2**	**8**	**10**	**12**
1997-98	**Philadelphia**	**NHL**	**77**	**6**	**27**	**33**	**36**	**5**	**0**	**1**	**1**	**0**
	Canada	Olympics	6	0	0	0	2	....	....	....	....	....
	NHL Totals		**678**	**73**	**255**	**328**	**494**	**122**	**15**	**39**	**54**	**79**

QMJHL Second All-Star Team (1987) • QMJHL First All-Star Team (1988)

Played in NHL All-Star Game (1992, 1996)

Traded to **Philadelphia** by **Montreal** with Gilbert Dionne and John LeClair for Mark Recchi and Philadelphia's 3rd round choice (Martin Hohenberger) in 1995 Entry Draft, February 9, 1995.

DESROCHES, JONATHAN (deh-ROHSH) — MTL.

Defense. Shoots left. 6', 206 lbs. Born, Granby, Que., May 23, 1979.
(Montreal's 7th choice, 145th overall, in 1997 Entry Draft).

			Regular Season					Playoffs				
Season	Club	Lea	GP	G	A	TP	PIM	GP	G	A	TP	PIM
1994-95	Magog	QAAA	42	6	15	21	38	....	....	....	....	....
1995-96	Granby	QMJHL	44	1	6	7	38	11	0	0	0	2
1996-97	Granby	QMJHL	58	7	15	22	36	5	0	1	1	2
1997-98	Moncton	QMJHL	63	4	27	31	56	10	0	2	2	4

DESSNER, JEFF — NYR

Defense. Shoots left. 6'2", 177 lbs. Born, Skokie, IL, April 16, 1977.
(NY Rangers' 6th choice, 185th overall, in 1996 Entry Draft).

			Regular Season					Playoffs				
Season	Club	Lea	GP	G	A	TP	PIM	GP	G	A	TP	PIM
1995-96	Taft High	H.S.	23	12	25	37	....	....	....	....	....	....
1996-97	U. of Wisconsin	WCHA	DID NOT PLAY – FRESHMAN									
1997-98	U. of Wisconsin	WCHA	19	1	3	4	43	....	....	....	....	....

DEULING, JARRETT — S.J.

Left wing. Shoots left. 6', 202 lbs. Born, Vernon, B.C., March 4, 1974.
(NY Islanders' 2nd choice, 56th overall, in 1992 Entry Draft).

			Regular Season					Playoffs				
Season	Club	Lea	GP	G	A	TP	PIM	GP	G	A	TP	PIM
1990-91	Kamloops	WHL	48	4	12	16	43	12	5	2	7	7
1991-92	Kamloops	WHL	68	28	26	54	79	17	10	6	16	18
1992-93	Kamloops	WHL	68	31	32	63	93	13	6	7	13	14
1993-94	Kamloops	WHL	70	44	59	103	171	18	*13	8	21	43
1994-95	Worcester	AHL	63	11	8	19	37	....	....	....	....	....
1995-96	**NY Islanders**	**NHL**	**14**	**0**	**1**	**1**	**11**	....	....	....	....	....
	Worcester	AHL	57	16	7	23	57	4	1	2	3	2
1996-97	**NY Islanders**	**NHL**	**1**	**0**	**0**	**0**	**0**	....	....	....	....	....
	Kentucky	AHL	58	15	31	46	57	4	3	0	3	8
1997-98	Milwaukee	IHL	64	18	18	36	84	10	4	3	7	36
	NHL Totals		**15**	**0**	**1**	**1**	**11**	....	....	....	....	....

Signed as a free agent by **San Jose**, August 27, 1998.

DEVEREAUX, BOYD (DEH-vuhr-oh) — EDM.

Center. Shoots left. 6'2", 195 lbs. Born, Seaforth, Ont., April 16, 1978.
(Edmonton's 1st choice, 6th overall, in 1996 Entry Draft).

			Regular Season					Playoffs				
Season	Club	Lea	GP	G	A	TP	PIM	GP	G	A	TP	PIM
1995-96	Kitchener	OHL	66	20	38	58	35	12	3	7	10	4
1996-97	Kitchener	OHL	54	28	41	69	37	13	4	11	15	8
	Hamilton	AHL	....	....	....	....	....	1	0	1	1	0
1997-98	**Edmonton**	**NHL**	**38**	**1**	**4**	**5**	**6**	....	....	....	....	....
	Hamilton	AHL	14	5	6	11	6	9	1	1	2	8
	NHL Totals		**38**	**1**	**4**	**5**	**6**	....	....	....	....	....

Canadian Major Junior Scholastic Player of the Year (1996)

de VRIES, GREG (deh-VREES) — EDM.

Defense. Shoots left. 6'3", 215 lbs. Born, Sundridge, Ont., January 4, 1973.

			Regular Season					Playoffs				
Season	Club	Lea	GP	G	A	TP	PIM	GP	G	A	TP	PIM
1991-92	Bowling Green	CCHA	24	0	3	3	20	....	....	....	....	....
1992-93	Niagara Falls	OHL	62	3	23	26	86	4	0	1	1	6
1993-94	Niagara Falls	OHL	64	5	40	45	135	....	....	....	....	....
	Cape Breton	AHL	9	0	0	0	11	1	0	0	0	0
1994-95	Cape Breton	AHL	77	5	19	24	68	....	....	....	....	....
1995-96	**Edmonton**	**NHL**	**13**	**1**	**1**	**2**	**12**	....	....	....	....	....
	Cape Breton	AHL	58	9	30	39	174	....	....	....	....	....
1996-97	**Edmonton**	**NHL**	**37**	**0**	**4**	**4**	**52**	**12**	**0**	**1**	**1**	**8**
	Hamilton	AHL	34	4	14	18	26	....	....	....	....	....
1997-98	**Edmonton**	**NHL**	**65**	**7**	**4**	**11**	**80**	**7**	**0**	**0**	**0**	**21**
	NHL Totals		**115**	**8**	**9**	**17**	**144**	**19**	**0**	**1**	**1**	**29**

Signed as a free agent by **Edmonton**, March 20, 1994.

DeWOLF, JOSH (duh-WOOLF) N.J.

Defense. Shoots left. 6'2", 190 lbs. Born, Bloomington, MN, July 25, 1977.
(New Jersey's 3rd choice, 41st overall, in 1996 Entry Draft).

			Regular Season					Playoffs				
Season	Club	Lea	GP	G	A	TP	PIM	GP	G	A	TP	PIM
1995-96	Twin Cities	USHL	40	11	15	26	38	....	....	....	....	....
1996-97	St. Cloud State	WCHA	31	3	11	14	62	....	....	....	....	....
1997-98	St. Cloud State	WCHA	37	9	9	18	78	....	....	....	....	....
	Albany	AHL	2	0	0	0	0	....	....	....	....	....

DEYELL, MARK (digh-EHL) TOR.

Center. Shoots right. 6', 180 lbs. Born, Regina, Sask., March 26, 1976.
(Toronto's 4th choice, 126th overall, in 1994 Entry Draft).

			Regular Season					Playoffs				
Season	Club	Lea	GP	G	A	TP	PIM	GP	G	A	TP	PIM
1993-94	Saskatoon	WHL	66	17	36	53	52	16	5	2	7	20
1994-95	Saskatoon	WHL	70	34	68	102	56	10	2	5	7	14
1995-96	Saskatoon	WHL	69	61	*98	*159	122	4	0	5	5	8
1996-97	St. John's	AHL	58	15	27	42	30	10	1	5	6	6
1997-98	St. John's	AHL	72	20	43	63	75	4	1	1	2	4

WHL East First All-Star Team (1996)

DHADPHALE, ANIKET (dahd-FAH-lee, AN-ih-keht) S.J.

Left wing. Shoots left. 6'3", 185 lbs. Born, Ann Arbor, MI, April 26, 1976.
(San Jose's 11th choice, 245th overall, in 1994 Entry Draft).

			Regular Season					Playoffs				
Season	Club	Lea	GP	G	A	TP	PIM	GP	G	A	TP	PIM
1993-94	Marquette	USHL	50	58	36	94	95	....	....	....	....	....
1994-95	Stratford	OJHL	46	31	33	64	74	....	....	....	....	....
1995-96	Notre Dame	CCHA	34	13	7	20	34	....	....	....	....	....
1996-97	Notre Dame	CCHA	34	5	16	21	20	....	....	....	....	....
1997-98	Notre Dame	CCHA	41	25	10	35	34	....	....	....	....	....

DIDUCK, GERALD (DIH-duhk) PHX.

Defense. Shoots right. 6'2", 217 lbs. Born, Edmonton, Alta., April 6, 1965.
(NY Islanders' 2nd choice, 16th overall, in 1983 Entry Draft).

			Regular Season					Playoffs				
Season	Club	Lea	GP	G	A	TP	PIM	GP	G	A	TP	PIM
1981-82	Lethbridge	WHL	71	1	15	16	81	12	0	3	3	27
1982-83	Lethbridge	WHL	67	8	16	24	151	20	3	12	15	49
1983-84	Lethbridge	WHL	65	10	24	34	133	5	1	4	5	27
	Indianapolis	CHL	....	....	....	....	....	10	1	6	7	19
1984-85	**NY Islanders**	**NHL**	**65**	**2**	**8**	**10**	**80**	....	....	....	....	....
1985-86	**NY Islanders**	**NHL**	**10**	**1**	**2**	**3**	**2**	....	....	....	....	....
	Springfield	AHL	61	6	14	20	173	....	....	....	....	....
1986-87	**NY Islanders**	**NHL**	**30**	**2**	**3**	**5**	**67**	**14**	**0**	**1**	**1**	**35**
	Springfield	AHL	45	6	8	14	120	....	....	....	....	....
1987-88	**NY Islanders**	**NHL**	**68**	**7**	**12**	**19**	**113**	**6**	**1**	**0**	**1**	**42**
1988-89	**NY Islanders**	**NHL**	**65**	**11**	**21**	**32**	**155**	....	....	....	....	....
1989-90	**NY Islanders**	**NHL**	**76**	**3**	**17**	**20**	**163**	**5**	**0**	**0**	**0**	**12**
1990-91	**Montreal**	**NHL**	**32**	**1**	**2**	**3**	**39**	....	....	....	....	....
	Vancouver	**NHL**	**31**	**3**	**7**	**10**	**66**	**6**	**1**	**0**	**1**	**11**
1991-92	**Vancouver**	**NHL**	**77**	**6**	**21**	**27**	**229**	**5**	**0**	**0**	**0**	**10**
1992-93	**Vancouver**	**NHL**	**80**	**6**	**14**	**20**	**171**	**12**	**4**	**2**	**6**	**12**
1993-94	**Vancouver**	**NHL**	**55**	**1**	**10**	**11**	**72**	**24**	**1**	**7**	**8**	**22**
1994-95	**Vancouver**	**NHL**	**22**	**1**	**3**	**4**	**15**	....	....	....	....	....
	Chicago	**NHL**	**13**	**1**	**0**	**1**	**48**	**16**	**1**	**3**	**4**	**22**
1995-96	**Hartford**	**NHL**	**79**	**1**	**9**	**10**	**88**	....	....	....	....	....
1996-97	**Hartford**	**NHL**	**56**	**1**	**10**	**11**	**40**	....	....	....	....	....
	Phoenix	**NHL**	**11**	**1**	**2**	**3**	**23**	**7**	**0**	**0**	**0**	**10**
1997-98	**Phoenix**	**NHL**	**78**	**8**	**10**	**18**	**118**	**6**	**0**	**2**	**2**	**20**
	NHL Totals		**848**	**56**	**151**	**207**	**1489**	**101**	**8**	**15**	**23**	**196**

Traded to **Montreal** by **NY Islanders** for Craig Ludwig, September 4, 1990. Traded to **Vancouver** by **Montreal** for Vancouver's 4th round choice (Vladimir Vujtek) in 1991 Entry Draft, January 12, 1991. Traded to **Chicago** by **Vancouver** for Bogdan Savenko and Hartford's 3rd round choice (previously acquired, Vancouver selected Larry Courville) in 1995 Entry Draft, April 7, 1995. Signed as a free agent by **Hartford**, August 24, 1995. Traded to **Phoenix** by **Hartford** for Chris Murray, March 18, 1997.

DIENER, DEREK ST.L.

Defense. Shoots left. 6'5", 197 lbs. Born, Burnaby, B.C., July 13, 1976.
(Philadelphia's 6th choice, 192nd overall, in 1994 Entry Draft).

			Regular Season					Playoffs				
Season	Club	Lea	GP	G	A	TP	PIM	GP	G	A	TP	PIM
1993-94	Lethbridge	WHL	62	1	8	9	64	3	0	0	0	7
1994-95	Lethbridge	WHL	68	13	29	42	104	....	....	....	....	....
1995-96	Lethbridge	WHL	56	6	27	33	78	4	0	1	1	4
1996-97	Kelowna	WHL	70	13	45	58	135	6	1	3	4	6
1997-98	Worcester	AHL	32	2	5	7	88	....	....	....	....	....

Signed as a free agent by **St. Louis**, March 20, 1997.

DiMAIO, ROB (duh-MIGH-oh) BOS.

Center. Shoots right. 5'10", 190 lbs. Born, Calgary, Alta., February 19, 1968.
(NY Islanders' 6th choice, 118th overall, in 1987 Entry Draft).

			Regular Season					Playoffs				
Season	Club	Lea	GP	G	A	TP	PIM	GP	G	A	TP	PIM
1986-87	Medicine Hat	WHL	70	27	43	70	130	20	7	11	18	46
1987-88	Medicine Hat	WHL	54	47	43	90	120	14	12	19	*31	59
1988-89	**NY Islanders**	**NHL**	**16**	**1**	**0**	**1**	**30**	....	....	....	....	....
	Springfield	AHL	40	13	18	31	67	....	....	....	....	....
1989-90	**NY Islanders**	**NHL**	**7**	**0**	**0**	**0**	**2**	**1**	**1**	**0**	**1**	**4**
	Springfield	AHL	54	25	27	52	69	16	4	7	11	45
1990-91	**NY Islanders**	**NHL**	**1**	**0**	**0**	**0**	**0**	....	....	....	....	....
	Capital District	AHL	12	3	4	7	22	....	....	....	....	....
1991-92	**NY Islanders**	**NHL**	**50**	**5**	**2**	**7**	**43**	....	....	....	....	....
1992-93	**Tampa Bay**	**NHL**	**54**	**9**	**15**	**24**	**62**	....	....	....	....	....
1993-94	**Tampa Bay**	**NHL**	**39**	**8**	**7**	**15**	**40**	....	....	....	....	....
	Philadelphia	**NHL**	**14**	**3**	**5**	**8**	**6**	....	....	....	....	....
1994-95	**Philadelphia**	**NHL**	**36**	**3**	**1**	**4**	**53**	**15**	**2**	**4**	**6**	**4**
1995-96	**Philadelphia**	**NHL**	**59**	**6**	**15**	**21**	**58**	**3**	**0**	**0**	**0**	**0**
1996-97	**Boston**	**NHL**	**72**	**13**	**15**	**28**	**82**	....	....	....	....	....
1997-98	**Boston**	**NHL**	**79**	**10**	**17**	**27**	**82**	**6**	**1**	**0**	**1**	**8**
	NHL Totals		**427**	**58**	**77**	**135**	**458**	**25**	**4**	**4**	**8**	**16**

Won Stafford Smythe Memorial Trophy (Memorial Cup Tournament MVP) (1988)

Claimed by **Tampa Bay** from **NY Islanders** in Expansion Draft, June 18, 1992. Traded to **Philadelphia** by **Tampa Bay** for Jim Cummins and Philadelphia's 4th round choice (later traded back to Philadelphia — Philadelphia selected Radovan Somik) in 1995 Entry Draft, March 18, 1994. Claimed by **San Jose** from **Philadelphia** in NHL Waiver Draft, September 30, 1996. Traded to **Boston** by **San Jose** for Boston's 5th round choice (Adam Nittel) in 1997 Entry Draft, September 30, 1996.

DINEEN, KEVIN CAR.

Right wing. Shoots right. 5'11", 190 lbs. Born, Quebec City, Que., October 28, 1963.
(Hartford's 3rd choice, 56th overall, in 1982 Entry Draft).

			Regular Season					Playoffs				
Season	Club	Lea	GP	G	A	TP	PIM	GP	G	A	TP	PIM
1980-81	St. Michael's	Jr. B	40	15	28	43	167	....	....	....	....	....
1981-82	U. of Denver	WCHA	26	10	10	20	70	....	....	....	....	....
1982-83	U. of Denver	WCHA	36	16	13	29	108	....	....	....	....	....
1983-84	Canada	Nat-Tm	52	5	11	16	2	....	....	....	....	....
	Canada	Olympics	7	0	0	0	8	....	....	....	....	....
1984-85	**Hartford**	**NHL**	**57**	**25**	**16**	**41**	**120**	....	....	....	....	....
	Binghamton	AHL	25	15	8	23	41	....	....	....	....	....
1985-86	**Hartford**	**NHL**	**57**	**33**	**35**	**68**	**124**	**10**	**6**	**7**	**13**	**18**
1986-87	**Hartford**	**NHL**	**78**	**40**	**39**	**79**	**110**	**6**	**2**	**1**	**3**	**31**
1987-88	**Hartford**	**NHL**	**74**	**25**	**25**	**50**	**217**	**6**	**4**	**4**	**8**	**8**
1988-89	**Hartford**	**NHL**	**79**	**45**	**44**	**89**	**167**	**4**	**1**	**0**	**1**	**10**
1989-90	**Hartford**	**NHL**	**67**	**25**	**41**	**66**	**164**	**6**	**3**	**2**	**5**	**18**
1990-91	**Hartford**	**NHL**	**61**	**17**	**30**	**47**	**104**	**6**	**1**	**0**	**1**	**16**
1991-92	**Hartford**	**NHL**	**16**	**4**	**2**	**6**	**23**	....	....	....	....	....
	Philadelphia	**NHL**	**64**	**26**	**30**	**56**	**130**	....	....	....	....	....
1992-93	**Philadelphia**	**NHL**	**83**	**35**	**28**	**63**	**201**	....	....	....	....	....
1993-94	**Philadelphia**	**NHL**	**71**	**19**	**23**	**42**	**113**	....	....	....	....	....
1994-95	**Philadelphia**	**NHL**	**40**	**8**	**5**	**13**	**39**	**15**	**6**	**4**	**10**	**18**
	Houston	IHL	17	6	4	10	42	....	....	....	....	....
1995-96	**Philadelphia**	**NHL**	**26**	**0**	**2**	**2**	**50**	....	....	....	....	....
	Hartford	**NHL**	**20**	**2**	**7**	**9**	**67**	....	....	....	....	....
1996-97	**Hartford**	**NHL**	**78**	**19**	**29**	**48**	**141**	....	....	....	....	....
1997-98	**Carolina**	**NHL**	**54**	**7**	**16**	**23**	**105**	....	....	....	....	....
	NHL Totals		**925**	**330**	**372**	**702**	**1875**	**53**	**23**	**18**	**41**	**119**

Won Bud Light/NHL Man of the Year Award (1991)

Played in NHL All-Star Game (1988, 1989)

Traded to **Philadelphia** by **Hartford** for Murray Craven and Philadelphia's 4th round choice (Kevin Smyth) in 1992 Entry Draft, November 13, 1991. Traded to **Hartford** by **Philadelphia** for Hartford's 3rd round choice (Kris Mallette) in 1997 Entry Draft, December 28, 1995. Transferred to **Carolina** after **Hartford** franchise relocated, June 25, 1997.

DINGMAN, CHRIS CGY.

Left wing. Shoots left. 6'4", 245 lbs. Born, Edmonton, Alta., July 6, 1976.
(Calgary's 1st choice, 19th overall, in 1994 Entry Draft).

			Regular Season					Playoffs				
Season	Club	Lea	GP	G	A	TP	PIM	GP	G	A	TP	PIM
1992-93	Brandon	WHL	50	10	17	27	64	4	0	0	0	0
1993-94	Brandon	WHL	45	21	20	41	77	13	1	7	8	39
1994-95	Brandon	WHL	66	40	43	83	201	3	1	0	1	9
1995-96	Brandon	WHL	40	16	29	45	109	19	12	11	23	60
	Saint John	AHL	....	....	....	....	....	1	0	0	0	0
1996-97	Saint John	AHL	71	5	6	11	195	....	....	....	....	....
1997-98	**Calgary**	**NHL**	**70**	**3**	**3**	**6**	**149**	....	....	....	....	....
	NHL Totals		**70**	**3**	**3**	**6**	**149**	....	....	....	....	....

DIONNE, GILBERT (dee-AHN, ZHIHL-bair)

Left wing. Shoots left. 6', 194 lbs. Born, Drummondville, Que., September 19, 1970.
(Montreal's 5th choice, 81st overall, in 1990 Entry Draft).

			Regular Season					Playoffs				
Season	Club	Lea	GP	G	A	TP	PIM	GP	G	A	TP	PIM
1988-89	Kitchener	OHL	66	11	33	44	13	5	1	1	2	4
1989-90	Kitchener	OHL	64	48	57	105	85	17	13	10	23	22
1990-91	**Montreal**	**NHL**	**2**	**0**	**0**	**0**	**0**	....	....	....	....	....
	Fredericton	AHL	77	40	47	87	62	9	6	5	11	8
1991-92	**Montreal**	**NHL**	**39**	**21**	**13**	**34**	**10**	**11**	**3**	**4**	**7**	**10**
	Fredericton	AHL	29	19	27	46	20	....	....	....	....	....
1992-93	**Montreal**	**NHL**	**75**	**20**	**28**	**48**	**63**	**20**	**6**	**6**	**12**	**20** ♦
	Fredericton	AHL	3	4	3	7	0	....	....	....	....	....
1993-94	**Montreal**	**NHL**	**74**	**19**	**26**	**45**	**31**	**5**	**1**	**2**	**3**	**0**
1994-95	**Montreal**	**NHL**	**6**	**0**	**3**	**3**	**2**	....	....	....	....	....
	Philadelphia	**NHL**	**20**	**0**	**6**	**6**	**2**	**3**	**0**	**0**	**0**	**4**
1995-96	**Philadelphia**	**NHL**	**2**	**0**	**1**	**1**	**0**	....	....	....	....	....
	Florida	**NHL**	**5**	**1**	**2**	**3**	**0**	....	....	....	....	....
	Carolina	AHL	55	43	58	101	29	....	....	....	....	....
1996-97	Carolina	AHL	72	41	47	88	69	....	....	....	....	....
1997-98	Cincinnati	IHL	76	42	57	99	54	9	3	4	7	28
	NHL Totals		**223**	**61**	**79**	**140**	**108**	**39**	**10**	**12**	**22**	**34**

NHL/Upper Deck All-Rookie Team (1992) • AHL Second All-Star Team (1996) • IHL First All-Star Team (1998)

Traded to **Philadelphia** by **Montreal** with Eric Desjardins and John LeClair for Mark Recchi and Philadelphia's 3rd round choice (Martin Hohenberger) in 1995 Entry draft, February 9, 1995. Signed as a free agent by **Florida**, January 29, 1996.

DIPENTA, JOE FLA.

Defense. Shoots right. 6'2", 205 lbs. Born, Barrie, Ont., February 25, 1979.
(Florida's 2nd choice, 61st overall, in 1998 Entry Draft).

			Regular Season					Playoffs				
Season	Club	Lea	GP	G	A	TP	PIM	GP	G	A	TP	PIM
1996-97	Smiths Falls	OJHL	54	13	22	35	92	....	....	....	....	....
1997-98	Boston University	H.E.	38	2	16	18	50	....	....	....	....	....

DIROBERTO, TORREY (DIH-raw-buhr-toh) BUF.

Center. Shoots left. 5'11", 180 lbs. Born, New York, NY, April 17, 1978.
(Buffalo's 6th choice, 128th overall, in 1997 Entry Draft).

			Regular Season					Playoffs				
Season	Club	Lea	GP	G	A	TP	PIM	GP	G	A	TP	PIM
1995-96	Seattle	WHL	70	16	19	35	118	5	0	2	2	8
1996-97	Seattle	WHL	72	37	44	81	91	15	9	5	14	8
1997-98	Seattle	WHL	43	14	21	35	48	5	0	2	2	14

DOAN, SHANE (DOHN) PHX.

Right wing. Shoots right. 6'2", 217 lbs. Born, Halkirk, Alta., October 10, 1976.
(Winnipeg's 1st choice, 7th overall, in 1995 Entry Draft).

			Regular Season					Playoffs				
Season	Club	Lea	GP	G	A	TP	PIM	GP	G	A	TP	PIM
1992-93	Kamloops	WHL	51	7	12	19	65	13	0	1	1	8
1993-94	Kamloops	WHL	52	24	24	48	88	....	....	....	....	....
1994-95	Kamloops	WHL	71	37	57	94	106	21	6	10	16	16
1995-96	**Winnipeg**	**NHL**	**74**	**7**	**10**	**17**	**101**	**6**	**0**	**0**	**0**	**6**
1996-97	**Phoenix**	**NHL**	**63**	**4**	**8**	**12**	**49**	**4**	**0**	**0**	**0**	**2**
1997-98	**Phoenix**	**NHL**	**33**	**5**	**6**	**11**	**35**	**6**	**1**	**0**	**1**	**6**
	Springfield	AHL	39	21	21	42	64	....	....	....	....	....
	NHL Totals		**170**	**16**	**24**	**40**	**185**	**16**	**1**	**0**	**1**	**14**

Memorial Cup All-Star Team (1995) • Won Stafford Smythe Memorial Trophy (Memorial Cup Tournament MVP) (1995)

Transferred to **Phoenix** after **Winnipeg** franchise relocated, July 1, 1996.

DOELL, CURTIS FLA.

Defense. Shoots right. 6'1", 220 lbs. Born, Saskatoon, Sask., October 3, 1976.

			Regular Season					Playoffs				
Season	Club	Lea	GP	G	A	TP	PIM	GP	G	A	TP	PIM
1996-97	U. Minn-Duluth	WCHA	37	6	20	26	114	....	....	....	....	....
1997-98	U. Minn-Duluth	WCHA	39	9	23	32	120	....	....	....	....	....

Signed as a free agent by **Florida**, June 5, 1998.

DOIG, JASON (DOIG) PHX.

Defense. Shoots right. 6'3", 220 lbs. Born, Montreal, Que., January 29, 1977.
(Winnipeg's 3rd choice, 34th overall, in 1995 Entry Draft).

			Regular Season					Playoffs				
Season	Club	Lea	GP	G	A	TP	PIM	GP	G	A	TP	PIM
1993-94	St-Jean	QMJHL	63	8	17	25	65	5	0	2	2	2
1994-95	Laval	QMJHL	55	13	42	55	259	20	4	13	17	39
1995-96	Laval	QMJHL	5	3	6	9	20	....	....	....	....	....
	Granby	QMJHL	24	4	30	34	91	20	10	22	32	*110
	Winnipeg	**NHL**	**15**	**1**	**1**	**2**	**28**	....	....	....	....	....
	Springfield	AHL	5	0	0	0	28	....	....	....	....	....
1996-97	Granby	QMJHL	39	14	33	47	211	5	0	4	4	27
	Las Vegas	IHL	6	0	1	1	19	....	....	....	....	....
	Springfield	AHL	5	0	3	3	2	17	1	4	5	37
1997-98	**Phoenix**	**NHL**	**4**	**0**	**1**	**1**	**12**	....	....	....	....	....
	Springfield	AHL	46	2	25	27	153	3	0	0	0	2
	NHL Totals		**19**	**1**	**2**	**3**	**40**	....	....	....	....	....

Memorial Cup All-Star Team (1996)

Transferred to **Phoenix** after **Winnipeg** franchise relocated, July 1, 1996.

DOLLAS, BOBBY (DAW-luhs) PIT.

Defense. Shoots left. 6'2", 212 lbs. Born, Montreal, Que., January 31, 1965.
(Winnipeg's 2nd choice, 14th overall, in 1983 Entry Draft).

			Regular Season					Playoffs				
Season	Club	Lea	GP	G	A	TP	PIM	GP	G	A	TP	PIM
1982-83	Laval	QMJHL	63	16	45	61	144	11	5	5	10	23
1983-84	Laval	QMJHL	54	12	33	45	80	14	1	8	9	23
	Winnipeg	**NHL**	**1**	**0**	**0**	**0**	**0**	....	....	....	....	....
1984-85	**Winnipeg**	**NHL**	**9**	**0**	**0**	**0**	**0**	....	....	....	....	....
	Sherbrooke	AHL	8	1	3	4	4	17	3	6	9	17
1985-86	**Winnipeg**	**NHL**	**46**	**0**	**5**	**5**	**66**	**3**	**0**	**0**	**0**	**2**
	Sherbrooke	AHL	25	4	7	11	29	....	....	....	....	....
1986-87	Sherbrooke	AHL	75	6	18	24	87	16	2	4	6	13
1987-88	**Quebec**	**NHL**	**9**	**0**	**0**	**0**	**2**	....	....	....	....	....
	Moncton	AHL	26	4	10	14	20	....	....	....	....	....
	Fredericton	AHL	33	4	8	12	27	15	2	2	4	24
1988-89	**Quebec**	**NHL**	**16**	**0**	**3**	**3**	**16**	....	....	....	....	....
	Halifax	AHL	57	5	19	24	65	4	1	0	1	14
1989-90	Canada	Nat-Tm	68	8	29	37	60	....	....	....	....	....
1990-91	**Detroit**	**NHL**	**56**	**3**	**5**	**8**	**20**	**7**	**1**	**0**	**1**	**13**
1991-92	**Detroit**	**NHL**	**27**	**3**	**1**	**4**	**20**	**2**	**0**	**1**	**1**	**0**
	Adirondack	AHL	19	1	6	7	33	18	7	4	11	22
1992-93	**Detroit**	**NHL**	**6**	**0**	**0**	**0**	**2**	....	....	....	....	....
	Adirondack	AHL	64	7	36	43	54	11	3	8	11	8
1993-94	**Anaheim**	**NHL**	**77**	**9**	**11**	**20**	**55**	....	....	....	....	....
1994-95	**Anaheim**	**NHL**	**45**	**7**	**13**	**20**	**12**	....	....	....	....	....
1995-96	**Anaheim**	**NHL**	**82**	**8**	**22**	**30**	**64**	....	....	....	....	....
1996-97	**Anaheim**	**NHL**	**79**	**4**	**14**	**18**	**55**	**11**	**0**	**0**	**0**	**4**
1997-98	**Anaheim**	**NHL**	**22**	**0**	**1**	**1**	**27**	....	....	....	....	....
	Edmonton	**NHL**	**30**	**2**	**5**	**7**	**22**	**11**	**0**	**0**	**0**	**16**
	NHL Totals		**505**	**36**	**80**	**116**	**361**	**34**	**1**	**1**	**2**	**35**

QMJHL Second All-Star Team (1983) • Won Eddie Shore Award (AHL's Outstanding Defenseman) (1993) • AHL First All-Star Team (1993)

Traded to **Quebec** by **Winnipeg** for Stu Kulak, December 17, 1987. Signed as a free agent by **Detroit**, October 18, 1990. Claimed by **Anaheim** from **Detroit** in Expansion Draft, June 24, 1993. Traded to **Edmonton** by **Anaheim** for Drew Bannister, January 9, 1998. Traded to **Pittsburgh** by **Edmonton** with Tony Hrkac for Josef Beranek, June 16, 1998.

DOME, ROBERT (doh-MAY) PIT.

Right wing. Shoots left. 6', 205 lbs. Born, Skalica, Czech., January 29, 1979.
(Pittsburgh's 1st choice, 17th overall, in 1997 Entry Draft).

			Regular Season					Playoffs				
Season	Club	Lea	GP	G	A	TP	PIM	GP	G	A	TP	PIM
1994-95	Dukla	Slov-Jr.	36	36	43	79	39	....	....	....	....	....
1995-96	Utah	IHL	56	10	9	19	28	....	....	....	....	....
1996-97	Long Beach	IHL	13	4	6	10	14	....	....	....	....	....
	Las Vegas	IHL	43	10	7	17	22	....	....	....	....	....
1997-98	**Pittsburgh**	**NHL**	**30**	**5**	**2**	**7**	**12**	....	....	....	....	....
	Syracuse	AHL	36	21	25	46	77	....	....	....	....	....
	NHL Totals		**30**	**5**	**2**	**7**	**12**	....	....	....	....	....

DOMENICHELLI, HNAT (daw-mehn-ih-CHEHL-ee, NAT) CGY.

Center. Shoots left. 6', 190 lbs. Born, Edmonton, Alta., February 17, 1976.
(Hartford's 2nd choice, 83rd overall, in 1994 Entry Draft).

			Regular Season					Playoffs				
Season	Club	Lea	GP	G	A	TP	PIM	GP	G	A	TP	PIM
1992-93	Kamloops	WHL	45	12	8	20	15	11	1	1	2	2
1993-94	Kamloops	WHL	69	27	40	67	31	19	10	12	22	0
1994-95	Kamloops	WHL	72	52	62	114	34	19	9	9	18	9
1995-96	Kamloops	WHL	62	59	89	148	37	16	7	9	16	29
1996-97	**Hartford**	**NHL**	**13**	**2**	**1**	**3**	**7**	....	....	....	....	....
	Springfield	AHL	39	24	24	48	12	....	....	....	....	....
	Calgary	**NHL**	**10**	**1**	**2**	**3**	**2**	....	....	....	....	....
	Saint John	AHL	1	1	1	2	0	5	5	0	5	2
1997-98	**Calgary**	**NHL**	**31**	**9**	**7**	**16**	**6**	....	....	....	....	....
	Saint John	AHL	48	33	13	46	24	19	7	8	15	14
	NHL Totals		**54**	**12**	**10**	**22**	**15**	....	....	....	....	....

WHL West Second All-Star Team (1995) • WHL West First All-Star Team (1996) • Canadian Major Junior First All-Star Team (1996) • Canadian Major Junior Most Sportsmanlike Player of the Year (1996)

Traded to **Calgary** by **Hartford** with Glen Featherstone, New Jersey's 2nd round choice (previously acquired, Calgary selected Dimitri Kokorev) in 1997 Entry Draft and Vancouver's 3rd round choice (previously acquired, Calgary selected Paul Manning) in 1998 Entry Draft for Steve Chiasson and Colorado's 3rd round choice (previously acquired, Carolina selected Francis Lessard) in 1997 Entry Draft, March 5, 1997.

DOMI, TIE (DOH-mee) TOR.

Right wing. Shoots right. 5'10", 200 lbs. Born, Windsor, Ont., November 1, 1969.
(Toronto's 2nd choice, 27th overall, in 1988 Entry Draft).

			Regular Season					Playoffs				
Season	Club	Lea	GP	G	A	TP	PIM	GP	G	A	TP	PIM
1986-87	Peterborough	OHL	18	1	1	2	79	....	....	....	....	....
1987-88	Peterborough	OHL	60	22	21	43	292	12	3	9	12	24
1988-89	Peterborough	OHL	43	14	16	30	175	17	10	9	19	70
1989-90	**Toronto**	**NHL**	**2**	**0**	**0**	**0**	**42**	....	....	....	....	....
	Newmarket	AHL	57	14	11	25	285	....	....	....	....	....
1990-91	**NY Rangers**	**NHL**	**28**	**1**	**0**	**1**	**185**	....	....	....	....	....
	Binghamton	AHL	25	11	6	17	219	7	3	2	5	16
1991-92	**NY Rangers**	**NHL**	**42**	**2**	**4**	**6**	**246**	**6**	**1**	**1**	**2**	**32**
1992-93	**NY Rangers**	**NHL**	**12**	**2**	**0**	**2**	**95**	....	....	....	....	....
	Winnipeg	**NHL**	**49**	**3**	**10**	**13**	**249**	**6**	**1**	**0**	**1**	**23**
1993-94	**Winnipeg**	**NHL**	**81**	**8**	**11**	**19**	***347**	....	....	....	....	....
1994-95	**Winnipeg**	**NHL**	**31**	**4**	**4**	**8**	**128**	....	....	....	....	....
	Toronto	**NHL**	**9**	**0**	**1**	**1**	**31**	**7**	**1**	**0**	**1**	**0**
1995-96	**Toronto**	**NHL**	**72**	**7**	**6**	**13**	**297**	**6**	**0**	**2**	**2**	**4**
1996-97	**Toronto**	**NHL**	**80**	**11**	**17**	**28**	**275**	....	....	....	....	....
1997-98	**Toronto**	**NHL**	**80**	**4**	**10**	**14**	**365**	....	....	....	....	....
	NHL Totals		**486**	**42**	**63**	**105**	**2260**	**25**	**3**	**3**	**6**	**59**

Traded to **NY Rangers** by **Toronto** with Mark LaForest for Greg Johnston, June 28, 1990. Traded to **Winnipeg** by **NY Rangers** with Kris King for Ed Olczyk, December 28, 1992. Traded to **Toronto** by **Winnipeg** for Mike Eastwood and Toronto's 3rd round choice (Brad Isbister) in 1995 Entry Draft, April 7, 1995.

DONATO, TED (duh-NAH-toh) BOS.

Left wing. Shoots left. 5'10", 181 lbs. Born, Boston, MA, April 28, 1969.
(Boston's 6th choice, 98th overall, in 1987 Entry Draft).

			Regular Season					Playoffs				
Season	Club	Lea	GP	G	A	TP	PIM	GP	G	A	TP	PIM
1986-87	Catholic Memorial	H.S.	22	29	34	63	30	....	....	....	....	....
1987-88	Harvard	ECAC	28	12	14	26	24	....	....	....	....	....
1988-89	Harvard	ECAC	34	14	37	51	30	....	....	....	....	....
1989-90	Harvard	ECAC	16	5	6	11	34	....	....	....	....	....
1990-91	Harvard	ECAC	27	19	*37	56	26	....	....	....	....	....
1991-92	United States	Nat-Tm	52	11	22	33	24	....	....	....	....	....
	United States	Olympics	8	4	3	7	8	....	....	....	....	....
	Boston	**NHL**	**10**	**1**	**2**	**3**	**8**	**15**	**3**	**4**	**7**	**4**
1992-93	**Boston**	**NHL**	**82**	**15**	**20**	**35**	**61**	**4**	**0**	**1**	**1**	....
1993-94	**Boston**	**NHL**	**84**	**22**	**32**	**54**	**59**	**13**	**4**	**2**	**6**	**10**
1994-95	TuTo Turku	Finland	14	5	5	10	47	....	....	....	....	....
	Boston	**NHL**	**47**	**10**	**10**	**20**	**10**	**5**	**0**	**0**	**0**	**4**
1995-96	**Boston**	**NHL**	**82**	**23**	**26**	**49**	**46**	**5**	**1**	**2**	**3**	**2**
1996-97	**Boston**	**NHL**	**67**	**25**	**26**	**51**	**37**	....	....	....	....	....
1997-98	**Boston**	**NHL**	**79**	**16**	**23**	**39**	**54**	**5**	**0**	**0**	**0**	**2**
	NHL Totals		**451**	**112**	**139**	**251**	**275**	**47**	**8**	**9**	**17**	**22**

NCAA Championship All-Tournament Team (1989) • NCAA Championship Tournament MVP (1989) • ECAC First All-Star Team (1991)

DONOVAN, SHEAN COL.

Right wing. Shoots right. 6'3", 210 lbs. Born, Timmins, Ont., January 22, 1975.
(San Jose's 2nd choice, 28th overall, in 1993 Entry Draft).

			Regular Season					Playoffs				
Season	Club	Lea	GP	G	A	TP	PIM	GP	G	A	TP	PIM
1991-92	Ottawa	OHL	58	11	8	19	14	11	1	0	1	5
1992-93	Ottawa	OHL	66	29	23	52	33	....	....	....	....	....
1993-94	Ottawa	OHL	62	35	49	84	63	17	10	11	21	14
1994-95	Ottawa	OHL	29	22	19	41	41	....	....	....	....	....
	San Jose	**NHL**	**14**	**0**	**0**	**0**	**6**	**7**	**0**	**1**	**1**	**6**
	Kansas City	IHL	5	0	2	2	7	14	5	3	8	23
1995-96	**San Jose**	**NHL**	**74**	**13**	**8**	**21**	**39**	....	....	....	....	....
	Kansas City	IHL	4	0	0	0	8	5	0	0	0	8
1996-97	**San Jose**	**NHL**	**73**	**9**	**6**	**15**	**42**	....	....	....	....	....
	Kentucky	AHL	3	1	3	4	18	....	....	....	....	....
1997-98	**San Jose**	**NHL**	**20**	**3**	**3**	**6**	**22**	....	....	....	....	....
	Colorado	**NHL**	**47**	**5**	**7**	**12**	**48**	....	....	....	....	....
	NHL Totals		**228**	**30**	**24**	**54**	**157**	**7**	**0**	**1**	**1**	**6**

Traded to **Colorado** by **San Jose** with San Jose's 1st round choice (Alex Tanguay) in 1998 Entry Draft for Mike Ricci and Colorado's 2nd round choice (later traded to Buffalo — Buffalo selected Jaroslav Kristek), in 1998 Entry Draft, November 21, 1997.

DOPITA, JIRI (doh-PEE-tuh, YIH-ree) NYI

Center. Shoots left. 6'3", 230 lbs. Born, Sumperk, Czechoslovakia, December 2, 1968.
(NY Islanders' 4th choice, 123rd overall, in 1998 Entry Draft).

			Regular Season					Playoffs				
Season	Club	Lea	GP	G	A	TP	PIM	GP	G	A	TP	PIM
1989-90	Dukla Jihlava	Czech.	5	1	2	3	0	....	....	....	....	....
1990-91	DS Olomouc	Czech.	42	11	13	24	26	....	....	....	....	....
1991-92	DS Olomouc	Czech.	38	24	20	44	28	3	1	4	5	0
1992-93	HC Olomouc	Czech.	28	12	17	29	16	....	....	....	....	....
	Eisbaren Berlin	Germany	11	7	8	15	49	....	....	....	....	....
1993-94	Eisbaren Berlin	Germany	42	23	21	44	52	....	....	....	....	....
	HC Olomouc	Cze-Rep.	....	....	....	....	....	12	4	7	11	....
1994-95	Eisbaren Berlin	Germany	42	28	40	68	55	....	....	....	....	....
1995-96	Petra Vsetin	Cze-Rep.	38	19	20	39	20	13	9	11	20	10
1996-97	Petra Vsetin	Cze-Rep.	52	30	31	61	55	10	7	4	11	22
1997-98	Petra Vsetin	Cze-Rep.	52	21	34	55	64	10	*12	6	18	4

DOURIS, PETER (DOOR-ihs)

Right wing. Shoots right. 6'1", 195 lbs. Born, Toronto, Ont., February 19, 1966.
(Winnipeg's 1st choice, 30th overall, in 1984 Entry Draft).

			Regular Season					Playoffs				
Season	Club	Lea	GP	G	A	TP	PIM	GP	G	A	TP	PIM
1983-84	New Hampshire	ECAC	37	19	15	34	14	....	....	....	....	....
1984-85	New Hampshire	H.E.	42	27	24	51	34	....	....	....	....	....
1985-86	Canada	Nat-Tm	33	16	7	23	18	....	....	....	....	....
	Winnipeg	NHL	11	0	0	0	0	....	....	....	....	....
1986-87	Winnipeg	NHL	6	0	0	0	0	....	....	....	....	....
	Sherbrooke	AHL	62	14	28	42	24	17	7	*15	*22	16
1987-88	Winnipeg	NHL	4	0	2	2	0	1	0	0	0	0
	Moncton	AHL	73	42	37	79	53	....	....	....	....	....
1988-89	Peoria	IHL	81	28	41	69	32	4	1	2	3	0
1989-90	Boston	NHL	36	5	6	11	15	8	0	1	1	8
	Maine	AHL	38	17	20	37	14	....	....	....	....	....
1990-91	Boston	NHL	39	5	2	7	9	7	0	1	1	6
	Maine	AHL	35	16	15	31	9	2	3	0	3	2
1991-92	Boston	NHL	54	10	13	23	10	7	2	3	5	0
	Maine	AHL	12	4	3	7	2	....	....	....	....	....
1992-93	Boston	NHL	19	4	4	8	4	4	1	0	1	0
	Providence	AHL	50	29	26	55	12	....	....	....	....	....
1993-94	Anaheim	NHL	74	12	22	34	21	....	....	....	....	....
1994-95	Anaheim	NHL	46	10	11	21	12	....	....	....	....	....
1995-96	Anaheim	NHL	31	8	7	15	9	....	....	....	....	....
1996-97	Milwaukee	IHL	80	36	36	72	14	3	2	2	4	2
1997-98	Dallas	NHL	1	0	0	0	0	....	....	....	....	....
	Michigan	IHL	78	26	31	57	29	4	0	5	5	2
	NHL Totals		321	54	67	121	80	27	3	5	8	14

Traded to **St. Louis** by **Winnipeg** for Kent Carlson and St. Louis' 12th round choice (Sergei Kharin) in 1989 Entry Draft and St. Louis' 4th round choice (Scott Levins) in 1990 Entry Draft, September 29, 1988. Signed as a free agent by **Boston**, June 27, 1989. Signed as a free agent by **Anaheim**, July 22, 1993. Signed as a free agent by **Dallas**, July 16, 1997.

DOWD, JIM (DOWD) NSH.

Center. Shoots right. 6'1", 190 lbs. Born, Brick, NJ, December 25, 1968.
(New Jersey's 7th choice, 149th overall, in 1987 Entry Draft).

			Regular Season					Playoffs				
Season	Club	Lea	GP	G	A	TP	PIM	GP	G	A	TP	PIM
1986-87	Brick High	H.S.	24	22	33	55	....	....	....	....	....	....
1987-88	Lake Superior	CCHA	45	18	27	45	16	....	....	....	....	....
1988-89	Lake Superior	CCHA	46	24	35	59	40	....	....	....	....	....
1989-90	Lake Superior	CCHA	46	25	*67	92	30	....	....	....	....	....
1990-91	Lake Superior	CCHA	44	24	*54	*78	53	....	....	....	....	....
1991-92	New Jersey	NHL	1	0	0	0	0	....	....	....	....	....
	Utica	AHL	78	17	42	59	47	4	2	2	4	4
1992-93	New Jersey	NHL	1	0	0	0	0	....	....	....	....	....
	Utica	AHL	78	27	45	72	62	5	1	7	8	10
1993-94	New Jersey	NHL	15	5	10	15	0	19	2	6	8	8
	Albany	AHL	58	26	37	63	76	....	....	....	....	....
1994-95	New Jersey	NHL	10	1	4	5	0	11	2	1	3	8 ♦
1995-96	New Jersey	NHL	28	4	9	13	17	....	....	....	....	....
	Vancouver	NHL	38	1	6	7	6	1	0	0	0	0
1996-97	NY Islanders	NHL	3	0	0	0	0	....	....	....	....	....
	Utah	IHL	48	10	21	31	27	....	....	....	....	....
	Saint John	AHL	24	5	11	16	18	5	1	2	3	0
1997-98	Calgary	NHL	48	6	8	14	12	....	....	....	....	....
	Saint John	AHL	35	8	30	38	20	19	3	13	16	10
	NHL Totals		144	17	37	54	35	31	4	7	11	16

CCHA Second All-Star Team (1990) • NCAA West Second All-American Team (1990) • CCHA First All-Star Team (1991) • NCAA West First All-American Team (1991)

Traded to **Hartford** by **New Jersey** with New Jersey's 2nd round choice (later traded to Calgary – Calgary selected Dmitri Kokorev) in 1997 Entry Draft for Jocelyn Lemieux and Hartford's 2nd round choice in 1998 Entry Draft, December 19, 1995. Traded to **Vancouver** by **Hartford** with Frantisek Kucera and Hartford's 2nd round choice (Ryan Bonni) in 1997 Entry Draft for Jeff Brown and Vancouver's 3rd round choice in 1998 Entry Draft, December 19, 1995. Claimed by **NY Islanders** from **Vancouver** in NHL Waiver Draft, September 30, 1996. Signed as a free agent by **Calgary**, August, 1997. Traded to **Nashville** by **Calgary** for future considerations, June 26, 1998.

DOWNEY, AARON BOS.

Right wing. Shoots right. 6', 210 lbs. Born, Shelburne, Ont., August 27, 1974.

			Regular Season					Playoffs				
Season	Club	Lea	GP	G	A	TP	PIM	GP	G	A	TP	PIM
1995-96	Hampton Roads	ECHL	65	12	11	23	354	....	....	....	....	....
1996-97	Hampton Roads	ECHL	64	8	8	16	338	9	0	3	3	26
	Portland	AHL	3	0	0	0	19	....	....	....	....	....
	Manitoba	IHL	2	0	0	0	17	....	....	....	....	....
1997-98	Providence	AHL	78	5	10	15	*407	....	....	....	....	....

Signed as a free agent by **Boston**, January 20, 1998.

DOYLE, JASON (DOIL) NYI

Right wing. Shoots right. 6'1", 200 lbs. Born, Toronto, Ont., May 15, 1978.
(NY Islanders' 9th choice, 242nd overall, in 1998 Entry Draft).

			Regular Season					Playoffs				
Season	Club	Lea	GP	G	A	TP	PIM	GP	G	A	TP	PIM
1994-95	London	OHL	45	4	10	14	7	4	1	1	2	0
1995-96	London	OHL	21	11	5	16	24	....	....	....	....	....
	S.S. Marie	OHL	44	17	17	34	30	4	1	1	2	6
1996-97	S.S. Marie	OHL	5	0	1	1	5	....	....	....	....	....
	Owen Sound	OHL	58	13	15	28	33	4	1	1	2	4
1997-98	Owen Sound	OHL	46	15	22	37	70	10	7	4	11	11

• Re-entered NHL draft. Originally Boston's 4th choice, 80th overall, in 1996 Entry Draft.

DRAKE, DALLAS PHX.

Right wing. Shoots left. 6', 185 lbs. Born, Trail, B.C., February 4, 1969.
(Detroit's 6th choice, 116th overall, in 1989 Entry Draft).

			Regular Season					Playoffs				
Season	Club	Lea	GP	G	A	TP	PIM	GP	G	A	TP	PIM
1988-89	North. Michigan	WCHA	38	17	22	39	22	....	....	....	....	....
1989-90	North. Michigan	WCHA	46	13	24	37	42	....	....	....	....	....
1990-91	North. Michigan	WCHA	44	22	36	58	89	....	....	....	....	....
1991-92	North. Michigan	WCHA	38	*39	41	*80	46	....	....	....	....	....
1992-93	Detroit	NHL	72	18	26	44	93	7	3	3	6	6
1993-94	Detroit	NHL	47	10	22	32	37	....	....	....	....	....
	Adirondack	AHL	1	2	0	2	0	....	....	....	....	....
	Winnipeg	NHL	15	3	5	8	12	....	....	....	....	....
1994-95	Winnipeg	NHL	43	8	18	26	30	....	....	....	....	....
1995-96	Winnipeg	NHL	69	19	20	39	36	3	0	0	0	0
1996-97	Phoenix	NHL	63	17	19	36	52	7	0	1	1	2
1997-98	Phoenix	NHL	60	11	29	40	71	4	0	1	1	2
	NHL Totals		369	86	139	225	331	21	3	5	8	10

WCHA First All-Star Team (1992) • NCAA West First All-American Team (1992)

Traded to **Winnipeg** by **Detroit** with Tim Cheveldae for Bob Essensa and Sergei Bautin, March 8, 1994. Transferred to **Phoenix** after **Winnipeg** franchise relocated, July 1, 1996.

DRAPER, KRIS (DRAY-puhr) DET.

Center. Shoots left. 5'11", 185 lbs. Born, Toronto, Ont., May 24, 1971.
(Winnipeg's 4th choice, 62nd overall, in 1989 Entry Draft).

			Regular Season					Playoffs				
Season	Club	Lea	GP	G	A	TP	PIM	GP	G	A	TP	PIM
1987-88	Don Mills	Midget	40	35	32	67	46	....	....	....	....	....
1988-89	Canada	Nat-Tm	60	11	15	26	16	....	....	....	....	....
1989-90	Canada	Nat-Tm	61	12	22	34	44	....	....	....	....	....
1990-91	Ottawa	OHL	39	19	42	61	35	17	8	11	19	20
	Winnipeg	NHL	3	1	0	1	5	....	....	....	....	....
	Moncton	AHL	7	2	1	3	2	....	....	....	....	....
1991-92	Winnipeg	NHL	10	2	0	2	2	2	0	0	0	0
	Moncton	AHL	61	11	18	29	113	4	0	1	1	6
1992-93	Winnipeg	NHL	7	0	0	0	2	....	....	....	....	....
	Moncton	AHL	67	12	23	35	40	5	2	2	4	18
1993-94	Detroit	NHL	39	5	8	13	31	7	2	2	4	4
	Adirondack	AHL	46	20	23	43	49	....	....	....	....	....
1994-95	Detroit	NHL	36	2	6	8	22	18	4	1	5	12
1995-96	Detroit	NHL	52	7	9	16	32	18	4	2	6	18
1996-97	Detroit	NHL	76	8	5	13	73	20	2	4	6	12 ♦
1997-98	Detroit	NHL	64	13	10	23	45	19	1	3	4	12 ♦
	NHL Totals		287	38	38	76	212	84	13	12	25	58

Traded to **Detroit** by **Winnipeg** for future considerations, June 30, 1993.

DRIVER, BRUCE

Defense. Shoots left. 6', 185 lbs. Born, Toronto, Ont., April 29, 1962.
(Colorado's 6th choice, 108th overall, in 1981 Entry Draft).

			Regular Season					Playoffs				
Season	Club	Lea	GP	G	A	TP	PIM	GP	G	A	TP	PIM
1979-80	Royal York	OJHL	43	13	57	70	102	....	....	....	....	....
1980-81	U. of Wisconsin	WCHA	42	5	15	20	42	....	....	....	....	....
1981-82	U. of Wisconsin	WCHA	46	7	37	44	84	....	....	....	....	....
1982-83	U. of Wisconsin	WCHA	49	19	42	61	100	....	....	....	....	....
1983-84	Canada	Nat-Tm	61	11	17	28	44	....	....	....	....	....
	Canada	Olympics	7	3	1	4	10	....	....	....	....	....
	New Jersey	NHL	4	0	2	2	0	....	....	....	....	....
	Maine	AHL	12	2	6	8	15	16	0	10	10	8
1984-85	New Jersey	NHL	67	9	23	32	36	....	....	....	....	....
1985-86	New Jersey	NHL	40	3	15	18	32	....	....	....	....	....
	Maine	AHL	15	4	7	11	16	....	....	....	....	....
1986-87	New Jersey	NHL	74	6	28	34	36	....	....	....	....	....
1987-88	New Jersey	NHL	74	15	40	55	68	20	3	7	10	14
1988-89	New Jersey	NHL	27	1	15	16	24	....	....	....	....	....
1989-90	New Jersey	NHL	75	7	46	53	63	6	1	5	6	6
1990-91	New Jersey	NHL	73	9	36	45	62	7	1	2	3	12
1991-92	New Jersey	NHL	78	7	35	42	66	7	0	4	4	2
1992-93	New Jersey	NHL	83	14	40	54	66	5	1	3	4	4
1993-94	New Jersey	NHL	66	8	24	32	63	20	3	5	8	12
1994-95	New Jersey	NHL	41	4	12	16	18	17	1	6	7	8 ♦
1995-96	NY Rangers	NHL	66	3	34	37	42	11	0	7	7	4
1996-97	NY Rangers	NHL	79	5	25	30	48	15	0	1	1	2
1997-98	NY Rangers	NHL	75	5	15	20	46	....	....	....	....	....
	NHL Totals		922	96	390	486	670	108	10	40	50	64

WCHA First All-Star Team (1982) • NCAA West First All-American Team (1982) • NCAA Championship All-Tournament Team (1982) • WCHA Second All-Star Team (1983)

Rights transferred to **New Jersey** after **Colorado** franchise relocated, June 30, 1982. Signed as a free agent by **NY Rangers**, September 28, 1995.

DROLET, JIMMY MTL.

Defense. Shoots left. 6', 190 lbs. Born, Vanier, Que., February 19, 1976.
(Montreal's 7th choice, 122nd overall, in 1994 Entry Draft).

			Regular Season					Playoffs				
Season	Club	Lea	GP	G	A	TP	PIM	GP	G	A	TP	PIM
1993-94	St-Hyacinthe	QMJHL	72	10	46	56	93	7	1	7	8	10
1994-95	St-Hyacinthe	QMJHL	68	9	27	36	126	5	0	2	2	12
1995-96	St-Hyacinthe	QMJHL	33	4	27	31	65	....	....	....	....	....
	Granby	QMJHL	29	4	26	30	70	21	7	18	25	28
1996-97	Fredericton	AHL	57	3	2	5	43	....	....	....	....	....
1997-98	Fredericton	AHL	28	1	3	4	38	....	....	....	....	....
	New Orleans	ECHL	10	1	3	4	2	4	1	4	5	0

DROUIN, P.C. (droo-IHN)

Left wing. Shoots left. 6'2", 208 lbs. Born, St. Lambert, Que., April 22, 1974.

			Regular Season					Playoffs				
Season	Club	Lea	GP	G	A	TP	PIM	GP	G	A	TP	PIM
1992-93	Cornell	ECAC	23	3	6	9	30	....	....	....	....	....
1993-94	Cornell	ECAC	21	6	13	19	32	....	....	....	....	....
1994-95	Cornell	ECAC	26	4	16	20	48	....	....	....	....	....
1995-96	Cornell	ECAC	31	18	14	32	60	....	....	....	....	....
1996-97	Boston	NHL	3	0	0	0	0	....	....	....	....	....
	Providence	AHL	42	12	11	23	10	....	....	....	....	....
1997-98	Providence	AHL	7	0	2	2	4	....	....	....	....	....
	Charlotte	ECHL	62	21	46	67	57	7	2	4	6	4
	NHL Totals		3	0	0	0	0					

Signed as a free agent by **Boston**, October 14, 1996.

DRUCE, JOHN (DROOS)

Right wing. Shoots right. 6'2", 195 lbs. Born, Peterborough, Ont., February 23, 1966.
(Washington's 2nd choice, 40th overall, in 1985 Entry Draft).

			Regular Season					Playoffs				
Season	Club	Lea	GP	G	A	TP	PIM	GP	G	A	TP	PIM
1984-85	Peterborough	OHL	54	12	14	26	90	17	6	2	8	21
1985-86	Peterborough	OHL	49	22	24	46	84	16	0	5	5	34
1986-87	Binghamton	AHL	77	13	9	22	131	12	0	3	3	28
1987-88	Binghamton	AHL	68	32	29	61	82	1	0	0	0	0
1988-89	**Washington**	**NHL**	**48**	**8**	**7**	**15**	**62**	**1**	**0**	**0**	**0**	**0**
	Baltimore	AHL	16	2	11	13	10	....	....	....	....	....
1989-90	**Washington**	**NHL**	**45**	**8**	**3**	**11**	**52**	**15**	**14**	**3**	**17**	**23**
	Baltimore	AHL	26	15	16	31	38	....	....	....	....	....
1990-91	**Washington**	**NHL**	**80**	**22**	**36**	**58**	**46**	**11**	**1**	**1**	**2**	**7**
1991-92	**Washington**	**NHL**	**67**	**19**	**18**	**37**	**39**	**7**	**1**	**0**	**1**	**2**
1992-93	**Winnipeg**	**NHL**	**50**	**6**	**14**	**20**	**37**	**2**	**0**	**0**	**0**	**0**
1993-94	**Los Angeles**	**NHL**	**55**	**14**	**17**	**31**	**50**	....	....	....	....	....
	Phoenix	IHL	8	5	6	11	9	....	....	....	....	....
1994-95	**Los Angeles**	**NHL**	**43**	**15**	**5**	**20**	**20**	....	....	....	....	....
1995-96	**Los Angeles**	**NHL**	**64**	**9**	**12**	**21**	**14**	....	....	....	....	....
	Philadelphia	**NHL**	**13**	**4**	**4**	**8**	**13**	**2**	**0**	**2**	**2**	**2**
1996-97	**Philadelphia**	**NHL**	**43**	**7**	**8**	**15**	**12**	**13**	**1**	**0**	**1**	**2**
1997-98	**Philadelphia**	**NHL**	**23**	**1**	**2**	**3**	**2**	**2**	**0**	**0**	**0**	**2**
	Philadelphia	AHL	39	21	28	49	45	....	....	....	....	....
	NHL Totals		**531**	**113**	**126**	**239**	**347**	**53**	**17**	**6**	**23**	**38**

Traded to **Winnipeg** by **Washington** with Toronto's 4th round choice (previously acquired by Washington — later traded to Detroit — Detroit selected John Jakopin) in 1993 Entry Draft for Pat Elynuik, October 1, 1992. Signed as a free agent by **LA Kings**, August 2, 1993. Traded to **Philadelphia** by **LA Kings** with LA Kings' 7th round choice (Todd Fedoruk) in 1997 Entry Draft for LA Kings' 4th round choice (previously acquired, LA Kings selected Mikael Simons) in 1996 Entry Draft, March 19, 1996.

DRUKEN, HAROLD VAN.

Center. Shoots left. 6', 205 lbs. Born, St. John's, Nfld., January 26, 1979.
(Vancouver's 3rd choice, 36th overall, in 1997 Entry Draft).

			Regular Season					Playoffs				
Season	Club	Lea	GP	G	A	TP	PIM	GP	G	A	TP	PIM
1996-97	Detroit	OHL	63	27	31	58	14	5	3	2	5	0
1997-98	Plymouth	OHL	64	38	44	82	12	15	9	11	20	4

DRURY, CHRIS COL.

Center. Shoots right. 5'10", 180 lbs. Born, Trumbull, CT, August 20, 1976.
(Quebec's 5th choice, 72nd overall, in 1994 Entry Draft).

			Regular Season					Playoffs				
Season	Club	Lea	GP	G	A	TP	PIM	GP	G	A	TP	PIM
1993-94	Fairfield Prep	H.S.	24	37	18	55	....	....	....	....	....	....
1994-95	Boston University	H.E.	39	12	15	27	38	....	....	....	....	....
1995-96	Boston University	H.E.	37	35	33	*68	46	....	....	....	....	....
1996-97	Boston University	H.E.	41	*38	24	62	64	....	....	....	....	....
1997-98	Boston University	H.E.	38	28	29	57	88	....	....	....	....	....

Hockey East Second All-Star Team (1996, 1997) • NCAA East Second All-American Team (1996) • NCAA East First All-American Team (1997, 1998) • NCAA Championship All-Tournament Team (1997) • Hockey East First All-Star Team (1998) • Won Hobey Baker Memorial Award (Top U.S. Collegiate Player) (1998)

Rights transferred to **Colorado** after **Quebec** franchise relocated, June 21, 1995.

DRURY, TED (DROO-ree) ANA.

Center. Shoots left. 6', 208 lbs. Born, Boston, MA, September 13, 1971.
(Calgary's 2nd choice, 42nd overall, in 1989 Entry Draft).

			Regular Season					Playoffs				
Season	Club	Lea	GP	G	A	TP	PIM	GP	G	A	TP	PIM
1988-89	Fairfield Prep	H.S.	25	35	31	66	....	....	....	....	....	....
1989-90	Harvard	ECAC	17	9	13	22	10	....	....	....	....	....
1990-91	Harvard	ECAC	25	18	18	36	22	....	....	....	....	....
1991-92	United States	Nat-Tm	53	11	23	34	30	....	....	....	....	....
	United States	Olympics	7	1	1	2	0	....	....	....	....	....
1992-93	Harvard	ECAC	31	22	*41	*63	28	....	....	....	....	....
1993-94	**Calgary**	**NHL**	**34**	**5**	**7**	**12**	**26**	....	....	....	....	....
	United States	Nat-Tm	11	1	4	5	11	....	....	....	....	....
	United States	Olympics	7	1	2	3	2	....	....	....	....	....
	Hartford	**NHL**	**16**	**1**	**5**	**6**	**10**	....	....	....	....	....
1994-95	**Hartford**	**NHL**	**34**	**3**	**6**	**9**	**21**	....	....	....	....	....
	Springfield	AHL	2	0	1	1	0	....	....	....	....	....
1995-96	**Ottawa**	**NHL**	**42**	**9**	**7**	**16**	**54**	....	....	....	....	....
1996-97	**Anaheim**	**NHL**	**73**	**9**	**9**	**18**	**54**	**10**	**1**	**0**	**1**	**4**
1997-98	**Anaheim**	**NHL**	**73**	**6**	**10**	**16**	**82**	....	....	....	....	....
	NHL Totals		**272**	**33**	**44**	**77**	**247**	**10**	**1**	**0**	**1**	**4**

ECAC First All-Star Team (1993) • NCAA East First All-America Team (1993)

Traded to **Hartford** by **Calgary** with Gary Suter and Paul Ranheim for James Patrick, Zarley Zalapski and Michael Nylander, March 10, 1994. Claimed by **Ottawa** from **Hartford** in NHL Waiver Draft, October 2, 1995. Traded to **Anaheim** by **Ottawa** with the rights to Marc Moro for Jason York and Shaun Van Allen, October 1, 1996.

DUBE, CHRISTIAN (doo-BAY) NYR

Center. Shoots right. 5'11", 170 lbs. Born, Sherbrooke, Que., April 25, 1977.
(NY Rangers' 1st choice, 39th overall, in 1995 Entry Draft).

			Regular Season					Playoffs				
Season	Club	Lea	GP	G	A	TP	PIM	GP	G	A	TP	PIM
1993-94	Sherbrooke	QMJHL	72	31	41	72	22	11	3	2	5	8
1994-95	Sherbrooke	QMJHL	71	36	65	101	43	7	1	7	8	8
1995-96	Sherbrooke	QMJHL	62	52	93	145	105	7	5	5	10	6
1996-97	Hull	QMJHL	19	15	22	37	37	14	7	16	23	14
	NY Rangers	**NHL**	**27**	**1**	**1**	**2**	**4**	**3**	**0**	**0**	**0**	**0**
1997-98	Hartford	AHL	79	11	46	57	46	9	0	4	4	6
	NHL Totals		**27**	**1**	**1**	**2**	**4**	**3**	**0**	**0**	**0**	**0**

QMJHL First All-Star Team (1996) • Canadian Major Junior First All-Star Team (1996) • Canadian Major Junior Player of the Year (1996) • Won Stafford Smythe Memorial Trophy (Memorial Cup Tournament MVP) (1997)

DUBINSKY, STEVE (doo-BIHN-skee) CHI.

Center. Shoots left. 6', 190 lbs. Born, Montreal, Que., July 9, 1970.
(Chicago's 9th choice, 226th overall, in 1990 Entry Draft).

			Regular Season					Playoffs				
Season	Club	Lea	GP	G	A	TP	PIM	GP	G	A	TP	PIM
1989-90	Clarkson	ECAC	35	7	10	17	24	....	....	....	....	....
1990-91	Clarkson	ECAC	39	13	23	36	26	....	....	....	....	....
1991-92	Clarkson	ECAC	32	20	31	51	40	....	....	....	....	....
1992-93	Clarkson	ECAC	35	18	26	44	58	....	....	....	....	....
1993-94	**Chicago**	**NHL**	**27**	**2**	**6**	**8**	**16**	**6**	**0**	**0**	**0**	**10**
	Indianapolis	IHL	54	15	25	40	63	....	....	....	....	....
1994-95	**Chicago**	**NHL**	**16**	**0**	**0**	**0**	**8**	....	....	....	....	....
	Indianapolis	IHL	62	16	11	27	29	....	....	....	....	....
1995-96	**Chicago**	**NHL**	**43**	**2**	**3**	**5**	**14**	....	....	....	....	....
	Indianapolis	IHL	16	8	8	16	10	....	....	....	....	....
1996-97	**Chicago**	**NHL**	**5**	**0**	**0**	**0**	**0**	**4**	**1**	**0**	**1**	**4**
	Indianapolis	IHL	77	32	40	72	53	1	3	1	4	0
1997-98	**Chicago**	**NHL**	**82**	**5**	**13**	**18**	**57**	....	....	....	....	....
	NHL Totals		**173**	**9**	**22**	**31**	**95**	**10**	**1**	**0**	**1**	**14**

DUCE, BRYAN N.J.

Right wing. Shoots right. 6', 190 lbs. Born, Thunder Bay, Ont., January 15, 1978.

			Regular Season					Playoffs				
Season	Club	Lea	GP	G	A	TP	PIM	GP	G	A	TP	PIM
1995-96	Kitchener	OHL	55	14	9	23	16	11	0	0	0	2
1996-97	Kitchener	OHL	62	27	30	57	36	11	5	3	8	2
1997-98	Kitchener	OHL	37	9	20	29	12	....	....	....	....	....
	S.S. Marie	OHL	21	3	2	5	4	....	....	....	....	....

Signed as a free agent by **New Jersey**, August 12, 1997.

DUCHESNE, STEVE (doo-SHAYN) L.A.

Defense. Shoots left. 5'11", 195 lbs. Born, Sept-Iles, Que., June 30, 1965.

			Regular Season					Playoffs				
Season	Club	Lea	GP	G	A	TP	PIM	GP	G	A	TP	PIM
1983-84	Drummondville	QMJHL	67	1	34	35	79	....	....	....	....	....
1984-85	Drummondville	QMJHL	65	22	54	76	94	5	4	7	11	8
1985-86	New Haven	AHL	75	14	35	49	76	5	0	2	2	9
1986-87	**Los Angeles**	**NHL**	**75**	**13**	**25**	**38**	**74**	**5**	**2**	**2**	**4**	**4**
1987-88	**Los Angeles**	**NHL**	**71**	**16**	**39**	**55**	**109**	**5**	**1**	**3**	**4**	**14**
1988-89	**Los Angeles**	**NHL**	**79**	**25**	**50**	**75**	**92**	**11**	**4**	**4**	**8**	**12**
1989-90	**Los Angeles**	**NHL**	**79**	**20**	**42**	**62**	**36**	**10**	**2**	**9**	**11**	**6**
1990-91	**Los Angeles**	**NHL**	**78**	**21**	**41**	**62**	**66**	**12**	**4**	**8**	**12**	**8**
1991-92	**Philadelphia**	**NHL**	**78**	**18**	**38**	**56**	**86**	....	....	....	....	....
1992-93	**Quebec**	**NHL**	**82**	**20**	**62**	**82**	**57**	**6**	**0**	**5**	**5**	**6**
1993-94	**St. Louis**	**NHL**	**36**	**12**	**19**	**31**	**14**	**4**	**0**	**2**	**2**	**2**
1994-95	**St. Louis**	**NHL**	**47**	**12**	**26**	**38**	**36**	**7**	**0**	**4**	**4**	**2**
1995-96	**Ottawa**	**NHL**	**62**	**12**	**24**	**36**	**42**	....	....	....	....	....
1996-97	**Ottawa**	**NHL**	**78**	**19**	**28**	**47**	**38**	**7**	**1**	**4**	**5**	**0**
1997-98	**St. Louis**	**NHL**	**80**	**14**	**42**	**56**	**32**	**10**	**0**	**4**	**4**	**6**
	NHL Totals		**845**	**202**	**436**	**638**	**682**	**77**	**14**	**45**	**59**	**60**

QMJHL First All-Star Team (1985) • NHL All-Rookie Team (1987)

Played in NHL All-Star Game (1989, 1990, 1993)

Signed as a free agent by **LA Kings**, October 1, 1984. Traded to **Philadelphia** by **LA Kings** with Steve Kasper and LA Kings' 4th round choice (Aris Brimanis) in 1991 Entry Draft for Jari Kurri and Jeff Chychrun, May 30, 1991. Traded to **Quebec** by **Philadelphia** with Peter Forsberg, Kerry Huffman, Mike Ricci, Ron Hextall, Chris Simon, Philadelphia's 1st round choice in the 1993 (Jocelyn Thibault) and 1994 (later traded to Toronto — later traded to Washington — Washington selected Nolan Baumgartner) Entry Drafts and cash for Eric Lindros, June 30, 1992. Traded to **St. Louis** by **Quebec** with Denis Chasse for Garth Butcher, Ron Sutter and Bob Bassen, January 23, 1994. Traded to **Ottawa** by **St. Louis** for Ottawa's 2nd round choice (later traded to Buffalo — Buffalo selected Cory Sarich) in 1996 Entry Draft, August 4, 1995. Traded to **St. Louis** by **Ottawa** for Igor Kravchuk, August 25, 1997. Signed as a free agent by **LA Kings**, July 2, 1998.

DUERDEN, DAVE FLA.

Left wing. Shoots left. 6'2", 200 lbs. Born, Oshawa, Ont., April 11, 1977.
(Florida's 4th choice, 80th overall, in 1995 Entry Draft).

			Regular Season					Playoffs				
Season	Club	Lea	GP	G	A	TP	PIM	GP	G	A	TP	PIM
1994-95	Peterborough	OHL	66	20	33	53	21	11	6	2	8	6
1995-96	Peterborough	OHL	66	35	35	70	47	24	14	13	27	16
1996-97	Peterborough	OHL	66	36	48	84	34	4	2	4	6	0
1997-98	Port Huron	UHL	7	0	4	4	10	....	....	....	....	....
	New Haven	AHL	36	6	7	13	10	....	....	....	....	....
	Fort Wayne	IHL	7	0	1	1	0	....	....	....	....	....

OHL Second All-Star Team (1997)

DUFRESNE, DONALD (doo-FRAYN, DOH-nal)

Defense. Shoots right. 6'1", 206 lbs. Born, Quebec City, Que., April 10, 1967.
(Montreal's 8th choice, 117th overall, in 1985 Entry Draft).

			Regular Season					Playoffs				
Season	Club	Lea	GP	G	A	TP	PIM	GP	G	A	TP	PIM
1983-84	Trois-Rivieres	QMJHL	67	7	12	19	97	....	....	....	....	....
1984-85	Trois-Rivieres	QMJHL	65	5	30	35	112	7	1	3	4	12
1985-86	Trois-Rivieres	QMJHL	63	8	32	40	160	1	0	0	0	0
1986-87	Trois-Rivieres	QMJHL	51	5	21	26	79	....	....	....	....	....
	Longueuil	QMJHL	16	0	8	8	18	20	1	8	9	38
1987-88	Sherbrooke	AHL	47	1	8	9	107	6	1	0	1	34
1988-89	**Montreal**	**NHL**	**13**	**0**	**1**	**1**	**43**	**6**	**1**	**1**	**2**	**4**
	Sherbrooke	AHL	47	0	12	12	170	....	....	....	....	....
1989-90	**Montreal**	**NHL**	**18**	**0**	**4**	**4**	**23**	**10**	**0**	**1**	**1**	**18**
	Sherbrooke	AHL	38	2	11	13	104	....	....	....	....	....
1990-91	**Montreal**	**NHL**	**53**	**2**	**13**	**15**	**55**	**10**	**0**	**1**	**1**	**21**
	Fredericton	AHL	10	1	4	5	35	1	0	0	0	0
1991-92	**Montreal**	**NHL**	**3**	**0**	**0**	**0**	**2**	....	....	....	....	....
	Fredericton	AHL	31	8	12	20	60	7	0	0	0	10
1992-93	**Montreal**	**NHL**	**32**	**1**	**2**	**3**	**32**	**2**	**0**	**0**	**0**	**0 ♦**
1993-94	**Tampa Bay**	**NHL**	**51**	**2**	**6**	**8**	**48**	....	....	....	....	....
	Los Angeles	**NHL**	**9**	**0**	**0**	**0**	**10**	....	....	....	....	....
1994-95	**St. Louis**	**NHL**	**22**	**0**	**3**	**3**	**10**	**3**	**0**	**0**	**0**	**4**
1995-96	**St. Louis**	**NHL**	**3**	**0**	**0**	**0**	**4**	....	....	....	....	....
	Worcester	AHL	13	1	1	2	14	....	....	....	....	....
	Edmonton	**NHL**	**42**	**1**	**6**	**7**	**16**	....	....	....	....	....
1996-97	**Edmonton**	**NHL**	**22**	**0**	**1**	**1**	**15**	**3**	**0**	**0**	**0**	**0**
1997-98	Quebec	IHL	15	0	4	4	20	....	....	....	....	....
	NHL Totals		**268**	**6**	**36**	**42**	**258**	**34**	**1**	**3**	**4**	**47**

QMJHL Second All-Star Team (1986, 1987)

Traded to **Tampa Bay** by **Montreal** to complete transaction that sent Rob Ramage to Montreal (March 20, 1993), June 20, 1993. Traded to **LA Kings** by **Tampa Bay** for LA Kings' 6th round choice (Daniel Juden) in 1994 Entry Draft, March 19, 1994. Claimed by **St. Louis** from **LA Kings** in NHL Waiver Draft, January 18, 1995. Traded to **Edmonton** by **St. Louis** with Jeff Norton for Igor Kravchuk and Ken Sutton, January 4, 1996.

DUMONT, JEAN-PIERRE CHI.

Right wing. Shoots left. 6'1", 187 lbs. Born, Montreal, Que., April 1, 1978.
(NY Islanders' 1st choice, 3rd overall, in 1996 Entry Draft).

			Regular Season					Playoffs				
Season	Club	Lea	GP	G	A	TP	PIM	GP	G	A	TP	PIM
1993-94	Val d'Or	QMJHL	25	9	11	20	10	....	....	....	....	....
1994-95	Val d'Or	QMJHL	48	5	14	19	24	....	....	....	....	....
1995-96	Val d'Or	QMJHL	66	48	57	105	109	13	12	8	20	22
1996-97	Val d'Or	QMJHL	62	44	64	108	86	13	9	7	16	12
1997-98	Val d'Or	QMJHL	55	57	42	99	63	19	31	15	46	18

QMJHL Second All-Star Team (1997)

Rights traded to **Chicago** by **NY Islanders** for Dmitri Nabokov, May 30, 1998.

DUSABEK, JOE S.J.

Right wing. Shoots right. 6'1", 200 lbs. Born, Fairbault, MN, May 1, 1978.
(San Jose's 5th choice, 163rd overall, in 1997 Entry Draft).

			Regular Season					Playoffs				
Season	Club	Lea	GP	G	A	TP	PIM	GP	G	A	TP	PIM
1996-97	Notre Dame	CCHA	35	13	12	25	74	....	....	....	....	....
1997-98	Notre Dame	CCHA	21	1	8	9	32	....	....	....	....	....

DUTIAUME, MARK (doo-TEE-owm) BUF.

Left wing. Shoots left. 6', 200 lbs. Born, Winnipeg, Man., January 31, 1977.
(Buffalo's 3rd choice, 42nd overall, in 1995 Entry Draft).

			Regular Season					Playoffs				
Season	Club	Lea	GP	G	A	TP	PIM	GP	G	A	TP	PIM
1993-94	Tri-City	WHL	3	2	0	2	0	....	....	....	....	....
	Brandon	WHL	55	4	7	11	43	12	0	2	2	6
1994-95	Brandon	WHL	62	23	21	44	80	17	1	2	3	33
1995-96	Brandon	WHL	7	0	4	4	6	9	2	1	3	12
1996-97	Brandon	WHL	48	12	11	23	73	6	2	2	4	13
	Rochester	AHL	6	1	1	2	0	....	....	....	....	....
1997-98	Rochester	AHL	11	1	0	1	4	....	....	....	....	....
	South Carolina	ECHL	28	3	4	7	24	2	0	0	0	2

DVORAK, RADEK (duh-VOHR-ak) FLA.

Right wing. Shoots right. 6'1", 194 lbs. Born, Tabor, Czech., March 9, 1977.
(Florida's 1st choice, 10th overall, in 1995 Entry Draft).

			Regular Season					Playoffs				
Season	Club	Lea	GP	G	A	TP	PIM	GP	G	A	TP	PIM
1993-94	Budejovice	Cze-Rep.	8	0	0	0	0	....	....	....	....	....
1994-95	Budejovice	Cze-Rep.	10	3	5	8	2	9	5	1	6	....
1995-96	**Florida**	**NHL**	**77**	**13**	**14**	**27**	**20**	**16**	**1**	**3**	**4**	**0**
1996-97	**Florida**	**NHL**	**78**	**18**	**21**	**39**	**30**	**3**	**0**	**0**	**0**	**0**
1997-98	**Florida**	**NHL**	**64**	**12**	**24**	**36**	**33**	....	....	....	....	....
	NHL Totals		**219**	**43**	**59**	**102**	**83**	**19**	**1**	**3**	**4**	**0**

DWYER, GORDIE (DWIGHR) MTL.

Left wing. Shoots left. 6'2", 190 lbs. Born, Dalhousie, NB, January 25, 1978.
(Montreal's 5th choice, 152nd overall, in 1998 Entry Draft).

			Regular Season					Playoffs				
Season	Club	Lea	GP	G	A	TP	PIM	GP	G	A	TP	PIM
1994-95	Hull	QMJHL	57	3	7	10	204	17	1	3	4	54
1995-96	Hull	QMJHL	25	5	9	14	199	....	....	....	....	....
	Laval	QMJHL	22	5	17	22	72	....	....	....	....	....
	Beauport	QMJHL	22	4	9	13	87	20	3	5	8	104
1996-97	Drummondville	QMJHL	66	21	48	69	393	8	6	1	7	39
1997-98	Quebec	QMJHL	59	18	27	45	365	14	4	9	13	67

• Re-entered NHL draft. Originally St. Louis' 2nd choice, 67th overall, in 1996 Entry Draft.

DYKHUIS, KARL (DIGH-kowz) T.B.

Defense. Shoots left. 6'3", 214 lbs. Born, Sept-Iles, Que., July 8, 1972.
(Chicago's 1st choice, 16th overall, in 1990 Entry Draft).

			Regular Season					Playoffs				
Season	Club	Lea	GP	G	A	TP	PIM	GP	G	A	TP	PIM
1988-89	Hull	QMJHL	63	2	29	31	59	9	1	9	10	6
1989-90	Hull	QMJHL	69	10	46	56	119	11	2	5	7	2
1990-91	Longueuil	QMJHL	3	1	4	5	6	8	2	5	7	6
	Canada	Nat-Tm	37	2	9	11	16	....	....	....	....	....
1991-92	Verdun	QMJHL	29	5	19	24	55	17	0	12	12	14
	Canada	Nat-Tm	19	1	2	3	16	....	....	....	....	....
	Chicago	**NHL**	**6**	**1**	**3**	**4**	**4**	....	....	....	....	....
1992-93	**Chicago**	**NHL**	**12**	**0**	**5**	**5**	**0**	....	....	....	....	....
	Indianapolis	IHL	59	5	18	23	76	5	1	1	2	8
1993-94	Indianapolis	IHL	73	7	25	32	132	....	....	....	....	....
1994-95	Indianapolis	IHL	52	2	21	23	63	....	....	....	....	....
	Philadelphia	**NHL**	**33**	**2**	**6**	**8**	**37**	**15**	**4**	**4**	**8**	**14**
	Hershey	AHL	1	0	0	0	0	....	....	....	....	....
1995-96	**Philadelphia**	**NHL**	**82**	**5**	**15**	**20**	**101**	**12**	**2**	**2**	**4**	**22**
1996-97	**Philadelphia**	**NHL**	**62**	**4**	**15**	**19**	**35**	**18**	**0**	**3**	**3**	**2**
1997-98	**Tampa Bay**	**NHL**	**78**	**5**	**9**	**14**	**110**	....	....	....	....	....
	NHL Totals		**273**	**17**	**53**	**70**	**287**	**45**	**6**	**9**	**15**	**38**

QMJHL First All-Star Team (1990)

Traded to **Philadelphia** by **Chicago** for Bob Wilkie and future considerations, February 16, 1995. Traded to **Tampa Bay** by **Philadelphia** with Mikael Renberg for Philadelphia's 1st round choices in 1998 (Simon Gagne), 1999, 2000, and 2001 Entry Drafts (previously acquired by Tampa Bay), August 20, 1997.

DZIEDZIC, JOE (zeed-ZIHK) PHX.

Left wing. Shoots left. 6'3", 227 lbs. Born, Minneapolis, MN, December 18, 1971.
(Pittsburgh's 2nd choice, 61st overall, in 1990 Entry Draft).

			Regular Season					Playoffs				
Season	Club	Lea	GP	G	A	TP	PIM	GP	G	A	TP	PIM
1989-90	Edison High	H.S.	17	29	19	48	10	....	....	....	....	....
1990-91	U. of Minnesota	WCHA	20	6	4	10	26	....	....	....	....	....
1991-92	U. of Minnesota	WCHA	34	8	9	17	68	....	....	....	....	....
1992-93	U. of Minnesota	WCHA	41	11	14	25	62	....	....	....	....	....
1993-94	U. of Minnesota	WCHA	18	7	10	17	48	....	....	....	....	....
1994-95	Cleveland	IHL	68	15	15	30	74	4	1	0	1	10
1995-96	**Pittsburgh**	**NHL**	**69**	**5**	**5**	**10**	**68**	**16**	**1**	**2**	**3**	**19**
1996-97	**Pittsburgh**	**NHL**	**59**	**9**	**9**	**18**	**63**	**5**	**0**	**1**	**1**	**4**
1997-98	Cleveland	IHL	65	21	20	41	176	10	3	4	7	28
	NHL Totals		**128**	**14**	**14**	**28**	**131**	**21**	**1**	**3**	**4**	**23**

Signed as a free agent by **Phoenix**, August 27, 1998.

EAGLES, MIKE WSH.

Center/Left wing. Shoots left. 5'10", 190 lbs. Born, Sussex, N.B., March 7, 1963.
(Quebec's 5th choice, 116th overall, in 1981 Entry Draft).

			Regular Season					Playoffs				
Season	Club	Lea	GP	G	A	TP	PIM	GP	G	A	TP	PIM
1980-81	Kitchener	OHA	56	11	27	38	64	18	4	2	6	36
1981-82	Kitchener	OHL	62	26	40	66	148	15	3	11	14	27
1982-83	Kitchener	OHL	58	26	36	62	133	12	5	7	12	27
	Quebec	**NHL**	**2**	**0**	**0**	**0**	**2**	....	....	....	....	....
1983-84	Fredericton	AHL	68	13	29	42	85	4	0	0	0	5
1984-85	Fredericton	AHL	36	4	20	24	80	3	0	0	0	2
1985-86	**Quebec**	**NHL**	**73**	**11**	**12**	**23**	**49**	**3**	**0**	**0**	**0**	**2**
1986-87	**Quebec**	**NHL**	**73**	**13**	**19**	**32**	**55**	**4**	**1**	**0**	**1**	**10**
1987-88	**Quebec**	**NHL**	**76**	**10**	**10**	**20**	**74**	....	....	....	....	....
1988-89	**Chicago**	**NHL**	**47**	**5**	**11**	**16**	**44**	....	....	....	....	....
1989-90	**Chicago**	**NHL**	**23**	**1**	**2**	**3**	**34**	....	....	....	....	....
	Indianapolis	IHL	24	11	13	24	47	13	*10	10	20	34
1990-91	**Winnipeg**	**NHL**	**44**	**0**	**9**	**9**	**79**	....	....	....	....	....
	Indianapolis	IHL	25	15	14	29	47	....	....	....	....	....
1991-92	**Winnipeg**	**NHL**	**65**	**7**	**10**	**17**	**118**	**7**	**0**	**0**	**0**	**8**
1992-93	**Winnipeg**	**NHL**	**84**	**8**	**18**	**26**	**131**	**5**	**0**	**1**	**1**	**6**
1993-94	**Winnipeg**	**NHL**	**73**	**4**	**8**	**12**	**96**	....	....	....	....	....
1994-95	**Winnipeg**	**NHL**	**27**	**2**	**1**	**3**	**40**	....	....	....	....	....
	Washington	**NHL**	**13**	**1**	**3**	**4**	**8**	**7**	**0**	**2**	**2**	**4**
1995-96	**Washington**	**NHL**	**70**	**4**	**7**	**11**	**75**	**6**	**1**	**1**	**2**	**2**
1996-97	**Washington**	**NHL**	**70**	**1**	**7**	**8**	**42**	....	....	....	....	....
1997-98	**Washington**	**NHL**	**36**	**1**	**3**	**4**	**16**	**12**	**0**	**2**	**2**	**2**
	NHL Totals		**776**	**68**	**120**	**188**	**863**	**44**	**2**	**6**	**8**	**34**

Traded to **Chicago** by **Quebec** for Bob Mason, July 5, 1988. Traded to **Winnipeg** by **Chicago** for Winnipeg's 4th round choice (Igor Kravchuk) in 1991 Entry Draft, December 14, 1990. Traded to **Washington** by **Winnipeg** with Igor Ulanov for Washington's 3rd (later traded to Dallas — Dallas selected Sergei Gusev) and 5th (Brian Elder) round choices in 1995 Entry Draft, April 7, 1995.

EAKINS, DALLAS (EE-kins) TOR.

Defense. Shoots left. 6'2", 195 lbs. Born, Dade City, FL, February 27, 1967.
(Washington's 11th choice, 208th overall, in 1985 Entry Draft).

			Regular Season					Playoffs				
Season	Club	Lea	GP	G	A	TP	PIM	GP	G	A	TP	PIM
1984-85	Peterborough	OHL	48	0	8	8	96	7	0	0	0	18
1985-86	Peterborough	OHL	60	6	16	22	134	16	0	1	1	30
1986-87	Peterborough	OHL	54	3	11	14	145	12	1	4	5	37
1987-88	Peterborough	OHL	64	11	27	38	129	12	3	12	15	16
1988-89	Baltimore	AHL	62	0	10	10	139	....	....	....	....	....
1989-90	Moncton	AHL	75	2	11	13	189	....	....	....	....	....
1990-91	Moncton	AHL	75	1	12	13	132	9	0	1	1	44
1991-92	Moncton	AHL	67	3	13	16	136	11	2	1	3	16
1992-93	**Winnipeg**	**NHL**	**14**	**0**	**2**	**2**	**38**	....	....	....	....	....
	Moncton	AHL	55	4	6	10	132	....	....	....	....	....
1993-94	**Florida**	**NHL**	**1**	**0**	**0**	**0**	**0**	....	....	....	....	....
	Cincinnati	IHL	80	1	18	19	143	8	0	1	1	41
1994-95	**Florida**	**NHL**	**17**	**0**	**1**	**1**	**35**	....	....	....	....	....
	Cincinnati	IHL	59	6	12	18	69	....	....	....	....	....
1995-96	**St. Louis**	**NHL**	**16**	**0**	**1**	**1**	**34**	....	....	....	....	....
	Worcester	AHL	4	0	0	0	12	....	....	....	....	....
	Winnipeg	**NHL**	**2**	**0**	**0**	**0**	**0**	....	....	....	....	....
1996-97	**Phoenix**	**NHL**	**4**	**0**	**0**	**0**	**10**	....	....	....	....	....
	Springfield	AHL	38	6	7	13	63	....	....	....	....	....
	NY Rangers	**NHL**	**3**	**0**	**0**	**0**	**6**	**4**	**0**	**0**	**0**	**4**
	Binghamton	AHL	19	1	7	8	15	....	....	....	....	....
1997-98	**Florida**	**NHL**	**23**	**0**	**1**	**1**	**44**	....	....	....	....	....
	New Haven	AHL	4	0	1	1	7	....	....	....	....	....
	NHL Totals		**80**	**0**	**5**	**5**	**167**	**4**	**0**	**0**	**0**	**4**

Signed as a free agent by **Winnipeg**, October 17, 1989. Signed as a free agent by **Florida**, July 8, 1993. Traded to **St. Louis** by **Florida** for St. Louis' 4th round choice (Ivan Novoseltsev) in 1997 Entry Draft, September 28, 1995. Claimed on waivers by **Winnipeg** from **St. Louis**, March 20, 1996. Transferred to **Phoenix** after **Winnipeg** franchise relocated, July 1, 1996. Traded to **NY Rangers** by **Phoenix** with Mike Eastwood for Jayson More, February 6, 1997. Signed as a free agent by **Florida**, July 30, 1997. Signed as a free agent by **Toronto**, July 28, 1998.

EASTWOOD, MIKE ST.L.

Center. Shoots right. 6'3", 205 lbs. Born, Ottawa, Ont., July 1, 1967.
(Toronto's 5th choice, 91st overall, in 1987 Entry Draft).

			Regular Season					Playoffs				
Season	Club	Lea	GP	G	A	TP	PIM	GP	G	A	TP	PIM
1986-87	Pembroke	OJHL			STATISTICS NOT AVAILABLE							
1987-88	Western Michigan	CCHA	42	5	8	13	14	....	....	....	....	....
1988-89	Western Michigan	CCHA	40	10	13	23	87	....	....	....	....	....
1989-90	Western Michigan	CCHA	40	25	27	52	36	....	....	....	....	....
1990-91	Western Michigan	CCHA	42	29	32	61	84	....	....	....	....	....
1991-92	**Toronto**	**NHL**	**9**	**0**	**2**	**2**	**4**	....	....	....	....	....
	St. John's	AHL	61	18	25	43	28	16	9	10	19	16
1992-93	**Toronto**	**NHL**	**12**	**1**	**6**	**7**	**21**	**10**	**1**	**2**	**3**	**8**
	St. John's	AHL	60	24	35	59	32	....	....	....	....	....
1993-94	**Toronto**	**NHL**	**54**	**8**	**10**	**18**	**28**	**18**	**3**	**2**	**5**	**12**
1994-95	**Toronto**	**NHL**	**36**	**5**	**5**	**10**	**32**	....	....	....	....	....
	Winnipeg	**NHL**	**13**	**3**	**6**	**9**	**4**	....	....	....	....	....
1995-96	**Winnipeg**	**NHL**	**80**	**14**	**14**	**28**	**20**	**6**	**0**	**1**	**1**	**2**
1996-97	**Phoenix**	**NHL**	**33**	**1**	**3**	**4**	**4**	....	....	....	....	....
	NY Rangers	**NHL**	**27**	**1**	**7**	**8**	**10**	**15**	**1**	**2**	**3**	**22**
1997-98	**NY Rangers**	**NHL**	**48**	**5**	**5**	**10**	**16**	....	....	....	....	....
	St. Louis	**NHL**	**10**	**1**	**0**	**1**	**6**	**3**	**1**	**0**	**1**	**0**
	NHL Totals		**322**	**39**	**58**	**97**	**145**	**52**	**6**	**7**	**13**	**44**

CCHA Second All-Star Team (1991)

Traded to **Winnipeg** by **Toronto** with Toronto's 3rd round choice (Brad Isbister) in 1995 Entry Draft for Tie Domi, April 7, 1995. Transferred to **Phoenix** after **Winnipeg** franchise relocated, July 1, 1996. Traded to **NY Rangers** by **Phoenix** with Dallas Eakins for Jayson More, February 6, 1997. Traded to **St. Louis** by **NY Rangers** for Harry York, March 24, 1998.

EATON, MARK PHI.

Defense. Shoots left. 6'3", 195 lbs. Born, Wilmington, DE, May 6, 1977.

			Regular Season					Playoffs				
Season	Club	Lea	GP	G	A	TP	PIM	GP	G	A	TP	PIM
1996-97	Waterloo	USHL	50	6	32	38	62	....	....	....	....	....
1997-98	Notre Dame	CCHA	41	12	17	29	32	....	....	....	....	....

Signed as a free agent by **Philadelphia**, July 28, 1998.

EDINGER, ADAM NYI

Center. Shoots left. 6'2", 210 lbs. Born, Toledo, OH, September 21, 1977.
(NY Islanders' 7th choice, 115th overall, in 1997 Entry Draft).

			Regular Season					Playoffs				
Season	Club	Lea	GP	G	A	TP	PIM	GP	G	A	TP	PIM
1994-95	Leamington	OJHL	38	19	62	81	100	....	....	....	....	....
1995-96	Leamington	OJHL	45	45	50	95	120	....	....	....	....	....
1996-97	Bowling Green	CCHA	34	11	18	29	42	....	....	....	....	....
1997-98	Bowling Green	CCHA	27	9	13	22	62	....	....	....	....	....

EGELAND, ALLAN (eh-GUH-luhnd)

Center. Shoots left. 6', 175 lbs. Born, Lethbridge, Alta., January 31, 1973.
(Tampa Bay's 3rd choice, 55th overall, in 1993 Entry Draft).

			Regular Season					Playoffs				
Season	Club	Lea	GP	G	A	TP	PIM	GP	G	A	TP	PIM
1990-91	Lethbridge	WHL	67	2	16	18	57	9	0	0	0	0
1991-92	Tacoma	WHL	72	35	39	74	135	4	0	1	1	18
1992-93	Tacoma	WHL	71	56	57	113	119	7	9	7	16	18
1993-94	Tacoma	WHL	70	47	76	123	204	8	5	3	8	26
1994-95	Atlanta	IHL	60	8	16	24	112	5	0	1	1	16
1995-96	**Tampa Bay**	**NHL**	**5**	**0**	**0**	**0**	**2**	....	....	....	....	....
	Atlanta	IHL	68	22	22	44	182	3	0	1	1	0
1996-97	**Tampa Bay**	**NHL**	**4**	**0**	**0**	**0**	**5**	....	....	....	....	....
	Adirondack	AHL	52	18	32	50	184	2	0	1	1	4
1997-98	**Tampa Bay**	**NHL**	**8**	**0**	**0**	**0**	**9**	....	....	....	....	....
	Adirondack	AHL	35	11	22	33	78	3	0	2	2	10
	NHL Totals		**17**	**0**	**0**	**0**	**16**	....	....	....	....	....

WHL West First All-Star Team (1993) • WHL West Second All-Star Team (1994)

EKLUND, PER (EHK-luhnd, PAIR)

Left wing. Shoots left. 5'11", 196 lbs. Born, Sollentuna, Sweden, July 9, 1970.
(Detroit's 8th choice, 182nd overall, in 1995 Entry Draft).

			Regular Season					Playoffs				
Season	Club	Lea	GP	G	A	TP	PIM	GP	G	A	TP	PIM
1991-92	Vasby	Sweden-2	29	13	24	37	26	....	....	....	....	....
1992-93	Huddinge	Sweden-2	36	22	23	45	14	....	....	....	....	....
1993-94	Huddinge	Sweden-2	35	20	11	31	40	....	....	....	....	....
1994-95	Djurgarden	Sweden	40	19	10	29	20	3	1	1	2	4
1995-96	Djurgarden	Sweden	39	17	10	27	10	1	0	0	0	0
1996-97	Djurgarden	Sweden	50	20	16	36	14	4	1	0	1	0
1997-98	Adirondack	AHL	73	21	29	50	12	3	0	0	0	0

EKMAN, NILS (EHK-mahn) CGY.

Left wing. Shoots left. 5'11", 175 lbs. Born, Stockholm, Sweden, March 11, 1976.
(Calgary's 6th choice, 107th overall, in 1994 Entry Draft).

			Regular Season					Playoffs				
Season	Club	Lea	GP	G	A	TP	PIM	GP	G	A	TP	PIM
1993-94	Hammarby	Sweden-2	18	7	2	9	4	....	....	....	....	....
1994-95	Hammarby	Sweden-2	29	10	7	17	18	....	....	....	....	....
1995-96	Hammarby	Sweden-2	26	9	7	16	53	1	0	0	0	0
1996-97	Kiekko	Finland	50	24	19	43	60	4	2	0	2	4
1997-98	Kiekko	Finland	43	14	14	28	86	7	2	2	4	27
	Saint John	AHL	....	....	....	....	....	1	0	0	0	2

ELFRING, CALVIN COL.

Defense. Shoots left. 6', 170 lbs. Born, Lethbridge, Alta., April 23, 1976.
(Quebec's 9th choice, 165th overall, in 1994 Entry Draft).

			Regular Season					Playoffs				
Season	Club	Lea	GP	G	A	TP	PIM	GP	G	A	TP	PIM
1993-94	Powell River	BCJHL	58	21	45	66	80	....	....	....	....	....
1994-95	Colorado	WCHA	43	3	23	26	34	....	....	....	....	....
1995-96	Colorado	WCHA	42	10	24	34	32	....	....	....	....	....
1996-97	Colorado	WCHA	44	9	22	31	26	....	....	....	....	....
1997-98	Colorado	WCHA	42	10	26	36	51	....	....	....	....	....

WCHA Second All-Star Team (1998) • NCAA West Second All-American Team (1998)

ELIAS, PATRIK (EH-lih-ahsh) N.J.

Left wing. Shoots left. 6', 195 lbs. Born, Trebic, Czech., April 13, 1976.
(New Jersey's 2nd choice, 51st overall, in 1994 Entry Draft).

			Regular Season					Playoffs				
Season	Club	Lea	GP	G	A	TP	PIM	GP	G	A	TP	PIM
1992-93	Poldi Kladno	Czech.	2	0	0	0	....	....	....	....	....	....
1993-94	Poldi Kladno	Cze-Rep.	15	1	2	3	....	11	2	2	4	....
1994-95	Poldi Kladno	Cze-Rep.	28	4	3	7	37	7	1	2	3	12
1995-96	**New Jersey**	**NHL**	**1**	**0**	**0**	**0**	**0**	....	....	....	....	....
	Albany	AHL	74	27	36	63	83	4	1	1	2	2
1996-97	**New Jersey**	**NHL**	**17**	**2**	**3**	**5**	**2**	**8**	**2**	**3**	**5**	**4**
	Albany	AHL	57	24	43	67	76	6	1	2	3	8
1997-98	**New Jersey**	**NHL**	**74**	**18**	**19**	**37**	**28**	**4**	**0**	**1**	**1**	**0**
	Albany	AHL	3	3	0	3	2	....	....	....	....	....
	NHL Totals		**92**	**20**	**22**	**42**	**30**	**12**	**2**	**4**	**6**	**4**

NHL All-Rookie Team (1998)

ELICH, MATT T.B.

Right wing. Shoots right. 6'3", 187 lbs. Born, Detroit, MI, September 22, 1979.
(Tampa Bay's 3rd choice, 61st overall, in 1997 Entry Draft).

			Regular Season					Playoffs				
Season	Club	Lea	GP	G	A	TP	PIM	GP	G	A	TP	PIM
1995-96	Windsor	OHL	52	10	2	12	17	5	1	0	1	2
1996-97	Windsor	OHL	58	15	13	28	19	5	0	1	1	6
1997-98	Windsor	OHL	20	9	12	21	8	....	....	....	....	....
	Kingston	OHL	34	14	4	18	2	12	2	4	6	2

ELICK, MICKEY (EHL-ihk) CGY.

Defense. Shoots left. 6'1", 200 lbs. Born, Calgary, Alta., March 17, 1974.
(NY Rangers' 8th choice, 192nd overall, in 1992 Entry Draft).

			Regular Season					Playoffs				
Season	Club	Lea	GP	G	A	TP	PIM	GP	G	A	TP	PIM
1991-92	Calgary	AJHL	41	18	32	50	54	....	....	....	....	....
1992-93	U. of Wisconsin	WCHA	33	1	6	7	24	....	....	....	....	....
1993-94	U. of Wisconsin	WCHA	42	7	12	19	54	....	....	....	....	....
1994-95	U. of Wisconsin	WCHA	43	5	24	29	52	....	....	....	....	....
1995-96	U. of Wisconsin	WCHA	39	14	26	40	60	....	....	....	....	....
1996-97	Charlotte	ECHL	70	25	36	61	79	3	1	0	1	14
	Binghamton	AHL	1	0	1	1	2	....	....	....	....	....
1997-98	Canada	Nat-Tm	61	20	28	48	60	....	....	....	....	....

Signed as a free agent by **Calgary**, July 6, 1998.

ELIK, TODD (EHL-ihk)

Center. Shoots left. 6'2", 195 lbs. Born, Brampton, Ont., April 15, 1966.

			Regular Season					Playoffs				
Season	Club	Lea	GP	G	A	TP	PIM	GP	G	A	TP	PIM
1984-85	Kingston	OHL	34	14	11	25	6	....	....	....	....	....
	North Bay	OHL	23	4	6	10	2	4	2	0	2	0
1985-86	North Bay	OHL	40	12	34	46	20	10	7	6	13	0
1986-87	U. of Regina	CWUAA	27	26	34	60	137	....	....	....	....	....
	Canada	Nat-Tm	1	0	0	0	0	....	....	....	....	....
1987-88	Colorado	IHL	81	44	56	100	83	12	8	12	20	9
1988-89	Denver	IHL	28	20	15	35	22	....	....	....	....	....
	New Haven	AHL	43	11	25	36	31	17	10	12	22	44
1989-90	**Los Angeles**	**NHL**	**48**	**10**	**23**	**33**	**41**	**10**	**3**	**9**	**12**	**10**
	New Haven	AHL	32	20	23	43	42	....	....	....	....	....
1990-91	**Los Angeles**	**NHL**	**74**	**21**	**37**	**58**	**58**	**12**	**2**	**7**	**9**	**6**
1991-92	**Minnesota**	**NHL**	**62**	**14**	**32**	**46**	**125**	**5**	**1**	**1**	**2**	**2**
1992-93	**Minnesota**	**NHL**	**46**	**13**	**18**	**31**	**48**	....	....	....	....	....
	Edmonton	**NHL**	**14**	**1**	**9**	**10**	**8**	....	....	....	....	....
1993-94	**Edmonton**	**NHL**	**4**	**0**	**0**	**0**	**6**	....	....	....	....	....
	San Jose	**NHL**	**75**	**25**	**41**	**66**	**89**	**14**	**5**	**5**	**10**	**12**
1994-95	**San Jose**	**NHL**	**22**	**7**	**10**	**17**	**18**	....	....	....	....	....
	St. Louis	**NHL**	**13**	**2**	**4**	**6**	**4**	**7**	**4**	**3**	**7**	**2**
1995-96	**Boston**	**NHL**	**59**	**13**	**33**	**46**	**40**	**4**	**0**	**2**	**2**	**16**
	Providence	AHL	7	2	7	9	10	....	....	....	....	....
1996-97	**Boston**	**NHL**	**31**	**4**	**12**	**16**	**16**	....	....	....	....	....
	Providence	AHL	37	16	29	45	63	10	1	6	7	33
1997-98	HC Lugano	Switz.	39	30	36	66	22	7	6	5	11	12
	NHL Totals		**448**	**110**	**219**	**329**	**453**	**52**	**15**	**27**	**42**	**48**

Signed as a free agent by **NY Rangers**, February 26, 1988. Traded to **LA Kings** by **NY Rangers** with Igor Liba, Michael Boyce and future considerations for Dean Kennedy and Denis Larocque, December 12, 1988. Traded to **Minnesota** by **LA Kings** for Randy Gilhen, Charlie Huddy, Jim Thomson and NY Rangers' 4th round choice (previously acquired, LA Kings selected Alexei Zhitnik) in 1991 Entry Draft, June 22, 1991. Traded to **Edmonton** by **Minnesota** for Brent Gilchrist, March 5, 1993. Claimed on waivers by **San Jose** from **Edmonton**, October 26, 1993. Traded to **St. Louis** by **San Jose** for Kevin Miller, March 23, 1995. Signed as a free agent by **Boston**, August 8, 1995.

ELLETT, DAVE — BOS.

Defense. Shoots left. 6'2", 205 lbs. Born, Cleveland, OH, March 30, 1964.
(Winnipeg's 3rd choice, 75th overall, in 1982 Entry Draft).

			Regular Season					Playoffs				
Season	Club	Lea	GP	G	A	TP	PIM	GP	G	A	TP	PIM
1981-82	Ottawa	OJHL	50	9	35	44	....	....	....	....	....	....
1982-83	Bowling Green	CCHA	40	4	13	17	34	....	....	....	....	....
1983-84	Bowling Green	CCHA	43	15	39	54	96	....	....	....	....	....
1984-85	**Winnipeg**	**NHL**	**80**	**11**	**27**	**38**	**85**	**8**	**1**	**5**	**6**	**4**
1985-86	**Winnipeg**	**NHL**	**80**	**15**	**31**	**46**	**96**	**3**	**0**	**1**	**1**	**0**
1986-87	**Winnipeg**	**NHL**	**78**	**13**	**31**	**44**	**53**	**10**	**0**	**8**	**8**	**2**
1987-88	**Winnipeg**	**NHL**	**68**	**13**	**45**	**58**	**106**	**5**	**1**	**2**	**3**	**10**
1988-89	**Winnipeg**	**NHL**	**75**	**22**	**34**	**56**	**62**	....	....	....	....	....
1989-90	**Winnipeg**	**NHL**	**77**	**17**	**29**	**46**	**96**	**7**	**2**	**0**	**2**	**6**
1990-91	**Winnipeg**	**NHL**	**17**	**4**	**7**	**11**	**6**	....	....	....	....	....
	Toronto	**NHL**	**60**	**8**	**30**	**38**	**69**	....	....	....	....	....
1991-92	**Toronto**	**NHL**	**79**	**18**	**33**	**51**	**95**	....	....	....	....	....
1992-93	**Toronto**	**NHL**	**70**	**6**	**34**	**40**	**46**	**21**	**4**	**8**	**12**	**8**
1993-94	**Toronto**	**NHL**	**68**	**7**	**36**	**43**	**42**	**18**	**3**	**15**	**18**	**31**
1994-95	**Toronto**	**NHL**	**33**	**5**	**10**	**15**	**26**	**7**	**0**	**2**	**2**	**0**
1995-96	**Toronto**	**NHL**	**80**	**3**	**19**	**22**	**59**	**6**	**0**	**0**	**0**	**4**
1996-97	**Toronto**	**NHL**	**56**	**4**	**10**	**14**	**34**	....	....	....	....	....
	New Jersey	**NHL**	**20**	**2**	**5**	**7**	**6**	**10**	**0**	**3**	**3**	**10**
1997-98	**Boston**	**NHL**	**82**	**3**	**20**	**23**	**67**	**6**	**0**	**1**	**1**	**6**
	NHL Totals		**1023**	**151**	**401**	**552**	**948**	**101**	**11**	**45**	**56**	**81**

CCHA Second All-Star Team (1984) • NCAA Championship All-Tournament Team (1984)

Played in NHL All-Star Game (1989, 1992)

Traded to **Toronto** by **Winnipeg** with Paul Fenton for Ed Olczyk and Mark Osborne, November 10, 1990. Traded to **New Jersey** by **Toronto** with Doug Gilmour and future considerations for Jason Smith, Steve Sullivan and the rights to Alyn McCauley, February 25, 1997. Signed as a free agent by **Boston**, July 29, 1997.

ELLIOTT, PAUL — EDM.

Defense. Shoots left. 6', 202 lbs. Born, White Rock, B.C., June 2, 1980.
(Edmonton's 5th choice, 128th overall, in 1998 Entry Draft).

			Regular Season					Playoffs				
Season	Club	Lea	GP	G	A	TP	PIM	GP	G	A	TP	PIM
1995-96	Lethbridge	WHL	2	0	0	0	0	....	....	....	....	....
1996-97	Lethbridge	WHL	46	0	8	8	17	1	0	0	0	0
1997-98	Lethbridge	WHL	48	4	18	22	35	....	....	....	....	....
	Medicine Hat	WHL	24	7	9	16	12	....	....	....	....	....

ELOFSSON, JONAS (EHL-uhf-suhn, YEW-nuhs) — EDM.

Defense. Shoots left. 6'1", 180 lbs. Born, Ulricehamn, Sweden, January 31, 1979.
(Edmonton's 4th choice, 94th overall, in 1997 Entry Draft).

			Regular Season					Playoffs				
Season	Club	Lea	GP	G	A	TP	PIM	GP	G	A	TP	PIM
1995-96	Farjestad	Sweden	26	6	11	17	18	....	....	....	....	....
1996-97	Farjestad	Sweden	3	0	0	0	0	5	0	1	1	0
1997-98	Farjestad	EuroHL	7	1	1	2	4	....	....	....	....	....
	Farjestad	Sweden	29	3	2	5	14	12	0	1	1	6

ELOMO, MIIKA (eh-LOH-moh, MEE-ka) — WSH.

Left wing. Shoots left. 6', 180 lbs. Born, Turku, Finland, April 21, 1977.
(Washington's 2nd choice, 23rd overall, in 1995 Entry Draft).

			Regular Season					Playoffs				
Season	Club	Lea	GP	G	A	TP	PIM	GP	G	A	TP	PIM
1994-95	Kiekko	Finland-2	14	9	2	11	39	....	....	....	....	....
	TPS Turku	Fin-Jr.	14	3	8	11	24	....	....	....	....	....
1995-96	TPS Turku	Fin-Jr.	6	0	2	2	18	....	....	....	....	....
	Kiekko	Finland-2	21	9	6	15	100	....	....	....	....	....
	TPS Turku	Finland	10	1	1	2	8	3	0	0	0	2
1996-97	Portland	AHL	52	8	9	17	37	....	....	....	....	....
1997-98	Portland	AHL	33	1	1	2	54	....	....	....	....	....
	Helsinki	Finland	16	4	1	5	6	9	4	3	7	6

ELOMO, TEEMU (eh-LOH-moh, TEE-moo) — DAL.

Left wing. Shoots left. 5'11", 176 lbs. Born, Turku, Finland, January 13, 1979.
(Dallas' 5th choice, 132nd overall, in 1997 Entry Draft).

			Regular Season					Playoffs				
Season	Club	Lea	GP	G	A	TP	PIM	GP	G	A	TP	PIM
1996-97	TPS Turku	Fin-Jr.	9	6	2	8	16	....	....	....	....	....
	Kiekko	Finland-2	15	4	3	7	24	....	....	....	....	....
	TPS Turku	Finland	6	0	1	1	0	3	0	0	0	2
1997-98	TPS Turku	EuroHL	3	0	0	0	2	....	....	....	....	....
	TPS Turku	Finland	26	3	3	6	14	3	1	0	1	2

EMERSON, NELSON — CAR.

Right wing. Shoots right. 5'11", 175 lbs. Born, Hamilton, Ont., August 17, 1967.
(New Jersey's 4th choice, 45th overall, in 1985 Entry Draft).

			Regular Season					Playoffs				
Season	Club	Lea	GP	G	A	TP	PIM	GP	G	A	TP	PIM
1984-85	Stratford	OJHL	40	23	38	61	70	....	....	....	....	....
1985-86	Stratford	OJHL	39	54	58	112	91	....	....	....	....	....
1986-87	Bowling Green	CCHA	45	26	35	61	28	....	....	....	....	....
1987-88	Bowling Green	CCHA	45	34	49	83	54	....	....	....	....	....
1988-89	Bowling Green	CCHA	44	22	46	68	46	....	....	....	....	....
1989-90	Bowling Green	CCHA	44	30	52	82	42	....	....	....	....	....
	Peoria	IHL	3	1	1	2	0	....	....	....	....	....
1990-91	**St. Louis**	**NHL**	**4**	**0**	**3**	**3**	**2**	....	....	....	....	....
	Peoria	IHL	73	36	79	115	91	17	9	12	21	16
1991-92	**St. Louis**	**NHL**	**79**	**23**	**36**	**59**	**66**	**6**	**3**	**3**	**6**	**21**
1992-93	**St. Louis**	**NHL**	**82**	**22**	**51**	**73**	**62**	**11**	**1**	**6**	**7**	**6**
1993-94	**Winnipeg**	**NHL**	**83**	**33**	**41**	**74**	**80**	....	....	....	....	....
1994-95	**Winnipeg**	**NHL**	**48**	**14**	**23**	**37**	**26**	....	....	....	....	....
1995-96	**Hartford**	**NHL**	**81**	**29**	**29**	**58**	**78**	....	....	....	....	....
1996-97	**Hartford**	**NHL**	**66**	**9**	**29**	**38**	**34**	....	....	....	....	....
1997-98	**Carolina**	**NHL**	**81**	**21**	**24**	**45**	**50**	....	....	....	....	....
	NHL Totals		**524**	**151**	**236**	**387**	**398**	**17**	**4**	**9**	**13**	**27**

NCAA West Second All-American Team (1988) • CCHA First All-Star Team (1988, 1990) • CCHA Second All-Star Team (1989) • NCAA West First All-American Team (1990) • IHL First All-Star Team (1991) • Won Garry F. Longman Memorial Trophy (Top Rookie - IHL) (1991)

Traded to **Winnipeg** by **St. Louis** with Stephane Quintal for Phil Housley, September 24, 1993. Traded to **Hartford** by **Winnipeg** for Darren Turcotte, October 6, 1995. Transferred to **Carolina** after **Hartford** franchise relocated, June 25, 1997.

EMMONS, JOHN — OTT.

Center. Shoots left. 6'2", 205 lbs. Born, San Jose, CA, August 17, 1974.
(Calgary's 7th choice, 122nd overall, in 1993 Entry Draft).

			Regular Season					Playoffs				
Season	Club	Lea	GP	G	A	TP	PIM	GP	G	A	TP	PIM
1992-93	Yale	ECAC	28	3	5	8	66	....	....	....	....	....
1993-94	Yale	ECAC	25	5	12	17	66	....	....	....	....	....
1994-95	Yale	ECAC	28	4	16	20	57	....	....	....	....	....
1995-96	Yale	ECAC	31	8	20	28	124	....	....	....	....	....
1996-97	Dayton	ECHL	69	20	37	57	62	....	....	....	....	....
1997-98	Michigan	IHL	81	9	25	34	85	4	1	1	2	10

Signed as a free agent by **Ottawa**, August 7, 1998.

ENGBLOM, DAVID (EHNG-blahm) — DET.

Center. Shoots left. 6'1", 183 lbs. Born, Vallentuna, Sweden, June 2, 1977.
(Detroit's 10th choice, 234th overall, in 1995 Entry Draft).

			Regular Season					Playoffs				
Season	Club	Lea	GP	G	A	TP	PIM	GP	G	A	TP	PIM
1993-94	Vallentuna	Sweden-2	27	0	0	0	4	....	....	....	....	....
1994-95	Vallentuna	Sweden-2	32	1	4	5	12	....	....	....	....	....
1995-96	AIK Solna	Sweden	39	0	4	4	6	....	....	....	....	....
1996-97	AIK Solna	Sweden	39	3	1	4	10	7	0	1	1	0
1997-98	AIK Solna	Sweden	44	4	2	6	24	....	....	....	....	....

ENGLEHART, BRAD — ANA.

Center. Shoots left. 5'11", 180 lbs. Born, Woodstock, N.B., September 16, 1975.
(Anaheim's 8th choice, 184th overall, in 1994 Entry Draft).

			Regular Season					Playoffs				
Season	Club	Lea	GP	G	A	TP	PIM	GP	G	A	TP	PIM
1993-94	Kimball Academy	H.S.	24	20	23	43	10	....	....	....	....	....
1994-95	U. of Wisconsin	WCHA	29	6	6	12	42	....	....	....	....	....
1995-96	U. of Wisconsin	WCHA	39	6	7	13	67	....	....	....	....	....
1996-97	U. of Wisconsin	WCHA	35	17	19	36	89	....	....	....	....	....
1997-98	U. of Wisconsin	WCHA	33	11	9	20	62	....	....	....	....	....
	Cincinnati	AHL	7	1	1	2	2	....	....	....	....	....

EPANCHINTSEV, VADIM (yeh-pah-CHIHN-tsehv)

Center. Shoots left. 5'10", 175 lbs. Born, Orsk, USSR, March 16, 1976.
(Tampa Bay's 3rd choice, 55th overall, in 1994 Entry Draft).

			Regular Season					Playoffs				
Season	Club	Lea	GP	G	A	TP	PIM	GP	G	A	TP	PIM
1993-94	Spartak	CIS	46	6	5	11	16	3	0	1	1	0
1994-95	Spartak	CIS	43	4	8	12	24	....	....	....	....	....
1995-96	Spartak	CIS	51	20	12	32	28	4	0	2	2	4
1996-97	Spartak	Russia	38	10	8	18	74	....	....	....	....	....
1997-98	Hampton Roads	ECHL	25	5	10	15	44	3	0	1	1	0
	Cleveland	IHL	34	3	6	9	18	....	....	....	....	....

ERIKSSON, ANDERS (AIR-ihk-suhn, AND-uhrs) — DET.

Defense. Shoots left. 6'3", 218 lbs. Born, Bollnas, Sweden, January 9, 1975.
(Detroit's 1st choice, 22nd overall, in 1993 Entry Draft).

			Regular Season					Playoffs				
Season	Club	Lea	GP	G	A	TP	PIM	GP	G	A	TP	PIM
1992-93	MoDo	Sweden	20	0	2	2	2	1	0	0	0	0
1993-94	MoDo	Sweden	38	2	8	10	42	11	0	0	0	8
1994-95	MoDo	Sweden	39	3	6	9	54	....	....	....	....	....
1995-96	**Detroit**	**NHL**	**1**	**0**	**0**	**0**	**2**	**3**	**0**	**0**	**0**	**0**
	Adirondack	AHL	75	6	36	42	64	3	0	0	0	0
1996-97	**Detroit**	**NHL**	**23**	**0**	**6**	**6**	**10**	....	....	....	....	....
	Adirondack	AHL	44	3	25	28	36	4	0	1	1	4
1997-98	**Detroit**	**NHL**	**66**	**7**	**14**	**21**	**32**	**18**	**0**	**5**	**5**	**16 ♦**
	NHL Totals		**90**	**7**	**20**	**27**	**44**	**21**	**0**	**5**	**5**	**16**

ERREY, BOB (AIRY) NYR

Left wing. Shoots left. 5'10", 185 lbs. Born, Montreal, Que., September 21, 1964.
(Pittsburgh's 1st choice, 15th overall, in 1983 Entry Draft).

			Regular Season					Playoffs				
Season	Club	Lea	GP	G	A	TP	PIM	GP	G	A	TP	PIM
1981-82	Peterborough	OHL	68	29	31	60	39	9	3	1	4	9
1982-83	Peterborough	OHL	67	53	47	100	74	4	1	3	4	7
1983-84	**Pittsburgh**	**NHL**	**65**	**9**	**13**	**22**	**29**	....	....	....	....	....
1984-85	**Pittsburgh**	**NHL**	**16**	**0**	**2**	**2**	**7**	....	....	....	....	....
	Baltimore	AHL	59	17	24	41	14	8	3	4	7	11
1985-86	**Pittsburgh**	**NHL**	**37**	**11**	**6**	**17**	**8**	....	....	....	....	....
	Baltimore	AHL	18	8	7	15	28	....	....	....	....	....
1986-87	**Pittsburgh**	**NHL**	**72**	**16**	**18**	**34**	**46**	....	....	....	....	....
1987-88	**Pittsburgh**	**NHL**	**17**	**3**	**6**	**9**	**18**	....	....	....	....	....
1988-89	**Pittsburgh**	**NHL**	**76**	**26**	**32**	**58**	**124**	**11**	**1**	**2**	**3**	**12**
1989-90	**Pittsburgh**	**NHL**	**78**	**20**	**19**	**39**	**109**	....	....	....	....	....
1990-91	**Pittsburgh**	**NHL**	**79**	**20**	**22**	**42**	**115**	**24**	**5**	**2**	**7**	**29 ♦**
1991-92	**Pittsburgh**	**NHL**	**78**	**19**	**16**	**35**	**119**	**14**	**3**	**0**	**3**	**10 ♦**
1992-93	**Pittsburgh**	**NHL**	**54**	**8**	**6**	**14**	**76**	....	....	....	....	....
	Buffalo	**NHL**	**8**	**1**	**3**	**4**	**4**	**4**	**0**	**1**	**1**	**10**
1993-94	**San Jose**	**NHL**	**64**	**12**	**18**	**30**	**126**	**14**	**3**	**2**	**5**	**10**
1994-95	**San Jose**	**NHL**	**13**	**2**	**2**	**4**	**27**	....	....	....	....	....
	Detroit	**NHL**	**30**	**6**	**11**	**17**	**31**	**18**	**1**	**5**	**6**	**30**
1995-96	**Detroit**	**NHL**	**71**	**11**	**21**	**32**	**66**	**14**	**0**	**4**	**4**	**8**
1996-97	**Detroit**	**NHL**	**36**	**1**	**2**	**3**	**27**	....	....	....	....	....
	San Jose	**NHL**	**30**	**3**	**6**	**9**	**20**	....	....	....	....	....
1997-98	**Dallas**	**NHL**	**59**	**2**	**9**	**11**	**46**	....	....	....	....	....
	NY Rangers	**NHL**	**12**	**0**	**0**	**0**	**7**	....	....	....	....	....
	NHL Totals		**895**	**170**	**212**	**382**	**1005**	**99**	**13**	**16**	**29**	**109**

OHL First All-Star Team (1983)

Traded to **Buffalo** by **Pittsburgh** for Mike Ramsey, March 22, 1993. Signed as a free agent by **San Jose**, August 17, 1993. Traded to **Detroit** by **San Jose** for Detroit's 5th round choice (Michal Bros) in 1995 Entry Draft, February 27, 1995. Claimed on waivers by **San Jose** from **Detroit**, February 8, 1997. Signed as a free agent by **Dallas**, July 28, 1997. Traded to **NY Rangers** by **Dallas** with Todd Harvey and Dallas' 4th round choice (Boyd Kane) in 1998 Entry Draft for Brian Skrudland, Mike Keane and NY Rangers' 6th round choice (Pavel Patera) in 1998 Entry Draft, March 24, 1998.

ERSKINE, JOHN DAL.

Defense. Shoots left. 6'4", 197 lbs. Born, Kingston, Ont., June 26, 1980.
(Dallas' 1st choice, 39th overall, in 1998 Entry Draft).

			Regular Season					Playoffs				
Season	Club	Lea	GP	G	A	TP	PIM	GP	G	A	TP	PIM
1996-97	Quinte Hawks	OJHL	48	4	16	20	241	....	....	....	....	....
1997-98	London	OHL	55	0	9	9	205	16	0	5	5	25

ESAU, LEONARD (EE-saw)

Defense. Shoots right. 6'3", 190 lbs. Born, Meadow Lake, Sask., June 3, 1968.
(Toronto's 5th choice, 86th overall, in 1988 Entry Draft).

			Regular Season					Playoffs				
Season	Club	Lea	GP	G	A	TP	PIM	GP	G	A	TP	PIM
1987-88	Humboldt	SJHL	57	16	37	53	229	....	....	....	....	....
1988-89	St. Cloud State	NCAA	35	12	27	39	69	....	....	....	....	....
1989-90	St. Cloud State	NCAA	29	8	11	19	83	....	....	....	....	....
1990-91	Newmarket	AHL	76	4	14	18	28	....	....	....	....	....
1991-92	**Toronto**	**NHL**	**2**	**0**	**0**	**0**	**0**	....	....	....	....	....
	St. John's	AHL	78	9	29	38	68	13	0	2	2	14
1992-93	**Quebec**	**NHL**	**4**	**0**	**1**	**1**	**2**	....	....	....	....	....
	Halifax	AHL	75	11	31	42	79	....	....	....	....	....
1993-94	**Calgary**	**NHL**	**6**	**0**	**3**	**3**	**7**	....	....	....	....	....
	Saint John	AHL	75	12	36	48	129	7	2	2	4	6
1994-95	Saint John	AHL	54	13	27	40	73	5	0	2	2	0
	Edmonton	**NHL**	**14**	**0**	**6**	**6**	**15**	....	....	....	....	....
	Calgary	**NHL**	**1**	**0**	**0**	**0**	**0**	....	....	....	....	....
1995-96	Cincinnati	IHL	82	15	21	36	150	17	5	6	11	26
1996-97	Milwaukee	IHL	49	6	16	22	70	....	....	....	....	....
	Detroit	IHL	30	6	8	14	36	13	1	4	5	38
1997-98	Milwaukee	IHL	26	3	9	12	32	....	....	....	....	....
	Indianapolis	IHL	55	6	33	39	28	5	0	0	0	4
	NHL Totals		**27**	**0**	**10**	**10**	**24**	....	....	....	....	....

Traded to **Quebec** by **Toronto** for Ken McRae, July 21, 1992. Signed as a free agent by **Calgary**, September 6, 1993. Claimed by **Edmonton** from **Calgary** in NHL Waiver Draft, January 18, 1995. Claimed on waivers by **Calgary** from **Edmonton**, March 7, 1995. Signed as a free agent by **Florida**, August 31, 1995.

ETTINGER, TREVOR EDM.

Defense. Shoots left. 6'5", 240 lbs. Born, Truro, N.S., July 13, 1980.
(Edmonton's 7th choice, 159th overall, in 1998 Entry Draft).

			Regular Season					Playoffs				
Season	Club	Lea	GP	G	A	TP	PIM	GP	G	A	TP	PIM
1997-98	Cape Breton	QMJHL	50	1	2	3	181	3	0	0	0	7

EWEN, TODD (YOO-ihn)

Right wing. Shoots right. 6'2", 230 lbs. Born, Saskatoon, Sask., March 22, 1966.
(Edmonton's 9th choice, 168th overall, in 1984 Entry Draft).

			Regular Season					Playoffs				
Season	Club	Lea	GP	G	A	TP	PIM	GP	G	A	TP	PIM
1982-83	Kamloops	WHL	3	0	0	0	2	2	0	0	0	0
1983-84	New Westminster	WHL	68	11	13	24	176	7	2	1	3	15
1984-85	New Westminster	WHL	56	11	20	31	304	10	1	8	9	60
1985-86	New Westminster	WHL	60	28	24	52	289	....	....	....	....	....
	Maine	AHL	....	....	....	....	....	3	0	0	0	7
1986-87	**St. Louis**	**NHL**	**23**	**2**	**0**	**2**	**84**	**4**	**0**	**0**	**0**	**23**
	Peoria	IHL	16	3	3	6	110	....	....	....	....	....
1987-88	**St. Louis**	**NHL**	**64**	**4**	**2**	**6**	**227**	**6**	**0**	**0**	**0**	**21**
1988-89	**St. Louis**	**NHL**	**34**	**4**	**5**	**9**	**171**	**2**	**0**	**0**	**0**	**21**
1989-90	**St. Louis**	**NHL**	**3**	**0**	**0**	**0**	**11**	....	....	....	....	....
	Peoria	IHL	2	0	0	0	12	....	....	....	....	....
	Montreal	**NHL**	**41**	**4**	**6**	**10**	**158**	**10**	**0**	**0**	**0**	**4**
1990-91	**Montreal**	**NHL**	**28**	**3**	**2**	**5**	**128**	....	....	....	....	....
1991-92	**Montreal**	**NHL**	**46**	**1**	**2**	**3**	**130**	**3**	**0**	**0**	**0**	**18**
1992-93	**Montreal**	**NHL**	**75**	**5**	**9**	**14**	**193**	**1**	**0**	**0**	**0**	**0 ♦**
1993-94	**Anaheim**	**NHL**	**76**	**9**	**9**	**18**	**272**	....	....	....	....	....
1994-95	**Anaheim**	**NHL**	**24**	**0**	**0**	**0**	**90**	....	....	....	....	....
1995-96	**Anaheim**	**NHL**	**53**	**4**	**3**	**7**	**285**	....	....	....	....	....
1996-97	**San Jose**	**NHL**	**51**	**0**	**2**	**2**	**162**	....	....	....	....	....
1997-98			DID NOT PLAY – INJURED									
	NHL Totals		**518**	**36**	**40**	**76**	**1911**	**26**	**0**	**0**	**0**	**87**

Traded to **St. Louis** by **Edmonton** for Shawn Evans, October 15, 1986. Traded to **Montreal** by **St. Louis** for future considerations, December 12, 1989. Traded to **Anaheim** by **Montreal** with Patrik Carnback for Anaheim's 3rd round choice (Chris Murray) in 1994 Entry Draft, August 10, 1993. Signed as a free agent by **San Jose**, September 4, 1996. • Missed entire 1997-98 season after undergoing knee surgery.

FADRNY, JAN (FUH-duhr-nee, YAN) PIT.

Center. Shoots right. 6', 176 lbs. Born, Brno, Czechoslovakia, June 14, 1980.
(Pittsburgh's 6th choice, 169th overall, in 1998 Entry Draft).

			Regular Season					Playoffs				
Season	Club	Lea	GP	G	A	TP	PIM	GP	G	A	TP	PIM
1995-96	Kometa Brno	Czech-Jr.	36	22	15	37	26	....	....	....	....	....
1996-97	HC Olomouc	Czech-Jr.	38	16	24	40	32	....	....	....	....	....
1997-98	Slavia Praha	Czech-Jr.	14	7	4	11	12	....	....	....	....	....
	Slavia Praha	Cze-Rep.	18	1	1	2	2	3	0	0	0	4

FAIRCHILD, KELLY DAL.

Center. Shoots left. 5'11", 180 lbs. Born, Hibbing, MN, April 9, 1973.
(Los Angeles' 6th choice, 152nd overall, in 1991 Entry Draft).

			Regular Season					Playoffs				
Season	Club	Lea	GP	G	A	TP	PIM	GP	G	A	TP	PIM
1990-91	Grand Rapids	H.S.	28	12	17	29	25	....	....	....	....	....
1991-92	U. of Wisconsin	WCHA	37	11	10	21	45	....	....	....	....	....
1992-93	U. of Wisconsin	WCHA	42	25	29	54	54	....	....	....	....	....
1993-94	U. of Wisconsin	WCHA	42	20	44	*64	81	....	....	....	....	....
1994-95	St. John's	AHL	53	27	23	50	51	4	0	2	2	4
1995-96	**Toronto**	**NHL**	**1**	**0**	**1**	**1**	**2**	....	....	....	....	....
	St. John's	AHL	78	29	49	78	85	2	0	1	1	4
1996-97	**Toronto**	**NHL**	**22**	**0**	**2**	**2**	**2**	....	....	....	....	....
	St. John's	AHL	29	9	22	31	36	....	....	....	....	....
	Orlando	IHL	25	9	6	15	20	9	6	5	11	16
1997-98	St. John's	AHL	17	5	2	7	24	....	....	....	....	....
	Orlando	IHL	22	2	6	8	20	....	....	....	....	....
	Milwaukee	IHL	40	20	24	44	32	10	5	2	7	4
	NHL Totals		**23**	**0**	**3**	**3**	**4**	....	....	....	....	....

WCHA First All-Star Team (1994)

Traded to **Toronto** by **LA Kings** with Dixon Ward, Guy Leveque and Shayne Toporowski for Eric Lacroix, Chris Snell and Toronto's 4th round choice (Eric Belanger) in 1996 Entry Draft, October 3, 1994. Signed as a free agent by **Dallas**, July 2, 1998.

FALLOON, PAT (fah-LOON) EDM.

Right wing. Shoots right. 5'11", 190 lbs. Born, Foxwarren, Man., September 22, 1972.
(San Jose's 1st choice, 2nd overall, in 1991 Entry Draft).

			Regular Season					Playoffs				
Season	Club	Lea	GP	G	A	TP	PIM	GP	G	A	TP	PIM
1988-89	Spokane	WHL	72	22	56	78	41	....	....	....	....	....
1989-90	Spokane	WHL	71	60	64	124	48	6	5	8	13	4
1990-91	Spokane	WHL	61	64	74	138	33	15	10	14	24	10
1991-92	**San Jose**	**NHL**	**79**	**25**	**34**	**59**	**16**	....	....	....	....	....
1992-93	**San Jose**	**NHL**	**41**	**14**	**14**	**28**	**12**	....	....	....	....	....
1993-94	**San Jose**	**NHL**	**83**	**22**	**31**	**53**	**18**	**14**	**1**	**2**	**3**	**6**
1994-95	**San Jose**	**NHL**	**46**	**12**	**7**	**19**	**25**	**11**	**3**	**1**	**4**	**0**
1995-96	**San Jose**	**NHL**	**9**	**3**	**0**	**3**	**4**	....	....	....	....	....
	Philadelphia	**NHL**	**62**	**22**	**26**	**48**	**6**	**12**	**3**	**2**	**5**	**2**
1996-97	**Philadelphia**	**NHL**	**52**	**11**	**12**	**23**	**10**	**14**	**3**	**1**	**4**	**2**
1997-98	**Philadelphia**	**NHL**	**30**	**5**	**7**	**12**	**8**	....	....	....	....	....
	Ottawa	**NHL**	**28**	**3**	**3**	**6**	**8**	**1**	**0**	**0**	**0**	**0**
	NHL Totals		**430**	**117**	**134**	**251**	**107**	**52**	**10**	**6**	**16**	**10**

WHL West Second All-Star Team (1989) • WHL West First All-Star Team (1991) • Canadian Major Junior Most Sportsmanlike Player of the Year (1991) • Memorial Cup All-Star Team (1991) • Won Stafford Smythe Memorial Trophy (Memorial Cup Tournament MVP) (1991)

Traded to **Philadelphia** by **San Jose** for Martin Spanhel, Philadelphia's 1st round choice (later traded to Phoenix — Phoenix selected Daniel Briere) in 1996 Entry Draft and Philadelphia's 4th round choice (later traded to Buffalo — Buffalo selected Mike Martone), in 1996 Entry Draft, November 16, 1995. Traded to **Ottawa** by **Philadelphia** with Vaclav Prospal and Dallas' 2nd round choice (previously acquired, Ottawa selected Chris Bala) in 1998 Entry Draft for Alexandre Daigle, January 17, 1998. Signed as a free agent by **Edmonton**, August 21, 1998.

FARKAS, JEFF (FAHR-kuhs) TOR.

Center. Shoots left. 6'1", 173 lbs. Born, Amherst, MA, January 24, 1978.
(Toronto's 1st choice, 57th overall, in 1997 Entry Draft).

			Regular Season					Playoffs				
Season	Club	Lea	GP	G	A	TP	PIM	GP	G	A	TP	PIM
1996-97	Boston College	H.E.	35	13	23	36	34	....	....	....	....	....
1997-98	Boston College	H.E.	40	11	28	39	42	....	....	....	....	....

FATA, RICO (FA-tuh, REE-koh) CGY.

Center. Shoots left. 5'11", 202 lbs. Born, Sault Ste. Marie, Ont., February 12, 1980.
(Calgary's 1st choice, 6th overall, in 1998 Entry Draft).

			Regular Season					Playoffs				
Season	Club	Lea	GP	G	A	TP	PIM	GP	G	A	TP	PIM
1995-96	S.S. Marie	OHL	62	11	15	26	52	4	0	0	0	0
1996-97	London	OHL	59	19	34	53	76	....	....	....	....	....
1997-98	London	OHL	64	43	33	76	110	16	9	5	14	*49

FEATHERSTONE, GLEN

Defense. Shoots left. 6'4", 209 lbs. Born, Toronto, Ont., July 8, 1968.
(St. Louis' 4th choice, 73rd overall, in 1986 Entry Draft).

			Regular Season					Playoffs				
Season	Club	Lea	GP	G	A	TP	PIM	GP	G	A	TP	PIM
1985-86	Windsor	OHL	49	0	6	6	135	14	1	1	2	23
1986-87	Windsor	OHL	47	6	11	17	154	14	2	6	8	19
1987-88	Windsor	OHL	53	7	27	34	201	12	6	9	15	47
1988-89	**St. Louis**	**NHL**	**18**	**0**	**2**	**2**	**22**	**6**	**0**	**0**	**0**	**25**
	Peoria	IHL	37	5	19	24	97	....	....	....	....	....
1989-90	**St. Louis**	**NHL**	**58**	**0**	**12**	**12**	**145**	**12**	**0**	**2**	**2**	**47**
	Peoria	IHL	15	1	4	5	43	....	....	....	....	....
1990-91	**St. Louis**	**NHL**	**68**	**5**	**15**	**20**	**204**	**9**	**0**	**0**	**0**	**31**
1991-92	**Boston**	**NHL**	**7**	**1**	**0**	**1**	**20**	....	....	....	....	....
1992-93	**Boston**	**NHL**	**34**	**5**	**5**	**10**	**102**	....	....	....	....	....
	Providence	AHL	8	3	4	7	60	....	....	....	....	....
1993-94	**Boston**	**NHL**	**58**	**1**	**8**	**9**	**152**	**1**	**0**	**0**	**0**	**0**
1994-95	**NY Rangers**	**NHL**	**6**	**1**	**0**	**1**	**18**	....	....	....	....	....
	Hartford	**NHL**	**13**	**1**	**1**	**2**	**32**	....	....	....	....	....
1995-96	**Hartford**	**NHL**	**68**	**2**	**10**	**12**	**138**	....	....	....	....	....
1996-97	**Hartford**	**NHL**	**41**	**2**	**5**	**7**	**87**	....	....	....	....	....
	Calgary	**NHL**	**13**	**1**	**3**	**4**	**19**	....	....	....	....	....
1997-98	Indianapolis	IHL	73	10	28	38	187	5	0	3	3	16
	NHL Totals		**384**	**19**	**61**	**80**	**939**	**28**	**0**	**2**	**2**	**103**

Signed as a free agent by **Boston**, July 25, 1991. Traded to **NY Rangers** by **Boston** for Daniel Lacroix, August 19, 1994. Traded to **Hartford** by **NY Rangers** with Michael Stewart, NY Rangers' 1st round choice (Jean-Sebastien Giguere) in 1995 Entry Draft and 4th round choice (Steve Wasylko) in 1996 Entry Draft for Pat Verbeek, March 23, 1995. Traded to **Calgary** by **Hartford** with Hnat Domenichelli, New Jersey's 2nd round choice (previously acquired, Calgary selected Dimitri Kokorev) in 1997 Entry Draft and Vancouver's 3rd round choice (previously acquired, Calgary selected Paul Manning) in 1998 Entry Draft for Steve Chiasson and Colorado's 3rd round choice (previously acquired, Carolina selected Francis Lessard) in 1997 Entry Draft, March 5, 1997.

FEDOROV, SERGEI (FEH-duh-rahf) DET.

Center. Shoots left. 6'1", 200 lbs. Born, Pskov, USSR, December 13, 1969.
(Detroit's 4th choice, 74th overall, in 1989 Entry Draft).

			Regular Season					Playoffs				
Season	Club	Lea	GP	G	A	TP	PIM	GP	G	A	TP	PIM
1986-87	CSKA Moscow	USSR	29	6	6	12	12	....	....	....	....	....
1987-88	CSKA Moscow	USSR	48	7	9	16	20	....	....	....	....	....
1988-89	CSKA Moscow	USSR	44	9	8	17	35	....	....	....	....	....
1989-90	CSKA Moscow	USSR	48	19	10	29	22	....	....	....	....	....
1990-91	**Detroit**	**NHL**	**77**	**31**	**48**	**79**	**66**	**7**	**1**	**5**	**6**	**4**
1991-92	**Detroit**	**NHL**	**80**	**32**	**54**	**86**	**72**	**11**	**5**	**5**	**10**	**8**
1992-93	**Detroit**	**NHL**	**73**	**34**	**53**	**87**	**72**	**7**	**3**	**6**	**9**	**23**
1993-94	**Detroit**	**NHL**	**82**	**56**	**64**	**120**	**34**	**7**	**1**	**7**	**8**	**6**
1994-95	**Detroit**	**NHL**	**42**	**20**	**30**	**50**	**24**	**17**	**7**	***17**	***24**	**6**
1995-96	**Detroit**	**NHL**	**78**	**39**	**68**	**107**	**48**	**19**	**2**	***18**	**20**	**10**
1996-97	**Detroit**	**NHL**	**74**	**30**	**33**	**63**	**30**	**20**	**8**	**12**	**20**	**12 ♦**
1997-98	**Detroit**	**NHL**	**21**	**6**	**11**	**17**	**25**	**22**	***10**	**10**	**20**	**12 ♦**
	Russia	Olympics	6	1	5	6	8	....	....	....	....	....
	NHL Totals		**527**	**248**	**361**	**609**	**371**	**110**	**37**	**80**	**117**	**81**

NHL/Upper Deck All-Rookie Team (1991) • NHL First All-Star Team (1994) • Won Frank J. Selke Trophy (1994, 1996) • Won Lester B. Pearson Award (1994) • Won Hart Trophy (1994)

Played in NHL All-Star Game (1992, 1994, 1996)

FEDORUK, TODD PHI.

Left wing. Shoots left. 6'1", 205 lbs. Born, Redwater, Alta., February 13, 1979.
(Philadelphia's 6th choice, 164th overall, in 1997 Entry Draft).

			Regular Season					Playoffs				
Season	Club	Lea	GP	G	A	TP	PIM	GP	G	A	TP	PIM
1996-97	Kelowna	WHL	31	1	5	6	87	6	0	0	0	13
1997-98	Kelowna	WHL	31	3	5	8	120	....	....	....	....	....
	Regina	WHL	21	4	3	7	80	9	1	2	3	23

FEDOTOV, SERGEI (feh-DAW-tahf) CAR.

Defense. Shoots left. 6'1", 185 lbs. Born, Moscow, USSR, January 24, 1977.
(Hartford's 2nd choice, 35th overall, in 1995 Entry Draft).

			Regular Season					Playoffs				
Season	Club	Lea	GP	G	A	TP	PIM	GP	G	A	TP	PIM
1994-95	Moscow D'amo	CIS	8	0	0	0	2	....	....	....	....	....
1995-96	Moscow D'amo 2	CIS-2	STATISTICS NOT AVAILABLE									
	Moscow D'amo	CIS	4	0	0	0	24	....	....	....	....	....
1996-97	Detroit	OHL	52	10	27	37	60	5	0	2	2	9
	Springfield	AHL	2	0	0	0	2	....	....	....	....	....
1997-98	Plymouth	OHL	38	5	11	16	33	15	3	2	5	10
	New Haven	AHL	5	0	0	0	0	....	....	....	....	....
	Richmond	ECHL	5	1	1	2	4	....	....	....	....	....

FEDYK, BRENT (FEH-dihk) NYR

Left wing. Shoots right. 6', 194 lbs. Born, Yorkton, Sask., March 8, 1967.
(Detroit's 1st choice, 8th overall, in 1985 Entry Draft).

			Regular Season					Playoffs				
Season	Club	Lea	GP	G	A	TP	PIM	GP	G	A	TP	PIM
1983-84	Regina	WHL	63	15	28	43	30	23	8	7	15	6
1984-85	Regina	WHL	66	35	35	70	48	8	5	4	9	0
1985-86	Regina	WHL	50	43	34	77	47	5	0	1	1	0
1986-87	Regina	WHL	12	9	6	15	9	....	....	....	....	....
	Seattle	WHL	13	5	11	16	9	....	....	....	....	....
	Portland	WHL	11	5	4	9	6	14	5	6	11	0
1987-88	**Detroit**	**NHL**	**2**	**0**	**1**	**1**	**2**	....	....	....	....	....
	Adirondack	AHL	34	9	11	20	22	5	0	2	2	6
1988-89	**Detroit**	**NHL**	**5**	**2**	**0**	**2**	**0**	....	....	....	....	....
	Adirondack	AHL	66	40	28	68	33	15	7	8	15	23
1989-90	**Detroit**	**NHL**	**27**	**1**	**4**	**5**	**6**	....	....	....	....	....
	Adirondack	AHL	33	14	15	29	24	6	2	1	3	4
1990-91	**Detroit**	**NHL**	**67**	**16**	**19**	**35**	**38**	**6**	**1**	**0**	**1**	**2**
1991-92	**Detroit**	**NHL**	**61**	**5**	**8**	**13**	**42**	**1**	**0**	**0**	**0**	**2**
	Adirondack	AHL	1	0	2	2	0	....	....	....	....	....
1992-93	**Philadelphia**	**NHL**	**74**	**21**	**38**	**59**	**48**	....	....	....	....	....
1993-94	**Philadelphia**	**NHL**	**72**	**20**	**18**	**38**	**74**	....	....	....	....	....
1994-95	**Philadelphia**	**NHL**	**30**	**8**	**4**	**12**	**14**	**9**	**2**	**2**	**4**	**8**
1995-96	**Philadelphia**	**NHL**	**24**	**10**	**5**	**15**	**24**	....	....	....	....	....
	Dallas	**NHL**	**41**	**10**	**9**	**19**	**30**	....	....	....	....	....
1996-97	Michigan	IHL	9	1	2	3	4	....	....	....	....	....
1997-98	Detroit	IHL	40	18	23	41	24	....	....	....	....	....
	Cincinnati	IHL	26	21	13	34	14	9	5	5	10	2
	NHL Totals		**403**	**93**	**106**	**199**	**278**	**16**	**3**	**2**	**5**	**12**

Traded to **Philadelphia** by **Detroit** for Philadelphia's 4th round choice (later traded to Boston — Boston selected Charles Paquette) in 1993 Entry Draft, October 1, 1992. Traded to **Dallas** by **Philadelphia** for Trent Klatt, December 13, 1995. Signed as a free agent by **NY Rangers**, August 13, 1998.

FEIL, CHRIS CHI.

Defense. Shoots left. 6'2", 180 lbs. Born, Orland Park, IL, April 25, 1978.
(Chicago's 11th choice, 230th overall, in 1997 Entry Draft).

			Regular Season					Playoffs				
Season	Club	Lea	GP	G	A	TP	PIM	GP	G	A	TP	PIM
1996-97	Ohio State	CCHA	33	5	4	9	119	....	....	....	....	....
1997-98	Barrie	OHL	40	3	16	19	51	6	0	0	0	15

FELSNER, BRIAN (FEHLZ-nuhr) OTT.

Left wing. Shoots left. 5'11", 189 lbs. Born, Mt. Clemens, MI, November 11, 1972.

			Regular Season					Playoffs				
Season	Club	Lea	GP	G	A	TP	PIM	GP	G	A	TP	PIM
1993-94	Lake Superior	CCHA	6	1	1	2	6	....	....	....	....	....
1994-95	Lake Superior	CCHA	41	24	28	52	51	....	....	....	....	....
1995-96	Lake Superior	CCHA	38	16	36	52	40	....	....	....	....	....
1996-97	Orlando	IHL	75	29	41	70	38	7	2	3	5	6
1997-98	**Chicago**	**NHL**	**12**	**1**	**3**	**4**	**12**	....	....	....	....	....
	Indianapolis	IHL	53	17	36	53	36	....	....	....	....	....
	Milwaukee	IHL	15	7	8	15	20	10	3	9	12	12
	NHL Totals		**12**	**1**	**3**	**4**	**12**	....	....	....	....	....

Signed as a free agent by **Chicago**, September 5, 1997. Traded to **Ottawa** by **Chicago** for Justin Hocking, August 21, 1998.

FERENCE, ANDREW (fuhr-EHNS) PIT.

Defense. Shoots left. 5'10", 187 lbs. Born, Edmonton, Alta., March 17, 1979.
(Pittsburgh's 8th choice, 208th overall, in 1997 Entry Draft).

			Regular Season					Playoffs				
Season	Club	Lea	GP	G	A	TP	PIM	GP	G	A	TP	PIM
1995-96	Portland	WHL	72	9	31	40	159	7	1	3	4	12
1996-97	Portland	WHL	72	12	32	44	163	6	1	2	3	12
1997-98	Portland	WHL	72	11	57	68	142	16	2	18	20	28

FERENCE, BRAD (fuhr-EHNS) VAN.

Defense. Shoots right. 6'3", 196 lbs. Born, Calgary, Alta., April 2, 1979.
(Vancouver's 1st choice, 10th overall, in 1997 Entry Draft).

			Regular Season					Playoffs				
Season	Club	Lea	GP	G	A	TP	PIM	GP	G	A	TP	PIM
1995-96	Spokane	WHL	5	0	2	2	18	....	....	....	....	....
1996-97	Spokane	WHL	67	6	20	26	324	9	0	4	4	21
1997-98	Spokane	WHL	54	9	30	39	213	18	0	7	7	59

Memorial Cup All-Star Team (1998)

FERGUSON, CRAIG FLA.

Center. Shoots left. 5'11", 190 lbs. Born, Castro Valley, CA, April 8, 1970.
(Montreal's 8th choice, 146th overall, in 1989 Entry Draft).

			Regular Season					Playoffs				
Season	Club	Lea	GP	G	A	TP	PIM	GP	G	A	TP	PIM
1988-89	Yale	ECAC	24	11	6	17	20	....	....	....	....	....
1989-90	Yale	ECAC	28	6	13	19	36	....	....	....	....	....
1990-91	Yale	ECAC	29	11	10	21	34	....	....	....	....	....
1991-92	Yale	ECAC	27	9	16	25	26	....	....	....	....	....
1992-93	Fredericton	AHL	55	15	13	28	20	5	0	1	1	2
	Wheeling	ECHL	9	6	5	11	24	....	....	....	....	....
1993-94	**Montreal**	**NHL**	**2**	**0**	**1**	**1**	**0**	....	....	....	....	....
	Fredericton	AHL	57	29	32	61	60	....	....	....	....	....
1994-95	Fredericton	AHL	80	27	35	62	62	17	6	2	8	6
	Montreal	**NHL**	**1**	**0**	**0**	**0**	**0**	....	....	....	....	....
1995-96	**Montreal**	**NHL**	**10**	**1**	**0**	**1**	**2**	....	....	....	....	....
	Calgary	**NHL**	**8**	**0**	**0**	**0**	**4**	....	....	....	....	....
	Saint John	AHL	18	5	13	18	8	....	....	....	....	....
	Phoenix	IHL	31	6	9	15	25	4	0	2	2	6
1996-97	**Florida**	**NHL**	**3**	**0**	**0**	**0**	**0**	....	....	....	....	....
	Carolina	AHL	74	29	41	70	57	....	....	....	....	....
1997-98	New Haven	AHL	64	24	28	52	41	3	2	1	3	2
	NHL Totals		**24**	**1**	**1**	**2**	**6**	....	....	....	....	....

Traded to **Calgary** by **Montreal** with Yves Sarault for Calgary's 8th round choice (Petr Kubos) in 1997 Entry Draft, November 26, 1995. Traded to **LA Kings** by **Calgary** for Pat Conacher, February 10, 1996. Signed as a free agent by **Florida**, July 24, 1996.

FERGUSON, SCOTT — ANA.

Defense. Shoots left. 6'1", 195 lbs. Born, Camrose, Alta., January 6, 1973.

Season	Club	Lea	Regular Season GP	G	A	TP	PIM	Playoffs GP	G	A	TP	PIM
1990-91	Kamloops	WHL	4	0	0	0	0	....	....	....	....	....
1991-92	Kamloops	WHL	62	4	10	14	138	12	0	2	2	21
1992-93	Kamloops	WHL	71	4	19	23	206	13	0	2	2	24
1993-94	Kamloops	WHL	68	5	49	54	180	19	5	11	16	48
1994-95	Cape Breton	AHL	58	4	6	10	103	....	....	....	....	....
	Wheeling	ECHL	5	1	5	6	16	....	....	....	....	....
1995-96	Cape Breton	AHL	80	5	16	21	196	....	....	....	....	....
1996-97	Hamilton	AHL	74	6	14	20	115	21	5	7	12	59
1997-98	**Edmonton**	**NHL**	**1**	**0**	**0**	**0**	**0**	....	....	....	....	....
	Hamilton	AHL	77	7	17	24	150	9	0	3	3	16
	NHL Totals		**1**	**0**	**0**	**0**	**0**	....	....	....	....	....

WHL West Second All-Star Team (1994)

Signed as a free agent by **Edmonton**, June 2, 1994. Traded to **Ottawa** by **Edmonton** for Frantisek Musil, March 9, 1998. Signed as a free agent by **Anaheim**, July 27, 1998.

FERONE, PAUL — VAN.

Right wing. Shoots right. 5'11", 180 lbs. Born, Vancouver, B.C., April 2, 1976.

Season	Club	Lea	Regular Season GP	G	A	TP	PIM	Playoffs GP	G	A	TP	PIM
1995-96	Seattle	WHL	63	14	19	33	241	5	0	1	1	31
1996-97	Seattle	WHL	59	20	21	41	155	15	1	4	5	41
1997-98	Syracuse	AHL	20	1	3	4	85	....	....	....	....	....
	Raleigh	ECHL	50	1	3	4	152	4	0	0	0	8

Signed as a free agent by **Vancouver**, September 19, 1997.

FERRARO, CHRIS — (fuh-RAHR-oh) EDM.

Right wing. Shoots right. 5'10", 185 lbs. Born, Port Jefferson, NY, January 24, 1973.
(NY Rangers' 4th choice, 85th overall, in 1992 Entry Draft).

Season	Club	Lea	Regular Season GP	G	A	TP	PIM	Playoffs GP	G	A	TP	PIM
1990-91	Dubuque	USHL	45	53	44	97	....	....	....	....	....	....
1991-92	Waterloo	USHL	38	49	50	99	106	....	....	....	....	....
1992-93	U. of Maine	H.E.	39	25	26	51	46	....	....	....	....	....
1993-94	U. of Maine	H.E.	4	0	1	1	8	....	....	....	....	....
	United States	Nat-Tm	48	8	34	42	58	....	....	....	....	....
1994-95	Atlanta	IHL	54	13	14	27	72	....	....	....	....	....
	Binghamton	AHL	13	6	4	10	38	10	2	3	5	16
1995-96	**NY Rangers**	**NHL**	**2**	**1**	**0**	**1**	**0**	....	....	....	....	....
	Binghamton	AHL	77	32	67	99	208	4	4	2	6	13
1996-97	**NY Rangers**	**NHL**	**12**	**1**	**1**	**2**	**6**	....	....	....	....	....
	Binghamton	AHL	53	29	34	63	94	....	....	....	....	....
1997-98	**Pittsburgh**	**NHL**	**46**	**3**	**4**	**7**	**43**	....	....	....	....	....
	NHL Totals		**60**	**5**	**5**	**10**	**49**	....	....	....	....	....

Claimed on waivers by **Pittsburgh** from **NY Rangers**, October 1, 1997. Signed as a free agent by **Edmonton**, August 13, 1998.

FERRARO, PETER — (fuh-RAHR-oh) BOS.

Center. Shoots right. 5'10", 180 lbs. Born, Port Jefferson, NY, January 24, 1973.
(NY Rangers' 1st choice, 24th overall, in 1992 Entry Draft).

Season	Club	Lea	Regular Season GP	G	A	TP	PIM	Playoffs GP	G	A	TP	PIM
1990-91	Dubuque	USHL	29	21	31	52	83	....	....	....	....	....
1991-92	Waterloo	USHL	42	48	53	101	168	....	....	....	....	....
1992-93	U. of Maine	H.E.	36	18	32	50	106	....	....	....	....	....
1993-94	U. of Maine	H.E.	4	3	6	9	16	....	....	....	....	....
	United States	Nat-Tm	60	30	34	64	87	....	....	....	....	....
	United States	Olympics	8	6	0	6	6	....	....	....	....	....
1994-95	Atlanta	IHL	61	15	24	39	118	....	....	....	....	....
	Binghamton	AHL	12	2	6	8	67	11	4	3	7	51
1995-96	**NY Rangers**	**NHL**	**5**	**0**	**1**	**1**	**0**	....	....	....	....	....
	Binghamton	AHL	68	48	53	101	157	4	1	6	7	22
1996-97	**NY Rangers**	**NHL**	**2**	**0**	**0**	**0**	**0**	**2**	**0**	**0**	**0**	**0**
	Binghamton	AHL	75	38	39	77	171	4	3	1	4	18
1997-98	**Pittsburgh**	**NHL**	**29**	**3**	**4**	**7**	**12**	....	....	....	....	....
	NY Rangers	**NHL**	**1**	**0**	**0**	**0**	**2**	....	....	....	....	....
	Hartford	AHL	36	17	23	40	54	15	8	6	14	59
	NHL Totals		**37**	**3**	**5**	**8**	**14**	**2**	**0**	**0**	**0**	**0**

• AHL First All-Star Team (1996)

Claimed on waivers by **Pittsburgh** from **NY Rangers**, October 1, 1997. Claimed on waivers by **NY Rangers** from **Pittsburgh**, January 9, 1997. Signed as a free agent by **Boston**, August 5, 1998.

FERRARO, RAY — (fuh-RAHR-oh) L.A.

Center. Shoots left. 5'9", 193 lbs. Born, Trail, B.C., August 23, 1964.
(Hartford's 5th choice, 88th overall, in 1982 Entry Draft).

Season	Club	Lea	Regular Season GP	G	A	TP	PIM	Playoffs GP	G	A	TP	PIM
1981-82	Penticton	BCJHL	40	65	67	132	90	....	....	....	....	....
1982-83	Portland	WHL	50	41	49	90	39	14	14	10	24	13
1983-84	Brandon	WHL	72	*108	84	*192	84	11	13	15	28	20
1984-85	**Hartford**	**NHL**	**44**	**11**	**17**	**28**	**40**	....	....	....	....	....
	Binghamton	AHL	37	20	13	33	29	....	....	....	....	....
1985-86	**Hartford**	**NHL**	**76**	**30**	**47**	**77**	**57**	**10**	**3**	**6**	**9**	**4**
1986-87	**Hartford**	**NHL**	**80**	**27**	**32**	**59**	**42**	**6**	**1**	**1**	**2**	**8**
1987-88	**Hartford**	**NHL**	**68**	**21**	**29**	**50**	**81**	**6**	**1**	**1**	**2**	**6**
1988-89	**Hartford**	**NHL**	**80**	**41**	**35**	**76**	**86**	**4**	**2**	**0**	**2**	**4**
1989-90	**Hartford**	**NHL**	**79**	**25**	**29**	**54**	**109**	**7**	**0**	**3**	**3**	**2**
1990-91	**Hartford**	**NHL**	**15**	**2**	**5**	**7**	**18**	....	....	....	....	....
	NY Islanders	**NHL**	**61**	**19**	**16**	**35**	**52**	....	....	....	....	....
1991-92	**NY Islanders**	**NHL**	**80**	**40**	**40**	**80**	**92**	....	....	....	....	....
1992-93	**NY Islanders**	**NHL**	**46**	**14**	**13**	**27**	**40**	**18**	**13**	**7**	**20**	**18**
	Capital District	AHL	1	0	2	2	2	....	....	....	....	....
1993-94	**NY Islanders**	**NHL**	**82**	**21**	**32**	**53**	**83**	**4**	**1**	**0**	**1**	**6**
1994-95	**NY Islanders**	**NHL**	**47**	**22**	**21**	**43**	**30**	....	....	....	....	....
1995-96	**NY Rangers**	**NHL**	**65**	**25**	**29**	**54**	**82**	....	....	....	....	....
	Los Angeles	**NHL**	**11**	**4**	**2**	**6**	**10**	....	....	....	....	....
1996-97	**Los Angeles**	**NHL**	**81**	**25**	**21**	**46**	**112**	....	....	....	....	....
1997-98	**Los Angeles**	**NHL**	**40**	**6**	**9**	**15**	**42**	**3**	**0**	**1**	**1**	**2**
	NHL Totals		**955**	**333**	**377**	**710**	**976**	**58**	**21**	**19**	**40**	**50**

WHL First All-Star Team (1984)

Played in NHL All-Star Game (1992)

Traded to **NY Islanders** by **Hartford** for Doug Crossman, November 13, 1990. Signed as a free agent by **NY Rangers**, August 9, 1995. Traded to **LA Kings** by **NY Rangers** with Ian Laperriere, Mattias Norstrom, Nathan Lafayette and NY Rangers' 4th round choice (Sean Blanchard) in 1997 Entry Draft for Marty McSorley, Jari Kurri and Shane Churla, March 14, 1996.

FETISOV, VIACHESLAV — (feh-TEE-sahf)

Defense. Shoots left. 6'1", 220 lbs. Born, Moscow, USSR, April 20, 1958.
(New Jersey's 6th choice, 150th overall, in 1983 Entry Draft).

Season	Club	Lea	Regular Season GP	G	A	TP	PIM	Playoffs GP	G	A	TP	PIM
1975-76	CSKA Moscow	USSR	1	0	0	0	0	....	....	....	....	....
1976-77	CSKA Moscow	USSR	28	3	4	7	14	....	....	....	....	....
1977-78	CSKA Moscow	USSR	35	9	18	27	46	....	....	....	....	....
1978-79	CSKA Moscow	USSR	29	10	19	29	40	....	....	....	....	....
1979-80	CSKA Moscow	USSR	37	10	14	24	46	....	....	....	....	....
	Soviet Union	Olympics	7	5	4	9	10	....	....	....	....	....
1980-81	CSKA Moscow	USSR	48	13	16	29	44	....	....	....	....	....
1981-82	CSKA Moscow	USSR	46	15	26	41	20	....	....	....	....	....
1982-83	CSKA Moscow	USSR	43	6	17	23	46	....	....	....	....	....
1983-84	CSKA Moscow	USSR	44	19	30	49	38	....	....	....	....	....
	Soviet Union	Olympics	7	3	8	11	8	....	....	....	....	....
1984-85	CSKA Moscow	USSR	20	13	12	25	6	....	....	....	....	....
1985-86	CSKA Moscow	USSR	40	15	19	34	12	....	....	....	....	....
1986-87	CSKA Moscow	USSR	39	13	20	33	18	....	....	....	....	....
1987-88	CSKA Moscow	USSR	46	18	17	35	26	....	....	....	....	....
	Soviet Union	Olympics	8	4	9	13	6	....	....	....	....	....
1988-89	CSKA Moscow	USSR	23	9	8	17	18	....	....	....	....	....
1989-90	**New Jersey**	**NHL**	**72**	**8**	**34**	**42**	**52**	**6**	**0**	**2**	**2**	**10**
1990-91	**New Jersey**	**NHL**	**67**	**3**	**16**	**19**	**62**	**7**	**0**	**0**	**0**	**17**
	Utica	AHL	1	1	1	2	0	....	....	....	....	....
1991-92	**New Jersey**	**NHL**	**70**	**3**	**23**	**26**	**108**	**6**	**0**	**3**	**3**	**8**
1992-93	**New Jersey**	**NHL**	**76**	**4**	**23**	**27**	**158**	**5**	**0**	**2**	**2**	**4**
1993-94	**New Jersey**	**NHL**	**52**	**1**	**14**	**15**	**30**	**14**	**1**	**0**	**1**	**8**
1994-95	Spartak	CIS	1	0	1	1	4	....	....	....	....	....
	New Jersey	**NHL**	**4**	**0**	**1**	**1**	**0**	....	....	....	....	....
	Detroit	**NHL**	**14**	**3**	**11**	**14**	**2**	**18**	**0**	**8**	**8**	**14**
1995-96	**Detroit**	**NHL**	**69**	**7**	**35**	**42**	**96**	**19**	**1**	**4**	**5**	**34**
1996-97	**Detroit**	**NHL**	**64**	**5**	**23**	**28**	**76**	**20**	**0**	**4**	**4**	**42 ♦**
1997-98	**Detroit**	**NHL**	**58**	**2**	**12**	**14**	**72**	**21**	**0**	**3**	**3**	**10 ♦**
	NHL Totals		**546**	**36**	**192**	**228**	**656**	**116**	**2**	**26**	**28**	**147**

USSR First All-Star Team (1979, 1980, 1982, 1983, 1984, 1985, 1986, 1987, 1988) • USSR Player of the Year (1982, 1986) • Leningradskaya-Pravda Trophy (Top Scoring Defenseman) (1984, 1986, 1987, 1988)

Played in NHL All-Star Game (1997, 1998)

• Re-entered NHL draft. Originally Montreal's 14th choice, 201st overall, in 1978 Amateur Draft.

Traded to **Detroit** by **New Jersey** for Detroit's 3rd round choice (David Gosselin) in 1995 Entry Draft, April 3, 1995.

FILATOV, ANATOLI — (fih LAH tohv) S.J.

Right wing. Shoots right. 5'10", 180 lbs. Born, Kamenogorsk, USSR, April 28, 1975.
(San Jose's 10th choice, 158th overall, in 1993 Entry Draft).

Season	Club	Lea	Regular Season GP	G	A	TP	PIM	Playoffs GP	G	A	TP	PIM
1992-93	Kamenogorsk	CIS	17	4	0	4	14	....	....	....	....	....
1993-94	Kamenogorsk	CIS	20	3	3	6	22	....	....	....	....	....
1994-95	Kamenogorsk	CIS	33	6	6	12	30	....	....	....	....	....
	Niagara Falls	OHL	12	2	3	5	6	....	....	....	....	....
1995-96	Kamenogorsk	CIS	48	9	15	24	78	....	....	....	....	....
1996-97	Kamenogorsk	Russia-2	25	14	14	28	28	....	....	....	....	....
1997-98	Novosibirsk	Russia	25	2	4	6	26	....	....	....	....	....

FINLEY, JEFF — NYR

Defense. Shoots left. 6'2", 205 lbs. Born, Edmonton, Alta., April 14, 1967.
(NY Islanders' 4th choice, 55th overall, in 1985 Entry Draft).

Season	Club	Lea	Regular Season GP	G	A	TP	PIM	Playoffs GP	G	A	TP	PIM
1983-84	Portland	WHL	5	0	0	0	5	5	0	1	1	4
1984-85	Portland	WHL	69	6	44	50	57	6	1	2	3	2
1985-86	Portland	WHL	70	11	59	70	83	15	1	7	8	16
1986-87	Portland	WHL	72	13	53	66	113	20	1	*21	22	27
1987-88	**NY Islanders**	**NHL**	**10**	**0**	**5**	**5**	**15**	**1**	**0**	**0**	**0**	**2**
	Springfield	AHL	52	5	18	23	50	....	....	....	....	....
1988-89	**NY Islanders**	**NHL**	**4**	**0**	**0**	**0**	**6**	....	....	....	....	....
	Springfield	AHL	65	3	16	19	55	....	....	....	....	....
1989-90	**NY Islanders**	**NHL**	**11**	**0**	**1**	**1**	**0**	**5**	**0**	**2**	**2**	**2**
	Springfield	AHL	57	1	15	16	41	13	1	4	5	23
1990-91	**NY Islanders**	**NHL**	**11**	**0**	**0**	**0**	**4**	....	....	....	....	....
	Capital District	AHL	67	10	34	44	34	....	....	....	....	....
1991-92	**NY Islanders**	**NHL**	**51**	**1**	**10**	**11**	**26**	....	....	....	....	....
	Capital District	AHL	20	1	9	10	6	....	....	....	....	....
1992-93	Capital District	AHL	61	6	29	35	34	4	0	1	1	0
1993-94	**Philadelphia**	**NHL**	**55**	**1**	**8**	**9**	**24**	....	....	....	....	....
1994-95	Hershey	AHL	36	2	9	11	33	6	0	1	1	8
1995-96	**Winnipeg**	**NHL**	**65**	**1**	**5**	**6**	**81**	**6**	**0**	**0**	**0**	**4**
	Springfield	AHL	14	3	12	15	22	....	....	....	....	....
1996-97	**Phoenix**	**NHL**	**65**	**3**	**7**	**10**	**40**	**1**	**0**	**0**	**0**	**2**
1997-98	**NY Rangers**	**NHL**	**63**	**1**	**6**	**7**	**55**	....	....	....	....	....
	NHL Totals		**335**	**7**	**42**	**49**	**251**	**13**	**0**	**2**	**2**	**10**

Traded to **Ottawa** by **NY Islanders** for Chris Luongo, June 30, 1993. Signed as a free agent by **Philadelphia**, July 30, 1993. Traded to **Winnipeg** by **Philadelphia** for Russ Romaniuk, June 27, 1995. Transferred to **Phoenix** after **Winnipeg** franchise relocated, July 1, 1996. Signed as a free agent by **NY Rangers**, August 18, 1997.

FINN, STEVEN

Defense. Shoots left. 6', 191 lbs. Born, Laval, Que., August 20, 1966.
(Quebec's 3rd choice, 57th overall, in 1984 Entry Draft).

			Regular Season					Playoffs				
Season	Club	Lea	GP	G	A	TP	PIM	GP	G	A	TP	PIM
1982-83	Laval	QMJHL	69	7	30	37	108	6	0	2	2	6
1983-84	Laval	QMJHL	68	7	39	46	159	14	1	6	7	27
1984-85	Laval	QMJHL	61	20	33	53	169	....	....	....	....	....
	Fredericton	AHL	4	0	0	0	14	6	1	1	2	4
1985-86	Laval	QMJHL	29	4	15	19	111	14	6	16	22	57
	Quebec	NHL	17	0	1	1	28	....	....	....	....	....
1986-87	Quebec	NHL	36	2	5	7	40	13	0	2	2	29
	Fredericton	AHL	38	7	19	26	73	....	....	....	....	....
1987-88	Quebec	NHL	75	3	7	10	198	....	....	....	....	....
1988-89	Quebec	NHL	77	2	6	8	235	....	....	....	....	....
1989-90	Quebec	NHL	64	3	9	12	208	....	....	....	....	....
1990-91	Quebec	NHL	71	6	13	19	228	....	....	....	....	....
1991-92	Quebec	NHL	65	4	7	11	194	....	....	....	....	....
1992-93	Quebec	NHL	80	5	9	14	160	6	0	1	1	8
1993-94	Quebec	NHL	80	4	13	17	159	....	....	....	....	....
1994-95	Quebec	NHL	40	0	3	3	64	4	0	1	1	2
1995-96	Tampa Bay	NHL	16	0	0	0	24	....	....	....	....	....
	Los Angeles	NHL	50	3	2	5	102	....	....	....	....	....
1996-97	Los Angeles	NHL	54	2	3	5	84	....	....	....	....	....
1997-98	Long Beach	IHL	75	6	14	20	134	17	1	4	5	48
	NHL Totals		725	34	78	112	1724	23	0	4	4	39

QMJHL First All-Star Team (1984) • QMJHL Second All-Star Team (1985)

Transferred to **Colorado** after **Quebec** franchise relocated, June 21, 1995. Traded to **Tampa Bay** by **Colorado** for Tampa Bay's 4th round choice (Brad Larsen) in 1997 Entry Draft, October 5, 1995. Traded to **LA Kings** by **Tampa Bay** for Michel Petit, November 13, 1995.

FINNSTROM, JOHAN (FIHN-struhm) CGY.

Defense. Shoots left. 6'3", 205 lbs. Born, Broby, Sweden, March 27, 1976.
(Calgary's 5th choice, 97th overall, in 1994 Entry Draft).

			Regular Season					Playoffs				
Season	Club	Lea	GP	G	A	TP	PIM	GP	G	A	TP	PIM
1993-94	Rogle	Sweden	7	1	1	2	2	....	....	....	....	....
1994-95	Rogle	Sweden	19	0	0	0	10	....	....	....	....	....
1995-96	Rogle	Sweden	18	0	0	0	10	....	....	....	....	....
1996-97	Rogle	Sweden-2	31	1	5	6	59	....	....	....	....	....
1997-98	Lulea HF	EuroHL	6	0	0	0	4	....	....	....	....	....
	Lulea HF	Sweden	45	0	1	1	17	3	0	0	0	0

FISCHER, JIRI (FIHSH-uhr, YIH-ree) DET.

Defense. Shoots left. 6'5", 210 lbs. Born, Horovice, Czechoslovakia, July 31, 1980.
(Detroit's 1st choice, 25th overall, in 1998 Entry Draft).

			Regular Season					Playoffs				
Season	Club	Lea	GP	G	A	TP	PIM	GP	G	A	TP	PIM
1995-96	Poldi Kladno	Czech-Jr.	39	6	10	16	....	....	....	....	....	....
1996-97	Poldi Kladno	Czech-Jr.	38	7	21	28	....	....	....	....	....	....
1997-98	Hull	QMJHL	70	3	19	22	112	11	1	4	5	16

FISHER, CRAIG BUF.

Center. Shoots left. 6'3", 180 lbs. Born, Oshawa, Ont., June 30, 1970.
(Philadelphia's 3rd choice, 56th overall, in 1988 Entry Draft).

			Regular Season					Playoffs				
Season	Club	Lea	GP	G	A	TP	PIM	GP	G	A	TP	PIM
1987-88	Ottawa	OJHL	36	42	34	76	48	....	....	....	....	....
1988-89	Miami-Ohio	CCHA	37	22	20	42	37	....	....	....	....	....
1989-90	Miami-Ohio	CCHA	39	37	29	66	38	....	....	....	....	....
	Philadelphia	NHL	2	0	0	0	0	....	....	....	....	....
1990-91	Philadelphia	NHL	2	0	0	0	0	....	....	....	....	....
	Hershey	AHL	77	43	36	79	46	7	5	3	8	2
1991-92	Cape Breton	AHL	60	20	25	45	28	1	0	0	0	0
1992-93	Cape Breton	AHL	75	32	29	61	74	1	0	0	0	2
1993-94	Cape Breton	AHL	16	5	5	10	11	....	....	....	....	....
	Winnipeg	NHL	4	0	0	0	2	....	....	....	....	....
	Moncton	AHL	46	26	35	61	36	21	11	11	22	28
1994-95	Indianapolis	IHL	77	53	40	93	65	....	....	....	....	....
1995-96	Orlando	IHL	82	*74	56	130	81	14	10	7	17	6
1996-97	Utah	IHL	15	6	7	13	4	....	....	....	....	....
	Florida	NHL	4	0	0	0	0	....	....	....	....	....
	Carolina	AHL	42	33	29	62	16	....	....	....	....	....
1997-98	Kolner Haie	EuroHL	4	0	0	0	4	....	....	....	....	....
	Kolner Haie	Germany	34	9	8	17	34	....	....	....	....	....
	NHL Totals		12	0	0	0	2	....	....	....	....	....

CCHA First All-Star Team (1990) • IHL First All-Star Team (1996)

Traded to **Edmonton** by **Philadelphia** with Scott Mellanby and Craig Berube for Dave Brown, Corey Foster and Jari Kurri, May 30, 1991. Traded to **Winnipeg** by **Edmonton** for cash, December 9, 1993. Signed as a free agent by **Chicago**, June 9, 1994. Signed as a free agent by **NY Islanders**, July 29, 1996. Traded to **Florida** by **NY Islanders** for cash, December 7, 1996. Signed as a free agent by **Buffalo**, July 30, 1998.

FISHER, MIKE OTT.

Center. Shoots right. 6', 180 lbs. Born, Peterborough, Ont., June 5, 1980.
(Ottawa's 2nd choice, 44th overall, in 1998 Entry Draft).

			Regular Season					Playoffs				
Season	Club	Lea	GP	G	A	TP	PIM	GP	G	A	TP	PIM
1996-97	Peterborough	OJHL	51	26	30	56	35	....	....	....	....	....
1997-98	Sudbury	OHL	66	24	25	49	65	9	2	2	4	13

FITZGERALD, RANDY CAR.

Left wing. Shoots left. 5'9", 175 lbs. Born, Toronto, Ont., September 5, 1979.
(Carolina's 8th choice, 199th overall, in 1997 Entry Draft).

			Regular Season					Playoffs				
Season	Club	Lea	GP	G	A	TP	PIM	GP	G	A	TP	PIM
1996-97	Detroit	OHL	65	12	18	30	123	5	0	1	1	13
1997-98	Plymouth	OHL	54	11	24	35	104	15	6	3	9	46

FITZGERALD, TOM NSH.

Right wing/Center. Shoots right. 6'1", 191 lbs. Born, Melrose, MA, August 28, 1968.
(NY Islanders' 1st choice, 17th overall, in 1986 Entry Draft).

			Regular Season					Playoffs				
Season	Club	Lea	GP	G	A	TP	PIM	GP	G	A	TP	PIM
1985-86	Austin Prep	H.S.	24	35	38	73	....	....	....	....	....	....
1986-87	Providence	H.E.	27	8	14	22	22	....	....	....	....	....
1987-88	Providence	H.E.	36	19	15	34	50	....	....	....	....	....
1988-89	NY Islanders	NHL	23	3	5	8	10	....	....	....	....	....
	Springfield	AHL	61	24	18	42	43	....	....	....	....	....
1989-90	NY Islanders	NHL	19	2	5	7	4	4	1	0	1	4
	Springfield	AHL	53	30	23	53	32	14	2	9	11	13
1990-91	NY Islanders	NHL	41	5	5	10	24	....	....	....	....	....
	Capital District	AHL	27	7	7	14	50	....	....	....	....	....
1991-92	NY Islanders	NHL	45	6	11	17	28	....	....	....	....	....
	Capital District	AHL	4	1	1	2	4	....	....	....	....	....
1992-93	NY Islanders	NHL	77	9	18	27	34	18	2	5	7	18
1993-94	Florida	NHL	83	18	14	32	54	....	....	....	....	....
1994-95	Florida	NHL	48	3	13	16	31	....	....	....	....	....
1995-96	Florida	NHL	82	13	21	34	75	22	4	4	8	34
1996-97	Florida	NHL	71	10	14	24	64	5	0	1	1	0
1997-98	Florida	NHL	69	10	5	15	57	....	....	....	....	....
	Colorado	NHL	11	2	1	3	22	7	0	1	1	20
	NHL Totals		569	81	112	193	403	56	7	11	18	76

Claimed by **Florida** from **NY Islanders** in Expansion Draft, June 24, 1993. Traded to **Colorado** by **Florida** for the rights to Mark Parrish and Anaheim's 3rd round choice (previously acquired, Florida selected Lance Ward) in 1998 Entry Draft, March 24, 1998. Signed as a free agent by **Nashville**, July 6, 1998.

FITZPATRICK, RORY ST.L.

Defense. Shoots right. 6'1", 205 lbs. Born, Rochester, NY, January 11, 1975.
(Montreal's 2nd choice, 47th overall, in 1993 Entry Draft).

			Regular Season					Playoffs				
Season	Club	Lea	GP	G	A	TP	PIM	GP	G	A	TP	PIM
1992-93	Sudbury	OHL	58	4	20	24	68	14	0	0	0	17
1993-94	Sudbury	OHL	65	12	34	46	112	10	2	5	7	10
1994-95	Sudbury	OHL	56	12	36	48	72	18	3	15	18	21
	Fredericton	AHL	....	....	....	....	....	10	1	2	3	5
1995-96	Montreal	NHL	42	0	2	2	18	6	1	1	2	0
	Fredericton	AHL	18	4	6	10	36	....	....	....	....	....
1996-97	Montreal	NHL	6	0	1	1	6	....	....	....	....	....
	St. Louis	NHL	2	0	0	0	2	....	....	....	....	....
	Worcester	AHL	49	4	13	17	78	5	1	2	3	0
1997-98	Worcester	AHL	62	8	22	30	111	11	0	3	3	26
	NHL Totals		50	0	3	3	26	6	1	1	2	0

Traded to **St. Louis** by **Montreal** with Pierre Turgeon and Craig Conroy for Murray Baron, Shayne Corson and St. Louis' 5th round choice (Gennady Razin) in 1997 Entry Draft, October 29, 1996.

FLEURY, THEOREN (FLUH-ree, THAIR-ihn) CGY.

Right wing. Shoots right. 5'6", 180 lbs. Born, Oxbow, Sask., June 29, 1968.
(Calgary's 9th choice, 166th overall, in 1987 Entry Draft).

			Regular Season					Playoffs				
Season	Club	Lea	GP	G	A	TP	PIM	GP	G	A	TP	PIM
1984-85	Moose Jaw	WHL	71	29	46	75	82	....	....	....	....	....
1985-86	Moose Jaw	WHL	72	43	65	108	124	....	....	....	....	....
1986-87	Moose Jaw	WHL	66	61	68	129	110	9	7	9	16	34
1987-88	Moose Jaw	WHL	65	68	92	*160	235	....	....	....	....	....
	Salt Lake	IHL	2	3	4	7	7	8	11	5	16	16
1988-89	Calgary	NHL	36	14	20	34	46	22	5	6	11	24 ♦
	Salt Lake	IHL	40	37	37	74	81	....	....	....	....	....
1989-90	Calgary	NHL	80	31	35	66	157	6	2	3	5	10
1990-91	Calgary	NHL	79	51	53	104	136	7	2	5	7	14
1991-92	Calgary	NHL	80	33	40	73	133	....	....	....	....	....
1992-93	Calgary	NHL	83	34	66	100	88	6	5	7	12	27
1993-94	Calgary	NHL	83	40	45	85	186	7	6	4	10	5
1994-95	Tappara	Finland	10	8	9	17	22	....	....	....	....	....
	Calgary	NHL	47	29	29	58	112	7	7	7	14	2
1995-96	Calgary	NHL	80	46	50	96	112	4	2	1	3	14
1996-97	Calgary	NHL	81	29	38	67	104	....	....	....	....	....
1997-98	Calgary	NHL	82	27	51	78	197	....	....	....	....	....
	Canada	Olympics	6	1	3	4	2	....	....	....	....	....
	NHL Totals		731	334	427	761	1271	59	29	33	62	96

WJC-A All-Star Team (1988) • WHL East Second All-Star Team (1988) • Co-winner of Alka-Seltzer Plus Award with Marty McSorley (1991) • NHL Second All-Star Team (1995)

Played in NHL All-Star Game (1991, 1992, 1996, 1997, 1998)

FLICHEL, MARTY (FLICK-ehl) DAL.

Right wing. Shoots left. 5'11", 175 lbs. Born, Hodgeville, Sask., March 6, 1976.
(Dallas' 6th choice, 228th overall, in 1994 Entry Draft).

			Regular Season					Playoffs				
Season	Club	Lea	GP	G	A	TP	PIM	GP	G	A	TP	PIM
1992-93	Tacoma	WHL	61	21	20	41	19	7	0	0	0	8
1993-94	Tacoma	WHL	72	27	48	75	69	8	1	4	5	13
1994-95	Tacoma	WHL	67	25	53	78	81	4	2	3	5	8
1995-96	Kelowna	WHL	69	28	79	107	107	6	1	6	7	10
1996-97	Daytona	ECHL	28	17	16	33	24	2	0	1	1	4
	Michigan	IHL	19	2	3	5	10	....	....	....	....	....
1997-98	Michigan	IHL	74	18	16	34	56	4	0	0	0	23

FLINN, RYAN N.J.

Left wing. Shoots left. 6'4", 210 lbs. Born, Halifax, N.S., April 20, 1980.
(New Jersey's 8th choice, 143rd overall, in 1998 Entry Draft).

			Regular Season					Playoffs				
Season	Club	Lea	GP	G	A	TP	PIM	GP	G	A	TP	PIM
1996-97	Laval	QMJHL	23	3	2	5	56	2	0	0	0	0
1997-98	Laval	QMJHL	59	4	12	16	217	15	1	0	1	63

FLODELL, JORDON (FLOH-dehl) PHI.

Defense. Shoots right. 6'2", 198 lbs. Born, Melfort, Sask., April 28, 1979.
(Philadelphia's 5th choice, 158th overall, in 1997 Entry Draft).

			Regular Season					Playoffs				
Season	Club	Lea	GP	G	A	TP	PIM	GP	G	A	TP	PIM
1995-96	Moose Jaw	WHL	17	0	0	0	7	....	....	....	....	....
1996-97	Moose Jaw	WHL	39	0	3	3	48	12	0	3	3	8
1997-98	Moose Jaw	WHL	71	2	2	4	164	4	0	0	0	10

FOCHT, DAN (FOHKT) PHX.

Defense. Shoots left. 6'6", 226 lbs. Born, Regina, Sask., December 31, 1977.
(Phoenix's 1st choice, 11th overall, in 1996 Entry Draft).

			Regular Season					Playoffs				
Season	Club	Lea	GP	G	A	TP	PIM	GP	G	A	TP	PIM
1995-96	Tri-City	WHL	63	6	12	18	161	11	1	1	2	23
1996-97	Tri-City	WHL	28	0	5	5	92	....	....	....	....	....
	Regina	WHL	22	2	2	4	59	5	0	2	2	8
	Springfield	AHL	1	0	0	0	2	....	....	....	....	....
1997-98	Springfield	AHL	61	2	5	7	125	3	0	0	0	4

FOGARTY, BRYAN CHI.

Defense. Shoots left. 6'2", 206 lbs. Born, Brantford, Ont., June 11, 1969.
(Quebec's 1st choice, 9th overall, in 1987 Entry Draft).

			Regular Season					Playoffs				
Season	Club	Lea	GP	G	A	TP	PIM	GP	G	A	TP	PIM
1985-86	Kingston	OHL	47	2	19	21	14	10	1	3	4	4
1986-87	Kingston	OHL	56	20	50	70	46	12	2	3	5	5
1987-88	Kingston	OHL	48	11	36	47	50	....	....	....	....	....
1988-89	Niagara Falls	OHL	60	47	*108	*155	88	17	10	22	32	36
1989-90	**Quebec**	**NHL**	**45**	**4**	**10**	**14**	**31**	....	....	....	....	....
	Halifax	AHL	22	5	14	19	6	6	2	4	6	0
1990-91	**Quebec**	**NHL**	**45**	**9**	**22**	**31**	**24**	....	....	....	....	....
	Halifax	AHL	5	0	2	2	0	....	....	....	....	....
1991-92	**Quebec**	**NHL**	**20**	**3**	**12**	**15**	**16**	....	....	....	....	....
	Halifax	AHL	2	0	0	0	2	....	....	....	....	....
	New Haven	AHL	4	0	1	1	6	....	....	....	....	....
	Muskegon	IHL	8	2	4	6	30	....	....	....	....	....
1992-93	**Pittsburgh**	**NHL**	**12**	**0**	**4**	**4**	**4**	....	....	....	....	....
	Cleveland	IHL	15	2	5	7	8	3	0	1	1	17
1993-94	Atlanta	IHL	8	1	5	6	4	....	....	....	....	....
	Las Vegas	IHL	33	3	16	19	38	....	....	....	....	....
	Kansas City	IHL	3	2	1	3	2	....	....	....	....	....
	Montreal	**NHL**	**13**	**1**	**2**	**3**	**10**	....	....	....	....	....
1994-95	**Montreal**	**NHL**	**21**	**5**	**2**	**7**	**34**	....	....	....	....	....
1995-96	Minnesota	IHL	17	3	12	15	24	....	....	....	....	....
	Detroit	IHL	18	1	5	6	14	....	....	....	....	....
	HC Davos	Switz.	....	....	....	....	....	3	1	1	2	0
1996-97	Kansas City	IHL	22	3	9	12	10	....	....	....	....	....
	HC Milano	Italy	16	8	20	28	30	....	....	....	....	....
	HC Milano	Alpen.	7	3	7	10	10	....	....	....	....	....
1997-98	Hannover	Germany	39	8	17	25	75	4	1	0	1	2
	NHL Totals		**156**	**22**	**52**	**74**	**119**	....	....	....	....	....

OHL First All-Star Team (1987, 1989) • Canadian Major Junior Defenseman of the Year (1989) • Canadian Major Junior Player of the Year (1989)

Traded to **Pittsburgh** by **Quebec** for Scott Young, March 10, 1992. Signed as a free agent by **Tampa Bay**, September 28, 1993. Signed as a free agent by **Montreal**, February 25, 1994. Signed as a free agent by **Buffalo**, September 8, 1995. Signed as a free agent by **Chicago**, September 2, 1998.

FOOTE, ADAM COL.

Defense. Shoots right. 6'1", 205 lbs. Born, Toronto, Ont., July 10, 1971.
(Quebec's 2nd choice, 22nd overall, in 1989 Entry Draft).

			Regular Season					Playoffs				
Season	Club	Lea	GP	G	A	TP	PIM	GP	G	A	TP	PIM
1988-89	S.S. Marie	OHL	66	7	32	39	120	....	....	....	....	....
1989-90	S.S. Marie	OHL	61	12	43	55	199	....	....	....	....	....
1990-91	S.S. Marie	OHL	59	18	51	69	93	14	5	12	17	28
1991-92	**Quebec**	**NHL**	**46**	**2**	**5**	**7**	**44**	....	....	....	....	....
	Halifax	AHL	6	0	1	1	2	....	....	....	....	....
1992-93	**Quebec**	**NHL**	**81**	**4**	**12**	**16**	**168**	**6**	**0**	**1**	**1**	**2**
1993-94	**Quebec**	**NHL**	**45**	**2**	**6**	**8**	**67**	....	....	....	....	....
1994-95	**Quebec**	**NHL**	**35**	**0**	**7**	**7**	**52**	**6**	**0**	**1**	**1**	**14**
1995-96	**Colorado**	**NHL**	**73**	**5**	**11**	**16**	**88**	**22**	**1**	**3**	**4**	**36 ♦**
1996-97	**Colorado**	**NHL**	**78**	**2**	**19**	**21**	**135**	**17**	**0**	**4**	**4**	**62**
1997-98	**Colorado**	**NHL**	**77**	**3**	**14**	**17**	**124**	**7**	**0**	**0**	**0**	**23**
	Canada	Olympics	6	0	1	1	4	....	....	....	....	....
	NHL Totals		**435**	**18**	**74**	**92**	**678**	**58**	**1**	**9**	**10**	**137**

OHL First All-Star Team (1991)

Transferred to **Colorado** after **Quebec** franchise relocated, June 21, 1995.

FORBES, COLIN PHI.

Left wing. Shoots left. 6'3", 205 lbs. Born, New Westminster, B.C., February 16, 1976.
(Philadelphia's 5th choice, 166th overall, in 1994 Entry Draft).

			Regular Season					Playoffs				
Season	Club	Lea	GP	G	A	TP	PIM	GP	G	A	TP	PIM
1993-94	Sherwood Park	AJHL	47	18	22	40	76	....	....	....	....	....
1994-95	Portland	WHL	72	24	31	55	108	9	1	3	4	10
1995-96	Portland	WHL	72	33	44	77	137	7	2	5	7	14
	Hershey	AHL	2	1	0	1	2	4	0	2	2	2
1996-97	**Philadelphia**	**NHL**	**3**	**1**	**0**	**1**	**0**	**3**	**0**	**0**	**0**	**0**
	Philadelphia	AHL	74	21	28	49	108	10	5	5	10	33
1997-98	**Philadelphia**	**NHL**	**63**	**12**	**7**	**19**	**59**	**5**	**0**	**0**	**0**	**2**
	Philadelphia	AHL	13	7	4	11	22	....	....	....	....	....
	NHL Totals		**66**	**13**	**7**	**20**	**59**	**8**	**0**	**0**	**0**	**2**

FORBES, IAN PHI.

Defense. Shoots left. 6'6", 180 lbs. Born, Brampton, Ont., August 2, 1980.
(Philadelphia's 3rd choice, 51st overall, in 1998 Entry Draft).

			Regular Season					Playoffs				
Season	Club	Lea	GP	G	A	TP	PIM	GP	G	A	TP	PIM
1996-97	Mississauga	OJHL	39	10	32	42	178	....	....	....	....	....
1997-98	Guelph	OHL	61	2	3	5	164	12	0	0	0	16

FORSANDER, JOHAN (fohr-SAHN-duhr, YOO-hahn) DET.

Left wing. Shoots left. 6'1", 174 lbs. Born, Jonkoping, Sweden, April 28, 1978.
(Detroit's 3rd choice, 108th overall, in 1996 Entry Draft).

			Regular Season					Playoffs				
Season	Club	Lea	GP	G	A	TP	PIM	GP	G	A	TP	PIM
1995-96	HV 71 Jonkoping	Swe-Jr.	27	15	8	23	12	....	....	....	....	....
	HV 71 Jonkoping	Sweden	6	0	0	0	0	3	0	0	0	2
1996-97	HV 71 Jonkoping	Sweden	44	3	2	5	6	5	0	0	0	0
1997-98	HV 71 Jonkoping	Sweden	46	3	2	5	12	5	0	0	0	0

FORSBERG, PETER (FOHRS-buhrg) COL.

Center. Shoots left. 6', 190 lbs. Born, Ornskoldsvik, Sweden, July 20, 1973.
(Philadelphia's 1st choice, 6th overall, in 1991 Entry Draft).

			Regular Season					Playoffs				
Season	Club	Lea	GP	G	A	TP	PIM	GP	G	A	TP	PIM
1990-91	MoDo	Sweden	23	7	10	17	22	....	....	....	....	....
1991-92	MoDo	Sweden	39	9	18	27	78	....	....	....	....	....
1992-93	MoDo	Sweden	39	23	24	47	92	3	4	1	5	0
1993-94	MoDo	Sweden	39	18	26	44	82	11	9	7	16	14
	Sweden	Olympics	8	2	6	8	6	....	....	....	....	....
1994-95	MoDo	Sweden	11	5	9	14	20	....	....	....	....	....
	Quebec	**NHL**	**47**	**15**	**35**	**50**	**16**	**6**	**2**	**4**	**6**	**4**
1995-96	**Colorado**	**NHL**	**82**	**30**	**86**	**116**	**47**	**22**	**10**	**11**	**21**	**18 ♦**
1996-97	**Colorado**	**NHL**	**65**	**28**	**58**	**86**	**73**	**14**	**5**	**12**	**17**	**10**
1997-98	**Colorado**	**NHL**	**72**	**25**	**66**	**91**	**94**	**7**	**6**	**5**	**11**	**12**
	Sweden	Olympics	4	1	4	5	6	....	....	....	....	....
	NHL Totals		**266**	**98**	**245**	**343**	**230**	**49**	**23**	**32**	**55**	**44**

NHL/Upper Deck All-Rookie Team (1995) • Won Calder Memorial Trophy (1995) • NHL First All-Star Team (1998)

Played in NHL All-Star Game (1996, 1998)

Traded to **Quebec** by **Philadelphia** with Steve Duchesne, Kerry Huffman, Mike Ricci, Ron Hextall, Chris Simon, Philadelphia's 1st round choice in the 1993 (Jocelyn Thibault) and 1994 (later traded to Toronto — later traded to Washington — Washington selected Nolan Baumgartner) Entry Drafts and cash for Eric Lindros, June 30, 1992. Transferred to **Colorado** after **Quebec** franchise relocated, June 21, 1995.

FORTIN, JEAN-FRANCOIS (fohr-TEHN) WSH.

Defense. Shoots right. 6'2", 190 lbs. Born, Laval, Que., March 15, 1979.
(Washington's 2nd choice, 35th overall, in 1997 Entry Draft).

			Regular Season					Playoffs				
Season	Club	Lea	GP	G	A	TP	PIM	GP	G	A	TP	PIM
1995-96	Sherbrooke	QMJHL	69	7	15	22	40	7	2	6	8	2
1996-97	Sherbrooke	QMJHL	59	7	30	37	89	2	0	1	1	14
1997-98	Sherbrooke	QMJHL	55	12	25	37	37	....	....	....	....	....

FRANCIS, RON CAR.

Center. Shoots left. 6'3", 200 lbs. Born, Sault Ste. Marie, Ont., March 1, 1963.
(Hartford's 1st choice, 4th overall, in 1981 Entry Draft).

			Regular Season					Playoffs				
Season	Club	Lea	GP	G	A	TP	PIM	GP	G	A	TP	PIM
1980-81	S.S. Marie	OHA	64	26	43	69	33	19	7	8	15	34
1981-82	S.S. Marie	OHL	25	18	30	48	46	....	....	....	....	....
	Hartford	**NHL**	**59**	**25**	**43**	**68**	**51**	....	....	....	....	....
1982-83	**Hartford**	**NHL**	**79**	**31**	**59**	**90**	**60**	....	....	....	....	....
1983-84	**Hartford**	**NHL**	**72**	**23**	**60**	**83**	**45**	....	....	....	....	....
1984-85	**Hartford**	**NHL**	**80**	**24**	**57**	**81**	**66**	....	....	....	....	....
1985-86	**Hartford**	**NHL**	**53**	**24**	**53**	**77**	**24**	**10**	**1**	**2**	**3**	**4**
1986-87	**Hartford**	**NHL**	**75**	**30**	**63**	**93**	**45**	**6**	**2**	**2**	**4**	**6**
1987-88	**Hartford**	**NHL**	**80**	**25**	**50**	**75**	**87**	**6**	**2**	**5**	**7**	**2**
1988-89	**Hartford**	**NHL**	**69**	**29**	**48**	**77**	**36**	**4**	**0**	**2**	**2**	**0**
1989-90	**Hartford**	**NHL**	**80**	**32**	**69**	**101**	**73**	**7**	**3**	**3**	**6**	**8**
1990-91	**Hartford**	**NHL**	**67**	**21**	**55**	**76**	**51**	....	....	....	....	....
	Pittsburgh	**NHL**	**14**	**2**	**9**	**11**	**21**	**24**	**7**	**10**	**17**	**24 ♦**
1991-92	**Pittsburgh**	**NHL**	**70**	**21**	**33**	**54**	**30**	**21**	**8**	***19**	**27**	**6 ♦**
1992-93	**Pittsburgh**	**NHL**	**84**	**24**	**76**	**100**	**68**	**12**	**6**	**11**	**17**	**19**
1993-94	**Pittsburgh**	**NHL**	**82**	**27**	**66**	**93**	**62**	**6**	**0**	**2**	**2**	**6**
1994-95	**Pittsburgh**	**NHL**	**44**	**11**	***48**	**59**	**18**	**12**	**6**	**13**	**19**	**4**
1995-96	**Pittsburgh**	**NHL**	**77**	**27**	***92**	**119**	**56**	**11**	**3**	**6**	**9**	**4**
1996-97	**Pittsburgh**	**NHL**	**81**	**27**	**63**	**90**	**20**	**5**	**1**	**2**	**3**	**2**
1997-98	**Pittsburgh**	**NHL**	**81**	**25**	**62**	**87**	**20**	**6**	**1**	**5**	**6**	**2**
	NHL Totals		**1247**	**428**	**1006**	**1434**	**833**	**130**	**40**	**82**	**122**	**87**

Won Alka-Seltzer Plus Award (1995) • Won Frank J. Selke Trophy (1995) • Won Lady Byng Trophy (1995, 1998)

Played in NHL All-Star Game (1983, 1985, 1990, 1996)

Traded to **Pittsburgh** by **Hartford** with Grant Jennings and Ulf Samuelsson for John Cullen, Jeff Parker and Zarley Zalapski, March 4, 1991. Signed as a free agent by **Carolina**, July 13, 1998.

FRANCZ, ROBERT (FRANZ) PHX.

Left wing. Shoots left. 6'1", 194 lbs. Born, Bad Muskau, East Germany, March 30, 1978.
(Phoenix's 4th choice, 151st overall, in 1997 Entry Draft).

			Regular Season					Playoffs				
Season	Club	Lea	GP	G	A	TP	PIM	GP	G	A	TP	PIM
1995-96	Augsburg	Ger-Jr.	7	1	1	2	62	....	....	....	....	....
	Augsburg	Germany	36	0	1	1	43	6	0	0	0	0
1996-97	Peterborough	OHL	60	9	21	30	149	8	1	1	2	17
1997-98	Peterborough	OHL	60	24	27	51	135	4	1	0	1	10

FRASER, IAIN

Center. Shoots left. 5'10", 175 lbs. Born, Scarborough, Ont., August 10, 1969.
(NY Islanders' 14th choice, 233rd overall, in 1989 Entry Draft).

			Regular Season					Playoffs				
Season	Club	Lea	GP	G	A	TP	PIM	GP	G	A	TP	PIM
1986-87	Oshawa	OHL	5	1	2	3	0	....	....	....	....	....
1987-88	Oshawa	OHL	16	4	4	8	22	6	2	3	5	2
1988-89	Oshawa	OHL	62	33	57	90	87	6	2	8	10	12
1989-90	Oshawa	OHL	56	40	65	105	75	17	10	*22	32	8
1990-91	Capital District	AHL	32	5	13	18	16	....	....	....	....	....
	Richmond	ECHL	3	1	1	2	0	....	....	....	....	....
1991-92	Capital District	AHL	45	9	11	20	24	....	....	....	....	....
1992-93	**NY Islanders**	**NHL**	**7**	**2**	**2**	**4**	**2**	....	....	....	....	....
	Capital District	AHL	74	41	69	110	16	4	0	1	1	0
1993-94	**Quebec**	**NHL**	**60**	**17**	**20**	**37**	**23**	....	....	....	....	....
1994-95	**Dallas**	**NHL**	**4**	**0**	**0**	**0**	**0**	....	....	....	....	....
	Edmonton	**NHL**	**9**	**3**	**0**	**3**	**0**	....	....	....	....	....
	Denver	IHL	1	0	0	0	0	....	....	....	....	....
1995-96	**Winnipeg**	**NHL**	**12**	**1**	**1**	**2**	**4**	**4**	**0**	**0**	**0**	**0**
	Springfield	AHL	53	24	47	71	27	6	0	6	6	2
1996-97	**San Jose**	**NHL**	**2**	**0**	**0**	**0**	**2**	....	....	....	....	....
	Kentucky	AHL	57	27	33	60	24	....	....	....	....	....
1997-98	Kansas City	IHL	77	16	44	60	45	11	2	6	8	6
	NHL Totals		**94**	**23**	**23**	**46**	**31**	**4**	**0**	**0**	**0**	**0**

Memorial Cup All-Star Team (1990) • Won Stafford Smythe Memorial Trophy (Memorial Cup Tournament MVP) (1990) • AHL Second All-Star Team (1993)

Signed as a free agent by **Quebec**, August 3, 1993. Traded to **Dallas** by **Quebec** for Dallas' 7th round choice (Dan Hinote) in 1996 Entry Draft, January 31, 1995. Claimed on waivers by **Edmonton** from **Dallas**, March 3, 1995. Signed as a free agent by **Winnipeg**, October 11, 1995. Signed as a free agent by **San Jose**, September 1, 1996.

FRASER, SCOTT — NYR

Center. Shoots right. 6'1", 178 lbs. Born, Moncton, N.B., May 3, 1972.
(Montreal's 12th choice, 193rd overall, in 1991 Entry Draft).

			Regular Season					Playoffs				
Season	Club	Lea	GP	G	A	TP	PIM	GP	G	A	TP	PIM
1990-91	Dartmouth	ECAC	24	10	10	20	30	....	....	....	....	....
1991-92	Dartmouth	ECAC	24	11	7	18	60	....	....	....	....	....
1992-93	Dartmouth	ECAC	26	21	23	44	13	....	....	....	....	....
	Canada	Nat-Tm	5	1	0	1	0	....	....	....	....	....
1993-94	Dartmouth	ECAC	24	17	13	30	34	....	....	....	....	....
	Canada	Nat-Tm	4	0	1	1	4	....	....	....	....	....
1994-95	Fredericton	AHL	65	23	25	48	36	16	3	5	8	14
	Wheeling	ECHL	8	4	2	6	8	....	....	....	....	....
1995-96	**Montreal**	**NHL**	**15**	**2**	**0**	**2**	**4**	....	....	....	....	....
	Fredericton	AHL	58	37	37	74	43	10	9	7	16	2
1996-97	Fredericton	AHL	7	3	8	11	0	....	....	....	....	....
	Saint John	AHL	37	22	10	32	24	....	....	....	....	....
	San Antonio	IHL	8	0	1	1	2	....	....	....	....	....
	Carolina	AHL	18	9	19	28	12	....	....	....	....	....
1997-98	**Edmonton**	**NHL**	**29**	**12**	**11**	**23**	**6**	**11**	**1**	**1**	**2**	**0**
	Hamilton	AHL	50	29	32	61	26	....	....	....	....	....
	NHL Totals		**44**	**14**	**11**	**25**	**10**	**11**	**1**	**1**	**2**	**0**

ECAC Second All-Star Team (1993)

Traded to **Calgary** by **Montreal** for David Ling and Calgary's 6th round choice in 1998 Entry Draft, October 24, 1996. Signed as a free agent by **Edmonton**, July 28, 1997. Signed as a free agent by **NY Rangers**, July 2, 1998.

FREADRICH, KYLE (FREE-drihk) — VAN.

Left wing. Shoots left. 6'6", 225 lbs. Born, Edmonton, Alta., December 28, 1978.
(Vancouver's 4th choice, 64th overall, in 1997 Entry Draft).

			Regular Season					Playoffs				
Season	Club	Lea	GP	G	A	TP	PIM	GP	G	A	TP	PIM
1996-97	Prince George	WHL	12	0	0	0	12	....	....	....	....	....
	Regina	WHL	50	1	3	4	152	4	0	0	0	8
1997-98	Regina	WHL	62	6	5	11	259	9	0	1	1	25

FREER, MARK (FRIHR)

Center. Shoots left. 5'10", 180 lbs. Born, Peterborough, Ont., July 14, 1968.

			Regular Season					Playoffs				
Season	Club	Lea	GP	G	A	TP	PIM	GP	G	A	TP	PIM
1985-86	Peterborough	OHL	65	16	28	44	24	14	3	4	7	13
1986-87	Peterborough	OHL	65	39	43	82	44	12	2	6	8	5
	Philadelphia	**NHL**	**1**	**0**	**1**	**1**	**0**	....	....	....	....	....
1987-88	Peterborough	OHL	63	38	70	108	63	12	5	12	17	4
	Philadelphia	**NHL**	**1**	**0**	**0**	**0**	**0**	....	....	....	....	....
1988-89	**Philadelphia**	**NHL**	**5**	**0**	**1**	**1**	**0**	....	....	....	....	....
	Hershey	AHL	75	30	49	79	77	12	4	6	10	2
1989-90	**Philadelphia**	**NHL**	**2**	**0**	**0**	**0**	**0**	....	....	....	....	....
	Hershey	AHL	65	28	36	64	31	....	....	....	....	....
1990-91	Hershey	AHL	77	18	44	62	45	7	1	3	4	17
1991-92	**Philadelphia**	**NHL**	**50**	**6**	**7**	**13**	**18**	....	....	....	....	....
	Hershey	AHL	31	13	11	24	38	6	0	3	3	2
1992-93	**Ottawa**	**NHL**	**63**	**10**	**14**	**24**	**39**	....	....	....	....	....
1993-94	**Calgary**	**NHL**	**2**	**0**	**0**	**0**	**4**	....	....	....	....	....
	Saint John	AHL	77	33	53	86	45	7	2	4	6	16
1994-95	Houston	IHL	80	38	42	80	54	4	0	1	1	4
1995-96	Houston	IHL	80	22	31	53	67	....	....	....	....	....
1996-97	Houston	IHL	81	21	36	57	43	12	2	3	5	4
1997-98	Houston	IHL	74	14	38	52	41	4	2	2	4	4
	NHL Totals		**124**	**16**	**23**	**39**	**61**	....	....	....	....	....

Signed as a free agent by **Philadelphia**, October 7, 1986. Claimed by **Ottawa** from **Philadelphia** in Expansion Draft, June 18, 1992. Signed as a free agent by **Calgary**, August 10, 1993.

FRIEDMAN, DOUG — NSH.

Left wing. Shoots left. 6'1", 195 lbs. Born, Cape Elizabeth, ME, September 1, 1971.
(Quebec's 13th choice, 222nd overall, in 1991 Entry Draft).

			Regular Season					Playoffs				
Season	Club	Lea	GP	G	A	TP	PIM	GP	G	A	TP	PIM
1989-90	Lawrence Acad.	H.S.	20	9	26	35	....	....	....	....	....	....
1990-91	Boston University	H.E.	36	6	6	12	37	....	....	....	....	....
1991-92	Boston University	H.E.	34	11	8	19	42	....	....	....	....	....
1992-93	Boston University	H.E.	38	17	24	41	62	....	....	....	....	....
1993-94	Boston University	H.E.	41	9	23	32	110	....	....	....	....	....
1994-95	Cornwall	AHL	55	6	9	15	56	3	0	0	0	0
1995-96	Cornwall	AHL	80	12	22	34	178	8	1	1	2	17
1996-97	Hershey	AHL	61	12	21	33	245	23	6	9	15	49
1997-98	**Edmonton**	**NHL**	**16**	**0**	**0**	**0**	**20**	....	....	....	....	....
	Hamilton	AHL	55	19	27	46	235	9	4	4	8	40
	NHL Totals		**16**	**0**	**0**	**0**	**20**	....	....	....	....	....

Rights transferred to **Colorado** after **Quebec** franchise relocated, June 21, 1995. Signed as a free agent by **Edmonton**, July 14, 1997. Claimed by **Nashville** from **Edmonton** in Expansion Draft, June 26, 1998. Signed as a free agent by **NY Rangers**, July 2, 1998.

FRIESEN, JEFF (FREE-zuhn) — S.J.

Center. Shoots left. 6'1", 200 lbs. Born, Meadow Lake, Sask., August 5, 1976.
(San Jose's 1st choice, 11th overall, in 1994 Entry Draft).

			Regular Season					Playoffs				
Season	Club	Lea	GP	G	A	TP	PIM	GP	G	A	TP	PIM
1991-92	Regina	WHL	4	3	1	4	2	....	....	....	....	....
1992-93	Regina	WHL	70	45	38	83	23	13	7	10	17	8
1993-94	Regina	WHL	66	51	67	118	48	4	3	2	5	2
1994-95	Regina	WHL	25	21	23	44	22	....	....	....	....	....
	San Jose	**NHL**	**48**	**15**	**10**	**25**	**14**	**11**	**1**	**5**	**6**	**4**
1995-96	**San Jose**	**NHL**	**79**	**15**	**31**	**46**	**42**	....	....	....	....	....
1996-97	**San Jose**	**NHL**	**82**	**28**	**34**	**62**	**75**	....	....	....	....	....
1997-98	**San Jose**	**NHL**	**79**	**31**	**32**	**63**	**40**	**6**	**0**	**1**	**1**	**2**
	NHL Totals		**288**	**89**	**107**	**196**	**171**	**17**	**1**	**6**	**7**	**6**

Canadian Major Junior Rookie of the Year (1993) • NHL/Upper Deck All-Rookie Team (1995)

FRYLEN, EDVIN (FRYUH-lehn) — ST.L.

Defense. Shoots left. 6', 211 lbs. Born, Jarfalla, Sweden, December 23, 1975.
(St. Louis' 3rd choice, 120th overall, in 1994 Entry Draft).

			Regular Season					Playoffs				
Season	Club	Lea	GP	G	A	TP	PIM	GP	G	A	TP	PIM
1991-92	Vasteras IK	Sweden	2	0	0	0	0	....	....	....	....	....
1992-93	Vasteras IK	Sweden	29	0	2	2	14	3	0	0	0	0
1993-94	Vasteras IK	Sweden	32	1	0	1	26	....	....	....	....	....
1994-95	Vasteras IK	Sweden	25	2	1	3	14	4	0	0	0	4
1995-96	Vasteras IK	Sweden	39	8	5	13	16	....	....	....	....	....
1996-97	Vasteras IK	Sweden	47	8	3	11	32	....	....	....	....	....
1997-98	Vasteras IK	Sweden	46	4	7	11	36	....	....	....	....	....

GAFFANEY, BRIAN — PIT.

Defense. Shoots left. 6'5", 205 lbs. Born, Alexandria, MN, October 4, 1977.
(Pittsburgh's 2nd choice, 44th overall, in 1997 Entry Draft).

			Regular Season					Playoffs				
Season	Club	Lea	GP	G	A	TP	PIM	GP	G	A	TP	PIM
1996-97	North Iowa	USHL	48	8	13	21	49	....	....	....	....	....
1997-98	St. Cloud State	WCHA	26	0	2	2	37	....	....	....	....	....

GAFFNEY, MIKE — OTT.

Defense. Shoots right. 6'1", 202 lbs. Born, Worchester, MA, June 19, 1976.
(Ottawa's 4th choice, 131st overall, in 1994 Entry Draft).

			Regular Season					Playoffs				
Season	Club	Lea	GP	G	A	TP	PIM	GP	G	A	TP	PIM
1993-94	St. John's High	H.S.	20	6	16	22	8	....	....	....	....	....
1994-95	U-Mass.-Amherst	H.E.	33	1	4	5	38	....	....	....	....	....
1995-96	U-Mass.-Amherst	H.E.	33	0	6	6	41	....	....	....	....	....
1996-97	U-Mass.-Amherst	H.E.	34	7	13	20	49	....	....	....	....	....
1997-98	U-Mass.-Amherst	H.E.	33	6	7	13	22	....	....	....	....	....

GAGNE, SIMON (GAH-nyay) — PHI.

Center. Shoots left. 6', 165 lbs. Born, Ste. Foy, Que., February 29, 1980.
(Philadelphia's 1st choice, 22nd overall, in 1998 Entry Draft).

			Regular Season					Playoffs				
Season	Club	Lea	GP	G	A	TP	PIM	GP	G	A	TP	PIM
1996-97	Beauport	QMJHL	51	9	22	31	49	....	....	....	....	....
1997-98	Quebec	QMJHL	53	30	39	69	26	12	11	5	16	23

GAGNER, DAVE (GAH-nyay) — FLA.

Center. Shoots left. 5'10", 188 lbs. Born, Chatham, Ont., December 11, 1964.
(NY Rangers' 1st choice, 12th overall, in 1983 Entry Draft).

			Regular Season					Playoffs				
Season	Club	Lea	GP	G	A	TP	PIM	GP	G	A	TP	PIM
1981-82	Brantford	OHL	68	30	46	76	31	11	3	6	9	6
1982-83	Brantford	OHL	70	55	66	121	57	8	5	5	10	4
1983-84	Brantford	OHL	12	7	13	20	4	6	0	4	4	6
	Canada	Nat-Tm	50	19	18	37	26	....	....	....	....	....
	Canada	Olympics	7	5	2	7	6	....	....	....	....	....
1984-85	**NY Rangers**	**NHL**	**38**	**6**	**6**	**12**	**16**	....	....	....	....	....
	New Haven	AHL	38	13	20	33	23	....	....	....	....	....
1985-86	**NY Rangers**	**NHL**	**32**	**4**	**6**	**10**	**19**	....	....	....	....	....
	New Haven	AHL	16	10	11	21	11	4	1	2	3	2
1986-87	**NY Rangers**	**NHL**	**10**	**1**	**4**	**5**	**12**	....	....	....	....	....
	New Haven	AHL	56	22	41	63	50	7	1	5	6	18
1987-88	**Minnesota**	**NHL**	**51**	**8**	**11**	**19**	**55**	....	....	....	....	....
	Kalamazoo	IHL	14	16	10	26	26	....	....	....	....	....
1988-89	**Minnesota**	**NHL**	**75**	**35**	**43**	**78**	**104**	....	....	....	....	....
	Kalamazoo	IHL	1	0	1	1	4	....	....	....	....	....
1989-90	**Minnesota**	**NHL**	**79**	**40**	**38**	**78**	**54**	**7**	**2**	**3**	**5**	**16**
1990-91	**Minnesota**	**NHL**	**73**	**40**	**42**	**82**	**114**	**23**	**12**	**15**	**27**	**28**
1991-92	**Minnesota**	**NHL**	**78**	**31**	**40**	**71**	**107**	**7**	**2**	**4**	**6**	**8**
1992-93	**Minnesota**	**NHL**	**84**	**33**	**43**	**76**	**143**	....	....	....	....	....
1993-94	**Dallas**	**NHL**	**76**	**32**	**29**	**61**	**83**	**9**	**5**	**1**	**6**	**2**
1994-95	Courmaosta	Italy	3	0	0	0	0	....	....	....	....	....
	Courmaosta	EuroHL	1	0	4	4	0	....	....	....	....	....
	Dallas	**NHL**	**48**	**14**	**28**	**42**	**42**	**5**	**1**	**1**	**2**	**4**
1995-96	**Dallas**	**NHL**	**45**	**14**	**13**	**27**	**44**	....	....	....	....	....
	Toronto	**NHL**	**28**	**7**	**15**	**22**	**59**	**6**	**0**	**2**	**2**	**6**
1996-97	**Calgary**	**NHL**	**82**	**27**	**33**	**60**	**48**	....	....	....	....	....
1997-98	**Florida**	**NHL**	**78**	**20**	**28**	**48**	**55**	....	....	....	....	....
	NHL Totals		**877**	**312**	**379**	**691**	**955**	**57**	**22**	**26**	**48**	**64**

OHL Second All-Star Team (1983)

Played in NHL All-Star Game (1991)

Traded to **Minnesota** by **NY Rangers** with Jay Caulfield for Jari Gronstrand and Paul Boutilier, October 8, 1987. Transferred to **Dallas** after **Minnesota** franchise relocated, June 9, 1993. Traded to **Toronto** by **Dallas** with Dallas' 6th round choice (Dmitriy Yakushin) in 1996 Entry Draft for Benoit Hogue and Randy Wood, January 29, 1996. Traded to **Calgary** by **Toronto** for Calgary's 3rd round choice (Mike Lankshear) in 1996 Entry Draft, June 22, 1996. Signed as a free agent by **Florida**, July 12, 1997.

GAGNON, SEAN (gah-NYAWN) — PHX.

Defense. Shoots Left. 6'2", 210 lbs. Born, Sault Ste. Marie, Ont., September 11, 1973.

			Regular Season					Playoffs				
Season	Club	Lea	GP	G	A	TP	PIM	GP	G	A	TP	PIM
1991-92	Sudbury	OHL	44	3	4	7	60	5	0	1	1	0
1992-93	Sudbury	OHL	6	1	1	2	16	....	....	....	....	....
	Ottawa	OHL	33	2	10	12	68	....	....	....	....	....
	S.S. Marie	OHL	24	1	5	6	65	15	2	2	4	25
1993-94	S.S. Marie	OHL	42	4	12	16	147	14	1	1	2	52
1994-95	Dayton	ECHL	68	9	23	32	339	8	0	3	3	69
1995-96	Dayton	ECHL	68	7	22	29	326	3	0	1	1	33
1996-97	Fort Wayne	IHL	72	7	7	14	457	....	....	....	....	....
1997-98	**Phoenix**	**NHL**	**5**	**0**	**1**	**1**	**14**	....	....	....	....	....
	Springfield	AHL	54	4	13	17	330	2	0	1	1	17
	NHL Totals		**5**	**0**	**1**	**1**	**14**	....	....	....	....	....

Signed as a free agent by **Phoenix**, May 14, 1997.

GAINEY, STEVE — DAL.

Center. Shoots left. 6', 180 lbs. Born, Montreal, Que., January 26, 1979.
(Dallas' 3rd choice, 77th overall, in 1997 Entry Draft).

			Regular Season					Playoffs				
Season	Club	Lea	GP	G	A	TP	PIM	GP	G	A	TP	PIM
1995-96	Kamloops	WHL	49	1	4	5	40	3	0	0	0	0
1996-97	Kamloops	WHL	60	9	18	27	60	2	0	0	0	9
1997-98	Kamloops	WHL	68	21	34	55	93	7	1	7	8	15

GALANOV, MAXIM (gah-LAH-nahf, mahx-EEM) NYR

Defense. Shoots left. 6'1", 195 lbs. Born, Krasnoyarsk, USSR, March 13, 1974.
(NY Rangers' 3rd choice, 61st overall, in 1993 Entry Draft).

			Regular Season					Playoffs				
Season	Club	Lea	GP	G	A	TP	PIM	GP	G	A	TP	PIM
1992-93	Lada	CIS	41	4	2	6	12	10	1	1	2	12
1993-94	Lada	CIS	7	1	0	1	4	12	1	0	1	8
1994-95	Lada	CIS	45	5	6	11	54	9	0	1	1	12
1995-96	Binghamton	AHL	72	17	36	53	24	4	1	1	2	0
1996-97	Binghamton	AHL	73	13	30	43	30	3	0	0	0	2
1997-98	NY Rangers	NHL	6	0	1	1	2	....	....	....	....	....
	Hartford	AHL	61	6	24	30	22	13	3	6	9	2
	NHL Totals		6	0	1	1	2	....	....	....	....	....

GALLEY, GARRY (GA-lee) L.A.

Defense. Shoots left. 6', 207 lbs. Born, Montreal, Que., April 16, 1963.
(Los Angeles' 4th choice, 103rd overall, in 1983 Entry Draft).

			Regular Season					Playoffs				
Season	Club	Lea	GP	G	A	TP	PIM	GP	G	A	TP	PIM
1981-82	Bowling Green	CCHA	42	3	36	39	48	....	....	....	....	....
1982-83	Bowling Green	CCHA	40	17	29	46	40	....	....	....	....	....
1983-84	Bowling Green	CCHA	44	15	52	67	61	....	....	....	....	....
1984-85	Los Angeles	NHL	78	8	30	38	82	3	1	0	1	2
1985-86	Los Angeles	NHL	49	9	13	22	46	....	....	....	....	....
	New Haven	AHL	4	2	6	8	6	....	....	....	....	....
1986-87	Los Angeles	NHL	30	5	11	16	57	....	....	....	....	....
	Washington	NHL	18	1	10	11	10	2	0	0	0	0
1987-88	Washington	NHL	58	7	23	30	44	13	2	4	6	13
1988-89	Boston	NHL	78	8	22	30	80	9	0	1	1	33
1989-90	Boston	NHL	71	8	27	35	75	21	3	3	6	34
1990-91	Boston	NHL	70	6	21	27	84	16	1	5	6	17
1991-92	Boston	NHL	38	2	12	14	83	....	....	....	....	....
	Philadelphia	NHL	39	3	15	18	34	....	....	....	....	....
1992-93	Philadelphia	NHL	83	13	49	62	115	....	....	....	....	....
1993-94	Philadelphia	NHL	81	10	60	70	91	....	....	....	....	....
1994-95	Philadelphia	NHL	33	2	20	22	20	....	....	....	....	....
	Buffalo	NHL	14	1	9	10	10	5	0	3	3	4
1995-96	Buffalo	NHL	78	10	44	54	81	....	....	....	....	....
1996-97	Buffalo	NHL	71	4	34	38	102	12	0	6	6	14
1997-98	Los Angeles	NHL	74	9	28	37	63	4	0	1	1	2
	NHL Totals		963	106	428	534	1077	85	7	23	30	119

CCHA First All-Star Team (1983, 1984) • NCAA East First All-American Team (1984) • NCAA Championship All-Tournament Team (1984)

Played in NHL All-Star Game (1991, 1994)

Traded to **Washington** by **LA Kings** for Al Jensen, February 14, 1987. Signed as a free agent by **Boston**, July 8, 1988. Traded to **Philadelphia** by **Boston** with Wes Walz and Boston's 3rd round choice (Milos Holan) in 1993 Entry Draft for Gord Murphy, Brian Dobbin, Philadelphia's 3rd round choice (Sergei Zholtok) in 1992 Entry Draft and 4th round choice (Charles Paquette) in 1993 Entry Draft, January 2, 1992. Traded to **Buffalo** by **Philadelphia** for Petr Svoboda, April 7, 1995. Signed as a free agent by **LA Kings**, July 15, 1997.

GARDINER, BRUCE OTT.

Center. Shoots right. 6'1", 193 lbs. Born, Barrie, Ont., February 11, 1972.
(St. Louis' 6th choice, 131st overall, in 1991 Entry Draft).

			Regular Season					Playoffs				
Season	Club	Lea	GP	G	A	TP	PIM	GP	G	A	TP	PIM
1990-91	Colgate	ECAC	27	4	9	13	72	....	....	....	....	....
1991-92	Colgate	ECAC	23	7	8	15	77	....	....	....	....	....
1992-93	Colgate	ECAC	33	17	12	29	64	....	....	....	....	....
1993-94	Colgate	ECAC	33	23	23	46	68	....	....	....	....	....
	Peoria	IHL	3	0	0	0	0	....	....	....	....	....
1994-95	P.E.I.	AHL	72	17	20	37	132	7	4	1	5	4
1995-96	P.E.I.	AHL	38	11	13	24	87	5	2	4	6	4
1996-97	Ottawa	NHL	67	11	10	21	49	7	0	1	1	2
1997-98	Ottawa	NHL	55	7	11	18	50	11	1	3	4	2
	NHL Totals		122	18	21	39	99	18	1	4	5	4

ECAC Second All-Star Team (1994)

Signed as a free agent by **Ottawa**, June 14, 1994.

GARDINER, PETER CHI.

Right wing. Shoots right. 6'5", 220 lbs. Born, Toronto, Ont., September 29, 1977.
(Chicago's 6th choice, 120th overall, in 1997 Entry Draft).

			Regular Season					Playoffs				
Season	Club	Lea	GP	G	A	TP	PIM	GP	G	A	TP	PIM
1996-97	RPI	ECAC	36	10	21	31	47	....	....	....	....	....
1997-98	RPI	ECAC	35	10	9	19	52	....	....	....	....	....

GARPENLOV, JOHAN (GAHR-pehn-LAHV, YOH-hahn) FLA.

Left wing. Shoots left. 5'11", 185 lbs. Born, Stockholm, Sweden, March 21, 1968.
(Detroit's 5th choice, 85th overall, in 1986 Entry Draft).

			Regular Season					Playoffs				
Season	Club	Lea	GP	G	A	TP	PIM	GP	G	A	TP	PIM
1986-87	Djurgarden	Sweden	29	5	8	13	22	2	0	0	0	0
1987-88	Djurgarden	Sweden	30	7	10	17	12	3	1	3	4	4
1988-89	Djurgarden	Sweden	36	12	19	31	20	8	3	4	7	10
1989-90	Djurgarden	Sweden	39	20	13	33	35	8	2	4	6	4
1990-91	Detroit	NHL	71	18	22	40	18	6	0	1	1	4
1991-92	Detroit	NHL	16	1	1	2	4	....	....	....	....	....
	Adirondack	AHL	9	3	3	6	6	....	....	....	....	....
	San Jose	NHL	12	5	6	11	4	....	....	....	....	....
1992-93	San Jose	NHL	79	22	44	66	56	....	....	....	....	....
1993-94	San Jose	NHL	80	18	35	53	28	14	4	6	10	6
1994-95	San Jose	NHL	13	1	1	2	2	....	....	....	....	....
	Florida	NHL	27	3	9	12	0	....	....	....	....	....
1995-96	Florida	NHL	82	23	28	51	36	20	4	2	6	8
1996-97	Florida	NHL	53	11	25	36	47	4	2	0	2	4
1997-98	Florida	NHL	39	2	3	5	8	....	....	....	....	....
	NHL Totals		472	104	174	278	203	44	10	9	19	22

Traded to **San Jose** by **Detroit** for Bob McGill and Vancouver's 8th round choice (previously acquired, San Jose selected C.J. Denomme) in 1992 Entry Draft, March 9, 1992. Traded to **Florida** by **San Jose** for future considerations, March 3, 1995.

GARTNER, MIKE

Right wing. Shoots right. 6', 187 lbs. Born, Ottawa, Ont., October 29, 1959.
(Washington's 1st choice, 4th overall, in 1979 Entry Draft).

			Regular Season					Playoffs				
Season	Club	Lea	GP	G	A	TP	PIM	GP	G	A	TP	PIM
1976-77	Niagara Falls	OHA	62	33	42	75	125	....	....	....	....	....
1977-78	Niagara Falls	OHA	64	41	49	90	56	....	....	....	....	....
1978-79	Cincinnati	WHA	78	27	25	52	123	3	0	2	2	2
1979-80	Washington	NHL	77	36	32	68	66	....	....	....	....	....
1980-81	Washington	NHL	80	48	46	94	100	....	....	....	....	....
1981-82	Washington	NHL	80	35	45	80	121	....	....	....	....	....
1982-83	Washington	NHL	73	38	38	76	54	4	0	0	0	4
1983-84	Washington	NHL	80	40	45	85	90	8	3	7	10	16
1984-85	Washington	NHL	80	50	52	102	71	5	4	3	7	9
1985-86	Washington	NHL	74	35	40	75	63	9	2	10	12	4
1986-87	Washington	NHL	78	41	32	73	61	7	4	3	7	14
1987-88	Washington	NHL	80	48	33	81	73	14	3	4	7	14
1988-89	Washington	NHL	56	26	29	55	71	....	....	....	....	....
	Minnesota	NHL	13	7	7	14	2	5	0	0	0	6
1989-90	Minnesota	NHL	67	34	36	70	32	....	....	....	....	....
	NY Rangers	NHL	12	11	5	16	6	10	5	3	8	12
1990-91	NY Rangers	NHL	79	49	20	69	53	6	1	1	2	0
1991-92	NY Rangers	NHL	76	40	41	81	55	13	8	8	16	4
1992-93	NY Rangers	NHL	84	45	23	68	59	....	....	....	....	....
1993-94	NY Rangers	NHL	71	28	24	52	58	....	....	....	....	....
	Toronto	NHL	10	6	6	12	4	18	5	6	11	14
1994-95	Toronto	NHL	38	12	8	20	6	5	2	2	4	2
1995-96	Toronto	NHL	82	35	19	54	52	6	4	1	5	4
1996-97	Phoenix	NHL	82	32	31	63	38	7	1	2	3	4
1997-98	Phoenix	NHL	60	12	15	27	24	5	1	0	1	18
	NHL Totals		1432	708	627	1335	1159	122	43	50	93	125

OHA First All-Star Team (1978)

Played in NHL All-Star Game (1981, 1985, 1986, 1988, 1990, 1993, 1996)

Signed as a underage free agent by **Birmingham** (WHA), May, 1978. Traded to **Minnesota** by **Washington** with Larry Murphy for Dino Ciccarelli and Bob Rouse, March 7, 1989. Traded to **NY Rangers** by **Minnesota** for Ulf Dahlen, LA Kings' 4th round choice (previously acquired, Minnesota selected Cal McGowan) in 1990 Entry Draft and future considerations, March 6, 1990. Traded to **Toronto** by **NY Rangers** for Glenn Anderson, the rights to Scott Malone and Toronto's 4th round choice (Alexander Korobolin) in 1994 Entry Draft, March 21, 1994. Traded to **Phoenix** by **Toronto** for Chicago's 4th round choice (previously acquired, Toronto selected Vladimir Antipov) in 1996 Entry Draft, June 22, 1996.

GASKINS, JON EDM.

Defense. Shoots left. 6'3", 205 lbs. Born, Dallas, TX, January 11, 1976.
(Edmonton's 8th choice, 110th overall, in 1994 Entry Draft).

			Regular Season					Playoffs				
Season	Club	Lea	GP	G	A	TP	PIM	GP	G	A	TP	PIM
1993-94	Dubuque	USHL	30	6	13	19	52	....	....	....	....	....
1994-95	Michigan State	CCHA	28	1	5	6	18	....	....	....	....	....
1995-96	Michigan State	CCHA	17	0	1	1	4	....	....	....	....	....
1996-97	Michigan State	CCHA	40	1	5	6	12	....	....	....	....	....
1997-98	Michigan State	CCHA	34	1	6	7	8	....	....	....	....	....

GAUDREAU, ROB (GUH-droh)

Right wing. Shoots right. 5'11", 185 lbs. Born, Lincoln, RI, January 20, 1970.
(Pittsburgh's 8th choice, 172nd overall, in 1988 Entry Draft).

			Regular Season					Playoffs				
Season	Club	Lea	GP	G	A	TP	PIM	GP	G	A	TP	PIM
1987-88	Bishop Hendrick	H.S.	32	52	60	112	....	....	....	....	....	....
1988-89	Providence	H.E.	42	28	29	57	32	....	....	....	....	....
1989-90	Providence	H.E.	32	20	18	38	12	....	....	....	....	....
1990-91	Providence	H.E.	36	34	27	61	20	....	....	....	....	....
1991-92	Providence	H.E.	36	21	34	55	22	....	....	....	....	....
1992-93	San Jose	NHL	59	23	20	43	18	....	....	....	....	....
	Kansas City	IHL	19	8	6	14	6	....	....	....	....	....
1993-94	San Jose	NHL	84	15	20	35	28	14	2	0	2	0
1994-95	Ottawa	NHL	36	5	9	14	8	....	....	....	....	....
1995-96	Ottawa	NHL	52	8	5	13	15	....	....	....	....	....
	P.E.I.	AHL	3	2	0	2	4	....	....	....	....	....
1996-97	Chaux-de-Fonds	Switz.	37	19	23	42	62	....	....	....	....	....
1997-98			STATISTICS NOT AVAILABLE									
	NHL Totals		231	51	54	105	69	14	2	0	2	0

Hockey East Second All-Star Team (1991) • Hockey East First All-Star Team (1992) • NCAA East Second All-American Team (1992)

Rights traded to **Minnesota** by **Pittsburgh** for Richard Zemlak, November 1, 1988. Claimed by **San Jose** from **Minnesota** in Dispersal Draft, May 30, 1991. Claimed by **Ottawa** from **San Jose** in Waiver Draft, January 18, 1995.

GAUL, MICHAEL NYI

Defense. Shoots right. 6'1", 200 lbs. Born, Lachine, Que., April 22, 1973.
(Los Angeles' 10th choice, 262nd overall, in 1991 Entry Draft).

			Regular Season					Playoffs				
Season	Club	Lea	GP	G	A	TP	PIM	GP	G	A	TP	PIM
1990-91	St. Lawrence	ECAC	31	1	3	4	46	....	....	....	....	....
1991-92	Laval	QMJHL	50	6	38	44	44	10	0	2	2	20
1992-93	Laval	QMJHL	57	16	57	73	66	13	3	10	13	10
1993-94	Laval	QMJHL	22	10	17	27	24	21	5	15	20	14
1994-95	Phoenix	IHL	4	0	1	1	2	....	....	....	....	....
	Knoxville	ECHL	68	13	41	54	51	4	2	1	3	2
1995-96	Knoxville	ECHL	54	13	48	61	44	....	....	....	....	....
1996-97	Timmendorf	Ger-2	51	40	52	92	100	....	....	....	....	....
1997-98	Hershey	AHL	60	12	47	59	69	7	0	7	7	6

Signed as a free agent by **NY Islanders**, July 16, 1998.

GAUTHIER, DENIS (GOH-tyay)

Defense. Shoots left. 6'2", 195 lbs. Born, Montreal, Que., October 1, 1976.
(Calgary's 1st choice, 20th overall, in 1995 Entry Draft).

			Regular Season					Playoffs				
Season	Club	Lea	GP	G	A	TP	PIM	GP	G	A	TP	PIM
1992-93	Drummondville	QMJHL	60	1	7	8	136	10	0	5	5	40
1993-94	Drummondville	QMJHL	60	0	7	7	176	9	2	0	2	41
1994-95	Drummondville	QMJHL	64	9	31	40	190	4	0	5	5	12
1995-96	Drummondville	QMJHL	53	25	49	74	140	6	4	4	8	32
	Saint John	AHL	5	2	0	2	8	16	1	6	7	20
1996-97	Saint John	AHL	73	3	28	31	74	5	0	0	0	6
1997-98	Calgary	NHL	10	0	0	0	16	....	....	....	....	....
	Saint John	AHL	68	4	20	24	154	21	0	4	4	83
	NHL Totals		10	0	0	0	16	....	....	....	....	....

QMJHL First All-Star Team (1996) • Canadian Major Junior First All-Star Team (1996)

GAUVREAU, BRENT — CGY.

Right wing. Shoots right. 6'3", 191 lbs. Born, Sudbury, Ont., June 29, 1980.
(Calgary's 6th choice, 120th overall, in 1998 Entry Draft).

			Regular Season					Playoffs				
Season	Club	Lea	GP	G	A	TP	PIM	GP	G	A	TP	PIM
1996-97	Oshawa	OHL	59	8	13	21	13	18	1	5	6	2
1997-98	Oshawa	OHL	66	25	42	67	39	7	3	1	4	2

GAVEY, AARON (GAY-vee) — DAL.

Center. Shoots left. 6'2", 200 lbs. Born, Sudbury, Ont., February 22, 1974.
(Tampa Bay's 4th choice, 74th overall, in 1992 Entry Draft).

			Regular Season					Playoffs				
Season	Club	Lea	GP	G	A	TP	PIM	GP	G	A	TP	PIM
1991-92	S.S. Marie	OHL	48	7	11	18	27	19	5	1	6	10
1992-93	S.S. Marie	OHL	62	45	39	84	116	18	5	9	14	36
1993-94	S.S. Marie	OHL	60	42	60	102	116	14	11	10	21	22
1994-95	Atlanta	IHL	66	18	17	35	85	5	0	1	1	9
1995-96	**Tampa Bay**	**NHL**	**73**	**8**	**4**	**12**	**56**	**6**	**0**	**0**	**0**	**4**
1996-97	**Tampa Bay**	**NHL**	**16**	**1**	**2**	**3**	**12**	....	....	....	....	....
	Calgary	**NHL**	**41**	**7**	**9**	**16**	**34**	....	....	....	....	....
1997-98	**Calgary**	**NHL**	**26**	**2**	**3**	**5**	**24**	....	....	....	....	....
	Saint John	AHL	8	4	3	7	28	....	....	....	....	....
	NHL Totals		**156**	**18**	**18**	**36**	**126**	**6**	**0**	**0**	**0**	**4**

Traded to **Calgary** by **Tampa Bay** for Rick Tabaracci, November 19, 1996. Traded to **Dallas** by **Calgary** for Bob Bassen, July 14, 1998.

GELINAS, MARTIN (ZHEHL-in-nuh, MAHR-ta) — CAR.

Left wing. Shoots left. 5'11", 195 lbs. Born, Shawinigan, Que., June 5, 1970.
(Los Angeles' 1st choice, 7th overall, in 1988 Entry Draft).

			Regular Season					Playoffs				
Season	Club	Lea	GP	G	A	TP	PIM	GP	G	A	TP	PIM
1987-88	Hull	QMJHL	65	63	68	131	74	17	15	18	33	32
1988-89	Hull	QMJHL	41	38	39	77	31	9	5	4	9	14
	Edmonton	**NHL**	**6**	**1**	**2**	**3**	**0**	....	....	....	....	....
1989-90	**Edmonton**	**NHL**	**46**	**17**	**8**	**25**	**30**	**20**	**2**	**3**	**5**	**6 ♦**
1990-91	**Edmonton**	**NHL**	**73**	**20**	**20**	**40**	**34**	**18**	**3**	**6**	**9**	**25**
1991-92	**Edmonton**	**NHL**	**68**	**11**	**18**	**29**	**62**	**15**	**1**	**3**	**4**	**10**
1992-93	**Edmonton**	**NHL**	**65**	**11**	**12**	**23**	**30**	....	....	....	....	....
1993-94	**Quebec**	**NHL**	**31**	**6**	**6**	**12**	**8**	....	....	....	....	....
	Vancouver	**NHL**	**33**	**8**	**8**	**16**	**26**	**24**	**5**	**4**	**9**	**14**
1994-95	**Vancouver**	**NHL**	**46**	**13**	**10**	**23**	**36**	**3**	**0**	**1**	**1**	**0**
1995-96	**Vancouver**	**NHL**	**81**	**30**	**26**	**56**	**59**	**6**	**1**	**1**	**2**	**12**
1996-97	**Vancouver**	**NHL**	**74**	**35**	**33**	**68**	**42**	....	....	....	....	....
1997-98	**Vancouver**	**NHL**	**24**	**4**	**4**	**8**	**10**	....	....	....	....	....
	Carolina	**NHL**	**40**	**12**	**14**	**26**	**30**	....	....	....	....	....
	NHL Totals		**587**	**168**	**161**	**329**	**367**	**86**	**12**	**18**	**30**	**67**

QMJHL First All-Star Team (1988) • Canadian Major Junior Rookie of the Year (1988) • Won George Parsons Trophy (Memorial Cup Tournament Most Sportsmanlike Player) (1988)

Traded to **Edmonton** by **LA Kings** with Jimmy Carson and LA Kings' 1st round choices in 1989 (previously acquired, New Jersey selected Jason Miller), 1991 (Martin Rucinsky) and 1993 (Nick Stajduhar) Entry Drafts and cash for Wayne Gretzky, Mike Krushelnyski and Marty McSorley, August 9, 1988. Traded to **Quebec** by **Edmonton** with Edmonton's 6th round choice (Nicholas Checco) in 1993 Entry Draft for Scott Pearson, June 20, 1993. Claimed on waivers by **Vancouver** from **Quebec**, January 15, 1994. Traded to **Carolina** by **Vancouver** with Kirk McLean for Sean Burke, Geoff Sanderson and Enrico Ciccone, January 3, 1998.

GENDRON, MARTIN (ZHEHN-drawn) — MTL.

Right wing. Shoots right. 5'9", 190 lbs. Born, Valleyfield, Que., February 15, 1974.
(Washington's 4th choice, 71st overall, in 1992 Entry Draft).

			Regular Season					Playoffs				
Season	Club	Lea	GP	G	A	TP	PIM	GP	G	A	TP	PIM
1990-91	St-Hyacinthe	QMJHL	55	34	23	57	33	4	1	2	3	0
1991-92	St-Hyacinthe	QMJHL	69	*71	66	137	45	6	7	4	11	14
1992-93	St-Hyacinthe	QMJHL	63	73	61	134	44	....	....	....	....	....
	Baltimore	AHL	10	1	2	3	2	3	0	0	0	0
1993-94	Hull	QMJHL	37	39	36	75	18	20	*21	17	38	8
	Canada	Nat-Tm	19	4	5	9	2	....	....	....	....	....
1994-95	**Washington**	**NHL**	**8**	**2**	**1**	**3**	**2**	....	....	....	....	....
	Portland	AHL	72	36	32	68	54	4	5	1	6	2
1995-96	**Washington**	**NHL**	**20**	**2**	**1**	**3**	**8**	....	....	....	....	....
	Portland	AHL	48	38	29	67	39	22	*15	18	33	8
1996-97	Las Vegas	IHL	81	51	39	90	20	3	2	1	3	0
1997-98	**Chicago**	**NHL**	**2**	**0**	**0**	**0**	**0**	....	....	....	....	....
	Indianapolis	IHL	17	8	6	14	16	....	....	....	....	....
	Milwaukee	IHL	40	20	19	39	14	....	....	....	....	....
	Fredericton	AHL	10	5	10	15	4	2	0	0	0	4
	NHL Totals		**30**	**4**	**2**	**6**	**10**	....	....	....	....	....

QMJHL First All-Star Team (1992) • Canadian Major Junior Most Sportsmanlike Player of the Year (1992) • QMJHL Second All-Star Team (1993) • Canadian Major Junior First All-Star Team (1993)

Traded to **Chicago** by **Washington** with Washington's 6th round choice (Jonathan Pelletier) in 1998 Entry Draft for Chicago's 5th round choice (Erik Wendell) in 1998 Entry Draft, October 10, 1997. Traded to **Montreal** by **Chicago** for David Ling, March 14, 1998.

GERNANDER, KEN (guhr-NAN-duhr) — NYR

Center. Shoots left. 5'10", 180 lbs. Born, Coleraine, MN, June 30, 1969.
(Winnipeg's 4th choice, 96th overall, in 1987 Entry Draft).

			Regular Season					Playoffs				
Season	Club	Lea	GP	G	A	TP	PIM	GP	G	A	TP	PIM
1986-87	Greenway High	H.S.	26	35	34	69	....	....	....	....	....	....
1987-88	U. of Minnesota	WCHA	44	14	14	28	14	....	....	....	....	....
1988-89	U. of Minnesota	WCHA	44	9	11	20	2	....	....	....	....	....
1989-90	U. of Minnesota	WCHA	44	32	17	49	24	....	....	....	....	....
1990-91	U. of Minnesota	WCHA	44	23	20	43	24	....	....	....	....	....
1991-92	Fort Wayne	IHL	13	7	6	13	2	....	....	....	....	....
	Moncton	AHL	43	8	18	26	9	8	1	1	2	2
1992-93	Moncton	AHL	71	18	29	47	20	5	1	4	5	0
1993-94	Moncton	AHL	71	22	25	47	12	19	6	1	7	0
1994-95	Binghamton	AHL	80	28	25	53	24	11	2	2	4	6
1995-96	**NY Rangers**	**NHL**	**10**	**2**	**3**	**5**	**4**	**6**	**0**	**0**	**0**	**0**
	Binghamton	AHL	63	44	29	73	38	....	....	....	....	....
1996-97	Binghamton	AHL	46	13	18	31	30	2	0	1	1	0
	NY Rangers	**NHL**	....	....	....	....	....	**9**	**0**	**0**	**0**	**0**
1997-98	Hartford	AHL	80	35	28	63	26	12	5	6	11	4
	NHL Totals		**10**	**2**	**3**	**5**	**4**	**15**	**0**	**0**	**0**	**0**

Won Fred Hunt Memorial Trophy (Sportsmanship - AHL) (1996)

Signed as a free agent by **NY Rangers**, July 4, 1994.

GILCHRIST, BRENT — DET.

Left wing. Shoots left. 5'11", 180 lbs. Born, Moose Jaw, Sask., April 3, 1967.
(Montreal's 6th choice, 79th overall, in 1985 Entry Draft).

			Regular Season					Playoffs				
Season	Club	Lea	GP	G	A	TP	PIM	GP	G	A	TP	PIM
1983-84	Kelowna	WHL	69	16	11	27	16	....	....	....	....	....
1984-85	Kelowna	WHL	51	35	38	73	58	6	5	2	7	8
1985-86	Spokane	WHL	52	45	45	90	57	9	6	7	13	19
1986-87	Spokane	WHL	46	45	55	100	71	5	2	7	9	6
	Sherbrooke	AHL	....	....	....	....	....	10	2	7	9	2
1987-88	Sherbrooke	AHL	77	26	48	74	83	6	1	3	4	6
1988-89	**Montreal**	**NHL**	**49**	**8**	**16**	**24**	**16**	**9**	**1**	**1**	**2**	**10**
	Sherbrooke	AHL	7	6	5	11	7	....	....	....	....	....
1989-90	**Montreal**	**NHL**	**57**	**9**	**15**	**24**	**28**	**8**	**2**	**0**	**2**	**2**
1990-91	**Montreal**	**NHL**	**51**	**6**	**9**	**15**	**10**	**13**	**5**	**3**	**8**	**6**
1991-92	**Montreal**	**NHL**	**79**	**23**	**27**	**50**	**57**	**11**	**2**	**4**	**6**	**6**
1992-93	**Edmonton**	**NHL**	**60**	**10**	**10**	**20**	**47**	....	....	....	....	....
	Minnesota	**NHL**	**8**	**0**	**1**	**1**	**2**	....	....	....	....	....
1993-94	**Dallas**	**NHL**	**76**	**17**	**14**	**31**	**31**	**9**	**3**	**1**	**4**	**2**
1994-95	**Dallas**	**NHL**	**32**	**9**	**4**	**13**	**16**	**5**	**0**	**1**	**1**	**2**
1995-96	**Dallas**	**NHL**	**77**	**20**	**22**	**42**	**36**	....	....	....	....	....
1996-97	**Dallas**	**NHL**	**67**	**10**	**20**	**30**	**24**	**6**	**2**	**2**	**4**	**2**
1997-98	**Detroit**	**NHL**	**61**	**13**	**14**	**27**	**40**	**15**	**2**	**1**	**3**	**12 ♦**
	NHL Totals		**617**	**125**	**152**	**277**	**307**	**76**	**17**	**13**	**30**	**42**

Traded to **Edmonton** by **Montreal** with Shayne Corson and Vladimir Vujtek for Vincent Damphousse and Edmonton's 4th round choice (Adam Wiesel) in 1993 Entry Draft, August 27, 1992. Traded to **Minnesota** by **Edmonton** for Todd Elik, March 5, 1993. Transferred to **Dallas** after **Minnesota** franchise relocated, June 9, 1993. Signed as a free agent by **Detroit**, August 1, 1997.

GILL, HAL (GIHL) — BOS.

Defense. Shoots left. 6'7", 240 lbs. Born, Concord, MA, April 6, 1975.
(Boston's 8th choice, 207th overall, in 1993 Entry Draft).

			Regular Season					Playoffs				
Season	Club	Lea	GP	G	A	TP	PIM	GP	G	A	TP	PIM
1992-93	Nashoba High	H.S.	20	25	25	50	....	....	....	....	....	....
1993-94	Providence	H.E.	31	1	2	3	26	....	....	....	....	....
1994-95	Providence	H.E.	26	1	3	4	22	....	....	....	....	....
1995-96	Providence	H.E.	39	5	12	17	54	....	....	....	....	....
1996-97	Providence	H.E.	35	5	16	21	52	....	....	....	....	....
1997-98	**Boston**	**NHL**	**68**	**2**	**4**	**6**	**47**	**6**	**0**	**0**	**0**	**4**
	Providence	AHL	4	1	0	1	23	....	....	....	....	....
	NHL Totals		**68**	**2**	**4**	**6**	**47**	**6**	**0**	**0**	**0**	**4**

GILL, TODD (GIHL) — ST.L.

Defense. Shoots left. 6', 180 lbs. Born, Cardinal, Ont., November 9, 1965.
(Toronto's 2nd choice, 25th overall, in 1984 Entry Draft).

			Regular Season					Playoffs				
Season	Club	Lea	GP	G	A	TP	PIM	GP	G	A	TP	PIM
1982-83	Windsor	OHL	70	12	24	36	108	3	0	0	0	11
1983-84	Windsor	OHL	68	9	48	57	184	3	1	1	2	10
1984-85	Windsor	OHL	53	17	40	57	148	4	0	1	1	14
	Toronto	**NHL**	**10**	**1**	**0**	**1**	**13**	....	....	....	....	....
1985-86	**Toronto**	**NHL**	**15**	**1**	**2**	**3**	**28**	**1**	**0**	**0**	**0**	**0**
	St. Catharines	AHL	58	8	25	33	90	10	1	6	7	17
1986-87	**Toronto**	**NHL**	**61**	**4**	**27**	**31**	**92**	**13**	**2**	**2**	**4**	**42**
	Newmarket	AHL	11	1	8	9	33	....	....	....	....	....
1987-88	**Toronto**	**NHL**	**65**	**8**	**17**	**25**	**131**	**6**	**1**	**3**	**4**	**20**
	Newmarket	AHL	2	0	1	1	2	....	....	....	....	....
1988-89	**Toronto**	**NHL**	**59**	**11**	**14**	**25**	**72**	....	....	....	....	....
1989-90	**Toronto**	**NHL**	**48**	**1**	**14**	**15**	**92**	**5**	**0**	**3**	**3**	**16**
1990-91	**Toronto**	**NHL**	**72**	**2**	**22**	**24**	**113**	....	....	....	....	....
1991-92	**Toronto**	**NHL**	**74**	**2**	**15**	**17**	**91**	....	....	....	....	....
1992-93	**Toronto**	**NHL**	**69**	**11**	**32**	**43**	**66**	**21**	**1**	**10**	**11**	**26**
1993-94	**Toronto**	**NHL**	**45**	**4**	**24**	**28**	**44**	**18**	**1**	**5**	**6**	**37**
1994-95	**Toronto**	**NHL**	**47**	**7**	**25**	**32**	**64**	**7**	**0**	**3**	**3**	**6**
1995-96	**Toronto**	**NHL**	**74**	**7**	**18**	**25**	**116**	**6**	**0**	**0**	**0**	**24**
1996-97	**San Jose**	**NHL**	**79**	**0**	**21**	**21**	**101**	....	....	....	....	....
1997-98	**San Jose**	**NHL**	**64**	**8**	**13**	**21**	**31**	....	....	....	....	....
	St. Louis	**NHL**	**11**	**5**	**4**	**9**	**10**	**10**	**2**	**2**	**4**	**10**
	NHL Totals		**793**	**72**	**248**	**320**	**1064**	**87**	**7**	**28**	**35**	**181**

Traded to **San Jose** by **Toronto** for Jamie Baker and San Jose's 5th round choice (Peter Cava) in 1996 Entry Draft, June 14, 1996. Traded to **St. Louis** by **San Jose** for Joe Murphy, March 24, 1998.

GILLAM, SEAN — DET.

Defense. Shoots right. 6'2", 187 lbs. Born, Lethbridge, Alta., May 7, 1976.
(Detroit's 3rd choice, 75th overall, in 1994 Entry Draft).

			Regular Season					Playoffs				
Season	Club	Lea	GP	G	A	TP	PIM	GP	G	A	TP	PIM
1992-93	Spokane	WHL	70	6	27	33	121	10	0	2	2	10
1993-94	Spokane	WHL	70	7	17	24	106	3	0	0	0	6
1994-95	Spokane	WHL	72	16	40	56	192	11	0	3	3	33
1995-96	Spokane	WHL	69	11	58	69	123	18	2	12	14	26
1996-97	Adirondack	AHL	64	1	7	8	50	....	....	....	....	....
1997-98	Adirondack	AHL	73	1	9	10	60	3	1	0	1	0

WHL West Second All-Star Team (1995, 1996)

GILLIS, NICK — OTT.

Right wing. Shoots right. 6', 188 lbs. Born, Cambridge, MA, February 20, 1978.
(Ottawa's 7th choice, 203rd overall, in 1997 Entry Draft).

			Regular Season					Playoffs				
Season	Club	Lea	GP	G	A	TP	PIM	GP	G	A	TP	PIM
1996-97	Cushing Academy	H.S.	32	30	54	84	27	....	....	....	....	....
1997-98	Boston University	H.E.	34	8	12	20	43	....	....	....	....	....

GILMOUR, DOUG — CHI.

Center. Shoots left. 5'11", 175 lbs. Born, Kingston, Ont., June 25, 1963.
(St. Louis' 4th choice, 134th overall, in 1982 Entry Draft).

			Regular Season					Playoffs				
Season	**Club**	**Lea**	**GP**	**G**	**A**	**TP**	**PIM**	**GP**	**G**	**A**	**TP**	**PIM**
1980-81	Cornwall	QMJHL	51	12	23	35	35	....	....	....	....	....
1981-82	Cornwall	OHL	67	46	73	119	42	5	6	9	15	2
1982-83	Cornwall	OHL	68	70	*107	*177	62	8	8	10	18	16
1983-84	**St. Louis**	**NHL**	**80**	**25**	**28**	**53**	**57**	**11**	**2**	**9**	**11**	**10**
1984-85	**St. Louis**	**NHL**	**78**	**21**	**36**	**57**	**49**	**3**	**1**	**1**	**2**	**2**
1985-86	**St. Louis**	**NHL**	**74**	**25**	**28**	**53**	**41**	**19**	**9**	**12**	***21**	**25**
1986-87	**St. Louis**	**NHL**	**80**	**42**	**63**	**105**	**58**	**6**	**2**	**2**	**4**	**16**
1987-88	**St. Louis**	**NHL**	**72**	**36**	**50**	**86**	**59**	**10**	**3**	**14**	**17**	**18**
1988-89	**Calgary**	**NHL**	**72**	**26**	**59**	**85**	**44**	**22**	**11**	**11**	**22**	**20** ♦
1989-90	**Calgary**	**NHL**	**78**	**24**	**67**	**91**	**54**	**6**	**3**	**1**	**4**	**8**
1990-91	**Calgary**	**NHL**	**78**	**20**	**61**	**81**	**144**	**7**	**1**	**1**	**2**	**0**
1991-92	**Calgary**	**NHL**	**38**	**11**	**27**	**38**	**46**	....	....	....	....	....
	Toronto	**NHL**	**40**	**15**	**34**	**49**	**32**	....	....	....	....	....
1992-93	**Toronto**	**NHL**	**83**	**32**	**95**	**127**	**100**	**21**	**10**	***25**	**35**	**30**
1993-94	**Toronto**	**NHL**	**83**	**27**	**84**	**111**	**105**	**18**	**6**	**22**	**28**	**42**
1994-95	Rapperswil	Switz.	9	2	13	15	16	....	....	....	....	....
	Toronto	**NHL**	**44**	**10**	**23**	**33**	**26**	**7**	**0**	**6**	**6**	**6**
1995-96	**Toronto**	**NHL**	**81**	**32**	**40**	**72**	**77**	**6**	**1**	**7**	**8**	**12**
1996-97	**Toronto**	**NHL**	**61**	**15**	**45**	**60**	**46**	....	....	....	....	....
	New Jersey	**NHL**	**20**	**7**	**15**	**22**	**22**	**10**	**0**	**4**	**4**	**14**
1997-98	**New Jersey**	**NHL**	**63**	**13**	**40**	**53**	**68**	**6**	**5**	**2**	**7**	**4**
	NHL Totals		**1125**	**381**	**795**	**1176**	**1028**	**152**	**54**	**117**	**171**	**207**

OHL First All-Star Team (1983) • Won Frank J. Selke Trophy (1993)

Played in NHL All-Star Game (1993, 1994)

Traded to **Calgary** by **St. Louis** with Mark Hunter, Steve Bozek and Michael Dark for Mike Bullard, Craig Coxe and Tim Corkery, September 6, 1988. Traded to **Toronto** by **Calgary** with Jamie Macoun, Ric Nattress, Kent Manderville and Rick Wamsley for Gary Leeman, Alexander Godynyuk, Jeff Reese, Michel Petit and Craig Berube, January 2, 1992. Traded to **New Jersey** by **Toronto** with Dave Ellett and future considerations for Jason Smith, Steve Sullivan and the rights to Alyn McCauley, February 25, 1997. Signed as a free agent by **Chicago**, July 28, 1998.

GIONTA, BRIAN — N.J.

Right wing. Shoots right. 5'7", 160 lbs. Born, Rochester, NY, January 18, 1979.
(New Jersey's 4th choice, 82nd overall, in 1998 Entry Draft).

			Regular Season					Playoffs				
Season	**Club**	**Lea**	**GP**	**G**	**A**	**TP**	**PIM**	**GP**	**G**	**A**	**TP**	**PIM**
1997-98	Boston College	H.E.	40	30	32	62	44	....	....	....	....	....

Hockey East Second All-Star Team (1998) • NCAA East Second All-American Team (1998)

GIRARD, JONATHAN (zhih-RAHR) — BOS.

Defense. Shoots right. 5'11", 192 lbs. Born, Joliette, Que., May 27, 1980.
(Boston's 1st choice, 48th overall, in 1998 Entry Draft).

			Regular Season					Playoffs				
Season	**Club**	**Lea**	**GP**	**G**	**A**	**TP**	**PIM**	**GP**	**G**	**A**	**TP**	**PIM**
1996-97	Laval	QMJHL	39	11	23	34	13	3	0	3	3	0
1997-98	Laval	QMJHL	64	20	47	67	44	16	2	16	18	13

QMJHL Second All-Star Team (1998)

GIROUX, RAY (zhih-ROO) — NYI

Defense. Shoots left. 6', 180 lbs. Born, North Bay, Ont., July 20, 1976.
(Philadelphia's 7th choice, 202nd overall, in 1994 Entry Draft).

			Regular Season					Playoffs				
Season	**Club**	**Lea**	**GP**	**G**	**A**	**TP**	**PIM**	**GP**	**G**	**A**	**TP**	**PIM**
1993-94	Powasson	Jr. A	36	10	40	50	42	....	....	....	....	....
1994-95	Yale	ECAC	27	1	3	4	8	....	....	....	....	....
1995-96	Yale	ECAC	30	3	16	19	36	....	....	....	....	....
1996-97	Yale	ECAC	32	9	12	21	38	....	....	....	....	....
1997-98	Yale	ECAC	35	9	*30	39	62	....	....	....	....	....

ECAC First All-Star Team (1998) • NCAA East First All-American Team (1998)

Rights traded to **NY Islanders** by **Philadelphia** for NY Islanders' 6th round choice in 2000 Entry Draft, August 25, 1998.

GLYNN, BRIAN (GLIHN)

Defense. Shoots left. 6'4", 218 lbs. Born, Iserlohn, West Germany, November 23, 1967.
(Calgary's 2nd choice, 37th overall, in 1986 Entry Draft).

			Regular Season					Playoffs				
Season	**Club**	**Lea**	**GP**	**G**	**A**	**TP**	**PIM**	**GP**	**G**	**A**	**TP**	**PIM**
1984-85	Saskatoon	WHL	12	1	0	1	2	3	0	0	0	0
1985-86	Saskatoon	WHL	66	7	25	32	131	13	0	3	3	30
1986-87	Saskatoon	WHL	44	2	26	28	163	11	1	3	4	19
1987-88	**Calgary**	**NHL**	**67**	**5**	**14**	**19**	**87**	**1**	**0**	**0**	**0**	**0**
1988-89	**Calgary**	**NHL**	**9**	**0**	**1**	**1**	**19**	....	....	....	....	....
	Salt Lake	IHL	31	3	10	13	105	14	3	7	10	31
1989-90	**Calgary**	**NHL**	**1**	**0**	**0**	**0**	**0**	....	....	....	....	....
	Salt Lake	IHL	80	17	44	61	164	....	....	....	....	....
1990-91	Salt Lake	IHL	8	1	3	4	18	....	....	....	....	....
	Minnesota	**NHL**	**66**	**8**	**11**	**19**	**83**	**23**	**2**	**6**	**8**	**18**
1991-92	**Minnesota**	**NHL**	**37**	**2**	**12**	**14**	**24**	....	....	....	....	....
	Edmonton	**NHL**	**25**	**2**	**6**	**8**	**6**	**16**	**4**	**1**	**5**	**12**
1992-93	**Edmonton**	**NHL**	**64**	**4**	**12**	**16**	**60**	....	....	....	....	....
1993-94	**Ottawa**	**NHL**	**48**	**2**	**13**	**15**	**41**	....	....	....	....	....
	Vancouver	**NHL**	**16**	**0**	**0**	**0**	**12**	**17**	**0**	**3**	**3**	**10**
1994-95	**Hartford**	**NHL**	**43**	**1**	**6**	**7**	**32**	....	....	....	....	....
1995-96	**Hartford**	**NHL**	**54**	**0**	**4**	**4**	**44**	....	....	....	....	....
1996-97	**Hartford**	**NHL**	**1**	**1**	**0**	**1**	**2**	....	....	....	....	....
	San Antonio	IHL	62	13	11	24	46	9	2	6	8	4
1997-98	Kolner Haie	EuroHL	6	3	2	5	10	....	....	....	....	....
	Kolner Haie	Germany	48	10	12	22	59	3	0	0	0	16
	NHL Totals		**431**	**25**	**79**	**104**	**410**	**57**	**6**	**10**	**16**	**40**

IHL First All-Star Team (1990) • Won Governors' Trophy (Outstanding Defenseman - IHL) (1990)

Traded to **Minnesota** by **Calgary** for Frantisek Musil, October 26, 1990. Traded to **Edmonton** by **Minnesota** for David Shaw, January 21, 1992. Traded to **Ottawa** by **Edmonton** for Ottawa's 8th round choice (Rob Quinn) in 1994 Entry Draft, September 15, 1993. Claimed on waivers by **Vancouver** from **Ottawa**, February 5, 1994. Claimed by **Hartford** from **Vancouver** in Waiver Draft, January 18, 1995. Traded to **Detroit** by **Hartford** with Brendan Shanahan for Paul Coffey, Keith Primeau and Detroit's 1st round choice (Nikos Tselios) in 1997 Entry Draft, October 9, 1996.

GOC, SASCHA (GAWCH, SA-shah) — N.J.

Defense. Shoots right. 6'2", 196 lbs. Born, Calw, Germany, April 17, 1979.
(New Jersey's 5th choice, 159th overall, in 1997 Entry Draft).

			Regular Season					Playoffs				
Season	**Club**	**Lea**	**GP**	**G**	**A**	**TP**	**PIM**	**GP**	**G**	**A**	**TP**	**PIM**
1995-96	Schwenningen	Ger-Jr.	11	3	6	9	77	....	....	....	....	....
	Schwenningen	Germany	1	0	0	0	0	....	....	....	....	....
1996-97	Schwenningen	Germany	41	3	1	4	28	5	0	0	0	0
1997-98	Schwenningen	Germany	49	5	5	10	45	....	....	....	....	....

GODBOUT, JASON — PIT.

Defense. Shoots left. 5'11", 180 lbs. Born, Woodbury, MN, August 5, 1976.
(Pittsburgh's 12th choice, 232nd overall, in 1994 Entry Draft).

			Regular Season					Playoffs				
Season	**Club**	**Lea**	**GP**	**G**	**A**	**TP**	**PIM**	**GP**	**G**	**A**	**TP**	**PIM**
1993-94	Hill-Murray	H.S.	25	18	16	44	....	....	....	....	....	....
1994-95	U. of Minnesota	WCHA	32	1	4	5	28	....	....	....	....	....
1995-96	U. of Minnesota	WCHA	39	6	7	13	24	....	....	....	....	....
1996-97	U. of Minnesota	WCHA	42	2	9	11	46	....	....	....	....	....
1997-98	U. of Minnesota	WCHA	24	2	1	3	38	....	....	....	....	....

GODYNYUK, ALEXANDER (goh-dih-NYOOK)

Defense. Shoots left. 6', 207 lbs. Born, Kiev, Ukraine, January 27, 1970.
(Toronto's 5th choice, 115th overall, in 1990 Entry Draft).

			Regular Season					Playoffs				
Season	**Club**	**Lea**	**GP**	**G**	**A**	**TP**	**PIM**	**GP**	**G**	**A**	**TP**	**PIM**
1986-87	Sokol Kiev	USSR	9	0	1	1	2	....	....	....	....	....
1987-88	Sokol Kiev	USSR	2	0	0	0	2	....	....	....	....	....
1988-89	Sokol Kiev	USSR	30	3	3	6	12	....	....	....	....	....
1989-90	Sokol Kiev	USSR	37	3	2	5	31	....	....	....	....	....
1990-91	Sokol Kiev	USSR	19	3	1	4	20	....	....	....	....	....
	Toronto	**NHL**	**18**	**0**	**3**	**3**	**16**	....	....	....	....	....
	Newmarket	AHL	11	0	1	1	29	....	....	....	....	....
1991-92	**Toronto**	**NHL**	**31**	**3**	**6**	**9**	**59**	....	....	....	....	....
	Calgary	**NHL**	**6**	**0**	**1**	**1**	**4**	....	....	....	....	....
	Salt Lake	IHL	17	2	1	3	24	....	....	....	....	....
1992-93	**Calgary**	**NHL**	**27**	**3**	**4**	**7**	**19**	....	....	....	....	....
1993-94	**Florida**	**NHL**	**26**	**0**	**10**	**10**	**35**	....	....	....	....	....
	Hartford	**NHL**	**43**	**3**	**9**	**12**	**40**	....	....	....	....	....
1994-95	**Hartford**	**NHL**	**14**	**0**	**0**	**0**	**8**	....	....	....	....	....
1995-96	**Hartford**	**NHL**	**3**	**0**	**0**	**0**	**2**	....	....	....	....	....
	Springfield	AHL	14	1	3	4	19	....	....	....	....	....
	Detroit	IHL	7	0	3	3	12	....	....	....	....	....
	Minnesota	IHL	45	9	17	26	81	....	....	....	....	....
1996-97	**Hartford**	**NHL**	**55**	**1**	**6**	**7**	**41**	....	....	....	....	....
1997-98	Chicago	IHL	50	5	11	16	85	1	0	0	0	0
	NHL Totals		**223**	**10**	**39**	**49**	**224**	....	....	....	....	....

Traded to **Calgary** by **Toronto** with Craig Berube, Gary Leeman, Michel Petit and Jeff Reese for Doug Gilmour, Jamie Macoun, Ric Nattress, Rick Wamsley and Kent Manderville, January 2, 1992. Claimed by **Florida** from **Calgary** in Expansion Draft, June 24, 1993. Traded to **Hartford** by **Florida** for Jim McKenzie, December 16, 1993. Transferred to **Carolina** after **Hartford** franchise relocated, June 25, 1997. Traded to **St. Louis** by **Carolina** with Carolina's 6th round choice (Brad Voth) in 1998 Entry Draft for Stephen Leach, June 27, 1997.

GOLDADE, AARON — BUF.

Center. Shoots left. 6', 180 lbs. Born, Prince Albert, Sask., July 30, 1980.
(Buffalo's 6th choice, 137th overall, in 1998 Entry Draft).

			Regular Season					Playoffs				
Season	**Club**	**Lea**	**GP**	**G**	**A**	**TP**	**PIM**	**GP**	**G**	**A**	**TP**	**PIM**
1996-97	Brandon	WHL	59	4	10	14	51	6	0	1	1	0
1997-98	Brandon	WHL	66	19	16	35	58	16	0	2	2	22

GOLDMANN, ERICH (GOHLD-mahn, AIR-ihkh) — OTT.

Defense. Shoots left. 6'3", 196 lbs. Born, Dingolfing, West Germany, April 7, 1976.
(Ottawa's 5th choice, 212th overall, in 1996 Entry Draft).

			Regular Season					Playoffs				
Season	**Club**	**Lea**	**GP**	**G**	**A**	**TP**	**PIM**	**GP**	**G**	**A**	**TP**	**PIM**
1993-94	Landshut	Germany	33	0	0	0	4	7	0	0	0	0
1994-95	Mannheim	Germany	31	0	0	0	22	10	1	0	1	2
1995-96	Mannheim	Germany	47	0	3	3	40	8	0	0	0	4
1996-97	Kaufbeuren	Germany	44	2	4	6	58	6	1	0	1	2
1997-98	Worcester	AHL	31	0	2	2	40	....	....	....	....	....
	Germany	Olympics	4	0	1	1	27	....	....	....	....	....
	Detroit	IHL	3	0	0	0	2	....	....	....	....	....
	Dayton	ECHL	3	0	2	2	5	5	0	0	0	8

GOLUBOVSKY, YAN (goh-luh-BOHV-skee) — DET.

Defense. Shoots right. 6'3", 183 lbs. Born, Novosibirsk, USSR, March 9, 1976.
(Detroit's 1st choice, 23rd overall, in 1994 Entry Draft).

			Regular Season					Playoffs				
Season	**Club**	**Lea**	**GP**	**G**	**A**	**TP**	**PIM**	**GP**	**G**	**A**	**TP**	**PIM**
1993-94	Moscow D'amo 2	CIS-3	10	0	1	1	....	....	....	....	....	....
	Russian Penguins	IHL	8	0	0	0	23	....	....	....	....	....
1994-95	Adirondack	AHL	57	4	2	6	39	....	....	....	....	....
1995-96	Adirondack	AHL	71	5	16	21	97	3	0	0	0	2
1996-97	Adirondack	AHL	62	2	11	13	67	4	0	0	0	0
1997-98	**Detroit**	**NHL**	**12**	**0**	**2**	**2**	**6**	....	....	....	....	....
	Adirondack	AHL	52	1	15	16	57	3	0	0	0	2
	NHL Totals		**12**	**0**	**2**	**2**	**6**	....	....	....	....	....

GOMEZ, SCOTT (GOH-mehz) — N.J.

Center. Shoots left. 5'11", 180 lbs. Born, Anchorage, Alaska, December 23, 1979.
(New Jersey's 2nd choice, 27th overall, in 1998 Entry Draft).

			Regular Season					Playoffs				
Season	**Club**	**Lea**	**GP**	**G**	**A**	**TP**	**PIM**	**GP**	**G**	**A**	**TP**	**PIM**
1996-97	Surrey	BCJHL	56	48	76	124	94	....	....	....	....	....
1997-98	Tri-City	WHL	45	12	37	49	57	....	....	....	....	....

GONCHAR, SERGEI (gohn-CHAR) WSH.

Defense. Shoots left. 6'2", 212 lbs. Born, Chelyabinsk, USSR, April 13, 1974.
(Washington's 1st choice, 14th overall, in 1992 Entry Draft).

			Regular Season					Playoffs				
Season	**Club**	**Lea**	**GP**	**G**	**A**	**TP**	**PIM**	**GP**	**G**	**A**	**TP**	**PIM**
1991-92	Chelyabinsk	CIS	31	1	0	1	6	....	....	....	....	....
1992-93	Moscow D'amo	CIS	31	1	3	4	70	10	0	0	0	12
1993-94	Moscow D'amo	CIS	44	4	5	9	36	10	0	3	3	14
	Portland	AHL	....	....	....	....	....	2	0	0	0	0
1994-95	Portland	AHL	61	10	32	42	67	....	....	....	....	....
	Washington	**NHL**	**31**	**2**	**5**	**7**	**22**	**7**	**2**	**2**	**4**	**2**
1995-96	**Washington**	**NHL**	**78**	**15**	**26**	**41**	**60**	**6**	**2**	**4**	**6**	**4**
1996-97	**Washington**	**NHL**	**57**	**13**	**17**	**30**	**36**	....	....	....	....	....
1997-98	Lada	Russia	7	3	2	5	4	....	....	....	....	....
	Lada	EuroHL	1	1	0	1	2	....	....	....	....	....
	Washington	**NHL**	**72**	**5**	**16**	**21**	**66**	**21**	**7**	**4**	**11**	**30**
	Russia	Olympics	6	0	2	2	0	....	....	....	....	....
	NHL Totals		**238**	**35**	**64**	**99**	**184**	**34**	**11**	**10**	**21**	**36**

GONEAU, DANIEL (guh-NOH) NYR

Left wing. Shoots left. 6', 194 lbs. Born, Montreal, Que., January 16, 1976.
(NY Rangers' 2nd choice, 48th overall, in 1996 Entry Draft).

			Regular Season					Playoffs				
Season	**Club**	**Lea**	**GP**	**G**	**A**	**TP**	**PIM**	**GP**	**G**	**A**	**TP**	**PIM**
1992-93	Laval	QMJHL	62	16	25	41	44	13	0	4	4	4
1993-94	Laval	QMJHL	68	29	57	86	81	19	8	21	29	45
1994-95	Laval	QMJHL	56	16	31	47	78	20	5	10	15	33
1995-96	Granby	QMJHL	67	54	51	105	115	21	11	22	33	40
1996-97	**NY Rangers**	**NHL**	**41**	**10**	**3**	**13**	**10**	....	....	....	....	....
	Binghamton	AHL	39	15	15	30	10	....	....	....	....	....
1997-98	**NY Rangers**	**NHL**	**11**	**2**	**0**	**2**	**4**	....	....	....	....	....
	Hartford	AHL	66	21	26	47	44	13	1	4	5	18
	NHL Totals		**52**	**12**	**3**	**15**	**14**	....	....	....	....	....

QMJHL First All-Star Team (1996)

• Re-entered NHL Entry Draft. Originally Boston's 2nd choice, 47th overall, in 1994 Entry Draft.

GOOLDY, ERIC TOR.

Left wing. Shoots left. 6'2", 200 lbs. Born, Utica, NY, February 10, 1979.
(Toronto's 4th choice, 138th overall, in 1997 Entry Draft).

			Regular Season					Playoffs				
Season	**Club**	**Lea**	**GP**	**G**	**A**	**TP**	**PIM**	**GP**	**G**	**A**	**TP**	**PIM**
1996-97	Detroit	OHL	66	7	11	18	131	5	0	1	1	15
1997-98	Plymouth	OHL	63	16	20	36	128	15	1	4	5	28

GORDON, HEATH CHI.

Left wing. Shoots left. 6'2", 197 lbs. Born, Boston, MA, May 28, 1978.
(Chicago's 8th choice, 147th overall, in 1997 Entry Draft).

			Regular Season					Playoffs				
Season	**Club**	**Lea**	**GP**	**G**	**A**	**TP**	**PIM**	**GP**	**G**	**A**	**TP**	**PIM**
1996-97	Green Bay	USHL	52	16	28	44	71	....	....	....	....	....
1997-98	Providence	H.E.	18	2	2	4	22	....	....	....	....	....

GORDON, RHETT PHX.

Right wing. Shoots right. 5'11", 175 lbs. Born, Regina, Sask., August 26, 1976.

			Regular Season					Playoffs				
Season	**Club**	**Lea**	**GP**	**G**	**A**	**TP**	**PIM**	**GP**	**G**	**A**	**TP**	**PIM**
1992-93	Regina	WHL	2	1	0	1	2	4	0	0	0	0
1993-94	Regina	WHL	60	19	28	47	14	4	0	0	0	7
1994-95	Regina	WHL	71	36	43	79	64	4	2	2	4	0
1995-96	Regina	WHL	66	53	50	103	68	11	9	4	13	10
	Springfield	AHL	2	0	0	0	2	1	0	0	0	0
1996-97	Springfield	AHL	54	11	11	22	54	8	1	2	3	6
1997-98	Springfield	AHL	75	17	11	28	54	4	1	1	2	0

WHL West First All-Star Team (1996)

Signed as a free agent by **Winnipeg**, September 29, 1994. Rights transferred to **Phoenix** after **Winnipeg** franchise relocated, July 1, 1996.

GORDON, ROBB VAN.

Center. Shoots right. 5'11", 190 lbs. Born, Murrayville, B.C., January 13, 1976.
(Vancouver's 2nd choice, 39th overall, in 1994 Entry Draft).

			Regular Season					Playoffs				
Season	**Club**	**Lea**	**GP**	**G**	**A**	**TP**	**PIM**	**GP**	**G**	**A**	**TP**	**PIM**
1993-94	Powell River	BCJHL	60	69	89	158	141	....	....	....	....	....
1994-95	U. of Michigan	CCHA	39	15	26	41	72	....	....	....	....	....
1995-96	Kelowna	WHL	58	51	63	114	84	6	3	6	9	19
1996-97	Syracuse	AHL	63	11	14	25	72	3	0	0	0	7
1997-98	Syracuse	AHL	40	4	6	10	35	....	....	....	....	....
	Raleigh	ECHL	7	3	10	13	28	....	....	....	....	....

GOREN, LEE BOS.

Right wing. Shoots right. 6'3", 190 lbs. Born, Winnipeg, Man., December 26, 1977.
(Boston's 5th choice, 63rd overall, in 1997 Entry Draft).

			Regular Season					Playoffs				
Season	**Club**	**Lea**	**GP**	**G**	**A**	**TP**	**PIM**	**GP**	**G**	**A**	**TP**	**PIM**
1995-96	Minot	SJHL	64	31	55	86	....	....	....	....	....	....
1996-97	North Dakota	WCHA			DID NOT PLAY – FRESHMAN							
1997-98	North Dakota	WCHA	29	3	13	16	26	....	....	....	....	....

GORENKO, DMITRI (goh-REHN-koh) CAR.

Left wing. Shoots left. 6', 165 lbs. Born, Barnaul, USSR, February 13, 1975.
(Hartford's 6th choice, 214th overall, in 1993 Entry Draft).

			Regular Season					Playoffs				
Season	**Club**	**Lea**	**GP**	**G**	**A**	**TP**	**PIM**	**GP**	**G**	**A**	**TP**	**PIM**
1991-92	CSKA Moscow	CIS	14	0	1	1	6	....	....	....	....	....
1992-93	CSKA Moscow	CIS	42	3	0	3	20	....	....	....	....	....
1993-94	CSKA Moscow	CIS	40	5	1	6	28	3	1	0	1	2
1994-95	CSKA Moscow	CIS	33	5	2	7	35	....	....	....	....	....
1995-96	Omsk	CIS	37	4	2	6	14	3	0	1	1	0
1996-97	Omsk	Russia	11	0	1	1	8	....	....	....	....	....
1997-98	Khabarovsk	Russia	42	11	8	19	24	....	....	....	....	....

GOROKHOV, ILJA (goh-ROH-khahf, ihl-YA) NYR

Defense. Shoots right. 6', 185 lbs. Born, Yaroslavl, USSR, August 23, 1977.
(NY Rangers' 8th choice, 195th overall, in 1995 Entry Draft).

			Regular Season					Playoffs				
Season	**Club**	**Lea**	**GP**	**G**	**A**	**TP**	**PIM**	**GP**	**G**	**A**	**TP**	**PIM**
1994-95	Yaroslavl	CIS	1	0	0	0	0	....	....	....	....	....
1995-96	Yaroslavl	CIS	43	0	3	3	10	2	0	0	0	0
1996-97	Las Vegas	IHL	1	0	0	0	0	....	....	....	....	....
	Yaroslavl	Russia	22	1	1	2	6	9	1	0	1	2
1997-98	Samara	Russia	7	0	1	1	6	....	....	....	....	....
	Yulayev	Russia	9	0	0	0	8	....	....	....	....	....
	Yaroslavl	Russia	5	0	1	1	4	....	....	....	....	....

GOSSELIN, CHRISTIAN S.J.

Defense. Shoots right. 6'5", 225 lbs. Born, Laval, Que., August 21, 1976.
(New Jersey's 5th choice, 129th overall, in 1994 Entry Draft).

			Regular Season					Playoffs				
Season	**Club**	**Lea**	**GP**	**G**	**A**	**TP**	**PIM**	**GP**	**G**	**A**	**TP**	**PIM**
1993-94	St-Hyacinthe	QMJHL	12	3	2	5	16	....	....	....	....	....
1994-95	St-Hyacinthe	QMJHL	60	5	10	15	202	5	0	0	0	11
1995-96	Laval	QMJHL	21	1	8	9	69	....	....	....	....	....
1996-97	Macon	CHL	63	8	10	18	229	....	....	....	....	....
1997-98	Pensacola	ECHL	42	6	5	11	181	18	0	1	1	52
	Fredericton	AHL	6	0	0	0	17	....	....	....	....	....

Signed as a free agent by **San Jose**, July 15, 1998.

GOSSELIN, DAVID NSH.

Right wing. Shoots right. 6', 175 lbs. Born, Levis, Que., June 22, 1977.
(New Jersey's 4th choice, 78th overall, in 1995 Entry Draft).

			Regular Season					Playoffs				
Season	**Club**	**Lea**	**GP**	**G**	**A**	**TP**	**PIM**	**GP**	**G**	**A**	**TP**	**PIM**
1994-95	Sherbrooke	QMJHL	58	8	8	16	36	7	0	0	0	2
1995-96	Sherbrooke	QMJHL	55	24	24	48	147	7	2	2	4	4
1996-97	Sherbrooke	QMJHL	23	11	15	26	52	....	....	....	....	....
	Chicoutimi	QMJHL	28	16	33	49	65	12	9	7	16	16
1997-98	Chicoutimi	QMJHL	69	46	64	110	139	6	1	4	5	8

Signed as a free agent by **Nashville**, July 1, 1998.

GRACHEV, VLADIMIR (grah-CHEHF) NYI

Left wing. Shoots left. 6', 178 lbs. Born, Moscow, USSR, January 28, 1973.
(NY Islanders' 6th choice, 152nd overall, in 1992 Entry Draft).

			Regular Season					Playoffs				
Season	**Club**	**Lea**	**GP**	**G**	**A**	**TP**	**PIM**	**GP**	**G**	**A**	**TP**	**PIM**
1991-92	Moscow D'amo 2	CIS-3	62	13	3	16	26	....	....	....	....	....
1992-93	Moscow D'amo	CIS	33	2	1	3	26	7	0	0	0	2
1993-94	Moscow D'amo	CIS	36	4	3	7	10	6	0	0	0	4
1994-95	Moscow D'amo	CIS	48	13	8	21	20	14	7	2	9	10
1995-96	Moscow D'amo	CIS	44	5	9	14	16	11	2	1	3	2
1996-97	Moscow D'amo	Russia	35	2	8	10	14	4	0	2	2	2
1997-98	Nizhnekamsk	Russia	46	10	10	20	12	....	....	....	....	....

GRANATO, TONY (gruh-NA-toh) S.J.

Right wing. Shoots right. 5'10", 185 lbs. Born, Downers Grove, IL, June 25, 1964.
(NY Rangers' 5th choice, 120th overall, in 1982 Entry Draft).

			Regular Season					Playoffs				
Season	**Club**	**Lea**	**GP**	**G**	**A**	**TP**	**PIM**	**GP**	**G**	**A**	**TP**	**PIM**
1981-82	Northwood Prep	H.S.			STATISTICS NOT AVAILABLE							
1982-83	Northwood Prep	H.S.			STATISTICS NOT AVAILABLE							
1983-84	U. of Wisconsin	WCHA	35	14	17	31	48	....	....	....	....	....
1984-85	U. of Wisconsin	WCHA	42	33	34	67	94	....	....	....	....	....
1985-86	U. of Wisconsin	WCHA	33	25	24	49	36	....	....	....	....	....
1986-87	U. of Wisconsin	WCHA	42	28	45	73	64	....	....	....	....	....
1987-88	United States	Nat-Tm	49	40	31	71	55	....	....	....	....	....
	United States	Olympics	6	1	7	8	4	....	....	....	....	....
	Colorado	IHL	22	13	14	27	36	8	9	4	13	16
1988-89	**NY Rangers**	**NHL**	**78**	**36**	**27**	**63**	**140**	**4**	**1**	**1**	**2**	**21**
1989-90	**NY Rangers**	**NHL**	**37**	**7**	**18**	**25**	**77**	....	....	....	....	....
	Los Angeles	**NHL**	**19**	**5**	**6**	**11**	**45**	**10**	**5**	**4**	**9**	**12**
1990-91	**Los Angeles**	**NHL**	**68**	**30**	**34**	**64**	**154**	**12**	**1**	**4**	**5**	**28**
1991-92	**Los Angeles**	**NHL**	**80**	**39**	**29**	**68**	**187**	**6**	**1**	**5**	**6**	**10**
1992-93	**Los Angeles**	**NHL**	**81**	**37**	**45**	**82**	**171**	**24**	**6**	**11**	**17**	**50**
1993-94	**Los Angeles**	**NHL**	**50**	**7**	**14**	**21**	**150**	....	....	....	....	....
1994-95	**Los Angeles**	**NHL**	**33**	**13**	**11**	**24**	**68**	....	....	....	....	....
1995-96	**Los Angeles**	**NHL**	**49**	**17**	**18**	**35**	**46**	....	....	....	....	....
1996-97	**San Jose**	**NHL**	**76**	**25**	**15**	**40**	**159**	....	....	....	....	....
1997-98	**San Jose**	**NHL**	**59**	**16**	**9**	**25**	**70**	**1**	**0**	**0**	**0**	**0**
	NHL Totals		**630**	**232**	**226**	**458**	**1267**	**57**	**14**	**25**	**39**	**121**

WCHA Second All-Star Team (1985, 1987) • NCAA West Second All-American Team (1985, 1987) • NHL All-Rookie Team (1989) • Won Bill Masterton Memorial Trophy (1997)

Played in NHL All-Star Game (1997)

Traded to **LA Kings** by **NY Rangers** with Tomas Sandstrom for Bernie Nicholls, January 20, 1990. Signed as a free agent by **San Jose**, September 1, 1996.

GRAND PIERRE, JEAN-LUC BUF.

Defense. Shoots right. 6'3", 207 lbs. Born, Montreal, Que., February 2, 1977.
(St. Louis' 6th choice, 179th overall, in 1995 Entry Draft).

			Regular Season					Playoffs				
Season	**Club**	**Lea**	**GP**	**G**	**A**	**TP**	**PIM**	**GP**	**G**	**A**	**TP**	**PIM**
1993-94	Beauport	QMJHL	46	1	4	5	27	1	0	0	0	0
1994-95	Val d'Or	QMJHL	59	10	13	23	126	....	....	....	....	....
1995-96	Val d'Or	QMJHL	67	13	21	34	209	13	1	4	5	47
1996-97	Val d'Or	QMJHL	58	9	24	33	186	13	5	8	13	46
1997-98	Rochester	AHL	75	4	6	10	211	4	0	0	0	2

Traded to **Buffalo** by **St. Louis** with Ottawa's 2nd round choice (previously acquired, Buffalo selected Cory Sarich) in 1996 Entry Draft and St. Louis' 3rd round choice (Maxim Afinogenov) in 1997 Entry Draft for Yuri Khmylev and Buffalo's 8th round choice (Andrei Podkonicky) in 1996 Entry Draft, March 20, 1996.

GRATTON, BENOIT (grah-TOHN) WSH.

Left wing. Shoots left. 5'10", 163 lbs. Born, Montreal, Que., December 28, 1976.
(Washington's 6th choice, 105th overall, in 1995 Entry Draft).

			Regular Season					Playoffs				
Season	**Club**	**Lea**	**GP**	**G**	**A**	**TP**	**PIM**	**GP**	**G**	**A**	**TP**	**PIM**
1993-94	Laval	QMJHL	51	9	14	23	70	20	2	1	3	19
1994-95	Laval	QMJHL	71	30	58	88	199	20	8	*21	29	42
1995-96	Laval	QMJHL	38	21	39	60	130	....	....	....	....	....
	Granby	QMJHL	27	12	46	58	97	21	13	26	39	68
1996-97	Portland	AHL	76	6	40	46	140	5	2	1	3	14
1997-98	**Washington**	**NHL**	**6**	**0**	**1**	**1**	**6**	....	....	....	....	....
	Portland	AHL	58	19	31	50	137	8	4	2	6	24
	NHL Totals		**6**	**0**	**1**	**1**	**6**	....	....	....	....	....

GRATTON, CHRIS (GRA-tuhn) PHI.

Center. Shoots left. 6'4", 218 lbs. Born, Brantford, Ont., July 5, 1975.
(Tampa Bay's 1st choice, 3rd overall, in 1993 Entry Draft).

			Regular Season					Playoffs				
Season	**Club**	**Lea**	**GP**	**G**	**A**	**TP**	**PIM**	**GP**	**G**	**A**	**TP**	**PIM**
1991-92	Kingston	OHL	62	27	29	66	37	....	....	....	....	....
1992-93	Kingston	OHL	58	55	54	109	125	16	11	18	29	42
1993-94	**Tampa Bay**	**NHL**	**84**	**13**	**29**	**42**	**123**	....	....	....	....	....
1994-95	**Tampa Bay**	**NHL**	**46**	**7**	**20**	**27**	**89**	....	....	....	....	....
1995-96	**Tampa Bay**	**NHL**	**82**	**17**	**21**	**38**	**105**	**6**	**0**	**2**	**2**	**27**
1996-97	**Tampa Bay**	**NHL**	**82**	**30**	**32**	**62**	**201**	....	....	....	....	....
1997-98	**Philadelphia**	**NHL**	**82**	**22**	**40**	**62**	**159**	**5**	**2**	**0**	**2**	**10**
	NHL Totals		**376**	**89**	**142**	**231**	**677**	**11**	**2**	**2**	**4**	**37**

Signed as a free agent by **Philadelphia**, August 14, 1997.

GRAVES, ADAM NYR

Center. Shoots left. 6', 210 lbs. Born, Toronto, Ont., April 12, 1968.
(Detroit's 2nd choice, 22nd overall, in 1986 Entry Draft).

			Regular Season					Playoffs				
Season	**Club**	**Lea**	**GP**	**G**	**A**	**TP**	**PIM**	**GP**	**G**	**A**	**TP**	**PIM**
1985-86	Windsor	OHL	62	27	37	64	35	16	5	11	16	10
1986-87	Windsor	OHL	66	45	55	100	70	14	9	8	17	32
	Adirondack	AHL	....	....	....	....	....	5	0	1	1	0
1987-88	Windsor	OHL	37	28	32	60	107	12	14	18	*32	16
	Detroit	**NHL**	**9**	**0**	**1**	**1**	**8**	....	....	....	....	....
1988-89	**Detroit**	**NHL**	**56**	**7**	**5**	**12**	**60**	**5**	**0**	**0**	**0**	**4**
	Adirondack	AHL	14	10	11	21	28	14	11	7	18	17
1989-90	**Detroit**	**NHL**	**13**	**0**	**1**	**1**	**13**	....	....	....	....	....
	Edmonton	**NHL**	**63**	**9**	**12**	**21**	**123**	**22**	**5**	**6**	**11**	**17** ♦
1990-91	**Edmonton**	**NHL**	**76**	**7**	**18**	**25**	**127**	**18**	**2**	**4**	**6**	**22**
1991-92	**NY Rangers**	**NHL**	**80**	**26**	**33**	**59**	**139**	**10**	**5**	**3**	**8**	**22**
1992-93	**NY Rangers**	**NHL**	**84**	**36**	**29**	**65**	**148**	....	....	....	....	....
1993-94	**NY Rangers**	**NHL**	**84**	**52**	**27**	**79**	**127**	**23**	**10**	**7**	**17**	**24** ♦
1994-95	**NY Rangers**	**NHL**	**47**	**17**	**14**	**31**	**51**	**10**	**4**	**4**	**8**	**8**
1995-96	**NY Rangers**	**NHL**	**82**	**22**	**36**	**58**	**100**	**10**	**7**	**1**	**8**	**4**
1996-97	**NY Rangers**	**NHL**	**82**	**33**	**28**	**61**	**66**	**15**	**2**	**1**	**3**	**12**
1997-98	**NY Rangers**	**NHL**	**72**	**23**	**12**	**35**	**41**	....	....	....	....	....
	NHL Totals		**748**	**232**	**216**	**448**	**1003**	**113**	**35**	**26**	**61**	**113**

NHL Second All-Star Team (1994) • Won King Clancy Memorial Trophy (1994)

Played in NHL All-Star Game (1994)

Traded to **Edmonton** by **Detroit** with Petr Klima, Joe Murphy and Jeff Sharples for Jimmy Carson, Kevin McClelland and Edmonton's 5th round choice (later traded to Montreal — Montreal selected Brad Layzell) in 1991 Entry Draft, November 2, 1989. Signed as a free agent by **NY Rangers**, September 3, 1991.

GREEN, JOSH L.A.

Left wing. Shoots left. 6'4", 212 lbs. Born, Camrose, Alta., November 16, 1977.
(Los Angeles' 1st choice, 30th overall, in 1996 Entry Draft).

			Regular Season					Playoffs				
Season	**Club**	**Lea**	**GP**	**G**	**A**	**TP**	**PIM**	**GP**	**G**	**A**	**TP**	**PIM**
1993-94	Medicine Hat	WHL	63	22	22	44	43	3	0	0	0	4
1994-95	Medicine Hat	WHL	68	32	23	55	64	5	5	1	6	2
1995-96	Medicine Hat	WHL	46	18	25	43	55	5	2	2	4	4
1996-97	Medicine Hat	WHL	51	25	32	57	61	....	....	....	....	....
	Swift Current	WHL	23	10	15	25	33	10	9	7	16	19
1997-98	Swift Current	WHL	5	9	1	10	9	....	....	....	....	....
	Portland	WHL	26	26	18	44	27	....	....	....	....	....
	Fredericton	AHL	43	16	15	31	14	4	1	3	4	6

GREEN, TRAVIS ANA.

Center. Shoots right. 6'1", 193 lbs. Born, Castlegar, B.C., December 20, 1970.
(NY Islanders' 2nd choice, 23rd overall, in 1989 Entry Draft).

			Regular Season					Playoffs				
Season	**Club**	**Lea**	**GP**	**G**	**A**	**TP**	**PIM**	**GP**	**G**	**A**	**TP**	**PIM**
1986-87	Spokane	WHL	64	8	17	25	27	3	0	0	0	0
1987-88	Spokane	WHL	72	33	54	87	42	15	10	10	20	13
1988-89	Spokane	WHL	75	51	51	102	79	....	....	....	....	....
1989-90	Spokane	WHL	50	45	44	89	80	....	....	....	....	....
	Medicine Hat	WHL	25	15	24	39	19	3	0	0	0	2
1990-91	Capital District	AHL	73	21	34	55	26	....	....	....	....	....
1991-92	Capital District	AHL	71	23	27	50	10	7	0	4	4	21
1992-93	**NY Islanders**	**NHL**	**61**	**7**	**18**	**25**	**43**	**12**	**3**	**1**	**4**	**6**
	Capital District	AHL	20	12	11	23	39	....	....	....	....	....
1993-94	**NY Islanders**	**NHL**	**83**	**18**	**22**	**40**	**44**	**4**	**0**	**0**	**0**	**2**
1994-95	**NY Islanders**	**NHL**	**42**	**5**	**7**	**12**	**25**	....	....	....	....	....
1995-96	**NY Islanders**	**NHL**	**69**	**25**	**45**	**70**	**42**	....	....	....	....	....
1996-97	**NY Islanders**	**NHL**	**79**	**23**	**41**	**64**	**38**	....	....	....	....	....
1997-98	**NY Islanders**	**NHL**	**54**	**14**	**12**	**26**	**66**	....	....	....	....	....
	Anaheim	**NHL**	**22**	**5**	**11**	**16**	**16**	....	....	....	....	....
	NHL Totals		**410**	**97**	**156**	**253**	**274**	**16**	**3**	**1**	**4**	**8**

Traded to **Anaheim** by **NY Islanders** with Doug Houda and Tony Tuzzolino for Joe Sacco, J.J. Daigneault and Mark Janssens, February 6, 1998.

GREIG, MARK (GREG) PHI.

Right wing. Shoots right. 5'11", 190 lbs. Born, High River, Alta., January 25, 1970.
(Hartford's 1st choice, 15th overall, in 1990 Entry Draft).

			Regular Season					Playoffs				
Season	**Club**	**Lea**	**GP**	**G**	**A**	**TP**	**PIM**	**GP**	**G**	**A**	**TP**	**PIM**
1987-88	Lethbridge	WHL	65	9	18	27	38	....	....	....	....	....
1988-89	Lethbridge	WHL	71	36	72	108	113	8	5	5	10	16
1989-90	Lethbridge	WHL	65	55	80	135	149	18	11	21	32	35
1990-91	**Hartford**	**NHL**	**4**	**0**	**0**	**0**	**0**	....	....	....	....	....
	Springfield	AHL	73	32	55	87	73	17	2	6	8	22
1991-92	**Hartford**	**NHL**	**17**	**0**	**5**	**5**	**6**	....	....	....	....	....
	Springfield	AHL	50	20	27	47	38	9	1	1	2	20
1992-93	**Hartford**	**NHL**	**22**	**1**	**7**	**8**	**27**	....	....	....	....	....
	Springfield	AHL	55	20	38	58	86	....	....	....	....	....
1993-94	**Hartford**	**NHL**	**31**	**4**	**5**	**9**	**31**	....	....	....	....	....
	Springfield	AHL	4	0	4	4	21	....	....	....	....	....
	Toronto	**NHL**	**13**	**2**	**2**	**4**	**10**	....	....	....	....	....
	St. John's	AHL	9	4	6	10	0	11	4	2	6	26
1994-95	**Calgary**	**NHL**	**8**	**1**	**1**	**2**	**2**	....	....	....	....	....
	Saint John	AHL	67	31	50	81	82	2	0	1	1	0
1995-96	Atlanta	IHL	71	25	48	73	104	3	2	1	3	4
1996-97	Quebec	IHL	5	1	2	3	0	....	....	....	....	....
	Houston	IHL	59	12	30	42	59	13	5	8	13	2
1997-98	Grand Rapids	IHL	69	26	36	62	103	3	0	4	4	4
	NHL Totals		**95**	**8**	**20**	**28**	**76**	....	....	....	....	....

WHL East First All-Star Team (1990)

Traded to **Toronto** by **Hartford** with Hartford's 6th round choice (later traded to NY Rangers — NY Rangers selected Yuri Litvinov) in 1994 Entry Draft for Ted Crowley, January 25, 1994. Signed as a free agent by **Calgary**, August 9, 1994. Signed as a free agent by **Philadelphia**, July 28, 1998.

GRETZKY, WAYNE (GRETZ-kee) NYR

Center. Shoots left. 6', 185 lbs. Born, Brantford, Ont., January 26, 1961.

			Regular Season					Playoffs				
Season	**Club**	**Lea**	**GP**	**G**	**A**	**TP**	**PIM**	**GP**	**G**	**A**	**TP**	**PIM**
1976-77	Peterborough	OHA	3	0	3	3	0	....	....	....	....	....
1977-78	S.S. Marie	OHA	64	70	112	182	14	13	6	20	26	0
1978-79	Indianapolis	WHA	8	3	3	6	0	....	....	....	....	....
	Edmonton	WHA	72	43	61	104	19	13	*10	10	*20	2
1979-80	**Edmonton**	**NHL**	**79**	**51**	***86**	***137**	**21**	**3**	**2**	**1**	**3**	**0**
1980-81	**Edmonton**	**NHL**	**80**	**55**	***109**	***164**	**28**	**9**	**7**	**14**	**21**	**4**
1981-82	**Edmonton**	**NHL**	**80**	***92**	***120**	***212**	**26**	**5**	**5**	**7**	**12**	**8**
1982-83	**Edmonton**	**NHL**	**80**	***71**	***125**	***196**	**59**	**16**	**12**	***26**	***38**	**4**
1983-84	**Edmonton**	**NHL**	**74**	***87**	***118**	***205**	**39**	**19**	**13**	***22**	***35**	**12** ♦
1984-85	**Edmonton**	**NHL**	**80**	***73**	***135**	***208**	**52**	**18**	**17**	***30**	***47**	**4** ♦
1985-86	**Edmonton**	**NHL**	**80**	**52**	***163**	***215**	**46**	**10**	**8**	**11**	**19**	**2**
1986-87	**Edmonton**	**NHL**	**79**	***62**	***121**	***183**	**28**	**21**	**5**	***29**	***34**	**6** ♦
1987-88	**Edmonton**	**NHL**	**64**	**40**	***109**	**149**	**24**	**19**	**12**	***31**	***43**	**16** ♦
1988-89	**Los Angeles**	**NHL**	**78**	**54**	***114**	**168**	**26**	**11**	**5**	**17**	**22**	**0**
1989-90	**Los Angeles**	**NHL**	**73**	**40**	***102**	***142**	**42**	**7**	**3**	**7**	**10**	**0**
1990-91	**Los Angeles**	**NHL**	**78**	**41**	***122**	***163**	**16**	**12**	**4**	**11**	**15**	**2**
1991-92	**Los Angeles**	**NHL**	**74**	**31**	***90**	**121**	**34**	**6**	**2**	**5**	**7**	**2**
1992-93	**Los Angeles**	**NHL**	**45**	**16**	**49**	**65**	**6**	**24**	***15**	***25**	***40**	**4**
1993-94	**Los Angeles**	**NHL**	**81**	**38**	***92**	***130**	**20**	....	....	....	....	....
1994-95	**Los Angeles**	**NHL**	**48**	**11**	**37**	**48**	**6**	....	....	....	....	....
1995-96	**Los Angeles**	**NHL**	**62**	**15**	**66**	**81**	**32**	....	....	....	....	....
	St. Louis	**NHL**	**18**	**8**	**13**	**21**	**2**	**13**	**2**	**14**	**16**	**0**
1996-97	**NY Rangers**	**NHL**	**82**	**25**	***72**	**97**	**28**	**15**	**10**	**10**	**20**	**2**
1997-98	**NY Rangers**	**NHL**	**82**	**23**	***67**	**90**	**28**	....	....	....	....	....
	Canada	Olympics	6	0	4	4	2	....	....	....	....	....
	NHL Totals		**1417**	***885**	***1910**	***2795**	**563**	**208**	***122**	***260**	***382**	**66**

OHA Second All-Star Team (1978) • WHA Second All-Star Team (1979) • Won Lou Kaplan Trophy (WHA Rookie of the Year) (1979) • Won Hart Trophy (1980, 1981, 1982, 1983, 1984, 1985, 1986, 1987, 1989) • Won Lady Byng Trophy (1980, 1991, 1992, 1994) • NHL Second All-Star Team (1980, 1988, 1989, 1990, 1994, 1997, 1998) • NHL First All-Star Team (1981, 1982, 1983, 1984, 1985, 1986, 1987, 1991) • Won Art Ross Trophy (1981, 1982, 1983, 1984, 1985, 1986, 1987, 1990, 1991, 1994) • NHL record for assists in regular season (1981, 1982, 1983, 1985, 1986) • NHL record for points in regular season (1981, 1982, 1986) • NHL record for goals in regular season (1982) • Won Lester B. Pearson Award (1982, 1983, 1984, 1985, 1987) • NHL record for assists in one playoff year (1983, 1985, 1988) • NHL record for points in one playoff year (1983, 1985) • Won Conn Smythe Trophy (1985, 1988) • NHL Plus/Minus Leader (1982, 1984, 1985, 1987) • Selected Chrysler-Dodge/NHL Performer of the Year (1985, 1986, 1987) • Won Dodge Performance of the Year Award (1989) • Won Lester Patrick Trophy (1994)

Played in NHL All-Star Game (1980, 1981, 1982, 1983, 1984, 1985, 1986, 1988, 1989, 1990, 1991, 1992, 1994, 1996, 1997, 1998)

Signed as an underage free agent by **Indianapolis** (WHA), June 12, 1978. Traded to **Edmonton** (WHA) by **Indianapolis** (WHA) with Eddie Mio and Peter Driscoll for cash, November, 1978. Reclaimed by **Edmonton** as an under-age junior prior to Expansion Draft, June 9, 1979. Claimed as priority selection by **Edmonton**, June 9, 1979. Traded to **LA Kings** by **Edmonton** with Mike Krushelnyski and Marty McSorley for Jimmy Carson, Martin Gelinas, LA Kings' 1st round choices in 1989 (acquired by New Jersey — New Jersey selected Jason Miller), 1991 (Martin Rucinsky) and 1993 (Nick Stajduhar) Entry Drafts and cash, August 9, 1988. Traded to **St. Louis** by **LA Kings** for Craig Johnson, Patrice Tardif, Roman Vopat, St. Louis 5th round choice (Peter Hogan) in 1996 Entry Draft and 1st round choice (Matt Zultek) in 1997 Entry Draft, February 27, 1996. Signed as a free agent by **NY Rangers**, July 21, 1996.

GRIER, MICHAEL (GREER) EDM.

Right wing. Shoots right. 6'1", 227 lbs. Born, Detroit, MI, January 5, 1975.
(St. Louis' 7th choice, 219th overall, in 1993 Entry Draft).

			Regular Season					Playoffs				
Season	**Club**	**Lea**	**GP**	**G**	**A**	**TP**	**PIM**	**GP**	**G**	**A**	**TP**	**PIM**
1992-93	St. Sebastian's	H.S.	22	16	27	43	32	....	....	....	....	....
1993-94	Boston University	H.E.	39	9	9	18	56	....	....	....	....	....
1994-95	Boston University	H.E.	37	*29	26	55	85	....	....	....	....	....
1995-96	Boston University	H.E.	38	21	25	46	82	....	....	....	....	....
1996-97	**Edmonton**	**NHL**	**79**	**15**	**17**	**32**	**45**	**12**	**3**	**1**	**4**	**4**
1997-98	**Edmonton**	**NHL**	**66**	**9**	**6**	**15**	**73**	**12**	**2**	**2**	**4**	**13**
	NHL Totals		**145**	**24**	**23**	**47**	**118**	**24**	**5**	**3**	**8**	**17**

Hockey East First All-Star Team (1995) • NCAA East First All-American Team (1995)

Rights traded to **Edmonton** by **St. Louis** with Curtis Joseph for St. Louis' 1st round choices in 1996 (previously acquired, St. Louis selected Marty Reasoner) and 1997 (later traded to LA Kings — LA Kings selected Matt Zultek) Entry Drafts, August 4, 1995.

GRIMES, KEVIN COL.

Defense. Shoots left. 6'2", 205 lbs. Born, Ottawa, Ont., August 19, 1979.
(Colorado's 1st choice, 26th overall, in 1997 Entry Draft).

			Regular Season					Playoffs				
Season	**Club**	**Lea**	**GP**	**G**	**A**	**TP**	**PIM**	**GP**	**G**	**A**	**TP**	**PIM**
1996-97	Kingston	OHL	57	2	12	14	188	1	0	0	0	0
1997-98	Kingston	OHL	62	1	27	28	179	12	0	1	1	16

GRIMSON, STU — ANA.

Left wing. Shoots left. 6'5", 227 lbs. Born, Kamloops, B.C., May 20, 1965.
(Calgary's 8th choice, 143rd overall, in 1985 Entry Draft).

			Regular Season					Playoffs				
Season	Club	Lea	GP	G	A	TP	PIM	GP	G	A	TP	PIM
1982-83	Regina	WHL	48	0	1	1	105	5	0	0	0	14
1983-84	Regina	WHL	63	8	8	16	131	21	0	1	1	29
1984-85	Regina	WHL	71	24	32	56	248	8	1	2	3	14
1985-86	U. of Manitoba	CWUAA	12	7	4	11	113	8	1	1	2	24
1986-87	U. of Manitoba	CWUAA	29	8	8	16	67	14	4	2	6	28
1987-88	Salt Lake	IHL	38	9	5	14	268	....	....	....	....	....
1988-89	**Calgary**	**NHL**	**1**	**0**	**0**	**0**	**5**	....	....	....	....	....
	Salt Lake	IHL	72	9	18	27	397	14	2	3	5	86
1989-90	**Calgary**	**NHL**	**3**	**0**	**0**	**0**	**17**	....	....	....	....	....
	Salt Lake	IHL	62	8	8	16	319	4	0	0	0	8
1990-91	**Chicago**	**NHL**	**35**	**0**	**1**	**1**	**183**	**5**	**0**	**0**	**0**	**46**
1991-92	**Chicago**	**NHL**	**54**	**2**	**2**	**4**	**234**	**14**	**0**	**1**	**1**	**10**
	Indianapolis	IHL	5	1	1	2	17	....	....	....	....	....
1992-93	**Chicago**	**NHL**	**78**	**1**	**1**	**2**	**193**	**2**	**0**	**0**	**0**	**4**
1993-94	**Anaheim**	**NHL**	**77**	**1**	**5**	**6**	**199**	....	....	....	....	....
1994-95	**Anaheim**	**NHL**	**31**	**0**	**1**	**1**	**110**	....	....	....	....	....
	Detroit	**NHL**	**11**	**0**	**0**	**0**	**37**	**11**	**1**	**0**	**1**	**26**
1995-96	**Detroit**	**NHL**	**56**	**0**	**1**	**1**	**128**	**2**	**0**	**0**	**0**	**0**
1996-97	**Detroit**	**NHL**	**1**	**0**	**0**	**0**	**0**	....	....	....	....	....
	Hartford	**NHL**	**75**	**2**	**2**	**4**	**218**	....	....	....	....	....
1997-98	**Carolina**	**NHL**	**82**	**3**	**4**	**7**	**204**	....	....	....	....	....
	NHL Totals		**504**	**9**	**17**	**26**	**1528**	**34**	**1**	**1**	**2**	**86**

• Re-entered NHL draft. Originally Detroit's 11th choice, 193rd overall, in 1983 Entry Draft.

Claimed on waivers by **Chicago** from **Calgary**, October 1, 1990. Claimed by **Anaheim** from **Chicago** in Expansion Draft, June 24, 1993. Traded to **Detroit** by **Anaheim** with Mark Ferner and Anaheim's 6th round choice (Magnus Nilsson) in 1996 Entry Draft for Mike Sillinger and Jason York, April 4, 1995. Claimed on waivers by **Hartford** from **Detroit**, October 13, 1996. Transferred to **Carolina** after **Hartford** franchise relocated, June 25, 1997. Traded to **Anaheim** by **Carolina** with Kevin Haller for David Karpa and a 4th round choice in 2000 Entry Draft, August 11, 1998.

GROLEAU, FRANCOIS — (groh-LOH)

Defense. Shoots left. 6', 197 lbs. Born, Longueuil, Que., January 23, 1973.
(Calgary's 2nd choice, 41st overall, in 1991 Entry Draft).

			Regular Season					Playoffs				
Season	Club	Lea	GP	G	A	TP	PIM	GP	G	A	TP	PIM
1989-90	Shawinigan	QMJHL	65	11	54	65	80	6	0	1	1	12
1990-91	Shawinigan	QMJHL	70	9	60	69	70	6	0	3	3	2
1991-92	Shawinigan	QMJHL	65	8	70	78	74	10	5	15	20	8
1992-93	St-Jean	QMJHL	48	7	38	45	66	4	0	1	1	14
1993-94	Saint John	AHL	73	8	14	22	49	7	0	1	1	2
1994-95	Saint John	AHL	65	6	34	40	28	....	....	....	....	....
	Cornwall	AHL	8	1	2	3	7	14	2	7	9	16
1995-96	**Montreal**	**NHL**	**2**	**0**	**1**	**1**	**2**	....	....	....	....	....
	San Francisco	IHL	63	6	26	32	60	....	....	....	....	....
	Fredericton	AHL	12	3	5	8	10	10	1	6	7	14
1996-97	**Montreal**	**NHL**	**5**	**0**	**0**	**0**	**4**	....	....	....	....	....
	Fredericton	AHL	47	8	24	32	43	....	....	....	....	....
1997-98	**Montreal**	**NHL**	**1**	**0**	**0**	**0**	**0**	....	....	....	....	....
	Fredericton	AHL	63	14	26	40	70	4	0	2	2	4
	NHL Totals		**8**	**0**	**1**	**1**	**6**	....	....	....	....	....

QMJHL Second All-Star Team (1990) • QMJHL First All-Star Team (1992)

Traded to **Quebec** by **Calgary** for Ed Ward, March 23, 1995. Signed as a free agent by **Montreal**, June 17, 1995.

GRON, STANISLAV — (GRAHN) N.J.

Center. Shoots left. 6'1", 190 lbs. Born, Bratislava, Czech., October 28, 1978.
(New Jersey's 2nd choice, 38th overall, in 1997 Entry Draft).

			Regular Season					Playoffs				
Season	Club	Lea	GP	G	A	TP	PIM	GP	G	A	TP	PIM
1996-97	Bratislava	Slovakia	7	0	0	0	....	....	....	....	....	....
	Bratislava	Slov-Jr.	22	20	16	36	....	....	....	....	....	....
1997-98	Seattle	WHL	61	9	29	38	21	5	1	5	6	0

GRONMAN, TUOMAS — (GROHN-mahn) PIT.

Defense. Shoots right. 6'3", 219 lbs. Born, Viitasaari, Finland, March 22, 1974.
(Quebec's 3rd choice, 29th overall, in 1992 Entry Draft).

			Regular Season					Playoffs				
Season	Club	Lea	GP	G	A	TP	PIM	GP	G	A	TP	PIM
1991-92	Tacoma	WHL	61	5	18	23	102	4	0	1	1	2
1992-93	Lukko Rauma	Finland	45	2	11	13	46	3	1	0	1	2
1993-94	Lukko Rauma	Finland	44	4	12	16	60	9	0	1	1	14
1994-95	TPS Turku	Finland	47	4	20	24	66	13	2	2	4	43
1995-96	TPS Turku	Finland	32	5	7	12	85	11	1	4	5	16
1996-97	**Chicago**	**NHL**	**16**	**0**	**1**	**1**	**13**	....	....	....	....	....
	Indianapolis	IHL	51	5	16	21	89	4	1	1	2	6
1997-98	Indianapolis	IHL	6	0	3	3	6	....	....	....	....	....
	Pittsburgh	**NHL**	**22**	**1**	**2**	**3**	**25**	**1**	**0**	**0**	**0**	**0**
	Syracuse	AHL	33	6	14	20	45	....	....	....	....	....
	Finland	Olympics	4	0	0	0	2	....	....	....	....	....
	NHL Totals		**38**	**1**	**3**	**4**	**38**	**1**	**0**	**0**	**0**	**0**

Rights traded to **Chicago** by **Colorado** for Chicago's 2nd round choice (Phillippe Sauve) in 1998 Entry Draft, July 10, 1996. Traded to **Pittsburgh** by **Chicago** for Greg Johnson, October 27, 1997.

GROSEK, MICHAL — (GROH-shehk) BUF.

Left wing. Shoots right. 6'2", 207 lbs. Born, Vyskov, Czech., June 1, 1975.
(Winnipeg's 7th choice, 145th overall, in 1993 Entry Draft).

			Regular Season					Playoffs				
Season	Club	Lea	GP	G	A	TP	PIM	GP	G	A	TP	PIM
1992-93	ZPS Zlin	Czech.	17	1	3	4	....	....	....	....	....	....
1993-94	Tacoma	WHL	30	25	20	45	106	7	2	2	4	30
	Winnipeg	**NHL**	**3**	**1**	**0**	**1**	**0**	....	....	....	....	....
	Moncton	AHL	20	1	2	3	47	2	0	0	0	0
1994-95	**Winnipeg**	**NHL**	**24**	**2**	**2**	**4**	**21**	....	....	....	....	....
	Springfield	AHL	45	10	22	32	98	....	....	....	....	....
1995-96	**Winnipeg**	**NHL**	**1**	**0**	**0**	**0**	**0**	....	....	....	....	....
	Springfield	AHL	39	16	19	35	68	....	....	....	....	....
	Buffalo	**NHL**	**22**	**6**	**4**	**10**	**31**	....	....	....	....	....
1996-97	**Buffalo**	**NHL**	**82**	**15**	**21**	**36**	**71**	**12**	**3**	**3**	**6**	**8**
1997-98	**Buffalo**	**NHL**	**67**	**10**	**20**	**30**	**60**	**15**	**6**	**4**	**10**	**28**
	NHL Totals		**199**	**34**	**47**	**81**	**183**	**27**	**9**	**7**	**16**	**36**

Traded to **Buffalo** by **Winnipeg** with Darryl Shannon for Craig Muni, February 15, 1996.

GROSS, PAVEL — NYI

Right wing. Shoots right. 6'3", 195 lbs. Born, Ustin Ogroh, Czech., May 11, 1968.
(NY Islanders' 7th choice, 111th overall, in 1988 Entry Draft).

			Regular Season					Playoffs				
Season	Club	Lea	GP	G	A	TP	PIM	GP	G	A	TP	PIM
1987-88	Sparta Praha	Czech.	29	4	6	10	10	....	....	....	....	....
1988-89	Sparta Praha	Czech.	39	13	9	22	22	....	....	....	....	....
1989-90	Sparta Praha	Czech.	36	10	9	19	....	....	....	....	....	....
1990-91	Freiburg	Germany	32	11	24	35	66	....	....	....	....	....
1991-92	Freiburg	Germany	43	15	22	37	59	....	....	....	....	....
1992-93	Freiburg	Germany	41	11	20	31	62	8	5	5	10	6
1993-94	Mannheim	Germany	42	14	24	38	30	....	....	....	....	....
1994-95	Mannheim	Germany	42	21	40	61	99	6	4	3	7	0
1995-96	Mannheim	Germany	49	29	43	72	81	8	4	2	6	14
1996-97	Mannheim	Germany	50	14	46	60	67	9	6	9	15	0
1997-98	Mannheim	Germany	35	7	15	22	41	10	1	6	7	24

GRUDEN, JOHN — OTT.

Defense. Shoots left. 6', 190 lbs. Born, Virginia, MN, June 4, 1970.
(Boston's 7th choice, 168th overall, in 1990 Entry Draft).

			Regular Season					Playoffs				
Season	Club	Lea	GP	G	A	TP	PIM	GP	G	A	TP	PIM
1989-90	Waterloo	OJHL	47	7	39	46	35	....	....	....	....	....
1990-91	Ferris State	CCHA	37	4	11	15	27	....	....	....	....	....
1991-92	Ferris State	CCHA	37	9	14	23	24	....	....	....	....	....
1992-93	Ferris State	CCHA	41	16	14	30	58	....	....	....	....	....
1993-94	Ferris State	CCHA	38	11	25	36	52	....	....	....	....	....
	Boston	**NHL**	**7**	**0**	**1**	**1**	**2**	....	....	....	....	....
1994-95	**Boston**	**NHL**	**38**	**0**	**6**	**6**	**22**	....	....	....	....	....
	Providence	AHL	1	0	1	1	0	....	....	....	....	....
1995-96	**Boston**	**NHL**	**14**	**0**	**0**	**0**	**4**	**3**	**0**	**1**	**1**	**0**
	Providence	AHL	39	5	19	24	29	....	....	....	....	....
1996-97	Providence	AHL	78	18	27	45	52	10	3	6	9	4
1997-98	Detroit	IHL	76	13	42	55	74	21	1	8	9	14
	NHL Totals		**59**	**0**	**7**	**7**	**28**	**3**	**0**	**1**	**1**	**0**

CCHA First All-Star Team (1994) • NCAA West First All-American Team (1994) • IHL Second All-Star Team (1998)

Signed as a free agent by **Ottawa**, August 7, 1998.

GUERIN, BILL — (GAIR-ihn) EDM.

Right wing. Shoots right. 6'2", 210 lbs. Born, Wilbraham, MA, November 9, 1970.
(New Jersey's 1st choice, 5th overall, in 1989 Entry Draft).

			Regular Season					Playoffs				
Season	Club	Lea	GP	G	A	TP	PIM	GP	G	A	TP	PIM
1988-89	Springfield	NEJHL	31	32	35	67	90	....	....	....	....	....
1989-90	Boston College	H.E.	39	14	11	25	54	....	....	....	....	....
1990-91	Boston College	H.E.	38	26	19	45	102	....	....	....	....	....
	United States	Nat-Tm	46	12	15	27	67	....	....	....	....	....
1991-92	**New Jersey**	**NHL**	**5**	**0**	**1**	**1**	**9**	**6**	**3**	**0**	**3**	**4**
	Utica	AHL	22	13	10	23	6	4	1	3	4	14
1992-93	**New Jersey**	**NHL**	**65**	**14**	**20**	**34**	**63**	**5**	**1**	**1**	**2**	**4**
	Utica	AHL	18	10	7	17	47	....	....	....	....	....
1993-94	**New Jersey**	**NHL**	**81**	**25**	**19**	**44**	**101**	**17**	**2**	**1**	**3**	**35**
1994-95	**New Jersey**	**NHL**	**48**	**12**	**13**	**25**	**72**	**20**	**3**	**8**	**11**	**30** ♦
1995-96	**New Jersey**	**NHL**	**80**	**23**	**30**	**53**	**116**	....	....	....	....	....
1996-97	**New Jersey**	**NHL**	**82**	**29**	**18**	**47**	**95**	**8**	**2**	**1**	**3**	**18**
1997-98	**New Jersey**	**NHL**	**19**	**5**	**5**	**10**	**13**	....	....	....	....	....
	Edmonton	**NHL**	**40**	**13**	**16**	**29**	**80**	**12**	**7**	**1**	**8**	**17**
	United States	Olympics	4	0	3	3	2	....	....	....	....	....
	NHL Totals		**420**	**121**	**122**	**243**	**549**	**68**	**18**	**12**	**30**	**108**

Traded to **Edmonton** by **New Jersey** with Valeri Zelepukin for Jason Arnott and Bryan Muir, January 4, 1998.

GUITE, BEN — MTL.

Right wing. Shoots right. 6', 202 lbs. Born, Montreal, Que., July 17, 1978.
(Montreal's 8th choice, 172nd overall, in 1997 Entry Draft).

			Regular Season					Playoffs				
Season	Club	Lea	GP	G	A	TP	PIM	GP	G	A	TP	PIM
1996-97	U. of Maine	H.E.	34	7	7	14	21	....	....	....	....	....
1997-98	U. of Maine	H.E.	32	6	12	18	20	....	....	....	....	....

GUNKO, YURI — (goon-KOH, YOO-ree) ST.L.

Defense. Shoots left. 6'1", 187 lbs. Born, Kiev, USSR, February 28, 1972.
(St. Louis' 11th choice, 230th overall, in 1992 Entry Draft).

			Regular Season					Playoffs				
Season	Club	Lea	GP	G	A	TP	PIM	GP	G	A	TP	PIM
1990-91	Sokol Kiev	USSR	14	0	0	0	8	....	....	....	....	....
1991-92	Sokol Kiev	CIS	22	1	0	1	16	....	....	....	....	....
1992-93	Sokol Kiev	CIS	40	2	3	5	28	....	....	....	....	....
1993-94	Sokol Kiev	CIS	42	0	8	8	28	....	....	....	....	....
1994-95	Sokol Kiev	CIS	25	4	0	4	18	....	....	....	....	....
1995-96	AK Bars Kazan	CIS	41	1	2	3	22	5	1	0	1	4
1996-97	AK Bars Kazan	Russia	42	6	7	13	42	3	1	0	1	4
1997-98	AK Bars Kazan	Russia	45	6	5	11	50	....	....	....	....	....

GUOLLA, STEPHEN — (GUH-wah-lah) S.J.

Left wing. Shoots left. 6', 190 lbs. Born, Scarborough, Ont., March 15, 1973.
(Ottawa's 1st choice, 3rd overall, in 1994 Supplemental Draft).

			Regular Season					Playoffs				
Season	Club	Lea	GP	G	A	TP	PIM	GP	G	A	TP	PIM
1991-92	Michigan State	CCHA	33	4	9	13	8	....	....	....	....	....
1992-93	Michigan State	CCHA	39	19	35	54	6	....	....	....	....	....
1993-94	Michigan State	CCHA	41	23	46	69	16	....	....	....	....	....
1994-95	Michigan State	CCHA	40	16	35	51	16	....	....	....	....	....
1995-96	P.E.I.	AHL	72	32	48	80	28	3	0	0	0	0
1996-97	**San Jose**	**NHL**	**43**	**13**	**8**	**21**	**14**	....	....	....	....	....
	Kentucky	AHL	34	22	22	44	10	4	2	1	3	0
1997-98	**San Jose**	**NHL**	**7**	**1**	**1**	**2**	**0**	....	....	....	....	....
	Kentucky	AHL	69	37	63	100	45	3	0	0	0	0
	NHL Totals		**50**	**14**	**9**	**23**	**14**	....	....	....	....	....

CCHA Second All-Star Team (1994) • NCAA West Second All-American Team (1994) • AHL Second All-Star Team (1998) • Won Les Cunningham Plaque (MVP - AHL) (1998)

Signed as a free agent by **San Jose**, August 22, 1996.

GUREN, MILOSLAV (GOO-rihn) MTL.

Defense. Shoots left. 6'2", 210 lbs. Born, Uherske. Hradiste, Czech., September 24, 1976.
(Montreal's 2nd choice, 60th overall, in 1995 Entry Draft).

			Regular Season					Playoffs				
Season	Club	Lea	GP	G	A	TP	PIM	GP	G	A	TP	PIM
1993-94	ZPS Zlin	Cze-Rep.	22	1	5	6	....	3	0	0	0	....
1994-95	ZPS Zlin	Cze-Rep.	32	3	7	10	10	12	1	0	1	6
1995-96	ZPS Zlin	Cze-Rep.	28	1	2	3	....	7	1	0	1	....
1996-97	Fredericton	AHL	79	6	26	32	26	....	....	....	....	....
1997-98	Fredericton	AHL	78	15	36	51	36	4	1	2	3	0

GUSAROV, ALEXEI (goo-SAH-rahf) COL.

Defense. Shoots left. 6'3", 185 lbs. Born, Leningrad, USSR, July 8, 1964.
(Quebec's 11th choice, 213th overall, in 1988 Entry Draft).

			Regular Season					Playoffs				
Season	Club	Lea	GP	G	A	TP	PIM	GP	G	A	TP	PIM
1981-82	Leningrad	USSR	20	1	2	3	16	....	....	....	....	....
1982-83	Leningrad	USSR	42	2	1	3	32	....	....	....	....	....
1983-84	Leningrad	USSR	43	2	3	5	32	....	....	....	....	....
1984-85	CSKA Moscow	USSR	36	3	2	5	26	....	....	....	....	....
1985-86	CSKA Moscow	USSR	40	3	5	8	30	....	....	....	....	....
1986-87	CSKA Moscow	USSR	38	4	7	11	24	....	....	....	....	....
1987-88	CSKA Moscow	USSR	39	3	2	5	28	....	....	....	....	....
	Soviet Union	Olympics	8	1	3	4	6	....	....	....	....	....
1988-89	CSKA Moscow	USSR	42	5	4	9	37	....	....	....	....	....
1989-90	CSKA Moscow	USSR	42	4	7	11	42	....	....	....	....	....
1990-91	CSKA Moscow	USSR	15	0	0	0	12	....	....	....	....	....
	Quebec	**NHL**	**36**	**3**	**9**	**12**	**12**	....	....	....	....	....
	Halifax	AHL	2	0	3	3	2	....	....	....	....	....
1991-92	**Quebec**	**NHL**	**68**	**5**	**18**	**23**	**22**	....	....	....	....	....
	Halifax	AHL	3	0	0	0	0	....	....	....	....	....
1992-93	**Quebec**	**NHL**	**79**	**8**	**22**	**30**	**57**	**5**	**0**	**1**	**1**	**0**
1993-94	**Quebec**	**NHL**	**76**	**5**	**20**	**25**	**38**	....	....	....	....	....
1994-95	**Quebec**	**NHL**	**14**	**1**	**2**	**3**	**6**	....	....	....	....	....
1995-96	**Colorado**	**NHL**	**65**	**5**	**15**	**20**	**56**	**21**	**0**	**9**	**9**	**12** ♦
1996-97	**Colorado**	**NHL**	**58**	**2**	**12**	**14**	**28**	**17**	**0**	**3**	**3**	**14**
1997-98	**Colorado**	**NHL**	**72**	**4**	**10**	**14**	**42**	**7**	**0**	**1**	**1**	**6**
	Russia	Olympics	6	0	1	1	8	....	....	....	....	....
	NHL Totals		**468**	**33**	**108**	**141**	**261**	**50**	**0**	**14**	**14**	**32**

Transferred to **Colorado** after **Quebec** franchise relocated, June 21, 1995.

GUSEV, SERGEY (GOO-sehv) DAL.

Defense. Shoots left. 6'1", 195 lbs. Born, Nizhny Tagil, USSR, July 31, 1975.
(Dallas' 4th choice, 69th overall, in 1995 Entry Draft).

			Regular Season					Playoffs				
Season	Club	Lea	GP	G	A	TP	PIM	GP	G	A	TP	PIM
1994-95	Samara	CIS	50	3	5	8	58	....	....	....	....	....
1995-96	Michigan	IHL	73	11	17	28	76	....	....	....	....	....
1996-97	Michigan	IHL	51	7	8	15	44	4	0	4	4	6
1997-98	**Dallas**	**NHL**	**9**	**0**	**0**	**0**	**2**	....	....	....	....	....
	Michigan	IHL	36	3	6	9	36	4	0	2	2	6
	NHL Totals		**9**	**0**	**0**	**0**	**2**	....	....	....	....	....

GUSMANOV, RAVIL (goos-MAN-ohv)

Left wing. Shoots left. 6'3", 185 lbs. Born, Naberezhnye Chelny, USSR, July 25, 1972.
(Winnipeg's 5th choice, 93rd overall, in 1993 Entry Draft).

			Regular Season					Playoffs				
Season	Club	Lea	GP	G	A	TP	PIM	GP	G	A	TP	PIM
1990-91	Chelyabinsk	USSR	15	0	0	0	10	....	....	....	....	....
1991-92	Chelyabinsk	CIS	38	4	4	8	20	....	....	....	....	....
1992-93	Chelyabinsk	CIS	39	15	8	23	30	8	4	0	4	2
1993-94	Chelyabinsk	CIS	43	18	9	27	51	6	4	3	7	10
	Russia	Olympics	8	3	1	4	0	....	....	....	....	....
1994-95	Springfield	AHL	72	18	15	33	14	....	....	....	....	....
1995-96	**Winnipeg**	**NHL**	**4**	**0**	**0**	**0**	**0**	....	....	....	....	....
	Springfield	AHL	60	36	32	68	20	....	....	....	....	....
	Indianapolis	IHL	11	6	10	16	4	5	2	3	5	4
1996-97	Indianapolis	IHL	60	21	27	48	14	....	....	....	....	....
	Saint John	AHL	12	4	4	8	2	3	0	1	1	2
1997-98	Chicago	IHL	56	27	28	55	26	11	1	3	4	19
	NHL Totals		**4**	**0**	**0**	**0**	**0**	....	....	....	....	....

Traded to **Chicago** by **Winnipeg** for Chicago's 4th round choice (later traded to Toronto — Toronto selected Vladimir Antipov) in 1996 Entry Draft, March 20, 1996. Traded to **Calgary** by **Chicago** for Marc Hussey, March 18, 1997.

GUSTAFSSON, JUHA (GOOS-tahf-suhn, YOO-huh) PHX.

Defense. Shoots left. 6'2", 200 lbs. Born, Helsinki, Finland, April 26, 1979.
(Phoenix's 1st choice, 43rd overall, in 1997 Entry Draft).

			Regular Season					Playoffs				
Season	Club	Lea	GP	G	A	TP	PIM	GP	G	A	TP	PIM
1995-96	Kiekko	Finland	1	0	0	0	0	....	....	....	....	....
	Kiekko	Fin-Jr.	33	1	5	6	28	4	0	0	0	2
1996-97	Kiekko	Fin-Jr.	32	1	3	4	30	....	....	....	....	....
	Kiekko	Finland	3	0	0	0	0	3	0	0	0	0
1997-98	Kiekko	Fin-Jr.	33	3	3	6	18	....	....	....	....	....
	Kiekko	Finland	2	0	0	0	0	....	....	....	....	....

GUSTAFSSON, PER (GOOS-tahf-suhn)

Defense. Shoots left. 6'2", 190 lbs. Born, Osterham, Sweden, June 6, 1970.
(Florida's 10th choice, 261st overall, in 1994 Entry Draft).

			Regular Season					Playoffs				
Season	Club	Lea	GP	G	A	TP	PIM	GP	G	A	TP	PIM
1993-94	HV 71 Jonkoping	Sweden	34	9	7	16	10	....	....	....	....	....
1994-95	HV 71 Jonkoping	Sweden	38	10	6	16	14	13	7	5	12	8
1995-96	HV 71 Jonkoping	Sweden	34	8	13	21	12	4	3	1	4	2
1996-97	**Florida**	**NHL**	**58**	**7**	**22**	**29**	**22**	....	....	....	....	....
1997-98	**Toronto**	**NHL**	**22**	**1**	**4**	**5**	**10**	....	....	....	....	....
	St. John's	AHL	25	7	18	25	10	....	....	....	....	....
	Ottawa	**NHL**	**9**	**0**	**1**	**1**	**6**	**1**	**0**	**0**	**0**	**0**
	NHL Totals		**89**	**8**	**27**	**35**	**38**	**1**	**0**	**0**	**0**	**0**

Swedish World All-Star Team (1996)

Traded to **Toronto** by **Florida** for Mike Lankshear, June 13, 1997. Traded to **Ottawa** by **Toronto** for Ottawa's 8th round choice (Dwight Wolfe) in 1998 Entry Draft, March 17, 1998.

HAGGERTY, SEAN NYI

Left wing. Shoots left. 6'1", 186 lbs. Born, Rye, NY, February 11, 1976.
(Toronto's 2nd choice, 48th overall, in 1994 Entry Draft).

			Regular Season					Playoffs				
Season	Club	Lea	GP	G	A	TP	PIM	GP	G	A	TP	PIM
1993-94	Detroit	OHL	60	31	32	63	21	17	9	10	19	11
1994-95	Detroit	OHL	61	40	49	89	37	21	13	24	37	18
1995-96	Detroit	OHL	66	*60	51	111	78	17	15	9	24	30
	Toronto	**NHL**	**1**	**0**	**0**	**0**	**0**	....	....	....	....	....
	Worcester	AHL	....	....	....	....	....	1	0	0	0	2
1996-97	Kentucky	AHL	77	13	22	35	60	4	1	0	1	4
1997-98	**NY Islanders**	**NHL**	**5**	**0**	**0**	**0**	**0**	....	....	....	....	....
	Kentucky	AHL	63	33	20	53	64	3	0	2	2	4
	NHL Totals		**6**	**0**	**0**	**0**	**0**	....	....	....	....	....

Memorial Cup All-Star Team (1995) • OHL Second All-Star Team (1996) • AHL Second All-Star Team (1998)

Traded to **NY Islanders** by **Toronto** with Darby Hendrickson, Kenny Jonsson and Toronto's 1st round choice (Roberto Luongo) in 1997 Entry Draft for Wendel Clark, Mathieu Schneider and D.J. Smith, March 13, 1996.

HAGLUND, BOBBY ST.L.

Left wing. Shoots left. 5'11", 195 lbs. Born, Worcester, MA, November 17, 1977.
(St. Louis' 7th choice, 206th overall, in 1997 Entry Draft).

			Regular Season					Playoffs				
Season	Club	Lea	GP	G	A	TP	PIM	GP	G	A	TP	PIM
1996-97	Des Moines	USHL	45	18	14	32	86	....	....	....	....	....
1997-98	Northeastern	H.E.	29	5	7	12	24	....	....	....	....	....

HAJT, CHRIS (HIGHT) EDM.

Defense. Shoots left. 6'3", 206 lbs. Born, Saskatoon, Sask., July 5, 1978.
(Edmonton's 3rd choice, 32nd overall, in 1996 Entry Draft).

			Regular Season					Playoffs				
Season	Club	Lea	GP	G	A	TP	PIM	GP	G	A	TP	PIM
1994-95	Guelph	OHL	57	1	7	8	35	14	0	2	2	9
1995-96	Guelph	OHL	63	8	27	35	69	16	0	6	6	13
1996-97	Guelph	OHL	58	11	15	26	62	18	0	8	8	25
1997-98	Guelph	OHL	44	2	21	23	46	12	1	5	6	11

OHL Second All-Star Team (1998)

HAKANEN, TIMO (HAW-kan-en, TEE-moo) S.J.

Center. Shoots left. 6'2", 195 lbs. Born, Pori, Finland, March 26, 1977.
(San Jose's 7th choice, 140th overall, in 1995 Entry Draft).

			Regular Season					Playoffs				
Season	Club	Lea	GP	G	A	TP	PIM	GP	G	A	TP	PIM
1994-95	Assat Pori	Fin-Jr.	36	23	21	44	6	5	0	0	0	0
1995-96	Assat Pori	Fin-Jr.	28	8	24	32	6	....	....	....	....	....
	Assat Pori	Finland	12	0	2	2	0	3	0	0	0	0
1996-97	Assat Pori	Fin-Jr.	20	10	12	22	22	....	....	....	....	....
	Assat Pori	Finland	22	0	2	2	2	2	0	0	0	0
1997-98	Assat Pori	Finland	48	1	6	7	14	3	0	0	0	0

HALFNIGHT, ASHLIN (HAF-night, ASH-lihn) CAR.

Defense. Shoots left. 6', 180 lbs. Born, Toronto, Ont., March 14, 1975.
(Hartford's 5th choice, 213th overall, in 1994 Entry Draft).

			Regular Season					Playoffs				
Season	Club	Lea	GP	G	A	TP	PIM	GP	G	A	TP	PIM
1992-93	Canada	Nat-Tm	3	1	0	1	2	....	....	....	....	....
1993-94	Harvard	ECAC	30	2	8	10	24	....	....	....	....	....
1994-95	Harvard	ECAC	24	5	15	20	42	....	....	....	....	....
1995-96	Harvard	ECAC	30	2	10	12	12	....	....	....	....	....
1996-97	Harvard	ECAC	31	6	6	12	50	....	....	....	....	....
1997-98	New Haven	AHL	64	3	11	14	26	3	0	1	1	2

Rights transferred to **Carolina** after **Hartford** franchise relocated, June 25, 1997.

HALKO, STEVEN (HAL-koh) CAR.

Defense. Shoots right. 6'1", 195 lbs. Born, Etobicoke, Ont., March 8, 1974.
(Hartford's 10th choice, 225th overall, in 1992 Entry Draft).

			Regular Season					Playoffs				
Season	Club	Lea	GP	G	A	TP	PIM	GP	G	A	TP	PIM
1991-92	Thornhill	OJHL	44	15	46	61	43	....	....	....	....	....
1992-93	U. of Michigan	CCHA	39	1	12	13	12	....	....	....	....	....
1993-94	U. of Michigan	CCHA	41	2	13	15	32	....	....	....	....	....
1994-95	U. of Michigan	CCHA	39	2	14	16	20	....	....	....	....	....
1995-96	U. of Michigan	CCHA	43	4	16	20	32	....	....	....	....	....
1996-97	Springfield	AHL	70	1	5	6	37	11	0	2	2	8
1997-98	**Carolina**	**NHL**	**18**	**0**	**2**	**2**	**10**	....	....	....	....	....
	New Haven	AHL	65	1	19	20	44	1	0	0	0	0
	NHL Totals		**18**	**0**	**2**	**2**	**10**	....	....	....	....	....

CCHA Second All-Star Team (1995, 1996) • NCAA Championship All-Tournament Team (1996)

Transferred to **Carolina** after **Hartford** franchise relocated, June 25, 1997.

HALL, TODD NYR

Left wing. Shoots left. 6'1", 212 lbs. Born, Hamden, CT, January 22, 1973.
(Hartford's 3rd choice, 53rd overall, in 1991 Entry Draft).

			Regular Season					Playoffs				
Season	Club	Lea	GP	G	A	TP	PIM	GP	G	A	TP	PIM
1990-91	Hamden High	H.S.	23	10	15	25	12	....	....	....	....	....
1991-92	Boston College	H.E.	33	2	10	12	14	....	....	....	....	....
1992-93	Boston College	H.E.	34	2	10	12	22	....	....	....	....	....
1993-94	New Hampshire	H.E.	DID NOT PLAY – TRANSFERRED COLLEGES									
1994-95	New Hampshire	H.E.	36	8	18	26	16	....	....	....	....	....
1995-96	New Hampshire	H.E.	31	4	26	30	10	....	....	....	....	....
1996-97	Binghamton	AHL	40	3	7	10	12	4	0	1	1	0
	Charlotte	ECHL	13	0	2	2	8	....	....	....	....	....
1997-98	Hartford	AHL	73	7	18	25	26	8	0	1	1	8

Hockey East Second All-Star Team (1996)

Signed as a free agent by **NY Rangers**, July 28, 1997.

HALLER, KEVIN (HAHL-ehr) ANA.

Defense. Shoots left. 6'2", 195 lbs. Born, Trochu, Alta., December 5, 1970.
(Buffalo's 1st choice, 14th overall, in 1989 Entry Draft).

			Regular Season					Playoffs				
Season	Club	Lea	GP	G	A	TP	PIM	GP	G	A	TP	PIM
1988-89	Regina	WHL	72	10	31	41	99	....	....	....	....	....
1989-90	Regina	WHL	58	16	37	53	93	11	2	9	11	16
	Buffalo	NHL	2	0	0	0	0	....	....	....	....	....
1990-91	Buffalo	NHL	21	1	8	9	20	6	1	4	5	10
	Rochester	AHL	52	2	8	10	53	10	2	1	3	6
1991-92	Buffalo	NHL	58	6	15	21	75	....	....	....	....	....
	Rochester	AHL	4	0	0	0	18	....	....	....	....	....
	Montreal	NHL	8	2	2	4	17	9	0	0	0	6
1992-93	Montreal	NHL	73	11	14	25	117	17	1	6	7	16 ♦
1993-94	Montreal	NHL	68	4	9	13	118	7	1	1	2	19
1994-95	Philadelphia	NHL	36	2	8	10	48	15	4	4	8	10
1995-96	Philadelphia	NHL	69	5	9	14	92	6	0	1	1	8
1996-97	Philadelphia	NHL	27	0	5	5	37	....	....	....	....	....
	Hartford	NHL	35	2	6	8	48	....	....	....	....	....
1997-98	Carolina	NHL	65	3	5	8	94	....	....	....	....	....
	NHL Totals		462	36	81	117	666	60	7	16	23	69

WHL East First All-Star Team (1990)

Traded to **Montreal** by **Buffalo** for Petr Svoboda, March 10, 1992. Traded to **Philadelphia** by **Montreal** for Yves Racine, June 29, 1994. Traded to **Hartford** by **Philadelphia** with Philadelphia's 1st round choice (later traded to San Jose — San Jose selected Scott Hannan) in 1997 Entry Draft and Hartford/Carolina's 7th round choice (previously acquired, Carolina selected Andrew Merrick) in 1997 Entry Draft for Paul Coffey and Hartford's 3rd round choice (Kris Mallette) in 1997 Entry Draft, December 15, 1996. Transferred to **Carolina** after **Hartford** franchise relocated, June 25, 1997. Traded to **Anaheim** by **Carolina** with Stu Grimson for David Karpa and a 4th round choice in 2000 Entry Draft, August 11, 1998.

HAMEL, DENIS (ha-MEHL, deh-NEE) BUF.

Left wing. Shoots left. 6'2", 200 lbs. Born, Lachute, Que., May 10, 1977.
(St. Louis' 5th choice, 153rd overall, in 1995 Entry Draft).

			Regular Season					Playoffs				
Season	Club	Lea	GP	G	A	TP	PIM	GP	G	A	TP	PIM
1994-95	Chicoutimi	QMJHL	66	15	12	27	155	12	2	0	2	27
1995-96	Chicoutimi	QMJHL	65	40	49	89	199	17	10	14	24	64
1996-97	Chicoutimi	QMJHL	70	50	50	100	357	20	15	10	25	58
1997-98	Rochester	AHL	74	10	15	25	98	4	1	2	3	0

Traded to **Buffalo** by **St. Louis** for Charlie Huddy and Buffalo's 7th round choice (Daniel Corso) in 1996 Entry Draft, March 19, 1996.

HAMILTON, HUGH CAR.

Defense. Shoots left. 6'1", 175 lbs. Born, Saskatoon, Sask., February 11, 1977.
(Hartford's 5th choice, 113th overall, in 1995 Entry Draft).

			Regular Season					Playoffs				
Season	Club	Lea	GP	G	A	TP	PIM	GP	G	A	TP	PIM
1993-94	Spokane	WHL	64	5	9	14	70	3	0	0	0	0
1994-95	Spokane	WHL	60	5	28	33	102	11	3	5	8	16
1995-96	Spokane	WHL	72	11	49	60	92	18	3	5	8	26
1996-97	Spokane	WHL	57	8	37	45	69	9	1	6	7	14
1997-98	New Haven	AHL	51	3	3	6	17	3	0	0	0	2

WHL West Second All-Star Team (1997)

Rights transferred to **Carolina** after **Hartford** franchise relocated, June 25, 1997.

HAMILTON, JASON CHI.

Defense. Shoots right. 6'2", 218 lbs. Born, Montreal, Que., January 25, 1977.

			Regular Season					Playoffs				
Season	Club	Lea	GP	G	A	TP	PIM	GP	G	A	TP	PIM
1995-96	Shawinigan	QMJHL	62	3	6	9	240	6	0	0	0	15
1996-97	Shawinigan	QMJHL	67	2	5	7	254	7	0	1	1	8
1997-98	Shawinigan	QMJHL	59	2	9	11	358	6	0	1	1	55

Signed as a free agent by **Chicago**, July 7, 1998.

HAMRLIK, ROMAN (HAHM-reh-lik) EDM.

Defense. Shoots left. 6'2", 215 lbs. Born, Gottwaldov, Czech., April 12, 1974.
(Tampa Bay's 1st choice, 1st overall, in 1992 Entry Draft).

			Regular Season					Playoffs				
Season	Club	Lea	GP	G	A	TP	PIM	GP	G	A	TP	PIM
1990-91	TJ Zlin	Czech.	14	2	2	4	18	....	....	....	....	....
1991-92	ZPS Zlin	Czech.	34	5	5	10	50	....	....	....	....	....
1992-93	Tampa Bay	NHL	67	6	15	21	71	....	....	....	....	....
	Atlanta	IHL	2	1	1	2	2	....	....	....	....	....
1993-94	Tampa Bay	NHL	64	3	18	21	135	....	....	....	....	....
1994-95	ZPS Zlin	Cze-Rep.	2	1	0	1	10	....	....	....	....	....
	Tampa Bay	NHL	48	12	11	23	86	....	....	....	....	....
1995-96	Tampa Bay	NHL	82	16	49	65	103	5	0	1	1	4
1996-97	Tampa Bay	NHL	79	12	28	40	57	....	....	....	....	....
1997-98	Tampa Bay	NHL	37	3	12	15	22	....	....	....	....	....
	Edmonton	NHL	41	6	20	26	48	12	0	6	6	12
	Czech.	Olympics	6	1	0	1	2	....	....	....	....	....
	NHL Totals		418	58	153	211	522	17	0	7	7	16

Played in NHL All-Star Game (1996)

Traded to **Edmonton** by **Tampa Bay** with Paul Comrie for Bryan Marchment, Steve Kelly and Jason Bonsignore, December 30, 1997.

HANDZUS, MICHAL (HAHND-zuhs, MEE-chal) ST.L.

Center. Shoots left. 6'3", 191 lbs. Born, Banska Bystrica, Czech., March 11, 1977.
(St. Louis' 3rd choice, 101st overall, in 1995 Entry Draft).

			Regular Season					Playoffs				
Season	Club	Lea	GP	G	A	TP	PIM	GP	G	A	TP	PIM
1994-95	Banska Bystrica	Slovak-2	22	15	14	29	10	....	....	....	....	....
1995-96	Banska Bystrica	Slovakia	19	3	1	4	8	....	....	....	....	....
1996-97	Poprad	Slovakia	44	15	18	33	....	....	....	....	....	....
1997-98	Worcester	AHL	69	27	36	63	54	11	2	6	8	10

HANKINSON, CASEY (HAN-kihn-suhn) CHI.

Left wing. Shoots left. 6'1", 187 lbs. Born, Edina, MN, May 8, 1976.
(Chicago's 9th choice, 201st overall, in 1995 Entry Draft).

			Regular Season					Playoffs				
Season	Club	Lea	GP	G	A	TP	PIM	GP	G	A	TP	PIM
1994-95	U. of Minnesota	WCHA	33	7	1	8	86	....	....	....	....	....
1995-96	U. of Minnesota	WCHA	39	16	19	35	101	....	....	....	....	....
1996-97	U. of Minnesota	WCHA	42	17	24	41	79	....	....	....	....	....
1997-98	U. of Minnesota	WCHA	35	10	12	22	81	....	....	....	....	....

HANNAN, SCOTT S.J.

Defense. Shoots left. 6'2", 210 lbs. Born, Richmond, B.C., January 23, 1979.
(San Jose's 2nd choice, 23rd overall, in 1997 Entry Draft).

			Regular Season					Playoffs				
Season	Club	Lea	GP	G	A	TP	PIM	GP	G	A	TP	PIM
1994-95	Tacoma	WHL	2	0	0	0	0	....	....	....	....	....
1995-96	Kelowna	WHL	69	4	5	9	76	6	0	1	1	4
1996-97	Kelowna	WHL	70	17	26	43	101	6	0	0	0	8
1997-98	Kelowna	WHL	47	10	30	40	70	7	2	7	9	14

HANSEN, TAVIS PHX.

Center. Shoots right. 6'1", 180 lbs. Born, Prince Albert, Sask., June 17, 1975.
(Winnipeg's 3rd choice, 58th overall, in 1994 Entry Draft).

			Regular Season					Playoffs				
Season	Club	Lea	GP	G	A	TP	PIM	GP	G	A	TP	PIM
1993-94	Tacoma	WHL	71	23	31	54	122	8	1	3	4	17
1994-95	Tacoma	WHL	71	32	41	73	142	4	1	1	2	8
	Winnipeg	NHL	1	0	0	0	0	....	....	....	....	....
1995-96	Springfield	AHL	67	6	16	22	85	5	1	2	3	2
1996-97	Phoenix	NHL	1	0	0	0	0	....	....	....	....	....
	Springfield	AHL	12	3	1	4	23	....	....	....	....	....
1997-98	Springfield	AHL	73	20	14	34	70	4	1	2	3	18
	NHL Totals		2	0	0	0	0	....	....	....	....	....

Transferred to **Phoenix** after **Winnipeg** franchise relocated, July 1, 1996.

HARDY, FRANCOIS

Defense. Shoots left. 6'2", 185 lbs. Born, Les Saules, Que., July 6, 1978.
(Ottawa's 4th choice, 163rd overall, in 1996 Entry Draft).

			Regular Season					Playoffs				
Season	Club	Lea	GP	G	A	TP	PIM	GP	G	A	TP	PIM
1995-96	Val d'Or	QMJHL	55	2	3	5	93	3	0	0	0	4
1996-97	Val d'Or	OMJHL	57	2	10	12	120	13	1	1	2	20
1997-98	Val d'Or	QMJHL	59	7	11	18	147	19	1	6	7	38

HARKINS, BRETT

Left wing. Shoots left. 6'1", 185 lbs. Born, North Ridgeville, OH, July 2, 1970.
(NY Islanders' 9th choice, 133rd overall, in 1989 Entry Draft).

			Regular Season					Playoffs				
Season	Club	Lea	GP	G	A	TP	PIM	GP	G	A	TP	PIM
1988-89	Detroit	NAJHL	38	23	46	69	94	....	....	....	....	....
1989-90	Bowling Green	CCHA	41	11	43	54	45	....	....	....	....	....
1990-91	Bowling Green	CCHA	40	22	38	60	30	....	....	....	....	....
1991-92	Bowling Green	CCHA	34	8	39	47	32	....	....	....	....	....
1992-93	Bowling Green	CCHA	35	19	28	47	28	....	....	....	....	....
1993-94	Adirondack	AHL	80	22	47	69	23	10	1	5	6	4
1994-95	Boston	NHL	1	0	1	1	0	....	....	....	....	....
	Providence	AHL	80	23	*69	92	32	13	8	14	22	4
1995-96	Florida	NHL	8	0	3	3	6	....	....	....	....	....
	Carolina	AHL	55	23	*71	94	44	....	....	....	....	....
1996-97	Boston	NHL	44	4	14	18	8	....	....	....	....	....
	Providence	AHL	28	9	31	40	32	10	2	10	12	0
1997-98	Cleveland	IHL	80	32	62	94	82	10	4	13	17	14
	NHL Totals		53	4	18	22	14	....	....	....	....	....

Signed as a free agent by **Boston**, July 1, 1994. Signed as a free agent by **Florida**, July 24, 1995. Signed as a free agent by **Boston**, September 4, 1996.

HARLOCK, DAVID (HAHR-lahk) NYI

Defense. Shoots left. 6'2", 205 lbs. Born, Toronto, Ont., March 16, 1971.
(New Jersey's 2nd choice, 24th overall, in 1990 Entry Draft).

			Regular Season					Playoffs				
Season	Club	Lea	GP	G	A	TP	PIM	GP	G	A	TP	PIM
1988-89	St. Michael's	Jr. B	25	4	16	20	34	27	3	12	15	14
1989-90	U. of Michigan	CCHA	42	2	13	15	44	....	....	....	....	....
1990-91	U. of Michigan	CCHA	39	2	8	10	70	....	....	....	....	....
1991-92	U. of Michigan	CCHA	44	1	6	7	80	....	....	....	....	....
1992-93	U. of Michigan	CCHA	38	3	9	12	58	....	....	....	....	....
	Canada	Nat-Tm	4	0	0	0	2	....	....	....	....	....
1993-94	Canada	Nat-Tm	41	0	3	3	28	....	....	....	....	....
	Canada	Olympics	8	0	0	0	8	....	....	....	....	....
	Toronto	NHL	6	0	0	0	0	....	....	....	....	....
	St. John's	AHL	10	0	3	3	2	9	0	0	0	6
1994-95	Toronto	NHL	1	0	0	0	0	....	....	....	....	....
	St. John's	AHL	58	0	6	6	44	5	0	0	0	0
1995-96	Toronto	NHL	1	0	0	0	0	....	....	....	....	....
	St. John's	AHL	77	0	12	12	92	4	0	1	1	2
1996-97	San Antonio	IHL	69	3	10	13	82	9	0	0	0	10
1997-98	Washington	NHL	6	0	0	0	4	....	....	....	....	....
	Portland	AHL	71	3	15	18	66	10	2	2	4	6
	NHL Totals		14	0	0	0	4	....	....	....	....	....

Signed as a free agent by **Toronto**, August 20, 1993. Signed as a free agent by **Washington**, August 20, 1997. Signed as a free agent by **NY Islanders**, August 24, 1998.

HARLTON, TYLER ST.L.

Defense. Shoots left. 6'3", 201 lbs. Born, Pense, Sask., January 11, 1976.
(St. Louis' 2nd choice, 94th overall, in 1994 Entry Draft).

			Regular Season					Playoffs				
Season	Club	Lea	GP	G	A	TP	PIM	GP	G	A	TP	PIM
1993-94	Vernon	BCJHL	60	3	18	21	102	....	....	....	....	....
1994-95	Michigan State	CCHA	39	1	3	4	55	....	....	....	....	....
1995-96	Michigan State	CCHA	39	1	6	7	51	....	....	....	....	....
1996-97	Michigan State	CCHA	39	2	9	11	75	....	....	....	....	....
1997-98	Michigan State	CCHA	44	1	12	13	68	....	....	....	....	....

CCHA First All-Star Team (1998) • NCAA West Second All-American Team (1998)

HARVEY, TODD — NYR

Center. Shoots right. 6', 195 lbs. Born, Hamilton, Ont., February 17, 1975.
(Dallas' 1st choice, 9th overall, in 1993 Entry Draft).

			Regular Season					Playoffs				
Season	Club	Lea	GP	G	A	TP	PIM	GP	G	A	TP	PIM
1991-92	Detroit	OHL	58	21	43	64	141	7	3	5	8	30
1992-93	Detroit	OHL	55	50	50	100	83	15	9	12	21	39
1993-94	Detroit	OHL	49	34	51	85	75	17	10	12	22	26
1994-95	Detroit	OHL	11	8	14	22	12	....	....	....	....	....
	Dallas	**NHL**	**40**	**11**	**9**	**20**	**67**	**5**	**0**	**0**	**0**	**8**
1995-96	**Dallas**	**NHL**	**69**	**9**	**20**	**29**	**136**	....	....	....	....	....
	Michigan	IHL	5	1	3	4	8	....	....	....	....	....
1996-97	**Dallas**	**NHL**	**71**	**9**	**22**	**31**	**142**	**7**	**0**	**1**	**1**	**10**
1997-98	**Dallas**	**NHL**	**59**	**9**	**10**	**19**	**104**	....	....	....	....	....
	NHL Totals		**239**	**38**	**61**	**99**	**449**	**12**	**0**	**1**	**1**	**18**

Traded to **NY Rangers** by **Dallas** with Bob Errey and Dallas' 4th round choice (Boyd Kane) in 1998 Entry Draft for Brian Skrudland, Mike Keane and NY Rangers' 6th round choice (Pavel Patera) in 1998 Entry Draft, March 24, 1998.

HATCHER, DERIAN — DAL.

Defense. Shoots left. 6'5", 225 lbs. Born, Sterling Heights, MI, June 4, 1972.
(Minnesota's 1st choice, 8th overall, in 1990 Entry Draft).

			Regular Season					Playoffs				
Season	Club	Lea	GP	G	A	TP	PIM	GP	G	A	TP	PIM
1989-90	North Bay	OHL	64	14	38	52	81	5	2	3	5	8
1990-91	North Bay	OHL	64	13	49	62	163	10	2	10	12	28
1991-92	**Minnesota**	**NHL**	**43**	**8**	**4**	**12**	**88**	**5**	**0**	**2**	**2**	**8**
1992-93	**Minnesota**	**NHL**	**67**	**4**	**15**	**19**	**178**	....	....	....	....	....
	Kalamazoo	IHL	2	1	2	3	21	....	....	....	....	....
1993-94	**Dallas**	**NHL**	**83**	**12**	**19**	**31**	**211**	**9**	**0**	**2**	**2**	**14**
1994-95	**Dallas**	**NHL**	**43**	**5**	**11**	**16**	**105**	....	....	....	....	....
1995-96	**Dallas**	**NHL**	**79**	**8**	**23**	**31**	**129**	....	....	....	....	....
1996-97	**Dallas**	**NHL**	**63**	**3**	**19**	**22**	**97**	**7**	**0**	**2**	**2**	**20**
1997-98	**Dallas**	**NHL**	**70**	**6**	**25**	**31**	**132**	**17**	**3**	**3**	**6**	**39**
	United States	Olympics	4	0	0	0	0	....	....	....	....	....
	NHL Totals		**448**	**46**	**116**	**162**	**940**	**38**	**3**	**9**	**12**	**81**

Played in NHL All-Star Game (1997)

Transferred to **Dallas** after **Minnesota** franchise relocated, June 9, 1993.

HATCHER, KEVIN — PIT.

Defense. Shoots right. 6'3", 232 lbs. Born, Detroit, MI, September 9, 1966.
(Washington's 1st choice, 17th overall, in 1984 Entry Draft).

			Regular Season					Playoffs				
Season	Club	Lea	GP	G	A	TP	PIM	GP	G	A	TP	PIM
1982-83	Detroit	NAJHL	75	30	45	75	120	....	....	....	....	....
1983-84	North Bay	OHL	67	10	39	49	61	4	2	2	4	11
1984-85	North Bay	OHL	58	26	37	63	75	8	3	8	11	9
	Washington	**NHL**	**2**	**1**	**0**	**1**	**0**	**1**	**0**	**0**	**0**	**0**
1985-86	**Washington**	**NHL**	**79**	**9**	**10**	**19**	**119**	**9**	**1**	**1**	**2**	**19**
1986-87	**Washington**	**NHL**	**78**	**8**	**16**	**24**	**144**	**7**	**1**	**0**	**1**	**20**
1987-88	**Washington**	**NHL**	**71**	**14**	**27**	**41**	**137**	**14**	**5**	**7**	**12**	**55**
1988-89	**Washington**	**NHL**	**62**	**13**	**27**	**40**	**101**	**6**	**1**	**4**	**5**	**20**
1989-90	**Washington**	**NHL**	**80**	**13**	**41**	**54**	**102**	**11**	**0**	**8**	**8**	**32**
1990-91	**Washington**	**NHL**	**79**	**24**	**50**	**74**	**69**	**11**	**3**	**3**	**6**	**8**
1991-92	**Washington**	**NHL**	**79**	**17**	**37**	**54**	**105**	**7**	**2**	**4**	**6**	**19**
1992-93	**Washington**	**NHL**	**83**	**34**	**45**	**79**	**114**	**6**	**0**	**1**	**1**	**14**
1993-94	**Washington**	**NHL**	**72**	**16**	**24**	**40**	**108**	**11**	**3**	**4**	**7**	**37**
1994-95	**Dallas**	**NHL**	**47**	**10**	**19**	**29**	**66**	**5**	**2**	**1**	**3**	**2**
1995-96	**Dallas**	**NHL**	**74**	**15**	**26**	**41**	**58**	....	....	....	....	....
1996-97	**Pittsburgh**	**NHL**	**80**	**15**	**39**	**54**	**103**	**5**	**1**	**1**	**2**	**4**
1997-98	**Pittsburgh**	**NHL**	**74**	**19**	**29**	**48**	**66**	**6**	**1**	**0**	**1**	**12**
	United States	Olympics	3	0	2	2	0	....	....	....	....	....
	NHL Totals		**960**	**208**	**390**	**598**	**1292**	**99**	**20**	**34**	**54**	**242**

OHL Second All-Star Team (1985)

Played in NHL All-Star Game (1990, 1991, 1992, 1996, 1997)

Traded to **Dallas** by **Washington** for Mark Tinordi and Rick Mrozik, January 18, 1995. Traded to **Pittsburgh** by **Dallas** for Sergei Zubov, June 22, 1996.

HAUER, BRETT — (HOW-uhr) EDM.

Defense. Shoots right. 6'2", 200 lbs. Born, Richfield, MN, July 11, 1971.
(Vancouver's 3rd choice, 71st overall, in 1989 Entry Draft).

			Regular Season					Playoffs				
Season	Club	Lea	GP	G	A	TP	PIM	GP	G	A	TP	PIM
1988-89	Richfield	H.S.	24	8	15	23	70	....	....	....	....	....
1989-90	U. Minn-Duluth	WCHA	37	2	6	8	44	....	....	....	....	....
1990-91	U. Minn-Duluth	WCHA	30	1	7	8	54	....	....	....	....	....
1991-92	U. Minn-Duluth	WCHA	33	8	14	22	40	....	....	....	....	....
1992-93	U. Minn-Duluth	WCHA	40	10	46	56	52	....	....	....	....	....
1993-94	United States	Nat-Tm	57	6	14	20	88	....	....	....	....	....
	United States	Olympics	8	0	0	0	10	....	....	....	....	....
	Las Vegas	IHL	21	0	7	7	8	1	0	0	0	0
1994-95	AIK Solna	Sweden	37	1	3	4	38	....	....	....	....	....
1995-96	**Edmonton**	**NHL**	**29**	**4**	**2**	**6**	**30**	....	....	....	....	....
	Cape Breton	AHL	17	3	5	8	29	....	....	....	....	....
1996-97	Chicago	IHL	81	10	30	40	50	4	2	0	2	4
1997-98	Manitoba	IHL	82	13	48	61	58	3	0	0	0	2
	NHL Totals		**29**	**4**	**2**	**6**	**30**	....	....	....	....	....

WCHA First All-Star Team (1993) • NCAA West First All-American Team (1993)

Traded to **Edmonton** by **Vancouver** for Edmonton's 7th round choice (Larry Shapley) in 1997 Entry Draft, August 24, 1995.

HAVELKA, PETR — (huh-VEHL-kah) PIT.

Left wing. Shoots left. 6'2", 187 lbs. Born, Most, Czech., March 4, 1979.
(Pittsburgh's 6th choice, 152nd overall, in 1997 Entry Draft).

			Regular Season					Playoffs				
Season	Club	Lea	GP	G	A	TP	PIM	GP	G	A	TP	PIM
1995-96	Sparta Praha	Czech-Jr.	40	15	10	25	....	....	....	....	....	....
1996-97	Sparta Praha	Czech-Jr.	22	14	13	27	....	....	....	....	....	....
	Sparta Praha	Cze-Rep.	....	....	....	....	....	1	0	0	0	0
1997-98	Sparta Praha	Czech-Jr.	DID NOT PLAY – INJURED									

HAWGOOD, GREG — (HAW-guhd)

Defense. Shoots left. 5'10", 190 lbs. Born, Edmonton, Alta., August 10, 1968.
(Boston's 9th choice, 202nd overall, in 1986 Entry Draft).

			Regular Season					Playoffs				
Season	Club	Lea	GP	G	A	TP	PIM	GP	G	A	TP	PIM
1983-84	Kamloops	WHL	49	10	23	33	39	....	....	....	....	....
1984-85	Kamloops	WHL	66	25	40	65	72	....	....	....	....	....
1985-86	Kamloops	WHL	71	34	85	119	86	16	9	22	31	16
1986-87	Kamloops	WHL	61	30	93	123	139	....	....	....	....	....
1987-88	Kamloops	WHL	63	48	85	133	142	16	10	16	26	33
	Boston	**NHL**	**1**	**0**	**0**	**0**	**0**	**3**	**1**	**0**	**1**	**0**
1988-89	**Boston**	**NHL**	**56**	**16**	**24**	**40**	**84**	**10**	**0**	**2**	**2**	**2**
	Maine	AHL	21	2	9	11	41	....	....	....	....	....
1989-90	**Boston**	**NHL**	**77**	**11**	**27**	**38**	**76**	**15**	**1**	**3**	**4**	**12**
1990-91	HC Asiago	Italy	2	3	0	3	9	....	....	....	....	....
	Maine	AHL	5	0	1	1	13	....	....	....	....	....
	Edmonton	**NHL**	**6**	**0**	**1**	**1**	**6**	....	....	....	....	....
	Cape Breton	AHL	55	10	32	42	73	4	0	3	3	23
1991-92	**Edmonton**	**NHL**	**20**	**2**	**11**	**13**	**22**	**13**	**0**	**3**	**3**	**23**
	Cape Breton	AHL	56	20	55	75	26	3	2	2	4	0
1992-93	**Edmonton**	**NHL**	**29**	**5**	**13**	**18**	**35**	....	....	....	....	....
	Philadelphia	**NHL**	**40**	**6**	**22**	**28**	**39**	....	....	....	....	....
1993-94	**Philadelphia**	**NHL**	**19**	**3**	**12**	**15**	**19**	....	....	....	....	....
	Florida	**NHL**	**33**	**2**	**14**	**16**	**9**	....	....	....	....	....
	Pittsburgh	**NHL**	**12**	**1**	**2**	**3**	**8**	**1**	**0**	**0**	**0**	**0**
1994-95	**Pittsburgh**	**NHL**	**21**	**1**	**4**	**5**	**25**	....	....	....	....	....
	Cleveland	IHL	....	....	....	....	....	3	1	0	1	4
1995-96	Las Vegas	IHL	78	20	65	85	101	15	5	11	16	24
1996-97	**San Jose**	**NHL**	**63**	**6**	**12**	**18**	**69**	....	....	....	....	....
1997-98	Kolner Haie	Germany	4	0	1	1	16	....	....	....	....	....
	Kolner Haie	EuroHL	1	0	0	0	2	....	....	....	....	....
	Houston	IHL	81	19	52	71	75	4	0	4	4	0
	NHL Totals		**377**	**53**	**142**	**195**	**392**	**42**	**2**	**8**	**10**	**37**

WHL West All-Star Team (1986, 1987, 1988) • Canadian Major Junior Defenseman of the Year (1988) • AHL First All-Star Team (1992) • Won Eddie Shore Award (Top Defenseman - AHL) (1992) • IHL First All-Star Team (1996, 1998) • Won Governors' Trophy (Top Defenseman - IHL) (1996)

Traded to **Edmonton** by **Boston** for Vladimir Ruzicka, October 22, 1990. Traded to **Philadelphia** by **Edmonton** with Josef Beranek for Brian Benning, January 16, 1993. Traded to **Florida** by **Philadelphia** for cash, November 30, 1993. Traded to **Pittsburgh** by **Florida** for Jeff Daniels, March 19, 1994. Signed as a free agent by **San Jose**, September 25, 1996.

HAWKINS, TODD

Left/Right wing. Shoots right. 6'1", 195 lbs. Born, Kingston, Ont., August 2, 1966.
(Vancouver's 10th choice, 217th overall, in 1986 Entry Draft).

			Regular Season					Playoffs				
Season	Club	Lea	GP	G	A	TP	PIM	GP	G	A	TP	PIM
1984-85	Belleville	OHL	58	7	16	23	117	12	1	0	1	10
1985-86	Belleville	OHL	60	14	13	27	172	24	9	7	16	60
1986-87	Belleville	OHL	60	47	40	87	187	6	3	5	8	16
1987-88	Flint	IHL	50	13	13	26	337	16	3	5	8	*174
	Fredericton	AHL	2	0	4	4	11	....	....	....	....	....
1988-89	**Vancouver**	**NHL**	**4**	**0**	**0**	**0**	**9**	....	....	....	....	....
	Milwaukee	IHL	63	12	14	26	307	9	1	0	1	33
1989-90	**Vancouver**	**NHL**	**4**	**0**	**0**	**0**	**6**	....	....	....	....	....
	Milwaukee	IHL	61	23	17	40	273	5	4	1	5	19
1990-91	Newmarket	AHL	22	2	5	7	66	....	....	....	....	....
	Milwaukee	IHL	39	9	11	20	134	....	....	....	....	....
1991-92	**Toronto**	**NHL**	**2**	**0**	**0**	**0**	**0**	....	....	....	....	....
	St. John's	AHL	66	30	27	57	139	7	1	0	1	10
1992-93	St. John's	AHL	72	21	41	62	103	9	1	3	4	10
1993-94	Cleveland	IHL	76	19	14	33	115	....	....	....	....	....
1994-95	Cleveland	IHL	4	2	0	2	29	....	....	....	....	....
	Minnesota	IHL	47	10	8	18	95	3	0	1	1	12
1995-96	Cincinnati	IHL	73	16	12	28	65	17	7	4	11	32
1996-97	Cincinnati	IHL	81	13	13	26	162	3	0	1	1	2
1997-98	Cincinnati	IHL	71	13	23	36	168	9	0	3	3	36
	NHL Totals		**10**	**0**	**0**	**0**	**15**	....	....	....	....	....

OHL Second All-Star Team (1987)

Traded to **Toronto** by **Vancouver** for Brian Blad, January 22, 1991. Signed as a free agent by **Pittsburgh**, August 20, 1993.

HAY, DWAYNE — FLA.

Left wing. Shoots left. 6'1", 183 lbs. Born, London, Ont., February 11, 1977.
(Washington's 3rd choice, 43rd overall, in 1995 Entry Draft).

			Regular Season					Playoffs				
Season	Club	Lea	GP	G	A	TP	PIM	GP	G	A	TP	PIM
1994-95	Guelph	OHL	65	26	28	54	37	14	5	7	12	6
1995-96	Guelph	OHL	60	28	30	58	49	16	4	9	13	18
1996-97	Guelph	OHL	32	17	17	34	21	11	4	6	10	0
1997-98	**Washington**	**NHL**	**2**	**0**	**0**	**0**	**2**	....	....	....	....	....
	Portland	AHL	58	6	7	13	35	....	....	....	....	....
	New Haven	AHL	10	3	2	5	4	2	0	0	0	0
	NHL Totals		**2**	**0**	**0**	**0**	**2**	....	....	....	....	....

Traded to **Florida** by **Washington** with future considerations for Esa Tikkanen, March 9, 1998.

HEALEY, PAUL — PHI.

Right wing. Shoots right. 6'2", 196 lbs. Born, Edmonton, Alta., March 20, 1975.
(Philadelphia's 7th choice, 192nd overall, in 1993 Entry Draft).

			Regular Season					Playoffs				
Season	Club	Lea	GP	G	A	TP	PIM	GP	G	A	TP	PIM
1992-93	Prince Albert	WHL	72	12	20	32	66	....	....	....	....	....
1993-94	Prince Albert	WHL	63	23	26	49	70	....	....	....	....	....
1994-95	Prince Albert	WHL	71	43	50	93	67	12	3	4	7	2
1995-96	Hershey	AHL	60	7	15	22	35	....	....	....	....	....
1996-97	**Philadelphia**	**NHL**	**2**	**0**	**0**	**0**	**0**	....	....	....	....	....
	Philadelphia	AHL	64	21	19	40	56	10	4	1	5	10
1997-98	**Philadelphia**	**NHL**	**4**	**0**	**0**	**0**	**12**	....	....	....	....	....
	Philadelphia	AHL	71	34	18	52	48	20	6	2	8	4
	NHL Totals		**6**	**0**	**0**	**0**	**12**	....	....	....	....	....

WHL East Second All-Star Team (1995)

HECHT, JOCHEN — ST.L.

Center. Shoots left. 6'1", 180 lbs. Born, Mannheim, Germany, June 21, 1977.
(St. Louis' 1st choice, 49th overall, in 1995 Entry Draft).

			Regular Season					Playoffs				
Season	Club	Lea	GP	G	A	TP	PIM	GP	G	A	TP	PIM
1994-95	Mannheim	Germany	43	11	12	23	68	10	5	4	9	12
1995-96	Mannheim	Germany	44	12	16	28	68	8	3	2	5	6
1996-97	Mannheim	Germany	46	21	21	42	36	9	3	3	6	4
1997-98	Mannheim	EuroHL	5	0	4	4	8	....	....	....	....	....
	Mannheim	Germany	44	7	19	26	42	10	1	1	2	14
	Germany	Olympics	4	1	0	1	6	....	....	....	....	....

HEDICAN, BRET — (HEH-dih-kan) VAN.

Defense. Shoots left. 6'2", 205 lbs. Born, St. Paul, MN, August 10, 1970.
(St. Louis' 10th choice, 198th overall, in 1988 Entry Draft).

			Regular Season					Playoffs				
Season	Club	Lea	GP	G	A	TP	PIM	GP	G	A	TP	PIM
1987-88	St. Paul High	H.S.	23	15	19	34	16	....	....	....	....	....
1988-89	St. Cloud State	NCAA	28	5	3	8	28	....	....	....	....	....
1989-90	St. Cloud State	NCAA	36	4	17	21	37	....	....	....	....	....
1990-91	St. Cloud State	WCHA	41	21	26	47	26	....	....	....	....	....
1991-92	United States	Nat-Tm	54	1	8	9	59	....	....	....	....	....
	United States	Olympics	8	0	0	0	4	....	....	....	....	....
	St. Louis	**NHL**	**4**	**1**	**0**	**1**	**0**	**5**	**0**	**0**	**0**	**0**
1992-93	**St. Louis**	**NHL**	**42**	**0**	**8**	**8**	**30**	**10**	**0**	**0**	**0**	**14**
	Peoria	IHL	19	0	8	8	10	....	....	....	....	....
1993-94	**St. Louis**	**NHL**	**61**	**0**	**11**	**11**	**64**	....	....	....	....	....
	Vancouver	**NHL**	**8**	**0**	**1**	**1**	**0**	**24**	**1**	**6**	**7**	**16**
1994-95	**Vancouver**	**NHL**	**45**	**2**	**11**	**13**	**34**	**11**	**0**	**2**	**2**	**6**
1995-96	**Vancouver**	**NHL**	**77**	**6**	**23**	**29**	**83**	**6**	**0**	**1**	**1**	**10**
1996-97	**Vancouver**	**NHL**	**67**	**4**	**15**	**19**	**51**	....	....	....	....	....
1997-98	**Vancouver**	**NHL**	**71**	**3**	**24**	**27**	**79**	....	....	....	....	....
	NHL Totals		**375**	**16**	**93**	**109**	**341**	**56**	**1**	**9**	**10**	**46**

WCHA First All-Star Team (1991)

Traded to **Vancouver** by **St. Louis** with Jeff Brown and Nathan Lafayette for Craig Janney, March 21, 1994.

HEDSTROM, JONATHAN — (HEHD-struhm) TOR.

Right wing. Shoots left. 6', 200 lbs. Born, Skelleftea, Sweden, December 27, 1977.
(Toronto's 8th choice, 221st overall, in 1997 Entry Draft).

			Regular Season					Playoffs				
Season	Club	Lea	GP	G	A	TP	PIM	GP	G	A	TP	PIM
1995-96	Skelleftea	Sweden-2	7	0	0	0	0	....	....	....	....	....
1996-97	Skelleftea	Sweden-2	12	1	1	2	10	6	0	0	0	2
	Skelleftea	Swe-Jr.	9	4	4	8	....	....	....	....	....	....
1997-98	Skelleftea	Sweden-2	16	2	3	5	....	....	....	....	....	....
	Skelleftea	Swe-Jr.	1	0	0	0	2	....	....	....	....	....

HEEREMA, JEFF — CAR.

Right wing. Shoots right. 6'1", 171 lbs. Born, Thunder Bay, Ont., January 17, 1980.
(Carolina's 1st choice, 11th overall, in 1998 Entry Draft).

			Regular Season					Playoffs				
Season	Club	Lea	GP	G	A	TP	PIM	GP	G	A	TP	PIM
1996-97	Thunder Bay	USHL	54	42	29	71	112	....	....	....	....	....
1997-98	Sarnia	OHL	63	32	40	72	88	5	4	1	5	10

HEINS, SHAWN — S.J.

Defense. Shoots left. 6'4", 215 lbs. Born, Eganville, Ont., December 24, 1973.

			Regular Season					Playoffs				
Season	Club	Lea	GP	G	A	TP	PIM	GP	G	A	TP	PIM
1995-96	Mobile	ECHL	62	7	20	27	152	....	....	....	....	....
1996-97	Mobile	ECHL	56	6	17	23	253	3	0	2	2	2
1997-98	Kansas City	IHL	82	22	28	50	303	11	1	0	1	49

Signed as a free agent by **San Jose**, January 5, 1997.

HEINZE, STEPHEN — (HIGHNS) BOS.

Right wing. Shoots right. 5'11", 202 lbs. Born, Lawrence, MA, January 30, 1970.
(Boston's 2nd choice, 60th overall, in 1988 Entry Draft).

			Regular Season					Playoffs				
Season	Club	Lea	GP	G	A	TP	PIM	GP	G	A	TP	PIM
1987-88	Lawrence Acad.	H.S.	23	30	25	55	....	....	....	....	....	....
1988-89	Boston College	H.E.	36	26	23	49	26	....	....	....	....	....
1989-90	Boston College	H.E.	40	27	36	63	41	....	....	....	....	....
1990-91	Boston College	H.E.	35	21	26	47	35	....	....	....	....	....
1991-92	United States	Nat-Tm	49	18	15	33	38	....	....	....	....	....
	United States	Olympics	8	1	3	4	8	....	....	....	....	....
	Boston	**NHL**	**14**	**3**	**4**	**7**	**6**	**7**	**0**	**3**	**3**	**17**
1992-93	**Boston**	**NHL**	**73**	**18**	**13**	**31**	**24**	**4**	**1**	**1**	**2**	**2**
1993-94	**Boston**	**NHL**	**77**	**10**	**11**	**21**	**32**	**13**	**2**	**3**	**5**	**7**
1994-95	**Boston**	**NHL**	**36**	**7**	**9**	**16**	**23**	**5**	**0**	**0**	**0**	**0**
1995-96	**Boston**	**NHL**	**76**	**16**	**12**	**28**	**43**	**5**	**1**	**1**	**2**	**4**
1996-97	**Boston**	**NHL**	**30**	**17**	**8**	**25**	**27**	....	....	....	....	....
1997-98	**Boston**	**NHL**	**61**	**26**	**20**	**46**	**54**	**6**	**0**	**0**	**0**	**6**
	NHL Totals		**367**	**97**	**77**	**174**	**209**	**40**	**4**	**8**	**12**	**36**

Hockey East First All-Star Team (1990) • NCAA East First All-American Team (1990)

HEJDUK, MILAN — (HEHI-duhk) COL.

Right wing. Shoots right. 5'11", 165 lbs. Born, Usti-nad-Labem, Czech., February 14, 1976.
(Quebec's 6th choice, 87th overall, in 1994 Entry Draft).

			Regular Season					Playoffs				
Season	Club	Lea	GP	G	A	TP	PIM	GP	G	A	TP	PIM
1993-94	Pardubice	Cze-Rep.	22	6	3	9	....	10	5	1	6	....
1994-95	Pardubice	Cze-Rep.	43	11	13	24	6	6	3	1	4	0
1995-96	Pardubice	Cze-Rep.	37	13	7	20	....	....	....	....	....	....
1996-97	Pardubice	Cze-Rep.	51	27	11	38	10	10	6	0	6	27
1997-98	Pardubice	Cze-Rep.	48	26	19	45	20	3	0	0	0	2
	Czech Republic	Olympics	4	0	0	0	2	....	....	....	....	....

Rights transferred to **Colorado** after **Quebec** franchise relocated, June 21, 1995.

HELENIUS, SAMI — (huh-LEHN-ee-uhs) CGY.

Defense. Shoots left. 6'5", 225 lbs. Born, Helsinki, Finland, January 22, 1974.
(Calgary's 5th choice, 102nd overall, in 1992 Entry Draft).

			Regular Season					Playoffs				
Season	Club	Lea	GP	G	A	TP	PIM	GP	G	A	TP	PIM
1992-93	Jokerit	Finland	1	0	0	0	0	....	....	....	....	....
1993-94	Reipas Lahti	Finland	37	2	3	5	46	....	....	....	....	....
1994-95	Saint John	AHL	69	2	5	7	217	....	....	....	....	....
1995-96	Saint John	AHL	68	0	3	3	231	10	0	0	0	9
1996-97	**Calgary**	**NHL**	**3**	**0**	**1**	**1**	**0**	....	....	....	....	....
	Saint John	AHL	72	5	10	15	218	2	0	0	0	0
1997-98	Saint John	AHL	63	1	2	3	185	....	....	....	....	....
	Las Vegas	IHL	10	0	1	1	19	4	0	0	0	25
	NHL Totals		**3**	**0**	**1**	**1**	**0**	....	....	....	....	....

HELMER, BRYAN — PHX.

Defense. Shoots right. 6'1", 200 lbs. Born, Sault Ste. Marie, Ont., July 15, 1972.

			Regular Season					Playoffs				
Season	Club	Lea	GP	G	A	TP	PIM	GP	G	A	TP	PIM
1992-93	Wellington	OJHL	57	25	62	87	62	....	....	....	....	....
1993-94	Albany	AHL	65	4	19	23	79	5	0	0	0	9
1994-95	Albany	AHL	77	7	36	43	101	7	1	0	1	0
1995-96	Albany	AHL	80	14	30	44	107	4	2	0	2	6
1996-97	Albany	AHL	77	12	27	39	113	16	1	7	8	10
1997-98	Albany	AHL	80	14	49	63	101	13	4	9	13	18

AHL First All-Star Team (1998)

Signed as a free agent by **New Jersey**, July 10, 1994. Signed as a free agent by **Phoenix**, July 17, 1998.

HENDERSON, JAY — BOS.

Left wing. Shoots left. 5'11", 188 lbs. Born, Edmonton, Alta., September 17, 1978.
(Boston's 12th choice, 246th overall, in 1997 Entry Draft).

			Regular Season					Playoffs				
Season	Club	Lea	GP	G	A	TP	PIM	GP	G	A	TP	PIM
1994-95	Red Deer	WHL	54	3	9	12	80	....	....	....	....	....
1995-96	Red Deer	WHL	71	15	13	28	139	10	1	1	2	11
1996-97	Edmonton	WHL	66	28	32	60	127	....	....	....	....	....
1997-98	Edmonton	WHL	72	49	45	94	130	....	....	....	....	....

HENDERSON, MATT — NSH.

Right wing. Shoots left. 6'1", 200 lbs. Born, White Bear Lake, MN, June 22, 1974.

			Regular Season					Playoffs				
Season	Club	Lea	GP	G	A	TP	PIM	GP	G	A	TP	PIM
1994-95	North Dakota	WCHA	19	1	3	4	16	....	....	....	....	....
1995-96	North Dakota	WCHA	36	9	10	19	34	2	0	1	1	0
1996-97	North Dakota	WCHA	42	14	17	31	71	7	5	4	9	10
1997-98	North Dakota	WCHA	38	24	14	38	74	5	2	2	4	4

NCAA Championship All-Tournament Team (1997) • NCAA Championship Tournament MVP (1997)

Signed as a free agent by **Nashville**, August, 1998.

HENDRICKSON, DARBY — TOR.

Center. Shoots left. 6', 185 lbs. Born, Richfield, MN, August 28, 1972.
(Toronto's 3rd choice, 73rd overall, in 1990 Entry Draft).

			Regular Season					Playoffs				
Season	Club	Lea	GP	G	A	TP	PIM	GP	G	A	TP	PIM
1989-90	Richfield	H.S.	24	23	27	50	49	....	....	....	....	....
1990-91	Richfield	H.S.	27	32	29	61	....	....	....	....	....	....
1991-92	U. of Minnesota	WCHA	41	25	28	53	61	....	....	....	....	....
1992-93	U. of Minnesota	WCHA	31	12	15	27	35	....	....	....	....	....
1993-94	United States	Nat-Tm	59	12	16	28	30	....	....	....	....	....
	United States	Olympics	8	0	0	0	6	....	....	....	....	....
	Toronto	**NHL**	....	....	....	....	....	**2**	**0**	**0**	**0**	**0**
	St. John's	AHL	6	4	1	5	4	3	1	1	2	0
1994-95	**Toronto**	**NHL**	**8**	**0**	**1**	**1**	**4**	....	....	....	....	....
	St. John's	AHL	59	16	20	36	48	....	....	....	....	....
1995-96	**Toronto**	**NHL**	**46**	**6**	**6**	**12**	**47**	....	....	....	....	....
	NY Islanders	**NHL**	**16**	**1**	**4**	**5**	**33**	....	....	....	....	....
1996-97	**Toronto**	**NHL**	**64**	**11**	**6**	**17**	**47**	....	....	....	....	....
	St. John's	AHL	12	5	4	9	21	....	....	....	....	....
1997-98	**Toronto**	**NHL**	**80**	**8**	**4**	**12**	**67**	....	....	....	....	....
	NHL Totals		**214**	**26**	**21**	**47**	**198**	**2**	**0**	**0**	**0**	**0**

Traded to **NY Islanders** by **Toronto** with Sean Haggerty, Kenny Jonsson and Toronto's 1st round choice (Roberto Luongo) in 1997 Entry Draft for Wendel Clark, Mathieu Schneider and D.J. Smith, March 13, 1996. Traded to **Toronto** by **NY Islanders** for a conditional choice in 1998 Entry Draft, October 11, 1996.

HENRICH, MICHAEL — EDM.

Right wing. Shoots right. 6'2", 206 lbs. Born, Thornhill, Ont., March 3, 1980.
(Edmonton's 1st choice, 13th overall, in 1998 Entry Draft).

			Regular Season					Playoffs				
Season	Club	Lea	GP	G	A	TP	PIM	GP	G	A	TP	PIM
1996-97	Barrie	OHL	52	9	15	24	19	9	0	5	5	0
1997-98	Barrie	OHL	66	41	22	63	75	5	1	3	4	0

HENRY, ALEX — EDM.

Defense. Shoots left. 6'5", 216 lbs. Born, Elliot Lake, Ont., October 18, 1979.
(Edmonton's 2nd choice, 67th overall, in 1998 Entry Draft).

			Regular Season					Playoffs				
Season	Club	Lea	GP	G	A	TP	PIM	GP	G	A	TP	PIM
1996-97	London	OHL	61	1	10	11	65	....	....	....	....	....
1997-98	London	OHL	62	5	9	14	97	16	0	3	3	14

HENRY, BURKE — NYR

Defense. Shoots left. 6'2", 190 lbs. Born, Ste. Rose, Man., January 21, 1979.
(NY Rangers' 3rd choice, 73rd overall, in 1997 Entry Draft).

			Regular Season					Playoffs				
Season	Club	Lea	GP	G	A	TP	PIM	GP	G	A	TP	PIM
1995-96	Brandon	WHL	50	6	11	17	58	19	0	4	4	19
1996-97	Brandon	WHL	55	6	25	31	81	6	1	3	4	4
1997-98	Brandon	WHL	72	18	65	83	153	18	3	16	19	37

WHL East First All-Star Team (1998)

HERBERS, IAN

Defense. Shoots left. 6'4", 225 lbs. Born, Jasper, Alta., July 18, 1967.
(Buffalo's 11th choice, 190th overall, in 1987 Entry Draft).

			Regular Season					Playoffs				
Season	Club	Lea	GP	G	A	TP	PIM	GP	G	A	TP	PIM
1984-85	Kelowna	WHL	68	3	14	17	120	6	0	1	1	9
1985-86	Spokane	WHL	29	1	6	7	85	....	....	....	....	....
	Lethbridge	WHL	32	1	4	5	109	10	1	0	1	37
1986-87	Swift Current	WHL	72	5	8	13	230	4	1	1	2	12
1987-88	Swift Current	WHL	56	5	14	19	238	4	0	2	2	4
1988-89	U. of Alberta	CWUAA	47	4	22	26	137	....	....	....	....	....
1989-90	U. of Alberta	CWUAA	45	5	31	36	83	....	....	....	....	....
1990-91	U. of Alberta	CWUAA	45	6	24	30	87	....	....	....	....	....
1991-92	U. of Alberta	CWUAA	43	14	34	48	86	....	....	....	....	....
1992-93	Cape Breton	AHL	77	7	15	22	129	10	0	1	1	16
1993-94	**Edmonton**	**NHL**	**22**	**0**	**2**	**2**	**32**	....	....	....	....	....
	Cape Breton	AHL	53	7	16	23	122	5	0	3	3	12
1994-95	Cape Breton	AHL	36	1	11	12	104	....	....	....	....	....
	Detroit	IHL	37	1	5	6	46	5	1	1	2	6
1995-96	Detroit	IHL	73	3	11	14	140	12	3	5	8	29
1996-97	Detroit	IHL	67	3	16	19	129	21	0	4	4	34
1997-98	Detroit	IHL	70	6	6	12	100	23	0	3	3	54
	NHL Totals		**22**	**0**	**2**	**2**	**32**	....	....	....	....	....

a CIAU All-Canadian Team (1991, 1992)

Signed as a free agent by **Edmonton**, September 9, 1992.

HERPERGER, CHRIS — CHI.

Left wing. Shoots left. 6', 190 lbs. Born, Esterhazy, Sask., February 24, 1974.
(Philadelphia's 9th choice, 223rd overall, in 1992 Entry Draft).

			Regular Season					Playoffs				
Season	Club	Lea	GP	G	A	TP	PIM	GP	G	A	TP	PIM
1990-91	Swift Current	WHL	10	0	1	1	5	....	....	....	....	....
1991-92	Swift Current	WHL	72	14	19	33	44	8	0	1	1	9
1992-93	Swift Current	WHL	20	9	7	16	31	....	....	....	....	....
	Seattle	WHL	46	20	11	31	30	5	1	1	2	6
1993-94	Seattle	WHL	71	44	51	95	110	9	12	10	22	12
1994-95	Seattle	WHL	59	49	52	101	106	4	4	0	4	6
	Hershey	AHL	4	0	0	0	0	....	....	....	....	....
1995-96	Hershey	AHL	46	8	12	20	36	....	....	....	....	....
	Baltimore	AHL	21	2	3	5	17	9	2	3	5	6
1996-97	Baltimore	AHL	67	19	22	41	88	3	0	0	0	0
1997-98	Canada	Nat-Tm	63	20	30	50	102	....	....	....	....	....

WHL West Second All-Star Team (1995)

Traded to **Anaheim** by **Philadelphia** with Winnipeg's 7th round choice (previously acquired, Anaheim selected Tony Mohagen) in 1997 Entry Draft for Bob Corkum, February 6, 1996. Signed as a free agent by **Chicago**, September 2, 1998.

HERR, MATT — WSH.

Center. Shoots left. 6'1", 180 lbs. Born, Hackensack, NJ, May 26, 1976.
(Washington's 4th choice, 93rd overall, in 1994 Entry Draft).

			Regular Season					Playoffs				
Season	Club	Lea	GP	G	A	TP	PIM	GP	G	A	TP	PIM
1993-94	Hotchkiss High	H.S.	24	28	19	47	....	....	....	....	....	....
1994-95	U. of Michigan	CCHA	37	11	8	19	51	....	....	....	....	....
1995-96	U. of Michigan	CCHA	40	18	13	31	55	....	....	....	....	....
1996-97	U. of Michigan	CCHA	43	29	23	52	67	....	....	....	....	....
1997-98	U. of Michigan	CCHA	31	14	17	31	62	....	....	....	....	....

HEWARD, JAMIE (HEW-uhrd) — NSH.

Defense. Shoots right. 6'2", 207 lbs. Born, Regina, Sask., March 30, 1971.
(Pittsburgh's 1st choice, 16th overall, in 1989 Entry Draft).

			Regular Season					Playoffs				
Season	Club	Lea	GP	G	A	TP	PIM	GP	G	A	TP	PIM
1987-88	Regina	WHL	68	10	17	27	17	4	1	1	2	2
1988-89	Regina	WHL	52	31	28	59	29	....	....	....	....	....
1989-90	Regina	WHL	72	14	44	58	42	11	2	2	4	10
1990-91	Regina	WHL	71	23	61	84	41	8	2	9	11	6
1991-92	Muskegon	IHL	54	6	21	27	37	14	1	4	5	4
1992-93	Cleveland	IHL	58	9	18	27	64	....	....	....	....	....
1993-94	Cleveland	IHL	73	8	16	24	72	....	....	....	....	....
1994-95	Canada	Nat-Tm	51	11	35	46	32	....	....	....	....	....
1995-96	**Toronto**	**NHL**	**5**	**0**	**0**	**0**	**0**	....	....	....	....	....
	St. John's	AHL	73	22	34	56	33	3	1	1	2	6
1996-97	**Toronto**	**NHL**	**20**	**1**	**4**	**5**	**6**	....	....	....	....	....
	St. John's	AHL	27	8	19	27	26	9	1	3	4	6
1997-98	Philadelphia	AHL	72	17	48	65	54	20	3	16	19	10
	NHL Totals		**25**	**1**	**4**	**5**	**6**	....	....	....	....	....

WHL East First All-Star Team (1991) • AHL First All-Star Team (1996, 1998) • Won Eddie Shore Award (Outstanding Defenseman - AHL) (1998)

Signed as a free agent by **Toronto**, May 4, 1995. Signed as a free agent by **Philadelphia**, July 31, 1997. Signed as a free agent by **Nashville**, August 10, 1998.

HICKS, ALEX

Left wing. Shoots left. 6'1", 195 lbs. Born, Calgary, Alta., September 4, 1969.

			Regular Season					Playoffs				
Season	Club	Lea	GP	G	A	TP	PIM	GP	G	A	TP	PIM
1988-89	Wisc.-Eau Claire	NCHA	30	21	26	47	42	....	....	....	....	....
1989-90	Wisc.-Eau Claire	NCHA	34	31	48	79	30	....	....	....	....	....
1990-91	Wisc.-Eau Claire	NCHA	26	22	35	57	43	....	....	....	....	....
1991-92	Wisc.-Eau Claire	NCHA	26	24	42	66	63	....	....	....	....	....
1992-93	Toledo	ECHL	50	26	34	60	100	16	5	10	15	79
	Adirondack	AHL	3	0	0	0	0	....	....	....	....	....
1993-94	Toledo	ECHL	60	31	49	80	240	14	10	10	20	56
	Adirondack	AHL	8	1	3	4	2	5	0	2	2	2
1994-95	Las Vegas	IHL	79	24	42	66	212	9	2	4	6	47
1995-96	**Anaheim**	**NHL**	**64**	**10**	**11**	**21**	**37**	....	....	....	....	....
	Baltimore	AHL	13	2	10	12	23	....	....	....	....	....
1996-97	**Anaheim**	**NHL**	**18**	**2**	**6**	**8**	**14**	....	....	....	....	....
	Pittsburgh	**NHL**	**55**	**5**	**15**	**20**	**76**	**5**	**0**	**1**	**1**	**2**
1997-98	**Pittsburgh**	**NHL**	**58**	**7**	**13**	**20**	**54**	**6**	**0**	**0**	**0**	**2**
	NHL Totals		**195**	**24**	**45**	**69**	**181**	**11**	**0**	**1**	**1**	**4**

NCAA (College Div.) West First All-American Team (1991, 1992)

Signed as a free agent by **Anaheim**, August 17, 1995. Traded to **Pittsburgh** by **Anaheim** with Fredrik Olausson for Shawn Antoski and Dmitri Mironov, November 19, 1996.

HIGGINS, MATT — MTL.

Center. Shoots left. 6'2", 182 lbs. Born, Calgary, Alta., October 29, 1977.
(Montreal's 1st choice, 18th overall, in 1996 Entry Draft).

			Regular Season					Playoffs				
Season	Club	Lea	GP	G	A	TP	PIM	GP	G	A	TP	PIM
1993-94	Moose Jaw	WHL	64	6	10	16	10	....	....	....	....	....
1994-95	Moose Jaw	WHL	72	36	34	70	26	10	1	2	3	2
1995-96	Moose Jaw	WHL	67	30	33	63	43	....	....	....	....	....
1996-97	Moose Jaw	WHL	71	33	57	90	51	12	3	5	8	2
1997-98	**Montreal**	**NHL**	**1**	**0**	**0**	**0**	**0**	....	....	....	....	....
	Fredericton	AHL	50	5	22	27	12	4	1	2	3	2
	NHL Totals		**1**	**0**	**0**	**0**	**0**	....	....	....	....	....

HILL, SEAN (HIHL, SHAWN) — CAR.

Defense. Shoots right. 6', 203 lbs. Born, Duluth, MN, February 14, 1970.
(Montreal's 9th choice, 167th overall, in 1988 Entry Draft).

			Regular Season					Playoffs				
Season	Club	Lea	GP	G	A	TP	PIM	GP	G	A	TP	PIM
1987-88	East Duluth	H.S.	24	10	17	27	....	....	....	....	....	....
1988-89	U. of Wisconsin	WCHA	45	2	23	25	69	....	....	....	....	....
1989-90	U. of Wisconsin	WCHA	42	14	39	53	78	....	....	....	....	....
1990-91	U. of Wisconsin	WCHA	37	19	32	51	122	....	....	....	....	....
	Montreal	**NHL**	....	....	....	....	....	**1**	**0**	**0**	**0**	**0**
	Fredericton	AHL	....	....	....	....	....	3	0	2	2	2
1991-92	Fredericton	AHL	42	7	20	27	65	7	1	3	4	6
	United States	Olympics	8	2	0	2	6	....	....	....	....	....
	United States	Nat-Tm	12	4	3	7	16	....	....	....	....	....
	Montreal	**NHL**	....	....	....	....	....	**4**	**1**	**0**	**1**	**2**
1992-93	**Montreal**	**NHL**	**31**	**2**	**6**	**8**	**54**	**3**	**0**	**0**	**0**	**4** ♦
	Fredericton	AHL	6	1	3	4	10	....	....	....	....	....
1993-94	**Anaheim**	**NHL**	**68**	**7**	**20**	**27**	**78**	....	....	....	....	....
1994-95	**Ottawa**	**NHL**	**45**	**1**	**14**	**15**	**30**	....	....	....	....	....
1995-96	**Ottawa**	**NHL**	**80**	**7**	**14**	**21**	**94**	....	....	....	....	....
1996-97	**Ottawa**	**NHL**	**5**	**0**	**0**	**0**	**4**	....	....	....	....	....
1997-98	**Ottawa**	**NHL**	**13**	**1**	**1**	**2**	**6**	....	....	....	....	....
	Carolina	**NHL**	**42**	**0**	**5**	**5**	**48**	....	....	....	....	....
	NHL Totals		**284**	**18**	**60**	**78**	**314**	**8**	**1**	**0**	**1**	**6**

WCHA Second All-Star Team (1990, 1991) • NCAA West Second All-American Team (1991)

Claimed by **Anaheim** from **Montreal** in Expansion Draft, June 24, 1993. Traded to **Ottawa** by **Anaheim** with Anaheim's 9th round choice (Frederic Cassivi) in 1994 Entry Draft for Ottawa's 3rd round choice (later traded to Tampa Bay — Tampa Bay selected Vadim Epanchintsev) in 1994 Entry Draft, June 29, 1994. Traded to **Carolina** by **Ottawa** for Chris Murray, November 18, 1997.

HINOTE, DAN — COL.

Right wing. Shoots right. 6', 187 lbs. Born, Leesburg, FL, January 30, 1977.
(Colorado's 9th choice, 167th overall, in 1996 Entry Draft).

			Regular Season					Playoffs				
Season	Club	Lea	GP	G	A	TP	PIM	GP	G	A	TP	PIM
1994-95	Army	NCAA	33	20	24	44	20	....	....	....	....	....
1995-96	Army	NCAA	34	21	24	45	22	....	....	....	....	....
1996-97	Oshawa	OHL	60	15	13	28	58	18	4	5	9	8
1997-98	Oshawa	OHL	35	12	15	27	39	5	2	2	4	7
	Hershey	AHL	24	1	4	5	25	....	....	....	....	....

HINZ, CHAD — EDM.

Right wing. Shoots right. 5'10", 185 lbs. Born, Saskatoon, Sask., March 21, 1979.
(Edmonton's 8th choice, 187th overall, in 1997 Entry Draft).

			Regular Season					Playoffs				
Season	Club	Lea	GP	G	A	TP	PIM	GP	G	A	TP	PIM
1995-96	Moose Jaw	WHL	70	22	32	54	65	....	....	....	....	....
1996-97	Moose Jaw	WHL	72	37	47	84	47	12	4	1	5	11
1997-98	Moose Jaw	WHL	72	20	57	77	45	4	1	2	3	2

HIRVONEN, TOMI (HIHR-voh-nehn) — COL.

Center. Shoots left. 5'11", 185 lbs. Born, Tampere, Finland, January 11, 1977.
(Colorado's 8th choice, 207th overall, in 1995 Entry Draft).

			Regular Season					Playoffs				
Season	Club	Lea	GP	G	A	TP	PIM	GP	G	A	TP	PIM
1994-95	Ilves	Fin-Jr.	28	9	13	22	30	8	4	2	6	14
1995-96	Ilves	Fin-Jr.	12	7	12	19	45	....	....	....	....	....
	KooVee	Finland-2	7	4	1	5	26	....	....	....	....	....
	Ilves	Finland	28	1	0	1	24	....	....	....	....	....
1996-97	Ilves	Finland	40	0	7	7	22	6	0	0	0	4
1997-98	Ilves	Finland	48	10	12	22	54	9	0	0	0	2

HLAVAC, JAN (huh-LAH-vahch, YAHN) — CGY.

Left wing. Shoots left. 6', 183 lbs. Born, Prague, Czech., September 20, 1976.
(NY Islanders' 2nd choice, 28th overall, in 1995 Entry Draft).

			Regular Season					Playoffs				
Season	Club	Lea	GP	G	A	TP	PIM	GP	G	A	TP	PIM
1993-94	HC Sparta	Cze-Rep.	9	1	1	2	....	....	....	....	....	....
1994-95	HC Sparta	Cze-Rep.	38	7	6	13	18	5	0	2	2	0
1995-96	HC Sparta	Cze-Rep.	34	8	5	13	....	12	1	2	3	....
1996-97	HC Sparta	Cze-Rep.	38	8	13	21	24	10	5	2	7	2
1997-98	Sparta Praha	EuroHL	5	0	3	3	4	....	....	....	....	....
	Sparta Praha	Cze-Rep.	48	17	30	47	40	5	1	0	1	2

HLUSHKO, TODD (huh-LUSH-koh) PIT.

Center. Shoots left. 5'11", 185 lbs. Born, Toronto, Ont., February 7, 1970.
(Washington's 14th choice, 240th overall, in 1990 Entry Draft).

			Regular Season					Playoffs				
Season	Club	Lea	GP	G	A	TP	PIM	GP	G	A	TP	PIM
1988-89	Guelph	OHL	66	28	18	46	71	7	5	3	8	18
1989-90	Owen Sound	OHL	25	9	17	26	31	....	....	....	....	....
	London	OHL	40	27	17	44	39	6	2	4	6	10
1990-91	Baltimore	AHL	66	9	14	23	55	....	....	....	....	....
1991-92	Baltimore	AHL	74	16	35	51	113	....	....	....	....	....
1992-93	Canada	Nat-Tm	58	22	26	48	10	....	....	....	....	....
1993-94	Canada	Nat-Tm	55	22	6	28	61	....	....	....	....	....
	Canada	Olympics	8	5	0	5	6	....	....	....	....	....
	Philadelphia	**NHL**	**2**	**1**	**0**	**1**	**0**	....	....	....	....	....
	Hershey	AHL	9	6	0	6	4	6	2	1	3	4
1994-95	**Calgary**	**NHL**	**2**	**0**	**1**	**1**	**2**	**1**	**0**	**0**	**0**	**2**
	Saint John	AHL	46	22	10	32	36	4	2	2	4	22
1995-96	**Calgary**	**NHL**	**4**	**0**	**0**	**0**	**6**	....	....	....	....	....
	Saint John	AHL	35	14	13	27	70	16	8	1	9	26
1996-97	**Calgary**	**NHL**	**58**	**7**	**11**	**18**	**49**	....	....	....	....	....
1997-98	**Calgary**	**NHL**	**13**	**0**	**1**	**1**	**27**	....	....	....	....	....
	Saint John	AHL	33	10	14	24	48	21	*13	4	17	61
	NHL Totals		**79**	**8**	**13**	**21**	**84**	**1**	**0**	**0**	**0**	**2**

Signed as a free agent by **Philadelphia**, March 7, 1994. Signed as a free agent by **Calgary**, June 17, 1994. Traded to **Pittsburgh** by **Calgary** with German Titov for Ken Wregget and Dave Roche, June 17, 1998.

HOBDAY, BRENT DET.

Center. Shoots left. 6'1", 192 lbs. Born, Winnipeg, Man., August 26, 1979.
(Detroit's 5th choice, 111th overall, in 1998 Entry Draft).

			Regular Season					Playoffs				
Season	Club	Lea	GP	G	A	TP	PIM	GP	G	A	TP	PIM
1997-98	Moose Jaw	WHL	68	21	22	43	122	4	2	0	2	4

HOCKING, JUSTIN CHI.

Defense. Shoots right. 6'4", 205 lbs. Born, Stettler, Alta., January 9, 1974.
(Los Angeles' 1st choice, 39th overall, in 1992 Entry Draft).

			Regular Season					Playoffs				
Season	Club	Lea	GP	G	A	TP	PIM	GP	G	A	TP	PIM
1991-92	Spokane	WHL	71	4	6	10	309	10	0	3	3	28
1992-93	Spokane	WHL	16	0	1	1	75	....	....	....	....	....
	Medicine Hat	WHL	54	1	9	10	119	10	0	1	1	13
1993-94	Medicine Hat	WHL	68	7	26	33	236	3	0	0	0	6
	Los Angeles	**NHL**	**1**	**0**	**0**	**0**	**0**	....	....	....	....	....
	Phoenix	IHL	3	0	0	0	15	....	....	....	....	....
1994-95	Syracuse	AHL	7	0	0	0	24	....	....	....	....	....
	Portland	AHL	9	0	1	1	34	....	....	....	....	....
	Knoxville	ECHL	20	0	6	6	70	4	0	0	0	26
	Phoenix	IHL	20	1	1	2	50	1	0	0	0	0
1995-96	P.E.I.	AHL	74	4	8	12	251	4	0	2	2	5
1996-97	Worcester	AHL	68	1	10	11	198	5	0	3	3	2
1997-98	Worcester	AHL	79	5	12	17	198	11	1	2	3	19
	NHL Totals		**1**	**0**	**0**	**0**	**0**	....	....	....	....	....

WHL East Second All-Star Team (1994)

Claimed by **Ottawa** from **LA Kings** in Waiver Draft, October 2, 1995. Traded to **Chicago** by **Ottawa** for Brian Felsner, August 21, 1998.

HOGAN, PETER L.A.

Defense. Shoots right. 6'3", 183 lbs. Born, Oshawa, Ont., January 10, 1978.
(Los Angeles' 7th choice, 123rd overall, in 1996 Entry Draft).

			Regular Season					Playoffs				
Season	Club	Lea	GP	G	A	TP	PIM	GP	G	A	TP	PIM
1995-96	Oshawa	OHL	66	3	25	28	54	5	2	0	2	2
1996-97	Oshawa	OHL	65	13	37	50	56	18	1	11	12	22
1997-98	Oshawa	OHL	63	10	28	38	104	....	....	....	....	....

HOGLUND, JONAS (HOHG-lund, YOH-nuhs) MTL.

Right wing. Shoots right. 6'3", 215 lbs. Born, Hammaro, Swe., August 29, 1972.
(Calgary's 11th choice, 222nd overall, in 1992 Entry Draft).

			Regular Season					Playoffs				
Season	Club	Lea	GP	G	A	TP	PIM	GP	G	A	TP	PIM
1988-89	Farjestad	Sweden	1	0	0	0	0	....	....	....	....	....
1989-90	Farjestad	Sweden	1	0	0	0	0	....	....	....	....	....
1990-91	Farjestad	Sweden	40	5	5	10	4	8	1	0	1	0
1991-92	Farjestad	Sweden	40	14	11	25	6	6	2	4	6	2
1992-93	Farjestad	Sweden	40	13	13	26	14	3	1	0	1	0
1993-94	Farjestad	Sweden	22	7	2	9	10	....	....	....	....	....
1994-95	Farjestad	Sweden	40	14	12	26	16	4	3	2	5	0
1995-96	Farjestad	Sweden	40	32	11	43	18	8	2	1	3	6
1996-97	**Calgary**	**NHL**	**68**	**19**	**16**	**35**	**12**	....	....	....	....	....
1997-98	**Calgary**	**NHL**	**50**	**6**	**8**	**14**	**16**	....	....	....	....	....
	Montreal	**NHL**	**28**	**6**	**5**	**11**	**6**	**10**	**2**	**0**	**2**	**0**
	NHL Totals		**146**	**31**	**29**	**60**	**34**	**10**	**2**	**0**	**2**	**0**

Traded to **Montreal** by **Calgary** with Zarley Zalapski for Valeri Bure and Montreal's 4th round choice (Shaun Sutter) in 1998 Entry Draft, February 1, 1998

HOGUE, BENOIT (HOHG) T.B.

Center. Shoots left. 5'10", 194 lbs. Born, Repentigny, Que., October 28, 1966.
(Buffalo's 2nd choice, 35th overall, in 1985 Entry Draft).

			Regular Season					Playoffs				
Season	Club	Lea	GP	G	A	TP	PIM	GP	G	A	TP	PIM
1983-84	St-Jean	QMJHL	59	14	11	25	42	....	....	....	....	....
1984-85	St-Jean	QMJHL	63	46	44	90	92	....	....	....	....	....
1985-86	St-Jean	QMJHL	65	54	54	108	115	9	6	4	10	26
1986-87	Rochester	AHL	52	14	20	34	52	12	5	4	9	8
1987-88	**Buffalo**	**NHL**	**3**	**1**	**1**	**2**	**0**	....	....	....	....	....
	Rochester	AHL	62	24	31	55	141	7	6	1	7	46
1988-89	**Buffalo**	**NHL**	**69**	**14**	**30**	**44**	**120**	**5**	**0**	**0**	**0**	**17**
1989-90	**Buffalo**	**NHL**	**45**	**11**	**7**	**18**	**79**	**3**	**0**	**0**	**0**	**10**
1990-91	**Buffalo**	**NHL**	**76**	**19**	**28**	**47**	**76**	**5**	**3**	**1**	**4**	**10**
1991-92	**Buffalo**	**NHL**	**3**	**0**	**1**	**1**	**0**	....	....	....	....	....
	NY Islanders	**NHL**	**72**	**30**	**45**	**75**	**67**	....	....	....	....	....
1992-93	**NY Islanders**	**NHL**	**70**	**33**	**42**	**75**	**108**	**18**	**6**	**6**	**12**	**31**
1993-94	**NY Islanders**	**NHL**	**83**	**36**	**33**	**69**	**73**	**4**	**0**	**1**	**1**	**4**
1994-95	**NY Islanders**	**NHL**	**33**	**6**	**4**	**10**	**34**	....	....	....	....	....
	Toronto	**NHL**	**12**	**3**	**3**	**6**	**0**	**7**	**0**	**0**	**0**	**6**
1995-96	**Toronto**	**NHL**	**44**	**12**	**25**	**37**	**68**	....	....	....	....	....
	Dallas	**NHL**	**34**	**7**	**20**	**27**	**36**	....	....	....	....	....
1996-97	**Dallas**	**NHL**	**73**	**19**	**24**	**43**	**54**	**7**	**2**	**2**	**4**	**6**
1997-98	**Dallas**	**NHL**	**53**	**6**	**16**	**22**	**35**	**17**	**4**	**2**	**6**	**16**
	NHL Totals		**670**	**197**	**279**	**476**	**750**	**66**	**15**	**12**	**27**	**100**

Traded to **NY Islanders** by **Buffalo** with Pierre Turgeon, Uwe Krupp and Dave McLlwain for Pat Lafontaine, Randy Hillier, Randy Wood and NY Islanders' 4th round choice (Dean Melanson) in 1992 Entry Draft, October 25, 1991. Traded to **Toronto** by **NY Islanders** with NY Islanders' 3rd round choice (Ryan Pepperall) in 1995 Entry Draft and 5th round choice (Brandon Sugden) in 1996 Entry Draft for Eric Fichaud, April 6, 1995. Traded to **Dallas** by **Toronto** with Randy Wood for Dave Gagner and Dallas' 6th round choice (Dmitriy Yakushin) in 1996 Entry Draft, January 29, 1996. Signed as a free agent by **Tampa Bay**, August 19, 1998.

HOHENBERGER, MARTIN (HOH-ehn-buhr-guhr) MTL.

Left wing. Shoots left. 6'1", 205 lbs. Born, Villach, Austria, January 29, 1977.
(Montreal's 3rd choice, 74th overall, in 1995 Entry Draft).

			Regular Season					Playoffs				
Season	Club	Lea	GP	G	A	TP	PIM	GP	G	A	TP	PIM
1993-94	Victoria	WHL	61	3	13	16	82	....	....	....	....	....
1994-95	Prince George	WHL	47	10	21	31	81	....	....	....	....	....
1995-96	Prince George	WHL	37	10	19	29	19	....	....	....	....	....
	Lethbridge	WHL	20	5	1	6	21	4	0	3	3	4
1996-97	Lethbridge	WHL	57	26	33	59	74	19	7	13	20	15
1997-98	Fredericton	AHL	9	0	1	1	2	....	....	....	....	....
	Austria	Olympics	4	0	0	0	2	....	....	....	....	....
	New Orleans	ECHL	9	1	2	3	15	3	0	0	0	0

HOLDEN, JOSH VAN.

Center. Shoots left. 6', 190 lbs. Born, Calgary, Alta., January 18, 1978.
(Vancouver's 1st choice, 12th overall, in 1996 Entry Draft).

			Regular Season					Playoffs				
Season	Club	Lea	GP	G	A	TP	PIM	GP	G	A	TP	PIM
1994-95	Regina	WHL	62	20	23	43	45	4	3	1	4	0
1995-96	Regina	WHL	70	57	55	112	105	11	4	5	9	23
1996-97	Regina	WHL	58	49	49	98	148	5	3	2	5	10
1997-98	Regina	WHL	56	41	58	99	134	2	2	2	4	10

WHL East Second All-Star Team (1998)

HOLDRIDGE, KEVIN CAR.

Defense. Shoots left. 6'2", 202 lbs. Born, Syracuse, NY, September 9, 1980.
(Carolina's 2nd choice, 70th overall, in 1998 Entry Draft).

			Regular Season					Playoffs				
Season	Club	Lea	GP	G	A	TP	PIM	GP	G	A	TP	PIM
1996-97	Detroit	OHL	55	0	9	9	49	5	0	0	0	2
1997-98	Plymouth	OHL	61	4	15	19	106	15	0	3	3	30

HOLIK, BOBBY (HOH-leek) N.J.

Left wing. Shoots right. 6'3", 225 lbs. Born, Jihlava, Czech., January 1, 1971.
(Hartford's 1st choice, 10th overall, in 1989 Entry Draft).

			Regular Season					Playoffs				
Season	Club	Lea	GP	G	A	TP	PIM	GP	G	A	TP	PIM
1987-88	Dukla Jihlava	Czech.	31	5	9	14	16	....	....	....	....	....
1988-89	Dukla Jihlava	Czech.	24	7	10	17	32	....	....	....	....	....
1989-90	Dukla Jihlava	Czech.	42	15	26	41	....	....	....	....	....	....
1990-91	**Hartford**	**NHL**	**78**	**21**	**22**	**43**	**113**	**6**	**0**	**0**	**0**	**7**
1991-92	**Hartford**	**NHL**	**76**	**21**	**24**	**45**	**44**	**7**	**0**	**1**	**1**	**6**
1992-93	**New Jersey**	**NHL**	**61**	**20**	**19**	**39**	**76**	**5**	**1**	**1**	**2**	**6**
	Utica	AHL	1	0	0	0	2	....	....	....	....	....
1993-94	**New Jersey**	**NHL**	**70**	**13**	**20**	**33**	**72**	**20**	**0**	**3**	**3**	**6**
1994-95	**New Jersey**	**NHL**	**48**	**10**	**10**	**20**	**18**	**20**	**4**	**4**	**8**	**22** ♦
1995-96	**New Jersey**	**NHL**	**63**	**13**	**17**	**30**	**58**	....	....	....	....	....
1996-97	**New Jersey**	**NHL**	**82**	**23**	**39**	**62**	**54**	**10**	**2**	**3**	**5**	**4**
1997-98	**New Jersey**	**NHL**	**82**	**29**	**36**	**65**	**100**	**5**	**0**	**0**	**0**	**8**
	NHL Totals		**560**	**150**	**187**	**337**	**535**	**73**	**7**	**12**	**19**	**59**

Played in NHL All-Star Game (1998)

Traded to **New Jersey** by **Hartford** with Hartford's 2nd round choice (Jay Pandolfo) in 1993 Entry Draft and future considerations for Sean Burke and Eric Weinrich, August 28, 1992.

HOLLAND, JASON BUF.

Defense. Shoots right. 6'2", 193 lbs. Born, Morinville, Alta., April 30, 1976.
(NY Islanders' 2nd choice, 38th overall, in 1994 Entry Draft).

			Regular Season					Playoffs				
Season	Club	Lea	GP	G	A	TP	PIM	GP	G	A	TP	PIM
1992-93	Kamloops	WHL	4	0	0	0	2	....	....	....	....	....
1993-94	Kamloops	WHL	59	14	15	29	80	18	2	3	5	4
1994-95	Kamloops	WHL	71	9	32	41	65	21	2	7	9	9
1995-96	Kamloops	WHL	63	24	33	57	98	16	4	9	13	22
1996-97	**NY Islanders**	**NHL**	**4**	**1**	**0**	**1**	**0**	....	....	....	....	....
	Kentucky	AHL	72	14	25	39	46	4	0	2	2	0
1997-98	**NY Islanders**	**NHL**	**8**	**0**	**0**	**0**	**4**	....	....	....	....	....
	Kentucky	AHL	50	10	16	26	29	....	....	....	....	....
	Rochester	AHL	9	0	4	4	10	4	0	3	3	4
	NHL Totals		**12**	**1**	**0**	**1**	**4**	....	....	....	....	....

WHL West First All-Star Team (1996)

Traded to **Buffalo** by **NY Islanders** with Paul Kruse for Jason Dawe, March 24, 1998.

HOLLINGER, TERRY

Defense. Shoots left. 6'1", 200 lbs. Born, Regina, Sask., February 24, 1971.
(St. Louis' 7th choice, 153rd overall, in 1991 Entry Draft).

			Regular Season					Playoffs				
Season	Club	Lea	GP	G	A	TP	PIM	GP	G	A	TP	PIM
1987-88	Regina	WHL	7	1	1	2	4	....	....	....	....	....
1988-89	Regina	WHL	65	2	27	29	49	....	....	....	....	....
1989-90	Regina	WHL	70	14	43	57	40	11	1	3	4	10
1990-91	Regina	WHL	8	1	6	7	6	....	....	....	....	....
	Lethbridge	WHL	62	9	32	41	113	16	3	14	17	22
1991-92	Lethbridge	WHL	65	23	62	85	155	5	1	2	3	13
	Peoria	IHL	1	0	2	2	0	5	0	1	1	0
1992-93	Peoria	IHL	72	2	28	30	67	4	1	1	2	0
1993-94	**St. Louis**	**NHL**	**2**	**0**	**0**	**0**	**0**	....	....	....	....	....
	Peoria	IHL	78	12	31	43	96	6	0	3	3	31
1994-95	**St. Louis**	**NHL**	**5**	**0**	**0**	**0**	**2**	....	....	....	....	....
	Peoria	IHL	69	7	25	32	137	4	2	4	6	8
1995-96	Rochester	AHL	62	5	50	55	71	19	3	11	14	12
1996-97	Rochester	AHL	73	12	51	63	54	10	2	7	9	27
1997-98	Worcester	AHL	55	8	24	32	34	....	....	....	....	....
	Houston	IHL	8	1	1	2	6	4	1	2	3	11
	NHL Totals		**7**	**0**	**0**	**0**	**2**	....	....	....	....	....

AHL Second All-Star Team (1996) • AHL First All-Star Team (1997)

Signed as a free agent by **Buffalo**, August 23, 1995. Signed as a free agent by **St. Louis**, July 28, 1997.

HOLMQVIST, MIKAEL (HOHLM-kvihst) ANA.

Center. Shoots left. 6'3", 189 lbs. Born, Stockholm, Sweden, June 8, 1979.
(Anaheim's 1st choice, 18th overall, in 1997 Entry Draft).

			Regular Season					Playoffs				
Season	Club	Lea	GP	G	A	TP	PIM	GP	G	A	TP	PIM
1995-96	Djurgarden	Swe-Jr.	24	7	2	9	4	....	....	....	....	....
1996-97	Djurgarden	Swe-Jr.	39	29	35	64	110	....	....	....	....	....
	Djurgarden	Sweden	9	0	0	0	0	....	....	....	....	....
1997-98	Farjestad	Sweden	41	2	3	5	6	7	0	0	0	0

HOLMSTROM, TOMAS (HOHLM-struhm) DET.

Left wing. Shoots left. 6', 200 lbs. Born, Pitea, Sweden, January 23, 1973.
(Detroit's 9th choice, 257th overall, in 1994 Entry Draft).

			Regular Season					Playoffs				
Season	Club	Lea	GP	G	A	TP	PIM	GP	G	A	TP	PIM
1994-95	Lulea HF	Sweden	40	14	14	28	56	8	1	2	3	20
1995-96	Lulea HF	Sweden	34	12	11	23	78	11	6	2	8	22
1996-97	**Detroit**	**NHL**	**47**	**6**	**3**	**9**	**33**	**1**	**0**	**0**	**0**	**0 ♦**
	Adirondack	AHL	6	3	1	4	7	....	....	....	....	....
1997-98	**Detroit**	**NHL**	**57**	**5**	**17**	**22**	**44**	**22**	**7**	**12**	**19**	**16 ♦**
	NHL Totals		**104**	**11**	**20**	**31**	**77**	**23**	**7**	**12**	**19**	**16**

HOLZINGER, BRIAN (HOHL-zihn-guhr) BUF.

Center. Shoots right. 5'11", 190 lbs. Born, Parma, OH, October 10, 1972.
(Buffalo's 7th choice, 124th overall, in 1991 Entry Draft).

			Regular Season					Playoffs				
Season	Club	Lea	GP	G	A	TP	PIM	GP	G	A	TP	PIM
1990-91	Detroit	NAJHL	37	45	41	86	16	....	....	....	....	....
1991-92	Bowling Green	CCHA	30	14	8	22	36	....	....	....	....	....
1992-93	Bowling Green	CCHA	41	31	26	57	44	....	....	....	....	....
1993-94	Bowling Green	CCHA	38	22	15	37	24	....	....	....	....	....
1994-95	Bowling Green	CCHA	38	35	33	68	42	....	....	....	....	....
	Buffalo	**NHL**	**4**	**0**	**3**	**3**	**0**	**4**	**2**	**1**	**3**	**2**
1995-96	**Buffalo**	**NHL**	**58**	**10**	**10**	**20**	**37**	....	....	....	....	....
	Rochester	AHL	17	10	11	21	14	19	10	14	24	10
1996-97	**Buffalo**	**NHL**	**81**	**22**	**29**	**51**	**54**	**12**	**2**	**5**	**7**	**8**
1997-98	**Buffalo**	**NHL**	**69**	**14**	**21**	**35**	**36**	**15**	**4**	**7**	**11**	**18**
	NHL Totals		**212**	**46**	**63**	**109**	**127**	**31**	**8**	**13**	**21**	**28**

CCHA Second All-Star Team (1993) • CCHA First All-Star Team (1995) • NCAA West First All-American Team (1995) • Won Hobey Baker Memorial Award (Top U.S. Collegiate Player) (1995)

HORACEK, JAN (HOHR-uh-chehk) ST.L.

Defense. Shoots right. 6'3", 198 lbs. Born, Benesov, Czech., May 22, 1979.
(St. Louis' 3rd choice, 98th overall, in 1997 Entry Draft).

			Regular Season					Playoffs				
Season	Club	Lea	GP	G	A	TP	PIM	GP	G	A	TP	PIM
1996-97	Slavia Praha	Czech-Jr.	25	4	14	18	....	....	....	....	....	....
	Slavia Praha	Cze-Rep.	9	0	0	0	6	3	0	0	0	0
	HC Beroun	Czech-2	2	0	0	0	....	....	....	....	....	....
1997-98	Moncton	QMJHL	54	3	18	21	146	10	1	5	6	20

HORCOFF, SHAWN EDM.

Center. Shoots left. 6'1", 194 lbs. Born, Trail, B.C., September 17, 1978.
(Edmonton's 3rd choice, 99th overall, in 1998 Entry Draft).

			Regular Season					Playoffs				
Season	Club	Lea	GP	G	A	TP	PIM	GP	G	A	TP	PIM
1996-97	Michigan State	CCHA	40	10	13	23	20	....	....	....	....	....
1997-98	Michigan State	CCHA	34	14	13	27	50	....	....	....	....	....

HORNUNG, TODD WSH.

Center. Shoots left. 6', 200 lbs. Born, Swift Current, Sask., September 3, 1980.
(Washington's 2nd choice, 59th overall, in 1998 Entry Draft).

			Regular Season					Playoffs				
Season	Club	Lea	GP	G	A	TP	PIM	GP	G	A	TP	PIM
1995-96	Portland	WHL	1	0	0	0	0	....	....	....	....	....
1996-97	Portland	WHL	59	3	3	6	51	6	0	0	0	0
1997-98	Portland	WHL	64	19	18	37	96	16	6	6	12	26

HOSSA, MARIAN (HOH-sah) OTT.

Left wing. Shoots left. 6'1", 194 lbs. Born, Stara Lubovna, Czech., January 12, 1979.
(Ottawa's 1st choice, 12th overall, in 1997 Entry Draft).

			Regular Season					Playoffs				
Season	Club	Lea	GP	G	A	TP	PIM	GP	G	A	TP	PIM
1995-96	Dukla Trencin	Slov-Jr.	53	42	49	91	26	....	....	....	....	....
1996-97	Dukla Trencin	Slovakia	46	25	19	44	33	7	5	5	10	....
1997-98	Portland	WHL	53	45	40	85	50	16	13	6	19	6
	Ottawa	**NHL**	**7**	**0**	**1**	**1**	**0**	....	....	....	....	....
	NHL Totals		**7**	**0**	**1**	**1**	**0**	....	....	....	....	....

WHL West First All-Star Team (1998) • Canadian Major Junior First All-Star Team (1998) • Memorial Cup All-Star Team (1998)

HOUDA, DOUG (HOO-duh) ANA.

Defense. Shoots right. 6'2", 190 lbs. Born, Blairmore, Alta., June 3, 1966.
(Detroit's 2nd choice, 28th overall, in 1984 Entry Draft).

			Regular Season					Playoffs				
Season	Club	Lea	GP	G	A	TP	PIM	GP	G	A	TP	PIM
1981-82	Calgary	WHL	3	0	0	0	0	....	....	....	....	....
1982-83	Calgary	WHL	71	5	23	28	99	16	1	3	4	44
1983-84	Calgary	WHL	69	6	30	36	195	4	0	0	0	7
1984-85	Calgary	WHL	65	20	54	74	182	8	3	4	7	29
	Kalamazoo	IHL	....	....	....	....	....	7	0	2	2	10
1985-86	Calgary	WHL	16	4	10	14	60	....	....	....	....	....
	Medicine Hat	WHL	35	9	23	32	80	25	4	19	23	64
	Detroit	**NHL**	**6**	**0**	**0**	**0**	**4**	....	....	....	....	....
1986-87	Adirondack	AHL	77	6	23	29	142	11	1	8	9	50
1987-88	**Detroit**	**NHL**	**11**	**1**	**1**	**2**	**10**	....	....	....	....	....
	Adirondack	AHL	71	10	32	42	169	11	0	3	3	44
1988-89	**Detroit**	**NHL**	**57**	**2**	**11**	**13**	**67**	**6**	**0**	**1**	**1**	**0**
	Adirondack	AHL	7	0	3	3	8	....	....	....	....	....
1989-90	**Detroit**	**NHL**	**73**	**2**	**9**	**11**	**127**	....	....	....	....	....
1990-91	**Detroit**	**NHL**	**22**	**0**	**4**	**4**	**43**	....	....	....	....	....
	Adirondack	AHL	38	9	17	26	67	....	....	....	....	....
	Hartford	**NHL**	**19**	**1**	**2**	**3**	**41**	**6**	**0**	**0**	**0**	**8**
1991-92	**Hartford**	**NHL**	**56**	**3**	**6**	**9**	**125**	**6**	**0**	**2**	**2**	**13**
1992-93	**Hartford**	**NHL**	**60**	**2**	**6**	**8**	**167**	....	....	....	....	....
1993-94	**Hartford**	**NHL**	**7**	**0**	**0**	**0**	**23**	....	....	....	....	....
	Los Angeles	**NHL**	**54**	**2**	**6**	**8**	**165**	....	....	....	....	....
1994-95	**Buffalo**	**NHL**	**28**	**1**	**2**	**3**	**68**	....	....	....	....	....
1995-96	**Buffalo**	**NHL**	**38**	**1**	**3**	**4**	**52**	....	....	....	....	....
	Rochester	AHL	21	1	6	7	41	19	3	5	8	30
1996-97	**NY Islanders**	**NHL**	**70**	**2**	**8**	**10**	**99**	....	....	....	....	....
	Utah	IHL	3	0	0	0	7	....	....	....	....	....
1997-98	**NY Islanders**	**NHL**	**31**	**1**	**2**	**3**	**47**	....	....	....	....	....
	Anaheim	**NHL**	**24**	**1**	**2**	**3**	**52**	....	....	....	....	....
	NHL Totals		**556**	**19**	**62**	**81**	**1090**	**18**	**0**	**3**	**3**	**21**

WHL East Second All-Star Team (1985) • AHL First All-Star Team (1988)

Traded to **Hartford** by **Detroit** for Doug Crossman, February 20, 1991. Traded to **LA Kings** by **Hartford** for Marc Potvin, November 3, 1993. Traded to **Buffalo** by **LA Kings** for Sean O'Donnell, July 26, 1994. Signed as a free agent by **NY Islanders**, October 26, 1996. Traded to **Anaheim** by **NY Islanders** with Travis Green and Tony Tuzzolino for Joe Sacco, J.J. Daigneault and Mark Janssens, February 6, 1998.

HOUDE, ERIC (OOD) MTL.

Center. Shoots left. 5'11", 191 lbs. Born, Montreal, Que., December 19, 1976.
(Montreal's 9th choice, 216th overall, in 1995 Entry Draft).

			Regular Season					Playoffs				
Season	Club	Lea	GP	G	A	TP	PIM	GP	G	A	TP	PIM
1993-94	St-Jean	QMJHL	71	16	16	32	14	5	1	1	2	4
1994-95	St-Jean	QMJHL	40	10	13	23	23	....	....	....	....	....
	Halifax	QMJHL	28	13	23	36	8	3	2	1	3	4
1995-96	Halifax	QMJHL	69	40	48	88	35	6	3	4	7	2
1996-97	**Montreal**	**NHL**	**13**	**0**	**2**	**2**	**2**	....	....	....	....	....
	Fredericton	AHL	66	30	36	66	20	....	....	....	....	....
1997-98	**Montreal**	**NHL**	**9**	**1**	**0**	**1**	**0**	....	....	....	....	....
	Fredericton	AHL	71	28	42	70	24	4	5	2	7	4
	NHL Totals		**22**	**1**	**2**	**3**	**2**	....	....	....	....	....

HOUGH, MIKE (HUHF) NYI

Left wing. Shoots left. 6'1", 197 lbs. Born, Montreal, Que., February 6, 1963.
(Quebec's 7th choice, 181st overall, in 1982 Entry Draft).

			Regular Season					Playoffs				
Season	Club	Lea	GP	G	A	TP	PIM	GP	G	A	TP	PIM
1981-82	Kitchener	OHL	58	14	24	38	172	14	4	1	5	16
1982-83	Kitchener	OHL	61	17	27	44	156	12	5	4	9	30
1983-84	Fredericton	AHL	69	11	16	27	142	1	0	0	0	7
1984-85	Fredericton	AHL	76	21	27	48	49	6	1	1	2	2
1985-86	Fredericton	AHL	74	21	33	54	68	6	0	3	3	8
1986-87	**Quebec**	**NHL**	**56**	**6**	**8**	**14**	**79**	**9**	**0**	**3**	**3**	**26**
	Fredericton	AHL	10	1	3	4	20	....	....	....	....	....
1987-88	**Quebec**	**NHL**	**17**	**3**	**2**	**5**	**2**	....	....	....	....	....
	Fredericton	AHL	46	16	25	41	133	15	4	8	12	55
1988-89	**Quebec**	**NHL**	**46**	**9**	**10**	**19**	**39**	....	....	....	....	....
	Halifax	AHL	22	11	10	21	87	....	....	....	....	....
1989-90	**Quebec**	**NHL**	**43**	**13**	**13**	**26**	**84**	....	....	....	....	....
1990-91	**Quebec**	**NHL**	**63**	**13**	**20**	**33**	**111**	....	....	....	....	....
1991-92	**Quebec**	**NHL**	**61**	**16**	**22**	**38**	**77**	....	....	....	....	....
1992-93	**Quebec**	**NHL**	**77**	**8**	**22**	**30**	**69**	**6**	**0**	**1**	**1**	**2**
1993-94	**Florida**	**NHL**	**78**	**6**	**23**	**29**	**62**	....	....	....	....	....
1994-95	**Florida**	**NHL**	**48**	**6**	**7**	**13**	**38**	....	....	....	....	....
1995-96	**Florida**	**NHL**	**64**	**7**	**16**	**23**	**37**	**22**	**4**	**1**	**5**	**8**
1996-97	**Florida**	**NHL**	**69**	**8**	**6**	**14**	**48**	**5**	**1**	**0**	**1**	**2**
1997-98	**NY Islanders**	**NHL**	**74**	**5**	**7**	**12**	**27**	....	....	....	....	....
	NHL Totals		**696**	**100**	**156**	**256**	**673**	**42**	**5**	**5**	**10**	**38**

Traded to **Washington** by **Quebec** for Reggie Savage and Paul MacDermid, June 20, 1993. Claimed by **Florida** from **Washington** in Expansion Draft, June 24, 1993. Signed as a free agent by **NY Islanders**, July 21, 1997.

HOULDER, BILL (HOHL-duhr) S.J.

Defense. Shoots left. 6'2", 210 lbs. Born, Thunder Bay, Ont., March 11, 1967.
(Washington's 4th choice, 82nd overall, in 1985 Entry Draft).

			Regular Season					Playoffs				
Season	Club	Lea	GP	G	A	TP	PIM	GP	G	A	TP	PIM
1984-85	North Bay	OHL	66	4	20	24	37	8	0	0	0	2
1985-86	North Bay	OHL	59	5	30	35	97	10	1	6	7	12
1986-87	North Bay	OHL	62	17	51	68	68	22	4	19	23	20
1987-88	Washington	NHL	30	1	2	3	10	....	....	....	....	....
	Fort Wayne	IHL	43	10	14	24	32	....	....	....	....	....
1988-89	Washington	NHL	8	0	3	3	4	....	....	....	....	....
	Baltimore	AHL	65	10	36	46	50	....	....	....	....	....
1989-90	Washington	NHL	41	1	11	12	28	....	....	....	....	....
	Baltimore	AHL	26	3	7	10	12	7	0	2	2	2
1990-91	Buffalo	NHL	7	0	2	2	4	....	....	....	....	....
	Rochester	AHL	69	13	53	66	28	15	5	13	18	4
1991-92	Buffalo	NHL	10	1	0	1	8	....	....	....	....	....
	Rochester	AHL	42	8	26	34	16	16	5	6	11	4
1992-93	Buffalo	NHL	15	3	5	8	6	8	0	2	2	4
	San Diego	IHL	64	24	48	72	39	....	....	....	....	....
1993-94	Anaheim	NHL	80	14	25	39	40	....	....	....	....	....
1994-95	St. Louis	NHL	41	5	13	18	20	4	1	1	2	0
1995-96	Tampa Bay	NHL	61	5	23	28	22	6	0	1	1	4
1996-97	Tampa Bay	NHL	79	4	21	25	30	....	....	....	....	....
1997-98	San Jose	NHL	82	7	25	32	48	6	1	2	3	2
	NHL Totals		454	41	130	171	220	24	2	6	8	10

AHL First All-Star Team (1991) • Won Governor's Trophy (Outstanding Defenseman - IHL) (1993) • IHL First All-Star Team (1993)

Traded to **Buffalo** by **Washington** for Shawn Anderson, September 30, 1990. Claimed by **Anaheim** from **Buffalo** in Expansion Draft, June 24, 1993. Traded to **St. Louis** by **Anaheim** for Jason Marshall, August 29, 1994. Signed as a free agent by **Tampa Bay**, July 26, 1995. Signed as a free agent by **San Jose**, July 16, 1997.

HOULE, JEAN-FRANCOIS (HOOL) MTL.

Left wing. Shoots left. 5'9", 185 lbs. Born, Charlesbourg, Que., January 14, 1975.
(Montreal's 5th choice, 99th overall, in 1993 Entry Draft).

			Regular Season					Playoffs				
Season	Club	Lea	GP	G	A	TP	PIM	GP	G	A	TP	PIM
1992-93	Northwood Prep	H.S.	28	37	45	82	....	....	....	....	....	....
1993-94	Clarkson	ECAC	34	6	19	25	20	....	....	....	....	....
1994-95	Clarkson	ECAC	34	8	11	19	42	....	....	....	....	....
1995-96	Clarkson	ECAC	38	14	15	29	46	....	....	....	....	....
1996-97	Clarkson	ECAC	37	21	*36	57	40	....	....	....	....	....
1997-98	Fredericton	AHL	7	1	0	1	8	....	....	....	....	....
	New Orleans	ECHL	53	25	37	62	119	4	1	1	2	16

HOUSE, BOBBY N.J.

Right wing. Shoots right. 6'1", 205 lbs. Born, Whitehorse, Yukon, January 7, 1973.
(Chicago's 4th choice, 66th overall, in 1991 Entry Draft).

			Regular Season					Playoffs				
Season	Club	Lea	GP	G	A	TP	PIM	GP	G	A	TP	PIM
1989-90	Spokane	WHL	64	18	16	34	74	5	0	0	0	6
1990-91	Spokane	WHL	38	11	19	30	63	....	....	....	....	....
	Brandon	WHL	23	18	7	25	14	....	....	....	....	....
1991-92	Brandon	WHL	71	35	42	77	133	....	....	....	....	....
1992-93	Brandon	WHL	61	57	39	96	87	4	2	2	4	0
1993-94	Indianapolis	IHL	42	10	8	18	51	....	....	....	....	....
	Flint	ColHL	4	3	3	6	0	....	....	....	....	....
1994-95	Columbus	ECHL	9	11	6	17	2	....	....	....	....	....
	Indianapolis	IHL	26	2	3	5	26	....	....	....	....	....
	Albany	AHL	26	4	7	11	12	8	1	1	2	0
1995-96	Albany	AHL	77	37	49	86	57	4	0	0	0	4
1996-97	Albany	AHL	68	18	16	34	65	16	3	2	5	23
1997-98	Albany	AHL	19	10	10	20	10	....	....	....	....	....
	Hershey	AHL	20	2	6	8	8	....	....	....	....	....
	Quebec	IHL	24	5	7	12	12	....	....	....	....	....
	Syracuse	AHL	9	5	6	11	6	5	2	0	2	4

WHL East Second All-Star Team (1993)

Traded to **New Jersey** by **Chicago** for cash, May 21, 1996.

HOUSLEY, PHIL (HOWZ-lee) CGY.

Defense. Shoots left. 5'10", 185 lbs. Born, St. Paul, MN, March 9, 1964.
(Buffalo's 1st choice, 6th overall, in 1982 Entry Draft).

			Regular Season					Playoffs				
Season	Club	Lea	GP	G	A	TP	PIM	GP	G	A	TP	PIM
1981-82	South St. Paul	H.S.	22	31	34	65	18	....	....	....	....	....
1982-83	Buffalo	NHL	77	19	47	66	39	10	3	4	7	2
1983-84	Buffalo	NHL	75	31	46	77	33	3	0	0	0	6
1984-85	Buffalo	NHL	73	16	53	69	28	5	3	2	5	2
1985-86	Buffalo	NHL	79	15	47	62	54	....	....	....	....	....
1986-87	Buffalo	NHL	78	21	46	67	57	....	....	....	....	....
1987-88	Buffalo	NHL	74	29	37	66	96	6	2	4	6	6
1988-89	Buffalo	NHL	72	26	44	70	47	5	1	3	4	2
1989-90	Buffalo	NHL	80	21	60	81	32	6	1	4	5	4
1990-91	Winnipeg	NHL	78	23	53	76	24	....	....	....	....	....
1991-92	Winnipeg	NHL	74	23	63	86	92	7	1	4	5	0
1992-93	Winnipeg	NHL	80	18	79	97	52	6	0	7	7	2
1993-94	St. Louis	NHL	26	7	15	22	12	4	2	1	3	4
1994-95	Zurcher SC	Switz.	10	6	8	14	34	....	....	....	....	....
	Calgary	NHL	43	8	35	43	18	7	0	9	9	0
1995-96	Calgary	NHL	59	16	36	52	22	....	....	....	....	....
	New Jersey	NHL	22	1	15	16	8	....	....	....	....	....
1996-97	Washington	NHL	77	11	29	40	24	....	....	....	....	....
1997-98	Washington	NHL	64	6	25	31	24	18	0	4	4	4
	NHL Totals		1131	291	730	1021	662	77	13	42	55	32

NHL All-Rookie Team (1983) • NHL Second All-Star Team (1992)

Played in NHL All-Star Game (1984, 1989, 1990, 1991, 1992, 1993)

Traded to **Winnipeg** by **Buffalo** with Scott Arniel, Jeff Parker and Buffalo's 1st round choice (Keith Tkachuk) in 1990 Entry Draft for Dale Hawerchuk, Winnipeg's 1st round choice (Brad May) in 1990 Entry Draft and future considerations, June 16, 1990. Traded to **St. Louis** by **Winnipeg** for Nelson Emerson and Stephane Quintal, September 24, 1993. Traded to **Calgary** by **St. Louis** with St. Louis' 2nd round choice (Steve Begin) in 1996 Entry Draft and 2nd round choice (John Tripp) in 1997 Entry Draft for Al MacInnis and Calgary's 4th round choice (Didier Tremblay) in 1997 Entry Draft, July 4, 1994. Traded to **New Jersey** by **Calgary** with Dan Keczmer for Tommy Albelin, Cale Hulse and Jocelyn Lemieux, February 26, 1996. Signed as a free agent by **Washington**, July 22, 1996. Claimed on waivers by **Calgary** from **Washington**, July 21, 1998.

HRDINA, JAN (rih-DEE-nah) PIT.

Center. Shoots right. 6', 197 lbs. Born, Hradec Kralove, Czech., February 5, 1976.
(Pittsburgh's 4th choice, 128th overall, in 1995 Entry Draft).

			Regular Season					Playoffs				
Season	Club	Lea	GP	G	A	TP	PIM	GP	G	A	TP	PIM
1993-94	Stadion	Cze-Rep.	23	1	5	6	....	4	0	1	1	....
1994-95	Seattle	WHL	69	41	59	100	79	4	0	1	1	8
1995-96	Seattle	WHL	30	19	28	47	37	....	....	....	....	....
	Spokane	WHL	18	10	16	26	25	18	5	14	19	49
1996-97	Cleveland	IHL	68	23	31	54	82	13	1	2	3	8
1997-98	Syracuse	AHL	72	20	24	44	82	5	1	3	4	10

HRKAC, TONY (HUHR-kuhz) DAL.

Center. Shoots left. 5'11", 170 lbs. Born, Thunder Bay, Ont., July 7, 1966.
(St. Louis' 2nd choice, 32nd overall, in 1984 Entry Draft).

			Regular Season					Playoffs				
Season	Club	Lea	GP	G	A	TP	PIM	GP	G	A	TP	PIM
1983-84	Orillia	OJHL	42	*52	54	*106	20	....	....	....	....	....
1984-85	North Dakota	WCHA	36	18	36	54	16	....	....	....	....	....
1985-86	Canada	Nat-Tm	62	19	30	49	36	....	....	....	....	....
1986-87	North Dakota	WCHA	48	46	79	125	48	....	....	....	....	....
	St. Louis	NHL	....	....	....	....	....	3	0	0	0	0
1987-88	St. Louis	NHL	67	11	37	48	22	10	6	1	7	4
1988-89	St. Louis	NHL	70	17	28	45	8	4	1	1	2	0
1989-90	St. Louis	NHL	28	5	12	17	8	....	....	....	....	....
	Quebec	NHL	22	4	8	12	2	....	....	....	....	....
	Halifax	AHL	20	12	21	33	4	6	5	9	14	4
1990-91	Quebec	NHL	70	16	32	48	16	....	....	....	....	....
	Halifax	AHL	3	4	1	5	2	....	....	....	....	....
1991-92	San Jose	NHL	22	2	10	12	4	....	....	....	....	....
	Chicago	NHL	18	1	2	3	6	3	0	0	0	2
1992-93	Indianapolis	IHL	80	45	*87	*132	70	5	0	2	2	2
1993-94	St. Louis	NHL	36	6	5	11	8	4	0	0	0	0
	Peoria	IHL	45	30	51	81	25	1	1	2	3	0
1994-95	Milwaukee	IHL	71	24	67	91	26	15	4	9	13	16
1995-96	Milwaukee	IHL	43	14	28	42	18	5	1	3	4	4
1996-97	Milwaukee	IHL	81	27	61	88	20	3	1	1	2	2
1997-98	Dallas	NHL	13	5	3	8	0	....	....	....	....	....
	Michigan	IHL	20	7	15	22	6	....	....	....	....	....
	Edmonton	NHL	36	8	11	19	10	12	0	3	3	2
	NHL Totals		382	75	148	223	84	36	7	5	12	8

WCHA First All-Star Team (1987) • NCAA West First All-American Team (1987) • NCAA Championship All-Tournament Team (1987) • NCAA Championship Tournament MVP (1987) • Won 1987 Hobey Baker Memorial Award (Top U.S. Collegiate Player) (1987) • Won James Gatschene Memorial Trophy (MVP - IHL) (1993) • Won Leo P. Lamoureux Memorial Trophy (Leading Scorer - IHL) (1993) • IHL First All-Star Team (1993)

Traded to **Quebec** by **St. Louis** with Greg Millen for Jeff Brown, December 13, 1989. Traded to **San Jose** by **Quebec** for Greg Paslawski, May 31, 1991. Traded to **Chicago** by **San Jose** for future considerations, February 7, 1992. Signed as a free agent by **St. Louis**, July 30, 1993. Signed as a free agent by **Dallas**, August 12, 1997. Claimed on waivers by **Edmonton** from **Dallas**, January 6, 1998. Traded to **Pittsburgh** by **Edmonton** with Bobby Dollas for Josef Beranek, June 16, 1998. Claimed by **Nashville** from **Pittsburgh** in Expansion Draft, June 26, 1998. Traded to **Dallas** by **Nashville** for future considerations, July 9, 1998.

HRUSKA, DAVID (huhr-OOSH-kah, dah-VEED) OTT.

Right wing. Shoots right. 6', 189 lbs. Born, Sokolov, Czech., January 8, 1977.
(Ottawa's 6th choice, 131st overall, in 1995 Entry Draft).

			Regular Season					Playoffs				
Season	Club	Lea	GP	G	A	TP	PIM	GP	G	A	TP	PIM
1994-95	Banik Sokolov	Czech-2	5	2	4	6	4	....	....	....	....	....
1995-96	Red Deer	WHL	28	14	14	28	6	....	....	....	....	....
	Vsetin	Cze-Rep.	5	1	0	1	....	1	0	0	0	....
1996-97	Vsetin	Cze-Rep.	20	4	2	6	4	6	2	4	6	0
	Sokolov	Czech-2	4	3	0	3	....	....	....	....	....	....
1997-98	Vsetin	EuroHL	5	0	0	0	0	....	....	....	....	....
	Vsetin	Cze-Rep.	14	5	1	6	0	....	....	....	....	....

HUARD, BILL (HEW-ahrd) EDM.

Left wing. Shoots left. 6'1", 215 lbs. Born, Welland, Ont., June 24, 1967.

			Regular Season					Playoffs				
Season	Club	Lea	GP	G	A	TP	PIM	GP	G	A	TP	PIM
1986-87	Peterborough	OHL	61	14	11	25	61	12	5	2	7	19
1987-88	Peterborough	OHL	66	28	33	61	132	12	7	8	15	33
1988-89	Carolina	ECHL	40	27	21	48	177	10	7	2	9	70
1989-90	Utica	AHL	27	1	7	8	67	5	0	1	1	33
	Nashville	ECHL	34	24	27	51	212	....	....	....	....	....
1990-91	Utica	AHL	72	11	16	27	359	....	....	....	....	....
1991-92	Utica	AHL	62	9	11	20	233	4	1	1	2	4
1992-93	Boston	NHL	2	0	0	0	0	....	....	....	....	....
	Providence	AHL	72	18	19	37	302	6	3	0	3	9
1993-94	Ottawa	NHL	63	2	2	4	162	....	....	....	....	....
1994-95	Ottawa	NHL	26	1	1	2	64	....	....	....	....	....
	Quebec	NHL	7	2	2	4	13	1	0	0	0	0
1995-96	Dallas	NHL	51	6	6	12	176	....	....	....	....	....
	Michigan	IHL	12	1	1	2	74	....	....	....	....	....
1996-97	Dallas	NHL	40	5	6	11	105	....	....	....	....	....
1997-98	Edmonton	NHL	30	0	1	1	72	4	0	0	0	2
	NHL Totals		219	16	18	34	592	5	0	0	0	2

Signed as a free agent by **New Jersey**, October 1, 1989. Signed as a free agent by **Boston**, December 4, 1992. Signed as a free agent by **Ottawa**, June 30, 1993. Traded to **Quebec** by **Ottawa** for Mika Stromberg and Quebec's 4th round choice (Kevin Boyd) in 1995 Entry Draft, April 7, 1995. Transferred to **Colorado** after **Quebec** franchise relocated, July 1, 1995. Claimed by **Dallas** from **Colorado** in NHL Waiver Draft, October 2, 1995. Signed as a free agent by **Edmonton**, July 22, 1997.

HUFFMAN, KERRY

Defense. Shoots left. 6'2", 200 lbs. Born, Peterborough, Ont., January 3, 1968.
(Philadelphia's 1st choice, 20th overall, in 1986 Entry Draft).

			Regular Season					Playoffs				
Season	Club	Lea	GP	G	A	TP	PIM	GP	G	A	TP	PIM
1985-86	Guelph	OHL	56	3	24	27	35	20	1	10	11	10
1986-87	Guelph	OHL	44	4	31	35	20	5	0	2	2	8
	Philadelphia	**NHL**	**9**	**0**	**0**	**0**	**2**	....	....	....	....	....
	Hershey	AHL	3	0	1	1	0	4	0	0	0	0
1987-88	**Philadelphia**	**NHL**	**52**	**6**	**17**	**23**	**34**	**2**	**0**	**0**	**0**	**0**
1988-89	**Philadelphia**	**NHL**	**29**	**0**	**11**	**11**	**31**	....	....	....	....	....
	Hershey	AHL	29	2	13	15	16	....	....	....	....	....
1989-90	**Philadelphia**	**NHL**	**43**	**1**	**12**	**13**	**34**	....	....	....	....	....
1990-91	**Philadelphia**	**NHL**	**10**	**1**	**2**	**3**	**10**	....	....	....	....	....
	Hershey	AHL	45	5	29	34	20	7	1	2	3	0
1991-92	**Philadelphia**	**NHL**	**60**	**14**	**18**	**32**	**41**	....	....	....	....	....
1992-93	**Quebec**	**NHL**	**52**	**4**	**18**	**22**	**54**	**3**	**0**	**0**	**0**	**0**
1993-94	**Quebec**	**NHL**	**28**	**0**	**6**	**6**	**28**	....	....	....	....	....
	Ottawa	**NHL**	**34**	**4**	**8**	**12**	**12**	....	....	....	....	....
1994-95	**Ottawa**	**NHL**	**37**	**2**	**4**	**6**	**46**	....	....	....	....	....
1995-96	**Ottawa**	**NHL**	**43**	**4**	**11**	**15**	**63**	....	....	....	....	....
	Philadelphia	**NHL**	**4**	**1**	**1**	**2**	**6**	**6**	**0**	**0**	**0**	**2**
1996-97	Las Vegas	IHL	44	5	19	24	38	3	0	0	0	2
1997-98	Grand Rapids	IHL	73	4	23	27	60	3	0	0	0	2
	NHL Totals		**401**	**37**	**108**	**145**	**361**	**11**	**0**	**0**	**0**	**2**

Won George Parsons Trophy (Memorial Cup Tournament Most Sportsmanlike Player) (1986) • OHL First All-Star Team (1987)

Traded to **Quebec** by **Philadelphia** with Peter Forsberg, Steve Duchesne, Mike Ricci, Ron Hextall, Chris Simon, Philadelphia's 1st round choice in the 1993 (Jocelyn Thibault) and 1994 (later traded to Toronto — later traded to Washington — Washington selected Nolan Baumgartner) — Entry Drafts and cash for Eric Lindros, June 30, 1992. Claimed on waivers by **Ottawa** from **Quebec**, January 15, 1994. Traded to **Philadelphia** by **Ottawa** for future considerations, March 19, 1996.

HUGHES, BRENT

Left wing. Shoots left. 5'11", 195 lbs. Born, New Westminster, B.C., April 5, 1966.

			Regular Season					Playoffs				
Season	Club	Lea	GP	G	A	TP	PIM	GP	G	A	TP	PIM
1983-84	New Westminster	WHL	67	21	18	39	133	9	2	2	4	27
1984-85	New Westminster	WHL	64	25	32	57	135	11	2	1	3	37
1985-86	New Westminster	WHL	71	28	52	80	180	....	....	....	....	....
1986-87	New Westminster	WHL	8	5	4	9	22	....	....	....	....	....
	Victoria	WHL	61	38	61	99	146	5	4	1	5	8
1987-88	Moncton	AHL	73	13	19	32	206	....	....	....	....	....
1988-89	**Winnipeg**	**NHL**	**28**	**3**	**2**	**5**	**82**	....	....	....	....	....
	Moncton	AHL	54	34	34	68	286	10	9	4	13	40
1989-90	**Winnipeg**	**NHL**	**11**	**1**	**2**	**3**	**33**	....	....	....	....	....
	Moncton	AHL	65	31	29	60	277	....	....	....	....	....
1990-91	Moncton	AHL	63	21	22	43	144	3	0	0	0	7
1991-92	Baltimore	AHL	55	25	29	54	190	....	....	....	....	....
	Boston	**NHL**	**8**	**1**	**1**	**2**	**38**	**10**	**2**	**0**	**2**	**20**
	Maine	AHL	12	6	4	10	34	....	....	....	....	....
1992-93	**Boston**	**NHL**	**62**	**5**	**4**	**9**	**191**	**1**	**0**	**0**	**0**	**2**
1993-94	**Boston**	**NHL**	**77**	**13**	**11**	**24**	**143**	**13**	**2**	**1**	**3**	**27**
	Providence	AHL	6	2	5	7	4	....	....	....	....	....
1994-95	**Boston**	**NHL**	**44**	**6**	**6**	**12**	**139**	**5**	**0**	**0**	**0**	**4**
1995-96	**Buffalo**	**NHL**	**76**	**5**	**10**	**15**	**148**	....	....	....	....	....
1996-97	**NY Islanders**	**NHL**	**51**	**7**	**3**	**10**	**57**	....	....	....	....	....
	Utah	IHL	5	2	2	4	11	....	....	....	....	....
1997-98	Houston	IHL	79	19	12	31	128	4	0	3	3	20
	NHL Totals		**357**	**41**	**39**	**80**	**831**	**29**	**4**	**1**	**5**	**53**

Signed as a free agent by **Winnipeg**, June 13, 1988. Traded to **Washington** by **Winnipeg** with Craig Duncanson and Simon Wheeldon for Bob Joyce, Tyler Larter and Kent Paynter, May 21, 1991. Traded to **Boston** by **Washington** with future considerations for John Byce and Dennis Smith, February 24, 1992. Claimed By **Buffalo** from **Boston** in NHL Waiver Draft, October 2, 1995. Signed as a free agent by **NY Islanders**, August 9, 1996.

HULBIG, JOE (HUHL-bihg) EDM.

Left wing. Shoots left. 6'3", 215 lbs. Born, Norwood, MA, September 29, 1973.
(Edmonton's 1st choice, 13th overall, in 1992 Entry Draft).

			Regular Season					Playoffs				
Season	Club	Lea	GP	G	A	TP	PIM	GP	G	A	TP	PIM
1991-92	St. Sebastian's	H.S.	17	19	24	43	30	....	....	....	....	....
1992-93	Providence	H.E.	26	3	13	16	22	....	....	....	....	....
1993-94	Providence	H.E.	28	6	4	10	36	....	....	....	....	....
1994-95	Providence	H.E.	37	14	21	35	36	....	....	....	....	....
1995-96	Providence	H.E.	31	14	22	36	56	....	....	....	....	....
1996-97	**Edmonton**	**NHL**	**6**	**0**	**0**	**0**	**0**	**6**	**0**	**1**	**1**	**2**
	Hamilton	AHL	73	18	28	46	59	16	6	10	16	6
1997-98	**Edmonton**	**NHL**	**17**	**2**	**2**	**4**	**2**	....	....	....	....	....
	Hamilton	AHL	46	15	16	31	52	3	0	1	1	2
	NHL Totals		**23**	**2**	**2**	**4**	**2**	**6**	**0**	**1**	**1**	**2**

HULL, BRETT DAL.

Right wing. Shoots right. 5'10", 201 lbs. Born, Belleville, Ont., August 9, 1964.
(Calgary's 6th choice, 117th overall, in 1984 Entry Draft).

			Regular Season					Playoffs				
Season	Club	Lea	GP	G	A	TP	PIM	GP	G	A	TP	PIM
1983-84	Penticton	BCJHL	56	*105	88	*188	20	....	....	....	....	....
1984-85	U. Minn-Duluth	WCHA	48	32	28	60	24	....	....	....	....	....
1985-86	U. Minn-Duluth	WCHA	42	52	32	84	46	....	....	....	....	....
	Calgary	**NHL**	....	....	....	....	....	**2**	**0**	**0**	**0**	**0**
1986-87	**Calgary**	**NHL**	**5**	**1**	**0**	**1**	**0**	**4**	**2**	**1**	**3**	**0**
	Moncton	AHL	67	50	42	92	16	3	2	2	4	2
1987-88	**Calgary**	**NHL**	**52**	**26**	**24**	**50**	**12**	....	....	....	....	....
	St. Louis	**NHL**	**13**	**6**	**8**	**14**	**4**	**10**	**7**	**2**	**9**	**4**
1988-89	**St. Louis**	**NHL**	**78**	**41**	**43**	**84**	**33**	**10**	**5**	**5**	**10**	**6**
1989-90	**St. Louis**	**NHL**	**80**	***72**	**41**	**113**	**24**	**12**	**13**	**8**	**21**	**17**
1990-91	**St. Louis**	**NHL**	**78**	***86**	**45**	**131**	**22**	**13**	**11**	**8**	**19**	**4**
1991-92	**St. Louis**	**NHL**	**73**	***70**	**39**	**109**	**48**	**6**	**4**	**4**	**8**	**4**
1992-93	**St. Louis**	**NHL**	**80**	**54**	**47**	**101**	**41**	**11**	**8**	**5**	**13**	**2**
1993-94	**St. Louis**	**NHL**	**81**	**57**	**40**	**97**	**38**	**4**	**2**	**1**	**3**	**0**
1994-95	**St. Louis**	**NHL**	**48**	**29**	**21**	**50**	**10**	**7**	**6**	**2**	**8**	**0**
1995-96	**St. Louis**	**NHL**	**70**	**43**	**40**	**83**	**30**	**13**	**6**	**5**	**11**	**10**
1996-97	**St. Louis**	**NHL**	**77**	**42**	**40**	**82**	**10**	**6**	**2**	**7**	**9**	**2**
1997-98	**St. Louis**	**NHL**	**66**	**27**	**45**	**72**	**26**	**10**	**3**	**3**	**6**	**2**
	United States	Olympics	4	2	1	3	0	....	....	....	....	....
	NHL Totals		**801**	**554**	**433**	**987**	**298**	**108**	**69**	**51**	**120**	**51**

WCHA First All-Star Team (1986) • AHL First All-Star Team (1987) • Won Dudley "Red" Garrett Memorial Trophy (Top Rookie - AHL) (1987) • NHL First All-Star Team (1990, 1991, 1992) • Won Lady Byng Trophy (1990) • Won Dodge Ram Tough Award (1990, 1991) • Won Hart Memorial Trophy (1991) • Won Lester B. Pearson Award (1991) • Won ProSet/NHL Player of the Year Award (1991)

Played in NHL All-Star Game (1989, 1990, 1992, 1993, 1994, 1996, 1997, 1998)

Traded to **St. Louis** by **Calgary** with Steve Bozek for Rob Ramage and Rick Wamsley, March 7, 1988. Signed as a free agent by **Dallas**, July 3, 1998.

HULL, JODY

Right wing. Shoots right. 6'2", 195 lbs. Born, Cambridge, Ont., February 2, 1969.
(Hartford's 1st choice, 18th overall, in 1987 Entry Draft).

			Regular Season					Playoffs				
Season	Club	Lea	GP	G	A	TP	PIM	GP	G	A	TP	PIM
1985-86	Peterborough	OHL	61	20	22	42	29	16	1	5	6	4
1986-87	Peterborough	OHL	49	18	34	52	22	12	4	9	13	14
1987-88	Peterborough	OHL	60	50	44	94	33	12	10	8	18	8
1988-89	**Hartford**	**NHL**	**60**	**16**	**18**	**34**	**10**	**1**	**0**	**0**	**0**	**2**
1989-90	**Hartford**	**NHL**	**38**	**7**	**10**	**17**	**21**	**5**	**0**	**1**	**1**	**2**
	Binghamton	AHL	21	7	10	17	6	....	....	....	....	....
1990-91	**NY Rangers**	**NHL**	**47**	**5**	**8**	**13**	**10**	....	....	....	....	....
1991-92	**NY Rangers**	**NHL**	**3**	**0**	**0**	**0**	**2**	....	....	....	....	....
	Binghamton	AHL	69	34	31	65	28	11	5	2	7	4
1992-93	**Ottawa**	**NHL**	**69**	**13**	**21**	**34**	**14**	....	....	....	....	....
1993-94	**Florida**	**NHL**	**69**	**13**	**13**	**26**	**8**	....	....	....	....	....
1994-95	**Florida**	**NHL**	**46**	**11**	**8**	**19**	**8**	....	....	....	....	....
1995-96	**Florida**	**NHL**	**78**	**20**	**17**	**37**	**25**	**14**	**3**	**2**	**5**	**0**
1996-97	**Florida**	**NHL**	**67**	**10**	**6**	**16**	**4**	**5**	**0**	**0**	**0**	**0**
1997-98	**Florida**	**NHL**	**21**	**2**	**0**	**2**	**4**	....	....	....	....	....
	Tampa Bay	**NHL**	**28**	**2**	**4**	**6**	**4**	....	....	....	....	....
	NHL Totals		**526**	**99**	**105**	**204**	**110**	**25**	**3**	**3**	**6**	**4**

OHL Second All-Star Team (1988)

Traded to **NY Rangers** by **Hartford** for Carey Wilson and NY Rangers' 3rd round choice (Mikael Nylander) in the 1991 Entry Draft, July 9, 1990. Traded to **Ottawa** by **NY Rangers** for future considerations, July 28, 1992. Signed as a free agent by **Florida**, August 10, 1993. Traded to **Tampa Bay** by **Florida** with Mark Fitzpatrick for Dino Ciccarelli and Jeff Norton, January 15, 1998.

HULSE, CALE (HULS) CGY.

Defense. Shoots right. 6'3", 215 lbs. Born, Edmonton, Alta., November 10, 1973.
(New Jersey's 3rd choice, 66th overall, in 1992 Entry Draft).

			Regular Season					Playoffs				
Season	Club	Lea	GP	G	A	TP	PIM	GP	G	A	TP	PIM
1991-92	Portland	WHL	70	4	18	22	250	6	0	2	2	27
1992-93	Portland	WHL	72	10	26	36	284	16	4	4	8	65
1993-94	Albany	AHL	79	7	14	21	186	5	0	3	3	11
1994-95	Albany	AHL	77	5	13	18	215	12	1	1	2	17
1995-96	**New Jersey**	**NHL**	**8**	**0**	**0**	**0**	**15**	....	....	....	....	....
	Albany	AHL	42	4	23	27	107	....	....	....	....	....
	Calgary	**NHL**	**3**	**0**	**0**	**0**	**5**	**1**	**0**	**0**	**0**	**0**
	Saint John	AHL	13	2	7	9	39	....	....	....	....	....
1996-97	**Calgary**	**NHL**	**63**	**1**	**6**	**7**	**91**	....	....	....	....	....
1997-98	**Calgary**	**NHL**	**79**	**5**	**22**	**27**	**169**	....	....	....	....	....
	NHL Totals		**153**	**6**	**28**	**34**	**280**	**1**	**0**	**0**	**0**	**0**

Traded to **Calgary** by **New Jersey** with Tommy Albelin and Jocelyn Lemieux for Phil Housley and Dan Keczmer, February 26, 1996.

HUNTER, DALE WSH.

Center. Shoots left. 5'10", 198 lbs. Born, Petrolia, Ont., July 31, 1960.
(Quebec's 2nd choice, 41st overall, in 1979 Entry Draft).

			Regular Season					Playoffs				
Season	Club	Lea	GP	G	A	TP	PIM	GP	G	A	TP	PIM
1977-78	Kitchener	OHA	68	22	42	64	115	....	....	....	....	....
1978-79	Sudbury	OHA	59	42	68	110	188	10	4	12	16	47
1979-80	Sudbury	OHA	61	34	51	85	189	9	6	9	15	45
1980-81	**Quebec**	**NHL**	**80**	**19**	**44**	**63**	**226**	**5**	**4**	**2**	**6**	**34**
1981-82	**Quebec**	**NHL**	**80**	**22**	**50**	**72**	**272**	**16**	**3**	**7**	**10**	**52**
1982-83	**Quebec**	**NHL**	**80**	**17**	**46**	**63**	**206**	**4**	**2**	**1**	**3**	**24**
1983-84	**Quebec**	**NHL**	**77**	**24**	**55**	**79**	**232**	**9**	**2**	**3**	**5**	**41**
1984-85	**Quebec**	**NHL**	**80**	**20**	**52**	**72**	**209**	**17**	**4**	**6**	**10**	***97**
1985-86	**Quebec**	**NHL**	**80**	**28**	**42**	**70**	**265**	**3**	**0**	**0**	**0**	**15**
1986-87	**Quebec**	**NHL**	**46**	**10**	**29**	**39**	**135**	**13**	**1**	**7**	**8**	**56**
1987-88	**Washington**	**NHL**	**79**	**22**	**37**	**59**	**240**	**14**	**7**	**5**	**12**	**98**
1988-89	**Washington**	**NHL**	**80**	**20**	**37**	**57**	**219**	**6**	**0**	**4**	**4**	**29**
1989-90	**Washington**	**NHL**	**80**	**23**	**39**	**62**	**233**	**15**	**4**	**8**	**12**	**61**
1990-91	**Washington**	**NHL**	**76**	**16**	**30**	**46**	**234**	**11**	**1**	**9**	**10**	**41**
1991-92	**Washington**	**NHL**	**80**	**28**	**50**	**78**	**205**	**7**	**1**	**4**	**5**	**16**
1992-93	**Washington**	**NHL**	**84**	**20**	**59**	**79**	**198**	**6**	**7**	**1**	**8**	**35**
1993-94	**Washington**	**NHL**	**52**	**9**	**29**	**38**	**131**	**7**	**0**	**3**	**3**	**14**
1994-95	**Washington**	**NHL**	**45**	**8**	**15**	**23**	**101**	**7**	**4**	**4**	**8**	**24**
1995-96	**Washington**	**NHL**	**82**	**13**	**24**	**37**	**112**	**6**	**1**	**5**	**6**	**24**
1996-97	**Washington**	**NHL**	**82**	**14**	**32**	**46**	**125**	....	....	....	....	....
1997-98	**Washington**	**NHL**	**82**	**8**	**18**	**26**	**103**	**21**	**0**	**4**	**4**	**30**
	NHL Totals		**1345**	**321**	**688**	**1009**	**3446**	**167**	**41**	**73**	**114**	**691**

Played in NHL All-Star Game (1997)

Traded to **Washington** by **Quebec** with Clint Malarchuk for Gaetan Duchesne, Alan Haworth and Washington's 1st round choice (Joe Sakic) in 1987 Entry Draft, June 13, 1987.

HUNTER, TRENT — ANA.

Right wing. Shoots right. 6'3", 191 lbs. Born, Red Deer, Alta., July 5, 1980.
(Anaheim's 4th choice, 150th overall, in 1998 Entry Draft).

			Regular Season					Playoffs				
Season	Club	Lea	GP	G	A	TP	PIM	GP	G	A	TP	PIM
1996-97	Red Deer	AJHL	42	30	25	55	50	....	....	....	....	....
1997-98	Prince George	WHL	60	13	14	27	34	8	1	0	1	4

HURLBUT, MIKE (HUHRL-buht) — BUF.

Defense. Shoots left. 6'2", 200 lbs. Born, Massena, NY, October 7, 1966.
(NY Rangers' 1st choice, 5th overall, in 1988 Supplemental Draft).

			Regular Season					Playoffs				
Season	Club	Lea	GP	G	A	TP	PIM	GP	G	A	TP	PIM
1985-86	St. Lawrence	ECAC	25	2	10	12	40	....	....	....	....	....
1986-87	St. Lawrence	ECAC	35	8	15	23	44	....	....	....	....	....
1987-88	St. Lawrence	ECAC	38	6	12	18	18	....	....	....	....	....
1988-89	St. Lawrence	ECAC	36	8	25	33	30	....	....	....	....	....
	Denver	IHL	8	0	2	2	13	4	1	2	3	2
1989-90	Flint	IHL	74	3	34	37	38	3	0	1	1	2
1990-91	San Diego	IHL	2	1	0	1	0	....	....	....	....	....
	Binghamton	AHL	33	2	11	13	27	3	0	1	1	0
1991-92	Binghamton	AHL	79	16	39	55	64	11	2	7	9	8
1992-93	**NY Rangers**	**NHL**	**23**	**1**	**8**	**9**	**16**	....	....	....	....	....
	Binghamton	AHL	45	11	25	36	46	14	2	5	7	12
1993-94	**Quebec**	**NHL**	**1**	**0**	**0**	**0**	**0**	....	....	....	....	....
	Cornwall	AHL	77	13	33	46	100	13	3	7	10	12
1994-95	Cornwall	AHL	74	11	49	60	69	3	1	0	1	15
1995-96	Minnesota	IHL	22	1	4	5	22	....	....	....	....	....
	Houston	IHL	38	3	12	15	33	....	....	....	....	....
1996-97	Houston	IHL	70	11	24	35	62	13	5	8	13	12
1997-98	**Buffalo**	**NHL**	**3**	**0**	**0**	**0**	**2**	....	....	....	....	....
	Rochester	AHL	45	10	20	30	48	4	1	1	2	2
	NHL Totals		**27**	**1**	**8**	**9**	**18**	....	....	....	....	....

ECAC First All-Star Team (1989) • NCAA East First All-American Team (1989) • AHL Second All-Star Team (1995)

Traded to **Quebec** by **NY Rangers** for Alexander Karpovtsev, September 7, 1993. Signed as a free agent by **Buffalo**, September 9, 1997.

HURLEY, MIKE

Right wing. Shoots right. 5'11", 173 lbs. Born, Charlottetown, P.E.I., November 17, 1977.
(Dallas' 3rd choice, 90th overall, in 1996 Entry Draft).

			Regular Season					Playoffs				
Season	Club	Lea	GP	G	A	TP	PIM	GP	G	A	TP	PIM
1994-95	Tri-City	WHL	47	2	4	6	10	10	0	1	1	0
1995-96	Tri-City	WHL	65	32	13	45	34	11	0	3	3	6
1996-97	Tri-City	WHL	59	36	22	58	54	....	....	....	....	....
1997-98	Tri-City	WHL	49	40	25	65	51	....	....	....	....	....
	Portland	WHL	27	10	17	27	28	16	4	5	9	12

HUSCROFT, JAMIE (HUHS-krawft) — VAN.

Defense. Shoots right. 6'2", 210 lbs. Born, Creston, B.C., January 9, 1967.
(New Jersey's 9th choice, 171st overall, in 1985 Entry Draft).

			Regular Season					Playoffs				
Season	Club	Lea	GP	G	A	TP	PIM	GP	G	A	TP	PIM
1983-84	Seattle	WHL	63	0	12	12	77	5	0	0	0	15
1984-85	Seattle	WHL	69	3	13	16	273	....	....	....	....	....
1985-86	Seattle	WHL	66	6	20	26	394	5	0	1	1	18
1986-87	Seattle	WHL	21	1	18	19	99	....	....	....	....	....
	Medicine Hat	WHL	35	4	21	25	170	20	0	3	3	*125
1987-88	Utica	AHL	71	5	7	12	316	....	....	....	....	....
	Flint	IHL	3	1	0	1	2	16	0	1	1	110
1988-89	**New Jersey**	**NHL**	**15**	**0**	**2**	**2**	**51**	....	....	....	....	....
	Utica	AHL	41	2	10	12	215	5	0	0	0	40
1989-90	**New Jersey**	**NHL**	**42**	**2**	**3**	**5**	**149**	**5**	**0**	**0**	**0**	**16**
	Utica	AHL	22	3	6	9	122	....	....	....	....	....
1990-91	**New Jersey**	**NHL**	**8**	**0**	**1**	**1**	**27**	**3**	**0**	**0**	**0**	**6**
	Utica	AHL	59	3	15	18	339	....	....	....	....	....
1991-92	Utica	AHL	50	4	7	11	224	....	....	....	....	....
1992-93	Providence	AHL	69	2	15	17	257	2	0	1	1	6
1993-94	**Boston**	**NHL**	**36**	**0**	**1**	**1**	**144**	**4**	**0**	**0**	**0**	**9**
	Providence	AHL	32	1	10	11	157	....	....	....	....	....
1994-95	**Boston**	**NHL**	**34**	**0**	**6**	**6**	**103**	**5**	**0**	**0**	**0**	**11**
1995-96	**Calgary**	**NHL**	**70**	**3**	**9**	**12**	**162**	**4**	**0**	**1**	**1**	**4**
1996-97	**Calgary**	**NHL**	**39**	**0**	**4**	**4**	**117**	....	....	....	....	....
	Tampa Bay	**NHL**	**13**	**0**	**1**	**1**	**34**	....	....	....	....	....
1997-98	**Tampa Bay**	**NHL**	**44**	**0**	**3**	**3**	**122**	....	....	....	....	....
	Vancouver	**NHL**	**7**	**0**	**1**	**1**	**55**	....	....	....	....	....
	NHL Totals		**308**	**5**	**31**	**36**	**964**	**21**	**0**	**1**	**1**	**46**

Signed as a free agent by **Boston**, July 23, 1992. Signed as a free agent by **Calgary**, August 22, 1995. Traded to **Tampa Bay** by **Calgary** for Tyler Moss, March 18, 1997. Traded to **Vancouver** by **Tampa Bay** for Enrico Ciccone, March 14, 1998.

HUSELIUS, KRISTIAN (hoo-SAY-lee-oos) — FLA.

Left wing. Shoots left. 6'1", 183 lbs. Born, Stockholm, Sweden, November 10, 1978.
(Florida's 2nd choice, 47th overall, in 1997 Entry Draft).

			Regular Season					Playoffs				
Season	Club	Lea	GP	G	A	TP	PIM	GP	G	A	TP	PIM
1996-97	Farjestad	Sweden	13	2	0	2	4	5	1	0	1	0
1997-98	Farjestad	EuroHL	5	2	3	5	0	....	....	....	....	....
	Farjestad	Sweden	34	2	1	3	2	11	0	0	0	0

HUSKA, RYAN (HUHS-kuh)

Left wing. Shoots left. 6'2", 194 lbs. Born, Cranbrook, B.C., July 2, 1975.
(Chicago's 4th choice, 76th overall, in 1993 Entry Draft).

			Regular Season					Playoffs				
Season	Club	Lea	GP	G	A	TP	PIM	GP	G	A	TP	PIM
1991-92	Kamloops	WHL	44	4	5	9	23	6	0	1	1	0
1992-93	Kamloops	WHL	68	17	15	32	50	13	2	6	8	4
1993-94	Kamloops	WHL	69	23	31	54	66	19	9	5	14	23
1994-95	Kamloops	WHL	66	27	40	67	78	17	7	8	15	12
1995-96	Indianapolis	IHL	28	2	3	5	15	5	1	1	2	27
1996-97	Indianapolis	IHL	80	18	12	30	100	4	0	0	0	4
1997-98	**Chicago**	**NHL**	**1**	**0**	**0**	**0**	**0**	....	....	....	....	....
	Indianapolis	IHL	80	19	16	35	115	5	0	3	3	10
	NHL Totals		**1**	**0**	**0**	**0**	**0**	....	....	....	....	....

HUSKINS, KENT — CHI.

Defense. Shoots left. 6'2", 190 lbs. Born, Ottawa, Ont., May 4, 1979.
(Chicago's 3rd choice, 156th overall, in 1998 Entry Draft).

			Regular Season					Playoffs				
Season	Club	Lea	GP	G	A	TP	PIM	GP	G	A	TP	PIM
1997-98	Clarkson	ECAC	35	2	8	10	46	....	....	....	....	....

HUSSEY, MARC

Defense. Shoots right. 6'4", 210 lbs. Born, Chatham, N.B., January 22, 1974.
(Pittsburgh's 2nd choice, 43rd overall, in 1992 Entry Draft).

			Regular Season					Playoffs				
Season	Club	Lea	GP	G	A	TP	PIM	GP	G	A	TP	PIM
1990-91	Moose Jaw	WHL	68	5	8	13	67	8	2	2	4	7
1991-92	Moose Jaw	WHL	72	7	27	34	203	4	1	1	2	0
1992-93	Moose Jaw	WHL	68	12	28	40	121	....	....	....	....	....
1993-94	Moose Jaw	WHL	17	4	5	9	33	....	....	....	....	....
	Tri-City	WHL	16	3	6	9	26	....	....	....	....	....
	Medicine Hat	WHL	41	6	24	30	90	3	0	1	1	4
1994-95	St. John's	AHL	11	0	1	1	20	....	....	....	....	....
	Canada	Nat-Tm	36	2	7	9	42	....	....	....	....	....
1995-96	Saint John	AHL	68	10	21	31	120	5	0	0	0	8
1996-97	Saint John	AHL	46	6	18	24	62	....	....	....	....	....
	Utah	IHL	8	0	1	1	6	....	....	....	....	....
	Indianapolis	IHL	14	0	2	2	17	4	0	1	1	10
1997-98	Indianapolis	IHL	23	2	5	7	14	....	....	....	....	....
	Milwaukee	IHL	50	3	15	18	81	10	2	3	5	14

Signed as a free agent by **Calgary**, March 10, 1996. Traded to **Chicago** by **Calgary** for Ravil Gusmanov, March 18, 1997.

HUTCHINS, TONY — ST.L.

Center. Shoots left. 6', 196 lbs. Born, Wolfeboro, NH, January 11, 1977.
(St. Louis' 9th choice, 203rd overall, in 1996 Entry Draft).

			Regular Season					Playoffs				
Season	Club	Lea	GP	G	A	TP	PIM	GP	G	A	TP	PIM
1995-96	Lawrence Acad.	H.S.	27	18	20	38	22	....	....	....	....	....
1996-97	Boston College	H.E.	26	8	0	8	10	....	....	....	....	....
1997-98	Boston College	H.E.	39	12	5	17	52	....	....	....	....	....

IAFRATE, AL (IGH-uh-FRAY-tee)

Defense. Shoots left. 6'3", 235 lbs. Born, Dearborn, MI, March 21, 1966.
(Toronto's 1st choice, 4th overall, in 1984 Entry Draft).

			Regular Season					Playoffs				
Season	Club	Lea	GP	G	A	TP	PIM	GP	G	A	TP	PIM
1983-84	United States	Nat-Tm	55	4	17	21	26	....	....	....	....	....
	United States	Olympics	6	0	0	0	2	....	....	....	....	....
	Belleville	OHL	10	2	4	6	2	3	0	1	1	5
1984-85	**Toronto**	**NHL**	**68**	**5**	**16**	**21**	**51**	....	....	....	....	....
1985-86	**Toronto**	**NHL**	**65**	**8**	**25**	**33**	**40**	**10**	**0**	**3**	**3**	**4**
1986-87	**Toronto**	**NHL**	**80**	**9**	**21**	**30**	**55**	**13**	**1**	**3**	**4**	**11**
1987-88	**Toronto**	**NHL**	**77**	**22**	**30**	**52**	**80**	**6**	**3**	**4**	**7**	**6**
1988-89	**Toronto**	**NHL**	**65**	**13**	**20**	**33**	**72**	....	....	....	....	....
1989-90	**Toronto**	**NHL**	**75**	**21**	**42**	**63**	**135**	....	....	....	....	....
1990-91	**Toronto**	**NHL**	**42**	**3**	**15**	**18**	**113**	....	....	....	....	....
	Washington	**NHL**	**30**	**6**	**8**	**14**	**124**	**10**	**1**	**3**	**4**	**22**
1991-92	**Washington**	**NHL**	**78**	**17**	**34**	**51**	**180**	**7**	**4**	**2**	**6**	**14**
1992-93	**Washington**	**NHL**	**81**	**25**	**41**	**66**	**169**	**6**	**6**	**0**	**6**	**4**
1993-94	**Washington**	**NHL**	**67**	**10**	**35**	**45**	**143**	....	....	....	....	....
	Boston	**NHL**	**12**	**5**	**8**	**13**	**20**	**13**	**3**	**1**	**4**	**6**
1994-95			DID NOT PLAY – INJURED									
1995-96			DID NOT PLAY – INJURED									
1996-97	**San Jose**	**NHL**	**38**	**6**	**9**	**15**	**91**	....	....	....	....	....
1997-98	**San Jose**	**NHL**	**21**	**2**	**7**	**9**	**28**	**6**	**1**	**0**	**1**	**10**
	NHL Totals		**799**	**152**	**311**	**463**	**1301**	**71**	**19**	**16**	**35**	**77**

NHL Second All-Star Team (1993)

Played in NHL All-Star Game (1988, 1990, 1993, 1994)

Traded to **Washington** by **Toronto** for Peter Zezel and Bob Rouse, January 16, 1991. Traded to **Boston** by **Washington** for Joe Juneau, March 21, 1994. • Missed entire 1994-95 and 1995-96 seasons recovering from knee surgery. Traded to **San Jose** by **Boston** for Jeff Odgers and Pittsburgh's 5th round choice (previously acquired, Boston selected Elias Abrahamsson) in 1996 Entry Draft, June 21, 1996. Claimed by **Nashville** from **San Jose** in Expansion Draft, June 26, 1998. Signed as a free agent by **Carolina**, July 14, 1998.

IGINLA, JAROME (ih-GIHN-lah, jah-ROHM) — CGY.

Right wing. Shoots right. 6'1", 202 lbs. Born, Edmonton, Alta., July 1, 1977.
(Dallas' 1st choice, 11th overall, in 1995 Entry Draft).

			Regular Season					Playoffs				
Season	Club	Lea	GP	G	A	TP	PIM	GP	G	A	TP	PIM
1993-94	Kamloops	WHL	48	6	23	39	33	19	3	6	9	10
1994-95	Kamloops	WHL	72	33	38	71	111	21	7	11	18	34
1995-96	Kamloops	WHL	63	63	73	136	120	16	16	13	29	44
	Calgary	**NHL**	....	....	....	....	....	**2**	**1**	**1**	**2**	**0**
1996-97	**Calgary**	**NHL**	**82**	**21**	**29**	**50**	**37**	....	....	....	....	....
1997-98	**Calgary**	**NHL**	**70**	**13**	**19**	**32**	**29**	....	....	....	....	....
	NHL Totals		**152**	**34**	**48**	**82**	**66**	**2**	**1**	**1**	**2**	**0**

Won George Parsons Trophy (Memorial Cup Tournament Most Sportsmanlike Player) (1995) • WHL West First All-Star Team (1996) • Canadian Major Junior First All-Star Team (1996) • NHL All-Rookie Team (1997)

Traded to **Calgary** by **Dallas** with Corey Millen for Joe Nieuwendyk, December 19, 1995.

IGNATJEV, VICTOR — PIT.

Defense. Shoots left. 6'4", 215 lbs. Born, Riga, USSR, April 26, 1970.
(San Jose's 11th choice, 243rd overall, in 1992 Entry Draft).

			Regular Season					Playoffs				
Season	Club	Lea	GP	G	A	TP	PIM	GP	G	A	TP	PIM
1989-90	Riga	USSR	40	0	0	0	26	....	....	....	....	....
1990-91	Riga	USSR	10	0	0	0	2	....	....	....	....	....
1991-92	Riga	CIS	22	4	5	9	22	....	....	....	....	....
1992-93	Kansas City	IHL	64	5	16	21	68	4	1	2	3	24
1993-94	Kansas City	IHL	67	1	24	25	123	....	....	....	....	....
1994-95	Oklahoma City	CHL	47	11	35	46	66	....	....	....	....	....
	Denver	IHL	23	2	11	13	4	17	3	8	11	8
1995-96	Utah	IHL	73	9	29	38	67	21	3	8	11	22
1996-97	Long Beach	IHL	82	16	53	69	112	12	3	4	7	18
1997-98	Long Beach	IHL	71	12	33	45	102	17	3	11	14	16

Signed as a free agent by **Pittsburgh**, August 11, 1998.

INTRANUOVO, RALPH (ihn-trah-NOO-voh) EDM.

Center. Shoots left. 5'8", 185 lbs. Born, East York, Ont., December 11, 1973.
(Edmonton's 5th choice, 96th overall, in 1992 Entry Draft).

			Regular Season					Playoffs				
Season	Club	Lea	GP	G	A	TP	PIM	GP	G	A	TP	PIM
1990-91	S.S. Marie	OHL	63	25	42	67	22	14	7	13	20	17
1991-92	S.S. Marie	OHL	65	50	63	113	44	18	10	14	24	12
1992-93	S.S. Marie	OHL	54	31	47	78	61	18	10	16	26	30
1993-94	Cape Breton	AHL	66	21	31	52	39	4	1	2	3	2
1994-95	**Edmonton**	**NHL**	**1**	**0**	**1**	**1**	**0**	....	....	....	....	....
	Cape Breton	AHL	70	46	47	93	62	....	....	....	....	....
1995-96	**Edmonton**	**NHL**	**13**	**1**	**2**	**3**	**4**	....	....	....	....	....
	Cape Breton	AHL	52	34	39	73	84	....	....	....	....	....
1996-97	**Toronto**	**NHL**	**3**	**0**	**1**	**1**	**0**	....	....	....	....	....
	Edmonton	**NHL**	**5**	**1**	**0**	**1**	**0**	....	....	....	....	....
	Hamilton	AHL	68	36	40	76	88	22	8	4	12	30
1997-98	Manitoba	IHL	81	26	35	61	68	3	2	0	2	4
	NHL Totals		**22**	**2**	**4**	**6**	**4**	....	....	....	....	....

Memorial Cup All-Star Team (1993) • Won Stafford Smythe Memorial Trophy (Memorial Cup Tournament MVP) (1993) • AHL Second All-Star Team (1995, 1997)

Claimed by **Toronto** from **Edmonton** in Waiver Draft, September 30, 1996. Claimed on waivers by **Edmonton** from **Toronto**, October 25, 1996.

IRVING, JOEL CGY.

Center. Shoots right. 6'3", 210 lbs. Born, Lumsden, Sask., January 2, 1976.
(Montreal's 8th choice, 148th overall, in 1994 Entry Draft).

			Regular Season					Playoffs				
Season	Club	Lea	GP	G	A	TP	PIM	GP	G	A	TP	PIM
1993-94	Regina	AJHL	32	16	46	62	22	....	....	....	....	....
1994-95	Western Michigan	CCHA	30	2	3	5	20	....	....	....	....	....
1995-96	Western Michigan	CCHA	39	7	6	13	58	....	....	....	....	....
1996-97	Western Michigan	CCHA	34	8	11	19	62	....	....	....	....	....
1997-98	Western Michigan	CCHA	36	8	10	18	82	....	....	....	....	....

Signed as a free agent by **Calgary**, July 28, 1998.

ISBISTER, BRAD (IHZ-bihs-tuhr) PHX.

Right wing. Shoots right. 6'3", 222 lbs. Born, Edmonton, Alta., May 7, 1977.
(Winnipeg's 4th choice, 67th overall, in 1995 Entry Draft).

			Regular Season					Playoffs				
Season	Club	Lea	GP	G	A	TP	PIM	GP	G	A	TP	PIM
1993-94	Portland	WHL	64	7	10	17	45	10	0	2	2	0
1994-95	Portland	WHL	67	16	20	36	123	....	....	....	....	....
1995-96	Portland	WHL	71	45	44	89	184	7	2	4	6	20
1996-97	Portland	WHL	24	15	18	33	45	6	2	1	3	16
	Springfield	AHL	7	3	1	4	14	9	1	2	3	10
1997-98	**Phoenix**	**NHL**	**66**	**9**	**8**	**17**	**102**	**5**	**0**	**0**	**0**	**2**
	Springfield	AHL	9	8	2	10	36	....	....	....	....	....
	NHL Totals		**66**	**9**	**8**	**17**	**102**	**5**	**0**	**0**	**0**	**2**

WHL West Second All-Star Team (1997)

Rights transferred to **Phoenix** after **Winnipeg** franchise relocated, July 1, 1996.

IVAN, MAREK (EE-vahn, MAH-rehk) ST.L.

Center. Shoots left. 6'1", 182 lbs. Born, Uhreske Hradiste, Czech., November 17, 1978.
(St. Louis' 9th choice, 244th overall, in 1997 Entry Draft).

			Regular Season					Playoffs				
Season	Club	Lea	GP	G	A	TP	PIM	GP	G	A	TP	PIM
1996-97	Lethbridge	WHL	69	14	10	24	127	19	0	0	0	20
1997-98	Lethbridge	WHL	14	8	6	14	26	....	....	....	....	....
	Moose Jaw	WHL	56	16	13	29	133	4	2	0	2	4

JACK, JUSTIN T.B.

Right wing. Shoots right. 6'4", 195 lbs. Born, Melfort, Sask., July 11, 1979.
(Tampa Bay's 8th choice, 168th overall, in 1997 Entry Draft).

			Regular Season					Playoffs				
Season	Club	Lea	GP	G	A	TP	PIM	GP	G	A	TP	PIM
1996-97	Kelowna	WHL	37	2	0	2	125	....	....	....	....	....
1997-98	Kelowna	WHL	37	1	3	4	93	7	0	0	0	23

JACKMAN, RICHARD DAL.

Defense. Shoots right. 6'2", 180 lbs. Born, Toronto, Ont., June 28, 1978.
(Dallas' 1st choice, 5th overall, in 1996 Entry Draft).

			Regular Season					Playoffs				
Season	Club	Lea	GP	G	A	TP	PIM	GP	G	A	TP	PIM
1995-96	S.S. Marie	OHL	66	13	29	42	97	4	1	0	1	15
1996-97	S.S. Marie	OHL	53	13	34	47	116	10	2	6	8	24
1997-98	S.S. Marie	OHL	60	33	40	73	111	....	....	....	....	....
	Michigan	IHL	14	1	5	6	10	4	0	0	0	10

OHL Second All-Star Team (1998)

JACKSON, DANE NYI

Right wing. Shoots right. 6'1", 200 lbs. Born, Castlegar, B.C., May 17, 1970.
(Vancouver's 3rd choice, 44th overall, in 1988 Entry Draft).

			Regular Season					Playoffs				
Season	Club	Lea	GP	G	A	TP	PIM	GP	G	A	TP	PIM
1987-88	Vernon	BCJHL	50	28	32	60	99	....	....	....	....	....
1988-89	North Dakota	WCHA	30	4	5	9	33	....	....	....	....	....
1989-90	North Dakota	WCHA	44	15	11	26	56	....	....	....	....	....
1990-91	North Dakota	WCHA	37	17	9	26	79	....	....	....	....	....
1991-92	North Dakota	WCHA	39	23	19	42	81	....	....	....	....	....
1992-93	Hamilton	AHL	68	23	20	43	59	....	....	....	....	....
1993-94	**Vancouver**	**NHL**	**12**	**5**	**1**	**6**	**9**	....	....	....	....	....
	Hamilton	AHL	60	25	35	60	75	4	2	2	4	16
1994-95	**Vancouver**	**NHL**	**3**	**1**	**0**	**1**	**4**	**6**	**0**	**0**	**0**	**10**
	Syracuse	AHL	78	30	28	58	162	....	....	....	....	....
1995-96	**Buffalo**	**NHL**	**22**	**5**	**4**	**9**	**41**	....	....	....	....	....
	Rochester	AHL	50	27	19	46	132	19	4	6	10	53
1996-97	Rochester	AHL	78	24	34	58	111	10	7	4	11	14
1997-98	**NY Islanders**	**NHL**	**8**	**1**	**1**	**2**	**4**	....	....	....	....	....
	Rochester	AHL	28	10	13	23	55	3	2	2	4	4
	NHL Totals		**45**	**12**	**6**	**18**	**58**	**6**	**0**	**0**	**0**	**10**

Signed as a free agent by **Buffalo**, September 20, 1995. Signed as a free agent by **NY Islanders**, July 21, 1997.

JACQUES, ALEXANDRE DET.

Center. Shoots right. 5'11", 165 lbs. Born, Laval, Que., September 27, 1977.
(Detroit's 6th choice, 162nd overall, in 1996 Entry Draft).

			Regular Season					Playoffs				
Season	Club	Lea	GP	G	A	TP	PIM	GP	G	A	TP	PIM
1994-95	Shawinigan	QMJHL	71	9	8	17	18	14	8	5	13	8
1995-96	Shawinigan	QMJHL	60	25	32	57	57	6	3	2	5	2
1996-97	Shawinigan	QMJHL	70	41	60	101	46	7	3	3	6	2
1997-98	Rimouski	QMJHL	24	17	23	40	47	10	12	10	22	6
	Adirondack	AHL	16	1	1	2	0	....	....	....	....	....
	Toledo	ECHL	9	6	4	10	6	....	....	....	....	....

JAGR, JAROMIR (YAH-guhr) PIT.

Right wing. Shoots left. 6'2", 228 lbs. Born, Kladno, Czech., February 15, 1972.
(Pittsburgh's 1st choice, 5th overall, in 1990 Entry Draft).

			Regular Season					Playoffs				
Season	Club	Lea	GP	G	A	TP	PIM	GP	G	A	TP	PIM
1988-89	Poldi Kladno	Czech.	39	8	10	18	4	....	....	....	....	....
1989-90	Poldi Kladno	Czech.	51	30	29	59	....	....	....	....	....	....
1990-91	**Pittsburgh**	**NHL**	**80**	**27**	**30**	**57**	**42**	**24**	**3**	**10**	**13**	**6 ♦**
1991-92	**Pittsburgh**	**NHL**	**70**	**32**	**37**	**69**	**34**	**21**	**11**	**13**	**24**	**6 ♦**
1992-93	**Pittsburgh**	**NHL**	**81**	**34**	**60**	**94**	**61**	**12**	**5**	**4**	**9**	**23**
1993-94	**Pittsburgh**	**NHL**	**80**	**32**	**67**	**99**	**61**	**6**	**2**	**4**	**6**	**16**
1994-95	Poldi Kladno	Cze-Rep.	11	8	14	22	10	....	....	....	....	....
	HC Bolzano	EuroHL	5	8	8	16	4	....	....	....	....	....
	HC Bolzano	Italy	1	0	0	0	0	....	....	....	....	....
	Schalke	Ger-2	1	1	10	11	0	....	....	....	....	....
	Pittsburgh	**NHL**	**48**	**32**	**38**	***70**	**37**	**12**	**10**	**5**	**15**	**6**
1995-96	**Pittsburgh**	**NHL**	**82**	**62**	**87**	**149**	**96**	**18**	**11**	**12**	**23**	**18**
1996-97	**Pittsburgh**	**NHL**	**63**	**47**	**48**	**95**	**40**	**5**	**4**	**4**	**8**	**4**
1997-98	**Pittsburgh**	**NHL**	**77**	**35**	***67**	***102**	**64**	**6**	**4**	**5**	**9**	**2**
	Czech Republic	Olympics	6	1	4	5	2	....	....	....	....	....
	NHL Totals		**581**	**301**	**434**	**735**	**435**	**104**	**50**	**57**	**107**	**81**

• NHL/Upper Deck All-Rookie Team (1991) • NHL First All-Star Team (1995, 1996, 1998) • Won Art Ross Trophy (1995, 1998) • NHL Second All-Star Team (1997)

Played in NHL All-Star Game (1992, 1993, 1996, 1998)

JAKOPIN, JOHN (JA-koh-pihn) FLA.

Defense. Shoots right. 6'5", 220 lbs. Born, Toronto, Ont., May 16, 1975.
(Detroit's 4th choice, 97th overall, in 1993 Entry Draft).

			Regular Season					Playoffs				
Season	Club	Lea	GP	G	A	TP	PIM	GP	G	A	TP	PIM
1992-93	St. Michael's	Jr. B	45	9	21	30	42	....	....	....	....	....
1993-94	Merrimack	H.E.	36	2	8	10	64	....	....	....	....	....
1994-95	Merrimack	H.E.	37	4	10	14	42	....	....	....	....	....
1995-96	Merrimack	H.E.	32	10	15	25	68	....	....	....	....	....
1996-97	Merrimack	H.E.	31	4	12	16	68	....	....	....	....	....
	Adirondack	AHL	3	0	0	0	9	....	....	....	....	....
1997-98	**Florida**	**NHL**	**2**	**0**	**0**	**0**	**4**	....	....	....	....	....
	New Haven	AHL	60	2	18	20	151	3	0	0	0	0
	NHL Totals		**2**	**0**	**0**	**0**	**4**	....	....	....	....	....

Signed as a free agent by **Florida**, May 14, 1997.

JANNEY, CRAIG T.B.

Center. Shoots left. 6'1", 190 lbs. Born, Hartford, CT, September 26, 1967.
(Boston's 1st choice, 13th overall, in 1986 Entry Draft).

			Regular Season					Playoffs				
Season	Club	Lea	GP	G	A	TP	PIM	GP	G	A	TP	PIM
1983-84	Deerfield Academy	H.S.	17	33	35	68	6	....	....	....	....	....
1985-86	Boston College	H.E.	34	13	14	27	8	....	....	....	....	....
1986-87	Boston College	H.E.	37	26	55	81	6	....	....	....	....	....
1987-88	United States	Nat-Tm	52	26	44	70	6	....	....	....	....	....
	United States	Olympics	5	3	3	6	2	....	....	....	....	....
	Boston	**NHL**	**15**	**7**	**9**	**16**	**0**	**23**	**6**	**10**	**16**	**11**
1988-89	**Boston**	**NHL**	**62**	**16**	**46**	**62**	**12**	**10**	**4**	**9**	**13**	**21**
1989-90	**Boston**	**NHL**	**55**	**24**	**38**	**62**	**4**	**18**	**3**	**19**	**22**	**2**
1990-91	**Boston**	**NHL**	**77**	**26**	**66**	**92**	**8**	**18**	**4**	**18**	**22**	**11**
1991-92	**St. Louis**	**NHL**	**25**	**6**	**30**	**36**	**2**	**6**	**0**	**6**	**6**	**0**
	Boston	**NHL**	**53**	**12**	**39**	**51**	**20**	....	....	....	....	....
1992-93	**St. Louis**	**NHL**	**84**	**24**	**82**	**106**	**12**	**11**	**2**	**9**	**11**	**0**
1993-94	**St. Louis**	**NHL**	**69**	**16**	**68**	**84**	**24**	**4**	**1**	**3**	**4**	**0**
1994-95	**St. Louis**	**NHL**	**8**	**2**	**5**	**7**	**0**	....	....	....	....	....
	San Jose	**NHL**	**27**	**5**	**15**	**20**	**10**	**11**	**3**	**4**	**7**	**4**
1995-96	**San Jose**	**NHL**	**71**	**13**	**49**	**62**	**26**	....	....	....	....	....
	Winnipeg	**NHL**	**13**	**7**	**13**	**20**	**0**	**6**	**1**	**2**	**3**	**0**
1996-97	**Phoenix**	**NHL**	**77**	**15**	**38**	**53**	**26**	**7**	**0**	**3**	**3**	**4**
1997-98	**Phoenix**	**NHL**	**68**	**10**	**43**	**53**	**12**	**6**	**0**	**3**	**3**	**0**
	NHL Totals		**704**	**183**	**541**	**724**	**156**	**120**	**24**	**86**	**110**	**53**

Hockey East First All-Star Team (1987) • NCAA East First All-American Team (1987)

Traded to **St. Louis** by **Boston** with Stephane Quintal for Adam Oates, February 7, 1992. Acquired by **Vancouver** from **St. Louis** with St. Louis' 2nd round choice (Dave Scathard) in 1994 Entry Draft as compensation for St. Louis' signing of free agent Petr Nedved, March 14, 1994. Traded to **St. Louis** by **Vancouver** for Jeff Brown, Bret Hedican and Nathan Lafayette, March 21, 1994. Traded to **San Jose** by **St. Louis** with cash for Jeff Norton and future considerations, March 6, 1995. Traded to **Winnipeg** by **San Jose** for Darren Turcotte and Dallas' 2nd round choice (previously acquired, later traded to Chicago — Chicago selected Remi Royer) in 1996 Entry Draft, March 18, 1996. Transferred to **Phoenix** after **Winnipeg** franchise relocated, July 1, 1996. Traded to **Tampa Bay** by **Phoenix** for Louie Debrusk and Tampa Bay's 5th round choice (Jay Leach) in 1998 Entry Draft, June 11, 1998.

JANSSENS, MARK — CHI.

Center. Shoots left. 6'3", 212 lbs. Born, Surrey, B.C., May 19, 1968.
(NY Rangers' 4th choice, 72nd overall, in 1986 Entry Draft).

			Regular Season					Playoffs				
Season	Club	Lea	GP	G	A	TP	PIM	GP	G	A	TP	PIM
1984-85	Regina	WHL	70	8	22	30	51	....	....	....	....	....
1985-86	Regina	WHL	71	25	38	63	146	9	0	2	2	17
1986-87	Regina	WHL	68	24	38	62	209	3	0	1	1	14
1987-88	Regina	WHL	71	39	51	90	202	4	3	4	7	6
	NY Rangers	**NHL**	**1**	**0**	**0**	**0**	**0**	....	....	....	....	....
	Colorado	IHL	6	2	2	4	24	12	3	2	5	20
1988-89	**NY Rangers**	**NHL**	**5**	**0**	**0**	**0**	**0**	....	....	....	....	....
	Denver	IHL	38	19	19	38	104	4	3	0	3	18
1989-90	**NY Rangers**	**NHL**	**80**	**5**	**8**	**13**	**161**	**9**	**2**	**1**	**3**	**10**
1990-91	**NY Rangers**	**NHL**	**67**	**9**	**7**	**16**	**172**	**6**	**3**	**0**	**3**	**6**
1991-92	**NY Rangers**	**NHL**	**4**	**0**	**0**	**0**	**5**	....	....	....	....	....
	Binghamton	AHL	55	10	23	33	109	....	....	....	....	....
	Minnesota	**NHL**	**3**	**0**	**0**	**0**	**0**	....	....	....	....	....
	Kalamazoo	IHL	2	0	0	0	2	11	1	2	3	22
1992-93	**Hartford**	**NHL**	**76**	**12**	**17**	**29**	**237**	....	....	....	....	....
1993-94	**Hartford**	**NHL**	**84**	**2**	**10**	**12**	**137**	....	....	....	....	....
1994-95	**Hartford**	**NHL**	**46**	**2**	**5**	**7**	**93**	....	....	....	....	....
1995-96	**Hartford**	**NHL**	**81**	**2**	**7**	**9**	**155**	....	....	....	....	....
1996-97	**Hartford**	**NHL**	**54**	**2**	**4**	**6**	**90**	....	....	....	....	....
	Anaheim	**NHL**	**12**	**0**	**2**	**2**	**47**	**11**	**0**	**0**	**0**	**15**
1997-98	**Anaheim**	**NHL**	**55**	**4**	**5**	**9**	**116**	....	....	....	....	....
	NY Islanders	**NHL**	**12**	**0**	**0**	**0**	**34**	....	....	....	....	....
	Phoenix	**NHL**	**7**	**1**	**2**	**3**	**4**	**1**	**0**	**0**	**0**	**2**
	NHL Totals		**587**	**39**	**67**	**106**	**1251**	**27**	**5**	**1**	**6**	**33**

Traded to **Minnesota** by **NY Rangers** for Mario Thyer and Minnesota's 3rd round choice (Maxim Galanov) in 1993 Entry Draft, March 10, 1992. Traded to **Hartford** by **Minnesota** for James Black, September 3, 1992. Traded to **Anaheim** by **Hartford** for Bates Battaglia and Anaheim's 4th round choice (Carolina selected Josef Vasicek) in 1998 Entry Draft, March 18, 1997. Traded to **NY Islanders** by **Anaheim** with Joe Sacco and J.J. Daigneault for Travis Green, Doug Houda and Tony Tuzzolino, February 6, 1998. Traded to **Phoenix** by **NY Islanders** for Phoenix's 9th round choice (Jason Doyle) in 1998 Entry Draft, March 24, 1998. Signed as a free agent by **Chicago**, July 28, 1998.

JANTUNEN, MARKO (YAN-too-nehn) — CGY.

Center. Shoots left. 5'10", 185 lbs. Born, Lahti, Finland, February 14, 1971.
(Calgary's 13th choice, 239th overall, in 1991 Entry Draft).

			Regular Season					Playoffs				
Season	Club	Lea	GP	G	A	TP	PIM	GP	G	A	TP	PIM
1990-91	Reipas Lahti	Finland	39	9	20	29	20	....	....	....	....	....
1991-92	Reipas Lahti	Finland	42	10	14	24	46	....	....	....	....	....
1992-93	KalPa	Finland	48	21	27	48	63	....	....	....	....	....
1993-94	TPS Turku	Finland	48	29	29	58	22	11	2	6	8	12
1994-95	V. Frolunda	Sweden	22	15	8	23	22	....	....	....	....	....
1995-96	V. Frolunda	Sweden	40	17	14	31	66	13	8	8	16	10
1996-97	**Calgary**	**NHL**	**3**	**0**	**0**	**0**	**0**	....	....	....	....	....
	Saint John	AHL	23	8	16	24	18	....	....	....	....	....
	V. Frolunda	Sweden	13	4	7	11	16	3	2	0	2	16
1997-98	V. Frolunda	Sweden	43	14	20	34	61	7	1	2	3	2
	NHL Totals		**3**	**0**	**0**	**0**	**0**	....	....	....	....	....

JARDINE, RYAN — FLA.

Left wing. Shoots left. 6', 178 lbs. Born, Ottawa, Ont., March 15, 1980.
(Florida's 4th choice, 89th overall, in 1998 Entry Draft).

			Regular Season					Playoffs				
Season	Club	Lea	GP	G	A	TP	PIM	GP	G	A	TP	PIM
1997-98	S.S. Marie	OHL	65	28	32	60	16	....	....	....	....	....

JARVIS, WES — NYR

Defense. Shoots left. 6'4", 203 lbs. Born, Toronto, Ont., April 16, 1979.
(NY Rangers' 2nd choice, 46th overall, in 1997 Entry Draft).

			Regular Season					Playoffs				
Season	Club	Lea	GP	G	A	TP	PIM	GP	G	A	TP	PIM
1996-97	Kitchener	OHL	56	4	8	12	108	13	0	4	4	25
1997-98	Kitchener	OHL	47	10	18	28	112	1	0	0	0	2

JINDRICH, ROBERT (IHN-drihkh) — S.J.

Defense. Shoots left. 5'11", 187 lbs. Born, Plzen, Czech., November 14, 1976.
(San Jose's 10th choice, 168th overall, in 1995 Entry Draft).

			Regular Season					Playoffs				
Season	Club	Lea	GP	G	A	TP	PIM	GP	G	A	TP	PIM
1993-94	Plzen	Cze-Rep.	18	0	2	2	....	....	....	....	....	....
1994-95	Plzen	Cze-Rep.	11	1	0	1	4	....	....	....	....	....
1995-96	Plzen	Cze-Rep.	37	1	3	4	....	3	0	0	0	....
1996-97	Plzen	Cze-Rep.	49	7	9	16	44	....	....	....	....	....
1997-98	Plzen	Cze-Rep.	39	1	6	7	18	4	0	0	0	0

JINMAN, LEE (JIHN-muhn) — DAL.

Center. Shoots right. 5'10", 160 lbs. Born, Toronto, Ont., January 10, 1976.
(Dallas' 2nd choice, 46th overall, in 1994 Entry Draft).

			Regular Season					Playoffs				
Season	Club	Lea	GP	G	A	TP	PIM	GP	G	A	TP	PIM
1993-94	North Bay	OHL	66	31	66	97	33	18	*18	19	37	8
1994-95	North Bay	OHL	63	39	65	104	41	6	5	5	10	4
1995-96	North Bay	OHL	38	19	33	52	23	....	....	....	....	....
	Detroit	OHL	26	10	35	45	26	17	6	15	21	16
1996-97	Michigan	IHL	81	17	40	57	65	4	1	1	2	2
1997-98	Dayton	ECHL	4	1	3	4	23	....	....	....	....	....
	Michigan	IHL	61	6	19	25	54	....	....	....	....	....

JOHANSSON, ANDREAS (yoh-HAHN-suhn, ahn-DRAY-uhs)

Center. Shoots left. 6', 205 lbs. Born, Hofors, Sweden, May 19, 1973.
(NY Islanders' 7th choice, 136th overall, in 1991 Entry Draft).

			Regular Season					Playoffs				
Season	Club	Lea	GP	G	A	TP	PIM	GP	G	A	TP	PIM
1990-91	Falun	Sweden-2	31	12	10	22	38	....	....	....	....	....
1991-92	Farjestad	Sweden	30	3	1	4	10	6	0	0	0	4
1992-93	Farjestad	Sweden	38	4	7	11	38	2	0	0	0	0
1993-94	Farjestad	Sweden	20	3	6	9	6	....	....	....	....	....
1994-95	Farjestad	Sweden	36	9	10	19	42	4	0	0	0	10
1995-96	**NY Islanders**	**NHL**	**3**	**0**	**1**	**1**	**0**	....	....	....	....	....
	Worcester	AHL	29	5	5	10	32	....	....	....	....	....
	Utah	IHL	22	4	13	17	28	12	0	5	5	6
1996-97	**NY Islanders**	**NHL**	**15**	**2**	**2**	**4**	**0**	....	....	....	....	....
	Pittsburgh	**NHL**	**27**	**2**	**7**	**9**	**20**	....	....	....	....	....
	Cleveland	IHL	10	2	4	6	42	11	1	5	6	8
1997-98	**Pittsburgh**	**NHL**	**50**	**5**	**10**	**15**	**20**	**1**	**0**	**0**	**0**	**0**
	Sweden	Olympics	3	0	0	0	2	....	....	....	....	....
	NHL Totals		**95**	**9**	**20**	**29**	**40**	**1**	**0**	**0**	**0**	**0**

Swedish World All-Star Team (1995)

Traded to **Pittsburgh** by **NY Islanders** with Darius Kasparaitis for Bryan Smolinski, November 17, 1996.

JOHANSSON, CALLE (yoh-HAHN-suhn, KAL-ee) — WSH.

Defense. Shoots left. 5'11", 200 lbs. Born, Goteborg, Sweden, February 14, 1967.
(Buffalo's 1st choice, 14th overall, in 1985 Entry Draft).

			Regular Season					Playoffs				
Season	Club	Lea	GP	G	A	TP	PIM	GP	G	A	TP	PIM
1983-84	V. Frolunda	Sweden	28	4	4	8	10	....	....	....	....	....
1984-85	V. Frolunda	Sweden-2	25	8	13	21	16	6	1	2	3	4
1985-86	Bjorkloven	Sweden	17	1	2	3	4	....	....	....	....	....
1986-87	Bjorkloven	Sweden	30	2	13	15	20	6	1	3	4	6
1987-88	**Buffalo**	**NHL**	**71**	**4**	**38**	**42**	**37**	**6**	**0**	**1**	**1**	**0**
1988-89	**Buffalo**	**NHL**	**47**	**2**	**11**	**13**	**33**	....	....	....	....	....
	Washington	**NHL**	**12**	**1**	**7**	**8**	**4**	**6**	**1**	**2**	**3**	**0**
1989-90	**Washington**	**NHL**	**70**	**8**	**31**	**39**	**25**	**15**	**1**	**6**	**7**	**4**
1990-91	**Washington**	**NHL**	**80**	**11**	**41**	**52**	**23**	**10**	**2**	**7**	**9**	**8**
1991-92	**Washington**	**NHL**	**80**	**14**	**42**	**56**	**49**	**7**	**0**	**5**	**5**	**4**
1992-93	**Washington**	**NHL**	**77**	**7**	**38**	**45**	**56**	**6**	**0**	**5**	**5**	**4**
1993-94	**Washington**	**NHL**	**84**	**9**	**33**	**42**	**59**	**6**	**1**	**3**	**4**	**4**
1994-95	EHC Kloten	Switz.	5	1	2	3	8	....	....	....	....	....
	Washington	**NHL**	**46**	**5**	**26**	**31**	**35**	**7**	**3**	**1**	**4**	**0**
1995-96	**Washington**	**NHL**	**78**	**10**	**25**	**35**	**50**	....	....	....	....	....
1996-97	**Washington**	**NHL**	**65**	**6**	**11**	**17**	**16**	....	....	....	....	....
1997-98	**Washington**	**NHL**	**73**	**15**	**20**	**35**	**30**	**21**	**2**	**8**	**10**	**16**
	Sweden	Olympics	4	0	0	0	2	....	....	....	....	....
	NHL Totals		**783**	**92**	**323**	**415**	**417**	**84**	**10**	**38**	**48**	**40**

• NHL All-Rookie Team (1988)

Traded to **Washington** by **Buffalo** with Buffalo's 2nd round choice (Byron Dafoe) in 1989 Entry Draft for Clint Malarchuk, Grant Ledyard and Washington's 6th round choice (Brian Holzinger) in 1991 Entry Draft, March 7, 1989.

JOHANSSON, DANIEL (yoh-HAHN-suhn) — NYI

Defense. Shoots right. 5'11", 180 lbs. Born, Glimakra, Sweden, September 10, 1974.
(NY Islanders' 9th choice, 222nd overall, in 1993 Entry Draft).

			Regular Season					Playoffs				
Season	Club	Lea	GP	G	A	TP	PIM	GP	G	A	TP	PIM
1991-92	Rogle	Sweden-2	33	4	9	13	30	....	....	....	....	....
1992-93	Rogle	Sweden	28	2	4	6	20	....	....	....	....	....
1993-94	Rogle	Sweden	37	5	10	15	34	3	0	0	0	0
1994-95	Rogle	Sweden	22	4	2	6	16	....	....	....	....	....
1995-96	HV 71 Jonkoping	Sweden	40	3	5	8	24	4	0	1	1	0
1996-97	HV 71 Jonkoping	Sweden	50	8	7	15	30	5	0	1	1	2
1997-98	HV 71 Jonkoping	Sweden	46	3	9	12	32	5	2	0	2	6

JOHANSSON, MATHIAS (yoh-HAHN-suhn) — CGY.

Center. Shoots left. 6'2", 190 lbs. Born, Oskarshamn, Sweden, February 22, 1974.
(Calgary's 3rd choice, 54th overall, in 1992 Entry Draft).

			Regular Season					Playoffs				
Season	Club	Lea	GP	G	A	TP	PIM	GP	G	A	TP	PIM
1990-91	Farjestad	Sweden	3	0	0	0	0	....	....	....	....	....
1991-92	Farjestad	Sweden	16	0	0	0	2	1	0	0	0	0
1992-93	Farjestad	Sweden	11	2	1	3	4	3	0	0	0	0
1993-94	Farjestad	Sweden	16	2	1	3	4	....	....	....	....	....
1994-95	Farjestad	Sweden	40	7	8	15	30	4	4	3	7	2
1995-96	Farjestad	Sweden	40	8	21	29	10	8	2	1	3	4
1996-97	Farjestad	Sweden	48	12	15	27	14	14	4	4	8	12
1997-98	Farjestad	EuroHL	8	3	4	7	2	....	....	....	....	....
	Farjestad	Sweden	46	8	21	29	36	12	2	1	3	10

JOHANSSON, MIKAEL (yoh-HAHN-suhn) — COL.

Center. Shoots left. 5'10", 185 lbs. Born, Stockholm, Swe., June 12, 1966.
(Quebec's 7th choice, 134th overall, in 1991 Entry Draft).

			Regular Season					Playoffs				
Season	Club	Lea	GP	G	A	TP	PIM	GP	G	A	TP	PIM
1986-87	Djurgarden	Sweden	32	9	16	25	8	....	....	....	....	....
1987-88	Djurgarden	Sweden	38	11	22	33	10	3	1	1	2	0
1988-89	Djurgarden	Sweden	29	6	15	21	10	....	....	....	....	....
1989-90	Djurgarden	Sweden	37	14	20	34	12	8	5	4	9	0
1990-91	Djurgarden	Sweden	39	13	27	40	21	7	2	7	9	0
1991-92	Djurgarden	Sweden	30	15	21	36	12	9	1	5	6	4
1992-93	Kloten	Switz.	36	18	30	48	2	....	....	....	....	....
1993-94	Kloten	Switz.	36	22	29	51	24	12	9	14	23	8
1994-95	Kloten	Switz.	35	14	36	50	8	12	4	9	13	8
1995-96	Kloten	Switz.	35	13	20	33	10	10	5	13	18	2
1996-97	Kloten	Switz.	46	17	27	44	10	4	1	2	3	2
1997-98	Djurgarden	Sweden	43	15	23	38	18	15	6	6	*12	4

JOHANSSON, TOBIAS (yoh-HAHN-suhn) — ANA.

Left wing. Shoots left. 5'11", 180 lbs. Born, Malmo, Sweden, October 31, 1977.
(Anaheim's 7th choice, 224th overall, in 1996 Entry Draft).

			Regular Season					Playoffs				
Season	Club	Lea	GP	G	A	TP	PIM	GP	G	A	TP	PIM
1995-96	Malmo IF	Swe-Jr.	30	7	13	20	38	....	....	....	....	....
1996-97	Malmo IF	Swe-Jr.	15	6	8	14	63	....	....	....	....	....
1997-98	Tranas	Sweden-2	31	7	2	9	18	....	....	....	....	....
	Fort Worth	CHL	3	0	0	0	4	....	....	....	....	....

JOHNSON, ANDY — CHI.

Defense. Shoots left. 6'3", 188 lbs. Born, Fredericton, N.B., March 6, 1978.
(Chicago's 4th choice, 130th overall, in 1996 Entry Draft).

			Regular Season					Playoffs				
Season	Club	Lea	GP	G	A	TP	PIM	GP	G	A	TP	PIM
1995-96	Peterborough	OHL	54	0	4	4	57	22	0	6	6	21
1996-97	Peterborough	OHL	57	4	24	28	82	7	1	2	3	10
1997-98	Peterborough	OHL	60	17	20	37	112	4	0	0	0	6

JOHNSON, CRAIG — L.A.

Left wing/Center. Shoots left. 6'2", 197 lbs. Born, St. Paul, MN, March 8, 1972.
(St. Louis' 1st choice, 33rd overall, in 1990 Entry Draft).

			Regular Season					Playoffs				
Season	Club	Lea	GP	G	A	TP	PIM	GP	G	A	TP	PIM
1989-90	Hill-Murray	H.S.	23	15	36	51	0	....	....	....	....	....
1990-91	U. of Minnesota	WCHA	33	13	18	31	34	....	....	....	....	....
1991-92	U. of Minnesota	WCHA	41	17	38	55	66	....	....	....	....	....
1992-93	U. of Minnesota	WCHA	42	22	24	46	70	....	....	....	....	....
1993-94	United States	Nat-Tm	54	25	26	51	64	....	....	....	....	....
	United States	Olympics	8	0	4	4	4	....	....	....	....	....
1994-95	**St. Louis**	**NHL**	**15**	**3**	**3**	**6**	**6**	**1**	**0**	**0**	**0**	**2**
	Peoria	IHL	16	2	6	8	25	9	0	4	4	10
1995-96	**St. Louis**	**NHL**	**49**	**8**	**7**	**15**	**30**	....	....	....	....	....
	Worcester	AHL	5	3	0	3	2	....	....	....	....	....
	Los Angeles	**NHL**	**11**	**5**	**4**	**9**	**6**	....	....	....	....	....
1996-97	**Los Angeles**	**NHL**	**31**	**4**	**3**	**7**	**26**	....	....	....	....	....
1997-98	**Los Angeles**	**NHL**	**74**	**17**	**21**	**38**	**42**	**4**	**1**	**0**	**1**	**4**
	NHL Totals		**180**	**37**	**38**	**75**	**110**	**5**	**1**	**0**	**1**	**6**

Traded to **LA Kings** by **St. Louis** with Patrice Tardif, Roman Vopat, St. Louis 5th round choice (Peter Hogan) in 1996 Entry Draft and 1st round choice (Matt Zultek) in 1997 Entry Draft for Wayne Gretzky, February 27, 1996.

JOHNSON, GREG — NSH.

Center. Shoots left. 5'10", 185 lbs. Born, Thunder Bay, Ont., March 16, 1971.
(Philadelphia's 1st choice, 33rd overall, in 1989 Entry Draft).

			Regular Season					Playoffs				
Season	Club	Lea	GP	G	A	TP	PIM	GP	G	A	TP	PIM
1988-89	Thunder Bay	USHL	47	32	64	96	4	12	5	13	18	0
1989-90	North Dakota	WCHA	44	17	38	55	11	....	....	....	....	....
1990-91	North Dakota	WCHA	38	18	*61	79	6	....	....	....	....	....
1991-92	North Dakota	WCHA	39	20	*54	74	8	....	....	....	....	....
1992-93	North Dakota	WCHA	34	19	45	64	18	....	....	....	....	....
	Canada	Nat-Tm	23	6	14	20	2	....	....	....	....	....
1993-94	**Detroit**	**NHL**	**52**	**6**	**11**	**17**	**22**	**7**	**2**	**2**	**4**	**2**
	Adirondack	AHL	3	2	4	6	0	4	0	4	4	2
	Canada	Nat-Tm	6	2	6	8	4	....	....	....	....	....
	Canada	Olympics	8	0	3	3	0	....	....	....	....	....
1994-95	**Detroit**	**NHL**	**22**	**3**	**5**	**8**	**14**	**1**	**0**	**0**	**0**	**0**
1995-96	**Detroit**	**NHL**	**60**	**18**	**22**	**40**	**30**	**13**	**3**	**1**	**4**	**8**
1996-97	**Detroit**	**NHL**	**43**	**6**	**10**	**16**	**12**	....	....	....	....	....
	Pittsburgh	**NHL**	**32**	**7**	**9**	**16**	**14**	**5**	**1**	**0**	**1**	**2**
1997-98	**Pittsburgh**	**NHL**	**5**	**1**	**0**	**1**	**2**	....	....	....	....	....
	Chicago	**NHL**	**69**	**11**	**22**	**33**	**38**	....	....	....	....	....
	NHL Totals		**283**	**52**	**79**	**131**	**132**	**26**	**6**	**3**	**9**	**12**

WCHA First All-Star Team (1991, 1992, 1993) • NCAA West First All-American Team (1991, 1993) • NCAA West Second All-American Team (1992)

Traded to **Detroit** by **Philadelphia** with Philadelphia's 5th round choice (Frederic Deschenes) in 1994 Entry Draft for Jim Cummins and Philadelphia's 4th round choice (previously acquired by Detroit — later traded to Boston — Boston selected Charles Paquette) in 1993 Entry Draft, June 20, 1993. Traded to **Pittsburgh** by **Detroit** for Tomas Sandstrom, January 27, 1997. Traded to **Chicago** by **Pittsburgh** for Tuomas Gronman, October 27, 1997. Claimed by **Nashville** from **Chicago** in Expansion Draft, June 26, 1998.

JOHNSON, JIM

Defense. Shoots left. 6'1", 190 lbs. Born, New Hope, MN, August 9, 1962.

			Regular Season					Playoffs				
Season	Club	Lea	GP	G	A	TP	PIM	GP	G	A	TP	PIM
1981-82	U. Minn-Duluth	WCHA	40	0	10	10	62	....	....	....	....	....
1982-83	U. Minn-Duluth	WCHA	44	3	18	21	118	....	....	....	....	....
1983-84	U. Minn-Duluth	WCHA	43	3	13	16	116	....	....	....	....	....
1984-85	U. Minn-Duluth	WCHA	47	7	29	36	49	....	....	....	....	....
1985-86	**Pittsburgh**	**NHL**	**80**	**3**	**26**	**29**	**115**	....	....	....	....	....
1986-87	**Pittsburgh**	**NHL**	**80**	**5**	**25**	**30**	**116**	....	....	....	....	....
1987-88	**Pittsburgh**	**NHL**	**55**	**1**	**12**	**13**	**87**	....	....	....	....	....
1988-89	**Pittsburgh**	**NHL**	**76**	**2**	**14**	**16**	**163**	**11**	**0**	**5**	**5**	**44**
1989-90	**Pittsburgh**	**NHL**	**75**	**3**	**13**	**16**	**154**	....	....	....	....	....
1990-91	**Pittsburgh**	**NHL**	**24**	**0**	**5**	**5**	**23**	....	....	....	....	....
	Minnesota	**NHL**	**44**	**1**	**9**	**10**	**100**	**14**	**0**	**1**	**1**	**52**
1991-92	**Minnesota**	**NHL**	**71**	**4**	**10**	**14**	**102**	**7**	**1**	**3**	**4**	**18**
1992-93	**Minnesota**	**NHL**	**79**	**3**	**20**	**23**	**105**	....	....	....	....	....
1993-94	**Dallas**	**NHL**	**53**	**0**	**7**	**7**	**51**	....	....	....	....	....
	Washington	**NHL**	**8**	**0**	**0**	**0**	**12**	....	....	....	....	....
1994-95	**Washington**	**NHL**	**47**	**0**	**13**	**13**	**43**	**7**	**0**	**2**	**2**	**8**
1995-96	**Washington**	**NHL**	**66**	**2**	**4**	**6**	**34**	**6**	**0**	**0**	**0**	**6**
1996-97	**Phoenix**	**NHL**	**55**	**3**	**7**	**10**	**74**	**6**	**0**	**0**	**0**	**4**
1997-98	**Phoenix**	**NHL**	**16**	**2**	**1**	**3**	**18**	....	....	....	....	....
	NHL Totals		**829**	**29**	**166**	**195**	**1197**	**51**	**1**	**11**	**12**	**132**

Signed as a free agent by **Pittsburgh**, June 9, 1985. Traded to **Minnesota** by **Pittsburgh** with Chris Dahlquist for Larry Murphy and Peter Taglianetti, December 11, 1990. Transferred to **Dallas** after **Minnesota** franchise relocated, June 9, 1993. Traded to **Washington** by **Dallas** for Alan May and Washington's 7th round choice (Jeff Dewar) in 1995 Entry Draft, March 21, 1994. Signed as a free agent by **Phoenix**, July 6, 1996.

JOHNSON, MATT — L.A.

Left wing. Shoots left. 6'5", 232 lbs. Born, Welland, Ont., November 23, 1975.
(Los Angeles' 2nd choice, 33rd overall, in 1994 Entry Draft).

			Regular Season					Playoffs				
Season	Club	Lea	GP	G	A	TP	PIM	GP	G	A	TP	PIM
1992-93	Peterborough	OHL	66	8	17	25	211	16	1	1	2	56
1993-94	Peterborough	OHL	50	13	24	37	233	....	....	....	....	....
1994-95	Peterborough	OHL	14	1	2	3	43	....	....	....	....	....
	Los Angeles	**NHL**	**14**	**1**	**0**	**1**	**102**	....	....	....	....	....
1995-96	**Los Angeles**	**NHL**	**1**	**0**	**0**	**0**	**5**	....	....	....	....	....
	Phoenix	IHL	29	4	4	8	87	....	....	....	....	....
1996-97	**Los Angeles**	**NHL**	**52**	**1**	**3**	**4**	**194**	....	....	....	....	....
1997-98	**Los Angeles**	**NHL**	**66**	**2**	**4**	**6**	**249**	**4**	**0**	**0**	**0**	**6**
	NHL Totals		**133**	**4**	**7**	**11**	**550**	**4**	**0**	**0**	**0**	**6**

JOHNSON, MIKE — TOR.

Right wing. Shoots right. 6'2", 190 lbs. Born, Scarborough, Ont., October 3, 1974.

			Regular Season					Playoffs				
Season	Club	Lea	GP	G	A	TP	PIM	GP	G	A	TP	PIM
1993-94	Bowling Green	CCHA	38	6	14	20	18	....	....	....	....	....
1994-95	Bowling Green	CCHA	37	16	33	49	35	....	....	....	....	....
1995-96	Bowling Green	CCHA	30	12	19	31	22	....	....	....	....	....
1996-97	Bowling Green	CCHA	38	30	32	62	46	....	....	....	....	....
	Toronto	**NHL**	**13**	**2**	**2**	**4**	**4**	....	....	....	....	....
1997-98	**Toronto**	**NHL**	**82**	**15**	**32**	**47**	**24**	....	....	....	....	....
	NHL Totals		**95**	**17**	**34**	**51**	**28**	....	....	....	....	....

NHL All-Rookie Team (1998)

Signed as a free agent by **Toronto**, March 16, 1997.

JOHNSON, RYAN — FLA.

Center. Shoots left. 6'2", 185 lbs. Born, Thunder Bay, Ont., June 14, 1976.
(Florida's 4th choice, 36th overall, in 1994 Entry Draft).

			Regular Season					Playoffs				
Season	Club	Lea	GP	G	A	TP	PIM	GP	G	A	TP	PIM
1993-94	Thunder Bay	USHL	48	14	36	50	28	....	....	....	....	....
1994-95	North Dakota	WCHA	38	6	22	28	39	....	....	....	....	....
1995-96	North Dakota	WCHA	21	2	17	19	14	....	....	....	....	....
	Canada	Nat-Tm	28	5	12	17	14	....	....	....	....	....
1996-97	Carolina	AHL	79	18	24	42	28	....	....	....	....	....
1997-98	**Florida**	**NHL**	**10**	**0**	**2**	**2**	**0**	....	....	....	....	....
	New Haven	AHL	64	19	48	67	12	3	0	1	1	0
	NHL Totals		**10**	**0**	**2**	**2**	**0**	....	....	....	....	....

JOHNSSON, KIM — (YAWN-suhn) — NYR

Defense. Shoots left. 6'1", 175 lbs. Born, Malmo, Sweden, March 16, 1976.
(NY Rangers' 15th choice, 286th overall, in 1994 Entry Draft).

			Regular Season					Playoffs				
Season	Club	Lea	GP	G	A	TP	PIM	GP	G	A	TP	PIM
1993-94	Malmo IF	Sweden	2	0	0	0	0	....	....	....	....	....
1994-95	Malmo IF	Sweden	13	0	0	0	4	1	0	0	0	0
1995-96	Malmo IF	Sweden	38	2	0	2	30	4	0	1	1	8
1996-97	Malmo IF	Sweden	49	4	9	13	42	4	0	0	0	2
1997-98	Malmo IF	Sweden	45	5	9	14	29	....	....	....	....	....

JOHNSTONE, ALEX — N.J.

Defense. Shoots left. 6'1", 170 lbs. Born, Halifax, N.S., December 28, 1979.

			Regular Season					Playoffs				
Season	Club	Lea	GP	G	A	TP	PIM	GP	G	A	TP	PIM
1996-97	Halifax	QMJHL	39	1	5	6	213	18	1	0	1	48
1997-98	Halifax	QMJHL	66	3	10	13	390	5	0	2	2	8

Signed as a free agent by **New Jersey**, August 8, 1998.

JOKELA, MIKKO — (YOH-kih-lah, MIH-koh) — N.J.

Defense. Shoots right. 6'1", 212 lbs. Born, Lappeenranta, Finland, March 4, 1980.
(New Jersey's 5th choice, 96th overall, in 1998 Entry Draft).

			Regular Season					Playoffs				
Season	Club	Lea	GP	G	A	TP	PIM	GP	G	A	TP	PIM
1995-96	KalPa Kuopio	Fin-Jr.	11	2	1	3	20	....	....	....	....	....
1996-97	KalPa Kuopio	Fin-Jr.	45	5	7	12	26	5	1	1	2	4
1997-98	HIFK Helsinki	Fin-Jr.	22	2	5	7	14	....	....	....	....	....
	HIFK Helsinki	Finland	16	0	0	0	0	....	....	....	....	....

JOKINEN, OLLI — (YOH-kih-nihn, OH-lee) — L.A.

Center. Shoots left. 6'3", 208 lbs. Born, Kuopio, Finland, December 5, 1978.
(Los Angeles' 1st choice, 3rd overall, in 1997 Entry Draft).

			Regular Season					Playoffs				
Season	Club	Lea	GP	G	A	TP	PIM	GP	G	A	TP	PIM
1995-96	KalPa	Fin-Jr.	25	20	14	34	47	7	4	4	8	20
	KalPa	Finland	15	1	1	2	2	....	....	....	....	....
1996-97	Helsinki	Finland	50	14	27	41	88	....	....	....	....	....
1997-98	**Los Angeles**	**NHL**	**8**	**0**	**0**	**0**	**6**	....	....	....	....	....
	Helsinki	Finland	30	11	28	39	8	9	*7	2	9	2
	NHL Totals		**8**	**0**	**0**	**0**	**6**	....	....	....	....	....

Finnish Rookie of the Year (1997)

JOMPHE, JEAN-FRANCOIS — (ZHAWMF) — PHX.

Center. Shoots left. 6'1", 195 lbs. Born, Harve' St. Pierre, Que., December 28, 1972.

			Regular Season					Playoffs				
Season	Club	Lea	GP	G	A	TP	PIM	GP	G	A	TP	PIM
1990-91	Shawinigan	QMJHL	42	17	22	39	14	6	2	1	3	2
1991-92	Shawinigan	QMJHL	44	28	33	61	69	10	6	10	16	10
1992-93	Sherbrooke	QMJHL	60	43	43	86	86	15	10	13	23	18
1993-94	San Diego	IHL	29	2	3	5	12	....	....	....	....	....
	Greensboro	ECHL	25	9	9	18	41	1	1	0	1	0
1994-95	Canada	Nat-Tm	52	33	25	58	85	....	....	....	....	....
1995-96	**Anaheim**	**NHL**	**31**	**2**	**12**	**14**	**39**	....	....	....	....	....
	Baltimore	AHL	47	21	34	55	75	....	....	....	....	....
1996-97	**Anaheim**	**NHL**	**64**	**7**	**14**	**21**	**53**	....	....	....	....	....
1997-98	**Anaheim**	**NHL**	**9**	**1**	**3**	**4**	**8**	....	....	....	....	....
	Cincinnati	AHL	38	9	19	28	32	....	....	....	....	....
	Quebec	IHL	17	6	4	10	24	....	....	....	....	....
	NHL Totals		**104**	**10**	**29**	**39**	**100**	....	....	....	....	....

Signed as a free agent by **Anaheim**, September 7, 1993. Traded to **Phoenix** by **Anaheim** for Jim McKenzie, June 18, 1998.

JONES, KEITH — COL.

Right wing. Shoots left. 6'2", 200 lbs. Born, Brantford, Ont., November 8, 1968.
(Washington's 7th choice, 141st overall, in 1988 Entry Draft).

			Regular Season					Playoffs				
Season	Club	Lea	GP	G	A	TP	PIM	GP	G	A	TP	PIM
1987-88	Niagara Falls	OJHL	40	50	80	130	....	....	....	....	....	....
1988-89	Western Michigan	CCHA	37	9	12	21	51	....	....	....	....	....
1989-90	Western Michigan	CCHA	40	19	18	37	82	....	....	....	....	....
1990-91	Western Michigan	CCHA	41	30	19	49	106	....	....	....	....	....
1991-92	Western Michigan	CCHA	35	25	31	56	77	....	....	....	....	....
	Baltimore	AHL	6	2	4	6	0	....	....	....	....	....
1992-93	**Washington**	**NHL**	**71**	**12**	**14**	**26**	**124**	**6**	**0**	**0**	**0**	**10**
	Baltimore	AHL	8	7	3	10	4	....	....	....	....	....
1993-94	**Washington**	**NHL**	**68**	**16**	**19**	**35**	**149**	**11**	**0**	**1**	**1**	**36**
	Portland	AHL	6	5	7	12	4	....	....	....	....	....
1994-95	**Washington**	**NHL**	**40**	**14**	**6**	**20**	**65**	**7**	**4**	**4**	**8**	**22**
1995-96	**Washington**	**NHL**	**68**	**18**	**23**	**41**	**103**	**2**	**0**	**0**	**0**	**7**
1996-97	**Washington**	**NHL**	**11**	**2**	**3**	**5**	**13**	....	....	....	....	....
	Colorado	**NHL**	**67**	**23**	**20**	**43**	**105**	**6**	**3**	**3**	**6**	**4**
1997-98	**Colorado**	**NHL**	**23**	**3**	**7**	**10**	**22**	**7**	**0**	**0**	**0**	**13**
	Hershey	AHL	4	2	1	3	2	....	....	....	....	....
	NHL Totals		**348**	**88**	**92**	**180**	**581**	**39**	**7**	**8**	**15**	**92**

CCHA First All-Star Team (1992)

Traded to **Colorado** by **Washington** with Washington's 1st round choice (Scott Parker) in 1998 Entry Draft and future considerations for Curtis Leschyshyn and Chris Simon, November 2, 1996.

JONES, TY — CHI.

Right wing. Shoots right. 6'3", 218 lbs. Born, Richland, WA, February 22, 1979.
(Chicago's 2nd choice, 16th overall, in 1997 Entry Draft).

			Regular Season					Playoffs				
Season	Club	Lea	GP	G	A	TP	PIM	GP	G	A	TP	PIM
1995-96	Spokane	WHL	34	1	0	1	77	3	0	0	0	6
1996-97	Spokane	WHL	67	20	34	54	202	9	2	4	6	10
1997-98	Spokane	WHL	60	36	48	84	161	18	2	14	16	35

JONSSON, HANS (YAWN-suhn) — PIT.

Defense. Shoots left. 6'1", 183 lbs. Born, Jarved, Sweden, August 2, 1973.
(Pittsburgh's 11th choice, 286th overall, in 1993 Entry Draft).

			Regular Season					Playoffs				
Season	Club	Lea	GP	G	A	TP	PIM	GP	G	A	TP	PIM
1991-92	MoDo	Sweden	6	0	1	1	4	....	....	....	....	....
1992-93	MoDo	Sweden	40	2	2	4	24	3	0	1	1	2
1993-94	MoDo	Sweden	23	4	1	5	18	10	0	1	1	12
1994-95	MoDo	Sweden	39	4	6	10	30	....	....	....	....	....
1995-96	MoDo	Sweden	36	10	6	16	30	8	2	1	3	24
1996-97	MoDo	Sweden	27	7	5	12	18	....	....	....	....	....
1997-98	MoDo	Sweden	40	8	6	14	40	8	1	1	2	12

JONSSON, JORGEN (YAWN-suhn) — NYI

Left wing. Shoots left. 6', 185 lbs. Born, Angelholm, Sweden, September 29, 1972.
(Calgary's 11th choice, 227th overall, in 1994 Entry Draft).

			Regular Season					Playoffs				
Season	Club	Lea	GP	G	A	TP	PIM	GP	G	A	TP	PIM
1992-93	Rogle	Sweden	40	17	11	28	28	....	....	....	....	....
1993-94	Rogle	Sweden	40	17	14	31	46	....	....	....	....	....
	Sweden	Olympics	6	0	0	0	0	....	....	....	....	....
1994-95	Rogle	Sweden	22	4	6	10	18	....	....	....	....	....
1995-96	Farjestad	Sweden	39	11	15	26	36	8	0	4	4	6
1996-97	Farjestad	Sweden	49	12	21	33	58	14	9	5	14	14
1997-98	Farjestad	EuroHL	7	2	4	6	6	....	....	....	....	....
	Farjestad	Sweden	45	22	25	47	53	12	2	*9	11	12
	Sweden	Olympics	1	0	0	0	0	....	....	....	....	....

JONSSON, KENNY (YAWN-suhn) — NYI

Defense. Shoots left. 6'3", 195 lbs. Born, Angelholm, Sweden, October 6, 1974.
(Toronto's 1st choice, 12th overall, in 1993 Entry Draft).

			Regular Season					Playoffs				
Season	Club	Lea	GP	G	A	TP	PIM	GP	G	A	TP	PIM
1991-92	Rogle	Sweden-2	30	4	11	15	24	....	....	....	....	....
1992-93	Rogle	Sweden	39	3	10	13	42	....	....	....	....	....
1993-94	Rogle	Sweden	36	4	13	17	40	3	1	1	2	2
	Sweden	Olympics	3	1	0	1	0	....	....	....	....	....
1994-95	Rogle	Sweden	8	3	1	4	20	....	....	....	....	....
	Toronto	**NHL**	**39**	**2**	**7**	**9**	**16**	**4**	**0**	**0**	**0**	**0**
	St. John's	AHL	10	2	5	7	2	....	....	....	....	....
1995-96	**Toronto**	**NHL**	**50**	**4**	**22**	**26**	**22**	....	....	....	....	....
	NY Islanders	**NHL**	**16**	**0**	**4**	**4**	**10**	....	....	....	....	....
1996-97	**NY Islanders**	**NHL**	**81**	**3**	**18**	**21**	**24**	....	....	....	....	....
1997-98	**NY Islanders**	**NHL**	**81**	**14**	**26**	**40**	**58**	....	....	....	....	....
	NHL Totals		**267**	**23**	**77**	**100**	**130**	**4**	**0**	**0**	**0**	**0**

Swedish Rookie of the Year (1993) • NHL/Upper Deck All-Rookie Team (1995)

Traded to **NY Islanders** by **Toronto** with Sean Haggerty, Darby Hendrickson and Toronto's 1st round choice (Roberto Luongo) in 1997 Entry Draft for Wendel Clark, Mathieu Schneider and D.J. Smith, March 13, 1996.

JOSEPH, CHRIS — PHI.

Defense. Shoots right. 6'2", 202 lbs. Born, Burnaby, B.C., September 10, 1969.
(Pittsburgh's 1st choice, 5th overall, in 1987 Entry Draft).

			Regular Season					Playoffs				
Season	Club	Lea	GP	G	A	TP	PIM	GP	G	A	TP	PIM
1985-86	Seattle	WHL	72	4	8	12	50	5	0	3	3	12
1986-87	Seattle	WHL	67	13	45	58	155	....	....	....	....	....
1987-88	**Pittsburgh**	**NHL**	**17**	**0**	**4**	**4**	**12**	....	....	....	....	....
	Edmonton	**NHL**	**7**	**0**	**4**	**4**	**6**	....	....	....	....	....
	Seattle	WHL	23	5	14	19	49	....	....	....	....	....
	Nova Scotia	AHL	8	0	2	2	8	4	0	0	0	9
1988-89	**Edmonton**	**NHL**	**44**	**4**	**5**	**9**	**54**	....	....	....	....	....
	Cape Breton	AHL	5	1	1	2	18	....	....	....	....	....
1989-90	**Edmonton**	**NHL**	**4**	**0**	**2**	**2**	**2**	....	....	....	....	....
	Cape Breton	AHL	61	10	20	30	69	6	2	1	3	4
1990-91	**Edmonton**	**NHL**	**49**	**5**	**17**	**22**	**59**	....	....	....	....	....
1991-92	**Edmonton**	**NHL**	**7**	**0**	**0**	**0**	**8**	**5**	**1**	**3**	**4**	**2**
	Cape Breton	AHL	63	14	29	43	72	5	0	2	2	8
1992-93	**Edmonton**	**NHL**	**33**	**2**	**10**	**12**	**48**	....	....	....	....	....
1993-94	**Edmonton**	**NHL**	**10**	**1**	**1**	**2**	**28**	....	....	....	....	....
	Tampa Bay	**NHL**	**66**	**10**	**19**	**29**	**108**	....	....	....	....	....
1994-95	**Pittsburgh**	**NHL**	**33**	**5**	**10**	**15**	**46**	**10**	**1**	**1**	**2**	**12**
1995-96	**Pittsburgh**	**NHL**	**70**	**5**	**14**	**19**	**71**	**15**	**1**	**0**	**1**	**8**
1996-97	**Vancouver**	**NHL**	**63**	**3**	**13**	**16**	**62**	....	....	....	....	....
1997-98	**Philadelphia**	**NHL**	**15**	**1**	**0**	**1**	**19**	**1**	**0**	**0**	**0**	**2**
	Philadelphia	AHL	6	2	3	5	2	....	....	....	....	....
	NHL Totals		**418**	**36**	**99**	**135**	**523**	**31**	**3**	**4**	**7**	**24**

WHL West Second All-Star Team (1987)

Traded to **Edmonton** by **Pittsburgh** with Craig Simpson, Dave Hannan and Moe Mantha for Paul Coffey, Dave Hunter and Wayne Van Dorp, November 24, 1987. Traded to **Tampa Bay** by **Edmonton** for Bob Beers, November 11, 1993. Claimed by **Pittsburgh** from **Tampa Bay** in NHL Waiver Draft, January 18, 1995. Claimed by **Vancouver** from **Pittsburgh** in NHL Waiver Draft, September 30, 1996. Signed as a free agent by **Philadelphia**, September 11, 1997.

JOVANOVSKI, ED (joh-van-OHV-skee) — FLA.

Defense. Shoots left. 6'2", 210 lbs. Born, Windsor, Ont., June 26, 1976.
(Florida's 1st choice, 1st overall, in 1994 Entry Draft).

			Regular Season					Playoffs				
Season	Club	Lea	GP	G	A	TP	PIM	GP	G	A	TP	PIM
1993-94	Windsor	OHL	62	15	36	51	221	4	0	0	0	15
1994-95	Windsor	OHL	50	23	42	65	198	9	2	7	9	39
1995-96	**Florida**	**NHL**	**70**	**10**	**11**	**21**	**137**	**22**	**1**	**8**	**9**	**52**
1996-97	**Florida**	**NHL**	**61**	**7**	**16**	**23**	**172**	**5**	**0**	**0**	**0**	**4**
1997-98	**Florida**	**NHL**	**81**	**9**	**14**	**23**	**158**	....	....	....	....	....
	NHL Totals		**212**	**26**	**41**	**67**	**467**	**27**	**1**	**8**	**9**	**56**

OHL Second All-Star Team (1994) • OHL First All-Star Team (1995) • NHL All-Rookie Team (1996)

JUHLIN, PATRIK (ew-LEEN)

Left wing. Shoots left. 6', 194 lbs. Born, Huddinge, Sweden, April 24, 1970.
(Philadelphia's 2nd choice, 34th overall, in 1989 Entry Draft).

			Regular Season					Playoffs				
Season	Club	Lea	GP	G	A	TP	PIM	GP	G	A	TP	PIM
1988-89	Vasteras IK	Sweden-2	30	29	13	42	....	....	....	....	....	....
1989-90	Vasteras IK	Sweden	35	10	13	23	18	2	0	0	0	0
1990-91	Vasteras IK	Sweden	40	13	9	22	24	4	3	1	4	0
1991-92	Vasteras IK	Sweden	39	15	12	27	40	....	....	....	....	....
1992-93	Vasteras IK	Sweden	34	14	12	26	22	3	0	1	1	2
1993-94	Vasteras IK	Sweden	40	15	16	31	20	4	1	1	2	2
	Sweden	Olympics	8	7	1	8	16	....	....	....	....	....
1994-95	Vasteras IK	Sweden	11	5	9	14	8	....	....	....	....	....
	Philadelphia	**NHL**	**42**	**4**	**3**	**7**	**6**	**13**	**1**	**0**	**1**	**2**
1995-96	**Philadelphia**	**NHL**	**14**	**3**	**3**	**6**	**17**	....	....	....	....	....
	Hershey	AHL	14	5	2	7	8	1	0	0	0	0
1996-97	Philadelphia	AHL	78	31	60	91	24	9	7	6	13	4
1997-98	Jokerit	EuroHL	6	2	3	5	2	....	....	....	....	....
	Jokerit	Finland	47	19	9	28	14	7	5	0	5	4
	NHL Totals		**56**	**7**	**6**	**13**	**23**	**13**	**1**	**0**	**1**	**2**

AHL First All-Star Team (1997)

JUNEAU, JOE (ZHOO-noh, ZHOH-ay) — WSH.

Center. Shoots left. 6', 195 lbs. Born, Pont-Rouge, Que., January 5, 1968.
(Boston's 3rd choice, 81st overall, in 1988 Entry Draft).

			Regular Season					Playoffs				
Season	Club	Lea	GP	G	A	TP	PIM	GP	G	A	TP	PIM
1987-88	RPI	ECAC	31	16	29	45	18	....	....	....	....	....
1988-89	RPI	ECAC	30	12	23	35	40	....	....	....	....	....
1989-90	RPI	ECAC	34	18	*52	*70	31	....	....	....	....	....
	Canada	Nat-Tm	3	0	2	2	4	....	....	....	....	....
1990-91	RPI	ECAC	29	23	40	63	68	....	....	....	....	....
	Canada	Nat-Tm	7	2	3	5	0	....	....	....	....	....
1991-92	Canada	Nat-Tm	60	20	49	69	35	....	....	....	....	....
	Canada	Olympics	8	6	9	15	4	....	....	....	....	....
	Boston	**NHL**	**14**	**5**	**14**	**19**	**4**	**15**	**4**	**8**	**12**	**21**
1992-93	**Boston**	**NHL**	**84**	**32**	**70**	**102**	**33**	**4**	**2**	**4**	**6**	**6**
1993-94	**Boston**	**NHL**	**63**	**14**	**58**	**72**	**35**	....	....	....	....	....
	Washington	**NHL**	**11**	**5**	**8**	**13**	**6**	**11**	**4**	**5**	**9**	**6**
1994-95	**Washington**	**NHL**	**44**	**5**	**38**	**43**	**8**	**7**	**2**	**6**	**8**	**2**
1995-96	**Washington**	**NHL**	**80**	**14**	**50**	**64**	**30**	**5**	**0**	**7**	**7**	**6**
1996-97	**Washington**	**NHL**	**58**	**15**	**27**	**42**	**8**	....	....	....	....	....
1997-98	**Washington**	**NHL**	**56**	**9**	**22**	**31**	**26**	**21**	**7**	**10**	**17**	**8**
	NHL Totals		**410**	**99**	**287**	**386**	**150**	**63**	**19**	**40**	**59**	**49**

NCAA East First All-American Team (1990) • ECAC Second All-Star Team (1991) • NCAA East Second All-American Team (1991) • NHL/Upper Deck All-Rookie Team (1993)

Traded to **Washington** by **Boston** for Al Iafrate, March 21, 1994.

KABERLE, TOMAS (ka-buhr-LAY) — TOR.

Defense. Shoots left. 6'1", 195 lbs. Born, Rakovnik, Czech., March 2, 1978.
(Toronto's 13th choice, 204th overall, in 1996 Entry Draft).

			Regular Season					Playoffs				
Season	Club	Lea	GP	G	A	TP	PIM	GP	G	A	TP	PIM
1995-96	Poldi Kladno	Czech-Jr.	23	6	13	19	....	....	....	....	....	....
	Poldi Kladno	Cze-Rep.	23	0	1	1	2	2	0	0	0	0
1996-97	Poldi Kladno	Cze-Rep.	49	0	5	5	26	3	0	0	0	0
1997-98	Poldi Kladno	Cze-Rep.	47	4	19	23	12	....	....	....	....	....
	St. John's	AHL	2	0	0	0	0	....	....	....	....	....

KALININ, DMITRI — BUF.

Defense. Shoots left. 6'2", 198 lbs. Born, Chelyabinsk, USSR, July 22, 1980.
(Buffalo's 1st choice, 18th overall, in 1998 Entry Draft).

			Regular Season					Playoffs				
Season	Club	Lea	GP	G	A	TP	PIM	GP	G	A	TP	PIM
1995-96	Chelyabinsk	Rus-Jr.	30	10	10	20	60	....	....	....	....	....
	Chelyabinsk	Russia-2	20	0	3	3	10	....	....	....	....	....
1996-97	Chelyabinsk	Russia	2	0	0	0	0	2	0	0	0	0
	Chelyabinsk 2	Russia-3	20	0	0	0	10	....	....	....	....	....
1997-98	Chelyabinsk	Russia	26	0	2	2	24	....	....	....	....	....

KALLARSSON, TOMI (KAL-ahr-suhn) — NYR

Defense. Shoots left. 6'3", 194 lbs. Born, Lempaala, Finland, March 15, 1979.
(NY Rangers' 4th choice, 93rd overall, in 1997 Entry Draft).

			Regular Season					Playoffs				
Season	Club	Lea	GP	G	A	TP	PIM	GP	G	A	TP	PIM
1996-97	Hameelinna	Fin-Jr.	31	1	3	4	26	....	....	....	....	....
1997-98	Hameelinna	Finland	12	0	0	0	2	....	....	....	....	....

KALLIO, TOMI (KAL-ee-oh) — COL.

Left wing. Shoots left. 6'1", 176 lbs. Born, Turku, Finland, January 27, 1977.
(Colorado's 4th choice, 81st overall, in 1995 Entry Draft).

			Regular Season					Playoffs				
Season	Club	Lea	GP	G	A	TP	PIM	GP	G	A	TP	PIM
1994-95	TPS Turku	Fin-Jr.	14	5	12	17	24	....	....	....	....	....
	Kiekko	Finland-2	25	8	5	13	16	7	3	1	4	6
1995-96	TPS Turku	Fin-Jr.	8	8	3	11	14	....	....	....	....	....
	Kiekko	Finland-2	29	10	11	21	28	....	....	....	....	....
	TPS Turku	Finland	8	2	3	5	10	4	0	0	0	2
1996-97	TPS Turku	Finland	47	9	10	19	18	8	2	0	2	2
1997-98	TPS Turku	EuroHL	6	0	1	1	2	....	....	....	....	....
	TPS Turku	Finland	47	10	10	20	8	4	0	2	2	0

KALMIKOV, KONSTANTIN (kahl-mih-KAHV) — TOR.

Left wing. Shoots right. 6'4", 205 lbs. Born, Kharkov, USSR, June 14, 1978.
(Toronto's 4th choice, 68th overall, in 1996 Entry Draft).

			Regular Season					Playoffs				
Season	Club	Lea	GP	G	A	TP	PIM	GP	G	A	TP	PIM
1994-95	Druzhba-78	Midget	65	51	55	106	45	....	....	....	....	....
1995-96	Flint	ColHL	38	4	12	16	16	....	....	....	....	....
	Detroit	ColHL	5	0	1	1	0	....	....	....	....	....
1996-97	Sudbury	OHL	66	22	34	56	25	....	....	....	....	....
	St. John's	AHL	2	0	0	0	0	....	....	....	....	....
1997-98	Sudbury	OHL	66	32	32	64	21	10	7	2	9	2

KAMENSKY, VALERI (kah-MEHN-skee) — COL.

Left wing. Shoots right. 6'2", 198 lbs. Born, Voskresensk, USSR, April 18, 1966.
(Quebec's 8th choice, 129th overall, in 1988 Entry Draft).

			Regular Season					Playoffs				
Season	Club	Lea	GP	G	A	TP	PIM	GP	G	A	TP	PIM
1982-83	Khimik	USSR	5	0	0	0	0	....	....	....	....	....
1983-84	Khimik	USSR	20	2	2	4	6	....	....	....	....	....
1984-85	Khimik	USSR	45	9	3	12	24	....	....	....	....	....
1985-86	CSKA Moscow	USSR	40	15	9	24	8	....	....	....	....	....
1986-87	CSKA Moscow	USSR	37	13	8	21	16	....	....	....	....	....
1987-88	CSKA Moscow	USSR	51	26	20	46	40	....	....	....	....	....
	Soviet Union	Olympics	8	4	2	6	4	....	....	....	....	....
1988-89	CSKA Moscow	USSR	40	18	10	28	30	....	....	....	....	....
1989-90	CSKA Moscow	USSR	45	19	18	37	40	....	....	....	....	....
1990-91	CSKA Moscow	USSR	46	20	26	46	66	....	....	....	....	....
1991-92	**Quebec**	**NHL**	**23**	**7**	**14**	**21**	**14**	....	....	....	....	....
1992-93	**Quebec**	**NHL**	**32**	**15**	**22**	**37**	**14**	**6**	**0**	**1**	**1**	**6**
1993-94	**Quebec**	**NHL**	**76**	**28**	**37**	**65**	**42**	....	....	....	....	....
1994-95	Ambri	Switz.	12	13	6	19	2	....	....	....	....	....
	Quebec	**NHL**	**40**	**10**	**20**	**30**	**22**	**2**	**1**	**0**	**1**	**0**
1995-96	**Colorado**	**NHL**	**81**	**38**	**47**	**85**	**85**	**22**	**10**	**12**	**22**	**28** ♦
1996-97	**Colorado**	**NHL**	**68**	**28**	**38**	**66**	**38**	**17**	**8**	**14**	**22**	**16**
1997-98	**Colorado**	**NHL**	**75**	**26**	**40**	**66**	**60**	**7**	**2**	**3**	**5**	**18**
	Russia	Olympics	6	1	2	3	0	....	....	....	....	....
	NHL Totals		**395**	**152**	**218**	**370**	**275**	**54**	**21**	**30**	**51**	**68**

USSR First All-Star Team (1990, 1991) • USSR Player of the Year (1991)

Played in NHL All-Star Game (1998)

Transferred to **Colorado** after **Quebec** franchise relocated, June 21, 1995.

KAMINSKI, ERIK (kay-MIHN-skee) — OTT.

Right wing. Shoots right. 6'3", 205 lbs. Born, Hudson, OH, March 23, 1976.
(Ottawa's 9th choice, 231st overall, in 1995 Entry Draft).

			Regular Season					Playoffs				
Season	Club	Lea	GP	G	A	TP	PIM	GP	G	A	TP	PIM
1994-95	Cleveland	NAJHL	42	34	33	67	99	....	....	....	....	....
1995-96	Northeastern	H.E.	34	5	8	13	30	....	....	....	....	....
1996-97	Northeastern	H.E.	34	11	7	18	30	....	....	....	....	....
1997-98	Winston-Salem	UHL	3	0	0	0	0	....	....	....	....	....
	Brantford	UHL	21	3	3	6	11	6	1	0	1	2

KAMINSKI, KEVIN (kah-MIHN-skee)

Center. Shoots left. 5'10", 190 lbs. Born, Churchbridge, Sask., March 13, 1969.
(Minnesota's 3rd choice, 48th overall, in 1987 Entry Draft).

			Regular Season					Playoffs				
Season	Club	Lea	GP	G	A	TP	PIM	GP	G	A	TP	PIM
1986-87	Saskatoon	WHL	67	26	44	70	325	11	5	6	11	45
1987-88	Saskatoon	WHL	55	38	61	99	247	10	5	7	12	37
1988-89	Saskatoon	WHL	52	25	43	68	199	8	4	9	13	25
	Minnesota	**NHL**	**1**	**0**	**0**	**0**	**0**	....	....	....	....	....
1989-90	**Quebec**	**NHL**	**1**	**0**	**0**	**0**	**0**	....	....	....	....	....
	Halifax	AHL	19	3	4	7	128	2	0	0	0	5
1990-91	Halifax	AHL	7	1	0	1	44	....	....	....	....	....
	Fort Wayne	IHL	56	9	15	24	*455	19	4	2	6	*169
1991-92	**Quebec**	**NHL**	**5**	**0**	**0**	**0**	**45**	....	....	....	....	....
	Halifax	AHL	63	18	27	45	329	....	....	....	....	....
1992-93	Halifax	AHL	79	27	37	64	*345	....	....	....	....	....
1993-94	**Washington**	**NHL**	**13**	**0**	**5**	**5**	**87**	....	....	....	....	....
	Portland	AHL	39	10	22	32	263	16	4	5	9	*91
1994-95	**Washington**	**NHL**	**27**	**1**	**1**	**2**	**102**	**5**	**0**	**0**	**0**	**36**
	Portland	AHL	34	15	20	35	292	....	....	....	....	....
1995-96	**Washington**	**NHL**	**54**	**1**	**2**	**3**	**164**	**3**	**0**	**0**	**0**	**16**
1996-97	**Washington**	**NHL**	**38**	**1**	**2**	**3**	**130**	....	....	....	....	....
1997-98	Portland	AHL	40	8	12	20	242	8	2	1	3	69
	NHL Totals		**139**	**3**	**10**	**13**	**528**	**8**	**0**	**0**	**0**	**52**

Traded to **Quebec** by **Minnesota** for Gaetan Duchesne, June 19, 1989. Traded to **Washington** by **Quebec** for Mark Matier, June 15, 1993.

KAMINSKY, YAN (kah-MIHN-skee)

Right wing. Shoots left. 6'1", 176 lbs. Born, Penza, USSR, July 28, 1971.
(Winnipeg's 4th choice, 99th overall, in 1991 Entry Draft).

			Regular Season					Playoffs				
Season	Club	Lea	GP	G	A	TP	PIM	GP	G	A	TP	PIM
1989-90	Moscow D'amo	USSR	6	1	0	1	4	....	....	....	....	....
1990-91	Moscow D'amo	USSR	25	10	5	15	2	....	....	....	....	....
1991-92	Moscow D'amo	CIS	42	9	7	16	22	....	....	....	....	....
1992-93	Moscow D'amo	CIS	39	15	14	29	12	10	2	5	7	8
1993-94	**Winnipeg**	**NHL**	**1**	**0**	**0**	**0**	**0**	....	....	....	....	....
	Moncton	AHL	33	9	13	22	6	....	....	....	....	....
	NY Islanders	**NHL**	**23**	**2**	**1**	**3**	**4**	**2**	**0**	**0**	**0**	**4**
1994-95	Denver	IHL	38	17	16	33	14	15	6	6	12	0
	NY Islanders	**NHL**	**2**	**1**	**1**	**2**	**0**	....	....	....	....	....
1995-96	Utah	IHL	16	3	3	6	8	21	3	5	8	4
1996-97	Utah	IHL	77	28	27	55	18	7	1	4	5	0
1997-98	Lukko Rauma	Finland	38	5	8	13	33	....	....	....	....	....
	NHL Totals		**26**	**3**	**2**	**5**	**4**	**2**	**0**	**0**	**0**	**4**

Traded to **NY Islanders** by **Winnipeg** for Wayne McBean, February 1, 1994.

KANE, BOYD — NYR

Left wing. Shoots left. 6'1", 207 lbs. Born, Swift Current, Sask., April 18, 1978.
(Pittsburgh's 4th choice, 114th overall, in 1998 Entry Draft).

			Regular Season					Playoffs				
Season	Club	Lea	GP	G	A	TP	PIM	GP	G	A	TP	PIM
1994-95	Regina	WHL	25	6	5	11	6	4	0	0	0	0
1995-96	Regina	WHL	72	21	42	63	155	11	5	7	12	12
1996-97	Regina	WHL	66	25	50	75	154	5	1	1	2	15
1997-98	Regina	WHL	68	48	45	93	133	9	5	7	12	29

• Re-entered NHL draft. Originally Pittsburgh's 3rd choice, 72nd overall, in 1996 Entry Draft.

KAPANEN, NIKO (KA-pah-nehn) — DAL.

Center. Shoots left. 5'9", 180 lbs. Born, Hattula, Finland, April 29, 1978.
(Dallas' 5th choice, 173rd overall, in 1998 Entry Draft).

			Regular Season					Playoffs				
Season	Club	Lea	GP	G	A	TP	PIM	GP	G	A	TP	PIM
1993-94	Hameenlinna	Fin-Jr.	31	17	33	50	34	....	....	....	....	....
1994-95	Hameenlinna	Fin-Jr.	37	19	44	63	40	....	....	....	....	....
1995-96	Hameenlinna	Fin-Jr.	26	15	22	37	34	....	....	....	....	....
	Hameenlinna	Finland	7	1	0	1	0	....	....	....	....	....
1996-97	Hameenlinna	Finland	41	6	9	15	12	10	4	5	9	2
	Hameenlinna	Fin-Jr.	5	1	7	8	2	2	0	1	1	2
1997-98	Hameenlinna	Finland	48	8	18	26	44	....	....	....	....	....
	Hameenlinna	Fin-Jr.	2	1	1	2	0	....	....	....	....	....

KAPANEN, SAMI (KA-pah-nehn) — CAR.

Left wing. Shoots left. 5'10", 170 lbs. Born, Vantaa, Finland, June 14, 1973.
(Hartford's 4th choice, 87th overall, in 1995 Entry Draft).

			Regular Season					Playoffs				
Season	Club	Lea	GP	G	A	TP	PIM	GP	G	A	TP	PIM
1990-91	KalPa	Finland	14	1	2	3	2	8	2	1	3	2
1991-92	KalPa	Finland	42	15	10	25	8	....	....	....	....	....
1992-93	KalPa	Finland	37	4	17	21	12	....	....	....	....	....
1993-94	KalPa	Finland	48	23	32	55	16	....	....	....	....	....
	Finland	Olympics	8	1	0	1	2	....	....	....	....	....
1994-95	Helsinki	Finland	49	14	28	42	42	3	0	0	0	0
1995-96	**Hartford**	**NHL**	**35**	**5**	**4**	**9**	**6**	....	....	....	....	....
	Springfield	AHL	28	14	17	31	4	3	1	2	3	0
1996-97	**Hartford**	**NHL**	**45**	**13**	**12**	**25**	**2**	....	....	....	....	....
1997-98	**Carolina**	**NHL**	**81**	**26**	**37**	**63**	**16**	....	....	....	....	....
	Finland	Olympics	6	0	1	1	0	....	....	....	....	....
	NHL Totals		**161**	**44**	**53**	**97**	**24**	....	....	....	....	....

Finnish First All-Star Team (1994)

Transferred to **Carolina** after **Hartford** franchise relocated, June 25, 1997.

KARALAHTI, JERE (kar-ah-LAHKH-tee, YEH-reh) — L.A.

Defense. Shoots right. 6'2", 210 lbs. Born, Helsinki, Finland, March 25, 1975.
(Los Angeles' 7th choice, 146th overall, in 1993 Entry Draft).

			Regular Season					Playoffs				
Season	Club	Lea	GP	G	A	TP	PIM	GP	G	A	TP	PIM
1993-94	Helsinki	Finland	46	1	10	11	36	3	0	0	0	6
1994-95	Helsinki	Finland	37	1	7	8	42	3	0	0	0	0
1995-96	Helsinki	Finland	36	4	6	10	102	3	0	0	0	4
1996-97	Helsinki	Finland	18	3	5	8	20	....	....	....	....	....
1997-98	Helsinki	Finland	43	14	16	30	32	9	2	0	2	8

KARIYA, PAUL (kah-REE-ah) ANA.

Left wing. Shoots left. 5'11", 180 lbs. Born, Vancouver, B.C., October 16, 1974.
(Anaheim's 1st choice, 4th overall, in 1993 Entry Draft).

			Regular Season					Playoffs				
Season	Club	Lea	GP	G	A	TP	PIM	GP	G	A	TP	PIM
1990-91	Penticton	BCJHL	54	45	67	112	8	....	....	....	....	....
1991-92	Penticton	BCJHL	40	46	86	132	18	....	....	....	....	....
1992-93	U. of Maine	H.E.	36	24	*69	*93	12	....	....	....	....	....
1993-94	U. of Maine	H.E.	12	8	16	24	4	....	....	....	....	....
	Canada	Nat-Tm	23	7	34	41	2	....	....	....	....	....
	Canada	Olympics	8	3	4	7	2	....	....	....	....	....
1994-95	**Anaheim**	**NHL**	**47**	**18**	**21**	**39**	**4**	....	....	....	....	....
1995-96	**Anaheim**	**NHL**	**82**	**50**	**58**	**108**	**20**	....	....	....	....	....
1996-97	**Anaheim**	**NHL**	**69**	**44**	**55**	**99**	**6**	**11**	**7**	**6**	**13**	**4**
1997-98	**Anaheim**	**NHL**	**22**	**17**	**14**	**31**	**23**	....	....	....	....	....
	NHL Totals		**220**	**129**	**148**	**277**	**53**	**11**	**7**	**6**	**13**	**4**

• Hockey East First All-Star Team (1993) • NCAA East First All-American Team (1993) • NCAA Championship All-Tournament Team (1993) • Won Hobey Baker Memorial Award (Top U.S. Collegiate Player) (1993) • NHL/Upper Deck All-Rookie Team (1995) • NHL First All-Star Team (1996, 1997) • Won Lady Byng Trophy (1996, 1997)

Played in NHL All-Star Game (1996, 1997)

KARLIN, MATTIAS (KAR-lihn) BOS.

Center/right wing. Shoots left. 5'11", 183 lbs. Born, Ornskoldsvik, Sweden, July 4, 1979.
(Boston's 4th choice, 54th overall, in 1997 Entry Draft).

			Regular Season					Playoffs				
Season	Club	Lea	GP	G	A	TP	PIM	GP	G	A	TP	PIM
1995-96	MoDo	Swe-Jr.	30	12	23	35	16	....	....	....	....	....
1996-97	MoDo	Swe-Jr.	STATISTICS NOT AVAILABLE									
	MoDo	Sweden	6	0	0	0	0	....	....	....	....	....
1997-98	MoDo	Sweden	32	0	2	2	8	1	0	0	0	0

KARLSSON, ANDREAS CGY.

Center. Shoots left. 6'2", 180 lbs. Born, Leksand, Sweden, August 19, 1975.
(Calgary's 8th choice, 148th overall, in 1993 Entry Draft).

			Regular Season					Playoffs				
Season	Club	Lea	GP	G	A	TP	PIM	GP	G	A	TP	PIM
1992-93	Leksand IF	Sweden	13	0	0	0	6	....	....	....	....	....
1993-94	Leksand IF	Sweden	21	0	0	0	10	3	0	0	0	0
1994-95	Leksand IF	Sweden	24	7	8	15	0	4	0	1	1	0
1995-96	Leksand IF	Sweden	40	10	13	23	10	....	....	....	....	....
1996-97	Leksand IF	Sweden	49	13	11	24	39	9	2	0	2	2
1997-98	Leksand IF	EuroHL	6	2	3	5	2	....	....	....	....	....
	Leksand IF	Sweden	33	9	14	23	20	4	1	0	1	0

KARLSSON, GABRIEL DAL.

Center. Shoots left. 6'1", 189 lbs. Born, Borlange, Sweden, January 22, 1980.
(Dallas' 3rd choice, 86th overall, in 1998 Entry Draft).

			Regular Season					Playoffs				
Season	Club	Lea	GP	G	A	TP	PIM	GP	G	A	TP	PIM
1996-97	HV 71 Jonkoping	Swe-Jr.	25	7	9	16	....	....	....	....	....	....
1997-98	HV 71 Jonkoping	Swe-Jr.	27	11	15	26	32	....	....	....	....	....
	HV 71 Jonkoping	Sweden	1	0	0	0	0	....	....	....	....	....

KARPA, DAVE (KAHR-puh) CAR.

Defense. Shoots right. 6'1", 210 lbs. Born, Regina, Sask., May 7, 1971.
(Quebec's 4th choice, 68th overall, in 1991 Entry Draft).

			Regular Season					Playoffs				
Season	Club	Lea	GP	G	A	TP	PIM	GP	G	A	TP	PIM
1990-91	Ferris State	CCHA	41	6	19	25	109	....	....	....	....	....
1991-92	Ferris State	CCHA	34	7	12	19	124	....	....	....	....	....
	Quebec	**NHL**	**4**	**0**	**0**	**0**	**14**	....	....	....	....	....
	Halifax	AHL	2	0	0	0	4	....	....	....	....	....
1992-93	**Quebec**	**NHL**	**12**	**0**	**1**	**1**	**13**	**3**	**0**	**0**	**0**	**0**
	Halifax	AHL	71	4	27	31	167	....	....	....	....	....
1993-94	**Quebec**	**NHL**	**60**	**5**	**12**	**17**	**148**	....	....	....	....	....
	Cornwall	AHL	1	0	0	0	0	12	2	2	4	27
1994-95	**Quebec**	**NHL**	**2**	**0**	**0**	**0**	**0**	....	....	....	....	....
	Cornwall	AHL	6	0	2	2	19	....	....	....	....	....
	Anaheim	**NHL**	**26**	**1**	**5**	**6**	**91**	....	....	....	....	....
1995-96	**Anaheim**	**NHL**	**72**	**3**	**16**	**19**	**270**	....	....	....	....	....
1996-97	**Anaheim**	**NHL**	**69**	**2**	**11**	**13**	**210**	**8**	**1**	**1**	**2**	**20**
1997-98	**Anaheim**	**NHL**	**78**	**1**	**11**	**12**	**217**	....	....	....	....	....
	NHL Totals		**323**	**12**	**56**	**68**	**963**	**11**	**1**	**1**	**2**	**20**

Traded to **Anaheim** by **Quebec** for Anaheim's 4th round choice (later traded to St. Louis — St. Louis selected Jan Horacek) in 1997 Entry Draft, March 9, 1995. Traded to **Carolina** by **Anaheim** with a 4th round choice in 2000 Entry Draft for Stu Grimson and Kevin Haller, August 11, 1998.

KARPOVTSEV, ALEXANDER (kar-POHV-tzehv) NYR

Defense. Shoots right. 6'1", 205 lbs. Born, Moscow, USSR, April 7, 1970.
(Quebec's 7th choice, 158th overall, in 1990 Entry Draft).

			Regular Season					Playoffs				
Season	Club	Lea	GP	G	A	TP	PIM	GP	G	A	TP	PIM
1989-90	Moscow D'amo	USSR	35	1	1	2	27	....	....	....	....	....
1990-91	Moscow D'amo	USSR	40	0	5	5	15	....	....	....	....	....
1991-92	Moscow D'amo	CIS	35	4	2	6	26	....	....	....	....	....
1992-93	Moscow D'amo	CIS	36	3	11	14	100	7	2	1	3	0
1993-94	**NY Rangers**	**NHL**	**67**	**3**	**15**	**18**	**58**	**17**	**0**	**4**	**4**	**12** ♦
1994-95	Moscow D'amo	CIS	13	0	2	2	10	....	....	....	....	....
	NY Rangers	**NHL**	**47**	**4**	**8**	**12**	**30**	**8**	**1**	**0**	**1**	**0**
1995-96	**NY Rangers**	**NHL**	**40**	**2**	**16**	**18**	**26**	**6**	**0**	**1**	**1**	**4**
1996-97	**NY Rangers**	**NHL**	**77**	**9**	**29**	**38**	**59**	**13**	**1**	**3**	**4**	**20**
1997-98	**NY Rangers**	**NHL**	**47**	**3**	**7**	**10**	**38**	....	....	....	....	....
	NHL Totals		**278**	**21**	**75**	**96**	**211**	**44**	**2**	**8**	**10**	**36**

Traded to **NY Rangers** by **Quebec** for Mike Hurlbut, September 7, 1993.

KASPARAITIS, DARIUS (KAZ-puhr-IGH-tihz) PIT.

Defense. Shoots left. 5'11", 209 lbs. Born, Elektrenai, USSR, October 16, 1972.
(NY Islanders' 1st choice, 5th overall, in 1992 Entry Draft).

			Regular Season					Playoffs				
Season	Club	Lea	GP	G	A	TP	PIM	GP	G	A	TP	PIM
1988-89	Moscow D'amo	USSR	3	0	0	0	0	....	....	....	....	....
1989-90	Moscow D'amo	USSR	1	0	0	0	0	....	....	....	....	....
1990-91	Moscow D'amo	USSR	17	0	1	1	10	....	....	....	....	....
1991-92	Moscow D'amo	CIS	31	2	10	12	14	....	....	....	....	....
1992-93	Moscow D'amo	CIS	7	1	3	4	8	....	....	....	....	....
	NY Islanders	**NHL**	**79**	**4**	**17**	**21**	**166**	**18**	**0**	**5**	**5**	**31**
1993-94	**NY Islanders**	**NHL**	**76**	**1**	**10**	**11**	**142**	**4**	**0**	**0**	**0**	**8**
1994-95	**NY Islanders**	**NHL**	**13**	**0**	**1**	**1**	**22**	....	....	....	....	....
1995-96	**NY Islanders**	**NHL**	**46**	**1**	**7**	**8**	**93**	....	....	....	....	....
1996-97	**NY Islanders**	**NHL**	**18**	**0**	**5**	**5**	**16**	....	....	....	....	....
	Pittsburgh	**NHL**	**57**	**2**	**16**	**18**	**84**	**5**	**0**	**0**	**0**	**6**
1997-98	**Pittsburgh**	**NHL**	**81**	**4**	**8**	**12**	**127**	**5**	**0**	**0**	**0**	**8**
	Russia	Olympics	6	0	2	2	6	....	....	....	....	....
	NHL Totals		**370**	**12**	**64**	**76**	**650**	**32**	**0**	**5**	**5**	**53**

Traded to **Pittsburgh** by **NY Islanders** with Andreas Johansson for Bryan Smolinski, November 17, 1996.

KATCHER, JEFF L.A.

Defense. Shoots right. 6'4", 188 lbs. Born, Winnipeg, Man., April 16, 1979.
(Los Angeles' 7th choice, 150th overall, in 1997 Entry Draft).

			Regular Season					Playoffs				
Season	Club	Lea	GP	G	A	TP	PIM	GP	G	A	TP	PIM
1996-97	Brandon	WHL	48	2	2	4	31	....	....	....	....	....
1997-98	Brandon	WHL	9	0	0	0	13	....	....	....	....	....
	Tri-City	WHL	54	1	12	13	104	....	....	....	....	....

KAUPPINEN, MARKO (KOW-pih-nehn) PHI.

Defense. Shoots left. 6', 178 lbs. Born, Mikkeli, Finland, March 23, 1979.
(Philadelphia's 7th choice, 214th overall, in 1997 Entry Draft).

			Regular Season					Playoffs				
Season	Club	Lea	GP	G	A	TP	PIM	GP	G	A	TP	PIM
1996-97	JyP HT	Fin-Jr.	29	2	3	5	14	7	0	0	0	29
1997-98	JyP HT	Fin-Jr.	16	2	4	6	16	....	....	....	....	....
	JyP HT	Finland	33	2	6	8	26	....	....	....	....	....

KAVANAGH, PAT (KA-vuh-naw) PHI.

Right wing. Shoots right. 6'3", 192 lbs. Born, Ottawa, Ont., March 14, 1979.
(Philadelphia's 2nd choice, 50th overall, in 1997 Entry Draft).

			Regular Season					Playoffs				
Season	Club	Lea	GP	G	A	TP	PIM	GP	G	A	TP	PIM
1996-97	Peterborough	OHL	43	6	8	14	53	11	1	1	2	12
1997-98	Peterborough	OHL	66	10	16	26	85	4	1	0	1	6

KAZAKEVICH, MIKHAIL (kah-zak-KAY-vihch) PIT.

Left wing. Shoots left. 6'1", 187 lbs. Born, Murmansk, USSR, January 14, 1976.
(Pittsburgh's 13th choice, 258th overall, in 1994 Entry Draft).

			Regular Season					Playoffs				
Season	Club	Lea	GP	G	A	TP	PIM	GP	G	A	TP	PIM
1992-93	Yaroslavl	CIS	7	0	1	1	0	3	0	0	0	0
1993-94	Yaroslavl	CIS	4	0	0	0	2	....	....	....	....	....
1994-95	Yaroslavl	CIS	11	1	3	4	2	....	....	....	....	....
1995-96	Moncton	QMJHL	41	7	13	20	16	....	....	....	....	....
	Shawinigan	QMJHL	14	1	3	4	8	4	0	1	1	2
1996-97	Khimik	Russia	1	0	0	0	0	....	....	....	....	....
1997-98	Saratov	Russia	10	0	1	1	8	....	....	....	....	....

KEALTY, JEFF COL.

Defense. Shoots left. 6'4", 175 lbs. Born, Boston, MA, April 9, 1976.
(Quebec's 2nd choice, 22nd overall, in 1994 Entry Draft).

			Regular Season					Playoffs				
Season	Club	Lea	GP	G	A	TP	PIM	GP	G	A	TP	PIM
1993-94	Catholic Memorial	H.S.	25	10	22	32	....	....	....	....	....	....
1994-95	Boston University	H.E.	25	0	5	5	29	....	....	....	....	....
1995-96	Boston University	H.E.	35	4	14	18	38	....	....	....	....	....
1996-97	Boston University	H.E.	40	4	9	13	42	....	....	....	....	....
1997-98	Boston University	H.E.	38	11	15	26	53	....	....	....	....	....

KEANE, MIKE DAL.

Right wing. Shoots right. 6', 185 lbs. Born, Winnipeg, Man., May 29, 1967.

			Regular Season					Playoffs				
Season	Club	Lea	GP	G	A	TP	PIM	GP	G	A	TP	PIM
1984-85	Moose Jaw	WHL	65	17	26	43	141	....	....	....	....	....
1985-86	Moose Jaw	WHL	67	34	49	83	162	13	6	8	14	9
1986-87	Moose Jaw	WHL	53	25	45	70	107	9	3	9	12	11
	Sherbrooke	AHL	....	....	....	....	....	9	2	2	4	16
1987-88	Sherbrooke	AHL	78	25	43	68	70	6	1	1	2	18
1988-89	**Montreal**	**NHL**	**69**	**16**	**19**	**35**	**69**	**21**	**4**	**3**	**7**	**17**
1989-90	**Montreal**	**NHL**	**74**	**9**	**15**	**24**	**78**	**11**	**0**	**1**	**1**	**8**
1990-91	**Montreal**	**NHL**	**73**	**13**	**23**	**36**	**50**	**12**	**3**	**2**	**5**	**6**
1991-92	**Montreal**	**NHL**	**67**	**11**	**30**	**41**	**64**	**8**	**1**	**1**	**2**	**16**
1992-93	**Montreal**	**NHL**	**77**	**15**	**45**	**60**	**95**	**19**	**2**	**13**	**15**	**6** ♦
1993-94	**Montreal**	**NHL**	**80**	**16**	**30**	**46**	**119**	**6**	**3**	**1**	**4**	**4**
1994-95	**Montreal**	**NHL**	**48**	**10**	**10**	**20**	**15**	....	....	....	....	....
1995-96	**Montreal**	**NHL**	**18**	**0**	**7**	**7**	**6**	....	....	....	....	....
	Colorado	**NHL**	**55**	**10**	**10**	**20**	**40**	**22**	**3**	**2**	**5**	**16** ♦
1996-97	**Colorado**	**NHL**	**81**	**10**	**17**	**27**	**63**	**17**	**3**	**1**	**4**	**24**
1997-98	**NY Rangers**	**NHL**	**70**	**8**	**10**	**18**	**47**	....	....	....	....	....
	Dallas	**NHL**	**13**	**2**	**3**	**5**	**5**	**17**	**4**	**4**	**8**	**0**
	NHL Totals		**725**	**120**	**219**	**339**	**651**	**133**	**23**	**28**	**51**	**97**

Signed as a free agent by **Montreal**, September 25, 1985. Traded to **Colorado** by **Montreal** with Patrick Roy for Andrei Kovalenko, Martin Rucinsky and Jocelyn Thibault, December 6, 1995. Signed as a free agent by **NY Rangers**, July 30, 1997. Traded to **Dallas** by **NY Rangers** with Brian Skrudland and NY Rangers' 6th round choice (Pavel Patera) in 1998 Entry Draft for Todd Harvey, Bob Errey and Dallas' 4th round choice (Boyd Kane) in 1998 Entry Draft, March 24, 1998.

KECZMER, DAN (KEHS-muhr) DAL.

Defense. Shoots left. 6'1", 190 lbs. Born, Mt. Clemens, MI, May 25, 1968.
(Minnesota's 11th choice, 201st overall, in 1986 Entry Draft).

			Regular Season					Playoffs				
Season	**Club**	**Lea**	**GP**	**G**	**A**	**TP**	**PIM**	**GP**	**G**	**A**	**TP**	**PIM**
1985-86	Detroit	NAJHL	65	6	48	54	116	....	....	....	....	....
1986-87	Lake Superior	CCHA	38	3	5	8	26	....	....	....	....	....
1987-88	Lake Superior	CCHA	41	2	15	17	34	....	....	....	....	....
1988-89	Lake Superior	CCHA	46	3	26	29	68	....	....	....	....	....
1989-90	Lake Superior	CCHA	43	13	23	36	48	....	....	....	....	....
1990-91	**Minnesota**	**NHL**	**9**	**0**	**1**	**1**	**6**	....	....	....	....	....
	Kalamazoo	IHL	60	4	20	24	60	9	1	2	3	10
1991-92	United States	Nat-Tm	51	3	11	14	56	....	....	....	....	....
	Hartford	**NHL**	**1**	**0**	**0**	**0**	**0**	....	....	....	....	....
	Springfield	AHL	18	3	4	7	10	4	0	0	0	6
1992-93	**Hartford**	**NHL**	**23**	**4**	**4**	**8**	**28**	....	....	....	....	....
	Springfield	AHL	37	1	13	14	38	12	0	4	4	14
1993-94	**Hartford**	**NHL**	**12**	**0**	**1**	**1**	**12**	....	....	....	....	....
	Springfield	AHL	7	0	1	1	4	....	....	....	....	....
	Calgary	**NHL**	**57**	**1**	**20**	**21**	**48**	**3**	**0**	**0**	**0**	**4**
1994-95	**Calgary**	**NHL**	**28**	**2**	**3**	**5**	**10**	**7**	**0**	**1**	**1**	**2**
1995-96	**Calgary**	**NHL**	**13**	**0**	**0**	**0**	**14**	....	....	....	....	....
	Saint John	AHL	22	3	11	14	14	....	....	....	....	....
	Albany	AHL	17	0	4	4	4	1	0	0	0	0
1996-97	**Dallas**	**NHL**	**13**	**0**	**1**	**1**	**6**	....	....	....	....	....
	Michigan	IHL	42	3	17	20	24	....	....	....	....	....
1997-98	**Dallas**	**NHL**	**17**	**1**	**2**	**3**	**26**	**2**	**0**	**0**	**0**	**2**
	Michigan	IHL	44	1	11	12	29	....	....	....	....	....
	NHL Totals		**173**	**8**	**32**	**40**	**150**	**12**	**0**	**1**	**1**	**8**

CCHA Second All-Star Team (1990)

Claimed by **San Jose** from **Minnesota** in Dispersal Draft, May 30, 1991. Traded to **Hartford** by **San Jose** for Dean Evason, October 2, 1991. Traded to **Calgary** by **Hartford** for Jeff Reese, November 19, 1993. Traded to **New Jersey** by **Calgary** with Phil Housley for Tommy Albelin, Cale Hulse and Jocelyn Lemieux, February 26, 1996. Signed as a free agent by **Dallas**, August 19, 1996.

KELLEHER, CHRIS PIT.

Defense. Shoots left. 6'1", 215 lbs. Born, Cambridge, MA, March 23, 1975.
(Pittsburgh's 5th choice, 130th overall, in 1993 Entry Draft).

			Regular Season					Playoffs				
Season	**Club**	**Lea**	**GP**	**G**	**A**	**TP**	**PIM**	**GP**	**G**	**A**	**TP**	**PIM**
1993-94	St. Sebastian's	H.S.	24	10	21	31	....	....	....	....	....	....
1994-95	Boston University	H.E.	35	3	17	20	62	....	....	....	....	....
1995-96	Boston University	H.E.	37	7	18	25	43	....	....	....	....	....
1996-97	Boston University	H.E.	39	10	24	34	54	....	....	....	....	....
1997-98	Boston University	H.E.	37	4	26	30	40	....	....	....	....	....

NCAA East Second All-American Team (1997, 1998) • Hockey East Second All-Star Team (1998)

KELLETT, KEVIN

Defense. Shoots right. 6', 196 lbs. Born, Prince Albert, Sask., July 23, 1978.
(Anaheim's 6th choice, 198th overall, in 1996 Entry Draft).

			Regular Season					Playoffs				
Season	**Club**	**Lea**	**GP**	**G**	**A**	**TP**	**PIM**	**GP**	**G**	**A**	**TP**	**PIM**
1994-95	Prince Albert	WHL	8	0	1	1	6	....	....	....	....	....
1995-96	Prince Albert	WHL	62	0	5	5	71	18	0	0	0	19
1996-97	Prince Albert	WHL	69	8	16	24	165	1	0	1	1	0
1997-98	Prince Albert	WHL	61	11	11	22	177	....	....	....	....	....

KELLY, STEVE T.B.

Center. Shoots left. 6'1", 190 lbs. Born, Vancouver, B.C., October 26, 1976.
(Edmonton's 1st choice, 6th overall, in 1995 Entry Draft).

			Regular Season					Playoffs				
Season	**Club**	**Lea**	**GP**	**G**	**A**	**TP**	**PIM**	**GP**	**G**	**A**	**TP**	**PIM**
1992-93	Prince Albert	WHL	65	11	9	20	75	....	....	....	....	....
1993-94	Prince Albert	WHL	65	19	42	61	106	....	....	....	....	....
1994-95	Prince Albert	WHL	68	31	41	72	153	15	7	9	16	35
1995-96	Prince Albert	WHL	70	27	74	101	203	18	13	18	31	47
1996-97	**Edmonton**	**NHL**	**8**	**1**	**0**	**1**	**6**	**6**	**0**	**0**	**0**	**2**
	Hamilton	AHL	48	9	29	38	111	11	3	3	6	24
1997-98	**Edmonton**	**NHL**	**19**	**0**	**2**	**2**	**8**	....	....	....	....	....
	Hamilton	AHL	11	2	8	10	18	....	....	....	....	....
	Tampa Bay	**NHL**	**24**	**2**	**1**	**3**	**15**	....	....	....	....	....
	Milwaukee	IHL	5	0	1	1	19	....	....	....	....	....
	Cleveland	IHL	5	1	1	2	29	1	0	1	1	0
	NHL Totals		**51**	**3**	**3**	**6**	**29**	**6**	**0**	**0**	**0**	**2**

Traded to **Tampa Bay** by **Edmonton** with Bryan Marchment and Jason Bonsignore for Roman Hamrlik and Paul Comrie, December 30, 1997.

KENADY, CHRIS ST.L.

Right wing. Shoots right. 6'2", 195 lbs. Born, Mound, MN, April 10, 1973.
(St. Louis' 8th choice, 175th overall, in 1991 Entry Draft).

			Regular Season					Playoffs				
Season	**Club**	**Lea**	**GP**	**G**	**A**	**TP**	**PIM**	**GP**	**G**	**A**	**TP**	**PIM**
1990-91	St. Paul	USHL	45	16	20	36	57	....	....	....	....	....
1991-92	U. of Denver	WCHA	36	8	5	13	56	....	....	....	....	....
1992-93	U. of Denver	WCHA	38	8	16	24	95	....	....	....	....	....
1993-94	U. of Denver	WCHA	37	14	11	25	125	....	....	....	....	....
1994-95	U. of Denver	WCHA	39	21	17	38	113	....	....	....	....	....
1995-96	Worcester	AHL	43	9	10	19	58	2	0	0	0	0
1996-97	Worcester	AHL	73	23	26	49	131	5	0	1	1	2
1997-98	**St. Louis**	**NHL**	**5**	**0**	**2**	**2**	**0**	....	....	....	....	....
	Worcester	AHL	63	23	22	45	84	11	1	5	6	26
	NHL Totals		**5**	**0**	**2**	**2**	**0**	....	....	....	....	....

KENNEDY, MIKE

Center. Shoots right. 6'1", 195 lbs. Born, Vancouver, B.C., April 13, 1972.
(Minnesota's 3rd choice, 97th overall, in 1991 Entry Draft).

			Regular Season					Playoffs				
Season	**Club**	**Lea**	**GP**	**G**	**A**	**TP**	**PIM**	**GP**	**G**	**A**	**TP**	**PIM**
1989-90	U.B.C.	CWUAA	9	5	7	12	0	....	....	....	....	....
1990-91	U.B.C.	CWUAA	28	17	17	34	18	....	....	....	....	....
1991-92	Seattle	WHL	71	42	47	89	134	15	11	6	17	20
1992-93	Kalamazoo	IHL	77	21	30	51	39	....	....	....	....	....
1993-94	Kalamazoo	IHL	63	20	18	38	42	3	1	2	3	2
1994-95	**Dallas**	**NHL**	**44**	**6**	**12**	**18**	**33**	**5**	**0**	**0**	**0**	**9**
	Kalamazoo	IHL	42	20	28	48	29	....	....	....	....	....
1995-96	**Dallas**	**NHL**	**61**	**9**	**17**	**26**	**48**	....	....	....	....	....
1996-97	**Dallas**	**NHL**	**24**	**1**	**6**	**7**	**13**	....	....	....	....	....
	Michigan	IHL	2	0	1	1	2	....	....	....	....	....
1997-98	**Toronto**	**NHL**	**13**	**0**	**1**	**1**	**14**	....	....	....	....	....
	St. John's	AHL	49	11	17	28	86	....	....	....	....	....
	Dallas	**NHL**	**2**	**0**	**0**	**0**	**2**	....	....	....	....	....
	NHL Totals		**144**	**16**	**36**	**52**	**110**	**5**	**0**	**0**	**0**	**9**

WHL West Second All-Star Team (1992)

Rights transferred to **Dallas** after **Minnesota** franchise relocated, June 9, 1993. Signed as a free agent by **Toronto**, July 2, 1997. Traded to **Dallas** by **Toronto** for Dallas' 8th round choice (Mikhail Travnicek) in 1998 Entry Draft, March 24, 1998.

KENNEDY, SHELDON

Right wing. Shoots right. 5'10", 180 lbs. Born, Elkhorn, Man., June 15, 1969.
(Detroit's 5th choice, 80th overall, in 1988 Entry Draft).

			Regular Season					Playoffs				
Season	**Club**	**Lea**	**GP**	**G**	**A**	**TP**	**PIM**	**GP**	**G**	**A**	**TP**	**PIM**
1986-87	Swift Current	WHL	49	23	41	64	43	4	0	3	3	4
1987-88	Swift Current	WHL	59	53	64	117	45	10	8	9	17	12
1988-89	Swift Current	WHL	51	58	48	106	92	12	9	15	24	22
1989-90	**Detroit**	**NHL**	**20**	**2**	**7**	**9**	**10**	....	....	....	....	....
	Adirondack	AHL	26	11	15	26	35	....	....	....	....	....
1990-91	**Detroit**	**NHL**	**7**	**1**	**0**	**1**	**12**	....	....	....	....	....
	Adirondack	AHL	11	1	3	4	8	....	....	....	....	....
1991-92	**Detroit**	**NHL**	**27**	**3**	**8**	**11**	**24**	....	....	....	....	....
	Adirondack	AHL	46	25	24	49	56	16	5	9	14	12
1992-93	**Detroit**	**NHL**	**68**	**19**	**11**	**30**	**46**	**7**	**1**	**1**	**2**	**2**
1993-94	**Detroit**	**NHL**	**61**	**6**	**7**	**13**	**30**	**7**	**1**	**2**	**3**	**0**
1994-95	**Calgary**	**NHL**	**30**	**7**	**8**	**15**	**45**	**7**	**3**	**1**	**4**	**16**
1995-96	**Calgary**	**NHL**	**41**	**3**	**7**	**10**	**36**	**3**	**1**	**0**	**1**	**2**
	Saint John	AHL	3	4	0	4	8	....	....	....	....	....
1996-97	**Boston**	**NHL**	**56**	**8**	**10**	**18**	**30**	....	....	....	....	....
	Providence	AHL	3	0	1	1	2	....	....	....	....	....
1997-98			DID NOT PLAY – INJURED									
	NHL Totals		**310**	**49**	**58**	**107**	**233**	**24**	**6**	**4**	**10**	**20**

WHL East Second All-Star Team (1989) • Memorial Cup All-Star Team (1989)

Traded to **Winnipeg** by **Detroit** for Winnipeg's 3rd round choice (Darryl Laplante) in 1995 Entry Draft, May 25, 1994. Claimed by **Calgary** from **Winnipeg** in NHL Waiver Draft, January 18, 1995. Signed as free agent by **Boston**, August 7, 1996. • Missed entire 1997-98 season recovering from off-season leg injury.

KESA, DAN (KEH-suh) PIT.

Right wing. Shoots right. 6', 198 lbs. Born, Vancouver, B.C., November 23, 1971.
(Vancouver's 4th choice, 95th overall, in 1991 Entry Draft).

			Regular Season					Playoffs				
Season	**Club**	**Lea**	**GP**	**G**	**A**	**TP**	**PIM**	**GP**	**G**	**A**	**TP**	**PIM**
1990-91	Prince Albert	WHL	69	30	23	53	116	3	1	1	2	0
1991-92	Prince Albert	WHL	62	46	51	97	201	10	9	10	19	27
1992-93	Hamilton	AHL	62	16	24	40	76	....	....	....	....	....
1993-94	**Vancouver**	**NHL**	**19**	**2**	**4**	**6**	**18**	....	....	....	....	....
	Hamilton	AHL	53	37	33	70	33	4	1	4	5	4
1994-95	Syracuse	AHL	70	34	44	78	81	....	....	....	....	....
1995-96	**Dallas**	**NHL**	**3**	**0**	**0**	**0**	**0**	....	....	....	....	....
	Michigan	IHL	15	4	11	15	33	....	....	....	....	....
	Springfield	AHL	22	10	5	15	13	....	....	....	....	....
	Detroit	IHL	27	9	6	15	22	12	6	4	10	4
1996-97	Detroit	IHL	60	22	21	43	19	20	7	5	12	20
1997-98	Detroit	IHL	76	40	37	77	40	20	*13	5	18	14
	NHL Totals		**22**	**2**	**4**	**6**	**18**	....	....	....	....	....

Traded to **Dallas** by **Vancouver** with Greg Adams and Vancouver's 5th round choice (later traded to LA Kings — LA Kings selected Jason Morgan) in 1995 Entry Draft for Russ Courtnall, April 7, 1995. Traded to **Hartford** by **Dallas** with future considerations for Robert Petrovicky, November 29, 1995. Signed as a free agent by **Pittsburgh**, August 20, 1998.

KHRISTICH, DMITRI (KRIH-stihch) BOS.

Left wing/Center. Shoots right. 6'2", 195 lbs. Born, Kiev, USSR, July 23, 1969.
(Washington's 6th choice, 120th overall, in 1988 Entry Draft).

			Regular Season					Playoffs				
Season	**Club**	**Lea**	**GP**	**G**	**A**	**TP**	**PIM**	**GP**	**G**	**A**	**TP**	**PIM**
1985-86	Sokol Kiev	USSR	4	0	0	0	0	....	....	....	....	....
1986-87	Sokol Kiev	USSR	20	3	0	3	4	....	....	....	....	....
1987-88	Sokol Kiev	USSR	37	9	1	10	18	....	....	....	....	....
1988-89	Sokol Kiev	USSR	42	17	10	27	15	....	....	....	....	....
1989-90	Sokol Kiev	USSR	47	14	22	36	32	....	....	....	....	....
1990-91	Sokol Kiev	USSR	28	10	12	22	20	....	....	....	....	....
	Washington	**NHL**	**40**	**13**	**14**	**27**	**21**	**11**	**1**	**3**	**4**	**6**
	Baltimore	AHL	3	0	0	0	0	....	....	....	....	....
1991-92	**Washington**	**NHL**	**80**	**36**	**37**	**73**	**35**	**7**	**3**	**2**	**5**	**15**
1992-93	**Washington**	**NHL**	**64**	**31**	**35**	**66**	**28**	**6**	**2**	**5**	**7**	**2**
1993-94	**Washington**	**NHL**	**83**	**29**	**29**	**58**	**73**	**11**	**2**	**3**	**5**	**10**
1994-95	**Washington**	**NHL**	**48**	**12**	**14**	**26**	**41**	**7**	**1**	**4**	**5**	**0**
1995-96	**Los Angeles**	**NHL**	**76**	**27**	**37**	**64**	**44**	....	....	....	....	....
1996-97	**Los Angeles**	**NHL**	**75**	**19**	**37**	**56**	**38**	....	....	....	....	....
1997-98	**Boston**	**NHL**	**82**	**29**	**37**	**66**	**42**	**6**	**2**	**2**	**4**	**2**
	NHL Totals		**548**	**196**	**240**	**436**	**322**	**48**	**11**	**19**	**30**	**35**

Played in NHL All-Star Game (1997)

Traded to **LA Kings** by **Washington** with Byron Dafoe for LA Kings' 1st round choice (Alexander Volchkov) and Dallas' 4th round choice (previously acquired, Washington selected Justin Davis) in 1996 Entry Draft, July 8, 1995. Traded to **Boston** by **LA Kings** with Byron Dafoe for Jozef Stumpel, Sandy Moger and Boston's 4th round choice (later traded to New Jersey - New Jersey selected Pierre Dagenais) in 1998 Entry Draft, August 29, 1997.

KIDNEY, KYLE — COL.

Left wing. Shoots left. 6'2", 223 lbs. Born, Ithaca, NY, January 11, 1978.
(Colorado's 9th choice, 243rd overall, in 1997 Entry Draft).

			Regular Season					Playoffs				
Season	Club	Lea	GP	G	A	TP	PIM	GP	G	A	TP	PIM
1996-97	Salisbury	H.S.	28	27	35	62	....	....	....	....	....	....
1997-98	U. Mass-Lowell	H.E.	33	3	8	11	38	....	....	....	....	....

KILGER, CHAD (KIHL-guhr) — CHI.

Center. Shoots left. 6'3", 204 lbs. Born, Cornwall, Ont., November 27, 1976.
(Anaheim's 1st choice, 4th overall, in 1995 Entry Draft).

			Regular Season					Playoffs				
Season	Club	Lea	GP	G	A	TP	PIM	GP	G	A	TP	PIM
1993-94	Kingston	OHL	66	17	35	52	23	6	7	2	9	8
1994-95	Kingston	OHL	65	42	53	95	95	6	5	2	7	10
1995-96	**Anaheim**	**NHL**	**45**	**5**	**7**	**12**	**22**	....	....	....	....	....
	Winnipeg	**NHL**	**29**	**2**	**3**	**5**	**12**	**4**	**1**	**0**	**1**	**0**
1996-97	**Phoenix**	**NHL**	**24**	**4**	**3**	**7**	**13**	....	....	....	....	....
	Springfield	AHL	52	17	28	45	36	16	5	7	12	56
1997-98	**Phoenix**	**NHL**	**10**	**0**	**1**	**1**	**4**	....	....	....	....	....
	Springfield	AHL	35	14	14	28	33	....	....	....	....	....
	Chicago	**NHL**	**22**	**3**	**8**	**11**	**6**	....	....	....	....	....
	NHL Totals		**130**	**14**	**22**	**36**	**57**	**4**	**1**	**0**	**1**	**0**

Traded to **Winnipeg** by **Anaheim** with Oleg Tverdovsky and Anaheim's 3rd round choice (Per-Anton Lundstrom) in 1996 Entry Draft for Teemu Selanne, Marc Chouinard and Winnipeg's 4th round choice (later traded to Toronto — later traded to Montreal — Montreal selected Kim Staal) in 1996 Entry Draft, February 7, 1996. Transferred to **Phoenix** after **Winnipeg** franchise relocated, July 1, 1996. Traded to **Chicago** by **Phoenix** with Jayson More for Keith Carney and Jim Cummins, March 4, 1998.

KING, DEREK — TOR.

Left wing. Shoots left. 6', 212 lbs. Born, Hamilton, Ont., February 11, 1967.
(NY Islanders' 2nd choice, 13th overall, in 1985 Entry Draft).

			Regular Season					Playoffs				
Season	Club	Lea	GP	G	A	TP	PIM	GP	G	A	TP	PIM
1984-85	S.S. Marie	OHL	63	35	38	73	106	16	3	13	16	11
1985-86	S.S. Marie	OHL	25	12	17	29	33	....	....	....	....	....
	Oshawa	OHL	19	8	13	21	15	6	3	2	5	13
1986-87	Oshawa	OHL	57	53	53	106	74	17	14	10	24	40
	NY Islanders	**NHL**	**2**	**0**	**0**	**0**	**0**	....	....	....	....	....
1987-88	**NY Islanders**	**NHL**	**55**	**12**	**24**	**36**	**30**	**5**	**0**	**2**	**2**	**2**
	Springfield	AHL	10	7	6	13	6	....	....	....	....	....
1988-89	**NY Islanders**	**NHL**	**60**	**14**	**29**	**43**	**14**	....	....	....	....	....
	Springfield	AHL	4	4	0	4	0	....	....	....	....	....
1989-90	**NY Islanders**	**NHL**	**46**	**13**	**27**	**40**	**20**	**4**	**0**	**0**	**0**	**4**
	Springfield	AHL	21	11	12	23	33	....	....	....	....	....
1990-91	**NY Islanders**	**NHL**	**66**	**19**	**26**	**45**	**44**	....	....	....	....	....
1991-92	**NY Islanders**	**NHL**	**80**	**40**	**38**	**78**	**46**	....	....	....	....	....
1992-93	**NY Islanders**	**NHL**	**77**	**38**	**38**	**76**	**47**	**18**	**3**	**11**	**14**	**14**
1993-94	**NY Islanders**	**NHL**	**78**	**30**	**40**	**70**	**59**	**4**	**0**	**1**	**1**	**0**
1994-95	**NY Islanders**	**NHL**	**43**	**10**	**16**	**26**	**41**	....	....	....	....	....
1995-96	**NY Islanders**	**NHL**	**61**	**12**	**20**	**32**	**23**	....	....	....	....	....
1996-97	**NY Islanders**	**NHL**	**70**	**23**	**30**	**53**	**20**	....	....	....	....	....
	Hartford	**NHL**	**12**	**3**	**3**	**6**	**2**	....	....	....	....	....
1997-98	**Toronto**	**NHL**	**77**	**21**	**25**	**46**	**43**	....	....	....	....	....
	NHL Totals		**727**	**235**	**316**	**551**	**389**	**31**	**3**	**14**	**17**	**20**

OHL First All-Star Team (1987)

Traded to **Hartford** by **NY Islanders** for Hartford's 5th round choice (Adam Edinger) in 1997 Entry Draft, March 18, 1997. Signed as a free agent by **Toronto**, July 4, 1997.

KING, KRIS — TOR.

Left wing. Shoots left. 5'11", 208 lbs. Born, Bracebridge, Ont., February 18, 1966.
(Washington's 4th choice, 80th overall, in 1984 Entry Draft).

			Regular Season					Playoffs				
Season	Club	Lea	GP	G	A	TP	PIM	GP	G	A	TP	PIM
1983-84	Peterborough	OHL	62	13	18	31	168	8	3	3	6	14
1984-85	Peterborough	OHL	61	18	35	53	222	16	2	8	10	28
1985-86	Peterborough	OHL	58	19	40	59	254	8	4	0	4	21
1986-87	Peterborough	OHL	46	23	33	56	160	12	5	8	13	41
	Binghamton	AHL	7	0	0	0	18	....	....	....	....	....
1987-88	**Detroit**	**NHL**	**3**	**1**	**0**	**1**	**2**	....	....	....	....	....
	Adirondack	AHL	76	21	32	53	337	10	4	4	8	53
1988-89	**Detroit**	**NHL**	**55**	**2**	**3**	**5**	**168**	**2**	**0**	**0**	**0**	**2**
1989-90	**NY Rangers**	**NHL**	**68**	**6**	**7**	**13**	**286**	**10**	**0**	**1**	**1**	**38**
1990-91	**NY Rangers**	**NHL**	**72**	**11**	**14**	**25**	**154**	**6**	**2**	**0**	**2**	**36**
1991-92	**NY Rangers**	**NHL**	**79**	**10**	**9**	**19**	**224**	**13**	**4**	**1**	**5**	**14**
1992-93	**NY Rangers**	**NHL**	**30**	**0**	**3**	**3**	**67**	....	....	....	....	....
	Winnipeg	**NHL**	**48**	**8**	**8**	**16**	**136**	**6**	**1**	**1**	**2**	**4**
1993-94	**Winnipeg**	**NHL**	**83**	**4**	**8**	**12**	**205**	....	....	....	....	....
1994-95	**Winnipeg**	**NHL**	**48**	**4**	**2**	**6**	**85**	....	....	....	....	....
1995-96	**Winnipeg**	**NHL**	**81**	**9**	**11**	**20**	**151**	**5**	**0**	**1**	**1**	**4**
1996-97	**Phoenix**	**NHL**	**81**	**3**	**11**	**14**	**185**	**7**	**0**	**0**	**0**	**17**
1997-98	**Toronto**	**NHL**	**82**	**3**	**3**	**6**	**199**	....	....	....	....	....
	NHL Totals		**730**	**61**	**79**	**140**	**1862**	**49**	**7**	**4**	**11**	**115**

Won King Clancy Memorial Trophy (1996)

Signed as a free agent by **Detroit**, March 23, 1987. Traded to **NY Rangers** by **Detroit** for Chris McRae and Detroit's 5th round choice (previously acquired, Detroit selected Tony Burns) in 1990 Entry Draft, September 7, 1989. Traded to **Winnipeg** by **NY Rangers** with Tie Domi for Ed Olczyk, December 28, 1992. Transferred to **Phoenix** after **Winnipeg** franchise relocated, July 1, 1996. Signed as a free agent by **Toronto**, July 23, 1997.

KING, STEVEN

Right wing. Shoots right. 6', 195 lbs. Born, Greenwich, RI, July 22, 1969.
(NY Rangers' 1st choice, 21st overall, in 1991 Supplemental Draft).

			Regular Season					Playoffs				
Season	Club	Lea	GP	G	A	TP	PIM	GP	G	A	TP	PIM
1989-90	Brown University	ECAC	27	19	8	27	53	....	....	....	....	....
1990-91	Brown University	ECAC	27	19	15	34	76	....	....	....	....	....
1991-92	Binghamton	AHL	66	27	15	42	56	10	2	0	2	14
1992-93	**NY Rangers**	**NHL**	**24**	**7**	**5**	**12**	**16**	....	....	....	....	....
	Binghamton	AHL	53	35	33	68	100	14	7	9	16	26
1993-94	**Anaheim**	**NHL**	**36**	**8**	**3**	**11**	**44**	....	....	....	....	....
1994-95			Did Not Play – Injured									
1995-96	**Anaheim**	**NHL**	**7**	**2**	**0**	**2**	**15**	....	....	....	....	....
	Baltimore	AHL	68	40	21	61	95	12	7	5	12	20
1996-97	Philadelphia	AHL	39	17	10	27	47	....	....	....	....	....
	Michigan	IHL	39	15	11	26	39	4	1	2	3	12
1997-98	Cincinnati	IHL	41	17	9	26	22	....	....	....	....	....
	Rochester	AHL	28	15	15	30	28	4	1	1	2	4
	NHL Totals		**67**	**17**	**8**	**25**	**75**	....	....	....	....	....

Claimed by **Anaheim** from **NY Rangers** in Expansion Draft, June 24, 1993. • Missed entire 1994-95 season after having reconstructive surgery on shoulder, January 5, 1994. Signed as a free agent by **Philadelphia**, July 31, 1996.

KINNEAR, GEORDIE — N.J.

Defense. Shoots left. 6'1", 195 lbs. Born, Simcoe, Ont., July 9, 1973.
(New Jersey's 8th choice, 162nd overall, in 1992 Entry Draft).

			Regular Season					Playoffs				
Season	Club	Lea	GP	G	A	TP	PIM	GP	G	A	TP	PIM
1990-91	Peterborough	OJHL	6	0	6	6	51	....	....	....	....	....
	Peterborough	OHL	37	1	0	1	76	2	0	0	0	10
1991-92	Peterborough	OHL	63	5	16	21	195	10	0	2	2	36
1992-93	Peterborough	OHL	58	6	22	28	161	19	1	5	6	43
1993-94	Albany	AHL	59	3	12	15	197	5	0	0	0	21
1994-95	Albany	AHL	68	5	11	16	136	9	1	1	2	7
1995-96	Albany	AHL	73	4	7	11	170	4	0	1	1	2
1996-97	Albany	AHL	59	2	9	11	175	10	0	1	1	15
1997-98	Albany	AHL	78	1	15	16	206	13	1	1	2	68

KJELLBERG, PATRIK (CHEHL-buhrg) — NSH.

Left wing. Shoots left. 6'2", 196 lbs. Born, Falun, Sweden, June 17, 1969.
(Montreal's 4th choice, 83rd overall, in 1988 Entry Draft).

			Regular Season					Playoffs				
Season	Club	Lea	GP	G	A	TP	PIM	GP	G	A	TP	PIM
1986-87	Falun	Sweden-2	27	11	13	24	14	....	....	....	....	....
1987-88	Falun	Sweden-2	29	15	10	25	6	....	....	....	....	....
1988-89	AIK Solna	Sweden	25	7	9	16	8	....	....	....	....	....
1989-90	AIK Solna	Sweden	33	8	16	24	6	3	1	0	1	0
1990-91	AIK Solna	Sweden	38	4	11	15	18	....	....	....	....	....
1991-92	AIK Solna	Sweden	40	20	13	33	14	3	1	0	1	2
	Sweden	Olympics	8	1	3	4	0	....	....	....	....	....
1992-93	**Montreal**	**NHL**	**7**	**0**	**0**	**0**	**2**	....	....	....	....	....
	Fredericton	AHL	41	10	27	37	14	5	2	2	4	0
1993-94	HV 71 Jonkoping	Sweden	40	11	17	28	18	....	....	....	....	....
	Sweden	Olympics	8	0	1	1	2	....	....	....	....	....
1994-95	HV 71 Jonkoping	Sweden	29	5	15	20	12	....	....	....	....	....
1995-96	Djurgarden	Sweden	40	9	7	16	10	4	0	2	2	2
1996-97	Djurgarden	Sweden	49	29	11	40	18	4	2	3	5	4
1997-98	Djurgarden	Sweden	46	*30	18	48	16	15	7	3	10	12
	NHL Totals		**7**	**0**	**0**	**0**	**2**	....	....	....	....	....

Signed as a free agent by **Nashville**, July 7, 1998.

KLATT, TRENT (KLAT) — PHI.

Right wing. Shoots right. 6'1", 205 lbs. Born, Robbinsdale, MN, January 30, 1971.
(Washington's 5th choice, 82nd overall, in 1989 Entry Draft).

			Regular Season					Playoffs				
Season	Club	Lea	GP	G	A	TP	PIM	GP	G	A	TP	PIM
1988-89	Ossea High	H.S.	22	24	39	63	....	....	....	....	....	....
1989-90	U. of Minnesota	WCHA	38	22	14	36	16	....	....	....	....	....
1990-91	U. of Minnesota	WCHA	39	16	28	44	58	....	....	....	....	....
1991-92	U. of Minnesota	WCHA	41	27	36	63	76	....	....	....	....	....
	Minnesota	**NHL**	**1**	**0**	**0**	**0**	**0**	**6**	**0**	**0**	**0**	**2**
1992-93	**Minnesota**	**NHL**	**47**	**4**	**19**	**23**	**38**	....	....	....	....	....
	Kalamazoo	IHL	31	8	11	19	18	....	....	....	....	....
1993-94	**Dallas**	**NHL**	**61**	**14**	**24**	**38**	**30**	**9**	**2**	**1**	**3**	**4**
	Kalamazoo	IHL	6	3	2	5	4	....	....	....	....	....
1994-95	**Dallas**	**NHL**	**47**	**12**	**10**	**22**	**26**	**5**	**1**	**0**	**1**	**0**
1995-96	**Dallas**	**NHL**	**22**	**4**	**4**	**8**	**23**	....	....	....	....	....
	Michigan	IHL	2	1	2	3	5	....	....	....	....	....
	Philadelphia	**NHL**	**49**	**3**	**8**	**11**	**21**	**12**	**4**	**1**	**5**	**0**
1996-97	**Philadelphia**	**NHL**	**76**	**24**	**21**	**45**	**20**	**19**	**4**	**3**	**7**	**12**
1997-98	**Philadelphia**	**NHL**	**82**	**14**	**28**	**42**	**16**	**5**	**0**	**0**	**0**	**0**
	NHL Totals		**385**	**75**	**114**	**189**	**174**	**56**	**11**	**5**	**16**	**18**

Traded to **Minnesota** by **Washington** with Steve Maltais for Shawn Chambers, June 21, 1991. Transferred to **Dallas** after **Minnesota** franchise relocated, June 9, 1993. Traded to **Philadelphia** by **Dallas** for Brent Fedyk, December 13, 1995.

KLEE, KEN — WSH.

Right wing. Shoots right. 6'1", 205 lbs. Born, Indianapolis, IN, April 24, 1971.
(Washington's 11th choice, 177th overall, in 1990 Entry Draft).

			Regular Season					Playoffs				
Season	Club	Lea	GP	G	A	TP	PIM	GP	G	A	TP	PIM
1989-90	Bowling Green	CCHA	39	0	5	5	52	....	....	....	....	....
1990-91	Bowling Green	CCHA	37	7	28	35	50	....	....	....	....	....
1991-92	Bowling Green	CCHA	10	0	1	1	14	....	....	....	....	....
1992-93	Baltimore	AHL	77	4	14	18	93	7	0	1	1	15
1993-94	Portland	AHL	65	2	9	11	87	17	1	2	3	14
1994-95	**Washington**	**NHL**	**23**	**3**	**1**	**4**	**41**	**7**	**0**	**0**	**0**	**4**
	Portland	AHL	49	5	7	12	89	....	....	....	....	....
1995-96	**Washington**	**NHL**	**66**	**8**	**3**	**11**	**60**	**1**	**0**	**0**	**0**	**0**
1996-97	**Washington**	**NHL**	**80**	**3**	**8**	**11**	**115**	....	....	....	....	....
1997-98	**Washington**	**NHL**	**51**	**4**	**2**	**6**	**46**	**9**	**1**	**0**	**1**	**10**
	NHL Totals		**220**	**18**	**14**	**32**	**262**	**17**	**1**	**0**	**1**	**14**

KLEMM, JON — COL.

Defense. Shoots right. 6'3", 200 lbs. Born, Cranbrook, B.C., January 8, 1970.

			Regular Season					Playoffs				
Season	Club	Lea	GP	G	A	TP	PIM	GP	G	A	TP	PIM
1987-88	Seattle	WHL	68	6	7	13	24	....	....	....	....	....
1988-89	Seattle	WHL	2	1	1	2	0	....	....	....	....	....
	Spokane	WHL	66	6	34	40	42	....	....	....	....	....
1989-90	Spokane	WHL	66	3	28	31	100	6	1	1	2	5
1990-91	Spokane	WHL	72	7	58	65	65	15	3	6	9	8
1991-92	Quebec	NHL	4	0	1	1	0	....	....	....	....	....
	Halifax	AHL	70	6	13	19	40	....	....	....	....	....
1992-93	Halifax	AHL	80	3	20	23	32	....	....	....	....	....
1993-94	Quebec	NHL	7	0	0	0	4	....	....	....	....	....
	Cornwall	AHL	66	4	26	30	78	13	1	2	3	6
1994-95	Quebec	NHL	4	1	0	1	2	....	....	....	....	....
	Cornwall	AHL	65	6	13	19	84	....	....	....	....	....
1995-96	Colorado	NHL	56	3	12	15	20	15	2	1	3	0 ♦
1996-97	Colorado	NHL	80	9	15	24	37	17	1	1	2	6
1997-98	Colorado	NHL	67	6	8	14	30	4	0	0	0	0
	NHL Totals		**218**	**19**	**36**	**55**	**93**	**36**	**3**	**2**	**5**	**6**

WHL West Second All-Star Team (1991)

Signed as a free agent by **Quebec**, May 14, 1991. Transferred to **Colorado** after **Quebec** franchise relocated, June 21, 1995.

KLIMA, PETR — (KLEE-muh)

Right/Left wing. Shoots right. 6', 190 lbs. Born, Chomutov, Czech., December 23, 1964.
(Detroit's 5th choice, 88th overall, in 1983 Entry Draft).

			Regular Season					Playoffs				
Season	Club	Lea	GP	G	A	TP	PIM	GP	G	A	TP	PIM
1981-82	Litvinov	Czech.	18	7	3	10	8	....	....	....	....	....
1982-83	Litvinov	Czech.	44	19	17	36	74	....	....	....	....	....
1983-84	Dukla Jihlava	Czech.	41	20	16	36	46	....	....	....	....	....
1984-85	Dukla Jihlava	Czech.	35	23	22	45	76	....	....	....	....	....
1985-86	Detroit	NHL	74	32	24	56	16	....	....	....	....	....
1986-87	Detroit	NHL	77	30	23	53	42	13	1	2	3	4
1987-88	Detroit	NHL	78	37	25	62	46	12	10	8	18	10
1988-89	Detroit	NHL	51	25	16	41	44	6	2	4	6	19
	Adirondack	AHL	5	5	1	6	4	....	....	....	....	....
1989-90	Detroit	NHL	13	5	5	10	6	....	....	....	....	....
	Edmonton	NHL	63	25	28	53	66	21	5	0	5	8 ♦
1990-91	Edmonton	NHL	70	40	28	68	113	18	7	6	13	16
1991-92	Edmonton	NHL	57	21	13	34	52	15	1	4	5	8
1992-93	Edmonton	NHL	68	32	16	48	100	....	....	....	....	....
1993-94	Tampa Bay	NHL	75	28	27	55	76	....	....	....	....	....
1994-95	Wolfsburg	Ger-2	12	27	11	38	28	....	....	....	....	....
	ZPS Zlin	Cze-Rep.	1	1	0	1	0	....	....	....	....	....
	Tampa Bay	NHL	47	13	13	26	26	....	....	....	....	....
1995-96	Tampa Bay	NHL	67	22	30	52	68	4	2	0	2	14
1996-97	Los Angeles	NHL	8	0	4	4	2	....	....	....	....	....
	Pittsburgh	NHL	9	1	3	4	4	....	....	....	....	....
	Cleveland	IHL	19	7	14	21	6	....	....	....	....	....
	Edmonton	NHL	16	1	5	6	6	6	0	0	0	4
1997-98	Krefeld	Germany	38	7	12	19	18	....	....	....	....	....
	NHL Totals		**773**	**312**	**260**	**572**	**667**	**95**	**28**	**24**	**52**	**83**

Traded to **Edmonton** by **Detroit** with Joe Murphy, Adam Graves and Jeff Sharples for Jimmy Carson, Kevin McClelland and Edmonton's 5th round choice (later traded to Montreal — Montreal selected Brad Layzell) in 1991 Entry Draft, November 2, 1989. Traded to **Tampa Bay** by **Edmonton** for Tampa Bay's 3rd round choice (Brad Symes) in 1994 Entry Draft, June 16, 1993. Traded to **LA Kings** by **Tampa Bay** for LA Kings' 5th round choice (Jan Sulc) in 1997 Entry Draft, August 22, 1996. Traded to **Pittsburgh** by **LA Kings** for future considerations, October 25, 1996. Signed as a free agent by **Edmonton**, February 26, 1997.

KLIMENTIEV, SERGEI — (klih-MEHN-tyehv) PHI.

Defense. Shoots left. 5'11", 200 lbs. Born, Kiev, USSR, April 5, 1975.
(Buffalo's 4th choice, 121st overall, in 1994 Entry Draft).

			Regular Season					Playoffs				
Season	Club	Lea	GP	G	A	TP	PIM	GP	G	A	TP	PIM
1991-92	SVSM Kiev	CIS-3	42	4	15	19	....	....	....	....	....	....
1992-93	Sokol Kiev	CIS	3	0	0	0	4	1	0	0	0	0
1993-94	Medicine Hat	WHL	72	16	26	42	165	3	0	0	0	4
1994-95	Medicine Hat	WHL	71	19	45	64	146	5	4	2	6	14
	Rochester	AHL	7	0	0	0	8	1	0	0	0	0
1995-96	Rochester	AHL	70	7	29	36	74	19	2	8	10	16
1996-97	Rochester	AHL	77	14	28	42	114	10	1	4	5	28
1997-98	Rochester	AHL	57	4	22	26	94	....	....	....	....	....

Signed as a free agent by **Philadelphia**, June 9, 1998.

KLIMOVICH, SERGEI — (klee-MOH-vich)

Center. Shoots right. 6'3", 189 lbs. Born, Novosibirsk, USSR, March 8, 1974.
(Chicago's 3rd choice, 41st overall, in 1992 Entry Draft).

			Regular Season					Playoffs				
Season	Club	Lea	GP	G	A	TP	PIM	GP	G	A	TP	PIM
1991-92	Moscow D'amo	CIS	3	0	0	0	0	....	....	....	....	....
1992-93	Moscow D'amo	CIS	30	4	1	5	14	10	1	0	1	2
1993-94	Moscow D'amo	CIS	39	7	4	11	14	12	2	3	5	6
1994-95	Moscow D'amo	CIS	4	1	0	1	2	....	....	....	....	....
	Indianapolis	IHL	71	14	30	44	20	....	....	....	....	....
1995-96	Indianapolis	IHL	68	17	21	38	28	5	1	1	2	6
1996-97	Chicago	NHL	1	0	0	0	2	....	....	....	....	....
	Indianapolis	IHL	75	20	37	57	98	3	1	2	3	0
1997-98	Idaho	WCHL	13	5	9	14	18	1	0	0	0	0
	Las Vegas	IHL	25	2	8	10	6	....	....	....	....	....
	Quebec	IHL	21	1	7	8	8	....	....	....	....	....
	NHL Totals		**1**	**0**	**0**	**0**	**2**	....	....	....	....	....

KLIMT, THOMAS — (KLIHMT, TAW-mahsh) NYI

Center. Shoots left. 6'1", 183 lbs. Born, Plzen, Czech., December 26, 1973.
(NY Islanders' 3rd choice, 104th overall, in 1992 Entry Draft).

			Regular Season					Playoffs				
Season	Club	Lea	GP	G	A	TP	PIM	GP	G	A	TP	PIM
1991-92	Skoda Plzen	Czech.	40	3	6	9	4	....	....	....	....	....
1992-93	Skoda Plzen	Czech.	34	3	8	11	....	....	....	....	....	....
1993-94	Skoda Plzen	Cze-Rep.	29	5	3	8	....	....	....	....	....	....
1994-95	STATISTICS NOT AVAILABLE											
1995-96	Skoda Plzen	Cze-Rep.	38	4	2	6	....	3	0	0	0	....
1996-97	Skoda Plzen	Cze-Rep.	27	5	3	8	6	....	....	....	....	....
1997-98	HC Becherovka	Cze-Rep.	51	6	10	16	20	....	....	....	....	....

KLOUCEK, TOMAS — (KLOH-chehk, TAW-mahsh) NYR

Defense. Shoots left. 6'2", 205 lbs. Born, Prague, Czechoslovakia, March 7, 1980.
(NY Rangers' 6th choice, 131st overall, in 1998 Entry Draft).

			Regular Season					Playoffs				
Season	Club	Lea	GP	G	A	TP	PIM	GP	G	A	TP	PIM
1995-96	Slavia Praha	Czech-Jr.	40	2	8	10	....	....	....	....	....	....
1996-97	Slavia Praha	Czech-Jr.	43	4	14	18	44	....	....	....	....	....
1997-98	Slavia Praha	Czech-Jr.	43	1	9	10	....	....	....	....	....	....

KNIPSCHEER, FRED — (kuh-NIHP-sheer)

Center. Shoots left. 5'11", 185 lbs. Born, Ft. Wayne, IN, September 3, 1969.

			Regular Season					Playoffs				
Season	Club	Lea	GP	G	A	TP	PIM	GP	G	A	TP	PIM
1990-91	St. Cloud State	WCHA	40	9	10	19	57	....	....	....	....	....
1991-92	St. Cloud State	WCHA	33	15	17	32	48	....	....	....	....	....
1992-93	St. Cloud State	WCHA	36	34	26	60	68	....	....	....	....	....
1993-94	Boston	NHL	11	3	2	5	14	12	2	1	3	6
	Providence	AHL	62	26	13	39	50	....	....	....	....	....
1994-95	Boston	NHL	16	3	1	4	2	4	0	0	0	0
	Providence	AHL	71	29	34	63	81	....	....	....	....	....
1995-96	St. Louis	NHL	1	0	0	0	2	....	....	....	....	....
	Worcester	AHL	68	36	37	73	93	3	0	0	0	2
1996-97	Phoenix	IHL	24	5	11	16	19	....	....	....	....	....
	Indianapolis	IHL	41	10	9	19	46	4	0	2	2	10
1997-98	Kentucky	AHL	17	0	7	7	8	3	0	1	1	7
	Utah	IHL	58	21	32	53	69	2	0	0	0	4
	NHL Totals		**28**	**6**	**3**	**9**	**18**	**16**	**2**	**1**	**3**	**6**

WCHA First All-Star Team (1993) • NCAA West Second All-American Team (1993)

Signed as a free agent by **Boston**, April 30, 1993. Traded to **St. Louis** by **Boston** for Rick Zombo, October 2, 1995. Signed as a free agent by **Chicago**, August 16, 1996.

KNUBLE, MICHAEL — (NOO-buhl) DET.

Right wing. Shoots right. 6'3", 208 lbs. Born, Toronto, Ont., July 4, 1972.
(Detroit's 4th choice, 76th overall, in 1991 Entry Draft).

			Regular Season					Playoffs				
Season	Club	Lea	GP	G	A	TP	PIM	GP	G	A	TP	PIM
1990-91	Kalamazoo	NAJHL	36	18	24	42	30	....	....	....	....	....
1991-92	U. of Michigan	CCHA	43	7	8	15	48	....	....	....	....	....
1992-93	U. of Michigan	CCHA	39	26	16	42	57	....	....	....	....	....
1993-94	U. of Michigan	CCHA	41	32	26	58	71	....	....	....	....	....
1994-95	U. of Michigan	CCHA	34	*38	22	60	62	....	....	....	....	....
	Adirondack	AHL	....	....	....	....	....	3	0	0	0	0
1995-96	Adirondack	AHL	80	22	23	45	59	3	1	0	1	0
1996-97	Detroit	NHL	9	1	0	1	0	....	....	....	....	....
	Adirondack	AHL	68	28	35	63	54	....	....	....	....	....
1997-98	Detroit	NHL	53	7	6	13	16	3	0	1	1	0 ♦
	NHL Totals		**62**	**8**	**6**	**14**	**16**	**3**	**0**	**1**	**1**	**0**

CCHA Second All-Star Team (1994, 1995) • NCAA West Second All-American Team (1995)

KNUTSEN, ESPEN — (kuh-NOOT-suhn)

Center. Shoots left. 5'11", 180 lbs. Born, Oslo, Norway, January 12, 1972.
(Hartford's 9th choice, 204th overall, in 1990 Entry Draft).

			Regular Season					Playoffs				
Season	Club	Lea	GP	G	A	TP	PIM	GP	G	A	TP	PIM
1989-90	Valerengen	Norway	34	22	26	48	....	....	....	....	....	....
1990-91	Valerengen	Norway	31	30	24	54	42	5	3	4	7	....
1991-92	Valerengen	Norway	30	28	26	54	37	8	7	8	15	....
1992-93	Valerengen	Norway	13	11	13	24	4	....	....	....	....	....
1993-94	Valerengen	Norway	38	32	26	58	20	....	....	....	....	....
	Norway	Olympics	7	1	3	4	2	....	....	....	....	....
1994-95	Djurgarden	Sweden	30	6	14	20	18	3	0	1	1	0
1995-96	Djurgarden	Sweden	32	10	23	33	50	4	1	0	1	2
1996-97	Djurgarden	Sweden	39	16	33	49	20	4	2	4	6	6
1997-98	Anaheim	NHL	19	3	0	3	6	....	....	....	....	....
	Cincinnati	AHL	41	4	13	17	18	....	....	....	....	....
	NHL Totals		**19**	**3**	**0**	**3**	**6**	....	....	....	....	....

Norwegian Player of the Year (1994)

Rights traded to **Anaheim** by **Hartford** for Kevin Brown, October 1, 1996.

KOCH, GEOFF — NSH.

Left wing. Shoots left. 6'1", 190 lbs. Born, Virginia, June 27, 1979.
(Nashville's 3rd choice, 85th overall, in 1998 Entry Draft).

			Regular Season					Playoffs				
Season	Club	Lea	GP	G	A	TP	PIM	GP	G	A	TP	PIM
1996-97	Exeter Prep	H.S.	27	22	38	60	45	....	....	....	....	....
1997-98	U. of Michigan	CCHA	43	5	6	11	51	....	....	....	....	....

KOCUR, JOE — (KOH-suhr) DET.

Right wing. Shoots right. 6', 205 lbs. Born, Calgary, Alta., December 21, 1964.
(Detroit's 6th choice, 91st overall, in 1983 Entry Draft).

			Regular Season					Playoffs				
Season	Club	Lea	GP	G	A	TP	PIM	GP	G	A	TP	PIM
1982-83	Saskatoon	WHL	62	23	17	40	289	6	2	3	5	25
1983-84	Saskatoon	WHL	69	40	41	81	258	....	....	....	....	....
	Adirondack	AHL	....	....	....	....	....	5	0	0	0	20
1984-85	Detroit	NHL	17	1	0	1	64	3	1	0	1	5
	Adirondack	AHL	47	12	7	19	171	....	....	....	....	....
1985-86	Detroit	NHL	59	9	6	15	*377	....	....	....	....	....
	Adirondack	AHL	9	6	2	8	34	....	....	....	....	....
1986-87	Detroit	NHL	77	9	9	18	276	16	2	3	5	71
1987-88	Detroit	NHL	63	7	7	14	263	10	0	1	1	13
1988-89	Detroit	NHL	60	9	9	18	213	3	0	1	1	6
1989-90	Detroit	NHL	71	16	20	36	268	....	....	....	....	....
1990-91	Detroit	NHL	52	5	4	9	253	....	....	....	....	....
	NY Rangers	NHL	5	0	0	0	36	6	0	2	2	21
1991-92	NY Rangers	NHL	51	7	4	11	121	12	1	1	2	38
1992-93	NY Rangers	NHL	65	3	6	9	131	....	....	....	....	....
1993-94	NY Rangers	NHL	71	2	1	3	129	20	1	1	2	17 ♦
1994-95	NY Rangers	NHL	48	1	2	3	71	10	0	0	0	8
1995-96	NY Rangers	NHL	38	1	2	3	49	....	....	....	....	....
	Vancouver	NHL	7	0	1	1	19	1	0	0	0	0
1996-97	San Antonio	IHL	5	1	1	2	24	....	....	....	....	....
	Detroit	NHL	34	2	1	3	70	19	1	3	4	22 ♦
1997-98	Detroit	NHL	63	6	5	11	92	18	4	0	4	30 ♦
	NHL Totals		**781**	**78**	**77**	**155**	**2432**	**118**	**10**	**12**	**22**	**231**

Traded to **NY Rangers** by **Detroit** with Per Djoos for Kevin Miller, Jim Cummins and Dennis Vial, March 5, 1991. Traded to **Vancouver** by **NY Rangers** for Kay Whitmore, March 20, 1996. Signed as a free agent by **Detroit**, December 27, 1996.

KOEHLER, GREG — CAR.

Center. Shoots left. 6'2", 195 lbs. Born, Scarborough, Ont., February 27, 1975.

			Regular Season					Playoffs				
Season	Club	Lea	GP	G	A	TP	PIM	GP	G	A	TP	PIM
1996-97	U. Mass-Lowell	H.E.	37	16	20	36	49	....	....	....	....	....
1997-98	U. Mass-Lowell	H.E.	33	20	17	37	62	....	....	....	....	....
	New Haven	AHL	3	0	0	0	2	....	....	....	....	....

Signed as a free agent by **Carolina**, March 31, 1998.

KOHN, LADISLAV (KOHN) — TOR.

Right wing. Shoots left. 5'10", 180 lbs. Born, Uherske Hradiste, Czech., March 4, 1975.
(Calgary's 9th choice, 175th overall, in 1994 Entry Draft).

			Regular Season					Playoffs				
Season	Club	Lea	GP	G	A	TP	PIM	GP	G	A	TP	PIM
1993-94	Brandon	WHL	2	0	0	0	0	....	....	....	....	....
	Swift Current	WHL	69	33	35	68	68	7	5	4	9	8
1994-95	Swift Current	WHL	65	32	60	92	122	6	2	6	8	14
	Saint John	AHL	1	0	0	0	0	....	....	....	....	....
1995-96	**Calgary**	**NHL**	**5**	**1**	**0**	**1**	**2**	....	....	....	....	....
	Saint John	AHL	73	28	45	73	97	16	6	5	11	12
1996-97	Saint John	AHL	76	28	29	57	81	5	0	0	0	0
1997-98	**Calgary**	**NHL**	**4**	**0**	**1**	**1**	**0**	....	....	....	....	....
	Saint John	AHL	65	25	31	56	90	21	14	6	20	20
	NHL Totals		**9**	**1**	**1**	**2**	**2**	....	....	....	....	....

Traded to **Toronto** by **Calgary** for David Cooper, July 2, 1998.

KOIVU, SAKU (KOY-voo, SA-koo) — MTL.

Center. Shoots left. 5'10", 183 lbs. Born, Turku, Finland, November 23, 1974.
(Montreal's 1st choice, 21st overall, in 1993 Entry Draft).

			Regular Season					Playoffs				
Season	Club	Lea	GP	G	A	TP	PIM	GP	G	A	TP	PIM
1992-93	TPS Turku	Finland	46	3	7	10	28	11	3	2	5	2
1993-94	TPS Turku	Finland	47	23	30	53	42	11	4	8	12	16
	Finland	Olympics	8	4	3	7	12	....	....	....	....	....
1994-95	TPS Turku	Finland	45	27	47	74	73	13	7	10	17	16
1995-96	**Montreal**	**NHL**	**82**	**20**	**25**	**45**	**40**	**6**	**3**	**1**	**4**	**8**
1996-97	**Montreal**	**NHL**	**50**	**17**	**39**	**56**	**38**	**5**	**1**	**3**	**4**	**10**
1997-98	**Montreal**	**NHL**	**69**	**14**	**43**	**57**	**48**	**6**	**2**	**3**	**5**	**2**
	Finland	Olympics	6	2	*8	*10	4	....	....	....	....	....
	NHL Totals		**201**	**51**	**107**	**158**	**126**	**17**	**6**	**7**	**13**	**20**

Finnish First All-Star Team (1995) • Finnish Player of the Year (1995)
Played in NHL All-Star Game (1998)

KOKOREV, DMITRI (KOH-koh-rehf) — CGY.

Defense. Shoots left. 6'3", 198 lbs. Born, Moscow, USSR, January 9, 1979.
(Calgary's 4th choice, 51st overall, in 1997 Entry Draft).

			Regular Season					Playoffs				
Season	Club	Lea	GP	G	A	TP	PIM	GP	G	A	TP	PIM
1996-97	Moscow D'amo 2	Russia-3	27	2	4	6	24	....	....	....	....	....
	Moscow D'amo	Russia	1	0	0	0	0	....	....	....	....	....
1997-98	Moscow D'amo 2	Russia-2	24	1	2	3	20	....	....	....	....	....

KOLESAR, MARK (kohl-UH-sahr)

Left wing. Shoots right. 6'1", 188 lbs. Born, Brampton, Ont., January 23, 1973.

			Regular Season					Playoffs				
Season	Club	Lea	GP	G	A	TP	PIM	GP	G	A	TP	PIM
1991-92	Brandon	WHL	56	6	7	13	36	....	....	....	....	....
1992-93	Brandon	WHL	68	27	33	60	110	4	0	0	0	4
1993-94	Brandon	WHL	59	29	37	66	131	14	8	3	11	48
1994-95	St. John's	AHL	65	12	18	30	62	5	1	0	1	2
1995-96	**Toronto**	**NHL**	**21**	**2**	**2**	**4**	**14**	**3**	**1**	**0**	**1**	**2**
	St. John's	AHL	52	22	13	35	47	....	....	....	....	....
1996-97	**Toronto**	**NHL**	**7**	**0**	**0**	**0**	**0**	....	....	....	....	....
	St. John's	AHL	62	22	28	50	64	10	1	3	4	6
1997-98	St. John's	AHL	2	0	0	0	2	....	....	....	....	....
	Manitoba	IHL	30	1	9	10	29	....	....	....	....	....
	Hamilton	AHL	27	2	12	14	47	6	1	1	2	0
	NHL Totals		**28**	**2**	**2**	**4**	**14**	**3**	**1**	**0**	**1**	**2**

Signed as a free agent by **Toronto**, May 24, 1994.

KOLKUNOV, ALEXEI (kohl-koo-NAHV) — PIT.

Center. Shoots right. 6'2", 185 lbs. Born, Belgorod, USSR, February 3, 1977.
(Pittsburgh's 5th choice, 154th overall, in 1995 Entry Draft).

			Regular Season					Playoffs				
Season	Club	Lea	GP	G	A	TP	PIM	GP	G	A	TP	PIM
1994-95	Soviet Wings	CIS	7	0	0	0	0	4	1	0	1	0
1995-96	Soviet Wings	CIS	43	9	3	12	35	....	....	....	....	....
1996-97	Soviet Wings	Russia	44	9	16	25	36	2	0	0	0	4
1997-98	Soviet Wings	Russia	20	6	4	10	22	....	....	....	....	....

KOMARNISKI, ZENITH (KOH-mahr-NIHS-kee, ZEE-nihth) — VAN.

Defense. Shoots left. 6', 200 lbs. Born, Edmonton, Alta., August 13, 1978.
(Vancouver's 2nd choice, 75th overall, in 1996 Entry Draft).

			Regular Season					Playoffs				
Season	Club	Lea	GP	G	A	TP	PIM	GP	G	A	TP	PIM
1994-95	Tri-City	WHL	66	5	19	24	110	17	1	2	3	47
1995-96	Tri-City	WHL	42	5	21	26	85	....	....	....	....	....
1996-97	Tri-City	WHL	58	12	44	56	112	....	....	....	....	....
1997-98	Tri-City	WHL	3	0	4	4	18	....	....	....	....	....
	Spokane	WHL	43	7	20	27	90	18	4	6	10	49

WHL West First All-Star Team (1997)

KOMAROV, ALEXEI (koh-muh-rahf) — DAL.

Defense. Shoots left. 6'6", 196 lbs. Born, Moscow, USSR, June 11, 1978.
(Dallas' 8th choice, 216th overall, in 1997 Entry Draft).

			Regular Season					Playoffs				
Season	Club	Lea	GP	G	A	TP	PIM	GP	G	A	TP	PIM
1996-97	Moscow D'amo 2	Russia-3	32	2	3	5	12	....	....	....	....	....
1997-98	Yekaterinburg	Russia	19	0	0	0	6	....	....	....	....	....
	Yekaterinburg	Russia-2	22	0	1	1	14	....	....	....	....	....

KONDRASHKIN, SERGEI (kohn-DRAHSH-kihn) — NYR

Right wing. Shoots left. 6', 192 lbs. Born, Cherepovets, USSR, April 2, 1975.
(NY Rangers' 7th choice, 162nd overall, in 1993 Entry Draft).

			Regular Season					Playoffs				
Season	Club	Lea	GP	G	A	TP	PIM	GP	G	A	TP	PIM
1992-93	Cherepovets	CIS	41	7	3	10	8	....	....	....	....	....
1993-94	Cherepovets	CIS	41	7	2	9	26	....	....	....	....	....
1994-95	Cherepovets	CIS	51	7	2	9	22	....	....	....	....	....
1995-96	Cherepovets	CIS	28	2	1	3	8	3	1	0	1	2
1996-97	Cherepovets	Russia	33	7	2	9	8	....	....	....	....	....
1997-98	Cherepovets	Russia	7	1	1	2	8	....	....	....	....	....

KONOWALCHUK, STEVE (kahn-uh-WAHL-chuhk) — WSH.

Center. Shoots left. 6'1", 195 lbs. Born, Salt Lake City, UT, November 11, 1972.
(Washington's 5th choice, 58th overall, in 1991 Entry Draft).

			Regular Season					Playoffs				
Season	Club	Lea	GP	G	A	TP	PIM	GP	G	A	TP	PIM
1990-91	Portland	WHL	72	43	49	92	78	....	....	....	....	....
1991-92	Portland	WHL	64	51	53	104	95	6	3	6	9	12
	Washington	**NHL**	**1**	**0**	**0**	**0**	**0**	....	....	....	....	....
	Baltimore	AHL	3	1	1	2	0	....	....	....	....	....
1992-93	**Washington**	**NHL**	**36**	**4**	**7**	**11**	**16**	**2**	**0**	**1**	**1**	**0**
	Baltimore	AHL	37	18	28	46	74	....	....	....	....	....
1993-94	**Washington**	**NHL**	**62**	**12**	**14**	**26**	**33**	**11**	**0**	**1**	**1**	**10**
	Portland	AHL	8	11	4	15	4	....	....	....	....	....
1994-95	**Washington**	**NHL**	**46**	**11**	**14**	**25**	**44**	**7**	**2**	**5**	**7**	**12**
1995-96	**Washington**	**NHL**	**70**	**23**	**22**	**45**	**92**	**2**	**0**	**2**	**2**	**0**
1996-97	**Washington**	**NHL**	**78**	**17**	**25**	**42**	**67**	....	....	....	....	....
1997-98	**Washington**	**NHL**	**80**	**10**	**24**	**34**	**80**	....	....	....	....	....
	NHL Totals		**373**	**77**	**106**	**183**	**332**	**22**	**2**	**9**	**11**	**22**

WHL First All-Star Team (1992)

KONSTANTINOV, VLADIMIR (kohn-stahn-TEE-nahf) — DET.

Defense. Shoots right. 5'11", 190 lbs. Born, Murmansk, USSR, March 19, 1967.
(Detroit's 12th choice, 221st overall, in 1989 Entry Draft).

			Regular Season					Playoffs				
Season	Club	Lea	GP	G	A	TP	PIM	GP	G	A	TP	PIM
1984-85	CSKA Moscow	USSR	40	1	4	5	10	....	....	....	....	....
1985-86	CSKA Moscow	USSR	26	4	3	7	12	....	....	....	....	....
1986-87	CSKA Moscow	USSR	35	2	2	4	19	....	....	....	....	....
1987-88	CSKA Moscow	USSR	50	3	6	9	32	....	....	....	....	....
1988-89	CSKA Moscow	USSR	37	7	8	15	20	....	....	....	....	....
1989-90	CSKA Moscow	USSR	47	14	14	28	44	....	....	....	....	....
1990-91	CSKA Moscow	USSR	45	5	12	17	42	....	....	....	....	....
1991-92	**Detroit**	**NHL**	**79**	**8**	**26**	**34**	**172**	**11**	**0**	**1**	**1**	**16**
1992-93	**Detroit**	**NHL**	**82**	**5**	**17**	**22**	**137**	**7**	**0**	**1**	**1**	**8**
1993-94	**Detroit**	**NHL**	**80**	**12**	**21**	**33**	**138**	**7**	**0**	**2**	**2**	**4**
1994-95	Wedemark	Ger-2	15	13	17	30	51	....	....	....	....	....
	Detroit	**NHL**	**47**	**3**	**11**	**14**	**101**	**18**	**1**	**1**	**2**	**22**
1995-96	**Detroit**	**NHL**	**81**	**14**	**20**	**34**	**139**	**19**	**4**	**5**	**9**	**28**
1996-97	**Detroit**	**NHL**	**77**	**5**	**33**	**38**	**151**	**20**	**0**	**4**	**4**	**29 •**
1997-98	**Detroit**	**NHL**	DID NOT PLAY – INJURED									
	NHL Totals		**446**	**47**	**128**	**175**	**838**	**82**	**5**	**14**	**19**	**107**

NHL/Upper Deck All-Rookie Team (1992) • NHL Second All-Star Team (1996) • Won Alka-Seltzer Plus Award (1996)

• Missed entire 1997-98 season recovering from injuries suffered in automobile accident, July 13, 1997.

KOPISCHKE, JAY — L.A.

Left wing. Shoots left. 6'3", 210 lbs. Born, Alexandria, MN, February 7, 1978.
(Los Angeles' 8th choice, 193rd overall, in 1997 Entry Draft).

			Regular Season					Playoffs				
Season	Club	Lea	GP	G	A	TP	PIM	GP	G	A	TP	PIM
1996-97	North Iowa	USHL	53	14	17	31	97	....	....	....	....	....
1997-98	Notre Dame	CCHA	40	2	4	6	24	....	....	....	....	....

KORDIC, DAN (KOHR-dihk) — PHI.

Left wing. Shoots left. 6'5", 234 lbs. Born, Edmonton, Alta., April 18, 1971.
(Philadelphia's 9th choice, 88th overall, in 1990 Entry Draft).

			Regular Season					Playoffs				
Season	Club	Lea	GP	G	A	TP	PIM	GP	G	A	TP	PIM
1987-88	Medicine Hat	WHL	63	1	5	6	75	....	....	....	....	....
1988-89	Medicine Hat	WHL	70	1	13	14	190	....	....	....	....	....
1989-90	Medicine Hat	WHL	59	4	12	16	182	3	0	0	0	9
1990-91	Medicine Hat	WHL	67	8	15	23	150	12	2	6	8	42
1991-92	**Philadelphia**	**NHL**	**46**	**1**	**3**	**4**	**126**	....	....	....	....	....
1992-93	Hershey	AHL	14	0	2	2	17	....	....	....	....	....
1993-94	**Philadelphia**	**NHL**	**4**	**0**	**0**	**0**	**5**	....	....	....	....	....
	Hershey	AHL	64	0	4	4	164	11	0	3	3	26
1994-95	Hershey	AHL	37	0	2	2	121	6	0	1	1	21
1995-96	**Philadelphia**	**NHL**	**9**	**1**	**0**	**1**	**31**	....	....	....	....	....
	Hershey	AHL	52	2	6	8	101	....	....	....	....	....
1996-97	**Philadelphia**	**NHL**	**75**	**1**	**4**	**5**	**210**	**12**	**1**	**0**	**1**	**22**
1997-98	**Philadelphia**	**NHL**	**61**	**1**	**1**	**2**	**210**	....	....	....	....	....
	NHL Totals		**195**	**4**	**8**	**12**	**582**	**12**	**1**	**0**	**1**	**22**

KOROBOLIN, ALEXANDER (koh-roh-BOH-lihn) — NYR

Defense. Shoots left. 6'2", 189 lbs. Born, Chelyabinsk, USSR, March 12, 1976.
(NY Rangers' 4th choice, 100th overall, in 1994 Entry Draft).

			Regular Season					Playoffs				
Season	Club	Lea	GP	G	A	TP	PIM	GP	G	A	TP	PIM
1993-94	Chelyabinsk	CIS	32	0	0	0	30	....	....	....	....	....
1994-95	Chelyabinsk	CIS-2	STATISTICS NOT AVAILABLE									
1995-96	Chelyabinsk	CIS-2	STATISTICS NOT AVAILABLE									
1996-97	Chelyabinsk	Russia-2	60	2	7	9	54	....	....	....	....	....
1997-98	Chelyabinsk	Russia	45	1	5	6	50	....	....	....	....	....

KOROLEV, EVGENY (koh-roh-LEHV) — NYI

Defense. Shoots left. 6'1", 186 lbs. Born, Moscow, USSR, July 24, 1978.
(NY Islanders' 9th choice, 192nd overall, in 1996 Entry Draft).

			Regular Season					Playoffs				
Season	Club	Lea	GP	G	A	TP	PIM	GP	G	A	TP	PIM
1995-96	Peterborough	OHL	60	2	12	14	60	6	0	0	0	2
1996-97	Peterborough	OHL	64	5	17	22	60	11	1	1	2	8
1997-98	Peterborough	OHL	37	5	21	26	39	....	....	....	....	....
	London	OHL	27	4	10	14	36	15	2	7	9	29

KOROLEV, IGOR (koh-roh-LEHV) TOR.

Right wing. Shoots left. 6'1", 187 lbs. Born, Moscow, USSR, September 6, 1970.
(St. Louis' 1st choice, 38th overall, in 1992 Entry Draft).

			Regular Season					Playoffs				
Season	Club	Lea	GP	G	A	TP	PIM	GP	G	A	TP	PIM
1988-89	Moscow D'amo	USSR	1	0	0	0	2					
1989-90	Moscow D'amo	USSR	17	3	2	5	2					
1990-91	Moscow D'amo	USSR	38	12	4	16	12					
1991-92	Moscow D'amo	CIS	39	15	12	27	16					
1992-93	Moscow D'amo	CIS	5	1	2	3	4					
	St. Louis	**NHL**	**74**	**4**	**23**	**27**	**20**	**3**	**0**	**0**	**0**	**0**
1993-94	**St. Louis**	**NHL**	**73**	**6**	**10**	**16**	**40**	**2**	**0**	**0**	**0**	**0**
1994-95	Moscow D'amo	CIS	13	4	6	10	18					
	Winnipeg	**NHL**	**45**	**8**	**22**	**30**	**10**					
1995-96	**Winnipeg**	**NHL**	**73**	**22**	**29**	**51**	**42**	**6**	**0**	**3**	**3**	**0**
1996-97	**Phoenix**	**NHL**	**41**	**3**	**7**	**10**	**28**	**1**	**0**	**0**	**0**	**0**
	Michigan	IHL	4	2	2	4	0					
	Phoenix	IHL	4	2	6	8	4					
1997-98	**Toronto**	**NHL**	**78**	**17**	**22**	**39**	**22**					
	NHL Totals		**384**	**60**	**113**	**173**	**162**	**12**	**0**	**3**	**3**	**0**

Claimed by **Winnipeg** from **St. Louis** in NHL Waiver Draft, January 18, 1995. Transferred to **Phoenix** after **Winnipeg** franchise relocated, July 1, 1996. Signed as a free agent by **Toronto**, September 29, 1997.

KOROLYUK, ALEXANDER (koh-roh-LYUHK) S.J.

Right wing. Shoots left. 5'9", 190 lbs. Born, Moscow, USSR, January 15, 1976.
(San Jose's 6th choice, 141st overall, in 1994 Entry Draft).

			Regular Season					Playoffs				
Season	Club	Lea	GP	G	A	TP	PIM	GP	G	A	TP	PIM
1993-94	Soviet Wings	CIS	22	4	4	8	20	3	1	0	1	4
1994-95	Soviet Wings	CIS	52	16	13	29	62	4	1	2	3	4
1995-96	Soviet Wings	CIS	50	30	19	49	77					
1996-97	Soviet Wings	Russia	17	8	5	13	46					
	Manitoba	IHL	42	20	16	36	71					
1997-98	**San Jose**	**NHL**	**19**	**2**	**3**	**5**	**6**					
	Kentucky	AHL	44	16	23	39	96	3	0	0	0	0
	NHL Totals		**19**	**2**	**3**	**5**	**6**					

KOS, KYLE (KOHS) T.B.

Defense. Shoots left. 6'3", 184 lbs. Born, Hope, B.C., May 25, 1979.
(Tampa Bay's 2nd choice, 33rd overall, in 1997 Entry Draft).

			Regular Season					Playoffs				
Season	Club	Lea	GP	G	A	TP	PIM	GP	G	A	TP	PIM
1996-97	Red Deer	WHL	64	2	18	20	40	10	0	0	0	8
1997-98	Red Deer	WHL	71	7	33	40	102	5	0	3	3	4

KOTALIK, ALES (KOH-tuh-lihk, AH-lehsh) BUF.

Right wing. Shoots right. 6'1", 198 lbs. Born, Jindrichuv Hradec, Czech., December 23, 1978.
(Buffalo's 7th choice, 164th overall, in 1998 Entry Draft).

			Regular Season					Playoffs				
Season	Club	Lea	GP	G	A	TP	PIM	GP	G	A	TP	PIM
1993-94	HC Budejovice	Czech-Jr.	28	12	12	24						
1994-95	HC Budejovice	Czech-Jr.	36	26	17	43						
1995-96	HC Budejovice	Czech-Jr.	28	6	7	13						
1996-97	HC Budejovice	Czech-Jr.	36	15	16	31	24					
1997-98	HC Budejovice	Cze-Rep.	47	9	7	16	14					

KOVALENKO, ANDREI (koh-vah-LEHN-koh) EDM.

Right wing. Shoots left. 5'10", 215 lbs. Born, Balakovo, USSR, June 7, 1970.
(Quebec's 6th choice, 148th overall, in 1990 Entry Draft).

			Regular Season					Playoffs				
Season	Club	Lea	GP	G	A	TP	PIM	GP	G	A	TP	PIM
1988-89	CSKA Moscow	USSR	10	1	0	1	0					
1989-90	CSKA Moscow	USSR	48	8	5	13	20					
1990-91	CSKA Moscow	USSR	45	13	8	21	26					
1991-92	CSKA Moscow	CIS	44	19	13	32	32					
	Russia	Olympics	8	1	1	2	2					
1992-93	CSKA Moscow	CIS	3	3	1	4	4					
	Quebec	**NHL**	**81**	**27**	**41**	**68**	**57**	**4**	**1**	**0**	**1**	**2**
1993-94	**Quebec**	**NHL**	**58**	**16**	**17**	**33**	**46**					
1994-95	Lada	CIS	11	9	2	11	14					
	Quebec	**NHL**	**45**	**14**	**10**	**24**	**31**	**6**	**0**	**1**	**1**	**2**
1995-96	**Colorado**	**NHL**	**26**	**11**	**11**	**22**	**16**					
	Montreal	**NHL**	**51**	**17**	**17**	**34**	**33**	**6**	**0**	**0**	**0**	**6**
1996-97	**Edmonton**	**NHL**	**74**	**32**	**27**	**59**	**81**	**12**	**4**	**3**	**7**	**6**
1997-98	**Edmonton**	**NHL**	**59**	**6**	**17**	**23**	**28**	**1**	**0**	**0**	**0**	**2**
	Russia	Olympics	6	4	1	5	14					
	NHL Totals		**394**	**123**	**140**	**263**	**292**	**29**	**5**	**4**	**9**	**18**

Transferred to **Colorado** after **Quebec** franchise relocated, June 21, 1995. Traded to **Montreal** by **Colorado** with Martin Rucinsky and Jocelyn Thibault for Patrick Roy and Mike Keane, December 6, 1995. Traded to **Edmonton** by **Montreal** for Scott Thornton, September 6, 1996.

KOVALEV, ALEXEI (koh-VAH-lehv) NYR

Right wing. Shoots left. 6', 210 lbs. Born, Togliatti, USSR, February 24, 1973.
(NY Rangers' 1st choice, 15th overall, in 1991 Entry Draft).

			Regular Season					Playoffs				
Season	Club	Lea	GP	G	A	TP	PIM	GP	G	A	TP	PIM
1989-90	Moscow D'amo	USSR	1	0	0	0	0					
1990-91	Moscow D'amo	USSR	18	1	2	3	4					
1991-92	Moscow D'amo	CIS	33	16	9	25	20					
	Russia	Olympics	8	1	2	3	14					
1992-93	**NY Rangers**	**NHL**	**65**	**20**	**18**	**38**	**79**					
	Binghamton	AHL	13	13	11	24	35	9	3	5	8	14
1993-94	**NY Rangers**	**NHL**	**76**	**23**	**33**	**56**	**154**	**23**	**9**	**12**	**21**	**18** ♦
1994-95	Lada	CIS	12	8	8	16	49					
	NY Rangers	**NHL**	**48**	**13**	**15**	**28**	**30**	**10**	**4**	**7**	**11**	**10**
1995-96	**NY Rangers**	**NHL**	**81**	**24**	**34**	**58**	**98**	**11**	**3**	**4**	**7**	**14**
1996-97	**NY Rangers**	**NHL**	**45**	**13**	**22**	**35**	**42**					
1997-98	**NY Rangers**	**NHL**	**73**	**23**	**30**	**53**	**44**					
	NHL Totals		**388**	**116**	**152**	**268**	**447**	**44**	**16**	**23**	**39**	**42**

KOZLOV, VIKTOR (KAHS-lahf) FLA.

Center. Shoots right. 6'5", 232 lbs. Born, Togliatti, USSR, February 14, 1975.
(San Jose's 1st choice, 6th overall, in 1993 Entry Draft).

			Regular Season					Playoffs				
Season	Club	Lea	GP	G	A	TP	PIM	GP	G	A	TP	PIM
1990-91	Lada	USSR-2	2	2	0	2	0					
1991-92	Lada	CIS	3	0	0	0	0					
1992-93	Moscow D'amo	CIS	30	6	5	11	4	10	3	0	3	0
1993-94	Moscow D'amo	CIS	42	16	9	25	14	7	3	2	5	0
1994-95	Moscow D'amo	CIS	3	1	1	2	2					
	San Jose	**NHL**	**16**	**2**	**0**	**2**	**2**					
	Kansas City	IHL	4	1	1	2	0	13	4	5	9	12
1995-96	**San Jose**	**NHL**	**62**	**6**	**13**	**19**	**6**					
	Kansas City	IHL	15	4	7	11	12					
1996-97	**San Jose**	**NHL**	**78**	**16**	**25**	**41**	**40**					
1997-98	**San Jose**	**NHL**	**18**	**5**	**2**	**7**	**2**					
	Florida	**NHL**	**46**	**12**	**11**	**23**	**14**					
	NHL Totals		**220**	**41**	**51**	**92**	**64**					

Traded to **Florida** by **San Jose** with Florida's 5th round choice (previously acquired, Florida selected Jaroslav Spacek) in 1998 Entry Draft for Dave Lowry and Florida's 1st round choice (later traded to Tampa Bay - Tampa Bay selected Vincent Lecavalier) in 1998 Entry Draft, November 13, 1997.

KOZLOV, VYACHESLAV (KAHS-lahf, VYACH-ih-slav) DET.

Center. Shoots left. 5'10", 180 lbs. Born, Voskresensk, USSR, May 3, 1972.
(Detroit's 2nd choice, 45th overall, in 1990 Entry Draft).

			Regular Season					Playoffs				
Season	Club	Lea	GP	G	A	TP	PIM	GP	G	A	TP	PIM
1987-88	Khimik	USSR	2	0	0	0	0					
1988-89	Khimik	USSR	14	0	1	1	2					
1989-90	Khimik	USSR	45	14	12	26	38					
1990-91	Khimik	USSR	45	11	13	24	46					
1991-92	CSKA Moscow	CIS	11	6	5	11	12					
	Detroit	**NHL**	**7**	**0**	**2**	**2**	**2**					
1992-93	**Detroit**	**NHL**	**17**	**4**	**1**	**5**	**14**	**4**	**0**	**2**	**2**	**2**
	Adirondack	AHL	45	23	36	59	54	4	1	1	2	4
1993-94	**Detroit**	**NHL**	**77**	**34**	**39**	**73**	**50**	**7**	**2**	**5**	**7**	**12**
	Adirondack	AHL	3	0	1	1	15					
1994-95	CSKA Moscow	CIS	10	3	4	7	14					
	Detroit	**NHL**	**46**	**13**	**20**	**33**	**45**	**18**	**9**	**7**	**16**	**10**
1995-96	**Detroit**	**NHL**	**82**	**36**	**37**	**73**	**70**	**19**	**5**	**7**	**12**	**10**
1996-97	**Detroit**	**NHL**	**75**	**23**	**22**	**45**	**46**	**20**	**8**	**5**	**13**	**14** ♦
1997-98	**Detroit**	**NHL**	**80**	**25**	**27**	**52**	**46**	**22**	**6**	**8**	**14**	**10** ♦
	NHL Totals		**384**	**135**	**148**	**283**	**273**	**90**	**30**	**34**	**64**	**58**

USSR Rookie of the Year (1990)

KOZYREV, ANDREI (KOH-zih-rehf) CHI.

Defense. Shoots left. 6'1", 200 lbs. Born, Cherepovets, USSR, June 17, 1973.
(Chicago's 7th choice, 236th overall, in 1996 Entry Draft).

			Regular Season					Playoffs				
Season	Club	Lea	GP	G	A	TP	PIM	GP	G	A	TP	PIM
1993-94	Cherepovets	CIS	43	0	2	2	84	2	0	0	0	0
1994-95	Cherepovets	CIS	40	0	0	0	36					
1995-96	Cherepovets	CIS	52	2	0	2	55	4	0	0	0	4
1996-97	Cherepovets	Russia	24	1	0	1	40	1	0	0	0	25
1997-98	Indianapolis	IHL	13	0	1	1	28					

KRAFT, MILAN PIT.

Center. Shoots right. 6'2", 191 lbs. Born, Plzen, Czechoslovakia, January 17, 1980.
(Pitsburgh's 1st choice, 23rd overall, in 1998 Entry Draft).

			Regular Season					Playoffs				
Season	Club	Lea	GP	G	A	TP	PIM	GP	G	A	TP	PIM
1995-96	ZKZ Plzen	Czech-Jr.	49	54	41	95						
1996-97	ZKZ Plzen	Czech-Jr.	29	24	12	36						
	ZKZ Plzen	Cze-Rep.	9	0	1	1	2					
1997-98	Keramika Plzen	Czech-Jr.	24	22	21	43	12					
	Keramika Plzen	Cze-Rep.	16	0	5	5	0	1	0	0	0	0

KRAFT, RYAN

Center. Shoots left. 5'9", 181 lbs. Born, Bottineau, ND, November 7, 1975.
(San Jose's 11th choice, 194th overall, in 1995 Entry Draft).

			Regular Season					Playoffs				
Season	Club	Lea	GP	G	A	TP	PIM	GP	G	A	TP	PIM
1994-95	U. of Minnesota	WCHA	44	13	33	46	44					
1995-96	U. of Minnesota	WCHA	41	13	24	37	24					
1996-97	U. of Minnesota	WCHA	42	25	21	46	37					
1997-98	U. of Minnesota	WCHA	32	11	26	37	16					

KRAVCHUK, IGOR (krahv-CHOOK) OTT.

Defense. Shoots left. 6'1", 200 lbs. Born, Ufa, USSR, September 13, 1966.
(Chicago's 5th choice, 71st overall, in 1991 Entry Draft).

			Regular Season					Playoffs				
Season	Club	Lea	GP	G	A	TP	PIM	GP	G	A	TP	PIM
1984-85	Yulayev	USSR-2	50	3	2	5	22					
1985-86	Yulayev	USSR	21	2	2	4	6					
1986-87	Yulayev	USSR	22	0	1	1	8					
1987-88	CSKA Moscow	USSR	48	1	8	9	12					
	Soviet Union	Olympics	6	1	0	1	0					
1988-89	CSKA Moscow	USSR	22	3	3	6	2					
1989-90	CSKA Moscow	USSR	48	1	3	4	16					
1990-91	CSKA Moscow	USSR	41	6	5	11	16					
1991-92	CSKA Moscow	CIS	30	3	8	11	6					
	Russia	Olympics	8	3	2	5	6					
	Chicago	**NHL**	**18**	**1**	**8**	**9**	**4**	**18**	**2**	**6**	**8**	**8**
1992-93	**Chicago**	**NHL**	**38**	**6**	**9**	**15**	**30**					
	Edmonton	**NHL**	**17**	**4**	**8**	**12**	**2**					
1993-94	**Edmonton**	**NHL**	**81**	**12**	**38**	**50**	**16**					
1994-95	**Edmonton**	**NHL**	**36**	**7**	**11**	**18**	**29**					
1995-96	**Edmonton**	**NHL**	**26**	**4**	**4**	**8**	**10**					
	St. Louis	**NHL**	**40**	**3**	**12**	**15**	**24**	**10**	**1**	**5**	**6**	**4**
1996-97	**St. Louis**	**NHL**	**82**	**4**	**24**	**28**	**35**	**2**	**0**	**0**	**0**	**2**
1997-98	**Ottawa**	**NHL**	**81**	**8**	**27**	**35**	**8**	**11**	**2**	**3**	**5**	**4**
	Russia	Olympics	6	0	2	2	2					
	NHL Totals		**419**	**49**	**141**	**190**	**158**	**41**	**5**	**14**	**19**	**18**

Played in NHL All-Star Game (1998)

Traded to **Edmonton** by **Chicago** with Dean McAmmond for Joe Murphy, February 24, 1993. Traded to **St. Louis** by **Edmonton** with Ken Sutton for Jeff Norton and Donald Dufresne, January 4, 1996. Traded to **Ottawa** by **St. Louis** for Steve Duchesne, August 25, 1997.

KRISTEK, JAROSLAV (KRIHSH-tehk, YAH-roh-slahv) BUF.

Right wing. Shoots left. 6', 183 lbs. Born, Zlin, Czechoslovakia, March 16, 1980.
(Buffalo's 4th choice, 50th overall, in 1998 Entry Draft).

			Regular Season					Playoffs				
Season	Club	Lea	GP	G	A	TP	PIM	GP	G	A	TP	PIM
1995-96	ZPS Zlin	Czech-Jr.	34	33	20	53	....	....	....	....	....	....
1996-97	ZPS Zlin	Czech-Jr.	44	28	27	55	....	....	....	....	....	....
1997-98	ZPS Zlin	Czech-Jr.	7	8	5	13	....	....	....	....	....	....
	ZPS Zlin	Cze-Rep.	37	2	8	10	20	....	....	....	....	....
	Prostejov	Czech 2	4	0	0	0	....	....	....	....	....	....

KRISTOFFERSON, MARC DAL.

Right wing. Shoots left. 6'3", 200 lbs. Born, Ostersund, Sweden, January 22, 1979.
(Dallas' 4th choice, 105th overall, in 1997 Entry Draft).

			Regular Season					Playoffs				
Season	Club	Lea	GP	G	A	TP	PIM	GP	G	A	TP	PIM
1996-97	Mora	Sweden-2	33	1	5	6	26	....	....	....	....	....
1997-98	Mora	Sweden-2	27	7	6	13	40	....	....	....	....	....

KRIVOKRASOV, SERGEI (krih-vuh-KRA-sahf) NSH.

Right wing. Shoots left. 5'11", 185 lbs. Born, Angarsk, USSR, April 15, 1974.
(Chicago's 1st choice, 12th overall, in 1992 Entry Draft).

			Regular Season					Playoffs				
Season	Club	Lea	GP	G	A	TP	PIM	GP	G	A	TP	PIM
1990-91	CSKA Moscow	USSR	41	4	0	4	8	....	....	....	....	....
1991-92	CSKA Moscow	CIS	42	10	8	18	35	....	....	....	....	....
1992-93	**Chicago**	**NHL**	**4**	**0**	**0**	**0**	**2**	....	....	....	....	....
	Indianapolis	IHL	78	36	33	69	157	5	3	1	4	2
1993-94	**Chicago**	**NHL**	**9**	**1**	**0**	**1**	**4**	....	....	....	....	....
	Indianapolis	IHL	53	19	26	45	145	....	....	....	....	....
1994-95	Indianapolis	IHL	29	12	15	27	41	....	....	....	....	....
	Chicago	**NHL**	**41**	**12**	**7**	**19**	**33**	**10**	**0**	**0**	**0**	**8**
1995-96	**Chicago**	**NHL**	**46**	**6**	**10**	**16**	**32**	**5**	**1**	**0**	**1**	**2**
	Indianapolis	IHL	9	4	5	9	28	....	....	....	....	....
1996-97	**Chicago**	**NHL**	**67**	**13**	**11**	**24**	**42**	**6**	**1**	**0**	**1**	**4**
1997-98	**Chicago**	**NHL**	**58**	**10**	**13**	**23**	**33**	....	....	....	....	....
	Russia	Olympics	6	0	0	0	4	....	....	....	....	....
	NHL Totals		**225**	**42**	**41**	**83**	**146**	**21**	**2**	**0**	**2**	**14**

Traded to **Nashville** by **Chicago** for future considerations, June 26, 1998.

KRON, ROBERT (KROHN) CAR.

Left wing. Shoots left. 5'11", 185 lbs. Born, Brno, Czech., February 27, 1967.
(Vancouver's 5th choice, 88th overall, in 1985 Entry Draft).

			Regular Season					Playoffs				
Season	Club	Lea	GP	G	A	TP	PIM	GP	G	A	TP	PIM
1983-84	Brno	Czech-2	3	0	1	1	0	....	....	....	....	....
1984-85	Zetor Brno	Czech.	40	6	8	14	6	....	....	....	....	....
1985-86	Zetor Brno	Czech.	44	5	6	11	....	....	....	....	....	....
1986-87	Zetor Brno	Czech.	34	18	11	29	10	....	....	....	....	....
1987-88	Zetor Brno	Czech.	44	14	7	21	30	....	....	....	....	....
1988-89	Dukla Trencin	Czech.	43	28	19	47	26	....	....	....	....	....
1989-90	Dukla Trencin	Czech.	39	22	22	44	....	....	....	....	....	....
1990-91	**Vancouver**	**NHL**	**76**	**12**	**20**	**32**	**21**	....	....	....	....	....
1991-92	**Vancouver**	**NHL**	**36**	**2**	**2**	**4**	**2**	**11**	**1**	**2**	**3**	**2**
1992-93	**Vancouver**	**NHL**	**32**	**10**	**11**	**21**	**14**	....	....	....	....	....
	Hartford	**NHL**	**13**	**4**	**2**	**6**	**4**	....	....	....	....	....
1993-94	**Hartford**	**NHL**	**77**	**24**	**26**	**50**	**8**	....	....	....	....	....
1994-95	**Hartford**	**NHL**	**37**	**10**	**8**	**18**	**10**	....	....	....	....	....
1995-96	**Hartford**	**NHL**	**77**	**22**	**28**	**50**	**6**	....	....	....	....	....
1996-97	**Hartford**	**NHL**	**68**	**10**	**12**	**22**	**10**	....	....	....	....	....
1997-98	**Carolina**	**NHL**	**81**	**16**	**20**	**36**	**12**	....	....	....	....	....
	NHL Totals		**497**	**110**	**129**	**239**	**87**	**11**	**1**	**2**	**3**	**2**

Traded to **Hartford** by **Vancouver** with Vancouver's 3rd round choice (Marek Malik) in 1993 Entry Draft and future considerations (Jim Sandlak, May 17, 1993) for Murray Craven and Vancouver's 5th round choice (previously acquired, Vancouver selected Scott Walker) in 1993 Entry Draft, March 22, 1993. Transferred to **Carolina** after **Hartford** franchise relocated, June 25, 1997.

KROPAC, RADOSLAV (KRO-pahch) NYR

Right wing. Shoots left. 6', 187 lbs. Born, Bratislava, Czech., April 5, 1975.
(NY Rangers' 13th choice, 260th overall, in 1994 Entry Draft).

			Regular Season					Playoffs				
Season	Club	Lea	GP	G	A	TP	PIM	GP	G	A	TP	PIM
1993-94	Bratislava	Slovakia	33	7	6	13	12	....	....	....	....	....
1994-95	Bratislava	Slovakia	35	17	8	25	38	7	1	2	3	4
1995-96	Bratislava	Slovakia	31	5	9	14	8	13	4	3	7	....
1996-97	Bratislava	Slovakia	43	8	7	15	....	2	1	1	2	....
1997-98	Bratislava	EuroHL	8	0	0	0	6	....	....	....	....	....
	Bratislava	Slovakia	33	12	12	24	8	11	3	3	6	4

KROUPA, VLASTIMIL (KROO-pah, VLAS-tuh-meel) N.J.

Defense. Shoots left. 6'3", 210 lbs. Born, Most, Czech., April 27, 1975.
(San Jose's 3rd choice, 45th overall, in 1993 Entry Draft).

			Regular Season					Playoffs				
Season	Club	Lea	GP	G	A	TP	PIM	GP	G	A	TP	PIM
1992-93	Litvinov	Czech.	9	0	1	1	....	....	....	....	....	....
1993-94	**San Jose**	**NHL**	**27**	**1**	**3**	**4**	**20**	**14**	**1**	**2**	**3**	**21**
	Kansas City	IHL	39	3	12	15	12	....	....	....	....	....
1994-95	**San Jose**	**NHL**	**14**	**0**	**2**	**2**	**16**	**6**	**0**	**0**	**0**	**4**
	Kansas City	IHL	51	4	8	12	49	12	2	4	6	22
1995-96	**San Jose**	**NHL**	**27**	**1**	**7**	**8**	**18**	....	....	....	....	....
	Kansas City	IHL	39	5	22	27	44	5	0	1	1	6
1996-97	**San Jose**	**NHL**	**35**	**2**	**6**	**8**	**12**	....	....	....	....	....
	Kentucky	AHL	5	0	3	3	0	....	....	....	....	....
1997-98	**New Jersey**	**NHL**	**2**	**0**	**1**	**1**	**0**	....	....	....	....	....
	Albany	AHL	71	5	29	34	48	12	0	3	3	6
	NHL Totals		**105**	**4**	**19**	**23**	**66**	**20**	**1**	**2**	**3**	**25**

Traded to **New Jersey** by **San Jose** for New Jersey's 3rd round choice (later traded to Nashville — Nashville selected Geoff Koch) in 1998 Entry Draft, August 22, 1997.

KRUPP, UWE (KROOP, OO-VAY) DET.

Defense. Shoots right. 6'6", 235 lbs. Born, Cologne, West Germany, June 24, 1965.
(Buffalo's 13th choice, 223rd overall, in 1983 Entry Draft).

			Regular Season					Playoffs				
Season	Club	Lea	GP	G	A	TP	PIM	GP	G	A	TP	PIM
1982-83	Kolner Haie	Germany	11	0	0	0	0	....	....	....	....	....
1983-84	Kolner Haie	Germany	26	0	4	4	22	....	....	....	....	....
1984-85	Kolner Haie	Germany	39	11	8	19	36	....	....	....	....	....
1985-86	Kolner Haie	Germany	45	10	21	31	83	....	....	....	....	....
1986-87	**Buffalo**	**NHL**	**26**	**1**	**4**	**5**	**23**	....	....	....	....	....
	Rochester	AHL	42	3	19	22	50	17	1	11	12	16
1987-88	**Buffalo**	**NHL**	**75**	**2**	**9**	**11**	**151**	**6**	**0**	**0**	**0**	**15**
1988-89	**Buffalo**	**NHL**	**70**	**5**	**13**	**18**	**55**	**5**	**0**	**1**	**1**	**4**
1989-90	**Buffalo**	**NHL**	**74**	**3**	**20**	**23**	**85**	**6**	**0**	**0**	**0**	**4**
1990-91	**Buffalo**	**NHL**	**74**	**12**	**32**	**44**	**66**	**6**	**1**	**1**	**2**	**6**
1991-92	**Buffalo**	**NHL**	**8**	**2**	**0**	**2**	**6**	....	....	....	....	....
	NY Islanders	**NHL**	**59**	**6**	**29**	**35**	**43**	....	....	....	....	....
1992-93	**NY Islanders**	**NHL**	**80**	**9**	**29**	**38**	**67**	**18**	**1**	**5**	**6**	**12**
1993-94	**NY Islanders**	**NHL**	**41**	**7**	**14**	**21**	**30**	**4**	**0**	**1**	**1**	**4**
1994-95	Landshut	Germany	5	1	2	3	6	....	....	....	....	....
	Quebec	**NHL**	**44**	**6**	**17**	**23**	**20**	**5**	**0**	**2**	**2**	**2**
1995-96	**Colorado**	**NHL**	**6**	**0**	**3**	**3**	**4**	**22**	**4**	**12**	**16**	**33** ♦
1996-97	**Colorado**	**NHL**	**60**	**4**	**17**	**21**	**48**	....	....	....	....	....
1997-98	**Colorado**	**NHL**	**78**	**9**	**22**	**31**	**38**	**7**	**0**	**1**	**1**	**4**
	Germany	Olympics	2	0	2	2	4	....	....	....	....	....
	NHL Totals		**695**	**66**	**209**	**275**	**636**	**79**	**6**	**23**	**29**	**84**

Played in NHL All-Star Game (1991)

Traded to **NY Islanders** by **Buffalo** with Pierre Turgeon, Benoit Hogue and Dave McLlwain for Pat Lafontaine, Randy Hillier, Randy Wood and NY Islanders' 4th round choice (Dean Melanson) in 1992 Entry Draft, October 25, 1991. Traded to **Quebec** by **NY Islanders** with NY Islanders' 1st round choice (Wade Belak) in 1994 Entry Draft for Ron Sutter and Quebec's 1st round choice (Brett Lindros) in 1994 Entry Draft, June 28, 1994. Transferred to **Colorado** after **Quebec** franchise relocated, June 21, 1995. Claimed by **Nashville** from **Colorado** in Expansion Draft, June 26, 1998. Signed as a free agent by **Detroit**, July 7, 1998.

KRUSE, PAUL (KROOZ) BUF.

Left wing. Shoots left. 6', 202 lbs. Born, Merritt, B.C., March 15, 1970.
(Calgary's 6th choice, 83rd overall, in 1990 Entry Draft).

			Regular Season					Playoffs				
Season	Club	Lea	GP	G	A	TP	PIM	GP	G	A	TP	PIM
1988-89	Kamloops	WHL	68	8	15	23	209	....	....	....	....	....
1989-90	Kamloops	WHL	67	22	23	45	291	17	3	5	8	79
1990-91	**Calgary**	**NHL**	**1**	**0**	**0**	**0**	**7**	....	....	....	....	....
	Salt Lake	IHL	83	24	20	44	313	4	1	1	2	4
1991-92	**Calgary**	**NHL**	**16**	**3**	**1**	**4**	**65**	....	....	....	....	....
	Salt Lake	IHL	57	14	15	29	267	5	1	2	3	19
1992-93	**Calgary**	**NHL**	**27**	**2**	**3**	**5**	**41**	....	....	....	....	....
	Salt Lake	IHL	35	1	4	5	206	....	....	....	....	....
1993-94	**Calgary**	**NHL**	**68**	**3**	**8**	**11**	**185**	**7**	**0**	**0**	**0**	**14**
1994-95	**Calgary**	**NHL**	**45**	**11**	**5**	**16**	**141**	**7**	**4**	**2**	**6**	**10**
1995-96	**Calgary**	**NHL**	**75**	**3**	**12**	**15**	**145**	**3**	**0**	**0**	**0**	**4**
1996-97	**Calgary**	**NHL**	**14**	**2**	**0**	**2**	**30**	....	....	....	....	....
	NY Islanders	**NHL**	**48**	**4**	**2**	**6**	**111**	....	....	....	....	....
1997-98	**NY Islanders**	**NHL**	**62**	**6**	**1**	**7**	**138**	....	....	....	....	....
	Buffalo	**NHL**	**12**	**1**	**1**	**2**	**49**	**1**	**1**	**0**	**1**	**4**
	NHL Totals		**368**	**35**	**33**	**68**	**912**	**18**	**5**	**2**	**7**	**32**

Traded to **NY Islanders** by **Calgary** for Colorado's 3rd round choice (previously acquired by NY Islanders — later traded to Hartford — Hartford selected Francis Lessard) in 1997 Entry Draft, November 27, 1996. Traded to **Buffalo** by **NY Islanders** with Jason Holland for Jason Dawe, March 24, 1998.

KRYGIER, TODD (KREE-guhr)

Left wing. Shoots left. 6', 185 lbs. Born, Chicago Heights, IL, October 12, 1965.
(Hartford's 1st choice, 16th overall, in 1988 Supplemental Draft).

			Regular Season					Playoffs				
Season	Club	Lea	GP	G	A	TP	PIM	GP	G	A	TP	PIM
1984-85	U. of Connecticut	NCAA	14	14	11	25	12	....	....	....	....	....
1985-86	U. of Connecticut	NCAA	32	29	27	56	46	....	....	....	....	....
1986-87	U. of Connecticut	NCAA	28	24	24	48	44	....	....	....	....	....
1987-88	U. of Connecticut	NCAA	27	32	39	71	28	....	....	....	....	....
	New Haven	AHL	13	1	5	6	34	....	....	....	....	....
1988-89	Binghamton	AHL	76	26	42	68	77	....	....	....	....	....
1989-90	**Hartford**	**NHL**	**58**	**18**	**12**	**30**	**52**	**7**	**2**	**1**	**3**	**4**
	Binghamton	AHL	12	1	9	10	16	....	....	....	....	....
1990-91	**Hartford**	**NHL**	**72**	**13**	**17**	**30**	**95**	**6**	**0**	**2**	**2**	**0**
1991-92	**Washington**	**NHL**	**67**	**13**	**17**	**30**	**107**	**5**	**2**	**1**	**3**	**4**
1992-93	**Washington**	**NHL**	**77**	**11**	**12**	**23**	**60**	**6**	**1**	**1**	**2**	**4**
1993-94	**Washington**	**NHL**	**66**	**12**	**18**	**30**	**60**	**5**	**2**	**0**	**2**	**10**
1994-95	**Anaheim**	**NHL**	**35**	**11**	**11**	**22**	**10**	....	....	....	....	....
1995-96	**Anaheim**	**NHL**	**60**	**9**	**28**	**37**	**70**	....	....	....	....	....
	Washington	**NHL**	**16**	**6**	**5**	**11**	**12**	**6**	**2**	**0**	**2**	**12**
1996-97	**Washington**	**NHL**	**47**	**5**	**11**	**16**	**37**	....	....	....	....	....
1997-98	**Washington**	**NHL**	**45**	**2**	**12**	**14**	**30**	**13**	**1**	**2**	**3**	**6**
	Portland	AHL	6	3	4	7	6	....	....	....	....	....
	NHL Totals		**543**	**100**	**143**	**243**	**533**	**48**	**10**	**7**	**17**	**40**

NCAA (College Div.) East Second All-American Team (1987)

Traded to **Washington** by **Hartford** for Washington's 4th round choice (later traded to Calgary — Calgary selected Jason Smith) in 1993 Entry Draft, October 3, 1991. Traded to **Anaheim** by **Washington** for Anaheim's 4th round choice (later traded to Dallas — Dallas selected Mike Hurley) in 1996 Entry Draft, February 2, 1995. Traded to **Washington** by **Anaheim** for Mike Torchia, March 8, 1996.

KUBA, FILIP (KOO-bah, FIHL-ihp) FLA.

Defense. Shoots left. 6'3", 202 lbs. Born, Ostrava, Czech., December 29, 1976.
(Florida's 8th choice, 192nd overall, in 1995 Entry Draft).

			Regular Season					Playoffs				
Season	Club	Lea	GP	G	A	TP	PIM	GP	G	A	TP	PIM
1994-95	Vitkovice	Czech-Jr.	35	10	15	25	....	....	....	....	....	....
	Vitkovice	Cze-Rep.	....	....	....	....	....	4	0	0	0	2
1995-96	Vitkovice	Cze-Rep.	19	0	1	1	....	....	....	....	....	....
1996-97	Carolina	AHL	51	0	12	12	38	....	....	....	....	....
1997-98	New Haven	AHL	77	4	13	17	58	3	1	1	2	0

KUBINA, PAVEL (koo-BEE-nuh) T.B.

Defense. Shoots right. 6'3", 213 lbs. Born, Celadna, Czech., April 15, 1977.
(Tampa Bay's 6th choice, 179th overall, in 1996 Entry Draft).

			Regular Season					Playoffs				
Season	Club	Lea	GP	G	A	TP	PIM	GP	G	A	TP	PIM
1993-94	Vitkovice	Czech-Jr.	35	4	3	7	....	....	....	....	....	....
	Vitkovice	Cze-Rep.	1	0	0	0	....	....	....	....	....	....
1994-95	Vitkovice	Czech-Jr.	20	6	10	16	....	....	....	....	....	....
	Vitkovice	Cze-Rep.	8	2	0	2	10	4	0	0	0	0
1995-96	Vitkovice	Cze-Rep.	33	3	4	7	32	4	0	0	0	0
	Vitkovice	Czech-Jr.	16	5	10	15	....	....	....	....	....	....
1996-97	Vitkovice	Cze-Rep.	1	0	0	0	0	....	....	....	....	....
	Moose Jaw	WHL	61	12	32	44	116	11	2	5	7	27
1997-98	**Tampa Bay**	**NHL**	**10**	**1**	**2**	**3**	**22**	....	....	....	....	....
	Adirondack	AHL	55	4	8	12	86	1	1	0	1	14
	NHL Totals		**10**	**1**	**2**	**3**	**22**	....	....	....	....	....

KUBOS, PETR (KOO-bawsh) MTL.

Defense. Shoots right. 6'2", 189 lbs. Born, Vsetin, Czechoslovakia, September 10, 1979.
(Montreal's 9th choice, 197th overall, in 1997 Entry Draft).

			Regular Season					Playoffs				
Season	Club	Lea	GP	G	A	TP	PIM	GP	G	A	TP	PIM
1994-95	Petra Vsetin	Czech-Jr.	19	8	11	19	14	....	....	....	....	....
1995-96	Petra Vsetin	Czech-Jr.	37	21	17	38	18	....	....	....	....	....
	Petra Vsetin	Cze-Rep.	2	0	0	0	0	....	....	....	....	....
1996-97	Petra Vsetin	Czech-Jr.	14	3	13	16	6	....	....	....	....	....
	Petra Vsetin	Cze-Rep.	16	0	1	1	2	....	....	....	....	....
1997-98	Prince George	WHL	58	3	17	20	12	11	1	0	1	0

KUCERA, FRANTISEK (koo-CHAIR-uh)

Defense. Shoots right. 6'2", 205 lbs. Born, Prague, Czech., February 3, 1968.
(Chicago's 3rd choice, 77th overall, in 1986 Entry Draft).

			Regular Season					Playoffs				
Season	Club	Lea	GP	G	A	TP	PIM	GP	G	A	TP	PIM
1985-86	Sparta Praha	Czech.	15	0	0	0	....	....	....	....	....	....
1986-87	Sparta Praha	Czech.	40	5	2	7	14	....	....	....	....	....
1987-88	Sparta Praha	Czech.	46	7	2	9	30	....	....	....	....	....
1988-89	Dukla Jihlava	Czech.	45	10	9	19	28	....	....	....	....	....
1989-90	Dukla Jihlava	Czech.	43	9	10	19	....	....	....	....	....	....
1990-91	**Chicago**	**NHL**	**40**	**2**	**12**	**14**	**32**	....	....	....	....	....
	Indianapolis	IHL	35	8	19	27	23	7	0	1	1	15
1991-92	**Chicago**	**NHL**	**61**	**3**	**10**	**13**	**36**	**6**	**0**	**0**	**0**	**0**
	Indianapolis	IHL	7	1	2	3	4	....	....	....	....	....
1992-93	**Chicago**	**NHL**	**71**	**5**	**14**	**19**	**59**	....	....	....	....	....
1993-94	**Chicago**	**NHL**	**60**	**4**	**13**	**17**	**34**	....	....	....	....	....
	Hartford	**NHL**	**16**	**1**	**3**	**4**	**14**	....	....	....	....	....
1994-95	Sparta Praha	Cze-Rep.	16	1	2	3	14	....	....	....	....	....
	Hartford	**NHL**	**48**	**3**	**17**	**20**	**30**	....	....	....	....	....
1995-96	**Hartford**	**NHL**	**30**	**2**	**6**	**8**	**10**	....	....	....	....	....
	Vancouver	**NHL**	**24**	**1**	**0**	**1**	**10**	**6**	**0**	**1**	**1**	**0**
1996-97	**Vancouver**	**NHL**	**2**	**0**	**0**	**0**	**0**	....	....	....	....	....
	Syracuse	AHL	42	6	29	35	36	....	....	....	....	....
	Houston	IHL	12	0	3	3	20	....	....	....	....	....
	Philadelphia	**NHL**	**2**	**0**	**0**	**0**	**2**	....	....	....	....	....
	Philadelphia	AHL	9	1	5	6	2	10	1	6	7	20
1997-98	Sparta Praha	EuroHL	4	0	1	1	2	....	....	....	....	....
	Sparta Praha	Cze-Rep.	43	8	12	20	49	9	3	1	4	*53
	Czech Republic	Olympics	6	0	0	0	0	....	....	....	....	....
	NHL Totals		**354**	**21**	**75**	**96**	**227**	**12**	**0**	**1**	**1**	**0**

Traded to **Hartford** by **Chicago** with Jocelyn Lemieux for Gary Suter, Randy Cunneyworth and Hartford's 3rd round choice (later traded to Vancouver — Vancouver selected Larry Courville) in 1995 Entry Draft, March 11, 1994. Traded to **Vancouver** by **Hartford** with Jim Dowd and Hartford's 2nd round choice (Ryan Bonni) in 1997 Entry Draft for Jeff Brown and Vancouver's 3rd round choice (later traded to Calgary — Calgary selected Paul Manning) in 1998 Entry Draft, December 19, 1995. Traded to **Philadelphia** by **Vancouver** for future considerations, March 18, 1997.

KUCERA, JIRI (kuh-CHEH-rah) PIT.

Center. Shoots left. 5'11", 180 lbs. Born, Plzen, Czech., March 28, 1966.
(Pittsburgh's 8th choice, 152nd overall, in 1987 Entry Draft).

			Regular Season					Playoffs				
Season	Club	Lea	GP	G	A	TP	PIM	GP	G	A	TP	PIM
1986-87	Dukla Jihlava	Czech.	43	13	12	25	18	....	....	....	....	....
1987-88	Skoda Plzen	Czech.	41	21	24	45	22	....	....	....	....	....
1988-89	Skoda Plzen	Czech.	40	20	15	35	22	....	....	....	....	....
1989-89	Skoda Plzen	Czech.	47	13	24	37	....	....	....	....	....	....
1990-91	Tappara	Finland	44	23	34	57	26	3	0	2	2	4
1991-92	Tappara	Finland	44	22	20	42	8	....	....	....	....	....
1992-93	Tappara	Finland	48	22	32	54	20	....	....	....	....	....
1993-94	Tappara	Finland	47	16	26	42	37	10	7	5	12	4
1994-95	Lulea	Sweden	40	15	12	27	24	9	2	7	9	8
1995-96	Lulea	Sweden	39	15	19	34	38	12	4	6	10	6
1996-97	ZKZ Plzen	Cze-Rep.	43	10	23	33	28	....	....	....	....	....
1997-98	EHC Kloten	Switz.	38	8	22	30	18	7	1	2	3	2

KUKI, ARTO (KUH-kee) MTL.

Center. Shoots left. 6'3", 205 lbs. Born, Espoo, Finland, February 22, 1976.
(Montreal's 6th choice, 96th overall, in 1994 Entry Draft).

			Regular Season					Playoffs				
Season	Club	Lea	GP	G	A	TP	PIM	GP	G	A	TP	PIM
1993-94	Kiekko	Fin-Jr.	26	1	10	11	28	....	....	....	....	....
1994-95	Kiekko	Finland	4	0	1	1	0	....	....	....	....	....
1995-96	Kiekko	Finland	47	6	3	9	16	....	....	....	....	....
1996-97	Kiekko	Finland	50	6	15	21	20	4	0	1	1	2
1997-98	Kiekko	Finland	17	2	1	3	0	8	1	1	2	2

KURRI, JARI (KUHR-ree, YAH-ree)

Right wing. Shoots right. 6'1", 195 lbs. Born, Helsinki, Finland, May 18, 1960.
(Edmonton's 3rd choice, 69th overall, in 1980 Entry Draft).

			Regular Season					Playoffs				
Season	Club	Lea	GP	G	A	TP	PIM	GP	G	A	TP	PIM
1977-78	Jokerit	Finland	29	2	9	11	12	....	....	....	....	....
1978-79	Jokerit	Finland	33	16	14	30	12	....	....	....	....	....
1979-80	Jokerit	Finland	33	23	16	39	22	6	7	2	9	13
	Finland	Olympics	7	2	1	3	6	....	....	....	....	....
1980-81	**Edmonton**	**NHL**	**75**	**32**	**43**	**75**	**40**	**9**	**5**	**7**	**12**	**4**
1981-82	**Edmonton**	**NHL**	**71**	**32**	**54**	**86**	**32**	**5**	**2**	**5**	**7**	**10**
1982-83	**Edmonton**	**NHL**	**80**	**45**	**59**	**104**	**22**	**16**	**8**	**15**	**23**	**8**
1983-84	**Edmonton**	**NHL**	**64**	**52**	**61**	**113**	**14**	**19**	***14**	**14**	**28**	**13** ♦
1984-85	**Edmonton**	**NHL**	**73**	**71**	**64**	**135**	**30**	**18**	***19**	**12**	**31**	**6** ♦
1985-86	**Edmonton**	**NHL**	**78**	***68**	**63**	**131**	**22**	**10**	**2**	**10**	**12**	**4**
1986-87	**Edmonton**	**NHL**	**79**	**54**	**54**	**108**	**41**	**21**	***15**	**10**	**25**	**20** ♦
1987-88	**Edmonton**	**NHL**	**80**	**43**	**53**	**96**	**30**	**19**	***14**	**17**	**31**	**12** ♦
1988-89	**Edmonton**	**NHL**	**76**	**44**	**58**	**102**	**69**	**7**	**3**	**5**	**8**	**6**
1989-90	**Edmonton**	**NHL**	**78**	**33**	**60**	**93**	**48**	**22**	**10**	**15**	**25**	**18** ♦
1990-91	HC Milano	Italy	30	27	48	75	6	10	10	12	22	2
1991-92	**Los Angeles**	**NHL**	**73**	**23**	**37**	**60**	**24**	**4**	**1**	**2**	**3**	**4**
1992-93	**Los Angeles**	**NHL**	**82**	**27**	**60**	**87**	**38**	**24**	**9**	**8**	**17**	**12**
1993-94	**Los Angeles**	**NHL**	**81**	**31**	**46**	**77**	**48**	....	....	....	....	....
1994-95	Jokerit	Finland	20	10	9	19	10	....	....	....	....	....
	Los Angeles	**NHL**	**38**	**10**	**19**	**29**	**24**	....	....	....	....	....
1995-96	**Los Angeles**	**NHL**	**57**	**17**	**23**	**40**	**37**	....	....	....	....	....
	NY Rangers	**NHL**	**14**	**1**	**4**	**5**	**2**	**11**	**3**	**5**	**8**	**2**
1996-97	**Anaheim**	**NHL**	**82**	**13**	**22**	**35**	**12**	**11**	**1**	**2**	**3**	**4**
1997-98	**Colorado**	**NHL**	**70**	**5**	**17**	**22**	**12**	**4**	**0**	**0**	**0**	**0**
	Finland	Olympics	6	1	4	5	2	....	....	....	....	....
	NHL Totals		**1251**	**601**	**797**	**1398**	**545**	**200**	**106**	**127**	**233**	**123**

NHL Second All-Star Team (1984, 1986, 1989) • Won Lady Byng Memorial Trophy (1985) • NHL First All-Star Team (1985, 1987)

Played in NHL All-Star Game (1983, 1985, 1986, 1988, 1989, 1990, 1993, 1998)

Traded to **Philadelphia** by **Edmonton** with Dave Brown and Corey Foster for Craig Fisher, Scott Mellanby and Craig Berube, May 30, 1991. Traded to **LA Kings** by **Philadelphia** with Jeff Chychrun for Steve Duchesne, Steve Kasper and LA Kings' 4th round choice (Aris Brimanis) in 1991 Entry Draft, May 30, 1991. Traded to **NY Rangers** by **LA Kings** with Marty McSorley and Shane Churla for Ray Ferraro, Ian Laperriere, Mattias Norstrom, Nathan Lafayette and NY Rangers' 4th round choice (Sean Blanchard) in 1997 Entry Draft, March 14, 1996. Signed as a free agent by **Anaheim**, September 10, 1996. Signed as a free agent by **Colorado**, September 15, 1997.

KUSTER, HENRY (KOO-stuhr)

Right wing. Shoots right. 6', 195 lbs. Born, Edmonton, Alta., November 11, 1977.
(Boston's 2nd choice, 45th overall, in 1996 Entry Draft).

			Regular Season					Playoffs				
Season	Club	Lea	GP	G	A	TP	PIM	GP	G	A	TP	PIM
1993-94	Medicine Hat	WHL	67	14	27	41	26	3	0	0	0	2
1994-95	Medicine Hat	WHL	71	28	26	54	61	5	1	3	4	6
1995-96	Medicine Hat	WHL	72	35	43	78	54	1	0	0	0	0
1996-97	Medicine Hat	WHL	72	26	35	61	47	4	0	1	1	4
1997-98	Medicine Hat	WHL	43	14	17	31	35	....	....	....	....	....
	Red Deer	WHL	25	9	23	32	16	5	1	3	4	4

KUZNETSOV, MAXIM (kooz-NEHT-zahv) DET.

Defense. Shoots left. 6'5", 198 lbs. Born, Pavlodar, USSR, March 24, 1977.
(Detroit's 1st choice, 26th overall, in 1995 Entry Draft).

			Regular Season					Playoffs				
Season	Club	Lea	GP	G	A	TP	PIM	GP	G	A	TP	PIM
1994-95	Moscow D'amo	CIS	11	0	0	0	8	....	....	....	....	....
1995-96	Moscow D'amo	CIS	9	1	1	2	22	4	0	0	0	0
1996-97	Moscow D'amo	Russia	23	0	2	2	16	....	....	....	....	....
	Adirondack	AHL	2	0	1	1	6	2	0	0	0	0
1997-98	Adirondack	AHL	51	5	5	10	43	3	0	1	1	4

KUZNETSOV, SERGEI (kooz-NEHT-zahv) T.B.

Center. Shoots left. 6', 180 lbs. Born, Yaroslavl, USSR, January 29, 1980.
(Tampa Bay's 6th choice, 146th overall, in 1998 Entry Draft).

			Regular Season					Playoffs				
Season	Club	Lea	GP	G	A	TP	PIM	GP	G	A	TP	PIM
1995-96	Yaroslavl	Rus-Jr.	28	14	14	28	20	....	....	....	....	....
1996-97	Yaroslavl 2	Russia-3	62	16	15	31	35	....	....	....	....	....
1997-98	Yaroslavl 2	Russia-2	42	10	13	23	30	....	....	....	....	....

KUZNIK, GREG CAR.

Defense. Shoots left. 6', 182 lbs. Born, Prince George, B.C., June 12, 1978.
(Hartford's 7th choice, 171st overall, in 1996 Entry Draft).

			Regular Season					Playoffs				
Season	Club	Lea	GP	G	A	TP	PIM	GP	G	A	TP	PIM
1995-96	Seattle	WHL	70	2	13	15	149	5	0	0	0	6
1996-97	Seattle	WHL	70	4	9	13	161	14	0	2	2	26
1997-98	Seattle	WHL	72	5	12	17	197	5	0	0	0	4

KVASHA, OLEG (kuh-VAH-shah) FLA.

Left wing. Shoots right. 6'5", 205 lbs. Born, Moscow, USSR, July 26, 1978.
(Florida's 3rd choice, 65th overall, in 1996 Entry Draft).

			Regular Season					Playoffs				
Season	Club	Lea	GP	G	A	TP	PIM	GP	G	A	TP	PIM
1995-96	CSKA Moscow	CIS	38	2	3	5	14	2	0	0	0	0
1996-97	CSKA Moscow	Russia	44	20	22	42	115	....	....	....	....	....
1997-98	New Haven	AHL	57	13	16	29	46	3	2	1	3	0

KWIATKOWSKI, JOEL (KWEE-at-KOW-skee) ANA.

Defense. Shoots left. 6'2", 200 lbs. Born, Maymont, Sask., March 22, 1977.
(Dallas' 7th choice, 194th overall, in 1996 Entry Draft).

			Regular Season					Playoffs				
Season	Club	Lea	GP	G	A	TP	PIM	GP	G	A	TP	PIM
1995-96	Prince George	WHL	72	12	28	40	133	....	....	....	....	....
1996-97	Prince George	WHL	72	15	37	52	94	15	4	2	6	24
1997-98	Prince George	WHL	62	21	43	64	65	11	3	6	9	6

WHL West Second All-Star Team (1997) • WHL West First All-Star Team (1998)

KYPREOS, NICK (KIH-pree-ohz)

Left wing. Shoots left. 6', 205 lbs. Born, Toronto, Ont., June 4, 1966.

			Regular Season					Playoffs				
Season	Club	Lea	GP	G	A	TP	PIM	GP	G	A	TP	PIM
1983-84	North Bay	OHL	51	12	11	23	36	4	3	2	5	9
1984-85	North Bay	OHL	64	41	36	77	71	8	2	2	4	15
1985-86	North Bay	OHL	64	62	35	97	112	....	....	....	....	....
1986-87	North Bay	OHL	46	49	41	90	54	24	11	5	16	78
	Hershey	AHL	10	0	1	1	4	....	....	....	....	....
1987-88	Hershey	AHL	71	24	20	44	101	12	0	2	2	17
1988-89	Hershey	AHL	28	12	15	27	19	12	4	5	9	11
1989-90	**Washington**	**NHL**	**31**	**5**	**4**	**9**	**82**	**7**	**1**	**0**	**1**	**15**
	Baltimore	AHL	14	6	5	11	6	7	4	1	5	17
1990-91	**Washington**	**NHL**	**79**	**9**	**9**	**18**	**196**	**9**	**0**	**1**	**1**	**38**
1991-92	**Washington**	**NHL**	**65**	**4**	**6**	**10**	**206**	....	....	....	....	....
1992-93	**Hartford**	**NHL**	**75**	**17**	**10**	**27**	**325**	....	....	....	....	....
1993-94	**Hartford**	**NHL**	**10**	**0**	**0**	**0**	**37**	....	....	....	....	....
	NY Rangers	**NHL**	**46**	**3**	**5**	**8**	**102**	**3**	**0**	**0**	**0**	**2 ♦**
1994-95	**NY Rangers**	**NHL**	**40**	**1**	**3**	**4**	**93**	**10**	**0**	**2**	**2**	**6**
1995-96	**NY Rangers**	**NHL**	**42**	**3**	**4**	**7**	**77**	....	....	....	....	....
	Toronto	**NHL**	**19**	**1**	**1**	**2**	**30**	**5**	**0**	**0**	**0**	**4**
1996-97	**Toronto**	**NHL**	**35**	**3**	**2**	**5**	**62**	....	....	....	....	....
	St. John's	AHL	4	0	0	0	4	....	....	....	....	....
1997-98	**Toronto**	**NHL**	DID NOT PLAY – INJURED									
	NHL Totals		**442**	**46**	**44**	**90**	**1210**	**34**	**1**	**3**	**4**	**65**

OHL First All-Star Team (1986) • OHL Second All-Star Team (1987)

Signed as a free agent by **Philadelphia,** September 30, 1984. Claimed by **Washington** from **Philadelphia** in NHL Waiver Draft, October 2, 1989. Traded to **Hartford** by **Washington** for Mark Hunter and future considerations (Yvon Corriveau, August 20, 1992), June 15, 1992. Traded to **NY Rangers** by **Hartford** with Steve Larmer, Barry Richter and Hartford's 6th round choice (Yuri Litvinov) in 1994 Entry Draft for Darren Turcotte and James Patrick, November 2, 1993. Traded to **Toronto** by **NY Rangers** for Bill Berg, February 29, 1996. • Suffered career-ending head injury in exhibition game vs. NY Rangers, September 17, 1997.

LAAKSONEN, ANTTI (lah-AHK-soh-nehn, AHN-tee) BOS.

Left wing. Shoots left. 6', 180 lbs. Born, Tammela, Finland, October 3, 1973.
(Boston's 10th choice, 191st overall, in 1997 Entry Draft).

			Regular Season					Playoffs				
Season	Club	Lea	GP	G	A	TP	PIM	GP	G	A	TP	PIM
1990-91	FoPS Forssa	Finland-2	2	0	0	0	0	....	....	....	....	....
1991-92	FoPS Forssa	Finland-2	41	16	15	31	8	....	....	....	....	....
1992-93	FoPS Forssa	Finland-2	34	11	19	30	36	....	....	....	....	....
	Hameenlinna	Finland	2	0	0	0	0	....	....	....	....	....
	Hameenlinna	Fin-Jr.	1	1	1	2	0	....	....	....	....	....
1993-94	U. of Denver	WCHA	36	12	9	21	38	....	....	....	....	....
1994-95	U. of Denver	WCHA	40	17	18	35	42	....	....	....	....	....
1995-96	U. of Denver	WCHA	39	25	28	53	71	....	....	....	....	....
1996-97	U. of Denver	WCHA	39	21	17	38	63	....	....	....	....	....
1997-98	Providence	AHL	38	3	2	5	14	....	....	....	....	....
	Charlotte	ECHL	15	4	3	7	12	6	0	3	3	0

LABELLE, MARC

Left wing. Shoots left. 6'1", 215 lbs. Born, Maniwaki, Que., December 20, 1969.

			Regular Season					Playoffs				
Season	Club	Lea	GP	G	A	TP	PIM	GP	G	A	TP	PIM
1987-88	Victoriaville	QMJHL	63	11	14	25	236	5	2	4	6	20
1988-89	Victoriaville	QMJHL	62	9	26	35	202	15	6	3	9	30
1989-90	Victoriaville	QMJHL	56	18	21	39	192	16	4	8	12	42
1990-91	Fredericton	AHL	25	1	4	5	95	4	0	2	2	25
	Richmond	ECHL	5	1	1	2	37	....	....	....	....	....
1991-92	Fredericton	AHL	62	7	10	17	238	3	0	0	0	6
1992-93	San Diego	IHL	5	0	2	2	5	....	....	....	....	....
	New Haven	AHL	31	5	4	9	124	....	....	....	....	....
	Thunder Bay	ColHL	9	0	5	5	17	7	0	1	1	11
1993-94	Cincinnati	IHL	37	2	1	3	133	4	0	1	1	6
1994-95	Cincinnati	IHL	54	3	4	7	173	8	0	0	0	7
1995-96	Cincinnati	IHL	57	6	11	17	218	....	....	....	....	....
	Milwaukee	IHL	20	5	3	8	50	5	1	1	2	4
1996-97	**Dallas**	**NHL**	**9**	**0**	**0**	**0**	**46**	....	....	....	....	....
	Milwaukee	IHL	14	1	1	2	33	....	....	....	....	....
	Michigan	IHL	46	4	7	11	148	3	0	0	0	6
1997-98	Cincinnati	IHL	60	2	1	3	160	9	0	1	1	38
	NHL Totals		**9**	**0**	**0**	**0**	**46**	....	....	....	....	....

Signed as a free agent by **Montreal**, January 21, 1991. Signed as a free agent by **Ottawa**, July 30, 1992. Claimed by **Florida** from **Ottawa** in Expansion Draft, June 24, 1993. Signed as a free agent by **Dallas**, April 15, 1996. Signed as a free agent by **Ottawa**, July 14, 1997.

LABRAATEN, JAN (la-BRA-tuhn) CGY.

Left wing. Shoots right. 6'2", 198 lbs. Born, Karlstad, Sweden, February 17, 1977.
(Calgary's 4th choice, 98th overall, in 1995 Entry Draft).

			Regular Season					Playoffs				
Season	Club	Lea	GP	G	A	TP	PIM	GP	G	A	TP	PIM
1994-95	Farjestad	Swe-Jr.	25	10	6	16	20	....	....	....	....	....
	Farjestad	Sweden	2	0	1	1	2	1	0	0	0	0
1995-96	Farjestad	Sweden	4	0	0	0	0	....	....	....	....	....
1996-97	Orebro	Sweden-2	30	9	6	15	51	....	....	....	....	....
1997-98	Raleigh	ECHL	41	5	12	17	26	....	....	....	....	....

LACEBY, MIKE DET.

Center. Shoots left. 6'1", 180 lbs. Born, Richmond Hill, Ont., April 6, 1978.
(Detroit's 6th choice, 186th overall, in 1997 Entry Draft).

			Regular Season					Playoffs				
Season	Club	Lea	GP	G	A	TP	PIM	GP	G	A	TP	PIM
1996-97	Kingston	OHL	64	5	11	16	29	....	....	....	....	....
1997-98	Kingston	OHL	35	5	7	12	24	....	....	....	....	....
	Toronto	OHL	28	1	2	3	4	....	....	....	....	....

LACHANCE, BOB

Right wing. Shoots right. 5'11", 180 lbs. Born, Northampton, MA, February 1, 1974.
(St. Louis' 5th choice, 134th overall, in 1992 Entry Draft).

			Regular Season					Playoffs				
Season	Club	Lea	GP	G	A	TP	PIM	GP	G	A	TP	PIM
1991-92	Springfield	NAJHL	46	40	98	138	87	....	....	....	....	....
1992-93	Boston University	H.E.	33	4	10	14	24	....	....	....	....	....
1993-94	Boston University	H.E.	32	13	19	32	42	....	....	....	....	....
1994-95	Boston University	H.E.	37	12	29	41	51	....	....	....	....	....
1995-96	Boston University	H.E.	39	15	37	52	67	....	....	....	....	....
	Worcester	AHL	7	1	0	1	6	....	....	....	....	....
1996-97	Worcester	AHL	74	21	35	56	66	5	0	2	2	4
1997-98	Worcester	AHL	70	15	33	48	56	11	6	10	16	12

LACHANCE, SCOTT NYI

Defense. Shoots left. 6'1", 196 lbs. Born, Charlottesville, VA, October 22, 1972.
(NY Islanders' 1st choice, 4th overall, in 1991 Entry Draft).

			Regular Season					Playoffs				
Season	Club	Lea	GP	G	A	TP	PIM	GP	G	A	TP	PIM
1989-90	Springfield	EJHL	34	25	41	66	62	....	....	....	....	....
1990-91	Boston University	H.E.	31	5	19	24	48	....	....	....	....	....
1991-92	United States	Nat-Tm	36	1	10	11	34	....	....	....	....	....
	United States	Olympics	8	0	1	1	6	....	....	....	....	....
	NY Islanders	**NHL**	**17**	**1**	**4**	**5**	**9**	....	....	....	....	....
1992-93	**NY Islanders**	**NHL**	**75**	**7**	**17**	**24**	**67**	....	....	....	....	....
1993-94	**NY Islanders**	**NHL**	**74**	**3**	**11**	**14**	**70**	**3**	**0**	**0**	**0**	**0**
1994-95	**NY Islanders**	**NHL**	**26**	**6**	**7**	**13**	**26**	....	....	....	....	....
1995-96	**NY Islanders**	**NHL**	**55**	**3**	**10**	**13**	**54**	....	....	....	....	....
1996-97	**NY Islanders**	**NHL**	**81**	**3**	**11**	**14**	**47**	....	....	....	....	....
1997-98	**NY Islanders**	**NHL**	**63**	**2**	**11**	**13**	**45**	....	....	....	....	....
	NHL Totals		**391**	**25**	**71**	**96**	**318**	**3**	**0**	**0**	**0**	**0**

Played in NHL All-Star Game (1997)

LACOUTURE, DAN (la-koo-TUHR) EDM.

Left wing. Shoots left. 6'3", 210 lbs. Born, Hyannis, MA, April 18, 1977.
(NY Islanders' 2nd choice, 29th overall, in 1996 Entry Draft).

			Regular Season					Playoffs				
Season	Club	Lea	GP	G	A	TP	PIM	GP	G	A	TP	PIM
1995-96	Springfield	EJHL	42	36	48	84	102	....	....	....	....	....
1996-97	Boston University	H.E.	31	13	12	25	18	....	....	....	....	....
1997-98	Hamilton	AHL	77	15	10	25	31	5	1	0	1	0

LACROIX, DANIEL (luh-KWAH) PHI.

Left wing. Shoots left. 6'2", 205 lbs. Born, Montreal, Que., March 11, 1969.
(NY Rangers' 2nd choice, 31st overall, in 1987 Entry Draft).

			Regular Season					Playoffs				
Season	Club	Lea	GP	G	A	TP	PIM	GP	G	A	TP	PIM
1986-87	Granby	QMJHL	54	9	16	25	311	8	1	2	3	22
1987-88	Granby	QMJHL	58	24	50	74	468	5	0	4	4	12
1988-89	Granby	QMJHL	70	45	49	94	320	4	1	1	2	57
	Denver	IHL	2	0	1	1	0	2	0	1	1	0
1989-90	Flint	IHL	61	12	16	28	128	4	2	0	2	24
1990-91	Binghamton	AHL	54	7	12	19	237	5	1	0	1	24
1991-92	Binghamton	AHL	52	12	20	32	149	11	2	4	6	28
1992-93	Binghamton	AHL	73	21	22	43	255	....	....	....	....	....
1993-94	**NY Rangers**	**NHL**	**4**	**0**	**0**	**0**	**0**	....	....	....	....	....
	Binghamton	AHL	59	20	23	43	278	....	....	....	....	....
1994-95	Providence	AHL	40	15	11	26	266	....	....	....	....	....
	Boston	**NHL**	**23**	**1**	**0**	**1**	**38**	....	....	....	....	....
	NY Rangers	**NHL**	**1**	**0**	**0**	**0**	**0**	....	....	....	....	....
1995-96	**NY Rangers**	**NHL**	**25**	**2**	**2**	**4**	**30**	....	....	....	....	....
	Binghamton	AHL	26	12	15	27	155	....	....	....	....	....
1996-97	**Philadelphia**	**NHL**	**74**	**7**	**1**	**8**	**163**	**12**	**0**	**1**	**1**	**22**
1997-98	**Philadelphia**	**NHL**	**56**	**1**	**4**	**5**	**135**	**4**	**0**	**0**	**0**	**4**
	NHL Totals		**183**	**11**	**7**	**18**	**366**	**16**	**0**	**1**	**1**	**26**

Traded to **Boston** by **NY Rangers** for Glen Featherstone, August 19, 1994. Claimed on waivers by **NY Rangers** from **Boston**, March 23, 1995. Signed as a free agent by **Philadelphia**, July 18, 1996.

LACROIX, ERIC (luh-KWAH) COL.

Left wing. Shoots left. 6'2", 210 lbs. Born, Montreal, Que., July 15, 1971.
(Toronto's 6th choice, 136th overall, in 1990 Entry Draft).

			Regular Season					Playoffs				
Season	Club	Lea	GP	G	A	TP	PIM	GP	G	A	TP	PIM
1989-90	Gov. Dummer	H.S.	25	23	18	41	....	....	....	....	....	....
1990-91	St. Lawrence	ECAC	35	13	11	24	35	....	....	....	....	....
1991-92	St. Lawrence	ECAC	34	11	20	31	40	....	....	....	....	....
1992-93	St. John's	AHL	76	15	19	34	59	9	5	3	8	4
1993-94	**Toronto**	**NHL**	**3**	**0**	**0**	**0**	**2**	**2**	**0**	**0**	**0**	**0**
	St. John's	AHL	59	17	22	39	69	11	5	3	8	6
1994-95	St. John's	AHL	1	0	0	0	2	....	....	....	....	....
	Phoenix	IHL	25	7	1	8	31	....	....	....	....	....
	Los Angeles	**NHL**	**45**	**9**	**7**	**16**	**54**	....	....	....	....	....
1995-96	**Los Angeles**	**NHL**	**72**	**16**	**16**	**32**	**110**	....	....	....	....	....
1996-97	**Colorado**	**NHL**	**81**	**18**	**18**	**36**	**26**	**17**	**1**	**4**	**5**	**19**
1997-98	**Colorado**	**NHL**	**82**	**16**	**15**	**31**	**84**	**7**	**0**	**0**	**0**	**6**
	NHL Totals		**283**	**59**	**56**	**115**	**276**	**26**	**1**	**4**	**5**	**25**

Traded to **LA Kings** by **Toronto** with Chris Snell and Toronto's 4th round choice (Eric Belanger) in 1996 Entry Draft for Dixon Ward, Guy Leveque, Kelly Fairchild and Shayne Toporowski, October 3, 1994. Traded to **Colorado** by **LA Kings** with LA Kings' 1st round choice (Martin Skoula) in 1998 Entry Draft for Stephane Fiset and Colorado's 1st round choice (Mathieu Biron) in 1998 Entry Draft, June 20, 1996.

LAFAYETTE, NATHAN (LAH-fay-eht) L.A.

Right wing. Shoots right. 6'1", 200 lbs. Born, New Westminster, B.C., February 17, 1973.
(St. Louis' 3rd choice, 65th overall, in 1991 Entry Draft).

			Regular Season					Playoffs				
Season	Club	Lea	GP	G	A	TP	PIM	GP	G	A	TP	PIM
1989-90	Kingston	OHL	53	6	8	14	14	7	0	1	1	0
1990-91	Kingston	OHL	35	13	13	26	10	....	....	....	....	....
	Cornwall	OHL	28	16	22	38	25	....	....	....	....	....
1991-92	Cornwall	OHL	66	28	45	73	26	6	2	5	7	15
1992-93	Newmarket	OHL	58	49	38	87	26	7	4	5	9	19
1993-94	**St. Louis**	**NHL**	**38**	**2**	**3**	**5**	**14**	....	....	....	....	....
	Peoria	IHL	27	13	11	24	20	....	....	....	....	....
	Vancouver	**NHL**	**11**	**1**	**1**	**2**	**4**	**20**	**2**	**7**	**9**	**4**
1994-95	Syracuse	AHL	27	9	9	18	10	....	....	....	....	....
	Vancouver	**NHL**	**27**	**4**	**4**	**8**	**2**	....	....	....	....	....
	NY Rangers	**NHL**	**12**	**0**	**0**	**0**	**0**	**8**	**0**	**0**	**0**	**2**
1995-96	**NY Rangers**	**NHL**	**5**	**0**	**0**	**0**	**2**	....	....	....	....	....
	Binghamton	AHL	57	21	27	48	32	....	....	....	....	....
	Los Angeles	**NHL**	**12**	**2**	**4**	**6**	**6**	....	....	....	....	....
1996-97	**Los Angeles**	**NHL**	**15**	**1**	**3**	**4**	**8**	....	....	....	....	....
	Phoenix	IHL	31	2	5	7	16	....	....	....	....	....
	Syracuse	AHL	26	14	11	25	18	3	1	0	1	2
1997-98	**Los Angeles**	**NHL**	**34**	**5**	**3**	**8**	**32**	**4**	**0**	**0**	**0**	**2**
	Fredericton	AHL	28	7	8	15	36	....	....	....	....	....
	NHL Totals		**154**	**15**	**18**	**33**	**68**	**32**	**2**	**7**	**9**	**8**

Canadian Major Junior Scholastic Player of the Year (1992)

Traded to **Vancouver** by **St. Louis** with Jeff Brown and Bret Hedican for Craig Janney, March 21, 1994. Traded to **NY Rangers** by **Vancouver** for Corey Hirsch, April 7, 1995. Traded to **LA Kings** by **NY Rangers** with Ray Ferraro, Mattias Norstrom, Ian Laperriere and NY Rangers' 4th round choice (Sean Blanchard) in 1997 Entry Draft for Marty McSorley, Jari Kurri and Shane Churla, March 14, 1996.

LAFLAMME, CHRISTIAN (lah-FLAM) CHI.

Defense. Shoots right. 6'1", 202 lbs. Born, St. Charles, Que., November 24, 1976.
(Chicago's 2nd choice, 45th overall, in 1995 Entry Draft).

			Regular Season					Playoffs				
Season	Club	Lea	GP	G	A	TP	PIM	GP	G	A	TP	PIM
1992-93	Verdun	QMJHL	69	2	17	19	85	3	0	2	2	6
1993-94	Verdun	QMJHL	72	4	34	38	85	4	0	3	3	4
1994-95	Beauport	QMJHL	67	6	41	47	82	8	1	4	5	6
1995-96	Beauport	QMJHL	41	13	23	36	63	20	7	17	24	32
1996-97	**Chicago**	**NHL**	**4**	**0**	**1**	**1**	**2**	....	....	....	....	....
	Indianapolis	IHL	62	5	15	20	60	4	1	1	2	16
1997-98	**Chicago**	**NHL**	**72**	**0**	**11**	**11**	**59**	....	....	....	....	....
	NHL Totals		**76**	**0**	**12**	**12**	**61**	....	....	....	....	....

QMJHL Second All-Star Team (1995)

LaFONTAINE, PAT (luh-FAHN-tayn)

Center. Shoots right. 5'10", 182 lbs. Born, St. Louis, MO, February 22, 1965.
(NY Islanders' 1st choice, 3rd overall, in 1983 Entry Draft).

			Regular Season					Playoffs				
Season	Club	Lea	GP	G	A	TP	PIM	GP	G	A	TP	PIM
1981-82	Detroit	NAJHL	79	175	149	324	....	....	....	....	....	....
1982-83	Verdun	QMJHL	70	*104	*130	*234	10	15	11	*24	*35	4
1983-84	United States	Nat-Tm	58	56	55	111	22	....	....	....	....	....
	United States	Olympics	6	5	3	8	0	....	....	....	....	....
	NY Islanders	**NHL**	**15**	**13**	**6**	**19**	**6**	**16**	**3**	**6**	**9**	**8**
1984-85	**NY Islanders**	**NHL**	**67**	**19**	**35**	**54**	**32**	**9**	**1**	**2**	**3**	**4**
1985-86	**NY Islanders**	**NHL**	**65**	**30**	**23**	**53**	**43**	**3**	**1**	**0**	**1**	**0**
1986-87	**NY Islanders**	**NHL**	**80**	**38**	**32**	**70**	**70**	**14**	**5**	**7**	**12**	**10**
1987-88	**NY Islanders**	**NHL**	**75**	**47**	**45**	**92**	**52**	**6**	**4**	**5**	**9**	**8**
1988-89	**NY Islanders**	**NHL**	**79**	**45**	**43**	**88**	**26**	....	....	....	....	....
1989-90	**NY Islanders**	**NHL**	**74**	**54**	**51**	**105**	**38**	**2**	**0**	**1**	**1**	**0**
1990-91	**NY Islanders**	**NHL**	**75**	**41**	**44**	**85**	**42**	....	....	....	....	....
1991-92	**Buffalo**	**NHL**	**57**	**46**	**47**	**93**	**98**	**7**	**8**	**3**	**11**	**4**
1992-93	**Buffalo**	**NHL**	**84**	**53**	**95**	**148**	**63**	**7**	**2**	**10**	**12**	**0**
1993-94	**Buffalo**	**NHL**	**16**	**5**	**13**	**18**	**2**	....	....	....	....	....
1994-95	**Buffalo**	**NHL**	**22**	**12**	**15**	**27**	**4**	**5**	**2**	**2**	**4**	**2**
1995-96	**Buffalo**	**NHL**	**76**	**40**	**51**	**91**	**36**	....	....	....	....	....
1996-97	**Buffalo**	**NHL**	**13**	**2**	**6**	**8**	**4**	....	....	....	....	....
1997-98	**NY Rangers**	**NHL**	**67**	**23**	**39**	**62**	**36**	....	....	....	....	....
	United States	Olympics	4	1	1	2	0	....	....	....	....	....
	NHL Totals		**865**	**468**	**545**	**1013**	**552**	**69**	**26**	**36**	**62**	**36**

QMJHL First All-Star Team (1983) • Canadian Major Junior Player of the Year (1983) • Won Dodge Performer of the Year Award (1990) • NHL Second All-Star Team (1993) • Won Bill Masterton Memorial Trophy (1995)

Played in NHL All-Star Game (1988, 1989, 1990, 1991, 1993)

Traded to **Buffalo** by **NY Islanders** with Randy Hillier, Randy Wood and NY Islanders' 4th round choice (Dean Melanson) in 1992 Entry Draft for Pierre Turgeon, Uwe Krupp, Benoit Hogue and Dave McLlwain, October 25, 1991. Traded to **NY Rangers** by **Buffalo** for NY Rangers' 2nd round choice (Andrew Peters) in 1998 Entry Draft and future considerations, September 29, 1997. • Suffered career-ending head injury in game vs. Ottawa, March 16, 1998.

LAFRANCE, BRANDON EDM.

Right wing. Shoots right. 6'1", 190 lbs. Born, Ottawa, Ont., November 1, 1976.
(Edmonton's 8th choice, 170th overall, in 1996 Entry Draft).

			Regular Season					Playoffs				
Season	Club	Lea	GP	G	A	TP	PIM	GP	G	A	TP	PIM
1995-96	Ohio State	CCHA	32	11	5	16	34	....	....	....	....	....
1996-97	Ohio State	CCHA	37	9	6	15	38	....	....	....	....	....
1997-98	Ohio State	CCHA	25	3	3	6	28	....	....	....	....	....

LAING, QUINTIN DET.

Left wing. Shoots left. 6'2", 175 lbs. Born, Rosetown, Sask., June 8, 1979.
(Detroit's 3rd choice, 102nd overall, in 1997 Entry Draft).

			Regular Season					Playoffs				
Season	Club	Lea	GP	G	A	TP	PIM	GP	G	A	TP	PIM
1996-97	Kelowna	WHL	63	13	24	37	54	1	0	0	0	0
1997-98	Kelowna	WHL	59	11	24	35	47	7	0	1	1	8

LAKOVIC, SASHA (LA-koh-vik) N.J.

Left wing. Shoots left. 6', 205 lbs. Born, Vancouver, B.C., September 7, 1971.

			Regular Season					Playoffs				
Season	Club	Lea	GP	G	A	TP	PIM	GP	G	A	TP	PIM
1992-93	Brant.–Chatham	ColHL	28	7	5	12	235	....	....	....	....	....
	Columbus	ECHL	27	7	9	16	162	....	....	....	....	....
	Binghamton	AHL	3	0	0	0	0	....	....	....	....	....
1993-94	Toledo	ECHL	24	5	10	15	198	....	....	....	....	....
	Chatham	ColHL	13	11	7	18	61	....	....	....	....	....
1994-95	Tulsa	CHL	40	20	24	44	214	5	1	3	4	88
1995-96	Las Vegas	IHL	49	1	2	3	416	13	1	1	2	*57
1996-97	**Calgary**	**NHL**	**19**	**0**	**1**	**1**	**54**	....	....	....	....	....
	St. John's	AHL	18	1	8	9	182	....	....	....	....	....
	Las Vegas	IHL	10	0	0	0	81	2	0	0	0	14
1997-98	**New Jersey**	**NHL**	**2**	**0**	**0**	**0**	**5**	....	....	....	....	....
	Albany	AHL	30	7	6	13	158	13	3	4	7	*84
	NHL Totals		**21**	**0**	**1**	**1**	**59**	....	....	....	....	....

Signed as a free agent by **Calgary**, October 10, 1996. Signed as a free agent by **New Jersey**, September 24, 1997.

LAMARCHE, MARTIN COL.

Left wing. Shoots left. 6'1", 205 lbs. Born, Ste. Justine, Que., October 2, 1975.

			Regular Season					Playoffs				
Season	Club	Lea	GP	G	A	TP	PIM	GP	G	A	TP	PIM
1991-92	Chicoutimi	QMJHL	62	2	6	8	62	4	0	0	0	0
1992-93	St-Jean	QMJHL	51	2	5	7	134	2	0	0	0	0
1993-94	Sherbrooke	QMJHL	53	10	20	30	121	10	2	1	3	44
1994-95	Shawinigan	QMJHL	58	20	29	49	353	14	3	10	13	65
1995-96	P.E.I.	AHL	30	0	1	1	88	....	....	....	....	....
1996-97	Saint John	AHL	33	4	5	9	114	4	0	0	0	21
1997-98	Binghamton	UHL	8	1	3	4	15	5	1	3	4	33
	Hershey	AHL	13	0	0	0	90	....	....	....	....	....

Signed as a free agent by **Ottawa**, March 3, 1995. Signed as a free agent by **Colorado**, January 6, 1998.

LAMBERT, DENNY (lahm-BAIR) NSH.

Left wing. Shoots left. 5'11", 200 lbs. Born, Wawa, Ont., January 7, 1970.

			Regular Season					Playoffs				
Season	Club	Lea	GP	G	A	TP	PIM	GP	G	A	TP	PIM
1988-89	S.S. Marie	OHL	61	14	15	29	203	....	....	....	....	....
1989-90	S.S. Marie	OHL	61	23	29	52	276	....	....	....	....	....
1990-91	S.S. Marie	OHL	59	28	39	67	169	14	7	9	16	48
1991-92	San Diego	IHL	71	17	14	31	229	3	0	0	0	10
	St. Thomas	ColHL	5	2	6	8	9	....	....	....	....	....
1992-93	San Diego	IHL	56	18	12	30	277	14	1	1	2	44
1993-94	San Diego	IHL	79	13	14	27	314	6	1	0	1	55
1994-95	San Diego	IHL	75	25	35	60	222	....	....	....	....	....
	Anaheim	**NHL**	**13**	**1**	**3**	**4**	**4**	....	....	....	....	....
1995-96	**Anaheim**	**NHL**	**33**	**0**	**8**	**8**	**55**	....	....	....	....	....
	Baltimore	AHL	44	14	28	42	126	12	3	9	12	39
1996-97	**Ottawa**	**NHL**	**80**	**4**	**16**	**20**	**217**	**6**	**0**	**1**	**1**	**9**
1997-98	**Ottawa**	**NHL**	**72**	**9**	**10**	**19**	**250**	**11**	**0**	**0**	**0**	**19**
	NHL Totals		**198**	**14**	**37**	**51**	**526**	**17**	**0**	**1**	**1**	**28**

Signed as a free agent by **Anaheim**, August 16, 1993. Signed as a free agent by **Ottawa**, July 29, 1996. Claimed by **Nashville** from **Ottawa** in Expansion Draft, June 26, 1998.

LANDRY, ERIC CGY.

Center. Shoots left. 5'11", 190 lbs. Born, Gatineau, Que., January 20, 1975.
(San Jose's 8th choice, 193rd overall, in 1994 Entry Draft).

			Regular Season					Playoffs				
Season	Club	Lea	GP	G	A	TP	PIM	GP	G	A	TP	PIM
1993-94	St-Hyacinthe	QMJHL	69	42	34	76	128	7	4	2	6	13
1994-95	St-Hyacinthe	QMJHL	68	38	36	74	249	5	2	1	3	10
1995-96	Cape Breton	AHL	74	19	33	52	187	....	....	....	....	....
1996-97	Hamilton	AHL	74	15	17	32	139	22	6	7	13	43
1997-98	**Calgary**	**NHL**	**12**	**1**	**0**	**1**	**4**	....	....	....	....	....
	Saint John	AHL	61	17	21	38	194	20	4	6	10	58
	NHL Totals		**12**	**1**	**0**	**1**	**4**	....	....	....	....	....

Signed as a free agent by **Calgary**, August 20, 1997.

LANG, ROBERT (LUHNG) PIT.

Center. Shoots right. 6'2", 216 lbs. Born, Teplice, Czech., December 19, 1970.
(Los Angeles' 6th choice, 133rd overall, in 1990 Entry Draft).

			Regular Season					Playoffs				
Season	Club	Lea	GP	G	A	TP	PIM	GP	G	A	TP	PIM
1988-89	Litvinov	Czech.	7	3	2	5	0	....	....	....	....	....
1989-90	Litvinov	Czech.	39	11	10	21	....	....	....	....	....	....
1990-91	Litvinov	Czech.	56	26	26	52	38	....	....	....	....	....
1991-92	Litvinov	Czech.	43	12	31	43	34	....	....	....	....	....
	Czechoslovakia	Olympics	8	5	8	13	8	....	....	....	....	....
1992-93	**Los Angeles**	**NHL**	**11**	**0**	**5**	**5**	**2**	....	....	....	....	....
	Phoenix	IHL	38	9	21	30	20	....	....	....	....	....
1993-94	**Los Angeles**	**NHL**	**32**	**9**	**10**	**19**	**10**	....	....	....	....	....
	Phoenix	IHL	44	11	24	35	34	....	....	....	....	....
1994-95	Litvinov	Cze-Rep.	16	4	19	23	28	....	....	....	....	....
	Los Angeles	**NHL**	**36**	**4**	**8**	**12**	**4**	....	....	....	....	....
1995-96	**Los Angeles**	**NHL**	**68**	**6**	**16**	**22**	**10**	....	....	....	....	....
1996-97	HC Sparta	Cze-Rep.	38	14	27	41	30	5	1	2	3	4
1997-98	**Boston**	**NHL**	**3**	**0**	**0**	**0**	**2**	....	....	....	....	....
	Czech Republic	Olympics	6	0	3	3	0	....	....	....	....	....
	Pittsburgh	**NHL**	**51**	**9**	**13**	**22**	**14**	**6**	**0**	**3**	**3**	**2**
	Houston	IHL	9	1	7	8	4	....	....	....	....	....
	NHL Totals		**201**	**28**	**52**	**80**	**42**	**6**	**0**	**3**	**3**	**2**

Signed as a free agent by **Pittsburgh**, September 2, 1997. Claimed by **Boston** from **Pittsburgh** in NHL Waiver Draft, September 28, 1997. Claimed on waivers by **Pittsburgh** from **Boston**, October 25, 1997.

LANGDON, DARREN NYR

Left wing. Shoots left. 6'1", 200 lbs. Born, Deer Lake, Nfld., January 8, 1971.

			Regular Season					Playoffs				
Season	Club	Lea	GP	G	A	TP	PIM	GP	G	A	TP	PIM
1991-92	Summerside	PEI Jr.	44	34	49	83	441	....	....	....	....	....
1992-93	Binghamton	AHL	18	3	4	7	115	8	0	1	1	14
	Dayton	ECHL	54	23	22	45	429	3	0	1	1	40
1993-94	Binghamton	AHL	54	2	7	9	327	....	....	....	....	....
1994-95	Binghamton	AHL	55	6	14	20	296	11	1	3	4	*84
	NY Rangers	**NHL**	**18**	**1**	**1**	**2**	**62**	....	....	....	....	....
1995-96	**NY Rangers**	**NHL**	**64**	**7**	**4**	**11**	**175**	**2**	**0**	**0**	**0**	**0**
	Binghamton	AHL	1	0	0	0	12	....	....	....	....	....
1996-97	**NY Rangers**	**NHL**	**60**	**3**	**6**	**9**	**195**	**10**	**0**	**0**	**0**	**2**
1997-98	**NY Rangers**	**NHL**	**70**	**3**	**3**	**6**	**197**	....	....	....	....	....
	NHL Totals		**212**	**14**	**14**	**28**	**629**	**12**	**0**	**0**	**0**	**2**

Signed as a free agent by **NY Rangers**, August 16, 1993.

LANGENBRUNNER, JAMIE (lan-gehn-BRUH-nuhr) DAL.

Center. Shoots right. 5'11", 185 lbs. Born, Duluth, MN, July 24, 1975.
(Dallas' 2nd choice, 35th overall, in 1993 Entry Draft).

			Regular Season					Playoffs				
Season	Club	Lea	GP	G	A	TP	PIM	GP	G	A	TP	PIM
1992-93	Cloquet High	H.S.	27	27	62	89	18	....	....	....	....	....
1993-94	Peterborough	OHL	62	33	58	91	53	7	4	6	10	2
1994-95	Peterborough	OHL	62	42	57	99	84	11	8	14	22	12
	Dallas	**NHL**	**2**	**0**	**0**	**0**	**2**	....	....	....	....	....
	Kalamazoo	IHL	....	....	....	....	....	11	1	3	4	2
1995-96	**Dallas**	**NHL**	**12**	**2**	**2**	**4**	**6**	....	....	....	....	....
	Michigan	IHL	59	25	40	65	129	10	3	10	13	8
1996-97	**Dallas**	**NHL**	**76**	**13**	**26**	**39**	**51**	**5**	**1**	**1**	**2**	**14**
1997-98	**Dallas**	**NHL**	**81**	**23**	**29**	**52**	**61**	**16**	**1**	**4**	**5**	**14**
	United States	Olympics	3	0	0	0	4	....	....	....	....	....
	NHL Totals		**171**	**38**	**57**	**95**	**120**	**21**	**2**	**5**	**7**	**28**

LANGFELD, JOSH OTT.

Right wing. Shoots right. 6'3", 205 lbs. Born, Fridley, MN, July 17, 1977.
(Ottawa's 3rd choice, 66th overall, in 1997 Entry Draft).

			Regular Season					Playoffs				
Season	Club	Lea	GP	G	A	TP	PIM	GP	G	A	TP	PIM
1996-97	Lincoln Stars	USHL	38	35	23	58	100	....	....	....	....	....
1997-98	U. of Michigan	CCHA	46	19	17	36	66	....	....	....	....	....

NCAA Championship All-Tournament Team (1998)

LANGKOW, DAYMOND (LAING-kow) T.B.

Center. Shoots left. 5'11", 175 lbs. Born, Edmonton, Alta, September 27, 1976.
(Tampa Bay's 1st choice, 5th overall, in 1995 Entry Draft).

			Regular Season					Playoffs				
Season	Club	Lea	GP	G	A	TP	PIM	GP	G	A	TP	PIM
1992-93	Tri-City	WHL	64	22	42	64	100	4	1	0	1	4
1993-94	Tri-City	WHL	61	40	43	83	174	4	2	2	4	15
1994-95	Tri-City	WHL	72	*67	73	*140	142	17	12	15	27	52
1995-96	Tri-City	WHL	48	30	61	91	103	11	14	13	27	20
	Tampa Bay	**NHL**	**4**	**0**	**1**	**1**	**0**	....	....	....	....	....
1996-97	**Tampa Bay**	**NHL**	**79**	**15**	**13**	**28**	**35**	....	....	....	....	....
	Adirondack	AHL	2	1	1	2	0	....	....	....	....	....
1997-98	**Tampa Bay**	**NHL**	**68**	**8**	**14**	**22**	**62**	....	....	....	....	....
	NHL Totals		**151**	**23**	**28**	**51**	**97**	....	....	....	....	....

WHL West First All-Star Team (1995) • Canadian Major Junior First All-Star Team (1995) • WHL West Second All-Star Team (1996)

LANK, JEFF PHI.

Defense. Shoots left. 6'3", 205 lbs. Born, Indian Head, Sask., March 1, 1975.
(Philadelphia's 9th choice, 230th overall, in 1995 Entry Draft).

			Regular Season					Playoffs				
Season	Club	Lea	GP	G	A	TP	PIM	GP	G	A	TP	PIM
1991-92	Prince Albert	WHL	56	2	8	10	26	9	0	0	0	2
1992-93	Prince Albert	WHL	63	1	11	12	60	....	....	....	....	....
1993-94	Prince Albert	WHL	72	9	38	47	62	....	....	....	....	....
1994-95	Prince Albert	WHL	68	12	25	37	60	13	2	10	12	8
1995-96	Hershey	AHL	72	7	13	20	70	5	0	0	0	8
1996-97	Philadelphia	AHL	44	2	12	14	49	7	2	1	3	4
1997-98	Philadelphia	AHL	69	7	9	16	59	20	1	4	5	22

• Re-entered NHL draft. Originally Montreal's 6th choice, 113th overall in 1993 Entry Draft.

LANKSHEAR, MIKE

Defense. Shoots left. 6'2", 185 lbs. Born, Calgary, Alta., September 8, 1978.
(Toronto's 3rd choice, 66th overall, in 1996 Entry Draft).

			Regular Season					Playoffs				
Season	Club	Lea	GP	G	A	TP	PIM	GP	G	A	TP	PIM
1995-96	Guelph	OHL	63	8	20	28	73	15	2	6	8	19
1996-97	Guelph	OHL	52	6	27	33	36	18	0	10	10	10
1997-98	Windsor	OHL	26	9	14	23	25	....	....	....	....	....
	Owen Sound	OHL	37	11	25	36	31	11	1	5	6	4

Traded to **Florida** by **Toronto** for Per Gustafsson, June 12, 1997.

LAPERRIERE, IAN (luh-PAIR-ee-YAIR, EE-ihn) L.A.

Center. Shoots right. 6'1", 197 lbs. Born, Montreal, Que., January 19, 1974.
(St. Louis' 6th choice, 158th overall, in 1992 Entry Draft).

			Regular Season					Playoffs				
Season	Club	Lea	GP	G	A	TP	PIM	GP	G	A	TP	PIM
1990-91	Drummondville	QMJHL	65	19	29	48	117	14	2	9	11	48
1991-92	Drummondville	QMJHL	70	28	49	77	160	4	2	2	4	9
1992-93	Drummondville	QMJHL	60	44	*96	140	188	10	6	13	19	20
1993-94	**St. Louis**	**NHL**	**1**	**0**	**0**	**0**	**0**	....	....	....	....	....
	Drummondville	QMJHL	62	41	72	113	150	9	4	6	10	35
	Peoria	IHL	....	....	....	....	....	5	1	3	4	2
1994-95	Peoria	IHL	51	16	32	48	111	....	....	....	....	....
	St. Louis	**NHL**	**37**	**13**	**14**	**27**	**85**	**7**	**0**	**4**	**4**	**21**
1995-96	**St. Louis**	**NHL**	**33**	**3**	**6**	**9**	**87**	....	....	....	....	....
	Worcester	AHL	3	2	1	3	22	....	....	....	....	....
	NY Rangers	**NHL**	**28**	**1**	**2**	**3**	**53**	....	....	....	....	....
	Los Angeles	**NHL**	**10**	**2**	**3**	**5**	**15**	....	....	....	....	....
1996-97	**Los Angeles**	**NHL**	**62**	**8**	**15**	**23**	**102**	....	....	....	....	....
1997-98	**Los Angeles**	**NHL**	**77**	**6**	**15**	**21**	**131**	**4**	**1**	**0**	**1**	**6**
	NHL Totals		**248**	**33**	**55**	**88**	**473**	**11**	**1**	**4**	**5**	**27**

QMJHL Second All-Star Team (1993)

Traded to **NY Rangers** by **St. Louis** for Stephane Matteau, December 28, 1995. Traded to **LA Kings** by **NY Rangers** with Ray Ferraro, Mattias Norstrom, Nathan Lafayette and NY Rangers' 4th round choice (Sean Blanchard) in 1997 Entry Draft for Marty McSorley, Jari Kurri and Shane Churla, March 14, 1996.

LAPLANTE, DARRYL DET.

Center. Shoots left. 6'1", 185 lbs. Born, Calgary, Alta., March 28, 1977.
(Detroit's 3rd choice, 58th overall, in 1995 Entry Draft).

			Regular Season					Playoffs				
Season	Club	Lea	GP	G	A	TP	PIM	GP	G	A	TP	PIM
1994-95	Moose Jaw	WHL	71	22	24	46	66	10	2	2	4	7
1995-96	Moose Jaw	WHL	72	42	40	82	76	....	....	....	....	....
1996-97	Moose Jaw	WHL	69	38	42	80	79	12	2	4	6	15
1997-98	**Detroit**	**NHL**	**2**	**0**	**0**	**0**	**0**	....	....	....	....	....
	Adirondack	AHL	77	15	10	25	51	3	0	1	1	4
	NHL Totals		**2**	**0**	**0**	**0**	**0**	....	....	....	....	....

LAPLANTE, ERIC S.J.

Left wing. Shoots left. 6', 185 lbs. Born, St. Maurice, Que., December 1, 1979.
(San Jose's 3rd choice, 65th overall, in 1998 Entry Draft).

			Regular Season					Playoffs				
Season	Club	Lea	GP	G	A	TP	PIM	GP	G	A	TP	PIM
1996-97	Halifax	QMJHL	68	20	30	50	245	18	3	11	14	28
1997-98	Halifax	QMJHL	40	19	22	41	193	....	....	....	....	....

LAPOINTE, CLAUDE (luh-PWAH, KLOHD) NYI

Center. Shoots left. 5'9", 181 lbs. Born, Lachine, Que., October 11, 1968.
(Quebec's 12th choice, 234th overall, in 1988 Entry Draft).

			Regular Season					Playoffs				
Season	Club	Lea	GP	G	A	TP	PIM	GP	G	A	TP	PIM
1986-87	Trois-Rivieres	QMJHL	70	47	57	104	123	....	....	....	....	....
1987-88	Laval	QMJHL	69	37	83	120	143	13	2	17	19	53
1988-89	Laval	QMJHL	63	32	72	104	158	17	5	14	19	66
1989-90	Halifax	AHL	63	18	19	37	51	6	1	1	2	34
1990-91	**Quebec**	**NHL**	**13**	**2**	**2**	**4**	**4**	....	....	....	....	....
	Halifax	AHL	43	17	17	34	46	....	....	....	....	....
1991-92	**Quebec**	**NHL**	**78**	**13**	**20**	**33**	**86**	....	....	....	....	....
1992-93	**Quebec**	**NHL**	**74**	**10**	**26**	**36**	**98**	**6**	**2**	**4**	**6**	**8**
1993-94	**Quebec**	**NHL**	**59**	**11**	**17**	**28**	**70**	....	....	....	....	....
1994-95	**Quebec**	**NHL**	**29**	**4**	**8**	**12**	**41**	**5**	**0**	**0**	**0**	**8**
1995-96	**Colorado**	**NHL**	**3**	**0**	**0**	**0**	**0**	....	....	....	....	....
	Calgary	**NHL**	**32**	**4**	**5**	**9**	**20**	**2**	**0**	**0**	**0**	**0**
	Saint John	AHL	12	5	3	8	10	....	....	....	....	....
1996-97	**NY Islanders**	**NHL**	**73**	**13**	**5**	**18**	**49**	....	....	....	....	....
	Utah	IHL	9	7	6	13	14	....	....	....	....	....
1997-98	**NY Islanders**	**NHL**	**78**	**10**	**10**	**20**	**47**	....	....	....	....	....
	NHL Totals		**439**	**67**	**93**	**160**	**415**	**13**	**2**	**4**	**6**	**16**

Transferred to **Colorado** after **Quebec** franchise relocated, June 21, 1995. Traded to **Calgary** by **Colorado** for Calgary's 7th round choice (Samuel Pahlsson) in 1996 Entry Draft, November 1, 1995. Signed as a free agent by **NY Islanders**, August 14, 1996.

LAPOINTE, MARTIN (luh-POYNT, MAHR-tai) DET.

Right wing. Shoots right. 5'11", 200 lbs. Born, Ville Ste. Pierre, Que., September 12, 1973.
(Detroit's 1st choice, 10th overall, in 1991 Entry Draft).

			Regular Season					Playoffs				
Season	Club	Lea	GP	G	A	TP	PIM	GP	G	A	TP	PIM
1989-90	Laval	QMJHL	65	42	54	96	77	14	8	17	25	54
1990-91	Laval	QMJHL	64	44	54	98	66	13	7	14	21	26
1991-92	Laval	QMJHL	31	25	30	55	84	10	4	10	14	32
	Detroit	**NHL**	**4**	**0**	**1**	**1**	**5**	**3**	**0**	**1**	**1**	**4**
	Adirondack	AHL	....	....	....	....	....	8	2	2	4	4
1992-93	Laval	QMJHL	35	38	51	89	41	13	*13	*17	*30	22
	Detroit	**NHL**	**3**	**0**	**0**	**0**	**0**	....	....	....	....	....
	Adirondack	AHL	8	1	2	3	9	....	....	....	....	....
1993-94	**Detroit**	**NHL**	**50**	**8**	**8**	**16**	**55**	**4**	**0**	**0**	**0**	**6**
	Adirondack	AHL	28	25	21	46	47	4	1	1	2	8
1994-95	Adirondack	AHL	39	29	16	45	80	....	....	....	....	....
	Detroit	**NHL**	**39**	**4**	**6**	**10**	**73**	**2**	**0**	**1**	**1**	**8**
1995-96	**Detroit**	**NHL**	**58**	**6**	**3**	**9**	**93**	**11**	**1**	**2**	**3**	**12**
1996-97	**Detroit**	**NHL**	**78**	**16**	**17**	**33**	**167**	**20**	**4**	**8**	**12**	**60** ♦
1997-98	**Detroit**	**NHL**	**79**	**15**	**19**	**34**	**106**	**21**	**9**	**6**	**15**	**20** ♦
	NHL Totals		**311**	**49**	**54**	**103**	**499**	**61**	**14**	**18**	**32**	**110**

QMJHL First All-Star Team (1990, 1993) • QMJHL Second All-Star Team (1991) • Memorial Cup All-Star Team (1993)

LARAQUE, GEORGES EDM.

Right wing. Shoots right. 6'3", 230 lbs. Born, Montreal, Que., December 7, 1976.
(Edmonton's 2nd choice, 31st overall, in 1995 Entry Draft).

			Regular Season					Playoffs				
Season	Club	Lea	GP	G	A	TP	PIM	GP	G	A	TP	PIM
1993-94	St-Jean	QMJHL	70	11	11	22	142	4	0	0	0	7
1994-95	St-Jean	QMJHL	62	19	22	41	259	7	1	1	2	42
1995-96	Laval	QMJHL	11	8	13	21	76	....	....	....	....	....
	St-Hyacinthe	QMJHL	8	3	4	7	59	....	....	....	....	....
	Granby	QMJHL	22	9	7	16	125	18	7	6	13	104
1996-97	Hamilton	AHL	73	14	20	34	179	15	1	3	4	12
1997-98	**Edmonton**	**NHL**	**11**	**0**	**0**	**0**	**59**	....	....	....	....	....
	Hamilton	AHL	46	10	20	30	154	3	0	0	0	11
	NHL Totals		**11**	**0**	**0**	**0**	**59**	....	....	....	....	....

LARIONOV, IGOR (LAIR-ee-AH-nohv) DET.

Center. Shoots left. 5'9", 170 lbs. Born, Voskresensk, USSR, December 3, 1960.
(Vancouver's 11th choice, 214th overall, in 1985 Entry Draft).

			Regular Season					Playoffs				
Season	Club	Lea	GP	G	A	TP	PIM	GP	G	A	TP	PIM
1977-78	Khimik	USSR	6	3	0	3	4	....	....	....	....	....
1978-79	Khimik	USSR	32	3	4	7	12	....	....	....	....	....
1979-80	Khimik	USSR	42	11	7	18	24	....	....	....	....	....
1980-81	Khimik	USSR	43	22	23	45	36	....	....	....	....	....
1981-82	CSKA Moscow	USSR	46	31	22	53	6	....	....	....	....	....
1982-83	CSKA Moscow	USSR	44	20	19	39	20	....	....	....	....	....
1983-84	CSKA Moscow	USSR	43	15	26	41	30	....	....	....	....	....
	Soviet Union	Olympics	6	1	4	5	6	....	....	....	....	....
1984-85	CSKA Moscow	USSR	40	18	28	46	20	....	....	....	....	....
1985-86	CSKA Moscow	USSR	40	21	31	52	33	....	....	....	....	....
1986-87	CSKA Moscow	USSR	39	20	26	46	34	....	....	....	....	....
1987-88	CSKA Moscow	USSR	51	25	32	57	54	....	....	....	....	....
	Soviet Union	Olympics	8	4	9	13	4	....	....	....	....	....
1988-89	CSKA Moscow	USSR	31	15	12	27	22	....	....	....	....	....
1989-90	**Vancouver**	**NHL**	**74**	**17**	**27**	**44**	**20**	....	....	....	....	....
1990-91	**Vancouver**	**NHL**	**64**	**13**	**21**	**34**	**14**	**6**	**1**	**0**	**1**	**6**
1991-92	**Vancouver**	**NHL**	**72**	**21**	**44**	**65**	**54**	**13**	**3**	**7**	**10**	**4**
1992-93	Lugano	Switz.	24	10	19	29	44	....	....	....	....	....
1993-94	**San Jose**	**NHL**	**60**	**18**	**38**	**56**	**40**	**14**	**5**	**13**	**18**	**10**
1994-95	**San Jose**	**NHL**	**33**	**4**	**20**	**24**	**14**	**11**	**1**	**8**	**9**	**2**
1995-96	**San Jose**	**NHL**	**4**	**1**	**1**	**2**	**0**	....	....	....	....	....
	Detroit	**NHL**	**69**	**21**	**50**	**71**	**34**	**19**	**6**	**7**	**13**	**6**
1996-97	**Detroit**	**NHL**	**64**	**12**	**42**	**54**	**26**	**20**	**4**	**8**	**12**	**8** ♦
1997-98	**Detroit**	**NHL**	**69**	**8**	**39**	**47**	**40**	**22**	**3**	**10**	**13**	**12** ♦
	NHL Totals		**509**	**115**	**282**	**397**	**242**	**105**	**23**	**53**	**76**	**48**

USSR First All-Star (1983, 1986, 1987, 1988) • USSR Player of the Year (1988)

Played in NHL All-Star Game (1998)

Claimed by **San Jose** from **Vancouver** in NHL Waiver Draft, October 4, 1992. Traded to **Detroit** by **San Jose** with future considerations for Ray Sheppard, October 24, 1995.

LARIVIERE, JACQUES N.J.

Left wing. Shoots left. 6'1", 210 lbs. Born, Sorel, Que., December 18, 1979.
(New Jersey's 9th choice, 172nd overall, in 1998 Entry Draft).

			Regular Season					Playoffs				
Season	Club	Lea	GP	G	A	TP	PIM	GP	G	A	TP	PIM
1996-97	Moncton	QMJHL	3	0	0	0	5	....	....	....	....	....
1997-98	Moncton	QMJHL	68	3	1	4	249	9	0	0	0	15

LAROCQUE, MARIO (luh-RAWK) T.B.

Defense. Shoots left. 6'2", 182 lbs. Born, Montreal, Que., April 24, 1978.
(Tampa Bay's 1st choice, 16th overall, in 1996 Entry Draft).

			Regular Season					Playoffs				
Season	Club	Lea	GP	G	A	TP	PIM	GP	G	A	TP	PIM
1995-96	Hull	QMJHL	68	7	19	26	196	14	2	5	7	16
1996-97	Hull	QMJHL	64	14	36	50	155	14	2	6	8	36
1997-98	Sherbrooke	QMJHL	28	6	10	16	125	....	....	....	....	....

LAROUCHE, STEVE (luh-ROOSH)

Center. Shoots right. 6', 180 lbs. Born, Rouyn, Que., April 14, 1971.
(Montreal's 3rd choice, 41st overall, in 1989 Entry Draft).

			Regular Season					Playoffs				
Season	Club	Lea	GP	G	A	TP	PIM	GP	G	A	TP	PIM
1987-88	Trois-Rivieres	QMJHL	66	11	29	40	25	....	....	....	....	....
1988-89	Trois-Rivieres	QMJHL	70	51	102	153	53	4	4	2	6	6
1989-90	Trois-Rivieres	QMJHL	60	55	90	145	40	7	3	5	8	8
	Canada	Nat-Tm	1	1	0	1	0	....	....	....	....	....
1990-91	Chicoutimi	QMJHL	45	35	41	76	64	17	*13	*20	*33	20
1991-92	Fredericton	AHL	74	21	35	56	41	7	1	0	1	0
1992-93	Fredericton	AHL	77	27	65	92	52	5	2	5	7	6
1993-94	Atlanta	IHL	80	43	53	96	73	14	*16	10	*26	16
1994-95	P.E.I.	AHL	70	*53	48	101	54	2	1	0	1	0
	Ottawa	**NHL**	**18**	**8**	**7**	**15**	**6**	....	....	....	....	....
1995-96	**NY Rangers**	**NHL**	**1**	**0**	**0**	**0**	**0**	....	....	....	....	....
	Binghamton	AHL	39	20	46	66	47	....	....	....	....	....
	Los Angeles	**NHL**	**7**	**1**	**2**	**3**	**4**	....	....	....	....	....
	Phoenix	IHL	33	19	17	36	14	4	0	1	1	8
1996-97	Quebec	IHL	79	49	53	102	78	9	3	10	13	18
1997-98	Quebec	IHL	68	23	44	67	40	....	....	....	....	....
	Chicago	IHL	13	9	10	19	20	22	9	11	20	14
	NHL Totals		**26**	**9**	**9**	**18**	**10**	....	....	....	....	....

QMJHL Second All-Star Team (1990) • AHL First All-Star Team (1995) • Won Fred Hunt Memorial Trophy (Sportsmanship - AHL) (1995) • Won Les Cunningham Plaque (MVP - AHL) (1995) • IHL First All-Star Team (1997)

Signed as a free agent by **Ottawa**, September 11, 1994. Traded to **NY Rangers** by **Ottawa** for Jean-Yves Roy, October 5, 1995. Traded to **LA Kings** by **NY Rangers** for Chris Snell, January 14, 1996.

LARSEN, BRAD COL.

Left wing. Shoots left. 5'11", 212 lbs. Born, Nakusp, B.C., January 28, 1977.
(Colorado's 5th choice, 87th overall, in 1997 Entry Draft).

			Regular Season					Playoffs				
Season	Club	Lea	GP	G	A	TP	PIM	GP	G	A	TP	PIM
1993-94	Swift Current	WHL	64	15	18	33	32	7	1	2	3	4
1994-95	Swift Current	WHL	62	24	33	57	73	6	0	1	1	2
1995-96	Swift Current	WHL	51	30	47	77	67	6	3	2	5	13
1996-97	Swift Current	WHL	61	36	46	82	61	....	....	....	....	....
1997-98	**Colorado**	**NHL**	**1**	**0**	**0**	**0**	**0**	....	....	....	....	....
	Hershey	AHL	65	12	10	22	80	7	3	2	5	2
	NHL Totals		**1**	**0**	**0**	**0**	**0**	....	....	....	....	....

WHL East Second All-Star Team (1997)

• Re-entered NHL draft. Originally Ottawa's 3rd choice, 53rd overall, in 1995 Entry Draft.

Rights traded to **Colorado** by **Ottawa** for Janne Laukkanen, January 26, 1996.

LAUER, BRAD (LAU-er)

Left wing. Shoots left. 6', 195 lbs. Born, Humboldt, Sask., October 27, 1966.
(NY Islanders' 3rd choice, 34th overall, in 1985 Entry Draft).

			Regular Season					Playoffs				
Season	Club	Lea	GP	G	A	TP	PIM	GP	G	A	TP	PIM
1983-84	Regina	WHL	60	5	7	12	51	16	0	1	1	24
1984-85	Regina	WHL	72	33	46	79	57	8	6	6	12	9
1985-86	Regina	WHL	57	36	38	74	69	10	4	5	9	2
1986-87	**NY Islanders**	**NHL**	**61**	**7**	**14**	**21**	**65**	**6**	**2**	**0**	**2**	**4**
1987-88	**NY Islanders**	**NHL**	**69**	**17**	**18**	**35**	**67**	**5**	**3**	**1**	**4**	**4**
1988-89	**NY Islanders**	**NHL**	**14**	**3**	**2**	**5**	**2**	....	....	....	....	....
	Springfield	AHL	8	1	5	6	0	....	....	....	....	....
1989-90	**NY Islanders**	**NHL**	**63**	**6**	**18**	**24**	**19**	**4**	**0**	**2**	**2**	**10**
	Springfield	AHL	7	4	2	6	0	....	....	....	....	....
1990-91	**NY Islanders**	**NHL**	**44**	**4**	**8**	**12**	**45**	....	....	....	....	....
	Capital District	AHL	11	5	11	16	14	....	....	....	....	....
1991-92	**NY Islanders**	**NHL**	**8**	**1**	**0**	**1**	**2**	....	....	....	....	....
	Chicago	**NHL**	**6**	**0**	**0**	**0**	**4**	**7**	**1**	**1**	**2**	**2**
	Indianapolis	IHL	57	24	30	54	46	....	....	....	....	....
1992-93	**Chicago**	**NHL**	**7**	**0**	**1**	**1**	**2**	....	....	....	....	....
	Indianapolis	IHL	62	*50	41	91	80	5	3	1	4	6
1993-94	**Ottawa**	**NHL**	**30**	**2**	**5**	**7**	**6**	....	....	....	....	....
	Las Vegas	IHL	32	21	21	42	30	4	1	0	1	2
1994-95	Cleveland	IHL	51	32	27	59	48	4	4	2	6	6
1995-96	**Pittsburgh**	**NHL**	**21**	**4**	**1**	**5**	**6**	**12**	**1**	**1**	**2**	**4**
	Cleveland	IHL	53	25	27	52	44	....	....	....	....	....
1996-97	Cleveland	IHL	64	27	21	48	61	14	4	6	10	8
1997-98	Cleveland	IHL	68	22	33	55	74	10	0	3	3	12
	NHL Totals		**323**	**44**	**67**	**111**	**218**	**34**	**7**	**5**	**12**	**24**

IHL First All-Star Team (1993)

Traded to **Chicago** by **NY Islanders** with Brent Sutter for Adam Creighton and Steve Thomas, October 25, 1991. Signed as a free agent by **Ottawa**, January 3, 1994. Signed as a free agent by **Pittsburgh**, August 10, 1995.

LAUKKANEN, JANNE (LOW-kah-nehn) OTT.

Defense. Shoots left. 6', 180 lbs. Born, Lahti, Finland, March 19, 1970.
(Quebec's 8th choice, 156th overall, in 1991 Entry Draft).

			Regular Season					Playoffs				
Season	Club	Lea	GP	G	A	TP	PIM	GP	G	A	TP	PIM
1989-90	Ilves	Finland	39	5	6	11	10	....	....	....	....	....
1990-91	Reipas Lahti	Finland	44	8	14	22	56	....	....	....	....	....
1991-92	Hameelinna	Finland	43	5	14	19	62	....	....	....	....	....
	Finland	Olympics	8	0	1	1	6	....	....	....	....	....
1992-93	Hameelinna	Finland	47	8	21	29	76	12	1	4	5	10
1993-94	Hameelinna	Finland	48	5	24	29	46	....	....	....	....	....
	Finland	Olympics	8	0	2	2	12	....	....	....	....	....
1994-95	Cornwall	AHL	55	8	26	34	41	....	....	....	....	....
	Quebec	**NHL**	**11**	**0**	**3**	**3**	**4**	**6**	**1**	**0**	**1**	**2**
1995-96	**Colorado**	**NHL**	**3**	**1**	**0**	**1**	**0**	....	....	....	....	....
	Cornwall	AHL	35	7	20	27	60	....	....	....	....	....
	Ottawa	**NHL**	**20**	**0**	**2**	**2**	**14**	....	....	....	....	....
1996-97	**Ottawa**	**NHL**	**76**	**3**	**18**	**21**	**76**	**7**	**0**	**1**	**1**	**6**
1997-98	**Ottawa**	**NHL**	**60**	**4**	**17**	**21**	**64**	**11**	**2**	**2**	**4**	**8**
	Finland	Olympics	6	0	0	0	4	....	....	....	....	....
	NHL Totals		**170**	**8**	**40**	**48**	**158**	**24**	**3**	**3**	**6**	**16**

Finnish First All-Star Team (1993)

Transferred to **Colorado** after **Quebec** franchise relocated, June 21, 1995. Traded to **Ottawa** by **Colorado** for the rights to Brad Larsen, January 26, 1996.

LAUS, PAUL (LOWZ) FLA.

Defense. Shoots right. 6'1", 212 lbs. Born, Beamsville, Ont., September 26, 1970.
(Pittsburgh's 2nd choice, 37th overall, in 1989 Entry Draft).

			Regular Season					Playoffs				
Season	Club	Lea	GP	G	A	TP	PIM	GP	G	A	TP	PIM
1987-88	Hamilton	OHL	56	1	9	10	171	14	0	0	0	28
1988-89	Niagara Falls	OHL	49	1	10	11	225	15	0	5	5	56
1989-90	Niagara Falls	OHL	60	13	35	48	231	16	6	16	22	71
1990-91	Albany	IHL	7	0	0	0	7	....	....	....	....	....
	Knoxville	ECHL	20	6	12	18	83	....	....	....	....	....
	Muskegon	IHL	35	3	4	7	103	4	0	0	0	13
1991-92	Muskegon	IHL	75	0	21	21	248	14	2	5	7	70
1992-93	Cleveland	IHL	76	8	18	26	427	4	1	0	1	27
1993-94	**Florida**	**NHL**	**39**	**2**	**0**	**2**	**109**	....	....	....	....	....
1994-95	**Florida**	**NHL**	**37**	**0**	**7**	**7**	**138**	....	....	....	....	....
1995-96	**Florida**	**NHL**	**78**	**3**	**6**	**9**	**236**	**21**	**2**	**6**	**8**	***62**
1996-97	**Florida**	**NHL**	**77**	**0**	**12**	**12**	**313**	**5**	**0**	**1**	**1**	**4**
1997-98	**Florida**	**NHL**	**77**	**0**	**11**	**11**	**293**	....	....	....	....	....
	NHL Totals		**308**	**5**	**36**	**41**	**1089**	**26**	**2**	**7**	**9**	**66**

Claimed by **Florida** from **Pittsburgh** in Expansion Draft, June 24, 1993.

LAWRENCE, MARK NYI

Right wing. Shoots right. 6'4", 215 lbs. Born, Burlington, Ont., January 27, 1972.
(Minnesota's 4th choice, 118th overall, in 1991 Entry Draft).

			Regular Season					Playoffs				
Season	Club	Lea	GP	G	A	TP	PIM	GP	G	A	TP	PIM
1988-89	Niagara Falls	OHL	63	9	27	36	142	....	....	....	....	....
1989-90	Niagara Falls	OHL	54	15	18	33	123	16	2	5	7	42
1990-91	Detroit	OHL	66	27	38	65	53	....	....	....	....	....
1991-92	Detroit	OHL	28	19	26	45	54	....	....	....	....	....
	North Bay	OHL	24	13	14	27	21	21	*23	12	35	36
1992-93	Dayton	ECHL	20	8	14	22	46	....	....	....	....	....
	Kalamazoo	IHL	57	22	13	35	47	....	....	....	....	....
1993-94	Kalamazoo	IHL	64	17	20	37	90	....	....	....	....	....
1994-95	Kalamazoo	IHL	77	21	29	50	92	16	3	7	10	28
	Dallas	**NHL**	**2**	**0**	**0**	**0**	**0**	....	....	....	....	....
1995-96	**Dallas**	**NHL**	**13**	**0**	**1**	**1**	**17**	....	....	....	....	....
	Michigan	IHL	55	15	14	29	92	10	3	4	7	30
1996-97	Michigan	IHL	68	15	21	36	141	4	0	0	0	18
1997-98	**NY Islanders**	**NHL**	**2**	**0**	**0**	**0**	**2**	....	....	....	....	....
	Utah	IHL	80	36	28	64	102	4	1	1	2	4
	NHL Totals		**17**	**0**	**1**	**1**	**19**	....	....	....	....	....

Rights transferred to **Dallas** after **Minnesota** franchise relocated, June 9, 1993. Signed as a free agent by **NY Islanders**, August 25, 1997.

LAZAREV, YEVGENY (LA-zahr-ehv, YEHV-geh-nee) COL.

Right wing. Shoots left. 6'2", 215 lbs. Born, Kharkov, USSR, April 25, 1980.
(Colorado's 8th choice, 79th overall, in 1998 Entry Draft).

			Regular Season					Playoffs				
Season	Club	Lea	GP	G	A	TP	PIM	GP	G	A	TP	PIM
1996-97	Yaroslavl	Russia	1	0	0	0	0	....	....	....	....	....
	Yaroslavl 2	Russia-3	44	18	15	33	38	....	....	....	....	....
1997-98	Kitchener	OJHL	11	9	13	22	19	5	5	2	7	17

LEACH, JAY PHX.

Defense. Shoots left. 6'3", 202 lbs. Born, Syracuse, NY, September 2, 1979.
(Phoenix's 5th choice, 115th overall, in 1998 Entry Draft).

			Regular Season					Playoffs				
Season	Club	Lea	GP	G	A	TP	PIM	GP	G	A	TP	PIM
1996-97	Capital District	NAJHL	57	8	50	58	140	....	....	....	....	....
1997-98	Providence College	H.E.	32	0	8	8	29	....	....	....	....	....

LEACH, STEPHEN — CAR.

Right wing. Shoots right. 5'11", 197 lbs. Born, Cambridge, MA, January 16, 1966.
(Washington's 2nd choice, 34th overall, in 1984 Entry Draft).

			Regular Season					Playoffs				
Season	Club	Lea	GP	G	A	TP	PIM	GP	G	A	TP	PIM
1983-84	Matignon	H.S.	21	27	22	49	49	....	....	....	....	....
1984-85	New Hampshire	H.E.	41	12	25	37	53	....	....	....	....	....
1985-86	New Hampshire	H.E.	25	22	6	28	30	....	....	....	....	....
	Washington	**NHL**	**11**	**1**	**1**	**2**	**2**	**6**	**0**	**1**	**1**	**0**
1986-87	**Washington**	**NHL**	**15**	**1**	**0**	**1**	**6**	....	....	....	....	....
	Binghamton	AHL	54	18	21	39	39	13	3	1	4	6
1987-88	United States	Nat-Tm	49	26	20	46	30	....	....	....	....	....
	United States	Olympics	6	1	2	3	0	....	....	....	....	....
	Washington	**NHL**	**8**	**1**	**1**	**2**	**17**	**9**	**2**	**1**	**3**	**0**
1988-89	**Washington**	**NHL**	**74**	**11**	**19**	**30**	**94**	**6**	**1**	**0**	**1**	**12**
1989-90	**Washington**	**NHL**	**70**	**18**	**14**	**32**	**104**	**14**	**2**	**2**	**4**	**8**
1990-91	**Washington**	**NHL**	**68**	**11**	**19**	**30**	**99**	**9**	**1**	**2**	**3**	**8**
1991-92	**Boston**	**NHL**	**78**	**31**	**29**	**60**	**147**	**15**	**4**	**0**	**4**	**10**
1992-93	**Boston**	**NHL**	**79**	**26**	**25**	**51**	**126**	**4**	**1**	**1**	**2**	**2**
1993-94	**Boston**	**NHL**	**42**	**5**	**10**	**15**	**74**	**5**	**0**	**1**	**1**	**2**
1994-95	**Boston**	**NHL**	**35**	**5**	**6**	**11**	**68**	....	....	....	....	....
1995-96	**Boston**	**NHL**	**59**	**9**	**13**	**22**	**86**	....	....	....	....	....
	St. Louis	**NHL**	**14**	**2**	**4**	**6**	**22**	**11**	**3**	**2**	**5**	**10**
1996-97	**St. Louis**	**NHL**	**17**	**2**	**1**	**3**	**24**	**6**	**0**	**0**	**0**	**33**
1997-98	**Carolina**	**NHL**	**45**	**4**	**5**	**9**	**42**	....	....	....	....	....
	NHL Totals		**615**	**127**	**147**	**274**	**911**	**85**	**14**	**10**	**24**	**85**

Traded to **Boston** by **Washington** for Randy Burridge, June 21, 1991. Traded to **St. Louis** by **Boston** for Kevin Sawyer and Steve Staios, March 8, 1996. Traded to **Carolina** by **St. Louis** for Alexander Godynyuk and Carolina's 6th round choice in 1998 Entry Draft, June 27, 1997.

LEAHY, PATRICK — NYR

Right wing. Shoots right. 6'3", 190 lbs. Born, Brighton, MA, June 9, 1979.
(NY Rangers' 5th choice, 122nd overall, in 1998 Entry Draft).

			Regular Season					Playoffs				
Season	Club	Lea	GP	G	A	TP	PIM	GP	G	A	TP	PIM
1997-98	Miami-Ohio	CCHA	28	0	1	1	24	....	....	....	....	....

LEBLANC, JOHN — (leh-BLAHNK)

Right wing. Shoots left. 6'1", 190 lbs. Born, Campbellton, N.B., January 21, 1964.

			Regular Season					Playoffs				
Season	Club	Lea	GP	G	A	TP	PIM	GP	G	A	TP	PIM
1982-83	Mount Allison	AUAA	20	21	26	47	10	....	....	....	....	....
1983-84	Hull	QMJHL	69	39	35	74	32	....	....	....	....	....
1984-85	New Brunswick	AUAA	24	25	34	59	32	....	....	....	....	....
1985-86	New Brunswick	AUAA	24	38	28	66	35	....	....	....	....	....
1986-87	**Vancouver**	**NHL**	**2**	**1**	**0**	**1**	**0**	....	....	....	....	....
	Fredericton	AHL	75	40	30	70	27	....	....	....	....	....
1987-88	**Vancouver**	**NHL**	**41**	**12**	**10**	**22**	**18**	....	....	....	....	....
	Fredericton	AHL	35	26	25	51	54	15	6	7	13	34
1988-89	Milwaukee	IHL	61	39	31	70	42	....	....	....	....	....
	Edmonton	**NHL**	**2**	**1**	**0**	**1**	**0**	**1**	**0**	**0**	**0**	**0**
	Cape Breton	AHL	3	4	0	4	0	....	....	....	....	....
1989-90	Cape Breton	AHL	77	*54	34	88	50	6	4	0	4	4
1990-91					DID NOT PLAY							
1991-92	**Winnipeg**	**NHL**	**16**	**6**	**1**	**7**	**6**	....	....	....	....	....
	Moncton	AHL	56	31	22	53	24	10	3	2	5	8
1992-93	**Winnipeg**	**NHL**	**3**	**0**	**0**	**0**	**2**	....	....	....	....	....
	Moncton	AHL	77	48	40	88	29	5	2	1	3	6
1993-94	**Winnipeg**	**NHL**	**17**	**6**	**2**	**8**	**2**	....	....	....	....	....
	Moncton	AHL	41	25	26	51	38	20	3	6	9	6
1994-95	**Winnipeg**	**NHL**	**2**	**0**	**0**	**0**	**0**	....	....	....	....	....
	Springfield	AHL	65	39	34	73	32	....	....	....	....	....
1995-96	Orlando	IHL	60	22	24	46	20	....	....	....	....	....
	Fort Wayne	IHL	16	12	11	23	4	5	0	2	2	14
1996-97	Fort Wayne	IHL	77	30	31	61	22	....	....	....	....	....
1997-98	Utah	IHL	69	25	17	42	16	2	0	0	0	2
	NHL Totals		**83**	**26**	**13**	**39**	**28**	**1**	**0**	**0**	**0**	**0**

Canadian University Player of the Year (1986)

Signed as a free agent by **Vancouver**, April 12, 1986. Traded to **Edmonton** by **Vancouver** with Vancouver's 5th round choice (Peter White) in 1989 Entry Draft for Doug Smith and Greg C. Adams, March 7, 1989. • Sat out entire 1990-91 season after failing to come to contract terms with Edmonton. Traded to **Winnipeg** by **Edmonton** with Edmonton's 10th round choice (Teemu Numminen) in 1992 Entry Draft for Winnipeg's 5th round choice (Ryan Haggerty) in 1991 Entry Draft, June 12, 1991.

LeBOUTILLIER, PETER — (lih-BOO-tihl-eer) ANA.

Right wing. Shoots right. 6'1", 205 lbs. Born, Neepawa, Man., January 11, 1975.
(Anaheim's 5th choice, 133rd overall, in 1995 Entry Draft).

			Regular Season					Playoffs				
Season	Club	Lea	GP	G	A	TP	PIM	GP	G	A	TP	PIM
1992-93	Red Deer	WHL	67	8	26	34	284	2	0	1	1	5
1993-94	Red Deer	WHL	66	19	20	39	300	2	0	1	1	4
1994-95	Red Deer	WHL	59	27	16	43	159	....	....	....	....	....
1995-96	Baltimore	AHL	68	7	9	16	228	11	0	0	0	33
1996-97	**Anaheim**	**NHL**	**23**	**1**	**0**	**1**	**121**	....	....	....	....	....
	Baltimore	AHL	47	6	12	18	175	....	....	....	....	....
1997-98	**Anaheim**	**NHL**	**12**	**1**	**1**	**2**	**55**	....	....	....	....	....
	Cincinnati	AHL	51	9	11	20	143	....	....	....	....	....
	NHL Totals		**35**	**2**	**1**	**3**	**176**	....	....	....	....	....

• Re-entered NHL draft. Originally NY Islanders' 6th choice, 144th overall, in 1993 Entry Draft.

LECAVALIER, VINCENT — (luh-KAV-uhl-YAY) T.B.

Center. Shoots left. 6'4", 180 lbs. Born, Ile Bizard, Que., April 21, 1980.
(Tampa Bay's 1st choice, 1st overall, in 1998 Entry Draft).

			Regular Season					Playoffs				
Season	Club	Lea	GP	G	A	TP	PIM	GP	G	A	TP	PIM
1996-97	Rimouski	QMJHL	64	42	61	103	38	4	4	3	7	2
1997-98	Rimouski	QMJHL	58	44	71	115	117	18	*15	*26	*41	46

QMJHL First All-Star Team (1998) • Canadian Major Junior First All-Star Team (1998)

LeCLAIR, JOHN — (luh-KLAIR) PHI.

Left wing. Shoots left. 6'3", 226 lbs. Born, St. Albans, VT, July 5, 1969.
(Montreal's 2nd choice, 33rd overall, in 1987 Entry Draft).

			Regular Season					Playoffs				
Season	Club	Lea	GP	G	A	TP	PIM	GP	G	A	TP	PIM
1986-87	Bellows Academy	H.S.	23	44	40	84	14	....	....	....	....	....
1987-88	U. of Vermont	ECAC	31	12	22	34	62	....	....	....	....	....
1988-89	U. of Vermont	ECAC	18	9	12	21	40	....	....	....	....	....
1989-90	U. of Vermont	ECAC	10	10	6	16	38	....	....	....	....	....
1990-91	U. of Vermont	ECAC	33	25	20	45	58	....	....	....	....	....
	Montreal	**NHL**	**10**	**2**	**5**	**7**	**2**	**3**	**0**	**0**	**0**	**0**
1991-92	**Montreal**	**NHL**	**59**	**8**	**11**	**19**	**14**	**8**	**1**	**1**	**2**	**4**
	Fredericton	AHL	8	7	7	14	10	2	0	0	0	4
1992-93	**Montreal**	**NHL**	**72**	**19**	**25**	**44**	**33**	**20**	**4**	**6**	**10**	**14 ♦**
1993-94	**Montreal**	**NHL**	**74**	**19**	**24**	**43**	**32**	**7**	**2**	**1**	**3**	**8**
1994-95	**Montreal**	**NHL**	**9**	**1**	**4**	**5**	**10**	....	....	....	....	....
	Philadelphia	**NHL**	**37**	**25**	**24**	**49**	**20**	**15**	**5**	**7**	**12**	**4**
1995-96	**Philadelphia**	**NHL**	**82**	**51**	**46**	**97**	**64**	**11**	**6**	**5**	**11**	**6**
1996-97	**Philadelphia**	**NHL**	**82**	**50**	**47**	**97**	**58**	**19**	**9**	**12**	**21**	**10**
1997-98	**Philadelphia**	**NHL**	**82**	**51**	**36**	**87**	**32**	**5**	**1**	**1**	**2**	**8**
	United States	Olympics	4	0	1	1	0	....	....	....	....	....
	NHL Totals		**507**	**226**	**222**	**448**	**265**	**88**	**28**	**33**	**61**	**54**

ECAC Second All-Star Team (1991) • NHL First All-Star Team (1995, 1998) • NHL Second All-Star Team (1996, 1997) • Won Bud Ice Plus/Minus Award (1997)

Played in NHL All-Star Game (1996, 1997, 1998)

Traded to **Philadelphia** by **Montreal** with Eric Desjardins and Gilbert Dionne for Mark Recchi and Philadelphia's 3rd round choice (Martin Hohenberger) in 1995 Entry Draft, February 9, 1995.

LECLERC, MIKE — ANA.

Left wing. Shoots left. 6'1", 205 lbs. Born, Winnipeg, Man., November 10, 1976.
(Anaheim's 3rd choice, 55th overall, in 1995 Entry Draft).

			Regular Season					Playoffs				
Season	Club	Lea	GP	G	A	TP	PIM	GP	G	A	TP	PIM
1992-93	Victoria	WHL	70	4	11	15	118	....	....	....	....	....
1993-94	Victoria	WHL	68	29	11	40	112	....	....	....	....	....
1994-95	Prince George	WHL	43	20	36	56	78	....	....	....	....	....
	Brandon	WHL	23	5	8	13	50	18	10	6	16	33
1995-96	Brandon	WHL	71	58	53	111	161	19	6	19	25	25
1996-97	**Anaheim**	**NHL**	**5**	**1**	**1**	**2**	**0**	**1**	**0**	**0**	**0**	**0**
	Baltimore	AHL	71	29	27	56	134	....	....	....	....	....
1997-98	**Anaheim**	**NHL**	**7**	**0**	**0**	**0**	**6**	....	....	....	....	....
	Cincinnati	AHL	48	18	22	40	83	....	....	....	....	....
	NHL Totals		**12**	**1**	**1**	**2**	**6**	**1**	**0**	**0**	**0**	**0**

WHL East Second All-Star Team (1996)

LECOMPTE, ERIC — (luh-COMP) ANA.

Left wing. Shoots left. 6'4", 190 lbs. Born, Montreal, Que., April 4, 1975.
(Chicago's 1st choice, 24th overall, in 1993 Entry Draft).

			Regular Season					Playoffs				
Season	Club	Lea	GP	G	A	TP	PIM	GP	G	A	TP	PIM
1991-92	Hull	QMJHL	60	16	17	33	138	6	1	0	1	4
1992-93	Hull	QMJHL	66	33	38	71	149	10	4	4	8	52
1993-94	Hull	QMJHL	62	39	49	88	171	20	10	10	20	68
1994-95	Hull	QMJHL	12	11	9	20	58	....	....	....	....	....
	St-Jean	QMJHL	18	9	10	19	54	....	....	....	....	....
	Sherbrooke	QMJHL	34	22	29	51	111	4	2	2	4	4
	Indianapolis	IHL	3	2	0	2	2	....	....	....	....	....
1995-96	Indianapolis	IHL	79	24	20	44	131	....	....	....	....	....
1996-97	Worcester	AHL	8	0	1	1	4	....	....	....	....	....
	Indianapolis	IHL	35	2	3	5	74	....	....	....	....	....
	Fort Wayne	IHL	14	1	2	3	62	....	....	....	....	....
1997-98	Indianapolis	IHL	46	7	11	18	52	....	....	....	....	....
	Cincinnati	AHL	26	11	8	19	68	....	....	....	....	....

Signed as a free agent by **Anaheim**, August 18, 1998.

LEDYARD, GRANT — BOS.

Defense. Shoots left. 6'2", 195 lbs. Born, Winnipeg, Man., November 19, 1961.

			Regular Season					Playoffs				
Season	Club	Lea	GP	G	A	TP	PIM	GP	G	A	TP	PIM
1980-81	Saskatoon	WHL	71	9	28	37	148	....	....	....	....	....
1981-82	Fort Garry	MJHL	63	25	45	70	150	....	....	....	....	....
1982-83	Tulsa	CHL	80	13	29	42	115	....	....	....	....	....
1983-84	Tulsa	CHL	58	9	17	26	71	9	5	4	9	10
1984-85	**NY Rangers**	**NHL**	**42**	**8**	**12**	**20**	**53**	**3**	**0**	**2**	**2**	**4**
	New Haven	AHL	36	6	20	26	18	....	....	....	....	....
1985-86	**NY Rangers**	**NHL**	**27**	**2**	**9**	**11**	**20**	....	....	....	....	....
	Los Angeles	**NHL**	**52**	**7**	**18**	**25**	**78**	....	....	....	....	....
1986-87	**Los Angeles**	**NHL**	**67**	**14**	**23**	**37**	**93**	**5**	**0**	**0**	**0**	**10**
1987-88	**Los Angeles**	**NHL**	**23**	**1**	**7**	**8**	**52**	....	....	....	....	....
	New Haven	AHL	3	2	1	3	4	....	....	....	....	....
	Washington	**NHL**	**21**	**4**	**3**	**7**	**14**	**14**	**1**	**0**	**1**	**30**
1988-89	**Washington**	**NHL**	**61**	**3**	**11**	**14**	**43**	....	....	....	....	....
	Buffalo	**NHL**	**13**	**1**	**5**	**6**	**8**	**5**	**1**	**2**	**3**	**2**
1989-90	**Buffalo**	**NHL**	**67**	**2**	**13**	**15**	**37**	....	....	....	....	....
1990-91	**Buffalo**	**NHL**	**60**	**8**	**23**	**31**	**46**	**6**	**3**	**3**	**6**	**10**
1991-92	**Buffalo**	**NHL**	**50**	**5**	**16**	**21**	**45**	....	....	....	....	....
1992-93	**Buffalo**	**NHL**	**50**	**2**	**14**	**16**	**45**	**8**	**0**	**0**	**0**	**8**
	Rochester	AHL	5	0	2	2	8	....	....	....	....	....
1993-94	**Dallas**	**NHL**	**84**	**9**	**37**	**46**	**42**	**9**	**1**	**2**	**3**	**6**
1994-95	**Dallas**	**NHL**	**38**	**5**	**13**	**18**	**20**	**3**	**0**	**0**	**0**	**2**
1995-96	**Dallas**	**NHL**	**73**	**5**	**19**	**24**	**20**	....	....	....	....	....
1996-97	**Dallas**	**NHL**	**67**	**1**	**15**	**16**	**61**	**7**	**0**	**2**	**2**	**0**
1997-98	**Vancouver**	**NHL**	**49**	**2**	**13**	**15**	**14**	....	....	....	....	....
	Boston	**NHL**	**22**	**2**	**7**	**9**	**6**	**6**	**0**	**0**	**0**	**2**
	NHL Totals		**866**	**81**	**258**	**339**	**697**	**66**	**6**	**11**	**17**	**74**

Won Bob Gassoff Trophy (CHL's Most Improved Defenseman) (1984)

Signed as a free agent by **NY Rangers**, July 7, 1982. Traded to **LA Kings** by **NY Rangers** with Roland Melanson for LA Kings' 4th round choice (Mike Sullivan) in 1987 Entry Draft and Brian MacLellan, December 7, 1985. Traded to **Washington** by **LA Kings** for Craig Laughlin, February 9, 1988. Traded to **Buffalo** by **Washington** with Clint Malarchuk and Washington's 6th round choice (Brian Holzinger) in 1991 Entry Draft for Calle Johansson and Buffalo's 2nd round choice (Byron Dafoe) in 1989 Entry Draft, March 7, 1989. Signed as a free agent by **Dallas**, August 12, 1993. Signed as a free agent by **Vancouver**, July 17, 1997. Traded to **Boston** by **Vancouver** for Boston's 8th round choice (Curtis Valentine) in 1998 Entry Draft, March 3, 1998.

LEEB, GREG — DAL.

Left wing. Shoots left. 5'9", 160 lbs. Born, Red Deer, Alta., May 31, 1977.

			Regular Season					Playoffs				
Season	Club	Lea	GP	G	A	TP	PIM	GP	G	A	TP	PIM
1994-95	Spokane	WHL	72	21	34	55	48	11	5	10	15	10
1995-96	Spokane	WHL	64	33	21	54	54	18	1	7	8	16
1996-97	Spokane	WHL	72	27	59	86	69	9	3	3	6	4
1997-98	Spokane	WHL	68	46	50	96	54	18	10	10	20	10

Signed as a free agent by **Dallas**, July 24, 1998.

LEETCH, BRIAN — NYR

Defense. Shoots left. 5'11", 190 lbs. Born, Corpus Christi, TX, March 3, 1968.
(NY Rangers' 1st choice, 9th overall, in 1986 Entry Draft).

			Regular Season					Playoffs				
Season	Club	Lea	GP	G	A	TP	PIM	GP	G	A	TP	PIM
1984-85	Avon Old Farms	H.S.	26	30	46	76	15	....	....	....	....	....
1985-86	Avon Old Farms	H.S.	28	40	44	84	18	....	....	....	....	....
1986-87	Boston College	H.E.	37	9	38	47	10	....	....	....	....	....
1987-88	United States	Nat-Tm	50	13	61	74	38	....	....	....	....	....
	United States	Olympics	6	1	5	6	4	....	....	....	....	....
	NY Rangers	**NHL**	**17**	**2**	**12**	**14**	**0**	....	....	....	....	....
1988-89	**NY Rangers**	**NHL**	**68**	**23**	**48**	**71**	**50**	**4**	**3**	**2**	**5**	**2**
1989-90	**NY Rangers**	**NHL**	**72**	**11**	**45**	**56**	**26**	....	....	....	....	....
1990-91	**NY Rangers**	**NHL**	**80**	**16**	**72**	**88**	**42**	**6**	**1**	**3**	**4**	**0**
1991-92	**NY Rangers**	**NHL**	**80**	**22**	**80**	**102**	**26**	**13**	**4**	**11**	**15**	**4**
1992-93	**NY Rangers**	**NHL**	**36**	**6**	**30**	**36**	**26**	....	....	....	....	....
1993-94	**NY Rangers**	**NHL**	**84**	**23**	**56**	**79**	**67**	**23**	**11**	***23**	***34**	**6** ♦
1994-95	**NY Rangers**	**NHL**	**48**	**9**	**32**	**41**	**18**	**10**	**6**	**8**	**14**	**8**
1995-96	**NY Rangers**	**NHL**	**82**	**15**	**70**	**85**	**30**	**11**	**1**	**6**	**7**	**4**
1996-97	**NY Rangers**	**NHL**	**82**	**20**	**58**	**78**	**40**	**15**	**2**	**8**	**10**	**6**
1997-98	**NY Rangers**	**NHL**	**76**	**17**	**33**	**50**	**32**	....	....	....	....	....
	United States	Olympics	4	1	1	2	0	....	....	....	....	....
	NHL Totals		**725**	**164**	**536**	**700**	**357**	**82**	**28**	**61**	**89**	**30**

Hockey East First All-Star Team (1987) • NCAA East First All-American Team (1987) • NHL All-Rookie Team (1989) • Won Calder Memorial Trophy (1989) • NHL Second All-Star Team (1991, 1994, 1996) • Won James Norris Memorial Trophy (1992, 1997) • NHL First All-Star Team (1992, 1997) • Won Conn Smythe Trophy (1994)

Played in NHL All-Star Game (1990, 1991, 1992, 1994, 1996, 1997, 1998)

LEFEBVRE, CHRISTIAN (luh-FAHV) — EDM.

Defense. Shoots left. 6'5", 212 lbs. Born, Montreal, Que., March 3, 1978.
(Edmonton's 8th choice, 213th overall, in 1998 Entry Draft).

			Regular Season					Playoffs				
Season	Club	Lea	GP	G	A	TP	PIM	GP	G	A	TP	PIM
1994-95	Granby	QMJHL	24	1	1	2	11	4	0	0	0	0
1995-96	Granby	QMJHL	36	4	6	10	41	20	2	2	4	30
1996-97						DID NOT PLAY						
1997-98	Baie-Comeau	QMJHL	8	0	0	0	18	....	....	....	....	....

• Re-entered draft. Originally Calgary's 6th choice, 94th overall, in 1996 Entry Draft.

LEFEBVRE, SYLVAIN (luh-FAYV) — COL.

Defense. Shoots left. 6'2", 205 lbs. Born, Richmond, Que., October 14, 1967.

			Regular Season					Playoffs				
Season	Club	Lea	GP	G	A	TP	PIM	GP	G	A	TP	PIM
1984-85	Laval	QMJHL	66	7	5	12	31	....	....	....	....	....
1985-86	Laval	QMJHL	71	8	17	25	48	14	1	0	1	25
1986-87	Laval	QMJHL	70	10	36	46	44	15	1	6	7	12
1987-88	Sherbrooke	AHL	79	3	24	27	73	6	2	3	5	4
1988-89	Sherbrooke	AHL	77	15	32	47	119	6	1	3	4	4
1989-90	**Montreal**	**NHL**	**68**	**3**	**10**	**13**	**61**	**6**	**0**	**0**	**0**	**2**
1990-91	**Montreal**	**NHL**	**63**	**5**	**18**	**23**	**30**	**11**	**1**	**0**	**1**	**6**
1991-92	**Montreal**	**NHL**	**69**	**3**	**14**	**17**	**91**	**2**	**0**	**0**	**0**	**2**
1992-93	**Toronto**	**NHL**	**81**	**2**	**12**	**14**	**90**	**21**	**3**	**3**	**6**	**20**
1993-94	**Toronto**	**NHL**	**84**	**2**	**9**	**11**	**79**	**18**	**0**	**3**	**3**	**16**
1994-95	**Quebec**	**NHL**	**48**	**2**	**11**	**13**	**17**	**6**	**0**	**2**	**2**	**2**
1995-96	**Colorado**	**NHL**	**75**	**5**	**11**	**16**	**49**	**22**	**0**	**5**	**5**	**12** ♦
1996-97	**Colorado**	**NHL**	**71**	**2**	**11**	**13**	**30**	**17**	**0**	**0**	**0**	**25**
1997-98	**Colorado**	**NHL**	**81**	**0**	**10**	**10**	**48**	**7**	**0**	**0**	**0**	**4**
	NHL Totals		**640**	**24**	**106**	**130**	**495**	**110**	**4**	**13**	**17**	**89**

AHL Second All-Star Team (1989)

Signed as a free agent by **Montreal**, September 24, 1986. Traded to **Toronto** by **Montreal** for Toronto's 3rd round choice (Martin Belanger) in 1994 Entry Draft, August 20, 1992. Traded to **Quebec** by **Toronto** with Wendel Clark, Landon Wilson and Toronto's 1st round choice (Jeffrey Kealty) in 1994 Entry Draft for Mats Sundin, Garth Butcher, Todd Warriner and Philadelphia's 1st round choice (previously acquired by Quebec — later traded to Washington — Washington selected Nolan Baumgartner) in 1994 Entry Draft, June 28, 1994. Transferred to **Colorado** after **Quebec** franchise relocated, June 21, 1995.

LEGAULT, JAY (LEH-goh) — ANA.

Left wing. Shoots left. 6'4", 205 lbs. Born, Peterborough, Ont., May 15, 1979.
(Anaheim's 3rd choice, 72nd overall, in 1997 Entry Draft).

			Regular Season					Playoffs				
Season	Club	Lea	GP	G	A	TP	PIM	GP	G	A	TP	PIM
1995-96	Oshawa	OHL	61	2	11	13	37	5	0	1	1	8
1996-97	Oshawa	OHL	39	13	26	39	50	....	....	....	....	....
	London	OHL	28	6	13	19	37	....	....	....	....	....
1997-98	London	OHL	61	39	56	95	87	16	1	8	9	34

LEGWAND, DAVID (LEHG-wuhnd) — NSH.

Center. Shoots left. 6'1", 175 lbs. Born, Detroit, MI, August 17, 1980.
(Nashville's 1st choice, 2nd overall, in 1998 Entry Draft).

			Regular Season					Playoffs				
Season	Club	Lea	GP	G	A	TP	PIM	GP	G	A	TP	PIM
1996-97	Detroit	USHL	44	21	41	62	58	....	....	....	....	....
1997-98	Plymouth	OHL	59	54	51	105	56	15	8	12	20	24

OHL First All-Star Team (1998) • Canadian Major Junior Rookie of the Year (1998)

LEHTERA, TERO (LEHKH-tuh-rah) — FLA.

Left wing. Shoots right. 6', 185 lbs. Born, Espoo, Finland, April 21, 1972.
(Florida's 9th choice, 235th overall, in 1994 Entry Draft).

			Regular Season					Playoffs				
Season	Club	Lea	GP	G	A	TP	PIM	GP	G	A	TP	PIM
1993-94	Espoo	Finland	48	19	27	46	2	....	....	....	....	....
	Finland	Olympics	4	0	1	1	0	....	....	....	....	....
1994-95	Malmo IF	Sweden	37	12	11	23	10	9	0	1	1	0
1995-96	Jokerit	Finland	48	11	12	23	27	11	2	5	7	2
1996-97	Jokerit	Finland	47	11	10	21	4	9	2	3	5	0
1997-98	Kiekko	Finland	47	9	13	22	4	8	1	1	2	0

LEHTINEN, JERE (lehkh-TIH-nehn) — DAL.

Right wing. Shoots right. 6', 192 lbs. Born, Espoo, Finland, June 24, 1973.
(Minnesota's 3rd choice, 88th overall, in 1992 Entry Draft).

			Regular Season					Playoffs				
Season	Club	Lea	GP	G	A	TP	PIM	GP	G	A	TP	PIM
1990-91	Espoo	Finland-2	32	15	9	24	12	....	....	....	....	....
1991-92	Espoo	Finland-2	43	32	17	49	6	....	....	....	....	....
1992-93	Kiekko	Finland	45	13	14	27	6	....	....	....	....	....
1993-94	TPS Turku	Finland	42	19	20	39	6	11	11	2	13	2
	Finland	Olympics	8	3	0	3	0	....	....	....	....	....
1994-95	TPS Turku	Finland	39	19	23	42	33	13	8	6	14	4
1995-96	**Dallas**	**NHL**	**57**	**6**	**22**	**28**	**16**	....	....	....	....	....
	Michigan	IHL	1	1	0	1	0	....	....	....	....	....
1996-97	**Dallas**	**NHL**	**63**	**16**	**27**	**43**	**2**	**7**	**2**	**2**	**4**	**0**
1997-98	**Dallas**	**NHL**	**72**	**23**	**19**	**42**	**20**	**12**	**3**	**5**	**8**	**2**
	Finland	Olympics	6	4	2	6	2	....	....	....	....	....
	NHL Totals		**192**	**45**	**68**	**113**	**38**	**19**	**5**	**7**	**12**	**2**

Finnish First All-Star Team (1995) • Won Frank J. Selke Trophy (1998)

Played in NHL All-Star Game (1998)

Rights transferred to **Dallas** after **Minnesota** franchise relocated, June 9, 1993.

LEMIEUX, CLAUDE (lehm-YOO) — COL.

Right wing. Shoots right. 6'1", 215 lbs. Born, Buckingham, Que., July 16, 1965.
(Montreal's 2nd choice, 26th overall, in 1983 Entry Draft).

			Regular Season					Playoffs				
Season	Club	Lea	GP	G	A	TP	PIM	GP	G	A	TP	PIM
1982-83	Trois-Rivieres	QMJHL	62	28	38	66	187	4	1	0	1	30
1983-84	Verdun	QMJHL	51	41	45	86	225	9	8	12	20	63
	Montreal	**NHL**	**8**	**1**	**1**	**2**	**12**	....	....	....	....	....
	Nova Scotia	AHL	....	....	....	....	....	2	1	0	1	0
1984-85	Verdun	QMJHL	52	58	66	124	152	14	23	17	40	38
	Montreal	**NHL**	**1**	**0**	**1**	**1**	**7**	....	....	....	....	....
1985-86	**Montreal**	**NHL**	**10**	**1**	**2**	**3**	**22**	**20**	**10**	**6**	**16**	**68** ♦
	Sherbrooke	AHL	58	21	32	53	145	....	....	....	....	....
1986-87	**Montreal**	**NHL**	**76**	**27**	**26**	**53**	**156**	**17**	**4**	**9**	**13**	**41**
1987-88	**Montreal**	**NHL**	**78**	**31**	**30**	**61**	**137**	**11**	**3**	**2**	**5**	**20**
1988-89	**Montreal**	**NHL**	**69**	**29**	**22**	**51**	**136**	**18**	**4**	**3**	**7**	**58**
1989-90	**Montreal**	**NHL**	**39**	**8**	**10**	**18**	**106**	**11**	**1**	**3**	**4**	**38**
1990-91	**New Jersey**	**NHL**	**78**	**30**	**17**	**47**	**105**	**7**	**4**	**0**	**4**	**34**
1991-92	**New Jersey**	**NHL**	**74**	**41**	**27**	**68**	**109**	**7**	**4**	**3**	**7**	**26**
1992-93	**New Jersey**	**NHL**	**77**	**30**	**51**	**81**	**155**	**5**	**2**	**0**	**2**	**19**
1993-94	**New Jersey**	**NHL**	**79**	**18**	**26**	**44**	**86**	**20**	**7**	**11**	**18**	**44**
1994-95	**New Jersey**	**NHL**	**45**	**6**	**13**	**19**	**86**	**20**	***13**	**3**	**16**	**20** ♦
1995-96	**Colorado**	**NHL**	**79**	**39**	**32**	**71**	**117**	**19**	**5**	**7**	**12**	**55** ♦
1996-97	**Colorado**	**NHL**	**45**	**11**	**17**	**28**	**43**	**17**	***13**	**10**	**23**	**32**
1997-98	**Colorado**	**NHL**	**78**	**26**	**27**	**53**	**115**	**7**	**3**	**3**	**6**	**8**
	NHL Totals		**836**	**298**	**302**	**600**	**1392**	**179**	**73**	**60**	**133**	**463**

QMJHL Second All-Star Team (1984) • QMJHL First All-Star Team (1985) • Won Conn Smythe Trophy (1995)

Traded to **New Jersey** by **Montreal** for Sylvain Turgeon, September 4, 1990. Traded to **NY Islanders** by **New Jersey** for Steve Thomas, October 3, 1995. Traded to **Colorado** by **NY Islanders** for Wendel Clark, October 3, 1995.

LEMIEUX, JOCELYN (lehm-YOO) — PHX.

Right wing. Shoots left. 5'11", 220 lbs. Born, Mont-Laurier, Que., November 18, 1967.
(St. Louis' 1st choice, 10th overall, in 1986 Entry Draft).

			Regular Season					Playoffs				
Season	Club	Lea	GP	G	A	TP	PIM	GP	G	A	TP	PIM
1984-85	Laval	QMJHL	68	13	19	32	92	....	....	....	....	....
1985-86	Laval	QMJHL	71	57	68	125	131	14	9	15	24	37
1986-87	**St. Louis**	**NHL**	**53**	**10**	**8**	**18**	**94**	**5**	**0**	**1**	**1**	**6**
1987-88	**St. Louis**	**NHL**	**23**	**1**	**0**	**1**	**42**	**5**	**0**	**0**	**0**	**15**
	Peoria	IHL	8	0	5	5	35	....	....	....	....	....
1988-89	**Montreal**	**NHL**	**1**	**0**	**1**	**1**	**0**	....	....	....	....	....
	Sherbrooke	AHL	73	25	28	53	134	4	3	1	4	6
1989-90	**Montreal**	**NHL**	**34**	**4**	**2**	**6**	**61**	....	....	....	....	....
	Chicago	**NHL**	**39**	**10**	**11**	**21**	**47**	**18**	**1**	**8**	**9**	**28**
1990-91	**Chicago**	**NHL**	**67**	**6**	**7**	**13**	**119**	**4**	**0**	**0**	**0**	**0**
1991-92	**Chicago**	**NHL**	**78**	**6**	**10**	**16**	**80**	**18**	**3**	**1**	**4**	**33**
1992-93	**Chicago**	**NHL**	**81**	**10**	**21**	**31**	**111**	**4**	**1**	**0**	**1**	**2**
1993-94	**Chicago**	**NHL**	**66**	**12**	**8**	**20**	**63**	....	....	....	....	....
	Hartford	**NHL**	**16**	**6**	**1**	**7**	**19**	....	....	....	....	....
1994-95	**Hartford**	**NHL**	**41**	**6**	**5**	**11**	**32**	....	....	....	....	....
1995-96	**Hartford**	**NHL**	**29**	**1**	**2**	**3**	**31**	....	....	....	....	....
	New Jersey	**NHL**	**18**	**0**	**1**	**1**	**4**	....	....	....	....	....
	Calgary	**NHL**	**20**	**4**	**4**	**8**	**10**	**4**	**0**	**0**	**0**	**0**
1996-97	Long Beach	IHL	28	4	10	14	54	....	....	....	....	....
	Phoenix	**NHL**	**2**	**1**	**0**	**1**	**0**	**2**	**0**	**0**	**0**	**4**
1997-98	**Phoenix**	**NHL**	**30**	**3**	**3**	**6**	**27**	....	....	....	....	....
	Long Beach	IHL	10	3	5	8	24	....	....	....	....	....
	Springfield	AHL	6	3	1	4	0	4	2	2	4	2
	NHL Totals		**598**	**80**	**84**	**164**	**740**	**60**	**5**	**10**	**15**	**88**

QMJHL First All-Star Team (1986)

Traded to **Montreal** by **St. Louis** with Darrell May and St. Louis' 2nd round choice (Patrice Brisebois) in the 1989 Entry Draft for Sergio Momesso and Vincent Riendeau, August 9, 1988. Traded to **Chicago** by **Montreal** for Chicago's 3rd round choice (Charles Poulin) in 1990 Entry Draft, January 5, 1990. Traded to **Hartford** by **Chicago** with Frantisek Kucera for Gary Suter, Randy Cunneyworth and Hartford's 3rd round choice (later traded to Vancouver — Vancouver selected Larry Courville) in 1995 Entry Draft, March 11, 1994. Traded to **New Jersey** by **Hartford** with Hartford's 2nd round choice in 1998 Entry Draft for Jim Dowd and New Jersey's 2nd round choice (later traded to Calgary — Calgary selected Dmitri Kokorev) in 1997 Entry Draft, December 19, 1995. Traded to **Calgary** by **New Jersey** with Tommy Albelin and Cale Hulse for Phil Housley and Dan Keczmer, February 26, 1996. Signed as a free agent by **Phoenix**, March 18, 1997.

LENT, NICHOLAS — PHX.

Right wing. Shoots right. 6'3", 210 lbs. Born, Boston, MA, June 10, 1977.
(Phoenix's 7th choice, 200th overall, in 1996 Entry Draft).

			Regular Season					Playoffs				
Season	Club	Lea	GP	G	A	TP	PIM	GP	G	A	TP	PIM
1995-96	Omaha	USHL	42	7	9	16	65	6	2	1	3	8
1996-97	Providence	H.E.	27	6	6	12	16	....	....	....	....	....
1997-98	Providence	H.E.	33	6	8	14	30	....	....	....	....	....

LEROUX, FRANCOIS (leh-ROO)

Defense. Shoots left. 6'6", 235 lbs. Born, Ste.-Adele, Que., April 18, 1970.
(Edmonton's 1st choice, 19th overall, in 1988 Entry Draft).

			Regular Season					Playoffs				
Season	Club	Lea	GP	G	A	TP	PIM	GP	G	A	TP	PIM
1987-88	St-Jean	QMJHL	58	3	8	11	143	7	2	0	2	21
1988-89	St-Jean	QMJHL	57	8	34	42	185	....	....	....	....	....
	Edmonton	**NHL**	**2**	**0**	**0**	**0**	**0**	....	....	....	....	....
1989-90	Victoriaville	QMJHL	54	4	33	37	169	....	....	....	....	....
	Edmonton	**NHL**	**3**	**0**	**1**	**1**	**0**	....	....	....	....	....
1990-91	**Edmonton**	**NHL**	**1**	**0**	**2**	**2**	**0**	....	....	....	....	....
	Cape Breton	AHL	71	2	7	9	124	4	0	1	1	19
1991-92	**Edmonton**	**NHL**	**4**	**0**	**0**	**0**	**7**	....	....	....	....	....
	Cape Breton	AHL	61	7	22	29	114	5	0	0	0	8
1992-93	**Edmonton**	**NHL**	**1**	**0**	**0**	**0**	**4**	....	....	....	....	....
	Cape Breton	AHL	55	10	24	34	139	16	0	5	5	29
1993-94	**Ottawa**	**NHL**	**23**	**0**	**1**	**1**	**70**	....	....	....	....	....
	P.E.I.	AHL	25	4	6	10	52	....	....	....	....	....
1994-95	P.E.I.	AHL	45	4	14	18	137	....	....	....	....	....
	Pittsburgh	**NHL**	**40**	**0**	**2**	**2**	**114**	**12**	**0**	**2**	**2**	**14**
1995-96	**Pittsburgh**	**NHL**	**66**	**2**	**9**	**11**	**161**	**18**	**1**	**1**	**2**	**20**
1996-97	**Pittsburgh**	**NHL**	**59**	**0**	**3**	**3**	**81**	**3**	**0**	**0**	**0**	**0**
1997-98	**Colorado**	**NHL**	**50**	**1**	**2**	**3**	**140**	....	....	....	....	....
	NHL Totals		**249**	**3**	**20**	**23**	**577**	**33**	**1**	**3**	**4**	**34**

Claimed on waivers by **Ottawa** from **Edmonton**, October 6, 1993. Claimed by **Pittsburgh** from **Ottawa** in Waiver Draft, January 18, 1995. Traded to **Colorado** by **Pittsburgh** for Colorado's 3rd round choice (David Cameron) in 1998 Entry Draft, September 28, 1997.

LEROUX, JEAN-YVES (leh-ROO) CHI.

Left wing. Shoots left. 6'2", 211 lbs. Born, Montreal, Que., June 24, 1976.
(Chicago's 2nd choice, 40th overall, in 1994 Entry Draft).

			Regular Season					Playoffs				
Season	Club	Lea	GP	G	A	TP	PIM	GP	G	A	TP	PIM
1992-93	Beauport	QMJHL	62	20	25	45	33	....	....	....	....	....
1993-94	Beauport	QMJHL	45	14	25	39	43	15	7	6	13	33
1994-95	Beauport	QMJHL	59	19	33	52	125	17	4	6	10	39
1995-96	Beauport	QMJHL	54	41	41	82	176	20	5	18	23	20
1996-97	**Chicago**	**NHL**	**1**	**0**	**1**	**1**	**5**	....	....	....	....	....
	Indianapolis	IHL	69	14	17	31	112	4	1	0	1	2
1997-98	**Chicago**	**NHL**	**66**	**6**	**7**	**13**	**55**	....	....	....	....	....
	NHL Totals		**67**	**6**	**8**	**14**	**60**	....	....	....	....	....

QMJHL Second All-Star Team (1994)

LEROUX, ROD (leh-ROO) VAN.

Defense. Shoots left. 6'4", 204 lbs. Born, Calgary, Alta., August 21, 1979.
(Vancouver's 10th choice, 171st overall, in 1997 Entry Draft).

			Regular Season					Playoffs				
Season	Club	Lea	GP	G	A	TP	PIM	GP	G	A	TP	PIM
1995-96	Seattle	WHL	4	0	1	1	2	....	....	....	....	....
1996-97	Seattle	WHL	46	0	4	4	90	13	0	0	0	4
1997-98	Seattle	WHL	45	0	11	11	100	1	0	0	0	0

LESCHYSHYN, CURTIS (luh-SIH-shuhn) CAR.

Defense. Shoots left. 6'1", 205 lbs. Born, Thompson, Man., September 21, 1969.
(Quebec's 1st choice, 3rd overall, in 1988 Entry Draft).

			Regular Season					Playoffs				
Season	Club	Lea	GP	G	A	TP	PIM	GP	G	A	TP	PIM
1986-87	Saskatoon	WHL	70	14	26	40	107	11	1	5	6	14
1987-88	Saskatoon	WHL	56	14	41	55	86	10	2	5	7	16
1988-89	**Quebec**	**NHL**	**71**	**4**	**9**	**13**	**71**	....	....	....	....	....
1989-90	**Quebec**	**NHL**	**68**	**2**	**6**	**8**	**44**	....	....	....	....	....
1990-91	**Quebec**	**NHL**	**55**	**3**	**7**	**10**	**49**	....	....	....	....	....
1991-92	**Quebec**	**NHL**	**42**	**5**	**12**	**17**	**42**	....	....	....	....	....
	Halifax	AHL	6	0	2	2	4	....	....	....	....	....
1992-93	**Quebec**	**NHL**	**82**	**9**	**23**	**32**	**61**	**6**	**1**	**1**	**2**	**6**
1993-94	**Quebec**	**NHL**	**72**	**5**	**17**	**22**	**65**	....	....	....	....	....
1994-95	**Quebec**	**NHL**	**44**	**2**	**13**	**15**	**20**	**3**	**0**	**1**	**1**	**4**
1995-96	**Colorado**	**NHL**	**77**	**4**	**15**	**19**	**73**	**17**	**1**	**2**	**3**	**8 ♦**
1996-97	**Colorado**	**NHL**	**11**	**0**	**5**	**5**	**6**	....	....	....	....	....
	Washington	**NHL**	**2**	**0**	**0**	**0**	**2**	....	....	....	....	....
	Hartford	**NHL**	**64**	**4**	**13**	**17**	**30**	....	....	....	....	....
1997-98	**Carolina**	**NHL**	**73**	**2**	**10**	**12**	**45**	....	....	....	....	....
	NHL Totals		**661**	**40**	**130**	**170**	**508**	**26**	**2**	**4**	**6**	**18**

Transferred to **Colorado** after **Quebec** franchise relocated, June 21, 1995. Traded to **Washington** by **Colorado** with Chris Simon for Keith Jones, Washington's 1st and 4th round choices in 1998 Entry Draft, November 2, 1996. Traded to **Hartford** by **Washington** for Andrei Nikolishin, November 9, 1996. Transferred to **Carolina** after **Hartford** franchise relocated, June 25, 1997.

LESSARD, FRANCIS (leh-SAHR) CAR.

Defense. Shoots right. 6'2", 184 lbs. Born, Montreal, Que., May 30, 1979.
(Carolina's 3rd choice, 80th overall, in 1997 Entry Draft).

			Regular Season					Playoffs				
Season	Club	Lea	GP	G	A	TP	PIM	GP	G	A	TP	PIM
1996-97	Val d'Or	QMJHL	66	1	9	10	287	....	....	....	....	....
1997-98	Val d'Or	QMJHL	63	3	20	23	338	19	1	6	7	*101

Memorial Cup All-Star Team (1998)

LETOWSKI, TREVOR (leh-TOW-skee) PHX.

Center. Shoots right. 5'10", 170 lbs. Born, Thunder Bay, Ont., April 5, 1977.
(Phoenix's 6th choice, 174th overall, in 1996 Entry Draft).

			Regular Season					Playoffs				
Season	Club	Lea	GP	G	A	TP	PIM	GP	G	A	TP	PIM
1994-95	Sarnia	OHL	66	22	19	41	33	4	0	1	1	9
1995-96	Sarnia	OHL	66	36	63	99	66	10	9	5	14	10
1996-97	Sarnia	OHL	55	35	73	108	51	12	9	12	21	20
1997-98	Springfield	AHL	75	11	20	31	26	4	1	0	1	2

LEVINS, SCOTT CAR.

Center/Right wing. Shoots right. 6'4", 210 lbs. Born, Spokane, WA, January 30, 1970.
(Winnipeg's 4th choice, 75th overall, in 1990 Entry Draft).

			Regular Season					Playoffs				
Season	Club	Lea	GP	G	A	TP	PIM	GP	G	A	TP	PIM
1988-89	Penticton	BCJHL	50	27	58	85	154	....	....	....	....	....
1989-90	Tri-City	WHL	71	25	37	62	132	6	2	3	5	18
1990-91	Moncton	AHL	74	12	26	38	133	4	0	0	0	4
1991-92	Moncton	AHL	69	15	18	33	271	11	3	4	7	30
1992-93	**Winnipeg**	**NHL**	**9**	**0**	**1**	**1**	**18**	....	....	....	....	....
	Moncton	AHL	54	22	26	48	158	5	1	3	4	14
1993-94	**Florida**	**NHL**	**29**	**5**	**6**	**11**	**69**	....	....	....	....	....
	Ottawa	**NHL**	**33**	**3**	**5**	**8**	**93**	....	....	....	....	....
1994-95	**Ottawa**	**NHL**	**24**	**5**	**6**	**11**	**51**	....	....	....	....	....
	P.E.I.	AHL	6	0	4	4	14	....	....	....	....	....
1995-96	**Ottawa**	**NHL**	**27**	**0**	**2**	**2**	**80**	....	....	....	....	....
	Detroit	IHL	9	0	0	0	9	....	....	....	....	....
1996-97	Springfield	AHL	68	24	23	47	267	11	5	4	9	37
1997-98	**Phoenix**	**NHL**	**2**	**0**	**0**	**0**	**5**	....	....	....	....	....
	Springfield	AHL	79	28	39	67	177	4	2	0	2	24
	NHL Totals		**124**	**13**	**20**	**33**	**316**	....	....	....	....	....

WHL West Second All-Star Team (1990)

Claimed by **Florida** from **Winnipeg** in Expansion Draft, June 24, 1993. Traded to **Ottawa** by **Florida** with Evgeny Davydov, Florida's 6th round choice (Mike Gaffney) in 1994 Entry Draft and Dallas' 4th round choice (previously acquired, Ottawa selected Kevin Bolibruck) in 1995 Entry Draft for Bob Kudelski, January 6, 1994. Signed as a free agent by **Phoenix**, October 3, 1996. Signed as a free agent by **Carolina**, August 18, 1998.

LIBBY, JEFF NYI

Defense. Shoots left. 6'3", 215 lbs. Born, Waterville, ME, March 1, 1974.

			Regular Season					Playoffs				
Season	Club	Lea	GP	G	A	TP	PIM	GP	G	A	TP	PIM
1993-94	U. of Maine	H.E.			DID NOT PLAY – FRESHMAN							
1994-95	U. of Maine	H.E.	22	2	4	6	6	....	....	....	....	....
1995-96	U. of Maine	H.E.	39	0	9	9	42	....	....	....	....	....
1996-97	U. of Maine	H.E.	34	6	25	31	41	....	....	....	....	....
1997-98	**NY Islanders**	**NHL**	**1**	**0**	**0**	**0**	**0**	....	....	....	....	....
	Kentucky	AHL	8	0	3	3	4	3	0	0	0	4
	Utah	IHL	47	1	5	6	25	1	0	0	0	0
	NHL Totals		**1**	**0**	**0**	**0**	**0**	....	....	....	....	....

Signed as a free agent by **NY Islanders**, May 12, 1997.

LIDSTER, DOUG

Defense. Shoots right. 6'1", 190 lbs. Born, Kamloops, B.C., October 18, 1960.
(Vancouver's 6th choice, 133rd overall, in 1980 Entry Draft).

			Regular Season					Playoffs				
Season	Club	Lea	GP	G	A	TP	PIM	GP	G	A	TP	PIM
1977-78	Seattle	WCJHL	2	0	0	0	0	....	....	....	....	....
1978-79	Kamloops	BCJHL	59	36	47	83	50	....	....	....	....	....
1979-80	Colorado	WCHA	39	18	25	43	52	....	....	....	....	....
1980-81	Colorado	WCHA	36	10	30	40	54	....	....	....	....	....
1981-82	Colorado	WCHA	36	13	22	35	32	....	....	....	....	....
1982-83	Colorado	WCHA	34	15	41	56	30	....	....	....	....	....
1983-84	Canada	Nat-Tm	59	6	20	26	28	....	....	....	....	....
	Canada	Olympics	7	0	2	2	2	....	....	....	....	....
	Vancouver	**NHL**	**8**	**0**	**0**	**0**	**4**	**2**	**0**	**1**	**1**	**0**
1984-85	**Vancouver**	**NHL**	**78**	**6**	**24**	**30**	**55**	....	....	....	....	....
1985-86	**Vancouver**	**NHL**	**78**	**12**	**16**	**28**	**56**	**3**	**0**	**1**	**1**	**2**
1986-87	**Vancouver**	**NHL**	**80**	**12**	**51**	**63**	**40**	....	....	....	....	....
1987-88	**Vancouver**	**NHL**	**64**	**4**	**32**	**36**	**105**	....	....	....	....	....
1988-89	**Vancouver**	**NHL**	**63**	**5**	**17**	**22**	**78**	**7**	**1**	**1**	**2**	**9**
1989-90	**Vancouver**	**NHL**	**80**	**8**	**28**	**36**	**36**	....	....	....	....	....
1990-91	**Vancouver**	**NHL**	**78**	**6**	**32**	**38**	**77**	**6**	**0**	**2**	**2**	**6**
1991-92	**Vancouver**	**NHL**	**66**	**6**	**23**	**29**	**39**	**11**	**1**	**2**	**3**	**11**
1992-93	**Vancouver**	**NHL**	**71**	**6**	**19**	**25**	**36**	**12**	**0**	**3**	**3**	**8**
1993-94	**NY Rangers**	**NHL**	**34**	**0**	**2**	**2**	**33**	**9**	**2**	**0**	**2**	**10 ♦**
1994-95	**St. Louis**	**NHL**	**37**	**2**	**7**	**9**	**12**	**4**	**0**	**0**	**0**	**2**
1995-96	**NY Rangers**	**NHL**	**59**	**5**	**9**	**14**	**50**	**7**	**1**	**0**	**1**	**6**
1996-97	**NY Rangers**	**NHL**	**48**	**3**	**4**	**7**	**24**	**15**	**1**	**5**	**6**	**8**
1997-98	**NY Rangers**	**NHL**	**36**	**0**	**4**	**4**	**24**	....	....	....	....	....
	NHL Totals		**880**	**75**	**268**	**343**	**669**	**76**	**6**	**15**	**21**	**62**

WCHA First All-Star Team (1982, 1983) • NCAA West First All-American Team (1983)

Traded to **NY Rangers** by **Vancouver** to complete transaction that sent John Vanbiesbrouck to Vancouver (June 30, 1993), June 25, 1993. Traded to **St. Louis** by **NY Rangers** with Esa Tikkanen for Petr Nedved, July 24, 1994. Traded to **NY Rangers** by **St. Louis** for Jay Wells, July 28, 1995.

LIDSTROM, NICKLAS (LID-struhm) DET.

Defense. Shoots left. 6'2", 185 lbs. Born, Vasteras, Sweden, April 28, 1970.
(Detroit's 3rd choice, 53rd overall, in 1989 Entry Draft).

			Regular Season					Playoffs				
Season	Club	Lea	GP	G	A	TP	PIM	GP	G	A	TP	PIM
1988-89	Vasteras IK	Sweden	19	0	2	2	4	....	....	....	....	....
1989-90	Vasteras IK	Sweden	39	8	8	16	14	2	0	1	1	2
1990-91	Vasteras IK	Sweden	38	4	19	23	2	4	0	0	0	4
1991-92	**Detroit**	**NHL**	**80**	**11**	**49**	**60**	**22**	**11**	**1**	**2**	**3**	**0**
1992-93	**Detroit**	**NHL**	**84**	**7**	**34**	**41**	**28**	**7**	**1**	**0**	**1**	**0**
1993-94	**Detroit**	**NHL**	**84**	**10**	**46**	**56**	**26**	**7**	**3**	**2**	**5**	**0**
1994-95	Vasteras IK	Sweden	13	2	10	12	4	....	....	....	....	....
	Detroit	**NHL**	**43**	**10**	**16**	**26**	**6**	**18**	**4**	**12**	**16**	**8**
1995-96	**Detroit**	**NHL**	**81**	**17**	**50**	**67**	**20**	**19**	**5**	**9**	**14**	**10**
1996-97	**Detroit**	**NHL**	**79**	**15**	**42**	**57**	**30**	**20**	**2**	**6**	**8**	**2 ♦**
1997-98	**Detroit**	**NHL**	**80**	**17**	**42**	**59**	**18**	**22**	**6**	**13**	**19**	**8 ♦**
	NHL Totals		**531**	**87**	**279**	**366**	**150**	**104**	**22**	**44**	**66**	**28**

NHL/Upper Deck All-Rookie Team (1992) • NHL First All-Star Team (1998)

Played in NHL All-Star Game (1996, 1998)

LILLEY, JOHN

Right wing. Shoots right. 5'9", 170 lbs. Born, Wakefield, MA, August 3, 1972.
(Winnipeg's 8th choice, 140th overall, in 1990 Entry Draft).

			Regular Season					Playoffs				
Season	Club	Lea	GP	G	A	TP	PIM	GP	G	A	TP	PIM
1989-90	Cushing Academy	H.S.	20	22	30	52	....	....	....	....	....	....
1990-91	Cushing Academy	H.S.	25	29	42	71	....	....	....	....	....	....
1991-92	Boston University	H.E.	23	9	9	18	43	....	....	....	....	....
1992-93	Boston University	H.E.	4	0	1	1	13	....	....	....	....	....
	Seattle	WHL	45	22	28	50	55	5	1	3	4	9
1993-94	United States	Nat-Tm	58	27	23	50	117	....	....	....	....	....
	United States	Olympics	8	3	1	4	16	....	....	....	....	....
	Anaheim	**NHL**	**13**	**1**	**6**	**7**	**8**	....	....	....	....	....
	San Diego	IHL	2	2	1	3	0	....	....	....	....	....
1994-95	San Diego	IHL	45	9	15	24	71	2	0	0	0	2
	Anaheim	**NHL**	**9**	**2**	**2**	**4**	**5**	....	....	....	....	....
1995-96	**Anaheim**	**NHL**	**1**	**0**	**0**	**0**	**0**	....	....	....	....	....
	Baltimore	AHL	12	2	4	6	34	....	....	....	....	....
	Los Angeles	IHL	64	12	20	32	112	....	....	....	....	....
1996-97	Rochester	AHL	1	0	2	2	15	....	....	....	....	....
	Providence	AHL	63	12	23	35	130	10	3	0	3	24
	Detroit	IHL	1	0	0	0	2	....	....	....	....	....
1997-98	Dusseldorf	Germany	44	9	14	23	120	3	0	0	0	4
	NHL Totals		**23**	**3**	**8**	**11**	**13**	....	....	....	....	....

Signed as a free agent by **Anaheim**, March 9, 1994.

LIND, ERIC — PIT.

Defense. Shoots right. 6'1", 198 lbs. Born, New Canaan, CT, March 12, 1978.
(Pittsburgh's 9th choice, 234th overall, in 1997 Entry Draft).

			Regular Season					Playoffs				
Season	Club	Lea	GP	G	A	TP	PIM	GP	G	A	TP	PIM
1996-97	Avon Old Farms	H.S.	55	18	39	57	50	....	....	....	....	....
1997-98	New Hampshire	H.E.	33	1	11	12	63	....	....	....	....	....

LIND, JUHA — (LIHND, YOO-huh) — DAL.

Center. Shoots left. 5'11", 178 lbs. Born, Helsinki, Finland, January 2, 1974.
(Minnesota's 6th choice, 178th overall, in 1992 Entry Draft).

			Regular Season					Playoffs				
Season	Club	Lea	GP	G	A	TP	PIM	GP	G	A	TP	PIM
1991-92	Jokerit	Fin-Jr.	28	16	24	40	10	....	....	....	....	....
1992-93	Vantaa	Finland-2	25	8	12	20	8	....	....	....	....	....
	Jokerit	Finland	6	0	0	0	2	1	0	0	0	0
1993-94	Jokerit	Finland	47	17	11	28	37	11	2	5	7	4
1994-95	Jokerit	Finland	50	10	8	18	12	11	1	2	3	6
1995-96	Jokerit	Finland	50	15	22	37	32	11	4	5	9	4
1996-97	Jokerit	Finland	50	16	22	38	28	9	5	3	8	0
1997-98	**Dallas**	**NHL**	**39**	**2**	**3**	**5**	**6**	**15**	**2**	**2**	**4**	**8**
	Michigan	IHL	8	2	2	4	2	....	....	....	....	....
	Finland	Olympics	6	0	1	1	6	....	....	....	....	....
	NHL Totals		**39**	**2**	**3**	**5**	**6**	**15**	**2**	**2**	**4**	**8**

Rights transferred to **Dallas** after **Minnesota** franchise relocated, June 9, 1993.

LINDBOM, JOHAN — (LIHND-buhm, YOO-hahn)

Left wing. Shoots left. 6'2", 216 lbs. Born, Alvesta, Sweden, July 8, 1971.
(NY Rangers' 6th choice, 134th overall, in 1997 Entry Draft).

			Regular Season					Playoffs				
Season	Club	Lea	GP	G	A	TP	PIM	GP	G	A	TP	PIM
1991-92	Tyngsryd	Sweden-2	30	10	11	21	68	....	....	....	....	....
1992-93	Troja	Sweden-2	30	10	16	26	20	10	6	3	9	18
1993-94	Troja	Sweden-2	33	16	11	27	30	11	6	6	12	2
1994-95	HV 71 Jonkoping	Sweden	39	9	7	16	30	13	2	5	7	12
1995-96	HV 71 Jonkoping	Sweden	37	12	14	26	30	4	0	0	0	4
1996-97	HV 71 Jonkoping	Sweden	49	20	14	34	26	5	1	0	1	6
1997-98	**NY Rangers**	**NHL**	**38**	**1**	**3**	**4**	**28**	....	....	....	....	....
	Hartford	AHL	7	1	5	6	6	....	....	....	....	....
	NHL Totals		**38**	**1**	**3**	**4**	**28**	....	....	....	....	....

LINDEN, TREVOR — NYI

Center/Right wing. Shoots right. 6'4", 210 lbs. Born, Medicine Hat, Alta., April 11, 1970.
(Vancouver's 1st choice, 2nd overall, in 1988 Entry Draft).

			Regular Season					Playoffs				
Season	Club	Lea	GP	G	A	TP	PIM	GP	G	A	TP	PIM
1986-87	Medicine Hat	WHL	72	14	22	36	59	20	5	4	9	17
1987-88	Medicine Hat	WHL	67	46	64	110	76	16	*13	12	25	19
1988-89	**Vancouver**	**NHL**	**80**	**30**	**29**	**59**	**41**	**7**	**3**	**4**	**7**	**8**
1989-90	**Vancouver**	**NHL**	**73**	**21**	**30**	**51**	**43**	....	....	....	....	....
1990-91	**Vancouver**	**NHL**	**80**	**33**	**37**	**70**	**65**	**6**	**0**	**7**	**7**	**2**
1991-92	**Vancouver**	**NHL**	**80**	**31**	**44**	**75**	**101**	**13**	**4**	**8**	**12**	**6**
1992-93	**Vancouver**	**NHL**	**84**	**33**	**39**	**72**	**64**	**12**	**5**	**8**	**13**	**16**
1993-94	**Vancouver**	**NHL**	**84**	**32**	**29**	**61**	**73**	**24**	**12**	**13**	**25**	**18**
1994-95	**Vancouver**	**NHL**	**48**	**18**	**22**	**40**	**40**	**11**	**2**	**6**	**8**	**12**
1995-96	**Vancouver**	**NHL**	**82**	**33**	**47**	**80**	**42**	**6**	**4**	**4**	**8**	**6**
1996-97	**Vancouver**	**NHL**	**49**	**9**	**31**	**40**	**27**	....	....	....	....	....
1997-98	**Vancouver**	**NHL**	**42**	**7**	**14**	**21**	**49**	....	....	....	....	....
	NY Islanders	**NHL**	**25**	**10**	**7**	**17**	**33**	....	....	....	....	....
	Canada	Olympics	6	1	0	1	10	....	....	....	....	....
	NHL Totals		**727**	**257**	**329**	**586**	**578**	**79**	**30**	**50**	**80**	**68**

WHL East Second All-Star Team (1988) • NHL All-Rookie Team (1989) • Won King Clancy Memorial Trophy (1997)

Played in NHL All-Star Game (1991, 1992)

Traded to **NY Islanders** by **Vancouver** for Todd Bertuzzi, Bryan McCabe and NY Islanders' 3rd round choice (Jarkko Ruutu) in 1998 Entry Draft, February 6, 1998.

LINDGREN, MATS — (LIHND-gruhn) — EDM.

Center. Shoots left. 6'2", 202 lbs. Born, Skelleftea, Sweden, October 1, 1974.
(Winnipeg's 1st choice, 15th overall, in 1993 Entry Draft).

			Regular Season					Playoffs				
Season	Club	Lea	GP	G	A	TP	PIM	GP	G	A	TP	PIM
1991-92	Skelleftea	Sweden-2	29	14	8	22	14	....	....	....	....	....
1992-93	Skelleftea	Sweden-2	32	20	14	34	18	....	....	....	....	....
1993-94	Farjestad	Sweden	22	11	6	17	26	....	....	....	....	....
1994-95	Farjestad	Sweden	37	17	15	32	20	3	0	0	0	4
1995-96	Cape Breton	AHL	13	7	5	12	6	....	....	....	....	....
1996-97	**Edmonton**	**NHL**	**69**	**11**	**14**	**25**	**12**	**12**	**0**	**4**	**4**	**0**
	Hamilton	AHL	9	6	7	13	6	....	....	....	....	....
1997-98	**Edmonton**	**NHL**	**82**	**13**	**13**	**26**	**42**	**12**	**1**	**1**	**2**	**10**
	Sweden	Olympics	4	0	0	0	2	....	....	....	....	....
	NHL Totals		**151**	**24**	**27**	**51**	**54**	**24**	**1**	**5**	**6**	**10**

Swedish Rookie of the Year (1994)

Traded to **Edmonton** by **Winnipeg** with Boris Mironov, Winnipeg's 1st round choice (Jason Bonsignore) in 1994 Entry Draft and Florida's 4th round choice (previously acquired, Edmonton selected Adam Copeland) in 1994 Entry Draft for Dave Manson and St. Louis' 6th round choice (previously acquired, Winnipeg selected Chris Kibermanis) in 1994 Entry Draft, March 15, 1994.

LINDQUIST, FREDRIK — (LIHND-kvihst) — EDM.

Center. Shoots left. 6', 190 lbs. Born, Sodertalje, Sweden, June 21, 1973.
(New Jersey's 4th choice, 55th overall, in 1991 Entry Draft).

			Regular Season					Playoffs				
Season	Club	Lea	GP	G	A	TP	PIM	GP	G	A	TP	PIM
1989-90	Huddinge	Sweden-2	2	0	0	0	0	....	....	....	....	....
1990-91	Djurgarden	Sweden	28	6	4	10	0	7	1	0	1	2
1991-92	Djurgarden	Sweden	39	9	6	15	14	10	1	1	2	2
1992-93	Djurgarden	Sweden	39	9	11	20	8	4	1	2	3	2
1993-94	Djurgarden	Sweden	25	5	8	13	8	6	2	1	3	2
1994-95	Djurgarden	Sweden	40	11	16	27	14	3	0	0	0	2
1995-96	Djurgarden	Sweden	33	12	19	31	16	1	0	0	0	0
1996-97	Djurgarden	Sweden	44	19	28	47	20	4	0	3	3	2
1997-98	Djurgarden	Sweden	42	10	*32	42	30	13	3	6	9	4

Traded to **Edmonton** by **New Jersey** with New Jersey's 4th (Kristian Antila) and 5th (Oleg Smirnov) round choices in 1998 Entry Draft for Pittsburgh's 3rd round choice (previously acquired, New Jersey selected Brian Gionta) in 1998 Entry Draft, June 27, 1998.

LINDROS, ERIC — (LIHND-rahz) — PHI.

Center. Shoots right. 6'4", 236 lbs. Born, London, Ont., February 28, 1973.
(Quebec's 1st choice, 1st overall, in 1991 Entry Draft).

			Regular Season					Playoffs				
Season	Club	Lea	GP	G	A	TP	PIM	GP	G	A	TP	PIM
1988-89	St. Michael's	Jr. B	37	24	43	67	193	27	23	25	48	155
	Canada	Nat-Tm	2	1	0	1	0	....	....	....	....	....
1989-90	Detroit	USHL	14	23	29	52	123	....	....	....	....	....
	Canada	Nat-Tm	3	1	0	1	4	....	....	....	....	....
	Oshawa	OHL	25	17	19	36	61	17	18	18	36	76
1990-91	Oshawa	OHL	57	*71	78	*149	189	16	*18	20	*38	*93
1991-92	Oshawa	OHL	13	9	22	31	54	....	....	....	....	....
	Canada	Nat-Tm	24	19	16	35	34	....	....	....	....	....
	Canada	Olympics	8	5	6	11	5	....	....	....	....	....
1992-93	**Philadelphia**	**NHL**	**61**	**41**	**34**	**75**	**147**	....	....	....	....	....
1993-94	**Philadelphia**	**NHL**	**65**	**44**	**53**	**97**	**103**	....	....	....	....	....
1994-95	**Philadelphia**	**NHL**	**46**	**29**	**41**	***70**	**60**	**12**	**4**	**11**	**15**	**18**
1995-96	**Philadelphia**	**NHL**	**73**	**47**	**68**	**115**	**163**	**12**	**6**	**6**	**12**	**43**
1996-97	**Philadelphia**	**NHL**	**52**	**32**	**47**	**79**	**136**	**19**	**12**	**14**	***26**	**40**
1997-98	**Philadelphia**	**NHL**	**63**	**30**	**41**	**71**	**134**	**5**	**1**	**2**	**3**	**17**
	Canada	Olympics	6	2	3	5	2	....	....	....	....	....
	NHL Totals		**360**	**223**	**284**	**507**	**743**	**48**	**23**	**33**	**56**	**118**

Memorial Cup All-Star Team (1990) • OHL First All-Star Team (1991) • Canadian Major Junior Player of the Year (1991) • NHL/Upper Deck All-Rookie Team (1993) • NHL First All-Star Team (1995) • Won Lester B. Pearson Award (1995) • Won Hart Trophy (1995) • NHL Second All-Star Team (1996)

Played in NHL All-Star Game (1994, 1996, 1997, 1998)

Traded to **Philadelphia** by **Quebec** for Peter Forsberg, Steve Duchesne, Kerry Huffman, Mike Ricci, Ron Hextall, Chris Simon, Philadelphia's 1st round choice in the 1993 (Jocelyn Thibault) and 1994 (later traded to Toronto — later traded to Washington — Washington selected Nolan Baumgartner) Entry Drafts and cash, June 30, 1992.

LINDSAY, BILL — FLA.

Left wing. Shoots left. 6', 195 lbs. Born, Big Fork, MT, May 17, 1971.
(Quebec's 6th choice, 103rd overall, in 1991 Entry Draft).

			Regular Season					Playoffs				
Season	Club	Lea	GP	G	A	TP	PIM	GP	G	A	TP	PIM
1989-90	Tri-City	WHL	72	40	45	85	84	7	3	0	3	17
1990-91	Tri-City	WHL	63	46	47	93	151	5	3	6	9	10
1991-92	Tri-City	WHL	42	34	59	93	111	3	2	3	5	16
	Quebec	**NHL**	**23**	**2**	**4**	**6**	**14**	....	....	....	....	....
1992-93	**Quebec**	**NHL**	**44**	**4**	**9**	**13**	**16**	....	....	....	....	....
	Halifax	AHL	20	11	13	24	18	....	....	....	....	....
1993-94	**Florida**	**NHL**	**84**	**6**	**6**	**12**	**97**	....	....	....	....	....
1994-95	**Florida**	**NHL**	**48**	**10**	**9**	**19**	**46**	....	....	....	....	....
1995-96	**Florida**	**NHL**	**73**	**12**	**22**	**34**	**57**	**22**	**5**	**5**	**10**	**18**
1996-97	**Florida**	**NHL**	**81**	**11**	**23**	**34**	**120**	**3**	**0**	**1**	**1**	**8**
1997-98	**Florida**	**NHL**	**82**	**12**	**16**	**28**	**80**	....	....	....	....	....
	NHL Totals		**435**	**57**	**89**	**146**	**430**	**25**	**5**	**6**	**11**	**26**

WHL West Second All-Star Team (1992)

Claimed by **Florida** from **Quebec** in Expansion Draft, June 24, 1993.

LING, DAVID

Right wing. Shoots right. 5'9", 185 lbs. Born, Halifax, N.S., January 9, 1975.
(Quebec's 9th choice, 179th overall, in 1993 Entry Draft).

			Regular Season					Playoffs				
Season	Club	Lea	GP	G	A	TP	PIM	GP	G	A	TP	PIM
1992-93	Kingston	OHL	64	17	46	63	275	16	3	12	15	*72
1993-94	Kingston	OHL	61	37	40	77	*254	6	4	2	6	16
1994-95	Kingston	OHL	62	*61	74	135	136	6	7	8	15	12
1995-96	Saint John	AHL	75	24	32	56	179	9	0	5	5	12
1996-97	Saint John	AHL	5	0	2	2	19	....	....	....	....	....
	Montreal	**NHL**	**2**	**0**	**0**	**0**	**0**	....	....	....	....	....
	Fredericton	AHL	48	22	36	58	229	....	....	....	....	....
1997-98	**Montreal**	**NHL**	**1**	**0**	**0**	**0**	**0**	....	....	....	....	....
	Fredericton	AHL	67	25	41	66	148	....	....	....	....	....
	Indianapolis	IHL	12	8	6	14	30	5	4	1	5	31
	NHL Totals		**3**	**0**	**0**	**0**	**0**	....	....	....	....	....

OHL First All-Star Team (1995) • Canadian Major Junior First All-Star Team (1995) • Canadian Junior Player of the Year (1995)

Rights transferred to **Colorado** after **Quebec** franchise relocated, June 21, 1995. Traded to **Calgary** by **Colorado** with Colorado's 9th round choice (Steve Shirreffs) in 1995 Entry Draft for Calgary's 9th round choice (Chris George) in 1995 Entry Draft, July 7, 1995. Traded to **Montreal** by **Calgary** with Calgary's 6th round choice (Gordie Dwyer) in 1998 Entry Draft for Scott Fraser, October 24, 1996. Traded to **Chicago** by **Montreal** for Martin Gendron, March 14, 1998.

LINGREN, STEVE — S.J.

Defense. Shoots left. 6', 193 lbs. Born, Lake Cowachin, B.C., July 23, 1973.

			Regular Season					Playoffs				
Season	Club	Lea	GP	G	A	TP	PIM	GP	G	A	TP	PIM
1991-92	Victoria	WHL	70	4	14	18	103	....	....	....	....	....
1992-93	Victoria	WHL	72	10	43	53	148	....	....	....	....	....
1993-94	Victoria	WHL	56	14	21	35	118	....	....	....	....	....
	Kalamazoo	IHL	2	0	0	0	0	....	....	....	....	....
1994-95	Dayton	ECHL	64	11	23	34	128	9	2	8	10	16
1995-96	Dayton	ECHL	51	15	28	43	83	....	....	....	....	....
	Cornwall	AHL	1	0	1	1	0	....	....	....	....	....
1996-97	Dayton	ECHL	9	2	5	7	15	....	....	....	....	....
	Hershey	AHL	40	3	10	13	67	12	1	2	3	8
1997-98	Hershey	AHL	63	12	18	30	89	....	....	....	....	....

ECHL First All-Star Team (1996)

Signed as a free agent by **San Jose**, July 23, 1998.

LINNIK, MAXIM (LIH-nihk, mahx-EEM) — ST.L.

Defense. Shoots left. 6'3", 190 lbs. Born, Kiev, USSR, September 6, 1979.
(St. Louis' 2nd choice, 41st overall, in 1998 Entry Draft).

			Regular Season					Playoffs				
Season	Club	Lea	GP	G	A	TP	PIM	GP	G	A	TP	PIM
1996-97	Sokol Kiev	Russia-2	7	0	0	0	0	....	....	....	....	....
1997-98	St. Thomas	OJHL	35	4	14	18	130	....	....	....	....	....

LINTNER, RICHARD (LIHNT-nuhr) — PHX.

Defense. Shoots right. 6'3", 194 lbs. Born, Trencin, Czech., November 15, 1977.
(Phoenix's 4th choice, 119th overall, in 1996 Entry Draft).

			Regular Season					Playoffs				
Season	Club	Lea	GP	G	A	TP	PIM	GP	G	A	TP	PIM
1994-95	Dukla Trencin	Slov-Jr.	42	12	13	25	20	....	....	....	....	....
1995-96	Dukla Trencin	Slov-Jr.	30	15	17	32	210	....	....	....	....	....
	Dukla Trencin	Slovakia	2	0	0	0	0	....	....	....	....	....
1996-97	Spisska	Slovakia	35	2	1	3	....	....	....	....	....	....
1997-98	Springfield	AHL	71	6	9	15	61	3	1	1	2	4

LIPUMA, CHRIS (lih-POO-muh)

Defense. Shoots left. 6', 183 lbs. Born, Bridgeview, IL, March 23, 1971.

			Regular Season					Playoffs				
Season	Club	Lea	GP	G	A	TP	PIM	GP	G	A	TP	PIM
1988-89	Kitchener	OHL	59	7	13	20	101	....	....	....	....	....
1989-90	Kitchener	OHL	63	11	26	37	125	17	1	4	5	6
1990-91	Kitchener	OHL	61	6	30	36	145	4	0	1	1	4
1991-92	Kitchener	OHL	61	13	59	72	115	14	4	9	13	34
1992-93	**Tampa Bay**	**NHL**	**15**	**0**	**5**	**5**	**34**	....	....	....	....	....
	Atlanta	IHL	66	4	14	18	379	9	1	1	2	35
1993-94	**Tampa Bay**	**NHL**	**27**	**0**	**4**	**4**	**77**	....	....	....	....	....
	Atlanta	IHL	42	2	10	12	254	11	1	1	2	28
1994-95	Atlanta	IHL	41	5	12	17	191	....	....	....	....	....
	Tampa Bay	**NHL**	**1**	**0**	**0**	**0**	**0**	....	....	....	....	....
	Nashville	ECHL	1	0	0	0	0	....	....	....	....	....
1995-96	**Tampa Bay**	**NHL**	**21**	**0**	**0**	**0**	**13**	....	....	....	....	....
	Atlanta	IHL	48	5	11	16	146	....	....	....	....	....
1996-97	**San Jose**	**NHL**	**8**	**0**	**0**	**0**	**22**	....	....	....	....	....
	Kentucky	AHL	48	6	17	23	93	4	0	3	3	6
1997-98	Orlando	IHL	13	1	4	5	63	....	....	....	....	....
	San Antonio	IHL	60	1	10	11	116	....	....	....	....	....
	NHL Totals		**72**	**0**	**9**	**9**	**146**	....	....	....	....	....

Signed as a free agent by **Tampa Bay**, June 29, 1992. Signed as a free agent by **San Jose**, August 23, 1996. Claimed on waivers by **New Jersey** from **San Jose**, March 18, 1997.

LOJKIN, ALEXEI — MTL.

Left wing. Shoots left. 5'9", 176 lbs. Born, Minsk, USSR, February 21, 1974.

			Regular Season					Playoffs				
Season	Club	Lea	GP	G	A	TP	PIM	GP	G	A	TP	PIM
1993-94	Chicoutimi	QMJHL	66	40	67	107	68	27	9	34	43	15
1994-95	Chicoutimi	QMJHL	57	43	58	101	26	11	6	5	11	2
1995-96	Fredericton	AHL	73	24	33	57	16	7	1	3	4	0
1996-97	Fredericton	AHL	79	33	56	89	41	....	....	....	....	....
1997-98	Fredericton	AHL	61	13	22	35	18	2	0	1	1	0

Signed as a free agent by **Montreal**, September 11, 1997.

LONG, ANDREW — FLA.

Center. Shoots right. 6'2", 181 lbs. Born, Toronto, Ont., August 10, 1978.
(Florida's 5th choice, 129th overall, in 1996 Entry Draft).

			Regular Season					Playoffs				
Season	Club	Lea	GP	G	A	TP	PIM	GP	G	A	TP	PIM
1994-95	Guelph	OHL	36	1	6	7	9	....	....	....	....	....
1995-96	Guelph	OHL	48	8	10	18	16	10	0	1	1	4
1996-97	Guelph	OHL	42	10	36	46	30	13	2	10	12	6
1997-98	Guelph	OHL	62	29	40	69	41	8	3	3	6	10

LOVEN, FREDRIK (LUH-vehn) — PHX.

Center. Shoots left. 6'2", 183 lbs. Born, Stockholm, Sweden, March 14, 1977.
(Winnipeg's 10th choice, 189th overall, in 1995 Entry Draft).

			Regular Season					Playoffs				
Season	Club	Lea	GP	G	A	TP	PIM	GP	G	A	TP	PIM
1994-95	Djurgarden	Swe-Jr.	29	6	10	16	14	....	....	....	....	....
1995-96	Djurgarden	Sweden	4	0	0	0	0	4	0	0	0	0
1996-97	Djurgarden	Sweden	7	0	0	0	0	....	....	....	....	....
	Djurgarden	Swe-Jr.	4	2	2	4	8	....	....	....	....	....
	Arlanda	Sweden-2	5	0	3	3	4	....	....	....	....	....
1997-98	Bjorkloven	Sweden-2	31	5	7	12	8	....	....	....	....	....

LOW, REED (LOH) — ST.L.

Right wing. Shoots right. 6'4", 220 lbs. Born, Moose Jaw, Sask., June 21, 1976.
(St. Louis' 7th choice, 177th overall, in 1996 Entry Draft).

			Regular Season					Playoffs				
Season	Club	Lea	GP	G	A	TP	PIM	GP	G	A	TP	PIM
1995-96	Moose Jaw	WHL	61	12	7	19	221	....	....	....	....	....
1996-97	Moose Jaw	WHL	62	16	11	27	228	12	2	1	3	50
1997-98	Worcester	AHL	17	1	1	2	75	3	0	0	0	0
	Baton Rouge	ECHL	39	4	2	6	145	....	....	....	....	....

LOWE, KEVIN (LOH)

Defense. Shoots left. 6'2", 200 lbs. Born, Lachute, Que., April 15, 1959.
(Edmonton's 1st choice, 21st overall, in 1979 Entry Draft).

			Regular Season					Playoffs				
Season	Club	Lea	GP	G	A	TP	PIM	GP	G	A	TP	PIM
1976-77	Quebec	QMJHL	69	3	19	22	39	....	....	....	....	....
1977-78	Quebec	QMJHL	64	13	52	65	86	4	1	2	3	6
1978-79	Quebec	QMJHL	68	26	60	86	120	6	1	7	8	36
1979-80	**Edmonton**	**NHL**	**64**	**2**	**19**	**21**	**70**	**3**	**0**	**1**	**1**	**0**
1980-81	**Edmonton**	**NHL**	**79**	**10**	**24**	**34**	**94**	**9**	**0**	**2**	**2**	**11**
1981-82	**Edmonton**	**NHL**	**80**	**9**	**31**	**40**	**63**	**5**	**0**	**3**	**3**	**0**
1982-83	**Edmonton**	**NHL**	**80**	**6**	**34**	**40**	**43**	**16**	**1**	**8**	**9**	**10**
1983-84	**Edmonton**	**NHL**	**80**	**4**	**42**	**46**	**59**	**19**	**3**	**7**	**10**	**16** ♦
1984-85	**Edmonton**	**NHL**	**80**	**4**	**21**	**25**	**104**	**16**	**0**	**5**	**5**	**8** ♦
1985-86	**Edmonton**	**NHL**	**74**	**2**	**16**	**18**	**90**	**10**	**1**	**3**	**4**	**15**
1986-87	**Edmonton**	**NHL**	**77**	**8**	**29**	**37**	**94**	**21**	**2**	**4**	**6**	**22** ♦
1987-88	**Edmonton**	**NHL**	**70**	**9**	**15**	**24**	**89**	**19**	**0**	**2**	**2**	**26** ♦
1988-89	**Edmonton**	**NHL**	**76**	**7**	**18**	**25**	**98**	**7**	**1**	**2**	**3**	**4**
1989-90	**Edmonton**	**NHL**	**78**	**7**	**26**	**33**	**140**	**20**	**0**	**2**	**2**	**10** ♦
1990-91	**Edmonton**	**NHL**	**73**	**3**	**13**	**16**	**113**	**14**	**1**	**1**	**2**	**14**
1991-92	**Edmonton**	**NHL**	**55**	**2**	**8**	**10**	**107**	**11**	**0**	**3**	**3**	**16**
1992-93	**NY Rangers**	**NHL**	**49**	**3**	**12**	**15**	**58**	....	....	....	....	....
1993-94	**NY Rangers**	**NHL**	**71**	**5**	**14**	**19**	**70**	**22**	**1**	**0**	**1**	**20** ♦
1994-95	**NY Rangers**	**NHL**	**44**	**1**	**7**	**8**	**58**	**10**	**0**	**1**	**1**	**12**
1995-96	**NY Rangers**	**NHL**	**53**	**1**	**5**	**6**	**76**	**10**	**0**	**4**	**4**	**4**
1996-97	**Edmonton**	**NHL**	**64**	**1**	**13**	**14**	**50**	**1**	**0**	**0**	**0**	**0**
1997-98	**Edmonton**	**NHL**	**7**	**0**	**0**	**0**	**22**	**1**	**0**	**0**	**0**	**4**
	NHL Totals		**1254**	**84**	**347**	**431**	**1498**	**214**	**10**	**48**	**58**	**192**

QMJHL Second All-Star Team (1978, 1979) • Won Bud Man of the Year Award (1990) • Won King Clancy Memorial Trophy (1990)

Played in NHL All-Star Game (1984, 1985, 1986, 1988, 1989, 1990, 1993)

Traded to **NY Rangers** by **Edmonton** for Roman Oksiuta and NY Rangers' 3rd round choice (Alexander Kerch) in 1993 Entry Draft, December 11, 1992. Signed as a free agent by **Edmonton**, September 28, 1996.

LOWRY, DAVE (LOW-ree)

Left wing. Shoots left. 6'1", 200 lbs. Born, Sudbury, Ont., February 14, 1965.
(Vancouver's 6th choice, 114th overall, in 1983 Entry Draft).

			Regular Season					Playoffs				
Season	Club	Lea	GP	G	A	TP	PIM	GP	G	A	TP	PIM
1982-83	London	OHL	42	11	16	27	48	3	0	0	0	14
1983-84	London	OHL	66	29	47	76	125	8	6	6	12	41
1984-85	London	OHL	61	60	60	120	94	8	6	5	11	10
1985-86	**Vancouver**	**NHL**	**73**	**10**	**8**	**18**	**143**	**3**	**0**	**0**	**0**	**0**
1986-87	**Vancouver**	**NHL**	**70**	**8**	**10**	**18**	**176**	....	....	....	....	....
1987-88	**Vancouver**	**NHL**	**22**	**1**	**3**	**4**	**38**	....	....	....	....	....
	Fredericton	AHL	46	18	27	45	59	14	7	3	10	72
1988-89	**St. Louis**	**NHL**	**21**	**3**	**3**	**6**	**11**	**10**	**0**	**5**	**5**	**4**
	Peoria	IHL	58	31	35	66	45	....	....	....	....	....
1989-90	**St. Louis**	**NHL**	**78**	**19**	**6**	**25**	**75**	**12**	**2**	**1**	**3**	**39**
1990-91	**St. Louis**	**NHL**	**79**	**19**	**21**	**40**	**168**	**13**	**1**	**4**	**5**	**35**
1991-92	**St. Louis**	**NHL**	**75**	**7**	**13**	**20**	**77**	**6**	**0**	**1**	**1**	**20**
1992-93	**St. Louis**	**NHL**	**58**	**5**	**8**	**13**	**101**	**11**	**2**	**0**	**2**	**14**
1993-94	**Florida**	**NHL**	**80**	**15**	**22**	**37**	**64**	....	....	....	....	....
1994-95	**Florida**	**NHL**	**45**	**10**	**10**	**20**	**25**	....	....	....	....	....
1995-96	**Florida**	**NHL**	**63**	**10**	**14**	**24**	**36**	**22**	**10**	**7**	**17**	**39**
1996-97	**Florida**	**NHL**	**77**	**15**	**14**	**29**	**51**	**5**	**0**	**0**	**0**	**0**
1997-98	**Florida**	**NHL**	**7**	**0**	**0**	**0**	**2**	....	....	....	....	....
	San Jose	**NHL**	**50**	**4**	**4**	**8**	**51**	**6**	**0**	**0**	**0**	**18**
	NHL Totals		**798**	**126**	**136**	**262**	**1018**	**88**	**15**	**18**	**33**	**169**

OHL First All-Star Team (1985)

Traded to **St. Louis** by **Vancouver** for Ernie Vargas, September 29, 1988. Claimed by **Florida** from **St. Louis** in Expansion Draft, June 24, 1993. Traded to **San Jose** by **Florida** with Florida's 1st round choice (later traded to Tampa Bay - Tampa Bay selected Vincent Lecavalier) for Viktor Kozlov and Florida's 5th round choice (previously acquired, Florida selected Jaroslav Spacek) in 1998 Entry Draft, November 13, 1997.

LUCHINKIN, SERGEI (loo-CHIHN-kihn) — DAL.

Right wing. Shoots left. 5'11", 172 lbs. Born, Dmitrov, USSR, October 16, 1976.
(Dallas' 9th choice, 202nd overall, in 1995 Entry Draft).

			Regular Season					Playoffs				
Season	Club	Lea	GP	G	A	TP	PIM	GP	G	A	TP	PIM
1994-95	Moscow D'amo	CIS	6	1	0	1	4	....	....	....	....	....
1995-96	Moscow D'amo	CIS	21	6	2	8	14	10	0	1	1	6
1996-97	Moscow D'amo	Russia	18	1	5	6	4	....	....	....	....	....
1997-98	Moscow D'amo	EuroHL	1	0	0	0	0	....	....	....	....	....
	Moscow D'amo	Russia	6	0	1	1	0	....	....	....	....	....
	Spartak	Russia	10	0	1	1	4	....	....	....	....	....

LUDWIG, CRAIG (9LUHD-wihg) DAL.

Defense. Shoots left. 6'3", 220 lbs. Born, Rhinelander, WI, March 15, 1961.
(Montreal's 5th choice, 61st overall, in 1980 Entry Draft).

			Regular Season					Playoffs				
Season	Club	Lea	GP	G	A	TP	PIM	GP	G	A	TP	PIM
1979-80	North Dakota	WCHA	33	1	8	9	32	....	....	....	....	....
1980-81	North Dakota	WCHA	34	4	8	12	48	....	....	....	....	....
1981-82	North Dakota	WCHA	37	4	17	21	42	....	....	....	....	....
1982-83	**Montreal**	**NHL**	**80**	**0**	**25**	**25**	**59**	**3**	**0**	**0**	**0**	**2**
1983-84	**Montreal**	**NHL**	**80**	**7**	**18**	**25**	**52**	**15**	**0**	**3**	**3**	**23**
1984-85	**Montreal**	**NHL**	**72**	**5**	**14**	**19**	**90**	**12**	**0**	**2**	**2**	**6**
1985-86	**Montreal**	**NHL**	**69**	**2**	**4**	**6**	**63**	**20**	**0**	**1**	**1**	**48** ♦
1986-87	**Montreal**	**NHL**	**75**	**4**	**12**	**16**	**105**	**17**	**2**	**3**	**5**	**30**
1987-88	**Montreal**	**NHL**	**74**	**4**	**10**	**14**	**69**	**11**	**1**	**1**	**2**	**6**
1988-89	**Montreal**	**NHL**	**74**	**3**	**13**	**16**	**73**	**21**	**0**	**2**	**2**	**24**
1989-90	**Montreal**	**NHL**	**73**	**1**	**15**	**16**	**108**	**11**	**0**	**1**	**1**	**16**
1990-91	**NY Islanders**	**NHL**	**75**	**1**	**8**	**9**	**77**	....	....	....	....	....
1991-92	**Minnesota**	**NHL**	**73**	**2**	**9**	**11**	**54**	**7**	**0**	**1**	**1**	**19**
1992-93	**Minnesota**	**NHL**	**78**	**1**	**10**	**11**	**153**	....	....	....	....	....
1993-94	**Dallas**	**NHL**	**84**	**1**	**13**	**14**	**123**	**9**	**0**	**3**	**3**	**8**
1994-95	**Dallas**	**NHL**	**47**	**2**	**7**	**9**	**61**	**4**	**0**	**1**	**1**	**2**
1995-96	**Dallas**	**NHL**	**65**	**1**	**2**	**3**	**70**	....	....	....	....	....
1996-97	**Dallas**	**NHL**	**77**	**2**	**11**	**13**	**62**	**7**	**0**	**2**	**2**	**18**
1997-98	**Dallas**	**NHL**	**80**	**0**	**7**	**7**	**131**	**17**	**0**	**1**	**1**	**22**
	NHL Totals		**1176**	**36**	**178**	**214**	**1350**	**154**	**3**	**21**	**24**	**224**

WCHA Second All-Star Team (1982)

Traded to **NY Islanders** by **Montreal** for Gerald Diduck, September 4, 1990. Traded to **Minnesota** by **NY Islanders** for Tom Kurvers, June 22, 1991. Transferred to **Dallas** after **Minnesota** franchise relocated, June 9, 1993.

LUHNING, WARREN (LOO-nihng) NYI

Right wing. Shoots right. 6'2", 185 lbs. Born, Edmonton, Alta., July 3, 1975.
(NY Islanders' 4th choice, 92nd overall, in 1993 Entry Draft).

			Regular Season					Playoffs				
Season	Club	Lea	GP	G	A	TP	PIM	GP	G	A	TP	PIM
1992-93	Calgary	AJHL	46	18	25	43	287	....	....	....	....	....
1993-94	U. of Michigan	CCHA	38	13	6	19	83	....	....	....	....	....
1994-95	U. of Michigan	CCHA	36	17	23	40	80	....	....	....	....	....
1995-96	U. of Michigan	CCHA	40	20	32	52	123	....	....	....	....	....
1996-97	U. of Michigan	CCHA	43	22	23	45	106	....	....	....	....	....
1997-98	**NY Islanders**	**NHL**	**8**	**0**	**0**	**0**	**0**	....	....	....	....	....
	Kentucky	AHL	51	6	7	13	82	....	....	....	....	....
	NHL Totals		**8**	**0**	**0**	**0**	**0**	....	....	....	....	....

LUKOWICH, BRAD (loo-KUH-wihch) DAL.

Defense. Shoots left. 6'1", 170 lbs. Born, Cranbrook, B.C., August 12, 1976.
(NY Islanders' 4th choice, 90th overall, in 1994 Entry Draft).

			Regular Season					Playoffs				
Season	Club	Lea	GP	G	A	TP	PIM	GP	G	A	TP	PIM
1992-93	Kamloops	WHL	1	0	0	0	0	....	....	....	....	....
1993-94	Kamloops	WHL	42	5	11	16	166	16	0	1	1	35
1994-95	Kamloops	WHL	63	10	35	45	125	18	0	7	7	21
1995-96	Kamloops	WHL	65	14	55	69	114	13	2	10	12	29
1996-97	Michigan	IHL	69	2	6	8	77	4	0	1	1	2
1997-98	**Dallas**	**NHL**	**4**	**0**	**1**	**1**	**2**	....	....	....	....	....
	Michigan	IHL	60	6	27	33	104	4	0	4	4	14
	NHL Totals		**4**	**0**	**1**	**1**	**2**	....	....	....	....	....

Traded to **Dallas** by **NY Islanders** for Dallas' 3rd round choice (Robert Schnabel) in 1997 Entry Draft, June 1, 1996.

LUMME, JYRKI (LOO-mee, YUHR-kee) PHX.

Defense. Shoots left. 6'1", 205 lbs. Born, Tampere, Finland, July 16, 1966.
(Montreal's 3rd choice, 57th overall, in 1986 Entry Draft).

			Regular Season					Playoffs				
Season	Club	Lea	GP	G	A	TP	PIM	GP	G	A	TP	PIM
1984-85	KooVee	Finland-3	30	6	4	10	44	....	....	....	....	....
1985-86	Ilves	Finland	31	1	4	5	4	....	....	....	....	....
1986-87	Ilves	Finland	43	12	12	24	52	4	0	1	1	2
1987-88	Ilves	Finland	43	8	22	30	75	....	....	....	....	....
	Finland	Olympics	6	0	1	1	2	....	....	....	....	....
1988-89	**Montreal**	**NHL**	**21**	**1**	**3**	**4**	**10**	....	....	....	....	....
	Sherbrooke	AHL	26	4	11	15	10	6	1	3	4	4
1989-90	**Montreal**	**NHL**	**54**	**1**	**19**	**20**	**41**	....	....	....	....	....
	Vancouver	**NHL**	**11**	**3**	**7**	**10**	**8**	....	....	....	....	....
1990-91	**Vancouver**	**NHL**	**80**	**5**	**27**	**32**	**59**	**6**	**2**	**3**	**5**	**0**
1991-92	**Vancouver**	**NHL**	**75**	**12**	**32**	**44**	**65**	**13**	**2**	**3**	**5**	**4**
1992-93	**Vancouver**	**NHL**	**74**	**8**	**36**	**44**	**55**	**12**	**0**	**5**	**5**	**6**
1993-94	**Vancouver**	**NHL**	**83**	**13**	**42**	**55**	**50**	**24**	**2**	**11**	**13**	**16**
1994-95	Ilves	Finland	12	4	4	8	24	....	....	....	....	....
	Vancouver	**NHL**	**36**	**5**	**12**	**17**	**26**	**11**	**2**	**6**	**8**	**8**
1995-96	**Vancouver**	**NHL**	**80**	**17**	**37**	**54**	**50**	**6**	**1**	**3**	**4**	**2**
1996-97	**Vancouver**	**NHL**	**66**	**11**	**24**	**35**	**32**	....	....	....	....	....
1997-98	**Vancouver**	**NHL**	**74**	**9**	**21**	**30**	**34**	....	....	....	....	....
	Finland	Olympics	6	1	0	1	16	....	....	....	....	....
	NHL Totals		**654**	**85**	**260**	**345**	**430**	**72**	**9**	**31**	**40**	**36**

Traded to **Vancouver** by **Montreal** for St. Louis' 2nd round choice (previously acquired, Montreal selected Craig Darby) in 1991 Entry Draft, March 6, 1990. Signed as a free agent by **Phoenix**, July 3, 1998.

LUNDSTROM, PER-ANTON PHX.

Defense. Shoots left. 6'2", 185 lbs. Born, Umea, Sweden, September 29, 1977.
(Phoenix's 3rd choice, 62nd overall, in 1996 Entry Draft).

			Regular Season					Playoffs				
Season	Club	Lea	GP	G	A	TP	PIM	GP	G	A	TP	PIM
1995-96	MoDo	Swe-Jr.	25	3	3	6	28	2	1	0	1	4
	MoDo	Sweden	19	1	1	2	29	4	0	0	0	2
1996-97	MoDo	Sweden	35	0	0	0	42	....	....	....	....	....
1997-98	Bjorkloven	Sweden-2	31	6	13	19	71	....	....	....	....	....

LUONGO, CHRIS (loo-WAHN-goh)

Defense. Shoots right. 5'10", 206 lbs. Born, Detroit, MI, March 17, 1967.
(Detroit's 5th choice, 92nd overall, in 1985 Entry Draft).

			Regular Season					Playoffs				
Season	Club	Lea	GP	G	A	TP	PIM	GP	G	A	TP	PIM
1984-85	Detroit	NAJHL	41	2	27	29	....	....	....	....	....	....
1985-86	Michigan State	CCHA	38	1	5	6	29	....	....	....	....	....
1986-87	Michigan State	CCHA	27	4	16	20	38	....	....	....	....	....
1987-88	Michigan State	CCHA	45	3	15	18	49	....	....	....	....	....
1988-89	Michigan State	CCHA	47	4	21	25	42	....	....	....	....	....
1989-90	Adirondack	AHL	53	9	14	23	37	3	0	0	0	0
	Phoenix	IHL	23	5	9	14	41	....	....	....	....	....
1990-91	**Detroit**	**NHL**	**4**	**0**	**1**	**1**	**4**	....	....	....	....	....
	Adirondack	AHL	76	14	25	39	71	2	0	0	0	7
1991-92	Adirondack	AHL	80	6	20	26	60	19	3	5	8	10
1992-93	**Ottawa**	**NHL**	**76**	**3**	**9**	**12**	**68**	....	....	....	....	....
	New Haven	AHL	7	0	2	2	2	....	....	....	....	....
1993-94	**NY Islanders**	**NHL**	**17**	**1**	**3**	**4**	**13**	....	....	....	....	....
	Salt Lake	IHL	51	9	31	40	54	....	....	....	....	....
1994-95	Denver	IHL	41	1	14	15	26	....	....	....	....	....
	NY Islanders	**NHL**	**47**	**1**	**3**	**4**	**36**	....	....	....	....	....
1995-96	**NY Islanders**	**NHL**	**74**	**3**	**7**	**10**	**55**	....	....	....	....	....
1996-97	Milwaukee	IHL	81	10	35	45	69	2	0	0	0	0
1997-98	EV Landshut	Germany	48	5	13	18	54	6	0	2	2	18
	NHL Totals		**218**	**8**	**23**	**31**	**176**	....	....	....	....	....

NCAA Championship All-Tournament Team (1987) • CCHA Second All-Star Team (1989)

Signed as a free agent by **Ottawa**, September 9, 1992. Traded to **NY Islanders** by **Ottawa** for Jeff Finley, June 30, 1993.

LYASHENKO, ROMAN (LIGH-a-SHEHN-koh) DAL.

Center. Shoots right. 6', 174 lbs. Born, Murmansk, Russia, May 2, 1979.
(Dallas' 2nd choice, 52nd overall, in 1997 Entry Draft).

			Regular Season					Playoffs				
Season	Club	Lea	GP	G	A	TP	PIM	GP	G	A	TP	PIM
1995-96	Yaroslavl 2	CIS-2	60	7	10	17	12	....	....	....	....	....
1996-97	Yaroslavl	Russia	42	5	7	12	16	9	3	0	3	6
	Yaroslavl 2	Russia-3	2	1	1	2	8	....	....	....	....	....
1997-98	Yaroslavl	EuroHL	10	1	1	2	2	....	....	....	....	....
	Yaroslavl	Russia	46	7	6	13	28	....	....	....	....	....

LYDMAN, TONI (LEED-man) CGY.

Defense. Shoots left. 6'1", 183 lbs. Born, Lahti, Finland, September 25, 1977.
(Calgary's 5th choice, 89th overall, in 1996 Entry Draft).

			Regular Season					Playoffs				
Season	Club	Lea	GP	G	A	TP	PIM	GP	G	A	TP	PIM
1995-96	Reipas Lahti	Fin-Jr.	9	2	2	4	6	....	....	....	....	....
	Reipas Lahti	Finland	39	5	2	7	30	3	0	1	1	0
1996-97	Tappara	Finland	49	1	2	3	65	3	0	0	0	6
1997-98	Tappara	Finland	48	4	10	14	48	4	0	2	2	0

MacDONALD, CRAIG CAR.

Center. Shoots left. 6'2", 180 lbs. Born, Antigonish, N.S., April 7, 1977.
(Hartford's 3rd choice, 88th overall, in 1996 Entry Draft).

			Regular Season					Playoffs				
Season	Club	Lea	GP	G	A	TP	PIM	GP	G	A	TP	PIM
1995-96	Harvard	ECAC	34	7	10	17	10	....	....	....	....	....
1996-97	Harvard	ECAC	32	6	10	16	20	....	....	....	....	....
1997-98	Canada	Nat-Tm	58	18	29	47	38	....	....	....	....	....

Rights transferred to **Carolina** after **Hartford** franchise relocated, June 25, 1997

MacDONALD, DOUG

Left wing. Shoots left. 6', 192 lbs. Born, Assiniboia, Sask., February 8, 1969.
(Buffalo's 3rd choice, 77th overall, in 1989 Entry Draft).

			Regular Season					Playoffs				
Season	Club	Lea	GP	G	A	TP	PIM	GP	G	A	TP	PIM
1988-89	U. of Wisconsin	WCHA	44	23	25	48	50	....	....	....	....	....
1989-90	U. of Wisconsin	WCHA	44	16	35	51	52	....	....	....	....	....
1990-91	U. of Wisconsin	WCHA	31	20	26	46	50	....	....	....	....	....
1991-92	U. of Wisconsin	WCHA	29	14	25	39	58	....	....	....	....	....
1992-93	**Buffalo**	**NHL**	**5**	**1**	**0**	**1**	**2**	....	....	....	....	....
	Rochester	AHL	64	25	33	58	58	7	0	2	2	4
1993-94	**Buffalo**	**NHL**	**4**	**0**	**0**	**0**	**0**	....	....	....	....	....
	Rochester	AHL	63	25	19	44	46	4	1	1	2	8
1994-95	Rochester	AHL	58	21	25	46	73	5	0	1	1	0
	Buffalo	**NHL**	**2**	**0**	**0**	**0**	**0**	....	....	....	....	....
1995-96	Cincinnati	IHL	71	19	40	59	66	15	1	3	4	14
1996-97	Cincinnati	IHL	65	20	34	54	36	3	0	0	0	0
1997-98	Cincinnati	IHL	70	17	19	36	64	4	0	4	4	0
	NHL Totals		**11**	**1**	**0**	**1**	**2**	....	....	....	....	....

MacINNIS, AL — ST.L.

Defense. Shoots right. 6'2", 196 lbs. Born, Inverness, N.S., July 11, 1963.
(Calgary's 1st choice, 15th overall, in 1981 Entry Draft).

			Regular Season					Playoffs				
Season	Club	Lea	GP	G	A	TP	PIM	GP	G	A	TP	PIM
1979-80	Regina	SJHL	59	20	28	48	110	....	....	....	....	....
1980-81	Kitchener	OHA	47	11	28	39	59	18	4	12	16	20
1981-82	Kitchener	OHL	59	25	50	75	145	15	5	10	15	44
	Calgary	NHL	2	0	0	0	0	....	....	....	....	....
1982-83	Kitchener	OHL	51	38	46	84	67	8	3	8	11	9
	Calgary	NHL	14	1	3	4	9	....	....	....	....	....
1983-84	Calgary	NHL	51	11	34	45	42	11	2	12	14	13
	Colorado	CHL	19	5	14	19	22	....	....	....	....	....
1984-85	Calgary	NHL	67	14	52	66	75	4	1	2	3	8
1985-86	Calgary	NHL	77	11	57	68	76	21	4	*15	19	30
1986-87	Calgary	NHL	79	20	56	76	97	4	1	0	1	0
1987-88	Calgary	NHL	80	25	58	83	114	7	3	6	9	18
1988-89	Calgary	NHL	79	16	58	74	126	22	7	*24	*31	46 ♦
1989-90	Calgary	NHL	79	28	62	90	82	6	2	3	5	8
1990-91	Calgary	NHL	78	28	75	103	90	7	2	3	5	8
1991-92	Calgary	NHL	72	20	57	77	83	....	....	....	....	....
1992-93	Calgary	NHL	50	11	43	54	61	6	1	6	7	10
1993-94	Calgary	NHL	75	28	54	82	95	7	2	6	8	12
1994-95	St. Louis	NHL	32	8	20	28	43	7	1	5	6	10
1995-96	St. Louis	NHL	82	17	44	61	88	13	3	4	7	20
1996-97	St. Louis	NHL	72	13	30	43	65	6	1	2	3	4
1997-98	St. Louis	NHL	71	19	30	49	80	8	2	6	8	12
	Canada	Olympics	6	2	0	2	2	....	....	....	....	....
	NHL Totals		1060	270	733	1003	1226	129	32	94	126	199

OHL First All-Star Team (1982, 1983) • NHL Second All-Star Team (1987, 1989, 1994) • Won Conn Smythe Trophy (1989) • NHL First All-Star Team (1990, 1991)

Played in NHL All-Star Game (1985, 1988, 1990, 1991, 1992, 1994, 1996, 1997, 1998)

Traded to **St. Louis** by **Calgary** with Calgary's 4th round choice (Didier Tremblay) in 1997 Entry Draft for Phil Housley, St. Louis' 2nd round choice (Steve Begin) in 1996 Entry Draft and 2nd round choice (John Tripp) in 1997 Entry Draft, July 4, 1994.

MacISAAC, DAVE — PHI.

Defense. Shoots left. 6'2", 225 lbs. Born, Arlington, MA, April 23, 1972.

			Regular Season					Playoffs				
Season	Club	Lea	GP	G	A	TP	PIM	GP	G	A	TP	PIM
1992-93	U. of Maine	H.E.	35	5	32	37	14	....	....	....	....	....
1993-94	U. of Maine	H.E.	31	4	20	24	22	....	....	....	....	....
1994-95	U. of Maine	H.E.	44	5	13	18	44	....	....	....	....	....
	Milwaukee	IHL	2	0	0	0	5	9	0	2	2	2
1995-96	Milwaukee	IHL	71	7	16	23	165	....	....	....	....	....
1996-97	Philadelphia	AHL	61	3	15	18	187	10	0	1	1	31
1997-98	Philadelphia	AHL	80	7	21	28	241	18	5	13	18	20

Signed as a free agent by **Philadelphia**, July 30, 1996.

MACIVER, NORM (mac-IGH-ver)

Defense. Shoots left. 5'11", 180 lbs. Born, Thunder Bay, Ont., September 8, 1964.

			Regular Season					Playoffs				
Season	Club	Lea	GP	G	A	TP	PIM	GP	G	A	TP	PIM
1982-83	U. Minn-Duluth	WCHA	45	1	26	27	40	6	0	2	2	2
1983-84	U. Minn-Duluth	WCHA	31	13	28	41	28	8	1	10	11	8
1984-85	U. Minn-Duluth	WCHA	47	14	47	61	63	10	3	3	6	6
1985-86	U. Minn-Duluth	WCHA	42	11	51	62	36	4	2	3	5	2
1986-87	NY Rangers	NHL	3	0	1	1	0	....	....	....	....	....
	New Haven	AHL	71	6	30	36	73	7	0	0	0	9
1987-88	NY Rangers	NHL	37	9	15	24	14	....	....	....	....	....
	Colorado	IHL	27	6	20	26	22	....	....	....	....	....
1988-89	NY Rangers	NHL	26	0	10	10	14	....	....	....	....	....
	Hartford	NHL	37	1	22	23	24	1	0	0	0	2
1989-90	Binghamton	AHL	2	0	0	0	0	....	....	....	....	....
	Edmonton	NHL	1	0	0	0	0	....	....	....	....	....
	Cape Breton	AHL	68	13	37	50	55	6	0	7	7	10
1990-91	Edmonton	NHL	21	2	5	7	14	18	0	4	4	8
	Cape Breton	AHL	56	13	46	59	60	....	....	....	....	....
1991-92	Edmonton	NHL	57	6	34	40	38	13	1	2	3	10
1992-93	Ottawa	NHL	80	17	46	63	84	....	....	....	....	....
1993-94	Ottawa	NHL	53	3	20	23	26	....	....	....	....	....
1994-95	Ottawa	NHL	28	4	7	11	10	....	....	....	....	....
	Pittsburgh	NHL	13	0	9	9	6	12	1	4	5	8
1995-96	Pittsburgh	NHL	32	2	21	23	32	....	....	....	....	....
	Winnipeg	NHL	39	5	25	30	26	6	1	0	1	2
1996-97	Phoenix	NHL	32	4	9	13	24	....	....	....	....	....
1997-98	Phoenix	NHL	41	2	6	8	38	6	0	1	1	2
	NHL Totals		500	55	230	285	350	56	3	11	14	32

WCHA First All-Star Team (1985, 1986) • NCAA West First All-American Team (1985, 1986) • AHL First All-Star Team (1991) • Won Eddie Shore Award (Top Defenseman - AHL) (1991)

Signed as a free agent by **NY Rangers**, September 8, 1986. Traded to **Hartford** by **NY Rangers** with Brian Lawton and Don Maloney for Carey Wilson and Hartford's 5th round choice (Lubos Rob) in 1990 Entry Draft, December 26, 1988. Traded to **Edmonton** by **Hartford** for Jim Ennis, October 10, 1989. Claimed by **Ottawa** from **Edmonton** in NHL Waiver Draft, October 4, 1992. Traded to **Pittsburgh** by **Ottawa** with Troy Murray for Martin Straka, April 7, 1995. Traded to **Winnipeg** by **Pittsburgh** for Neil Wilkinson, December 28, 1995. Transferred to **Phoenix** after **Winnipeg** franchise relocated, July 1, 1996.

MACKINNON, STEPHEN — OTT.

Left wing. Shoots left. 6'4", 200 lbs. Born, Lowell, MA, August 20, 1976.
(Ottawa's 9th choice, 237th overall, in 1994 Entry Draft).

			Regular Season					Playoffs				
Season	Club	Lea	GP	G	A	TP	PIM	GP	G	A	TP	PIM
1993-94	Cushing Academy	H.S.	25	13	15	28	....	....	....	....	....	....
1994-95	Cushing Academy	H.S.	25	26	29	55	....	....	....	....	....	....
1995-96	Mass.-Amherst	H.E.	18	1	0	1	61	....	....	....	....	....
1996-97	Mass.-Amherst	H.E.	34	14	12	26	52	....	....	....	....	....
1997-98	Mass.-Amherst	H.E.	17	2	5	7	39	....	....	....	....	....

MacLEAN, DONALD — L.A.

Center. Shoots left. 6'2", 199 lbs. Born, Sydney, N.S., January 14, 1977.
(Los Angeles' 2nd choice, 33rd overall, in 1995 Entry Draft).

			Regular Season					Playoffs				
Season	Club	Lea	GP	G	A	TP	PIM	GP	G	A	TP	PIM
1994-95	Beauport	QMJHL	64	15	27	42	37	17	4	4	8	6
1995-96	Beauport	QMJHL	1	0	1	1	0	....	....	....	....	....
	Laval	QMJHL	21	17	11	28	29	....	....	....	....	....
	Hull	QMJHL	39	26	34	60	44	17	6	7	13	14
1996-97	Hull	QMJHL	69	34	47	81	67	14	11	10	21	39
1997-98	Los Angeles	NHL	22	5	2	7	4	....	....	....	....	....
	Fredericton	AHL	39	9	5	14	32	4	1	3	4	2
	NHL Totals		22	5	2	7	4	....	....	....	....	....

MacLEAN, JOHN — NYR

Right wing. Shoots right. 6', 210 lbs. Born, Oshawa, Ont., November 20, 1964.
(New Jersey's 1st choice, 6th overall, in 1983 Entry Draft).

			Regular Season					Playoffs				
Season	Club	Lea	GP	G	A	TP	PIM	GP	G	A	TP	PIM
1981-82	Oshawa	OHL	67	17	22	39	197	12	3	6	9	63
1982-83	Oshawa	OHL	66	47	51	98	138	17	*18	20	*38	35
1983-84	Oshawa	OHL	30	23	36	59	58	7	2	5	7	18
	New Jersey	NHL	23	1	0	1	10	....	....	....	....	....
1984-85	New Jersey	NHL	61	13	20	33	44	....	....	....	....	....
1985-86	New Jersey	NHL	74	21	36	57	112	....	....	....	....	....
1986-87	New Jersey	NHL	80	31	36	67	120	....	....	....	....	....
1987-88	New Jersey	NHL	76	23	16	39	147	20	7	11	18	60
1988-89	New Jersey	NHL	74	42	45	87	122	....	....	....	....	....
1989-90	New Jersey	NHL	80	41	38	79	80	6	4	1	5	12
1990-91	New Jersey	NHL	78	45	33	78	150	7	5	3	8	20
1991-92			DID NOT PLAY – INJURED									
1992-93	New Jersey	NHL	80	24	24	48	102	5	0	1	1	10
1993-94	New Jersey	NHL	80	37	33	70	95	20	6	10	16	22
1994-95	New Jersey	NHL	46	17	12	29	32	20	5	13	18	14 ♦
1995-96	New Jersey	NHL	76	20	28	48	91	....	....	....	....	....
1996-97	New Jersey	NHL	80	29	25	54	49	10	4	5	9	4
1997-98	New Jersey	NHL	26	3	8	11	14	....	....	....	....	....
	San Jose	NHL	51	13	19	32	28	6	2	3	5	4
	NHL Totals		985	360	373	733	1196	94	33	47	80	146

Memorial Cup All-Star Team (1983)

Played in NHL All-Star Game (1989, 1991)

• Missed entire 1991-92 season with torn ligament in right knee. Traded to **San Jose** by **New Jersey** with Ken Sutton for Doug Bodger and Dody Wood, December 7, 1997. Signed as a free agent by **NY Rangers**, July 22, 1998.

MACNEIL, IAN — CAR.

Center. Shoots left. 6'2", 171 lbs. Born, Halifax, N.S., April 27, 1977.
(Hartford's 3rd choice, 85th overall, in 1995 Entry Draft).

			Regular Season					Playoffs				
Season	Club	Lea	GP	G	A	TP	PIM	GP	G	A	TP	PIM
1994-95	Oshawa	OHL	60	7	21	28	62	7	0	2	2	0
1995-96	Oshawa	OHL	49	15	17	32	54	5	1	2	3	8
1996-97	Oshawa	OHL	64	23	20	43	96	18	2	3	5	37
1997-98	New Haven	AHL	68	12	21	33	67	3	1	0	1	10

MacNEVIN, JOSH — N.J.

Defense. Shoots right. 6'2", 185 lbs. Born, Calgary, Alta., July 14, 1977.
(New Jersey's 8th choice, 101st overall, in 1996 Entry Draft).

			Regular Season					Playoffs				
Season	Club	Lea	GP	G	A	TP	PIM	GP	G	A	TP	PIM
1995-96	Vernon	BCJHL	51	13	45	58	54	....	....	....	....	....
1996-97	Providence	H.E.	30	5	9	14	18	....	....	....	....	....
1997-98	Providence	H.E.	33	5	14	19	39	....	....	....	....	....

MACOUN, JAMIE (muh-KOW-uhn) — DET.

Defense. Shoots left. 6'2", 200 lbs. Born, Newmarket, Ont., August 17, 1961.

			Regular Season					Playoffs				
Season	Club	Lea	GP	G	A	TP	PIM	GP	G	A	TP	PIM
1980-81	Ohio State	CCHA	38	9	20	29	83	....	....	....	....	....
1981-82	Ohio State	CCHA	25	2	18	20	89	....	....	....	....	....
1982-83	Ohio State	CCHA	19	6	21	27	54	....	....	....	....	....
	Calgary	NHL	22	1	4	5	25	9	0	2	2	8
1983-84	Calgary	NHL	72	9	23	32	97	11	1	0	1	0
1984-85	Calgary	NHL	70	9	30	39	67	4	1	0	1	4
1985-86	Calgary	NHL	77	11	21	32	81	22	1	6	7	23
1986-87	Calgary	NHL	79	7	33	40	111	3	0	1	1	8
1987-88			DID NOT PLAY – INJURED									
1988-89	Calgary	NHL	72	8	19	27	76	22	3	6	9	30 ♦
1989-90	Calgary	NHL	78	8	27	35	70	6	0	3	3	10
1990-91	Calgary	NHL	79	7	15	22	84	7	0	1	1	4
1991-92	Calgary	NHL	37	2	12	14	53	....	....	....	....	....
	Toronto	NHL	39	3	13	16	18	....	....	....	....	....
1992-93	Toronto	NHL	77	4	15	19	55	21	0	6	6	36
1993-94	Toronto	NHL	82	3	27	30	115	18	1	1	2	12
1994-95	Toronto	NHL	46	2	8	10	75	7	1	2	3	8
1995-96	Toronto	NHL	82	0	8	8	87	6	0	2	2	8
1996-97	Toronto	NHL	73	1	10	11	93	....	....	....	....	....
1997-98	Toronto	NHL	67	0	7	7	63	....	....	....	....	....
	Detroit	NHL	7	0	0	0	2	22	2	2	4	18 ♦
	NHL Totals		1059	75	272	347	1172	158	10	32	42	169

NHL All-Rookie Team (1984)

Signed as a free agent by **Calgary**, January 30, 1983. • Missed entire 1987-88 season recovering from nerve damage to arm after automobile accident, May, 1987. Traded to **Toronto** by **Calgary** with Doug Gilmour, Ric Natress, Kent Manderville and Rick Wamsley for Gary Leeman, Alexander Godynyuk, Jeff Reese, Michel Petit and Craig Berube, January 2, 1992. Traded to **Detroit** by **Toronto** for Tampa Bay's 4th round choice (previously acquired, Toronto selected Alexei Ponikarovsky) in 1998 Entry Draft, March 24, 1998.

MADDEN, JOHN — N.J.

Left wing. Shoots left. 5'11", 185 lbs. Born, Barrie, Ont., May 4, 1975.

			Regular Season					Playoffs				
Season	Club	Lea	GP	G	A	TP	PIM	GP	G	A	TP	PIM
1993-94	U. of Michigan	CCHA	36	6	11	17	14	....	....	....	....	....
1994-95	U. of Michigan	CCHA	39	21	22	43	8	....	....	....	....	....
1995-96	U. of Michigan	CCHA	43	27	30	57	45	....	....	....	....	....
1996-97	U. of Michigan	CCHA	42	26	37	63	56	....	....	....	....	....
1997-98	Albany	AHL	74	20	36	56	40	13	3	13	16	14

CCHA First All-Star Team (1997) • NCAA West First All-American Team (1997)

Signed as a free agent by **New Jersey**, June 26, 1997.

MADER, MIKE — PHX.

Defense. Shoots right. 6'2", 183 lbs. Born, Manchester, CT, November 7, 1975.
(Winnipeg's 10th choice, 238th overall, in 1994 Entry Draft).

			Regular Season					Playoffs				
Season	Club	Lea	GP	G	A	TP	PIM	GP	G	A	TP	PIM
1993-94	Loomis High	H.S.	26	12	35	47	....	....	....	....	....	....
1994-95	Providence	H.E.	29	1	5	6	26	....	....	....	....	....
1995-96	Providence	H.E.	37	3	6	9	33	....	....	....	....	....
1996-97	Providence	H.E.	35	4	10	14	48	....	....	....	....	....
1997-98	Providence	H.E.	34	7	13	20	50	....	....	....	....	....
	Springfield	AHL	2	0	0	0	0	....	....	....	....	....

MAIR, ADAM — TOR.

Center. Shoots right. 6', 189 lbs. Born, Hamilton, Ont., February 15, 1979.
(Toronto's 2nd choice, 84th overall, in 1997 Entry Draft).

			Regular Season					Playoffs				
Season	Club	Lea	GP	G	A	TP	PIM	GP	G	A	TP	PIM
1995-96	Owen Sound	OHL	62	12	15	27	63	6	0	0	0	2
1996-97	Owen Sound	OHL	65	16	35	51	113	4	1	0	1	2
1997-98	Owen Sound	OHL	56	25	27	52	179	11	6	3	9	31

MAJOR, MARK — WSH.

Left wing. Shoots left. 6'3", 223 lbs. Born, Toronto, Ont., March 20, 1970.
(Pittsburgh's 2nd choice, 25th overall, in 1988 Entry Draft).

			Regular Season					Playoffs				
Season	Club	Lea	GP	G	A	TP	PIM	GP	G	A	TP	PIM
1987-88	North Bay	OHL	57	16	17	33	272	4	0	2	2	8
1988-89	North Bay	OHL	11	3	2	5	58	....	....	....	....	....
	Kingston	OHL	53	22	29	51	193	....	....	....	....	....
1989-90	Kingston	OHL	62	29	32	61	168	6	3	3	6	12
1990-91	Muskegon	IHL	60	8	10	18	160	5	0	0	0	0
1991-92	Muskegon	IHL	80	13	18	31	302	12	1	3	4	29
1992-93	Cleveland	IHL	82	13	15	28	155	3	0	0	0	0
1993-94	Providence	AHL	61	17	9	26	176	....	....	....	....	....
1994-95	Detroit	IHL	78	17	19	36	229	5	0	1	1	23
1995-96	Adirondack	AHL	78	10	19	29	234	3	0	0	0	21
1996-97	**Detroit**	**NHL**	**2**	**0**	**0**	**0**	**5**	....	....	....	....	....
	Adirondack	AHL	78	17	18	35	213	4	0	0	0	13
1997-98	Portland	AHL	79	13	2	15	355	10	2	1	3	52
	NHL Totals		**2**	**0**	**0**	**0**	**5**	....	....	....	....	....

Signed as a free agent by **Boston**, July 22, 1993. Signed as a free agent by **Detroit**, June 26, 1995. Signed as a free agent by **Washington**, August 20, 1997.

MAKINEN, MARKO (mya-KIH-nehn) — S.J.

Right wing. Shoots right. 6'5", 200 lbs. Born, Turku, Finland, March 31, 1977.
(San Jose's 3rd choice, 64th overall, in 1995 Entry Draft).

			Regular Season					Playoffs				
Season	Club	Lea	GP	G	A	TP	PIM	GP	G	A	TP	PIM
1994-95	TPS Turku	Fin-Jr.	26	7	1	8	34	....	....	....	....	....
	Kiekko	Finland-2	4	0	0	0	6	....	....	....	....	....
1995-96	TPS Turku	Fin-Jr.	11	5	1	6	28	....	....	....	....	....
	Kiekko	Fin-Jr.	4	4	2	6	12	....	....	....	....	....
	Kiekko	Finland-2	21	6	2	8	98	6	2	2	4	6
1996-97	Kiekko	Finland	15	2	1	3	34	4	0	0	0	0
	Kiekko	Finland-2	30	2	8	10	63	....	....	....	....	....
1997-98	Kentucky	AHL	26	2	2	4	15	....	....	....	....	....
	Louisville	ECHL	38	10	6	16	19	....	....	....	....	....

Signed as a free agent by **Chicago**, September 2, 1998.

MALAKHOV, VLADIMIR (mah-LAH-kahf) — MTL.

Defense. Shoots left. 6'4", 229 lbs. Born, Ekaterinburg, USSR, August 30, 1968.
(NY Islanders' 12th choice, 191st overall, in 1989 Entry Draft).

			Regular Season					Playoffs				
Season	Club	Lea	GP	G	A	TP	PIM	GP	G	A	TP	PIM
1986-87	Spartak	USSR	22	0	1	1	12	....	....	....	....	....
1987-88	Spartak	USSR	28	2	2	4	26	....	....	....	....	....
1988-89	CSKA Moscow	USSR	34	6	2	8	16	....	....	....	....	....
1989-90	CSKA Moscow	USSR	48	2	10	12	34	....	....	....	....	....
1990-91	CSKA Moscow	USSR	46	5	13	18	22	....	....	....	....	....
1991-92	CSKA Moscow	CIS	40	1	9	10	12	....	....	....	....	....
	Russia	Olympics	8	3	0	3	4	....	....	....	....	....
1992-93	**NY Islanders**	**NHL**	**64**	**14**	**38**	**52**	**59**	**17**	**3**	**6**	**9**	**12**
	Capital District	AHL	3	2	1	3	11	....	....	....	....	....
1993-94	**NY Islanders**	**NHL**	**76**	**10**	**47**	**57**	**80**	**4**	**0**	**0**	**0**	**6**
1994-95	**NY Islanders**	**NHL**	**26**	**3**	**13**	**16**	**32**	....	....	....	....	....
	Montreal	**NHL**	**14**	**1**	**4**	**5**	**14**	....	....	....	....	....
1995-96	**Montreal**	**NHL**	**61**	**5**	**23**	**28**	**79**	....	....	....	....	....
1996-97	**Montreal**	**NHL**	**65**	**10**	**20**	**30**	**43**	**5**	**0**	**0**	**0**	**6**
1997-98	**Montreal**	**NHL**	**74**	**13**	**31**	**44**	**70**	**9**	**3**	**4**	**7**	**10**
	NHL Totals		**380**	**56**	**176**	**232**	**377**	**35**	**6**	**10**	**16**	**34**

NHL/Upper Deck All-Rookie Team (1993)

Traded to **Montreal** by **NY Islanders** with Pierre Turgeon for Kirk Muller, Mathieu Schneider and Craig Darby, April 5, 1995.

MALGUNAS, STEWART (mal-GOO-nuhs) — WSH.

Defense. Shoots left. 6', 200 lbs. Born, Prince George, B.C., April 21, 1970.
(Detroit's 3rd choice, 66th overall, in 1990 Entry Draft).

			Regular Season					Playoffs				
Season	Club	Lea	GP	G	A	TP	PIM	GP	G	A	TP	PIM
1987-88	New Westminster	WHL	6	0	0	0	0	....	....	....	....	....
1988-89	Seattle	WHL	72	11	41	52	51	....	....	....	....	....
1989-90	Seattle	WHL	63	15	48	63	116	13	2	9	11	32
1990-91	Adirondack	AHL	78	5	19	24	70	2	0	0	0	4
1991-92	Adirondack	AHL	69	4	28	32	82	18	2	6	8	28
1992-93	Adirondack	AHL	45	3	12	15	39	11	3	3	6	8
1993-94	**Philadelphia**	**NHL**	**67**	**1**	**3**	**4**	**86**	....	....	....	....	....
1994-95	**Philadelphia**	**NHL**	**4**	**0**	**0**	**0**	**4**	....	....	....	....	....
	Hershey	AHL	32	3	5	8	28	6	2	1	3	31
1995-96	**Winnipeg**	**NHL**	**29**	**0**	**1**	**1**	**32**	....	....	....	....	....
	Washington	**NHL**	**1**	**0**	**0**	**0**	**0**	....	....	....	....	....
	Portland	AHL	16	2	5	7	18	13	1	3	4	19
1996-97	**Washington**	**NHL**	**6**	**0**	**0**	**0**	**2**	....	....	....	....	....
	Portland	AHL	68	6	12	18	59	5	0	0	0	8
1997-98	**Washington**	**NHL**	**8**	**0**	**0**	**0**	**12**	....	....	....	....	....
	Portland	AHL	69	14	25	39	73	9	1	1	2	19
	NHL Totals		**115**	**1**	**4**	**5**	**136**	....	....	....	....	....

WHL West First All-Star Team (1990)

Traded to **Philadelphia** by **Detroit** for Philadelphia's 5th round choice (David Arsenault) in 1995 Entry Draft, September 9, 1993. Signed as a free agent by **Winnipeg**, August 9, 1995. Traded to **Washington** by **Winnipeg** for Denis Chasse, February 15, 1996.

MALHOTRA, MANNY (mal-HOH-truh) — NYR

Center. Shoots left. 6'1", 210 lbs. Born, Mississauga, Ont., May 18, 1980.
(NY Rangers' 1st choice, 7th overall, in 1998 Entry Draft).

			Regular Season					Playoffs				
Season	Club	Lea	GP	G	A	TP	PIM	GP	G	A	TP	PIM
1996-97	Guelph	OHL	61	16	28	44	26	18	7	7	14	11
1997-98	Guelph	OHL	57	16	35	51	29	12	7	6	13	8

Memorial Cup All-Star Team (1998) • Won George Parsons Trophy (Memorial Cup Tournament Most Sportsmanlike Player) (1998)

MALIK, MAREK (MAW-leck) — CAR.

Defense. Shoots left. 6'5", 190 lbs. Born, Ostrava, Czech., June 24, 1975.
(Hartford's 2nd choice, 72nd overall, in 1993 Entry Draft).

			Regular Season					Playoffs				
Season	Club	Lea	GP	G	A	TP	PIM	GP	G	A	TP	PIM
1992-93	Vitkovice	Czech-Jr.	20	5	10	15	16	....	....	....	....	....
1993-94	Vitkovice	Cze-Rep.	38	3	3	6	0	3	0	1	1	0
1994-95	Springfield	AHL	58	11	30	41	91	....	....	....	....	....
	Hartford	**NHL**	**1**	**0**	**1**	**1**	**0**	....	....	....	....	....
1995-96	**Hartford**	**NHL**	**7**	**0**	**0**	**0**	**4**	....	....	....	....	....
	Springfield	AHL	68	8	14	22	135	8	1	3	4	20
1996-97	**Hartford**	**NHL**	**47**	**1**	**5**	**6**	**50**	....	....	....	....	....
	Springfield	AHL	3	0	3	3	4	....	....	....	....	....
1997-98	Malmo IF	Sweden	37	1	5	6	21	....	....	....	....	....
	NHL Totals		**55**	**1**	**6**	**7**	**54**	....	....	....	....	....

Transferred to **Carolina** after **Hartford** franchise relocated, June 25, 1997.

MALKOC, DEAN (mal-KAWK) — NYI

Defense. Shoots left. 6'3", 215 lbs. Born, Vancouver, B.C., January 26, 1970.
(New Jersey's 7th choice, 95th overall, in 1990 Entry Draft).

			Regular Season					Playoffs				
Season	Club	Lea	GP	G	A	TP	PIM	GP	G	A	TP	PIM
1989-90	Kamloops	WHL	48	3	18	21	209	17	0	3	3	56
1990-91	Kamloops	WHL	8	1	4	5	47	....	....	....	....	....
	Swift Current	WHL	56	10	23	33	248	3	0	2	2	5
	Utica	AHL	1	0	0	0	0	....	....	....	....	....
1991-92	Utica	AHL	66	1	11	12	274	4	0	2	2	6
1992-93	Utica	AHL	73	5	19	24	255	5	0	1	1	8
1993-94	Albany	AHL	79	0	9	9	296	5	0	0	0	21
1994-95	Albany	AHL	9	0	1	1	52	....	....	....	....	....
	Indianapolis	IHL	62	1	3	4	193	....	....	....	....	....
1995-96	**Vancouver**	**NHL**	**41**	**0**	**2**	**2**	**136**	....	....	....	....	....
1996-97	**Boston**	**NHL**	**33**	**0**	**0**	**0**	**70**	....	....	....	....	....
	Providence	AHL	4	0	2	2	28	....	....	....	....	....
1997-98	**Boston**	**NHL**	**40**	**1**	**0**	**1**	**86**	....	....	....	....	....
	NHL Totals		**114**	**1**	**2**	**3**	**292**	....	....	....	....	....

Traded to **Chicago** by **New Jersey** for Rob Conn, January 30, 1995. Signed as a free agent by **Vancouver**, September 8, 1995. Claimed by **Boston** from **Vancouver** in NHL Waiver Draft, September 30, 1996. Signed as a free agent by **NY Islanders**, August 19, 1998.

MALLETTE, KRIS (muh-LEHT) — PHI.

Defense. Shoots right. 6'3", 220 lbs. Born, North Bay, Ont., January 19, 1979.
(Philadelphia's 3rd choice, 62nd overall, in 1997 Entry Draft).

			Regular Season					Playoffs				
Season	Club	Lea	GP	G	A	TP	PIM	GP	G	A	TP	PIM
1996-97	Kelowna	WHL	67	0	3	3	206	6	0	0	0	8
1997-98	Kelowna	WHL	63	4	9	13	220	7	0	0	0	20

MALLETTE, TROY (muh-LEHT)

Left wing. Shoots left. 6'2", 210 lbs. Born, Sudbury, Ont., February 25, 1970.
(NY Rangers' 1st choice, 22nd overall, in 1988 Entry Draft).

			Regular Season					Playoffs				
Season	Club	Lea	GP	G	A	TP	PIM	GP	G	A	TP	PIM
1986-87	S.S. Marie	OHL	65	20	25	45	157	4	0	2	2	12
1987-88	S.S. Marie	OHL	62	18	30	48	186	6	1	3	4	12
1988-89	S.S. Marie	OHL	64	39	37	76	172	....	....	....	....	....
1989-90	**NY Rangers**	**NHL**	**79**	**13**	**16**	**29**	**305**	**10**	**2**	**2**	**4**	**81**
1990-91	**NY Rangers**	**NHL**	**71**	**12**	**10**	**22**	**252**	**5**	**0**	**0**	**0**	**18**
1991-92	**Edmonton**	**NHL**	**15**	**1**	**3**	**4**	**36**	....	....	....	....	....
	New Jersey	**NHL**	**17**	**3**	**4**	**7**	**43**	....	....	....	....	....
1992-93	**New Jersey**	**NHL**	**34**	**4**	**3**	**7**	**56**	....	....	....	....	....
	Utica	AHL	5	3	3	6	17	....	....	....	....	....
1993-94	**Ottawa**	**NHL**	**82**	**7**	**16**	**23**	**166**	....	....	....	....	....
1994-95	**Ottawa**	**NHL**	**23**	**3**	**5**	**8**	**35**	....	....	....	....	....
	P.E.I.	AHL	5	1	5	6	9	....	....	....	....	....
1995-96	**Ottawa**	**NHL**	**64**	**2**	**3**	**5**	**171**	....	....	....	....	....
1996-97	**Boston**	**NHL**	**68**	**6**	**8**	**14**	**155**	....	....	....	....	....
1997-98	**Tampa Bay**	**NHL**	**3**	**0**	**0**	**0**	**7**	....	....	....	....	....
	NHL Totals		**456**	**51**	**68**	**119**	**1226**	**15**	**2**	**2**	**4**	**99**

Transferred to **Edmonton** by **NY Rangers** as compensation for NY Rangers' signing of free agent Adam Graves, September 12, 1991. Traded to **New Jersey** by **Edmonton** for David Maley, January 12, 1992. Traded to **Ottawa** by **New Jersey** with Craig Billington and New Jersey's 4th round choice (Cosmo Dupaul) in 1993 Entry Draft for Peter Sidorkiewicz and future considerations (Mike Peluso, June 26, 1993), June 20, 1993. Signed as a free agent by **Boston**, July 24, 1996. Signed as a free agent by **Tampa Bay**, October 2, 1997.

MALTAIS, STEVE (MAHL-tay)

Left wing. Shoots left. 6'2", 205 lbs. Born, Arvida, Que., January 25, 1969.
(Washington's 2nd choice, 57th overall, in 1987 Entry Draft).

			Regular Season					Playoffs				
Season	Club	Lea	GP	G	A	TP	PIM	GP	G	A	TP	PIM
1986-87	Cornwall	OHL	65	32	12	44	29	5	0	0	0	2
1987-88	Cornwall	OHL	59	39	46	85	30	11	9	6	15	33
1988-89	Cornwall	OHL	58	53	70	123	67	18	14	16	30	16
	Fort Wayne	IHL	....	....	....	....	....	4	2	1	3	0
1989-90	**Washington**	**NHL**	**8**	**0**	**0**	**0**	**2**	**1**	**0**	**0**	**0**	**0**
	Baltimore	AHL	67	29	37	66	54	12	6	10	16	6
1990-91	**Washington**	**NHL**	**7**	**0**	**0**	**0**	**2**	....	....	....	....	....
	Baltimore	AHL	73	36	43	79	97	6	1	4	5	10
1991-92	**Minnesota**	**NHL**	**12**	**2**	**1**	**3**	**2**	....	....	....	....	....
	Kalamazoo	IHL	48	25	31	56	51	....	....	....	....	....
	Halifax	AHL	10	3	3	6	0	....	....	....	....	....
1992-93	**Tampa Bay**	**NHL**	**63**	**7**	**13**	**20**	**35**	....	....	....	....	....
	Atlanta	IHL	16	14	10	24	22	....	....	....	....	....
1993-94	**Detroit**	**NHL**	**4**	**0**	**1**	**1**	**0**	....	....	....	....	....
	Adirondack	AHL	73	35	49	84	79	12	5	11	16	14
1994-95	Chicago	IHL	79	*57	40	97	145	3	1	1	2	0
1995-96	Chicago	IHL	81	56	66	122	161	9	7	7	14	20
1996-97	Chicago	IHL	81	*60	54	114	62	4	2	0	2	4
1997-98	Chicago	IHL	82	*46	57	103	120	22	8	11	19	28
	NHL Totals		**94**	**9**	**15**	**24**	**41**	**1**	**0**	**0**	**0**	**0**

OHL Second All-Star Team (1989) • IHL First All-Star Team (1995) • IHL Second All-Star Team (1996, 1997)

Traded to **Minnesota** by **Washington** with Trent Klatt for Shawn Chambers, June 21, 1991. Traded to **Quebec** by **Minnesota** for Kip Miller, March 8, 1992. Claimed by **Tampa Bay** from **Quebec** in Expansion Draft, June 18, 1992. Traded to **Detroit** by **Tampa Bay** for Dennis Vial, June 8, 1993.

MALTBY, KIRK (MAHLT-bee) **DET.**

Right wing. Shoots right. 6', 180 lbs. Born, Guelph, Ont., December 22, 1972.
(Edmonton's 4th choice, 65th overall, in 1992 Entry Draft).

			Regular Season					Playoffs				
Season	Club	Lea	GP	G	A	TP	PIM	GP	G	A	TP	PIM
1989-90	Owen Sound	OHL	61	12	15	27	90	12	1	6	7	15
1990-91	Owen Sound	OHL	66	34	32	66	100	....	....	....	....	....
1991-92	Owen Sound	OHL	66	50	41	91	99	5	3	3	6	18
1992-93	Cape Breton	AHL	73	22	23	45	130	16	3	3	6	45
1993-94	**Edmonton**	**NHL**	**68**	**11**	**8**	**19**	**74**	....	....	....	....	....
1994-95	**Edmonton**	**NHL**	**47**	**8**	**3**	**11**	**49**	....	....	....	....	....
1995-96	**Edmonton**	**NHL**	**49**	**2**	**6**	**8**	**61**	....	....	....	....	....
	Cape Breton	AHL	4	1	2	3	6	....	....	....	....	....
	Detroit	**NHL**	**6**	**1**	**0**	**1**	**6**	**8**	**0**	**1**	**1**	**4**
1996-97	**Detroit**	**NHL**	**66**	**3**	**5**	**8**	**75**	**20**	**5**	**2**	**7**	**24 ♦**
1997-98	**Detroit**	**NHL**	**65**	**14**	**9**	**23**	**89**	**22**	**3**	**1**	**4**	**30 ♦**
	NHL Totals		**301**	**39**	**31**	**70**	**354**	**50**	**8**	**4**	**12**	**58**

Traded to **Detroit** by **Edmonton** for Dan McGillis, March 20, 1996.

MANDERVILLE, KENT **CAR.**

Left wing. Shoots left. 6'3", 210 lbs. Born, Edmonton, Alta., April 12, 1971.
(Calgary's 1st choice, 24th overall, in 1989 Entry Draft).

			Regular Season					Playoffs				
Season	Club	Lea	GP	G	A	TP	PIM	GP	G	A	TP	PIM
1988-89	Notre Dame	SJHL	58	39	36	75	165	....	....	....	....	....
1989-90	Cornell	ECAC	26	11	15	26	28	....	....	....	....	....
1990-91	Cornell	ECAC	28	17	14	31	60	....	....	....	....	....
	Canada	Nat-Tm	3	1	2	3	0	....	....	....	....	....
1991-92	Canada	Nat-Tm	63	16	24	40	78	....	....	....	....	....
	Canada	Olympics	8	1	2	3	0	....	....	....	....	....
	Toronto	**NHL**	**15**	**0**	**4**	**4**	**0**	....	....	....	....	....
	St. John's	AHL	....	....	....	....	....	12	5	9	14	14
1992-93	**Toronto**	**NHL**	**18**	**1**	**1**	**2**	**17**	**18**	**1**	**0**	**1**	**8**
	St. John's	AHL	56	19	28	47	86	2	0	2	2	0
1993-94	**Toronto**	**NHL**	**67**	**7**	**9**	**16**	**63**	**12**	**1**	**0**	**1**	**4**
1994-95	**Toronto**	**NHL**	**36**	**0**	**1**	**1**	**22**	**7**	**0**	**0**	**0**	**6**
1995-96	**Edmonton**	**NHL**	**37**	**3**	**5**	**8**	**38**	....	....	....	....	....
	St. John's	AHL	27	16	12	28	26	....	....	....	....	....
1996-97	**Hartford**	**NHL**	**44**	**6**	**5**	**11**	**18**	....	....	....	....	....
	Springfield	AHL	23	5	20	25	18	....	....	....	....	....
1997-98	**Carolina**	**NHL**	**77**	**4**	**4**	**8**	**31**	....	....	....	....	....
	NHL Totals		**294**	**21**	**29**	**50**	**189**	**37**	**2**	**0**	**2**	**18**

Traded to **Toronto** by **Calgary** with Doug Gilmour, Jamie Macoun, Rick Wamsley and Ric Nattress for Gary Leeman, Alexander Godynyuk, Jeff Reese, Michel Petit and Craig Berube, January 2, 1992. Traded to **Edmonton** by **Toronto** for Peter White and Edmonton's 4th round choice (Jason Sessa) in 1996 Entry Draft, December 4, 1995. Signed as a free agent by **Hartford**, October 2, 1996. Transferred to **Carolina** after **Hartford** franchise relocated, June 25, 1997.

MANELUK, MIKE **PHI.**

Left wing. Shoots right. 5'11", 188 lbs. Born, Winnipeg, Man., October 1, 1973.

			Regular Season					Playoffs				
Season	Club	Lea	GP	G	A	TP	PIM	GP	G	A	TP	PIM
1991-92	Brandon	WHL	68	23	30	53	102	....	....	....	....	....
1992-93	Brandon	WHL	72	36	51	87	75	4	2	1	3	2
1993-94	Brandon	WHL	63	50	47	97	112	13	11	3	14	23
	San Diego	IHL	....	....	....	....	....	1	0	0	0	0
1994-95	Canada	Nat-Tm	44	36	24	60	34	....	....	....	....	....
	San Diego	IHL	10	0	1	1	4	....	....	....	....	....
1995-96	Baltimore	AHL	74	33	38	71	73	6	4	3	7	14
1996-97	Worcester	AHL	70	27	27	54	89	5	1	2	3	14
1997-98	Worcester	AHL	5	3	3	6	4	....	....	....	....	....
	Philadelphia	AHL	66	27	35	62	62	20	*13	*21	*34	30

Won Jack A. Butterfield Trophy (Playoff MVP - AHL) (1998)

Signed as a free agent by **Anaheim**, January 28, 1994. Traded to **Ottawa** by **Anaheim** for Kevin Brown, July 1, 1996.

MANN, CAMERON **BOS.**

Right wing. Shoots right. 6', 194 lbs. Born, Thompson, Man., April 20, 1977.
(Boston's 5th choice, 99th overall, in 1995 Entry Draft).

			Regular Season					Playoffs				
Season	Club	Lea	GP	G	A	TP	PIM	GP	G	A	TP	PIM
1993-94	Peterborough	OHL	49	8	17	25	18	7	1	1	2	2
1994-95	Peterborough	OHL	64	19	24	43	40	11	3	8	11	4
1995-96	Peterborough	OHL	66	42	60	102	108	24	*27	16	*43	33
1996-97	Peterborough	OHL	51	33	50	83	91	11	10	18	28	16
1997-98	**Boston**	**NHL**	**9**	**0**	**1**	**1**	**4**	....	....	....	....	....
	Providence	AHL	71	21	26	47	99	....	....	....	....	....
	NHL Totals		**9**	**0**	**1**	**1**	**4**	....	....	....	....	....

OHL First All-Star Team (1996, 1997) • Memorial Cup All-Star Team (1996) • Won Stafford Smythe Memorial Trophy (Memorial Cup Tournament MVP) (1996)

MANNING, PAUL **CGY.**

Defense. Shoots left. 6'4", 193 lbs. Born, Red Deer, Alta., April 15, 1979.
(Calgary's 3rd choice, 62nd overall, in 1998 Entry Draft).

			Regular Season					Playoffs				
Season	Club	Lea	GP	G	A	TP	PIM	GP	G	A	TP	PIM
1996-97	Red Deer	AJHL	36	9	33	42	....	....	....	....	....	....
1997-98	Colorado College	WCHA	30	1	5	6	16	....	....	....	....	....

MANSON, DAVE **MTL.**

Defense. Shoots left. 6'2", 219 lbs. Born, Prince Albert, Sask., January 27, 1967.
(Chicago's 1st choice, 11th overall, in 1985 Entry Draft).

			Regular Season					Playoffs				
Season	Club	Lea	GP	G	A	TP	PIM	GP	G	A	TP	PIM
1983-84	Prince Albert	WHL	70	2	7	9	233	5	0	0	0	4
1984-85	Prince Albert	WHL	72	8	30	38	247	13	1	0	1	34
1985-86	Prince Albert	WHL	70	14	34	48	177	20	1	8	9	63
1986-87	**Chicago**	**NHL**	**63**	**1**	**8**	**9**	**146**	**3**	**0**	**0**	**0**	**10**
1987-88	**Chicago**	**NHL**	**54**	**1**	**6**	**7**	**185**	**5**	**0**	**0**	**0**	**27**
	Saginaw	IHL	6	0	3	3	37	....	....	....	....	....
1988-89	**Chicago**	**NHL**	**79**	**18**	**36**	**54**	**352**	**16**	**0**	**8**	**8**	**84**
1989-90	**Chicago**	**NHL**	**59**	**5**	**23**	**28**	**301**	**20**	**2**	**4**	**6**	**46**
1990-91	**Chicago**	**NHL**	**75**	**14**	**15**	**29**	**191**	**6**	**0**	**1**	**1**	**36**
1991-92	**Edmonton**	**NHL**	**79**	**15**	**32**	**47**	**220**	**16**	**3**	**9**	**12**	**44**
1992-93	**Edmonton**	**NHL**	**83**	**15**	**30**	**45**	**210**	....	....	....	....	....
1993-94	**Edmonton**	**NHL**	**57**	**3**	**13**	**16**	**140**	....	....	....	....	....
	Winnipeg	**NHL**	**13**	**1**	**4**	**5**	**51**	....	....	....	....	....
1994-95	**Winnipeg**	**NHL**	**44**	**3**	**15**	**18**	**139**	....	....	....	....	....
1995-96	**Winnipeg**	**NHL**	**82**	**7**	**23**	**30**	**205**	**6**	**2**	**1**	**3**	**30**
1996-97	**Phoenix**	**NHL**	**66**	**3**	**17**	**20**	**164**	....	....	....	....	....
	Montreal	**NHL**	**9**	**1**	**1**	**2**	**23**	**5**	**0**	**0**	**0**	**17**
1997-98	**Montreal**	**NHL**	**81**	**4**	**30**	**34**	**122**	**10**	**0**	**1**	**1**	**14**
	NHL Totals		**844**	**91**	**253**	**344**	**2449**	**87**	**7**	**24**	**31**	**308**

WHL East Second All-Star Team (1986)

Played in NHL All-Star Game (1989, 1993)

Traded to **Edmonton** by **Chicago** with Chicago's 3rd round choice (Kirk Maltby) in 1992 Entry Draft for Steve Smith, October 2, 1991. Traded to **Winnipeg** by **Edmonton** with St. Louis' 6th round choice (previously acquired, Winnipeg selected Chris Kibermanis) in 1994 Entry Draft for Boris Mironov, Mats Lindgren, Winnipeg's 1st round choice (Jason Bonsignore) in 1994 Entry Draft and Florida's 4th round choice (previously acquired, Edmonton selected Adam Copeland) in 1994 Entry Draft, March 15, 1994. Transferred to **Phoenix** after **Winnipeg** franchise relocated, July 1, 1996. Traded to **Montreal** by **Phoenix** for Murray Baron and Chris Murray, March 18, 1997.

MARA, PAUL (MA-rah) **T.B.**

Defense. Shoots left. 6'4", 202 lbs. Born, Ridgewood, NJ, September 7, 1979.
(Tampa Bay's 1st choice, 7th overall, in 1997 Entry Draft).

			Regular Season					Playoffs				
Season	Club	Lea	GP	G	A	TP	PIM	GP	G	A	TP	PIM
1996-97	Sudbury	OHL	44	9	34	43	61	....	....	....	....	....
1997-98	Sudbury	OHL	25	8	18	26	79	....	....	....	....	....
	Plymouth	OHL	25	8	15	23	30	15	3	14	17	30

MARA, ROB (MA-rah) **CHI.**

Right wing. Shoots right. 6'1", 175 lbs. Born, Boston, MA, September 25, 1975.
(Chicago's 10th choice, 263rd overall, in 1994 Entry Draft).

			Regular Season					Playoffs				
Season	Club	Lea	GP	G	A	TP	PIM	GP	G	A	TP	PIM
1993-94	Belmont Hill	H.S.	28	18	28	46	....	....	....	....	....	....
1994-95	Colgate	ECAC	33	6	8	14	33	....	....	....	....	....
1995-96	Colgate	ECAC	33	8	6	14	36	....	....	....	....	....
1996-97	Colgate	ECAC	32	18	15	33	44	....	....	....	....	....
1997-98	Colgate	ECAC	32	13	11	24	66	....	....	....	....	....

MARCHAND, HUGO (mahr-SHAHNT) **TOR.**

Defense. Shoots left. 6'4", 210 lbs. Born, Montreal, Que., July 16, 1979.
(Toronto's 5th choice, 165th overall, in 1997 Entry Draft).

			Regular Season					Playoffs				
Season	Club	Lea	GP	G	A	TP	PIM	GP	G	A	TP	PIM
1996-97	Victoriaville	QMJHL	61	0	4	4	101	6	0	0	0	6
1997-98	Victoriaville	QMJHL	58	2	3	5	119	6	0	0	0	0

MARCHANT, TERRY (mahr-SHAHNT) **EDM.**

Left wing. Shoots left. 6'2", 205 lbs. Born, Buffalo, NY, February 24, 1976.
(Edmonton's 9th choice, 136th overall, in 1994 Entry Draft).

			Regular Season					Playoffs				
Season	Club	Lea	GP	G	A	TP	PIM	GP	G	A	TP	PIM
1993-94	Niagara Scenics	NAJHL	42	27	40	67	43	....	....	....	....	....
1994-95	Lake Superior	CCHA	23	2	5	7	12	....	....	....	....	....
1995-96	Lake Superior	CCHA	36	8	5	13	15	....	....	....	....	....
1996-97	Lake Superior	CCHA	38	12	14	26	26	....	....	....	....	....
1997-98	Lake Superior	CCHA	36	17	22	39	24	....	....	....	....	....

CCHA Second All-Star Team (1998)

MARCHANT, TODD (mahr-SHAHNT) EDM.

Center. Shoots left. 5'10", 178 lbs. Born, Buffalo, NY, August 12, 1973.
(NY Rangers' 8th choice, 164th overall, in 1993 Entry Draft).

			Regular Season					Playoffs				
Season	Club	Lea	GP	G	A	TP	PIM	GP	G	A	TP	PIM
1991-92	Clarkson	ECAC	32	20	12	32	32	....	....	....	....	....
1992-93	Clarkson	ECAC	33	18	28	46	38	....	....	....	....	....
1993-94	United States	Nat-Tm	59	28	39	67	48	....	....	....	....	....
	United States	Olympics	8	1	1	2	6	....	....	....	....	....
	NY Rangers	**NHL**	**1**	**0**	**0**	**0**	**0**	....	....	....	....	....
	Binghamton	AHL	8	2	7	9	6	....	....	....	....	....
	Edmonton	**NHL**	**3**	**0**	**1**	**1**	**2**	....	....	....	....	....
	Cape Breton	AHL	3	1	4	5	2	5	1	1	2	0
1994-95	Cape Breton	AHL	38	22	25	47	25	....	....	....	....	....
	Edmonton	**NHL**	**45**	**13**	**14**	**27**	**32**	....	....	....	....	....
1995-96	**Edmonton**	**NHL**	**81**	**19**	**19**	**38**	**66**	....	....	....	....	....
1996-97	**Edmonton**	**NHL**	**79**	**14**	**19**	**33**	**44**	**12**	**4**	**2**	**6**	**12**
1997-98	**Edmonton**	**NHL**	**76**	**14**	**21**	**35**	**71**	**12**	**1**	**1**	**2**	**10**
	NHL Totals		**285**	**60**	**74**	**134**	**215**	**24**	**5**	**3**	**8**	**22**

ECAC Second All-Star Team (1993)

Traded to **Edmonton** by **NY Rangers** for Craig MacTavish, March 21, 1994.

MARCHMENT, BRYAN (MAHRCH-mehnt) S.J.

Defense. Shoots left. 6'1", 205 lbs. Born, Scarborough, Ont., May 1, 1969.
(Winnipeg's 1st choice, 16th overall, in 1987 Entry Draft).

			Regular Season					Playoffs				
Season	Club	Lea	GP	G	A	TP	PIM	GP	G	A	TP	PIM
1985-86	Belleville	OHL	57	5	15	20	225	21	0	7	7	83
1986-87	Belleville	OHL	52	6	38	44	238	6	0	4	4	17
1987-88	Belleville	OHL	56	7	51	58	200	6	1	3	4	19
1988-89	Belleville	OHL	43	14	36	50	118	5	0	1	1	12
	Winnipeg	**NHL**	**2**	**0**	**0**	**0**	**2**	....	....	....	....	....
1989-90	**Winnipeg**	**NHL**	**7**	**0**	**2**	**2**	**28**	....	....	....	....	....
	Moncton	AHL	56	4	19	23	217	....	....	....	....	....
1990-91	**Winnipeg**	**NHL**	**28**	**2**	**2**	**4**	**91**	....	....	....	....	....
	Moncton	AHL	33	2	11	13	101	....	....	....	....	....
1991-92	**Chicago**	**NHL**	**58**	**5**	**10**	**15**	**168**	**16**	**1**	**0**	**1**	**36**
1992-93	**Chicago**	**NHL**	**78**	**5**	**15**	**20**	**313**	**4**	**0**	**0**	**0**	**12**
1993-94	**Chicago**	**NHL**	**13**	**1**	**4**	**5**	**42**	....	....	....	....	....
	Hartford	**NHL**	**42**	**3**	**7**	**10**	**124**	....	....	....	....	....
1994-95	**Edmonton**	**NHL**	**40**	**1**	**5**	**6**	**184**	....	....	....	....	....
1995-96	**Edmonton**	**NHL**	**78**	**3**	**15**	**18**	**202**	....	....	....	....	....
1996-97	**Edmonton**	**NHL**	**71**	**3**	**13**	**16**	**132**	**3**	**0**	**0**	**0**	**4**
1997-98	**Edmonton**	**NHL**	**27**	**0**	**4**	**4**	**58**	....	....	....	....	....
	Tampa Bay	**NHL**	**22**	**2**	**4**	**6**	**43**	....	....	....	....	....
	San Jose	**NHL**	**12**	**0**	**3**	**3**	**43**	**6**	**0**	**0**	**0**	**10**
	NHL Totals		**478**	**25**	**84**	**109**	**1430**	**29**	**1**	**0**	**1**	**62**

OHL Second All-Star Team (1989)

Traded to **Chicago** by **Winnipeg** with Chris Norton for Troy Murray and Warren Rychel, July 22, 1991. Traded to **Hartford** by **Chicago** with Steve Larmer for Eric Weinrich and Patrick Poulin, November 2, 1993. Transferred to **Edmonton** from **Hartford** as compensation for Hartford's signing of free agent Steven Rice, August 30, 1994. Traded to **Tampa Bay** by **Edmonton** with Steve Kelly and Jason Bonsignore for Roman Hamrlik and Paul Comrie, December 30, 1997. Traded to **San Jose** by **Tampa Bay** with David Shaw and Tampa Bay's 1st round choice (later traded to Nashville - Nashville selected David Legwand) in 1998 Entry Draft for Andrei Nazarov and Florida's 1st round choice (previously acquired, Tampa Bay selected Vincent Lecavallier) in 1998 Entry Draft, March 24, 1998.

MARHA, JOSEF (MAHR-hah) ANA.

Center. Shoots left. 6', 176 lbs. Born, Havlickuv Brod, Czech., June 2, 1976.
(Quebec's 3rd choice, 35th overall, in 1994 Entry Draft).

			Regular Season					Playoffs				
Season	Club	Lea	GP	G	A	TP	PIM	GP	G	A	TP	PIM
1992-93	Dukla Jihlava	Czech.	7	2	2	4	....	....	....	....	....	....
1993-94	Dukla Jihlava	Cze-Rep.	41	7	2	9	....	3	0	1	1	....
1994-95	Dukla Jihlava	Cze-Rep.	35	3	7	10	6	....	....	....	....	....
1995-96	**Colorado**	**NHL**	**2**	**0**	**1**	**1**	**0**	....	....	....	....	....
	Cornwall	AHL	74	18	30	48	30	8	1	2	3	10
1996-97	**Colorado**	**NHL**	**6**	**0**	**1**	**1**	**0**	....	....	....	....	....
	Hershey	AHL	67	23	49	72	44	19	6	*16	*22	10
1997-98	**Colorado**	**NHL**	**11**	**2**	**5**	**7**	**4**	....	....	....	....	....
	Hershey	AHL	55	6	46	52	30	....	....	....	....	....
	Anaheim	**NHL**	**12**	**7**	**4**	**11**	**0**	....	....	....	....	....
	NHL Totals		**31**	**9**	**11**	**20**	**4**	....	....	....	....	....

Rights transferred to **Colorado** after **Quebec** franchise relocated, June 21, 1995. Traded to **Anaheim** by **Colorado** for Warren Rychel and future considerations, March 24, 1998.

MARINUCCI, CHRIS (mair-ihn-OO-chee)

Center. Shoots left. 6', 188 lbs. Born, Grand Rapids, MN, December 29, 1971.
(NY Islanders' 4th choice, 90th overall, in 1990 Entry Draft).

			Regular Season					Playoffs				
Season	Club	Lea	GP	G	A	TP	PIM	GP	G	A	TP	PIM
1989-90	Grand Rapids	H.S.	28	24	39	63	12	....	....	....	....	....
1990-91	U. Minn-Duluth	WCHA	36	6	10	16	20	....	....	....	....	....
1991-92	U. Minn-Duluth	WCHA	37	6	13	19	41	....	....	....	....	....
1992-93	U. Minn-Duluth	WCHA	40	35	42	77	52	....	....	....	....	....
1993-94	U. Minn-Duluth	WCHA	38	*30	31	61	65	....	....	....	....	....
1994-95	**NY Islanders**	**NHL**	**12**	**1**	**4**	**5**	**2**	....	....	....	....	....
	Denver	IHL	74	29	40	69	42	14	3	4	7	12
1995-96	Utah	IHL	8	3	5	8	8	....	....	....	....	....
1996-97	Utah	IHL	21	3	13	16	6	....	....	....	....	....
	Los Angeles	**NHL**	**1**	**0**	**0**	**0**	**0**	....	....	....	....	....
	Phoenix	IHL	62	23	29	52	26	....	....	....	....	....
1997-98	Chicago	IHL	78	27	48	75	35	22	7	6	13	12
	NHL Totals		**13**	**1**	**4**	**5**	**2**	....	....	....	....	....

WCHA Second All-Star Team (1993) • WCHA First All-Star Team (1994) • NCAA West First All-American Team (1994) • Won Hobey Baker Memorial Award (Top U.S. Collegiate Player) (1994)

Traded to **LA Kings** by **NY Islanders** for Nick Vachon, November 19, 1996.

MARKKANEN, MIKKO (MAHR-kah-nehn, MEE-koh) S.J.

Right wing. Shoots right. 5'9", 165 lbs. Born, Turku, Finland, January 9, 1977.
(San Jose's 12th choice, 220th overall, in 1995 Entry Draft).

			Regular Season					Playoffs				
Season	Club	Lea	GP	G	A	TP	PIM	GP	G	A	TP	PIM
1994-95	TPS Turku	Fin-Jr.	32	10	8	18	28	....	....	....	....	....
	Kiekko	Finland-2	1	0	1	1	0	....	....	....	....	....
1995-96	TPS Turku	Fin-Jr.	7	2	3	5	16	....	....	....	....	....
	Kiekko	Finland-2	38	9	11	20	34	6	1	1	2	6
1996-97	Kiekko	Finland-2	43	15	3	18	51	....	....	....	....	....
1997-98	TuTo	Finland-2	24	2	4	6	12	....	....	....	....	....
	Nordhorn	Ger-2	21	9	6	15	8	....	....	....	....	....

MARKOV, ANDREI (MAHR-kahf) MTL.

Defense. Shoots left. 6', 185 lbs. Born, Voskresensk, USSR, December 20, 1978.
(Montreal's 6th choice, 162nd overall, in 1998 Entry Draft).

			Regular Season					Playoffs				
Season	Club	Lea	GP	G	A	TP	PIM	GP	G	A	TP	PIM
1995-96	Khimik	CIS	38	0	0	0	14	....	....	....	....	....
1996-97	Khimik	Russia	43	8	4	12	32	2	1	1	2	0
1997-98	Khimik	Russia	43	10	5	15	83	....	....	....	....	....

MARKOV, DANIIL (MAHR-kahf, dan-EEL) TOR.

Defense. Shoots left. 6'1", 196 lbs. Born, Moscow, USSR, July 11, 1976.
(Toronto's 7th choice, 223rd overall, in 1995 Entry Draft).

			Regular Season					Playoffs				
Season	Club	Lea	GP	G	A	TP	PIM	GP	G	A	TP	PIM
1993-94	Spartak	CIS	13	1	0	1	6	1	0	0	0	0
1994-95	Spartak	CIS	39	0	1	1	36	....	....	....	....	....
1995-96	Spartak	CIS	38	2	0	2	12	2	0	0	0	2
1996-97	Spartak	Russia	39	3	6	9	41	....	....	....	....	....
	St. John's	AHL	10	2	4	6	18	11	2	6	8	14
1997-98	**Toronto**	**NHL**	**25**	**2**	**5**	**7**	**28**	....	....	....	....	....
	St. John's	AHL	52	3	23	26	124	2	0	1	1	0
	NHL Totals		**25**	**2**	**5**	**7**	**28**	....	....	....	....	....

MARLEAU, PATRICK (mahr-LOH) S.J.

Center. Shoots left. 6'2", 200 lbs. Born, Swift Current, Sask., September 15, 1979.
(San Jose's 1st choice, 2nd overall, in 1997 Entry Draft).

			Regular Season					Playoffs				
Season	Club	Lea	GP	G	A	TP	PIM	GP	G	A	TP	PIM
1995-96	Seattle	WHL	72	32	42	74	22	5	3	4	7	4
1996-97	Seattle	WHL	71	51	74	125	37	15	7	16	23	12
1997-98	**San Jose**	**NHL**	**74**	**13**	**19**	**32**	**14**	**5**	**0**	**1**	**1**	**0**
	NHL Totals		**74**	**13**	**19**	**32**	**14**	**5**	**0**	**1**	**1**	**0**

WHL West First All-Star Team (1997)

MARSHALL, GRANT DAL.

Right wing. Shoots right. 6'1", 193 lbs. Born, Mississauga, Ont., June 9, 1973.
(Toronto's 2nd choice, 23rd overall, in 1992 Entry Draft).

			Regular Season					Playoffs				
Season	Club	Lea	GP	G	A	TP	PIM	GP	G	A	TP	PIM
1990-91	Ottawa	OHL	26	6	11	17	25	1	0	0	0	0
1991-92	Ottawa	OHL	61	32	51	83	132	11	6	11	17	11
1992-93	Ottawa	OHL	30	14	29	43	83	....	....	....	....	....
	Newmarket	OHL	31	11	25	36	89	7	4	7	11	20
	St. John's	AHL	2	0	0	0	0	2	0	0	0	2
1993-94	St. John's	AHL	67	11	29	40	155	11	1	5	6	17
1994-95	**Dallas**	**NHL**	**2**	**0**	**1**	**1**	**0**	....	....	....	....	....
	Kalamazoo	IHL	61	17	29	46	96	16	9	3	12	27
1995-96	**Dallas**	**NHL**	**70**	**9**	**19**	**28**	**111**	....	....	....	....	....
1996-97	**Dallas**	**NHL**	**56**	**6**	**4**	**10**	**98**	**5**	**0**	**2**	**2**	**8**
1997-98	**Dallas**	**NHL**	**72**	**9**	**10**	**19**	**96**	**17**	**0**	**2**	**2**	***47**
	NHL Totals		**200**	**24**	**34**	**58**	**305**	**22**	**0**	**4**	**4**	**55**

Transferred to **Dallas** from **Toronto** with Peter Zezel as compensation for Toronto's signing of free agent Mike Craig, August 10, 1994.

MARSHALL, JASON ANA.

Defense. Shoots right. 6'2", 200 lbs. Born, Cranbrook, B.C., February 22, 1971.
(St. Louis' 1st choice, 9th overall, in 1989 Entry Draft).

			Regular Season					Playoffs				
Season	Club	Lea	GP	G	A	TP	PIM	GP	G	A	TP	PIM
1988-89	Vernon	BCJHL	48	10	30	40	197	31	6	6	12	14
	Canada	Nat-Tm	2	0	1	1	0	....	....	....	....	....
1989-90	Canada	Nat-Tm	73	1	11	12	57	....	....	....	....	....
1990-91	Tri-City	WHL	59	10	34	44	236	7	1	2	3	20
	Peoria	IHL	....	....	....	....	....	18	0	1	1	48
1991-92	**St. Louis**	**NHL**	**2**	**1**	**0**	**1**	**4**	....	....	....	....	....
	Peoria	IHL	78	4	18	22	178	10	0	1	1	16
1992-93	Peoria	IHL	77	4	16	20	229	4	0	0	0	20
1993-94	Canada	Nat-Tm	41	3	10	13	60	....	....	....	....	....
	Peoria	IHL	20	1	1	2	72	3	2	0	2	2
1994-95	**Anaheim**	**NHL**	**1**	**0**	**0**	**0**	**0**	....	....	....	....	....
	San Diego	IHL	80	7	18	25	218	5	0	1	1	8
1995-96	**Anaheim**	**NHL**	**24**	**0**	**1**	**1**	**42**	....	....	....	....	....
	Baltimore	AHL	57	1	13	14	150	....	....	....	....	....
1996-97	**Anaheim**	**NHL**	**73**	**1**	**9**	**10**	**140**	**7**	**0**	**1**	**1**	**4**
1997-98	**Anaheim**	**NHL**	**72**	**3**	**6**	**9**	**189**	....	....	....	....	....
	NHL Totals		**172**	**5**	**16**	**21**	**375**	**7**	**0**	**1**	**1**	**4**

Traded to **Anaheim** by **St. Louis** for Bill Houlder, August 29, 1994.

MARTIN, CRAIG

Right wing. Shoots right. 6'2", 215 lbs. Born, Amherst, N.S., January 21, 1971.
(Winnipeg's 6th choice, 98th overall, in 1990 Entry Draft).

			Regular Season					Playoffs				
Season	Club	Lea	GP	G	A	TP	PIM	GP	G	A	TP	PIM
1987-88	Hull	QMJHL	66	5	5	10	137	....	....	....	....	....
1988-89	Hull	QMJHL	70	14	29	43	260	....	....	....	....	....
1989-90	Hull	QMJHL	66	14	31	45	299	11	2	1	3	65
1990-91	Hull	QMJHL	18	5	6	11	87	....	....	....	....	....
	St-Hyacinthe	QMJHL	36	8	9	17	166	....	....	....	....	....
1991-92	Moncton	AHL	11	1	1	2	70	....	....	....	....	....
	Fort Wayne	IHL	24	0	0	0	115	....	....	....	....	....
1992-93	Moncton	AHL	64	5	13	18	198	5	0	1	1	22
1993-94	Adirondack	AHL	76	15	24	39	297	12	2	2	4	63
1994-95	**Winnipeg**	**NHL**	**20**	**0**	**1**	**1**	**19**	....	....	....	....	....
	Springfield	AHL	6	0	1	1	21	....	....	....	....	....
1995-96	Springfield	AHL	48	6	5	11	245	8	0	1	1	34
1996-97	**Florida**	**NHL**	**1**	**0**	**0**	**0**	**5**	....	....	....	....	....
	Carolina	AHL	44	1	2	3	239	....	....	....	....	....
	San Antonio	IHL	15	3	3	6	99	6	0	1	1	25
1997-98	Quebec	IHL	24	1	3	4	115	....	....	....	....	....
	San Antonio	IHL	6	1	1	2	21	....	....	....	....	....
	Manitoba	IHL	30	4	3	7	202	1	0	0	0	10
	NHL Totals		**21**	**0**	**1**	**1**	**24**	....	....	....	....	....

Signed as a free agent by **Detroit**, July 28, 1993. Claimed on waivers by **Winnipeg** from **Detroit**, January 20, 1995. Signed as a free agent by **Florida**, August 1, 1996.

MARTIN, JEFF — BUF.

Center. Shoots left. 6'1", 177 lbs. Born, Stratford, Ont., April 26, 1979.
(Buffalo's 4th choice, 75th overall, in 1997 Entry Draft).

			Regular Season					Playoffs				
Season	Club	Lea	GP	G	A	TP	PIM	GP	G	A	TP	PIM
1995-96	Windsor	OHL	63	9	5	14	8	7	1	1	2	4
1996-97	Windsor	OHL	65	24	23	47	37	5	2	0	2	2
1997-98	Windsor	OHL	65	40	54	94	48	....	....	....	....	....

MARTIN, JUSTIN — L.A.

Right wing. Shoots right. 6'4", 210 lbs. Born, Syracuse, NY, May 1, 1975.
(Los Angeles' 8th choice, 172nd overall, in 1993 Entry Draft).

			Regular Season					Playoffs				
Season	Club	Lea	GP	G	A	TP	PIM	GP	G	A	TP	PIM
1993-94	Taft Prep School	H.S.	20	16	10	26	26	....	....	....	....	....
1994-95	U. of Vermont	ECAC	23	4	2	6	20	....	....	....	....	....
1995-96	U. of Vermont	ECAC	28	1	0	1	20	....	....	....	....	....
1996-97	U. of Vermont	ECAC	35	3	6	9	49	....	....	....	....	....
1997-98	U. of Vermont	ECAC	34	8	7	15	45	....	....	....	....	....

MARTIN, MATT — DAL.

Defense. Shoots left. 6'3", 205 lbs. Born, Hamden, CT, April 30, 1971.
(Toronto's 4th choice, 66th overall, in 1989 Entry Draft).

			Regular Season					Playoffs				
Season	Club	Lea	GP	G	A	TP	PIM	GP	G	A	TP	PIM
1988-89	Avon Old Farms	H.S.	25	9	23	32	....	....	....	....	....	....
1989-90	Avon Old Farms	H.S.	STATISTICS NOT AVAILABLE									
1990-91	U. of Maine	H.E.	35	3	12	15	48	....	....	....	....	....
1991-92	U. of Maine	H.E.	30	4	14	18	46	....	....	....	....	....
1992-93	U. of Maine	H.E.	44	6	26	32	88	....	....	....	....	....
	St. John's	AHL	2	0	0	0	2	9	1	5	6	4
1993-94	United States	Nat-Tm	39	7	8	15	127	....	....	....	....	....
	United States	Olympics	8	0	2	2	8	....	....	....	....	....
	Toronto	**NHL**	**12**	**0**	**1**	**1**	**6**	....	....	....	....	....
	St. John's	AHL	12	1	5	6	9	11	1	5	6	33
1994-95	**Toronto**	**NHL**	**15**	**0**	**0**	**0**	**13**	....	....	....	....	....
	St. John's	AHL	49	2	16	18	54	....	....	....	....	....
1995-96	**Toronto**	**NHL**	**13**	**0**	**0**	**0**	**14**	....	....	....	....	....
1996-97	**Toronto**	**NHL**	**36**	**0**	**4**	**4**	**38**	....	....	....	....	....
	St. John's	AHL	12	1	3	4	4	....	....	....	....	....
1997-98	Chicago	IHL	78	7	22	29	95	19	0	5	5	24
	NHL Totals		**76**	**0**	**5**	**5**	**71**	....	....	....	....	....

Signed as a free agent by **Dallas**, July 24, 1998.

MARTIN, MIKE — NYR

Defense. Shoots right. 6'2", 204 lbs. Born, Stratford, Ont., October 27, 1976.
(NY Rangers' 2nd choice, 65th overall, in 1995 Entry Draft).

			Regular Season					Playoffs				
Season	Club	Lea	GP	G	A	TP	PIM	GP	G	A	TP	PIM
1992-93	Windsor	OHL	61	2	7	9	80	....	....	....	....	....
1993-94	Windsor	OHL	64	2	29	31	94	4	1	2	3	4
1994-95	Windsor	OHL	53	9	28	37	79	10	1	3	4	21
1995-96	Windsor	OHL	65	19	48	67	128	7	0	6	6	14
1996-97	Binghamton	AHL	62	2	7	9	45	3	0	1	1	2
1997-98	Hartford	AHL	60	4	11	15	70	4	0	0	0	2

MARTINS, STEVE — OTT.

Center. Shoots left. 5'9", 175 lbs. Born, Gatineau, Que., April 13, 1972.
(Hartford's 1st choice, 5th overall, in 1994 Supplemental Draft).

			Regular Season					Playoffs				
Season	Club	Lea	GP	G	A	TP	PIM	GP	G	A	TP	PIM
1991-92	Harvard	ECAC	20	13	14	27	26	....	....	....	....	....
1992-93	Harvard	ECAC	18	6	8	14	40	....	....	....	....	....
1993-94	Harvard	ECAC	32	25	35	60	*93	....	....	....	....	....
1994-95	Harvard	ECAC	28	15	23	38	93	....	....	....	....	....
1995-96	**Hartford**	**NHL**	**23**	**1**	**3**	**4**	**8**	....	....	....	....	....
	Springfield	AHL	30	9	20	29	10	....	....	....	....	....
1996-97	**Hartford**	**NHL**	**2**	**0**	**1**	**1**	**0**	....	....	....	....	....
	Springfield	AHL	63	12	31	43	78	17	1	3	4	26
1997-98	**Carolina**	**NHL**	**3**	**0**	**0**	**0**	**0**	....	....	....	....	....
	Chicago	IHL	78	20	41	61	122	21	6	14	20	28
	NHL Totals		**28**	**1**	**4**	**5**	**8**	....	....	....	....	....

ECAC First All-Star Team (1994) • NCAA East First All-American Team (1994) • NCAA Final Four All-Tournament Team (1994)

Transferred to **Carolina** after **Hartford** franchise relocated, June 25, 1997. Signed as a free agent by **Ottawa**, July 20, 1998.

MARTONE, MIKE (mahr-TOHN) — PHX.

Defense. Shoots right. 6'2", 200 lbs. Born, Sault Ste. Marie, Ont., September 26, 1977.
(Buffalo's 6th choice, 106th overall, in 1996 Entry Draft).

			Regular Season					Playoffs				
Season	Club	Lea	GP	G	A	TP	PIM	GP	G	A	TP	PIM
1994-95	Peterborough	OHL	62	3	9	12	99	10	0	2	2	4
1995-96	Peterborough	OHL	64	3	12	15	127	24	7	5	12	37
1996-97	Peterborough	OHL	50	9	21	30	104	10	0	6	6	30
1997-98	Peterborough	OHL	48	5	17	22	88	4	0	2	2	10

Signed as a free agent by **Phoenix**, August 12, 1998.

MARTYNYUK, DENIS — VAN.

Left wing. Shoots left. 6'3", 190 lbs. Born, Kapfenberg, Austria, July 26, 1979.
(Vancouver's 11th choice, 201st overall, in 1997 Entry Draft).

			Regular Season					Playoffs				
Season	Club	Lea	GP	G	A	TP	PIM	GP	G	A	TP	PIM
1994-95	CSKA Moscow	Rus-Jr.	34	25	25	50	20	....	....	....	....	....
1995-96	CSKA Moscow	Rus-Jr.	36	10	15	25	20	....	....	....	....	....
	CSKA Moscow 2	Russia-2	25	2	5	7	20	....	....	....	....	....
1996-97	CSKA Moscow 2	Russia-3	41	7	4	11	12	....	....	....	....	....
	CSKA Moscow	Russia	3	1	0	1	0	....	....	....	....	....
1997-98	Spartak-2	Russia-3	45	9	5	14	34	....	....	....	....	....

MATHIEU, ALEXANDRE (mah-TYOO) — PIT.

Left wing. Shoots left. 6'1", 176 lbs. Born, Repentigny, Que., February 12, 1979.
(Pittsburgh's 4th choice, 97th overall, in 1997 Entry Draft).

			Regular Season					Playoffs				
Season	Club	Lea	GP	G	A	TP	PIM	GP	G	A	TP	PIM
1996-97	Halifax	QMJHL	70	12	22	34	16	18	2	5	7	2
1997-98	Halifax	QMJHL	68	35	41	76	52	5	1	1	2	4

MATTE, CHRISTIAN — COL.

Right wing. Shoots right. 5'11", 170 lbs. Born, Hull, Que., January 20, 1975.
(Quebec's 8th choice, 153rd overall, in 1993 Entry Draft).

			Regular Season					Playoffs				
Season	Club	Lea	GP	G	A	TP	PIM	GP	G	A	TP	PIM
1992-93	Granby	QMJHL	68	17	36	53	59	....	....	....	....	....
1993-94	Granby	QMJHL	59	50	47	97	103	7	5	5	10	12
	Cornwall	AHL	1	0	0	0	0	....	....	....	....	....
1994-95	Granby	QMJHL	66	50	66	116	86	13	11	7	18	12
	Cornwall	AHL	....	....	....	....	....	3	0	1	1	2
1995-96	Cornwall	AHL	64	20	32	52	51	7	1	1	2	6
1996-97	**Colorado**	**NHL**	**5**	**1**	**1**	**2**	**0**	....	....	....	....	....
	Hershey	AHL	49	18	18	36	78	22	8	3	11	25
1997-98	**Colorado**	**NHL**	**5**	**0**	**0**	**0**	**6**	....	....	....	....	....
	Hershey	AHL	71	33	40	73	109	7	3	2	5	4
	NHL Totals		**10**	**1**	**1**	**2**	**6**	....	....	....	....	....

QMJHL Second All-Star Team (1994)

Rights transferred to **Colorado** after **Quebec** franchise relocated, June 21, 1995.

MATTEAU, STEPHANE (mah-TOH) — S.J.

Left wing. Shoots left. 6'4", 220 lbs. Born, Rouyn-Noranda, Que., September 2, 1969.
(Calgary's 2nd choice, 25th overall, in 1987 Entry Draft).

			Regular Season					Playoffs				
Season	Club	Lea	GP	G	A	TP	PIM	GP	G	A	TP	PIM
1985-86	Hull	QMJHL	60	6	8	14	19	4	0	0	0	0
1986-87	Hull	QMJHL	69	27	48	75	113	8	3	7	10	8
1987-88	Hull	QMJHL	57	17	40	57	179	18	5	14	19	94
1988-89	Hull	QMJHL	59	44	45	89	202	9	8	6	14	30
	Salt Lake	IHL	....	....	....	....	....	9	0	4	4	13
1989-90	Salt Lake	IHL	81	23	35	58	130	10	6	3	9	38
1990-91	**Calgary**	**NHL**	**78**	**15**	**19**	**34**	**93**	**5**	**0**	**1**	**1**	**0**
1991-92	**Calgary**	**NHL**	**4**	**1**	**0**	**1**	**19**	....	....	....	....	....
	Chicago	**NHL**	**20**	**5**	**8**	**13**	**45**	**18**	**4**	**6**	**10**	**24**
1992-93	**Chicago**	**NHL**	**79**	**15**	**18**	**33**	**98**	**3**	**0**	**1**	**1**	**2**
1993-94	**Chicago**	**NHL**	**65**	**15**	**16**	**31**	**55**	....	....	....	....	....
	NY Rangers	**NHL**	**12**	**4**	**3**	**7**	**2**	**23**	**6**	**3**	**9**	**20** ♦
1994-95	**NY Rangers**	**NHL**	**41**	**3**	**5**	**8**	**25**	**9**	**0**	**1**	**1**	**10**
1995-96	**NY Rangers**	**NHL**	**32**	**4**	**2**	**6**	**22**	....	....	....	....	....
	St. Louis	**NHL**	**46**	**7**	**13**	**20**	**65**	**11**	**0**	**2**	**2**	**8**
1996-97	**St. Louis**	**NHL**	**74**	**16**	**20**	**36**	**50**	**5**	**0**	**0**	**0**	**0**
1997-98	**San Jose**	**NHL**	**73**	**15**	**14**	**29**	**60**	**4**	**0**	**1**	**1**	**0**
	NHL Totals		**524**	**100**	**118**	**218**	**534**	**78**	**10**	**15**	**25**	**64**

Traded to **Chicago** by **Calgary** for Trent Yawney, December 16, 1991. Traded to **NY Rangers** by **Chicago** with Brian Noonan for Tony Amonte and the rights to Matt Oates, March 21, 1994. Traded to **St. Louis** by **NY Rangers** for Ian Laperriere, December 28, 1995. Traded to **San Jose** by **St. Louis** for Darren Turcotte, July 24, 1997.

MATTSSON, JESPER (MAT-suhn) — CGY.

Center. Shoots right. 6', 185 lbs. Born, Malmo, Sweden, May 13, 1975.
(Calgary's 1st choice, 18th overall, in 1993 Entry Draft).

			Regular Season					Playoffs				
Season	Club	Lea	GP	G	A	TP	PIM	GP	G	A	TP	PIM
1991-92	Malmo IF	Sweden	24	0	1	1	2	....	....	....	....	....
1992-93	Malmo IF	Sweden	40	9	8	17	14	5	0	0	0	0
1993-94	Malmo IF	Sweden	40	3	6	9	14	9	1	2	3	2
1994-95	Malmo IF	Sweden	37	9	6	15	18	9	2	0	2	18
1995-96	Saint John	AHL	73	12	26	38	18	9	1	1	2	2
1996-97	Saint John	AHL	72	22	18	40	32	3	1	1	2	0
1997-98	Saint John	AHL	29	7	11	18	30	....	....	....	....	....
	Malmo IF	Sweden	16	3	5	8	8	....	....	....	....	....

MATVICHUK, RICHARD (MAT-vih-chuhk) DAL.

Defense. Shoots left. 6'2", 200 lbs. Born, Edmonton, Alta., February 5, 1973.
(Minnesota's 1st choice, 8th overall, in 1991 Entry Draft).

			Regular Season					Playoffs				
Season	**Club**	**Lea**	**GP**	**G**	**A**	**TP**	**PIM**	**GP**	**G**	**A**	**TP**	**PIM**
1989-90	Saskatoon	WHL	56	8	24	32	126	10	2	8	10	16
1990-91	Saskatoon	WHL	68	13	36	49	117	....	....	....	....	....
1991-92	Saskatoon	WHL	58	14	40	54	126	22	1	9	10	61
1992-93	**Minnesota**	**NHL**	**53**	**2**	**3**	**5**	**26**	....	....	....	....	....
	Kalamazoo	IHL	3	0	1	1	6	....	....	....	....	....
1993-94	**Dallas**	**NHL**	**25**	**0**	**3**	**3**	**22**	**7**	**1**	**1**	**2**	**12**
	Kalamazoo	IHL	43	8	17	25	84	....	....	....	....	....
1994-95	**Dallas**	**NHL**	**14**	**0**	**2**	**2**	**14**	**5**	**0**	**2**	**2**	**4**
	Kalamazoo	IHL	17	0	6	6	16	....	....	....	....	....
1995-96	**Dallas**	**NHL**	**73**	**6**	**16**	**22**	**71**	....	....	....	....	....
1996-97	**Dallas**	**NHL**	**57**	**5**	**7**	**12**	**87**	**7**	**0**	**1**	**1**	**20**
1997-98	**Dallas**	**NHL**	**74**	**3**	**15**	**18**	**63**	**16**	**1**	**1**	**2**	**14**
	NHL Totals		**296**	**16**	**46**	**62**	**283**	**35**	**2**	**5**	**7**	**50**

WHL East First All-Star Team (1992)

Transferred to **Dallas** after **Minnesota** franchise relocated, June 9, 1993.

MAY, BRAD VAN.

Left wing. Shoots left. 6'1", 210 lbs. Born, Toronto, Ont., November 29, 1971.
(Buffalo's 1st choice, 14th overall, in 1990 Entry Draft).

			Regular Season					Playoffs				
Season	**Club**	**Lea**	**GP**	**G**	**A**	**TP**	**PIM**	**GP**	**G**	**A**	**TP**	**PIM**
1988-89	Niagara Falls	OHL	65	8	14	22	304	17	0	1	1	55
1989-90	Niagara Falls	OHL	61	32	58	90	223	16	9	13	22	64
1990-91	Niagara Falls	OHL	34	37	32	69	93	14	11	14	25	53
1991-92	**Buffalo**	**NHL**	**69**	**11**	**6**	**17**	**309**	**7**	**1**	**4**	**5**	**2**
1992-93	**Buffalo**	**NHL**	**82**	**13**	**13**	**26**	**242**	**8**	**1**	**1**	**2**	**14**
1993-94	**Buffalo**	**NHL**	**84**	**18**	**27**	**45**	**171**	**7**	**0**	**2**	**2**	**9**
1994-95	**Buffalo**	**NHL**	**33**	**3**	**3**	**6**	**87**	**4**	**0**	**0**	**0**	**2**
1995-96	**Buffalo**	**NHL**	**79**	**15**	**29**	**44**	**295**	....	....	....	....	....
1996-97	**Buffalo**	**NHL**	**42**	**3**	**4**	**7**	**106**	**10**	**1**	**1**	**2**	**32**
1997-98	**Buffalo**	**NHL**	**36**	**4**	**7**	**11**	**113**	....	....	....	....	....
	Vancouver	**NHL**	**27**	**9**	**3**	**12**	**41**	....	....	....	....	....
	NHL Totals		**452**	**76**	**92**	**168**	**1364**	**36**	**3**	**8**	**11**	**59**

OHL Second All-Star Team (1990, 1991)

Traded to **Vancouver** by **Buffalo** with future considerations for Geoff Sanderson, February 4, 1998.

MAYERS, JAMAL ST.L.

Center. Shoots right. 6', 190 lbs. Born, Toronto, Ont., October 24, 1974.
(St. Louis' 3rd choice, 89th overall, in 1993 Entry Draft).

			Regular Season					Playoffs				
Season	**Club**	**Lea**	**GP**	**G**	**A**	**TP**	**PIM**	**GP**	**G**	**A**	**TP**	**PIM**
1991-92	Thornhill	OJHL	56	38	69	107	36	....	....	....	....	....
1992-93	Western Michigan	CCHA	38	8	17	25	26	....	....	....	....	....
1993-94	Western Michigan	CCHA	40	17	32	49	40	....	....	....	....	....
1994-95	Western Michigan	CCHA	39	13	32	45	40	....	....	....	....	....
1995-96	Western Michigan	CCHA	38	17	22	39	75	....	....	....	....	....
1996-97	**St. Louis**	**NHL**	**6**	**0**	**1**	**1**	**2**	....	....	....	....	....
	Worcester	AHL	62	12	14	26	104	5	4	5	9	4
1997-98	Worcester	AHL	61	19	24	43	117	11	3	4	7	10
	NHL Totals		**6**	**0**	**1**	**1**	**2**	....	....	....	....	....

McALLISTER, CHRIS VAN.

Defense. Shoots left. 6'7", 235 lbs. Born, Saskatoon, Sask., June 16, 1975.
(Vancouver's 1st choice, 40th overall, in 1995 Entry Draft).

			Regular Season					Playoffs				
Season	**Club**	**Lea**	**GP**	**G**	**A**	**TP**	**PIM**	**GP**	**G**	**A**	**TP**	**PIM**
1993-94	Saskatoon	WHL	2	0	0	0	5	....	....	....	....	....
1994-95	Saskatoon	WHL	65	2	8	10	134	10	0	0	0	28
1995-96	Syracuse	AHL	68	0	2	2	142	16	0	0	0	34
1996-97	Syracuse	AHL	43	3	1	4	108	3	0	0	0	6
1997-98	**Vancouver**	**NHL**	**36**	**1**	**2**	**3**	**106**	....	....	....	....	....
	Syracuse	AHL	23	0	1	1	71	5	0	0	0	21
	NHL Totals		**36**	**1**	**2**	**3**	**106**	....	....	....	....	....

McALPINE, CHRIS ST.L.

Defense. Shoots right. 6', 210 lbs. Born, Roseville, MN, December 1, 1971.
(New Jersey's 10th choice, 137th overall, in 1990 Entry Draft).

			Regular Season					Playoffs				
Season	**Club**	**Lea**	**GP**	**G**	**A**	**TP**	**PIM**	**GP**	**G**	**A**	**TP**	**PIM**
1989-90	Roseville Prep	H.S.	25	15	13	28	....	....	....	....	....	....
1990-91	U. of Minnesota	WCHA	38	7	9	16	112	....	....	....	....	....
1991-92	U. of Minnesota	WCHA	39	3	9	12	126	....	....	....	....	....
1992-93	U. of Minnesota	WCHA	41	14	9	23	82	....	....	....	....	....
1993-94	U. of Minnesota	WCHA	36	12	18	30	121	....	....	....	....	....
1994-95	Albany	AHL	48	4	18	22	49	....	....	....	....	....
	New Jersey	**NHL**	**24**	**0**	**3**	**3**	**17**	....	....	....	....	.... ♦
1995-96	Albany	AHL	57	5	14	19	72	4	0	0	0	13
1996-97	Albany	AHL	44	1	9	10	48	....	....	....	....	....
	St. Louis	**NHL**	**15**	**0**	**0**	**0**	**24**	**4**	**0**	**1**	**1**	**0**
1997-98	**St. Louis**	**NHL**	**54**	**3**	**7**	**10**	**36**	**10**	**0**	**0**	**0**	**16**
	NHL Totals		**93**	**3**	**10**	**13**	**77**	**14**	**0**	**1**	**1**	**16**

WCHA First All-Star Team (1994) • NCAA West Second All-American Team (1994)

Traded to **St. Louis** by **New Jersey** with New Jersey's 9th round choice in 1999 Entry Draft for Peter Zezel, February 11, 1997.

McAMMOND, DEAN EDM.

Center. Shoots left. 5'11", 200 lbs. Born, Grand Cache, Alta., June 15, 1973.
(Chicago's 1st choice, 22nd overall, in 1991 Entry Draft).

			Regular Season					Playoffs				
Season	**Club**	**Lea**	**GP**	**G**	**A**	**TP**	**PIM**	**GP**	**G**	**A**	**TP**	**PIM**
1989-90	Prince Albert	WHL	53	11	11	22	49	14	2	3	5	18
1990-91	Prince Albert	WHL	71	33	35	68	108	2	0	1	1	6
1991-92	Prince Albert	WHL	63	37	54	91	189	10	12	11	23	26
	Chicago	**NHL**	**5**	**0**	**2**	**2**	**0**	**3**	**0**	**0**	**0**	**2**
1992-93	Prince Albert	WHL	30	19	29	48	44	....	....	....	....	....
	Swift Current	WHL	18	10	13	23	24	17	*16	19	35	20
1993-94	**Edmonton**	**NHL**	**45**	**6**	**21**	**27**	**16**	....	....	....	....	....
	Cape Breton	AHL	28	9	12	21	38	....	....	....	....	....
1994-95	**Edmonton**	**NHL**	**6**	**0**	**0**	**0**	**0**	....	....	....	....	....
1995-96	**Edmonton**	**NHL**	**53**	**15**	**15**	**30**	**23**	....	....	....	....	....
	Cape Breton	AHL	22	9	15	24	55	....	....	....	....	....
1996-97	**Edmonton**	**NHL**	**57**	**12**	**17**	**29**	**28**	....	....	....	....	....
1997-98	**Edmonton**	**NHL**	**77**	**19**	**31**	**50**	**46**	**12**	**1**	**4**	**5**	**12**
	NHL Totals		**243**	**52**	**86**	**138**	**113**	**15**	**1**	**4**	**5**	**14**

Traded to **Edmonton** by **Chicago** with Igor Kravchuk for Joe Murphy, February 24, 1993.

McBAIN, JASON

Defense. Shoots left. 6'2", 180 lbs. Born, Ilion, NY, April 12, 1974.
(Hartford's 5th choice, 81st overall, in 1992 Entry Draft).

			Regular Season					Playoffs				
Season	**Club**	**Lea**	**GP**	**G**	**A**	**TP**	**PIM**	**GP**	**G**	**A**	**TP**	**PIM**
1990-91	Lethbridge	WHL	52	2	7	9	39	1	0	0	0	0
1991-92	Lethbridge	WHL	13	0	1	1	12	....	....	....	....	....
	Portland	WHL	54	9	23	32	95	6	1	0	1	13
1992-93	Portland	WHL	71	9	35	44	76	16	2	12	14	14
1993-94	Portland	WHL	63	15	51	66	86	10	2	7	9	14
1994-95	Springfield	AHL	77	16	28	44	92	....	....	....	....	....
1995-96	**Hartford**	**NHL**	**3**	**0**	**0**	**0**	**0**	....	....	....	....	....
	Springfield	AHL	73	11	33	44	43	8	1	1	2	2
1996-97	**Hartford**	**NHL**	**6**	**0**	**0**	**0**	**0**	....	....	....	....	....
	Springfield	AHL	58	8	26	34	40	16	0	8	8	12
1997-98	Cleveland	IHL	65	8	22	30	62	3	0	2	2	2
	NHL Totals		**9**	**0**	**0**	**0**	**0**	....	....	....	....	....

Transferred to **Carolina** after **Hartford** franchise relocated, June 25, 1997.

McBAIN, MIKE T.B.

Defense. Shoots left. 6'2", 195 lbs. Born, Kimberley, B.C., January 12, 1977.
(Tampa Bay's 2nd choice, 30th overall, in 1995 Entry Draft).

			Regular Season					Playoffs				
Season	**Club**	**Lea**	**GP**	**G**	**A**	**TP**	**PIM**	**GP**	**G**	**A**	**TP**	**PIM**
1993-94	Red Deer	WHL	58	4	13	17	41	4	0	0	0	0
1994-95	Red Deer	WHL	68	6	28	34	55	....	....	....	....	....
1995-96	Red Deer	WHL	68	7	34	41	68	10	1	7	8	10
1996-97	Red Deer	WHL	59	14	35	49	55	15	1	6	7	9
1997-98	**Tampa Bay**	**NHL**	**27**	**0**	**1**	**1**	**8**	....	....	....	....	....
	Adirondack	AHL	42	2	13	15	28	....	....	....	....	....
	NHL Totals		**27**	**0**	**1**	**1**	**8**	....	....	....	....	....

McCABE, BRYAN VAN.

Defense. Shoots left. 6'1", 210 lbs. Born, St. Catharines, Ont., June 8, 1975.
(NY Islanders' 2nd choice, 40th overall, in 1993 Entry Draft).

			Regular Season					Playoffs				
Season	**Club**	**Lea**	**GP**	**G**	**A**	**TP**	**PIM**	**GP**	**G**	**A**	**TP**	**PIM**
1991-92	Medicine Hat	WHL	68	6	24	30	157	4	0	0	0	6
1992-93	Medicine Hat	WHL	14	0	13	13	83	....	....	....	....	....
	Spokane	WHL	46	3	44	47	134	6	1	5	6	28
1993-94	Spokane	WHL	64	22	62	84	218	3	0	4	4	4
1994-95	Spokane	WHL	42	14	39	53	115	....	....	....	....	....
	Brandon	WHL	20	6	10	16	38	18	4	13	17	59
1995-96	**NY Islanders**	**NHL**	**82**	**7**	**16**	**23**	**156**	....	....	....	....	....
1996-97	**NY Islanders**	**NHL**	**82**	**8**	**20**	**28**	**165**	....	....	....	....	....
1997-98	**NY Islanders**	**NHL**	**56**	**3**	**9**	**12**	**145**	....	....	....	....	....
	Vancouver	**NHL**	**26**	**1**	**11**	**12**	**64**	....	....	....	....	....
	NHL Totals		**246**	**19**	**56**	**75**	**530**	....	....	....	....	....

WHL West Second All-Star Team (1993) • WHL West First All-Star Team (1994) • WHL East First All-Star Team (1995) • Memorial Cup All-Star Team (1995)

Traded to **Vancouver** by **NY Islanders** with Todd Bertuzzi and NY Islanders' 3rd round choice (Jarkko Ruutu) in 1998 Entry Draft for Trevor Linden, February 6, 1998.

McCALLUM, SCOTT PHX.

Defense. Shoots left. 6'3", 220 lbs. Born, Dauphin, Man., February 15, 1979.
(Phoenix's 2nd choice, 96th overall, in 1997 Entry Draft).

			Regular Season					Playoffs				
Season	**Club**	**Lea**	**GP**	**G**	**A**	**TP**	**PIM**	**GP**	**G**	**A**	**TP**	**PIM**
1995-96	Tri-City	WHL	45	1	1	2	27	6	0	0	0	0
1996-97	Tri-City	WHL	56	1	16	17	119	....	....	....	....	....
1997-98	Tri-City	WHL	9	0	3	3	18	....	....	....	....	....
	Brandon	WHL	32	1	7	8	52	10	0	2	2	14

McCAMBRIDGE, KEITH

Defense. Shoots left. 6'2", 205 lbs. Born, Thompson, Man., February 1, 1974.
(Calgary's 10th choice, 201st overall, in 1994 Entry Draft).

			Regular Season					Playoffs				
Season	**Club**	**Lea**	**GP**	**G**	**A**	**TP**	**PIM**	**GP**	**G**	**A**	**TP**	**PIM**
1991-92	Swift Current	WHL	72	1	4	5	84	8	0	0	0	2
1992-93	Swift Current	WHL	70	0	6	6	87	17	0	1	1	27
1993-94	Swift Current	WHL	71	0	10	10	179	7	0	0	0	4
1994-95	Swift Current	WHL	48	5	7	12	120	....	....	....	....	....
	Kamloops	WHL	21	0	6	6	90	21	0	5	5	49
1995-96	Saint John	AHL	48	1	3	4	89	16	0	0	0	6
1996-97	Saint John	AHL	56	2	1	3	109	....	....	....	....	....
1997-98	Saint John	AHL	56	4	4	8	118	....	....	....	....	....
	Las Vegas	IHL	10	0	1	1	16	4	0	0	0	9

McCARTHY, SANDY — T.B.

Right wing. Shoots right. 6'3", 225 lbs. Born, Toronto, Ont., June 15, 1972.
(Calgary's 3rd choice, 52nd overall, in 1991 Entry Draft).

			Regular Season					Playoffs				
Season	**Club**	**Lea**	**GP**	**G**	**A**	**TP**	**PIM**	**GP**	**G**	**A**	**TP**	**PIM**
1989-90	Laval	QMJHL	65	10	11	21	269	14	3	3	6	60
1990-91	Laval	QMJHL	68	21	19	40	297	13	6	5	11	67
1991-92	Laval	QMJHL	62	39	51	90	326	8	4	5	9	81
1992-93	Salt Lake	IHL	77	18	20	38	220	....	....	....	....	....
1993-94	**Calgary**	**NHL**	**79**	**5**	**5**	**10**	**173**	**7**	**0**	**0**	**0**	**34**
1994-95	**Calgary**	**NHL**	**37**	**5**	**3**	**8**	**101**	**6**	**0**	**1**	**1**	**17**
1995-96	**Calgary**	**NHL**	**75**	**9**	**7**	**16**	**173**	**4**	**0**	**0**	**0**	**10**
1996-97	**Calgary**	**NHL**	**33**	**3**	**5**	**8**	**113**	....	....	....	....	....
1997-98	**Calgary**	**NHL**	**52**	**8**	**5**	**13**	**170**	....	....	....	....	....
	Tampa Bay	**NHL**	**14**	**0**	**5**	**5**	**71**	....	....	....	....	....
	NHL Totals		**290**	**30**	**30**	**60**	**801**	**17**	**0**	**1**	**1**	**61**

Traded to **Tampa Bay** by **Calgary** with Calgary's 3rd (Brad Richards) and 5th (Curtis Rich) round choices in 1998 Entry Draft for Jason Wiemer, March 24, 1998.

McCARTY, DARREN — DET.

Right wing. Shoots right. 6'1", 210 lbs. Born, Burnaby, B.C., April 1, 1972.
(Detroit's 2nd choice, 46th overall, in 1992 Entry Draft).

			Regular Season					Playoffs				
Season	**Club**	**Lea**	**GP**	**G**	**A**	**TP**	**PIM**	**GP**	**G**	**A**	**TP**	**PIM**
1989-90	Belleville	OHL	63	12	15	27	142	11	1	1	2	21
1990-91	Belleville	OHL	60	30	37	67	151	6	2	2	4	13
1991-92	Belleville	OHL	65	*55	72	127	177	5	1	4	5	13
1992-93	Adirondack	AHL	73	17	19	36	278	11	0	1	1	33
1993-94	**Detroit**	**NHL**	**67**	**9**	**17**	**26**	**181**	**7**	**2**	**2**	**4**	**8**
1994-95	**Detroit**	**NHL**	**31**	**5**	**8**	**13**	**88**	**18**	**3**	**2**	**5**	**14**
1995-96	**Detroit**	**NHL**	**63**	**15**	**14**	**29**	**158**	**19**	**3**	**2**	**5**	**20**
1996-97	**Detroit**	**NHL**	**68**	**19**	**30**	**49**	**126**	**20**	**3**	**4**	**7**	**34 ♦**
1997-98	**Detroit**	**NHL**	**71**	**15**	**22**	**37**	**157**	**22**	**3**	**8**	**11**	**34 ♦**
	NHL Totals		**300**	**63**	**91**	**154**	**710**	**86**	**14**	**18**	**32**	**110**

OHL First All-Star Team (1992)

McCAULEY, ALYN — TOR.

Center. Shoots left. 5'11", 185 lbs. Born, Brockville, Ont., May 29, 1977.
(New Jersey's 5th choice, 79th overall, in 1995 Entry Draft).

			Regular Season					Playoffs				
Season	**Club**	**Lea**	**GP**	**G**	**A**	**TP**	**PIM**	**GP**	**G**	**A**	**TP**	**PIM**
1993-94	Ottawa	OHL	38	13	23	36	10	13	5	14	19	4
1994-95	Ottawa	OHL	65	16	38	54	20	....	....	....	....	....
1995-96	Ottawa	OHL	55	34	48	82	24	2	0	0	0	0
1996-97	Ottawa	OHL	50	*56	56	112	16	22	14	22	36	14
	St. John's	AHL	....	....	....	....	....	3	0	1	1	0
1997-98	**Toronto**	**NHL**	**60**	**6**	**10**	**16**	**6**	....	....	....	....	....
	NHL Totals		**60**	**6**	**10**	**16**	**6**	....	....	....	....	....

OHL First All-Star Team (1996, 1997) • Canadian Major Junior First All-Star Team (1997) • Canadian Major Junior Player of the Year (1997)

Rights traded to **Toronto** by **New Jersey** with Jason Smith and Steve Sullivan for Doug Gilmour, Dave Ellett and future considerations, February 25, 1997.

McCLEARY, TRENT

Right wing. Shoots right. 6', 180 lbs. Born, Swift Current, Sask., September 8, 1972.

			Regular Season					Playoffs				
Season	**Club**	**Lea**	**GP**	**G**	**A**	**TP**	**PIM**	**GP**	**G**	**A**	**TP**	**PIM**
1989-90	Swift Current	WHL	70	3	15	18	43	4	1	0	1	0
1990-91	Swift Current	WHL	70	16	24	40	53	3	0	0	0	2
1991-92	Swift Current	WHL	72	23	22	45	240	8	1	2	3	16
1992-93	Swift Current	WHL	63	17	33	50	138	17	5	4	9	16
	New Haven	AHL	2	1	0	1	6	....	....	....	....	....
1993-94	P.E.I.	AHL	4	0	0	0	6	....	....	....	....	....
	Thunder Bay	ColHL	51	23	17	40	123	9	2	11	13	15
1994-95	P.E.I.	AHL	51	9	20	29	60	9	2	3	5	26
1995-96	**Ottawa**	**NHL**	**75**	**4**	**10**	**14**	**68**	....	....	....	....	....
1996-97	**Boston**	**NHL**	**59**	**3**	**5**	**8**	**33**	....	....	....	....	....
1997-98	Detroit	IHL	21	1	1	2	45	....	....	....	....	....
	Las Vegas	IHL	54	7	6	13	120	3	1	0	1	2
	NHL Totals		**134**	**7**	**15**	**22**	**101**	....	....	....	....	....

Signed as a free agent by **Ottawa**, October 9, 1992. Traded to **Boston** by **Ottawa** with Ottawa's 3rd round choice (Eric Naud) in 1996 Entry Draft for Shawn McEachern, June 22, 1996.

McCOSH, SHAWN — PHI.

Center. Shoots right. 6', 197 lbs. Born, Oshawa, Ont., June 5, 1969.
(Detroit's 5th choice, 95th overall, in 1989 Entry Draft).

			Regular Season					Playoffs				
Season	**Club**	**Lea**	**GP**	**G**	**A**	**TP**	**PIM**	**GP**	**G**	**A**	**TP**	**PIM**
1986-87	Hamilton	OHL	50	11	17	28	49	6	1	0	1	2
1987-88	Hamilton	OHL	64	17	36	53	96	14	6	8	14	14
1988-89	Niagara Falls	OHL	56	41	62	103	75	14	4	13	17	23
1989-90	Niagara Falls	OHL	9	6	10	16	24	....	....	....	....	....
	Hamilton	OHL	39	24	28	52	65	....	....	....	....	....
1990-91	New Haven	AHL	66	16	21	37	104	....	....	....	....	....
1991-92	**Los Angeles**	**NHL**	**4**	**0**	**0**	**0**	**4**	....	....	....	....	....
	Phoenix	IHL	71	21	32	53	118	....	....	....	....	....
	New Haven	AHL	....	....	....	....	....	5	0	1	1	0
1992-93	Phoenix	IHL	22	9	8	17	36	....	....	....	....	....
	New Haven	AHL	46	22	32	54	54	....	....	....	....	....
1993-94	Binghamton	AHL	75	31	44	75	68	....	....	....	....	....
1994-95	**NY Rangers**	**NHL**	**5**	**1**	**0**	**1**	**2**	....	....	....	....	....
	Binghamton	AHL	67	23	60	83	73	8	3	9	12	6
1995-96	Hershey	AHL	71	31	52	83	82	5	1	5	6	8
1996-97	Philadelphia	AHL	79	30	51	81	110	10	3	9	12	23
1997-98	Philadelphia	AHL	80	24	54	78	102	20	6	13	19	14
	NHL Totals		**9**	**1**	**0**	**1**	**6**	....	....	....	....	....

Traded to **LA Kings** by **Detroit** for LA Kings' 8th round choice (Justin Krall) in 1992 Entry Draft, August 15, 1990. Traded to **Ottawa** by **LA Kings** with Bob Kudelski for Marc Fortier and Jim Thomson, December 19, 1992. Signed as a free agent by **NY Rangers**, July 30, 1993. Signed as a free agent by **Philadelphia**, July 31, 1995.

McDONELL, KENT — CAR.

Right wing. Shoots right. 6', 175 lbs. Born, Cornwall, Ont., March 1, 1979.
(Carolina's 9th choice, 225th overall, in 1997 Entry Draft).

			Regular Season					Playoffs				
Season	**Club**	**Lea**	**GP**	**G**	**A**	**TP**	**PIM**	**GP**	**G**	**A**	**TP**	**PIM**
1996-97	Guelph	OHL	56	7	5	12	57	16	0	2	2	4
1997-98	Guelph	OHL	64	28	23	51	76	12	7	4	11	18

McEACHERN, SHAWN — (muh-GEH-kruhn) OTT.

Left wing. Shoots left. 5'11", 195 lbs. Born, Waltham, MA, February 28, 1969.
(Pittsburgh's 6th choice, 110th overall, in 1987 Entry Draft).

			Regular Season					Playoffs				
Season	**Club**	**Lea**	**GP**	**G**	**A**	**TP**	**PIM**	**GP**	**G**	**A**	**TP**	**PIM**
1986-87	Matignon	H.S.	16	29	28	57	....	....	....	....	....	....
1987-88	Matignon	H.S.	22	52	40	92	....	....	....	....	....	....
1988-89	Boston University	H.E.	36	20	28	48	32	....	....	....	....	....
1989-90	Boston University	H.E.	43	25	31	56	78	....	....	....	....	....
1990-91	Boston University	H.E.	41	34	48	82	43	....	....	....	....	....
1991-92	United States	Nat-Tm	57	26	23	49	38	....	....	....	....	....
	United States	Olympics	8	1	0	1	10	....	....	....	....	....
	Pittsburgh	**NHL**	**15**	**0**	**4**	**4**	**0**	**19**	**2**	**7**	**9**	**4 ♦**
1992-93	**Pittsburgh**	**NHL**	**84**	**28**	**33**	**61**	**46**	**12**	**3**	**2**	**5**	**10**
1993-94	**Los Angeles**	**NHL**	**49**	**8**	**13**	**21**	**24**	....	....	....	....	....
	Pittsburgh	**NHL**	**27**	**12**	**9**	**21**	**10**	**6**	**1**	**0**	**1**	**2**
1994-95	Kiekko	Finland	8	1	3	4	6	....	....	....	....	....
	Pittsburgh	**NHL**	**44**	**13**	**13**	**26**	**22**	**11**	**0**	**2**	**2**	**8**
1995-96	**Boston**	**NHL**	**82**	**24**	**29**	**53**	**34**	**5**	**2**	**1**	**3**	**8**
1996-97	**Ottawa**	**NHL**	**65**	**11**	**20**	**31**	**18**	**7**	**2**	**0**	**2**	**8**
1997-98	**Ottawa**	**NHL**	**81**	**24**	**24**	**48**	**42**	**11**	**0**	**4**	**4**	**8**
	NHL Totals		**447**	**120**	**145**	**265**	**196**	**71**	**10**	**16**	**26**	**48**

Hockey East Second All-Star Team (1990) • Hockey East First All-Star Team (1991) • NCAA East First All-American Team (1991)

Traded to **LA Kings** by **Pittsburgh** for Marty McSorley, August 27, 1993. Traded to **Pittsburgh** by **LA Kings** with Tomas Sandstrom for Marty McSorley and Jim Paek, February 16, 1994. Traded to **Boston** by **Pittsburgh** with Kevin Stevens for Glen Murray, Bryan Smolinski and Boston's 3rd round choice (Boyd Kane) in 1996 Entry Draft, August 2, 1995. Traded to **Ottawa** by **Boston** for Trent McCleary and Ottawa's 3rd round choice (Eric Naud) in 1996 Entry Draft, June 22, 1996.

McGILLIS, DANIEL — PHI.

Defense. Shoots left. 6'2", 225 lbs. Born, Hawkesbury, Ont., July 1, 1972.
(Detroit's 10th choice, 238th overall, in 1992 Entry Draft).

			Regular Season					Playoffs				
Season	**Club**	**Lea**	**GP**	**G**	**A**	**TP**	**PIM**	**GP**	**G**	**A**	**TP**	**PIM**
1991-92	Hawkesbury	OJHL	36	5	19	24	106	....	....	....	....	....
1992-93	Northeastern	H.E.	35	5	12	17	42	....	....	....	....	....
1993-94	Northeastern	H.E.	38	4	25	29	82	....	....	....	....	....
1994-95	Northeastern	H.E.	34	9	22	31	70	....	....	....	....	....
1995-96	Northeastern	H.E.	34	12	24	36	50	....	....	....	....	....
1996-97	**Edmonton**	**NHL**	**73**	**6**	**16**	**22**	**52**	**12**	**0**	**5**	**5**	**24**
1997-98	**Edmonton**	**NHL**	**67**	**10**	**15**	**25**	**74**	....	....	....	....	....
	Philadelphia	**NHL**	**13**	**1**	**5**	**6**	**35**	**5**	**1**	**2**	**3**	**10**
	NHL Totals		**153**	**17**	**36**	**53**	**161**	**17**	**1**	**7**	**8**	**34**

Hockey East First All-Star Team (1995, 1996) • NCAA East First All-American Team (1996)

Traded to **Edmonton** by **Detroit** for Kirk Maltby, March 20, 1996. Traded to **Philadelphia** by **Edmonton** with Edmonton's 2nd round choice (Jason Beckett) in 1998 Entry Draft for Janne Niinimaa, March 24, 1998.

McINNIS, MARTY — CGY.

Center. Shoots right. 5'11", 190 lbs. Born, Hingham, MA., June 2, 1970.
(NY Islanders' 10th choice, 163rd overall, in 1988 Entry Draft).

			Regular Season					Playoffs				
Season	**Club**	**Lea**	**GP**	**G**	**A**	**TP**	**PIM**	**GP**	**G**	**A**	**TP**	**PIM**
1987-88	Milton Academy	H.S.	25	26	25	51	....	....	....	....	....	....
1988-89	Boston College	H.E.	39	13	19	32	8	....	....	....	....	....
1989-90	Boston College	H.E.	41	24	29	53	43	....	....	....	....	....
1990-91	Boston College	H.E.	38	21	36	57	40	....	....	....	....	....
1991-92	United States	Nat-Tm	54	15	19	34	20	....	....	....	....	....
	United States	Olympics	8	5	2	7	4	....	....	....	....	....
	NY Islanders	**NHL**	**15**	**3**	**5**	**8**	**0**	....	....	....	....	....
1992-93	**NY Islanders**	**NHL**	**56**	**10**	**20**	**30**	**24**	**3**	**0**	**1**	**1**	**0**
	Capital District	AHL	10	4	12	16	2	....	....	....	....	....
1993-94	**NY Islanders**	**NHL**	**81**	**25**	**31**	**56**	**24**	**4**	**0**	**0**	**0**	**0**
1994-95	**NY Islanders**	**NHL**	**41**	**9**	**7**	**16**	**8**	....	....	....	....	....
1995-96	**NY Islanders**	**NHL**	**74**	**12**	**34**	**46**	**39**	....	....	....	....	....
1996-97	**NY Islanders**	**NHL**	**70**	**20**	**22**	**42**	**20**	....	....	....	....	....
	Calgary	**NHL**	**10**	**3**	**4**	**7**	**2**	....	....	....	....	....
1997-98	**Calgary**	**NHL**	**75**	**19**	**25**	**44**	**34**	....	....	....	....	....
	NHL Totals		**422**	**101**	**148**	**249**	**151**	**7**	**0**	**1**	**1**	**0**

Traded to **Calgary** by **NY Islanders** with Tyrone Garner and Calgary's 6th round choice (previously acquired, Calgary selected Ilja Demidov) in 1997 Entry Draft for Robert Reichel, March 18, 1997.

McKAY, RANDY — N.J.

Right wing. Shoots right. 6'2", 210 lbs. Born, Montreal, Que., January 25, 1967.
(Detroit's 6th choice, 113th overall, in 1985 Entry Draft).

			Regular Season					Playoffs				
Season	**Club**	**Lea**	**GP**	**G**	**A**	**TP**	**PIM**	**GP**	**G**	**A**	**TP**	**PIM**
1983-84	Lac St-Louis	QAAA	38	18	28	46	62	....	....	....	....	....
1984-85	Michigan Tech	WCHA	25	4	5	9	32	....	....	....	....	....
1985-86	Michigan Tech	WCHA	40	12	22	34	46	....	....	....	....	....
1986-87	Michigan Tech	WCHA	39	5	11	16	46	....	....	....	....	....
1987-88	Michigan Tech	WCHA	41	17	24	41	70	....	....	....	....	....
	Adirondack	AHL	10	0	3	3	12	6	0	4	4	0
1988-89	**Detroit**	**NHL**	**3**	**0**	**0**	**0**	**0**	**2**	**0**	**0**	**0**	**2**
	Adirondack	AHL	58	29	34	63	170	14	4	7	11	60
1989-90	**Detroit**	**NHL**	**33**	**3**	**6**	**9**	**51**	....	....	....	....	....
	Adirondack	AHL	36	16	23	39	99	6	3	0	3	35
1990-91	**Detroit**	**NHL**	**47**	**1**	**7**	**8**	**183**	**5**	**0**	**1**	**1**	**41**
1991-92	**New Jersey**	**NHL**	**80**	**17**	**16**	**33**	**246**	**7**	**1**	**3**	**4**	**10**
1992-93	**New Jersey**	**NHL**	**73**	**11**	**11**	**22**	**206**	**5**	**0**	**0**	**0**	**16**
1993-94	**New Jersey**	**NHL**	**78**	**12**	**15**	**27**	**244**	**20**	**1**	**2**	**3**	**24**
1994-95	**New Jersey**	**NHL**	**33**	**5**	**7**	**12**	**44**	**19**	**8**	**4**	**12**	**11 ♦**
1995-96	**New Jersey**	**NHL**	**76**	**11**	**10**	**21**	**145**	....	....	....	....	....
1996-97	**New Jersey**	**NHL**	**77**	**9**	**18**	**27**	**109**	**10**	**1**	**1**	**2**	**0**
1997-98	**New Jersey**	**NHL**	**74**	**24**	**24**	**48**	**86**	**6**	**0**	**1**	**1**	**0**
	NHL Totals		**574**	**93**	**114**	**207**	**1314**	**74**	**11**	**12**	**23**	**104**

Transferred to **New Jersey** by **Detroit** with Dave Barr as compensation for Detroit's signing of free agent Troy Crowder, September 9, 1991.

McKEE, JAY — BUF.

Defense. Shoots left. 6'3", 195 lbs. Born, Kingston, Ont., September 8, 1977.
(Buffalo's 1st choice, 14th overall, in 1995 Entry Draft).

			Regular Season					Playoffs				
Season	Club	Lea	GP	G	A	TP	PIM	GP	G	A	TP	PIM
1993-94	Sudbury	OHL	51	0	1	1	51	3	0	0	0	0
1994-95	Sudbury	OHL	39	6	6	12	91	....	....	....	....	....
	Niagara Falls	OHL	26	3	13	16	60	6	2	3	5	10
1995-96	Niagara Falls	OHL	64	5	41	46	129	10	1	5	6	16
	Buffalo	**NHL**	**1**	**0**	**1**	**1**	**2**	....	....	....	....	....
	Rochester	AHL	4	0	1	1	15	....	....	....	....	....
1996-97	**Buffalo**	**NHL**	**43**	**1**	**9**	**10**	**35**	**3**	**0**	**0**	**0**	**0**
	Rochester	AHL	7	2	5	7	4	....	....	....	....	....
1997-98	**Buffalo**	**NHL**	**56**	**1**	**13**	**14**	**42**	**1**	**0**	**0**	**0**	**0**
	Rochester	AHL	13	1	7	8	11	....	....	....	....	....
	NHL Totals		**100**	**2**	**23**	**25**	**79**	**4**	**0**	**0**	**0**	**0**

OHL Second All-Star Team (1996)

McKENNA, STEVE — L.A.

Left wing. Shoots left. 6'8", 247 lbs. Born, Toronto, Ont., August 21, 1973.

			Regular Season					Playoffs				
Season	Club	Lea	GP	G	A	TP	PIM	GP	G	A	TP	PIM
1993-94	Merrimack	H.E.	37	1	2	3	74	....	....	....	....	....
1994-95	Merrimack	H.E.	37	1	9	10	74	....	....	....	....	....
1995-96	Merrimack	H.E.	33	3	11	14	67	....	....	....	....	....
1996-97	**Los Angeles**	**NHL**	**9**	**0**	**0**	**0**	**37**	....	....	....	....	....
	Phoenix	IHL	66	6	5	11	187	....	....	....	....	....
1997-98	**Los Angeles**	**NHL**	**62**	**4**	**4**	**8**	**150**	**3**	**0**	**1**	**1**	**8**
	Fredericton	AHL	6	2	1	3	48	....	....	....	....	....
	NHL Totals		**71**	**4**	**4**	**8**	**187**	**3**	**0**	**1**	**1**	**8**

Signed as a free agent by **LA Kings**, May 23, 1996.

McKENZIE, JIM — ANA.

Left wing. Shoots left. 6'3", 205 lbs. Born, Gull Lake, Sask., November 3, 1969.
(Hartford's 3rd choice, 73rd overall, in 1989 Entry Draft).

			Regular Season					Playoffs				
Season	Club	Lea	GP	G	A	TP	PIM	GP	G	A	TP	PIM
1985-86	Moose Jaw	WHL	3	0	2	2	0	....	....	....	....	....
1986-87	Moose Jaw	WHL	65	5	3	8	125	9	0	0	0	7
1987-88	Moose Jaw	WHL	62	1	17	18	134	....	....	....	....	....
1988-89	Victoria	WHL	67	15	27	42	176	8	1	4	5	30
1989-90	**Hartford**	**NHL**	**5**	**0**	**0**	**0**	**4**	....	....	....	....	....
	Binghamton	AHL	56	4	12	16	149	....	....	....	....	....
1990-91	**Hartford**	**NHL**	**41**	**4**	**3**	**7**	**108**	**6**	**0**	**0**	**0**	**8**
	Springfield	AHL	24	3	4	7	102	....	....	....	....	....
1991-92	**Hartford**	**NHL**	**67**	**5**	**1**	**6**	**87**	....	....	....	....	....
1992-93	**Hartford**	**NHL**	**64**	**3**	**6**	**9**	**202**	....	....	....	....	....
1993-94	**Hartford**	**NHL**	**26**	**1**	**2**	**3**	**67**	....	....	....	....	....
	Dallas	**NHL**	**34**	**2**	**3**	**5**	**63**	....	....	....	....	....
	Pittsburgh	**NHL**	**11**	**0**	**0**	**0**	**16**	**3**	**0**	**0**	**0**	**0**
1994-95	**Pittsburgh**	**NHL**	**39**	**2**	**1**	**3**	**63**	**5**	**0**	**0**	**0**	**4**
1995-96	**Winnipeg**	**NHL**	**73**	**4**	**2**	**6**	**202**	**1**	**0**	**0**	**0**	**2**
1996-97	**Phoenix**	**NHL**	**65**	**5**	**3**	**8**	**200**	**7**	**0**	**0**	**0**	**2**
1997-98	**Phoenix**	**NHL**	**64**	**3**	**4**	**7**	**146**	**1**	**0**	**0**	**0**	**0**
	NHL Totals		**489**	**29**	**25**	**54**	**1158**	**23**	**0**	**0**	**0**	**16**

Traded to **Florida** by **Hartford** for Alexander Godynyuk, December 16, 1993. Traded to **Dallas** by **Florida** for Dallas' 4th round choice (later traded to Ottawa — Ottawa selected Kevin Bolibruck) in 1995 Entry Draft, December 16, 1993. Traded to **Pittsburgh** by **Dallas** for Mike Needham, March 21, 1994. Signed as a free agent by **NY Islanders**, August 2, 1995. Claimed by **Winnipeg** from **NY Islanders** in NHL Waiver Draft, October 2, 1995. Transferred to **Phoenix** after **Winnipeg** franchise relocated, July 1, 1996. Traded to **Anaheim** by **Phoenix** for J.F. Jomphe, June 18, 1998.

McKERCHER, JEFF — DAL.

Defense. Shoots right. 6'2", 197 lbs. Born, Cornwall, Ont., January 14, 1979.
(Dallas' 7th choice, 189th overall, in 1997 Entry Draft).

			Regular Season					Playoffs				
Season	Club	Lea	GP	G	A	TP	PIM	GP	G	A	TP	PIM
1996-97	Barrie	OHL	60	1	4	5	32	9	0	1	1	13
1997-98	Barrie	OHL	51	0	2	2	21	6	0	0	0	2

McKIE, RYAN

Defense. Shoots right. 6'2", 198 lbs. Born, Kenora, Ont., March 30, 1978.
(NY Rangers' 7th choice, 211th overall, in 1996 Entry Draft).

			Regular Season					Playoffs				
Season	Club	Lea	GP	G	A	TP	PIM	GP	G	A	TP	PIM
1995-96	London	OHL	65	2	7	9	64	....	....	....	....	....
1996-97	London	OHL	33	2	6	8	40	....	....	....	....	....
	Sudbury	OHL	30	2	7	9	27	....	....	....	....	....
1997-98	Sudbury	OHL	66	8	15	23	116	10	0	2	2	17

McLAREN, KYLE — BOS.

Defense. Shoots left. 6'4", 219 lbs. Born, Humboldt, Sask., June 18, 1977.
(Boston's 1st choice, 9th overall, in 1995 Entry Draft).

			Regular Season					Playoffs				
Season	Club	Lea	GP	G	A	TP	PIM	GP	G	A	TP	PIM
1993-94	Tacoma	WHL	62	1	9	10	53	6	1	4	5	6
1994-95	Tacoma	WHL	47	13	19	32	68	4	1	1	2	4
1995-96	**Boston**	**NHL**	**74**	**5**	**12**	**17**	**73**	**5**	**0**	**0**	**0**	**14**
1996-97	**Boston**	**NHL**	**58**	**5**	**9**	**14**	**54**	....	....	....	....	....
1997-98	**Boston**	**NHL**	**66**	**5**	**20**	**25**	**56**	**6**	**1**	**0**	**1**	**4**
	NHL Totals		**198**	**15**	**41**	**56**	**183**	**11**	**1**	**0**	**1**	**18**

NHL All-Rookie Team (1996)

McLAREN, STEVE — PHI.

Defense. Shoots left. 6', 194 lbs. Born, Owen Sound, Ont., February 3, 1975.
(Chicago's 3rd choice, 85th overall, in 1994 Entry Draft).

			Regular Season					Playoffs				
Season	Club	Lea	GP	G	A	TP	PIM	GP	G	A	TP	PIM
1993-94	North Bay	OHL	55	2	15	17	130	18	0	3	3	50
1994-95	North Bay	OHL	27	3	10	13	119	6	2	1	3	23
1995-96	Indianapolis	IHL	54	1	2	3	170	3	0	0	0	2
1996-97	Indianapolis	IHL	63	2	5	7	309	4	0	0	0	10
1997-98	Indianapolis	IHL	61	3	5	8	208	5	0	0	0	24

Signed as a free agent by **Philadelphia**, August 24, 1998.

McLEOD, GAVIN — OTT.

Defense. Shoots left. 6'4", 187 lbs. Born, Fort Sasaktchewan, Alta., January 1, 1980.
(Ottawa's 6th choice, 130th overall, in 1998 Entry Draft).

			Regular Season					Playoffs				
Season	Club	Lea	GP	G	A	TP	PIM	GP	G	A	TP	PIM
1996-97	Kelowna	WHL	60	0	6	6	44	....	....	....	....	....
1997-98	Kelowna	WHL	70	3	17	20	98	7	0	0	0	14

McMAHON, MARK (muhk-MAN) — CAR.

Defense. Shoots left. 6'1", 179 lbs. Born, Geralton, Ont., February 10, 1978.
(Hartford's 5th choice, 116th overall, in 1996 Entry Draft).

			Regular Season					Playoffs				
Season	Club	Lea	GP	G	A	TP	PIM	GP	G	A	TP	PIM
1995-96	Kitchener	OHL	55	1	8	9	105	5	0	1	1	17
1996-97	Kitchener	OHL	63	4	18	22	155	13	0	6	6	31
1997-98	Kitchener	OHL	61	12	38	50	175	6	1	5	6	27
	New Haven	AHL	4	0	1	1	6	2	0	0	0	16

McNEIL, SHAWN

Center. Shoots left. 5'11", 175 lbs. Born, Pembroke, Ont., March 17, 1978.
(Washington's 6th choice, 78th overall, in 1996 Entry Draft).

			Regular Season					Playoffs				
Season	Club	Lea	GP	G	A	TP	PIM	GP	G	A	TP	PIM
1993-94	Kamloops	WHL	1	0	0	0	0	....	....	....	....	....
1994-95	Kamloops	WHL	43	4	3	7	11	9	0	1	1	0
1995-96	Kamloops	WHL	67	15	30	45	24	16	4	12	16	17
1996-97	Kamloops	WHL	70	38	47	85	37	5	1	3	4	2
1997-98	Red Deer	WHL	72	47	62	109	69	5	1	3	4	9

McSORLEY, MARTY

Defense. Shoots right. 6'1", 235 lbs. Born, Hamilton, Ont., May 18, 1963.

			Regular Season					Playoffs				
Season	Club	Lea	GP	G	A	TP	PIM	GP	G	A	TP	PIM
1981-82	Belleville	OHL	58	6	13	19	234	....	....	....	....	....
1982-83	Belleville	OHL	70	10	41	51	183	4	0	0	0	7
	Baltimore	AHL	2	0	0	0	22	....	....	....	....	....
1983-84	**Pittsburgh**	**NHL**	**72**	**2**	**7**	**9**	**224**	....	....	....	....	....
1984-85	**Pittsburgh**	**NHL**	**15**	**0**	**0**	**0**	**15**	....	....	....	....	....
	Baltimore	AHL	58	6	24	30	154	14	0	7	7	47
1985-86	**Edmonton**	**NHL**	**59**	**11**	**12**	**23**	**265**	**8**	**0**	**2**	**2**	**50**
	Nova Scotia	AHL	9	2	4	6	34	....	....	....	....	....
1986-87	**Edmonton**	**NHL**	**41**	**2**	**4**	**6**	**159**	**21**	**4**	**3**	**7**	**65** ♦
	Nova Scotia	AHL	7	2	2	4	48	....	....	....	....	....
1987-88	**Edmonton**	**NHL**	**60**	**9**	**17**	**26**	**223**	**16**	**0**	**3**	**3**	**67** ♦
1988-89	**Los Angeles**	**NHL**	**66**	**10**	**17**	**27**	**350**	**11**	**0**	**2**	**2**	**33**
1989-90	**Los Angeles**	**NHL**	**75**	**15**	**21**	**36**	**322**	**10**	**1**	**3**	**4**	**18**
1990-91	**Los Angeles**	**NHL**	**61**	**7**	**32**	**39**	**221**	**12**	**0**	**0**	**0**	**58**
1991-92	**Los Angeles**	**NHL**	**71**	**7**	**22**	**29**	**268**	**6**	**1**	**0**	**1**	**21**
1992-93	**Los Angeles**	**NHL**	**81**	**15**	**26**	**41**	***399**	**24**	**4**	**6**	**10**	***60**
1993-94	**Pittsburgh**	**NHL**	**47**	**3**	**18**	**21**	**139**	....	....	....	....	....
	Los Angeles	**NHL**	**18**	**4**	**6**	**10**	**55**	....	....	....	....	....
1994-95	**Los Angeles**	**NHL**	**41**	**3**	**18**	**21**	**83**	....	....	....	....	....
1995-96	**Los Angeles**	**NHL**	**59**	**10**	**21**	**31**	**148**	....	....	....	....	....
	NY Rangers	**NHL**	**9**	**0**	**2**	**2**	**21**	**4**	**0**	**0**	**0**	**0**
1996-97	**San Jose**	**NHL**	**57**	**4**	**12**	**16**	**186**	....	....	....	....	....
1997-98	**San Jose**	**NHL**	**56**	**2**	**10**	**12**	**140**	....	....	....	....	....
	NHL Totals		**888**	**104**	**245**	**349**	**3218**	**112**	**10**	**19**	**29**	**372**

Co-winner of Alka-Seltzer Plus Award with Theoren Fleury (1991)

Signed as a free agent by **Pittsburgh**, July 30, 1982. Traded to **Edmonton** by **Pittsburgh** with Tim Hrynewich and future considerations (Craig Muni, October 6, 1986) for Gilles Meloche, September 12, 1985. Traded to **LA Kings** by **Edmonton** with Wayne Gretzky and Mike Krushelnyski for Jimmy Carson, Martin Gelinas, LA Kings' 1st round choices in 1989 (later traded to New Jersey — New Jersey selected Jason Miller), 1991 (Martin Rucinsky) and 1993 (Nick Stajduhar) Entry Drafts and cash, August 9, 1988. Traded to **Pittsburgh** by **LA Kings**, for Shawn McEachern, August 27, 1993. Traded to **LA Kings** by **Pittsburgh** with Jim Paek for Tomas Sandstrom and Shawn McEachern, February 16, 1994. Traded to **NY Rangers** by **LA Kings** with Jari Kurri and Shane Churla for Ray Ferraro, Ian Laperriere, Mattias Norstrom, Nathan Lafayette and NY Rangers' 4th round choice (Sean Blanchard) in 1997 Entry Draft, March 14, 1996. Traded to **San Jose** by **NY Rangers** for Jayson More, Brian Swanson and future considerations, August 20, 1996.

McTAVISH, DALE — CGY.

Center. Shoots left. 6'1", 200 lbs. Born, Eganville, Ont., February 28, 1972.

			Regular Season					Playoffs				
Season	Club	Lea	GP	G	A	TP	PIM	GP	G	A	TP	PIM
1989-90	Peterborough	OHL	66	26	35	61	34	12	1	5	6	2
1990-91	Peterborough	OHL	66	21	27	48	44	4	1	0	1	0
1991-92	Peterborough	OHL	60	25	31	56	59	10	2	5	7	11
1992-93	Peterborough	OHL	66	31	50	81	98	21	9	8	17	22
1993-94	St. FX University	AUAA	27	30	24	54	71	....	....	....	....	....
1994-95	St. FX University	AUAA	27	25	27	52	59	....	....	....	....	....
1995-96	Canada	Nat-Tm	53	24	32	56	91	....	....	....	....	....
	Saint John	AHL	4	2	3	5	5	15	5	4	9	15
1996-97	**Calgary**	**NHL**	**9**	**1**	**2**	**3**	**2**	....	....	....	....	....
	Saint John	AHL	53	16	21	37	65	3	0	1	1	0
1997-98	SaiPa	Finland	47	*25	18	43	73	3	0	3	3	4
	NHL Totals		**9**	**1**	**2**	**3**	**2**	....	....	....	....	....

Signed as a free agent by **Calgary**, August 1, 1996.

MELANSON, DEAN (meh-LAHN-suhn)

Defense. Shoots right. 5'11", 211 lbs. Born, Antigonish, N.S., November 19, 1973.
(Buffalo's 4th choice, 80th overall, in 1992 Entry Draft).

			Regular Season					Playoffs				
Season	Club	Lea	GP	G	A	TP	PIM	GP	G	A	TP	PIM
1990-91	St-Hyacinthe	QMJHL	69	10	17	27	110	4	0	1	1	2
1991-92	St-Hyacinthe	QMJHL	42	8	19	27	158	6	1	2	3	25
1992-93	St-Hyacinthe	QMJHL	57	13	29	42	253	....	....	....	....	....
	Rochester	AHL	8	0	1	1	6	14	1	6	7	18
1993-94	Rochester	AHL	80	1	21	22	138	4	0	1	1	2
1994-95	**Buffalo**	**NHL**	**5**	**0**	**0**	**0**	**4**	....	....	....	....	....
	Rochester	AHL	43	4	7	11	84	....	....	....	....	....
1995-96	Rochester	AHL	70	3	13	16	204	14	3	3	6	22
1996-97	Quebec	IHL	72	3	21	24	95	7	0	2	2	12
1997-98	Rochester	AHL	73	7	9	16	228	4	0	2	2	0
	NHL Totals		**5**	**0**	**0**	**0**	**4**	....	....	....	....	....

MELENOVSKY, MAREK (meh-leh-NAHF-skee) TOR.

Center. Shoots left. 5'9", 176 lbs. Born, Humpolec, Czech., March 30, 1977.
(Toronto's 5th choice, 171st overall, in 1995 Entry Draft).

			Regular Season					Playoffs				
Season	Club	Lea	GP	G	A	TP	PIM	GP	G	A	TP	PIM
1993-94	Dukla Jihlava	Cze-Rep.	1	0	0	0	....	....	....	....	....	....
1994-95	Dukla Jihlava	Czech-Jr	28	23	11	34	....	....	....	....	....	....
	Dukla Jihlava	Cze-Rep.	3	0	0	0	0	5	1	3	4	0
1995-96	Dukla Jihlava	Cze-Rep.	33	3	3	6	....	5	1	2	3	....
1996-97	Dukla Jihlava	Cze-Rep.	46	5	13	18	22	....	....	....	....	....
	St. John's	AHL	2	1	2	3	0	2	0	0	0	0
1997-98	Dukla Jihlava	Cze-Rep.	18	10	14	24	30	....	....	....	....	....

MELICHAR, JOSEF (mehl-ee-KHAHR, YOH-sehf) PIT.

Defense. Shoots left. 6'3", 198 lbs. Born, Budejovice, Czech., January 20, 1979.
(Pittsburgh's 3rd choice, 71st overall, in 1997 Entry Draft).

			Regular Season					Playoffs				
Season	Club	Lea	GP	G	A	TP	PIM	GP	G	A	TP	PIM
1995-96	Budejovice	Czech-Jr.	38	3	4	7	....	....	....	....	....	....
1996-97	Budejovice	Cze-Rep.	41	2	3	5	10	....	....	....	....	....
1997-98	Tri-City	WHL	67	9	24	33	154	....	....	....	....	....

MELLANBY, SCOTT FLA.

Right wing. Shoots right. 6'1", 205 lbs. Born, Montreal, Que., June 11, 1966.
(Philadelphia's 2nd choice, 27th overall, in 1984 Entry Draft).

			Regular Season					Playoffs				
Season	Club	Lea	GP	G	A	TP	PIM	GP	G	A	TP	PIM
1983-84	Henry Carr	H.S.	39	37	37	74	97	....	....	....	....	....
1984-85	U. of Wisconsin	WCHA	40	14	24	38	60	....	....	....	....	....
1985-86	U. of Wisconsin	WCHA	32	21	23	44	89	....	....	....	....	....
	Philadelphia	**NHL**	**2**	**0**	**0**	**0**	**0**	....	....	....	....	....
1986-87	**Philadelphia**	**NHL**	**71**	**11**	**21**	**32**	**94**	**24**	**5**	**5**	**10**	**46**
1987-88	**Philadelphia**	**NHL**	**75**	**25**	**26**	**51**	**185**	**7**	**0**	**1**	**1**	**16**
1988-89	**Philadelphia**	**NHL**	**76**	**21**	**29**	**50**	**183**	**19**	**4**	**5**	**9**	**28**
1989-90	**Philadelphia**	**NHL**	**57**	**6**	**17**	**23**	**77**	....	....	....	....	....
1990-91	**Philadelphia**	**NHL**	**74**	**20**	**21**	**41**	**155**	....	....	....	....	....
1991-92	**Edmonton**	**NHL**	**80**	**23**	**27**	**50**	**197**	**16**	**2**	**1**	**3**	**29**
1992-93	**Edmonton**	**NHL**	**69**	**15**	**17**	**32**	**147**	....	....	....	....	....
1993-94	**Florida**	**NHL**	**80**	**30**	**30**	**60**	**149**	....	....	....	....	....
1994-95	**Florida**	**NHL**	**48**	**13**	**12**	**25**	**90**	....	....	....	....	....
1995-96	**Florida**	**NHL**	**79**	**32**	**38**	**70**	**160**	**22**	**3**	**6**	**9**	**44**
1996-97	**Florida**	**NHL**	**82**	**27**	**29**	**56**	**170**	**5**	**0**	**2**	**2**	**4**
1997-98	**Florida**	**NHL**	**79**	**15**	**24**	**39**	**127**	....	....	....	....	....
	NHL Totals		**872**	**238**	**291**	**529**	**1734**	**93**	**14**	**20**	**34**	**167**

Played in NHL All-Star Game (1996)

Traded to **Edmonton** by **Philadelphia** with Craig Fisher and Craig Berube for Dave Brown, Corey Foster and Jari Kurri, May 30, 1991. Claimed by **Florida** from **Edmonton** in Expansion Draft, June 24, 1993.

MELOCHE, ERIC (muh-LAWSH) PIT.

Right wing. Shoots right. 5'11", 195 lbs. Born, Montreal, Que., May 1, 1976.
(Pittsburgh's 7th choice, 186th overall, in 1996 Entry Draft).

			Regular Season					Playoffs				
Season	Club	Lea	GP	G	A	TP	PIM	GP	G	A	TP	PIM
1995-96	Cornwall	OJHL	64	68	53	121	162	....	....	....	....	....
1996-97	Ohio State	CCHA	39	12	11	23	78	....	....	....	....	....
1997-98	Ohio State	CCHA	42	26	22	48	86	....	....	....	....	....

MERRICK, ANDREW CAR.

Center. Shoots left. 5'11", 202 lbs. Born, Syosset, NY, March 23, 1978.
(Carolina's 6th choice, 169th overall, in 1997 Entry Draft).

			Regular Season					Playoffs				
Season	Club	Lea	GP	G	A	TP	PIM	GP	G	A	TP	PIM
1996-97	U. of Michigan	CCHA	36	3	10	13	42	....	....	....	....	....
1997-98	U. of Michigan	CCHA	33	4	3	7	74	....	....	....	....	....

MERTZIG, JAN NYR

Defense. Shoots left. 6'4", 218 lbs. Born, Huddinge, Sweden, July 18, 1970.
(NY Rangers' 9th choice, 235th overall, in 1998 Entry Draft).

			Regular Season					Playoffs				
Season	Club	Lea	GP	G	A	TP	PIM	GP	G	A	TP	PIM
1991-92	Huddinge	Sweden-2	28	1	6	7	10	4	2	0	2	4
1992-93	Huddinge	Sweden-2	35	3	7	10	18	9	1	0	1	10
1993-94	Huddinge	Sweden-2	35	5	7	12	26	2	1	0	1	4
1994-95	Huddinge	Sweden-2	34	10	8	18	16	2	0	1	1	0
1995-96	Lulea	Sweden	38	7	10	17	14	13	3	3	6	6
1996-97	Lulea	Sweden	47	15	10	25	30	9	0	2	2	4
1997-98	Lulea	Sweden	45	7	8	15	27	3	1	0	1	4

MESSIER, ERIC (MEHS-see-ay) COL.

Defense. Shoots left. 6'2", 200 lbs. Born, Drummondville, Que., October 29, 1973.

			Regular Season					Playoffs				
Season	Club	Lea	GP	G	A	TP	PIM	GP	G	A	TP	PIM
1991-92	Trois-Rivieres	QMJHL	58	2	10	12	28	15	2	2	4	13
1992-93	Sherbrooke	QMJHL	51	4	17	21	82	15	0	4	4	18
1993-94	Sherbrooke	QMJHL	67	4	24	28	69	12	1	7	8	14
1994-95	U. of Quebec	OUAA	13	8	5	13	20	4	0	3	3	8
1995-96	Cornwall	AHL	72	5	9	14	111	8	1	1	2	20
1996-97	**Colorado**	**NHL**	**21**	**0**	**0**	**0**	**4**	**6**	**0**	**0**	**0**	**4**
	Hershey	AHL	55	16	26	42	69	5	2	4	6	12
1997-98	**Colorado**	**NHL**	**62**	**4**	**12**	**16**	**20**	....	....	....	....	....
	NHL Totals		**83**	**4**	**12**	**16**	**24**	**6**	**0**	**0**	**0**	**4**

QMJHL Second All-Star Team (1994)

Signed as a free agent by **Colorado**, June 14, 1995.

MESSIER, MARK (MEHS-see-ay) VAN.

Center. Shoots left. 6'1", 205 lbs. Born, Edmonton, Alta., January 18, 1961.
(Edmonton's 2nd choice, 48th overall, in 1979 Entry Draft).

			Regular Season					Playoffs				
Season	Club	Lea	GP	G	A	TP	PIM	GP	G	A	TP	PIM
1976-77	Spruce Grove	AJHL	57	27	39	55	91	....	....	....	....	....
1977-78	St. Albert	AJHL	STATISTICS NOT AVAILABLE									
	Portland	WHL	....	....	....	....	....	7	4	1	5	2
1978-79	Indianapolis	WHA	5	0	0	0	0	....	....	....	....	....
	Cincinnati	WHA	47	1	10	11	58	....	....	....	....	....
1979-80	**Edmonton**	**NHL**	**75**	**12**	**21**	**33**	**120**	**3**	**1**	**2**	**3**	**2**
	Houston	CHL	4	0	3	3	4	....	....	....	....	....
1980-81	**Edmonton**	**NHL**	**72**	**23**	**40**	**63**	**102**	**9**	**2**	**5**	**7**	**13**
1981-82	**Edmonton**	**NHL**	**78**	**50**	**38**	**88**	**119**	**5**	**1**	**2**	**3**	**8**
1982-83	**Edmonton**	**NHL**	**77**	**48**	**58**	**106**	**72**	**15**	**15**	**6**	**21**	**14**
1983-84	**Edmonton**	**NHL**	**73**	**37**	**64**	**101**	**165**	**19**	**8**	**18**	**26**	**19** ♦
1984-85	**Edmonton**	**NHL**	**55**	**23**	**31**	**54**	**57**	**18**	**12**	**13**	**25**	**12** ♦
1985-86	**Edmonton**	**NHL**	**63**	**35**	**49**	**84**	**68**	**10**	**4**	**6**	**10**	**18**
1986-87	**Edmonton**	**NHL**	**77**	**37**	**70**	**107**	**73**	**21**	**12**	**16**	**28**	**16** ♦
1987-88	**Edmonton**	**NHL**	**77**	**37**	**74**	**111**	**103**	**19**	**11**	**23**	**34**	**29** ♦
1988-89	**Edmonton**	**NHL**	**72**	**33**	**61**	**94**	**130**	**7**	**1**	**11**	**12**	**8**
1989-90	**Edmonton**	**NHL**	**79**	**45**	**84**	**129**	**79**	**22**	**9**	***22**	**31**	**20** ♦
1990-91	**Edmonton**	**NHL**	**53**	**12**	**52**	**64**	**34**	**18**	**4**	**11**	**15**	**16**
1991-92	**NY Rangers**	**NHL**	**79**	**35**	**72**	**107**	**76**	**11**	**7**	**7**	**14**	**6**
1992-93	**NY Rangers**	**NHL**	**75**	**25**	**66**	**91**	**72**	....	....	....	....	....
1993-94	**NY Rangers**	**NHL**	**76**	**26**	**58**	**84**	**76**	**23**	**12**	**18**	**30**	**33** ♦
1994-95	**NY Rangers**	**NHL**	**46**	**14**	**39**	**53**	**40**	**10**	**3**	**10**	**13**	**8**
1995-96	**NY Rangers**	**NHL**	**74**	**47**	**52**	**99**	**122**	**11**	**4**	**7**	**11**	**16**
1996-97	**NY Rangers**	**NHL**	**71**	**36**	**48**	**84**	**88**	**15**	**3**	**9**	**12**	**6**
1997-98	**Vancouver**	**NHL**	**82**	**22**	**38**	**60**	**58**	....	....	....	....	....
	NHL Totals		**1354**	**597**	**1015**	**1612**	**1654**	***236**	**109**	**186**	**295**	**244**

NHL First All-Star Team (1982, 1983, 1990, 1992) • NHL Second All-Star Team (1984) • Won Conn Smythe Trophy (1984) • Won Hart Trophy (1990, 1992) • Won Lester B. Pearson Award (1990, 1992)

Played in NHL All-Star Game (1982, 1983, 1984, 1986, 1988, 1989, 1990, 1991, 1992, 1994, 1996, 1997, 1998)

Signed as an underage free agent by **Indianapolis** (WHA) to 10-game tryout contract, November 5, 1978. Signed as a free agent by **Cincinnati** (WHA) after **Indianapolis** (WHA) franchise folded, December, 1978. Traded to **NY Rangers** by **Edmonton** with future considerations for Bernie Nicholls, Steven Rice and Louie DeBrusk, October 4, 1991. Signed as a free agent by **Vancouver**, July 30, 1997.

METHOT, FRANCOIS BUF.

Center. Shoots right. 6', 175 lbs. Born, Montreal, Que., April 26, 1978.
(Buffalo's 4th choice, 54th overall, in 1996 Entry Draft).

			Regular Season					Playoffs				
Season	Club	Lea	GP	G	A	TP	PIM	GP	G	A	TP	PIM
1994-95	St-Hyacinthe	QMJHL	60	14	38	52	22	5	0	1	1	0
1995-96	St-Hyacinthe	QMJHL	68	32	62	94	22	12	6	6	12	4
1996-97	Rouyn-Noranda	QMJHL	47	21	30	51	22	....	....	....	....	....
	Shawinigan	QMJHL	18	8	17	25	2	7	2	6	8	2
1997-98	Shawinigan	QMJHL	36	23	42	65	10	6	1	3	4	5

MIETTINEN, TOMMI (mih-EHT-tih-nehn) ANA.

Center. Shoots left. 5'10", 165 lbs. Born, Kuopio, Finland, December 3, 1975.
(Anaheim's 9th choice, 236th overall, in 1994 Entry Draft).

			Regular Season					Playoffs				
Season	Club	Lea	GP	G	A	TP	PIM	GP	G	A	TP	PIM
1992-93	KalPa	Finland	14	0	0	0	0	....	....	....	....	....
1993-94	KalPa	Finland	47	5	7	12	14	....	....	....	....	....
1994-95	KalPa	Finland	48	13	16	29	26	3	1	1	2	2
1995-96	TPS Turku	Finland	36	3	10	13	10	10	2	1	3	29
1996-97	TPS Turku	Finland	41	6	15	21	6	12	3	4	7	8
1997-98	TPS Turku	EuroHL	3	0	0	0	2	....	....	....	....	....
	TPS Turku	Finland	42	8	6	14	26	4	0	0	0	0

MIKA, PETR (MEE-kah) NYI

Left wing. Shoots right. 6'4", 194 lbs. Born, Prague, Czech., February 12, 1979.
(NY Islanders' 6th choice, 85th overall, in 1997 Entry Draft).

			Regular Season					Playoffs				
Season	Club	Lea	GP	G	A	TP	PIM	GP	G	A	TP	PIM
1996-97	Slavia Praha	Cze-Rep.	15	8	0	8	....	....	....	....	....	....
	HC Beroun	Czech-2	9	1	0	1	....	....	....	....	....	....
	Slavia Praha	Cze-Rep.	20	1	2	3	6	....	....	....	....	....
1997-98	Ottawa	OHL	41	10	8	18	28	....	....	....	....	....

MIKKOLA, ILKKA (mih-KOHLA-, IHL-ka) MTL.

Defense. Shoots left. 6', 189 lbs. Born, Oulu, Finland, January 18, 1979.
(Montreal's 3rd choice, 65th overall, in 1997 Entry Draft).

			Regular Season					Playoffs				
Season	Club	Lea	GP	G	A	TP	PIM	GP	G	A	TP	PIM
1995-96	Karpat Oulu	Fin-Jr.	21	2	3	5	20	....	....	....	....	....
	Karpat Oulu	Finland-2	10	0	4	4	29	2	0	0	0	2
1996-97	Karpat Oulu	Finland-2	40	7	12	19	32	6	0	0	0	4
1997-98	Karpat Oulu	Finland-2	27	7	2	9	34	....	....	....	....	....
	Karpat Oulu	Fin-Jr.	8	4	2	6	10	....	....	....	....	....

MILANOVIC, RYAN BOS.

Left wing. Shoots left. 6'2", 201 lbs. Born, Toronto, Ont., September 3, 1980.
(Boston's 5th choice, 165th overall, in 1998 Entry Draft).

			Regular Season					Playoffs				
Season	Club	Lea	GP	G	A	TP	PIM	GP	G	A	TP	PIM
1996-97	Kitchener	OHL	58	3	10	13	78	13	1	1	2	4
1997-98	Kitchener	OHL	42	1	8	9	72	6	1	3	4	19

MILLAR, CRAIG — EDM.

Defense. Shoots left. 6'2", 205 lbs. Born, Winnipeg, Man., July 12, 1976.
(Buffalo's 10th choice, 225th overall, in 1994 Entry Draft).

			Regular Season					Playoffs				
Season	Club	Lea	GP	G	A	TP	PIM	GP	G	A	TP	PIM
1992-93	Swift Current	WHL	43	2	1	3	8	....	....	....	....	....
1993-94	Swift Current	WHL	66	2	9	11	53	7	0	3	3	4
1994-95	Swift Current	WHL	72	8	42	50	80	6	1	1	2	10
1995-96	Swift Current	WHL	72	31	46	77	151	6	1	0	1	22
1996-97	Rochester	AHL	64	7	18	25	65	....	....	....	....	....
	Edmonton	**NHL**	**1**	**0**	**0**	**0**	**2**	....	....	....	....	....
	Hamilton	AHL	10	1	3	4	10	22	4	4	8	21
1997-98	**Edmonton**	**NHL**	**11**	**4**	**0**	**4**	**8**	....	....	....	....	....
	Hamilton	AHL	60	10	22	32	113	9	3	1	4	22
	NHL Totals		**12**	**4**	**0**	**4**	**10**	....	....	....	....	....

WHL East First All-Star Team (1996)

Traded to **Edmonton** by **Buffalo** with Barrie Moore for Miroslav Satan, March 18, 1997.

MILLEN, COREY

Center. Shoots right. 5'7", 170 lbs. Born, Cloquet, MN, March 30, 1964.
(NY Rangers' 3rd choice, 57th overall, in 1982 Entry Draft).

			Regular Season					Playoffs				
Season	Club	Lea	GP	G	A	TP	PIM	GP	G	A	TP	PIM
1981-82	Cloquet High	H.S.	18	46	35	81	....	....	....	....	....	....
1982-83	U. of Minnesota	WCHA	21	14	15	29	18	....	....	....	....	....
1983-84	United States	Nat-Tm	45	15	11	26	10	....	....	....	....	....
	United States	Olympics	6	0	0	0	2	....	....	....	....	....
1984-85	U. of Minnesota	WCHA	38	28	36	64	60	....	....	....	....	....
1985-86	U. of Minnesota	WCHA	48	41	42	83	64	....	....	....	....	....
1986-87	U. of Minnesota	WCHA	42	36	29	65	62	....	....	....	....	....
1987-88	United States	Nat-Tm	47	41	43	84	26	....	....	....	....	....
	United States	Olympics	6	6	5	11	4	....	....	....	....	....
1988-89	Ambri	Switz.	36	32	22	54	18	6	4	3	7	0
1989-90	**NY Rangers**	**NHL**	**4**	**0**	**0**	**0**	**2**	....	....	....	....	....
	Flint	IHL	11	4	5	9	2	....	....	....	....	....
1990-91	**NY Rangers**	**NHL**	**4**	**3**	**1**	**4**	**0**	**6**	**1**	**2**	**3**	**0**
	Binghamton	AHL	40	19	37	56	68	6	0	7	7	6
1991-92	**NY Rangers**	**NHL**	**11**	**1**	**4**	**5**	**10**	....	....	....	....	....
	Binghamton	AHL	15	8	7	15	44	....	....	....	....	....
	Los Angeles	**NHL**	**46**	**20**	**21**	**41**	**44**	**6**	**0**	**1**	**1**	**6**
1992-93	**Los Angeles**	**NHL**	**42**	**23**	**16**	**39**	**42**	**23**	**2**	**4**	**6**	**12**
1993-94	**New Jersey**	**NHL**	**78**	**20**	**30**	**50**	**52**	**7**	**1**	**0**	**1**	**2**
1994-95	**New Jersey**	**NHL**	**17**	**2**	**3**	**5**	**8**	....	....	....	....	....
	Dallas	**NHL**	**28**	**3**	**15**	**18**	**28**	**5**	**1**	**0**	**1**	**2**
1995-96	**Dallas**	**NHL**	**13**	**3**	**4**	**7**	**8**	....	....	....	....	....
	Michigan	IHL	11	8	11	19	14	....	....	....	....	....
	Calgary	**NHL**	**31**	**4**	**10**	**14**	**10**	....	....	....	....	....
1996-97	**Calgary**	**NHL**	**61**	**11**	**15**	**26**	**32**	....	....	....	....	....
1997-98	Kolner Haie	EuroHL	5	1	5	6	10	....	....	....	....	....
	Kolner Haie	Germany	30	17	17	34	52	3	2	1	3	6
	NHL Totals		**335**	**90**	**119**	**209**	**236**	**47**	**5**	**7**	**12**	**22**

WCHA Second All-Star Team (1985, 1986, 1987) • NCAA West Second All-American Team (1986) • NCAA Championship All-Tournament Team (1987)

Traded to **LA Kings** by **NY Rangers** for Randy Gilhen, December 23, 1991. Traded to **New Jersey** by **LA Kings** for New Jersey's 5th round choice (Jason Saal) in 1993 Entry Draft, June 26, 1993. Traded to **Dallas** by **New Jersey** for Neal Broten, February 27, 1995. Traded to **Calgary** by **Dallas** with Jarome Iginla for Joe Nieuwendyk, December 19, 1995.

MILLER, AARON — COL.

Defense. Shoots right. 6'3", 200 lbs. Born, Buffalo, NY, August 11, 1971.
(NY Rangers' 6th choice, 88th overall, in 1989 Entry Draft).

			Regular Season					Playoffs				
Season	Club	Lea	GP	G	A	TP	PIM	GP	G	A	TP	PIM
1988-89	Niagara Scenics	NAJHL	59	24	38	62	60	....	....	....	....	....
1989-90	U. of Vermont	ECAC	31	1	15	16	24	....	....	....	....	....
1990-91	U. of Vermont	ECAC	30	3	7	10	22	....	....	....	....	....
1991-92	U. of Vermont	ECAC	31	3	16	19	28	....	....	....	....	....
1992-93	U. of Vermont	ECAC	30	4	13	17	16	....	....	....	....	....
1993-94	**Quebec**	**NHL**	**1**	**0**	**0**	**0**	**0**	....	....	....	....	....
	Cornwall	AHL	64	4	10	14	49	13	0	2	2	10
1994-95	**Quebec**	**NHL**	**9**	**0**	**3**	**3**	**6**	....	....	....	....	....
	Cornwall	AHL	76	4	18	22	69	....	....	....	....	....
1995-96	**Colorado**	**NHL**	**5**	**0**	**0**	**0**	**0**	....	....	....	....	....
	Cornwall	AHL	62	4	23	27	77	8	0	1	1	6
1996-97	**Colorado**	**NHL**	**56**	**5**	**12**	**17**	**15**	**17**	**1**	**2**	**3**	**10**
1997-98	**Colorado**	**NHL**	**55**	**2**	**2**	**4**	**51**	**7**	**0**	**0**	**0**	**8**
	NHL Totals		**126**	**7**	**17**	**24**	**72**	**24**	**1**	**2**	**3**	**18**

ECAC First All-Star Team (1993) • NCAA East Second All-American Team (1993)

Traded to **Quebec** by **NY Rangers** with NY Rangers' 5th round choice (Bill Lindsay) in 1991 Entry Draft for Joe Cirella, January 17, 1991. Transferred to **Colorado** after **Quebec** franchise relocated, June 21, 1996.

MILLER, KELLY — WSH.

Left wing. Shoots left. 5'11", 197 lbs. Born, Lansing, MI, March 3, 1963.
(NY Rangers' 9th choice, 183rd overall, in 1982 Entry Draft).

			Regular Season					Playoffs				
Season	Club	Lea	GP	G	A	TP	PIM	GP	G	A	TP	PIM
1981-82	Michigan State	CCHA	38	11	18	29	17	....	....	....	....	....
1982-83	Michigan State	CCHA	36	16	19	35	12	....	....	....	....	....
1983-84	Michigan State	CCHA	46	28	21	49	12	....	....	....	....	....
1984-85	Michigan State	CCHA	43	27	23	50	21	....	....	....	....	....
	NY Rangers	**NHL**	**5**	**0**	**2**	**2**	**2**	**3**	**0**	**0**	**0**	**2**
1985-86	**NY Rangers**	**NHL**	**74**	**13**	**20**	**33**	**52**	**16**	**3**	**4**	**7**	**4**
1986-87	**NY Rangers**	**NHL**	**38**	**6**	**14**	**20**	**22**	....	....	....	....	....
	Washington	**NHL**	**39**	**10**	**12**	**22**	**26**	**7**	**2**	**2**	**4**	**0**
1987-88	**Washington**	**NHL**	**80**	**9**	**23**	**32**	**35**	**14**	**4**	**4**	**8**	**10**
1988-89	**Washington**	**NHL**	**78**	**19**	**21**	**40**	**45**	**6**	**1**	**0**	**1**	**2**
1989-90	**Washington**	**NHL**	**80**	**18**	**22**	**40**	**49**	**15**	**3**	**5**	**8**	**23**
1990-91	**Washington**	**NHL**	**80**	**24**	**26**	**50**	**29**	**11**	**4**	**2**	**6**	**6**
1991-92	**Washington**	**NHL**	**78**	**14**	**38**	**52**	**49**	**7**	**1**	**2**	**3**	**4**
1992-93	**Washington**	**NHL**	**84**	**18**	**27**	**45**	**32**	**6**	**0**	**3**	**3**	**2**
1993-94	**Washington**	**NHL**	**84**	**14**	**25**	**39**	**32**	**11**	**2**	**7**	**9**	**0**
1994-95	**Washington**	**NHL**	**48**	**10**	**13**	**23**	**6**	**7**	**0**	**3**	**3**	**4**
1995-96	**Washington**	**NHL**	**74**	**7**	**13**	**20**	**30**	**6**	**0**	**1**	**1**	**4**
1996-97	**Washington**	**NHL**	**77**	**10**	**14**	**24**	**33**	....	....	....	....	....
1997-98	**Washington**	**NHL**	**76**	**7**	**7**	**14**	**41**	**10**	**0**	**1**	**1**	**4**
	NHL Totals		**995**	**179**	**277**	**456**	**483**	**119**	**20**	**34**	**54**	**65**

CCHA First All-Star Team (1985) • NCAA West First All-American Team (1985)

Traded to **Washington** by **NY Rangers** with Bob Crawford and Mike Ridley for Bob Carpenter and Washington's 2nd round choice (Jason Prosofsky) in 1989 Entry Draft, January 1, 1987.

MILLER, KEVIN

Center. Shoots right. 5'11", 190 lbs. Born, Lansing, MI, September 2, 1965.
(NY Rangers' 10th choice, 202nd overall, in 1984 Entry Draft).

			Regular Season					Playoffs				
Season	Club	Lea	GP	G	A	TP	PIM	GP	G	A	TP	PIM
1983-84	Redford	NAJHL	STATISTICS NOT AVAILABLE									
1984-85	Michigan State	CCHA	44	11	29	40	84	....	....	....	....	....
1985-86	Michigan State	CCHA	45	19	52	71	112	....	....	....	....	....
1986-87	Michigan State	CCHA	42	25	56	81	63	....	....	....	....	....
1987-88	Michigan State	CCHA	9	6	3	9	18	....	....	....	....	....
	United States	Nat-Tm	48	31	32	63	33	....	....	....	....	....
	United States	Olympics	5	1	3	4	4	....	....	....	....	....
1988-89	**NY Rangers**	**NHL**	**24**	**3**	**5**	**8**	**2**	....	....	....	....	....
	Denver	IHL	55	29	47	76	19	4	2	1	3	2
1989-90	**NY Rangers**	**NHL**	**16**	**0**	**5**	**5**	**2**	**1**	**0**	**0**	**0**	**0**
	Flint	IHL	48	19	23	42	41	....	....	....	....	....
1990-91	**NY Rangers**	**NHL**	**63**	**17**	**27**	**44**	**63**	....	....	....	....	....
	Detroit	**NHL**	**11**	**5**	**2**	**7**	**4**	**7**	**3**	**2**	**5**	**20**
1991-92	**Detroit**	**NHL**	**80**	**20**	**26**	**46**	**53**	**9**	**0**	**2**	**2**	**4**
1992-93	**Washington**	**NHL**	**10**	**0**	**3**	**3**	**35**	....	....	....	....	....
	St. Louis	**NHL**	**72**	**24**	**22**	**46**	**65**	**10**	**0**	**3**	**3**	**11**
1993-94	**St. Louis**	**NHL**	**75**	**23**	**25**	**48**	**83**	**3**	**1**	**0**	**1**	**4**
1994-95	**St. Louis**	**NHL**	**15**	**2**	**5**	**7**	**0**	....	....	....	....	....
	San Jose	**NHL**	**21**	**6**	**7**	**13**	**13**	**6**	**0**	**0**	**0**	**2**
1995-96	**San Jose**	**NHL**	**68**	**22**	**20**	**42**	**41**	....	....	....	....	....
	Pittsburgh	**NHL**	**13**	**6**	**5**	**11**	**4**	**18**	**3**	**2**	**5**	**8**
1996-97	**Chicago**	**NHL**	**69**	**14**	**17**	**31**	**41**	**6**	**0**	**1**	**1**	**0**
1997-98	**Chicago**	**NHL**	**37**	**4**	**7**	**11**	**8**	....	....	....	....	....
	Indianapolis	IHL	26	11	11	22	41	2	1	1	2	0
	NHL Totals		**574**	**146**	**176**	**322**	**414**	**60**	**7**	**10**	**17**	**49**

Traded to **Detroit** by **NY Rangers** with Jim Cummins and Dennis Vial for Joey Kocur and Per Djoos, March 5, 1991. Traded to **Washington** by **Detroit** for Dino Ciccarelli, June 20, 1992. Traded to **St. Louis** by **Washington** for Paul Cavallini, November 2, 1992. Traded to **San Jose** by **St. Louis** for Todd Elik, March 23, 1995. Traded to **Pittsburgh** by **San Jose** for Pittsburgh's 5th round choice (later traded to Boston — Boston selected Elias Abrahamsson) in 1996 Entry Draft and future considerations, March 20, 1996. Signed as a free agent by **Chicago**, July 18, 1996.

MILLER, KIP

Center. Shoots left. 5'10", 190 lbs. Born, Lansing, MI, June 11, 1969.
(Quebec's 4th choice, 72nd overall, in 1987 Entry Draft).

			Regular Season					Playoffs				
Season	Club	Lea	GP	G	A	TP	PIM	GP	G	A	TP	PIM
1986-87	Michigan State	CCHA	41	20	19	39	92	....	....	....	....	....
1987-88	Michigan State	CCHA	39	16	25	41	51	....	....	....	....	....
1988-89	Michigan State	CCHA	47	32	45	77	94	....	....	....	....	....
1989-90	Michigan State	CCHA	45	*48	53	*101	60	....	....	....	....	....
1990-91	**Quebec**	**NHL**	**13**	**4**	**3**	**7**	**7**	....	....	....	....	....
	Halifax	AHL	66	36	33	69	40	....	....	....	....	....
1991-92	**Quebec**	**NHL**	**36**	**5**	**10**	**15**	**12**	....	....	....	....	....
	Halifax	AHL	24	9	17	26	8	....	....	....	....	....
	Minnesota	**NHL**	**3**	**1**	**2**	**3**	**2**	....	....	....	....	....
	Kalamazoo	IHL	6	1	8	9	4	12	3	9	12	12
1992-93	Kalamazoo	IHL	61	17	39	56	59	....	....	....	....	....
1993-94	**San Jose**	**NHL**	**11**	**2**	**2**	**4**	**6**	....	....	....	....	....
	Kansas City	IHL	71	38	54	92	51	....	....	....	....	....
1994-95	Denver	IHL	71	46	60	106	54	17	*15	14	29	8
	NY Islanders	**NHL**	**8**	**0**	**1**	**1**	**0**	....	....	....	....	....
1995-96	**Chicago**	**NHL**	**10**	**1**	**4**	**5**	**2**	....	....	....	....	....
	Indianapolis	IHL	73	32	59	91	46	5	2	6	8	2
1996-97	Chicago	IHL	43	11	41	52	32	....	....	....	....	....
	Indianapolis	IHL	37	17	24	41	18	4	2	2	4	2
1997-98	Utah	IHL	72	38	59	97	30	4	3	2	5	10
	NY Islanders	**NHL**	**9**	**1**	**3**	**4**	**2**	....	....	....	....	....
	NHL Totals		**90**	**14**	**25**	**39**	**31**	....	....	....	....	....

CCHA First All-Star Team (1989, 1990) • NCAA West First All-American Team (1989, 1990) • Won Hobey Baker Memorial Award (Top U.S. Collegiate Player) (1990)

Traded to **Minnesota** by **Quebec** for Steve Maltais, March 8, 1992. Signed as a free agent by **San Jose**, August 10, 1993. Signed as a free agent by **NY Islanders**, July 7, 1994. Signed as a free agent by **Chicago**, July 21, 1995. Signed as a free agent by **NY Islanders**, November 26, 1997.

MILLER, RICHARD — NYR

Defense. Shoots right. 6'3", 200 lbs. Born, Meriden, CN, January 12, 1978.
(NY Rangers' 12th choice, 236th overall, in 1997 Entry Draft).

			Regular Season					Playoffs				
Season	Club	Lea	GP	G	A	TP	PIM	GP	G	A	TP	PIM
1996-97	Providence	H.E.	12	1	4	5	6	....	....	....	....	....
1997-98	Providence	H.E.	27	1	5	6	32	....	....	....	....	....

MILLEY, NORMAN — BUF.

Right wing. Shoots right. 5'11", 185 lbs. Born, Toronto, Ont., February 14, 1980.
(Buffalo's 3rd choice, 47th overall, in 1998 Entry Draft).

			Regular Season					Playoffs				
Season	Club	Lea	GP	G	A	TP	PIM	GP	G	A	TP	PIM
1996-97	Sudbury	OHL	61	30	32	62	15	....	....	....	....	....
1997-98	Sudbury	OHL	62	33	41	74	48	10	0	1	1	4

MILLS, CRAIG — CHI.

Right wing. Shoots right. 6', 190 lbs. Born, Toronto, Ont., August 27, 1976.
(Winnipeg's 5th choice, 108th overall, in 1994 Entry Draft).

			Regular Season					Playoffs				
Season	Club	Lea	GP	G	A	TP	PIM	GP	G	A	TP	PIM
1993-94	Belleville	OHL	63	15	18	33	88	12	2	1	3	11
1994-95	Belleville	OHL	62	39	41	80	104	13	7	9	16	8
1995-96	Belleville	OHL	48	10	19	29	113	14	4	5	9	32
	Winnipeg	**NHL**	**4**	**0**	**2**	**2**	**0**	**1**	**0**	**0**	**0**	**0**
	Springfield	AHL	....	....	....	....	....	2	0	0	0	0
1996-97	Indianapolis	IHL	80	12	7	19	199	4	0	0	0	4
1997-98	**Chicago**	**NHL**	**20**	**0**	**3**	**3**	**34**	....	....	....	....	....
	Indianapolis	IHL	42	8	11	19	119	5	0	0	0	27
	NHL Totals		**24**	**0**	**5**	**5**	**34**	**1**	**0**	**0**	**0**	**0**

Canadian Major Junior Humanitarian Player of the Year (1996)

Rights transferred to **Phoenix** after **Winnipeg** franchise relocated, July 1, 1996. Traded to **Chicago** by **Phoenix** with Alexei Zhamnov and Phoenix's 1st round choice (Ty Jones) in 1997 Entry Draft for Jeremy Roenick, August 16, 1996.

MIRONOV, BORIS (mih-RAWN-ohv) EDM.

Defense. Shoots right. 6'3", 223 lbs. Born, Moscow, USSR, March 21, 1972.
(Winnipeg's 2nd choice, 27th overall, in 1992 Entry Draft).

			Regular Season					Playoffs				
Season	Club	Lea	GP	G	A	TP	PIM	GP	G	A	TP	PIM
1988-89	CSKA Moscow	USSR	1	0	0	0	0	....	....	....	....	....
1989-90	CSKA Moscow	USSR	7	0	0	0	0	....	....	....	....	....
1990-91	CSKA Moscow	USSR	36	1	5	6	16	....	....	....	....	....
1991-92	CSKA Moscow	CIS	36	2	1	3	22	....	....	....	....	....
1992-93	CSKA Moscow	CIS	19	0	5	5	20	....	....	....	....	....
1993-94	**Winnipeg**	**NHL**	**65**	**7**	**22**	**29**	**96**	....	....	....	....	....
	Edmonton	**NHL**	**14**	**0**	**2**	**2**	**14**	....	....	....	....	....
1994-95	**Edmonton**	**NHL**	**29**	**1**	**7**	**8**	**40**	....	....	....	....	....
	Cape Breton	AHL	4	2	5	7	23	....	....	....	....	....
1995-96	**Edmonton**	**NHL**	**78**	**8**	**24**	**32**	**101**	....	....	....	....	....
1996-97	**Edmonton**	**NHL**	**55**	**6**	**26**	**32**	**85**	**12**	**2**	**8**	**10**	**16**
1997-98	**Edmonton**	**NHL**	**81**	**16**	**30**	**46**	**100**	**12**	**3**	**3**	**6**	**27**
	Russia	Olympics	6	0	2	2	2	....	....	....	....	....
	NHL Totals		**322**	**38**	**111**	**149**	**436**	**24**	**5**	**11**	**16**	**43**

NHL/Upper Deck All-Rookie Team (1994)

Traded to **Edmonton** by **Winnipeg** with Mats Lindgren, Winnipeg's 1st round choice (Jason Bonsignore) in 1994 Entry Draft and Florida's 4th round choice (previously acquired, Edmonton selected Adam Copeland) in 1994 Entry Draft for Dave Manson and St. Louis' 6th round choice (previously acquired, Winnipeg selected Chris Kibermanis) in 1994 Entry Draft, March 15, 1994.

MIRONOV, DMITRI (mih-RAWN-ohv) WSH.

Defense. Shoots right. 6'3", 215 lbs. Born, Moscow, USSR, December 25, 1965.
(Toronto's 7th choice, 160th overall, in 1991 Entry Draft).

			Regular Season					Playoffs				
Season	Club	Lea	GP	G	A	TP	PIM	GP	G	A	TP	PIM
1985-86	CSKA Moscow	USSR	9	0	1	1	8	....	....	....	....	....
1986-87	CSKA Moscow	USSR	20	1	3	4	10	....	....	....	....	....
1987-88	Soviet Wings	USSR	44	12	6	18	30	....	....	....	....	....
1988-89	Soviet Wings	USSR	44	5	6	11	44	....	....	....	....	....
1989-90	Soviet Wings	USSR	45	4	11	15	34	....	....	....	....	....
1990-91	Soviet Wings	USSR	45	16	12	28	22	....	....	....	....	....
1991-92	Soviet Wings	CIS	35	15	16	31	62	....	....	....	....	....
	Toronto	**NHL**	**7**	**1**	**0**	**1**	**0**	....	....	....	....	....
	Russia	Olympics	8	3	1	4	6	....	....	....	....	....
1992-93	**Toronto**	**NHL**	**59**	**7**	**24**	**31**	**40**	**14**	**1**	**2**	**3**	**2**
1993-94	**Toronto**	**NHL**	**76**	**9**	**27**	**36**	**78**	**18**	**6**	**9**	**15**	**6**
1994-95	**Toronto**	**NHL**	**33**	**5**	**12**	**17**	**28**	**6**	**2**	**1**	**3**	**2**
1995-96	**Pittsburgh**	**NHL**	**72**	**3**	**31**	**34**	**88**	**15**	**0**	**1**	**1**	**10**
1996-97	**Pittsburgh**	**NHL**	**15**	**1**	**5**	**6**	**24**	....	....	....	....	....
	Anaheim	**NHL**	**62**	**12**	**34**	**46**	**77**	**11**	**1**	**10**	**11**	**10**
1997-98	**Anaheim**	**NHL**	**66**	**6**	**30**	**36**	**115**	....	....	....	....	....
	Russia	Olympics	6	0	3	3	0	....	....	....	....	....
	Detroit	**NHL**	**11**	**2**	**5**	**7**	**4**	**7**	**0**	**3**	**3**	**14 ♦**
	NHL Totals		**401**	**46**	**168**	**214**	**454**	**71**	**10**	**26**	**36**	**44**

Played in NHL All-Star Game (1998)

Traded to **Pittsburgh** by **Toronto** with Toronto's 2nd round choice (later traded to New Jersey — New Jersey selected Joshua Dewolf) in 1996 Entry Draft for Larry Murphy, July 8, 1995. Traded to **Anaheim** by **Pittsburgh** with Shawn Antoski for Alex Hicks and Fredrik Olausson, November 19, 1996. Traded to **Detroit** by **Anaheim** for Jamie Pushor and Detroit's 4th round choice (Viktor Wallin) in 1998 Entry Draft, March 24, 1998. Signed as a free agent by **Washington**, July 29, 1998.

MISKOVICH, AARON (MIHS-kuh-vihch) COL.

Center. Shoots left. 5'10", 185 lbs. Born, Grand Rapids, MN, April 28, 1978.
(Colorado's 6th choice, 133rd overall, in 1997 Entry Draft).

			Regular Season					Playoffs				
Season	Club	Lea	GP	G	A	TP	PIM	GP	G	A	TP	PIM
1996-97	Green Bay	USHL	14	4	9	13	14	....	....	....	....	....
1997-98	U. of Minnesota	WCHA	28	4	8	12	14	....	....	....	....	....

MITCHELL, JEFF DAL.

Center/Right wing. Shoots right. 6'1", 190 lbs. Born, Wayne, MI, May 16, 1975.
(Los Angeles' 2nd choice, 68th overall, in 1993 Entry Draft).

			Regular Season					Playoffs				
Season	Club	Lea	GP	G	A	TP	PIM	GP	G	A	TP	PIM
1992-93	Detroit	OHL	62	10	15	25	100	15	3	3	6	16
1993-94	Detroit	OHL	59	25	18	43	99	17	3	5	8	22
1994-95	Detroit	OHL	61	30	30	60	121	21	9	12	21	48
1995-96	Michigan	IHL	50	5	4	9	119	....	....	....	....	....
1996-97	Michigan	IHL	24	0	3	3	40	....	....	....	....	....
	Philadelphia	AHL	31	7	5	12	103	10	1	1	2	20
1997-98	**Dallas**	**NHL**	**7**	**0**	**0**	**0**	**7**	....	....	....	....	....
	Michigan	IHL	62	9	8	17	206	4	0	0	0	30
	NHL Totals		**7**	**0**	**0**	**0**	**7**	....	....	....	....	....

Rights traded to **Dallas** by **LA Kings** for Vancouver's 5th round choice (previously acquired, LA Kings selected Jason Morgan) in 1995 Entry Draft, June 7, 1995.

MITCHELL, WILLIE N.J.

Defense. Shoots left. 6'3", 210 lbs. Born, Ft. McNeill, B.C., April 23, 1977.
(New Jersey's 12th choice, 199th overall, in 1996 Entry Draft).

			Regular Season					Playoffs				
Season	Club	Lea	GP	G	A	TP	PIM	GP	G	A	TP	PIM
1995-96	Melfort	SJHL	19	2	6	8	....	14	0	2	2	12
1996-97	Melfort	SJHL	64	14	42	56	227	4	0	1	1	23
1997-98	Clarkson	ECAC	34	9	17	26	105	....	....	....	....	....

ECAC Second All-Star Team (1998)

MODANO, MIKE (moh-DAN-oh) DAL.

Center. Shoots left. 6'3", 200 lbs. Born, Livonia, MI, June 7, 1970.
(Minnesota's 1st choice, 1st overall, in 1988 Entry Draft).

			Regular Season					Playoffs				
Season	Club	Lea	GP	G	A	TP	PIM	GP	G	A	TP	PIM
1986-87	Prince Albert	WHL	70	32	30	62	96	8	1	4	5	4
1987-88	Prince Albert	WHL	65	47	80	127	80	9	7	11	18	18
1988-89	Prince Albert	WHL	41	39	66	105	74	....	....	....	....	....
	Minnesota	**NHL**	....	....	....	....	....	**2**	**0**	**0**	**0**	**0**
1989-90	**Minnesota**	**NHL**	**80**	**29**	**46**	**75**	**63**	**7**	**1**	**1**	**2**	**12**
1990-91	**Minnesota**	**NHL**	**79**	**28**	**36**	**64**	**65**	**23**	**8**	**12**	**20**	**16**
1991-92	**Minnesota**	**NHL**	**76**	**33**	**44**	**77**	**46**	**7**	**3**	**2**	**5**	**4**
1992-93	**Minnesota**	**NHL**	**82**	**33**	**60**	**93**	**83**	....	....	....	....	....
1993-94	**Dallas**	**NHL**	**76**	**50**	**43**	**93**	**54**	**9**	**7**	**3**	**10**	**16**
1994-95	**Dallas**	**NHL**	**30**	**12**	**17**	**29**	**8**	....	....	....	....	....
1995-96	**Dallas**	**NHL**	**78**	**36**	**45**	**81**	**63**	....	....	....	....	....
1996-97	**Dallas**	**NHL**	**80**	**35**	**48**	**83**	**42**	**7**	**4**	**1**	**5**	**0**
1997-98	**Dallas**	**NHL**	**52**	**21**	**38**	**59**	**32**	**17**	**4**	**10**	**14**	**12**
	United States	Olympics	4	2	0	2	0	....	....	....	....	....
	NHL Totals		**633**	**277**	**377**	**654**	**456**	**72**	**27**	**29**	**56**	**60**

WHL East All-Star Team (1989) • NHL All-Rookie Team (1990)

Played in NHL All-Star Game (1993, 1998)

Transferred to **Dallas** after **Minnesota** franchise relocated, June 9, 1993.

MODIN, FREDRIK (muh-DEEN) TOR.

Left wing. Shoots left. 6'3", 222 lbs. Born, Sundsvall, Sweden, October 8, 1974.
(Toronto's 3rd choice, 64th overall, in 1994 Entry Draft).

			Regular Season					Playoffs				
Season	Club	Lea	GP	G	A	TP	PIM	GP	G	A	TP	PIM
1991-92	Sundsvall	Sweden-2	11	1	0	1	0	....	....	....	....	....
1992-93	Sundsvall	Sweden-2	30	5	7	12	12	....	....	....	....	....
1993-94	Sundsvall	Sweden-2	30	16	15	31	36	....	....	....	....	....
1994-95	Brynas IF	Sweden	38	9	10	19	33	14	4	4	8	6
1995-96	Brynas IF	Sweden	22	4	8	12	22	....	....	....	....	....
1996-97	**Toronto**	**NHL**	**76**	**6**	**7**	**13**	**24**	....	....	....	....	....
1997-98	**Toronto**	**NHL**	**74**	**16**	**16**	**32**	**32**	....	....	....	....	....
	NHL Totals		**150**	**22**	**23**	**45**	**56**	....	....	....	....	....

MODRY, JAROSLAV (MOHD-ree) L.A.

Defense. Shoots left. 6'2", 219 lbs. Born, Ceske-Budejovice, Czech., February 27, 1971.
(New Jersey's 11th choice, 179th overall, in 1990 Entry Draft).

			Regular Season					Playoffs				
Season	Club	Lea	GP	G	A	TP	PIM	GP	G	A	TP	PIM
1987-88	Budejovice	Czech.	3	0	0	0	0	....	....	....	....	....
1988-89	Budejovice	Czech.	28	0	1	1	8	....	....	....	....	....
1989-90	Budejovice	Czech.	41	2	2	4	....	....	....	....	....	....
1990-91	Dukla Trencin	Czech.	33	1	9	10	6	....	....	....	....	....
1991-92	Dukla Trencin	Czech.	18	0	4	4	6	....	....	....	....	....
	Budejovice	Czech-2	14	4	10	14	....	....	....	....	....	....
1992-93	Utica	AHL	80	7	35	42	62	5	0	2	2	2
1993-94	**New Jersey**	**NHL**	**41**	**2**	**15**	**17**	**18**	....	....	....	....	....
	Albany	AHL	19	1	5	6	25	....	....	....	....	....
1994-95	Budejovice	Cze-Rep.	19	1	3	4	30	....	....	....	....	....
	New Jersey	**NHL**	**11**	**0**	**0**	**0**	**0**	....	....	....	....	....
	Albany	AHL	18	5	6	11	14	14	3	3	6	4
1995-96	**Ottawa**	**NHL**	**64**	**4**	**14**	**18**	**38**	....	....	....	....	....
	Los Angeles	**NHL**	**9**	**0**	**3**	**3**	**6**	....	....	....	....	....
1996-97	**Los Angeles**	**NHL**	**30**	**3**	**3**	**6**	**25**	....	....	....	....	....
	Phoenix	IHL	23	3	12	15	17	....	....	....	....	....
	Utah	IHL	11	1	4	5	20	7	0	1	1	6
1997-98	Utah	IHL	74	12	21	33	72	4	0	2	2	6
	NHL Totals		**155**	**9**	**35**	**44**	**87**	....	....	....	....	....

Traded to **Ottawa** by **New Jersey** for Ottawa's 4th round choice (Alyn McCauley) in 1995 Entry Draft, July 8, 1995. Traded to **LA Kings** by **Ottawa** with Ottawa's 8th round choice (Stephen Valiquette) in 1996 Entry Draft for Kevin Brown, March 20, 1996.

MOGER, SANDY (MOH-guhr) L.A.

Center. Shoots right. 6'4", 220 lbs. Born, 100 Mile House, B.C., March 21, 1969.
(Vancouver's 7th choice, 176th overall, in 1989 Entry Draft).

			Regular Season					Playoffs				
Season	Club	Lea	GP	G	A	TP	PIM	GP	G	A	TP	PIM
1987-88	Yorkton	SJHL	60	39	41	80	144	....	....	....	....	....
1988-89	Lake Superior	CCHA	21	3	5	8	26	....	....	....	....	....
1989-90	Lake Superior	CCHA	46	17	15	32	76	....	....	....	....	....
1990-91	Lake Superior	CCHA	45	27	21	48	*172	....	....	....	....	....
1991-92	Lake Superior	CCHA	38	24	24	48	93	....	....	....	....	....
1992-93	Hamilton	AHL	78	23	26	49	57	....	....	....	....	....
1993-94	Hamilton	AHL	29	9	8	17	41	....	....	....	....	....
1994-95	**Boston**	**NHL**	**18**	**2**	**6**	**8**	**6**	....	....	....	....	....
	Providence	AHL	63	32	29	61	105	....	....	....	....	....
1995-96	**Boston**	**NHL**	**80**	**15**	**14**	**29**	**65**	**5**	**2**	**2**	**4**	**12**
1996-97	**Boston**	**NHL**	**34**	**10**	**3**	**13**	**45**	....	....	....	....	....
	Providence	AHL	3	0	2	2	19	....	....	....	....	....
1997-98	**Los Angeles**	**NHL**	**62**	**11**	**13**	**24**	**70**	....	....	....	....	....
	NHL Totals		**194**	**38**	**36**	**74**	**186**	**5**	**2**	**2**	**4**	**12**

CCHA Second All-Star Team (1992)

Signed as a free agent by **Boston**, June 22, 1994. Traded to **LA Kings** by **Boston** with Jozef Stumpel and Boston's 4th round choice (later traded to New Jersey — New Jersey selected Pierre Dagenais) in 1998 Entry Draft for Dimitri Khristich and Byron Dafoe, August 29, 1997.

MOGILNY, ALEXANDER (moh-GIHL-nee) VAN.

Right wing. Shoots left. 5'11", 200 lbs. Born, Khabarovsk, USSR, February 18, 1969.
(Buffalo's 4th choice, 89th overall, in 1988 Entry Draft).

			Regular Season					Playoffs				
Season	Club	Lea	GP	G	A	TP	PIM	GP	G	A	TP	PIM
1986-87	CSKA Moscow	USSR	28	15	1	16	4	....	....	....	....	....
1987-88	CSKA Moscow	USSR	39	12	8	20	14	....	....	....	....	....
	Soviet Union	Olympics	6	3	2	5	2	....	....	....	....	....
1988-89	CSKA Moscow	USSR	31	11	11	22	24	....	....	....	....	....
1989-90	**Buffalo**	**NHL**	**65**	**15**	**28**	**43**	**16**	**4**	**0**	**1**	**1**	**2**
1990-91	**Buffalo**	**NHL**	**62**	**30**	**34**	**64**	**16**	**6**	**0**	**6**	**6**	**2**
1991-92	**Buffalo**	**NHL**	**67**	**39**	**45**	**84**	**73**	**2**	**0**	**2**	**2**	**0**
1992-93	**Buffalo**	**NHL**	**77**	***76**	**51**	**127**	**40**	**7**	**7**	**3**	**10**	**6**
1993-94	**Buffalo**	**NHL**	**66**	**32**	**47**	**79**	**22**	**7**	**4**	**2**	**6**	**6**
1994-95	Spartak	CIS	1	0	1	1	0	....	....	....	....	....
	Buffalo	**NHL**	**44**	**19**	**28**	**47**	**36**	**5**	**3**	**2**	**5**	**2**
1995-96	**Vancouver**	**NHL**	**79**	**55**	**52**	**107**	**16**	**6**	**1**	**8**	**9**	**8**
1996-97	**Vancouver**	**NHL**	**76**	**31**	**42**	**73**	**18**	....	....	....	....	....
1997-98	**Vancouver**	**NHL**	**51**	**18**	**27**	**45**	**36**	....	....	....	....	....
	NHL Totals		**587**	**315**	**354**	**669**	**273**	**37**	**15**	**24**	**39**	**26**

NHL Second All-Star Team (1993, 1996)

Played in NHL All-Star Game (1992, 1993, 1994, 1996)

Traded to **Vancouver** by **Buffalo** with Buffalo's 5th round choice (Todd Norman) in 1995 Entry Draft for Mike Peca, Mike Wilson and Vancouver's 1st round choice (Jay McKee) in 1995 Entry Draft, July 8, 1995.

MOHAGEN, TONY ANA.

Left wing. Shoots left. 6'4", 220 lbs. Born, Regina, Sask., July 13, 1978.
(Anaheim's 5th choice, 178th overall, in 1997 Entry Draft).

			Regular Season					Playoffs				
Season	Club	Lea	GP	G	A	TP	PIM	GP	G	A	TP	PIM
1995-96	Seattle	WHL	58	2	2	4	131	2	0	0	0	0
1996-97	Seattle	WHL	55	5	6	11	191	15	0	1	1	50
1997-98	Swift Current	WHL	52	7	11	18	299	11	3	0	3	*70

MOISE, MARTIN (MOIZ) CGY.

Left wing. Shoots left. 6', 197 lbs. Born, Valleyfield, Que., January 18, 1979.
(Calgary's 9th choice, 113th overall, in 1997 Entry Draft).

			Regular Season					Playoffs				
Season	Club	Lea	GP	G	A	TP	PIM	GP	G	A	TP	PIM
1995-96	St-Hyacinthe	QMJHL	67	6	19	25	11	10	1	1	2	0
1996-97	Beauport	QMJHL	70	21	23	44	23	4	4	1	5	0
1997-98	Quebec	QMJHL	70	32	43	75	37	14	3	3	6	17

MOMESSO, SERGIO (moh-MESS-oh)

Left wing. Shoots left. 6'3", 215 lbs. Born, Montreal, Que., September 4, 1965.
(Montreal's 3rd choice, 27th overall, in 1983 Entry Draft).

			Regular Season					Playoffs				
Season	Club	Lea	GP	G	A	TP	PIM	GP	G	A	TP	PIM
1982-83	Shawinigan	QMJHL	70	27	42	69	93	10	5	4	9	55
1983-84	Shawinigan	QMJHL	68	42	88	130	235	6	4	4	8	13
	Montreal	**NHL**	**1**	**0**	**0**	**0**	**0**	....	....	....	....	....
	Nova Scotia	AHL	....	....	....	....	....	8	0	2	2	4
1984-85	Shawinigan	QMJHL	64	56	90	146	216	8	7	8	15	17
1985-86	**Montreal**	**NHL**	**24**	**8**	**7**	**15**	**46**	....	....	....	....	....
1986-87	**Montreal**	**NHL**	**59**	**14**	**17**	**31**	**96**	**11**	**1**	**3**	**4**	**31**
	Sherbrooke	AHL	6	1	6	7	10	....	....	....	....	....
1987-88	**Montreal**	**NHL**	**53**	**7**	**14**	**21**	**101**	**6**	**0**	**2**	**2**	**16**
1988-89	**St. Louis**	**NHL**	**53**	**9**	**17**	**26**	**139**	**10**	**2**	**5**	**7**	**24**
1989-90	**St. Louis**	**NHL**	**79**	**24**	**32**	**56**	**199**	**12**	**3**	**2**	**5**	**63**
1990-91	**St. Louis**	**NHL**	**59**	**10**	**18**	**28**	**131**	....	....	....	....	....
	Vancouver	**NHL**	**11**	**6**	**2**	**8**	**43**	**6**	**0**	**3**	**3**	**25**
1991-92	**Vancouver**	**NHL**	**58**	**20**	**23**	**43**	**198**	**13**	**0**	**5**	**5**	**30**
1992-93	**Vancouver**	**NHL**	**84**	**18**	**20**	**38**	**200**	**12**	**3**	**0**	**3**	**30**
1993-94	**Vancouver**	**NHL**	**68**	**14**	**13**	**27**	**149**	**24**	**3**	**4**	**7**	**56**
1994-95	HC Milano	Italy	2	1	4	5	2	....	....	....	....	....
	HC Milano	EuroHL	2	2	3	5	0	....	....	....	....	....
	Vancouver	**NHL**	**48**	**10**	**15**	**25**	**65**	**11**	**3**	**1**	**4**	**16**
1995-96	**Toronto**	**NHL**	**54**	**7**	**8**	**15**	**112**	....	....	....	....	....
	NY Rangers	**NHL**	**19**	**4**	**4**	**8**	**30**	**11**	**3**	**1**	**4**	**14**
1996-97	**NY Rangers**	**NHL**	**9**	**0**	**0**	**0**	**11**	....	....	....	....	....
	St. Louis	**NHL**	**31**	**1**	**3**	**4**	**37**	**3**	**0**	**0**	**0**	**6**
1997-98	Kolner Haie	Germany	42	14	18	32	*193	3	1	2	3	4
	Kolner Haie	EuroHL	6	4	4	8	29	....	....	....	....	....
	NHL Totals		**710**	**152**	**193**	**345**	**1557**	**119**	**18**	**26**	**44**	**311**

QMJHL First All-Star Team (1985)

Traded to **St. Louis** by **Montreal** with Vincent Riendeau for Jocelyn Lemieux, Darrell May and St. Louis' 2nd round choice (Patrice Brisebois) in the 1989 Entry Draft, August 9, 1988. Traded to **Vancouver** by **St. Louis** with Geoff Courtnall, Robert Dirk, Cliff Ronning and St. Louis' 5th round choice (Brian Loney) in 1992 Entry Draft for Dan Quinn and Garth Butcher, March 5, 1991. Traded to **Toronto** by **Vancouver** for Mike Ridley, July 8, 1995. Traded by **NY Rangers** by **Toronto** for Wayne Presley, February 29, 1996. Traded to **St. Louis** by **NY Rangers** for Brian Noonan, November 13, 1996.

MONTGOMERY, JIM PHI.

Center. Shoots right. 5'10", 185 lbs. Born, Montreal, Que., June 30, 1969.

			Regular Season					Playoffs				
Season	Club	Lea	GP	G	A	TP	PIM	GP	G	A	TP	PIM
1989-90	U. of Maine	H.E.	45	26	34	60	35	....	....	....	....	....
1990-91	U. of Maine	H.E.	43	24	*57	81	44	....	....	....	....	....
1991-92	U. of Maine	H.E.	37	21	44	65	46	....	....	....	....	....
1992-93	U. of Maine	H.E.	45	32	63	95	40	....	....	....	....	....
1993-94	**St. Louis**	**NHL**	**67**	**6**	**14**	**20**	**44**	....	....	....	....	....
	Peoria	IHL	12	7	8	15	10	....	....	....	....	....
1994-95	**Montreal**	**NHL**	**5**	**0**	**0**	**0**	**2**	....	....	....	....	....
	Philadelphia	**NHL**	**8**	**1**	**1**	**2**	**6**	**7**	**1**	**0**	**1**	**2**
	Hershey	AHL	16	8	6	14	14	6	3	2	5	25
1995-96	**Philadelphia**	**NHL**	**5**	**1**	**2**	**3**	**9**	**1**	**0**	**0**	**0**	**0**
	Hershey	AHL	78	34	*71	105	95	4	3	2	5	6
1996-97	Kolner Haie	Germany	50	12	35	47	111	4	0	1	1	6
1997-98	Philadelphia	AHL	68	19	43	62	75	20	*13	16	29	55
	NHL Totals		**85**	**8**	**17**	**25**	**61**	**8**	**1**	**0**	**1**	**2**

Hockey East Second All-Star Team (1991, 1992) • Hockey East First All-Star Team (1993) • NCAA East Second All-American Team (1993) • NCAA Championship All-Tournament Team (1993) • NCAA Championship Tournament MVP (1993) • AHL Second All-Star Team (1996)

Signed as a free agent by **St. Louis**, June 2, 1993. Traded to **Montreal** by **St. Louis** for Guy Carbonneau, August 19, 1994. Claimed on waivers by **Philadelphia** from **Montreal**, February 10, 1995.

MOORE, BARRIE EDM.

Left wing. Shoots left. 5'11", 175 lbs. Born, London, Ont., May 22, 1975.
(Buffalo's 7th choice, 220th overall, in 1993 Entry Draft).

			Regular Season					Playoffs				
Season	Club	Lea	GP	G	A	TP	PIM	GP	G	A	TP	PIM
1991-92	Sudbury	OHL	62	15	38	53	57	11	0	7	7	12
1992-93	Sudbury	OHL	57	13	26	39	71	14	4	3	7	19
1993-94	Sudbury	OHL	65	36	49	85	69	10	3	5	8	14
1994-95	Sudbury	OHL	60	47	42	89	67	18	*15	14	29	24
1995-96	**Buffalo**	**NHL**	**3**	**0**	**0**	**0**	**0**	....	....	....	....	....
	Rochester	AHL	64	26	30	56	40	18	3	6	9	18
1996-97	**Buffalo**	**NHL**	**31**	**2**	**6**	**8**	**18**	....	....	....	....	....
	Rochester	AHL	32	14	15	29	14	....	....	....	....	....
	Edmonton	**NHL**	**4**	**0**	**0**	**0**	**0**	....	....	....	....	....
	Hamilton	AHL	9	5	2	7	0	22	2	6	8	15
1997-98	Hamilton	AHL	70	22	29	51	64	8	0	1	1	4
	NHL Totals		**38**	**2**	**6**	**8**	**18**	....	....	....	....	....

Traded to **Edmonton** by **Buffalo** with Craig Millar for Miroslav Satan, March 18, 1997.

MOORE, MARK PIT.

Defense. Shoots right. 6'3", 185 lbs. Born, Windsor, Ont., February 18, 1977.
(Pittsburgh's 7th choice, 179th overall, in 1997 Entry Draft).

			Regular Season					Playoffs				
Season	Club	Lea	GP	G	A	TP	PIM	GP	G	A	TP	PIM
1996-97	Harvard	ECAC	22	5	2	7	16	....	....	....	....	....
1997-98	Harvard	ECAC	32	1	3	4	90	....	....	....	....	....

MOORE, STEVE COL.

Center. Shoots right. 6'2", 190 lbs. Born, Windsor, Ont., September 22, 1978.
(Colorado's 7th choice, 53rd overall, in 1998 Entry Draft).

			Regular Season					Playoffs				
Season	Club	Lea	GP	G	A	TP	PIM	GP	G	A	TP	PIM
1996-97	Thornhill	OJHL	50	34	52	86	52	....	....	....	....	....
1997-98	Harvard	ECAC	33	10	23	33	46	....	....	....	....	....

MORAN, IAN (moh-RAN) PIT.

Right wing. Shoots right. 6', 206 lbs. Born, Cleveland, OH, August 24, 1972.
(Pittsburgh's 5th choice, 107th overall, in 1990 Entry Draft).

			Regular Season					Playoffs				
Season	Club	Lea	GP	G	A	TP	PIM	GP	G	A	TP	PIM
1989-90	Belmont Hill	H.S.	23	10	36	46	....	....	....	....	....	....
1990-91	Belmont Hill	H.S.	23	7	44	51	12	....	....	....	....	....
1991-92	Boston College	H.E.	30	2	16	18	44	....	....	....	....	....
1992-93	Boston College	H.E.	31	8	12	20	32	....	....	....	....	....
1993-94	United States	Nat-Tm	50	8	15	23	69	....	....	....	....	....
	Cleveland	IHL	33	5	13	18	39	....	....	....	....	....
1994-95	Cleveland	IHL	64	7	31	38	94	4	0	1	1	2
	Pittsburgh	**NHL**	....	....	....	....	....	**8**	**0**	**0**	**0**	**0**
1995-96	**Pittsburgh**	**NHL**	**51**	**1**	**1**	**2**	**47**	....	....	....	....	....
1996-97	**Pittsburgh**	**NHL**	**36**	**4**	**5**	**9**	**22**	**5**	**1**	**2**	**3**	**4**
	Cleveland	IHL	36	6	23	29	26	....	....	....	....	....
1997-98	**Pittsburgh**	**NHL**	**37**	**1**	**6**	**7**	**19**	**6**	**0**	**0**	**0**	**2**
	NHL Totals		**124**	**6**	**12**	**18**	**88**	**19**	**1**	**2**	**3**	**6**

MORE, JAYSON (MOHR) NSH.

Defense. Shoots right. 6'1", 210 lbs. Born, Souris, Man., January 12, 1969.
(NY Rangers' 1st choice, 10th overall, in 1987 Entry Draft).

			Regular Season					Playoffs				
Season	Club	Lea	GP	G	A	TP	PIM	GP	G	A	TP	PIM
1984-85	Lethbridge	WHL	71	3	9	12	101	4	1	0	1	7
1985-86	Lethbridge	WHL	61	7	18	25	155	9	0	2	2	36
1986-87	Brandon	WHL	21	4	6	10	62	....	....	....	....	....
	New Westminster	WHL	43	4	23	27	155	....	....	....	....	....
1987-88	New Westminster	WHL	70	13	47	60	270	5	0	2	2	26
1988-89	**NY Rangers**	**NHL**	**1**	**0**	**0**	**0**	**0**	....	....	....	....	....
	Denver	IHL	62	7	15	22	138	3	0	1	1	26
1989-90	Flint	IHL	9	1	5	6	41	....	....	....	....	....
	Minnesota	**NHL**	**5**	**0**	**0**	**0**	**16**	....	....	....	....	....
	Kalamazoo	IHL	64	9	25	34	316	10	0	3	3	13
1990-91	Kalamazoo	IHL	10	0	5	5	46	....	....	....	....	....
	Fredericton	AHL	57	7	17	24	152	9	1	1	2	34
1991-92	**San Jose**	**NHL**	**46**	**4**	**13**	**17**	**85**	....	....	....	....	....
	Kansas City	IHL	2	0	2	2	4	....	....	....	....	....
1992-93	**San Jose**	**NHL**	**73**	**5**	**6**	**11**	**179**	....	....	....	....	....
1993-94	**San Jose**	**NHL**	**49**	**1**	**6**	**7**	**63**	**13**	**0**	**2**	**2**	**32**
	Kansas City	IHL	2	1	0	1	25	....	....	....	....	....
1994-95	**San Jose**	**NHL**	**45**	**0**	**6**	**6**	**71**	**11**	**0**	**4**	**4**	**6**
1995-96	**San Jose**	**NHL**	**74**	**2**	**7**	**9**	**147**	....	....	....	....	....
1996-97	**NY Rangers**	**NHL**	**14**	**0**	**1**	**1**	**25**	....	....	....	....	....
	Phoenix	**NHL**	**23**	**1**	**6**	**7**	**37**	**7**	**0**	**0**	**0**	**7**
1997-98	**Phoenix**	**NHL**	**41**	**5**	**5**	**10**	**53**	....	....	....	....	....
	Chicago	**NHL**	**17**	**0**	**2**	**2**	**8**	....	....	....	....	....
	NHL Totals		**388**	**18**	**52**	**70**	**684**	**31**	**0**	**6**	**6**	**45**

WHL All-Star Team (1988)

Traded to **Minnesota** by **NY Rangers** for Dave Archibald, November 1, 1989. Traded to **Montreal** by **Minnesota** for Brian Hayward, November 7, 1990. Claimed by **San Jose** from **Montreal** in Expansion Draft, May 30, 1991. Traded to **NY Rangers** by **San Jose** with Brian Swanson and future considerations for Marty McSorley, August 20, 1996. Traded to **Phoenix** by **NY Rangers** for Mike Eastwood and Dallas Eakins, February 6, 1997. Traded to **Chicago** by **Phoenix** with Chad Kilger for Keith Carney and Jim Cummins, March 4, 1998. Signed as a free agent by **Nashville**, June 4, 1998.

MOREAU, ETHAN (moh-ROH, EE-than) CHI.

Left wing. Shoots left. 6'2", 205 lbs. Born, Huntsville, Ont., September 22, 1975.
(Chicago's 1st choice, 14th overall, in 1994 Entry Draft).

			Regular Season					Playoffs				
Season	Club	Lea	GP	G	A	TP	PIM	GP	G	A	TP	PIM
1991-92	Niagara Falls	OHL	62	20	35	55	39	17	4	6	10	4
1992-93	Niagara Falls	OHL	65	32	41	73	69	4	0	3	3	4
1993-94	Niagara Falls	OHL	59	44	54	98	100	....	....	....	....	....
1994-95	Niagara Falls	OHL	39	25	41	66	69	....	....	....	....	....
	Sudbury	OHL	23	13	17	30	22	18	6	12	18	26
1995-96	**Chicago**	**NHL**	**8**	**0**	**1**	**1**	**4**	....	....	....	....	....
	Indianapolis	IHL	71	21	20	41	126	5	4	0	4	8
1996-97	**Chicago**	**NHL**	**82**	**15**	**16**	**31**	**123**	**6**	**1**	**0**	**1**	**9**
1997-98	**Chicago**	**NHL**	**54**	**9**	**9**	**18**	**73**	....	....	....	....	....
	NHL Totals		**144**	**24**	**26**	**50**	**200**	**6**	**1**	**0**	**1**	**9**

MORGAN, JASON — L.A.

Center. Shoots left. 6'1", 200 lbs. Born, St. John's, Nfld., October 9, 1976.
(Los Angeles' 5th choice, 118th overall, in 1995 Entry Draft).

			Regular Season					Playoffs				
Season	Club	Lea	GP	G	A	TP	PIM	GP	G	A	TP	PIM
1993-94	Kitchener	OHL	65	6	15	21	16	5	1	0	1	0
1994-95	Kitchener	OHL	35	3	15	18	25	....	....	....	....	....
	Kingston	OHL	20	0	3	3	14	6	0	2	2	0
1995-96	Kingston	OHL	66	16	38	54	50	6	1	2	3	0
1996-97	**Los Angeles**	**NHL**	**3**	**0**	**0**	**0**	**0**	....	....	....	....	....
	Phoenix	IHL	57	3	6	9	29	....	....	....	....	....
	Mississippi	ECHL	6	3	0	3	0	3	1	1	2	6
1997-98	**Los Angeles**	**NHL**	**11**	**1**	**0**	**1**	**4**	....	....	....	....	....
	Springfield	AHL	58	13	22	35	66	3	1	0	1	18
	NHL Totals		**14**	**1**	**0**	**1**	**4**	....	....	....	....	....

MORIN, JEAN-PHILIPPE — PHI.

Defense. Shoots left. 6'1", 188 lbs. Born, Gaspe, Que., February 6, 1980.
(Philadelphia's 4th choice, 109th overall, in 1998 Entry Draft).

			Regular Season					Playoffs				
Season	Club	Lea	GP	G	A	TP	PIM	GP	G	A	TP	PIM
1996-97	Victoriaville	QMJHL	56	3	5	8	20	1	0	0	0	0
1997-98	Victoriaville	QMJHL	35	3	11	14	79	....	....	....	....	....
	Drummondville	QMJHL	18	1	4	5	16	....	....	....	....	....

MORIN, OLIVIER — MTL.

Right wing. Shoots right. 6', 176 lbs. Born, Montreal, Que., April 2, 1978.

			Regular Season					Playoffs				
Season	Club	Lea	GP	G	A	TP	PIM	GP	G	A	TP	PIM
1995-96	Chicoutimi	QMJHL	68	17	32	49	102	17	6	5	11	51
1996-97	Chicoutimi	QMJHL	70	22	44	66	152	21	5	8	13	24
1997-98	Val d'Or	QMJHL	56	20	31	51	73	4	4	3	7	4

Signed as a free agent by **Montreal**, October 3, 1996.

MORISSETTE, DAVE — MTL.

Left wing. Shoots left. 6'1", 220 lbs. Born, Baie Comeau, Que., December 24, 1971.
(Washington's 7th choice, 146th overall, in 1991 Entry Draft).

			Regular Season					Playoffs				
Season	Club	Lea	GP	G	A	TP	PIM	GP	G	A	TP	PIM
1989-90	Shawinigan	QMJHL	66	2	9	11	269	....	....	....	....	....
1990-91	Shawinigan	QMJHL	64	20	26	46	224	6	1	1	2	17
1991-92	Hampton Roads	ECHL	47	6	10	16	293	13	1	3	4	74
	Baltimore	AHL	2	0	0	0	6	....	....	....	....	....
1992-93	Hampton Roads	ECHL	54	9	13	22	226	2	0	0	0	2
1993-94	Roanoke	ECHL	45	8	10	18	278	2	0	1	1	4
1994-95	Minnesota	IHL	50	1	4	5	174	....	....	....	....	....
1995-96	Minnesota	IHL	33	3	2	5	104	....	....	....	....	....
1996-97	Houston	IHL	59	2	1	3	214	2	0	0	0	0
1997-98	Houston	IHL	67	4	4	8	254	2	0	0	0	2

Signed as a free agent by **Montreal**, June 10, 1998.

MORO, MARC (MOH-roh) — ANA.

Defense. Shoots left. 6'1", 225 lbs. Born, Toronto, Ont., July 17, 1977.
(Ottawa's 2nd choice, 27th overall, in 1995 Entry Draft).

			Regular Season					Playoffs				
Season	Club	Lea	GP	G	A	TP	PIM	GP	G	A	TP	PIM
1993-94	Kingston	OHL	43	0	3	3	81	....	....	....	....	....
1994-95	Kingston	OHL	64	4	12	16	255	6	0	0	0	23
1995-96	Kingston	OHL	66	4	17	21	261	6	0	0	0	12
	P.E.I.	AHL	2	0	0	0	7	2	0	0	0	4
1996-97	Kingston	OHL	37	4	8	12	97	....	....	....	....	....
	S.S. Marie	OHL	26	0	5	5	74	11	1	6	7	38
1997-98	**Anaheim**	**NHL**	**1**	**0**	**0**	**0**	**0**	....	....	....	....	....
	Cincinnati	AHL	74	1	6	7	181	....	....	....	....	....
	NHL Totals		**1**	**0**	**0**	**0**	**0**	....	....	....	....	....

Rights traded to **Anaheim** by **Ottawa** with Ted Drury for Jason York and Shaun Van Allen, October 1, 1996.

MOROZOV, ALEXEI (moh-ROH-zohv) — PIT.

Right wing. Shoots left. 6'1", 180 lbs. Born, Moscow, USSR, February 16, 1977.
(Pittsburgh's 1st choice, 24th overall, in 1995 Entry Draft).

			Regular Season					Playoffs				
Season	Club	Lea	GP	G	A	TP	PIM	GP	G	A	TP	PIM
1993-94	Soviet Wings	CIS	7	0	0	0	0	3	0	0	0	2
1994-95	Soviet Wings	CIS	48	15	12	27	53	4	0	3	3	0
1995-96	Soviet Wings	CIS	47	13	9	22	26	....	....	....	....	....
1996-97	Soviet Wings	Russia	44	21	11	32	32	2	0	1	1	2
1997-98	Soviet Wings	Russia	6	2	1	3	4	....	....	....	....	....
	Pittsburgh	**NHL**	**76**	**13**	**13**	**26**	**8**	**6**	**0**	**1**	**1**	**2**
	Russia	Olympics	6	2	2	4	0	....	....	....	....	....
	NHL Totals		**76**	**13**	**13**	**26**	**8**	**6**	**0**	**1**	**1**	**2**

CIS Rookie of the Year (1995)

MOROZOV, VALENTIN (moh-ROH-zohv) — PIT.

Center. Shoots left. 5'11", 176 lbs. Born, Moscow, USSR, June 1, 1975.
(Pittsburgh's 8th choice, 154th overall, in 1994 Entry Draft).

			Regular Season					Playoffs				
Season	Club	Lea	GP	G	A	TP	PIM	GP	G	A	TP	PIM
1992-93	CSKA Moscow	CIS	17	0	0	0	6	....	....	....	....	....
1993-94	CSKA Moscow	CIS	18	4	1	5	8	3	0	1	1	0
1994-95	CSKA Moscow	CIS	47	9	4	13	10	2	2	0	2	0
1995-96	CSKA Moscow	CIS	51	30	11	41	28	3	1	0	1	2
1996-97	CSKA Moscow	Russia	22	8	5	13	8	....	....	....	....	....
	CSKA Moscow	EuroHL	4	2	1	3	0	....	....	....	....	....
1997-98	Soviet Wings	Russia	34	5	15	20	8	....	....	....	....	....

MORRIS, DEREK — CGY.

Defense. Shoots right. 6', 200 lbs. Born, Edmonton, Alta., August 24, 1978.
(Calgary's 1st choice, 13th overall, in 1996 Entry Draft).

			Regular Season					Playoffs				
Season	Club	Lea	GP	G	A	TP	PIM	GP	G	A	TP	PIM
1995-96	Regina	WHL	67	8	44	52	70	11	1	7	8	26
1996-97	Regina	WHL	67	18	57	75	180	5	0	3	3	9
	Saint John	AHL	7	0	3	3	7	5	0	3	3	7
1997-98	**Calgary**	**NHL**	**82**	**9**	**20**	**29**	**88**	....	....	....	....	....
	NHL Totals		**82**	**9**	**20**	**29**	**88**	....	....	....	....	....

WHL East First All-Star Team (1997) • NHL All-Rookie Team (1998)

MORRISON, BRENDAN — N.J.

Center. Shoots left. 5'11", 180 lbs. Born, N. Vancouver, B.C., August 12, 1975.
(New Jersey's 3rd choice, 39th overall, in 1993 Entry Draft).

			Regular Season					Playoffs				
Season	Club	Lea	GP	G	A	TP	PIM	GP	G	A	TP	PIM
1992-93	Penticton	BCJHL	56	35	59	94	45	....	....	....	....	....
1993-94	U. of Michigan	CCHA	38	20	28	48	24	....	....	....	....	....
1994-95	U. of Michigan	CCHA	39	23	*53	*76	42	....	....	....	....	....
1995-96	U. of Michigan	CCHA	35	28	44	*72	41	....	....	....	....	....
1996-97	U. of Michigan	CCHA	43	31	*57	*88	52	....	....	....	....	....
1997-98	**New Jersey**	**NHL**	**11**	**5**	**4**	**9**	**0**	**3**	**0**	**1**	**1**	**0**
	Albany	AHL	72	35	49	84	44	8	3	4	7	19
	NHL Totals		**11**	**5**	**4**	**9**	**0**	**3**	**0**	**1**	**1**	**0**

CCHA First All-Star Team (1995, 1996, 1997) • NCAA West First All-American Team (1995, 1996, 1997) • NCAA Championship All-Tournament Team (1996) • NCAA Championship Tournament MVP (1996) • Won Hobey Baker Memorial Award (Top U.S. Collegiate Player) (1997)

MORRISON, JUSTIN — VAN.

Right wing. Shoots right. 6'3", 205 lbs. Born, Los Angeles, CA, September 10, 1979.
(Vancouver's 4th choice, 81st overall, in 1998 Entry Draft).

			Regular Season					Playoffs				
Season	Club	Lea	GP	G	A	TP	PIM	GP	G	A	TP	PIM
1996-97	Omaha	USHL	62	12	24	36	44	....	....	....	....	....
1997-98	Colorado College	WCHA	42	4	9	13	8	....	....	....	....	....

MORRONE, MIKE — CAR.

Left wing. Shoots left. 5'11", 215 lbs. Born, Windsor, Ont., January 3, 1976.

			Regular Season					Playoffs				
Season	Club	Lea	GP	G	A	TP	PIM	GP	G	A	TP	PIM
1993-94	Owen Sound	OHL	57	0	7	7	99	6	0	0	0	4
1994-95	Owen Sound	OHL	8	1	1	2	14	....	....	....	....	....
	Detroit	OHL	47	4	21	25	129	21	1	1	2	11
1995-96	Detroit	OHL	65	9	20	29	207	17	3	6	9	42
1996-97	Detroit	OHL	46	5	13	18	164	5	1	1	2	42
1997-98	Richmond	ECHL	65	4	4	8	281	....	....	....	....	....
	New Haven	AHL	1	0	0	0	4	....	....	....	....	....

Signed as a free agent by **Carolina**, June 9, 1997.

MORROW, BRENDEN — DAL.

Left wing. Shoots left. 5'11", 196 lbs. Born, Carlisle, Sask., January 16, 1979.
(Dallas' 1st choice, 25th overall, in 1997 Entry Draft).

			Regular Season					Playoffs				
Season	Club	Lea	GP	G	A	TP	PIM	GP	G	A	TP	PIM
1995-96	Portland	WHL	65	13	12	25	61	7	0	0	0	8
1996-97	Portland	WHL	71	39	49	88	178	6	2	1	3	4
1997-98	Portland	WHL	68	34	52	86	184	16	10	8	18	65

MOTTAU, MIKE — NYR

Defense. Shoots left. 6', 188 lbs. Born, Quincy, MA, March 19, 1978.
(NY Rangers' 10th choice, 182nd overall, in 1997 Entry Draft).

			Regular Season					Playoffs				
Season	Club	Lea	GP	G	A	TP	PIM	GP	G	A	TP	PIM
1996-97	Boston College	H.E.	38	5	18	23	77	....	....	....	....	....
1997-98	Boston College	H.E.	40	13	36	49	50	....	....	....	....	....

MOWERS, MARK — NSH.

Right wing. Shoots right. 5'11", 188 lbs. Born, Whitesboro, NY, January 6, 1974.

			Regular Season					Playoffs				
Season	Club	Lea	GP	G	A	TP	PIM	GP	G	A	TP	PIM
1994-95	New Hampshire	H.E.	36	13	23	36	16	....	....	....	....	....
1995-96	New Hampshire	H.E.	34	21	26	47	18	....	....	....	....	....
1996-97	New Hampshire	H.E.	39	26	32	58	52	....	....	....	....	....
1997-98	New Hampshire	H.E.	35	25	31	56	32	....	....	....	....	....

Signed as a free agent by **Nashville**, August, 1988.

MRAZEK, FRANTISEK (muh-RA-zehk) — TOR.

Left wing. Shoots left. 6'4", 211 lbs. Born, Ceske-Budejovice, Czech., May 16, 1979.
(Toronto's 3rd choice, 111th overall, in 1997 Entry Draft).

			Regular Season					Playoffs				
Season	Club	Lea	GP	G	A	TP	PIM	GP	G	A	TP	PIM
1996-97	Budejovice	Czech-Jr.	40	18	15	33	....	....	....	....	....	....
1997-98	Red Deer	WHL	65	30	24	54	71	5	1	0	1	2

MROZIK, RICK (muh-ROH-zihk) — WSH.

Defense. Shoots left. 6'2", 185 lbs. Born, Duluth, MN, January 2, 1975.
(Dallas' 4th choice, 136th overall, in 1993 Entry Draft).

			Regular Season					Playoffs				
Season	Club	Lea	GP	G	A	TP	PIM	GP	G	A	TP	PIM
1992-93	Cloquet High	H.S.	28	9	38	47	12	....	....	....	....	....
1993-94	U. Minn-Duluth	WCHA	38	2	9	11	38	....	....	....	....	....
1994-95	U. Minn-Duluth	WCHA	3	0	0	0	2	....	....	....	....	....
1995-96	U. Minn-Duluth	WCHA	35	3	19	22	63	....	....	....	....	....
1996-97	U. Minn-Duluth	WCHA	38	11	23	34	56	....	....	....	....	....
1997-98	Portland	AHL	75	2	15	17	52	10	1	3	4	2

WCHA Second All-Star Team (1997)

Traded to **Washington** by **Dallas** with Mark Tinordi for Kevin Hatcher, January 18, 1995.

MUCKALT, BILL (MUH-kawlt) — VAN.

Right wing. Shoots right. 6', 190 lbs. Born, Surrey, B.C., July 15, 1974.
(Vancouver's 9th choice, 221st overall, in 1994 Entry Draft).

			Regular Season					Playoffs				
Season	Club	Lea	GP	G	A	TP	PIM	GP	G	A	TP	PIM
1993-94	Merritt	BCJHL	43	58	51	109	99	....	....	....	....	....
	Kelowna	BCJHL	15	12	10	22	20	....	....	....	....	....
1994-95	U. of Michigan	CCHA	39	19	18	37	42	....	....	....	....	....
1995-96	U. of Michigan	CCHA	41	28	30	58	34	....	....	....	....	....
1996-97	U. of Michigan	CCHA	36	26	38	64	69	....	....	....	....	....
1997-98	U. of Michigan	CCHA	46	32	*35	*67	94	....	....	....	....	....

CCHA First All-Star Team (1998) • NCAA West First All-American Team (1998)

MUIR, BRYAN — N.J.

Defense. Shoots left. 6'4", 220 lbs. Born, Winnipeg, Man., June 8, 1973.

			Regular Season					Playoffs				
Season	Club	Lea	GP	G	A	TP	PIM	GP	G	A	TP	PIM
1992-93	New Hampshire	H.E.	26	1	2	3	24	....	....	....	....	....
1993-94	New Hampshire	H.E.	40	0	4	4	48	....	....	....	....	....
1994-95	New Hampshire	H.E.	28	9	9	18	46	....	....	....	....	....
1995-96	Canada	Nat-Tm	42	6	12	18	38	....	....	....	....	....
	Edmonton	**NHL**	**5**	**0**	**0**	**0**	**6**	....	....	....	....	....
1996-97	Hamilton	AHL	75	8	16	24	80	14	0	5	5	12
	Edmonton	**NHL**	....	....	....	....	....	**5**	**0**	**0**	**0**	**4**
1997-98	**Edmonton**	**NHL**	**7**	**0**	**0**	**0**	**17**	....	....	....	....	....
	Hamilton	AHL	28	3	10	13	62	....	....	....	....	....
	Albany	AHL	41	3	10	13	67	13	3	0	3	12
	NHL Totals		**12**	**0**	**0**	**0**	**23**	**5**	**0**	**0**	**0**	**4**

Signed as a free agent by **Edmonton**, April 30, 1996.

Traded to **New Jersey** by **Edmonton** with Jason Arnott for Valeri Zelepukin and Bill Guerin, January 4, 1998.

MULHERN, RYAN — WSH.

Center. Shoots right. 6'1", 180 lbs. Born, Philadelphia, PA, January 11, 1973.
(Calgary's 9th choice, 174th overall, in 1992 Entry Draft).

			Regular Season					Playoffs				
Season	Club	Lea	GP	G	A	TP	PIM	GP	G	A	TP	PIM
1991-92	Canterbury Prep	H.S.	37	51	27	78	50	....	....	....	....	....
1992-93	Brown University	ECAC	31	15	9	24	46	....	....	....	....	....
1993-94	Brown University	ECAC	27	18	17	35	48	....	....	....	....	....
1994-95	Brown University	ECAC	30	18	16	34	*108	....	....	....	....	....
1995-96	Brown University	ECAC	32	10	16	26	78	....	....	....	....	....
1996-97	Hampton Roads	ECHL	40	22	16	38	52	....	....	....	....	....
	Portland	AHL	38	19	15	34	16	5	1	1	2	2
1997-98	**Washington**	**NHL**	**3**	**0**	**0**	**0**	**0**	....	....	....	....	....
	Portland	AHL	71	25	40	65	85	6	1	0	1	12
	NHL Totals		**3**	**0**	**0**	**0**	**0**	....	....	....	....	....

AHL First All-Star Team (1998)

Signed as a free agent by **Washington**, March 17, 1997.

MULLER, KIRK — FLA.

Left wing. Shoots left. 6', 205 lbs. Born, Kingston, Ont., February 8, 1966.
(New Jersey's 1st choice, 2nd overall, in 1984 Entry Draft).

			Regular Season					Playoffs				
Season	Club	Lea	GP	G	A	TP	PIM	GP	G	A	TP	PIM
1981-82	Kingston	OHL	67	12	39	51	27	4	5	1	6	4
1982-83	Guelph	OHL	66	52	60	112	41	....	....	....	....	....
1983-84	Guelph	OHL	49	31	63	94	27	....	....	....	....	....
	Canada	Nat-Tm	15	2	2	4	6	....	....	....	....	....
	Canada	Olympics	7	2	1	3	0	....	....	....	....	....
1984-85	**New Jersey**	**NHL**	**80**	**17**	**37**	**54**	**69**	....	....	....	....	....
1985-86	**New Jersey**	**NHL**	**77**	**25**	**41**	**66**	**45**	....	....	....	....	....
1986-87	**New Jersey**	**NHL**	**79**	**26**	**50**	**76**	**75**	....	....	....	....	....
1987-88	**New Jersey**	**NHL**	**80**	**37**	**57**	**94**	**114**	**20**	**4**	**8**	**12**	**37**
1988-89	**New Jersey**	**NHL**	**80**	**31**	**43**	**74**	**119**	....	....	....	....	....
1989-90	**New Jersey**	**NHL**	**80**	**30**	**56**	**86**	**74**	**6**	**1**	**3**	**4**	**11**
1990-91	**New Jersey**	**NHL**	**80**	**19**	**51**	**70**	**76**	**7**	**0**	**2**	**2**	**10**
1991-92	**Montreal**	**NHL**	**78**	**36**	**41**	**77**	**86**	**11**	**4**	**3**	**7**	**31**
1992-93	**Montreal**	**NHL**	**80**	**37**	**57**	**94**	**77**	**20**	**10**	**7**	**17**	**18** ♦
1993-94	**Montreal**	**NHL**	**76**	**23**	**34**	**57**	**96**	**7**	**6**	**2**	**8**	**4**
1994-95	**Montreal**	**NHL**	**33**	**8**	**11**	**19**	**33**	....	....	....	....	....
	NY Islanders	**NHL**	**12**	**3**	**5**	**8**	**14**	....	....	....	....	....
1995-96	**NY Islanders**	**NHL**	**15**	**4**	**3**	**7**	**15**	....	....	....	....	....
	Toronto	**NHL**	**36**	**9**	**16**	**25**	**42**	**6**	**3**	**2**	**5**	**0**
1996-97	**Toronto**	**NHL**	**66**	**20**	**17**	**37**	**85**	....	....	....	....	....
	Florida	**NHL**	**10**	**1**	**2**	**3**	**4**	**5**	**1**	**2**	**3**	**4**
1997-98	**Florida**	**NHL**	**70**	**8**	**21**	**29**	**54**	....	....	....	....	....
	NHL Totals		**1032**	**334**	**542**	**876**	**1078**	**82**	**29**	**29**	**58**	**115**

Played in NHL All-Star Game (1985, 1986, 1988, 1990, 1992, 1993)

Traded to **Montreal** by **New Jersey** with Roland Melanson for Stephane Richer and Tom Chorske, September 20, 1991. Traded to **NY Islanders** by **Montreal** with Mathieu Schneider and Craig Darby for Pierre Turgeon and Vladimir Malakhov, April 5, 1995. Traded to **Toronto** by **NY Islanders** with Don Beaupre to complete transaction that sent Damian Rhodes and Ken Belanger to NY Islanders (January 23, 1996), January 23, 1996. Traded to **Florida** by **Toronto** for Jason Podollan, March 18, 1997.

MUNI, CRAIG — (MYOO-ne)

Defense. Shoots left. 6'3", 208 lbs. Born, Toronto, Ont., July 19, 1962.
(Toronto's 1st choice, 25th overall, in 1980 Entry Draft).

			Regular Season					Playoffs				
Season	Club	Lea	GP	G	A	TP	PIM	GP	G	A	TP	PIM
1979-80	Kingston	OHA	66	6	28	34	114	....	....	....	....	....
1980-81	Kingston	OHA	38	2	14	16	65	....	....	....	....	....
	Windsor	OHA	25	5	11	16	41	11	1	4	5	14
	New Brunswick	AHL	....	....	....	....	....	2	0	1	1	10
1981-82	Windsor	OHL	49	5	32	37	92	9	2	3	5	16
	Toronto	**NHL**	**3**	**0**	**0**	**0**	**2**	....	....	....	....	....
	Cincinnati	CHL	....	....	....	....	....	3	0	2	2	2
1982-83	**Toronto**	**NHL**	**2**	**0**	**1**	**1**	**0**	....	....	....	....	....
	St. Catharines	AHL	64	6	32	38	52	....	....	....	....	....
1983-84	St. Catharines	AHL	64	4	16	20	79	7	0	1	1	0
1984-85	**Toronto**	**NHL**	**8**	**0**	**0**	**0**	**0**	....	....	....	....	....
	St. Catharines	AHL	68	7	17	24	54	....	....	....	....	....
1985-86	**Toronto**	**NHL**	**6**	**0**	**1**	**1**	**4**	....	....	....	....	....
	St. Catharines	AHL	73	3	34	37	91	13	0	5	5	16
1986-87	**Edmonton**	**NHL**	**79**	**7**	**22**	**29**	**85**	**14**	**0**	**2**	**2**	**17** ♦
1987-88	**Edmonton**	**NHL**	**72**	**4**	**15**	**19**	**77**	**19**	**0**	**4**	**4**	**31** ♦
1988-89	**Edmonton**	**NHL**	**69**	**5**	**13**	**18**	**71**	**7**	**0**	**3**	**3**	**8**
1989-90	**Edmonton**	**NHL**	**71**	**5**	**12**	**17**	**81**	**22**	**0**	**3**	**3**	**16** ♦
1990-91	**Edmonton**	**NHL**	**76**	**1**	**9**	**10**	**77**	**18**	**0**	**3**	**3**	**20**
1991-92	**Edmonton**	**NHL**	**54**	**2**	**5**	**7**	**34**	**3**	**0**	**0**	**0**	**2**
1992-93	**Edmonton**	**NHL**	**72**	**0**	**11**	**11**	**67**	....	....	....	....	....
	Chicago	**NHL**	**9**	**0**	**0**	**0**	**8**	**4**	**0**	**0**	**0**	**2**
1993-94	**Chicago**	**NHL**	**9**	**0**	**4**	**4**	**4**	....	....	....	....	....
	Buffalo	**NHL**	**73**	**2**	**8**	**10**	**62**	**7**	**0**	**0**	**0**	**4**
1994-95	**Buffalo**	**NHL**	**40**	**0**	**6**	**6**	**36**	**5**	**0**	**1**	**1**	**2**
1995-96	**Buffalo**	**NHL**	**47**	**0**	**4**	**4**	**69**	....	....	....	....	....
	Winnipeg	**NHL**	**25**	**1**	**3**	**4**	**37**	**6**	**0**	**1**	**1**	**2**
1996-97	**Pittsburgh**	**NHL**	**64**	**0**	**4**	**4**	**36**	**3**	**0**	**0**	**0**	**0**
1997-98	**Dallas**	**NHL**	**40**	**1**	**1**	**2**	**25**	**5**	**0**	**0**	**0**	**4**
	NHL Totals		**819**	**28**	**119**	**147**	**775**	**113**	**0**	**17**	**17**	**108**

Signed as a free agent by **Edmonton,** August 18, 1986. Traded to **Buffalo** by **Edmonton** for cash, October 2, 1986. Traded to **Pittsburgh** by **Buffalo** for future considerations, October 3, 1986. Traded to **Edmonton** by **Pittsburgh** to complete September 11, 1985 transaction which sent Gilles Meloche to Pittsburgh, October 6, 1986. Traded to **Chicago** by **Edmonton** for Mike Hudson, March 22, 1993. Traded to **Buffalo** by **Chicago** with Chicago's 5th round choice (Daniel Bienvenue) in 1995 Entry Draft for Keith Carney and Buffalo's 6th round choice (Marc Magliarditi) in 1995 Entry Draft, October 26, 1993. Traded to **Winnipeg** by **Buffalo** for Darryl Shannon and Michael Grosek, February 15, 1996. Signed as a free agent by **Pittsburgh**, October 2, 1996.

MURPHY, BURKE

Left wing. Shoots left. 6', 180 lbs. Born, Gloucester, Ont., June 5, 1973.
(Calgary's 11th choice, 278th overall, in 1993 Entry Draft).

			Regular Season					Playoffs				
Season	Club	Lea	GP	G	A	TP	PIM	GP	G	A	TP	PIM
1992-93	St. Lawrence	ECAC	32	19	10	29	32	....	....	....	....	....
1993-94	St. Lawrence	ECAC	30	20	17	37	42	....	....	....	....	....
1994-95	St. Lawrence	ECAC	33	27	23	50	61	....	....	....	....	....
1995-96	St. Lawrence	ECAC	35	*33	25	58	37	....	....	....	....	....
1996-97	Saint John	AHL	54	8	18	26	20	....	....	....	....	....
1997-98	Saint John	AHL	35	4	7	11	28	....	....	....	....	....
	Cleveland	IHL	11	3	2	5	2	....	....	....	....	....
	Quebec	IHL	13	10	6	16	4	....	....	....	....	....

ECAC Second All-Star Team (1995) • ECAC First All-Star Team (1996) • NCAA East Second All-American Team (1996)

MURPHY, GORD — FLA.

Defense. Shoots right. 6'2", 195 lbs. Born, Willowdale, Ont., March 23, 1967.
(Philadelphia's 10th choice, 189th overall, in 1985 Entry Draft).

			Regular Season					Playoffs				
Season	Club	Lea	GP	G	A	TP	PIM	GP	G	A	TP	PIM
1984-85	Oshawa	OHL	59	3	12	15	25	....	....	....	....	....
1985-86	Oshawa	OHL	64	7	15	22	56	6	1	1	2	6
1986-87	Oshawa	OHL	56	7	30	37	95	24	6	16	22	22
1987-88	Hershey	AHL	62	8	20	28	44	12	0	8	8	12
1988-89	**Philadelphia**	**NHL**	**75**	**4**	**31**	**35**	**68**	**19**	**2**	**7**	**9**	**13**
1989-90	**Philadelphia**	**NHL**	**75**	**14**	**27**	**41**	**95**	....	....	....	....	....
1990-91	**Philadelphia**	**NHL**	**80**	**11**	**31**	**42**	**58**	....	....	....	....	....
1991-92	**Philadelphia**	**NHL**	**31**	**2**	**8**	**10**	**33**	....	....	....	....	....
	Boston	**NHL**	**42**	**3**	**6**	**9**	**51**	**15**	**1**	**0**	**1**	**12**
1992-93	**Boston**	**NHL**	**49**	**5**	**12**	**17**	**62**	....	....	....	....	....
	Providence	AHL	2	1	3	4	2	....	....	....	....	....
1993-94	**Florida**	**NHL**	**84**	**14**	**29**	**43**	**71**	....	....	....	....	....
1994-95	**Florida**	**NHL**	**46**	**6**	**16**	**22**	**24**	....	....	....	....	....
1995-96	**Florida**	**NHL**	**70**	**8**	**22**	**30**	**30**	**14**	**0**	**4**	**4**	**6**
1996-97	**Florida**	**NHL**	**80**	**8**	**15**	**23**	**51**	**5**	**0**	**5**	**5**	**4**
1997-98	**Florida**	**NHL**	**79**	**6**	**11**	**17**	**46**	....	....	....	....	....
	NHL Totals		**711**	**81**	**208**	**289**	**589**	**53**	**3**	**16**	**19**	**35**

Traded to **Boston** by **Philadelphia** with Brian Dobbin, Philadelphia's 3rd round choice (Sergei Zholtok) in 1992 Entry Draft and Philadelphia's 4th round choice (Charles Paquette) in 1993 Entry Draft, for Garry Galley, Wes Walz and Boston's 3rd round choice (Milos Holan) in 1993 Entry Draft, January 2, 1992. Traded to **Dallas** by **Boston** for future considerations (Jon Casey, June 25, 1993), June 20, 1993. Claimed by **Florida** from **Dallas** in Expansion Draft, June 24, 1993.

MURPHY, JOE — S.J.

Right wing. Shoots left. 6', 190 lbs. Born, London, Ont., October 16, 1967.
(Detroit's 1st choice, 1st overall, in 1986 Entry Draft).

			Regular Season					Playoffs				
Season	Club	Lea	GP	G	A	TP	PIM	GP	G	A	TP	PIM
1984-85	Penticton	BCJHL	51	68	84	*152	92	....	....	....	....	....
1985-86	Michigan State	CCHA	35	24	37	61	50	....	....	....	....	....
	Canada	Nat-Tm	8	3	3	6	2	....	....	....	....	....
1986-87	**Detroit**	**NHL**	5	0	1	1	2	....	....	....	....	....
	Adirondack	AHL	71	21	38	59	61	10	2	1	3	33
1987-88	**Detroit**	**NHL**	50	10	9	19	37	8	0	1	1	6
	Adirondack	AHL	6	5	6	11	4	....	....	....	....	....
1988-89	**Detroit**	**NHL**	26	1	7	8	28	....	....	....	....	....
	Adirondack	AHL	47	31	35	66	66	16	6	11	17	17
1989-90	**Detroit**	**NHL**	9	3	1	4	4	....	....	....	....	....
	Edmonton	**NHL**	62	7	18	25	56	22	6	8	14	16 ♦
1990-91	**Edmonton**	**NHL**	80	27	35	62	35	15	2	5	7	14
1991-92	**Edmonton**	**NHL**	80	35	47	82	52	16	8	16	24	12
1992-93	**Chicago**	**NHL**	19	7	10	17	18	4	0	0	0	8
1993-94	**Chicago**	**NHL**	81	31	39	70	111	6	1	3	4	25
1994-95	**Chicago**	**NHL**	40	23	18	41	89	16	9	3	12	29
1995-96	**Chicago**	**NHL**	70	22	29	51	86	10	6	2	8	33
1996-97	**St. Louis**	**NHL**	75	20	25	45	69	6	1	1	2	10
1997-98	**St. Louis**	**NHL**	27	4	9	13	22	....	....	....	....	....
	San Jose	**NHL**	10	5	4	9	14	6	1	1	2	20
	NHL Totals		634	195	252	447	623	109	34	40	74	173

Traded to **Edmonton** by **Detroit** with Petr Klima, Adam Graves and Jeff Sharples for Jimmy Carson, Kevin McClelland and Edmonton's 5th round choice (later traded to Montreal — Montreal selected Brad Layzell) in 1991 Entry Draft, November 2, 1989. Traded to **Chicago** by **Edmonton** for Igor Kravchuk and Dean McAmmond, February 24, 1993. Signed as a free agent by **St. Louis**, July 8, 1996. Traded to **San Jose** by **St. Louis** for Todd Gill, March 24, 1998.

MURPHY, LARRY — DET.

Defense. Shoots right. 6'2", 210 lbs. Born, Scarborough, Ont., March 8, 1961.
(Los Angeles' 1st choice, 4th overall, in 1980 Entry Draft).

			Regular Season					Playoffs				
Season	Club	Lea	GP	G	A	TP	PIM	GP	G	A	TP	PIM
1978-79	Peterborough	OHA	66	6	21	27	82	19	1	9	10	42
1979-80	Peterborough	OHA	68	21	68	89	88	14	4	13	17	20
1980-81	**Los Angeles**	**NHL**	80	16	60	76	79	4	3	0	3	2
1981-82	**Los Angeles**	**NHL**	79	22	44	66	95	10	2	8	10	12
1982-83	**Los Angeles**	**NHL**	77	14	48	62	81	....	....	....	....	....
1983-84	**Los Angeles**	**NHL**	6	0	3	3	0	....	....	....	....	....
	Washington	**NHL**	72	13	33	46	50	8	0	3	3	6
1984-85	**Washington**	**NHL**	79	13	42	55	51	5	2	3	5	0
1985-86	**Washington**	**NHL**	78	21	44	65	50	9	1	5	6	6
1986-87	**Washington**	**NHL**	80	23	58	81	39	7	2	2	4	6
1987-88	**Washington**	**NHL**	79	8	53	61	72	13	4	4	8	33
1988-89	**Washington**	**NHL**	65	7	29	36	70	....	....	....	....	....
	Minnesota	**NHL**	13	4	6	10	12	5	0	2	2	8
1989-90	**Minnesota**	**NHL**	77	10	58	68	44	7	1	2	3	31
1990-91	**Pittsburgh**	**NHL**	44	5	23	28	30	23	5	18	23	44 ♦
	Minnesota	**NHL**	31	4	11	15	38	....	....	....	....	....
1991-92	**Pittsburgh**	**NHL**	77	21	56	77	48	21	6	10	16	19 ♦
1992-93	**Pittsburgh**	**NHL**	83	22	63	85	73	12	2	11	13	10
1993-94	**Pittsburgh**	**NHL**	84	17	56	73	44	6	0	5	5	0
1994-95	**Pittsburgh**	**NHL**	48	13	25	38	18	12	2	13	15	0
1995-96	**Toronto**	**NHL**	82	12	49	61	34	6	0	2	2	4
1996-97	**Toronto**	**NHL**	69	7	32	39	20	....	....	....	....	....
	Detroit	**NHL**	12	2	4	6	0	20	2	9	11	8 ♦
1997-98	**Detroit**	**NHL**	82	11	41	52	37	22	3	12	15	2 ♦
	NHL Totals		1397	265	838	1103	985	190	35	109	144	191

OHA First All-Star Team (1980) • NHL Second All-Star Team (1987, 1993, 1995)

Played in NHL All-Star Game (1994, 1996)

Traded to **Washington** by **LA Kings** for Ken Houston and Brian Engblom, October 18, 1983. Traded to **Minnesota** by **Washington** with Mike Gartner for Dino Ciccarelli and Bob Rouse, March 7, 1989. Traded to **Pittsburgh** by **Minnesota** with Peter Taglianetti for Chris Dahlquist and Jim Johnson, December 11, 1990. Traded to **Toronto** by **Pittsburgh** for Dmitri Mironov and Toronto's 2nd round choice (later traded to New Jersey — New Jersey selected Joshua Dewolf) in 1996 Entry Draft, July 8, 1995. Traded to **Detroit** by **Toronto** for future considerations, March 18, 1997.

MURPHY, MARK

Left wing. Shoots left. 5'11", 200 lbs. Born, Stoughton, MA, August 6, 1976.
(Toronto's 6th choice, 197th overall, in 1995 Entry Draft).

			Regular Season					Playoffs				
Season	Club	Lea	GP	G	A	TP	PIM	GP	G	A	TP	PIM
1994-95	Stratford	OJHL	47	52	56	108	64	....	....	....	....	....
1995-96	Stratford	OJHL	1	0	0	0	0	....	....	....	....	....
	RPI	ECAC	32	1	1	2	50	....	....	....	....	....
1996-97	RPI	ECAC	34	9	18	27	56	....	....	....	....	....
1997-98	RPI	ECAC	35	8	27	35	63	....	....	....	....	....

MURRAY, CHRIS — OTT.

Right wing. Shoots right. 6'2", 209 lbs. Born, Port Hardy, B.C., October 25, 1974.
(Montreal's 3rd choice, 54th overall, in 1994 Entry Draft).

			Regular Season					Playoffs				
Season	Club	Lea	GP	G	A	TP	PIM	GP	G	A	TP	PIM
1991-92	Kamloops	WHL	33	1	1	2	218	5	0	0	0	10
1992-93	Kamloops	WHL	62	6	10	16	217	13	0	4	4	34
1993-94	Kamloops	WHL	59	14	16	30	260	15	4	2	6	*107
1994-95	**Montreal**	**NHL**	3	0	0	0	4	....	....	....	....	....
	Fredericton	AHL	55	6	12	18	234	12	1	1	2	50
1995-96	**Montreal**	**NHL**	48	3	4	7	163	4	0	0	0	4
	Fredericton	AHL	30	13	13	26	217	....	....	....	....	....
1996-97	**Montreal**	**NHL**	56	4	2	6	114	....	....	....	....	....
	Hartford	**NHL**	8	1	1	2	10	....	....	....	....	....
1997-98	**Carolina**	**NHL**	7	0	1	1	22	....	....	....	....	....
	Ottawa	**NHL**	46	5	3	8	96	11	1	0	1	8
	NHL Totals		168	13	11	24	409	15	1	0	1	12

Traded to **Phoenix** by **Montreal** with Murray Baron for Dave Manson, March 18, 1997. Traded to **Hartford** by **Phoenix** for Gerald Diduck, March 18, 1997. Transferred to **Carolina** after **Hartford** franchise relocated, June 25, 1997. Traded to **Ottawa** by **Carolina** for Sean Hill, November 18, 1997.

MURRAY, GLEN — L.A.

Right wing. Shoots right. 6'3", 222 lbs. Born, Halifax, N.S., November 1, 1972.
(Boston's 1st choice, 18th overall, in 1991 Entry Draft).

			Regular Season					Playoffs				
Season	Club	Lea	GP	G	A	TP	PIM	GP	G	A	TP	PIM
1989-90	Sudbury	OHL	62	8	28	36	17	7	0	0	0	4
1990-91	Sudbury	OHL	66	27	38	65	82	5	8	4	12	10
1991-92	Sudbury	OHL	54	37	47	84	93	11	7	4	11	18
	Boston	**NHL**	5	3	1	4	0	15	4	2	6	10
1992-93	**Boston**	**NHL**	27	3	4	7	8	....	....	....	....	....
	Providence	AHL	48	30	26	56	42	6	1	4	5	4
1993-94	**Boston**	**NHL**	81	18	13	31	48	13	4	5	9	14
1994-95	**Boston**	**NHL**	35	5	2	7	46	2	0	0	0	2
1995-96	**Pittsburgh**	**NHL**	69	14	15	29	57	18	2	6	8	10
1996-97	**Pittsburgh**	**NHL**	66	11	11	22	24	....	....	....	....	....
	Los Angeles	**NHL**	11	5	3	8	8	....	....	....	....	....
1997-98	**Los Angeles**	**NHL**	81	29	31	60	54	4	2	0	2	6
	NHL Totals		375	88	80	168	245	52	12	13	25	42

Traded to **Pittsburgh** by **Boston** with Bryan Smolinski and Boston's 3rd round choice (Boyd Kane) in 1996 Entry Draft for Kevin Stevens and Shawn McEachern, August 2, 1995. Traded to **LA Kings** by **Pittsburgh** for Ed Olczyk, March 18, 1997.

MURRAY, MARTY — CGY.

Center. Shoots left. 5'9", 178 lbs. Born, Deloraine, Man., February 16, 1975.
(Calgary's 5th choice, 96th overall, in 1993 Entry Draft).

			Regular Season					Playoffs				
Season	Club	Lea	GP	G	A	TP	PIM	GP	G	A	TP	PIM
1991-92	Brandon	WHL	68	20	36	56	22	....	....	....	....	....
1992-93	Brandon	WHL	67	29	65	94	50	4	1	3	4	0
1993-94	Brandon	WHL	64	43	71	114	33	14	6	14	20	14
1994-95	Brandon	WHL	65	40	*88	128	53	18	9	*20	29	16
1995-96	**Calgary**	**NHL**	15	3	3	6	0	....	....	....	....	....
	Saint John	AHL	58	25	31	56	20	14	2	4	6	4
1996-97	**Calgary**	**NHL**	2	0	0	0	4	....	....	....	....	....
	Saint John	AHL	67	19	39	58	40	5	2	3	5	4
1997-98	**Calgary**	**NHL**	2	0	0	0	2	....	....	....	....	....
	Saint John	AHL	41	10	30	40	16	21	10	10	20	12
	NHL Totals		19	3	3	6	6	....	....	....	....	....

WHL East First All-Star Team (1994, 1995) • Canadian Major Junior Second All-Star Team (1994)

MURRAY, REM — EDM.

Left wing. Shoots left. 6'2", 195 lbs. Born, Stratford, Ont., October 9, 1972.
(Los Angeles' 5th choice, 135th overall, in 1992 Entry Draft).

			Regular Season					Playoffs				
Season	Club	Lea	GP	G	A	TP	PIM	GP	G	A	TP	PIM
1990-91	Stratford	OJHL	48	39	59	98	22	....	....	....	....	....
1991-92	Michigan State	CCHA	41	12	36	48	16	....	....	....	....	....
1992-93	Michigan State	CCHA	40	22	35	57	24	....	....	....	....	....
1993-94	Michigan State	CCHA	41	16	38	54	18	....	....	....	....	....
1994-95	Michigan State	CCHA	40	20	36	56	21	....	....	....	....	....
1995-96	Cape Breton	AHL	79	31	59	90	40	....	....	....	....	....
1996-97	**Edmonton**	**NHL**	82	11	20	31	16	12	1	2	3	4
1997-98	**Edmonton**	**NHL**	61	9	9	18	39	11	1	4	5	2
	NHL Totals		143	20	29	49	55	23	2	6	8	6

CCHA Second All-Star Team (1995)

Signed as a free agent by **Edmonton**, September 19, 1995.

MURRAY, ROB — PHX.

Center. Shoots right. 6'1", 180 lbs. Born, Toronto, Ont., April 4, 1967.
(Washington's 3rd choice, 61st overall, in 1985 Entry Draft).

			Regular Season					Playoffs				
Season	Club	Lea	GP	G	A	TP	PIM	GP	G	A	TP	PIM
1984-85	Peterborough	OHL	63	12	9	21	155	17	2	7	9	45
1985-86	Peterborough	OHL	52	14	18	32	125	16	1	2	3	50
1986-87	Peterborough	OHL	62	17	37	54	204	3	1	4	5	8
1987-88	Fort Wayne	IHL	80	12	21	33	139	6	0	2	2	16
1988-89	Baltimore	AHL	80	11	23	34	235	....	....	....	....	....
1989-90	**Washington**	**NHL**	41	2	7	9	58	9	0	0	0	18
	Baltimore	AHL	23	5	4	9	63	....	....	....	....	....
1990-91	**Washington**	**NHL**	17	0	3	3	19	....	....	....	....	....
	Baltimore	AHL	48	6	20	26	177	4	0	0	0	12
1991-92	**Winnipeg**	**NHL**	9	0	1	1	18	....	....	....	....	....
	Moncton	AHL	60	16	15	31	247	8	0	1	1	56
1992-93	**Winnipeg**	**NHL**	10	1	0	1	6	....	....	....	....	....
	Moncton	AHL	56	16	21	37	147	3	0	0	0	6
1993-94	**Winnipeg**	**NHL**	6	0	0	0	2	....	....	....	....	....
	Moncton	AHL	69	25	32	57	280	21	2	3	5	60
1994-95	Springfield	AHL	78	16	38	54	373	....	....	....	....	....
	Winnipeg	**NHL**	10	0	2	2	2	....	....	....	....	....
1995-96	**Winnipeg**	**NHL**	1	0	0	0	2	....	....	....	....	....
	Springfield	AHL	74	10	28	38	263	10	1	6	7	32
1996-97	Springfield	AHL	78	16	27	43	234	17	2	3	5	66
1997-98	Springfield	AHL	80	7	30	37	255	4	0	2	2	2
	NHL Totals		94	3	13	16	107	9	0	0	0	18

Claimed by **Minnesota** from **Washington** in Expansion Draft, May 30, 1991. Traded to **Winnipeg** by **Minnesota** with future considerations for Winnipeg's 7th round choice (Geoff Finch) in 1991 Entry Draft and future considerations, May 31, 1991.

MURZYN, DANA (MUHR-zihn) **VAN.**

Defense. Shoots left. 6'2", 200 lbs. Born, Calgary, Alta., December 9, 1966.
(Hartford's 1st choice, 5th overall, in 1985 Entry Draft).

			Regular Season					Playoffs				
Season	Club	Lea	GP	G	A	TP	PIM	GP	G	A	TP	PIM
1983-84	Calgary	WHL	65	11	20	31	135	2	0	0	0	10
1984-85	Calgary	WHL	72	32	60	92	233	8	1	11	12	16
1985-86	**Hartford**	**NHL**	**78**	**3**	**23**	**26**	**125**	**4**	**0**	**0**	**0**	**10**
1986-87	**Hartford**	**NHL**	**74**	**9**	**19**	**28**	**95**	**6**	**2**	**1**	**3**	**29**
1987-88	**Hartford**	**NHL**	**33**	**1**	**6**	**7**	**45**	....	....	....	....	....
	Calgary	**NHL**	**41**	**6**	**5**	**11**	**94**	**5**	**2**	**0**	**2**	**13**
1988-89	**Calgary**	**NHL**	**63**	**3**	**19**	**22**	**142**	**21**	**0**	**3**	**3**	**20** ♦
1989-90	**Calgary**	**NHL**	**78**	**7**	**13**	**20**	**140**	**6**	**2**	**2**	**4**	**2**
1990-91	**Calgary**	**NHL**	**19**	**0**	**2**	**2**	**30**	....	....	....	....	....
	Vancouver	**NHL**	**10**	**1**	**0**	**1**	**8**	**6**	**0**	**1**	**1**	**8**
1991-92	**Vancouver**	**NHL**	**70**	**3**	**11**	**14**	**147**	**1**	**0**	**0**	**0**	**15**
1992-93	**Vancouver**	**NHL**	**79**	**5**	**11**	**16**	**196**	**12**	**3**	**2**	**5**	**18**
1993-94	**Vancouver**	**NHL**	**80**	**6**	**14**	**20**	**109**	**7**	**0**	**0**	**0**	**4**
1994-95	**Vancouver**	**NHL**	**40**	**0**	**8**	**8**	**129**	**8**	**0**	**1**	**1**	**22**
1995-96	**Vancouver**	**NHL**	**69**	**2**	**10**	**12**	**130**	**6**	**0**	**0**	**0**	**25**
1996-97	**Vancouver**	**NHL**	**61**	**1**	**7**	**8**	**118**	....	....	....	....	....
1997-98	**Vancouver**	**NHL**	**31**	**5**	**2**	**7**	**42**	....	....	....	....	....
	NHL Totals		**826**	**52**	**150**	**202**	**1550**	**82**	**9**	**10**	**19**	**166**

WHL East First All-Star Team, (1985) • NHL All-Rookie Team (1986)

Traded to **Calgary** by **Hartford** with Shane Churla for Neil Sheehy, Carey Wilson and the rights to Lane MacDonald, January 3, 1988. Traded to **Vancouver** by **Calgary** for Ron Stern, Kevan Guy and future considerations, March 5, 1991.

MUSIL, FRANTISEK (moo-SIHL) **EDM.**

Defense. Shoots left. 6'3", 215 lbs. Born, Pardubice, Czech., December 17, 1964.
(Minnesota's 3rd choice, 38th overall, in 1983 Entry Draft).

			Regular Season					Playoffs				
Season	Club	Lea	GP	G	A	TP	PIM	GP	G	A	TP	PIM
1980-81	Pardubice	Czech.	2	0	0	0	0	....	....	....	....	....
1981-82	Pardubice	Czech.	35	1	3	4	34	....	....	....	....	....
1982-83	Pardubice	Czech.	33	1	2	3	44	....	....	....	....	....
1983-84	Pardubice	Czech.	37	4	8	12	72	....	....	....	....	....
1984-85	Dukla Jihlava	Czech.	44	4	6	10	76	....	....	....	....	....
1985-86	Dukla Jihlava	Czech.	34	4	7	11	42	....	....	....	....	....
1986-87	**Minnesota**	**NHL**	**72**	**2**	**9**	**11**	**148**	....	....	....	....	....
1987-88	**Minnesota**	**NHL**	**80**	**9**	**8**	**17**	**213**	....	....	....	....	....
1988-89	**Minnesota**	**NHL**	**55**	**1**	**19**	**20**	**54**	**5**	**1**	**1**	**2**	**4**
1989-90	**Minnesota**	**NHL**	**56**	**2**	**8**	**10**	**109**	**4**	**0**	**0**	**0**	**14**
1990-91	**Minnesota**	**NHL**	**8**	**0**	**2**	**2**	**23**	....	....	....	....	....
	Calgary	**NHL**	**67**	**7**	**14**	**21**	**160**	**7**	**0**	**0**	**0**	**10**
1991-92	**Calgary**	**NHL**	**78**	**4**	**8**	**12**	**103**	....	....	....	....	....
1992-93	**Calgary**	**NHL**	**80**	**6**	**10**	**16**	**131**	**6**	**1**	**1**	**2**	**7**
1993-94	**Calgary**	**NHL**	**75**	**1**	**8**	**9**	**50**	**7**	**0**	**1**	**1**	**4**
1994-95	Sparta Praha	Cze-Rep.	19	1	4	5	50	....	....	....	....	....
	Saxonia	Germany	1	0	0	0	2	....	....	....	....	....
	Calgary	**NHL**	**35**	**0**	**5**	**5**	**61**	**5**	**0**	**1**	**1**	**0**
1995-96	Karlovy	Czech-2	16	7	4	11	16	....	....	....	....	....
	Ottawa	**NHL**	**65**	**1**	**3**	**4**	**85**	....	....	....	....	....
1996-97	**Ottawa**	**NHL**	**57**	**0**	**5**	**5**	**58**	....	....	....	....	....
1997-98	Indianapolis	IHL	52	5	8	13	122	....	....	....	....	....
	Detroit	IHL	9	0	0	0	6	....	....	....	....	....
	Edmonton	**NHL**	**17**	**1**	**2**	**3**	**8**	**7**	**0**	**0**	**0**	**6**
	NHL Totals		**745**	**34**	**101**	**135**	**1203**	**41**	**2**	**4**	**6**	**45**

Traded to **Calgary** by **Minnesota** for Brian Glynn, October 26, 1990. Traded to **Ottawa** by **Calgary** for Ottawa's 4th round choice (Chris St. Croix) in 1997 Entry Draft, October 7, 1995. Traded to **Edmonton** by **Ottawa** for Scott Ferguson, March 9, 1998.

MYHRES, BRANTT (MIGH-uhrs) **S.J.**

Right wing. Shoots right. 6'4", 222 lbs. Born, Edmonton, Alta., March 18, 1974.
(Tampa Bay's 5th choice, 97th overall, in 1992 Entry Draft).

			Regular Season					Playoffs				
Season	Club	Lea	GP	G	A	TP	PIM	GP	G	A	TP	PIM
1990-91	Portland	WHL	59	2	7	9	125	....	....	....	....	....
1991-92	Portland	WHL	4	0	2	2	22	....	....	....	....	....
	Lethbridge	WHL	53	4	11	15	359	5	0	0	0	36
1992-93	Lethbridge	WHL	64	13	35	48	277	3	0	0	0	11
1993-94	Lethbridge	WHL	34	10	21	31	103	....	....	....	....	....
	Spokane	WHL	27	10	22	32	139	3	1	4	5	7
	Atlanta	IHL	2	0	0	0	17	....	....	....	....	....
1994-95	Atlanta	IHL	40	5	5	10	213	....	....	....	....	....
	Tampa Bay	**NHL**	**15**	**2**	**0**	**2**	**81**	....	....	....	....	....
1995-96	Atlanta	IHL	12	0	2	2	58	....	....	....	....	....
1996-97	**Tampa Bay**	**NHL**	**47**	**3**	**1**	**4**	**136**	....	....	....	....	....
	San Antonio	IHL	12	0	0	0	98	....	....	....	....	....
1997-98	**Philadelphia**	**NHL**	**23**	**0**	**0**	**0**	**169**	....	....	....	....	....
	Philadelphia	AHL	18	4	4	8	67	....	....	....	....	....
	NHL Totals		**85**	**5**	**1**	**6**	**386**	....	....	....	....	....

Traded to **Edmonton** by **Tampa Bay** with Toronto's 3rd round choice (previously acquired, Edmonton selected Alex Henry) in 1998 Entry Draft for Vladimir Vujtek and Edmonton's 3rd round choice (Dimitri Afanasenkov) in 1998 Entry Draft, July 16, 1997. Traded to **Philadelphia** by **Edmonton** for Jason Bowen, October 15, 1997. Signed as a free agent by **San Jose**, August, 1998.

MYRVOLD, ANDERS (MYOOR-vohld)

Defense. Shoots left. 6'2", 200 lbs. Born, Lorenskog, Norway, August 12, 1975.
(Quebec's 6th choice, 127th overall, in 1993 Entry Draft).

			Regular Season					Playoffs				
Season	Club	Lea	GP	G	A	TP	PIM	GP	G	A	TP	PIM
1992-93	Farjestad	Sweden	2	0	0	0	0	....	....	....	....	....
1993-94	Grum	Sweden-2	24	1	0	1	59	....	....	....	....	....
1994-95	Laval	QMJHL	64	14	50	64	173	20	4	10	14	68
	Cornwall	AHL	....	....	....	....	....	3	0	1	1	2
1995-96	**Colorado**	**NHL**	**4**	**0**	**1**	**1**	**6**	....	....	....	....	....
	Cornwall	AHL	70	5	24	29	125	5	1	0	1	19
1996-97	Hershey	AHL	20	0	3	3	16	....	....	....	....	....
	Boston	**NHL**	**9**	**0**	**2**	**2**	**4**	....	....	....	....	....
	Providence	AHL	53	6	15	21	107	10	0	1	1	6
1997-98	Providence	AHL	75	4	21	25	91	....	....	....	....	....
	NHL Totals		**13**	**0**	**3**	**3**	**10**	....	....	....	....	....

Rights transferred to **Colorado** after **Quebec** franchise relocated, June 21, 1995. Traded to **Boston** by **Colorado** with Landon Wilson for Boston's 1st round choice (Robyn Regehr) in 1998 Entry Draft, November 22, 1996.

NABOKOV, DMITRI (nuh-BAW-kahv) **NYI**

Center. Shoots right. 6'2", 216 lbs. Born, Novosibirsk, USSR, January 4, 1977.
(Chicago's 1st choice, 19th overall, in 1995 Entry Draft).

			Regular Season					Playoffs				
Season	Club	Lea	GP	G	A	TP	PIM	GP	G	A	TP	PIM
1993-94	Soviet Wings	CIS	17	0	2	2	6	3	0	0	0	0
1994-95	Soviet Wings	CIS	49	15	12	27	32	4	5	0	5	6
1995-96	Soviet Wings	CIS	50	12	14	26	51	....	....	....	....	....
1996-97	Soviet Wings	Russia	1	0	0	0	0	....	....	....	....	....
	Regina	WHL	50	39	56	95	61	5	2	3	5	2
	Indianapolis	IHL	2	0	0	0	0	....	....	....	....	....
1997-98	**Chicago**	**NHL**	**25**	**7**	**4**	**11**	**10**	....	....	....	....	....
	Indianapolis	IHL	46	6	15	21	16	5	2	1	3	0
	NHL Totals		**25**	**7**	**4**	**11**	**10**	....	....	....	....	....

WHL East Second All-Star Team (1997)

Traded to **NY Islanders** by **Chicago** for Jean-Pierre Dumont and Chicago's 5th round choice (later traded to Philadelphia - Philadelphia selected Francis Belanger) in 1998 Entry Draft, June 1, 1998.

NAGY, LADISLAV (NA-gee, LA-dih-slahv) **ST.L.**

Center. Shoots left. 5'11", 183 lbs. Born, Saca, Czechoslovakia, June 1, 1979.
(St. Louis' 6th choice, 177th overall, in 1997 Entry Draft).

			Regular Season					Playoffs				
Season	Club	Lea	GP	G	A	TP	PIM	GP	G	A	TP	PIM
1996-97	Dragon Presov	Slovak-2	11	6	5	11	....	....	....	....	....	....
1997-98	HC Kosice	Slovakia	29	19	15	34	41	11	2	4	6	6

NAMESTNIKOV, YEVGENY (nah-MEST-nih-kov, yev-GAIN-ee)

Defense. Shoots right. 5'11", 190 lbs. Born, Arzamis-lg, USSR, October 9, 1971.
(Vancouver's 5th choice, 117th overall, in 1991 Entry Draft).

			Regular Season					Playoffs				
Season	Club	Lea	GP	G	A	TP	PIM	GP	G	A	TP	PIM
1988-89	Torpedo Gorky	USSR	2	0	0	0	2	....	....	....	....	....
1989-90	Torpedo Gorky	USSR	23	0	0	0	25	....	....	....	....	....
1990-91	Torpedo Nizhny	USSR	42	1	2	3	49	....	....	....	....	....
1991-92	CSKA Moscow	CIS	42	1	1	2	47	....	....	....	....	....
1992-93	CSKA Moscow	CIS	42	5	5	10	68	....	....	....	....	....
1993-94	**Vancouver**	**NHL**	**17**	**0**	**5**	**5**	**10**	....	....	....	....	....
	Hamilton	AHL	59	7	27	34	97	4	0	2	2	19
1994-95	Syracuse	AHL	59	11	22	33	59	....	....	....	....	....
	Vancouver	**NHL**	**16**	**0**	**3**	**3**	**4**	**1**	**0**	**0**	**0**	**2**
1995-96	Syracuse	AHL	59	13	34	47	85	15	1	8	9	16
	Vancouver	**NHL**	....	....	....	....	....	**1**	**0**	**0**	**0**	**0**
1996-97	**Vancouver**	**NHL**	**2**	**0**	**0**	**0**	**4**	....	....	....	....	....
	Syracuse	AHL	55	9	37	46	73	3	2	0	2	0
1997-98	**NY Islanders**	**NHL**	**6**	**0**	**1**	**1**	**4**	....	....	....	....	....
	Utah	IHL	62	6	19	25	48	4	1	0	1	2
	NHL Totals		**41**	**0**	**9**	**9**	**22**	**2**	**0**	**0**	**0**	**2**

Signed as a free agent by **NY Islanders**, July 21, 1997.

NASH, TYSON **ST.L.**

Left wing. Shoots left. 6', 185 lbs. Born, Edmonton, Alta., March 11, 1975.
(Vancouver's 10th choice, 247th overall, in 1994 Entry Draft).

			Regular Season					Playoffs				
Season	Club	Lea	GP	G	A	TP	PIM	GP	G	A	TP	PIM
1991-92	Kamloops	WHL	33	1	6	7	62	4	0	0	0	0
1992-93	Kamloops	WHL	61	10	16	26	78	13	3	2	5	32
1993-94	Kamloops	WHL	65	20	36	56	135	16	3	4	7	12
1994-95	Kamloops	WHL	63	34	41	75	70	21	10	7	17	30
1995-96	Syracuse	AHL	50	4	7	11	58	4	0	0	0	11
	Raleigh	ECHL	6	1	1	2	8	....	....	....	....	....
1996-97	Syracuse	AHL	77	17	17	34	105	3	0	2	2	0
1997-98	Syracuse	AHL	74	20	20	40	184	5	0	2	2	28

NASLUND, MARKUS (NAZ-luhnd) **VAN.**

Right wing. Shoots left. 6', 186 lbs. Born, Ornskoldsvik, Sweden, July 30, 1973.
(Pittsburgh's 1st choice, 16th overall, in 1991 Entry Draft).

			Regular Season					Playoffs				
Season	Club	Lea	GP	G	A	TP	PIM	GP	G	A	TP	PIM
1990-91	MoDo	Sweden	32	10	9	19	14	....	....	....	....	....
1991-92	MoDo	Sweden	39	22	18	40	54	....	....	....	....	....
1992-93	MoDo	Sweden	39	22	17	39	67	3	3	2	5	0
1993-94	**Pittsburgh**	**NHL**	**71**	**4**	**7**	**11**	**27**	....	....	....	....	....
	Cleveland	IHL	5	1	6	7	4	....	....	....	....	....
1994-95	**Pittsburgh**	**NHL**	**14**	**2**	**2**	**4**	**2**	....	....	....	....	....
	Cleveland	IHL	7	3	4	7	6	4	1	3	4	8
1995-96	**Pittsburgh**	**NHL**	**66**	**19**	**33**	**52**	**36**	....	....	....	....	....
	Vancouver	**NHL**	**10**	**3**	**0**	**3**	**6**	**6**	**1**	**2**	**3**	**8**
1996-97	**Vancouver**	**NHL**	**78**	**21**	**20**	**41**	**30**	....	....	....	....	....
1997-98	**Vancouver**	**NHL**	**76**	**14**	**20**	**34**	**56**	....	....	....	....	....
	NHL Totals		**315**	**63**	**82**	**145**	**157**	**6**	**1**	**2**	**3**	**8**

Traded to **Vancouver** by **Pittsburgh** for Alek Stojanov, March 20, 1996.

NASREDDINE, ALAIN (NAS-ruh-deen, AL-ay) **CHI.**

Defense. Shoots left. 6'1", 201 lbs. Born, Montreal, Que., July 10, 1975.
(Florida's 8th choice, 135th overall, in 1993 Entry Draft).

			Regular Season					Playoffs				
Season	Club	Lea	GP	G	A	TP	PIM	GP	G	A	TP	PIM
1991-92	Drummondville	QMJHL	61	1	9	10	78	4	0	0	0	17
1992-93	Drummondville	QMJHL	64	0	14	14	137	10	0	1	1	36
1993-94	Chicoutimi	QMJHL	60	3	24	27	218	26	2	10	12	118
1994-95	Chicoutimi	QMJHL	67	8	31	39	342	13	3	5	8	40
1995-96	Carolina	AHL	63	0	5	5	245	....	....	....	....	....
1996-97	Carolina	AHL	26	0	4	4	109	....	....	....	....	....
	Indianapolis	IHL	49	0	2	2	248	4	1	1	2	27
1997-98	Indianapolis	IHL	75	1	12	13	258	5	0	2	2	12

QMJHL Second All-Star Team (1995)

Traded to **Chicago** by **Florida** with a conditional choice in 1999 Entry Draft for Ivan Droppa, December 18, 1996.

NAUD, ERIC (NOH)

Left wing. Shoots left. 6'1", 187 lbs. Born, Lasarre, Que., October 2, 1977.
(Boston's 3rd choice, 53rd overall, in 1996 Entry Draft).

			Regular Season					Playoffs				
Season	Club	Lea	GP	G	A	TP	PIM	GP	G	A	TP	PIM
1995-96	Laval	QMJHL	9	4	3	7	37	....	....	....	....	....
	St-Hyacinthe	QMJHL	54	7	18	25	193	12	1	2	3	19
1996-97	Rouyn-Noranda	QMJHL	34	8	11	19	159	....	....	....	....	....
	Hull	QMJHL	2	0	0	0	15	12	4	2	6	73
1997-98	Providence	AHL	27	1	2	3	54	....	....	....	....	....
	Charlotte	ECHL	16	0	0	0	42	....	....	....	....	....

NAUMENKO, NICK (NAH-mehn-koh)

Defense. Shoots right. 5'11", 180 lbs. Born, Chicago, IL, July 7, 1974.
(St. Louis' 9th choice, 182nd overall, in 1992 Entry Draft).

			Regular Season					Playoffs				
Season	Club	Lea	GP	G	A	TP	PIM	GP	G	A	TP	PIM
1991-92	Dubuque	USHL	24	6	19	25	4	....	....	....	....	....
1992-93	North Dakota	WCHA	38	10	24	34	26	....	....	....	....	....
1993-94	North Dakota	WCHA	32	4	22	26	22	....	....	....	....	....
1994-95	North Dakota	WCHA	39	13	26	39	78	....	....	....	....	....
1995-96	North Dakota	WCHA	37	11	30	41	32	....	....	....	....	....
1996-97	Worcester	AHL	54	6	22	28	72	1	0	0	0	0
1997-98	Worcester	AHL	71	12	34	46	63	11	1	7	8	8

WCHA First All-Star Team (1995, 1996)

NAZAROV, ANDREI (nah-ZAH-rohv) T.B.

Left wing. Shoots right. 6'5", 230 lbs. Born, Chelyabinsk, USSR, May 22, 1974.
(San Jose's 2nd choice, 10th overall, in 1992 Entry Draft).

			Regular Season					Playoffs				
Season	Club	Lea	GP	G	A	TP	PIM	GP	G	A	TP	PIM
1991-92	Moscow D'amo	CIS	2	1	0	1	2	....	....	....	....	....
1992-93	Moscow D'amo	CIS	42	8	2	10	79	10	1	1	2	8
1993-94	Moscow D'amo	CIS	6	2	2	4	0	....	....	....	....	....
	San Jose	**NHL**	**1**	**0**	**0**	**0**	**0**	....	....	....	....	....
	Kansas City	IHL	71	15	18	33	64	....	....	....	....	....
1994-95	Kansas City	IHL	43	15	10	25	55	....	....	....	....	....
	San Jose	**NHL**	**26**	**3**	**5**	**8**	**94**	**6**	**0**	**0**	**0**	**9**
1995-96	**San Jose**	**NHL**	**42**	**7**	**7**	**14**	**62**	....	....	....	....	....
	Kansas City	IHL	27	4	6	10	118	2	0	0	0	2
1996-97	**San Jose**	**NHL**	**60**	**12**	**15**	**27**	**222**	....	....	....	....	....
	Kentucky	AHL	3	1	2	3	4	....	....	....	....	....
1997-98	**San Jose**	**NHL**	**40**	**1**	**1**	**2**	**112**	....	....	....	....	....
	Tampa Bay	**NHL**	**14**	**1**	**1**	**2**	**58**	....	....	....	....	....
	NHL Totals		**183**	**24**	**29**	**53**	**548**	**6**	**0**	**0**	**0**	**9**

Traded to **Tampa Bay** by **San Jose** with Florida's 1st round choice (previously acquired, Tampa Bay selected Vincent Lecavalier) for Bryan Marchment, David Shaw and Tampa Bay's 1st round choice (later traded to Nashville — Nashville selected David Legwand) in 1998 Entry Draft, March 24, 1998.

NDUR, RUMUN (nih-DOOR, ROO-muhn) BUF.

Defense. Shoots left. 6'2", 200 lbs. Born, Zaria, Nigeria, July 7, 1975.
(Buffalo's 3rd choice, 69th overall, in 1994 Entry Draft).

			Regular Season					Playoffs				
Season	Club	Lea	GP	G	A	TP	PIM	GP	G	A	TP	PIM
1992-93	Guelph	OHL	22	1	3	4	30	4	0	1	1	4
1993-94	Guelph	OHL	61	6	33	39	176	9	4	1	5	24
1994-95	Guelph	OHL	63	10	21	31	187	14	0	4	4	28
1995-96	Rochester	AHL	73	2	12	14	306	17	1	2	3	33
1996-97	**Buffalo**	**NHL**	**2**	**0**	**0**	**0**	**2**	....	....	....	....	....
	Rochester	AHL	68	5	11	16	282	10	3	1	4	21
1997-98	**Buffalo**	**NHL**	**1**	**0**	**0**	**0**	**2**	....	....	....	....	....
	Rochester	AHL	50	1	12	13	207	4	0	2	2	16
	NHL Totals		**3**	**0**	**0**	**0**	**4**	....	....	....	....	....

NECKAR, STANISLAV (NEHTS-kahrzh) OTT.

Defense. Shoots left. 6'1", 212 lbs. Born, Ceske Budejovice, Czech., December 22, 1975.
(Ottawa's 2nd choice, 29th overall, in 1994 Entry Draft).

			Regular Season					Playoffs				
Season	Club	Lea	GP	G	A	TP	PIM	GP	G	A	TP	PIM
1992-93	Budejovice	Czech.	42	2	9	11	12	....	....	....	....	....
1993-94	Budejovice	Cze-Rep.	12	3	2	5	2	3	0	0	0	....
1994-95	Detroit	IHL	15	2	2	4	15	....	....	....	....	....
	Ottawa	**NHL**	**48**	**1**	**3**	**4**	**37**	....	....	....	....	....
1995-96	**Ottawa**	**NHL**	**82**	**3**	**9**	**12**	**54**	....	....	....	....	....
1996-97	**Ottawa**	**NHL**	**5**	**0**	**0**	**0**	**2**	....	....	....	....	....
1997-98	**Ottawa**	**NHL**	**60**	**2**	**2**	**4**	**31**	**9**	**0**	**0**	**0**	**2**
	NHL Totals		**195**	**6**	**14**	**20**	**124**	**9**	**0**	**0**	**0**	**2**

NEDVED, PETR (NEHD-VEHD) PIT.

Center. Shoots left. 6'3", 195 lbs. Born, Liberec, Czech., December 9, 1971.
(Vancouver's 1st choice, 2nd overall, in 1990 Entry Draft).

			Regular Season					Playoffs				
Season	Club	Lea	GP	G	A	TP	PIM	GP	G	A	TP	PIM
1989-90	Seattle	WHL	71	65	80	145	80	11	4	9	13	2
1990-91	**Vancouver**	**NHL**	**61**	**10**	**6**	**16**	**20**	**6**	**0**	**1**	**1**	**0**
1991-92	**Vancouver**	**NHL**	**77**	**15**	**22**	**37**	**36**	**10**	**1**	**4**	**5**	**16**
1992-93	**Vancouver**	**NHL**	**84**	**38**	**33**	**71**	**96**	**12**	**2**	**3**	**5**	**2**
1993-94	Canada	Nat-Tm	17	19	12	31	16	....	....	....	....	....
	Canada	Olympics	8	5	1	6	6	....	....	....	....	....
	St. Louis	**NHL**	**19**	**6**	**14**	**20**	**8**	**4**	**0**	**1**	**1**	**4**
1994-95	**NY Rangers**	**NHL**	**46**	**11**	**12**	**23**	**26**	**10**	**3**	**2**	**5**	**6**
1995-96	**Pittsburgh**	**NHL**	**80**	**45**	**54**	**99**	**68**	**18**	**10**	**10**	**20**	**16**
1996-97	**Pittsburgh**	**NHL**	**74**	**33**	**38**	**71**	**66**	**5**	**1**	**2**	**3**	**12**
1997-98	Sparta Praha	Cze-Rep.	5	2	3	5	8	6	0	2	2	52
	Las Vegas	IHL	3	3	3	6	4	....	....	....	....	....
	NHL Totals		**441**	**158**	**179**	**337**	**320**	**65**	**17**	**23**	**40**	**56**

Canadian Major Junior Rookie of the Year (1990)

Signed as a free agent by **St. Louis**, March 5, 1994. Traded to **NY Rangers** by **St. Louis** for Esa Tikkanen and Doug Lidster, July 24, 1994. Traded to **Pittsburgh** by **NY Rangers** with Sergei Zubov for Luc Robitaille and Ulf Samuelsson, August 31, 1995.

NEDVED, ZDENEK (NEHD-VEHD)

Right wing. Shoots left. 6', 180 lbs. Born, Lany, Czech., March 3, 1975.
(Toronto's 3rd choice, 123rd overall, in 1993 Entry Draft).

			Regular Season					Playoffs				
Season	Club	Lea	GP	G	A	TP	PIM	GP	G	A	TP	PIM
1991-92	Poldi Kladno	Czech.	19	15	12	27	22	....	....	....	....	....
1992-93	Sudbury	OHL	18	3	9	12	6	....	....	....	....	....
1993-94	Sudbury	OHL	60	50	50	100	42	10	7	8	15	10
1994-95	Sudbury	OHL	59	47	51	98	36	18	12	16	28	16
	Toronto	**NHL**	**1**	**0**	**0**	**0**	**2**	....	....	....	....	....
1995-96	**Toronto**	**NHL**	**7**	**1**	**1**	**2**	**6**	....	....	....	....	....
	St. John's	AHL	41	13	14	27	22	4	2	0	2	0
1996-97	**Toronto**	**NHL**	**23**	**3**	**5**	**8**	**6**	....	....	....	....	....
	St. John's	AHL	51	9	25	34	34	7	2	2	4	6
1997-98	St. John's	AHL	45	7	8	15	24	3	1	0	1	2
	Long Beach	IHL	19	3	8	11	18	....	....	....	....	....
	NHL Totals		**31**	**4**	**6**	**10**	**14**	....	....	....	....	....

NEHRLING, LUCAS N.J.

Defense. Shoots right. 6'4", 195 lbs. Born, Peterborough, Ont., August 14, 1979.
(New Jersey's 3rd choice, 104th overall, in 1997 Entry Draft).

			Regular Season					Playoffs				
Season	Club	Lea	GP	G	A	TP	PIM	GP	G	A	TP	PIM
1996-97	Sarnia	OHL	63	3	12	15	74	12	0	2	2	23
1997-98	Sarnia	OHL	22	0	2	2	46	....	....	....	....	....
	Kingston	OHL	39	1	8	9	83	12	0	1	1	19

NEIL, CHRISTOPHER OTT.

Right wing. Shoots right. 6', 210 lbs. Born, Markdale, Ont., June 18, 1979.
(Ottawa's 7th choice, 161st overall, in 1998 Entry Draft).

			Regular Season					Playoffs				
Season	Club	Lea	GP	G	A	TP	PIM	GP	G	A	TP	PIM
1996-97	North Bay	OHL	65	13	16	29	150	....	....	....	....	....
1997-98	North Bay	OHL	59	26	29	55	231	....	....	....	....	....

NELSON, JEFF NSH.

Center. Shoots left. 6', 190 lbs. Born, Prince Albert, Sask., December 18, 1972.
(Washington's 4th choice, 36th overall, in 1991 Entry Draft).

			Regular Season					Playoffs				
Season	Club	Lea	GP	G	A	TP	PIM	GP	G	A	TP	PIM
1988-89	Prince Albert	WHL	71	30	57	87	74	4	0	3	3	4
1989-90	Prince Albert	WHL	72	28	69	97	79	14	2	11	13	10
1990-91	Prince Albert	WHL	72	46	74	120	58	3	1	1	2	4
1991-92	Prince Albert	WHL	64	48	65	113	84	9	7	14	21	18
1992-93	Baltimore	AHL	72	14	38	52	12	7	1	3	4	2
1993-94	Portland	AHL	80	34	73	107	92	17	10	5	15	20
1994-95	Portland	AHL	64	33	50	83	57	7	1	4	5	8
	Washington	**NHL**	**10**	**1**	**0**	**1**	**2**	....	....	....	....	....
1995-96	**Washington**	**NHL**	**33**	**0**	**7**	**7**	**16**	**3**	**0**	**0**	**0**	**4**
	Portland	AHL	39	15	32	47	62	....	....	....	....	....
1996-97	Grand Rapids	IHL	82	34	55	89	85	5	0	4	4	4
1997-98	Milwaukee	IHL	52	20	34	54	30	10	2	7	9	15
	NHL Totals		**43**	**1**	**7**	**8**	**18**	**3**	**0**	**0**	**0**	**4**

Canadian Major Junior Scholastic Player of the Year (1989, 1990) • WHL East Second All-Star Team (1991, 1992)

Traded to **Nashville** by **Washington** for future considerations, August 19, 1998.

NEMCHINOV, SERGEI (nehm-CHEE-nahf, SAIR-gay) NYI

Center. Shoots left. 6', 200 lbs. Born, Moscow, USSR, January 14, 1964.
(NY Rangers' 14th choice, 244th overall, in 1990 Entry Draft).

			Regular Season					Playoffs				
Season	Club	Lea	GP	G	A	TP	PIM	GP	G	A	TP	PIM
1981-82	Soviet Wings	USSR	15	1	0	1	0	....	....	....	....	....
1982-83	CSKA Moscow	USSR	11	0	0	0	2	....	....	....	....	....
1983-84	CSKA Moscow	USSR	20	6	5	11	4	....	....	....	....	....
1984-85	CSKA Moscow	USSR	31	2	4	6	4	....	....	....	....	....
1985-86	Soviet Wings	USSR	39	7	12	19	28	....	....	....	....	....
1986-87	Soviet Wings	USSR	40	13	9	22	24	....	....	....	....	....
1987-88	Soviet Wings	USSR	48	17	11	28	26	....	....	....	....	....
1988-89	Soviet Wings	USSR	43	15	14	29	28	....	....	....	....	....
1989-90	Soviet Wings	USSR	48	17	16	33	34	....	....	....	....	....
1990-91	Soviet Wings	USSR	46	21	24	45	30	....	....	....	....	....
1991-92	**NY Rangers**	**NHL**	**73**	**30**	**28**	**58**	**15**	**13**	**1**	**4**	**5**	**8**
1992-93	**NY Rangers**	**NHL**	**81**	**23**	**31**	**54**	**34**	....	....	....	....	....
1993-94	**NY Rangers**	**NHL**	**76**	**22**	**27**	**49**	**36**	**23**	**2**	**5**	**7**	**6** ◆
1994-95	**NY Rangers**	**NHL**	**47**	**7**	**6**	**13**	**16**	**10**	**4**	**5**	**9**	**2**
1995-96	**NY Rangers**	**NHL**	**78**	**17**	**15**	**32**	**38**	**6**	**0**	**1**	**1**	**2**
1996-97	**NY Rangers**	**NHL**	**63**	**6**	**13**	**19**	**12**	....	....	....	....	....
	Vancouver	**NHL**	**6**	**2**	**3**	**5**	**4**	....	....	....	....	....
1997-98	**NY Islanders**	**NHL**	**74**	**10**	**19**	**29**	**24**	....	....	....	....	....
	Russia	Olympics	6	1	0	1	0	....	....	....	....	....
	NHL Totals		**498**	**117**	**142**	**259**	**179**	**52**	**7**	**15**	**22**	**18**

Traded to **Vancouver** by **NY Rangers** with Brian Noonan for Esa Tikkanen and Russ Courtnall, March 8, 1997. Signed as a free agent by **NY Islanders**, July 10, 1997.

NEMECEK, JAN (NEHM-eh-chehk, YAHN) L.A.

Defense. Shoots right. 6'1", 215 lbs. Born, Pisek, Czech., February 14, 1976.
(Los Angeles' 7th choice, 215th overall, in 1994 Entry Draft).

			Regular Season					Playoffs				
Season	Club	Lea	GP	G	A	TP	PIM	GP	G	A	TP	PIM
1992-93	Budejovice	Czech.	15	0	0	0	....	....	....	....	....	....
1993-94	Budejovice	Cze-Rep.	16	0	1	1	16	....	....	....	....	....
1994-95	Hull	QMJHL	49	10	16	26	48	21	5	9	14	10
1995-96	Hull	QMJHL	57	17	49	66	58	17	2	13	15	10
1996-97	Mississippi	ECHL	20	3	9	12	16	3	0	0	0	4
	Phoenix	IHL	24	1	1	2	2	....	....	....	....	....
1997-98	Fredericton	AHL	65	7	24	31	43	2	0	0	0	0

QMJHL Second All-Star Team (1996)

NEMIROVSKY, DAVID (neh-mih-ROHV-skee) FLA.

Right wing. Shoots right. 6'1", 192 lbs. Born, Toronto, Ont., August 1, 1976.
(Florida's 5th choice, 84th overall, in 1994 Entry Draft).

			Regular Season					Playoffs				
Season	Club	Lea	GP	G	A	TP	PIM	GP	G	A	TP	PIM
1993-94	Ottawa	OHL	64	21	31	52	18	17	10	10	20	2
1994-95	Ottawa	OHL	59	27	29	56	25	....	....	....	....	....
1995-96	Sarnia	OHL	26	18	27	45	14	10	8	8	16	6
	Florida	**NHL**	**9**	**0**	**2**	**2**	**2**	....	....	....	....	....
	Carolina	AHL	5	1	2	3	0	....	....	....	....	....
1996-97	**Florida**	**NHL**	**39**	**7**	**7**	**14**	**32**	**3**	**1**	**0**	**1**	**0**
	Carolina	AHL	34	21	21	42	18	....	....	....	....	....
1997-98	**Florida**	**NHL**	**41**	**9**	**12**	**21**	**8**	....	....	....	....	....
	New Haven	AHL	29	10	15	25	10	1	1	0	1	0
	NHL Totals		**89**	**16**	**21**	**37**	**42**	**3**	**1**	**0**	**1**	**0**

NICHOL, SCOTT BUF.

Center. Shoots right. 5'8", 160 lbs. Born, Edmonton, Alta., December 31, 1974.
(Buffalo's 9th choice, 272nd overall, in 1993 Entry Draft).

			Regular Season					Playoffs				
Season	Club	Lea	GP	G	A	TP	PIM	GP	G	A	TP	PIM
1992-93	Portland	WHL	67	31	33	64	146	16	8	8	16	41
1993-94	Portland	WHL	65	40	53	93	144	10	3	8	11	16
1994-95	Rochester	AHL	71	11	16	27	136	5	0	3	3	14
1995-96	**Buffalo**	**NHL**	**2**	**0**	**0**	**0**	**10**	....	....	....	....	....
	Rochester	AHL	62	14	18	32	170	19	7	6	13	36
1996-97	Rochester	AHL	68	22	21	43	133	10	2	1	3	26
1997-98	**Buffalo**	**NHL**	**3**	**0**	**0**	**0**	**4**	....	....	....	....	....
	Rochester	AHL	35	13	7	20	113	....	....	....	....	....
	NHL Totals		**5**	**0**	**0**	**0**	**14**	....	....	....	....	....

NICHOLLS, BERNIE (NICK-uhls) S.J.

Center. Shoots right. 6', 185 lbs. Born, Haliburton, Ont., June 24, 1961.
(Los Angeles' 6th choice, 73rd overall, in 1980 Entry Draft).

			Regular Season					Playoffs				
Season	Club	Lea	GP	G	A	TP	PIM	GP	G	A	TP	PIM
1979-80	Kingston	OHA	68	36	43	79	85	3	1	0	1	10
1980-81	Kingston	OHA	65	63	89	152	109	14	8	10	18	17
1981-82	**Los Angeles**	**NHL**	**22**	**14**	**18**	**32**	**27**	**10**	**4**	**0**	**4**	**23**
	New Haven	AHL	55	41	30	71	31	....	....	....	....	....
1982-83	**Los Angeles**	**NHL**	**71**	**28**	**22**	**50**	**124**	....	....	....	....	....
1983-84	**Los Angeles**	**NHL**	**78**	**41**	**54**	**95**	**83**	....	....	....	....	....
1984-85	**Los Angeles**	**NHL**	**80**	**46**	**54**	**100**	**76**	**3**	**1**	**1**	**2**	**9**
1985-86	**Los Angeles**	**NHL**	**80**	**36**	**61**	**97**	**78**	....	....	....	....	....
1986-87	**Los Angeles**	**NHL**	**80**	**33**	**48**	**81**	**101**	**5**	**2**	**5**	**7**	**6**
1987-88	**Los Angeles**	**NHL**	**65**	**32**	**46**	**78**	**114**	**5**	**2**	**6**	**8**	**11**
1988-89	**Los Angeles**	**NHL**	**79**	**70**	**80**	**150**	**96**	**11**	**7**	**9**	**16**	**12**
1989-90	**Los Angeles**	**NHL**	**47**	**27**	**48**	**75**	**66**	....	....	....	....	....
	NY Rangers	**NHL**	**32**	**12**	**25**	**37**	**20**	**10**	**7**	**5**	**12**	**16**
1990-91	**NY Rangers**	**NHL**	**71**	**25**	**48**	**73**	**96**	**5**	**4**	**3**	**7**	**8**
1991-92	**NY Rangers**	**NHL**	**1**	**0**	**0**	**0**	**0**	....	....	....	....	....
	Edmonton	**NHL**	**49**	**20**	**29**	**49**	**60**	**16**	**8**	**11**	**19**	**25**
1992-93	**Edmonton**	**NHL**	**46**	**8**	**32**	**40**	**40**	....	....	....	....	....
	New Jersey	**NHL**	**23**	**5**	**15**	**20**	**40**	**5**	**0**	**0**	**0**	**6**
1993-94	**New Jersey**	**NHL**	**61**	**19**	**27**	**46**	**86**	**16**	**4**	**9**	**13**	**28**
1994-95	**Chicago**	**NHL**	**48**	**22**	**29**	**51**	**32**	**16**	**1**	**11**	**12**	**8**
1995-96	**Chicago**	**NHL**	**59**	**19**	**41**	**60**	**60**	**10**	**2**	**7**	**9**	**4**
1996-97	**San Jose**	**NHL**	**65**	**12**	**33**	**45**	**63**	....	....	....	....	....
1997-98	**San Jose**	**NHL**	**60**	**6**	**22**	**28**	**26**	**6**	**0**	**5**	**5**	**8**
	NHL Totals		**1117**	**475**	**732**	**1207**	**1288**	**118**	**42**	**72**	**114**	**164**

Played in NHL All-Star Game (1984, 1989, 1990)

Traded to **NY Rangers** by **LA Kings** for Tomas Sandstrom and Tony Granato, January 20, 1990. Traded to **Edmonton** by **NY Rangers** with Steven Rice and Louie DeBrusk for Mark Messier and future considerations, October 4, 1991. Traded to **New Jersey** by **Edmonton** for Zdeno Ciger and Kevin Todd, January 13, 1993. Signed as a free agent by **Chicago**, July 14, 1994. Signed as a free agent by **San Jose**, August 5, 1996.

NICKULAS, ERIC BOS.

Center. Shoots right. 5'11", 190 lbs. Born, Cape Cod, MA, March 25, 1975.
(Boston's 3rd choice, 99th overall, in 1994 Entry Draft).

			Regular Season					Playoffs				
Season	Club	Lea	GP	G	A	TP	PIM	GP	G	A	TP	PIM
1993-94	Cushing Academy	H.S.	25	46	36	82	....	....	....	....	....	....
1994-95	New Hampshire	H.E.	33	15	9	24	32	....	....	....	....	....
1995-96	New Hampshire	H.E.	34	26	12	38	66	....	....	....	....	....
1996-97	New Hampshire	H.E.	39	29	22	51	80	....	....	....	....	....
1997-98	Orlando	IHL	76	22	9	31	77	6	0	0	0	10

NIECKAR, BARRY (NIGH-kahr) PHX.

Left wing. Shoots left. 6'3", 205 lbs. Born, Rama, Sask., December 16, 1967.

			Regular Season					Playoffs				
Season	Club	Lea	GP	G	A	TP	PIM	GP	G	A	TP	PIM
1991-92	Phoenix	IHL	5	0	0	0	9	....	....	....	....	....
	Raleigh	ECHL	46	10	18	28	229	4	4	0	4	22
1992-93	**Hartford**	**NHL**	**2**	**0**	**0**	**0**	**2**	....	....	....	....	....
	Springfield	AHL	21	2	4	6	65	6	1	0	1	14
1993-94	Springfield	AHL	30	0	2	2	67	....	....	....	....	....
	Raleigh	ECHL	18	4	6	10	126	15	5	7	12	51
1994-95	Saint John	AHL	65	8	7	15	*491	4	0	0	0	22
	Calgary	**NHL**	**3**	**0**	**0**	**0**	**12**	....	....	....	....	....
1995-96	Utah	IHL	53	9	15	24	194	....	....	....	....	....
	Peoria	IHL	10	3	3	6	72	12	4	6	10	48
1996-97	**Anaheim**	**NHL**	**2**	**0**	**0**	**0**	**5**	....	....	....	....	....
	Long Beach	IHL	63	3	10	13	386	5	0	0	0	22
1997-98	**Anaheim**	**NHL**	**1**	**0**	**0**	**0**	**2**	....	....	....	....	....
	Cincinnati	AHL	75	10	14	24	295	....	....	....	....	....
	NHL Totals		**8**	**0**	**0**	**0**	**21**	....	....	....	....	....

Signed as a free agent by **Hartford**, September 25, 1992. Signed as a free agent by **Calgary**, February 11, 1995. Signed as a free agent by **NY Islanders**, August 8, 1995. Signed as a free agent by **Anaheim**, October 2, 1996. Signed as a free agent by **Phoenix**, August 12, 1998.

NIEDERMAYER, ROB (nee-duhr-MIGH-uhr) FLA.

Center. Shoots left. 6'2", 204 lbs. Born, Cassiar, B.C., December 28, 1974.
(Florida's 1st choice, 5th overall, in 1993 Entry Draft).

			Regular Season					Playoffs				
Season	Club	Lea	GP	G	A	TP	PIM	GP	G	A	TP	PIM
1990-91	Medicine Hat	WHL	71	24	26	50	8	12	3	7	10	2
1991-92	Medicine Hat	WHL	71	32	46	78	77	4	2	3	5	2
1992-93	Medicine Hat	WHL	52	43	34	77	67	....	....	....	....	....
1993-94	**Florida**	**NHL**	**65**	**9**	**17**	**26**	**51**	....	....	....	....	....
1994-95	Medicine Hat	WHL	13	9	15	24	14	....	....	....	....	....
	Florida	**NHL**	**48**	**4**	**6**	**10**	**36**	....	....	....	....	....
1995-96	**Florida**	**NHL**	**82**	**26**	**35**	**61**	**107**	**22**	**5**	**3**	**8**	**12**
1996-97	**Florida**	**NHL**	**60**	**14**	**24**	**38**	**54**	**5**	**2**	**1**	**3**	**6**
1997-98	**Florida**	**NHL**	**33**	**8**	**7**	**15**	**41**	....	....	....	....	....
	NHL Totals		**288**	**61**	**89**	**150**	**289**	**27**	**7**	**4**	**11**	**18**

WHL East First All-Star Team (1993)

NIEDERMAYER, SCOTT (NEE-duhr-MIGH-uhr) N.J.

Defense. Shoots left. 6', 205 lbs. Born, Edmonton, Alta., August 31, 1973.
(New Jersey's 1st choice, 3rd overall, in 1991 Entry Draft).

			Regular Season					Playoffs				
Season	Club	Lea	GP	G	A	TP	PIM	GP	G	A	TP	PIM
1989-90	Kamloops	WHL	64	14	55	69	64	17	2	14	16	35
1990-91	Kamloops	WHL	57	26	56	82	52	....	....	....	....	....
1991-92	Kamloops	WHL	35	7	32	39	61	17	9	14	23	28
	New Jersey	**NHL**	**4**	**0**	**1**	**1**	**2**	....	....	....	....	....
1992-93	**New Jersey**	**NHL**	**80**	**11**	**29**	**40**	**47**	**5**	**0**	**3**	**3**	**2**
1993-94	**New Jersey**	**NHL**	**81**	**10**	**36**	**46**	**42**	**20**	**2**	**2**	**4**	**8**
1994-95	**New Jersey**	**NHL**	**48**	**4**	**15**	**19**	**18**	**20**	**4**	**7**	**11**	**10** ♦
1995-96	**New Jersey**	**NHL**	**79**	**8**	**25**	**33**	**46**	....	....	....	....	....
1996-97	**New Jersey**	**NHL**	**81**	**5**	**30**	**35**	**64**	**10**	**2**	**4**	**6**	**6**
1997-98	**New Jersey**	**NHL**	**81**	**14**	**43**	**57**	**27**	**6**	**0**	**2**	**2**	**4**
	NHL Totals		**454**	**52**	**179**	**231**	**246**	**61**	**8**	**18**	**26**	**30**

WHL West First All-Star Team (1991, 1992) • Canadian Major Junior Scholastic Player of the Year (1991) • Memorial Cup All-Star Team (1992) • Won Stafford Smythe Memorial Trophy (Memorial Cup Tournament MVP) (1992) • NHL/Upper Deck All-Rookie Team (1993) • NHL Second All-Star Team (1998)

Played in NHL All-Star Game (1998)

NIELSEN, CHRIS NYI

Center. Shoots right. 6'2", 185 lbs. Born, Moshi, Tanzania, February 16, 1980.
(NY Islanders' 2nd choice, 36th overall, in 1998 Entry Draft).

			Regular Season					Playoffs				
Season	Club	Lea	GP	G	A	TP	PIM	GP	G	A	TP	PIM
1995-96	Calgary	WHL	6	0	0	0	0	....	....	....	....	....
1996-97	Calgary	WHL	62	11	19	30	39	....	....	....	....	....
1997-98	Calgary	WHL	68	22	29	51	31	18	2	4	6	10

NIELSEN, JEFF ANA.

Right wing. Shoots left. 6', 200 lbs. Born, Grand Rapids, MN, September 20, 1971.
(NY Rangers' 4th choice, 69th overall, in 1990 Entry Draft).

			Regular Season					Playoffs				
Season	Club	Lea	GP	G	A	TP	PIM	GP	G	A	TP	PIM
1989-90	Grand Rapids	H.S.	28	32	25	57	....	....	....	....	....	....
1990-91	U. of Minnesota	WCHA	45	11	14	25	50	....	....	....	....	....
1991-92	U. of Minnesota	WCHA	41	14	14	28	70	....	....	....	....	....
1992-93	U. of Minnesota	WCHA	42	21	20	41	80	....	....	....	....	....
1993-94	U. of Minnesota	WCHA	41	29	16	45	94	....	....	....	....	....
1994-95	Binghamton	AHL	76	24	13	37	139	7	0	0	0	22
1995-96	Binghamton	AHL	64	22	20	42	56	4	1	1	2	4
1996-97	**NY Rangers**	**NHL**	**2**	**0**	**0**	**0**	**2**	....	....	....	....	....
	Binghamton	AHL	76	27	26	53	71	4	0	0	0	7
1997-98	**Anaheim**	**NHL**	**32**	**4**	**5**	**9**	**16**	....	....	....	....	....
	Cincinnati	AHL	18	4	8	12	37	....	....	....	....	....
	NHL Totals		**34**	**4**	**5**	**9**	**18**	....	....	....	....	....

WCHA Second All-Star Team (1994)

Signed as a free agent by **Anaheim**, August 18, 1997.

NIELSEN, KIRK

Right wing. Shoots right. 6'1", 205 lbs. Born, Grand Rapids, MN, October 19, 1973.
(Philadelphia's 1st choice, 10th overall, in 1994 Supplemental Draft).

			Regular Season					Playoffs				
Season	Club	Lea	GP	G	A	TP	PIM	GP	G	A	TP	PIM
1992-93	Harvard	ECAC	30	2	2	4	38	....	....	....	....	....
1993-94	Harvard	ECAC	32	6	9	15	41	....	....	....	....	....
1994-95	Harvard	ECAC	30	13	8	21	24	....	....	....	....	....
1995-96	Harvard	ECAC	31	12	16	28	66	....	....	....	....	....
1996-97	Providence	AHL	68	12	23	35	30	9	2	1	3	2
1997-98	**Boston**	**NHL**	**6**	**0**	**0**	**0**	**0**	....	....	....	....	....
	Providence	AHL	72	19	29	48	40	....	....	....	....	....
	NHL Totals		**6**	**0**	**0**	**0**	**0**	....	....	....	....	....

Signed as a free agent by **Boston**, June 7, 1996.

NIEMI, ANTTI-JUSSI (nee-mee, AN-tee-YOO-see) OTT.

Defense. Shoots left. 6'1", 183 lbs. Born, Vantaa, Finland, September 22, 1977.
(Ottawa's 2nd choice, 81st overall, in 1996 Entry Draft).

			Regular Season					Playoffs				
Season	Club	Lea	GP	G	A	TP	PIM	GP	G	A	TP	PIM
1995-96	Jokerit	Fin-Jr.	34	11	18	29	56	8	0	4	4	39
	Jarvenpaa	Finland-2	4	0	2	2	8	....	....	....	....	....
	Jokerit	Finland	6	0	2	2	6	1	0	0	0	0
1996-97	Jokerit	Finland	44	2	9	11	38	9	0	2	2	2
1997-98	Jokerit	EuroHL	6	0	1	1	6	....	....	....	....	....
	Jokerit	Finland	46	2	6	8	24	8	0	1	1	0

NIEMINEN, VILLE (nee-EHM-ih-nehn, VIHL-ee) COL.

Right wing. Shoots left. 5'11", 205 lbs. Born, Tampere, Finland, April 6, 1977.
(Colorado's 4th choice, 78th overall, in 1997 Entry Draft).

			Regular Season					Playoffs				
Season	Club	Lea	GP	G	A	TP	PIM	GP	G	A	TP	PIM
1994-95	Tappara	Fin-Jr.	16	11	21	32	47	....	....	....	....	....
	Tappara	Finland	16	0	0	0	0	....	....	....	....	....
1995-96	Tappara	Fin-Jr.	20	20	23	43	63	....	....	....	....	....
	Tappara	Finland	4	0	1	1	8	....	....	....	....	....
	KooVee	Finland-2	7	2	1	3	4	....	....	....	....	....
1996-97	Tappara	Finland	49	10	13	23	120	3	1	0	1	8
1997-98	Hershey	AHL	74	14	22	36	85	....	....	....	....	....

NIEUWENDYK, JOE (NOO-ihn-DIGHK) DAL.

Center. Shoots left. 6'1", 195 lbs. Born, Oshawa, Ont., September 10, 1966.
(Calgary's 2nd choice, 27th overall, in 1985 Entry Draft).

			Regular Season					Playoffs				
Season	Club	Lea	GP	G	A	TP	PIM	GP	G	A	TP	PIM
1983-84	Pickering	OJHL	38	30	28	58	35	....	....	....	....	....
1984-85	Cornell	ECAC	29	21	24	45	30	....	....	....	....	....
1985-86	Cornell	ECAC	29	26	28	54	67	....	....	....	....	....
1986-87	Cornell	ECAC	23	26	26	52	26	....	....	....	....	....
	Canada	Nat-Tm	5	2	0	2	0	....	....	....	....	....
	Calgary	**NHL**	**9**	**5**	**1**	**6**	**0**	**6**	**2**	**2**	**4**	**0**
1987-88	**Calgary**	**NHL**	**75**	**51**	**41**	**92**	**23**	**8**	**3**	**4**	**7**	**2**
1988-89	**Calgary**	**NHL**	**77**	**51**	**31**	**82**	**40**	**22**	**10**	**4**	**14**	**10 ♦**
1989-90	**Calgary**	**NHL**	**79**	**45**	**50**	**95**	**40**	**6**	**4**	**6**	**10**	**4**
1990-91	**Calgary**	**NHL**	**79**	**45**	**40**	**85**	**36**	**7**	**4**	**1**	**5**	**10**
1991-92	**Calgary**	**NHL**	**69**	**22**	**34**	**56**	**55**	....	....	....	....	....
1992-93	**Calgary**	**NHL**	**79**	**38**	**37**	**75**	**52**	**6**	**3**	**6**	**9**	**10**
1993-94	**Calgary**	**NHL**	**64**	**36**	**39**	**75**	**51**	**6**	**2**	**2**	**4**	**0**
1994-95	**Calgary**	**NHL**	**46**	**21**	**29**	**50**	**33**	**5**	**4**	**3**	**7**	**0**
1995-96	**Dallas**	**NHL**	**52**	**14**	**18**	**32**	**41**	....	....	....	....	....
1996-97	**Dallas**	**NHL**	**66**	**30**	**21**	**51**	**32**	**7**	**2**	**2**	**4**	**6**
1997-98	**Dallas**	**NHL**	**73**	**39**	**30**	**69**	**30**	**1**	**1**	**0**	**1**	**0**
	NHL Totals		**768**	**397**	**371**	**768**	**433**	**74**	**35**	**30**	**65**	**42**

NCAA East First All-American Team (1986, 1987) • ECAC First All-Star Team (1986, 1987) • NHL All-Rookie Team (1988) • Won Calder Memorial Trophy (1988) • Won Dodge Ram Tough Award (1988) • Won King Clancy Memorial Trophy (1995)

Played in NHL All-Star Game (1988, 1989, 1990, 1994)

Traded to **Dallas** by **Calgary** for Corey Millen and Jarome Iginla, December 19, 1995.

NIINIMAA, JANNE (nihn-EE-mah, YAH-nee) EDM.

Defense. Shoots left. 6'2", 220 lbs. Born, Raahe, Finland, May 22, 1975.
(Philadelphia's 1st choice, 36th overall, in 1993 Entry Draft).

			Regular Season					Playoffs				
Season	Club	Lea	GP	G	A	TP	PIM	GP	G	A	TP	PIM
1991-92	Karpat Oulu	Finland-2	41	2	11	13	49	....	....	....	....	....
1992-93	Karpat Oulu	Finland-2	29	2	3	5	14	....	....	....	....	....
1993-94	Jokerit	Finland	45	3	8	11	24	12	1	1	2	4
1994-95	Jokerit	Finland	42	7	10	17	36	10	1	4	5	35
1995-96	Jokerit	Finland	49	5	15	20	79	11	0	2	2	12
1996-97	**Philadelphia**	**NHL**	**77**	**4**	**40**	**44**	**58**	**19**	**1**	**12**	**13**	**16**
1997-98	**Philadelphia**	**NHL**	**66**	**3**	**31**	**34**	**56**	....	....	....	....	....
	Finland	Olympics	6	0	3	3	8	....	....	....	....	....
	Edmonton	**NHL**	**11**	**1**	**8**	**9**	**6**	**11**	**1**	**1**	**2**	**12**
	NHL Totals		**154**	**8**	**79**	**87**	**120**	**30**	**2**	**13**	**15**	**28**

NHL All-Rookie Team (1997)

Traded to **Edmonton** by **Philadelphia** for Dan McGillis and Edmonton's 2nd round choice (Jason Beckett) in 1998 Entry Draft, March 24, 1998.

NIKOLISHIN, ANDREI (nee-koh-LEE-shin) WSH.

Left wing. Shoots left. 5'11", 200 lbs. Born, Vorkuta, USSR, March 25, 1973.
(Hartford's 2nd choice, 47th overall, in 1992 Entry Draft).

			Regular Season					Playoffs				
Season	Club	Lea	GP	G	A	TP	PIM	GP	G	A	TP	PIM
1990-91	Moscow D'amo	USSR	2	0	0	0	0	....	....	....	....	....
1991-92	Moscow D'amo	CIS	18	1	0	1	4	....	....	....	....	....
1992-93	Moscow D'amo	CIS	42	5	7	12	30	10	2	1	3	8
1993-94	Moscow D'amo	CIS	41	8	12	20	30	9	1	3	4	4
	Russia	Olympics	8	2	5	7	6	....	....	....	....	....
1994-95	Moscow D'amo	CIS	12	7	2	9	6	....	....	....	....	....
	Hartford	**NHL**	**39**	**8**	**10**	**18**	**10**	....	....	....	....	....
1995-96	**Hartford**	**NHL**	**61**	**14**	**37**	**51**	**34**	....	....	....	....	....
1996-97	**Hartford**	**NHL**	**12**	**2**	**5**	**7**	**2**	....	....	....	....	....
	Washington	**NHL**	**59**	**7**	**14**	**21**	**30**	....	....	....	....	....
1997-98	**Washington**	**NHL**	**38**	**6**	**10**	**16**	**14**	**21**	**1**	**13**	**14**	**12**
	Portland	AHL	2	0	0	0	2	....	....	....	....	....
	NHL Totals		**209**	**37**	**76**	**113**	**90**	**21**	**1**	**13**	**14**	**12**

CIS First All-Star Team (1994) • CIS Player of the Year (1994)

Traded to **Washington** by **Hartford** for Curtis Leschyshyn, November 9, 1996.

NIKOLOV, ANGEL (NIH-koh-lohv) S.J.

Defense. Shoots left. 6'1", 178 lbs. Born, Most, Czech., November 18, 1975.
(San Jose's 2nd choice, 37th overall, in 1994 Entry Draft).

			Regular Season					Playoffs				
Season	Club	Lea	GP	G	A	TP	PIM	GP	G	A	TP	PIM
1993-94	Litvinov	Cze-Rep.	10	2	2	4	....	3	0	0	0	....
1994-95	Litvinov	Cze-Rep.	41	1	4	5	18	4	0	0	0	27
1995-96	Litvinov	Cze-Rep.	40	1	7	8	....	10	0	1	1	....
1996-97	Litvinov	Cze-Rep.	47	0	9	9	44	....	....	....	....	....
1997-98	Litvinov	Cze-Rep.	51	1	4	5	53	4	0	3	3	27

NIKULIN, IGOR (nih-KOO-lihn) ANA.

Right wing. Shoots left. 6'1", 200 lbs. Born, Cherepovets, USSR, August 26, 1972.
(Anaheim's 4th choice, 107th overall, in 1995 Entry Draft).

			Regular Season					Playoffs				
Season	Club	Lea	GP	G	A	TP	PIM	GP	G	A	TP	PIM
1992-93	Cherepovets	CIS	42	11	11	22	22	....	....	....	....	....
1993-94	Cherepovets	CIS	44	14	15	29	52	2	1	0	1	0
1994-95	Cherepovets	CIS	52	14	12	26	28	....	....	....	....	....
1995-96	Cherepovets	CIS	47	20	13	33	28	4	1	0	1	0
	Baltimore	AHL	4	2	2	4	2	....	....	....	....	....
1996-97	Baltimore	AHL	61	27	25	52	14	3	2	1	3	2
	Fort Wayne	IHL	10	1	2	3	4	....	....	....	....	....
	Anaheim	**NHL**	....	....	....	....	....	**1**	**0**	**0**	**0**	**0**
1997-98	Cincinnati	AHL	54	14	11	25	40	....	....	....	....	....
	NHL Totals		**0**	**0**	**0**	**0**	**0**	**1**	**0**	**0**	**0**	**0**

NILSON, MARCUS FLA.

Right wing. Shoots right. 6'1", 183 lbs. Born, Stockholm, Sweden, March 1, 1978.
(Florida's 1st choice, 20th overall, in 1996 Entry Draft).

			Regular Season					Playoffs				
Season	Club	Lea	GP	G	A	TP	PIM	GP	G	A	TP	PIM
1995-96	Djurgarden	Swe-Jr.	25	19	17	36	46	2	1	1	2	12
	Djurgarden	Sweden	12	0	0	0	0	1	0	0	0	0
1996-97	Djurgarden	Sweden	37	0	3	3	33	4	0	0	0	0
1997-98	Djurgarden	Sweden	41	4	7	11	18	15	2	1	3	16

NILSSON, MAGNUS DET.

Right wing. Shoots left. 6'1", 187 lbs. Born, Finspang, Sweden, February 1, 1978.
(Detroit's 5th choice, 144th overall, in 1996 Entry Draft).

			Regular Season					Playoffs				
Season	Club	Lea	GP	G	A	TP	PIM	GP	G	A	TP	PIM
1995-96	Vita Hasten	Sweden-2	28	3	3	6	16	....	....	....	....	....
1996-97	Malmo IF	Swe-Jr.	14	10	9	19	45	....	....	....	....	....
	Malmo IF	Sweden	12	0	0	0	0	....	....	....	....	....
1997-98	Malmo IF	Sweden	45	6	1	7	6	....	....	....	....	....

NITTEL, ADAM (nih-TEHL) S.J.

Right wing. Shoots right. 6', 215 lbs. Born, Kitchener, Ont., July 17, 1978.
(San Jose's 4th choice, 107th overall, in 1997 Entry Draft).

			Regular Season					Playoffs				
Season	Club	Lea	GP	G	A	TP	PIM	GP	G	A	TP	PIM
1995-96	Niagara Falls	OHL	39	3	3	6	74	10	0	3	3	39
1996-97	Erie	OHL	46	8	11	19	194	....	....	....	....	....
1997-98	Erie	OHL	48	11	17	28	*309	7	0	0	0	19

NOBLE, STEVE ST.L.

Center. Shoots left. 6'1", 185 lbs. Born, Sault Ste. Marie, Ont., July 17, 1976.
(St. Louis' 5th choice, 198th overall, in 1994 Entry Draft).

			Regular Season					Playoffs				
Season	Club	Lea	GP	G	A	TP	PIM	GP	G	A	TP	PIM
1993-94	Stratford	OJHL	25	14	19	33	45	....	....	....	....	....
1994-95	Notre Dame	CCHA	37	6	8	14	25	....	....	....	....	....
1995-96	Notre Dame	CCHA	36	5	15	20	48	....	....	....	....	....
1996-97	Notre Dame	CCHA	34	9	7	16	34	....	....	....	....	....
1997-98	Notre Dame	CCHA	41	8	17	25	18	....	....	....	....	....

NOLAN, OWEN S.J.

Right wing. Shoots right. 6'1", 205 lbs. Born, Belfast, Ireland, February 12, 1972.
(Quebec's 1st choice, 1st overall, in 1990 Entry Draft).

			Regular Season					Playoffs				
Season	Club	Lea	GP	G	A	TP	PIM	GP	G	A	TP	PIM
1988-89	Cornwall	OHL	62	34	25	59	213	18	5	11	16	41
1989-90	Cornwall	OHL	58	51	59	110	240	6	7	5	12	26
1990-91	**Quebec**	**NHL**	**59**	**3**	**10**	**13**	**109**	....	....	....	....	....
	Halifax	AHL	6	4	4	8	11	....	....	....	....	....
1991-92	**Quebec**	**NHL**	**75**	**42**	**31**	**73**	**183**	....	....	....	....	....
1992-93	**Quebec**	**NHL**	**73**	**36**	**41**	**77**	**185**	**5**	**1**	**0**	**1**	**2**
1993-94	**Quebec**	**NHL**	**6**	**2**	**2**	**4**	**8**	....	....	....	....	....
1994-95	**Quebec**	**NHL**	**46**	**30**	**19**	**49**	**46**	**6**	**2**	**3**	**5**	**6**
1995-96	**Colorado**	**NHL**	**9**	**4**	**4**	**8**	**9**	....	....	....	....	....
	San Jose	**NHL**	**72**	**29**	**32**	**61**	**137**	....	....	....	....	....
1996-97	**San Jose**	**NHL**	**72**	**31**	**32**	**63**	**155**	....	....	....	....	....
1997-98	**San Jose**	**NHL**	**75**	**14**	**27**	**41**	**144**	**6**	**2**	**2**	**4**	**26**
	NHL Totals		**487**	**191**	**198**	**389**	**976**	**17**	**5**	**5**	**10**	**34**

OHL First All-Star Team (1990)

Played in NHL All-Star Game (1992, 1996, 1997)

Transferred to **Colorado** after **Quebec** franchise relocated, June 21, 1995. Traded to **San Jose** by **Colorado** for Sandis Ozolinsh, October 26, 1995.

NOONAN, BRIAN

Right wing. Shoots right. 6'1", 200 lbs. Born, Boston, MA, May 29, 1965.
(Chicago's 10th choice, 186th overall, in 1983 Entry Draft).

			Regular Season					Playoffs				
Season	Club	Lea	GP	G	A	TP	PIM	GP	G	A	TP	PIM
1982-83	Arch. Wiliams	H.S.	21	26	17	43	....	....	....	....	....	....
1983-84	Arch. Wiliams	H.S.	17	14	23	32	....	....	....	....	....	....
1984-85	New Westminster	WHL	72	50	66	116	76	11	8	7	15	4
1985-86	Nova Scotia	AHL	2	0	0	0	0	....	....	....	....	....
	Saginaw	IHL	76	39	39	78	69	11	6	3	9	6
1986-87	Nova Scotia	AHL	70	25	26	51	30	5	3	1	4	4
1987-88	**Chicago**	**NHL**	**77**	**10**	**20**	**30**	**44**	**3**	**0**	**0**	**0**	**4**
1988-89	**Chicago**	**NHL**	**45**	**4**	**12**	**16**	**28**	**1**	**0**	**0**	**0**	**0**
	Saginaw	IHL	19	18	13	31	36	1	0	0	0	0
1989-90	**Chicago**	**NHL**	**8**	**0**	**2**	**2**	**6**	....	....	....	....	....
	Indianapolis	IHL	56	40	36	76	85	14	6	9	15	20
1990-91	**Chicago**	**NHL**	**7**	**0**	**4**	**4**	**2**	....	....	....	....	....
	Indianapolis	IHL	59	38	53	91	67	7	6	4	10	18
1991-92	**Chicago**	**NHL**	**65**	**19**	**12**	**31**	**81**	**18**	**6**	**9**	**15**	**30**
1992-93	**Chicago**	**NHL**	**63**	**16**	**14**	**30**	**82**	**4**	**3**	**0**	**3**	**4**
1993-94	**Chicago**	**NHL**	**64**	**14**	**21**	**35**	**57**	....	....	....	....	....
	NY Rangers	**NHL**	**12**	**4**	**2**	**6**	**12**	**22**	**4**	**7**	**11**	**17 ♦**
1994-95	**NY Rangers**	**NHL**	**45**	**14**	**13**	**27**	**26**	**5**	**0**	**0**	**0**	**8**
1995-96	**St. Louis**	**NHL**	**81**	**13**	**22**	**35**	**84**	**13**	**4**	**1**	**5**	**10**
1996-97	**St. Louis**	**NHL**	**13**	**2**	**5**	**7**	**0**	....	....	....	....	....
	NY Rangers	**NHL**	**44**	**6**	**9**	**15**	**28**	....	....	....	....	....
	Vancouver	**NHL**	**16**	**4**	**8**	**12**	**6**	....	....	....	....	....
1997-98	**Vancouver**	**NHL**	**82**	**10**	**15**	**25**	**62**	....	....	....	....	....
	NHL Totals		**622**	**116**	**159**	**275**	**518**	**66**	**17**	**17**	**34**	**73**

IHL Second All-Star Team (1990) • IHL First All-Star Team (1991)

Traded to **NY Rangers** by **Chicago** with Stephane Matteau for Tony Amonte and the rights to Matt Oates, March 21, 1994. Signed as a free agent by **St. Louis**, July 24, 1995. Traded to **NY Rangers** by **St. Louis** for Sergio Momesso, November 13, 1996. Traded to **Vancouver** by **NY Rangers** with Sergei Nemchinov for Esa Tikkanen and Russ Courtnall, March 8, 1997.

NORDGREN, NIKLAS CAR.

Left wing. Shoots right. 5'11", 183 lbs. Born, Ornskoldsvik, Sweden, June 28, 1979.
(Carolina's 7th choice, 195th overall, in 1997 Entry Draft).

			Regular Season					Playoffs				
Season	Club	Lea	GP	G	A	TP	PIM	GP	G	A	TP	PIM
1996-97	MoDo	Swe-Jr.	22	14	6	20	....	....	....	....	....	....
	MoDo	Sweden	5	0	0	0	0	....	....	....	....	....
1997-98	MoDo	Swe-Jr.	28	15	15	30	52	....	....	....	....	....

NORDSTROM, PETER BOS.

Center. Shoots left. 6'1", 200 lbs. Born, Munkfors, Sweden, July 26, 1974.
(Boston's 3rd choice, 78th overall, in 1998 Entry Draft).

			Regular Season					Playoffs				
Season	Club	Lea	GP	G	A	TP	PIM	GP	G	A	TP	PIM
1991-92	Munkfors	Sweden-3	31	12	20	32	42	....	....	....	....	....
1992-93	Munkfors	Sweden-3	35	19	11	30	44	....	....	....	....	....
1993-94	Munkfors	Sweden-3	31	17	26	43	87	....	....	....	....	....
1994-95	Munkfors	Sweden-2	21	8	17	25	30	....	....	....	....	....
1995-96	Farjestad	Sweden	40	6	5	11	36	8	0	3	3	12
1996-97	Farjestad	Sweden	44	9	5	14	32	14	1	2	3	6
1997-98	Farjestad	Sweden	45	6	19	25	46	12	5	7	*12	8

NORRIS, CLAYTON

Right wing. Shoots right. 6'2", 205 lbs. Born, Edmonton, Alta., March 8, 1972.
(Philadelphia's 5th choice, 116th overall, in 1991 Entry Draft).

			Regular Season					Playoffs				
Season	Club	Lea	GP	G	A	TP	PIM	GP	G	A	TP	PIM
1988-89	Medicine Hat	WHL	66	4	9	13	122	3	0	0	0	2
1989-90	Medicine Hat	WHL	72	13	18	31	176	3	0	0	0	15
1990-91	Medicine Hat	WHL	71	26	27	53	165	12	5	4	9	41
1991-92	Medicine Hat	WHL	69	26	39	65	300	2	0	0	0	9
1992-93	Medicine Hat	WHL	41	21	16	37	128	10	3	2	5	14
	Hershey	AHL	4	0	0	0	5	....	....	....	....	....
	Roanoke	ECHL	4	0	0	0	0	....	....	....	....	....
1993-94	Hershey	AHL	62	8	10	18	217	10	1	0	1	18
1994-95	Hershey	AHL	76	12	21	33	287	4	0	0	0	8
1995-96	Hershey	AHL	57	8	8	16	163	5	0	1	1	4
1996-97	Philadelphia	AHL	1	0	0	0	17	....	....	....	....	....
	Orlando	IHL	69	9	9	18	261	10	2	3	5	17
1997-98	St. John's	AHL	59	4	11	15	265	4	0	0	0	10
	Orlando	IHL	13	0	3	3	51	....	....	....	....	....

WHL East Second All-Star Team (1992)

NORRIS, DWAYNE

Right wing. Shoots right. 5'10", 175 lbs. Born, St. John's, Nfld., January 8, 1970.
(Quebec's 5th choice, 127th overall, in 1990 Entry Draft).

			Regular Season					Playoffs				
Season	Club	Lea	GP	G	A	TP	PIM	GP	G	A	TP	PIM
1988-89	Michigan State	CCHA	40	16	21	37	32	....	....	....	....	....
1989-90	Michigan State	CCHA	33	18	25	43	30	....	....	....	....	....
1990-91	Michigan State	CCHA	40	26	25	51	60	....	....	....	....	....
1991-92	Michigan State	CCHA	41	40	38	78	58	....	....	....	....	....
1992-93	Halifax	AHL	50	25	28	53	62	....	....	....	....	....
1993-94	Canada	Nat-Tm	48	18	14	32	22	....	....	....	....	....
	Canada	Olympics	8	2	2	4	4	....	....	....	....	....
	Quebec	**NHL**	**4**	**1**	**1**	**2**	**4**	....	....	....	....	....
	Cornwall	AHL	9	2	9	11	0	13	7	4	11	17
1994-95	Cornwall	AHL	60	30	43	73	61	12	7	8	15	4
	Quebec	**NHL**	**13**	**1**	**2**	**3**	**2**	....	....	....	....	....
1995-96	Los Angeles	IHL	14	7	16	23	22	....	....	....	....	....
	Anaheim	**NHL**	**3**	**0**	**1**	**1**	**2**	....	....	....	....	....
	Baltimore	AHL	62	31	55	86	16	12	6	9	15	12
1996-97	Kolner Haie	Germany	49	16	28	44	24	4	3	0	3	0
1997-98	Kolner Haie	EuroHL	6	1	3	4	2	....	....	....	....	....
	Kolner Haie	Germany	42	13	14	27	34	3	0	0	0	0
	NHL Totals		**20**	**2**	**4**	**6**	**8**	....	....	....	....	....

CCHA First All-Star Team (1992) • NCAA West First All-American Team (1992) • AHL First All-Star Team (1995) • AHL Second All-Star Team (1996)

Signed as a free agent by **Anaheim**, November 3, 1995.

NORRIS, WARREN

Center. Shoots left. 6'1", 185 lbs. Born, St. John's, Nfld., September 19, 1974.

			Regular Season					Playoffs				
Season	Club	Lea	GP	G	A	TP	PIM	GP	G	A	TP	PIM
1993-94	U. Mass-Amherst	H.E.	29	20	27	47	12	....	....	....	....	....
1994-95	U. Mass-Amherst	H.E.	35	13	8	21	12	....	....	....	....	....
1995-96	U. Mass-Amherst	H.E.	33	20	20	40	64	....	....	....	....	....
1996-97	U. Mass-Amherst	H.E.	35	20	26	46	48	....	....	....	....	....
	St. John's	AHL	9	1	0	1	4	....	....	....	....	....
1997-98	St. John's	AHL	35	2	2	4	4	....	....	....	....	....

Signed as a free agent by **Toronto**, April 10, 1997.

NORSTROM, MATTIAS (NOHR-struhm) L.A.

Defense. Shoots left. 6'2", 201 lbs. Born, Stockholm, Sweden, January 2, 1972.
(NY Rangers' 2nd choice, 48th overall, in 1992 Entry Draft).

			Regular Season					Playoffs				
Season	Club	Lea	GP	G	A	TP	PIM	GP	G	A	TP	PIM
1991-92	AIK Solna	Sweden	39	4	3	7	28	3	0	2	2	2
1992-93	AIK Solna	Sweden	22	0	1	1	16	....	....	....	....	....
1993-94	**NY Rangers**	**NHL**	**9**	**0**	**2**	**2**	**6**	....	....	....	....	....
	Binghamton	AHL	55	1	9	10	70	....	....	....	....	....
1994-95	Binghamton	AHL	63	9	10	19	91	....	....	....	....	....
	NY Rangers	**NHL**	**9**	**0**	**3**	**3**	**2**	**3**	**0**	**0**	**0**	**0**
1995-96	**NY Rangers**	**NHL**	**25**	**2**	**1**	**3**	**22**	....	....	....	....	....
	Los Angeles	**NHL**	**11**	**0**	**1**	**1**	**18**	....	....	....	....	....
1996-97	**Los Angeles**	**NHL**	**80**	**1**	**21**	**22**	**84**	....	....	....	....	....
1997-98	**Los Angeles**	**NHL**	**73**	**1**	**12**	**13**	**90**	**4**	**0**	**0**	**0**	**2**
	Sweden	Olympics	4	0	1	1	2	....	....	....	....	....
	NHL Totals		**207**	**4**	**40**	**44**	**222**	**7**	**0**	**0**	**0**	**2**

Traded to **LA Kings** by **NY Rangers** with Ray Ferraro, Ian Laperriere, Nathan Lafayette and NY Rangers' 4th round choice (Sean Blanchard) in 1997 Entry Draft for Marty McSorley, Jari Kurri and Shane Churla, March 14, 1996.

NORTON, BRAD EDM.

Defense. Shoots left. 6'4", 225 lbs. Born, Cambridge, MA, February 13, 1975.
(Edmonton's 9th choice, 215th overall, in 1993 Entry Draft).

			Regular Season					Playoffs				
Season	Club	Lea	GP	G	A	TP	PIM	GP	G	A	TP	PIM
1992-93	Cushing Academy	H.S.	31	10	26	36	....	....	....	....	....	....
1993-94	Cushing Academy	H.S.	STATISTICS NOT AVAILABLE									
1994-95	U. Mass-Amherst	H.E.	30	0	6	6	89	....	....	....	....	....
1995-96	U. Mass-Amherst	H.E.	34	4	12	16	99	....	....	....	....	....
1996-97	U. Mass-Amherst	H.E.	35	2	16	18	88	....	....	....	....	....
1997-98	U. Mass-Amherst	H.E.	20	2	13	15	28	....	....	....	....	....
	Detroit	IHL	33	1	4	5	56	22	0	2	2	87

NORTON, JEFF FLA.

Defense. Shoots left. 6'2", 200 lbs. Born, Acton, MA, November 25, 1965.
(NY Islanders' 3rd choice, 62nd overall, in 1984 Entry Draft).

			Regular Season					Playoffs				
Season	Club	Lea	GP	G	A	TP	PIM	GP	G	A	TP	PIM
1983-84	Cushing Academy	H.S.	21	22	33	55	....	....	....	....	....	....
1984-85	U. of Michigan	CCHA	37	8	16	24	103	....	....	....	....	....
1985-86	U. of Michigan	CCHA	37	15	30	45	99	....	....	....	....	....
1986-87	U. of Michigan	CCHA	39	12	36	48	92	....	....	....	....	....
1987-88	United States	Nat-Tm	54	7	22	29	52	....	....	....	....	....
	United States	Olympics	6	0	4	4	4	....	....	....	....	....
	NY Islanders	**NHL**	**15**	**1**	**6**	**7**	**14**	**3**	**0**	**2**	**2**	**13**
1988-89	**NY Islanders**	**NHL**	**69**	**1**	**30**	**31**	**74**	....	....	....	....	....
1989-90	**NY Islanders**	**NHL**	**60**	**4**	**49**	**53**	**65**	**4**	**1**	**3**	**4**	**17**
1990-91	**NY Islanders**	**NHL**	**44**	**3**	**25**	**28**	**16**	....	....	....	....	....
1991-92	**NY Islanders**	**NHL**	**28**	**1**	**18**	**19**	**18**	....	....	....	....	....
1992-93	**NY Islanders**	**NHL**	**66**	**12**	**38**	**50**	**45**	**10**	**1**	**1**	**2**	**4**
1993-94	**San Jose**	**NHL**	**64**	**7**	**33**	**40**	**36**	**14**	**1**	**5**	**6**	**20**
1994-95	**San Jose**	**NHL**	**20**	**1**	**9**	**10**	**39**	....	....	....	....	....
	St. Louis	**NHL**	**28**	**2**	**18**	**20**	**33**	**7**	**1**	**1**	**2**	**11**
1995-96	**St. Louis**	**NHL**	**36**	**4**	**7**	**11**	**26**	....	....	....	....	....
	Edmonton	**NHL**	**30**	**4**	**16**	**20**	**16**	....	....	....	....	....
1996-97	**Edmonton**	**NHL**	**62**	**2**	**11**	**13**	**42**	....	....	....	....	....
	Tampa Bay	**NHL**	**13**	**0**	**5**	**5**	**16**	....	....	....	....	....
1997-98	**Tampa Bay**	**NHL**	**37**	**4**	**6**	**10**	**26**	....	....	....	....	....
	Florida	**NHL**	**19**	**0**	**7**	**7**	**18**	....	....	....	....	....
	NHL Totals		**591**	**46**	**278**	**324**	**484**	**38**	**4**	**12**	**16**	**65**

CCHA Second All-Star Team (1987)

Traded to **San Jose** by **NY Islanders** for San Jose's 3rd round choice (Jason Strudwick) in 1994 Entry Draft, June 20, 1993. Traded to **St. Louis** by **San Jose** with San Jose's 3rd round choice (later traded to Colorado — Colorado selected Rick Berry) in 1997 Entry Draft for Craig Janney and cash, March 6, 1995. Traded to **Edmonton** by **St. Louis** with Donald Dufresne for Igor Kravchuk and Ken Sutton, January 4, 1996. Traded to **Tampa Bay** by **Edmonton** for Drew Bannister and Tampa Bay's 6th round choice (Peter Sarno) in 1997 Entry Draft, March 18, 1997. Traded to **Florida** by **Tampa Bay** with Dino Ciccarelli for Mark Fitzpatrick and Jody Hull, January 15, 1998.

NOVOSELTSEV, IVAN (noh-voh-SEHLT-sehv, ee-VAHN) FLA.

Left wing. Shoots left. 6'1", 183 lbs. Born, Golitsino, USSR, January 23, 1979.
(Florida's 5th choice, 95th overall, in 1997 Entry Draft).

			Regular Season					Playoffs				
Season	Club	Lea	GP	G	A	TP	PIM	GP	G	A	TP	PIM
1995-96	Soviet Wings	CIS	1	0	0	0	2	....	....	....	....	....
1996-97	Soviet Wings	Russia	30	0	3	3	18	2	0	0	0	4
	Soviet Wings 2	Russia-3	19	5	3	8	39	....	....	....	....	....
1997-98	Sarnia	OHL	53	26	22	48	41	5	1	1	2	8

NUMMINEN, TEPPO (NOO-mih-nehn, TEH-poh) PHX.

Defense. Shoots right. 6'1", 190 lbs. Born, Tampere, Finland, July 3, 1968.
(Winnipeg's 2nd choice, 29th overall, in 1986 Entry Draft).

			Regular Season					Playoffs				
Season	Club	Lea	GP	G	A	TP	PIM	GP	G	A	TP	PIM
1985-86	Tappara	Finland	31	2	4	6	6	8	0	0	0	0
1986-87	Tappara	Finland	44	9	9	18	16	9	4	1	5	4
1987-88	Tappara	Finland	40	10	10	20	29	10	6	6	12	6
	Finland	Olympics	6	1	4	5	0	....	....	....	....	....
1988-89	**Winnipeg**	**NHL**	**69**	**1**	**14**	**15**	**36**	....	....	....	....	....
1989-90	**Winnipeg**	**NHL**	**79**	**11**	**32**	**43**	**20**	**7**	**1**	**2**	**3**	**10**
1990-91	**Winnipeg**	**NHL**	**80**	**8**	**25**	**33**	**28**	....	....	....	....	....
1991-92	**Winnipeg**	**NHL**	**80**	**5**	**34**	**39**	**32**	**7**	**0**	**0**	**0**	**0**
1992-93	**Winnipeg**	**NHL**	**66**	**7**	**30**	**37**	**33**	**6**	**1**	**1**	**2**	**2**
1993-94	**Winnipeg**	**NHL**	**57**	**5**	**18**	**23**	**28**	....	....	....	....	....
1994-95	TuTo Turku	Finland	12	3	8	11	4	....	....	....	....	....
	Winnipeg	**NHL**	**42**	**5**	**16**	**21**	**16**	....	....	....	....	....
1995-96	**Winnipeg**	**NHL**	**74**	**11**	**43**	**54**	**22**	**6**	**0**	**0**	**0**	**2**
1996-97	**Phoenix**	**NHL**	**82**	**2**	**25**	**27**	**28**	**7**	**3**	**3**	**6**	**0**
1997-98	**Phoenix**	**NHL**	**82**	**11**	**40**	**51**	**30**	**1**	**0**	**0**	**0**	**0**
	Finland	Olympics	6	1	1	2	2	....	....	....	....	....
	NHL Totals		**711**	**66**	**277**	**343**	**273**	**34**	**5**	**6**	**11**	**14**

Transferred to **Phoenix** after **Winnipeg** franchise relocated, July 1, 1996.

NURMINEN, KAI (NUHR-mih-nehn, KIGH)

Left wing. Shoots left. 6'1", 198 lbs. Born, Turku, Finland, March 29, 1969.
(Los Angeles' 9th choice, 193rd overall, in 1996 Entry Draft).

			Regular Season					Playoffs				
Season	Club	Lea	GP	G	A	TP	PIM	GP	G	A	TP	PIM
1990-91	TuTo Turku	Finland-2	33	26	20	46	14	....	....	....	....	....
1991-92	Kiekko	Finland-2	44	44	19	63	34	....	....	....	....	....
1992-93	TPS Turku	Finland	31	4	6	10	13	7	1	2	3	0
	Kiekko	Finland-2	8	6	4	10	2	....	....	....	....	....
1993-94	TPS Turku	Finland	45	23	12	35	20	11	0	3	3	4
1994-95	Hameelinna	Finland	49	30	25	55	40	....	....	....	....	....
1995-96	HV 71 Jonkoping	Finland	40	31	24	55	30	4	3	1	4	8
1996-97	**Los Angeles**	**NHL**	**67**	**16**	**11**	**27**	**22**	....	....	....	....	....
1997-98	V. Frolunda	Sweden	23	9	7	16	24	....	....	....	....	....
	Jokerit	Finland	20	7	9	16	30	8	5	3	8	4
	NHL Totals		**67**	**16**	**11**	**27**	**22**	....	....	....	....	....

Finnish First All-Star Team (1995)

NUUTINEN, SAMI (NOO-tih-nehn) EDM.

Defense. Shoots left. 6'1", 189 lbs. Born, Espoo, Finland, June 11, 1971.
(Edmonton's 12th choice, 248th overall, in 1990 Entry Draft).

			Regular Season					Playoffs				
Season	Club	Lea	GP	G	A	TP	PIM	GP	G	A	TP	PIM
1988-89	Espoo	Finland-2	39	18	10	28	46	....	....	....	....	....
1989-90	Espoo	Finland-2	40	8	15	23	....	....	....	....	....	....
1990-91	K-Kissat	Finland-2	3	1	0	1	0	....	....	....	....	....
	Helsinki	Finland	27	1	3	4	6	3	0	0	0	0
1991-92	Helsinki	Finland	44	5	6	11	10	9	0	1	1	4
1992-93	Kiekko	Finland	48	7	11	18	59	....	....	....	....	....
1993-94	Kiekko	Finland	46	9	15	24	36	....	....	....	....	....
1994-95	Kiekko	Finland	50	8	24	32	38	4	0	1	1	0
1995-96	Kiekko	Finland	49	7	7	14	54	....	....	....	....	....
1996-97	Vasteras IK	Sweden	50	7	7	14	22	....	....	....	....	....
1997-98	Kiekko	Finland	48	4	17	21	51	8	0	2	2	6

NYLANDER, MICHAEL (NEE-lan-duhr) CGY.

Center. Shoots left. 5'11", 195 lbs. Born, Stockholm, Sweden, October 3, 1972.
(Hartford's 4th choice, 59th overall, in 1991 Entry Draft).

			Regular Season					Playoffs				
Season	Club	Lea	GP	G	A	TP	PIM	GP	G	A	TP	PIM
1989-90	Huddinge	Sweden-2	31	7	15	22	4	....	....	....	....	....
1990-91	Huddinge	Sweden-2	33	14	20	34	10	....	....	....	....	....
1991-92	AIK Solna	Sweden	40	11	17	28	30	3	1	4	5	4
1992-93	**Hartford**	**NHL**	**59**	**11**	**22**	**33**	**36**	....	....	....	....	....
	Springfield	AHL	....	....	....	....	....	3	3	3	6	2
1993-94	**Hartford**	**NHL**	**58**	**11**	**33**	**44**	**24**	....	....	....	....	....
	Springfield	AHL	4	0	9	9	0	....	....	....	....	....
	Calgary	**NHL**	**15**	**2**	**9**	**11**	**6**	**3**	**0**	**0**	**0**	**0**
1994-95	JyP HT	Finland	16	11	19	30	63	....	....	....	....	....
	Calgary	**NHL**	**6**	**0**	**1**	**1**	**2**	**6**	**0**	**6**	**6**	**2**
1995-96	**Calgary**	**NHL**	**73**	**17**	**38**	**55**	**20**	**4**	**0**	**0**	**0**	**0**
1996-97	HC Lugano	Switz.	36	12	43	55	28	8	3	8	11	8
1997-98	**Calgary**	**NHL**	**65**	**13**	**23**	**36**	**24**	....	....	....	....	....
	Sweden	Olympics	4	0	0	0	6	....	....	....	....	....
	NHL Totals		**276**	**54**	**126**	**180**	**112**	**13**	**0**	**6**	**6**	**2**

Swedish Rookie of the Year (1992) • Swedish World All-Star Team (1996, 1997)

Traded to **Calgary** by **Hartford** with James Patrick and Zarley Zalapski for Gary Suter, Paul Ranheim and Ted Drury, March 10, 1994.

OATES, ADAM WSH.

Center. Shoots right. 5'11", 185 lbs. Born, Weston, Ont., August 27, 1962.

			Regular Season					Playoffs				
Season	Club	Lea	GP	G	A	TP	PIM	GP	G	A	TP	PIM
1982-83	RPI	ECAC	22	9	33	42	8	....	....	....	....	....
1983-84	RPI	ECAC	38	26	57	83	15	....	....	....	....	....
1984-85	RPI	ECAC	38	31	60	91	29	....	....	....	....	....
1985-86	**Detroit**	**NHL**	**38**	**9**	**11**	**20**	**10**	....	....	....	....	....
	Adirondack	AHL	34	18	28	46	4	17	7	14	21	4
1986-87	**Detroit**	**NHL**	**76**	**15**	**32**	**47**	**21**	**16**	**4**	**7**	**11**	**6**
1987-88	**Detroit**	**NHL**	**63**	**14**	**40**	**54**	**20**	**16**	**8**	**12**	**20**	**6**
1988-89	**Detroit**	**NHL**	**69**	**16**	**62**	**78**	**14**	**6**	**0**	**8**	**8**	**2**
1989-90	**St. Louis**	**NHL**	**80**	**23**	**79**	**102**	**30**	**12**	**2**	**12**	**14**	**4**
1990-91	**St. Louis**	**NHL**	**61**	**25**	**90**	**115**	**29**	**13**	**7**	**13**	**20**	**10**
1991-92	**St. Louis**	**NHL**	**54**	**10**	**59**	**69**	**12**	....	....	....	....	....
	Boston	**NHL**	**26**	**10**	**20**	**30**	**10**	**15**	**5**	**14**	**19**	**4**
1992-93	**Boston**	**NHL**	**84**	**45**	***97**	**142**	**32**	**4**	**0**	**9**	**9**	**4**
1993-94	**Boston**	**NHL**	**77**	**32**	**80**	**112**	**45**	**13**	**3**	**9**	**12**	**8**
1994-95	**Boston**	**NHL**	**48**	**12**	**41**	**53**	**8**	**5**	**1**	**0**	**1**	**2**
1995-96	**Boston**	**NHL**	**70**	**25**	**67**	**92**	**18**	**5**	**2**	**5**	**7**	**2**
1996-97	**Boston**	**NHL**	**63**	**18**	**52**	**70**	**10**	....	....	....	....	....
	Washington	**NHL**	**17**	**4**	**8**	**12**	**4**	....	....	....	....	....
1997-98	**Washington**	**NHL**	**82**	**18**	**58**	**76**	**36**	**21**	**6**	**11**	**17**	**8**
	NHL Totals		**908**	**276**	**796**	**1072**	**299**	**126**	**38**	**100**	**138**	**56**

ECAC Second All-Star Team (1984) • NCAA East First All-American Team (1984, 1985) • ECAC First All-Star Team (1985) • NCAA Championship All-Tournament Team (1985) • NHL Second All-Star Team (1991)

Played in NHL All-Star Game (1991, 1992, 1993, 1994, 1997)

Signed as a free agent by **Detroit,** June 28, 1985. Traded to **St. Louis** by **Detroit** with Paul MacLean for Bernie Federko and Tony McKegney, June 15, 1989. Traded to **Boston** by **St. Louis** for Craig Janney and Stephane Quintal, February 7, 1992. Traded to **Washington** by **Boston** with Bill Ranford and Rick Tocchet for Jim Carey, Anson Carter, Jason Allison and Washington's 3rd round choice (Lee Goren) in 1997 Entry Draft, March 1, 1997.

O'BRIEN, SEAN PIT.

Left wing. Shoots left. 6'1", 200 lbs. Born, Belmont, MA, February 9, 1972.

			Regular Season					Playoffs				
Season	Club	Lea	GP	G	A	TP	PIM	GP	G	A	TP	PIM
1990-91	Princeton	ECAC	24	0	6	6	12	....	....	....	....	....
1991-92	Princeton	ECAC	27	3	10	13	38	....	....	....	....	....
1992-93	Princeton	ECAC	29	2	22	24	54	....	....	....	....	....
1993-94	Princeton	ECAC	28	8	15	23	40	....	....	....	....	....
1994-95	Richmond	ECHL	52	5	18	23	147	17	2	5	7	77
	Houston	IHL	13	2	1	3	23	....	....	....	....	....
1995-96	Las Vegas	IHL	1	0	0	0	2	....	....	....	....	....
	Utah	IHL	7	2	2	4	12	....	....	....	....	....
	Houston	IHL	4	0	1	1	12	....	....	....	....	....
	Tallahasee	ECHL	54	9	19	28	179	8	0	2	2	23
1996-97	Tallahasee	ECHL	10	7	3	10	29	....	....	....	....	....
	Utah	IHL	50	21	10	31	135	....	....	....	....	....
	Phoenix	IHL	10	3	3	6	20	....	....	....	....	....
1997-98	Fayetteville	CHL	1	0	0	0	0	....	....	....	....	....
	Philadelphia	AHL	33	7	10	17	88	20	4	2	6	48
	Utah	IHL	36	3	8	11	77	....	....	....	....	....

ECAC Second All-Star Team (1994)

Signed as a free agent by **LA Kings**, June 26, 1997. Signed as a free agent by **Pittsburgh**, August 11, 1998.

O'CONNELL, ALBERT NYI

Left wing. Shoots left. 6', 188 lbs. Born, Cambridge, MA, May 20, 1976.
(NY Islanders' 6th choice, 116th overall, in 1994 Entry Draft).

			Regular Season					Playoffs				
Season	Club	Lea	GP	G	A	TP	PIM	GP	G	A	TP	PIM
1993-94	St. Sebastian's	H.S.	24	16	23	39	26	....	....	....	....	....
1994-95	St. Sebastian's	H.S.	26	19	25	44	....	....	....	....	....	....
1995-96	Boston University	H.E.	38	9	8	17	34	....	....	....	....	....
1996-97	Boston University	H.E.	41	12	12	24	72	....	....	....	....	....
1997-98	Boston University	H.E.	34	12	16	28	60	....	....	....	....	....

ODELEIN, LYLE (OH-duh-LIGHN) N.J.

Defense. Shoots right. 5'11", 210 lbs. Born, Quill Lake, Sask., July 21, 1968.
(Montreal's 8th choice, 141st overall, in 1986 Entry Draft).

			Regular Season					Playoffs				
Season	Club	Lea	GP	G	A	TP	PIM	GP	G	A	TP	PIM
1985-86	Moose Jaw	WHL	67	9	37	46	117	13	1	6	7	34
1986-87	Moose Jaw	WHL	59	9	50	59	70	9	2	5	7	26
1987-88	Moose Jaw	WHL	63	15	43	58	166	....	....	....	....	....
1988-89	Sherbrooke	AHL	33	3	4	7	120	3	0	2	2	5
	Peoria	IHL	36	2	8	10	116	....	....	....	....	....
1989-90	**Montreal**	**NHL**	**8**	**0**	**2**	**2**	**33**	....	....	....	....	....
	Sherbrooke	AHL	68	7	24	31	265	12	6	5	11	79
1990-91	**Montreal**	**NHL**	**52**	**0**	**2**	**2**	**259**	**12**	**0**	**0**	**0**	**54**
1991-92	**Montreal**	**NHL**	**71**	**1**	**7**	**8**	**212**	**7**	**0**	**0**	**0**	**11**
1992-93	**Montreal**	**NHL**	**83**	**2**	**14**	**16**	**205**	**20**	**1**	**5**	**6**	**30** ♦
1993-94	**Montreal**	**NHL**	**79**	**11**	**29**	**40**	**276**	**7**	**0**	**0**	**0**	**17**
1994-95	**Montreal**	**NHL**	**48**	**3**	**7**	**10**	**152**	....	....	....	....	....
1995-96	**Montreal**	**NHL**	**79**	**3**	**14**	**17**	**230**	**6**	**1**	**1**	**2**	**6**
1996-97	**New Jersey**	**NHL**	**79**	**3**	**13**	**16**	**110**	**10**	**2**	**2**	**4**	**19**
1997-98	**New Jersey**	**NHL**	**79**	**4**	**19**	**23**	**171**	**6**	**1**	**1**	**2**	**21**
	NHL Totals		**578**	**27**	**107**	**134**	**1648**	**68**	**5**	**9**	**14**	**158**

Traded to **New Jersey** by **Montreal** for Stephane Richer, August 22, 1996.

ODGERS, JEFF (AWD-juhrs) COL.

Right wing. Shoots right. 6', 200 lbs. Born, Spy Hill, Sask., May 31, 1969.

			Regular Season					Playoffs				
Season	Club	Lea	GP	G	A	TP	PIM	GP	G	A	TP	PIM
1986-87	Brandon	WHL	70	7	14	21	150	....	....	....	....	....
1987-88	Brandon	WHL	70	17	18	35	202	4	1	1	2	14
1988-89	Brandon	WHL	71	31	29	60	277	....	....	....	....	....
1989-90	Brandon	WHL	64	37	28	65	209	....	....	....	....	....
1990-91	Kansas City	IHL	77	12	19	31	318	....	....	....	....	....
1991-92	**San Jose**	**NHL**	**61**	**7**	**4**	**11**	**217**	....	....	....	....	....
	Kansas City	IHL	12	2	2	4	56	4	2	1	3	0
1992-93	**San Jose**	**NHL**	**66**	**12**	**15**	**27**	**253**	....	....	....	....	....
1993-94	**San Jose**	**NHL**	**81**	**13**	**8**	**21**	**222**	**11**	**0**	**0**	**0**	**11**
1994-95	**San Jose**	**NHL**	**48**	**4**	**3**	**7**	**117**	**11**	**1**	**1**	**2**	**23**
1995-96	**San Jose**	**NHL**	**78**	**12**	**4**	**16**	**192**	....	....	....	....	....
1996-97	**Boston**	**NHL**	**80**	**7**	**8**	**15**	**197**	....	....	....	....	....
1997-98	Providence	AHL	4	0	0	0	31	....	....	....	....	....
	Colorado	**NHL**	**68**	**5**	**8**	**13**	**213**	**6**	**0**	**0**	**0**	**25**
	NHL Totals		**482**	**60**	**50**	**110**	**1411**	**28**	**1**	**1**	**2**	**59**

Signed as a free agent by **San Jose**, September 3, 1991. Traded to **Boston** by **San Jose** with Pittsburgh's 5th round choice (previously acquired, Boston selected Elias Abrahamsson) in 1996 Entry Draft for Al Iafrate, June 21, 1996. Signed as a free agent by **Colorado**, October 24, 1997.

ODJICK, GINO (OH-jihk) NYI

Left wing. Shoots left. 6'3", 210 lbs. Born, Maniwaki, Que., September 7, 1970.
(Vancouver's 5th choice, 86th overall, in 1990 Entry Draft).

			Regular Season					Playoffs				
Season	Club	Lea	GP	G	A	TP	PIM	GP	G	A	TP	PIM
1988-89	Laval	QMJHL	50	9	15	24	278	16	0	9	9	129
1989-90	Laval	QMJHL	51	12	26	38	280	13	6	5	11	110
1990-91	**Vancouver**	**NHL**	**45**	**7**	**1**	**8**	**296**	**6**	**0**	**0**	**0**	**18**
	Milwaukee	IHL	17	7	3	10	102	....	....	....	....	....
1991-92	**Vancouver**	**NHL**	**65**	**4**	**6**	**10**	**348**	**4**	**0**	**0**	**0**	**6**
1992-93	**Vancouver**	**NHL**	**75**	**4**	**13**	**17**	**370**	**1**	**0**	**0**	**0**	**0**
1993-94	**Vancouver**	**NHL**	**76**	**16**	**13**	**29**	**271**	**10**	**0**	**0**	**0**	**18**
1994-95	**Vancouver**	**NHL**	**23**	**4**	**5**	**9**	**109**	**5**	**0**	**0**	**0**	**47**
1995-96	**Vancouver**	**NHL**	**55**	**3**	**4**	**7**	**181**	**6**	**3**	**1**	**4**	**6**
1996-97	**Vancouver**	**NHL**	**70**	**5**	**8**	**13**	***371**	....	....	....	....	....
1997-98	**Vancouver**	**NHL**	**35**	**3**	**2**	**5**	**181**	....	....	....	....	....
	NY Islanders	**NHL**	**13**	**0**	**0**	**0**	**31**	....	....	....	....	....
	NHL Totals		**457**	**46**	**52**	**98**	**2158**	**32**	**3**	**1**	**4**	**95**

Traded to **NY Islanders** by **Vancouver** for Jason Strudwick, March 23, 1998.

O'DONNELL, SEAN L.A.

Defense. Shoots left. 6'3", 230 lbs. Born, Ottawa, Ont., October 13, 1971.
(Buffalo's 6th choice, 123rd overall, in 1991 Entry Draft).

			Regular Season					Playoffs				
Season	Club	Lea	GP	G	A	TP	PIM	GP	G	A	TP	PIM
1990-91	Sudbury	OHL	66	8	23	31	114	5	1	4	5	10
1991-92	Rochester	AHL	73	4	9	13	193	16	1	2	3	21
1992-93	Rochester	AHL	74	3	18	21	203	17	1	6	7	38
1993-94	Rochester	AHL	64	2	10	12	242	4	0	1	1	21
1994-95	Phoenix	IHL	61	2	18	20	132	9	0	1	1	21
	Los Angeles	**NHL**	**15**	**0**	**2**	**2**	**49**	....	....	....	....	....
1995-96	**Los Angeles**	**NHL**	**71**	**2**	**5**	**7**	**127**	....	....	....	....	....
1996-97	**Los Angeles**	**NHL**	**55**	**5**	**12**	**17**	**144**	....	....	....	....	....
1997-98	**Los Angeles**	**NHL**	**80**	**2**	**15**	**17**	**179**	**4**	**1**	**0**	**1**	**36**
	NHL Totals		**221**	**9**	**34**	**43**	**499**	**4**	**1**	**0**	**1**	**36**

Traded to **LA Kings** by **Buffalo** for Doug Houda, July 26, 1994.

ODUYA, FREDRIK (oh-DOO-yuh) S.J.

Left wing. Shoots left. 6'3", 220 lbs. Born, Stockholm, Sweden, May 31, 1975.
(San Jose's 8th choice, 154th overall, in 1993 Entry Draft).

			Regular Season					Playoffs				
Season	Club	Lea	GP	G	A	TP	PIM	GP	G	A	TP	PIM
1992-93	Guelph	OHL	23	2	4	6	29	....	....	....	....	....
	Ottawa	OHL	17	0	3	3	70	....	....	....	....	....
1993-94	Ottawa	OHL	51	11	12	23	181	17	0	3	3	22
1994-95	Ottawa	OHL	61	2	13	15	175	....	....	....	....	....
1995-96	Kansas City	IHL	56	2	6	8	235	3	0	0	0	2
1996-97	Kentucky	AHL	69	2	9	11	241	....	....	....	....	....
1997-98	Kentucky	AHL	72	6	10	16	300	....	....	....	....	....

O'GRADY, MIKE FLA.

Defense. Shoots left. 6'3", 227 lbs. Born, Neilburg, Sask., March 22, 1977.
(Florida's 3rd choice, 62nd overall, in 1995 Entry Draft).

			Regular Season					Playoffs				
Season	Club	Lea	GP	G	A	TP	PIM	GP	G	A	TP	PIM
1993-94	Saskatoon	WHL	13	0	1	1	29	....	....	....	....	....
1994-95	Saskatoon	WHL	39	0	7	7	157	....	....	....	....	....
	Lethbridge	WHL	21	1	2	3	124	....	....	....	....	....
1995-96	Lethbridge	WHL	61	2	9	11	242	4	1	0	1	8
1996-97	Lethbridge	WHL	61	8	25	33	262	18	1	5	6	41
1997-98	Port Huron	UHL	12	2	3	5	30	....	....	....	....	....
	Tallahasee	ECHL	4	0	0	0	18	....	....	....	....	....
	New Haven	AHL	32	1	4	5	58	2	0	0	0	0

OHLUND, MATTIAS (OH-luhnd) VAN.

Defense. Shoots left. 6'3", 209 lbs. Born, Pitea, Sweden, September 9, 1976.
(Vancouver's 1st choice, 13th overall, in 1994 Entry Draft).

			Regular Season					Playoffs				
Season	Club	Lea	GP	G	A	TP	PIM	GP	G	A	TP	PIM
1992-93	Pitea	Sweden-2	22	0	6	6	16	....	....	....	....	....
1993-94	Pitea	Sweden-2	28	7	10	17	62	....	....	....	....	....
1994-95	Lulea HF	Sweden	34	6	10	16	34	9	4	0	4	16
1995-96	Lulea HF	Sweden	38	4	10	14	26	13	1	0	1	47
1996-97	Lulea HF	Sweden	47	7	9	16	38	10	1	2	3	8
1997-98	**Vancouver**	**NHL**	**77**	**7**	**23**	**30**	**76**	....	....	....	....	....
	Sweden	Olympics	4	0	1	1	4	....	....	....	....	....
	NHL Totals		**77**	**7**	**23**	**30**	**76**	....	....	....	....	....

NHL All-Rookie Team (1998)

OIKAWA, MATT (oh-ee-kah-wah) WSH.

Right wing. Shoots right. 6'2", 205 lbs. Born, Hamilton, Ont., October 27, 1977.
(Washington's 7th choice, 226th overall, in 1997 Entry Draft).

			Regular Season					Playoffs				
Season	Club	Lea	GP	G	A	TP	PIM	GP	G	A	TP	PIM
1995-96	St. Lawrence	ECAC	13	3	1	4	15	....	....	....	....	....
1996-97	St. Lawrence	ECAC	34	9	10	19	18	....	....	....	....	....
1997-98	St. Lawrence	ECAC	16	2	5	7	6	....	....	....	....	....

OKSIUTA, ROMAN (ohk-SEW-tah)

Right wing. Shoots left. 6'3", 230 lbs. Born, Murmansk, USSR, August 21, 1970.
(NY Rangers' 11th choice, 202nd overall, in 1989 Entry Draft).

			Regular Season					Playoffs				
Season	Club	Lea	GP	G	A	TP	PIM	GP	G	A	TP	PIM
1987-88	Khimik	USSR	11	1	0	1	4	....	....	....	....	....
1988-89	Khimik	USSR	34	13	3	16	14	....	....	....	....	....
1989-90	Khimik	USSR	37	13	6	19	16	....	....	....	....	....
1990-91	Khimik	USSR	41	12	8	20	24	....	....	....	....	....
1991-92	Khimik	CIS	42	24	20	44	28	....	....	....	....	....
1992-93	Khimik	CIS	20	11	2	13	42	....	....	....	....	....
	Cape Breton	AHL	43	26	25	51	22	16	9	19	28	12
1993-94	**Edmonton**	**NHL**	**10**	**1**	**2**	**3**	**4**	....	....	....	....	....
	Cape Breton	AHL	47	31	22	53	90	4	2	2	4	22
1994-95	Cape Breton	AHL	25	9	7	16	20	....	....	....	....	....
	Edmonton	**NHL**	**26**	**11**	**2**	**13**	**8**	....	....	....	....	....
	Vancouver	**NHL**	**12**	**5**	**2**	**7**	**2**	**10**	**2**	**3**	**5**	**0**
1995-96	**Vancouver**	**NHL**	**56**	**16**	**23**	**39**	**42**	....	....	....	....	....
	Anaheim	**NHL**	**14**	**7**	**5**	**12**	**18**	....	....	....	....	....
1996-97	**Anaheim**	**NHL**	**28**	**6**	**7**	**13**	**22**	....	....	....	....	....
	Pittsburgh	**NHL**	**7**	**0**	**0**	**0**	**4**	....	....	....	....	....
1997-98	Fort Wayne	IHL	19	5	8	13	50	3	0	0	0	12
	NHL Totals		**153**	**46**	**41**	**87**	**100**	**10**	**2**	**3**	**5**	**0**

Won Izvestia Trophy (CIS Top Scorer) (1992)

Traded to **Edmonton** by **NY Rangers** with NY Rangers' 3rd round choice (Alexander Kerch) in 1993 Entry Draft for Kevin Lowe, December 11, 1992. Traded to **Vancouver** by **Edmonton** for Jiri Slegr, April 7, 1995. Traded to **Anaheim** by **Vancouver** for Mike Sillinger, March 15, 1996. Traded to **Pittsburgh** by **Anaheim** for Richard Park, March 18, 1997.

OLAUSSON, FREDRIK (OHL-ah-suhn) ANA.

Defense. Shoots right. 6'2", 198 lbs. Born, Dadesjo, Sweden, October 5, 1966.
(Winnipeg's 4th choice, 81st overall, in 1985 Entry Draft).

			Regular Season					Playoffs				
Season	Club	Lea	GP	G	A	TP	PIM	GP	G	A	TP	PIM
1982-83	Nybro	Sweden-2	31	4	4	8	12	....	....	....	....	....
1983-84	Nybro	Sweden-2	28	8	14	22	32	....	....	....	....	....
1984-85	Farjestad	Sweden	29	5	12	17	22	3	1	0	1	0
1985-86	Farjestad	Sweden	33	4	12	16	22	8	3	2	5	6
1986-87	**Winnipeg**	**NHL**	**72**	**7**	**29**	**36**	**24**	**10**	**2**	**3**	**5**	**4**
1987-88	**Winnipeg**	**NHL**	**38**	**5**	**10**	**15**	**18**	**5**	**1**	**1**	**2**	**0**
1988-89	**Winnipeg**	**NHL**	**75**	**15**	**47**	**62**	**32**	....	....	....	....	....
1989-90	**Winnipeg**	**NHL**	**77**	**9**	**46**	**55**	**32**	**7**	**0**	**2**	**2**	**2**
1990-91	**Winnipeg**	**NHL**	**71**	**12**	**29**	**41**	**24**	....	....	....	....	....
1991-92	**Winnipeg**	**NHL**	**77**	**20**	**42**	**62**	**34**	**7**	**1**	**5**	**6**	**4**
1992-93	**Winnipeg**	**NHL**	**68**	**16**	**41**	**57**	**22**	**6**	**0**	**2**	**2**	**2**
1993-94	**Winnipeg**	**NHL**	**18**	**2**	**5**	**7**	**10**	....	....	....	....	....
	Edmonton	**NHL**	**55**	**9**	**19**	**28**	**20**	....	....	....	....	....
1994-95	Ehrwald	Austria	10	4	3	7	8	....	....	....	....	....
	Edmonton	**NHL**	**33**	**0**	**10**	**10**	**20**	....	....	....	....	....
1995-96	**Edmonton**	**NHL**	**20**	**0**	**6**	**6**	**14**	....	....	....	....	....
	Anaheim	**NHL**	**36**	**2**	**16**	**18**	**24**	....	....	....	....	....
1996-97	**Anaheim**	**NHL**	**20**	**2**	**9**	**11**	**8**	....	....	....	....	....
	Pittsburgh	**NHL**	**51**	**7**	**20**	**27**	**24**	**4**	**0**	**1**	**1**	**0**
1997-98	**Pittsburgh**	**NHL**	**76**	**6**	**27**	**33**	**42**	**6**	**0**	**3**	**3**	**2**
	NHL Totals		**787**	**112**	**356**	**468**	**348**	**45**	**4**	**17**	**21**	**14**

Swedish World All-Star Team (1986)

Traded to **Edmonton** by **Winnipeg** with Winnipeg's 7th round choice (Curtis Sheptak) in 1994 Entry Draft for Edmonton's 3rd round choice (Tavis Hansen) in 1994 Entry Draft, December 6, 1993. Claimed on waivers by **Anaheim** from **Edmonton**, January 16, 1996. Traded to **Pittsburgh** by **Anaheim** with Alex Hicks for Shawn Antoski and Dmitri Mironov, November 19, 1996. Signed as a free agent by **Anaheim**, August 28, 1998.

OLCZYK, ED (OHL-chehk) CHI.

Center. Shoots left. 6'1", 205 lbs. Born, Chicago, IL, August 16, 1966.
(Chicago's 1st choice, 3rd overall, in 1984 Entry Draft).

			Regular Season					Playoffs				
Season	Club	Lea	GP	G	A	TP	PIM	GP	G	A	TP	PIM
1983-84	United States	Nat-Tm	62	21	47	68	36	....	....	....	....	....
	United States	Olympics	6	2	5	7	0	....	....	....	....	....
1984-85	**Chicago**	**NHL**	**70**	**20**	**30**	**50**	**67**	**15**	**6**	**5**	**11**	**11**
1985-86	**Chicago**	**NHL**	**79**	**29**	**50**	**79**	**47**	**3**	**0**	**0**	**0**	**0**
1986-87	**Chicago**	**NHL**	**79**	**16**	**35**	**51**	**119**	**4**	**1**	**1**	**2**	**4**
1987-88	**Toronto**	**NHL**	**80**	**42**	**33**	**75**	**55**	**6**	**5**	**4**	**9**	**2**
1988-89	**Toronto**	**NHL**	**80**	**38**	**52**	**90**	**75**	....	....	....	....	....
1989-90	**Toronto**	**NHL**	**79**	**32**	**56**	**88**	**78**	**5**	**1**	**2**	**3**	**14**
1990-91	**Toronto**	**NHL**	**18**	**4**	**10**	**14**	**13**	....	....	....	....	....
	Winnipeg	**NHL**	**61**	**26**	**31**	**57**	**69**	....	....	....	....	....
1991-92	**Winnipeg**	**NHL**	**64**	**32**	**33**	**65**	**67**	**6**	**2**	**1**	**3**	**4**
1992-93	**Winnipeg**	**NHL**	**25**	**8**	**12**	**20**	**26**	....	....	....	....	....
	NY Rangers	**NHL**	**46**	**13**	**16**	**29**	**26**	....	....	....	....	....
1993-94	**NY Rangers**	**NHL**	**37**	**3**	**5**	**8**	**28**	**1**	**0**	**0**	**0**	**0** ♦
1994-95	**NY Rangers**	**NHL**	**20**	**2**	**1**	**3**	**4**	....	....	....	....	....
	Winnipeg	**NHL**	**13**	**2**	**8**	**10**	**8**	....	....	....	....	....
1995-96	**Winnipeg**	**NHL**	**51**	**27**	**22**	**49**	**65**	**6**	**1**	**2**	**3**	**6**
1996-97	**Los Angeles**	**NHL**	**67**	**21**	**23**	**44**	**45**	....	....	....	....	....
	Pittsburgh	**NHL**	**12**	**4**	**7**	**11**	**6**	**5**	**1**	**0**	**1**	**12**
1997-98	**Pittsburgh**	**NHL**	**56**	**11**	**11**	**22**	**35**	**6**	**2**	**0**	**2**	**4**
	NHL Totals		**937**	**330**	**435**	**765**	**833**	**57**	**19**	**15**	**34**	**57**

Traded to **Toronto** by **Chicago** with Al Secord for Rick Vaive, Steve Thomas and Bob McGill, September 3, 1987. Traded to **Winnipeg** by **Toronto** with Mark Osborne for Dave Ellett and Paul Fenton, November 10, 1990. Traded to **NY Rangers** by **Winnipeg** for Kris King and Tie Domi, December 28, 1992. Traded to **Winnipeg** by **NY Rangers** for Winnipeg's 5th round choice (Alexei Vasiliev) in 1995 Entry Draft, April 7, 1995. Signed as a free agent by **LA Kings**, July 8, 1996. Traded to **Pittsburgh** by **LA Kings** for Glen Murray, March 18, 1997. Signed as a free agent by **Chicago**, August 26, 1998.

O'LEARY, PAT PHX.

Center. Shoots left. 6'2", 190 lbs. Born, Minneapolis, MN, September 2, 1979.
(Phoenix's 3rd choice, 73rd overall, in 1998 Entry Draft).

			Regular Season					Playoffs				
Season	Club	Lea	GP	G	A	TP	PIM	GP	G	A	TP	PIM
1996-97	Robbinsdale	H.S.	22	28	27	55	42	....	....	....	....	....
1997-98	Robbinsdale	H.S.	24	22	27	49	28	....	....	....	....	....

OLIVER, DAVID OTT.

Right wing. Shoots right. 6', 190 lbs. Born, Sechelt, B.C., April 17, 1971.
(Edmonton's 7th choice, 144th overall, in 1991 Entry Draft).

			Regular Season					Playoffs				
Season	Club	Lea	GP	G	A	TP	PIM	GP	G	A	TP	PIM
1990-91	U. of Michigan	CCHA	27	13	11	24	34	....	....	....	....	....
1991-92	U. of Michigan	CCHA	44	31	27	58	32	....	....	....	....	....
1992-93	U. of Michigan	CCHA	40	35	20	55	18	....	....	....	....	....
1993-94	U. of Michigan	CCHA	41	28	40	68	16	....	....	....	....	....
1994-95	Cape Breton	AHL	32	11	18	29	8	....	....	....	....	....
	Edmonton	**NHL**	**44**	**16**	**14**	**30**	**20**	....	....	....	....	....
1995-96	**Edmonton**	**NHL**	**80**	**20**	**19**	**39**	**34**	....	....	....	....	....
1996-97	**Edmonton**	**NHL**	**17**	**1**	**2**	**3**	**4**	....	....	....	....	....
	NY Rangers	**NHL**	**14**	**2**	**1**	**3**	**4**	**3**	**0**	**0**	**0**	**0**
1997-98	Houston	IHL	78	38	27	65	60	4	3	0	3	4
	NHL Totals		**155**	**39**	**36**	**75**	**62**	**3**	**0**	**0**	**0**	**0**

CCHA Second All-Star Team (1993) • CCHA First All-Star Team (1994) • NCAA West First All-American Team (1994)

Claimed on waivers by **NY Rangers** from **Edmonton**, February 21, 1997. Signed as a free agent by **Ottawa**, July 2, 1998.

OLIWA, KRZYSZTOF (oh-LEE-vuh, KHRIH-stahf) N.J.

Left wing. Shoots left. 6'5", 235 lbs. Born, Tychy, Poland, April 12, 1973.
(New Jersey's 4th choice, 65th overall, in 1993 Entry Draft).

			Regular Season					Playoffs				
Season	Club	Lea	GP	G	A	TP	PIM	GP	G	A	TP	PIM
1991-92	Tychy	Poland	10	3	7	10	6	....	....	....	....	....
1992-93	Welland	OJHL	30	13	21	34	127	....	....	....	....	....
1993-94	Albany	AHL	33	2	4	6	151	....	....	....	....	....
	Raleigh	ECHL	15	0	2	2	65	9	0	0	0	35
1994-95	Albany	AHL	20	1	1	2	77	....	....	....	....	....
	Saint John	AHL	14	1	4	5	79	....	....	....	....	....
	Raleigh	ECHL	5	0	2	2	32	....	....	....	....	....
	Detroit	IHL	4	0	1	1	24	....	....	....	....	....
1995-96	Albany	AHL	51	5	11	16	217	....	....	....	....	....
	Raleigh	ECHL	9	1	0	1	53	....	....	....	....	....
1996-97	**New Jersey**	**NHL**	**1**	**0**	**0**	**0**	**5**	....	....	....	....	....
	Albany	AHL	60	13	14	27	322	15	7	1	8	49
1997-98	**New Jersey**	**NHL**	**73**	**2**	**3**	**5**	**295**	**6**	**0**	**0**	**0**	**23**
	NHL Totals		**74**	**2**	**3**	**5**	**300**	**6**	**0**	**0**	**0**	**23**

OLSON, BOYD MTL.

Center. Shoots left. 6'1", 187 lbs. Born, Edmonton, Alta., April 4, 1976.
(Montreal's 6th choice, 138th overall, in 1995 Entry Draft).

			Regular Season					Playoffs				
Season	Club	Lea	GP	G	A	TP	PIM	GP	G	A	TP	PIM
1993-94	Tri-City	WHL	2	0	1	1	0	....	....	....	....	....
1994-95	Tri-City	WHL	69	16	16	32	87	17	6	2	8	22
1995-96	Tri-City	WHL	62	13	12	25	105	11	1	4	5	16
	Fredericton	AHL	....	....	....	....	....	2	1	0	1	0
1996-97	Fredericton	AHL	74	8	12	20	43	....	....	....	....	....
1997-98	Fredericton	AHL	57	4	9	13	43	....	....	....	....	....

OLSSON, CHRISTER (OOL-suhn) OTT.

Defense. Shoots left. 5'11", 190 lbs. Born, Arboga, Sweden, July 24, 1970.
(St. Louis' 10th choice, 275th overall, in 1993 Entry Draft).

			Regular Season					Playoffs				
Season	Club	Lea	GP	G	A	TP	PIM	GP	G	A	TP	PIM
1991-92	Mora	Sweden-2	36	6	10	16	38	....	....	....	....	....
1992-93	Brynas IF	Sweden	22	4	4	8	18	....	....	....	....	....
1993-94	Brynas IF	Sweden	38	7	3	10	50	7	0	3	3	6
1994-95	Brynas IF	Sweden	39	6	5	11	18	14	1	3	4	8
1995-96	**St. Louis**	**NHL**	**26**	**2**	**8**	**10**	**14**	**3**	**0**	**0**	**0**	**0**
	Worcester	AHL	39	7	7	14	22	....	....	....	....	....
1996-97	**St. Louis**	**NHL**	**5**	**0**	**1**	**1**	**0**	....	....	....	....	....
	Worcester	AHL	2	0	0	0	0	....	....	....	....	....
	Ottawa	**NHL**	**25**	**2**	**3**	**5**	**10**	....	....	....	....	....
1997-98	V. Frolunda	Sweden	45	13	8	21	54	7	0	1	1	18
	NHL Totals		**56**	**4**	**12**	**16**	**24**	**3**	**0**	**0**	**0**	**0**

Traded to **Ottawa** by **St. Louis** for Pavol Demitra, November 27, 1996.

O'NEILL, JEFF CAR.

Center. Shoots right. 6'1", 190 lbs. Born, Richmond Hill, Ont., February 23, 1976.
(Hartford's 1st choice, 5th overall, in 1994 Entry Draft).

			Regular Season					Playoffs				
Season	Club	Lea	GP	G	A	TP	PIM	GP	G	A	TP	PIM
1992-93	Guelph	OHL	65	32	47	79	88	5	2	2	4	6
1993-94	Guelph	OHL	66	45	81	126	95	9	2	11	13	31
1994-95	Guelph	OHL	57	43	81	124	56	14	8	18	26	34
1995-96	**Hartford**	**NHL**	**65**	**8**	**19**	**27**	**40**	....	....	....	....	....
1996-97	**Hartford**	**NHL**	**72**	**14**	**16**	**30**	**40**	....	....	....	....	....
	Springfield	AHL	1	0	0	0	0	....	....	....	....	....
1997-98	**Carolina**	**NHL**	**74**	**19**	**20**	**39**	**67**	....	....	....	....	....
	NHL Totals		**211**	**41**	**55**	**96**	**147**	....	....	....	....	....

OHL First All-Star Team (1995)
Transferred to **Carolina** after **Hartford** franchise relocated, June 25, 1997.

OREKHOVSKY, OLEG (oh-reh-KHOHV-skee) WSH.

Defense. Shoots right. 6', 183 lbs. Born, Krasnoyarsk, USSR, November 3, 1977.
(Washington's 11th choice, 206th overall, in 1996 Entry Draft).

			Regular Season					Playoffs				
Season	Club	Lea	GP	G	A	TP	PIM	GP	G	A	TP	PIM
1994-95	Moscow D'amo	CIS	30	0	1	1	18	....	....	....	....	....
1995-96	Moscow D'amo	CIS	22	1	2	3	14	8	0	0	0	6
1996-97	Moscow D'amo	Russia	32	4	2	6	16	4	2	1	3	2
1997-98	Moscow D'amo	EuroHL	7	2	1	3	12	....	....	....	....	....
	Moscow D'amo	Russia	40	4	5	9	34	....	....	....	....	....

ORSZAGH, VLADIMIR (OHR-sahk) NYI

Right wing. Shoots left. 5'11", 173 lbs. Born, Banska Bystrica, Czech., May 24, 1977.
(NY Islanders' 4th choice, 106th overall, in 1995 Entry Draft).

			Regular Season					Playoffs				
Season	Club	Lea	GP	G	A	TP	PIM	GP	G	A	TP	PIM
1994-95	Banska Bystrica	Slovak-2	38	18	12	30	....	....	....	....	....	....
1995-96	Banska Bystrica	Slovakia	31	9	5	14	22	....	....	....	....	....
1996-97	Utah	IHL	68	12	15	27	30	3	0	1	1	4
1997-98	**NY Islanders**	**NHL**	**11**	**0**	**1**	**1**	**2**	....	....	....	....	....
	Utah	IHL	62	13	10	23	60	4	2	0	2	0
	NHL Totals		**11**	**0**	**1**	**1**	**2**	....	....	....	....	....

O'SULLIVAN, CHRIS CGY.

Defense. Shoots left. 6'2", 205 lbs. Born, Dorchester, MA, May 15, 1974.
(Calgary's 2nd choice, 30th overall, in 1992 Entry Draft).

			Regular Season					Playoffs				
Season	Club	Lea	GP	G	A	TP	PIM	GP	G	A	TP	PIM
1991-92	Catholic Memorial	H.S.	26	26	23	49	65	....	....	....	....	....
1992-93	Boston University	H.E.	5	0	2	2	4	....	....	....	....	....
1993-94	Boston University	H.E.	32	5	18	23	25	....	....	....	....	....
1994-95	Boston University	H.E.	40	23	33	56	48	....	....	....	....	....
1995-96	Boston University	H.E.	37	12	35	47	50	....	....	....	....	....
1996-97	**Calgary**	**NHL**	**27**	**2**	**8**	**10**	**2**	....	....	....	....	....
	Saint John	AHL	29	3	8	11	17	5	0	4	4	0
1997-98	**Calgary**	**NHL**	**12**	**0**	**2**	**2**	**10**	....	....	....	....	....
	Saint John	AHL	32	4	10	14	2	21	2	17	19	18
	NHL Totals		**39**	**2**	**10**	**12**	**12**	....	....	....	....	....

Hockey East First All-Star Team (1995) • NCAA East Second All-American Team (1995) • NCAA Championship All-Tournament Team (1995) • NCAA Championship Tournament MVP (1995)

OTTO, JOEL (AW-toh)

Center. Shoots right. 6'4", 220 lbs. Born, Elk River, MN, October 29, 1961.

			Regular Season					Playoffs				
Season	Club	Lea	GP	G	A	TP	PIM	GP	G	A	TP	PIM
1980-81	Bemidji State	NCAA	23	5	11	16	10	....	....	....	....	....
1981-82	Bemidji State	NCAA	31	19	33	52	24	....	....	....	....	....
1982-83	Bemidji State	NCAA	37	33	28	61	68	....	....	....	....	....
1983-84	Bemidji State	NCAA	31	32	43	75	32	....	....	....	....	....
1984-85	**Calgary**	**NHL**	**17**	**4**	**8**	**12**	**30**	**3**	**2**	**1**	**3**	**10**
	Moncton	AHL	56	27	36	63	89	....	....	....	....	....
1985-86	**Calgary**	**NHL**	**79**	**25**	**34**	**59**	**188**	**22**	**5**	**10**	**15**	**80**
1986-87	**Calgary**	**NHL**	**68**	**19**	**31**	**50**	**185**	**2**	**0**	**2**	**2**	**6**
1987-88	**Calgary**	**NHL**	**62**	**13**	**39**	**52**	**194**	**9**	**3**	**2**	**5**	**26**
1988-89	**Calgary**	**NHL**	**72**	**23**	**30**	**53**	**213**	**22**	**6**	**13**	**19**	**46 ♦**
1989-90	**Calgary**	**NHL**	**75**	**13**	**20**	**33**	**116**	**6**	**2**	**2**	**4**	**2**
1990-91	**Calgary**	**NHL**	**76**	**19**	**20**	**39**	**183**	**7**	**1**	**2**	**3**	**8**
1991-92	**Calgary**	**NHL**	**78**	**13**	**21**	**34**	**161**	....	....	....	....	....
1992-93	**Calgary**	**NHL**	**75**	**19**	**33**	**52**	**150**	**6**	**4**	**2**	**6**	**4**
1993-94	**Calgary**	**NHL**	**81**	**11**	**12**	**23**	**92**	**3**	**0**	**1**	**1**	**4**
1994-95	**Calgary**	**NHL**	**47**	**8**	**13**	**21**	**130**	**7**	**0**	**3**	**3**	**2**
1995-96	**Philadelphia**	**NHL**	**67**	**12**	**29**	**41**	**115**	**12**	**3**	**4**	**7**	**11**
1996-97	**Philadelphia**	**NHL**	**78**	**13**	**19**	**32**	**99**	**18**	**1**	**5**	**6**	**8**
1997-98	**Philadelphia**	**NHL**	**68**	**3**	**4**	**7**	**78**	**5**	**0**	**0**	**0**	**0**
	United States	Olympics	4	0	0	0	0	....	....	....	....	....
	NHL Totals		**943**	**195**	**313**	**508**	**1934**	**122**	**27**	**47**	**74**	**207**

NCAA (College Div.) West All-American Team (1983, 1984)
Signed as a free agent by **Calgary,** September 11, 1984. Signed as a free agent by **Philadelphia**, July 31, 1995.

OVINGTON, CHRIS FLA.

Defense. Shoots right. 6'3", 173 lbs. Born, Vernon, B.C., August 15, 1980.
(Florida's 6th choice, 148th overall, in 1998 Entry Draft).

			Regular Season					Playoffs				
Season	Club	Lea	GP	G	A	TP	PIM	GP	G	A	TP	PIM
1996-97	Red Deer	WHL	33	0	3	3	17	7	0	1	1	2
1997-98	Red Deer	WHL	68	2	13	15	72	5	0	0	0	2

OZOLINSH, SANDIS (OH-zoh-LIHNCH, SAN-dihz) COL.

Defense. Shoots left. 6'3", 205 lbs. Born, Riga, Latvia, August 3, 1972.
(San Jose's 3rd choice, 30th overall, in 1991 Entry Draft).

			Regular Season					Playoffs				
Season	Club	Lea	GP	G	A	TP	PIM	GP	G	A	TP	PIM
1990-91	Dynamo Riga	USSR	44	0	3	3	51	....	....	....	....	....
1991-92	Dynamo Riga	CIS	30	6	0	6	42	....	....	....	....	....
	Kansas City	IHL	34	6	9	15	20	15	2	5	7	22
1992-93	**San Jose**	**NHL**	**37**	**7**	**16**	**23**	**40**	....	....	....	....	....
1993-94	**San Jose**	**NHL**	**81**	**26**	**38**	**64**	**24**	**14**	**0**	**10**	**10**	**8**
1994-95	**San Jose**	**NHL**	**48**	**9**	**16**	**25**	**30**	**11**	**3**	**2**	**5**	**6**
1995-96	San Francisco	IHL	2	1	0	1	0	....	....	....	....	....
	San Jose	**NHL**	**7**	**1**	**3**	**4**	**4**	....	....	....	....	....
	Colorado	**NHL**	**66**	**13**	**37**	**50**	**50**	**22**	**5**	**14**	**19**	**16 ♦**
1996-97	**Colorado**	**NHL**	**80**	**23**	**45**	**68**	**88**	**17**	**4**	**13**	**17**	**24**
1997-98	**Colorado**	**NHL**	**66**	**13**	**38**	**51**	**65**	**7**	**0**	**7**	**7**	**14**
	NHL Totals		**385**	**92**	**193**	**285**	**301**	**71**	**12**	**46**	**58**	**68**

NHL First All-Star Team (1997)
Played in NHL All-Star Game (1994, 1997, 1998)
Traded to **Colorado** by **San Jose** for Owen Nolan, October 26, 1995.

PAEK, JIM (PAK)

Defense. Shoots left. 6'1", 195 lbs. Born, Seoul, South Korea, April 7, 1967.
(Pittsburgh's 9th choice, 170th overall, in 1985 Entry Draft).

			Regular Season					Playoffs				
Season	Club	Lea	GP	G	A	TP	PIM	GP	G	A	TP	PIM
1984-85	Oshawa	OHL	54	2	13	15	57	5	1	0	1	9
1985-86	Oshawa	OHL	64	5	21	26	122	6	0	1	1	9
1986-87	Oshawa	OHL	57	5	17	22	75	26	1	14	15	43
1987-88	Muskegon	IHL	82	7	52	59	141	6	0	0	0	29
1988-89	Muskegon	IHL	80	3	54	57	96	14	1	10	11	24
1989-90	Muskegon	IHL	81	9	41	50	115	15	1	10	11	41
1990-91	Canada	Nat-Tm	48	2	12	14	24	....	....	....	....	....
	Pittsburgh	**NHL**	**3**	**0**	**0**	**0**	**9**	**8**	**1**	**0**	**1**	**2 ♦**
1991-92	**Pittsburgh**	**NHL**	**49**	**1**	**7**	**8**	**36**	**19**	**0**	**4**	**4**	**6 ♦**
1992-93	**Pittsburgh**	**NHL**	**77**	**3**	**15**	**18**	**64**	....	....	....	....	....
1993-94	**Pittsburgh**	**NHL**	**41**	**0**	**4**	**4**	**8**	....	....	....	....	....
	Los Angeles	**NHL**	**18**	**1**	**1**	**2**	**10**	....	....	....	....	....
1994-95	**Ottawa**	**NHL**	**29**	**0**	**2**	**2**	**28**	....	....	....	....	....
1995-96	Houston	IHL	25	2	5	7	20	....	....	....	....	....
	Minnesota	IHL	42	1	11	12	54	....	....	....	....	....
1996-97	Manitoba	IHL	9	0	2	2	12	....	....	....	....	....
	Cleveland	IHL	74	3	25	28	36	14	0	1	1	2
1997-98	Cleveland	IHL	75	7	9	16	48	10	2	1	3	4
	NHL Totals		**217**	**5**	**29**	**34**	**155**	**27**	**1**	**4**	**5**	**8**

Traded to **LA Kings** by **Pittsburgh** with Marty McSorley for Tomas Sandstrom and Shawn McEachern, February 16, 1994. Traded to **Ottawa** by **LA Kings** for Ottawa's 7th round choice (Benoit Larose) in 1995 Entry Draft, June 26, 1994.

PAHLSSON, SAMUAL (PAWL-suhn) COL.

Center. Shoots left. 5'11", 190 lbs. Born, Ornskoldsvik, Sweden, December 17, 1977.
(Colorado's 10th choice, 176th overall, in 1996 Entry Draft).

			Regular Season					Playoffs				
Season	Club	Lea	GP	G	A	TP	PIM	GP	G	A	TP	PIM
1994-95	MoDo	Sweden	1	0	0	0	0	....	....	....	....	....
	MoDo	Swe-Jr.	30	10	11	21	26	....	....	....	....	....
1995-96	MoDo	Sweden	36	1	3	4	8	4	0	0	0	0
	MoDo	Swe-Jr.	5	2	6	8	2	....	....	....	....	....
1996-97	MoDo	Sweden	49	8	9	17	83	....	....	....	....	....
1997-98	MoDo	Sweden	23	6	11	17	24	9	3	0	3	6

PALFFY, ZIGMUND (PAHL-fee) NYI

Right wing. Shoots left. 5'10", 183 lbs. Born, Skalica, Czech., May 5, 1972.
(NY Islanders' 2nd choice, 26th overall, in 1991 Entry Draft).

			Regular Season					Playoffs				
Season	Club	Lea	GP	G	A	TP	PIM	GP	G	A	TP	PIM
1990-91	AC Nitra	Czech.	50	34	16	50	18	....	....	....	....	....
1991-92	Dukla Trencin	Czech.	45	41	33	74	36	....	....	....	....	....
1992-93	Dukla Trencin	Czech.	43	38	41	79	....	....	....	....	....	....
1993-94	**NY Islanders**	**NHL**	**5**	**0**	**0**	**0**	**0**	....	....	....	....	....
	Salt Lake	IHL	57	25	32	57	83	....	....	....	....	....
	Slovakia	Olympics	8	3	7	10	8	....	....	....	....	....
1994-95	Denver	IHL	33	20	23	43	40	....	....	....	....	....
	NY Islanders	**NHL**	**33**	**10**	**7**	**17**	**6**	....	....	....	....	....
1995-96	**NY Islanders**	**NHL**	**81**	**43**	**44**	**87**	**56**	....	....	....	....	....
1996-97	Dukla Trencin	Slovakia	1	0	0	0	....	....	....	....	....	....
	NY Islanders	**NHL**	**80**	**48**	**42**	**90**	**43**	....	....	....	....	....
1997-98	**NY Islanders**	**NHL**	**82**	**45**	**42**	**87**	**34**	....	....	....	....	....
	NHL Totals		**281**	**146**	**135**	**281**	**139**	....	....	....	....	....

Czechoslovakian Rookie of the Year (1991) • Czechoslovakian First All-Star Team (1992)
Played in NHL All-Star Game (1998)

PANDOLFO, JAY (pan-DAHL-foh) N.J.

Left wing. Shoots left. 6'1", 200 lbs. Born, Winchester, MA, December 27, 1974.
(New Jersey's 2nd choice, 32nd overall, in 1993 Entry Draft).

			Regular Season					Playoffs				
Season	Club	Lea	GP	G	A	TP	PIM	GP	G	A	TP	PIM
1991-92	Burlington Prep	H.S.	20	35	34	69	20	....	....	....	....	....
1992-93	Boston University	H.E.	37	16	22	38	16	....	....	....	....	....
1993-94	Boston University	H.E.	37	17	25	42	27	....	....	....	....	....
1994-95	Boston University	H.E.	20	7	13	20	6	....	....	....	....	....
1995-96	Boston University	H.E.	39	*38	29	67	6	....	....	....	....	....
	Albany	AHL	5	3	1	4	0	3	0	0	0	0
1996-97	**New Jersey**	**NHL**	**46**	**6**	**8**	**14**	**6**	**6**	**0**	**1**	**1**	**0**
	Albany	AHL	12	3	9	12	0	....	....	....	....	....
1997-98	**New Jersey**	**NHL**	**23**	**1**	**3**	**4**	**4**	**3**	**0**	**2**	**2**	**0**
	Albany	AHL	51	18	19	37	24	....	....	....	....	....
	NHL Totals		**69**	**7**	**11**	**18**	**10**	**9**	**0**	**3**	**3**	**0**

Hockey East First All-Star Team (1996) • NCAA East First All-American Team (1996)

PANDOLFO, MIKE (pan-DAHL-foh) BUF.

Left wing. Shoots left. 6'3", 226 lbs. Born, Winchester, MA, September 15, 1979.
(Buffalo's 5th choice, 77th overall, in 1998 Entry Draft).

			Regular Season					Playoffs				
Season	Club	Lea	GP	G	A	TP	PIM	GP	G	A	TP	PIM
1996-97	St. Sebastians	H.S.	32	27	28	55	30	....	....	....	....	....
1997-98	St. Sebastians	H.S.	28	29	23	52	18	....	....	....	....	....

PAPINEAU, JUSTIN L.A.

Center. Shoots left. 5'10", 160 lbs. Born, Ottawa, Ont., January 15, 1980.
(Los Angeles' 2nd choice, 46th overall, in 1998 Entry Draft).

			Regular Season					Playoffs				
Season	Club	Lea	GP	G	A	TP	PIM	GP	G	A	TP	PIM
1996-97	Belleville	OHL	50	10	32	42	32	....	....	....	....	....
1997-98	Belleville	OHL	66	41	53	94	34	10	5	9	14	6

PARK, RICHARD PHI.

Center. Shoots right. 5'11", 190 lbs. Born, Seoul, S. Korea, May 27, 1976.
(Pittsburgh's 2nd choice, 50th overall, in 1994 Entry Draft).

			Regular Season					Playoffs				
Season	Club	Lea	GP	G	A	TP	PIM	GP	G	A	TP	PIM
1992-93	Belleville	OHL	66	23	38	61	38	5	0	0	0	14
1993-94	Belleville	OHL	59	27	49	76	70	12	3	5	8	18
1994-95	Belleville	OHL	45	28	51	79	35	16	9	18	27	12
	Pittsburgh	**NHL**	**1**	**0**	**1**	**1**	**2**	**3**	**0**	**0**	**0**	**2**
1995-96	Belleville	OHL	6	7	6	13	2	14	18	12	30	10
	Pittsburgh	**NHL**	**56**	**4**	**6**	**10**	**36**	**1**	**0**	**0**	**0**	**0**
1996-97	**Pittsburgh**	**NHL**	**1**	**0**	**0**	**0**	**0**	....	....	....	....	....
	Cleveland	IHL	50	12	15	27	30	....	....	....	....	....
	Anaheim	**NHL**	**11**	**1**	**1**	**2**	**10**	**11**	**0**	**1**	**1**	**2**
1997-98	**Anaheim**	**NHL**	**15**	**0**	**2**	**2**	**8**	....	....	....	....	....
	Cincinnati	AHL	56	17	26	43	36	....	....	....	....	....
	NHL Totals		**84**	**5**	**10**	**15**	**56**	**15**	**0**	**1**	**1**	**4**

Traded to **Anaheim** by **Pittsburgh** for Roman Oksiuta, March 18, 1997. Signed as a free agent by **Philadelphia**, August 24, 1998.

PARKER, SCOTT COL.

Right wing. Shoots right. 6'4", 220 lbs. Born, Hanford, CA, January 29, 1978.
(Colorado's 4th choice, 20th overall, in 1998 Entry Draft).

			Regular Season					Playoffs				
Season	Club	Lea	GP	G	A	TP	PIM	GP	G	A	TP	PIM
1995-96	Kelowna	WHL	64	3	4	7	159	6	0	0	0	12
1996-97	Kelowna	WHL	68	18	8	26	*330	6	0	2	2	4
1997-98	Kelowna	WHL	71	30	22	52	243	7	6	0	6	23

• Re-entered NHL draft. Originally New Jersey's 6th choice, 63rd overall, in 1996 Entry Draft.

PARRISH, MARK FLA.

Left wing. Shoots right. 6', 185 lbs. Born, Edina, MN, February 2, 1977.
(Colorado's 3rd choice, 79th overall, in 1996 Entry Draft).

			Regular Season					Playoffs				
Season	Club	Lea	GP	G	A	TP	PIM	GP	G	A	TP	PIM
1995-96	St. Cloud State	WCHA	39	15	13	28	30	....	....	....	....	....
1996-97	St. Cloud State	WCHA	35	*27	15	42	60	....	....	....	....	....
1997-98	Seattle	WHL	54	54	38	92	29	5	2	3	5	2

NCAA West Second All-American Team (1997) • WHL West First All-Star Team (1998)

PARTHENAIS, PAT (PAR-thehn-ay) FLA.

Defense. Shoots left. 6'4", 212 lbs. Born, Rochester, NY, July 17, 1979.
(Florida's 6th choice, 127th overall, in 1997 Entry Draft).

			Regular Season					Playoffs				
Season	Club	Lea	GP	G	A	TP	PIM	GP	G	A	TP	PIM
1996-97	Detroit	OHL	58	0	4	4	88	5	0	0	0	5
1997-98	Plymouth	OHL	63	2	7	9	155	1	0	0	0	0

PATERA, PAVEL (puh-TEHR-uh) DAL.

Center. Shoots left. 6'1", 176 lbs. Born, Kladno, Czechoslovakia, September 6, 1971.
(Dallas' 4th choice, 153rd overall, in 1998 Entry Draft).

			Regular Season					Playoffs				
Season	Club	Lea	GP	G	A	TP	PIM	GP	G	A	TP	PIM
1990-91	Poldi Kladno	Czech.	3	0	0	0	....	....	....	....	....	....
1991-92	Poldi Kladno	Czech.	38	12	13	25	26	8	8	4	12	0
1992-93	Poldi Kladno	Czech.	42	9	23	32	....	....	....	....	....	....
1993-94	HC Kladno	Cze-Rep.	43	21	39	60	....	11	5	10	15	....
1994-95	HC Kladno	Cze-Rep.	43	26	49	75	24	11	5	7	12	6
1995-96	Poldi Kladno	Cze-Rep.	40	24	31	55	38	8	3	1	4	34
1996-97	AIK Solna	Sweden	50	19	24	43	44	7	2	3	5	6
1997-98	AIK Solna	Sweden	46	8	17	25	50	....	....	....	....	....

PATRICK, JAMES

Defense. Shoots right. 6'2", 198 lbs. Born, Winnipeg, Man., June 14, 1963.
(NY Rangers' 1st choice, 9th overall, in 1981 Entry Draft).

			Regular Season					Playoffs				
Season	Club	Lea	GP	G	A	TP	PIM	GP	G	A	TP	PIM
1980-81	Prince Albert	SJHL	59	21	61	82	162	....	....	....	....	....
1981-82	North Dakota	WCHA	42	5	24	29	26	....	....	....	....	....
1982-83	North Dakota	WCHA	36	12	36	48	29	....	....	....	....	....
1983-84	Canada	Nat-Tm	63	7	24	31	52	....	....	....	....	....
	Canada	Olympics	7	0	3	3	4	....	....	....	....	....
	NY Rangers	**NHL**	**12**	**1**	**7**	**8**	**2**	**5**	**0**	**3**	**3**	**2**
1984-85	**NY Rangers**	**NHL**	**75**	**8**	**28**	**36**	**71**	**3**	**0**	**0**	**0**	**4**
1985-86	**NY Rangers**	**NHL**	**75**	**14**	**29**	**43**	**88**	**16**	**1**	**5**	**6**	**34**
1986-87	**NY Rangers**	**NHL**	**78**	**10**	**45**	**55**	**62**	**6**	**1**	**2**	**3**	**2**
1987-88	**NY Rangers**	**NHL**	**70**	**17**	**45**	**62**	**52**	....	....	....	....	....
1988-89	**NY Rangers**	**NHL**	**68**	**11**	**36**	**47**	**41**	**4**	**0**	**1**	**1**	**2**
1989-90	**NY Rangers**	**NHL**	**73**	**14**	**43**	**57**	**50**	**10**	**3**	**8**	**11**	**0**
1990-91	**NY Rangers**	**NHL**	**74**	**10**	**49**	**59**	**58**	**6**	**0**	**0**	**0**	**6**
1991-92	**NY Rangers**	**NHL**	**80**	**14**	**57**	**71**	**54**	**13**	**0**	**7**	**7**	**12**
1992-93	**NY Rangers**	**NHL**	**60**	**5**	**21**	**26**	**61**	....	....	....	....	....
1993-94	**NY Rangers**	**NHL**	**6**	**0**	**3**	**3**	**2**	....	....	....	....	....
	Hartford	**NHL**	**47**	**8**	**20**	**28**	**32**	....	....	....	....	....
	Calgary	**NHL**	**15**	**2**	**2**	**4**	**6**	**7**	**0**	**1**	**1**	**6**
1994-95	**Calgary**	**NHL**	**43**	**0**	**10**	**10**	**14**	**5**	**0**	**1**	**1**	**0**
1995-96	**Calgary**	**NHL**	**80**	**3**	**32**	**35**	**30**	**4**	**0**	**0**	**0**	**2**
1996-97	**Calgary**	**NHL**	**19**	**3**	**1**	**4**	**6**	....	....	....	....	....
1997-98	**Calgary**	**NHL**	**60**	**6**	**11**	**17**	**26**	....	....	....	....	....
	NHL Totals		**935**	**126**	**439**	**565**	**655**	**79**	**5**	**28**	**33**	**70**

WCHA Second All-Star Team (1982) • NCAA Chamionship All-Tournament Team (1982) • WCHA First All-Star Team (1983) • NCAA West All American Team (1983)

Traded to **Hartford** by **NY Rangers** with Darren Turcotte for Steve Larmer, Nick Kypreos, Barry Richter and Hartford's 6th round choice (Yuri Litvinov) in 1994 Entry Draft, November 2, 1993. Traded to **Calgary** by **Hartford** with Zarley Zalapski and Michael Nylander for Gary Suter, Paul Ranheim and Ted Drury, March 10, 1994.

PATTERSON, ED

Right wing. Shoots right. 6'2", 213 lbs. Born, Delta, B.C., November 14, 1972.
(Pittsburgh's 7th choice, 148th overall, in 1991 Entry Draft).

			Regular Season					Playoffs				
Season	Club	Lea	GP	G	A	TP	PIM	GP	G	A	TP	PIM
1988-89	Seattle	WHL	46	4	6	10	55	....	....	....	....	....
1989-90	Seattle	WHL	18	9	2	11	19	....	....	....	....	....
	Swift Current	WHL	15	1	3	4	0	4	0	0	0	2
1990-91	Swift Current	WHL	7	2	7	9	0	....	....	....	....	....
	Kamloops	WHL	55	14	33	47	134	5	0	0	0	7
1991-92	Kamloops	WHL	38	19	25	44	120	1	0	0	0	0
1992-93	Cleveland	IHL	63	4	16	20	131	3	1	1	2	2
1993-94	**Pittsburgh**	**NHL**	**27**	**3**	**1**	**4**	**10**	....	....	....	....	....
	Cleveland	IHL	55	21	32	53	73	....	....	....	....	....
1994-95	Cleveland	IHL	58	13	17	30	93	4	1	2	3	6
1995-96	**Pittsburgh**	**NHL**	**35**	**0**	**2**	**2**	**38**	....	....	....	....	....
1996-97	**Pittsburgh**	**NHL**	**6**	**0**	**0**	**0**	**8**	....	....	....	....	....
	Cleveland	IHL	40	6	12	18	75	13	2	4	6	61
1997-98	Grand Rapids	IHL	81	12	31	43	226	3	2	1	3	8
	NHL Totals		**68**	**3**	**3**	**6**	**56**	....	....	....	....	....

PAUL, DUSTIN CGY.

Right wing. Shoots right. 5'11", 195 lbs. Born, Calgary, Alta., April 22, 1979.
(Calgary's 12th choice, 223rd overall, in 1997 Entry Draft).

			Regular Season					Playoffs				
Season	Club	Lea	GP	G	A	TP	PIM	GP	G	A	TP	PIM
1996-97	Moose Jaw	WHL	70	19	13	32	33	12	7	2	9	2
1997-98	Moose Jaw	WHL	71	36	31	67	46	4	1	2	3	8

PAUL, JEFF CHI.

Defense. Shoots right. 6'3", 196 lbs. Born, London, Ont., March 1, 1978.
(Chicago's 2nd choice, 42nd overall, in 1996 Entry Draft).

			Regular Season					Playoffs				
Season	Club	Lea	GP	G	A	TP	PIM	GP	G	A	TP	PIM
1994-95	Niagara Falls	OHL	57	3	10	13	64	6	0	2	2	0
1995-96	Niagara Falls	OHL	48	1	7	8	81	10	0	4	4	37
1996-97	Erie	OHL	60	4	23	27	152	5	2	0	2	12
1997-98	Erie	OHL	48	3	17	20	108	7	0	2	2	13

PAYER, SERGE FLA.

Center. Shoots left. 6', 185 lbs. Born, Rockland, Ont., May 7, 1979.

			Regular Season					Playoffs				
Season	Club	Lea	GP	G	A	TP	PIM	GP	G	A	TP	PIM
1995-96	Kitchener	OHL	66	8	16	24	18	12	0	2	2	2
1996-97	Kitchener	OHL	63	7	16	23	27	13	1	3	4	2
1997-98	Kitchener	OHL	44	20	21	41	51	6	3	0	3	7

Signed as a free agent by **Florida**, September 30, 1997.

PAYETTE, ANDRE PHI.

Center. Shoots left. 6'2", 205 lbs. Born, Cornwall, Ont., July 29, 1976.
(Philadelphia's 9th choice, 244th overall, in 1994 Entry Draft).

			Regular Season					Playoffs				
Season	Club	Lea	GP	G	A	TP	PIM	GP	G	A	TP	PIM
1993-94	S.S. Marie	OHL	40	2	3	5	98	....	....	....	....	....
1994-95	S.S. Marie	OHL	50	15	15	30	177	....	....	....	....	....
1995-96	S.S. Marie	OHL	57	20	19	39	257	4	0	0	0	5
1996-97	S.S. Marie	OHL	4	3	0	3	19	....	....	....	....	....
	Kingston	OHL	29	10	13	23	143	2	0	0	0	2
1997-98	Philadelphia	AHL	56	5	5	10	209	4	0	0	0	9

PAYNE, DAVIS

Left wing. Shoots left. 6'2", 205 lbs. Born, Port Alberni, B.C., September 24, 1970.
(Edmonton's 6th choice, 140th overall, in 1989 Entry Draft).

			Regular Season					Playoffs				
Season	Club	Lea	GP	G	A	TP	PIM	GP	G	A	TP	PIM
1988-89	Michigan Tech	WCHA	35	5	3	8	39	....	....	....	....	....
1989-90	Michigan Tech	WCHA	30	11	10	21	81	....	....	....	....	....
1990-91	Michigan Tech	WCHA	41	15	20	35	82	....	....	....	....	....
1991-92	Michigan Tech	WCHA	24	6	1	7	71	....	....	....	....	....
1992-93	Greensboro	ECHL	57	15	20	35	178	1	0	0	0	4
1993-94	Greensboro	ECHL	36	17	17	34	139	8	2	1	3	27
	Phoenix	IHL	22	6	3	9	51	....	....	....	....	....
	Rochester	AHL	2	0	0	0	5	3	0	2	2	0
1994-95	Greensboro	ECHL	62	25	36	61	195	17	7	10	17	38
	Providence	AHL	2	1	0	1	0	....	....	....	....	....
1995-96	**Boston**	**NHL**	**7**	**0**	**0**	**0**	**7**	....	....	....	....	....
	Providence	AHL	51	17	22	39	72	4	1	4	5	2
1996-97	**Boston**	**NHL**	**15**	**0**	**1**	**1**	**7**	....	....	....	....	....
	Providence	AHL	57	18	15	33	104	....	....	....	....	....
1997-98	Providence	AHL	3	0	0	0	0	....	....	....	....	....
	San Antonio	IHL	59	15	10	25	117	....	....	....	....	....
	NHL Totals		**22**	**0**	**1**	**1**	**14**	....	....	....	....	....

Signed as a free agent by **Boston**, September 6, 1995.

PEAKE, PAT

Center. Shoots right. 6'1", 195 lbs. Born, Rochester, MI, May 28, 1973.
(Washington's 1st choice, 14th overall, in 1991 Entry Draft).

			Regular Season					Playoffs				
Season	Club	Lea	GP	G	A	TP	PIM	GP	G	A	TP	PIM
1990-91	Detroit	OHL	63	39	51	90	54	....	....	....	....	....
1991-92	Detroit	OHL	53	41	52	93	44	7	8	9	17	10
	Baltimore	AHL	3	1	0	1	4	....	....	....	....	....
1992-93	Detroit	OHL	46	58	78	136	64	2	1	3	4	2
1993-94	**Washington**	**NHL**	**49**	**11**	**18**	**29**	**39**	**8**	**0**	**1**	**1**	**8**
	Portland	AHL	4	0	5	5	2	....	....	....	....	....
1994-95	**Washington**	**NHL**	**18**	**0**	**4**	**4**	**12**	....	....	....	....	....
	Portland	AHL	5	1	3	4	2	4	0	3	3	6
1995-96	**Washington**	**NHL**	**62**	**17**	**19**	**36**	**46**	**5**	**2**	**1**	**3**	**12**
1996-97	**Washington**	**NHL**	**4**	**0**	**0**	**0**	**4**	....	....	....	....	....
	Portland	AHL	3	0	2	2	0	....	....	....	....	....
1997-98	**Washington**	**NHL**	**1**	**0**	**0**	**0**	**4**	....	....	....	....	....
	NHL Totals		**134**	**28**	**41**	**69**	**105**	**13**	**2**	**2**	**4**	**20**

Canadian Major Junior Player of the Year (1993) • Canadian Major Junior First All-Star Team (1993) • OHL First All-Star Team (1993)

PEARSON, ROB

Right wing. Shoots right. 6'3", 198 lbs. Born, Oshawa, Ont., March 8, 1971.
(Toronto's 2nd choice, 12th overall, in 1989 Entry Draft).

			Regular Season					Playoffs				
Season	Club	Lea	GP	G	A	TP	PIM	GP	G	A	TP	PIM
1988-89	Belleville	OHL	26	8	12	20	51	....	....	....	....	....
1989-90	Belleville	OHL	58	48	40	88	174	11	5	5	10	26
1990-91	Belleville	OHL	10	6	3	9	27	....	....	....	....	....
	Oshawa	OHL	41	57	52	109	76	16	16	17	33	39
	Newmarket	AHL	3	0	0	0	29	....	....	....	....	....
1991-92	**Toronto**	**NHL**	**47**	**14**	**10**	**24**	**58**	....	....	....	....	....
	St. John's	AHL	27	15	14	29	107	13	5	4	9	40
1992-93	**Toronto**	**NHL**	**78**	**23**	**14**	**37**	**211**	**14**	**2**	**2**	**4**	**31**
1993-94	**Toronto**	**NHL**	**67**	**12**	**18**	**30**	**189**	**14**	**1**	**0**	**1**	**32**
1994-95	**Washington**	**NHL**	**32**	**0**	**6**	**6**	**96**	**3**	**1**	**0**	**1**	**17**
1995-96	Portland	AHL	44	18	24	42	143	....	....	....	....	....
	St. Louis	**NHL**	**27**	**6**	**4**	**10**	**54**	**2**	**0**	**0**	**0**	**14**
1996-97	**St. Louis**	**NHL**	**18**	**1**	**2**	**3**	**37**	....	....	....	....	....
	Worcester	AHL	46	11	16	27	199	5	3	0	3	16
1997-98	Cleveland	IHL	46	17	14	31	118	10	6	4	10	43
	NHL Totals		**269**	**56**	**54**	**110**	**645**	**33**	**4**	**2**	**6**	**94**

OHL First All-Star Team (1991)

Traded to **Washington** by **Toronto** with Philadelphia's 1st round choice (previously acquired by Toronto — Washington selected Nolan Baumgartner) in 1994 Entry Draft for Mike Ridley and St. Louis' 1st round choice (previously acquired, Toronto selected Eric Fichaud) in 1994 Entry Draft, June 28, 1994. Traded to **St. Louis** by **Washington** for Denis Chasse, January 29, 1996.

PEARSON, SCOTT — TOR.

Left wing. Shoots left. 6'1", 205 lbs. Born, Cornwall, Ont., December 19, 1969.
(Toronto's 1st choice, 6th overall, in 1988 Entry Draft).

			Regular Season					Playoffs				
Season	Club	Lea	GP	G	A	TP	PIM	GP	G	A	TP	PIM
1985-86	Kingston	OHL	63	16	23	39	56	....	....	....	....	....
1986-87	Kingston	OHL	62	30	24	54	101	9	3	3	6	42
1987-88	Kingston	OHL	46	26	32	58	117	....	....	....	....	....
1988-89	Kingston	OHL	13	9	8	17	34	....	....	....	....	....
	Niagara Falls	OHL	32	26	34	60	90	17	14	10	24	53
	Toronto	**NHL**	**9**	**0**	**1**	**1**	**2**	....	....	....	....	....
1989-90	**Toronto**	**NHL**	**41**	**5**	**10**	**15**	**90**	**2**	**2**	**0**	**2**	**10**
	Newmarket	AHL	18	12	11	23	64	....	....	....	....	....
1990-91	**Toronto**	**NHL**	**12**	**0**	**0**	**0**	**20**	....	....	....	....	....
	Quebec	**NHL**	**35**	**11**	**4**	**15**	**86**	....	....	....	....	....
	Halifax	AHL	24	12	15	27	44	....	....	....	....	....
1991-92	**Quebec**	**NHL**	**10**	**1**	**2**	**3**	**14**	....	....	....	....	....
	Halifax	AHL	5	2	1	3	4	....	....	....	....	....
1992-93	**Quebec**	**NHL**	**41**	**13**	**1**	**14**	**95**	**3**	**0**	**0**	**0**	**0**
	Halifax	AHL	5	3	1	4	25	....	....	....	....	....
1993-94	**Edmonton**	**NHL**	**72**	**19**	**18**	**37**	**165**	....	....	....	....	....
1994-95	**Edmonton**	**NHL**	**28**	**1**	**4**	**5**	**54**	....	....	....	....	....
	Buffalo	**NHL**	**14**	**2**	**1**	**3**	**20**	**5**	**0**	**0**	**0**	**4**
1995-96	**Buffalo**	**NHL**	**27**	**4**	**0**	**4**	**67**	....	....	....	....	....
	Rochester	AHL	26	8	8	16	113	....	....	....	....	....
1996-97	**Toronto**	**NHL**	**1**	**0**	**0**	**0**	**2**	....	....	....	....	....
	St. John's	AHL	14	5	2	7	26	9	5	2	7	14
1997-98	Chicago	IHL	78	34	17	51	225	22	12	6	18	50
	NHL Totals		**290**	**56**	**41**	**97**	**615**	**10**	**2**	**0**	**2**	**14**

Traded to **Quebec** by **Toronto** with Toronto's 2nd round choices in 1991 (later traded to Washington — Washington selected Eric Lavigne) and 1992 (Tuomas Gronman) Entry Drafts for Aaron Broten, Lucien Deblois and Michel Petit, November 17, 1990. Traded to **Edmonton** by **Quebec** for Martin Gelinas and Edmonton's 6th round choice (Nicholas Checco) in 1993 Entry Draft, June 20, 1993. Traded to **Buffalo** by **Edmonton** for Ken Sutton, April 7, 1995. Signed as a free agent by **Toronto**, July 24, 1996.

PEAT, STEPHEN — ANA.

Defense. Shoots right. 6'3", 210 lbs. Born, Princeton, B.C., March 18, 1980.
(Anaheim's 2nd choice, 32nd overall, in 1998 Entry Draft).

			Regular Season					Playoffs				
Season	Club	Lea	GP	G	A	TP	PIM	GP	G	A	TP	PIM
1995-96	Red Deer	WHL	1	0	0	0	0	....	....	....	....	....
1996-97	Red Deer	WHL	68	3	14	17	161	16	0	2	2	22
1997-98	Red Deer	WHL	63	6	12	18	189	5	0	0	0	8

PECA, MICHAEL — (PEH-kuh) — BUF.

Center. Shoots right. 5'11", 181 lbs. Born, Toronto, Ont., March 26, 1974.
(Vancouver's 2nd choice, 40th overall, in 1992 Entry Draft).

			Regular Season					Playoffs				
Season	Club	Lea	GP	G	A	TP	PIM	GP	G	A	TP	PIM
1990-91	Sudbury	OHL	62	14	27	41	24	5	1	0	1	7
1991-92	Sudbury	OHL	39	16	34	50	61	....	....	....	....	....
	Ottawa	OHL	27	8	17	25	32	11	6	10	16	6
1992-93	Ottawa	OHL	55	38	64	102	80	....	....	....	....	....
	Hamilton	AHL	9	6	3	9	11	....	....	....	....	....
1993-94	Ottawa	OHL	55	50	63	113	101	17	7	22	29	30
	Vancouver	**NHL**	**4**	**0**	**0**	**0**	**2**	....	....	....	....	....
1994-95	Syracuse	AHL	35	10	24	34	75	....	....	....	....	....
	Vancouver	**NHL**	**33**	**6**	**6**	**12**	**30**	**5**	**0**	**1**	**1**	**8**
1995-96	**Buffalo**	**NHL**	**68**	**11**	**20**	**31**	**67**	....	....	....	....	....
1996-97	**Buffalo**	**NHL**	**79**	**20**	**29**	**49**	**80**	**10**	**0**	**2**	**2**	**8**
1997-98	**Buffalo**	**NHL**	**61**	**18**	**22**	**40**	**57**	**13**	**3**	**2**	**5**	**8**
	NHL Totals		**245**	**55**	**77**	**132**	**236**	**28**	**3**	**5**	**8**	**24**

Won Frank J. Selke Trophy (1997)

Traded to **Buffalo** by **Vancouver** with Mike Wilson and Vancouver's 1st round choice (Jay McKee) in 1995 Entry Draft for Alexander Mogilny and Buffalo's 5th round choice (Todd Norman) in 1995 Entry Draft, July 8, 1995.

PEDERSON, DENIS — N.J.

Center. Shoots right. 6'2", 205 lbs. Born, Prince Albert, Sask., September 10, 1975.
(New Jersey's 1st choice, 13th overall, in 1993 Entry Draft).

			Regular Season					Playoffs				
Season	Club	Lea	GP	G	A	TP	PIM	GP	G	A	TP	PIM
1991-92	Prince Albert	Midget	21	33	25	58	40	....	....	....	....	....
	Prince Albert	WHL	10	0	0	0	6	7	0	1	1	13
1992-93	Prince Albert	WHL	72	33	40	73	134	....	....	....	....	....
1993-94	Prince Albert	WHL	71	53	45	98	157	....	....	....	....	....
1994-95	Prince Albert	WHL	63	30	38	68	122	15	11	14	25	14
	Albany	AHL	....	....	....	....	....	3	0	0	0	2
1995-96	**New Jersey**	**NHL**	**10**	**3**	**1**	**4**	**0**	....	....	....	....	....
	Albany	AHL	68	28	43	71	104	4	1	2	3	0
1996-97	**New Jersey**	**NHL**	**70**	**12**	**20**	**32**	**62**	**9**	**0**	**0**	**0**	**2**
	Albany	AHL	3	1	3	4	7	....	....	....	....	....
1997-98	**New Jersey**	**NHL**	**80**	**15**	**13**	**28**	**97**	**6**	**1**	**1**	**2**	**2**
	NHL Totals		**160**	**30**	**34**	**64**	**159**	**15**	**1**	**1**	**2**	**4**

WHL East Second All-Star Team (1994)

PEDERSON, TOM

Defense. Shoots right. 5'9", 175 lbs. Born, Bloomington, MN, January 14, 1970.
(Minnesota's 12th choice, 217th overall, in 1989 Entry Draft).

			Regular Season					Playoffs				
Season	Club	Lea	GP	G	A	TP	PIM	GP	G	A	TP	PIM
1987-88	Jefferson High	H.S.	22	16	27	43	....	....	....	....	....	....
1988-89	U. of Minnesota	WCHA	36	4	20	24	40	....	....	....	....	....
1989-90	U. of Minnesota	WCHA	43	8	30	38	58	....	....	....	....	....
1990-91	U. of Minnesota	WCHA	36	12	20	32	46	....	....	....	....	....
1991-92	United States	Nat-Tm	44	3	11	14	41	....	....	....	....	....
	Kansas City	IHL	20	6	9	15	16	13	1	6	7	14
1992-93	**San Jose**	**NHL**	**44**	**7**	**13**	**20**	**31**	....	....	....	....	....
	Kansas City	IHL	26	6	15	21	10	12	1	6	7	2
1993-94	**San Jose**	**NHL**	**74**	**6**	**19**	**25**	**31**	**14**	**1**	**6**	**7**	**2**
	Kansas City	IHL	7	3	1	4	0	....	....	....	....	....
1994-95	**San Jose**	**NHL**	**47**	**5**	**11**	**16**	**31**	**10**	**0**	**5**	**5**	**8**
1995-96	**San Jose**	**NHL**	**60**	**1**	**4**	**5**	**40**	....	....	....	....	....
1996-97	Seibu	Japan	29	10	28	38	24	....	....	....	....	....
	Toronto	**NHL**	**15**	**1**	**2**	**3**	**9**	....	....	....	....	....
	St. John's	AHL	1	0	4	4	2	....	....	....	....	....
	Utah	IHL	10	1	2	3	8	7	1	3	4	4
1997-98	Fort Wayne	IHL	78	12	24	36	87	4	2	0	2	4
	NHL Totals		**240**	**20**	**49**	**69**	**142**	**24**	**1**	**11**	**12**	**10**

Claimed by **San Jose** from **Minnesota** in Dispersal Draft, May 30, 1991. Signed as a free agent by **Toronto**, December 11, 1996.

PELLERIN, SCOTT — (PEHL-ih-rihn) — ST.L.

Left wing. Shoots left. 5'11", 180 lbs. Born, Shediac, N.B., January 9, 1970.
(New Jersey's 4th choice, 47th overall, in 1989 Entry Draft).

			Regular Season					Playoffs				
Season	Club	Lea	GP	G	A	TP	PIM	GP	G	A	TP	PIM
1987-88	Notre Dame	SJHL	57	37	49	86	139	....	....	....	....	....
1988-89	U. of Maine	H.E.	45	29	33	62	92	....	....	....	....	....
1989-90	U. of Maine	H.E.	42	22	34	56	68	....	....	....	....	....
1990-91	U. of Maine	H.E.	43	23	25	48	60	....	....	....	....	....
1991-92	U. of Maine	H.E.	37	*32	25	57	54	....	....	....	....	....
	Utica	AHL	....	....	....	....	....	3	1	0	1	0
1992-93	**New Jersey**	**NHL**	**45**	**10**	**11**	**21**	**41**	....	....	....	....	....
	Utica	AHL	27	15	18	33	33	2	0	1	1	0
1993-94	**New Jersey**	**NHL**	**1**	**0**	**0**	**0**	**2**	....	....	....	....	....
	Albany	AHL	73	28	46	74	84	5	2	1	3	11
1994-95	Albany	AHL	74	23	33	56	95	14	6	4	10	8
1995-96	**New Jersey**	**NHL**	**6**	**2**	**1**	**3**	**0**	....	....	....	....	....
	Albany	AHL	75	35	47	82	142	4	0	3	3	10
1996-97	**St. Louis**	**NHL**	**54**	**8**	**10**	**18**	**35**	**6**	**0**	**0**	**0**	**6**
	Worcester	AHL	24	10	16	26	37	....	....	....	....	....
1997-98	**St. Louis**	**NHL**	**80**	**8**	**21**	**29**	**62**	**10**	**0**	**2**	**2**	**10**
	NHL Totals		**186**	**28**	**43**	**71**	**140**	**16**	**0**	**2**	**2**	**16**

Hockey East First All-Star Team (1992) • NCAA East First All-American Team (1992) • Won Hobey Baker Memorial Award (Top U.S. Collegiate Player) (1992)

Signed as a free agent by **St. Louis**, July 10, 1996.

PELTONEN, VILLE (PEHL-TOH-ner) **NSH.**

Left wing. Shoots left. 5'11", 180 lbs. Born, Vantaa, Finland, May 24, 1973.
(San Jose's 4th choice, 58th overall, in 1993 Entry Draft).

			Regular Season					Playoffs				
Season	Club	Lea	GP	G	A	TP	PIM	GP	G	A	TP	PIM
1991-92	Helsinki	Finland	6	0	0	0	0	....	....	....	....	....
1992-93	Helsinki	Finland	46	13	24	37	16	4	0	2	2	2
1993-94	Helsinki	Finland	43	16	22	38	14	3	0	0	0	2
	Finland	Olympics	8	4	3	7	0	....	....	....	....	....
1994-95	Helsinki	Finland	45	20	16	36	16	3	0	0	0	0
1995-96	**San Jose**	**NHL**	**31**	**2**	**11**	**13**	**14**	....	....	....	....	....
	Kansas City	IHL	29	5	13	18	8	....	....	....	....	....
1996-97	**San Jose**	**NHL**	**28**	**2**	**3**	**5**	**0**	....	....	....	....	....
	Kentucky	AHL	40	22	30	52	21	....	....	....	....	....
1997-98	V. Frolunda	Sweden	45	22	29	51	44	7	4	2	6	0
	Finland	Olympics	6	2	1	3	6	....	....	....	....	....
	NHL Totals		**59**	**4**	**14**	**18**	**14**	....	....	....	....	....

Finnish Rookie of the Year (1993)

Traded to **Nashville** by **San Jose** for Nashville's 5th round choice (later traded to Phoenix - Phoenix selected Josh Blackburn) in 1998 Entry Draft, June 26, 1998.

PELUSO, MIKE (puh-LOO-soh)

Left wing. Shoots left. 6'4", 225 lbs. Born, Pengilly, MN, November 8, 1965.
(New Jersey's 10th choice, 190th overall, in 1984 Entry Draft).

			Regular Season					Playoffs				
Season	Club	Lea	GP	G	A	TP	PIM	GP	G	A	TP	PIM
1983-84	Greenway High	H.S.	12	5	15	20	30	....	....	....	....	....
1984-85	Stratford	OJHL	52	11	45	56	114	....	....	....	....	....
1985-86	Alaska-Anchorage	G.N.	32	2	11	13	59	....	....	....	....	....
1986-87	Alaska-Anchorage	G.N.	30	5	21	26	68	....	....	....	....	....
1987-88	Alaska-Anchorage	G.N.	35	4	33	37	76	....	....	....	....	....
1988-89	Alaska-Anchorage	G.N.	33	10	27	37	75	....	....	....	....	....
1989-90	**Chicago**	**NHL**	**2**	**0**	**0**	**0**	**15**	....	....	....	....	....
	Indianapolis	IHL	75	7	10	17	279	14	0	1	1	58
1990-91	**Chicago**	**NHL**	**53**	**6**	**1**	**7**	**320**	**3**	**0**	**0**	**0**	**2**
	Indianapolis	IHL	6	2	1	3	21	5	0	2	2	40
1991-92	**Chicago**	**NHL**	**63**	**6**	**3**	**9**	***408**	**17**	**1**	**2**	**3**	**8**
	Indianapolis	IHL	4	0	1	1	15	....	....	....	....	....
1992-93	**Ottawa**	**NHL**	**81**	**15**	**10**	**25**	**318**	....	....	....	....	....
1993-94	**New Jersey**	**NHL**	**69**	**4**	**16**	**20**	**238**	**17**	**1**	**0**	**1**	***64**
1994-95	**New Jersey**	**NHL**	**46**	**2**	**9**	**11**	**167**	**20**	**1**	**2**	**3**	**8** ♦
1995-96	**New Jersey**	**NHL**	**57**	**3**	**8**	**11**	**146**	....	....	....	....	....
1996-97	**New Jersey**	**NHL**	**20**	**0**	**2**	**2**	**68**	....	....	....	....	....
	St. Louis	**NHL**	**44**	**2**	**3**	**5**	**158**	**5**	**0**	**0**	**0**	**25**
1997-98	**Calgary**	**NHL**	**23**	**0**	**0**	**0**	**113**	....	....	....	....	....
	NHL Totals		**458**	**38**	**52**	**90**	**1951**	**62**	**3**	**4**	**7**	**107**

Signed as a free agent by **Chicago**, September 7, 1989. Claimed by **Ottawa** from **Chicago** in Expansion Draft, June 18, 1992. Traded to **New Jersey** by **Ottawa** to complete transaction that sent Craig Billington, Troy Mallette and New Jersey's 4th round choice (Cosmo Dupaul) in 1993 Entry Draft to Ottawa (June 20, 1993), June 26, 1993. Traded to **St. Louis** by **New Jersey** with Ricard Persson for Ken Sutton and St. Louis' 2nd round choice in 1999 Entry Draft, November 26, 1996. Transferred to **NY Rangers** from **St. Louis** as compensation for St. Louis' signing of Larry Pleau as head coach, June 21, 1997. Claimed by **Calgary** from **NY Rangers** in NHL Waiver Draft, September 28, 1997.

PEPPERALL, COLIN **CHI.**

Left wing. Shoots left. 5'11", 160 lbs. Born, Niagara Falls, Ont., April 28, 1978.
(NY Rangers' 4th choice, 131st overall, in 1996 Entry Draft).

			Regular Season					Playoffs				
Season	Club	Lea	GP	G	A	TP	PIM	GP	G	A	TP	PIM
1995-96	Niagara Falls	OHL	66	26	26	52	47	10	3	4	7	8
1996-97	Erie	OHL	66	36	36	72	39	5	3	2	5	2
1997-98	Erie	OHL	60	31	60	91	151	7	4	4	8	16
	Hartford	AHL	3	1	0	1	2	....	....	....	....	....

OHL Second All-Star Team (1988)

PEPPERALL, RYAN **TOR.**

Right wing. Shoots right. 6'1", 185 lbs. Born, Niagara Falls, Ont., January 26, 1977.
(Toronto's 2nd choice, 54th overall, in 1995 Entry Draft).

			Regular Season					Playoffs				
Season	Club	Lea	GP	G	A	TP	PIM	GP	G	A	TP	PIM
1994-95	Kitchener	OHL	62	17	16	33	86	5	2	2	4	8
1995-96	Kitchener	OHL	66	31	26	57	173	12	3	4	7	34
1996-97	Kitchener	OHL	65	35	36	71	201	13	9	6	15	17
1997-98	St. John's	AHL	63	3	4	7	50	1	0	0	0	0

OHL Second All-Star Team (1998)

PERREAULT, YANIC (puh-ROH, YAH-nihk) **L.A.**

Center. Shoots left. 5'11", 188 lbs. Born, Sherbrooke, Que., April 4, 1971.
(Toronto's 1st choice, 47th overall, in 1991 Entry Draft).

			Regular Season					Playoffs				
Season	Club	Lea	GP	G	A	TP	PIM	GP	G	A	TP	PIM
1988-89	Trois-Rivieres	QMJHL	70	53	55	108	48	....	....	....	....	....
1989-90	Trois-Rivieres	QMJHL	63	51	63	114	75	7	6	5	11	19
1990-91	Trois-Rivieres	QMJHL	67	*87	98	*185	103	6	4	7	11	6
1991-92	St. John's	AHL	62	38	38	76	19	16	7	8	15	4
1992-93	St. John's	AHL	79	49	46	95	56	9	4	5	9	2
1993-94	**Toronto**	**NHL**	**13**	**3**	**3**	**6**	**0**	....	....	....	....	....
	St. John's	AHL	62	45	60	105	38	11	*12	6	18	14
1994-95	Phoenix	IHL	68	51	48	99	52	....	....	....	....	....
	Los Angeles	**NHL**	**26**	**2**	**5**	**7**	**20**	....	....	....	....	....
1995-96	**Los Angeles**	**NHL**	**78**	**25**	**24**	**49**	**16**	....	....	....	....	....
1996-97	**Los Angeles**	**NHL**	**41**	**11**	**14**	**25**	**20**	....	....	....	....	....
1997-98	**Los Angeles**	**NHL**	**79**	**28**	**20**	**48**	**32**	**4**	**1**	**2**	**3**	**6**
	NHL Totals		**237**	**69**	**66**	**135**	**88**	**4**	**1**	**2**	**3**	**6**

Canadian Major Junior Rookie of the Year (1989) • QMJHL First All-Star Team (1991)

Traded to **LA Kings** by **Toronto** for LA Kings' 4th round choice (later traded to Philadelphia — later traded to LA Kings — LA Kings selected Mikael Simons) in 1996 Entry Draft, July 11, 1994.

PERROTT, NATHAN **CHI.**

Right wing. Shoots right. 6', 215 lbs. Born, Owen Sound, Ont., December 8, 1976.
(New Jersey's 2nd choice, 44th overall, in 1995 Entry Draft).

			Regular Season					Playoffs				
Season	Club	Lea	GP	G	A	TP	PIM	GP	G	A	TP	PIM
1994-95	Oshawa	OHL	63	18	28	46	233	2	1	1	2	9
1995-96	Oshawa	OHL	59	30	32	62	158	5	2	3	5	8
	Albany	AHL	4	0	0	0	12	....	....	....	....	....
1996-97	Oshawa	OHL	5	1	0	1	17	....	....	....	....	....
	S.S. Marie	OHL	37	18	23	41	120	11	5	5	10	60
1997-98	Indianapolis	IHL	31	4	3	7	76	....	....	....	....	....
	Jacksonville	ECHL	30	6	8	14	135	....	....	....	....	....

Signed as a free agent by **Chicago**, August 27, 1997.

PERSHIN, EDUARD (PEHR-shihn, ehd-WUHRD) **T.B.**

Right wing. Shoots left. 6', 191 lbs. Born, Nizhnekamsk, USSR, September 1, 1977.
(Tampa Bay's 5th choice, 134th overall, in 1995 Entry Draft).

			Regular Season					Playoffs				
Season	Club	Lea	GP	G	A	TP	PIM	GP	G	A	TP	PIM
1994-95	Moscow D'amo	CIS	4	1	1	2	2	3	0	0	0	2
1995-96	Moscow D'amo	CIS	38	4	10	14	18	2	0	0	0	0
1996-97	Moscow D'amo	Russia	31	4	9	13	16	3	0	2	2	0
1997-98	Chesapeake	ECHL	38	12	21	33	38	3	0	0	0	4

PERSSON, RICARD (PAIR-suhn, RIH-kahrd) **ST.L.**

Defense. Shoots left. 6'2", 205 lbs. Born, Ostersund, Sweden, August 24, 1969.
(New Jersey's 2nd choice, 23rd overall, in 1987 Entry Draft).

			Regular Season					Playoffs				
Season	Club	Lea	GP	G	A	TP	PIM	GP	G	A	TP	PIM
1985-86	Ostersund	Sweden-2	24	2	2	4	16	....	....	....	....	....
1986-87	Ostersund	Sweden-2	31	10	11	21	28	....	....	....	....	....
1987-88	Leksand IF	Sweden	31	2	0	2	8	2	0	1	1	2
1988-89	Leksand IF	Sweden	33	2	4	6	28	9	0	1	1	6
1989-90	Leksand IF	Sweden	43	9	10	19	62	3	0	0	0	6
1990-91	Leksand IF	Sweden	37	6	9	15	42	....	....	....	....	....
1991-92	Leksand IF	Sweden	21	0	7	7	28	....	....	....	....	....
1992-93	Leksand IF	Sweden	36	7	15	22	63	2	0	2	2	0
1993-94	Malmo IF	Sweden	40	11	9	20	38	11	2	0	2	12
1994-95	Malmo IF	Sweden	31	3	13	16	38	9	0	2	2	8
	Albany	AHL	3	0	0	0	0	9	3	5	8	7
1995-96	**New Jersey**	**NHL**	**12**	**2**	**1**	**3**	**8**	....	....	....	....	....
	Albany	AHL	67	15	31	46	59	4	0	0	0	7
1996-97	**New Jersey**	**NHL**	**1**	**0**	**0**	**0**	**0**	....	....	....	....	....
	Albany	AHL	13	1	4	5	8	....	....	....	....	....
	St. Louis	**NHL**	**53**	**4**	**8**	**12**	**45**	**6**	**0**	**0**	**0**	**27**
1997-98	**St. Louis**	**NHL**	**1**	**0**	**0**	**0**	**0**	....	....	....	....	....
	Worcester	AHL	32	2	16	18	58	10	3	7	10	24
	NHL Totals		**67**	**6**	**9**	**15**	**53**	**6**	**0**	**0**	**0**	**27**

Traded to **St. Louis** by **New Jersey** with Mike Peluso for Ken Sutton and St. Louis' 2nd round choice in 1999 Entry Draft, November 26, 1996.

PETERS, ANDREW **BUF.**

Left wing. Shoots left. 6'4", 195 lbs. Born, St. Catharines, Ont., May 5, 1980.
(Buffalo's 2nd choice, 34th overall, in 1998 Entry Draft).

			Regular Season					Playoffs				
Season	Club	Lea	GP	G	A	TP	PIM	GP	G	A	TP	PIM
1996-97	Georgetown	OJHL	46	11	16	27	65	....	....	....	....	....
1997-98	Oshawa	OHL	60	11	7	18	220	7	2	0	2	19

PETERS, GEOFF **CHI.**

Center. Shoots left. 6', 174 lbs. Born, Hamilton, Ont., April 30, 1978.
(Chicago's 3rd choice, 46th overall, in 1996 Entry Draft).

			Regular Season					Playoffs				
Season	Club	Lea	GP	G	A	TP	PIM	GP	G	A	TP	PIM
1994-95	Niagara Falls	OHL	57	11	9	20	37	6	2	0	2	4
1995-96	Niagara Falls	OHL	64	25	34	59	51	10	4	4	8	8
1996-97	Erie	OHL	28	12	10	22	39	5	1	3	4	7
1997-98	Erie	OHL	31	15	11	26	36	....	....	....	....	....
	North Bay	OHL	20	11	14	25	22	....	....	....	....	....
	Indianapolis	IHL	2	0	0	0	10	....	....	....	....	....

PETERSON, BRENT **T.B.**

Left wing. Shoots left. 6'3", 200 lbs. Born, Calgary, Alta., July 20, 1972.
(Tampa Bay's 1st choice, 3rd overall, in 1993 Supplemental Draft).

			Regular Season					Playoffs				
Season	Club	Lea	GP	G	A	TP	PIM	GP	G	A	TP	PIM
1991-92	Michigan Tech	WCHA	39	11	9	20	18	....	....	....	....	....
1992-93	Michigan Tech	WCHA	37	24	18	42	32	....	....	....	....	....
1993-94	Michigan Tech	WCHA	43	25	21	46	30	....	....	....	....	....
1994-95	Michigan Tech	WCHA	39	20	16	36	27	....	....	....	....	....
1995-96	Atlanta	IHL	69	9	19	28	33	3	0	0	0	0
1996-97	**Tampa Bay**	**NHL**	**17**	**2**	**0**	**2**	**4**	....	....	....	....	....
	Adirondack	AHL	52	22	23	45	56	4	3	1	4	2
1997-98	**Tampa Bay**	**NHL**	**19**	**5**	**0**	**5**	**2**	....	....	....	....	....
	Milwaukee	IHL	63	20	39	59	48	8	5	3	8	22
	NHL Totals		**36**	**7**	**0**	**7**	**6**	....	....	....	....	....

PETERSON, KYLE **EDM.**

Center. Shoots left. 6'4", 220 lbs. Born, Calgary, Alta., April 17, 1974.
(Minnesota's 5th choice, 154th overall, in 1992 Entry Draft).

			Regular Season					Playoffs				
Season	Club	Lea	GP	G	A	TP	PIM	GP	G	A	TP	PIM
1991-92	Thunder Bay	USHL	23	5	7	12	18	....	....	....	....	....
1992-93	Thunder Bay	USHL	24	8	23	31	22	....	....	....	....	....
1993-94	Michigan Tech	WCHA	45	5	9	14	82	....	....	....	....	....
1994-95	Michigan Tech	WCHA	36	7	11	18	52	....	....	....	....	....
1995-96	Michigan Tech	WCHA	23	8	7	15	18	....	....	....	....	....
1996-97	Michigan Tech	WCHA	38	15	10	25	44	....	....	....	....	....
1997-98	New Orleans	ECHL	25	5	9	14	37	....	....	....	....	....

Signed as a free agent by **Edmonton**, June 5, 1997.

PETERSON, MATT

Defense. Shoots left. 6'1", 190 lbs. Born, Maple Grove, MN, February 15, 1975.
(Anaheim's 7th choice, 160th overall, in 1993 Entry Draft).

			Regular Season					Playoffs				
Season	Club	Lea	GP	G	A	TP	PIM	GP	G	A	TP	PIM
1992-93	Osseo High	H.S.	24	13	17	30	....	....	....	....	....	....
1993-94	U. of Wisconsin	WCHA	DID NOT PLAY – FRESHMAN									
1994-95	U. of Wisconsin	WCHA	20	0	0	0	10	....	....	....	....	....
1995-96	U. of Wisconsin	WCHA	21	0	0	0	24	....	....	....	....	....
1996-97	U. of Wisconsin	WCHA	32	2	1	3	22	....	....	....	....	....
1997-98	U. of Wisconsin	WCHA	41	3	4	7	36	....	....	....	....	....

PETIT, MICHEL (puh-TEE) PHX.

Defense. Shoots right. 6'1", 205 lbs. Born, St. Malo, Que., February 12, 1964.
(Vancouver's 1st choice, 11th overall, in 1982 Entry Draft).

			Regular Season					Playoffs				
Season	Club	Lea	GP	G	A	TP	PIM	GP	G	A	TP	PIM
1981-82	Sherbrooke	QMJHL	63	10	39	49	106	22	5	20	25	24
1982-83	St-Jean	QMJHL	62	19	67	86	196	3	0	0	0	35
	Vancouver	**NHL**	**2**	**0**	**0**	**0**	**0**	....	....	....	....	....
1983-84	Canada	Nat-Tm	19	3	10	13	58	....	....	....	....	....
	Vancouver	**NHL**	**44**	**6**	**9**	**15**	**53**	**1**	**0**	**0**	**0**	**0**
1984-85	**Vancouver**	**NHL**	**69**	**5**	**26**	**31**	**127**	....	....	....	....	....
1985-86	**Vancouver**	**NHL**	**32**	**1**	**6**	**7**	**27**	....	....	....	....	....
	Fredericton	AHL	25	0	13	13	79	....	....	....	....	....
1986-87	**Vancouver**	**NHL**	**69**	**12**	**13**	**25**	**131**	....	....	....	....	....
1987-88	**Vancouver**	**NHL**	**10**	**0**	**3**	**3**	**35**	....	....	....	....	....
	NY Rangers	**NHL**	**64**	**9**	**24**	**33**	**223**	....	....	....	....	....
1988-89	**NY Rangers**	**NHL**	**69**	**8**	**25**	**33**	**154**	**4**	**0**	**2**	**2**	**27**
1989-90	**Quebec**	**NHL**	**63**	**12**	**24**	**36**	**215**	....	....	....	....	....
1990-91	**Quebec**	**NHL**	**19**	**4**	**7**	**11**	**47**	....	....	....	....	....
	Toronto	**NHL**	**54**	**9**	**19**	**28**	**132**	....	....	....	....	....
1991-92	**Toronto**	**NHL**	**34**	**1**	**13**	**14**	**85**	....	....	....	....	....
	Calgary	**NHL**	**36**	**3**	**10**	**13**	**79**	....	....	....	....	....
1992-93	**Calgary**	**NHL**	**35**	**3**	**9**	**12**	**54**	....	....	....	....	....
1993-94	**Calgary**	**NHL**	**63**	**2**	**21**	**23**	**110**	....	....	....	....	....
1994-95	**Los Angeles**	**NHL**	**40**	**5**	**12**	**17**	**84**	....	....	....	....	....
1995-96	**Los Angeles**	**NHL**	**9**	**0**	**1**	**1**	**27**	....	....	....	....	....
	Tampa Bay	**NHL**	**45**	**4**	**7**	**11**	**108**	**6**	**0**	**0**	**0**	**20**
1996-97	**Edmonton**	**NHL**	**18**	**2**	**4**	**6**	**20**	....	....	....	....	....
	Philadelphia	**NHL**	**20**	**0**	**3**	**3**	**51**	**3**	**0**	**0**	**0**	**6**
1997-98	Detroit	IHL	9	2	3	5	24	....	....	....	....	....
	Phoenix	**NHL**	**32**	**4**	**2**	**6**	**77**	**5**	**0**	**0**	**0**	**8**
	NHL Totals		**827**	**90**	**238**	**328**	**1839**	**19**	**0**	**2**	**2**	**61**

QMJHL First All-Star Team (1982, 1983)

Traded to **NY Rangers** by **Vancouver** for Willie Huber and Larry Melnyk, November 4, 1987. Traded to **Quebec** by **NY Rangers** for Randy Moller, October 5, 1989. Traded to **Toronto** by **Quebec** with Aaron Broten and Lucien Deblois for Scott Pearson and Toronto's 2nd round choices in 1991 (later traded to Washington — Washington selected Eric Lavigne) and 1992 (Tuomas Gronman) Entry Drafts, November 17, 1990. Traded to **Calgary** by **Toronto** with Craig Berube, Alexander Godynyuk, Gary Leeman and Jeff Reese for Doug Gilmour, Jamie Macoun, Ric Nattress, Rick Wamsley and Kent Manderville, January 2, 1992. Signed as a free agent by **LA Kings**, June 16, 1994. Traded to **Tampa Bay** by **LA Kings** for Steven Finn, November 13, 1995. Signed as a free agent by **Edmonton**, October 24, 1996. Claimed on waivers by **Philadelphia** from **Edmonton**, January 17, 1997. Signed as a free agent by **Phoenix**, November 25, 1997.

PETRAKOV, ANDREI (peh-trah-KAHF) ST.L.

Right wing. Shoots left. 6', 198 lbs. Born, Sverdlovsk, USSR, April 26, 1976.
(St. Louis' 4th choice, 97th overall, in 1996 Entry Draft).

			Regular Season					Playoffs				
Season	Club	Lea	GP	G	A	TP	PIM	GP	G	A	TP	PIM
1992-93	Yekaterinburg	CIS	5	0	0	0	0	1	0	0	0	0
1993-94	Yekaterinburg	CIS	35	4	2	6	10	....	....	....	....	....
1994-95	Yekaterinburg	CIS	11	1	1	2	6	1	0	0	0	0
1995-96	Yekaterinburg	CIS-2	52	17	6	23	14	....	....	....	....	....
1996-97	Yekaterinburg	Russia	14	6	1	7	6	....	....	....	....	....
	Magnitogorsk	Russia	18	4	0	4	8	6	0	0	0	0
1997-98	Samara	Russia	9	0	0	0	4	....	....	....	....	....
	Magnitogorsk	Russia	29	9	11	20	0	....	....	....	....	....

PETRE, HENRIK (PEH-treh) WSH.

Defense. Shoots left. 6'1", 187 lbs. Born, Stockholm, Sweden, April 9, 1979.
(Washington's 5th choice, 143rd overall, in 1997 Entry Draft).

			Regular Season					Playoffs				
Season	Club	Lea	GP	G	A	TP	PIM	GP	G	A	TP	PIM
1995-96	Djurgarden	Swe-Jr.	21	6	4	10	8	....	....	....	....	....
1996-97	Djurgarden	Swe-Jr.	20	7	6	13	....	....	....	....	....	....
1997-98	Huddinge	Sweden-2	30	4	4	8	30	....	....	....	....	....

PETRILAINEN, PASI (peh-trih-LAI-nehn, PAH-see) N.J.

Defense. Shoots left. 5'10", 185 lbs. Born, Tampere, Finland, May 5, 1978.
(New Jersey's 14th choice, 225th overall, in 1996 Entry Draft).

			Regular Season					Playoffs				
Season	Club	Lea	GP	G	A	TP	PIM	GP	G	A	TP	PIM
1994-95	Tappara	Finland	25	3	0	3	14	....	....	....	....	....
	Tappara	Fin-Jr.	14	3	4	7	6	....	....	....	....	....
1995-96	Tappara	Finland	40	0	4	4	18	4	0	0	0	2
	Tappara	Fin-Jr.	5	0	2	2	4	....	....	....	....	....
1996-97	Tappara	Finland	43	2	9	11	46	3	0	0	0	2
1997-98	Tappara	Finland	48	4	7	11	34	4	0	0	0	4

PETROCHININ, YEVGENY (peht-roh-CHIH-nihn) DAL.

Defense. Shoots left. 6'2", 190 lbs. Born, Murmansk, USSR, February 7, 1976.
(Dallas' 5th choice, 150th overall, in 1994 Entry Draft).

			Regular Season					Playoffs				
Season	Club	Lea	GP	G	A	TP	PIM	GP	G	A	TP	PIM
1993-94	Spartak	CIS	2	0	0	0	0	....	....	....	....	....
1994-95	Spartak	CIS	45	0	2	2	14	....	....	....	....	....
1995-96	Spartak	CIS	50	5	17	22	18	5	3	0	3	0
1996-97	Spartak	Russia	32	5	6	11	52	....	....	....	....	....
1997-98	Spartak	Russia	46	12	6	18	100	....	....	....	....	....

PETROVICKY, ROBERT (PEHT-roh-VEETS-kee)

Center. Shoots left. 5'11", 172 lbs. Born, Kosice, Czech., October 26, 1973.
(Hartford's 1st choice, 9th overall, in 1992 Entry Draft).

			Regular Season					Playoffs				
Season	Club	Lea	GP	G	A	TP	PIM	GP	G	A	TP	PIM
1990-91	Dukla Trencin	Czech.	33	9	14	23	12	....	....	....	....	....
1991-92	Dukla Trencin	Czech.	46	25	36	61	28	....	....	....	....	....
1992-93	**Hartford**	**NHL**	**42**	**3**	**6**	**9**	**45**	....	....	....	....	....
	Springfield	AHL	16	5	3	8	39	15	5	6	11	14
1993-94	Dukla Trencin	Slovakia	1	0	0	0	0	....	....	....	....	....
	Hartford	**NHL**	**33**	**6**	**5**	**11**	**39**	....	....	....	....	....
	Springfield	AHL	30	16	8	24	39	4	0	2	2	4
	Slovakia	Olympics	8	1	6	7	18	....	....	....	....	....
1994-95	Springfield	AHL	74	30	52	82	121	....	....	....	....	....
	Hartford	**NHL**	**2**	**0**	**0**	**0**	**0**	....	....	....	....	....
1995-96	Springfield	AHL	9	4	8	12	18	....	....	....	....	....
	Detroit	IHL	12	5	3	8	16	....	....	....	....	....
	Dallas	**NHL**	**5**	**1**	**1**	**2**	**0**	....	....	....	....	....
	Michigan	IHL	50	23	23	46	63	7	3	1	4	16
1996-97	**St. Louis**	**NHL**	**44**	**7**	**12**	**19**	**10**	**2**	**0**	**0**	**0**	**0**
	Worcester	AHL	12	5	4	9	19	....	....	....	....	....
1997-98	Worcester	AHL	65	27	34	61	97	10	3	4	7	12
	Slovakia	Olympics	4	2	1	3	0	....	....	....	....	....
	NHL Totals		**126**	**17**	**24**	**41**	**94**	**2**	**0**	**0**	**0**	**0**

Czechoslovakian First All-Star Team (1992)

Traded to **Dallas** by **Hartford** for Dan Kesa and future considerations, November 29, 1995. Signed as a free agent by **St. Louis**, September 6, 1996.

PETROVICKY, RONALD (PEHT-roh-VEETS-kee) CGY.

Right wing. Shoots right. 5'11", 185 lbs. Born, Zilina, Czech., February 15, 1977.
(Calgary's 9th choice, 228th overall, in 1996 Entry Draft).

			Regular Season					Playoffs				
Season	Club	Lea	GP	G	A	TP	PIM	GP	G	A	TP	PIM
1993-94	Dukla Trencin	Slov-Jr.	36	28	27	55	42	....	....	....	....	....
	Dukla Trencin	Slovakia	1	0	0	0	0	....	....	....	....	....
1994-95	Tri-City	WHL	39	4	11	15	86	....	....	....	....	....
	Prince George	WHL	21	4	6	10	37	....	....	....	....	....
1995-96	Prince George	WHL	39	19	21	40	61	....	....	....	....	....
1996-97	Prince George	WHL	72	32	37	69	119	15	4	9	13	31
1997-98	Regina	WHL	71	64	49	113	168	9	2	4	6	11

WHL East Second All-Star Team (1998)

PETRUNIN, ANDREI (puh-TROO-nihn) CAR.

Right wing. Shoots left. 5'9", 169 lbs. Born, Moscow, USSR, February 2, 1978.
(Hartford's 2nd choice, 61st overall, in 1996 Entry Draft).

			Regular Season					Playoffs				
Season	Club	Lea	GP	G	A	TP	PIM	GP	G	A	TP	PIM
1994-95	CSKA Moscow	CIS	7	0	1	1	0	2	0	0	0	0
1995-96	CSKA Moscow	CIS	52	12	8	20	22	2	0	0	0	2
1996-97	CSKA Moscow	Russia-2	55	36	32	68	73	....	....	....	....	....
1997-98	CSKA Moscow	Russia	45	7	13	20	71	....	....	....	....	....

PHILLIPS, CHRIS OTT.

Defense. Shoots left. 6'2", 200 lbs. Born, Fort McMurray, Alta., March 9, 1978.
(Ottawa's 1st choice, 1st overall, in 1996 Entry Draft).

			Regular Season					Playoffs				
Season	Club	Lea	GP	G	A	TP	PIM	GP	G	A	TP	PIM
1995-96	Prince Albert	WHL	61	10	30	40	97	18	2	12	14	30
1996-97	Prince Albert	WHL	32	3	23	26	58	....	....	....	....	....
	Lethbridge	WHL	26	4	18	22	28	19	4	*21	25	20
1997-98	**Ottawa**	**NHL**	**72**	**5**	**11**	**16**	**38**	**11**	**0**	**2**	**2**	**2**
	NHL Totals		**72**	**5**	**11**	**16**	**38**	**11**	**0**	**2**	**2**	**2**

WHL East First All-Star Team (1997) • Canadian Major Junior First All-Star Team (1997)

PHILLIPS, GREG L.A.

Center. Shoots right. 6'2", 205 lbs. Born, Winnipeg, Man., March 27, 1978.
(Los Angeles' 3rd choice, 57th overall, in 1996 Entry Draft).

			Regular Season					Playoffs				
Season	Club	Lea	GP	G	A	TP	PIM	GP	G	A	TP	PIM
1994-95	Saskatoon	WHL	64	3	5	8	94	10	0	0	0	4
1995-96	Saskatoon	WHL	67	21	24	45	132	4	1	2	3	2
1996-97	Saskatoon	WHL	34	17	19	36	64	....	....	....	....	....
1997-98	Saskatoon	WHL	47	24	28	52	116	....	....	....	....	....
	Brandon	WHL	22	10	21	31	49	18	11	11	22	58

PHILPOTT, ETHAN

Right wing. Shoots right. 6'4", 230 lbs. Born, Rochester, MN, February 11, 1975.
(Buffalo's 2nd choice, 64th overall, in 1993 Entry Draft).

			Regular Season					Playoffs				
Season	Club	Lea	GP	G	A	TP	PIM	GP	G	A	TP	PIM
1992-93	Phillips Andover	H.S.	18	17	19	36	....	....	....	....	....	....
1993-94	Harvard	ECAC	3	1	0	1	8	....	....	....	....	....
1994-95	Des Moines	USHL	48	19	42	61	57	....	....	....	....	....
1995-96	Harvard	ECAC	34	6	4	10	39	....	....	....	....	....
1996-97	Harvard	ECAC	25	3	9	12	38	....	....	....	....	....
1997-98	New Haven	AHL	64	3	11	14	26	3	0	1	1	2
	Richmond	ECHL	8	1	0	1	7	....	....	....	....	....

Signed as a free agent by **Carolina**, August 30, 1997.

PICARD, MICHEL (PEE-cahr) ST.L.

Left wing. Shoots left. 5'11", 190 lbs. Born, Beauport, Que., November 7, 1969.
(Hartford's 8th choice, 178th overall, in 1989 Entry Draft).

			Regular Season					Playoffs				
Season	Club	Lea	GP	G	A	TP	PIM	GP	G	A	TP	PIM
1986-87	Trois-Rivieres	QMJHL	66	33	35	68	53					
1987-88	Trois-Rivieres	QMJHL	69	40	55	95	71					
1988-89	Trois-Rivieres	QMJHL	66	59	81	140	170	4	1	3	4	2
1989-90	Binghamton	AHL	67	16	24	40	98					
1990-91	**Hartford**	**NHL**	**5**	**1**	**0**	**1**	**2**					
	Springfield	AHL	77	*56	40	96	61	18	8	13	21	18
1991-92	**Hartford**	**NHL**	**25**	**3**	**5**	**8**	**6**					
	Springfield	AHL	40	21	17	38	44	11	2	0	2	34
1992-93	**San Jose**	**NHL**	**25**	**4**	**0**	**4**	**24**					
	Kansas City	IHL	33	7	10	17	51	12	3	2	5	20
1993-94	Portland	AHL	61	41	44	85	99	17	11	10	21	22
1994-95	P.E.I.	AHL	57	32	57	89	58	8	4	4	8	6
	Ottawa	**NHL**	**24**	**5**	**8**	**13**	**14**					
1995-96	**Ottawa**	**NHL**	**17**	**2**	**6**	**8**	**10**					
	P.E.I.	AHL	55	37	45	82	79	5	5	1	6	2
1996-97	V. Frolunda	Sweden	3	0	1	1	0					
	Grand Rapids	IHL	82	46	55	101	58	5	2	0	2	10
1997-98	Grand Rapids	IHL	58	28	41	69	42					
	St. Louis	**NHL**	**16**	**1**	**8**	**9**	**29**					
	NHL Totals		**112**	**16**	**27**	**43**	**85**					

QMJHL Second All-Star Team (1989) • AHL First All-Star Team (1991, 1995) • AHL Second All-Star Team (1994) • IHL First All-Star Team (1997)

Traded to **San Jose** by **Hartford** for future considerations (Yvon Corriveau, January 21, 1993), October 9, 1992. Signed as a free agent by **Ottawa**, June 16, 1994. Traded to **Washington** by **Ottawa** for cash, May 21, 1996. Signed as a free agent by **St. Louis**, January 3, 1998.

PIETROPAULO, DIDIER (pee-EHT-roh-PAW-loh) S.J.

Defense. Shoots left. 6'1", 204 lbs. Born, Laval, Que., February 9, 1979.

			Regular Season					Playoffs				
Season	Club	Lea	GP	G	A	TP	PIM	GP	G	A	TP	PIM
1995-96	St-Hyacinthe	QMJHL	55	0	1	1	124					
1996-97	Rouyn-Noranda	QMJHL	33	1	2	3	145					
1997-98	Rouyn-Noranda	QMJHL	60	7	18	25	320	6	0	2	2	26

Signed as a free agent by **San Jose**, September 19, 1997.

PILON, RICHARD (PEE-lahn) NYI

Defense. Shoots left. 6', 205 lbs. Born, Saskatoon, Sask., April 30, 1968.
(NY Islanders' 9th choice, 143rd overall, in 1986 Entry Draft).

			Regular Season					Playoffs				
Season	Club	Lea	GP	G	A	TP	PIM	GP	G	A	TP	PIM
1985-86	Prince Albert	Midget	35	3	28	31	142					
1986-87	Prince Albert	WHL	68	4	21	25	192	7	1	6	7	17
1987-88	Prince Albert	WHL	65	13	34	47	177	9	0	6	6	38
1988-89	**NY Islanders**	**NHL**	**62**	**0**	**14**	**14**	**242**					
1989-90	**NY Islanders**	**NHL**	**14**	**0**	**2**	**2**	**31**					
1990-91	**NY Islanders**	**NHL**	**60**	**1**	**4**	**5**	**126**					
1991-92	**NY Islanders**	**NHL**	**65**	**1**	**6**	**7**	**183**					
1992-93	**NY Islanders**	**NHL**	**44**	**1**	**3**	**4**	**164**	**15**	**0**	**0**	**0**	**50**
	Capital District	AHL	6	0	1	1	8					
1993-94	**NY Islanders**	**NHL**	**28**	**1**	**4**	**5**	**75**					
	Salt Lake	IHL	2	0	0	0	8					
1994-95	**NY Islanders**	**NHL**	**20**	**1**	**1**	**2**	**40**					
1995-96	**NY Islanders**	**NHL**	**27**	**0**	**3**	**3**	**72**					
1996-97	**NY Islanders**	**NHL**	**52**	**1**	**4**	**5**	**179**					
1997-98	**NY Islanders**	**NHL**	**76**	**0**	**7**	**7**	**291**					
	NHL Totals		**448**	**6**	**48**	**54**	**1403**	**15**	**0**	**0**	**0**	**50**

WHL East Second All-Star Team (1988)

PIROS, KAMIL (PIH-ruhsh, KA-mihl) BUF.

Center. Shoots left. 6'1", 183 lbs. Born, Most, Czechoslovakia, November 20, 1978.
(Buffalo's 9th choice, 212th overall, in 1997 Entry Draft).

			Regular Season					Playoffs				
Season	Club	Lea	GP	G	A	TP	PIM	GP	G	A	TP	PIM
1993-94	Most	Czech-Jr.	16	12	10	22	....					
	Litvinov	Czech-Jr.	22	6	13	19	....					
1994-95	Litvinov	Czech-Jr.	40	27	16	43	....					
1995-96	Litvinov	Czech-Jr.	42	16	13	29	....					
1996-97	Litvinov	Cze-Rep.	38	4	9	13	10					
	Litvinov	Czech-Jr.	3	2	1	3	....					
1997-98	Litvinov	Cze-Rep.	14	0	1	1	2					

PISANI, FERNANDO EDM.

Center/left wing. Shoots left. 6'1", 180 lbs. Born, Edmonton, Alta., December 27, 1976.
(Edmonton's 9th choice, 195th overall, in 1996 Entry Draft).

			Regular Season					Playoffs				
Season	Club	Lea	GP	G	A	TP	PIM	GP	G	A	TP	PIM
1995-96	St. Albert	AJHL	58	40	63	103	134	18	7	22	29	28
1996-97	Providence	H.E.	35	12	18	30	36					
1997-98	Providence	H.E.	36	16	18	34	20					

PITLICK, LANCE (PIHT-lihk) OTT.

Defense. Shoots right. 6', 203 lbs. Born, Minneapolis, MN, November 5, 1967.
(Minnesota's 10th choice, 180th overall, in 1986 Entry Draft).

			Regular Season					Playoffs				
Season	Club	Lea	GP	G	A	TP	PIM	GP	G	A	TP	PIM
1985-86	Cooper High	H.S.	21	17	8	25	....					
1986-87	U. of Minnesota	WCHA	45	0	9	9	88					
1987-88	U. of Minnesota	WCHA	38	3	9	12	76					
1988-89	U. of Minnesota	WCHA	47	4	9	13	95					
1989-90	U. of Minnesota	WIAA	14	3	2	5	26					
1990-91	Hershey	AHL	64	6	15	21	75	3	0	0	0	9
1991-92	United States	Nat-Tm	19	0	1	1	38					
	Hershey	AHL	4	0	0	0	6	3	0	0	0	4
1992-93	Hershey	AHL	53	5	10	15	77					
1993-94	Hershey	AHL	58	4	13	17	93	11	1	0	1	11
1994-95	P.E.I.	AHL	61	8	19	27	55	11	1	4	5	10
	Ottawa	**NHL**	**15**	**0**	**1**	**1**	**6**					
1995-96	**Ottawa**	**NHL**	**28**	**1**	**6**	**7**	**20**					
	P.E.I.	AHL	29	4	10	14	39	5	0	0	0	0
1996-97	**Ottawa**	**NHL**	**66**	**5**	**5**	**10**	**91**	**7**	**0**	**0**	**0**	**4**
1997-98	**Ottawa**	**NHL**	**69**	**2**	**7**	**9**	**50**	**11**	**0**	**1**	**1**	**17**
	NHL Totals		**178**	**8**	**19**	**27**	**167**	**18**	**0**	**1**	**1**	**21**

Signed as a free agent by **Philadelphia**, September 5, 1990. Signed as a free agent by **Ottawa**, June 22, 1994.

PITTIS, DOMENIC BUF.

Center. Shoots left. 5'11", 190 lbs. Born, Calgary, Alta., October 1, 1974.
(Pittsburgh's 2nd choice, 52nd overall, in 1993 Entry Draft).

			Regular Season					Playoffs				
Season	Club	Lea	GP	G	A	TP	PIM	GP	G	A	TP	PIM
1991-92	Lethbridge	WHL	65	6	17	23	48	5	0	2	2	4
1992-93	Lethbridge	WHL	66	46	73	119	69	4	3	3	6	8
1993-94	Lethbridge	WHL	72	58	69	127	93	8	4	11	15	16
1994-95	Cleveland	IHL	62	18	32	50	66	3	0	2	2	2
1995-96	Cleveland	IHL	74	10	28	38	100	3	0	0	0	2
1996-97	**Pittsburgh**	**NHL**	**1**	**0**	**0**	**0**	**0**					
	Long Beach	IHL	65	23	43	66	91	18	5	9	14	26
1997-98	Syracuse	AHL	75	23	41	64	90	5	1	3	4	4
	NHL Totals		**1**	**0**	**0**	**0**	**0**					

WHL East Second All-Star Team (1994)

Signed as a free agent by **Buffalo**, August 10, 1998.

PIVONKA, MICHAL (pih-VAHN-kuh) WSH.

Center. Shoots left. 6'2", 195 lbs. Born, Kladno, Czech., January 28, 1966.
(Washington's 3rd choice, 59th overall, in 1984 Entry Draft).

			Regular Season					Playoffs				
Season	Club	Lea	GP	G	A	TP	PIM	GP	G	A	TP	PIM
1984-85	Dukla Jihlava	Czech.	33	8	11	19	18					
1985-86	Dukla Jihlava	Czech.	42	5	13	18	18					
1986-87	**Washington**	**NHL**	**73**	**18**	**25**	**43**	**41**	**7**	**1**	**1**	**2**	**2**
1987-88	**Washington**	**NHL**	**71**	**11**	**23**	**34**	**28**	**14**	**4**	**9**	**13**	**4**
1988-89	**Washington**	**NHL**	**52**	**8**	**19**	**27**	**30**	**6**	**3**	**1**	**4**	**10**
	Baltimore	AHL	31	12	24	36	19					
1989-90	**Washington**	**NHL**	**77**	**25**	**39**	**64**	**54**	**11**	**0**	**2**	**2**	**6**
1990-91	**Washington**	**NHL**	**79**	**20**	**50**	**70**	**34**	**11**	**2**	**3**	**5**	**8**
1991-92	**Washington**	**NHL**	**80**	**23**	**57**	**80**	**47**	**7**	**1**	**5**	**6**	**13**
1992-93	**Washington**	**NHL**	**69**	**21**	**53**	**74**	**66**	**6**	**0**	**2**	**2**	**0**
1993-94	**Washington**	**NHL**	**82**	**14**	**36**	**50**	**38**	**7**	**4**	**4**	**8**	**4**
1994-95	Klagenfurt	Austria	7	2	4	6	4					
	Washington	**NHL**	**46**	**10**	**23**	**33**	**50**	**7**	**1**	**4**	**5**	**21**
1995-96	Detroit	IHL	7	1	9	10	19					
	Washington	**NHL**	**73**	**16**	**65**	**81**	**36**	**6**	**3**	**2**	**5**	**18**
1996-97	**Washington**	**NHL**	**54**	**7**	**16**	**23**	**22**					
1997-98	**Washington**	**NHL**	**33**	**3**	**6**	**9**	**20**	**13**	**0**	**3**	**3**	**0**
	NHL Totals		**789**	**176**	**412**	**588**	**466**	**95**	**19**	**36**	**55**	**86**

PLANTE, DAN (PLAHNT)

Right wing. Shoots right. 5'11", 202 lbs. Born, Hayward, WI, October 5, 1971.
(NY Islanders' 3rd choice, 48th overall, in 1990 Entry Draft).

			Regular Season					Playoffs				
Season	Club	Lea	GP	G	A	TP	PIM	GP	G	A	TP	PIM
1989-90	Edina High	H.S.	24	8	18	26	12					
1990-91	U. of Wisconsin	WCHA	33	1	2	3	54					
1991-92	U. of Wisconsin	WCHA	36	13	13	26	107					
1992-93	U. of Wisconsin	WCHA	42	26	31	57	142					
1993-94	**NY Islanders**	**NHL**	**12**	**0**	**1**	**1**	**4**	**1**	**1**	**0**	**1**	**2**
	Salt Lake	IHL	66	7	17	24	148					
1994-95	Denver	IHL	2	0	0	0	4					
1995-96	**NY Islanders**	**NHL**	**73**	**5**	**3**	**8**	**50**					
1996-97	**NY Islanders**	**NHL**	**67**	**4**	**9**	**13**	**75**					
1997-98	**NY Islanders**	**NHL**	**7**	**0**	**1**	**1**	**6**					
	Utah	IHL	73	22	27	49	125	4	0	2	2	14
	NHL Totals		**159**	**9**	**14**	**23**	**135**	**1**	**1**	**0**	**1**	**2**

PLANTE, DEREK (PLAHNT) BUF.

Center. Shoots left. 5'11", 181 lbs. Born, Cloquet, MN, January 17, 1971.
(Buffalo's 7th choice, 161st overall, in 1989 Entry Draft).

			Regular Season					Playoffs				
Season	Club	Lea	GP	G	A	TP	PIM	GP	G	A	TP	PIM
1988-89	Cloquet High	H.S.	24	30	33	63	....					
1989-90	U. Minn-Duluth	WCHA	28	10	11	21	12					
1990-91	U. Minn-Duluth	WCHA	36	23	20	43	6					
1991-92	U. Minn-Duluth	WCHA	37	27	36	63	28					
1992-93	U. Minn-Duluth	WCHA	37	*36	*56	*92	30					
1993-94	**Buffalo**	**NHL**	**77**	**21**	**35**	**56**	**24**	**7**	**1**	**0**	**1**	**0**
	United States	Nat-Tm	2	0	1	1	0					
1994-95	**Buffalo**	**NHL**	**47**	**3**	**19**	**22**	**12**					
1995-96	**Buffalo**	**NHL**	**76**	**23**	**33**	**56**	**28**					
1996-97	**Buffalo**	**NHL**	**82**	**27**	**26**	**53**	**24**	**12**	**4**	**6**	**10**	**4**
1997-98	**Buffalo**	**NHL**	**72**	**13**	**21**	**34**	**26**	**11**	**0**	**3**	**3**	**10**
	NHL Totals		**354**	**87**	**134**	**221**	**114**	**30**	**5**	**9**	**14**	**14**

WCHA Second All-Star Team (1992) • WCHA First All-Star Team (1993) • NCAA West First All-American Team (1993)

PLEKHANOV, DMITRI (plih-KHAH-nahv) ST.L.

Defense. Shoots left. 6'2", 176 lbs. Born, Nizhnekamsk, USSR, March 13, 1978.
(St. Louis' 8th choice, 232nd overall, in 1997 Entry Draft).

			Regular Season					Playoffs				
Season	Club	Lea	GP	G	A	TP	PIM	GP	G	A	TP	PIM
1995-96	Nizhnekamsk	CIS	30	1	2	3	28					
1996-97	Nizhnekamsk	Russia	26	0	0	0	18	2	0	0	0	2
1997-98	Nizhnekamsk	Russia	18	0	0	0	6					

POAPST, STEVE (POHPST)

Defense. Shoots left. 6', 200 lbs. Born, Cornwall, Ont., January 3, 1969.

			Regular Season					Playoffs				
Season	Club	Lea	GP	G	A	TP	PIM	GP	G	A	TP	PIM
1987-88	Colgate	ECAC	32	3	13	16	22					
1988-89	Colgate	ECAC	30	0	5	5	38					
1989-90	Colgate	ECAC	38	4	15	19	54					
1990-91	Colgate	ECAC	32	6	15	21	43					
1991-92	Hampton Roads	ECHL	55	8	20	28	29	14	1	4	5	12
1992-93	Hampton Roads	ECHL	63	10	35	45	57	4	0	1	1	4
	Baltimore	AHL	7	0	1	1	4	7	0	3	3	6
1993-94	Portland	AHL	78	14	21	35	47	12	0	3	3	8
1994-95	Portland	AHL	71	8	22	30	60	7	0	1	1	16
1995-96	**Washington**	**NHL**	**3**	**1**	**0**	**1**	**0**	**6**	**0**	**0**	**0**	**0**
	Portland	AHL	70	10	24	34	79	20	2	6	8	16
1996-97	Portland	AHL	47	1	20	21	34	5	0	1	1	6
1997-98	Portland	AHL	76	8	29	37	46	10	2	3	5	8
	NHL Totals		**3**	**1**	**0**	**1**	**0**	**6**	**0**	**0**	**0**	**0**

ECHL First All-Star Team (1993)

Signed as a free agent by **Washington**, February 4, 1995.

PODEIN, SHJON (poh-DEEN, SHAWN) PHI.

Left wing. Shoots left. 6'2", 200 lbs. Born, Rochester, MN, March 5, 1968.
(Edmonton's 9th choice, 166th overall, in 1988 Entry Draft).

			Regular Season					Playoffs				
Season	Club	Lea	GP	G	A	TP	PIM	GP	G	A	TP	PIM
1987-88	U. Minn-Duluth	WCHA	30	4	4	8	48	....	....	....	....	....
1988-89	U. Minn-Duluth	WCHA	36	7	5	12	46	....	....	....	....	....
1989-90	U. Minn-Duluth	WCHA	35	21	18	39	36	....	....	....	....	....
1990-91	Cape Breton	AHL	63	14	15	29	65	4	0	0	0	5
1991-92	Cape Breton	AHL	80	30	24	54	46	5	3	1	4	2
1992-93	**Edmonton**	**NHL**	**40**	**13**	**6**	**19**	**25**	....	....	....	....	....
	Cape Breton	AHL	38	18	21	39	32	9	2	2	4	29
1993-94	**Edmonton**	**NHL**	**28**	**3**	**5**	**8**	**8**	....	....	....	....	....
	Cape Breton	AHL	5	4	4	8	4	....	....	....	....	....
1994-95	**Philadelphia**	**NHL**	**44**	**3**	**7**	**10**	**33**	**15**	**1**	**3**	**4**	**10**
1995-96	**Philadelphia**	**NHL**	**79**	**15**	**10**	**25**	**89**	**12**	**1**	**2**	**3**	**50**
1996-97	**Philadelphia**	**NHL**	**82**	**14**	**18**	**32**	**41**	**19**	**4**	**3**	**7**	**16**
1997-98	**Philadelphia**	**NHL**	**82**	**11**	**13**	**24**	**53**	**5**	**0**	**0**	**0**	**10**
	NHL Totals		**355**	**59**	**59**	**118**	**249**	**51**	**6**	**8**	**14**	**86**

Signed as a free agent by **Philadelphia**, July 27, 1994.

PODKONICKY, ANDREJ (pohd-koh-NIHTZ-kee) ST.L.

Center. Shoots left. 6', 174 lbs. Born, Zvolen, Czech., May 9, 1978.
(St. Louis' 8th choice, 196th overall, in 1996 Entry Draft).

			Regular Season					Playoffs				
Season	Club	Lea	GP	G	A	TP	PIM	GP	G	A	TP	PIM
1994-95	Zvolen	Slovak-2	17	0	4	4	6	....	....	....	....	....
1995-96	Zvolen	Slovak-2	38	18	12	30	18	....	....	....	....	....
1996-97	Portland	WHL	71	25	46	71	127	6	1	1	2	8
1997-98	Portland	WHL	64	30	44	74	81	16	4	12	16	20

Memorial Cup All-Star Team (1998) • Won Ed Chynoweth Award (Memorial Cup Tournament Top Scorer) (1998)

PODOLLAN, JASON (poh-DOH-luhn) TOR.

Right wing. Shoots right. 6'1", 192 lbs. Born, Vernon, B.C., February 18, 1976.
(Florida's 3rd choice, 31st overall, in 1994 Entry Draft).

			Regular Season					Playoffs				
Season	Club	Lea	GP	G	A	TP	PIM	GP	G	A	TP	PIM
1991-92	Spokane	WHL	2	0	0	0	2	10	3	1	4	16
1992-93	Spokane	WHL	72	36	33	69	108	10	4	4	8	14
1993-94	Spokane	WHL	69	29	37	66	108	3	3	0	3	2
1994-95	Spokane	WHL	72	43	41	84	102	11	5	7	12	18
	Cincinnati	IHL	....	....	....	....	....	3	0	0	0	2
1995-96	Spokane	WHL	56	37	25	62	103	18	*21	12	33	28
1996-97	**Florida**	**NHL**	**19**	**1**	**1**	**2**	**4**	....	....	....	....	....
	Carolina	AHL	39	21	25	46	36	....	....	....	....	....
	Toronto	**NHL**	**10**	**0**	**3**	**3**	**6**	....	....	....	....	....
	St. John's	AHL	....	....	....	....	....	11	2	3	5	6
1997-98	St. John's	AHL	70	30	31	61	116	4	1	0	1	10
	NHL Totals		**29**	**1**	**4**	**5**	**10**	....	....	....	....	....

WHL West Second All-Star Team (1996)
Traded to **Toronto** by **Florida** for Kirk Muller, March 18, 1997.

POESCHEK, RUDY (POH-shehk) ST.L.

Right wing/Defense. Shoots right. 6'2", 218 lbs. Born, Kamloops, B.C., September 29, 1966.
(NY Rangers' 12th choice, 238th overall, in 1985 Entry Draft).

			Regular Season					Playoffs				
Season	Club	Lea	GP	G	A	TP	PIM	GP	G	A	TP	PIM
1983-84	Kamloops	WHL	47	3	9	12	93	8	0	2	2	7
1984-85	Kamloops	WHL	34	6	7	13	100	15	0	3	3	56
1985-86	Kamloops	WHL	32	3	13	16	92	16	3	7	10	40
1986-87	Kamloops	WHL	54	13	18	31	153	15	2	4	6	37
1987-88	**NY Rangers**	**NHL**	**1**	**0**	**0**	**0**	**2**	....	....	....	....	....
	Colorado	IHL	82	7	31	38	210	12	2	2	4	31
1988-89	**NY Rangers**	**NHL**	**52**	**0**	**2**	**2**	**199**	....	....	....	....	....
	Colorado	IHL	2	0	0	0	6	....	....	....	....	....
1989-90	**NY Rangers**	**NHL**	**15**	**0**	**0**	**0**	**55**	....	....	....	....	....
	Flint	IHL	38	8	13	21	109	4	0	0	0	16
1990-91	Binghamton	AHL	38	1	3	4	162	....	....	....	....	....
	Winnipeg	**NHL**	**1**	**0**	**0**	**0**	**5**	....	....	....	....	....
	Moncton	AHL	23	2	4	6	67	9	1	1	2	41
1991-92	**Winnipeg**	**NHL**	**4**	**0**	**0**	**0**	**17**	....	....	....	....	....
	Moncton	AHL	63	4	18	22	170	11	0	2	2	48
1992-93	St. John's	AHL	78	7	24	31	189	9	0	4	4	13
1993-94	**Tampa Bay**	**NHL**	**71**	**3**	**6**	**9**	**118**	....	....	....	....	....
1994-95	**Tampa Bay**	**NHL**	**25**	**1**	**1**	**2**	**92**	....	....	....	....	....
1995-96	**Tampa Bay**	**NHL**	**57**	**1**	**3**	**4**	**88**	**3**	**0**	**0**	**0**	**12**
1996-97	**Tampa Bay**	**NHL**	**60**	**0**	**6**	**6**	**120**	....	....	....	....	....
1997-98	**St. Louis**	**NHL**	**50**	**1**	**7**	**8**	**64**	**2**	**0**	**0**	**0**	**6**
	NHL Totals		**336**	**6**	**25**	**31**	**760**	**5**	**0**	**0**	**0**	**18**

Traded to **Winnipeg** by **NY Rangers** for Guy Larose, January 22, 1991. Signed as a free agent by **Toronto**, July 8, 1992. Signed as a free agent by **Tampa Bay**, August 10, 1993. Signed as a free agent by **St. Louis**, July 31, 1997.

POLLOCK, JAME ST.L.

Defense. Shoots right. 6'1", 190 lbs. Born, Quebec City, Que., June 16, 1979.
(St. Louis' 4th choice, 106th overall, in 1997 Entry Draft).

			Regular Season					Playoffs				
Season	Club	Lea	GP	G	A	TP	PIM	GP	G	A	TP	PIM
1995-96	Seattle	WHL	32	0	1	1	15	....	....	....	....	....
1996-97	Seattle	WHL	66	15	19	34	94	15	3	5	8	16
1997-98	Seattle	WHL	66	11	36	47	78	5	0	1	1	17

PONIKAROVSKY, ALEXEI (poh-NIH-kahr-ohv-skee) TOR.

Right wing. Shoots left. 6'4", 196 lbs. Born, Kiev, USSR, April 9, 1980.
(Toronto's 4th choice, 87th overall, in 1998 Entry Draft).

			Regular Season					Playoffs				
Season	Club	Lea	GP	G	A	TP	PIM	GP	G	A	TP	PIM
1995-96	Moscow D'amo	Rus-Jr.	70	14	10	24	20	....	....	....	....	....
1996-97	Moscow D'amo	Rus-Jr.	60	12	15	27	30	....	....	....	....	....
	Moscow D'amo 2	Russia-3	2	0	0	0	2	....	....	....	....	....
1997-98	Moscow D'amo 2	Russia-2	24	1	2	3	30	....	....	....	....	....

POPOVIC, PETER (puh-PUH-vihch) NYR

Defense. Shoots left. 6'6", 235 lbs. Born, Koping, Sweden, February 10, 1968.
(Montreal's 5th choice, 93rd overall, in 1988 Entry Draft).

			Regular Season					Playoffs				
Season	Club	Lea	GP	G	A	TP	PIM	GP	G	A	TP	PIM
1986-87	Vasteras IK	Sweden-2	24	1	2	3	10	....	....	....	....	....
1987-88	Vasteras IK	Sweden-2	28	3	17	20	16	....	....	....	....	....
1988-89	Vasteras IK	Sweden	22	1	4	5	32	....	....	....	....	....
1989-90	Vasteras IK	Sweden	30	2	10	12	24	2	0	1	1	2
1990-91	Vasteras IK	Sweden	40	3	2	5	62	4	0	0	0	4
1991-92	Vasteras IK	Sweden	34	7	10	17	30	....	....	....	....	....
1992-93	Vasteras IK	Sweden	39	6	12	18	46	3	0	1	1	2
1993-94	**Montreal**	**NHL**	**47**	**2**	**12**	**14**	**26**	**6**	**0**	**1**	**1**	**0**
1994-95	Vasteras IK	Sweden	11	0	3	3	10	....	....	....	....	....
	Montreal	**NHL**	**33**	**0**	**5**	**5**	**8**	....	....	....	....	....
1995-96	**Montreal**	**NHL**	**76**	**2**	**12**	**14**	**69**	**6**	**0**	**2**	**2**	**4**
1996-97	**Montreal**	**NHL**	**78**	**1**	**13**	**14**	**32**	**3**	**0**	**0**	**0**	**2**
1997-98	**Montreal**	**NHL**	**69**	**2**	**6**	**8**	**38**	**10**	**1**	**1**	**2**	**2**
	NHL Totals		**303**	**7**	**48**	**55**	**173**	**25**	**1**	**4**	**5**	**8**

Traded to **NY Rangers** by **Montreal** for Sylvain Blouin and NY Rangers' 6th round choice in 1999 Entry Draft, June 30, 1998.

POSMYK, MAREK (PAWZ-mihk) TOR.

Defense. Shoots right. 6'5", 220 lbs. Born, Jihlava, Czech., September 15, 1978.
(Toronto's 1st choice, 36th overall, in 1996 Entry Draft).

			Regular Season					Playoffs				
Season	Club	Lea	GP	G	A	TP	PIM	GP	G	A	TP	PIM
1994-95	Dukla Jihlava	Czech-Jr.	16	1	3	4	....	....	....	....	....	....
1995-96	Dukla Jihlava	Czech-Jr.	16	6	5	11	....	....	....	....	....	....
	Dukla Jihlava	Cze-Rep.	18	1	2	3	....	1	0	0	0	....
1996-97	Dukla Jihlava	Cze-Rep.	24	1	7	8	44	....	....	....	....	....
	St. John's	AHL	2	0	0	0	2	....	....	....	....	....
1997-98	Sarnia	OHL	48	8	16	24	94	5	0	2	2	6
	St. John's	AHL	3	0	0	0	4	....	....	....	....	....

POTI, TOM (POH-tee) EDM.

Defense. Shoots left. 6'3", 215 lbs. Born, Worcester, MA, March 22, 1977.
(Edmonton's 4th choice, 59th overall, in 1996 Entry Draft).

			Regular Season					Playoffs				
Season	Club	Lea	GP	G	A	TP	PIM	GP	G	A	TP	PIM
1995-96	Cushing Academy	H.S.	29	14	59	73	18	....	....	....	....	....
1996-97	Boston University	H.E.	38	4	17	21	54	....	....	....	....	....
1997-98	Boston University	H.E.	38	13	29	42	60	....	....	....	....	....

NCAA Championship All-Tournament Team (1997) • Hockey East First All-Star Team (1998) • NCAA East First All-American Team (1998)

POTOMSKI, BARRY (poh-TAWM-skee) DET.

Left wing. Shoots left. 6'2", 215 lbs. Born, Windsor, Ont., November 24, 1972.

			Regular Season					Playoffs				
Season	Club	Lea	GP	G	A	TP	PIM	GP	G	A	TP	PIM
1989-90	London	OHL	9	0	2	2	18	....	....	....	....	....
1990-91	London	OHL	65	14	17	31	202	7	0	2	2	10
1991-92	London	OHL	61	19	32	51	224	10	5	1	6	22
1992-93	Erie	ECHL	5	1	1	2	31	....	....	....	....	....
	Toledo	ECHL	43	5	18	23	184	14	5	2	7	73
1993-94	Toledo	ECHL	13	9	4	13	81	....	....	....	....	....
	Adirondack	AHL	50	9	5	14	224	11	1	1	2	44
1994-95	Phoenix	IHL	42	5	6	11	171	....	....	....	....	....
1995-96	**Los Angeles**	**NHL**	**33**	**3**	**2**	**5**	**104**	....	....	....	....	....
	Phoenix	IHL	24	5	2	7	74	3	1	0	1	8
1996-97	**Los Angeles**	**NHL**	**26**	**3**	**2**	**5**	**93**	....	....	....	....	....
	Phoenix	IHL	28	2	11	13	58	....	....	....	....	....
1997-98	**San Jose**	**NHL**	**9**	**0**	**1**	**1**	**30**	....	....	....	....	....
	Las Vegas	IHL	31	3	2	5	143	4	1	0	1	13
	NHL Totals		**68**	**6**	**5**	**11**	**227**	....	....	....	....	....

Signed as a free agent by **LA Kings**, July 7, 1994. Signed as a free agent by **San Jose**, August 15, 1997. Signed as a free agent by **Detroit**, August 13, 1998.

POTVIN, MARC (PAHT-vahn)

Right wing. Shoots right. 6'1", 200 lbs. Born, Ottawa, Ont., January 29, 1967.
(Detroit's 9th choice, 169th overall, in 1986 Entry Draft).

			Regular Season					Playoffs				
Season	Club	Lea	GP	G	A	TP	PIM	GP	G	A	TP	PIM
1985-86	Stratford	OJHL	63	5	6	11	117	....	....	....	....	....
1986-87	Bowling Green	CCHA	43	5	15	20	74	....	....	....	....	....
1987-88	Bowling Green	CCHA	45	15	21	36	80	....	....	....	....	....
1988-89	Bowling Green	CCHA	46	23	12	35	63	....	....	....	....	....
1989-90	Bowling Green	CCHA	40	19	17	36	72	....	....	....	....	....
	Adirondack	AHL	5	2	1	3	9	4	0	1	1	23
1990-91	**Detroit**	**NHL**	**9**	**0**	**0**	**0**	**55**	**6**	**0**	**0**	**0**	**32**
	Adirondack	AHL	63	9	13	22	*365	....	....	....	....	....
1991-92	**Detroit**	**NHL**	**5**	**1**	**0**	**1**	**52**	**1**	**0**	**0**	**0**	**0**
	Adirondack	AHL	51	13	16	29	314	19	5	4	9	57
1992-93	Adirondack	AHL	37	8	12	20	109	....	....	....	....	....
	Los Angeles	**NHL**	**20**	**0**	**1**	**1**	**61**	**1**	**0**	**0**	**0**	**0**
1993-94	**Los Angeles**	**NHL**	**3**	**0**	**0**	**0**	**26**	....	....	....	....	....
	Hartford	**NHL**	**51**	**2**	**3**	**5**	**246**	....	....	....	....	....
1994-95	**Boston**	**NHL**	**6**	**0**	**1**	**1**	**4**	....	....	....	....	....
	Providence	AHL	21	4	14	18	84	12	2	4	6	25
1995-96	**Boston**	**NHL**	**27**	**0**	**0**	**0**	**12**	**5**	**0**	**1**	**1**	**18**
	Providence	AHL	48	9	9	18	118	....	....	....	....	....
1996-97	Portland	AHL	71	17	15	32	222	5	0	0	0	12
1997-98	Chicago	IHL	81	4	8	12	170	10	0	0	0	22
	NHL Totals		**121**	**3**	**5**	**8**	**456**	**13**	**0**	**1**	**1**	**50**

Traded to **LA Kings** by **Detroit** with Jimmy Carson and Gary Shuchuk for Paul Coffey, Sylvain Couturier and Jim Hiller, January 29, 1993. Traded to **Hartford** by **LA Kings** for Doug Houda, November 3, 1993. Signed as a free agent by **Boston**, June 29, 1994.

POULIN, PATRICK (poo-LIHN) MTL.

Left wing. Shoots left. 6'1", 210 lbs. Born, Vanier, Que., April 23, 1973.
(Hartford's 1st choice, 9th overall, in 1991 Entry Draft).

			Regular Season					Playoffs				
Season	Club	Lea	GP	G	A	TP	PIM	GP	G	A	TP	PIM
1989-90	St-Hyacinthe	QMJHL	60	25	26	51	55	12	1	9	10	5
1990-91	St-Hyacinthe	QMJHL	56	32	38	70	82	4	0	2	2	23
1991-92	St-Hyacinthe	QMJHL	56	52	86	*138	58	5	2	2	4	4
	Hartford	**NHL**	**1**	**0**	**0**	**0**	**2**	**7**	**2**	**1**	**3**	**0**
	Springfield	AHL	....	....	....	....	....	1	0	0	0	0
1992-93	**Hartford**	**NHL**	**81**	**20**	**31**	**51**	**37**	....	....	....	....	....
1993-94	**Hartford**	**NHL**	**9**	**2**	**1**	**3**	**11**	....	....	....	....	....
	Chicago	**NHL**	**58**	**12**	**13**	**25**	**40**	**4**	**0**	**0**	**0**	**0**
1994-95	**Chicago**	**NHL**	**45**	**15**	**15**	**30**	**53**	**16**	**4**	**1**	**5**	**8**
1995-96	**Chicago**	**NHL**	**38**	**7**	**8**	**15**	**16**	....	....	....	....	....
	Indianapolis	IHL	1	0	1	1	0	....	....	....	....	....
	Tampa Bay	**NHL**	**8**	**0**	**1**	**1**	**0**	**2**	**0**	**0**	**0**	**0**
1996-97	**Tampa Bay**	**NHL**	**73**	**12**	**14**	**26**	**56**	....	....	....	....	....
1997-98	**Tampa Bay**	**NHL**	**44**	**2**	**7**	**9**	**19**	....	....	....	....	....
	Montreal	**NHL**	**34**	**4**	**6**	**10**	**8**	**3**	**0**	**0**	**0**	**0**
	NHL Totals		**391**	**74**	**96**	**170**	**242**	**32**	**6**	**2**	**8**	**8**

QMJHL First All-Star Team (1992) • Canadian Major Junior Player of the Year (1992)

Traded to **Chicago** by **Hartford** with Eric Weinrich for Steve Larmer and Bryan Marchment, November 2, 1993. Traded to **Tampa Bay** by **Chicago** with Igor Ulanov and Chicago's 2nd round choice (later traded to New Jersey — New Jersey selected Pierre Dagenais) in 1996 Entry Draft for Enrico Ciccone and Tampa Bay's 2nd round choice (Jeff Paul) in 1996 Entry Draft, March 20, 1996. Traded to **Montreal** by **Tampa Bay** with Mick Vukota and Igor Ulanov for Stephane Richer, Darcy Tucker and David Wilkie, January 15, 1998.

PRATT, HARLAN PIT.

Defense. Shoots right. 6'2", 191 lbs. Born, Fort McMurray, Alta., December 10, 1978.
(Pittsburgh's 5th choice, 124th overall, in 1997 Entry Draft).

			Regular Season					Playoffs				
Season	Club	Lea	GP	G	A	TP	PIM	GP	G	A	TP	PIM
1994-95	Seattle	WHL	33	1	0	1	17	1	0	0	0	0
1995-96	Red Deer	WHL	60	2	3	5	22	10	0	0	0	4
1996-97	Red Deer	WHL	2	0	0	0	2	....	....	....	....	....
	Prince Albert	WHL	65	7	26	33	49	4	1	1	2	4
1997-98	Prince Albert	WHL	37	6	14	20	12	....	....	....	....	....
	Regina	WHL	24	2	6	8	23	9	2	2	4	2

PRATT, NOLAN CAR.

Defense. Shoots left. 6'2", 195 lbs. Born, Fort McMurray, Alta., August 14, 1975.
(Hartford's 4th choice, 115th overall, in 1993 Entry Draft).

			Regular Season					Playoffs				
Season	Club	Lea	GP	G	A	TP	PIM	GP	G	A	TP	PIM
1991-92	Portland	WHL	22	2	9	11	13	6	1	3	4	12
1992-93	Portland	WHL	70	4	19	23	97	16	2	7	9	31
1993-94	Portland	WHL	72	4	32	36	105	10	1	2	3	14
1994-95	Portland	WHL	72	6	37	43	196	9	1	6	7	10
1995-96	Springfield	AHL	62	2	6	8	72	2	0	0	0	0
	Richmond	ECHL	4	1	0	1	2	....	....	....	....	....
1996-97	**Hartford**	**NHL**	**9**	**0**	**2**	**2**	**6**	....	....	....	....	....
	Springfield	AHL	66	1	18	19	127	17	0	3	3	18
1997-98	**Carolina**	**NHL**	**23**	**0**	**2**	**2**	**44**	....	....	....	....	....
	New Haven	AHL	54	3	15	18	135	....	....	....	....	....
	NHL Totals		**32**	**0**	**4**	**4**	**50**	....	....	....	....	....

Transferred to **Carolina** after **Hartford** franchise relocated, June 25, 1997.

PRIER, BOB (PRIGH-uhr) BOS.

Right wing. Shoots right. 6'1", 210 lbs. Born, Pembroke, Ont., August 5, 1976.
(Boston's 9th choice, 208th overall, in 1996 Entry Draft).

			Regular Season					Playoffs				
Season	Club	Lea	GP	G	A	TP	PIM	GP	G	A	TP	PIM
1995-96	St. Lawrence	ECAC	32	10	8	18	31	....	....	....	....	....
1996-97	St. Lawrence	ECAC	33	15	9	24	14	....	....	....	....	....
1997-98	St. Lawrence	ECAC	31	15	13	28	34	....	....	....	....	....

PRIMEAU, KEITH (PREE-moh) CAR.

Center. Shoots left. 6'4", 210 lbs. Born, Toronto, Ont., November 24, 1971.
(Detroit's 1st choice, 3rd overall, in 1990 Entry Draft).

			Regular Season					Playoffs				
Season	Club	Lea	GP	G	A	TP	PIM	GP	G	A	TP	PIM
1987-88	Hamilton	OHL	47	6	6	12	69	11	0	2	2	2
1988-89	Niagara Falls	OHL	48	20	35	55	56	17	9	16	25	12
1989-90	Niagara Falls	OHL	65	*57	70	*127	97	16	*16	17	*33	49
1990-91	**Detroit**	**NHL**	**58**	**3**	**12**	**15**	**106**	**5**	**1**	**1**	**2**	**25**
	Adirondack	AHL	6	3	5	8	8	....	....	....	....	....
1991-92	**Detroit**	**NHL**	**35**	**6**	**10**	**16**	**83**	**11**	**0**	**0**	**0**	**14**
	Adirondack	AHL	42	21	24	45	89	9	1	7	8	27
1992-93	**Detroit**	**NHL**	**73**	**15**	**17**	**32**	**152**	**7**	**0**	**2**	**2**	**26**
1993-94	**Detroit**	**NHL**	**78**	**31**	**42**	**73**	**173**	**7**	**0**	**2**	**2**	**6**
1994-95	**Detroit**	**NHL**	**45**	**15**	**27**	**42**	**99**	**17**	**4**	**5**	**9**	**45**
1995-96	**Detroit**	**NHL**	**74**	**27**	**25**	**52**	**168**	**17**	**1**	**4**	**5**	**28**
1996-97	**Hartford**	**NHL**	**75**	**26**	**25**	**51**	**161**	....	....	....	....	....
1997-98	**Carolina**	**NHL**	**81**	**26**	**37**	**63**	**110**	....	....	....	....	....
	Canada	Olympics	6	2	1	3	4	....	....	....	....	....
	NHL Totals		**519**	**149**	**195**	**344**	**1052**	**64**	**6**	**14**	**20**	**144**

OHL Second All-Star Team (1990)

Traded to **Hartford** by **Detroit** with Paul Coffey and Detroit's 1st round choice (Nikos Tselios) in 1997 Entry Draft for Brendan Shanahan and Brian Glynn, October 9, 1996. Transferred to **Carolina** after **Hartford** franchise relocated, June 25, 1997.

PRIMEAU, WAYNE (PREE-moh) BUF.

Center. Shoots left. 6'3", 220 lbs. Born, Scarborough, Ont., June 4, 1976.
(Buffalo's 1st choice, 17th overall, in 1994 Entry Draft).

			Regular Season					Playoffs				
Season	Club	Lea	GP	G	A	TP	PIM	GP	G	A	TP	PIM
1992-93	Owen Sound	OHL	66	10	27	37	108	8	1	4	5	0
1993-94	Owen Sound	OHL	65	25	50	75	75	9	1	6	7	8
1994-95	Owen Sound	OHL	66	34	62	96	84	10	4	9	13	15
	Buffalo	**NHL**	**1**	**1**	**0**	**1**	**0**	....	....	....	....	....
1995-96	Owen Sound	OHL	28	15	29	44	52	....	....	....	....	....
	Oshawa	OHL	24	12	13	25	33	3	2	3	5	2
	Buffalo	**NHL**	**2**	**0**	**0**	**0**	**0**	....	....	....	....	....
	Rochester	AHL	8	2	3	5	6	17	3	1	4	11
1996-97	**Buffalo**	**NHL**	**45**	**2**	**4**	**6**	**64**	**9**	**0**	**0**	**0**	**6**
	Rochester	AHL	24	9	5	14	27	1	0	0	0	0
1997-98	**Buffalo**	**NHL**	**69**	**6**	**6**	**12**	**87**	**14**	**1**	**3**	**4**	**6**
	NHL Totals		**117**	**9**	**10**	**19**	**151**	**23**	**1**	**3**	**4**	**12**

PROBERT, BOB (PROH-buhrt) CHI.

Left wing. Shoots left. 6'3", 225 lbs. Born, Windsor, Ont., June 5, 1965.
(Detroit's 3rd choice, 46th overall, in 1983 Entry Draft).

			Regular Season					Playoffs				
Season	Club	Lea	GP	G	A	TP	PIM	GP	G	A	TP	PIM
1982-83	Brantford	OHL	51	12	16	28	133	8	2	2	4	23
1983-84	Brantford	OHL	65	35	28	63	189	6	0	3	3	16
1984-85	Hamilton	OHL	4	0	1	1	21	....	....	....	....	....
	S.S. Marie	OHL	44	20	52	72	172	15	6	11	17	60
1985-86	**Detroit**	**NHL**	**44**	**8**	**13**	**21**	**186**	....	....	....	....	....
	Adirondack	AHL	32	12	15	27	152	10	2	3	5	68
1986-87	**Detroit**	**NHL**	**63**	**13**	**11**	**24**	**221**	**16**	**3**	**4**	**7**	**63**
	Adirondack	AHL	7	1	4	5	15	....	....	....	....	....
1987-88	**Detroit**	**NHL**	**74**	**29**	**33**	**62**	***398**	**16**	**8**	**13**	**21**	**51**
1988-89	**Detroit**	**NHL**	**25**	**4**	**2**	**6**	**106**	....	....	....	....	....
1989-90	**Detroit**	**NHL**	**4**	**3**	**0**	**3**	**21**	....	....	....	....	....
1990-91	**Detroit**	**NHL**	**55**	**16**	**23**	**39**	**315**	**6**	**1**	**2**	**3**	**50**
1991-92	**Detroit**	**NHL**	**63**	**20**	**24**	**44**	**276**	**11**	**1**	**6**	**7**	**28**
1992-93	**Detroit**	**NHL**	**80**	**14**	**29**	**43**	**292**	**7**	**0**	**3**	**3**	**10**
1993-94	**Detroit**	**NHL**	**66**	**7**	**10**	**17**	**275**	**7**	**1**	**1**	**2**	**8**
1994-95						DID NOT PLAY						
1995-96	**Chicago**	**NHL**	**78**	**19**	**21**	**40**	**237**	**10**	**0**	**2**	**2**	**23**
1996-97	**Chicago**	**NHL**	**82**	**9**	**14**	**23**	**326**	**6**	**2**	**1**	**3**	**41**
1997-98	**Chicago**	**NHL**	**14**	**2**	**1**	**3**	**48**	....	....	....	....	....
	NHL Totals		**648**	**144**	**181**	**325**	**2701**	**79**	**16**	**32**	**48**	**274**

Played in NHL All-Star Game (1988)

Signed as a free agent by **Chicago**, July 23, 1994. • Missed entire 1994-95 season after being placed on inactive list by NHL.

PROCHAZKA, LIBOR (proh-HAHZ-kah) ST.L.

Defense. Shoots right. 6', 185 lbs. Born, Vlasim, Czech., April 25, 1974.
(St. Louis' 8th choice, 245th overall, in 1993 Entry Draft).

			Regular Season					Playoffs				
Season	Club	Lea	GP	G	A	TP	PIM	GP	G	A	TP	PIM
1991-92	Poldi Kladno	Czech.	7	0	0	0	0	....	....	....	....	....
1992-93	Poldi Kladno	Czech.	34	2	2	4	....	....	....	....	....	....
1993-94	Poldi Kladno	Cze-Rep.	41	4	7	11	....	8	0	3	3	....
1994-95	Poldi Kladno	Cze-Rep.	40	4	16	20	81	11	2	1	3	14
1995-96	Poldi Kladno	Cze-Rep.	38	6	10	16	....	8	2	1	3	....
1996-97	Poldi Kladno	Cze-Rep.	49	4	15	19	108	3	0	0	0	4
1997-98	AIK Solna	Sweden	43	3	4	7	92	....	....	....	....	....
	Czech Republic	Olympics	1	0	0	0	0	....	....	....	....	....

PROCHAZKA, MARTIN (pro-HAHS-kah)

Right wing. Shoots right. 5'11", 180 lbs. Born, Slany, Czech., March 3, 1972.
(Toronto's 6th choice, 135th overall, in 1991 Entry Draft).

			Regular Season					Playoffs				
Season	Club	Lea	GP	G	A	TP	PIM	GP	G	A	TP	PIM
1989-90	Poldi Kladno	Czech.	49	18	12	30	....	....	....	....	....	....
1990-91	Poldi Kladno	Czech.	50	19	10	29	21	....	....	....	....	....
1991-92	Dukla Jihlava	Czech.	44	18	11	29	2	....	....	....	....	....
1992-93	Poldi Kladno	Czech.	46	26	12	38	....	....	....	....	....	....
1993-94	Poldi Kladno	Cze-Rep.	43	24	16	40	0	2	2	0	2	....
1994-95	Poldi Kladno	Cze-Rep.	41	25	33	58	18	11	8	4	12	4
1995-96	Poldi Kladno	Cze-Rep.	37	15	27	42	....	8	2	4	6	....
1996-97	AIK Solna	Sweden	49	16	23	39	38	7	2	3	5	8
1997-98	**Toronto**	**NHL**	**29**	**2**	**4**	**6**	**8**	....	....	....	....	....
	Czech.	Olympics	6	1	1	2	0	....	....	....	....	....
	NHL Totals		**29**	**2**	**4**	**6**	**8**	....	....	....	....	....

PROKOPEC, MIKE (PROH-koh-pehk) OTT.

Right wing. Shoots right. 6'2", 190 lbs. Born, Toronto, Ont., May 17, 1974.
(Chicago's 7th choice, 161st overall, in 1992 Entry Draft).

			Regular Season					Playoffs				
Season	Club	Lea	GP	G	A	TP	PIM	GP	G	A	TP	PIM
1991-92	Cornwall	OHL	59	12	15	27	75	6	0	0	0	0
1992-93	Newmarket	OHL	40	6	14	20	70	....	....	....	....	....
	Guelph	OHL	28	10	14	24	27	5	1	0	1	14
1993-94	Guelph	OHL	66	52	58	110	93	9	12	4	16	17
1994-95	Indianapolis	IHL	70	21	12	33	80	....	....	....	....	....
1995-96	**Chicago**	**NHL**	**9**	**0**	**0**	**0**	**5**	....	....	....	....	....
	Indianapolis	IHL	67	18	22	40	131	5	2	0	2	4
1996-97	**Chicago**	**NHL**	**6**	**0**	**0**	**0**	**6**	....	....	....	....	....
	Indianapolis	IHL	57	13	18	31	143	....	....	....	....	....
	Detroit	IHL	3	2	0	2	4	8	2	1	3	14
1997-98	Worcester	AHL	62	21	25	46	112	11	1	2	3	10
	NHL Totals		**15**	**0**	**0**	**0**	**11**	....	....	....	....	....

Traded to **Ottawa** by **Chicago** for Denis Chasse, the rights to Kevin Bolibruck and future considerations, March 18, 1997.

PRONGER, CHRIS (PRAHN-guhr) ST.L.

Defense. Shoots left. 6'5", 220 lbs. Born, Dryden, Ont., October 10, 1974.
(Hartford's 1st choice, 2nd overall, in 1993 Entry Draft).

			Regular Season					Playoffs				
Season	Club	Lea	GP	G	A	TP	PIM	GP	G	A	TP	PIM
1991-92	Peterborough	OHL	63	17	45	62	90	10	1	8	9	28
1992-93	Peterborough	OHL	61	15	62	77	108	21	15	25	40	51
1993-94	**Hartford**	**NHL**	**81**	**5**	**25**	**30**	**113**	....	....	....	....	....
1994-95	**Hartford**	**NHL**	**43**	**5**	**9**	**14**	**54**	....	....	....	....	....
1995-96	**St. Louis**	**NHL**	**78**	**7**	**18**	**25**	**110**	**13**	**1**	**5**	**6**	**16**
1996-97	**St. Louis**	**NHL**	**79**	**11**	**24**	**35**	**143**	**6**	**1**	**1**	**2**	**22**
1997-98	**St. Louis**	**NHL**	**81**	**9**	**27**	**36**	**180**	**10**	**1**	**9**	**10**	**26**
	Canada	Olympics	6	0	0	0	4	....	....	....	....	....
	NHL Totals		**362**	**37**	**103**	**140**	**600**	**29**	**3**	**15**	**18**	**64**

OHL First All-Star Team (1993) • Canadian Major Junior First All-Star Team (1993) • Canadian Major Junior Defenseman of the Year (1993) • NHL/Upper Deck All-Rookie Team (1994) • NHL Second All-Star Team (1998) • Won Bud Ice Plus/Minus Award (1998)

Traded to **St. Louis** by **Hartford** for Brendan Shanahan, July 27, 1995.

PRONGER, SEAN (PRAHN-guhr) PIT.

Center. Shoots left. 6'2", 205 lbs. Born, Dryden, Ont., November 30, 1972.
(Vancouver's 3rd choice, 51st overall, in 1991 Entry Draft).

			Regular Season					Playoffs				
Season	Club	Lea	GP	G	A	TP	PIM	GP	G	A	TP	PIM
1989-90	Thunder Bay	USHL	48	18	34	52	61	....	....	....	....	....
1990-91	Bowling Green	CCHA	40	3	7	10	30	....	....	....	....	....
1991-92	Bowling Green	CCHA	34	9	7	16	28	....	....	....	....	....
1992-93	Bowling Green	CCHA	39	23	23	46	35	....	....	....	....	....
1993-94	Bowling Green	CCHA	38	17	17	34	38	....	....	....	....	....
1994-95	Knoxville	ECHL	34	18	23	41	55	....	....	....	....	....
	Greensboro	ECHL	2	0	2	2	0	....	....	....	....	....
	San Diego	IHL	8	0	0	0	2	....	....	....	....	....
1995-96	**Anaheim**	**NHL**	**7**	**0**	**1**	**1**	**6**	....	....	....	....	....
	Baltimore	AHL	72	16	17	33	61	12	3	7	10	16
1996-97	**Anaheim**	**NHL**	**39**	**7**	**7**	**14**	**20**	**9**	**0**	**2**	**2**	**4**
	Baltimore	AHL	41	26	17	43	17	....	....	....	....	....
1997-98	**Anaheim**	**NHL**	**62**	**5**	**15**	**20**	**30**	....	....	....	....	....
	Pittsburgh	**NHL**	**5**	**1**	**0**	**1**	**2**	**5**	**0**	**0**	**0**	**4**
	NHL Totals		**113**	**13**	**23**	**36**	**58**	**14**	**0**	**2**	**2**	**8**

Signed as a free agent by **Anaheim**, February 14, 1995. Traded to **Pittsburgh** by **Anaheim** for the rights to Patrick Lalime, March 24, 1998.

PROSKURNICKI, ANDREW NYR

Left wing. Shoots left. 6'3", 201 lbs. Born, Hamilton, Ont., July 24, 1978.
(NY Rangers' 11th choice, 210th overall, in 1997 Entry Draft).

			Regular Season					Playoffs				
Season	Club	Lea	GP	G	A	TP	PIM	GP	G	A	TP	PIM
1995-96	Sarnia	OHL	60	3	11	14	96	10	1	3	4	12
1996-97	Sarnia	OHL	62	9	26	35	191	12	2	4	6	28
1997-98	Sarnia	OHL	66	20	33	53	229	5	1	1	2	28
	Hartford	AHL	4	0	1	1	7	....	....	....	....	....

PROSOFSKY, GARRETT PHI.

Center. Shoots left. 5'11", 180 lbs. Born, Saskatoon, Sask., May 19, 1980.
(Philadelphia's 6th choice, 139th overall, in 1998 Entry Draft).

			Regular Season					Playoffs				
Season	Club	Lea	GP	G	A	TP	PIM	GP	G	A	TP	PIM
1995-96	Saskatoon	WHL	4	0	0	0	0	....	....	....	....	....
1996-97	Saskatoon	WHL	66	20	45	65	67	....	....	....	....	....
1997-98	Saskatoon	WHL	71	28	42	70	76	6	6	3	9	4

PROSPAL, VACLAV (PRAWS-pahl, VAHT-slahv) OTT.

Center. Shoots left. 6'2", 185 lbs. Born, Ceske-Budejovice, Czech., February 17, 1975.
(Philadelphia's 2nd choice, 71st overall, in 1993 Entry Draft).

			Regular Season					Playoffs				
Season	Club	Lea	GP	G	A	TP	PIM	GP	G	A	TP	PIM
1992-93	Budejovice	Czech-Jr.	32	26	31	57	24	....	....	....	....	....
1993-94	Hershey	AHL	55	14	21	35	38	2	0	0	0	2
1994-95	Hershey	AHL	69	13	32	45	36	2	1	0	1	4
1995-96	Hershey	AHL	68	15	36	51	59	5	2	4	6	2
1996-97	**Philadelphia**	**NHL**	**18**	**5**	**10**	**15**	**4**	**5**	**1**	**3**	**4**	**4**
	Philadelphia	AHL	63	32	63	95	70	....	....	....	....	....
1997-98	**Philadelphia**	**NHL**	**41**	**5**	**13**	**18**	**17**	....	....	....	....	....
	Ottawa	**NHL**	**15**	**1**	**6**	**7**	**4**	**6**	**0**	**0**	**0**	**0**
	NHL Totals		**74**	**11**	**29**	**40**	**25**	**11**	**1**	**3**	**4**	**4**

AHL First All-Star Team (1997)

Traded to **Ottawa** by **Philadelphia** with Pat Falloon and Dallas' 2nd round choice (previously acquired, Ottawa selected Chris Bala) in 1998 Entry Draft for Alexandre Daigle, January 17, 1998.

PROTSENKO, BORIS (proht-SEHN-koh) PIT.

Right wing. Shoots right. 5'11", 194 lbs. Born, Kiev, USSR, August 21, 1978.
(Pittsburgh's 4th choice, 77th overall, in 1996 Entry Draft).

			Regular Season					Playoffs				
Season	Club	Lea	GP	G	A	TP	PIM	GP	G	A	TP	PIM
1995-96	Calgary	WHL	71	46	29	75	68	....	....	....	....	....
1996-97	Calgary	WHL	67	35	32	67	136	....	....	....	....	....
1997-98	Calgary	WHL	70	40	47	87	124	18	6	8	14	30

PRPIC, JOEL (puhr-PIHCH) BOS.

Center. Shoots left. 6'7", 225 lbs. Born, Sudbury, Ont., September 25, 1974.
(Boston's 9th choice, 233rd overall, in 1993 Entry Draft).

			Regular Season					Playoffs				
Season	Club	Lea	GP	G	A	TP	PIM	GP	G	A	TP	PIM
1992-93	Waterloo	OJHL	45	17	43	60	160	....	....	....	....	....
1993-94	St. Lawrence	ECAC	31	2	4	6	90	....	....	....	....	....
1994-95	St. Lawrence	ECAC	32	7	10	17	62	....	....	....	....	....
1995-96	St. Lawrence	ECAC	32	3	10	13	77	....	....	....	....	....
1996-97	St. Lawrence	ECAC	34	10	8	18	57	....	....	....	....	....
1997-98	**Boston**	**NHL**	**1**	**0**	**0**	**0**	**2**	....	....	....	....	....
	Providence	AHL	73	17	18	35	53	....	....	....	....	....
	NHL Totals		**1**	**0**	**0**	**0**	**2**	....	....	....	....	....

PURINTON, DALE NYR

Defense. Shoots left. 6'2", 190 lbs. Born, Fort Wayne, IN, October 11, 1976.
(NY Rangers' 5th choice, 117th overall, in 1995 Entry Draft).

			Regular Season					Playoffs				
Season	Club	Lea	GP	G	A	TP	PIM	GP	G	A	TP	PIM
1994-95	Tacoma	WHL	65	0	8	8	291	3	0	0	0	13
1995-96	Kelowna	WHL	22	1	4	5	88	....	....	....	....	....
	Lethbridge	WHL	37	3	6	9	144	4	1	1	2	25
1996-97	Lethbridge	WHL	51	6	26	32	254	18	3	5	8	*88
1997-98	Hartford	AHL	17	0	0	0	95	....	....	....	....	....
	Charlotte	ECHL	34	3	5	8	186	....	....	....	....	....

PUSHOR, JAMIE (PUH-shohr) ANA.

Defense. Shoots right. 6'3", 225 lbs. Born, Lethbridge, Alta., February 11, 1973.
(Detroit's 2nd choice, 32nd overall, in 1991 Entry Draft).

			Regular Season					Playoffs				
Season	Club	Lea	GP	G	A	TP	PIM	GP	G	A	TP	PIM
1989-90	Lethbridge	WHL	10	0	2	2	2	....	....	....	....	....
1990-91	Lethbridge	WHL	71	1	13	14	193	....	....	....	....	....
1991-92	Lethbridge	WHL	49	2	15	17	232	5	0	0	0	33
1992-93	Lethbridge	WHL	72	6	22	28	200	4	0	1	1	9
1993-94	Adirondack	AHL	73	1	17	18	124	12	0	0	0	22
1994-95	Adirondack	AHL	58	2	11	13	129	4	0	1	1	0
1995-96	**Detroit**	**NHL**	**5**	**0**	**1**	**1**	**17**	....	....	....	....	....
	Adirondack	AHL	65	2	16	18	126	3	0	0	0	5
1996-97	**Detroit**	**NHL**	**75**	**4**	**7**	**11**	**129**	**5**	**0**	**1**	**1**	**5** ♦
1997-98	**Detroit**	**NHL**	**54**	**2**	**5**	**7**	**71**	....	....	....	....	....
	Anaheim	**NHL**	**10**	**0**	**2**	**2**	**10**	....	....	....	....	....
	NHL Totals		**144**	**6**	**15**	**21**	**227**	**5**	**0**	**1**	**1**	**5**

Traded to **Anaheim** by **Detroit** with Detroit's 4th round choice (Viktor Wallin) in 1998 Entry Draft for Dmitri Mironov, March 24, 1998.

QUINT, DERON (KWIHNT) PHX.

Defense. Shoots left. 6'2", 201 lbs. Born, Durham, NH, March 12, 1976.
(Winnipeg's 1st choice, 30th overall, in 1994 Entry Draft).

			Regular Season					Playoffs				
Season	Club	Lea	GP	G	A	TP	PIM	GP	G	A	TP	PIM
1993-94	Seattle	WHL	63	15	29	44	47	9	4	12	16	8
1994-95	Seattle	WHL	65	29	60	89	82	3	1	2	3	6
1995-96	**Winnipeg**	**NHL**	**51**	**5**	**13**	**18**	**22**	....	....	....	....	....
	Springfield	AHL	11	2	3	5	4	10	2	3	5	6
	Seattle	WHL	....	....	....	....	....	5	4	1	5	6
1996-97	**Phoenix**	**NHL**	**27**	**3**	**11**	**14**	**4**	**7**	**0**	**2**	**2**	**0**
	Springfield	AHL	43	6	18	24	20	12	2	7	9	4
1997-98	**Phoenix**	**NHL**	**32**	**4**	**7**	**11**	**16**	....	....	....	....	....
	Springfield	AHL	8	1	7	8	10	1	0	0	0	0
	NHL Totals		**110**	**12**	**31**	**43**	**42**	**7**	**0**	**2**	**2**	**0**

WHL West First All-Star Team (1995)

Transferred to **Phoenix** after **Winnipeg** franchise relocated, July 1, 1996.

QUINTAL, STEPHANE (KAYN-tahl) MTL.

Defense. Shoots right. 6'3", 230 lbs. Born, Boucherville, Que., October 22, 1968.
(Boston's 2nd choice, 14th overall, in 1987 Entry Draft).

			Regular Season					Playoffs				
Season	Club	Lea	GP	G	A	TP	PIM	GP	G	A	TP	PIM
1985-86	Granby	QMJHL	67	2	17	19	144	....	....	....	....	....
1986-87	Granby	QMJHL	67	13	41	54	178	8	0	9	9	10
1987-88	Hull	QMJHL	38	13	23	36	138	19	7	12	19	30
1988-89	**Boston**	**NHL**	**26**	**0**	**1**	**1**	**29**	....	....	....	....	....
	Maine	AHL	16	4	10	14	28	....	....	....	....	....
1989-90	**Boston**	**NHL**	**38**	**2**	**2**	**4**	**22**	....	....	....	....	....
	Maine	AHL	37	4	16	20	27	....	....	....	....	....
1990-91	**Boston**	**NHL**	**45**	**2**	**6**	**8**	**89**	**3**	**0**	**1**	**1**	**7**
	Maine	AHL	23	1	5	6	30	....	....	....	....	....
1991-92	**Boston**	**NHL**	**49**	**4**	**10**	**14**	**77**	....	....	....	....	....
	St. Louis	**NHL**	**26**	**0**	**6**	**6**	**32**	**4**	**1**	**2**	**3**	**6**
1992-93	**St. Louis**	**NHL**	**75**	**1**	**10**	**11**	**100**	**9**	**0**	**0**	**0**	**8**
1993-94	**Winnipeg**	**NHL**	**81**	**8**	**18**	**26**	**119**	....	....	....	....	....
1994-95	**Winnipeg**	**NHL**	**43**	**6**	**17**	**23**	**78**	....	....	....	....	....
1995-96	**Montreal**	**NHL**	**68**	**2**	**14**	**16**	**117**	**6**	**0**	**1**	**1**	**6**
1996-97	**Montreal**	**NHL**	**71**	**7**	**15**	**22**	**100**	**5**	**0**	**1**	**1**	**6**
1997-98	**Montreal**	**NHL**	**71**	**6**	**10**	**16**	**97**	**9**	**0**	**2**	**2**	**4**
	NHL Totals		**593**	**38**	**109**	**147**	**860**	**36**	**1**	**7**	**8**	**37**

QMJHL First All-Star Team (1987)

Traded to **St. Louis** by **Boston** with Craig Janney for Adam Oates, February 7, 1992. Traded to **Winnipeg** by **St. Louis** with Nelson Emerson for Phil Housley, September 24, 1993. Traded to **Montreal** by **Winnipeg** for Montreal's 2nd round choice (Jason Doig) in 1995 Entry Draft, July 8, 1995.

RACHUNEK, KAREL (ra-KHOO-nehk, KAH-rehl) OTT.

Defense. Shoots right. 6', 183 lbs. Born, Gottwaldov, Czechoslovakia, August 27, 1979.
(Ottawa's 8th choice, 229th overall, in 1997 Entry Draft).

			Regular Season					Playoffs				
Season	Club	Lea	GP	G	A	TP	PIM	GP	G	A	TP	PIM
1995-96	ZPS Zlin	Czech-Jr.	38	8	11	19	....	....	....	....	....	....
1996-97	ZPS Zlin	Czech-Jr.	27	2	11	13	....	....	....	....	....	....
1997-98	ZPS Zlin	Cze-Rep.	27	1	2	3	16	....	....	....	....	....

RACINE, YVES (ruh-SEEN, EEV)

Defense. Shoots left. 6', 205 lbs. Born, Matane, Que., February 7, 1969.
(Detroit's 1st choice, 11th overall, in 1987 Entry Draft).

			Regular Season					Playoffs				
Season	Club	Lea	GP	G	A	TP	PIM	GP	G	A	TP	PIM
1986-87	Longueuil	QMJHL	70	7	43	50	50	20	3	11	14	14
1987-88	Victoriaville	QMJHL	69	10	84	94	150	5	0	0	0	13
	Adirondack	AHL	....	....	....	....	....	9	4	2	6	2
1988-89	Victoriaville	QMJHL	63	23	85	108	95	16	3	*30	*33	41
	Adirondack	AHL	....	....	....	....	....	2	1	1	2	0
1989-90	**Detroit**	**NHL**	**28**	**4**	**9**	**13**	**23**	....	....	....	....	....
	Adirondack	AHL	46	8	27	35	31	....	....	....	....	....
1990-91	**Detroit**	**NHL**	**62**	**7**	**40**	**47**	**33**	**7**	**2**	**0**	**2**	**0**
	Adirondack	AHL	16	3	9	12	10	....	....	....	....	....
1991-92	**Detroit**	**NHL**	**61**	**2**	**22**	**24**	**94**	**11**	**2**	**1**	**3**	**10**
1992-93	**Detroit**	**NHL**	**80**	**9**	**31**	**40**	**80**	**7**	**1**	**3**	**4**	**27**
1993-94	**Philadelphia**	**NHL**	**67**	**9**	**43**	**52**	**48**	....	....	....	....	....
1994-95	**Montreal**	**NHL**	**47**	**4**	**7**	**11**	**42**	....	....	....	....	....
1995-96	**Montreal**	**NHL**	**25**	**0**	**3**	**3**	**26**	....	....	....	....	....
	San Jose	**NHL**	**32**	**1**	**16**	**17**	**28**	....	....	....	....	....
1996-97	Kentucky	AHL	4	0	1	1	2	....	....	....	....	....
	Quebec	IHL	6	0	4	4	4	....	....	....	....	....
	Calgary	**NHL**	**46**	**1**	**15**	**16**	**24**	....	....	....	....	....
1997-98	**Tampa Bay**	**NHL**	**60**	**0**	**8**	**8**	**41**	....	....	....	....	....
	NHL Totals		**508**	**37**	**194**	**231**	**439**	**25**	**5**	**4**	**9**	**37**

QMJHL First-All Star Team (1988, 1989)

Traded to **Philadelphia** by **Detroit** with Detroit's 4th round choice (Sebastien Vallee) in 1994 Entry Draft for Terry Carkner, October 5, 1993. Traded to **Montreal** by **Philadelphia** for Kevin Haller, June 29, 1994. Claimed on waivers by **San Jose** from **Montreal**, January 23, 1996. Traded to **Calgary** by **San Jose** for cash, December 17, 1996. Signed as a free agent by **Tampa Bay**, July 16, 1997.

RAGNARSSON, MARCUS (RAG-nahr-suhn) S.J.

Defense. Shoots left. 6'1", 215 lbs. Born, Ostervala, Sweden, August 13, 1971.
(San Jose's 5th choice, 99th overall, in 1992 Entry Draft).

			Regular Season					Playoffs				
Season	Club	Lea	GP	G	A	TP	PIM	GP	G	A	TP	PIM
1989-90	Djurgarden	Sweden	13	0	2	2	0	1	0	0	0	0
1990-91	Djurgarden	Sweden	35	4	1	5	12	7	0	0	0	6
1991-92	Djurgarden	Sweden	40	8	5	13	14	10	0	1	1	4
1992-93	Djurgarden	Sweden	35	3	3	6	53	6	0	3	3	8
1993-94	Djurgarden	Sweden	19	0	4	4	24	....	....	....	....	....
1994-95	Djurgarden	Sweden	38	7	9	16	20	3	0	0	0	4
1995-96	**San Jose**	**NHL**	**71**	**8**	**31**	**39**	**42**	....	....	....	....	....
1996-97	**San Jose**	**NHL**	**69**	**3**	**14**	**17**	**63**	....	....	....	....	....
1997-98	**San Jose**	**NHL**	**79**	**5**	**20**	**25**	**65**	**6**	**0**	**0**	**0**	**4**
	Sweden	Olympics	3	0	1	1	0	....	....	....	....	....
	NHL Totals		**219**	**16**	**65**	**81**	**170**	**6**	**0**	**0**	**0**	**4**

RAJNOHA, PAVEL (righ-NOH-kha) CGY.

Defense. Shoots right. 6', 185 lbs. Born, Gottwaldov, Czech., February 23, 1974.
(Calgary's 8th choice, 150th overall, in 1992 Entry Draft).

			Regular Season					Playoffs				
Season	Club	Lea	GP	G	A	TP	PIM	GP	G	A	TP	PIM
1990-91	TJ Zlin	Czech.	6	0	0	0	4	....	....	....	....	....
1991-92	ZPS Zlin	Czech.	24	0	1	1	4	....	....	....	....	....
1992-93	ZPS Zlin	Czech.	26	2	1	3	....	....	....	....	....	....
1993-94	ZPS Zlin	Cze-Rep.	28	2	1	3	0	3	0	4	4	....
1994-95	ZPS Zlin	Cze-Rep.	29	0	6	6	22	....	....	....	....	....
1995-96	Dukla Jihlava	Cze-Rep.	38	0	2	2	....	8	0	0	0	....
1996-97	ZPS Zlin	Cze-Rep.	32	6	5	11	4	....	....	....	....	....
1997-98	ZPS Zlin	Cze-Rep.	15	1	2	3	12	....	....	....	....	....

RAKHMATULLIN, ASKHAT (rahkh-ma-TOO-lihn, ahs-KHAHT) CAR.

Left wing. Shoots left. 5'11", 165 lbs. Born, Ufa, USSR, May 31, 1978.
(Hartford's 10th choice, 231st overall, in 1996 Entry Draft).

			Regular Season					Playoffs				
Season	Club	Lea	GP	G	A	TP	PIM	GP	G	A	TP	PIM
1996-97	Ufa Salavat	Russia	28	1	3	4	8	3	0	0	0	0
1997-98	Ufa Salavat	Russia	14	0	1	1	6	....	....	....	....	....

Rights transferred to **Carolina** after **Hartford** franchise relocated, June 25, 1997.

RAMSAY, BRUCE

Left wing. Shoots left. 6', 180 lbs. Born, Dryden, Ont., May 13, 1969.

			Regular Season					Playoffs				
Season	Club	Lea	GP	G	A	TP	PIM	GP	G	A	TP	PIM
1991-92	Thunder Bay	ColHL	54	7	16	23	313	12	1	2	3	55
1992-93	Thunder Bay	ColHL	52	3	16	19	234	....	....	....	....	....
1993-94	Thunder Bay	ColHL	63	9	22	31	313	8	1	2	3	45
1994-95	Thunder Bay	ColHL	62	14	29	43	462	11	0	3	3	83
	P.E.I.	AHL	2	0	1	1	10	1	0	0	0	2
1995-96	Thunder Bay	ColHL	56	6	15	21	400	18	2	3	5	142
	Milwaukee	IHL	3	0	0	0	5	....	....	....	....	....
1996-97	Thunder Bay	ColHL	9	6	4	10	71	....	....	....	....	....
	Grand Rapids	IHL	66	3	5	8	306	4	0	0	0	2
1997-98	Grand Rapids	IHL	62	5	6	11	310	....	....	....	....	....

Signed as a free agent by **St. Louis**, July 31, 1997.

RANDALL, BRYAN

Center. Shoots left. 6'3", 190 lbs. Born, Winnipeg, Man., August 8, 1978.
(Edmonton's 6th choice, 141st overall, in 1996 Entry Draft).

			Regular Season					Playoffs				
Season	Club	Lea	GP	G	A	TP	PIM	GP	G	A	TP	PIM
1995-96	Medicine Hat	WHL	64	4	5	9	51	5	0	0	0	7
1996-97	Medicine Hat	WHL	2	0	0	0	7	....	....	....	....	....
	Regina	WHL	48	5	18	23	55	2	0	1	1	2
1997-98	Regina	WHL	43	2	8	10	58	....	....	....	....	....
	Kelowna	WHL	25	8	12	20	26	7	0	2	2	2

RANHEIM, PAUL (RAN-highm) CAR.

Left wing. Shoots right. 6'1", 210 lbs. Born, St. Louis, MO, January 25, 1966.
(Calgary's 3rd choice, 38th overall, in 1984 Entry Draft).

			Regular Season					Playoffs				
Season	Club	Lea	GP	G	A	TP	PIM	GP	G	A	TP	PIM
1983-84	Edina High	H.S.	26	16	24	40	6	....	....	....	....	....
1984-85	U. of Wisconsin	WCHA	42	11	11	22	40	....	....	....	....	....
1985-86	U. of Wisconsin	WCHA	33	17	17	34	34	....	....	....	....	....
1986-87	U. of Wisconsin	WCHA	42	24	35	59	54	....	....	....	....	....
1987-88	U. of Wisconsin	WCHA	44	36	26	62	63	....	....	....	....	....
1988-89	**Calgary**	**NHL**	**5**	**0**	**0**	**0**	**0**	....	....	....	....	....
	Salt Lake	IHL	75	*68	29	97	16	14	5	5	10	8
1989-90	**Calgary**	**NHL**	**80**	**26**	**28**	**54**	**23**	**6**	**1**	**3**	**4**	**2**
1990-91	**Calgary**	**NHL**	**39**	**14**	**16**	**30**	**4**	**7**	**2**	**2**	**4**	**0**
1991-92	**Calgary**	**NHL**	**80**	**23**	**20**	**43**	**32**	....	....	....	....	....
1992-93	**Calgary**	**NHL**	**83**	**21**	**22**	**43**	**26**	**6**	**0**	**1**	**1**	**0**
1993-94	**Calgary**	**NHL**	**67**	**10**	**14**	**24**	**20**	....	....	....	....	....
	Hartford	**NHL**	**15**	**0**	**3**	**3**	**2**	....	....	....	....	....
1994-95	**Hartford**	**NHL**	**47**	**6**	**14**	**20**	**10**	....	....	....	....	....
1995-96	**Hartford**	**NHL**	**73**	**10**	**20**	**30**	**14**	....	....	....	....	....
1996-97	**Hartford**	**NHL**	**67**	**10**	**11**	**21**	**18**	....	....	....	....	....
1997-98	**Carolina**	**NHL**	**73**	**5**	**9**	**14**	**28**	....	....	....	....	....
	NHL Totals		**629**	**125**	**157**	**282**	**177**	**19**	**3**	**6**	**9**	**2**

WCHA Second All-Star Team (1987) • NCAA West First All-American Team (1988) • WCHA First All-Star Team (1988) • IHL Second All-Star Team (1989) • Won Garry F. Longman Memorial Trophy (Top Rookie - IHL) (1989)

Traded to **Hartford** by **Calgary** with Gary Suter and Ted Drury for James Patrick, Zarley Zalapski and Michael Nylander, March 10, 1994. Transferred to **Carolina** after **Hartford** franchise relocated, June 25, 1997.

RASMUSSEN, ERIK (RAS-moo-suhn) BUF.

Center. Shoots left. 6'2", 205 lbs. Born, Minneapolis, MN, March 28, 1977.
(Buffalo's 1st choice, 7th overall, in 1996 Entry Draft).

			Regular Season					Playoffs				
Season	Club	Lea	GP	G	A	TP	PIM	GP	G	A	TP	PIM
1995-96	U. of Minnesota	WCHA	40	16	32	48	55	....	....	....	....	....
1996-97	U. of Minnesota	WCHA	34	15	12	27	*123	....	....	....	....	....
1997-98	**Buffalo**	**NHL**	**21**	**2**	**3**	**5**	**14**	....	....	....	....	....
	Rochester	AHL	53	9	14	23	83	1	0	0	0	5
	NHL Totals		**21**	**2**	**3**	**5**	**14**	....	....	....	....	....

RATCHUK, PETER (RAT-chuhk) FLA.

Defense. Shoots left. 6'1", 180 lbs. Born, Buffalo, NY, September 10, 1977.
(Colorado's 1st choice, 25th overall, in 1996 Entry Draft).

			Regular Season					Playoffs				
Season	Club	Lea	GP	G	A	TP	PIM	GP	G	A	TP	PIM
1995-96	Shattuck	H.S.	35	22	28	50	24	....	....	....	....	....
1996-97	Bowling Green	CCHA	35	9	12	21	14	....	....	....	....	....
1997-98	Hull	QMJHL	60	23	31	54	34	11	3	6	9	8

Signed as a free agent by **Florida**, June 15, 1998.

RATHJE, MIKE (RATH-jee) S.J.

Defense. Shoots left. 6'5", 230 lbs. Born, Mannville, Alta., May 11, 1974.
(San Jose's 1st choice, 3rd overall, in 1992 Entry Draft).

			Regular Season					Playoffs				
Season	Club	Lea	GP	G	A	TP	PIM	GP	G	A	TP	PIM
1990-91	Medicine Hat	WHL	64	1	16	17	28	12	0	4	4	2
1991-92	Medicine Hat	WHL	67	11	23	34	109	4	0	1	1	2
1992-93	Medicine Hat	WHL	57	12	37	49	103	10	3	3	6	12
	Kansas City	IHL	....	....	....	....	....	5	0	0	0	12
1993-94	**San Jose**	**NHL**	**47**	**1**	**9**	**10**	**59**	**1**	**0**	**0**	**0**	**0**
	Kansas City	IHL	6	0	2	2	0	....	....	....	....	....
1994-95	**San Jose**	**NHL**	**42**	**2**	**7**	**9**	**29**	**11**	**5**	**2**	**7**	**4**
	Kansas City	IHL	6	0	1	1	7	....	....	....	....	....
1995-96	**San Jose**	**NHL**	**27**	**0**	**7**	**7**	**14**	....	....	....	....	....
	Kansas City	IHL	36	6	11	17	34	....	....	....	....	....
1996-97	**San Jose**	**NHL**	**31**	**0**	**8**	**8**	**21**	....	....	....	....	....
1997-98	**San Jose**	**NHL**	**81**	**3**	**12**	**15**	**59**	**6**	**1**	**0**	**1**	**6**
	NHL Totals		**228**	**6**	**43**	**49**	**182**	**18**	**6**	**2**	**8**	**10**

WHL East Second All-Star Team (1992, 1993)

RAY, ROB BUF.

Right wing. Shoots left. 6', 203 lbs. Born, Stirling, Ont., June 8, 1968.
(Buffalo's 5th choice, 97th overall, in 1988 Entry Draft).

			Regular Season					Playoffs				
Season	Club	Lea	GP	G	A	TP	PIM	GP	G	A	TP	PIM
1985-86	Cornwall	OHL	53	6	13	19	253	6	0	0	0	26
1986-87	Cornwall	OHL	46	17	20	37	158	5	1	1	2	16
1987-88	Cornwall	OHL	61	11	41	52	179	11	2	3	5	33
1988-89	Rochester	AHL	74	11	18	29	*446	....	....	....	....	....
1989-90	**Buffalo**	**NHL**	**27**	**2**	**1**	**3**	**99**	....	....	....	....	....
	Rochester	AHL	43	2	13	15	335	17	1	3	4	115
1990-91	**Buffalo**	**NHL**	**66**	**8**	**8**	**16**	***350**	**6**	**1**	**1**	**2**	**56**
	Rochester	AHL	8	1	1	2	15	....	....	....	....	....
1991-92	**Buffalo**	**NHL**	**63**	**5**	**3**	**8**	**354**	**7**	**0**	**0**	**0**	**2**
1992-93	**Buffalo**	**NHL**	**68**	**3**	**2**	**5**	**211**	....	....	....	....	....
1993-94	**Buffalo**	**NHL**	**82**	**3**	**4**	**7**	**274**	**7**	**1**	**0**	**1**	**43**
1994-95	**Buffalo**	**NHL**	**47**	**0**	**3**	**3**	**173**	**5**	**0**	**0**	**0**	**14**
1995-96	**Buffalo**	**NHL**	**71**	**3**	**6**	**9**	**287**	....	....	....	....	....
1996-97	**Buffalo**	**NHL**	**82**	**7**	**3**	**10**	**286**	**12**	**0**	**1**	**1**	**28**
1997-98	**Buffalo**	**NHL**	**63**	**2**	**4**	**6**	**234**	**10**	**0**	**0**	**0**	**24**
	NHL Totals		**569**	**33**	**34**	**67**	**2268**	**47**	**2**	**2**	**4**	**167**

RAZIN, GENNADY (RAH-zihn, gen-AH-dee) MTL.

Defense. Shoots left. 6'3", 175 lbs. Born, Kharkov, USSR, February 3, 1978.
(Montreal's 6th choice, 122nd overall, in 1997 Entry Draft).

			Regular Season					Playoffs				
Season	Club	Lea	GP	G	A	TP	PIM	GP	G	A	TP	PIM
1996-97	Kamloops	WHL	63	7	19	26	56	3	0	0	0	4
1997-98	Kamloops	WHL	70	2	11	13	64	7	0	0	0	4

READY, RYAN CGY.

Left wing. Shoots left. 6'2", 185 lbs. Born, Peterborough, Ont., November 7, 1978.
(Calgary's 8th choice, 100th overall, in 1997 Entry Draft).

			Regular Season					Playoffs				
Season	Club	Lea	GP	G	A	TP	PIM	GP	G	A	TP	PIM
1995-96	Belleville	OHL	63	5	13	18	54	10	0	2	2	2
1996-97	Belleville	OHL	66	23	24	47	102	6	1	3	4	4
1997-98	Belleville	OHL	66	33	39	72	80	10	5	2	7	12

REASONER, MARTY ST.L.

Center. Shoots left. 6'1", 185 lbs. Born, Rochester, NY, February 26, 1977.
(St. Louis' 1st choice, 14th overall, in 1996 Entry Draft).

			Regular Season					Playoffs				
Season	Club	Lea	GP	G	A	TP	PIM	GP	G	A	TP	PIM
1995-96	Boston College	H.E.	34	16	29	45	32	....	....	....	....	....
1996-97	Boston College	H.E.	35	20	24	44	31	....	....	....	....	....
1997-98	Boston College	H.E.	42	*33	40	*73	56	....	....	....	....	....

Hockey East First All-Star Team (1997, 1998) • NCAA East First All-American Team (1998) • NCAA Championship All-Tournament Team (1998)

RECCHI, MARK (REH-kee) **MTL.**

Right wing. Shoots left. 5'10", 185 lbs. Born, Kamloops, B.C., February 1, 1968.
(Pittsburgh's 4th choice, 67th overall, in 1988 Entry Draft).

			Regular Season					Playoffs				
Season	Club	Lea	GP	G	A	TP	PIM	GP	G	A	TP	PIM
1985-86	New Westminster	WHL	72	21	40	61	55	....	....	....	....	....
1986-87	Kamloops	WHL	40	26	50	76	63	13	3	16	19	17
1987-88	Kamloops	WHL	62	61	*93	154	75	17	10	*21	*31	18
1988-89	**Pittsburgh**	**NHL**	**15**	**1**	**1**	**2**	**0**	....	....	....	....	....
	Muskegon	IHL	63	50	49	99	86	14	7	*14	*21	28
1989-90	**Pittsburgh**	**NHL**	**74**	**30**	**37**	**67**	**44**	....	....	....	....	....
	Muskegon	IHL	4	7	4	11	2	....	....	....	....	....
1990-91	**Pittsburgh**	**NHL**	**78**	**40**	**73**	**113**	**48**	**24**	**10**	**24**	**34**	**33 ♦**
1991-92	**Pittsburgh**	**NHL**	**58**	**33**	**37**	**70**	**78**	....	....	....	....	....
	Philadelphia	**NHL**	**22**	**10**	**17**	**27**	**18**	....	....	....	....	....
1992-93	**Philadelphia**	**NHL**	**84**	**53**	**70**	**123**	**95**	....	....	....	....	....
1993-94	**Philadelphia**	**NHL**	**84**	**40**	**67**	**107**	**46**	....	....	....	....	....
1994-95	**Philadelphia**	**NHL**	**10**	**2**	**3**	**5**	**12**	....	....	....	....	....
	Montreal	**NHL**	**39**	**14**	**29**	**43**	**16**	....	....	....	....	....
1995-96	**Montreal**	**NHL**	**82**	**28**	**50**	**78**	**69**	**6**	**3**	**3**	**6**	**0**
1996-97	**Montreal**	**NHL**	**82**	**34**	**46**	**80**	**58**	**5**	**4**	**2**	**6**	**2**
1997-98	**Montreal**	**NHL**	**82**	**32**	**42**	**74**	**51**	**10**	**4**	**8**	**12**	**6**
	Canada	Olympics	5	0	2	2	0	....	....	....	....	....
	NHL Totals		**710**	**317**	**472**	**789**	**535**	**45**	**21**	**37**	**58**	**41**

WHL West All-Star Team (1988) • IHL Second All-Star Team (1989) • NHL Second All-Star Team (1992)

Played in NHL All-Star Game (1991, 1993, 1994, 1997, 1998)

Traded to **Philadelphia** by **Pittsburgh** with Brian Benning and LA Kings' 1st round choice (previously acquired, Philadelphia selected Jason Bowen) in 1992 Entry Draft for Rick Tocchet, Kjell Samuelsson, Ken Wregget and Philadelphia's 3rd round choice (Dave Roche) in 1993 Entry Draft, February 19, 1992. Traded to **Montreal** by **Philadelphia** with Philadelphia's 3rd round choice (Martin Hohenberger) in 1995 Entry Draft for Eric Desjardins, Gilbert Dionne and John LeClair, February 9, 1995.

REDDEN, WADE **OTT.**

Defense. Shoots left. 6'2", 193 lbs. Born, Lloydminster, Sask., June 12, 1977.
(NY Islanders' 1st choice, 2nd overall, in 1995 Entry Draft).

			Regular Season					Playoffs				
Season	Club	Lea	GP	G	A	TP	PIM	GP	G	A	TP	PIM
1993-94	Brandon	WHL	63	4	35	39	98	14	2	4	6	10
1994-95	Brandon	WHL	64	14	46	60	83	18	5	10	15	8
1995-96	Brandon	WHL	51	9	45	54	55	19	5	10	15	19
1996-97	**Ottawa**	**NHL**	**82**	**6**	**24**	**30**	**41**	**7**	**1**	**3**	**4**	**2**
1997-98	**Ottawa**	**NHL**	**80**	**8**	**14**	**22**	**27**	**9**	**0**	**2**	**2**	**2**
	NHL Totals		**162**	**14**	**38**	**52**	**68**	**16**	**1**	**5**	**6**	**4**

WHL East Second All-Star Team (1995) • WHL East First All-Star Team (1996) • Memorial Cup All-Star Team (1996)

Traded to **Ottawa** by **NY Islanders** with Damian Rhodes for Don Beaupre, Martin Straka and Bryan Berard, January 23, 1996.

REEKIE, JOE (REE-kee) **WSH.**

Defense. Shoots left. 6'3", 220 lbs. Born, Victoria, B.C., February 22, 1965.
(Buffalo's 6th choice, 119th overall, in 1985 Entry Draft).

			Regular Season					Playoffs				
Season	Club	Lea	GP	G	A	TP	PIM	GP	G	A	TP	PIM
1982-83	North Bay	OHL	59	2	9	11	49	8	0	1	1	11
1983-84	North Bay	OHL	9	1	0	1	18	....	....	....	....	....
	Cornwall	OHL	53	6	27	33	166	3	0	0	0	4
1984-85	Cornwall	OHL	65	19	63	82	134	9	4	13	17	18
1985-86	**Buffalo**	**NHL**	**3**	**0**	**0**	**0**	**14**	....	....	....	....	....
	Rochester	AHL	77	3	25	28	178	....	....	....	....	....
1986-87	**Buffalo**	**NHL**	**56**	**1**	**8**	**9**	**82**	....	....	....	....	....
	Rochester	AHL	22	0	6	6	52	....	....	....	....	....
1987-88	**Buffalo**	**NHL**	**30**	**1**	**4**	**5**	**68**	**2**	**0**	**0**	**0**	**4**
1988-89	**Buffalo**	**NHL**	**15**	**1**	**3**	**4**	**26**	....	....	....	....	....
	Rochester	AHL	21	1	2	3	56	....	....	....	....	....
1989-90	**NY Islanders**	**NHL**	**31**	**1**	**8**	**9**	**43**	....	....	....	....	....
	Springfield	AHL	15	1	4	5	24	....	....	....	....	....
1990-91	**NY Islanders**	**NHL**	**66**	**3**	**16**	**19**	**96**	....	....	....	....	....
	Capital District	AHL	2	1	0	1	0	....	....	....	....	....
1991-92	**NY Islanders**	**NHL**	**54**	**4**	**12**	**16**	**85**	....	....	....	....	....
	Capital District	AHL	3	2	2	4	2	....	....	....	....	....
1992-93	**Tampa Bay**	**NHL**	**42**	**2**	**11**	**13**	**69**	....	....	....	....	....
1993-94	**Tampa Bay**	**NHL**	**73**	**1**	**11**	**12**	**127**	....	....	....	....	....
	Washington	**NHL**	**12**	**0**	**5**	**5**	**29**	**11**	**2**	**1**	**3**	**29**
1994-95	**Washington**	**NHL**	**48**	**1**	**6**	**7**	**97**	**7**	**0**	**0**	**0**	**2**
1995-96	**Washington**	**NHL**	**78**	**3**	**7**	**10**	**149**	....	....	....	....	....
1996-97	**Washington**	**NHL**	**65**	**1**	**8**	**9**	**107**	....	....	....	....	....
1997-98	**Washington**	**NHL**	**68**	**2**	**8**	**10**	**70**	**21**	**1**	**2**	**3**	**20**
	NHL Totals		**641**	**21**	**107**	**128**	**1062**	**41**	**3**	**3**	**6**	**55**

• Re-entered NHL draft. Originally Hartford's 8th choice, 128th overall, in 1983 Entry Draft.

Traded to **NY Islanders** by **Buffalo** for NY Islanders' 6th round choice (Bill Pye) in 1989 Entry Draft, June 17, 1989. Claimed by **Tampa Bay** from **NY Islanders** in Expansion Draft, June 18, 1992. Traded to **Washington** by **Tampa Bay** for Enrico Ciccone, Washington's 3rd round choice (later traded to Anaheim — Anaheim selected Craig Reichert) in 1994 Entry Draft and the return of draft choices transferred in the Pat Elynuik trade, March 21, 1994.

REGEHR, ROBYN **COL.**

Defense. Shoots left. 6'2", 210 lbs. Born, Recife, Brazil, April 19, 1980.
(Colorado's 3rd choice, 19th overall, in 1998 Entry Draft).

			Regular Season					Playoffs				
Season	Club	Lea	GP	G	A	TP	PIM	GP	G	A	TP	PIM
1996-97	Kamloops	WHL	64	4	19	23	96	5	0	1	1	18
1997-98	Kamloops	WHL	65	4	10	14	120	5	0	3	3	8

REHNBERG, HENRIK (REHN-buhrg) **N.J.**

Defense. Shoots left. 6'2", 195 lbs. Born, Grava, Sweden, July 20, 1977.
(New Jersey's 6th choice, 96th overall, in 1995 Entry Draft).

			Regular Season					Playoffs				
Season	Club	Lea	GP	G	A	TP	PIM	GP	G	A	TP	PIM
1994-95	Farjestad	Swe-Jr.	24	1	2	3	62	....	....	....	....	....
1995-96	Farjestad	Swe-Jr.	21	1	4	5	38	....	....	....	....	....
	Farjestad	Sweden	4	0	0	0	0	....	....	....	....	....
1996-97	Farjestad	Sweden	42	2	3	5	38	14	1	1	2	16
1997-98	Farjestad	EuroHL	6	0	0	0	39	....	....	....	....	....
	Farjestad	Sweden	32	0	1	1	24	10	0	0	0	12

REICH, JEREMY (RIGHK) **CHI.**

Center. Shoots left. 6'1", 198 lbs. Born, Craik, Sask., February 11, 1979.
(Chicago's 3rd choice, 39th overall, in 1997 Entry Draft).

			Regular Season					Playoffs				
Season	Club	Lea	GP	G	A	TP	PIM	GP	G	A	TP	PIM
1995-96	Seattle	WHL	65	11	11	22	88	5	0	1	1	10
1996-97	Seattle	WHL	62	19	31	50	134	15	2	5	7	36
1997-98	Seattle	WHL	43	24	23	47	121	....	....	....	....	....
	Swift Current	WHL	22	8	8	16	47	12	5	6	11	37

REICHEL, MARTIN (RIGH-khul) **EDM.**

Right wing. Shoots left. 6'1", 183 lbs. Born, Most, Czech., November 7, 1973.
(Edmonton's 2nd choice, 37th overall, in 1992 Entry Draft).

			Regular Season					Playoffs				
Season	Club	Lea	GP	G	A	TP	PIM	GP	G	A	TP	PIM
1990-91	Freiburg	Germany	23	7	8	15	19	....	....	....	....	....
1991-92	Freiburg	Germany	27	15	16	31	8	4	1	1	2	4
1992-93	Freiburg	Germany	37	13	9	22	27	9	4	4	8	11
1993-94	Rosenheim	Germany	20	5	15	20	6	....	....	....	....	....
1994-95	Rosenheim	Germany	43	11	26	37	36	7	3	3	6	37
1995-96	Rosenheim	Germany	50	17	28	45	40	4	3	0	3	2
1996-97	Rosenheim	Germany	45	8	14	22	30	3	0	0	0	4
1997-98	Nurnberg	Germany	49	13	24	37	35	....	....	....	....	....

REICHEL, ROBERT (RIGH-khul) **NYI**

Center. Shoots left. 5'10", 185 lbs. Born, Litvinov, Czech., June 25, 1971.
(Calgary's 5th choice, 70th overall, in 1989 Entry Draft).

			Regular Season					Playoffs				
Season	Club	Lea	GP	G	A	TP	PIM	GP	G	A	TP	PIM
1987-88	Litvinov	Czech.	36	17	10	27	8	....	....	....	....	....
1988-89	Litvinov	Czech.	44	23	25	48	32	....	....	....	....	....
1989-90	Litvinov	Czech.	52	*49	34	*83	....	....	....	....	....	....
1990-91	**Calgary**	**NHL**	**66**	**19**	**22**	**41**	**22**	**6**	**1**	**1**	**2**	**0**
1991-92	**Calgary**	**NHL**	**77**	**20**	**34**	**54**	**32**	....	....	....	....	....
1992-93	**Calgary**	**NHL**	**80**	**40**	**48**	**88**	**54**	**6**	**2**	**4**	**6**	**2**
1993-94	**Calgary**	**NHL**	**84**	**40**	**53**	**93**	**58**	**7**	**0**	**5**	**5**	**0**
1994-95	Frankfurt	Germany	21	19	24	43	41	....	....	....	....	....
	Calgary	**NHL**	**48**	**18**	**17**	**35**	**28**	**7**	**2**	**4**	**6**	**4**
1995-96	Frankfurt	Germany	46	47	54	101	84	3	1	3	4	0
1996-97	**Calgary**	**NHL**	**70**	**16**	**27**	**43**	**22**	....	....	....	....	....
	NY Islanders	**NHL**	**12**	**5**	**14**	**19**	**4**	....	....	....	....	....
1997-98	**NY Islanders**	**NHL**	**82**	**25**	**40**	**65**	**32**	....	....	....	....	....
	Czech.	Olympics	6	3	0	3	0	....	....	....	....	....
	NHL Totals		**519**	**183**	**255**	**438**	**252**	**26**	**5**	**14**	**19**	**6**

Czechoslovakian First All-Star Team (1990)

Traded to **NY Islanders** by **Calgary** for Marty McInnis, Tyrone Garner and Calgary's 6th round choice (previously acquired, Calgary selected Ilja Demidov) in 1997 Entry Draft, March 18, 1997.

REICHERT, CRAIG (RIGH-kuhrt) **ANA.**

Right wing. Shoots right. 6'1", 200 lbs. Born, Winnipeg, Man., May 11, 1974.
(Anaheim's 3rd choice, 67th overall, in 1994 Entry Draft).

			Regular Season					Playoffs				
Season	Club	Lea	GP	G	A	TP	PIM	GP	G	A	TP	PIM
1991-92	Spokane	WHL	68	13	20	33	86	4	1	0	1	4
1992-93	Red Deer	WHL	66	32	33	65	62	4	3	1	4	2
1993-94	Red Deer	WHL	72	52	67	119	153	4	2	2	4	8
1994-95	San Diego	IHL	49	4	12	16	28	....	....	....	....	....
1995-96	Baltimore	AHL	68	10	17	27	50	1	0	0	0	0
1996-97	**Anaheim**	**NHL**	**3**	**0**	**0**	**0**	**0**	....	....	....	....	....
	Baltimore	AHL	77	22	53	75	54	3	0	2	2	0
1997-98	Cincinnati	AHL	78	28	59	87	28	....	....	....	....	....
	NHL Totals		**3**	**0**	**0**	**0**	**0**	....	....	....	....	....

REID, DAVID **DAL.**

Left wing. Shoots left. 6'1", 217 lbs. Born, Toronto, Ont., May 15, 1964.
(Boston's 4th choice, 60th overall, in 1982 Entry Draft).

			Regular Season					Playoffs				
Season	Club	Lea	GP	G	A	TP	PIM	GP	G	A	TP	PIM
1981-82	Peterborough	OHL	68	10	32	42	41	9	2	3	5	11
1982-83	Peterborough	OHL	70	23	34	57	33	4	3	1	4	0
1983-84	Peterborough	OHL	60	33	64	97	12	....	....	....	....	....
	Boston	**NHL**	**8**	**1**	**0**	**1**	**2**	....	....	....	....	....
1984-85	**Boston**	**NHL**	**35**	**14**	**13**	**27**	**27**	**5**	**1**	**0**	**1**	**0**
	Hershey	AHL	43	10	14	24	6	....	....	....	....	....
1985-86	**Boston**	**NHL**	**37**	**10**	**10**	**20**	**10**	....	....	....	....	....
	Moncton	AHL	26	14	18	32	4	....	....	....	....	....
1986-87	**Boston**	**NHL**	**12**	**3**	**3**	**6**	**0**	**2**	**0**	**0**	**0**	**0**
	Moncton	AHL	40	12	22	34	23	5	0	1	1	0
1987-88	**Boston**	**NHL**	**3**	**0**	**0**	**0**	**0**	....	....	....	....	....
	Maine	AHL	63	21	37	58	40	10	6	7	13	0
1988-89	**Toronto**	**NHL**	**77**	**9**	**21**	**30**	**22**	....	....	....	....	....
1989-90	**Toronto**	**NHL**	**70**	**9**	**19**	**28**	**9**	**3**	**0**	**0**	**0**	**0**
1990-91	**Toronto**	**NHL**	**69**	**15**	**13**	**28**	**18**	....	....	....	....	....
1991-92	**Boston**	**NHL**	**43**	**7**	**7**	**14**	**27**	**15**	**2**	**5**	**7**	**4**
	Maine	AHL	12	1	5	6	4	....	....	....	....	....
1992-93	**Boston**	**NHL**	**65**	**20**	**16**	**36**	**10**	....	....	....	....	....
1993-94	**Boston**	**NHL**	**83**	**6**	**17**	**23**	**25**	**13**	**2**	**1**	**3**	**2**
1994-95	**Boston**	**NHL**	**38**	**5**	**5**	**10**	**10**	**5**	**0**	**0**	**0**	**0**
	Providence	AHL	7	3	0	3	0	....	....	....	....	....
1995-96	**Boston**	**NHL**	**63**	**23**	**21**	**44**	**4**	**5**	**0**	**2**	**2**	**2**
1996-97	**Dallas**	**NHL**	**82**	**19**	**20**	**39**	**10**	**7**	**1**	**0**	**1**	**4**
1997-98	**Dallas**	**NHL**	**65**	**6**	**12**	**18**	**14**	**5**	**0**	**3**	**3**	**2**
	NHL Totals		**750**	**147**	**177**	**324**	**188**	**60**	**6**	**11**	**17**	**14**

Signed as a free agent by **Toronto**, June 23, 1988. Signed as a free agent by **Boston**, December 1, 1991. Signed as a free agent by **Dallas**, July 11, 1996.

RENBERG, MIKAEL (REHN-buhrg) T.B.

Right wing. Shoots left. 6'2", 218 lbs. Born, Pitea, Sweden, May 5, 1972.
(Philadelphia's 3rd choice, 40th overall, in 1990 Entry Draft).

			Regular Season					Playoffs				
Season	Club	Lea	GP	G	A	TP	PIM	GP	G	A	TP	PIM
1988-89	Pitea	Sweden-2	12	6	3	9	....	....	....	....	....	....
1989-90	Pitea	Sweden-2	29	15	19	34	....	....	....	....	....	....
1990-91	Lulea HF	Sweden	29	11	6	17	12	5	1	1	2	4
1991-92	Lulea HF	Sweden	38	8	15	23	20	2	0	0	0	0
1992-93	Lulea HF	Sweden	39	19	13	32	61	11	4	4	8	4
1993-94	**Philadelphia**	**NHL**	**83**	**38**	**44**	**82**	**36**	....	....	....	....	....
1994-95	Lulea HF	Sweden	10	9	4	13	16	....	....	....	....	....
	Philadelphia	**NHL**	**47**	**26**	**31**	**57**	**20**	**15**	**6**	**7**	**13**	**6**
1995-96	**Philadelphia**	**NHL**	**51**	**23**	**20**	**43**	**45**	**11**	**3**	**6**	**9**	**14**
1996-97	**Philadelphia**	**NHL**	**77**	**22**	**37**	**59**	**65**	**18**	**5**	**6**	**11**	**4**
1997-98	**Tampa Bay**	**NHL**	**68**	**16**	**22**	**38**	**34**	....	....	....	....	....
	Sweden	Olympics	4	1	2	3	4	....	....	....	....	....
	NHL Totals		**326**	**125**	**154**	**279**	**200**	**44**	**14**	**19**	**33**	**24**

NHL/Upper Deck All-Rookie Team (1994)

Traded to **Tampa Bay** by **Philadelphia** with Karl Dykhuis for Philadelphia's 1st round choices in 1998 (Simon Gagne), 1999, 2000 and 2001 Entry Drafts (previously acquired by Tampa Bay), August 20, 1997.

RENNETTE, TYLER ST.L.

Center. Shoots right. 6'1", 175 lbs. Born, North Bay, Ont., April 16, 1979.
(St. Louis' 1st choice, 40th overall, in 1997 Entry Draft).

			Regular Season					Playoffs				
Season	Club	Lea	GP	G	A	TP	PIM	GP	G	A	TP	PIM
1996-97	North Bay	OHL	63	24	34	58	42	....	....	....	....	....
1997-98	North Bay	OHL	31	17	14	31	37	....	....	....	....	....
	Erie	OHL	24	16	17	33	20	6	3	3	6	2

RHEAUME, PASCAL (RAY-awm) ST.L.

Center. Shoots left. 6'1", 200 lbs. Born, Quebec, Que., June 21, 1973.

			Regular Season					Playoffs				
Season	Club	Lea	GP	G	A	TP	PIM	GP	G	A	TP	PIM
1991-92	Trois-Rivieres	QMJHL	65	17	20	37	84	14	5	4	9	23
1992-93	Sherbrooke	QMJHL	65	28	34	62	88	14	6	5	11	31
1993-94	Albany	AHL	55	17	18	35	43	5	0	1	1	0
1994-95	Albany	AHL	78	19	25	44	46	14	3	6	9	19
1995-96	Albany	AHL	68	26	42	68	50	4	1	2	3	2
1996-97	**New Jersey**	**NHL**	**2**	**1**	**0**	**1**	**0**	....	....	....	....	....
	Albany	AHL	51	22	23	45	40	16	2	8	10	16
1997-98	**St. Louis**	**NHL**	**48**	**6**	**9**	**15**	**35**	**10**	**1**	**3**	**4**	**8**
	NHL Totals		**50**	**7**	**9**	**16**	**35**	**10**	**1**	**3**	**4**	**8**

Signed as a free agent by **New Jersey**, October 1, 1993. Claimed by **St. Louis** from **New Jersey** in NHL Waiver Draft, September 28, 1997.

RIBEIRO, MIKE MTL.

Center. Shoots left. 5'11", 150 lbs. Born, Montreal, Que., February 10, 1980.
(Montreal's 2nd choice, 45th overall, in 1998 Entry Draft).

			Regular Season					Playoffs				
Season	Club	Lea	GP	G	A	TP	PIM	GP	G	A	TP	PIM
1996-97	Montreal	QAAA	43	32	57	89	48	....	....	....	....	....
1997-98	Rouyn Noranda	QMJHL	67	40	*85	125	55	6	3	1	4	0

QMJHL Second All-Star Team (1998)

RICCI, MIKE (REE-CHEE) S.J.

Center. Shoots left. 6', 190 lbs. Born, Scarborough, Ont., October 27, 1971.
(Philadelphia's 1st choice, 4th overall, in 1990 Entry Draft).

			Regular Season					Playoffs				
Season	Club	Lea	GP	G	A	TP	PIM	GP	G	A	TP	PIM
1987-88	Peterborough	OHL	41	24	37	61	20	8	5	5	10	4
1988-89	Peterborough	OHL	60	54	52	106	43	17	19	16	35	18
1989-90	Peterborough	OHL	60	52	64	116	39	12	5	7	12	26
1990-91	**Philadelphia**	**NHL**	**68**	**21**	**20**	**41**	**64**	....	....	....	....	....
1991-92	**Philadelphia**	**NHL**	**78**	**20**	**36**	**56**	**93**	....	....	....	....	....
1992-93	**Quebec**	**NHL**	**77**	**27**	**51**	**78**	**123**	**6**	**0**	**6**	**6**	**8**
1993-94	**Quebec**	**NHL**	**83**	**30**	**21**	**51**	**113**	....	....	....	....	....
1994-95	**Quebec**	**NHL**	**48**	**15**	**21**	**36**	**40**	**6**	**1**	**3**	**4**	**8**
1995-96	**Colorado**	**NHL**	**62**	**6**	**21**	**27**	**52**	**22**	**6**	**11**	**17**	**18** ♦
1996-97	**Colorado**	**NHL**	**63**	**13**	**19**	**32**	**59**	**17**	**2**	**4**	**6**	**17**
1997-98	**Colorado**	**NHL**	**6**	**0**	**4**	**4**	**2**	....	....	....	....	....
	San Jose	**NHL**	**59**	**9**	**14**	**23**	**30**	**6**	**1**	**3**	**4**	**6**
	NHL Totals		**544**	**141**	**207**	**348**	**576**	**57**	**10**	**27**	**37**	**57**

OHL Second All-Star Team (1989) • Canadian Major Junior Player of the Year (1990) • OHL First All-Star Team (1990)

Traded to **Quebec** by **Philadelphia** with Peter Forsberg, Steve Duchesne, Kerry Huffman, Ron Hextall, Chris Simon, Philadelphia's 1st round choice in the 1993 (Jocelyn Thibault) and 1994 (later traded to Toronto — later traded to Washington — Washington selected Nolan Baumgartner) Entry Drafts and cash for Eric Lindros, June 30, 1992. Transferred to **Colorado** after **Quebec** franchise relocated, June 21, 1995. Traded to **San Jose** by **Colorado** with Colorado's 2nd round choice (later traded to Buffalo - Buffalo selected Jaroslav Kristek) in 1998 Entry Draft for Shean Donovan and San Jose's 1st round choice (Alex Tanguay) in 1998 Entry Draft, November 21, 1997.

RICE, STEVEN

Right wing. Shoots right. 6', 217 lbs. Born, Kitchener, Ont., May 26, 1971.
(NY Rangers' 1st choice, 20th overall, in 1989 Entry Draft).

			Regular Season					Playoffs				
Season	Club	Lea	GP	G	A	TP	PIM	GP	G	A	TP	PIM
1987-88	Kitchener	OHL	59	11	14	25	43	4	0	1	1	0
1988-89	Kitchener	OHL	64	36	30	66	42	5	2	1	3	8
1989-90	Kitchener	OHL	58	39	37	76	102	16	4	8	12	24
1990-91	Kitchener	OHL	29	30	30	60	43	6	5	6	11	2
	NY Rangers	**NHL**	**11**	**1**	**1**	**2**	**4**	**2**	**2**	**1**	**3**	**6**
	Binghamton	AHL	8	4	1	5	12	5	2	0	2	2
1991-92	**Edmonton**	**NHL**	**3**	**0**	**0**	**0**	**2**	....	....	....	....	....
	Cape Breton	AHL	45	32	20	52	38	5	4	4	8	10
1992-93	**Edmonton**	**NHL**	**28**	**2**	**5**	**7**	**28**	....	....	....	....	....
	Cape Breton	AHL	51	34	28	62	63	14	4	6	10	22
1993-94	**Edmonton**	**NHL**	**63**	**17**	**15**	**32**	**36**	....	....	....	....	....
1994-95	**Hartford**	**NHL**	**40**	**11**	**10**	**21**	**61**	....	....	....	....	....
1995-96	**Hartford**	**NHL**	**59**	**10**	**12**	**22**	**47**	....	....	....	....	....
1996-97	**Hartford**	**NHL**	**78**	**21**	**14**	**35**	**59**	....	....	....	....	....
1997-98	**Carolina**	**NHL**	**47**	**2**	**4**	**6**	**38**	....	....	....	....	....
	NHL Totals		**329**	**64**	**61**	**125**	**275**	**2**	**2**	**1**	**3**	**6**

Memorial Cup All-Star Team (1990) • OHL Second All-Star Team (1991) • AHL Second All-Star Team (1993)

Traded to **Edmonton** by **NY Rangers** with Bernie Nicholls and Louie DeBrusk for Mark Messier and future considerations, October 4, 1991. Signed as a free agent by **Hartford**, August 18, 1994. Transferred to **Carolina** after **Hartford** franchise relocated, June 25, 1997.

RICH, CURTIS T.B.

Defense. Shoots left. 6'4", 200 lbs. Born, Edmonton, Alta., October 6, 1979.
(Tampa Bay's 5th choice, 121st overall, in 1998 Entry Draft).

			Regular Season					Playoffs				
Season	Club	Lea	GP	G	A	TP	PIM	GP	G	A	TP	PIM
1995-96	Calgary	WHL	24	0	0	0	10	....	....	....	....	....
1996-97	Calgary	WHL	45	1	6	7	73	....	....	....	....	....
1997-98	Calgary	WHL	70	3	12	15	204	17	0	0	0	36

RICHARDS, BRAD T.B.

Left wing. Shoots left. 6', 170 lbs. Born, Montague, P.E.I., May 2, 1980.
(Tampa Bay's 2nd choice, 64th overall, in 1998 Entry Draft).

			Regular Season					Playoffs				
Season	Club	Lea	GP	G	A	TP	PIM	GP	G	A	TP	PIM
1996-97	Notre Dame	SJHL	63	39	48	87	73	....	....	....	....	....
1997-98	Rimouski	QJMHL	68	33	82	115	44	19	8	24	32	2

RICHARDSON, LUKE PHI.

Defense. Shoots left. 6'4", 210 lbs. Born, Ottawa, Ont., March 26, 1969.
(Toronto's 1st choice, 7th overall, in 1987 Entry Draft).

			Regular Season					Playoffs				
Season	Club	Lea	GP	G	A	TP	PIM	GP	G	A	TP	PIM
1985-86	Peterborough	OHL	63	6	18	24	57	16	2	1	3	50
1986-87	Peterborough	OHL	59	13	32	45	70	12	0	5	5	24
1987-88	**Toronto**	**NHL**	**78**	**4**	**6**	**10**	**90**	**2**	**0**	**0**	**0**	**0**
1988-89	**Toronto**	**NHL**	**55**	**2**	**7**	**9**	**106**	....	....	....	....	....
1989-90	**Toronto**	**NHL**	**67**	**4**	**14**	**18**	**122**	**5**	**0**	**0**	**0**	**22**
1990-91	**Toronto**	**NHL**	**78**	**1**	**9**	**10**	**238**	....	....	....	....	....
1991-92	**Edmonton**	**NHL**	**75**	**2**	**19**	**21**	**118**	**16**	**0**	**5**	**5**	**45**
1992-93	**Edmonton**	**NHL**	**82**	**3**	**10**	**13**	**142**	....	....	....	....	....
1993-94	**Edmonton**	**NHL**	**69**	**2**	**6**	**8**	**131**	....	....	....	....	....
1994-95	**Edmonton**	**NHL**	**46**	**3**	**10**	**13**	**40**	....	....	....	....	....
1995-96	**Edmonton**	**NHL**	**82**	**2**	**9**	**11**	**108**	....	....	....	....	....
1996-97	**Edmonton**	**NHL**	**82**	**1**	**11**	**12**	**91**	**12**	**0**	**2**	**2**	**14**
1997-98	**Philadelphia**	**NHL**	**81**	**2**	**3**	**5**	**139**	**5**	**0**	**0**	**0**	**0**
	NHL Totals		**795**	**26**	**104**	**130**	**1325**	**40**	**0**	**7**	**7**	**81**

Traded to **Edmonton** by **Toronto** with Vincent Damphousse, Peter Ing, Scott Thornton, future considerations and cash for Grant Fuhr, Glenn Anderson and Craig Berube, September 19, 1991. Signed as a free agent by **Philadelphia**, July 23, 1997.

RICHER, STEPHANE (REE-shay) T.B.

Right wing. Shoots right. 6'2", 215 lbs. Born, Ripon, Que., June 7, 1966.
(Montreal's 3rd choice, 29th overall, in 1984 Entry Draft).

			Regular Season					Playoffs				
Season	Club	Lea	GP	G	A	TP	PIM	GP	G	A	TP	PIM
1983-84	Granby	QMJHL	67	39	37	76	58	3	1	1	2	4
1984-85	Granby	QMJHL	30	30	27	57	31	....	....	....	....	....
	Chicoutimi	QMJHL	27	31	32	63	40	12	13	13	26	25
	Montreal	**NHL**	**1**	**0**	**0**	**0**	**0**	....	....	....	....	....
	Sherbrooke	AHL	....	....	....	....	....	9	6	3	9	10
1985-86	**Montreal**	**NHL**	**65**	**21**	**16**	**37**	**50**	**16**	**4**	**1**	**5**	**23** ♦
1986-87	**Montreal**	**NHL**	**57**	**20**	**19**	**39**	**80**	**5**	**3**	**2**	**5**	**0**
	Sherbrooke	AHL	12	10	4	14	11	....	....	....	....	....
1987-88	**Montreal**	**NHL**	**72**	**50**	**28**	**78**	**72**	**8**	**7**	**5**	**12**	**6**
1988-89	**Montreal**	**NHL**	**68**	**25**	**35**	**60**	**61**	**21**	**6**	**5**	**11**	**14**
1989-90	**Montreal**	**NHL**	**75**	**51**	**40**	**91**	**46**	**9**	**7**	**3**	**10**	**2**
1990-91	**Montreal**	**NHL**	**75**	**31**	**30**	**61**	**53**	**13**	**9**	**5**	**14**	**6**
1991-92	**New Jersey**	**NHL**	**74**	**29**	**35**	**64**	**25**	**7**	**1**	**2**	**3**	**0**
1992-93	**New Jersey**	**NHL**	**78**	**38**	**35**	**73**	**44**	**5**	**2**	**2**	**4**	**2**
1993-94	**New Jersey**	**NHL**	**80**	**36**	**36**	**72**	**16**	**20**	**7**	**5**	**12**	**6**
1994-95	**New Jersey**	**NHL**	**45**	**23**	**16**	**39**	**10**	**19**	**6**	**15**	**21**	**2** ♦
1995-96	**New Jersey**	**NHL**	**73**	**20**	**12**	**32**	**30**	....	....	....	....	....
1996-97	**Montreal**	**NHL**	**63**	**22**	**24**	**46**	**32**	**5**	**0**	**0**	**0**	**0**
1997-98	**Montreal**	**NHL**	**14**	**5**	**4**	**9**	**5**	....	....	....	....	....
	Tampa Bay	**NHL**	**26**	**9**	**11**	**20**	**36**	....	....	....	....	....
	NHL Totals		**866**	**380**	**341**	**721**	**560**	**128**	**52**	**45**	**97**	**61**

QMJHL Rookie of the Year (1984) • QMJHL Second All-Star Team (1985)

Played in NHL All-Star Game (1990)

Traded to **New Jersey** by **Montreal** with Tom Chorske for Kirk Muller and Roland Melanson, September 20, 1991. Traded to **Montreal** by **New Jersey** for Lyle Odelein, August 22, 1996. Traded to **Tampa Bay** by **Montreal** with Darcy Tucker and David Wilkie for Patrick Poulin, Mick Vukota and Igor Ulanov, January 15, 1998.

RICHTER, BARRY (RIHK-tuhr) **NYI**

Defense. Shoots left. 6'2", 200 lbs. Born, Madison, WI, September 11, 1970.
(Hartford's 2nd choice, 32nd overall, in 1988 Entry Draft).

			Regular Season					Playoffs				
Season	Club	Lea	GP	G	A	TP	PIM	GP	G	A	TP	PIM
1987-88	Culver Academy	H.S.	35	24	29	53	18	....	....	....	....	....
1988-89	Culver Academy	H.S.	19	21	29	50	16	....	....	....	....	....
1989-90	U. of Wisconsin	WCHA	42	13	23	36	36	....	....	....	....	....
1990-91	U. of Wisconsin	WCHA	43	15	20	35	42	....	....	....	....	....
1991-92	U. of Wisconsin	WCHA	39	10	25	35	62	....	....	....	....	....
1992-93	U. of Wisconsin	WCHA	42	14	32	46	74	....	....	....	....	....
1993-94	United States	Nat-Tm	56	7	16	23	50	....	....	....	....	....
	United States	Olympics	8	0	3	3	4	....	....	....	....	....
	Binghamton	AHL	21	0	9	9	12	....	....	....	....	....
1994-95	Binghamton	AHL	73	15	41	56	54	11	4	5	9	12
1995-96	**NY Rangers**	**NHL**	**4**	**0**	**1**	**1**	**0**	....	....	....	....	....
	Binghamton	AHL	69	20	61	81	64	3	0	3	3	0
1996-97	**Boston**	**NHL**	**50**	**5**	**13**	**18**	**32**	....	....	....	....	....
	Providence	AHL	19	2	6	8	4	10	4	4	8	4
1997-98	Providence	AHL	75	16	29	45	47	....	....	....	....	....
	NHL Totals		**54**	**5**	**14**	**19**	**32**	....	....	....	....	....

NCAA Championship All-Tournament Team (1992) • WCHA First All-Star Team (1993) • NCAA West First All-American Team (1993) • AHL First All-Star Team (1996) • Won Eddie Shore Award (Outstanding Defenseman - AHL) (1996)

Traded to **NY Rangers** by **Hartford** with Steve Larmer, Nick Kypreos and Hartford's 6th round choice (Yuri Litvinov) in 1994 Entry Draft for Darren Turcotte and James Patrick, November 2, 1993. Signed as a free agent by **Boston**, July 19, 1996. Signed as a free agent by **NY Islanders**, August 17, 1998.

RIESEN, MICHEL (REE-sehn, MEE-shehl) **EDM.**

Left wing. Shoots right. 6'2", 190 lbs. Born, Oberbalm, Switzerland, April 11, 1979.
(Edmonton's 1st choice, 14th overall, in 1997 Entry Draft).

			Regular Season					Playoffs				
Season	Club	Lea	GP	G	A	TP	PIM	GP	G	A	TP	PIM
1994-95	EC Biel	Switz.	12	0	2	2	0	6	2	0	2	0
1995-96	EC Biel	Switz-2	34	9	6	15	2	3	1	0	1	0
1996-97	EC Biel	Switz-2	38	16	16	32	49	....	....	....	....	....
1997-98	HC Davos	Switz.	32	16	9	25	8	18	5	5	10	4

RIIHIJARVI, TEEMU (REE-ee-hee-jahr-vee) **S.J.**

Left wing. Shoots left. 6'6", 200 lbs. Born, Espoo, Finland, March 1, 1977.
(San Jose's 1st choice, 12th overall, in 1995 Entry Draft).

			Regular Season					Playoffs				
Season	Club	Lea	GP	G	A	TP	PIM	GP	G	A	TP	PIM
1993-94	Kiekko	Finland	13	1	1	2	6	....	....	....	....	....
1994-95	Kiekko	Finland	13	1	0	1	4	....	....	....	....	....
1995-96	Kiekko	Finland	2	0	0	0	0	....	....	....	....	....
	Haukat	Finland-2	4	0	0	0	2	....	....	....	....	....
	Kiekko	Fin-Jr.	19	2	4	6	46	4	0	2	2	6
1996-97	Kiekko	Finland	47	3	1	4	8	4	0	0	0	2
1997-98	Kiekko	Finland	12	0	1	1	6	....	....	....	....	....
	Lukko Rauma	Finland	37	5	3	8	61	....	....	....	....	....

RISIDORE, RYAN (RIHZ-ih-daws) **NYR**

Defense. Shoots left. 6'4", 195 lbs. Born, Hamilton, Ont., April 4, 1976.
(Hartford's 3rd choice, 109th overall, in 1994 Entry Draft).

			Regular Season					Playoffs				
Season	Club	Lea	GP	G	A	TP	PIM	GP	G	A	TP	PIM
1993-94	Guelph	OHL	51	2	9	11	39	9	0	0	0	12
1994-95	Guelph	OHL	65	2	30	32	102	14	2	2	4	19
1995-96	Guelph	OHL	66	12	38	50	186	16	4	5	9	*48
1996-97	Springfield	AHL	63	1	9	10	90	15	0	1	1	12
1997-98	Indianapolis	IHL	75	3	8	11	123	4	0	1	1	6

Rights transferred to **Carolina** after **Hartford** franchise relocated, June 25, 1997. Traded to **Chicago** by **Carolina** with Carolina's 5th round choice in 1998 Entry Draft for Enrico Ciccone, July 25, 1997. Traded to **NY Rangers** by **Chicago** for Ryan Vandenbussche, March 24, 1998.

RITCHIE, BYRON **CAR.**

Center. Shoots left. 5'10", 180 lbs. Born, Burnaby, B.C., April 24, 1977.
(Hartford's 6th choice, 165th overall, in 1995 Entry Draft).

			Regular Season					Playoffs				
Season	Club	Lea	GP	G	A	TP	PIM	GP	G	A	TP	PIM
1993-94	Lethbridge	WHL	44	4	11	15	44	6	0	0	0	14
1994-95	Lethbridge	WHL	58	22	28	50	132	....	....	....	....	....
1995-96	Lethbridge	WHL	66	55	51	106	163	4	0	2	2	4
	Springfield	AHL	6	2	1	3	4	8	0	3	3	0
1996-97	Lethbridge	WHL	63	50	76	126	115	18	*16	12	*28	28
1997-98	New Haven	AHL	65	13	18	31	97	....	....	....	....	....

WHL East Second All-Star Team (1996, 1997)

Rights transferred to **Carolina** after **Hartford** franchise relocated, June 25, 1997.

RITCHLIN, SEAN (RIHCH-lihn, SHAWN) **N.J.**

Right wing. Shoots right. 6', 200 lbs. Born, Rochester, NY, June 14, 1977.
(New Jersey's 10th choice, 145th overall, in 1996 Entry Draft).

			Regular Season					Playoffs				
Season	Club	Lea	GP	G	A	TP	PIM	GP	G	A	TP	PIM
1995-96	U. of Michigan	CCHA	27	7	7	14	24	....	....	....	....	....
1996-97	U. of Michigan	CCHA	38	10	10	20	48	....	....	....	....	....
1997-98	U. of Michigan	CCHA	27	3	3	6	29	....	....	....	....	....

RIVERS, JAMIE **ST.L.**

Defense. Shoots left. 6', 190 lbs. Born, Ottawa, Ont., March 16, 1975.
(St. Louis' 2nd choice, 63rd overall, in 1993 Entry Draft).

			Regular Season					Playoffs				
Season	Club	Lea	GP	G	A	TP	PIM	GP	G	A	TP	PIM
1991-92	Sudbury	OHL	55	3	13	16	20	8	0	0	0	0
1992-93	Sudbury	OHL	62	12	43	55	20	14	7	19	26	4
1993-94	Sudbury	OHL	65	32	*89	121	58	10	1	9	10	14
1994-95	Sudbury	OHL	46	9	56	65	30	18	7	26	33	22
1995-96	**St. Louis**	**NHL**	**3**	**0**	**0**	**0**	**2**	....	....	....	....	....
	Worcester	AHL	75	7	45	52	130	4	0	1	1	4
1996-97	**St. Louis**	**NHL**	**15**	**2**	**5**	**7**	**6**	....	....	....	....	....
	Worcester	AHL	63	8	35	43	83	5	1	2	3	14
1997-98	**St. Louis**	**NHL**	**59**	**2**	**4**	**6**	**36**	....	....	....	....	....
	NHL Totals		**77**	**4**	**9**	**13**	**44**	....	....	....	....	....

OHL First All-Star Team (1994) • Canadian Major Junior Second All-Star Team (1994) • OHL Second All-Star Team (1995) • AHL Second All-Star Team (1997)

RIVET, CRAIG (rih-VAY) **MTL.**

Defense. Shoots right. 6'2", 195 lbs. Born, North Bay, Ont., September 13, 1974.
(Montreal's 4th choice, 68th overall, in 1992 Entry Draft).

			Regular Season					Playoffs				
Season	Club	Lea	GP	G	A	TP	PIM	GP	G	A	TP	PIM
1991-92	Kingston	OHL	66	5	21	26	97	....	....	....	....	....
1992-93	Kingston	OHL	64	19	55	74	117	16	5	7	12	39
1993-94	Kingston	OHL	61	12	52	64	100	6	0	3	3	6
	Fredericton	AHL	4	0	2	2	2	....	....	....	....	....
1994-95	Fredericton	AHL	78	5	27	32	126	12	0	4	4	17
	Montreal	**NHL**	**5**	**0**	**1**	**1**	**5**	....	....	....	....	....
1995-96	**Montreal**	**NHL**	**19**	**1**	**4**	**5**	**54**	....	....	....	....	....
	Fredericton	AHL	49	5	18	23	189	6	0	0	0	12
1996-97	**Montreal**	**NHL**	**35**	**0**	**4**	**4**	**54**	**5**	**0**	**1**	**1**	**14**
	Fredericton	AHL	23	3	12	15	99	....	....	....	....	....
1997-98	**Montreal**	**NHL**	**61**	**0**	**2**	**2**	**93**	**5**	**0**	**0**	**0**	**2**
	NHL Totals		**120**	**1**	**11**	**12**	**206**	**10**	**0**	**1**	**1**	**16**

ROBERTS, DAVID **DAL.**

Left wing. Shoots left. 6', 185 lbs. Born, Alameda, CA, May 28, 1970.
(St. Louis' 5th choice, 114th overall, in 1989 Entry Draft).

			Regular Season					Playoffs				
Season	Club	Lea	GP	G	A	TP	PIM	GP	G	A	TP	PIM
1988-89	Avon Old Farms	H.S.	25	28	48	76	....	....	....	....	....	....
1989-90	U. of Michigan	CCHA	42	21	32	53	46	....	....	....	....	....
1990-91	U. of Michigan	CCHA	43	26	45	71	58	....	....	....	....	....
1991-92	U. of Michigan	CCHA	44	16	42	58	68	....	....	....	....	....
1992-93	U. of Michigan	CCHA	40	27	38	65	40	....	....	....	....	....
1993-94	United States	Nat-Tm	49	17	28	45	68	....	....	....	....	....
	United States	Olympics	8	1	5	6	4	....	....	....	....	....
	St. Louis	**NHL**	**1**	**0**	**0**	**0**	**2**	**3**	**0**	**0**	**0**	**12**
	Peoria	IHL	10	4	6	10	4	....	....	....	....	....
1994-95	Peoria	IHL	65	30	38	68	65	....	....	....	....	....
	St. Louis	**NHL**	**19**	**6**	**5**	**11**	**10**	**6**	**0**	**0**	**0**	**4**
1995-96	**St. Louis**	**NHL**	**28**	**1**	**6**	**7**	**12**	....	....	....	....	....
	Worcester	AHL	22	8	17	25	46	....	....	....	....	....
	Edmonton	**NHL**	**6**	**2**	**4**	**6**	**6**	....	....	....	....	....
1996-97	**Vancouver**	**NHL**	**58**	**10**	**17**	**27**	**51**	....	....	....	....	....
1997-98	**Vancouver**	**NHL**	**13**	**1**	**1**	**2**	**4**	....	....	....	....	....
	Syracuse	AHL	37	17	22	39	44	5	2	1	3	2
	NHL Totals		**125**	**20**	**33**	**53**	**85**	**9**	**0**	**0**	**0**	**16**

CCHA Second All-Star Team (1991, 1993) • NCAA West Second All-American Team (1991)

Traded to **Edmonton** by **St. Louis** for future considerations, March 12, 1996. Signed as a free agent by **Vancouver**, July 31, 1996. Signed as a free agent by **Dallas**, July 31, 1998.

ROBERTS, GARY **CAR.**

Left wing. Shoots left. 6'1", 190 lbs. Born, North York, Ont., May 23, 1966.
(Calgary's 1st choice, 12th overall, in 1984 Entry Draft).

			Regular Season					Playoffs				
Season	Club	Lea	GP	G	A	TP	PIM	GP	G	A	TP	PIM
1982-83	Ottawa	OHL	53	12	8	20	83	5	1	0	1	19
1983-84	Ottawa	OHL	48	27	30	57	144	13	10	7	17	62
1984-85	Ottawa	OHL	59	44	62	106	186	5	2	8	10	10
	Moncton	AHL	7	4	2	6	7	....	....	....	....	....
1985-86	Ottawa	OHL	24	26	25	51	83	....	....	....	....	....
	Guelph	OHL	23	18	15	33	65	20	18	13	31	43
1986-87	**Calgary**	**NHL**	**32**	**5**	**10**	**15**	**85**	**2**	**0**	**0**	**0**	**4**
	Moncton	AHL	38	20	18	38	72	....	....	....	....	....
1987-88	**Calgary**	**NHL**	**74**	**13**	**15**	**28**	**282**	**9**	**2**	**3**	**5**	**29**
1988-89	**Calgary**	**NHL**	**71**	**22**	**16**	**38**	**250**	**22**	**5**	**7**	**12**	**57** ♦
1989-90	**Calgary**	**NHL**	**78**	**39**	**33**	**72**	**222**	**6**	**2**	**5**	**7**	**41**
1990-91	**Calgary**	**NHL**	**80**	**22**	**31**	**53**	**252**	**7**	**1**	**3**	**4**	**18**
1991-92	**Calgary**	**NHL**	**76**	**53**	**37**	**90**	**207**	....	....	....	....	....
1992-93	**Calgary**	**NHL**	**58**	**38**	**41**	**79**	**172**	**5**	**1**	**6**	**7**	**43**
1993-94	**Calgary**	**NHL**	**73**	**41**	**43**	**84**	**145**	**7**	**2**	**6**	**8**	**24**
1994-95	**Calgary**	**NHL**	**8**	**2**	**2**	**4**	**43**	....	....	....	....	....
1995-96	**Calgary**	**NHL**	**35**	**22**	**20**	**42**	**78**	....	....	....	....	....
1996-97			DID NOT PLAY – INJURED									
1997-98	**Carolina**	**NHL**	**61**	**20**	**29**	**49**	**103**	....	....	....	....	....
	NHL Totals		**646**	**277**	**277**	**554**	**1839**	**58**	**13**	**30**	**43**	**216**

OHL Second All-Star Team (1985, 1986) • Won Bill Masterton Memorial Trophy (1996)

Played in NHL All-Star Game (1992, 1993)

• Missed entire 1996-97 season after being placed on voluntary retired list to recover from neck and shoulder injuries, June 17, 1996. Traded to **Carolina** by **Calgary** with Trevor Kidd for Andrew Cassels and Jean-Sebastien Giguere, August 25, 1997.

ROBERTSSON, BERT (ROH-behrt-suhn) **VAN.**

Defense. Shoots left. 6'3", 205 lbs. Born, Sodertalje, Sweden, June 30, 1974.
(Vancouver's 8th choice, 254th overall, in 1993 Entry Draft).

			Regular Season					Playoffs				
Season	Club	Lea	GP	G	A	TP	PIM	GP	G	A	TP	PIM
1992-93	Sodertalje	Sweden-2	23	2	1	3	24	....	....	....	....	....
1993-94	Sodertalje	Sweden-2	28	0	1	1	12	....	....	....	....	....
1994-95	Sodertalje	Sweden-2	23	1	2	3	24	....	....	....	....	....
1995-96	Syracuse	AHL	65	1	7	8	109	16	0	1	1	26
1996-97	Syracuse	AHL	80	4	9	13	132	3	1	0	1	4
1997-98	**Vancouver**	**NHL**	**30**	**2**	**4**	**6**	**24**	....	....	....	....	....
	Syracuse	AHL	42	5	9	14	87	3	0	0	0	6
	NHL Totals		**30**	**2**	**4**	**6**	**24**	....	....	....	....	....

ROBIDAS, STEPHANE (ROH-bih-dah) **MTL.**

Defense. Shoots right. 5'11", 195 lbs. Born, Sherbrooke, Que., March 3, 1977.
(Montreal's 7th choice, 164th overall, in 1995 Entry Draft).

			Regular Season					Playoffs				
Season	Club	Lea	GP	G	A	TP	PIM	GP	G	A	TP	PIM
1993-94	Shawinigan	QMJHL	67	3	18	21	33	1	0	0	0	0
1994-95	Shawinigan	QMJHL	71	13	56	69	44	15	7	12	19	4
1995-96	Shawinigan	QMJHL	67	23	56	79	53	6	1	5	6	10
1996-97	Shawinigan	QMJHL	67	24	51	75	59	7	4	6	10	14
1997-98	Fredericton	AHL	79	10	21	31	50	4	0	2	2	0

QMJHL First All-Star Team (1996, 1997)

ROBINSON, JASON — T.B.

Defense. Shoots left. 6'2", 190 lbs. Born, Goderich, Ont., August 22, 1978.
(Tampa Bay's 3rd choice, 125th overall, in 1996 Entry Draft).

			Regular Season					Playoffs				
Season	Club	Lea	GP	G	A	TP	PIM	GP	G	A	TP	PIM
1995-96	Niagara Falls	OHL	51	2	4	6	100	10	0	0	0	16
1996-97	Erie	OHL	19	0	7	7	58	....	....	....	....	....
1997-98	Erie	OHL	49	5	15	20	97	7	0	1	1	14

ROBITAILLE, LUC (ROH-buh-tigh) — L.A.

Left wing. Shoots left. 6'1", 205 lbs. Born, Montreal, Que., February 17, 1966.
(Los Angeles' 9th choice, 171st overall, in 1984 Entry Draft).

			Regular Season					Playoffs				
Season	Club	Lea	GP	G	A	TP	PIM	GP	G	A	TP	PIM
1983-84	Hull	QMJHL	70	32	53	85	48	....	....	....	....	....
1984-85	Hull	QMJHL	64	55	94	149	115	5	4	2	6	27
1985-86	Hull	QMJHL	63	68	123	191	91	15	17	27	44	28
1986-87	**Los Angeles**	**NHL**	**79**	**45**	**39**	**84**	**28**	**5**	**1**	**4**	**5**	**2**
1987-88	**Los Angeles**	**NHL**	**80**	**53**	**58**	**111**	**82**	**5**	**2**	**5**	**7**	**18**
1988-89	**Los Angeles**	**NHL**	**78**	**46**	**52**	**98**	**65**	**11**	**2**	**6**	**8**	**10**
1989-90	**Los Angeles**	**NHL**	**80**	**52**	**49**	**101**	**38**	**10**	**5**	**5**	**10**	**10**
1990-91	**Los Angeles**	**NHL**	**76**	**45**	**46**	**91**	**68**	**12**	**12**	**4**	**16**	**22**
1991-92	**Los Angeles**	**NHL**	**80**	**44**	**63**	**107**	**95**	**6**	**3**	**4**	**7**	**12**
1992-93	**Los Angeles**	**NHL**	**84**	**63**	**62**	**125**	**100**	**24**	**9**	**13**	**22**	**28**
1993-94	**Los Angeles**	**NHL**	**83**	**44**	**42**	**86**	**86**	....	....	....	....	....
1994-95	**Pittsburgh**	**NHL**	**46**	**23**	**19**	**42**	**37**	**12**	**7**	**4**	**11**	**26**
1995-96	**NY Rangers**	**NHL**	**77**	**23**	**46**	**69**	**80**	**11**	**1**	**5**	**6**	**8**
1996-97	**NY Rangers**	**NHL**	**69**	**24**	**24**	**48**	**48**	**15**	**4**	**7**	**11**	**4**
1997-98	**Los Angeles**	**NHL**	**57**	**16**	**24**	**40**	**66**	**4**	**1**	**2**	**3**	**6**
	NHL Totals		**889**	**478**	**524**	**1002**	**793**	**115**	**47**	**59**	**106**	**146**

QMJHL Second All-Star Team (1985) • QMJHL First All-Star Team (1986) • Canadian Major Junior Player of the Year (1986) • NHL All-Rookie Team (1987) • Won Calder Memorial Trophy (1987) • NHL Second All-Star Team (1987, 1992) • NHL First All-Star Team (1988, 1989, 1990, 1991, 1993)

Played in NHL All-Star Game (1988, 1989, 1990, 1991, 1992, 1993)

Traded to **Pittsburgh** by **LA Kings** for Rick Tocchet and Pittsburgh's 2nd round choice (Pavel Rosa) in 1995 Entry Draft, July 29, 1994. Traded to **NY Rangers** by **Pittsburgh** with Ulf Samuelsson for Petr Nedved and Sergei Zubov, August 31, 1995. Traded to **LA Kings** by **NY Rangers** for Kevin Stevens, August 28, 1997.

ROBITAILLE, RANDY (ROH-buh-tigh) — BOS.

Center. Shoots left. 5'11", 190 lbs. Born, Ottawa, Ont., October 12, 1975.

			Regular Season					Playoffs				
Season	Club	Lea	GP	G	A	TP	PIM	GP	G	A	TP	PIM
1995-96	Miami-Ohio	CCHA	36	14	31	45	26	....	....	....	....	....
1996-97	Miami-Ohio	CCHA	39	27	34	61	44	....	....	....	....	....
	Boston	**NHL**	**1**	**0**	**0**	**0**	**0**	....	....	....	....	....
1997-98	**Boston**	**NHL**	**4**	**0**	**0**	**0**	**0**	....	....	....	....	....
	Providence	AHL	48	15	29	44	16	....	....	....	....	....
	NHL Totals		**5**	**0**	**0**	**0**	**0**	....	....	....	....	....

CCHA First All-Star Team (1997) • NCAA West First All-American Team (1997)

Signed as a free agent by **Boston**, March 27, 1997.

ROCHE, DAVE (ROHSH) — CGY.

Center. Shoots left. 6'4", 234 lbs. Born, Lindsay, Ont., June 13, 1975.
(Pittsburgh's 3rd choice, 62nd overall, in 1993 Entry Draft).

			Regular Season					Playoffs				
Season	Club	Lea	GP	G	A	TP	PIM	GP	G	A	TP	PIM
1991-92	Peterborough	OHL	62	10	17	27	134	10	0	0	0	34
1992-93	Peterborough	OHL	56	40	60	100	105	21	14	15	29	42
1993-94	Peterborough	OHL	34	15	22	37	127	....	....	....	....	....
	Windsor	OHL	29	14	20	34	73	4	1	1	2	15
1994-95	Windsor	OHL	66	55	59	114	180	10	9	6	15	16
1995-96	**Pittsburgh**	**NHL**	**71**	**7**	**7**	**14**	**130**	**16**	**2**	**7**	**9**	**26**
1996-97	**Pittsburgh**	**NHL**	**61**	**5**	**5**	**10**	**155**	....	....	....	....	....
	Cleveland	IHL	18	5	5	10	25	13	6	3	9	*87
1997-98	Syracuse	AHL	73	12	20	32	307	5	2	0	2	10
	NHL Totals		**132**	**12**	**12**	**24**	**285**	**16**	**2**	**7**	**9**	**26**

OHL First All-Star Team (1995)

Traded to **Calgary** by **Pittsburgh** with Ken Wregget for German Titov and Todd Hlushko, June 17, 1998.

ROCHEFORT, RICHARD — N.J.

Center. Shoots right. 5'10", 185 lbs. Born, North Bay, Ont., January 7, 1977.
(New Jersey's 9th choice, 174th overall, in 1995 Entry Draft).

			Regular Season					Playoffs				
Season	Club	Lea	GP	G	A	TP	PIM	GP	G	A	TP	PIM
1994-95	Sudbury	OHL	57	21	44	65	26	13	3	7	10	6
1995-96	Sudbury	OHL	56	25	40	65	38	....	....	....	....	....
1996-97	Sudbury	OHL	28	18	24	42	40	....	....	....	....	....
	Sarnia	OHL	18	5	23	28	23	12	3	9	12	8
1997-98	Albany	AHL	59	7	14	21	16	13	1	0	1	4

RODGERS, MARC — DET.

Right wing. Shoots right. 5'9", 185 lbs. Born, Shawville, Que., March 16, 1972.

			Regular Season					Playoffs				
Season	Club	Lea	GP	G	A	TP	PIM	GP	G	A	TP	PIM
1989-90	Granby	QMJHL	61	24	31	55	155	....	....	....	....	....
1990-91	Granby	QMJHL	64	28	49	77	41	....	....	....	....	....
1991-92	Granby	QMJHL	36	30	57	87	49	....	....	....	....	....
	Verdun	QMJHL	29	14	19	33	0	18	3	13	16	26
1992-93	Wheeling	ECHL	64	23	40	63	91	6	1	1	2	8
1993-94	Las Vegas	IHL	40	7	7	14	110	4	0	2	2	17
1994-95	Las Vegas	IHL	58	17	19	36	131	10	2	6	8	25
1995-96	Las Vegas	IHL	51	13	16	29	65	....	....	....	....	....
	Utah	IHL	31	6	14	20	51	21	4	4	8	16
1996-97	Utah	IHL	5	2	2	4	10	....	....	....	....	....
	Quebec	IHL	70	25	42	67	115	9	1	9	10	14
1997-98	Quebec	IHL	61	20	22	42	61	....	....	....	....	....
	Chicago	IHL	11	5	5	10	22	22	9	9	18	10

Signed as a free agent by **Detroit**, August 3, 1998.

ROED, PETER — S.J.

Center. Shoots left. 5'11", 190 lbs. Born, St. Paul, MN, November 15, 1976.
(San Jose's 2nd choice, 38th overall, in 1995 Entry Draft).

			Regular Season					Playoffs				
Season	Club	Lea	GP	G	A	TP	PIM	GP	G	A	TP	PIM
1994-95	White Bear Lake	H.S.	28	20	39	59	22	....	....	....	....	....
1995-96	Prince George	WHL	66	18	19	37	36	....	....	....	....	....
1996-97	Prince George	WHL	51	21	16	37	8	14	5	2	7	9
	Louisville	ECHL	7	1	0	1	4	....	....	....	....	....
1997-98	Kentucky	AHL	67	6	7	13	44	....	....	....	....	....
	Louisville	ECHL	4	0	2	2	10	....	....	....	....	....

ROENICK, JEREMY (ROH-nihk) — PHX.

Center. Shoots right. 6', 192 lbs. Born, Boston, MA, January 17, 1970.
(Chicago's 1st choice, 8th overall, in 1988 Entry Draft).

			Regular Season					Playoffs				
Season	Club	Lea	GP	G	A	TP	PIM	GP	G	A	TP	PIM
1987-88	Thayer Academy	H.S.	24	34	50	84	....	....	....	....	....	....
1988-89	Hull	QMJHL	28	34	36	70	14	....	....	....	....	....
	Chicago	**NHL**	**20**	**9**	**9**	**18**	**4**	**10**	**1**	**3**	**4**	**7**
1989-90	**Chicago**	**NHL**	**78**	**26**	**40**	**66**	**54**	**20**	**11**	**7**	**18**	**8**
1990-91	**Chicago**	**NHL**	**79**	**41**	**53**	**94**	**80**	**6**	**3**	**5**	**8**	**4**
1991-92	**Chicago**	**NHL**	**80**	**53**	**50**	**103**	**98**	**18**	**12**	**10**	**22**	**12**
1992-93	**Chicago**	**NHL**	**84**	**50**	**57**	**107**	**86**	**4**	**1**	**2**	**3**	**2**
1993-94	**Chicago**	**NHL**	**84**	**46**	**61**	**107**	**125**	**6**	**1**	**6**	**7**	**2**
1994-95	Kolner Haie	Germany	3	3	1	4	2	....	....	....	....	....
	Chicago	**NHL**	**33**	**10**	**24**	**34**	**14**	**8**	**1**	**2**	**3**	**16**
1995-96	**Chicago**	**NHL**	**66**	**32**	**35**	**67**	**109**	**10**	**5**	**7**	**12**	**2**
1996-97	**Phoenix**	**NHL**	**72**	**29**	**40**	**69**	**115**	**6**	**2**	**4**	**6**	**4**
1997-98	**Phoenix**	**NHL**	**79**	**24**	**32**	**56**	**103**	**6**	**5**	**3**	**8**	**4**
	United States	Olympics	4	0	1	1	6	....	....	....	....	....
	NHL Totals		**675**	**320**	**401**	**721**	**788**	**94**	**42**	**49**	**91**	**61**

QMJHL Second All-Star Team (1989)

Played in NHL All-Star Game (1991, 1992, 1993, 1994)

Traded to **Phoenix** by **Chicago** for Alexei Zhamnov, Craig Mills and Phoenix's 1st round choice (Ty Jones) in 1997 Entry Draft, August 16, 1996.

ROEST, STACY (ROHST) — DET.

Center. Shoots right. 5'9", 192 lbs. Born, Lethbridge, Alta., March 15, 1974.

			Regular Season					Playoffs				
Season	Club	Lea	GP	G	A	TP	PIM	GP	G	A	TP	PIM
1992-93	Medicine Hat	WHL	72	33	73	106	30	10	3	10	13	6
1993-94	Medicine Hat	WHL	72	48	72	120	48	3	1	0	1	4
1994-95	Medicine Hat	WHL	69	37	78	115	32	5	2	7	9	2
	Adirondack	AHL	3	0	0	0	0	....	....	....	....	....
1995-96	Adirondack	AHL	76	16	39	55	40	3	0	0	0	0
1996-97	Adirondack	AHL	78	25	41	66	30	4	1	1	2	0
1997-98	Adirondack	AHL	80	34	58	92	30	3	2	1	3	6

WHL East First All-Star Team (1994) • WHL East Second All-Star Team (1995)

Signed as a free agent by **Detroit**, June 9, 1997.

ROHLIN, LEIF (roh-LEEN) — VAN.

Defense. Shoots left. 6'1", 198 lbs. Born, Vasteras, Sweden, February 26, 1968.
(Vancouver's 2nd choice, 33rd overall, in 1988 Entry Draft).

			Regular Season					Playoffs				
Season	Club	Lea	GP	G	A	TP	PIM	GP	G	A	TP	PIM
1986-87	Vasteras IK	Sweden-2	27	2	5	7	12	12	0	2	2	8
1987-88	Vasteras IK	Sweden-2	30	2	15	17	46	7	0	4	4	8
1988-89	Vasteras IK	Sweden	22	3	7	10	18	....	....	....	....	....
1989-90	Vasteras IK	Sweden	32	3	6	9	40	2	0	0	0	2
1990-91	Vasteras IK	Sweden	40	4	10	14	46	4	0	1	1	8
1991-92	Vasteras IK	Sweden	39	4	6	10	52	....	....	....	....	....
1992-93	Vasteras IK	Sweden	37	5	7	12	24	2	0	0	0	0
1993-94	Vasteras IK	Sweden	40	6	14	20	26	4	0	1	1	6
	Sweden	Olympics	8	0	1	1	10	....	....	....	....	....
1994-95	Vasteras IK	Sweden	39	15	15	30	46	4	2	0	2	2
1995-96	**Vancouver**	**NHL**	**56**	**6**	**16**	**22**	**32**	**5**	**0**	**0**	**0**	**0**
1996-97	**Vancouver**	**NHL**	**40**	**2**	**8**	**10**	**8**	....	....	....	....	....
1997-98	Ambri	Switz.	40	7	29	36	28	14	3	4	7	32
	NHL Totals		**96**	**8**	**24**	**32**	**40**	**5**	**0**	**0**	**0**	**0**

ROHLOFF, JON (ROH-lawf) — S.J.

Defense. Shoots right. 5'11", 221 lbs. Born, Mankato, MN, October 3, 1969.
(Boston's 7th choice, 186th overall, in 1988 Entry Draft).

			Regular Season					Playoffs				
Season	Club	Lea	GP	G	A	TP	PIM	GP	G	A	TP	PIM
1987-88	Grand Rapids	H.S.	23	10	13	23	....	....	....	....	....	....
1988-89	U. Minn-Duluth	WCHA	39	1	2	3	44	....	....	....	....	....
1989-90	U. Minn-Duluth	WCHA	5	0	1	1	6	....	....	....	....	....
1990-91	U. Minn-Duluth	WCHA	32	6	11	17	38	....	....	....	....	....
1991-92	U. Minn-Duluth	WCHA	27	9	9	18	48	....	....	....	....	....
1992-93	U. Minn-Duluth	WCHA	36	15	20	35	87	....	....	....	....	....
1993-94	Providence	AHL	55	12	23	35	59	....	....	....	....	....
1994-95	Providence	AHL	4	2	1	3	6	....	....	....	....	....
	Boston	**NHL**	**34**	**3**	**8**	**11**	**39**	**5**	**0**	**0**	**0**	**6**
1995-96	**Boston**	**NHL**	**79**	**1**	**12**	**13**	**59**	**5**	**1**	**2**	**3**	**2**
1996-97	**Boston**	**NHL**	**37**	**3**	**5**	**8**	**31**	....	....	....	....	....
	Providence	AHL	3	1	1	2	0	....	....	....	....	....
1997-98	Providence	AHL	58	6	17	23	46	....	....	....	....	....
	NHL Totals		**150**	**7**	**25**	**32**	**129**	**10**	**1**	**2**	**3**	**8**

WCHA Second All-Star Team (1993)

Signed as a free agent by **San Jose**, July 22, 1998.

ROHLOFF, TODD (ROH-lawf) — CHI.

Defense. Shoots left. 6'3", 213 lbs. Born, Grand Rapids, MN, January 16, 1974.

			Regular Season					Playoffs				
Season	Club	Lea	GP	G	A	TP	PIM	GP	G	A	TP	PIM
1994-95	Miami-Ohio	CCHA	38	1	6	7	22	....	....	....	....	....
1995-96	Miami-Ohio	CCHA	23	2	4	6	24	....	....	....	....	....
1996-97	Miami-Ohio	CCHA	38	2	12	14	48	....	....	....	....	....
1997-98	Miami-Ohio	CCHA	17	2	5	7	38	....	....	....	....	....
	Indianapolis	IHL	5	0	1	1	6	1	0	0	0	0

Signed as a free agent by **Chicago**, July 8, 1998.

ROLSTON, BRIAN (ROHL-stuhn) N.J.

Center. Shoots left. 6'2", 200 lbs. Born, Flint, MI, February 21, 1973.
(New Jersey's 2nd choice, 11th overall, in 1991 Entry Draft).

			Regular Season					Playoffs				
Season	Club	Lea	GP	G	A	TP	PIM	GP	G	A	TP	PIM
1990-91	Detroit	NAJHL	36	49	46	95	14	....	....	....	....	....
1991-92	Lake Superior	CCHA	37	14	23	37	14	....	....	....	....	....
1992-93	Lake Superior	CCHA	39	33	31	64	20	....	....	....	....	....
1993-94	United States	Nat-Tm	41	20	28	48	36	....	....	....	....	....
	United States	Olympics	8	7	0	7	8	....	....	....	....	....
	Albany	AHL	17	5	5	10	8	5	1	2	3	0
1994-95	Albany	AHL	18	9	11	20	10	....	....	....	....	....
	New Jersey	**NHL**	**40**	**7**	**11**	**18**	**17**	**6**	**2**	**1**	**3**	**4 ♦**
1995-96	**New Jersey**	**NHL**	**58**	**13**	**11**	**24**	**8**	....	....	....	....	....
1996-97	**New Jersey**	**NHL**	**81**	**18**	**27**	**45**	**20**	**10**	**4**	**1**	**5**	**6**
1997-98	**New Jersey**	**NHL**	**76**	**16**	**14**	**30**	**16**	**6**	**1**	**0**	**1**	**2**
	NHL Totals		**255**	**54**	**63**	**117**	**61**	**22**	**7**	**2**	**9**	**12**

NCAA Championship All-Tournament Team (1992, 1993) • CCHA First All-Star Team (1993) • NCAA West Second All-American Team (1993)

ROMANIUK, RUSSELL (ROH-muh-NUHK)

Left wing. Shoots left. 6', 195 lbs. Born, Winnipeg, Man., June 9, 1970.
(Winnipeg's 2nd choice, 31st overall, in 1988 Entry Draft).

			Regular Season					Playoffs				
Season	Club	Lea	GP	G	A	TP	PIM	GP	G	A	TP	PIM
1987-88	St. Boniface	MJHL			STATISTICS NOT AVAILABLE							
1988-89	North Dakota	WCHA	39	17	14	31	32	....	....	....	....	....
	Canada	Nat-Tm	3	1	0	1	0	....	....	....	....	....
1989-90	North Dakota	WCHA	45	36	15	51	54	....	....	....	....	....
1990-91	North Dakota	WCHA	39	40	28	68	30	....	....	....	....	....
1991-92	**Winnipeg**	**NHL**	**27**	**3**	**5**	**8**	**18**	....	....	....	....	....
	Moncton	AHL	45	16	15	31	25	10	5	4	9	19
1992-93	**Winnipeg**	**NHL**	**28**	**3**	**1**	**4**	**22**	**1**	**0**	**0**	**0**	**0**
	Moncton	AHL	28	18	8	26	40	5	0	4	4	2
	Fort Wayne	IHL	4	2	0	2	7	....	....	....	....	....
1993-94	Canada	Nat-Tm	34	8	9	17	17	....	....	....	....	....
	Winnipeg	**NHL**	**24**	**4**	**8**	**12**	**6**	....	....	....	....	....
	Moncton	AHL	18	16	8	24	24	17	2	6	8	30
1994-95	**Winnipeg**	**NHL**	**6**	**0**	**0**	**0**	**0**	....	....	....	....	....
	Springfield	AHL	17	5	7	12	29	....	....	....	....	....
1995-96	**Philadelphia**	**NHL**	**17**	**3**	**0**	**3**	**17**	**1**	**0**	**0**	**0**	**0**
	Hershey	AHL	27	19	10	29	43	....	....	....	....	....
1996-97	Manitoba	IHL	46	14	13	27	43	....	....	....	....	....
1997-98	Long Beach	IHL	49	16	11	27	37	....	....	....	....	....
	Manitoba	IHL	5	0	1	1	8	....	....	....	....	....
	Las Vegas	IHL	22	6	4	10	10	4	2	2	4	4
	NHL Totals		**102**	**13**	**14**	**27**	**63**	**2**	**0**	**0**	**0**	**0**

WCHA First All-Star Team (1991)

Traded to **Philadelphia** by **Winnipeg** for Jeff Finley, June 27, 1995.

RONAN, ED (ROH-nan)

Right wing. Shoots right. 6', 197 lbs. Born, Quincy, MA, March 21, 1968.
(Montreal's 13th choice, 227th overall, in 1987 Entry Draft).

			Regular Season					Playoffs				
Season	Club	Lea	GP	G	A	TP	PIM	GP	G	A	TP	PIM
1986-87	Andover Academy	H.S.	22	10	22	32	10	....	....	....	....	....
1987-88	Boston University	H.E.	31	2	5	7	20	....	....	....	....	....
1988-89	Boston University	H.E.	36	4	11	15	34	....	....	....	....	....
1989-90	Boston University	H.E.	44	17	23	40	50	....	....	....	....	....
1990-91	Boston University	H.E.	41	16	19	35	38	....	....	....	....	....
1991-92	**Montreal**	**NHL**	**3**	**0**	**0**	**0**	**0**	....	....	....	....	....
	Fredericton	AHL	78	25	34	59	82	7	5	1	6	6
1992-93	**Montreal**	**NHL**	**53**	**5**	**7**	**12**	**20**	**14**	**2**	**3**	**5**	**10 ♦**
	Fredericton	AHL	16	10	5	15	15	5	2	4	6	6
1993-94	**Montreal**	**NHL**	**61**	**6**	**8**	**14**	**42**	**7**	**1**	**0**	**1**	**0**
1994-95	**Montreal**	**NHL**	**30**	**1**	**4**	**5**	**12**	....	....	....	....	....
1995-96	**Winnipeg**	**NHL**	**17**	**0**	**0**	**0**	**16**	....	....	....	....	....
	Springfield	AHL	31	8	16	24	50	10	7	6	13	4
1996-97	**Buffalo**	**NHL**	**18**	**1**	**4**	**5**	**11**	**6**	**1**	**0**	**1**	**6**
	Rochester	AHL	47	13	21	34	62	....	....	....	....	....
1997-98	Providence	AHL	49	13	15	28	48	....	....	....	....	....
	NHL Totals		**182**	**13**	**23**	**36**	**101**	**27**	**4**	**3**	**7**	**16**

Signed as a free agent by **Winnipeg**, October 13, 1995. Signed as a free agent by **Buffalo**, September 5, 1996.

RONDEAU, JEREMY CGY.

Left wing. Shoots left. 6'2", 220 lbs. Born, Vermillion, Alta., November 30, 1978.
(Calgary's 11th choice, 167th overall, in 1997 Entry Draft).

			Regular Season					Playoffs				
Season	Club	Lea	GP	G	A	TP	PIM	GP	G	A	TP	PIM
1995-96	Swift Current	WHL	42	4	2	6	22	....	....	....	....	....
1996-97	Swift Current	WHL	70	11	15	26	64	10	1	1	2	8
1997-98	Swift Current	WHL	70	19	24	43	84	12	0	4	4	4

RONNING, CLIFF PHX.

Center. Shoots left. 5'8", 167 lbs. Born, Burnaby, B.C., October 1, 1965.
(St. Louis' 9th choice, 134th overall, in 1984 Entry Draft).

			Regular Season					Playoffs				
Season	Club	Lea	GP	G	A	TP	PIM	GP	G	A	TP	PIM
1983-84	New Westminster	WHL	71	69	67	136	10	9	8	13	21	10
1984-85	New Westminster	WHL	70	*89	108	*197	20	11	10	14	24	4
1985-86	Canada	Nat-Tm	71	55	63	118	....	....	....	....	....	....
	St. Louis	**NHL**	....	....	....	....	....	**5**	**1**	**1**	**2**	**2**
1986-87	Canada	Nat-Tm	26	17	16	33	12	....	....	....	....	....
	St. Louis	**NHL**	**42**	**11**	**14**	**25**	**6**	**4**	**0**	**1**	**1**	**0**
1987-88	**St. Louis**	**NHL**	**26**	**5**	**8**	**13**	**12**	....	....	....	....	....
1988-89	**St. Louis**	**NHL**	**64**	**24**	**31**	**55**	**18**	**7**	**1**	**3**	**4**	**0**
	Peoria	IHL	12	11	20	31	8	....	....	....	....	....
1989-90	HC Asiago	Italy	36	67	49	116	25	6	7	12	19	4
1990-91	**St. Louis**	**NHL**	**48**	**14**	**18**	**32**	**10**	....	....	....	....	....
	Vancouver	**NHL**	**11**	**6**	**6**	**12**	**0**	**6**	**6**	**3**	**9**	**12**
1991-92	**Vancouver**	**NHL**	**80**	**24**	**47**	**71**	**42**	**13**	**8**	**5**	**13**	**6**
1992-93	**Vancouver**	**NHL**	**79**	**29**	**56**	**85**	**30**	**12**	**2**	**9**	**11**	**6**
1993-94	**Vancouver**	**NHL**	**76**	**25**	**43**	**68**	**42**	**24**	**5**	**10**	**15**	**16**
1994-95	**Vancouver**	**NHL**	**41**	**6**	**19**	**25**	**27**	**11**	**3**	**5**	**8**	**2**
1995-96	**Vancouver**	**NHL**	**79**	**22**	**45**	**67**	**42**	**6**	**0**	**2**	**2**	**6**
1996-97	**Phoenix**	**NHL**	**69**	**19**	**32**	**51**	**26**	**7**	**0**	**7**	**7**	**12**
1997-98	**Phoenix**	**NHL**	**80**	**11**	**44**	**55**	**36**	**6**	**1**	**3**	**4**	**4**
	NHL Totals		**695**	**196**	**363**	**559**	**291**	**101**	**27**	**49**	**76**	**66**

WHL First All-Star Team (1985)

Traded to **Vancouver** by **St. Louis** with Geoff Courtnall, Robert Dirk, Sergio Momesso and St. Louis' 5th round choice (Brian Loney) in 1992 Entry Draft for Dan Quinn and Garth Butcher, March 5, 1991. Signed as a free agent by **Phoenix**, July 1, 1996.

ROSA, PAVEL (ROHZA) L.A.

Right wing. Shoots right. 6', 195 lbs. Born, Most, Czech., June 7, 1977.
(Los Angeles' 3rd choice, 50th overall, in 1995 Entry Draft).

			Regular Season					Playoffs				
Season	Club	Lea	GP	G	A	TP	PIM	GP	G	A	TP	PIM
1994-95	Litvinov	Czech-Jr.	40	56	42	98	....	....	....	....	....	....
	Litvinov	Cze-Rep.	2	0	0	0	0	1	0	0	0	0
1995-96	Hull	QMJHL	61	46	70	116	39	18	14	22	36	25
1996-97	Hull	QMJHL	68	*63	*90	*153	66	14	18	13	31	16
1997-98	Fredericton	AHL	1	0	0	0	0	....	....	....	....	....
	Long Beach	IHL	2	0	1	1	0	1	1	1	2	0

QMJHL First All-Star Team (1997) • Canadian Major Junior First All-Star Team (1997)

ROSSITER, KYLE FLA.

Defense. Shoots left. 6'2", 200 lbs. Born, Edmonton, Alta., June 9, 1980.
(Florida's 1st choice, 30th overall, in 1998 Entry Draft).

			Regular Season					Playoffs				
Season	Club	Lea	GP	G	A	TP	PIM	GP	G	A	TP	PIM
1996-97	Spokane	WHL	50	0	2	2	65	9	0	0	0	6
1997-98	Spokane	WHL	61	6	16	22	190	15	0	3	3	28

Canadian Major Junior Scholastic Player of the Year (1998)

ROURKE, ALLAN TOR.

Defense. Shoots left. 6'1", 214 lbs. Born, Mississauga, Ont., March 6, 1980.
(Toronto's 6th choice, 154th overall, in 1998 Entry Draft).

			Regular Season					Playoffs				
Season	Club	Lea	GP	G	A	TP	PIM	GP	G	A	TP	PIM
1996-97	Kitchener	OHL	25	1	1	2	12	6	0	0	0	0
1997-98	Kitchener	OHL	48	5	17	22	59	6	1	1	2	6

ROUSE, BOB (ROWS) S.J.

Defense. Shoots right. 6'2", 220 lbs. Born, Surrey, B.C., June 18, 1964.
(Minnesota's 3rd choice, 80th overall, in 1982 Entry Draft).

			Regular Season					Playoffs				
Season	Club	Lea	GP	G	A	TP	PIM	GP	G	A	TP	PIM
1980-81	Billings	WHL	70	0	13	13	116	5	0	0	0	2
1981-82	Billings	WHL	71	7	22	29	209	5	0	2	2	10
1982-83	Nanaimo	WHL	29	7	20	27	86	....	....	....	....	....
	Lethbridge	WHL	42	8	30	38	82	20	2	13	15	55
1983-84	Lethbridge	WHL	71	18	42	60	101	5	0	1	1	28
	Minnesota	**NHL**	**1**	**0**	**0**	**0**	**0**	....	....	....	....	....
1984-85	**Minnesota**	**NHL**	**63**	**2**	**9**	**11**	**113**	....	....	....	....	....
	Springfield	AHL	8	0	3	3	6	....	....	....	....	....
1985-86	**Minnesota**	**NHL**	**75**	**1**	**14**	**15**	**151**	**3**	**0**	**0**	**0**	**0**
1986-87	**Minnesota**	**NHL**	**72**	**2**	**10**	**12**	**179**	....	....	....	....	....
1987-88	**Minnesota**	**NHL**	**74**	**0**	**12**	**12**	**168**	....	....	....	....	....
1988-89	**Minnesota**	**NHL**	**66**	**4**	**13**	**17**	**124**	....	....	....	....	....
	Washington	**NHL**	**13**	**0**	**2**	**2**	**36**	**6**	**2**	**0**	**2**	**4**
1989-90	**Washington**	**NHL**	**70**	**4**	**16**	**20**	**123**	**15**	**2**	**3**	**5**	**47**
1990-91	**Washington**	**NHL**	**47**	**5**	**15**	**20**	**65**	....	....	....	....	....
	Toronto	**NHL**	**13**	**2**	**4**	**6**	**10**	....	....	....	....	....
1991-92	**Toronto**	**NHL**	**79**	**3**	**19**	**22**	**97**	....	....	....	....	....
1992-93	**Toronto**	**NHL**	**82**	**3**	**11**	**14**	**130**	**21**	**3**	**8**	**11**	**29**
1993-94	**Toronto**	**NHL**	**63**	**5**	**11**	**16**	**101**	**18**	**0**	**3**	**3**	**29**
1994-95	**Detroit**	**NHL**	**48**	**1**	**7**	**8**	**36**	**18**	**0**	**3**	**3**	**8**
1995-96	**Detroit**	**NHL**	**58**	**0**	**6**	**6**	**48**	**7**	**0**	**1**	**1**	**4**
1996-97	**Detroit**	**NHL**	**70**	**4**	**9**	**13**	**58**	**20**	**0**	**0**	**0**	**55 ♦**
1997-98	**Detroit**	**NHL**	**71**	**1**	**11**	**12**	**57**	**22**	**0**	**3**	**3**	**16 ♦**
	NHL Totals		**965**	**37**	**169**	**206**	**1496**	**130**	**7**	**21**	**28**	**192**

WHL East First All-Star Team (1984)

Traded to **Washington** by **Minnesota** with Dino Ciccarelli for Mike Gartner and Larry Murphy, March 7, 1989. Traded to **Toronto** by **Washington** with Peter Zezel for Al Iafrate, January 16, 1991. Signed as a free agent by **Detroit**, August 5, 1994. Signed as a free agent by **San Jose**, June 14, 1998.

ROY, ANDRE (WAH, AHN-dray)

Left wing. Shoots left. 6'3", 202 lbs. Born, Port Chester, NY, February 8, 1975.
(Boston's 5th choice, 151st overall, in 1994 Entry Draft).

			Regular Season					Playoffs				
Season	**Club**	**Lea**	**GP**	**G**	**A**	**TP**	**PIM**	**GP**	**G**	**A**	**TP**	**PIM**
1993-94	Beauport	QMJHL	33	6	7	13	125	....	....	....	....	....
	Chicoutimi	QMJHL	32	4	14	18	152	25	3	6	9	94
1994-95	Chicoutimi	QMJHL	20	15	8	23	90	....	....	....	....	....
	Drummondville	QMJHL	34	18	13	31	233	4	2	0	2	34
1995-96	**Boston**	**NHL**	**3**	**0**	**0**	**0**	**0**	....	....	....	....	....
	Providence	AHL	58	7	8	15	167	1	0	0	0	10
1996-97	**Boston**	**NHL**	**10**	**0**	**2**	**2**	**12**	....	....	....	....	....
	Providence	AHL	50	17	11	28	234	....	....	....	....	....
1997-98	Providence	AHL	36	3	11	14	154	....	....	....	....	....
	Charlotte	ECHL	27	10	8	18	132	7	2	3	5	34
	NHL Totals		**13**	**0**	**2**	**2**	**12**	....	....	....	....	....

ROY, JEAN-YVES (WAH)

Right wing. Shoots left. 5'10", 180 lbs. Born, Rosemere, Que., February 17, 1969.

			Regular Season					Playoffs				
Season	**Club**	**Lea**	**GP**	**G**	**A**	**TP**	**PIM**	**GP**	**G**	**A**	**TP**	**PIM**
1989-90	U. of Maine	H.E.	46	*39	26	65	52	....	....	....	....	....
1990-91	U. of Maine	H.E.	43	37	45	82	62	....	....	....	....	....
1991-92	U. of Maine	H.E.	35	32	24	56	62	....	....	....	....	....
	Canada	Nat-Tm	13	10	4	14	6	....	....	....	....	....
1992-93	Canada	Nat-Tm	23	9	6	15	35	....	....	....	....	....
	Binghamton	AHL	49	13	15	28	21	14	5	2	7	4
1993-94	Binghamton	AHL	65	41	24	65	33	....	....	....	....	....
	Canada	Nat-Tm	6	3	2	5	2	....	....	....	....	....
	Canada	Olympics	8	1	0	1	0	....	....	....	....	....
1994-95	Binghamton	AHL	67	41	36	77	28	11	4	6	10	12
	NY Rangers	**NHL**	**3**	**1**	**0**	**1**	**2**	....	....	....	....	....
1995-96	**Ottawa**	**NHL**	**4**	**1**	**1**	**2**	**2**	....	....	....	....	....
	P.E.I.	AHL	67	40	55	95	64	5	4	8	12	6
1996-97	**Boston**	**NHL**	**52**	**10**	**15**	**25**	**22**	....	....	....	....	....
	Providence	AHL	27	9	16	25	30	10	2	7	9	2
1997-98	**Boston**	**NHL**	**2**	**0**	**0**	**0**	**0**	....	....	....	....	....
	Providence	AHL	65	28	34	62	60	....	....	....	....	....
	NHL Totals		**61**	**12**	**16**	**28**	**26**	....	....	....	....	....

NCAA East Second All-American Team (1990) • Hockey East First All-Star Team (1991) • NCAA East First All-American Team (1991, 1992) • NCAA Championship All-Tournament Team (1991) • Hockey East Second All-Star Team (1992)

Signed as a free agent by **NY Rangers**, July 20, 1992. Traded to **Ottawa** by **NY Rangers** for Steve Larouche, October 5, 1995. Signed as a free agent by **Boston**, July 15, 1996.

ROY, JIMMY (ROI)

Center. Shoots right. 5'11", 170 lbs. Born, Sioux Lookout, Ont., September 22, 1975.
(Dallas' 7th choice, 254th overall, in 1994 Entry Draft).

			Regular Season					Playoffs				
Season	**Club**	**Lea**	**GP**	**G**	**A**	**TP**	**PIM**	**GP**	**G**	**A**	**TP**	**PIM**
1993-94	Thunder Bay	USHL	46	21	33	54	101	....	....	....	....	....
1994-95	Michigan Tech	WCHA	38	5	11	16	62	....	....	....	....	....
1995-96	Michigan Tech	WCHA	42	17	17	34	84	....	....	....	....	....
1996-97	Canada	Nat-Tm	55	10	17	27	82	....	....	....	....	....
1997-98	Manitoba	IHL	61	8	10	18	133	3	0	0	0	6

ROY, STEPHANE (WAH) **ST.L.**

Center. Shoots left. 5'10", 173 lbs. Born, Ste-Martine, Que., January 26, 1976.
(St. Louis' 1st choice, 68th overall, in 1994 Entry Draft).

			Regular Season					Playoffs				
Season	**Club**	**Lea**	**GP**	**G**	**A**	**TP**	**PIM**	**GP**	**G**	**A**	**TP**	**PIM**
1993-94	Val d'Or	QMJHL	72	25	28	53	116	....	....	....	....	....
1994-95	Val d'Or	QMJHL	68	19	52	71	113	....	....	....	....	....
1995-96	Val d'Or	QMJHL	62	43	72	115	89	13	9	15	24	10
	Worcester	AHL	1	0	0	0	2	....	....	....	....	....
1996-97	Worcester	AHL	66	24	23	47	57	5	2	0	2	4
1997-98	Worcester	AHL	77	21	27	48	95	10	4	4	8	10

ROYER, REMI (ROHY-uhr) **CHI.**

Defense. Shoots right. 6'1", 183 lbs. Born, Donnacona, Que., February 12, 1978.
(Chicago's 1st choice, 31st overall, in 1996 Entry Draft).

			Regular Season					Playoffs				
Season	**Club**	**Lea**	**GP**	**G**	**A**	**TP**	**PIM**	**GP**	**G**	**A**	**TP**	**PIM**
1994-95	Victoriaville	QMJHL	57	3	17	20	144	4	0	1	1	7
1995-96	Victoriaville	QMJHL	43	12	14	26	209	....	....	....	....	....
	St-Hyacinthe	QMJHL	19	10	9	19	80	12	1	4	5	29
1996-97	Rouyn-Noranda	QMJHL	29	3	12	15	85	....	....	....	....	....
	Indianapolis	IHL	10	0	1	1	17	....	....	....	....	....
1997-98	Rouyn-Noranda	QMJHL	66	20	48	68	205	6	1	3	4	8
	Indianapolis	IHL	5	0	2	2	4	5	1	2	3	12

QMJHL First All-Star Team (1998)

ROZSIVAL, MICHAL (ROH-see-vahl) **PIT.**

Defense. Shoots right. 6'1", 194 lbs. Born, Vlasim, Czech., September 3, 1978.
(Pittsburgh's 5th choice, 105th overall, in 1996 Entry Draft).

			Regular Season					Playoffs				
Season	**Club**	**Lea**	**GP**	**G**	**A**	**TP**	**PIM**	**GP**	**G**	**A**	**TP**	**PIM**
1994-95	Dukla Jihlava	Czech-Jr.	31	8	13	21	....	....	....	....	....	....
1995-96	Dukla Jihlava	Cze-Rep.	36	3	4	7	....	....	....	....	....	....
1996-97	Swift Current	WHL	63	8	31	39	80	10	0	6	6	15
1997-98	Swift Current	WHL	71	14	55	69	122	12	0	5	5	33

WHL East First All-Star Team (1998)

RUCCHIN, STEVE (ROO-chihn) **ANA.**

Center. Shoots left. 6'3", 215 lbs. Born, Thunder Bay, Ont., July 4, 1971.
(Anaheim's 1st choice, 2nd overall, in 1994 Supplemental Draft).

			Regular Season					Playoffs				
Season	**Club**	**Lea**	**GP**	**G**	**A**	**TP**	**PIM**	**GP**	**G**	**A**	**TP**	**PIM**
1990-91	Western Ontario	OUAA	34	13	16	29	14	....	....	....	....	....
1991-92	Western Ontario	OUAA	37	28	34	62	36	....	....	....	....	....
1992-93	Western Ontario	OUAA	34	22	26	48	16	....	....	....	....	....
1993-94	Western Ontario	OUAA	35	30	23	53	30	....	....	....	....	....
1994-95	San Diego	IHL	41	11	15	26	14	....	....	....	....	....
	Anaheim	**NHL**	**43**	**6**	**11**	**17**	**23**	....	....	....	....	....
1995-96	**Anaheim**	**NHL**	**64**	**19**	**25**	**44**	**12**	....	....	....	....	....
1996-97	**Anaheim**	**NHL**	**79**	**19**	**48**	**67**	**24**	**8**	**1**	**2**	**3**	**10**
1997-98	**Anaheim**	**NHL**	**72**	**17**	**36**	**53**	**13**	....	....	....	....	....
	NHL Totals		**258**	**61**	**120**	**181**	**72**	**8**	**1**	**2**	**3**	**10**

RUCINSKI, MIKE (roo-SIHN-skee) **CAR.**

Defense. Shoots left. 5'11", 179 lbs. Born, Trenton, MI, March 30, 1975.
(Hartford's 8th choice, 217th overall, in 1995 Entry Draft).

			Regular Season					Playoffs				
Season	**Club**	**Lea**	**GP**	**G**	**A**	**TP**	**PIM**	**GP**	**G**	**A**	**TP**	**PIM**
1992-93	Detroit	OHL	66	6	13	19	59	15	0	4	4	12
1993-94	Detroit	OHL	66	2	26	28	58	17	0	7	7	15
1994-95	Detroit	OHL	64	9	18	27	61	21	3	3	6	8
1995-96	Detroit	OHL	51	10	26	36	65	11	2	4	6	14
1996-97	Richmond	ECHL	61	20	23	43	85	8	2	6	8	18
	Springfield	AHL	6	0	1	1	0	....	....	....	....	....
1997-98	**Carolina**	**NHL**	**9**	**0**	**1**	**1**	**2**	....	....	....	....	....
	New Haven	AHL	65	5	17	22	50	1	0	0	0	0
	Cleveland	IHL	2	0	0	0	4	....	....	....	....	....
	NHL Totals		**9**	**0**	**1**	**1**	**2**	....	....	....	....	....

• Rights transferred to **Carolina** after **Hartford** franchise relocated, June 25, 1997.

RUCINSKY, MARTIN (roo-SHIHN-skee) **MTL.**

Left wing. Shoots left. 6'1", 205 lbs. Born, Most, Czech., March 11, 1971.
(Edmonton's 2nd choice, 20th overall, in 1991 Entry Draft).

			Regular Season					Playoffs				
Season	**Club**	**Lea**	**GP**	**G**	**A**	**TP**	**PIM**	**GP**	**G**	**A**	**TP**	**PIM**
1988-89	Litvinov	Czech.	3	1	0	1	2	....	....	....	....	....
1989-90	Litvinov	Czech.	47	17	9	26	....	....	....	....	....	....
1990-91	Litvinov	Czech.	56	24	20	44	69	....	....	....	....	....
1991-92	**Edmonton**	**NHL**	**2**	**0**	**0**	**0**	**0**	....	....	....	....	....
	Cape Breton	AHL	35	11	12	23	34	....	....	....	....	....
	Quebec	**NHL**	**4**	**1**	**1**	**2**	**2**	....	....	....	....	....
	Halifax	AHL	7	1	1	2	6	....	....	....	....	....
1992-93	**Quebec**	**NHL**	**77**	**18**	**30**	**48**	**51**	**6**	**1**	**1**	**2**	**4**
1993-94	**Quebec**	**NHL**	**60**	**9**	**23**	**32**	**58**	....	....	....	....	....
1994-95	Litvinov	Cze-Rep.	13	12	10	22	54	....	....	....	....	....
	Quebec	**NHL**	**20**	**3**	**6**	**9**	**14**	....	....	....	....	....
1995-96	Vsetin	Cze-Rep.	1	1	1	2	0	....	....	....	....	....
	Colorado	**NHL**	**22**	**4**	**11**	**15**	**14**	....	....	....	....	....
	Montreal	**NHL**	**56**	**25**	**35**	**60**	**54**	....	....	....	....	....
1996-97	**Montreal**	**NHL**	**70**	**28**	**27**	**55**	**62**	**5**	**0**	**0**	**0**	**4**
1997-98	**Montreal**	**NHL**	**78**	**21**	**32**	**53**	**84**	**10**	**3**	**0**	**3**	**4**
	Czech Republic	Olympics	6	3	1	4	4	....	....	....	....	....
	NHL Totals		**389**	**109**	**165**	**274**	**339**	**21**	**4**	**1**	**5**	**12**

Traded to **Quebec** by **Edmonton** for Ron Tugnutt and Brad Zavisha, March 10, 1992. Transferred to **Colorado** after **Quebec** franchise relocated, June 21, 1995. Traded to **Montreal** by **Colorado** with Andrei Kovalenko and Jocelyn Thibault for Patrick Roy and Mike Keane, December 6, 1995.

RUFF, JASON

Left wing. Shoots left. 6'2", 192 lbs. Born, Kelowna, B.C., January 27, 1970.
(St Louis' 3rd choice, 96th overall, in 1990 Entry Draft).

			Regular Season					Playoffs				
Season	**Club**	**Lea**	**GP**	**G**	**A**	**TP**	**PIM**	**GP**	**G**	**A**	**TP**	**PIM**
1987-88	Lethbridge	WHL	69	25	22	47	109	....	....	....	....	....
1988-89	Lethbridge	WHL	69	42	38	80	127	....	....	....	....	....
1989-90	Lethbridge	WHL	72	55	64	119	114	19	9	10	19	18
1990-91	Lethbridge	WHL	66	61	75	136	154	16	12	17	29	18
	Peoria	IHL	....	....	....	....	....	5	0	0	0	2
1991-92	Peoria	IHL	67	27	45	72	148	10	7	7	14	19
1992-93	**St. Louis**	**NHL**	**7**	**2**	**1**	**3**	**8**	....	....	....	....	....
	Peoria	IHL	40	22	21	43	81	....	....	....	....	....
	Tampa Bay	**NHL**	**1**	**0**	**0**	**0**	**0**	....	....	....	....	....
	Atlanta	IHL	26	11	14	25	90	7	2	1	3	26
1993-94	**Tampa Bay**	**NHL**	**6**	**1**	**2**	**3**	**2**	....	....	....	....	....
	Atlanta	IHL	71	24	25	49	122	14	6	*17	23	41
1994-95	Atlanta	IHL	64	42	34	76	161	3	3	1	4	10
1995-96	Atlanta	IHL	59	39	33	72	135	2	0	0	0	16
1996-97	Quebec	IHL	80	35	50	85	93	9	8	5	13	10
1997-98	Quebec	IHL	54	21	24	45	77	....	....	....	....	....
	Cleveland	IHL	6	2	3	5	9	10	6	6	12	4
	NHL Totals		**14**	**3**	**3**	**6**	**10**	....	....	....	....	....

WHL East First All-Star Team (1991)

Traded to **Tampa Bay** by **St. Louis** with future considerations for Doug Crossman, Basil McRae and Tampa Bay's 4th round choice (Andrei Petrakov) in 1996 Entry Draft, January 28, 1993.

RULLIER, JOE **L.A.**

Defense. Shoots right. 6'3", 198 lbs. Born, Montreal, Que., January 28, 1980.
(Los Angeles' 5th choice, 133rd overall, in 1998 Entry Draft).

			Regular Season					Playoffs				
Season	**Club**	**Lea**	**GP**	**G**	**A**	**TP**	**PIM**	**GP**	**G**	**A**	**TP**	**PIM**
1996-97	Rimouski	QMJHL	23	0	3	3	87	4	0	0	0	11
1997-98	Rimouski	QMJHL	55	1	10	11	176	16	1	4	5	34

RUMBLE, DARREN

Defense. Shoots left. 6'1", 200 lbs. Born, Barrie, Ont., January 23, 1969.
(Philadelphia's 1st choice, 20th overall, in 1987 Entry Draft).

			Regular Season					Playoffs				
Season	**Club**	**Lea**	**GP**	**G**	**A**	**TP**	**PIM**	**GP**	**G**	**A**	**TP**	**PIM**
1986-87	Kitchener	OHL	64	11	32	43	44	4	0	1	1	9
1987-88	Kitchener	OHL	55	15	50	65	64	....	....	....	....	....
1988-89	Kitchener	OHL	46	11	28	39	25	5	1	0	1	2
1989-90	Hershey	AHL	57	2	13	15	31	....	....	....	....	....
1990-91	**Philadelphia**	**NHL**	**3**	**1**	**0**	**1**	**0**	....	....	....	....	....
	Hershey	AHL	73	6	35	41	48	3	0	5	5	2
1991-92	Hershey	AHL	79	12	54	66	118	6	0	3	3	2
1992-93	**Ottawa**	**NHL**	**69**	**3**	**13**	**16**	**61**	....	....	....	....	....
	New Haven	AHL	2	1	0	1	0	....	....	....	....	....
1993-94	**Ottawa**	**NHL**	**70**	**6**	**9**	**15**	**116**	....	....	....	....	....
	P.E.I.	AHL	3	2	0	2	0	....	....	....	....	....
1994-95	P.E.I.	AHL	70	7	46	53	77	11	0	6	6	4
1995-96	**Philadelphia**	**NHL**	**5**	**0**	**0**	**0**	**4**	....	....	....	....	....
	Hershey	AHL	58	13	37	50	83	5	0	0	0	6
1996-97	**Philadelphia**	**NHL**	**10**	**0**	**0**	**0**	**0**	....	....	....	....	....
	Philadelphia	AHL	72	18	44	62	83	7	0	3	3	19
1997-98	Mannheim	EuroHL	4	0	1	1	4	....	....	....	....	....
	Mannheim	Germany	21	2	7	9	18	....	....	....	....	....
	San Antonio	IHL	46	7	22	29	47	....	....	....	....	....
	NHL Totals		**157**	**10**	**22**	**32**	**181**	....	....	....	....	....

AHL Second All-Star Team (1995) • AHL First All-Star Team (1997) • Won Eddie Shore Award (Outstanding Defenseman - AHL) (1997)

Claimed by **Ottawa** from **Philadelphia** in Expansion Draft, June 18, 1992. Signed as a free agent by **Philadelphia**, July 31, 1995.

RUPP, MICHAEL — NYI

Left wing. Shoots left. 6'5", 218 lbs. Born, Cleveland, OH, January 13, 1980.
(NY Islanders' 1st choice, 9th overall, in 1998 Entry Draft).

			Regular Season					Playoffs				
Season	Club	Lea	GP	G	A	TP	PIM	GP	G	A	TP	PIM
1997-98	Windsor	OHL	38	9	8	17	60	....	....	....	....	....
	Erie	OHL	26	7	3	10	57	7	3	1	4	6

RUSSELL, CAM — CHI.

Defense. Shoots left. 6'4", 200 lbs. Born, Halifax, N.S., January 12, 1969.
(Chicago's 3rd choice, 50th overall, in 1987 Entry Draft).

			Regular Season					Playoffs				
Season	Club	Lea	GP	G	A	TP	PIM	GP	G	A	TP	PIM
1985-86	Hull	QMJHL	56	3	4	7	24	15	0	2	2	4
1986-87	Hull	QMJHL	66	3	16	19	119	8	0	1	1	16
1987-88	Hull	QMJHL	53	9	18	27	141	19	2	5	7	39
1988-89	Hull	QMJHL	66	8	32	40	109	9	2	6	8	6
1989-90	**Chicago**	**NHL**	**19**	**0**	**1**	**1**	**27**	**1**	**0**	**0**	**0**	**0**
	Indianapolis	IHL	46	3	15	18	114	9	0	1	1	24
1990-91	**Chicago**	**NHL**	**3**	**0**	**0**	**0**	**5**	**1**	**0**	**0**	**0**	**0**
	Indianapolis	IHL	53	5	9	14	125	6	0	2	2	30
1991-92	**Chicago**	**NHL**	**19**	**0**	**0**	**0**	**34**	**12**	**0**	**2**	**2**	**2**
	Indianapolis	IHL	41	4	9	13	78	....	....	....	....	....
1992-93	**Chicago**	**NHL**	**67**	**2**	**4**	**6**	**151**	**4**	**0**	**0**	**0**	**0**
1993-94	**Chicago**	**NHL**	**67**	**1**	**7**	**8**	**200**	....	....	....	....	....
1994-95	**Chicago**	**NHL**	**33**	**1**	**3**	**4**	**88**	**16**	**0**	**3**	**3**	**8**
1995-96	**Chicago**	**NHL**	**61**	**2**	**2**	**4**	**129**	**6**	**0**	**0**	**0**	**2**
1996-97	**Chicago**	**NHL**	**44**	**1**	**1**	**2**	**65**	**4**	**0**	**0**	**0**	**4**
1997-98	**Chicago**	**NHL**	**41**	**1**	**1**	**2**	**79**	....	....	....	....	....
	NHL Totals		**354**	**8**	**19**	**27**	**778**	**44**	**0**	**5**	**5**	**16**

RUUTU, JARKKO — (ROO-too, YAHR-koh) — VAN.

Left wing. Shoots left. 6'2", 194 lbs. Born, Vantaa, Finland, August 23, 1975.
(Vancouver's 3rd choice, 68th overall, in 1998 Entry Draft).

			Regular Season					Playoffs				
Season	Club	Lea	GP	G	A	TP	PIM	GP	G	A	TP	PIM
1991-92	HIFK Helsinki	Fin-Jr.	1	0	0	0	0	....	....	....	....	....
1992-93	HIFK Helsinki	Fin-Jr.	34	26	21	47	53	....	....	....	....	....
1993-94	HIFK Helsinki	Fin-Jr.	19	9	12	21	44	....	....	....	....	....
1994-95	HIFK Helsinki	Fin-Jr.	35	26	22	48	117	....	....	....	....	....
1995-96	Michigan Tech	WCHA	39	12	10	22	96	....	....	....	....	....
1996-97	HIFK Helsinki	Finland	48	11	10	21	155	....	....	....	....	....
1997-98	HIFK Helsinki	Finland	37	10	10	20	87	8	*7	4	11	10

RYAN, TERRY — MTL.

Left wing. Shoots left. 6'1", 201 lbs. Born, St. John's, Nfld., January 14, 1977.
(Montreal's 1st choice, 8th overall, in 1995 Entry Draft).

			Regular Season					Playoffs				
Season	Club	Lea	GP	G	A	TP	PIM	GP	G	A	TP	PIM
1993-94	Tri-City	WHL	61	16	17	33	176	4	0	1	1	25
1994-95	Tri-City	WHL	70	50	60	110	207	17	12	15	27	36
1995-96	Tri-City	WHL	59	32	37	69	133	5	0	0	0	4
	Fredericton	AHL	....	....	....	....	....	3	0	0	0	2
1996-97	Red Deer	WHL	16	13	22	35	10	16	18	6	24	32
	Montreal	**NHL**	**3**	**0**	**0**	**0**	**0**	....	....	....	....	....
1997-98	**Montreal**	**NHL**	**4**	**0**	**0**	**0**	**31**	....	....	....	....	....
	Fredericton	AHL	71	21	18	39	256	3	1	1	2	0
	NHL Totals		**7**	**0**	**0**	**0**	**31**	....	....	....	....	....

WHL West Second All-Star Team (1995)

RYAZANTSEV, ALEXANDER — (ree-ZAHNT-sehv) — COL.

Defense. Shoots right. 5'11", 200 lbs. Born, Moscow, USSR, March 15, 1980.
(Colorado's 10th choice, 167th overall, in 1998 Entry Draft).

			Regular Season					Playoffs				
Season	Club	Lea	GP	G	A	TP	PIM	GP	G	A	TP	PIM
1996-97	Spartak	Russia	20	1	2	3	4	....	....	....	....	....
	SAK Moscow	Russia-3	18	0	0	0	8	....	....	....	....	....
1997-98	Spartak 2	Russia-3	31	3	8	11	26	....	....	....	....	....
	Victoriaville	QMJHL	22	6	9	15	14	....	....	....	....	....

RYCHEL, WARREN — (RIGH-kuhl) — COL.

Left wing. Shoots left. 6', 205 lbs. Born, Tecumseh, Ont., May 12, 1967.

			Regular Season					Playoffs				
Season	Club	Lea	GP	G	A	TP	PIM	GP	G	A	TP	PIM
1984-85	Sudbury	OHL	35	5	8	13	74	....	....	....	....	....
	Guelph	OHL	29	1	3	4	48	....	....	....	....	....
1985-86	Guelph	OHL	38	14	5	19	119	....	....	....	....	....
	Ottawa	OHL	29	11	18	29	54	....	....	....	....	....
1986-87	Ottawa	OHL	28	11	7	18	57	....	....	....	....	....
	Kitchener	OHL	21	5	5	10	39	4	0	0	0	9
1987-88	Peoria	IHL	7	2	1	3	7	....	....	....	....	....
	Saginaw	IHL	51	2	7	9	113	1	0	0	0	0
1988-89	**Chicago**	**NHL**	**2**	**0**	**0**	**0**	**17**	....	....	....	....	....
	Saginaw	IHL	50	15	14	29	226	6	0	0	0	51
1989-90	Indianapolis	IHL	77	23	16	39	374	14	1	3	4	64
1990-91	Indianapolis	IHL	68	33	30	63	338	5	2	1	3	30
	Chicago	**NHL**	....	....	....	....	....	**3**	**1**	**3**	**4**	**2**
1991-92	Moncton	AHL	36	14	15	29	211	....	....	....	....	....
	Kalamazoo	IHL	45	15	20	35	165	8	0	3	3	51
1992-93	**Los Angeles**	**NHL**	**70**	**6**	**7**	**13**	**314**	**23**	**6**	**7**	**13**	**39**
1993-94	**Los Angeles**	**NHL**	**80**	**10**	**9**	**19**	**322**	....	....	....	....	....
1994-95	**Los Angeles**	**NHL**	**7**	**0**	**0**	**0**	**19**	....	....	....	....	....
	Toronto	**NHL**	**26**	**1**	**6**	**7**	**101**	**3**	**0**	**0**	**0**	**0**
1995-96	**Colorado**	**NHL**	**52**	**6**	**2**	**8**	**147**	**12**	**1**	**0**	**1**	**23 ♦**
1996-97	**Anaheim**	**NHL**	**70**	**10**	**7**	**17**	**218**	**11**	**0**	**2**	**2**	**19**
1997-98	**Anaheim**	**NHL**	**63**	**5**	**6**	**11**	**198**	....	....	....	....	....
	Colorado	**NHL**	**8**	**0**	**0**	**0**	**23**	**6**	**0**	**0**	**0**	**24**
	NHL Totals		**378**	**38**	**37**	**75**	**1359**	**58**	**8**	**12**	**20**	**107**

Signed as a free agent by **Chicago**, September 19, 1986. Traded to **Winnipeg** by **Chicago** with Troy Murray for Bryan Marchment and Chris Norton, July 22, 1991. Traded to **Minnesota** by **Winnipeg** for Tony Joseph, December 30, 1991. Signed as a free agent by **LA Kings**, October 1, 1992. Traded to **Washington** by **LA Kings** for Randy Burridge, February 10, 1995. Traded to **Toronto** by **Washington** for Toronto's 4th round choice (Sebastien Charpentier) in 1995 Entry Draft, February 10, 1995. Traded to **Colorado** by **Toronto** for cash, October 2, 1995. Signed as a free agent by **Anaheim**, August 21, 1996. Traded to **Colorado** by **Anaheim** with future considerations for Josef Marha, March 24, 1998.

SACCO, JOE — (SAK-oh) — NYI

Right wing. Shoots left. 6'1", 195 lbs. Born, Medford, MA, February 4, 1969.
(Toronto's 4th choice, 71st overall, in 1987 Entry Draft).

			Regular Season					Playoffs				
Season	Club	Lea	GP	G	A	TP	PIM	GP	G	A	TP	PIM
1986-87	Medford Prep	H.S.	21	22	32	54	....	....	....	....	....	....
1987-88	Boston University	H.E.	34	16	20	36	40	....	....	....	....	....
1988-89	Boston University	H.E.	33	21	19	40	66	....	....	....	....	....
1989-90	Boston University	H.E.	44	28	24	52	70	....	....	....	....	....
1990-91	**Toronto**	**NHL**	**20**	**0**	**5**	**5**	**2**	....	....	....	....	....
	Newmarket	AHL	49	18	17	35	24	....	....	....	....	....
1991-92	United States	Nat-Tm	50	11	26	37	61	....	....	....	....	....
	United States	Olympics	8	0	2	2	0	....	....	....	....	....
	Toronto	**NHL**	**17**	**7**	**4**	**11**	**4**	....	....	....	....	....
	St. John's	AHL	....	....	....	....	....	1	1	1	2	0
1992-93	**Toronto**	**NHL**	**23**	**4**	**4**	**8**	**8**	....	....	....	....	....
	St. John's	AHL	37	14	16	30	45	7	6	4	10	2
1993-94	**Anaheim**	**NHL**	**84**	**19**	**18**	**37**	**61**	....	....	....	....	....
1994-95	**Anaheim**	**NHL**	**41**	**10**	**8**	**18**	**23**	....	....	....	....	....
1995-96	**Anaheim**	**NHL**	**76**	**13**	**14**	**27**	**40**	....	....	....	....	....
1996-97	**Anaheim**	**NHL**	**77**	**12**	**17**	**29**	**35**	**11**	**2**	**0**	**2**	**2**
1997-98	**Anaheim**	**NHL**	**55**	**8**	**11**	**19**	**24**	....	....	....	....	....
	NY Islanders	**NHL**	**25**	**3**	**3**	**6**	**10**	....	....	....	....	....
	NHL Totals		**418**	**76**	**84**	**160**	**207**	**11**	**2**	**0**	**2**	**2**

Claimed by **Anaheim** from **Toronto** in Expansion Draft, June 24, 1993. Traded to **NY Islanders** by **Anaheim** with J.J. Daigneault and Mark Janssens for Travis Green, Doug Houda and Tony Tuzzolino, February 6, 1998.

ST. CROIX, CHRIS — (SAINT KWAH) — CGY.

Defense. Shoots right. 6'1", 186 lbs. Born, Voorhees, NJ, May 2, 1979.
(Calgary's 7th choice, 92nd overall, in 1997 Entry Draft).

			Regular Season					Playoffs				
Season	Club	Lea	GP	G	A	TP	PIM	GP	G	A	TP	PIM
1995-96	Kamloops	WHL	61	4	5	9	29	13	0	2	2	4
1996-97	Kamloops	WHL	67	11	39	50	67	5	0	1	1	2
1997-98	Kamloops	WHL	46	3	13	16	51	7	1	1	2	6

ST. PIERRE, SAMUEL — T.B.

Right wing. Shoots right. 6'1", 170 lbs. Born, Laurierville, Que., June 28, 1979.
(Tampa Bay's 10th choice, 185th overall, in 1997 Entry Draft).

			Regular Season					Playoffs				
Season	Club	Lea	GP	G	A	TP	PIM	GP	G	A	TP	PIM
1996-97	Victoriaville	QMJHL	61	13	10	23	24	6	0	1	1	2
1997-98	Victoriaville	QMJHL	34	8	10	18	32	....	....	....	....	....
	Drummondville	QMJHL	35	28	15	43	16	....	....	....	....	....

SAKIC, JOE — (SAK-ihk) — COL.

Center. Shoots left. 5'11", 185 lbs. Born, Burnaby, B.C., July 7, 1969.
(Quebec's 2nd choice, 15th overall, in 1987 Entry Draft).

			Regular Season					Playoffs				
Season	Club	Lea	GP	G	A	TP	PIM	GP	G	A	TP	PIM
1986-87	Swift Current	WHL	72	60	73	133	31	4	0	1	1	0
	Canada	Nat-Tm	1	0	0	0	0	....	....	....	....	....
1987-88	Swift Current	WHL	64	*78	82	*160	64	10	11	13	24	12
1988-89	**Quebec**	**NHL**	**70**	**23**	**39**	**62**	**24**	....	....	....	....	....
1989-90	**Quebec**	**NHL**	**80**	**39**	**63**	**102**	**27**	....	....	....	....	....
1990-91	**Quebec**	**NHL**	**80**	**48**	**61**	**109**	**24**	....	....	....	....	....
1991-92	**Quebec**	**NHL**	**69**	**29**	**65**	**94**	**20**	....	....	....	....	....
1992-93	**Quebec**	**NHL**	**78**	**48**	**57**	**105**	**40**	**6**	**3**	**3**	**6**	**2**
1993-94	**Quebec**	**NHL**	**84**	**28**	**64**	**92**	**18**	....	....	....	....	....
1994-95	**Quebec**	**NHL**	**47**	**19**	**43**	**62**	**30**	**6**	**4**	**1**	**5**	**0**
1995-96	**Colorado**	**NHL**	**82**	**51**	**69**	**120**	**44**	**22**	***18**	**16**	***34**	**14 ♦**
1996-97	**Colorado**	**NHL**	**65**	**22**	**52**	**74**	**34**	**17**	**8**	***17**	**25**	**14**
1997-98	**Colorado**	**NHL**	**64**	**27**	**36**	**63**	**50**	**6**	**2**	**3**	**5**	**6**
	Canada	Olympics	4	1	2	3	4	....	....	....	....	....
	NHL Totals		**719**	**334**	**549**	**883**	**311**	**57**	**35**	**40**	**75**	**36**

WHL East Second All-Star Team (1987) • Canadian Major Junior Player of the Year (1988) • WHL East First All-Star Team (1988) • Won Conn Smythe Trophy (1996)

Played in NHL All-Star Game (1990, 1991, 1992, 1993, 1994, 1996, 1998)

Transferred to **Colorado** after **Quebec** franchise relocated, June 21, 1995.

SALEI, RUSLAN — (sah-LEE, ROOS-luhn) — ANA.

Defense. Shoots left. 6'2", 205 lbs. Born, Minsk, USSR, November 2, 1974.
(Anaheim's 1st choice, 9th overall, in 1996 Entry Draft).

			Regular Season					Playoffs				
Season	Club	Lea	GP	G	A	TP	PIM	GP	G	A	TP	PIM
1992-93	Minsk	CIS	9	1	0	1	10	....	....	....	....	....
1993-94	Minsk	CIS	39	2	3	5	50	....	....	....	....	....
1994-95	Minsk	CIS	51	4	2	6	44	....	....	....	....	....
1995-96	Las Vegas	IHL	76	7	23	30	123	15	3	7	10	18
1996-97	**Anaheim**	**NHL**	**30**	**0**	**1**	**1**	**37**	....	....	....	....	....
	Baltimore	AHL	12	1	4	5	12	....	....	....	....	....
	Las Vegas	IHL	8	0	2	2	24	3	2	1	3	6
1997-98	**Anaheim**	**NHL**	**66**	**5**	**10**	**15**	**70**	....	....	....	....	....
	Cincinnati	AHL	6	3	6	9	14	....	....	....	....	....
	Belarus	Olympics	7	1	0	1	4	....	....	....	....	....
	NHL Totals		**96**	**5**	**11**	**16**	**107**	....	....	....	....	....

SALO, SAMI — (SA-loh) — OTT.

Defense. Shoots right. 6'3", 190 lbs. Born, Turku, Finland, September 2, 1974.
(Ottawa's 7th choice, 239th overall, in 1996 Entry Draft).

			Regular Season					Playoffs				
Season	Club	Lea	GP	G	A	TP	PIM	GP	G	A	TP	PIM
1994-95	TPS Turku	Fin-Jr.	14	1	3	4	6	....	....	....	....	....
	Kiekko	Finland-2	19	4	2	6	4	....	....	....	....	....
	TPS Turku	Finland	7	1	2	3	8	1	0	0	0	0
1995-96	TPS Turku	Finland	47	7	14	21	32	11	1	3	4	8
1996-97	TPS Turku	Finland	48	9	6	15	10	10	2	3	5	4
1997-98	Jokerit	Finland	35	3	5	8	10	8	0	1	1	2

SALVADOR, BRYCE — ST.L.

Defense. Shoots left. 6'2", 194 lbs. Born, Brandon, Man., February 11, 1976.
(Tampa Bay's 6th choice, 138th overall, in 1994 Entry Draft).

			Regular Season					Playoffs				
Season	Club	Lea	GP	G	A	TP	PIM	GP	G	A	TP	PIM
1992-93	Lethbridge	WHL	64	1	4	5	29	4	0	0	0	0
1993-94	Lethbridge	WHL	61	4	14	18	36	9	0	1	1	2
1994-95	Lethbridge	WHL	67	1	9	10	88	....	....	....	....	....
1995-96	Lethbridge	WHL	56	4	12	16	75	3	0	1	1	2
1996-97	Lethbridge	WHL	63	8	32	40	81	19	0	7	7	14
1997-98	Worcester	AHL	46	2	8	10	74	11	0	1	1	45

Signed as a free agent by **St. Louis**, December 16, 1996.

SAMSONOV, SERGEI (sam-SAWN-nahf) — BOS.

Left wing. Shoots right. 5'8", 184 lbs. Born, Moscow, USSR, October 27, 1978.
(Boston's 2nd choice, 8th overall, in 1997 Entry Draft).

			Regular Season					Playoffs				
Season	Club	Lea	GP	G	A	TP	PIM	GP	G	A	TP	PIM
1994-95	CSKA Moscow	CIS-Jr.	50	110	72	182	....	....	....	....	....	....
	CSKA Moscow	CIS	13	2	2	4	14	2	0	0	0	0
1995-96	CSKA Moscow	CIS	51	21	17	38	12	3	1	1	2	4
1996-97	Detroit	IHL	73	29	35	64	18	19	8	4	12	12
1997-98	**Boston**	**NHL**	**81**	**22**	**25**	**47**	**8**	**6**	**2**	**5**	**7**	**0**
	NHL Totals		**81**	**22**	**25**	**47**	**8**	**6**	**2**	**5**	**7**	**0**

Won Garry F. Longman Memorial Trophy (Top Rookie - IHL) (1997) • NHL All-Rookie Team (1998) • Won Calder Memorial Trophy (1998)

SAMUELSSON, KJELL (SAM-yuhl-suhn, SHEHL)

Defense. Shoots right. 6'6", 235 lbs. Born, Tyngsryd, Sweden, October 18, 1958.
(NY Rangers' 5th choice, 119th overall, in 1984 Entry Draft).

			Regular Season					Playoffs				
Season	Club	Lea	GP	G	A	TP	PIM	GP	G	A	TP	PIM
1977-78	Tyngsryd	Sweden-2	20	3	0	3	41	....	....	....	....	....
1978-79	Tyngsryd	Sweden-2	24	3	4	7	67	....	....	....	....	....
1979-80	Tyngsryd	Sweden-2	26	5	4	9	45	....	....	....	....	....
1980-81	Tyngsryd	Sweden-2	35	6	7	13	61	2	0	1	1	14
1981-82	Tyngsryd	Sweden-2	33	11	14	25	68	3	0	2	2	2
1982-83	Tyngsryd	Sweden-2	32	11	6	17	57	....	....	....	....	....
1983-84	Leksand IF	Sweden	36	6	6	12	59	....	....	....	....	....
1984-85	Leksand IF	Sweden	35	9	5	14	34	....	....	....	....	....
1985-86	NY Rangers	NHL	9	0	0	0	10	9	0	1	1	8
	New Haven	AHL	56	6	21	27	87	3	0	0	0	10
1986-87	NY Rangers	NHL	30	2	6	8	50	....	....	....	....	....
	Philadelphia	NHL	46	1	6	7	86	26	0	4	4	25
1987-88	Philadelphia	NHL	74	6	24	30	184	7	2	5	7	23
1988-89	Philadelphia	NHL	69	3	14	17	140	19	1	3	4	24
1989-90	Philadelphia	NHL	66	5	17	22	91	....	....	....	....	....
1990-91	Philadelphia	NHL	78	9	19	28	82	....	....	....	....	....
1991-92	Philadelphia	NHL	54	4	9	13	76	....	....	....	....	....
	Pittsburgh	NHL	20	1	2	3	34	15	0	3	3	12 ♦
1992-93	Pittsburgh	NHL	63	3	6	9	106	12	0	3	3	2
1993-94	Pittsburgh	NHL	59	5	8	13	118	6	0	0	0	26
1994-95	Pittsburgh	NHL	41	1	6	7	54	11	0	1	1	32
1995-96	Philadelphia	NHL	75	3	11	14	81	12	1	0	1	24
1996-97	Philadelphia	NHL	34	4	3	7	47	5	0	0	0	2
1997-98	Philadelphia	NHL	49	0	3	3	28	1	0	0	0	0
	NHL Totals		**767**	**47**	**134**	**181**	**1187**	**123**	**4**	**20**	**24**	**178**

Played in NHL All-Star Game (1988)

Traded to **Philadelphia** by **NY Rangers** with NY Rangers' 2nd round choice (Patrik Juhlin) in 1989 Entry Draft for Bob Froese, December 18, 1986. Traded to **Pittsburgh** by **Philadelphia** with Rick Tocchet, Ken Wregget and Philadelphia's 3rd round choice (Dave Roche) in 1993 Entry Draft for Mark Recchi, Brian Benning and LA Kings' 1st round choice (previously acquired, Philadelphia selected Jason Bowen) in 1992 Entry Draft, February 19, 1992. Signed as a free agent by **Philadelphia**, August 31, 1995.

SAMUELSSON, MIKAEL (SAM-yuhl-suhn, MIH-kigh-ehl) — S.J.

Right wing. Shoots left. 6'1", 194 lbs. Born, Mariefred, Sweden, December 23, 1976.
(San Jose's 7th choice, 145th overall, in 1998 Entry Draft).

			Regular Season					Playoffs				
Season	Club	Lea	GP	G	A	TP	PIM	GP	G	A	TP	PIM
1994-95	Sodertalje	Swe-Jr.	30	8	6	14	12	....	....	....	....	....
1995-96	Sodertalje	Swe-Jr.	22	13	12	25	20	....	....	....	....	....
	Sodertalje	Sweden-2	18	5	1	6	0	4	0	0	0	0
1996-97	Sodertalje	Swe-Jr.	2	2	1	3	....	....	....	....	....	....
	Sodertalje	Sweden	29	3	2	5	10	....	....	....	....	....
1997-98	Sodertalje	Sweden	31	8	8	16	47	....	....	....	....	....

SAMUELSSON, ULF (SAM-yuhl-suhn, UHLF) — NYR

Defense. Shoots left. 6'1", 205 lbs. Born, Fagersta, Sweden, March 26, 1964.
(Hartford's 4th choice, 67th overall, in 1982 Entry Draft).

			Regular Season					Playoffs				
Season	Club	Lea	GP	G	A	TP	PIM	GP	G	A	TP	PIM
1981-82	Leksand IF	Sweden	31	3	1	4	40	....	....	....	....	....
1982-83	Leksand IF	Sweden	33	9	6	15	72	....	....	....	....	....
1983-84	Leksand IF	Sweden	36	5	11	16	53	....	....	....	....	....
1984-85	Hartford	NHL	41	2	6	8	83	....	....	....	....	....
	Binghamton	AHL	36	5	11	16	92	....	....	....	....	....
1985-86	Hartford	NHL	80	5	19	24	174	10	1	2	3	38
1986-87	Hartford	NHL	78	2	31	33	162	5	0	1	1	41
1987-88	Hartford	NHL	76	8	33	41	159	5	0	0	0	8
1988-89	Hartford	NHL	71	9	26	35	181	4	0	2	2	4
1989-90	Hartford	NHL	55	2	11	13	177	7	1	0	1	2
1990-91	Hartford	NHL	62	3	18	21	174	....	....	....	....	....
	Pittsburgh	NHL	14	1	4	5	37	20	3	2	5	34 ♦
1991-92	Pittsburgh	NHL	62	1	14	15	206	21	0	2	2	39 ♦
1992-93	Pittsburgh	NHL	77	3	26	29	249	12	1	5	6	24
1993-94	Pittsburgh	NHL	80	5	24	29	199	6	0	1	1	18
1994-95	Leksand IF	Sweden	2	0	0	0	8	....	....	....	....	....
	Pittsburgh	NHL	44	1	15	16	113	7	0	2	2	8
1995-96	NY Rangers	NHL	74	1	18	19	122	11	1	5	6	16
1996-97	NY Rangers	NHL	73	6	11	17	138	15	0	2	2	30
1997-98	NY Rangers	NHL	73	3	9	12	122	....	....	....	....	....
	Sweden	Olympics	3	0	1	1	4	....	....	....	....	....
	NHL Totals		**960**	**52**	**265**	**317**	**2296**	**123**	**7**	**24**	**31**	**262**

Traded to **Pittsburgh** by **Hartford** with Ron Francis and Grant Jennings for John Cullen, Jeff Parker and Zarley Zalapski, March 4, 1991. Traded to **NY Rangers** by **Pittsburgh** with Luc Robitaille for Petr Nedved and Sergei Zubov, August 31, 1995.

SANDBERG, OLA — NYR

Defense. Shoots left. 6'1", 189 lbs. Born, Djurgarden, Sweden, February 23, 1977.
(NY Rangers' 5th choice, 158th overall, in 1996 Entry Draft).

			Regular Season					Playoffs				
Season	Club	Lea	GP	G	A	TP	PIM	GP	G	A	TP	PIM
1995-96	Djurgarden	Swe-Jr.	26	3	5	8	46	....	....	....	....	....
1996-97	Arlanda	Sweden-2	17	1	0	1	24	....	....	....	....	....
	Djurgarden	Sweden	4	0	0	0	0	....	....	....	....	....
1997-98	Pensacola	ECHL	52	2	5	7	56	....	....	....	....	....
	Quebec	IHL	7	0	0	0	8	....	....	....	....	....

SANDERSON, GEOFF — BUF.

Left wing. Shoots left. 6', 190 lbs. Born, Hay River, N.W.T., February 1, 1972.
(Hartford's 2nd choice, 36th overall, in 1990 Entry Draft).

			Regular Season					Playoffs				
Season	Club	Lea	GP	G	A	TP	PIM	GP	G	A	TP	PIM
1988-89	Swift Current	WHL	58	17	11	28	16	12	3	5	8	6
1989-90	Swift Current	WHL	70	32	62	94	56	4	1	4	5	8
1990-91	Swift Current	WHL	70	62	50	112	57	3	1	2	3	4
	Hartford	NHL	2	1	0	1	0	3	0	0	0	0
	Springfield	AHL	....	....	....	....	....	1	0	0	0	2
1991-92	Hartford	NHL	64	13	18	31	18	7	1	0	1	2
1992-93	Hartford	NHL	82	46	43	89	28	....	....	....	....	....
1993-94	Hartford	NHL	82	41	26	67	42	....	....	....	....	....
1994-95	Hameelinna	Finland	12	6	4	10	24	....	....	....	....	....
	Hartford	NHL	46	18	14	32	24	....	....	....	....	....
1995-96	Hartford	NHL	81	34	31	65	40	....	....	....	....	....
1996-97	Hartford	NHL	82	36	31	67	29	....	....	....	....	....
1997-98	Carolina	NHL	40	7	10	17	14	....	....	....	....	....
	Vancouver	NHL	9	0	3	3	4	....	....	....	....	....
	Buffalo	NHL	26	4	5	9	20	14	3	1	4	4
	NHL Totals		**514**	**200**	**181**	**381**	**219**	**24**	**4**	**1**	**5**	**6**

Played in NHL All-Star Game (1994, 1997)

Transferred to **Carolina** after **Hartford** franchise relocated, June 25, 1997. Traded to **Vancouver** by **Carolina** with Sean Burke and Enrico Ciccone for Kirk McLean and Martin Gelinas, January 3, 1998. Traded to **Buffalo** by **Vancouver** for Brad May and future considerations, February 4, 1998.

SANDSTROM, TOMAS (SAND-struhm) — ANA.

Right wing. Shoots left. 6'2", 205 lbs. Born, Jakobstad, Finland, September 4, 1964.
(NY Rangers' 2nd choice, 36th overall, in 1982 Entry Draft).

			Regular Season					Playoffs				
Season	Club	Lea	GP	G	A	TP	PIM	GP	G	A	TP	PIM
1981-82	Fagersta	Sweden-2	32	28	11	39	74	....	....	....	....	....
1982-83	Brynas IF	Sweden	36	23	14	37	50	....	....	....	....	....
1983-84	Brynas IF	Sweden	34	19	10	29	81	....	....	....	....	....
	Sweden	Olympics	7	2	1	3	6	....	....	....	....	....
1984-85	NY Rangers	NHL	74	29	29	58	51	3	0	2	2	0
1985-86	NY Rangers	NHL	73	25	29	54	109	16	4	6	10	20
1986-87	NY Rangers	NHL	64	40	34	74	60	6	1	2	3	20
1987-88	NY Rangers	NHL	69	28	40	68	95	....	....	....	....	....
1988-89	NY Rangers	NHL	79	32	56	88	148	4	3	2	5	12
1989-90	NY Rangers	NHL	48	19	19	38	100	....	....	....	....	....
	Los Angeles	NHL	28	13	20	33	28	10	5	4	9	19
1990-91	Los Angeles	NHL	68	45	44	89	106	10	4	4	8	14
1991-92	Los Angeles	NHL	49	17	22	39	70	6	0	3	3	8
1992-93	Los Angeles	NHL	39	25	27	52	57	24	8	17	25	12
1993-94	Los Angeles	NHL	51	17	24	41	59	....	....	....	....	....
	Pittsburgh	NHL	27	6	11	17	24	6	0	0	0	4
1994-95	Malmo IF	Sweden	12	10	5	15	14	....	....	....	....	....
	Pittsburgh	NHL	47	21	23	44	42	12	3	3	6	16
1995-96	Pittsburgh	NHL	58	35	35	70	69	18	4	2	6	30
1996-97	Pittsburgh	NHL	40	9	15	24	33	....	....	....	....	....
	Detroit	NHL	34	9	9	18	36	20	0	4	4	24 ♦
1997-98	Anaheim	NHL	77	9	8	17	64	....	....	....	....	....
	Sweden	Olympics	4	0	1	1	0	....	....	....	....	....
	NHL Totals		**925**	**379**	**445**	**824**	**1151**	**135**	**32**	**49**	**81**	**179**

NHL All-Rookie Team (1985)

Played in NHL All-Star Game (1988, 1991)

Traded to **LA Kings** by **NY Rangers** with Tony Granato for Bernie Nicholls, January 20, 1990. Traded to **Pittsburgh** by **LA Kings** with Shawn McEachern for Marty McSorley and Jim Paek, February 16, 1994. Traded to **Detroit** by **Pittsburgh** for Greg Johnson, January 27, 1997. Signed as a free agent by **Anaheim**, October 20, 1997.

SANDWITH, TERRAN — ANA.

Defense. Shoots left. 6'4", 210 lbs. Born, Edmonton, Alta., April 17, 1972.
(Philadelphia's 4th choice, 42nd overall, in 1990 NHL Entry Draft).

			Regular Season					Playoffs				
Season	Club	Lea	GP	G	A	TP	PIM	GP	G	A	TP	PIM
1988-89	Tri-City	WHL	31	0	0	0	29	6	0	0	0	4
1989-90	Tri-City	WHL	70	4	14	18	92	7	0	2	2	14
1990-91	Tri-City	WHL	46	5	17	22	132	7	1	0	1	14
1991-92	Brandon	WHL	41	6	14	20	145	....	....	....	....	....
	Saskatoon	WHL	18	2	5	7	53	18	2	1	3	28
1992-93	Hershey	AHL	61	1	12	13	140	....	....	....	....	....
1993-94	Hershey	AHL	62	3	5	8	169	2	0	1	1	4
1994-95	Hershey	AHL	11	1	1	2	32	....	....	....	....	....
	Kansas City	IHL	25	0	3	3	73	....	....	....	....	....
1995-96	Canada	Nat-Tm	47	3	12	15	63	....	....	....	....	....
	Cape Breton	AHL	5	0	2	2	4	....	....	....	....	....
1996-97	Hamilton	AHL	78	3	6	9	213	22	0	2	2	27
1997-98	Edmonton	NHL	8	0	0	0	6	....	....	....	....	....
	Hamilton	AHL	54	4	8	12	131	9	0	0	0	10
	NHL Totals		**8**	**0**	**0**	**0**	**6**	....	....	....	....	....

Signed as a free agent by **Edmonton**, April 10, 1996. Signed as a free agent by **Anaheim**, July 13, 1998.

SARAULT, YVES (sah-ROH, EEV) OTT.

Left wing. Shoots left. 6'1", 185 lbs. Born, Valleyfield, Que., December 23, 1972.
(Montreal's 4th choice, 61st overall, in 1991 Entry Draft).

			Regular Season					Playoffs				
Season	**Club**	**Lea**	**GP**	**G**	**A**	**TP**	**PIM**	**GP**	**G**	**A**	**TP**	**PIM**
1989-90	Victoriaville	QMJHL	70	12	28	40	140	16	0	3	3	26
1990-91	St-Jean	QMJHL	56	22	24	46	113	....	....	....	....	....
1991-92	St-Jean	QMJHL	50	28	38	66	96	....	....	....	....	....
	Trois-Rivieres	QMJHL	18	15	14	29	12	15	10	10	20	18
1992-93	Fredericton	AHL	59	14	17	31	41	3	0	1	1	2
	Wheeling	ECHL	2	1	3	4	0	....	....	....	....	....
1993-94	Fredericton	AHL	60	13	14	27	72	....	....	....	....	....
1994-95	Fredericton	AHL	69	24	21	45	96	13	2	1	3	33
	Montreal	**NHL**	**8**	**0**	**1**	**1**	**0**	....	....	....	....	....
1995-96	**Montreal**	**NHL**	**14**	**0**	**0**	**0**	**4**	....	....	....	....	....
	Calgary	**NHL**	**11**	**2**	**1**	**3**	**4**	....	....	....	....	....
	Saint John	AHL	26	10	12	22	34	16	6	2	8	33
1996-97	**Colorado**	**NHL**	**28**	**2**	**1**	**3**	**6**	**5**	**0**	**0**	**0**	**2**
	Hershey	AHL	6	2	3	5	8	....	....	....	....	....
1997-98	**Colorado**	**NHL**	**2**	**1**	**0**	**1**	**0**	....	....	....	....	....
	Hershey	AHL	63	23	36	59	43	7	1	2	3	14
	NHL Totals		**63**	**5**	**3**	**8**	**14**	**5**	**0**	**0**	**0**	**2**

QMJHL Second All-Star Team (1992)

Traded to **Calgary** by **Montreal** with Craig Ferguson for Calgary's 8th round choice (Petr Kubos) in 1997 Entry Draft, November 26, 1995. Signed as a free agent by **Colorado**, September 13, 1996. Signed as a free agent by **Ottawa**, August 7, 1998.

SARICH, CORY (SAHR-ihch) BUF.

Defense. Shoots right. 6'3", 175 lbs. Born, Saskatoon, Sask., August 16, 1978.
(Buffalo's 2nd choice, 27th overall, in 1996 Entry Draft).

			Regular Season					Playoffs				
Season	**Club**	**Lea**	**GP**	**G**	**A**	**TP**	**PIM**	**GP**	**G**	**A**	**TP**	**PIM**
1995-96	Saskatoon	WHL	59	5	18	23	54	3	0	0	0	4
1996-97	Saskatoon	WHL	58	6	27	33	158	....	....	....	....	....
1997-98	Saskatoon	WHL	33	5	24	29	90	....	....	....	....	....
	Seattle	WHL	13	3	16	19	47	....	....	....	....	....

WHL West Second All-Star Team (1998)

SARNO, PETER EDM.

Center. Shoots left. 5'11", 185 lbs. Born, Toronto, Ont., July 26, 1979.
(Edmonton's 6th choice, 141st overall, in 1997 Entry Draft).

			Regular Season					Playoffs				
Season	**Club**	**Lea**	**GP**	**G**	**A**	**TP**	**PIM**	**GP**	**G**	**A**	**TP**	**PIM**
1996-97	Windsor	OHL	66	20	63	83	59	5	0	3	3	6
1997-98	Windsor	OHL	64	33	88	121	18	....	....	....	....	....
	Hamilton	AHL	8	1	1	2	2	....	....	....	....	....

SATAN, MIROSLAV (SHA-tuhn) BUF.

Left wing. Shoots left. 6'1", 195 lbs. Born, Topolcany, Czech., October 22, 1974.
(Edmonton's 6th choice, 111th overall, in 1993 Entry Draft).

			Regular Season					Playoffs				
Season	**Club**	**Lea**	**GP**	**G**	**A**	**TP**	**PIM**	**GP**	**G**	**A**	**TP**	**PIM**
1991-92	Topocalny	Czech-2	9	2	1	3	6	....	....	....	....	....
1992-93	Dukla Trencin	Czech.	38	11	6	17	....	....	....	....	....	....
1993-94	Dukla Trencin	Slovakia	30	32	16	48	16	....	....	....	....	....
	Slovakia	Olympics	8	9	0	9	0	....	....	....	....	....
1994-95	Cape Breton	AHL	25	24	16	40	15	....	....	....	....	....
	Detroit	IHL	8	1	3	4	4	....	....	....	....	....
	San Diego	IHL	6	0	2	2	6	....	....	....	....	....
1995-96	**Edmonton**	**NHL**	**62**	**18**	**17**	**35**	**22**	....	....	....	....	....
1996-97	**Edmonton**	**NHL**	**64**	**17**	**11**	**28**	**22**	....	....	....	....	....
	Buffalo	**NHL**	**12**	**8**	**2**	**10**	**4**	**7**	**0**	**0**	**0**	**0**
1997-98	**Buffalo**	**NHL**	**79**	**22**	**24**	**46**	**34**	**14**	**5**	**4**	**9**	**4**
	NHL Totals		**217**	**65**	**54**	**119**	**82**	**21**	**5**	**4**	**9**	**4**

Traded to **Buffalo** by **Edmonton** for Barrie Moore and Craig Millar, March 18, 1997.

SAUER, KENT NSH.

Defense. Shoots right. 6'2", 226 lbs. Born, St. Cloud, MN, May 10, 1979.
(Nashville's 4th choice, 88th overall, in 1998 Entry Draft).

			Regular Season					Playoffs				
Season	**Club**	**Lea**	**GP**	**G**	**A**	**TP**	**PIM**	**GP**	**G**	**A**	**TP**	**PIM**
1996-97	St. Cloud-Apollo	H.S.	23	14	15	29	20	....	....	....	....	....
1997-98	North Iowa	USHL	54	4	19	23	99	....	....	....	....	....

SAVAGE, ANDRE BOS.

Center. Shoots right. 6', 195 lbs. Born, Ottawa, Ont., May 27, 1975.

			Regular Season					Playoffs				
Season	**Club**	**Lea**	**GP**	**G**	**A**	**TP**	**PIM**	**GP**	**G**	**A**	**TP**	**PIM**
1994-95	Michigan Tech	WCHA	39	7	17	24	56	....	....	....	....	....
1995-96	Michigan Tech	WCHA	38	13	27	40	42	....	....	....	....	....
1996-97	Michigan Tech	WCHA	37	18	20	38	34	....	....	....	....	....
1997-98	Michigan Tech	WCHA	33	14	27	41	34	....	....	....	....	....

Signed as a free agent by **Boston**, June 18, 1998.

SAVAGE, BRIAN MTL.

Left wing. Shoots left. 6'2", 192 lbs. Born, Sudbury, Ont., February 24, 1971.
(Montreal's 11th choice, 171st overall, in 1991 Entry Draft).

			Regular Season					Playoffs				
Season	**Club**	**Lea**	**GP**	**G**	**A**	**TP**	**PIM**	**GP**	**G**	**A**	**TP**	**PIM**
1990-91	Miami-Ohio	CCHA	28	5	6	11	26	....	....	....	....	....
1991-92	Miami-Ohio	CCHA	40	24	16	40	43	....	....	....	....	....
1992-93	Miami-Ohio	CCHA	38	*37	21	58	44	....	....	....	....	....
	Canada	Nat-Tm	9	3	0	3	12	....	....	....	....	....
1993-94	Canada	Nat-Tm	51	20	26	46	38	....	....	....	....	....
	Canada	Olympics	8	2	2	4	6	....	....	....	....	....
	Montreal	**NHL**	**3**	**1**	**0**	**1**	**0**	**3**	**0**	**2**	**2**	**0**
	Fredericton	AHL	17	12	15	27	4	....	....	....	....	....
1994-95	**Montreal**	**NHL**	**37**	**12**	**7**	**19**	**27**	....	....	....	....	....
1995-96	**Montreal**	**NHL**	**75**	**25**	**8**	**33**	**28**	**6**	**0**	**2**	**2**	**2**
1996-97	**Montreal**	**NHL**	**81**	**23**	**37**	**60**	**39**	**5**	**1**	**1**	**2**	**0**
1997-98	**Montreal**	**NHL**	**64**	**26**	**17**	**43**	**36**	**9**	**0**	**2**	**2**	**6**
	NHL Totals		**260**	**87**	**69**	**156**	**130**	**23**	**1**	**7**	**8**	**8**

CCHA First All-Star Team (1993) • NCAA West Second All-American Team (1993)

SAVARD, MARC (sa-VAHR) NYR

Center. Shoots left. 5'10", 174 lbs. Born, Ottawa, Ont., July 17, 1977.
(NY Rangers' 3rd choice, 91st overall, in 1995 Entry Draft).

			Regular Season					Playoffs				
Season	**Club**	**Lea**	**GP**	**G**	**A**	**TP**	**PIM**	**GP**	**G**	**A**	**TP**	**PIM**
1993-94	Oshawa	OHL	61	18	39	57	20	5	4	3	7	8
1994-95	Oshawa	OHL	66	43	96	*139	78	7	5	6	11	8
1995-96	Oshawa	OHL	48	28	59	87	77	5	4	5	9	6
1996-97	Oshawa	OHL	64	43	*87	*130	94	18	13	*24	*37	20
1997-98	**NY Rangers**	**NHL**	**28**	**1**	**5**	**6**	**4**	....	....	....	....	....
	Hartford	AHL	58	21	53	74	66	15	8	19	27	24
	NHL Totals		**28**	**1**	**5**	**6**	**4**	....	....	....	....	....

OHL Second All-Star Team (1995)

SAVOIA, RYAN (sa-VOI-ah) PIT.

Center. Shoots right. 6'1", 204 lbs. Born, Thorold, Ont., May 6, 1973.

			Regular Season					Playoffs				
Season	**Club**	**Lea**	**GP**	**G**	**A**	**TP**	**PIM**	**GP**	**G**	**A**	**TP**	**PIM**
1994-95	Brock University	OUAA	38	35	48	83	24	....	....	....	....	....
	Cleveland	IHL	1	0	0	0	0	....	....	....	....	....
1995-96	Cleveland	IHL	49	6	7	13	31	....	....	....	....	....
1996-97	Johnstown	ECHL	60	35	44	79	100	....	....	....	....	....
	Cleveland	IHL	4	1	0	1	2	....	....	....	....	....
	Fort Wayne	IHL	8	0	2	2	2	....	....	....	....	....
1997-98	Helsinki	Finland	1	0	0	0	0	....	....	....	....	....
	Syracuse	AHL	7	0	4	4	2	....	....	....	....	....
	Johnstown	ECHL	6	1	5	6	0	....	....	....	....	....

Signed as a free agent by **Pittsburgh**, April 7, 1995.

SAWYER, KEVIN

Left wing. Shoots left. 6'2", 205 lbs. Born, Christina Lake, B.C., February 21, 1974.

			Regular Season					Playoffs				
Season	**Club**	**Lea**	**GP**	**G**	**A**	**TP**	**PIM**	**GP**	**G**	**A**	**TP**	**PIM**
1992-93	Spokane	WHL	62	4	3	7	274	8	1	1	2	13
1993-94	Spokane	WHL	60	10	15	25	350	3	0	1	1	6
1994-95	Spokane	WHL	54	7	9	16	365	11	2	0	2	58
	Peoria	IHL	....	....	....	....	....	2	0	0	0	12
1995-96	**St. Louis**	**NHL**	**6**	**0**	**0**	**0**	**23**	....	....	....	....	....
	Worcester	AHL	41	3	4	7	268	....	....	....	....	....
	Boston	**NHL**	**2**	**0**	**0**	**0**	**5**	....	....	....	....	....
	Providence	AHL	4	0	0	0	29	4	0	1	1	9
1996-97	**Boston**	**NHL**	**2**	**0**	**0**	**0**	**0**	....	....	....	....	....
	Providence	AHL	60	8	9	17	367	6	0	0	0	32
1997-98	Michigan	IHL	60	2	5	7	*398	3	0	0	0	23
	NHL Totals		**10**	**0**	**0**	**0**	**28**	....	....	....	....	....

Signed as a free agent by **St. Louis**, February 28, 1995. Traded to **Boston** by **St. Louis** with Steve Staios for Steve Leach, March 8, 1996. Signed as a free agent by **Dallas**, August 19, 1997.

SCATCHARD, DAVE (SKAT-chuhrd) VAN.

Center. Shoots right. 6'2", 220 lbs. Born, Hinton, Alta., February 20, 1976.
(Vancouver's 3rd choice, 42nd overall, in 1994 Entry Draft).

			Regular Season					Playoffs				
Season	**Club**	**Lea**	**GP**	**G**	**A**	**TP**	**PIM**	**GP**	**G**	**A**	**TP**	**PIM**
1993-94	Portland	WHL	47	9	11	20	46	10	2	1	3	4
1994-95	Portland	WHL	71	20	30	50	148	8	0	3	3	21
1995-96	Portland	WHL	59	19	28	47	146	7	1	8	9	14
	Syracuse	AHL	1	0	0	0	0	15	2	5	7	29
1996-97	Syracuse	AHL	26	8	7	15	65	....	....	....	....	....
1997-98	**Vancouver**	**NHL**	**76**	**13**	**11**	**24**	**165**	....	....	....	....	....
	NHL Totals		**76**	**13**	**11**	**24**	**165**	....	....	....	....	....

SCHAEFER, PETER (SHAY-fuhr) VAN.

Left wing. Shoots left. 5'11", 190 lbs. Born, Yellow Grass, Sask., July 12, 1977.
(Vancouver's 3rd choice, 66th overall, in 1995 Entry Draft).

			Regular Season					Playoffs				
Season	**Club**	**Lea**	**GP**	**G**	**A**	**TP**	**PIM**	**GP**	**G**	**A**	**TP**	**PIM**
1993-94	Brandon	WHL	2	1	0	1	0	....	....	....	....	....
1994-95	Brandon	WHL	68	27	32	59	34	18	5	3	8	18
1995-96	Brandon	WHL	69	47	61	108	53	19	10	13	23	5
1996-97	Brandon	WHL	61	49	74	123	85	6	1	4	5	4
	Syracuse	AHL	5	0	3	3	0	3	1	3	4	14
1997-98	Syracuse	AHL	73	19	44	63	41	5	2	1	3	2

WHL East First All-Star Team (1996, 1997) • Canadian Major Junior First All-Star Team (1997)

SCHASTLIVY, PETR (schust-LEE-vee, PEH-tuhr) OTT.

Left wing. Shoots left. 6', 191 lbs. Born, Angarsk, USSR, April 18, 1979.
(Ottawa's 5th choice, 101st overall, in 1998 Entry Draft).

			Regular Season					Playoffs				
Season	**Club**	**Lea**	**GP**	**G**	**A**	**TP**	**PIM**	**GP**	**G**	**A**	**TP**	**PIM**
1996-97	Yermak Angarsk	Russia-3			STATISTICS NOT AVAILABLE							
1997-98	Yaroslavl 2	Russia-2	47	15	9	24	34	....	....	....	....	....
	Yaroslavl	Russia	4	0	0	0	0	....	....	....	....	....

SCHMIDT, CHRIS L.A.

Center. Shoots left. 6'3", 212 lbs. Born, Beaverlodge, Alta., March 1, 1976.
(Los Angeles' 4th choice, 111th overall, in 1994 Entry Draft).

			Regular Season					Playoffs				
Season	**Club**	**Lea**	**GP**	**G**	**A**	**TP**	**PIM**	**GP**	**G**	**A**	**TP**	**PIM**
1992-93	Seattle	WHL	61	6	7	13	17	5	0	1	1	0
1993-94	Seattle	WHL	68	7	17	24	26	9	3	1	4	2
1994-95	Seattle	WHL	61	21	11	32	31	3	0	0	0	0
1995-96	Seattle	WHL	61	39	23	62	135	5	1	5	6	9
1996-97	Mississippi	ECHL	18	7	7	14	35	....	....	....	....	....
	Phoenix	IHL	37	3	6	9	60	....	....	....	....	....
1997-98	Fredericton	AHL	69	8	5	13	67	4	0	0	0	2

SCHMIDT, DOUG COL.

Defense. Shoots right. 5'10", 205 lbs. Born, Pompton Plains, NJ, January 19, 1978.
(Colorado's 8th choice, 217th overall, in 1997 Entry Draft).

			Regular Season					Playoffs				
Season	**Club**	**Lea**	**GP**	**G**	**A**	**TP**	**PIM**	**GP**	**G**	**A**	**TP**	**PIM**
1996-97	Waterloo	USHL	48	18	26	44	201	....	....	....	....	....
1997-98	Northern Michigan	WCHA	34	7	12	19	100	....	....	....	....	....

SCHNABEL, ROBERT (SHNAH-buhl) PHX.

Defense. Shoots left. 6'6", 216 lbs. Born, Prague, Czechoslovakia, November 10, 1978.
(Phoenix's 7th choice, 129th overall, in 1998 Entry Draft).

			Regular Season					Playoffs				
Season	Club	Lea	GP	G	A	TP	PIM	GP	G	A	TP	PIM
1995-96	Slavia Praha	Czech-Jr.	38	3	5	8	....	....	....	....	....	....
1996-97	Slavia Praha	Czech-Jr.	36	5	2	7	....	....	....	....	....	....
	Slavia Praha	Cze-Rep.	4	0	0	0	4	1	0	0	0	0
1997-98	Red Deer	WHL	61	1	22	23	143	5	0	0	0	16

• Re-entered NHL draft. Originally NY Islanders' 5th choice, 79th overall, in 1997 Entry Draft.

SCHNEIDER, ANDY OTT.

Left wing. Shoots left. 5'9", 170 lbs. Born, Edmonton, Alta., March 29, 1972.

			Regular Season					Playoffs				
Season	Club	Lea	GP	G	A	TP	PIM	GP	G	A	TP	PIM
1990-91	Swift Current	WHL	69	12	74	86	103	3	0	0	0	2
1991-92	Swift Current	WHL	63	44	60	104	120	8	4	9	13	8
1992-93	Swift Current	WHL	38	19	66	85	78	17	13	*26	*39	40
	New Haven	AHL	19	2	2	4	13	....	....	....	....	....
1993-94	**Ottawa**	**NHL**	**10**	**0**	**0**	**0**	**15**	....	....	....	....	....
	P.E.I.	AHL	61	15	46	61	119	....	....	....	....	....
1994-95	Leksand IF	Sweden	39	6	8	14	71	4	1	1	2	31
	Canada	Nat-Tm	3	1	0	1	0	....	....	....	....	....
	P.E.I.	AHL	10	1	5	6	25	11	5	5	10	11
1995-96	Minnesota	IHL	81	12	28	40	85	....	....	....	....	....
1996-97	Manitoba	IHL	79	14	37	51	142	....	....	....	....	....
1997-98	Revier Lowen	Germany	26	3	12	15	46	....	....	....	....	....
	Schwenningen	Germany	22	7	13	20	91	....	....	....	....	....
	NHL Totals		**10**	**0**	**0**	**0**	**15**	....	....	....	....	....

WHL East Second All-Star Team (1993)

Signed as a free agent by **Ottawa**, October 9, 1992.

SCHNEIDER, MATHIEU TOR.

Defense. Shoots left. 5'10", 192 lbs. Born, New York, NY, June 12, 1969.
(Montreal's 4th choice, 44th overall, in 1987 Entry Draft).

			Regular Season					Playoffs				
Season	Club	Lea	GP	G	A	TP	PIM	GP	G	A	TP	PIM
1986-87	Cornwall	OHL	63	7	29	36	75	5	0	0	0	22
1987-88	Cornwall	OHL	48	21	40	61	83	11	2	6	8	14
	Montreal	**NHL**	**4**	**0**	**0**	**0**	**2**	....	....	....	....	....
	Sherbrooke	AHL	....	....	....	....	....	3	0	3	3	12
1988-89	Cornwall	OHL	59	16	57	73	96	18	7	20	27	30
1989-90	**Montreal**	**NHL**	**44**	**7**	**14**	**21**	**25**	**9**	**1**	**3**	**4**	**31**
	Sherbrooke	AHL	28	6	13	19	20	....	....	....	....	....
1990-91	**Montreal**	**NHL**	**69**	**10**	**20**	**30**	**63**	**13**	**2**	**7**	**9**	**18**
1991-92	**Montreal**	**NHL**	**78**	**8**	**24**	**32**	**72**	**10**	**1**	**4**	**5**	**6**
1992-93	**Montreal**	**NHL**	**60**	**13**	**31**	**44**	**91**	**11**	**1**	**2**	**3**	**16** ♦
1993-94	**Montreal**	**NHL**	**75**	**20**	**32**	**52**	**62**	**1**	**0**	**0**	**0**	**0**
1994-95	**Montreal**	**NHL**	**30**	**5**	**15**	**20**	**49**	....	....	....	....	....
	NY Islanders	**NHL**	**13**	**3**	**6**	**9**	**30**	....	....	....	....	....
1995-96	**NY Islanders**	**NHL**	**65**	**11**	**36**	**47**	**93**	....	....	....	....	....
	Toronto	**NHL**	**13**	**2**	**5**	**7**	**10**	**6**	**0**	**4**	**4**	**8**
1996-97	**Toronto**	**NHL**	**26**	**5**	**7**	**12**	**20**	....	....	....	....	....
1997-98	**Toronto**	**NHL**	**76**	**11**	**26**	**37**	**44**	....	....	....	....	....
	United States	Olympics	4	0	0	0	6	....	....	....	....	....
	NHL Totals		**553**	**95**	**216**	**311**	**561**	**50**	**5**	**20**	**25**	**79**

OHL First All-Star Team (1988, 1989)

Played in NHL All-Star Game (1996)

Traded to **NY Islanders** by **Montreal** with Kirk Muller and Craig Darby for Pierre Turgeon and Vladimir Malakhov, April 5, 1995. Traded to **Toronto** by **NY Islanders** with Wendel Clark and D.J. Smith for Darby Hendrickson, Sean Haggerty, Kenny Jonsson and Toronto's 1st round choice (Roberto Luongo) in 1997 Entry Draft, March 13, 1996.

SCHULTE, PAXTON (SHUHL-tee)

Left wing. Shoots left. 6'2", 217 lbs. Born, Onaway, Alta., July 16, 1972.
(Quebec's 7th choice, 124th overall, in 1992 Entry Draft).

			Regular Season					Playoffs				
Season	Club	Lea	GP	G	A	TP	PIM	GP	G	A	TP	PIM
1990-91	North Dakota	WCHA	38	2	4	6	32	....	....	....	....	....
1991-92	Spokane	WHL	70	42	42	84	222	10	2	8	10	48
1992-93	Spokane	WHL	45	38	35	73	142	10	5	6	11	12
1993-94	**Quebec**	**NHL**	**1**	**0**	**0**	**0**	**2**	....	....	....	....	....
	Cornwall	AHL	56	15	15	30	102	....	....	....	....	....
1994-95	Cornwall	AHL	74	14	22	36	217	14	3	3	6	29
1995-96	Cornwall	AHL	69	25	31	56	171	....	....	....	....	....
	Saint John	AHL	14	4	5	9	25	14	4	7	11	40
1996-97	**Calgary**	**NHL**	**1**	**0**	**0**	**0**	**2**	....	....	....	....	....
	Saint John	AHL	71	14	23	37	274	4	2	0	2	35
1997-98	Saint John	AHL	59	8	17	25	133	....	....	....	....	....
	Las Vegas	IHL	10	0	1	1	32	4	0	0	0	4
	NHL Totals		**2**	**0**	**0**	**0**	**4**	....	....	....	....	....

Transferred to **Colorado** after **Quebec** franchise relocated, July 1, 1995. Traded to **Calgary** by **Colorado** for Vesa Viitakoski, March 19, 1996.

SCHULTZ, RAY NYI

Defense. Shoots left. 6'2", 200 lbs. Born, Red Deer, Alta., November 14, 1976.
(Ottawa's 8th choice, 184th overall, in 1995 Entry Draft).

			Regular Season					Playoffs				
Season	Club	Lea	GP	G	A	TP	PIM	GP	G	A	TP	PIM
1993-94	Tri-City	WHL	3	0	0	0	11	....	....	....	....	....
1994-95	Tri-City	WHL	63	1	8	9	209	11	0	0	0	16
1995-96	Calgary	WHL	66	3	17	20	282	....	....	....	....	....
1996-97	Calgary	WHL	32	3	17	20	141	....	....	....	....	....
	Kelowna	WHL	23	3	11	14	63	6	0	2	2	12
1997-98	**NY Islanders**	**NHL**	**13**	**0**	**1**	**1**	**45**	....	....	....	....	....
	Kentucky	AHL	51	2	4	6	179	1	0	0	0	25
	NHL Totals		**13**	**0**	**1**	**1**	**45**	....	....	....	....	....

Signed as a free agent by **NY Islanders**, June 9, 1997.

SCHUTZ, DEREK (SHOOTS) CGY.

Center. Shoots right. 6'2", 185 lbs. Born, Yorkton, Sask., March 5, 1979.
(Calgary's 5th choice, 60th overall, in 1997 Entry Draft).

			Regular Season					Playoffs				
Season	Club	Lea	GP	G	A	TP	PIM	GP	G	A	TP	PIM
1994-95	Spokane	WHL	2	0	0	0	2	....	....	....	....	....
1995-96	Spokane	WHL	70	10	7	17	121	18	1	4	5	37
1996-97	Spokane	WHL	61	20	21	41	126	9	1	3	4	9
1997-98	Spokane	WHL	67	22	34	56	113	18	1	5	6	21

SCISSONS, JEFF (SKIH-zuhns) VAN.

Center. Shoots left. 6'1", 190 lbs. Born, Saskatoon, Sask., November 24, 1976.
(Vancouver's 7th choice, 201st overall, in 1996 Entry Draft).

			Regular Season					Playoffs				
Season	Club	Lea	GP	G	A	TP	PIM	GP	G	A	TP	PIM
1995-96	Vernon	BCJHL	60	26	48	74	28	....	....	....	....	....
1996-97	U. Minn-Duluth	WCHA	38	3	14	17	30	....	....	....	....	....
1997-98	U. Minn-Duluth	WCHA	40	17	24	41	50	....	....	....	....	....

SCORSUNE, MATTHEW (SKOHR-soon) COL.

Defense. Shoots right. 6'3", 190 lbs. Born, Morristown, NJ, June 27, 1977.
(Colorado's 12th choice, 214th overall, in 1996 Entry Draft).

			Regular Season					Playoffs				
Season	Club	Lea	GP	G	A	TP	PIM	GP	G	A	TP	PIM
1995-96	Hotchkiss	H.S.	24	7	22	29	24	....	....	....	....	....
1996-97	Harvard	ECAC	30	3	8	11	28	....	....	....	....	....
1997-98	Harvard	ECAC	33	9	10	19	30	....	....	....	....	....

SCUDERI, ROBERT PIT.

Defense. Shoots left. 6'1", 194 lbs. Born, Syosset, NY, December 30, 1978.
(Pittsburgh's 5th choice, 134th overall, in 1998 Entry Draft).

			Regular Season					Playoffs				
Season	Club	Lea	GP	G	A	TP	PIM	GP	G	A	TP	PIM
1996-97	Apple Collegiate	H.S.	80	42	70	112	52	....	....	....	....	....
1997-98	Boston College	H.E.	42	0	24	24	12	....	....	....	....	....

SEELEY, RICHARD L.A.

Defense. Shoots left. 6'2", 199 lbs. Born, Powell River, B.C., April 30, 1979.
(Los Angeles' 6th choice, 137th overall, in 1997 Entry Draft).

			Regular Season					Playoffs				
Season	Club	Lea	GP	G	A	TP	PIM	GP	G	A	TP	PIM
1995-96	Powell River	BCJHL	44	1	8	9	42	....	....	....	....	....
1996-97	Lethbridge	WHL	3	0	0	0	11	....	....	....	....	....
	Prince Albert	WHL	18	0	1	1	9	4	0	0	0	2
1997-98	Prince Albert	WHL	65	8	21	29	114	....	....	....	....	....

SEIKKULA, TIMO (SAY-koo-lah, TEE-moh) PIT.

Center. Shoots left. 6'2", 183 lbs. Born, Kalajoki, Finland, May 27, 1978.
(Pittsburgh's 8th choice, 238th overall, in 1996 Entry Draft).

			Regular Season					Playoffs				
Season	Club	Lea	GP	G	A	TP	PIM	GP	G	A	TP	PIM
1994-95	Junkkarit	Finland-2	44	1	2	3	8	....	....	....	....	....
1995-96	Junkkarit	Finland-2	46	10	11	21	80	....	....	....	....	....
1996-97	Kiekko	Finland-2	43	5	5	10	38	....	....	....	....	....
1997-98	TPS Turku	Finland	1	0	1	1	0	....	....	....	....	....

SELANNE, TEEMU (SEH-lahn-nay, TEE-moo) ANA.

Right wing. Shoots right. 6', 200 lbs. Born, Helsinki, Finland, July 3, 1970.
(Winnipeg's 1st choice, 10th overall, in 1988 Entry Draft).

			Regular Season					Playoffs				
Season	Club	Lea	GP	G	A	TP	PIM	GP	G	A	TP	PIM
1987-88	Jokerit	Fin-Jr.	33	43	23	66	18	5	4	3	7	2
	Jokerit	Finland-2	5	1	1	2	0	....	....	....	....	....
1988-89	Jokerit	Finland-2	34	35	33	68	12	5	7	3	10	4
1989-90	Jokerit	Finland	11	4	8	12	0	....	....	....	....	....
1990-91	Jokerit	Finland	42	33	25	58	12	....	....	....	....	....
1991-92	Jokerit	Finland	44	*39	23	62	20	10	10	7	17	18
	Finland	Olympics	8	7	4	11	6	....	....	....	....	....
1992-93	**Winnipeg**	**NHL**	**84**	*76	**56**	**132**	**45**	**6**	**4**	**2**	**6**	**2**
1993-94	**Winnipeg**	**NHL**	**51**	**25**	**29**	**54**	**22**	....	....	....	....	....
1994-95	Jokerit	Finland	20	7	12	19	6	....	....	....	....	....
	Winnipeg	**NHL**	**45**	**22**	**26**	**48**	**2**	....	....	....	....	....
1995-96	**Winnipeg**	**NHL**	**51**	**24**	**48**	**72**	**18**	....	....	....	....	....
	Anaheim	**NHL**	**28**	**16**	**20**	**36**	**4**	....	....	....	....	....
1996-97	**Anaheim**	**NHL**	**78**	**51**	**58**	**109**	**34**	**11**	**7**	**3**	**10**	**4**
1997-98	**Anaheim**	**NHL**	**73**	*52	**34**	**86**	**30**	....	....	....	....	....
	Finland	Olympics	5	4	6	*10	8	....	....	....	....	....
	NHL Totals		**410**	**266**	**271**	**537**	**155**	**17**	**11**	**5**	**16**	**6**

Won Calder Memorial Trophy (1993) • NHL First All-Star Team (1993, 1997) • NHL/Upper Deck All-Rookie Team (1993) • NHL Second All-Star Team (1998)

Played in NHL All-Star Game (1993, 1994, 1996, 1997, 1998)

Traded to **Anaheim** by **Winnipeg** with Marc Chouinard and Winnipeg's 4th round choice (later traded to Toronto — later traded to Montreal — Montreal selected Kim Staal) in 1996 Entry Draft for Chad Kilger, Oleg Tverdovsky and Anaheim's 3rd round choice (Per-Anton Lundstrom) in 1996 Entry Draft, February 7, 1996.

SELIVANOV, ALEX (seh-lih-VAH-nohv) T.B.

Right wing. Shoots left. 6', 206 lbs. Born, Moscow, USSR, March 23, 1971.
(Philadelphia's 4th choice, 140th overall, in 1994 Entry Draft).

			Regular Season					Playoffs				
Season	Club	Lea	GP	G	A	TP	PIM	GP	G	A	TP	PIM
1988-89	Spartak	USSR	1	0	0	0	0	....	....	....	....	....
1989-90	Spartak	USSR	4	0	0	0	0	....	....	....	....	....
1990-91	Spartak	USSR	21	3	1	4	6	....	....	....	....	....
1991-92	Spartak	CIS	31	6	7	13	16	....	....	....	....	....
1992-93	Spartak	CIS	42	12	19	31	66	3	2	0	2	2
1993-94	Spartak	CIS	45	30	11	41	50	6	5	1	6	2
1994-95	Atlanta	IHL	4	0	3	3	2	....	....	....	....	....
	Chicago	IHL	14	4	1	5	8	....	....	....	....	....
	Tampa Bay	**NHL**	**43**	**10**	**6**	**16**	**14**	....	....	....	....	....
1995-96	**Tampa Bay**	**NHL**	**79**	**31**	**21**	**52**	**93**	**6**	**2**	**2**	**4**	**6**
1996-97	**Tampa Bay**	**NHL**	**69**	**15**	**18**	**33**	**61**	....	....	....	....	....
1997-98	**Tampa Bay**	**NHL**	**70**	**16**	**19**	**35**	**85**	....	....	....	....	....
	NHL Totals		**261**	**72**	**64**	**136**	**253**	**6**	**2**	**2**	**4**	**6**

Traded to **Tampa Bay** by **Philadelphia** for Philadelphia's 4th round choice (previously acquired, Philadelphia selected Radovan Somik) in 1995 Entry Draft, September 6, 1994.

SEMAK, ALEXANDER (seh-MAHK)

Center. Shoots right. 5'10", 185 lbs. Born, Ufa, USSR, February 11, 1966.
(New Jersey's 12th choice, 207th overall, in 1988 Entry Draft).

			Regular Season					Playoffs				
Season	Club	Lea	GP	G	A	TP	PIM	GP	G	A	TP	PIM
1984-85	Ufa Salavat	USSR-2	47	19	17	36	64					
1985-86	Ufa Salavat	USSR	22	9	7	16	22					
1986-87	Moscow D'amo	USSR	40	20	8	28	32					
1987-88	Moscow D'amo	USSR	47	21	14	35	40					
1988-89	Moscow D'amo	USSR	44	18	10	28	22					
1989-90	Moscow D'amo	USSR	43	23	11	34	33					
1990-91	Moscow D'amo	USSR	46	17	21	38	48					
1991-92	Moscow D'amo	CIS	26	10	13	23	26					
	New Jersey	**NHL**	**25**	**5**	**6**	**11**	**0**	**1**	**0**	**0**	**0**	**0**
	Utica	AHL	7	3	2	5	0					
1992-93	**New Jersey**	**NHL**	**82**	**37**	**42**	**79**	**70**	**5**	**1**	**1**	**2**	**0**
1993-94	**New Jersey**	**NHL**	**54**	**12**	**17**	**29**	**22**	**2**	**0**	**0**	**0**	**0**
1994-95	Ufa Salavat	CIS	9	9	6	15	4					
	New Jersey	**NHL**	**19**	**2**	**6**	**8**	**13**					
	Tampa Bay	**NHL**	**22**	**5**	**5**	**10**	**12**					
1995-96	**NY Islanders**	**NHL**	**69**	**20**	**14**	**34**	**68**					
1996-97	**Vancouver**	**NHL**	**18**	**2**	**1**	**3**	**2**					
	Syracuse	AHL	23	10	14	24	12					
	Las Vegas	IHL	13	11	13	24	10	3	0	4	4	4
1997-98	Chicago	IHL	67	26	35	61	90	22	10	*17	*27	35
	NHL Totals		**289**	**83**	**91**	**174**	**187**	**8**	**1**	**1**	**2**	**0**

USSR First All-Star Team (1991) • Won "Bud" Poile Trophy (Playoff MVP - IHL) (1998)

Traded to **Tampa Bay** by **New Jersey** with Ben Hankinson for Shawn Chambers and Danton Cole, March 14, 1995. Traded to **NY Islanders** by **Tampa Bay** for NY Islanders' 5th round choice (Karel Betik) in 1997 Entry Draft, September 14, 1995. Claimed by **Vancouver** from **NY Islanders** in NHL Waiver Draft, September 30, 1996.

SESSA, JASON (SEH-sa) TOR.

Right wing. Shoots right. 6'1", 173 lbs. Born, Long Island, NY, July 17, 1977.
(Toronto's 5th choice, 86th overall, in 1996 Entry Draft).

			Regular Season					Playoffs				
Season	Club	Lea	GP	G	A	TP	PIM	GP	G	A	TP	PIM
1995-96	Lake Superior	CCHA	30	9	5	14	12					
1996-97	Lake Superior	CCHA	34	22	22	44	91					
1997-98	Lake Superior	CCHA	32	16	13	29	55					
	St. John's	AHL	5	0	0	0	6					

CCHA Second All-Star Team (1997)

SEVERSON, CAM S.J.

Left wing. Shoots left. 6'1", 215 lbs. Born, Canora, Sask., January 15, 1978.
(San Jose's 6th choice, 192nd overall, in 1997 Entry Draft).

			Regular Season					Playoffs				
Season	Club	Lea	GP	G	A	TP	PIM	GP	G	A	TP	PIM
1996-97	Lethbridge	WHL	45	12	13	25	169					
	Prince Albert	WHL	16	5	13	18	54	4	4	0	4	8
1997-98	Prince Albert	WHL	41	23	25	48	129					
	Spokane	WHL	23	9	11	20	88	18	11	4	15	51

SEVERYN, BRENT (SEH-vuh-rihn) DAL.

Left wing. Shoots left. 6'2", 211 lbs. Born, Vegreville, Alta., February 22, 1966.
(Winnipeg's 5th choice, 99th overall, in 1984 Entry Draft).

			Regular Season					Playoffs				
Season	Club	Lea	GP	G	A	TP	PIM	GP	G	A	TP	PIM
1983-84	Seattle	WHL	72	14	22	36	49					
1984-85	Seattle	WHL	38	8	32	40	54					
	Brandon	WHL	26	7	16	23	57					
1985-86	Seattle	WHL	33	11	20	31	164					
	Saskatoon	WHL	9	1	4	5	38					
1986-87	U. of Alberta	CWUAA	43	7	19	26	171					
1987-88	U. of Alberta	CWUAA	46	21	29	50	178					
1988-89	Halifax	AHL	47	2	12	14	141					
1989-90	**Quebec**	**NHL**	**35**	**0**	**2**	**2**	**42**					
	Halifax	AHL	43	6	9	15	105	6	1	2	3	49
1990-91	Halifax	AHL	50	7	26	33	202					
1991-92	Utica	AHL	80	11	33	44	211	4	0	1	1	4
1992-93	Utica	AHL	77	20	32	52	240	5	0	0	0	35
1993-94	**Florida**	**NHL**	**67**	**4**	**7**	**11**	**156**					
1994-95	**Florida**	**NHL**	**9**	**1**	**1**	**2**	**37**					
	NY Islanders	**NHL**	**19**	**1**	**3**	**4**	**34**					
1995-96	**NY Islanders**	**NHL**	**65**	**1**	**8**	**9**	**180**					
1996-97	**Colorado**	**NHL**	**66**	**1**	**4**	**5**	**193**	**8**	**0**	**0**	**0**	**12**
1997-98	**Anaheim**	**NHL**	**37**	**1**	**3**	**4**	**133**					
	NHL Totals		**298**	**9**	**28**	**37**	**775**	**8**	**0**	**0**	**0**	**12**

AHL First All-Star Team (1993)

Signed as a free agent by **Quebec**, July 15, 1988. Traded to **New Jersey** by **Quebec** for Dave Marcinyshyn, June 3, 1991. Traded to **Winnipeg** by **New Jersey** for Winnipeg's 6th round choice (Ryan Smart) in 1994 Entry Draft, September 30, 1993. Traded to **Florida** by **Winnipeg** for Milan Tichy, October 3, 1993. Traded to **NY Islanders** by **Florida** for NY Islanders' 4th round choice (Dave Duerden) in 1995 Entry Draft, March 3, 1995. Traded to **Colorado** by **NY Islanders** for Colorado's 3rd round choice (later traded to Calgary — later traded to Hartford/Carolina — Carolina selected Francis Lessard) in 1997 Entry Draft, September 4, 1996. Claimed by **Anaheim** from **Colorado** in NHL Waiver Draft, September 28, 1997. Signed as a free agent by **Dallas**, August 26, 1998.

SEVIGNY, PIERRE (seh-VIH-nee)

Left wing. Shoots left. 6', 195 lbs. Born, Trois-Rivières, Que., September 8, 1971.
(Montreal's 4th choice, 51st overall, in 1989 Entry Draft).

			Regular Season					Playoffs				
Season	Club	Lea	GP	G	A	TP	PIM	GP	G	A	TP	PIM
1988-89	Verdun	QMJHL	67	27	43	70	88					
1989-90	St-Hyacinthe	QMJHL	67	47	72	119	205	12	8	8	16	42
1990-91	St-Hyacinthe	QMJHL	60	36	46	82	203					
1991-92	Fredericton	AHL	74	22	37	59	145	7	1	1	2	26
1992-93	Fredericton	AHL	80	36	40	76	113	5	1	1	2	2
1993-94	**Montreal**	**NHL**	**43**	**4**	**5**	**9**	**42**	**3**	**0**	**1**	**1**	**0**
1994-95	**Montreal**	**NHL**	**19**	**0**	**0**	**0**	**15**					
1995-96	Fredericton	AHL	76	39	42	81	188	10	5	9	14	20
1996-97	**Montreal**	**NHL**	**13**	**0**	**0**	**0**	**5**					
	Fredericton	AHL	32	9	17	26	58					
1997-98	**NY Rangers**	**NHL**	**3**	**0**	**0**	**0**	**2**					
	Hartford	AHL	40	18	13	31	94	12	3	5	8	14
	NHL Totals		**78**	**4**	**5**	**9**	**64**	**3**	**0**	**1**	**1**	**0**

QMJHL First All-Star Team (1981)

QMJHL Second All-Star Team (1990, 1991)

Signed as a free agent by **NY Rangers**, August 26, 1997

SHAFIKOV, RUSLAN (SHAH-fee-kahv, roos-LAHN) PHI.

Center. Shoots right. 6'1", 176 lbs. Born, Ufa, USSR, May 11, 1976.
(Philadelphia's 8th choice, 204th overall, in 1995 Entry Draft).

			Regular Season					Playoffs				
Season	Club	Lea	GP	G	A	TP	PIM	GP	G	A	TP	PIM
1994-95	Ufa Salavat	CIS	30	2	0	2	10	7	1	1	2	4
1995-96	Ufa Salavat	CIS	51	9	2	11	18	3	0	0	0	4
1996-97	Ufa Salavat	Russia	31	11	7	18	22	10	3	2	5	12
1997-98	Ufa Salavat	Russia	40	12	4	16	16					

SHAFRANOV, KONSTANTIN (shahf-RAH-nahv)

Right wing. Shoots left. 5'11", 176 lbs. Born, Kamengorsk, USSR, September 11, 1968.
(St. Louis' 10th choice, 229th overall, in 1996 Entry Draft).

			Regular Season					Playoffs				
Season	Club	Lea	GP	G	A	TP	PIM	GP	G	A	TP	PIM
1989-90	Kamenogorsk	USSR	28	6	8	14	16					
1990-91	Kamenogorsk	USSR	40	16	6	22	32					
1991-92	Kamenogorsk	CIS	36	10	6	16	40					
1992-93	Kamenogorsk	CIS	42	19	19	38	26	1	0	1	1	0
1993-94	Detroit	ColHL	4	3	2	5	0					
	Kamenogorsk	CIS	27	18	21	39	6					
1994-95	Magnitogorsk	CIS	47	21	30	51	24	7	5	4	9	12
1995-96	Magnitogorsk	CIS	6	3	3	6	0					
	Fort Wayne	IHL	74	46	28	74	26	5	1	2	3	4
1996-97	**St. Louis**	**NHL**	**5**	**2**	**1**	**3**	**0**					
	Worcester	AHL	62	23	25	48	16	5	0	2	2	0
1997-98	Fort Wayne	IHL	67	28	52	80	50	4	2	4	6	2
	Kazakhstan	Olympics	7	4	3	7	6					
	NHL Totals		**5**	**2**	**1**	**3**	**0**					

Won Garry F. Longman Memorial Trophy (Top Rookie - IHL) (1996) • IHL Second All-Star Team (1998)

SHALDYBIN, YEVGENY (shahl-DAY-bihn, yehv-GEH-nee) BOS.

Defense. Shoots left. 6'2", 198 lbs. Born, Novosibirsk, USSR, July 29, 1975.
(Boston's 6th choice, 151st overall, in 1995 Entry Draft).

			Regular Season					Playoffs				
Season	Club	Lea	GP	G	A	TP	PIM	GP	G	A	TP	PIM
1993-94	Yaroslavl	CIS	14	0	0	0	0					
1994-95	Yaroslavl	CIS	42	2	5	7	10	4	0	1	1	0
1995-96	Yaroslavl	CIS	41	0	2	2	10	3	0	1	1	2
1996-97	**Boston**	**NHL**	**3**	**1**	**0**	**1**	**0**					
	Providence	AHL	65	4	13	17	28	3	0	0	0	0
1997-98	Providence	AHL	63	5	7	12	54					
	NHL Totals		**3**	**1**	**0**	**1**	**0**					

SHANAHAN, BRENDAN DET.

Left wing. Shoots right. 6'3", 218 lbs. Born, Mimico, Ont., January 23, 1969.
(New Jersey's 1st choice, 2nd overall, in 1987 Entry Draft).

			Regular Season					Playoffs				
Season	Club	Lea	GP	G	A	TP	PIM	GP	G	A	TP	PIM
1985-86	London	OHL	59	28	34	62	70	5	5	5	10	5
1986-87	London	OHL	56	39	53	92	92					
1987-88	**New Jersey**	**NHL**	**65**	**7**	**19**	**26**	**131**	**12**	**2**	**1**	**3**	**44**
1988-89	**New Jersey**	**NHL**	**68**	**22**	**28**	**50**	**115**					
1989-90	**New Jersey**	**NHL**	**73**	**30**	**42**	**72**	**137**	**6**	**3**	**3**	**6**	**20**
1990-91	**New Jersey**	**NHL**	**75**	**29**	**37**	**66**	**141**	**7**	**3**	**5**	**8**	**12**
1991-92	**St. Louis**	**NHL**	**80**	**33**	**36**	**69**	**171**	**6**	**2**	**3**	**5**	**14**
1992-93	**St. Louis**	**NHL**	**71**	**51**	**43**	**94**	**174**	**11**	**4**	**3**	**7**	**18**
1993-94	**St. Louis**	**NHL**	**81**	**52**	**50**	**102**	**211**	**4**	**2**	**5**	**7**	**4**
1994-95	Dusseldorf	Germany	3	5	3	8	4					
	St. Louis	**NHL**	**45**	**20**	**21**	**41**	**136**	**5**	**4**	**5**	**9**	**14**
1995-96	**Hartford**	**NHL**	**74**	**44**	**34**	**78**	**125**					
1996-97	**Hartford**	**NHL**	**2**	**1**	**0**	**1**	**0**					
	Detroit	**NHL**	**79**	**46**	**41**	**87**	**131**	**20**	**9**	**8**	**17**	**43 ♦**
1997-98	**Detroit**	**NHL**	**75**	**28**	**29**	**57**	**154**	**20**	**5**	**4**	**9**	**22 ♦**
	Canada	Olympics	6	2	0	2	0					
	NHL Totals		**788**	**363**	**380**	**743**	**1626**	**91**	**34**	**37**	**71**	**191**

NHL First All-Star Team (1994)

Played in NHL All-Star Game (1994, 1996, 1997, 1998)

Signed as a free agent by **St. Louis**, July 25, 1991. Traded to **Hartford** by **St. Louis** for Chris Pronger, July 27, 1995. Traded to **Detroit** by **Hartford** with Brian Glynn for Paul Coffey, Keith Primeau and Detroit's 1st round choice (Nikos Tselios) in 1997 Entry Draft, October 9, 1996.

SHANNON, DARRIN

Left wing. Shoots left. 6'2", 210 lbs. Born, Barrie, Ont., December 8, 1969.
(Pittsburgh's 1st choice, 4th overall, in 1988 Entry Draft).

			Regular Season					Playoffs				
Season	Club	Lea	GP	G	A	TP	PIM	GP	G	A	TP	PIM
1986-87	Windsor	OHL	60	16	67	83	116	14	4	6	10	8
1987-88	Windsor	OHL	43	33	41	74	49	12	6	12	18	9
1988-89	Windsor	OHL	54	33	48	81	47	4	1	6	7	2
	Buffalo	**NHL**	**3**	**0**	**0**	**0**	**0**	**2**	**0**	**0**	**0**	**0**
1989-90	**Buffalo**	**NHL**	**17**	**2**	**7**	**9**	**4**	**6**	**0**	**1**	**1**	**4**
	Rochester	AHL	50	20	23	43	25	9	4	1	5	2
1990-91	**Buffalo**	**NHL**	**34**	**8**	**6**	**14**	**12**	**6**	**1**	**2**	**3**	**4**
	Rochester	AHL	49	26	34	60	56	10	3	5	8	22
1991-92	**Buffalo**	**NHL**	**1**	**0**	**1**	**1**	**0**					
	Winnipeg	**NHL**	**68**	**13**	**26**	**39**	**41**	**7**	**0**	**1**	**1**	**10**
1992-93	**Winnipeg**	**NHL**	**84**	**20**	**40**	**60**	**91**	**6**	**2**	**4**	**6**	**6**
1993-94	**Winnipeg**	**NHL**	**77**	**21**	**37**	**58**	**87**					
1994-95	**Winnipeg**	**NHL**	**19**	**5**	**3**	**8**	**14**					
1995-96	**Winnipeg**	**NHL**	**63**	**5**	**18**	**23**	**28**	**6**	**1**	**0**	**1**	**6**
1996-97	**Phoenix**	**NHL**	**82**	**11**	**13**	**24**	**41**	**7**	**3**	**1**	**4**	**4**
1997-98	**Phoenix**	**NHL**	**58**	**2**	**12**	**14**	**26**	**5**	**0**	**1**	**1**	**4**
	NHL Totals		**506**	**87**	**163**	**250**	**344**	**45**	**7**	**10**	**17**	**38**

Canadian Major Junior Scholastic Player of the Year (1988)

Traded to **Buffalo** by **Pittsburgh** with Doug Bodger for Tom Barrasso and Buffalo's 3rd round choice (Joe Dziedzic) in 1990 Entry Draft, November 12, 1988. Traded to **Winnipeg** by **Buffalo** with Mike Hartman and Dean Kennedy for Dave McLlwain, Gord Donnelly, Winnipeg's 5th round choice (Yuri Khmylev) in 1992 Entry Draft and future considerations, October 11, 1991. Transferred to **Phoenix** after **Winnipeg** franchise relocated, July 1, 1996.

SHANNON, DARRYL — BUF.

Defense. Shoots left. 6'2", 208 lbs. Born, Barrie, Ont., June 21, 1968.
(Toronto's 2nd choice, 36th overall, in 1986 Entry Draft).

			Regular Season					Playoffs				
Season	Club	Lea	GP	G	A	TP	PIM	GP	G	A	TP	PIM
1985-86	Windsor	OHL	57	6	21	27	52	16	5	6	11	22
1986-87	Windsor	OHL	64	23	27	50	83	14	4	8	12	18
1987-88	Windsor	OHL	60	16	67	83	116	12	3	8	11	17
1988-89	**Toronto**	**NHL**	14	1	3	4	6	....	....	....	....	....
	Newmarket	AHL	61	5	24	29	37	5	0	3	3	10
1989-90	**Toronto**	**NHL**	10	0	1	1	12	....	....	....	....	....
	Newmarket	AHL	47	4	15	19	58	....	....	....	....	....
1990-91	**Toronto**	**NHL**	10	0	1	1	0	....	....	....	....	....
	Newmarket	AHL	47	2	14	16	51	....	....	....	....	....
1991-92	**Toronto**	**NHL**	48	2	8	10	23	....	....	....	....	....
1992-93	**Toronto**	**NHL**	16	0	0	0	11	....	....	....	....	....
	St. John's	AHL	7	1	1	2	4	....	....	....	....	....
1993-94	**Winnipeg**	**NHL**	20	0	4	4	18	....	....	....	....	....
	Moncton	AHL	37	1	10	11	62	20	1	7	8	32
1994-95	**Winnipeg**	**NHL**	40	5	9	14	48	....	....	....	....	....
1995-96	**Winnipeg**	**NHL**	48	2	7	9	72	....	....	....	....	....
	Buffalo	**NHL**	26	2	6	8	20	....	....	....	....	....
1996-97	**Buffalo**	**NHL**	82	4	19	23	112	12	2	3	5	8
1997-98	**Buffalo**	**NHL**	76	3	19	22	56	15	2	4	6	8
	NHL Totals		**390**	**19**	**77**	**96**	**378**	**27**	**4**	**7**	**11**	**16**

OHL Second All-Star Team (1987) • OHL First All-Star Team (1988)

Signed as a free agent by **Winnipeg**, June 30, 1993. Traded to **Buffalo** by **Winnipeg** with Michal Grosek for Craig Muni, February 15, 1996.

SHANTZ, JEFF — CHI.

Center. Shoots right. 6', 195 lbs. Born, Duchess, Alta., October 10, 1973.
(Chicago's 2nd choice, 36th overall, in 1992 Entry Draft).

			Regular Season					Playoffs				
Season	Club	Lea	GP	G	A	TP	PIM	GP	G	A	TP	PIM
1990-91	Regina	WHL	69	16	21	37	22	8	2	2	4	2
1991-92	Regina	WHL	72	39	50	89	75	....	....	....	....	....
1992-93	Regina	WHL	64	29	54	83	75	13	2	12	14	14
1993-94	**Chicago**	**NHL**	52	3	13	16	30	6	0	0	0	6
	Indianapolis	IHL	19	5	9	14	20	....	....	....	....	....
1994-95	Indianapolis	IHL	32	9	15	24	20	....	....	....	....	....
	Chicago	**NHL**	45	6	12	18	33	16	3	1	4	2
1995-96	**Chicago**	**NHL**	78	6	14	20	24	10	2	3	5	6
1996-97	**Chicago**	**NHL**	69	9	21	30	28	6	0	4	4	6
1997-98	**Chicago**	**NHL**	61	11	20	31	36	....	....	....	....	....
	NHL Totals		**305**	**35**	**80**	**115**	**151**	**38**	**5**	**8**	**13**	**20**

WHL East First All-Star Team (1993)

SHAPLEY, LARRY (SHAP-lee) — VAN.

Defense. Shoots right. 6'6", 215 lbs. Born, Dunnville, Ont., February 6, 1978.
(Vancouver's 9th choice, 148th overall, in 1997 Entry Draft).

			Regular Season					Playoffs				
Season	Club	Lea	GP	G	A	TP	PIM	GP	G	A	TP	PIM
1996-97	Welland	OJHL	35	3	10	13	270	....	....	....	....	....
1997-98	Peterborough	OHL	63	1	1	2	211	4	0	0	0	0

SHARIFJANOV, VADIM (shah-rih-FYAH-nohv) — N.J.

Right wing. Shoots left. 6', 205 lbs. Born, Ufa, USSR, December 23, 1975.
(New Jersey's 1st choice, 25th overall, in 1994 Entry Draft).

			Regular Season					Playoffs				
Season	Club	Lea	GP	G	A	TP	PIM	GP	G	A	TP	PIM
1992-93	Ufa Salavat	CIS	37	6	4	10	16	2	1	0	1	0
1993-94	Ufa Salavat	CIS	46	10	6	16	36	5	3	0	3	4
1994-95	CSKA Moscow	CIS	34	7	3	10	26	2	0	0	0	0
	Albany	AHL	1	1	1	2	0	9	3	3	6	10
1995-96	Albany	AHL	69	14	28	42	28	....	....	....	....	....
1996-97	**New Jersey**	**NHL**	2	0	0	0	0	....	....	....	....	....
	Albany	AHL	70	14	27	41	89	10	3	3	6	6
1997-98	Albany	AHL	72	23	27	50	69	12	4	9	13	6
	NHL Totals		**2**	**0**	**0**	**0**	**0**	....	....	....	....	....

SHAW, DAVID — S.J.

Defense. Shoots right. 6'2", 205 lbs. Born, St. Thomas, Ont., May 25, 1964.
(Quebec's 1st choice, 13th overall, in 1982 Entry Draft).

			Regular Season					Playoffs				
Season	Club	Lea	GP	G	A	TP	PIM	GP	G	A	TP	PIM
1981-82	Kitchener	OHL	68	6	25	31	94	15	2	2	4	51
1982-83	Kitchener	OHL	57	18	56	74	78	12	2	10	12	18
	Quebec	**NHL**	2	0	0	0	0	....	....	....	....	....
1983-84	Kitchener	OHL	58	14	34	48	73	16	4	9	13	12
	Quebec	**NHL**	3	0	0	0	0	....	....	....	....	....
1984-85	**Quebec**	**NHL**	14	0	0	0	11	....	....	....	....	....
	Fredericton	AHL	48	7	6	13	73	2	0	0	0	7
1985-86	**Quebec**	**NHL**	73	7	19	26	78	....	....	....	....	....
1986-87	**Quebec**	**NHL**	75	0	19	19	69	....	....	....	....	....
1987-88	**NY Rangers**	**NHL**	68	7	25	32	100	....	....	....	....	....
1988-89	**NY Rangers**	**NHL**	63	6	11	17	88	4	0	2	2	30
1989-90	**NY Rangers**	**NHL**	22	2	10	12	22	....	....	....	....	....
1990-91	**NY Rangers**	**NHL**	77	2	10	12	89	6	0	0	0	11
1991-92	**NY Rangers**	**NHL**	10	0	1	1	15	....	....	....	....	....
	Edmonton	**NHL**	12	1	1	2	8	....	....	....	....	....
	Minnesota	**NHL**	37	0	7	7	49	7	2	2	4	10
1992-93	**Boston**	**NHL**	77	10	14	24	108	4	0	1	1	6
1993-94	**Boston**	**NHL**	55	1	9	10	85	13	1	2	3	16
1994-95	**Boston**	**NHL**	44	3	4	7	36	5	0	1	1	4
1995-96	**Tampa Bay**	**NHL**	66	1	11	12	64	6	0	1	1	4
1996-97	**Tampa Bay**	**NHL**	57	1	10	11	72	....	....	....	....	....
1997-98	**Tampa Bay**	**NHL**	14	0	2	2	12	....	....	....	....	....
	Las Vegas	IHL	26	6	13	19	28	....	....	....	....	....
	NHL Totals		**769**	**41**	**153**	**194**	**906**	**45**	**3**	**9**	**12**	**81**

OHL First All-Star Team (1984) • Memorial Cup All-Star Team (1984)

Traded to **NY Rangers** by **Quebec** with John Ogrodnick for Jeff Jackson and Terry Carkner, September 30, 1987. Traded to **Edmonton** by **NY Rangers** for Jeff Beukeboom, November 12, 1991. Traded to **Minnesota** by **Edmonton** for Brian Glynn, January 21, 1992. Traded to **Boston** by **Minnesota** for future considerations, September 2, 1992. Traded to **Tampa Bay** by **Boston** for Detroit's 3rd round choice (previously acquired, Boston selected Jason Doyle) in 1996 Entry Draft, August 17, 1995. Traded to **San Jose** by **Tampa Bay** with Bryan Marchment and Tampa Bay's 1st round choice (later traded to Nashville - Nashville selected David Legwand) in 1998 Entry Draft for Andrei Nazarov and Florida's 1st round choice (previously acquired, Tampa Bay selected Vincent Lecavalier) in 1998 Entry Draft, March 24, 1998.

SHAW, LLOYD — ANA.

Defense. Shoots right. 6'3", 220 lbs. Born, Regina, Sask., September 26, 1976.
(Vancouver's 4th choice, 92nd overall, in 1995 Entry Draft).

			Regular Season					Playoffs				
Season	Club	Lea	GP	G	A	TP	PIM	GP	G	A	TP	PIM
1993-94	Seattle	WHL	47	0	4	4	107	8	0	0	0	23
1994-95	Seattle	WHL	66	3	12	15	313	3	0	0	0	13
1995-96	Seattle	WHL	27	0	1	1	92	....	....	....	....	....
	Red Deer	WHL	37	2	4	6	120	10	0	2	2	25
1996-97	Red Deer	WHL	66	8	16	24	257	16	0	6	6	60
1997-98	Cincinnati	AHL	60	1	2	3	138	....	....	....	....	....
	Columbus	ECHL	4	0	0	0	7	....	....	....	....	....

Signed as a free agent by **Anaheim**, July 7, 1997.

SHEARER, ROB — COL.

Center. Shoots right. 5'10", 190 lbs. Born, Kitchener, Ont., October 19, 1976.

			Regular Season					Playoffs				
Season	Club	Lea	GP	G	A	TP	PIM	GP	G	A	TP	PIM
1993-94	Windsor	OHL	66	17	25	42	46	4	0	2	2	6
1994-95	Windsor	OHL	59	28	28	56	48	10	4	4	8	10
1995-96	Windsor	OHL	63	40	53	93	74	7	6	3	9	8
1996-97	Hershey	AHL	78	12	16	28	88	23	0	4	4	9
1997-98	Hershey	AHL	79	30	30	60	44	7	0	5	5	6

Signed as a free agent by **Colorado**, October 5, 1995.

SHEPPARD, RAY — CAR.

Right wing. Shoots right. 6'1", 195 lbs. Born, Pembroke, Ont., May 27, 1966.
(Buffalo's 3rd choice, 60th overall, in 1984 Entry Draft).

			Regular Season					Playoffs				
Season	Club	Lea	GP	G	A	TP	PIM	GP	G	A	TP	PIM
1983-84	Cornwall	OHL	68	44	36	80	69	....	....	....	....	....
1984-85	Cornwall	OHL	49	25	33	58	51	9	2	12	14	4
1985-86	Cornwall	OHL	63	*81	61	*142	25	6	7	4	11	0
1986-87	Rochester	AHL	55	18	13	31	11	15	12	3	15	2
1987-88	**Buffalo**	**NHL**	74	38	27	65	14	6	1	1	2	2
1988-89	**Buffalo**	**NHL**	67	22	21	43	15	1	0	1	1	0
1989-90	**Buffalo**	**NHL**	18	4	2	6	0	....	....	....	....	....
	Rochester	AHL	5	3	5	8	2	17	8	7	15	9
1990-91	**NY Rangers**	**NHL**	59	24	23	47	21	....	....	....	....	....
1991-92	**Detroit**	**NHL**	74	36	26	62	27	11	6	2	8	4
1992-93	**Detroit**	**NHL**	70	32	34	66	29	7	2	3	5	0
1993-94	**Detroit**	**NHL**	82	52	41	93	26	7	2	1	3	4
1994-95	**Detroit**	**NHL**	43	30	10	40	17	17	4	3	7	5
1995-96	**Detroit**	**NHL**	5	2	2	4	2	....	....	....	....	....
	San Jose	**NHL**	51	27	19	46	10	....	....	....	....	....
	Florida	**NHL**	14	8	2	10	4	21	8	8	16	4
1996-97	**Florida**	**NHL**	68	29	31	60	4	5	2	0	2	0
1997-98	**Florida**	**NHL**	61	14	17	31	21	....	....	....	....	....
	Carolina	**NHL**	10	4	2	6	2	....	....	....	....	....
	NHL Totals		**696**	**322**	**257**	**579**	**192**	**75**	**25**	**19**	**44**	**19**

OHL First All-Star Team (1986) • NHL All-Rookie Team (1988)

Traded to **NY Rangers** by **Buffalo** for cash and future considerations, July 9, 1990. Signed as a free agent by **Detroit**, August 5, 1991. Traded to **San Jose** by **Detroit** for Igor Larionov and future considerations, October 24, 1995. Traded to **Florida** by **San Jose** with San Jose's 4th round choice (Joey Tetarenko) in 1996 Entry Draft for Florida's 2nd (later traded to Chicago — Chicago selected Geoff Peters) and 4th (Matt Bradley) round choices in 1996 Entry Draft, March 16, 1996. Traded to **Carolina** by **Florida** for Kirk McLean, March 24, 1998.

SHEVALIER, JEFF (sheh-VAL-ee-ay)

Left wing. Shoots left. 5'11", 180 lbs. Born, Mississauga, Ont., March 14, 1974.
(Los Angeles' 4th choice, 111th overall, in 1992 Entry Draft).

			Regular Season					Playoffs				
Season	Club	Lea	GP	G	A	TP	PIM	GP	G	A	TP	PIM
1991-92	North Bay	OHL	64	28	29	57	26	21	5	11	16	25
1992-93	North Bay	OHL	62	59	54	113	46	2	1	2	3	4
1993-94	North Bay	OHL	64	52	49	101	52	17	8	14	22	18
1994-95	Phoenix	IHL	68	31	39	70	44	9	5	4	9	0
	Los Angeles	**NHL**	1	1	0	1	0	....	....	....	....	....
1995-96	Phoenix	IHL	79	29	38	67	72	4	2	2	4	2
1996-97	**Los Angeles**	**NHL**	26	4	9	13	6	....	....	....	....	....
	Phoenix	IHL	46	16	21	37	26	....	....	....	....	....
1997-98	Springfield	AHL	66	23	30	53	38	4	1	1	2	0
	NHL Totals		**27**	**5**	**9**	**14**	**6**	....	....	....	....	....

OHL First All-Star Team (1994)

SHIKHANOV, SERGEI (shih-KHAHN-ohf) — CHI.

Right wing. Shoots left. 6'1", 187 lbs. Born, Togliatti, USSR, April 8, 1978.
(Chicago's 10th choice, 204th overall, in 1997 Entry Draft).

			Regular Season					Playoffs				
Season	Club	Lea	GP	G	A	TP	PIM	GP	G	A	TP	PIM
1996-97	Togliatti	Russia	19	4	4	8	20	8	1	0	1	10
	Neftekhimik	Russia	5	1	1	2	2	....	....	....	....	....
1997-98	Togliatti	Russia	19	3	0	3	4	....	....	....	....	....

SHIRREFFS, STEVE (SHUHR-ehfs) — CGY.

Defense. Shoots left. 6'3", 200 lbs. Born, Boston, MA, February 18, 1976.
(Calgary's 7th choice, 233rd overall, in 1995 Entry Draft).

			Regular Season					Playoffs				
Season	Club	Lea	GP	G	A	TP	PIM	GP	G	A	TP	PIM
1995-96	Princeton	ECAC	25	0	3	3	6	....	....	....	....	....
1996-97	Princeton	ECAC	34	5	4	9	12	....	....	....	....	....
1997-98	Princeton	ECAC	36	9	24	33	54	....	....	....	....	....

ECAC First All-Star Team (1998) • NCAA East Second All-American Team (1998)

SHUCHUK, GARY (SHOO-chuhk)

Right wing. Shoots right. 5'11", 190 lbs. Born, Edmonton, Alta., February 17, 1967.
(Detroit's 1st choice, 22nd overall, in 1988 Supplemental Draft).

			Regular Season					Playoffs				
Season	Club	Lea	GP	G	A	TP	PIM	GP	G	A	TP	PIM
1986-87	U. of Wisconsin	WCHA	42	19	11	30	72	....	....	....	....	....
1987-88	U. of Wisconsin	WCHA	44	7	22	29	70	....	....	....	....	....
1988-89	U. of Wisconsin	WCHA	46	18	19	37	102	....	....	....	....	....
1989-90	U. of Wisconsin	WCHA	45	*41	39	*80	70	....	....	....	....	....
1990-91	**Detroit**	**NHL**	**6**	**1**	**2**	**3**	**6**	**3**	**0**	**0**	**0**	**0**
	Adirondack	AHL	59	23	24	47	32	....	....	....	....	....
1991-92	Adirondack	AHL	79	32	48	80	48	19	4	9	13	18
1992-93	Adirondack	AHL	47	24	53	77	66	....	....	....	....	....
	Los Angeles	**NHL**	**25**	**2**	**4**	**6**	**16**	**17**	**2**	**2**	**4**	**12**
1993-94	**Los Angeles**	**NHL**	**56**	**3**	**4**	**7**	**30**	....	....	....	....	....
1994-95	**Los Angeles**	**NHL**	**22**	**3**	**6**	**9**	**6**	....	....	....	....	....
	Phoenix	IHL	13	8	7	15	12	....	....	....	....	....
1995-96	**Los Angeles**	**NHL**	**33**	**4**	**10**	**14**	**12**	....	....	....	....	....
	Phoenix	IHL	33	8	21	29	76	4	1	0	1	4
1996-97	Houston	IHL	55	18	23	41	48	13	5	2	7	18
1997-98	Herisau	Switz.	40	15	33	48	60	....	....	....	....	....
	NHL Totals		**142**	**13**	**26**	**39**	**70**	**20**	**2**	**2**	**4**	**12**

WCHA First All-Star Team (1990) • NCAA West First All-American Team (1990)

Traded to **LA Kings** by **Detroit** with Jimmy Carson and Marc Potvin for Paul Coffey, Sylvain Couturier and Jim Hiller, January 29, 1993.

SIDULOV, KONSTANTIN (sih-DOO-lahf) MTL.

Defense. Shoots right. 6'1", 176 lbs. Born, Chelyabinsk, USSR, January 1, 1977.
(Montreal's 5th choice, 118th overall, in 1997 Entry Draft).

			Regular Season					Playoffs				
Season	Club	Lea	GP	G	A	TP	PIM	GP	G	A	TP	PIM
1994-95	Chelyabinsk	CIS	2	0	0	0	0	....	....	....	....	....
1995-96	Chelyabinsk	CIS	52	1	0	1	58	....	....	....	....	....
1996-97	Chelyabinsk	Russia	42	0	0	0	28	2	0	0	0	0
1997-98	Chelyabinsk	Russia	43	1	3	4	36	....	....	....	....	....

SIDYAKIN, ANDREI (sihd-YA-kihn) MTL.

Right wing. Shoots left. 5'11", 169 lbs. Born, Ufa, USSR, January 20, 1979.
(Montreal's 10th choice, 202nd overall, in 1997 Entry Draft).

			Regular Season					Playoffs				
Season	Club	Lea	GP	G	A	TP	PIM	GP	G	A	TP	PIM
1994-95	Yulayev	CIS	7	0	1	1	0	....	....	....	....	....
1995-96	Yulayev	CIS	25	1	0	1	4	3	0	0	0	2
1996-97	Yulayev	Russia	29	3	5	8	4	....	....	....	....	....
1997-98	Yulayev	Russia	42	5	4	9	32	....	....	....	....	....

SIKLENKA, MIKE WSH.

Defense. Shoots right. 6'4", 215 lbs. Born, Meadow Lake, Sask., December 18, 1979.
(Washington's 5th choice, 118th overall, in 1998 Entry Draft).

			Regular Season					Playoffs				
Season	Club	Lea	GP	G	A	TP	PIM	GP	G	A	TP	PIM
1997-98	Lloydminster	SJHL	54	10	17	27	120	....	....	....	....	....

SILLINGER, MIKE PHI.

Center. Shoots right. 5'10", 190 lbs. Born, Regina, Sask., June 29, 1971.
(Detroit's 1st choice, 11th overall, in 1989 Entry Draft).

			Regular Season					Playoffs				
Season	Club	Lea	GP	G	A	TP	PIM	GP	G	A	TP	PIM
1987-88	Regina	WHL	67	18	25	43	17	4	2	2	4	0
1988-89	Regina	WHL	72	53	78	131	52	....	....	....	....	....
1989-90	Regina	WHL	70	57	72	129	41	11	12	10	22	2
	Adirondack	AHL	....	....	....	....	....	1	0	0	0	0
1990-91	Regina	WHL	57	50	66	116	42	8	6	9	15	4
	Detroit	**NHL**	**3**	**0**	**1**	**1**	**0**	**3**	**0**	**1**	**1**	**0**
1991-92	Adirondack	AHL	64	25	41	66	26	15	9	*19	*28	12
	Detroit	**NHL**	....	....	....	....	....	**8**	**2**	**2**	**4**	**2**
1992-93	**Detroit**	**NHL**	**51**	**4**	**17**	**21**	**16**	....	....	....	....	....
	Adirondack	AHL	15	10	20	30	31	11	5	13	18	10
1993-94	**Detroit**	**NHL**	**62**	**8**	**21**	**29**	**10**	....	....	....	....	....
1994-95	CE Wien	Austria	13	13	14	27	10	....	....	....	....	....
	Detroit	**NHL**	**13**	**2**	**6**	**8**	**2**	....	....	....	....	....
	Anaheim	**NHL**	**15**	**2**	**5**	**7**	**6**	....	....	....	....	....
1995-96	**Anaheim**	**NHL**	**62**	**13**	**21**	**34**	**32**	....	....	....	....	....
	Vancouver	**NHL**	**12**	**1**	**3**	**4**	**6**	**6**	**0**	**0**	**0**	**2**
1996-97	**Vancouver**	**NHL**	**78**	**17**	**20**	**37**	**25**	....	....	....	....	....
1997-98	**Vancouver**	**NHL**	**48**	**10**	**9**	**19**	**34**	....	....	....	....	....
	Philadelphia	**NHL**	**27**	**11**	**11**	**22**	**16**	**3**	**1**	**0**	**1**	**0**
	NHL Totals		**371**	**68**	**114**	**182**	**147**	**20**	**3**	**3**	**6**	**4**

WHL East Second All-Star Team (1990) • WHL East First All-Star Team (1991)

Traded to **Anaheim** by **Detroit** with Jason York for Stu Grimson, Mark Ferner and Anaheim's 6th round choice (Magnus Nilsson) in 1996 Entry Draft, April 4, 1995. Traded to **Vancouver** by **Anaheim** for Roman Oksiuta, March 15, 1996. Traded to **Philadelphia** by **Vancouver** for Philadelphia's 5th round choice (traded back to Philadelphia — Philadelphia selected Garrett Prosofsky) in 1998 Entry Draft, February 5, 1998.

SIM, JONATHAN DAL.

Center. Shoots left. 5'9", 175 lbs. Born, New Glasgow, N.S., September 29, 1977.
(Dallas' 2nd choice, 70th overall, in 1996 Entry Draft).

			Regular Season					Playoffs				
Season	Club	Lea	GP	G	A	TP	PIM	GP	G	A	TP	PIM
1994-95	Sarnia	OHL	25	9	12	21	19	4	3	2	5	2
1995-96	Sarnia	OHL	63	56	46	102	130	10	8	7	15	26
1996-97	Sarnia	OHL	64	*56	39	95	109	12	9	5	14	32
1997-98	Sarnia	OHL	59	44	50	94	95	5	1	4	5	14

OHL Second All-Star Team (1998)

SIMON, BENJAMIN CHI.

Center. Shoots left. 5'11", 178 lbs. Born, Shaker Heights, OH, June 14, 1978.
(Chicago's 5th choice, 110th overall, in 1997 Entry Draft).

			Regular Season					Playoffs				
Season	Club	Lea	GP	G	A	TP	PIM	GP	G	A	TP	PIM
1996-97	Notre Dame	CCHA	30	4	15	19	79	....	....	....	....	....
1997-98	Notre Dame	CCHA	37	9	28	37	91	....	....	....	....	....

SIMON, CHRIS WSH.

Left wing. Shoots left. 6'3", 225 lbs. Born, Wawa, Ont., January 30, 1972.
(Philadelphia's 2nd choice, 25th overall, in 1990 Entry Draft).

			Regular Season					Playoffs				
Season	Club	Lea	GP	G	A	TP	PIM	GP	G	A	TP	PIM
1988-89	Ottawa	OHL	36	4	2	6	31	....	....	....	....	....
1989-90	Ottawa	OHL	57	36	38	74	146	3	2	1	3	4
1990-91	Ottawa	OHL	20	16	6	22	69	17	5	9	14	59
1991-92	Ottawa	OHL	2	1	1	2	24	....	....	....	....	....
	S.S. Marie	OHL	31	19	25	44	143	11	5	8	13	49
1992-93	**Quebec**	**NHL**	**16**	**1**	**1**	**2**	**67**	**5**	**0**	**0**	**0**	**26**
	Halifax	AHL	36	12	6	18	131	....	....	....	....	....
1993-94	**Quebec**	**NHL**	**37**	**4**	**4**	**8**	**132**	....	....	....	....	....
1994-95	**Quebec**	**NHL**	**29**	**3**	**9**	**12**	**106**	**6**	**1**	**1**	**2**	**19**
1995-96	**Colorado**	**NHL**	**64**	**16**	**18**	**34**	**250**	**12**	**1**	**2**	**3**	**11 ♦**
1996-97	**Washington**	**NHL**	**42**	**9**	**13**	**22**	**165**	....	....	....	....	....
1997-98	**Washington**	**NHL**	**28**	**7**	**10**	**17**	**38**	**18**	**1**	**0**	**1**	**26**
	NHL Totals		**216**	**40**	**55**	**95**	**758**	**41**	**3**	**3**	**6**	**82**

Traded to **Quebec** by **Philadelphia** with Peter Forsberg, Steve Duchesne, Kerry Huffman, Mike Ricci, Ron Hextall, Philadelphia's 1st round choice in the 1993 (Jocelyn Thibault) and 1994 (later traded to Toronto — later traded to Washington — Washington selected Nolan Baumgartner) Entry Drafts and cash for Eric Lindros, June 30, 1992. Transferred to **Coloradeo** after **Quebec** franchise relocated, July 1, 1995. Traded to **Washington** by **Colorado** with Curtis Leschyshyn for Keith Jones and Washington's 1st (Scott Parker) and 4th (later traded back to Washington — Washington selected Krys Barch) round choices in 1998 Entry Draft, November 2, 1996.

SIMON, JASON

Left wing. Shoots left. 6'1", 210 lbs. Born, Sarnia, Ont., March 21, 1969.
(New Jersey's 9th choice, 215th overall, in 1989 Entry Draft).

			Regular Season					Playoffs				
Season	Club	Lea	GP	G	A	TP	PIM	GP	G	A	TP	PIM
1986-87	London	OHL	33	1	2	3	33	....	....	....	....	....
	Sudbury	OHL	26	2	3	5	50	....	....	....	....	....
1987-88	Sudbury	OHL	26	5	7	12	35	....	....	....	....	....
	Hamilton	OHL	29	5	13	18	124	11	0	2	2	15
1988-89	Windsor	OHL	62	23	39	62	193	4	1	4	5	13
1989-90	Utica	AHL	16	3	4	7	28	2	0	0	0	12
	Nashville	ECHL	13	4	3	7	81	5	1	3	4	17
1990-91	Utica	AHL	50	2	12	14	189	....	....	....	....	....
	Johnstown	ECHL	22	11	9	20	55	....	....	....	....	....
1991-92	Utica	AHL	1	0	0	0	12	....	....	....	....	....
	San Diego	IHL	13	1	4	5	45	3	0	1	1	9
1992-93	Detroit	ColHL	11	7	13	20	38	....	....	....	....	....
	Flint	ColHL	44	17	32	49	202	....	....	....	....	....
1993-94	Salt Lake	IHL	50	7	7	14	*323	....	....	....	....	....
	NY Islanders	**NHL**	**4**	**0**	**0**	**0**	**34**	....	....	....	....	....
	Detroit	ColHL	13	9	16	25	87	....	....	....	....	....
1994-95	Denver	IHL	61	3	6	9	300	1	0	0	0	12
1995-96	Springfield	AHL	18	2	2	4	90	7	1	0	1	26
1996-97	**Phoenix**	**NHL**	**1**	**0**	**0**	**0**	**0**	....	....	....	....	....
	Las Vegas	IHL	64	4	3	7	402	3	0	0	0	0
1997-98	Hershey	AHL	26	0	1	1	170	....	....	....	....	....
	Quebec	IHL	30	6	3	9	127	....	....	....	....	....
	NHL Totals		**5**	**0**	**0**	**0**	**34**	....	....	....	....	....

Signed as a free agent by **NY Islanders**, January 6, 1994. Signed as a free agent by **Winnipeg**, August 9, 1995. Transferred to **Phoenix** after **Winnipeg** franchise relocated, July 1, 1996. Signed as a free agent by **Colorado**, August 22, 1997.

SIMPSON, REID CHI.

Left wing. Shoots left. 6'2", 220 lbs. Born, Flin Flon, Man., May 21, 1969.
(Philadelphia's 3rd choice, 72nd overall, in 1989 Entry Draft).

			Regular Season					Playoffs				
Season	Club	Lea	GP	G	A	TP	PIM	GP	G	A	TP	PIM
1985-86	Flin Flon	AJHL	40	20	21	41	200	....	....	....	....	....
	New Westminster	WHL	2	0	0	0	0	....	....	....	....	....
1986-87	Prince Albert	WHL	47	3	8	11	105	....	....	....	....	....
1987-88	Prince Albert	WHL	72	13	14	27	164	10	1	0	1	43
1988-89	Prince Albert	WHL	59	26	29	55	264	4	2	1	3	30
1989-90	Prince Albert	WHL	29	15	17	32	121	14	4	7	11	34
	Hershey	AHL	28	2	2	4	175	....	....	....	....	....
1990-91	Hershey	AHL	54	9	15	24	183	1	0	0	0	0
1991-92	**Philadelphia**	**NHL**	**1**	**0**	**0**	**0**	**0**	....	....	....	....	....
	Hershey	AHL	60	11	7	18	145	....	....	....	....	....
1992-93	**Minnesota**	**NHL**	**1**	**0**	**0**	**0**	**5**	....	....	....	....	....
	Kalamazoo	IHL	45	5	5	10	193	....	....	....	....	....
1993-94	Kalamazoo	IHL	5	0	0	0	16	....	....	....	....	....
	Albany	AHL	37	9	5	14	135	5	1	1	2	18
1994-95	Albany	AHL	70	18	25	43	268	14	1	8	9	13
	New Jersey	**NHL**	**9**	**0**	**0**	**0**	**27**	....	....	....	....	....
1995-96	**New Jersey**	**NHL**	**23**	**1**	**5**	**6**	**79**	....	....	....	....	....
	Albany	AHL	6	1	3	4	17	....	....	....	....	....
1996-97	**New Jersey**	**NHL**	**27**	**0**	**4**	**4**	**60**	**5**	**0**	**0**	**0**	**29**
	Albany	AHL	3	0	0	0	10	....	....	....	....	....
1997-98	**New Jersey**	**NHL**	**6**	**0**	**0**	**0**	**16**	....	....	....	....	....
	Chicago	**NHL**	**38**	**3**	**2**	**5**	**102**	....	....	....	....	....
	NHL Totals		**105**	**4**	**11**	**15**	**289**	**5**	**0**	**0**	**0**	**29**

Signed as a free agent by **Minnesota**, December 14, 1992. Transferred to **Dallas** after **Minnesota** franchise relocated, June 9, 1993. Traded to **New Jersey** by **Dallas** with Roy Mitchell for future considerations, March 21, 1994. Traded to **Chicago** by **New Jersey** for Chicago's 4th round choice (Mikko Jokela) in 1998 Entry Draft and future considerations, January 8, 1998.

SIMPSON, TODD CGY.

Defense. Shoots left. 6'3", 215 lbs. Born, North Vancouver, B.C., May 28, 1973.

			Regular Season					Playoffs				
Season	Club	Lea	GP	G	A	TP	PIM	GP	G	A	TP	PIM
1991-92	Brown University	ECAC	14	1	3	4	18	....	....	....	....	....
1992-93	Tri-City	WHL	69	5	18	23	196	4	0	0	0	13
1993-94	Tri-City	WHL	12	2	3	5	32	....	....	....	....	....
	Saskatoon	WHL	51	7	19	26	175	16	1	5	6	42
1994-95	Saint John	AHL	80	3	10	13	321	5	0	0	0	4
1995-96	**Calgary**	**NHL**	**6**	**0**	**0**	**0**	**32**	....	....	....	....	....
	Saint John	AHL	66	4	13	17	277	16	2	3	5	32
1996-97	**Calgary**	**NHL**	**82**	**1**	**13**	**14**	**208**	....	....	....	....	....
1997-98	**Calgary**	**NHL**	**53**	**1**	**5**	**6**	**109**	....	....	....	....	....
	NHL Totals		**141**	**2**	**18**	**20**	**349**	....	....	....	....	....

Signed as free agent by **Calgary**, July 6, 1994.

SINCLAIR, DARREN — VAN.

Center/Left wing. Shoots left. 6', 200 lbs. Born, Brooks, Alta., August 24, 1976.

			Regular Season					Playoffs				
Season	Club	Lea	GP	G	A	TP	PIM	GP	G	A	TP	PIM
1993-94	Spokane	WHL	66	9	15	24	54	3	0	0	0	0
1994-95	Spokane	WHL	71	16	20	36	81	11	2	3	5	8
1995-96	Spokane	WHL	72	35	47	82	52	18	8	12	20	25
1996-97	Syracuse	AHL	68	12	16	28	32	3	0	2	2	0
1997-98	Syracuse	AHL	57	5	15	20	23	4	0	0	0	2
	Raleigh	ECHL	6	2	0	2	0	....	....	....	....	....

Signed as a free agent by **Vancouver**, October 5, 1995.

SKALDE, JARROD (SKAHL-dee) — S.J.

Center. Shoots left. 6', 175 lbs. Born, Niagara Falls, Ont., February 26, 1971.
(New Jersey's 3rd choice, 26th overall, in 1989 Entry Draft).

			Regular Season					Playoffs				
Season	Club	Lea	GP	G	A	TP	PIM	GP	G	A	TP	PIM
1987-88	Oshawa	OHL	60	12	16	28	24	7	2	1	3	2
1988-89	Oshawa	OHL	65	38	38	76	36	6	1	5	6	2
1989-90	Oshawa	OHL	62	40	52	92	66	17	10	7	17	6
1990-91	Oshawa	OHL	15	8	14	22	14	....	....	....	....	....
	Belleville	OHL	40	30	52	82	21	6	9	6	15	10
	New Jersey	**NHL**	**1**	**0**	**1**	**1**	**0**	....	....	....	....	....
	Utica	AHL	3	3	2	5	0	....	....	....	....	....
1991-92	**New Jersey**	**NHL**	**15**	**2**	**4**	**6**	**4**	....	....	....	....	....
	Utica	AHL	62	20	20	40	56	4	3	1	4	8
1992-93	**New Jersey**	**NHL**	**11**	**0**	**2**	**2**	**4**	....	....	....	....	....
	Utica	AHL	59	21	39	60	76	5	0	2	2	19
	Cincinnati	IHL	4	1	2	3	4	....	....	....	....	....
1993-94	**Anaheim**	**NHL**	**20**	**5**	**4**	**9**	**10**	....	....	....	....	....
	San Diego	IHL	57	25	38	63	79	9	3	12	15	10
1994-95	Las Vegas	IHL	74	34	41	75	103	9	2	4	6	8
1995-96	Baltimore	AHL	11	2	6	8	55	....	....	....	....	....
	Calgary	**NHL**	**1**	**0**	**0**	**0**	**0**	....	....	....	....	....
	Saint John	AHL	68	27	40	67	98	16	4	9	13	6
1996-97	Saint John	AHL	65	32	36	68	94	3	0	0	0	14
1997-98	**San Jose**	**NHL**	**22**	**4**	**6**	**10**	**14**	....	....	....	....	....
	Kentucky	AHL	6	2	6	8	10	....	....	....	....	....
	Chicago	**NHL**	**4**	**0**	**1**	**1**	**2**	....	....	....	....	....
	Indianapolis	IHL	2	0	2	2	0	....	....	....	....	....
	Dallas	**NHL**	**1**	**0**	**0**	**0**	**0**	....	....	....	....	....
	Chicago	**NHL**	**3**	**0**	**0**	**0**	**2**	....	....	....	....	....
	Kentucky	AHL	17	3	9	12	38	3	3	0	3	6
	NHL Totals		**78**	**11**	**18**	**29**	**36**	....	....	....	....	....

OHL Second All-Star Team (1991)

Claimed by **Anaheim** from **New Jersey** in Expansion Draft, June 24, 1993. Traded to **Calgary** by **Anaheim** for Bobby Marshall, October 30, 1995. Signed as a free agent by **San Jose**, August 14, 1997. Claimed on waivers by **Chicago** from **San Jose**, January 8, 1998. Claimed on waivers by **San Jose** from **Chicago**, January 23, 1998. Claimed on waivers by **Dallas** from **San Jose**, January 27, 1998. Claimed on waivers by **Chicago** from **Dallas**, February 10, 1998. Claimed on waivers by **San Jose** from **Chicago**, March 6, 1998.

SKOLNEY, SHAWN — T.B.

Defense. Shoots left. 6'2", 185 lbs. Born, Humboldt, Sask., July 15, 1979.
(Tampa Bay's 11th choice, 198th overall, in 1997 Entry Draft).

			Regular Season					Playoffs				
Season	Club	Lea	GP	G	A	TP	PIM	GP	G	A	TP	PIM
1996-97	Seattle	WHL	37	0	6	6	24	....	....	....	....	....
1997-98	Seattle	WHL	22	0	3	3	40	....	....	....	....	....
	Moose Jaw	WHL	39	5	2	7	22	3	0	0	0	2

SKOPINTSEV, ANDREI (skuh-PIHN-sehf) — T.B.

Defense. Shoots right. 6', 185 lbs. Born, Elekrostal, USSR, September 28, 1971.
(Tampa Bay's 7th choice, 153rd overall, in 1997 Entry Draft).

			Regular Season					Playoffs				
Season	Club	Lea	GP	G	A	TP	PIM	GP	G	A	TP	PIM
1989-90	Soviet Wings	USSR	20	0	0	0	10	....	....	....	....	....
1990-91	Soviet Wings	USSR	16	0	1	1	2	....	....	....	....	....
1991-92	Soviet Wings	CIS	36	1	1	2	14	....	....	....	....	....
1992-93	Soviet Wings	CIS	12	1	0	1	4	7	1	0	1	2
1993-94	Soviet Wings	CIS	43	4	8	12	14	3	1	0	1	0
1994-95	Soviet Wings	CIS	52	8	12	20	55	4	1	1	2	0
1995-96	Augsburg	Germany	46	10	20	30	32	7	3	2	5	22
1996-97	TPS Turku	Finland	46	3	6	9	80	10	1	1	2	4
1997-98	TPS Turku	EuroHL	5	0	1	1	4	....	....	....	....	....
	TPS Turku	Finland	48	2	9	11	8	4	0	1	1	4

SKOREPA, ZDENEK (SKOHR-zheh-pah) — N.J.

Right wing. Shoots left. 6', 185 lbs. Born, Duchcov, Czech., August 10, 1976.
(New Jersey's 4th choice, 103rd overall, in 1994 Entry Draft).

			Regular Season					Playoffs				
Season	Club	Lea	GP	G	A	TP	PIM	GP	G	A	TP	PIM
1993-94	Litvinov	Cze-Rep.	20	4	7	11	....	4	0	0	0	....
1994-95	Litvinov	Cze-Rep.	28	3	3	6	20	3	0	0	0	2
1995-96	Kingston	OHL	37	21	18	39	13	6	5	2	7	5
1996-97	Albany	AHL	60	12	12	24	38	13	3	2	5	14
1997-98	Detroit	IHL	8	0	0	0	2	....	....	....	....	....
	Albany	AHL	28	2	2	4	4	1	0	0	0	0

SKOULA, MARTIN (SHKOH-la) — COL.

Defense. Shoots left. 6'2", 195 lbs. Born, Litvinov, Czechoslovakia, October 28, 1979.
(Colorado's 2nd choice, 17th overall, in 1998 Entry Draft).

			Regular Season					Playoffs				
Season	Club	Lea	GP	G	A	TP	PIM	GP	G	A	TP	PIM
1995-96	Litvinov	Czech-Jr.	38	0	4	4	....	....	....	....	....	....
	Litvinov	Cze-Rep.	....	....	....	....	....	1	0	0	0	0
1996-97	Litvinov	Czech-Jr.	38	2	9	11	....	....	....	....	....	....
	Litvinov	Cze-Rep.	1	0	0	0	0	....	....	....	....	....
1997-98	Barrie	OHL	66	8	36	44	36	6	1	3	4	4

SKRBEK, PAVEL (skuh-BEHK) — PIT.

Defense. Shoots left. 6'3", 191 lbs. Born, Kladno, Czech., August 9, 1978.
(Pittsburgh's 2nd choice, 28th overall, in 1996 Entry Draft).

			Regular Season					Playoffs				
Season	Club	Lea	GP	G	A	TP	PIM	GP	G	A	TP	PIM
1994-95	Poldi Kladno	Czech-Jr.	29	7	6	13	....	....	....	....	....	....
1995-96	Poldi Kladno	Czech-Jr.	29	10	12	22	....	....	....	....	....	....
	Poldi Kladno	Cze-Rep.	13	0	1	1	....	5	0	0	0	....
1996-97	Poldi Kladno	Cze-Rep.	35	1	5	6	26	3	0	0	0	4
1997-98	Poldi Kladno	Cze-Rep.	47	4	10	14	126	....	....	....	....	....

SKRLAC, ROB (SKUHR-lak) — N.J.

Left wing. Shoots left. 6'5", 250 lbs. Born, Campbell, B.C., June 10, 1976.
(Buffalo's 11th choice, 224th overall, in 1995 Entry Draft).

			Regular Season					Playoffs				
Season	Club	Lea	GP	G	A	TP	PIM	GP	G	A	TP	PIM
1994-95	Kamloops	WHL	23	0	1	1	177	....	....	....	....	....
1995-96	Kamloops	WHL	63	1	4	5	216	13	0	0	0	52
1996-97	Kamloops	WHL	61	8	10	18	278	5	0	0	0	35
1997-98	Albany	AHL	53	0	2	2	256	....	....	....	....	....

Signed as a free agent by **New Jersey**, June 17, 1997.

SKRUDLAND, BRIAN (SKROOD-luhnd) — DAL.

Center. Shoots left. 6', 195 lbs. Born, Peace River, Alta., July 31, 1963.

			Regular Season					Playoffs				
Season	Club	Lea	GP	G	A	TP	PIM	GP	G	A	TP	PIM
1980-81	Saskatoon	WHL	66	15	27	42	97	....	....	....	....	....
1981-82	Saskatoon	WHL	71	27	29	56	135	5	0	1	1	2
1982-83	Saskatoon	WHL	71	35	59	94	42	6	1	3	4	19
1983-84	Nova Scotia	AHL	56	13	12	25	55	12	2	8	10	14
1984-85	Sherbrooke	AHL	70	22	28	50	109	17	9	8	17	23
1985-86	**Montreal**	**NHL**	**65**	**9**	**13**	**22**	**57**	**20**	**2**	**4**	**6**	**76** ♦
1986-87	**Montreal**	**NHL**	**79**	**11**	**17**	**28**	**107**	**14**	**1**	**5**	**6**	**29**
1987-88	**Montreal**	**NHL**	**79**	**12**	**24**	**36**	**112**	**11**	**1**	**5**	**6**	**24**
1988-89	**Montreal**	**NHL**	**71**	**12**	**29**	**41**	**84**	**21**	**3**	**7**	**10**	**40**
1989-90	**Montreal**	**NHL**	**59**	**11**	**31**	**42**	**56**	**11**	**3**	**5**	**8**	**30**
1990-91	**Montreal**	**NHL**	**57**	**15**	**19**	**34**	**85**	**13**	**3**	**10**	**13**	**42**
1991-92	**Montreal**	**NHL**	**42**	**3**	**3**	**6**	**36**	**11**	**1**	**1**	**2**	**20**
1992-93	**Montreal**	**NHL**	**23**	**5**	**3**	**8**	**55**	....	....	....	....	....
	Calgary	**NHL**	**16**	**2**	**4**	**6**	**10**	**6**	**0**	**3**	**3**	**12**
1993-94	**Florida**	**NHL**	**79**	**15**	**25**	**40**	**136**	....	....	....	....	....
1994-95	**Florida**	**NHL**	**47**	**5**	**9**	**14**	**88**	....	....	....	....	....
1995-96	**Florida**	**NHL**	**79**	**7**	**20**	**27**	**129**	**21**	**1**	**3**	**4**	**18**
1996-97	**Florida**	**NHL**	**51**	**5**	**13**	**18**	**48**	....	....	....	....	....
1997-98	**NY Rangers**	**NHL**	**59**	**5**	**6**	**11**	**39**	....	....	....	....	....
	Dallas	**NHL**	**13**	**2**	**0**	**2**	**10**	**17**	**0**	**1**	**1**	**16**
	NHL Totals		**819**	**119**	**216**	**335**	**1052**	**145**	**15**	**44**	**59**	**307**

Won Jack A. Butterfield Trophy (Playoff MVP - AHL) (1985)

Signed as a free agent by **Montreal**, September 13, 1983. Traded to **Calgary** by **Montreal** for Gary Leeman, January 28, 1993. Claimed by **Florida** from **Calgary** in Expansion Draft, June 24, 1993. Signed as a free agent by **NY Rangers**, August 21, 1997. Traded to **Dallas** by **NY Rangers** with Mike Keane and NY Rangers' 6th round choice (Pavel Patera) in 1998 Entry Draft for Todd Harvey, Bob Errey and Dallas' 4th round choice (Boyd Kane) in 1998 Entry Draft, March 24, 1998.

SLANEY, JOHN — NSH.

Defense. Shoots left. 6', 185 lbs. Born, St. John's, Nfld., February 7, 1972.
(Washington's 1st choice, 9th overall, in 1990 Entry Draft).

			Regular Season					Playoffs				
Season	Club	Lea	GP	G	A	TP	PIM	GP	G	A	TP	PIM
1988-89	Cornwall	OHL	66	16	43	59	23	18	8	16	24	10
1989-90	Cornwall	OHL	64	38	59	97	68	6	0	8	8	11
1990-91	Cornwall	OHL	34	21	25	46	28	....	....	....	....	....
1991-92	Cornwall	OHL	34	19	41	60	43	6	3	8	11	0
	Baltimore	AHL	6	2	4	6	0	....	....	....	....	....
1992-93	Baltimore	AHL	79	20	46	66	60	7	0	7	7	8
1993-94	**Washington**	**NHL**	**47**	**7**	**9**	**16**	**27**	**11**	**1**	**1**	**2**	**2**
	Portland	AHL	29	14	13	27	17	....	....	....	....	....
1994-95	**Washington**	**NHL**	**16**	**0**	**3**	**3**	**6**	....	....	....	....	....
	Portland	AHL	8	3	10	13	4	7	1	3	4	4
1995-96	**Colorado**	**NHL**	**7**	**0**	**3**	**3**	**4**	....	....	....	....	....
	Cornwall	AHL	5	0	4	4	2	....	....	....	....	....
	Los Angeles	**NHL**	**31**	**6**	**11**	**17**	**10**	....	....	....	....	....
1996-97	**Los Angeles**	**NHL**	**32**	**3**	**11**	**14**	**4**	....	....	....	....	....
	Phoenix	IHL	35	9	25	34	8	....	....	....	....	....
1997-98	**Phoenix**	**NHL**	**55**	**3**	**14**	**17**	**24**	....	....	....	....	....
	Las Vegas	IHL	5	2	2	4	10	....	....	....	....	....
	NHL Totals		**188**	**19**	**51**	**70**	**75**	**11**	**1**	**1**	**2**	**2**

OHL First All-Star Team (1990) • Canadian Major Junior Defenseman of the Year (1990) • OHL Second All-Star Team (1991)

Traded to **Colorado** by **Washington** for Philadelphia's 3rd round choice (previously acquired, Washington selected Shawn McNeil) in 1996 Entry Draft, July 12, 1995. Traded to **LA Kings** by **Colorado** for Winnipeg's 6th round choice (previously acquired, Colorado selected Brian Willsie) in 1996 Entry Draft, December 28, 1995. Signed as a free agent by **Phoenix**, August 19, 1997. Claimed by **Nashville** from **Phoenix** in Expansion Draft, June 26, 1998.

SLEGR, JIRI (SLAY-guhr, YOO-ree) — PIT.

Defense. Shoots left. 6', 207 lbs. Born, Jihlava, Czech., May 30, 1971.
(Vancouver's 3rd choice, 23rd overall, in 1990 Entry Draft).

			Regular Season					Playoffs				
Season	Club	Lea	GP	G	A	TP	PIM	GP	G	A	TP	PIM
1987-88	Litvinov	Czech.	4	1	1	2	0	....	....	....	....	....
1988-89	Litvinov	Czech.	8	0	0	0	4	....	....	....	....	....
1989-90	Litvinov	Czech.	51	4	15	19	....	....	....	....	....	....
1990-91	Litvinov	Czech.	47	11	36	47	26	....	....	....	....	....
1991-92	Litvinov	Czech.	42	9	23	32	38	....	....	....	....	....
	Czechoslovakia	Olympics	8	1	1	2	14	....	....	....	....	....
1992-93	**Vancouver**	**NHL**	**41**	**4**	**22**	**26**	**109**	**5**	**0**	**3**	**3**	**4**
	Hamilton	AHL	21	4	14	18	42	....	....	....	....	....
1993-94	**Vancouver**	**NHL**	**78**	**5**	**33**	**38**	**86**	....	....	....	....	....
1994-95	Litvinov	Cze-Rep.	11	3	10	13	80	....	....	....	....	....
	Vancouver	**NHL**	**19**	**1**	**5**	**6**	**32**	....	....	....	....	....
	Edmonton	**NHL**	**12**	**1**	**5**	**6**	**14**	....	....	....	....	....
1995-96	**Edmonton**	**NHL**	**57**	**4**	**13**	**17**	**74**	....	....	....	....	....
	Cape Breton	AHL	4	1	2	3	4	....	....	....	....	....
1996-97	Litvinov	Cze-Rep.	1	0	0	0	0	....	....	....	....	....
	Sodertalje	Sweden	30	4	14	18	62	....	....	....	....	....
1997-98	**Pittsburgh**	**NHL**	**73**	**5**	**12**	**17**	**109**	**6**	**0**	**4**	**4**	**2**
	Czech Republic	Olympics	6	1	0	1	8	....	....	....	....	....
	NHL Totals		**280**	**20**	**90**	**110**	**424**	**11**	**0**	**7**	**7**	**6**

Czechoslovakian First All-Star Team (1991)

Traded to **Edmonton** by **Vancouver** for Roman Oksiuta, April 7, 1995. Traded to **Pittsburgh** by **Edmonton** for Pittsburgh's 3rd round choice (later traded to New Jersey — New Jersey selected Brian Gionta) in 1998 Entry Draft, August 12, 1997.

SMART, RYAN — N.J.

Center. Shoots right. 6', 175 lbs. Born, Meadville, PA, September 22, 1975.
(New Jersey's 6th choice, 134th overall, in 1994 Entry Draft).

			Regular Season					Playoffs				
Season	Club	Lea	GP	G	A	TP	PIM	GP	G	A	TP	PIM
1993-94	Meadville	H.S.	46	59	57	116	....	....	....	....	....	....
1994-95	Cornell	ECAC	26	13	7	20	10	....	....	....	....	....
1995-96	Cornell	ECAC	34	8	19	27	22	....	....	....	....	....
1996-97	Cornell	ECAC	35	5	12	17	20	....	....	....	....	....
1997-98	Cornell	ECAC	20	5	6	11	20	....	....	....	....	....

SMEHLIK, RICHARD (SHMEH-lihk) — BUF.

Defense. Shoots left. 6'3", 222 lbs. Born, Ostrava, Czech., January 23, 1970.
(Buffalo's 3rd choice, 97th overall, in 1990 Entry Draft).

			Regular Season					Playoffs				
Season	Club	Lea	GP	G	A	TP	PIM	GP	G	A	TP	PIM
1988-89	Vitkovice	Czech.	38	2	5	7	12	....	....	....	....	....
1989-90	Vitkovice	Czech.	51	5	4	9	....	....	....	....	....	....
1990-91	Dukla Jihlava	Czech.	58	4	3	7	22	....	....	....	....	....
1991-92	Vitkovice	Czech.	47	9	10	19	42	....	....	....	....	....
	Czechoslovakia	Olympics	8	0	1	1	2	....	....	....	....	....
1992-93	**Buffalo**	**NHL**	**80**	**4**	**27**	**31**	**59**	**8**	**0**	**4**	**4**	**2**
1993-94	**Buffalo**	**NHL**	**84**	**14**	**27**	**41**	**69**	**7**	**0**	**2**	**2**	**10**
1994-95	Vitkovice	Cze-Rep.	13	5	2	7	12	....	....	....	....	....
	Buffalo	**NHL**	**39**	**4**	**7**	**11**	**46**	**5**	**0**	**0**	**0**	**2**
1995-96			DID NOT PLAY – INJURED									
1996-97	**Buffalo**	**NHL**	**62**	**11**	**19**	**30**	**43**	**12**	**0**	**2**	**2**	**4**
1997-98	**Buffalo**	**NHL**	**72**	**3**	**17**	**20**	**62**	**15**	**0**	**2**	**2**	**6**
	Czech Republic	Olympics	6	0	1	1	4	....	....	....	....	....
	NHL Totals		**337**	**36**	**97**	**133**	**279**	**47**	**0**	**10**	**10**	**24**

• Missed entire 1995-96 season after undergoing off-season knee surgery, August 11, 1995.

SMIRNOV, OLEG (smihr-NOHF) — EDM.

Left wing. Shoots right. 5'11", 176 lbs. Born, Elektrostal, USSR, April 8, 1980.
(Edmonton's 6th choice, 144th overall, in 1998 Entry Draft).

			Regular Season					Playoffs				
Season	Club	Lea	GP	G	A	TP	PIM	GP	G	A	TP	PIM
1996-97	Kristall 2	Russia-3	38	2	2	4	8	....	....	....	....	....
1997-98	Kristall	Russia	6	0	2	2	0	....	....	....	....	....
	Kristall	Russia-2	10	0	0	0	2	....	....	....	....	....

SMITH, ADAM — NYR

Defense. Shoots left. 6', 190 lbs. Born, Digby, N.S., May 24, 1976.
(NY Rangers' 3rd choice, 78th overall, in 1994 Entry Draft).

			Regular Season					Playoffs				
Season	Club	Lea	GP	G	A	TP	PIM	GP	G	A	TP	PIM
1992-93	Tacoma	WHL	67	0	12	12	43	7	0	1	1	4
1993-94	Tacoma	WHL	66	4	19	23	119	8	0	0	0	10
1994-95	Tacoma	WHL	69	2	19	21	96	4	0	1	1	9
1995-96	Kelowna	WHL	67	8	15	23	125	6	1	1	2	8
1996-97	Binghamton	AHL	56	0	8	8	59	2	0	0	0	0
1997-98	Hartford	AHL	64	7	5	12	120	4	0	0	0	12

SMITH, BRANDON — BOS.

Defense. Shoots left. 6'1", 196 lbs. Born, Hazelton, B.C., February 25, 1973.

			Regular Season					Playoffs				
Season	Club	Lea	GP	G	A	TP	PIM	GP	G	A	TP	PIM
1989-90	Portland	WHL	59	2	17	19	16	....	....	....	....	....
1990-91	Portland	WHL	17	8	5	13	8	....	....	....	....	....
1991-92	Portland	WHL	70	12	32	44	63	....	....	....	....	....
1992-93	Portland	WHL	72	20	54	74	38	16	4	9	13	6
1993-94	Portland	WHL	72	19	63	82	47	10	2	10	12	8
1994-95	Dayton	ECHL	60	16	49	65	57	4	2	3	5	0
	Adirondack	AHL	14	1	2	3	7	3	0	0	0	2
1995-96	Adirondack	AHL	48	4	13	17	22	3	0	1	1	2
1996-97	Adirondack	AHL	80	8	26	34	30	4	0	0	0	0
1997-98	Adirondack	AHL	64	9	27	36	26	1	0	1	1	0

WHL West Second All-Star Team (1993, 1994) • ECHL First All-Star Team (1995) • Top Defenseman - ECHL (1995)

Signed as a free agent by **Detroit**, July 22, 1997. Signed as a free agent by **Boston**, August 5, 1998.

SMITH, DAN — COL.

Defense. Shoots left. 6'2", 195 lbs. Born, Fernie, B.C., October 19, 1976.
(Colorado's 7th choice, 181st overall, in 1995 Entry Draft).

			Regular Season					Playoffs				
Season	Club	Lea	GP	G	A	TP	PIM	GP	G	A	TP	PIM
1994-95	U.B.C.	CWUAA	28	1	3	4	26	....	....	....	....	....
1995-96	Tri-City	WHL	58	1	21	22	70	11	1	3	4	14
1996-97	Tri-City	WHL	72	5	19	24	174	....	....	....	....	....
	Hershey	AHL	8	0	1	1	6	15	0	1	1	25
1997-98	Hershey	AHL	50	1	2	3	71	6	0	0	0	4

SMITH, DENIS — TOR.

Defense. Shoots left. 6'1", 200 lbs. Born, Windsor, Ont., May 13, 1977.
(NY Islanders' 3rd choice, 41st overall, in 1995 Entry Draft).

			Regular Season					Playoffs				
Season	Club	Lea	GP	G	A	TP	PIM	GP	G	A	TP	PIM
1994-95	Windsor	OHL	61	4	13	17	201	10	1	3	4	41
1995-96	Windsor	OHL	64	14	45	59	260	7	1	7	8	23
	St. John's	AHL	1	0	0	0	0	....	....	....	....	....
1996-97	Windsor	OHL	63	15	52	67	190	5	1	7	8	11
	Toronto	**NHL**	**8**	**0**	**1**	**1**	**7**	....	....	....	....	....
	St. John's	AHL	....	....	....	....	....	1	0	0	0	0
1997-98	St. John's	AHL	65	4	11	15	237	4	0	0	0	4
	NHL Totals		**8**	**0**	**1**	**1**	**7**	....	....	....	....	....

OHL Second All-Star Team (1997)

Traded to **Toronto** by **NY Islanders** with Wendel Clark and Mathieu Schneider for Darby Hendrickson, Sean Haggerty, Kenny Jonsson and Toronto's 1st round choice (Roberto Luongo) in 1997 Entry Draft, March 13, 1996.

SMITH, GEOFF — NYR

Defense. Shoots left. 6'3", 194 lbs. Born, Edmonton, Alta., March 7, 1969.
(Edmonton's 3rd choice, 63rd overall, in 1987 Entry Draft).

			Regular Season					Playoffs				
Season	Club	Lea	GP	G	A	TP	PIM	GP	G	A	TP	PIM
1986-87	St. Albert	AJHL	57	7	28	35	101	....	....	....	....	....
1987-88	North Dakota	WCHA	42	4	12	16	34	....	....	....	....	....
1988-89	North Dakota	WCHA	9	0	1	1	8	....	....	....	....	....
	Kamloops	WHL	32	4	31	35	29	6	1	3	4	12
1989-90	**Edmonton**	**NHL**	**74**	**4**	**11**	**15**	**52**	**3**	**0**	**0**	**0**	**0 ♦**
1990-91	**Edmonton**	**NHL**	**59**	**1**	**12**	**13**	**55**	**4**	**0**	**0**	**0**	**0**
1991-92	**Edmonton**	**NHL**	**74**	**2**	**16**	**18**	**43**	**5**	**0**	**1**	**1**	**6**
1992-93	**Edmonton**	**NHL**	**78**	**4**	**14**	**18**	**30**	....	....	....	....	....
1993-94	**Edmonton**	**NHL**	**21**	**0**	**3**	**3**	**12**	....	....	....	....	....
	Florida	**NHL**	**56**	**1**	**5**	**6**	**38**	....	....	....	....	....
1994-95	**Florida**	**NHL**	**47**	**2**	**4**	**6**	**22**	....	....	....	....	....
1995-96	**Florida**	**NHL**	**31**	**3**	**7**	**10**	**20**	**1**	**0**	**0**	**0**	**2**
1996-97	**Florida**	**NHL**	**3**	**0**	**0**	**0**	**2**	....	....	....	....	....
	Carolina	AHL	27	3	4	7	20	....	....	....	....	....
1997-98	**NY Rangers**	**NHL**	**15**	**1**	**1**	**2**	**6**	....	....	....	....	....
	Hartford	AHL	59	1	12	13	34	....	....	....	....	....
	NHL Totals		**458**	**18**	**73**	**91**	**280**	**13**	**0**	**1**	**1**	**8**

WHL West Second All-Star Team (1989) • NHL All-Rookie Team (1990)

Traded to **Florida** by **Edmonton** with Edmonton's 4th round choice (David Nemirovsky) in 1994 Entry Draft for Florida's 3rd round choice (Corey Neilson) in 1994 Entry Draft and St. Louis' 6th round choice (previously acquired and later traded to Winnipeg — Winnipeg selected Chris Kibermanis) in 1994 Entry Draft, December 6, 1993.

SMITH, JARRETT — NYI

Center. Shoots left. 6'1", 190 lbs. Born, Edmonton, Alta., June 15, 1979.
(NY Islanders' 4th choice, 59th overall, in 1997 Entry Draft).

			Regular Season					Playoffs				
Season	Club	Lea	GP	G	A	TP	PIM	GP	G	A	TP	PIM
1994-95	Prince George	WHL	1	0	0	0	0	....	....	....	....	....
1995-96	Prince George	WHL	18	2	0	2	6	....	....	....	....	....
1996-97	Prince George	WHL	67	20	22	42	58	15	2	2	4	5
1997-98	Prince George	WHL	42	12	22	34	21	11	3	1	4	8

SMITH, JASON — TOR.

Defense. Shoots right. 6'3", 205 lbs. Born, Calgary, Alta., November 2, 1973.
(New Jersey's 1st choice, 18th overall, in 1992 Entry Draft).

			Regular Season					Playoffs				
Season	Club	Lea	GP	G	A	TP	PIM	GP	G	A	TP	PIM
1990-91	Calgary	AJHL	45	3	15	18	69	....	....	....	....	....
	Regina	WHL	2	0	0	0	7	4	0	0	0	2
1991-92	Regina	WHL	62	9	29	38	168	....	....	....	....	....
1992-93	Regina	WHL	64	14	52	66	175	13	4	8	12	39
	Utica	AHL	....	....	....	....	....	1	0	0	0	2
1993-94	**New Jersey**	**NHL**	**41**	**0**	**5**	**5**	**43**	**6**	**0**	**0**	**0**	**7**
	Albany	AHL	20	6	3	9	31	....	....	....	....	....
1994-95	**New Jersey**	**NHL**	**2**	**0**	**0**	**0**	**0**	....	....	....	....	....
	Albany	AHL	7	0	2	2	15	11	2	2	4	19
1995-96	**New Jersey**	**NHL**	**64**	**2**	**1**	**3**	**86**	....	....	....	....	....
1996-97	**New Jersey**	**NHL**	**57**	**1**	**2**	**3**	**38**	....	....	....	....	....
	Toronto	**NHL**	**21**	**0**	**5**	**5**	**16**	....	....	....	....	....
1997-98	**Toronto**	**NHL**	**81**	**3**	**13**	**16**	**100**	....	....	....	....	....
	NHL Totals		**266**	**6**	**26**	**32**	**283**	**6**	**0**	**0**	**0**	**7**

WHL East First All-Star Team (1993) • Canadian Major Junior First All-Star Team (1993)

Traded to **Toronto** by **New Jersey** with Steve Sullivan and the rights to Alyn McCauley for Doug Gilmour, Dave Ellett and New Jersey's 4th round choice (previously acquired — later traded to Edmonton — Edmonton selected Kristian Antila) in 1998 Entry Draft, February 25, 1997.

SMITH, JERAD — CHI.

Defense. Shoots right. 6'3", 205 lbs. Born, Lethbridge, Alta., January 5, 1979.
(Chicago's 9th choice, 174th overall, in 1997 Entry Draft).

			Regular Season					Playoffs				
Season	Club	Lea	GP	G	A	TP	PIM	GP	G	A	TP	PIM
1996-97	Portland	WHL	41	2	1	3	28	4	0	0	0	0
1997-98	Portland	WHL	23	0	1	1	14	....	....	....	....	....

SMITH, MARK — S.J.

Center. Shoots left. 5'10", 190 lbs. Born, Edmonton, Alta., October 24, 1977.
(San Jose's 7th choice, 219th overall, in 1997 Entry Draft).

			Regular Season					Playoffs				
Season	Club	Lea	GP	G	A	TP	PIM	GP	G	A	TP	PIM
1995-96	Lethbridge	WHL	71	11	24	35	59	4	2	0	2	2
1996-97	Lethbridge	WHL	62	19	38	57	125	19	7	13	20	51
1997-98	Lethbridge	WHL	70	42	67	109	206	3	0	2	2	18

WHL East Second All-Star Team (1998)

SMITH, MATT — ST.L.

Defense. Shoots right. 6'6", 215 lbs. Born, Kent, England, December 23, 1976.

			Regular Season					Playoffs				
Season	Club	Lea	GP	G	A	TP	PIM	GP	G	A	TP	PIM
1997-98	U-Mass.-Amherst	H.E.	33	5	8	13	48	....	....	....	....	....
	Worcester	AHL	4	1	0	1	4	3	0	0	0	10

Signed as a free agent by **St. Louis**, March 27, 1998.

SMITH, NICK — FLA.

Center. Shoots left. 6'1", 165 lbs. Born, Hamilton, Ont., March 23, 1979.
(Florida's 4th choice, 74th overall, in 1997 Entry Draft).

			Regular Season					Playoffs				
Season	Club	Lea	GP	G	A	TP	PIM	GP	G	A	TP	PIM
1995-96	Shelburne	MJHL	42	13	18	31	12	....	....	....	....	....
1996-97	Barrie	OHL	63	10	18	28	15	9	3	8	11	13
1997-98	Barrie	OHL	63	13	21	34	21	6	1	2	3	4

SMITH, STEVE — CGY.

Defense. Shoots left. 6'4", 215 lbs. Born, Glasgow, Scotland, April 30, 1963.
(Edmonton's 5th choice, 111th overall, in 1981 Entry Draft).

			Regular Season					Playoffs				
Season	Club	Lea	GP	G	A	TP	PIM	GP	G	A	TP	PIM
1980-81	London	OHA	62	4	12	16	141	....	....	....	....	....
1981-82	London	OHL	58	10	36	46	207	4	1	2	3	13
1982-83	London	OHL	50	6	35	41	133	3	1	0	1	10
	Moncton	AHL	2	0	0	0	0	....	....	....	....	....
1983-84	Moncton	AHL	64	1	8	9	176	....	....	....	....	....
1984-85	**Edmonton**	**NHL**	**2**	**0**	**0**	**0**	**2**	....	....	....	....	....
	Nova Scotia	AHL	68	2	28	30	161	5	0	3	3	40
1985-86	**Edmonton**	**NHL**	**55**	**4**	**20**	**24**	**166**	**6**	**0**	**1**	**1**	**14**
	Nova Scotia	AHL	4	0	2	2	11	....	....	....	....	....
1986-87	**Edmonton**	**NHL**	**62**	**7**	**15**	**22**	**165**	**15**	**1**	**3**	**4**	**45 ♦**
1987-88	**Edmonton**	**NHL**	**79**	**12**	**43**	**55**	**286**	**19**	**1**	**11**	**12**	**55 ♦**
1988-89	**Edmonton**	**NHL**	**35**	**3**	**19**	**22**	**97**	**7**	**2**	**2**	**4**	**20**
1989-90	**Edmonton**	**NHL**	**75**	**7**	**34**	**41**	**171**	**22**	**5**	**10**	**15**	**37 ♦**
1990-91	**Edmonton**	**NHL**	**77**	**13**	**41**	**54**	**193**	**18**	**1**	**2**	**3**	**45**
1991-92	**Chicago**	**NHL**	**76**	**9**	**21**	**30**	**304**	**18**	**1**	**11**	**12**	**16**
1992-93	**Chicago**	**NHL**	**78**	**10**	**47**	**57**	**214**	**4**	**0**	**0**	**0**	**10**
1993-94	**Chicago**	**NHL**	**57**	**5**	**22**	**27**	**174**	....	....	....	....	....
1994-95	**Chicago**	**NHL**	**48**	**1**	**12**	**13**	**128**	**16**	**0**	**1**	**1**	**26**
1995-96	**Chicago**	**NHL**	**37**	**0**	**9**	**9**	**71**	**6**	**0**	**0**	**0**	**16**
1996-97	**Chicago**	**NHL**	**21**	**0**	**0**	**0**	**29**	**3**	**0**	**0**	**0**	**4**
1997-98			DID NOT PLAY – RETIRED									
	NHL Totals		**702**	**71**	**283**	**354**	**2000**	**134**	**11**	**41**	**52**	**288**

Played in NHL All-Star Game (1991)

Traded to **Chicago** by **Edmonton** for Dave Manson and Chicago's 3rd round choice (Kirk Maltby) in 1992 Entry Draft, October 2, 1991. Signed as a free agent by **Calgary**, August 18, 1998.

SMITH, WYATT — PHX.

Center. Shoots left. 5'11", 198 lbs. Born, Thief River Falls, MN, February 13, 1977.
(Phoenix's 6th choice, 233rd overall, in 1997 Entry Draft).

			Regular Season					Playoffs				
Season	Club	Lea	GP	G	A	TP	PIM	GP	G	A	TP	PIM
1995-96	U. of Minnesota	WCHA	32	4	5	9	32	....	....	....	....	....
1996-97	U. of Minnesota	WCHA	38	16	14	30	44	....	....	....	....	....
1997-98	U. of Minnesota	WCHA	39	24	23	47	62	....	....	....	....	....

SMOLINSKI, BRYAN — (smoh-LIHN-skee) NYI

Center/Right wing. Shoots right. 6'1", 202 lbs. Born, Toledo, OH, December 27, 1971.
(Boston's 1st choice, 21st overall, in 1990 Entry Draft).

			Regular Season					Playoffs				
Season	Club	Lea	GP	G	A	TP	PIM	GP	G	A	TP	PIM
1988-89	Stratford	OJHL	46	32	62	94	132	....	....	....	....	....
1989-90	Michigan State	CCHA	35	9	13	22	34	....	....	....	....	....
1990-91	Michigan State	CCHA	35	9	12	21	24	....	....	....	....	....
1991-92	Michigan State	CCHA	41	28	33	61	55	....	....	....	....	....
1992-93	Michigan State	CCHA	40	31	37	*68	93	....	....	....	....	....
	Boston	**NHL**	**9**	**1**	**3**	**4**	**0**	**4**	**1**	**0**	**1**	**2**
1993-94	**Boston**	**NHL**	**83**	**31**	**20**	**51**	**82**	**13**	**5**	**4**	**9**	**4**
1994-95	**Boston**	**NHL**	**44**	**18**	**13**	**31**	**31**	**5**	**0**	**1**	**1**	**4**
1995-96	**Pittsburgh**	**NHL**	**81**	**24**	**40**	**64**	**69**	**18**	**5**	**4**	**9**	**10**
1996-97	Detroit	IHL	6	5	7	12	10	....	....	....	....	....
	NY Islanders	**NHL**	**64**	**28**	**28**	**56**	**25**	....	....	....	....	....
1997-98	**NY Islanders**	**NHL**	**81**	**13**	**30**	**43**	**34**	....	....	....	....	....
	NHL Totals		**362**	**115**	**134**	**249**	**241**	**40**	**11**	**9**	**20**	**20**

CCHA First All-Star Team (1993) • NCAA West First All-American Team (1993)

Traded to **Pittsburgh** by **Boston** with Glen Murray and Boston's 3rd round choice (Boyd Kane) in 1996 Entry Draft for Kevin Stevens and Shawn McEachern, August 2, 1995. Traded to **NY Islanders** by **Pittsburgh** for Darius Kasparaitis and Andreas Johansson, November 17, 1996.

SMYTH, BRAD — (SMIHTH) NSH.

Right wing. Shoots right. 6', 200 lbs. Born, Ottawa, Ont., March 13, 1973.

			Regular Season					Playoffs				
Season	Club	Lea	GP	G	A	TP	PIM	GP	G	A	TP	PIM
1990-91	London	OHL	29	2	6	8	22	....	....	....	....	....
1991-92	London	OHL	58	17	18	35	93	10	2	0	2	8
1992-93	London	OHL	66	54	55	109	118	12	7	8	15	25
1993-94	Cincinnati	IHL	30	7	3	10	54	....	....	....	....	....
	Birmingham	ECHL	29	26	30	56	38	10	8	8	16	19
1994-95	Springfield	AHL	3	0	0	0	7	....	....	....	....	....
	Birmingham	ECHL	36	33	35	68	52	3	5	2	7	0
	Cincinnati	IHL	26	2	11	13	34	1	0	0	0	2
1995-96	**Florida**	**NHL**	**7**	**1**	**1**	**2**	**4**	....	....	....	....	....
	Carolina	AHL	68	*68	58	*126	80	....	....	....	....	....
1996-97	**Florida**	**NHL**	**8**	**1**	**0**	**1**	**2**	....	....	....	....	....
	Los Angeles	**NHL**	**44**	**8**	**8**	**16**	**74**	....	....	....	....	....
	Phoenix	IHL	3	5	2	7	0	....	....	....	....	....
1997-98	**Los Angeles**	**NHL**	**9**	**1**	**3**	**4**	**4**	....	....	....	....	....
	NY Rangers	**NHL**	**1**	**0**	**0**	**0**	**0**	....	....	....	....	....
	Hartford	AHL	57	29	33	62	79	15	12	8	20	11
	NHL Totals		**69**	**11**	**12**	**23**	**84**	....	....	....	....	....

AHL First All-Star Team (1996) • Won John B. Sollenberger Trophy (Top Scorer - AHL) (1996) • Won Les Cunningham Plaque (MVP - AHL) (1996)

Signed as a free agent by **Florida**, October 4, 1993. Traded to **LA Kings** by **Florida** for LA Kings' 3rd round choice (Vratislav Czech) in 1997 Entry Draft, November 28, 1996. Traded to **NY Rangers** by **LA Kings** for future considerations, November 14, 1997. Signed as a free agent by **Nashville**, July 16, 1998.

SMYTH, GREG — (SMIHTH) TOR.

Defense. Shoots right. 6'3", 212 lbs. Born, Oakville, Ont., April 23, 1966.
(Philadelphia's 1st choice, 22nd overall, in 1984 Entry Draft).

			Regular Season					Playoffs				
Season	Club	Lea	GP	G	A	TP	PIM	GP	G	A	TP	PIM
1983-84	London	OHL	64	4	21	25	252	6	1	0	1	24
1984-85	London	OHL	47	7	16	23	188	8	2	2	4	27
1985-86	London	OHL	46	12	42	54	199	4	1	2	3	28
	Hershey	AHL	2	0	1	1	5	8	0	0	0	60
1986-87	**Philadelphia**	**NHL**	**1**	**0**	**0**	**0**	**0**	**1**	**0**	**0**	**0**	**2**
	Hershey	AHL	35	0	2	2	158	2	0	0	0	19
1987-88	**Philadelphia**	**NHL**	**48**	**1**	**6**	**7**	**192**	**5**	**0**	**0**	**0**	**38**
	Hershey	AHL	21	0	10	10	102	....	....	....	....	....
1988-89	**Quebec**	**NHL**	**10**	**0**	**1**	**1**	**70**	....	....	....	....	....
	Halifax	AHL	43	3	9	12	310	4	0	1	1	35
1989-90	**Quebec**	**NHL**	**13**	**0**	**0**	**0**	**57**	....	....	....	....	....
	Halifax	AHL	49	5	14	19	235	6	1	0	1	52
1990-91	**Quebec**	**NHL**	**1**	**0**	**0**	**0**	**0**	....	....	....	....	....
	Halifax	AHL	56	6	23	29	340	....	....	....	....	....
1991-92	**Quebec**	**NHL**	**29**	**0**	**2**	**2**	**138**	....	....	....	....	....
	Halifax	AHL	9	1	3	4	35	....	....	....	....	....
	Calgary	**NHL**	**7**	**1**	**1**	**2**	**15**	....	....	....	....	....
1992-93	**Calgary**	**NHL**	**35**	**1**	**2**	**3**	**95**	....	....	....	....	....
	Salt Lake	IHL	5	0	1	1	31	....	....	....	....	....
1993-94	**Florida**	**NHL**	**12**	**1**	**0**	**1**	**37**	....	....	....	....	....
	Toronto	**NHL**	**11**	**0**	**1**	**1**	**38**	....	....	....	....	....
	Chicago	**NHL**	**38**	**0**	**0**	**0**	**108**	**6**	**0**	**0**	**0**	**0**
1994-95	**Chicago**	**NHL**	**22**	**0**	**3**	**3**	**33**	....	....	....	....	....
	Indianapolis	IHL	2	0	0	0	0	....	....	....	....	....
1995-96	Chicago	IHL	15	1	3	4	53	....	....	....	....	....
	Los Angeles	IHL	41	2	7	9	231	....	....	....	....	....
1996-97	**Toronto**	**NHL**	**2**	**0**	**0**	**0**	**0**	....	....	....	....	....
	St. John's	AHL	43	2	4	6	273	5	0	1	1	14
1997-98	St. John's	AHL	63	5	6	11	353	4	0	1	1	6
	NHL Totals		**229**	**4**	**16**	**20**	**783**	**12**	**0**	**0**	**0**	**40**

OHL Second All-Star Team (1986)

Traded to **Quebec** by **Philadelphia** with Philadelphia's 3rd round choice (John Tanner) in the 1989 Entry Draft for Terry Carkner, July 25, 1988. Traded to **Calgary** by **Quebec** for Martin Simard, March 10, 1992. Signed as a free agent by **Florida**, August 10, 1993. Traded to **Toronto** by **Florida** for cash, December 7, 1993. Claimed on waivers by **Chicago** from **Toronto**, January 8, 1994. Signed as a free agent by **Toronto**, August 22, 1996.

SMYTH, KEVIN — (SMIHTH)

Left wing. Shoots left. 6'2", 217 lbs. Born, Banff, Alta., November 22, 1973.
(Hartford's 4th choice, 79th overall, in 1992 Entry Draft).

			Regular Season					Playoffs				
Season	Club	Lea	GP	G	A	TP	PIM	GP	G	A	TP	PIM
1990-91	Moose Jaw	WHL	66	30	45	75	96	6	1	1	2	0
1991-92	Moose Jaw	WHL	71	30	55	85	114	4	1	3	4	6
1992-93	Moose Jaw	WHL	64	44	38	82	111	....	....	....	....	....
1993-94	**Hartford**	**NHL**	**21**	**3**	**2**	**5**	**10**	....	....	....	....	....
	Springfield	AHL	42	22	27	49	72	6	4	5	9	0
1994-95	Springfield	AHL	57	17	22	39	72	....	....	....	....	....
	Hartford	**NHL**	**16**	**1**	**5**	**6**	**13**	....	....	....	....	....
1995-96	**Hartford**	**NHL**	**21**	**2**	**1**	**3**	**8**	....	....	....	....	....
	Springfield	AHL	47	15	33	48	87	10	5	5	10	8
1996-97	Orlando	IHL	38	14	17	31	49	10	1	2	3	6
1997-98	Orlando	IHL	43	10	5	15	59	1	0	0	0	2
	NHL Totals		**58**	**6**	**8**	**14**	**31**	....	....	....	....	....

Rights transferred to **Carolina** after **Hartford** franchise relocated, June 25, 1997.

SMYTH, RYAN — (SMIHTH) EDM.

Left wing. Shoots left. 6'1", 195 lbs. Born, Banff, Alta., February 21, 1976.
(Edmonton's 2nd choice, 6th overall, in 1994 Entry Draft).

			Regular Season					Playoffs				
Season	Club	Lea	GP	G	A	TP	PIM	GP	G	A	TP	PIM
1991-92	Moose Jaw	WHL	2	0	0	0	0	....	....	....	....	....
1992-93	Moose Jaw	WHL	64	19	14	33	59	....	....	....	....	....
1993-94	Moose Jaw	WHL	72	50	55	105	88	....	....	....	....	....
1994-95	Moose Jaw	WHL	50	41	45	86	66	10	6	9	15	22
	Edmonton	**NHL**	**3**	**0**	**0**	**0**	**0**	....	....	....	....	....
1995-96	**Edmonton**	**NHL**	**48**	**2**	**9**	**11**	**28**	....	....	....	....	....
	Cape Breton	AHL	9	6	5	11	4	....	....	....	....	....
1996-97	**Edmonton**	**NHL**	**82**	**39**	**22**	**61**	**76**	**12**	**5**	**5**	**10**	**12**
1997-98	**Edmonton**	**NHL**	**65**	**20**	**13**	**33**	**44**	**12**	**1**	**3**	**4**	**16**
	NHL Totals		**198**	**61**	**44**	**105**	**148**	**24**	**6**	**8**	**14**	**28**

WHL East Second All-Star Team (1995)

SNESRUD, MAT — ANA.

Defense. Shoots right. 6'1", 205 lbs. Born, Minneapolis, MN, January 28, 1977.
(Anaheim's 6th choice, 181st overall, in 1997 Entry Draft).

			Regular Season					Playoffs				
Season	Club	Lea	GP	G	A	TP	PIM	GP	G	A	TP	PIM
1996-97	North Iowa	USHL	50	12	22	34	76	....	....	....	....	....
1997-98	Michigan Tech	WCHA	39	0	18	18	44	....	....	....	....	....

SODERBERG, ANDERS — (SOH-dehr-buhrg) BOS.

Right wing. Shoots right. 5'6", 161 lbs. Born, Ornskoldsvik, Sweden, October 7, 1975.
(Boston's 10th choice, 234th overall, in 1996 Entry Draft).

			Regular Season					Playoffs				
Season	Club	Lea	GP	G	A	TP	PIM	GP	G	A	TP	PIM
1992-93	MoDo	Swe-Jr.	13	6	12	18	2	....	....	....	....	....
	MoDo	Sweden	1	0	0	0	0	....	....	....	....	....
1993-94	MoDo	Swe-Jr.	9	8	5	13	10	....	....	....	....	....
	MoDo	Sweden	19	0	0	0	2	9	0	0	0	0
1994-95	MoDo	Sweden	38	9	14	23	2	....	....	....	....	....
1995-96	MoDo	Sweden	40	10	18	28	10	8	3	3	6	0
1996-97	MoDo	Sweden	39	9	13	22	16	....	....	....	....	....
1997-98	MoDo	Sweden	44	15	10	25	4	9	5	1	6	2

SOLING, JONAS — (SOH-lihng, YOH-nahs) VAN.

Right wing. Shoots left. 6'4", 192 lbs. Born, Stockholm, Sweden, September 7, 1978.
(Vancouver's 3rd choice, 93rd overall, in 1996 Entry Draft).

			Regular Season					Playoffs				
Season	Club	Lea	GP	G	A	TP	PIM	GP	G	A	TP	PIM
1995-96	Huddinge	Swe-Jr.	24	8	4	12	18	....	....	....	....	....
	Huddinge	Sweden-2	5	0	0	0	0	....	....	....	....	....
1996-97	Sudbury	OHL	66	18	22	40	60	....	....	....	....	....
1997-98	Sudbury	OHL	56	9	25	34	67	10	0	7	7	10

SOMERVUORI, EERO (soh-muhr-VOH-ree, ai-AIR-oh) T.B.

Right wing. Shoots right. 5'10", 167 lbs. Born, Jarvenpaa, Finland, February 7, 1979.
(Tampa Bay's 9th choice, 170th overall, in 1997 Entry Draft).

			Regular Season					Playoffs				
Season	**Club**	**Lea**	**GP**	**G**	**A**	**TP**	**PIM**	**GP**	**G**	**A**	**TP**	**PIM**
1994-95	Jokerit	Fin-Jr.	26	9	12	21	6	....	....	....	....	....
1995-96	Jokerit	Fin-Jr.	28	14	12	26	10	9	4	1	5	4
	Jokerit	Finland	6	1	2	3	0	....	....	....	....	....
	Jarvenpaa	Finland-2	1	0	0	0	0	....	....	....	....	....
1996-97	Jokerit	Finland	35	1	1	2	2	5	0	0	0	0
	Jokerit	Fin-Jr.	28	20	19	39	30	5	3	0	3	4
1997-98	Jokerit	Fin-Jr.	14	4	8	12	2	....	....	....	....	....
	Jokerit	Finland	42	3	7	10	46	8	2	1	3	6

SOMIK, RADOVAN (SAW-mihk, RAH-doh-vahn) PHI.

Left wing. Shoots right. 6'2", 194 lbs. Born, Martin, Czech., May 5, 1977.
(Philadelphia's 3rd choice, 100th overall, in 1995 Entry Draft).

			Regular Season					Playoffs				
Season	**Club**	**Lea**	**GP**	**G**	**A**	**TP**	**PIM**	**GP**	**G**	**A**	**TP**	**PIM**
1993-94	Martin	Slovakia	1	0	0	0	0	....	....	....	....	....
1994-95	Martin	Slovakia	25	3	0	3	39	3	1	0	1	2
1995-96	Martin	Slovakia	25	3	6	9	8	9	1	0	1	....
1996-97	Martin	Slovakia	35	3	5	8	....	3	0	0	0	....
1997-98	Martin	Slovakia	26	6	9	15	10	3	0	0	0	0

SOPEL, BRENT (SOH-puhl) VAN.

Defense. Shoots right. 6'1", 190 lbs. Born, Calgary, Alta., January 7, 1977.
(Vancouver's 6th choice, 144th overall, in 1995 Entry Draft).

			Regular Season					Playoffs				
Season	**Club**	**Lea**	**GP**	**G**	**A**	**TP**	**PIM**	**GP**	**G**	**A**	**TP**	**PIM**
1993-94	Saskatoon	WHL	11	2	2	4	2	....	....	....	....	....
1994-95	Saskatoon	WHL	22	1	10	11	31	....	....	....	....	....
	Swift Current	WHL	41	4	19	23	50	3	0	3	3	0
1995-96	Swift Current	WHL	71	13	48	61	87	6	1	2	3	4
	Syracuse	AHL	1	0	0	0	0	....	....	....	....	....
1996-97	Swift Current	WHL	62	15	41	56	109	10	5	11	16	32
	Syracuse	AHL	2	0	0	0	0	3	0	0	0	0
1997-98	Syracuse	AHL	76	10	33	43	70	5	0	7	7	12

SOROCHAN, LEE (soh-RAW-kihn) NYR

Defense. Shoots left. 5'11", 210 lbs. Born, Edmonton, Alta., September 9, 1975.
(NY Rangers' 2nd choice, 34th overall, in 1993 Entry Draft).

			Regular Season					Playoffs				
Season	**Club**	**Lea**	**GP**	**G**	**A**	**TP**	**PIM**	**GP**	**G**	**A**	**TP**	**PIM**
1991-92	Lethbridge	WHL	67	2	9	11	105	5	0	2	2	6
1992-93	Lethbridge	WHL	69	8	32	40	208	4	0	1	1	12
1993-94	Lethbridge	WHL	46	5	27	32	123	9	4	3	7	16
1994-95	Lethbridge	WHL	29	4	15	19	93	....	....	....	....	....
	Saskatoon	WHL	24	5	13	18	63	10	3	6	9	34
	Binghamton	AHL	....	....	....	....	....	8	0	0	0	11
1995-96	Binghamton	AHL	45	2	8	10	26	1	0	0	0	0
1996-97	Binghamton	AHL	77	4	27	31	160	4	0	2	2	18
1997-98	Hartford	AHL	73	7	11	18	197	13	0	2	2	51

SOURAY, SHELDON (SUHR-ee) N.J.

Defense. Shoots left. 6'4", 235 lbs. Born, Elk Point, Alta., July 13, 1976.
(New Jersey's 3rd choice, 71st overall, in 1994 Entry Draft).

			Regular Season					Playoffs				
Season	**Club**	**Lea**	**GP**	**G**	**A**	**TP**	**PIM**	**GP**	**G**	**A**	**TP**	**PIM**
1992-93	Tri-City	WHL	2	0	0	0	0	....	....	....	....	....
1993-94	Tri-City	WHL	42	3	6	9	122	....	....	....	....	....
1994-95	Tri-City	WHL	40	2	24	26	140	....	....	....	....	....
	Prince George	WHL	11	2	3	5	23	....	....	....	....	....
	Albany	AHL	7	0	2	2	8	....	....	....	....	....
1995-96	Prince George	WHL	32	9	18	27	91	....	....	....	....	....
	Kelowna	WHL	27	7	20	27	94	6	0	5	5	2
	Albany	AHL	6	0	2	2	12	4	0	1	1	4
1996-97	Albany	AHL	70	2	11	13	160	16	2	3	5	47
1997-98	**New Jersey**	**NHL**	**60**	**3**	**7**	**10**	**85**	**3**	**0**	**1**	**1**	**2**
	Albany	AHL	6	0	0	0	8	....	....	....	....	....
	NHL Totals		**60**	**3**	**7**	**10**	**85**	**3**	**0**	**1**	**1**	**2**

WHL West Second All-Star Team (1996)

SOUZA, MIKE (SOO-zah) CHI.

Left wing. Shoots left. 6'1", 190 lbs. Born, Melrose, MA, January 28, 1978.
(Chicago's 4th choice, 67th overall, in 1997 Entry Draft).

			Regular Season					Playoffs				
Season	**Club**	**Lea**	**GP**	**G**	**A**	**TP**	**PIM**	**GP**	**G**	**A**	**TP**	**PIM**
1996-97	New Hampshire	H.E.	39	15	11	26	20	....	....	....	....	....
1997-98	New Hampshire	H.E.	38	13	12	25	36	....	....	....	....	....

SPACEK, JAROSLAV (SPAH-chehk, YA-roh-slahv) FLA.

Defense. Shoots left. 5'11", 198 lbs. Born, Rokycany, Czechoslovakia, February 11, 1974.
(Florida's 5th choice, 117th overall, in 1998 Entry Draft).

			Regular Season					Playoffs				
Season	**Club**	**Lea**	**GP**	**G**	**A**	**TP**	**PIM**	**GP**	**G**	**A**	**TP**	**PIM**
1992-93	Skoda Plzen	Czech.	16	1	3	4	....	....	....	....	....	....
1993-94	Skoda Plzen	Cze-Rep.	34	2	10	2	....	....	....	....	....	....
1994-95	Plzen	Cze-Rep.	38	4	8	12	14	3	1	0	1	2
1995-96	ZKZ Plzen	Cze-Rep.	40	3	10	13	42	3	0	1	1	4
1996-97	ZKZ Plzen	Cze-Rep.	52	9	29	38	44	....	....	....	....	....
1997-98	Farjestad	Sweden	45	10	16	26	63	12	2	5	7	14

SPRING, COREY

Right wing. Shoots right. 6'4", 214 lbs. Born, Cranbrook, B.C., May 31, 1971.

			Regular Season					Playoffs				
Season	**Club**	**Lea**	**GP**	**G**	**A**	**TP**	**PIM**	**GP**	**G**	**A**	**TP**	**PIM**
1990-91	Vernon	BCJHL	60	43	43	86	104	....	....	....	....	....
1991-92	Alaska-Anchorage	NCAA	35	3	8	11	30	....	....	....	....	....
1992-93	Alaska-Anchorage	CCHA	28	5	5	10	20	....	....	....	....	....
1993-94	Alaska-Anchorage	CCHA	38	19	18	37	34	....	....	....	....	....
1994-95	Alaska-Anchorage	CCHA	33	18	14	32	56	....	....	....	....	....
1995-96	Atlanta	IHL	73	14	14	28	104	2	0	0	0	0
1996-97	Adirondack	AHL	69	20	26	46	118	4	0	0	0	14
1997-98	**Tampa Bay**	**NHL**	**8**	**1**	**0**	**1**	**10**	....	....	....	....	....
	Adirondack	AHL	57	19	25	44	120	3	0	0	0	6
	NHL Totals		**8**	**1**	**0**	**1**	**10**	....	....	....	....	....

Signed as a free agent by **Tampa Bay**, July 24, 1995.

SPROULE, DOUG (SPROOL) OTT.

Left wing. Shoots left. 6'3", 190 lbs. Born, Red Bank, NJ, February 16, 1976.
(Ottawa's 6th choice, 159th overall, in 1994 Entry Draft).

			Regular Season					Playoffs				
Season	**Club**	**Lea**	**GP**	**G**	**A**	**TP**	**PIM**	**GP**	**G**	**A**	**TP**	**PIM**
1993-94	Hotchkiss High	H.S.	23	28	39	67	....	....	....	....	....	....
1994-95	Harvard	ECAC	30	7	2	9	28	....	....	....	....	....
1995-96	Harvard	ECAC	12	1	0	1	6	....	....	....	....	....
1996-97	Harvard	ECAC	32	6	10	16	46	....	....	....	....	....
1997-98	Harvard	ECAC	33	3	5	8	46	....	....	....	....	....

SRDINKO, JAN (suhr-DIHN-koh, YAN) N.J.

Defense. Shoots left. 5'11", 195 lbs. Born, Vsetin, Czech., February 22, 1974.
(New Jersey's 8th choice, 241st overall, in 1997 Entry Draft).

			Regular Season					Playoffs				
Season	**Club**	**Lea**	**GP**	**G**	**A**	**TP**	**PIM**	**GP**	**G**	**A**	**TP**	**PIM**
1994-95	Vsetin	Cze-Rep.	1	0	0	0	....	....	....	....	....	....
1995-96	Vsetin	Cze-Rep.	31	0	3	3	....	9	0	0	0	....
1996-97	Vsetin	Cze-Rep.	49	2	8	10	71	10	0	3	3	29
1997-98	Vsetin	EuroHL	9	0	1	1	4	....	....	....	....	....
	Vsetin	Cze-Rep.	47	1	4	5	95	10	0	3	3	4

STAAL, KIM (STOHL) MTL.

Center. Shoots right. 6', 185 lbs. Born, Herlev, Denmark, March 10, 1978.
(Montreal's 4th choice, 92nd overall, in 1996 Entry Draft).

			Regular Season					Playoffs				
Season	**Club**	**Lea**	**GP**	**G**	**A**	**TP**	**PIM**	**GP**	**G**	**A**	**TP**	**PIM**
1995-96	Malmo IF	Swe-Jr.	30	24	20	44	14	....	....	....	....	....
1996-97	Malmo IF	Sweden	4	0	1	1	2	....	....	....	....	....
	Malmo IF	Swe-Jr.	3	6	4	10	2	....	....	....	....	....
1997-98	Malmo IF	Sweden	13	0	1	1	1	....	....	....	....	....

STAIOS, STEVE (STAY-uhs) VAN.

Right wing. Shoots right. 6', 200 lbs. Born, Hamilton, Ont., July 28, 1973.
(St. Louis' 1st choice, 27th overall, in 1991 Entry Draft).

			Regular Season					Playoffs				
Season	**Club**	**Lea**	**GP**	**G**	**A**	**TP**	**PIM**	**GP**	**G**	**A**	**TP**	**PIM**
1990-91	Niagara Falls	OHL	66	17	29	46	115	12	2	3	5	10
1991-92	Niagara Falls	OHL	65	11	42	53	122	17	7	8	15	27
1992-93	Niagara Falls	OHL	12	4	14	18	30	....	....	....	....	....
	Sudbury	OHL	53	13	44	57	67	11	5	6	11	22
1993-94	Peoria	IHL	38	3	9	12	42	....	....	....	....	....
1994-95	Peoria	IHL	60	3	13	16	64	6	0	0	0	10
1995-96	Peoria	IHL	6	0	1	1	14	....	....	....	....	....
	Worcester	AHL	57	1	11	12	114	....	....	....	....	....
	Boston	**NHL**	**12**	**0**	**0**	**0**	**4**	**3**	**0**	**0**	**0**	**0**
	Providence	AHL	7	1	4	5	8	....	....	....	....	....
1996-97	**Boston**	**NHL**	**54**	**3**	**8**	**11**	**71**	....	....	....	....	....
	Vancouver	**NHL**	**9**	**0**	**6**	**6**	**20**	....	....	....	....	....
1997-98	**Vancouver**	**NHL**	**77**	**3**	**4**	**7**	**134**	....	....	....	....	....
	NHL Totals		**152**	**6**	**18**	**24**	**229**	**3**	**0**	**0**	**0**	**0**

Traded to **Boston** by **St. Louis** with Kevin Sawyer for Steve Leach, March 8, 1996. Claimed on waivers by **Vancouver** from **Boston**, March 18, 1997.

STANLEY, CHRIS VAN.

Center. Shoots left. 6'1", 200 lbs. Born, Parry Sound, Ont., June 18, 1979.
(Vancouver's 5th choice, 90th overall, in 1997 Entry Draft).

			Regular Season					Playoffs				
Season	**Club**	**Lea**	**GP**	**G**	**A**	**TP**	**PIM**	**GP**	**G**	**A**	**TP**	**PIM**
1996-97	Belleville	OHL	66	19	24	43	16	6	1	0	1	0
1997-98	Belleville	OHL	66	21	23	44	31	10	3	2	5	4

STAPLES, JEFF NSH.

Defense. Shoots left. 6'2", 207 lbs. Born, Kitimat, B.C., March 4, 1975.
(Philadelphia's 10th choice, 244th overall, in 1993 Entry Draft).

			Regular Season					Playoffs				
Season	**Club**	**Lea**	**GP**	**G**	**A**	**TP**	**PIM**	**GP**	**G**	**A**	**TP**	**PIM**
1991-92	Brandon	WHL	3	0	0	0	0	....	....	....	....	....
1992-93	Brandon	WHL	40	0	5	5	114	4	0	1	1	4
1993-94	Brandon	WHL	37	0	7	7	126	....	....	....	....	....
1994-95	Brandon	WHL	57	3	16	19	176	18	0	2	2	23
1995-96	Hershey	AHL	61	7	3	10	100	5	0	1	1	0
1996-97	Philadelphia	AHL	74	4	11	15	157	8	0	2	2	10
1997-98	Philadelphia	AHL	63	4	16	20	187	19	0	0	0	23

STAPLETON, MIKE PHX.

Center. Shoots right. 5'10", 183 lbs. Born, Sarnia, Ont., May 5, 1966.
(Chicago's 7th choice, 132nd overall, in 1984 Entry Draft).

			Regular Season					Playoffs				
Season	**Club**	**Lea**	**GP**	**G**	**A**	**TP**	**PIM**	**GP**	**G**	**A**	**TP**	**PIM**
1983-84	Cornwall	OHL	70	24	45	69	94	3	1	2	3	4
1984-85	Cornwall	OHL	56	41	44	85	68	9	2	4	6	23
1985-86	Cornwall	OHL	56	39	64	103	74	6	2	3	5	2
1986-87	Canada	Nat-Tm	21	2	4	6	4	....	....	....	....	....
	Chicago	**NHL**	**39**	**3**	**6**	**9**	**6**	**4**	**0**	**0**	**0**	**2**
1987-88	**Chicago**	**NHL**	**53**	**2**	**9**	**11**	**59**	....	....	....	....	....
	Saginaw	IHL	31	11	19	30	52	10	5	6	11	10
1988-89	**Chicago**	**NHL**	**7**	**0**	**1**	**1**	**7**	....	....	....	....	....
	Saginaw	IHL	69	21	47	68	162	6	1	3	4	4
1989-90	Indianapolis	IHL	16	5	10	15	6	13	9	10	19	38
1990-91	**Chicago**	**NHL**	**7**	**0**	**1**	**1**	**2**	....	....	....	....	....
	Indianapolis	IHL	75	29	52	81	76	7	1	4	5	0
1991-92	**Chicago**	**NHL**	**19**	**4**	**4**	**8**	**8**	....	....	....	....	....
	Indianapolis	IHL	59	18	40	58	65	....	....	....	....	....
1992-93	**Pittsburgh**	**NHL**	**78**	**4**	**9**	**13**	**10**	**4**	**0**	**0**	**0**	**0**
1993-94	**Pittsburgh**	**NHL**	**58**	**7**	**4**	**11**	**18**	....	....	....	....	....
	Edmonton	**NHL**	**23**	**5**	**9**	**14**	**28**	....	....	....	....	....
1994-95	**Edmonton**	**NHL**	**46**	**6**	**11**	**17**	**21**	....	....	....	....	....
1995-96	**Winnipeg**	**NHL**	**58**	**10**	**14**	**24**	**37**	**6**	**0**	**0**	**0**	**21**
1996-97	**Phoenix**	**NHL**	**55**	**4**	**11**	**15**	**36**	**7**	**0**	**0**	**0**	**14**
1997-98	**Phoenix**	**NHL**	**64**	**5**	**5**	**10**	**36**	**6**	**0**	**0**	**0**	**2**
	NHL Totals		**507**	**50**	**84**	**134**	**268**	**27**	**0**	**0**	**0**	**39**

Signed as a free agent by **Pittsburgh**, September 30, 1992. Claimed on waivers by **Edmonton** from **Pittsburgh**, February 19, 1994. Signed as a free agent by **Winnipeg**, August 18, 1995. Transferred to **Phoenix** after **Winnipeg** franchise relocated, July 1, 1996.

STEEN, CALLE — DET.

Right wing. Shoots left. 5'11", 198 lbs. Born, Stockholm, Sweden, May 16, 1980.
(Detroit's 6th choice, 142nd overall, in 1998 Entry Draft).

			Regular Season					Playoffs				
Season	Club	Lea	GP	G	A	TP	PIM	GP	G	A	TP	PIM
1995-96	Hammarby	Swe-Jr.	5	0	0	0	....	....	....	....	....	....
1996-97	Hammarby	Swe-Jr.	24	4	9	13	....	....	....	....	....	....
1997-98	Hammarby	Swe-Jr.	STATISTICS NOT AVAILABLE									

STERN, RON — S.J.

Right wing. Shoots right. 6', 195 lbs. Born, Ste. Agathe, Que., January 11, 1967.
(Vancouver's 3rd choice, 70th overall, in 1986 Entry Draft).

			Regular Season					Playoffs				
Season	Club	Lea	GP	G	A	TP	PIM	GP	G	A	TP	PIM
1984-85	Longueuil	QMJHL	67	6	14	20	176	....	....	....	....	....
1985-86	Longueuil	QMJHL	70	39	33	72	317	....	....	....	....	....
1986-87	Longueuil	QMJHL	56	32	39	71	266	19	11	9	20	55
1987-88	**Vancouver**	**NHL**	**15**	**0**	**0**	**0**	**52**	....	....	....	....	....
	Fredericton	AHL	2	1	0	1	4	....	....	....	....	....
	Flint	IHL	55	14	19	33	294	16	8	8	16	94
1988-89	**Vancouver**	**NHL**	**17**	**1**	**0**	**1**	**49**	**3**	**0**	**1**	**1**	**17**
	Milwaukee	IHL	45	19	23	42	280	5	1	0	1	11
1989-90	**Vancouver**	**NHL**	**34**	**2**	**3**	**5**	**208**	....	....	....	....	....
	Milwaukee	IHL	26	8	9	17	165	....	....	....	....	....
1990-91	**Vancouver**	**NHL**	**31**	**2**	**3**	**5**	**171**	....	....	....	....	....
	Milwaukee	IHL	7	2	2	4	81	....	....	....	....	....
	Calgary	**NHL**	**13**	**1**	**3**	**4**	**69**	**7**	**1**	**3**	**4**	**14**
1991-92	**Calgary**	**NHL**	**72**	**13**	**9**	**22**	**338**	....	....	....	....	....
1992-93	**Calgary**	**NHL**	**70**	**10**	**15**	**25**	**207**	**6**	**0**	**0**	**0**	**43**
1993-94	**Calgary**	**NHL**	**71**	**9**	**20**	**29**	**243**	**7**	**2**	**0**	**2**	**12**
1994-95	**Calgary**	**NHL**	**39**	**9**	**4**	**13**	**163**	**7**	**3**	**1**	**4**	**8**
1995-96	**Calgary**	**NHL**	**52**	**10**	**5**	**15**	**111**	**4**	**0**	**2**	**2**	**8**
1996-97	**Calgary**	**NHL**	**79**	**7**	**10**	**17**	**157**	....	....	....	....	....
1997-98	**Calgary**	**NHL**	DID NOT PLAY – INJURED									
	NHL Totals		**493**	**64**	**72**	**136**	**1768**	**34**	**6**	**7**	**13**	**102**

Traded to **Calgary** by **Vancouver** with Kevan Guy for Dana Murzyn, March 5, 1991. • Missed entire 1997-98 season after undergoing knee surgery, October, 1997. Signed as a free agent by **San Jose**, August 25, 1998.

STEVENS, JOHN — PHI.

Defense. Shoots left. 6'1", 195 lbs. Born, Campbellton, N.B., May 4, 1966.
(Philadelphia's 5th choice, 47th overall, in 1984 Entry Draft).

			Regular Season					Playoffs				
Season	Club	Lea	GP	G	A	TP	PIM	GP	G	A	TP	PIM
1983-84	Oshawa	OHL	70	1	10	11	71	7	0	1	1	6
1984-85	Oshawa	OHL	44	2	10	12	61	5	0	2	2	4
	Hershey	AHL	3	0	0	0	0	....	....	....	....	....
1985-86	Oshawa	OHL	65	1	7	8	146	6	0	2	2	14
	Kalamazoo	IHL	6	0	1	1	8	6	0	3	3	9
1986-87	**Philadelphia**	**NHL**	**6**	**0**	**2**	**2**	**14**	....	....	....	....	....
	Hershey	AHL	63	1	15	16	131	3	0	0	0	7
1987-88	**Philadelphia**	**NHL**	**3**	**0**	**0**	**0**	**0**	....	....	....	....	....
	Hershey	AHL	59	1	15	16	108	....	....	....	....	....
1988-89	Hershey	AHL	78	3	13	16	129	12	1	1	2	29
1989-90	Hershey	AHL	79	3	10	13	193	....	....	....	....	....
1990-91	**Hartford**	**NHL**	**14**	**0**	**1**	**1**	**11**	....	....	....	....	....
	Springfield	AHL	65	0	12	12	139	18	0	6	6	35
1991-92	**Hartford**	**NHL**	**21**	**0**	**4**	**4**	**19**	....	....	....	....	....
	Springfield	AHL	45	1	12	13	73	11	1	3	4	27
1992-93	Springfield	AHL	74	1	19	20	111	15	0	1	1	18
1993-94	**Hartford**	**NHL**	**9**	**0**	**3**	**3**	**4**	....	....	....	....	....
	Springfield	AHL	71	3	9	12	85	3	0	0	0	0
1994-95	Springfield	AHL	79	5	15	20	122	....	....	....	....	....
1995-96	Springfield	AHL	69	0	19	19	95	10	0	1	1	31
1996-97	Philadelphia	AHL	74	2	18	20	116	10	0	2	2	8
1997-98	Philadelphia	AHL	50	1	9	10	76	20	0	6	6	44
	NHL Totals		**53**	**0**	**10**	**10**	**48**	....	....	....	....	....

Signed as a free agent by **Hartford**, July 30, 1990. Signed as a free agent by **Philadelphia**, August 6, 1996.

STEVENS, KEVIN — NYR

Left wing. Shoots left. 6'3", 217 lbs. Born, Brockton, MA, April 15, 1965.
(Los Angeles' 6th choice, 112th overall, in 1983 Entry Draft).

			Regular Season					Playoffs				
Season	Club	Lea	GP	G	A	TP	PIM	GP	G	A	TP	PIM
1982-83	Silver Lake	H.S.	18	24	27	51	....	....	....	....	....	....
1983-84	Boston College	ECAC	37	6	14	20	36	....	....	....	....	....
1984-85	Boston College	H.E.	40	13	23	36	36	....	....	....	....	....
1985-86	Boston College	H.E.	42	17	27	44	56	....	....	....	....	....
1986-87	Boston College	H.E.	39	35	35	70	54	....	....	....	....	....
1987-88	United States	Nat-Tm	44	22	23	45	52	....	....	....	....	....
	United States	Olympics	5	1	3	4	2	....	....	....	....	....
	Pittsburgh	**NHL**	**16**	**5**	**2**	**7**	**8**	....	....	....	....	....
1988-89	**Pittsburgh**	**NHL**	**24**	**12**	**3**	**15**	**19**	**11**	**3**	**7**	**10**	**16**
	Muskegon	IHL	45	24	41	65	113	....	....	....	....	....
1989-90	**Pittsburgh**	**NHL**	**76**	**29**	**41**	**70**	**171**	....	....	....	....	....
1990-91	**Pittsburgh**	**NHL**	**80**	**40**	**46**	**86**	**133**	**24**	***17**	**16**	**33**	**53 ♦**
1991-92	**Pittsburgh**	**NHL**	**80**	**54**	**69**	**123**	**254**	**21**	**13**	**15**	**28**	**28 ♦**
1992-93	**Pittsburgh**	**NHL**	**72**	**55**	**56**	**111**	**177**	**12**	**5**	**11**	**16**	**22**
1993-94	**Pittsburgh**	**NHL**	**83**	**41**	**47**	**88**	**155**	**6**	**1**	**1**	**2**	**10**
1994-95	**Pittsburgh**	**NHL**	**27**	**15**	**12**	**27**	**51**	**12**	**4**	**7**	**11**	**21**
1995-96	**Boston**	**NHL**	**41**	**10**	**13**	**23**	**49**	....	....	....	....	....
	Los Angeles	**NHL**	**20**	**3**	**10**	**13**	**22**	....	....	....	....	....
1996-97	**Los Angeles**	**NHL**	**69**	**14**	**20**	**34**	**96**	....	....	....	....	....
1997-98	**NY Rangers**	**NHL**	**80**	**14**	**27**	**41**	**130**	....	....	....	....	....
	NHL Totals		**668**	**292**	**346**	**638**	**1265**	**86**	**43**	**57**	**100**	**150**

Hockey East First All-Star Team (1987) • NCAA East Second All-American Team (1987) • NHL Second All-Star Team (1991, 1993) • NHL First All-Star Team (1992)

Played in NHL All-Star Game (1991, 1992, 1993)

Rights traded to **Pittsburgh** by **LA Kings** for Anders Hakansson, September 9, 1983. Traded to **Boston** by **Pittsburgh** with Shawn McEachern for Glen Murray, Bryan Smolinski and Boston's 3rd round choice (Boyd Kane) in 1996 Entry Draft, August 2, 1995. Traded to **LA Kings** by **Boston** for Rick Tocchet, January 25, 1996. Traded to **NY Rangers** by **LA Kings** for Luc Robitaille, August 28, 1997.

STEVENS, SCOTT — N.J.

Defense. Shoots left. 6'1", 215 lbs. Born, Kitchener, Ont., April 1, 1964.
(Washington's 1st choice, 5th overall, in 1982 Entry Draft).

			Regular Season					Playoffs				
Season	Club	Lea	GP	G	A	TP	PIM	GP	G	A	TP	PIM
1980-81	Kitchener	OJHL	39	7	33	40	82	....	....	....	....	....
	Kitchener	OHA	1	0	0	0	0	....	....	....	....	....
1981-82	Kitchener	OHL	68	6	36	42	158	15	1	10	11	71
1982-83	**Washington**	**NHL**	**77**	**9**	**16**	**25**	**195**	**4**	**1**	**0**	**1**	**26**
1983-84	**Washington**	**NHL**	**78**	**13**	**32**	**45**	**201**	**8**	**1**	**8**	**9**	**21**
1984-85	**Washington**	**NHL**	**80**	**21**	**44**	**65**	**221**	**5**	**0**	**1**	**1**	**20**
1985-86	**Washington**	**NHL**	**73**	**15**	**38**	**53**	**165**	**9**	**3**	**8**	**11**	**12**
1986-87	**Washington**	**NHL**	**77**	**10**	**51**	**61**	**283**	**7**	**0**	**5**	**5**	**19**
1987-88	**Washington**	**NHL**	**80**	**12**	**60**	**72**	**184**	**13**	**1**	**11**	**12**	**46**
1988-89	**Washington**	**NHL**	**80**	**7**	**61**	**68**	**225**	**6**	**1**	**4**	**5**	**11**
1989-90	**Washington**	**NHL**	**56**	**11**	**29**	**40**	**154**	**15**	**2**	**7**	**9**	**25**
1990-91	**St. Louis**	**NHL**	**78**	**5**	**44**	**49**	**150**	**13**	**0**	**3**	**3**	**36**
1991-92	**New Jersey**	**NHL**	**68**	**17**	**42**	**59**	**124**	**7**	**2**	**1**	**3**	**29**
1992-93	**New Jersey**	**NHL**	**81**	**12**	**45**	**57**	**120**	**5**	**2**	**2**	**4**	**10**
1993-94	**New Jersey**	**NHL**	**83**	**18**	**60**	**78**	**112**	**20**	**2**	**9**	**11**	**42**
1994-95	**New Jersey**	**NHL**	**48**	**2**	**20**	**22**	**56**	**20**	**1**	**7**	**8**	**24 ♦**
1995-96	**New Jersey**	**NHL**	**82**	**5**	**23**	**28**	**100**	....	....	....	....	....
1996-97	**New Jersey**	**NHL**	**79**	**5**	**19**	**24**	**70**	**10**	**0**	**4**	**4**	**2**
1997-98	**New Jersey**	**NHL**	**80**	**4**	**22**	**26**	**80**	**6**	**1**	**0**	**1**	**8**
	Canada	Olympics	6	0	0	0	2	....	....	....	....	....
	NHL Totals		**1200**	**166**	**606**	**772**	**2440**	**148**	**17**	**70**	**87**	**331**

NHL All-Rookie Team (1983) • NHL First All-Star Team (1988, 1994) • NHL Second All-Star Team (1992, 1997) • Won Alka-Seltzer Plus Award (1994)

Played in NHL All-Star Game (1985, 1989, 1991, 1992, 1993, 1994, 1996, 1997, 1998)

Signed as a free agent by **St. Louis**, July 16, 1990. Transferred to **New Jersey** from **St. Louis** as compensation for St. Louis' signing of free agent Brendan Shanahan, September 3, 1991.

STEVENSON, JEREMY — ANA.

Left wing. Shoots left. 6'2", 220 lbs. Born, San Bernadino, CA, July 28, 1974.
(Anaheim's 10th choice, 262nd overall, in 1994 Entry Draft).

			Regular Season					Playoffs				
Season	Club	Lea	GP	G	A	TP	PIM	GP	G	A	TP	PIM
1990-91	Cornwall	OHL	58	13	20	33	124	....	....	....	....	....
1991-92	Cornwall	OHL	63	15	23	38	176	6	3	1	4	4
1992-93	Newmarket	OHL	54	28	28	56	144	5	5	1	6	28
1993-94	Newmarket	OHL	9	2	4	6	27	....	....	....	....	....
	S.S. Marie	OHL	48	18	19	37	183	14	1	1	2	23
1994-95	Greensboro	ECHL	43	14	13	27	231	17	6	11	17	64
1995-96	**Anaheim**	**NHL**	**3**	**0**	**1**	**1**	**12**	....	....	....	....	....
	Baltimore	AHL	60	11	10	21	295	12	4	2	6	23
1996-97	**Anaheim**	**NHL**	**5**	**0**	**0**	**0**	**14**	....	....	....	....	....
	Baltimore	AHL	25	8	8	16	125	3	0	0	0	8
1997-98	**Anaheim**	**NHL**	**45**	**3**	**5**	**8**	**101**	....	....	....	....	....
	Cincinnati	AHL	10	5	0	5	34	....	....	....	....	....
	NHL Totals		**53**	**3**	**6**	**9**	**127**	....	....	....	....	....

• Re-entered NHL draft. Originally Winnipeg's 3rd choice, 60th overall, in 1992 Entry Draft.

STEVENSON, TURNER — MTL.

Right wing. Shoots right. 6'3", 220 lbs. Born, Prince George, B.C., May 18, 1972.
(Montreal's 1st choice, 12th overall, in 1990 Entry Draft).

			Regular Season					Playoffs				
Season	Club	Lea	GP	G	A	TP	PIM	GP	G	A	TP	PIM
1988-89	Seattle	WHL	69	15	12	27	84	....	....	....	....	....
1989-90	Seattle	WHL	62	29	32	61	276	13	3	2	5	35
1990-91	Seattle	WHL	57	36	27	63	222	6	1	5	6	15
	Fredericton	AHL	....	....	....	....	....	4	0	0	0	5
1991-92	Seattle	WHL	58	20	32	52	264	15	9	3	12	55
1992-93	**Montreal**	**NHL**	**1**	**0**	**0**	**0**	**0**	....	....	....	....	....
	Fredericton	AHL	79	25	34	59	102	5	2	3	5	11
1993-94	**Montreal**	**NHL**	**2**	**0**	**0**	**0**	**2**	**3**	**0**	**2**	**2**	**0**
	Fredericton	AHL	66	19	28	47	155	....	....	....	....	....
1994-95	Fredericton	AHL	37	12	12	24	109	....	....	....	....	....
	Montreal	**NHL**	**41**	**6**	**1**	**7**	**86**	....	....	....	....	....
1995-96	**Montreal**	**NHL**	**80**	**9**	**16**	**25**	**167**	**6**	**0**	**1**	**1**	**2**
1996-97	**Montreal**	**NHL**	**65**	**8**	**13**	**21**	**97**	**5**	**1**	**1**	**2**	**2**
1997-98	**Montreal**	**NHL**	**63**	**4**	**6**	**10**	**110**	**10**	**3**	**4**	**7**	**12**
	NHL Totals		**252**	**27**	**36**	**63**	**462**	**24**	**4**	**8**	**12**	**16**

WHL West First All-Star Team (1992) • Memorial Cup All-Star Team (1992)

STEWART, CAM

Left wing. Shoots left. 5'11", 196 lbs. Born, Kitchener, Ont., September 18, 1971.
(Boston's 2nd choice, 63rd overall, in 1990 Entry Draft).

			Regular Season					Playoffs				
Season	Club	Lea	GP	G	A	TP	PIM	GP	G	A	TP	PIM
1989-90	Elmira	OJHL	46	44	95	139	172	....	....	....	....	....
1990-91	U. of Michigan	CCHA	44	8	24	32	122	....	....	....	....	....
1991-92	U. of Michigan	CCHA	44	13	15	28	106	....	....	....	....	....
1992-93	U. of Michigan	CCHA	39	20	39	59	69	....	....	....	....	....
1993-94	**Boston**	**NHL**	**57**	**3**	**6**	**9**	**66**	**8**	**0**	**3**	**3**	**7**
	Providence	AHL	14	3	2	5	5	....	....	....	....	....
1994-95	**Boston**	**NHL**	**5**	**0**	**0**	**0**	**2**	....	....	....	....	....
	Providence	AHL	31	13	11	24	38	9	2	5	7	0
1995-96	**Boston**	**NHL**	**6**	**0**	**0**	**0**	**0**	**5**	**1**	**0**	**1**	**2**
	Providence	AHL	54	17	25	42	39	....	....	....	....	....
1996-97	**Boston**	**NHL**	**15**	**0**	**1**	**1**	**4**	....	....	....	....	....
	Providence	AHL	18	4	3	7	37	....	....	....	....	....
	Cincinnati	IHL	7	3	2	5	8	1	0	0	0	0
1997-98	Houston	IHL	63	18	27	45	51	4	0	1	1	18
	NHL Totals		**83**	**3**	**7**	**10**	**72**	**13**	**1**	**3**	**4**	**9**

STEWART, JASON — NYI

Right wing. Shoots right. 5'11", 185 lbs. Born, St. Paul, MN, April 30, 1976.
(NY Islanders' 7th choice, 142nd overall, in 1994 Entry Draft).

			Regular Season					Playoffs				
Season	Club	Lea	GP	G	A	TP	PIM	GP	G	A	TP	PIM
1993-94	Simley High	H.S.	23	15	15	30	32	....	....	....	....	....
1994-95	St. Cloud State	WCHA	28	1	3	4	16	....	....	....	....	....
1995-96	St. Cloud State	WCHA	36	4	7	11	40	....	....	....	....	....
1996-97	St. Cloud State	WCHA	40	6	5	11	32	....	....	....	....	....
1997-98	St. Cloud State	WCHA	36	14	15	29	53	....	....	....	....	....

STILLMAN, CORY — CGY.

Center. Shoots left. 6', 190 lbs. Born, Peterborough, Ont., December 20, 1973.
(Calgary's 1st choice, 6th overall, in 1992 Entry Draft).

			Regular Season					Playoffs				
Season	Club	Lea	GP	G	A	TP	PIM	GP	G	A	TP	PIM
1990-91	Windsor	OHL	64	31	70	101	31	11	3	6	9	8
1991-92	Windsor	OHL	53	29	61	90	59	7	2	4	6	8
1992-93	Peterborough	OHL	61	25	55	80	55	18	3	8	11	18
	Canada	Nat-Tm	1	0	0	0	0					
1993-94	Saint John	AHL	79	35	48	83	52	7	2	4	6	16
1994-95	Saint John	AHL	63	28	53	81	70	5	0	2	2	2
	Calgary	NHL	10	0	2	2	2					
1995-96	Calgary	NHL	74	16	19	35	41	2	1	1	2	0
1996-97	Calgary	NHL	58	6	20	26	14					
1997-98	Calgary	NHL	72	27	22	49	40					
	NHL Totals		214	49	63	112	97	2	1	1	2	0

STOCK, P.J. — NYR

Left wing. Shoots left. 5'10", 190 lbs. Born, Victoriaville, Que., May 26, 1975.

			Regular Season					Playoffs				
Season	Club	Lea	GP	G	A	TP	PIM	GP	G	A	TP	PIM
1994-95	Victoriaville	QMJHL	70	9	46	55	386	4	0	0	0	60
1995-96	Victoriaville	QMJHL	67	19	43	62	432	12	5	4	9	79
1996-97	St. FX University	AUAA	27	11	20	31	110	3	0	4	4	14
1997-98	Hartford	AHL	41	8	8	16	202	11	1	3	4	79
	NY Rangers	NHL	38	2	3	5	114					
	NHL Totals		38	2	3	5	114					

Signed as a free agent by **NY Rangers**, November 18, 1997.

STOJANOV, ALEK (STOY-uh-nahf)

Right wing. Shoots left. 6'4", 225 lbs. Born, Windsor, Ont., April 25, 1973.
(Vancouver's 1st choice, 7th overall, in 1991 Entry Draft).

			Regular Season					Playoffs				
Season	Club	Lea	GP	G	A	TP	PIM	GP	G	A	TP	PIM
1989-90	Hamilton	OHL	37	4	4	8	91					
1990-91	Hamilton	OHL	62	25	20	45	181	4	1	1	2	14
1991-92	Guelph	OHL	33	12	15	27	91					
1992-93	Guelph	OHL	36	27	28	55	62					
	Newmarket	OHL	14	9	7	16	26	7	1	3	4	26
	Hamilton	AHL	4	4	0	4	0					
1993-94	Hamilton	AHL	4	0	1	1	5					
1994-95	Syracuse	AHL	73	18	12	30	270					
	Vancouver	NHL	4	0	0	0	13	5	0	0	0	2
1995-96	Vancouver	NHL	58	0	1	1	123					
	Pittsburgh	NHL	10	1	0	1	7	9	0	0	0	19
1996-97	Pittsburgh	NHL	35	1	4	5	79					
1997-98	Syracuse	AHL	41	5	4	9	215	3	1	0	1	4
	NHL Totals		107	2	5	7	222	14	0	0	0	21

Traded to **Pittsburgh** by **Vancouver** for Markus Naslund, March 20, 1996.

STOREY, BEN — COL.

Defense. Shoots left. 6'2", 180 lbs. Born, Ottawa, Ont., June 22, 1977.
(Colorado's 4th choice, 98th overall, in 1996 Entry Draft).

			Regular Season					Playoffs				
Season	Club	Lea	GP	G	A	TP	PIM	GP	G	A	TP	PIM
1994-95	Ottawa	OJHL	51	6	33	39	83					
1995-96	Harvard	ECAC	33	2	11	13	44					
1996-97	Harvard	ECAC	25	0	6	6	40					
1997-98	Harvard	ECAC	33	9	16	25	56					

STORM, JIM

Left wing. Shoots left. 6'2", 200 lbs. Born, Milford, MI, February 5, 1971.
(Hartford's 5th choice, 75th overall, in 1991 Entry Draft).

			Regular Season					Playoffs				
Season	Club	Lea	GP	G	A	TP	PIM	GP	G	A	TP	PIM
1989-90	Detroit	NAJHL	55	38	73	111	58					
1990-91	Michigan Tech	WCHA	36	16	18	34	46					
1991-92	Michigan Tech	WCHA	39	25	33	58	12					
1992-93	Michigan Tech	WCHA	33	22	32	54	30					
1993-94	Hartford	NHL	68	6	10	16	27					
	United States	Nat-Tm	28	8	12	20	14					
1994-95	Hartford	NHL	6	0	3	3	0					
	Springfield	AHL	33	11	11	22	29					
1995-96	Dallas	NHL	10	1	2	3	17					
	Michigan	IHL	60	18	33	51	27	10	4	8	12	2
1996-97	Michigan	IHL	75	25	24	49	27	4	0	1	1	4
1997-98	Utah	IHL	5	0	0	0	2					
	NHL Totals		84	7	15	22	44					

Signed as a free agent by **Dallas**, September 13, 1995. Signed as a free agent by **NY Islanders**, July 21, 1997.

STRAKA, JOSEF (STRAH-kuh) — CGY.

Center. Shoots right. 5'11", 183 lbs. Born, Jindrichuv Hradec, Czech., February 11, 1978.
(Calgary's 7th choice, 122nd overall, in 1996 Entry Draft).

			Regular Season					Playoffs				
Season	Club	Lea	GP	G	A	TP	PIM	GP	G	A	TP	PIM
1995-96	Litvinov	Cze-Rep.	33	5	6	11	14	15	3	1	4	
1996-97	Litvinov	Cze-Rep.	52	14	16	30	32					
1997-98	Litvinov	Cze-Rep.	17	2	4	6	8					

STRAKA, MARTIN (STRAH-kuh) — PIT.

Center. Shoots left. 5'10", 175 lbs. Born, Plzen, Czech., September 3, 1972.
(Pittsburgh's 1st choice, 19th overall, in 1992 Entry Draft).

			Regular Season					Playoffs				
Season	Club	Lea	GP	G	A	TP	PIM	GP	G	A	TP	PIM
1989-90	Skoda Plzen	Czech.	1	0	3	3						
1990-91	Skoda Plzen	Czech.	47	7	24	31	6					
1991-92	Skoda Plzen	Czech.	50	27	28	55	20					
1992-93	Pittsburgh	NHL	42	3	13	16	29	11	2	1	3	2
	Cleveland	IHL	4	4	3	7	0					
1993-94	Pittsburgh	NHL	84	30	34	64	24	6	1	0	1	2
1994-95	Plzen	Cze-Rep.	19	10	11	21	18					
	Pittsburgh	NHL	31	4	12	16	16					
	Ottawa	NHL	6	1	1	2	0					
1995-96	Ottawa	NHL	43	9	16	25	29					
	NY Islanders	NHL	22	2	10	12	6					
	Florida	NHL	12	2	4	6	6	13	2	2	4	2
1996-97	Florida	NHL	55	7	22	29	12	4	0	0	0	0
1997-98	Pittsburgh	NHL	75	19	23	42	28	6	2	0	2	2
	Czech Republic	Olympics	6	1	2	3	0					
	NHL Totals		370	77	135	212	150	40	7	3	10	8

Czechoslovakian First All-Star Team (1992)

Traded to **Ottawa** by **Pittsburgh** for Troy Murray and Norm Maciver, April 7, 1995. Traded to **NY Islanders** by **Ottawa** with Don Beaupre and Bryan Berard for Damian Rhodes and Wade Redden, January 23, 1996. Claimed on waivers by **Florida** from **NY Islanders**, March 15, 1996. Signed as a free agent by **Pittsburgh**, August 6, 1997.

STREIT, MARTIN (STRIGHT) — PHI.

Left wing. Shoots right. 6'2", 191 lbs. Born, Vyskov, Czech., February 2, 1977.
(Philadelphia's 7th choice, 178th overall, in 1995 Entry Draft).

			Regular Season					Playoffs				
Season	Club	Lea	GP	G	A	TP	PIM	GP	G	A	TP	PIM
1994-95	HC Olomouc	Czech-Jr.	STATISTICS NOT AVAILABLE									
1995-96	HC Olomouc	Czech-Jr.	19	10	6	16						
	HC Olomouc	Cze-Rep.	10	0	0	0						
1996-97	HC Olomouc	Cze-Rep.	18	1	2	3	14					
1997-98	Karlovy	Cze-Rep.	48	5	13	18	24					

STROM, PETER (STRUHM) — MTL.

Left wing. Shoots right. 6', 178 lbs. Born, Snotorp, Sweden, January 14, 1975.
(Montreal's 10th choice, 200th overall, in 1994 Entry Draft).

			Regular Season					Playoffs				
Season	Club	Lea	GP	G	A	TP	PIM	GP	G	A	TP	PIM
1993-94	V. Frolunda	Sweden	29	0	0	0	8					
1994-95	V. Frolunda	Sweden	16	0	3	3	10					
	V. Frolunda	Sweden-2	12	8	10	18	10					
1995-96	V. Frolunda	Sweden	35	7	8	15	10	13	0	3	3	0
1996-97	V. Frolunda	Sweden	49	7	16	23	24	3	0	0	0	2
1997-98	V. Frolunda	Sweden	46	6	15	21	22	7	0	4	4	0

STRUDWICK, JASON (STRUHD-wihk) — VAN.

Defense. Shoots left. 6'3", 215 lbs. Born, Edmonton, Alta., July 17, 1975.
(NY Islanders' 3rd choice, 63rd overall, in 1994 Entry Draft).

			Regular Season					Playoffs				
Season	Club	Lea	GP	G	A	TP	PIM	GP	G	A	TP	PIM
1993-94	Kamloops	WHL	61	6	8	14	118	19	0	4	4	24
1994-95	Kamloops	WHL	72	3	11	14	183	21	1	1	2	39
1995-96	NY Islanders	NHL	1	0	0	0	7					
	Worcester	AHL	60	2	7	9	119	4	0	1	1	0
1996-97	Kentucky	AHL	80	1	9	10	198	4	0	0	0	0
1997-98	NY Islanders	NHL	17	0	1	1	36					
	Kentucky	AHL	39	3	1	4	87					
	Vancouver	NHL	11	0	1	1	29					
	Syracuse	AHL						3	0	0	0	6
	NHL Totals		29	0	2	2	72					

Traded to **Vancouver** by **NY Islanders** for Gino Odjick, March 23, 1998.

STUART, BRAD — S.J.

Defense. Shoots left. 6'2", 215 lbs. Born, Rocky Mountain House, Alta., November 6, 1979.
(San Jose's 1st choice, 3rd overall, in 1998 Entry Draft).

			Regular Season					Playoffs				
Season	Club	Lea	GP	G	A	TP	PIM	GP	G	A	TP	PIM
1996-97	Regina	WHL	57	7	36	43	58	5	0	4	4	14
1997-98	Regina	WHL	72	20	45	65	82	9	3	4	7	10

WHL East Second All-Star Team (1998)

STUMPEL, JOZEF (STUM-puhl) — L.A.

Center. Shoots right. 6'3", 216 lbs. Born, Nitra, Czech., July 20, 1972.
(Boston's 2nd choice, 40th overall, in 1991 Entry Draft).

			Regular Season					Playoffs				
Season	Club	Lea	GP	G	A	TP	PIM	GP	G	A	TP	PIM
1989-90	AC Nitra	Czech-2	38	12	11	23						
1990-91	AC Nitra	Czech.	49	23	22	45	14					
1991-92	Kolner Haie	Germany	37	20	19	39	35					
	Boston	NHL	4	1	0	1	0					
1992-93	Boston	NHL	13	1	3	4	4					
	Providence	AHL	56	31	61	92	26	6	4	4	8	0
1993-94	Boston	NHL	59	8	15	23	14	13	1	7	8	4
	Providence	AHL	17	5	12	17	4					
1994-95	Kolner Haie	Germany	25	16	23	39	18					
	Boston	NHL	44	5	13	18	8	5	0	0	0	0
1995-96	Boston	NHL	76	18	36	54	14	5	1	2	3	0
1996-97	Boston	NHL	78	21	55	76	14					
1997-98	Los Angeles	NHL	77	21	58	79	53	4	1	2	3	2
	NHL Totals		351	75	180	255	107	27	3	11	14	6

Traded to **LA Kings** by **Boston** with Sandy Moger and Boston's 4th round choice (later traded to New Jersey — New Jersey selected Pierre Dagenais) in 1998 Entry Draft for Dimitri Kristich and Byron Dafoe, August 29, 1997.

STURM, MARCO (STURHM) — S.J.

Center. Shoots left. 6', 190 lbs. Born, Dingolfing, Germany, September 8, 1978.
(San Jose's 2nd choice, 21st overall, in 1996 Entry Draft).

			Regular Season					Playoffs				
Season	Club	Lea	GP	G	A	TP	PIM	GP	G	A	TP	PIM
1995-96	EV Landshut	Germany	47	12	20	32	50	11	1	3	4	18
1996-97	EV Landshut	Germany	46	16	27	43	40	7	1	4	5	6
1997-98	San Jose	NHL	74	10	20	30	40	2	0	0	0	0
	Germany	Olympics	2	0	0	0	0					
	NHL Totals		74	10	20	30	40	2	0	0	0	0

STUSSI, RENE (SHTOO-see) ANA.

Left wing. Shoots right. 5'11", 183 lbs. Born, Muri, Switzerland, December 13, 1978.
(Anaheim's 7th choice, 209th overall, in 1997 Entry Draft).

			Regular Season					Playoffs				
Season	Club	Lea	GP	G	A	TP	PIM	GP	G	A	TP	PIM
1995-96	Thurgau	Switz-2	34	2	4	6	10	7	3	0	3	2
1996-97	Thurgau	Switz-2	42	20	31	51	24	8	5	4	9	4
1997-98	Kloten	Switz.	38	9	8	17	10	7	1	0	1	4

STYF, PAR (STOOF) PHI.

Defense. Shoots left. 6', 187 lbs. Born, Harnosand, Sweden, April 11, 1979.
(Philadelphia's 8th choice, 240th overall, in 1997 Entry Draft).

			Regular Season					Playoffs				
Season	Club	Lea	GP	G	A	TP	PIM	GP	G	A	TP	PIM
1996-97	MoDo	Swe-Jr.	11	2	4	6	....	....	....	....	....	....
1997-98	MoDo	Swe-Jr.	17	7	5	12	60	....	....	....	....	....

SUBBOTIN, DMITRI (soo-BOH-tihn) NYR

Left wing. Shoots left. 6'1", 183 lbs. Born, Tomsk, USSR, October 20, 1977.
(NY Rangers' 3rd choice, 76th overall, in 1996 Entry Draft).

			Regular Season					Playoffs				
Season	Club	Lea	GP	G	A	TP	PIM	GP	G	A	TP	PIM
1993-94	Yekaterinburg	CIS	12	0	3	3	4	....	....	....	....	....
1994-95	Yekaterinburg	CIS	52	9	6	15	75	2	0	0	0	2
1995-96	CSKA Moscow	CIS	41	6	5	11	62	3	0	0	0	0
1996-97	CSKA Moscow	Russia	17	5	3	8	22	2	0	0	0	2
	CSKA Moscow	Russia-2	8	1	0	1	8	....	....	....	....	....
1997-98	CSKA Moscow	Russia	16	1	1	2	47	....	....	....	....	....

SUCHY, RADOSLAV (soo-KHEE) PHX.

Defense. Shoots left. 6'1", 185 lbs. Born, Poprad, Czechoslovakia, July 4, 1976.

			Regular Season					Playoffs				
Season	Club	Lea	GP	G	A	TP	PIM	GP	G	A	TP	PIM
1993-94	SKP PS Poprad	Slovakia	3	0	0	0	0	....	....	....	....	....
1994-95	Sherbrooke	QMJHL	69	12	32	44	30	7	0	3	3	2
1995-96	Sherbrooke	QMJHL	68	15	53	68	68	7	0	3	3	2
1996-97	Sherbrooke	QMJHL	32	6	34	40	14	....	....	....	....	....
	Chicoutimi	QMJHL	28	5	24	29	26	19	6	15	21	12
1997-98	Las Vegas	IHL	26	1	4	5	10	....	....	....	....	....
	Springfield	AHL	41	6	15	21	16	4	0	1	1	2

QMJHL Second All-Star Team (1997) • Won George Parsons Trophy (Memorial Cup Tournament Most Sportsmanlike Player) (1997)

Signed as a free agent by **Phoenix**, September 26, 1997.

SUGDEN, BRANDON (SUHG-duhn)

Defense. Shoots right. 6'2", 178 lbs. Born, Toronto, Ont., June 23, 1978.
(Toronto's 8th choice, 111th overall, in 1996 Entry Draft).

			Regular Season					Playoffs				
Season	Club	Lea	GP	G	A	TP	PIM	GP	G	A	TP	PIM
1995-96	London	OHL	55	2	7	9	*264	....	....	....	....	....
1996-97	London	OHL	31	4	10	14	158	....	....	....	....	....
	Sudbury	OHL	20	0	4	4	70	....	....	....	....	....
1997-98	Sudbury	OHL	11	2	3	5	62	....	....	....	....	....
	Barrie	OHL	49	6	21	27	191	6	0	0	0	18

SULC, JAN (SOOLTZ, YAN) T.B.

Center. Shoots right. 6'3", 180 lbs. Born, Litvinov, Czech., February 17, 1979.
(Tampa Bay's 5th choice, 109th overall, in 1997 Entry Draft).

			Regular Season					Playoffs				
Season	Club	Lea	GP	G	A	TP	PIM	GP	G	A	TP	PIM
1996-97	Litvinov	Cze-Rep.	37	14	17	31	....	....	....	....	....	....
1997-98	St. Michael's	OHL	34	3	10	13	11	....	....	....	....	....
	Kingston	OHL	29	6	8	14	7	12	0	0	0	0

SULLIVAN, JEFF

Defense. Shoots left. 6'1", 185 lbs. Born, St. John's, Nfld., September 18, 1978.
(Ottawa's 5th choice, 146th overall, in 1997 Entry Draft).

			Regular Season					Playoffs				
Season	Club	Lea	GP	G	A	TP	PIM	GP	G	A	TP	PIM
1996-97	Granby	QMJHL	25	4	8	12	47	....	....	....	....	....
	Halifax	QMJHL	45	4	23	27	200	18	0	5	5	96
1997-98	Halifax	QMJHL	69	9	27	36	377	5	0	1	1	21

SULLIVAN, MIKE PHX.

Center. Shoots left. 6'2", 190 lbs. Born, Marshfield, MA, February 27, 1968.
(NY Rangers' 4th choice, 69th overall, in 1987 Entry Draft).

			Regular Season					Playoffs				
Season	Club	Lea	GP	G	A	TP	PIM	GP	G	A	TP	PIM
1985-86	Boston College	H.S.	22	26	33	59	....	....	....	....	....	....
1986-87	Boston University	H.E.	37	13	18	31	18	....	....	....	....	....
1987-88	Boston University	H.E.	30	18	22	40	30	....	....	....	....	....
1988-89	Boston University	H.E.	36	19	17	36	30	....	....	....	....	....
1989-90	Boston University	H.E.	38	11	20	31	26	....	....	....	....	....
1990-91	San Diego	IHL	74	12	23	35	27	....	....	....	....	....
1991-92	**San Jose**	**NHL**	**64**	**8**	**11**	**19**	**15**	....	....	....	....	....
	Kansas City	IHL	10	2	8	10	8	....	....	....	....	....
1992-93	**San Jose**	**NHL**	**81**	**6**	**8**	**14**	**30**	....	....	....	....	....
1993-94	**San Jose**	**NHL**	**26**	**2**	**2**	**4**	**4**	....	....	....	....	....
	Kansas City	IHL	6	3	3	6	0	....	....	....	....	....
	Calgary	**NHL**	**19**	**2**	**3**	**5**	**6**	**7**	**1**	**1**	**2**	**8**
	Saint John	AHL	5	2	0	2	4	....	....	....	....	....
1994-95	**Calgary**	**NHL**	**38**	**4**	**7**	**11**	**14**	**7**	**3**	**5**	**8**	**2**
1995-96	**Calgary**	**NHL**	**81**	**9**	**12**	**21**	**24**	**4**	**0**	**0**	**0**	**0**
1996-97	**Calgary**	**NHL**	**67**	**5**	**6**	**11**	**10**	....	....	....	....	....
1997-98	**Boston**	**NHL**	**77**	**5**	**13**	**18**	**34**	**6**	**0**	**1**	**1**	**2**
	NHL Totals		**453**	**41**	**62**	**103**	**137**	**24**	**4**	**7**	**11**	**12**

Rights traded to **Minnesota** by **NY Rangers** with Paul Jerrard, the rights to Bret Barnett, and LA Kings' 3rd round choice (previously acquired, Minnesota selected Murray Garbutt) in 1989 Entry Draft for Brian Lawton, Igor Liba and the rights to Eric Bennett, October 11, 1988. Signed as a free agent by **San Jose**, August 9, 1991. Claimed on waivers by **Calgary** from **San Jose**, January 6, 1994. Traded to **Boston** by **Calgary** for Boston's 7th round choice (Radek Duda) in 1998 Entry Draft, June 21, 1997. Claimed by **Nashville** from **Boston** in Expansion Draft, June 26, 1998. Traded to **Phoenix** by **Nashville** for Phoenix's 7th round choice in 1999 Entry Draft, June 30, 1998.

SULLIVAN, STEVE TOR.

Center. Shoots right. 5'9", 155 lbs. Born, Timmins, Ont., July 6, 1974.
(New Jersey's 10th choice, 233rd overall, in 1994 Entry Draft).

			Regular Season					Playoffs				
Season	Club	Lea	GP	G	A	TP	PIM	GP	G	A	TP	PIM
1992-93	S.S. Marie	OHL	62	36	27	63	44	16	3	8	11	18
1993-94	S.S. Marie	OHL	63	51	62	113	82	14	9	16	25	22
1994-95	Albany	AHL	75	31	50	81	124	14	4	7	11	10
1995-96	**New Jersey**	**NHL**	**16**	**5**	**4**	**9**	**8**	....	....	....	....	....
	Albany	AHL	53	33	42	75	127	4	3	0	3	6
1996-97	**New Jersey**	**NHL**	**33**	**8**	**14**	**22**	**14**	....	....	....	....	....
	Albany	AHL	15	8	7	15	16	....	....	....	....	....
	Toronto	**NHL**	**21**	**5**	**11**	**16**	**23**	....	....	....	....	....
1997-98	**Toronto**	**NHL**	**63**	**10**	**18**	**28**	**40**	....	....	....	....	....
	NHL Totals		**133**	**28**	**47**	**75**	**85**	....	....	....	....	....

AHL First All-Star Team (1996)

Traded to **Toronto** by **New Jersey** with Jason Smith and the rights to Alyn McCauley for Doug Gilmour, Dave Ellett and future considerations, February 25, 1997.

SUNDIN, MATS (SUHN-deen) TOR.

Center/Right wing. Shoots right. 6'4", 228 lbs. Born, Bromma, Sweden, February 13, 1971.
(Quebec's 1st choice, 1st overall, in 1989 Entry Draft).

			Regular Season					Playoffs				
Season	Club	Lea	GP	G	A	TP	PIM	GP	G	A	TP	PIM
1988-89	Nacka	Sweden-2	25	10	8	18	18	....	....	....	....	....
1989-90	Djurgarden	Sweden	34	10	8	18	16	8	7	0	7	4
1990-91	**Quebec**	**NHL**	**80**	**23**	**36**	**59**	**58**	....	....	....	....	....
1991-92	**Quebec**	**NHL**	**80**	**33**	**43**	**76**	**103**	....	....	....	....	....
1992-93	**Quebec**	**NHL**	**80**	**47**	**67**	**114**	**96**	**6**	**3**	**1**	**4**	**6**
1993-94	**Quebec**	**NHL**	**84**	**32**	**53**	**85**	**60**	....	....	....	....	....
1994-95	Djurgarden	Sweden	12	7	2	9	14	....	....	....	....	....
	Toronto	**NHL**	**47**	**23**	**24**	**47**	**14**	**7**	**5**	**4**	**9**	**4**
1995-96	**Toronto**	**NHL**	**76**	**33**	**50**	**83**	**46**	**6**	**3**	**1**	**4**	**4**
1996-97	**Toronto**	**NHL**	**82**	**41**	**53**	**94**	**59**	....	....	....	....	....
1997-98	**Toronto**	**NHL**	**82**	**33**	**41**	**74**	**49**	....	....	....	....	....
	Sweden	Olympics	4	3	0	3	4	....	....	....	....	....
	NHL Totals		**611**	**265**	**367**	**632**	**485**	**19**	**11**	**6**	**17**	**14**

Swedish World All-Star Team (1991, 1992, 1994, 1997)

Played in NHL All-Star Game (1996, 1997, 1998)

Traded to **Toronto** by **Quebec** with Garth Butcher, Todd Warriner and Philadelphia's 1st round choice (previously acquired by Quebec — later traded to Washington — Washington selected Nolan Baumgartner) in 1994 Entry Draft for Wendel Clark, Sylvain Lefebvre, Landon Wilson and Toronto's 1st round choice (Jeffrey Kealty) in 1994 Entry Draft, June 28, 1994.

SUNDIN, RONNIE (SUHN-deen)

Defense. Shoots left. 6'1", 220 lbs. Born, Ludvika, Sweden, October 3, 1970.
(NY Rangers' 8th choice, 237th overall, in 1996 Entry Draft).

			Regular Season					Playoffs				
Season	Club	Lea	GP	G	A	TP	PIM	GP	G	A	TP	PIM
1991-92	Mora	Sweden-2	35	2	5	7	18	2	0	0	0	0
1992-93	V. Frolunda	Sweden	17	2	3	5	12	....	....	....	....	....
1993-94	V. Frolunda	Sweden	38	0	9	9	42	4	0	0	0	0
1994-95	V. Frolunda	Sweden	11	3	4	7	6	....	....	....	....	....
1995-96	V. Frolunda	Sweden	40	3	6	9	18	13	1	4	5	10
1996-97	V. Frolunda	Sweden	47	3	14	17	24	3	1	0	1	2
1997-98	**NY Rangers**	**NHL**	**1**	**0**	**0**	**0**	**0**	....	....	....	....	....
	Hartford	AHL	67	3	19	22	59	14	2	5	7	15
	NHL Totals		**1**	**0**	**0**	**0**	**0**	....	....	....	....	....

SUNDSTROM, NIKLAS (SUHN-struhm) NYR

Left wing. Shoots left. 6', 185 lbs. Born, Ornskoldsvik, Sweden, June 6, 1975.
(NY Rangers' 1st choice, 8th overall, in 1993 Entry Draft).

			Regular Season					Playoffs				
Season	Club	Lea	GP	G	A	TP	PIM	GP	G	A	TP	PIM
1991-92	MoDo	Sweden	9	1	3	4	0	....	....	....	....	....
1992-93	MoDo	Sweden	40	7	11	18	18	3	0	0	0	0
1993-94	MoDo	Sweden	37	7	12	19	28	11	4	3	7	2
1994-95	MoDo	Sweden	33	8	13	21	30	....	....	....	....	....
1995-96	**NY Rangers**	**NHL**	**82**	**9**	**12**	**21**	**14**	**11**	**4**	**3**	**7**	**4**
1996-97	**NY Rangers**	**NHL**	**82**	**24**	**28**	**52**	**20**	**9**	**0**	**5**	**5**	**2**
1997-98	**NY Rangers**	**NHL**	**70**	**19**	**28**	**47**	**24**	....	....	....	....	....
	Sweden	Olympics	4	1	1	2	2	....	....	....	....	....
	NHL Totals		**234**	**52**	**68**	**120**	**58**	**20**	**4**	**8**	**12**	**6**

SUTER, CURTIS (SOO-tuhr) PHX.

Left wing. Shoots left. 6'4", 220 lbs. Born, Kerrobert, Sask., August 5, 1979.
(Phoenix's 3rd choice, 123rd overall, in 1997 Entry Draft).

			Regular Season					Playoffs				
Season	Club	Lea	GP	G	A	TP	PIM	GP	G	A	TP	PIM
1996-97	Spokane	WHL	56	2	2	4	133	2	0	0	0	0
1997-98	Spokane	WHL	62	9	8	17	216	18	0	1	1	9

SUTER, GARY (SOO-tuhr) S.J.

Defense. Shoots left. 6', 205 lbs. Born, Madison, WI, June 24, 1964.
(Calgary's 9th choice, 180th overall, in 1984 Entry Draft).

			Regular Season					Playoffs				
Season	Club	Lea	GP	G	A	TP	PIM	GP	G	A	TP	PIM
1983-84	U. of Wisconsin	WCHA	35	4	18	22	32	....	....	....	....	....
1984-85	U. of Wisconsin	WCHA	39	12	39	51	110	....	....	....	....	....
1985-86	**Calgary**	**NHL**	**80**	**18**	**50**	**68**	**141**	**10**	**2**	**8**	**10**	**8**
1986-87	**Calgary**	**NHL**	**68**	**9**	**40**	**49**	**70**	**6**	**0**	**3**	**3**	**10**
1987-88	**Calgary**	**NHL**	**75**	**21**	**70**	**91**	**124**	**9**	**1**	**9**	**10**	**6**
1988-89	**Calgary**	**NHL**	**63**	**13**	**49**	**62**	**78**	**5**	**0**	**3**	**3**	**10 ♦**
1989-90	**Calgary**	**NHL**	**76**	**16**	**60**	**76**	**97**	**6**	**0**	**1**	**1**	**14**
1990-91	**Calgary**	**NHL**	**79**	**12**	**58**	**70**	**102**	**7**	**1**	**6**	**7**	**12**
1991-92	**Calgary**	**NHL**	**70**	**12**	**43**	**55**	**128**	....	....	....	....	....
1992-93	**Calgary**	**NHL**	**81**	**23**	**58**	**81**	**112**	**6**	**2**	**3**	**5**	**8**
1993-94	**Calgary**	**NHL**	**25**	**4**	**9**	**13**	**20**	....	....	....	....	....
	Chicago	**NHL**	**16**	**2**	**3**	**5**	**18**	**6**	**3**	**2**	**5**	**6**
1994-95	**Chicago**	**NHL**	**48**	**10**	**27**	**37**	**42**	**12**	**2**	**5**	**7**	**10**
1995-96	**Chicago**	**NHL**	**82**	**20**	**47**	**67**	**80**	**10**	**3**	**3**	**6**	**8**
1996-97	**Chicago**	**NHL**	**82**	**7**	**21**	**28**	**70**	**6**	**1**	**4**	**5**	**8**
1997-98	**Chicago**	**NHL**	**73**	**14**	**28**	**42**	**74**	....	....	....	....	....
	United States	Olympics	4	0	0	0	2	....	....	....	....	....
	NHL Totals		**918**	**181**	**563**	**744**	**1156**	**83**	**15**	**47**	**62**	**100**

Won Calder Memorial Trophy (1986) • NHL All-Rookie Team (1986) • NHL Second All-Star Team (1988)

Played in NHL All-Star Game (1986, 1988, 1989, 1991)

Traded to **Hartford** by **Calgary** with Paul Ranheim and Ted Drury for James Patrick, Zarley Zalapski and Michael Nylander, March 10, 1994. Traded to **Chicago** by **Hartford** with Randy Cunneyworth and Hartford's 3rd round choice (later traded to Vancouver — Vancouver selected Larry Courville) in 1995 Entry Draft for Frantisek Kucera and Jocelyn Lemieux, March 11, 1994. Signed as a free agent by **San Jose**, July 1, 1998.

SUTTER, BRENT (SUH-tuhr)

Center. Shoots right. 6', 188 lbs. Born, Viking, Alta., June 10, 1962.
(NY Islanders' 1st choice, 17th overall, in 1980 Entry Draft).

			Regular Season					Playoffs				
Season	Club	Lea	GP	G	A	TP	PIM	GP	G	A	TP	PIM
1977-78	Red Deer	AJHL	60	12	18	30	33	....	....	....	....	....
1978-79	Red Deer	AJHL	60	42	42	84	79	....	....	....	....	....
1979-80	Red Deer	AJHL	59	70	101	171	....	....	....	....	....	....
	Lethbridge	WHL	5	1	0	1	2	....	....	....	....	....
1980-81	Lethbridge	WHL	68	54	54	108	116	9	6	4	10	51
	NY Islanders	**NHL**	**3**	**2**	**2**	**4**	**0**	....	....	....	....	....
1981-82	Lethbridge	WHL	34	46	33	79	162	....	....	....	....	....
	NY Islanders	**NHL**	**43**	**21**	**22**	**43**	**114**	**19**	**2**	**6**	**8**	**36 ♦**
1982-83	**NY Islanders**	**NHL**	**80**	**21**	**19**	**40**	**128**	**20**	**10**	**11**	**21**	**26 ♦**
1983-84	**NY Islanders**	**NHL**	**69**	**34**	**15**	**49**	**69**	**20**	**4**	**10**	**14**	**18**
1984-85	**NY Islanders**	**NHL**	**72**	**42**	**60**	**102**	**51**	**10**	**3**	**3**	**6**	**14**
1985-86	**NY Islanders**	**NHL**	**61**	**24**	**31**	**55**	**74**	**3**	**0**	**1**	**1**	**2**
1986-87	**NY Islanders**	**NHL**	**69**	**27**	**36**	**63**	**73**	**5**	**1**	**0**	**1**	**4**
1987-88	**NY Islanders**	**NHL**	**70**	**29**	**31**	**60**	**55**	**6**	**2**	**1**	**3**	**18**
1988-89	**NY Islanders**	**NHL**	**77**	**29**	**34**	**63**	**77**	....	....	....	....	....
1989-90	**NY Islanders**	**NHL**	**67**	**33**	**35**	**68**	**65**	**5**	**2**	**3**	**5**	**2**
1990-91	**NY Islanders**	**NHL**	**75**	**21**	**32**	**53**	**49**	....	....	....	....	....
1991-92	**Chicago**	**NHL**	**61**	**18**	**32**	**50**	**30**	**18**	**3**	**5**	**8**	**22**
	NY Islanders	**NHL**	**8**	**4**	**6**	**10**	**6**	....	....	....	....	....
1992-93	**Chicago**	**NHL**	**65**	**20**	**34**	**54**	**67**	**4**	**1**	**1**	**2**	**4**
1993-94	**Chicago**	**NHL**	**73**	**9**	**29**	**38**	**43**	**6**	**0**	**0**	**0**	**2**
1994-95	**Chicago**	**NHL**	**47**	**7**	**8**	**15**	**51**	**16**	**1**	**2**	**3**	**4**
1995-96	**Chicago**	**NHL**	**80**	**13**	**27**	**40**	**56**	**10**	**1**	**1**	**2**	**6**
1996-97	**Chicago**	**NHL**	**39**	**7**	**7**	**14**	**18**	**2**	**0**	**0**	**0**	**6**
1997-98	**Chicago**	**NHL**	**52**	**2**	**6**	**8**	**28**	....	....	....	....	....
	NHL Totals		**1111**	**363**	**466**	**829**	**1054**	**144**	**30**	**44**	**74**	**164**

Played in NHL All-Star Game (1985)

Traded to **Chicago** by **NY Islanders** with Brad Lauer for Adam Creighton and Steve Thomas, October 25, 1991.

SUTTER, RON (SUH-tuhr) S.J.

Center. Shoots right. 6', 180 lbs. Born, Viking, Alta., December 2, 1963.
(Philadelphia's 1st choice, 4th overall, in 1982 Entry Draft).

			Regular Season					Playoffs				
Season	Club	Lea	GP	G	A	TP	PIM	GP	G	A	TP	PIM
1979-80	Red Deer	AJHL	60	12	33	45	44	....	....	....	....	....
1980-81	Lethbridge	WHL	72	13	32	45	152	9	2	5	7	29
1981-82	Lethbridge	WHL	59	38	54	92	207	12	6	5	11	28
1982-83	**Philadelphia**	**NHL**	**10**	**1**	**1**	**2**	**9**	....	....	....	....	....
	Lethbridge	WHL	58	35	48	83	98	20	*22	*19	*41	45
1983-84	**Philadelphia**	**NHL**	**79**	**19**	**32**	**51**	**101**	**3**	**0**	**0**	**0**	**22**
1984-85	**Philadelphia**	**NHL**	**73**	**16**	**29**	**45**	**94**	**19**	**4**	**8**	**12**	**28**
1985-86	**Philadelphia**	**NHL**	**75**	**18**	**42**	**60**	**159**	**5**	**0**	**2**	**2**	**10**
1986-87	**Philadelphia**	**NHL**	**39**	**10**	**17**	**27**	**69**	**16**	**1**	**7**	**8**	**12**
1987-88	**Philadelphia**	**NHL**	**69**	**8**	**25**	**33**	**146**	**7**	**0**	**1**	**1**	**26**
1988-89	**Philadelphia**	**NHL**	**55**	**26**	**22**	**48**	**80**	**19**	**1**	**9**	**10**	**51**
1989-90	**Philadelphia**	**NHL**	**75**	**22**	**26**	**48**	**104**	....	....	....	....	....
1990-91	**Philadelphia**	**NHL**	**80**	**17**	**28**	**45**	**92**	....	....	....	....	....
1991-92	**St. Louis**	**NHL**	**68**	**19**	**27**	**46**	**91**	**6**	**1**	**3**	**4**	**8**
1992-93	**St. Louis**	**NHL**	**59**	**12**	**15**	**27**	**99**	....	....	....	....	....
1993-94	**St. Louis**	**NHL**	**36**	**6**	**12**	**18**	**46**	....	....	....	....	....
	Quebec	**NHL**	**37**	**9**	**13**	**22**	**44**	....	....	....	....	....
1994-95	**NY Islanders**	**NHL**	**27**	**1**	**4**	**5**	**21**	....	....	....	....	....
1995-96	Phoenix	IHL	25	6	13	19	28	....	....	....	....	....
	Boston	**NHL**	**18**	**5**	**7**	**12**	**24**	**5**	**0**	**0**	**0**	**8**
1996-97	**San Jose**	**NHL**	**78**	**5**	**7**	**12**	**65**	....	....	....	....	....
1997-98	**San Jose**	**NHL**	**57**	**2**	**7**	**9**	**22**	**6**	**1**	**0**	**1**	**14**
	NHL Totals		**935**	**196**	**314**	**510**	**1266**	**86**	**8**	**30**	**38**	**179**

Traded to **St. Louis** by **Philadelphia** with Murray Baron for Dan Quinn and Rod Brind'Amour, September 22, 1991. Traded to **Quebec** by **St. Louis** with Garth Butcher and Bob Bassen for Steve Duchesne and Denis Chasse, January 23, 1994. Traded to **NY Islanders** by **Quebec** with Quebec's 1st round choice (Brett Lindros) in 1994 Entry Draft for Uwe Krupp and NY Islanders' 1st round choice (Wade Belak) in 1994 Entry Draft, June 28, 1994. Signed as a free agent by **Boston**, March 9, 1996. Signed as a free agent by **San Jose**, October 12, 1996.

SUTTER, SHAUN (SUH-tuhr) CGY.

Center. Shoots right. 5'11", 160 lbs. Born, Red Deer, Alta., June 2, 1980.
(Calgary's 4th choice, 102nd overall, in 1998 Entry Draft).

			Regular Season					Playoffs				
Season	Club	Lea	GP	G	A	TP	PIM	GP	G	A	TP	PIM
1996-97	Lethbridge	WHL	1	0	0	0	0	....	....	....	....	....
1997-98	Lethbridge	WHL	69	11	9	20	146	4	0	0	0	4

SUTTON, ANDY S.J.

Defense. Shoots left. 5'10", 192 lbs. Born, Edmonton, Alta., October 24, 1977.

			Regular Season					Playoffs				
Season	Club	Lea	GP	G	A	TP	PIM	GP	G	A	TP	PIM
1994-95	Michigan Tech	WCHA	19	2	1	3	42	....	....	....	....	....
1995-96	Michigan Tech	WCHA	33	2	2	4	58	....	....	....	....	....
1996-97	Michigan Tech	WCHA	32	2	7	9	73	....	....	....	....	....
1997-98	Michigan Tech	WCHA	38	16	24	40	97	....	....	....	....	....
	Kentucky	AHL	7	0	0	0	33	....	....	....	....	....

Signed as a free agent by **San Jose**, March 20, 1998.

SUTTON, KEN N.J.

Defense. Shoots left. 6', 205 lbs. Born, Edmonton, Alta., November 5, 1969.
(Buffalo's 4th choice, 98th overall, in 1989 Entry Draft).

			Regular Season					Playoffs				
Season	Club	Lea	GP	G	A	TP	PIM	GP	G	A	TP	PIM
1987-88	Calgary	AJHL	53	13	43	56	228	....	....	....	....	....
1988-89	Saskatoon	WHL	71	22	31	53	104	8	2	5	7	12
1989-90	Rochester	AHL	57	5	14	19	83	11	1	6	7	15
1990-91	**Buffalo**	**NHL**	**15**	**3**	**6**	**9**	**13**	**6**	**0**	**1**	**1**	**2**
	Rochester	AHL	62	7	24	31	65	3	1	1	2	14
1991-92	**Buffalo**	**NHL**	**64**	**2**	**18**	**20**	**71**	**7**	**0**	**2**	**2**	**4**
1992-93	**Buffalo**	**NHL**	**63**	**8**	**14**	**22**	**30**	**8**	**3**	**1**	**4**	**8**
1993-94	**Buffalo**	**NHL**	**78**	**4**	**20**	**24**	**71**	**4**	**0**	**0**	**0**	**2**
1994-95	**Buffalo**	**NHL**	**12**	**1**	**2**	**3**	**30**	....	....	....	....	....
	Edmonton	**NHL**	**12**	**3**	**1**	**4**	**12**	....	....	....	....	....
1995-96	**Edmonton**	**NHL**	**32**	**0**	**8**	**8**	**39**	....	....	....	....	....
	St. Louis	**NHL**	**6**	**0**	**0**	**0**	**4**	**1**	**0**	**0**	**0**	**0**
	Worcester	AHL	32	4	16	20	60	4	0	2	2	21
1996-97	Manitoba	IHL	20	3	10	13	48	....	....	....	....	....
	Albany	AHL	61	6	13	19	79	16	4	8	12	55
1997-98	**New Jersey**	**NHL**	**13**	**0**	**0**	**0**	**6**	....	....	....	....	....
	Albany	AHL	10	0	7	7	15	....	....	....	....	....
	San Jose	**NHL**	**8**	**0**	**0**	**0**	**15**	....	....	....	....	....
	NHL Totals		**303**	**21**	**69**	**90**	**291**	**26**	**3**	**4**	**7**	**16**

Memorial Cup All-Star Team (1989)

Traded to **Edmonton** by **Buffalo** for Scott Pearson, April 7, 1995. Traded to **St. Louis** by **Edmonton** with Igor Kravchuk for Jeff Norton and Donald Dufresne, January 4, 1996. Traded to **New Jersey** by **St. Louis** with St. Louis' 2nd round choice in 1999 Entry Draft for Mike Peluso and Ricard Persson, November 26, 1996. Traded to **San Jose** by **New Jersey** with John MacLean for Doug Bodger and Dody Wood, December 7, 1997. Traded to **New Jersey** by **San Jose** for future considerations, August 26, 1998.

SUURSOO, TOIVO (SUH-uhr-soh-oh) DET.

Left wing. Shoots right. 6', 175 lbs. Born, Tallinn, USSR, November 23, 1975.
(Detroit's 10th choice, 283rd overall, in 1994 Entry Draft).

			Regular Season					Playoffs				
Season	Club	Lea	GP	G	A	TP	PIM	GP	G	A	TP	PIM
1993-94	Soviet Wings	CIS	33	3	0	3	8	....	....	....	....	....
1994-95	Soviet Wings	CIS	47	10	5	15	36	4	0	0	0	4
1995-96	Soviet Wings	CIS	47	6	4	10	36	....	....	....	....	....
1996-97	TPS Turku	Finland	50	11	8	19	64	12	2	3	5	4
1997-98	TPS Turku	EuroHL	4	2	0	2	0	....	....	....	....	....
	TPS Turku	Finland	38	17	5	22	46	4	2	1	3	2

SVARTVADET, PER (svahrt-VAH-deht) DAL.

Center. Shoots left. 6'1", 180 lbs. Born, Solleftea, Sweden, May 17, 1975.
(Dallas' 5th choice, 139th overall, in 1993 Entry Draft).

			Regular Season					Playoffs				
Season	Club	Lea	GP	G	A	TP	PIM	GP	G	A	TP	PIM
1992-93	MoDo	Sweden	2	0	0	0	0	....	....	....	....	....
1993-94	MoDo	Sweden	36	2	1	3	4	11	0	0	0	6
1994-95	MoDo	Sweden	40	6	9	15	31	....	....	....	....	....
1995-96	MoDo	Sweden	40	9	14	23	26	8	2	3	5	0
1996-97	MoDo	Sweden	50	7	18	25	38	....	....	....	....	....
1997-98	MoDo	Sweden	46	6	12	18	28	7	3	2	5	2

SVEHLA, ROBERT (SHVEH-lah) FLA.

Defense. Shoots right. 6'1", 210 lbs. Born, Martin, Czech., January 2, 1969.
(Calgary's 4th choice, 78th overall, in 1992 Entry Draft).

			Regular Season					Playoffs				
Season	Club	Lea	GP	G	A	TP	PIM	GP	G	A	TP	PIM
1989-90	Dukla Trencin	Czech.	29	4	3	7	....	....	....	....	....	....
1990-91	Dukla Trencin	Czech.	52	16	9	25	62	....	....	....	....	....
1991-92	Dukla Trencin	Czech.	51	23	28	51	74	....	....	....	....	....
	Czechoslovakia	Olympics	8	2	1	3	8	....	....	....	....	....
1992-93	Malmo IF	Sweden	40	19	10	29	86	6	0	1	1	14
1993-94	Malmo IF	Sweden	37	14	25	39	127	10	5	1	6	23
	Slovakia	Olympics	8	2	4	6	26	....	....	....	....	....
1994-95	Malmo IF	Sweden	32	11	13	24	83	9	2	3	5	6
	Florida	**NHL**	**5**	**1**	**1**	**2**	**0**	....	....	....	....	....
1995-96	**Florida**	**NHL**	**81**	**8**	**49**	**57**	**94**	**22**	**0**	**6**	**6**	**32**
1996-97	**Florida**	**NHL**	**82**	**13**	**32**	**45**	**86**	**5**	**1**	**4**	**5**	**4**
1997-98	**Florida**	**NHL**	**79**	**9**	**34**	**43**	**113**	....	....	....	....	....
	Slovakia	Olympics	2	0	1	1	0	....	....	....	....	....
	NHL Totals		**247**	**31**	**116**	**147**	**293**	**27**	**1**	**10**	**11**	**36**

Czechoslovakian First All-Star Team (1992)

Played in NHL All-Star Game (1997)

Traded to **Florida** by **Calgary** with Magnus Svensson for Florida's 3rd round choice (Dmitri Vlasenkov) in 1996 Entry Draft and 4th round choice (Ryan Ready) in 1997 Entry Draft, September 29, 1994.

SVEJKOVSKY, JAROSLAV (svehzh-KOHV-skee) WSH.

Right wing. Shoots right. 5'11", 185 lbs. Born, Plzen, Czech., October 1, 1976.
(Washington's 2nd choice, 17th overall, in 1996 Entry Draft).

			Regular Season					Playoffs				
Season	Club	Lea	GP	G	A	TP	PIM	GP	G	A	TP	PIM
1993-94	Skoda Plzen	Cze-Rep.	8	0	0	0	8	....	....	....	....	....
1994-95	Tabor	Czech-2	11	6	7	13	....	....	....	....	....	....
1995-96	Tri-City	WHL	70	58	43	101	118	11	10	9	19	8
1996-97	**Washington**	**NHL**	**19**	**7**	**3**	**10**	**4**	....	....	....	....	....
	Portland	AHL	54	38	28	66	56	5	2	0	2	6
1997-98	**Washington**	**NHL**	**17**	**4**	**1**	**5**	**10**	**1**	**0**	**0**	**0**	**2**
	Portland	AHL	16	12	7	19	16	7	1	2	3	2
	NHL Totals		**36**	**11**	**4**	**15**	**14**	**1**	**0**	**0**	**0**	**2**

WHL West Second All-Star Team (1996) • Won Dudley "Red" Garrett Memorial Trophy (Top Rookie - AHL) (1997)

SVOBODA, PETR (svah-BOH-duh) PHI.

Defense. Shoots left. 6'1", 195 lbs. Born, Most, Czech., February 14, 1966.
(Montreal's 1st choice, 5th overall, in 1984 Entry Draft).

			Regular Season					Playoffs				
Season	Club	Lea	GP	G	A	TP	PIM	GP	G	A	TP	PIM
1982-83	Litvinov	Czech.	4	0	0	0	2	....	....	....	....	....
1983-84	Litvinov	Czech.	18	3	1	4	20	....	....	....	....	....
1984-85	Montreal	NHL	73	4	27	31	65	7	1	1	2	12
1985-86	Montreal	NHL	73	1	18	19	93	8	0	0	0	21 ♦
1986-87	Montreal	NHL	70	5	17	22	63	14	0	5	5	10
1987-88	Montreal	NHL	69	7	22	29	149	10	0	5	5	12
1988-89	Montreal	NHL	71	8	37	45	147	21	1	11	12	16
1989-90	Montreal	NHL	60	5	31	36	98	10	0	5	5	7
1990-91	Montreal	NHL	60	4	22	26	52	2	0	1	1	2
1991-92	Montreal	NHL	58	5	16	21	94	....	....	....	....	....
	Buffalo	NHL	13	1	6	7	52	7	1	4	5	6
1992-93	Buffalo	NHL	40	2	24	26	59	....	....	....	....	....
1993-94	Buffalo	NHL	60	2	14	16	89	3	0	0	0	4
1994-95	Litvinov	Cze-Rep.	8	2	0	2	50	....	....	....	....	....
	Buffalo	NHL	26	0	5	5	60	....	....	....	....	....
	Philadelphia	NHL	11	0	3	3	10	14	0	4	4	8
1995-96	Philadelphia	NHL	73	1	28	29	105	12	0	6	6	22
1996-97	Philadelphia	NHL	67	2	12	14	94	16	1	2	3	16
1997-98	Philadelphia	NHL	56	3	15	18	83	3	0	1	1	4
	Czech.	Olympics	6	1	1	2	*39	....	....	....	....	....
	NHL Totals		880	50	297	347	1313	127	4	45	49	140

Traded to **Buffalo** by **Montreal** for Kevin Haller, March 10, 1992. Traded to **Philadelphia** by **Buffalo** for Garry Galley, April 7, 1995.

SVOBODA, PETR (svah-BOH-duh) TOR.

Defense. Shoots right. 6'2", 194 lbs. Born, Jihlava, Czechoslovakia, June 20, 1980.
(Toronto's 2nd choice, 35th overall, in 1998 Entry Draft).

			Regular Season					Playoffs				
Season	Club	Lea	GP	G	A	TP	PIM	GP	G	A	TP	PIM
1995-96	SK Jihlava	Czech-Jr.	38	4	12	16	50	....	....	....	....	....
1996-97	SK Jihlava	Czech-Jr.	29	1	3	4	....	....	....	....	....	....
1997-98	Dukla Jihlava	Cze-Rep.	1	0	0	0	0	....	....	....	....	....
	Havlickuv Brod	Czech-2	18	1	2	3	16	....	....	....	....	....
	SK Jihlava	Czech-Jr.	12	0	2	2	....	....	....	....	....	....

SWANSON, BRIAN NYR

Center. Shoots left. 5'10", 180 lbs. Born, Anchorage, AK, March 24, 1976.
(San Jose's 5th choice, 115th overall, in 1994 Entry Draft).

			Regular Season					Playoffs				
Season	Club	Lea	GP	G	A	TP	PIM	GP	G	A	TP	PIM
1993-94	Omaha	USHL	47	38	42	80	40	....	....	....	....	....
1994-95	Omaha	USHL	33	14	35	49	12	....	....	....	....	....
1995-96	Colorado	WCHA	40	26	33	59	24	....	....	....	....	....
1996-97	Colorado	WCHA	43	19	32	51	47	....	....	....	....	....
1997-98	Colorado	WCHA	42	18	*38	*56	26	....	....	....	....	....

WCHA Second All-Star Team (1996) • WCHA First All-Star Team (1997, 1998) • NCAA West Second All-American Team (1998)

Traded to **NY Rangers** by **San Jose** with Jayson More and a conditional choice in 1998 Entry Draft for Marty McSorley, August 20, 1996.

SWANSON, SCOTT WSH.

Defense. Shoots left. 6'2", 190 lbs. Born, St. Paul, MN, February 15, 1975.
(Washington's 10th choice, 225th overall, in 1995 Entry Draft).

			Regular Season					Playoffs				
Season	Club	Lea	GP	G	A	TP	PIM	GP	G	A	TP	PIM
1994-95	Omaha	USHL	48	14	46	60	22	....	....	....	....	....
1995-96	Omaha	USHL	1	0	0	0	0	....	....	....	....	....
	Colorado	WCHA	42	13	35	48	16	....	....	....	....	....
1996-97	Colorado	WCHA	44	4	16	20	22	....	....	....	....	....
1997-98	Colorado	WCHA	42	7	32	39	24	....	....	....	....	....

WCHA Second All-Star Team (1996)

SWEENEY, DON BOS.

Defense. Shoots left. 5'10", 184 lbs. Born, St. Stephen, N.B., August 17, 1966.
(Boston's 8th choice, 166th overall, in 1984 Entry Draft).

			Regular Season					Playoffs				
Season	Club	Lea	GP	G	A	TP	PIM	GP	G	A	TP	PIM
1983-84	St. Paul	H.S.	22	33	26	59	....	....	....	....	....	....
1984-85	Harvard	ECAC	29	3	7	10	30	....	....	....	....	....
1985-86	Harvard	ECAC	31	4	5	9	12	....	....	....	....	....
1986-87	Harvard	ECAC	34	7	4	11	22	....	....	....	....	....
1987-88	Harvard	ECAC	30	6	23	29	37	....	....	....	....	....
	Maine	AHL	....	....	....	....	....	6	1	3	4	0
1988-89	Boston	NHL	36	3	5	8	20	....	....	....	....	....
	Maine	AHL	42	8	17	25	24	....	....	....	....	....
1989-90	Boston	NHL	58	3	5	8	58	21	1	5	6	18
	Maine	AHL	11	0	8	8	8	....	....	....	....	....
1990-91	Boston	NHL	77	8	13	21	67	19	3	0	3	25
1991-92	Boston	NHL	75	3	11	14	74	15	0	0	0	10
1992-93	Boston	NHL	84	7	27	34	68	4	0	0	0	4
1993-94	Boston	NHL	75	6	15	21	50	12	2	1	3	4
1994-95	Boston	NHL	47	3	19	22	24	5	0	0	0	4
1995-96	Boston	NHL	77	4	24	28	42	5	0	2	2	6
1996-97	Boston	NHL	82	3	23	26	39	....	....	....	....	....
1997-98	Boston	NHL	59	1	15	16	24	....	....	....	....	....
	NHL Totals		670	41	157	198	466	81	6	8	14	71

NCAA East All-American Team (1988) • ECAC First All-Star Team (1988)

SWEENEY, TIM

Left wing. Shoots left. 5'11", 185 lbs. Born, Boston, MA, April 12, 1967.
(Calgary's 7th choice, 122nd overall, in 1985 Entry Draft).

			Regular Season					Playoffs				
Season	Club	Lea	GP	G	A	TP	PIM	GP	G	A	TP	PIM
1984-85	Weymouth	H.S.	22	32	56	88	....	....	....	....	....	....
1985-86	Boston College	H.E.	32	8	4	12	8	....	....	....	....	....
1986-87	Boston College	H.E.	38	31	18	49	28	....	....	....	....	....
1987-88	Boston College	H.E.	18	9	11	20	18	....	....	....	....	....
1988-89	Boston College	H.E.	39	29	44	73	26	....	....	....	....	....
1989-90	Salt Lake	IHL	81	46	51	97	32	11	5	4	9	4
1990-91	Calgary	NHL	42	7	9	16	8	....	....	....	....	....
	Salt Lake	IHL	31	19	16	35	8	4	3	3	6	0
1991-92	United States	Nat-Tm	21	9	11	20	10	....	....	....	....	....
	United States	Olympics	8	3	4	7	6	....	....	....	....	....
	Calgary	NHL	11	1	2	3	4	....	....	....	....	....
1992-93	Boston	NHL	14	1	7	8	6	3	0	0	0	0
	Providence	AHL	60	41	55	96	32	3	2	2	4	0
1993-94	Anaheim	NHL	78	16	27	43	49	....	....	....	....	....
1994-95	Anaheim	NHL	13	1	1	2	2	....	....	....	....	....
	Providence	AHL	2	2	2	4	0	13	8	*17	*25	6
1995-96	Boston	NHL	41	8	8	16	14	1	0	0	0	2
	Providence	AHL	34	17	22	39	12	....	....	....	....	....
1996-97	Boston	NHL	36	10	11	21	14	....	....	....	....	....
	Providence	AHL	23	11	22	33	6	....	....	....	....	....
1997-98	NY Rangers	NHL	56	11	18	29	26	....	....	....	....	....
	Hartford	AHL	7	2	6	8	8	....	....	....	....	....
	NHL Totals		291	55	83	138	123	4	0	0	0	2

Hockey East First All-Star Team (1989) • NCAA East Second All-American Team (1989) • IHL Second All-Star Team (1990) • AHL Second All-Star Team (1993)

Signed as a free agent by **Boston**, September 16, 1992. Claimed by **Anaheim** from **Boston** in Expansion Draft, June 24, 1993. Signed as a free agent by **Boston**, August 9, 1995. Signed as a free agent by **NY Rangers**, September 15, 1997.

SYDOR, DARRYL (sih-DOHR) DAL.

Defense. Shoots left. 6', 195 lbs. Born, Edmonton, Alta., May 13, 1972.
(Los Angeles' 1st choice, 7th overall, in 1990 Entry Draft).

			Regular Season					Playoffs				
Season	Club	Lea	GP	G	A	TP	PIM	GP	G	A	TP	PIM
1987-88	Edmonton	AJHL	38	10	11	21	54	....	....	....	....	....
1988-89	Kamloops	WHL	65	12	14	26	86	15	1	4	5	19
1989-90	Kamloops	WHL	67	29	66	95	129	17	2	9	11	28
1990-91	Kamloops	WHL	66	27	78	105	88	12	3	*22	25	10
1991-92	Kamloops	WHL	29	9	39	48	43	17	3	15	18	18
	Los Angeles	NHL	18	1	5	6	22	....	....	....	....	....
1992-93	Los Angeles	NHL	80	6	23	29	63	24	3	8	11	16
1993-94	Los Angeles	NHL	84	8	27	35	94	....	....	....	....	....
1994-95	Los Angeles	NHL	48	4	19	23	36	....	....	....	....	....
1995-96	Los Angeles	NHL	58	1	11	12	34	....	....	....	....	....
	Dallas	NHL	26	2	6	8	41	....	....	....	....	....
1996-97	Dallas	NHL	82	8	40	48	51	7	0	2	2	0
1997-98	Dallas	NHL	79	11	35	46	51	17	0	5	5	14
	NHL Totals		475	41	166	207	392	48	3	15	18	30

Played in NHL All-Star Game (1998)

WHL West First All-Star Team (1990, 1991, 1992)

Traded to **Dallas** by **LA Kings** with LA Kings' 5th round choice (Ryan Christie) in 1996 Entry Draft for Shane Churla and Doug Zmolek, February 17, 1996.

SYKORA, MICHAL (SEE-koh-ra) T.B.

Defense. Shoots left. 6'5", 225 lbs. Born, Pardubice, Czech., July 5, 1973.
(San Jose's 6th choice, 123rd overall, in 1992 Entry Draft).

			Regular Season					Playoffs				
Season	Club	Lea	GP	G	A	TP	PIM	GP	G	A	TP	PIM
1990-91	Pardubice	Czech.	2	0	0	0	....	....	....	....	....	....
1991-92	Tacoma	WHL	61	13	23	36	66	4	0	2	2	2
1992-93	Tacoma	WHL	70	23	50	73	73	7	4	8	12	2
1993-94	San Jose	NHL	22	1	4	5	14	....	....	....	....	....
	Kansas City	IHL	47	5	11	16	30	....	....	....	....	....
1994-95	Kansas City	IHL	36	1	10	11	30	....	....	....	....	....
	San Jose	NHL	16	0	4	4	10	....	....	....	....	....
1995-96	San Jose	NHL	79	4	16	20	54	....	....	....	....	....
1996-97	San Jose	NHL	35	2	5	7	59	....	....	....	....	....
	Chicago	NHL	28	1	9	10	10	1	0	0	0	0
1997-98	Chicago	NHL	28	1	3	4	12	....	....	....	....	....
	Indianapolis	IHL	6	0	0	0	4	....	....	....	....	....
	Pardubice	Cze-Rep.	1	1	0	1	2	....	....	....	....	....
	NHL Totals		208	9	41	50	159	1	0	0	0	0

WHL West First All-Star Team (1993)

Traded to **Chicago** by **San Jose** with Chris Terreri and Ulf Dahlen for Ed Belfour, January 25, 1997. Traded to **Tampa Bay** by **Chicago** for Mark Fitzpatrick and Tampa Bay's 4th round choice in 1999 Entry Draft, July 17, 1998.

SYKORA, PETR (SEE-koh-ra) N.J.

Center. Shoots left. 5'11", 185 lbs. Born, Plzen, Czech., November 19, 1976.
(New Jersey's 1st choice, 18th overall, in 1995 Entry Draft).

			Regular Season					Playoffs				
Season	Club	Lea	GP	G	A	TP	PIM	GP	G	A	TP	PIM
1992-93	Skoda Plzen	Czech.	19	12	5	17	....	....	....	....	....	....
1993-94	Skoda Plzen	Cze-Rep.	37	10	16	26	....	4	0	1	1	....
	Cleveland	IHL	13	4	5	9	8	....	....	....	....	....
1994-95	Detroit	IHL	29	12	17	29	16	....	....	....	....	....
1995-96	New Jersey	NHL	63	18	24	42	32	....	....	....	....	....
	Albany	AHL	5	4	1	5	0	....	....	....	....	....
1996-97	New Jersey	NHL	19	1	2	3	4	2	0	0	0	2
	Albany	AHL	43	20	25	45	48	4	1	4	5	2
1997-98	New Jersey	NHL	58	16	20	36	22	2	0	0	0	0
	Albany	AHL	2	4	1	5	0	....	....	....	....	....
	NHL Totals		140	35	46	81	58	4	0	0	0	2

NHL All-Rookie Team (1996)

SYKORA, PETR (SEE-koh-ra) NSH.

Center. Shoots right. 6'2", 180 lbs. Born, Pardubice, Czech., December 21, 1978.
(Detroit's 2nd choice, 76th overall, in 1997 Entry Draft).

			Regular Season					Playoffs				
Season	Club	Lea	GP	G	A	TP	PIM	GP	G	A	TP	PIM
1995-96	Pardubice	Czech-Jr.	26	13	9	22	....	....	....	....	....	....
1996-97	Pardubice	Czech-Jr.	12	14	4	18	....	....	....	....	....	....
	Pardubice	Cze-Rep.	29	1	3	4	4	....	....	....	....	....
1997-98	Pardubice	Cze-Rep.	39	4	5	9	8	3	0	0	0	....

Traded to **Nashville** by **Detroit** with Detroit's 3rd round choice in 1999 Entry Draft for Doug Brown, July 14, 1998.

SYMES, BRAD EDM.

Defense. Shoots left. 6'2", 210 lbs. Born, Edmonton, Alta., April 26, 1976.
(Edmonton's 5th choice, 60th overall, in 1994 Entry Draft).

			Regular Season					Playoffs				
Season	Club	Lea	GP	G	A	TP	PIM	GP	G	A	TP	PIM
1992-93	Portland	WHL	68	4	2	6	107	16	0	1	1	7
1993-94	Portland	WHL	71	7	15	22	170	7	0	0	0	21
1994-95	Portland	WHL	70	8	16	24	134	9	0	2	2	27
1995-96	Portland	WHL	62	9	12	21	118	7	1	2	3	14
1996-97	Wheeling	ECHL	51	6	17	23	63	1	0	0	0	0
	Hamilton	AHL	5	0	0	0	7	....	....	....	....	....
1997-98	New Orleans	ECHL	18	1	4	5	28	....	....	....	....	....

TALLAIRE, SEAN (tuh-LAIR, SHAWN)

Right wing. Shoots right. 5'10", 185 lbs. Born, Steinbach, MN, October 3, 1973.
(Vancouver's 7th choice, 202nd overall, in 1993 Entry Draft).

			Regular Season					Playoffs				
Season	Club	Lea	GP	G	A	TP	PIM	GP	G	A	TP	PIM
1992-93	Lake Superior	CCHA	43	26	26	52	26	....	....	....	....	....
1993-94	Lake Superior	CCHA	45	23	32	55	22	....	....	....	....	....
1994-95	Lake Superior	CCHA	41	21	29	50	38	....	....	....	....	....
1995-96	Lake Superior	CCHA	40	*32	18	50	36	....	....	....	....	....
1996-97	Manitoba	IHL	74	21	29	50	67	....	....	....	....	....
1997-98	Grand Rapids	IHL	73	13	17	30	65	....	....	....	....	....
	Cleveland	IHL	7	1	1	2	4	10	2	2	4	4

CCHA First All-Star Team (1996) • NCAA West Second All-American Team (1996)

TALLINDER, HENRIK (tah-LIHN-duhr) BUF.

Defense. Shoots left. 6'3", 194 lbs. Born, Stockholm, Sweden, January 10, 1979.
(Buffalo's 2nd choice, 48th overall, in 1997 Entry Draft).

			Regular Season					Playoffs				
Season	Club	Lea	GP	G	A	TP	PIM	GP	G	A	TP	PIM
1996-97	AIK Solna	Swe-Jr.	40	4	13	17	55	....	....	....	....	....
	AIK Solna	Sweden	1	0	0	0	0	....	....	....	....	....
1997-98	AIK Solna	Sweden	34	0	0	0	26	....	....	....	....	....

TAMER, CHRIS (TAY-muhr) PIT.

Defense. Shoots left. 6'1", 207 lbs. Born, Dearborn, MI, November 17, 1970.
(Pittsburgh's 3rd choice, 68th overall, in 1990 Entry Draft).

			Regular Season					Playoffs				
Season	Club	Lea	GP	G	A	TP	PIM	GP	G	A	TP	PIM
1988-89	Redford	NAJHL	31	6	13	19	79	....	....	....	....	....
1989-90	U. of Michigan	CCHA	42	2	7	9	147	....	....	....	....	....
1990-91	U. of Michigan	CCHA	45	8	19	27	130	....	....	....	....	....
1991-92	U. of Michigan	CCHA	43	4	15	19	125	....	....	....	....	....
1992-93	U. of Michigan	CCHA	39	5	18	23	113	....	....	....	....	....
1993-94	**Pittsburgh**	**NHL**	**12**	**0**	**0**	**0**	**9**	**5**	**0**	**0**	**0**	**2**
	Cleveland	IHL	53	1	2	3	160	....	....	....	....	....
1994-95	Cleveland	IHL	48	4	10	14	204	....	....	....	....	....
	Pittsburgh	**NHL**	**36**	**2**	**0**	**2**	**82**	**4**	**0**	**0**	**0**	**18**
1995-96	**Pittsburgh**	**NHL**	**70**	**4**	**10**	**14**	**153**	**18**	**0**	**7**	**7**	**24**
1996-97	**Pittsburgh**	**NHL**	**45**	**2**	**4**	**6**	**131**	**4**	**0**	**0**	**0**	**4**
1997-98	**Pittsburgh**	**NHL**	**79**	**0**	**7**	**7**	**181**	**6**	**0**	**1**	**1**	**4**
	NHL Totals		**242**	**8**	**21**	**29**	**556**	**37**	**0**	**8**	**8**	**52**

TANCILL, CHRIS (TAN-sihl)

Center. Shoots left. 5'10", 185 lbs. Born, Livonia, MI, February 7, 1968.
(Hartford's 1st choice, 15th overall, in 1989 Supplemental Draft).

			Regular Season					Playoffs				
Season	Club	Lea	GP	G	A	TP	PIM	GP	G	A	TP	PIM
1986-87	U. of Wisconsin	WCHA	40	9	23	32	26	....	....	....	....	....
1987-88	U. of Wisconsin	WCHA	44	13	14	27	48	....	....	....	....	....
1988-89	U. of Wisconsin	WCHA	44	20	23	43	50	....	....	....	....	....
1989-90	U. of Wisconsin	WCHA	45	39	32	71	44	....	....	....	....	....
1990-91	**Hartford**	**NHL**	**9**	**1**	**1**	**2**	**4**	....	....	....	....	....
	Springfield	AHL	72	37	35	72	46	17	8	4	12	32
1991-92	**Hartford**	**NHL**	**10**	**0**	**0**	**0**	**2**	....	....	....	....	....
	Springfield	AHL	17	12	7	19	20	....	....	....	....	....
	Detroit	**NHL**	**1**	**0**	**0**	**0**	**0**	....	....	....	....	....
	Adirondack	AHL	50	36	34	70	42	19	7	9	16	31
1992-93	**Detroit**	**NHL**	**4**	**1**	**0**	**1**	**2**	....	....	....	....	....
	Adirondack	AHL	68	*59	43	102	62	10	7	7	14	10
1993-94	**Dallas**	**NHL**	**12**	**1**	**3**	**4**	**8**	....	....	....	....	....
	Kalamazoo	IHL	60	41	54	95	55	5	0	2	2	8
1994-95	Kansas City	IHL	64	31	28	59	40	....	....	....	....	....
	San Jose	**NHL**	**26**	**3**	**11**	**14**	**10**	**11**	**1**	**1**	**2**	**8**
1995-96	**San Jose**	**NHL**	**45**	**7**	**16**	**23**	**20**	....	....	....	....	....
	Kansas City	IHL	27	12	16	28	18	....	....	....	....	....
1996-97	**San Jose**	**NHL**	**25**	**4**	**0**	**4**	**8**	....	....	....	....	....
	Kentucky	AHL	42	19	26	45	31	4	2	0	2	2
1997-98	**Dallas**	**NHL**	**2**	**0**	**1**	**1**	**0**	....	....	....	....	....
	Michigan	IHL	70	30	39	69	86	4	3	0	3	14
	NHL Totals		**134**	**17**	**32**	**49**	**54**	**11**	**1**	**1**	**2**	**8**

NCAA Championship All-Tournament Team (1990) • NCAA Championship Tournament MVP (1990) • AHL First All-Star Team (1992, 1993)

Traded to **Detroit** by **Hartford** for Daniel Shank, December 18, 1991. Signed as a free agent by **Dallas**, August 28, 1993. Signed as a free agent by **San Jose**, August 24, 1994. Signed as a free agent by **Dallas**, August 6, 1997.

TANGUAY, ALEX (TAN-guay) COL.

Center. Shoots left. 6', 180 lbs. Born, Ste-Justine, Que., November 21, 1979.
(Colorado's 1st choice, 12th overall, in 1998 Entry Draft).

			Regular Season					Playoffs				
Season	Club	Lea	GP	G	A	TP	PIM	GP	G	A	TP	PIM
1996-97	Halifax	QMJHL	70	27	42	68	60	12	5	8	13	8
1997-98	Halifax	QMJHL	51	47	38	85	32	5	7	6	13	4

TARDIF, PATRICE (tahr-DIHF)

Center. Shoots left. 6'2", 202 lbs. Born, Thetford Mines, Que., October 30, 1970.
(St. Louis' 2nd choice, 54th overall, in 1990 Entry Draft).

			Regular Season					Playoffs				
Season	Club	Lea	GP	G	A	TP	PIM	GP	G	A	TP	PIM
1989-90	Champlain College	QCAA	27	58	36	94	36	....	....	....	....	....
1990-91	U. of Maine	H.E.	36	13	12	25	18	....	....	....	....	....
1991-92	U. of Maine	H.E.	31	18	20	38	14	....	....	....	....	....
1992-93	U. of Maine	H.E.	45	23	25	48	22	....	....	....	....	....
1993-94	U. of Maine	H.E.	34	18	15	33	42	....	....	....	....	....
	Peoria	IHL	11	4	4	8	21	4	2	0	2	4
1994-95	Peoria	IHL	53	27	18	45	83	....	....	....	....	....
	St. Louis	**NHL**	**27**	**3**	**10**	**13**	**29**	....	....	....	....	....
1995-96	**St. Louis**	**NHL**	**23**	**3**	**0**	**3**	**12**	....	....	....	....	....
	Worcester	AHL	30	13	13	26	69	....	....	....	....	....
	Los Angeles	**NHL**	**15**	**1**	**1**	**2**	**37**	....	....	....	....	....
1996-97	Phoenix	IHL	9	0	3	3	13	....	....	....	....	....
	Detroit	IHL	66	24	23	47	70	11	0	1	1	8
1997-98	Rochester	AHL	41	13	13	26	68	....	....	....	....	....
	Detroit	IHL	28	10	9	19	24	15	3	7	10	14
	NHL Totals		**65**	**7**	**11**	**18**	**78**	....	....	....	....	....

Traded to **LA Kings** by **St. Louis** with Craig Johnson, Roman Vopat, St. Louis' 5th round choice (Peter Hogan) in 1996 Entry Draft and 1st round choice (Matt Zultek) in 1997 Entry Draft for Wayne Gretzky, February 27, 1996. Signed as a free agent by **Buffalo**, September 9, 1997.

TARDIF, STEVE (tahr-DIHF) CHI.

Center. Shoots left. 5'11", 178 lbs. Born, St-Agnes, Que., March 29, 1977.
(Chicago's 8th choice, 175th overall, in 1995 Entry Draft).

			Regular Season					Playoffs				
Season	Club	Lea	GP	G	A	TP	PIM	GP	G	A	TP	PIM
1993-94	Drummondville	QMJHL	71	5	16	21	117	10	0	1	1	19
1994-95	Drummondville	QMJHL	64	10	33	43	313	4	1	2	3	9
1995-96	Drummondville	QMJHL	54	17	33	50	291	6	2	3	5	58
1996-97	Drummondville	QMJHL	65	24	40	64	377	6	1	5	6	62
1997-98	Jacksonville	ECHL	15	4	3	7	48	....	....	....	....	....
	Indianapolis	IHL	42	3	4	7	113	....	....	....	....	....

TARNSTROM, DICK (TAHRN-struhm) NYI

Defense. Shoots left. 6', 180 lbs. Born, Sundbyberg, Sweden, January 20, 1975.
(NY Islanders' 12th choice, 272nd overall, in 1994 Entry Draft).

			Regular Season					Playoffs				
Season	Club	Lea	GP	G	A	TP	PIM	GP	G	A	TP	PIM
1992-93	AIK Solna	Sweden	3	0	0	0	0	....	....	....	....	....
1993-94	AIK Solna	Sweden	33	1	4	5	....	....	....	....	....	....
1994-95	AIK Solna	Sweden	37	8	4	12	26	....	....	....	....	....
1995-96	AIK Solna	Sweden	40	0	5	5	32	....	....	....	....	....
1996-97	AIK Solna	Sweden	49	5	3	8	38	7	0	1	1	6
1997-98	AIK Solna	Sweden	45	2	12	14	30	....	....	....	....	....

TARVAINEN, JUSSI (tahr-VIGH-nehn) EDM.

Center. Shoots right. 6'2", 185 lbs. Born, Lahti, Finland, May 31, 1976.
(Edmonton's 7th choice, 95th overall, in 1994 Entry Draft).

			Regular Season					Playoffs				
Season	Club	Lea	GP	G	A	TP	PIM	GP	G	A	TP	PIM
1993-94	KalPa	Finland	42	3	4	7	20	....	....	....	....	....
1994-95	KalPa	Finland	45	10	7	17	34	3	0	0	0	2
1995-96	KalPa	Finland	47	8	11	19	50	....	....	....	....	....
1996-97	KalPa	Finland	49	14	26	40	62	....	....	....	....	....
1997-98	JyP HT	Finland	43	12	26	38	59	....	....	....	....	....

TAYLOR, ANDREW

Left wing. Shoots left. 6'1", 182 lbs. Born, Stratford, Ont., January 17, 1977.
(NY Islanders' 5th choice, 158th overall, in 1995 Entry Draft).

			Regular Season					Playoffs				
Season	Club	Lea	GP	G	A	TP	PIM	GP	G	A	TP	PIM
1993-94	Kitchener	OHL	62	1	8	9	60	5	0	1	1	6
1994-95	Kitchener	OHL	42	4	5	9	65	....	....	....	....	....
	Detroit	OHL	18	2	2	4	11	9	0	0	0	7
1995-96	Detroit	OHL	63	14	24	38	82	17	2	5	7	13
1996-97	Detroit	OHL	66	32	39	71	106	5	3	0	3	8
1997-98	Plymouth	OHL	61	33	38	71	124	15	7	9	16	25

TAYLOR, CHRIS BOS.

Center. Shoots left. 6', 189 lbs. Born, Stratford, Ont., March 6, 1972.
(NY Islanders' 2nd choice, 27th overall, in 1990 Entry Draft).

			Regular Season					Playoffs				
Season	Club	Lea	GP	G	A	TP	PIM	GP	G	A	TP	PIM
1988-89	London	OHL	62	7	16	23	52	15	0	2	2	15
1989-90	London	OHL	66	45	60	105	60	6	3	2	5	6
1990-91	London	OHL	65	50	78	128	50	7	4	8	12	6
1991-92	London	OHL	66	48	74	122	57	10	8	16	24	9
1992-93	Capital District	AHL	77	19	43	62	32	4	0	1	1	2
1993-94	Salt Lake	IHL	79	21	20	41	38	....	....	....	....	....
1994-95	Denver	IHL	78	38	48	86	47	14	7	6	13	10
	NY Islanders	**NHL**	**10**	**0**	**3**	**3**	**2**	....	....	....	....	....
1995-96	**NY Islanders**	**NHL**	**11**	**0**	**1**	**1**	**2**	....	....	....	....	....
	Utah	IHL	50	18	23	41	60	22	5	11	16	26
1996-97	**NY Islanders**	**NHL**	**1**	**0**	**0**	**0**	**0**	....	....	....	....	....
	Utah	IHL	71	27	40	67	24	7	1	2	3	0
1997-98	Utah	IHL	79	28	56	84	66	4	0	2	2	6
	NHL Totals		**22**	**0**	**4**	**4**	**4**	....	....	....	....	....

Signed as a free agent by **LA Kings**, July 25, 1997. Signed as a free agent by **Boston**, August 5, 1998.

TAYLOR, TIM — BOS.

Center. Shoots left. 6'1", 185 lbs. Born, Stratford, Ont., February 6, 1969.
(Washington's 2nd choice, 36th overall, in 1988 Entry Draft).

			Regular Season					Playoffs				
Season	Club	Lea	GP	G	A	TP	PIM	GP	G	A	TP	PIM
1986-87	London	OHL	34	7	9	16	11	....	....	....	....	....
1987-88	London	OHL	64	46	50	96	66	12	9	9	18	26
1988-89	London	OHL	61	34	80	114	93	21	*21	25	*46	58
1989-90	Baltimore	AHL	79	31	36	67	124	9	2	2	4	13
1990-91	Baltimore	AHL	79	25	42	67	75	5	0	1	1	4
1991-92	Baltimore	AHL	65	9	18	27	131	....	....	....	....	....
1992-93	Baltimore	AHL	41	15	16	31	49	....	....	....	....	....
	Hamilton	AHL	36	15	22	37	37	....	....	....	....	....
1993-94	**Detroit**	**NHL**	**1**	**1**	**0**	**1**	**0**	....	....	....	....	....
	Adirondack	AHL	79	36	*81	*117	86	12	2	10	12	12
1994-95	**Detroit**	**NHL**	**22**	**0**	**4**	**4**	**16**	**6**	**0**	**1**	**1**	**12**
1995-96	**Detroit**	**NHL**	**72**	**11**	**14**	**25**	**39**	**18**	**0**	**4**	**4**	**4**
1996-97	**Detroit**	**NHL**	**44**	**3**	**4**	**7**	**52**	**2**	**0**	**0**	**0**	**0** ♦
1997-98	**Boston**	**NHL**	**79**	**20**	**11**	**31**	**57**	**6**	**0**	**0**	**0**	**10**
	NHL Totals		**218**	**35**	**33**	**68**	**164**	**32**	**0**	**5**	**5**	**26**

AHL First All-Star Team (1994) • Won John B. Sollenberger Trophy (Top Scorer - AHL) (1994)

Traded to **Vancouver** by **Washington** for Eric Murano, January 29, 1993. Signed as a free agent by **Detroit**, July 28, 1993. Claimed by **Boston** from **Detroit** in NHL Waiver Draft, September 28, 1998.

TERTYSHNY, DIMITRI — (tuhr-TIHSH-nee) PHI.

Defense. Shoots left. 6'1", 176 lbs. Born, Chelyabinsk, USSR, December 26, 1976.
(Philadelphia's 4th choice, 132nd overall, in 1995 Entry Draft).

			Regular Season					Playoffs				
Season	Club	Lea	GP	G	A	TP	PIM	GP	G	A	TP	PIM
1994-95	Chelyabinsk	CIS	38	0	3	3	14	1	0	0	0	0
1995-96	Chelyabinsk	CIS	44	1	5	6	50	....	....	....	....	....
1996-97	Chelyabinsk	Russia	40	2	5	7	32	2	0	0	0	2
1997-98	Chelyabinsk	Russia	46	3	7	10	18	....	....	....	....	....

TETARENKO, JOEY — (teh-tar-EHN-koh) FLA.

Defense. Shoots right. 6'1", 215 lbs. Born, Prince Albert, Sask., March 3, 1978.
(Florida's 4th choice, 82nd overall, in 1996 Entry Draft).

			Regular Season					Playoffs				
Season	Club	Lea	GP	G	A	TP	PIM	GP	G	A	TP	PIM
1994-95	Portland	WHL	59	0	1	1	134	9	0	0	0	8
1995-96	Portland	WHL	71	4	11	15	190	7	0	1	1	17
1996-97	Portland	WHL	68	8	18	26	182	2	0	0	0	2
1997-98	Portland	WHL	49	2	12	14	148	16	0	2	2	30

TETRAULT, DANIEL — (teh-TROH) MTL.

Defense. Shoots right. 6', 198 lbs. Born, St. Boniface, Man., September 4, 1979.
(Montreal's 4th choice, 91st overall, in 1997 Entry Draft).

			Regular Season					Playoffs				
Season	Club	Lea	GP	G	A	TP	PIM	GP	G	A	TP	PIM
1995-96	Brandon	WHL	72	6	13	19	91	19	1	1	2	25
1996-97	Brandon	WHL	64	5	24	29	136	6	0	0	0	14
1997-98	Brandon	WHL	16	2	3	5	32	18	0	5	5	25

TEZIKOV, ALEXEI — (TEH-zih-kahf) BUF.

Defense. Shoots left. 6'1", 198 lbs. Born, Togliatti, USSR, June 22, 1978.
(Buffalo's 7th choice, 115th overall, in 1996 Entry Draft).

			Regular Season					Playoffs				
Season	Club	Lea	GP	G	A	TP	PIM	GP	G	A	TP	PIM
1995-96	Lada	CIS	14	0	0	0	8	....	....	....	....	....
1996-97	Lada	Russia	7	0	0	0	4	....	....	....	....	....
	Torpedo Nizhny	Russia	5	0	2	2	2	....	....	....	....	....
1997-98	Moncton	QMJHL	60	15	33	48	144	10	3	8	11	20

QMJHL Second All-Star Team (1998)

THEORET, LUC — (THEE-ohr-eht) BUF.

Defense. Shoots left. 6'1", 197 lbs. Born, Winnipeg, Man., July 30, 1979.
(Buffalo's 5th choice, 101st overall, in 1997 Entry Draft).

			Regular Season					Playoffs				
Season	Club	Lea	GP	G	A	TP	PIM	GP	G	A	TP	PIM
1995-96	Lethbridge	WHL	47	4	13	17	41	4	0	0	0	6
1996-97	Lethbridge	WHL	43	3	7	10	51	19	1	5	6	8
1997-98	Lethbridge	WHL	65	12	37	49	98	4	0	1	1	8

THERIAULT, JOEL — (TEH-ree-oh) WSH.

Defense. Shoots right. 6'3", 201 lbs. Born, Montreal, Que., October 30, 1976.
(Washington's 5th choice, 95th overall, in 1995 Entry Draft).

			Regular Season					Playoffs				
Season	Club	Lea	GP	G	A	TP	PIM	GP	G	A	TP	PIM
1993-94	St-Jean	QMJHL	57	3	0	3	63	5	0	1	1	0
1994-95	St-Jean	QMJHL	18	2	7	9	94	....	....	....	....	....
	Beauport	QMJHL	51	2	5	7	293	18	3	6	9	*162
1995-96	Halifax	QMJHL	39	5	15	20	*358	....	....	....	....	....
	Drummondville	QMJHL	24	1	5	6	*215	6	0	2	2	45
1996-97	Hampton Roads	ECHL	50	2	4	6	206	6	0	0	0	10
1997-98	Portland	AHL	15	0	2	2	89	....	....	....	....	....
	Hampton Roads	ECHL	32	2	4	6	161	....	....	....	....	....
	Mobile	ECHL	10	1	1	2	43	2	2	1	3	18

THERIEN, CHRIS — (TEH-ree-ehn) PHI.

Defense. Shoots left. 6'5", 230 lbs. Born, Ottawa, Ont., December 14, 1971.
(Philadelphia's 7th choice, 47th overall, in 1990 Entry Draft).

			Regular Season					Playoffs				
Season	Club	Lea	GP	G	A	TP	PIM	GP	G	A	TP	PIM
1989-90	Northwood Prep	H.S.	31	35	37	72	54	....	....	....	....	....
1990-91	Providence	H.E.	36	4	18	22	36	....	....	....	....	....
1991-92	Providence	H.E.	36	16	25	41	38	....	....	....	....	....
1992-93	Providence	H.E.	33	8	11	19	52	....	....	....	....	....
	Canada	Nat-Tm	8	1	4	5	8	....	....	....	....	....
1993-94	Canada	Nat-Tm	59	7	15	22	46	....	....	....	....	....
	Canada	Olympics	4	0	0	0	4	....	....	....	....	....
	Hershey	AHL	6	0	0	0	2	....	....	....	....	....
1994-95	Hershey	AHL	34	3	13	16	27	....	....	....	....	....
	Philadelphia	**NHL**	**48**	**3**	**10**	**13**	**38**	**15**	**0**	**0**	**0**	**10**
1995-96	**Philadelphia**	**NHL**	**82**	**6**	**17**	**23**	**89**	**12**	**0**	**0**	**0**	**18**
1996-97	**Philadelphia**	**NHL**	**71**	**2**	**22**	**24**	**64**	**19**	**1**	**6**	**7**	**6**
1997-98	**Philadelphia**	**NHL**	**78**	**3**	**16**	**19**	**80**	**5**	**0**	**1**	**1**	**4**
	NHL Totals		**279**	**14**	**65**	**79**	**271**	**51**	**1**	**7**	**8**	**38**

Hockey East Second All-Star Team (1993) • NHL/Upper Deck All-Rookie Team (1995)

THIBEAULT, DAVID — (TEE-boh)

Left wing. Shoots left. 6'1", 190 lbs. Born, Trois-Rivieres, Que., May 12, 1978.
(San Jose's 8th choice, 217th overall, in 1996 Entry Draft).

			Regular Season					Playoffs				
Season	Club	Lea	GP	G	A	TP	PIM	GP	G	A	TP	PIM
1994-95	Drummondville	QMJHL	61	10	19	29	101	4	0	0	0	0
1995-96	Drummondville	QMJHL	57	23	35	58	99	6	0	3	3	12
1996-97	Victoriaville	QMJHL	58	39	38	77	37	6	3	3	6	4
	Kentucky	AHL	1	0	0	0	0	....	....	....	....	....
1997-98	Victoriaville	QMJHL	70	46	56	102	95	6	3	4	7	6

THOMAS, STEVE — TOR.

Left wing. Shoots left. 5'11", 190 lbs. Born, Stockport, England, July 15, 1963.

			Regular Season					Playoffs				
Season	Club	Lea	GP	G	A	TP	PIM	GP	G	A	TP	PIM
1981-82	Markham	MTHL	48	68	57	125	113	....	....	....	....	....
1982-83	Toronto	OHL	61	18	20	38	42	....	....	....	....	....
1983-84	Toronto	OHL	70	51	54	105	77	....	....	....	....	....
1984-85	St. Catharines	AHL	64	42	48	90	56	....	....	....	....	....
	Toronto	**NHL**	**18**	**1**	**1**	**2**	**2**	....	....	....	....	....
1985-86	**Toronto**	**NHL**	**65**	**20**	**37**	**57**	**36**	**10**	**6**	**8**	**14**	**9**
	St. Catharines	AHL	19	18	14	32	35	....	....	....	....	....
1986-87	**Toronto**	**NHL**	**78**	**35**	**27**	**62**	**114**	**13**	**2**	**3**	**5**	**13**
1987-88	**Chicago**	**NHL**	**30**	**13**	**13**	**26**	**40**	**3**	**1**	**2**	**3**	**6**
1988-89	**Chicago**	**NHL**	**45**	**21**	**19**	**40**	**69**	**12**	**3**	**5**	**8**	**10**
1989-90	**Chicago**	**NHL**	**76**	**40**	**30**	**70**	**91**	**20**	**7**	**6**	**13**	**33**
1990-91	**Chicago**	**NHL**	**69**	**19**	**35**	**54**	**129**	**6**	**1**	**2**	**3**	**15**
1991-92	**Chicago**	**NHL**	**11**	**2**	**6**	**8**	**26**	....	....	....	....	....
	NY Islanders	**NHL**	**71**	**28**	**42**	**70**	**71**	....	....	....	....	....
1992-93	**NY Islanders**	**NHL**	**79**	**37**	**50**	**87**	**111**	**18**	**9**	**8**	**17**	**37**
1993-94	**NY Islanders**	**NHL**	**78**	**42**	**33**	**75**	**139**	**4**	**1**	**0**	**1**	**8**
1994-95	**NY Islanders**	**NHL**	**47**	**11**	**15**	**26**	**60**	....	....	....	....	....
1995-96	**New Jersey**	**NHL**	**81**	**26**	**35**	**61**	**98**	....	....	....	....	....
1996-97	**New Jersey**	**NHL**	**57**	**15**	**19**	**34**	**46**	**10**	**1**	**1**	**2**	**18**
1997-98	**New Jersey**	**NHL**	**55**	**14**	**10**	**24**	**32**	**6**	**0**	**3**	**3**	**2**
	NHL Totals		**860**	**324**	**372**	**696**	**1064**	**102**	**31**	**38**	**69**	**151**

Won Dudley "Red" Garrett Memorial Trophy (Top Rookie - AHL) (1985) • AHL First All-Star Team (1985)

Signed as a free agent by **Toronto,** May 12, 1984. Traded to **Chicago** by **Toronto** with Rick Vaive and Bob McGill for Al Secord and Ed Olczyk, September 3, 1987. Traded to **NY Islanders** by **Chicago** with Adam Creighton for Brent Sutter and Brad Lauer, October 25, 1991. Traded to **New Jersey** by **NY Islanders** for Claude Lemieux, October 3, 1995. Signed as a free agent by **Toronto**, July 30, 1998.

THOMPSON, BRENT — NYR

Defense. Shoots left. 6'2", 200 lbs. Born, Calgary, Alta., January 9, 1971.
(Los Angeles' 1st choice, 39th overall, in 1989 Entry Draft).

			Regular Season					Playoffs				
Season	Club	Lea	GP	G	A	TP	PIM	GP	G	A	TP	PIM
1988-89	Medicine Hat	WHL	72	3	10	13	160	3	0	0	0	2
1989-90	Medicine Hat	WHL	68	10	35	45	167	3	0	1	1	14
1990-91	Medicine Hat	WHL	51	5	40	45	87	12	1	7	8	16
	Phoenix	IHL	....	....	....	....	....	4	0	1	1	6
1991-92	**Los Angeles**	**NHL**	**27**	**0**	**5**	**5**	**89**	**4**	**0**	**0**	**0**	**4**
	Phoenix	IHL	42	4	13	17	139	....	....	....	....	....
1992-93	**Los Angeles**	**NHL**	**30**	**0**	**4**	**4**	**76**	....	....	....	....	....
	Phoenix	IHL	22	0	5	5	112	....	....	....	....	....
1993-94	**Los Angeles**	**NHL**	**24**	**1**	**0**	**1**	**81**	....	....	....	....	....
	Phoenix	IHL	26	1	11	12	118	....	....	....	....	....
1994-95	**Winnipeg**	**NHL**	**29**	**0**	**0**	**0**	**78**	....	....	....	....	....
1995-96	**Winnipeg**	**NHL**	**10**	**0**	**1**	**1**	**21**	....	....	....	....	....
	Springfield	AHL	58	2	10	12	203	10	1	4	5	*55
1996-97	**Phoenix**	**NHL**	**1**	**0**	**0**	**0**	**7**	....	....	....	....	....
	Springfield	AHL	64	2	15	17	215	17	0	2	2	31
	Phoenix	IHL	12	0	1	1	67	....	....	....	....	....
1997-98	Hartford	AHL	77	4	15	19	308	15	0	4	4	25
	NHL Totals		**121**	**1**	**10**	**11**	**352**	**4**	**0**	**0**	**0**	**4**

WHL East Second All-Star Team (1991)

Traded to **Winnipeg** by **LA Kings** with future considerations for the rights to Ruslan Batyrshin and Winnipeg's 2nd round choice (Marian Cisar) in 1996 Entry Draft, August 8, 1994. Transferred to **Phoenix** after **Winnipeg** franchise relocated, July 1, 1996. Signed as a free agent by **NY Rangers**, August 26, 1997.

THOMPSON, CHRIS — N.J.

Right wing. Shoots left. 6', 180 lbs. Born, Prince Albert, Sask., April 10, 1978.

			Regular Season					Playoffs				
Season	Club	Lea	GP	G	A	TP	PIM	GP	G	A	TP	PIM
1995-96	Seattle	WHL	56	8	5	13	86	5	0	0	0	21
1996-97	Seattle	WHL	65	3	14	17	191	15	1	1	2	67
1997-98	Seattle	WHL	70	16	32	48	339	5	0	0	0	18

Signed as a free agent by **New Jersey**, July 23, 1998.

THOMPSON, MARK — T.B.

Defense. Shoots right. 6'6", 205 lbs. Born, St. Albert, Alta., April 26, 1979.
(Tampa Bay's 4th choice, 108th overall, in 1997 Entry Draft).

			Regular Season					Playoffs				
Season	Club	Lea	GP	G	A	TP	PIM	GP	G	A	TP	PIM
1996-97	Regina	WHL	32	1	5	6	20	3	0	1	1	2
1997-98	Regina	WHL	46	0	2	2	44	2	0	0	0	0

THOMPSON, ROCKY — CGY.

Defense. Shoots right. 6'2", 205 lbs. Born, Calgary, Alta., August 8, 1977.
(Calgary's 3rd choice, 72nd overall, in 1995 Entry Draft).

			Regular Season					Playoffs				
Season	Club	Lea	GP	G	A	TP	PIM	GP	G	A	TP	PIM
1993-94	Medicine Hat	WHL	68	1	4	5	166	3	0	0	0	2
1994-95	Medicine Hat	WHL	63	1	6	7	220	5	0	0	0	17
1995-96	Medicine Hat	WHL	71	9	20	29	260	5	2	3	5	26
	Saint John	AHL	4	0	0	0	33	....	....	....	....	....
1996-97	Medicine Hat	WHL	47	6	9	15	170	....	....	....	....	....
	Swift Current	WHL	22	3	5	8	90	10	1	2	3	22
1997-98	**Calgary**	**NHL**	**12**	**0**	**0**	**0**	**61**	....	....	....	....	....
	Saint John	AHL	51	3	0	3	187	18	1	1	2	47
	NHL Totals		**12**	**0**	**0**	**0**	**61**	....	....	....	....	....

THORNTON, JOE — BOS.

Center. Shoots left. 6'4", 225 lbs. Born, London, Ont., July 2, 1979.
(Boston's 1st choice, 1st overall, in 1997 Entry Draft).

			Regular Season					Playoffs				
Season	Club	Lea	GP	G	A	TP	PIM	GP	G	A	TP	PIM
1995-96	S.S. Marie	OHL	66	30	46	76	53	4	1	1	2	11
1996-97	S.S. Marie	OHL	59	41	81	122	123	11	11	8	19	24
1997-98	**Boston**	**NHL**	**55**	**3**	**4**	**7**	**19**	**6**	**0**	**0**	**0**	**9**
	NHL Totals		**55**	**3**	**4**	**7**	**19**	**6**	**0**	**0**	**0**	**9**

Canadian Major Junior Rookie of the Year (1996) • OHL Second All-Star Team (1997)

THORNTON, SCOTT — MTL.

Center. Shoots left. 6'3", 219 lbs. Born, London, Ont., January 9, 1971.
(Toronto's 1st choice, 3rd overall, in 1989 Entry Draft).

			Regular Season					Playoffs				
Season	Club	Lea	GP	G	A	TP	PIM	GP	G	A	TP	PIM
1987-88	Belleville	OHL	62	11	19	30	54	6	0	1	1	2
1988-89	Belleville	OHL	59	28	34	62	103	5	1	1	2	6
1989-90	Belleville	OHL	47	21	28	49	91	11	2	10	12	15
1990-91	Belleville	OHL	3	2	1	3	2	6	0	7	7	14
	Toronto	**NHL**	**33**	**1**	**3**	**4**	**30**	....	....	....	....	....
	Newmarket	AHL	5	1	0	1	4	....	....	....	....	....
1991-92	**Edmonton**	**NHL**	**15**	**0**	**1**	**1**	**43**	**1**	**0**	**0**	**0**	**0**
	Cape Breton	AHL	49	9	14	23	40	5	1	0	1	8
1992-93	**Edmonton**	**NHL**	**9**	**0**	**1**	**1**	**0**	....	....	....	....	....
	Cape Breton	AHL	58	23	27	50	102	16	1	2	3	35
1993-94	**Edmonton**	**NHL**	**61**	**4**	**7**	**11**	**104**	....	....	....	....	....
	Cape Breton	AHL	2	1	1	2	31	....	....	....	....	....
1994-95	**Edmonton**	**NHL**	**47**	**10**	**12**	**22**	**89**	....	....	....	....	....
1995-96	**Edmonton**	**NHL**	**77**	**9**	**9**	**18**	**149**	....	....	....	....	....
1996-97	**Montreal**	**NHL**	**73**	**10**	**10**	**20**	**128**	**5**	**1**	**0**	**1**	**2**
1997-98	**Montreal**	**NHL**	**67**	**6**	**9**	**15**	**158**	**9**	**0**	**2**	**2**	**10**
	NHL Totals		**382**	**40**	**52**	**92**	**701**	**15**	**1**	**2**	**3**	**12**

Traded to **Edmonton** by **Toronto** with Vincent Damphousse, Peter Ing, Luke Richardson, future considerations and cash for Grant Fuhr, Glenn Anderson and Craig Berube, September 19, 1991. Traded to **Montreal** by **Edmonton** for Andrei Kovalenko, September 6, 1996.

THORNTON, SHAWN — TOR.

Right wing. Shoots right. 6'1", 196 lbs. Born, Oshawa, Ont., July 23, 1979.
(Toronto's 6th choice, 190th overall, in 1997 Entry Draft).

			Regular Season					Playoffs				
Season	Club	Lea	GP	G	A	TP	PIM	GP	G	A	TP	PIM
1995-96	Peterborough	OHL	63	4	10	14	192	24	3	0	3	25
1996-97	Peterborough	OHL	61	19	10	29	204	11	2	4	6	20
1997-98	St. John's	AHL	59	0	3	3	225	....	....	....	....	....

THURESSON, MARCUS (TOO-reh-suhn) — S.J.

Center. Shoots left. 6'1", 180 lbs. Born, Jonkoping, Sweden, May 31, 1971.
(NY Islanders' 11th choice, 224th overall, in 1991 Entry Draft).

			Regular Season					Playoffs				
Season	Club	Lea	GP	G	A	TP	PIM	GP	G	A	TP	PIM
1989-90	Leksand IF	Sweden	28	8	7	15	18	3	2	0	2	12
1990-91	Leksand IF	Sweden	22	3	2	5	20	....	....	....	....	....
1991-92	Leksand IF	Sweden	21	2	4	6	22	....	....	....	....	....
1992-93	Leksand IF	Sweden	31	6	10	16	22	2	2	0	2	2
1993-94	Leksand IF	Sweden	32	3	4	7	28	4	0	1	1	0
1994-95	Leksand IF	Sweden	39	3	10	13	42	4	1	0	1	0
1995-96	HV 71 Jonkoping	Sweden	32	7	6	13	28	....	....	....	....	....
1996-97	TPS Turku	Finland	44	14	25	39	44	12	1	1	2	8
1997-98	Malmo IF	Sweden	44	9	23	32	24	....	....	....	....	....

Rights traded to **San Jose** by **NY Islanders** for Brian Mullen, August 24, 1992.

TIKKANEN, ESA (TEE-kuh-nehn, EHZ-uh)

Left wing. Shoots left. 6'1", 190 lbs. Born, Helsinki, Finland, January 25, 1965.
(Edmonton's 4th choice, 82nd overall, in 1983 Entry Draft).

			Regular Season					Playoffs				
Season	Club	Lea	GP	G	A	TP	PIM	GP	G	A	TP	PIM
1981-82	Regina	SJHL	59	38	37	75	216	....	....	....	....	....
	Regina	WHL	2	0	0	0	0	....	....	....	....	....
1982-83	Helsinki	Fin-Jr.	30	34	31	65	104	4	4	3	7	10
	Helsinki	Finland	....	....	....	....	....	1	0	0	0	2
1983-84	Helsinki	Fin-Jr.	6	5	9	14	13	4	4	3	7	8
	Helsinki	Finland	36	19	11	30	30	2	0	0	0	0
1984-85	Helsinki	Finland	36	21	33	54	42	....	....	....	....	....
	Edmonton	**NHL**	....	....	....	....	....	**3**	**0**	**0**	**0**	**2 ♦**
1985-86	**Edmonton**	**NHL**	**35**	**7**	**6**	**13**	**28**	**8**	**3**	**2**	**5**	**7**
	Nova Scotia	AHL	15	4	8	12	17	....	....	....	....	....
1986-87	**Edmonton**	**NHL**	**76**	**34**	**44**	**78**	**120**	**21**	**7**	**2**	**9**	**22 ♦**
1987-88	**Edmonton**	**NHL**	**80**	**23**	**51**	**74**	**153**	**19**	**10**	**17**	**27**	**72 ♦**
1988-89	**Edmonton**	**NHL**	**67**	**31**	**47**	**78**	**92**	**7**	**1**	**3**	**4**	**12**
1989-90	**Edmonton**	**NHL**	**79**	**30**	**33**	**63**	**161**	**22**	**13**	**11**	**24**	**26 ♦**
1990-91	**Edmonton**	**NHL**	**79**	**27**	**42**	**69**	**85**	**18**	**12**	**8**	**20**	**24**
1991-92	**Edmonton**	**NHL**	**40**	**12**	**16**	**28**	**44**	**16**	**5**	**3**	**8**	**8**
1992-93	**Edmonton**	**NHL**	**66**	**14**	**19**	**33**	**76**	....	....	....	....	....
	NY Rangers	**NHL**	**15**	**2**	**5**	**7**	**18**	....	....	....	....	....
1993-94	**NY Rangers**	**NHL**	**83**	**22**	**32**	**54**	**114**	**23**	**4**	**4**	**8**	**34 ♦**
1994-95	Helsinki	Finland	19	2	11	13	16	....	....	....	....	....
	St. Louis	**NHL**	**43**	**12**	**23**	**35**	**22**	**7**	**2**	**2**	**4**	**20**
1995-96	**St. Louis**	**NHL**	**11**	**1**	**4**	**5**	**18**	....	....	....	....	....
	New Jersey	**NHL**	**9**	**0**	**2**	**2**	**4**	....	....	....	....	....
	Vancouver	**NHL**	**38**	**13**	**24**	**37**	**14**	**6**	**3**	**2**	**5**	**2**
1996-97	**Vancouver**	**NHL**	**62**	**12**	**15**	**27**	**66**	....	....	....	....	....
	NY Rangers	**NHL**	**14**	**1**	**2**	**3**	**6**	**15**	**9**	**3**	**12**	**26**
1997-98	**Florida**	**NHL**	**28**	**1**	**8**	**9**	**16**	....	....	....	....	....
	Finland	Olympics	6	1	1	2	0	....	....	....	....	....
	Washington	**NHL**	**20**	**2**	**10**	**12**	**2**	**21**	**3**	**3**	**6**	**20**
	NHL Totals		**845**	**244**	**383**	**627**	**1039**	**186**	**72**	**60**	**132**	**275**

Traded to **NY Rangers** by **Edmonton** for Doug Weight, March 17, 1993. Traded to **St. Louis** by **NY Rangers** with Doug Lidster for Petr Nedved, July 24, 1994. Traded to **New Jersey** by **St. Louis** for New Jersey's 3rd round choice (later traded to Colorado — Colorado selected Ville Nielnen) in 1997 Entry Draft, November 1, 1995. Traded to **Vancouver** by **New Jersey** for Vancouver's 2nd round choice (Wesley Mason) in 1996 Entry Draft, November 23, 1995. Traded to **NY Rangers** by **Vancouver** with Russ Courtnall for Sergei Nemchinov and Brian Noonan, March 8, 1997. Signed as a free agent by **Florida**, September 17, 1997. Traded to **Washington** by **Florida** for Dwayne Hay and future considerations, March 9, 1998.

TILEY, BRAD — PHX.

Defense. Shoots left. 6'1", 185 lbs. Born, Markdale, Ont., July 5, 1971.
(Boston's 4th choice, 84th overall, in 1991 Entry Draft).

			Regular Season					Playoffs				
Season	Club	Lea	GP	G	A	TP	PIM	GP	G	A	TP	PIM
1988-89	S.S. Marie	OHL	50	4	11	15	31	....	....	....	....	....
1989-90	S.S. Marie	OHL	66	9	32	41	47	....	....	....	....	....
1990-91	S.S. Marie	OHL	66	11	55	66	29	14	4	15	19	12
1991-92	Maine	AHL	62	7	22	29	36	....	....	....	....	....
1992-93	Phoenix	IHL	46	11	27	38	35	....	....	....	....	....
	Binghamton	AHL	26	6	10	16	19	8	0	1	1	2
1993-94	Binghamton	AHL	29	6	10	16	6	....	....	....	....	....
	Phoenix	IHL	35	8	15	23	21	....	....	....	....	....
1994-95	Detroit	IHL	56	7	19	26	32	....	....	....	....	....
	Fort Wayne	IHL	14	1	6	7	2	3	1	2	3	0
1995-96	Orlando	IHL	69	11	23	34	82	23	2	4	6	16
1996-97	Phoenix	IHL	66	8	28	36	34	....	....	....	....	....
	Long Beach	IHL	3	1	0	1	2	....	....	....	....	....
1997-98	**Phoenix**	**NHL**	**1**	**0**	**0**	**0**	**0**	....	....	....	....	....
	Springfield	AHL	60	10	31	41	36	4	0	4	4	2
	NHL Totals		**1**	**0**	**0**	**0**	**0**	....	....	....	....	....

Memorial Cup All-Star Team (1991)

Signed as a free agent by **NY Rangers**, September 4, 1992. Traded to **LA Kings** by **NY Rangers** for LA Kings' 11th round choice (Jamie Butt) in 1994 Entry Draft, January 28, 1994. Signed as a free agent by **Phoenix**, September 4, 1997.

TIMANDER, MATTIAS (tih-MAHN-duhr, MA-tee-uhs) — BOS.

Defense. Shoots left. 6'3", 210 lbs. Born, Solleftea, Sweden, April 16, 1974.
(Boston's 7th choice, 208th overall, in 1992 Entry Draft).

			Regular Season					Playoffs				
Season	Club	Lea	GP	G	A	TP	PIM	GP	G	A	TP	PIM
1992-93	MoDo	Sweden	1	0	0	0	0	....	....	....	....	....
1993-94	MoDo	Sweden	23	2	2	4	6	11	2	0	2	10
1994-95	MoDo	Sweden	39	8	9	17	24	....	....	....	....	....
1995-96	MoDo	Sweden	37	4	10	14	34	7	1	1	2	8
1996-97	**Boston**	**NHL**	**41**	**1**	**8**	**9**	**14**	....	....	....	....	....
	Providence	AHL	32	3	11	14	20	10	1	1	2	12
1997-98	**Boston**	**NHL**	**23**	**1**	**1**	**2**	**6**	....	....	....	....	....
	Providence	AHL	31	3	7	10	25	....	....	....	....	....
	NHL Totals		**64**	**2**	**9**	**11**	**20**	....	....	....	....	....

TIMKIN, ALEXEI (TIHM-kihn) — DAL.

Right wing. Shoots left. 6'2", 194 lbs. Born, Kirov, USSR, April 21, 1979.
(Dallas' 6th choice, 160th overall, in 1997 Entry Draft).

			Regular Season					Playoffs				
Season	Club	Lea	GP	G	A	TP	PIM	GP	G	A	TP	PIM
1996-97	Yaroslavl 2	Russia-3	47	16	6	22	54	....	....	....	....	....
	Yaroslavl	Russia	3	0	1	1	0	....	....	....	....	....
1997-98	Yaroslavl 2	Russia-2	16	4	5	9	14	....	....	....	....	....

TIMMONS, K.C. — COL.

Left wing. Shoots left. 6'2", 205 lbs. Born, Victoria, B.C., April 6, 1980.
(Colorado's 9th choice, 141st overall, in 1998 Entry Draft).

			Regular Season					Playoffs				
Season	Club	Lea	GP	G	A	TP	PIM	GP	G	A	TP	PIM
1996-97	Tri-City	WHL	52	0	5	5	27	....	....	....	....	....
1997-98	Tri-City	WHL	72	11	7	18	139	....	....	....	....	....

TIMONEN, KIMMO (TIH-moh-nehn) — NSH.

Defense. Shoots left. 5'9", 180 lbs. Born, Kuopio, Finland, March 18, 1975.
(Los Angeles' 11th choice, 250th overall, in 1993 Entry Draft).

			Regular Season					Playoffs				
Season	Club	Lea	GP	G	A	TP	PIM	GP	G	A	TP	PIM
1991-92	KalPa	Finland	5	0	0	0	0	....	....	....	....	....
1992-93	KalPa	Finland	33	0	2	2	4	....	....	....	....	....
1993-94	KalPa	Finland	46	6	7	13	55	....	....	....	....	....
1994-95	TPS Turku	Finland	45	3	4	7	10	13	0	1	1	6
1995-96	TPS Turku	Finland	48	3	21	24	22	9	1	2	3	12
1996-97	TPS Turku	Finland	50	10	14	24	18	12	2	7	9	8
1997-98	Helsinki	Finland	45	10	15	25	59	9	3	4	7	8
	Finland	Olympics	6	0	1	1	2	....	....	....	....	....

TINORDI, MARK (tih-NOHR-dee) — WSH.

Defense. Shoots left. 6'4", 213 lbs. Born, Red Deer, Alta., May 9, 1966.

			Regular Season					Playoffs				
Season	Club	Lea	GP	G	A	TP	PIM	GP	G	A	TP	PIM
1982-83	Lethbridge	WHL	64	0	4	4	50	20	1	1	2	6
1983-84	Lethbridge	WHL	72	5	14	19	53	5	0	1	1	7
1984-85	Lethbridge	WHL	58	10	15	25	134	4	0	2	2	12
1985-86	Lethbridge	WHL	58	8	30	38	139	8	1	3	4	15
1986-87	Calgary	WHL	61	29	37	66	148	....	....	....	....	....
	New Haven	AHL	2	0	0	0	2	2	0	0	0	0
1987-88	**NY Rangers**	**NHL**	**24**	**1**	**2**	**3**	**50**	....	....	....	....	....
	Colorado	IHL	41	8	19	27	150	11	1	5	6	31
1988-89	**Minnesota**	**NHL**	**47**	**2**	**3**	**5**	**107**	**5**	**0**	**0**	**0**	**0**
	Kalamazoo	IHL	10	0	0	0	35	....	....	....	....	....
1989-90	**Minnesota**	**NHL**	**66**	**3**	**7**	**10**	**240**	**7**	**0**	**1**	**1**	**16**
1990-91	**Minnesota**	**NHL**	**69**	**5**	**27**	**32**	**189**	**23**	**5**	**6**	**11**	**78**
1991-92	**Minnesota**	**NHL**	**63**	**4**	**24**	**28**	**179**	**7**	**1**	**2**	**3**	**11**
1992-93	**Minnesota**	**NHL**	**69**	**15**	**27**	**42**	**157**	....	....	....	....	....
1993-94	**Dallas**	**NHL**	**61**	**6**	**18**	**24**	**143**	....	....	....	....	....
1994-95	**Washington**	**NHL**	**42**	**3**	**9**	**12**	**71**	**1**	**0**	**0**	**0**	**2**
1995-96	**Washington**	**NHL**	**71**	**3**	**10**	**13**	**113**	**6**	**0**	**0**	**0**	**16**
1996-97	**Washington**	**NHL**	**56**	**2**	**6**	**8**	**118**	....	....	....	....	....
1997-98	**Washington**	**NHL**	**47**	**8**	**9**	**17**	**39**	**21**	**1**	**2**	**3**	**42**
	NHL Totals		**615**	**52**	**142**	**194**	**1406**	**70**	**7**	**11**	**18**	**165**

Played in NHL All-Star Game (1992)

Signed as a free agent by **NY Rangers**, January 4, 1987. Traded to **Minnesota** by **NY Rangers** with Paul Jerrard, the rights to Bret Barnett and Mike Sullivan, and LA Kings' 3rd round choice (previously acquired, Minnesota selected Murray Garbutt) in 1989 Entry Draft for Brian Lawton, Igor Liba and the rights to Eric Bennett, October 11, 1988. Transferred to **Dallas** after **Minnesota** franchise relocated, June 9, 1993. Traded to **Washington** by **Dallas** with Rich Mrozik for Kevin Hatcher, January 18, 1995.

TIPLER, CURTIS — T.B.

Right wing. Shoots right. 6'5", 205 lbs. Born, Wainwright, Alta., May 9, 1978.
(Tampa Bay's 2nd choice, 69th overall, in 1996 Entry Draft).

			Regular Season					Playoffs				
Season	Club	Lea	GP	G	A	TP	PIM	GP	G	A	TP	PIM
1995-96	Regina	WHL	69	27	38	65	65	11	3	1	4	4
1996-97	Regina	WHL	47	18	18	36	35	5	1	2	3	4
1997-98	Prince George	WHL	68	26	32	58	43	11	0	3	3	4

TITOV, GERMAN — (TEE-tahf, GUHR-mihn) PIT.

Center. Shoots left. 6'1", 190 lbs. Born, Moscow, USSR, October 16, 1965.
(Calgary's 10th choice, 252nd overall, in 1993 Entry Draft).

			Regular Season					Playoffs				
Season	Club	Lea	GP	G	A	TP	PIM	GP	G	A	TP	PIM
1986-87	Khimik	USSR	23	1	0	1	10	....	....	....	....	....
1987-88	Khimik	USSR	39	6	5	11	10	....	....	....	....	....
1988-89	Khimik	USSR	44	10	3	13	24	....	....	....	....	....
1989-90	Khimik	USSR	44	6	14	20	19	....	....	....	....	....
1990-91	Khimik	USSR	45	13	11	24	28	....	....	....	....	....
1991-92	Khimik	CIS	42	18	13	31	35	....	....	....	....	....
1992-93	TPS Turku	Finland	47	25	19	44	49	12	5	12	17	10
1993-94	**Calgary**	**NHL**	**76**	**27**	**18**	**45**	**28**	**7**	**2**	**1**	**3**	**4**
1994-95	TPS Turku	Finland	14	6	6	12	20	....	....	....	....	....
	Calgary	**NHL**	**40**	**12**	**12**	**24**	**16**	**7**	**5**	**3**	**8**	**10**
1995-96	**Calgary**	**NHL**	**82**	**28**	**39**	**67**	**24**	**4**	**0**	**2**	**2**	**0**
1996-97	**Calgary**	**NHL**	**79**	**22**	**30**	**52**	**36**	....	....	....	....	....
1997-98	**Calgary**	**NHL**	**68**	**18**	**22**	**40**	**38**	....	....	....	....	....
	Russia	Olympics	6	1	0	1	6	....	....	....	....	....
	NHL Totals		**345**	**107**	**121**	**228**	**142**	**18**	**7**	**6**	**13**	**14**

Traded to **Pittsburgh** by **Calgary** with Todd Hlushko for Ken Wregget and Dave Roche, June 17, 1998.

TJARNQVIST, DANIEL — (TUH-yahrn-kvihst) FLA.

Defense. Shoots left. 6'2", 178 lbs. Born, Umea, Sweden, October 14, 1976.
(Florida's 5th choice, 88th overall, in 1995 Entry Draft).

			Regular Season					Playoffs				
Season	Club	Lea	GP	G	A	TP	PIM	GP	G	A	TP	PIM
1994-95	Rogle	Sweden	18	0	1	1	2	....	....	....	....	....
	Rogle	Sweden-2	15	2	3	5	0	....	....	....	....	....
1995-96	Rogle	Sweden	22	1	7	8	6	....	....	....	....	....
1996-97	Jokerit	Finland	44	3	8	11	4	9	0	3	3	4
1997-98	Djurgarden	Sweden	40	5	9	14	12	15	1	1	2	2

TKACHUK, KEITH — (kuh-CHUK) PHX.

Left wing. Shoots left. 6'2", 220 lbs. Born, Melrose, MA, March 28, 1972.
(Winnipeg's 1st choice, 19th overall, in 1990 Entry Draft).

			Regular Season					Playoffs				
Season	Club	Lea	GP	G	A	TP	PIM	GP	G	A	TP	PIM
1989-90	Malden	H.S.	6	12	14	26	....	....	....	....	....	....
1990-91	Boston University	H.E.	36	17	23	40	70	....	....	....	....	....
1991-92	United States	Nat-Tm	45	10	10	20	141	....	....	....	....	....
	United States	Olympics	8	1	1	2	12	....	....	....	....	....
	Winnipeg	**NHL**	**17**	**3**	**5**	**8**	**28**	**7**	**3**	**0**	**3**	**30**
1992-93	**Winnipeg**	**NHL**	**83**	**28**	**23**	**51**	**201**	**6**	**4**	**0**	**4**	**14**
1993-94	**Winnipeg**	**NHL**	**84**	**41**	**40**	**81**	**255**	....	....	....	....	....
1994-95	**Winnipeg**	**NHL**	**48**	**22**	**29**	**51**	**152**	....	....	....	....	....
1995-96	**Winnipeg**	**NHL**	**76**	**50**	**48**	**98**	**156**	**6**	**1**	**2**	**3**	**22**
1996-97	**Phoenix**	**NHL**	**81**	***52**	**34**	**86**	**228**	**7**	**6**	**0**	**6**	**7**
1997-98	**Phoenix**	**NHL**	**69**	**40**	**26**	**66**	**147**	**6**	**3**	**3**	**6**	**10**
	United States	Olympics	4	0	2	2	6	....	....	....	....	....
	NHL Totals		**458**	**236**	**205**	**441**	**1167**	**32**	**17**	**5**	**22**	**83**

NHL Second All-Star Team (1995, 1998)

Played in NHL All-Star Game (1997, 1998)

Transferred to **Phoenix** after **Winnipeg** franchise relocated, July 1, 1996.

TKACZUK, DANIEL — (kuh-CHUK) CGY.

Center. Shoots left. 6', 190 lbs. Born, Toronto, Ont., June 10, 1979.
(Calgary's 1st choice, 6th overall, in 1997 Entry Draft).

			Regular Season					Playoffs				
Season	Club	Lea	GP	G	A	TP	PIM	GP	G	A	TP	PIM
1995-96	Barrie	OHL	61	22	39	61	38	7	1	2	3	8
1996-97	Barrie	OHL	62	45	48	93	49	9	7	2	9	2
1997-98	Barrie	OHL	57	35	40	75	38	6	2	3	5	8

TOCCHET, RICK — (TAH-keht) PHX.

Right wing. Shoots right. 6', 214 lbs. Born, Scarborough, Ont., April 9, 1964.
(Philadelphia's 5th choice, 125th overall, in 1983 Entry Draft).

			Regular Season					Playoffs				
Season	Club	Lea	GP	G	A	TP	PIM	GP	G	A	TP	PIM
1981-82	S.S. Marie	OHL	59	7	15	22	184	11	1	1	2	28
1982-83	S.S. Marie	OHL	66	32	34	66	146	16	4	13	17	67
1983-84	S.S. Marie	OHL	64	44	64	108	209	16	*22	14	*36	41
1984-85	**Philadelphia**	**NHL**	**75**	**14**	**25**	**39**	**181**	**19**	**3**	**4**	**7**	**72**
1985-86	**Philadelphia**	**NHL**	**69**	**14**	**21**	**35**	**284**	**5**	**1**	**2**	**3**	**26**
1986-87	**Philadelphia**	**NHL**	**69**	**21**	**26**	**47**	**288**	**26**	**11**	**10**	**21**	**72**
1987-88	**Philadelphia**	**NHL**	**65**	**31**	**33**	**64**	**301**	**5**	**1**	**4**	**5**	**55**
1988-89	**Philadelphia**	**NHL**	**66**	**45**	**36**	**81**	**183**	**16**	**6**	**6**	**12**	**69**
1989-90	**Philadelphia**	**NHL**	**75**	**37**	**59**	**96**	**196**	....	....	....	....	....
1990-91	**Philadelphia**	**NHL**	**70**	**40**	**31**	**71**	**150**	....	....	....	....	....
1991-92	**Pittsburgh**	**NHL**	**19**	**14**	**16**	**30**	**49**	**14**	**6**	**13**	**19**	**24** ♦
	Philadelphia	**NHL**	**42**	**13**	**16**	**29**	**102**	....	....	....	....	....
1992-93	**Pittsburgh**	**NHL**	**80**	**48**	**61**	**109**	**252**	**12**	**7**	**6**	**13**	**24**
1993-94	**Pittsburgh**	**NHL**	**51**	**14**	**26**	**40**	**134**	**6**	**2**	**3**	**5**	**20**
1994-95	**Los Angeles**	**NHL**	**36**	**18**	**17**	**35**	**70**	....	....	....	....	....
1995-96	**Los Angeles**	**NHL**	**44**	**13**	**23**	**36**	**117**	....	....	....	....	....
	Boston	**NHL**	**27**	**16**	**8**	**24**	**64**	**5**	**4**	**0**	**4**	**21**
1996-97	**Boston**	**NHL**	**40**	**16**	**14**	**30**	**67**	....	....	....	....	....
	Washington	**NHL**	**13**	**5**	**5**	**10**	**31**	....	....	....	....	....
1997-98	**Phoenix**	**NHL**	**68**	**26**	**19**	**45**	**157**	**6**	**6**	**2**	**8**	**25**
	NHL Totals		**909**	**385**	**436**	**821**	**2626**	**114**	**47**	**50**	**97**	**408**

Played in NHL All-Star Game (1989, 1990, 1991, 1993)

Traded to **Pittsburgh** by **Philadelphia** with Kjell Samuelsson, Ken Wregget and Philadelphia's 3rd round choice (Dave Roche) in 1993 Entry Draft for Mark Recchi, Brian Benning and LA Kings' 1st round choice (previously acquired, Philadelphia selected Jason Bowen) in 1992 Entry Draft, February 19, 1992 Traded to **LA Kings** by **Pittsburgh** with Pittsburgh's 2nd round choice (Pavel Rosa) in 1995 Entry Draft for Luc Robitaille, July 29, 1994. Traded to **Boston** by **LA Kings** for Kevin Stevens, January 25, 1996. Traded to **Washington** by **Boston** with Bill Ranford and Adam Oates for Jim Carey, Anson Carter, Jason Allison and Washington's 3rd round choice (Lee Goren) in 1997 Entry Draft, March 1, 1997. Signed as a free agent by **Phoenix**, July 23, 1997.

TODD, KEVIN

Center. Shoots left. 5'10", 180 lbs. Born, Winnipeg, Man., May 4, 1968.
(New Jersey's 7th choice, 129th overall, in 1986 Entry Draft).

			Regular Season					Playoffs				
Season	Club	Lea	GP	G	A	TP	PIM	GP	G	A	TP	PIM
1985-86	Prince Albert	WHL	55	14	25	39	19	20	7	6	13	29
1986-87	Prince Albert	WHL	71	39	46	85	92	8	2	5	7	17
1987-88	Prince Albert	WHL	72	49	72	121	83	10	8	11	19	27
1988-89	**New Jersey**	**NHL**	**1**	**0**	**0**	**0**	**0**	....	....	....	....	....
	Utica	AHL	78	26	45	71	62	4	2	0	2	6
1989-90	Utica	AHL	71	18	36	54	72	5	2	4	6	2
1990-91	**New Jersey**	**NHL**	**1**	**0**	**0**	**0**	**0**	**1**	**0**	**0**	**0**	**6**
	Utica	AHL	75	37	*81	*118	75	....	....	....	....	....
1991-92	**New Jersey**	**NHL**	**80**	**21**	**42**	**63**	**69**	**7**	**3**	**2**	**5**	**8**
1992-93	**New Jersey**	**NHL**	**30**	**5**	**5**	**10**	**16**	....	....	....	....	....
	Utica	AHL	2	2	1	3	0	....	....	....	....	....
	Edmonton	**NHL**	**25**	**4**	**9**	**13**	**10**	....	....	....	....	....
1993-94	**Chicago**	**NHL**	**35**	**5**	**6**	**11**	**16**	....	....	....	....	....
	Los Angeles	**NHL**	**12**	**3**	**8**	**11**	**8**	....	....	....	....	....
1994-95	**Los Angeles**	**NHL**	**33**	**3**	**8**	**11**	**12**	....	....	....	....	....
1995-96	**Los Angeles**	**NHL**	**74**	**16**	**27**	**43**	**38**	....	....	....	....	....
1996-97	**Anaheim**	**NHL**	**65**	**9**	**21**	**30**	**44**	**4**	**0**	**0**	**0**	**2**
1997-98	**Anaheim**	**NHL**	**27**	**4**	**7**	**11**	**12**	....	....	....	....	....
	Long Beach	IHL	30	18	28	46	54	13	1	10	11	38
	NHL Totals		**383**	**70**	**133**	**203**	**225**	**12**	**3**	**2**	**5**	**16**

AHL First All-Star Team (1991) • Won John B. Sollenberger Trophy (Leading Scorer - AHL) (1991) • Won Les Cunningham Plaque (MVP - AHL) (1992) • NHL/Upper Deck All-Rookie Team (1992)

Traded to **Edmonton** by **New Jersey** with Zdeno Ciger for Bernie Nicholls, January 13, 1993. Traded to **Chicago** by **Edmonton** for Adam Bennett, October 7, 1993. Traded to **LA Kings** by **Chicago** for LA Kings' 4th round choice (Steve McLaren) in 1994 Entry Draft, March 21, 1994. Signed as a free agent by **Pittsburgh**, July 10, 1996. Claimed on waivers by **Anaheim** from **Pittsburgh**, October 4, 1996.

TOMS, JEFF — WSH.

Left wing. Shoots left. 6'5", 200 lbs. Born, Swift Current, Sask., June 4, 1974.
(New Jersey's 10th choice, 210th overall, in 1992 Entry Draft).

			Regular Season					Playoffs				
Season	Club	Lea	GP	G	A	TP	PIM	GP	G	A	TP	PIM
1991-92	S.S. Marie	OHL	36	9	5	14	0	16	0	1	1	2
1992-93	S.S. Marie	OHL	59	16	23	39	20	16	4	4	8	7
1993-94	S.S. Marie	OHL	64	52	45	97	19	14	11	4	15	2
1994-95	Atlanta	IHL	40	7	8	15	10	4	0	0	0	4
1995-96	**Tampa Bay**	**NHL**	**1**	**0**	**0**	**0**	**0**	....	....	....	....	....
	Atlanta	IHL	68	16	18	34	18	1	0	0	0	0
1996-97	**Tampa Bay**	**NHL**	**34**	**2**	**8**	**10**	**10**	....	....	....	....	....
	Adirondack	AHL	37	11	16	27	8	4	1	2	3	0
1997-98	**Tampa Bay**	**NHL**	**13**	**1**	**2**	**3**	**7**	....	....	....	....	....
	Washington	**NHL**	**33**	**3**	**4**	**7**	**8**	**1**	**0**	**0**	**0**	**0**
	NHL Totals		**81**	**6**	**14**	**20**	**25**	**1**	**0**	**0**	**0**	**0**

Traded to **Tampa Bay** by **New Jersey** for Vancouver's 4th round choice (previously acquired by Tampa Bay — later traded to Calgary — Calgary selected Ryan Duthie) in 1994 Entry Draft, May 31, 1994. Claimed by on waivers by **Washington** from **Tampa Bay**, November 19, 1997.

TOPOROWSKI, SHAYNE — (toh-poh-ROW-skee) ST.L.

Right wing. Shoots right. 6'2", 210 lbs. Born, Paddockwood, Sask., August 6, 1975.
(Los Angeles' 1st choice, 42nd overall, in 1993 Entry Draft).

			Regular Season					Playoffs				
Season	Club	Lea	GP	G	A	TP	PIM	GP	G	A	TP	PIM
1991-92	Prince Albert	WHL	6	2	0	2	2	7	2	1	3	6
1992-93	Prince Albert	WHL	72	25	32	57	235	....	....	....	....	....
1993-94	Prince Albert	WHL	68	37	45	82	183	....	....	....	....	....
1994-95	Prince Albert	WHL	72	36	38	74	151	15	10	8	18	25
1995-96	St. John's	AHL	72	11	26	37	216	4	1	1	2	4
1996-97	**Toronto**	**NHL**	**3**	**0**	**0**	**0**	**7**	....	....	....	....	....
	St. John's	AHL	72	20	17	37	210	11	3	2	5	16
1997-98	Worcester	AHL	73	9	21	30	128	11	5	3	8	44
	NHL Totals		**3**	**0**	**0**	**0**	**7**	....	....	....	....	....

Traded to **Toronto** by **LA Kings** with Dixon Ward, Guy Leveque and Kelly Fairchild for Eric Lacroix, Chris Snell and Toronto's 4th round choice (Eric Belanger) in 1996 Entry Draft, October 3, 1994. Signed as a free agent by **St. Louis**, September 9, 1997.

TORMANEN, ANTTI — (TOHR-mah-nehn) OTT.

Right wing. Shoots left. 6'1", 198 lbs. Born, Espoo, Finland, September 19, 1970.
(Ottawa's 10th choice, 274th overall, in 1994 Entry Draft).

			Regular Season					Playoffs				
Season	Club	Lea	GP	G	A	TP	PIM	GP	G	A	TP	PIM
1990-91	Jokerit	Finland	44	12	9	21	70	....	....	....	....	....
1991-92	Jokerit	Finland	40	18	11	29	18	....	....	....	....	....
1992-93	Jokerit	Finland	21	2	0	2	8	....	....	....	....	....
1993-94	Jokerit	Finland	46	20	18	38	46	....	....	....	....	....
1994-95	Jokerit	Finland	50	19	13	32	32	11	7	3	11	20
1995-96	**Ottawa**	**NHL**	**50**	**7**	**8**	**15**	**28**	....	....	....	....	....
	P.E.I.	AHL	22	6	11	17	17	5	2	3	5	2
1996-97	Jokerit	Finland	50	18	14	32	54	9	3	5	8	10
1997-98	Jokerit	Finland	48	20	14	34	37	8	3	2	5	12
	Finland	Olympics	5	0	0	0	0	....	....	....	....	....
	NHL Totals		**50**	**7**	**8**	**15**	**28**	....	....	....	....	....

TRATTNIG, MATTHIAS — (TRAT-nihg, MAH-tee-uhs) CHI.

Center. Shoots left. 6'1", 208 lbs. Born, Graz, Austria, April 22, 1979.
(Chicago's 2nd choice, 94th overall, in 1998 Entry Draft).

			Regular Season					Playoffs				
Season	Club	Lea	GP	G	A	TP	PIM	GP	G	A	TP	PIM
1995-96	Graz	Austria	17	0	1	1	0	....	....	....	....	....
1996-97	Capital District	NYJHL	51	30	54	84	64	....	....	....	....	....
1997-98	U. of Maine	H.E.	34	8	9	17	30	....	....	....	....	....

TRAVERSE, PATRICK — OTT.

Defense. Shoots left. 6'3", 190 lbs. Born, Montreal, Que., March 14, 1974.
(Ottawa's 3rd choice, 50th overall, in 1992 Entry Draft).

			Regular Season					Playoffs				
Season	Club	Lea	GP	G	A	TP	PIM	GP	G	A	TP	PIM
1991-92	Shawinigan	QMJHL	59	3	11	14	12	10	0	0	0	4
1992-93	St-Jean	QMJHL	68	6	30	36	24	4	0	1	1	2
	New Haven	AHL	2	0	0	0	2	....	....	....	....	....
1993-94	St-Jean	QMJHL	66	15	37	52	30	5	0	4	4	4
	P.E.I.	AHL	3	0	1	1	2	....	....	....	....	....
1994-95	P.E.I.	AHL	70	5	13	18	19	7	0	2	2	0
1995-96	**Ottawa**	**NHL**	**5**	**0**	**0**	**0**	**2**	....	....	....	....	....
	P.E.I.	AHL	55	4	21	25	32	5	1	2	3	2
1996-97	Worcester	AHL	24	0	4	4	23	....	....	....	....	....
	Grand Rapids	IHL	10	2	1	3	10	2	0	1	1	2
1997-98	Hershey	AHL	71	14	15	29	67	7	1	3	4	4
	NHL Totals		**5**	**0**	**0**	**0**	**2**	....	....	....	....	....

TREBIL, DANIEL (TREH-bihl) — ANA.

Defense. Shoots right. 6'3", 210 lbs. Born, Bloomington, MN, April 10, 1974.
(New Jersey's 7th choice, 138th overall, in 1992 Entry Draft).

			Regular Season					Playoffs				
Season	Club	Lea	GP	G	A	TP	PIM	GP	G	A	TP	PIM
1991-92	Jefferson High	H.S.	28	7	26	33	6	....	....	....	....	....
1992-93	U. of Minnesota	WCHA	36	2	11	13	16	....	....	....	....	....
1993-94	U. of Minnesota	WCHA	42	1	21	22	24	....	....	....	....	....
1994-95	U. of Minnesota	WCHA	44	10	33	43	10	....	....	....	....	....
1995-96	U. of Minnesota	WCHA	42	11	35	46	36	....	....	....	....	....
1996-97	**Anaheim**	**NHL**	**29**	**3**	**3**	**6**	**23**	**9**	**0**	**1**	**1**	**6**
	Baltimore	AHL	49	4	20	24	38	....	....	....	....	....
1997-98	**Anaheim**	**NHL**	**21**	**0**	**1**	**1**	**2**	....	....	....	....	....
	Cincinnati	AHL	32	5	15	20	21	....	....	....	....	....
	NHL Totals		**50**	**3**	**4**	**7**	**25**	**9**	**0**	**1**	**1**	**6**

WCHA Second All-Star Team (1996) • NCAA West Second All-American Team (1996)

Signed as a free agent by **Anaheim**, May 30, 1996.

TREMBLAY, DIDIER (TRAHM-blay) — ST.L.

Defense. Shoots left. 6'1", 190 lbs. Born, Laval, Que., May 4, 1979.
(St. Louis' 2nd choice, 86th overall, in 1997 Entry Draft).

			Regular Season					Playoffs				
Season	Club	Lea	GP	G	A	TP	PIM	GP	G	A	TP	PIM
1995-96	Halifax	QMJHL	56	4	10	14	80	6	0	3	3	4
1996-97	Halifax	QMJHL	68	11	26	37	79	12	1	3	4	6
1997-98	Halifax	QMJHL	39	6	19	25	26	....	....	....	....	....
	Val d'Or	QMJHL	31	6	24	30	43	19	5	13	18	8

TREMBLAY, MICHEL (TRAHM-blay)

Left wing. Shoots left. 6'1", 185 lbs. Born, Alma, Que., April 8, 1978.
(Montreal's 10th choice, 233rd overall, in 1996 Entry Draft).

			Regular Season					Playoffs				
Season	Club	Lea	GP	G	A	TP	PIM	GP	G	A	TP	PIM
1995-96	Shawinigan	QMJHL	52	11	11	22	52	6	0	1	1	6
1996-97	Shawinigan	QMJHL	63	14	12	26	81	7	0	4	4	8
1997-98	Shawinigan	QMJHL	59	27	38	65	51	6	1	0	1	12

TREMBLAY, YANNICK (TRAHM-blay) — TOR.

Defense. Shoots right. 6'2", 185 lbs. Born, Pointe-aux-Trembles, Que., November 15, 1975.
(Toronto's 4th choice, 145th overall, in 1995 Entry Draft).

			Regular Season					Playoffs				
Season	Club	Lea	GP	G	A	TP	PIM	GP	G	A	TP	PIM
1993-94	St. Thomas	AUAA	25	2	3	5	10	....	....	....	....	....
1994-95	Beauport	QMJHL	70	10	32	42	22	17	6	8	14	6
1995-96	Beauport	QMJHL	61	12	33	45	42	20	3	16	19	18
	St. John's	AHL	3	0	1	1	0	....	....	....	....	....
1996-97	**Toronto**	**NHL**	**5**	**0**	**0**	**0**	**0**	....	....	....	....	....
	St. John's	AHL	67	7	25	32	34	11	2	9	11	0
1997-98	**Toronto**	**NHL**	**38**	**2**	**4**	**6**	**6**	....	....	....	....	....
	St. John's	AHL	17	3	7	10	4	4	0	1	1	5
	NHL Totals		**43**	**2**	**4**	**6**	**6**	....	....	....	....	....

TREPANIER, PASCAL (truh-PAN-yai) — COL.

Defense. Shoots right. 6', 205 lbs. Born, Gaspe, Que., April 9, 1973.

			Regular Season					Playoffs				
Season	Club	Lea	GP	G	A	TP	PIM	GP	G	A	TP	PIM
1990-91	Hull	QMJHL	46	3	3	6	56	4	0	2	2	7
1991-92	Trois-Rivieres	QMJHL	53	4	18	22	125	15	3	5	8	21
1992-93	Sherbrooke	QMJHL	59	15	33	48	130	15	5	7	12	36
1993-94	Sherbrooke	QMJHL	48	16	41	57	67	12	1	8	9	14
1994-95	Dayton	ECHL	36	16	28	44	113	9	2	4	6	20
	Kalamazoo	IHL	14	1	2	3	47	....	....	....	....	....
	Cornwall	AHL	4	0	0	0	9	14	2	7	9	32
1995-96	Cornwall	AHL	70	13	20	33	142	8	1	2	3	24
1996-97	Hershey	AHL	73	14	39	53	151	23	6	13	19	59
1997-98	**Colorado**	**NHL**	**15**	**0**	**1**	**1**	**18**	....	....	....	....	....
	Hershey	AHL	43	13	18	31	105	7	4	2	6	8
	NHL Totals		**15**	**0**	**1**	**1**	**18**	....	....	....	....	....

AHL Second All-Star Team (1997)

Signed as a free agent by **Colorado**, August 30, 1995.

TRIPP, JOHN — CGY.

Right wing. Shoots right. 6'2", 207 lbs. Born, Kingston, Ont., May 4, 1977.
(Calgary's 3rd choice, 42nd overall, in 1997 Entry Draft).

			Regular Season					Playoffs				
Season	Club	Lea	GP	G	A	TP	PIM	GP	G	A	TP	PIM
1994-95	Oshawa	OHL	58	6	11	17	53	7	0	1	1	4
1995-96	Oshawa	OHL	56	13	14	27	95	5	1	1	2	13
1996-97	Oshawa	OHL	59	28	20	48	126	18	*16	10	26	42
1997-98	Roanoke	ECHL	9	0	2	2	22	....	....	....	....	....
	Saint John	AHL	61	1	11	12	66	2	0	1	1	0

• Re-entered NHL draft. Originally Colorado's 3rd choice, 77th overall, in 1995 Entry Draft.

TRNKA, PAVEL (truhn-KAH) — ANA.

Defense. Shoots left. 6'3", 200 lbs. Born, Plzen, Czech., July 27, 1976.
(Anaheim's 5th choice, 106th overall, in 1994 Entry Draft).

			Regular Season					Playoffs				
Season	Club	Lea	GP	G	A	TP	PIM	GP	G	A	TP	PIM
1993-94	Skoda Plzen	Cze-Rep.	12	0	1	1	....	....	....	....	....	....
1994-95	Poldi Kladno	Cze-Rep.	28	0	5	5	24	....	....	....	....	....
	Plzen	Cze-Rep.	6	0	0	0	0	....	....	....	....	....
1995-96	Baltimore	AHL	69	2	6	8	44	6	0	0	0	2
1996-97	Baltimore	AHL	69	6	14	20	86	3	0	0	0	2
1997-98	**Anaheim**	**NHL**	**48**	**3**	**4**	**7**	**40**	....	....	....	....	....
	Cincinnati	AHL	23	3	5	8	28	....	....	....	....	....
	NHL Totals		**48**	**3**	**4**	**7**	**40**	....	....	....	....	....

TROSCHINSKY, ANDREI (troh-SCHIHN-skee) — ST.L.

Center. Shoots left. 6'5", 187 lbs. Born, Ust-Kamenogorsk, USSR, February 14, 1978.
(St. Louis' 5th choice, 170th overall, in 1998 Entry Draft).

			Regular Season					Playoffs				
Season	Club	Lea	GP	G	A	TP	PIM	GP	G	A	TP	PIM
1996-97	Torpedo	Russia-2	9	1	1	2	8	....	....	....	....	....
1997-98	Torpedo	Russia-2	47	10	16	26	34	....	....	....	....	....

TROTTIER, JOEL — BOS.

Right wing. Shoots right. 6', 190 lbs. Born, Alexandria, Ont., February 11, 1977.
(Boston's 8th choice, 162nd overall, in 1997 Entry Draft).

			Regular Season					Playoffs				
Season	Club	Lea	GP	G	A	TP	PIM	GP	G	A	TP	PIM
1994-95	Ottawa	OHL	53	7	10	17	13	....	....	....	....	....
1995-96	Ottawa	OHL	63	25	19	44	57	4	4	1	5	7
1996-97	Ottawa	OHL	56	41	39	80	57	22	14	12	26	23
1997-98	Plymouth	OHL	10	4	6	10	17	....	....	....	....	....
	Belleville	OHL	43	23	32	55	51	10	5	6	11	9

TSELIOS, NIKOS (TSEHL-ee-ohs) — CAR.

Defense. Shoots left. 6'4", 187 lbs. Born, Oak Park, IL, January 20, 1979.
(Carolina's 1st choice, 22nd overall, in 1997 Entry Draft).

			Regular Season					Playoffs				
Season	Club	Lea	GP	G	A	TP	PIM	GP	G	A	TP	PIM
1996-97	Belleville	OHL	64	9	37	46	61	6	1	1	2	2
1997-98	Belleville	OHL	20	2	10	12	16	....	....	....	....	....
	Plymouth	OHL	41	8	20	28	27	15	1	8	9	27

TSULYGIN, NIKOLAI (tsoo-LEE-gihn)

Defense. Shoots right. 6'3", 210 lbs. Born, Ufa, USSR, May 29, 1975.
(Anaheim's 2nd choice, 30th overall, in 1993 Entry Draft).

			Regular Season					Playoffs				
Season	Club	Lea	GP	G	A	TP	PIM	GP	G	A	TP	PIM
1992-93	Ufa Salavat	CIS	42	5	4	9	21	2	0	0	0	0
1993-94	Ufa Salavat	CIS	43	0	14	14	24	5	0	1	1	0
1994-95	CSKA Moscow	CIS	16	0	0	0	12	....	....	....	....	....
	Ufa Salavat	CIS	13	2	2	4	10	7	0	0	0	4
1995-96	Baltimore	AHL	78	3	18	21	109	12	0	5	5	18
1996-97	**Anaheim**	**NHL**	**22**	**0**	**1**	**1**	**8**	....	....	....	....	....
	Fort Wayne	IHL	5	2	1	3	8	....	....	....	....	....
	Baltimore	AHL	17	4	13	17	8	3	0	0	0	0
1997-98	Cincinnati	AHL	77	5	31	36	63	....	....	....	....	....
	NHL Totals		**22**	**0**	**1**	**1**	**8**	....	....	....	....	....

TSYBUK, YEVGENY (tsee-BUHK) — DAL.

Defense. Shoots left. 6', 183 lbs. Born, Chebarkul, USSR, February 2, 1978.
(Dallas' 5th choice, 113th overall, in 1996 Entry Draft).

			Regular Season					Playoffs				
Season	Club	Lea	GP	G	A	TP	PIM	GP	G	A	TP	PIM
1995-96	Yaroslavl 2	CIS-2	STATISTICS NOT AVAILABLE									
1996-97	Lethbridge	WHL	10	0	1	1	13	....	....	....	....	....
1997-98	Lethbridge	WHL	41	5	13	18	129	4	1	1	2	12

TSYPLAKOV, VLADIMIR (tsih-plah-KAHF) — L.A.

Left wing. Shoots left. 6'1", 197 lbs. Born, Moscow, USSR, April 18, 1969.
(Los Angeles' 4th choice, 59th overall, in 1995 Entry Draft).

			Regular Season					Playoffs				
Season	Club	Lea	GP	G	A	TP	PIM	GP	G	A	TP	PIM
1988-89	Minsk D'amo	USSR	19	6	1	7	4	....	....	....	....	....
1989-90	Minsk D'amo	USSR	47	11	6	17	20	....	....	....	....	....
1990-91	Minsk D'amo	USSR	28	6	5	11	14	....	....	....	....	....
1991-92	Minsk D'amo	CIS	29	10	9	19	16	....	....	....	....	....
1992-93	Detroit	ColHL	44	33	43	76	20	6	5	4	9	6
	Indianapolis	IHL	11	6	7	13	4	5	1	1	2	2
1993-94	Fort Wayne	IHL	63	31	32	63	51	14	6	8	14	16
1994-95	Fort Wayne	IHL	79	38	40	78	39	4	2	4	6	2
1995-96	**Los Angeles**	**NHL**	**23**	**5**	**5**	**10**	**4**	....	....	....	....	....
	Las Vegas	IHL	9	5	6	11	4	....	....	....	....	....
1996-97	**Los Angeles**	**NHL**	**67**	**16**	**23**	**39**	**12**	....	....	....	....	....
1997-98	**Los Angeles**	**NHL**	**73**	**18**	**34**	**52**	**18**	**4**	**0**	**1**	**1**	**8**
	Belarus	Olympics	5	1	1	2	2	....	....	....	....	....
	NHL Totals		**163**	**39**	**62**	**101**	**34**	**4**	**0**	**1**	**1**	**8**

TUCKER, DARCY — T.B.

Center. Shoots left. 5'10", 179 lbs. Born, Castor, Alta., March 15, 1975.
(Montreal's 8th choice, 151st overall, in 1993 Entry Draft).

			Regular Season					Playoffs				
Season	Club	Lea	GP	G	A	TP	PIM	GP	G	A	TP	PIM
1991-92	Kamloops	WHL	26	3	10	13	32	9	0	1	1	16
1992-93	Kamloops	WHL	67	31	58	89	155	13	7	6	13	34
1993-94	Kamloops	WHL	66	52	88	140	143	19	9	*18	*27	43
1994-95	Kamloops	WHL	64	64	73	137	94	21	*16	15	*31	19
1995-96	**Montreal**	**NHL**	**3**	**0**	**0**	**0**	**0**	....	....	....	....	....
	Fredericton	AHL	74	29	64	93	174	7	7	3	10	14
1996-97	**Montreal**	**NHL**	**73**	**7**	**13**	**20**	**110**	**4**	**0**	**0**	**0**	**0**
1997-98	**Montreal**	**NHL**	**39**	**1**	**5**	**6**	**57**	....	....	....	....	....
	Tampa Bay	**NHL**	**35**	**6**	**8**	**14**	**89**	....	....	....	....	....
	NHL Totals		**150**	**14**	**26**	**40**	**256**	**4**	**0**	**0**	**0**	**0**

WHL West First All-Star Team (1994, 1995) • Canadian Major Junior First All-Star Team (1994) • Memorial Cup All-Star Team (1994, 1995) • Won Stafford Smythe Memorial Trophy (Memorial Cup Tournament MVP) (1994) • Won Dudley "Red" Garrett Memorial Trophy (Top Rookie - AHL) (1996)

Traded to **Tampa Bay** by **Montreal** with Stephane Richer and David Wilkie for Patrick Poulin, Mick Vukota and Igor Ulanov, January 15, 1998.

TURCOTTE, DARREN — NSH.

Center. Shoots left. 6', 178 lbs. Born, Boston, MA, March 2, 1968.
(NY Rangers' 6th choice, 114th overall, in 1986 Entry Draft).

			Regular Season					Playoffs				
Season	Club	Lea	GP	G	A	TP	PIM	GP	G	A	TP	PIM
1984-85	North Bay	OHL	62	33	32	65	28	8	0	2	2	0
1985-86	North Bay	OHL	62	35	37	72	35	10	3	4	7	8
1986-87	North Bay	OHL	55	30	48	78	20	18	12	8	20	6
1987-88	North Bay	OHL	32	30	33	63	16	4	3	0	3	4
	Colorado	IHL	8	4	3	7	9	6	2	6	8	8
1988-89	**NY Rangers**	**NHL**	**20**	**7**	**3**	**10**	**4**	**1**	**0**	**0**	**0**	**0**
	Denver	IHL	40	21	28	49	32	....	....	....	....	....
1989-90	**NY Rangers**	**NHL**	**76**	**32**	**34**	**66**	**32**	**10**	**1**	**6**	**7**	**4**
1990-91	**NY Rangers**	**NHL**	**74**	**26**	**41**	**67**	**37**	**6**	**1**	**2**	**3**	**0**
1991-92	**NY Rangers**	**NHL**	**71**	**30**	**23**	**53**	**57**	**8**	**4**	**0**	**4**	**6**
1992-93	**NY Rangers**	**NHL**	**71**	**25**	**28**	**53**	**40**	....	....	....	....	....
1993-94	**NY Rangers**	**NHL**	**13**	**2**	**4**	**6**	**13**	....	....	....	....	....
	Hartford	**NHL**	**19**	**2**	**11**	**13**	**4**	....	....	....	....	....
1994-95	**Hartford**	**NHL**	**47**	**17**	**18**	**35**	**22**	....	....	....	....	....
1995-96	**Winnipeg**	**NHL**	**59**	**16**	**16**	**32**	**26**	....	....	....	....	....
	San Jose	**NHL**	**9**	**6**	**5**	**11**	**4**	....	....	....	....	....
1996-97	**San Jose**	**NHL**	**65**	**16**	**21**	**37**	**16**	....	....	....	....	....
1997-98	**St. Louis**	**NHL**	**62**	**12**	**6**	**18**	**26**	**10**	**0**	**0**	**0**	**2**
	NHL Totals		**586**	**191**	**210**	**401**	**281**	**35**	**6**	**8**	**14**	**12**

Played in NHL All-Star Game (1991)

Traded to **Hartford** by **NY Rangers** with James Patrick for Steve Larmer, Nick Kypreos, Barry Richter and Hartford's 6th round choice (Yuri Litvinov) in 1994 Entry Draft, November 2, 1993. Traded to **Winnipeg** by **Hartford** for Nelson Emerson, October 6, 1995. Traded to **San Jose** by **Winnipeg** with Dallas' 2nd round choice (previously acquired and later traded to Chicago — Chicago selected Remi Royer) in 1996 Entry Draft for Craig Janney, March 18, 1996. Traded to **St. Louis** by **San Jose** for Stephane Matteau, July 24, 1997. Traded to **Nashville** by **St. Louis** for future considerations, June 26, 1998.

TURGEON, PIERRE — (TUHR-zhaw) — ST.L.

Center. Shoots left. 6'1", 195 lbs. Born, Rouyn, Que., August 28, 1969.
(Buffalo's 1st choice, 1st overall, in 1987 Entry Draft).

			Regular Season					Playoffs				
Season	Club	Lea	GP	G	A	TP	PIM	GP	G	A	TP	PIM
1985-86	Granby	QMJHL	69	47	67	114	31	....	....	....	....	....
	Canada	Nat-Tm	11	2	4	6	2	....	....	....	....	....
1986-87	Granby	QMJHL	58	69	85	154	8	7	9	6	15	15
1987-88	**Buffalo**	**NHL**	**76**	**14**	**28**	**42**	**34**	**6**	**4**	**3**	**7**	**4**
1988-89	**Buffalo**	**NHL**	**80**	**34**	**54**	**88**	**26**	**5**	**3**	**5**	**8**	**2**
1989-90	**Buffalo**	**NHL**	**80**	**40**	**66**	**106**	**29**	**6**	**2**	**4**	**6**	**2**
1990-91	**Buffalo**	**NHL**	**78**	**32**	**47**	**79**	**26**	**6**	**3**	**1**	**4**	**6**
1991-92	**Buffalo**	**NHL**	**8**	**2**	**6**	**8**	**4**	....	....	....	....	....
	NY Islanders	**NHL**	**69**	**38**	**49**	**87**	**16**	....	....	....	....	....
1992-93	**NY Islanders**	**NHL**	**83**	**58**	**74**	**132**	**26**	**11**	**6**	**7**	**13**	**0**
1993-94	**NY Islanders**	**NHL**	**69**	**38**	**56**	**94**	**18**	**4**	**0**	**1**	**1**	**0**
1994-95	**NY Islanders**	**NHL**	**34**	**13**	**14**	**27**	**10**	....	....	....	....	....
	Montreal	**NHL**	**15**	**11**	**9**	**20**	**4**	....	....	....	....	....
1995-96	**Montreal**	**NHL**	**80**	**38**	**58**	**96**	**44**	**6**	**2**	**4**	**6**	**2**
1996-97	**Montreal**	**NHL**	**9**	**1**	**10**	**11**	**2**	....	....	....	....	....
	St. Louis	**NHL**	**69**	**25**	**49**	**74**	**12**	**5**	**1**	**1**	**2**	**2**
1997-98	**St. Louis**	**NHL**	**60**	**22**	**46**	**68**	**24**	**10**	**4**	**4**	**8**	**2**
	NHL Totals		**810**	**366**	**566**	**932**	**275**	**59**	**25**	**30**	**55**	**20**

Won Lady Byng Memorial Trophy (1993)

Played in NHL All-Star Game (1990, 1993, 1994, 1996)

Traded to **NY Islanders** by **Buffalo** with Uwe Krupp, Benoit Hogue and Dave McLlwain for Pat Lafontaine, Randy Hillier, Randy Wood and NY Islanders' 4th round choice (Dean Melanson) in 1992 Entry Draft, October 25, 1991. Traded to **Montreal** by **NY Islanders** with Vladimir Malakhov for Kirk Muller, Mathieu Schneider and Craig Darby, April 5, 1995. Traded to **St. Louis** by **Montreal** with Rory Fitzpatrick and Craig Conroy for Murray Baron, Shayne Corson and St. Louis' 5th round choice (Gennady Razin) in 1997 Entry Draft, October 29, 1996.

TUZZOLINO, TONY — ANA.

Right wing. Shoots right. 6'2", 190 lbs. Born, Buffalo, NY, October 9, 1975.
(Quebec's 7th choice, 113th overall, in 1994 Entry Draft).

			Regular Season					Playoffs				
Season	Club	Lea	GP	G	A	TP	PIM	GP	G	A	TP	PIM
1993-94	Michigan State	CCHA	35	4	3	7	46	....	....	....	....	....
1994-95	Michigan State	CCHA	39	9	18	27	81	....	....	....	....	....
1995-96	Michigan State	CCHA	41	12	17	29	120	....	....	....	....	....
1996-97	Michigan State	CCHA	39	14	18	32	120	....	....	....	....	....
1997-98	Kentucky	AHL	35	9	14	23	83	....	....	....	....	....
	Anaheim	**NHL**	**1**	**0**	**0**	**0**	**2**	....	....	....	....	....
	Cincinnati	AHL	13	3	3	6	6	....	....	....	....	....
	NHL Totals		**1**	**0**	**0**	**0**	**2**	....	....	....	....	....

Rights transferred to **Colorado** after **Quebec** franchise relocated, June 21, 1995. Signed as a free agent by **NY Islanders**, April 26, 1997. Traded to **Anaheim** by **NY Islanders** with Travis Green and Doug Houda for Joe Sacco, J.J. Daigneault and Mark Janssens, February 6, 1998.

TVERDOVSKY, OLEG — (tvehr-DOHV-skee) — PHX.

Defense. Shoots left. 6', 195 lbs. Born, Donetsk, USSR, May 18, 1976.
(Anaheim's 1st choice, 2nd overall, in 1994 Entry Draft).

			Regular Season					Playoffs				
Season	Club	Lea	GP	G	A	TP	PIM	GP	G	A	TP	PIM
1992-93	Soviet Wings	CIS	21	0	1	1	6	6	0	0	0	0
1993-94	Soviet Wings	CIS	46	4	10	14	22	3	1	0	1	2
1994-95	Brandon	WHL	7	1	4	5	4	....	....	....	....	....
	Anaheim	**NHL**	**36**	**3**	**9**	**12**	**14**	....	....	....	....	....
1995-96	**Anaheim**	**NHL**	**51**	**7**	**15**	**22**	**35**	....	....	....	....	....
	Winnipeg	**NHL**	**31**	**0**	**8**	**8**	**6**	**6**	**0**	**1**	**1**	**0**
1996-97	**Phoenix**	**NHL**	**82**	**10**	**45**	**55**	**30**	**7**	**0**	**1**	**1**	**0**
1997-98	Hamilton	AHL	9	8	6	14	2	....	....	....	....	....
	Phoenix	**NHL**	**46**	**7**	**12**	**19**	**12**	**6**	**0**	**7**	**7**	**0**
	NHL Totals		**246**	**27**	**89**	**116**	**97**	**19**	**0**	**9**	**9**	**0**

Played in NHL All-Star Game (1997)

Traded to **Winnipeg** by **Anaheim** with Chad Kilger and Anaheim's 3rd round choice (Per-Anton Lundstrom) in 1996 Entry Draft for Teemu Selanne, Marc Chouinard and Winnipeg's 4th round choice (later traded to Toronto — later traded to Montreal — Montreal selected Kim Staal) in 1996 Entry Draft, February 7, 1996. Transferred to **Phoenix** after **Winnipeg** franchise relocated, July 1, 1996.

TWERDUN, CHRIS

Defense. Shoots right. 6', 200 lbs. Born, Saskatoon, Sask., February 11, 1978.
(Chicago's 6th choice, 210th overall, in 1996 Entry Draft).

			Regular Season					Playoffs				
Season	Club	Lea	GP	G	A	TP	PIM	GP	G	A	TP	PIM
1994-95	Moose Jaw	WHL	70	5	12	17	25	10	0	3	3	2
1995-96	Moose Jaw	WHL	72	5	16	21	93	....	....	....	....	....
1996-97	Moose Jaw	WHL	63	8	15	23	66	12	0	2	2	10
1997-98	Moose Jaw	WHL	69	11	10	21	93	4	0	3	3	6

TWIST, TONY — ST.L.

Left wing. Shoots left. 6'1", 220 lbs. Born, Sherwood Park, Alta., May 9, 1968.
(St. Louis' 9th choice, 177th overall, in 1988 Entry Draft).

			Regular Season					Playoffs				
Season	Club	Lea	GP	G	A	TP	PIM	GP	G	A	TP	PIM
1986-87	Saskatoon	WHL	64	0	8	8	181	....	....	....	....	....
1987-88	Saskatoon	WHL	55	1	8	9	226	10	1	1	2	6
1988-89	Peoria	IHL	67	3	8	11	312	....	....	....	....	....
1989-90	**St. Louis**	**NHL**	**28**	**0**	**0**	**0**	**124**	....	....	....	....	....
	Peoria	IHL	36	1	5	6	200	5	0	1	1	8
1990-91	Peoria	IHL	38	2	10	12	244	....	....	....	....	....
	Quebec	**NHL**	**24**	**0**	**0**	**0**	**104**	....	....	....	....	....
1991-92	**Quebec**	**NHL**	**44**	**0**	**1**	**1**	**164**	....	....	....	....	....
1992-93	**Quebec**	**NHL**	**34**	**0**	**2**	**2**	**64**	....	....	....	....	....
1993-94	**Quebec**	**NHL**	**49**	**0**	**4**	**4**	**101**	....	....	....	....	....
1994-95	**St. Louis**	**NHL**	**28**	**3**	**0**	**3**	**89**	**1**	**0**	**0**	**0**	**6**
1995-96	**St. Louis**	**NHL**	**51**	**3**	**2**	**5**	**100**	**10**	**1**	**1**	**2**	**16**
1996-97	**St. Louis**	**NHL**	**64**	**1**	**2**	**3**	**121**	**6**	**0**	**0**	**0**	**0**
1997-98	**St. Louis**	**NHL**	**60**	**1**	**1**	**2**	**105**	....	....	....	....	....
	NHL Totals		**382**	**8**	**12**	**20**	**972**	**17**	**1**	**1**	**2**	**22**

Traded to **Quebec** by **St. Louis** with Herb Raglan and Andy Rymsha for Darin Kimble, February 4, 1991. Signed as a free agent by **St. Louis**, August 16, 1994.

ULANOV, IGOR — (yoo-LAH-nahf, EE-gohr) — MTL.

Defense. Shoots left. 6'2", 205 lbs. Born, Krasnokamsk, USSR, October 1, 1969.
(Winnipeg's 8th choice, 203rd overall, in 1991 Entry Draft).

			Regular Season					Playoffs				
Season	Club	Lea	GP	G	A	TP	PIM	GP	G	A	TP	PIM
1990-91	Khimik	USSR	41	2	2	4	52	....	....	....	....	....
1991-92	Khimik	CIS	27	1	4	5	24	....	....	....	....	....
	Winnipeg	**NHL**	**27**	**2**	**9**	**11**	**67**	**7**	**0**	**0**	**0**	**39**
	Moncton	AHL	3	0	1	1	16	....	....	....	....	....
1992-93	**Winnipeg**	**NHL**	**56**	**2**	**14**	**16**	**124**	**4**	**0**	**0**	**0**	**4**
	Moncton	AHL	9	1	3	4	26	....	....	....	....	....
	Fort Wayne	IHL	3	0	1	1	29	....	....	....	....	....
1993-94	**Winnipeg**	**NHL**	**74**	**0**	**17**	**17**	**165**	....	....	....	....	....
1994-95	**Winnipeg**	**NHL**	**19**	**1**	**3**	**4**	**27**	....	....	....	....	....
	Washington	**NHL**	**3**	**0**	**1**	**1**	**2**	**2**	**0**	**0**	**0**	**4**
1995-96	**Chicago**	**NHL**	**53**	**1**	**8**	**9**	**92**	....	....	....	....	....
	Indianapolis	IHL	1	0	0	0	0	....	....	....	....	....
	Tampa Bay	**NHL**	**11**	**2**	**1**	**3**	**24**	**5**	**0**	**0**	**0**	**15**
1996-97	**Tampa Bay**	**NHL**	**59**	**1**	**7**	**8**	**108**	....	....	....	....	....
1997-98	**Tampa Bay**	**NHL**	**45**	**2**	**7**	**9**	**85**	....	....	....	....	....
	Montreal	**NHL**	**4**	**0**	**1**	**1**	**12**	**10**	**1**	**4**	**5**	**12**
	NHL Totals		**351**	**11**	**68**	**79**	**706**	**28**	**1**	**4**	**5**	**74**

Traded to **Washington** by **Winnipeg** with Mike Eagles for Washington's 3rd (later traded to Dallas — Dallas selected Sergei Gusev) and 5th (Brian Elder) round choices in 1995 Entry Draft, April 7, 1995. Traded to **Chicago** by **Washington** for Chicago's 3rd round choice (Dave Weninger) in 1996 Entry Draft, October 17, 1995. Traded to **Tampa Bay** by **Chicago** with Patrick Poulin and Chicago's 2nd round choice (later traded to New Jersey — New Jersey selected Pierre Dagenais) in 1996 Entry Draft for Enrico Ciccone and Tampa Bay's 2nd round choice (Jeff Paul) in 1996 Entry Draft, March 20, 1996. Traded to **Montreal** by **Tampa Bay** with Patrick Poulin and Mick Vukota for Stephane Richer, Darcy Tucker and David Wilkie, January 15, 1998.

URICK, BRIAN — (YOOR-ihk) — EDM.

Right wing. Shoots right. 6'1", 190 lbs. Born, Minneapolis, MN, January 25, 1977.
(Edmonton's 5th choice, 114th overall, in 1996 Entry Draft).

			Regular Season					Playoffs				
Season	Club	Lea	GP	G	A	TP	PIM	GP	G	A	TP	PIM
1994-95	Minnetonka High	H.S.	24	30	29	59	28	....	....	....	....	....
1995-96	Notre Dame	CCHA	36	12	15	27	66	....	....	....	....	....
1996-97	Notre Dame	CCHA	34	13	12	25	88	....	....	....	....	....
1997-98	Notre Dame	CCHA	41	16	18	34	40	....	....	....	....	....

USTORF, STEFAN — (OOSH-tohrf, SHTEH-fuhn) — WSH.

Center. Shoots left. 6', 185 lbs. Born, Kaufbeuren, Germany, January 3, 1974.
(Washington's 3rd choice, 53rd overall, in 1992 Entry Draft).

			Regular Season					Playoffs				
Season	Club	Lea	GP	G	A	TP	PIM	GP	G	A	TP	PIM
1990-91	Kaufbeuren	Germany	37	33	34	67	78	....	....	....	....	....
1991-92	Kaufbeuren	Germany	41	2	22	24	46	5	2	7	9	6
1992-93	Kaufbeuren	Germany	37	14	18	32	32	3	1	0	1	10
1993-94	Kaufbeuren	Germany	38	10	20	30	21	3	0	0	0	4
	Germany	Olympics	8	1	2	3	2	....	....	....	....	....
1994-95	Portland	AHL	63	21	38	59	51	7	1	6	7	7
1995-96	**Washington**	**NHL**	**48**	**7**	**10**	**17**	**14**	**5**	**0**	**0**	**0**	**0**
	Portland	AHL	8	1	4	5	6	....	....	....	....	....
1996-97	**Washington**	**NHL**	**6**	**0**	**0**	**0**	**2**	....	....	....	....	....
	Portland	AHL	36	7	17	24	27	....	....	....	....	....
1997-98	Berlin	Germany	45	17	23	40	54	....	....	....	....	....
	Germany	Olympics	4	0	0	0	0	....	....	....	....	....
	NHL Totals		**54**	**7**	**10**	**17**	**16**	**5**	**0**	**0**	**0**	**0**

USTYUGOV, ANATOLI — (oos-too-gahv) — DET.

Left wing. Shoots left. 5'10", 165 lbs. Born, Usole Siberskoye, USSR, June 26, 1977.
(Detroit's 4th choice, 104th overall, in 1995 Entry Draft).

			Regular Season					Playoffs				
Season	Club	Lea	GP	G	A	TP	PIM	GP	G	A	TP	PIM
1994-95	Yaroslavl	CIS	5	0	0	0	0	....	....	....	....	....
1995-96	Yaroslavl	CIS	9	1	0	1	4	....	....	....	....	....
1996-97	Yaroslavl 2	Russia-3	32	9	12	21	52	....	....	....	....	....
	Yaroslavl	Russia	4	0	0	0	2	....	....	....	....	....
1997-98	Novgorod	Russia	13	2	0	2	2	....	....	....	....	....

VAANANEN, OSSI (VAN-ih-nehn, AW-see) PHX.

Defense. Shoots left. 6'3", 200 lbs. Born, Vantaa, Finland, August 18, 1980.
(Phoenix's 2nd choice, 43rd overall, in 1998 Entry Draft).

			Regular Season					Playoffs				
Season	**Club**	**Lea**	**GP**	**G**	**A**	**TP**	**PIM**	**GP**	**G**	**A**	**TP**	**PIM**
1995-96	Jokerit	Fin-Jr.	2	0	0	0	0	....	....	....	....	....
1996-97	Jokerit	Fin-Jr.	17	1	2	3	43	....	....	....	....	....
1997-98	Jokerit	Fin-Jr.	31	0	6	6	24	....	....	....	....	....

VACHON, NICK (VA-shawn)

Center. Shoots left. 5'10", 185 lbs. Born, Montreal, Que., July 20, 1972.
(Toronto's 11th choice, 241st overall, in 1990 Entry Draft).

			Regular Season					Playoffs				
Season	**Club**	**Lea**	**GP**	**G**	**A**	**TP**	**PIM**	**GP**	**G**	**A**	**TP**	**PIM**
1989-90	Gov. Dummer	H.S.	20	20	22	42	....	....	....	....	....	....
1990-91	Boston University	H.E.	8	0	1	1	4	....	....	....	....	....
1991-92	Boston University	H.E.	16	6	7	13	10	....	....	....	....	....
	Portland	WHL	25	9	19	28	46	6	0	3	3	14
1992-93	Portland	WHL	66	33	58	91	100	16	11	7	18	34
1993-94	Atlanta	IHL	3	1	1	2	0	....	....	....	....	....
	Knoxville	ECHL	61	29	57	86	139	3	0	0	0	2
1994-95	Phoenix	IHL	64	13	26	39	137	9	1	2	3	24
1995-96	Phoenix	IHL	73	13	17	30	168	1	0	0	0	2
1996-97	Phoenix	IHL	16	3	3	6	18	....	....	....	....	....
	NY Islanders	**NHL**	**1**	**0**	**0**	**0**	**0**	....	....	....	....	....
	Utah	IHL	33	3	5	8	110	....	....	....	....	....
	Long Beach	IHL	13	1	2	3	42	18	1	2	3	43
1997-98	Springfield	AHL	7	0	0	0	16	....	....	....	....	....
	Long Beach	IHL	56	3	6	9	113	....	....	....	....	....
	NHL Totals		**1**	**0**	**0**	**0**	**0**	....	....	....	....	....

Signed as a free agent by **LA Kings**, September 12, 1995. Traded to **NY Islanders** by **LA Kings** for Chris Marinucci, November 19, 1996.

VAIC, LUBOMIR (VIGHTZ) VAN.

Center. Shoots left. 5'9", 178 lbs. Born, Spisska Nova Ves, Czech., March 6, 1977.
(Vancouver's 8th choice, 227th overall, in 1996 Entry Draft).

			Regular Season					Playoffs				
Season	**Club**	**Lea**	**GP**	**G**	**A**	**TP**	**PIM**	**GP**	**G**	**A**	**TP**	**PIM**
1993-94	Poprad	Slovakia	28	10	6	16	10	....	....	....	....	....
1994-95	Spisska	Slovakia	19	5	4	9	2	....	....	....	....	....
1995-96	HC Kosice	Slovakia	36	7	19	26	10	13	0	7	7	....
1996-97	HC Kosice	Slovakia	36	13	12	25	....	7	2	0	2	....
1997-98	**Vancouver**	**NHL**	**5**	**1**	**1**	**2**	**2**	....	....	....	....	....
	Syracuse	AHL	50	12	15	27	22	3	0	0	0	4
	NHL Totals		**5**	**1**	**1**	**2**	**2**	....	....	....	....	....

VALICEVIC, ROBERT NSH.

Right wing. Shoots right. 6'2", 197 lbs. Born, Detroit, MI, January 6, 1971.
(NY Islanders' 6th choice, 114th overall, in 1991 Entry Draft).

			Regular Season					Playoffs				
Season	**Club**	**Lea**	**GP**	**G**	**A**	**TP**	**PIM**	**GP**	**G**	**A**	**TP**	**PIM**
1990-91	Detroit	USHL	39	31	44	75	54	....	....	....	....	....
1991-92	Lake Superior	CCHA	32	8	4	12	12	....	....	....	....	....
1992-93	Lake Superior	CCHA	43	21	20	41	28	....	....	....	....	....
1993-94	Lake Superior	CCHA	45	18	20	38	46	....	....	....	....	....
1994-95	Lake Superior	CCHA	37	10	21	31	40	....	....	....	....	....
1995-96	Springfield	AHL	2	0	0	0	2	....	....	....	....	....
1996-97	Houston	IHL	58	11	12	23	42	12	1	3	4	11
1997-98	Houston	IHL	72	29	28	57	47	4	2	0	2	2

Signed as a free agent by **Nashville**, May 28, 1998.

VALILA, MIKA (VA-lih-lah, MEE-ka) PIT.

Center. Shoots left. 6', 187 lbs. Born, Sodertalje, Sweden, February 20, 1970.
(Pittsburgh's 7th choice, 130th overall, in 1990 Entry Draft).

			Regular Season					Playoffs				
Season	**Club**	**Lea**	**GP**	**G**	**A**	**TP**	**PIM**	**GP**	**G**	**A**	**TP**	**PIM**
1988-89	Tappara	Finland	14	2	5	7	8	3	1	0	1	2
1989-90	Tappara	Finland	44	8	16	24	16	7	2	2	4	4
1990-91	Tappara	Finland	41	10	9	19	16	3	0	1	1	0
1991-92	Jokerit	Finland	30	4	3	7	4	8	1	1	2	2
1992-93	Lukko	Finland	48	8	10	18	24	3	0	0	0	0
1993-94	Lukko	Finland	45	7	7	14	18	9	0	0	0	8
1994-95	Troja-Ljunby	Sweden-2	33	14	14	28	54	....	....	....	....	....
1995-96	Troja-Ljunby	Sweden-2	29	4	6	10	36	....	....	....	....	....
1996-97	Boden	Sweden-2	19	6	8	14	47	....	....	....	....	....
1997-98	Boden	Sweden-2	STATISTICS NOT AVAILABLE									

VALK, GARRY (VAHLK)

Left wing. Shoots left. 6'1", 205 lbs. Born, Edmonton, Alta., November 27, 1967.
(Vancouver's 5th choice, 108th overall, in 1987 Entry Draft).

			Regular Season					Playoffs				
Season	**Club**	**Lea**	**GP**	**G**	**A**	**TP**	**PIM**	**GP**	**G**	**A**	**TP**	**PIM**
1986-87	Sherwood Park	AJHL	59	42	44	86	204	....	....	....	....	....
1987-88	North Dakota	WCHA	38	23	12	35	64	....	....	....	....	....
1988-89	North Dakota	WCHA	40	14	17	31	71	....	....	....	....	....
1989-90	North Dakota	WCHA	43	22	17	39	92	....	....	....	....	....
1990-91	**Vancouver**	**NHL**	**59**	**10**	**11**	**21**	**67**	**5**	**0**	**0**	**0**	**20**
	Milwaukee	IHL	10	12	4	16	13	3	0	0	0	2
1991-92	**Vancouver**	**NHL**	**65**	**8**	**17**	**25**	**56**	**4**	**0**	**0**	**0**	**5**
1992-93	**Vancouver**	**NHL**	**48**	**6**	**7**	**13**	**77**	**7**	**0**	**1**	**1**	**12**
	Hamilton	AHL	7	3	6	9	6	....	....	....	....	....
1993-94	**Anaheim**	**NHL**	**78**	**18**	**27**	**45**	**100**	....	....	....	....	....
1994-95	**Anaheim**	**NHL**	**36**	**3**	**6**	**9**	**34**	....	....	....	....	....
1995-96	**Anaheim**	**NHL**	**79**	**12**	**12**	**24**	**125**	....	....	....	....	....
1996-97	**Anaheim**	**NHL**	**53**	**7**	**7**	**14**	**53**	....	....	....	....	....
	Pittsburgh	**NHL**	**17**	**3**	**4**	**7**	**25**	....	....	....	....	....
1997-98	**Pittsburgh**	**NHL**	**39**	**2**	**1**	**3**	**33**	....	....	....	....	....
	NHL Totals		**474**	**69**	**92**	**161**	**570**	**16**	**0**	**1**	**1**	**37**

OHA First All-Star Team (1974)

Claimed by **Anaheim** from **Vancouver** in NHL Waiver Draft, October 3, 1993. Traded to **Pittsburgh** by **Anaheim** for Jean-Jacques Daigneault, February 21, 1997.

VALTONEN, TOMEK DET.

Left wing. Shoots left. 6'1", 198 lbs. Born, Piotrkow Trybunalski, Poland, January 8, 1980.
(Detroit's 3rd choice, 56th overall, in 1998 Entry Draft).

			Regular Season					Playoffs				
Season	**Club**	**Lea**	**GP**	**G**	**A**	**TP**	**PIM**	**GP**	**G**	**A**	**TP**	**PIM**
1995-96	Ilves	Fin-Jr.	12	7	7	14	28	....	....	....	....	....
1996-97	Ilves	Fin-Jr.	27	10	9	19	82	3	0	1	1	6
1997-98	Kiekko	Finland-2	6	1	2	3	39	....	....	....	....	....
	Ilves	Fin-Jr.	13	3	2	5	36	....	....	....	....	....
	Ilves	Finland	19	1	0	1	14	3	0	0	0	0

VAN ACKER, ERIC BOS.

Defense. Shoots left. 6'5", 220 lbs. Born, St. Jean, Que., March 1, 1979.
(Boston's 11th choice, 218th overall, in 1997 Entry Draft).

			Regular Season					Playoffs				
Season	**Club**	**Lea**	**GP**	**G**	**A**	**TP**	**PIM**	**GP**	**G**	**A**	**TP**	**PIM**
1996-97	Chicoutimi	QMJHL	69	2	5	7	153	16	0	0	0	4
1997-98	Chicoutimi	QMJHL	49	1	5	6	136	6	0	0	0	14

VAN ALLEN, SHAUN OTT.

Center. Shoots left. 6'1", 200 lbs. Born, Calgary, Alta., August 29, 1967.
(Edmonton's 5th choice, 105th overall, in 1987 Entry Draft).

			Regular Season					Playoffs				
Season	**Club**	**Lea**	**GP**	**G**	**A**	**TP**	**PIM**	**GP**	**G**	**A**	**TP**	**PIM**
1984-85	Swift Current	WHL	61	12	20	32	136	....	....	....	....	....
1985-86	Saskatoon	WHL	55	12	11	23	43	13	4	8	12	28
1986-87	Saskatoon	WHL	72	38	59	97	116	11	4	6	10	24
1987-88	Milwaukee	IHL	40	14	28	42	34	....	....	....	....	....
	Nova Scotia	AHL	19	4	10	14	17	4	1	1	2	4
1988-89	Cape Breton	AHL	76	32	42	74	81	....	....	....	....	....
1989-90	Cape Breton	AHL	61	25	44	69	83	4	0	2	2	8
1990-91	**Edmonton**	**NHL**	**2**	**0**	**0**	**0**	**0**	....	....	....	....	....
	Cape Breton	AHL	76	25	75	100	182	4	0	1	1	8
1991-92	Cape Breton	AHL	77	29	*84	*113	80	5	3	7	10	14
1992-93	**Edmonton**	**NHL**	**21**	**1**	**4**	**5**	**6**	....	....	....	....	....
	Cape Breton	AHL	43	14	62	76	68	15	8	9	17	18
1993-94	**Anaheim**	**NHL**	**80**	**8**	**25**	**33**	**64**	....	....	....	....	....
1994-95	**Anaheim**	**NHL**	**45**	**8**	**21**	**29**	**32**	....	....	....	....	....
1995-96	**Anaheim**	**NHL**	**49**	**8**	**17**	**25**	**41**	....	....	....	....	....
1996-97	**Ottawa**	**NHL**	**80**	**11**	**14**	**25**	**35**	**7**	**0**	**1**	**1**	**4**
1997-98	**Ottawa**	**NHL**	**80**	**4**	**15**	**19**	**48**	**11**	**0**	**1**	**1**	**10**
	NHL Totals		**357**	**40**	**96**	**136**	**226**	**18**	**0**	**2**	**2**	**14**

AHL Second All-Star Team (1991) • AHL First All-Star Team (1992) • Won John B. Sollenberger Trophy (Top Scorer - AHL) (1992)

Signed as a free agent by **Anaheim**, July 22, 1993. Traded to **Ottawa** by **Anaheim** with Jason York for Ted Drury and the rights to Marc Moro, October 1, 1996.

VANBUSKIRK, RYAN PHX.

Defense. Shoots left. 6'1", 190 lbs. Born, Sault Ste. Marie, MI, January 12, 1980.
(Phoenix's 4th choice, 100th overall, in 1998 Entry Draft).

			Regular Season					Playoffs				
Season	**Club**	**Lea**	**GP**	**G**	**A**	**TP**	**PIM**	**GP**	**G**	**A**	**TP**	**PIM**
1996-97	Petrolia	OJHL	43	7	28	35	133	....	....	....	....	....
1997-98	Sarnia	OHL	61	8	17	25	84	5	1	2	3	4

VANDENBUSSCHE, RYAN (van-dehn-BUHSH) CHI.

Right wing. Shoots right. 5'11", 187 lbs. Born, Simcoe, Ont., February 28, 1973.
(Toronto's 9th choice, 173rd overall, in 1992 Entry Draft).

			Regular Season					Playoffs				
Season	**Club**	**Lea**	**GP**	**G**	**A**	**TP**	**PIM**	**GP**	**G**	**A**	**TP**	**PIM**
1990-91	Cornwall	OHL	49	3	8	11	139	....	....	....	....	....
1991-92	Cornwall	OHL	61	13	15	28	232	6	0	2	2	9
1992-93	Newmarket	OHL	30	15	12	27	161	....	....	....	....	....
	Guelph	OHL	29	3	14	17	99	5	1	3	4	13
	St. John's	AHL	1	0	0	0	0	....	....	....	....	....
1993-94	St. John's	AHL	44	4	10	14	124	....	....	....	....	....
	Springfield	AHL	9	1	2	3	29	5	0	0	0	16
1994-95	St. John's	AHL	53	2	13	15	239	3	0	0	0	17
1995-96	Binghamton	AHL	68	3	17	20	240	4	0	0	0	9
1996-97	**NY Rangers**	**NHL**	**11**	**1**	**0**	**1**	**30**	....	....	....	....	....
	Binghamton	AHL	38	8	11	19	133	....	....	....	....	....
1997-98	**NY Rangers**	**NHL**	**16**	**1**	**0**	**1**	**38**	....	....	....	....	....
	Hartford	AHL	15	2	0	2	45	....	....	....	....	....
	Chicago	**NHL**	**4**	**0**	**1**	**1**	**5**	....	....	....	....	....
	Indianapolis	IHL	3	1	1	2	4	....	....	....	....	....
	NHL Totals		**31**	**2**	**1**	**3**	**73**	....	....	....	....	....

Signed as a free agent by **NY Rangers**, August 22, 1995. Traded to **Chicago** by **NY Rangers** for Ryan Risidore, March 24, 1998.

VAN DRUNEN, DAVID OTT.

Defense. Shoots right. 6', 200 lbs. Born, Sherwood Park, Alta., January 31, 1976.

			Regular Season					Playoffs				
Season	**Club**	**Lea**	**GP**	**G**	**A**	**TP**	**PIM**	**GP**	**G**	**A**	**TP**	**PIM**
1993-94	Prince Albert	WHL	63	3	10	13	95	....	....	....	....	....
1994-95	Prince Albert	WHL	71	2	14	16	132	15	3	4	7	36
1995-96	Prince Albert	WHL	70	10	23	33	172	18	1	5	6	37
1996-97	Prince Albert	WHL	72	18	47	65	218	4	0	4	4	24
1997-98	Hershey	AHL	5	0	0	0	2	....	....	....	....	....
	Portland	AHL	4	0	0	0	2	....	....	....	....	....
	Baton Rouge	ECHL	59	8	22	30	107	....	....	....	....	....

WHL East Second All-Star Team (1997)

Signed as a free agent by **Ottawa**, May 2, 1997.

VAN IMPE, DARREN (van-IHMP) BOS.

Defense. Shoots left. 6'1", 205 lbs. Born, Saskatoon, Sask., May 18, 1973.
(NY Islanders' 7th choice, 170th overall, in 1993 Entry Draft).

			Regular Season					Playoffs				
Season	Club	Lea	GP	G	A	TP	PIM	GP	G	A	TP	PIM
1990-91	Prince Albert	WHL	70	15	45	60	57	3	1	1	2	2
1991-92	Prince Albert	WHL	69	9	37	46	129	8	1	5	6	10
1992-93	Red Deer	WHL	54	23	47	70	118	4	2	5	7	16
1993-94	Red Deer	WHL	58	20	64	84	125	4	2	4	6	6
1994-95	San Diego	IHL	76	6	17	23	74	5	0	0	0	0
	Anaheim	**NHL**	**1**	**0**	**1**	**1**	**4**	....	....	....	....	....
1995-96	**Anaheim**	**NHL**	**16**	**1**	**2**	**3**	**14**	....	....	....	....	....
	Baltimore	AHL	63	11	47	58	79	....	....	....	....	....
1996-97	**Anaheim**	**NHL**	**74**	**4**	**19**	**23**	**90**	**9**	**0**	**2**	**2**	**16**
1997-98	**Anaheim**	**NHL**	**19**	**1**	**3**	**4**	**4**	....	....	....	....	....
	Boston	**NHL**	**50**	**2**	**8**	**10**	**36**	**6**	**2**	**1**	**3**	**0**
	NHL Totals		**160**	**8**	**33**	**41**	**148**	**15**	**2**	**3**	**5**	**16**

WHL East First All-Star Team (1993, 1994)

Traded to **Anaheim** by **NY Islanders** for Anaheim's 8th round choice (Mike Broda) in 1995 Entry Draft, August 31, 1994. Claimed on waivers by **Boston** from **Anaheim**, November 26, 1997.

VAN OENE, DARREN (van OH-uhn) BUF.

Left wing. Shoots left. 6'3", 207 lbs. Born, Edmonton, Alta., January 18, 1978.
(Buffalo's 3rd choice, 33rd overall, in 1996 Entry Draft).

			Regular Season					Playoffs				
Season	Club	Lea	GP	G	A	TP	PIM	GP	G	A	TP	PIM
1994-95	Brandon	WHL	58	5	13	18	106	18	1	1	2	34
1995-96	Brandon	WHL	47	10	18	28	126	18	1	6	7	*78
1996-97	Brandon	WHL	56	21	27	48	139	6	2	3	5	19
1997-98	Brandon	WHL	51	23	24	47	161	18	6	8	14	51

VAN RYN, MIKE N.J.

Defense. Shoots right. 6'1", 190 lbs. Born, London, Ont., May 14, 1979.
(New Jersey's 1st choice, 26th overall, in 1998 Entry Draft).

			Regular Season					Playoffs				
Season	Club	Lea	GP	G	A	TP	PIM	GP	G	A	TP	PIM
1996-97	London	OJHL	46	14	31	45	32	....	....	....	....	....
1997-98	U. of Michigan	CCHA	38	4	14	18	44	....	....	....	....	....

VARADA, VACLAV (VAH-rah-dah) BUF.

Right wing. Shoots left. 6', 200 lbs. Born, Vsetin, Czech., April 26, 1976.
(San Jose's 4th choice, 89th overall, in 1994 Entry Draft).

			Regular Season					Playoffs				
Season	Club	Lea	GP	G	A	TP	PIM	GP	G	A	TP	PIM
1992-93	Vitkovice	Czech.	1	0	0	0	....	....	....	....	....	....
1993-94	Vitkovice	Cze-Rep.	24	6	7	13	....	5	1	1	2	....
1994-95	Tacoma	WHL	68	50	38	88	108	4	4	3	7	11
1995-96	Kelowna	WHL	59	39	46	85	100	6	3	3	6	16
	Buffalo	**NHL**	**1**	**0**	**0**	**0**	**0**	....	....	....	....	....
	Rochester	AHL	5	3	0	3	4	....	....	....	....	....
1996-97	**Buffalo**	**NHL**	**5**	**0**	**0**	**0**	**2**	....	....	....	....	....
	Rochester	AHL	53	23	25	48	81	10	1	6	7	27
1997-98	**Buffalo**	**NHL**	**27**	**5**	**6**	**11**	**15**	**15**	**3**	**4**	**7**	**18**
	Rochester	AHL	45	30	26	56	74	....	....	....	....	....
	NHL Totals		**33**	**5**	**6**	**11**	**17**	**15**	**3**	**4**	**7**	**18**

Traded to **Buffalo** by **San Jose** with Martin Spahnel and Philadelphia's 1st (previously acquired by San Jose — later traded to Phoenix — Phoenix selected Daniel Briere) and 4th (previously acquired, Buffalo selected Mike Martone) round choices in 1996 Entry Draft for Doug Bodger, November 16, 1995.

VARIS, PETRI (VAH-rihs)

Left wing. Shoots left. 6'1", 200 lbs. Born, Varkaus, Finland, May 13, 1969.
(San Jose's 7th choice, 132nd overall, in 1993 Entry Draft).

			Regular Season					Playoffs				
Season	Club	Lea	GP	G	A	TP	PIM	GP	G	A	TP	PIM
1990-91	KooKoo Espoo	Finland-2	44	20	31	51	42	....	....	....	....	....
1991-92	Assat Pori	Finland	36	13	23	36	24	....	....	....	....	....
1992-93	Assat Pori	Finland	46	14	35	49	42	8	2	2	4	12
1993-94	Jokerit	Finland	31	14	15	29	16	11	3	4	7	6
	Finland	Olympics	5	1	1	2	2	....	....	....	....	....
1994-95	Jokerit	Finland	47	21	20	41	53	11	7	2	9	10
1995-96	Jokerit	Finland	50	28	28	56	22	11	12	7	19	6
1996-97	Jokerit	Finland	50	*36	23	*59	38	9	7	4	11	14
1997-98	**Chicago**	**NHL**	**1**	**0**	**0**	**0**	**0**	....	....	....	....	....
	Indianapolis	IHL	77	18	54	72	32	5	3	4	7	4
	NHL Totals		**1**	**0**	**0**	**0**	**0**	....	....	....	....	....

Finnish Rookie of the Year (1992)

Rights traded to **Chicago** by **San Jose** with San Jose's 6th round choice (Jari Viuhkola) in 1998 Entry Draft for Murray Craven, July 25, 1997.

VARLAMOV, SERGEI (vahr-LAHM-uhf) CGY.

Left wing. Shoots left. 5'11", 190 lbs. Born, Kiev, USSR, July 21, 1978.

			Regular Season					Playoffs				
Season	Club	Lea	GP	G	A	TP	PIM	GP	G	A	TP	PIM
1995-96	Swift Current	WHL	55	23	21	44	65	....	....	....	....	....
1996-97	Swift Current	WHL	72	46	39	85	94	10	3	8	11	10
	Saint John	AHL	1	0	0	0	0	....	....	....	....	....
1997-98	Swift Current	WHL	72	*66	53	*119	132	12	10	5	15	28
	Calgary	**NHL**	**1**	**0**	**0**	**0**	**0**	....	....	....	....	....
	Saint John	AHL	....	....	....	....	....	3	0	0	0	0
	NHL Totals		**1**	**0**	**0**	**0**	**0**	....	....	....	....	....

WHL East First All-Star Team (1998) • Canadian Major Junior First All-Star Team (1998) • Canadian Major Junior Player of the Year (1998)

Signed as a free agent by **Calgary**, September 18, 1996.

VASICEK, JOSEF (VAHSH-ih-chehk, YOH-zehf) CAR.

Center. Shoots left. 6'4", 189 lbs. Born, Havlickuv Brod, Czechoslovakia, September 12, 1980.
(Carolina's 4th choice, 91st overall, in 1998 Entry Draft).

			Regular Season					Playoffs				
Season	Club	Lea	GP	G	A	TP	PIM	GP	G	A	TP	PIM
1995-96	Havlickuv Brod	Czech-Jr.	36	25	25	50	....	....	....	....	....	....
1996-97	Slavia Praha	Czech-Jr.	37	20	40	60	....	....	....	....	....	....
1997-98	Slavia Praha	Czech-Jr.	34	13	20	33	....	....	....	....	....	....

VASILEVSKI, ALEXANDER (vah-sih-LEHV-skee)

Right wing. Shoots left. 5'11", 190 lbs. Born, Kiev, USSR, January 8, 1975.
(St. Louis' 9th choice, 271st overall, in 1993 Entry Draft).

			Regular Season					Playoffs				
Season	Club	Lea	GP	G	A	TP	PIM	GP	G	A	TP	PIM
1992-93	Victoria	WHL	71	27	25	52	52	....	....	....	....	....
1993-94	Victoria	WHL	69	34	51	85	78	....	....	....	....	....
1994-95	Prince George	WHL	48	32	34	66	52	....	....	....	....	....
	Brandon	WHL	23	6	11	17	39	18	3	6	9	34
1995-96	**St. Louis**	**NHL**	**1**	**0**	**0**	**0**	**0**	....	....	....	....	....
	Worcester	AHL	69	18	21	39	112	4	2	1	3	10
1996-97	**St. Louis**	**NHL**	**3**	**0**	**0**	**0**	**2**	....	....	....	....	....
	Worcester	AHL	61	9	23	32	100	....	....	....	....	....
	Grand Rapids	IHL	10	1	5	6	43	5	0	1	1	19
1997-98	Hamilton	AHL	41	3	14	17	60	....	....	....	....	....
	Detroit	IHL	9	1	1	2	7	....	....	....	....	....
	NHL Totals		**4**	**0**	**0**	**0**	**2**	....	....	....	....	....

VASILIEV, ALEXEI (vah-SEE-lee-ehf) NYR

Defense. Shoots left. 6'1", 190 lbs. Born, Yaroslavl, USSR, September 1, 1977.
(NY Rangers' 4th choice, 110th overall, in 1995 Entry Draft).

			Regular Season					Playoffs				
Season	Club	Lea	GP	G	A	TP	PIM	GP	G	A	TP	PIM
1993-94	Yaroslavl	CIS	2	0	1	1	4	....	....	....	....	....
1994-95	Yaroslavl 2	CIS-2	STATISTICS NOT AVAILABLE									
1995-96	Yaroslavl	CIS	40	4	7	11	4	....	....	....	....	....
1996-97	Yaroslavl	Russia	44	2	8	10	10	9	1	1	2	8
1997-98			DID NOT PLAY – INJURED									

• Missed entire 1997-98 season after suffering knee injury at conclusion of training camp, October, 1997.

VASILJEVS, HERBERT (vah-SEE-lee-ehf) FLA.

Center. Shoots right. 5'11", 170 lbs. Born, Riga, USSR, May 27, 1976.

			Regular Season					Playoffs				
Season	Club	Lea	GP	G	A	TP	PIM	GP	G	A	TP	PIM
1995-96	Guelph	OHL	65	34	33	67	63	16	6	13	19	6
1996-97	Carolina	AHL	54	13	18	31	30	....	....	....	....	....
	Port Huron	ColHL	3	3	2	5	4	....	....	....	....	....
1997-98	New Haven	AHL	76	36	30	66	60	3	1	0	1	2

Signed as a free agent by **Florida**, October 3, 1996.

VASILYEV, ANDREI (vah-SEE-lee-ehf) PHX.

Left wing. Shoots right. 5'9", 180 lbs. Born, Voskresensk, USSR, March 30, 1972.
(NY Islanders' 11th choice, 248th overall, in 1992 Entry Draft).

			Regular Season					Playoffs				
Season	Club	Lea	GP	G	A	TP	PIM	GP	G	A	TP	PIM
1991-92	CSKA Moscow	CIS	28	7	2	9	2	....	....	....	....	....
1992-93	Khimik	CIS	34	4	8	12	20	....	....	....	....	....
1993-94	CSKA Moscow	CIS	46	17	6	23	8	3	1	0	1	0
1994-95	Denver	IHL	74	28	37	65	48	13	9	4	13	22
	NY Islanders	**NHL**	**2**	**0**	**0**	**0**	**2**	....	....	....	....	....
1995-96	**NY Islanders**	**NHL**	**10**	**2**	**5**	**7**	**2**	....	....	....	....	....
	Utah	IHL	43	26	20	46	34	22	12	4	16	18
1996-97	**NY Islanders**	**NHL**	**3**	**0**	**0**	**0**	**2**	....	....	....	....	....
	Utah	IHL	56	16	18	34	42	7	4	1	5	0
1997-98	Long Beach	IHL	62	33	34	67	60	17	9	4	13	14
	NHL Totals		**15**	**2**	**5**	**7**	**6**	....	....	....	....	....

Signed as a free agent by **Phoenix**, August 5, 1998.

VASKE, DENNIS (VAS-kee)

Defense. Shoots left. 6'2", 210 lbs. Born, Rockford, IL, October 11, 1967.
(NY Islanders' 2nd choice, 38th overall, in 1986 Entry Draft).

			Regular Season					Playoffs				
Season	Club	Lea	GP	G	A	TP	PIM	GP	G	A	TP	PIM
1985-86	Armstrong	H.S.	20	9	13	22	....	....	....	....	....	....
1986-87	U. Minn-Duluth	WCHA	33	0	2	2	40	....	....	....	....	....
1987-88	U. Minn-Duluth	WCHA	39	1	6	7	90	....	....	....	....	....
1988-89	U. Minn-Duluth	WCHA	37	9	19	28	86	....	....	....	....	....
1989-90	U. Minn-Duluth	WCHA	37	5	24	29	72	....	....	....	....	....
1990-91	**NY Islanders**	**NHL**	**5**	**0**	**0**	**0**	**2**	....	....	....	....	....
	Capital District	AHL	67	10	10	20	65	....	....	....	....	....
1991-92	**NY Islanders**	**NHL**	**39**	**0**	**1**	**1**	**39**	....	....	....	....	....
	Capital District	AHL	31	1	11	12	59	....	....	....	....	....
1992-93	**NY Islanders**	**NHL**	**27**	**1**	**5**	**6**	**32**	**18**	**0**	**6**	**6**	**14**
	Capital District	AHL	42	4	15	19	70	....	....	....	....	....
1993-94	**NY Islanders**	**NHL**	**65**	**2**	**11**	**13**	**76**	**4**	**0**	**1**	**1**	**2**
1994-95	**NY Islanders**	**NHL**	**41**	**1**	**11**	**12**	**53**	....	....	....	....	....
1995-96	**NY Islanders**	**NHL**	**19**	**1**	**6**	**7**	**21**	....	....	....	....	....
1996-97	**NY Islanders**	**NHL**	**17**	**0**	**4**	**4**	**12**	....	....	....	....	....
1997-98	**NY Islanders**	**NHL**	**19**	**0**	**3**	**3**	**12**	....	....	....	....	....
	NHL Totals		**232**	**5**	**41**	**46**	**247**	**22**	**0**	**7**	**7**	**16**

VAUCLAIR, JULIEN (voh-KLAIR) OTT.

Defense. Shoots left. 6'1" 198 lbs. Born, Delemont, Switzerland, October 2, 1979.
(Ottawa's 4th choice, 74th overall, in 1998 Entry Draft).

			Regular Season					Playoffs				
Season	Club	Lea	GP	G	A	TP	PIM	GP	G	A	TP	PIM
1995-96	Ajoie	Switz-3	20	4	10	14	....	....	....	....	....	....
1996-97	Ajoie	Switz-2	40	0	6	6	24	9	0	2	2	8
1997-98	Lugano	Switz.	36	1	2	3	12	7	0	0	0	25

VELLINGA, MIKE CGY.

Defense. Shoots right. 6'1", 218 lbs. Born, Chatham, Ont., August 19, 1978.
(Chicago's 5th choice, 184th overall, in 1996 Entry Draft).

			Regular Season					Playoffs				
Season	Club	Lea	GP	G	A	TP	PIM	GP	G	A	TP	PIM
1995-96	Guelph	OHL	57	3	8	11	32	16	2	6	8	6
1996-97	Guelph	OHL	66	6	30	36	73	18	1	9	10	34
1997-98	Guelph	OHL	63	6	22	28	101	12	1	8	9	28

Signed as a free agent by **Calgary**, July 21, 1998.

VERBEEK, PAT (vuhr-BEEK) DAL.

Right/Left wing. Shoots right. 5'9", 192 lbs. Born, Sarnia, Ont., May 24, 1964.
(New Jersey's 3rd choice, 43rd overall, in 1982 Entry Draft).

			Regular Season					Playoffs				
Season	Club	Lea	GP	G	A	TP	PIM	GP	G	A	TP	PIM
1980-81	Petrolia Jets	OJHL	42	44	44	88	155	....	....	....	....	....
1981-82	Sudbury	OHL	66	37	51	88	180	....	....	....	....	....
1982-83	Sudbury	OHL	61	40	67	107	184	....	....	....	....	....
	New Jersey	**NHL**	**6**	**3**	**2**	**5**	**8**	....	....	....	....	....
1983-84	**New Jersey**	**NHL**	**79**	**20**	**27**	**47**	**158**	....	....	....	....	....
1984-85	**New Jersey**	**NHL**	**78**	**15**	**18**	**33**	**162**	....	....	....	....	....
1985-86	**New Jersey**	**NHL**	**76**	**25**	**28**	**53**	**79**	....	....	....	....	....
1986-87	**New Jersey**	**NHL**	**74**	**35**	**24**	**59**	**120**	....	....	....	....	....
1987-88	**New Jersey**	**NHL**	**73**	**46**	**31**	**77**	**227**	**20**	**4**	**8**	**12**	**51**
1988-89	**New Jersey**	**NHL**	**77**	**26**	**21**	**47**	**189**	....	....	....	....	....
1989-90	**Hartford**	**NHL**	**80**	**44**	**45**	**89**	**228**	**7**	**2**	**2**	**4**	**26**
1990-91	**Hartford**	**NHL**	**80**	**43**	**39**	**82**	**246**	**6**	**3**	**2**	**5**	**40**
1991-92	**Hartford**	**NHL**	**76**	**22**	**35**	**57**	**243**	**7**	**0**	**2**	**2**	**12**
1992-93	**Hartford**	**NHL**	**84**	**39**	**43**	**82**	**197**	....	....	....	....	....
1993-94	**Hartford**	**NHL**	**84**	**37**	**38**	**75**	**177**	....	....	....	....	....
1994-95	**Hartford**	**NHL**	**29**	**7**	**11**	**18**	**53**	....	....	....	....	....
	NY Rangers	**NHL**	**19**	**10**	**5**	**15**	**18**	**10**	**4**	**6**	**10**	**20**
1995-96	**NY Rangers**	**NHL**	**69**	**41**	**41**	**82**	**129**	**11**	**3**	**6**	**9**	**12**
1996-97	**Dallas**	**NHL**	**81**	**17**	**36**	**53**	**128**	**7**	**1**	**3**	**4**	**16**
1997-98	**Dallas**	**NHL**	**82**	**31**	**26**	**57**	**170**	**17**	**3**	**2**	**5**	**26**
	NHL Totals		**1147**	**461**	**470**	**931**	**2532**	**85**	**20**	**31**	**51**	**203**

Played in NHL All-Star Game (1991, 1996)

Traded to **Hartford** by **New Jersey** for Sylvain Turgeon, June 17, 1989. Traded to **NY Rangers** by **Hartford** for Glen Featherstone, Michael Stewart, NY Rangers' 1st round choice (Jean-Sebastien Giguere) in 1995 Entry Draft and 4th round choice (Steve Wasylko) in 1996 Entry Draft, March 23, 1995. Signed as a free agent by **Dallas**, August 21, 1996.

VERCIK, RUDOLF (VEHR-chihk) NYR

Left wing. Shoots left. 6'1", 189 lbs. Born, Bratislava, Czech., March 19, 1976.
(NY Rangers' 2nd choice, 52nd overall, in 1994 Entry Draft).

			Regular Season					Playoffs				
Season	Club	Lea	GP	G	A	TP	PIM	GP	G	A	TP	PIM
1993-94	Bratislava	Slovakia	17	1	4	5	14	....	....	....	....	....
1994-95	Bratislava	Slovakia	33	14	9	23	22	....	....	....	....	....
1995-96	Bratislava	Slovakia	28	7	3	10	61	13	1	0	1	....
1996-97	Bratislava	Slovakia	40	8	3	11	....	2	0	0	0	....
1997-98	Nova Ves	Slovakia	36	8	5	13	36	3	1	1	2	0

VERTALA, TIMO (vehr-TAH-lah, TEE-moh) MTL.

Right wing. Shoots left. 6'1", 180 lbs. Born, Jyvaskyla, Finland, May 2, 1978.
(Montreal's 8th choice, 181st overall, in 1996 Entry Draft).

			Regular Season					Playoffs				
Season	Club	Lea	GP	G	A	TP	PIM	GP	G	A	TP	PIM
1995-96	JyP HT	Finland	3	0	1	1	2	....	....	....	....	....
	JyP HT	Fin-Jr.	35	15	10	25	54	6	1	1	2	6
1996-97	JyP HT	Finland	46	8	5	13	39	4	0	0	0	0
	JyP HT	Fin-Jr.	7	4	4	8	12	....	....	....	....	....
1997-98	JyP HT	Finland	43	4	8	12	34	....	....	....	....	....

VIAL, DENNIS (vee-AL)

Left wing. Shoots left. 6'1", 220 lbs. Born, Sault Ste. Marie, Ont., April 10, 1969.
(NY Rangers' 5th choice, 110th overall, in 1988 Entry Draft).

			Regular Season					Playoffs				
Season	Club	Lea	GP	G	A	TP	PIM	GP	G	A	TP	PIM
1985-86	Hamilton	OHL	31	1	1	2	66	....	....	....	....	....
1986-87	Hamilton	OHL	53	1	8	9	194	8	0	0	0	8
1987-88	Hamilton	OHL	52	3	17	20	229	13	2	2	4	49
1988-89	Niagara Falls	OHL	50	10	27	37	227	15	1	7	8	44
1989-90	Flint	IHL	79	6	29	35	351	4	0	0	0	10
1990-91	**NY Rangers**	**NHL**	**21**	**0**	**0**	**0**	**61**	....	....	....	....	....
	Binghamton	AHL	40	2	7	9	250	....	....	....	....	....
	Detroit	**NHL**	**9**	**0**	**0**	**0**	**16**	....	....	....	....	....
1991-92	**Detroit**	**NHL**	**27**	**1**	**0**	**1**	**72**	....	....	....	....	....
	Adirondack	AHL	20	2	4	6	107	17	1	3	4	43
1992-93	**Detroit**	**NHL**	**9**	**0**	**1**	**1**	**20**	....	....	....	....	....
	Adirondack	AHL	30	2	11	13	177	11	1	1	2	14
1993-94	**Ottawa**	**NHL**	**55**	**2**	**5**	**7**	**214**	....	....	....	....	....
1994-95	**Ottawa**	**NHL**	**27**	**0**	**4**	**4**	**65**	....	....	....	....	....
1995-96	**Ottawa**	**NHL**	**64**	**1**	**4**	**5**	**276**	....	....	....	....	....
1996-97	**Ottawa**	**NHL**	**11**	**0**	**1**	**1**	**25**	....	....	....	....	....
1997-98	**Ottawa**	**NHL**	**19**	**0**	**0**	**0**	**45**	....	....	....	....	....
	Chicago	IHL	24	1	3	4	86	1	0	0	0	2
	NHL Totals		**242**	**4**	**15**	**19**	**794**	....	....	....	....	....

Traded to **Detroit** by **NY Rangers** with Kevin Miller and Jim Cummins for Joey Kocur and Per Djoos, March 5, 1991. Traded to **Quebec** by **Detroit** with Doug Crossman for cash, June 15, 1992. Traded to **Detroit** by **Quebec** for cash, September 9, 1992. Traded to **Tampa Bay** by **Detroit** for Steve Maltais, June 8, 1993. Claimed by **Anaheim** from **Tampa Bay** in Expansion Draft, June 24, 1993. Claimed by **Ottawa** from **Anaheim** in Phase II of Expansion Draft, June 25, 1993.

VISHEAU, MARK (VEE-SHOO) L.A.

Defense. Shoots right. 6'6", 222 lbs. Born, Burlington, Ont., June 27, 1973.
(Winnipeg's 4th choice, 84th overall, in 1992 Entry Draft).

			Regular Season					Playoffs				
Season	Club	Lea	GP	G	A	TP	PIM	GP	G	A	TP	PIM
1990-91	London	OHL	59	4	11	15	40	7	0	1	1	6
1991-92	London	OHL	66	5	31	36	104	10	0	4	4	27
1992-93	London	OHL	62	8	52	60	88	12	0	5	5	26
1993-94	**Winnipeg**	**NHL**	**1**	**0**	**0**	**0**	**0**	....	....	....	....	....
	Moncton	AHL	48	4	5	9	58	....	....	....	....	....
1994-95	Springfield	AHL	35	0	4	4	94	....	....	....	....	....
1995-96	Cape Breton	AHL	8	0	0	0	30	....	....	....	....	....
	Minnesota	IHL	10	0	0	0	25	....	....	....	....	....
	Wheeling	ECHL	7	1	2	3	14	7	0	3	3	4
1996-97	Raleigh	ECHL	15	1	5	6	61	....	....	....	....	....
	Quebec	IHL	64	3	10	13	173	9	1	1	2	11
1997-98	Milwaukee	IHL	72	4	12	16	227	....	....	....	....	....
	NHL Totals		**1**	**0**	**0**	**0**	**0**	....	....	....	....	....

Signed as a free agent by **LA Kings**, July 30, 1997.

VISHNEVSKY, VITALI (vihsh-NEHV-skee, vih-TAL-ee) ANA.

Defense. Shoots left. 6'1", 190 lbs. Born, Kharkov, USSR, March 18, 1980.
(Anaheim's 1st choice, 5th overall, in 1998 Entry Draft).

			Regular Season					Playoffs				
Season	Club	Lea	GP	G	A	TP	PIM	GP	G	A	TP	PIM
1995-96	Yaroslavl 2	Russia-2	40	4	4	8	20	....	....	....	....	....
1996-97	Yaroslavl 2	Russia-3	45	0	2	2	30	....	....	....	....	....
1997-98	Yaroslavl 2	Russia-2	47	8	9	17	164	....	....	....	....	....

VIUHKOLA, JARI (VEW-koh-lak, YA-ree) CHI.

Center. Shoots left. 6', 165 lbs. Born, Oulu, Finland, February 27, 1980.
(Chicago's 4th choice, 158th overall, in 1998 Entry Draft).

			Regular Season					Playoffs				
Season	Club	Lea	GP	G	A	TP	PIM	GP	G	A	TP	PIM
1996-97	Karpat Oulu	Fin-Jr.	32	8	11	19	74	....	....	....	....	....
1997-98	Karpat Oulu	Fin-Jr.	28	8	18	26	57	....	....	....	....	....

VLASENKOV, DMITRI (vlah-SEHN-khahf) CGY.

Left wing. Shoots left. 5'11", 183 lbs. Born, Olenigorsk, USSR, January 1, 1978.
(Calgary's 4th choice, 73rd overall, in 1996 Entry Draft).

			Regular Season					Playoffs				
Season	Club	Lea	GP	G	A	TP	PIM	GP	G	A	TP	PIM
1995-96	Yaroslavl	CIS	17	1	1	2	4	1	0	0	0	0
1996-97	Yaroslavl 2	Russia-3	18	10	2	12	6	....	....	....	....	....
	Yaroslavl	Russia	28	3	2	5	10	8	1	1	2	2
1997-98	Yaroslavl	EuroHL	6	0	0	0	2	....	....	....	....	....
	Yaroslavl	Russia	44	10	3	13	12	....	....	....	....	....

VOLCHKOV, ALEXANDER (VOHLCH-kahf) WSH.

Center. Shoots left. 6'1", 205 lbs. Born, Moscow, USSR, September 25, 1977.
(Washington's 1st choice, 4th overall, in 1996 Entry Draft).

			Regular Season					Playoffs				
Season	Club	Lea	GP	G	A	TP	PIM	GP	G	A	TP	PIM
1994-95	CSKA Moscow	CIS	1	0	0	0	0	....	....	....	....	....
1995-96	Barrie	OHL	47	37	27	64	36	7	2	3	5	12
1996-97	Barrie	OHL	56	29	53	82	76	9	6	9	15	12
	Portland	AHL	....	....	....	....	....	4	0	0	0	0
1997-98	Portland	AHL	34	2	5	7	20	1	0	0	0	0

OHL Second All-Star Team (1997)

VOPAT, JAN (VOH-paht) NSH.

Defense. Shoots left. 6', 205 lbs. Born, Most, Czech., March 22, 1973.
(Hartford's 3rd choice, 57th overall, in 1992 Entry Draft).

			Regular Season					Playoffs				
Season	Club	Lea	GP	G	A	TP	PIM	GP	G	A	TP	PIM
1990-91	Litvinov	Czech.	25	1	4	5	4	....	....	....	....	....
1991-92	Litvinov	Czech.	46	4	2	6	16	....	....	....	....	....
1992-93	Litvinov	Czech.	45	12	10	22	....	....	....	....	....	....
1993-94	Litvinov	Cze-Rep.	41	9	19	28	0	4	1	1	2	....
	Czech Republic	Olympics	8	0	1	1	8	....	....	....	....	....
1994-95	Litvinov	Cze-Rep.	42	7	18	25	49	4	0	2	2	2
1995-96	**Los Angeles**	**NHL**	**11**	**1**	**4**	**5**	**4**	....	....	....	....	....
	Phoenix	IHL	47	0	9	9	34	4	0	2	2	4
1996-97	**Los Angeles**	**NHL**	**33**	**4**	**5**	**9**	**22**	....	....	....	....	....
	Phoenix	IHL	4	0	6	6	6	....	....	....	....	....
1997-98	**Los Angeles**	**NHL**	**21**	**1**	**5**	**6**	**10**	**2**	**0**	**1**	**1**	**2**
	Utah	IHL	38	8	13	21	24	....	....	....	....	....
	NHL Totals		**65**	**6**	**14**	**20**	**36**	**2**	**0**	**1**	**1**	**2**

Rights traded to **LA Kings** by **Hartford** for LA Kings' 4th round choice (Ian MacNeil) in 1995 Entry Draft, May 31, 1995. Traded to **Nashville** by **LA Kings** with Kimmo Timonen for future considerations, June 26, 1998.

VOPAT, ROMAN (VOH-paht) L.A.

Center. Shoots left. 6'3", 223 lbs. Born, Litvinov, Czech., April 21, 1976.
(St. Louis' 4th choice, 172nd overall, in 1994 Entry Draft).

			Regular Season					Playoffs				
Season	Club	Lea	GP	G	A	TP	PIM	GP	G	A	TP	PIM
1993-94	Litvinov	Cze-Rep.	7	0	0	0	0	....	....	....	....	....
1994-95	Moose Jaw	WHL	72	23	20	43	141	10	4	1	5	28
	Peoria	IHL	....	....	....	....	....	6	0	2	2	2
1995-96	Moose Jaw	WHL	7	0	4	4	34	....	....	....	....	....
	Prince Albert	WHL	22	15	5	20	81	18	9	8	17	57
	St. Louis	**NHL**	**25**	**2**	**3**	**5**	**48**	....	....	....	....	....
	Worcester	AHL	5	2	0	2	14	....	....	....	....	....
1996-97	**Los Angeles**	**NHL**	**29**	**4**	**5**	**9**	**60**	....	....	....	....	....
	Phoenix	IHL	50	8	8	16	139	....	....	....	....	....
1997-98	**Los Angeles**	**NHL**	**25**	**0**	**3**	**3**	**55**	....	....	....	....	....
	Fredericton	AHL	29	10	10	20	93	....	....	....	....	....
	NHL Totals		**79**	**6**	**11**	**17**	**163**	....	....	....	....	....

Traded to **LA Kings** by **St. Louis** with Craig Johnson, Patrice Tardif, St. Louis 5th round choice (Peter Hogan) in 1996 Entry Draft and 1st round choice (Matt Zultek) in 1997 Entry Draft for Wayne Gretzky, February 27, 1996.

VOROBIEV, VLADIMIR (vah-roh-BEE-ehf) NYR

Left wing. Shoots right. 6', 185 lbs. Born, Cherepovets, USSR, October 2, 1972.
(NY Rangers' 10th choice, 240th overall, in 1992 Entry Draft).

			Regular Season					Playoffs				
Season	Club	Lea	GP	G	A	TP	PIM	GP	G	A	TP	PIM
1992-93	Cherepovets	CIS	42	18	5	23	18	....	....	....	....	....
1993-94	Moscow D'amo	CIS	11	3	1	4	2	....	....	....	....	....
1994-95	Moscow D'amo	CIS	48	9	20	29	28	14	1	7	8	2
1995-96	Moscow D'amo	CIS	42	19	9	28	49	9	2	8	10	2
1996-97	**NY Rangers**	**NHL**	**16**	**5**	**5**	**10**	**6**	....	....	....	....	....
	Binghamton	AHL	61	22	27	49	6	4	1	1	2	2
1997-98	**NY Rangers**	**NHL**	**15**	**2**	**2**	**4**	**6**	....	....	....	....	....
	Hartford	AHL	56	20	28	48	18	15	11	8	19	4
	NHL Totals		**31**	**7**	**7**	**14**	**12**	....	....	....	....	....

VOTH, BRAD ST.L.

Defense. Shoots right. 6'4", 223 lbs. Born, Saskatoon, Sask., February 25, 1980.
(St. Louis' 4th choice, 157th overall, in 1998 Entry Draft).

			Regular Season					Playoffs				
Season	Club	Lea	GP	G	A	TP	PIM	GP	G	A	TP	PIM
1996-97	Medicine Hat	WHL	2	0	0	0	2	....	....	....	....	....
1997-98	Medicine Hat	WHL	70	8	5	13	244	....	....	....	....	....

VUJTEK, VLADIMIR (VYOO-tehk)

Left wing. Shoots left. 6'1", 190 lbs. Born, Ostrava, Czech., February 17, 1972.
(Montreal's 5th choice, 73rd overall, in 1991 Entry Draft).

			Regular Season					Playoffs				
Season	**Club**	**Lea**	**GP**	**G**	**A**	**TP**	**PIM**	**GP**	**G**	**A**	**TP**	**PIM**
1988-89	Vitkovice	Czech.	3	0	1	1	0	....	....	....	....	....
1989-90	Vitkovice	Czech.	29	7	7	14	....	....	....	....	....	....
1990-91	Vitkovice	Czech.	26	7	4	11	....	....	....	....	....	....
	Tri-City	WHL	37	26	18	44	25	7	2	3	5	4
1991-92	Tri-City	WHL	53	41	61	102	114	....	....	....	....	....
	Montreal	**NHL**	**2**	**0**	**0**	**0**	**0**	....	....	....	....	....
1992-93	**Edmonton**	**NHL**	**30**	**1**	**10**	**11**	**8**	....	....	....	....	....
	Cape Breton	AHL	20	10	9	19	14	1	0	0	0	0
1993-94	**Edmonton**	**NHL**	**40**	**4**	**15**	**19**	**14**	....	....	....	....	....
1994-95	Vitkovice	Cze-Rep.	18	5	7	12	51	....	....	....	....	....
	Cape Breton	AHL	30	10	11	21	30	....	....	....	....	....
	Las Vegas	IHL	1	0	0	0	0	....	....	....	....	....
1995-96	Vitkovice	Cze-Rep.	26	6	7	13	....	4	1	1	2	....
1996-97	Assat Pori	Finland	50	27	31	58	48	4	1	2	3	2
1997-98	**Tampa Bay**	**NHL**	**30**	**2**	**4**	**6**	**16**	....	....	....	....	....
	Adirondack	AHL	2	1	2	3	0	....	....	....	....	....
	NHL Totals		**102**	**7**	**29**	**36**	**38**	....	....	....	....	....

WHL West First All-Star Team (1992)

Traded to **Edmonton** by **Montreal** with Shayne Corson and Brent Gilchrist for Vincent Damphousse and Edmonton's 4th round choice (Adam Wiesel) in 1993 Entry Draft, August 27, 1992. Traded to **Tampa Bay** by **Edmonton** with Edmonton's 3rd round choice (Dmitri Afanasenkov) in 1998 Entry Draft for Brantt Myhres and Toronto's 3rd round choice (previously acquired, Edmonton selected Alex Henry) in 1998 Entry Draft, July 16, 1997.

VUKOTA, MICK (vuh-KOH-tuh)

Right wing. Shoots right. 6'1", 225 lbs. Born, Saskatoon, Sask., September 14, 1966.

			Regular Season					Playoffs				
Season	**Club**	**Lea**	**GP**	**G**	**A**	**TP**	**PIM**	**GP**	**G**	**A**	**TP**	**PIM**
1983-84	Winnipeg	WHL	3	1	1	2	10	....	....	....	....	....
1984-85	Kelowna	WHL	66	10	6	16	247	....	....	....	....	....
1985-86	Spokane	WHL	64	19	14	33	369	9	6	4	10	68
1986-87	Spokane	WHL	61	25	28	53	*337	4	0	0	0	40
1987-88	**NY Islanders**	**NHL**	**17**	**1**	**0**	**1**	**82**	**2**	**0**	**0**	**0**	**23**
	Springfield	AHL	52	7	9	16	375	....	....	....	....	....
1988-89	**NY Islanders**	**NHL**	**48**	**2**	**2**	**4**	**237**	....	....	....	....	....
	Springfield	AHL	3	1	0	1	33	....	....	....	....	....
1989-90	**NY Islanders**	**NHL**	**76**	**4**	**8**	**12**	**290**	**1**	**0**	**0**	**0**	**17**
1990-91	**NY Islanders**	**NHL**	**60**	**2**	**4**	**6**	**238**	....	....	....	....	....
	Capital District	AHL	2	0	0	0	9	....	....	....	....	....
1991-92	**NY Islanders**	**NHL**	**74**	**0**	**6**	**6**	**293**	....	....	....	....	....
1992-93	**NY Islanders**	**NHL**	**74**	**2**	**5**	**7**	**216**	**15**	**0**	**0**	**0**	**16**
1993-94	**NY Islanders**	**NHL**	**72**	**3**	**1**	**4**	**237**	**4**	**0**	**0**	**0**	**17**
1994-95	**NY Islanders**	**NHL**	**40**	**0**	**2**	**2**	**109**	....	....	....	....	....
1995-96	**NY Islanders**	**NHL**	**32**	**1**	**1**	**2**	**106**	....	....	....	....	....
1996-97	**NY Islanders**	**NHL**	**17**	**1**	**0**	**1**	**71**	....	....	....	....	....
	Utah	IHL	43	11	11	22	185	7	1	2	3	20
1997-98	**Tampa Bay**	**NHL**	**42**	**1**	**0**	**1**	**116**	....	....	....	....	....
	Montreal	**NHL**	**22**	**0**	**0**	**0**	**76**	**1**	**0**	**0**	**0**	**0**
	NHL Totals		**574**	**17**	**29**	**46**	**2071**	**23**	**0**	**0**	**0**	**73**

Signed as a free agent by **NY Islanders**, March 2, 1987. Claimed by **Tampa Bay** from **NY Islanders** in NHL Waiver Draft, September 28, 1997. Traded to **Montreal** by **Tampa Bay** with Patrick Poulin and Igor Ulanov for Stephane Richer, Darcy Tucker and David Wilkie, January 15, 1998.

VYSHEDKEVICH, SERGEI (vee-shehd-KAY-vihch) N.J.

Defense. Shoots left. 6', 195 lbs. Born, Dedovsk, USSR, January 3, 1975.
(New Jersey's 3rd choice, 70th overall, in 1995 Entry Draft).

			Regular Season					Playoffs				
Season	**Club**	**Lea**	**GP**	**G**	**A**	**TP**	**PIM**	**GP**	**G**	**A**	**TP**	**PIM**
1994-95	Moscow D'amo	CIS	49	6	7	13	67	14	2	0	2	12
1995-96	Moscow D'amo	CIS	49	5	4	9	12	13	1	1	2	6
1996-97	Albany	AHL	65	8	27	35	16	12	0	6	6	0
1997-98	Albany	AHL	54	12	16	28	12	13	0	10	10	4

WALBY, STEFFON BUF.

Right wing. Shoots right. 6'1", 198 lbs. Born, Madison, WI, November 22, 1972.

			Regular Season					Playoffs				
Season	**Club**	**Lea**	**GP**	**G**	**A**	**TP**	**PIM**	**GP**	**G**	**A**	**TP**	**PIM**
1992-93	Kelowna	BCJHL	59	53	68	121	76	....	....	....	....	....
1993-94	St. John's	AHL	63	15	22	37	79	2	0	0	0	2
1994-95	St. John's	AHL	70	23	23	46	30	5	1	1	2	4
1995-96	St. John's	AHL	57	23	31	54	61	4	2	2	4	17
1996-97	Hershey	AHL	74	24	23	47	61	19	7	3	10	34
1997-98	Fort Wayne	IHL	77	28	26	54	53	4	1	1	2	6

Signed as a free agent by **Toronto**, August 20, 1993. Signed as a free agent by **Buffalo**, August 31, 1998.

WALKER, MATT ST.L.

Defense. Shoots right. 6'2", 212 lbs. Born, Beaverlodge, Alta., April 7, 1980.
(St. Louis' 3rd choice, 83rd overall, in 1998 Entry Draft).

			Regular Season					Playoffs				
Season	**Club**	**Lea**	**GP**	**G**	**A**	**TP**	**PIM**	**GP**	**G**	**A**	**TP**	**PIM**
1997-98	Portland	WHL	64	2	13	15	124	16	0	0	0	21

WALKER, SCOTT NSH.

Center. Shoots right. 5'10", 189 lbs. Born, Montreal, Que., July 19, 1973.
(Vancouver's 4th choice, 124th overall, in 1993 Entry Draft).

			Regular Season					Playoffs				
Season	**Club**	**Lea**	**GP**	**G**	**A**	**TP**	**PIM**	**GP**	**G**	**A**	**TP**	**PIM**
1991-92	Owen Sound	OHL	53	7	31	38	128	5	0	7	7	8
1992-93	Owen Sound	OHL	57	23	68	91	110	8	1	5	6	16
	Canada	Nat-Tm	2	3	0	3	0	....	....	....	....	....
1993-94	Hamilton	AHL	77	10	29	39	272	4	0	1	1	25
1994-95	Syracuse	AHL	74	14	38	52	334	....	....	....	....	....
	Vancouver	**NHL**	**11**	**0**	**1**	**1**	**33**	....	....	....	....	....
1995-96	**Vancouver**	**NHL**	**63**	**4**	**8**	**12**	**137**	....	....	....	....	....
	Syracuse	AHL	15	3	12	15	52	16	9	8	17	39
1996-97	**Vancouver**	**NHL**	**64**	**3**	**15**	**18**	**132**	....	....	....	....	....
1997-98	**Vancouver**	**NHL**	**59**	**3**	**10**	**13**	**164**	....	....	....	....	....
	NHL Totals		**197**	**10**	**34**	**44**	**466**	....	....	....	....	....

OHL Second All-Star Team (1993)

Claimed by **Nashville** from **Vancouver** in Expansion Draft, June 26, 1998.

WALLIN, JESSE (WAHL-ihn) DET.

Defense. Shoots left. 6'2", 190 lbs. Born, Saskatoon, Sask., March 10, 1978.
(Detroit's 1st choice, 26th overall, in 1996 Entry Draft).

			Regular Season					Playoffs				
Season	**Club**	**Lea**	**GP**	**G**	**A**	**TP**	**PIM**	**GP**	**G**	**A**	**TP**	**PIM**
1994-95	Red Deer	WHL	72	4	20	24	72	....	....	....	....	....
1995-96	Red Deer	WHL	70	5	19	24	61	9	0	3	3	4
1996-97	Red Deer	WHL	59	6	33	39	70	16	1	4	5	10
1997-98	Red Deer	WHL	14	1	6	7	17	5	0	1	1	2

WALLIN, RICKARD (WAHL-in) PHX.

Center. Shoots left. 6'2", 183 lbs. Born, Stockholm, Sweden, April 19, 1980.
(Phoenix's 8th choice, 160th overall, in 1998 Entry Draft).

			Regular Season					Playoffs				
Season	**Club**	**Lea**	**GP**	**G**	**A**	**TP**	**PIM**	**GP**	**G**	**A**	**TP**	**PIM**
1996-97	Farjestad	Swe-Jr.	26	3	3	6	....	....	....	....	....	....
1997-98	Farjestad	Swe-Jr.	29	20	30	50	32	2	1	1	2	2

WALLIN, VIKTOR (WAHL-in) ANA.

Center. Shoots left. 6'3", 200 lbs. Born, Jonkoping, Sweden, January 17, 1980.
(Anaheim's 3rd choice, 112th overall, in 1998 Entry Draft).

			Regular Season					Playoffs				
Season	**Club**	**Lea**	**GP**	**G**	**A**	**TP**	**PIM**	**GP**	**G**	**A**	**TP**	**PIM**
1996-97	HV 71 Jonkoping	Swe-Jr.	16	1	2	3	....	....	....	....	....	....
1997-98	HV 71 Jonkoping	Swe-Jr.	28	9	15	24	42	....	....	....	....	....

WALSH, KURT

Right wing. Shoots right. 6'2", 205 lbs. Born, St. John's, Nfld., September 26, 1977.
(Buffalo's 5th choice, 87th overall, in 1996 Entry Draft).

			Regular Season					Playoffs				
Season	**Club**	**Lea**	**GP**	**G**	**A**	**TP**	**PIM**	**GP**	**G**	**A**	**TP**	**PIM**
1993-94	Newmarket	OHL	35	1	2	3	23	....	....	....	....	....
1994-95	Sarnia	OHL	17	0	4	4	18	....	....	....	....	....
	Oshawa	OHL	42	6	10	16	31	....	....	....	....	....
1995-96	Oshawa	OHL	41	19	18	37	63	....	....	....	....	....
	Owen Sound	OHL	26	8	9	17	20	6	0	2	2	4
1996-97	Owen Sound	OHL	63	17	16	33	73	4	0	0	0	11
1997-98	Kingston	OHL	12	5	5	10	18	....	....	....	....	....

WALZ, WES (WAHLZ)

Center. Shoots right. 5'10", 185 lbs. Born, Calgary, Alta., May 15, 1970.
(Boston's 3rd choice, 57th overall, in 1989 Entry Draft).

			Regular Season					Playoffs				
Season	**Club**	**Lea**	**GP**	**G**	**A**	**TP**	**PIM**	**GP**	**G**	**A**	**TP**	**PIM**
1988-89	Lethbridge	WHL	63	29	75	104	32	8	1	5	6	6
1989-90	Lethbridge	WHL	56	54	86	140	69	19	13	*24	*37	33
	Boston	**NHL**	**2**	**1**	**1**	**2**	**0**	....	....	....	....	....
1990-91	**Boston**	**NHL**	**56**	**8**	**8**	**16**	**32**	**2**	**0**	**0**	**0**	**0**
	Maine	AHL	20	8	12	20	19	2	0	0	0	21
1991-92	**Boston**	**NHL**	**15**	**0**	**3**	**3**	**12**	....	....	....	....	....
	Maine	AHL	21	13	11	24	38	....	....	....	....	....
	Philadelphia	**NHL**	**2**	**1**	**0**	**1**	**0**	....	....	....	....	....
	Hershey	AHL	41	13	28	41	37	6	1	2	3	0
1992-93	Hershey	AHL	78	35	45	80	106	....	....	....	....	....
1993-94	**Calgary**	**NHL**	**53**	**11**	**27**	**38**	**16**	**6**	**3**	**0**	**3**	**2**
	Saint John	AHL	15	6	6	12	14	....	....	....	....	....
1994-95	**Calgary**	**NHL**	**39**	**6**	**12**	**18**	**11**	**1**	**0**	**0**	**0**	**0**
1995-96	**Detroit**	**NHL**	**2**	**0**	**0**	**0**	**0**	....	....	....	....	....
	Adirondack	AHL	38	20	35	55	58	....	....	....	....	....
1996-97	EV Zug	Switz.	41	24	22	46	67	9	5	1	6	39
1997-98	EV Zug	Switz.	38	18	34	52	32	20	*16	*12	*28	18
	NHL Totals		**169**	**27**	**51**	**78**	**71**	**9**	**3**	**0**	**3**	**2**

WHL East First All-Star Team (1990)

Traded to **Philadelphia** by **Boston** with Garry Galley and Boston's 3rd round choice (Milos Holan) in 1993 Entry Draft for Gord Murphy, Brian Dobbin, Philadelphia's 3rd round choice (Sergei Zholtok) in 1992 Entry Draft and Philadelphia's 4th round choice (Charles Paquette) in 1993 Entry Draft, January 2, 1992. Signed as a free agent by **Calgary**, August 26, 1993. Signed as a free agent by **Detroit**, September 6, 1995.

WARD, AARON DET.

Defense. Shoots right. 6'2", 200 lbs. Born, Windsor, Ont., January 17, 1973.
(Winnipeg's 1st choice, 5th overall, in 1991 Entry Draft).

			Regular Season					Playoffs				
Season	**Club**	**Lea**	**GP**	**G**	**A**	**TP**	**PIM**	**GP**	**G**	**A**	**TP**	**PIM**
1989-90	Nepean	COJHL	52	6	33	39	85	....	....	....	....	....
1990-91	U. of Michigan	CCHA	46	8	11	19	126	....	....	....	....	....
1991-92	U. of Michigan	CCHA	42	7	12	19	64	....	....	....	....	....
1992-93	U. of Michigan	CCHA	30	5	8	13	73	....	....	....	....	....
	Canada	Nat-Tm	4	0	0	0	8	....	....	....	....	....
1993-94	**Detroit**	**NHL**	**5**	**1**	**0**	**1**	**4**	....	....	....	....	....
	Adirondack	AHL	58	4	12	16	87	9	2	6	8	6
1994-95	Adirondack	AHL	76	11	24	35	87	4	0	1	1	0
	Detroit	**NHL**	**1**	**0**	**1**	**1**	**2**	....	....	....	....	....
1995-96	Adirondack	AHL	74	5	10	15	133	3	0	0	0	6
1996-97	**Detroit**	**NHL**	**49**	**2**	**5**	**7**	**52**	**19**	**0**	**0**	**0**	**17** ♦
1997-98	**Detroit**	**NHL**	**52**	**5**	**5**	**10**	**47**	....	....	....	....	.... ♦
	NHL Totals		**107**	**8**	**11**	**19**	**105**	**19**	**0**	**0**	**0**	**17**

Traded to **Detroit** by **Winnipeg** with Toronto's 4th round choice (previously acquired by Winnipeg — later traded to Detroit — Detroit selected John Jakopin) in 1993 Entry Draft for Paul Ysebaert and future considerations (Alan Kerr, June 18, 1993), June 11, 1993.

WARD, DIXON — BUF.

Right wing. Shoots right. 6', 200 lbs. Born, Leduc, Alta., September 23, 1968.
(Vancouver's 6th choice, 128th overall, in 1988 Entry Draft).

			Regular Season					Playoffs				
Season	Club	Lea	GP	G	A	TP	PIM	GP	G	A	TP	PIM
1987-88	Red Deer	AJHL	51	60	71	131	167	....	....	....	....	....
1988-89	North Dakota	WCHA	37	8	9	17	26	....	....	....	....	....
1989-90	North Dakota	WCHA	45	35	34	69	44	....	....	....	....	....
1990-91	North Dakota	WCHA	43	34	35	69	84	....	....	....	....	....
1991-92	North Dakota	WCHA	38	33	31	64	90	....	....	....	....	....
1992-93	**Vancouver**	**NHL**	**70**	**22**	**30**	**52**	**82**	**9**	**2**	**3**	**5**	**0**
1993-94	**Vancouver**	**NHL**	**33**	**6**	**1**	**7**	**37**	....	....	....	....	....
	Los Angeles	**NHL**	**34**	**6**	**2**	**8**	**45**	....	....	....	....	....
1994-95	**Toronto**	**NHL**	**22**	**0**	**3**	**3**	**31**	....	....	....	....	....
	St. John's	AHL	6	3	3	6	19	....	....	....	....	....
	Detroit	IHL	7	3	6	9	7	5	3	0	3	7
1995-96	**Buffalo**	**NHL**	**8**	**2**	**2**	**4**	**6**	....	....	....	....	....
	Rochester	AHL	71	38	56	94	74	19	11	*24	*35	8
1996-97	**Buffalo**	**NHL**	**79**	**13**	**32**	**45**	**36**	**12**	**2**	**3**	**5**	**6**
1997-98	**Buffalo**	**NHL**	**71**	**10**	**13**	**23**	**42**	**15**	**3**	**8**	**11**	**6**
	NHL Totals		**317**	**59**	**83**	**142**	**279**	**36**	**7**	**14**	**21**	**12**

WCHA Second All-Star Team (1991, 1992) • Won Jack A. Butterfield Trophy (Playoff MVP - AHL) (1996)

Traded to **LA Kings** by **Vancouver** for Jimmy Carson, January 8, 1994. Traded to **Toronto** by **LA Kings** with Guy Leveque, Kelly Fairchild and Shayne Toporowski for Eric Lacroix, Chris Snell and Toronto's 4th round choice (Eric Belanger) in 1996 Entry draft, October 3, 1994. Signed as a free agent by **Buffalo**, September 20, 1995.

WARD, ED — CGY.

Right wing. Shoots right. 6'3", 215 lbs. Born, Edmonton, Alta., November 10, 1969.
(Quebec's 7th choice, 108th overall, in 1988 Entry Draft).

			Regular Season					Playoffs				
Season	Club	Lea	GP	G	A	TP	PIM	GP	G	A	TP	PIM
1986-87	Sherwood Park	AJHL	60	18	28	46	272	....	....	....	....	....
1987-88	North. Michigan	WCHA	25	0	2	2	40	....	....	....	....	....
1988-89	North. Michigan	WCHA	42	5	15	20	36	....	....	....	....	....
1989-90	North. Michigan	WCHA	39	5	11	16	77	....	....	....	....	....
1990-91	North. Michigan	WCHA	46	13	18	31	109	....	....	....	....	....
1991-92	Greensboro	ECHL	12	4	8	12	21	....	....	....	....	....
	Halifax	AHL	51	7	11	18	65	....	....	....	....	....
1992-93	Halifax	AHL	70	13	19	32	56	....	....	....	....	....
1993-94	**Quebec**	**NHL**	**7**	**1**	**0**	**1**	**5**	....	....	....	....	....
	Cornwall	AHL	60	12	30	42	65	12	1	3	4	14
1994-95	Cornwall	AHL	56	10	14	24	118	....	....	....	....	....
	Calgary	**NHL**	**2**	**1**	**1**	**2**	**2**	....	....	....	....	....
	Saint John	AHL	11	4	5	9	20	5	1	0	1	10
1995-96	**Calgary**	**NHL**	**41**	**3**	**5**	**8**	**44**	....	....	....	....	....
	Saint John	AHL	12	1	2	3	45	16	4	4	8	27
1996-97	**Calgary**	**NHL**	**40**	**5**	**8**	**13**	**49**	....	....	....	....	....
	Saint John	AHL	1	0	0	0	0	....	....	....	....	....
	Detroit	IHL	31	7	6	13	45	....	....	....	....	....
1997-98	**Calgary**	**NHL**	**64**	**4**	**5**	**9**	**122**	....	....	....	....	....
	NHL Totals		**154**	**14**	**19**	**33**	**222**	....	....	....	....	....

Traded to **Calgary** by **Quebec** for Francois Groleau, March 23, 1995.

WARD, JASON — MTL.

Right wing/center. Shoots right. 6'2", 184 lbs. Born, Chapleau, Ont., January 16, 1979.
(Montreal's 1st choice, 11th overall, in 1997 Entry Draft).

			Regular Season					Playoffs				
Season	Club	Lea	GP	G	A	TP	PIM	GP	G	A	TP	PIM
1995-96	Niagara Falls	OHL	64	15	35	50	139	10	6	4	10	23
1996-97	Erie	OHL	58	25	39	64	137	5	1	2	3	2
1997-98	Erie	OHL	21	7	9	16	42	....	....	....	....	....
	Windsor	OHL	26	19	27	46	34	....	....	....	....	....
	Fredericton	AHL	7	1	0	1	2	1	0	0	0	2

WARD, LANCE — FLA.

Defense. Shoots left. 6'3", 195 lbs. Born, Lloydminster, Alta., June 2, 1978.
(Florida's 3rd choice, 63rd overall, in 1998 Entry Draft).

			Regular Season					Playoffs				
Season	Club	Lea	GP	G	A	TP	PIM	GP	G	A	TP	PIM
1994-95	Red Deer	WHL	28	0	0	0	57	....	....	....	....	....
1995-96	Red Deer	WHL	72	4	13	17	127	10	0	4	4	10
1996-97	Red Deer	WHL	70	5	34	39	229	16	0	3	3	36
1997-98	Red Deer	WHL	71	8	25	33	233	5	0	0	0	16

• Re-entered NHL draft. Originally New Jersey's 1st choice, 10th overall, in 1996 Entry Draft.

WARE, JEFF — (WAIR) TOR.

Defense. Shoots left. 6'4", 220 lbs. Born, Toronto, Ont., May 19, 1977.
(Toronto's 1st choice, 15th overall, in 1995 Entry Draft).

			Regular Season					Playoffs				
Season	Club	Lea	GP	G	A	TP	PIM	GP	G	A	TP	PIM
1994-95	Oshawa	OHL	55	2	11	13	86	7	1	1	2	6
1995-96	Oshawa	OHL	62	4	19	23	128	5	0	1	1	8
	St. John's	AHL	4	0	0	0	4	4	0	0	0	2
1996-97	Oshawa	OHL	24	1	10	11	38	13	0	3	3	34
	Toronto	**NHL**	**13**	**0**	**0**	**0**	**6**	....	....	....	....	....
1997-98	**Toronto**	**NHL**	**2**	**0**	**0**	**0**	**0**	....	....	....	....	....
	St. John's	AHL	67	0	3	3	182	4	0	0	0	4
	NHL Totals		**15**	**0**	**0**	**0**	**6**	....	....	....	....	....

WARREN, MORGAN — TOR.

Right wing. Shoots right. 6'1", 190 lbs. Born, Summerside, P.E.I., March 6, 1980.
(Toronto's 5th choice, 126th overall, in 1998 Entry Draft).

			Regular Season					Playoffs				
Season	Club	Lea	GP	G	A	TP	PIM	GP	G	A	TP	PIM
1996-97	Quinte Hawks	OJHL	49	32	38	70	65	....	....	....	....	....
1997-98	Moncton	QMJHL	58	11	10	21	80	10	2	2	4	2

WARRENER, RHETT — (WAHR-ihn-uhr, REHT) FLA.

Defense. Shoots left. 6'1", 209 lbs. Born, Shaunavon, Sask., January 27, 1976.
(Florida's 2nd choice, 27th overall, in 1994 Entry Draft).

			Regular Season					Playoffs				
Season	Club	Lea	GP	G	A	TP	PIM	GP	G	A	TP	PIM
1991-92	Saskatoon	WHL	2	0	0	0	0	....	....	....	....	....
1992-93	Saskatoon	WHL	68	2	17	19	100	9	0	0	0	14
1993-94	Saskatoon	WHL	61	7	19	26	131	16	0	5	5	33
1994-95	Saskatoon	WHL	66	13	26	39	137	10	0	3	3	6
1995-96	**Florida**	**NHL**	**28**	**0**	**3**	**3**	**46**	**21**	**0**	**1**	**1**	**0**
	Carolina	AHL	9	0	0	0	4	....	....	....	....	....
1996-97	**Florida**	**NHL**	**62**	**4**	**9**	**13**	**88**	**5**	**0**	**0**	**0**	**0**
1997-98	**Florida**	**NHL**	**79**	**0**	**4**	**4**	**99**	....	....	....	....	....
	NHL Totals		**169**	**4**	**16**	**20**	**233**	**26**	**0**	**1**	**1**	**0**

WARRINER, TODD — (WAHR-ihn-uhr) TOR.

Left wing. Shoots left. 6'1", 188 lbs. Born, Blenheim, Ont., January 3, 1974.
(Quebec's 1st choice, 4th overall, in 1992 Entry Draft).

			Regular Season					Playoffs				
Season	Club	Lea	GP	G	A	TP	PIM	GP	G	A	TP	PIM
1990-91	Windsor	OHL	57	36	28	64	26	11	5	6	11	12
1991-92	Windsor	OHL	50	41	41	82	64	7	5	4	9	6
1992-93	Windsor	OHL	23	13	21	34	29	....	....	....	....	....
	Kitchener	OHL	32	19	24	43	35	7	5	14	19	14
1993-94	Canada	Nat-Tm	50	11	20	31	33	....	....	....	....	....
	Canada	Olympics	4	1	1	2	0	....	....	....	....	....
	Kitchener	OHL	....	....	....	....	....	1	0	1	1	0
	Cornwall	AHL	....	....	....	....	....	10	1	4	5	4
1994-95	St. John's	AHL	46	8	10	18	22	4	1	0	1	2
	Toronto	**NHL**	**5**	**0**	**0**	**0**	**0**	....	....	....	....	....
1995-96	**Toronto**	**NHL**	**57**	**7**	**8**	**15**	**26**	**6**	**1**	**1**	**2**	**2**
	St. John's	AHL	11	5	6	11	16	....	....	....	....	....
1996-97	**Toronto**	**NHL**	**75**	**12**	**21**	**33**	**41**	....	....	....	....	....
1997-98	**Toronto**	**NHL**	**45**	**5**	**8**	**13**	**20**	....	....	....	....	....
	NHL Totals		**182**	**24**	**37**	**61**	**87**	**6**	**1**	**1**	**2**	**2**

OHL First All-Star Team (1992)

Traded to **Toronto** by **Quebec** with Mats Sundin, Garth Butcher and Philadelphia's 1st round choice (previously acquired by Quebec — later traded to Washington — Washington selected Nolan Baumgartner) in 1994 Entry Draft for Wendel Clark, Sylvain Lefebvre, Landon Wilson and Toronto's 1st round choice (Jeffrey Kealty) in 1994 Entry Draft, June 28, 1994.

WASHBURN, STEVE — FLA.

Center. Shoots left. 6'2", 198 lbs. Born, Ottawa, Ont., April 10, 1975.
(Florida's 5th choice, 78th overall, in 1993 Entry Draft).

			Regular Season					Playoffs				
Season	Club	Lea	GP	G	A	TP	PIM	GP	G	A	TP	PIM
1991-92	Ottawa	OHL	59	5	17	22	10	11	2	3	5	4
1992-93	Ottawa	OHL	66	20	38	58	54	....	....	....	....	....
1993-94	Ottawa	OHL	65	30	50	80	88	17	7	16	23	10
1994-95	Ottawa	OHL	63	43	63	106	72	....	....	....	....	....
	Cincinnati	IHL	6	3	1	4	0	9	1	3	4	4
1995-96	**Florida**	**NHL**	**1**	**0**	**1**	**1**	**0**	**1**	**0**	**1**	**1**	**0**
	Carolina	AHL	78	29	54	83	45	....	....	....	....	....
1996-97	**Florida**	**NHL**	**18**	**3**	**6**	**9**	**4**	....	....	....	....	....
	Carolina	AHL	60	23	40	63	66	....	....	....	....	....
1997-98	**Florida**	**NHL**	**58**	**11**	**8**	**19**	**32**	....	....	....	....	....
	New Haven	AHL	6	3	5	8	4	3	2	0	2	15
	NHL Totals		**77**	**14**	**15**	**29**	**36**	**1**	**0**	**1**	**1**	**0**

WATT, MIKE — NYI

Left wing. Shoots left. 6'2", 212 lbs. Born, Seaforth, Ont., March 31, 1976.
(Edmonton's 3rd choice, 32nd overall, in 1994 Entry Draft).

			Regular Season					Playoffs				
Season	Club	Lea	GP	G	A	TP	PIM	GP	G	A	TP	PIM
1993-94	Stratford	OJHL	48	34	34	68	165	....	....	....	....	....
1994-95	Michigan State	CCHA	39	12	6	18	64	....	....	....	....	....
1995-96	Michigan State	CCHA	37	17	22	39	60	....	....	....	....	....
1996-97	Michigan State	CCHA	39	24	17	41	109	....	....	....	....	....
1997-98	**Edmonton**	**NHL**	**14**	**1**	**2**	**3**	**4**	....	....	....	....	....
	Hamilton	AHL	63	24	25	49	65	9	2	2	4	8
	NHL Totals		**14**	**1**	**2**	**3**	**4**	....	....	....	....	....

Traded to **NY Islanders** by **Edmonton** for Eric Fichaud, June 18, 1998.

WEBB, STEVE — NYI

Right wing. Shoots right. 6', 195 lbs. Born, Peterborough, Ont., April 20, 1975.
(Buffalo's 8th choice, 176th overall, in 1994 Entry Draft).

			Regular Season					Playoffs				
Season	Club	Lea	GP	G	A	TP	PIM	GP	G	A	TP	PIM
1992-93	Windsor	OHL	60	14	25	39	190	....	....	....	....	....
1993-94	Peterborough	OHL	35	6	16	22	126	6	1	1	2	10
1994-95	Peterborough	OHL	42	8	16	24	109	11	3	3	6	22
1995-96	Muskegon	ColHL	58	18	24	42	263	5	1	2	3	22
	Detroit	IHL	4	0	0	0	24	....	....	....	....	....
1996-97	**NY Islanders**	**NHL**	**41**	**1**	**4**	**5**	**144**	....	....	....	....	....
	Kentucky	AHL	25	6	6	12	103	2	0	0	0	19
1997-98	**NY Islanders**	**NHL**	**20**	**0**	**0**	**0**	**35**	....	....	....	....	....
	Kentucky	AHL	37	5	13	18	139	3	0	1	1	10
	NHL Totals		**61**	**1**	**4**	**5**	**179**	....	....	....	....	....

Signed as a free agent by **NY Islanders**, October 10, 1996.

WEIGHT, DOUG (WAYT) EDM.

Center. Shoots left. 5'11", 200 lbs. Born, Warren, MI, January 21, 1971.
(NY Rangers' 2nd choice, 34th overall, in 1990 Entry Draft).

			Regular Season					Playoffs				
Season	Club	Lea	GP	G	A	TP	PIM	GP	G	A	TP	PIM
1988-89	Bloomfield	NAJHL	34	26	53	79	105	....	....	....	....	....
1989-90	Lake Superior	CCHA	46	21	48	69	44	....	....	....	....	....
1990-91	Lake Superior	CCHA	42	29	46	75	86	....	....	....	....	....
	NY Rangers	**NHL**	....	....	....	....	....	**1**	**0**	**0**	**0**	**0**
1991-92	**NY Rangers**	**NHL**	**53**	**8**	**22**	**30**	**23**	**7**	**2**	**2**	**4**	**0**
	Binghamton	AHL	9	3	14	17	2	4	1	4	5	6
1992-93	**NY Rangers**	**NHL**	**65**	**15**	**25**	**40**	**55**	....	....	....	....	....
	Edmonton	**NHL**	**13**	**2**	**6**	**8**	**10**	....	....	....	....	....
1993-94	**Edmonton**	**NHL**	**84**	**24**	**50**	**74**	**47**	....	....	....	....	....
1994-95	Rosenheim	Germany	8	2	3	5	18	....	....	....	....	....
	Edmonton	**NHL**	**48**	**7**	**33**	**40**	**69**	....	....	....	....	....
1995-96	**Edmonton**	**NHL**	**82**	**25**	**79**	**104**	**95**	....	....	....	....	....
1996-97	**Edmonton**	**NHL**	**80**	**21**	**61**	**82**	**80**	**12**	**3**	**8**	**11**	**8**
1997-98	**Edmonton**	**NHL**	**79**	**26**	**44**	**70**	**69**	**12**	**2**	**7**	**9**	**14**
	United States	Olympics	4	0	2	2	2	....	....	....	....	....
	NHL Totals		**504**	**128**	**320**	**448**	**448**	**32**	**7**	**17**	**24**	**22**

CCHA First All-Star Team (1991) • NCAA West Second All-American Team (1991)

Played in NHL All-Star Game (1996, 1998)

Traded to **Edmonton** by **NY Rangers** for Esa Tikkanen, March 17, 1993.

WEINRICH, ERIC (WIGHN-rihc) CHI.

Defense. Shoots left. 6'1", 210 lbs. Born, Roanoke, VA, December 19, 1966.
(New Jersey's 3rd choice, 32nd overall, in 1985 Entry Draft).

			Regular Season					Playoffs				
Season	Club	Lea	GP	G	A	TP	PIM	GP	G	A	TP	PIM
1984-85	Yarmouth Acad.	H.S.	20	6	21	27	....	....	....	....	....	....
1985-86	U. of Maine	H.E.	34	0	14	14	26	....	....	....	....	....
1986-87	U. of Maine	H.E.	41	12	32	44	59	....	....	....	....	....
1987-88	U. of Maine	H.E.	8	4	7	11	22	....	....	....	....	....
	United States	Nat-Tm	38	3	9	12	24	....	....	....	....	....
	United States	Olympics	3	0	0	0	0	....	....	....	....	....
1988-89	**New Jersey**	**NHL**	**2**	**0**	**0**	**0**	**0**	....	....	....	....	....
	Utica	AHL	80	17	27	44	70	5	0	1	1	4
1989-90	**New Jersey**	**NHL**	**19**	**2**	**7**	**9**	**11**	**6**	**1**	**3**	**4**	**17**
	Utica	AHL	57	12	48	60	38	....	....	....	....	....
1990-91	**New Jersey**	**NHL**	**76**	**4**	**34**	**38**	**48**	**7**	**1**	**2**	**3**	**6**
1991-92	**New Jersey**	**NHL**	**76**	**7**	**25**	**32**	**55**	**7**	**0**	**2**	**2**	**4**
1992-93	**Hartford**	**NHL**	**79**	**7**	**29**	**36**	**76**	....	....	....	....	....
1993-94	**Hartford**	**NHL**	**8**	**1**	**1**	**2**	**2**	....	....	....	....	....
	Chicago	**NHL**	**54**	**3**	**23**	**26**	**31**	**6**	**0**	**2**	**2**	**6**
1994-95	**Chicago**	**NHL**	**48**	**3**	**10**	**13**	**33**	**16**	**1**	**5**	**6**	**4**
1995-96	**Chicago**	**NHL**	**77**	**5**	**10**	**15**	**65**	**10**	**1**	**4**	**5**	**10**
1996-97	**Chicago**	**NHL**	**81**	**7**	**25**	**32**	**62**	**6**	**0**	**1**	**1**	**4**
1997-98	**Chicago**	**NHL**	**82**	**2**	**21**	**23**	**106**	....	....	....	....	....
	NHL Totals		**602**	**41**	**185**	**226**	**489**	**58**	**4**	**19**	**23**	**51**

Hockey East First All-Star Team (1987) • NCAA East Second All-American Team (1987) • AHL First All-Star Team (1990) • Won Eddie Shore Award (Outstanding Defenseman - AHL) (1990) • NHL/Upper Deck All-Rookie Team (1991)

Traded to **Hartford** by **New Jersey** with Sean Burke for Bobby Holik, Hartford's 2nd round choice (Jay Pandolfo) in 1993 Entry Draft and future considerations, August 28, 1992. Traded to **Chicago** by **Hartford** with Patrick Poulin for Steve Larmer and Bryan Marchment, November 2, 1993.

WELLS, CHRIS FLA.

Center. Shoots left. 6'6", 223 lbs. Born, Calgary, Alta., November 12, 1975.
(Pittsburgh's 1st choice, 24th overall, in 1994 Entry Draft).

			Regular Season					Playoffs				
Season	Club	Lea	GP	G	A	TP	PIM	GP	G	A	TP	PIM
1991-92	Seattle	WHL	64	13	8	21	80	11	0	0	0	15
1992-93	Seattle	WHL	63	18	37	55	111	5	2	3	5	4
1993-94	Seattle	WHL	69	30	44	74	150	9	6	5	11	23
1994-95	Seattle	WHL	69	45	63	108	148	3	0	1	1	4
	Cleveland	IHL	3	0	1	1	2	....	....	....	....	....
1995-96	**Pittsburgh**	**NHL**	**54**	**2**	**2**	**4**	**59**	....	....	....	....	....
1996-97	Cleveland	IHL	15	4	6	10	9	....	....	....	....	....
	Florida	**NHL**	**47**	**2**	**6**	**8**	**42**	**3**	**0**	**0**	**0**	**0**
1997-98	**Florida**	**NHL**	**61**	**5**	**10**	**15**	**47**	....	....	....	....	....
	NHL Totals		**162**	**9**	**18**	**27**	**148**	**3**	**0**	**0**	**0**	**0**

WHL West First All-Star Team (1995)

Traded to **Florida** by **Pittsburgh** for Stu Barnes and Jason Woolley, November 19, 1996.

WELSING, ROCKY ANA.

Defense. Shoots left. 6'3", 196 lbs. Born, Beloit, WI, February 8, 1976.
(Anaheim's 7th choice, 158th overall, in 1994 Entry Draft).

			Regular Season					Playoffs				
Season	Club	Lea	GP	G	A	TP	PIM	GP	G	A	TP	PIM
1993-94	Wisconsin	USHL	40	5	21	26	262	....	....	....	....	....
1994-95	North. Michigan	WCHA	38	0	8	8	129	....	....	....	....	....
1995-96	North. Michigan	WCHA	38	0	6	6	84	....	....	....	....	....
1996-97	North. Michigan	WCHA	33	2	1	3	77	....	....	....	....	....
1997-98	North. Michigan	CCHA	38	3	8	11	83	....	....	....	....	....

WENDELL, ERIK WSH.

Center. Shoots left. 6'1", 197 lbs. Born, Minneapolis, MN, August 23, 1979.
(Washington's 6th choice, 125th overall, in 1998 Entry Draft).

			Regular Season					Playoffs				
Season	Club	Lea	GP	G	A	TP	PIM	GP	G	A	TP	PIM
1997-98	Maple Grove	H.S.	24	24	23	47	38	....	....	....	....	....

WERENKA, BRAD (wuh-REHN-kuh) PIT.

Defense. Shoots left. 6'1", 221 lbs. Born, Two Hills, Alta., February 12, 1969.
(Edmonton's 2nd choice, 42nd overall, in 1987 Entry Draft).

			Regular Season					Playoffs				
Season	Club	Lea	GP	G	A	TP	PIM	GP	G	A	TP	PIM
1986-87	North. Michigan	WCHA	30	4	4	8	35	....	....	....	....	....
1987-88	North. Michigan	WCHA	34	7	23	30	26	....	....	....	....	....
1988-89	North. Michigan	WCHA	28	7	13	20	16	....	....	....	....	....
1989-90	North. Michigan	WCHA	8	2	5	7	8	....	....	....	....	....
1990-91	North. Michigan	WCHA	47	20	43	63	36	....	....	....	....	....
1991-92	Cape Breton	AHL	66	6	21	27	95	5	0	3	3	6
1992-93	Canada	Nat-Tm	18	3	7	10	10	....	....	....	....	....
	Edmonton	**NHL**	**27**	**5**	**4**	**9**	**24**	....	....	....	....	....
	Cape Breton	AHL	4	1	1	2	4	16	4	17	21	12
1993-94	**Edmonton**	**NHL**	**15**	**0**	**4**	**4**	**14**	....	....	....	....	....
	Cape Breton	AHL	25	6	17	23	19	....	....	....	....	....
	Canada	Olympics	8	2	2	4	8	....	....	....	....	....
	Quebec	**NHL**	**11**	**0**	**7**	**7**	**8**	....	....	....	....	....
	Cornwall	AHL	....	....	....	....	....	12	2	10	12	22
1994-95	Milwaukee	IHL	80	8	45	53	161	15	3	10	13	36
1995-96	**Chicago**	**NHL**	**9**	**0**	**0**	**0**	**8**	....	....	....	....	....
	Indianapolis	IHL	73	15	42	57	85	5	1	3	4	8
1996-97	Indianapolis	IHL	82	20	56	76	83	4	1	4	5	6
1997-98	**Pittsburgh**	**NHL**	**71**	**3**	**15**	**18**	**46**	**6**	**1**	**0**	**1**	**8**
	NHL Totals		**133**	**8**	**30**	**38**	**100**	**6**	**1**	**0**	**1**	**8**

WCHA First All-Star Team (1991) • NCAA West First All-American Team (1991) • NCAA Championship All-Tournament Team (1991) • IHL First All-Star Team (1997) • Won Governors' Trophy (Top Defenseman - IHL) (1997)

Traded to **Quebec** by **Edmonton** for Steve Passmore, March 21, 1994. Signed as a free agent by **Chicago**, July 20, 1995. Signed as a free agent by **Pittsburgh**, July 31, 1997.

WESENBERG, BRIAN (WEE-sehn-buhrg) PHI.

Right wing. Shoots right. 6'3", 187 lbs. Born, Peterborough, Ont., May 9, 1977.
(Anaheim's 2nd choice, 29th overall, in 1995 Entry Draft).

			Regular Season					Playoffs				
Season	Club	Lea	GP	G	A	TP	PIM	GP	G	A	TP	PIM
1994-95	Guelph	OHL	66	17	27	44	81	14	2	3	5	18
1995-96	Guelph	OHL	66	25	33	58	161	16	4	11	15	34
1996-97	Guelph	OHL	64	37	43	80	186	18	4	9	13	59
	Philadelphia	AHL	....	....	....	....	....	3	0	0	0	7
1997-98	Philadelphia	AHL	74	17	22	39	93	19	1	4	5	34

Traded to **Philadelphia** by **Anaheim** for Anatoli Semenov and Mike Crowley, March 19, 1996.

WESLEY, GLEN CAR.

Defense. Shoots left. 6'1", 197 lbs. Born, Red Deer, Alta., October 2, 1968.
(Boston's 1st choice, 3rd overall, in 1987 Entry Draft).

			Regular Season					Playoffs				
Season	Club	Lea	GP	G	A	TP	PIM	GP	G	A	TP	PIM
1983-84	Portland	WHL	3	1	2	3	0	....	....	....	....	....
1984-85	Portland	WHL	67	16	52	68	76	6	1	6	7	8
1985-86	Portland	WHL	69	16	75	91	96	15	3	11	14	29
1986-87	Portland	WHL	63	16	46	62	72	20	8	18	26	27
1987-88	**Boston**	**NHL**	**79**	**7**	**30**	**37**	**69**	**23**	**6**	**8**	**14**	**22**
1988-89	**Boston**	**NHL**	**77**	**19**	**35**	**54**	**61**	**10**	**0**	**2**	**2**	**4**
1989-90	**Boston**	**NHL**	**78**	**9**	**27**	**36**	**48**	**21**	**2**	**6**	**8**	**36**
1990-91	**Boston**	**NHL**	**80**	**11**	**32**	**43**	**78**	**19**	**2**	**9**	**11**	**19**
1991-92	**Boston**	**NHL**	**78**	**9**	**37**	**46**	**54**	**15**	**2**	**4**	**6**	**16**
1992-93	**Boston**	**NHL**	**64**	**8**	**25**	**33**	**47**	**4**	**0**	**0**	**0**	**0**
1993-94	**Boston**	**NHL**	**81**	**14**	**44**	**58**	**64**	**13**	**3**	**3**	**6**	**12**
1994-95	**Hartford**	**NHL**	**48**	**2**	**14**	**16**	**50**	....	....	....	....	....
1995-96	**Hartford**	**NHL**	**68**	**8**	**16**	**24**	**88**	....	....	....	....	....
1996-97	**Hartford**	**NHL**	**68**	**6**	**26**	**32**	**40**	....	....	....	....	....
1997-98	**Carolina**	**NHL**	**82**	**6**	**19**	**25**	**36**	....	....	....	....	....
	NHL Totals		**803**	**99**	**305**	**404**	**635**	**105**	**15**	**32**	**47**	**109**

WHL West All-Star Team (1986, 1987) • NHL All-Rookie Team (1988)

Played in NHL All-Star Game (1989)

Traded to **Hartford** by **Boston** for Hartford/Carolina's 1st round choices in 1995 (Kyle McLaren), 1996 (Jonathan Aitken) and 1997 (Sergei Samsonov) Entry Drafts, August 26, 1994. Transferred to **Carolina** after **Hartford** franchise relocated, June 25, 1997.

WESTLUND, TOMMY CAR.

Right wing. Shoots right. 6', 210 lbs. Born, Fors, Sweden, December 29, 1974.
(Carolina's 5th choice, 93rd overall, in 1998 Entry Draft).

			Regular Season					Playoffs				
Season	Club	Lea	GP	G	A	TP	PIM	GP	G	A	TP	PIM
1991-92	Avesta	Sweden-3	27	11	9	20	8	....	....	....	....	....
1992-93	Avesta	Sweden-2	32	9	5	14	32	....	....	....	....	....
1993-94	Avesta	Sweden-2	31	20	11	31	34	....	....	....	....	....
1994-95	Avesta	Sweden-2	32	17	13	30	22	....	....	....	....	....
1995-96	Brynas Gavle	Sweden	18	2	1	3	2	....	....	....	....	....
	Brynas Gavle	Sweden-2	18	10	10	20	4	8	1	0	1	4
1996-97	Brynas Gavle	Sweden	50	21	13	34	16	....	....	....	....	....
1997-98	Brynas Gavle	Sweden	46	29	9	38	45	3	0	1	1	0

WHITE, BRIAN COL.

Defense. Shoots right. 6'1", 180 lbs. Born, Winchester, MA, February 7, 1976.
(Tampa Bay's 11th choice, 268th overall, in 1994 Entry Draft).

			Regular Season					Playoffs				
Season	Club	Lea	GP	G	A	TP	PIM	GP	G	A	TP	PIM
1993-94	Coburg	OJHL	40	14	18	32	81	....	....	....	....	....
1994-95	U. of Maine	H.E.	28	1	1	2	16	....	....	....	....	....
1995-96	U. of Maine	H.E.	39	0	4	4	18	....	....	....	....	....
1996-97	U. of Maine	H.E.	35	4	12	16	36	....	....	....	....	....
1997-98	U. of Maine	H.E.	33	0	12	12	45	....	....	....	....	....
	Long Beach	IHL	1	0	0	0	0	....	....	....	....	....

Signed as a free agent by **Colorado**, July 7, 1998.

WHITE, COLIN N.J.

Defense. Shoots left. 6'3", 215 lbs. Born, New Glasgow, N.S., December 12, 1977.
(New Jersey's 5th choice, 49th overall, in 1996 Entry Draft).

			Regular Season					Playoffs				
Season	Club	Lea	GP	G	A	TP	PIM	GP	G	A	TP	PIM
1994-95	Laval	QMJHL	7	0	1	1	32	....	....	....	....	....
	Hull	QMJHL	5	0	1	1	4	12	0	0	0	23
1995-96	Hull	QMJHL	62	2	8	10	303	18	0	4	4	42
1996-97	Hull	QMJHL	63	3	12	15	297	14	3	12	15	65
1997-98	Albany	AHL	76	3	13	16	235	13	0	0	0	55

WHITE, PETER — PHI.

Center. Shoots left. 5'11", 200 lbs. Born, Montreal, Que., March 15, 1969.
(Edmonton's 4th choice, 92nd overall, in 1989 Entry Draft).

			Regular Season					Playoffs				
Season	Club	Lea	GP	G	A	TP	PIM	GP	G	A	TP	PIM
1987-88	Pembroke	OJHL	56	90	136	226	32	....	....	....	....	....
1988-89	Michigan State	CCHA	46	20	33	53	17	....	....	....	....	....
1989-90	Michigan State	CCHA	45	22	40	62	6	....	....	....	....	....
1990-91	Michigan State	CCHA	37	7	31	38	28	....	....	....	....	....
1991-92	Michigan State	CCHA	41	26	49	75	32	....	....	....	....	....
1992-93	Cape Breton	AHL	64	12	28	40	10	16	3	3	6	12
1993-94	**Edmonton**	**NHL**	**26**	**3**	**5**	**8**	**2**	....	....	....	....	....
	Cape Breton	AHL	45	21	49	70	12	5	2	3	5	2
1994-95	Cape Breton	AHL	65	36	*69	*105	30	....	....	....	....	....
	Edmonton	**NHL**	**9**	**2**	**4**	**6**	**0**	....	....	....	....	....
1995-96	**Edmonton**	**NHL**	**26**	**5**	**3**	**8**	**0**	....	....	....	....	....
	Toronto	**NHL**	**1**	**0**	**0**	**0**	**0**	....	....	....	....	....
	St. John's	AHL	17	6	7	13	6	....	....	....	....	....
	Atlanta	IHL	36	21	20	41	4	3	0	3	3	2
1996-97	Philadelphia	AHL	80	*44	61	*105	28	10	6	8	14	6
1997-98	Philadelphia	AHL	80	27	*78	*105	28	20	9	9	18	6
	NHL Totals		**62**	**10**	**12**	**22**	**2**	....	....	....	....	....

AHL Second All-Star Team (1995, 1997) • Won John B. Sollenberger Trophy (Top Scorer - AHL) (1995, 1997, 1998)

Traded to **Toronto** by **Edmonton** with Edmonton's 4th round choice (Jason Sessa) in 1996 Entry Draft for Kent Manderville, December 4, 1995. Signed as a free agent by **Philadelphia**, August 19, 1996.

WHITE, TODD — CHI.

Center. Shoots left. 5'10", 181 lbs. Born, Kanata, Ont., May 21, 1975.

			Regular Season					Playoffs				
Season	Club	Lea	GP	G	A	TP	PIM	GP	G	A	TP	PIM
1993-94	Clarkson	ECAC	33	10	12	22	28	....	....	....	....	....
1994-95	Clarkson	ECAC	34	13	16	29	44	....	....	....	....	....
1995-96	Clarkson	ECAC	38	29	43	72	36	....	....	....	....	....
1996-97	Clarkson	ECAC	37	*38	*36	*74	22	....	....	....	....	....
1997-98	**Chicago**	**NHL**	**7**	**1**	**0**	**1**	**2**	....	....	....	....	....
	Indianapolis	IHL	65	46	36	82	28	5	2	3	5	4
	NHL Totals		**7**	**1**	**0**	**1**	**2**	....	....	....	....	....

ECAC Second All-Star Team (1996) • NCAA East Second All-American Team (1996) • ECAC First All-Star Team (1997) • NCAA East First All-American Team (1997) • Won Garry F. Longman Memorial Trophy (Top Rookie - IHL) (1998)

Signed as a free agent by **Chicago**, August 27, 1997.

WHITFIELD, TRENT

Center. Shoots left. 5'11", 176 lbs. Born, Estevan, Sask., June 17, 1977.
(Boston's 5th choice, 100th overall, in 1996 Entry Draft).

			Regular Season					Playoffs				
Season	Club	Lea	GP	G	A	TP	PIM	GP	G	A	TP	PIM
1993-94	Spokane	WHL	5	1	1	2	0	....	....	....	....	....
1994-95	Spokane	WHL	48	8	17	25	26	11	7	6	13	5
1995-96	Spokane	WHL	72	33	51	84	75	18	8	10	18	10
1996-97	Spokane	WHL	58	34	42	76	74	9	5	7	12	10
1997-98	Spokane	WHL	65	38	44	82	97	18	9	10	19	15

WHL West First All-Star Team (1997) • WHL West Second All-Star Team (1998)

WHITNEY, RAY — FLA.

Left wing. Shoots right. 5'10", 175 lbs. Born, Fort Saskatchewan, Alta., May 8, 1972.
(San Jose's 2nd choice, 23rd overall, in 1991 Entry Draft).

			Regular Season					Playoffs				
Season	Club	Lea	GP	G	A	TP	PIM	GP	G	A	TP	PIM
1988-89	Spokane	WHL	71	17	33	50	16	....	....	....	....	....
1989-90	Spokane	WHL	71	57	56	113	50	6	3	4	7	6
1990-91	Spokane	WHL	72	67	118	*185	36	15	13	18	*31	12
1991-92	Kolner Haie	Germany	10	3	6	9	4	....	....	....	....	....
	Canada	Nat-Tm	5	1	0	1	6	....	....	....	....	....
	San Jose	**NHL**	**2**	**0**	**3**	**3**	**0**	....	....	....	....	....
	San Diego	IHL	63	36	54	90	12	4	0	0	0	0
1992-93	**San Jose**	**NHL**	**26**	**4**	**6**	**10**	**4**	....	....	....	....	....
	Kansas City	IHL	46	20	33	53	14	12	5	7	12	2
1993-94	**San Jose**	**NHL**	**61**	**14**	**26**	**40**	**14**	**14**	**0**	**4**	**4**	**8**
1994-95	**San Jose**	**NHL**	**39**	**13**	**12**	**25**	**14**	**11**	**4**	**4**	**8**	**2**
1995-96	**San Jose**	**NHL**	**60**	**17**	**24**	**41**	**16**	....	....	....	....	....
1996-97	**San Jose**	**NHL**	**12**	**0**	**2**	**2**	**4**	....	....	....	....	....
	Kentucky	AHL	9	1	7	8	2	....	....	....	....	....
	Utah	IHL	43	13	35	48	34	7	3	1	4	6
1997-98	**Edmonton**	**NHL**	**9**	**1**	**3**	**4**	**0**	....	....	....	....	....
	Florida	**NHL**	**68**	**32**	**29**	**61**	**28**	....	....	....	....	....
	NHL Totals		**277**	**81**	**105**	**186**	**80**	**25**	**4**	**8**	**12**	**10**

WHL West First All-Star Team (1991) • Memorial Cup All-Star Team (1991) • Won George Parsons Trophy (Memorial Cup Tournament Most Sportsmanlike Player) (1991)

Claimed on waivers by **Florida** from **Edmonton**, November 6, 1997.

WIDMER, JASON — ST.L.

Defense. Shoots left. 6', 200 lbs. Born, Calgary, Alta., August 1, 1973.
(NY Islanders' 8th choice, 176th overall, in 1992 Entry Draft).

			Regular Season					Playoffs				
Season	Club	Lea	GP	G	A	TP	PIM	GP	G	A	TP	PIM
1989-90	Moose Jaw	WHL	58	1	8	9	33	....	....	....	....	....
1990-91	Lethbridge	WHL	58	2	12	14	55	16	0	1	1	12
1991-92	Lethbridge	WHL	40	2	19	21	181	5	0	4	4	9
1992-93	Lethbridge	WHL	55	3	15	18	140	4	0	3	3	2
	Capital District	AHL	4	0	0	0	2	....	....	....	....	....
1993-94	Lethbridge	WHL	64	11	31	42	191	9	3	5	8	34
1994-95	Canada	Nat-Tm	6	1	4	5	4	....	....	....	....	....
	NY Islanders	**NHL**	**1**	**0**	**0**	**0**	**0**	....	....	....	....	....
	Worcester	AHL	73	8	26	34	136	....	....	....	....	....
1995-96	**NY Islanders**	**NHL**	**4**	**0**	**0**	**0**	**7**	....	....	....	....	....
	Worcester	AHL	76	6	21	27	129	4	2	0	2	9
1996-97	**San Jose**	**NHL**	**2**	**0**	**1**	**1**	**0**	....	....	....	....	....
	Kentucky	AHL	76	4	24	28	105	4	0	0	0	8
1997-98	Kentucky	AHL	71	5	13	18	176	3	0	0	0	6
	NHL Totals		**7**	**0**	**1**	**1**	**7**	....	....	....	....	....

Signed as a free agent by **San Jose**, September 11, 1996. Signed as a free agent by **St. Louis**, July 28, 1998.

WIEMER, JASON — (WEE-muhr) CGY.

Center. Shoots left. 6'2", 219 lbs. Born, Kimberley, B.C., April 14, 1976.
(Tampa Bay's 1st choice, 8th overall, in 1994 Entry Draft).

			Regular Season					Playoffs				
Season	Club	Lea	GP	G	A	TP	PIM	GP	G	A	TP	PIM
1991-92	Portland	WHL	2	0	1	1	0	....	....	....	....	....
1992-93	Portland	WHL	68	18	34	52	159	16	7	3	10	27
1993-94	Portland	WHL	72	45	51	96	236	10	4	4	8	32
1994-95	Portland	WHL	16	10	14	24	63	....	....	....	....	....
	Tampa Bay	**NHL**	**36**	**1**	**4**	**5**	**44**	....	....	....	....	....
1995-96	**Tampa Bay**	**NHL**	**66**	**9**	**9**	**18**	**81**	**6**	**1**	**0**	**1**	**28**
1996-97	**Tampa Bay**	**NHL**	**63**	**9**	**5**	**14**	**134**	....	....	....	....	....
	Adirondack	AHL	4	1	0	1	7	....	....	....	....	....
1997-98	**Tampa Bay**	**NHL**	**67**	**8**	**9**	**17**	**132**	....	....	....	....	....
	Calgary	**NHL**	**12**	**4**	**1**	**5**	**28**	....	....	....	....	....
	NHL Totals		**244**	**31**	**28**	**59**	**419**	**6**	**1**	**0**	**1**	**28**

Traded to **Calgary** by **Tampa Bay** for Sandy McCarthy and Calgary's 3rd (Brad Richards) and 5th (Curtis Rich) round choices in 1998 Entry Draft, March 24, 1998.

WIKSTROM, JOHN — DET.

Defense. Shoots left. 6'3", 200 lbs. Born, Lulea, Sweden, January 30, 1979.
(Detroit's 4th choice, 129th overall, in 1997 Entry Draft).

			Regular Season					Playoffs				
Season	Club	Lea	GP	G	A	TP	PIM	GP	G	A	TP	PIM
1995-96	Lulea HF	Sweden	9	0	0	0	2	....	....	....	....	....
1996-97	Lulea HF	Sweden	9	0	0	0	0	3	0	0	0	0
1997-98	Lulea HF	EuroHL	1	0	0	0	0	....	....	....	....	....
	Lulea HF	Sweden	1	0	0	0	0	....	....	....	....	....

WILFORD, MARTY — CHI.

Defense. Shoots left. 6', 207 lbs. Born, Cobourg, Ont., April 17, 1977.
(Chicago's 7th choice, 149th overall, in 1995 Entry Draft).

			Regular Season					Playoffs				
Season	Club	Lea	GP	G	A	TP	PIM	GP	G	A	TP	PIM
1994-95	Oshawa	OHL	63	1	6	7	95	7	1	1	2	4
1995-96	Oshawa	OHL	65	3	24	27	107	5	0	1	1	4
1996-97	Oshawa	OHL	62	19	43	62	126	16	2	18	20	28
1997-98	Columbus	ECHL	46	8	27	35	123	....	....	....	....	....
	Indianapolis	IHL	26	0	4	4	16	....	....	....	....	....

OHL Second All-Star Team (1997)

WILKIE, DAVID — T.B.

Defense. Shoots right. 6'2", 210 lbs. Born, Ellensburgh, WA, May 30, 1974.
(Montreal's 1st choice, 20th overall, in 1992 Entry Draft).

			Regular Season					Playoffs				
Season	Club	Lea	GP	G	A	TP	PIM	GP	G	A	TP	PIM
1990-91	Seattle	WHL	25	1	1	2	22	....	....	....	....	....
1991-92	Kamloops	WHL	71	12	28	40	153	16	6	5	11	19
1992-93	Kamloops	WHL	53	11	26	37	109	6	4	2	6	2
1993-94	Kamloops	WHL	27	11	18	29	18	....	....	....	....	....
	Regina	WHL	29	27	21	48	16	4	1	4	5	4
1994-95	Fredericton	AHL	70	10	43	53	34	1	0	0	0	0
	Montreal	**NHL**	**1**	**0**	**0**	**0**	**0**	....	....	....	....	....
1995-96	**Montreal**	**NHL**	**24**	**1**	**5**	**6**	**10**	**6**	**1**	**2**	**3**	**12**
	Fredericton	AHL	23	5	12	17	20	....	....	....	....	....
1996-97	**Montreal**	**NHL**	**61**	**6**	**9**	**15**	**63**	**2**	**0**	**0**	**0**	**2**
1997-98	**Montreal**	**NHL**	**5**	**1**	**0**	**1**	**4**	....	....	....	....	....
	Tampa Bay	**NHL**	**29**	**1**	**5**	**6**	**17**	....	....	....	....	....
	NHL Totals		**120**	**9**	**19**	**28**	**94**	**8**	**1**	**2**	**3**	**14**

Traded to **Tampa Bay** by **Montreal** with Stephane Richer and Darcy Tucker for Patrick Poulin, Mick Vukota and Igor Ulanov, January 15, 1998.

WILKINSON, NEIL — PIT.

Defense. Shoots right. 6'3", 194 lbs. Born, Selkirk, Man., August 15, 1967.
(Minnesota's 2nd choice, 30th overall, in 1986 Entry Draft).

			Regular Season					Playoffs				
Season	Club	Lea	GP	G	A	TP	PIM	GP	G	A	TP	PIM
1985-86	Selkirk	MJHL	42	14	35	49	91	....	....	....	....	....
1986-87	Michigan State	CCHA	19	3	4	7	18	....	....	....	....	....
1987-88	Medicine Hat	WHL	55	11	21	32	157	5	1	0	1	2
1988-89	Kalamazoo	IHL	39	5	15	20	96	....	....	....	....	....
1989-90	**Minnesota**	**NHL**	**36**	**0**	**5**	**5**	**100**	**7**	**0**	**2**	**2**	**11**
	Kalamazoo	IHL	20	6	7	13	62	....	....	....	....	....
1990-91	**Minnesota**	**NHL**	**50**	**2**	**9**	**11**	**117**	**22**	**3**	**3**	**6**	**12**
	Kalamazoo	IHL	10	0	3	3	38	....	....	....	....	....
1991-92	**San Jose**	**NHL**	**60**	**4**	**15**	**19**	**107**	....	....	....	....	....
1992-93	**San Jose**	**NHL**	**59**	**1**	**7**	**8**	**96**	....	....	....	....	....
1993-94	**Chicago**	**NHL**	**72**	**3**	**9**	**12**	**116**	**4**	**0**	**0**	**0**	**0**
1994-95	**Winnipeg**	**NHL**	**40**	**1**	**4**	**5**	**75**	....	....	....	....	....
1995-96	**Winnipeg**	**NHL**	**21**	**1**	**4**	**5**	**33**	....	....	....	....	....
	Pittsburgh	**NHL**	**41**	**2**	**10**	**12**	**87**	**15**	**0**	**1**	**1**	**14**
1996-97	**Pittsburgh**	**NHL**	**23**	**0**	**0**	**0**	**36**	**5**	**0**	**0**	**0**	**4**
	Cleveland	IHL	2	0	1	1	0	....	....	....	....	....
1997-98	**Pittsburgh**	**NHL**	**34**	**2**	**4**	**6**	**24**	....	....	....	....	....
	NHL Totals		**436**	**16**	**67**	**83**	**791**	**53**	**3**	**6**	**9**	**41**

Claimed by **San Jose** from **Minnesota** in Dispersal Draft, May 30, 1991. Traded to **Chicago** by **San Jose** to complete transaction that sent Jimmy Waite to San Jose (June 18, 1993), July 9, 1993. Traded to **Winnipeg** by **Chicago** for Chicago's 3rd round choice (previously acquired, Chicago selected Kevin McKay) in 1995 Entry Draft, June 3, 1994. Traded to **Pittsburgh** by **Winnipeg** for Norm Maciver, December 28, 1995.

WILLEJTO, STEVE — DET.

Center. Shoots left. 5'10", 178 lbs. Born, Burn's Lake, B.C., January 26, 1979.
(Detroit's 7th choice, 213th overall, in 1997 Entry Draft).

			Regular Season					Playoffs				
Season	Club	Lea	GP	G	A	TP	PIM	GP	G	A	TP	PIM
1996-97	Prince Albert	WHL	69	11	13	24	32	4	1	1	2	0
1997-98	Prince Albert	WHL	71	15	15	30	35	....	....	....	....	....

WILLERS, GREG — DET.

Defense. Shoots right. 6'1", 195 lbs. Born, Scarborough, Ont., August 8, 1979.
(Detroit's 8th choice, 239th overall, in 1997 Entry Draft).

			Regular Season					Playoffs				
Season	Club	Lea	GP	G	A	TP	PIM	GP	G	A	TP	PIM
1996-97	Kingston	OHL	51	4	7	11	37	5	1	0	1	0
1997-98	Kingston	OHL	19	1	5	6	8	....	....	....	....	....
	Sarnia	OHL	40	12	16	28	26	5	2	1	3	6

WILLIAMS, JEFF — N.J.

Center. Shoots left. 6', 195 lbs. Born, Pointe-Claire, Que., February 11, 1976.
(New Jersey's 8th choice, 181st overall, in 1994 Entry Draft).

			Regular Season					Playoffs				
Season	Club	Lea	GP	G	A	TP	PIM	GP	G	A	TP	PIM
1993-94	Guelph	OHL	62	14	12	26	19	9	2	1	3	4
1994-95	Guelph	OHL	52	15	32	47	21	14	5	5	10	0
1995-96	Guelph	OHL	63	15	49	64	42	16	13	15	28	10
1996-97	Raleigh	ECHL	20	4	8	12	8	....	....	....	....	....
	Albany	AHL	46	13	20	33	12	15	1	2	3	15
1997-98	Albany	AHL	58	13	12	25	20	12	5	6	11	2

Canadian Major Junior Most Sportsmanlike Player of the Year (1996)

WILLIS, SHANE — CAR.

Right wing. Shoots right. 6', 176 lbs. Born, Edmonton, Alta., June 13, 1977.
(Carolina's 4th choice, 88th overall, in 1997 Entry Draft).

			Regular Season					Playoffs				
Season	Club	Lea	GP	G	A	TP	PIM	GP	G	A	TP	PIM
1994-95	Prince Albert	WHL	65	24	19	43	38	13	3	4	7	6
1995-96	Prince Albert	WHL	69	41	40	81	47	18	11	10	21	18
1996-97	Prince Albert	WHL	41	34	22	56	63	....	....	....	....	....
	Lethbridge	WHL	26	22	17	39	24	19	13	11	24	20
1997-98	Lethbridge	WHL	64	58	54	112	73	4	2	3	5	6
	New Haven	AHL	1	0	1	1	2	....	....	....	....	....

WHL East First All-Star Team (1997, 1998)

• Re-entered NHL Entry Draft. Tampa Bay's 3rd choice, 56th overall, in 1995 Entry Draft.

WILLIS, TYLER — ST.L.

Right wing. Shoots right. 5'8", 167 lbs. Born, Princeton, B.C., April 8, 1977.
(Vancouver's 8th choice, 196th overall, in 1995 Entry Draft).

			Regular Season					Playoffs				
Season	Club	Lea	GP	G	A	TP	PIM	GP	G	A	TP	PIM
1993-94	Swift Current	WHL	71	19	26	45	263	....	....	....	....	....
1994-95	Swift Current	WHL	71	21	29	50	284	6	0	0	0	20
1995-96	Swift Current	WHL	40	9	38	47	196	....	....	....	....	....
	Seattle	WHL	15	1	3	4	71	5	1	5	6	13
1996-97	Seattle	WHL	72	12	40	52	302	15	1	7	8	68
1997-98	Worcester	AHL	24	2	1	3	140	....	....	....	....	....
	Baton Rouge	ECHL	21	4	10	14	112	....	....	....	....	....

Signed as a free agent by **St. Louis**, October 3, 1997.

WILLSIE, BRIAN — COL.

Right wing. Shoots right. 6', 190 lbs. Born, London, Ont., March 16, 1978.
(Colorado's 7th choice, 146th overall, in 1996 Entry Draft).

			Regular Season					Playoffs				
Season	Club	Lea	GP	G	A	TP	PIM	GP	G	A	TP	PIM
1995-96	Guelph	OHL	65	13	21	34	18	16	4	2	6	6
1996-97	Guelph	OHL	64	37	31	68	37	18	15	4	19	10
1997-98	Guelph	OHL	57	45	31	76	41	12	9	5	14	18

OHL First All-Star Team (1998)

WILM, CLARKE — (WIHLM) CGY.

Center. Shoots left. 6', 202 lbs. Born, Central Butte, Sask., October 24, 1976.
(Calgary's 5th choice, 150th overall, in 1995 Entry Draft).

			Regular Season					Playoffs				
Season	Club	Lea	GP	G	A	TP	PIM	GP	G	A	TP	PIM
1992-93	Saskatoon	WHL	69	14	19	33	71	9	4	2	6	13
1993-94	Saskatoon	WHL	70	18	32	50	181	16	0	9	9	19
1994-95	Saskatoon	WHL	71	20	39	59	179	10	6	1	7	21
1995-96	Saskatoon	WHL	72	49	61	110	83	4	1	1	2	4
1996-97	Saint John	AHL	62	9	19	28	107	5	2	0	2	15
1997-98	Saint John	AHL	68	13	26	39	112	21	5	9	14	8

WILSON, LANDON — BOS.

Right wing. Shoots right. 6'2", 216 lbs. Born, St. Louis, MO, March 13, 1975.
(Toronto's 2nd choice, 19th overall, in 1993 Entry Draft).

			Regular Season					Playoffs				
Season	Club	Lea	GP	G	A	TP	PIM	GP	G	A	TP	PIM
1992-93	Dubuque	USHL	43	29	36	65	284	....	....	....	....	....
1993-94	North Dakota	WCHA	35	18	15	33	*147	....	....	....	....	....
1994-95	North Dakota	WCHA	31	7	16	23	141	....	....	....	....	....
	Cornwall	AHL	8	4	4	8	25	13	3	4	7	68
1995-96	**Colorado**	**NHL**	**7**	**1**	**0**	**1**	**6**	....	....	....	....	....
	Cornwall	AHL	53	21	13	34	154	8	1	3	4	22
1996-97	**Colorado**	**NHL**	**9**	**1**	**2**	**3**	**23**	....	....	....	....	....
	Boston	**NHL**	**40**	**7**	**10**	**17**	**49**	....	....	....	....	....
	Providence	AHL	2	2	1	3	2	10	3	4	7	16
1997-98	**Boston**	**NHL**	**28**	**1**	**5**	**6**	**7**	**1**	**0**	**0**	**0**	**0**
	Providence	AHL	42	18	10	28	146	....	....	....	....	....
	NHL Totals		**84**	**10**	**17**	**27**	**85**	**1**	**0**	**0**	**0**	**0**

Traded to **Quebec** by **Toronto** with Wendel Clark, Sylvain Lefebvre and Toronto's 1st round choice (Jeffrey Kealty) in 1994 Entry Draft for Mats Sundin, Garth Butcher, Todd Warriner and Philadelphia's 1st round choice (previously acquired by Quebec — later traded to Washington — Washington selected Nolan Baumgartner) in 1994 Entry Draft, June 28, 1994. Traded to **Boston** by **Colorado** with Anders Myrvold for Boston's 1st round choice (Robyn Regehr) in 1998 Entry Draft, November 22, 1996.

WILSON, MIKE — BUF.

Defense. Shoots left. 6'6", 212 lbs. Born, Brampton, Ont., February 26, 1975.
(Vancouver's 1st choice, 20th overall, in 1993 Entry Draft).

			Regular Season					Playoffs				
Season	Club	Lea	GP	G	A	TP	PIM	GP	G	A	TP	PIM
1991-92	Georgetown	OJHL	41	9	13	22	65	....	....	....	....	....
1992-93	Sudbury	OHL	53	6	7	13	58	14	1	1	2	2
1993-94	Sudbury	OHL	60	4	22	26	62	9	1	3	4	8
1994-95	Sudbury	OHL	64	13	34	47	46	18	1	8	9	10
1995-96	**Buffalo**	**NHL**	**58**	**4**	**8**	**12**	**41**	....	....	....	....	....
	Rochester	AHL	15	0	5	5	38	....	....	....	....	....
1996-97	**Buffalo**	**NHL**	**77**	**2**	**9**	**11**	**51**	**10**	**0**	**1**	**1**	**2**
1997-98	**Buffalo**	**NHL**	**66**	**4**	**4**	**8**	**48**	**15**	**0**	**1**	**1**	**13**
	NHL Totals		**201**	**10**	**21**	**31**	**140**	**25**	**0**	**2**	**2**	**15**

Traded to **Buffalo** by **Vancouver** with Mike Peca and Vancouver's 1st round choice (Jay McKee) in 1995 Entry Draft for Alexander Mogilny and Buffalo's 5th round choice (Todd Norman) in 1995 Entry Draft, July 8, 1995.

WINNES, CHRIS — (WIHN-ehs) NYR

Right wing. Shoots right. 6', 201 lbs. Born, Ridgefield, CT, February 12, 1968.
(Boston's 9th choice, 161st overall, in 1987 Entry Draft).

			Regular Season					Playoffs				
Season	Club	Lea	GP	G	A	TP	PIM	GP	G	A	TP	PIM
1986-87	Northwood Prep	H.S.	27	25	25	50	....	....	....	....	....	....
1987-88	New Hampshire	H.E.	30	17	19	36	28	....	....	....	....	....
1988-89	New Hampshire	H.E.	30	11	20	31	22	....	....	....	....	....
1989-90	New Hampshire	H.E.	24	10	13	23	12	....	....	....	....	....
1990-91	New Hampshire	H.E.	33	15	16	31	24	....	....	....	....	....
	Maine	AHL	7	3	1	4	0	1	0	2	2	0
	Boston	**NHL**	....	....	....	....	....	**1**	**0**	**0**	**0**	**0**
1991-92	**Boston**	**NHL**	**24**	**1**	**3**	**4**	**6**	....	....	....	....	....
	Maine	AHL	45	12	35	47	30	....	....	....	....	....
1992-93	**Boston**	**NHL**	**5**	**0**	**1**	**1**	**0**	....	....	....	....	....
	Providence	AHL	64	23	36	59	34	4	0	2	2	5
1993-94	**Philadelphia**	**NHL**	**4**	**0**	**2**	**2**	**0**	....	....	....	....	....
	Hershey	AHL	70	29	21	50	20	7	1	3	4	0
1994-95	Hershey	AHL	78	26	40	66	39	6	2	2	4	17
1995-96	Michigan	IHL	27	6	13	19	14	....	....	....	....	....
	Fort Wayne	IHL	39	6	7	13	12	2	0	0	0	0
1996-97	Utah	IHL	5	0	0	0	0	....	....	....	....	....
	HC Merano	Italy	12	11	5	16	10	....	....	....	....	....
1997-98	San Antonio	IHL	3	0	0	0	0	....	....	....	....	....
	Hartford	AHL	64	17	23	40	16	13	1	4	5	2
	NHL Totals		**33**	**1**	**6**	**7**	**6**	**1**	**0**	**0**	**0**	**0**

Signed as a free agent by **Philadelphia**, August 4, 1993. Signed as a free agent by **NY Rangers**, July 21, 1998.

WISEMAN, BRIAN

Center. Shoots left. 5'8", 175 lbs. Born, Chatham, Ont., July 13, 1971.
(NY Rangers' 11th choice, 257th overall, in 1991 Entry Draft).

			Regular Season					Playoffs				
Season	Club	Lea	GP	G	A	TP	PIM	GP	G	A	TP	PIM
1990-91	U. of Michigan	CCHA	47	25	33	58	58	....	....	....	....	....
1991-92	U. of Michigan	CCHA	44	27	44	71	38	....	....	....	....	....
1992-93	U. of Michigan	CCHA	35	13	37	50	40	....	....	....	....	....
1993-94	U. of Michigan	CCHA	40	19	50	69	44	....	....	....	....	....
1994-95	Chicago	IHL	75	17	55	72	52	3	1	1	2	4
1995-96	Chicago	IHL	73	33	55	88	117	....	....	....	....	....
1996-97	**Toronto**	**NHL**	**3**	**0**	**0**	**0**	**0**	....	....	....	....	....
	St. John's	AHL	71	33	62	95	83	7	5	4	9	8
1997-98	Houston	IHL	78	26	72	98	86	4	0	3	3	8
	NHL Totals		**3**	**0**	**0**	**0**	**0**	....	....	....	....	....

CCHA First All-Star Team (1994) • NCAA West First All-American Team (1994) • IHL First All-Star Team (1998)

Signed as a free agent by **Toronto**, August 14, 1996.

WITEHALL, JOHAN — NYR

Left wing. Shoots left. 6'1", 198 lbs. Born, Kungsbacka, Sweden, January 7, 1972.
(NY Rangers' 8th choice, 207th overall, in 1998 Entry Draft).

			Regular Season					Playoffs				
Season	Club	Lea	GP	G	A	TP	PIM	GP	G	A	TP	PIM
1991-92	Hanhals Kungs.	Sweden	32	23	14	37	52	....	....	....	....	....
1992-93	Hanhals Kungs.	Sweden-2	29	12	7	19	34	....	....	....	....	....
1993-94	Hanhals Kungs.	Sweden-2	30	13	12	25	66	....	....	....	....	....
1994-95	Hanhals Kungs.	Sweden-2	32	38	13	51	44	....	....	....	....	....
1995-96	Hanhals Kungs.	Sweden-2	36	43	17	60	48	....	....	....	....	....
1996-97	Oskarshamn	Sweden-2	32	19	16	35	38	....	....	....	....	....
1997-98	Leksand	Sweden	42	12	4	16	34	2	0	0	0	2

WITT, BRENDAN — WSH.

Defense. Shoots left. 6'1", 205 lbs. Born, Humbolt, Sask., February 20, 1975.
(Washington's 1st choice, 11th overall, in 1993 Entry Draft).

			Regular Season					Playoffs				
Season	Club	Lea	GP	G	A	TP	PIM	GP	G	A	TP	PIM
1991-92	Seattle	WHL	67	3	9	12	212	15	1	1	2	84
1992-93	Seattle	WHL	70	2	26	28	239	5	1	2	3	30
1993-94	Seattle	WHL	56	8	31	39	235	9	3	8	11	23
1994-95					DID NOT PLAY							
1995-96	**Washington**	**NHL**	**48**	**2**	**3**	**5**	**85**	....	....	....	....	....
1996-97	**Washington**	**NHL**	**44**	**3**	**2**	**5**	**88**	....	....	....	....	....
	Portland	AHL	30	2	4	6	56	5	1	0	1	30
1997-98	**Washington**	**NHL**	**64**	**1**	**7**	**8**	**112**	**16**	**1**	**0**	**1**	**14**
	NHL Totals		**156**	**6**	**12**	**18**	**285**	**16**	**1**	**0**	**1**	**14**

WHL West First All-Star Team (1993, 1994) • Canadian Major Junior First All-Star Team (1994)

• Sat out entire 1994-95 season after failing to come to contract terms with Washington.

WOLANIN, CRAIG — (wuh-LAN-ihn)

Defense. Shoots left. 6'4", 215 lbs. Born, Grosse Pointe, MI, July 27, 1967.
(New Jersey's 1st choice, 3rd overall, in 1985 Entry Draft).

			Regular Season					Playoffs				
Season	Club	Lea	GP	G	A	TP	PIM	GP	G	A	TP	PIM
1983-84	Detroit	NAJHL	69	8	42	50	86	....	....	....	....	....
1984-85	Kitchener	OHL	60	5	16	21	95	4	1	1	2	2
1985-86	**New Jersey**	**NHL**	**44**	**2**	**16**	**18**	**74**	....	....	....	....	....
1986-87	**New Jersey**	**NHL**	**68**	**4**	**6**	**10**	**109**	....	....	....	....	....
1987-88	**New Jersey**	**NHL**	**78**	**6**	**25**	**31**	**170**	**18**	**2**	**5**	**7**	**51**
1988-89	**New Jersey**	**NHL**	**56**	**3**	**8**	**11**	**69**	....	....	....	....	....
1989-90	**New Jersey**	**NHL**	**37**	**1**	**7**	**8**	**47**	....	....	....	....	....
	Utica	AHL	6	2	4	6	2	....	....	....	....	....
	Quebec	**NHL**	**13**	**0**	**3**	**3**	**10**	....	....	....	....	....
1990-91	**Quebec**	**NHL**	**80**	**5**	**13**	**18**	**89**	....	....	....	....	....
1991-92	**Quebec**	**NHL**	**69**	**2**	**11**	**13**	**80**	....	....	....	....	....
1992-93	**Quebec**	**NHL**	**24**	**1**	**4**	**5**	**49**	**4**	**0**	**0**	**0**	**4**
1993-94	**Quebec**	**NHL**	**63**	**6**	**10**	**16**	**80**	....	....	....	....	....
1994-95	**Quebec**	**NHL**	**40**	**3**	**6**	**9**	**40**	**6**	**1**	**1**	**2**	**4**
1995-96	**Colorado**	**NHL**	**75**	**7**	**20**	**27**	**50**	**7**	**1**	**0**	**1**	**8** ♦
1996-97	**Tampa Bay**	**NHL**	**15**	**0**	**0**	**0**	**8**	....	....	....	....	....
	Toronto	**NHL**	**23**	**0**	**4**	**4**	**13**	....	....	....	....	....
1997-98	**Toronto**	**NHL**	**10**	**0**	**0**	**0**	**6**	....	....	....	....	....
	NHL Totals		**695**	**40**	**133**	**173**	**894**	**35**	**4**	**6**	**10**	**67**

Traded to **Quebec** by **New Jersey** with future considerations (Randy Velischek, August 13, 1990) for Peter Stastny, March 6, 1990. Transferred to **Colorado** after **Quebec** franchise relocated, July 1, 1995. Traded to **Tampa Bay** by **Colorado** for Tampa Bay's 2nd round choice (Ramzi Abid) in 1998 Entry Draft, July 29, 1996. Traded to **Toronto** by **Tampa Bay** for Toronto's 3rd round choice (later traded to Edmonton — Edmonton Selected Alex Henry) in 1998 Entry Draft, January 31, 1997.

WOOD, DODY

Center. Shoots left. 6', 200 lbs. Born, Chetwynd, B.C., March 18, 1972.
(San Jose's 4th choice, 45th overall, in 1991 Entry Draft).

			Regular Season					Playoffs				
Season	Club	Lea	GP	G	A	TP	PIM	GP	G	A	TP	PIM
1989-90	Fort St. John	PCJHL	44	51	73	124	270	....	....	....	....	....
	Seattle	WHL	....	....	....	....	....	5	0	0	0	2
1990-91	Seattle	WHL	69	28	37	65	272	6	0	1	1	2
1991-92	Seattle	WHL	37	13	19	32	232	....	....	....	....	....
	Swift Current	WHL	3	0	2	2	14	7	2	1	3	37
1992-93	**San Jose**	**NHL**	**13**	**1**	**1**	**2**	**71**	....	....	....	....	....
	Kansas City	IHL	36	3	2	5	216	6	0	1	1	15
1993-94	Kansas City	IHL	48	5	15	20	320	....	....	....	....	....
1994-95	Kansas City	IHL	44	5	13	18	255	21	7	10	17	87
	San Jose	**NHL**	**9**	**1**	**1**	**2**	**29**	....	....	....	....	....
1995-96	**San Jose**	**NHL**	**32**	**3**	**6**	**9**	**138**	....	....	....	....	....
1996-97	**San Jose**	**NHL**	**44**	**3**	**2**	**5**	**193**	....	....	....	....	....
	Kansas City	IHL	6	3	6	9	35	....	....	....	....	....
1997-98	**San Jose**	**NHL**	**8**	**0**	**0**	**0**	**40**	....	....	....	....	....
	Kansas City	IHL	2	0	1	1	31	....	....	....	....	....
	Albany	AHL	34	4	13	17	185	13	2	0	2	55
	NHL Totals		**106**	**8**	**10**	**18**	**471**	....	....	....	....	....

Traded to **New Jersey** by **San Jose** with Doug Bodger for John MacLean and Ken Sutton, December 7, 1997.

WOOLLEY, JASON (WOO-lee) BUF.

Defense. Shoots left. 6'1", 188 lbs. Born, Toronto, Ont., July 27, 1969.
(Washington's 4th choice, 61st overall, in 1989 Entry Draft).

			Regular Season					Playoffs				
Season	Club	Lea	GP	G	A	TP	PIM	GP	G	A	TP	PIM
1987-88	St. Michael's	Jr. B	31	19	37	56	22	....	....	....	....	....
1988-89	Michigan State	CCHA	47	12	25	37	26	....	....	....	....	....
1989-90	Michigan State	CCHA	45	10	38	48	26	....	....	....	....	....
1990-91	Michigan State	CCHA	40	15	44	59	24	....	....	....	....	....
1991-92	Canada	Nat-Tm	60	14	30	44	36	....	....	....	....	....
	Canada	Olympics	8	0	5	5	4	....	....	....	....	....
	Washington	**NHL**	**1**	**0**	**0**	**0**	**0**	....	....	....	....	....
	Baltimore	AHL	15	1	10	11	6	....	....	....	....	....
1992-93	**Washington**	**NHL**	**26**	**0**	**2**	**2**	**10**	....	....	....	....	....
	Baltimore	AHL	29	14	27	41	22	1	0	2	2	0
1993-94	**Washington**	**NHL**	**10**	**1**	**2**	**3**	**4**	**4**	**1**	**0**	**1**	**4**
	Portland	AHL	41	12	29	41	14	9	2	2	4	4
1994-95	Detroit	IHL	48	8	28	36	38	....	....	....	....	....
	Florida	**NHL**	**34**	**4**	**9**	**13**	**18**	....	....	....	....	....
1995-96	**Florida**	**NHL**	**52**	**6**	**28**	**34**	**32**	**13**	**2**	**6**	**8**	**14**
1996-97	**Florida**	**NHL**	**3**	**0**	**0**	**0**	**2**	....	....	....	....	....
	Pittsburgh	**NHL**	**57**	**6**	**30**	**36**	**28**	**5**	**0**	**3**	**3**	**0**
1997-98	**Buffalo**	**NHL**	**71**	**9**	**26**	**35**	**35**	**15**	**2**	**9**	**11**	**12**
	NHL Totals		**254**	**26**	**97**	**123**	**129**	**37**	**5**	**18**	**23**	**30**

CCHA First All-Star Team (1991) • NCAA West First All-American Team (1991)

Signed as a free agent by **Florida**, February 15, 1995. Traded to **Pittsburgh** by **Florida** with Stu Barnes for Chris Wells, November 19, 1996. Traded to **Buffalo** by **Pittsburgh** for Buffalo's 5th round choice (Robert Scuderi) in 1998 Entry Draft, September 24, 1997.

WORRELL, PETER (woh-REHL) FLA.

Left wing. Shoots left. 6'6", 225 lbs. Born, Pierre Fonds, Que., August 18, 1977.
(Florida's 7th choice, 166th overall, in 1995 Entry Draft).

			Regular Season					Playoffs				
Season	Club	Lea	GP	G	A	TP	PIM	GP	G	A	TP	PIM
1994-95	Hull	QMJHL	56	1	8	9	243	21	0	1	1	91
1995-96	Hull	QMJHL	63	23	36	59	464	18	11	8	19	81
1996-97	Hull	QMJHL	62	17	46	63	437	14	3	13	16	83
1997-98	**Florida**	**NHL**	**19**	**0**	**0**	**0**	**153**	....	....	....	....	....
	New Haven	AHL	50	15	12	27	309	1	0	1	1	6
	NHL Totals		**19**	**0**	**0**	**0**	**153**	....	....	....	....	....

WOTTON, MARK (WAH-tuhn) VAN.

Defense. Shoots left. 6', 190 lbs. Born, Foxwarren, Man., November 16, 1973.
(Vancouver's 11th choice, 237th overall, in 1992 Entry Draft).

			Regular Season					Playoffs				
Season	Club	Lea	GP	G	A	TP	PIM	GP	G	A	TP	PIM
1990-91	Saskatoon	WHL	45	4	11	15	37	....	....	....	....	....
1991-92	Saskatoon	WHL	64	11	25	36	92	....	....	....	....	....
1992-93	Saskatoon	WHL	71	15	51	66	90	9	6	5	11	18
1993-94	Saskatoon	WHL	65	12	34	46	108	16	3	12	15	32
1994-95	Syracuse	AHL	75	12	29	41	50	....	....	....	....	....
	Vancouver	**NHL**	**1**	**0**	**0**	**0**	**0**	**5**	**0**	**0**	**0**	**4**
1995-96	Syracuse	AHL	80	10	35	45	96	15	1	12	13	20
1996-97	**Vancouver**	**NHL**	**36**	**3**	**6**	**9**	**19**	....	....	....	....	....
	Syracuse	AHL	27	2	8	10	25	2	0	0	0	4
1997-98	**Vancouver**	**NHL**	**5**	**0**	**0**	**0**	**6**	....	....	....	....	....
	Syracuse	AHL	56	12	21	33	80	5	0	0	0	12
	NHL Totals		**42**	**3**	**6**	**9**	**25**	**5**	**0**	**0**	**0**	**4**

WHL East Second All-Star Team (1994)

WREN, BOB (REHN) ANA.

Left wing. Shoots left. 5'10", 185 lbs. Born, Preston, Ont., September 16, 1974.
(Los Angeles' 3rd choice, 94th overall, in 1993 Entry Draft).

			Regular Season					Playoffs				
Season	Club	Lea	GP	G	A	TP	PIM	GP	G	A	TP	PIM
1991-92	Detroit	OHL	62	13	36	49	58	7	3	4	7	19
1992-93	Detroit	OHL	63	57	88	145	91	15	4	11	15	20
1993-94	Detroit	OHL	57	45	64	109	81	17	12	18	30	20
1994-95	Springfield	AHL	61	16	15	31	118	....	....	....	....	....
	Richmond	ECHL	2	0	1	1	0	....	....	....	....	....
1995-96	Detroit	IHL	1	0	0	0	0	....	....	....	....	....
	Knoxville	ECHL	50	21	35	56	257	8	4	11	15	32
1996-97	Baltimore	AHL	72	23	36	59	97	3	1	1	2	0
1997-98	**Anaheim**	**NHL**	**3**	**0**	**0**	**0**	**0**	....	....	....	....	....
	Cincinnati	AHL	77	*42	58	100	151	....	....	....	....	....
	NHL Totals		**3**	**0**	**0**	**0**	**0**	....	....	....	....	....

OHL Second All-Star Team (1993, 1994)

Signed as a free agent by **Hartford**, September 6, 1994. Signed as a free agent by **Anaheim**, August 1, 1997.

WRIGHT, JAMIE DAL.

Left wing. Shoots left. 6', 172 lbs. Born, Kitchener, Ont., May 13, 1976.
(Dallas' 3rd choice, 98th overall, in 1994 Entry Draft).

			Regular Season					Playoffs				
Season	Club	Lea	GP	G	A	TP	PIM	GP	G	A	TP	PIM
1993-94	Guelph	OHL	65	17	15	32	34	8	2	1	3	10
1994-95	Guelph	OHL	65	43	39	82	36	14	6	8	14	6
1995-96	Guelph	OHL	55	30	36	66	45	16	10	12	22	35
1996-97	Michigan	IHL	60	6	8	14	34	1	0	0	0	0
1997-98	**Dallas**	**NHL**	**21**	**4**	**2**	**6**	**2**	**5**	**0**	**0**	**0**	**0**
	Michigan	IHL	53	15	11	26	31	....	....	....	....	....
	NHL Totals		**21**	**4**	**2**	**6**	**2**	**5**	**0**	**0**	**0**	**0**

WRIGHT, SHAYNE

Defense. Shoots left. 6', 189 lbs. Born, Welland, Ont., June 30, 1975.
(Buffalo's 12th choice, 277th overall, in 1994 Entry Draft).

			Regular Season					Playoffs				
Season	Club	Lea	GP	G	A	TP	PIM	GP	G	A	TP	PIM
1992-93	Owen Sound	OHL	62	9	21	30	101	8	2	0	2	5
1993-94	Owen Sound	OHL	64	11	24	35	95	9	1	10	11	4
1994-95	Owen Sound	OHL	63	11	50	61	114	10	1	9	10	34
	Rochester	AHL	2	0	0	0	0	4	0	1	1	0
1995-96	Rochester	AHL	48	0	7	7	99	5	0	1	1	8
1996-97	Rochester	AHL	80	7	30	37	124	10	2	3	5	6
1997-98	Rochester	AHL	70	2	18	20	122	4	0	2	2	0

WRIGHT, TYLER PIT.

Center. Shoots right. 5'11", 185 lbs. Born, Canora, Sask., April 6, 1973.
(Edmonton's 1st choice, 12th overall, in 1991 Entry Draft).

			Regular Season					Playoffs				
Season	Club	Lea	GP	G	A	TP	PIM	GP	G	A	TP	PIM
1989-90	Swift Current	WHL	67	14	18	32	139	4	0	0	0	12
1990-91	Swift Current	WHL	66	41	51	92	157	3	0	0	0	6
1991-92	Swift Current	WHL	63	36	46	82	295	8	2	5	7	16
1992-93	Swift Current	WHL	37	24	41	65	76	17	9	17	26	*49
	Edmonton	**NHL**	**7**	**1**	**1**	**2**	**19**	....	....	....	....	....
1993-94	**Edmonton**	**NHL**	**5**	**0**	**0**	**0**	**4**	....	....	....	....	....
	Cape Breton	AHL	65	14	27	41	160	5	2	0	2	11
1994-95	Cape Breton	AHL	70	16	15	31	184	....	....	....	....	....
	Edmonton	**NHL**	**6**	**1**	**0**	**1**	**14**	....	....	....	....	....
1995-96	**Edmonton**	**NHL**	**23**	**1**	**0**	**1**	**33**	....	....	....	....	....
	Cape Breton	AHL	31	6	12	18	158	....	....	....	....	....
1996-97	**Pittsburgh**	**NHL**	**45**	**2**	**2**	**4**	**70**	....	....	....	....	....
	Cleveland	IHL	10	4	3	7	34	14	4	2	6	44
1997-98	**Pittsburgh**	**NHL**	**82**	**3**	**4**	**7**	**112**	**6**	**0**	**1**	**1**	**4**
	NHL Totals		**168**	**8**	**7**	**15**	**252**	**6**	**0**	**1**	**1**	**4**

Traded to **Pittsburgh** by **Edmonton** for Pittsburgh's 7th round choice (Brandon Lafrance) in 1996 Entry Draft, June 22, 1996.

YACHMENEV, VITALI (yach-meh-NEHV) NSH.

Right wing. Shoots left. 5'9", 180 lbs. Born, Chelyabinsk, USSR, January 8, 1975.
(Los Angeles' 3rd choice, 59th overall, in 1994 Entry Draft).

			Regular Season					Playoffs				
Season	Club	Lea	GP	G	A	TP	PIM	GP	G	A	TP	PIM
1992-93	Chelyabinsk	CIS-2	51	23	20	43	12	....	....	....	....	....
1993-94	North Bay	OHL	66	*61	52	113	18	18	13	19	32	12
1994-95	North Bay	OHL	59	53	52	105	8	6	1	8	9	2
	Phoenix	IHL	....	....	....	....	....	4	1	0	1	0
1995-96	**Los Angeles**	**NHL**	**80**	**19**	**34**	**53**	**16**	....	....	....	....	....
1996-97	**Los Angeles**	**NHL**	**65**	**10**	**22**	**32**	**10**	....	....	....	....	....
1997-98	**Los Angeles**	**NHL**	**4**	**0**	**1**	**1**	**4**	....	....	....	....	....
	Long Beach	IHL	59	23	28	51	14	17	8	9	17	4
	NHL Totals		**149**	**29**	**57**	**86**	**30**	....	....	....	....	....

Canadian Major Junior Rookie of the Year (1994)

Traded to **Nashville** by **LA Kings** for future considerations, July 7, 1998.

YAKE, TERRY (YAYK) ST.L.

Right wing. Shoots right. 5'11", 190 lbs. Born, New Westminster, B.C., October 22, 1968.
(Hartford's 3rd choice, 81st overall, in 1987 Entry Draft).

			Regular Season					Playoffs				
Season	Club	Lea	GP	G	A	TP	PIM	GP	G	A	TP	PIM
1984-85	Brandon	WHL	11	1	1	2	0	....	....	....	....	....
1985-86	Brandon	WHL	72	26	26	52	49	....	....	....	....	....
1986-87	Brandon	WHL	71	44	58	102	64	....	....	....	....	....
1987-88	Brandon	WHL	72	55	85	140	59	3	4	2	6	7
1988-89	**Hartford**	**NHL**	**2**	**0**	**0**	**0**	**0**	....	....	....	....	....
	Binghamton	AHL	75	39	56	95	57	....	....	....	....	....
1989-90	**Hartford**	**NHL**	**2**	**0**	**1**	**1**	**0**	....	....	....	....	....
	Binghamton	AHL	77	13	42	55	37	....	....	....	....	....
1990-91	**Hartford**	**NHL**	**19**	**1**	**4**	**5**	**10**	**6**	**1**	**1**	**2**	**16**
	Springfield	AHL	60	35	42	77	56	15	9	9	18	10
1991-92	**Hartford**	**NHL**	**15**	**1**	**1**	**2**	**4**	....	....	....	....	....
	Springfield	AHL	53	21	34	55	63	8	3	4	7	2
1992-93	**Hartford**	**NHL**	**66**	**22**	**31**	**53**	**46**	....	....	....	....	....
	Springfield	AHL	16	8	14	22	27	....	....	....	....	....
1993-94	**Anaheim**	**NHL**	**82**	**21**	**31**	**52**	**44**	....	....	....	....	....
1994-95	**Toronto**	**NHL**	**19**	**3**	**2**	**5**	**2**	....	....	....	....	....
	Denver	IHL	2	0	3	3	2	17	4	11	15	16
1995-96	Milwaukee	IHL	70	32	56	88	70	5	3	6	9	4
1996-97	Rochester	AHL	78	34	*67	101	77	10	8	8	16	2
1997-98	**St. Louis**	**NHL**	**65**	**10**	**15**	**25**	**38**	**10**	**2**	**1**	**3**	**6**
	NHL Totals		**270**	**58**	**85**	**143**	**144**	**16**	**3**	**2**	**5**	**22**

Claimed by **Anaheim** from **Hartford** in Expansion Draft, June 24, 1993. Traded to **Toronto** by **Anaheim** for David Sacco, September 28, 1994. Signed as a free agent by **Buffalo**, September 17, 1996. Signed as a free agent by **St. Louis**, July 24, 1997.

YAKUSHIN, DMITRI (yah-KOO-shihn) TOR.

Defense. Shoots left. 6', 200 lbs. Born, Kharkov, USSR, January 21, 1978.
(Toronto's 9th choice, 140th overall, in 1996 Entry Draft).

			Regular Season					Playoffs				
Season	Club	Lea	GP	G	A	TP	PIM	GP	G	A	TP	PIM
1995-96	Pembroke	OJHL	31	8	5	13	62	....	....	....	....	....
1996-97	Edmonton	WHL	63	3	14	17	103	....	....	....	....	....
1997-98	Edmonton	WHL	29	1	10	11	41	....	....	....	....	....
	Regina	WHL	13	0	14	14	16	9	2	8	10	12

YASHIN, ALEXEI (YAH-shin) OTT.

Center. Shoots right. 6'3", 225 lbs. Born, Sverdlovsk, USSR, November 5, 1973.
(Ottawa's 1st choice, 2nd overall, in 1992 Entry Draft).

			Regular Season					Playoffs				
Season	Club	Lea	GP	G	A	TP	PIM	GP	G	A	TP	PIM
1990-91	Sverdlovsk	USSR	26	2	1	3	10	....	....	....	....	....
1991-92	Moscow D'amo	CIS	35	7	5	12	19	....	....	....	....	....
1992-93	Moscow D'amo	CIS	27	10	12	22	18	10	7	3	10	18
1993-94	**Ottawa**	**NHL**	**83**	**30**	**49**	**79**	**22**	....	....	....	....	....
1994-95	Las Vegas	IHL	24	15	20	35	32	....	....	....	....	....
	Ottawa	**NHL**	**47**	**21**	**23**	**44**	**20**	....	....	....	....	....
1995-96	CSKA Moscow	CIS	4	2	2	4	4	....	....	....	....	....
	Ottawa	**NHL**	**46**	**15**	**24**	**39**	**28**	....	....	....	....	....
1996-97	**Ottawa**	**NHL**	**82**	**35**	**40**	**75**	**44**	**7**	**1**	**5**	**6**	**2**
1997-98	**Ottawa**	**NHL**	**82**	**33**	**39**	**72**	**24**	**11**	**5**	**3**	**8**	**8**
	Russia	Olympics	6	3	3	6	0	....	....	....	....	....
	NHL Totals		**340**	**134**	**175**	**309**	**138**	**18**	**6**	**8**	**14**	**10**

CIS First All-Star Team (1993)
Played in NHL All-Star Game (1994)

YAWNEY, TRENT (YAW-nee) CHI.

Defense. Shoots left. 6'3", 195 lbs. Born, Hudson Bay, Sask., September 29, 1965.
(Chicago's 2nd choice, 45th overall, in 1984 Entry Draft).

			Regular Season					Playoffs				
Season	Club	Lea	GP	G	A	TP	PIM	GP	G	A	TP	PIM
1982-83	Saskatoon	WHL	59	6	31	37	44	6	0	2	2	0
1983-84	Saskatoon	WHL	73	13	46	59	81	....	....	....	....	....
1984-85	Saskatoon	WHL	72	16	51	67	158	3	1	6	7	7
1985-86	Canada	Nat-Tm	73	6	15	21	60	....	....	....	....	....
1986-87	Canada	Nat-Tm	51	4	15	19	37	....	....	....	....	....
1987-88	Canada	Nat-Tm	60	4	12	16	81	....	....	....	....	....
	Canada	Olympics	8	1	1	2	6	....	....	....	....	....
	Chicago	**NHL**	**15**	**2**	**8**	**10**	**15**	**5**	**0**	**4**	**4**	**8**
1988-89	**Chicago**	**NHL**	**69**	**5**	**19**	**24**	**116**	**15**	**3**	**6**	**9**	**20**
1989-90	**Chicago**	**NHL**	**70**	**5**	**15**	**20**	**82**	**20**	**3**	**5**	**8**	**27**
1990-91	**Chicago**	**NHL**	**61**	**3**	**13**	**16**	**77**	**1**	**0**	**0**	**0**	**0**
1991-92	**Calgary**	**NHL**	**47**	**4**	**9**	**13**	**45**	....	....	....	....	....
	Indianapolis	IHL	9	2	3	5	12	....	....	....	....	....
1992-93	**Calgary**	**NHL**	**63**	**1**	**16**	**17**	**67**	**6**	**3**	**2**	**5**	**6**
1993-94	**Calgary**	**NHL**	**58**	**6**	**15**	**21**	**60**	**7**	**0**	**0**	**0**	**16**
1994-95	**Calgary**	**NHL**	**37**	**0**	**2**	**2**	**108**	**2**	**0**	**0**	**0**	**2**
1995-96	**Calgary**	**NHL**	**69**	**0**	**3**	**3**	**88**	**4**	**0**	**0**	**0**	**2**
1996-97	**St. Louis**	**NHL**	**39**	**0**	**2**	**2**	**17**	....	....	....	....	....
1997-98	**Chicago**	**NHL**	**45**	**1**	**0**	**1**	**76**	....	....	....	....	....
	NHL Totals		**573**	**27**	**102**	**129**	**751**	**60**	**9**	**17**	**26**	**81**

Traded to **Calgary** by **Chicago** for Stephane Matteau, December 16, 1991. Signed as a free agent by **St. Louis**, July 31, 1996. Signed as a free agent by **Chicago**, September 25, 1997.

YEGOROV, ALEXEI (yeh-GOH-rohv) S.J.

Right wing. Shoots left. 5'11", 185 lbs. Born, St. Petersburg, USSR, May 21, 1975.
(San Jose's 3rd choice, 66th overall, in 1994 Entry Draft).

			Regular Season					Playoffs				
Season	Club	Lea	GP	G	A	TP	PIM	GP	G	A	TP	PIM
1992-93	St. Peterburg	CIS	17	1	2	3	10	6	3	1	4	6
1993-94	St. Peterburg	CIS	23	5	3	8	18	6	0	0	0	4
1994-95	St. Peterburg	CIS	10	2	1	3	10	....	....	....	....	....
	Fort Worth	CHL	18	4	10	14	15	....	....	....	....	....
1995-96	**San Jose**	**NHL**	**9**	**3**	**2**	**5**	**2**	....	....	....	....	....
	Kansas City	IHL	65	31	25	56	84	5	2	0	2	8
1996-97	**San Jose**	**NHL**	**2**	**0**	**1**	**1**	**0**	....	....	....	....	....
	Kentucky	AHL	75	26	32	58	59	4	0	1	1	2
1997-98	Kentucky	AHL	79	32	52	84	56	3	2	0	2	0
	NHL Totals		**11**	**3**	**3**	**6**	**2**	....	....	....	....	....

YELLE, STEPHANE (YEHL) COL.

Center. Shoots left. 6'1", 190 lbs. Born, Ottawa, Ont., May 9, 1974.
(New Jersey's 9th choice, 186th overall, in 1992 Entry Draft).

			Regular Season					Playoffs				
Season	Club	Lea	GP	G	A	TP	PIM	GP	G	A	TP	PIM
1991-92	Oshawa	OHL	55	12	14	26	20	7	2	0	2	1
1992-93	Oshawa	OHL	66	24	50	74	20	10	2	4	6	4
1993-94	Oshawa	OHL	66	35	69	104	22	5	1	7	8	2
1994-95	Cornwall	AHL	40	18	15	33	22	13	7	7	14	8
1995-96	**Colorado**	**NHL**	**71**	**13**	**14**	**27**	**30**	**22**	**1**	**4**	**5**	**8** ♦
1996-97	**Colorado**	**NHL**	**79**	**9**	**17**	**26**	**38**	**12**	**1**	**6**	**7**	**2**
1997-98	**Colorado**	**NHL**	**81**	**7**	**15**	**22**	**48**	**7**	**1**	**0**	**1**	**12**
	NHL Totals		**231**	**29**	**46**	**75**	**116**	**41**	**3**	**10**	**13**	**22**

Traded to **Quebec** by **New Jersey** with New Jersey's 11th round choice (Steven Low) in 1994 Entry Draft for Quebec's 11th round choice (Mike Hansen) in 1994 Entry Draft, June 1, 1994. Transferred to **Colorado** after **Quebec** franchise relocated, June 21, 1995.

YERKOVICH, SERGEI (yehr-KOH-vihch) EDM.

Defense. Shoots left. 6'3", 210 lbs. Born, Minsk, USSR, September 3, 1974.
(Edmonton's 3rd choice, 68th overall, in 1997 Entry Draft).

			Regular Season					Playoffs				
Season	Club	Lea	GP	G	A	TP	PIM	GP	G	A	TP	PIM
1993-94	Minsk	CIS	39	2	1	3	34	....	....	....	....	....
1994-95	Minsk	CIS	45	3	1	4	52	....	....	....	....	....
1995-96	Minsk	CIS	41	5	3	8	30	....	....	....	....	....
1996-97	Las Vegas	IHL	76	6	19	25	167	....	....	....	....	....
1997-98	Las Vegas	IHL	69	7	15	22	130	4	0	0	0	6
	Belarus	Olympics	6	2	0	2	16	....	....	....	....	....

YGRANES, JARL ESPEN (yoo-GRAH-nehs, YARL, EHS-pehn) MTL.

Defense. Shoots left. 6'1", 187 lbs. Born, Oslo, Norway, January 23, 1979.
(Montreal's 11th choice, 228th overall, in 1997 Entry Draft).

			Regular Season					Playoffs				
Season	Club	Lea	GP	G	A	TP	PIM	GP	G	A	TP	PIM
1996-97	Furuset Oslo	Norway	34	4	4	8	63	....	....	....	....	....
1997-98	Furuset Oslo	Norway	13	0	2	2	10	....	....	....	....	....
	London	OHL	25	0	7	7	19	....	....	....	....	....

YLONEN, YUHA (YOO-lih-nehn, YOO-hah) PHX.

Center. Shoots left. 6', 180 lbs. Born, Helsinki, Finland, February 13, 1972.
(Winnipeg's 3rd choice, 91st overall, in 1991 Entry Draft).

			Regular Season					Playoffs				
Season	Club	Lea	GP	G	A	TP	PIM	GP	G	A	TP	PIM
1990-91	Kiekko-Espoo	Finland-2	40	12	21	33	4	....	....	....	....	....
1991-92	Hameelinna	Finland	43	7	11	18	8	....	....	....	....	....
1992-93	Hameelinna	Finland	48	8	18	26	22	12	3	5	8	2
1993-94	Jokerit	Finland	37	5	11	16	2	12	1	3	4	8
1994-95	Jokerit	Finland	50	13	15	28	10	11	3	2	5	0
1995-96	Jokerit	Finland	24	3	13	16	20	11	4	5	9	4
1996-97	**Phoenix**	**NHL**	**2**	**0**	**0**	**0**	**0**	....	....	....	....	....
	Springfield	AHL	70	20	41	61	6	17	5	*16	21	4
1997-98	**Phoenix**	**NHL**	**55**	**1**	**11**	**12**	**10**	....	....	....	....	....
	Finland	Olympics	6	0	0	0	8	....	....	....	....	....
	NHL Totals		**57**	**1**	**11**	**12**	**10**	....	....	....	....	....

Rights transferred to **Phoenix** after **Winnipeg** franchise relocated, July 1, 1996.

YORK, HARRY NYR

Center. Shoots left. 6'2", 215 lbs. Born, Ponoka, Alta., April 16, 1974.

			Regular Season					Playoffs				
Season	Club	Lea	GP	G	A	TP	PIM	GP	G	A	TP	PIM
1994-95	Fort McMurray	AJHL	54	35	73	108	....	....	....	....	....	....
1995-96	Nashville	ECHL	64	33	50	83	122	....	....	....	....	....
	Atlanta	IHL	2	0	0	0	15	....	....	....	....	....
	Worcester	AHL	13	8	5	13	2	4	0	4	4	4
1996-97	**St. Louis**	**NHL**	**74**	**14**	**18**	**32**	**24**	**5**	**0**	**0**	**0**	**2**
1997-98	**St. Louis**	**NHL**	**58**	**4**	**6**	**10**	**31**	....	....	....	....	....
	NY Rangers	**NHL**	**2**	**0**	**0**	**0**	**0**	....	....	....	....	....
	NHL Totals		**134**	**18**	**24**	**42**	**55**	**5**	**0**	**0**	**0**	**2**

Signed as a free agent by **St. Louis**, May 1, 1996. Traded to **NY Rangers** by **St. Louis** for Mike Eastwood, March 24, 1998.

YORK, JASON OTT.

Defense. Shoots right. 6'2", 198 lbs. Born, Nepean, Ont., May 20, 1970.
(Detroit's 6th choice, 129th overall, in 1990 Entry Draft).

			Regular Season					Playoffs				
Season	Club	Lea	GP	G	A	TP	PIM	GP	G	A	TP	PIM
1989-90	Windsor	OHL	39	9	30	39	38	....	....	....	....	....
	Kitchener	OHL	25	11	25	36	17	17	3	19	22	10
1990-91	Windsor	OHL	66	13	80	93	40	11	3	10	13	12
1991-92	Adirondack	AHL	49	4	20	24	32	5	0	1	1	0
1992-93	**Detroit**	**NHL**	**2**	**0**	**0**	**0**	**0**	....	....	....	....	....
	Adirondack	AHL	77	15	40	55	86	11	0	3	3	18
1993-94	**Detroit**	**NHL**	**7**	**1**	**2**	**3**	**2**	....	....	....	....	....
	Adirondack	AHL	74	10	56	66	98	12	3	11	14	22
1994-95	**Detroit**	**NHL**	**10**	**1**	**2**	**3**	**2**	....	....	....	....	....
	Adirondack	AHL	5	1	3	4	4	....	....	....	....	....
	Anaheim	**NHL**	**15**	**0**	**8**	**8**	**12**	....	....	....	....	....
1995-96	**Anaheim**	**NHL**	**79**	**3**	**21**	**24**	**88**	....	....	....	....	....
1996-97	**Ottawa**	**NHL**	**75**	**4**	**17**	**21**	**67**	**7**	**0**	**0**	**0**	**4**
1997-98	**Ottawa**	**NHL**	**73**	**3**	**13**	**16**	**62**	**7**	**1**	**1**	**2**	**7**
	NHL Totals		**261**	**12**	**63**	**75**	**233**	**14**	**1**	**1**	**2**	**11**

AHL First All-Star Team (1994)

Traded to **Anaheim** by **Detroit** with Mike Sillinger for Stu Grimson, Mark Ferner and Anaheim's 6th round choice (Magnus Nilsson) in 1996 Entry Draft, April 4, 1995. Traded to **Ottawa** by **Anaheim** with Shaun Van Allen for Ted Drury and the rights to Marc Moro, October 1, 1996.

YORK, MICHAEL NYR

Center. Shoots right. 5'9", 179 lbs. Born, Pontiac, MI, January 3, 1978.
(NY Rangers' 7th choice, 136th overall, in 1997 Entry Draft).

			Regular Season					Playoffs				
Season	Club	Lea	GP	G	A	TP	PIM	GP	G	A	TP	PIM
1995-96	Michigan State	CCHA	39	12	27	39	20	....	....	....	....	....
1996-97	Michigan State	CCHA	37	18	29	47	42	....	....	....	....	....
1997-98	Michigan State	CCHA	40	27	34	61	38	....	....	....	....	....

CCHA Second All-Star Team (1998) • NCAA West First All-American Team (1998)

YOUNG, B.J. DET.

Right wing. Shoots right. 5'10", 178 lbs. Born, Anchorage, AK, July 23, 1977.
(Detroit's 5th choice, 157th overall, in 1997 Entry Draft).

			Regular Season					Playoffs				
Season	Club	Lea	GP	G	A	TP	PIM	GP	G	A	TP	PIM
1993-94	Tri-City	WHL	54	19	24	43	66	2	1	1	2	2
1994-95	Tri-City	WHL	30	6	3	9	39	....	....	....	....	....
	Red Deer	WHL	21	5	9	14	33	....	....	....	....	....
1995-96	Red Deer	WHL	67	49	45	94	144	8	4	9	13	12
1996-97	Red Deer	WHL	63	58	56	114	97	16	8	14	22	26
1997-98	Adirondack	AHL	65	15	22	37	191	3	0	2	2	6

WHL East First All-Star Team (1997)

YOUNG, SCOTT — ST.L.

Right wing. Shoots right. 6', 190 lbs. Born, Clinton, MA, October 1, 1967.
(Hartford's 1st choice, 11th overall, in 1986 Entry Draft).

			Regular Season					Playoffs				
Season	Club	Lea	GP	G	A	TP	PIM	GP	G	A	TP	PIM
1984-85	St. Marks High	H.S.	23	28	41	69	....	....	....	....	....	....
1985-86	Boston University	H.E.	38	16	13	29	31	....	....	....	....	....
1986-87	Boston University	H.E.	33	15	21	36	24	....	....	....	....	....
1987-88	United States	Nat-Tm	56	11	47	58	31	....	....	....	....	....
	United States	Olympics	6	2	6	8	4	....	....	....	....	....
	Hartford	**NHL**	**7**	**0**	**0**	**0**	**2**	**4**	**1**	**0**	**1**	**0**
1988-89	**Hartford**	**NHL**	**76**	**19**	**40**	**59**	**27**	**4**	**2**	**0**	**2**	**4**
1989-90	**Hartford**	**NHL**	**80**	**24**	**40**	**64**	**47**	**7**	**2**	**0**	**2**	**2**
1990-91	**Hartford**	**NHL**	**34**	**6**	**9**	**15**	**8**	....	....	....	....	....
	Pittsburgh	**NHL**	**43**	**11**	**16**	**27**	**33**	**17**	**1**	**6**	**7**	**2** ♦
1991-92	HC Bolzano	Italy	18	22	17	39	6	5	4	3	7	7
	United States	Nat-Tm	10	2	4	6	21	....	....	....	....	....
	United States	Olympics	8	2	1	3	2	....	....	....	....	....
1992-93	**Quebec**	**NHL**	**82**	**30**	**30**	**60**	**20**	**6**	**4**	**1**	**5**	**0**
1993-94	**Quebec**	**NHL**	**76**	**26**	**25**	**51**	**14**	....	....	....	....	....
1994-95	EV Landshut	Germany	4	6	1	7	6	....	....	....	....	....
	Frankfurt	Germany	1	1	0	1	0	....	....	....	....	....
	Quebec	**NHL**	**48**	**18**	**21**	**39**	**14**	**6**	**3**	**3**	**6**	**2**
1995-96	**Colorado**	**NHL**	**81**	**21**	**39**	**60**	**50**	**22**	**3**	**12**	**15**	**10** ♦
1996-97	**Colorado**	**NHL**	**72**	**18**	**19**	**37**	**14**	**17**	**4**	**2**	**6**	**14**
1997-98	**Anaheim**	**NHL**	**73**	**13**	**20**	**33**	**22**	....	....	....	....	....
	NHL Totals		**672**	**186**	**259**	**445**	**251**	**83**	**20**	**24**	**44**	**34**

ECAC First All-Star Team (1989)

Traded to **Pittsburgh** by **Hartford** for Rob Brown, December 21, 1990. Traded to **Quebec** by **Pittsburgh** for Bryan Fogarty, March 10, 1992. Transferred to **Colorado** after **Quebec** franchise relocated, June 21, 1995. Traded to **Anaheim** by **Colorado** for Anaheim's 3rd round choice (later traded to Florida - Florida selected Lance Ward) in 1998 Entry Draft, September 17, 1997. Signed as a free agent by **St. Louis**, July 28, 1998.

YSEBAERT, PAUL (IGHS-bahrt) — T.B.

Center. Shoots left. 6'1", 194 lbs. Born, Sarnia, Ont., May 15, 1966.
(New Jersey's 4th choice, 74th overall, in 1984 Entry Draft).

			Regular Season					Playoffs				
Season	Club	Lea	GP	G	A	TP	PIM	GP	G	A	TP	PIM
1983-84	Petrolia	OJHL	33	35	42	77	20	....	....	....	....	....
1984-85	Bowling Green	CCHA	42	23	32	55	54	....	....	....	....	....
1985-86	Bowling Green	CCHA	42	23	45	68	50	....	....	....	....	....
1986-87	Bowling Green	CCHA	45	27	58	85	44	....	....	....	....	....
	Canada	Nat-Tm	5	1	0	1	4	....	....	....	....	....
1987-88	Utica	AHL	78	30	49	79	60	....	....	....	....	....
1988-89	**New Jersey**	**NHL**	**5**	**0**	**4**	**4**	**0**	....	....	....	....	....
	Utica	AHL	56	36	44	80	22	5	0	1	1	4
1989-90	**New Jersey**	**NHL**	**5**	**1**	**2**	**3**	**0**	....	....	....	....	....
	Utica	AHL	74	53	52	*105	61	5	2	4	6	0
1990-91	**New Jersey**	**NHL**	**11**	**4**	**3**	**7**	**6**	....	....	....	....	....
	Detroit	**NHL**	**51**	**15**	**18**	**33**	**16**	**2**	**0**	**2**	**2**	**0**
1991-92	**Detroit**	**NHL**	**79**	**35**	**40**	**75**	**55**	**10**	**1**	**0**	**1**	**10**
1992-93	**Detroit**	**NHL**	**80**	**34**	**28**	**62**	**42**	**7**	**3**	**1**	**4**	**2**
1993-94	**Winnipeg**	**NHL**	**60**	**9**	**18**	**27**	**18**	....	....	....	....	....
	Chicago	**NHL**	**11**	**5**	**3**	**8**	**8**	**6**	**0**	**0**	**0**	**8**
1994-95	**Chicago**	**NHL**	**15**	**4**	**5**	**9**	**6**	....	....	....	....	....
	Tampa Bay	**NHL**	**29**	**8**	**11**	**19**	**12**	....	....	....	....	....
1995-96	**Tampa Bay**	**NHL**	**55**	**16**	**15**	**31**	**16**	**5**	**0**	**0**	**0**	**0**
1996-97	**Tampa Bay**	**NHL**	**39**	**5**	**12**	**17**	**4**	....	....	....	....	....
1997-98	**Tampa Bay**	**NHL**	**82**	**13**	**27**	**40**	**32**	....	....	....	....	....
	NHL Totals		**522**	**149**	**186**	**335**	**215**	**30**	**4**	**3**	**7**	**20**

CCHA Second All-Star Team (1986, 1987) • AHL First All-Star Team (1990) • Won John B. Sollenberger Trophy (Top Scorer - AHL) (1990) • Won Les Cunningham Plaque (MVP - AHL) (1990) • Won Alka-Seltzer Plus Award (1992)

Traded to **Detroit** by **New Jersey** for Lee Norwood and Detroit's 4th round choice (Scott McCabe) in 1992 Entry Draft, November 27, 1990. Traded to **Winnipeg** by **Detroit** with future considerations (Alan Kerr, June 18, 1993) for Aaron Ward and Toronto's 4th round choice (previously acquired by Winnipeg — later traded to Detroit — Detroit selected John Jakopin) in 1993 Entry Draft, June 11, 1993. Traded to **Chicago** by **Winnipeg** for Chicago's 3rd round choice (later traded back to Chicago — Chicago selected Kevin McKay) in 1995 Entry Draft, March 21, 1994. Traded to **Tampa Bay** by **Chicago** with Rich Sutter for Jim Cummins, Tom Tilley and Jeff Buchanan, February 22, 1995.

YTFELDT, DAVID (YOOT-fehld) — VAN.

Defense. Shoots left. 6', 187 lbs. Born, Ornskoldsvik, Sweden, September 29, 1979.
(Vancouver's 6th choice, 136th overall, in 1998 Entry Draft).

			Regular Season					Playoffs				
Season	Club	Lea	GP	G	A	TP	PIM	GP	G	A	TP	PIM
1996-97	Leksand	Swe-Jr.	25	3	5	8	....	....	....	....	....	....
1997-98	Leksand	Sweden	10	0	0	0	2	....	....	....	....	....
	Leksand	Swe-Jr.	23	13	10	23	101	....	....	....	....	....

• Name when drafted was David Jonsson. His last name was legally changed to Ytfeldt.

YUSHKEVICH, DIMITRI (yoosh-KAY-vihch) — TOR.

Defense. Shoots right. 5'11", 208 lbs. Born, Yaroslavl, USSR, November 19, 1971.
(Philadelphia's 6th choice, 122nd overall, in 1991 Entry Draft).

			Regular Season					Playoffs				
Season	Club	Lea	GP	G	A	TP	PIM	GP	G	A	TP	PIM
1988-89	Yaroslavl	USSR	23	2	1	3	8	....	....	....	....	....
1989-90	Yaroslavl	USSR	41	2	3	5	39	....	....	....	....	....
1990-91	Yaroslavl	USSR	41	10	4	14	22	....	....	....	....	....
1991-92	Moscow D'amo	CIS	35	5	7	12	14	....	....	....	....	....
	Russia	Olympics	8	1	2	3	4	....	....	....	....	....
1992-93	**Philadelphia**	**NHL**	**82**	**5**	**27**	**32**	**71**	....	....	....	....	....
1993-94	**Philadelphia**	**NHL**	**75**	**5**	**25**	**30**	**86**	....	....	....	....	....
1994-95	Yaroslavl	CIS	10	3	4	7	8	....	....	....	....	....
	Philadelphia	**NHL**	**40**	**5**	**9**	**14**	**47**	**15**	**1**	**5**	**6**	**12**
1995-96	**Toronto**	**NHL**	**69**	**1**	**10**	**11**	**54**	**4**	**0**	**0**	**0**	**0**
1996-97	**Toronto**	**NHL**	**74**	**4**	**10**	**14**	**56**	....	....	....	....	....
1997-98	**Toronto**	**NHL**	**72**	**0**	**12**	**12**	**78**	....	....	....	....	....
	NHL Totals		**412**	**20**	**93**	**113**	**392**	**19**	**1**	**5**	**6**	**12**

Traded to **Toronto** by **Philadelphia** with Philadelphia's 2nd round choice (Francis Larivee) in 1996 Entry Draft for Toronto's 1st round choice (Dainius Zubrus) in 1996 Entry Draft, 2nd round choice (Jean-Marc Pelletier) in 1997 Entry Draft and LA Kings' 4th round choice (previously acquired by Toronto — later traded to LA Kings — LA Kings selected Mikael Simons) in 1996 Entry Draft, August 30, 1995.

YZERMAN, STEVE (IGH-zuhr-muhn) — DET.

Center. Shoots right. 5'11", 185 lbs. Born, Cranbrook, B.C., May 9, 1965.
(Detroit's 1st choice, 4th overall, in 1983 Entry Draft).

			Regular Season					Playoffs				
Season	Club	Lea	GP	G	A	TP	PIM	GP	G	A	TP	PIM
1981-82	Peterborough	OHL	58	21	43	64	65	6	0	1	1	16
1982-83	Peterborough	OHL	56	42	49	91	33	4	1	4	5	0
1983-84	**Detroit**	**NHL**	**80**	**39**	**48**	**87**	**33**	**4**	**3**	**3**	**6**	**0**
1984-85	**Detroit**	**NHL**	**80**	**30**	**59**	**89**	**58**	**3**	**2**	**1**	**3**	**2**
1985-86	**Detroit**	**NHL**	**51**	**14**	**28**	**42**	**16**	....	....	....	....	....
1986-87	**Detroit**	**NHL**	**80**	**31**	**59**	**90**	**43**	**16**	**5**	**13**	**18**	**8**
1987-88	**Detroit**	**NHL**	**64**	**50**	**52**	**102**	**44**	**3**	**1**	**3**	**4**	**6**
1988-89	**Detroit**	**NHL**	**80**	**65**	**90**	**155**	**61**	**6**	**5**	**5**	**10**	**2**
1989-90	**Detroit**	**NHL**	**79**	**62**	**65**	**127**	**79**	....	....	....	....	....
1990-91	**Detroit**	**NHL**	**80**	**51**	**57**	**108**	**34**	**7**	**3**	**3**	**6**	**4**
1991-92	**Detroit**	**NHL**	**79**	**45**	**58**	**103**	**64**	**11**	**3**	**5**	**8**	**12**
1992-93	**Detroit**	**NHL**	**84**	**58**	**79**	**137**	**44**	**7**	**4**	**3**	**7**	**4**
1993-94	**Detroit**	**NHL**	**58**	**24**	**58**	**82**	**36**	**3**	**1**	**3**	**4**	**0**
1994-95	**Detroit**	**NHL**	**47**	**12**	**26**	**38**	**40**	**15**	**4**	**8**	**12**	**0**
1995-96	**Detroit**	**NHL**	**80**	**36**	**59**	**95**	**64**	**18**	**8**	**12**	**20**	**4**
1996-97	**Detroit**	**NHL**	**81**	**22**	**63**	**85**	**78**	**20**	**7**	**6**	**13**	**4** ♦
1997-98	**Detroit**	**NHL**	**75**	**24**	**45**	**69**	**46**	**22**	**6**	***18**	***24**	**22** ♦
	Canada	Olympics	6	1	1	2	10	....	....	....	....	....
	NHL Totals		**1098**	**563**	**846**	**1409**	**740**	**135**	**52**	**83**	**135**	**68**

NHL All-Rookie Team (1984) • Won Lester B. Pearson Award (1989) • Won Conn Smythe Trophy (1998)

Played in NHL All-Star Game (1984, 1988, 1989, 1990, 1991, 1992, 1993, 1997)

ZABRANSKY, LIBOR (zah-BRAN-skee) — ST.L.

Defense. Shoots left. 6'3", 196 lbs. Born, Brno, Czech., November 25, 1973.
(St. Louis' 8th choice, 209th overall, in 1995 Entry Draft).

			Regular Season					Playoffs				
Season	Club	Lea	GP	G	A	TP	PIM	GP	G	A	TP	PIM
1994-95	Budejovice	Cze-Rep.	44	2	6	8	54	9	0	4	4	6
1995-96	Budejovice	Cze-Rep.	40	4	7	11	....	10	0	1	1	....
1996-97	**St. Louis**	**NHL**	**34**	**1**	**5**	**6**	**44**	....	....	....	....	....
	Worcester	AHL	23	3	6	9	24	5	2	5	7	6
1997-98	**St. Louis**	**NHL**	**6**	**0**	**1**	**1**	**6**	....	....	....	....	....
	Worcester	AHL	54	2	17	19	61	6	1	1	2	8
	NHL Totals		**40**	**1**	**6**	**7**	**50**	....	....	....	....	....

ZALAPSKI, ZARLEY (zah-LAP-skee, ZAHR-lee) — NYR

Defense. Shoots left. 6'1", 215 lbs. Born, Edmonton, Alta., April 22, 1968.
(Pittsburgh's 1st choice, 4th overall, in 1986 Entry Draft).

			Regular Season					Playoffs				
Season	Club	Lea	GP	G	A	TP	PIM	GP	G	A	TP	PIM
1984-85	Ft. Saskatchewan	AJHL	23	17	30	47	14	....	....	....	....	....
1985-86	Ft. Saskatchewan	AJHL	27	20	33	53	46	....	....	....	....	....
	Canada	Nat-Tm	32	2	4	6	10	....	....	....	....	....
1986-87	Canada	Nat-Tm	74	11	29	40	28	....	....	....	....	....
1987-88	Canada	Nat-Tm	47	3	13	16	32	....	....	....	....	....
	Canada	Olympics	8	1	3	4	2	....	....	....	....	....
	Pittsburgh	**NHL**	**15**	**3**	**8**	**11**	**7**	....	....	....	....	....
1988-89	**Pittsburgh**	**NHL**	**58**	**12**	**33**	**45**	**57**	**11**	**1**	**8**	**9**	**13**
1989-90	**Pittsburgh**	**NHL**	**51**	**6**	**25**	**31**	**37**	....	....	....	....	....
1990-91	**Pittsburgh**	**NHL**	**66**	**12**	**36**	**48**	**59**	....	....	....	....	....
	Hartford	**NHL**	**11**	**3**	**3**	**6**	**6**	**6**	**1**	**3**	**4**	**8**
1991-92	**Hartford**	**NHL**	**79**	**20**	**37**	**57**	**120**	**7**	**2**	**3**	**5**	**6**
1992-93	**Hartford**	**NHL**	**83**	**14**	**51**	**65**	**94**	....	....	....	....	....
1993-94	**Hartford**	**NHL**	**56**	**7**	**30**	**37**	**56**	....	....	....	....	....
	Calgary	**NHL**	**13**	**3**	**7**	**10**	**18**	**7**	**0**	**3**	**3**	**2**
1994-95	**Calgary**	**NHL**	**48**	**4**	**24**	**28**	**46**	**7**	**0**	**4**	**4**	**4**
1995-96	**Calgary**	**NHL**	**80**	**12**	**17**	**29**	**115**	**4**	**0**	**1**	**1**	**10**
1996-97	**Calgary**	**NHL**	**2**	**0**	**0**	**0**	**0**	....	....	....	....	....
1997-98	**Calgary**	**NHL**	**35**	**2**	**7**	**9**	**41**	....	....	....	....	....
	Montreal	**NHL**	**28**	**1**	**5**	**6**	**22**	**6**	**0**	**1**	**1**	**4**
	NHL Totals		**625**	**99**	**283**	**382**	**678**	**48**	**4**	**23**	**27**	**47**

NHL All-Rookie Team (1989)

Played in NHL All-Star Game (1993)

Traded to **Hartford** by **Pittsburgh** with John Cullen and Jeff Parker for Ron Francis, Grant Jennings and Ulf Samuelsson, March 4, 1991. Traded to **Calgary** by **Hartford** with James Patrick and Michael Nylander for Gary Suter, Paul Ranheim and Ted Drury, March 10, 1994. Traded to **Montreal** by **Calgary** with Jonas Hoglund for Valeri Bure and Montreal's 4th round choice (Shaun Sutter) in 1998 Entry Draft, February 1, 1998. Signed as a free agent by **NY Rangers**, August 31, 1998.

ZALESAK, MIROSLAV (zah-LIH-sahk) — S.J.

Right wing. Shoots left. 6', 183 lbs. Born, Skalica, Czechoslovakia, January 2, 1980.
(San Jose's 5th choice, 104th overall, in 1998 Entry Draft).

			Regular Season					Playoffs				
Season	Club	Lea	GP	G	A	TP	PIM	GP	G	A	TP	PIM
1995-96	HC Nitra	Slov-Jr.	49	53	29	82	....	....	....	....	....	....
1996-97	HC Nitra	Slov-Jr.	58	51	31	82	....	....	....	....	....	....
1997-98	HC Nitra	Slov-Jr.	23	33	23	56	16	....	....	....	....	....
	Plastika Nitra	Slovakia	30	8	6	14	0	....	....	....	....	....

ZAMUNER, ROB (ZAM-nuhr) — T.B.

Left wing. Shoots left. 6'2", 206 lbs. Born, Oakville, Ont., September 17, 1969.
(NY Rangers' 3rd choice, 45th overall, in 1989 Entry Draft).

			Regular Season					Playoffs				
Season	Club	Lea	GP	G	A	TP	PIM	GP	G	A	TP	PIM
1986-87	Guelph	OHL	62	6	15	21	8	....	....	....	....	....
1987-88	Guelph	OHL	58	20	41	61	18	....	....	....	....	....
1988-89	Guelph	OHL	66	46	65	111	38	7	5	5	10	9
1989-90	Flint	IHL	77	44	35	79	32	4	1	0	1	6
1990-91	Binghamton	AHL	80	25	58	83	50	9	7	6	13	35
1991-92	**NY Rangers**	**NHL**	**9**	**1**	**2**	**3**	**2**	....	....	....	....	....
	Binghamton	AHL	61	19	53	72	42	11	8	9	17	8
1992-93	**Tampa Bay**	**NHL**	**84**	**15**	**28**	**43**	**74**	....	....	....	....	....
1993-94	**Tampa Bay**	**NHL**	**59**	**6**	**6**	**12**	**42**	....	....	....	....	....
1994-95	**Tampa Bay**	**NHL**	**43**	**9**	**6**	**15**	**24**	....	....	....	....	....
1995-96	**Tampa Bay**	**NHL**	**72**	**15**	**20**	**35**	**62**	**6**	**2**	**3**	**5**	**10**
1996-97	**Tampa Bay**	**NHL**	**82**	**17**	**33**	**50**	**56**	....	....	....	....	....
1997-98	**Tampa Bay**	**NHL**	**77**	**14**	**12**	**26**	**41**	....	....	....	....	....
	Canada	Olympics	6	1	0	1	8	....	....	....	....	....
	NHL Totals		**426**	**77**	**107**	**184**	**301**	**6**	**2**	**3**	**5**	**10**

Signed as a free agent by **Tampa Bay**, July 13, 1992.

ZANUTTO, MIKE — BUF.

Center. Shoots left. 6', 190 lbs. Born, Burlington, Ont., January 1, 1977.
(Buffalo's 10th choice, 198th overall, in 1995 Entry Draft).

			Regular Season					Playoffs				
Season	Club	Lea	GP	G	A	TP	PIM	GP	G	A	TP	PIM
1994-95	North Bay	OHL	13	1	1	2	2	....	....	....	....	....
	Oshawa	OHL	42	13	17	30	2	7	4	1	5	0
1995-96	Oshawa	OHL	66	32	38	70	6	5	0	2	2	0
1996-97	Oshawa	OHL	62	23	33	56	18	18	6	6	12	12
1997-98	Rochester	AHL	9	0	0	0	0	....	....	....	....	....
	South Carolina	ECHL	49	18	17	35	6	5	0	0	0	0

ZEDNIK, RICHARD (ZEHD-nihk, REE-khahrd) — WSH.

Left wing. Shoots left. 5'11", 190 lbs. Born, Bystrica, Czech., January 6, 1976.
(Washington's 10th choice, 249th overall, in 1994 Entry Draft).

			Regular Season					Playoffs				
Season	Club	Lea	GP	G	A	TP	PIM	GP	G	A	TP	PIM
1993-94	Banska Bystrica	Slovak-2	25	3	6	9	....	....	....	....	....	....
1994-95	Portland	WHL	65	35	51	86	89	9	5	5	10	20
1995-96	Portland	WHL	61	44	37	81	154	7	8	4	12	23
	Washington	NHL	1	0	0	0	0	....	....	....	....	....
	Portland	AHL	1	1	1	2	0	21	4	5	9	26
1996-97	Washington	NHL	11	2	1	3	4	....	....	....	....	....
	Portland	AHL	56	15	20	35	70	5	1	0	1	6
1997-98	Washington	NHL	65	17	9	26	28	17	7	3	10	16
	NHL Totals		77	19	10	29	32	17	7	3	10	16

WHL West Second All-Star Team (1996)

ZEHR, JEFF (ZAIR) — NYI

Left wing. Shoots left. 6'3", 195 lbs. Born, Woodstock, Ont., December 10, 1978.
(NY Islanders' 3rd choice, 31st overall, in 1997 Entry Draft).

			Regular Season					Playoffs				
Season	Club	Lea	GP	G	A	TP	PIM	GP	G	A	TP	PIM
1995-96	Windsor	OHL	56	4	21	25	103	7	0	1	1	2
1996-97	Windsor	OHL	57	27	32	59	196	5	2	1	3	4
1997-98	Windsor	OHL	20	12	18	30	67	....	....	....	....	....
	Erie	OHL	32	15	24	39	91	5	0	3	3	24

ZELENKO, BORIS (zeh-LEHN-koh) — PIT.

Left wing. Shoots right. 6'1", 172 lbs. Born, Moscow, USSR, September 12, 1975.
(Pittsburgh's 11th choice, 206th overall, in 1994 Entry Draft).

			Regular Season					Playoffs				
Season	Club	Lea	GP	G	A	TP	PIM	GP	G	A	TP	PIM
1993-94	CSKA Moscow	CIS	34	5	1	6	10	1	0	0	0	0
1994-95	CSKA Moscow	CIS	35	5	1	6	12	1	0	0	0	0
1995-96	CSKA Moscow	CIS	26	4	2	6	8	3	1	0	1	0
1996-97	CSKA Moscow	Russia	23	2	5	7	8	2	0	0	0	0
1997-98	CSKA Moscow	Russia	25	5	5	10	14	....	....	....	....	....
	Hampton Roads	ECHL	37	9	17	26	18	20	7	8	15	6

ZELEPUKIN, VALERI (zeh-leh-POO-kin) — EDM.

Left wing. Shoots left. 6'1", 200 lbs. Born, Voskresensk, USSR, September 17, 1968.
(New Jersey's 13th choice, 221st overall, in 1990 Entry Draft).

			Regular Season					Playoffs				
Season	Club	Lea	GP	G	A	TP	PIM	GP	G	A	TP	PIM
1984-85	Khimik	USSR	5	0	0	0	2	....	....	....	....	....
1985-86	Khimik	USSR	33	2	2	4	10	....	....	....	....	....
1986-87	Khimik	USSR	19	1	0	1	4	....	....	....	....	....
1987-88	CSKA Moscow	USSR	19	3	1	4	8	....	....	....	....	....
1988-89	CSKA Moscow	USSR	17	2	3	5	2	....	....	....	....	....
1989-90	Khimik	USSR	46	17	14	31	26	....	....	....	....	....
1990-91	Khimik	USSR	34	11	6	17	38	....	....	....	....	....
1991-92	New Jersey	NHL	44	13	18	31	28	4	1	1	2	2
	Utica	AHL	22	20	9	29	8	....	....	....	....	....
1992-93	New Jersey	NHL	78	23	41	64	70	5	0	2	2	0
1993-94	New Jersey	NHL	82	26	31	57	70	20	5	2	7	14
1994-95	New Jersey	NHL	4	1	2	3	6	18	1	2	3	12 ♦
1995-96	New Jersey	NHL	61	6	9	15	107	....	....	....	....	....
1996-97	New Jersey	NHL	71	14	24	38	36	8	3	2	5	2
1997-98	New Jersey	NHL	35	2	8	10	32	....	....	....	....	....
	Edmonton	NHL	33	2	10	12	57	8	1	2	3	2
	Russia	Olympics	6	1	2	3	0	....	....	....	....	....
	NHL Totals		408	87	143	230	406	63	11	11	22	32

Traded to **Edmonton** by **New Jersey** with Bill Guerin for Jason Arnott and Bryan Muir, January 4, 1998.

ZENT, JASON — PHI.

Left wing. Shoots left. 5'11", 204 lbs. Born, Buffalo, NY, April 15, 1971.
(NY Islanders' 3rd choice, 44th overall, in 1989 Entry Draft).

			Regular Season					Playoffs				
Season	Club	Lea	GP	G	A	TP	PIM	GP	G	A	TP	PIM
1987-88	Nichols High	H.S.	21	20	16	36	28	....	....	....	....	....
1988-89	Nichols High	H.S.	29	49	32	81	26	....	....	....	....	....
1989-90	Nichols High	H.S.	STATISTICS NOT AVAILABLE									
1990-91	U. of Wisconsin	WCHA	39	19	18	37	51	....	....	....	....	....
1991-92	U. of Wisconsin	WCHA	39	22	17	39	128	....	....	....	....	....
1992-93	U. of Wisconsin	WCHA	40	26	12	38	92	....	....	....	....	....
1993-94	U. of Wisconsin	WCHA	42	20	21	41	120	....	....	....	....	....
1994-95	P.E.I.	AHL	55	15	11	26	46	9	6	1	7	6
1995-96	P.E.I.	AHL	68	14	5	19	61	5	2	1	3	4
1996-97	Ottawa	NHL	22	3	3	6	9	....	....	....	....	....
	Worcester	AHL	45	14	10	24	45	5	3	3	6	4
1997-98	Ottawa	NHL	3	0	0	0	4	....	....	....	....	....
	Detroit	IHL	4	1	0	1	0	....	....	....	....	....
	Worcester	AHL	66	25	17	42	67	11	2	0	2	6
	NHL Totals		25	3	3	6	13	....	....	....	....	....

NCAA Championship All-Tournament Team (1992)

Traded to **Ottawa** by **NY Islanders** for Ottawa's 5th round choice (Andy Berenzweig) in 1996 Entry Draft, October 15, 1994. Signed as a free agent by **Philadelphia**, July 28, 1998.

ZETTLER, ROB — NSH.

Defense. Shoots left. 6'3", 200 lbs. Born, Sept Iles, Que., March 8, 1968.
(Minnesota's 5th choice, 55th overall, in 1986 Entry Draft).

			Regular Season					Playoffs				
Season	Club	Lea	GP	G	A	TP	PIM	GP	G	A	TP	PIM
1984-85	S.S. Marie	OHL	60	2	14	16	37	....	....	....	....	....
1985-86	S.S. Marie	OHL	57	5	23	28	92	....	....	....	....	....
1986-87	S.S. Marie	OHL	64	13	22	35	89	4	0	0	0	0
1987-88	S.S. Marie	OHL	64	7	41	48	77	6	2	2	4	9
	Kalamazoo	IHL	2	0	1	1	0	7	0	2	2	2
1988-89	Minnesota	NHL	2	0	0	0	0	....	....	....	....	....
	Kalamazoo	IHL	80	5	21	26	79	6	0	1	1	26
1989-90	Minnesota	NHL	31	0	8	8	45	....	....	....	....	....
	Kalamazoo	IHL	41	6	10	16	64	7	0	0	0	6
1990-91	Minnesota	NHL	47	1	4	5	119	....	....	....	....	....
	Kalamazoo	IHL	1	0	0	0	2	....	....	....	....	....
1991-92	San Jose	NHL	74	1	8	9	99	....	....	....	....	....
1992-93	San Jose	NHL	80	0	7	7	150	....	....	....	....	....
1993-94	San Jose	NHL	42	0	3	3	65	....	....	....	....	....
	Philadelphia	NHL	33	0	4	4	69	....	....	....	....	....
1994-95	Philadelphia	NHL	32	0	1	1	34	1	0	0	0	2
1995-96	Toronto	NHL	29	0	1	1	48	2	0	0	0	0
1996-97	Toronto	NHL	48	2	12	14	51	....	....	....	....	....
	Utah	IHL	30	0	10	10	60	....	....	....	....	....
1997-98	Toronto	NHL	59	0	7	7	108	....	....	....	....	....
	NHL Totals		477	4	55	59	788	3	0	0	0	2

Claimed by **San Jose** from **Minnesota** in Dispersal Draft, May 30, 1991. Traded to **Philadelphia** by **San Jose** for Viacheslav Butsayev, February 1, 1994. Traded to **Toronto** by **Philadelphia** for Toronto's 5th round choice (Per-Ragna Bergqvist) in 1996 Entry Draft, July 8, 1995. Claimed by **Nashville** from **Toronto** in Expansion Draft, June 26, 1998.

ZEVAKHIN, ALEXANDER (zeh-VAH-khin) — PIT.

Right wing. Shoots left. 6', 187 lbs. Born, Perm, USSR, June 4, 1980.
(Pittsburgh's 2nd choice, 54th overall, in 1998 Entry Draft).

			Regular Season					Playoffs				
Season	Club	Lea	GP	G	A	TP	PIM	GP	G	A	TP	PIM
1995-96	CSKA Moscow	Rus-Jr.	65	52	30	82	30	....	....	....	....	....
1996-97	CSKA Moscow	Russia	29	7	3	10	10	....	....	....	....	....
	CSKA Moscow 2	Russia-3	30	15	18	33	10	....	....	....	....	....
1997-98	CSKA Moscow 2	Russia-3	32	13	14	27	20	....	....	....	....	....
	CSKA Moscow	Russia	10	1	0	1	0	....	....	....	....	....

ZEZEL, PETER (ZEH-zehl) — VAN.

Center. Shoots left. 5'11", 220 lbs. Born, Toronto, Ont., April 22, 1965.
(Philadelphia's 1st choice, 41st overall, in 1983 Entry Draft).

			Regular Season					Playoffs				
Season	Club	Lea	GP	G	A	TP	PIM	GP	G	A	TP	PIM
1982-83	Toronto	OHL	66	35	39	74	28	4	2	4	6	0
1983-84	Toronto	OHL	68	47	86	133	31	9	7	5	12	4
1984-85	Philadelphia	NHL	65	15	46	61	26	19	1	8	9	28
1985-86	Philadelphia	NHL	79	17	37	54	76	5	3	1	4	4
1986-87	Philadelphia	NHL	71	33	39	72	71	25	3	10	13	10
1987-88	Philadelphia	NHL	69	22	35	57	42	7	3	2	5	7
1988-89	Philadelphia	NHL	26	4	13	17	15	....	....	....	....	....
	St. Louis	NHL	52	17	36	53	27	10	6	6	12	4
1989-90	St. Louis	NHL	73	25	47	72	30	12	1	7	8	4
1990-91	Washington	NHL	20	7	5	12	10	....	....	....	....	....
	Toronto	NHL	32	14	14	28	4	....	....	....	....	....
1991-92	Toronto	NHL	64	16	33	49	26	....	....	....	....	....
1992-93	Toronto	NHL	70	12	23	35	24	20	2	1	3	6
1993-94	Toronto	NHL	41	8	8	16	19	18	2	4	6	8
1994-95	Dallas	NHL	30	6	5	11	19	3	1	0	1	0
	Kalamazoo	IHL	2	0	0	0	0	....	....	....	....	....
1995-96	St. Louis	NHL	57	8	13	21	12	10	3	0	3	2
1996-97	St. Louis	NHL	35	4	9	13	12	....	....	....	....	....
	New Jersey	NHL	18	0	3	3	4	2	0	0	0	10
1997-98	New Jersey	NHL	5	0	3	3	0	....	....	....	....	....
	Albany	AHL	35	13	37	50	18	....	....	....	....	....
	Vancouver	NHL	25	5	12	17	2	....	....	....	....	....
	NHL Totals		832	213	381	594	419	131	25	39	64	83

Traded to **St. Louis** by **Philadelphia** for Mike Bullard, November 29, 1988. Traded to **Washington** by **St. Louis** with Mike Lalor for Geoff Courtnall, July 13, 1990. Traded to **Toronto** by **Washington** with Bob Rouse for Al Iafrate, January 16, 1991. Transferred to **Dallas** by **Toronto** with Grant Marshall as compensation for Toronto's signing of free agent Mike Craig, August 10, 1994. Signed as a free agent by **St. Louis**, October 19, 1995. Traded to **New Jersey** by **St. Louis** for Chris McAlpine and New Jersey's 9th round choice in 1999 Entry Draft, February 11, 1997. Traded to **Vancouver** by **New Jersey** for Vancouver's 5th round choice (Anton But) in 1998 Entry Draft, February 5, 1998.

ZHAMNOV, ALEXEI (ZHAHM-nahf) — CHI.

Center. Shoots left. 6'1", 195 lbs. Born, Moscow, USSR, October 1, 1970.
(Winnipeg's 5th choice, 77th overall, in 1990 Entry Draft).

			Regular Season					Playoffs				
Season	Club	Lea	GP	G	A	TP	PIM	GP	G	A	TP	PIM
1988-89	Moscow D'amo	USSR	4	0	0	0	0	....	....	....	....	....
1989-90	Moscow D'amo	USSR	43	11	6	17	21	....	....	....	....	....
1990-91	Moscow D'amo	USSR	46	16	12	28	24	....	....	....	....	....
1991-92	Moscow D'amo	CIS	39	15	21	36	28	....	....	....	....	....
	Russia	Olympics	8	0	3	3	8	....	....	....	....	....
1992-93	Winnipeg	NHL	68	25	47	72	58	6	0	2	2	2
1993-94	Winnipeg	NHL	61	26	45	71	62	....	....	....	....	....
1994-95	Winnipeg	NHL	48	30	35	65	20	....	....	....	....	....
1995-96	Winnipeg	NHL	58	22	37	59	65	6	2	1	3	8
1996-97	Chicago	NHL	74	20	42	62	56	....	....	....	....	....
1997-98	Chicago	NHL	70	21	28	49	61	....	....	....	....	....
	Russia	Olympics	6	2	1	3	2	....	....	....	....	....
	NHL Totals		379	144	234	378	322	12	2	3	5	10

NHL Second All-Star Team (1995)

Traded to **Chicago** by **Phoenix** with Craig Mills and Phoenix's 1st round choice (Ty Jones) in 1997 Entry Draft for Jeremy Roenick, August 16, 1996.

ZHITNIK, ALEXEI (ZHIHT-nihk) BUF.

Defense. Shoots left. 5'11", 204 lbs. Born, Kiev, USSR, October 10, 1972.
(Los Angeles' 3rd choice, 81st overall, in 1991 Entry Draft).

			Regular Season					Playoffs				
Season	Club	Lea	GP	G	A	TP	PIM	GP	G	A	TP	PIM
1989-90	Sokol Kiev	USSR	31	3	4	7	16	....	....	....	....	....
1990-91	Sokol Kiev	USSR	46	1	4	5	46	....	....	....	....	....
1991-92	CSKA Moscow	CIS	44	2	7	9	52	....	....	....	....	....
	Russia	Olympics	8	1	0	1	0	....	....	....	....	....
1992-93	**Los Angeles**	**NHL**	**78**	**12**	**36**	**48**	**80**	**24**	**3**	**9**	**12**	**26**
1993-94	**Los Angeles**	**NHL**	**81**	**12**	**40**	**52**	**101**	....	....	....	....	....
1994-95	**Los Angeles**	**NHL**	**11**	**2**	**5**	**7**	**27**	....	....	....	....	....
	Buffalo	**NHL**	**21**	**2**	**5**	**7**	**34**	**5**	**0**	**1**	**1**	**14**
1995-96	**Buffalo**	**NHL**	**80**	**6**	**30**	**36**	**58**	....	....	....	....	....
1996-97	**Buffalo**	**NHL**	**80**	**7**	**28**	**35**	**95**	**12**	**1**	**0**	**1**	**16**
1997-98	**Buffalo**	**NHL**	**78**	**15**	**30**	**45**	**102**	**15**	**0**	**3**	**3**	**36**
	Russia	Olympics	6	0	2	2	2	....	....	....	....	....
	NHL Totals		**429**	**56**	**174**	**230**	**497**	**56**	**4**	**13**	**17**	**92**

Traded to **Buffalo** by **LA Kings** with Robb Stauber, Charlie Huddy and LA Kings' 5th round choice (Marian Menhart) in 1995 Entry Draft for Philippe Boucher, Denis Tsygurov and Grant Fuhr, February 14, 1995.

ZHOLTOK, SERGEI (ZHOL-tok)

Center. Shoots right. 6', 190 lbs. Born, Riga, Latvia, December 2, 1972.
(Boston's 2nd choice, 55th overall, in 1992 Entry Draft).

			Regular Season					Playoffs				
Season	Club	Lea	GP	G	A	TP	PIM	GP	G	A	TP	PIM
1990-91	Dynamo Riga	USSR	39	4	0	4	16	....	....	....	....	....
1991-92	HC Riga	CIS	27	6	3	9	6	....	....	....	....	....
1992-93	**Boston**	**NHL**	**1**	**0**	**1**	**1**	**0**	....	....	....	....	....
	Providence	AHL	64	31	35	66	57	6	3	5	8	4
1993-94	**Boston**	**NHL**	**24**	**2**	**1**	**3**	**2**	....	....	....	....	....
	Providence	AHL	54	29	33	62	16	....	....	....	....	....
1994-95	Providence	AHL	78	23	35	58	42	13	8	5	13	6
1995-96	Las Vegas	IHL	82	51	50	101	30	15	7	13	20	6
1996-97	**Ottawa**	**NHL**	**57**	**12**	**16**	**28**	**19**	**7**	**1**	**1**	**2**	**0**
	Las Vegas	IHL	19	13	14	27	20	....	....	....	....	....
1997-98	**Ottawa**	**NHL**	**78**	**10**	**13**	**23**	**16**	**11**	**0**	**2**	**2**	**0**
	NHL Totals		**160**	**24**	**31**	**55**	**37**	**18**	**1**	**3**	**4**	**0**

EJC-A All-Star Team (1990)

Signed as a free agent by **Ottawa**, July 10, 1996.

ZHURIK, ALEXANDER (ZHUH-rihk) EDM.

Defense. Shoots left. 6'3", 195 lbs. Born, Minsk, USSR, May 29, 1975.
(Edmonton's 7th choice, 163rd overall, in 1993 Entry Draft).

			Regular Season					Playoffs				
Season	Club	Lea	GP	G	A	TP	PIM	GP	G	A	TP	PIM
1993-94	Kingston	OHL	59	7	23	30	92	6	0	0	0	4
1994-95	Kingston	OHL	54	3	21	24	51	6	0	0	0	0
1995-96	Cape Breton	AHL	80	5	36	41	85	....	....	....	....	....
1996-97	Hamilton	AHL	72	5	16	21	49	22	2	11	13	14
1997-98	Hamilton	AHL	63	1	23	24	84	9	0	4	4	8
	Belarus	Olympics	4	0	0	0	10	....	....	....	....	....

ZIB, LUKAS (ZIHB, LOO-kahsh) EDM.

Defense. Shoots right. 6'1", 200 lbs. Born, Ceske Budejovice, Czech., February 24, 1977.
(Edmonton's 3rd choice, 57th overall, in 1995 Entry Draft).

			Regular Season					Playoffs				
Season	Club	Lea	GP	G	A	TP	PIM	GP	G	A	TP	PIM
1994-95	Budejovice	Cze-Rep.	13	2	0	2	16	9	1	0	1	6
1995-96	Budejovice	Czech-Jr.	11	5	1	6	....	....	....	....	....	....
	Budejovice	Cze-Rep.	7	1	0	1	....	2	0	0	0	....
1996-97	Budejovice	Cze-Rep.	13	0	0	0	4	2	0	0	0	0
1997-98	Budejovice	Cze-Rep.	47	5	6	11	22	....	....	....	....	....

ZIMAKOV, SERGEI (zih-MAH-kahv) WSH.

Defense. Shoots left. 6'1", 194 lbs. Born, Moscow, USSR, January 15, 1978.
(Washington's 4th choice, 58th overall, in 1996 Entry Draft).

			Regular Season					Playoffs				
Season	Club	Lea	GP	G	A	TP	PIM	GP	G	A	TP	PIM
1995-96	Soviet Wings	CIS	49	2	7	9	36	....	....	....	....	....
1996-97	Soviet Wings	Russia	39	4	3	7	57	2	0	0	0	0
1997-98	Soviet Wings	Russia	42	4	1	5	48	....	....	....	....	....

ZIZKA, TOMAS (ZHIHZH-kuh, TAW-mahsh) L.A.

Defense. Shoots left. 6'1", 198 lbs. Born, Sternberk, Czechoslovakia, October 10, 1979.
(Los Angeles' 6th choice, 163rd overall, in 1998 Entry Draft).

			Regular Season					Playoffs				
Season	Club	Lea	GP	G	A	TP	PIM	GP	G	A	TP	PIM
1994-95	ZPS Zlin	Czech-Jr.	39	1	10	11	....	....	....	....	....	....
1995-96	ZPS Zlin	Czech-Jr.	47	2	8	10	....	....	....	....	....	....
1996-97	ZPS Zlin	Czech-Jr.	14	1	0	1	....	....	....	....	....	....
1997-98	ZPS Zlin	Czech-Jr.	11	3	4	7	....	....	....	....	....	....
	ZPS Zlin	Cze-Rep.	33	0	3	3	2	....	....	....	....	....

ZMOLEK, DOUG (zuh-MOH-lehk) CHI.

Defense. Shoots left. 6'2", 222 lbs. Born, Rochester, MN, November 3, 1970.
(Minnesota's 1st choice, 7th overall, in 1989 Entry Draft).

			Regular Season					Playoffs				
Season	Club	Lea	GP	G	A	TP	PIM	GP	G	A	TP	PIM
1988-89	John Marshall	H.S.	29	17	41	58	....	....	....	....	....	....
1989-90	U. of Minnesota	WCHA	40	1	10	11	52	....	....	....	....	....
1990-91	U. of Minnesota	WCHA	34	11	6	17	38	....	....	....	....	....
1991-92	U. of Minnesota	WCHA	41	6	20	26	84	....	....	....	....	....
1992-93	**San Jose**	**NHL**	**84**	**5**	**10**	**15**	**229**	....	....	....	....	....
1993-94	**San Jose**	**NHL**	**68**	**0**	**4**	**4**	**122**	....	....	....	....	....
	Dallas	**NHL**	**7**	**1**	**0**	**1**	**11**	**7**	**0**	**1**	**1**	**4**
1994-95	**Dallas**	**NHL**	**42**	**0**	**5**	**5**	**67**	**5**	**0**	**0**	**0**	**10**
1995-96	**Dallas**	**NHL**	**42**	**1**	**5**	**6**	**65**	....	....	....	....	....
	Los Angeles	**NHL**	**16**	**1**	**0**	**1**	**22**	....	....	....	....	....
1996-97	**Los Angeles**	**NHL**	**57**	**1**	**0**	**1**	**116**	....	....	....	....	....
1997-98	**Los Angeles**	**NHL**	**46**	**0**	**8**	**8**	**111**	**2**	**0**	**0**	**0**	**2**
	NHL Totals		**362**	**9**	**32**	**41**	**743**	**14**	**0**	**1**	**1**	**16**

WCHA Second All-Star Team (1992) • NCAA West Second All-American Team (1992)

Claimed by **San Jose** from **Minnesota** in Dispersal Draft, May 30, 1991. Traded to **Dallas** by **San Jose** with Mike Lalor and cash for Ulf Dahlen and Dallas' 7th round choice (Brad Mehalko) in 1995 Entry Draft, March 19, 1994. Traded to **LA Kings** by **Dallas** with Shane Churla for Darryl Sydor and LA Kings' 5th round choice (Ryan Christie) in 1996 Entry Draft, February 17, 1996. Traded to **Chicago** by **LA Kings** for Chicago's 3rd round choice in 1999 Entry Draft, September 3, 1998.

ZOLOTOV, ROMAN (ZOH-loh-tov) CGY.

Defense. Shoots left. 6'1", 191 lbs. Born, Moscow, USSR, February 13, 1974.
(Philadelphia's 5th choice, 127th overall, in 1992 Entry Draft).

			Regular Season					Playoffs				
Season	Club	Lea	GP	G	A	TP	PIM	GP	G	A	TP	PIM
1991-92	Moscow D'amo	CIS	1	0	0	0	0	....	....	....	....	....
1992-93	Moscow D'amo	CIS-Jr.	STATISTICS NOT AVAILABLE									
1993-94	Moscow D'amo	CIS	33	0	2	2	20	5	0	1	1	6
1994-95	Moscow D'amo	CIS	25	0	2	2	24	8	1	2	3	6
1995-96	Moscow D'amo	CIS	41	0	2	2	94	9	0	1	1	6
1996-97	Moscow D'amo	Russia	34	3	2	5	34	3	0	0	0	4
1997-98	Moscow D'amo	EuroHL	5	0	2	2	31	....	....	....	....	....
	Moscow D'amo	Russia	31	2	4	6	12	....	....	....	....	....

ZUBOV, SERGEI (ZOO-bahf) DAL.

Defense. Shoots right. 6'1", 200 lbs. Born, Moscow, USSR, July 22, 1970.
(NY Rangers' 6th choice, 85th overall, in 1990 Entry Draft).

			Regular Season					Playoffs				
Season	Club	Lea	GP	G	A	TP	PIM	GP	G	A	TP	PIM
1988-89	CSKA Moscow	USSR	29	1	4	5	10	....	....	....	....	....
1989-90	CSKA Moscow	USSR	48	6	2	8	16	....	....	....	....	....
1990-91	CSKA Moscow	USSR	41	6	5	11	12	....	....	....	....	....
1991-92	CSKA Moscow	CIS	44	4	7	11	8	....	....	....	....	....
	Russia	Olympics	8	0	1	1	0	....	....	....	....	....
1992-93	CSKA Moscow	CIS	1	0	1	1	0	....	....	....	....	....
	NY Rangers	**NHL**	**49**	**8**	**23**	**31**	**4**	....	....	....	....	....
	Binghamton	AHL	30	7	29	36	14	11	5	5	10	2
1993-94	**NY Rangers**	**NHL**	**78**	**12**	**77**	**89**	**39**	**22**	**5**	**14**	**19**	**0** ♦
	Binghamton	AHL	2	1	2	3	0	....	....	....	....	....
1994-95	**NY Rangers**	**NHL**	**38**	**10**	**26**	**36**	**18**	**10**	**3**	**8**	**11**	**2**
1995-96	**Pittsburgh**	**NHL**	**64**	**11**	**55**	**66**	**22**	**18**	**1**	**14**	**15**	**26**
1996-97	**Dallas**	**NHL**	**78**	**13**	**30**	**43**	**24**	**7**	**0**	**3**	**3**	**2**
1997-98	**Dallas**	**NHL**	**73**	**10**	**47**	**57**	**16**	**17**	**4**	**5**	**9**	**2**
	NHL Totals		**380**	**64**	**258**	**322**	**123**	**74**	**13**	**44**	**57**	**32**

Played in NHL All-Star Game (1998)

Traded to **Pittsburgh** by **NY Rangers** with Petr Nedved for Luc Robitaille and Ulf Samuelsson, August 31, 1995. Traded to **Dallas** by **Pittsburgh** for Kevin Hatcher, June 22, 1996.

ZUBRUS, DAINIUS (ZOO-bruhs) PHI.

Right wing. Shoots left. 6'3", 215 lbs. Born, Elektrenai, USSR, June 16, 1978.
(Philadelphia's 1st choice, 15th overall, in 1996 Entry Draft).

			Regular Season					Playoffs				
Season	Club	Lea	GP	G	A	TP	PIM	GP	G	A	TP	PIM
1995-96	Pembroke	OJHL	28	19	13	32	73	....	....	....	....	....
	Caledon	OJHL	7	3	7	10	2	17	11	12	23	4
1996-97	**Philadelphia**	**NHL**	**68**	**8**	**13**	**21**	**22**	**19**	**5**	**4**	**9**	**12**
1997-98	**Philadelphia**	**NHL**	**69**	**8**	**25**	**33**	**42**	**5**	**0**	**1**	**1**	**2**
	NHL Totals		**137**	**16**	**38**	**54**	**64**	**24**	**5**	**5**	**10**	**14**

ZULTEK, MATT (ZUHL-tehk) L.A.

Center. Shoots left. 6'3", 218 lbs. Born, Windsor, Ont., March 12, 1979.
(Los Angeles' 2nd choice, 15th overall, in 1997 Entry Draft).

			Regular Season					Playoffs				
Season	Club	Lea	GP	G	A	TP	PIM	GP	G	A	TP	PIM
1996-97	Ottawa	OHL	63	27	13	40	76	21	7	6	13	27
1997-98	Ottawa	OHL	62	28	28	56	156	13	6	12	18	20

ZYUZIN, ANDREI (ZYOO-zin) S.J.

Defense. Shoots left. 6'1", 195 lbs. Born, Ufa, USSR, January 21, 1978.
(San Jose's 1st choice, 2nd overall, in 1996 Entry Draft).

			Regular Season					Playoffs				
Season	Club	Lea	GP	G	A	TP	PIM	GP	G	A	TP	PIM
1994-95	Ufa Salavat	CIS	30	3	0	3	16	....	....	....	....	....
1995-96	Ufa Salavat	CIS	41	6	3	9	24	....	....	....	....	....
1996-97	Ufa Salavat	Russia	32	7	10	17	28	7	1	1	2	4
1997-98	**San Jose**	**NHL**	**56**	**6**	**7**	**13**	**66**	**6**	**1**	**0**	**1**	**14**
	Kentucky	AHL	17	4	5	9	28	....	....	....	....	....
	NHL Totals		**56**	**6**	**7**	**13**	**66**	**6**	**1**	**0**	**1**	**14**

Notes

Retired NHL Player Index

Abbreviations: Teams/Cities: — **Ana.** – Anaheim; **Atl.** – Atlanta; **Bos.** – Boston, **Bro.** – Brooklyn; **Buf.** – Buffalo; **Cal.** – California; **Cgy.** – Calgary; **Cle.** – Cleveland; **Col.** – Colorado; **Dal.** – Dallas; **Det.** – Detroit; **Edm.** – Edmonton; **Fla.** – Florida; **Ham.** – Hamilton; **Hfd.** – Hartford; **K.C.** – Kansas City; **L.A.** – Los Angeles; **Min.** — Minnesota; **Mtl.** - Montreal; **Mtl. M.** – Montreal Maroons; **Mtl. W.** – Montreal Wanderers; **N.J.** – New Jersey; **NYA** – NY Americans; **NYI** – New York Islanders; **NYR** – New York Rangers; **Oak.** – Oakland; **Ott.** – Ottawa; **Phi.** – Philadelphia; **Phx.** – Phoenix; **Pit.** – Pittsburgh; **Que.** - Quebec; **St. L.** – St. Louis; **S.J.** – San Jose; **T.B.** – Tampa Bay; **Tor.** – Toronto; **Van.** – Vancouver; **Wpg.** – Winnipeg; **Wsh.** – Washington.

Total seasons are rounded off to the nearest full season. **A** – assists; **G** – goals; **GP** – games played; **PIM** – penalties in minutes; **TP** – total points.
• – deceased. Assists not recorded during 1917-18 season.

Keith Allen

Glenn Anderson

Mark Astley

Don Awrey

			Regular Schedule					Playoffs					NHL	First	Last
Name	NHL Teams	NHL Seasons	GP	G	A	TP	PIM	GP	G	A	TP	PIM	Cup Wins	NHL Season	NHL Season
A															
Abbott, Reg	Mtl.	1	3	0	0	0	0	....	....	....	....	....		1952-53	1952-53
• Abel, Clarence	NYR, Chi.	8	333	18	18	36	359	38	1	1	2	58	2	1926-27	1933-34
Abel, Gerry	Det.	1	1	0	0	0	0	....	....	....	....	....		1966-67	1966-67
Abel, Sid	Det., Chi.	14	612	189	283	472	376	97	28	30	58	79	3	1938-39	1953-54
Abgrall, Dennis	L.A.	1	13	0	2	2	4	....	....	....	....	....		1975-76	1975-76
Abrahamsson, Thommy	Hfd.	1	32	6	11	17	16	....	....	....	....	....		1980-81	1980-81
Achtymichuk, Gene	Mtl., Det.	4	32	3	5	8	2	....	....	....	....	....		1951-52	1958-59
Acomb, Doug	Tor.	1	2	0	1	1	0	....	....	....	....	....		1969-70	1969-70
Acton, Keith	Mtl., Min., Edm., Phi., Wsh., NYI	15	1023	226	358	584	1172	66	12	21	33	88	1	1979-80	1993-94
Adam, Douglas	NYR	1	4	0	1	1	0	....	....	....	....	....		1949-50	1949-50
Adam, Russ	Tor.	1	8	1	2	3	11	....	....	....	....	....		1982-83	1982-83
Adams, Greg C.	Phi., Hfd., Wsh., Edm., Van., Que., Det.	10	545	84	143	227	1173	43	2	11	13	153		1980-81	1989-90
• Adams, Jack	Tor., Ott.	7	174	82	29	111	353	10	2	0	2	15	2	1917-18	1926-27
Adams, John	Mtl.	1	42	6	12	18	11	3	0	0	0	0		1940-41	1940-41
• Adams, Stew	Chi., Tor.	4	106	9	26	35	60	11	3	3	6	14		1929-30	1932-33
Adduono, Rick	Bos., Atl.	2	4	0	0	0	2	....	....	....	....	....		1975-76	1979-80
Affleck, Bruce	St.L., Van., NYI	7	280	14	66	80	86	8	0	0	0	0		1974-75	1983-84
Agnew, Jim	Van., Hfd.	6	81	0	1	1	257	4	0	0	0	6		1986-87	1992-93
Ahern, Fred	Cal., Cle., Col.	4	146	31	30	61	130	2	0	1	1	2		1974-75	1977-78
Ahlin, Tony	Chi.	1	1	0	0	0	0	....	....	....	....	....		1937-38	1937-38
Ahola, Peter	L.A., Pit., S.J., Cgy.	3	123	10	17	27	137	6	0	0	0	2		1991-92	1993-94
Ahrens, Chris	Min.	6	52	0	3	3	84	1	0	0	0	0		1973-74	1977-78
• Ailsby, Lloyd	NYR	1	3	0	0	0	2	....	....	....	....	....		1951-52	1951-52
Aitken, Brad	Pit., Edm.	2	14	1	3	4	25	....	....	....	....	....		1987-88	1990-91
Albright, Clint	NYR	1	59	14	5	19	19	....	....	....	....	....		1948-49	1948-49
Aldcorn, Gary	Tor., Det., Bos.	5	226	41	56	97	78	6	1	2	3	4		1956-57	1960-61
Alexander, Claire	Tor., Van.	4	155	18	47	65	36	16	2	4	6	4		1974-75	1977-78
• Alexandre, Art	Mtl.	2	11	0	2	2	8	4	0	0	0	0		1931-32	1932-33
Allan, Jeff	Cle.	1	4	0	0	0	2	....	....	....	....	....		1977-78	1977-78
• Allen, George	NYR, Chi., Mtl.	8	339	82	115	197	179	41	9	10	19	32		1938-39	1946-47
Allen, Keith	Det.	2	28	0	4	4	8	5	0	0	0	0	1	1953-54	1954-55
• Allen, Viv	NYA	1	6	0	1	1	0	....	....	....	....	....		1940-41	1940-41
Alley, Steve	Hfd.	2	15	3	3	6	11	3	0	1	1	0		1979-80	1980-81
Allison, Dave	Mtl.	1	3	0	0	0	12	....	....	....	....	....		1983-84	1983-84
Allison, Mike	NYR, Tor., L.A.	10	499	102	166	268	630	82	9	17	26	135		1980-81	1989-90
Allison, Ray	Hfd., Phi.	7	238	64	93	157	223	12	2	3	5	20		1979-80	1986-87
• Allum, Bill	Chi, NYR	2	2	0	1	1	0	....	....	....	....	....		1939-40	1940-41
• Amadio, Dave	Det., L.A.	3	125	5	11	16	163	16	1	2	3	18		1957-58	1968-69
Ambroziak, Peter	Buf.	1	12	0	1	1	0	....	....	....	....	....		1994-95	1994-95
Amodeo, Mike	Wpg.	1	19	0	0	0	2	....	....	....	....	....		1979-80	1979-80
• Anderson, Bill	Bos.	1	....	....	....	....	....	1	0	0	0	0		1942-43	1942-43
Anderson, Dale	Det.	1	13	0	0	0	6	2	0	0	0	0		1956-57	1956-57
Anderson, Doug	Mtl.	1	....	....	....	....	....	2	0	0	0	0	1	1952-53	1952-53
Anderson, Earl	Det., Bos.	3	109	19	19	38	22	5	0	1	1	0		1974-75	1976-77
Anderson, Glenn	Edm., Tor., NYR, St.L.	16	1129	498	601	1099	1120	225	93	121	214	442	6	1980-81	1995-96
Anderson, Jim	L.A.	1	7	1	2	3	2	....	....	....	....	....		1967-68	1967-68
Anderson, John	Tor., Que., Hfd.	12	814	282	349	631	263	37	9	18	27	2		1977-78	1988-89
Anderson, Murray	Wsh.	1	40	0	1	1	68	....	....	....	....	....		1974-75	1974-75
Anderson, Perry	St.L., N.J., S.J.	10	400	50	59	109	1051	36	2	1	3	161		1981-82	1991-92
Anderson, Ron C.	Det., L.A., St.L., Buf.	5	251	28	30	58	146	5	0	0	0	4		1967-68	1971-72
Anderson, Ron H.	Wsh.	1	28	9	7	16	8	....	....	....	....	....		1974-75	1974-75
Anderson, Russ	Pit., Hfd., L.A.	9	519	22	99	121	1086	10	0	3	3	28		1976-77	1984-85
• Anderson, Tom	Det., NYA, Bro.	8	319	62	127	189	190	16	2	7	9	8		1934-35	1941-42
Andersson, Kent-Erik	Min., NYR	7	456	72	103	175	78	50	4	11	15	4		1977-78	1983-84
Andersson, Peter	Wsh., Que.	3	172	10	41	51	81	7	0	2	2	2		1983-84	1985-86
Andersson, Peter	NYR, Fla.	2	47	6	13	19	20	....	....	....	....	....		1992-93	1993-94
Andrascik, Steve	NYR	1	....	....	....	....	....	1	0	0	0	0		1971-72	1971-72
Andrea, Paul	NYR, Pit., Cal., Buf.	4	150	31	49	80	10	....	....	....	....	....		1965-66	1970-71
• Andrews, Lloyd	Tor.	4	53	8	5	13	10	7	2	0	2	5		1921-22	1924-25
Andrijevski, Alexander	Chi.	1	1	0	0	0	0	....	....	....	....	....		1992-93	1992-93
Andruff, Ron	Mtl., Col.,	5	153	19	36	55	54	2	0	0	0	0		1974-75	1978-79
Andrusak, Greg	Pit.	3	12	0	4	4	8	....	....	....	....	....		1993-94	1995-96
Angotti, Lou	NYR, Chi., Phi., Pit., St.L.	10	653	103	186	289	228	65	8	8	16	17		1964-65	1973-74
Anholt, Darrel	Chi.	1	1	0	0	0	0	....	....	....	....	....		1983-84	1983-84
Anslow, Bert	NYR	1	2	0	0	0	0	....	....	....	....	....		1947-48	1947-48
Antonovich, Mike	Min., Hfd., N.J.	5	87	10	15	25	37	....	....	....	....	....		1975-76	1983-84
Apps Jr., Syl	NYR, Pit., L.A.	10	727	183	423	606	311	23	5	5	10	23		1970-71	1979-80
Apps Sr., Syl	Tor.	10	423	201	231	432	56	69	25	29	54	8	3	1936-37	1947-48
Arbour, Al	Det., Chi., Tor., St.L.	16	626	12	58	70	617	86	1	8	9	92	3	1953-54	1970-71
• Arbour, Amos	Mtl., Ham., Tor.	6	111	51	17	68	71	....	....	....	....	....		1918-19	1923-24
• Arbour, Jack	Det., Tor.	2	47	5	1	6	56	....	....	....	....	....		1926-27	1928-29
Arbour, John	Bos., Pit., Van., St.L.	5	106	1	9	10	149	5	0	0	0	0		1965-66	1971-72
• Arbour, Ty	Pit., Chi.	5	207	28	28	56	112	11	2	0	2	6		1926-27	1930-31
Archambault, Michel	Chi.	1	3	0	0	0	0	....	....	....	....	....		1976-77	1976-77
Archibald, Jim	Min.	3	16	1	2	3	45	....	....	....	....	....		1984-85	1986-87
Areshenkoff, Ronald	Edm.	1	4	0	0	0	0	....	....	....	....	....		1979-80	1979-80
Armstrong, Bill H.	Phi.	1	1	0	1	1	0	....	....	....	....	....		1990-91	1990-91
• Armstrong, Bob	Bos.	12	542	13	86	99	671	42	1	7	8	28		1950-51	1961-62
Armstrong, George	Tor.	21	1187	296	417	713	721	110	26	34	60	52	4	1949-50	1970-71
Armstrong, Murray	Tor., NYA, Bro., Det.	8	270	67	121	188	72	30	4	6	10	2		1937-38	1945-46
• Armstrong, Norm	Tor.	1	7	1	1	2	2	....	....	....	....	....		1962-63	1962-63
Armstrong, Tim	Tor.	1	11	1	0	1	6	....	....	....	....	....		1988-89	1988-89
Arnason, Chuck	Mtl., Atl., Pit., K.C., Col., Cle., Min., Wsh.	8	401	109	90	199	122	9	2	4	6	4		1971-72	1978-79
Arniel, Scott	Wpg., Buf., Bos.	11	730	149	189	338	599	34	3	3	6	39		1981-82	1991-92
Arthur, Fred	Hfd., Phi.	3	80	1	8	9	49	4	0	0	0	2		1980-81	1982-83
Arundel, John	Tor.	1	3	0	0	0	9	....	....	....	....	....		1949-50	1949-50
• Ashbee, Barry	Bos., Phi.	5	284	15	70	85	291	17	0	4	4	22	1	1965-66	1973-74
• Ashby, Don	Tor., Col., Edm.	6	188	40	56	96	40	12	1	0	1	4		1975-76	1980-81
Ashton, Brent	Van., Col., N.J., Min., Que., Det., Wpg., Bos., Cgy.	14	998	284	345	629	635	85	24	25	49	70		1979-80	1992-93
Ashworth, Frank	Chi.	1	18	5	4	9	2	....	....	....	....	....		1946-47	1946-47
Asmundson, Oscar	NYR, Det., St.L., NYA, Mtl.	5	111	11	23	34	30	9	0	2	2	4	1	1932-33	1937-38
Astley, Mark	Buf.	3	75	4	19	23	92	2	0	0	0	0		1993-94	1995-96
• Atanas, Walt	NYR	1	49	13	8	21	40	....	....	....	....	....		1944-45	1944-45
Atkinson, Steve	Bos., Buf., Wsh.	6	302	60	51	111	104	1	0	0	0	0		1968-69	1974-75
Attwell, Bob	Col.	2	22	1	5	6	0	....	....	....	....	....		1979-80	1980-81
Attwell, Ron	St.L., NYR	1	22	1	7	8	8	....	....	....	....	....		1967-68	1967-68
Aubin, Norm	Tor.	2	69	18	13	31	30	1	0	0	0	0		1981-82	1982-83
Aubry, Pierre	Que., Det.	5	202	24	26	50	133	20	1	1	2	32		1980-81	1984-85
Aubuchon, Ossie	Bos., NYR	2	50	19	12	31	4	6	1	0	1	0		1942-43	1943-44

Norm Barnes

Dave Barr

Bob Beers

Jean Beliveau

Name	NHL Teams	NHL Seasons	Regular Schedule GP	G	A	TP	PIM	Playoffs GP	G	A	TP	PIM	NHL Cup Wins	First NHL Season	Last NHL Season
Auge, Les	Col.	1	6	0	3	3	4	....	....	....	....	....		1980-81	1980-81
• Aurie, Larry	Det.	12	489	147	129	276	279	24	6	9	15	10	2	1927-28	1938-39
Awrey, Don	Bos., St.L., Mtl., Pit., NYR, Col.	16	979	31	158	189	1065	71	0	18	18	150	2	1963-64	1978-79
• Ayres, Vern	NYA, Mtl.M., St.L., NYR	6	211	6	14	20	350	....	....	....	....	....		1930-31	1935-36

B

Name	NHL Teams	NHL Seasons	Regular Schedule GP	G	A	TP	PIM	Playoffs GP	G	A	TP	PIM	NHL Cup Wins	First NHL Season	Last NHL Season
Babando, Pete	Bos., Det., Chi., NYR	6	351	86	73	159	194	17	3	3	6	6	1	1947-48	1952-53
Babcock, Bobby	Wsh.	2	2	0	0	0	2	....	....	....	....	....		1990-91	1992-93
Babe, Warren	Min.	3	21	2	5	7	23	2	0	0	0	0		1987-88	1990-91
Babin, Mitch	St.L.	1	8	0	0	0	0	....	....	....	....	....		1975-76	1975-76
Baby, John	Cle., Min.	2	26	2	8	10	26	....	....	....	....	....		1977-78	1978-79
Babych, Wayne	St.L., Pit., Que., Hfd.	9	519	192	246	438	498	41	7	9	16	24		1978-79	1986-87
Baca, Jergus	Hfd.	2	10	0	2	2	14	....	....	....	....	....		1990-91	1991-92
Backman, Mike	NYR	3	18	1	6	7	18	10	2	2	4	2		1981-82	1983-84
Backor, Peter	Tor.	1	36	4	5	9	6	....	....	....	....	....	1	1944-45	1944-45
Backstrom, Ralph	Mtl., L.A., Chi.	17	1032	278	361	639	386	116	27	32	59	68	6	1956-57	1972-73
• Bailey, Ace	Tor.	8	313	111	82	193	472	21	3	4	7	12	1	1926-27	1933-34
Bailey, Bob	Tor., Det., Chi.	5	150	15	21	36	207	15	0	4	4	22		1953-54	1957-58
Bailey, Garnet	Bos., Det., St.L., Wsh.	10	568	107	171	278	633	15	2	4	6	28	1	1968-69	1977-78
Bailey, Reid	Phi., Tor., Hfd.	4	40	1	3	4	105	16	0	2	2	25		1980-81	1983-84
Baillargeon, Joel	Wpg., Que.	3	20	0	2	2	31	....	....	....	....	....		1986-87	1988-89
Baird, Ken	Cal.	1	10	0	2	2	15	....	....	....	....	....		1971-72	1971-72
Baker, Bill	Mtl., Col., St.L., NYR	3	143	7	25	32	175	6	0	0	0	0		1980-81	1982-83
Bakovic, Peter	Van.	1	10	2	0	2	48	....	....	....	....	....		1987-88	1987-88
Balderis, Helmut	Min.	1	26	3	6	9	2	....	....	....	....	....		1989-90	1989-90
Baldwin, Doug	Tor., Det., Chi.	3	24	0	1	1	8	....	....	....	....	....		1945-46	1947-48
Balfour, Earl	Tor., Chi.,	7	288	30	22	52	78	26	0	3	3	4	1	1951-52	1960-61
• Balfour, Murray	Mtl., Chi., Bos.	8	306	67	90	157	393	40	9	10	19	45	1	1956-57	1964-65
Ball, Terry	Phi., Buf.	4	74	7	19	26	26	....	....	....	....	....		1967-68	1971-72
Balon, Dave	NYR, Mtl., Min., Van.	14	776	192	222	414	607	78	14	21	35	109	2	1959-60	1972-73
Baltimore, Bryon	Edm.	1	2	0	0	0	4	....	....	....	....	....		1979-80	1979-80
Baluik, Stanley	Bos.	1	7	0	0	0	2	....	....	....	....	....		1959-60	1959-60
Bandura, Jeff	NYR	1	2	0	1	1	0	....	....	....	....	....		1980-81	1980-81
Banks, Darren	Bos.	2	20	2	2	4	73	....	....	....	....	....		1992-93	1993-94
Barahona, Ralph	Bos.	2	6	2	2	4	0	....	....	....	....	....		1990-91	1991-92
Barbe, Andy	Tor.	1	1	0	0	0	2	....	....	....	....	....		1950-51	1950-51
Barber, Bill	Phi.	12	903	420	463	883	623	129	53	55	108	109	2	1972-73	1984-85
Barber, Don	Min., Wpg., Que., S.J.	4	115	25	32	57	64	11	4	4	8	10		1988-89	1991-92
• Barilko, Bill	Tor.	5	252	26	36	62	456	47	5	7	12	104	4	1946-47	1950-51
Barkley, Doug	Chi., Det.	6	253	24	80	104	382	30	0	9	9	63		1957-58	1965-66
Barlow, Bob	Min.	2	77	16	17	33	10	6	2	2	4	6		1969-70	1970-71
Barnes, Blair	L.A.	1	1	0	0	0	0	....	....	....	....	....		1982-83	1982-83
Barnes, Norm	Phi., Hfd.	5	156	6	38	44	178	12	0	0	0	8		1976-77	1981-82
Baron, Normand	Mtl., St.L.	2	27	2	0	2	51	3	0	0	0	22		1983-84	1985-86
Barr, Dave	Bos., NYR, St.L., Hfd., Det., N.J., Dal.	13	614	128	204	332	520	71	12	10	22	70		1981-82	1993-94
Barrault, Doug	Min., Fla.	2	4	0	0	0	2	....	....	....	....	....		1992-93	1993-94
Barrett, Fred	Min., L.A.	13	745	25	123	148	671	44	0	2	2	60		1970-71	1983-84
Barrett, John	Det., Wsh., Min.	8	488	20	77	97	604	16	2	2	4	50		1980-81	1987-88
Barrie, Doug	Pit., Buf., L.A.	3	158	10	42	52	268	....	....	....	....	....		1968-69	1971-72
Barry, Ed	Bos.	1	19	1	3	4	2	....	....	....	....	....		1946-47	1946-47
• Barry, Marty	NYA, Bos., Det., Mtl.	12	509	195	192	387	231	43	15	18	33	34	2	1927-28	1939-40
Barry, Ray	Bos.	1	18	1	2	3	6	....	....	....	....	....		1951-52	1951-52
Bartel, Robin	Cgy., Van.	2	41	0	1	1	14	6	0	0	0	16		1985-86	1986-87
Bartlett, Jim	Mtl., NYR, Bos.	5	191	34	23	57	273	2	0	0	0	0		1954-55	1960-61
• Barton, Cliff	Pit., Phi., NYR	3	85	10	9	19	22	....	....	....	....	....		1929-30	1939-40
Bathe, Frank	Det., Phi.,	9	224	3	28	31	542	27	1	3	4	42		1974-75	1983-84
Bathgate, Andy	NYR, Tor., Det., Pit.	17	1069	349	624	973	624	54	21	14	35	76	1	1952-53	1970-71
Bathgate, Frank	NYR	1	2	0	0	0	2	....	....	....	....	....		1952-53	1952-53
• Batters, Jeff	St.L.	2	16	0	0	0	28	....	....	....	....	....		1993-94	1994-95
Batyrshin, Ruslan	L.A.	1	2	0	0	0	6	....	....	....	....	....		1995-96	1995-96
• Bauer, Bobby	Bos.	9	327	123	137	260	36	48	11	8	19	6	2	1935-36	1951-52
Baumgartner, Mike	K.C.	1	17	0	0	0	0	....	....	....	....	....		1974-75	1974-75
Baun, Bob	Tor., Oak., Det.	17	964	37	187	224	1493	96	3	12	15	171	4	1956-57	1972-73
Bautin, Sergei	Wpg., Det., S.J.	3	132	5	25	30	176	6	0	0	0	2		1992-93	1995-96
Bawa, Robin	Wsh., Van., S.J., Ana.	4	61	6	1	7	60	1	0	0	0	0		1989-90	1993-94
Baxter, Paul	Que., Pit., Cgy.	8	472	48	121	169	1564	40	0	5	5	162		1979-80	1986-87
Beadle, Sandy	Wpg.	1	6	1	0	1	2	....	....	....	....	....		1980-81	1980-81
Beaton, Frank	NYR	2	25	1	1	2	43	....	....	....	....	....		1978-79	1979-80
• Beattie, Red	Bos., Det., NYA	9	334	62	85	147	137	24	4	2	6	8		1930-31	1938-39
Beaudin, Norm	St.L., Min.	2	25	1	2	3	4	....	....	....	....	....		1967-68	1970-71
Beaudoin, Serge	Atl.	1	3	0	0	0	0	....	....	....	....	....		1979-80	1979-80
Beaudoin, Yves	Wsh.	3	11	0	0	0	5	....	....	....	....	....		1985-86	1987-88
Beck, Barry	Col., NYR, L.A.	10	615	104	251	355	1016	51	10	23	33	77		1977-78	1989-90
Beckett, Bob	Bos.	4	68	7	6	13	18	....	....	....	....	....		1956-57	1963-64
Bedard, James	Chi.	2	22	1	1	2	8	....	....	....	....	....		1949-50	1950-51
Bednarski, John	NYR, Edm.	4	100	2	18	20	114	1	0	0	0	17		1974-75	1979-80
Beers, Bob	Bos., T.B., Edm., NYI	8	258	28	79	107	225	21	1	1	2	22		1989-90	1996-97
Beers, Eddy	Cgy., St.L.	5	250	94	116	210	256	41	7	10	17	47		1981-82	1985-86
• Behling, Dick	Det.	2	5	1	0	1	2	....	....	....	....	....		1940-41	1942-43
Beisler, Frank	NYA	2	2	0	0	0	0	....	....	....	....	....		1936-37	1939-40
Belanger, Alain	Tor.	1	9	0	1	1	6	....	....	....	....	....		1977-78	1977-78
Belanger, Roger	Pit.	1	44	3	5	8	32	....	....	....	....	....		1984-85	1984-85
Belisle, Danny	NYR	1	4	2	0	2	0	....	....	....	....	....		1960-61	1960-61
Beliveau, Jean	Mtl.	20	1125	507	712	1219	1029	162	79	97	176	211	10	1950-51	1970-71
• Bell, Billy	Mtl.W, Mtl., Ott.	6	61	3	2	5	10	8	0	0	0	0		1917-18	1923-24
Bell, Bruce	Que., St.L., NYR, Edm.	5	209	12	64	76	113	34	3	5	8	41		1984-85	1989-90
Bell, Harry	NYR	1	1	0	1	1	0	....	....	....	....	....		1946-47	1946-47
Bell, Joe	NYR	2	62	8	9	17	18	....	....	....	....	....		1942-43	1946-47
Belland, Neil	Van., Pit.	6	109	13	32	45	54	21	2	9	11	23		1981-82	1986-87
• Bellefeuille, Pete	Tor., Det.	4	92	26	4	30	58	....	....	....	....	....		1925-26	1929-30
• Bellemer, Andy	Mtl.M.	1	15	0	0	0	0	....	....	....	....	....		1932-33	1932-33
• Bend, Lin	NYR	1	8	3	1	4	2	....	....	....	....	....		1942-43	1942-43
Bennett, Adam	Chi., Edm.	3	69	3	8	11	69	....	....	....	....	....		1991-92	1993-94
Bennett, Bill	Bos., Hfd.	2	31	4	7	11	65	....	....	....	....	....		1978-79	1979-80
Bennett, Curt	St.L., NYR, Atl.	10	580	152	182	334	347	21	1	1	2	57		1970-71	1979-80
Bennett, Frank	Det.	1	7	0	1	1	2	....	....	....	....	....		1943-44	1943-44
Bennett, Harvey	Pit., Wsh., Phi., Min., St.L.	5	268	44	46	90	347	4	0	0	0	2		1974-75	1978-79
• Bennett, Max	Mtl.	1	1	0	0	0	0	....	....	....	....	....		1935-36	1935-36
Bennett, Rick	NYR	3	15	1	1	2	13	....	....	....	....	....		1989-90	1991-92
Benning, Brian	St.L., L.A., Phi., Edm., Fla.	11	568	63	233	296	963	48	3	20	23	74		1984-85	1994-95
Benning, Jim	Tor., Van.	9	605	52	191	243	461	7	1	1	2	2		1981-82	1989-90
• Benoit, Joe	Mtl.	5	185	75	69	144	94	11	6	3	9	11	1	1940-41	1946-47
Benson, Bill	NYA, Bro.	2	67	11	25	36	35	....	....	....	....	....		1940-41	1941-42
• Benson, Bobby	Bos.	1	8	0	1	1	4	....	....	....	....	....		1924-25	1924-25
• Bentley, Doug	Chi., NYR	13	566	219	324	543	217	23	9	8	17	8		1939-40	1953-54
• Bentley, Max	Chi., Tor., NYR	12	646	245	299	544	179	51	18	27	45	14	3	1940-41	1953-54
Bentley, Reggie	Chi.	1	11	1	2	3	2	....	....	....	....	....		1942-43	1942-43
Beraldo, Paul	Bos.	2	10	0	0	0	4	....	....	....	....	....		1987-88	1988-89
Berenson, Red	Mtl., NYR, St.L., Det.	17	987	261	397	658	305	85	23	14	37	49	2	1961-62	1977-78
Berezan, Perry	Cgy., Min., S.J.	9	378	61	75	136	279	31	4	7	11	34		1984-85	1992-93
• Bergdinon, Fred	Bos.	1	2	0	0	0	0	....	....	....	....	....		1925-26	1925-26
Bergen, Todd	Phi.	1	14	11	5	16	4	17	4	9	13	8		1984-85	1984-85
Berger, Mike	Min.	2	30	3	1	4	67	....	....	....	....	....		1987-88	1988-89
Bergeron, Michel	Det., NYI, Wsh.	5	229	80	58	138	165	....	....	....	....	....		1974-75	1978-79
Bergeron, Yves	Pit.	2	3	0	0	0	0	....	....	....	....	....		1974-75	1976-77
Bergland, Tim	Wsh., T.B.	5	182	17	26	43	75	26	2	2	4	22		1989-90	1993-94
Bergloff, Bob	Min.	1	2	0	0	0	5	....	....	....	....	....		1982-83	1982-83
Berglund, Bo	Que., Min., Phi.	3	130	28	39	67	40	9	2	0	2	6		1983-84	1985-86
Bergman, Gary	Det., Min., K.C.	12	838	68	299	367	1249	21	0	5	5	20		1964-65	1975-76
Bergman, Thommie	Det.	6	246	21	44	65	243	7	0	2	2	2		1972-73	1979-80
Bergqvist, Jonas	Cgy.	1	22	2	5	7	10	....	....	....	....	....		1989-90	1989-90

			Regular Schedule					Playoffs							
Name	NHL Teams	NHL Seasons	GP	G	A	TP	PIM	GP	G	A	TP	PIM	NHL Cup Wins	First NHL Season	Last NHL Season
● Berlinquette, Louis	Mtl., Mtl.M., Pit.	8	193	46	33	79	128	16	1	4	5	9		1917-18	1925-26
Bernier, Serge	Phi., L.A., Que.	7	302	78	119	197	234	5	1	1	2	0		1968-69	1980-81
Berry, Bob	Mtl., L.A.	8	541	159	191	350	344	26	2	6	8	6		1968-69	1976-77
Berry, Doug	Col.	2	121	10	33	43	25	....	....	....	....	....		1979-80	1980-81
Berry, Fred	Det.	1	3	0	0	0	0	....	....	....	....	....		1976-77	1976-77
Berry, Ken	Edm., Van.	4	55	8	10	18	30	....	....	....	....	....		1981-82	1988-89
● Besler, Phil	Bos., Chi., Det.	2	30	1	4	5	18	....	....	....	....	....		1935-36	1938-39
● Bessone, Pete	Det.	1	6	0	1	1	6	....	....	....	....	....		1937-38	1937-38
Bethel, John	Wpg.	1	17	0	2	2	4	....	....	....	....	....		1979-80	1979-80
Bets, Maxim	Ana.	1	3	0	0	0	0	....	....	....	....	....		1993-94	1993-94
Bettio, Sam	Bos.	1	44	9	12	21	32	....	....	....	....	....		1949-50	1949-50
Beverley, Nick	Bos., Pit., NYR, Min., L.A., Col.	11	502	18	94	112	156	7	0	1	1	0		1966-67	1979-80
Bialowas, Dwight	Atl., Min.	4	164	11	46	57	46	....	....	....	....	....		1973-74	1976-77
Bianchin, Wayne	Pit., Edm.	7	276	68	41	109	137	3	0	1	1	6		1973-74	1979-80
Bidner, Todd	Wsh.	1	12	2	1	3	7	....	....	....	....	....		1981-82	1981-82
Biggs, Don	Min., Phi.	2	12	2	0	2	8	....	....	....	....	....		1984-85	1989-90
Bignell, Larry	Pit.	2	20	0	3	3	2	3	0	0	0	2		1973-74	1974-75
Bilodeau, Gilles	Que.	1	9	0	1	1	25	....	....	....	....	....		1979-80	1979-80
Bionda, Jack	Tor., Bos.	4	93	3	9	12	113	11	0	1	1	14		1955-56	1958-59
Bissett, Tom	Det.	1	5	0	0	0	0	....	....	....	....	....		1990-91	1990-91
Bjugstad, Scott	Min., Pit., L.A.	9	317	76	68	144	144	9	0	1	1	2		1983-84	1991-92
Black, Stephen	Det., Chi.	2	113	11	20	31	77	13	0	0	0	13	1	1949-50	1950-51
Blackburn, Bob	NYR., Pit.	3	135	8	12	20	105	6	0	0	0	4		1968-69	1970-71
Blackburn, Don	Bos., Phi., NYR, NYI, Min.	6	185	23	44	67	87	12	3	0	3	10		1962-63	1972-73
Blade, Hank	Chi.	2	24	2	3	5	2	....	....	....	....	....		1946-47	1947-48
Bladon, Tom	Phi., Pit., Edm., Wpg., Det.	9	610	73	197	270	392	86	8	29	37	70	2	1972-73	1980-81
Blaine, Gary	Mtl.	1	1	0	0	0	0	....	....	....	....	....		1954-55	1954-55
● Blair, Andy	Tor., Chi.	9	402	74	86	160	323	38	6	6	12	32	1	1928-29	1936-37
Blair, Chuck	Tor.	1	1	0	0	0	0	....	....	....	....	....		1948-49	1950-51
Blair, George	Tor.	1	2	0	0	0	0	....	....	....	....	....		1950-51	1950-51
Blaisdell, Mike	Det., NYR, Pit., Tor.	9	343	70	84	154	166	6	1	2	3	10		1980-81	1988-89
Blake, Bob	Bos.	1	12	0	0	0	0	....	....	....	....	....		1935-36	1935-36
● Blake, Mickey	St.L., Bos., Tor.	3	10	1	1	2	4	....	....	....	....	....		1934-35	1935-36
● Blake, Toe	Mtl.M., Mtl.	14	577	235	292	527	272	58	25	37	62	23	3	1932-33	1947-48
Blight, Rick	Van., L.A.	7	326	96	125	221	170	5	0	5	5	2		1975-76	1982-83
● Blinco, Russ	Mtl.M, Chi.	6	268	59	66	125	24	19	3	3	6	4	1	1933-34	1938-39
Block, Ken	Van.	1	1	0	0	0	0	....	....	....	....	....		1970-71	1970-71
Blomqvist, Timo	Wsh., N.J.	5	243	4	53	57	293	13	0	0	0	24		1981-82	1986-87
Blomsten, Arto	Wpg., L.A.	3	25	0	4	4	8	....	....	....	....	....		1993-94	1995-96
Bloom, Mike	Wsh., Det.	3	201	30	47	77	215	....	....	....	....	....		1974-75	1976-77
Blum, John	Edm., Bos., Wsh., Det.	8	250	7	34	41	610	20	0	2	2	27		1982-83	1989-90
Bodak, Bob	Cgy., Hfd.	2	4	0	0	0	29	....	....	....	....	....		1987-88	1989-90
Boddy, Gregg	Van.	5	273	23	44	67	263	3	0	0	0	0		1971-72	1975-76
Bodnar, Gus	Tor., Chi., Bos.	12	667	142	254	396	207	32	4	3	7	10	2	1943-44	1954-55
Boehm, Ron	Oak.	1	16	2	1	3	10	....	....	....	....	....		1967-68	1967-68
● Boesch, Garth	Tor.	4	197	9	28	37	205	34	2	5	7	18	3	1946-47	1949-50
Boh, Rick	Min.	1	8	2	1	3	4	....	....	....	....	....		1987-88	1987-88
Boileau, Marc	Det.	1	54	5	6	11	8	....	....	....	....	....		1961-62	1961-62
Boileau, Rene	NYA	1	7	0	0	0	0	....	....	....	....	....		1925-26	1925-26
Boimistruck, Fred	Tor.	2	83	4	14	18	45	....	....	....	....	....		1981-82	1982-83
Boisvert, Serge	Tor., Mtl.	5	46	5	7	12	8	23	3	7	10	4	1	1982-83	1987-88
Boivin, Claude	Phi., Ott.	4	132	12	19	31	364	....	....	....	....	....		1991-92	1994-95
Boivin, Leo	Tor., Bos., Det., Pit., Min.	19	1150	72	250	322	1192	54	3	10	13	59		1951-52	1969-70
Boland, Mike A.	Phi.	1	2	0	0	0	0	....	....	....	....	....		1974-75	1974-75
Boland, Mike J.	K.C., Buf.	2	23	1	2	3	29	3	1	0	1	2		1974-75	1978-79
Boldirev, Ivan	Bos., Cal., Chi., Atl., Van., Det.	15	1052	361	505	866	507	48	13	20	33	14		1970-71	1984-85
Bolduc, Danny	Det., Cgy.	3	102	22	19	41	33	1	0	0	0	0		1978-79	1983-84
Bolduc, Michel	Que.	2	10	0	0	0	6	....	....	....	....	....		1981-82	1982-83
● Boll, Frank	Tor., NYA, Bro., Bos.	12	437	133	130	263	148	31	7	3	10	13		1932-33	1943-44
Bolonchuk, Larry	Van., Wsh.	4	74	3	9	12	97	....	....	....	....	....		1972-73	1977-78
Bolton, Hugh	Tor.	8	235	10	51	61	221	17	0	5	5	14		1949-50	1956-57
Bonar, Dan	L.A.	3	170	25	39	64	208	14	3	4	7	22		1980-81	1982-83
Bonin, Marcel	Det., Bos., Mtl.	9	454	97	175	272	336	50	11	14	25	51	4	1952-53	1961-62
Boo, Jim	Min.	1	6	0	0	0	22	....	....	....	....	....		1977-78	1977-78
Boone, Buddy	Bos.	2	34	5	3	8	28	22	2	1	3	25		1956-57	1957-58
Boothman, George	Tor.	2	58	17	19	36	18	5	2	1	3	2		1942-43	1943-44
Bordeleau, Christian	Mtl., St.L., Chi.,	4	205	38	65	103	82	19	4	7	11	17	1	1968-69	1971-72
Bordeleau, J.P.	Chi.	10	519	97	126	223	143	48	3	6	9	12		1969-70	1979-80
Bordeleau, Paulin	Van.	3	183	33	56	89	47	5	2	1	3	0		1973-74	1975-76
Borotsik, Jack	St.L.	1	1	0	0	0	0	....	....	....	....	....		1974-75	1974-75
Borsato, Luciano	Wpg.	5	203	35	55	90	113	7	1	0	1	4		1990-91	1994-95
Boschman, Laurie	Tor., Edm., Wpg., N.J., Ott.	14	1009	229	348	577	2265	57	8	13	21	140		1979-80	1992-93
Bossy, Mike	NYI	10	752	573	553	1126	210	129	85	75	160	38	4	1977-78	1986-87
Bostrom, Helge	Chi.	4	96	3	3	6	58	13	0	0	0	16		1929-30	1932-33
Botell, Mark	Phi.	1	32	4	10	14	31	....	....	....	....	....		1981-82	1981-82
Bothwell, Tim	NYR, St.L., Hfd.	11	502	28	93	121	382	49	0	3	3	56		1978-79	1988-89
Botting, Cam	Atl.	1	2	0	1	1	0	....	....	....	....	....		1975-76	1975-76
Boucha, Henry	Det., Min., K.C., Col.	6	247	53	49	102	157	....	....	....	....	....		1971-72	1976-77
Bouchard, Butch	Mtl.	15	785	49	144	193	863	113	11	21	32	121	4	1941-42	1955-56
Bouchard, Dick	NYR	1	1	0	0	0	0	....	....	....	....	....		1954-55	1954-55
● Bouchard, Edmond	Mtl., Ham., NYA, Pit.	8	220	19	21	40	105	....	....	....	....	....		1921-22	1928-29
Bouchard, Pierre	Mtl., Wsh.	12	595	24	82	106	433	76	3	10	13	56	5	1970-71	1981-82
● Boucher, Billy	Mtl., Bos., NYA	7	213	93	35	128	391	21	9	3	12	35		1921-22	1927-28
● Boucher, Clarence	NYA	2	47	2	2	4	133	....	....	....	....	....		1926-27	1927-28
● Boucher, Frank	Ott., NYR	14	557	160	263	423	119	55	16	18	34	12	2	1921-22	1943-44
● Boucher, George	Ott., Mtl.M, Chi.	15	449	120	81	201	802	44	9	3	12	99	4	1917-18	1931-32
● Boucher, Robert	Mtl.	1	12	0	0	0	0	....	....	....	....	....		1923-24	1923-24
Boudreau, Bruce	Tor., Chi.	8	141	28	42	70	46	9	2	0	2	0		1976-77	1985-86
Boudrias, Andre	Mtl., Min., Chi., St.L., Van.	12	662	151	340	491	218	34	6	10	16	12		1963-64	1975-76
Boughner, Barry	Oak., Cal.	2	20	0	0	0	11	....	....	....	....	....		1969-70	1970-71
Bourbonnais, Dan	Hfd.	2	59	3	25	28	11	....	....	....	....	....		1981-82	1983-84
Bourbonnais, Rick	St.L.	3	71	9	15	24	29	4	0	1	1	0		1975-76	1977-78
● Bourcier, Conrad	Mtl.	1	6	0	0	0	0	....	....	....	....	....		1935-36	1935-36
Bourcier, Jean	Mtl.	1	9	0	1	1	0	....	....	....	....	....		1935-36	1935-36
● Bourgeault, Leo	Tor. NYR, Ott., Mtl.	8	307	24	20	44	269	24	1	1	2	18	1	1926-27	1934-35
Bourgeois, Charlie	Cgy., St.L., Hfd.	7	290	16	54	70	788	40	2	3	5	194		1981-82	1987-88
Bourne, Bob	NYI, L.A.	14	964	258	324	582	605	139	40	56	96	108	4	1974-75	1987-88
Bourque, Phil	Pit., NYR, Ott.	12	477	88	111	199	516	56	13	12	25	107	2	1983-84	1995-96
Boutette, Pat	Tor., Hfd., Pit.	10	756	171	282	453	1354	46	10	14	24	109		1975-76	1984-85
Boutilier, Paul	NYI, Bos., Min., NYR, Wpg.	8	288	27	83	110	358	41	1	9	10	45	1	1981-82	1988-89
Bowman, Kirk	Chi.	3	88	11	17	28	19	7	1	0	1	0		1976-77	1978-79
● Bowman, Ralph	Ott., St.L., Det.	7	274	8	17	25	260	22	2	2	4	6	2	1933-34	1939-40
Bownass, Jack	Mtl., NYR	4	80	3	8	11	58	....	....	....	....	....		1957-58	1961-62
Bowness, Rick	Atl., Det., St. L, Wpg.	7	173	18	37	55	191	5	0	0	0	2		1975-76	1981-82
● Boyd, Bill	NYR, NYA	4	138	15	7	22	72	9	0	0	0	2	1	1926-27	1929-30
Boyd, Irwin	Bos., Det.	4	97	18	19	37	51	5	0	1	1	4		1931-32	1943-44
Boyd, Randy	Pit., Chi., NYI, Van.	8	257	20	67	87	328	13	0	2	2	26		1981-82	1988-89
Boyer, Wally	Tor., Chi., Oak. Pit.	7	365	54	105	159	163	15	1	3	4	0		1965-66	1971-72
Boyer, Zac	Dal.	2	3	0	0	0	0	2	0	0	0	0		1994-95	1995-96
Boyko, Darren	Wpg.	1	1	0	0	0	0	....	....	....	....	....		1988-89	1988-89
Bozek, Steve	L.A., Cgy., St.L., Van., S.J.	11	641	164	167	331	309	58	12	11	23	69		1981-82	1991-92
Bozon, Philippe	St.L.	4	144	16	25	41	101	19	2	0	2	31		1991-92	1994-95
● Brackenborough, John	Bos.	1	7	0	0	0	0	....	....	....	....	....		1925-26	1925-26
Brackenbury, Curt	Que., Edm., St.L.	4	141	9	17	26	226	2	0	0	0	0		1979-80	1982-83
Bradley, Barton	Bos.	1	1	0	0	0	0	....	....	....	....	....		1949-50	1949-50
Bradley, Lyle	Cal. Cle.	2	6	1	0	1	2	....	....	....	....	....		1973-74	1976-77
Bragnalo, Rick	Wsh.	4	145	15	35	50	46	....	....	....	....	....		1975-76	1978-79
● Branigan, Andy	NYA, Bro.	2	27	1	2	3	31	....	....	....	....	....		1940-41	1941-42
Brasar, Per-Olov	Min., Van.	5	348	64	142	206	33	13	1	2	3	0		1977-78	1981-82
Brayshaw, Russ	Chi.	1	43	5	9	14	24	....	....	....	....	....		1944-45	1944-45
Breault, Francois	L.A.	3	27	2	4	6	42	....	....	....	....	....		1990-91	1992-93
Breitenbach, Ken	Buf.	3	68	1	13	14	49	8	0	1	1	4		1975-76	1978-79
Brennan, Dan	L.A.	2	8	0	1	1	9	....	....	....	....	....		1983-84	1985-86

Perry Berezan

Gus Bodnar

Mike Bossy

Mel Bridgman

Neal Broten

Jeff Brubaker

Wayne Carleton

Randy Carlyle

			Regular Schedule					Playoffs							
Name	NHL Teams	NHL Seasons	GP	G	A	TP	PIM	GP	G	A	TP	PIM	NHL Cup Wins	First NHL Season	Last NHL Season
Brennan, Doug	NYR	3	123	9	7	16	152	16	1	0	1	21	1	1931-32	1933-34
Brennan, Tom	Bos.	2	22	2	2	4	2	....	....	....	....	....		1943-44	1944-45
Brenneman, John	Chi., NYR, Tor., Det., Oak.	5	152	21	19	40	46	....	....	....	....	....		1964-65	1968-69
Bretto, Joe	Chi.	1	3	0	0	0	4	....	....	....	....	....		1944-45	1944-45
Brewer, Carl	Tor., Det., St.L.	12	604	25	198	223	1037	72	3	17	20	146	3	1957-58	1979-80
Brickley, Andy	Phi., Pit., N.J., Bos., Wpg.	11	385	82	140	222	81	17	1	4	5	4		1982-83	1993-94
● Briden, Archie	Det., Pit.	2	72	9	5	14	56	....	....	....	....	....		1926-27	1929-30
Bridgman, Mel	Phi., Cgy., N.J., Det., Van.	14	977	252	449	701	1625	125	28	39	67	298		1975-76	1988-89
● Briere, Michel	Pit.	1	76	12	32	44	20	10	5	3	8	17		1969-70	1969-70
Brindley, Doug	Tor.	1	3	0	0	0	0	....	....	....	....	....		1970-71	1970-71
● Brink, Milt	Chi.	1	5	0	0	0	0	....	....	....	....	....		1936-37	1936-37
Brisson, Gerry	Mtl.	1	4	0	2	2	4	....	....	....	....	....		1962-63	1962-63
Britz, Greg	Tor., Hfd.	3	8	0	0	0	4	....	....	....	....	....		1983-84	1986-87
● Broadbent, Harry	Ott. Mt.M, NYA	11	303	122	48	170	562	42	12	7	19	111	4	1918-19	1928-29
Brochu, Stephane	NYR	1	1	0	0	0	0	....	....	....	....	....		1988-89	1988-89
Broden, Connie	Mtl.	3	6	2	1	3	2	7	0	1	1	0	2	1955-56	1957-58
Brooke, Bob	NYR, Min., N.J.	7	447	69	97	166	520	34	9	9	18	59		1983-84	1989-90
Brooks, Gord	St.L., Wsh.	3	70	7	18	25	37	....	....	....	....	....		1971-72	1974-75
● Brophy, Bernie	Mtl.M, Det.	3	62	4	4	8	25	2	0	0	0	2		1925-26	1929-30
Brossart, Willie	Phi., Tor., Wsh.	6	129	1	14	15	88	1	0	0	0	0		1970-71	1975-76
Broten, Aaron	Col., N.J., Min., Que., Tor., Wpg.	12	748	186	329	515	441	34	7	18	25	40		1980-81	1991-92
Broten, Neal	Min., Dal., N.J., L.A.	17	1099	289	634	923	569	135	35	63	98	77	1	1980-81	1996-97
Broten, Paul	NYR, Dal., St.L.	7	322	46	55	101	264	38	4	6	10	18		1989-90	1995-96
● Brown, Adam	Det. Chi. Bos.	10	391	104	113	217	378	26	2	4	6	14	1	1941-42	1951-52
Brown, Arnie	Tor. NYR, Det., NYI, Atl.	12	681	44	141	185	738	22	0	6	6	23		1961-62	1973-74
Brown, Cam	Van.	1	1	0	0	0	7	....	....	....	....	....		1990-91	1990-91
Brown, Connie	Det.	5	73	15	24	39	12	14	2	3	5	0		1938-39	1942-43
Brown, David	Phi., Edm., S.J.	14	729	45	52	97	1789	80	2	3	5	209	1	1982-83	1995-96
● Brown, Fred	Mtl.M	1	19	1	0	1	0	9	0	0	0	0		1927-28	1927-28
Brown, George	Mtl.	3	79	6	22	28	34	7	0	0	0	2		1936-37	1938-39
Brown, Gerry	Det.	2	23	4	5	9	2	12	2	1	3	4		1941-42	1945-46
Brown, Greg	Bos., Buf., Pit., Wpg.	4	94	4	14	18	86	6	0	1	1	4		1990-91	1994-95
Brown, Harold	NYR	1	13	2	1	3	2	....	....	....	....	....		1945-46	1945-46
Brown, Jim	L.A.	1	3	0	1	1	5	....	....	....	....	....		1982-83	1982-83
Brown, Keith	Chi., Fla.	16	876	68	274	342	916	103	4	32	36	184		1979-80	1994-95
Brown, Larry	NYR, Det., Phi., L.A.	9	455	7	53	60	180	35	0	4	4	10		1969-70	1977-78
● Brown, Stan	NYR, Det.	2	48	8	2	10	18	2	0	0	0	0		1926-27	1927-28
Brown, Wayne	Bos.	1	....	....	....	....	....	4	0	0	0	2		1953-54	1953-54
● Browne, Cecil	Chi.	1	13	2	0	2	4	....	....	....	....	....		1927-28	1927-28
Brownschidle, Jack	St.L., Hfd.	9	494	39	162	201	151	26	0	5	5	18		1977-78	1985-86
Brownschidle, Jeff	Hfd.	2	7	0	1	1	2	....	....	....	....	....		1981-82	1982-83
Brubaker, Jeff	Hfd., Mtl., Cgy., Tor., Edm., NYR, Det.	8	178	16	9	25	512	2	0	0	0	27		1979-80	1988-89
● Bruce, Gordie	Bos.	3	28	4	9	13	13	7	2	3	5	4		1940-41	1945-46
● Bruce, Morley	Ott.	4	74	8	3	11	27	13	0	0	0	2	2	1917-18	1921-22
Brumwell, Murray	Min., N.J.,	7	128	12	31	43	70	2	0	0	0	2		1980-81	1987-88
Bruneteau, Eddie	Det.	7	180	40	42	82	35	31	7	6	13	0		1940-41	1948-49
● Bruneteau, Mud	Det.	11	411	139	138	277	80	77	23	14	37	22	3	1935-36	1945-46
● Brydge, Bill	Tor., Det., NYA	9	368	26	52	78	506	2	0	0	0	4		1926-27	1935-36
Brydges, Paul	Buf.	1	15	2	2	4	6	....	....	....	....	....		1986-87	1986-87
● Brydson, Glenn	Mtl.M, St.L., NYR, Chi.	8	299	56	79	135	203	11	0	0	0	8		1930-31	1937-38
● Brydson, Gord	Tor.	1	8	2	0	2	8	....	....	....	....	....		1929-30	1929-30
Bubla, Jiri	Van.	5	256	17	101	118	202	6	0	0	0	7		1981-82	1985-86
Buchanan, Al	Tor.	2	4	0	1	1	2	....	....	....	....	....		1948-49	1949-50
Buchanan, Bucky	NYR	1	2	0	0	0	0	....	....	....	....	....		1948-49	1948-49
Buchanan, Mike	Chi.	1	1	0	0	0	0	....	....	....	....	....		1951-52	1951-52
Buchanan, Ron	Bos., St.L.	2	5	0	0	0	0	....	....	....	....	....		1966-67	1969-70
Bucyk, John	Det., Bos.,	23	1540	556	813	1369	497	124	41	62	103	42	2	1955-56	1977-78
Bucyk, Randy	Mtl., Cgy.	2	19	4	2	6	8	2	0	0	0	0		1985-86	1987-88
Buhr, Doug	K.C.	1	6	0	2	2	4	....	....	....	....	....		1974-75	1974-75
Bukovich, Tony	Det.	2	17	7	3	10	6	6	0	1	1	0		1943-44	1944-45
Bullard, Mike	Pit., Cgy., St.L., Phi., Tor.	11	727	329	345	674	703	40	11	18	29	44		1980-81	1991-92
● Buller, Hy	Det., NYR	5	188	22	58	80	215	....	....	....	....	....		1943-44	1953-54
Bulley, Ted	Chi., Wsh., Pit.	8	414	101	113	214	704	29	5	5	10	24		1976-77	1983-84
Burakovsky, Robert	Ott.	1	23	2	3	5	6	....	....	....	....	....		1993-94	1993-94
● Burch, Billy	Ham., NYA, Bos., Chi.	11	390	137	53	190	251	2	0	0	0	0		1922-23	1932-33
● Burchell, Fred	Mtl.	2	4	0	0	0	2	....	....	....	....	....		1950-51	1953-54
Burdon, Glen	K.C.	1	11	0	2	2	0	....	....	....	....	....		1974-75	1974-75
Burega, Bill	Tor.	1	4	0	1	1	4	....	....	....	....	....		1955-56	1955-56
● Burke, Eddie	Bos., NYA	4	106	29	20	49	55	....	....	....	....	....		1931-32	1934-35
● Burke, Marty	Mtl., Pit., Ott., Chi.	11	494	19	47	66	560	31	2	4	6	44		1927-28	1937-38
● Burmeister, Roy	NYA	3	67	4	3	7	2	....	....	....	....	....		1929-30	1931-32
Burnett, Kelly	NYR	1	3	1	0	1	0	....	....	....	....	....		1952-53	1952-53
Burns, Bobby	Chi.	3	20	1	0	1	8	....	....	....	....	....		1927-28	1929-30
Burns, Charlie	Det., Bos., Oak., Pit., Min.	11	749	106	198	304	252	31	5	4	9	6		1958-59	1972-73
Burns, Gary	NYR	2	11	2	2	4	18	5	0	0	0	2		1980-81	1981-82
● Burns, Norm	NYR	1	11	0	4	4	2	....	....	....	....	....		1941-42	1941-42
Burns, Robin	Pit., K.C.	5	190	31	38	69	139	....	....	....	....	....		1970-71	1975-76
Burrows, Dave	Pit., Tor.	10	724	29	135	164	373	29	1	5	6	25		1971-72	1980-81
● Burry, Bert	Ott.	1	4	0	0	0	0	....	....	....	....	....		1932-33	1932-33
Burton, Cummy	Det.	3	43	0	2	2	21	3	0	0	0	0		1955-56	1958-59
Burton, Nelson	Wsh.	2	8	1	0	1	21	....	....	....	....	....		1977-78	1978-79
● Bush, Eddie	Det.	2	26	4	6	10	40	11	1	6	7	23		1938-39	1941-42
Buskas, Rod	Pit., Van., L.A., Chi.	11	556	19	63	82	1294	18	0	3	3	45		1982-83	1992-93
Busniuk, Mike	Phi.	2	143	3	23	26	297	25	2	5	7	34		1979-80	1980-81
Busniuk, Ron	Buf.	2	6	0	3	3	13	....	....	....	....	....		1972-73	1973-74
● Buswell, Walt	Det., Mtl.	8	368	10	40	50	164	24	2	1	3	10		1932-33	1939-40
Butcher, Garth	Van., St.L., Que., Tor.	14	897	48	158	206	2302	50	6	5	11	122		1981-82	1994-95
Butler, Dick	Chi.	1	7	2	0	2	0	....	....	....	....	....		1947-48	1947-48
Butler, Jerry	NYR, St.L., Tor., Van., Wpg.	11	641	99	120	219	515	48	3	3	6	79		1972-73	1982-83
Butters, Bill	Min.	2	72	1	4	5	77	....	....	....	....	....		1977-78	1978-79
Buttrey, Gord	Chi.	1	10	0	0	0	0	....	....	....	....	....		1943-44	1943-44
Buynak, Gordon	St. L	1	4	0	0	0	2	....	....	....	....	....		1974-75	1974-75
Byakin, Ilja	Edm., S.J.	2	57	8	25	33	44	....	....	....	....	....		1993-94	1994-95
Byce, John	Bos.	3	21	2	3	5	6	8	2	0	2	2		1989-90	1991-92
Byers, Gord	Bos.	1	1	0	1	1	0	....	....	....	....	....		1949-50	1949-50
Byers, Jerry	Min., Atl, NYR	4	43	3	4	7	15	....	....	....	....	....		1972-73	1977-78
Byers, Lyndon	Bos., S.J.	10	279	28	43	71	1081	37	2	2	4	96		1983-84	1992-93
Byers, Mike	Tor., Phi., Buf., L.A.	4	166	42	34	76	39	4	0	1	1	0		1967-68	1971-72
Byram, Shawn	NYI, Chi.	2	5	0	0	0	14	....	....	....	....	....		1990-91	1991-92

C

● Caffery, Jack	Tor., Bos.	3	57	3	2	5	22	10	1	0	1	4		1954-55	1957-58
Caffery, Terry	Chi., Min.	2	14	0	0	0	0	1	0	0	0	0		1969-70	1970-71
● Cahan, Larry	Tor., NYR, Oak., L.A.	13	666	38	92	130	700	29	1	1	2	38		1954-55	1970-71
● Cahill, Chuck	Bos.	2	32	0	1	1	4	....	....	....	....	....		1925-26	1926-27
● Cain, Francis	Mtl.M, Tor.	2	61	4	0	4	35	....	....	....	....	....	1	1924-25	1925-26
● Cain, Herb	Mtl.M, Mtl., Bos.	13	570	206	194	400	178	67	16	13	29	13	2	1933-34	1945-46
Cairns, Don	K.C., Col.	2	9	0	1	1	2	....	....	....	....	....		1975-76	1976-77
Calder, Eric	Wsh.	2	2	0	0	0	0	....	....	....	....	....		1981-82	1982-83
● Calladine, Norm	Bos.	3	63	19	29	48	8	....	....	....	....	....		1942-43	1944-45
Callander, Drew	Phi., Van.	4	39	6	2	8	7	....	....	....	....	....		1976-77	1979-80
Callander, John	Pit., T.B.	5	109	22	29	51	116	22	3	8	11	12	1	1987-88	1992-93
Callighen, Brett	Edm.	3	160	56	89	145	132	14	4	6	10	8		1979-80	1981-82
Callighen, Patsy	NYR	1	36	0	0	0	32	9	0	0	0	0	1	1927-28	1927-28
Camazzola, James	Chi.	2	3	0	0	0	0	....	....	....	....	....		1983-84	1986-87
Camazzola, Tony	Wsh.	1	3	0	0	0	4	....	....	....	....	....		1981-82	1981-82
Cameron, Al	Det., Wpg.	6	282	11	44	55	356	7	0	1	1	2		1975-76	1980-81
● Cameron, Billy	Mtl., NYA	2	39	0	0	0	2	6	0	0	0	0		1923-24	1925-26
Cameron, Craig	Det., St.L., Min., NYI	9	552	87	65	152	196	27	3	1	4	17		1966-67	1975-76
Cameron, Dave	Col., N.J.	3	168	25	28	53	238	....	....	....	....	....		1981-82	1983-84

Name	NHL Teams	NHL Seasons	Regular Schedule GP	G	A	TP	PIM	Playoffs GP	G	A	TP	PIM	NHL Cup Wins	First NHL Season	Last NHL Season
● Cameron, Harry	Tor., Ott., Mtl.	6	128	88	51	139	195	20	10	7	17	39	2	1917-18	1922-23
● Cameron, Scotty	NYR	1	35	8	11	19	0	....	....	....	....	....		1942-43	1942-43
Campbell, Bryan	L.A., Chi.	5	260	35	71	106	74	22	3	4	7	2		1967-68	1971-72
Campbell, Colin	Pit., Col., Edm., Van., Det.	11	636	25	103	128	1292	45	4	10	14	181		1974-75	1984-85
● Campbell, Dave	Mtl.	1	2	0	0	0	0	....	....	....	....	....		1920-21	1920-21
Campbell, Don	Chi.	1	17	1	3	4	8	....	....	....	....	....		1943-44	1943-44
● Campbell, Earl	Ott., NYA	3	77	5	1	6	12	2	0	0	0	0		1923-24	1925-26
Campbell, Scott	Wpg., St.L.	3	80	4	21	25	243	....	....	....	....	....		1979-80	1981-82
Campbell, Wade	Wpg., Bos.	6	213	9	27	36	305	10	0	0	0	20		1982-83	1987-88
Campeau, Tod	Mtl.	3	42	5	9	14	16	1	0	0	0	0		1943-44	1948-49
Campedelli, Dom	Mtl.	1	2	0	0	0	0	....	....	....	....	....		1985-86	1985-86
Capuano, Dave	Pit., Van., T.B., S.J.	4	104	17	38	55	56	6	1	1	2	5		1989-90	1993-94
Capuano, Jack	Tor., Van., Bos.	3	6	0	0	0	0	....	....	....	....	....		1989-90	1991-92
Carbol, Leo	Chi.	1	6	0	1	1	4	....	....	....	....	....		1942-43	1942-43
Cardin, Claude	St.L.	1	1	0	0	0	0	....	....	....	....	....		1967-68	1967-68
Cardwell, Steve	Pit.	3	53	9	11	20	35	4	0	0	0	2		1970-71	1972-73
● Carey, George	Que, Ham., Tor.	5	72	21	12	33	20	....	....	....	....	....		1919-20	1923-24
Carleton, Wayne	Tor., Bos., Cal.	7	278	55	73	128	172	18	2	4	6	14	1	1965-66	1971-72
Carlin, Brian	L.A.	1	5	1	0	1	0	....	....	....	....	....		1971-72	1971-72
Carlson, Jack	Min., St.L.	6	236	30	15	45	417	25	1	2	3	72		1978-79	1986-87
Carlson, Kent	Mtl., St.L., Wsh.	5	113	7	11	18	148	8	0	0	0	13		1983-84	1988-89
Carlson, Steve	L.A.	1	52	9	12	21	23	4	1	1	2	7		1979-80	1979-80
Carlsson, Anders	N.J.	3	104	7	26	33	34	3	1	0	1	2		1986-87	1988-89
Carlyle, Randy	Tor., Pit., Wpg.	17	1055	148	499	647	1400	69	9	24	33	120		1976-77	1992-93
Carnback, Patrik	Mtl., Ana.	4	154	24	38	62	122	....	....	....	....	....		1992-93	1995-96
● Caron, Alain	Oak., Mtl.	2	60	9	13	22	18	....	....	....	....	....		1967-68	1968-69
● Carpenter, Eddie	Que, Ham.	2	45	10	5	15	31	....	....	....	....	....		1919-20	1920-21
Carr, Al	Tor.	1	5	0	1	1	2	....	....	....	....	....		1943-44	1943-44
Carr, Gene	St.L., NYR, L.A., Pit., Atl.	8	465	79	136	215	365	35	5	8	13	66		1971-72	1978-79
Carr, Lorne	NYR, NYA, Tor.	13	580	204	222	426	132	53	10	9	19	13	2	1933-34	1945-46
Carriere, Larry	Buf. Atl, Van., L.A., Tor.	7	367	16	74	90	462	27	0	3	3	42		1972-73	1979-80
● Carrigan, Gene	NYR, StL, Det.	3	37	2	1	3	13	4	0	0	0	0		1930-31	1934-35
Carroll, Billy	NYI, Edm., Det.	7	322	30	54	84	113	71	6	12	18	18	4	1980-81	1986-87
● Carroll, George	Mtl.M, Bos.	1	15	0	0	0	9	....	....	....	....	....		1924-25	1924-25
Carroll, Greg	Wsh., Det., Hfd.	2	131	20	34	54	44	....	....	....	....	....		1978-79	1979-80
Carruthers, Dwight	Det. Phi.	2	2	0	0	0	0	....	....	....	....	....		1965-66	1967-68
Carse, Bill	NYR, Chi.	4	124	28	43	71	38	13	3	2	5	0		1938-39	1941-42
Carse, Bob	Chi., Mtl.	5	167	32	55	87	52	10	0	2	2	2		1939-40	1947-48
● Carson, Bill	Tor., Bos.	4	159	54	24	78	156	11	3	0	3	14	1	1926-27	1929-30
● Carson, Frank	Mtl.M., NYA, Det.	7	248	42	48	90	166	31	0	2	2	9	1	1925-26	1933-34
● Carson, Gerry	Mtl., NYR, Mtl.M.	6	261	12	11	23	205	22	0	0	0	12		1928-29	1936-37
Carson, Lindsay	Phi., Hfd.	7	373	66	80	146	524	49	4	10	14	56		1981-82	1987-88
Carter, Billy	Mtl., Bos.	3	16	0	0	0	6	....	....	....	....	....		1957-58	1961-62
Carter, John	Bos., S.J.	8	244	40	50	90	201	31	7	5	12	51		1985-86	1992-93
Carter, Ron	Edm.	1	2	0	0	0	0	....	....	....	....	....		1979-80	1979-80
● Carveth, Joe	Det., Bos., Mtl.	11	504	150	189	339	81	69	21	16	37	28	2	1940-41	1950-51
Cashman, Wayne	Bos.	17	1027	277	516	793	1041	145	31	57	88	250	2	1964-65	1982-83
Cassidy, Bruce	Chi.	6	36	4	13	17	10	1	0	0	0	0		1983-84	1989-90
Cassidy, Tom	Pit.	1	26	3	4	7	15	....	....	....	....	....		1977-78	1977-78
Cassolato, Tony	Wsh.	3	23	1	6	7	4	....	....	....	....	....		1979-80	1981-82
Caufield, Jay	NYR, Min., Pit.	7	208	5	8	13	759	17	0	0	0	42	2	1986-87	1992-93
Cavallini, Gino	Cgy., St.L., Que.	9	593	114	159	273	507	74	14	19	33	66		1984-85	1992-93
Cavallini, Paul	Wsh., St.L., Dal.	10	564	56	177	233	750	69	8	27	35	114		1986-87	1995-96
Ceresino, Ray	Tor.	1	12	1	1	2	2	....	....	....	....	....		1948-49	1948-49
Cernik, Frantisek	Det.	1	49	5	4	9	13	....	....	....	....	....		1984-85	1984-85
Chabot, John	Mtl., Pit., Det.	8	508	84	228	312	85	33	6	20	26	2		1983-84	1990-91
● Chad, John	Chi.	3	80	15	22	37	29	10	0	1	1	2		1939-40	1945-46
● Chalmers, Bill	NYR	1	1	0	0	0	0	....	....	....	....	....		1953-54	1953-54
Chalupa, Milan	Det.	1	14	0	5	5	6	....	....	....	....	....		1984-85	1984-85
● Chamberlain, Murph	Tor., Mtl., Bro., Bos.	12	510	100	175	275	769	66	14	17	31	96	2	1937-38	1948-49
Champagne, Andre	Tor.	1	2	0	0	0	0	....	....	....	....	....		1962-63	1962-63
Chapdelaine, Rene	L.A.	3	32	0	2	2	32	....	....	....	....	....		1990-91	1992-93
● Chapman, Art	Bos., NYA	10	438	62	176	238	140	26	1	5	6	9		1930-31	1939-40
Chapman, Blair	Pit., St.L.	7	402	106	125	231	158	25	4	6	10	15		1976-77	1982-83
Chapman, Brian	Hfd.	1	3	0	0	0	29	....	....	....	....	....		1990-91	1990-91
Charbonneau, Jose	Mtl., Van.	4	71	9	13	22	67	11	1	0	1	8		1987-88	1994-95
Charbonneau, Stephane	Que.	1	2	0	0	0	0	....	....	....	....	....		1991-92	1991-92
Charlebois, Bob	Min.	1	7	1	0	1	0	....	....	....	....	....		1967-68	1967-68
Charlesworth, Todd	Pit., NYR	6	93	3	9	12	47	....	....	....	....	....		1983-84	1989-90
Charron, Guy	Mtl., Det., K.C., Wsh.	12	734	221	309	530	146	....	....	....	....	....		1969-70	1980-81
Chartier, Dave	Wpg.	1	1	0	0	0	0	....	....	....	....	....		1980-81	1980-81
Chartraw, Rick	Mtl., L.A., NYR, Edm.	10	420	28	64	92	399	75	7	9	16	80	4	1974-75	1983-84
Check, Lude	Det., Chi.	2	27	6	2	8	4	....	....	....	....	....		1943-44	1944-45
Chernoff, Mike	Min.	1	1	0	0	0	0	....	....	....	....	....		1968-69	1968-69
Chernomaz, Rich	Col., N.J., Cgy.	7	51	9	7	16	18	....	....	....	....	....		1981-82	1991-92
Cherry, Dick	Bos., Phi.	3	145	12	10	22	45	4	1	0	1	4		1956-57	1969-70
Cherry, Don	Bos.	1	....	....	....	....	....	1	0	0	0	0		1954-55	1954-55
Chervyakov, Denis	Bos.	1	2	0	0	0	2	....	....	....	....	....		1992-93	1992-93
● Chevrefils, Real	Bos., Det.	8	387	104	97	201	185	30	5	4	9	20		1951-52	1958-59
Chibirev, Igor	Hfd.	2	45	7	12	19	2	....	....	....	....	....		1993-94	1994-95
Chicoine, Dan	Cle. Min.	3	31	1	2	3	12	1	0	0	0	0		1977-78	1979-80
Chinnick, Rick	Min.	2	4	0	2	2	0	....	....	....	....	....		1973-74	1974-75
Chipperfield, Ron	Edm., Que.,	2	83	22	24	46	34	....	....	....	....	....		1979-80	1980-81
Chisholm, Art	Bos.	1	3	0	0	0	0	....	....	....	....	....		1960-61	1960-61
Chisholm, Colin	Min.	1	1	0	0	0	0	....	....	....	....	....		1986-87	1986-87
● Chisholm, Lex	Tor.	2	54	10	8	18	19	3	1	0	1	0		1939-40	1940-41
Chorney, Marc	Pit. L.A.	4	210	8	27	35	209	7	0	1	1	2		1980-81	1983-84
● Chouinard, Gene	Ott.	1	8	0	0	0	0	....	....	....	....	....		1927-28	1927-28
Chouinard, Guy	Atl, Cgy., St.L.	10	578	205	370	575	120	46	9	28	37	12		1974-75	1983-84
Christian, Dave	Wpg., Wsh., Bos., St.L., Chi.	15	1009	340	433	773	284	102	32	25	57	27		1979-80	1993-94
Christie, Mike	Cal., Cle., Col., Van.	7	412	15	101	116	550	2	0	0	0	0		1974-75	1980-81
Christoff, Steve	Min. Cgy., L.A.	5	248	77	64	141	108	35	16	12	28	25		1979-80	1983-84
Chrystal, Bob	NYR	2	132	11	14	25	112	....	....	....	....	....		1953-54	1954-55
● Church, Jack	Tor., Bro., Bos.	5	130	4	19	23	154	25	1	1	2	18		1938-39	1945-46
Chychrun, Jeff	Phi., L.A., Pit., Edm.	8	262	3	22	25	744	19	0	2	2	65	1	1986-87	1993-94
Cichocki, Chris	Det., N.J.	4	68	11	12	23	27	....	....	....	....	....		1985-86	1988-89
● Ciesla, Hank	Chi., NYR	4	269	26	51	77	87	6	0	2	2	0		1955-56	1958-59
Cimellaro, Tony	Ott.	1	2	0	0	0	0	....	....	....	....	....		1992-93	1992-93
Cimetta, Robert	Bos., Tor.	4	103	16	16	32	66	1	0	0	0	15		1988-89	1991-92
Cirella, Joe	Col., N.J., Que., NYR, Fla., Ott.	15	828	64	211	275	1446	38	0	13	13	98		1981-82	1995-96
Cirone, Jason	Wpg.	1	3	0	0	0	2	....	....	....	....	....		1991-92	1991-92
Clackson, Kim	Pit., Que.	2	106	0	8	8	370	8	0	0	0	70		1979-80	1980-81
● Clancy, King	Ott., Tor.	16	592	137	144	281	906	61	9	8	17	92	3	1921-22	1936-37
Clancy, Terry	Oak., Tor.	4	93	6	6	12	39	....	....	....	....	....		1967-68	1972-73
● Clapper, Dit	Bos.	20	833	228	246	474	462	82	13	17	30	50	3	1927-28	1946-47
Clark, Dan	NYR	1	4	0	1	1	6	....	....	....	....	....		1978-79	1978-79
Clark, Dean	Edm.	1	1	0	0	0	0	....	....	....	....	....		1983-84	1983-84
Clark, Gordie	Bos.	2	8	0	1	1	0	1	0	0	0	0		1974-75	1975-76
● Clark, Nobby	Bos.	1	5	0	0	0	0	....	....	....	....	....		1927-28	1927-28
Clarke, Bobby	Phi.	15	1144	358	852	1210	1453	136	42	77	119	152	2	1969-70	1983-84
● Cleghorn, Odie	Mtl., Pit.	10	182	94	30	124	147	24	8	3	11	11		1918-19	1927-28
● Cleghorn, Sprague	Ott. Tor. Mtl., Bos.	10	262	85	47	132	534	39	7	8	15	66	2	1918-19	1927-28
Clement, Bill	Phi., Wsh., Atl., Cgy.	11	719	148	208	356	383	50	5	3	8	26	2	1971-72	1981-82
Cline, Bruce	NYR	1	30	2	3	5	10	....	....	....	....	....		1956-57	1956-57
Clippingdale, Steve	L.A., Wsh.	2	19	1	2	3	9	1	0	0	0	0		1976-77	1979-80
Cloutier, Real	Que. Buf.	6	317	146	198	344	119	25	7	5	12	20		1979-80	1984-85
Cloutier, Rejean	Det.	2	5	0	2	2	2	....	....	....	....	....		1979-80	1981-82
Cloutier, Roland	Det., Que.	3	34	8	9	17	2	....	....	....	....	....		1977-78	1979-80
● Clune, Wally	Mtl.	1	5	0	0	0	6	....	....	....	....	....		1955-56	1955-56
Coalter, Gary	Cal., K.C.	2	34	2	4	6	2	....	....	....	....	....		1973-74	1974-75
Coates, Steve	Det.	1	5	1	0	1	24	....	....	....	....	....		1976-77	1976-77
Cochrane, Glen	Phi., Van., Chi., Edm.	10	411	17	72	89	1556	18	1	1	2	31		1978-79	1988-89

Murph Chamberlain

Steve Christoff

Shawn Cronin

Troy Crowder

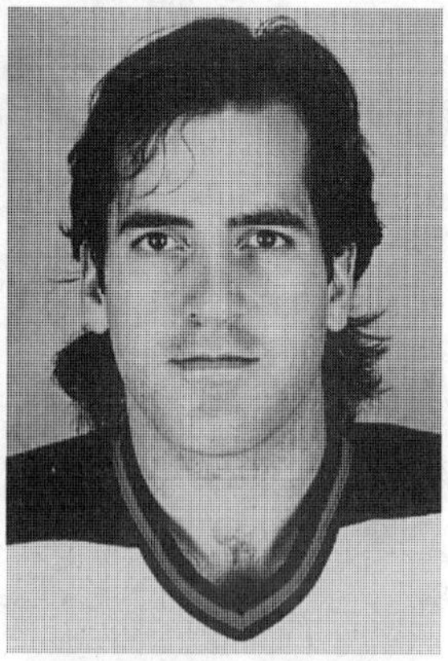

Rob Conn

Sylvain Couturier

Chris Dahlquist

Dan Daoust

Name	NHL Teams	NHL Seasons	Regular Schedule GP	G	A	TP	PIM	Playoffs GP	G	A	TP	PIM	NHL Cup Wins	First NHL Season	Last NHL Season
Coflin, Hugh	Chi.	1	31	0	3	3	33	....	....	....	....	....		1950-51	1950-51
Colley, Tom	Min.	1	1	0	0	0	2	....	....	....	....	....		1974-75	1974-75
Collings, Norm	Mtl.	1	1	0	1	1	0	....	....	....	....	....		1934-35	1934-35
Collins, Bill	Min., Mtl., Det., St. L, NYR, Phi., Wsh.	11	768	157	154	311	415	18	3	5	8	12		1967-68	1977-78
Collins, Gary	Tor.	1	....	....	....	....	....	2	0	0	0	0		1958-59	1958-59
Collyard, Bob	St.L.	1	10	1	3	4	4	....	....	....	....	....		1973-74	1973-74
• Colman, Michael	S.J.	1	15	0	1	1	32	....	....	....	....	....		1991-92	1991-92
Colville, Mac	NYR	9	353	71	104	175	130	40	9	10	19	14	1	1935-36	1946-47
• Colville, Neil	NYR	12	464	99	166	265	213	46	7	19	26	32	1	1935-36	1948-49
Colwill, Les	NYR	1	69	7	6	13	16	....	....	....	....	....		1958-59	1958-59
Comeau, Rey	Mtl., Atl, Col.	9	564	98	141	239	175	9	2	1	3	8		1971-72	1979-80
Conacher, Brian	Tor., Det.	5	155	28	28	56	84	12	3	2	5	21	1	1961-62	1971-72
• Conacher, Charlie	Tor., Det., NYA	12	459	225	173	398	523	49	17	18	35	49	1	1929-30	1940-41
Conacher, Jim	Det., Chi., NYR	8	328	85	117	202	91	19	5	2	7	4		1945-46	1952-53
• Conacher, Lionel	Pit., NYA, Mtl.M., Chi.	12	498	80	105	185	882	35	2	2	4	34	2	1925-26	1936-37
Conacher, Pat	NYR, Edm., N.J., L.A., Cgy., NYI	13	521	63	76	139	235	66	11	10	21	40	1	1979-80	1995-96
Conacher, Pete	Chi., NYR, Tor.	6	229	47	39	86	57	7	0	0	0	0		1951-52	1957-58
• Conacher, Roy	Bos., Det., Chi.	11	490	226	200	426	90	42	15	15	30	14	2	1938-39	1951-52
• Conn, Hugh	NYA	2	96	9	28	37	22	....	....	....	....	....		1933-34	1934-35
Conn, Rob	Chi., Buf.	2	30	2	5	7	20	....	....	....	....	....		1991-92	1995-96
• Connelly, Bert	NYR, Chi.	3	87	13	15	28	37	14	1	0	1	0	1	1934-35	1937-38
Connelly, Wayne	Mtl., Bos., Min., Det., St. L, Van.	10	543	133	174	307	156	24	11	7	18	4		1960-61	1971-72
Connor, Cam	Mtl., Edm., NYR	5	89	9	22	31	256	20	5	0	5	6	1	1978-79	1982-83
• Connor, Harry	Bos., NYA, Ott.	4	134	16	5	21	149	10	0	0	0	2		1927-28	1930-31
• Connors, Bobby	NYA, Det.	3	78	17	10	27	110	2	0	0	0	10		1926-27	1929-30
Conroy, Al	Phi.	3	114	9	14	23	156	....	....	....	....	....		1991-92	1993-94
Contini, Joe	Col., Min.	3	68	17	21	38	34	2	0	0	0	0		1977-78	1980-81
• Convey, Eddie	NYR	3	36	1	1	2	33	....	....	....	....	....		1930-31	1932-33
• Cook, Bill	NYR	11	474	229	138	367	386	46	13	11	24	68	2	1926-27	1936-37
• Cook, Bob	Van., Det., NYI, Min.	4	72	13	9	22	22	....	....	....	....	....		1970-71	1974-75
• Cook, Bud	Bos., Ott., St.L.	3	50	5	4	9	22	....	....	....	....	....		1931-32	1934-35
• Cook, Bun	NYR, Bos.	11	473	158	144	302	444	46	15	3	18	50	2	1926-27	1936-37
• Cook, Lloyd	Bos.	1	4	1	0	1	0	....	....	....	....	....		1924-25	1924-25
• Cook, Tom	Chi., Mtl.M.	9	349	77	98	175	184	24	2	4	6	19	1	1929-30	1937-38
• Cooper, Carson	Bos., Mtl., Det.	8	294	110	57	167	111	7	0	0	0	2		1924-25	1931-32
Cooper, Ed	Col.	2	49	8	7	15	46	....	....	....	....	....		1980-81	1981-82
• Cooper, Hal	NYR	1	8	0	0	0	2	....	....	....	....	....		1944-45	1944-45
• Cooper, Joe	NYR, Chi.	11	420	30	66	96	442	35	3	5	8	58		1935-36	1946-47
Copp, Bob	Tor.	2	40	3	9	12	26	....	....	....	....	....		1942-43	1950-51
• Corbeau, Bert	Mtl., Ham., Tor.,	10	259	64	44	108	639	14	2	2	4	31		1917-18	1926-27
Corbett, Michael	L.A.	1	....	....	....	....	....	2	0	1	1	2		1967-68	1967-68
Corcoran, Norm	Bos., Det., Chi.	4	29	1	3	4	21	4	0	0	0	6		1949-50	1955-56
• Cormier, Roger	Mtl.	1	1	0	0	0	0	....	....	....	....	....		1925-26	1925-26
Corrigan, Chuck	Tor., NYA	2	19	2	2	4	2	....	....	....	....	....		1937-38	1940-41
Corrigan, Mike	L.A., Van., Pit.	10	594	152	195	347	698	17	2	3	5	20		1967-68	1977-78
Corriveau, Andre	Mtl.	1	3	0	1	1	0	....	....	....	....	....		1953-54	1953-54
Corriveau, Yvon	Wsh., Hfd., S.J.	9	280	48	40	88	310	29	5	7	12	50		1985-86	1993-94
Cory, Ross	Wpg.	2	51	2	10	12	41	....	....	....	....	....		1979-80	1980-81
Cossete, Jacques	Pit.	3	64	8	6	14	29	3	0	1	1	4		1975-76	1978-79
Costello, Les	Tor.	3	15	2	3	5	11	6	2	2	4	2	1	1947-48	1949-50
Costello, Murray	Chi., Bos., Det.	4	162	13	19	32	54	5	0	0	0	2		1953-54	1956-57
Costello, Rich	Tor.	2	12	2	2	4	2	....	....	....	....	....		1983-84	1985-86
• Cotch, Charlie	Ham., Tor.	1	11	1	0	1	0	....	....	....	....	....		1924-25	1924-25
Cote, Alain	Que.	10	696	103	190	293	383	67	9	15	24	44		1979-80	1988-89
Cote, Alain G.	Bos., Wsh., Mtl., T.B., Que.	9	119	2	18	20	124	11	0	2	2	26		1985-86	1993-94
Cote, Ray	Edm.	3	15	0	0	0	4	14	3	2	5	0		1982-83	1984-85
• Cotton, Baldy	Pit., Tor., NYA	12	503	101	103	204	419	43	4	9	13	46	1	1925-26	1936-37
• Coughlin, Jack	Tor., Que, Mtl., Ham.	3	18	2	0	2	3	....	....	....	....	....		1917-18	1920-21
Coulis, Tim	Wsh., Min.	4	47	4	5	9	138	3	1	0	1	2		1979-80	1985-86
Coulson, D'arcy	Phi.	1	28	0	0	0	103	....	....	....	....	....		1930-31	1930-31
• Coulter, Art	Chi., NYR	11	465	30	82	112	543	49	4	5	9	61	2	1931-32	1941-42
Coulter, Neal	NYI	3	26	5	5	10	11	....	....	....	....	....		1985-86	1987-88
Cournoyer, Yvan	Mtl.	16	968	428	435	863	255	147	64	63	127	47	10	1963-64	1978-79
Courteau, Yves	Cgy., Hfd.	3	22	2	5	7	4	1	0	0	0	0		1984-85	1986-87
Courtenay, Ed	S.J.	2	44	7	13	20	10	....	....	....	....	....		1991-92	1992-93
• Coutu, Billy	Mtl., Ham., Bos.	10	246	33	21	54	443	32	2	2	4	40		1917-18	1926-27
• Couture, Gerry	Det., Mtl., Chi.,	10	385	86	70	156	89	45	9	7	16	4	1	1944-45	1953-54
• Couture, Rosie	Chi., Mtl.	8	309	48	56	104	184	23	1	5	6	15		1928-29	1935-36
Couturier, Sylvain	L.A.	3	33	4	5	9	4	....	....	....	....	....		1988-89	1991-92
Cowick, Bruce	Phi., Wsh., St.L.	3	70	5	6	11	43	8	0	0	0	9	1	1973-74	1975-76
Cowie, Rob	L.A.	2	78	7	12	19	52	....	....	....	....	....		1994-95	1995-96
• Cowley, Bill	St.L., Bos.	13	549	195	353	548	143	64	12	34	46	22	2	1934-35	1946-47
• Cox, Danny	Tor., Ott., Det., NYR, St.L.	8	319	47	49	96	128	10	0	1	1	6		1926-27	1934-35
Coxe, Craig	Van., Cgy., St.L., S.J.	8	235	14	31	45	713	5	1	0	1	18		1984-85	1991-92
Crashley, Bart	Det., K.C., L.A.	6	140	7	36	43	50	....	....	....	....	....		1965-66	1975-76
Crawford, Bob	St.L., Hfd., NYR, Wsh.	7	246	71	71	142	72	11	0	1	1	8		1979-80	1986-87
Crawford, Bobby	Col., Det.	2	16	1	3	4	6	....	....	....	....	....		1980-81	1982-83
• Crawford, Jack	Bos.	13	548	38	140	178	202	66	4	13	17	36	2	1937-38	1949-50
Crawford, Lou	Bos.	2	26	2	1	3	29	....	....	....	....	....		1989-90	1991-92
Crawford, Marc	Van.	6	176	19	31	50	229	20	1	2	3	44		1981-82	1986-87
• Crawford, Rusty	Ott., Tor.,	2	39	10	8	18	118	2	2	1	3	9	1	1917-18	1918-19
Creighton, Adam	Buf., Chi., NYI, T.B., St.L.	14	708	187	216	403	1077	61	11	14	25	137		1983-84	1996-97
Creighton, Dave	Bos., Chi., Tor., NYR	12	616	140	174	314	223	51	11	13	24	20		1948-49	1959-60
• Creighton, Jimmy	Det.	1	11	1	0	1	2	....	....	....	....	....		1930-31	1930-31
Cressman, Dave	Min.	2	85	6	8	14	37	....	....	....	....	....		1974-75	1975-76
Cressman, Glen	Mtl.	1	4	0	0	0	2	....	....	....	....	....		1956-57	1956-57
Crisp, Terry	Bos., St.L., Phi., NYI	11	536	67	134	201	135	110	15	28	43	40	2	1965-66	1976-77
Cristofoli, Ed	Mtl.	1	9	0	1	1	4	....	....	....	....	....		1989-90	1989-90
• Croghen, Maurice	Mtl.M.	1	16	0	0	0	4	....	....	....	....	....		1937-38	1937-38
Crombeen, Mike	Cle., St.L., Hfd.	8	475	55	68	123	218	27	6	2	8	32		1977-78	1984-85
Cronin, Shawn	Wsh., Wpg., Phi., S.J.	7	292	3	18	21	877	32	1	0	1	38		1988-89	1994-95
• Crossett, Stan	Phi.,	1	21	0	0	0	10	....	....	....	....	....		1930-31	1930-31
Crossman, Doug	Chi., Phi., NYI, Hfd., Det., T.B., St.L.	14	914	105	359	464	534	97	12	39	51	105		1980-81	1993-94
Croteau, Gary	L.A., Det., Cal., K.C., Col.	12	684	144	175	319	143	11	3	2	5	8		1968-69	1979-80
Crowder, Bruce	Bos., Pit.	4	243	47	51	98	156	31	8	4	12	41		1981-82	1984-85
Crowder, Keith	Bos., L.A.	10	662	223	271	494	1344	85	14	22	36	218		1980-81	1989-90
Crowder, Troy	N.J., Det., L.A., Van.	7	150	9	7	16	433	4	0	0	0	22		1987-88	1996-97
Crozier, Joe	Tor.,	1	5	0	3	3	2	....	....	....	....	....		1959-60	1959-60
• Crutchfield, Nels	Mtl.	1	41	5	5	10	20	2	0	1	1	22		1934-35	1934-35
Culhane, Jim	Hfd.	1	6	0	1	1	4	....	....	....	....	....		1989-90	1989-90
Cullen, Barry	Tor., Det.	5	219	32	52	84	111	6	0	0	0	2		1955-56	1959-60
Cullen, Brian	Tor., NYR	7	326	56	100	156	92	19	3	0	3	2		1954-55	1960-61
Cullen, Ray	NYR, Det., Min., Van.	6	313	92	123	215	120	20	3	10	13	2		1965-66	1970-71
Cummins, Barry	Cal.	1	36	1	2	3	39	....	....	....	....	....		1973-74	1973-74
Cunningham, Bob	NYR	2	4	0	1	1	0	....	....	....	....	....		1960-61	1961-62
Cunningham, Jim	Phi.	1	1	0	0	0	4	....	....	....	....	....		1977-78	1977-78
Cunningham, Les	NYA, Chi.	2	60	7	19	26	21	1	0	0	0	0		1936-37	1939-40
Cupolo, Bill	Bos.	1	47	11	13	24	10	7	1	2	3	0		1944-45	1944-45
Curran, Brian	Bos., NYI, Tor., Buf., Wsh.	10	381	7	33	40	1461	24	0	1	1	122		1983-84	1993-94
Currie, Dan	Edm., L.A.	4	22	2	1	3	4	....	....	....	....	....		1990-91	1993-94
Currie, Glen	Wsh., L.A.	8	326	39	79	118	100	12	1	3	4	4		1979-80	1987-88
Currie, Hugh	Mtl.	1	1	0	0	0	0	....	....	....	....	....		1950-51	1950-51
Currie, Tony	St.L., Hfd., Van.	8	290	92	119	211	83	16	4	12	16	14		1977-78	1984-85
Curry, Floyd	Mtl.	11	601	105	99	204	147	91	23	17	40	38	4	1947-48	1957-58
Curtale, Tony	Cgy.	1	2	0	0	0	0	....	....	....	....	....		1980-81	1980-81
Curtis, Paul	Mtl., L.A., St.L.	4	185	3	34	37	161	5	0	0	0	2		1969-70	1972-73
Cushenan, Ian	Chi., Mtl., NYR, Det.	5	129	3	11	14	134	....	....	....	....	....		1956-57	1963-64
Cusson, Jean	Oak.	1	2	0	0	0	0	....	....	....	....	....		1967-68	1967-68
Cyr, Denis	Cgy., Chi., St.L.	6	193	41	43	84	36	4	0	0	0	0		1980-81	1985-86
Cyr, Paul	Buf., NYR, Hfd.	9	470	101	140	241	623	24	4	6	10	31		1982-83	1991-92

			Regular Schedule					Playoffs					NHL Cup	First NHL	Last NHL
Name	NHL Teams	NHL Seasons	GP	G	A	TP	PIM	GP	G	A	TP	PIM	Wins	Season	Season
D															
Dahlin, Kjell	Mtl.	3	166	57	59	116	10	35	6	11	17	6	1	1985-86	1987-88
Dahlquist, Chris	Pit., Min., Cgy., Ott.	11	532	19	71	90	488	39	4	7	11	30		1985-86	1995-96
Dahlstrom, Cully	Chi.	8	342	88	118	206	58	29	6	8	14	4	1	1937-38	1944-45
Daigle, Alain	Chi.	6	389	56	50	106	122	17	0	1	1	0		1974-75	1979-80
Dailey, Bob	Van., Phi.	9	561	94	231	325	814	63	12	34	46	105		1973-74	1981-82
● Daley, Frank	Det.	1	5	0	0	0	0	2	0	0	0	0		1928-29	1928-29
Daley, Pat	Wpg.	2	12	1	0	1	13	....	....	....	....	....		1979-80	1980-81
Dalgarno, Brad	NYI	10	321	49	71	120	332	27	2	4	6	37		1985-86	1995-96
Dallman, Marty	Tor.	2	6	0	1	1	0	....	....	....	....	....		1987-88	1988-89
Dallman, Rod	NYI, Phi.	4	6	1	0	1	26	1	0	1	1	0		1987-88	1991-92
● Dame, Napoleon	Mtl.	1	34	2	5	7	4	....	....	....	....	....		1941-42	1941-42
Damore, Hank	NYR	1	4	1	0	1	2	....	....	....	....	....		1943-44	1943-44
Daniels, Kimbi	Phi.	2	27	1	2	3	4	....	....	....	....	....		1990-91	1991-92
Daoust, Dan	Mtl., Tor.	8	522	87	167	254	544	32	7	5	12	83		1982-83	1989-90
Dark, Michael	St.L.	2	43	5	6	11	14	....	....	....	....	....		1986-87	1987-88
● Darragh, Harold	Pit., Phi., Bos., Tor.	8	308	68	49	117	50	16	1	3	4	4	1	1925-26	1932-33
● Darragh, Jack	Ott.	6	121	67	45	112	113	23	15	2	17	17	3	1917-18	1923-24
David, Richard	Que.	3	31	4	4	8	10	1	0	0	0	0		1979-80	1982-83
● Davidson, Bob	Tor.	12	491	94	160	254	398	82	5	17	22	79	2	1934-35	1945-46
● Davidson, Gord	NYR	2	51	3	6	9	8	....	....	....	....	....		1942-43	1943-44
● Davie, Bob	Bos.	3	41	0	1	1	25	....	....	....	....	....		1933-34	1935-36
Davies, Buck	NYR	1	....	....	....	....	....	1	0	0	0	0		1947-48	1947-48
● Davis, Bob	Det.	1	3	0	0	0	0	....	....	....	....	....		1932-33	1932-33
Davis, Kim	Pit., Tor.	4	36	5	7	12	51	4	0	0	0	0		1977-78	1980-81
Davis, Lorne	Mtl., Chi., Det., Bos.	6	95	8	12	20	20	18	3	1	4	10	1	1951-52	1959-60
Davis, Mal	Det., Buf.	6	100	31	22	53	34	7	1	0	1	0		1980-81	1985-86
Davison, Murray	Bos.	1	1	0	0	0	0	....	....	....	....	....		1965-66	1965-66
Davydov, Evgeny	Wpg., Fla., Ott.	4	155	40	39	79	120	11	2	2	4	2		1991-92	1994-95
Dawes, Robert	Tor., Mtl.	4	32	2	7	9	6	10	0	0	0	2	1	1946-47	1950-51
● Day, Hap	Tor., NYA	14	581	86	116	202	601	53	4	7	11	56	1	1924-25	1937-38
Day, Joe	Hfd., NYI	3	72	1	10	11	87	....	....	....	....	....		1991-92	1993-94
Dea, Billy	Chi., NYR, Det., Pit.	8	397	67	54	121	44	11	2	1	3	6		1953-54	1970-71
● Deacon, Don	Det.	3	30	6	4	10	6	2	2	1	3	0		1936-37	1939-40
Deadmarsh, Butch	Buf., ATL, K.C.	5	137	12	5	17	155	4	0	0	0	17		1970-71	1974-75
Dean, Barry	Col., Phi.	3	165	25	56	81	146	....	....	....	....	....		1976-77	1978-79
Debenedet, Nelson	Det., Pit.	2	46	10	4	14	13	....	....	....	....	....		1973-74	1974-75
DeBlois, Lucien	NYR, Col., Wpg., Mtl., Que., Tor.	15	993	249	276	525	814	52	7	6	13	38		1977-78	1991-92
Debol, David	Hfd.	2	92	26	26	52	4	3	0	0	0	0		1979-80	1980-81
Defazio, Dean	Pit.	1	22	0	2	2	28	....	....	....	....	....		1983-84	1983-84
DeGray, Dale	Cgy., Tor. L.A., Buf.	5	153	18	47	65	195	13	1	3	4	28		1985-86	1989-90
● Delmonte, Armand	Bos.	1	1	0	0	0	0	....	....	....	....	....		1945-46	1945-46
Delorme, Gilbert	Mtl., St.L., Que., Det., Pit.	9	541	31	92	123	520	56	1	9	10	56		1981-82	1989-90
Delorme, Ron	Col., Van.	9	524	83	83	166	667	25	1	2	3	59		1976-77	1984-85
Delory, Valentine	NYR	1	1	0	0	0	0	....	....	....	....	....		1948-49	1948-49
Delparte, Guy	Col.	1	48	1	8	9	18	....	....	....	....	....		1976-77	1976-77
Delvecchio, Alex	Det.	24	1549	456	825	1281	383	121	35	69	104	29	3	1950-51	1973-74
DeMarco, Ab Jr.	NYR, St.L., Pit., Van., L.A., Bos.	9	344	44	80	124	75	25	1	2	3	17		1969-70	1978-79
● DeMarco, Ab Sr.	Chi., Tor., Bos., NYR	7	209	72	93	165	53	11	3	0	3	2		1938-39	1946-47
● Demers, Tony	Mtl., NYR	6	83	20	22	42	23	2	0	0	0	0		1937-38	1943-44
Denis, Jean-Paul	NYR	2	10	0	2	2	2	....	....	....	....	....		1946-47	1949-50
Denis, Lulu	Mtl.	2	3	0	1	1	0	....	....	....	....	....		1949-50	1950-51
● Denneny, Corb	Tor., Ham., Chi.	9	176	103	41	144	148	16	7	3	10	9	2	1917-18	1927-28
● Denneny, Cy	Ott., Bos.	12	326	246	85	331	290	43	21	8	29	51	5	1917-18	1928-29
Dennis, Norm	St.L.	4	12	3	0	3	11	5	0	0	0	2		1968-69	1971-72
● Denoird, Gerry	Tor.	1	15	0	0	0	0	....	....	....	....	....		1922-23	1922-23
DePalma, Larry	Min., S.J., Pit.	7	148	21	20	41	408	3	0	0	0	6		1985-86	1993-94
Derlago, Bill	Van., Bos., Wpg., Que., Tor.	9	555	189	227	416	247	13	5	0	5	8		1978-79	1986-87
● Desaulniers, Gerard	Mtl.	3	8	0	2	2	4	....	....	....	....	....		1950-51	1953-54
● Desilets, Joffre	Mtl., Chi.	5	192	37	45	82	57	7	1	0	1	7		1935-36	1939-40
Desjardins, Martin	Mtl.	1	8	0	2	2	2	....	....	....	....	....		1989-90	1989-90
● Desjardins, Vic	Chi., NYR	2	87	6	15	21	27	16	0	0	0	0		1930-31	1931-32
Deslauriers, Jacques	Mtl.	1	2	0	0	0	0	....	....	....	....	....		1955-56	1955-56
Devine, Kevin	NYI	1	2	0	1	1	8	....	....	....	....	....		1982-83	1982-83
● Dewar, Tom	NYR	1	9	0	2	2	4	....	....	....	....	....		1943-44	1943-44
Dewsbury, Al	Det., Chi.	9	347	30	78	108	365	14	1	5	6	16	1	1946-47	1955-56
Deziel, Michel	Buf.	1	....	....	....	....	....	1	0	0	0	0		1974-75	1974-75
Dheere, Marcel	Mtl.	1	11	1	2	3	2	5	0	0	0	6		1942-43	1942-43
Diachuk, Edward	Det.	1	12	0	0	0	19	....	....	....	....	....		1960-61	1960-61
Dick, Harry	Chi.	1	12	0	1	1	12	....	....	....	....	....		1946-47	1946-47
Dickens, Ernie	Tor., Chi.	6	278	12	44	56	98	13	0	0	0	4	1	1941-42	1950-51
Dickenson, Herb	NYR	2	48	18	17	35	10	....	....	....	....	....		1951-52	1952-53
Dietrich, Don	Chi., N.J.	2	28	0	7	7	10	....	....	....	....	....		1983-84	1985-86
● Dill, Bob	NYR	2	76	15	15	30	135	....	....	....	....	....		1943-44	1944-45
● Dillabough, Bob	Det., Bos., Pit., Oak.	9	283	32	54	86	76	17	3	0	3	0		1961-62	1969-70
● Dillon, Cecil	NYR, Det.	10	453	167	131	298	105	43	14	9	23	14	1	1930-31	1939-40
Dillon, Gary	Col.	1	13	1	1	2	29	....	....	....	....	....		1980-81	1980-81
Dillon, Wayne	NYR, Wpg.	4	229	43	66	109	60	3	0	1	1	0		1975-76	1979-80
Dineen, Bill	Det., Chi.	5	323	51	44	95	122	37	1	1	2	18	2	1953-54	1957-58
Dineen, Gary	Min.	1	4	0	1	1	0	....	....	....	....	....		1968-69	1968-69
Dineen, Gord	NYI, Min., Pit., Ott.	13	528	16	90	106	693	40	1	7	8	68		1982-83	1994-95
Dineen, Peter	L.A., Det.	2	13	0	2	2	13	....	....	....	....	....		1986-87	1989-90
● Dinsmore, Chuck	Mtl.M	4	100	6	2	8	50	12	1	0	1	6	1	1924-25	1929-30
Dionne, Marcel	Det., L.A., NYR	18	1348	731	1040	1771	600	49	21	24	45	17		1971-72	1988-89
Di Pietro, Paul	Mtl., Tor., L.A.	6	192	31	49	80	96	31	11	10	21	10	1	1991-92	1996-97
Dirk, Robert	St.L., Van., Chi., Ana., Mtl.	9	402	13	29	42	786	39	0	1	1	56		1987-88	1995-96
Djoos, Per	Det., NYR	3	82	2	31	33	58	....	....	....	....	....		1990-91	1992-93
Doak, Gary	Det., Bos., Van., NYR	16	789	23	107	130	908	78	2	4	6	121	1	1965-66	1980-81
Dobbin, Brian	Phi., Bos.	5	63	7	8	15	61	2	0	0	0	17		1986-87	1991-92
Dobson, Jim	Min., Col., Que.	4	12	0	0	0	6	....	....	....	....	....		1979-80	1983-84
● Doherty, Fred	Mtl.	1	2	0	0	0	0	....	....	....	....	....		1918-19	1918-19
Donaldson, Gary	Chi.	1	1	0	0	0	0	....	....	....	....	....		1973-74	1973-74
Donatelli, Clark	Min., Bos.	2	35	3	4	7	39	2	0	0	0	0		1989-90	1991-92
● Donnelly, Babe	Mtl.M.	1	34	0	1	1	14	2	0	0	0	0		1926-27	1926-27
Donnelly, Dave	Bos., Chi., Edm.	5	137	15	24	39	150	5	0	0	0	0		1983-84	1987-88
Donnelly, Gord	Que., Wpg., Buf., Dal.	12	554	28	41	69	2069	26	0	2	2	61		1983-84	1994-95
Donnelly, Mike	NYR, Buf., L.A., Dal., NYI	11	465	114	121	235	255	47	12	12	24	30		1986-87	1996-97
● Doran, John	NYA., Det., Mtl.	5	98	5	10	15	110	3	0	0	0	0		1933-34	1939-40
Doran, Lloyd	Det.	1	24	3	2	5	10	....	....	....	....	....		1946-47	1946-47
● Doraty, Ken	Chi., Tor., Det.	5	103	15	26	41	24	15	7	2	9	2		1926-27	1937-38
Dore, Andre	NYR, St.L., Que.	7	257	14	81	95	261	23	1	2	3	32		1978-79	1984-85
Dore, Daniel	Que.	2	17	2	3	5	59	....	....	....	....	....		1989-90	1990-91
Dorey, Jim	Tor., NYR	4	232	25	74	99	553	11	0	2	2	40		1968-69	1971-72
Dorion, Dan	N.J.	2	4	1	1	2	2	....	....	....	....	....		1985-86	1987-88
Dornhoefer, Gary	Bos., Phi.	14	787	214	328	542	1291	80	17	19	36	203	2	1963-64	1977-78
Dorohoy, Eddie	Mtl.	1	16	0	0	0	6	....	....	....	....	....		1948-49	1948-49
Douglas, Jordy	Hfd., Min., Wpg.	6	268	76	62	138	160	6	0	0	0	4		1979-80	1984-85
Douglas, Kent	Tor., Oak., Det.	7	428	33	115	148	631	19	1	3	4	33	1	1962-63	1968-69
Douglas, Les	Det.	4	52	6	12	18	8	10	3	2	5	2	1	1940-41	1946-47
● Downie, Dave	Tor.	1	11	0	1	1	2	....	....	....	....	....		1932-33	1932-33
Doyon, Mario	Chi., Que.	3	28	3	4	7	16	....	....	....	....	....		1988-89	1990-91
● Draper, Bruce	Tor.	1	1	0	0	0	0	....	....	....	....	....		1962-63	1962-63
● Drillon, Gordie	Tor., Mtl.	7	311	155	139	294	56	50	26	15	41	10	1	1936-37	1942-43
Driscoll, Pete	Edm.	2	60	3	8	11	97	3	0	0	0	0		1979-80	1980-81
Drolet, Rene	Phi., Det.	2	2	0	0	0	0	....	....	....	....	....		1971-72	1974-75
Droppa, Ivan	Chi.	2	19	0	1	1	14	....	....	....	....	....		1993-94	1995-96
● Drouillard, Clarence	Det.	1	10	0	1	1	0	....	....	....	....	....		1937-38	1937-38
Drouin, Jude	Mtl., Min., NYI, Wpg.	12	666	151	305	456	346	72	27	41	68	33		1968-69	1980-81
● Drouin, Polly	Mtl.	7	160	23	50	73	80	5	0	1	1	5		1935-36	1940-41
Drulia, Stan	T.B.	1	24	2	1	3	10	....	....	....	....	....		1992-93	1992-93

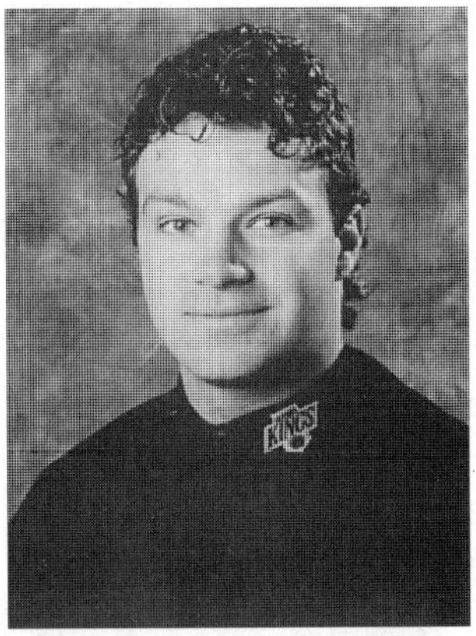
Paul DiPietro

Robert Dirk

Gord Donnelly

Mike Donnelly

Kent Douglas

Craig Duncanson

David Emma

Bernie Federko

Name	NHL Teams	NHL Seasons	Regular Schedule GP	G	A	TP	PIM	Playoffs GP	G	A	TP	PIM	NHL Cup Wins	First NHL Season	Last NHL Season
• Drummond, Jim	NYR	1	2	0	0	0	0	....	....	....	....	....		1944-45	1944-45
• Drury, Herb	Pit., Phi.	6	213	24	13	37	203	4	1	1	2	0		1925-26	1930-31
Dube, Gilles	Mtl., Det.	2	12	1	2	3	2	2	0	0	0	0	1	1949-50	1953-54
Dube, Norm	K.C.	2	57	8	10	18	54	....	....	....	....	....		1974-75	1975-76
Duberman, Justin	Pit.	1	4	0	0	0	0	....	....	....	....	....		1993-94	1993-94
Duchesne, Gaetan	Wsh., Que., Min., S.J., Fla.	14	1028	179	254	433	617	84	14	13	27	97		1981-82	1994-95
Dudley, Rick	Buf., Wpg.	6	309	75	99	174	292	25	7	2	9	69		1972-73	1980-81
Duff, Dick	Tor., NYR, Mtl., L.A., Buf.	18	1030	283	289	572	743	114	30	49	79	78	6	1954-55	1971-72
Dufour, Luc	Bos., Que., St.L.	3	167	23	21	44	199	18	1	0	1	32		1982-83	1984-85
Dufour, Marc	NYR, L.A.	3	14	1	0	1	2	....	....	....	....	....		1963-64	1968-69
• Duggan, Jack	Ott.	1	27	0	0	0	0	2	0	0	0	0		1925-26	1925-26
Duggan, Ken	Min.	1	1	0	0	0	0	....	....	....	....	....		1987-88	1987-88
Duguay, Ron	NYR, Det., Pit., L.A.	12	864	274	346	620	582	89	31	22	53	118		1977-78	1988-89
• Duguid, Lorne	Mtl.M, Det., Bos.	6	135	9	15	24	57	2	0	0	0	4		1931-32	1936-37
• Dukowski, Duke	Chi., NYA, NYR	5	200	16	30	46	172	6	0	0	0	6		1926-27	1933-34
Dumart, Woody	Bos.	16	772	211	218	429	99	88	12	15	27	23	2	1935-36	1953-54
Dunbar, Dale	Van., Bos.	2	2	0	0	0	2	....	....	....	....	....		1985-86	1988-89
• Duncan, Art	Det., Tor.	5	156	18	16	34	225	5	0	0	0	4		1926-27	1930-31
Duncan, Iain	Wpg.	4	127	34	55	89	149	11	0	3	3	6		1986-87	1990-91
Duncanson, Craig	L.A., Wpg., NYR	7	38	5	4	9	61	....	....	....	....	....		1985-86	1992-93
Dundas, Rocky	Tor.	1	5	0	0	0	14	....	....	....	....	....		1989-90	1989-90
• Dunlap, Frank	Tor.	1	15	0	1	1	2	....	....	....	....	....		1943-44	1943-44
Dunlop, Blake	Min., Phi., St.L., Det.	11	550	130	274	404	172	40	4	10	14	18		1973-74	1983-84
Dunn, Dave	Van., Tor.	3	184	14	41	55	313	10	1	1	2	41		1973-74	1975-76
Dunn, Richie	Buf., Cgy., Hfd.	12	483	36	140	176	314	36	3	15	18	24		1977-78	1988-89
Dupere, Denis	Tor., Wsh., St.L., K.C., Col.	8	421	80	99	179	66	16	1	0	1	0		1970-71	1977-78
Dupont, Andre	NYR, St.L., Phi., Que.	13	800	59	185	244	1986	140	14	18	32	352	2	1970-71	1982-83
Dupont, Jerome	Chi., Tor.	6	214	7	29	36	468	20	0	2	2	56		1981-82	1986-87
Dupont, Norm	Mtl., Wpg., Hfd.	5	256	55	85	140	52	13	4	2	6	0		1979-80	1983-84
• Dupre, Yanick	Phi.	3	35	2	0	2	16	....	....	....	....	....		1991-92	1995-96
Durbano, Steve	St.L., Pit., K.C., Col.	6	220	13	60	73	1127	5	0	2	2	8		1972-73	1978-79
Duris, Vitezslav	Tor.	2	89	3	20	23	62	3	0	1	1	2		1980-81	1982-83
Dussault, Norm	Mtl.	4	206	31	62	93	47	7	3	1	4	0		1947-48	1950-51
• Dutton, Red	Mtl.M, NYA	10	449	29	67	96	871	18	1	0	1	33		1926-27	1935-36
Dvorak, Miroslav	Phi.	3	193	11	74	85	51	18	0	2	2	6		1982-83	1984-85
Dwyer, Mike	Col., Cgy.	4	31	2	6	8	25	1	1	0	1	0		1978-79	1981-82
• Dyck, Henry	NYR	1	1	0	0	0	0	....	....	....	....	....		1943-44	1943-44
• Dye, Babe	Tor., Ham., Chi., NYA	11	271	202	44	246	221	15	11	1	12	14	1	1919-20	1930-31
Dykstra, Steven	Buf., Edm., Pit., Hfd.	5	217	8	32	40	545	1	0	0	0	2		1985-86	1989-90
Dyte, John	Chi.	1	27	1	0	1	31	....	....	....	....	....		1943-44	1943-44

E

Name	NHL Teams	NHL Seasons	Regular Schedule GP	G	A	TP	PIM	Playoffs GP	G	A	TP	PIM	NHL Cup Wins	First NHL Season	Last NHL Season
Eakin, Bruce	Cgy., Det.	4	13	2	2	4	4	....	....	....	....	....		1981-82	1985-86
Eatough, Jeff	Buf.	1	1	0	0	0	0	....	....	....	....	....		1981-82	1981-82
Eaves, Mike	Min., Cgy.	8	324	83	143	226	80	43	7	10	17	14		1978-79	1985-86
Eaves, Murray	Wpg., Det.	8	57	4	13	17	9	4	0	1	1	2		1980-81	1989-90
Ecclestone, Tim	St.L., Det., Tor., Atl.	11	692	126	233	359	344	48	6	11	17	76		1967-68	1977-78
Edberg, Rolf	Wsh.	3	184	45	58	103	24	....	....	....	....	....		1978-79	1980-81
• Eddolls, Frank	Mtl., NYR	8	317	23	43	66	114	31	0	2	2	10	1	1944-45	1951-52
Edestrand, Darryl	St.L., Phi., Pit., Bos., L.A.	10	455	34	90	124	404	42	3	9	12	57		1967-68	1978-79
Edmundson, Garry	Mtl., Tor.	3	43	4	6	10	49	11	0	1	1	8		1951-52	1960-61
Edur, Tom	Col., Pit	2	158	17	70	87	67	....	....	....	....	....		1976-77	1977-78
Egan, Pat	NYA, Bro., Det., Bos., NYR	11	554	77	153	230	776	44	9	4	13	44		1939-40	1950-51
Egers, Jack	NYR, St.L., Wsh.	7	284	64	69	133	154	32	5	6	11	32		1969-70	1975-76
Ehman, Gerry	Bos., Det., Tor., Oak, Cal.	9	429	96	118	214	100	41	10	10	20	12	1	1957-58	1970-71
Eisenhut, Neil	Van., Cgy.	2	16	1	3	4	21	....	....	....	....	....		1993-94	1994-95
Eklund, Pelle	Phi., Dal.	9	594	120	335	455	109	66	10	36	46	8		1985-86	1993-94
Eldebrink, Anders	Van., Que.	2	55	3	11	14	29	14	0	0	0	10		1981-82	1982-83
Elik, Boris	Det.	1	3	0	0	0	0	....	....	....	....	....		1962-63	1962-63
• Elliot, Fred	Ott.	1	43	2	0	2	6	....	....	....	....	....		1928-29	1928-29
Ellis, Ron	Tor.	16	1034	332	308	640	207	70	18	8	26	20	1	1963-64	1980-81
Eloranta, Kari	Cgy., St.L.	5	267	13	103	116	155	26	1	7	8	19		1981-82	1986-87
Elynuik, Pat	Wpg., Wsh., T.B., Ott.	9	506	154	188	342	459	20	6	9	15	25		1987-88	1995-96
Emberg, Eddie	Mtl.	1	....	....	....	....	....	2	1	0	1	0		1944-45	1944-45
Emma, David	N.J., Bos.	4	28	5	6	11	2	....	....	....	....	....		1992-93	1996-97
Emmons, Gary	S.J.	1	3	1	0	1	0	....	....	....	....	....		1993-94	1993-94
• Emms, Hap	Mtl.M, NYA, Det., Bos.	10	320	36	53	89	311	14	0	0	0	12		1926-27	1937-38
Endean, Craig	Wpg.	1	2	0	1	1	0	....	....	....	....	....		1986-87	1986-87
Engblom, Brian	Mtl., Wsh., L.A., Buf., Cgy.	11	659	29	177	206	599	48	3	9	12	43	3	1976-77	1986-87
Engele, Jerry	Min.	3	100	2	13	15	162	2	0	1	1	0		1975-76	1977-78
English, John	L.A.	1	3	1	3	4	4	1	0	0	0	0		1987-88	1987-88
Ennis, Jim	Edm.	1	5	1	0	1	10	....	....	....	....	....		1987-88	1987-88
Erickson, Aut	Bos., Chi., Oak., Tor.	7	226	7	24	31	182	7	0	0	0	2	1	1959-60	1969-70
Erickson, Bryan	Wsh., L.A., Pit., Wpg.	9	351	80	125	205	141	14	3	4	7	7		1983-84	1993-94
Erickson, Grant	Bos., Min.	2	6	1	0	1	0	....	....	....	....	....		1968-69	1969-70
Eriksson, Peter	Edm.	1	20	3	3	6	24	....	....	....	....	....		1989-90	1989-90
Eriksson, Roland	Min., Van.	3	193	48	95	143	26	2	1	0	1	0		1976-77	1978-79
Eriksson, Thomas	Phi.	5	208	22	76	98	107	19	0	3	3	12		1980-81	1985-86
Erixon, Jan	NYR	10	556	57	159	216	167	58	7	7	14	16		1983-84	1992-93
Esposito, Phil	Chi., Bos., NYR	18	1282	717	873	1590	910	130	61	76	137	138	2	1963-64	1980-81
Evans, Chris	Tor., Buf., St.L., Det., K.C.	5	241	19	42	61	143	12	1	1	2	8		1969-70	1974-75
Evans, Daryl	L.A., Wsh., Tor.	6	113	22	30	52	25	11	5	8	13	12		1981-82	1986-87
Evans, Doug	St.L., Wpg., Phi.	8	355	48	87	135	502	22	3	4	7	38		1985-86	1992-93
Evans, J. Paul	Phi.	3	103	14	25	39	34	1	0	0	0	0		1978-79	1982-83
• Evans, Jack	NYR, Chi.	14	752	19	80	99	989	56	2	2	4	97	1	1948-49	1962-63
Evans, Kevin	Min., S.J.	2	9	0	1	1	44	....	....	....	....	....		1990-91	1991-92
Evans, Paul E.	Tor.	2	11	1	1	2	21	2	0	0	0	0		1976-77	1977-78
Evans, Shawn	St. L., NYI	2	9	1	0	1	2	....	....	....	....	....		1985-86	1989-90
• Evans, Stewart	Det., Mtl.M., Mtl.	8	367	28	49	77	425	26	0	0	0	20	1	1930-31	1938-39
Evason, Dean	Wsh., Hfd., S.J., Dal., Cgy.	13	803	139	233	372	1002	55	9	20	29	132		1983-84	1995-96
Ezinicki, Bill	Tor., Bos., NYR	9	368	79	105	184	713	40	5	8	13	87	3	1944-45	1954-55

F

Name	NHL Teams	NHL Seasons	Regular Schedule GP	G	A	TP	PIM	Playoffs GP	G	A	TP	PIM	NHL Cup Wins	First NHL Season	Last NHL Season
Fahey, Trevor	NYR	1	1	0	0	0	0	....	....	....	....	....		1964-65	1964-65
Fairbairn, Bill	NYR, Min. St.L.	11	658	162	261	423	173	54	13	22	35	42		1968-69	1978-79
Falkenberg, Bob	Det.	5	54	1	5	6	26	....	....	....	....	....		1966-67	1971-72
Farrant, Walt	Chi.	1	1	0	0	0	0	....	....	....	....	....		1943-44	1943-44
Farrish, Dave	NYR, Que, Tor.	7	430	17	110	127	440	14	0	2	2	24		1976-77	1983-84
Fashoway, Gordie	Chi.	1	13	3	2	5	14	....	....	....	....	....		1950-51	1950-51
Faubert, Mario	Pit.	7	231	21	90	111	292	10	2	2	4	6		1974-75	1981-82
Faulkner, Alex	Tor., Det.	3	101	15	17	32	15	12	5	0	5	2		1961-62	1963-64
Fauss, Ted	Tor.	2	28	0	2	2	15	....	....	....	....	....		1986-87	1987-88
Faust, Andre	Phi.	2	47	10	7	17	14	....	....	....	....	....		1992-93	1993-94
Feamster, Dave	Chi.	4	169	13	24	37	154	33	3	5	8	61		1981-82	1984-85
Featherstone, Tony	Oak., Cal., Min.	3	130	17	21	38	65	2	0	0	0	0		1969-70	1973-74
Federko, Bernie	St.L., Det.	14	1000	369	761	1130	487	91	35	66	101	83		1976-77	1989-90
Fedotov, Anatoli	Wpg., Ana.	2	4	0	2	2	0	....	....	....	....	....		1992-93	1993-94
Felix, Chris	Wsh.	4	35	1	12	13	10	2	0	1	1	0		1987-88	1990-91
Felsner, Denny	St.L.	4	18	1	4	5	6	10	2	3	5	2		1991-92	1994-95
Feltrin, Tony	Pit., NYR	4	48	3	3	6	65	....	....	....	....	....		1980-81	1985-86
Fenton, Paul	Hfd., NYR, L.A., Wpg., Tor., Cgy., S.J.	8	411	100	83	183	198	17	4	1	5	27		1984-85	1991-92
Fenyves, David	Buf., Phi.	9	206	3	32	35	119	11	0	0	0	9		1982-83	1990-91
Fergus, Tom	Bos., Tor., Van.	12	726	235	346	581	499	65	21	17	38	48		1981-82	1992-93
Ferguson, George	Tor., Pit, Min	12	797	160	238	398	431	86	14	23	37	44		1972-73	1983-84
Ferguson, John	Mtl.	8	500	145	158	303	1214	85	20	18	38	260	5	1963-64	1970-71
Ferguson, Lorne	Bos., Det., Chi.	8	422	82	80	162	193	31	6	3	9	24		1949-50	1958-59
Ferguson, Norm	Oak., Cal.	4	279	73	66	139	72	10	1	4	5	7		1968-69	1971-72
Ferner, Mark	Buf., Wsh., Ana., Det.	6	91	3	10	13	51	....	....	....	....	....		1986-87	1994-95
Fidler, Mike	Cle., Min, Hfd., Chi.	7	271	84	97	181	124	....	....	....	....	....		1976-77	1982-83
• Field, Wilf	Bro., Mtl., Chi., NYA	6	219	17	25	42	151	5	0	0	0	2		1936-37	1944-45

Name	NHL Teams	NHL Seasons	Regular Schedule					Playoffs					NHL Cup Wins	First NHL Season	Last NHL Season
			GP	G	A	TP	PIM	GP	G	A	TP	PIM			
Fielder, Guyle	Det., Chi., Bos.	4	9	0	0	0	2	6	0	0	0	2		1950-51	1957-58
Filimonov, Dmitri	Ott.	1	30	1	4	5	18	....	....	....	....	....		1993-94	1993-94
Fillion, Bob	Mtl.	7	327	42	61	103	84	33	7	4	11	10	2	1943-44	1949-50
Fillion, Marcel	Bos.	1	1	0	0	0	0	....	....	....	....	....		1944-45	1944-45
• Filmore, Tommy	Det., NYA, Bos.	4	117	15	12	27	33	....	....	....	....	....		1930-31	1933-34
Finkbeiner, Lloyd	NYA	1	2	0	0	0	0	....	....	....	....	....		1940-41	1940-41
Finney, Sid	Chi.	3	59	10	7	17	4	7	0	2	2	0		1951-52	1953-54
• Finnigan, Ed	St.L., Bos.	2	15	1	1	2	2	....	....	....	....	....		1934-35	1935-36
• Finnigan, Frank	Ott., Tor., St.L.	14	553	115	88	203	405	38	6	9	15	22	2	1923-24	1936-37
Fiorentino, Peter	NYR	1	1	0	0	0	0	....	....	....	....	....		1991-92	1991-92
Fischer, Ron	Buf.	2	18	0	7	7	6	....	....	....	....	....		1981-82	1982-83
• Fisher, Alvin	Tor.	1	9	1	0	1	4	....	....	....	....	....		1924-25	1924-25
Fisher, Dunc	NYR, Bos., Det.	7	275	45	70	115	104	21	4	4	8	14	1	1947-48	1958-59
Fisher, Joe	Det.	4	65	8	12	20	13	12	2	1	3	6	1	1939-40	1942-43
Fitchner, Bob	Que	2	78	12	20	32	59	3	0	0	0	10		1979-80	1980-81
Fitzgerald, Rusty	Pit.	2	25	2	2	4	12	5	0	0	0	4		1994-95	1995-96
Fitzpatrick, Ross	Phi.	4	20	5	2	7	0	....	....	....	....	....		1982-83	1985-86
Fitzpatrick, Sandy	NYR, Min.	2	22	3	6	9	8	12	0	0	0	0		1964-65	1967-68
Flaman, Fernie	Bos., Tor.	17	910	34	174	208	1370	63	4	8	12	93	1	1944-45	1960-61
Flatley, Pat	NYI, NYR	14	780	170	340	510	686	70	18	15	33	75		1983-84	1996-97
Fleming, Gerry	Mtl.	2	11	0	0	0	42	....	....	....	....	....		1993-94	1994-95
Fleming, Reggie	Mtl., Chi., Bos., NYR, Phi., Buf.	12	749	108	132	240	1468	50	3	6	9	106	1	1959-60	1970-71
Flesch, John	Min, Pit, Col.	4	124	18	23	41	117	....	....	....	....	....		1974-75	1979-80
Fletcher, Steven	Mtl., Wpg.	2	3	0	0	0	5	1	0	0	0	5		1987-88	1988-89
Flett, Bill	L.A., Phi., Tor., Atl, Edm.	11	689	202	215	417	501	52	7	16	23	42	1	1967-68	1979-80
Flichel, Todd	Wpg.	3	6	0	1	1	4	....	....	....	....	....		1987-88	1989-90
Flockhart, Rob	Van., Min	5	55	2	5	7	14	1	1	0	1	2		1976-77	1980-81
Flockhart, Ron	Phi., Pit., Mtl., St.L., Bos.	9	453	145	183	328	208	19	4	6	10	14		1980-81	1988-89
Floyd, Larry	N.J.	2	12	2	3	5	9	....	....	....	....	....		1982-83	1983-84
Fogolin, Lee	Buf., Edm.	13	924	44	195	239	1318	108	5	19	24	173	2	1974-75	1986-87
Fogolin, Lidio	Det., Chi.	9	427	10	48	58	575	28	0	2	2	30	1	1947-48	1955-56
Folco, Peter	Van.	1	2	0	0	0	0	....	....	....	....	....		1973-74	1973-74
Foley, Gerry	Tor., NYR, L.A.	4	142	9	14	23	99	9	0	1	1	2		1954-55	1968-69
Foley, Rick	Chi., Phi., Det.	3	67	11	26	37	180	4	0	1	1	4		1970-71	1973-74
Foligno, Mike	Det., Buf., Tor., Fla.	15	1018	355	372	727	2049	57	15	17	32	185		1979-80	1993-94
Folk, Bill	Det.	2	12	0	0	0	4	....	....	....	....	....		1951-52	1952-53
Fontaine, Len	Det.	2	46	8	11	19	10	....	....	....	....	....		1972-73	1973-74
Fontas, Jon	Min.	2	2	0	0	0	0	....	....	....	....	....		1979-80	1980-81
Fonteyne, Val	Det., NYR, Pit.	13	820	75	154	229	26	59	3	10	13	8		1959-60	1971-72
Fontinato, Lou	NYR, Mtl.	9	535	26	78	104	1247	21	0	2	2	42		1954-55	1962-63
Forbes, Dave	Bos., Wsh.	6	363	64	64	128	341	45	1	4	5	13		1973-74	1978-79
Forbes, Mike	Bos., Edm.	3	50	1	11	12	41	....	....	....	....	....		1977-78	1981-82
Forey, Connie	St.L.	1	4	0	0	0	2	....	....	....	....	....		1973-74	1973-74
• Forsey, Jack	Tor.	1	19	7	9	16	10	3	0	1	1	0		1942-43	1942-43
• Forslund, Gus	Ott.	1	48	4	9	13	2	....	....	....	....	....		1932-33	1932-33
Forslund, Tomas	Cgy.	2	44	5	11	16	12	....	....	....	....	....		1991-92	1992-93
Forsyth, Alex	Wsh.	1	1	0	0	0	0	....	....	....	....	....		1976-77	1976-77
• Fortier, Charles	Mtl.	1	1	0	0	0	0	....	....	....	....	....		1923-24	1923-24
Fortier, Dave	Tor., NYI, Van.	4	205	8	21	29	335	20	0	2	2	33		1972-73	1976-77
Fortier, Marc	Que., Ott., L.A.	6	212	42	60	102	135	....	....	....	....	....		1987-88	1992-93
Fortin, Ray	St.L.	3	92	2	6	8	33	6	0	0	0	8		1967-68	1969-70
Foster, Corey	N.J., Phi., Pit., NYI	4	45	5	6	11	24	3	0	0	0	4		1988-89	1996-97
Foster, Dwight	Bos., Col., N.J., Det.	10	541	111	163	274	420	35	5	12	17	4		1977-78	1986-87
Foster, Herb	NYR	2	6	1	0	1	5	....	....	....	....	....		1940-41	1947-48
• Foster, Yip	NYR, Bos., Det.	4	83	3	2	5	32	....	....	....	....	....		1929-30	1934-35
Fotiu, Nick	NYR, Hfd., Cgy., Phi., Edm.	13	646	60	77	137	1362	38	0	4	4	67		1976-77	1988-89
• Fowler, Jimmy	Tor.	3	135	18	29	47	39	18	0	3	3	2		1936-37	1938-39
Fowler, Tom	Chi.	1	24	0	1	1	18	....	....	....	....	....		1946-47	1946-47
Fox, Greg	Atl, Chi., Pit.	8	494	14	92	106	637	44	1	9	10	67		1977-78	1984-85
Fox, Jim	L.A.	9	578	186	293	479	143	22	4	8	12	0		1980-81	1989-90
• Foyston, Frank	Det.	2	64	17	7	24	32	....	....	....	....	....		1926-27	1927-28
Frampton, Bob	Mtl.	1	2	0	0	0	0	3	0	0	0	0		1949-50	1949-50
Franceschetti, Lou	Wsh., Tor., Buf.	10	459	59	81	140	747	44	3	2	5	111		1981-82	1991-92
Francis, Bobby	Det.	1	14	2	0	2	0	....	....	....	....	....		1982-83	1982-83
• Fraser, Archie	NYR	1	3	0	1	1	0	....	....	....	....	....		1943-44	1943-44
• Fraser, Charles	Ham.	1	1	0	0	0	0	....	....	....	....	....		1923-24	1923-24
Fraser, Curt	Van., Chi., Min.	12	704	193	240	433	1306	65	15	18	33	198		1978-79	1989-90
• Fraser, Gord	Chi., Det., Mtl., Pit., Phi.	5	144	24	12	36	224	2	1	0	1	6		1926-27	1930-31
Fraser, Harvey	Chi.	1	21	5	4	9	0	....	....	....	....	....		1944-45	1944-45
Frawley, Dan	Chi., Pit.	6	273	37	40	77	674	1	0	0	0	0		1983-84	1988-89
• Fredrickson, Frank	Det., Bos., Pit.	5	161	39	34	73	206	10	2	5	7	26	1	1926-27	1930-31
• Frew, Irv	Mtl.M, St.L., Mtl.	3	96	2	5	7	146	4	0	0	0	6		1933-34	1935-36
Friday, Tim	Det.	1	23	0	3	3	6	....	....	....	....	....		1985-86	1985-86
Fridgen, Dan	Hfd.	2	13	2	3	5	2	....	....	....	....	....		1981-82	1982-83
Friest, Ron	Min.	3	64	7	7	14	191	6	1	0	1	7		1980-81	1982-83
Frig, Len	Chi., Cal., Cle., St.L.	7	311	13	51	64	479	14	2	1	3	0		1972-73	1979-80
Frost, Harry	Bos.	1	4	0	0	0	0	1	0	0	0	0		1938-39	1938-39
Frycer, Miroslav	Que., Tor., Det., Edm.	8	415	147	183	330	486	17	3	8	11	16		1981-82	1988-89
Fryday, Bob	Mtl.	2	5	1	0	1	0	....	....	....	....	....		1949-50	1951-52
Ftorek, Robbie	Det., Que, NYR	8	334	77	150	227	262	19	9	6	15	28		1972-73	1984-85
Fullan, Larry	Wsh.	1	4	1	0	1	0	....	....	....	....	....		1974-75	1974-75
Fusco, Mark	Hfd.	2	80	3	12	15	42	....	....	....	....	....		1983-84	1984-85

G

Name	NHL Teams	NHL Seasons	GP	G	A	TP	PIM	GP	G	A	TP	PIM	NHL Cup Wins	First NHL Season	Last NHL Season
Gadsby, Bill	Chi., NYR, Det.	20	1248	130	438	568	1539	67	4	23	27	92		1946-47	1965-66
Gaetz, Link	Min., S.J.	3	65	6	8	14	412	....	....	....	....	....		1988-89	1991-92
Gage, Jody	Det., Buf.	6	68	14	15	29	26	....	....	....	....	....		1980-81	1991-92
• Gagne, Art	Mtl., Bos., Ott., Det.	6	228	67	33	100	257	11	2	1	3	20		1926-27	1931-32
Gagne, Paul	Col., N.J., Tor., NYI	8	390	110	101	211	127	....	....	....	....	....		1980-81	1989-90
Gagne, Pierre	Bos.	1	2	0	0	0	0	....	....	....	....	....		1959-60	1959-60
Gagnon, Germaine	Mtl., NYI, Chi., K.C.	5	259	40	101	141	72	19	2	3	5	2		1971-72	1975-76
• Gagnon, Johnny	Mtl., Bos., NYA	10	454	120	141	261	295	32	12	12	24	37		1930-31	1939-40
Gainey, Bob	Mtl.	16	1160	239	262	501	585	182	25	48	73	151	5	1973-74	1988-89
• Gainor, Norm	Bos., NYR, Ott., Mtl.M	7	246	51	56	107	129	22	2	1	3	14	2	1927-28	1934-35
Galarneau, Michel	Hfd.	3	78	7	10	17	34	....	....	....	....	....		1980-81	1982-83
• Galbraith, Percy	Bos., Ott.	8	347	29	31	60	224	31	4	7	11	24		1926-27	1933-34
• Gallagher, John	Mtl.M, Det., NYA	7	205	14	19	33	153	24	2	3	5	27	1	1930-31	1938-39
Gallant, Gerard	Det., T.B.	11	615	211	269	480	1674	58	18	21	39	178		1984-85	1994-95
Gallimore, Jamie	Min.	1	2	0	0	0	0	....	....	....	....	....		1977-78	1977-78
• Gallinger, Don	Bos.	5	222	65	88	153	89	23	5	5	10	19		1942-43	1947-48
Gamble, Dick	Mtl., Chi., Tor.	8	195	41	41	82	66	14	1	2	3	4	2	1950-51	1966-67
Gambucci, Gary	Min.	2	51	2	7	9	9	....	....	....	....	....		1971-72	1973-74
Ganchar, Perry	St. L., Mtl., Pit.	4	42	3	7	10	36	7	3	1	4	0		1983-84	1988-89
Gans, Dave	L.A.	2	6	0	0	0	2	....	....	....	....	....		1982-83	1985-86
• Gardiner, Herb	Mtl., Chi.	3	101	10	9	19	52	9	0	1	1	14		1926-27	1928-29
Gardner, Bill	Chi., Hfd.	9	380	73	115	188	68	45	3	8	11	17		1980-81	1988-89
Gardner, Cal	NYR, Tor., Chi., Bos.	12	696	154	238	392	517	61	7	10	17	20	2	1945-46	1956-57
Gardner, Dave	Mtl., St.L., Cal., Cle., Phi.	7	350	75	115	190	41	....	....	....	....	....		1972-73	1979-80
Gardner, Paul	Col., Tor., Pit., Wsh., Buf.	10	447	201	201	402	207	16	2	6	8	14		1976-77	1985-86
Gare, Danny	Buf., Det., Edm.	13	827	354	331	685	1285	64	25	21	46	195		1974-75	1986-87
Gariepy, Ray	Bos., Tor.	2	36	1	6	7	43	....	....	....	....	....		1953-54	1955-56
• Garland, Scott	Tor., L.A.	3	91	13	24	37	115	7	1	2	3	35		1975-76	1978-79
Garner, Rob	Pit.	1	1	0	0	0	0	....	....	....	....	....		1982-83	1982-83
• Garrett, Red	NYR	1	23	1	1	2	18	....	....	....	....	....		1942-43	1942-43
• Gassoff, Bob	St.L.	4	245	11	47	58	866	9	0	1	1	16		1973-74	1976-77
Gassoff, Brad	Van.	4	122	19	17	36	163	3	0	0	0	0		1975-76	1978-79
Gatzos, Steve	Pit.	4	89	15	20	35	83	1	0	0	0	0		1981-82	1984-85
Gaudreault, Armand	Bos.	1	44	15	9	24	27	7	0	2	2	8		1944-45	1944-45
• Gaudreault, Leo	Mtl.	3	67	8	4	12	30	....	....	....	....	....		1927-28	1932-33
Gaulin, Jean-Marc	Que.	4	26	4	3	7	8	1	0	0	0	0		1982-83	1985-86
Gaume, Dallas	Hfd.	1	4	1	1	2	0	....	....	....	....	....		1988-89	1988-89

Frank Finnegan

Pat Flatley

Dwight Foster

Bernie Geoffrion

Randy Gilhen

Ebbie Goodfellow

Brent Gretzky

Brent Grieve

Name	NHL Teams	NHL Seasons	Regular Schedule GP	G	A	TP	PIM	Playoffs GP	G	A	TP	PIM	NHL Cup Wins	First NHL Season	Last NHL Season
● Gauthier, Art	Mtl.	1	13	0	0	0	0	1	0	0	0	0		1926-27	1926-27
Gauthier, Daniel	Chi.	1	5	0	0	0	0	....	....	....	....	....		1994-95	1994-95
● Gauthier, Fern	NYR, Mtl., Det.	6	229	46	50	96	35	22	5	1	6	7		1943-44	1948-49
Gauthier, Jean	Mtl., Phi., Bos.	10	166	6	29	35	150	14	1	3	4	22	1	1960-61	1969-70
Gauthier, Luc	Mtl.	1	3	0	0	0	2	....	....	....	....	....		1990-91	1990-91
Gauvreau, Jocelyn	Mtl.	1	2	0	0	0	0	....	....	....	....	....		1983-84	1983-84
Gavin, Stewart	Tor., Hfd., Min.	13	768	130	155	285	584	66	14	20	34	75		1980-81	1992-93
Geale, Bob	Pit.	1	1	0	0	0	2	....	....	....	....	....		1984-85	1984-85
● Gee, George	Chi., Det.	9	551	135	183	318	345	41	6	13	19	32	1	1945-46	1953-54
Geldart, Gary	Min.	1	4	0	0	0	5	....	....	....	....	....		1970-71	1970-71
Gendron, Jean-Guy	NYR, Mtl., Bos., Phi.	14	863	182	201	383	701	42	7	4	11	47		1955-56	1971-72
Geoffrion, Bernie	Mtl., NYR	16	883	393	429	822	689	132	58	60	118	88	6	1950-51	1967-68
Geoffrion, Danny	Mtl., Wpg.	3	111	20	32	52	99	2	0	0	0	7		1979-80	1981-82
● Geran, Gerry	Mtl.W., Bos.	2	34	5	1	6	6	....	....	....	....	....		1917-18	1925-26
● Gerard, Eddie	Ott., Tor.	6	128	50	47	97	120	27	7	1	8	71	4	1917-18	1922-23
Germain, Eric	L.A.	1	4	0	1	1	13	1	0	0	0	4		1987-88	1987-88
Getliffe, Ray	Bos., Mtl.	10	393	136	137	273	250	45	9	10	19	30	2	1935-36	1944-45
Giallonardo, Mario	Col.	2	23	0	3	3	6	....	....	....	....	....		1979-80	1980-81
Gibbs, Barry	Bos., Min., Atl., St.L., L.A.	13	797	58	224	282	945	36	4	2	6	67		1967-68	1979-80
Gibson, Don	Van.	1	14	0	3	3	20	....	....	....	....	....		1990-91	1990-91
Gibson, Doug	Bos., Wsh.	3	63	9	19	28	0	1	0	0	0	0		1973-74	1977-78
Gibson, John	L.A., Tor., Wpg.	3	48	0	2	2	120	....	....	....	....	....		1980-81	1983-84
Giesebrecht, Gus	Det.	4	135	27	51	78	13	17	2	3	5	0		1938-39	1941-42
Giffin, Lee	Pit.	2	27	1	3	4	9	....	....	....	....	....		1986-87	1987-88
Gilbert, Ed	K.C., Pit.	3	166	21	31	52	22	....	....	....	....	....		1974-75	1976-77
Gilbert, Greg	NYI, Chi., NYR, St.L.	15	837	150	228	378	576	133	17	33	50	162	3	1981-82	1995-96
Gilbert, Jeannot	Bos.	2	9	0	1	1	4	....	....	....	....	....		1962-63	1964-65
Gilbert, Rod	NYR	18	1065	406	615	1021	508	79	34	33	67	43		1960-61	1977-78
Gilbertson, Stan	Cal., St.L., Wsh., Pit.	6	428	85	89	174	148	3	1	1	2	2		1971-72	1976-77
Giles, Curt	Min., NYR, St.L.	14	895	43	199	242	733	103	6	16	22	118		1979-80	1992-93
Gilhen, Randy	Hfd., Wpg., Pit., L.A., NYR, T.B., Fla.	11	457	55	60	115	314	33	3	2	5	26	1	1982-83	1995-96
Gillen, Don	Phi., Hfd.	2	35	2	4	6	22	....	....	....	....	....		1979-80	1981-82
● Gillie, Farrand	Det.	1	1	0	0	0	0	....	....	....	....	....		1928-29	1928-29
Gillies, Clark	NYI, Buf.	14	958	319	378	697	1023	164	47	47	94	287	4	1974-75	1987-88
Gillis, Jere	Que., Buf., Phi., Van., NYR	9	386	78	95	173	230	19	4	7	11	9		1977-78	1986-87
Gillis, Mike	Col., Bos.	6	246	33	43	76	186	27	2	5	7	10		1978-79	1983-84
Gillis, Paul	Que., Chi., Hfd.	11	624	88	154	242	1498	42	3	14	17	156		1982-83	1992-93
Gingras, Gaston	Mtl., Tor., St.L.	10	476	61	174	235	161	52	6	18	24	20	1	1979-80	1988-89
Girard, Bob	Cal., Cle., Wsh.	5	305	45	69	114	140	....	....	....	....	....		1975-76	1979-80
Girard, Kenny	Tor.	3	7	0	1	1	2	....	....	....	....	....		1956-57	1959-60
● Giroux, Art	Mtl., Bos., Det.	3	54	6	4	10	14	2	0	0	0	0		1932-33	1935-36
Giroux, Larry	St.L., K.C., Det., Hfd.	7	274	15	74	89	333	5	0	0	0	4		1973-74	1979-80
Giroux, Pierre	L.A.	1	6	1	0	1	17	....	....	....	....	....		1982-83	1982-83
Gladney, Bob	L.A., Pit.	2	14	1	5	6	4	....	....	....	....	....		1982-83	1983-84
Gladu, Jean-Paul	Bos.	1	40	6	14	20	2	7	2	2	4	0		1944-45	1944-45
Glennie, Brian	Tor., L.A.	10	572	14	100	114	621	32	0	1	1	66		1969-70	1978-79
Glennon, Matt	Bos.	1	3	0	0	0	2	....	....	....	....	....		1991-92	1991-92
Gloeckner, Lorry	Det.	1	13	0	2	2	6	....	....	....	....	....		1978-79	1978-79
Gloor, Dan	Van.	1	2	0	0	0	0	....	....	....	....	....		1973-74	1973-74
Glover, Fred	Det., Chi.	5	92	13	11	24	62	8	0	0	0	0	1	1948-49	1952-53
Glover, Howie	Chi., Det., NYR, Mtl.	5	144	29	17	46	101	11	1	2	3	2		1958-59	1968-69
Godden, Ernie	Tor.	1	5	1	1	2	6	....	....	....	....	....		1981-82	1981-82
Godfrey, Warren	Bos., Det.	16	786	32	125	157	752	52	1	4	5	42		1952-53	1967-68
Godin, Eddy	Wsh.	2	27	3	6	9	12	....	....	....	....	....		1977-78	1978-79
● Godin, Sammy	Ott., Mtl.	3	83	4	3	7	36	....	....	....	....	....		1927-28	1933-34
Goegan, Pete	Det., NYR, Min.	11	383	19	67	86	365	33	1	3	4	61		1957-58	1967-68
Goertz, Dave	Pit.	1	2	0	0	0	2	....	....	....	....	....		1987-88	1987-88
● Goldham, Bob	Tor., Chi., Det.	12	650	28	143	171	400	66	3	14	17	53	5	1941-42	1955-56
● Goldsworthy, Bill	Bos., Min., NYR	14	771	283	258	541	793	40	18	19	37	30		1964-65	1977-78
● Goldsworthy, Leroy	NYR, Det., Chi., Mtl., Bos., NYA	10	336	66	57	123	79	24	1	0	1	4	1	1929-30	1938-39
Goldup, Glenn	Mtl., L.A.	9	291	52	67	119	303	16	4	3	7	22		1973-74	1981-82
Goldup, Hank	Tor., NYR	6	202	63	80	143	97	26	5	1	6	6	1	1939-40	1945-46
Gooden, Bill	NYR	2	53	9	11	20	15	....	....	....	....	....		1942-43	1943-44
Goodenough, Larry	Phi., Van.	6	242	22	77	99	179	22	3	15	18	10	1	1974-75	1979-80
● Goodfellow, Ebbie	Det.	14	557	134	190	324	511	45	8	8	16	65	3	1929-30	1942-43
Gordiouk, Viktor	Buf.	2	26	3	8	11	0	....	....	....	....	....		1992-93	1994-95
Gordon, Fred	Det., Bos.	2	81	8	7	15	68	2	0	0	0	0		1926-27	1927-28
Gordon, Jackie	NYR	3	36	3	10	13	0	9	1	1	2	7		1948-49	1950-51
Gorence, Tom	Phi., Edm.	6	303	58	53	111	89	37	9	6	15	47		1978-79	1983-84
Goring, Butch	L.A., NYI, Bos.	16	1107	375	513	888	102	134	38	50	88	32	4	1969-70	1984-85
Gorman, Dave	Atl.	1	3	0	0	0	0	....	....	....	....	....		1979-80	1979-80
● Gorman, Ed	Ott., Tor.	4	113	14	5	19	108	8	0	0	0	2	1	1924-25	1927-28
Gosselin, Benoit	NYR	1	7	0	0	0	33	....	....	....	....	....		1977-78	1977-78
Gosselin, Guy	Wpg.	1	5	0	0	0	6	....	....	....	....	....		1987-88	1987-88
Gotaas, Steve	Pit., Min.	3	49	6	9	15	53	3	0	1	1	5		1987-88	1990-91
● Gottselig, Johnny	Chi.	16	589	176	195	371	203	43	13	13	26	18	2	1928-29	1944-45
Gould, Bobby	Atl., Cgy., Wsh., Bos.	11	697	145	159	304	572	78	15	13	28	58		1979-80	1989-90
Gould, John	Buf., Van., Atl.	9	504	131	138	269	113	14	3	2	5	4		1971-72	1979-80
Gould, Larry	Van.	1	2	0	0	0	0	....	....	....	....	....		1973-74	1973-74
Goulet, Michel	Que., Chi.	15	1089	548	604	1152	825	92	39	39	78	110		1979-80	1993-94
Goupille, Red	Mtl.	8	222	12	28	40	256	8	2	0	2	6		1935-36	1942-43
Govedaris, Chris	Hfd., Tor.	4	45	4	6	10	24	4	0	0	0	2		1989-90	1993-94
Goyer, Gerry	Chi.	1	40	1	2	3	4	3	0	0	0	2		1967-68	1967-68
Goyette, Phil	Mtl., NYR, St.L., Buf.	16	941	207	467	674	131	94	17	29	46	26	4	1956-57	1971-72
Graboski, Tony	Mtl.	3	66	6	10	16	24	3	0	0	0	6		1940-41	1942-43
● Gracie, Bob	Tor., Bos., NYA, Mtl.M., Mtl., Chi.	9	379	82	109	191	205	33	4	7	11	4	2	1930-31	1938-39
Gradin, Thomas	Van., Bos.	9	677	209	384	593	298	42	17	25	42	20		1978-79	1986-87
Graham, Dirk	Min., Chi.	12	772	219	270	489	917	90	17	27	44	92		1983-84	1994-95
● Graham, Leth	Ott., Ham.	6	26	3	0	3	0	1	0	0	0	0	1	1920-21	1925-26
Graham, Pat	Pit., Tor.	3	103	11	17	28	136	4	0	0	0	2		1981-82	1983-84
Graham, Rod	Bos.	1	14	2	1	3	7	....	....	....	....	....		1974-75	1974-75
● Graham, Ted	Chi., Mtl.M., Det., St.L., Bos., NYA	9	346	14	25	39	300	24	3	1	4	30		1927-28	1936-37
Grant, Danny	Mtl., Min., Det., L.A.	13	736	263	273	536	239	43	10	14	24	19	1	1965-66	1978-79
Gratton, Dan	L.A.	1	7	1	0	1	5	....	....	....	....	....		1987-88	1987-88
Gratton, Norm	NYR, Atl., Buf., Min.	5	201	39	44	83	64	6	0	1	1	2		1971-72	1975-76
Gravelle, Leo	Mtl., Det.	5	223	44	34	78	42	17	4	1	5	2		1946-47	1950-51
Graves, Hilliard	Cal., Atl., Van., Wpg.	9	556	118	163	281	209	2	0	0	0	0		1970-71	1979-80
Graves, Steve	Edm.	3	35	5	4	9	10	....	....	....	....	....		1983-84	1987-88
● Gray, Alex	NYR, Tor.	2	50	7	0	7	32	13	1	0	1	0	1	1927-28	1928-29
Gray, Terry	Bos., Mtl., L.A., St.L.	6	147	26	28	54	64	35	5	5	10	22		1961-62	1970-71
● Green, Red	Ham., NYA, Bos., Det.	6	195	59	13	72	261	1	0	0	0	0	1	1923-24	1928-29
Green, Rick	Wsh., Mtl., Det., NYI	15	845	43	220	263	588	100	3	16	19	73	1	1976-77	1991-92
● Green, Shorty	Ham., NYA	4	103	36	8	44	220	....	....	....	....	....		1923-24	1926-27
Green, Ted	Bos.	11	620	48	206	254	1029	31	4	8	12	54	1	1960-61	1971-72
Greenlaw, Jeff	Wsh., Fla.	6	57	3	6	9	108	2	0	0	0	21		1986-87	1993-94
Gregg, Randy	Edm., Van.	10	474	41	152	193	333	137	13	38	51	127	5	1981-82	1991-92
Greig, Bruce	Cal.	2	9	0	1	1	46	....	....	....	....	....		1973-74	1974-75
Grenier, Lucien	Mtl., L.A.	4	151	14	14	28	18	2	0	0	0	0	1	1968-69	1971-72
Grenier, Richard	NYI	1	10	1	1	2	2	....	....	....	....	....		1972-73	1972-73
Greschner, Ron	NYR	16	982	179	431	610	1226	84	17	32	49	106		1974-75	1989-90
Gretzky, Brent	T.B.	2	13	1	3	4	2	....	....	....	....	....		1993-94	1994-95
Grieve, Brent	NYI, Edm., Chi., L.A.	4	97	20	16	36	87	....	....	....	....	....		1993-94	1996-97
Grigor, George	Chi.	1	2	1	0	1	0	1	0	0	0	0		1943-44	1943-44
Grisdale, John	Tor., Van.	6	250	4	39	43	346	10	0	1	1	15		1972-73	1978-79
Gronsdahl, Lloyd	Bos.	1	10	1	2	3	0	....	....	....	....	....		1941-42	1941-42
Gronstrand, Jari	Min., NYR, Que., NYI	5	185	8	26	34	135	3	0	0	0	4		1986-87	1990-91
Gross, Lloyd	Tor., NYA, Bos., Det.	3	62	11	5	16	20	1	0	0	0	0		1926-27	1934-35
● Grosso, Don	Det., Chi., Bos.	9	336	87	117	204	90	48	15	14	29	63	1	1938-39	1946-47
Grosvenor, Len	Ott., NYA, Mtl.	6	149	9	11	20	78	4	0	0	0	2		1927-28	1932-33
Groulx, Wayne	Que.	1	1	0	0	0	0	....	....	....	....	....		1984-85	1984-85
Gruen, Danny	Det., Col.	3	49	9	13	22	19	....	....	....	....	....		1972-73	1976-77
Gruhl, Scott	L.A., Pit.	3	20	3	3	6	6	....	....	....	....	....		1981-82	1987-88
Gryp, Bob	Bos., Wsh.	3	74	11	13	24	33	....	....	....	....	....		1973-74	1975-76

Name	NHL Teams	NHL Seasons	Regular Schedule					Playoffs					NHL Cup Wins	First NHL Season	Last NHL Season
			GP	G	A	TP	PIM	GP	G	A	TP	PIM			
Guay, Francois	Buf.	1	1	0	0	0	0	....	....	....	....	....		1989-90	1989-90
Guay, Paul	Phi., L.A., Bos., NYI	7	117	11	23	34	92	9	0	1	1	12		1983-84	1990-91
Guerard, Daniel	Ott.	1	2	0	0	0	0	....	....	....	....	....		1994-95	1994-95
Guerard, Stephane	Que.	2	34	0	0	0	40	....	....	....	....	....		1987-88	1989-90
Guevremont, Jocelyn	Van., Buf., NYR	9	571	84	223	307	319	40	4	17	21	18		1971-72	1979-80
Guidolin, Aldo	NYR	4	182	9	15	24	117	....	....	....	....	....		1952-53	1955-56
Guidolin, Bep	Bos., Det., Chi.	9	519	107	171	278	606	24	5	7	12	35		1942-43	1951-52
Guindon, Bobby	Wpg.	1	6	0	1	1	0	....	....	....	....	....		1979-80	1979-80
Gustafsson, Bengt	Wsh.	9	629	196	359	555	196	32	9	19	28	16		1979-80	1988-89
Gustavsson, Peter	Col.	1	2	0	0	0	0	....	....	....	....	....		1981-82	1981-82
Guy, Kevan	Cgy., Van.	6	156	5	20	25	138	5	0	1	1	23		1986-87	1991-92

H

Name	NHL Teams	NHL Seasons	GP	G	A	TP	PIM	GP	G	A	TP	PIM	NHL Cup Wins	First NHL Season	Last NHL Season
Haanpaa, Ari	NYI	3	60	6	11	17	37	6	0	0	0	10		1985-86	1987-88
Haas, David	Edm., Cgy.	2	7	2	1	3	7	....	....	....	....	....		1990-91	1993-94
Habscheid, Marc	Edm., Min., Det., Cgy.	11	345	72	91	163	171	12	1	3	4	13		1981-82	1991-92
Hachborn, Len	Phi., L.A.	3	102	20	39	59	29	7	0	3	3	7		1983-84	1985-86
Haddon, Lloyd	Det.	1	8	0	0	0	2	1	0	0	0	0		1959-60	1959-60
Hadfield, Vic	NYR, Pit.	16	1002	323	389	712	1154	73	27	21	48	117		1961-62	1976-77
Haggarty, Jim	Mtl.	1	5	1	1	2	0	3	2	1	3	0		1941-42	1941-42
● Hagglund, Roger	Que.	1	3	0	0	0	0	....	....	....	....	....		1984-85	1984-85
Hagman, Matti	Bos., Edm.	4	237	56	89	145	36	20	5	2	7	6		1976-77	1981-82
Haidy, Gord	Det.	1	....	....	....	....	....	1	0	0	0	0	1	1949-50	1949-50
Hajdu, Richard	Buf.	2	5	0	0	0	4	....	....	....	....	....		1985-86	1986-87
Hajt, Bill	Buf.	14	854	42	202	244	433	80	2	16	18	70		1973-74	1986-87
Hakansson, Anders	Min., Pit., L.A.	5	330	52	46	98	141	6	0	0	0	2		1981-82	1985-86
● Halderson, Harold	Det., Tor.	1	44	3	2	5	65	....	....	....	....	....		1926-27	1926-27
Hale, Larry	Phi.	4	196	5	37	42	90	8	0	0	0	12		1968-69	1971-72
Haley, Len	Det.	2	30	2	2	4	14	6	1	3	4	6		1959-60	1960-61
Halkidis, Bob	Buf., L.A., Tor., Det., T.B., NYI	11	256	8	32	40	825	20	0	1	1	51		1984-85	1995-96
Hall, Bob	NYA	1	8	0	0	0	0	....	....	....	....	....		1925-26	1925-26
Hall, Del	Cal.	3	9	2	0	2	2	....	....	....	....	....		1971-72	1973-74
● Hall, Joe	Mtl.	2	37	15	9	24	235	12	0	1	1	39		1917-18	1918-19
Hall, Murray	Chi., Det., Min., Van.	9	164	35	48	83	46	6	0	0	0	0		1961-62	1971-72
Hall, Taylor	Van., Bos.	5	41	7	9	16	29	....	....	....	....	....		1983-84	1987-88
Hall, Wayne	NYR	1	4	0	0	0	0	....	....	....	....	....		1960-61	1960-61
● Halliday, Milt	Ott.	3	67	1	0	1	4	6	0	0	0	0	1	1926-27	1928-29
Hallin, Mats	NYI, Min.	5	152	17	14	31	193	15	1	0	1	13	1	1982-83	1986-87
Halward, Doug	Bos., L.A., Van., Det., Edm.	14	653	69	224	293	774	47	7	10	17	113		1975-76	1988-89
Hamel, Gilles	Buf., Wpg., L.A.	9	519	127	147	274	276	27	4	5	9	10		1980-81	1988-89
● Hamel, Herb	Tor.	1	2	0	0	0	4	....	....	....	....	....		1930-31	1930-31
Hamel, Jean	St.L., Det., Que., Mtl.	12	699	26	95	121	766	33	0	2	2	44		1972-73	1983-84
● Hamill, Red	Bos., Chi.	12	419	128	94	222	160	24	1	2	3	20	2	1937-38	1950-51
Hamilton, Al	NYR, Buf., Edm.	7	257	10	78	88	258	7	0	0	0	2		1965-66	1979-80
Hamilton, Chuck	Mtl., St.L.	2	4	0	2	2	2	....	....	....	....	....		1961-62	1972-73
● Hamilton, Jack	Tor.	3	138	31	48	79	76	11	2	1	3	0		1942-43	1945-46
Hamilton, Jim	Pit.	8	95	14	18	32	28	6	3	0	3	0		1977-78	1984-85
● Hamilton, Reg	Tor., Chi.	12	424	21	87	108	412	64	3	8	11	46	2	1935-36	1946-47
Hammarstrom, Inge	Tor., St.L.	6	427	116	123	239	86	13	2	3	5	4		1973-74	1978-79
Hammond, Ken	L.A., Edm., NYR, Tor., Bos., S.J., Van., Ott.	8	193	18	29	47	290	15	0	0	0	24		1984-85	1992-93
Hampson, Gord	Cgy.	1	4	0	0	0	5	....	....	....	....	....		1982-83	1982-83
Hampson, Ted	Tor., NYR, Det., Oak., Cal., Min.	12	676	108	245	353	94	35	7	10	17	2		1959-60	1971-72
Hampton, Rick	Cal., Cle., L.A.	6	337	59	113	172	147	2	0	0	0	0		1974-75	1979-80
Hamr, Radek	Ott.	2	11	0	0	0	0	....	....	....	....	....		1992-93	1993-94
Hamway, Mark	NYI	3	53	5	13	18	9	1	0	0	0	0		1984-85	1986-87
Handy, Ron	NYI, St.L.	2	14	0	3	3	0	....	....	....	....	....		1984-85	1987-88
Hangsleben, Al	Hfd., Wsh., L.A.	3	185	21	48	69	396	....	....	....	....	....		1979-80	1981-82
Hankinson, Ben	N.J., T.B.	3	43	3	3	6	45	2	1	0	1	4		1992-93	1994-95
Hanna, John	NYR, Mtl., Phi.	5	198	6	26	32	206	....	....	....	....	....		1958-59	1967-68
Hannan, Dave	Pit., Edm., Tor., Buf., Col., Ott.	16	841	114	191	305	942	63	6	7	13	46	2	1981-82	1996-97
● Hannigan, Gord	Tor.	4	161	29	31	60	117	9	2	0	2	8		1952-53	1955-56
Hannigan, Pat	Tor., NYR, Phi.	5	182	30	39	69	116	11	1	2	3	11		1959-60	1968-69
Hannigan, Ray	Tor.	1	3	0	0	0	2	....	....	....	....	....		1948-49	1948-49
Hansen, Ritchie	NYI, St.L.	4	20	2	8	10	4	....	....	....	....	....		1976-77	1981-82
Hanson, Dave	Det., Min.	2	33	1	1	2	65	....	....	....	....	....		1978-79	1979-80
● Hanson, Emil	Det.	1	7	0	0	0	6	....	....	....	....	....		1932-33	1932-33
Hanson, Keith	Cgy.	1	25	0	2	2	77	....	....	....	....	....		1983-84	1983-84
Hanson, Oscar	Chi.	1	8	0	0	0	0	....	....	....	....	....		1937-38	1937-38
Harbaruk, Nick	Pit., St.L.	5	364	45	75	120	273	14	3	1	4	20		1969-70	1973-74
Harding, Jeff	Phi.	2	15	0	0	0	47	....	....	....	....	....		1988-89	1989-90
Hardy, Joe	Oak., Cal.	2	63	9	14	23	51	4	0	0	0	0		1969-70	1970-71
Hardy, Mark	L.A., NYR, Min.	15	915	62	306	368	1293	67	5	16	21	158		1979-80	1993-94
Hargreaves, Jim	Van.	2	66	1	7	8	105	....	....	....	....	....		1970-71	1972-73
Harkins, Todd	Cgy., Hfd.	3	48	3	3	6	78	....	....	....	....	....		1991-92	1993-94
Harlow, Scott	St.L.	1	1	0	1	1	0	....	....	....	....	....		1987-88	1987-88
Harmon, Glen	Mtl.	9	452	50	96	146	334	53	5	10	15	37	2	1942-43	1950-51
Harms, John	Chi.	2	44	5	5	10	21	4	3	0	3	2		1943-44	1944-45
● Harnott, Walter	Bos.	1	6	0	0	0	2	....	....	....	....	....		1933-34	1933-34
Harper, Terry	Mtl., L.A., Det., St.L., Col.	19	1066	35	221	256	1362	112	4	13	17	140	5	1962-63	1980-81
Harrer, Tim	Cgy.	1	3	0	0	0	2	....	....	....	....	....		1982-83	1982-83
● Harrington, Leland	Bos., Mtl.	3	72	9	3	12	15	4	1	0	1	2		1925-26	1932-33
Harris, Bill	NYI, L.A., Tor.	12	897	231	327	558	394	71	19	19	38	48		1972-73	1983-84
Harris, Billy	Tor., Det., Oak., Pit.	13	769	126	219	345	205	62	8	10	18	30	3	1955-56	1968-69
Harris, Duke	Min., Tor.	1	26	1	4	5	4	....	....	....	....	....		1967-68	1967-68
● Harris, Henry	Bos.	1	32	2	4	6	20	....	....	....	....	....		1930-31	1930-31
Harris, Hugh	Buf.	1	60	12	26	38	17	3	0	0	0	0		1972-73	1972-73
Harris, Ron	Det., Oak., Atl., NYR	11	476	20	91	111	474	28	4	3	7	33		1962-63	1975-76
Harris, Ted	Mtl., Min., Det., St.L., Phi.	12	788	30	168	198	1000	100	1	22	23	230	5	1963-64	1974-75
● Harris, Thomas	Bos.	1	6	3	1	4	8	....	....	....	....	....		1924-25	1930-31
Harrison, Ed	Bos., NYR	4	194	27	24	51	53	9	1	0	1	2		1947-48	1950-51
Harrison, Jim	Bos., Tor., Chi., Edm.	8	324	67	86	153	435	13	1	1	2	43		1968-69	1979-80
Hart, Gerry	Det., NYI, Que., St.L.	15	730	29	150	179	1240	78	3	12	15	175		1968-69	1982-83
● Hart, Wilf	Det., Mtl.	3	104	6	8	14	12	8	0	1	1	0		1926-27	1932-33
Hartman, Mike	Buf., Wpg., T.B., NYR	9	397	43	35	78	1388	21	0	0	0	106	1	1986-87	1994-95
Hartsburg, Craig	Min.	10	570	98	315	413	818	61	15	27	42	70		1979-80	1988-89
● Harvey, Doug	Mtl., NYR, Det., St.L.	20	1113	88	452	540	1216	137	8	64	72	152	6	1947-48	1968-69
Harvey, Fred	Min., Atl., K.C., Det.	7	407	90	118	208	131	14	0	2	2	8		1970-71	1976-77
Harvey, Hugh	K.C.	2	18	1	1	2	4	....	....	....	....	....		1974-75	1975-76
Hassard, Bob	Tor., Chi.	5	126	9	28	37	22	....	....	....	....	....		1949-50	1954-55
Hatoum, Ed	Det., Van.	3	47	3	6	9	25	....	....	....	....	....		1968-69	1970-71
Hawerchuk, Dale	Wpg., Buf., St.L., Phi.	16	1188	518	891	1409	730	97	30	69	99	67		1981-82	1996-97
Haworth, Alan	Buf., Wsh., Que.	8	524	189	211	400	425	42	12	16	28	28		1980-81	1987-88
Haworth, Gord	NYR	1	2	0	1	1	0	....	....	....	....	....		1952-53	1952-53
Hawryliw, Neil	NYI	1	1	0	0	0	0	....	....	....	....	....		1981-82	1981-82
Hay, Bill	Chi.	8	506	113	273	386	244	67	15	21	36	62		1959-60	1966-67
● Hay, George	Chi., Det.	7	239	74	60	134	84	8	2	3	5	2		1926-27	1933-34
Hay, Jim	Det.	3	75	1	5	6	22	9	1	0	1	2	1	1952-53	1954-55
Hayek, Peter	Min.	1	1	0	0	0	0	....	....	....	....	....		1981-82	1981-82
Hayes, Chris	Bos.	1	....	....	....	....	....	1	0	0	0	0	1	1971-72	1971-72
● Haynes, Paul	Mtl.M., Bos., Mtl.	11	391	61	134	195	164	24	2	8	10	13		1930-31	1940-41
Hayward, Rick	L.A.	1	4	0	0	0	5	....	....	....	....	....		1990-91	1990-91
Hazlett, Steve	Van.	1	1	0	0	0	0	....	....	....	....	....		1979-80	1979-80
Head, Galen	Det.	1	1	0	0	0	0	....	....	....	....	....		1967-68	1967-68
● Headley, Fern	Bos., Mtl.	1	27	1	1	2	6	5	0	0	0	0		1924-25	1924-25
Healey, Dick	Det.	1	1	0	0	0	2	....	....	....	....	....		1960-61	1960-61
Heaphy, Shawn	Cgy.	1	1	0	0	0	0	....	....	....	....	....		1992-93	1992-93
Heaslip, Mark	NYR, L.A.	3	117	10	19	29	110	5	0	0	0	2		1976-77	1978-79
Heath, Randy	NYR	2	13	2	4	6	15	....	....	....	....	....		1984-85	1985-86
Hebenton, Andy	NYR, Bos.	9	630	189	202	391	83	22	6	5	11	8		1955-56	1963-64
Hedberg, Anders	NYR	7	465	172	225	397	144	58	22	24	46	31		1978-79	1984-85
● Heffernan, Frank	Tor.	1	19	0	1	1	10	....	....	....	....	....		1919-20	1919-20

Bob Halkidis

Ted Hampson

Dave Hannan

Craig Hartsburg

Dale Hawerchuk

Camille Henry

Gordie Howe

Tim Hunter

			Regular Schedule					Playoffs					NHL	First	Last
Name	NHL Teams	NHL Seasons	GP	G	A	TP	PIM	GP	G	A	TP	PIM	Cup Wins	NHL Season	NHL Season
Heffernan, Gerry	Mtl.	3	83	33	35	68	27	11	3	3	6	8	1	1941-42	1943-44
Heidt, Michael	L.A.	1	6	0	1	1	7	....	....	....	....	....		1983-84	1983-84
• Heindl, Bill	Min., NYR	3	18	2	1	3	0	....	....	....	....	....		1970-71	1972-73
Heinrich, Lionel	Bos.	1	35	1	1	2	33	....	....	....	....	....		1955-56	1955-56
Heiskala, Earl	Phi.	3	127	13	11	24	294	....	....	....	....	....		1968-69	1970-71
Helander, Peter	L.A.	1	7	0	1	1	0	....	....	....	....	....		1982-83	1982-83
• Heller, Ott	NYR	15	647	55	176	231	465	61	6	8	14	61	2	1931-32	1945-46
Helman, Harry	Ott.	3	42	1	0	1	7	4	0	0	0	0	1	1922-23	1924-25
Helminen, Raimo	NYR, Min., NYI	3	117	13	46	59	16	2	0	0	0	0		1985-86	1988-89
• Hemmerling, Tony	NYA	2	22	3	3	6	4	....	....	....	....	....		1935-36	1936-37
Henderson, Archie	Wsh., Min., Hfd.	3	23	3	1	4	92	....	....	....	....	....		1980-81	1982-83
Henderson, Murray	Bos.	8	405	24	62	86	305	41	2	3	5	23		1944-45	1951-52
Henderson, Paul	Det., Tor., Atl.	13	707	236	241	477	304	56	11	14	25	28		1962-63	1979-80
Hendrickson, John	Det.	3	5	0	0	0	4	....	....	....	....	....		1957-58	1961-62
Henning, Lorne	NYI	9	544	73	111	184	102	81	7	7	14	8	2	1972-73	1980-81
• Henry, Camille	NYR, Chi., St.L.	14	727	279	249	528	88	47	6	12	18	7		1953-54	1969-70
Henry, Dale	NYI	6	132	13	26	39	263	14	1	0	1	19		1984-85	1989-90
Hepple, Alan	N.J.	3	3	0	0	0	7	....	....	....	....	....		1983-84	1985-86
• Herberts, Jimmy	Bos., Tor., Det.	6	206	83	29	112	248	9	3	0	3	10		1924-25	1929-30
Herchenratter, Art	Det.	1	10	1	2	3	2	....	....	....	....	....		1940-41	1940-41
Hergerts, Fred	NYA	2	20	2	4	6	2	....	....	....	....	....		1934-35	1935-36
Hergesheimer, Philip	Chi., Bos.	4	125	21	41	62	19	6	0	0	0	2		1939-40	1942-43
Hergesheimer, Wally	NYR, Chi.	7	351	114	85	199	106	5	1	0	1	0		1951-52	1958-59
Heron, Red	Tor., Bro., Mtl.	4	106	21	19	40	38	21	2	2	4	6		1938-39	1941-42
Heroux, Yves	Que.	1	1	0	0	0	0	....	....	....	....	....		1986-87	1986-87
Herter, Jason	NYI	1	1	0	1	1	0	....	....	....	....	....		1995-96	1995-96
Hervey, Matt	Wpg., Bos., T.B.	3	35	0	5	5	97	5	0	0	0	6		1988-89	1992-93
Hess, Bob	St.L., Buf., Hfd.	8	329	27	95	122	178	4	1	1	2	2		1974-75	1983-84
Heximer, Orville	NYR, Bos., NYA	3	84	13	7	20	16	5	0	0	0	2		1929-30	1934-35
Hextall, Bryan Jr.	NYR, Pit., Atl., Det., Min.	8	549	99	161	260	738	18	0	4	4	59		1962-63	1975-76
• Hextall, Bryan Sr.	NYR	11	449	187	175	362	227	37	8	9	17	19	1	1936-37	1947-48
Hextall, Dennis	NYR, L.A., Cal., Min., Det., Wsh.	13	681	153	350	503	1398	22	3	3	6	45		1968-69	1979-80
Heyliger, Vic	Chi.	2	33	2	3	5	2	....	....	....	....	....		1937-38	1943-44
Hicke, Bill	Mtl., NYR, Oak., Cal., Pit.	14	729	168	234	402	395	42	3	10	13	41	2	1958-59	1971-72
Hicke, Ernie	Cal., Atl., NYI, Min., L.A.	8	520	132	140	272	407	2	1	0	1	0		1970-71	1977-78
Hickey, Greg	NYR	1	1	0	0	0	0	....	....	....	....	....		1977-78	1977-78
Hickey, Pat	NYR, Col., Tor., Que., St.L.	10	646	192	212	404	351	55	5	11	16	37		1975-76	1984-85
Hicks, Doug	Min., Chi., Edm., Wsh.	9	561	37	131	168	442	18	2	1	3	15		1974-75	1982-83
Hicks, Glenn	Det.	2	108	6	12	18	127	....	....	....	....	....		1979-80	1980-81
• Hicks, Harold	Mtl.M., Det.	3	96	7	2	9	72	....	....	....	....	....		1928-29	1930-31
Hicks, Wayne	Chi., Bos., Mtl., Phi., Pit.	5	115	13	23	36	22	2	0	1	1	2	1	1959-60	1967-68
Hidi, Andre	Wsh.	2	7	2	1	3	9	2	0	0	0	0		1983-84	1984-85
Hiemer, Uli	N.J.	3	143	19	54	73	176	....	....	....	....	....		1984-85	1986-87
Higgins, Paul	Tor.	2	25	0	0	0	152	1	0	0	0	0		1981-82	1982-83
Higgins, Tim	Chi., N.J., Det.	11	706	154	198	352	719	65	5	8	13	77		1978-79	1988-89
Hildebrand, Ike	NYR, Chi.	2	41	7	11	18	16	....	....	....	....	....		1953-54	1954-55
Hill, Al	Phi.	8	221	40	55	95	227	51	8	11	19	43		1976-77	1987-88
Hill, Brian	Hfd.	1	19	1	1	2	4	....	....	....	....	....		1979-80	1979-80
• Hill, Mel	Bos., Bro., Tor.	9	324	89	109	198	128	43	12	7	19	18	3	1937-38	1945-46
Hiller, Dutch	NYR, Det., Bos., Mtl.	9	383	91	113	204	163	48	9	8	17	21	2	1937-38	1945-46
Hiller, Jim	L.A., Det., NYR	2	63	8	12	20	116	2	0	0	0	4		1992-93	1993-94
Hillier, Randy	Bos., Pit., NYI, Buf.	11	543	16	110	126	906	28	0	2	2	93	1	1981-82	1991-92
Hillman, Floyd	Bos.	1	6	0	0	0	10	....	....	....	....	....		1956-57	1956-57
Hillman, Larry	Det., Bos., Tor., Min., Mtl., Phi., L.A., Buf.	19	790	36	196	232	579	74	2	9	11	30	6	1954-55	1972-73
• Hillman, Wayne	Chi., NYR, Min., Phi.	13	691	18	86	104	534	28	0	3	3	19	1	1960-61	1972-73
Hilworth, John	Det.	3	57	1	1	2	89	....	....	....	....	....		1977-78	1979-80
• Himes, Normie	NYA	9	402	106	113	219	127	2	0	0	0	0		1926-27	1934-35
Hindmarch, Dave	Cgy.	4	99	21	17	38	25	10	0	0	0	6		1980-81	1983-84
Hinse, Andre	Tor.	1	4	0	0	0	0	....	....	....	....	....		1967-68	1967-68
Hinton, Dan	Chi.	1	14	0	0	0	16	....	....	....	....	....		1976-77	1976-77
Hirsch, Tom	Min.	3	31	1	7	8	30	12	0	0	0	6		1983-84	1987-88
• Hirschfeld, Bert	Mtl.	2	33	1	4	5	2	5	1	0	1	0		1949-50	1950-51
Hislop, Jamie	Que., Cgy.	5	345	75	103	178	86	28	3	2	5	11		1979-80	1983-84
• Hitchman, Lionel	Ott., Bos.	12	416	28	33	61	523	40	4	1	5	77	2	1922-23	1933-34
Hlinka, Ivan	Van.	2	137	42	81	123	28	16	3	10	13	8		1981-82	1982-83
Hodge, Ken	Min., Bos., T.B.	4	142	39	48	87	32	15	4	6	10	6		1988-89	1992-93
Hodge, Ken	Chi., Bos., NYR	14	881	328	472	800	779	97	34	47	81	120	2	1965-66	1977-78
Hodgson, Dan	Tor., Van.	4	114	29	45	74	64	....	....	....	....	....		1985-86	1988-89
Hodgson, Rick	Hfd.	1	6	0	0	0	6	1	0	0	0	0		1979-80	1979-80
Hodgson, Ted	Bos.	1	4	0	0	0	0	....	....	....	....	....		1966-67	1966-67
Hoekstra, Cecil	Mtl.	1	4	0	0	0	0	....	....	....	....	....		1959-60	1959-60
Hoekstra, Ed	Phi.	1	70	15	21	36	6	7	0	1	1	0		1967-68	1967-68
Hoene, Phil	L.A.	3	37	2	4	6	22	....	....	....	....	....		1972-73	1974-75
Hoffinger, Val	Chi.	2	28	0	1	1	30	....	....	....	....	....		1927-28	1928-29
Hoffman, Mike	Hfd.	3	9	1	3	4	2	....	....	....	....	....		1982-83	1985-86
Hoffmeyer, Bob	Chi., Phi., N.J.	6	198	14	52	66	325	3	0	1	1	25		1977-78	1984-85
Hofford, Jim	Buf., L.A.	3	18	0	0	0	47	....	....	....	....	....		1985-86	1988-89
Hogaboam, Bill	Atl., Det., Min.	8	332	80	109	189	100	2	0	0	0	0		1972-73	1979-80
Hoganson, Dale	L.A., Mtl., Que.	7	343	13	77	90	186	11	0	3	3	12		1969-70	1981-82
Holan, Milos	Phi., Ana.	3	49	5	11	16	42	....	....	....	....	....		1993-94	1995-96
Holbrook, Terry	Min.	2	43	3	6	9	4	6	0	0	0	0		1972-73	1973-74
Holland, Jerry	NYR	2	37	8	4	12	6	....	....	....	....	....		1974-75	1975-76
• Hollett, Flash	Tor., Ott., Bos., Det.	13	562	132	181	313	358	79	8	26	34	38	2	1933-34	1945-46
• Hollingworth, Gord	Chi., Det.	4	163	4	14	18	201	3	0	0	0	2		1954-55	1957-58
Holloway, Bruce	Van.	1	2	0	0	0	0	....	....	....	....	....		1984-85	1984-85
• Holmes, Bill	Mtl., NYA.	3	52	6	4	10	35	....	....	....	....	....		1925-26	1929-30
Holmes, Chuck	Det.	2	23	1	3	4	10	....	....	....	....	....		1958-59	1961-62
Holmes, Lou	Chi.	2	59	1	4	5	6	2	0	0	0	2		1931-32	1932-33
Holmes, Warren	L.A.	3	45	8	18	26	7	....	....	....	....	....		1981-82	1983-84
Holmgren, Paul	Phi., Min.	10	527	144	179	323	1684	82	19	32	51	195		1975-76	1984-85
• Holota, John	Det.	2	15	2	0	2	0	....	....	....	....	....		1942-43	1945-46
Holst, Greg	NYR	3	11	0	0	0	0	....	....	....	....	....		1975-76	1977-78
Holt, Gary	Cal., Clev., St.L.	5	101	13	11	24	133	....	....	....	....	....		1973-74	1977-78
Holt, Randy	Chi., Clev., Van., L.A., Cgy., Wsh., Phi.	10	395	4	37	41	1438	21	2	3	5	83		1974-75	1983-84
• Holway, Albert	Tor., Mtl.M., Pit.	5	113	7	2	9	48	8	0	0	0	2	1	1923-24	1928-29
Homenuke, Ron	Van.	1	1	0	0	0	0	....	....	....	....	....		1972-73	1972-73
Hoover, Ron	Bos., St.L.	3	18	4	0	4	31	8	0	0	0	18		1989-90	1991-92
Hopkins, Dean	L.A., Edm., Que.	6	223	23	51	74	306	18	1	5	6	29		1979-80	1988-89
Hopkins, Larry	Tor., Wpg.	4	60	13	16	29	26	6	0	0	0	2		1977-78	1982-83
Horacek, Tony	Phi., Chi.	5	154	10	19	29	316	2	1	0	1	2		1989-90	1994-95
Horava, Miloslav	NYR	3	80	5	17	22	38	2	0	1	1	0		1988-89	1990-91
Horbul, Doug	K.C.	1	4	1	0	1	2	....	....	....	....	....		1974-75	1974-75
Hordy, Mike	NYI	2	11	0	0	0	7	....	....	....	....	....		1978-79	1979-80
Horeck, Pete	Chi., Det., Bos.	8	426	106	118	224	340	34	6	8	14	43		1944-45	1951-52
• Horne, George	Mtl.M, Tor.	3	54	9	3	12	34	4	0	0	0	4	1	1925-26	1928-29
Horner, Red	Tor.	12	490	42	110	152	1254	71	7	10	17	170	1	1928-29	1939-40
Hornung, Larry	St.L.	2	48	2	9	11	10	11	0	2	2	2		1970-71	1971-72
• Horton, Tim	Tor., NYR, Buf., Pit.	24	1446	115	403	518	1611	126	11	39	50	183	4	1949-50	1973-74
Horvath, Bronco	NYR, Mtl., Bos., Chi., Tor., Min.	9	434	141	185	326	319	36	12	9	21	18		1955-56	1967-68
Hospodar, Ed	NYR, Hfd., Phi., Min., Buf.	9	450	17	51	68	1314	44	4	1	5	208		1979-80	1987-88
Hostak, Martin	Phi.	2	55	3	11	14	24	....	....	....	....	....		1990-91	1991-92
Hotham, Greg	Tor., Pit.	6	230	15	74	89	139	5	0	3	3	6		1979-80	1984-85
Houck, Paul	Min.	3	16	1	2	3	2	....	....	....	....	....		1985-86	1987-88
Houde, Claude	K.C.	2	59	3	6	9	40	....	....	....	....	....		1974-75	1975-76
Houle, Rejean	Mtl.	11	635	161	247	408	395	90	14	34	48	66	5	1969-70	1982-83
Houston, Ken	Atl., Cgy., Wsh., L.A.	9	570	161	167	328	624	35	10	9	19	66		1975-76	1983-84
Howard, John Francis	Tor.	1	2	0	0	0	0	....	....	....	....	....		1936-37	1936-37
Howatt, Garry	NYI, Hfd., N.J.	12	720	112	156	268	1836	87	12	14	26	289	2	1972-73	1983-84
Howe, Gordie	Det., Hfd.	26	1767	801	1049	1850	1685	157	68	92	160	220	4	1946-47	1979-80
Howe, Mark	Hfd., Phi., Det.	16	929	197	545	742	455	101	10	51	61	34		1979-80	1994-95
Howe, Marty	Hfd., Bos.	6	197	2	29	31	99	15	1	2	3	9		1979-80	1984-85
• Howe, Syd	Ott., Phi., Tor., St.L., Det.	17	698	237	291	528	212	70	17	27	44	10	3	1929-30	1945-46

Name	NHL Teams	NHL Seasons	Regular Schedule GP	G	A	TP	PIM	Playoffs GP	G	A	TP	PIM	NHL Cup Wins	First NHL Season	Last NHL Season
Howe, Vic	NYR	3	33	3	4	7	10	....	....	....	....	....		1950-51	1954-55
Howell, Harry	NYR, Oak., L.A.	21	1411	94	324	418	1298	38	3	3	6	32		1952-53	1972-73
Howell, Ron	NYR	2	4	0	0	0	0	....	....	....	....	....		1954-55	1955-56
Howse, Don	L.A.	1	33	2	5	7	6	2	0	0	0	0		1979-80	1979-80
Howson, Scott	NYI	2	18	5	3	8	4	....	....	....	....	....		1984-85	1985-86
Hoyda, Dave	Phi., Wpg.	4	132	6	17	23	299	12	0	0	0	17		1977-78	1980-81
Hrdina, Jiri	Cgy., Pit.	5	250	45	85	130	92	46	2	5	7	24	3	1987-88	1991-92
Hrechkosy, Dave	Cal., St.L.	4	140	42	24	66	41	3	1	0	1	2		1973-74	1976-77
Hrycuik, Jim	Wsh.	1	21	5	5	10	12	....	....	....	....	....		1974-75	1974-75
Hrymnak, Steve	Chi., Det.	2	18	2	1	3	4	2	0	0	0	0		1951-52	1952-53
Hrynewich, Tim	Pit.	2	55	6	8	14	82	....	....	....	....	....		1982-83	1983-84
Huard, Rolly	Tor.	1	1	1	0	1	0	....	....	....	....	....		1930-31	1930-31
Huber, Willie	Det., NYR, Van., Phi.	10	655	104	217	321	950	33	5	5	10	35		1978-79	1987-88
Hubick, Greg	Tor., Van.	2	77	6	9	15	10	....	....	....	....	....		1975-76	1979-80
Huck, Fran	Mtl., St.L.	3	94	24	30	54	38	11	3	4	7	2		1969-70	1972-73
Hucul, Fred	Chi., St.L.	5	164	11	30	41	113	6	1	0	1	10		1950-51	1967-68
Huddy, Charlie	Edm., L.A., Buf., St.L.	17	1017	99	354	453	785	183	19	66	85	135	5	1980-81	1996-97
Hudson, Dave	NYI, K.C., Col.	6	409	59	124	183	89	2	1	1	2	0		1972-73	1977-78
Hudson, Lex	Pit.	1	2	0	0	0	0	2	0	0	0	0		1978-79	1978-79
Hudson, Mike	Chi., Edm., NYR, Pit., Tor., St.L., Phx.	9	416	49	87	136	414	49	4	10	14	64	1	1988-89	1996-97
Hudson, Ron	Det.	2	33	5	2	7	2	....	....	....	....	....		1937-38	1939-40
Huggins, Al	Mtl.M	1	20	1	1	2	2	....	....	....	....	....		1930-31	1930-31
Hughes, Al	NYA	2	60	6	8	14	22	....	....	....	....	....		1930-31	1931-32
Hughes, Brent	L.A., Phi., St.L., Det., K.C.	8	435	15	117	132	440	22	1	3	4	53		1967-68	1974-75
Hughes, Frank	Cal.	1	5	0	0	0	0	....	....	....	....	....		1971-72	1971-72
Hughes, Howie	L.A.	3	168	25	32	57	30	14	2	0	2	2		1967-68	1969-70
Hughes, Jack	Col.	2	46	2	5	7	104	....	....	....	....	....		1980-81	1981-82
Hughes, James	Det.	1	40	0	1	1	48	....	....	....	....	....		1929-30	1929-30
Hughes, John	Van., Edm., NYR	2	70	2	14	16	211	7	0	1	1	16		1979-80	1980-81
Hughes, Pat	Mtl., Pit., Edm., Buf., St.L., Hfd.	10	573	130	128	258	646	71	8	25	33	77	3	1977-78	1986-87
Hughes, Ryan	Bos.	1	3	0	0	0	0	....	....	....	....	....		1995-96	1995-96
Hull, Bobby	Chi., Wpg., Hfd.	16	1063	610	560	1170	640	119	62	67	129	102	1	1957-58	1979-80
Hull, Dennis	Chi., Det.	14	959	303	351	654	261	104	33	34	67	30		1964-65	1977-78
• Hunt, Fred	NYA, NYR	2	59	15	14	29	6	....	....	....	....	....		1940-41	1944-45
Hunter, Dave	Edm., Pit., Wpg.	10	746	133	190	323	918	105	16	24	40	211	3	1979-80	1988-89
Hunter, Mark	Mtl., St.L., Cgy., Hfd., Wsh.	12	628	213	171	384	1426	79	18	20	38	230	1	1981-82	1992-93
Hunter, Tim	Cgy., Que., Van., S.J.	16	815	62	76	138	3146	132	5	7	12	426	1	1981-82	1996-97
Huras, Larry	NYR	1	2	0	0	0	0	....	....	....	....	....		1976-77	1976-77
Hurlburt, Bob	Van.	1	1	0	0	0	2	....	....	....	....	....		1974-75	1974-75
Hurley, Paul	Bos.	1	1	0	1	1	0	....	....	....	....	....		1968-69	1968-69
Hurst, Ron	Tor.	2	64	9	7	16	70	3	0	2	2	4		1955-56	1956-57
Huston, Ron	Cal.	2	79	15	31	46	8	....	....	....	....	....		1973-74	1974-75
Hutchinson, Ronald	NYR	1	9	0	0	0	0	....	....	....	....	....		1960-61	1960-61
Hutchison, Dave	L.A., Tor., Chi., N.J.	10	584	19	97	116	1550	48	2	12	14	149		1974-75	1983-84
• Hutton, Bill	Bos., Ott., Phi.	2	64	3	2	5	8	2	0	0	0	0		1929-30	1930-31
• Hyland, Harry	Mtl.W, Ott.	1	17	14	2	16	65	....	....	....	....	....		1917-18	1917-18
Hynes, Dave	Bos.	2	22	4	0	4	2	....	....	....	....	....		1973-74	1974-75
Hynes, Gord	Bos., Phi.	2	52	3	9	12	22	12	1	2	3	6		1991-92	1992-93

I

Name	NHL Teams	NHL Seasons	Regular Schedule GP	G	A	TP	PIM	Playoffs GP	G	A	TP	PIM	NHL Cup Wins	First NHL Season	Last NHL Season
Ihnacak, Miroslav	Tor., Det.	3	56	8	9	17	39	1	0	0	0	0		1985-86	1988-89
Ihnacak, Peter	Tor.	8	417	102	165	267	175	28	4	10	14	25		1982-83	1989-90
Imlach, Brent	Tor.	2	3	0	0	0	0	....	....	....	....	....		1965-66	1966-67
Ingarfield, Earl	NYR, Pit., Oak., Cal.	13	746	179	226	405	239	21	9	8	17	10		1958-59	1970-71
Ingarfield, Earl Jr.	Atl., Cgy., Det.	2	39	4	4	8	22	2	0	1	1	0		1979-80	1980-81
Inglis, Bill	L.A., Buf.	3	36	1	3	4	4	11	1	2	3	4		1967-68	1970-71
• Ingoldsby, Johnny	Tor.	2	29	5	1	6	15	....	....	....	....	....		1942-43	1943-44
Ingram, Frank	Chi.	3	101	24	16	40	69	11	0	1	1	2		1929-30	1931-32
• Ingram, John J.	Bos.	1	1	0	0	0	0	....	....	....	....	....		1924-25	1924-25
Ingram, Ron	Chi., Det., NYR	4	114	5	15	20	81	2	0	0	0	0		1956-57	1964-65
• Irvin, Dick	Chi.	3	94	29	23	52	78	2	2	0	2	4		1926-27	1928-29
Irvine, Ted	Bos., L.A., NYR, St.L.	11	724	154	177	331	657	83	16	24	40	115		1963-64	1976-77
Irwin, Ivan	Mtl., NYR	5	155	2	27	29	214	5	0	0	0	8		1952-53	1957-58
Isaksson, Ulf	L.A.	1	50	7	15	22	10	....	....	....	....	....		1982-83	1982-83
Issel, Kim	Edm.	1	4	0	0	0	0	....	....	....	....	....		1988-89	1988-89

J

Name	NHL Teams	NHL Seasons	Regular Schedule GP	G	A	TP	PIM	Playoffs GP	G	A	TP	PIM	NHL Cup Wins	First NHL Season	Last NHL Season
• Jackson, Art	Tor., Bos., NYA	11	468	123	178	301	144	52	8	12	20	29	2	1934-35	1944-45
Jackson, Don	Min., Edm., NYR	10	311	16	52	68	640	53	4	5	9	147	2	1977-78	1986-87
• Jackson, Harold	Chi., Det.	8	219	17	34	51	208	31	1	2	3	33	2	1936-37	1946-47
• Jackson, Harvey	Tor., Bos., NYA	15	633	241	234	475	437	71	18	12	30	53	1	1929-30	1943-44
Jackson, Jeff	Tor., NYR, Que., Chi.	8	263	38	48	86	313	6	1	1	2	16		1984-85	1991-92
Jackson, Jim	Cgy., Buf.	4	112	17	30	47	20	14	3	2	5	6		1982-83	1987-88
Jackson, John	Chi.	1	48	2	5	7	38	....	....	....	....	....		1946-47	1946-47
Jackson, Lloyd	NYA	1	14	1	1	2	0	....	....	....	....	....		1936-37	1936-37
• Jackson, Stan	Tor., Bos., Ott.	5	85	9	4	13	74	....	....	....	....	....	1	1921-22	1926-27
Jackson, Walter	NYA, Bos.	4	84	16	11	27	18	....	....	....	....	....		1932-33	1934-35
• Jacobs, Paul	Tor.	1	1	0	0	0	0	....	....	....	....	....		1918-19	1918-19
Jacobs, Tim	Cal.	1	46	0	10	10	35	....	....	....	....	....		1975-76	1975-76
Jalo, Risto	Edm.	1	3	0	3	3	0	....	....	....	....	....		1985-86	1985-86
Jalonen, Kari	Cgy., Edm.	2	37	9	6	15	4	5	1	0	1	0		1982-83	1983-84
James, Gerry	Tor.	5	149	14	26	40	257	15	1	0	1	8		1954-55	1959-60
James, Val	Buf., Tor.	2	11	0	0	0	30	....	....	....	....	....		1981-82	1986-87
Jamieson, Jim	NYR	1	1	0	1	1	0	....	....	....	....	....		1943-44	1943-44
Jankowski, Lou	Det., Chi.	4	127	19	18	37	15	1	0	0	0	0		1950-51	1954-55
Jarrett, Doug	Chi., NYR	13	775	38	182	220	631	99	7	16	23	82		1964-65	1976-77
Jarrett, Gary	Tor., Det., Oak., Cal.	7	341	72	92	164	131	11	3	1	4	9		1960-61	1971-72
Jarry, Pierre	NYR, Tor., Det., Min.	7	344	88	117	205	142	5	0	1	1	0		1971-72	1977-78
Jarvenpaa, Hannu	Wpg.	3	114	11	26	37	83	....	....	....	....	....		1986-87	1988-89
Jarvi, Iiro	Que.	2	116	18	43	61	58	....	....	....	....	....		1988-89	1989-90
Jarvis, Doug	Mtl., Wsh., Hfd.	13	964	139	264	403	263	105	14	27	41	42	4	1975-76	1987-88
Jarvis, James	Pit., Phi., Tor.	3	112	17	15	32	62	....	....	....	....	....		1929-30	1936-37
Jarvis, Wes	Wsh., Min., L.A., Tor.	9	237	31	55	86	98	2	0	0	0	2		1979-80	1987-88
Javanainen, Arto	Pit.	1	14	4	1	5	2	....	....	....	....	....		1984-85	1984-85
Jay, Bob	L.A.	1	3	0	1	1	0	....	....	....	....	....		1993-94	1993-94
Jeffrey, Larry	Det., Tor., NYR	8	368	39	62	101	293	38	4	10	14	42	1	1961-62	1968-69
Jelinek, Tomas	Ott.	1	49	7	6	13	52	....	....	....	....	....		1992-93	1992-93
Jenkins, Dean	L.A.	1	5	0	0	0	2	....	....	....	....	....		1983-84	1983-84
Jenkins, Roger	Tor., Chi., Mtl., Bos., Mtl.M., NYA	8	325	15	39	54	253	25	1	7	8	12	2	1930-31	1938-39
Jennings, Bill	Det., Bos.	5	108	32	33	65	45	20	4	4	8	6		1940-41	1944-45
Jennings, Grant	Wsh., Hfd., Pit., Tor., Buf.	9	389	14	43	57	804	54	2	1	3	68	2	1987-88	1995-96
Jensen, Chris	NYR, Phi.	6	74	9	12	21	27	....	....	....	....	....		1985-86	1991-92
Jensen, David A.	Hfd., Wsh.	4	69	9	13	22	22	11	0	0	0	2		1983-84	1987-88
Jensen, David H.	Min.	3	18	0	2	2	11	....	....	....	....	....		1983-84	1985-86
Jensen, Steve	Min., L.A.	7	438	113	107	220	318	12	0	3	3	9		1975-76	1981-82
• Jeremiah, Ed	NYA, Bos.	1	15	0	1	1	0	....	....	....	....	....		1931-32	1931-32
Jerrard, Paul	Min.	1	5	0	0	0	4	....	....	....	....	....		1988-89	1988-89
Jerwa, Frank	Bos.	4	81	11	16	27	53	....	....	....	....	....		1931-32	1934-35
• Jerwa, Joe	NYR, Bos., St.L., NYA	7	234	29	58	87	309	17	2	3	5	16		1930-31	1938-39
Jirik, Jaroslav	St.L.	1	3	0	0	0	0	....	....	....	....	....		1969-70	1969-70
Joanette, Rosario	Mtl.	1	2	0	1	1	4	....	....	....	....	....		1944-45	1944-45
Jodzio, Rick	Col., Clev.	1	70	2	8	10	71	....	....	....	....	....		1977-78	1977-78
Johannesen, Glenn	NYI	1	2	0	0	0	0	....	....	....	....	....		1985-86	1985-86
Johannson, John	N.J.	1	5	0	0	0	0	....	....	....	....	....		1983-84	1983-84
Johansen, Bill	Tor.	1	1	0	0	0	0	....	....	....	....	....		1949-50	1949-50
Johansen, Trevor	Tor., Col., L.A.	5	286	11	46	57	282	13	0	3	3	21		1977-78	1981-82
Johansson, Bjorn	Clev.	2	15	1	1	2	10	....	....	....	....	....		1976-77	1977-78
Johansson, Roger	Cgy., Chi.	4	161	9	34	43	163	5	0	1	1	2		1989-90	1994-95
Johns, Don	NYR, Mtl., Min.	6	153	2	21	23	76	....	....	....	....	....		1960-61	1967-68
Johnson, Al	Mtl., Det.	4	105	21	28	49	30	11	2	2	4	6		1956-57	1962-63
Johnson, Brian	Det.	1	3	0	0	0	5	....	....	....	....	....		1983-84	1983-84

Charlie Huddy

Earl Ingarfield

Doug Jarvis

Grant Jennings

Ching Johnson

Dave Keon

Yuri Khmylev

Marko Kiprusoff

Name	NHL Teams	NHL Seasons	Regular Schedule					Playoffs					NHL Cup Wins	First NHL Season	Last NHL Season
			GP	G	A	TP	PIM	GP	G	A	TP	PIM			
• Johnson, Danny	Tor., Van., Det.	3	121	18	19	37	24	....	....	....	....	....		1969-70	1971-72
Johnson, Earl	Det.	1	1	0	0	0	0	....	....	....	....	....		1953-54	1953-54
• Johnson, Ivan	NYR, NYA	12	436	38	48	86	808	61	5	2	7	161	2	1926-27	1937-38
Johnson, Jim	NYR, Phi., L.A.	8	302	75	111	186	73	7	0	2	2	2		1964-65	1971-72
Johnson, Mark	Pit., Min., Hfd., St.L., N.J.	11	669	203	305	508	260	37	16	12	28	10		1979-80	1989-90
Johnson, Norm	Bos., Chi.	3	61	5	20	25	41	14	4	0	4	6		1957-58	1959-60
Johnson, Terry	Que., St.L., Cgy., Tor.	9	285	3	24	27	580	38	0	4	4	118		1979-80	1987-88
Johnson, Tom	Mtl., Bos.	17	978	51	213	264	960	111	8	15	23	109	6	1947-48	1964-65
• Johnson, Virgil	Chi.	3	75	2	9	11	27	19	0	3	3	4	1	1937-38	1944-45
Johnston, Bernie	Hfd.	2	57	12	24	36	16	3	0	1	1	0		1979-80	1980-81
Johnston, George	Chi.	4	58	20	12	32	2	....	....	....	....	....		1941-42	1946-47
Johnston, Greg	Bos., Tor.	9	187	26	29	55	124	22	2	1	3	12		1983-84	1991-92
Johnston, Jay	Wsh.	2	8	0	0	0	13	....	....	....	....	....		1980-81	1981-82
Johnston, Joey	Min., Cal., Chi.	6	331	85	106	191	320	....	....	....	....	....		1968-69	1975-76
Johnston, Larry	L.A., Det., K.C., Col.	7	320	9	64	73	580	....	....	....	....	....		1967-68	1976-77
Johnston, Marshall	Min., Cal.	7	251	14	52	66	58	6	0	0	0	2		1967-68	1973-74
Johnston, Randy	NYI	1	4	0	0	0	4	....	....	....	....	....		1979-80	1979-80
Johnstone, Eddie	NYR, Det.	10	426	122	136	258	375	55	13	10	23	83		1975-76	1986-87
Johnstone, Ross	Tor.	2	42	5	4	9	14	3	0	0	0	0	1	1943-44	1944-45
• Joliat, Aurel	Mtl.	16	654	270	190	460	757	54	14	19	33	89		1922-23	1937-38
• Joliat, Rene	Mtl.	1	1	0	0	0	0	....	....	....	....	....		1924-25	1924-25
Joly, Greg	Wsh., Det.	9	365	21	76	97	250	5	0	0	0	8		1974-75	1982-83
Joly, Yvan	Mtl.	3	2	0	0	0	0	1	0	0	0	0		1979-80	1982-83
Jonathan, Stan	Bos., Pit.	8	411	91	110	201	751	63	8	4	12	137		1975-76	1982-83
Jones, Bob	NYR	1	2	0	0	0	0	....	....	....	....	....		1968-69	1968-69
Jones, Brad	Wpg., L.A., Phi.	6	148	25	31	56	122	9	1	1	2	2		1986-87	1991-92
Jones, Buck	Det., Tor.	4	50	2	2	4	36	12	0	1	1	18		1938-39	1942-43
Jones, Jim	Cal.	1	2	0	0	0	0	....	....	....	....	....		1971-72	1971-72
Jones, Jimmy	Tor.	3	148	13	18	31	68	19	1	5	6	11		1977-78	1979-80
Jones, Ron	Bos., Pit., Wsh.	5	54	1	4	5	31	....	....	....	....	....		1971-72	1975-76
Jonsson, Tomas	NYI, Edm.	8	552	85	259	344	482	80	11	26	37	97	2	1981-82	1988-89
Joseph, Anthony	Wpg.	1	2	1	0	1	0	....	....	....	....	....		1988-89	1988-89
Joyal, Eddie	Det., Tor., L.A., Phi.	9	466	128	134	262	103	50	11	8	19	18		1962-63	1971-72
Joyce, Bob	Bos., Wsh., Wpg.	6	158	34	49	83	90	46	15	9	24	29		1987-88	1992-93
Joyce, Duane	Dal.	1	3	0	0	0	0	....	....	....	....	....		1993-94	1993-94
Juckes, Bing	NYR	2	16	2	1	3	6	....	....	....	....	....		1947-48	1949-50
Julien, Claude	Que.	2	14	0	1	1	25	....	....	....	....	....		1984-85	1985-86
Junker, Steve	NYI	2	5	0	0	0	0	3	0	1	1	0		1992-93	1993-94
Jutila, Timo	Buf.	1	10	1	5	6	13	....	....	....	....	....		1984-85	1984-85
Juzda, Bill	NYR, Tor.	9	398	14	54	68	398	42	0	3	3	46	2	1940-41	1951-52

K

Name	NHL Teams	NHL Seasons	GP	G	A	TP	PIM	GP	G	A	TP	PIM	NHL Cup Wins	First NHL Season	Last NHL Season
Kabel, Bob	NYR	2	48	5	13	18	34	....	....	....	....	....		1959-60	1960-61
Kachowski, Mark	Pit.	3	64	6	5	11	209	....	....	....	....	....		1987-88	1989-90
Kachur, Ed	Chi.	2	96	10	14	24	35	....	....	....	....	....		1956-57	1957-58
Kaese, Trent	Buf.	1	1	0	0	0	0	....	....	....	....	....		1988-89	1988-89
Kaiser, Vern	Mtl.	1	50	7	5	12	33	2	0	0	0	0		1950-51	1950-51
• Kalbfleish, Walter	Ott., St.L., NYA, Bos.	4	36	0	4	4	32	5	0	0	0	2		1933-34	1936-37
• Kaleta, Alex	Chi., NYR	7	387	92	121	213	190	17	1	6	7	2		1941-42	1950-51
Kallur, Anders	NYI	6	383	101	110	211	149	78	12	23	35	32	4	1979-80	1984-85
• Kaminsky, Max	Ott., St.L., Bos., Mtl.M.	4	130	22	34	56	38	4	0	0	0	0		1933-34	1936-37
• Kampman, Rudolph	Tor.	5	189	14	30	44	287	47	1	4	5	38	1	1937-38	1941-42
Kane, Francis	Det.	1	2	0	0	0	0	....	....	....	....	....		1943-44	1943-44
Kannegiesser, Gord	St.L.	2	23	0	1	1	15	....	....	....	....	....		1967-68	1971-72
Kannegiesser, Sheldon	Pit., NYR, L.A., Van.	8	366	14	67	81	292	18	0	2	2	10		1970-71	1977-78
Karabin, Ladislav	Pit.	1	9	0	0	0	2	....	....	....	....	....		1993-94	1993-94
Karamnov, Vitali	St.L.	3	92	12	20	32	65	2	0	0	0	2		1992-93	1994-95
Karjalainen, Kyosti	L.A.	1	28	1	8	9	12	3	0	1	1	2		1991-92	1991-92
Karlander, Al	Det.	4	212	36	56	92	70	4	0	1	1	0		1969-70	1972-73
Karpov, Valeri	Ana.	3	76	14	15	29	32	....	....	....	....	....		1994-95	1996-97
Kasatonov, Alexei	N.J., Ana., St.L., Bos.	7	383	38	122	160	326	33	4	7	11	40		1989-90	1995-96
Kasper, Steve	Bos., L.A., Phi., T.B.	13	821	177	291	468	554	94	20	28	48	82		1980-81	1992-93
Kastelic, Ed	Wsh., Hfd.	7	220	11	10	21	719	8	1	0	1	32		1985-86	1991-92
Kaszycki, Mike	NYI, Wsh., Tor.	5	226	42	80	122	108	19	2	6	8	10		1977-78	1982-83
Kea, Ed	Atl., St.L.	10	583	30	145	175	508	32	2	4	6	39		1973-74	1982-83
Kearns, Dennis	Van.	10	677	31	290	321	386	11	1	2	3	8		1971-72	1980-81
• Keating, Jack	NYA	2	35	5	5	10	17	....	....	....	....	....		1931-32	1932-33
Keating, John	Det.	2	11	2	1	3	4	....	....	....	....	....		1938-39	1939-40
Keating, Mike	NYR	1	1	0	0	0	0	....	....	....	....	....		1977-78	1977-78
• Keats, Duke	Bos., Det., Chi.	3	82	30	19	49	113	....	....	....	....	....		1926-27	1928-29
• Keeling, Butch	Tor., NYR	12	525	157	63	220	331	47	11	11	22	34	1	1926-27	1937-38
Keenan, Larry	Tor., St.L., Buf., Phi.	6	233	38	64	102	28	46	15	16	31	12		1961-62	1971-72
Kehoe, Rick	Tor., Pit.	14	906	371	396	767	120	39	4	17	21	4		1971-72	1984-85
Kekalainen, Jarmo	Bos., Ott.	3	55	5	8	13	28	....	....	....	....	....		1989-90	1993-94
Keller, Ralph	NYR	1	3	1	0	1	6	....	....	....	....	....		1962-63	1962-63
Kellgren, Christer	Col.	1	5	0	0	0	0	....	....	....	....	....		1981-82	1981-82
Kelly, Bob	St.L., Pit., Chi.	6	425	87	109	196	687	23	6	3	9	40		1973-74	1978-79
Kelly, Bob	Phi., Wsh.	12	837	154	208	362	1454	101	9	14	23	172	2	1970-71	1981-82
Kelly, Dave	Det.	1	16	2	0	2	4	....	....	....	....	....		1976-77	1976-77
Kelly, John Paul	L.A.	7	400	54	70	124	366	18	1	1	2	41		1979-80	1985-86
Kelly, Pete	St.L., Det., NYA, Bro.	7	177	21	38	59	68	19	3	1	4	2	2	1934-35	1941-42
Kelly, Red	Det., Tor.	20	1316	281	542	823	327	164	33	59	92	51	8	1947-48	1966-67
• Kelly, Regis	Tor., Chi., Bro.	8	288	74	53	127	105	38	7	6	13	10		1934-35	1941-42
Kemp, Kevin	Hfd.	1	3	0	0	0	4	....	....	....	....	....		1980-81	1980-81
Kemp, Stan	Tor.	1	1	0	0	0	2	....	....	....	....	....		1948-49	1948-49
• Kendall, Bill	Chi., Tor.	5	131	16	10	26	28	6	0	0	0	0	1	1933-34	1937-38
Kennedy, Dean	L.A., NYR, Buf., Wpg., Edm.	12	717	26	108	134	1118	36	1	7	8	59		1982-83	1994-95
Kennedy, Forbes	Chi., Det., Bos., Phi., Tor.	11	603	70	108	178	988	12	2	4	6	64		1956-57	1968-69
Kennedy, Ted	Tor.	14	696	231	329	560	432	78	29	31	60	32	5	1942-43	1956-57
• Kenny, Ernest	NYR, Chi.	2	10	0	0	0	18	....	....	....	....	....		1930-31	1934-35
Keon, Dave	Tor., Hfd.	18	1296	396	590	986	117	92	32	36	68	6	4	1960-61	1981-82
Kerch, Alexander	Edm.	1	5	0	0	0	2	....	....	....	....	....		1993-94	1993-94
Kerr, Alan	NYI, Det., Wpg.	9	391	72	94	166	826	38	5	4	9	70		1984-85	1992-93
Kerr, Reg	Cle., Chi., Edm.	6	263	66	94	160	169	7	1	0	1	7		1977-78	1983-84
Kerr, Tim	Phi., NYR, Hfd.	13	655	370	304	674	596	81	40	31	71	58		1980-81	1992-93
Kessell, Rick	Pit., Cal.	5	135	4	24	28	6	....	....	....	....	....		1969-70	1973-74
Ketola, Veli-Pekka	Col.	1	44	9	5	14	4	....	....	....	....	....		1981-82	1981-82
Ketter, Kerry	Atl.	1	41	0	2	2	58	....	....	....	....	....		1972-73	1972-73
Kharin, Sergei	Wpg.	1	7	2	3	5	2	....	....	....	....	....		1990-91	1990-91
Khmylev, Yuri	Buf., St.L.	5	263	64	88	152	133	26	8	6	14	24		1992-93	1996-97
Kidd, Ian	Van.	2	20	4	7	11	25	....	....	....	....	....		1987-88	1988-89
Kiessling, Udo	Min.	1	1	0	0	0	2	....	....	....	....	....		1981-82	1981-82
Kilrea, Brian	Det., L.A.	2	26	3	5	8	12	....	....	....	....	....		1957-58	1967-68
• Kilrea, Hec	Ott., Det., Tor.	15	633	167	129	296	438	48	8	7	15	18	3	1925-26	1939-40
• Kilrea, Ken	Det.	5	91	16	23	39	8	15	2	2	4	4		1938-39	1943-44
Kilrea, Wally	Ott., Phi., NYA, Mtl.M., Det.	9	329	35	58	93	87	25	2	4	6	6	2	1929-30	1937-38
Kimble, Darin	Que., St.L., Bos., Chi.	7	311	23	20	43	1082	23	0	0	0	52		1988-89	1994-95
Kindrachuk, Orest	Phi., Pit., Wsh.	10	508	118	261	379	648	76	20	20	40	53	2	1972-73	1981-82
King, Frank	Mtl.	1	10	1	0	1	2	....	....	....	....	....		1950-51	1950-51
King, Wayne	Cal.	3	73	5	18	23	34	....	....	....	....	....		1973-74	1975-76
Kinsella, Brian	Wsh.	2	10	0	1	1	0	....	....	....	....	....		1975-76	1976-77
• Kinsella, Ray	Ott.	1	14	0	0	0	0	....	....	....	....	....		1930-31	1930-31
Kiprusoff, Marko	Mtl.	1	24	0	4	4	8	....	....	....	....	....		1995-96	1995-96
• Kirk, Bobby	NYR	1	39	4	8	12	14	....	....	....	....	....		1937-38	1937-38
Kirkpatrick, Bob	NYR	1	49	12	12	24	6	....	....	....	....	....		1942-43	1942-43
Kirton, Mark	Tor., Det., Van.	6	266	57	56	113	121	4	1	2	3	7		1979-80	1984-85
Kisio, Kelly	Det., NYR, S.J., Cgy.	13	761	229	429	658	768	39	6	15	21	52		1982-83	1994-95
Kitchen, Bill	Mtl., Tor.	4	41	1	4	5	40	3	0	1	1	0		1981-82	1984-85
• Kitchen, Hobie	Mtl.M., Det.	2	47	5	4	9	58	....	....	....	....	....		1925-26	1926-27
Kitchen, Mike	Col., N.J.	8	474	12	62	74	370	2	0	0	0	2		1976-77	1983-84
Klassen, Ralph	Cal., Clev., Col., St.L.	9	497	52	93	145	120	26	4	2	6	12		1975-76	1983-84
• Klein, Jim	Bos., NYA	8	164	30	24	54	68	5	0	0	0	2		1928-29	1937-38

Name	NHL Teams	NHL Seasons	Regular Schedule GP	G	A	TP	PIM	Playoffs GP	G	A	TP	PIM	NHL Cup Wins	First NHL Season	Last NHL Season
Kleinendorst, Scot	NYR, Hfd., Wsh.	8	281	12	46	58	452	26	2	7	9	40		1982-83	1989-90
Klingbeil, Ike	Chi.	1	5	1	2	3	2	....	....	....	....	....		1936-37	1936-37
Klukay, Joe	Tor., Bos.	11	566	109	127	236	189	71	13	10	23	23	4	1942-43	1955-56
Kluzak, Gord	Bos.	7	299	25	98	123	543	46	6	13	19	129		1982-83	1990-91
Knibbs, Bill	Bos.	1	53	7	10	17	4	....	....	....	....	....		1964-65	1964-65
● Knott, William	Bro.	1	14	3	1	4	9	....	....	....	....	....		1941-42	1941-42
Knox, Paul	Tor.	1	1	0	0	0	0	....	....	....	....	....		1954-55	1954-55
Kolstad, Dean	Min., S.J.	3	40	1	7	8	69	....	....	....	....	....		1988-89	1992-93
Komadoski, Neil	L.A., St.L.	8	502	16	76	92	632	23	0	2	2	47		1972-73	1979-80
Konik, George	Pit.	1	52	7	8	15	26	....	....	....	....	....		1967-68	1967-68
Konroyd, Steve	Cgy., NYI, Chi., Hfd., Det., Ott.	15	895	41	195	236	863	97	10	15	25	99		1980-81	1994-95
Kontos, Chris	NYR, Pit., L.A., T.B.	8	230	54	69	123	103	20	11	0	11	12		1982-83	1992-93
Kopak, Russ	Bos.	1	24	7	9	16	0	....	....	....	....	....		1943-44	1943-44
Korab, Jerry	Chi., Van., Buf., L.A.	15	975	114	341	455	1629	93	8	18	26	201		1970-71	1984-85
● Kordic, John	Mtl., Tor., Wsh., Que.	7	244	17	18	35	997	41	4	3	7	131	1	1985-86	1991-92
Korn, Jim	Det., Tor., Buf., N.J., Cgy.	10	597	66	122	188	1801	16	1	2	3	109		1979-80	1989-90
Korney, Mike	Det., NYR	4	77	9	10	19	59	....	....	....	....	....		1973-74	1978-79
Koroll, Cliff	Chi.	11	814	208	254	462	376	85	19	29	48	67		1969-70	1979-80
Kortko, Roger	NYI	2	79	7	17	24	28	10	0	3	3	17		1984-85	1985-86
Kostynski, Doug	Bos.	2	15	3	1	4	4	....	....	....	....	....		1983-84	1984-85
Kotanen, Dick	NYR	1	1	0	0	0	0	....	....	....	....	....		1950-51	1950-51
Kotsopoulos, Chris	NYR, Hfd.,Tor., Det.	10	479	44	109	153	827	31	1	3	4	91		1980-81	1989-90
Kowal, Joe	Buf.	2	22	0	5	5	13	2	0	0	0	0		1976-77	1977-78
Kozak, Don	L.A., Van.	7	437	96	86	182	480	29	7	2	9	69		1972-73	1978-79
Kozak, Les	Tor.	1	12	1	0	1	2	....	....	....	....	....		1961-62	1961-62
● Kraftcheck, Stephen	Bos., NYR, Tor.	4	157	11	18	29	83	6	0	0	0	7		1950-51	1958-59
Krake, Skip	Bos., L.A., Buf.	7	249	23	40	63	182	10	1	0	1	17		1963-64	1970-71
Kravets, Mikhail	S.J.	2	2	0	0	0	0	....	....	....	....	....		1991-92	1992-93
Krentz, Dale	Det.	3	30	5	3	8	9	2	0	0	0	0		1986-87	1988-89
● Krol, Joe	NYR, Bro.	3	26	10	4	14	8	....	....	....	....	....		1936-37	1941-42
Kromm, Rich	Cgy., NYI	9	372	70	103	173	138	36	2	6	8	22		1983-84	1992-93
Krook, Kevin	Col.	1	3	0	0	0	2	....	....	....	....	....		1978-79	1978-79
Krulicki, Jim	NYR, Det.	1	41	0	3	3	6	....	....	....	....	....		1970-71	1970-71
Kruppke, Gord	Det.	3	23	0	0	0	32	....	....	....	....	....		1990-91	1993-94
Krushelnyski, Mike	Bos., Edm., L.A., Tor., Det.	14	897	241	328	569	699	139	29	43	72	106	3	1981-82	1994-95
Krutov, Vladimir	Van.	1	61	11	23	34	20	....	....	....	....	....		1989-90	1989-90
Kryskow, Dave	Chi., Wsh., Det., Atl.	4	231	33	56	89	174	12	2	0	2	4		1972-73	1975-76
Kryznowski, Edward	Bos., Chi.	5	237	15	22	37	65	18	0	1	1	4		1948-49	1952-53
Kudashov, Alexei	Tor.	1	25	1	0	1	4	....	....	....	....	....		1993-94	1993-94
Kudelski, Bob	L.A., Ott., Fla.	9	442	139	102	241	218	22	4	4	8	4		1987-88	1995-96
● Kuhn, Gord	NYA	1	12	1	1	2	4	....	....	....	....	....		1932-33	1932-33
Kukulowicz, Aggie	NYR	2	4	1	0	1	0	....	....	....	....	....		1952-53	1953-54
Kulak, Stu	Van., Edm., NYR, Que., Wpg.	4	90	8	4	12	130	3	0	0	0	2		1982-83	1988-89
Kullman, Arnie	Bos.	2	13	0	1	1	11	....	....	....	....	....		1947-48	1949-50
● Kullman, Eddie	NYR	6	343	56	70	126	298	6	1	0	1	2		1947-48	1953-54
Kumpel, Mark	Que., Det., Wpg.	6	288	38	46	84	113	39	6	4	10	14		1984-85	1990-91
● Kuntz, Alan	NYR	2	45	10	12	22	12	6	1	0	1	2		1941-42	1945-46
Kuntz, Murray	St.L.	1	7	1	2	3	0	....	....	....	....	....		1974-75	1974-75
Kurtenbach, Orland	NYR, Bos., Tor., Van.	13	639	119	213	332	628	19	2	4	6	70		1960-61	1973-74
Kurvers, Tom	Mtl., Buf., N.J., Tor., Van., NYI, Ana.	11	659	93	328	421	350	57	8	22	30	68	1	1984-85	1994-95
Kuryluk, Mervin	Chi.	1	....	....	....	....	....	2	0	0	0	0		1961-62	1961-62
Kushner, Dale	NYI, Phi.	3	84	10	13	23	215	....	....	....	....	....		1989-90	1991-92
Kuzyk, Ken	Clev.	2	41	5	9	14	8	....	....	....	....	....		1976-77	1977-78
Kvartalnov, Dmitri	Bos.	2	112	42	49	91	26	4	0	0	0	0		1992-93	1993-94
Kwong, Larry	NYR	1	1	0	0	0	0	....	....	....	....	....		1947-48	1947-48
● Kyle, Bill	NYR	2	3	0	3	3	0	....	....	....	....	....		1949-50	1950-51
● Kyle, Gus	NYR, Bos.	3	203	6	20	26	362	14	1	2	3	34		1949-50	1951-52
Kyllonen, Markku	Wpg.	1	9	0	2	2	2	....	....	....	....	....		1988-89	1988-89
Kyte, Jim	Wpg., Pit., Cgy., Ott., S.J.	13	598	17	49	66	1342	42	0	6	6	94		1982-83	1995-96

Chris Kontos

Jim Kyte

L

Name	NHL Teams	NHL Seasons	Regular Schedule GP	G	A	TP	PIM	Playoffs GP	G	A	TP	PIM	NHL Cup Wins	First NHL Season	Last NHL Season
Labadie, Mike	NYR	1	3	0	0	0	0	....	....	....	....	....		1952-53	1952-53
Labatte, Neil	St.L.	2	26	0	2	2	19	....	....	....	....	....		1978-79	1981-82
L'Abbe, Moe	Chi.	1	5	0	1	1	0	....	....	....	....	....		1972-73	1972-73
Labine, Leo	Bos., Det.	11	643	128	193	321	730	60	11	12	23	82		1951-52	1961-62
Labossierre, Gord	NYR, L.A., Min.	6	215	44	62	106	75	10	2	3	5	28		1963-64	1971-72
Labovitch, Max	NYR	1	5	0	0	0	4	....	....	....	....	....		1943-44	1943-44
Labraaten, Daniel	Det., Cgy.	4	268	71	73	144	47	8	1	0	1	4		1978-79	1981-82
Labre, Yvon	Pit., Wsh.	9	371	14	87	101	788	....	....	....	....	....		1970-71	1980-81
Labrie, Guy	Bos., NYR	2	42	4	9	13	16	....	....	....	....	....		1943-44	1944-45
Lach, Elmer	Mtl.	14	664	215	408	623	478	76	19	45	64	36	3	1940-41	1953-54
Lachance, Michel	Col.	1	21	0	4	4	22	....	....	....	....	....		1978-79	1978-79
Lacombe, Francois	Oak., Buf., Que.	4	78	2	17	19	54	3	1	0	1	0		1968-69	1979-80
Lacombe, Normand	Buf., Edm., Phi	7	319	53	62	115	196	26	5	1	6	49	1	1984-85	1990-91
Lacroix, Andre	Phi., Chi., Hfd.	6	325	79	119	198	44	16	2	5	7	0		1967-68	1979-80
Lacroix, Pierre	Que., Hfd.	4	274	24	108	132	197	8	0	2	2	10		1979-80	1982-83
Ladouceur, Randy	Det., Hfd., Ana.	14	930	30	126	156	1322	40	5	8	13	59		1982-83	1995-96
Lafleur, Guy	Mtl., NYR, Que.	17	1126	560	793	1353	399	128	58	76	134	67	5	1971-72	1990-91
● Lafleur, Roland	Mtl.	1	1	0	0	0	0	....	....	....	....	....		1924-25	1924-25
Laforce, Ernie	Mtl.	1	1	0	0	0	0	....	....	....	....	....		1942-43	1942-43
LaForest, Bob	L.A.	1	5	1	0	1	2	....	....	....	....	....		1983-84	1983-84
Laforge, Claude	Mtl., Det., Phi.	8	193	24	33	57	82	5	1	2	3	15		1957-58	1968-69
Laforge, Marc	Hfd., Edm.	2	14	0	0	0	64	....	....	....	....	....		1989-90	1993-94
Laframboise, Pete	Cal., Wsh., Pit.	4	227	33	55	88	70	9	1	0	1	0		1971-72	1974-75
Lafrance, Adie	Mtl.	1	3	0	0	0	2	2	0	0	0	0		1933-34	1933-34
Lafrance, Leo	Mtl., Chi.	2	33	2	0	2	6	....	....	....	....	....		1926-27	1927-28
Lafreniere, Jason	Que., NYR, T.B.	5	146	34	53	87	22	15	1	5	6	19		1986-87	1993-94
Lafreniere, Roger	Det., St.L.	2	13	0	0	0	4	....	....	....	....	....		1962-63	1972-73
Lagace, Jean-Guy	Pit., Buf., K.C.	6	197	9	39	48	251	....	....	....	....	....		1968-69	1975-76
Laidlaw, Tom	NYR, L.A.	10	705	25	139	164	717	69	4	17	21	78		1980-81	1989-90
Laird, Robbie	Min.	1	1	0	0	0	0	....	....	....	....	....		1979-80	1979-80
Lajeunesse, Serge	Det., Phi.	5	103	1	4	5	103	....	....	....	....	....		1970-71	1974-75
Lalande, Hec	Chi., Det.	4	151	21	39	60	120	....	....	....	....	....		1953-54	1957-58
Lalonde, Bobby	Van., Atl., Bos., Cgy.	11	641	124	210	334	298	16	4	2	6	6		1971-72	1981-82
● Lalonde, Newsy	Mtl., NYA	6	99	124	42	166	151	12	21	3	24	35		1917-18	1926-27
Lalonde, Ron	Pit., Wsh.	7	397	45	78	123	106	....	....	....	....	....		1972-73	1978-79
Lalor, Mike	Mtl., St.L., Wsh., Wpg., S.J., Dal.	12	687	17	88	105	677	92	5	10	15	167	1	1985-86	1996-97
● Lamb, Joe	Mtl.M., Ott., NYA, Bos., Mtl., St.L., Det.	11	443	108	101	209	601	18	1	1	2	51		1927-28	1937-38
Lamb, Mark	Cgy., Det., Edm., Ott., Phi., Mtl.	11	403	46	100	146	291	70	7	19	26	51	1	1985-86	1995-96
Lambert, Dan	Que.	2	29	6	9	15	22	....	....	....	....	....		1990-91	1991-92
Lambert, Lane	Det., NYR, Que.	6	283	58	66	124	521	17	2	4	6	40		1983-84	1988-89
Lambert, Yvon	Mtl., Buf.	10	683	206	273	479	340	90	27	22	49	67	4	1972-73	1981-82
Lamby, Dick	St.L.	3	22	0	5	5	22	....	....	....	....	....		1978-79	1980-81
● Lamirande, Jean-Paul	NYR, Mtl.	4	49	5	5	10	26	8	0	0	0	4		1946-47	1954-55
Lammens, Hank	Ott.	1	27	1	2	3	22	....	....	....	....	....		1993-94	1993-94
● Lamoureux, Leo	Mtl.	6	235	19	79	98	175	28	1	6	7	16	2	1941-42	1946-47
Lamoureux, Mitch	Pit., Phi.	3	73	11	9	20	59	....	....	....	....	....		1983-84	1987-88
Lampman, Mike	St.L., Van., Wsh.	4	96	17	20	37	34	....	....	....	....	....		1972-73	1976-77
Lancien, Jack	NYR	4	63	1	5	6	35	6	0	1	1	2		1946-47	1950-51
Landon, Larry	Mtl., Tor.	2	9	0	0	0	2	....	....	....	....	....		1983-84	1984-85
Lane, Gord	Wsh., NYI	10	539	19	94	113	1228	75	3	14	17	214	4	1975-76	1984-85
● Lane, Myles	NYR, Bos.	3	71	4	1	5	41	11	0	0	0	0	1	1928-29	1933-34
Langdon, Steve	Bos.	3	7	0	1	1	2	4	0	0	0	0		1974-75	1977-78
Langelle, Pete	Tor.	4	136	22	51	73	11	41	5	9	14	4	1	1938-39	1941-42
Langevin, Chris	Buf.	2	22	3	1	4	22	....	....	....	....	....		1983-84	1985-86
Langevin, Dave	NYI, Min., L.A.	8	513	12	107	119	530	87	2	17	19	106	4	1979-80	1986-87
Langlais, Alain	Min.	2	25	4	4	8	10	....	....	....	....	....		1973-74	1974-75
Langlois, Albert	Mtl., NYR, Det., Bos.	9	497	21	91	112	488	53	1	5	6	50	3	1957-58	1965-66
● Langlois, Charlie	Ham., NYA., Pit., Mtl.	4	151	22	3	25	201	2	0	0	0	0		1924-25	1927-28
Langway, Rod	Mtl., Wsh.	15	994	51	278	329	849	104	5	22	27	97	1	1978-79	1992-93
Lanthier, Jean-Marc	Van.	4	105	16	16	32	29	....	....	....	....	....		1983-84	1987-88
Lanyon, Ted	Pit.	1	5	0	0	0	4	....	....	....	....	....		1967-68	1967-68

Mike Lalor

Mark Lamb

Dan Laperriere

Hal Laycoe

Stephan Lebeau

Mario Lemieux

Name	NHL Teams	NHL Seasons	Regular Schedule					Playoffs					NHL Cup Wins	First NHL Season	Last NHL Season
			GP	G	A	TP	PIM	GP	G	A	TP	PIM			
Lanz, Rick	Van., Tor., Chi.	10	569	65	221	286	448	28	3	8	11	35		1980-81	1991-92
Laperriere, Daniel	St.L., Ott.	4	48	2	5	7	27	....	....	....	....	....		1992-93	1995-96
Laperriere, Jacques	Mtl.	12	691	40	242	282	674	88	9	22	31	101	6	1962-63	1973-74
Lapointe, Guy	Mtl., St.L., Bos.	16	884	171	451	622	893	123	26	44	70	138	6	1968-69	1983-84
Lapointe, Rick	Det., Phi., St.L., Que., L.A.	11	664	44	176	220	831	46	2	7	9	64		1975-76	1985-86
Lappin, Peter	Min., S.J.	2	7	0	0	0	2	....	....	....	....	....		1989-90	1991-92
Laprade, Edgar	NYR	10	500	108	172	280	42	18	4	9	13	4		1945-46	1954-55
LaPrairie, Benjamin	Chi.	1	7	0	0	0	0	....	....	....	....	....		1936-37	1936-37
Lariviere, Garry	Que., Edm.	4	219	6	57	63	167	14	0	5	5	8		1979-80	1982-83
Larmer, Jeff	Col., N.J., Chi.	5	158	37	51	88	57	5	1	0	1	2		1981-82	1985-86
Larmer, Steve	Chi., NYR	15	1006	441	571	1012	532	140	56	75	131	89	1	1980-81	1994-95
• Larochelle, Wildor	Mtl., Chi.	12	474	92	74	166	211	34	6	4	10	24		1925-26	1936-37
Larocque, Denis	L.A.	1	8	0	1	1	18	....	....	....	....	....		1987-88	1987-88
• Larose, Charles	Bos.	1	6	0	0	0	0	....	....	....	....	....		1925-26	1925-26
Larose, Claude	NYR	2	25	4	7	11	2	2	0	0	0	0		1979-80	1981-82
Larose, Claude	Mtl., Min., St.L.	16	943	226	257	483	887	97	14	18	32	143	5	1962-63	1977-78
Larose, Guy	Wpg., Tor., Cgy., Bos.	6	70	10	9	19	63	4	0	0	0	0		1988-89	1994-95
Larouche, Pierre	Pit., Mtl., Hfd., NYR	14	812	395	427	822	237	64	20	34	54	16	2	1974-75	1987-88
Larson, Norman	NYA., Bro., NYR	3	89	25	18	43	12	....	....	....	....	....		1940-41	1946-47
Larson, Reed	Det., Bos., Edm., NYI, Min., Buf.	14	904	222	463	685	1391	32	4	7	11	63		1976-77	1989-90
Larter, Tyler	Wsh.	1	1	0	0	0	0	....	....	....	....	....		1989-90	1989-90
Latal, Jiri	Phi.	3	92	12	36	48	24	....	....	....	....	....		1989-90	1990-91
Latos, James	NYR	1	1	0	0	0	0	....	....	....	....	....		1988-89	1988-89
Latreille, Phil	NYR	1	4	0	0	0	2	....	....	....	....	....		1960-61	1960-61
Latta, David	Que.	4	36	4	8	12	4	....	....	....	....	....		1985-86	1990-91
Lauder, Martin	Bos.	1	3	0	0	0	2	....	....	....	....	....		1927-28	1927-28
Lauen, Mike	Wpg.	1	4	0	1	1	0	....	....	....	....	....		1983-84	1983-84
Laughlin, Craig	Mtl., Wsh., L.A., Tor.	8	549	136	205	341	364	33	6	6	12	20		1981-82	1988-89
Laughton, Mike	Oak., Cal.	4	189	39	48	87	101	11	2	4	6	0		1967-68	1970-71
Laurence, Don	Atl., St.L.	2	79	15	22	37	14	....	....	....	....	....		1978-79	1979-80
LaVallee, Kevin	Cgy., L.A., St.L., Pit.	7	366	110	125	235	85	32	5	8	13	21		1980-81	1986-87
Lavarre, Mark	Chi.	3	78	9	16	25	58	1	0	0	0	2		1985-86	1987-88
Lavender, Brian	St.L., NYI, Det., Cal.	4	184	16	26	42	174	3	0	0	0	2		1971-72	1974-75
Lavigne, Eric	L.A.	1	1	0	0	0	0	....	....	....	....	....		1994-95	1994-95
• Laviolette, Jack	Mtl.	1	18	2	1	3	6	2	0	0	0	0		1917-18	1917-18
Laviolette, Peter	NYR	1	12	0	0	0	6	....	....	....	....	....		1988-89	1988-89
Lavoie, Dominic	St.L., Ott., Bos., L.A.	6	38	5	8	13	32	....	....	....	....	....		1988-89	1993-94
Lawless, Paul	Hfd., Phi., Van., Tor.	7	239	49	77	126	54	3	0	2	2	2		1982-83	1989-90
Lawson, Danny	Det., Min., Buf.	5	219	28	29	57	61	16	0	1	1	2		1967-68	1971-72
Lawton, Brian	Min., NYR, Hfd., Que., Bos., S.J.	9	483	112	154	266	401	11	1	1	2	12		1983-84	1992-93
Laxdal, Derek	Tor., NYI	6	67	12	7	19	88	1	0	2	2	2		1984-85	1990-91
• Laycoe, Hal	NYR, Mtl., Bos.	11	531	25	77	102	292	40	2	5	7	39		1945-46	1955-56
Lazaro, Jeff	Bos., Ott.	3	102	14	23	37	114	28	3	3	6	32		1990-91	1992-93
Leach, Jamie	Pit., Hfd., Fla.	5	81	11	9	20	12	....	....	....	....	....	1	1989-90	1993-94
Leach, Larry	Bos.	3	126	13	29	42	91	7	1	1	2	8		1958-59	1961-62
Leach, Reggie	Bos., Cal., Phi., Det.	13	934	381	285	666	387	94	47	22	69	22	1	1970-71	1982-83
Leavins, Jim	Det., NYR	2	41	2	12	14	30	....	....	....	....	....		1985-86	1986-87
Lebeau, Patrick	Mtl., Cgy., Fla.	3	7	2	2	4	4	....	....	....	....	....		1990-91	1993-94
Lebeau, Stephan	Mtl., Ana.	7	373	118	159	277	105	30	9	7	16	12	1	1988-89	1994-95
LeBlanc, Fern	Det.	3	34	5	6	11	0	....	....	....	....	....		1976-77	1978-79
LeBlanc, J.P.	Chi., Det.	5	153	14	30	44	87	2	0	0	0	0		1968-69	1978-79
LeBrun, Al	NYR	2	6	0	2	2	4	....	....	....	....	....		1960-61	1965-66
Lecaine, Bill	Pit.	1	4	0	0	0	0	....	....	....	....	....		1968-69	1968-69
Leclair, Jackie	Mtl.	3	160	20	40	60	56	20	6	1	7	6	1	1954-55	1956-57
Leclerc, Rene	Det.	2	87	10	11	21	105	....	....	....	....	....		1968-69	1970-71
Lecuyer, Doug	Chi., Wpg., Pit.	4	126	11	31	42	178	7	4	0	4	15		1978-79	1982-83
Ledingham, Walt	Chi., NYI	3	15	0	2	2	4	....	....	....	....	....		1972-73	1976-77
• LeDuc, Albert	Mtl., Ott., NYR	10	383	57	35	92	614	28	5	6	11	32		1925-26	1934-35
LeDuc, Rich	Bos., Que.	4	130	28	38	66	69	5	0	0	0	9		1972-73	1980-81
• Lee, Bobby	Mtl.	1	1	0	0	0	0	....	....	....	....	....		1942-43	1942-43
Lee, Edward	Que.	1	2	0	0	0	5	....	....	....	....	....		1984-85	1984-85
Lee, Peter	Pit.	6	431	114	131	245	257	19	0	8	8	4		1977-78	1982-83
Leeman, Gary	Tor., Cgy., Mtl., Van., St.L.	14	667	199	267	466	531	36	8	16	24	36	1	1982-83	1996-97
• Lefley, Bryan	N.Y.I., K.C., Col.	5	228	7	29	36	101	2	0	0	0	0		1972-73	1977-78
Lefley, Chuck	Mtl., St.L.	9	407	128	164	292	137	29	5	8	13	10	2	1970-71	1980-81
• Leger, Roger	NYR, Mtl.	5	187	18	53	71	71	20	0	7	7	14		1943-44	1949-50
Legge, Barry	Que., Wpg.	3	107	1	11	12	144	....	....	....	....	....		1979-80	1981-82
Legge, Randy	NYR	1	12	0	2	2	2	....	....	....	....	....		1972-73	1972-73
Lehmann, Tommy	Bos., Edm.	3	36	5	5	10	16	....	....	....	....	....		1987-88	1989-90
Lehto, Petteri	Pit.	1	6	0	0	0	4	....	....	....	....	....		1984-85	1984-85
Lehtonen, Antero	Wsh.	1	65	9	12	21	14	....	....	....	....	....		1979-80	1979-80
Lehvonen, Henri	K.C.	1	4	0	0	0	0	....	....	....	....	....		1974-75	1974-75
Leier, Edward	Chi.	2	16	2	1	3	2	....	....	....	....	....		1949-50	1950-51
Leinonen, Mikko	NYR, Wsh.	4	162	31	78	109	71	20	2	11	13	28		1981-82	1984-85
Leiter, Bobby	Bos., Pit., Atl.	10	447	98	126	224	144	8	3	0	3	2		1962-63	1975-76
Leiter, Ken	NYI, Min.	5	143	14	36	50	62	15	0	6	6	8		1984-85	1989-90
Lemaire, Jacques	Mtl.	12	853	366	469	835	217	145	61	78	139	63	8	1967-68	1978-79
Lemay, Moe	Van., Edm., Bos., Wpg.	8	317	72	94	166	442	28	6	3	9	55	1	1981-82	1988-89
Lemelin, Roger	K.C., Col.	4	36	1	2	3	27	....	....	....	....	....		1974-75	1977-78
Lemieux, Alain	St.L., Que., Pit.	6	119	28	44	72	38	19	4	6	10	0		1981-82	1986-87
Lemieux, Bob	Oak.	1	19	0	1	1	12	....	....	....	....	....		1967-68	1967-68
Lemieux, Jacques	L.A.	3	19	0	4	4	8	1	0	0	0	0		1967-68	1969-70
Lemieux, Jean	L.A., Atl., Wsh.	5	204	23	63	86	39	3	1	1	2	0		1969-70	1977-78
Lemieux, Mario	Pit.	12	745	613	881	1494	737	89	70	85	155	83	2	1984-85	1996-97
• Lemieux, Real	Det., L.A., NYR, Buf.	8	456	51	104	155	262	18	2	4	6	10		1966-67	1973-74
Lemieux, Richard	Van., K.C., Atl.	5	274	39	82	121	132	2	0	0	0	0		1971-72	1975-76
Lenardon, Tim	N.J., Van.	2	15	2	1	3	4	....	....	....	....	....		1986-87	1989-90
• Lepine, Hec	Mtl.	1	33	5	2	7	2	....	....	....	....	....		1925-26	1925-26
• Lepine, Pit	Mtl.	13	526	143	98	241	392	41	7	5	12	26		1925-26	1937-38
Leroux, Gaston	Mtl.	1	2	0	0	0	0	....	....	....	....	....		1935-36	1935-36
Lesieur, Art	Mtl., Chi.	4	100	4	2	6	50	14	0	0	0	4		1928-29	1935-36
Lessard, Rick	Cgy., S.J.	3	15	0	4	4	18	....	....	....	....	....		1988-89	1991-92
Lesuk, Bill	Bos., Phi., L.A., Wsh., Wpg.	8	388	44	63	107	368	9	1	0	1	12	1	1968-69	1979-80
• Leswick, Jack	Chi.	1	3	1	7	8	16	....	....	....	....	....		1933-34	1933-34
Leswick, Pete	NYA, Bos.	2	3	1	0	1	0	....	....	....	....	....		1936-37	1944-45
Leswick, Tony	NYR, Det., Chi.	12	740	165	159	324	900	59	13	10	23	91	3	1945-46	1957-58
Levandoski, Joseph	NYR	1	8	1	1	2	0	....	....	....	....	....		1946-47	1946-47
Leveille, Normand	Bos.	2	75	17	25	42	49	....	....	....	....	....		1981-82	1982-83
Leveque, Guy	L.A.	2	17	2	2	4	21	....	....	....	....	....		1992-93	1993-94
Lever, Don	Van., Atl., Cgy., Col., N.J., Buf.	15	1020	313	367	680	593	30	7	10	17	26		1972-73	1986-87
Levie, Craig	Wpg., Min., Van., St.L.	6	183	22	53	75	177	16	2	3	5	32		1981-82	1986-87
• Levinsky, Alex	Tor., Chi., NYR	9	367	19	49	68	307	37	2	1	3	26	2	1930-31	1938-39
Levo, Tapio	Col., N.J.,	2	107	16	53	69	36	....	....	....	....	....		1981-82	1982-83
Lewicki, Danny	Tor., NYR, Chi.	9	461	105	135	240	177	28	0	4	4	8	1	1950-51	1958-59
Lewis, Dale	NYR	1	8	0	0	0	0	....	....	....	....	....		1975-76	1975-76
Lewis, Dave	NYI, L.A., N.J., Det.	15	1008	36	187	223	953	91	1	20	21	143		1973-74	1987-88
Lewis, Douglas	Mtl.	1	3	0	0	0	0	....	....	....	....	....		1946-47	1946-47
• Lewis, Herbie	Det.	11	483	148	161	309	248	38	13	10	23	6	2	1928-29	1938-39
Ley, Rick	Tor., Hfd.	6	310	12	72	84	528	14	0	2	2	20		1968-69	1980-81
Liba, Igor	NYR, L.A.	1	37	7	18	25	36	2	0	0	0	2		1988-89	1988-89
Libett, Nick	Det., Pit.	14	982	237	268	505	472	16	6	2	8	2		1967-68	1980-81
Licari, Tony	Det.	1	9	0	1	1	0	....	....	....	....	....		1946-47	1946-47
Liddington, Bob	Tor.	1	11	0	1	1	2	....	....	....	....	....		1970-71	1970-71
Lindberg, Chris	Cgy., Que.	3	116	17	25	42	47	2	0	1	1	2		1991-92	1993-94
Linden, Jamie	Fla.	1	4	0	0	0	17	....	....	....	....	....		1994-95	1994-95
Lindgren, Lars	Van., Min.	6	394	25	113	138	325	40	5	6	11	20		1978-79	1983-84
Lindholm, Mikael	L.A.	1	18	2	2	4	2	....	....	....	....	....		1989-90	1989-90
Lindros, Brett	NYI	2	51	2	5	7	147	....	....	....	....	....		1994-95	1995-96
Lindsay, Ted	Det., Chi.	17	1068	379	472	851	1808	133	47	49	96	194	4	1944-45	1964-65
Lindstrom, Willy	Wpg., Edm., Pit.	8	582	161	162	323	200	57	14	18	32	24	2	1979-80	1986-87
Linseman, Ken	Phi., Edm., Bos., Tor.	14	860	256	551	807	1727	113	43	77	120	325	1	1978-79	1991-92
Liscombe, Carl	Det.	9	373	137	140	277	117	59	22	19	41	20	1	1937-38	1945-46
Litzenberger, Ed	Mtl., Chi., Det., Tor.	12	618	178	238	416	283	40	5	13	18	34	4	1952-53	1963-64
Loach, Lonnie	Ott., L.A., Ana.	2	56	10	13	23	29	1	0	0	0	0		1992-93	1993-94

Name	NHL Teams	NHL Seasons	Regular Schedule GP	G	A	TP	PIM	Playoffs GP	G	A	TP	PIM	NHL Cup Wins	First NHL Season	Last NHL Season
• Locas, Jacques	Mtl.	2	59	7	8	15	66	....	....	....	....	....		1947-48	1948-49
Lochead, Bill	NYR, Det., Col.	6	330	69	62	131	180	7	3	0	3	6		1974-75	1979-80
• Locking, Norm	Chi.	2	48	2	6	8	26	....	....	....	....	....		1934-35	1935-36
Loewen, Darcy	Buf., Ott.	5	135	4	8	12	211	....	....	....	....	....		1989-90	1993-94
Lofthouse, Mark	Wsh., Det.	6	181	42	38	80	73	....	....	....	....	....		1977-78	1982-83
Logan, Dave	Chi., Van.	6	218	5	29	34	470	12	0	0	0	10		1975-76	1980-81
Logan, Robert	Buf., L.A.	3	42	10	5	15	0	....	....	....	....	....		1986-87	1988-89
Loiselle, Claude	Det., N.J., Que., Tor., NYI	13	616	92	117	209	1149	41	4	11	15	60		1981-82	1993-94
Lomakin, Andrei	Phi., Fla.	4	215	42	62	104	92	....	....	....	....	....		1991-92	1994-95
Loney, Brian	Van.	1	12	2	3	5	6	....	....	....	....	....		1995-96	1995-96
Loney, Troy	Pit., Ana., NYI, NYR	12	624	87	110	197	1091	67	8	14	22	97	2	1983-84	1994-95
Long, Barry	L.A., Det., Wpg.	5	280	11	68	79	250	5	0	1	1	18		1972-73	1981-82
• Long, Stanley	Mtl.	1	....	....	....	....	....	3	0	0	0	0		1951-52	1951-52
Lonsberry, Ross	Phi., Pit., Bos., L.A.	15	968	256	310	566	806	100	21	25	46	87	2	1966-67	1980-81
Loob, Hakan	Cgy.	6	450	193	236	429	189	73	26	28	54	16	1	1983-84	1988-89
Loob, Peter	Que.	1	8	1	2	3	0	....	....	....	....	....		1984-85	1984-85
Lorentz, Jim	NYR, Buf., Bos., St.L.	10	659	161	238	399	208	54	12	10	22	30	1	1968-69	1977-78
Lorimer, Bob	NYI, Col., N.J.	10	529	22	90	112	431	49	3	10	13	83	2	1976-77	1985-86
• Lorrain, Rod	Mtl.	6	179	28	39	67	30	11	0	3	3	0		1935-36	1941-42
• Loughlin, Clem	Det., Chi.	3	101	8	6	14	77	....	....	....	....	....		1926-27	1928-29
• Loughlin, Wilf	Tor.	1	14	0	0	0	2	....	....	....	....	....		1923-24	1923-24
Lovsin, Ken	Wsh.	1	1	0	0	0	0	....	....	....	....	....		1990-91	1990-91
Lowdermilk, Dwayne	Wsh.	1	2	0	1	1	2	....	....	....	....	....		1980-81	1980-81
Lowe, Darren	Pit.	1	8	1	2	3	0	....	....	....	....	....		1983-84	1983-84
Lowe, Norm	NYR	1	4	1	1	2	0	....	....	....	....	....		1948-49	1949-50
• Lowe, Ross	Bos., Mtl.	3	77	6	8	14	82	2	0	0	0	0		1949-50	1951-52
• Lowrey, Eddie	Ott., Ham.	3	26	2	2	4	6	....	....	....	....	....		1917-18	1920-21
• Lowrey, Fred	Mtl.M., Pit.	2	54	1	0	1	10	2	0	0	0	6		1924-25	1925-26
• Lowrey, Gerry	Tor., Pit., Phi., Chi., Ott.	6	211	48	48	96	148	2	1	0	1	2		1927-28	1932-33
Lucas, Danny	Phi.	1	6	1	0	1	0	....	....	....	....	....		1978-79	1978-79
Lucas, Dave	Det.	1	1	0	0	0	0	....	....	....	....	....		1962-63	1962-63
Luce, Don	NYR, Det., Buf., L.A., Tor.	13	894	225	329	554	364	71	17	22	39	52		1969-70	1981-82
Ludvig, Jan	N.J., Buf.	7	314	54	87	141	418	....	....	....	....	....		1982-83	1988-89
Ludzik, Steve	Chi., Buf.	9	424	46	93	139	333	44	4	8	12	70		1981-82	1989-90
Lukowich, Bernie	Pit., St.L.	2	79	13	15	28	34	2	0	0	0	0		1973-74	1974-75
Lukowich, Morris	Wpg., Bos., L.A.	8	582	199	219	418	584	11	0	2	2	24		1979-80	1986-87
Luksa, Charlie	Hfd.	1	8	0	1	1	4	....	....	....	....	....		1979-80	1979-80
Lumley, Dave	Mtl., Edm., Hfd.	9	437	98	160	258	680	61	6	8	14	131	2	1978-79	1986-87
Lund, Pentti	NYR, Bos.	7	259	44	55	99	40	19	7	5	12	0		1946-47	1952-53
Lundberg, Brian	Pit.	1	1	0	0	0	2	....	....	....	....	....		1982-83	1982-83
Lunde, Len	Min., Van., Det., Chi.	8	321	39	83	122	75	20	3	2	5	2		1958-59	1970-71
Lundholm, Bengt	Wpg.	5	275	48	95	143	72	14	3	4	7	14		1981-82	1985-86
Lundrigan, Joe	Tor., Wsh.	2	52	2	8	10	22	....	....	....	....	....		1972-73	1974-75
Lundstrom, Tord	Det.	1	11	1	1	2	0	....	....	....	....	....		1973-74	1973-74
Lundy, Pat	Det. Chi.	5	150	37	32	69	31	16	2	2	4	2		1945-46	1950-51
Lupien, Gilles	Mtl., Pit., Hfd.	5	226	5	25	30	416	25	0	0	0	21	2	1977-78	1981-82
Lupul, Gary	Van.	7	293	70	75	145	243	25	4	7	11	11		1979-80	1985-86
Lyle, George	Det., Hfd.	4	99	24	38	62	51	....	....	....	....	....		1979-80	1982-83
Lynch, Jack	Pit., Det., Wsh.	7	382	24	106	130	336	....	....	....	....	....		1972-73	1978-79
Lynn, Vic	Det., Mtl., Tor., Bos., Chi.	10	326	49	76	125	274	47	7	10	17	46	3	1943-44	1953-54
Lyon, Steve	Pit.	1	3	0	0	0	2	....	....	....	....	....		1976-77	1976-77
Lyons, Ron	Bos., Phi.	1	36	2	4	6	27	5	0	0	0	0		1930-31	1930-31
Lysiak, Tom	Atl., Chi.	13	919	292	551	843	567	76	25	38	63	49		1973-74	1985-86

M

Name	NHL Teams	NHL Seasons	Regular Schedule GP	G	A	TP	PIM	Playoffs GP	G	A	TP	PIM	NHL Cup Wins	First NHL Season	Last NHL Season
MacAdam, Al	Phi., Cal., Cle., Min., Van.	12	864	240	351	591	509	64	20	24	44	21	1	1973-74	1984-85
MacDermid, Paul	Hfd., Wpg., Wsh., Que.	14	690	116	142	258	1303	43	5	11	16	116		1981-82	1994-95
MacDonald, Blair	Edm., Van.	4	219	91	100	191	65	11	0	6	6	2		1979-80	1982-83
MacDonald, Brett	Van.	1	1	0	0	0	0	....	....	....	....	....		1987-88	1987-88
• MacDonald, Jack	Mtl.W, Mtl., Que., Tor.	5	68	26	14	40	30	14	3	4	7	6		1917-18	1921-22
MacDonald, Kevin	Ott.	1	1	0	0	0	2	....	....	....	....	....		1993-94	1993-94
• MacDonald, Kilby	NYR	4	151	36	34	70	47	15	1	2	3	4	1	1939-40	1944-45
MacDonald, Lowell	Det., L.A., Pit.	13	506	180	210	390	92	30	11	11	22	12		1961-62	1977-78
MacDonald, Parker	Tor., NYR, Det., Bos., Min.	14	676	144	179	323	253	75	14	14	28	20		1952-53	1968-69
• MacDonnell, Moylan	Ham.	1	22	1	2	3	2	....	....	....	....	....		1920-21	1920-21
MacDougall, Kim	Min.	1	1	0	0	0	0	....	....	....	....	....		1974-75	1974-75
MacEachern, Shane	St.L.	1	1	0	0	0	0	....	....	....	....	....		1987-88	1987-88
Macey, Hubert	NYR, Mtl.	3	30	6	9	15	0	8	0	0	0	0		1941-42	1946-47
MacGregor, Bruce	Det., NYR	14	893	213	257	470	217	107	19	28	47	44		1960-61	1973-74
MacGregor, Randy	Hfd.	1	2	1	1	2	2	....	....	....	....	....		1981-82	1981-82
MacGuigan, Garth	NYI	2	5	0	1	1	2	....	....	....	....	....		1979-80	1979-80
MacIver, Don	Wpg.	1	6	0	0	0	2	....	....	....	....	....		1979-80	1979-80
MacKasey, Blair	Tor.	1	1	0	0	0	2	....	....	....	....	....		1976-77	1976-77
MacKay, Calum	Det., Mtl.	8	237	50	55	105	214	38	5	13	18	20	1	1946-47	1954-55
Mackay, Dave	Chi.	1	29	3	0	3	26	5	0	1	1	2		1940-41	1940-41
• MacKay, Mickey	Chi., Pit., Bos.	4	147	44	19	63	79	11	0	0	0	6	1	1926-27	1929-30
MacKay, Murdo	Mtl.	4	19	0	3	3	0	15	1	2	3	0		1945-46	1947-48
Mackell, Fleming	Tor., Bos.	13	665	149	220	369	562	80	22	41	63	75	2	1947-48	1959-60
• MacKell, Jack	Ott.	2	46	4	2	6	59	11	0	0	0	0	1	1919-20	1920-21
MacKenzie, Barry	Min.	1	6	0	1	1	6	....	....	....	....	....		1968-69	1968-69
• MacKenzie, Bill	Chi., Mtl.M., Mtl., NYR	7	264	15	14	29	145	21	1	1	2	11	1	1932-33	1939-40
Mackey, David	Chi., Min., St.L.	6	126	8	12	20	305	3	0	0	0	2		1987-88	1993-94
• MacKey, Reg	NYR	1	34	0	0	0	16	1	0	0	0	0		1926-27	1926-27
• Mackie, Howie	Det.	2	20	1	0	1	4	8	0	0	0	0	1	1936-37	1937-38
MacKinnon, Paul	Wsh.	5	147	5	23	28	91	....	....	....	....	....		1979-80	1983-84
MackIntosh, Ian	NYR	1	4	0	0	0	4	....	....	....	....	....		1952-53	1952-53
MacLean, Paul	St.L., Wpg., Det.	11	719	324	349	673	968	53	21	14	35	110		1980-81	1990-91
MacLeish, Rick	Phi., Hfd., Pit., Det.	14	846	349	410	759	434	114	54	53	107	38	2	1970-71	1983-84
MacLellan, Brian	L.A., NYR, Min., Cgy., Det.	10	606	172	241	413	551	47	5	9	14	42		1982-83	1991-92
MacLeod, Pat	Min., S.J., Dal.	4	53	5	13	18	14	....	....	....	....	....		1990-91	1995-96
MacMillan, Billy	Tor., Atl., NYI	7	446	74	77	151	184	53	6	6	12	40		1970-71	1976-77
MacMillan, Bob	NYR, St.L., Atl., Cgy., Col., N.J., Chi.	11	753	228	349	577	260	31	8	11	19	16		1974-75	1984-85
MacMillan, John	Tor., Det.	5	104	5	10	15	32	12	0	1	1	2	2	1960-61	1964-65
MacNeil, Bernie	St.L.	1	4	0	0	0	0	....	....	....	....	....		1973-74	1973-74
MacNeil, Al	Tor., Mtl., Chi., NYR, Pit.	11	524	17	75	92	617	37	0	4	4	67		1955-56	1967-68
• MacPherson, Bud	Mtl.	7	259	5	33	38	233	29	0	3	3	21	1	1948-49	1956-57
• MacSweyn, Ralph	Phi.	5	47	0	5	5	10	8	0	0	0	6		1967-68	1971-72
MacTavish, Craig	Bos., Edm., NYR, Phi., St.L.	17	1093	213	267	480	891	193	20	38	58	218	4	1979-80	1996-97
MacWilliam, Mike	NYI	1	6	0	0	0	14	....	....	....	....	....		1995-96	1995-96
Madigan, Connie	St.L.	1	20	0	3	3	25	5	0	0	0	4		1972-73	1972-73
Madill, Jeff	N.J.	1	14	4	0	4	46	7	0	2	2	8		1990-91	1990-91
Magee, Dean	Min.	1	7	0	0	0	4	....	....	....	....	....		1977-78	1977-78
Maggs, Daryl	Chi., Cal., Tor.	3	135	14	19	33	54	4	0	0	0	0		1971-72	1979-80
Magnan, Marc	Tor.	1	4	0	1	1	5	....	....	....	....	....		1982-83	1982-83
Magnuson, Keith	Chi.	11	589	14	125	139	1442	68	3	9	12	164		1969-70	1979-80
Maguire, Kevin	Tor., Buf., Phi.	6	260	29	30	59	782	11	0	0	0	86		1986-87	1991-92
Mahaffy, John	Mtl., NYR	3	37	11	25	36	4	1	0	1	1	0		1942-43	1944-45
Mahovlich, Frank	Tor., Det., Mtl.	18	1181	533	570	1103	1056	137	51	67	118	163	6	1956-57	1973-74
Mahovlich, Pete	Det., Mtl., Pit.	16	884	288	485	773	916	88	30	42	72	134	4	1965-66	1980-81
Mailhot, Jacques	Que.	1	5	0	0	0	33	....	....	....	....	....		1988-89	1988-89
Mailley, Frank	Mtl.	1	1	0	0	0	0	....	....	....	....	....		1942-43	1942-43
Mair, Jim	Phi., NYI, Van.	5	76	4	15	19	49	3	1	2	3	4		1970-71	1974-75
• Majeau, Fern	Mtl.	2	56	22	24	46	43	1	0	0	0	0	1	1943-44	1944-45
Major, Bruce	Que.	1	4	0	0	0	0	....	....	....	....	....		1990-91	1990-91
Makarov, Sergei	Cgy., S.J., Dal.	7	424	134	250	384	317	34	12	11	23	8		1989-90	1996-97
Makela, Mikko	NYI, L.A., Buf., Bos.	7	423	118	147	265	139	18	3	8	11	14		1985-86	1994-95
Maki, Chico	Chi.	15	841	143	292	435	345	113	17	36	53	43	1	1960-61	1975-76
• Maki, Wayne	Chi., St.L., Van.	6	246	57	79	136	184	2	1	0	1	2		1967-68	1972-73
Makkonen, Kari	Edm.	1	9	2	2	4	0	....	....	....	....	....		1979-80	1979-80
Maley, David	Mtl., N.J., Edm., S.J., NYI	9	466	43	81	124	1043	46	5	5	10	111	1	1985-86	1993-94
Malinowski, Merlin	Col., N.J., Hfd.	5	282	54	111	165	121	....	....	....	....	....		1978-79	1982-83

Craig MacTavish

Sergei Makarov

Phil Maloney

Alan May

Brad McCrimmon

Rick McLeish

Dave McLlwain

Basil McRae

			Regular Schedule					Playoffs					NHL	First	Last
Name	NHL Teams	NHL Seasons	GP	G	A	TP	PIM	GP	G	A	TP	PIM	Cup Wins	NHL Season	NHL Season
Malone, Cliff	Mtl.	1	3	0	0	0	0	....	....	....	....	....		1951-52	1951-52
Malone, Greg	Pit., Hfd., Que.	11	704	191	310	501	661	20	3	5	8	32		1976-77	1986-87
• Malone, Joe	Mtl., Que., Ham.	7	125	143	32	175	57	9	5	1	6	3		1917-18	1923-24
Maloney, Dan	Chi., L.A., Det., Tor.	11	737	192	259	451	1489	40	4	7	11	35		1970-71	1981-82
Maloney, Dave	NYR, Buf.	11	657	71	246	317	1154	49	7	17	24	91		1974-75	1984-85
Maloney, Don	NYR, Hfd., NYI	13	765	214	350	564	815	94	22	35	57	101		1978-79	1990-91
Maloney, Phil	Bos., Tor., Chi.	5	158	28	43	71	16	6	0	0	0	0		1949-50	1959-60
Maluta, Ray	Bos.	2	25	2	3	5	6	2	0	0	0	0		1975-76	1976-77
Manastersky, Tom	Mtl.	1	6	0	0	0	11	....	....	....	....	....		1950-51	1950-51
• Mancuso, Gus	Mtl., NYR	4	42	7	9	16	17	....	....	....	....	....		1937-38	1942-43
Mandich, Dan	Min.	4	111	5	11	16	303	7	0	0	0	2		1982-83	1985-86
Manery, Kris	Van., Wpg., Clev., Min.	4	250	63	64	127	91	....	....	....	....	....		1977-78	1980-81
Manery, Randy	L.A., Det., Atl.	10	582	50	206	256	415	13	0	2	2	12		1970-71	1979-80
Mann, Jack	NYR	2	9	3	4	7	0	....	....	....	....	....		1943-44	1944-45
Mann, Jimmy	Wpg., Que., Pit.	8	293	10	20	30	895	22	0	0	0	89		1979-80	1987-88
Mann, Ken	Det.	1	1	0	0	0	0	....	....	....	....	....		1975-76	1975-76
Mann, Norm	Tor.	3	31	0	3	3	4	2	0	0	0	0		1935-36	1940-41
• Manners, Rennison	Pit., Phi.	2	37	3	2	5	14	....	....	....	....	....		1929-30	1930-31
Manno, Bob	Van., Tor., Det.	8	371	41	131	172	274	17	2	4	6	12		1976-77	1984-85
Manson, Ray	Bos., NYR	2	2	0	1	1	0	....	....	....	....	....		1947-48	1948-49
• Mantha, Georges	Mtl.	13	488	89	102	191	148	36	6	2	8	24		1928-29	1940-41
Mantha, Moe	Wpg., Pit., Edm., Min., Phi.	12	656	81	289	370	501	17	5	10	15	18		1980-81	1991-92
• Mantha, Sylvio	Mtl., Bos.	14	542	63	72	135	667	46	5	4	9	66		1923-24	1936-37
• Maracle, Bud	NYR	1	11	1	3	4	4	4	0	0	0	0		1930-31	1930-31
Marcetta, Milan	Tor., Min.	3	54	7	15	22	10	17	7	7	14	4	1	1966-67	1968-69
• March, Mush	Chi.	17	759	153	230	383	540	45	12	15	27	41	2	1928-29	1944-45
Marchinko, Brian	Tor., NYI	4	47	2	6	8	0	....	....	....	....	....		1970-71	1973-74
Marcinyshyn, David	N.J., Que., NYR	3	16	0	1	1	49	....	....	....	....	....		1990-91	1992-93
Marcon, Lou	Det.	3	60	0	4	4	42	....	....	....	....	....		1958-59	1962-63
Marcotte, Don	Bos.	15	868	230	254	484	317	132	34	27	61	81	2	1965-66	1981-82
Marini, Hector	NYI, N.J.	5	154	27	46	73	246	10	3	6	9	14	2	1978-79	1983-84
• Mario, Frank	Bos.	2	53	9	19	28	24	....	....	....	....	....		1941-42	1944-45
• Mariucci, John	Chi.	5	223	11	34	45	308	12	0	3	3	26		1940-41	1947-48
Mark, Gordon	N.J., Edm.	4	85	3	10	13	187	....	....	....	....	....		1986-87	1994-95
Markell, John	Wpg., St. L., Min.	4	55	11	10	21	36	....	....	....	....	....		1979-80	1984-85
• Marker, Gus	Det., Mtl.M., Tor., Bro.	10	322	64	69	133	133	46	5	7	12	36	1	1932-33	1941-42
Markham, Ray	NYR	1	14	1	1	2	21	7	1	0	1	24		1979-80	1979-80
• Markle, Jack	Tor.	1	8	0	1	1	0	....	....	....	....	....		1935-36	1935-36
• Marks, Jack	Mtl.W, Tor., Que.	2	7	0	0	0	4	....	....	....	....	....		1917-18	1919-20
Marks, John	Chi.	10	657	112	163	275	330	57	5	9	14	60		1972-73	1981-82
Markwart, Nevin	Bos., Cgy.	8	309	41	68	109	794	19	1	0	1	33		1983-84	1991-92
Marois, Daniel	Tor., NYI, Bos., Dal.	8	350	117	93	210	419	19	3	3	6	28		1987-88	1995-96
Marois, Mario	NYR, Van., Que., Wpg., St.L.	15	955	76	357	433	1746	100	4	34	38	182		1977-78	1991-92
Marotte, Gilles	Bos., Chi., L.A., NYR, St.L.	12	808	56	265	321	919	29	3	3	6	26		1965-66	1976-77
Marquess, Mark	Bos.	1	27	5	4	9	6	4	0	0	0	0		1946-47	1946-47
Marsh, Brad	Atl., Cgy., Phi., Tor., Det., Ott.	15	1086	23	175	198	1241	97	6	18	24	124		1978-79	1992-93
Marsh, Gary	Det., Tor.	2	7	1	3	4	4	....	....	....	....	....		1967-68	1968-69
Marsh, Peter	Wpg., Chi.	5	278	48	71	119	224	26	1	5	6	33		1979-80	1983-84
Marshall, Bert	Det., Oak., Cal., NYR, NYI	14	868	17	181	198	926	72	4	22	26	99		1965-66	1978-79
Marshall, Don	Mtl., NYR, Buf., Tor.	19	1176	265	324	589	127	94	8	15	23	14	5	1951-52	1971-72
Marshall, Paul	Pit., Tor., Hfd.	4	95	15	18	33	17	1	0	0	0	0		1979-80	1982-83
Marshall, Willie	Tor.	4	33	1	5	6	2	....	....	....	....	....		1952-53	1958-59
Marson, Mike	Wsh., L.A.	6	196	24	24	48	233	....	....	....	....	....		1974-75	1979-80
• Martin, Clare	Bos., Det., Chi., NYR	6	237	12	28	40	78	27	0	2	2	6	1	1941-42	1951-52
Martin, Frank	Bos., Chi.	6	282	11	46	57	122	10	0	2	2	2		1952-53	1957-58
Martin, Grant	Van., Wsh.	4	44	0	4	4	55	1	1	0	1	2		1983-84	1986-87
Martin, Jack	Tor.	1	1	0	0	0	0	....	....	....	....	....		1960-61	1960-61
Martin, Pit	Det., Bos., Chi., Van.	17	1101	324	485	809	609	100	27	31	58	56		1961-62	1978-79
Martin, Rick	Buf., L.A.	11	685	384	317	701	477	63	24	29	53	74		1971-72	1981-82
• Martin, Ron	NYA	2	94	13	16	29	36	....	....	....	....	....		1932-33	1933-34
Martin, Terry	Buf., Que., Tor., Edm., Min.	10	479	104	101	205	202	21	4	2	6	26		1975-76	1984-85
Martin, Thomas	Tor.	1	3	1	0	1	0	....	....	....	....	....		1967-68	1967-68
Martin, Tom	Wpg., Hfd., Min.	6	92	12	11	23	249	4	0	0	0	6		1984-85	1989-90
Martineau, Don	Atl., Min., Det.	4	90	6	10	16	63	....	....	....	....	....		1973-74	1976-77
Martini, Darcy	Edm.	1	2	0	0	0	0	....	....	....	....	....		1993-94	1993-94
Martinson, Steven	Det., Mtl., Min.	4	49	2	1	3	244	1	0	0	0	10		1987-88	1991-92
Maruk, Dennis	Cal., Clev., Min., Wsh.	14	888	356	522	878	761	34	14	22	36	26		1975-76	1988-89
Masnick, Paul	Mtl., Chi., Tor.	6	232	18	41	59	139	33	4	5	9	27	1	1950-51	1957-58
• Mason, Charley	NYR, NYA, Det., Chi.	4	95	7	18	25	44	4	0	1	1	0		1934-35	1938-39
• Massecar, George	NYA	3	100	12	11	23	46	....	....	....	....	....		1929-30	1931-32
Masters, Jamie	St.L.	3	33	1	13	14	2	2	0	0	0	0		1975-76	1978-79
• Masterton, Bill	Min.	1	38	4	8	12	4	....	....	....	....	....		1967-68	1967-68
Mathers, Frank	Tor.	3	23	1	3	4	4	....	....	....	....	....		1948-49	1951-52
Mathiasen, Dwight	Pit.	3	33	1	7	8	18	....	....	....	....	....		1985-86	1987-88
Mathieson, Jim	Wsh.	1	2	0	0	0	4	....	....	....	....	....		1989-90	1989-90
• Matte, Joe	Tor., Ham., Bos., Mtl.	4	68	17	15	32	54	....	....	....	....	....		1919-20	1925-26
• Matte, Roland Joseph	Chi., Det.	2	24	0	3	3	8	....	....	....	....	....		1929-30	1942-43
Mattiussi, Dick	Pit., Oak., Cal.	4	200	8	31	39	124	8	0	1	1	6		1967-68	1970-71
• Matz, Johnny	Mtl.	1	30	3	2	5	0	5	0	0	0	2		1924-25	1924-25
Maxner, Wayne	Bos.	2	62	8	9	17	48	....	....	....	....	....		1964-65	1965-66
Maxwell, Brad	Min., Que., Tor., Van., NYR	10	612	98	270	368	1292	79	12	49	61	178		1977-78	1986-87
Maxwell, Bryan	Min., St.L., Wpg., Pit.	8	331	18	77	95	745	15	1	1	2	86		1977-78	1984-85
Maxwell, Kevin	Min., Col., N.J.	3	66	6	15	21	61	16	3	4	7	24		1980-81	1983-84
Maxwell, Wally	Tor.	1	2	0	0	0	0	....	....	....	....	....		1952-53	1952-53
May, Alan	Bos., Edm., Wsh., Dal., Cgy.	8	393	31	45	76	1348	40	1	2	3	80		1987-88	1994-95
Mayer, Derek	Ott.	1	17	2	2	4	8	....	....	....	....	....		1993-94	1993-94
Mayer, Jim	NYR	1	4	0	0	0	0	....	....	....	....	....		1979-80	1979-80
Mayer, Pat	Pit.	1	1	0	0	0	4	....	....	....	....	....		1987-88	1987-88
Mayer, Shep	Tor.	1	12	1	2	3	4	....	....	....	....	....		1942-43	1942-43
• Mazur, Eddie	Mtl., Chi.	6	107	8	20	28	120	25	4	5	9	22	1	1950-51	1956-57
Mazur, Jay	Van.	4	47	11	7	18	20	6	0	1	1	8		1988-89	1991-92
McAdam, Gary	Buf., Pit., Det., Cgy., Wsh., N.J., Tor.	11	534	96	132	228	243	30	6	5	11	16		1975-76	1985-86
• McAdam, Sam	NYR	1	5	0	0	0	0	....	....	....	....	....		1930-31	1930-31
• McAndrew, Hazen	Bro.	1	7	0	1	1	6	....	....	....	....	....		1941-42	1941-42
McAneeley, Ted	Cal.	3	158	8	35	43	141	....	....	....	....	....		1972-73	1974-75
McAtee, Jud	Det.	3	46	15	13	28	6	14	2	1	3	0		1942-43	1944-45
McAtee, Norm	Bos.	1	13	0	1	1	0	....	....	....	....	....		1946-47	1946-47
McAvoy, George	Mtl.	1	....	....	....	....	....	4	0	0	0	0		1954-55	1954-55
McBain, Andrew	Wpg., Pit., Van., Ott.	11	608	129	172	301	633	24	5	7	12	39		1983-84	1993-94
McBean, Wayne	L.A., NYI, Wpg.	6	211	10	39	49	168	2	1	1	2	0		1987-88	1993-94
McBride, Cliff	Mtl.M., Tor.	2	2	0	0	0	0	....	....	....	....	....		1928-29	1929-30
McBurney, Jim	Chi.	1	1	0	1	1	0	....	....	....	....	....		1952-53	1952-53
• McCabe, Stan	Det., Mtl.M.	4	78	9	4	13	49	....	....	....	....	....		1929-30	1933-34
• McCaffrey, Bert	Tor., Pit., Mtl.	7	260	42	30	72	202	8	2	1	3	12		1924-25	1930-31
McCahill, John	Col.	1	1	0	0	0	0	....	....	....	....	....		1977-78	1977-78
McCaig, Douglas	Det., Chi.	7	263	8	21	29	255	7	0	1	1	10		1941-42	1950-51
• McCallum, Dunc	NYR, Pit.	5	187	14	35	49	230	10	1	2	3	12		1965-66	1970-71
• McCalmon, Eddie	Chi., Phi.	2	39	5	0	5	14	....	....	....	....	....		1927-28	1930-31
McCann, Rick	Det.	6	43	1	4	5	6	....	....	....	....	....		1967-68	1974-75
McCarthy, Dan	NYR	1	5	4	0	4	4	....	....	....	....	....		1980-81	1980-81
McCarthy, Kevin	Phi., Van., Pit.	10	537	67	191	258	527	21	2	3	5	20		1977-78	1986-87
• McCarthy, Thomas	Que., Ham.	2	34	22	7	29	10	....	....	....	....	....		1919-20	1920-21
McCarthy, Thomas Patrick	Det., Bos.	4	60	8	9	17	8	....	....	....	....	....		1956-57	1960-61
McCarthy, Tom	Min., Bos.	9	460	178	221	399	330	68	12	26	38	67		1979-80	1987-88
• McCartney, Walt	Mtl.	1	2	0	0	0	0	....	....	....	....	....		1932-33	1932-33
McCaskill, Ted	Min.	1	4	0	2	2	0	....	....	....	....	....		1967-68	1967-68
McClanahan, Rob	Buf., Hfd., NYR	5	224	38	63	101	126	34	4	12	16	31		1979-80	1983-84
McClelland, Kevin	Pit., Edm., Det., Tor., Wpg.	12	588	68	112	180	1672	98	11	18	29	281	4	1981-82	1993-94
McCord, Bob	Bos., Det., Min., St.L.	7	316	10	58	68	262	14	2	5	7	10		1963-64	1972-73
McCord, Dennis	Van.	1	3	0	0	0	6	....	....	....	....	....		1973-74	1973-74
McCormack, John	Tor., Mtl., Chi.	8	311	25	49	74	35	22	1	1	2	0	2	1947-48	1954-55
McCourt, Dale	Det., Buf., Tor.	7	532	194	284	478	124	21	9	7	16	6		1977-78	1983-84

Name	NHL Teams	NHL Seasons	Regular Schedule GP	G	A	TP	PIM	Playoffs GP	G	A	TP	PIM	NHL Cup Wins	First NHL Season	Last NHL Season
McCreary, Bill Jr.	Tor.	1	12	1	0	1	4	....	....	....	....	....		1980-81	1980-81
McCreary, Bill Sr.	NYR, Det., Mtl., St.L.	8	309	53	62	115	108	48	6	16	22	14		1953-54	1970-71
McCreary, Keith	Mtl., Pit., Atl.	10	532	131	112	243	294	16	0	4	4	6		1961-62	1974-75
• McCreedy, Johnny	Tor.	2	64	17	12	29	25	21	4	3	7	16	2	1941-42	1944-45
McCrimmon, Brad	Bos., Phi., Cgy., Det., Hfd., Pho.	18	1222	81	322	403	1416	116	11	18	29	176	1	1979-80	1996-97
McCrimmon, Jim	St.L.	1	2	0	0	0	0	....	....	....	....	....		1974-75	1974-75
McCulley, Bob	Mtl.	1	1	0	0	0	0	....	....	....	....	....		1934-35	1934-35
• McCurry, Duke	Pit.	4	148	21	11	32	119	4	0	2	2	4		1925-26	1928-29
McCutcheon, Brian	Det.	3	37	3	1	4	7	....	....	....	....	....		1974-75	1976-77
McCutcheon, Darwin	Tor.	1	1	0	0	0	2	....	....	....	....	....		1981-82	1981-82
McDill, Jeff	Chi.	1	1	0	0	0	0	....	....	....	....	....		1976-77	1976-77
McDonagh, Bill	NYR	1	4	0	0	0	2	....	....	....	....	....		1949-50	1949-50
McDonald, Ab	Mtl., Chi., Bos., Det., Pit., St.L.	15	762	182	248	430	200	84	21	29	50	42	4	1957-58	1971-72
McDonald, Brian	Chi., Buf.	2	12	0	0	0	29	8	0	0	0	2		1967-68	1970-71
• McDonald, Bucko	Det., Tor., NYR	11	446	35	88	123	206	50	6	1	7	24	3	1934-35	1944-45
McDonald, Butch	Det., Chi.	2	66	8	20	28	2	5	0	2	2	10		1939-40	1944-45
McDonald, Gerry	Hfd.	2	8	0	0	0	4	....	....	....	....	....		1981-82	1981-82
• McDonald, John	NYR	1	43	10	9	19	6	....	....	....	....	....		1943-44	1943-44
McDonald, Lanny	Tor., Col., Cgy.	16	1111	500	506	1006	899	117	44	40	84	120	1	1973-74	1988-89
McDonald, Robert	NYR	1	1	0	0	0	0	....	....	....	....	....		1943-44	1943-44
McDonald, Terry	K.C.	1	8	0	1	1	6	....	....	....	....	....		1975-76	1975-76
McDonnell, Joe	Van., Pit.	3	50	2	10	12	34	....	....	....	....	....		1981-82	1985-86
McDonough, Al	L.A., Pit., Atl., Det.	5	237	73	88	161	73	8	0	1	1	2		1970-71	1977-78
McDonough, Hubie	L.A., NYI, S.J.	5	195	40	26	66	67	5	1	0	1	4		1988-89	1992-93
McDougal, Mike	NYR, Hfd.	4	61	8	10	18	43	....	....	....	....	....		1978-79	1982-83
McDougall, Bill	Det., Edm., T.B.	3	28	5	5	10	12	1	0	0	0	0		1990-91	1993-94
McElmury, Jim	Min., K.C., Col.	5	180	14	47	61	49	....	....	....	....	....		1972-73	1977-78
McEwen, Mike	NYR, Col., NYI, L.A., Wsh., Det., Hfd.	12	716	108	296	404	460	78	12	36	48	48	3	1976-77	1987-88
McFadden, Jim	Det., Chi.	8	412	100	126	226	89	49	10	9	19	30	1	1947-48	1953-54
McFadyen, Don	Chi.	4	179	12	33	45	77	11	2	2	4	5	1	1932-33	1935-36
McFall, Dan	Wpg.	2	9	0	1	1	0	....	....	....	....	....		1984-85	1985-86
• McFarlane, Gordon	Chi.	1	2	0	0	0	0	....	....	....	....	....		1926-27	1926-27
McGeough, Jim	Wsh., Pit.	4	57	7	10	17	32	....	....	....	....	....		1981-82	1986-87
• McGibbon, Irv	Mtl.	1	1	0	0	0	2	....	....	....	....	....		1942-43	1942-43
McGill, Bob	Tor., Chi., S.J., Det., NYI, Hfd.	13	705	17	55	72	1766	49	0	0	0	88		1981-82	1993-94
• McGill, Jack	Mtl.	3	134	27	10	37	71	3	2	0	2	0		1934-35	1936-37
McGill, John	Bos.	4	97	23	36	59	42	27	7	4	11	17		1941-42	1946-47
McGill, Ryan	Chi., Phi., Edm.	4	151	4	15	19	391	....	....	....	....	....		1991-92	1994-95
McGregor, Sandy	NYR	1	2	0	0	0	2	....	....	....	....	....		1963-64	1963-64
• McGuire, Mickey	Pit.	2	36	3	0	3	6	....	....	....	....	....		1926-27	1927-28
McHugh, Mike	Min., S.J.	4	20	1	0	1	16	....	....	....	....	....		1988-89	1991-92
McIlhargey, Jack	Phi., Van., Hfd.	8	393	11	36	47	1102	27	0	3	3	68		1974-75	1981-82
• McInenly, Bert	Det., NYA, Ott., Bos.	6	166	19	15	34	144	4	0	0	0	2		1930-31	1935-36
McIntosh, Bruce	Min.	1	2	0	0	0	0	....	....	....	....	....		1972-73	1972-73
McIntosh, Paul	Buf.	2	48	0	2	2	66	2	0	0	0	7		1974-75	1975-76
McIntyre, Jack	Bos., Chi., Det.	11	499	109	102	211	173	29	7	6	13	4		1949-50	1959-60
McIntyre, John	Tor., L.A., NYR, Van.	6	351	24	54	78	516	44	0	6	6	54		1989-90	1994-95
McIntyre, Larry	Tor.	2	41	0	3	3	26	....	....	....	....	....		1969-70	1972-73
McKay, Doug	Det.	1	....	....	....	....	....	1	0	0	0	0	1	1949-50	1949-50
McKay, Ray	Chi., Buf., Cal.	6	140	2	16	18	102	....	....	....	....	....		1968-69	1973-74
McKay, Scott	Ana.	1	1	0	0	0	0	....	....	....	....	....		1993-94	1993-94
McKechnie, Walt	Min., Cal., Bos., Det., Wsh., Clev., Tor., Col.	16	955	214	392	606	469	15	7	5	12	7		1967-68	1982-83
McKee, Mike	Que.	1	48	3	12	15	41	....	....	....	....	....		1993-94	1993-94
McKegney, Ian	Chi.	1	3	0	0	0	2	....	....	....	....	....		1976-77	1976-77
McKegney, Tony	Buf., Que., Min., NYR, St.L., Det., Chi.	13	912	320	319	639	517	79	24	23	47	56		1978-79	1990-91
McKendry, Alex	NYI, Cgy.	4	46	3	6	9	21	6	2	2	4	0	1	1977-78	1980-81
McKenna, Sean	Buf., L.A., Tor.	9	414	82	80	162	181	15	1	2	3	2		1981-82	1989-90
McKenney, Don	Bos., NYR, Tor., Det., St.L.	13	798	237	345	582	211	58	18	29	47	10	1	1954-55	1967-68
McKenny, Jim	Tor., Min.	14	604	82	247	329	294	37	7	9	16	10		1965-66	1978-79
McKenzie, Brian	Pit.	1	6	1	1	2	4	....	....	....	....	....		1971-72	1971-72
McKenzie, John	Chi., Det., NYR, Bos.	12	691	206	268	474	917	69	15	32	47	133	2	1958-59	1971-72
McKim, Andrew	Bos., Det.	3	38	1	4	5	6	....	....	....	....	....		1992-93	1994-95
• McKinnon, Alex	Ham., NYA, Chi.	5	194	19	10	29	235	....	....	....	....	....		1924-25	1928-29
• McKinnon, John	Mtl., Pit., Phi.	6	208	28	11	39	224	2	0	0	0	4		1925-26	1930-31
McLean, Don	Wsh.	1	9	0	0	0	6	....	....	....	....	....		1975-76	1975-76
• McLean, Fred	Que., Ham.	2	11	0	0	0	2	....	....	....	....	....		1919-20	1920-21
McLean, Jack	Tor.	3	67	14	24	38	76	13	2	2	4	8	1	1942-43	1944-45
McLean, Jeff	S.J.	1	6	1	0	1	0	....	....	....	....	....		1993-94	1993-94
• McLellan, John	Tor.	1	2	0	0	0	0	....	....	....	....	....		1951-52	1951-52
McLellan, Scott	Bos.	1	2	0	0	0	0	....	....	....	....	....		1982-83	1982-83
McLellan, Todd	NYI	1	5	1	1	2	0	....	....	....	....	....		1987-88	1987-88
• McLenahan, Rollie	Det.	1	9	2	1	3	10	2	0	0	0	0		1945-46	1945-46
McLeod, Al	Det.	1	26	2	2	4	24	....	....	....	....	....		1973-74	1973-74
McLeod, Jackie	NYR	5	106	14	23	37	12	7	0	0	0	0		1949-50	1954-55
McLlwain, Dave	Pit., Wpg., Buf., NYI, Tor., Ott.	10	501	100	107	207	292	20	0	2	2	2		1987-88	1996-97
McMahon, Mike Jr.	NYR, Min., Chi., Det., Pit., Buf.	8	224	15	68	83	171	14	3	7	10	4		1963-64	1971-72
• McMahon, Mike Sr.	Mtl., Bos.	3	57	7	18	25	102	13	1	2	3	30	1	1942-43	1945-46
McManama, Bob	Pit.	3	99	11	25	36	28	8	0	1	1	6		1973-74	1975-76
• McManus, Sammy	Mtl.M., Bos.	2	26	0	1	1	8	1	0	0	0	0	1	1934-35	1936-37
McMurchy, Tom	Chi., Edm.	4	55	8	4	12	65	....	....	....	....	....		1983-84	1987-88
McNab, Max	Det.	4	128	16	19	35	24	25	1	0	1	4	1	1947-48	1950-51
McNab, Peter	Buf., Bos., Van., N.J.	14	954	363	450	813	179	107	40	42	82	20		1973-74	1986-87
McNabney, Sid	Mtl.	1	....	....	....	....	....	5	0	1	1	2		1950-51	1950-51
• McNamara, Howard	Mtl.	1	12	1	0	1	6	....	....	....	....	....		1919-20	1919-20
• McNaughton, George	Que.B.	1	1	0	0	0	0	....	....	....	....	....		1919-20	1919-20
McNeill, Billy	Det.	6	257	21	46	67	142	4	1	1	2	4		1956-57	1963-64
McNeill, Mike	Chi., Que.	2	63	5	11	16	18	....	....	....	....	....		1990-91	1991-92
McNeill, Stu	Det.	3	10	1	1	2	2	....	....	....	....	....		1957-58	1959-60
McPhee, George	NYR, N.J.	7	115	24	25	49	257	29	5	3	8	69		1982-83	1988-89
McPhee, Mike	Mtl., Min., Dal.	11	744	200	199	399	661	134	28	27	55	193	1	1983-84	1993-94
McRae, Basil	Que., Tor., Det., Min., T.B., St.L., Chi.	16	576	53	83	136	2457	78	8	4	12	349		1981-82	1996-97
McRae, Chris	Tor., Det.	3	21	1	0	1	122	....	....	....	....	....		1987-88	1989-90
McRae, Ken	Que., Tor.	7	137	14	21	35	364	6	0	0	0	4		1987-88	1993-94
McReavy, Pat	Bos., Det.	4	55	5	10	15	4	22	3	3	6	9	1	1938-39	1941-42
McReynolds, Brian	Wpg., NYR, L.A.	3	30	1	5	6	8	....	....	....	....	....		1989-90	1993-94
McSheffrey, Bryan	Van., Buf.	3	90	13	7	20	44	....	....	....	....	....		1972-73	1974-75
McSween, Don	Buf., Ana.	5	47	3	10	13	55	....	....	....	....	....		1987-88	1995-96
McTaggart, Jim	Wsh.	2	71	3	10	13	205	....	....	....	....	....		1980-81	1981-82
McTavish, Gordon	St.L., Wpg.	2	11	1	3	4	2	....	....	....	....	....		1978-79	1979-80
• McVeigh, Charley	Chi., NYA	9	397	84	88	172	138	4	0	0	0	2		1926-27	1934-35
• McVicar, Jack	Mtl.M.	2	88	2	4	6	63	6	0	0	0	2		1930-31	1931-32
Meagher, Rick	Mtl., Hfd., N.J., St.L.	12	691	144	165	309	383	62	8	7	15	41		1979-80	1990-91
Meehan, Gerry	Tor., Phi., Buf., Van., Atl., Wsh.	10	670	180	243	423	111	10	0	1	1	0		1968-69	1978-79
Meeke, Brent	Cal., Clev.	5	75	9	22	31	8	....	....	....	....	....		1972-73	1976-77
Meeker, Howie	Tor.	8	346	83	102	185	329	42	6	9	15	50	4	1946-47	1953-54
Meeker, Mike	Pit.	1	4	0	0	0	5	....	....	....	....	....		1978-79	1978-79
• Meeking, Harry	Tor., Det., Bos.	3	65	18	13	31	66	14	4	2	6	21	1	1917-18	1926-27
Meger, Paul	Mtl.	6	212	39	52	91	118	35	3	8	11	16	1	1949-50	1954-55
Meighan, Ron	Min., Pit.	2	48	3	7	10	18	....	....	....	....	....		1981-82	1982-83
Meissner, Barrie	Min.	2	6	0	1	1	4	....	....	....	....	....		1967-68	1968-69
Meissner, Dick	Bos., NYR	5	171	11	15	26	37	....	....	....	....	....		1959-60	1964-65
Melametsa, Anssi	Wpg.	1	27	0	3	3	2	....	....	....	....	....		1985-86	1985-86
Melin, Roger	Min.	2	3	0	0	0	0	....	....	....	....	....		1980-81	1981-82
Mellor, Tom	Det.	2	26	2	4	6	25	....	....	....	....	....		1973-74	1974-75
Melnyk, Gerry	Det., Chi., St.L.	6	269	39	77	116	34	53	6	6	12	6		1955-56	1967-68
Melnyk, Larry	Bos., Edm., NYR, Van.	10	432	11	63	74	686	66	2	9	11	127	1	1980-81	1989-90
Melrose, Barry	Wpg., Tor., Det.	6	300	10	23	33	728	7	0	2	2	38		1979-80	1985-86
Menard, Hillary	Chi.	1	1	0	0	0	0	....	....	....	....	....		1953-54	1953-54
Menard, Howie	Det., L.A., Chi., Oak.	4	151	23	42	65	87	19	3	7	10	36		1963-64	1969-70
Mercredi, Vic	Atl.	1	2	0	0	0	0	....	....	....	....	....		1974-75	1974-75
Meredith, Greg	Cgy.	2	38	6	4	10	8	5	3	1	4	4		1980-81	1982-83
Merkosky, Glenn	Hfd., N.J., Det.	5	66	5	12	17	22	....	....	....	....	....		1981-82	1989-90

Joby Messier

Stan Mikita

Ken Morrow

Bill Mosienko

Joe Mullen

Troy Murray

Frank Nighbor

Ulf Nilsson

			Regular Schedule					Playoffs					NHL	First	Last
Name	NHL Teams	NHL Seasons	GP	G	A	TP	PIM	GP	G	A	TP	PIM	Cup Wins	NHL Season	NHL Season
Meronek, Bill	Mtl.	2	19	5	8	13	0	1	0	0	0	0		1939-40	1942-43
Merrick, Wayne	St.L., Cal., Clev., NYI	12	774	191	265	456	303	102	19	30	49	30	4	1972-73	1983-84
• Merrill, Horace	Ott.	2	8	0	0	0	3	....	....	....	....	....	1	1917-18	1919-20
Messier, Joby	NYR	3	25	0	4	4	24	....	....	....	....	....		1992-93	1994-95
Messier, Mitch	Min.	4	20	0	2	2	11	....	....	....	....	....		1987-88	1990-91
Messier, Paul	Col.	1	9	0	0	0	4	....	....	....	....	....		1978-79	1978-79
Metcalfe, Scott	Edm., Buf.	3	19	1	2	3	18	....	....	....	....	....		1987-88	1989-90
Metz, Don	Tor.	9	172	20	35	55	42	42	7	8	15	12	5	1939-40	1948-49
• Metz, Nick	Tor.	12	518	131	119	250	149	76	19	20	39	31	4	1934-35	1947-48
Michaluk, Art	Chi.	1	5	0	0	0	0	....	....	....	....	....		1947-48	1947-48
Michaluk, John	Chi.	1	1	0	0	0	0	....	....	....	....	....		1950-51	1950-51
Michayluk, Dave	Phi., Pit.	3	14	2	6	8	8	7	1	1	2	0	1	1981-82	1991-92
Micheletti, Joe	St.L., Col.	3	158	11	60	71	114	11	1	11	12	10		1979-80	1981-82
Micheletti, Pat	Min.	1	12	2	0	2	8	....	....	....	....	....		1987-88	1987-88
• Mickey, Larry	Chi., NYR., Tor., Mtl., L.A., Phi., Buf.	11	292	39	53	92	160	9	1	0	1	10		1964-65	1974-75
Mickoski, Nick	NYR, Chi., Det., Bos.	13	703	158	185	343	319	18	1	6	7	6		1947-48	1959-60
Middendorf, Max	Que., Edm.	4	13	2	4	6	6	....	....	....	....	....		1986-87	1990-91
Middleton, Rick	NYR, Bos.	14	1005	448	540	988	157	114	45	55	100	19		1974-75	1987-88
Miehm, Kevin	St.L.	2	22	1	4	5	8	2	0	1	1	0		1992-93	1993-94
Migay, Rudy	Tor.	10	418	59	92	151	293	15	1	0	1	20		1949-50	1959-60
Mikita, Stan	Chi.	22	1394	541	926	1467	1270	155	59	91	150	169	1	1958-59	1979-80
Mikkelson, Bill	L.A., N.Y.I., Wsh.	4	147	4	18	22	105	....	....	....	....	....		1971-72	1976-77
Mikol, Jim	Tor., NYR	2	34	1	4	5	8	....	....	....	....	....		1962-63	1964-65
Mikulchik, Oleg	Wpg., Ana.	3	37	0	3	3	33	....	....	....	....	....		1993-94	1995-96
Milbury, Mike	Bos.	12	754	49	189	238	1552	86	4	24	28	219		1975-76	1986-87
• Milks, Hib	Pit., Phi., NYR, Ott.	8	317	87	41	128	179	11	0	0	0	2		1925-26	1932-33
Millar, Hugh	Det.	1	4	0	0	0	0	1	0	0	0	0		1946-47	1946-47
Millar, Mike	Hfd., Wsh., Bos., Tor.	5	78	18	18	36	12	....	....	....	....	....		1986-87	1990-91
Miller, Bill	Mtl.M., Mtl.	3	95	7	3	10	16	12	0	0	0	0	1	1934-35	1936-37
Miller, Bob	Bos., Col., L.A.	6	404	75	119	194	220	36	4	7	11	27		1977-78	1984-85
Miller, Brad	Buf., Ott., Cgy.	6	82	1	5	6	321	....	....	....	....	....		1988-89	1993-94
• Miller, Earl	Chi., Tor.	5	109	19	14	33	124	10	1	0	1	6	1	1927-28	1931-32
Miller, Jack	Chi.	2	17	0	0	0	4	....	....	....	....	....		1949-50	1950-51
Miller, Jason	N.J.	3	6	0	0	0	0	....	....	....	....	....		1990-91	1992-93
Miller, Jay	Bos., L.A.	7	446	40	44	84	1723	48	2	3	5	243		1985-86	1991-92
Miller, Paul	Col.	1	3	0	3	3	0	....	....	....	....	....		1981-82	1981-82
Miller, Perry	Det.	4	217	10	51	61	387	....	....	....	....	....		1977-78	1980-81
Miller, Tom	Det., NYI	4	118	16	25	41	34	....	....	....	....	....		1970-71	1974-75
Miller, Warren	NYR, Hfd.	4	262	40	50	90	137	6	1	0	1	0		1979-80	1982-83
Miner, John	Edm.	1	14	2	3	5	16	....	....	....	....	....		1987-88	1987-88
Minor, Gerry	Van.	5	140	11	21	32	173	12	1	3	4	25		1979-80	1983-84
Miszuk, John	Det., Chi., Phi., Min.	6	237	7	39	46	232	19	0	3	3	19		1963-64	1969-70
Mitchell, Bill	Det.	1	1	0	0	0	0	....	....	....	....	....		1963-64	1963-64
• Mitchell, Herb	Bos.	2	53	6	0	6	38	....	....	....	....	....		1924-25	1925-26
Mitchell, Red	Chi.	3	83	4	5	9	67	....	....	....	....	....		1941-42	1944-45
Mitchell, Roy	Min.	1	3	0	0	0	0	....	....	....	....	....		1992-93	1992-93
Moe, Billy	NYR	5	261	11	42	53	163	1	0	0	0	0		1944-45	1948-49
Moffat, Lyle	Tor., Wpg.	3	97	12	16	28	51	....	....	....	....	....		1972-73	1979-80
• Moffat, Ron	Det.	3	37	1	1	2	8	7	0	0	0	0		1932-33	1934-35
Moher, Mike	N.J.	1	9	0	1	1	28	....	....	....	....	....		1982-83	1982-83
Mohns, Doug	Bos., Chi., Min., Atl., Wsh.	22	1390	248	462	710	1250	94	14	36	50	122		1953-54	1974-75
Mohns, Lloyd	NYR	1	1	0	0	0	0	....	....	....	....	....		1943-44	1943-44
Mokosak, Carl	Cgy., L.A., Phi., Pit., Bos.	6	83	11	15	26	170	1	0	0	0	0		1981-82	1988-89
Mokosak, John	Det.	2	41	0	2	2	96	....	....	....	....	....		1988-89	1989-90
Molin, Lars	Van.	3	172	33	65	98	37	19	2	9	11	7		1981-82	1983-84
Moller, Mike	Buf., Edm.	7	134	15	28	43	41	3	0	1	1	0		1980-81	1986-87
Moller, Randy	Que., NYR, Buf., Fla.	14	815	45	180	225	1692	78	6	16	22	197		1981-82	1994-95
Molloy, Mitch	Buf.	1	2	0	0	0	10	....	....	....	....	....		1989-90	1989-90
Molyneaux, Larry	NYR	2	45	0	1	1	20	10	0	0	0	8		1937-38	1938-39
Monahan, Garry	Mtl., Det., L.A., Tor., Van.	12	748	116	169	285	484	22	3	1	4	13		1967-68	1978-79
Monahan, Hartland	Cal., NYR, Wsh., Pit., L.A., St.L.	7	334	61	80	141	163	6	0	0	0	4		1973-74	1980-81
• Mondou, Armand	Mtl.	12	386	47	71	118	99	32	3	5	8	12		1928-29	1939-40
Mondou, Pierre	Mtl.	9	548	194	262	456	179	69	17	28	45	26	3	1976-77	1984-85
Mongeau, Michel	St.L., T.B.	4	54	6	19	25	10	2	0	1	1	0		1989-90	1992-93
Mongrain, Bob	Buf., L.A.	6	81	13	14	27	14	11	1	2	3	2		1979-80	1985-86
Monteith, Hank	Det.	3	77	5	12	17	6	4	0	0	0	0		1968-69	1970-71
Moore, Dickie	Mtl., Tor., St.L.	14	719	261	347	608	652	135	46	64	110	122	6	1951-52	1967-68
• Moran, Amby	Mtl., Chi.	2	35	1	1	2	24	....	....	....	....	....		1926-27	1927-28
• Morenz, Howie	Mtl., Chi., NYR	14	550	270	197	467	531	47	21	11	32	68		1923-24	1936-37
Moretto, Angelo	Clev.	1	5	1	2	3	2	....	....	....	....	....		1976-77	1976-77
• Morin, Pete	Mtl.	1	31	10	12	22	7	1	0	0	0	0		1941-42	1941-42
Morin, Stephane	Que., Van.	5	90	16	39	55	52	....	....	....	....	....		1989-90	1993-94
• Morris, Bernie	Bos.	1	6	2	0	2	0	....	....	....	....	....		1924-25	1924-25
Morris, Elwyn	Tor., NYR	4	135	13	29	42	58	18	4	2	6	16	1	1943-44	1948-49
Morris, Jon	N.J., S.J., Bos.	6	103	16	33	49	47	11	1	7	8	25		1988-89	1993-94
Morrison, Dave	L.A., Van.	4	39	3	3	6	4	....	....	....	....	....		1980-81	1984-85
Morrison, Don	Det., Chi.	3	112	18	28	46	12	3	0	1	1	0		1947-48	1950-51
Morrison, Doug	Bos.	4	23	7	3	10	15	....	....	....	....	....		1979-80	1984-85
Morrison, Gary	Phi.	3	43	1	15	16	70	5	0	1	1	2		1979-80	1981-82
Morrison, George	St.L.	2	115	17	21	38	13	3	0	0	0	0		1970-71	1971-72
Morrison, Jim	Bos., Tor., Det., NYR, Pit.	12	704	40	160	200	542	36	0	12	12	38		1951-52	1970-71
• Morrison, John	NYA	1	18	0	0	0	0	....	....	....	....	....		1925-26	1925-26
Morrison, Kevin	Col.	1	41	4	11	15	23	....	....	....	....	....		1979-80	1979-80
Morrison, Lew	Phi., Atl., Wsh., Pit.	9	564	39	52	91	107	17	0	0	0	2		1969-70	1977-78
Morrison, Mark	NYR	2	10	1	1	2	0	....	....	....	....	....		1981-82	1983-84
Morrison, Rod	Det.	1	34	8	7	15	4	3	0	0	0	0		1947-48	1947-48
Morrow, Ken	NYI	10	550	17	88	105	309	127	11	22	33	97	4	1979-80	1988-89
Morrow, Scott	Cgy.	1	4	0	0	0	0	....	....	....	....	....		1994-95	1994-95
Morton, Dean	Det.	1	1	1	0	1	2	....	....	....	....	....		1989-90	1989-90
Mortson, Gus	Tor., Chi., Det.	13	797	46	152	198	1380	54	5	8	13	68	4	1946-47	1958-59
Mosdell, Kenny	Bro., Mtl., Chi.	16	693	141	168	309	475	80	16	13	29	48	4	1941-42	1958-59
• Mosienko, Bill	Chi.	14	711	258	282	540	121	22	10	4	14	15		1941-42	1954-55
Mott, Morris	Cal.	3	199	18	32	50	49	....	....	....	....	....		1972-73	1974-75
• Motter, Alex	Bos., Det.	8	256	39	64	103	135	41	3	9	12	41	1	1934-35	1942-43
Moxey, Jim	Cal., Clev., L.A.	3	127	22	27	49	59	....	....	....	....	....		1974-75	1976-77
Mulhern, Richard	Atl., L.A., Tor., Wpg.	6	303	27	93	120	217	7	0	3	3	5		1975-76	1980-81
Mullen, Brian	Wpg., NYR, S.J., NYI	11	832	260	362	622	414	62	12	18	30	30		1982-83	1992-93
Mullen, Joe	St.L., Cgy., Pit., Bos.	17	1062	502	561	1063	241	143	60	46	106	42	3	1979-80	1996-97
Muloin, Wayne	Det., Oak., Cal., Min.	3	147	3	21	24	93	11	0	0	0	2		1963-64	1970-71
Mulvenna, Glenn	Pit., Phi.	2	2	0	0	0	4	....	....	....	....	....		1991-92	1992-93
Mulvey, Grant	Chi., N.J.	10	586	149	135	284	816	42	10	5	15	70		1974-75	1983-84
Mulvey, Paul	Wsh., Pit., L.A.	4	225	30	51	81	613	....	....	....	....	....		1978-79	1981-82
• Mummery, Harry	Tor., Que., Mtl., Ham.	6	107	33	19	52	230	7	1	7	8	38	1	1917-18	1922-23
• Munro, Dunc	Mtl. M., Mtl.	8	239	28	18	46	170	25	3	2	5	24	1	1924-25	1931-32
• Munro, Gerry	Mtl. M., Tor.	2	33	1	0	1	22	....	....	....	....	....		1924-25	1925-26
Murdoch, Bob	Mtl., L.A., Atl., Cgy.	12	757	60	218	278	764	69	4	18	22	92	2	1970-71	1981-82
Murdoch, Bob	Cal., Clev., St.L.	4	260	72	85	157	127	....	....	....	....	....		1975-76	1978-79
Murdoch, Don	NYR, Edm., Det.	6	320	121	117	238	155	24	10	8	18	16		1976-77	1981-82
Murdoch, Murray	NYR	11	508	84	108	192	197	55	9	12	21	28	2	1926-27	1936-37
Murphy, Brian	Det.	1	1	0	0	0	0	....	....	....	....	....		1974-75	1974-75
Murphy, Mike	St.L. NYR, L.A.	12	831	238	318	556	514	66	13	23	36	54		1971-72	1982-83
Murphy, Rob	Van., Ott., L.A.	7	125	9	12	21	152	4	0	0	0	2		1987-88	1993-94
Murphy, Ron	NYR, Chi., Det., Bos.	18	889	205	274	479	460	53	7	8	15	26	1	1952-53	1969-70
Murray, Allan	NYA	7	271	5	9	14	163	14	0	0	0	10		1933-34	1939-40
Murray, Bob	Chi.	15	1008	132	382	514	873	112	19	37	56	106		1975-76	1989-90
Murray, Bob	Atl., Van.	4	194	6	16	22	98	10	1	1	2	15		1973-74	1976-77
Murray, Jim	L.A.	1	30	0	2	2	14	....	....	....	....	....		1967-68	1967-68
Murray, Ken	Tor., N.Y.I., Det., K.C.	5	106	1	10	11	135	....	....	....	....	....		1969-70	1975-76
• Murray, Leo	Mtl.	1	6	0	0	0	2	....	....	....	....	....		1932-33	1932-33
Murray, Mike	Phi.	1	1	0	0	0	0	....	....	....	....	....		1987-88	1987-88
Murray, Pat	Phi.	2	25	3	1	4	15	....	....	....	....	....		1990-91	1991-92
Murray, Randy	Tor.	1	3	0	0	0	2	....	....	....	....	....		1969-70	1969-70
Murray, Terry	Cal., Phi., Det., Wsh.	8	302	4	76	80	199	18	2	2	4	10		1972-73	1981-82

Name	NHL Teams	NHL Seasons	Regular Schedule GP	G	A	TP	PIM	Playoffs GP	G	A	TP	PIM	NHL Cup Wins	First NHL Season	Last NHL Season
Murray, Troy	Chi., Wpg., Ott., Pit., Col.	15	915	230	354	584	875	113	17	26	43	145	1	1981-82	1995-96
Myers, Hap	Buf.	1	13	0	0	0	6	....	....	....	....	....		1970-71	1970-71
Myles, Vic	NYR	1	45	6	9	15	57	....	....	....	....	....		1942-43	1942-43

N

Name	NHL Teams	NHL Seasons	Regular Schedule GP	G	A	TP	PIM	Playoffs GP	G	A	TP	PIM	NHL Cup Wins	First NHL Season	Last NHL Season
Nachbaur, Don	Hfd., Edm., Phi.	8	223	23	46	69	465	11	1	1	2	24		1980-81	1989-90
Nahrgang, Jim	Det.	3	57	5	12	17	34	....	....	....	....	....		1974-75	1976-77
Nanne, Lou	Min.	11	635	68	157	225	356	32	4	10	14	8		1967-68	1977-78
Nantais, Richard	Min.	3	63	5	4	9	79	....	....	....	....	....		1974-75	1976-77
Napier, Mark	Mtl., Min., Edm., Buf.	11	767	235	306	541	157	82	18	24	42	11	2	1978-79	1988-89
Naslund, Mats	Mtl., Bos.	9	651	251	383	634	111	102	35	57	92	33	1	1982-83	1994-95
Nattrass, Ralph	Chi.	4	223	18	38	56	308	....	....	....	....	....		1946-47	1949-50
Nattress, Ric	Mtl., St.L., Cgy., Tor., Phi.	11	536	29	135	164	377	67	5	10	15	60	1	1982-83	1992-93
Natyshak, Mike	Que.	1	4	0	0	0	0	....	....	....	....	....		1987-88	1987-88
Neaton, Pat	Pit.	1	9	1	1	2	12	....	....	....	....	....		1993-94	1993-94
Nechayev, Viktor	L.A.	1	3	1	0	1	0	....	....	....	....	....		1982-83	1982-83
Nedomansky, Vaclav	Det., NYR, St.L.	6	421	122	156	278	88	7	3	5	8	0		1977-78	1982-83
Needham, Mike	Pit., Dal.	3	86	9	5	14	16	14	2	0	2	4	1	1991-92	1993-94
Neely, Bob	Tor., Col.	5	283	39	59	98	266	26	5	7	12	15		1973-74	1977-78
Neely, Cam	Van., Bos.	13	726	395	299	694	1241	93	57	32	89	168		1983-84	1995-96
Neilson, Jim	NYR, Cal., Clev.	16	1023	69	299	368	904	65	1	17	18	61		1962-63	1977-78
Nelson, Gordie	Tor.	1	3	0	0	0	11	....	....	....	....	....		1969-70	1969-70
Nelson, Todd	Wsh.	2	3	1	0	1	2	4	0	0	0	0		1994-95	1995-96
Nemeth, Steve	NYR	1	12	2	0	2	2	....	....	....	....	....		1987-88	1987-88
Nesterenko, Eric	Tor., Chi.	21	1219	250	324	574	1273	124	13	24	37	127	1	1951-52	1971-72
Nethery, Lance	NYR, Edm.	2	41	11	14	25	14	14	5	3	8	9		1980-81	1981-82
Neufeld, Ray	Hfd., Win., Bos.	11	595	157	200	357	816	28	8	6	14	55		1979-80	1989-90
• Neville, Mike	Tor., NYA	3	64	5	3	8	14	2	0	0	0	0	1	1917-18	1930-31
Nevin, Bob	Tor., NYR, Min., L.A.	18	1128	307	419	726	211	84	16	18	34	24	2	1957-58	1975-76
Newberry, John	Mtl., Hfd.	4	22	0	4	4	6	2	0	0	0	0		1982-83	1985-86
Newell, Rick	Det.	2	6	0	0	0	0	....	....	....	....	....		1972-73	1973-74
Newman, Dan	NYR, Mtl., Edm.	4	126	17	24	41	63	3	0	0	0	4		1976-77	1979-80
• Newman, John	Det.	1	8	1	1	2	0	....	....	....	....	....		1930-31	1930-31
Nicholson, Al	Bos.	2	19	0	1	1	4	....	....	....	....	....		1955-56	1956-57
Nicholson, Edward	Det.	1	1	0	0	0	0	....	....	....	....	....		1947-48	1947-48
• Nicholson, Hickey	Chi.	1	2	1	0	1	0	....	....	....	....	....		1937-38	1937-38
Nicholson, Neil	Oak., N.Y.I.	4	39	3	1	4	23	2	0	0	0	0		1969-70	1977-78
Nicholson, Paul	Wsh.	3	62	4	8	12	18	....	....	....	....	....		1974-75	1976-77
Nicolson, Graeme	Bos., Col., NYR	3	52	2	7	9	60	....	....	....	....	....		1978-79	1982-83
Niekamp, Jim	Det.	2	29	0	2	2	37	....	....	....	....	....		1970-71	1971-72
Nienhuis, Kraig	Bos.	3	87	20	16	36	39	2	0	0	0	14		1985-86	1987-88
• Nighbor, Frank	Ott., Tor.	13	349	137	92	229	252	36	11	12	23	27	4	1917-18	1929-30
Nigro, Frank	Tor.	2	68	8	18	26	39	3	0	0	0	2		1982-83	1983-84
Nilan, Chris	Mtl., NYR, Bos.	13	688	110	115	225	3043	111	8	9	17	541	1	1979-80	1991-92
Nill, Jim	St.L., Van., Bos., Wpg., Det.	9	524	58	87	145	854	59	10	5	15	203		1981-82	1989-90
Nilsson, Kent	Atl., Cgy., Min., Edm.	9	553	264	422	686	116	59	11	41	52	14	1	1979-80	1994-95
Nilsson, Ulf	NYR	4	170	57	112	169	85	25	8	14	22	27		1978-79	1982-83
Nistico, Lou	Col.	1	3	0	0	0	0	....	....	....	....	....		1977-78	1977-78
• Noble, Reg	Tor., Mtl.M., Det.	16	509	167	97	264	859	32	4	4	8	61	3	1917-18	1932-33
Noel, Claude	Wsh.	1	7	0	0	0	0	....	....	....	....	....		1979-80	1979-80
• Nolan, Paddy	Tor.	1	2	0	0	0	0	....	....	....	....	....	1	1921-22	1921-22
Nolan, Ted	Det., Pit.	3	78	6	16	22	105	....	....	....	....	....		1981-82	1985-86
Nolet, Simon	Phi., K.C., Pit., Col.	10	562	150	182	332	187	34	6	3	9	8	1	1967-68	1976-77
Nordmark, Robert	St. L., Van.	4	236	13	70	83	254	7	3	2	5	8		1987-88	1990-91
Noris, Joe	Pit., St.L., Buf.	3	55	2	5	7	22	....	....	....	....	....		1971-72	1973-74
Norrish, Rod	Min.	2	21	3	3	6	2	....	....	....	....	....		1973-74	1974-75
• Northcott, Baldy	Mtl.M., Chi.	11	446	133	112	245	273	31	8	5	13	14	1	1928-29	1938-39
Norwich, Craig	Wpg., St.L., Col.	2	104	17	58	75	60	....	....	....	....	....		1979-80	1980-81
Norwood, Lee	Que., Wsh., St.L., Det., N.J., Hfd., Cgy.	12	503	58	153	211	1099	65	6	22	28	171		1980-81	1993-94
Novy, Milan	Wsh.	1	73	18	30	48	16	2	0	0	0	0		1982-83	1982-83
Nowak, Hank	Pit., Det., Bos.	4	180	26	29	55	161	13	1	0	1	8		1973-74	1976-77
Nykoluk, Mike	Tor.	1	32	3	1	4	20	....	....	....	....	....		1956-57	1956-57
Nylund, Gary	Tor., Chi., NYI	11	608	32	139	171	1235	24	0	6	6	63		1982-83	1992-93
• Nyrop, Bill	Mtl., Min.	4	207	12	51	63	101	35	1	7	8	22	3	1975-76	1981-82
Nystrom, Bob	NYI	14	900	235	278	513	1248	157	39	44	83	236	4	1972-73	1985-86

O

Name	NHL Teams	NHL Seasons	Regular Schedule GP	G	A	TP	PIM	Playoffs GP	G	A	TP	PIM	NHL Cup Wins	First NHL Season	Last NHL Season
• Oatman, Russell	Det., Mtl.M., NYR	3	120	20	9	29	100	15	1	0	1	18		1926-27	1928-29
O'Brien, Dennis	Min., Col., Clev., Bos.	10	592	31	91	122	1017	34	1	2	3	101		1970-71	1979-80
O'Brien, Ellard	Bos.	1	2	0	0	0	0	....	....	....	....	....		1955-56	1955-56
O'Callahan, Jack	Chi., N.J.	7	389	27	104	131	541	32	4	11	15	41		1982-83	1988-89
O'Connell, Mike	Chi., Bos., Det.	13	860	105	334	439	605	82	8	24	32	64		1977-78	1989-90
• O'Connor, Buddy	Mtl., NYR	10	509	140	257	397	34	53	15	21	36	6	2	1941-42	1950-51
O'Connor, Myles	N.J., Ana.	4	43	3	4	7	69	....	....	....	....	....		1990-91	1993-94
Oddleifson, Chris	Bos., Van.	9	524	95	191	286	464	14	1	6	7	8		1972-73	1980-81
Odelein, Selmar	Edm.	3	18	0	2	2	35	....	....	....	....	....		1985-86	1988-89
O'Donnell, Fred	Bos.	2	115	15	11	26	98	5	0	1	1	5		1972-73	1973-74
O'Donoghue, Don	Oak., Cal.	3	125	18	17	35	35	3	0	0	0	0		1969-70	1971-72
Odrowski, Gerry	Det., Oak., St.L.	6	309	12	19	31	111	30	0	1	1	16		1960-61	1971-72
O'Dwyer, Bill	L.A., Bos.	5	120	9	13	22	108	10	0	0	0	2		1983-84	1989-90
O'Flaherty, Gerry	Tor., Van., Atl.	8	438	99	95	194	168	7	2	2	4	6		1971-72	1978-79
O'Flaherty, Peanuts	NYA, Bro.	2	21	5	1	6	0	....	....	....	....	....		1940-41	1941-42
Ogilvie, Brian	Chi., St.L.	6	90	15	21	36	29	....	....	....	....	....		1972-73	1978-79
• O'Grady, George	Mtl.M.	1	4	0	0	0	0	....	....	....	....	....		1917-18	1917-18
Ogrodnick, John	Det., Que., NYR	14	928	402	425	827	260	41	18	8	26	6		1979-80	1992-93
Ojanen, Janne	N.J.	4	98	21	23	44	28	3	0	2	2	0		1988-89	1992-93
Okerlund, Todd	NYI	1	4	0	0	0	2	....	....	....	....	....		1987-88	1987-88
• Oliver, Harry	Bos., NYA	11	463	127	85	212	147	35	10	6	16	24	1	1926-27	1936-37
Oliver, Murray	Det., Bos., Tor., Min.	17	1127	274	454	728	320	35	9	16	25	10		1957-58	1974-75
Olmstead, Bert	Chi., Mtl., Tor.	14	848	181	421	602	884	115	16	43	59	101	5	1948-49	1961-62
Olsen, Darryl	Cgy.	1	1	0	0	0	0	....	....	....	....	....		1991-92	1991-92
Olson, Dennis	Det.	1	4	0	0	0	0	....	....	....	....	....		1957-58	1957-58
O'Neil, Paul	Van., Bos.	2	6	0	0	0	0	....	....	....	....	....		1973-74	1975-76
• O'Neill, Jim	Bos., Mtl.	6	156	6	30	36	109	9	1	1	2	13		1933-34	1941-42
• O'Neill, Tom	Tor.	2	66	10	12	22	53	4	0	0	0	6	1	1943-44	1944-45
Orban, Bill	Chi., Min.	3	114	8	15	23	67	3	0	0	0	0		1967-68	1969-70
O'Ree, Willie	Bos.	2	45	4	10	14	26	....	....	....	....	....		1957-58	1960-61
O'Regan, Tom	Pit.	3	61	5	12	17	10	....	....	....	....	....		1983-84	1985-86
O'Reilly, Terry	Bos.	14	891	204	402	606	2095	108	25	42	67	335		1971-72	1984-85
Orlando, Gaetano	Buf.	3	98	18	26	44	51	5	0	4	4	14		1984-85	1986-87
Orlando, Jimmy	Det.	6	199	6	25	31	375	36	0	9	9	105	1	1936-37	1942-43
Orleski, Dave	Mtl.	2	2	0	0	0	0	....	....	....	....	....		1980-81	1981-82
Orr, Bobby	Bos., Chi.	12	657	270	645	915	953	74	26	66	92	107	2	1966-67	1978-79
Osborne, Keith	St.L., T.B.	2	16	1	3	4	16	....	....	....	....	....		1989-90	1992-93
Osborne, Mark	Det., NYR, Tor., Wpg.	14	919	212	319	531	1152	87	12	16	28	141		1981-82	1994-95
Osburn, Randy	Tor., Phi.	2	27	0	2	2	0	....	....	....	....	....		1972-73	1974-75
O'Shea, Danny	Min., Chi., St.L.	5	369	64	115	179	265	39	3	7	10	61		1968-69	1972-73
O'Shea, Kevin	Buf., St.L.	3	134	13	18	31	85	12	2	1	3	10		1970-71	1972-73
Osiecki, Mark	Cgy., Ott., Wpg., Min.	2	93	3	11	14	43	....	....	....	....	....		1991-92	1992-93
Otevrel, Jaroslav	S.J.	2	16	3	4	7	2	....	....	....	....	....		1992-93	1993-94
Ouelette, Eddie	Chi.	1	43	3	2	5	11	1	0	0	0	0		1935-36	1935-36
Ouelette, Gerry	Bos.	1	34	5	4	9	0	....	....	....	....	....		1960-61	1960-61
Owchar, Dennis	Pit., Col.	6	288	30	85	115	200	10	1	1	2	8		1974-75	1979-80
• Owen, George	Bos.	5	183	44	33	77	151	21	2	5	7	25	1	1928-29	1932-33

P

Name	NHL Teams	NHL Seasons	Regular Schedule GP	G	A	TP	PIM	Playoffs GP	G	A	TP	PIM	NHL Cup Wins	First NHL Season	Last NHL Season
Pachal, Clayton	Bos., Col.	3	35	2	3	5	95	....	....	....	....	....		1976-77	1978-79
Paddock, John	Wsh., Phi., Que.	5	87	8	14	22	86	5	2	0	2	0		1975-76	1982-83
Paiement, Rosaire	Phi., Van.	5	190	48	52	100	343	3	3	0	3	0		1967-68	1971-72

Gerry Odrowski

Dennis Owchar

George Parsons

Steve Payne

Cliff Pennington

Denis Potvin

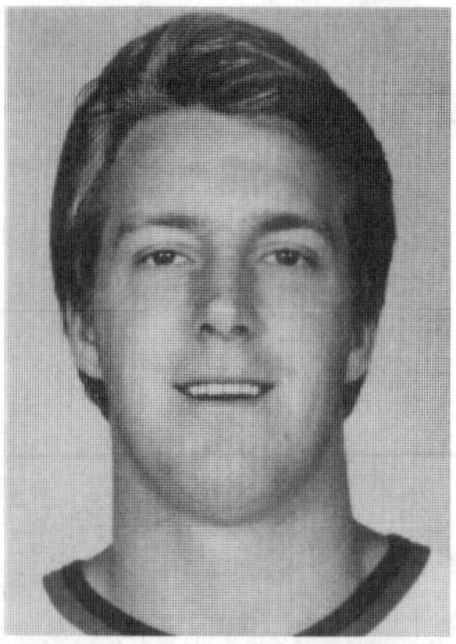

Wayne Presley

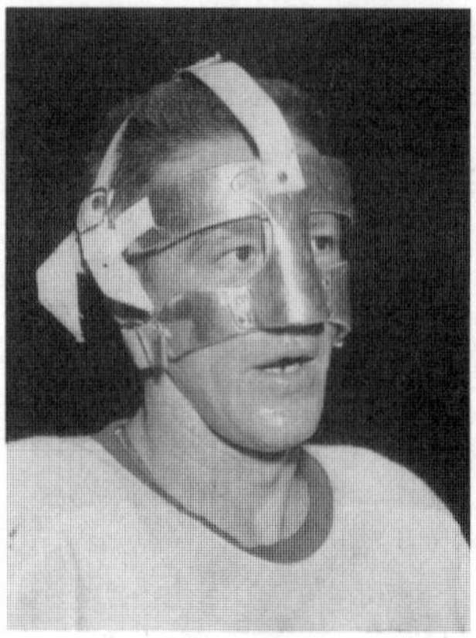

Marcel Pronovost

Name	NHL Teams	NHL Seasons	Regular Schedule GP	G	A	TP	PIM	Playoffs GP	G	A	TP	PIM	NHL Cup Wins	First NHL Season	Last NHL Season
Paiement, Wilf	K.C. Col., Tor., Que., NYR, Buf., Pit.	14	946	356	458	814	1757	69	18	17	35	185		1974-75	1987-88
Palangio, Peter	Mtl., Det., Chi.	5	71	13	10	23	28	7	0	0	0	0	1	1926-27	1937-38
Palazzari, Aldo	Bos., NYR	1	35	8	3	11	4	....	....	....	....	....		1943-44	1943-44
Palazzari, Doug	St.L.	4	108	18	20	38	23	2	0	0	0	0		1974-75	1978-79
Palmer, Brad	Min., Bos.	3	168	32	38	70	58	29	9	5	14	16		1980-81	1982-83
Palmer, Rob	Chi.	3	16	0	3	3	2	....	....	....	....	....		1973-74	1975-76
Palmer, Robert Ross	L.A., N.J.	7	320	9	101	110	115	8	1	2	3	6		1977-78	1983-84
● Panagabko, Ed	Bos.	2	29	0	3	3	38	....	....	....	....	....		1955-56	1956-57
Panteleev, Grigori	Bos., NYI	4	54	8	6	14	12	....	....	....	....	....		1992-93	1995-96
● Papike, Joe	Chi.	3	20	3	3	6	4	5	0	2	2	0		1940-41	1944-45
Pappin, Jim	Tor., Chi., Cal., Clev.	14	767	278	295	573	667	92	33	34	67	101	2	1963-64	1976-77
Paradise, Bob	Min., Atl., Pit., Wsh.	8	368	8	54	62	393	12	0	1	1	19		1971-72	1978-79
Pargeter, George	Mtl.	1	4	0	0	0	0	....	....	....	....	....		1946-47	1946-47
Parise, Jean-Paul	Bos., Tor., Min., NYI, Clev.	14	890	238	356	594	706	86	27	31	58	87		1965-66	1978-79
Parizeau, Michel	St.L., Phi.	1	58	3	14	17	18	....	....	....	....	....		1971-72	1971-72
Park, Brad	NYR, Bos., Det.	17	1113	213	683	896	1429	161	35	90	125	217		1968-69	1984-85
Parker, Jeff	Buf., Hfd.	5	141	16	19	35	163	5	0	0	0	26		1986-87	1990-91
● Parkes, Ernie	Mtl.M.	1	17	0	0	0	2	....	....	....	....	....		1924-25	1924-25
Parks, Greg	NYI	3	23	1	2	3	6	2	0	0	0	0		1990-91	1992-93
● Parsons, George	Tor.	3	78	12	13	25	20	7	3	2	5	11		1936-37	1938-39
● Pasek, Dusan	Min.	1	48	4	10	14	30	2	1	0	1	0		1988-89	1988-89
Pasin, Dave	Bos., L.A.	2	76	18	19	37	50	3	0	1	1	0		1985-86	1988-89
Paslawski, Greg	Mtl., St.L., Wpg., Buf., Que., Phi., Cgy.	11	650	187	185	372	169	60	19	13	32	25		1983-84	1993-94
Paterson, Joe	Det., Phi., L.A., NYR	9	291	19	37	56	829	22	3	4	7	77		1980-81	1988-89
Paterson, Mark	Hfd.	4	29	3	3	6	33	....	....	....	....	....		1982-83	1985-86
Paterson, Rick	Chi.	9	430	50	43	93	136	61	7	10	17	51		1978-79	1986-87
Patey, Doug	Wsh.	3	45	4	2	6	8	....	....	....	....	....		1976-77	1978-79
Patey, Larry	Cal., St.L., NYR	12	717	153	163	316	631	40	8	10	18	57		1973-74	1984-85
Patrick, Craig	Cal., St.L., K.C., Wsh.	8	401	72	91	163	61	2	0	1	1	0		1971-72	1978-79
Patrick, Glenn	St.L., Cal., Clev.	3	38	2	3	5	72	....	....	....	....	....		1973-74	1976-77
● Patrick, Lester	NYR	1	1	0	0	0	2	....	....	....	....	....		1926-27	1926-27
● Patrick, Lynn	NYR	10	455	145	190	335	240	44	10	6	16	22	1	1934-35	1945-46
● Patrick, Muzz	NYR	5	166	5	26	31	133	25	4	0	4	34	1	1937-38	1945-46
Patrick, Steve	Buf., NYR, Que.	6	250	40	68	108	242	12	0	1	1	12		1980-81	1985-86
Patterson, Colin	Cgy., Buf.	9	504	96	109	205	239	85	12	17	29	57	1	1983-84	1992-93
Patterson, Dennis	K.C., Phi.	3	138	6	22	28	67	....	....	....	....	....		1974-75	1979-80
● Patterson, George	Bos., Det., St.L., Tor., Mtl., NYA	9	284	51	27	78	218	3	0	0	0	2		1926-27	1934-35
● Paul, Butch	Det.	1	3	0	0	0	0	....	....	....	....	....		1964-65	1964-65
● Paulhus, Rollie	Mtl.	1	33	0	0	0	0	....	....	....	....	....		1925-26	1925-26
Pavelich, Mark	NYR, Min., S.J.	7	355	137	192	329	340	23	7	17	24	14		1981-82	1991-92
Pavelich, Marty	Det.	10	634	93	159	252	454	91	13	15	28	74	4	1947-48	1956-57
Pavese, Jim	St.L., NYR, Det., Hfd.	8	328	13	44	57	689	34	0	6	6	81		1981-82	1988-89
● Payer, Evariste	Mtl.	1	1	0	0	0	0	....	....	....	....	....		1917-18	1917-18
Payne, Steve	Min.	10	613	228	238	466	435	71	35	35	70	60		1978-79	1987-88
Paynter, Kent	Chi., Wsh., Wpg., Ott.	7	37	1	3	4	69	4	0	0	0	10		1987-88	1993-94
Pearson, Mel	NYR, Pit.	5	38	2	6	8	25	....	....	....	....	....		1949-50	1967-68
Pedersen, Allen	Bos., Min., Hfd.	8	428	5	36	41	487	64	0	0	0	91		1986-87	1993-94
Pederson, Barry	Bos., Van., Pit., Hfd.	12	701	238	416	654	472	34	22	30	52	25		1980-81	1991-92
Pederson, Mark	Mtl., Phi., S.J., Det.	5	169	35	50	85	77	2	0	0	0	0		1989-90	1993-94
Peer, Bert	Det.	1	1	0	0	0	0	....	....	....	....	....		1939-40	1939-40
Peirson, Johnny	Bos.	11	545	153	173	326	315	49	9	17	26	26		1946-47	1957-58
Pelensky, Perry	Chi.	1	4	0	0	0	5	....	....	....	....	....		1983-84	1983-84
Pelletier, Roger	Phi.	1	1	0	0	0	0	....	....	....	....	....		1967-68	1967-68
Peloffy, Andre	Wsh.	1	9	0	0	0	0	....	....	....	....	....		1974-75	1974-75
Pelyk, Mike	Tor.	9	441	26	88	114	566	40	0	3	3	41		1967-68	1977-78
Penney, Chad	Ott.	1	3	0	0	0	2	....	....	....	....	....		1993-94	1993-94
Pennington, Cliff	Mtl., Bos.	3	101	17	42	59	6	....	....	....	....	....		1960-61	1962-63
Peplinski, Jim	Cgy.	11	711	161	263	424	1467	99	15	31	46	382	1	1980-81	1994-95
Perlini, Fred	Tor.	2	8	2	3	5	0	....	....	....	....	....		1981-82	1983-84
Perreault, Fern	NYR	2	3	0	0	0	0	....	....	....	....	....		1947-48	1949-50
Perreault, Gilbert	Buf.	17	1191	512	814	1326	500	90	33	70	103	44		1970-71	1986-87
Perry, Brian	Oak., Buf.	3	96	16	29	45	24	8	1	1	2	4		1968-69	1970-71
Persson, Stefan	NYI	9	622	52	317	369	574	102	7	50	57	69	4	1977-78	1985-86
Pesut, George	Cal.	2	92	3	22	25	130	....	....	....	....	....		1974-75	1975-76
● Peters, Frank	NYR	1	43	0	0	0	59	4	0	0	0	2		1930-31	1930-31
Peters, Garry	Mtl., NYR, Phi., Bos.	8	311	34	34	68	261	9	2	2	4	31	1	1964-65	1971-72
Peters, Jimmy Jr.	Det., L.A.	9	309	37	36	73	48	11	0	2	2	2		1964-65	1974-75
Peters, Jimmy Sr.	Det., Chi., Mtl., Bos.	9	574	125	150	275	186	60	5	9	14	22	3	1945-46	1953-54
Peters, Steve	Col.	1	2	0	1	1	0	....	....	....	....	....		1979-80	1979-80
Peterson, Brent	Det., Buf., Van., Hfd.	11	620	72	141	213	484	31	4	4	8	65		1979-80	1988-89
Petrenko, Sergei	Buf.	1	14	0	4	4	0	....	....	....	....	....		1993-94	1993-94
Petrov, Oleg	Mtl.	4	112	20	26	46	39	8	0	1	1	0	1	1992-93	1995-96
Pettersson, Jorgen	St.L., Hfd., Wsh.	6	435	174	192	366	117	44	15	12	27	4		1980-81	1985-86
● Pettinger, Eric	Ott., Bos., Tor.	3	98	7	12	19	83	4	1	0	1	8		1928-29	1930-31
Pettinger, Gord	Det., NYR, Bos.	8	292	42	74	116	77	47	4	5	9	11	4	1932-33	1939-40
Phair, Lyle	L.A.	3	48	6	7	13	12	1	0	0	0	0		1985-86	1987-88
Phillipoff, Harold	Atl., Chi.,	3	141	26	57	83	267	6	0	2	2	9		1977-78	1979-80
● Phillips, Batt	Mtl.M.	2	28	1	1	2	6	4	0	0	0	2		1929-30	1929-30
Phillips, Charlie	Mtl.	1	17	0	0	0	6	....	....	....	....	....		1942-43	1942-43
● Phillips, Meryn J.	Mtl.M., NYA.	8	302	52	31	83	232	28	6	2	8	19	1	1925-26	1932-33
Picard, Noel	Atl., Mtl., St.L.	7	335	12	63	75	616	50	2	11	13	167	1	1964-65	1972-73
Picard, Robert	Wsh. Tor., Mtl., Wpg., Que., Det.	13	899	104	319	423	1025	36	5	15	20	39		1977-78	1989-90
Picard, Roger	St.L.	1	15	2	2	4	21	....	....	....	....	....		1967-68	1967-68
Pichette, Dave	Que., St.L., N.J., NYR	7	322	41	140	181	348	28	3	7	10	54		1980-81	1987-88
Picketts, Hal	NYA.	1	48	3	1	4	32	....	....	....	....	....		1933-34	1933-34
Pidhirny, Harry	Bos.	1	2	0	0	0	0	....	....	....	....	....		1957-58	1957-58
Pierce, Randy	Col., N.J., Hfd.	8	277	62	76	138	223	2	0	0	0	0		1977-78	1984-85
Pike, Alf	NYR	6	234	42	77	119	145	21	4	2	6	12	1	1939-40	1946-47
Pilote, Pierre	Chi., Tor.	14	890	80	418	498	1251	86	8	53	61	102	1	1955-56	1968-69
Pinder, Gerry	Chi., Cal.	3	223	55	69	124	135	17	0	4	4	6		1969-70	1971-72
Pirus, Alex	Min., Det.	4	159	30	28	58	94	2	0	1	1	2		1976-77	1979-80
● Pitre, Didier	Mtl.	6	129	63	29	91	85	14	2	6	8	19		1917-18	1922-23
● Plager, Barclay	St.L.	10	614	44	187	231	1115	68	3	20	23	182		1967-68	1976-77
Plager, Bill	Min., St.L., Atl.	9	263	4	34	38	294	31	0	2	2	26		1967-68	1975-76
Plager, Bob	NYR, St.L.	14	644	20	126	146	802	74	2	17	19	195		1964-65	1977-78
Plamondon, Gerry	Mtl.	5	74	7	13	20	10	11	5	2	7	2	1	1945-46	1950-51
Plante, Cam	Tor.	1	2	0	0	0	0	....	....	....	....	....		1984-85	1984-85
Plante, Pierre	NYR, Que., Phi., St.L., Chi.	9	599	125	172	297	599	33	2	6	8	51		1971-72	1979-80
Plantery, Mark	Wpg.	1	25	1	5	6	14	....	....	....	....	....		1980-81	1980-81
Plavsic, Adrien	St.L., Van., T.B., Ana.	8	214	16	56	72	161	13	1	7	8	4		1989-90	1996-97
● Plaxton, Hugh	Mtl.M.	1	15	1	2	3	4	....	....	....	....	....		1932-33	1932-33
Playfair, Jim	Edm., Chi.	3	21	2	4	6	51	....	....	....	....	....		1983-84	1988-89
Playfair, Larry	Buf., L.A.	12	688	26	94	120	1812	43	0	6	6	111		1978-79	1989-90
Pleau, Larry	Mtl.	3	94	9	15	24	27	4	0	0	0	0		1969-70	1971-72
Pletsch, Charles	Ham.	1	1	0	0	0	0	....	....	....	....	....		1920-21	1920-21
Plett, Willi	Atl., Cgy., Min., Bos.	13	834	222	215	437	2572	83	24	22	46	466		1975-76	1987-88
Plumb, Rob	Det.	2	14	3	2	5	2	....	....	....	....	....		1977-78	1977-78
Plumb, Ron	Hfd.	1	26	3	4	7	14	....	....	....	....	....		1979-80	1979-80
Pocza, Harvie	Wsh.	2	3	0	0	0	2	....	....	....	....	....		1979-80	1981-82
Poddubny, Walt	Edm., Tor., NYR, Que., N.J.	11	468	184	238	422	454	19	7	2	9	12		1981-82	1991-92
Podloski, Ray	Bos.	1	8	0	1	1	22	....	....	....	....	....		1988-89	1988-89
Podolsky, Nels	Det.	1	1	0	0	0	0	7	0	0	0	4		1948-49	1948-49
Poeta, Tony	Chi.	1	1	0	0	0	0	....	....	....	....	....		1951-52	1951-52
Poile, Bud	NYR, Bos., Det., Tor., Chi.,	7	311	107	122	229	91	23	4	5	9	8	1	1942-43	1949-50
Poile, Don	Det.	2	66	7	9	16	12	4	0	0	0	0		1954-55	1957-58
Poirer, Gordie	Mtl.	1	10	0	0	0	0	....	....	....	....	....		1939-40	1939-40
Polanic, Tom	Min.	2	19	0	2	2	53	5	1	1	2	4		1969-70	1970-71
Polich, John	NYR	2	3	0	1	1	0	....	....	....	....	....		1939-40	1940-41
Polich, Mike	Mtl., Min.	5	226	24	29	53	57	23	2	1	3	2	1	1976-77	1980-81
Polis, Greg	Pit., St.L., NYR, Wsh.	10	615	174	169	343	391	7	0	2	2	6		1970-71	1979-80
Poliziani, Daniel	Bos.	1	1	0	0	0	0	3	0	0	0	0		1958-59	1958-59
Polonich, Dennis	Det.	8	390	59	82	141	1242	7	1	0	1	19		1974-75	1982-83

Name	NHL Teams	NHL Seasons	Regular Schedule GP	G	A	TP	PIM	Playoffs GP	G	A	TP	PIM	NHL Cup Wins	First NHL Season	Last NHL Season
Pooley, Paul	Wpg.	2	15	0	3	3	0	....	....	....	....	....		1984-85	1985-86
Popein, Larry	NYR, Oak.	8	449	80	141	221	162	16	1	4	5	6		1954-55	1967-68
Popiel, Poul	Bos., L.A., Det., Van., Edm.	7	224	13	41	54	210	4	1	0	1	4		1965-66	1979-80
● Portland, Jack	Mtl., Bos., Chi.	10	381	15	56	71	323	33	1	3	4	25	1	1933-34	1942-43
Porvari, Jukka	Col., N.J.	2	39	3	9	12	4	....	....	....	....	....		1981-82	1982-83
Posa, Victor	Chi.	1	2	0	0	0	2	....	....	....	....	....		1985-86	1985-86
Posavad, Mike	St.L.	2	8	0	0	0	0	....	....	....	....	....		1985-86	1986-87
Potvin, Denis	NYI	15	1060	310	742	1052	1356	185	56	108	164	253	4	1973-74	1987-88
Potvin, Jean	L.A., Min., Phi., NYI, Cle.	11	613	63	224	287	478	39	2	9	11	17	1	1970-71	1980-81
Poudrier, Daniel	Que.	3	25	1	5	6	10	....	....	....	....	....		1985-86	1987-88
Poulin, Dan	Min.	1	3	1	1	2	2	....	....	....	....	....		1981-82	1981-82
Poulin, Dave	Phi., Bos., Wsh.	13	724	205	325	530	482	129	31	42	73	132		1982-83	1994-95
Pouzar, Jaroslav	Edm.	4	186	34	48	82	135	29	6	4	10	16	3	1982-83	1986-87
Powell, Ray	Chi.	1	31	7	15	22	2	....	....	....	....	....		1950-51	1950-51
Powis, Geoff	Chi.	1	2	0	0	0	0	....	....	....	....	....		1967-68	1967-68
Powis, Lynn	Chi., K.C.	2	130	19	33	52	25	1	0	0	0	0		1973-74	1974-75
Prajsler, Petr	L.A., Bos.	4	46	3	10	13	51	4	0	0	0	0		1987-88	1991-92
● Pratt, Babe	Bos., NYR, Tor.	12	517	83	209	292	463	63	12	17	29	90	2	1935-36	1946-47
Pratt, Jack	Bos.	2	37	2	0	2	42	4	0	0	0	0		1930-31	1931-32
Pratt, Kelly	Pit.	1	22	0	6	6	15	....	....	....	....	....		1974-75	1974-75
Pratt, Tracy	Van., Col., Buf., Pit. Tor., Oak.	10	580	17	97	114	1026	25	0	1	1	62		1967-68	1976-77
Prentice, Dean	Pit., Min., Det., NYR, Bos.	22	1378	391	469	860	484	54	13	17	30	38		1952-53	1973-74
Prentice, Eric	Tor.	1	5	0	0	0	4	....	....	....	....	....		1943-44	1943-44
Presley, Wayne	Chi., S.J., Buf., NYR, Tor.	12	684	155	147	302	953	83	26	17	43	142		1984-85	1995-96
Preston, Rich	Chi., N.J.	8	580	127	164	291	348	47	4	18	22	56		1979-80	1986-87
Preston, Yves	Phi.	2	28	7	3	10	4	....	....	....	....	....		1978-79	1980-81
Priakin, Sergei	Cgy.	3	46	3	8	11	2	1	0	0	0	0		1988-89	1990-91
Price, Jack	Chi.	3	57	4	6	10	24	4	0	0	0	0		1951-52	1953-54
Price, Noel	Pit., L.A., Det., Tor., NYR, Mtl., Atl.	14	499	14	114	128	333	12	0	1	1	8	1	1957-58	1975-76
Price, Pat	NYI, Edm., Pit., Que., NYR, Min.	13	726	43	218	261	1456	74	2	10	12	195		1975-76	1987-88
Price, Tom	Cal., Clev., Pit.	5	29	0	2	2	12	....	....	....	....	....		1974-75	1978-79
Priestlay, Ken	Buf., Pit.	6	168	27	34	61	63	14	0	0	0	21	1	1986-87	1991-92
● Primeau, Joe	Tor.	9	310	66	177	243	105	38	5	18	23	12	1	1927-28	1935-36
Primeau, Kevin	Van.	1	2	0	0	0	4	....	....	....	....	....		1980-81	1980-81
● Pringle, Ellie	NYA	1	6	0	0	0	0	....	....	....	....	....		1930-31	1930-31
● Prodgers, Goldie	Tor., Ham.	6	111	63	25	88	35	....	....	....	....	....		1919-20	1924-25
Prokhorov, Vitali	St.L.	3	83	19	11	30	35	4	0	0	0	0		1992-93	1994-95
Pronovost, Andre	Mtl., Bos., Det., Min.	10	556	94	104	198	408	70	11	11	22	58	4	1956-57	1967-68
Pronovost, Jean	Wsh., Pit., Atl.	14	998	391	383	774	413	35	11	9	20	14		1968-69	1981-82
Pronovost, Marcel	Det., Tor.	21	1206	88	257	345	851	134	8	23	31	104	5	1949-50	1969-70
Propp, Brian	Phi., Bos., Min., Hfd.	15	1016	425	579	1004	830	160	64	84	148	151		1979-80	1993-94
Proulx, Christian	Mtl.	1	7	1	2	3	20	....	....	....	....	....		1993-94	1993-94
● Provost, Claude	Mtl.	15	1005	254	335	589	469	126	25	38	63	86	9	1955-56	1969-70
Pryor, Chris	Min., NYI	6	82	1	4	5	122	....	....	....	....	....		1984-85	1989-90
Prystai, Metro	Chi., Det.	11	674	151	179	330	231	43	12	14	26	8	2	1947-48	1957-58
● Pudas, Al	Tor.	1	4	0	0	0	0	....	....	....	....	....		1926-27	1926-27
Pulford, Bob	Tor., L.A.	16	1079	281	362	643	792	89	25	26	51	126	4	1956-57	1971-72
Pulkkinen, Dave	NYI	1	2	0	0	0	0	....	....	....	....	....		1972-73	1972-73
Purpur, Fido	Det., Chi., St.L.	5	144	25	35	60	46	16	1	2	3	4		1934-35	1944-45
Purves, John	Wsh.	1	7	1	0	1	0	....	....	....	....	....		1990-91	1990-91
● Pusie, Jean	Mtl., NYR, Bos.	5	61	1	4	5	28	7	0	0	0	0		1930-31	1935-36
Pyatt, Nelson	Det., Wsh., Col.	7	296	71	63	134	69	....	....	....	....	....		1973-74	1979-80

Q

Name	NHL Teams	NHL Seasons	Regular Schedule GP	G	A	TP	PIM	Playoffs GP	G	A	TP	PIM	NHL Cup Wins	First NHL Season	Last NHL Season
Quackenbush, Bill	Det., Bos.	14	774	62	222	284	95	80	2	19	21	8		1942-43	1955-56
Quackenbush, Max	Bos., Chi.,	2	61	4	7	11	30	6	0	0	0	4		1950-51	1951-52
Quenneville, Joel	Tor., Col., N.J., Hfd., Wsh.	13	803	54	136	190	705	32	0	8	8	22		1978-79	1990-91
● Quenneville, Leo	NYR	1	25	0	3	3	10	3	0	0	0	0		1929-30	1929-30
● Quilty, John	Mtl., Bos.	4	125	36	34	70	81	13	3	5	8	9		1940-41	1947-48
Quinn, Dan	Cgy., Pit., Van., St.L., Phi., Min., Ott., L.A.	14	805	266	419	685	533	65	22	26	48	62		1983-84	1996-97
Quinn, Pat	Tor., Van., Atl.	9	606	18	113	131	950	11	0	1	1	21		1968-69	1976-77
Quinney, Ken	Que.	3	59	7	13	20	23	....	....	....	....	....		1986-87	1990-91
Quintin, Jean-Francois	S.J.	2	22	5	5	10	4	....	....	....	....	....		1991-92	1992-93

R

Name	NHL Teams	NHL Seasons	Regular Schedule GP	G	A	TP	PIM	Playoffs GP	G	A	TP	PIM	NHL Cup Wins	First NHL Season	Last NHL Season
● Radley, Yip	NYA, Mtl.M.	2	18	0	1	1	13	....	....	....	....	....		1930-31	1936-37
Raglan, Clare	Det., Chi.	3	100	4	9	13	52	3	0	0	0	0		1950-51	1952-53
Raglan, Herb	St.L., Que., T.B., Ott.	9	343	33	56	89	775	32	3	6	9	50		1985-86	1993-94
Raleigh, Don	NYR	10	535	101	219	320	96	18	6	5	11	6		1943-44	1955-56
Ramage, Rob	Col., St.L., Cgy., Tor., Min., T.B., Mtl., Phi.	15	1044	139	425	564	2226	84	8	42	50	218	2	1979-80	1993-94
● Ramsay, Beattie	Tor.,	1	43	0	2	2	10	....	....	....	....	....		1927-28	1927-28
Ramsay, Craig	Buf.	14	1070	252	420	672	201	89	17	31	48	27		1971-72	1984-85
Ramsay, Les	Chi.	1	11	2	2	4	2	....	....	....	....	....		1944-45	1944-45
Ramsey, Mike	Buf., Pit., Det.	18	1070	79	266	345	1012	115	8	29	37	176		1979-80	1996-97
Ramsey, Wayne	Buf.	1	2	0	0	0	0	....	....	....	....	....		1977-78	1977-78
● Randall, Ken	Tor., Ham., NYA	10	217	69	35	104	503	15	4	1	5	67	2	1917-18	1926-27
Ranieri, George	Bos.	1	2	0	0	0	0	....	....	....	....	....		1956-57	1956-57
Ratelle, Jean	NYR, Bos.	21	1281	491	776	1267	276	123	32	66	98	24		1960-61	1980-81
Rathwell, John	Bos.	1	1	0	0	0	0	....	....	....	....	....		1974-75	1974-75
Ratushny, Dan	Van.	1	1	0	1	1	2	....	....	....	....	....		1992-93	1992-93
Rausse, Errol	Wsh.	3	31	7	3	10	0	....	....	....	....	....		1979-80	1981-82
Rautakallio, Pekka	Atl., Cgy.	3	235	33	121	154	122	23	2	5	7	8		1979-80	1981-82
Ravlich, Matt	Bos., Chi., Det., L.A.	10	410	12	78	90	364	24	1	5	6	16		1962-63	1972-73
● Raymond, Armand	Mtl.	2	22	0	2	2	10	....	....	....	....	....		1937-38	1939-40
● Raymond, Paul	Mtl.	4	76	2	3	5	6	5	0	0	0	2		1932-33	1937-38
Read, Mel	NYR	1	1	0	0	0	0	....	....	....	....	....		1946-47	1946-47
Reardon, Ken	Mtl.	7	341	26	96	122	604	31	2	5	7	62	1	1940-41	1949-50
● Reardon, Terry	Bos., Mtl.	7	193	47	53	100	73	30	8	10	18	12	1	1938-39	1946-47
Reaume, Marc	Tor., Det., Mtl., Van.	9	344	8	43	51	273	21	0	2	2	8		1954-55	1970-71
Reay, Billy	Det., Mtl.	10	479	105	162	267	202	63	13	16	29	43	2	1943-44	1952-53
Redahl, Gord	Bos.	1	18	0	1	1	2	....	....	....	....	....		1958-59	1958-59
● Redding, George	Bos.	2	35	3	2	5	10	....	....	....	....	....		1924-25	1925-26
Redmond, Craig	L.A., Edm.	5	191	16	68	84	134	3	1	0	1	2		1984-85	1988-89
Redmond, Dick	Min., Cal., Chi., St.L., Atl., Bos.	13	771	133	312	445	504	66	9	22	31	27		1969-70	1981-82
Redmond, Keith	L.A.	1	12	1	0	1	20	....	....	....	....	....		1993-94	1993-94
Redmond, Mickey	Mtl., Det.	9	538	233	195	428	219	16	2	3	5	2	2	1967-68	1975-76
Reeds, Mark	St.L., Hfd.	8	365	45	114	159	135	53	8	9	17	23		1981-82	1988-89
● Regan, Bill	NYR, NYA	3	67	3	2	5	67	8	0	0	0	2		1929-30	1932-33
Regan, Larry	Bos., Tor.,	5	280	41	95	136	71	42	7	14	21	18		1956-57	1960-61
Regier, Darcy	Clev., NYI	3	26	0	2	2	35	....	....	....	....	....		1977-78	1983-84
Reibel, Earl	Det., Chi., Bos.	6	409	84	161	245	75	39	6	14	20	4	2	1953-54	1958-59
Reid, Dave	Tor.	3	7	0	0	0	0	....	....	....	....	....		1952-53	1955-56
Reid, Gerry	Det.	1	....	....	....	....	....	2	0	0	0	2		1948-49	1948-49
Reid, Gord	NYA	1	1	0	0	0	2	....	....	....	....	....		1936-37	1936-37
● Reid, Reg	Tor.	2	40	2	0	2	4	2	0	0	0	0		1924-25	1925-26
Reid, Tom	Chi., Min.	11	701	17	113	130	654	42	1	13	14	49		1967-68	1977-78
Reierson, Dave	Cgy.	1	2	0	0	0	2	....	....	....	....	....		1988-89	1988-89
Reigle, Ed	Bos.	1	17	0	2	2	25	....	....	....	....	....		1950-51	1950-51
Reinhart, Paul	Atl., Cgy., Van.	11	648	133	426	559	277	83	23	54	77	42		1979-80	1989-90
● Reinikka, Ollie	NYR	1	16	0	0	0	0	....	....	....	....	....		1926-27	1926-27
Reise, Leo Jr.	Chi., Det., NYR	9	494	28	81	109	399	52	8	5	13	68	2	1945-46	1953-54
● Reise, Leo Sr.	Ham., NYA, NYR	8	223	36	29	65	180	6	0	0	0	16		1920-21	1929-30
Renaud, Mark	Hfd., Buf.	5	152	6	50	56	86	....	....	....	....	....		1979-80	1983-84
Reynolds, Bobby	Tor.	1	7	1	1	2	0	....	....	....	....	....		1989-90	1989-90
Ribble, Pat	Atl., Chi., Tor., Wsh., Cgy.	8	349	19	60	79	365	8	0	1	1	12		1975-76	1982-83
Richard, Henri	Mtl.	20	1256	358	688	1046	928	180	49	80	129	181	11	1955-56	1974-75
Richard, Jacques	Alt., Buf., Que.	10	556	160	187	347	307	35	5	5	10	34		1972-73	1982-83
Richard, Jean-Marc	Que.	2	5	2	1	3	2	....	....	....	....	....		1987-88	1989-90

Dan Quinn

Don Raleigh

Mike Ramsey

Earl Reibel

Art Ross

Darcy Rota

Terry Ruskowski

David Sacco

			Regular Schedule					Playoffs					NHL	First	Last
Name	NHL Teams	NHL Seasons	GP	G	A	TP	PIM	GP	G	A	TP	PIM	Cup Wins	NHL Season	NHL Season
Richard, Maurice	Mtl.	18	978	544	421	965	1285	133	82	44	126	188	8	1942-43	1959-60
Richard, Mike	Wsh.	2	7	0	2	2	0	....	....	....	....	....		1987-88	1989-90
Richards, Todd	Hfd.	2	8	0	4	4	4	11	0	3	3	6		1990-91	1991-92
Richards, Travis	Dal.	2	3	0	0	0	2	....	....	....	....	....		1994-95	1995-96
Richardson, Dave	NYR, Chi., Det.	4	45	3	2	5	27	....	....	....	....	....		1963-64	1967-68
Richardson, Glen	Van.	1	24	3	6	9	19	....	....	....	....	....		1975-76	1975-76
Richardson, Ken	St.L.	3	49	8	13	21	16	....	....	....	....	....		1974-75	1978-79
Richer, Bob	Buf.	1	3	0	0	0	0	....	....	....	....	....		1972-73	1972-73
Richer, Stephane J. G.	T.B., Bos., Fla.	3	27	1	5	6	20	3	0	0	0	0		1992-93	1994-95
Richmond, Steve	NYR, Det., N.J., L.A.	5	159	4	23	27	514	4	0	0	0	12		1983-84	1988-89
Richter, Dave	Min., Phi., Van., St.L.	9	365	9	40	49	1030	22	1	0	1	80		1981-82	1989-90
Ridley, Mike	NYR, Wsh., Tor., Van.	12	866	292	466	758	424	104	28	50	78	70		1985-86	1996-97
Riley, Bill	Wsh., Wpg.	5	139	31	30	61	320	....	....	....	....	....		1974-75	1979-80
Riley, Jack	Det., Mtl., Bos.,	4	104	10	22	32	8	4	0	3	3	0		1932-33	1935-36
• Riley, Jim	Det., Chi.	1	9	0	2	2	14	....	....	....	....	....		1926-27	1926-27
Riopelle, Rip	Mtl.	3	169	27	16	43	73	8	1	1	2	2		1947-48	1949-50
Rioux, Gerry	Wpg.	1	8	0	0	0	6	....	....	....	....	....		1979-80	1979-80
Rioux, Pierre	Cgy.	1	14	1	2	3	4	....	....	....	....	....		1982-83	1982-83
• Ripley, Vic	Chi., Bos., NYR, St.L.	7	278	51	49	100	173	20	4	1	5	10		1928-29	1934-35
Risebrough, Doug	Mtl., Cgy.	13	740	185	286	471	1542	124	21	37	58	238	4	1974-75	1986-87
Rissling, Gary	Wsh., Pit.	7	221	23	30	53	1008	5	0	1	1	4		1978-79	1984-85
Ritchie, Bob	Phi., Det.	2	29	8	4	12	10	....	....	....	....	....		1976-77	1977-78
• Ritchie, Dave	Mtl.W, Ott., Tor., Que., Mtl.	6	57	15	11	26	48	1	0	0	0	0		1917-18	1925-26
Ritson, Alex	NYR	1	1	0	0	0	0	....	....	....	....	....		1944-45	1944-45
Rittinger, Alan	Bos.	1	19	3	7	10	0	....	....	....	....	....		1943-44	1943-44
Rivard, Bob	Pit.	1	27	5	12	17	4	....	....	....	....	....		1967-68	1967-68
• Rivers, Gus	Mtl.	3	88	4	5	9	12	16	2	0	2	2		1929-30	1931-32
Rivers, Shawn	T.B.	1	4	0	2	2	2	....	....	....	....	....		1992-93	1992-93
Rivers, Wayne	Det., Bos., St.L., NYR	7	108	15	30	45	94	....	....	....	....	....		1961-62	1968-69
Rizzuto, Garth	Van.	1	37	3	4	7	16	....	....	....	....	....		1970-71	1970-71
• Roach, Mickey	Tor., Ham., NYA	8	211	77	32	109	43	....	....	....	....	....		1919-20	1926-27
Roberge, Mario	Mtl.	5	112	7	7	14	314	15	0	0	0	24	1	1990-91	1994-95
Roberge, Serge	Que.	1	9	0	0	0	24	....	....	....	....	....		1990-91	1990-91
Robert, Claude	Mtl.	1	23	1	0	1	9	....	....	....	....	....		1950-51	1950-51
Robert, Rene	Tor., Pit., Buf., Col.	12	744	284	418	702	597	50	22	19	41	73		1970-71	1981-82
Roberto, Phil	Mtl., St.L., Det., K.C., Col., Clev.	8	385	75	106	181	464	31	9	8	17	69	1	1969-70	1976-77
Roberts, Doug	Det., Oak., Cal., Bos.	10	419	43	104	147	342	16	2	3	5	46		1965-66	1974-75
Roberts, Gordie	Hfd., Min., Phi., St.L., Pit., Bos.	15	1097	61	359	420	1582	153	10	47	57	273	2	1979-80	1993-94
Roberts, Jim	Min.	3	106	17	23	40	33	2	0	0	0	0		1976-77	1978-79
Roberts, Jimmy	Mtl., St.L.	15	1006	126	194	320	621	153	20	16	36	160	5	1963-64	1977-78
• Robertson, Fred	Tor., Det.,	2	34	1	0	1	35	7	0	0	0	0	1	1931-32	1933-34
Robertson, Geordie	Buf.	1	5	1	2	3	7	....	....	....	....	....		1982-83	1982-83
Robertson, George	Mtl.	2	31	2	5	7	6	....	....	....	....	....		1947-48	1948-49
Robertson, Torrie	Wsh., Hfd., Det.	10	442	49	99	148	1751	22	2	1	3	90		1980-81	1989-90
Robidoux, Florent	Chi.	3	52	7	4	11	75	....	....	....	....	....		1980-81	1983-84
Robinson, Doug	Chi., NYR, L.A.	7	239	44	67	111	34	11	4	3	7	0		1963-64	1970-71
• Robinson, Earl	Mtl.M., Chi., Mtl.	11	417	83	98	181	133	25	5	4	9	0	1	1928-29	1939-40
Robinson, Larry	Mtl., L.A.	20	1384	208	750	958	793	227	28	116	144	211	6	1972-73	1991-92
Robinson, Moe	Mtl	1	1	0	0	0	0	....	....	....	....	....		1979-80	1979-80
Robinson, Rob	St.L.	1	22	0	1	1	8	....	....	....	....	....		1991-92	1991-92
Robinson, Scott	Min.	1	1	0	0	0	2	....	....	....	....	....		1989-90	1989-90
Robitaille, Mike	NYR, Det., Buf., Van.	8	382	23	105	128	280	13	0	1	1	4		1969-70	1976-77
• Roche, Des	Mtl.M., Ott., St.L., Mtl., Det.	4	113	20	18	38	44	....	....	....	....	....		1930-31	1934-35
• Roche, Earl	Mtl.M., Bos., Ott., St.L., Det.	4	147	25	27	52	48	2	0	0	0	0		1930-31	1934-35
Roche, Ernest	Mtl.	1	4	0	0	0	2	....	....	....	....	....		1950-51	1950-51
Rochefort, Dave	Det	1	1	0	0	0	0	....	....	....	....	....		1966-67	1966-67
Rochefort, Leon	NYR, Mtl., Phi., L.A., Det., Atl., Van.	15	617	121	147	268	93	39	4	4	8	16	2	1960-61	1975-76
Rochefort, Normand	Que., NYR, T.B.	13	598	39	119	158	570	69	7	5	12	82		1980-81	1993-94
• Rockburn, Harvey	Det., Ott.	3	94	4	2	6	254	....	....	....	....	....		1929-30	1932-33
• Rodden, Eddie	Chi., Tor., Bos., NYR	4	97	6	14	20	60	2	0	1	1	0	1	1926-27	1930-31
Rogers, John	Min.	2	14	2	4	6	0	....	....	....	....	....		1973-74	1974-75
Rogers, Mike	Hfd., NYR, Edm.	7	484	202	317	519	184	17	1	13	14	6		1979-80	1985-86
Rohlicek, Jeff	Van.	2	9	0	0	0	8	....	....	....	....	....		1987-88	1988-89
Rolfe, Dale	Bos., L.A., Det., NYR	9	509	25	125	150	556	71	5	24	29	89		1959-60	1974-75
Romanchych, Larry	Chi., Atl	6	298	68	97	165	102	7	2	2	4	4		1970-71	1976-77
Rombough, Doug	Buf., NYI, Min.	4	150	24	27	51	80	....	....	....	....	....		1972-73	1975-76
• Romnes, Doc	Chi., Tor., NYA	10	360	68	136	204	42	45	7	18	25	4	2	1930-31	1939-40
• Ronan, Skene	Ott.	1	10	0	0	0	9	....	....	....	....	....		1918-19	1918-19
Ronson, Len	NYR, Oak.	2	18	2	1	3	10	....	....	....	....	....		1960-61	1968-69
Ronty, Paul	Bos., NYR, Mtl.	8	488	101	211	312	103	21	1	7	8	6		1947-48	1954-55
Rooney, Steve	Mtl., Wpg., N.J.	5	154	15	13	28	496	25	3	2	5	86	1	1984-85	1988-89
Root, Bill	Mtl., Tor., St.L., Phi.	6	247	11	23	34	180	22	1	2	3	25		1982-83	1987-88
• Ross, Art	Mtl.W	1	3	1	0	1	12	....	....	....	....	....		1917-18	1917-18
Ross, Jim	NYR	2	62	2	11	13	29	....	....	....	....	....		1951-52	1952-53
Rossignol, Roland	Det., Mtl.	3	14	3	5	8	6	1	0	0	0	2		1943-44	1945-46
Rota, Darcy	Chi., Atl., Van.	11	794	256	239	495	973	60	14	7	21	147		1973-74	1983-84
Rota, Randy	Mtl., L.A., K.C., Col.	5	212	38	39	77	60	5	0	1	1	0		1972-73	1976-77
• Rothschild, Sam	Mtl.M., NYA	4	99	8	6	14	24	10	0	0	0	0	1	1924-25	1927-28
• Roulston, Rolly	Det.	3	24	0	6	6	10	....	....	....	....	....		1935-36	1937-38
Roulston, Tom	Edm., Pit.	5	195	47	49	96	74	21	2	2	4	2		1980-81	1985-86
Roupe, Magnus	Phi.	2	40	3	5	8	42	....	....	....	....	....		1987-88	1988-89
Rousseau, Bobby	Mtl., Min., NYR	15	942	245	458	703	359	128	27	57	84	69	4	1960-61	1974-75
Rousseau, Guy	Mtl.	2	4	0	1	1	0	....	....	....	....	....		1954-55	1956-57
Rousseau, Roland	Mtl.	1	2	0	0	0	0	....	....	....	....	....		1952-53	1952-53
Routhier, Jean-Marc	Que.	1	8	0	0	0	9	....	....	....	....	....		1989-90	1989-90
• Rowe, Bobby	Bos.	1	4	1	0	1	0	....	....	....	....	....		1924-25	1924-25
Rowe, Mike	Pit.	3	11	0	0	0	11	....	....	....	....	....		1984-85	1986-87
Rowe, Ron	NYR	1	5	1	0	1	0	....	....	....	....	....		1947-48	1947-48
Rowe, Tom	Wsh., Hfd., Det.	7	357	85	100	185	615	3	2	0	2	0		1976-77	1982-83
Roy, Stephane	Min.	1	12	1	0	1	0	....	....	....	....	....		1987-88	1987-88
Rozzini, Gino	Bos.	1	31	5	10	15	20	6	1	2	3	6		1944-45	1944-45
Rucinski, Mike	Chi.	2	1	0	0	0	0	2	0	0	0	0		1987-88	1988-89
Ruelle, Bernie	Det.	1	2	1	0	1	0	....	....	....	....	....		1943-44	1943-44
Ruff, Lindy	Buf., NYR	12	691	105	195	300	1264	52	11	13	24	193		1979-80	1990-91
Ruhnke, Kent	Bos.	1	2	0	1	1	0	....	....	....	....	....		1975-76	1975-76
Rundqvist, Thomas	Mtl.	1	2	0	1	1	0	....	....	....	....	....		1984-85	1984-85
• Runge, Paul	Bos., Mtl.M., Mtl.	7	140	18	22	40	57	7	0	0	0	6		1930-31	1937-38
Ruotsalainen, Reijo	NYR, Edm., N.J.	7	446	107	237	344	180	86	15	32	47	44	2	1981-82	1989-90
Rupp, Duane	NYR, Tor., Min., Pit.	10	374	24	93	117	220	10	2	2	4	8		1962-63	1972-73
Ruskowski, Terry	Chi., L.A., Pit., Min.	10	630	113	313	426	1354	21	1	6	7	86		1979-80	1988-89
• Russell, Church	NYR	3	90	20	16	36	12	....	....	....	....	....		1945-46	1947-48
Russell, Phil	Chi., Atl., Cgy., N.J., Buf.	15	1016	99	325	424	2038	73	4	22	26	202		1972-73	1986-87
Ruuttu, Christian	Buf., Chi., Van.	9	621	134	298	432	714	42	4	9	13	49		1986-87	1994-95
Ruzicka, Vladimir	Edm., Bos., Ott.	5	233	82	85	167	129	30	4	14	18	2		1989-90	1993-94
Rymsha, Andy	Que.	1	6	0	0	0	23	....	....	....	....	....		1991-92	1991-92

S

Name	NHL Teams	NHL Seasons	GP	G	A	TP	PIM	GP	G	A	TP	PIM	NHL Cup Wins	First NHL Season	Last NHL Season
Saarinen, Simo	NYR	1	8	0	0	0	0	....	....	....	....	....		1984-85	1984-85
Sabol, Shaun	Phi.	1	2	0	0	0	0	....	....	....	....	....		1989-90	1989-90
Sabourin, Bob	Tor.	1	1	0	0	0	2	....	....	....	....	....		1951-52	1951-52
Sabourin, Gary	St.L., Tor., Cal., Clev.	10	627	169	188	357	397	62	19	11	30	58		1967-68	1976-77
Sabourin, Ken	Cgy., Wsh.	4	74	2	8	10	201	12	0	0	0	34	1	1988-89	1991-92
Sacco, David	Tor., Ana.	3	35	5	13	18	22	....	....	....	....	....		1993-94	1995-96
Sacharuk, Lawrence	NYR, St.L.	5	151	29	33	62	42	2	1	1	2	2		1972-73	1976-77
Saganiuk, Rocky	Tor., Pit.	6	259	57	65	122	201	6	1	0	1	15		1978-79	1983-84
St. Amour, Martin	Ott.	1	1	0	0	0	2	....	....	....	....	....		1992-93	1992-93
St. Laurent, Andre	NYI, Det., L.A., Pit.	11	644	129	187	316	749	59	8	12	20	48		1973-74	1983-84
St. Laurent, Dollard	Mtl., Chi.	12	652	29	133	162	496	92	2	22	24	87	5	1950-51	1961-62
St. Marseille, Frank	St.L., L.A.	10	707	140	285	425	242	88	20	25	45	18		1967-68	1976-77
St. Sauveur, Claude	Atl.	1	79	24	24	48	23	2	0	0	0	0		1975-76	1975-76
Saleski, Don	Phi., Col.	9	543	128	125	253	629	82	13	17	30	131	2	1971-72	1979-80
Salming, Borje	Tor., Det.	17	1148	150	637	787	1344	81	12	37	49	91		1973-74	1989-90

Name	NHL Teams	NHL Seasons	Regular Schedule GP	G	A	TP	PIM	Playoffs GP	G	A	TP	PIM	NHL Cup Wins	First NHL Season	Last NHL Season
Salovaara, John Barry	Det.	2	90	2	13	15	70	....	....	....	....	....		1974-75	1975-76
Salvian, Dave	NYI	1	....	....	....	....	....	1	0	1	1	2		1976-77	1976-77
Samis, Phil	Tor.	2	2	0	0	0	0	5	0	1	1	2	1	1947-48	1949-50
Sampson, Gary	Wsh.	4	105	13	22	35	25	12	1	0	1	0		1983-84	1986-87
Sandelin, Scott	Mtl., Phi., Min.	4	25	0	4	4	2	....	....	....	....	....		1986-87	1991-92
Sanderson, Derek	Bos., NYR, St.L., Van., Pit.	13	598	202	250	452	911	56	18	12	30	187	2	1965-66	1977-78
Sandford, Ed	Bos., Det., Chi.	9	502	106	145	251	355	42	13	11	24	27		1947-48	1955-56
Sandlak, Jim	Van., Hfd.	11	549	110	119	229	821	33	7	10	17	30		1985-86	1995-96
• Sands, Charlie	Tor., Bos., Mtl., NYR	12	427	99	109	208	58	34	6	6	12	4	1	1932-33	1943-44
Sanipass, Everett	Chi., Que.	5	164	25	34	59	358	5	2	0	2	4		1986-87	1990-91
Sargent, Gary	L.A., Min.	8	402	61	161	222	273	20	5	7	12	8		1975-76	1982-83
Sarner, Craig	Bos.	1	7	0	0	0	0	....	....	....	....	....		1974-75	1974-75
Sarrazin, Dick	Phi.	3	100	20	35	55	22	4	0	0	0	0		1968-69	1971-72
Saskamoose, Fred	Chi.	1	11	0	0	0	6	....	....	....	....	....		1953-54	1953-54
Sasser, Grant	Pit.	1	3	0	0	0	0	....	....	....	....	....		1983-84	1983-84
Sather, Glen	Bos., Pit., NYR, St.L., Mtl., Min.	10	658	80	113	193	724	72	1	5	6	86		1966-67	1975-76
Saunders, Bernie	Que.	2	10	0	1	1	8	....	....	....	....	....		1979-80	1980-81
Saunders, David	Van.	1	56	7	13	20	10	....	....	....	....	....		1987-88	1987-88
Saunders, Ted	Ott.	1	18	1	3	4	4	....	....	....	....	....		1933-34	1933-34
Sauve, Jean-Francois	Buf., Que.	7	290	65	138	203	114	36	9	12	21	10		1980-81	1986-87
Savage, Joel	Buf.	1	3	0	1	1	0	....	....	....	....	....		1990-91	1990-91
Savage, Reggie	Wsh., Que.	3	34	5	7	12	28	....	....	....	....	....		1990-91	1993-94
• Savage, Tony	Bos., Mtl.	1	49	1	5	6	6	2	0	0	0	0		1934-35	1934-35
Savard, Andre	Bos., Buf., Que.	12	790	211	271	482	411	85	13	18	31	77		1973-74	1984-85
Savard, Denis	Chi., Mtl., T.B.	17	1196	473	865	1338	1336	169	66	109	175	256	1	1980-81	1996-97
Savard, Jean	Chi, Hfd.	3	43	7	12	19	29	....	....	....	....	....		1977-78	1979-80
Savard, Serge	Mtl., Wpg.	17	1040	106	333	439	592	130	19	49	68	88	7	1966-67	1982-83
Scamurra, Peter	Wsh.	4	132	8	25	33	59	....	....	....	....	....		1975-76	1979-80
Sceviour, Darin	Chi.	1	1	0	0	0	0	....	....	....	....	....		1986-87	1986-87
Schaeffer, Butch	Chi.,	1	5	0	0	0	6	....	....	....	....	....		1936-37	1936-37
Schamehorn, Kevin	Det., L.A.	3	10	0	0	0	17	....	....	....	....	....		1976-77	1980-81
Schella, John	Van.	2	115	2	18	20	224	....	....	....	....	....		1970-71	1971-72
Scherza, Chuck	Bos., NYR	2	36	6	6	12	35	....	....	....	....	....		1943-44	1944-45
Schinkel, Ken	NYR, Pit.	12	636	127	198	325	163	19	7	2	9	4		1959-60	1972-73
Schlegel, Brad	Wsh., Cgy.	3	48	1	8	9	10	7	0	1	1	2		1991-92	1993-94
Schliebener, Andy	Van.	3	84	2	11	13	74	6	0	0	0	0		1981-82	1984-85
Schmautz, Bobby	Chi., Bos., Edm., Col., Van.	13	764	271	286	557	988	84	28	33	61	92		1967-68	1980-81
Schmautz, Cliff	Buf., Phi.	1	56	13	19	32	33	....	....	....	....	....		1970-71	1970-71
Schmidt, Clarence	Bos.,	1	7	1	0	1	2	....	....	....	....	....		1943-44	1943-44
Schmidt, Jackie	Bos.	1	45	6	7	13	6	5	0	0	0	0		1942-43	1942-43
Schmidt, Joseph	Bos.	1	2	0	0	0	0	....	....	....	....	....		1943-44	1943-44
Schmidt, Milt	Bos.	16	776	229	346	575	466	86	24	25	49	60	2	1936-37	1954-55
Schmidt, Norm	Pit.	4	125	23	33	56	73	....	....	....	....	....		1983-84	1987-88
• Schnarr, Werner	Bos.	2	25	0	0	0	0	....	....	....	....	....		1924-25	1925-26
Schock, Danny	Bos., Phi.	2	20	1	2	3	0	1	0	0	0	0	1	1969-70	1970-71
Schock, Ron	Bos., St.L., Pit., Buf.	15	909	166	351	517	260	55	4	16	20	29		1963-64	1977-78
Schoenfeld, Jim	Buf., Det., Bos.	13	719	51	204	255	1132	75	3	13	16	151		1972-73	1984-85
Schofield, Dwight	Det., Mtl., St.L., Wsh., Pit., Wpg.	7	211	8	22	30	631	9	0	0	0	55		1976-77	1987-88
Schreiber, Wally	Min.	2	41	8	10	18	12	....	....	....	....	....		1987-88	1988-89
• Schriner, Sweeney	NYA, Tor.	11	484	201	204	405	148	59	18	11	29	54	2	1934-35	1945-46
Schultz, Dave	Phi., L.A., Pit., Buf.	9	535	79	121	200	2294	73	8	12	20	412	2	1971-72	1979-80
Schurman, Maynard	Hfd.	1	7	0	0	0	0	....	....	....	....	....		1979-80	1979-80
Schutt, Rod	Mtl., Pit., Tor.	8	286	77	92	169	177	22	8	6	14	26		1977-78	1985-86
Scissons, Scott	NYI	3	2	0	0	0	0	1	0	0	0	0		1990-91	1993-94
Sclisizzi, Enio	Det., Chi.	6	81	12	11	23	26	13	0	0	0	6		1946-47	1952-53
• Scott, Ganton	Tor., Ham., Mtl.M.	3	53	1	1	2	0	....	....	....	....	....		1922-23	1924-25
• Scott, Laurie	NYA, NYR	2	62	6	3	9	28	....	....	....	....	....	1	1926-27	1927-28
Scremin, Claudio	S.J.	2	17	0	1	1	29	....	....	....	....	....		1991-92	1992-93
Scruton, Howard	L.A.	1	4	0	4	4	9	....	....	....	....	....		1982-83	1982-83
Seabrooke, Glen	Phi.	3	19	1	6	7	4	....	....	....	....	....		1986-87	1988-89
Secord, Al	Bos., Chi., Tor, Phi.	12	766	273	222	495	2093	102	21	34	55	382		1978-79	1989-90
Sedlbauer, Ron	Van., Chi., Tor.	7	430	143	86	229	210	19	1	3	4	27		1974-75	1980-81
Seftel, Steve	Wsh.	1	4	0	0	0	2	....	....	....	....	....		1990-91	1990-91
Seguin, Dan	Min., Van.	2	37	2	6	8	50	....	....	....	....	....		1970-71	1973-74
Seguin, Steve	L.A.	1	5	0	0	0	9	....	....	....	....	....		1984-85	1984-85
• Seibert, Earl	NYR, Chi., Det.	15	645	89	187	276	746	66	11	8	19	76	2	1931-32	1945-46
Seiling, Ric	Buf., Det.	10	738	179	208	387	573	62	14	14	28	36		1977-78	1986-87
Seiling, Rod	Tor., NYR, Wsh., St.L., Atl.	17	979	62	269	331	601	77	4	8	12	55		1962-63	1978-79
Sejba, Jiri	Buf.	1	11	0	2	2	8	....	....	....	....	....		1990-91	1990-91
Selby, Brit	Tor., Phi., St.L.	8	350	55	62	117	163	16	1	1	2	8		1964-65	1971-72
Self, Steve	Wsh.	1	3	0	0	0	0	....	....	....	....	....		1976-77	1976-77
Selwood, Brad	Tor., L.A.	3	163	7	40	47	153	6	0	0	0	4		1970-71	1979-80
Semchuk, Brandy	L.A.	1	1	0	0	0	2	....	....	....	....	....		1992-93	1992-93
Semenko, Dave	Edm., Hfd., Tor.	9	575	65	88	153	1175	73	6	6	12	208	2	1979-80	1987-88
Semenov, Anatoli	Edm., T.B., Van., Ana., Phi., Buf.	8	362	68	126	194	122	49	9	13	22	12	1	1989-90	1996-97
Senick, George	NYR	1	13	2	3	5	8	....	....	....	....	....		1952-53	1952-53
Seppa, Jyrki	Wpg.	1	13	0	2	2	6	....	....	....	....	....		1983-84	1983-84
Serafini, Ron	Cal.	1	2	0	0	0	2	....	....	....	....	....		1973-74	1973-74
Serowik, Jeff	Tor., Bos.	2	2	0	0	0	0	....	....	....	....	....		1990-91	1994-95
Servinis, George	Min.	1	5	0	0	0	0	....	....	....	....	....		1987-88	1987-88
Sevcik, Jaroslav	Que.	1	13	0	2	2	2	....	....	....	....	....		1989-90	1989-90
Shack, Eddie	NYR, Tor., Bos., L.A., Buf., Pit.	17	1047	239	226	465	1437	74	6	7	13	151	4	1958-59	1974-75
• Shack, Joe	NYR	2	70	9	27	36	20	....	....	....	....	....		1942-43	1944-45
Shakes, Paul	Cal.	1	21	0	4	4	12	....	....	....	....	....		1973-74	1973-74
Shanahan, Sean	Mtl., Col., Bos.	3	40	1	3	4	47	....	....	....	....	....		1975-76	1977-78
Shand, Dave	Atl., Tor., Wsh.	8	421	19	84	103	544	26	1	2	3	83		1976-77	1984-85
Shank, Daniel	Det., Hfd.	3	77	13	14	27	175	5	0	0	0	22		1989-90	1991-92
Shannon, Chuck	NYA	1	4	0	0	0	2	....	....	....	....	....		1939-40	1939-40
• Shannon, Gerry	Ott., St.L., Bos., Mtl.M.	5	180	23	29	52	80	9	0	1	1	2		1933-34	1937-38
Sharples, Jeff	Det.	3	105	14	35	49	70	7	0	3	3	6		1986-87	1988-89
Sharpley, Glen	Min., Chi.	6	389	117	161	278	199	27	7	11	18	24		1976-77	1981-82
Shaunessy, Scott	Que.	2	7	0	0	0	23	....	....	....	....	....		1986-87	1988-89
Shaw, Brad	Hfd., Ott.	10	361	22	137	159	200	19	4	8	12	6		1985-86	1994-95
• Shay, Norman	Bos., Tor.	2	53	5	2	7	34	....	....	....	....	....		1924-25	1925-26
• Shea, Pat	Chi.	1	10	0	1	1	0	....	....	....	....	....		1931-32	1931-32
Shedden, Doug	Pit., Det., Que., Tor.	8	416	139	186	325	176	....	....	....	....	....		1981-82	1990-91
Sheehan, Bobby	Mtl., Cal., Chi., Det., NYR, Col., L.A.	9	310	48	63	111	50	25	4	3	7	8	1	1969-70	1981-82
Sheehy, Neil	Cgy., Hfd., Wsh.	9	379	18	47	65	1311	54	0	3	3	241		1983-84	1991-92
Sheehy, Tim	Det., Hfd.	2	27	2	1	3	0	....	....	....	....	....		1977-78	1979-80
Shelton, Doug	Chi.	1	5	0	1	1	2	....	....	....	....	....		1967-68	1967-68
• Sheppard, Frank	Det.	1	8	1	1	2	0	....	....	....	....	....		1927-28	1927-28
Sheppard, Gregg	Bos., Pit.	10	657	205	293	498	243	82	32	40	72	31		1972-73	1981-82
• Sheppard, Johnny	Det., NYA, Bos., Chi.	8	308	68	58	126	224	10	0	0	0	0	1	1926-27	1933-34
• Sherf, John	Det.	5	19	0	0	0	8	8	0	1	1	2	1	1935-36	1943-44
• Shero, Fred	NYR	3	145	6	14	20	137	13	0	2	2	8		1947-48	1949-50
Sherritt, Gordon	Det.	1	8	0	0	0	12	....	....	....	....	....		1943-44	1943-44
Sherven, Gord	Edm., Min., Hfd.	5	97	13	22	35	33	3	0	0	0	0		1983-84	1987-88
• Shewchuck, Jack	Bos.	6	187	9	19	28	160	20	0	1	1	19	1	1938-39	1944-45
Shibicky, Alex	NYR	8	324	110	91	201	161	39	12	12	24	12	1	1935-36	1945-46
• Shields, Al	Ott., Phi., NYA, Mtl.M., Bos.	11	459	42	46	88	637	17	0	1	1	14	1	1927-28	1937-38
Shill, Bill	Bos.	3	79	21	13	34	18	7	1	2	3	2		1942-43	1946-47
• Shill, Jack	Tor., Bos., NYA, Chi.	6	160	15	20	35	70	25	1	6	7	23	1	1933-34	1938-39
Shinske, Rick	Clev., St.L.	3	63	5	16	21	10	....	....	....	....	....		1976-77	1978-79
Shires, Jim	Det., St.L., Pit.	3	56	3	6	9	32	....	....	....	....	....		1970-71	1972-73
Shmyr, Paul	Chi., Cal., Min., Hfd.	7	343	13	72	85	528	34	3	3	6	44		1968-69	1981-82
Shoebottom, Bruce	Bos.	4	35	1	4	5	53	14	1	2	3	77		1987-88	1990-91
• Shore, Eddie	Bos., NYA	14	550	105	179	284	1047	55	6	13	19	181	2	1926-27	1939-40
• Shore, Hamby	Ott.	1	20	3	8	11	51	....	....	....	....	....		1917-18	1917-18
Short, Steve	L.A., Det.	2	6	0	0	0	2	....	....	....	....	....		1977-78	1978-79
Shudra, Ron	Edm.	1	10	0	5	5	6	....	....	....	....	....		1987-88	1987-88
Shutt, Steve	Mtl., L.A.	13	930	424	393	817	410	99	50	48	98	65	5	1972-73	1984-85
• Siebert, Babe	Mtl.M., NYR, Bos., Mtl.	14	592	140	156	296	982	53	8	7	15	64	2	1925-26	1938-39
Silk, Dave	NYR, Bos., Wpg., Det.	7	249	54	59	113	271	13	2	4	6	13		1979-80	1985-86

Borje Salming

Denis Savard

Brit Selby

Anatoli Semenov

Peter Stastny

Nels Stewart

Bob Sweeney

Steve Tambellini

			Regular Schedule					Playoffs							
Name	NHL Teams	NHL Seasons	GP	G	A	TP	PIM	GP	G	A	TP	PIM	NHL Cup Wins	First NHL Season	Last NHL Season
Siltala, Mike	Wsh., NYR	3	7	1	0	1	2	....	....	....	....	....		1981-82	1987-88
Siltanen, Risto	Edm., Hfd., Que.	8	562	90	265	355	266	32	6	12	18	30		1979-80	1986-87
Sim, Trevor	Edm.	1	3	0	1	1	2	....	....	....	....	....		1989-90	1989-90
Simard, Martin	Cgy., T.B.	3	44	1	5	6	183	....	....	....	....	....		1990-91	1992-93
Simmer, Charlie	Cal., Cle., L.A., Bos., Pit.	14	712	342	369	711	544	24	9	9	18	32		1974-75	1987-88
Simmons, Al	Cal., Bos.	3	11	0	1	1	21	1	0	0	0	0		1971-72	1975-76
• Simon, Cully	Det., Chi.	3	130	4	11	15	121	14	0	1	1	6	1	1942-43	1944-45
Simon, Thain	Det.	1	3	0	0	0	0	....	....	....	....	....		1946-47	1946-47
Simon, Todd	Buf.	1	15	0	1	1	0	5	1	0	1	0		1993-94	1993-94
Simonetti, Frank	Bos.	4	115	5	8	13	76	12	0	1	1	8		1984-85	1987-88
Simpson, Bobby	Atl., St.L., Pit.	5	175	35	29	64	98	6	0	1	1	2		1976-77	1982-83
• Simpson, Cliff	Det.	2	6	0	1	1	0	2	0	0	0	2		1946-47	1947-48
Simpson, Craig	Pit., Edm., Buf.	10	634	247	250	497	659	67	36	32	68	56	2	1985-86	1994-95
• Simpson, Joe	NYA	6	228	21	19	40	156	2	0	0	0	0		1925-26	1930-31
Sims, Al	Bos., Hfd., L.A.	10	475	49	116	165	286	41	0	2	2	14		1973-74	1982-83
Sinclair, Reg	NYR, Det.	3	208	49	43	92	139	3	1	0	1	0		1950-51	1952-53
• Singbush, Alex	Mtl.	1	32	0	5	5	15	3	0	0	0	4		1940-41	1940-41
Sinisalo, Ilkka	Phi., Min., L.A.	11	582	204	222	426	208	68	21	11	32	6		1981-82	1991-92
Siren, Ville	Pit., Min.	5	290	14	68	82	276	7	0	0	0	6		1985-86	1989-90
Sirois, Bob	Phi., Wsh.	6	286	92	120	212	42	....	....	....	....	....		1974-75	1979-80
Sittler, Darryl	Tor., Phi., Det.	15	1096	484	637	1121	948	76	29	45	74	137		1970-71	1984-85
• Sjoberg, Lars-Erik	Wpg.	1	79	7	27	34	48	....	....	....	....	....		1979-80	1979-80
Sjodin, Tommy	Min., Dal., Que.	2	106	8	40	48	52	....	....	....	....	....		1992-93	1993-94
• Skaare, Bjorne	Det.	1	1	0	0	0	0	....	....	....	....	....		1978-79	1978-79
Skarda, Randy	St.L.	2	26	0	5	5	11	....	....	....	....	....		1989-90	1991-92
• Skilton, Raymie	Mtl.W	1	1	0	0	0	0	....	....	....	....	....		1917-18	1917-18
• Skinner, Alf	Tor., Bos., Mtl.M., Pit.	4	70	26	11	37	90	7	8	3	11	27	1	1917-18	1925-26
Skinner, Larry	Col.	4	47	10	12	22	8	2	0	0	0	0		1976-77	1979-80
Skov, Glen	Det., Chi., Mtl.	12	650	106	136	242	413	53	7	7	14	48	3	1949-50	1960-61
Skriko, Petri	Van., Bos., Wpg., S.J.	9	541	183	222	405	246	28	5	9	14	4		1984-85	1992-93
Sleaver, John	Chi.	2	13	1	0	1	6	....	....	....	....	....		1953-54	1956-57
Sleigher, Louis	Que., Bos.	6	194	46	53	99	146	17	1	1	2	64		1979-80	1985-86
Sloan, Tod	Tor., Chi.	13	745	220	262	482	831	47	9	12	21	47	2	1947-48	1960-61
• Slobodian, Peter	NYA	1	41	3	2	5	54	....	....	....	....	....		1940-41	1940-41
Slowinski, Eddie	NYR	6	291	58	74	132	63	16	2	6	8	6		1947-48	1952-53
Sly, Darryl	Tor., Min., Van.	4	79	1	2	3	20	....	....	....	....	....		1965-66	1970-71
Smail, Doug	Wpg., Min., Que., Ott.	13	845	210	249	459	602	42	9	2	11	49		1980-81	1992-93
Smart, Alex	Mtl.	1	8	5	2	7	0	....	....	....	....	....		1942-43	1942-43
Smedsmo, Dale	Tor.	1	4	0	0	0	0	....	....	....	....	....		1972-73	1972-73
Smillie, Don	Bos.	1	12	2	2	4	4	....	....	....	....	....		1933-34	1933-34
• Smith, Alex	Ott., Det., Bos., NYA	11	443	41	50	91	643	19	0	2	2	40	1	1924-25	1934-35
• Smith, Art	Tor., Ott.	4	144	15	10	25	249	4	1	1	2	8		1927-28	1930-31
Smith, Barry	Bos., Col.	3	114	7	7	14	10	....	....	....	....	....		1975-76	1980-81
Smith, Bobby	Min., Mtl.	15	1077	357	679	1036	917	184	64	96	160	245	1	1978-79	1992-93
Smith, Brad	Van., Atl., Cgy., Det., Tor.	9	222	28	34	62	591	20	3	3	6	49		1978-79	1986-87
• Smith, Brian D.	L.A., Min.	2	67	10	10	20	33	7	0	0	0	0		1967-68	1968-69
Smith, Brian S.	Det.	3	61	2	8	10	12	5	0	0	0	0		1957-58	1960-61
• Smith, Carl	Det.	1	7	1	1	2	2	....	....	....	....	....		1943-44	1943-44
Smith, Clint	NYR, Chi.	11	483	161	236	397	24	42	10	14	24	2	1	1936-37	1946-47
Smith, Dallas	Bos., NYR	16	890	55	252	307	959	86	3	29	32	128	2	1959-60	1977-78
Smith, Dennis	Wsh., L.A.	2	8	0	0	0	4	....	....	....	....	....		1989-90	1990-91
Smith, Derek	Buf., Det.	8	335	78	116	194	60	30	9	14	23	13		1975-76	1982-83
Smith, Derrick	Phi., Min., Dal.	10	537	82	92	174	373	82	14	11	25	79		1984-85	1993-94
Smith, Des	Mtl.M., Mtl., Chi., Bos.	5	196	22	25	47	236	25	1	4	5	18	1	1937-38	1941-42
• Smith, Don	Mtl.	1	12	1	0	1	6	....	....	....	....	....		1919-20	1919-20
Smith, Don A.	NYR	1	11	1	1	2	0	1	0	0	0	0		1949-50	1949-50
Smith, Doug	L.A., Buf., Edm., Van., Pit.	9	535	115	138	253	624	18	4	2	6	21		1981-82	1989-90
Smith, Floyd	Bos., NYR, Det., Tor., Buf.	13	616	129	178	307	207	48	12	11	23	16		1954-55	1971-72
Smith, Glen	Chi.	1	2	0	0	0	0	....	....	....	....	....		1950-51	1950-51
• Smith, Glenn Grafton	Tor.	1	9	0	0	0	0	....	....	....	....	....		1921-22	1921-22
Smith, Gord	Wsh., Wpg.	6	299	9	30	39	284	....	....	....	....	....		1974-75	1979-80
Smith, Greg	Cal., Clev., Min., Det., Wsh.	13	829	56	232	288	1110	63	4	7	11	106		1975-76	1987-88
• Smith, Hooley	Ott., Mtl.M., Bos., NYA	17	715	200	215	415	1013	54	11	8	19	109	2	1924-25	1940-41
Smith, Kenny	Bos.	7	331	78	93	171	49	30	8	13	21	6		1944-45	1950-51
Smith, Nakina	NYA, Det.	1	10	1	2	3	0	....	....	....	....	....		1936-37	1943-44
Smith, Randy	Min.	2	3	0	0	0	0	....	....	....	....	....		1985-86	1986-87
Smith, Rick	Bos., Cal., St.L., Det., Wsh.	11	687	52	167	219	560	78	3	23	26	73	1	1968-69	1980-81
• Smith, Rodger	Pit., Phi.	6	210	20	4	24	172	4	3	0	3	0		1925-26	1930-31
Smith, Ron	NYI	1	11	1	1	2	14	....	....	....	....	....		1972-73	1972-73
Smith, Sid	Tor.	12	601	186	183	369	94	44	17	10	27	2	3	1946-47	1957-58
Smith, Stan	NYR	2	9	2	1	3	0	1	0	0	0	0	1	1939-40	1940-41
Smith, Steve	Phi., Buf.	6	18	0	1	1	15	....	....	....	....	....		1981-82	1988-89
Smith, Stu	Mtl.	2	4	2	2	4	2	1	0	0	0	0		1940-41	1941-42
Smith, Stu G.	Hfd.	4	77	2	10	12	95	....	....	....	....	....		1979-80	1982-83
• Smith, Tommy	Que.B.	1	10	0	1	1	11	....	....	....	....	....		1919-20	1919-20
Smith, Vern	NYI	1	1	0	0	0	0	....	....	....	....	....		1984-85	1984-85
Smith, Wayne	Chi.	1	2	1	1	2	2	1	0	0	0	0		1966-67	1966-67
Smrke, John	St.L., Que.	3	103	11	17	28	33	....	....	....	....	....		1977-78	1979-80
• Smrke, Stan	Mtl.	2	9	0	3	3	0	....	....	....	....	....		1956-57	1957-58
Smyl, Stan	Van.	13	896	262	411	673	1556	41	16	17	33	64		1978-79	1990-91
• Smylie, Rod	Tor., Ott.	6	75	3	2	5	10	9	1	3	4	2	1	1920-21	1925-26
Snell, Chris	Tor., L.A.	2	34	2	7	9	24	....	....	....	....	....		1993-94	1994-95
Snell, Ron	Pit.	2	7	3	2	5	6	....	....	....	....	....		1968-69	1969-70
Snell, Ted	Pit., K.C., Det.	2	104	7	18	25	22	....	....	....	....	....		1973-74	1974-75
Snepsts, Harold	Van., Min., Det., St.L.	17	1033	38	195	233	2009	93	1	14	15	231		1974-75	1990-91
Snow, Sandy	Det.	1	3	0	0	0	2	....	....	....	....	....		1968-69	1968-69
Snuggerud, Dave	Buf., S.J., Phi.	4	265	30	54	84	127	12	1	3	4	6		1989-90	1992-93
Sobchuk, Dennis	Det., Que.	2	35	5	6	11	2	....	....	....	....	....		1979-80	1982-83
• Sobchuk, Gene	Van.	1	1	0	0	0	0	....	....	....	....	....		1973-74	1973-74
Solheim, Ken	Chi., Min., Det., Edm.	5	135	19	20	39	34	3	1	1	2	2		1980-81	1985-86
Solinger, Bob	Tor., Det.	5	99	10	11	21	19	....	....	....	....	....		1951-52	1959-60
• Somers, Art	Chi., NYR	6	222	33	56	89	189	30	1	5	6	20	1	1929-30	1934-35
Sommer, Roy	Edm.	1	3	1	0	1	7	....	....	....	....	....		1980-81	1980-81
Songin, Tom	Bos.	3	43	5	5	10	22	....	....	....	....	....		1978-79	1980-81
Sonmor, Glen	NYR	2	28	2	0	2	21	....	....	....	....	....		1953-54	1954-55
• Sorrell, John	Det., NYA	11	490	127	119	246	100	42	12	15	27	10	2	1930-31	1940-41
• Sparrow, Emory	Bos.	1	6	0	0	0	4	....	....	....	....	....		1924-25	1924-25
Speck, Fred	Det., Van.	3	28	1	2	3	2	....	....	....	....	....		1968-69	1971-72
• Speer, Bill	Pit., Bos.	4	130	5	20	25	79	8	1	0	1	4	1	1967-68	1970-71
Speers, Ted	Det.	1	4	1	1	2	0	....	....	....	....	....		1985-86	1985-86
• Spence, Gordon	Tor.	1	3	0	0	0	0	....	....	....	....	....		1925-26	1925-26
• Spencer, Brian	Tor., NYI, Buf., Pit.	10	553	80	143	223	634	37	1	5	6	29		1969-70	1978-79
Spencer, Irv	NYR, Bos., Det.	8	230	12	38	50	127	16	0	0	0	8		1959-60	1967-68
• Speyer, Chris	Tor., NYA	3	14	0	0	0	0	....	....	....	....	....		1923-24	1933-34
Spring, Don	Wpg.	4	259	1	54	55	80	6	0	0	0	10		1980-81	1983-84
Spring, Frank	Bos., St.L., Cal., Clev.	5	61	14	20	34	12	....	....	....	....	....		1969-70	1976-77
• Spring, Jesse	Ham., Pit., Tor., NYA	6	162	11	2	13	62	2	0	2	2	2		1923-24	1929-30
Spruce, Andy	Van., Col.	3	172	31	42	73	111	2	0	2	2	0		1976-77	1978-79
Srsen, Tomas	Edm.	1	2	0	0	0	0	....	....	....	....	....		1990-91	1990-91
Stackhouse, Ron	Cal., Det., Pit.	12	889	87	372	459	824	32	5	8	13	38		1970-71	1981-82
• Stackhouse, Ted	Tor.	1	13	0	0	0	2	5	0	0	0	0	1	1921-22	1921-22
• Stahan, Butch	Mtl.	1	....	....	....	....	....	3	0	1	1	2		1944-45	1944-45
Stajduhar, Nick	Edm.	1	2	0	0	0	4	....	....	....	....	....		1995-96	1995-96
Staley, Al	NYR	1	1	0	1	1	0	....	....	....	....	....		1948-49	1948-49
Stamler, Lorne	L.A., Tor., Wpg.	4	116	14	11	25	16	....	....	....	....	....		1976-77	1979-80
Standing, George	Min.	1	2	0	0	0	0	....	....	....	....	....		1967-68	1967-68
Stanfield, Fred	Chi., Bos., Min., Buf.	14	914	211	405	616	134	106	21	35	56	10	2	1964-65	1977-78
Stanfield, Jack	Chi.	1	....	....	....	....	....	1	0	0	0	0		1965-66	1965-66
Stanfield, Jim	L.A.	3	7	0	1	1	0	....	....	....	....	....		1969-70	1971-72
Stankiewicz, Ed	Det.	2	6	0	0	0	2	....	....	....	....	....		1953-54	1955-56
Stankiewicz, Myron	St.L., Phi.	1	35	0	7	7	36	1	0	0	0	0		1968-69	1968-69
Stanley, Allan	NYR, Chi., Bos., Tor., Phi.	21	1244	100	333	433	792	109	7	36	43	80	4	1948-49	1968-69

Name	NHL Teams	NHL Seasons	Regular Schedule GP	G	A	TP	PIM	Playoffs GP	G	A	TP	PIM	NHL Cup Wins	First NHL Season	Last NHL Season
• Stanley, Barney	Chi.	1	1	0	0	0	0	....	....	....	....	....		1927-28	1927-28
Stanley, Daryl	Phi., Van.	6	189	8	17	25	408	17	0	0	0	30		1983-84	1989-90
Stanowski, Wally	Tor., NYR	10	428	23	88	111	160	60	3	14	17	13	4	1939-40	1950-51
Stanton, Paul	Pit., Bos., NYI	5	295	14	49	63	262	44	2	10	12	66	2	1990-91	1994-95
Stapleton, Brian	Wsh.	1	1	0	0	0	0	....	....	....	....	....		1975-76	1975-76
Stapleton, Pat	Bos., Chi.	10	635	43	294	337	353	65	10	39	49	38		1961-62	1972-73
Starikov, Sergei	N.J.	1	16	0	1	1	8	....	....	....	....	....		1989-90	1989-90
Starr, Harold	Ott., Mtl.M., Mtl., NYR	7	205	6	5	11	186	15	1	0	1	4		1929-30	1935-36
Starr, Wilf	NYA, Det.	4	87	8	6	14	25	7	0	2	2	2	1	1932-33	1935-36
Stasiuk, Vic	Chi., Det., Bos.	14	745	183	254	437	669	69	16	18	34	40	2	1949-50	1962-63
Stastny, Anton	Que.	9	650	252	384	636	150	66	20	32	52	31		1980-81	1988-89
Stastny, Marian	Que., Tor.	5	322	121	173	294	110	32	5	17	22	7		1981-82	1985-86
Stastny, Peter	Que., N.J., St.L.	15	977	450	789	1239	824	93	33	72	105	123		1980-81	1994-95
Staszak, Ray	Det.	1	4	0	1	1	7	....	....	....	....	....		1985-86	1985-86
• Steele, Frank	Det.	1	1	0	0	0	0	....	....	....	....	....		1930-31	1930-31
Steen, Anders	Wpg.	1	42	5	11	16	22	....	....	....	....	....		1980-81	1980-81
Steen, Thomas	Wpg.	14	950	264	553	817	753	56	12	32	44	62		1981-82	1994-95
Stefaniw, Morris	Atl.	1	13	1	1	2	2	....	....	....	....	....		1972-73	1972-73
Stefanski, Bud	NYR	1	1	0	0	0	0	....	....	....	....	....		1977-78	1977-78
Stemkowski, Pete	Tor., Det., NYR, L.A.	15	967	206	349	555	866	83	25	29	54	136	1	1963-64	1977-78
Stenlund, Vern	Clev.	1	4	0	0	0	0	....	....	....	....	....		1976-77	1976-77
• Stephens, Phil	Mtl.W, Mtl.	3	25	1	0	1	3	....	....	....	....	....		1917-18	1921-22
Stephenson, Bob	Hfd., Tor.	1	18	2	3	5	4	....	....	....	....	....		1979-80	1979-80
Sterner, Ulf	NYR	1	4	0	0	0	0	....	....	....	....	....		1964-65	1964-65
Stevens, Mike	Van., NYI, Tor.	4	23	1	4	5	29	....	....	....	....	....		1984-85	1989-90
Stevenson, Shayne	Bos., T.B.	3	27	0	2	2	35	....	....	....	....	....		1990-91	1992-93
Stewart, Allan	N.J., Bos.	6	64	6	4	10	243	....	....	....	....	....		1985-86	1991-92
Stewart, Bill	Buf., St.L., Tor., Min.	8	261	7	64	71	424	13	1	3	4	11		1977-78	1985-86
Stewart, Blair	Det., Wsh., Que.	7	229	34	44	78	326	....	....	....	....	....		1973-74	1979-80
Stewart, Gaye	Tor., Chi., Det., NYR, Mtl.	11	502	185	159	344	274	25	2	9	11	16	2	1941-42	1953-54
• Stewart, Jack	Det., Chi.	12	565	31	84	115	765	80	5	14	19	143	2	1938-39	1951-52
Stewart, John A.	Pit., Atl., Cal.	5	258	58	60	118	158	4	0	0	0	10		1970-71	1974-75
Stewart, John C.	Que.	1	2	0	0	0	0	....	....	....	....	....		1979-80	1979-80
• Stewart, Ken	Chi.	1	6	1	1	2	2	....	....	....	....	....		1941-42	1941-42
• Stewart, Nels	Mtl.M., Bos., NYA	15	650	324	191	515	953	54	15	13	28	61	1	1925-26	1939-40
Stewart, Paul	Que.	1	21	2	0	2	74	....	....	....	....	....		1979-80	1979-80
Stewart, Ralph	Van., NYI	7	252	57	73	130	28	19	4	4	8	2		1970-71	1977-78
Stewart, Robert	Bos., Cal., Clev., St.L., Pit.	9	575	27	101	128	809	5	1	1	2	2		1971-72	1979-80
Stewart, Ron	Tor., Bos., St.L., NYR, Van., NYI	21	1353	276	253	529	560	119	14	21	35	60	3	1952-53	1972-73
Stewart, Ryan	Wpg.	1	3	1	0	1	0	....	....	....	....	....		1985-86	1985-86
Stienburg, Trevor	Que.	4	71	8	4	12	161	1	0	0	0	0		1985-86	1988-89
Stiles, Tony	Cgy.	1	30	2	7	9	20	....	....	....	....	....		1983-84	1983-84
Stoddard, Jack	NYR	2	80	16	15	31	31	....	....	....	....	....		1951-52	1952-53
Stoltz, Roland	Wsh.	1	14	2	2	4	14	....	....	....	....	....		1981-82	1981-82
Stone, Steve	Van.	1	2	0	0	0	0	....	....	....	....	....		1973-74	1973-74
Stothers, Mike	Phi., Tor.	4	30	0	2	2	65	5	0	0	0	11		1984-85	1987-88
Stoughton, Blaine	Pit., Tor., Hfd., NYR	8	526	258	191	449	204	8	4	2	6	2		1973-74	1983-84
Stoyanovich, Steve	Hfd.	1	23	3	5	8	11	....	....	....	....	....		1983-84	1983-84
• Strain, Neil	NYR	1	52	11	13	24	12	....	....	....	....	....		1952-53	1952-53
Strate, Gord	Det.	3	61	0	0	0	34	....	....	....	....	....		1956-57	1958-59
Stratton, Art	NYR, Det., Chi., Pit., Phi.	4	95	18	33	51	24	5	0	0	0	0		1959-60	1967-68
Strobel, Art	NYR	1	7	0	0	0	0	....	....	....	....	....		1943-44	1943-44
Strong, Ken	Tor.	3	15	2	2	4	6	....	....	....	....	....		1982-83	1984-85
Struch, David	Cgy.	1	4	0	0	0	4	....	....	....	....	....		1993-94	1993-94
Strueby, Todd	Edm.	3	5	0	1	1	2	....	....	....	....	....		1981-82	1983-84
• Stuart, Billy	Tor., Bos.	7	195	30	18	48	145	17	1	3	4	12	1	1920-21	1926-27
Stumpf, Robert	St.L., Pit.	1	10	1	1	2	20	....	....	....	....	....		1974-75	1974-75
Sturgeon, Peter	Col.	2	6	0	1	1	2	....	....	....	....	....		1979-80	1980-81
Suikkanen, Kai	Buf.	2	2	0	0	0	0	....	....	....	....	....		1981-82	1982-83
Sulliman, Doug	NYR, Hfd., N.J., Phi.	11	631	160	168	328	175	16	1	3	4	2		1979-80	1989-90
Sullivan, Barry	Det.	1	1	0	0	0	0	....	....	....	....	....		1947-48	1947-48
Sullivan, Bob	Hfd.	1	62	18	19	37	18	....	....	....	....	....		1982-83	1982-83
Sullivan, Brian	N.J.	1	2	0	1	1	0	....	....	....	....	....		1992-93	1992-93
Sullivan, Frank	Tor., Chi.	4	8	0	0	0	2	....	....	....	....	....		1949-50	1955-56
Sullivan, Peter	Wpg.	2	126	28	54	82	40	....	....	....	....	....		1979-80	1980-81
Sullivan, Red	Bos., Chi., NYR	11	557	107	239	346	441	18	1	2	3	6		1949-50	1960-61
Summanen, Raimo	Edm., Van.	5	151	36	40	76	35	10	2	5	7	0		1983-84	1987-88
• Summerhill, Bill	Mtl., Bro.	4	72	14	17	31	70	3	0	0	0	2		1938-39	1941-42
Sundblad, Niklas	Cgy.	1	2	0	0	0	0	....	....	....	....	....		1995-96	1995-96
Sundstrom, Patrik	Van., N.J.	10	679	219	369	588	349	37	9	17	26	25		1982-83	1991-92
Sundstrom, Peter	NYR, Wsh., N.J.	6	338	61	83	144	120	23	3	3	6	8		1983-84	1989-90
• Suomi, Al	Chi.	1	5	0	0	0	0	....	....	....	....	....		1936-37	1936-37
Sutherland, Bill	Mtl., Phi., Tor., St.L., Det.	6	250	70	58	128	99	14	2	4	6	0		1962-63	1971-72
• Sutherland, Max	Bos.	1	2	0	0	0	0	....	....	....	....	....		1931-32	1931-32
Sutter, Brian	St.L.	12	779	303	333	636	1786	65	21	21	42	249		1976-77	1987-88
Sutter, Darryl	Chi.	8	406	161	118	279	288	51	24	19	43	26		1979-80	1986-87
Sutter, Duane	NYI, Chi.	11	731	139	203	342	1333	161	26	32	58	405	4	1979-80	1989-90
Sutter, Rich	Pit., Phi., Van., St. L., Chi., T.B., Tor.	13	874	149	166	315	1411	78	13	5	18	133		1982-83	1994-95
Suzor, Mark	Phi., Col.	2	64	4	16	20	60	....	....	....	....	....		1976-77	1977-78
Svensson, Leif	Wsh.	2	121	6	40	46	49	....	....	....	....	....		1978-79	1979-80
Svensson, Magnus	Fla.	2	46	4	14	18	31	....	....	....	....	....		1994-95	1995-96
Swain, Garry	Pit.	1	9	1	1	2	0	....	....	....	....	....		1968-69	1968-69
Swarbrick, George	Oak., Pit., Phi.	4	132	17	25	42	173	....	....	....	....	....		1967-68	1970-71
• Sweeney, Bill	NYR	1	4	1	0	1	0	....	....	....	....	....		1959-60	1959-60
Sweeney, Bob	Bos., Buf., NYI, Cgy.	10	639	125	163	288	799	103	15	18	33	197		1986-87	1995-96
Sykes, Bob	Tor.	1	2	0	0	0	0	....	....	....	....	....		1974-75	1974-75
Sykes, Phil	L.A., Wpg.	10	456	79	85	164	519	26	0	3	3	29		1982-83	1991-92
Szura, Joe	Oak.	2	90	10	15	25	30	7	2	3	5	2		1967-68	1968-69

T

Name	NHL Teams	NHL Seasons	Regular Schedule GP	G	A	TP	PIM	Playoffs GP	G	A	TP	PIM	NHL Cup Wins	First NHL Season	Last NHL Season
Taft, John	Det.	1	15	0	2	2	4	....	....	....	....	....		1978-79	1978-79
Taglianetti, Peter	Wpg., Min., Pit., T.B.	11	451	18	74	92	1106	53	2	8	10	103	2	1984-85	1994-95
Talafous, Dean	Atl., Min., NYR	8	497	104	154	258	163	21	4	7	11	11		1974-75	1981-82
Talakoski, Ron	NYR	2	9	0	1	1	33	....	....	....	....	....		1986-87	1987-88
Talbot, Jean-Guy	Mtl., Min., Det., St.L., Buf.	17	1056	43	242	285	1006	150	4	26	30	142	7	1954-55	1970-71
Tallon, Dale	Van., Chi., Pit.	10	642	98	238	336	568	33	2	10	12	45		1970-71	1979-80
Tambellini, Steve	NYI, Col., N.J., Cgy., Van.	10	553	160	150	310	105	2	0	1	1	0	1	1978-79	1987-88
Tanguay, Chris	Que.	1	2	0	0	0	0	....	....	....	....	....		1981-82	1981-82
Tannahill, Don	Van.	2	111	30	33	63	25	....	....	....	....	....		1972-73	1973-74
Tanti, Tony	Chi., Van., Pit., Buf.	11	697	287	273	560	661	30	3	12	15	27		1981-82	1991-92
Tardif, Marc	Mtl., Que.	8	517	194	207	401	443	62	13	15	28	75	2	1969-70	1982-83
Tatarinov, Mikhail	Wsh., Que., Bos.	4	161	21	48	69	184	....	....	....	....	....		1990-91	1993-94
Tatchell, Spence	NYR	1	1	0	0	0	0	....	....	....	....	....		1942-43	1942-43
• Taylor, Billy	Tor., Det., Bos., NYR	7	323	87	180	267	120	33	6	18	24	13	1	1939-40	1947-48
• Taylor, Billy Jr.	NYR	1	2	0	0	0	0	....	....	....	....	....		1964-65	1964-65
• Taylor, Bob	Bos.	1	8	0	0	0	6	....	....	....	....	....		1929-30	1929-30
Taylor, Dave	L.A.	17	1111	431	638	1069	1589	92	26	33	59	145		1977-78	1993-94
Taylor, Harry	Tor., Chi.	3	66	5	10	15	30	1	0	0	0	0	1	1946-47	1951-52
Taylor, Mark	Phi., Pit., Wsh.	5	209	42	68	110	73	6	0	0	0	0		1981-82	1985-86
• Taylor, Ralph	Chi., NYR	3	99	4	1	5	169	4	0	0	0	10		1927-28	1929-30
Taylor, Ted	NYR, Det., Min., Van.	6	166	23	35	58	181	....	....	....	....	....		1964-65	1971-72
Teal, Jeff	Mtl.	1	6	0	1	1	0	....	....	....	....	....		1984-85	1984-85
Teal, Skip	Bos.	1	1	0	0	0	0	....	....	....	....	....		1954-55	1954-55
Teal, Victor	NYI	1	1	0	0	0	0	....	....	....	....	....		1973-74	1973-74
Tebbutt, Greg	Que., Pit.	2	26	0	3	3	35	....	....	....	....	....		1979-80	1983-84
Tepper, Stephen	Chi.	1	1	0	0	0	0	....	....	....	....	....		1992-93	1992-93
Terbenche, Paul	Chi., Buf.	5	189	5	26	31	28	12	0	0	0	0		1967-68	1973-74
Terrion, Greg	L.A., Tor.	8	561	93	150	243	339	35	2	9	11	41		1980-81	1987-88
Terry, Bill	Min.	1	5	0	0	0	0	....	....	....	....	....		1987-88	1987-88
Tessier, Orval	Mtl., Bos.	3	59	5	7	12	6	....	....	....	....	....		1954-55	1960-61
Theberge, Greg	Wsh.	5	153	15	63	78	73	4	0	1	1	0		1979-80	1983-84
Thelin, Mats	Bos.	3	163	8	19	27	107	5	0	0	0	6		1984-85	1986-87

Fred Thurier

Zellio Toppazzini

Sylvain Turgeon

Ian Turnbull

Garry Unger

Phil Von Stefenelli

Cooney Weiland

			Regular Schedule					Playoffs					NHL	First	Last
Name	NHL Teams	NHL Seasons	GP	G	A	TP	PIM	GP	G	A	TP	PIM	Cup Wins	NHL Season	NHL Season
Thelven, Michael	Bos.	5	207	20	80	100	217	34	4	10	14	34		1985-86	1989-90
Therrien, Gaston	Que.	3	22	0	8	8	12	9	0	1	1	4		1980-81	1982-83
Thibaudeau, Gilles	Mtl., NYI, Tor.	5	119	25	37	62	40	8	3	3	6	2		1986-87	1990-91
Thibeault, Lorran	Det., Mtl.	2	5	0	2	2	2	....	....	....	....	....		1944-45	1945-46
Thiffault, Leo	Min.	1	....	....	....	....	....	5	0	0	0	0		1967-68	1967-68
Thomas, Cy	Chi., Tor.	1	14	2	2	4	12	....	....	....	....	....		1947-48	1947-48
Thomas, Reg	Que.	1	39	9	7	16	6	....	....	....	....	....		1979-80	1979-80
Thomas, Scott	Buf.	2	39	3	3	6	23	....	....	....	....	....		1992-93	1993-94
Thomlinson, Dave	St.L., Bos., L.A.	5	42	1	3	4	50	9	3	1	4	4		1989-90	1994-95
Thompson, Cliff	Bos.	2	13	0	1	1	2	....	....	....	....	....		1941-42	1948-49
Thompson, Errol	Tor., Det., Pit.	10	599	208	185	393	184	34	7	5	12	11		1970-71	1980-81
• Thompson, Kenneth	Mtl.W	1	1	0	0	0	0	....	....	....	....	....		1917-18	1917-18
• Thompson, Paul	NYR, Chi.	13	582	153	179	332	336	48	11	11	22	54	3	1926-27	1938-39
• Thompson, Rhys	Mtl., Tor.	2	25	0	2	2	38	....	....	....	....	....		1939-40	1942-43
• Thoms, Bill	Tor., Chi., Bos.	13	548	135	206	341	154	44	6	10	16	6		1932-33	1944-45
Thomson, Bill	Det., Chi.	2	9	2	2	4	0	2	0	0	0	0		1938-39	1943-44
Thomson, Floyd	St.L.	8	411	56	97	153	341	10	0	2	2	6		1971-72	1979-80
Thomson, Jim	Wsh., Hfd., N.J., L.A., Ott., Ana.	7	115	4	3	7	416	1	0	0	0	0		1986-87	1993-94
• Thomson, Jimmy	Tor., Chi.	13	787	19	215	234	920	63	2	13	15	135	4	1945-46	1957-58
Thornbury, Tom	Pit.	1	14	1	8	9	16	....	....	....	....	....		1983-84	1983-84
• Thorsteinson, Joe	NYA	1	4	0	0	0	0	....	....	....	....	....		1932-33	1932-33
• Thurier, Fred	NYA, Bro., NYR	3	80	25	27	52	18	....	....	....	....	....		1940-41	1944-45
Thurlby, Tom	Oak.	1	20	1	1	2	4	....	....	....	....	....		1967-68	1967-68
Thyer, Mario	Min.	1	5	0	0	0	0	1	0	0	0	2		1989-90	1989-90
Tichy, Milan	Chi., NYI	3	23	0	5	5	40	....	....	....	....	....		1992-93	1995-96
Tidey, Alex	Buf., Edm.	3	9	0	0	0	8	2	0	0	0	0		1976-77	1979-80
Tilley, Tom	St.L.	4	174	4	38	42	89	14	1	3	4	19		1988-89	1993-94
Timgren, Ray	Tor., Chi.	6	251	14	44	58	70	30	3	9	12	6	2	1948-49	1954-55
Tippett, Dave	Hfd., Wsh., Pit., Phi.	11	721	93	169	262	317	62	6	16	22	34		1983-84	1993-94
Titanic, Morris	Buf.	2	19	0	0	0	0	....	....	....	....	....		1974-75	1975-76
Tkaczuk, Walt	NYR	14	945	227	451	678	556	93	19	32	51	119		1967-68	1980-81
Toal, Mike	Edm.	1	3	0	0	0	0	....	....	....	....	....		1979-80	1979-80
Tomalty, Glenn	Wpg.	1	1	0	0	0	0	....	....	....	....	....		1979-80	1979-80
Tomlak, Mike	Hfd.	4	141	15	22	37	103	10	0	1	1	4		1989-90	1993-94
Tomlinson, Dave	Tor., Wpg., Fla.	4	42	1	3	4	28	....	....	....	....	....		1991-92	1994-95
Tomlinson, Kirk	Min.	1	1	0	0	0	0	....	....	....	....	....		1987-88	1987-88
Tomson, Jack	NYA	3	15	1	1	2	0	2	0	0	0	0		1938-39	1940-41
Tonelli, John	NYI, Cgy., L.A., Chi., Que.	14	1028	325	511	836	911	172	40	75	115	200	4	1978-79	1991-92
Tookey, Tim	Wsh., Que., Pit., Phi., L.A.	7	106	22	36	58	71	10	1	3	4	2		1980-81	1988-89
Toomey, Sean	Min.	1	1	0	0	0	0	....	....	....	....	....		1986-87	1986-87
Toppazzini, Jerry	Bos., Chi., Det.	12	783	163	244	407	436	40	13	9	22	13		1952-53	1963-64
Toppazzini, Zellio	Bos., NYR, Chi.	5	123	21	22	43	49	2	0	0	0	0		1948-49	1956-57
Torgayev, Pavel	Cgy.	1	41	6	10	16	14	1	0	0	0	0		1995-96	1995-96
Torkki, Jari	Chi.	1	4	1	0	1	0	....	....	....	....	....		1988-89	1988-89
Touhey, Bill	Mtl.M., Ott., Bos.	7	280	65	40	105	107	2	1	0	1	0		1927-28	1933-34
• Toupin, Jacques	Chi.	1	8	1	2	3	0	4	0	0	0	0		1943-44	1943-44
• Townsend, Art	Chi.	1	5	0	0	0	0	....	....	....	....	....		1926-27	1926-27
Townshend, Graeme	Bos., NYI, Ott.	5	45	3	7	10	28	....	....	....	....	....		1989-90	1993-94
Trader, Larry	Det., St.L., Mtl.	4	91	5	13	18	74	3	0	0	0	0		1982-83	1987-88
• Trainor, Wes	NYR	1	17	1	2	3	6	....	....	....	....	....		1948-49	1948-49
• Trapp, Bob	Chi.	2	82	4	4	8	129	2	0	0	0	4		1926-27	1927-28
Trapp, Doug	Buf.	1	2	0	0	0	0	....	....	....	....	....		1986-87	1986-87
• Traub, Percy	Chi., Det.	3	130	3	3	6	217	4	0	0	0	6		1926-27	1928-29
Tredway, Brock	L.A.	1	....	....	....	....	....	1	0	0	0	0		1981-82	1981-82
Tremblay, Brent	Wsh.	2	10	1	0	1	6	....	....	....	....	....		1978-79	1979-80
Tremblay, Gilles	Mtl.	9	509	168	162	330	161	48	9	14	23	4	2	1960-61	1968-69
• Tremblay, J.C.	Mtl.	13	794	57	306	363	204	108	14	51	65	58	5	1959-60	1971-72
Tremblay, Marcel	Mtl.	1	10	0	2	2	0	....	....	....	....	....		1938-39	1938-39
Tremblay, Mario	Mtl.	12	852	258	326	584	1043	101	20	29	49	187	5	1974-75	1985-86
• Tremblay, Nils	Mtl.	2	3	0	1	1	0	2	0	0	0	0		1944-45	1945-46
Trimper, Tim	Chi., Wpg., Min.	6	190	30	36	66	153	2	0	0	0	2		1979-80	1984-85
Trottier, Bryan	NYI, Pit.	18	1279	524	901	1425	912	221	71	113	184	277	6	1975-76	1993-94
• Trottier, Dave	Mtl.M., Det.	11	446	121	113	234	517	31	4	3	7	39	1	1928-29	1938-39
Trottier, Guy	NYR, Tor.	3	115	28	17	45	37	9	1	0	1	16		1968-69	1971-72
Trottier, Rocky	N.J.	2	38	6	4	10	2	....	....	....	....	....		1983-84	1984-85
• Trudel, Louis	Chi., Mtl.	8	306	49	69	118	122	24	1	3	4	4	2	1933-34	1940-41
• Trudell, Rene	NYR	3	129	24	28	52	72	5	0	0	0	2		1945-46	1947-48
Tsygurov, Denis	Buf., L.A.	3	51	1	5	6	45	....	....	....	....	....		1993-94	1995-96
Tucker, John	Buf., Wsh., NYI, T.B.	12	656	177	259	436	285	31	10	18	28	24		1983-84	1995-96
• Tudin, Connie	Mtl.	1	4	0	1	1	4	....	....	....	....	....		1941-42	1941-42
Tudor, Rob	Van., St.L.	3	28	4	4	8	19	3	0	0	0	0		1978-79	1982-83
Tuer, Allan	L.A., Min., Hfd.	4	57	1	1	2	208	....	....	....	....	....		1985-86	1989-90
Tuomainen, Marko	Edm.	1	4	0	0	0	0	....	....	....	....	....		1994-95	1994-95
Turcotte, Alfie	Mtl., Wpg., Wsh.	7	112	17	29	46	49	5	0	0	0	0		1983-84	1990-91
Turgeon, Sylvain	Hfd., N.J., Mtl., Ott.	12	669	269	226	495	691	36	4	7	11	22		1983-84	1994-95
Turlick, Gord	Bos.	1	2	0	0	0	2	....	....	....	....	....		1959-60	1959-60
Turnbull, Ian	Tor., L.A., Pit.	10	628	123	317	440	736	55	13	32	45	94		1973-74	1982-83
Turnbull, Perry	St.L., Mtl., Wpg.	9	608	188	163	351	1245	34	6	7	13	86		1979-80	1987-88
Turnbull, Randy	Cgy.	1	1	0	0	0	2	....	....	....	....	....		1981-82	1981-82
Turner, Bob	Mtl., Chi.	8	478	19	51	70	307	68	1	4	5	44	5	1955-56	1962-63
Turner, Brad	NYI	1	3	0	0	0	0	....	....	....	....	....		1991-92	1991-92
Turner, Dean	NYR, Col., L.A.	4	35	1	0	1	59	....	....	....	....	....		1978-79	1982-83
• Tustin, Norman	NYR	1	18	2	4	6	0	....	....	....	....	....		1941-42	1941-42
Tuten, Aut	Chi.	2	39	4	8	12	48	....	....	....	....	....		1941-42	1942-43
Tutt, Brian	Wsh.	1	7	1	0	1	2	....	....	....	....	....		1989-90	1989-90
Tuttle, Steve	St.L.	3	144	28	28	56	12	17	1	6	7	2		1988-89	1990-91

U V

Jay Wells

Ubriaco, Gene	Pit., Oak., Chi.	3	177	39	35	74	50	11	2	0	2	4		1967-68	1969-70
Ullman, Norm	Det., Tor.	20	1410	490	739	1229	712	106	30	53	83	67		1955-56	1974-75
Unger, Garry	Tor., Det., St.L., Atl., L.A., Edm.	16	1105	413	391	804	1075	52	12	18	30	105		1967-68	1982-83
Vadnais, Carol	Mtl., Oak., Cal., Bos., NYR, N.J.	17	1087	169	418	587	1813	106	10	40	50	185	2	1966-67	1982-83
Vail, Eric	Atl, Cgy., Det.	9	591	216	260	476	281	20	5	6	11	6		1973-74	1981-82
• Vail, Melville	NYR	2	50	4	1	5	18	10	0	0	0	2		1928-29	1929-30
Vaive, Rick	Van., Tor., Chi., Buf.	13	876	441	347	788	1445	54	27	16	43	111		1979-80	1991-92
Valentine, Chris	Wsh.	3	105	43	52	95	127	2	0	0	0	4		1981-82	1983-84
Valiquette, Jack	Tor., Col.	7	350	84	134	218	79	23	3	6	9	4		1974-75	1980-81
Vallis, Lindsay	Mtl.	1	1	0	0	0	0	....	....	....	....	....		1993-94	1993-94
Van Boxmeer, John	Mtl., Col., Buf., Que.	11	588	84	274	358	465	38	5	15	20	37		1973-74	1983-84
Van Dorp, Wayne	Edm., Pit., Chi., Que.	6	125	12	12	24	565	27	0	1	1	42		1986-87	1991-92
Van Impe, Ed	Chi., Phi., Pit.	11	700	27	126	153	1025	66	1	12	13	131	2	1966-67	1976-77
Varvio, Jarkko	Dal.	2	13	3	4	7	4	....	....	....	....	....		1993-94	1994-95
Vasko, Elmer	Chi., Min.	13	786	34	166	200	719	78	2	7	9	73	1	1956-57	1969-70
Vasko, Rick	Det.	3	31	3	7	10	29	....	....	....	....	....		1977-78	1980-81
Vautour, Yvon	NYI, Col., N.J., Que.	6	204	26	33	59	401	....	....	....	....	....		1979-80	1984-85
Vaydik, Greg	Chi.	1	5	0	0	0	0	....	....	....	....	....		1976-77	1976-77
Veitch, Darren	Wsh., Det., Tor.	10	511	48	209	257	296	33	4	11	15	33		1980-81	1990-91
Velischek, Randy	Min., N.J., Que.	10	509	21	76	97	401	44	2	5	7	32		1982-83	1991-92
Vellucci, Mike	Hfd.	1	2	0	0	0	11	....	....	....	....	....		1987-88	1987-88
Venasky, Vic	L.A.	7	430	61	101	162	66	21	1	5	6	12		1972-73	1978-79
Veneruzzo, Gary	St.L.	2	7	1	1	2	0	9	0	2	2	2		1967-68	1971-72
Vermette, Mark	Que.	4	67	5	13	18	33	....	....	....	....	....		1988-89	1991-92
Verret, Claude	Buf.	2	14	2	5	7	2	....	....	....	....	....		1983-84	1984-85
Verstraete, Leigh	Tor.	3	8	0	1	1	14	....	....	....	....	....		1982-83	1987-88
Ververgaert, Dennis	Van., Phi., Wsh.	8	583	176	216	392	247	8	1	2	3	6		1973-74	1980-81
Vesey, Jim	St.L., Bos.	3	15	1	2	3	7	....	....	....	....	....		1988-89	1991-92
Veysey, Sid	Van.	1	1	0	0	0	0	....	....	....	....	....		1977-78	1977-78
Vickers, Steve	NYR	10	698	246	340	586	330	68	24	25	49	58		1972-73	1981-82
Vigneault, Alain	St.L.	2	42	2	5	7	82	4	0	1	1	26		1981-82	1982-83
Viitakoski, Vesa	Cgy.	3	23	2	4	6	8	....	....	....	....	....		1993-94	1995-96
Vilgrain, Claude	Van., N.J., Phi.	5	89	21	32	53	78	11	1	1	2	17		1987-88	1993-94
Vincelette, Daniel	Chi., Que.	6	193	20	22	42	351	12	0	0	0	4		1986-87	1991-92

Name	NHL Teams	NHL Seasons	Regular Schedule GP	G	A	TP	PIM	Playoffs GP	G	A	TP	PIM	NHL Cup Wins	First NHL Season	Last NHL Season
Vipond, Pete	Cal.	1	3	0	0	0	0	....	....	....	....	....		1972-73	1972-73
Virta, Hannu	Buf.	5	245	25	101	126	66	17	1	3	4	6		1981-82	1985-86
Vitolinsh, Harijs	Wpg.	1	8	0	0	0	4	....	....	....	....	....		1993-94	1993-94
Viveiros, Emanuel	Min.	3	29	1	11	12	6	....	....	....	....	....		1985-86	1987-88
• Vokes, Ed	Chi.	1	5	0	0	0	0	....	....	....	....	....		1930-31	1930-31
Volcan, Mickey	Hfd., Cgy.	4	162	8	33	41	146	....	....	....	....	....		1980-81	1983-84
Volek, David	NYI	6	396	95	154	249	201	15	5	5	10	2		1988-89	1993-94
Volmar, Doug	Det., L.A.	4	62	13	8	21	26	2	1	0	1	0		1969-70	1972-73
Von Stefenelli, Phil	Bos., Ott.	2	43	0	5	5	23	....	....	....	....	....		1995-96	1996-97
• Voss, Carl	Tor., NYR, Det., Ott., St.L., Mtl.M., NYA, Chi.	8	261	34	70	104	50	24	5	3	8	0	1	1926-27	1937-38
Vyazmikin, Igor	Edm.	1	4	1	0	1	0	....	....	....	....	....		1990-91	1990-91

W

Name	NHL Teams	NHL Seasons	Regular Schedule GP	G	A	TP	PIM	Playoffs GP	G	A	TP	PIM	NHL Cup Wins	First NHL Season	Last NHL Season
Waddell, Don	L.A.	1	1	0	0	0	0	....	....	....	....	....		1980-81	1980-81
• Waite, Frank	NYR	1	17	1	3	4	4	....	....	....	....	....		1930-31	1930-31
Walker, Gord	NYR, L.A.	4	31	3	4	7	23	....	....	....	....	....		1986-87	1989-90
Walker, Howard	Wsh., Cgy.	3	83	2	13	15	133	....	....	....	....	....		1980-81	1982-83
• Walker, Jack	Det.	2	80	5	8	13	18	....	....	....	....	....		1926-27	1927-28
Walker, Kurt	Tor.	3	71	4	5	9	142	16	0	0	0	34		1975-76	1977-78
Walker, Russ	L.A.	2	17	1	0	1	41	....	....	....	....	....		1976-77	1977-78
Wall, Bob	Det., L.A., St.L.	8	322	30	55	85	155	22	0	3	3	2		1964-65	1971-72
Wallin, Peter	NYR	2	52	3	14	17	14	14	2	6	8	6		1980-81	1981-82
Walsh, Jim	Buf.	1	4	0	1	1	4	....	....	....	....	....		1981-82	1981-82
Walsh, Mike	NYI	2	14	2	0	2	4	....	....	....	....	....		1987-88	1988-89
Walter, Ryan	Wsh., Mtl., Van.	15	1003	264	382	646	946	113	16	35	51	62	1	1978-79	1992-93
Walton, Bobby	Mtl.	1	4	0	0	0	0	....	....	....	....	....		1943-44	1943-44
Walton, Mike	Tor., Bos., Van., Chi., St.L.	12	588	201	247	448	357	47	14	10	24	45	2	1965-66	1978-79
Wappel, Gord	Atl., Cgy.	3	20	1	1	2	10	2	0	0	0	4		1979-80	1981-82
Ward, Don	Chi., Bos.	2	34	0	1	1	16	....	....	....	....	....		1957-58	1959-60
• Ward, Jimmy	Mtl.M., Mtl.	12	527	147	127	274	455	36	4	4	8	26	1	1927-28	1938-39
Ward, Joe	Col.	1	4	0	0	0	2	....	....	....	....	....		1980-81	1980-81
Ward, Ron	Tor., Van.,	2	89	2	5	7	6	....	....	....	....	....		1969-70	1971-72
Ware, Michael	Edm.	2	5	0	1	1	15	....	....	....	....	....		1988-89	1989-90
Wares, Eddie	NYR, Det., Chi.	9	321	60	102	162	161	45	5	7	12	34	1	1936-37	1946-47
Warner, Bob	Tor.	2	10	1	1	2	4	4	0	0	0	0		1975-76	1976-77
Warner, Jim	Hfd.	1	32	0	3	3	10	....	....	....	....	....		1979-80	1979-80
Warwick, Bill	NYR	2	14	3	3	6	16	....	....	....	....	....		1942-43	1943-44
Warwick, Grant	NYR, Bos., Mtl.	9	395	147	142	289	220	16	2	4	6	6		1941-42	1949-50
• Wasnie, Nick	Chi., Mtl., NYA, Ott., St.L.	7	248	57	34	91	176	14	6	3	9	20		1927-28	1934-35
Watson, Bill	Chi.	4	115	23	36	59	12	6	0	2	2	0		1985-86	1988-89
Watson, Bryan	Mtl., Oak., Pit., Det., St.L., Wsh.	16	878	17	135	152	2212	32	2	0	2	70		1963-64	1978-79
Watson, Dave	Col.	2	18	0	1	1	10	....	....	....	....	....		1979-80	1980-81
Watson, Harry	Bro., Det., Tor., Chi.	14	809	236	207	443	150	62	16	9	25	27	5	1941-42	1956-57
Watson, Jim A.	Det., Buf.	8	221	4	19	23	345	....	....	....	....	....		1963-64	1971-72
Watson, Jimmy	Phi.	10	613	38	148	186	492	101	5	34	39	89	2	1972-73	1981-82
Watson, Joe	Bos., Phi., Col.	14	835	38	178	216	447	84	3	12	15	82	2	1964-65	1978-79
• Watson, Phil	NYR, Mtl.	13	590	144	265	409	532	45	10	25	35	67	2	1935-36	1947-48
Watters, Tim	Wpg., L.A.	14	741	26	151	177	1289	82	1	5	6	115		1981-82	1994-95
Watts, Brian	Det.	1	4	0	0	0	0	....	....	....	....	....		1975-76	1975-76
• Webster, Aubrey	Phi., Mtl.M.	2	5	0	0	0	0	....	....	....	....	....		1930-31	1934-35
• Webster, Don	Tor.	1	27	7	6	13	28	5	0	0	0	12		1943-44	1943-44
Webster, John	NYR	1	14	0	0	0	4	....	....	....	....	....		1949-50	1949-50
Webster, Tom	Bos., Det., Cal.	5	102	33	42	75	61	1	0	0	0	0		1968-69	1979-80
• Weiland, Cooney	Bos., Ott., Det.	11	509	173	160	333	147	45	12	10	22	12	2	1928-29	1938-39
Weir, Stan	Cal., Tor., Edm., Col., Det.	10	642	139	207	346	183	37	6	5	11	4		1972-73	1982-83
Weir, Wally	Que., Hfd., Pit.	6	320	21	45	66	625	23	0	1	1	96		1979-80	1984-85
• Wellington, Alex	Que.	1	1	0	0	0	0	....	....	....	....	....		1919-20	1919-20
Wells, Jay	L.A., Phi., Buf., NYR, St.L., T.B.	18	1098	47	216	263	2359	114	3	14	17	213	1	1979-80	1996-97
Wensink, John	Bos., Que., Col., N.J., St.L.	8	403	70	68	138	840	43	2	6	8	86		1973-74	1982-83
• Wentworth, Cy	Chi., Mtl.M., Mtl.	13	575	39	68	107	355	35	5	6	11	20	1	1927-28	1939-40
Wesley, Blake	Phi., Hfd., Que., Tor.	7	298	18	46	64	486	19	2	2	4	30		1979-80	1985-86
Westfall, Ed	Bos., NYI	18	1220	231	394	625	544	95	22	37	59	41	2	1961-62	1978-79
Wharram, Kenny	Chi.	14	766	252	281	533	222	80	16	27	43	38	1	1951-52	1968-69
Wharton, Len	NYR	1	1	0	0	0	0	....	....	....	....	....		1944-45	1944-45
Wheeldon, Simon	NYR, Wpg.	3	15	0	2	2	10	....	....	....	....	....		1987-88	1990-91
• Wheldon, Donald	St.L.	1	2	0	0	0	0	....	....	....	....	....		1974-75	1974-75
Whelton, Bill	Wpg.	1	2	0	0	0	0	....	....	....	....	....		1980-81	1980-81
Whistle, Rob	NYR, St.L.	2	51	7	5	12	16	4	0	0	0	2		1985-86	1987-88
White, Bill	L.A., Chi.	9	604	50	215	265	495	91	7	32	39	76		1967-68	1975-76
White, Moe	Mtl.	1	4	0	1	1	2	....	....	....	....	....		1945-46	1945-46
• White, Sherman	NYR	2	4	0	2	2	0	....	....	....	....	....		1946-47	1949-50
• White, Tex	Pit., NYA, Phi.	6	203	33	12	45	141	4	0	0	0	4		1925-26	1930-31
White, Tony	Wsh., Min.	5	164	37	28	65	104	....	....	....	....	....		1974-75	1979-80
Whitelaw, Bob	Det.	2	32	0	2	2	2	8	0	0	0	0		1940-41	1941-42
Whitlock, Bob	Min.	1	1	0	0	0	0	....	....	....	....	....		1969-70	1969-70
Whyte, Sean	L.A.	2	21	0	2	2	12	....	....	....	....	....		1991-92	1992-93
Wickenheiser, Doug	Mtl., St.L., Van., NYR, Wsh.	10	556	111	165	276	286	41	4	7	11	18		1980-81	1989-90
• Widing, Juha	NYR, L.A., Clev.	8	575	144	226	370	208	8	1	2	3	2		1969-70	1976-77
• Wiebe, Art	Chi.	11	414	14	27	41	201	31	1	3	4	10	1	1932-33	1943-44
Wiemer, Jim	Buf., NYR, Edm., L.A., Bos.	11	325	29	72	101	378	62	5	8	13	63	1	1982-83	1993-94
• Wilcox, Archie	Mtl.M., Bos., St.L.	6	208	8	14	22	158	12	1	0	1	8		1929-30	1934-35
Wilcox, Barry	Van.	2	33	3	2	5	15	....	....	....	....	....		1972-73	1974-75
Wilder, Arch	Det.	1	18	0	2	2	2	....	....	....	....	....		1940-41	1940-41
Wiley, Jim	Pit., Van.	5	63	4	10	14	8	....	....	....	....	....		1972-73	1976-77
Wilkie, Bob	Det., Phi.	2	18	2	5	7	10	....	....	....	....	....		1990-91	1993-94
Wilkins, Barry	Bos., Van., Pit.	9	418	27	125	152	663	6	0	1	1	4		1966-67	1975-76
• Wilkinson, John	Bos.	1	9	0	0	0	6	....	....	....	....	....		1943-44	1943-44
Wilks, Brian	L.A.	4	48	4	8	12	27	....	....	....	....	....		1984-85	1988-89
Willard, Rod	Tor.	1	1	0	0	0	0	....	....	....	....	....		1982-83	1982-83
• Williams, Burr	Det., St.L., Bos.	3	19	0	1	1	28	7	0	0	0	8		1933-34	1936-37
Williams, Darryl	L.A.	1	2	0	0	0	10	....	....	....	....	....		1992-93	1992-93
Williams, Dave	Tor., Van., Det., L.A., Hfd.	14	962	241	272	513	3966	83	12	23	35	455		1974-75	1987-88
Williams, David	S.J., Ana.	4	173	11	53	64	157	....	....	....	....	....		1991-92	1994-95
Williams, Fred	Det.	1	44	2	5	7	10	....	....	....	....	....		1976-77	1976-77
Williams, Gord	Phi.	2	2	0	0	0	2	....	....	....	....	....		1981-82	1982-83
Williams, Sean	Chi.	1	2	0	0	0	4	....	....	....	....	....		1991-92	1991-92
Williams, Tom	NYR, L.A.	8	397	115	138	253	73	29	8	7	15	4		1971-72	1978-79
• Williams, Tommy	Bos., Min., Cal., Wsh.	13	663	161	269	430	177	10	2	5	7	2		1961-62	1975-76
Williams, Warren	St.L., Cal.	3	108	14	35	49	131	....	....	....	....	....		1973-74	1975-76
Willson, Don	Mtl.	2	22	2	7	9	0	3	0	0	0	0		1937-38	1938-39
Wilson, Behn	Phi., Chi.	9	601	98	260	358	1480	67	12	29	41	190		1978-79	1987-88
• Wilson, Bert	NYR, L.A., St.L., Cgy.	8	478	37	44	81	646	21	0	2	2	42		1973-74	1980-81
Wilson, Bob	Chi.	1	1	0	0	0	0	....	....	....	....	....		1953-54	1953-54
Wilson, Carey	Cgy., Hfd., NYR	10	552	169	258	427	314	52	11	13	24	14		1983-84	1992-93
• Wilson, Cully	Tor., Mtl., Ham., Chi.	5	125	59	24	83	238	2	1	0	1	6		1919-20	1926-27
Wilson, Doug	Chi., S.J.	16	1024	237	590	827	830	95	19	61	80	88		1977-78	1992-93
Wilson, Gord	Bos.	1	....	....	....	....	....	2	0	0	0	0		1954-55	1954-55
Wilson, Hub	NYA	1	2	0	0	0	0	....	....	....	....	....		1931-32	1931-32
Wilson, Jerry	Mtl.	1	3	0	0	0	2	....	....	....	....	....		1956-57	1956-57
Wilson, Johnny	Det., Chi., Tor., NYR	13	688	161	171	332	190	66	14	13	27	11	4	1949-50	1961-62
• Wilson, Larry	Det., Chi.	6	152	21	48	69	75	4	0	0	0	0	1	1949-50	1955-56
Wilson, Mitch	N.J., Pit.	2	26	2	3	5	104	....	....	....	....	....		1984-85	1986-87
Wilson, Murray	Mtl., L.A.	7	386	94	95	189	162	53	5	14	19	32	4	1972-73	1978-79
Wilson, Rick	Mtl., St.L., Det.	4	239	6	26	32	165	3	0	0	0	0		1973-74	1976-77
Wilson, Rik	St.L., Cgy., Chi.	6	251	25	65	90	220	22	0	4	4	23		1981-82	1987-88
Wilson, Roger	Chi.	1	7	0	2	2	6	....	....	....	....	....		1974-75	1974-75
Wilson, Ron	Wpg., St.L., Mtl.	14	832	110	216	326	415	63	10	12	22	64		1979-80	1993-94
Wilson, Ron	Tor., Min.	7	177	26	67	93	68	20	4	13	17	8		1977-78	1987-88
Wilson, Wally	Bos.	1	53	11	8	19	18	1	0	0	0	0		1947-48	1947-48
Wing, Murray	Det.	1	1	0	1	1	0	....	....	....	....	....		1973-74	1973-74

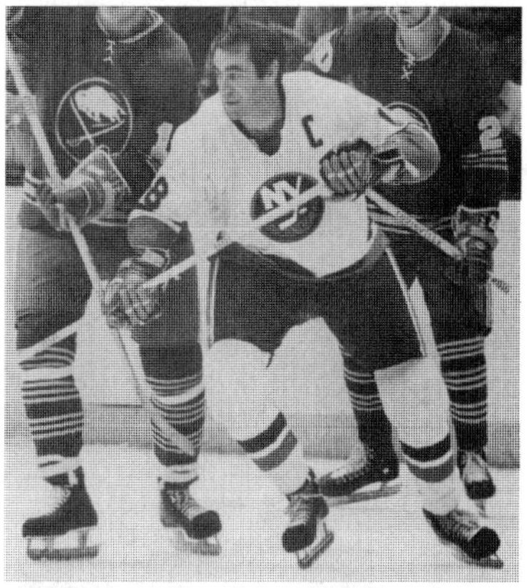

Ed Westfall

Doug Wickenheiser

Dave Williams

Randy Wood

Ross Yates

Rick Zombo

			Regular Schedule					Playoffs							
Name	**NHL Teams**	**NHL Seasons**	**GP**	**G**	**A**	**TP**	**PIM**	**GP**	**G**	**A**	**TP**	**PIM**	**NHL Cup Wins**	**First NHL Season**	**Last NHL Season**
• Wiseman, Eddie	Det., NYA, Bos.	10	456	115	165	280	136	43	10	10	20	16	1	1932-33	1941-42
Wiste, Jim	Chi., Van.	3	52	1	10	11	8	....	....	....	....	....		1968-69	1970-71
Witherspoon, Jim	L.A.	1	2	0	0	0	2	....	....	....	....	....		1975-76	1975-76
Witiuk, Steve	Chi.	1	33	3	8	11	14	....	....	....	....	....		1951-52	1951-52
Woit, Benny	Det., Chi.	7	334	7	26	33	170	41	2	6	8	18	3	1950-51	1956-57
Wojciechowski, Steven	Det.	2	54	19	20	39	17	6	0	1	1	0		1944-45	1946-47
Wolf, Bennett	Pit.	3	30	0	1	1	133	....	....	....	....	....		1980-81	1982-83
Wong, Mike	Det.	1	22	1	1	2	12	....	....	....	....	....		1975-76	1975-76
Wood, Randy	NYI, Buf., Tor., Dal.	11	741	175	159	334	603	51	8	9	17	40		1986-87	1996-97
Wood, Robert	NYR	1	1	0	0	0	0	....	....	....	....	....		1950-51	1950-51
Woodley, Dan	Van.	1	5	2	0	2	17	....	....	....	....	....		1987-88	1987-88
Woods, Paul	Det.	7	501	72	124	196	276	7	0	5	5	4		1977-78	1983-84
Wortman, Kevin	Cgy.	1	5	0	0	0	2	....	....	....	....	....		1993-94	1993-94
• Woytowich, Bob	Bos., Min., Pit., L.A.	8	503	32	126	158	352	24	1	3	4	20		1964-65	1971-72
Wright, John	Van., St.L., K.C.	3	127	16	36	52	67	....	....	....	....	....		1972-73	1974-75
Wright, Keith	Phi.	1	1	0	0	0	0	....	....	....	....	....		1967-68	1967-68
Wright, Larry	Phi., Cal., Det.	5	106	4	8	12	19	....	....	....	....	....		1971-72	1977-78
Wycherley, Ralph	NYA, Bro.	2	28	4	7	11	6	....	....	....	....	....		1940-41	1941-42
Wylie, Duane	Chi.	2	14	3	3	6	2	....	....	....	....	....		1974-75	1976-77
• Wylie, William	NYR	1	1	0	0	0	0	....	....	....	....	....		1950-51	1950-51
Wyrozub, Randy	Buf.	4	100	8	10	18	10	....	....	....	....	....		1970-71	1973-74

Y Z

• Yackel, Ken	Bos.	1	6	0	0	0	2	2	0	0	0	2		1958-59	1958-59
Yaremchuk, Gary	Tor.	4	34	1	4	5	28	....	....	....	....	....		1981-82	1984-85
Yaremchuk, Ken	Chi., Tor.	6	235	36	56	92	106	31	6	8	14	49		1983-84	1988-89
Yates, Ross	Hfd.	1	7	1	1	2	4	....	....	....	....	....		1983-84	1983-84
Young, Brian	Chi.	1	8	0	2	2	6	....	....	....	....	....		1980-81	1980-81
Young, C.J.	Cgy., Bos.	1	43	7	7	14	32	....	....	....	....	....		1992-93	1992-93
• Young, Doug	Mtl., Det.	10	388	35	45	80	303	28	1	5	6	16	2	1931-32	1940-41
Young, Howie	Det., Chi., Van.	8	336	12	62	74	851	19	2	4	6	46		1960-61	1970-71
Young, Tim	Min., Wpg., Phi.	10	628	195	341	536	438	36	7	24	31	27		1975-76	1984-85
Young, Warren	Min., Pit., Det.	7	236	72	77	149	472	....	....	....	....	....		1981-82	1987-88
Younghans, Tom	Min., NYR	6	429	44	41	85	373	24	2	1	3	21		1976-77	1981-82
Zaharko, Miles	Atl., Chi.	4	129	5	32	37	84	3	0	0	0	0		1977-78	1981-82
Zaine, Rod	Pit., Buf.	2	61	10	6	16	25	....	....	....	....	....		1970-71	1971-72
Zanussi, Joe	NYR, Bos., St.L.	3	87	1	13	14	46	4	0	1	1	2		1974-75	1976-77
Zanussi, Ron	Min., Tor.	5	299	52	83	135	373	17	0	4	4	17		1977-78	1981-82
Zavisha, Brad	Edm.	1	2	0	0	0	0	....	....	....	....	....		1993-94	1993-94
Zeidel, Larry	Det., Chi., Phi.	5	158	3	16	19	198	12	0	1	1	12	1	1951-52	1968-69
Zemlak, Richard	Que., Min., Pit., Cgy.	5	132	2	12	14	587	1	0	0	0	10		1986-87	1991-92
Zeniuk, Ed	Det.	1	2	0	0	0	0	....	....	....	....	....		1954-55	1954-55
Zetterstrom, Lars	Van.	1	14	0	1	1	2	....	....	....	....	....		1978-79	1978-79
Zoborosky, Marty	Chi.	1	1	0	0	0	2	....	....	....	....	....		1944-45	1944-45
Zombo, Rick	Det., St.L., Bos.	12	652	24	130	154	728	60	1	11	12	127		1984-85	1995-96
Zuke, Mike	St.L., Hfd.	8	455	86	196	282	220	26	6	6	12	12		1978-79	1985-86
Zunich, Rudy	Det.	1	2	0	0	0	2	....	....	....	....	....		1943-44	1943-44

NOTE: Some players added to the Retired Player Index remain active in other leagues in North America and Europe. Players with NHL experience playing outside the NHL are placed in the Retired Player Index when they have completed one or more seasons of play after having been removed from an NHL club's reserve list. A player's age and his performance outside the NHL are considered in determining when he is moved from the active Player Register to the Retired Player Index.

Retired Players and Goaltenders Research Project

Throughout the Retired Players and Retired Goaltenders sections of this book, you will notice many players with a bullet (•) by their names. These players, according to our records, are deceased. The editors recognize that our information on the death dates of NHLers is incomplete. If you have documented information on the passing of any player not marked with a bullet (•) in this edition, we would like to hear from you. Please send this information to:

Retired Player Research Project
c/o NHL Publishing
194 Dovercourt Road
Toronto, Ontario
M6J 3C8 Canada
Fax: 416/531-3939

Many thanks to the following contributors in 1997-98:

Kevin Bixby, Paul R. Carroll, Jr., Bob Duff, Peter Fillman, Ernie Fitzsimmons, Al Mason, Scott Miller, Gary J. Pearce, Ed Sweeney.

1998-99 Goaltender Register

Note: The 1998-99 Goaltender Register lists every goaltender who appeared in an NHL game in the 1997-98 season, every goaltender drafted in the first six rounds of the 1998 Entry Draft, goaltenders on NHL Reserve Lists and other goaltenders.

Trades and roster changes are current as of September 5, 1998

To calculate a goaltender's goals-against-per-game average **(AVG)**, divide goals against **(GA)** by minutes played **(Mins)** and multiply this result by **60**.

Abbreviations: A list of league names can be found at the beginning of the Player Register. **Avg.** – goals against per game average; **GA** – goals against; **GP** – games played; **L** – losses; **Lea** – league; **SO** – shutouts; **T** – ties; **W** – wins; ♦ – member of Stanley Cup-winning team.

Player Register begins on page 259.

AEBISCHER, DAVID (IGH-bih-shuhr) COL.

Goaltender. Catches left. 6'1", 185 lbs. Born, Fribourg, Switz., February 7, 1978.
(Colorado's 7th choice, 161st overall, in 1997 Entry Draft).

			Regular Season								Playoffs						
Season	**Club**	**Lea**	**GP**	**W**	**L**	**T**	**Mins**	**GA**	**SO**	**Avg**	**GP**	**W**	**L**	**Mins**	**GA**	**SO**	**Avg**
1996-97	Fribourg	Switz.	10	....	....	....	577	34	....	3.53	3	....	....	184	13	....	4.24
1997-98	Hershey	AHL	2	0	0	1	79	5	0	3.76	....	....	....	....	....	....	....
	Chesapeake	ECHL	17	5	7	2	930	52	0	3.35	....	....	....	....	....	....	....
	Wheeling	ECHL	10	5	3	1	564	30	1	3.19	....	....	....	....	....	....	....
	Fribourg	Switz.	1	....	....	....	60	1	....	1.00	4	....	....	240	17	....	4.25

ANTILA, KRISTIAN (AN-tih-luh) EDM.

Goaltender. Catches left. 6'3", 207 lbs. Born, Vammala, Finland, January 10, 1980.
(Edmonton's 4th choice, 113th overall, in 1998 Entry Draft).

			Regular Season								Playoffs						
Season	**Club**	**Lea**	**GP**	**W**	**L**	**T**	**Mins**	**GA**	**SO**	**Avg**	**GP**	**W**	**L**	**Mins**	**GA**	**SO**	**Avg**
1997-98	Ilves Tampere	Fin-Jr.	11	....	....	....	564	28	0	2.97	....	....	....	....	....	....	....

ARSENAULT, DAVID (AR-seh-noh) DET.

Goaltender. Catches left. 6'2", 165 lbs. Born, Frankfurt, Germany, March 21, 1977.
(Detroit's 6th choice, 126th overall, in 1995 Entry Draft).

			Regular Season								Playoffs						
Season	**Club**	**Lea**	**GP**	**W**	**L**	**T**	**Mins**	**GA**	**SO**	**Avg**	**GP**	**W**	**L**	**Mins**	**GA**	**SO**	**Avg**
1994-95	St-Hyacinthe	QMJHL	19	3	10	0	858	75	0	5.24	....	....	....	....	....	....	....
	Drummondville	QMJHL	12	2	5	0	475	40	0	5.06	2	0	2	122	8	0	3.93
1995-96	Drummondville	QMJHL	21	8	10	1	1182	89	0	4.52	....	....	....	....	....	....	....
	Chicoutimi	QMJHL	6	1	1	1	208	14	0	4.04	5	0	1	108	10	0	5.61
1996-97	Chicoutimi	QMJHL	4	2	2	0	219	12	0	3.27	....	....	....	....	....	....	....
	Oshawa	OHL	41	24	9	5	2316	106	2	2.75	17	*11	6	1027	46	*1	*2.69
1997-98	Toledo	ECHL	22	13	4	3	1261	60	0	2.85	....	....	....	....	....	....	....
	Adirondack	AHL	10	3	5	0	563	41	0	4.37	....	....	....	....	....	....	....

ASKEY, TOM ANA.

Goaltender. Catches left. 6'2", 185 lbs. Born, Kenmore, NY, October 4, 1974.
(Anaheim's 8th choice, 186th overall, in 1993 Entry Draft).

			Regular Season								Playoffs						
Season	**Club**	**Lea**	**GP**	**W**	**L**	**T**	**Mins**	**GA**	**SO**	**Avg**	**GP**	**W**	**L**	**Mins**	**GA**	**SO**	**Avg**
1992-93	Ohio State	CCHA	25	2	19	0	1235	125	1	6.07	....	....	....	....	....	....	....
1993-94	Ohio State	CCHA	27	3	19	4	1488	103	1	4.15	....	....	....	....	....	....	....
1994-95	Ohio State	CCHA	26	4	19	2	1387	121	0	5.23	....	....	....	....	....	....	....
1995-96	Ohio State	CCHA	26	8	11	4	1340	68	1	3.05	....	....	....	....	....	....	....
1996-97	Baltimore	AHL	40	17	18	2	2239	140	1	3.75	3	0	3	138	11	0	4.79
1997-98	**Anaheim**	**NHL**	**7**	**0**	**1**	**2**	**273**	**12**	**0**	**2.64**	....	....	....	....	....	....	....
	Cincinnati	AHL	32	10	16	4	1753	104	3	3.56	....	....	....	....	....	....	....
	NHL Totals		**7**	**0**	**1**	**2**	**273**	**12**	**0**	**2.64**	....	....	....	....	....	....	....

CCHA Second All-Star Team (1996)

AUBIN, JEAN-SEBASTIEN (OH-behn) PIT.

Goaltender. Catches right. 5'11", 179 lbs. Born, Montreal, Que., July 19, 1977.
(Pittsburgh's 2nd choice, 76th overall, in 1995 Entry Draft).

			Regular Season								Playoffs						
Season	**Club**	**Lea**	**GP**	**W**	**L**	**T**	**Mins**	**GA**	**SO**	**Avg**	**GP**	**W**	**L**	**Mins**	**GA**	**SO**	**Avg**
1994-95	Sherbrooke	QMJHL	27	13	10	1	1287	73	1	3.40	3	1	2	185	11	0	3.57
1995-96	Sherbrooke	QMJHL	40	18	14	2	2140	127	0	3.57	4	1	3	238	23	0	5.55
1996-97	Laval	QMJHL	11	2	6	1	532	41	0	4.62	....	....	....	....	....	....	....
	Moncton	QMJHL	22	9	12	0	1252	67	1	3.21	....	....	....	....	....	....	....
	Sherbrooke	QMJHL	4	3	1	0	249	8	0	1.93	1	0	1	60	4	0	4.00
1997-98	Syracuse	AHL	8	2	4	1	380	26	0	4.10	....	....	....	....	....	....	....
	Dayton	ECHL	21	15	2	2	1177	59	1	3.01	3	1	1	142	4	0	1.69

BACH, RYAN (BAWK) DET.

Goaltender. Catches left. 6'1", 180 lbs. Born, Sherwood Park, Alta., October 21, 1973.
(Detroit's 11th choice, 262nd overall, in 1992 Entry Draft).

			Regular Season								Playoffs						
Season	**Club**	**Lea**	**GP**	**W**	**L**	**T**	**Mins**	**GA**	**SO**	**Avg**	**GP**	**W**	**L**	**Mins**	**GA**	**SO**	**Avg**
1991-92	Notre Dame	SJHL	33	....	....	....	1062	124	0	4.00	....	....	....	....	....	....	....
1992-93	Colorado	WCHA	4	1	3	0	239	11	0	2.76	....	....	....	....	....	....	....
1993-94	Colorado	WCHA	30	17	7	5	1733	105	0	3.64	....	....	....	....	....	....	....
1994-95	Colorado	WCHA	27	18	5	1	1522	83	0	3.27	....	....	....	....	....	....	....
1995-96	Colorado	WCHA	23	*17	4	2	1390	62	2	2.68	....	....	....	....	....	....	....
1996-97	Utica	ColHL	2	0	1	1	119	8	0	4.03	....	....	....	....	....	....	....
	Toledo	ECHL	20	5	11	3	1168	74	0	3.80	....	....	....	....	....	....	....
	Adirondack	AHL	13	2	3	1	451	29	0	3.86	1	0	0	46	3	0	3.92
1997-98	Houston	IHL	43	26	9	6	2452	95	5	2.32	....	....	....	....	....	....	....

WCHA First All-Star Team (1995, 1996) • NCAA West Second All-American Team (1995) • NCAA West First All-American Team (1996)

BAILEY, SCOTT

Goaltender. Catches left. 6', 195 lbs. Born, Calgary, Alta., May 2, 1972.
(Boston's 3rd choice, 112th overall, in 1992 Entry Draft).

			Regular Season								Playoffs						
Season	**Club**	**Lea**	**GP**	**W**	**L**	**T**	**Mins**	**GA**	**SO**	**Avg**	**GP**	**W**	**L**	**Mins**	**GA**	**SO**	**Avg**
1990-91	Spokane	WHL	46	33	11	0	2537	157	*4	3.71	....	....	....	....	....	....	....
1991-92	Spokane	WHL	65	34	23	5	3798	206	1	3.30	10	5	5	605	43	0	4.26
1992-93	Johnstown	ECHL	36	13	15	3	1750	112	1	3.84	....	....	....	....	....	....	....
1993-94	Providence	AHL	7	2	2	2	377	24	0	3.82	....	....	....	....	....	....	....
	Charlotte	ECHL	36	22	11	3	2180	130	1	3.58	3	1	2	187	12	0	3.83
1994-95	Providence	AHL	52	25	16	9	2936	147	2	3.00	9	4	4	504	31	*2	3.69
1995-96	**Boston**	**NHL**	**11**	**5**	**1**	**2**	**571**	**31**	**0**	**3.26**	....	....	....	....	....	....	....
	Providence	AHL	37	15	19	3	2210	120	1	3.26	2	1	1	119	6	0	3.03
1996-97	**Boston**	**NHL**	**8**	**1**	**5**	**0**	**394**	**24**	**0**	**3.65**	....	....	....	....	....	....	....
	Providence	AHL	31	11	17	2	1735	112	0	3.87	7	3	4	453	23	0	3.05
1997-98	San Antonio	IHL	37	11	17	3	1898	118	1	3.73	....	....	....	....	....	....	....
	NHL Totals		**19**	**6**	**6**	**2**	**965**	**55**	**0**	**3.42**	....	....	....	....	....	....	....

WHL West Second All-Star Team (1991, 1992)

BAKER, AARON

Goaltender. Catches right. 6'1", 174 lbs. Born, Eckville, Alta., February 17, 1978.
(Hartford's 6th choice, 143rd overall, in 1996 Entry Draft).

			Regular Season								Playoffs						
Season	**Club**	**Lea**	**GP**	**W**	**L**	**T**	**Mins**	**GA**	**SO**	**Avg**	**GP**	**W**	**L**	**Mins**	**GA**	**SO**	**Avg**
1995-96	Tri-City	WHL	20	11	6	0	1082	61	2	3.38	1	0	0	20	1	0	3.00
1996-97	Tri-City	WHL	34	11	19	1	1898	131	1	4.14	....	....	....	....	....	....	....
1997-98	Tri-City	WHL	65	15	42	4	3424	275	1	4.82	....	....	....	....	....	....	....

BALES, MIKE DAL.

Goaltender. Catches left. 6'1", 180 lbs. Born, Prince Albert, Sask., August 6, 1971.
(Boston's 4th choice, 105th overall, in 1990 Entry Draft).

			Regular Season								Playoffs						
Season	**Club**	**Lea**	**GP**	**W**	**L**	**T**	**Mins**	**GA**	**SO**	**Avg**	**GP**	**W**	**L**	**Mins**	**GA**	**SO**	**Avg**
1988-89	Estevan	SJHL	44	....	....	....	2412	197	1	4.90	....	....	....	....	....	....	....
1989-90	Ohio State	CCHA	21	6	13	2	1117	95	0	5.11	....	....	....	....	....	....	....
1990-91	Ohio State	CCHA	*39	11	24	3	*2180	184	0	5.06	....	....	....	....	....	....	....
1991-92	Ohio State	CCHA	36	11	20	5	2060	180	0	5.24	....	....	....	....	....	....	....
1992-93	**Boston**	**NHL**	**1**	**0**	**0**	**0**	**25**	**1**	**0**	**2.40**	....	....	....	....	....	....	....
	Providence	AHL	44	22	17	0	2363	166	1	4.21	2	0	2	118	8	0	4.07
1993-94	Providence	AHL	33	9	15	4	1757	130	0	4.44	....	....	....	....	....	....	....
1994-95	P.E.I.	AHL	45	25	16	3	2649	160	2	3.62	9	6	3	530	24	*2	2.72
	Ottawa	**NHL**	**1**	**0**	**0**	**0**	**3**	**0**	**0**	**0.00**	....	....	....	....	....	....	....
1995-96	**Ottawa**	**NHL**	**20**	**2**	**14**	**1**	**1040**	**72**	**0**	**4.15**	....	....	....	....	....	....	....
	P.E.I.	AHL	2	0	2	0	118	11	0	5.58	....	....	....	....	....	....	....
1996-97	**Ottawa**	**NHL**	**1**	**0**	**1**	**0**	**52**	**4**	**0**	**4.62**	....	....	....	....	....	....	....
	Baltimore	AHL	46	13	21	8	2544	130	3	3.07	....	....	....	....	....	....	....
1997-98	Rochester	AHL	39	13	19	5	2229	127	0	3.42	....	....	....	....	....	....	....
	NHL Totals		**23**	**2**	**15**	**1**	**1120**	**77**	**0**	**4.12**	....	....	....	....	....	....	....

Signed as a free agent by **Ottawa**, July 4, 1994. Signed as a free agent by **Buffalo**, September 9, 1997. Signed as a free agent by **Dallas**, July 8, 1998.

BARRASSO, TOM (buh-RAH-soh) PIT.

Goaltender. Catches right. 6'3", 211 lbs. Born, Boston, MA, March 31, 1965.
(Buffalo's 1st choice, 5th overall, in 1983 Entry Draft).

			Regular Season								Playoffs						
Season	**Club**	**Lea**	**GP**	**W**	**L**	**T**	**Mins**	**GA**	**SO**	**Avg**	**GP**	**W**	**L**	**Mins**	**GA**	**SO**	**Avg**
1981-82	Acton-Boxboro	H.S.	23	....	....	....	1035	32	7	1.86	....	....	....	....	....	....	....
1982-83	Acton-Boxboro	H.S.	23	....	....	....	1035	17	10	0.74	....	....	....	....	....	....	....
1983-84	**Buffalo**	**NHL**	**42**	**26**	**12**	**3**	**2475**	**117**	**2**	**2.84**	**3**	**0**	**2**	**139**	**8**	**0**	**3.45**
1984-85	**Buffalo**	**NHL**	**54**	**25**	**18**	**10**	**3248**	**144**	***5**	***2.66**	**5**	**2**	**3**	**300**	**22**	**0**	**4.40**
	Rochester	AHL	5	3	1	1	267	6	1	1.35	....	....	....	....	....	....	....
1985-86	**Buffalo**	**NHL**	**60**	**29**	**24**	**5**	**3561**	**214**	**2**	**3.61**	....	....	....	....	....	....	....
1986-87	**Buffalo**	**NHL**	**46**	**17**	**23**	**2**	**2501**	**152**	**2**	**3.65**	....	....	....	....	....	....	....
1987-88	**Buffalo**	**NHL**	**54**	**25**	**18**	**8**	**3133**	**173**	**2**	**3.31**	**4**	**1**	**3**	**224**	**16**	**0**	**4.29**
1988-89	**Buffalo**	**NHL**	**10**	**2**	**7**	**0**	**545**	**45**	**0**	**4.95**	....	....	....	....	....	....	....
	Pittsburgh	**NHL**	**44**	**18**	**15**	**7**	**2406**	**162**	**0**	**4.04**	**11**	**7**	**4**	**631**	**40**	**0**	**3.80**
1989-90	**Pittsburgh**	**NHL**	**24**	**7**	**12**	**3**	**1294**	**101**	**0**	**4.68**	....	....	....	....	....	....	....
1990-91	**Pittsburgh**	**NHL**	**48**	**27**	**16**	**3**	**2754**	**165**	**1**	**3.59**	**20**	**12**	**7**	**1175**	**51**	***1**	***2.60** ♦
1991-92	**Pittsburgh**	**NHL**	**57**	**25**	**22**	**9**	**3329**	**196**	**1**	**3.53**	***21**	***16**	**5**	***1233**	**58**	**1**	**2.82** ♦
1992-93	**Pittsburgh**	**NHL**	**63**	***43**	**14**	**5**	**3702**	**186**	**4**	**3.01**	**12**	**7**	**5**	**722**	**35**	***2**	**2.91**
1993-94	**Pittsburgh**	**NHL**	**44**	**22**	**15**	**5**	**2482**	**139**	**2**	**3.36**	**6**	**2**	**4**	**356**	**17**	**0**	**2.87**
1994-95	**Pittsburgh**	**NHL**	**2**	**0**	**1**	**1**	**125**	**8**	**0**	**3.84**	**2**	**0**	**1**	**80**	**8**	**0**	**6.00**
1995-96	**Pittsburgh**	**NHL**	**49**	**29**	**16**	**2**	**2799**	**160**	**2**	**3.43**	**10**	**4**	**5**	**558**	**26**	**1**	**2.80**
1996-97	**Pittsburgh**	**NHL**	**5**	**0**	**5**	**0**	**270**	**26**	**0**	**5.78**	....	....	....	....	....	....	....
1997-98	**Pittsburgh**	**NHL**	**63**	**31**	**14**	**13**	**3542**	**122**	**7**	**2.07**	**6**	**2**	**4**	**376**	**17**	**0**	**2.71**
	NHL Totals		**665**	**326**	**232**	**76**	**38166**	**2110**	**30**	**3.32**	**100**	**53**	**43**	**5794**	**298**	**5**	**3.09**

NHL All-Rookie Team (1984) • NHL First All-Star Team (1984) • Won Calder Memorial Trophy (1984) • Won Vezina Trophy (1984) • NHL Second All-Star Team (1985, 1993) • Shared William Jennings Trophy with Bob Sauve (1985)

Played in NHL All-Star Game (1985)

Traded to **Pittsburgh** by **Buffalo** with Buffalo's 3rd round choice (Joe Dziedzic) in 1990 Entry Draft for Doug Bodger and Darrin Shannon, November 12, 1988.

BEAUREGARD, STEPHANE (BOH-reh-gahrd)

Goaltender. Catches right. 5'11", 190 lbs. Born, Cowansville, Que., January 10, 1968.
(Winnipeg's 3rd choice, 52nd overall, in 1988 Entry Draft).

			Regular Season								Playoffs						
Season	Club	Lea	GP	W	L	T	Mins	GA	SO	Avg	GP	W	L	Mins	GA	SO	Avg
1986-87	St-Jean	QMJHL	13	6	7	0	785	58	0	4.43	5	1	3	260	26	0	6.00
1987-88	St-Jean	QMJHL	66	38	20	3	3766	229	2	3.65	7	3	4	423	34	0	4.82
1988-89	Moncton	AHL	15	4	8	2	824	62	0	4.51	....	....	....	....	....	....	....
	Fort Wayne	IHL	16	9	5	0	830	43	0	3.10	9	4	4	484	21	*1	*2.60
1989-90	**Winnipeg**	**NHL**	**19**	**7**	**8**	**3**	**1079**	**59**	**0**	**3.28**	**4**	**1**	**3**	**238**	**12**	**0**	**3.03**
	Fort Wayne	IHL	33	20	8	3	1949	115	0	3.54	....	....	....	....	....	....	....
1990-91	**Winnipeg**	**NHL**	**16**	**3**	**10**	**1**	**836**	**55**	**0**	**3.95**	....	....	....	....	....	....	....
	Moncton	AHL	9	3	4	1	504	20	1	2.38	1	1	0	60	1	0	1.00
	Fort Wayne	IHL	32	14	13	2	1761	109	0	3.71	*19	*10	9	*1158	57	0	2.95
1991-92	**Winnipeg**	**NHL**	**26**	**6**	**8**	**6**	**1267**	**61**	**2**	**2.89**	....	....	....	....	....	....	....
1992-93	**Philadelphia**	**NHL**	**16**	**3**	**9**	**0**	**802**	**59**	**0**	**4.41**	....	....	....	....	....	....	....
	Hershey	AHL	13	5	5	3	794	48	0	3.63	....	....	....	....	....	....	....
1993-94	**Winnipeg**	**NHL**	**13**	**0**	**4**	**1**	**418**	**34**	**0**	**4.88**	....	....	....	....	....	....	....
	Moncton	AHL	37	18	11	6	2082	121	1	3.49	*21	*12	9	*1305	57	*2	2.62
1994-95	Springfield	AHL	24	10	11	3	1381	73	2	3.17	....	....	....	....	....	....	....
1995-96	San Francisco	IHL	*69	*36	24	8	*4022	207	1	3.09	4	1	3	241	10	0	2.49
1996-97	Quebec	IHL	67	35	20	11	3945	174	4	2.65	9	5	3	498	19	0	2.29
1997-98	Chicago	IHL	18	10	6	0	917	49	1	3.20	14	10	4	820	36	1	2.63
	NHL Totals		**90**	**19**	**39**	**11**	**4402**	**268**	**2**	**3.65**	**4**	**1**	**3**	**238**	**12**	**0**	**3.03**

QMJHL First All-Star Team (1988) • Canadian Major Junior Goaltender of the year (1988) • IHL First All-Star Team (1996) • Won James Gatschene Memorial Trophy (MVP - IHL) (1996)

Traded to **Buffalo** by **Winnipeg** for Christian Ruuttu and future considerations, June 15, 1992. Traded to **Chicago** by **Buffalo** with Buffalo's 4th round choice (Eric Daze) in 1993 Entry Draft for Dominik Hasek, August 7, 1992. Traded to **Winnipeg** by **Chicago** for Christian Ruuttu, August 10, 1992. Traded to **Philadelphia** by **Winnipeg** for future considerations, October 1, 1992. Traded to **Winnipeg** by **Philadelphia** for future considerations, June 11, 1993. Signed as a free agent by **Washington**, August 20, 1997.

BELFOUR, ED (BEHL-fohr) DAL.

Goaltender. Catches left. 5'11", 182 lbs. Born, Carman, Man., April 21, 1965.

			Regular Season								Playoffs						
Season	Club	Lea	GP	W	L	T	Mins	GA	SO	Avg	GP	W	L	Mins	GA	SO	Avg
1985-86	Winkler	MJHL	48	....	....	....	2880	124	1	2.58	....	....	....	....	....	....	....
1986-87	North Dakota	WCHA	34	29	4	0	2049	81	3	2.43	....	....	....	....	....	....	....
1987-88	Saginaw	IHL	61	32	25	0	*3446	183	3	3.19	9	4	5	561	33	0	3.53
1988-89	**Chicago**	**NHL**	**23**	**4**	**12**	**3**	**1148**	**74**	**0**	**3.87**	....	....	....	....	....	....	....
	Saginaw	IHL	29	12	10	0	1760	92	0	3.10	5	2	3	298	14	0	2.82
1989-90	Canada	Nat-Tm	33	13	12	6	1808	93	0	3.08	....	....	....	....	....	....	....
	Chicago	**NHL**	....	....	....	....	....	....	....	....	**9**	**4**	**2**	**409**	**17**	**0**	**2.49**
1990-91	**Chicago**	**NHL**	***74**	***43**	**19**	**7**	***4127**	**170**	**4**	***2.47**	**6**	**2**	**4**	**295**	**20**	**0**	**4.07**
1991-92	**Chicago**	**NHL**	**52**	**21**	**18**	**10**	**2928**	**132**	***5**	**2.70**	**18**	**12**	**4**	**949**	**39**	**1**	***2.47**
1992-93	**Chicago**	**NHL**	***71**	**41**	**18**	**11**	***4106**	**177**	***7**	**2.59**	**4**	**0**	**4**	**249**	**13**	**0**	**3.13**
1993-94	**Chicago**	**NHL**	**70**	**37**	**24**	**6**	**3998**	**178**	***7**	**2.67**	**6**	**2**	**4**	**360**	**15**	**0**	**2.50**
1994-95	**Chicago**	**NHL**	**42**	**22**	**15**	**3**	**2450**	**93**	***5**	**2.28**	**16**	**9**	**7**	**1014**	**37**	**1**	**2.19**
1995-96	**Chicago**	**NHL**	**50**	**22**	**17**	**10**	**2956**	**135**	**1**	**2.74**	**9**	**6**	**3**	**666**	**23**	**1**	**2.07**
1996-97	**Chicago**	**NHL**	**33**	**11**	**15**	**6**	**1966**	**88**	**1**	**2.69**	....	....	....	....	....	....	....
	San Jose	**NHL**	**13**	**3**	**9**	**0**	**757**	**43**	**1**	**3.41**	....	....	....	....	....	....	....
1997-98	**Dallas**	**NHL**	**61**	**37**	**12**	**10**	**3581**	**112**	**9**	***1.88**	**17**	**10**	**7**	**1039**	**31**	**1**	***1.79**
	NHL Totals		**489**	**241**	**159**	**66**	**28017**	**1202**	**40**	**2.57**	**85**	**45**	**35**	**4981**	**195**	**4**	**2.35**

WCHA First All-Star Team (1987) • NCAA Championship All-Tournament Team (1987) • IHL First All-Star Team (1988) • Shared Garry F. Longman Memorial Trophy (Top Rookie - IHL) with John Cullen (1988) • NHL/Upper Deck All-Rookie Team (1991) • NHL First All-Star Team (1991, 1993) • Won Trico Goaltender Award (1991) • Won Calder Memorial Trophy (1991) • Won William M. Jennings Trophy (1991, 1993, 1995) • Won Vezina Trophy (1991, 1993) • NHL Second All-Star Team (1995)

Played in NHL All-Star Game (1992, 1993, 1996, 1998)

Signed as a free agent by **Chicago**, September 25, 1987. Traded to **San Jose** by **Chicago** for Chris Terreri, Ulf Dahlen and Michal Sykora, January 25, 1997. Signed as a free agent by **Dallas**, July 2, 1997.

BERGQVIST, PER-RAGNAR (BUHRG-kvihst) PHI.

Goaltender. Catches left. 5'11", 183 lbs. Born, Leksand, Sweden, April 11, 1976.
(Philadelphia's 3rd choice, 124th overall, in 1996 Entry Draft).

			Regular Season								Playoffs						
Season	Club	Lea	GP	W	L	T	Mins	GA	SO	Avg	GP	W	L	Mins	GA	SO	Avg
1995-96	Leksand IF	Swe-Jr.	3	....	....	....	180	17	0	5.67	....	....	....	....	....	....	....
	Leksand IF	Sweden	6	....	....	....	327	17	0	3.12	1	....	....	60	1	0	1.00
1996-97	Leksand IF	Sweden	11	....	....	....	660	32	1	2.91	1	....	....	86	5	0	3.49
1997-98	Leksand IF	Sweden	16	....	....	....	909	53	....	3.50	1	0	1	59	5	0	5.08

BIERK, ZAC (BUHRK, ZAK) T.B.

Goaltender. Catches left. 6'4", 186 lbs. Born, Peterborough, Ont., September 17, 1976.
(Tampa Bay's 8th choice, 212th overall, in 1995 Entry Draft).

			Regular Season								Playoffs						
Season	Club	Lea	GP	W	L	T	Mins	GA	SO	Avg	GP	W	L	Mins	GA	SO	Avg
1993-94	Peterborough	OHL	9	0	4	2	423	37	0	5.22	1	0	0	33	7	0	12.70
1994-95	Peterborough	OHL	35	11	15	5	1779	117	0	3.95	6	2	3	301	24	0	4.78
1995-96	Peterborough	OHL	58	31	16	6	3292	174	2	3.17	*22	*14	7	*1383	83	0	3.60
1996-97	Peterborough	OHL	49	*28	16	0	2744	151	2	3.30	11	6	5	666	35	0	3.15
1997-98	**Tampa Bay**	**NHL**	**13**	**1**	**4**	**1**	**433**	**30**	**0**	**4.16**	....	....	....	....	....	....	....
	Adirondack	AHL	12	1	6	1	557	36	0	3.87	....	....	....	....	....	....	....
	NHL Totals		**13**	**1**	**4**	**1**	**433**	**30**	**0**	**4.16**	....	....	....	....	....	....	....

OHL First All-Star Team (1997)

BILLINGTON, CRAIG COL.

Goaltender. Catches left. 5'10", 170 lbs. Born, London, Ont., September 11, 1966.
(New Jersey's 2nd choice, 23rd overall, in 1984 Entry Draft).

			Regular Season								Playoffs						
Season	Club	Lea	GP	W	L	T	Mins	GA	SO	Avg	GP	W	L	Mins	GA	SO	Avg
1983-84	Belleville	OHL	44	20	19	0	2335	162	1	4.16	1	0	0	30	3	0	6.00
1984-85	Belleville	OHL	47	26	19	0	2544	180	1	4.25	14	7	5	761	47	1	3.71
1985-86	**New Jersey**	**NHL**	**18**	**4**	**9**	**1**	**901**	**77**	**0**	**5.13**	....	....	....	....	....	....	....
	Belleville	OHL	3	2	1	0	180	11	0	3.67	20	9	6	1133	68	0	3.60
1986-87	**New Jersey**	**NHL**	**22**	**4**	**13**	**2**	**1114**	**89**	**0**	**4.79**	....	....	....	....	....	....	....
	Maine	AHL	20	9	8	2	1151	70	0	3.65	....	....	....	....	....	....	....
1987-88	Utica	AHL	*59	22	27	8	*3404	208	1	3.67	....	....	....	....	....	....	....
1988-89	**New Jersey**	**NHL**	**3**	**1**	**1**	**0**	**140**	**11**	**0**	**4.71**	....	....	....	....	....	....	....
	Utica	AHL	41	17	18	6	2432	150	2	3.70	4	1	3	220	18	0	4.91
1989-90	Utica	AHL	38	20	13	1	2087	138	0	3.97	....	....	....	....	....	....	....
1990-91	Canada	Nat-Tm	34	17	14	2	1879	110	2	3.51	....	....	....	....	....	....	....
1991-92	**New Jersey**	**NHL**	**26**	**13**	**7**	**1**	**1363**	**69**	**2**	**3.04**	....	....	....	....	....	....	....
1992-93	**New Jersey**	**NHL**	**42**	**21**	**16**	**4**	**2389**	**146**	**2**	**3.67**	**2**	**0**	**1**	**78**	**5**	**0**	**3.85**
1993-94	**Ottawa**	**NHL**	**63**	**11**	**41**	**4**	**3319**	**254**	**0**	**4.59**	....	....	....	....	....	....	....
1994-95	**Ottawa**	**NHL**	**9**	**0**	**6**	**2**	**472**	**32**	**0**	**4.07**	....	....	....	....	....	....	....
	Boston	**NHL**	**8**	**5**	**1**	**0**	**373**	**19**	**0**	**3.06**	**1**	**0**	**0**	**25**	**1**	**0**	**2.40**
1995-96	**Boston**	**NHL**	**27**	**10**	**13**	**3**	**1380**	**79**	**1**	**3.43**	**1**	**0**	**1**	**60**	**6**	**0**	**6.00**
1996-97	**Colorado**	**NHL**	**23**	**11**	**8**	**2**	**1200**	**53**	**1**	**2.65**	**1**	**0**	**0**	**20**	**1**	**0**	**3.00**
1997-98	**Colorado**	**NHL**	**23**	**8**	**7**	**4**	**1162**	**45**	**1**	**2.32**	**1**	**0**	**0**	**1**	**0**	**0**	**0.00**
	NHL Totals		**264**	**88**	**122**	**23**	**13813**	**874**	**7**	**3.80**	**6**	**0**	**2**	**184**	**13**	**0**	**4.24**

OHL First All-Star Team (1985)

Played in NHL All-Star Game (1993)

Traded to **Ottawa** by **New Jersey** with Troy Mallette and New Jersey's 4th round choice (Cosmo Dupaul) in 1993 Entry Draft for Peter Sidorkiewicz and future considerations (Mike Peluso, June 26, 1993), June 20, 1993. Traded to **Boston** by **Ottawa** for NY Islanders' 8th round choice (previously acquired, Ottawa selected Ray Schultz) in 1995 Entry Draft, April 7, 1995. Signed as a free agent by **Florida**, September 5, 1996. Claimed by **Colorado** from **Florida** in NHL Waiver Draft, September 30, 1996.

BIRON, MARTIN (BIH-rohn) BUF.

Goaltender. Catches left. 6'1", 154 lbs. Born, Lac St. Charles, Que., August 15, 1977.
(Buffalo's 2nd choice, 16th overall, in 1995 Entry Draft).

			Regular Season								Playoffs						
Season	Club	Lea	GP	W	L	T	Mins	GA	SO	Avg	GP	W	L	Mins	GA	SO	Avg
1994-95	Beauport	QMJHL	56	29	16	9	3193	132	3	*2.48	16	8	7	900	37	*4	2.47
1995-96	Beauport	QMJHL	55	29	17	7	3201	152	1	2.85	*19	*12	7	1134	64	0	3.39
	Buffalo	**NHL**	**3**	**0**	**2**	**0**	**119**	**10**	**0**	**5.04**	....	....	....	....	....	....	....
1996-97	Beauport	QMJHL	18	6	9	1	928	61	1	3.94	....	....	....	....	....	....	....
	Hull	QMJHL	16	11	4	1	974	43	2	2.65	6	3	1	325	19	0	3.51
1997-98	South Carolina	ECHL	2	0	1	1	86	3	0	2.09	....	....	....	....	....	....	....
	Rochester	AHL	41	14	18	6	2312	113	*5	2.93	4	1	3	239	16	0	4.01
	NHL Totals		**3**	**0**	**2**	**0**	**119**	**10**	**0**	**5.04**	....	....	....	....	....	....	....

Canadian Major Junior First All-Star Team (1995) • Canadian Major Junior Goaltender of the Year (1995)

BLACKBURN, JOSH PHX.

Goaltender. Catches left. 6', 185 lbs. Born, Delrio, TX, November 13, 1978.
(Phoenix's 6th choice, 116th overall, in 1998 Entry Draft).

			Regular Season								Playoffs						
Season	Club	Lea	GP	W	L	T	Mins	GA	SO	Avg	GP	W	L	Mins	GA	SO	Avg
1997-98	Lincoln Stars	USHL	45	....	....	....	2609	135	1	3.10	....	....	....	....	....	....	....

BONNER, DOUG TOR.

Goaltender. Catches left. 5'10", 175 lbs. Born, Tacoma, WA, October 15, 1976.
(Toronto's 3rd choice, 139th overall, in 1995 Entry Draft).

			Regular Season								Playoffs						
Season	Club	Lea	GP	W	L	T	Mins	GA	SO	Avg	GP	W	L	Mins	GA	SO	Avg
1992-93	Seattle	WHL	30	7	15	0	1212	93	1	4.60	....	....	....	....	....	....	....
1993-94	Seattle	WHL	29	9	15	0	1481	111	1	4.50	....	....	....	....	....	....	....
1994-95	Seattle	WHL	59	33	23	1	3386	205	1	3.63	3	0	3	193	10	0	3.11
1995-96	Seattle	WHL	58	20	27	7	3219	190	2	3.54	5	1	4	317	19	0	3.60
1996-97	St. John's	AHL	11	0	4	1	366	26	0	4.27	....	....	....	....	....	....	....
	Peoria	ECHL	23	13	8	1	1315	63	1	2.87	10	6	3	541	28	0	3.10
1997-98	St. John's	AHL	2	2	0	0	120	3	1	1.50	....	....	....	....	....	....	....
	Louisiana	ECHL	*54	*36	11	6	*3164	160	1	3.03	12	8	4	772	47	1	3.65

BOUCHER, BRIAN (BOO-shay) PHI.

Goaltender. Catches left. 6'1", 190 lbs. Born, Woonsocket, RI, January 2, 1977.
(Philadelphia's 1st choice, 22nd overall, in 1995 Entry Draft).

			Regular Season								Playoffs						
Season	Club	Lea	GP	W	L	T	Mins	GA	SO	Avg	GP	W	L	Mins	GA	SO	Avg
1994-95	Tri-City	WHL	35	17	11	2	1969	108	1	3.29	13	6	5	795	50	0	3.77
1995-96	Tri-City	WHL	55	33	19	2	3183	181	1	3.41	11	6	5	653	37	*2	3.40
1996-97	Tri-City	WHL	41	10	24	6	2458	149	1	3.64	....	....	....	....	....	....	....
1997-98	Philadelphia	AHL	34	16	12	3	1901	101	0	3.19	2	0	0	30	1	0	1.95

WHL West Second All-Star Team (1996) • WHL West First All-Star Team (1997)

BRADY, PETER VAN.

Goaltender. Catches left. 6'1", 175 lbs. Born, Cap-Rouge, Que., October 25, 1977.
(Vancouver's 12th choice, 227th overall, in 1997 Entry Draft).

			Regular Season								Playoffs						
Season	Club	Lea	GP	W	L	T	Mins	GA	SO	Avg	GP	W	L	Mins	GA	SO	Avg
1996-97	Powell River	BCJHL	37	....	....	....	2268	90	0	2.38	....	....	....	....	....	....	....
1997-98	Alaska-Anchorage	WCHA	7	0	5	1	345	23	0	4.00	....	....	....	....	....	....	....

BRATHWAITE, FRED (BRAYTH-wayt)

Goaltender. Catches left. 5'7", 170 lbs. Born, Ottawa, Ont., November 24, 1972.

							Regular Season								Playoffs		
Season	Club	Lea	GP	W	L	T	Mins	GA	SO	Avg	GP	W	L	Mins	GA	SO	Avg
1989-90	Oshawa	OHL	20	11	2	1	886	43	1	2.91	10	4	2	451	22	0	*2.93
1990-91	Oshawa	OHL	39	25	6	3	1986	112	1	3.38	13	*9	2	677	43	0	3.81
1991-92	Oshawa	OHL	24	12	7	2	1248	81	0	3.89	....	....	....	....	....	....	....
	London	OHL	23	15	6	2	1325	61	*4	2.76	10	5	5	615	36	0	3.51
1992-93	Detroit	OHL	37	23	10	4	2192	134	0	3.67	15	9	6	858	48	1	3.36
1993-94	Edmonton	NHL	19	3	10	3	982	58	0	3.54	....	....	....	....	....	....	....
	Cape Breton	AHL	2	1	1	0	119	6	0	3.04	....	....	....	....	....	....	....
1994-95	Edmonton	NHL	14	2	5	1	601	40	0	3.99	....	....	....	....	....	....	....
1995-96	Edmonton	NHL	7	0	2	0	293	12	0	2.46	....	....	....	....	....	....	....
	Cape Breton	AHL	31	12	16	0	1699	110	1	3.88	....	....	....	....	....	....	....
1996-97	Manitoba	IHL	58	22	22	5	2945	167	1	3.40	....	....	....	....	....	....	....
1997-98	Manitoba	IHL	51	23	18	4	2736	138	1	3.03	2	0	1	72	4	0	3.30
	NHL Totals		40	5	17	4	1876	110	0	3.52	....	....	....	....	....	....	....

• Scored a goal while with Detroit (OHL), April 20, 1993. • Scored a goal while with Manitoba (IHL), November 9, 1996.

Signed as a free agent by **Edmonton**, October 6, 1993.

BROCHU, MARTIN (broh-SHOO) WSH.

Goaltender. Catches left. 5'10", 200 lbs. Born, Anjou, Que., March 10, 1973.

							Regular Season								Playoffs		
Season	Club	Lea	GP	W	L	T	Mins	GA	SO	Avg	GP	W	L	Mins	GA	SO	Avg
1990-91	Granby	QMJHL	16	6	5	0	622	39	....	3.76	....	....	....	....	....	....	....
1991-92	Granby	QMJHL	52	15	29	2	2772	278	0	4.72	....	....	....	....	....	....	....
1992-93	Hull	QMJHL	29	9	15	1	1453	137	0	5.66	2	0	1	69	7	0	6.07
1993-94	Fredericton	AHL	32	10	11	3	1505	76	2	3.03	....	....	....	....	....	....	....
1994-95	Fredericton	AHL	44	18	18	4	2475	145	0	3.51	....	....	....	....	....	....	....
1995-96	Fredericton	AHL	17	6	8	2	986	70	0	4.26	....	....	....	....	....	....	....
	Wheeling	ECHL	19	10	6	2	1060	51	1	2.89	....	....	....	....	....	....	....
	Portland	AHL	5	2	2	1	287	15	0	3.14	12	7	4	700	28	*2	*2.40
1996-97	Portland	AHL	55	23	17	7	2962	150	2	3.04	5	2	3	324	13	0	2.41
1997-98	Portland	AHL	37	16	14	1	1926	96	2	2.99	6	3	2	296	16	0	3.24

Signed as a free agent by **Montreal**, September 22, 1992. Traded to **Washington** by **Montreal** for future considerations, March 15, 1996.

BRODEUR, MARTIN (broh-DOOR, MAHR-tihn) N.J.

Goaltender. Catches left. 6'1", 205 lbs. Born, Montreal, Que., May 6, 1972.
(New Jersey's 1st choice, 20th overall, in 1990 Entry Draft).

							Regular Season								Playoffs		
Season	Club	Lea	GP	W	L	T	Mins	GA	SO	Avg	GP	W	L	Mins	GA	SO	Avg
1988-89	Montreal	QAAA	27	....	....	....	1580	98	0	3.72	....	....	....	....	....	....	....
1989-90	St-Hyacinthe	QMJHL	42	23	13	2	2333	156	0	4.01	12	5	7	678	46	0	4.07
1990-91	St-Hyacinthe	QMJHL	52	22	24	4	2946	162	2	3.30	4	0	4	232	16	0	4.14
1991-92	St-Hyacinthe	QMJHL	48	27	16	4	2846	161	2	3.39	5	2	3	317	14	0	2.65
	New Jersey	NHL	4	2	1	0	179	10	0	3.35	1	0	1	32	3	0	5.63
1992-93	Utica	AHL	32	14	13	5	1952	131	0	4.03	4	1	3	258	18	0	4.19
1993-94	New Jersey	NHL	47	27	11	8	2625	105	3	2.40	17	8	9	1171	38	1	1.95
1994-95	New Jersey	NHL	40	19	11	6	2184	89	3	2.45	*20	*16	4	*1222	34	*3	*1.67
1995-96	New Jersey	NHL	77	34	30	12	*4433	173	6	2.34	....	....	....	....	....	....	....
1996-97	New Jersey	NHL	67	37	14	13	3838	120	*10	*1.88	10	5	5	659	19	2	*1.73
1997-98	New Jersey	NHL	70	*43	17	8	4128	130	10	1.89	6	2	4	366	12	0	1.97
	Canada	Olympics					DID NOT PLAY – SPARE GOALTENDER										
	NHL Totals		305	162	84	47	17387	627	32	2.16	54	31	23	3450	106	6	1.84

QMJHL Second All-Star Team (1992) • NHL/Upper Deck All-Rookie Team (1994) • Won Calder Memorial Trophy (1994) • NHL Second All-Star Team (1997, 1998) • Shared William M. Jennings Trophy with Mike Dunham (1997) • Won William M. Jennings Trophy (1998)

Played in NHL All-Star Game (1996, 1997, 1998)

• Scored a goal in playoffs vs. Montreal, April 17, 1997.

BURKE, SEAN

Goaltender. Catches left. 6'4", 208 lbs. Born, Windsor, Ont., January 29, 1967.
(New Jersey's 2nd choice, 24th overall, in 1985 Entry Draft).

							Regular Season								Playoffs		
Season	Club	Lea	GP	W	L	T	Mins	GA	SO	Avg	GP	W	L	Mins	GA	SO	Avg
1983-84	St. Michael's	Jr. B	25	....	....	....	1482	120	0	4.86	....	....	....	....	....	....	....
1984-85	Toronto	OHL	49	25	21	3	2987	211	0	4.24	5	1	3	266	25	0	5.64
1985-86	Toronto	OHL	47	16	27	3	2840	233	0	4.92	4	0	4	238	24	0	6.05
1986-87	Canada	Nat-Tm	42	27	13	2	2550	130	0	3.05	....	....	....	....	....	....	....
1987-88	Canada	Nat-Tm	37	19	9	2	1962	92	1	2.81	....	....	....	....	....	....	....
	Canada	Olympics	4	1	2	1	238	12	....	3.02	....	....	....	....	....	....	....
	New Jersey	NHL	13	10	1	0	689	35	1	3.05	17	9	8	1001	57	*1	3.42
1988-89	New Jersey	NHL	62	22	31	9	3590	230	3	3.84	....	....	....	....	....	....	....
1989-90	New Jersey	NHL	52	22	22	6	2914	175	0	3.60	2	0	2	125	8	0	3.84
1990-91	New Jersey	NHL	35	8	12	8	1870	112	0	3.59	....	....	....	....	....	....	....
1991-92	Canada	Nat-Tm	31	18	6	4	1721	75	1	2.61	....	....	....	....	....	....	....
	Canada	Olympics	7	5	2	0	429	17	0	2.37	....	....	....	....	....	....	....
	San Diego	IHL	7	4	2	1	424	17	0	2.41	3	0	3	160	13	0	4.88
1992-93	Hartford	NHL	50	16	27	3	2656	184	0	4.16	....	....	....	....	....	....	....
1993-94	Hartford	NHL	47	17	24	5	2750	137	2	2.99	....	....	....	....	....	....	....
1994-95	Hartford	NHL	42	17	19	4	2418	108	0	2.68	....	....	....	....	....	....	....
1995-96	Hartford	NHL	66	28	28	6	3669	190	4	3.11	....	....	....	....	....	....	....
1996-97	Hartford	NHL	51	22	22	6	2985	134	4	2.69	....	....	....	....	....	....	....
1997-98	Carolina	NHL	25	7	11	5	1415	66	1	2.80	....	....	....	....	....	....	....
	Vancouver	NHL	16	2	9	4	838	49	0	3.51	....	....	....	....	....	....	....
	Philadelphia	NHL	11	7	3	0	632	27	1	2.56	5	1	4	283	17	0	3.60
	NHL Totals		470	178	209	56	26426	1447	16	3.29	24	10	14	1409	82	1	3.49

Played in NHL All-Star Game (1989)

Traded to **Hartford** by **New Jersey** with Eric Weinrich for Bobby Holik, Hartford's 2nd round choice (Jay Pandolfo) in 1993 Entry Draft and future considerations, August 28, 1992. Transferred to **Carolina** after **Hartford** franchise relocated, June 25, 1997. Traded to **Vancouver** by **Carolina** with Geoff Sanderson and Enrico Ciccone for Kirk McLean and Martin Gelinas, January 3, 1998. Traded to **Philadelphia** by **Vancouver** for Garth Snow, March 4, 1998.

BUZAK, MIKE N.J.

Goaltender. Catches left. 6'3", 215 lbs. Born, Edson, Alta., February 10, 1973.
(St. Louis' 5th choice, 167th overall, in 1993 Entry Draft).

							Regular Season								Playoffs		
Season	Club	Lea	GP	W	L	T	Mins	GA	SO	Avg	GP	W	L	Mins	GA	SO	Avg
1991-92	Michigan State	CCHA	7	4	0	0	311	22	0	4.25	....	....	....	....	....	....	....
1992-93	Michigan State	CCHA	38	22	10	2	*2090	102	0	2.93	....	....	....	....	....	....	....
1993-94	Michigan State	CCHA	*39	21	12	5	*2297	104	2	2.72	....	....	....	....	....	....	....
1994-95	Michigan State	CCHA	31	17	10	3	1796	94	0	3.14	....	....	....	....	....	....	....
1995-96	Worcester	AHL	30	9	10	5	1672	85	0	3.05	....	....	....	....	....	....	....
1996-97	Baton Rouge	ECHL	3	0	2	0	108	7	0	3.87	....	....	....	....	....	....	....
	Worcester	AHL	19	9	4	3	972	41	1	2.53	1	0	1	58	3	0	3.06
1997-98	Long Beach	IHL	31	18	6	5	1763	58	*6	*1.97	5	0	3	215	11	0	3.06

CCHA Second All-Star Team (1994, 1995) • Shared James Norris Memorial Trophy (fewest goals against - IHL) with Kay Whitmore (1998)

Signed as a free agent by **New Jersey**, August 14, 1998.

CAREY, JIM (CAIR-ee) BOS.

Goaltender. Catches left. 6'2", 205 lbs. Born, Dorchester, MA, May 31, 1974.
(Washington's 2nd choice, 32nd overall, in 1992 Entry Draft).

							Regular Season								Playoffs		
Season	Club	Lea	GP	W	L	T	Mins	GA	SO	Avg	GP	W	L	Mins	GA	SO	Avg
1991-92	Catholic Mem.	H.S.	21	....	....	....	940	34	8	1.63	....	....	....	....	....	....	....
1992-93	U. of Wisconsin	WCHA	26	15	8	1	1525	78	1	3.07	....	....	....	....	....	....	....
1993-94	U. of Wisconsin	WCHA	*40	*24	13	1	*2247	114	*1	*3.04	....	....	....	....	....	....	....
1994-95	Portland	AHL	55	30	14	11	3281	151	*6	2.76	....	....	....	....	....	....	....
	Washington	NHL	28	18	6	3	1604	57	4	2.13	7	2	4	358	25	0	4.19
1995-96	Washington	NHL	71	35	24	9	4069	153	*9	2.26	3	0	1	97	10	0	6.19
1996-97	Washington	NHL	40	17	18	3	2293	105	1	2.75	....	....	....	....	....	....	....
	Boston	NHL	19	5	13	0	1004	64	0	3.82	....	....	....	....	....	....	....
1997-98	Boston	NHL	10	3	2	1	496	24	2	2.90	....	....	....	....	....	....	....
	Providence	AHL	10	2	7	1	604	40	0	3.97	....	....	....	....	....	....	....
	NHL Totals		168	78	63	16	9466	403	16	2.55	10	2	5	455	35	0	4.62

WCHA Second All-Star Team (1993) • AHL First All-Star Team (1995) • Won Dudley "Red" Garrett Memorial Trophy (Top Rookie - AHL) (1995) • Won Baz Bastien Memorial Trophy (Top Goaltender - AHL) (1995) • NHL/Upper Deck All-Rookie Team (1995) • NHL First All-Star Team (1996) • Won Vezina Trophy (1996)

Traded to **Boston** by **Washington** with Anson Carter, Jason Allison and Washington's 3rd round choice (Lee Goren) in 1997 Entry Draft for Bill Ranford, Adam Oates and Rick Tocchet, March 1, 1997.

CASEY, JON (CAY-see)

Goaltender. Catches left. 5'10", 155 lbs. Born, Grand Rapids, MN, March 29, 1962.

							Regular Season								Playoffs		
Season	Club	Lea	GP	W	L	T	Mins	GA	SO	Avg	GP	W	L	Mins	GA	SO	Avg
1980-81	North Dakota	WCHA	5	3	1	0	300	19	0	3.80	....	....	....	....	....	....	....
1981-82	North Dakota	WCHA	18	15	3	0	1038	48	1	2.77	....	....	....	....	....	....	....
1982-83	North Dakota	WCHA	17	9	6	2	1020	42	0	2.51	....	....	....	....	....	....	....
1983-84	North Dakota	WCHA	37	25	10	2	2180	115	2	3.13	....	....	....	....	....	....	....
	Minnesota	NHL	2	1	0	0	84	6	0	4.29	....	....	....	....	....	....	....
1984-85	Baltimore	AHL	46	30	11	4	2646	116	*4	*2.63	*13	8	3	689	38	0	3.31
1985-86	Minnesota	NHL	26	11	11	1	1402	91	0	3.89	....	....	....	....	....	....	....
	Springfield	AHL	9	4	3	1	464	30	0	3.88	....	....	....	....	....	....	....
1986-87	Springfield	AHL	13	1	8	0	770	56	0	4.36	....	....	....	....	....	....	....
	Indianapolis	IHL	31	14	15	0	1794	133	0	4.45	....	....	....	....	....	....	....
1987-88	Minnesota	NHL	14	1	7	4	663	41	0	3.71	....	....	....	....	....	....	....
	Kalamazoo	IHL	42	24	13	5	2541	154	2	3.64	7	3	3	382	26	0	4.08
1988-89	Minnesota	NHL	55	18	17	12	2961	151	1	3.06	4	1	3	211	16	0	4.55
1989-90	Minnesota	NHL	61	*31	22	4	3407	183	3	3.22	7	3	4	415	21	1	3.04
1990-91	Minnesota	NHL	55	21	20	11	3185	158	3	2.98	*23	*14	7	*1205	61	*1	3.04
1991-92	Minnesota	NHL	52	19	23	5	2911	165	2	3.40	7	3	4	437	22	0	3.02
	Kalamazoo	IHL	4	2	1	1	250	11	0	2.64	....	....	....	....	....	....	....
1992-93	Minnesota	NHL	60	26	26	5	3476	193	3	3.33	....	....	....	....	....	....	....
1993-94	Boston	NHL	57	30	15	9	3192	153	4	2.88	11	5	6	698	34	0	2.92
1994-95	St. Louis	NHL	19	7	5	4	872	40	0	2.75	2	0	1	30	2	0	4.00
1995-96	St. Louis	NHL	9	2	3	0	395	25	0	3.80	12	6	6	747	36	1	2.89
	Peoria	IHL	43	21	19	2	2514	128	3	3.05	....	....	....	....	....	....	....
1996-97	St. Louis	NHL	15	3	8	0	707	40	0	3.39	....	....	....	....	....	....	....
	Worcester	AHL	4	2	1	1	245	10	0	2.45	....	....	....	....	....	....	....
1997-98	Kansas City	IHL	24	9	13	2	1340	62	2	2.78	....	....	....	....	....	....	....
	NHL Totals		425	170	157	55	23255	1246	16	3.21	66	32	31	3743	192	3	3.08

WCHA First All-Star Team (1982, 1984) • WCHA Second All-Star Team (1983) • NCAA West First All-American Team (1984) • AHL First All-Star Team (1985) • Won Harry "Hap" Holmes Memorial Trophy (fewest goals against - AHL) (1985) • Won Baz Bastien Memorial Trophy (Top Goaltender - AHL) (1985)

Played in NHL All-Star Game (1993)

Signed as a free agent by **Minnesota**, April 1, 1984. Transferred to **Dallas** after **Minnesota** franchise relocated, June 9, 1993. Traded to **Boston** by **Dallas** for Andy Moog and (Gord Murphy, June 20, 1993), June 25, 1993. Signed as a free agent by **St. Louis**, June 29, 1994.

CASSIVI, FREDERIC (KASS-ih-vee) OTT.

Goaltender. Catches left. 6'4", 205 lbs. Born, Sorel, Que., June 12, 1975.
(Ottawa's 7th choice, 210th overall, in 1994 Entry Draft).

							Regular Season								Playoffs		
Season	Club	Lea	GP	W	L	T	Mins	GA	SO	Avg	GP	W	L	Mins	GA	SO	Avg
1993-94	St-Hyacinthe	QMJHL	35	15	13	3	1751	127	1	4.35	....	....	....	....	....	....	....
1994-95	Halifax	QMJHL	24	9	12	1	1362	105	0	4.63	....	....	....	....	....	....	....
	St-Jean	QMJHL	19	12	6	0	1021	55	1	3.23	5	2	3	258	18	0	4.19
1995-96	Thunder Bay	ColHL	12	6	4	2	715	51	0	4.28	....	....	....	....	....	....	....
	P.E.I.	AHL	41	20	14	3	2347	128	1	3.27	5	2	3	317	24	0	4.54
1996-97	Syracuse	AHL	55	23	22	8	3069	164	2	3.21	1	0	1	60	3	0	3.01
1997-98	Worcester	AHL	45	20	22	2	2593	140	1	3.24	6	3	3	326	18	0	3.31

CHABOT, FREDERIC (shah-BOH) L.A.

Goaltender. Catches left. 5'11", 187 lbs. Born, Hebertville-Station, Que., February 12, 1968.
(New Jersey's 10th choice, 192nd overall, in 1986 Entry Draft).

			Regular Season								Playoffs						
Season	Club	Lea	GP	W	L	T	Mins	GA	SO	Avg	GP	W	L	Mins	GA	SO	Avg
1985-86	Ste-Foy	QAAA					STATISTICS NOT AVAILABLE										
1986-87	Drummondville	QMJHL	62	31	29	0	3508	293	1	5.01	8	2	6	481	40	0	4.99
1987-88	Drummondville	QMJHL	58	27	24	4	3276	237	1	4.34	16	10	6	1019	56	*1	*3.30
1988-89	Prince Albert	WHL	54	21	29	0	2957	202	2	4.10	4	1	1	199	16	0	4.82
1989-90	Sherbrooke	AHL	2	1	1	0	119	8	0	4.03	....	....	....	....	....	....	....
	Fort Wayne	IHL	23	6	13	3	1208	87	1	4.32	....	....	....	....	....	....	....
1990-91	**Montreal**	**NHL**	**3**	**0**	**0**	**1**	**108**	**6**	**0**	**3.33**	....	....	....	....	....	....	....
	Fredericton	AHL	35	9	15	5	1800	122	0	4.07	....	....	....	....	....	....	....
1991-92	Fredericton	AHL	30	17	9	4	1761	79	2	*2.69	7	3	4	457	20	0	2.63
	Winston-Salem	ECHL	24	15	7	2	1449	71	0	*2.94	....	....	....	....	....	....	....
1992-93	**Montreal**	**NHL**	**1**	**0**	**0**	**0**	**40**	**1**	**0**	**1.50**	....	....	....	....	....	....	....
	Fredericton	AHL	45	22	17	4	2544	141	0	3.33	4	1	3	261	16	0	3.68
1993-94	**Montreal**	**NHL**	**1**	**0**	**1**	**0**	**60**	**5**	**0**	**5.00**	....	....	....	....	....	....	....
	Fredericton	AHL	3	0	1	1	143	12	0	5.03	....	....	....	....	....	....	....
	Las Vegas	IHL	2	1	1	0	110	5	0	2.72	....	....	....	....	....	....	....
	Philadelphia	**NHL**	**4**	**0**	**1**	**1**	**70**	**5**	**0**	**4.29**	....	....	....	....	....	....	....
	Hershey	AHL	28	13	5	6	1464	63	2	*2.58	11	7	4	665	32	0	2.89
1994-95	Cincinnati	IHL	48	25	12	7	2622	128	1	2.93	5	3	2	326	16	0	2.94
1995-96	Cincinnati	IHL	38	23	9	4	2147	88	3	*2.46	14	9	5	854	37	1	2.60
1996-97	Houston	IHL	*72	*39	26	7	*4265	180	*7	2.53	13	8	5	777	34	*2	2.63
1997-98	**Los Angeles**	**NHL**	**12**	**3**	**3**	**2**	**554**	**29**	**0**	**3.14**	....	....	....	....	....	....	....
	Houston	IHL	22	12	7	2	1237	46	1	2.23	4	1	3	238	11	0	2.77
	NHL Totals		**21**	**3**	**5**	**4**	**832**	**46**	**0**	**3.32**	....	....	....	....	....	....	....

WHL East All-Star Team (1989) • Won Baz Bastien Award (Top Goaltender - AHL) (1994) • IHL Second All-Star Team (1996) • IHL First All-Star Team (1997) • Won James Gatschene Memorial Trophy (MVP - IHL) (1997)

Signed as a free agent by **Montreal**, January 16, 1990. Claimed by **Tampa Bay** from **Montreal** in Expansion Draft, June 18, 1992. Traded to **Montreal** by **Tampa Bay** for J.C. Bergeron, June 19, 1992. Traded to **Philadelphia** by **Montreal** for cash, February 21, 1994. Signed as a free agent by **Florida**, August 11, 1994. Signed as a free agent by **LA Kings**, September 3, 1997. Claimed by **Nashville** from **LA Kings** in Expansion Draft, June 26, 1998. Claimed on waivers by **LA Kings** from **Nashville**, July 18, 1998.

CHARPENTIER, SEBASTIEN (shahr-PUHNT-yay) WSH.

Goaltender. Catches left. 5'9", 161 lbs. Born, Drummondville, Que., April 18, 1977.
(Washington's 4th choice, 93rd overall, in 1995 Entry Draft).

			Regular Season								Playoffs						
Season	Club	Lea	GP	W	L	T	Mins	GA	SO	Avg	GP	W	L	Mins	GA	SO	Avg
1994-95	Laval	QMJHL	41	25	12	1	2152	99	2	2.76	16	9	4	886	45	0	3.05
1995-96	Laval	QMJHL	18	4	10	0	938	97	0	6.20	....	....	....	....	....	....	....
	Val d'Or	QMJHL	33	21	9	1	1906	87	1	2.74	13	7	5	740	45	0	3.64
1996-97	Shawinigan	QMJHL	*62	*37	17	4	*3480	177	1	3.05	4	2	1	196	13	0	3.98
1997-98	Portland	AHL	4	1	3	0	229	10	0	2.61	....	....	....	....	....	....	....
	Hampton Roads	ECHL	43	20	16	6	2388	114	0	2.86	18	*14	4	*1183	38	1	*1.93

Playoff MVP - ECHL (1998)

CHEVELDAE, TIM (SHEH-vehl-day)

Goaltender. Catches left. 5'10", 195 lbs. Born, Melville, Sask., February 15, 1968.
(Detroit's 4th choice, 64th overall, in 1986 Entry Draft).

			Regular Season								Playoffs						
Season	Club	Lea	GP	W	L	T	Mins	GA	SO	Avg	GP	W	L	Mins	GA	SO	Avg
1985-86	Saskatoon	WHL	36	21	10	3	2030	165	0	4.88	8	6	2	480	29	0	3.63
1986-87	Saskatoon	WHL	33	20	11	0	1909	133	2	4.18	5	4	1	308	20	0	3.90
1987-88	Saskatoon	WHL	66	44	19	3	3798	235	1	3.71	6	4	2	364	27	0	4.45
1988-89	**Detroit**	**NHL**	**2**	**0**	**2**	**0**	**122**	**9**	**0**	**4.43**	....	....	....	....	....	....	....
	Adirondack	AHL	30	20	8	0	1694	98	1	3.47	2	1	0	99	9	0	5.45
1989-90	**Detroit**	**NHL**	**28**	**10**	**9**	**8**	**1600**	**101**	**0**	**3.79**	....	....	....	....	....	....	....
	Adirondack	AHL	31	17	8	6	1848	116	0	3.77	....	....	....	....	....	....	....
1990-91	**Detroit**	**NHL**	**65**	**30**	**26**	**5**	**3615**	**214**	**2**	**3.55**	**7**	**3**	**4**	**398**	**22**	**0**	**3.32**
1991-92	**Detroit**	**NHL**	***72**	***38**	**23**	**9**	***4236**	**226**	**2**	**3.20**	**11**	**3**	**7**	**597**	**25**	***2**	**2.51**
1992-93	**Detroit**	**NHL**	**67**	**34**	**24**	**7**	**3880**	**210**	**4**	**3.25**	**7**	**3**	**4**	**423**	**24**	**0**	**3.40**
1993-94	**Detroit**	**NHL**	**30**	**16**	**9**	**1**	**1572**	**91**	**1**	**3.47**	....	....	....	....	....	....	....
	Adirondack	AHL	2	1	0	1	125	7	0	3.36	....	....	....	....	....	....	....
	Winnipeg	**NHL**	**14**	**5**	**8**	**1**	**788**	**52**	**1**	**3.96**	....	....	....	....	....	....	....
1994-95	**Winnipeg**	**NHL**	**30**	**8**	**16**	**3**	**1571**	**97**	**0**	**3.70**	....	....	....	....	....	....	....
1995-96	**Winnipeg**	**NHL**	**30**	**8**	**18**	**3**	**1695**	**111**	**0**	**3.93**	....	....	....	....	....	....	....
	Hershey	AHL	8	4	3	0	457	31	0	4.07	4	2	2	250	14	0	3.36
1996-97	**Boston**	**NHL**	**2**	**0**	**1**	**0**	**93**	**5**	**0**	**3.23**	....	....	....	....	....	....	....
	Fort Wayne	IHL	21	6	9	4	1137	75	0	3.96	....	....	....	....	....	....	....
1997-98	Las Vegas	IHL	38	9	17	5	1942	128	0	3.95	....	....	....	....	....	....	....
	NHL Totals		**340**	**149**	**136**	**37**	**19172**	**1116**	**10**	**3.49**	**25**	**9**	**15**	**1418**	**71**	**2**	**3.00**

WHL East All-Star Team (1988)

Played in NHL All-Star Game (1992)

Traded to **Winnipeg** by **Detroit** with Dallas Drake for Bob Essensa and Sergei Bautin, March 8, 1994. Traded to **Philadelphia** by **Winnipeg** with Winnipeg's 3rd round choice (Chester Gallant) in 1996 Entry Draft for Dominic Roussel, February 27, 1996. Signed as a free agent by **Boston**, August 27, 1996.

CHOUINARD, MATHIEU (shwee-NAHR) OTT.

Goaltender. Catches left. 6'1", 200 lbs. Born, Laval, Que., April 11, 1980.
(Ottawa's 1st choice, 15th overall, in 1998 Entry Draft).

			Regular Season								Playoffs						
Season	Club	Lea	GP	W	L	T	Mins	GA	SO	Avg	GP	W	L	Mins	GA	SO	Avg
1996-97	Shawinigan	QMJHL	17	4	7	1	795	51	0	3.85	4	1	3	264	15	0	3.41
1997-98	Shawinigan	QMJHL	55	*32	18	3	3055	142	2	2.79	6	2	4	348	24	0	4.14

CLEMMENSEN, SCOTT N.J.

Goaltender. Catches left. 6'2", 185 lbs. Born, Des Moines, IA, July 23, 1977.
(New Jersey's 7th choice, 215th overall, in 1997 Entry Draft).

			Regular Season								Playoffs						
Season	Club	Lea	GP	W	L	T	Mins	GA	SO	Avg	GP	W	L	Mins	GA	SO	Avg
1996-97	Des Moines	USHL	36	....	....	....	2042	111	1	3.26	....	....	....	....	....	....	....
1997-98	Boston College	H.E.	37	24	9	4	2205	102	*4	2.78	....	....	....	....	....	....	....

CLOUTIER, DAN (KLOO-tyay) NYR

Goaltender. Catches left. 6'1", 182 lbs. Born, Mont-Laurier, Que., April 22, 1976.
(NY Rangers' 1st choice, 26th overall, in 1994 Entry Draft).

			Regular Season								Playoffs						
Season	Club	Lea	GP	W	L	T	Mins	GA	SO	Avg	GP	W	L	Mins	GA	SO	Avg
1992-93	S.S. Marie	OHL	12	4	6	0	572	44	0	4.62	4	1	2	231	12	0	3.12
1993-94	S.S. Marie	OHL	55	28	14	6	2934	174	*2	3.56	14	*10	4	833	52	0	3.75
1994-95	S.S. Marie	OHL	45	15	26	2	2518	185	1	4.41	....	....	....	....	....	....	....
1995-96	S.S. Marie	OHL	13	9	3	0	641	43	0	4.02	....	....	....	....	....	....	....
	Guelph	OHL	17	12	2	2	1004	35	2	2.09	16	11	5	993	52	*2	3.14
1996-97	Binghamton	AHL	60	23	28	8	3367	199	3	3.55	4	1	3	236	13	0	3.31
1997-98	**NY Rangers**	**NHL**	**12**	**4**	**5**	**1**	**551**	**23**	**0**	**2.50**	....	....	....	....	....	....	....
	Hartford	AHL	24	12	8	3	1417	62	0	2.63	8	5	3	478	24	0	3.01
	NHL Totals		**12**	**4**	**5**	**1**	**551**	**23**	**0**	**2.50**	....	....	....	....	....	....	....

OHL Second All-Star Team (1996)

COCKELL, MATT VAN.

Goaltender. Catches left. 5'11", 195 lbs. Born, Calgary, Alta., May 4, 1979.
(Vancouver's 7th choice, 117th overall, in 1997 Entry Draft).

			Regular Season								Playoffs						
Season	Club	Lea	GP	W	L	T	Mins	GA	SO	Avg	GP	W	L	Mins	GA	SO	Avg
1996-97	Saskatoon	WHL	47	14	26	4	2609	175	0	4.02	....	....	....	....	....	....	....
1997-98	Saskatoon	WHL	22	6	11	1	1085	99	1	5.47	....	....	....	....	....	....	....
	Seattle	WHL	10	3	4	0	484	33	0	4.09	1	0	0	20	2	0	6.00

COUSINEAU, MARCEL (koo-ZEE-noh) NYI

Goaltender. Catches left. 5'9", 180 lbs. Born, Delson, Que., April 30, 1973.
(Boston's 3rd choice, 62nd overall, in 1991 Entry Draft).

			Regular Season								Playoffs						
Season	Club	Lea	GP	W	L	T	Mins	GA	SO	Avg	GP	W	L	Mins	GA	SO	Avg
1990-91	Beauport	QMJHL	49	13	29	3	2739	196	1	4.29	....	....	....	....	....	....	....
1991-92	Beauport	QMJHL	*67	26	32	5	*3673	241	0	3.94	....	....	....	....	....	....	....
1992-93	Drummondville	QMJHL	60	20	32	2	3298	225	0	4.09	9	3	6	498	37	*1	4.45
1993-94	St. John's	AHL	37	13	11	9	2015	118	0	3.51	....	....	....	....	....	....	....
1994-95	St. John's	AHL	58	22	27	6	3342	171	4	3.07	3	0	3	179	9	0	3.01
1995-96	St. John's	AHL	62	21	26	13	3629	192	1	3.17	4	1	3	258	11	0	2.56
1996-97	**Toronto**	**NHL**	**13**	**3**	**5**	**1**	**566**	**31**	**1**	**3.29**	....	....	....	....	....	....	....
	St. John's	AHL	19	7	8	3	1053	58	0	3.30	11	6	5	658	28	0	2.55
1997-98	**Toronto**	**NHL**	**2**	**0**	**0**	**0**	**17**	**0**	**0**	**0.00**	....	....	....	....	....	....	....
	St. John's	AHL	57	17	25	13	3306	167	1	3.03	4	1	3	254	10	0	2.36
	NHL Totals		**15**	**3**	**5**	**1**	**583**	**31**	**1**	**3.19**	....	....	....	....	....	....	....

Signed as a free agent by **Toronto**, November 13, 1993. Signed as a free agent by **NY Islanders**, July 29, 1998.

CRUICKSHANK, CURTIS (KRUHK-shank) WSH.

Goaltender. Catches left. 6'2", 209 lbs. Born, Ottawa, Ont., March 21, 1979.
(Washington's 3rd choice, 89th overall, in 1997 Entry Draft).

			Regular Season								Playoffs						
Season	Club	Lea	GP	W	L	T	Mins	GA	SO	Avg	GP	W	L	Mins	GA	SO	Avg
1996-97	Kingston	OHL	35	13	16	1	1792	118	2	3.95	1	0	1	26	4	0	9.23
1997-98	Kingston	OHL	57	30	20	4	3166	207	2	3.92	12	5	6	702	45	0	3.85

CRUZ, JOMAR WSH.

Goaltender. Catches left. 6'1", 177 lbs. Born, The Pas, Man., April 5, 1980.
(Washington's 1st choice, 49th overall, in 1998 Entry Draft).

			Regular Season								Playoffs						
Season	Club	Lea	GP	W	L	T	Mins	GA	SO	Avg	GP	W	L	Mins	GA	SO	Avg
1996-97	Notre Dame	SJHL	20	13	6	0	1107	71	2	3.84	....	....	....	....	....	....	....
1997-98	Brandon	WHL	30	16	19	1	1596	81	3	3.05	14	7	6	749	41	0	3.28

DAFOE, BYRON (day-FOH) BOS.

Goaltender. Catches left. 5'11", 190 lbs. Born, Sussex, England, February 25, 1971.
(Washington's 2nd choice, 35th overall, in 1989 Entry Draft).

			Regular Season								Playoffs						
Season	Club	Lea	GP	W	L	T	Mins	GA	SO	Avg	GP	W	L	Mins	GA	SO	Avg
1988-89	Portland	WHL	59	29	24	3	3279	291	1	5.32	*18	10	8	*1091	81	*1	4.45
1989-90	Portland	WHL	40	14	21	3	2265	193	0	5.11	....	....	....	....	....	....	....
1990-91	Portland	WHL	8	1	5	1	414	41	0	5.94	....	....	....	....	....	....	....
	Prince Albert	WHL	32	13	12	4	1839	124	0	4.05	....	....	....	....	....	....	....
1991-92	Baltimore	AHL	33	12	16	4	1847	119	0	3.87	....	....	....	....	....	....	....
	New Haven	AHL	7	3	2	1	364	22	0	3.63	....	....	....	....	....	....	....
	Hampton Roads	ECHL	10	6	4	0	562	26	0	2.78	....	....	....	....	....	....	....
1992-93	**Washington**	**NHL**	**1**	**0**	**0**	**0**	**1**	**0**	**0**	**0.00**	....	....	....	....	....	....	....
	Baltimore	AHL	48	16	20	7	2617	191	1	4.38	5	2	3	241	22	0	5.48
1993-94	**Washington**	**NHL**	**5**	**2**	**2**	**0**	**230**	**13**	**0**	**3.39**	**2**	**0**	**2**	**118**	**5**	**0**	**2.54**
	Portland	AHL	47	24	16	4	2661	148	1	3.34	1	0	0	9	1	0	6.79
1994-95	Phoenix	IHL	49	25	16	6	2743	169	2	3.70	....	....	....	....	....	....	....
	Washington	**NHL**	**4**	**1**	**1**	**1**	**187**	**11**	**0**	**3.53**	**1**	**0**	**0**	**20**	**1**	**0**	**3.00**
	Portland	AHL	6	5	0	0	330	16	0	2.91	7	3	4	416	29	0	4.18
1995-96	**Los Angeles**	**NHL**	**47**	**14**	**24**	**8**	**2666**	**172**	**1**	**3.87**	....	....	....	....	....	....	....
1996-97	**Los Angeles**	**NHL**	**40**	**13**	**17**	**5**	**2162**	**112**	**0**	**3.11**	....	....	....	....	....	....	....
1997-98	**Boston**	**NHL**	**65**	**30**	**25**	**9**	**3693**	**138**	**6**	**2.24**	**6**	**2**	**4**	**422**	**14**	**1**	**1.99**
	NHL Totals		**162**	**60**	**69**	**23**	**8939**	**446**	**7**	**2.99**	**9**	**2**	**6**	**560**	**20**	**1**	**2.14**

AHL First All-Star Team (1994) • Shared Harry "Hap" Holmes Trophy (fewest goals-against - AHL) with Olaf Kolzig (1994)

Traded to **Los Angeles** by **Washington** with Dimitri Khristich for Los Angeles' 1st round choice (Alexander Volchkov) and Dallas' 4th round choice (previously acquired, Washington selected Justin Davis) in 1996 Entry Draft, July 8, 1995. Traded to **Boston** by **Los Angeles** with Dimitri Khristich for Jozef Stumpel, Sandy Moger and Boston's 4th round choice (later traded to New Jersey - New Jersey selected Pierre Dagenais) in 1998 Entry Draft, August 29, 1997.

DAIGLE, SYLVAIN (DAYG) PHX.

Goaltender. Catches right. 5'8", 185 lbs. Born, St-Hyacinthe, Que., October 20, 1976.
(Winnipeg's 7th choice, 136th overall, in 1995 Entry Draft).

			Regular Season								Playoffs						
Season	Club	Lea	GP	W	L	T	Mins	GA	SO	Avg	GP	W	L	Mins	GA	SO	Avg
1993-94	Shawinigan	QMJHL	31	14	11	3	1645	113	0	4.12	....	....	....	....	....	....	....
1994-95	Shawinigan	QMJHL	48	27	17	3	2831	159	3	3.37	14	7	6	824	57	0	4.15
1995-96	Shawinigan	QMJHL	49	23	14	5	2708	159	*3	3.52	6	2	4	389	22	0	3.39
1996-97	Springfield	AHL	13	8	3	0	691	23	1	2.00	6	1	4	311	18	0	3.47
	Mississippi	ECHL	34	20	8	5	1951	100	2	3.08	....	....	....	....	....	....	....
	Las Vegas	IHL	1	0	0	0	41	5	0	7.17	....	....	....	....	....	....	....
1997-98	Springfield	AHL	21	7	9	2	1093	68	0	3.73	2	0	0	23	0	0	0.00

Transfered to **Phoenix** after **Winnipeg** franchise relocated, July 1, 1996.

DAMPHOUSSE, JEAN-FRANCOIS (DAHM-fooz) N.J.

Goaltender. Catches left. 6', 175 lbs. Born, St-Alexis-des-Monts, Que., July 21, 1979.
(New Jersey's 1st choice, 24th overall, in 1997 Entry Draft).

			Regular Season								Playoffs						
Season	**Club**	**Lea**	**GP**	**W**	**L**	**T**	**Mins**	**GA**	**SO**	**Avg**	**GP**	**W**	**L**	**Mins**	**GA**	**SO**	**Avg**
1996-97	Moncton	QMJHL	39	6	25	2	2063	190	0	5.53	....	....	....	....	....	....	....
1997-98	Moncton	QMJHL	59	24	26	6	3400	174	1	3.07	10	5	5	595	28	0	2.82

DAUBENSPECK, KIRK (DAW-behn-spehk) CHI.

Goaltender. Catches left. 6', 190 lbs. Born, Madison, WI, July 16, 1974.
(Philadelphia's 6th choice, 151st overall, in 1992 Entry Draft).

			Regular Season								Playoffs						
Season	**Club**	**Lea**	**GP**	**W**	**L**	**T**	**Mins**	**GA**	**SO**	**Avg**	**GP**	**W**	**L**	**Mins**	**GA**	**SO**	**Avg**
1991-92	Culver Academy	H.S.	20	....	....	....	1190	57	0	2.88	....	....	....	....	....	....	....
1992-93	U. of Wisconsin	WCHA						DID NOT PLAY – FRESHMAN									
1993-94	U. of Wisconsin	WCHA	7	2	2	0	280	19	0	4.07	....	....	....	....	....	....	....
1994-95	U. of Wisconsin	WCHA	42	*23	15	4	*2503	146	0	3.51	....	....	....	....	....	....	....
1995-96	U. of Wisconsin	WCHA	*39	*17	20	2	*2357	151	0	3.84	....	....	....	....	....	....	....
1996-97	U. of Wisconsin	WCHA	33	13	18	2	1925	124	1	3.86	....	....	....	....	....	....	....
1997-98	Jacksonville	ECHL	32	20	9	2	1865	92	1	2.96	....	....	....	....	....	....	....
	Indianapolis	IHL	18	6	9	0	953	58	0	3.65	....	....	....	....	....	....	....

WCHA Second All-Star Team (1997) • NCAA West Second All-American Team (1997)

Traded to **Ottawa** by **Philadelphia** with Claude Boivin for Mark Lamb, March 5, 1994. Traded to **Chicago** by **Ottawa** for Ottawa's 6th round choice (previously acquired, Ottawa selected Christopher Neil) in 1998 Entry Draft and future considerations, September 23, 1997.

DEGAGNE, SHAWN (duh-GAH-nyay) NYR

Goaltender. Catches left. 5'11", 164 lbs. Born, North Bay, Ont., December 18, 1978.
(NY Rangers' 8th choice, 154th overall, in 1997 Entry Draft).

			Regular Season								Playoffs						
Season	**Club**	**Lea**	**GP**	**W**	**L**	**T**	**Mins**	**GA**	**SO**	**Avg**	**GP**	**W**	**L**	**Mins**	**GA**	**SO**	**Avg**
1995-96	Kitchener	OHL	3	0	1	0	53	5	0	5.66	....	....	....	....	....	....	....
1996-97	Kitchener	OHL	25	12	5	1	1111	61	0	3.29	6	0	1	168	8	0	2.86
1997-98	Kitchener	OHL	38	12	15	5	1863	125	0	4.03	4	0	1	132	9	0	4.09

DENIS, MARC (deh-NEE) COL.

Goaltender. Catches left. 6', 188 lbs. Born, Montreal, Que., August 1, 1977.
(Colorado's 1st choice, 25th overall, in 1995 Entry Draft).

			Regular Season								Playoffs						
Season	**Club**	**Lea**	**GP**	**W**	**L**	**T**	**Mins**	**GA**	**SO**	**Avg**	**GP**	**W**	**L**	**Mins**	**GA**	**SO**	**Avg**
1994-95	Chicoutimi	QMJHL	32	17	9	1	1688	98	0	3.48	6	4	2	372	19	1	3.06
1995-96	Chicoutimi	QMJHL	51	23	21	4	2951	157	2	3.19	16	8	8	957	69	0	4.33
1996-97	Chicoutimi	QMJHL	41	22	15	2	2323	104	4	*2.69	*21	*11	10	*1229	70	*1	3.42
	Colorado	**NHL**	**1**	**0**	**1**	**0**	**60**	**3**	**0**	**3.00**	....	....	....	....	....	....	....
	Hershey	AHL	....	....	....	....	....	....	....	....	4	1	0	56	1	0	1.08
1997-98	Hershey	AHL	47	17	23	4	2588	125	1	2.90	6	3	3	346	15	0	2.59
	NHL Totals		**1**	**0**	**1**	**0**	**60**	**3**	**0**	**3.00**	....	....	....	....	....	....	....

QMJHL First All-Star Team (1997) • Canadian Major Junior First All-Star Team (1997) • Canadian Major Junior Goaltender of the Year (1997)

DeROUVILLE, PHILIPPE (deh-ROO-vihl)

Goaltender. Catches left. 6'1", 185 lbs. Born, Victoriaville, Que., August 7, 1974.
(Pittsburgh's 5th choice, 115th overall, in 1992 Entry Draft).

			Regular Season								Playoffs						
Season	**Club**	**Lea**	**GP**	**W**	**L**	**T**	**Mins**	**GA**	**SO**	**Avg**	**GP**	**W**	**L**	**Mins**	**GA**	**SO**	**Avg**
1990-91	Longueuil	QMJHL	20	13	6	0	1030	50	0	2.91	....	....	....	....	....	....	....
1991-92	Verdun	QMJHL	34	20	6	3	1854	99	2	3.20	11	7	3	593	28	1	2.83
1992-93	Verdun	QMJHL	61	30	27	2	3491	210	1	3.61	4	0	4	256	18	0	3.61
1993-94	Verdun	QMJHL	51	28	22	0	2845	145	1	*3.06	4	0	4	210	14	0	4.00
1994-95	Cleveland	IHL	41	24	10	5	2369	131	1	3.32	4	1	3	263	18	0	4.09
	Pittsburgh	**NHL**	**1**	**1**	**0**	**0**	**60**	**3**	**0**	**3.00**	....	....	....	....	....	....	....
1995-96	Cleveland	IHL	38	19	11	3	2008	129	1	3.86	....	....	....	....	....	....	....
1996-97	**Pittsburgh**	**NHL**	**2**	**0**	**2**	**0**	**111**	**6**	**0**	**3.24**	....	....	....	....	....	....	....
	Kansas City	IHL	26	11	11	4	1470	69	2	2.82	2	0	1	32	4	0	7.35
1997-98	Louisville	ECHL	8	5	2	1	480	27	0	3.38	....	....	....	....	....	....	....
	Hartford	AHL	3	0	2	1	184	10	0	3.26	....	....	....	....	....	....	....
	Utica	IHL	30	18	9	1	1524	65	3	2.56	2	1	1	129	7	0	3.25
	NHL Totals		**3**	**1**	**2**	**0**	**171**	**9**	**0**	**3.16**	....	....	....	....	....	....	....

QMJHL Second All-Star Team (1993, 1994)

DESROCHERS, PATRICK PHX.

Goaltender. Catches left. 6'3", 195 lbs. Born, Penetang, Ont., October 27, 1979.
(Phoenix's 1st choice, 14th overall, in 1998 Entry Draft).

			Regular Season								Playoffs						
Season	**Club**	**Lea**	**GP**	**W**	**L**	**T**	**Mins**	**GA**	**SO**	**Avg**	**GP**	**W**	**L**	**Mins**	**GA**	**SO**	**Avg**
1995-96	Sarnia	OHL	29	12	6	2	1265	96	0	4.55	3	0	1	71	5	0	4.23
1996-97	Sarnia	OHL	50	22	17	4	2667	154	4	3.46	11	6	5	576	42	0	4.38
1997-98	Sarnia	OHL	56	26	17	11	3205	179	1	3.35	4	1	2	160	12	0	4.50

DOVIGI, PATRICK EDM.

Goaltender. Catches left. 6', 180 lbs. Born, Sault Ste. Marie, Ont., July 2, 1979.
(Edmonton's 2nd choice, 41st overall, in 1997 Entry Draft).

			Regular Season								Playoffs						
Season	**Club**	**Lea**	**GP**	**W**	**L**	**T**	**Mins**	**GA**	**SO**	**Avg**	**GP**	**W**	**L**	**Mins**	**GA**	**SO**	**Avg**
1995-96	Elmira	OJHL	33	10	12	1	....	....	4	4.53	....	....	....	....	....	....	....
1996-97	Erie	OHL	36	11	14	4	1764	114	3	3.88	5	1	4	303	18	0	3.56
1997-98	Erie	OHL	41	17	17	2	2174	161	0	4.44	....	....	....	....	....	....	....

DUNHAM, MICHAEL (DUHN-uhm) NSH.

Goaltender. Catches left. 6'3", 200 lbs. Born, Johnson City, NY, June 1, 1972.
(New Jersey's 4th choice, 53rd overall, in 1990 Entry Draft).

			Regular Season								Playoffs						
Season	**Club**	**Lea**	**GP**	**W**	**L**	**T**	**Mins**	**GA**	**SO**	**Avg**	**GP**	**W**	**L**	**Mins**	**GA**	**SO**	**Avg**
1989-90	Canterbury	H.S.	32	....	....	....	1558	68	3	1.96	....	....	....	....	....	....	....
1990-91	U. of Maine	H.E.	23	14	5	2	1275	63	0	*2.96	....	....	....	....	....	....	....
1991-92	U. of Maine	H.E.	7	6	0	0	382	14	1	2.20	....	....	....	....	....	....	....
	United States	Nat-Tm	3	0	1	1	157	10	0	3.82	....	....	....	....	....	....	....
	United States	Olympics						DID NOT PLAY – SPARE GOALTENDER									
1992-93	U. of Maine	H.E.	25	*21	1	1	1429	63	0	2.65	....	....	....	....	....	....	....
1993-94	United States	Nat-Tm	33	22	9	2	1983	125	2	3.78	....	....	....	....	....	....	....
	United States	Olympics	3	0	1	2	180	15	0	5.00	....	....	....	....	....	....	....
	Albany	AHL	5	2	2	1	304	26	0	5.12	....	....	....	....	....	....	....
1994-95	Albany	AHL	35	20	7	8	2120	99	1	2.80	7	6	1	419	20	1	2.86
1995-96	Albany	AHL	44	30	10	2	2592	109	1	2.52	3	1	2	182	5	1	1.65
1996-97	**New Jersey**	**NHL**	**26**	**8**	**7**	**1**	**1013**	**43**	**2**	**2.55**	....	....	....	....	....	....	....
	Albany	AHL	3	1	1	1	184	12	0	3.91	....	....	....	....	....	....	....
1997-98	**New Jersey**	**NHL**	**15**	**5**	**5**	**3**	**773**	**29**	**1**	**2.25**	....	....	....	....	....	....	....
	NHL Totals		**41**	**13**	**12**	**4**	**1786**	**72**	**3**	**2.42**	....	....	....	....	....	....	....

Hockey East First All-Star Team (1993) • NCAA East First All-American Team (1993) • Shared Harry "Hap" Holmes Memorial Trophy (fewest goals against - AHL) with Corey Schwab (1995) • Shared Jack A. Butterfield Trophy (Playoff MVP - AHL) with Corey Schwab (1995) • AHL Second All-Star Team (1996) • Shared William M. Jennings Trophy with Martin Brodeur (1997)

Claimed by **Nashville** from **New Jersey** in Expansion Draft, June 26, 1998.

ELLIOT, JASON DET.

Goaltender. Catches left. 6'2", 183 lbs. Born, Inuvik, N.W.T., November 10, 1975.
(Detroit's 7th choice, 205th overall, in 1994 Entry Draft).

			Regular Season								Playoffs						
Season	**Club**	**Lea**	**GP**	**W**	**L**	**T**	**Mins**	**GA**	**SO**	**Avg**	**GP**	**W**	**L**	**Mins**	**GA**	**SO**	**Avg**
1993-94	Kimberley	RMJHL						STATISTICS NOT AVAILABLE									
1994-95	Cornell	ECAC	16	3	11	1	877	62	0	4.24	....	....	....	....	....	....	....
1995-96	Cornell	ECAC	19	12	2	1	971	38	2	2.35	....	....	....	....	....	....	....
1996-97	Cornell	ECAC	27	16	7	2	1475	67	0	2.73	....	....	....	....	....	....	....
1997-98	Cornell	ECAC	29	14	12	2	1683	74	2	2.64	....	....	....	....	....	....	....

ECAC Second All-Star Team (1998)

ESCHE, ROBERT (EHSH) PHX.

Goaltender. Catches left. 6', 188 lbs. Born, Utica, NY, January 22, 1978.
(Phoenix's 5th choice, 139th overall, in 1996 Entry Draft).

			Regular Season								Playoffs						
Season	**Club**	**Lea**	**GP**	**W**	**L**	**T**	**Mins**	**GA**	**SO**	**Avg**	**GP**	**W**	**L**	**Mins**	**GA**	**SO**	**Avg**
1995-96	Detroit	OHL	23	13	6	0	1219	76	1	3.74	3	0	2	105	4	0	2.29
1996-97	Detroit	OHL	58	24	28	2	3241	206	2	3.81	5	1	4	317	19	0	3.60
1997-98	Plymouth	OHL	48	29	13	4	2810	135	3	2.88	15	8	7	869	45	0	3.11

OHL Second All-Star Team (1998)

ESSENSA, BOB (EH-sehn-suh) EDM.

Goaltender. Catches left. 6', 188 lbs. Born, Toronto, Ont., January 14, 1965.
(Winnipeg's 5th choice, 71st overall, in 1983 Entry Draft).

			Regular Season								Playoffs						
Season	**Club**	**Lea**	**GP**	**W**	**L**	**T**	**Mins**	**GA**	**SO**	**Avg**	**GP**	**W**	**L**	**Mins**	**GA**	**SO**	**Avg**
1982-83	Henry Carr	H.S.	31	....	....	....	1840	98	2	3.20	....	....	....	....	....	....	....
1983-84	Michigan State	CCHA	17	11	4	0	946	44	2	2.79	....	....	....	....	....	....	....
1984-85	Michigan State	CCHA	18	15	2	0	1059	29	2	1.64	....	....	....	....	....	....	....
1985-86	Michigan State	CCHA	23	17	4	1	1333	74	1	3.33	....	....	....	....	....	....	....
1986-87	Michigan State	CCHA	25	19	3	1	1383	64	2	2.78	....	....	....	....	....	....	....
1987-88	Moncton	AHL	27	7	11	1	1287	100	1	4.66	....	....	....	....	....	....	....
1988-89	**Winnipeg**	**NHL**	**20**	**6**	**8**	**3**	**1102**	**68**	**1**	**3.70**	....	....	....	....	....	....	....
	Fort Wayne	IHL	22	14	7	0	1287	70	0	3.26	....	....	....	....	....	....	....
1989-90	**Winnipeg**	**NHL**	**36**	**18**	**9**	**5**	**2035**	**107**	**1**	**3.15**	**4**	**2**	**1**	**206**	**12**	**0**	**3.50**
	Moncton	AHL	6	3	3	0	358	15	0	2.51	....	....	....	....	....	....	....
1990-91	**Winnipeg**	**NHL**	**55**	**19**	**24**	**6**	**2916**	**153**	**4**	**3.15**	....	....	....	....	....	....	....
	Moncton	AHL	2	1	0	1	125	6	0	2.88	....	....	....	....	....	....	....
1991-92	**Winnipeg**	**NHL**	**47**	**21**	**17**	**6**	**2627**	**126**	***5**	**2.88**	**1**	**0**	**0**	**33**	**3**	**0**	**5.45**
1992-93	**Winnipeg**	**NHL**	**67**	**33**	**26**	**6**	**3855**	**227**	**2**	**3.53**	**6**	**2**	**4**	**367**	**20**	**0**	**3.27**
1993-94	**Winnipeg**	**NHL**	**56**	**19**	**30**	**6**	**3136**	**201**	**1**	**3.85**	....	....	....	....	....	....	....
	Detroit	**NHL**	**13**	**4**	**7**	**2**	**778**	**34**	**1**	**2.62**	**2**	**0**	**2**	**109**	**9**	**0**	**4.95**
1994-95	San Diego	IHL	16	6	8	1	919	52	0	3.39	1	0	1	59	3	0	3.05
1995-96	Adirondack	AHL	3	1	2	0	179	11	0	3.69	....	....	....	....	....	....	....
	Fort Wayne	IHL	45	24	14	5	2529	122	1	2.89	5	2	3	299	12	0	2.41
1996-97	**Edmonton**	**NHL**	**19**	**4**	**8**	**0**	**868**	**41**	**1**	**2.83**	....	....	....	....	....	....	....
1997-98	**Edmonton**	**NHL**	**16**	**6**	**6**	**1**	**825**	**35**	**0**	**2.55**	**1**	**0**	**0**	**27**	**1**	**0**	**2.22**
	NHL Totals		**329**	**130**	**135**	**35**	**18142**	**992**	**16**	**3.28**	**14**	**4**	**7**	**742**	**45**	**0**	**3.64**

CCHA First All-Star Team (1985) • CCHA Second All-Star Team (1986) • NHL All-Rookie Team (1990)

Traded to **Detroit** by **Winnipeg** with Sergei Bautin for Tim Cheveldae and Dallas Drake, March 8, 1994. Traded to **Edmonton** by **Detroit** for future considerations, June 14, 1996.

FANKHOUSER, SCOTT ST.L.

Goaltender. Catches left. 6'2", 195 lbs. Born, Bismark, ND, July 1, 1975.
(St. Louis' 8th choice, 276th overall, in 1994 Entry Draft).

			Regular Season								Playoffs						
Season	**Club**	**Lea**	**GP**	**W**	**L**	**T**	**Mins**	**GA**	**SO**	**Avg**	**GP**	**W**	**L**	**Mins**	**GA**	**SO**	**Avg**
1993-94	Loomis-Chaffe	H.S.						STATISTICS NOT AVAILABLE									
1994-95	Lowell	H.E.	11	4	4	1	499	37	0	4.44	....	....	....	....	....	....	....
1995-96	Melfort	SJHL	45	....	....	....	2544	109	....	2.57	....	....	....	....	....	....	....
1996-97	Lowell	H.E.	11	2	4	1	517	38	0	4.41	....	....	....	....	....	....	....
1997-98	Lowell	H.E.	16	4	7	2	798	48	0	3.61	....	....	....	....	....	....	....

FERNANDEZ, MANNY — DAL.

Goaltender. Catches left. 6', 185 lbs. Born, Etobicoke, Ont., August 27, 1974.
(Quebec's 4th choice, 52nd overall, in 1992 Entry Draft).

			Regular Season								Playoffs						
Season	Club	Lea	GP	W	L	T	Mins	GA	SO	Avg	GP	W	L	Mins	GA	SO	Avg
1991-92	Laval	QMJHL	31	14	13	2	1593	99	1	3.73	9	3	5	468	39	0	5.00
1992-93	Laval	QMJHL	43	26	14	2	2347	141	1	3.60	13	*12	1	818	42	0	3.08
1993-94	Laval	QMJHL	51	29	14	1	2776	143	*5	3.09	19	14	5	1116	49	*1	*2.63
1994-95	Kalamazoo	IHL	46	21	10	9	2470	115	2	2.79	14	10	2	753	34	1	2.71
	Dallas	**NHL**	**1**	**0**	**1**	**0**	**59**	**3**	**0**	**3.05**	....	....	....	....	....	....	....
1995-96	**Dallas**	**NHL**	**5**	**0**	**1**	**1**	**249**	**19**	**0**	**4.58**	....	....	....	....	....	....	....
	Michigan	IHL	47	22	15	9	2664	133	*4	3.00	6	5	1	372	14	0	*2.26
1996-97	Michigan	IHL	48	20	24	2	2720	142	2	3.13	4	1	3	277	15	0	3.25
1997-98	**Dallas**	**NHL**	**2**	**1**	**0**	**0**	**69**	**2**	**0**	**1.74**	**1**	**0**	**0**	**2**	**0**	**0**	**0.00**
	Michigan	IHL	55	27	17	5	3022	139	5	2.76	2	0	2	88	7	0	4.73
	NHL Totals		**8**	**1**	**2**	**1**	**377**	**24**	**0**	**3.82**	**1**	**0**	**0**	**2**	**0**	**0**	**0.00**

QMJHL First All-Star Team (1994) • IHL Second All-Star Team (1995)

Rights traded to **Dallas** by **Quebec** for Tommy Sjodin and Dallas' 3rd round choice (Chris Drury) in 1994 Entry Draft, February 13, 1994.

FICHAUD, ERIC — (FEE-shoh) EDM.

Goaltender. Catches left. 5'11", 171 lbs. Born, Anjou, Que., November 4, 1975.
(Toronto's 1st choice, 16th overall, in 1994 Entry Draft).

			Regular Season								Playoffs						
Season	Club	Lea	GP	W	L	T	Mins	GA	SO	Avg	GP	W	L	Mins	GA	SO	Avg
1992-93	Chicoutimi	QMJHL	43	18	13	1	2039	149	0	4.38	....	....	....	....	....	....	....
1993-94	Chicoutimi	QMJHL	*63	*37	21	3	*3493	192	4	3.30	*26	*16	10	*1560	86	*1	3.31
1994-95	Chicoutimi	QMJHL	46	21	19	4	2637	151	4	3.44	7	2	5	428	20	0	2.80
1995-96	**NY Islanders**	**NHL**	**24**	**7**	**12**	**2**	**1234**	**68**	**1**	**3.31**	....	....	....	....	....	....	....
	Worcester	AHL	34	13	15	6	1989	97	1	2.93	2	1	1	127	7	0	3.30
1996-97	**NY Islanders**	**NHL**	**34**	**9**	**14**	**4**	**1759**	**91**	**0**	**3.10**	....	....	....	....	....	....	....
1997-98	**NY Islanders**	**NHL**	**17**	**3**	**8**	**3**	**807**	**40**	**0**	**2.97**	....	....	....	....	....	....	....
	Utica	IHL	1	0	0	0	40	3	0	4.45	....	....	....	....	....	....	....
	NHL Totals		**75**	**19**	**34**	**9**	**3800**	**199**	**1**	**3.14**	....	....	....	....	....	....	....

Canadian Major Junior Second All-Star Team (1994) • Memorial Cup All-Star Team (1994) • Won Hap Emms Memorial Trophy (Memorial Cup Tournament Top Goaltender) (1994) • QMJHL First All-Star Team (1995)

Traded to **NY Islanders** by **Toronto** for Benoit Hogue, NY Islanders' 3rd round choice (Ryan Pepperall) in 1995 Entry Draft and 5th round choice (Brandon Sugden) in 1996 Entry Draft, April 6, 1995. Traded to **Edmonton** by **NY Islanders** for Mike Watt, June 14, 1998.

FISCHER, KAI — (FIH-shuhr, KIGH) COL.

Goaltender. Catches left. 5'11", 176 lbs. Born, Forst, Germany, March 25, 1977.
(Colorado's 8th choice, 160th overall, in 1996 Entry Draft).

			Regular Season								Playoffs						
Season	Club	Lea	GP	W	L	T	Mins	GA	SO	Avg	GP	W	L	Mins	GA	SO	Avg
1995-96	Dusseldorf	Ger-Jr.						STATISTICS NOT AVAILABLE									
1996-97	Dusseldorf	Germany	2	....	....	....	125	7	0	3.36	....	....	....	....	....	....	....
1997-98	Bremerhaven	Ger-2	45	....	....	....	2674	172	....	3.86	....	....	....	....	....	....	....

FISET, STEPHANE — (fih-SEHT) L.A.

Goaltender. Catches left. 6'1", 198 lbs. Born, Montreal, Que., June 17, 1970.
(Quebec's 3rd choice, 24th overall, in 1988 Entry Draft).

			Regular Season								Playoffs						
Season	Club	Lea	GP	W	L	T	Mins	GA	SO	Avg	GP	W	L	Mins	GA	SO	Avg
1987-88	Victoriaville	QMJHL	40	15	17	4	2221	146	1	3.94	2	0	2	163	10	0	3.68
1988-89	Victoriaville	QMJHL	43	25	14	0	2401	138	1	*3.45	12	*9	2	711	33	0	*2.78
1989-90	**Quebec**	**NHL**	**6**	**0**	**5**	**1**	**342**	**34**	**0**	**5.96**	....	....	....	....	....	....	....
	Victoriaville	QMJHL	24	14	6	3	1383	63	1	*2.73	*14	7	6	*790	49	0	3.72
1990-91	**Quebec**	**NHL**	**3**	**0**	**2**	**1**	**186**	**12**	**0**	**3.87**	....	....	....	....	....	....	....
	Halifax	AHL	36	10	15	8	1902	131	0	4.13	....	....	....	....	....	....	....
1991-92	**Quebec**	**NHL**	**23**	**7**	**10**	**2**	**1133**	**71**	**1**	**3.76**	....	....	....	....	....	....	....
	Halifax	AHL	29	8	14	6	1675	110	*3	3.94	....	....	....	....	....	....	....
1992-93	**Quebec**	**NHL**	**37**	**18**	**9**	**4**	**1939**	**110**	**0**	**3.40**	**1**	**0**	**0**	**21**	**1**	**0**	**2.86**
	Halifax	AHL	3	2	1	0	180	11	0	3.67	....	....	....	....	....	....	....
1993-94	**Quebec**	**NHL**	**50**	**20**	**25**	**4**	**2798**	**158**	**2**	**3.39**	....	....	....	....	....	....	....
	Cornwall	AHL	1	0	1	0	60	4	0	4.00	....	....	....	....	....	....	....
1994-95	**Quebec**	**NHL**	**32**	**17**	**10**	**3**	**1879**	**87**	**2**	**2.78**	**4**	**1**	**2**	**209**	**16**	**0**	**4.59**
1995-96	**Colorado**	**NHL**	**37**	**22**	**6**	**7**	**2107**	**103**	**1**	**2.93**	**1**	**0**	**0**	**1**	**0**	**0**	**0.00** ♦
1996-97	**Los Angeles**	**NHL**	**44**	**13**	**24**	**5**	**2482**	**132**	**4**	**3.19**	....	....	....	....	....	....	....
1997-98	**Los Angeles**	**NHL**	**60**	**26**	**25**	**8**	**3497**	**158**	**2**	**2.71**	**2**	**0**	**2**	**93**	**7**	**0**	**4.52**
	NHL Totals		**292**	**123**	**116**	**35**	**16363**	**865**	**12**	**3.17**	**8**	**1**	**4**	**324**	**24**	**0**	**4.44**

QMJHL First All-Star Team (1989) • Canadian Major Junior Goaltender of the Year (1989)

Transferred to **Colorado** after **Quebec** franchise relocated, June 21, 1995. Traded to **Los Angeles** by **Colorado** with Colorado's 1st round choice (Mathieu Biron) in 1998 Entry Draft for Eric Lacroix and Los Angeles' 1st round choice (Martin Skoula) in 1998 Entry Draft, June 20, 1996.

FITZPATRICK, MARK — CHI.

Goaltender. Catches left. 6'2", 198 lbs. Born, Toronto, Ont., November 13, 1968.
(Los Angeles' 2nd choice, 27th overall, in 1987 Entry Draft).

			Regular Season								Playoffs						
Season	Club	Lea	GP	W	L	T	Mins	GA	SO	Avg	GP	W	L	Mins	GA	SO	Avg
1984-85	Medicine Hat	WHL	3	1	2	0	180	9	0	3.00	1	0	0	20	2	0	6.00
1985-86	Medicine Hat	WHL	41	26	6	1	2074	99	1	*2.86	*19	*11	5	*986	58	0	3.53
1986-87	Medicine Hat	WHL	50	31	11	4	2844	159	4	3.35	20	12	8	1224	71	1	3.48
1987-88	Medicine Hat	WHL	63	36	15	6	3600	194	2	3.23	16	12	4	959	52	*1	*3.25
1988-89	**Los Angeles**	**NHL**	**17**	**6**	**7**	**3**	**957**	**64**	**0**	**4.01**	....	....	....	....	....	....	....
	New Haven	AHL	18	10	5	1	980	54	1	3.31	....	....	....	....	....	....	....
	NY Islanders	**NHL**	**11**	**3**	**5**	**2**	**627**	**41**	**0**	**3.92**	....	....	....	....	....	....	....
1989-90	**NY Islanders**	**NHL**	**47**	**19**	**19**	**5**	**2653**	**150**	**3**	**3.39**	**4**	**0**	**2**	**152**	**13**	**0**	**5.13**
1990-91	**NY Islanders**	**NHL**	**2**	**1**	**1**	**0**	**120**	**6**	**0**	**3.00**	....	....	....	....	....	....	....
	Capital District	AHL	12	3	7	2	734	47	0	3.84	....	....	....	....	....	....	....
1991-92	**NY Islanders**	**NHL**	**30**	**11**	**13**	**5**	**1743**	**93**	**0**	**3.20**	....	....	....	....	....	....	....
	Capital District	AHL	14	6	5	1	782	39	0	2.99	....	....	....	....	....	....	....
1992-93	**NY Islanders**	**NHL**	**39**	**17**	**15**	**5**	**2253**	**130**	**0**	**3.46**	**3**	**0**	**1**	**77**	**4**	**0**	**3.12**
	Capital District	AHL	5	1	3	1	284	18	0	3.80	....	....	....	....	....	....	....
1993-94	**Florida**	**NHL**	**28**	**12**	**8**	**6**	**1603**	**73**	**1**	**2.73**	....	....	....	....	....	....	....
1994-95	**Florida**	**NHL**	**15**	**6**	**7**	**2**	**819**	**36**	**2**	**2.64**	....	....	....	....	....	....	....
1995-96	**Florida**	**NHL**	**34**	**15**	**11**	**3**	**1786**	**88**	**0**	**2.96**	**2**	**0**	**0**	**60**	**6**	**0**	**6.00**
1996-97	**Florida**	**NHL**	**30**	**8**	**9**	**9**	**1680**	**66**	**0**	**2.36**	....	....	....	....	....	....	....
1997-98	**Florida**	**NHL**	**12**	**2**	**7**	**2**	**640**	**32**	**1**	**3.00**	....	....	....	....	....	....	....
	Fort Wayne	IHL	2	1	1	0	119	8	0	4.03	....	....	....	....	....	....	....
	Tampa Bay	**NHL**	**34**	**7**	**24**	**1**	**1938**	**102**	**1**	**3.16**	....	....	....	....	....	....	....
	NHL Totals		**299**	**107**	**126**	**43**	**16819**	**881**	**8**	**3.14**	**9**	**0**	**3**	**289**	**23**	**0**	**4.78**

WHL East Second All-Star Team (1986, 1988) • Won Hap Emms Memorial Trophy (Memorial Cup Tournament Top Goaltender) (1987, 1988) • Won Bill Masterton Memorial Trophy (1992)

Traded to **NY Islanders** by **Los Angeles** with Wayne McBean and future considerations (Doug Crossman, May 23, 1989) for Kelly Hrudey, February 22, 1989. Traded to **Quebec** by **NY Islanders** with NY Islanders' 1st round choice (Adam Deadmarsh) in 1993 Entry Draft for Ron Hextall and Quebec's 1st round choice (Todd Bertuzzi) in 1993 Entry Draft, June 20, 1993. Claimed by **Florida** from **Quebec** in Expansion Draft, June 24, 1993. Traded to **Tampa Bay** by **Florida** with Jody Hull for Dino Ciccarelli and Jeff Norton, January 15, 1998. Traded to **Chicago** by **Tampa Bay** with Tampa Bay's 4th round choice in 1999 Entry Draft for Michal Sykora, July 17, 1998.

FLAHERTY, WADE — (FLAY-uhr-tee) NYI

Goaltender. Catches left. 6', 170 lbs. Born, Terrace, B.C., January 11, 1968.
(Buffalo's 10th choice, 181st overall, in 1988 Entry Draft).

			Regular Season								Playoffs						
Season	Club	Lea	GP	W	L	T	Mins	GA	SO	Avg	GP	W	L	Mins	GA	SO	Avg
1984-85	Kelowna	WHL	1	0	0	0	55	5	0	5.45	....	....	....	....	....	....	....
1985-86	Seattle	WHL	9	1	3	0	271	36	0	7.97	....	....	....	....	....	....	....
	Spokane	WHL	5	0	3	0	161	21	0	7.83	....	....	....	....	....	....	....
1986-87	Victoria	WHL	3	0	2	0	127	16	0	7.56	....	....	....	....	....	....	....
1987-88	Victoria	WHL	36	20	15	0	2052	135	0	3.95	5	2	3	300	18	0	3.60
1988-89	Victoria	WHL	42	21	19	0	2408	180	4	4.49	....	....	....	....	....	....	....
1989-90	Greensboro	ECHL	27	12	10	0	1308	96	0	4.40	....	....	....	....	....	....	....
1990-91	Kansas City	IHL	*56	16	31	4	2990	224	0	4.49	....	....	....	....	....	....	....
1991-92	**San Jose**	**NHL**	**3**	**0**	**3**	**0**	**178**	**13**	**0**	**4.38**	....	....	....	....	....	....	....
	Kansas City	IHL	43	26	14	3	2603	140	1	3.23	1	0	0	1	0	0	0.00
1992-93	**San Jose**	**NHL**	**1**	**0**	**1**	**0**	**60**	**5**	**0**	**5.00**	....	....	....	....	....	....	....
	Kansas City	IHL	*61	*34	19	7	*3642	195	2	3.21	*12	6	6	733	34	*1	2.78
1993-94	Kansas City	IHL	*60	32	19	9	*3564	202	0	3.40	....	....	....	....	....	....	....
1994-95	**San Jose**	**NHL**	**18**	**5**	**6**	**1**	**852**	**44**	**1**	**3.10**	**7**	**2**	**3**	**377**	**31**	**0**	**4.93**
1995-96	**San Jose**	**NHL**	**24**	**3**	**12**	**1**	**1137**	**92**	**0**	**4.85**	....	....	....	....	....	....	....
1996-97	**San Jose**	**NHL**	**7**	**2**	**4**	**0**	**359**	**31**	**0**	**5.18**	....	....	....	....	....	....	....
	Kentucky	AHL	19	8	6	2	1032	54	1	3.14	3	1	2	200	11	0	3.30
1997-98	**NY Islanders**	**NHL**	**16**	**4**	**4**	**3**	**694**	**23**	**3**	**1.99**	....	....	....	....	....	....	....
	Utah	IHL	24	16	5	3	1341	40	3	1.79	....	....	....	....	....	....	....
	NHL Totals		**69**	**14**	**30**	**5**	**3280**	**208**	**4**	**3.80**	**7**	**2**	**3**	**377**	**31**	**0**	**4.93**

WHL West Second All-Star Team (1988) • Playoff MVP - ECHL (1990) • Shared James Norris Memorial Trophy (fewest goals against - IHL) with Arturs Irbe (1992) • IHL Second All-Star Team (1993, 1994)

Signed as a free agent by **San Jose**, September 3, 1991. Signed as a free agent by **NY Islanders**, July 22, 1997.

FORSBERG, JONAS — (FOHRZ-buhrg, YOH-nuhs) S.J.

Goaltender. Catches left. 5'10", 160 lbs. Born, Stockholm, Sweden, June 15, 1975.
(San Jose's 12th choice, 210th overall, in 1993 Entry Draft).

			Regular Season								Playoffs						
Season	Club	Lea	GP	W	L	T	Mins	GA	SO	Avg	GP	W	L	Mins	GA	SO	Avg
1992-93	Djurgarden	Swe-Jr.	41	....	....	....	....	....	....	2.78	....	....	....	....	....	....	....
1993-94	Djurgarden	Sweden	1	....	....	....	60	4	....	4.00	....	....	....	....	....	....	....
1994-95	Djurgarden	Sweden	1	....	....	....	60	6	....	6.00	....	....	....	....	....	....	....
1995-96	Djurgarden	Sweden						DID NOT PLAY – INJURED									
1996-97	Manglerud Star	Norway						STATISTICS NOT AVAILABLE									
1997-98	Sodertalje	Sweden	23	....	....	....	1252	60	....	2.88	....	....	....	....	....	....	....

FOUNTAIN, MIKE — CAR.

Goaltender. Catches left. 6'1", 176 lbs. Born, North York, Ont., January 26, 1972.
(Vancouver's 3rd choice, 45th overall, in 1992 Entry Draft).

			Regular Season								Playoffs						
Season	Club	Lea	GP	W	L	T	Mins	GA	SO	Avg	GP	W	L	Mins	GA	SO	Avg
1990-91	S.S. Marie	OHL	7	5	2	0	380	19	0	3.00	....	....	....	....	....	....	....
	Oshawa	OHL	30	17	5	1	1483	84	0	3.40	8	1	4	292	26	0	5.34
1991-92	Oshawa	OHL	40	18	13	6	2260	149	1	3.96	7	3	4	429	26	0	3.64
1992-93	Canada	Nat-Tm	13	7	5	1	745	37	1	2.98	....	....	....	....	....	....	....
	Hamilton	AHL	12	2	8	0	618	46	0	4.47	....	....	....	....	....	....	....
1993-94	Hamilton	AHL	*70	*34	28	6	*4005	241	*4	3.61	3	0	2	146	12	0	4.92
1994-95	Syracuse	AHL	61	25	29	7	3618	225	2	3.73	....	....	....	....	....	....	....
1995-96	Syracuse	AHL	54	21	27	3	3060	184	1	3.61	15	8	7	915	57	*2	3.74
1996-97	**Vancouver**	**NHL**	**6**	**2**	**2**	**0**	**245**	**14**	**1**	**3.43**	....	....	....	....	....	....	....
	Syracuse	AHL	25	8	14	2	1462	78	1	3.20	2	0	2	120	12	0	6.02
1997-98	**Carolina**	**NHL**	**3**	**0**	**3**	**0**	**163**	**10**	**0**	**3.68**	....	....	....	....	....	....	....
	New Haven	AHL	50	25	19	5	2922	139	3	2.85	....	....	....	....	....	....	....
	NHL Totals		**9**	**2**	**5**	**0**	**408**	**24**	**1**	**3.53**	....	....	....	....	....	....	....

OHL First All-Star Team (1992) • AHL Second All-Star Team (1994)

Signed as a free agent by **Carolina**, August 19, 1997.

FRANEK, PETR (FRAH-nehk) COL.

Goaltender. Catches left. 5'11", 187 lbs. Born, Most, Czech., April 6, 1975.
(Quebec's 10th choice, 205th overall, in 1993 Entry Draft).

			Regular Season								Playoffs						
Season	Club	Lea	GP	W	L	T	Mins	GA	SO	Avg	GP	W	L	Mins	GA	SO	Avg
1992-93	Litvinov	Czech.	5	....	....	....	273	15	....	3.29							
1993-94	Litvinov	Cze-Rep.	11	....	....	....	535	34	....	3.81	2	....	....	61	10	....	9.83
1994-95	Litvinov	Cze-Rep.	12	....	....	....	657	47	....	4.29	1	0	0	16	0	0	0.00
1995-96	Litvinov	Cze-Rep.	36	....	....	....	2096	85	3	2.43	16	....	....	948	47	....	2.97
1996-97	Hershey	AHL	15	4	1	0	457	23	3	3.02							
	Brantford	ColHL	6	4	1	0	321	14	0	2.61							
	Quebec	IHL	6	3	3	0	357	18	0	3.02	1	0	1	40	4	0	6.00
1997-98	Hershey	AHL	43	19	14	2	2169	98	2	2.71	1	0	1	60	4	0	4.00

Transferred to **Colorado** after **Quebec** franchise relocated, June 21, 1995.

FRIESEN, TERRY S.J.

Goaltender. Catches left. 5'11", 190 lbs. Born, Winkler, Man., October 29, 1977.
(San Jose's 3rd choice, 55th overall, in 1996 Entry Draft).

			Regular Season								Playoffs						
Season	Club	Lea	GP	W	L	T	Mins	GA	SO	Avg	GP	W	L	Mins	GA	SO	Avg
1995-96	Swift Current	WHL	42	19	17	3	2504	155	2	3.71	6	2	4	338	21	0	3.73
1996-97	Swift Current	WHL	53	28	19	3	3090	170	1	3.30	10	6	4	592	27	0	2.74
1997-98	Swift Current	WHL	44	26	10	7	2639	124	1	2.82	12	7	5	754	28	1	*2.23

WHL East Second All-Star Team (1996) • WHL East First All-Star Team (1998)

FUHR, GRANT (FYOOR) ST.L.

Goaltender. Catches right. 5'9", 190 lbs. Born, Spruce Grove, Alta., September 28, 1962.
(Edmonton's 1st choice, 8th overall, in 1981 Entry Draft).

			Regular Season								Playoffs						
Season	Club	Lea	GP	W	L	T	Mins	GA	SO	Avg	GP	W	L	Mins	GA	SO	Avg
1979-80	Victoria	WHL	43	30	12	0	2488	130	2	3.14	8	5	3	465	22	0	2.84
1980-81	Victoria	WHL	59	48	9	1	3448	160	*4	*2.78	15	12	3	899	45	*1	*3.00
1981-82	Edmonton	NHL	48	28	5	14	2847	157	0	3.31	5	2	3	309	26	0	5.05
1982-83	Edmonton	NHL	32	13	12	5	1803	129	0	4.29	1	0	0	11	0	0	0.00
	Moncton	AHL	10	4	5	1	604	40	0	3.98							
1983-84	Edmonton	NHL	45	30	10	4	2625	171	1	3.91	16	11	4	883	44	1	2.99 ♦
1984-85	Edmonton	NHL	46	26	8	7	2559	165	1	3.87	*18	*15	3	1064	55	0	3.10 ♦
1985-86	Edmonton	NHL	40	29	8	0	2184	143	0	3.93	9	5	4	541	28	0	3.11
1986-87	Edmonton	NHL	44	22	13	3	2388	137	0	3.44	19	14	5	1148	47	0	2.46 ♦
1987-88	Edmonton	NHL	*75	*40	24	9	*4304	246	*4	3.43	*19	*16	2	*1136	55	0	2.90 ♦
1988-89	Edmonton	NHL	59	23	26	6	3341	213	1	3.83	7	3	4	417	24	1	3.45
1989-90	Edmonton	NHL	21	9	7	3	1081	70	1	3.89							♦
	Cape Breton	AHL	2	2	0	0	120	6	0	3.01							
1990-91	Edmonton	NHL	13	6	4	3	778	39	1	3.01	17	8	7	1019	51	0	3.00
	Cape Breton	AHL	4	2	2	0	240	17	0	4.25							
1991-92	Toronto	NHL	66	25	33	5	3774	230	2	3.66							
1992-93	Toronto	NHL	29	13	9	4	1665	87	1	3.14							
	Buffalo	NHL	29	11	15	2	1694	98	0	3.47	8	3	4	474	27	1	3.42
1993-94	Buffalo	NHL	32	13	12	3	1726	106	2	3.68							
	Rochester	AHL	5	3	0	2	310	10	0	1.94							
1994-95	Buffalo	NHL	3	1	2	0	180	12	0	4.00							
	Los Angeles	NHL	14	1	7	3	698	47	0	4.04							
1995-96	St. Louis	NHL	*79	30	28	16	4365	209	3	2.87	2	1	0	69	1	0	0.87
1996-97	St. Louis	NHL	73	33	27	11	4261	193	3	2.72	6	2	4	357	13	2	2.18
1997-98	St. Louis	NHL	58	29	21	6	3274	138	3	2.53	10	6	4	616	28	0	2.73
	NHL Totals		**806**	**382**	**271**	**104**	**45547**	**2590**	**23**	**3.41**	**137**	**86**	**44**	**8044**	**399**	**5**	**2.98**

WHL First All-Star Team (1980, 1981) • NHL Second All-Star Team (1982) • NHL First All-Star Team (1988) • Won Vezina Trophy (1988) • Shared William M. Jennings Trophy with Dominik Hasek (1994)

Played in NHL All-Star Game (1982, 1984, 1985, 1986, 1988, 1989)

• Statistics (Mins., GA) for suspended game on May 24, 1988 are included in playoff record.

Traded to **Toronto** by **Edmonton** with Glenn Anderson and Craig Berube for Vincent Damphousse, Peter Ing, Scott Thornton, Luke Richardson, future considerations and cash, September 19, 1991. Traded to **Buffalo** by **Toronto** with Toronto's 5th round choice (Kevin Popp) in 1995 Entry Draft for Dave Andreychuk, Daren Puppa and Buffalo's 1st round choice (Kenny Jonsson) in 1993 Entry Draft, February 2, 1993. Traded to **Los Angeles** by **Buffalo** with Philippe Boucher and Denis Tsygurov for Alexei Zhitnik, Robb Stauber, Charlie Huddy and Los Angeles' 5th round choice (Marian Menhart) in 1995 Entry Draft, February 14, 1995. Signed as a free agent by **St. Louis**, July 14, 1995.

GARNER, TYRONE CGY.

Goaltender. Catches left. 6'1", 170 lbs. Born, Stoney Creek, Ont., July 27, 1978.
(NY Islanders' 4th choice, 83rd overall, in 1996 Entry Draft).

			Regular Season								Playoffs						
Season	Club	Lea	GP	W	L	T	Mins	GA	SO	Avg	GP	W	L	Mins	GA	SO	Avg
1995-96	Oshawa	OHL	32	11	15	4	1697	112	0	3.96							
1996-97	Oshawa	OHL	9	6	1	0	434	20	0	2.76	3	1	0	88	6	0	4.09
1997-98	Oshawa	OHL	54	23	17	8	2946	162	1	3.30	7	3	4	450	25	0	3.33

Traded to **Calgary** by **NY Islanders** with Marty McInnis and Calgary's sixth round choice (previously acquired, Calgary selected Ilja Demidov) in 1997 Entry Draft for Robert Reichel, March 18, 1997.

GARON, MATHIEU (gah-ROHN) MTL.

Goaltender. Catches right. 6'1", 187 lbs. Born, Chandler, Que., January 9, 1978.
(Montreal's 2nd choice, 44th overall, in 1996 Entry Draft).

			Regular Season								Playoffs						
Season	Club	Lea	GP	W	L	T	Mins	GA	SO	Avg	GP	W	L	Mins	GA	SO	Avg
1995-96	Victoriaville	QMJHL	51	18	27	0	2709	189	1	4.19	12	7	4	676	38	1	3.39
1996-97	Victoriaville	QMJHL	53	29	18	3	3032	150	*6	2.97	6	2	4	330	23	0	4.18
1997-98	Victoriaville	QMJHL	47	27	18	2	2802	125	5	2.68	6	2	4	345	22	0	3.82

QMJHL First All-Star Team (1998) • Canadian Major Junior First All-Star Team (1998) • Canadian Major Junior Goaltender of the Year (1998)

GAUTHIER, SEAN S.J.

Goaltender. Catches left. 5'11", 195 lbs. Born, Sudbury, Ont., March 28, 1971.
(Winnipeg's 7th choice, 181st overall, in 1991 Entry Draft).

			Regular Season								Playoffs						
Season	Club	Lea	GP	W	L	T	Mins	GA	SO	Avg	GP	W	L	Mins	GA	SO	Avg
1988-89	Kingston	OHL	37	7	18	1	1528	141	0	5.54							
1989-90	Kingston	OHL	32	17	9	0	1602	101	0	3.78	2	0	1	76	6	0	4.74
1990-91	Kingston	OHL	59	16	36	3	3200	282	0	5.29							
1991-92	Moncton	AHL	25	8	10	5	1415	88	1	3.73	2	0	0	26	2	0	4.62
	Fort Wayne	IHL	18	10	4	2	978	59	1	3.62	2	0	0	48	7	0	8.74
1992-93	Moncton	AHL	38	10	16	9	2196	145	0	3.96	2	0	1	75	6	0	4.80
1993-94	Moncton	AHL	13	3	5	1	616	41	0	3.99							
	Fort Wayne	IHL	22	9	9	3	1139	66	0	3.48							
1994-95	Fort Wayne	IHL	5	0	2	1	217	15	0	4.13							
1995-96	South Carolina	ECHL	49	31	11	7	2891	149	0	3.09	8	5	3	478	24	0	3.01
1996-97	Pensacola	ECHL	46	23	21	1	2692	168	1	3.74	12	8	4	749	44	1	3.52
1997-98	Pensacola	ECHL	54	29	17	7	3213	194	0	3.62	19	12	7	1180	58	1	2.95

ECHL Second All-Star Team (1998)

Signed as a free agent by **San Jose**, July 23, 1998.

GIGUERE, JEAN-SEBASTIEN (ZHEE-gair) CGY.

Goaltender. Catches left. 6', 175 lbs. Born, Montreal, Que., May 16, 1977.
(Hartford's 1st choice, 13th overall, in 1995 Entry Draft).

			Regular Season								Playoffs						
Season	Club	Lea	GP	W	L	T	Mins	GA	SO	Avg	GP	W	L	Mins	GA	SO	Avg
1993-94	Verdun	QMJHL	25	13	5	2	1234	66	1	3.21							
1994-95	Halifax	QMJHL	47	14	27	5	2755	181	2	3.94	7	3	4	417	17	1	*2.45
1995-96	Halifax	QMJHL	55	26	23	2	3230	185	1	3.44	6	1	5	354	24	0	4.07
1996-97	Hartford	NHL	8	1	4	0	394	24	0	3.65							
	Halifax	QMJHL	50	28	19	3	3014	170	2	3.38	16	9	7	954	58	0	3.65
1997-98	Saint John	AHL	31	16	10	3	1758	72	2	2.46	10	5	3	536	27	0	3.02
	NHL Totals		**8**	**1**	**4**	**0**	**394**	**24**	**0**	**3.65**							

QMJHL Second All-Star Team (1997) • Shared Harry "Hap" Holmes Memorial Trophy (fewest goals against - AHL) with Tyler Moss (1998)

Transferred to **Carolina** after **Hartford** franchise relocated, June 25, 1997. Traded to **Calgary** by **Carolina** with Andrew Cassels for Gary Roberts and Trevor Kidd, August 25, 1997.

GORDON, IAN

Goaltender. Catches left. 5'10", 160 lbs. Born, Yorkton, Sask., May 15, 1975.

			Regular Season								Playoffs						
Season	Club	Lea	GP	W	L	T	Mins	GA	SO	Avg	GP	W	L	Mins	GA	SO	Avg
1992-93	Swift Current	WHL	10	1	6	0	365	31	0	5.10	2	0	0	53	3	0	3.40
1993-94	Swift Current	WHL	65	29	27	4	3657	204	6	3.35	7	3	4	420	21	1	3.00
1994-95	Swift Current	WHL	17	6	9	1	994	62	1	3.74							
	Saskatoon	WHL	41	24	9	7	2476	129	1	3.13	10	4	6	633	29	1	2.75
1995-96	Saint John	AHL	19	2	12	0	768	56	0	4.37							
1996-97	Saint John	AHL	21	5	9	1	988	50	0	3.03							
	Grand Rapids	IHL	5	2	2	0	257	15	0	3.50	1	0	0	0	0	0	0.00
1997-98	Grand Rapids	IHL	49	23	16	4	2573	115	1	2.68	2	0	2	118	7	0	3.54

Signed as a free agent by **Calgary**, October 6, 1995.

GRAHAME, JOHN BOS.

Goaltender. Catches left. 6'2", 210 lbs. Born, Denver, CO, August 31, 1975.
(Boston's 7th choice, 229th overall, in 1994 Entry Draft).

			Regular Season								Playoffs						
Season	Club	Lea	GP	W	L	T	Mins	GA	SO	Avg	GP	W	L	Mins	GA	SO	Avg
1993-94	Sioux City	USHL	20	....	....	....	1200	73	0	3.70							
1994-95	Lake Superior	CCHA	28	16	7	3	1616	75	2	2.79							
1995-96	Lake Superior	CCHA	29	21	4	2	1558	66	2	2.54							
1996-97	Lake Superior	CCHA	37	19	13	4	2197	134	3	3.66							
1997-98	Providence	AHL	55	15	31	4	3053	164	3	3.22							

HACKETT, JEFF CHI.

Goaltender. Catches left. 6'1", 195 lbs. Born, London, Ont., June 1, 1968.
(NY Islanders' 2nd choice, 34th overall, in 1987 Entry Draft).

			Regular Season								Playoffs						
Season	Club	Lea	GP	W	L	T	Mins	GA	SO	Avg	GP	W	L	Mins	GA	SO	Avg
1986-87	Oshawa	OHL	31	18	9	2	1672	85	2	3.05	15	8	7	895	40	0	2.68
1987-88	Oshawa	OHL	53	30	21	2	3165	205	0	3.89	7	3	4	438	31	0	4.25
1988-89	NY Islanders	NHL	13	4	7	0	662	39	0	3.53							
	Springfield	AHL	29	12	14	2	1677	116	0	4.15							
1989-90	Springfield	AHL	54	24	25	3	3045	187	1	3.68	*17	*10	5	934	60	0	3.85
1990-91	NY Islanders	NHL	30	5	18	1	1508	91	0	3.62							
1991-92	San Jose	NHL	42	11	27	1	2314	148	0	3.84							
1992-93	San Jose	NHL	36	2	30	1	2000	176	0	5.28							
1993-94	Chicago	NHL	22	2	12	3	1084	62	0	3.43							
1994-95	Chicago	NHL	7	1	3	2	328	13	0	2.38	2	0	0	26	1	0	2.31
1995-96	Chicago	NHL	35	18	11	4	2000	80	4	2.40	1	0	1	60	5	0	5.00
1996-97	Chicago	NHL	41	19	18	4	2473	89	2	2.16	6	2	4	345	25	0	4.35
1997-98	Chicago	NHL	58	21	25	11	3441	126	8	2.20							
	NHL Totals		**284**	**83**	**151**	**27**	**15810**	**824**	**14**	**3.13**	**9**	**2**	**5**	**431**	**31**	**0**	**4.32**

Won Jack A. Butterfield Trophy (Playoff MVP - AHL) (1990)

Claimed by **San Jose** from **NY Islanders** in Expansion Draft, May 30, 1991. Traded to **Chicago** by **San Jose** for Chicago's 3rd round choice (Alexei Yegorov) in 1994 Entry Draft, July 13, 1993.

HASEK, DOMINIK (HAH-shihk) BUF.

Goaltender. Catches left. 5'11", 168 lbs. Born, Pardubice, Czech., January 29, 1965.
(Chicago's 11th choice, 207th overall, in 1983 Entry Draft).

			Regular Season								Playoffs						
Season	Club	Lea	GP	W	L	T	Mins	GA	SO	Avg	GP	W	L	Mins	GA	SO	Avg
1981-82	Pardubice	Czech.	12	....	....	....	661	34	....	3.09	....	....	....	....	....	....	....
1982-83	Pardubice	Czech.	42	....	....	....	2358	105	....	2.67	....	....	....	....	....	....	....
1983-84	Pardubice	Czech.	40	....	....	....	2304	108	....	2.81	....	....	....	....	....	....	....
1984-85	Pardubice	Czech.	42	....	....	....	2419	131	....	3.25	....	....	....	....	....	....	....
1985-86	Pardubice	Czech.	45	....	....	....	2689	138	....	3.08	....	....	....	....	....	....	....
1986-87	Pardubice	Czech.	43	....	....	....	2515	103	....	2.46	....	....	....	....	....	....	....
1987-88	Pardubice	Czech.	31	....	....	....	1862	93	....	3.00	....	....	....	....	....	....	....
	Czechoslovakia	Olympics	5	....	....	....	217	18	....	4.98	....	....	....	....	....	....	....
1988-89	Pardubice	Czech.	42	....	....	....	2507	114	....	2.73	....	....	....	....	....	....	....
1989-90	Dukla Jihlava	Czech.	40	....	....	....	2251	80	....	2.13	....	....	....	....	....	....	....
1990-91	**Chicago**	**NHL**	**5**	**3**	**0**	**1**	**195**	**8**	**0**	**2.46**	**3**	**0**	**0**	**69**	**3**	**0**	**2.61**
	Indianapolis	IHL	33	20	11	1	1903	80	*5	*2.52	1	1	0	60	3	0	3.00
1991-92	**Chicago**	**NHL**	**20**	**10**	**4**	**1**	**1014**	**44**	**1**	**2.60**	**3**	**0**	**2**	**158**	**8**	**0**	**3.04**
	Indianapolis	IHL	20	7	10	3	1162	69	1	3.56	....	....	....	....	....	....	....
1992-93	**Buffalo**	**NHL**	**28**	**11**	**10**	**4**	**1429**	**75**	**0**	**3.15**	**1**	**1**	**0**	**45**	**1**	**0**	**1.33**
1993-94	**Buffalo**	**NHL**	**58**	**30**	**20**	**6**	**3358**	**109**	***7**	***1.95**	**7**	**3**	**4**	**484**	**13**	**2**	***1.61**
1994-95	Pardubice	Cze-Rep.	2	....	....	....	124	6	0	2.90	....	....	....	....	....	....	....
	Buffalo	**NHL**	**41**	**19**	**14**	**7**	**2416**	**85**	***5**	***2.11**	**5**	**1**	**4**	**309**	**18**	**0**	**3.50**
1995-96	**Buffalo**	**NHL**	**59**	**22**	**30**	**6**	**3417**	**161**	**2**	**2.83**	....	....	....	....	....	....	....
1996-97	**Buffalo**	**NHL**	**67**	**37**	**20**	**10**	**4037**	**153**	**5**	**2.27**	**3**	**1**	**1**	**153**	**5**	**0**	**1.96**
1997-98	**Buffalo**	**NHL**	***72**	**33**	**23**	**13**	***4220**	**147**	***13**	**2.09**	**15**	**10**	**5**	**948**	**32**	**1**	**2.03**
	Czech Republic	Olympics	6	*5	1	0	*369	6	*2	*0.97	....	....	....	....	....	....	....
	NHL Totals		**350**	**165**	**121**	**48**	**20086**	**782**	**33**	**2.34**	**37**	**16**	**16**	**2166**	**80**	**3**	**2.22**

Czechoslovakian Goaltender-of-the-Year (1986, 1987, 1988, 1989, 1990) • Czechoslovakian Player-of-the-Year (1987, 1989, 1990) • Czechoslovakian First All-Star Team (1988, 1989, 1990) • IHL First All-Star Team (1991) • NHL/Upper Deck All-Rookie Team (1992) • NHL First All-Star Team (1994, 1995, 1997, 1998) • Shared William M. Jennings Trophy with Grant Fuhr (1994) • Won Vezina Trophy (1994, 1995, 1997, 1998) • Won Lester B. Pearson Award (1997, 1998) • Won Hart Trophy (1997, 1998)

Played in NHL All-Star Game (1996, 1997, 1998)

Traded to **Buffalo** by **Chicago** for Stephane Beauregard and Buffalo's 4th round choice (Eric Daze) in 1993 Entry Draft, August 7, 1992.

HEALY, GLENN TOR.

Goaltender. Catches left. 5'10", 185 lbs. Born, Pickering, Ont., August 23, 1962.

			Regular Season								Playoffs						
Season	Club	Lea	GP	W	L	T	Mins	GA	SO	Avg	GP	W	L	Mins	GA	SO	Avg
1981-82	Western Michigan	CCHA	27	7	19	1	1569	116	0	4.44	....	....	....	....	....	....	....
1982-83	Western Michigan	CCHA	30	8	19	2	1732	116	0	4.01	....	....	....	....	....	....	....
1983-84	Western Michigan	CCHA	38	19	16	3	2241	146	0	3.90	....	....	....	....	....	....	....
1984-85	Western Michigan	CCHA	37	21	14	2	2171	118	0	3.26	....	....	....	....	....	....	....
1985-86	**Los Angeles**	**NHL**	**1**	**0**	**0**	**0**	**51**	**6**	**0**	**7.06**	....	....	....	....	....	....	....
	New Haven	AHL	43	21	15	4	2410	160	0	3.98	2	0	2	49	11	0	5.55
1986-87	New Haven	AHL	47	21	15	0	2828	173	1	3.67	7	3	4	427	19	0	2.67
1987-88	**Los Angeles**	**NHL**	**34**	**12**	**18**	**1**	**1869**	**135**	**1**	**4.33**	**4**	**1**	**3**	**240**	**20**	**0**	**5.00**
1988-89	**Los Angeles**	**NHL**	**48**	**25**	**19**	**2**	**2699**	**192**	**0**	**4.27**	**3**	**0**	**1**	**97**	**6**	**0**	**3.71**
1989-90	**NY Islanders**	**NHL**	**39**	**12**	**19**	**6**	**2197**	**128**	**2**	**3.50**	**4**	**1**	**2**	**166**	**9**	**0**	**3.25**
1990-91	**NY Islanders**	**NHL**	**53**	**18**	**24**	**9**	**2999**	**166**	**0**	**3.32**	....	....	....	....	....	....	....
1991-92	**NY Islanders**	**NHL**	**37**	**14**	**16**	**4**	**1960**	**124**	**1**	**3.80**	....	....	....	....	....	....	....
1992-93	**NY Islanders**	**NHL**	**47**	**22**	**20**	**2**	**2655**	**146**	**1**	**3.30**	**18**	**9**	**8**	**1109**	**59**	**0**	**3.19**
1993-94	**NY Rangers**	**NHL**	**29**	**10**	**12**	**2**	**1368**	**69**	**2**	**3.03**	**2**	**0**	**0**	**68**	**1**	**0**	**0.88** ♦
1994-95	**NY Rangers**	**NHL**	**17**	**8**	**6**	**1**	**888**	**35**	**1**	**2.36**	**5**	**2**	**1**	**230**	**13**	**0**	**3.39**
1995-96	**NY Rangers**	**NHL**	**44**	**17**	**14**	**11**	**2564**	**124**	**2**	**2.90**	....	....	....	....	....	....	....
1996-97	**NY Rangers**	**NHL**	**23**	**5**	**12**	**4**	**1357**	**59**	**1**	**2.61**	....	....	....	....	....	....	....
1997-98	**Toronto**	**NHL**	**21**	**4**	**10**	**2**	**1068**	**53**	**0**	**2.98**	....	....	....	....	....	....	....
	NHL Totals		**393**	**147**	**170**	**44**	**21675**	**1237**	**11**	**3.42**	**36**	**13**	**15**	**1910**	**108**	**0**	**3.39**

CCHA Second All-Star Team (1985) • NCAA West Second All-American Team (1985)

Signed as a free agent by **Los Angeles**, June 13, 1985. Signed as a free agent by **NY Islanders**, August 16, 1989. Claimed by **Anaheim** from **NY Islanders** in Expansion Draft, June 24, 1993. Claimed by **Tampa Bay** from **Anaheim** in Phase II of Expansion Draft, June 25, 1993. Traded to **NY Rangers** by **Tampa Bay** for Tampa Bay's 3rd round choice (previously acquired, Tampa Bay selected Allan Egeland) in 1993 Entry Draft, June 25, 1993. Signed as a free agent by **Toronto**, August 8, 1997.

HEBERT, GUY (ay-BAIR, GEE) ANA.

Goaltender. Catches left. 5'11", 185 lbs. Born, Troy, NY, January 7, 1967.
(St. Louis' 8th choice, 159th overall, in 1987 Entry Draft).

			Regular Season								Playoffs						
Season	Club	Lea	GP	W	L	T	Mins	GA	SO	Avg	GP	W	L	Mins	GA	SO	Avg
1985-86	Hamilton College	NCAA	18	4	12	2	1011	69	2	4.09	....	....	....	....	....	....	....
1986-87	Hamilton College	NCAA	18	12	5	0	1070	40	3	2.19	2	1	1	134	6	0	2.69
1987-88	Hamilton College	NCAA	9	5	3	0	510	22	1	2.58	1	0	1	60	3	0	3.00
1988-89	Hamilton College	NCAA	25	18	7	0	1454	62	2	2.56	2	1	1	126	4	0	1.90
1989-90	Peoria	IHL	30	7	13	7	1706	124	1	4.36	2	0	1	76	5	0	3.95
1990-91	Peoria	IHL	36	24	10	1	2093	100	2	2.87	8	3	4	458	32	0	4.19
1991-92	**St. Louis**	**NHL**	**13**	**5**	**5**	**1**	**738**	**36**	**0**	**2.93**	....	....	....	....	....	....	....
	Peoria	IHL	29	20	9	0	1731	98	0	3.40	4	3	1	239	9	0	2.26
1992-93	**St. Louis**	**NHL**	**24**	**8**	**8**	**2**	**1210**	**74**	**1**	**3.67**	**1**	**0**	**0**	**2**	**0**	**0**	**0.00**
1993-94	**Anaheim**	**NHL**	**52**	**20**	**27**	**3**	**2991**	**141**	**2**	**2.83**	....	....	....	....	....	....	....
1994-95	**Anaheim**	**NHL**	**39**	**12**	**20**	**4**	**2092**	**109**	**2**	**3.13**	....	....	....	....	....	....	....
1995-96	**Anaheim**	**NHL**	**59**	**28**	**23**	**5**	**3326**	**157**	**4**	**2.83**	....	....	....	....	....	....	....
1996-97	**Anaheim**	**NHL**	**67**	**29**	**25**	**12**	**3863**	**172**	**4**	**2.67**	**9**	**4**	**4**	**534**	**18**	**1**	**2.02**
1997-98	**Anaheim**	**NHL**	**46**	**13**	**24**	**6**	**2660**	**130**	**3**	**2.93**	....	....	....	....	....	....	....
	NHL Totals		**300**	**115**	**132**	**33**	**16880**	**819**	**16**	**2.91**	**10**	**4**	**4**	**536**	**18**	**1**	**2.01**

IHL Second All-Star Team (1991) • Shared James Norris Memorial Trophy (fewest goals against - IHL) with Pat Jablonski (1991)

Played in NHL All-Star Game (1997)

Claimed by **Anaheim** from **St. Louis** in Expansion Draft, June 24, 1993.

HEDBERG, JOHAN (HEHD-buhrg) S.J.

Goaltender. Catches left. 5'11", 180 lbs. Born, Leksand, Sweden, May 5, 1973.
(Philadelphia's 8th choice, 218th overall, in 1994 Entry Draft).

			Regular Season								Playoffs						
Season	Club	Lea	GP	W	L	T	Mins	GA	SO	Avg	GP	W	L	Mins	GA	SO	Avg
1992-93	Leksand IF	Sweden	10	....	....	....	600	24	....	2.40	....	....	....	....	....	....	....
1993-94	Leksand IF	Sweden	17	....	....	....	1020	48	....	2.81	....	....	....	....	....	....	....
1994-95	Leksand IF	Sweden	17	....	....	....	986	58	....	3.53	....	....	....	....	....	....	....
1995-96	Leksand IF	Sweden	34	....	....	....	2013	95	....	2.83	4	....	....	240	13	....	3.25
1996-97	Leksand IF	Sweden	38	....	....	....	2260	95	3	2.52	8	....	....	581	18	1	1.86
1997-98	Baton Rouge	ECHL	2	1	1	0	100	7	0	4.20	....	....	....	....	....	....	....
	Detroit	IHL	16	7	2	2	726	32	1	2.64	....	....	....	....	....	....	....
	Manitoba	IHL	14	8	4	1	745	32	1	2.58	2	0	2	105	6	0	3.40
	Sweden	Olympics	DID NOT PLAY – SPARE GOALTENDER														

Traded to **San Jose** by **Philadelphia** for San Jose's 7th round choice in 1999 Entry Draft, August 6, 1998.

HEIL, JEFF NYR

Goaltender. Catches left. 6'1", 190 lbs. Born, Bloomington, MN, September 17, 1975.
(NY Rangers' 7th choice, 169th overall, in 1995 Entry Draft).

			Regular Season								Playoffs						
Season	Club	Lea	GP	W	L	T	Mins	GA	SO	Avg	GP	W	L	Mins	GA	SO	Avg
1994-95	Wisc-Fall River	NCHA	25	13	7	3	1399	64	2	2.74	....	....	....	....	....	....	....
1995-96	Wisc-Fall River	NCHA	16	13	2	0	943	28	2	1.78	....	....	....	....	....	....	....
1996-97	Wisc-Fall River	NCHA	23	15	8	0	1335	52	4	2.34	....	....	....	....	....	....	....
1997-98	Charlotte	ECHL	22	12	5	4	1240	69	2	3.34	....	....	....	....	....	....	....
	Hartford	AHL	1	0	0	1	35	0	0	0.00	....	....	....	....	....	....	....

HENRY, FREDERIC N.J.

Goaltender. Catches left. 5'11", 170 lbs. Born, Cap-Rouge, Que., August 9, 1977.
(New Jersey's 10th choice, 200th overall, in 1995 Entry Draft).

			Regular Season								Playoffs						
Season	Club	Lea	GP	W	L	T	Mins	GA	SO	Avg	GP	W	L	Mins	GA	SO	Avg
1994-95	Granby	QMJHL	15	8	5	0	866	47	0	3.26	6	1	2	232	21	0	5.43
1995-96	Granby	QMJHL	28	19	5	2	1530	69	*3	2.71	12	9	2	610	21	2	*2.08
1996-97	Granby	QMJHL	57	33	16	6	3330	162	4	2.92	5	1	4	251	17	0	4.06
	Albany	AHL	1	1	0	0	60	3	0	3.00	....	....	....	....	....	....	....
1997-98	Raleigh	ECHL	34	13	17	2	1889	119	2	3.78	....	....	....	....	....	....	....
	Albany	AHL	4	2	0	1	199	8	0	2.41	....	....	....	....	....	....	....

HEXTALL, RON PHI.

Goaltender. Catches left. 6'3", 192 lbs. Born, Brandon, Man., May 3, 1964.
(Philadelphia's 6th choice, 119th overall, in 1982 Entry Draft).

			Regular Season								Playoffs						
Season	Club	Lea	GP	W	L	T	Mins	GA	SO	Avg	GP	W	L	Mins	GA	SO	Avg
1981-82	Brandon	WHL	30	12	11	0	1398	133	0	5.71	3	0	2	103	16	0	9.32
1982-83	Brandon	WHL	44	13	30	0	2589	249	0	5.77	....	....	....	....	....	....	....
1983-84	Brandon	WHL	46	29	13	2	2670	190	0	4.27	10	5	5	592	37	0	3.75
1984-85	Hershey	AHL	11	4	6	0	555	34	0	3.68	....	....	....	....	....	....	....
	Kalamazoo	IHL	19	6	11	1	1103	80	0	4.35	....	....	....	....	....	....	....
1985-86	Hershey	AHL	*53	30	19	2	*3061	174	*5	3.41	13	5	7	780	42	*1	3.23
1986-87	**Philadelphia**	**NHL**	***66**	**37**	**21**	**6**	***3799**	**190**	**1**	**3.00**	***26**	**15**	**11**	***1540**	**71**	***2**	**2.77**
1987-88	**Philadelphia**	**NHL**	**62**	**30**	**22**	**7**	**3561**	**208**	**0**	**3.50**	**7**	**2**	**4**	**379**	**30**	**0**	**4.75**
1988-89	**Philadelphia**	**NHL**	**64**	**30**	**28**	**6**	**3756**	**202**	**0**	**3.23**	**15**	**8**	**7**	**886**	**49**	**0**	**3.32**
1989-90	**Philadelphia**	**NHL**	**8**	**4**	**2**	**1**	**419**	**29**	**0**	**4.15**	....	....	....	....	....	....	....
	Hershey	AHL	1	1	0	0	49	3	0	3.67	....	....	....	....	....	....	....
1990-91	**Philadelphia**	**NHL**	**36**	**13**	**16**	**5**	**2035**	**106**	**0**	**3.13**	....	....	....	....	....	....	....
1991-92	**Philadelphia**	**NHL**	**45**	**16**	**21**	**6**	**2668**	**151**	**3**	**3.40**	....	....	....	....	....	....	....
1992-93	**Quebec**	**NHL**	**54**	**29**	**16**	**5**	**2988**	**172**	**0**	**3.45**	**6**	**2**	**4**	**372**	**18**	**0**	**2.90**
1993-94	**NY Islanders**	**NHL**	**65**	**27**	**26**	**6**	**3581**	**184**	**5**	**3.08**	**3**	**0**	**3**	**158**	**16**	**0**	**6.08**
1994-95	**Philadelphia**	**NHL**	**31**	**17**	**9**	**4**	**1824**	**88**	**1**	**2.89**	**15**	**10**	**5**	**897**	**42**	**0**	**2.81**
1995-96	**Philadelphia**	**NHL**	**53**	**31**	**13**	**7**	**3102**	**112**	**4**	***2.17**	**12**	**6**	**6**	**760**	**27**	**0**	**2.13**
1996-97	**Philadelphia**	**NHL**	**55**	**31**	**16**	**5**	**3094**	**132**	**5**	**2.56**	**8**	**4**	**3**	**444**	**22**	**0**	**2.97**
1997-98	**Philadelphia**	**NHL**	**46**	**21**	**17**	**7**	**2688**	**97**	**4**	**2.17**	**1**	**0**	**0**	**20**	**1**	**0**	**3.00**
	NHL Totals		**585**	**286**	**207**	**65**	**33515**	**1671**	**23**	**2.99**	**93**	**47**	**43**	**5456**	**276**	**2**	**3.04**

AHL First All-Star Team (1986) • Won Dudley "Red" Garrett Memorial Trophy (Top Rookie - AHL) (1986) • NHL All-Rookie Team (1987) • NHL First All-Star Team (1987) • Won Vezina Trophy (1987) • Won Conn Smythe Trophy (1987)

• Scored a goal vs. Boston, December 8, 1987 • Scored a goal in playoffs vs. Washington, April 11, 1989.

Played in NHL All-Star Game (1988)

Traded to **Quebec** by **Philadelphia** with Peter Forsberg, Steve Duchesne, Kerry Huffman, Mike Ricci, Chris Simon, Philadelphia's 1st round choice in the 1993 (Jocelyn Thibault) and 1994 (later traded to Toronto — later traded to Washington — Washington selected Nolan Baumgartner) Entry Drafts and cash for Eric Lindros, June 30, 1992. Traded to **NY Islanders** by **Quebec** with Quebec's 1st round choice (Todd Bertuzzi) in 1993 Entry Draft for Mark Fitzpatrick and NY Islanders' 1st round choice (Adam Deadmarsh) in 1993 Entry Draft, June 20, 1993. Traded to **Philadelphia** by **NY Islanders** with NY Islanders' 6th round choice (Dimitri Tertyshny) in 1995 Entry Draft for Tommy Soderstrom, September 22, 1994.

HILLIER, CRAIG PIT.

Goaltender. Catches left. 6'1", 176 lbs. Born, Cole Harbour, N.S., February 28, 1978.
(Pittsburgh's 1st choice, 23rd overall, in 1996 Entry Draft).

			Regular Season								Playoffs						
Season	Club	Lea	GP	W	L	T	Mins	GA	SO	Avg	GP	W	L	Mins	GA	SO	Avg
1994-95	Ottawa	OHL	24	6	7	2	1078	69	1	3.84	....	....	....	....	....	....	....
1995-96	Ottawa	OHL	44	24	14	3	2439	117	2	2.88	3	0	2	130	12	0	5.54
1996-97	Ottawa	OHL	36	23	6	4	2007	89	2	2.66	10	4	5	540	33	0	3.67
1997-98	Ottawa	OHL	46	27	12	4	2587	108	*6	*2.50	9	6	2	447	20	1	2.68

OHL First All-Star Team (1996)

HIRSCH, COREY (HUHRSH) VAN.

Goaltender. Catches left. 5'10", 175 lbs. Born, Medicine Hat, Alta., July 1, 1972.
(NY Rangers' 7th choice, 169th overall, in 1991 Entry Draft).

			Regular Season								Playoffs						
Season	Club	Lea	GP	W	L	T	Mins	GA	SO	Avg	GP	W	L	Mins	GA	SO	Avg
1988-89	Kamloops	WHL	32	11	12	2	1516	106	2	4.20	5	3	2	245	19	0	4.65
1989-90	Kamloops	WHL	*63	*48	13	0	3608	230	*3	3.82	*17	*14	3	*1043	60	0	*3.45
1990-91	Kamloops	WHL	38	26	7	1	1970	100	3	*3.05	11	5	6	623	42	0	4.04
1991-92	Kamloops	WHL	48	35	10	2	2732	124	*5	*2.72	*16	*11	5	954	35	*2	*2.20
1992-93	**NY Rangers**	**NHL**	**4**	**1**	**2**	**1**	**224**	**14**	**0**	**3.75**	....	....	....	....	....	....	....
	Binghamton	AHL	46	*35	4	5	2692	125	1	*2.79	14	7	7	831	46	0	3.32
1993-94	Canada	Nat-Tm	45	24	17	3	2653	124	0	2.80	....	....	....	....	....	....	....
	Canada	Olympics	8	5	2	1	495	18	....	2.18	....	....	....	....	....	....	....
	Binghamton	AHL	10	5	4	1	610	38	0	3.73	....	....	....	....	....	....	....
1994-95	Binghamton	AHL	57	31	20	5	3371	175	0	3.11	....	....	....	....	....	....	....
1995-96	**Vancouver**	**NHL**	**41**	**17**	**14**	**6**	**2338**	**114**	**1**	**2.93**	**6**	**2**	**3**	**338**	**21**	**0**	**3.73**
1996-97	**Vancouver**	**NHL**	**39**	**12**	**20**	**4**	**2127**	**116**	**2**	**3.27**	....	....	....	....	....	....	....
1997-98	**Vancouver**	**NHL**	**1**	**0**	**0**	**0**	**50**	**5**	**0**	**6.00**	....	....	....	....	....	....	....
	Syracuse	AHL	60	30	22	6	3512	187	1	3.19	5	2	3	297	10	1	*2.02
	NHL Totals		**85**	**30**	**36**	**11**	**4739**	**249**	**3**	**3.15**	**6**	**2**	**3**	**338**	**21**	**0**	**3.73**

WHL West Second All-Star Team (1990) • WHL West First All-Star Team (1991, 1992) • Canadian Major Junior Goaltender of the Year (1992) • Memorial Cup All-Star Team (1992) • Memorial Cup Tournament Top Goaltender (1992) • AHL First All-Star Team (1993) • Won Dudley "Red" Garrett Memorial Trophy (AHL Rookie of the Year) (1993) • Shared Harry "Hap" Holmes Memorial Trophy (fewest goals-against - AHL) with Boris Rousson (1993) • NHL All-Rookie Team (1996)

Traded to **Vancouver** by **NY Rangers** for Nathan Lafayette, April 7, 1995.

HITCHEN, ALLAN VAN.

Goaltender. Catches left. 6'1", 195 lbs. Born, North York, Ont., March 6, 1978.

			Regular Season								Playoffs						
Season	Club	Lea	GP	W	L	T	Mins	GA	SO	Avg	GP	W	L	Mins	GA	SO	Avg
1995-96	Peterborough	OHL	17	4	6	3	727	60	0	4.95	3	2	1	126	9	0	4.29
1996-97	Peterborough	OHL	5	2	2	0	186	16	0	5.16	....	....	....	....	....	....	....
	London	OHL	25	5	15	0	1335	113	1	5.08	....	....	....	....	....	....	....
1997-98	London	OHL	11	4	4	0	449	28	0	3.74	....	....	....	....	....	....	....
	North Bay	OHL	6	0	1	0	62	6	0	5.81	....	....	....	....	....	....	....

Signed as a free agent by **Vancouver**, October 3, 1996.

HODSON, JAMIE TOR.

Goaltender. Catches left. 6'1", 180 lbs. Born, Brandon, Man., April 8, 1980.
(Toronto's 3rd choice, 69th overall, in 1998 Entry Draft).

			Regular Season								Playoffs						
Season	Club	Lea	GP	W	L	T	Mins	GA	SO	Avg	GP	W	L	Mins	GA	SO	Avg
1996-97	Yellowhead	Midget	12	....	....	....	720	58	1	4.83	....	....	....	....	....	....	....
1997-98	Brandon	WHL	20	12	2	2	964	52	2	3.24	6	5	0	337	16	0	2.85

HODSON, KEVIN DET.

Goaltender. Catches left. 6', 182 lbs. Born, Winnipeg, Man., March 27, 1972.

			Regular Season								Playoffs						
Season	Club	Lea	GP	W	L	T	Mins	GA	SO	Avg	GP	W	L	Mins	GA	SO	Avg
1990-91	S.S. Marie	OHL	30	18	11	0	1638	88	*2	*3.22	10	*9	1	581	28	0	*2.89
1991-92	S.S. Marie	OHL	50	28	12	4	2722	151	0	3.33	18	12	6	1116	54	1	2.90
1992-93	S.S. Marie	OHL	26	18	5	2	1470	76	1	*3.10	14	11	2	755	34	0	2.70
	Indianapolis	IHL	14	5	9	0	777	53	0	4.09	....	....	....	....	....	....	....
1993-94	Adirondack	AHL	37	20	10	5	2082	102	2	2.94	3	0	2	89	10	0	6.77
1994-95	Adirondack	AHL	51	19	22	8	2731	161	1	3.54	4	0	4	237	14	0	3.53
1995-96	**Detroit**	**NHL**	**4**	**2**	**0**	**0**	**163**	**3**	**1**	**1.10**	....	....	....	....	....	....	....
	Adirondack	AHL	32	13	13	2	1654	87	0	3.16	3	0	2	150	8	0	3.21
1996-97	**Detroit**	**NHL**	**6**	**2**	**2**	**1**	**294**	**8**	**1**	**1.63**	....	....	....	....	....	....	....
	Quebec	IHL	2	1	1	0	118	7	0	3.54	....	....	....	....	....	....	....
1997-98	**Detroit**	**NHL**	**21**	**9**	**3**	**3**	**988**	**44**	**2**	**2.67**	**1**	**0**	**0**	**1**	**0**	**0**	**0.00** ♦
	NHL Totals		**31**	**13**	**5**	**4**	**1445**	**55**	**4**	**2.28**	**1**	**0**	**0**	**1**	**0**	**0**	**0.00**

Memorial Cup All-Star Team (1993) • Won Hap Emms Memorial Trophy (Memorial Cup Tournament Top Goaltender) (1993)

Signed as a free agent by **Chicago**, August 17, 1992. Signed as a free agent by **Detroit**, June 16, 1993. • Played 16 seconds in playoff game vs. Chicago, May 17, 1998.

HOLMQVIST, JOHAN NYR

Goaltender. Catches left. 6'1", 200 lbs. Born, Tolfta, Sweden, May 24, 1978.
(NY Rangers' 9th choice, 175th overall, in 1997 Entry Draft).

			Regular Season								Playoffs						
Season	Club	Lea	GP	W	L	T	Mins	GA	SO	Avg	GP	W	L	Mins	GA	SO	Avg
1996-97	Brynas Gavle	Sweden	2	0	0	0	80	4	0	3.00	....	....	....	....	....	....	....
1997-98	Brynas Gavle	Sweden	33	....	....	....	1897	82	....	2.59	3	....	....	180	14	....	4.67

HRUDEY, KELLY (ROO-dee)

Goaltender. Catches left. 5'10", 189 lbs. Born, Edmonton, Alta., January 13, 1961.
(NY Islanders' 2nd choice, 38th overall, in 1980 Entry Draft).

			Regular Season								Playoffs						
Season	Club	Lea	GP	W	L	T	Mins	GA	SO	Avg	GP	W	L	Mins	GA	SO	Avg
1978-79	Medicine Hat	WHL	57	12	34	7	3093	318	0	6.17	....	....	....	....	....	....	....
1979-80	Medicine Hat	WHL	57	25	23	4	3049	212	1	4.17	13	6	6	638	48	0	4.51
1980-81	Medicine Hat	WHL	55	32	19	1	3023	200	4	3.97	4	1	3	244	17	0	4.18
	Indianapolis	CHL	....	....	....	....	....	....	....	....	2	....	....	135	8	0	3.56
1981-82	Indianapolis	CHL	51	27	19	4	3033	149	1	*2.95	13	11	2	842	34	*1	*2.42
1982-83	Indianapolis	CHL	47	*26	17	1	2744	139	2	3.04	10	*7	3	*637	28	0	*2.64
1983-84	**NY Islanders**	**NHL**	**12**	**7**	**2**	**0**	**535**	**28**	**0**	**3.14**	....	....	....	....	....	....	....
	Indianapolis	CHL	6	3	2	1	370	21	0	3.40	....	....	....	....	....	....	....
1984-85	**NY Islanders**	**NHL**	**41**	**19**	**17**	**3**	**2335**	**141**	**2**	**3.62**	**5**	**1**	**3**	**281**	**8**	**0**	**1.71**
1985-86	**NY Islanders**	**NHL**	**45**	**19**	**15**	**8**	**2563**	**137**	**1**	**3.21**	**2**	**0**	**2**	**120**	**6**	**0**	**3.00**
1986-87	**NY Islanders**	**NHL**	**46**	**21**	**15**	**7**	**2634**	**145**	**0**	**3.30**	**14**	**7**	**7**	**842**	**38**	**0**	**2.71**
1987-88	**NY Islanders**	**NHL**	**47**	**22**	**17**	**5**	**2751**	**153**	**3**	**3.34**	**6**	**2**	**4**	**381**	**23**	**0**	**3.62**
1988-89	**NY Islanders**	**NHL**	***50**	**18**	**24**	**3**	***2800**	**183**	**0**	**3.92**	....	....	....	....	....	....	....
	Los Angeles	**NHL**	***16**	**10**	**4**	**2**	***974**	**47**	**1**	**2.90**	**10**	**4**	**6**	**566**	**35**	**0**	**3.71**
1989-90	**Los Angeles**	**NHL**	**52**	**22**	**21**	**6**	**2860**	**194**	**2**	**4.07**	**9**	**4**	**4**	**539**	**39**	**0**	**4.34**
1990-91	**Los Angeles**	**NHL**	**47**	**26**	**13**	**6**	**2730**	**132**	**3**	**2.90**	**12**	**6**	**6**	**798**	**37**	**0**	**2.78**
1991-92	**Los Angeles**	**NHL**	**60**	**26**	**17**	**13**	**3509**	**197**	**1**	**3.37**	**6**	**2**	**4**	**355**	**22**	**0**	**3.72**
1992-93	**Los Angeles**	**NHL**	**50**	**18**	**21**	**6**	**2718**	**175**	**2**	**3.86**	**20**	**10**	**10**	**1261**	**74**	**0**	**3.52**
1993-94	**Los Angeles**	**NHL**	**64**	**22**	**31**	**7**	**3713**	**228**	**1**	**3.68**	....	....	....	....	....	....	....
1994-95	**Los Angeles**	**NHL**	**35**	**14**	**13**	**5**	**1894**	**99**	**0**	**3.14**	....	....	....	....	....	....	....
1995-96	**Los Angeles**	**NHL**	**36**	**7**	**15**	**10**	**2077**	**113**	**0**	**3.26**	....	....	....	....	....	....	....
	Phoenix	IHL	1	0	1	0	50	5	0	5.95	....	....	....	....	....	....	....
1996-97	**San Jose**	**NHL**	**48**	**16**	**24**	**5**	**2631**	**140**	**0**	**3.19**	....	....	....	....	....	....	....
1997-98	**San Jose**	**NHL**	**28**	**4**	**16**	**2**	**1360**	**62**	**1**	**2.74**	**1**	**0**	**0**	**20**	**1**	**0**	**3.00**
	NHL Totals		**677**	**271**	**265**	**88**	**38084**	**2174**	**17**	**3.43**	**85**	**36**	**46**	**5163**	**283**	**0**	**3.29**

WHL Second All-Star Team (1981) • CHL First All-Star Team (1982, 1983) • Shared Terry Sawchuk Trophy (fewest goals against - CHL) with Rob Holland (1982, 1983) • Won Tommy Ivan Trophy (CHL's MVP) (1983)

Traded to **LA Kings** by **NY Islanders** for Mark Fitzpatrick, Wayne McBean and future considerations (Doug Crossman, May 23, 1989) February 22, 1989. Signed as a free agent by **San Jose**, August 18, 1996.

HURME, JANI (HOOR-meh) OTT.

Goaltender. Catches left. 6', 187 lbs. Born, Turku, Finland, January 7, 1975.
(Ottawa's 2nd choice, 58th overall, in 1997 Entry Draft).

			Regular Season								Playoffs						
Season	Club	Lea	GP	W	L	T	Mins	GA	SO	Avg	GP	W	L	Mins	GA	SO	Avg
1995-96	TPS Turku	Finland	16	....	....	....	946	34	2	2.16	10	....	....	545	22	2	2.42
	Kiekko-67	Finland-2	16	....	....	....	968	39	1	2.42	....	....	....	....	....	....	....
	TPS Turku	Fin-Jr.	13	....	....	....	777	34	1	2.63	....	....	....	....	....	....	....
1996-97	TPS Turku	Finland	48	31	11	6	2917	101	6	2.08	12	6	6	722	39	0	3.24
1997-98	Detroit	IHL	6	2	2	2	290	20	0	4.13	....	....	....	....	....	....	....
	Indianapolis	IHL	29	11	11	3	1506	83	1	3.30	3	1	0	129	10	0	4.62

IRBE, ARTURS (UHR-bay, AHR-tuhrs)

Goaltender. Catches left. 5'8", 175 lbs. Born, Riga, Latvia, February 2, 1967.
(Minnesota's 11th choice, 196th overall, in 1989 Entry Draft).

			Regular Season								Playoffs						
Season	Club	Lea	GP	W	L	T	Mins	GA	SO	Avg	GP	W	L	Mins	GA	SO	Avg
1986-87	Dynamo Riga	USSR	2	....	....	....	27	1	0	2.22	....	....	....	....	....	....	....
1987-88	Dynamo Riga	USSR	34	....	....	....	1870	86	4	2.69	....	....	....	....	....	....	....
1988-89	Dynamo Riga	USSR	40	....	....	....	2460	116	4	2.85	....	....	....	....	....	....	....
1989-90	Dynamo Riga	USSR	48	....	....	....	2880	115	2	2.42	....	....	....	....	....	....	....
1990-91	Dynamo Riga	USSR	46	....	....	....	2713	133	5	2.94	....	....	....	....	....	....	....
1991-92	**San Jose**	**NHL**	**13**	**2**	**6**	**3**	**645**	**48**	**0**	**4.47**	....	....	....	....	....	....	....
	Kansas City	IHL	32	24	7	1	1955	80	0	*2.46	*15	*12	3	914	44	0	*2.89
1992-93	**San Jose**	**NHL**	**36**	**7**	**26**	**0**	**2074**	**142**	**1**	**4.11**	....	....	....	....	....	....	....
	Kansas City	IHL	6	3	3	0	364	20	0	3.30	....	....	....	....	....	....	....
1993-94	**San Jose**	**NHL**	***74**	**30**	**28**	**16**	***4412**	**209**	**3**	**2.84**	**14**	**7**	**7**	**806**	**50**	**0**	**3.72**
1994-95	**San Jose**	**NHL**	**38**	**14**	**19**	**3**	**2043**	**111**	**4**	**3.26**	**6**	**2**	**4**	**316**	**27**	**0**	**5.13**
1995-96	**San Jose**	**NHL**	**22**	**4**	**12**	**4**	**1112**	**85**	**0**	**4.59**	....	....	....	....	....	....	....
	Kansas City	IHL	4	1	2	1	226	16	0	4.24	....	....	....	....	....	....	....
1996-97	**Dallas**	**NHL**	**35**	**17**	**12**	**3**	**1965**	**88**	**3**	**2.69**	**1**	**0**	**0**	**13**	**0**	**0**	**0.00**
1997-98	**Vancouver**	**NHL**	**41**	**14**	**11**	**6**	**1999**	**91**	**2**	**2.73**	....	....	....	....	....	....	....
	NHL Totals		**259**	**88**	**114**	**35**	**14250**	**774**	**13**	**3.26**	**21**	**9**	**11**	**1135**	**77**	**0**	**4.07**

USSR Rookie-of-the-Year (1988) • IHL First All-Star Team (1992) • Shared James Norris Memorial Trophy (fewest goals against - IHL) with Wade Flaherty (1992)

Played in NHL All-Star Game (1994)

Claimed by **San Jose** from **Minnesota** in Dispersal Draft, May 30, 1991. Signed as a free agent by **Dallas**, August 19, 1996. Signed as a free agent by **Vancouver**, August 25, 1997.

JABLONSKI, PAT CAR.

Goaltender. Catches right. 6', 180 lbs. Born, Toledo, OH, June 20, 1967.
(St. Louis' 6th choice, 138th overall, in 1985 Entry Draft).

			Regular Season								Playoffs						
Season	Club	Lea	GP	W	L	T	Mins	GA	SO	Avg	GP	W	L	Mins	GA	SO	Avg
1984-85	Detroit	NAJHL	29	....	....	....	1483	95	0	3.84	....	....	....	....	....	....	....
1985-86	Windsor	OHL	29	6	16	4	1600	119	1	4.46	6	0	3	263	20	0	4.56
1986-87	Windsor	OHL	41	22	14	2	2328	128	*3	3.30	12	8	4	710	38	0	3.21
1987-88	Peoria	IHL	5	2	2	1	285	17	0	3.58	....	....	....	....	....	....	....
	Windsor	OHL	18	14	3	0	994	48	2	2.90	9	*8	0	537	28	0	3.13
1988-89	Peoria	IHL	35	11	20	0	2051	163	1	4.77	3	0	2	130	13	0	6.00
1989-90	**St. Louis**	**NHL**	**4**	**0**	**3**	**0**	**208**	**17**	**0**	**4.90**	....	....	....	....	....	....	....
	Peoria	IHL	36	14	17	4	2023	165	0	4.89	4	1	3	223	19	0	5.11
1990-91	**St. Louis**	**NHL**	**8**	**2**	**3**	**3**	**492**	**25**	**0**	**3.05**	**3**	**0**	**0**	**90**	**5**	**0**	**3.33**
	Peoria	IHL	29	23	3	2	1738	87	0	3.00	10	7	2	532	23	0	2.59
1991-92	**St. Louis**	**NHL**	**10**	**3**	**6**	**0**	**468**	**38**	**0**	**4.87**	....	....	....	....	....	....	....
	Peoria	IHL	8	6	1	1	493	29	1	3.53	....	....	....	....	....	....	....
1992-93	**Tampa Bay**	**NHL**	**43**	**8**	**24**	**4**	**2268**	**150**	**1**	**3.97**	....	....	....	....	....	....	....
1993-94	**Tampa Bay**	**NHL**	**15**	**5**	**6**	**3**	**834**	**54**	**0**	**3.88**	....	....	....	....	....	....	....
	St. John's	AHL	16	12	3	1	962	49	1	3.05	11	6	5	676	36	0	3.19
1994-95	Chicago	IHL	4	0	4	0	216	17	0	4.71	....	....	....	....	....	....	....
	Houston	IHL	3	1	1	1	179	9	0	3.01	....	....	....	....	....	....	....
1995-96	**St. Louis**	**NHL**	**1**	**0**	**0**	**0**	**8**	**1**	**0**	**7.50**	....	....	....	....	....	....	....
	Montreal	**NHL**	**23**	**5**	**9**	**6**	**1264**	**62**	**0**	**2.94**	**1**	**0**	**0**	**49**	**1**	**0**	**1.22**
1996-97	**Montreal**	**NHL**	**17**	**4**	**6**	**2**	**754**	**50**	**0**	**3.98**	....	....	....	....	....	....	....
	Phoenix	**NHL**	**2**	**0**	**1**	**0**	**59**	**2**	**0**	**2.03**	....	....	....	....	....	....	....
1997-98	**Carolina**	**NHL**	**5**	**1**	**4**	**0**	**279**	**14**	**0**	**3.01**	....	....	....	....	....	....	....
	Cleveland	IHL	34	13	13	6	1950	98	0	3.01	....	....	....	....	....	....	....
	Quebec	IHL	7	3	3	0	368	21	0	3.42	....	....	....	....	....	....	....
	NHL Totals		**128**	**28**	**62**	**18**	**6634**	**413**	**1**	**3.74**	**4**	**0**	**0**	**139**	**6**	**0**	**2.59**

Shared James Norris Memorial Trophy (fewest goals against - IHL) with Guy Hebert (1991)

Traded to **Tampa Bay** by **St. Louis** with Steve Tuttle and Darin Kimble for future considerations, June 19, 1992. Traded to **Toronto** by **Tampa Bay** for cash, February 21, 1994. Claimed by **St. Louis** from **Toronto** in NHL Waiver Draft, October 2, 1995. Traded to **Montreal** by **St. Louis** for J.J. Daigneault, November 7, 1995. Traded to **Phoenix** by **Montreal** for Steve Cheredaryk, March 18, 1997. Signed as a free agent by **Carolina**, August 12, 1997.

JOHNSON, BRENT — ST.L.

Goaltender. Catches left. 6'1", 175 lbs. Born, Farmington, MI, March 12, 1977.
(Colorado's 5th choice, 129th overall, in 1995 Entry Draft).

			Regular Season								Playoffs						
Season	Club	Lea	GP	W	L	T	Mins	GA	SO	Avg	GP	W	L	Mins	GA	SO	Avg
1994-95	Owen Sound	OHL	18	3	9	1	904	75	0	4.98	....	....	....	....	....	....	....
1995-96	Owen Sound	OHL	58	24	28	1	3211	243	1	4.54	6	2	4	371	29	0	4.69
1996-97	Owen Sound	OHL	50	20	28	1	2798	201	1	4.31	4	0	4	253	24	0	5.69
1997-98	Worcester	AHL	42	14	15	7	2240	119	0	3.19	6	3	2	332	19	0	3.43

Traded to **St. Louis** by **Colorado** for San Jose's third round choice (previously acquired, Colorado selected Rick Berry) in 1997 Entry Draft and a conditional choice in 2000 Entry Draft, May 30, 1997.

JOSEPH, CURTIS — TOR.

Goaltender. Catches left. 5'10", 185 lbs. Born, Keswick, Ont., April 29, 1967.

			Regular Season								Playoffs						
Season	Club	Lea	GP	W	L	T	Mins	GA	SO	Avg	GP	W	L	Mins	GA	SO	Avg
1987-88	Notre Dame	SJHL	36	25	4	7	2174	94	1	2.59	....	....	....	....	....	....	....
1988-89	U. of Wisconsin	WCHA	38	21	11	5	2267	94	1	2.49	....	....	....	....	....	....	....
1989-90	**St. Louis**	**NHL**	**15**	**9**	**5**	**1**	**852**	**48**	**0**	**3.38**	**6**	**4**	**1**	**327**	**18**	**0**	**3.30**
	Peoria	IHL	23	10	8	2	1241	80	0	3.87	....	....	....	....	....	....	....
1990-91	**St. Louis**	**NHL**	**30**	**16**	**10**	**2**	**1710**	**89**	**0**	**3.12**	....	....	....	....	....	....	....
1991-92	**St. Louis**	**NHL**	**60**	**27**	**20**	**10**	**3494**	**175**	**2**	**3.01**	**6**	**2**	**4**	**379**	**23**	**0**	**3.64**
1992-93	**St. Louis**	**NHL**	**68**	**29**	**28**	**9**	**3890**	**196**	**1**	**3.02**	**11**	**7**	**4**	**715**	**27**	***2**	**2.27**
1993-94	**St. Louis**	**NHL**	**71**	**36**	**23**	**11**	**4127**	**213**	**1**	**3.10**	**4**	**0**	**4**	**246**	**15**	**0**	**3.66**
1994-95	**St. Louis**	**NHL**	**36**	**20**	**10**	**1**	**1914**	**89**	**1**	**2.79**	**7**	**3**	**3**	**392**	**24**	**0**	**3.67**
1995-96	Las Vegas	IHL	15	12	2	1	874	29	1	1.99	....	....	....	....	....	....	....
	Edmonton	**NHL**	**34**	**15**	**16**	**2**	**1936**	**111**	**0**	**3.44**	....	....	....	....	....	....	....
1996-97	**Edmonton**	**NHL**	**72**	**32**	**29**	**9**	**4100**	**200**	**6**	**2.93**	**12**	**5**	**7**	**767**	**36**	**2**	**2.82**
1997-98	**Edmonton**	**NHL**	**71**	**29**	**31**	**9**	**4132**	**181**	**8**	**2.63**	**12**	**5**	**7**	**716**	**23**	**3**	**1.93**
	Canada	Olympics	DID NOT PLAY – SPARE GOALTENDER														
	NHL Totals		**457**	**213**	**172**	**54**	**26155**	**1302**	**19**	**2.99**	**58**	**26**	**30**	**3542**	**166**	**7**	**2.81**

WCHA First All-Star Team (1989) • NCAA West Second All-American Team (1989)

Played in NHL All-Star Game (1994)

Signed as a free agent by **St. Louis**, June 16, 1989. Traded to **Edmonton** by **St. Louis** with the rights to Michael Grier for St. Louis' 1st round choices (previously acquired) in 1996 (St. Louis selected Marty Reasoner) and 1997 (later traded to Los Angeles — Los Angeles selected Matt Zultek) Entry Drafts, August 4, 1995. Signed as a free agent by **Toronto**, July 15, 1998.

KEYES, TIM — VAN.

Goaltender. Catches left. 5'11", 185 lbs. Born, Ganonoque, Ont., May 28, 1976.

			Regular Season								Playoffs						
Season	Club	Lea	GP	W	L	T	Mins	GA	SO	Avg	GP	W	L	Mins	GA	SO	Avg
1993-94	Kingston	OHL	6	0	2	0	171	16	0	5.61	....	....	....	....	....	....	....
1994-95	Kingston	OHL	16	7	2	2	750	56	0	4.48	1	0	0	27	5	0	11.11
1995-96	Ottawa	OHL	27	15	7	2	1497	73	1	2.93	3	0	2	110	12	0	6.55
1996-97	Ottawa	OHL	37	26	5	2	1990	87	2	2.62	17	10	5	929	50	0	3.23
1997-98	Syracuse	AHL	15	2	7	4	831	59	0	4.26	....	....	....	....	....	....	....
	Raleigh	ECHL	1	0	1	0	60	4	0	4.00	....	....	....	....	....	....	....
	Dayton	ECHL	9	1	6	2	534	33	0	3.70	....	....	....	....	....	....	....

Signed as a free agent by **Vancouver**, September 8, 1997.

KHABIBULIN, NIKOLAI — (khah-bee-BOO-lihn) PHX.

Goaltender. Catches left. 6'1", 176 lbs. Born, Sverdlovsk, USSR, January 13, 1973.
(Winnipeg's 8th choice, 204th overall, in 1992 Entry Draft).

			Regular Season								Playoffs						
Season	Club	Lea	GP	W	L	T	Mins	GA	SO	Avg	GP	W	L	Mins	GA	SO	Avg
1991-92	CSKA Moscow	CIS	2	....	....	....	34	2	0	3.52	....	....	....	....	....	....	....
	Russia	Olympics	DID NOT PLAY – SPARE GOALTENDER														
1992-93	CSKA Moscow	CIS	13	....	....	....	491	27	....	3.29	....	....	....	....	....	....	....
1993-94	CSKA Moscow	CIS	46	....	....	....	2625	116	....	2.65	3	....	....	193	11	....	3.42
	Russian Pens	IHL	12	2	7	2	639	47	0	4.41	....	....	....	....	....	....	....
1994-95	Springfield	AHL	23	9	9	3	1240	80	0	3.87	....	....	....	....	....	....	....
	Winnipeg	**NHL**	**26**	**8**	**9**	**4**	**1339**	**76**	**0**	**3.41**	....	....	....	....	....	....	....
1995-96	**Winnipeg**	**NHL**	**53**	**26**	**20**	**3**	**2914**	**152**	**2**	**3.13**	**6**	**2**	**4**	**359**	**19**	**0**	**3.18**
1996-97	**Phoenix**	**NHL**	**72**	**30**	**33**	**6**	**4091**	**193**	**7**	**2.83**	**7**	**3**	**4**	**426**	**15**	**1**	**2.11**
1997-98	**Phoenix**	**NHL**	**70**	**30**	**28**	**10**	**4026**	**184**	**4**	**2.74**	**4**	**2**	**1**	**185**	**13**	**0**	**4.22**
	NHL Totals		**221**	**94**	**90**	**23**	**12370**	**605**	**13**	**2.93**	**17**	**7**	**9**	**970**	**47**	**1**	**2.91**

Played in NHL All-Star Game (1998)

Transferred to **Phoenix** after **Winnipeg** franchise relocated, July 1, 1996.

KHLOPTONOV, DENIS — (khloh-POHT-nahv) FLA.

Goaltender. Catches left. 6'4", 198 lbs. Born, Moscow, USSR, January 27, 1978.
(Florida's 8th choice, 209th overall, in 1996 Entry Draft).

			Regular Season								Playoffs						
Season	Club	Lea	GP	W	L	T	Mins	GA	SO	Avg	GP	W	L	Mins	GA	SO	Avg
1995-96	CSKA Moscow	CIS-Jr.	STATISTICS NOT AVAILABLE														
1996-97	CSKA Moscow	Russia	21	....	....	....	1260	42	0	2.00	....	....	....	....	....	....	....
1997-98	CSKA Moscow	Russia	20	....	....	....	987	58	....	3.53	....	....	....	....	....	....	....

KIDD, TREVOR — CAR.

Goaltender. Catches left. 6'2", 190 lbs. Born, Dugald, Man., March 29, 1972.
(Calgary's 1st choice, 11th overall, in 1990 Entry Draft).

			Regular Season								Playoffs						
Season	Club	Lea	GP	W	L	T	Mins	GA	SO	Avg	GP	W	L	Mins	GA	SO	Avg
1988-89	Brandon	WHL	32	11	13	1	1509	102	0	4.06	....	....	....	....	....	....	....
1989-90	Brandon	WHL	*63	24	32	2	*3676	254	2	4.15	....	....	....	....	....	....	....
1990-91	Brandon	WHL	30	10	19	1	1730	117	0	4.06	....	....	....	....	....	....	....
	Spokane	WHL	14	8	3	0	749	44	0	3.52	15	*14	1	926	32	2	*2.07
1991-92	Canada	Nat-Tm	28	18	4	4	1349	79	2	3.51	....	....	....	....	....	....	....
	Canada	Olympics	1	1	0	0	60	0	1	0.00	....	....	....	....	....	....	....
	Calgary	**NHL**	**2**	**1**	**1**	**0**	**120**	**8**	**0**	**4.00**	....	....	....	....	....	....	....
1992-93	Salt Lake	IHL	29	10	16	1	1696	111	1	3.93	....	....	....	....	....	....	....
1993-94	**Calgary**	**NHL**	**31**	**13**	**7**	**6**	**1614**	**85**	**0**	**3.16**	....	....	....	....	....	....	....
1994-95	**Calgary**	**NHL**	***43**	**22**	**14**	**6**	***2463**	**107**	**3**	**2.61**	**7**	**3**	**4**	**434**	**26**	**1**	**3.59**
1995-96	**Calgary**	**NHL**	**47**	**15**	**21**	**8**	**2570**	**119**	**3**	**2.78**	**2**	**0**	**1**	**83**	**9**	**0**	**6.51**
1996-97	**Calgary**	**NHL**	**55**	**21**	**23**	**6**	**2979**	**141**	**4**	**2.84**	....	....	....	....	....	....	....
1997-98	**Carolina**	**NHL**	**47**	**21**	**21**	**3**	**2685**	**97**	**3**	**2.17**	....	....	....	....	....	....	....
	NHL Totals		**225**	**93**	**87**	**29**	**12431**	**557**	**13**	**2.69**	**9**	**3**	**5**	**517**	**35**	**1**	**4.06**

WHL East First All-Star Team (1990) • Canadian Major Junior Goaltender of the Year (1990)

Traded to **Carolina** by **Calgary** with Gary Roberts for Andrew Cassels and Jean-Sebastien Giguere, August 25, 1997.

KIPRUSOFF, MIIKKA — (KIHP-ruh-sohf, MEE-kah) S.J.

Goaltender. Catches left. 6', 176 lbs. Born, Turku, Finland, October 26, 1976.
(San Jose's 5th choice, 116th overall, in 1995 Entry Draft).

			Regular Season								Playoffs						
Season	Club	Lea	GP	W	L	T	Mins	GA	SO	Avg	GP	W	L	Mins	GA	SO	Avg
1994-95	TPS Turku	Fin-Jr.	31	....	....	....	1896	92	....	2.91	....	....	....	....	....	....	....
	TPS Turku	Finland	4	....	....	....	240	12	0	3.00	2	....	....	120	7	....	3.50
1995-96	TPS Turku	Fin-Jr.	3	....	....	....	180	9	....	3.00	....	....	....	....	....	....	....
	Kiekko-67	Finland-2	5	....	....	....	300	7	....	1.40	....	....	....	....	....	....	....
	TPS Turku	Finland	12	....	....	....	550	38	0	4.14	3	....	....	114	4	....	2.11
1996-97	AIK Solna	Sweden	42	....	....	....	2466	104	3	2.53	7	....	....	420	23	0	3.28
1997-98	AIK Solna	Sweden	42	....	....	....	2457	110	....	2.69	....	....	....	....	....	....	....

KOLZIG, OLAF — (KOHLT-zihg, OH-lahf) WSH.

Goaltender. Catches left. 6'3", 225 lbs. Born, Johannesburg, South Africa, April 9, 1970.
(Washington's 1st choice, 19th overall, in 1989 Entry Draft).

			Regular Season								Playoffs						
Season	Club	Lea	GP	W	L	T	Mins	GA	SO	Avg	GP	W	L	Mins	GA	SO	Avg
1987-88	New Westminster	WHL	15	6	5	0	650	48	1	4.43	3	0	3	149	11	0	4.43
1988-89	Tri-City	WHL	30	16	10	2	1671	97	1	*3.48	....	....	....	....	....	....	....
1989-90	**Washington**	**NHL**	**2**	**0**	**2**	**0**	**120**	**12**	**0**	**6.00**	....	....	....	....	....	....	....
	Tri-City	WHL	48	27	27	3	2504	250	1	4.38	6	4	0	318	27	0	5.09
1990-91	Baltimore	AHL	26	10	12	1	1367	72	0	3.16	....	....	....	....	....	....	....
	Hampton Roads	ECHL	21	11	9	1	1248	71	2	3.41	3	1	2	180	14	0	4.66
1991-92	Baltimore	AHL	28	5	17	2	1503	105	1	4.19	....	....	....	....	....	....	....
	Hampton Roads	ECHL	14	11	3	0	847	41	0	2.90	....	....	....	....	....	....	....
1992-93	**Washington**	**NHL**	**1**	**0**	**0**	**0**	**20**	**2**	**0**	**6.00**	....	....	....	....	....	....	....
	Rochester	AHL	49	25	16	4	2737	168	0	3.68	*17	9	8	*1040	61	0	3.52
1993-94	**Washington**	**NHL**	**7**	**0**	**3**	**0**	**224**	**20**	**0**	**5.36**	....	....	....	....	....	....	....
	Portland	AHL	29	16	8	5	1725	88	3	3.06	17	*12	5	1035	44	0	*2.55
1994-95	**Washington**	**NHL**	**14**	**2**	**8**	**2**	**724**	**30**	**0**	**2.49**	**2**	**1**	**0**	**44**	**1**	**0**	**1.36**
	Portland	AHL	2	1	0	1	125	3	0	1.44	....	....	....	....	....	....	....
1995-96	**Washington**	**NHL**	**18**	**4**	**8**	**2**	**897**	**46**	**0**	**3.08**	**5**	**2**	**3**	**341**	**11**	**0**	***1.94**
	Portland	AHL	5	5	0	0	300	7	1	1.40	....	....	....	....	....	....	....
1996-97	**Washington**	**NHL**	**29**	**8**	**15**	**4**	**1645**	**71**	**2**	**2.59**	....	....	....	....	....	....	....
1997-98	**Washington**	**NHL**	**64**	**33**	**18**	**10**	**3788**	**139**	**5**	**2.20**	**21**	**12**	**9**	**1351**	**44**	***4**	**1.95**
	Germany	Olympics	2	2	0	0	120	2	1	1.00	....	....	....	....	....	....	....
	NHL Totals		**135**	**47**	**54**	**18**	**7418**	**320**	**7**	**2.59**	**28**	**15**	**12**	**1736**	**56**	**4**	**1.94**

WHL West Second All-Star Team (1989) • Shared Harry "Hap" Holmes Trophy (fewest goals-against - AHL) with Byron Dafoe (1994) • Won Jack Butterfield Trophy (Playoff MVP - IHL) (1994)

Played in NHL All-Star Game (1998)

• Scored a goal while with Tri-City (WHL), November 29, 1989.

LABARBERA, JASON — NYR

Goaltender. Catches left. 6'2", 205 lbs. Born, Burnaby, B.C., January 18, 1980.
(NY Rangers' 3rd choice, 66th overall, in 1998 Entry Draft).

			Regular Season								Playoffs						
Season	Club	Lea	GP	W	L	T	Mins	GA	SO	Avg	GP	W	L	Mins	GA	SO	Avg
1996-97	Tri-City	WHL	2	1	0	0	63	4	0	3.81	....	....	....	....	....	....	....
	Portland	WHL	9	5	1	1	443	18	0	2.44	....	....	....	....	....	....	....
1997-98	Portland	WHL	23	18	4	0	1305	72	1	3.31	....	....	....	....	....	....	....

LABBE, JEAN-FRANCOIS — (lah-BAY) NYR

Goaltender. Catches left. 5'9", 170 lbs. Born, Sherbrooke, Que., June 15, 1972.

			Regular Season								Playoffs						
Season	Club	Lea	GP	W	L	T	Mins	GA	SO	Avg	GP	W	L	Mins	GA	SO	Avg
1989-90	Trois-Rivieres	QMJHL	28	13	10	0	1499	106	1	4.24	3	1	1	132	8	0	3.64
1990-91	Trois-Rivieres	QMJHL	54	*35	14	0	2870	158	5	3.30	5	1	4	230	19	0	4.96
1991-92	Trois-Rivieres	QMJHL	48	*31	13	3	2749	142	1	3.10	*15	*10	3	791	33	*1	*2.50
1992-93	Hull	QMJHL	46	26	18	2	2701	156	2	3.46	10	6	3	518	24	*1	*2.78
1993-94	Thunder Bay	ColHL	52	*35	11	4	*2900	150	*2	*3.10	8	7	1	493	18	*2	*2.19
	P.E.I.	AHL	7	4	3	0	389	22	0	3.39	....	....	....	....	....	....	....
1994-95	P.E.I.	AHL	32	13	14	3	1817	94	2	3.10	....	....	....	....	....	....	....
1995-96	Cornwall	AHL	55	25	21	5	2972	144	3	2.91	8	3	5	471	21	1	2.68
1996-97	Hershey	AHL	66	*34	22	9	3811	160	*6	*2.52	*23	*14	8	*1364	59	1	2.60
1997-98	Hamilton	AHL	52	24	17	11	3138	149	2	2.85	7	3	4	413	20	0	2.90

QMJHL First All-Star Team (1992) • ColHL First All-Star Team (1994) • Named ColHL's Rookie of the Year (1994) • Named ColHL's Outstanding Goaltender (1994) • AHL First All-Star Team (1997) • Won Harry "Hap" Holmes Memorial Trophy (fewest goals against - AHL) (1997) • Won Baz Bastien Memorial Trophy (Top Goaltender - AHL) (1997) • Won Les Cunningham Award (MVP - AHL) (1997)

Signed as a free agent by **Ottawa**, May 12, 1994. Traded to **Colorado** by **Ottawa** for future considerations, September 20, 1995. Signed as a free agent by **Edmonton**, September 2, 1997. Signed as a free agent by **NY Rangers**, July 30, 1998.

LABRECQUE, PATRICK — (lah-BREHK)

Goaltender. Catches left. 6', 190 lbs. Born, Laval, Que., March 6, 1971.
(Quebec's 5th choice, 90th overall, in 1991 Entry Draft).

			Regular Season								Playoffs						
Season	Club	Lea	GP	W	L	T	Mins	GA	SO	Avg	GP	W	L	Mins	GA	SO	Avg
1990-91	St-Jean	QMJHL	59	17	34	6	3375	216	1	3.84	....	....	....	....	....	....	....
1991-92	Halifax	AHL	29	5	12	8	1570	114	0	4.36	....	....	....	....	....	....	....
1992-93	Greensboro	ECHL	11	6	3	2	650	31	0	2.86	1	0	1	59	5	0	5.08
	Halifax	AHL	20	3	12	2	914	76	0	4.99	....	....	....	....	....	....	....
1993-94	Cornwall	AHL	4	1	2	0	198	8	1	2.42	....	....	....	....	....	....	....
	Greensboro	ECHL	29	17	8	2	1609	89	0	3.32	1	0	0	22	4	0	10.80
1994-95	Fredericton	AHL	35	15	17	1	1913	104	1	3.26	*16	*10	6	*967	40	1	2.48
	Wheeling	ECHL	5	2	3	0	281	22	0	4.69	....	....	....	....	....	....	....
1995-96	**Montreal**	**NHL**	**2**	**0**	**1**	**0**	**98**	**7**	**0**	**4.29**	....	....	....	....	....	....	....
	Fredericton	AHL	48	23	18	6	2686	153	3	3.42	7	3	3	405	31	0	4.59
1996-97	Fredericton	AHL	12	1	7	1	602	31	0	3.09	....	....	....	....	....	....	....
	Quebec	IHL	9	2	6	0	482	29	0	3.61	....	....	....	....	....	....	....
1997-98	Baton Rouge	ECHL	34	17	13	4	1935	107	0	3.32	....	....	....	....	....	....	....
	Hershey	AHL	....	....	....	....	....	....	....	....	1	0	0	10	0	0	0.00
	NHL Totals		**2**	**0**	**1**	**0**	**98**	**7**	**0**	**4.29**	....	....	....	....	....	....	....

Signed as a free agent by **Montreal**, June 21, 1994.

LAGRAND, SCOTT

Goaltender. Catches left. 6', 165 lbs. Born, Potsdam, NY, February 11, 1970.
(Philadelphia's 5th choice, 77th overall, in 1988 Entry Draft).

			Regular Season								Playoffs						
Season	**Club**	**Lea**	**GP**	**W**	**L**	**T**	**Mins**	**GA**	**SO**	**Avg**	**GP**	**W**	**L**	**Mins**	**GA**	**SO**	**Avg**
1987-88	Hotchkiss High	H.S.	25	....	....	....	1560	36	2	2.50	....	....	....	....	....	....	....
1988-89	Boston College	H.E.						DID NOT PLAY – FRESHMAN									
1989-90	Boston College	H.E.	24	17	4	0	1268	57	0	2.70	....	....	....	....	....	....	....
1990-91	Boston College	H.E.	23	12	8	0	1153	63	2	3.28	....	....	....	....	....	....	....
1991-92	Boston College	H.E.	30	11	16	2	1750	108	1	3.70	....	....	....	....	....	....	....
1992-93	Hershey	AHL	32	8	17	4	1854	145	0	4.69	....	....	....	....	....	....	....
1993-94	Hershey	AHL	40	16	13	3	2032	117	2	3.45	....	....	....	....	....	....	....
1994-95	Atlanta	IHL	21	7	7	3	993	67	0	4.04	3	0	2	101	10	0	5.91
	Hershey	AHL	21	7	9	3	1104	71	1	3.86	....	....	....	....	....	....	....
1995-96	Orlando	IHL	33	17	7	3	1618	103	1	3.82	3	0	0	51	1	0	1.17
1996-97	Orlando	IHL	35	16	10	2	1746	85	2	2.92	4	0	2	153	5	0	1.96
1997-98	Orlando	IHL	23	8	9	3	1264	68	0	3.23	....	....	....	....	....	....	....
	Utah	IHL	7	1	1	2	360	18	0	3.00	....	....	....	....	....	....	....
	Fort Wayne	IHL	11	3	5	0	488	28	0	3.44	2	0	1	94	7	0	4.47

Hockey East First All-Star Team (1991) • NCAA East Second All-American Team (1992)

Traded to **Tampa Bay** by **Philadelphia** for Mike Greenlay, February 2, 1995.

LALIME, PATRICK (lah-LEEM) ANA.

Goaltender. Catches left. 6'2", 170 lbs. Born, St. Bonaventure, Que., July 7, 1974.
(Pittsburgh's 6th choice, 156th overall, in 1993 Entry Draft).

			Regular Season								Playoffs						
Season	**Club**	**Lea**	**GP**	**W**	**L**	**T**	**Mins**	**GA**	**SO**	**Avg**	**GP**	**W**	**L**	**Mins**	**GA**	**SO**	**Avg**
1992-93	Shawinigan	QMJHL	44	10	24	4	2467	192	0	4.67	....	....	....	....	....	....	....
1993-94	Shawinigan	QMJHL	48	22	20	0	2733	192	1	4.22	5	1	3	223	25	0	6.73
1994-95	Hampton Roads	ECHL	26	15	7	3	1470	82	2	3.35	....	....	....	....	....	....	....
	Cleveland	IHL	23	7	10	4	1230	91	0	4.44	....	....	....	....	....	....	....
1995-96	Cleveland	IHL	41	20	12	7	2314	149	0	3.86	....	....	....	....	....	....	....
1996-97	**Pittsburgh**	**NHL**	**39**	**21**	**12**	**2**	**2058**	**101**	**3**	**2.94**	....	....	....	....	....	....	....
	Cleveland	IHL	14	6	6	2	834	45	1	3.24	....	....	....	....	....	....	....
1997-98	Grand Rapids	IHL	31	10	10	9	1749	76	2	2.61	1	0	1	77	4	0	3.11
	NHL Totals		**39**	**21**	**12**	**2**	**2058**	**101**	**3**	**2.94**	....	....	....	....	....	....	....

NHL All-Rookie Team (1997)

Rights traded to **Anaheim** by **Pittsburgh** for Sean Pronger, March 24, 1998.

LAMBERT, JUDD N.J.

Goaltender. Catches left. 6'1", 175 lbs. Born, Richmond, B.C., June 3, 1974.
(New Jersey's 9th choice, 221st overall, in 1993 Entry Draft).

			Regular Season								Playoffs						
Season	**Club**	**Lea**	**GP**	**W**	**L**	**T**	**Mins**	**GA**	**SO**	**Avg**	**GP**	**W**	**L**	**Mins**	**GA**	**SO**	**Avg**
1992-93	Chilliwack	BCJHL	50	....	....	....	2488	234	0	5.84	....	....	....	....	....	....	....
1993-94	Colorado	WCHA	11	6	4	0	620	33	0	3.19	....	....	....	....	....	....	....
1994-95	Colorado	WCHA	21	12	7	0	1060	57	*1	3.23	....	....	....	....	....	....	....
1995-96	Colorado	WCHA	19	16	1	2	1179	43	1	*2.19	....	....	....	....	....	....	....
1996-97	Colorado	WCHA	34	19	12	1	1993	101	3	3.04	....	....	....	....	....	....	....
1997-98	Dayton	ECHL	23	9	10	4	1373	75	0	3.28	3	1	2	176	10	0	3.39
	Albany	AHL	4	0	3	1	213	16	0	4.51	....	....	....	....	....	....	....
	Fort Wayne	IHL	4	1	2	0	196	12	0	3.66	....	....	....	....	....	....	....

LAMOTHE, MARC (luh-MAWTH) CHI.

Goaltender. Catches left. 6'1", 204 lbs. Born, New Liskeard, Ont., February 27, 1974.
(Montreal's 6th choice, 92nd overall, in 1992 Entry Draft).

			Regular Season								Playoffs						
Season	**Club**	**Lea**	**GP**	**W**	**L**	**T**	**Mins**	**GA**	**SO**	**Avg**	**GP**	**W**	**L**	**Mins**	**GA**	**SO**	**Avg**
1991-92	Kingston	OHL	42	10	25	2	2378	189	1	4.77	....	....	....	....	....	....	....
1992-93	Kingston	OHL	45	23	12	6	2489	162	1	3.91	15	8	5	753	48	1	3.82
1993-94	Kingston	OHL	48	23	20	5	2828	177	*2	3.76	6	2	2	224	12	0	3.21
1994-95	Fredericton	AHL	9	2	5	0	428	32	0	4.48	....	....	....	....	....	....	....
	Wheeling	ECHL	13	9	2	1	737	38	0	3.10	....	....	....	....	....	....	....
1995-96	Fredericton	AHL	23	5	9	3	1166	73	1	3.76	3	1	2	161	9	0	3.36
1996-97	Indianapolis	IHL	38	20	14	4	2271	100	1	2.64	1	0	0	20	1	0	3.00
1997-98	Indianapolis	IHL	31	18	10	2	1772	72	3	2.44	4	1	3	177	10	0	3.38

Signed as a free agent by **Chicago**, September 26, 1996.

LANGKOW, SCOTT (LAING-kow) PHX.

Goaltender. Catches left. 5'11", 190 lbs. Born, Sherwood Park, Alta., April 21, 1975.
(Winnipeg's 2nd choice, 31st overall, in 1993 Entry Draft).

			Regular Season								Playoffs						
Season	**Club**	**Lea**	**GP**	**W**	**L**	**T**	**Mins**	**GA**	**SO**	**Avg**	**GP**	**W**	**L**	**Mins**	**GA**	**SO**	**Avg**
1991-92	Portland	WHL	1	0	0	0	33	2	0	3.46	....	....	....	....	....	....	....
1992-93	Portland	WHL	34	24	8	2	2064	119	2	3.46	9	6	3	535	31	0	3.48
1993-94	Portland	WHL	39	27	9	1	2302	121	2	3.15	10	6	4	600	34	0	3.40
1994-95	Portland	WHL	63	20	36	5	*3638	240	1	3.96	8	3	5	510	30	0	3.53
1995-96	**Winnipeg**	**NHL**	**1**	**0**	**0**	**0**	**6**	**0**	**0**	**0.00**	....	....	....	....	....	....	....
	Springfield	AHL	39	18	15	6	2329	116	3	2.99	7	4	2	393	23	0	3.51
1996-97	Springfield	AHL	33	15	9	7	1929	85	0	2.64	....	....	....	....	....	....	....
1997-98	**Phoenix**	**NHL**	**3**	**0**	**1**	**1**	**137**	**10**	**0**	**4.38**	....	....	....	....	....	....	....
	Springfield	AHL	51	30	13	5	2874	128	3	2.67	4	1	3	216	14	0	3.88
	NHL Totals		**4**	**0**	**1**	**1**	**143**	**10**	**0**	**4.20**	....	....	....	....	....	....	....

WHL West Second All-Star Team (1994, 1995) • Shared Harry "Hap" Holmes Memorial Trophy (fewest goals against - AHL) with Manny Legace (1996) • AHL First All-Star Team (1998) • Won Baz Bastien Memorial Trophy (Top Goaltender - AHL) (1998)

Transferred to **Phoenix** after **Winnipeg** franchise relocated, July 1, 1996.

LARIVEE, FRANCIS (la-RIHV-ay) TOR.

Goaltender. Catches left. 6'2", 198 lbs. Born, Montreal, Que., November 8, 1977.
(Toronto's 2nd choice, 50th overall, in 1996 Entry Draft).

			Regular Season								Playoffs						
Season	**Club**	**Lea**	**GP**	**W**	**L**	**T**	**Mins**	**GA**	**SO**	**Avg**	**GP**	**W**	**L**	**Mins**	**GA**	**SO**	**Avg**
1993-94	Val d'Or	QMJHL	36	5	20	1	1706	162	0	5.71	....	....	....	....	....	....	....
1994-95	Val d'Or	QMJHL	38	9	21	1	1795	132	0	4.41	....	....	....	....	....	....	....
1995-96	Val d'Or	QMJHL	*22	12	4	2	1162	73	0	3.77	....	....	....	....	....	....	....
	Laval	QMJHL	*39	9	24	1	2085	178	0	5.12	....	....	....	....	....	....	....
1996-97	Granby	QMJHL	1	1	0	0	60	1	0	1.00	1	0	0	50	4	0	4.80
	Laval	QMJHL	21	6	11	1	1068	77	1	4.33	....	....	....	....	....	....	....
	St. John's	AHL	4	3	1	0	244	9	0	2.21	2	0	0	1	0	0	0.00
1997-98	St. John's	AHL	30	6	12	5	1460	79	0	3.25	....	....	....	....	....	....	....

LAROCQUE, MICHEL (lah-RAWK) S.J.

Goaltender. Catches left. 5'11", 198 lbs. Born, Lahr, West Germany, October 3, 1976.
(San Jose's 5th choice, 137th overall, in 1996 Entry Draft).

			Regular Season								Playoffs						
Season	**Club**	**Lea**	**GP**	**W**	**L**	**T**	**Mins**	**GA**	**SO**	**Avg**	**GP**	**W**	**L**	**Mins**	**GA**	**SO**	**Avg**
1995-96	Boston U.	H.E.	14	10	1	1	735	42	0	3.43	....	....	....	....	....	....	....
1996-97	Boston U.	H.E.	24	16	4	4	1466	58	0	*2.37	....	....	....	....	....	....	....
1997-98	Boston U.	H.E.	24	17	4	1	1370	50	1	2.19	....	....	....	....	....	....	....

Hockey East Second All-Star Team (1998)

LEGACE, MANNY (LEH-gah-see) L.A.

Goaltender. Catches left. 5'9", 162 lbs. Born, Toronto, Ont., February 4, 1973.
(Hartford's 5th choice, 188th overall, in 1993 Entry Draft).

			Regular Season								Playoffs						
Season	**Club**	**Lea**	**GP**	**W**	**L**	**T**	**Mins**	**GA**	**SO**	**Avg**	**GP**	**W**	**L**	**Mins**	**GA**	**SO**	**Avg**
1989-90	Vaughn	OJHL	29	....	....	....	1660	119	1	4.30	....	....	....	....	....	....	....
1990-91	Niagara Falls	OHL	30	13	11	2	1515	107	0	4.24	4	1	1	119	10	0	5.04
1991-92	Niagara Falls	OHL	43	21	16	3	2384	143	0	3.60	14	8	5	791	56	0	4.25
1992-93	Niagara Falls	OHL	48	22	19	3	2630	171	0	3.90	4	0	4	240	18	0	4.50
1993-94	Canada	Nat-Tm	16	8	6	0	859	36	2	2.51	....	....	....	....	....	....	....
	Canada	Olympics						DID NOT PLAY – SPARE GOALTENDER									
1994-95	Springfield	AHL	39	12	17	6	2169	128	2	3.54	....	....	....	....	....	....	....
1995-96	Springfield	AHL	37	20	12	4	2196	83	*5	*2.27	4	1	3	220	18	0	4.91
1996-97	Springfield	AHL	36	17	14	5	2119	107	1	3.03	12	9	3	745	25	*2	2.01
	Richmond	ECHL	3	2	1	0	157	8	0	3.05	....	....	....	....	....	....	....
1997-98	Springfield	AHL	6	4	2	0	345	16	0	2.78	....	....	....	....	....	....	....
	Las Vegas	IHL	41	18	16	4	2106	111	1	3.16	4	1	3	237	16	0	4.05

OHL First All-Star Team (1993) • AHL First All-Star Team (1996) • Shared Harry "Hap" Holmes Memorial Trophy (fewest goals against - AHL) with Scott Langkow (1996) • Won Baz Bastien Memorial Trophy (Top Goaltender - AHL) (1996)

Rights transferred to **Carolina** after **Hartford** franchise relocated, June 25, 1997. • Traded to **LA Kings** by **Carolina** for a conditional choice in 1999 Entry Draft, July 31, 1998.

LEITZA, BRIAN

Goaltender. Catches left. 6'2", 185 lbs. Born, Waukegin, IL, March 16, 1974.
(Pittsburgh's 14th choice, 284th overall, in 1994 Entry Draft).

			Regular Season								Playoffs						
Season	**Club**	**Lea**	**GP**	**W**	**L**	**T**	**Mins**	**GA**	**SO**	**Avg**	**GP**	**W**	**L**	**Mins**	**GA**	**SO**	**Avg**
1993-94	Sioux City	USHL	32	....	....	....	1793	98	0	3.28	....	....	....	....	....	....	....
1994-95	St. Cloud State	WCHA	30	13	15	0	1626	93	0	3.43	....	....	....	....	....	....	....
1995-96	St. Cloud State	WCHA	35	12	19	4	2068	129	2	3.74	....	....	....	....	....	....	....
1996-97	St. Cloud State	WCHA	30	19	8	1	1738	93	0	3.21	....	....	....	....	....	....	....
1997-98	St. Cloud State	WCHA	38	22	14	2	2238	115	2	3.08	....	....	....	....	....	....	....

WCHA Second All-Star Team (1998)

LINDSAY, EVAN CGY.

Goaltender. Catches left. 6'1", 180 lbs. Born, Calgary, Alta., May 15, 1979.
(Calgary's 2nd choice, 32nd overall, in 1997 Entry Draft).

			Regular Season								Playoffs						
Season	**Club**	**Lea**	**GP**	**W**	**L**	**T**	**Mins**	**GA**	**SO**	**Avg**	**GP**	**W**	**L**	**Mins**	**GA**	**SO**	**Avg**
1995-96	Olds Grizzlys	AJHL	11	4	5	0	....	....	0	3.64	....	....	....	....	....	....	....
1996-97	Prince Albert	WHL	44	20	17	6	2651	153	1	3.46	4	0	4	240	16	0	4.00
1997-98	Prince Albert	WHL	52	14	30	4	3005	193	1	3.85	....	....	....	....	....	....	....

WHL East Second All-Star Team (1998)

LITTLE, NEIL PHI.

Goaltender. Catches left. 6'1", 193 lbs. Born, Medicine Hat, Alta., December 18, 1971.
(Philadelphia's 10th choice, 226th overall, in 1991 Entry Draft).

			Regular Season								Playoffs						
Season	**Club**	**Lea**	**GP**	**W**	**L**	**T**	**Mins**	**GA**	**SO**	**Avg**	**GP**	**W**	**L**	**Mins**	**GA**	**SO**	**Avg**
1989-90	Estevan	SJHL	46	21	19	4	2707	150	1	3.32	....	....	....	....	....	....	....
1990-91	RPI	ECAC	18	9	8	0	1032	71	0	4.13	....	....	....	....	....	....	....
1991-92	RPI	ECAC	28	11	11	3	1532	96	0	3.76	....	....	....	....	....	....	....
1992-93	RPI	ECAC	*31	*19	9	3	*1801	88	0	2.93	....	....	....	....	....	....	....
1993-94	RPI	ECAC	27	16	7	4	1570	88	0	3.36	....	....	....	....	....	....	....
	Hershey	AHL	1	0	0	0	18	1	0	3.33	....	....	....	....	....	....	....
1994-95	Hershey	AHL	19	5	7	3	919	60	0	3.91	....	....	....	....	....	....	....
	Johnstown	ECHL	16	7	6	1	897	55	0	3.68	3	0	2	145	11	0	4.55
1995-96	Hershey	AHL	48	21	18	6	2680	149	0	3.34	1	0	1	60	4	0	4.02
1996-97	Philadelphia	AHL	54	31	12	7	3007	145	0	2.89	10	6	4	620	20	1	*1.94
1997-98	Philadelphia	AHL	51	*31	11	7	2960	145	0	2.94	*20	*15	5	*1193	48	*3	2.41

ECAC First All-Star Team (1993) • NCAA East Second All-American Team (1993)

LITTMAN, DAVID

Goaltender. Catches left. 6', 183 lbs. Born, Cranston, RI, June 13, 1967.
(Buffalo's 12th choice, 211th overall, in 1987 Entry Draft).

			Regular Season								Playoffs						
Season	**Club**	**Lea**	**GP**	**W**	**L**	**T**	**Mins**	**GA**	**SO**	**Avg**	**GP**	**W**	**L**	**Mins**	**GA**	**SO**	**Avg**
1985-86	Boston College	H.E.	7	4	0	1	312	18	0	3.46	....	....	....	....	....	....	....
1986-87	Boston College	H.E.	21	15	5	0	1182	68	0	3.45	....	....	....	....	....	....	....
1987-88	Boston College	H.E.	30	11	16	2	1726	116	0	4.03	....	....	....	....	....	....	....
1988-89	Boston College	H.E.	*32	19	9	4	*1945	107	0	3.30	....	....	....	....	....	....	....
1989-90	Rochester	AHL	14	5	6	1	681	37	0	3.26	....	....	....	....	....	....	....
	Phoenix	IHL	18	8	7	2	1047	64	0	3.67	....	....	....	....	....	....	....
1990-91	**Buffalo**	**NHL**	**1**	**0**	**0**	**0**	**36**	**3**	**0**	**5.00**	....	....	....	....	....	....	....
	Rochester	AHL	*56	*33	13	5	*3155	160	3	3.04	8	4	2	378	16	0	2.54
1991-92	**Buffalo**	**NHL**	**1**	**0**	**1**	**0**	**60**	**4**	**0**	**4.00**	....	....	....	....	....	....	....
	Rochester	AHL	*61	*29	20	9	*3558	174	*3	2.93	15	8	7	879	43	*1	2.94
1992-93	**Tampa Bay**	**NHL**	**1**	**0**	**1**	**0**	**45**	**7**	**0**	**9.33**	....	....	....	....	....	....	....
	Atlanta	IHL	44	23	12	4	2390	134	0	3.36	3	1	2	178	8	0	2.70
1993-94	Fredericton	AHL	16	8	7	0	872	63	0	4.33	....	....	....	....	....	....	....
	Providence	AHL	25	10	11	3	1385	83	0	3.60	....	....	....	....	....	....	....
1994-95	Richmond	ECHL	8	4	2	0	346	13	1	2.25	*17	*12	4	*953	37	*3	*2.33
1995-96	Los Angeles	IHL	43	17	16	5	2245	145	1	3.88	....	....	....	....	....	....	....
1996-97	San Antonio	IHL	45	20	16	5	2437	138	2	3.40	4	1	3	230	11	0	2.87
1997-98	Orlando	IHL	44	21	13	6	2303	102	0	2.66	16	8	8	966	48	1	2.98
	NHL Totals		**3**	**0**	**2**	**0**	**141**	**14**	**0**	**5.96**	....	....	....	....	....	....	....

Hockey East Second All-Star Team (1988) • Hockey East First All-Star Team (1989) • NCAA East Second All-American Team (1989) • AHL First All-Star Team (1991) • Shared Harry "Hap" Holmes Memorial Trophy (fewest goals against - AHL) with Darcy Wakaluk (1991) • AHL Second All-Star Team (1992) • Won Harry "Hap" Holmes Memorial Trophy (fewest goals against - AHL) (1992)

Signed as a free agent by **Tampa Bay**, August 27, 1992. Signed as a free agent by **Boston**, August 6, 1993.

LUONGO, ROBERTO (loo-WAHN-goh) NYI

Goaltender. Catches left. 6'2", 175 lbs. Born, St-Leonard, Que., April 4, 1979.
(NY Islanders' 1st choice, 4th overall, in 1997 Entry Draft).

			Regular Season								Playoffs						
Season	Club	Lea	GP	W	L	T	Mins	GA	SO	Avg	GP	W	L	Mins	GA	SO	Avg
1995-96	Val d'Or	QMJHL	23	6	11	4	1201	74	0	3.70	3	0	1	68	5	0	4.41
1996-97	Val d'Or	QMJHL	60	32	22	2	3305	171	2	3.10	13	8	5	777	44	0	3.40
1997-98	Val d'Or	QMJHL	54	27	20	5	3046	157	*7	3.09	*17	*14	3	*1019	37	*2	*2.18

MacDONALD, AARON FLA.

Goaltender. Catches left. 6'1", 193 lbs. Born, Grand Prairie, Alta., August 29, 1977.
(Florida's 2nd choice, 36th overall, in 1995 Entry Draft).

			Regular Season								Playoffs						
Season	Club	Lea	GP	W	L	T	Mins	GA	SO	Avg	GP	W	L	Mins	GA	SO	Avg
1993-94	Swift Current	WHL	18	6	6	0	710	48	0	4.06	....	....	....	....	....	....	....
1994-95	Swift Current	WHL	53	24	20	6	2957	177	4	3.59	6	2	4	393	18	0	2.75
1995-96	Swift Current	WHL	29	14	12	2	1657	98	0	3.55	....	....	....	....	....	....	....
	Calgary	WHL	19	2	14	1	1025	84	0	4.92	....	....	....	....	....	....	....
1996-97	Calgary	WHL	30	6	19	3	1679	112	0	4.00	....	....	....	....	....	....	....
	Kelowna	WHL	23	17	6	0	1364	76	0	3.34	6	2	4	360	24	0	4.00
1997-98	Tallahassee	ECHL	37	11	19	2	1832	127	0	4.16	....	....	....	....	....	....	....

MacDONALD, TODD FLA.

Goaltender. Catches left. 6', 167 lbs. Born, Charlottetown, P.E.I., July 5, 1975.
(Florida's 7th choice, 109th overall, in 1993 Entry Draft).

			Regular Season								Playoffs						
Season	Club	Lea	GP	W	L	T	Mins	GA	SO	Avg	GP	W	L	Mins	GA	SO	Avg
1992-93	Tacoma	WHL	19	6	6	0	823	59	0	4.30	....	....	....	....	....	....	....
1993-94	Tacoma	WHL	29	13	10	2	1606	109	1	4.07	....	....	....	....	....	....	....
1994-95	Tacoma	WHL	60	*35	21	2	3433	179	3	3.13	4	1	3	255	13	0	3.06
1995-96	Carolina	AHL	18	3	12	2	980	78	0	4.78	....	....	....	....	....	....	....
	Detroit	ColHL	2	1	1	0	120	8	0	4.01	2	1	1	133	3	0	1.36
1996-97	Carolina	AHL	1	0	1	0	58	4	0	4.14	....	....	....	....	....	....	....
	Cincinnati	IHL	31	11	9	5	1616	73	2	2.71	1	0	0	20	1	0	3.00
1997-98	Birmingham	ECHL	3	1	1	1	180	8	0	2.67	....	....	....	....	....	....	....
	Cincinnati	IHL	15	4	6	3	796	46	0	3.46	....	....	....	....	....	....	....
	New Haven	AHL	13	8	3	2	790	30	1	2.28	3	0	3	177	15	0	5.07

WHL West First All-Star Team (1995)

MADDEN, CHRIS CAR.

Goaltender. Catches left. 6', 177 lbs. Born, Syracuse, NY, March 10, 1979.
(Carolina's 6th choice, 97th overall, in 1998 Entry Draft).

			Regular Season								Playoffs						
Season	Club	Lea	GP	W	L	T	Mins	GA	SO	Avg	GP	W	L	Mins	GA	SO	Avg
1996-97	Guelph	OHL	21	11	5	1	1128	68	1	3.62	3	1	1	72	4	0	3.33
1997-98	Guelph	OHL	51	*33	11	3	2906	132	4	2.73	12	*11	1	688	20	0	*1.74

Memorial Cup All-Star Team (1998) • Won Hap Emms Memorial Trophy (Memorial Cup Tournament Top Goaltender) (1998) • Won Stafford Smythe Memorial Trophy (Memorial Cup Tournament MVP) (1998)

MARACLE, NORM (MAHR-ah-cuhl) DET.

Goaltender. Catches left. 5'9", 175 lbs. Born, Belleville, Ont., October 2, 1974.
(Detroit's 6th choice, 126th overall, in 1993 Entry Draft).

			Regular Season								Playoffs						
Season	Club	Lea	GP	W	L	T	Mins	GA	SO	Avg	GP	W	L	Mins	GA	SO	Avg
1991-92	Saskatoon	WHL	29	13	6	3	1529	87	1	3.41	15	9	5	860	37	0	3.38
1992-93	Saskatoon	WHL	53	27	18	3	1939	160	1	3.27	9	4	5	569	33	0	3.48
1993-94	Saskatoon	WHL	56	*41	13	1	3219	148	2	2.76	16	*11	5	940	48	*1	3.06
1994-95	Adirondack	AHL	39	12	15	2	1997	119	0	3.57	....	....	....	....	....	....	....
1995-96	Adirondack	AHL	54	24	18	6	2949	135	2	2.75	1	0	1	30	4	0	8.11
1996-97	Adirondack	AHL	*68	*34	22	9	*3843	173	5	2.70	4	1	3	192	10	1	3.13
1997-98	**Detroit**	**NHL**	**4**	**2**	**0**	**1**	**178**	**6**	**0**	**2.02**	....	....	....	....	....	....	....
	Adirondack	AHL	*66	27	29	8	*3709	190	1	3.07	3	0	3	180	10	0	3.33
	NHL Totals		**4**	**2**	**0**	**1**	**178**	**6**	**0**	**2.02**	....	....	....	....	....	....	....

WHL East Second All-Star Team (1993) • WHL East First All-Star Team (1994) • Canadian Major Junior First All-Star Team (1994) • Canadian Major Junior Goaltender of the Year (1994) • AHL Second All-Star Team (1997, 1998)

MASON, CHRIS ANA.

Goaltender. Catches left. 6', 200 lbs. Born, Red Deer, Alta., April 20, 1976.
(New Jersey's 7th choice, 122nd overall, in 1995 Entry Draft).

			Regular Season								Playoffs						
Season	Club	Lea	GP	W	L	T	Mins	GA	SO	Avg	GP	W	L	Mins	GA	SO	Avg
1993-94	Victoria	WHL	5	1	4	0	237	27	0	6.84	....	....	....	....	....	....	....
1994-95	Prince George	WHL	44	8	30	1	2288	192	1	5.03	....	....	....	....	....	....	....
1995-96	Prince George	WHL	59	16	37	1	3289	236	1	4.31	....	....	....	....	....	....	....
1996-97	Prince George	WHL	50	19	24	4	2851	172	2	3.62	15	9	6	938	44	*1	2.81
1997-98	Cincinnati	AHL	47	13	19	7	2368	136	0	3.45	....	....	....	....	....	....	....

Signed as a free agent by **Anaheim**, June 27, 1997.

McARTHUR, MARK NYI

Goaltender. Catches left. 5'10", 175 lbs. Born, East York, Ont., November 16, 1975.
(NY Islanders' 5th choice, 112th overall, in 1994 Entry Draft).

			Regular Season								Playoffs						
Season	Club	Lea	GP	W	L	T	Mins	GA	SO	Avg	GP	W	L	Mins	GA	SO	Avg
1992-93	Guelph	OHL	35	14	14	3	1853	180	0	5.83	....	....	....	....	....	....	....
1993-94	Guelph	OHL	51	25	18	5	2936	201	0	4.11	9	4	5	561	38	0	4.06
1994-95	Guelph	OHL	48	*34	8	4	2776	130	1	*2.81	13	9	4	797	44	0	3.31
1995-96	Utah	IHL	26	12	12	0	1482	77	0	3.12	....	....	....	....	....	....	....
1996-97	Utah	IHL	56	28	20	6	3111	155	3	2.99	....	....	....	....	....	....	....
1997-98	Utah	IHL	20	7	7	2	1059	60	0	3.40	1	0	1	63	4	0	3.78

OHL Second All-Star Team (1995) • Shared James Norris Memorial Trophy (fewest goals against - IHL) with Tommy Salo (1996)

McCRACKEN, JAKE DET.

Goaltender. Catches left. 5'10", 180 lbs. Born, London, Ont., January 15, 1980.
(Detroit's 4th choice, 84th overall, in 1998 Entry Draft).

			Regular Season								Playoffs						
Season	Club	Lea	GP	W	L	T	Mins	GA	SO	Avg	GP	W	L	Mins	GA	SO	Avg
1996-97	S.S. Marie	OHL	29	13	3	6	1389	80	0	3.46	1	0	1	28	4	0	8.57
1997-98	S.S. Marie	OHL	55	16	31	5	3102	216	0	4.18	....	....	....	....	....	....	....

McLEAN, JASON NYR

Goaltender. Catches left. 6', 200 lbs. Born, Regina, Sask., September 3, 1979.
(NY Rangers' 5th choice, 126th overall, in 1997 Entry Draft).

			Regular Season								Playoffs						
Season	Club	Lea	GP	W	L	T	Mins	GA	SO	Avg	GP	W	L	Mins	GA	SO	Avg
1995-96	Moose Jaw	WHL	11	1	7	1	544	38	0	4.19	....	....	....	....	....	....	....
1996-97	Moose Jaw	WHL	19	7	7	2	1014	60	0	3.55	....	....	....	....	....	....	....
1997-98	Moose Jaw	WHL	5	1	3	0	243	21	0	5.19	....	....	....	....	....	....	....
	Lethbridge	WHL	46	19	18	6	2610	131	2	3.01	4	0	3	190	17	0	5.37

McLEAN, KIRK FLA.

Goaltender. Catches left. 6', 180 lbs. Born, Willowdale, Ont., June 26, 1966.
(New Jersey's 6th choice, 107th overall, in 1984 Entry Draft).

			Regular Season								Playoffs						
Season	Club	Lea	GP	W	L	T	Mins	GA	SO	Avg	GP	W	L	Mins	GA	SO	Avg
1983-84	Oshawa	OHL	17	5	9	0	940	67	0	4.28	....	....	....	....	....	....	....
1984-85	Oshawa	OHL	47	23	17	2	2581	143	1	*3.32	5	1	3	271	21	0	4.65
1985-86	**New Jersey**	**NHL**	**2**	**1**	**1**	**0**	**111**	**11**	**0**	**5.95**	....	....	....	....	....	....	....
	Oshawa	OHL	51	24	21	2	2830	169	1	3.58	4	1	2	201	18	0	5.37
1986-87	**New Jersey**	**NHL**	**4**	**1**	**1**	**0**	**160**	**10**	**0**	**3.75**	....	....	....	....	....	....	....
	Maine	AHL	45	15	23	4	2606	140	1	3.22	....	....	....	....	....	....	....
1987-88	**Vancouver**	**NHL**	**41**	**11**	**27**	**3**	**2380**	**147**	**1**	**3.71**	....	....	....	....	....	....	....
1988-89	**Vancouver**	**NHL**	**42**	**20**	**17**	**3**	**2477**	**127**	**4**	**3.08**	**5**	**2**	**3**	**302**	**18**	**0**	**3.58**
1989-90	**Vancouver**	**NHL**	***63**	**21**	**30**	**10**	***3739**	**216**	**0**	**3.47**	....	....	....	....	....	....	....
1990-91	**Vancouver**	**NHL**	**41**	**10**	**22**	**3**	**1969**	**131**	**0**	**3.99**	**2**	**1**	**1**	**123**	**7**	**0**	**3.41**
1991-92	**Vancouver**	**NHL**	**65**	***38**	**17**	**9**	**3852**	**176**	***5**	**2.74**	**13**	**6**	**7**	**785**	**33**	***2**	**2.52**
1992-93	**Vancouver**	**NHL**	**54**	**28**	**21**	**5**	**3261**	**184**	**3**	**3.39**	**12**	**6**	**6**	**754**	**42**	**0**	**3.34**
1993-94	**Vancouver**	**NHL**	**52**	**23**	**26**	**3**	**3128**	**156**	**3**	**2.99**	***24**	**15**	**9**	***1544**	**59**	***4**	**2.29**
1994-95	**Vancouver**	**NHL**	**40**	**18**	**12**	**10**	**2374**	**109**	**1**	**2.75**	**11**	**4**	**7**	**660**	**36**	**0**	**3.27**
1995-96	**Vancouver**	**NHL**	**45**	**15**	**21**	**9**	**2645**	**156**	**2**	**3.54**	**1**	**0**	**1**	**21**	**3**	**0**	**8.57**
1996-97	**Vancouver**	**NHL**	**44**	**21**	**18**	**3**	**2581**	**138**	**0**	**3.21**	....	....	....	....	....	....	....
1997-98	**Vancouver**	**NHL**	**29**	**6**	**17**	**4**	**1583**	**97**	**1**	**3.68**	....	....	....	....	....	....	....
	Carolina	**NHL**	**8**	**4**	**2**	**0**	**401**	**22**	**0**	**3.29**	....	....	....	....	....	....	....
	Florida	**NHL**	**7**	**4**	**2**	**1**	**406**	**22**	**0**	**3.25**	....	....	....	....	....	....	....
	NHL Totals		**537**	**221**	**234**	**63**	**31067**	**1702**	**20**	**3.29**	**68**	**34**	**34**	**4189**	**198**	**6**	**2.84**

NHL Second All-Star Team (1992)

Played in NHL All-Star Game (1990, 1992)

Traded to **Vancouver** by **New Jersey** with Greg Adams and New Jersey's 2nd round choice (Leif Rohlin) in 1988 Entry Draft for Patrik Sundstrom and Vancouver's 2nd (Jeff Christian) and 4th (Matt Ruchty) round choices in 1988 Entry Draft, September 10, 1987. Traded to **Carolina** by **Vancouver** with Martin Gelinas for Sean Burke, Geoff Sanderson and Enrico Ciccone, January 3, 1998. Traded to **Florida** by **Carolina** for Ray Sheppard, March 24, 1998.

McLENNAN, JAMIE ST.L.

Goaltender. Catches left. 6', 190 lbs. Born, Edmonton, Alta., June 30, 1971.
(NY Islanders' 3rd choice, 48th overall, in 1991 Entry Draft).

			Regular Season								Playoffs						
Season	Club	Lea	GP	W	L	T	Mins	GA	SO	Avg	GP	W	L	Mins	GA	SO	Avg
1989-90	Lethbridge	WHL	34	20	4	2	1690	110	1	3.91	13	6	5	677	44	0	3.90
1990-91	Lethbridge	WHL	56	32	18	4	3230	205	0	3.81	*16	8	8	*970	56	0	3.46
1991-92	Capital District	AHL	18	4	10	2	952	60	1	3.78	....	....	....	....	....	....	....
	Richmond	ECHL	32	16	12	2	1837	114	0	3.72	....	....	....	....	....	....	....
1992-93	Capital District	AHL	38	17	14	6	2171	117	1	3.23	1	0	1	20	5	0	15.00
1993-94	**NY Islanders**	**NHL**	**22**	**8**	**7**	**6**	**1287**	**61**	**0**	**2.84**	**2**	**0**	**1**	**82**	**6**	**0**	**4.39**
	Salt Lake	IHL	24	8	12	2	1320	80	0	3.64	....	....	....	....	....	....	....
1994-95	**NY Islanders**	**NHL**	**21**	**6**	**11**	**2**	**1185**	**67**	**0**	**3.39**	....	....	....	....	....	....	....
	Denver	IHL	4	3	0	1	239	12	0	3.00	11	8	2	640	23	1	*2.15
1995-96	**NY Islanders**	**NHL**	**13**	**3**	**9**	**1**	**636**	**39**	**0**	**3.68**	....	....	....	....	....	....	....
	Utah	IHL	14	9	2	2	728	29	0	2.39	....	....	....	....	....	....	....
	Worcester	AHL	22	14	7	1	1216	57	0	2.81	2	0	2	119	8	0	4.04
1996-97	Worcester	AHL	39	18	13	4	2152	100	2	2.79	4	2	2	262	16	0	3.67
1997-98	**St. Louis**	**NHL**	**30**	**16**	**8**	**2**	**1658**	**60**	**2**	**2.17**	**1**	**0**	**0**	**14**	**1**	**0**	**4.29**
	NHL Totals		**86**	**33**	**35**	**11**	**4766**	**227**	**2**	**2.86**	**3**	**0**	**1**	**96**	**7**	**0**	**4.38**

WHL East First All-Star Team (1991) • Won Bill Masterton Memorial Trophy (1998)

Signed as a free agent by **St. Louis**, July 15, 1996.

MIKLENDA, JAROSLAV (mih-KLEHN-da) OTT.

Goaltender. Catches left. 6'1", 176 lbs. Born, Uherske Hradiste, Czech., March 7, 1974.
(Ottawa's 7th choice, 146th overall, in 1992 Entry Draft).

			Regular Season								Playoffs						
Season	Club	Lea	GP	W	L	T	Mins	GA	SO	Avg	GP	W	L	Mins	GA	SO	Avg
1991-92	HC Olomouc	Czech.	1	....	....	....	36	6	0	9.99	....	....	....	....	....	....	....
1992-93	HC Olomouc	Czech.	5	....	....	....	285	22	....	4.63	....	....	....	....	....	....	....
1993-94	Vitkovice	Cze-Rep.	10	....	....	....	555	25	0	2.71	....	....	....	....	....	....	....
1994-95	Presov	Czech-2	8	....	....	....	428	20	....	2.80	....	....	....	....	....	....	....
1995-96	HC Olomouc	Cze-Rep.	1	....	....	....	60	6	0	6.00	....	....	....	....	....	....	....
	Sternberk	Czech-2	20	....	....	....	1200	54	....	2.70	....	....	....	....	....	....	....
1996-97	Sternberk	Czech-2	21	....	....	....	1260	43	....	2.05	....	....	....	....	....	....	....
1997-98	Sternberk	Czech-3	5	....	....	....	300	3	....	0.60	....	....	....	....	....	....	....

MILLER, AREN DET.

Goaltender. Catches left. 6'2", 208 lbs. Born, Oxbow, Sask., January 13, 1978.
(Detroit's 2nd choice, 52nd overall, in 1996 Entry Draft).

			Regular Season								Playoffs						
Season	Club	Lea	GP	W	L	T	Mins	GA	SO	Avg	GP	W	L	Mins	GA	SO	Avg
1995-96	Spokane	WHL	23	8	7	2	965	50	1	3.11	3	0	3	81	8	0	5.93
1996-97	Spokane	WHL	52	22	20	3	2834	151	3	3.20	9	4	5	555	28	*1	3.03
1997-98	Spokane	WHL	*64	*38	22	3	*3466	187	3	3.24	7	2	3	318	24	0	4.53

MINARD, MIKE EDM.

Goaltender. Catches left. 6'3", 205 lbs. Born, Owen Sound, Ont., November 1, 1976.
(Edmonton's 4th choice, 83rd overall, in 1995 Entry Draft).

			Regular Season								Playoffs						
Season	Club	Lea	GP	W	L	T	Mins	GA	SO	Avg	GP	W	L	Mins	GA	SO	Avg
1993-94	St. Mary's	OJHL	31	....	....	....	1710	78	1	2.74	....	....	....	....	....	....	....
1994-95	Chilliwack	BCJHL	40	....	....	....	2330	136	0	3.50	....	....	....	....	....	....	....
1995-96	Barrie	OHL	1	0	1	0	52	8	0	9.23	....	....	....	....	....	....	....
	Detroit	OHL	42	25	10	4	2314	128	2	3.32	17	9	6	922	55	1	3.58
1996-97	Hamilton	AHL	3	1	1	0	100	7	0	4.20	....	....	....	....	....	....	....
	Wheeling	ECHL	23	3	7	1	899	69	0	4.60	3	0	2	148	16	0	6.47
1997-98	Brantford	UHL	2	1	1	0	74	7	0	5.63	....	....	....	....	....	....	....
	Hamilton	AHL	2	1	0	0	80	2	0	1.50	....	....	....	....	....	....	....
	New Orleans	ECHL	11	6	2	0	429	30	0	4.19	....	....	....	....	....	....	....
	Milwaukee	IHL	8	2	2	0	362	19	0	3.15	....	....	....	....	....	....	....

MOOG, ANDY (MOHG)

Goaltender. Catches left. 5'8", 175 lbs. Born, Penticton, B.C., February 18, 1960.
(Edmonton's 6th choice, 132nd overall, in 1980 Entry Draft).

			Regular Season								Playoffs						
Season	**Club**	**Lea**	**GP**	**W**	**L**	**T**	**Mins**	**GA**	**SO**	**Avg**	**GP**	**W**	**L**	**Mins**	**GA**	**SO**	**Avg**
1978-79	Billings	WHL	26	13	5	4	1306	90	4	4.13	5	1	3	229	21	0	5.50
1979-80	Billings	WHL	46	23	14	1	2435	149	1	3.67	3	2	1	190	10	0	3.16
1980-81	**Edmonton**	**NHL**	**7**	**3**	**3**	**0**	**313**	**20**	**0**	**3.83**	**9**	**5**	**4**	**526**	**32**	**0**	**3.65**
	Wichita	CHL	29	14	13	1	1602	89	0	3.33	5	3	2	300	16	0	3.20
1981-82	**Edmonton**	**NHL**	**8**	**3**	**5**	**0**	**399**	**32**	**0**	**4.81**	....	....	....	....	....	....	....
	Wichita	CHL	40	23	13	3	2391	119	1	2.99	7	3	4	434	23	0	3.18
1982-83	**Edmonton**	**NHL**	**50**	**33**	**8**	**7**	**2833**	**167**	**1**	**3.54**	**16**	**11**	**5**	**949**	**48**	**0**	**3.03**
1983-84	**Edmonton**	**NHL**	**38**	**27**	**8**	**1**	**2212**	**139**	**1**	**3.77**	**7**	**4**	**0**	**263**	**12**	**0**	**2.74** ♦
1984-85	**Edmonton**	**NHL**	**39**	**22**	**9**	**3**	**2019**	**111**	**1**	**3.30**	**2**	**0**	**0**	**20**	**0**	**0**	**0.00** ♦
1985-86	**Edmonton**	**NHL**	**47**	**27**	**9**	**7**	**2664**	**164**	**1**	**3.69**	**1**	**1**	**0**	**60**	**1**	**0**	**1.00**
1986-87	**Edmonton**	**NHL**	**46**	**28**	**11**	**3**	**2461**	**144**	**0**	**3.51**	**2**	**2**	**0**	**120**	**8**	**0**	**4.00** ♦
1987-88	Canada	Nat-Tm	27	10	7	5	1438	86	0	3.58	....	....	....	....	....	....	....
	Canada	Olympics	4	4	0	0	240	9	1	2.25	....	....	....	....	....	....	....
	Boston	**NHL**	**6**	**4**	**2**	**0**	**360**	**17**	**1**	**2.83**	**7**	**1**	**4**	**354**	**25**	**0**	**4.24**
1988-89	**Boston**	**NHL**	**41**	**18**	**14**	**8**	**2482**	**133**	**1**	**3.22**	**6**	**4**	**2**	**359**	**14**	**0**	**2.34**
1989-90	**Boston**	**NHL**	**46**	**24**	**10**	**7**	**2536**	**122**	**3**	**2.89**	**20**	**13**	**7**	**1195**	**44**	***2**	***2.21**
1990-91	**Boston**	**NHL**	**51**	**25**	**13**	**9**	**2844**	**136**	**4**	**2.87**	**19**	**10**	**9**	**1133**	**60**	**0**	**3.18**
1991-92	**Boston**	**NHL**	**62**	**28**	**22**	**9**	**3640**	**196**	**1**	**3.23**	**15**	**8**	**7**	**866**	**46**	**1**	**3.19**
1992-93	**Boston**	**NHL**	**55**	**37**	**14**	**3**	**3194**	**168**	**3**	**3.16**	**3**	**0**	**3**	**161**	**14**	**0**	**5.22**
1993-94	**Dallas**	**NHL**	**55**	**24**	**20**	**7**	**3121**	**170**	**2**	**3.27**	**4**	**1**	**3**	**246**	**12**	**0**	**2.93**
1994-95	**Dallas**	**NHL**	**31**	**10**	**12**	**7**	**1770**	**72**	**2**	**2.44**	**5**	**1**	**4**	**277**	**16**	**0**	**3.47**
1995-96	**Dallas**	**NHL**	**41**	**13**	**19**	**7**	**2228**	**111**	**1**	**2.99**	....	....	....	....	....	....	....
1996-97	**Dallas**	**NHL**	**48**	**28**	**13**	**5**	**2738**	**98**	**3**	**2.15**	**7**	**3**	**4**	**449**	**21**	**0**	**2.81**
1997-98	**Montreal**	**NHL**	**42**	**18**	**17**	**5**	**2337**	**97**	**3**	**2.49**	**9**	**4**	**5**	**474**	**24**	**1**	**3.04**
	NHL Totals		**713**	**372**	**209**	**88**	**40151**	**2097**	**28**	**3.13**	**132**	**68**	**57**	**7452**	**377**	**4**	**3.04**

WHL Second All-Star Team (1980) • CHL Second All-Star Team (1982) • Shared William Jennings Trophy with Rejean Lemelin (1990)

Played in NHL All-Star Game (1985, 1986, 1991, 1997)

• Statistics (Mins., GA) for suspended game on May 24, 1988 are included in playoff record.

Traded to **Boston** by **Edmonton** for Geoff Courtnall, Bill Ranford and Boston's 2nd round choice (Petro Koivunen) in 1988 Entry Draft, March 8, 1988. Traded to **Dallas** by **Boston** with (Gord Murphy, June 20, 1993) for Jon Casey, June 25, 1993. Signed as a free agent by **Montreal**, July 17, 1997.

MOSS, TYLER — CGY.

Goaltender. Catches right. 6', 184 lbs. Born, Ottawa, Ont., June 29, 1975.
(Tampa Bay's 2nd choice, 29th overall, in 1993 Entry Draft).

			Regular Season								Playoffs						
Season	**Club**	**Lea**	**GP**	**W**	**L**	**T**	**Mins**	**GA**	**SO**	**Avg**	**GP**	**W**	**L**	**Mins**	**GA**	**SO**	**Avg**
1992-93	Kingston	OHL	31	13	7	5	1537	97	0	3.79	6	1	2	228	19	0	5.00
1993-94	Kingston	OHL	13	6	4	3	795	42	1	3.17	3	0	2	136	8	0	3.53
1994-95	Kingston	OHL	*57	33	17	5	*3249	164	1	3.03	6	2	4	333	27	0	4.86
1995-96	Atlanta	IHL	40	11	19	4	2030	138	1	4.08	3	0	3	213	11	0	3.10
1996-97	Adirondack	AHL	11	1	5	2	507	42	1	4.97	....	....	....	....	....	....	....
	Grand Rapids	IHL	15	5	6	1	715	35	0	2.94	....	....	....	....	....	....	....
	Muskegon	ColHL	2	1	1	0	119	5	0	2.51	....	....	....	....	....	....	....
	Saint John	AHL	9	6	1	1	534	17	0	1.91	5	2	3	242	15	0	3.72
1997-98	**Calgary**	**NHL**	**6**	**2**	**3**	**1**	**367**	**20**	**0**	**3.27**	....	....	....	....	....	....	....
	Saint John	AHL	39	19	10	7	2194	91	0	2.49	15	8	5	761	37	0	2.91
	NHL Totals		**6**	**2**	**3**	**1**	**367**	**20**	**0**	**3.27**	....	....	....	....	....	....	....

OHL First All-Star Team (1995) • Shared Harry "Hap" Holmes Memorial Trophy (fewest goals against - AHL) with Jean-Sebastien Giguere (1998)

Traded to **Calgary** by **Tampa Bay** for Jamie Huscroft, March 18, 1997.

MUZZATTI, JASON (moo-ZAH-tee)

Goaltender. Catches left. 6'2", 210 lbs. Born, Toronto, Ont., February 3, 1970.
(Calgary's 1st choice, 21st overall, in 1988 Entry Draft).

			Regular Season								Playoffs						
Season	**Club**	**Lea**	**GP**	**W**	**L**	**T**	**Mins**	**GA**	**SO**	**Avg**	**GP**	**W**	**L**	**Mins**	**GA**	**SO**	**Avg**
1986-87	St. Michael's	Jr. B	20	....	....	....	1054	69	1	3.93	....	....	....	....	....	....	....
1987-88	Michigan State	CCHA	33	19	9	3	1915	109	0	3.41	....	....	....	....	....	....	....
1988-89	Michigan State	CCHA	42	32	9	1	2515	127	3	*3.03	....	....	....	....	....	....	....
1989-90	Michigan State	CCHA	33	*24	6	0	1976	99	0	3.01	....	....	....	....	....	....	....
1990-91	Michigan State	CCHA	22	8	10	2	1204	75	1	3.74	....	....	....	....	....	....	....
1991-92	Salt Lake	IHL	52	24	22	5	3033	167	2	3.30	4	1	3	247	18	0	4.37
1992-93	Canada	Nat-Tm	16	6	9	0	880	53	0	3.84	....	....	....	....	....	....	....
	Indianapolis	IHL	12	5	6	1	707	48	0	4.07	....	....	....	....	....	....	....
	Salt Lake	IHL	13	5	6	1	747	52	0	4.18	....	....	....	....	....	....	....
1993-94	**Calgary**	**NHL**	**1**	**0**	**1**	**0**	**60**	**8**	**0**	**8.00**	....	....	....	....	....	....	....
	Saint John	AHL	51	26	21	3	2939	183	2	3.74	7	3	4	415	19	0	2.75
1994-95	Saint John	AHL	31	10	14	4	1741	101	2	3.48	....	....	....	....	....	....	....
	Calgary	**NHL**	**1**	**0**	**0**	**0**	**10**	**0**	**0**	**0.00**	....	....	....	....	....	....	....
1995-96	**Hartford**	**NHL**	**22**	**4**	**8**	**3**	**1013**	**49**	**1**	**2.90**	....	....	....	....	....	....	....
	Springfield	AHL	5	4	0	1	300	12	1	2.40	....	....	....	....	....	....	....
1996-97	**Hartford**	**NHL**	**31**	**9**	**13**	**5**	**1591**	**91**	**0**	**3.43**	....	....	....	....	....	....	....
1997-98	**NY Rangers**	**NHL**	**6**	**0**	**3**	**2**	**313**	**17**	**0**	**3.26**	....	....	....	....	....	....	....
	Hartford	AHL	17	11	5	1	999	57	0	3.42	....	....	....	....	....	....	....
	San Jose	**NHL**	**1**	**0**	**0**	**0**	**27**	**2**	**0**	**4.44**	....	....	....	....	....	....	....
	Kentucky	AHL	7	2	3	2	430	25	0	3.49	3	0	3	153	13	0	5.07
	NHL Totals		**62**	**13**	**25**	**10**	**3014**	**167**	**1**	**3.32**	....	....	....	....	....	....	....

CCHA Second All-Star Team (1988) • CCHA First All-Star Team (1990) • NCAA West Second All-American Team (1990)

Claimed on waivers by **Hartford** from **Calgary**, October 6, 1995. Transferred to **Carolina** after **Hartford** franchise relocated, June 25, 1997. Traded to **NY Rangers** by **Carolina** for NY Rangers' 4th round choice (Tommy Westlund) in 1998 Entry Draft, August 8, 1997. Traded to **San Jose** by **NY Rangers** for Rich Brennan, March 24, 1998.

MYERS, SCOTT — PIT.

Goaltender. Catches right. 5'10", 172 lbs. Born, Winnipeg, Man., June 11, 1979.
(Pittsburgh's 4th choice, 110th overall, in 1998 Entry Draft).

			Regular Season								Playoffs						
Season	**Club**	**Lea**	**GP**	**W**	**L**	**T**	**Mins**	**GA**	**SO**	**Avg**	**GP**	**W**	**L**	**Mins**	**GA**	**SO**	**Avg**
1996-97	Prince George	WHL	25	6	14	1	1284	94	0	4.39	....	....	....	....	....	....	....
1997-98	Prince George	WHL	48	29	13	4	2822	139	2	2.96	11	5	6	665	25	*2	2.26

NABOKOV, YEVGENI (nuh-BAW-kahv, yehv-GEH-nee) — S.J.

Goaltender. Catches left. 6', 180 lbs. Born, Ust-Kamenogorsk, USSR, July 25, 1975.
(San Jose's 9th choice, 219th overall, in 1994 Entry Draft).

			Regular Season								Playoffs						
Season	**Club**	**Lea**	**GP**	**W**	**L**	**T**	**Mins**	**GA**	**SO**	**Avg**	**GP**	**W**	**L**	**Mins**	**GA**	**SO**	**Avg**
1992-93	Kamenogorsk	CIS	4	....	....	....	109	5	0	2.75	....	....	....	....	....	....	....
1993-94	Kamenogorsk	CIS	11	....	....	....	539	29	0	3.22	....	....	....	....	....	....	....
1994-95	Moscow D'amo	CIS	24	....	....	....	1265	40	....	1.89	....	....	....	....	....	....	....
1995-96	Moscow D'amo	CIS	39	....	....	....	2008	67	5	2.00	6	....	....	298	7	....	1.41
1996-97	Moscow D'amo	Russia	27	....	....	....	1588	56	2	2.11	4	....	....	255	12	0	2.82
1997-98	Kentucky	AHL	33	10	21	2	1866	122	0	3.92	1	0	0	23	1	0	2.59

NIITTYMAKI, ANTERO — PHI.

Goaltender. Catches left. 6', 176 lbs. Born, Turku, Finland, June 18, 1980.
(Philadelphia's 7th choice, 168th overall, in 1998 Entry Draft).

			Regular Season								Playoffs						
Season	**Club**	**Lea**	**GP**	**W**	**L**	**T**	**Mins**	**GA**	**SO**	**Avg**	**GP**	**W**	**L**	**Mins**	**GA**	**SO**	**Avg**
1996-97	TPS Turku	Fin-Jr.	22	....	....	....	....	....	....	....	6	....	....	....	....	....	....
1997-98	TPS Turku	Fin-Jr.	33	....	....	....	....	....	....	....	....	....	....	....	....	....	....

NORONEN, MIKA (NOH-rah-nehn, MEE-kah) — BUF.

Goaltender. Catches left. 6'1", 191 lbs. Born, Tampere, Finland, June 17, 1979.
(Buffalo's 1st choice, 21st overall, in 1997 Entry Draft).

			Regular Season								Playoffs						
Season	**Club**	**Lea**	**GP**	**W**	**L**	**T**	**Mins**	**GA**	**SO**	**Avg**	**GP**	**W**	**L**	**Mins**	**GA**	**SO**	**Avg**
1996-97	Tappara	Finland	5	1	3	0	215	17	0	4.73	....	....	....	....	....	....	....
1997-98	Tappara	Finland	37	14	12	3	1704	83	1	2.92	4	1	2	196	12	0	3.67

O'NEILL, MIKE

Goaltender. Catches left. 5'7", 160 lbs. Born, LaSalle, Que., November 3, 1967.
(Winnipeg's 1st choice, 15th overall, in 1988 Supplemental Draft).

			Regular Season								Playoffs						
Season	**Club**	**Lea**	**GP**	**W**	**L**	**T**	**Mins**	**GA**	**SO**	**Avg**	**GP**	**W**	**L**	**Mins**	**GA**	**SO**	**Avg**
1985-86	Yale	ECAC	6	3	1	0	389	17	0	3.53	....	....	....	....	....	....	....
1986-87	Yale	ECAC	16	9	6	1	964	55	2	3.42	....	....	....	....	....	....	....
1987-88	Yale	ECAC	24	6	17	0	1385	101	0	4.37	....	....	....	....	....	....	....
1988-89	Yale	ECAC	25	10	14	1	1490	93	0	3.74	....	....	....	....	....	....	....
1989-90	Tappara	Finland	41	23	13	5	2369	127	2	3.22	....	....	....	....	....	....	....
1990-91	Fort Wayne	IHL	8	5	2	1	490	31	0	3.80	....	....	....	....	....	....	....
	Moncton	AHL	30	13	7	6	1613	84	0	3.12	8	3	4	435	29	0	4.00
1991-92	**Winnipeg**	**NHL**	**1**	**0**	**0**	**0**	**13**	**1**	**0**	**4.62**	....	....	....	....	....	....	....
	Moncton	AHL	32	14	16	2	1902	108	1	3.41	11	4	7	670	43	*1	3.85
	Fort Wayne	IHL	33	22	6	3	1858	97	*4	3.13	....	....	....	....	....	....	....
1992-93	**Winnipeg**	**NHL**	**2**	**0**	**0**	**1**	**73**	**6**	**0**	**4.93**	....	....	....	....	....	....	....
	Moncton	AHL	30	13	10	4	1649	88	1	3.20	....	....	....	....	....	....	....
1993-94	**Winnipeg**	**NHL**	**17**	**0**	**9**	**1**	**738**	**51**	**0**	**4.15**	....	....	....	....	....	....	....
	Moncton	AHL	12	8	4	0	716	33	1	2.76	....	....	....	....	....	....	....
	Fort Wayne	IHL	11	4	4	3	642	38	0	3.55	....	....	....	....	....	....	....
1994-95	Fort Wayne	IHL	28	11	12	4	1603	109	0	4.08	....	....	....	....	....	....	....
	Phoenix	IHL	21	13	4	4	1256	64	1	3.06	9	4	5	535	33	0	3.70
1995-96	Baltimore	AHL	*74	31	31	7	*4250	250	2	3.53	12	6	6	689	43	0	3.75
1996-97	**Anaheim**	**NHL**	**1**	**0**	**0**	**0**	**31**	**3**	**0**	**5.81**	....	....	....	....	....	....	....
	Long Beach	IHL	45	26	12	6	2644	145	1	3.29	1	0	0	7	0	0	0.00
1997-98	Portland	AHL	47	16	18	10	2640	135	1	3.07	6	2	3	305	16	0	3.15
	NHL Totals		**21**	**0**	**9**	**2**	**855**	**61**	**0**	**4.28**	....	....	....	....	....	....	....

ECAC First All-Star Team (1987, 1989) • NCAA East First All-American Team (1989)

Signed as a free agent by **Anaheim**, July 14, 1995. Signed as a free agent by **Washington**, August 20, 1997.

OSGOOD, CHRIS (AWS-gud) — DET.

Goaltender. Catches left. 5'10", 160 lbs. Born, Peace River, Alta., November 26, 1972.
(Detroit's 3rd choice, 54th overall, in 1991 Entry Draft).

			Regular Season								Playoffs						
Season	**Club**	**Lea**	**GP**	**W**	**L**	**T**	**Mins**	**GA**	**SO**	**Avg**	**GP**	**W**	**L**	**Mins**	**GA**	**SO**	**Avg**
1989-90	Medicine Hat	WHL	57	24	28	2	3094	228	0	4.42	3	0	3	173	17	0	5.91
1990-91	Medicine Hat	WHL	46	23	18	3	2630	173	2	3.95	12	7	5	712	42	0	3.54
1991-92	Medicine Hat	WHL	15	10	3	0	819	44	0	3.22	....	....	....	....	....	....	....
	Brandon	WHL	16	3	10	1	890	60	1	4.04	....	....	....	....	....	....	....
	Seattle	WHL	21	12	7	1	1217	65	1	3.20	15	9	6	904	51	0	3.38
1992-93	Adirondack	AHL	45	19	19	4	2438	159	0	3.91	1	0	1	59	2	0	2.03
1993-94	**Detroit**	**NHL**	**41**	**23**	**8**	**5**	**2206**	**105**	**2**	**2.86**	**6**	**3**	**2**	**307**	**12**	**1**	**2.35**
	Adirondack	AHL	4	3	1	0	239	13	0	3.26	....	....	....	....	....	....	....
1994-95	**Detroit**	**NHL**	**19**	**14**	**5**	**0**	**1087**	**41**	**1**	**2.26**	**2**	**0**	**0**	**68**	**2**	**0**	**1.76**
	Adirondack	AHL	2	1	1	0	120	6	0	3.00	....	....	....	....	....	....	....
1995-96	**Detroit**	**NHL**	**50**	***39**	**6**	**5**	**2933**	**106**	**5**	**2.17**	**15**	**8**	**7**	**936**	**33**	**2**	**2.12**
1996-97	**Detroit**	**NHL**	**47**	**23**	**13**	**9**	**2769**	**106**	**6**	**2.30**	**2**	**0**	**0**	**47**	**2**	**0**	**2.55** ♦
1997-98	**Detroit**	**NHL**	**64**	**33**	**20**	**11**	**3807**	**140**	**6**	**2.21**	***22**	***16**	**6**	***1361**	**48**	**2**	**2.12** ♦
	NHL Totals		**221**	**132**	**52**	**30**	**12802**	**498**	**20**	**2.33**	**47**	**27**	**15**	**2719**	**97**	**5**	**2.14**

WHL East Second All-Star Team (1991) • NHL Second All-Star Team (1996) • Shared William M. Jennings Trophy with Mike Vernon (1996)

Played in NHL All-Star Game (1996, 1997, 1998)

• Scored a goal while with Medicine Hat (WHL), January 3, 1991. • Scored a goal vs. Hartford, March 6, 1996.

PARENT, RICH (PEH-ruhn) — ST.L.

Goaltender. Catches left. 6'3", 195 lbs. Born, Montreal, Que., January 12, 1973.

			Regular Season								Playoffs						
Season	**Club**	**Lea**	**GP**	**W**	**L**	**T**	**Mins**	**GA**	**SO**	**Avg**	**GP**	**W**	**L**	**Mins**	**GA**	**SO**	**Avg**
1994-95	Muskegon	ColHL	35	17	11	3	1867	112	1	3.60	13	7	3	725	47	1	3.89
1995-96	Muskegon	ColHL	36	23	7	4	2087	85	2	2.44	....	....	....	....	....	....	....
	Detroit	IHL	19	16	0	1	1040	48	2	2.77	7	3	3	363	22	0	3.64
1996-97	Detroit	IHL	53	31	13	4	2815	104	4	2.22	15	8	3	786	21	1	*1.60
1997-98	**St. Louis**	**NHL**	**1**	**0**	**0**	**0**	**12**	**0**	**0**	**0.00**	....	....	....	....	....	....	....
	Manitoba	IHL	26	8	12	2	1334	69	3	3.10	....	....	....	....	....	....	....
	Detroit	IHL	7	4	0	3	417	15	0	2.15	5	1	0	157	6	0	2.29
	NHL Totals		**1**	**0**	**0**	**0**	**12**	**0**	**0**	**0.00**	....	....	....	....	....	....	....

ColHL First All-Star Team (1996) • Named ColHL's Outstanding Goaltender (1996) • Shared James Norris Memorial Trophy (fewest goals against - IHL) with Jeff Reese (1997)

Signed as a free agent by **St. Louis**, July 31, 1997.

PASSMORE, STEVE — EDM.

Goaltender. Catches left. 5'9", 165 lbs. Born, Thunder Bay, Ont., January 29, 1973.
(Quebec's 10th choice, 196th overall, in 1992 Entry Draft).

			Regular Season								Playoffs						
Season	**Club**	**Lea**	**GP**	**W**	**L**	**T**	**Mins**	**GA**	**SO**	**Avg**	**GP**	**W**	**L**	**Mins**	**GA**	**SO**	**Avg**
1990-91	Victoria	WHL	35	3	25	1	1838	190	0	6.20	....	....	....	....	....	....	....
1991-92	Victoria	WHL	*71	15	50	5	*4228	347	0	4.92	....	....	....	....	....	....	....
1992-93	Victoria	WHL	43	14	24	2	2402	150	1	3.75	....	....	....	....	....	....	....
	Kamloops	WHL	25	19	6	0	1479	69	1	2.80	7	4	2	401	22	1	3.29
1993-94	Kamloops	WHL	36	22	9	2	1927	88	1	*2.74	*18	*11	7	*1099	60	0	3.28
1994-95	Cape Breton	AHL	25	8	13	3	1455	93	0	3.83	....	....	....	....	....	....	....
1995-96	Cape Breton	AHL	2	1	0	0	90	2	0	1.33	....	....	....	....	....	....	....
1996-97	Hamilton	AHL	27	12	12	3	1568	70	1	2.68	22	12	10	1325	61	*2	2.76
	Raleigh	ECHL	2	1	1	0	118	13	0	6.56	....	....	....	....	....	....	....
1997-98	San Antonio	IHL	14	3	8	2	736	56	0	4.56	....	....	....	....	....	....	....
	Hamilton	AHL	27	11	10	6	1655	87	2	3.15	3	0	2	132	14	0	6.33

WHL West First All-Star Team (1993, 1994) • Won Fred Hunt Memorial Trophy (Sportsmanship - AHL) (1997)

Traded to **Edmonton** by **Quebec** for Brad Werenka, March 21, 1994.

PELLETIER, JEAN-MARC (PEHL-tyay) PHI.

Goaltender. Catches left. 6'3", 200 lbs. Born, Atlanta, GA, March 4, 1978.
(Philadelphia's 1st choice, 30th overall, in 1997 Entry Draft).

			Regular Season								Playoffs						
Season	Club	Lea	GP	W	L	T	Mins	GA	SO	Avg	GP	W	L	Mins	GA	SO	Avg
1995-96	Cornell	ECAC	5	1	2	0	179	15	0	5.03	....	....	....	....	....	....	....
1996-97	Cornell	ECAC	11	5	2	3	679	28	1	2.47	....	....	....	....	....	....	....
1997-98	Rimouski	QMJHL	34	17	11	3	1913	118	0	3.70	16	11	3	895	51	1	3.42

PELLETIER, JONATHAN CHI.

Goaltender. Catches left. 5'11", 165 lbs. Born, Riviere-du-loop, Que., April 15, 1980.
(Chicago's 5th choice, 166th overall, in 1998 Entry Draft).

			Regular Season								Playoffs						
Season	Club	Lea	GP	W	L	T	Mins	GA	SO	Avg	GP	W	L	Mins	GA	SO	Avg
1996-97	Victoriaville	QMJHL	25	14	5	1	1226	64	0	3.13	2	0	0	30	1	0	2.00
1997-98	Victoriaville	QMJHL	16	7	4	3	902	58	0	3.86	....	....	....	....	....	....	....
	Drummondville	QMJHL	29	5	17	1	1571	116	0	4.43	....	....	....	....	....	....	....

PERSSON, JOAKIM (PEHR-suhn) BOS.

Goaltender. Catches left. 5'11", 176 lbs. Born, Ostervala, Sweden, May 4, 1970.
(Boston's 10th choice, 259th overall, in 1993 Entry Draft).

			Regular Season								Playoffs						
Season	Club	Lea	GP	W	L	T	Mins	GA	SO	Avg	GP	W	L	Mins	GA	SO	Avg
1992-93	Hammarby	Swe-2	40	....	....	....	2395	108	....	2.71	....	....	....	....	....	....	....
1993-94	Hammarby	Swe-2	23	....	....	....	1380	59	....	2.57	....	....	....	....	....	....	....
	Providence	AHL	1	0	0	0	24	0	0	0.00	....	....	....	....	....	....	....
1994-95	AIK Solna	Sweden	30	....	....	....	1800	103	1	3.43	....	....	....	....	....	....	....
1995-96	AIK Solna	Sweden	24	....	....	....	1344	64	....	2.86	....	....	....	....	....	....	....
1996-97	Ratingen	Germany	35	....	....	....	2111	154	0	4.37	6	....	....	360	29	0	4.83
1997-98	Vasteras IK	Sweden	7	....	....	....	291	24	....	4.95	....	....	....	....	....	....	....

PETRUK, RANDY CAR.

Goaltender. Catches right. 5'9", 178 lbs. Born, Cranbrook, B.C., April 23, 1978.
(Colorado's 5th choice, 107th overall, in 1996 Entry Draft).

			Regular Season								Playoffs						
Season	Club	Lea	GP	W	L	T	Mins	GA	SO	Avg	GP	W	L	Mins	GA	SO	Avg
1994-95	Kamloops	WHL	27	16	3	4	1462	71	1	2.91	7	5	2	423	19	0	2.70
1995-96	Kamloops	WHL	52	34	15	1	3071	181	1	3.54	16	9	6	990	58	0	3.52
1996-97	Kamloops	WHL	*60	25	28	5	*3475	210	0	3.63	....	....	....	....	....	....	....
1997-98	Kamloops	WHL	57	31	21	1	3097	157	3	3.04	7	3	4	425	21	0	2.96

WHL West Second All-Star Team (1998)

Traded to **Carolina** by **Colorado** for Carolina's 5th round choice in 1999 Entry Draft, June 1, 1998.

POTVIN, FELIX (PAHT-vihn) TOR.

Goaltender. Catches left. 6'1", 190 lbs. Born, Anjou, Que., June 23, 1971.
(Toronto's 2nd choice, 31st overall, in 1990 Entry Draft).

			Regular Season								Playoffs						
Season	Club	Lea	GP	W	L	T	Mins	GA	SO	Avg	GP	W	L	Mins	GA	SO	Avg
1988-89	Chicoutimi	QMJHL	*65	25	31	1	*3489	271	*2	4.66	....	....	....	....	....	....	....
1989-90	Chicoutimi	QMJHL	*62	*31	26	2	*3478	231	*2	3.99	....	....	....	....	....	....	....
1990-91	Chicoutimi	QMJHL	54	33	15	4	3216	145	*6	*2.70	*16	*11	5	*992	46	0	*2.78
1991-92	Toronto	NHL	4	0	2	1	210	8	0	2.29	....	....	....	....	....	....	....
	St. John's	AHL	35	18	10	6	2070	101	2	2.93	11	7	4	642	41	0	3.83
1992-93	Toronto	NHL	48	25	15	7	2781	116	2	*2.50	*21	11	10	*1308	62	1	2.84
	St. John's	AHL	5	3	0	2	309	18	0	3.50	....	....	....	....	....	....	....
1993-94	Toronto	NHL	66	34	22	9	3883	187	3	2.89	18	9	9	1124	46	3	2.46
1994-95	Toronto	NHL	36	15	13	7	2144	104	0	2.91	7	3	4	424	20	1	2.83
1995-96	Toronto	NHL	69	30	26	11	4009	192	2	2.87	6	2	4	350	19	0	3.26
1996-97	Toronto	NHL	*74	27	36	7	*4271	224	0	3.15	....	....	....	....	....	....	....
1997-98	Toronto	NHL	67	26	33	7	3864	176	5	2.73	....	....	....	....	....	....	....
	NHL Totals		**364**	**157**	**147**	**49**	**21162**	**1007**	**12**	**2.86**	**52**	**25**	**27**	**3206**	**147**	**5**	**2.75**

QMJHL Second All-Star Team (1990) • QMJHL First All-Star Team (1991) • Canadian Major Junior Goaltender of the Year (1991) • Memorial Cup All-Star Team (1991) • Won Hap Emms Memorial Trophy (Memorial Cup Top Goaltender) (1991) • AHL First All-Star Team (1992) • Won Dudley "Red" Garrett Memorial Trophy (Top Rookie - AHL) (1992) • Won Baz Bastien Memorial Trophy (Top Goaltender - AHL) (1992) • NHL/Upper Deck All-Rookie Team (1993)

Played in NHL All-Star Game (1994, 1996)

PRESTIFILIPPO, J.R. (PREHS-tee-fihl-ih-poh) NYI

Goaltender. Catches left. 5'10", 170 lbs. Born, Newark, NJ, March 23, 1977.
(NY Islanders' 8th choice, 165th overall, in 1996 Entry Draft).

			Regular Season								Playoffs						
Season	Club	Lea	GP	W	L	T	Mins	GA	SO	Avg	GP	W	L	Mins	GA	SO	Avg
1995-96	Hotchkiss	H.S.	24	....	....	....	1440	56	3	2.33	....	....	....	....	....	....	....
1996-97	Harvard	ECAC	31	10	18	3	1866	99	1	3.18	....	....	....	....	....	....	....
1997-98	Harvard	ECAC	23	9	12	2	1394	80	0	3.44	....	....	....	....	....	....	....

PUPPA, DAREN (POO-puh) T.B.

Goaltender. Catches right. 6'4", 205 lbs. Born, Kirkland Lake, Ont., March 23, 1965.
(Buffalo's 6th choice, 76th overall, in 1983 Entry Draft).

			Regular Season								Playoffs						
Season	Club	Lea	GP	W	L	T	Mins	GA	SO	Avg	GP	W	L	Mins	GA	SO	Avg
1982-83	Kirkland Lake	NOHA	STATISTICS NOT AVAILABLE														
1983-84	RPI	ECAC	32	24	6	0	1816	89	0	2.94	....	....	....	....	....	....	....
1984-85	RPI	ECAC	32	31	1	0	1830	78	0	2.56	....	....	....	....	....	....	....
1985-86	Buffalo	NHL	7	3	4	0	401	21	1	3.14	....	....	....	....	....	....	....
	Rochester	AHL	20	8	11	0	1092	79	0	4.34	....	....	....	....	....	....	....
1986-87	Buffalo	NHL	3	0	2	1	185	13	0	4.22	....	....	....	....	....	....	....
	Rochester	AHL	57	*33	14	0	3129	146	1	2.80	*16	*10	6	*944	48	*1	3.05
1987-88	Buffalo	NHL	17	8	6	1	874	61	0	4.19	3	1	1	142	11	0	4.65
	Rochester	AHL	26	14	8	2	1415	65	2	2.76	2	0	1	108	5	0	2.78
1988-89	Buffalo	NHL	37	17	10	6	1908	107	1	3.36	....	....	....	....	....	....	....
1989-90	Buffalo	NHL	56	*31	16	6	3241	156	1	2.89	6	2	4	370	15	0	2.43
1990-91	Buffalo	NHL	38	15	11	6	2092	118	2	3.38	2	0	1	81	10	0	7.41
1991-92	Buffalo	NHL	33	11	14	4	1757	114	0	3.89	....	....	....	....	....	....	....
	Rochester	AHL	2	0	2	0	119	9	0	4.54	....	....	....	....	....	....	....
1992-93	Buffalo	NHL	24	11	5	4	1306	78	0	3.58	....	....	....	....	....	....	....
	Toronto	NHL	8	6	2	0	479	18	2	2.25	1	0	0	20	1	0	3.00
1993-94	Tampa Bay	NHL	63	22	33	6	3653	165	4	2.71	....	....	....	....	....	....	....
1994-95	Tampa Bay	NHL	36	14	19	2	2013	90	1	2.68	....	....	....	....	....	....	....
1995-96	Tampa Bay	NHL	57	29	16	9	3189	131	5	2.46	4	1	3	173	14	0	4.86
1996-97	Tampa Bay	NHL	6	1	1	2	325	14	0	2.58	....	....	....	....	....	....	....
	Adirondack	AHL	1	1	0	0	62	3	0	2.90	....	....	....	....	....	....	....
1997-98	Tampa Bay	NHL	26	5	14	6	1456	66	0	2.72	....	....	....	....	....	....	....
	NHL Totals		**411**	**173**	**153**	**53**	**22879**	**1152**	**17**	**3.02**	**16**	**4**	**9**	**786**	**51**	**0**	**3.89**

AHL First All-Star Team (1987) • NHL Second All-Star Team (1990)

Played in NHL All-Star Game (1990)

Traded to **Toronto** by **Buffalo** with Dave Andreychuk and Buffalo's 1st round choice (Kenny Jonsson) in 1993 Entry Draft for Grant Fuhr and Toronto's 5th round choice (Kevin Popp) in 1995 Entry Draft, February 2, 1993. Claimed by **Florida** from **Toronto** in Expansion Draft, June 24, 1993. Claimed by **Tampa Bay** from **Florida** in Phase II of Expansion Draft, June 25, 1993.

RACINE, BRUCE

Goaltender. Catches left. 6', 170 lbs. Born, Cornwall, Ont., August 9, 1966.
(Pittsburgh's 3rd choice, 58th overall, in 1985 Entry Draft).

			Regular Season								Playoffs						
Season	Club	Lea	GP	W	L	T	Mins	GA	SO	Avg	GP	W	L	Mins	GA	SO	Avg
1984-85	Northeastern	H.E.	26	11	14	1	1615	103	1	3.83	....	....	....	....	....	....	....
1985-86	Northeastern	H.E.	32	17	14	1	1920	147	0	4.56	....	....	....	....	....	....	....
1986-87	Northeastern	H.E.	33	12	18	3	1966	133	0	4.06	....	....	....	....	....	....	....
1987-88	Northeastern	H.E.	30	15	11	4	1808	108	1	3.58	....	....	....	....	....	....	....
1988-89	Muskegon	IHL	51	*37	11	0	*3039	184	*3	3.63	5	4	1	300	15	0	3.00
1989-90	Muskegon	IHL	49	29	15	4	2911	182	1	3.75	9	5	4	566	32	1	3.34
1990-91	Albany	IHL	29	7	18	1	1567	104	0	3.98	....	....	....	....	....	....	....
	Muskegon	IHL	9	4	4	1	516	40	0	4.65	....	....	....	....	....	....	....
1991-92	Muskegon	IHL	27	13	10	3	1559	91	1	3.50	1	0	1	60	6	0	6.00
1992-93	Cleveland	IHL	35	13	16	6	1949	140	1	4.31	2	0	0	37	2	0	3.24
1993-94	St. John's	AHL	37	20	9	2	1875	116	0	3.71	1	0	0	20	1	0	0.00
1994-95	St. John's	AHL	27	11	10	4	1492	85	1	3.42	2	1	1	119	3	0	1.51
1995-96	St. Louis	NHL	11	0	3	0	230	12	0	3.13	1	0	0	1	0	0	0.00
	Peoria	IHL	22	11	10	1	1228	69	1	3.37	1	0	1	59	3	0	3.05
1996-97	San Antonio	IHL	44	25	14	2	2426	122	6	3.02	6	3	2	325	17	0	3.13
1997-98	San Antonio	IHL	*15	*4	9	1	*836	51	0	3.66	....	....	....	....	....	....	....
	Fort Wayne	IHL	*45	*30	10	4	*2605	109	1	2.51	3	1	2	152	10	0	3.95
	NHL Totals		**11**	**0**	**3**	**0**	**230**	**12**	**0**	**3.13**	**1**	**0**	**0**	**1**	**0**	**0**	**0.00**

Hockey East Second All-Star Team (1985) • Hockey East First All-Star Team (1987) • NCAA East First All-American Team (1987, 1988) • IHL First All-Star Team (1998)

Signed as a free agent by **Toronto**, August 11, 1993. Signed as a free agent by **St. Louis**, August 10, 1995.

RAM, JAMIE ANA.

Goaltender. Catches left. 5'11", 175 lbs. Born, Scarborough, Ont., January 18, 1971.
(NY Rangers' 9th choice, 213th overall, in 1991 Entry Draft).

			Regular Season								Playoffs						
Season	Club	Lea	GP	W	L	T	Mins	GA	SO	Avg	GP	W	L	Mins	GA	SO	Avg
1990-91	Michigan Tech	WCHA	14	5	9	0	826	57	0	4.14	....	....	....	....	....	....	....
1991-92	Michigan Tech	WCHA	23	9	9	1	1144	83	0	4.35	....	....	....	....	....	....	....
1992-93	Michigan Tech	WCHA	*36	16	14	5	*2078	115	0	3.32	....	....	....	....	....	....	....
1993-94	Michigan Tech	WCHA	39	12	20	5	2192	117	*1	3.20	....	....	....	....	....	....	....
1994-95	Binghamton	AHL	26	12	10	2	1472	81	1	3.30	11	6	5	663	29	1	2.62
1995-96	NY Rangers	NHL	1	0	0	0	27	0	0	0.00	....	....	....	....	....	....	....
	Binghamton	AHL	40	18	16	3	2262	151	1	4.01	1	0	0	34	1	0	1.75
1996-97	Kentucky	AHL	50	25	19	5	2937	161	4	3.29	1	0	1	60	3	0	3.00
1997-98	Kentucky	AHL	44	17	18	5	2553	124	3	2.91	....	....	....	....	....	....	....
	Utica	IHL	7	3	4	0	398	24	0	3.61	1	0	1	59	3	0	3.04
	NHL Totals		**1**	**0**	**0**	**0**	**27**	**0**	**0**	**0.00**	....	....	....	....	....	....	....

WCHA First All-Star Team (1993, 1994) • NCAA West First All-American Team (1993, 1994)

Signed as a free agent by **San Jose**, August 19, 1997. Signed as a free agent by **Anaheim**, July 30, 1998.

RANFORD, BILL — T.B.

Goaltender. Catches left. 5'11", 185 lbs. Born, Brandon, Man., December 14, 1966.
(Boston's 2nd choice, 52nd overall, in 1985 Entry Draft).

			Regular Season								Playoffs						
Season	Club	Lea	GP	W	L	T	Mins	GA	SO	Avg	GP	W	L	Mins	GA	SO	Avg
1983-84	New Westminster	WHL	27	10	14	0	1450	130	0	5.38	1	0	0	27	2	0	4.44
1984-85	New Westminster	WHL	38	19	17	0	2034	142	0	4.19	7	2	3	309	26	0	5.05
1985-86	**Boston**	**NHL**	**4**	**3**	**1**	**0**	**240**	**10**	**0**	**2.50**	**2**	**0**	**2**	**120**	**7**	**0**	**3.50**
	New Westminster	WHL	53	17	29	1	2791	225	1	4.84	....	....	....	....	....	....	....
1986-87	**Boston**	**NHL**	**41**	**16**	**20**	**2**	**2234**	**124**	**3**	**3.33**	**2**	**0**	**2**	**123**	**8**	**0**	**3.90**
	Moncton	AHL	3	3	0	0	180	6	0	2.00	....	....	....	....	....	....	....
1987-88	Maine	AHL	51	27	16	6	2856	165	1	3.47	....	....	....	....	....	....	....
	Edmonton	**NHL**	**6**	**3**	**0**	**2**	**325**	**16**	**0**	**2.95**	....	....	....	....	....	....	.... ♦
1988-89	**Edmonton**	**NHL**	**29**	**15**	**8**	**2**	**1509**	**88**	**1**	**3.50**	....	....	....	....	....	....	....
1989-90	**Edmonton**	**NHL**	**56**	**24**	**16**	**9**	**3107**	**165**	**1**	**3.19**	***22**	***16**	**6**	***1401**	**59**	**1**	**2.53** ♦
1990-91	**Edmonton**	**NHL**	**60**	**27**	**27**	**3**	**3415**	**182**	**0**	**3.20**	**3**	**1**	**2**	**135**	**8**	**0**	**3.56**
1991-92	**Edmonton**	**NHL**	**67**	**27**	**26**	**10**	**3822**	**228**	**1**	**3.58**	**16**	**8**	**8**	**909**	**51**	***2**	**3.37**
1992-93	**Edmonton**	**NHL**	**67**	**17**	**38**	**6**	**3753**	**240**	**1**	**3.84**	....	....	....	....	....	....	....
1993-94	**Edmonton**	**NHL**	**71**	**22**	**34**	**11**	**4070**	**236**	**1**	**3.48**	....	....	....	....	....	....	....
1994-95	**Edmonton**	**NHL**	**40**	**15**	**20**	**3**	**2203**	**133**	**2**	**3.62**	....	....	....	....	....	....	....
1995-96	**Edmonton**	**NHL**	**37**	**13**	**18**	**5**	**2015**	**128**	**1**	**3.81**	....	....	....	....	....	....	....
	Boston	**NHL**	**40**	**21**	**12**	**4**	**2307**	**109**	**1**	**2.83**	**4**	**1**	**3**	**239**	**16**	**0**	**4.02**
1996-97	**Boston**	**NHL**	**37**	**12**	**16**	**8**	**2147**	**125**	**2**	**3.49**	....	....	....	....	....	....	....
	Washington	**NHL**	**18**	**8**	**7**	**2**	**1009**	**46**	**0**	**2.74**	....	....	....	....	....	....	....
1997-98	**Washington**	**NHL**	**22**	**7**	**12**	**2**	**1183**	**55**	**0**	**2.79**	....	....	....	....	....	....	....
	NHL Totals		**595**	**230**	**255**	**69**	**33339**	**1885**	**14**	**3.39**	**49**	**26**	**23**	**2927**	**149**	**3**	**3.05**

WHL West Second All-Star Team (1986) • Won Conn Smythe Trophy (1990)

Played in NHL All-Star Game (1991)

Traded to **Edmonton** by **Boston** with Geoff Courtnall and future considerations for Andy Moog, March 8, 1988. Traded to **Boston** by **Edmonton** for Mariusz Czerkawski, Sean Brown and Boston's 1st round choice (Matthieu Descoteaux) in 1996 Entry Draft, January 11, 1996. Traded to **Washington** by **Boston** with Adam Oates and Rick Tocchet for Jim Carey, Anson Carter, Jason Allison and Washington's 3rd round choice (Lee Goren) in 1997 Entry Draft, March 1, 1997. Traded to **Tampa Bay** by **Washington** for Tampa Bay's 3rd round choice (Todd Hornung) in 1998 Entry Draft and 2nd round choice in 1999 Entry Draft, June 18, 1998.

RAYCROFT, ANDREW — BOS.

Goaltender. Catches left. 6', 150 lbs. Born, Belleville, Ont., May 4, 1980.
(Boston's 4th choice, 135th overall, in 1998 Entry Draft).

			Regular Season								Playoffs						
Season	Club	Lea	GP	W	L	T	Mins	GA	SO	Avg	GP	W	L	Mins	GA	SO	Avg
1997-98	Sudbury	OHL	33	8	16	5	1802	125	0	4.16	2	0	1	89	8	0	5.39

REESE, JEFF

Goaltender. Catches left. 5'9", 180 lbs. Born, Brantford, Ont., March 24, 1966.
(Toronto's 3rd choice, 67th overall, in 1984 Entry Draft).

			Regular Season								Playoffs						
Season	Club	Lea	GP	W	L	T	Mins	GA	SO	Avg	GP	W	L	Mins	GA	SO	Avg
1983-84	London	OHL	43	18	19	1	2308	173	0	4.50	6	3	3	327	27	0	4.95
1984-85	London	OHL	50	31	15	1	2878	186	1	3.88	8	5	2	440	20	1	2.73
1985-86	London	OHL	*57	25	26	3	*3281	215	0	3.93	5	0	4	299	25	0	5.02
1986-87	Newmarket	AHL	50	11	29	0	2822	193	1	4.10	....	....	....	....	....	....	....
1987-88	**Toronto**	**NHL**	**5**	**1**	**2**	**1**	**249**	**17**	**0**	**4.10**	....	....	....	....	....	....	....
	Newmarket	AHL	28	10	14	3	1587	103	0	3.89	....	....	....	....	....	....	....
1988-89	**Toronto**	**NHL**	**10**	**2**	**6**	**1**	**486**	**40**	**0**	**4.94**	....	....	....	....	....	....	....
	Newmarket	AHL	37	17	14	3	2072	132	0	3.82	....	....	....	....	....	....	....
1989-90	**Toronto**	**NHL**	**21**	**9**	**6**	**3**	**1101**	**81**	**0**	**4.41**	**2**	**1**	**1**	**108**	**6**	**0**	**3.33**
	Newmarket	AHL	7	3	2	2	431	29	0	4.04	....	....	....	....	....	....	....
1990-91	**Toronto**	**NHL**	**30**	**6**	**13**	**3**	**1430**	**92**	**1**	**3.86**	....	....	....	....	....	....	....
	Newmarket	AHL	3	2	1	0	180	7	0	2.33	....	....	....	....	....	....	....
1991-92	**Toronto**	**NHL**	**8**	**1**	**5**	**1**	**413**	**20**	**1**	**2.91**	....	....	....	....	....	....	....
	Calgary	**NHL**	**12**	**3**	**2**	**2**	**587**	**37**	**0**	**3.78**	....	....	....	....	....	....	....
1992-93	**Calgary**	**NHL**	**26**	**14**	**4**	**1**	**1311**	**70**	**1**	**3.20**	**4**	**1**	**3**	**209**	**17**	**0**	**4.88**
1993-94	**Calgary**	**NHL**	**1**	**0**	**0**	**0**	**13**	**1**	**0**	**4.62**	....	....	....	....	....	....	....
	Hartford	**NHL**	**19**	**5**	**9**	**3**	**1086**	**56**	**1**	**3.09**	....	....	....	....	....	....	....
1994-95	**Hartford**	**NHL**	**11**	**2**	**5**	**1**	**477**	**26**	**0**	**3.27**	....	....	....	....	....	....	....
1995-96	**Hartford**	**NHL**	**7**	**2**	**3**	**0**	**275**	**14**	**1**	**3.05**	....	....	....	....	....	....	....
	Tampa Bay	**NHL**	**19**	**7**	**7**	**1**	**994**	**54**	**0**	**3.26**	**5**	**1**	**1**	**198**	**12**	**0**	**3.64**
1996-97	**New Jersey**	**NHL**	**3**	**0**	**2**	**0**	**139**	**13**	**0**	**5.61**	....	....	....	....	....	....	....
	Detroit	IHL	32	23	4	3	1763	55	4	*1.87	11	7	3	518	22	0	2.55
1997-98	Detroit	IHL	46	27	9	8	2570	95	4	2.22	*22	*13	9	*1276	52	*2	2.44
	NHL Totals		**172**	**52**	**64**	**17**	**8561**	**521**	**5**	**3.65**	**11**	**3**	**5**	**515**	**35**	**0**	**4.08**

IHL Second All-Star Team (1997, 1998) • Shared James Norris Memorial Trophy (fewest goals against - IHL) with Rich Parent (1997)

Traded to **Calgary** by **Toronto** with Craig Berube, Alexander Godynyuk, Gary Leeman and Michel Petit for Doug Gilmour, Jamie Macoun, Ric Nattress, Rick Wamsley and Kent Manderville, January 2, 1992. Traded to **Hartford** by **Calgary** for Dan Keczmer, November 19, 1993. Traded to **Tampa Bay** by **Hartford** for Tampa Bay's 9th round choice (Ashhat Rakhmatullin) in 1996 Entry Draft, December 1, 1995. Traded to **New Jersey** by **Tampa Bay** with Chicago's 2nd round choice (previously acquired, New Jersey selected Pierre Dagenais) in 1996 Entry Draft and Tampa Bay's 8th round choice (Jason Bertsch) in 1996 Entry Draft for Corey Schwab, June 22, 1996.

RHODES, DAMIAN — (ROHDZ) OTT.

Goaltender. Catches left. 6', 180 lbs. Born, St. Paul, MN, May 28, 1969.
(Toronto's 6th choice, 112th overall, in 1987 Entry Draft).

			Regular Season								Playoffs						
Season	Club	Lea	GP	W	L	T	Mins	GA	SO	Avg	GP	W	L	Mins	GA	SO	Avg
1986-87	Richfield High	H.S.	19	....	....	....	673	51	1	4.55	....	....	....	....	....	....	....
1987-88	Michigan Tech	WCHA	29	16	10	1	1625	114	0	4.20	....	....	....	....	....	....	....
1988-89	Michigan Tech	WCHA	37	15	22	0	2216	163	0	4.41	....	....	....	....	....	....	....
1989-90	Michigan Tech	WCHA	25	6	17	0	1358	119	0	6.26	....	....	....	....	....	....	....
1990-91	**Toronto**	**NHL**	**1**	**1**	**0**	**0**	**60**	**1**	**0**	**1.00**	....	....	....	....	....	....	....
	Newmarket	AHL	38	8	24	3	2154	144	1	4.01	....	....	....	....	....	....	....
1991-92	St. John's	AHL	43	20	16	5	2454	148	0	3.62	6	4	1	331	16	0	2.90
1992-93	St. John's	AHL	*52	27	16	8	*3074	184	1	3.59	9	4	5	538	37	0	4.13
1993-94	**Toronto**	**NHL**	**22**	**9**	**7**	**3**	**1213**	**53**	**0**	**2.62**	**1**	**0**	**0**	**1**	**0**	**0**	**0.00**
1994-95	**Toronto**	**NHL**	**13**	**6**	**6**	**1**	**760**	**34**	**0**	**2.68**	....	....	....	....	....	....	....
1995-96	**Toronto**	**NHL**	**11**	**4**	**5**	**1**	**624**	**29**	**0**	**2.79**	....	....	....	....	....	....	....
	Ottawa	**NHL**	**36**	**10**	**22**	**4**	**2123**	**98**	**2**	**2.77**	....	....	....	....	....	....	....
1996-97	**Ottawa**	**NHL**	**50**	**14**	**20**	**14**	**2934**	**133**	**1**	**2.72**	....	....	....	....	....	....	....
1997-98	**Ottawa**	**NHL**	**50**	**19**	**19**	**7**	**2743**	**107**	**5**	**2.34**	**10**	**5**	**5**	**590**	**21**	**0**	**2.14**
	NHL Totals		**183**	**63**	**79**	**30**	**10457**	**455**	**8**	**2.61**	**11**	**5**	**5**	**591**	**21**	**0**	**2.13**

• Credited with scoring a goal while with Michigan Tech (WCHA), January 21, 1989.

• Played 10 seconds in playoff game vs. San Jose, May 6, 1994. Traded to **NY Islanders** by **Toronto** with Ken Belanger for future considerations (Kirk Muller and Don Beaupre, January 23, 1996), January 23, 1996. Traded to **Ottawa** by **NY Islanders** with Wade Redden for Don Beaupre, Martin Straka and Bryan Berard, January 23, 1996.

RICHTER, MIKE — (RIHK-tuhr) NYR

Goaltender. Catches left. 5'11", 187 lbs. Born, Abington, PA, September 22, 1966.
(NY Rangers' 2nd choice, 28th overall, in 1985 Entry Draft).

			Regular Season								Playoffs						
Season	Club	Lea	GP	W	L	T	Mins	GA	SO	Avg	GP	W	L	Mins	GA	SO	Avg
1984-85	Northwood	H.S.	24	....	....	....	1374	52	2	2.27	....	....	....	....	....	....	....
1985-86	U. of Wisconsin	WCHA	24	14	9	0	1394	92	1	3.96	....	....	....	....	....	....	....
1986-87	U. of Wisconsin	WCHA	36	19	16	1	2136	126	0	3.54	....	....	....	....	....	....	....
1987-88	United States	Nat-Tm	29	17	7	2	1559	86	0	3.31	....	....	....	....	....	....	....
	United States	Olympics	4	....	....	....	230	15	....	3.91	....	....	....	....	....	....	....
	Colorado	IHL	22	16	5	0	1298	68	1	3.14	10	5	3	536	35	0	3.92
1988-89	Denver	IHL	*57	23	26	0	3031	217	1	4.30	4	0	4	210	21	0	6.00
	NY Rangers	**NHL**	....	....	....	....	....	....	....	....	**1**	**0**	**1**	**58**	**4**	**0**	**4.14**
1989-90	**NY Rangers**	**NHL**	**23**	**12**	**5**	**5**	**1320**	**66**	**0**	**3.00**	**6**	**3**	**2**	**330**	**19**	**0**	**3.45**
	Flint	IHL	13	7	4	2	782	49	0	3.76	....	....	....	....	....	....	....
1990-91	**NY Rangers**	**NHL**	**45**	**21**	**13**	**7**	**2596**	**135**	**0**	**3.12**	**6**	**2**	**4**	**313**	**14**	***1**	**2.68**
1991-92	**NY Rangers**	**NHL**	**41**	**23**	**12**	**2**	**2298**	**119**	**3**	**3.11**	**7**	**4**	**2**	**412**	**24**	**1**	**3.50**
1992-93	**NY Rangers**	**NHL**	**38**	**13**	**19**	**3**	**2105**	**134**	**1**	**3.82**	....	....	....	....	....	....	....
	Binghamton	AHL	5	4	0	1	305	6	0	1.18	....	....	....	....	....	....	....
1993-94	**NY Rangers**	**NHL**	**68**	***42**	**12**	**6**	**3710**	**159**	**5**	**2.57**	**23**	***16**	**7**	**1417**	**49**	***4**	**2.07** ♦
1994-95	**NY Rangers**	**NHL**	**35**	**14**	**17**	**2**	**1993**	**97**	**2**	**2.92**	**7**	**2**	**5**	**384**	**23**	**0**	**3.59**
1995-96	**NY Rangers**	**NHL**	**41**	**24**	**13**	**3**	**2396**	**107**	**3**	**2.68**	**11**	**5**	**6**	**661**	**36**	**0**	**3.27**
1996-97	**NY Rangers**	**NHL**	**61**	**33**	**22**	**6**	**3598**	**161**	**4**	**2.68**	**15**	**9**	**6**	**939**	**33**	***3**	**2.11**
1997-98	**NY Rangers**	**NHL**	***72**	**21**	**31**	**15**	**4143**	**184**	**0**	**2.66**	....	....	....	....	....	....	....
	United States	Olympics	4	1	3	0	237	14	0	3.55	....	....	....	....	....	....	....
	NHL Totals		**424**	**203**	**144**	**49**	**24159**	**1162**	**18**	**2.89**	**76**	**41**	**33**	**4514**	**202**	**9**	**2.68**

WCHA Second All-Star Team (1987) • World Cup All-Star Team (1996) • Named World Cup MVP (1996)

Played in NHL All-Star Game (1992, 1994)

Claimed by **Nashville** from **NY Rangers** in Expansion Draft, June 26, 1998. Signed as a free agent by **NY Rangers**, July 15, 1998.

ROBITAILLE, MARC — (ROH-buh-tigh) TOR.

Goaltender. Catches left. 5'10", 185 lbs. Born, Gloucester, Ont., June 7, 1976.

			Regular Season								Playoffs						
Season	Club	Lea	GP	W	L	T	Mins	GA	SO	Avg	GP	W	L	Mins	GA	SO	Avg
1996-97	Northeastern	H.E.	34	7	24	3	1928	135	3	4.20	....	....	....	....	....	....	....
1997-98	Northeastern	H.E.	*39	21	15	3	*2313	123	1	3.19	....	....	....	....	....	....	....

Hockey East First All-Star Team (1998) • NCAA East First All-American Team (1998)

Signed as a free agent by **Toronto**, June 4, 1998.

ROCHE, SCOTT — (ROHSH) ST.L.

Goaltender. Catches left. 6'4", 220 lbs. Born, Lindsay, Ont., March 19, 1977.
(St. Louis' 2nd choice, 75th overall, in 1995 Entry Draft).

			Regular Season								Playoffs						
Season	Club	Lea	GP	W	L	T	Mins	GA	SO	Avg	GP	W	L	Mins	GA	SO	Avg
1993-94	North Bay	OHL	32	15	5	4	1587	93	0	3.52	5	2	1	191	10	0	*3.14
1994-95	North Bay	OHL	47	24	17	2	2599	167	2	3.86	6	2	4	348	30	0	5.17
1995-96	North Bay	OHL	53	12	29	5	2859	232	1	4.87	....	....	....	....	....	....	....
1996-97	North Bay	OHL	3	0	3	0	122	21	0	10.30	....	....	....	....	....	....	....
	Windsor	OHL	44	20	16	4	2496	152	1	3.65	5	1	4	267	26	0	5.84
1997-98	Peoria	ECHL	38	23	11	3	2228	109	1	2.93	2	0	2	121	6	0	2.95
	Detroit	IHL	4	0	1	0	146	8	0	3.27	....	....	....	....	....	....	....

ROLOSON, DWAYNE — (ROH-loh-suhn) BUF.

Goaltender. Catches left. 6'1", 190 lbs. Born, Simcoe, Ont., October 12, 1969.

			Regular Season								Playoffs						
Season	Club	Lea	GP	W	L	T	Mins	GA	SO	Avg	GP	W	L	Mins	GA	SO	Avg
1990-91	U Mass-Lowell	H.E.	15	5	9	0	823	63	0	4.59	....	....	....	....	....	....	....
1991-92	U Mass-Lowell	H.E.	12	3	8	0	660	52	0	4.73	....	....	....	....	....	....	....
1992-93	U Mass-Lowell	H.E.	*39	20	17	2	*2342	150	0	3.84	....	....	....	....	....	....	....
1993-94	U Mass-Lowell	H.E.	*40	*23	10	7	*2305	106	0	2.76	....	....	....	....	....	....	....
1994-95	Saint John	AHL	46	16	21	8	2734	156	1	3.42	5	1	4	298	13	0	2.61
1995-96	Saint John	AHL	67	*33	22	11	4026	190	1	2.83	16	10	6	1027	49	1	2.86
1996-97	**Calgary**	**NHL**	**31**	**9**	**14**	**3**	**1618**	**78**	**1**	**2.89**	....	....	....	....	....	....	....
	Saint John	AHL	8	6	2	0	481	22	1	2.75	....	....	....	....	....	....	....
1997-98	**Calgary**	**NHL**	**39**	**11**	**16**	**8**	**2205**	**110**	**0**	**2.99**	....	....	....	....	....	....	....
	Saint John	AHL	4	3	0	1	245	8	0	1.96	....	....	....	....	....	....	....
	NHL Totals		**70**	**20**	**30**	**11**	**3823**	**188**	**1**	**2.95**	....	....	....	....	....	....	....

Hockey East First All-Star Team (1994) • NCAA East First All-Ameircan Team (1994)

Signed as a free agent by **Calgary**, July 4, 1994. Signed as a free agent by **Buffalo**, July 15, 1998.

ROSATI, MIKE — (roh-ZA-tee) WSH.

Goaltender. Catches left. 5'10", 170 lbs. Born, Toronto, Ont., January 7, 1968.
(NY Rangers' 6th choice, 131st overall, in 1988 Entry Draft).

			Regular Season								Playoffs						
Season	Club	Lea	GP	W	L	T	Mins	GA	SO	Avg	GP	W	L	Mins	GA	SO	Avg
1986-87	Hamilton	OHL	26	....	....	....	1334	85	1	3.82	....	....	....	....	....	....	....
1987-88	Hamilton	OHL	62	29	25	3	3468	233	1	4.03	14	8	6	833	66	0	4.75
1988-89	Niagara Falls	OHL	52	*28	15	2	2339	174	1	4.46	16	10	4	861	62	0	4.32
1989-90	Erie	ECHL	18	12	5	0	1056	73	0	4.14	....	....	....	....	....	....	....
1990-91	Bolzano	Italy	46	....	....	....	2700	212	0	4.71	....	....	....	....	....	....	....
1991-92	Bolzano	Italy	18	11	6	1	1022	58	2	3.22	7	5	2	409	30	0	4.28
1992-93	Bolzano	Italy								Statistics Not Available							
1993-94	Bolzano	Italy								Statistics Not Available							
1994-95	Bolzano	Italy	47	....	....	....	2705	149	1	3.30	....	....	....	....	....	....	....
1995-96	Bolzano	Italy	42	....	....	....	2465	137	3	3.33	....	....	....	....	....	....	....
1996-97	Mannheim	Germany	44	....	....	....	2625	104	6	2.38	9	....	....	514	24	0	2.80
1997-98	Mannheim	Germany	43	....	....	....	2567	116	2	2.71	*10	*9	1	569	17	*1	*2.00

Signed as a free agent by **Washington**, July 15, 1998.

ROUSSEL, DOMINIC (roo-SEHL) NSH.

Goaltender. Catches left. 6'1", 191 lbs. Born, Hull, Que., February 22, 1970.
(Philadelphia's 4th choice, 63rd overall, in 1988 Entry Draft).

			Regular Season								Playoffs						
Season	Club	Lea	GP	W	L	T	Mins	GA	SO	Avg	GP	W	L	Mins	GA	SO	Avg
1987-88	Trois-Rivieres	QMJHL	51	18	25	4	2905	251	0	5.18	....	....	....	....	....	....	....
1988-89	Shawinigan	QMJHL	46	24	15	2	2555	171	0	4.02	10	6	4	638	36	0	3.39
1989-90	Shawinigan	QMJHL	37	20	14	1	1985	133	0	4.02	2	1	1	120	12	0	6.00
1990-91	Hershey	AHL	45	20	14	7	2507	151	1	3.61	7	3	4	366	21	0	3.44
1991-92	**Philadelphia**	**NHL**	**17**	**7**	**8**	**2**	**922**	**40**	**1**	**2.60**	....	....	....	....	....	....	....
	Hershey	AHL	35	15	11	6	2040	121	1	3.56	....	....	....	....	....	....	....
1992-93	**Philadelphia**	**NHL**	**34**	**13**	**11**	**5**	**1769**	**111**	**1**	**3.76**	....	....	....	....	....	....	....
	Hershey	AHL	6	0	3	3	372	23	0	3.71	....	....	....	....	....	....	....
1993-94	**Philadelphia**	**NHL**	**60**	**29**	**20**	**5**	**3285**	**183**	**1**	**3.34**	....	....	....	....	....	....	....
1994-95	**Philadelphia**	**NHL**	**19**	**11**	**7**	**0**	**1075**	**42**	**1**	**2.34**	**1**	**0**	**0**	**23**	**0**	**0**	**0.00**
	Hershey	AHL	1	0	1	0	59	5	0	5.07	....	....	....	....	....	....	....
1995-96	**Philadelphia**	**NHL**	**9**	**2**	**3**	**2**	**456**	**22**	**1**	**2.89**	....	....	....	....	....	....	....
	Hershey	AHL	12	4	4	3	690	32	0	2.78	....	....	....	....	....	....	....
	Winnipeg	**NHL**	**7**	**2**	**2**	**0**	**285**	**16**	**0**	**3.37**	....	....	....	....	....	....	....
1996-97	Philadelphia	AHL	36	18	9	3	1852	82	2	2.66	1	0	0	26	3	0	6.93
1997-98	Canada	Nat-Tm	41	25	12	1	2307	86	5	2.24	....	....	....	....	....	....	....
	Rosenheim	Germany	2	....	....	....	120	12	0	6.00	....	....	....	....	....	....	....
	NHL Totals		**146**	**64**	**51**	**14**	**7792**	**414**	**5**	**3.19**	**1**	**0**	**0**	**23**	**0**	**0**	**0.00**

Traded to **Winnipeg** by **Philadelphia** for Tim Cheveldae and Winnipeg's 3rd round choice (Chester Gallant) in 1996 Entry Draft, February 27, 1996. Signed as a free agent by **Philadelphia**, July 3, 1996. Traded to **Nashville** by **Philadelphia** with Jeff Staples for Nashville's 7th round choice (Cam Ondrik) in 1998 Entry Draft, June 26, 1998.

ROY, PATRICK (WAH) COL.

Goaltender. Catches left. 6', 192 lbs. Born, Quebec City, Que., October 5, 1965.
(Montreal's 4th choice, 51st overall, in 1984 Entry Draft).

			Regular Season								Playoffs						
Season	Club	Lea	GP	W	L	T	Mins	GA	SO	Avg	GP	W	L	Mins	GA	SO	Avg
1982-83	Granby	QMJHL	54	13	35	1	2808	293	0	6.26	....	....	....	....	....	....	....
1983-84	Granby	QMJHL	61	29	29	1	3585	265	0	4.44	4	0	4	244	22	0	5.41
1984-85	**Montreal**	**NHL**	**1**	**1**	**0**	**0**	**20**	**0**	**0**	**0.00**	....	....	....	....	....	....	....
	Granby	QMJHL	44	16	25	1	2463	228	0	5.55	....	....	....	....	....	....	....
	Sherbrooke	AHL	1	1	0	0	60	4	0	4.00	13	10	3	*769	37	0	*2.89
1985-86	**Montreal**	**NHL**	**47**	**23**	**18**	**3**	**2651**	**148**	**1**	**3.35**	**20**	***15**	**5**	**1218**	**39**	***1**	**1.92** ♦
1986-87	**Montreal**	**NHL**	**46**	**22**	**16**	**6**	**2686**	**131**	**1**	**2.93**	**6**	**4**	**2**	**330**	**22**	**0**	**4.00**
1987-88	**Montreal**	**NHL**	**45**	**23**	**12**	**9**	**2586**	**125**	**3**	**2.90**	**8**	**3**	**4**	**430**	**24**	**0**	**3.35**
1988-89	**Montreal**	**NHL**	**48**	**33**	**5**	**6**	**2744**	**113**	**4**	***2.47**	**19**	**13**	**6**	**1206**	**42**	**2**	***2.09**
1989-90	**Montreal**	**NHL**	**54**	***31**	**16**	**5**	**3173**	**134**	**3**	**2.53**	**11**	**5**	**6**	**641**	**26**	**1**	**2.43**
1990-91	**Montreal**	**NHL**	**48**	**25**	**15**	**6**	**2835**	**128**	**1**	**2.71**	**13**	**7**	**5**	**785**	**40**	**0**	**3.06**
1991-92	**Montreal**	**NHL**	**67**	**36**	**22**	**8**	**3935**	**155**	***5**	***2.36**	**11**	**4**	**7**	**686**	**30**	**1**	**2.62**
1992-93	**Montreal**	**NHL**	**62**	**31**	**25**	**5**	**3595**	**192**	**2**	**3.20**	**20**	***16**	**4**	**1293**	**46**	**0**	***2.13** ♦
1993-94	**Montreal**	**NHL**	**68**	**35**	**17**	**11**	**3867**	**161**	***7**	**2.50**	**6**	**3**	**3**	**375**	**16**	**0**	**2.56**
1994-95	**Montreal**	**NHL**	**43**	**17**	**20**	**6**	**2566**	**127**	**1**	**2.97**	....	....	....	....	....	....	....
1995-96	**Montreal**	**NHL**	**22**	**12**	**9**	**1**	**1260**	**62**	**1**	**2.95**	....	....	....	....	....	....	....
	Colorado	**NHL**	**39**	**22**	**15**	**1**	**2305**	**103**	**1**	**2.68**	***22**	***16**	**6**	***1454**	**51**	***3**	**2.10** ♦
1996-97	**Colorado**	**NHL**	**62**	***38**	**15**	**7**	**3698**	**143**	**7**	**2.32**	**17**	**10**	**7**	**1034**	**38**	***3**	**2.21**
1997-98	**Colorado**	**NHL**	**65**	**31**	**19**	**13**	**3835**	**153**	**4**	**2.39**	**7**	**3**	**4**	**430**	**18**	**0**	**2.51**
	Canada	Olympics	6	3	3	0	*369	9	1	1.46	....	....	....	....	....	....	....
	NHL Totals		**717**	**380**	**224**	**87**	**41756**	**1875**	**41**	**2.69**	***160**	***99**	**59**	***9882**	**392**	**11**	**2.38**

NHL All-Rookie Team (1986) • Won Conn Smythe Trophy (1986, 1993) • Shared William Jennings Trophy with Brian Hayward (1987, 1988, 1989) • NHL Second All-Star Team (1988, 1991) • NHL First All-Star Team (1989, 1990, 1992) • Won Trico Goaltending Award (1989, 1990) • Won Vezina Trophy (1989, 1990, 1992) • Won William M. Jennings Trophy (1992)

Played in NHL All-Star Game (1988, 1990, 1991, 1992, 1993, 1994, 1997, 1998)

Traded to **Colorado** by **Montreal** with Mike Keane for Andrei Kovalenko, Martin Rucinsky and Jocelyn Thibault, December 6, 1995.

RUSSELL, BLAINE ANA.

Goaltender. Catches left. 5'11", 180 lbs. Born, Wetaskawin, Sask., January 11, 1977.
(Anaheim's 4th choice, 149th overall, in 1996 Entry Draft).

			Regular Season								Playoffs						
Season	Club	Lea	GP	W	L	T	Mins	GA	SO	Avg	GP	W	L	Mins	GA	SO	Avg
1995-96	Spokane	WHL	1	0	1	0	37	5	0	8.11	....	....	....	....	....	....	....
	Prince Albert	WHL	34	25	5	2	1920	98	2	3.06	7	4	2	380	20	0	3.16
1996-97	Prince Albert	WHL	29	9	15	3	1690	99	2	3.51	....	....	....	....	....	....	....
	Lethbridge	WHL	6	4	1	1	370	17	0	2.76	14	*13	1	817	29	0	*2.13
1997-98	Columbus	ECHL	4	1	2	0	199	19	0	5.71	....	....	....	....	....	....	....
	Cincinnati	AHL	20	0	9	2	748	58	0	4.65	....	....	....	....	....	....	....
	Huntington	ECHL	1	0	1	0	60	6	0	6.00	....	....	....	....	....	....	....
	New Orleans	ECHL	4	0	0	2	183	11	0	3.59	....	....	....	....	....	....	....

SABOURIN, DANY (SA-boo-rihn) CGY.

Goaltender. Catches left. 6'2", 165 lbs. Born, Val D'or, Que., September 2, 1980.
(Calgary's 5th choice, 108th overall, in 1998 Entry Draft).

			Regular Season								Playoffs						
Season	Club	Lea	GP	W	L	T	Mins	GA	SO	Avg	GP	W	L	Mins	GA	SO	Avg
1997-98	Sherbrooke	QMJHL	37	15	15	2	1906	128	1	4.03	....	....	....	....	....	....	....

SALO, TOMMY (SAH-loh) NYI

Goaltender. Catches left. 5'11", 173 lbs. Born, Surahammar, Sweden, February 1, 1971.
(NY Islanders' 5th choice, 118th overall, in 1993 Entry Draft).

			Regular Season								Playoffs						
Season	Club	Lea	GP	W	L	T	Mins	GA	SO	Avg	GP	W	L	Mins	GA	SO	Avg
1990-91	Vasteras IK	Sweden	2	....	....	....	100	11	0	6.60	....	....	....	....	....	....	....
1991-92	Vasteras IK	Sweden	DID NOT PLAY – INJURED														
1992-93	Vasteras IK	Sweden	24	....	....	....	1431	59	2	2.47	2	....	....	120	6	0	3.00
1993-94	Vasteras IK	Sweden	32	....	....	....	1896	106	0	3.35	....	....	....	....	....	....	....
	Sweden	Olympics	6	5	1	0	370	13	....	2.11	....	....	....	....	....	....	....
1994-95	Denver	IHL	*65	*45	14	4	*3810	165	*3	*2.60	8	7	0	390	20	0	3.07
	NY Islanders	**NHL**	**6**	**1**	**5**	**0**	**358**	**18**	**0**	**3.02**	....	....	....	....	....	....	....
1995-96	**NY Islanders**	**NHL**	**10**	**1**	**7**	**1**	**523**	**35**	**0**	**4.02**	....	....	....	....	....	....	....
	Utah	IHL	45	28	15	2	2695	119	*4	2.65	22	*15	7	1342	51	*3	2.28
1996-97	**NY Islanders**	**NHL**	**58**	**20**	**27**	**8**	**3208**	**151**	**5**	**2.82**	....	....	....	....	....	....	....
1997-98	**NY Islanders**	**NHL**	**62**	**23**	**29**	**5**	**3461**	**152**	**4**	**2.64**	....	....	....	....	....	....	....
	Sweden	Olympics	4	2	2	0	238	9	0	2.27	....	....	....	....	....	....	....
	NHL Totals		**136**	**45**	**68**	**14**	**7550**	**356**	**9**	**2.83**	....	....	....	....	....	....	....

IHL First All-Star Team (1995) • Won Garry F. Longman Memorial Trophy (Top Rookie - IHL) (1995) • Won James Norris Memorial Trophy (Fewest goals against - IHL) (1995) • Won James Gatschene Memorial Trophy (MVP - IHL) (1995) • Shared James Norris Memorial Trophy (fewest goals against - IHL) with Mark McArthur (1996) • Won "Bud" Poile Trophy (Playoff MVP - IHL) (1996)

SARJEANT, GEOFF (SAHR-jehnt)

Goaltender. Catches left. 5'9", 180 lbs. Born, Newmarket, Ont., November 30, 1969.
(St. Louis' 1st choice, 17th overall, in 1990 Supplemental Draft).

			Regular Season								Playoffs						
Season	Club	Lea	GP	W	L	T	Mins	GA	SO	Avg	GP	W	L	Mins	GA	SO	Avg
1988-89	Michigan Tech	WCHA	6	0	3	2	329	22	0	4.01	....	....	....	....	....	....	....
1989-90	Michigan Tech	WCHA	19	4	13	0	1043	94	0	5.41	....	....	....	....	....	....	....
1990-91	Michigan Tech	WCHA	23	5	15	3	1540	97	0	3.78	....	....	....	....	....	....	....
1991-92	Michigan Tech	WCHA	23	7	13	0	1201	90	1	4.50	....	....	....	....	....	....	....
1992-93	Peoria	IHL	41	22	14	3	2356	130	0	3.31	3	0	3	179	13	0	4.36
1993-94	Peoria	IHL	41	25	9	2	2275	93	*2	*2.45	4	2	2	211	13	0	3.69
1994-95	Peoria	IHL	55	32	12	8	3146	158	0	3.01	4	0	3	206	20	0	5.81
	St. Louis	**NHL**	**4**	**1**	**0**	**0**	**120**	**6**	**0**	**3.00**	....	....	....	....	....	....	....
1995-96	**San Jose**	**NHL**	**4**	**0**	**2**	**1**	**171**	**14**	**0**	**4.91**	....	....	....	....	....	....	....
	Kansas City	IHL	41	18	18	1	2167	140	1	3.88	2	0	1	99	3	0	1.82
1996-97	Cincinnati	IHL	59	32	20	5	3287	157	1	2.87	3	0	3	158	12	0	4.55
1997-98	Cincinnati	IHL	54	25	19	9	3118	142	5	2.73	5	4	1	353	14	0	2.38
	NHL Totals		**8**	**1**	**2**	**1**	**291**	**20**	**0**	**4.12**	....	....	....	....	....	....	....

IHL First All-Star Team (1994)

Signed as a free agent by **San Jose**, September 23, 1995.

SAUVE, PHILLIPE (SOH-vay) COL.

Goaltender. Catches left. 6', 175 lbs. Born, Buffalo, NY, February 27, 1980.
(Colorado's 6th choice, 38th overall, in 1998 Entry Draft).

			Regular Season								Playoffs						
Season	Club	Lea	GP	W	L	T	Mins	GA	SO	Avg	GP	W	L	Mins	GA	SO	Avg
1996-97	Rimouski	QMJHL	26	11	9	2	1334	84	0	3.78	1	0	0	14	3	0	12.90
1997-98	Rimouski	QMJHL	40	23	16	0	2326	131	1	3.38	7	0	5	262	33	0	7.55

SCHAFER, PAXTON BOS.

Goaltender. Catches left. 5'9", 164 lbs. Born, Medicine Hat, Alta., February 26, 1976.
(Boston's 3rd choice, 47th overall, in 1995 Entry Draft).

			Regular Season								Playoffs						
Season	Club	Lea	GP	W	L	T	Mins	GA	SO	Avg	GP	W	L	Mins	GA	SO	Avg
1993-94	Medicine Hat	WHL	19	6	9	1	909	67	0	4.42	....	....	....	....	....	....	....
1994-95	Medicine Hat	WHL	61	32	26	2	3519	185	0	3.15	5	1	4	339	18	0	3.19
1995-96	Medicine Hat	WHL	60	24	30	3	3256	200	1	3.69	5	1	4	251	25	0	5.98
1996-97	**Boston**	**NHL**	**3**	**0**	**0**	**0**	**77**	**6**	**0**	**4.68**	....	....	....	....	....	....	....
	Providence	AHL	22	9	10	0	1206	75	1	3.73	....	....	....	....	....	....	....
	Charlotte	ECHL	4	3	1	0	239	7	0	1.75	....	....	....	....	....	....	....
1997-98	Providence	AHL	3	1	1	0	158	11	0	4.16	....	....	....	....	....	....	....
	Charlotte	ECHL	44	21	17	5	2538	131	1	3.10	7	3	4	428	21	0	2.94
	NHL Totals		**3**	**0**	**0**	**0**	**77**	**6**	**0**	**4.68**	....	....	....	....	....	....	....

WHL East First All-Star Team (1995)

SCHWAB, COREY (SHWAHB) T.B.

Goaltender. Catches left. 6', 180 lbs. Born, North Battleford, Sask., November 4, 1970.
(New Jersey's 12th choice, 200th overall, in 1990 Entry Draft).

			Regular Season								Playoffs						
Season	Club	Lea	GP	W	L	T	Mins	GA	SO	Avg	GP	W	L	Mins	GA	SO	Avg
1988-89	Seattle	WHL	10	2	2	0	386	31	0	4.82	....	....	....	....	....	....	....
1989-90	Seattle	WHL	27	15	2	1	1150	69	1	3.60	3	0	0	49	2	0	2.45
1990-91	Seattle	WHL	*58	32	18	3	*3289	224	0	4.09	6	1	5	382	25	0	3.93
1991-92	Utica	AHL	24	9	12	1	1322	95	0	4.31	....	....	....	....	....	....	....
	Cincinnati	ECHL	8	6	0	1	450	31	0	4.13	9	6	3	540	29	0	3.22
1992-93	Utica	AHL	40	18	16	5	2387	169	*2	4.25	1	0	1	59	6	0	6.10
	Cincinnati	IHL	3	1	2	0	185	17	0	5.51	....	....	....	....	....	....	....
1993-94	Albany	AHL	51	27	21	3	3058	184	0	3.61	5	1	4	298	20	0	4.02
1994-95	Albany	AHL	45	25	10	9	2711	117	3	*2.59	7	6	1	425	19	0	2.68
1995-96	**New Jersey**	**NHL**	**10**	**0**	**3**	**0**	**331**	**12**	**0**	**2.18**	....	....	....	....	....	....	....
	Albany	AHL	5	3	2	0	299	13	0	2.61	....	....	....	....	....	....	....
1996-97	**Tampa Bay**	**NHL**	**31**	**11**	**12**	**1**	**1462**	**74**	**2**	**3.04**	....	....	....	....	....	....	....
1997-98	**Tampa Bay**	**NHL**	**16**	**2**	**9**	**1**	**821**	**40**	**1**	**2.92**	....	....	....	....	....	....	....
	NHL Totals		**57**	**13**	**24**	**2**	**2614**	**126**	**3**	**2.89**	....	....	....	....	....	....	....

AHL Second All-Star Team (1995) • Shared Harry "Hap" Holmes Memorial Trophy (fewest goals against - AHL) with Mike Dunham (1995) • Shared Jack A. Butterfield Trophy (Playoff MVP - AHL) with Mike Dunham (1995)

Traded to **Tampa Bay** by **New Jersey** for Jeff Reese, Chicago's 2nd round choice (previously acquired, New Jersey selected Pierre Dagenais) in 1996 Entry Draft and Tampa Bay's 8th round choice (Jason Bertsch) in 1996 Entry Draft, June 22, 1996.

SCOTT, TRAVIS ST.L.

Goaltender. Catches left. 6'2", 185 lbs. Born, Kanata, Ont., September 14, 1975.

			Regular Season								Playoffs						
Season	Club	Lea	GP	W	L	T	Mins	GA	SO	Avg	GP	W	L	Mins	GA	SO	Avg
1993-94	Windsor	OHL	45	20	18	0	2312	158	1	4.10	4	0	4	240	16	0	4.00
1994-95	Windsor	OHL	48	26	14	3	2644	147	3	3.34	3	0	1	94	6	1	3.83
1995-96	Oshawa	OHL	31	15	9	4	1763	78	3	2.65	5	1	4	315	23	0	4.38
1996-97	Baton Rouge	ECHL	10	5	2	1	501	22	0	2.63	....	....	....	....	....	....	....
	Worcester	AHL	29	14	10	1	1482	75	1	3.04	....	....	....	....	....	....	....
1997-98	Baton Rouge	ECHL	36	14	11	6	1949	96	1	2.96	....	....	....	....	....	....	....

Signed as a free agent by **St. Louis**, December 30, 1996.

SHIELDS, STEVE S.J.

Goaltender. Catches left. 6'3", 210 lbs. Born, Toronto, Ont., July 19, 1972.
(Buffalo's 5th choice, 101st overall, in 1991 Entry Draft).

			Regular Season								Playoffs						
Season	Club	Lea	GP	W	L	T	Mins	GA	SO	Avg	GP	W	L	Mins	GA	SO	Avg
1990-91	U. of Michigan	CCHA	37	26	6	3	1963	106	0	3.24	....	....	....	....	....	....	....
1991-92	U. of Michigan	CCHA	*37	*27	7	2	*2090	99	1	2.84	....	....	....	....	....	....	....
1992-93	U. of Michigan	CCHA	*39	*30	6	2	2027	75	2	*2.22	....	....	....	....	....	....	....
1993-94	U. of Michigan	CCHA	36	*28	6	1	1961	87	0	2.66	....	....	....	....	....	....	....
1994-95	Rochester	AHL	13	3	8	0	673	53	0	4.72	1	0	0	20	3	0	9.00
	South Carolina	ECHL	21	11	5	2	1158	52	2	2.69	3	0	2	144	11	0	4.58
1995-96	**Buffalo**	**NHL**	**2**	**1**	**0**	**0**	**75**	**4**	**0**	**3.20**	....	....	....	....	....	....	....
	Rochester	AHL	43	20	17	2	2357	140	1	3.56	*19	*15	3	*1127	47	1	2.50
1996-97	**Buffalo**	**NHL**	**13**	**3**	**8**	**2**	**789**	**39**	**0**	**2.97**	**10**	**4**	**6**	**570**	**26**	**1**	**2.74**
	Rochester	AHL	23	14	6	2	1331	60	1	2.70	....	....	....	....	....	....	....
1997-98	**Buffalo**	**NHL**	**16**	**3**	**6**	**4**	**785**	**37**	**0**	**2.83**	....	....	....	....	....	....	....
	Rochester	AHL	1	0	1	0	59	3	0	3.04	....	....	....	....	....	....	....
	NHL Totals		**31**	**7**	**14**	**6**	**1649**	**80**	**0**	**2.91**	**10**	**4**	**6**	**570**	**26**	**1**	**2.74**

CCHA First All-Star Team (1993, 1994) • NCAA West Second All-American Team (1993, 1994)

Traded to **San Jose** by **Buffalo** with Buffalo's 4th round choice (Miroskav Zalesak) in 1998 Entry Draft for Kay Whitmore, Colorado's 2nd round choice (previously acquired, Buffalo selected Jaroslav Kristek) in 1998 Entry Draft and San Jose's 5th round choice in 2000 Entry Draft, June 18, 1998.

SHTALENKOV, MIKHAIL (shtuh-LEHN-kahf, mihk-HAIL) NSH.

Goaltender. Catches left. 6'2", 185 lbs. Born, Moscow, USSR, October 20, 1965.
(Anaheim's 5th choice, 108th overall, in 1993 Entry Draft).

			Regular Season								Playoffs						
Season	**Club**	**Lea**	**GP**	**W**	**L**	**T**	**Mins**	**GA**	**SO**	**Avg**	**GP**	**W**	**L**	**Mins**	**GA**	**SO**	**Avg**
1986-87	Moscow D'amo	USSR	17	....	....	....	893	36	1	2.41	....	....	....	....	....	....	....
1987-88	Moscow D'amo	USSR	25	....	....	....	1302	72	1	3.31	....	....	....	....	....	....	....
1988-89	Moscow D'amo	USSR	4	....	....	....	80	3	0	2.25	....	....	....	....	....	....	....
1989-90	Moscow D'amo	USSR	6	....	....	....	20	1	0	3.00	....	....	....	....	....	....	....
1990-91	Moscow D'amo	USSR	31	....	....	....	1568	56	2	2.14	....	....	....	....	....	....	....
1991-92	Moscow D'amo	CIS	27	....	....	....	1268	45	1	2.12	....	....	....	....	....	....	....
	Russia	Olympics	8	7	1	0	440	12	....	1.64	....	....	....	....	....	....	....
1992-93	Milwaukee	IHL	47	26	14	5	2669	135	2	3.03	3	1	2	209	11	0	3.16
1993-94	**Anaheim**	**NHL**	**10**	**3**	**4**	**1**	**543**	**24**	**0**	**2.65**	....	....	....	....	....	....	....
	San Diego	IHL	28	15	11	2	1616	93	0	3.45	....	....	....	....	....	....	....
1994-95	**Anaheim**	**NHL**	**18**	**4**	**7**	**1**	**810**	**49**	**0**	**3.63**	....	....	....	....	....	....	....
1995-96	**Anaheim**	**NHL**	**30**	**7**	**16**	**3**	**1637**	**85**	**0**	**3.12**	....	....	....	....	....	....	....
1996-97	**Anaheim**	**NHL**	**24**	**7**	**8**	**1**	**1079**	**52**	**2**	**2.89**	**4**	**0**	**3**	**211**	**10**	**0**	**2.84**
1997-98	**Anaheim**	**NHL**	**40**	**13**	**18**	**5**	**2049**	**110**	**1**	**3.22**	....	....	....	....	....	....	....
	Russia	Olympics	5	4	1	0	290	8	0	1.65	....	....	....	....	....	....	....
	NHL Totals		**122**	**34**	**53**	**11**	**6118**	**320**	**3**	**3.14**	**4**	**0**	**3**	**211**	**10**	**0**	**2.84**

USSR Rookie of the Year (1987) • Won Garry F. Longman Memorial Trophy (Top Rookie - IHL) (1993)

Claimed by **Nashville** from **Anaheim** in Expansion Draft, June 26, 1998.

SHULMISTRA, RICHARD (shuhl-MIHS-trah) N.J.

Goaltender. Catches right. 6'2", 185 lbs. Born, Sudbury, Ont., April 1, 1971.
(Quebec's 1st choice, 4th overall, in 1992 Supplemental Draft).

			Regular Season								Playoffs						
Season	**Club**	**Lea**	**GP**	**W**	**L**	**T**	**Mins**	**GA**	**SO**	**Avg**	**GP**	**W**	**L**	**Mins**	**GA**	**SO**	**Avg**
1990-91	Miami-Ohio	CCHA	20	2	12	2	920	80	0	5.21	....	....	....	....	....	....	....
1991-92	Miami-Ohio	CCHA	19	3	5	2	850	67	0	4.72	....	....	....	....	....	....	....
1992-93	Miami-Ohio	CCHA	33	22	6	4	1949	88	1	2.71	....	....	....	....	....	....	....
1993-94	Miami-Ohio	CCHA	27	13	12	1	1521	74	0	2.92	....	....	....	....	....	....	....
1994-95	Cornwall	AHL	20	4	9	2	937	58	0	3.71	8	4	3	446	22	0	2.95
1995-96	Cornwall	AHL	36	9	18	2	1844	100	0	3.25	1	0	0	9	1	0	6.76
1996-97	Albany	AHL	23	5	9	2	1062	43	2	2.43	2	1	0	77	2	0	1.56
1997-98	Fort Wayne	IHL	11	3	8	0	656	34	1	3.11	....	....	....	....	....	....	....
	New Jersey	**NHL**	**1**	**0**	**1**	**0**	**62**	**2**	**0**	**1.94**	....	....	....	....	....	....	....
	Albany	AHL	35	20	8	4	2022	78	2	*2.31	13	8	3	696	32	1	2.76
	NHL Totals		**1**	**0**	**1**	**0**	**62**	**2**	**0**	**1.94**	....	....	....	....	....	....	....

CCHA Second All-Star Team (1993) • AHL Second All-Star Team (1998)

Transferred to **Colorado** after **Quebec** franchise relocated, June 21, 1995. Signed as a free agent by **New Jersey**, December 31, 1997.

SIDORKIEWICZ, PETER (sih-DOHR-kuh-vihch)

Goaltender. Catches left. 5'9", 180 lbs. Born, Dabrowa Bialostocka, Pol., June 29, 1963.
(Washington's 5th choice, 91st overall, in 1981 Entry Draft).

			Regular Season								Playoffs						
Season	**Club**	**Lea**	**GP**	**W**	**L**	**T**	**Mins**	**GA**	**SO**	**Avg**	**GP**	**W**	**L**	**Mins**	**GA**	**SO**	**Avg**
1980-81	Oshawa	OHA	7	3	3	0	308	24	0	4.68	5	2	2	266	20	0	4.52
1981-82	Oshawa	OHL	29	14	11	1	1553	123	*2	4.75	1	0	0	13	1	0	4.62
1982-83	Oshawa	OHL	60	36	20	3	3536	213	0	3.61	17	15	1	1020	60	0	3.53
1983-84	Oshawa	OHL	52	28	21	1	2966	250	1	4.15	7	3	4	420	27	*1	3.86
1984-85	Binghamton	AHL	45	31	9	5	2691	137	3	3.05	8	4	4	481	31	0	3.87
	Fort Wayne	IHL	10	4	4	2	590	43	0	4.37	....	....	....	....	....	....	....
1985-86	Binghamton	AHL	49	21	22	3	2819	150	2	*3.19	4	1	3	235	12	0	3.06
1986-87	Binghamton	AHL	57	23	16	0	3304	161	4	2.92	13	6	7	794	36	0	*2.72
1987-88	**Hartford**	**NHL**	**1**	**0**	**1**	**0**	**60**	**6**	**0**	**6.00**	....	....	....	....	....	....	....
	Binghamton	AHL	42	19	17	3	2345	144	0	3.68	3	0	2	147	8	0	3.27
1988-89	**Hartford**	**NHL**	**44**	**22**	**18**	**4**	**2635**	**133**	**4**	**3.03**	**2**	**0**	**2**	**124**	**8**	**0**	**3.87**
1989-90	**Hartford**	**NHL**	**46**	**19**	**19**	**7**	**2703**	**161**	**1**	**3.57**	**7**	**3**	**4**	**429**	**23**	**0**	**3.22**
1990-91	**Hartford**	**NHL**	**52**	**21**	**22**	**7**	**2953**	**164**	**1**	**3.33**	**6**	**2**	**4**	**359**	**24**	**0**	**4.01**
1991-92	**Hartford**	**NHL**	**35**	**9**	**19**	**6**	**1995**	**111**	**2**	**3.34**	....	....	....	....	....	....	....
1992-93	**Ottawa**	**NHL**	**64**	**8**	**46**	**3**	**3388**	**250**	**0**	**4.43**	....	....	....	....	....	....	....
1993-94	**New Jersey**	**NHL**	**3**	**0**	**3**	**0**	**130**	**6**	**0**	**2.77**	....	....	....	....	....	....	....
	Albany	AHL	15	6	7	2	907	60	0	3.97	....	....	....	....	....	....	....
	Fort Wayne	IHL	11	6	3	0	591	27	*2	2.74	*18	10	8	*1054	59	*1	3.36
1994-95	Fort Wayne	IHL	16	8	6	1	941	58	1	3.70	3	1	2	144	12	0	5.00
1995-96	Albany	AHL	32	19	7	5	1809	89	3	2.95	1	0	1	59	3	0	3.06
1996-97	Albany	AHL	62	31	23	6	3539	171	2	2.90	16	7	8	920	48	0	3.13
1997-98	**New Jersey**	**NHL**	**1**	**0**	**0**	**0**	**20**	**1**	**0**	**3.00**	....	....	....	....	....	....	....
	Albany	AHL	43	21	15	5	2422	115	3	2.85	2	1	1	89	6	0	4.01
	NHL Totals		**246**	**79**	**128**	**27**	**13884**	**832**	**8**	**3.60**	**15**	**5**	**10**	**912**	**55**	**0**	**3.62**

AHL Second All-Star Team (1987) • NHL All-Rookie Team (1989)

Played in NHL All-Star Game (1993)

Traded to **Hartford** by **Washington** with Dean Evason for David Jensen, March 12, 1985. Claimed by **Ottawa** from **Hartford** in Expansion Draft, June 18, 1992. Traded to **New Jersey** by **Ottawa** with future considerations (Mike Peluso, June 26, 1993) for Craig Billington, Troy Mallette and New Jersey's 4th round choice (Cosmo Dupaul) in 1993 Entry Draft, June 20, 1993.

SKUDRA, PETER PIT.

Goaltender. Catches left. 6'1", 182 lbs. Born, Riga, USSR, April 24, 1973.

			Regular Season								Playoffs						
Season	**Club**	**Lea**	**GP**	**W**	**L**	**T**	**Mins**	**GA**	**SO**	**Avg**	**GP**	**W**	**L**	**Mins**	**GA**	**SO**	**Avg**
1992-93	Pardaugava Riga	CIS	27	....	....	....	1498	74	....	2.96	1	....	....	60	5	0	5.00
1993-94	Pardaugava Riga	CIS	14	....	....	....	783	42	....	3.22	1	....	....	55	4	0	4.36
1994-95	Greensboro	ECHL	33	13	9	5	1612	113	0	4.20	6	2	2	341	28	0	4.92
	Memphis	CHL	2	0	1	0	60	8	0	6.01	....	....	....	....	....	....	....
1995-96	Erie	ECHL	12	3	8	1	681	47	0	4.14	....	....	....	....	....	....	....
	Johnstown	ECHL	30	12	11	4	1657	98	0	3.55	....	....	....	....	....	....	....
1996-97	Hamilton	AHL	32	8	16	2	1615	101	0	3.75	....	....	....	....	....	....	....
	Johnstown	ECHL	4	2	1	1	200	11	0	3.30	....	....	....	....	....	....	....
1997-98	**Pittsburgh**	**NHL**	**17**	**6**	**4**	**3**	**851**	**26**	**0**	**1.83**	....	....	....	....	....	....	....
	Houston	IHL	9	5	3	1	499	23	0	2.77	....	....	....	....	....	....	....
	Kansas City	IHL	13	10	3	0	775	37	0	2.86	8	4	4	512	20	1	*2.34
	NHL Totals		**17**	**6**	**4**	**3**	**851**	**26**	**0**	**1.83**	....	....	....	....	....	....	....

Signed as a free agent by **Pittsburgh**, September 24, 1997.

SMANGS, HENRIK (SMOHNGS) PHX.

Goaltender. Catches left. 5'11", 174 lbs. Born, Leksand, Sweden, January 19, 1976.
(Winnipeg's 9th choice, 212th overall, in 1994 Entry Draft).

			Regular Season								Playoffs						
Season	**Club**	**Lea**	**GP**	**W**	**L**	**T**	**Mins**	**GA**	**SO**	**Avg**	**GP**	**W**	**L**	**Mins**	**GA**	**SO**	**Avg**
1994-95	Leksand IF	Swe-Jr.						STATISTICS NOT AVAILABLE									
1995-96	Leksand IF	Swe-Jr.						STATISTICS NOT AVAILABLE									
1996-97	Mora	Swe-2	5	....	....	....	260	12	....	2.70	....	....	....	....	....	....	....
1997-98	Mora	Swe-2						STATISTICS NOT AVAILABLE									

Transferred to **Phoenix** after **Winnipeg** franchise relocated, July 1, 1996.

SNOW, GARTH VAN.

Goaltender. Catches left. 6'3", 200 lbs. Born, Wrentham, MA, July 28, 1969.
(Quebec's 6th choice, 114th overall, in 1987 Entry Draft).

			Regular Season								Playoffs						
Season	**Club**	**Lea**	**GP**	**W**	**L**	**T**	**Mins**	**GA**	**SO**	**Avg**	**GP**	**W**	**L**	**Mins**	**GA**	**SO**	**Avg**
1986-87	Mt. St. Charles	H.S.	30	....	....	....	1795	53	10	1.77	....	....	....	....	....	....	....
1987-88	Mt. St. Charles	H.S.						STATISTICS NOT AVAILABLE									
1988-89	U. of Maine	H.E.	5	2	2	0	241	14	1	3.49	....	....	....	....	....	....	....
1989-90								DID NOT PLAY									
1990-91	U. of Maine	H.E.	25	*18	4	0	1290	64	2	2.98	....	....	....	....	....	....	....
1991-92	U. of Maine	H.E.	31	*25	4	2	1792	73	*2	*2.44	....	....	....	....	....	....	....
1992-93	U. of Maine	H.E.	23	*21	0	1	1210	42	1	*2.08	....	....	....	....	....	....	....
1993-94	United States	Nat-Tm	23	13	5	3	1324	71	1	3.22	....	....	....	....	....	....	....
	United States	Olympics	5	....	....	....	299	17	....	3.41	....	....	....	....	....	....	....
	Quebec	**NHL**	**5**	**3**	**2**	**0**	**279**	**16**	**0**	**3.44**	....	....	....	....	....	....	....
	Cornwall	AHL	16	6	5	3	927	51	0	3.30	13	8	5	790	42	0	3.19
1994-95	Cornwall	AHL	*62	*32	20	7	*3558	162	3	2.73	8	4	3	402	14	*2	*2.09
	Quebec	**NHL**	**2**	**1**	**1**	**0**	**119**	**11**	**0**	**5.55**	**1**	**0**	**0**	**9**	**1**	**0**	**6.67**
1995-96	**Philadelphia**	**NHL**	**26**	**12**	**8**	**4**	**1437**	**69**	**0**	**2.88**	**1**	**0**	**0**	**1**	**0**	**0**	**0.00**
1996-97	**Philadelphia**	**NHL**	**35**	**14**	**8**	**8**	**1884**	**79**	**2**	**2.52**	**12**	**8**	**4**	**699**	**33**	**0**	**2.83**
1997-98	**Philadelphia**	**NHL**	**29**	**14**	**9**	**4**	**1651**	**67**	**1**	**2.43**	....	....	....	....	....	....	....
	Vancouver	**NHL**	**12**	**3**	**6**	**0**	**504**	**26**	**0**	**3.10**	....	....	....	....	....	....	....
	NHL Totals		**109**	**47**	**34**	**16**	**5874**	**268**	**3**	**2.74**	**14**	**8**	**4**	**709**	**34**	**0**	**2.88**

Hockey East Second All-Star Team (1992, 1993) • NCAA Championship All-Tournament Team (1993)

Transferred to **Colorado** after **Quebec** franchise relocated, June 21, 1995. Traded to **Philadelphia** by **Colorado** for Philadelphia's 3rd (later traded to Washington — Washington selected Shawn McNeil) and 6th (Kai Fischer) round choices in 1996 Entry Draft, July 12, 1995. Traded to **Vancouver** by **Philadelphia** for Sean Burke, March 4, 1998.

SODERSTROM, TOMMY (SAH-duhr-struhm)

Goaltender. Catches left. 5'7", 157 lbs. Born, Stockholm, Sweden, July 17, 1969.
(Philadelphia's 14th choice, 214th overall, in 1990 Entry Draft).

			Regular Season								Playoffs						
Season	**Club**	**Lea**	**GP**	**W**	**L**	**T**	**Mins**	**GA**	**SO**	**Avg**	**GP**	**W**	**L**	**Mins**	**GA**	**SO**	**Avg**
1989-90	Djurgarden	Sweden	4	....	....	....	240	14	0	3.50	....	....	....	....	....	....	....
1990-91	Djurgarden	Sweden	39	22	12	6	2340	104	3	2.67	7	....	....	423	10	2	1.42
1991-92	Djurgarden	Sweden	39	15	8	11	2340	109	4	2.79	10	....	....	635	28	0	2.65
	Sweden	Olympics	5	3	1	1	298	13	....	2.62	....	....	....	....	....	....	....
1992-93	**Philadelphia**	**NHL**	**44**	**20**	**17**	**6**	**2512**	**143**	**5**	**3.42**	....	....	....	....	....	....	....
	Hershey	AHL	7	4	1	0	373	15	0	2.41	....	....	....	....	....	....	....
1993-94	**Philadelphia**	**NHL**	**34**	**6**	**18**	**4**	**1736**	**116**	**2**	**4.01**	....	....	....	....	....	....	....
	Hershey	AHL	9	3	4	1	461	37	0	4.81	....	....	....	....	....	....	....
1994-95	**NY Islanders**	**NHL**	**26**	**8**	**12**	**3**	**1350**	**70**	**1**	**3.11**	....	....	....	....	....	....	....
1995-96	**NY Islanders**	**NHL**	**51**	**11**	**22**	**6**	**2590**	**167**	**2**	**3.87**	....	....	....	....	....	....	....
1996-97	**NY Islanders**	**NHL**	**1**	**0**	**0**	**0**	**1**	**0**	**0**	**0.00**	....	....	....	....	....	....	....
	Rochester	AHL	2	2	0	0	120	8	0	4.00	....	....	....	....	....	....	....
	Utica	IHL	26	12	11	0	1463	76	0	3.12	....	....	....	....	....	....	....
1997-98	Djurgarden	Sweden	*46	....	....	....	*2760	103	....	*2.24	*15	....	....	*936	34	....	2.18
	Sweden	Olympics						DID NOT PLAY – SPARE GOALTENDER									
	NHL Totals		**156**	**45**	**69**	**19**	**8189**	**496**	**10**	**3.63**	....	....	....	....	....	....	....

Swedish Rookie of the Year (1991) • Swedish World All-Star Team (1992)

Traded to **NY Islanders** by **Philadelphia** for Ron Hextall and NY Islanders' 6th round choice (Dmitry Tertyshny) in 1995 Entry Draft, September 22, 1994. • Played 10 seconds in game on March 31, 1997.

STAUBER, ROBB (STAW-buhr)

Goaltender. Catches left. 5'11", 180 lbs. Born, Duluth, MN, November 25, 1967.
(Los Angeles' 5th choice, 107th overall, in 1986 Entry Draft).

			Regular Season								Playoffs						
Season	**Club**	**Lea**	**GP**	**W**	**L**	**T**	**Mins**	**GA**	**SO**	**Avg**	**GP**	**W**	**L**	**Mins**	**GA**	**SO**	**Avg**
1985-86	Duluth	H.S.	27	....	....	....	1215	66	0	3.26	....	....	....	....	....	....	....
1986-87	U. of Minnesota	WCHA	20	13	5	0	1072	63	0	3.53	....	....	....	....	....	....	....
1987-88	U. of Minnesota	WCHA	44	34	10	0	2621	119	5	2.72	....	....	....	....	....	....	....
1988-89	U. of Minnesota	WCHA	34	26	8	0	2024	82	0	2.43	....	....	....	....	....	....	....
1989-90	**Los Angeles**	**NHL**	**2**	**0**	**1**	**0**	**83**	**11**	**0**	**7.95**	....	....	....	....	....	....	....
	New Haven	AHL	14	6	6	2	851	43	0	3.03	5	2	3	302	24	0	4.77
1990-91	New Haven	AHL	33	13	16	4	1882	115	1	3.67	....	....	....	....	....	....	....
	Phoenix	IHL	4	1	2	0	160	11	0	4.13	....	....	....	....	....	....	....
1991-92	Phoenix	IHL	22	8	12	1	1242	80	0	3.86	....	....	....	....	....	....	....
1992-93	**Los Angeles**	**NHL**	**31**	**15**	**8**	**4**	**1735**	**111**	**0**	**3.84**	**4**	**3**	**1**	**240**	**16**	**0**	**4.00**
1993-94	**Los Angeles**	**NHL**	**22**	**4**	**11**	**5**	**1144**	**65**	**1**	**3.41**	....	....	....	....	....	....	....
	Phoenix	IHL	3	1	1	0	121	13	0	6.42	....	....	....	....	....	....	....
1994-95	**Los Angeles**	**NHL**	**1**	**0**	**0**	**0**	**16**	**2**	**0**	**7.50**	....	....	....	....	....	....	....
	Buffalo	**NHL**	**6**	**2**	**3**	**0**	**317**	**20**	**0**	**3.79**	....	....	....	....	....	....	....
1995-96	Rochester	AHL	16	6	7	1	833	49	0	3.53	....	....	....	....	....	....	....
1996-97	Portland	AHL	30	13	13	2	1606	82	0	3.06	....	....	....	....	....	....	....
1997-98	Hartford	AHL	39	20	10	6	2221	89	2	2.40	7	3	4	419	30	0	4.29
	NHL Totals		**62**	**21**	**23**	**9**	**3295**	**209**	**1**	**3.81**	**4**	**3**	**1**	**240**	**16**	**0**	**4.00**

WCHA First All-Star Team (1988) • NCAA West First All-American Team (1988) • Won Hobey Baker Memorial Award (Top U.S. Collegiate Player) (1988) • WCHA Second All-Star Team (1989)

• Scored a goal while with Rochester (AHL), October 9, 1995.

Traded to **Buffalo** by **Los Angeles** with Alexei Zhitnik, Charlie Huddy and Los Angeles' 5th round choice (Marian Menhart) in 1995 Entry Draft for Philippe Boucher, Denis Tsygurov and Grant Fuhr, February 14, 1995. Signed as a free agent by **Washington**, August 27, 1996. Signed as a free agent by **NY Rangers**, September 2, 1997.

STORR, JAMIE (STOHR) L.A.

Goaltender. Catches left. 6'2", 198 lbs. Born, Brampton, Ont., December 28, 1975.
(Los Angeles' 1st choice, 7th overall, in 1994 Entry Draft).

			Regular Season								Playoffs						
Season	**Club**	**Lea**	**GP**	**W**	**L**	**T**	**Mins**	**GA**	**SO**	**Avg**	**GP**	**W**	**L**	**Mins**	**GA**	**SO**	**Avg**
1991-92	Owen Sound	OHL	34	11	16	1	1732	128	0	4.43	5	1	4	299	28	0	5.62
1992-93	Owen Sound	OHL	41	20	17	3	2362	180	0	4.57	8	4	4	454	35	0	4.63
1993-94	Owen Sound	OHL	35	21	11	1	2004	120	1	3.59	9	4	5	547	44	0	4.83
1994-95	Owen Sound	OHL	17	5	9	2	977	64	0	3.93	....	....	....	....	....	....	....
	Los Angeles	**NHL**	**5**	**1**	**3**	**1**	**263**	**17**	**0**	**3.88**	....	....	....	....	....	....	....
	Windsor	OHL	4	3	1	0	241	8	1	1.99	10	6	3	520	34	1	3.92
1995-96	**Los Angeles**	**NHL**	**5**	**3**	**1**	**0**	**262**	**12**	**0**	**2.75**	....	....	....	....	....	....	....
	Phoenix	IHL	48	22	20	4	2711	139	2	3.08	2	1	1	118	4	1	2.03
1996-97	**Los Angeles**	**NHL**	**5**	**2**	**1**	**1**	**265**	**11**	**0**	**2.49**	....	....	....	....	....	....	....
	Phoenix	IHL	44	16	22	4	2441	147	0	3.61	....	....	....	....	....	....	....
1997-98	**Los Angeles**	**NHL**	**17**	**9**	**5**	**1**	**920**	**34**	**2**	**2.22**	**3**	**0**	**2**	**145**	**9**	**0**	**3.72**
	Long Beach	IHL	11	7	2	1	629	31	0	2.96	....	....	....	....	....	....	....
	NHL Totals		**32**	**15**	**10**	**3**	**1710**	**74**	**2**	**2.60**	**3**	**0**	**2**	**145**	**9**	**0**	**3.72**

OHL First All-Star Team (1994) • NHL All-Rookie Team (1998)

SYMINGTON, JEREMY — NYI

Goaltender. Catches left. 6'2", 185 lbs. Born, Petrolia, Ont., August 17, 1978.
(NY Islanders' 10th choice, 196th overall, in 1997 Entry Draft).

			Regular Season								Playoffs						
Season	Club	Lea	GP	W	L	T	Mins	GA	SO	Avg	GP	W	L	Mins	GA	SO	Avg
1996-97	Petrolia	OJHL	33	....	....	....	1953	111	1	3.41	....	....	....	....	....	....	....
1997-98	St. Lawrence	ECAC	7	0	6	0	370	41	0	6.74	....	....	....	....	....	....	....

TABARACCI, RICK (tab-uh-RA-chee) — WSH.

Goaltender. Catches left. 6'1", 180 lbs. Born, Toronto, Ont., January 2, 1969.
(Pittsburgh's 2nd choice, 26th overall, in 1987 Entry Draft).

			Regular Season								Playoffs						
Season	Club	Lea	GP	W	L	T	Mins	GA	SO	Avg	GP	W	L	Mins	GA	SO	Avg
1986-87	Cornwall	OHL	*59	23	32	3	*3347	290	1	5.20	5	1	4	303	26	0	3.17
1987-88	Cornwall	OHL	58	*33	18	6	3448	200	*3	3.48	11	5	6	642	37	0	3.46
	Muskegon	IHL	....	....	....	....	....	....	....	....	1	0	0	13	1	0	4.62
1988-89	**Pittsburgh**	**NHL**	**1**	**0**	**0**	**0**	**33**	**4**	**0**	**7.27**	....	....	....	....	....	....	....
	Cornwall	OHL	50	24	20	5	2974	210	1	4.24	18	10	8	1080	65	*1	3.61
1989-90	Moncton	AHL	27	10	15	2	1580	107	2	4.06	....	....	....	....	....	....	....
	Fort Wayne	IHL	22	8	9	1	1064	73	0	4.12	3	1	2	159	19	0	7.17
1990-91	**Winnipeg**	**NHL**	**24**	**4**	**9**	**4**	**1093**	**71**	**1**	**3.90**	....	....	....	....	....	....	....
	Moncton	AHL	11	4	5	2	645	41	0	3.81	....	....	....	....	....	....	....
1991-92	**Winnipeg**	**NHL**	**18**	**6**	**7**	**3**	**966**	**52**	**0**	**3.23**	**7**	**3**	**4**	**387**	**26**	**0**	**4.03**
	Moncton	AHL	23	10	11	1	1313	80	0	3.66	....	....	....	....	....	....	....
1992-93	**Winnipeg**	**NHL**	**19**	**5**	**10**	**0**	**959**	**70**	**0**	**4.38**	....	....	....	....	....	....	....
	Moncton	AHL	5	2	1	2	290	18	0	3.72	....	....	....	....	....	....	....
	Washington	**NHL**	**6**	**3**	**2**	**0**	**343**	**10**	**2**	**1.75**	**4**	**1**	**3**	**304**	**14**	**0**	**2.76**
1993-94	**Washington**	**NHL**	**32**	**13**	**14**	**2**	**1770**	**91**	**2**	**3.08**	**2**	**0**	**2**	**111**	**6**	**0**	**3.24**
	Portland	AHL	3	3	0	0	176	8	0	2.72	....	....	....	....	....	....	....
1994-95	**Washington**	**NHL**	**8**	**1**	**3**	**2**	**394**	**16**	**0**	**2.44**	....	....	....	....	....	....	....
	Chicago	IHL	2	1	1	0	119	9	0	4.51	....	....	....	....	....	....	....
	Calgary	**NHL**	**5**	**2**	**0**	**1**	**202**	**5**	**0**	**1.49**	**1**	**0**	**0**	**19**	**0**	**0**	**0.00**
1995-96	**Calgary**	**NHL**	**43**	**19**	**16**	**3**	**2391**	**117**	**3**	**2.94**	**3**	**0**	**3**	**204**	**7**	**0**	**2.06**
1996-97	**Calgary**	**NHL**	**7**	**2**	**4**	**0**	**361**	**14**	**1**	**2.33**	....	....	....	....	....	....	....
	Tampa Bay	**NHL**	**55**	**20**	**25**	**6**	**3012**	**138**	**4**	**2.75**	....	....	....	....	....	....	....
1997-98	**Calgary**	**NHL**	**42**	**13**	**22**	**6**	**2419**	**116**	**0**	**2.88**	....	....	....	....	....	....	....
	NHL Totals		**260**	**88**	**112**	**27**	**13943**	**704**	**13**	**3.03**	**17**	**4**	**12**	**1025**	**53**	**0**	**3.10**

OHL First All-Star Team (1988) • OHL Second All-Star Team (1989)

Traded to **Winnipeg** by **Pittsburgh** with Randy Cunneyworth and Dave McLlwain for Jim Kyte, Andrew McBain and Randy Gilhen, June 17, 1989. Traded to **Washington** by **Winnipeg** for Jim Hrivnak and Washington's 2nd round choice (Alexei Budayev) in 1993 Entry Draft, March 22, 1993. Traded to **Calgary** by **Washington** for Calgary's 5th round choice (Joel Cort) in 1995 Entry Draft, April 7, 1995. Traded to **Tampa Bay** by **Calgary** for Aaron Gavey, November 19, 1996. Traded to **Calgary** by **Tampa Bay** for Calgary's 4th round choice (Eric Beaudoin) in 1998 Entry Draft, June 21, 1997. Traded to **Washington** by **Calgary** for future considerations, August 7, 1998.

TALLAS, ROBBIE (TAL-as) — BOS.

Goaltender. Catches left. 6', 163 lbs. Born, Edmonton, Alta., March 20, 1973.

			Regular Season								Playoffs						
Season	Club	Lea	GP	W	L	T	Mins	GA	SO	Avg	GP	W	L	Mins	GA	SO	Avg
1991-92	Seattle	WHL	14	4	7	0	708	52	0	4.41	....	....	....	....	....	....	....
1992-93	Seattle	WHL	58	24	23	3	3151	194	2	3.69	5	1	4	333	18	0	3.24
1993-94	Seattle	WHL	51	23	21	3	2849	188	0	3.96	9	5	4	567	40	0	4.23
1994-95	Charlotte	ECHL	36	21	9	3	2011	114	0	3.40	....	....	....	....	....	....	....
	Providence	AHL	2	1	0	0	82	4	1	2.90	....	....	....	....	....	....	....
1995-96	**Boston**	**NHL**	**1**	**1**	**0**	**0**	**60**	**3**	**0**	**3.00**	....	....	....	....	....	....	....
	Providence	AHL	37	12	16	7	2136	117	1	3.29	2	0	2	135	9	0	4.01
1996-97	**Boston**	**NHL**	**28**	**8**	**12**	**1**	**1244**	**69**	**1**	**3.33**	....	....	....	....	....	....	....
	Providence	AHL	24	9	14	1	1424	83	0	3.50	....	....	....	....	....	....	....
1997-98	**Boston**	**NHL**	**14**	**6**	**3**	**3**	**788**	**24**	**1**	**1.83**	....	....	....	....	....	....	....
	Providence	AHL	10	1	8	1	575	39	0	4.07	....	....	....	....	....	....	....
	NHL Totals		**43**	**15**	**15**	**4**	**2092**	**96**	**2**	**2.75**	....	....	....	....	....	....	....

Signed as a free agent by **Boston**, September 13, 1995.

TERRERI, CHRIS (tuh-RAIR-ee) — N.J.

Goaltender. Catches left. 5'8", 160 lbs. Born, Providence, RI, November 15, 1964.
(New Jersey's 3rd choice, 87th overall, in 1983 Entry Draft).

			Regular Season								Playoffs						
Season	Club	Lea	GP	W	L	T	Mins	GA	SO	Avg	GP	W	L	Mins	GA	SO	Avg
1982-83	Providence	ECAC	11	7	1	0	528	17	2	1.93	....	....	....	....	....	....	....
1983-84	Providence	ECAC	10	4	2	0	391	20	0	3.07	....	....	....	....	....	....	....
1984-85	Providence	H.E.	33	15	13	5	1956	116	1	3.35	....	....	....	....	....	....	....
1985-86	Providence	H.E.	22	6	16	0	1320	84	0	3.74	....	....	....	....	....	....	....
1986-87	**New Jersey**	**NHL**	**7**	**0**	**3**	**1**	**286**	**21**	**0**	**4.41**	....	....	....	....	....	....	....
	Maine	AHL	14	4	9	1	765	57	0	4.47	....	....	....	....	....	....	....
1987-88	Utica	AHL	7	5	1	0	399	18	0	2.71	....	....	....	....	....	....	....
	United States	Nat-Tm	26	17	7	2	1430	81	0	3.40	....	....	....	....	....	....	....
	United States	Olympics	3	....	....	....	127	14	....	6.58	....	....	....	....	....	....	....
1988-89	**New Jersey**	**NHL**	**8**	**0**	**4**	**2**	**402**	**18**	**0**	**2.69**	....	....	....	....	....	....	....
	Utica	AHL	39	20	15	3	2314	132	0	3.42	2	0	1	80	6	0	4.50
1989-90	**New Jersey**	**NHL**	**35**	**15**	**12**	**3**	**1931**	**110**	**0**	**3.42**	**4**	**2**	**2**	**238**	**13**	**0**	**3.28**
1990-91	**New Jersey**	**NHL**	**53**	**24**	**21**	**7**	**2970**	**144**	**1**	**2.91**	**7**	**3**	**4**	**428**	**21**	**0**	**2.94**
1991-92	**New Jersey**	**NHL**	**54**	**22**	**22**	**10**	**3186**	**169**	**1**	**3.18**	**7**	**3**	**3**	**386**	**23**	**0**	**3.58**
1992-93	**New Jersey**	**NHL**	**48**	**19**	**21**	**3**	**2672**	**151**	**2**	**3.39**	**4**	**1**	**3**	**219**	**17**	**0**	**4.66**
1993-94	**New Jersey**	**NHL**	**44**	**20**	**11**	**4**	**2340**	**106**	**2**	**2.72**	**4**	**3**	**0**	**200**	**9**	**0**	**2.70**
1994-95	**New Jersey**	**NHL**	**15**	**3**	**7**	**2**	**734**	**31**	**0**	**2.53**	**1**	**0**	**0**	**8**	**0**	**0**	**0.00** ♦
1995-96	**New Jersey**	**NHL**	**4**	**3**	**0**	**0**	**210**	**9**	**0**	**2.57**	....	....	....	....	....	....	....
	San Jose	**NHL**	**46**	**13**	**29**	**1**	**2516**	**155**	**0**	**3.70**	....	....	....	....	....	....	....
1996-97	**San Jose**	**NHL**	**22**	**6**	**10**	**3**	**1200**	**55**	**0**	**2.75**	....	....	....	....	....	....	....
	Chicago	**NHL**	**7**	**4**	**1**	**2**	**429**	**19**	**0**	**2.66**	**2**	**0**	**0**	**44**	**3**	**0**	**4.09**
1997-98	**Chicago**	**NHL**	**21**	**8**	**10**	**2**	**1222**	**49**	**2**	**2.41**	....	....	....	....	....	....	....
	Indianapolis	IHL	3	2	0	1	180	3	1	1.00	....	....	....	....	....	....	....
	NHL Totals		**364**	**137**	**151**	**40**	**20098**	**1037**	**8**	**3.10**	**29**	**12**	**12**	**1523**	**86**	**0**	**3.39**

Hockey East First All-Star Team (1985) • NCAA East First All-American Team (1985) • NCAA Championship All-Tournament Team (1985) • NCAA Championship Tournament MVP (1985)

Traded to **San Jose** by **New Jersey** for San Jose's 2nd round choice (later traded to Pittsburgh — Pittsburgh selected Pavel Skrbek) in 1996 Entry Draft, November 15, 1995. Traded to **Chicago** by **San Jose** with Ulf Dahlen and Michal Sykora for Ed Belfour, January 25, 1997. Traded to **New Jersey** by **Chicago** for a conditional choice in 1999 Entry Draft, August 25, 1998.

THEODORE, JOSE (THEE-uh-dohr, joh-SAY) — MTL.

Goaltender. Catches right. 5'8", 177 lbs. Born, Laval, Que., September 13, 1976.
(Montreal's 2nd choice, 44th overall, in 1994 Entry Draft).

			Regular Season								Playoffs						
Season	Club	Lea	GP	W	L	T	Mins	GA	SO	Avg	GP	W	L	Mins	GA	SO	Avg
1992-93	St-Jean	QMJHL	34	12	16	2	1776	112	0	3.78	3	0	2	175	11	0	3.77
1993-94	St-Jean	QMJHL	57	20	29	6	3225	194	0	3.61	5	1	4	296	18	0	3.65
1994-95	Hull	QMJHL	*58	*32	22	2	*3348	193	5	3.46	*21	*15	6	*1263	59	*1	2.80
	Fredericton	AHL	....	....	....	....	....	....	....	....	1	0	1	60	3	0	3.00
1995-96	**Montreal**	**NHL**	**1**	**0**	**0**	**0**	**9**	**1**	**0**	**6.67**	....	....	....	....	....	....	....
	Hull	QMJHL	48	33	11	2	2807	158	0	3.38	5	2	3	299	20	0	4.01
1996-97	**Montreal**	**NHL**	**16**	**5**	**6**	**2**	**821**	**53**	**0**	**3.87**	**2**	**1**	**1**	**168**	**7**	**0**	**2.50**
	Fredericton	AHL	26	12	12	0	1469	87	0	3.55	....	....	....	....	....	....	....
1997-98	Fredericton	AHL	53	20	23	8	3053	145	2	2.85	4	1	3	237	13	0	3.28
	Montreal	**NHL**	....	....	....	....	....	....	....	....	**3**	**0**	**1**	**120**	**1**	**0**	**0.50**
	NHL Totals		**17**	**5**	**6**	**2**	**830**	**54**	**0**	**3.90**	**5**	**1**	**2**	**288**	**8**	**0**	**1.67**

QMJHL Second All-Star Team (1995, 1996)

THERRIEN, PIERRE-LUC — WSH.

Goaltender. Catches left. 6', 170 lbs. Born, Terrebonne, Que., September 3, 1979.
(Washington's 6th choice, 200th overall, in 1997 Entry Draft).

			Regular Season								Playoffs						
Season	Club	Lea	GP	W	L	T	Mins	GA	SO	Avg	GP	W	L	Mins	GA	SO	Avg
1996-96	Drummondville	QMJHL	37	15	17	1	2073	117	1	3.40	6	1	5	367	39	0	6.38
1996-97	Drummondville	QMJHL	42	16	17	1	2235	147	2	3.94	5	1	0	154	16	0	6.22
1997-98	Drummondville	QMJHL	16	5	8	0	857	68	0	4.76	....	....	....	....	....	....	....
	Victoriaville	QMJHL	10	6	1	2	571	26	0	2.73	1	0	0	16	5	0	18.40

THIBAULT, JOCELYN (tee-BOW) — MTL.

Goaltender. Catches left. 5'11", 170 lbs. Born, Montreal, Que., January 12, 1975.
(Quebec's 1st choice, 10th overall, in 1993 Entry Draft).

			Regular Season								Playoffs						
Season	Club	Lea	GP	W	L	T	Mins	GA	SO	Avg	GP	W	L	Mins	GA	SO	Avg
1991-92	Trois-Rivieres	QMJHL	30	14	7	1	1496	77	0	3.09	3	1	1	110	4	0	2.19
1992-93	Sherbrooke	QMJHL	56	34	14	5	3190	159	3	2.99	15	9	6	882	57	0	3.87
1993-94	**Quebec**	**NHL**	**29**	**8**	**13**	**3**	**1504**	**83**	**0**	**3.31**	....	....	....	....	....	....	....
	Cornwall	AHL	4	4	0	0	240	9	1	2.25	....	....	....	....	....	....	....
1994-95	Sherbrooke	QMJHL	13	6	6	1	776	38	1	2.94	....	....	....	....	....	....	....
	Quebec	**NHL**	**18**	**12**	**2**	**2**	**898**	**35**	**1**	**2.34**	**3**	**1**	**2**	**148**	**8**	**0**	**3.24**
1995-96	**Colorado**	**NHL**	**10**	**3**	**4**	**2**	**558**	**28**	**0**	**3.01**	....	....	....	....	....	....	....
	Montreal	**NHL**	**40**	**23**	**13**	**3**	**2334**	**110**	**3**	**2.83**	**6**	**2**	**4**	**311**	**18**	**0**	**3.47**
1996-97	**Montreal**	**NHL**	**61**	**22**	**24**	**11**	**3397**	**164**	**1**	**2.90**	**3**	**0**	**3**	**179**	**13**	**0**	**4.36**
1997-98	**Montreal**	**NHL**	**47**	**19**	**15**	**8**	**2652**	**109**	**2**	**2.47**	**2**	**0**	**0**	**43**	**4**	**0**	**5.58**
	NHL Totals		**205**	**87**	**71**	**29**	**11343**	**529**	**7**	**2.80**	**14**	**3**	**9**	**681**	**43**	**0**	**3.79**

QMJHL First All-Star Team (1993) • Canadian Major Junior First All-Star Team (1993) • Canadian Major Junior Goaltender of the Year (1993)

Transferred to **Colorado** after **Quebec** franchise relocated, June 21, 1995. Traded to **Montreal** by **Colorado** with Andrei Kovalenko and Martin Rucinsky for Patrick Roy and Mike Keane, December 6, 1995.

THOMAS, TIM — EDM.

Goaltender. Catches left. 5'11", 180 lbs. Born, Flint, MI, April 15, 1974.
(Quebec's 11th choice, 217th overall, in 1994 Entry Draft).

			Regular Season								Playoffs						
Season	Club	Lea	GP	W	L	T	Mins	GA	SO	Avg	GP	W	L	Mins	GA	SO	Avg
1993-94	U. of Vermont	ECAC	*33	15	12	6	1864	94	0	3.03	....	....	....	....	....	....	....
1994-95	U. of Vermont	ECAC	34	18	13	2	2010	90	*4	*2.69	....	....	....	....	....	....	....
1995-96	U. of Vermont	ECAC	37	*26	7	4	*2254	88	*3	*2.34	....	....	....	....	....	....	....
1996-97	U. of Vermont	ECAC	36	22	11	3	2158	101	2	2.81	....	....	....	....	....	....	....
1997-98	Helsinki	Finland	18	13	4	1	1035	28	2	*1.62	*9	*9	0	*551	14	*3	*1.52
	Birmingham	ECHL	6	4	1	1	360	13	1	2.17	....	....	....	....	....	....	....
	Houston	IHL	1	0	1	0	59	4	0	4.01	....	....	....	....	....	....	....

ECAC First All-Star Team (1995, 1996) • NCAA East Second All-American Team (1995) • NCAA East First All-American Team (1996)

Signed as a free agent by **Edmonton**, June 4, 1998.

TORCHIA, MIKE (TOR-chee-ah)

Goaltender. Catches left. 5'11", 215 lbs. Born, Toronto, Ont., February 23, 1972.
(Minnesota's 2nd choice, 74th overall, in 1991 Entry Draft).

			Regular Season								Playoffs						
Season	Club	Lea	GP	W	L	T	Mins	GA	SO	Avg	GP	W	L	Mins	GA	SO	Avg
1988-89	Kitchener	OHL	30	14	9	4	1672	112	0	4.02	2	0	2	126	8	0	3.81
1989-90	Kitchener	OHL	40	25	11	2	2280	136	1	3.58	*17	*11	6	*1023	60	0	3.52
1990-91	Kitchener	OHL	57	25	24	7	*3317	219	0	3.96	6	2	4	382	30	0	4.71
1991-92	Kitchener	OHL	*55	25	24	3	*3042	203	1	4.00	14	7	7	900	47	0	3.13
1992-93	Canada	Nat-Tm	5	5	0	0	300	11	1	2.20	....	....	....	....	....	....	....
	Kalamazoo	IHL	48	19	17	9	2729	173	0	3.80	....	....	....	....	....	....	....
1993-94	Kalamazoo	IHL	43	23	12	2	2168	133	0	3.68	4	1	3	221	14	*1	3.80
1994-95	Kalamazoo	IHL	41	19	14	5	2140	106	*3	2.97	6	0	4	257	17	0	3.97
	Dallas	**NHL**	**6**	**3**	**2**	**1**	**327**	**18**	**0**	**3.30**	....	....	....	....	....	....	....
1995-96	Portland	AHL	12	2	6	2	577	46	0	4.79	....	....	....	....	....	....	....
	Hampton Roads	ECHL	5	2	2	0	260	17	0	3.92	....	....	....	....	....	....	....
	Michigan	IHL	1	1	0	0	60	1	0	1.00	....	....	....	....	....	....	....
	Orlando	IHL	7	3	1	1	341	17	0	2.99	....	....	....	....	....	....	....
	Baltimore	AHL	5	2	1	1	256	18	0	4.21	1	0	0	40	0	0	0.00
1996-97	Fort Wayne	IHL	57	20	31	3	2970	172	1	3.47	....	....	....	....	....	....	....
	Baltimore	AHL	....	....	....	....	....	....	....	....	1	0	0	40	4	0	6.00
1997-98	Milwaukee	IHL	34	13	14	1	1828	94	1	3.09	....	....	....	....	....	....	....
	San Antonio	IHL	2	0	2	0	118	12	0	6.07	....	....	....	....	....	....	....
	Peoria	ECHL	5	4	1	0	299	16	0	3.21	1	0	1	60	7	0	7.00
	NHL Totals		**6**	**3**	**2**	**1**	**327**	**18**	**0**	**3.30**	....	....	....	....	....	....	....

Memorial Cup All-Star Team (1990) • Won Hap Emms Memorial Trophy (Memorial Cup Tournament Top Goaltender) (1990) • OHL First All-Star Team (1991)

Transferred to **Dallas** after **Minnesota** franchise relocated, June 9, 1993. Traded to **Washington** by **Dallas** for cash, July 14, 1995. Traded to **Anaheim** by **Washington** for Todd Krygier, March 8, 1996.

TOSKALA, VESA (TAWS-kah-lah) — S.J.

Goaltender. Catches left. 5'9", 172 lbs. Born, Tampere, Finland, May 20, 1977.
(San Jose's 4th choice, 90th overall, in 1995 Entry Draft).

			Regular Season								Playoffs						
Season	Club	Lea	GP	W	L	T	Mins	GA	SO	Avg	GP	W	L	Mins	GA	SO	Avg
1994-95	Ilves	Fin-Jr.	17	....	....	....	956	36	....	2.26	....	....	....	....	....	....	....
1995-96	Ilves	Fin-Jr.	3	....	....	....	180	3	....	1.00	....	....	....	....	....	....	....
	KooVee	Finland-2	2	....	....	....	119	5	....	2.51	....	....	....	....	....	....	....
	Ilves	Finland	37	....	....	....	2073	109	1	3.16	2	....	....	78	11	....	8.49
1996-97	Ilves	Finland	40	22	12	5	2270	108	0	2.85	8	3	5	479	29	0	3.63
1997-98	Ilves	Finland	43	*26	13	3	2555	118	1	2.77	*9	6	3	519	18	1	2.08

TREFILOV, ANDREI (TREH-fee-lahf) CHI.

Goaltender. Catches left. 6', 190 lbs. Born, Kirovo-Chepetsk, USSR, August 31, 1969.
(Calgary's 14th choice, 261st overall, in 1991 Entry Draft).

			Regular Season								Playoffs						
Season	Club	Lea	GP	W	L	T	Mins	GA	SO	Avg	GP	W	L	Mins	GA	SO	Avg
1990-91	Moscow D'amo	USSR	20	....	....	....	1070	36	0	2.01	....	....	....	....	....	....	....
1991-92	Moscow D'amo	CIS	28	....	....	....	1326	35	0	1.58	....	....	....	....	....	....	....
	Russia	Olympics	4	0	0	0	39	2	0	3.08	....	....	....	....	....	....	....
1992-93	**Calgary**	**NHL**	**1**	**0**	**0**	**1**	**65**	**5**	**0**	**4.62**	....	....	....	....	....	....	....
	Salt Lake	IHL	44	23	17	3	2536	135	0	3.19	....	....	....	....	....	....	....
1993-94	**Calgary**	**NHL**	**11**	**3**	**4**	**2**	**623**	**26**	**2**	**2.50**	....	....	....	....	....	....	....
	Saint John	AHL	28	10	10	7	1629	93	0	3.42	....	....	....	....	....	....	....
1994-95	**Calgary**	**NHL**	**6**	**0**	**3**	**0**	**236**	**16**	**0**	**4.07**	....	....	....	....	....	....	....
	Saint John	AHL	7	1	5	1	383	20	0	3.13	....	....	....	....	....	....	....
1995-96	**Buffalo**	**NHL**	**22**	**8**	**8**	**1**	**1094**	**64**	**0**	**3.51**	....	....	....	....	....	....	....
	Rochester	AHL	5	4	1	0	299	13	0	2.61	....	....	....	....	....	....	....
1996-97	**Buffalo**	**NHL**	**3**	**0**	**2**	**0**	**159**	**10**	**0**	**3.77**	**1**	**0**	**0**	**5**	**0**	**0**	**0.00**
1997-98	Rochester	AHL	3	1	0	1	138	6	0	2.60	....	....	....	....	....	....	....
	Chicago	**NHL**	**6**	**1**	**4**	**0**	**299**	**17**	**0**	**3.41**	....	....	....	....	....	....	....
	Indianapolis	IHL	1	0	1	0	59	3	0	3.03	....	....	....	....	....	....	....
	Russia	Olympics	2	1	0	0	69	4	0	3.45	....	....	....	....	....	....	....
	NHL Totals		**49**	**12**	**21**	**4**	**2476**	**138**	**2**	**3.34**	**1**	**0**	**0**	**5**	**0**	**0**	**0.00**

Signed as a free agent by **Buffalo**, July 11, 1995. Traded to **Chicago** by **Buffalo** for future considerations, November 12, 1997.

TUGNUTT, RON OTT.

Goaltender. Catches left. 5'11", 155 lbs. Born, Scarborough, Ont., October 22, 1967.
(Quebec's 4th choice, 81st overall, in 1986 Entry Draft).

			Regular Season								Playoffs						
Season	Club	Lea	GP	W	L	T	Mins	GA	SO	Avg	GP	W	L	Mins	GA	SO	Avg
1984-85	Peterborough	OHL	18	7	4	2	938	59	0	3.77	....	....	....	....	....	....	....
1985-86	Peterborough	OHL	26	18	7	0	1543	74	1	2.88	3	2	0	133	6	0	2.71
1986-87	Peterborough	OHL	31	21	7	2	1891	88	2	*2.79	6	3	3	374	21	1	3.37
1987-88	**Quebec**	**NHL**	**6**	**2**	**3**	**0**	**284**	**16**	**0**	**3.38**	....	....	....	....	....	....	....
	Fredericton	AHL	34	20	9	4	1964	118	1	3.60	4	1	2	204	11	0	3.24
1988-89	**Quebec**	**NHL**	**26**	**10**	**10**	**3**	**1367**	**82**	**0**	**3.60**	....	....	....	....	....	....	....
	Halifax	AHL	24	14	7	2	1368	79	1	3.46	....	....	....	....	....	....	....
1989-90	**Quebec**	**NHL**	**35**	**5**	**24**	**3**	**1978**	**152**	**0**	**4.61**	....	....	....	....	....	....	....
	Halifax	AHL	6	1	5	0	366	23	0	3.77	....	....	....	....	....	....	....
1990-91	**Quebec**	**NHL**	**56**	**12**	**29**	**10**	**3144**	**212**	**0**	**4.05**	....	....	....	....	....	....	....
	Halifax	AHL	2	0	1	0	100	8	0	4.80	....	....	....	....	....	....	....
1991-92	**Quebec**	**NHL**	**30**	**6**	**17**	**3**	**1583**	**106**	**1**	**4.02**	....	....	....	....	....	....	....
	Halifax	AHL	8	3	3	1	447	30	0	4.03	....	....	....	....	....	....	....
	Edmonton	**NHL**	**3**	**1**	**1**	**0**	**124**	**10**	**0**	**4.84**	**2**	**0**	**0**	**60**	**3**	**0**	**3.00**
1992-93	**Edmonton**	**NHL**	**26**	**9**	**12**	**2**	**1338**	**93**	**0**	**4.17**	....	....	....	....	....	....	....
1993-94	**Anaheim**	**NHL**	**28**	**10**	**15**	**1**	**1520**	**76**	**1**	**3.00**	....	....	....	....	....	....	....
	Montreal	**NHL**	**8**	**2**	**3**	**1**	**378**	**24**	**0**	**3.81**	**1**	**0**	**1**	**59**	**5**	**0**	**5.08**
1994-95	**Montreal**	**NHL**	**7**	**1**	**3**	**1**	**346**	**18**	**0**	**3.12**	....	....	....	....	....	....	....
1995-96	Portland	AHL	58	21	23	6	3068	171	2	3.34	13	7	6	782	36	1	2.76
1996-97	**Ottawa**	**NHL**	**37**	**17**	**15**	**1**	**1991**	**93**	**3**	**2.80**	**7**	**3**	**4**	**425**	**14**	**1**	**1.98**
1997-98	**Ottawa**	**NHL**	**42**	**15**	**14**	**8**	**2236**	**84**	**3**	**2.25**	**2**	**0**	**1**	**74**	**6**	**0**	**4.86**
	NHL Totals		**304**	**90**	**146**	**33**	**16289**	**966**	**8**	**3.56**	**12**	**3**	**6**	**618**	**28**	**1**	**2.72**

OHL First All-Star Team (1987)

Traded to **Edmonton** by **Quebec** with Brad Zavisha for Martin Rucinsky, March 10, 1992. Claimed by **Anaheim** from **Edmonton** in Expansion Draft, June 24, 1993. Traded to **Montreal** by **Anaheim** for Stephan Lebeau, February 20, 1994. Signed as a free agent by **Washington**, September 25, 1995. Signed as a free agent by **Ottawa**, August 14, 1996.

TURCO, MARTY DAL.

Goaltender. Catches left. 5'11", 175 lbs. Born, Sault Ste. Marie, Ont., August 13, 1975.
(Dallas' 4th choice, 124th overall, in 1994 Entry Draft).

			Regular Season								Playoffs						
Season	Club	Lea	GP	W	L	T	Mins	GA	SO	Avg	GP	W	L	Mins	GA	SO	Avg
1993-94	Cambridge	OJHL	34	....	....	....	1973	114	0	3.47	....	....	....	....	....	....	....
1994-95	U. of Michigan	CCHA	37	*27	7	1	2063	95	1	2.76	....	....	....	....	....	....	....
1995-96	U. of Michigan	CCHA	*42	*34	7	1	*2335	84	*5	*2.16	....	....	....	....	....	....	....
1996-97	U. of Michigan	CCHA	*41	*33	4	4	*2296	87	*4	*2.27	....	....	....	....	....	....	....
1997-98	U. of Michigan	CCHA	*45	*33	10	1	*2640	95	4	2.16	....	....	....	....	....	....	....

CCHA First All-Star Team (1997) • NCAA West First All-American Team (1997) • CCHA Second All-Star Team (1998) • NCAA Championship All-Tournament Team (1998) • NCAA Championship Tournament MVP (1988)

TUREK, ROMAN (TOOR-ehk) DAL.

Goaltender. Catches right. 6'3", 190 lbs. Born, Pisek, Czech., May 21, 1970.
(Minnesota's 6th choice, 113th overall, in 1990 Entry Draft).

			Regular Season								Playoffs						
Season	Club	Lea	GP	W	L	T	Mins	GA	SO	Avg	GP	W	L	Mins	GA	SO	Avg
1990-91	Budejovice	Czech.	26	....	....	....	1244	98	0	4.70	....	....	....	....	....	....	....
1991-92	Budejovice	Czech-2	STATISTICS NOT AVAILABLE														
1992-93	Budejovice	Czech.	43	....	....	....	2555	121	....	2.84	....	....	....	....	....	....	....
1993-94	Budejovice	Cze-Rep.	44	....	....	....	2584	111	....	2.51	3	....	....	180	12	0	4.00
	Czech Republic	Olympics	2	....	....	....	120	3	....	1.50	....	....	....	....	....	....	....
1994-95	Budejovice	Cze-Rep.	44	....	....	....	2587	119	....	2.76	9	....	....	498	25	....	3.01
1995-96	Nurnberg	Germany	48	....	....	....	2787	154	....	3.31	5	....	....	338	14	....	2.48
1996-97	**Dallas**	**NHL**	**6**	**3**	**1**	**0**	**263**	**9**	**0**	**2.05**	....	....	....	....	....	....	....
	Michigan	IHL	29	8	13	4	1555	77	0	2.97	....	....	....	....	....	....	....
1997-98	**Dallas**	**NHL**	**23**	**11**	**10**	**1**	**1324**	**49**	**1**	**2.22**	....	....	....	....	....	....	....
	Michigan	IHL	2	1	1	0	119	5	0	2.51	....	....	....	....	....	....	....
	NHL Totals		**29**	**14**	**11**	**1**	**1587**	**58**	**1**	**2.19**	....	....	....	....	....	....	....

Czech Republic Player of the Year (1994)

Transferred to **Dallas** after **Minnesota** franchise relocated, June 9, 1993.

VAILLANCOURT, LUC (VIGH-an-koor) ANA.

Goaltender. Catches left. 6'1", 190 lbs. Born, Ferme-Neuve, Que., June 13, 1978.
(Anaheim's 4th choice, 125th overall, in 1997 Entry Draft).

			Regular Season								Playoffs						
Season	Club	Lea	GP	W	L	T	Mins	GA	SO	Avg	GP	W	L	Mins	GA	SO	Avg
1995-96	Beauport	QMJHL	22	7	8	0	882	71	0	4.83	2	1	0	80	3	0	2.25
1996-97	Beauport	QMJHL	51	18	27	1	2684	163	0	3.64	4	1	3	240	20	0	5.00
1997-98	Quebec	QMJHL	22	11	8	1	1196	73	0	3.66	....	....	....	....	....	....	....
	Rouyn-Noranda	QMJHL	30	19	10	1	1762	93	0	3.17	6	2	4	362	26	0	4.31

VALIQUETTE, STEPHEN (val-ih-KEHT) NYI

Goaltender. Catches left. 6'5", 205 lbs. Born, Etobicoke, Ont., August 20, 1977.
(Los Angeles' 8th choice, 190th overall, in 1996 Entry Draft).

			Regular Season								Playoffs						
Season	Club	Lea	GP	W	L	T	Mins	GA	SO	Avg	GP	W	L	Mins	GA	SO	Avg
1994-95	Sudbury	OHL	4	2	0	0	138	6	0	2.61	....	....	....	....	....	....	....
1995-96	Sudbury	OHL	39	13	16	2	1887	123	0	3.91	....	....	....	....	....	....	....
1996-97	Sudbury	OHL	61	21	29	7	3311	232	1	4.20	....	....	....	....	....	....	....
	Dayton	ECHL	3	1	0	0	89	6	0	4.03	2	1	1	118	5	0	2.54
1997-98	Sudbury	OHL	14	5	7	1	807	50	0	3.72	....	....	....	....	....	....	....
	Erie	OHL	28	16	7	3	1525	65	3	2.56	7	3	4	467	15	1	1.93

VALLEY, MIKE VAN.

Goaltender. Catches left. 6', 190 lbs. Born, Delta, B.C., September 3, 1976.

			Regular Season								Playoffs						
Season	Club	Lea	GP	W	L	T	Mins	GA	SO	Avg	GP	W	L	Mins	GA	SO	Avg
1997-98	U. of Wisconsin	WCHA	21	11	9	1	1202	88	0	3.09	....	....	....	....	....	....	....

Signed as a free agent by **Vancouver**, June 9, 1998.

VANBIESBROUCK, JOHN (van-BEES-bruhk) PHI.

Goaltender. Catches left. 5'8", 176 lbs. Born, Detroit, MI, September 4, 1963.
(NY Rangers' 5th choice, 72nd overall, in 1981 Entry Draft).

			Regular Season								Playoffs						
Season	Club	Lea	GP	W	L	T	Mins	GA	SO	Avg	GP	W	L	Mins	GA	SO	Avg
1980-81	S.S. Marie	OHA	56	31	16	1	2941	203	0	4.14	11	3	3	457	24	1	3.15
1981-82	**NY Rangers**	**NHL**	**1**	**1**	**0**	**0**	**60**	**1**	**0**	**1.00**	....	....	....	....	....	....	....
	S.S. Marie	OHL	31	12	12	2	1686	102	0	3.62	7	1	4	276	20	0	4.35
1982-83	S.S. Marie	OHL	*62	39	21	1	3471	209	0	3.61	16	7	6	944	56	*1	3.56
1983-84	**NY Rangers**	**NHL**	**3**	**2**	**1**	**0**	**180**	**10**	**0**	**3.33**	**1**	**0**	**0**	**1**	**0**	**0**	**0.00**
	Tulsa	CHL	37	20	13	2	2153	124	*3	3.46	4	4	0	240	10	0	*2.50
1984-85	**NY Rangers**	**NHL**	**42**	**12**	**24**	**3**	**2358**	**166**	**1**	**4.22**	**1**	**0**	**0**	**20**	**0**	**0**	**0.00**
1985-86	**NY Rangers**	**NHL**	**61**	***31**	**21**	**5**	**3326**	**184**	**3**	**3.32**	**16**	**8**	**8**	**899**	**49**	***1**	**3.27**
1986-87	**NY Rangers**	**NHL**	**50**	**18**	**20**	**5**	**2656**	**161**	**0**	**3.64**	**4**	**1**	**3**	**195**	**11**	**1**	**3.38**
1987-88	**NY Rangers**	**NHL**	**56**	**27**	**22**	**7**	**3319**	**187**	**2**	**3.38**	....	....	....	....	....	....	....
1988-89	**NY Rangers**	**NHL**	**56**	**28**	**21**	**4**	**3207**	**197**	**0**	**3.69**	**2**	**0**	**1**	**107**	**6**	**0**	**3.36**
1989-90	**NY Rangers**	**NHL**	**47**	**19**	**19**	**7**	**2734**	**154**	**1**	**3.38**	**6**	**2**	**3**	**298**	**15**	**0**	**3.02**
1990-91	**NY Rangers**	**NHL**	**40**	**15**	**18**	**6**	**2257**	**126**	**3**	**3.35**	**1**	**0**	**0**	**52**	**1**	**0**	**1.15**
1991-92	**NY Rangers**	**NHL**	**45**	**27**	**13**	**3**	**2526**	**120**	**2**	**2.85**	**7**	**2**	**5**	**368**	**23**	**0**	**3.75**
1992-93	**NY Rangers**	**NHL**	**48**	**20**	**18**	**7**	**2757**	**152**	**4**	**3.31**	....	....	....	....	....	....	....
1993-94	**Florida**	**NHL**	**57**	**21**	**25**	**11**	**3440**	**145**	**1**	**2.53**	....	....	....	....	....	....	....
1994-95	**Florida**	**NHL**	**37**	**14**	**15**	**4**	**2087**	**86**	**4**	**2.47**	....	....	....	....	....	....	....
1995-96	**Florida**	**NHL**	**57**	**26**	**20**	**7**	**3178**	**142**	**2**	**2.68**	***22**	**12**	**10**	**1332**	**50**	**1**	**2.25**
1996-97	**Florida**	**NHL**	**57**	**27**	**19**	**10**	**3347**	**128**	**2**	**2.29**	**5**	**1**	**4**	**328**	**13**	**1**	**2.38**
1997-98	**Florida**	**NHL**	**60**	**18**	**29**	**11**	**3451**	**165**	**4**	**2.87**	....	....	....	....	....	....	....
	United States	Olympics	1	0	0	0	1	0	0	0.00	....	....	....	....	....	....	....
	NHL Totals		**717**	**306**	**285**	**90**	**40883**	**2124**	**29**	**3.12**	**65**	**26**	**34**	**3600**	**168**	**4**	**2.80**

OHL Second All-Star Team (1983) • CHL First All-Star Team (1984) • Shared Terry Sawchuk Trophy (fewest goals against - CHL) with Ron Scott (1984) • Shared Tommy Ivan Trophy (CHL's MVP) with Bruce Affleck (1984) • NHL First All-Star Team (1986) • Won Vezina Trophy (1986) • NHL Second All-Star Team (1994)

Played in NHL All-Star Game (1994, 1996, 1997)

Traded to **Vancouver** by **NY Rangers** for future considerations (Doug Lidster, June 25, 1993), June 20, 1993. Claimed by **Florida** from **Vancouver** in Expansion Draft, June 24, 1993. Signed as a free agent by **Philadelphia**, July 16, 1998.

VERNON, MIKE S.J.

Goaltender. Catches left. 5'9", 170 lbs. Born, Calgary, Alta., February 24, 1963.
(Calgary's 2nd choice, 56th overall, in 1981 Entry Draft).

			Regular Season								Playoffs						
Season	Club	Lea	GP	W	L	T	Mins	GA	SO	Avg	GP	W	L	Mins	GA	SO	Avg
1980-81	Calgary	WHL	59	33	17	1	3154	198	1	3.77	22	14	8	1271	82	1	3.87
1981-82	Calgary	WHL	42	22	14	2	2329	143	3	3.68	9	5	4	527	30	0	3.42
	Oklahoma City	CHL	....	....	....	....	....	....	....	....	1	0	1	70	4	0	3.43
1982-83	**Calgary**	**NHL**	**2**	**0**	**2**	**0**	**100**	**11**	**0**	**6.59**	....	....	....	....	....	....	....
	Calgary	WHL	50	29	18	2	2856	155	*3	*3.26	16	9	7	925	60	0	3.89
1983-84	**Calgary**	**NHL**	**1**	**0**	**1**	**0**	**11**	**4**	**0**	**22.22**	....	....	....	....	....	....	....
	Colorado	CHL	46	30	13	2	2648	148	1	*3.35	6	2	4	347	21	0	3.63
1984-85	Moncton	AHL	41	10	20	4	2050	134	0	3.92	....	....	....	....	....	....	....
1985-86	**Calgary**	**NHL**	**18**	**9**	**3**	**3**	**921**	**52**	**1**	**3.39**	***21**	**12**	***9**	***1229**	**60**	**0**	**2.93**
	Moncton	AHL	6	3	1	2	374	21	0	3.37	....	....	....	....	....	....	....
	Salt Lake	IHL	10	6	4	0	600	34	1	3.40	....	....	....	....	....	....	....
1986-87	**Calgary**	**NHL**	**54**	**30**	**21**	**1**	**2957**	**178**	**1**	**3.61**	**5**	**2**	**3**	**263**	**16**	**0**	**3.65**
1987-88	**Calgary**	**NHL**	**64**	**39**	**16**	**7**	**3565**	**210**	**1**	**3.53**	**9**	**4**	**4**	**515**	**34**	**0**	**3.96**
1988-89	**Calgary**	**NHL**	**52**	***37**	**6**	**5**	**2938**	**130**	**0**	**2.65**	***22**	***16**	**5**	***1381**	**52**	***3**	**2.26** ♦
1989-90	**Calgary**	**NHL**	**47**	**23**	**14**	**9**	**2795**	**146**	**0**	**3.13**	**6**	**2**	**3**	**342**	**19**	**0**	**3.33**
1990-91	**Calgary**	**NHL**	**54**	**31**	**19**	**3**	**3121**	**172**	**1**	**3.31**	**7**	**3**	**4**	**427**	**21**	**0**	**2.95**
1991-92	**Calgary**	**NHL**	**63**	**24**	**30**	**9**	**3640**	**217**	**0**	**3.58**	....	....	....	....	....	....	....
1992-93	**Calgary**	**NHL**	**64**	**29**	**26**	**9**	**3732**	**203**	**2**	**3.26**	**4**	**1**	**1**	**150**	**15**	**0**	**6.00**
1993-94	**Calgary**	**NHL**	**48**	**26**	**17**	**5**	**2798**	**131**	**3**	**2.81**	**7**	**3**	**4**	**466**	**23**	**0**	**2.96**
1994-95	**Detroit**	**NHL**	**30**	**19**	**6**	**4**	**1807**	**76**	**1**	**2.52**	**18**	**12**	**6**	**1063**	**41**	**1**	**2.31**
1995-96	**Detroit**	**NHL**	**32**	**21**	**7**	**2**	**1855**	**70**	**3**	**2.26**	**4**	**2**	**2**	**243**	**11**	**0**	**2.72**
1996-97	**Detroit**	**NHL**	**33**	**13**	**11**	**8**	**1952**	**79**	**0**	**2.43**	***20**	***16**	**4**	***1229**	**36**	**1**	**1.76** ♦
1997-98	**San Jose**	**NHL**	**62**	**30**	**22**	**8**	**3564**	**146**	**5**	**2.46**	**6**	**2**	**4**	**348**	**14**	**1**	**2.41**
	NHL Totals		**624**	**331**	**201**	**73**	**35756**	**1825**	**18**	**3.06**	**129**	**75**	**49**	**7656**	**342**	**6**	**2.68**

WHL First All-Star Team (1982, 1983) • Won Hap Emms Memorial Trophy (Memorial Cup Tournament Top Goaltender) (1983) • CHL Second All-Star Team (1984) • NHL Second All-Star Team (1989) • Shared William M. Jennings Trophy with Chris Osgood (1996) • Won Conn Smythe Trophy (1997)

Played in NHL All-Star Game (1988, 1989, 1990, 1991, 1993)

Traded to **Detroit** by **Calgary** for Steve Chiasson, June 29, 1994. Traded to **San Jose** by **Detroit** with Detroit's 5th round choice in 1999 Entry Draft for San Jose's 2nd round choice (later traded to St. Louis - St. Louis selected Maxim Linnik) in 1998 Entry Draft and San Jose's 2nd round choice in 1999 Entry Draft, August 18, 1997.

VOKOUN, TOMAS (voh-KOHN) NSH.

Goaltender. Catches right. 5'11", 208 lbs. Born, Karlovy Vary, Czech., July 2, 1976.
(Montreal's 11th choice, 226th overall, in 1994 Entry Draft).

			Regular Season								Playoffs						
Season	Club	Lea	GP	W	L	T	Mins	GA	SO	Avg	GP	W	L	Mins	GA	SO	Avg
1993-94	Poldi Kladno	Cze-Rep.	1	0	0	0	20	2	0	6.01	....	....	....	....	....	....	....
1994-95	Poldi Kladno	Cze-Rep.	26	....	....	....	1368	70	....	3.07	5	....	....	240	19	....	4.75
1995-96	Wheeling	ECHL	35	20	10	2	1912	117	0	3.67	7	4	3	436	19	0	2.61
	Fredericton	AHL	....	....	....	....	....	....	....	....	1	0	1	59	4	0	4.09
1996-97	**Montreal**	**NHL**	**1**	**0**	**0**	**0**	**20**	**4**	**0**	**12.00**	....	....	....	....	....	....	....
	Fredericton	AHL	47	12	26	7	2645	154	2	3.49	....	....	....	....	....	....	....
1997-98	Fredericton	AHL	31	13	13	2	1735	90	0	3.11	....	....	....	....	....	....	....
	NHL Totals		**1**	**0**	**0**	**0**	**20**	**4**	**0**	**12.00**	....	....	....	....	....	....	....

Claimed by **Nashville** from **Montreal** in Expansion Draft, June 26, 1998.

VOLKOV, ALEXEY (VOHL-kawf) L.A.

Goaltender. Catches left. 6'1", 185 lbs. Born, Sverdlovsk, USSR, March 15, 1980.
(Los Angeles' 3rd choice, 76th overall, in 1998 Entry Draft).

			Regular Season								Playoffs						
Season	Club	Lea	GP	W	L	T	Mins	GA	SO	Avg	GP	W	L	Mins	GA	SO	Avg
1995-96	SKA Yekaterinburg	Russia-2	42	....	....	....	....	78	....	....	....	....	....	....	....	....	....
1996-97	SKA Yekaterinburg	Russia-3	34	....	....	....	....	66	....	....	....	....	....	....	....	....	....
	Soviet Wings	Rus-Jr.	8	....	....	....	....	9	....	....	....	....	....	....	....	....	....
1997-98	Soviet Wings	Russia-3	27	....	....	....	....	72	....	....	....	....	....	....	....	....	....

WAGNER, STEPHEN ST.L.

Goaltender. Catches left. 6'2", 200 lbs. Born, Red Deer, Alta., January 17, 1977.
(St. Louis' 5th choice, 159th overall, in 1996 Entry Draft).

			Regular Season								Playoffs						
Season	Club	Lea	GP	W	L	T	Mins	GA	SO	Avg	GP	W	L	Mins	GA	SO	Avg
1995-96	Olds Grizzlys	AJHL	47	....	....	....	2787	139	2	2.99	....	....	....	....	....	....	....
1996-97	U. of Denver	WCHA	22	13	6	0	1202	57	1	2.85	....	....	....	....	....	....	....
1997-98	U. of Denver	WCHA	29	9	17	1	1615	113	0	4.20	....	....	....	....	....	....	....

WAITE, JIMMY (WAYT) PHX.

Goaltender. Catches left. 6'1", 180 lbs. Born, Sherbrooke, Que., April 15, 1969.
(Chicago's 1st choice, 8th overall, in 1987 Entry Draft).

			Regular Season								Playoffs						
Season	Club	Lea	GP	W	L	T	Mins	GA	SO	Avg	GP	W	L	Mins	GA	SO	Avg
1986-87	Chicoutimi	QMJHL	50	23	17	3	2569	209	2	4.48	11	4	6	576	54	1	5.63
1987-88	Chicoutimi	QMJHL	36	17	16	1	2000	150	0	4.50	4	1	2	222	17	0	4.59
1988-89	**Chicago**	**NHL**	**11**	**0**	**7**	**1**	**494**	**43**	**0**	**5.22**	....	....	....	....	....	....	....
	Saginaw	IHL	5	3	1	0	304	10	0	1.97	....	....	....	....	....	....	....
1989-90	**Chicago**	**NHL**	**4**	**2**	**0**	**0**	**183**	**14**	**0**	**4.59**	....	....	....	....	....	....	....
	Indianapolis	IHL	54	*34	14	5	*3207	135	*5	*2.53	*10	*9	1	*602	19	*1	*1.89
1990-91	**Chicago**	**NHL**	**1**	**1**	**0**	**0**	**60**	**2**	**0**	**2.00**	....	....	....	....	....	....	....
	Indianapolis	IHL	49	*26	18	4	2888	167	3	3.47	6	2	4	369	20	0	3.25
1991-92	**Chicago**	**NHL**	**17**	**4**	**7**	**4**	**877**	**54**	**0**	**3.69**	....	....	....	....	....	....	....
	Indianapolis	IHL	13	4	7	1	702	53	0	4.53	....	....	....	....	....	....	....
	Hershey	AHL	11	6	4	1	631	44	0	4.18	6	2	4	360	19	0	3.17
1992-93	**Chicago**	**NHL**	**20**	**6**	**7**	**1**	**996**	**49**	**2**	**2.95**	....	....	....	....	....	....	....
1993-94	**San Jose**	**NHL**	**15**	**3**	**7**	**0**	**697**	**50**	**0**	**4.30**	**2**	**0**	**0**	**40**	**3**	**0**	**4.50**
1994-95	**Chicago**	**NHL**	**2**	**1**	**1**	**0**	**119**	**5**	**0**	**2.52**	....	....	....	....	....	....	....
	Indianapolis	IHL	4	2	1	1	239	13	0	3.25	....	....	....	....	....	....	....
1995-96	**Chicago**	**NHL**	**1**	**0**	**0**	**0**	**31**	**0**	**0**	**0.00**	....	....	....	....	....	....	....
	Indianapolis	IHL	56	28	18	6	3157	179	0	3.40	5	2	3	298	15	1	3.02
1996-97	**Chicago**	**NHL**	**2**	**0**	**1**	**1**	**105**	**7**	**0**	**4.00**	....	....	....	....	....	....	....
	Indianapolis	IHL	41	22	15	4	2450	112	4	2.74	4	1	3	222	13	0	3.51
1997-98	**Phoenix**	**NHL**	**17**	**5**	**6**	**1**	**793**	**28**	**1**	**2.12**	**4**	**0**	**3**	**171**	**11**	**0**	**3.86**
	NHL Totals		**90**	**22**	**36**	**8**	**4355**	**252**	**3**	**3.47**	**6**	**0**	**3**	**211**	**14**	**0**	**3.98**

QMJHL Second All-Star Team (1987) • IHL First All-Star Team (1990) • Won James Norris Memorial Trophy (fewest goals against - IHL) (1990)

Traded to **San Jose** by **Chicago** for future considerations (Neil Wilkinson, July 9, 1993), June 19, 1993. Traded to **Chicago** by **San Jose** for Chicago's 4th round choice (later traded to NY Rangers — NY Rangers selected Tomi Kallarsson) in 1997 Entry Draft, February 5, 1995. Claimed by **Phoenix** from **Chicago** in NHL Waiver Draft, September 28, 1997.

WAKALUK, DARCY (WAHK-uh-luhk)

Goaltender. Catches left. 5'11", 180 lbs. Born, Pincher Creek, Alta., March 14, 1966.
(Buffalo's 7th choice, 144th overall, in 1984 Entry Draft).

			Regular Season								Playoffs						
Season	Club	Lea	GP	W	L	T	Mins	GA	SO	Avg	GP	W	L	Mins	GA	SO	Avg
1983-84	Kelowna	WHL	31	2	22	0	1555	163	0	6.29	....	....	....	....	....	....	....
1984-85	Kelowna	WHL	54	19	30	4	3094	244	0	4.73	5	1	4	282	22	0	4.68
1985-86	Spokane	WHL	47	21	22	1	2562	224	1	5.25	7	3	4	419	37	0	5.30
1986-87	Rochester	AHL	11	2	2	0	545	26	0	2.86	5	2	0	141	11	0	4.68
1987-88	Rochester	AHL	55	27	16	3	2763	159	0	3.45	6	3	3	328	22	0	4.02
1988-89	**Buffalo**	**NHL**	**6**	**1**	**3**	**0**	**214**	**15**	**0**	**4.21**	....	....	....	....	....	....	....
	Rochester	AHL	33	11	14	0	1566	97	1	3.72	....	....	....	....	....	....	....
1989-90	Rochester	AHL	56	31	16	4	3095	173	2	3.35	*17	*10	6	*1001	50	0	*3.01
1990-91	**Buffalo**	**NHL**	**16**	**4**	**5**	**3**	**630**	**35**	**0**	**3.33**	**2**	**0**	**1**	**37**	**2**	**0**	**3.24**
	Rochester	AHL	26	10	10	3	1363	68	4	*2.99	9	6	3	544	30	0	3.31
1991-92	**Minnesota**	**NHL**	**36**	**13**	**19**	**1**	**1905**	**104**	**1**	**3.28**	....	....	....	....	....	....	....
	Kalamazoo	IHL	1	1	0	0	60	7	0	7.00	....	....	....	....	....	....	....
1992-93	**Minnesota**	**NHL**	**29**	**10**	**12**	**5**	**1596**	**97**	**1**	**3.65**	....	....	....	....	....	....	....
1993-94	**Dallas**	**NHL**	**36**	**18**	**9**	**6**	**2000**	**88**	**3**	**2.64**	**5**	**4**	**1**	**307**	**15**	**0**	**2.93**
1994-95	**Dallas**	**NHL**	**15**	**4**	**8**	**0**	**754**	**40**	**2**	**3.18**	**1**	**0**	**0**	**20**	**1**	**0**	**3.00**
1995-96	**Dallas**	**NHL**	**37**	**9**	**16**	**5**	**1875**	**106**	**1**	**3.39**	....	....	....	....	....	....	....
1996-97	**Phoenix**	**NHL**	**16**	**8**	**3**	**1**	**782**	**39**	**1**	**2.99**	....	....	....	....	....	....	....
1997-98			DID NOT PLAY – INJURED														
	NHL Totals		**191**	**67**	**75**	**21**	**9756**	**524**	**9**	**3.22**	**8**	**4**	**2**	**364**	**18**	**0**	**2.97**

Shared Harry "Hap" Holmes Memorial Trophy (fewest goals against - AHL) with David Littman (1991)

• Scored a goal while with Rochester (AHL), December 6, 1987.

Traded to **Minnesota** by **Buffalo** for Minnesota's 8th round choice (Jiri Kuntos) in 1991 Entry Draft and Minnesota's 5th round choice (later traded to Toronto — Toronto selected Chris Deruiter) in 1992 Entry Draft, May 26, 1991. Transferred to **Dallas** after **Minnesota** franchise relocated, June 9, 1993. Signed as a free agent by **Phoenix**, July 23, 1996. • Missed entire 1997-98 season recovering from right knee surgery, April, 1997.

WEEKES, KEVIN FLA.

Goaltender. Catches left. 6', 195 lbs. Born, Toronto, Ont., April 4, 1975.
(Florida's 2nd choice, 41st overall, in 1993 Entry Draft).

			Regular Season								Playoffs						
Season	Club	Lea	GP	W	L	T	Mins	GA	SO	Avg	GP	W	L	Mins	GA	SO	Avg
1991-92	Toronto	Jr. B	35	....	....	....	1575	68	4	1.94	....	....	....	....	....	....	....
	St. Michael's	Jr. B	2	....	....	....	127	11	0	5.20	....	....	....	....	....	....	....
1992-93	Owen Sound	OHL	29	9	12	5	1645	143	0	5.22	1	0	0	26	5	0	11.50
1993-94	Owen Sound	OHL	34	13	19	1	1974	158	0	4.80	....	....	....	....	....	....	....
1994-95	Ottawa	OHL	41	13	23	4	2266	153	1	4.05	....	....	....	....	....	....	....
1995-96	Carolina	AHL	60	24	25	8	3404	229	2	4.04	....	....	....	....	....	....	....
1996-97	Carolina	AHL	51	17	28	4	2899	172	1	3.56	....	....	....	....	....	....	....
1997-98	**Florida**	**NHL**	**11**	**0**	**5**	**1**	**485**	**32**	**0**	**3.96**	....	....	....	....	....	....	....
	Fort Wayne	IHL	12	9	2	1	719	34	1	2.84	....	....	....	....	....	....	....
	NHL Totals		**11**	**0**	**5**	**1**	**485**	**32**	**0**	**3.96**	....	....	....	....	....	....	....

WENINGER, DAVE WSH.

Goaltender. Catches left. 6'1", 160 lbs. Born, Calgary, Alta., February 8, 1976.
(Washington's 5th choice, 74th overall, in 1996 Entry Draft).

			Regular Season								Playoffs						
Season	Club	Lea	GP	W	L	T	Mins	GA	SO	Avg	GP	W	L	Mins	GA	SO	Avg
1995-96	Michigan Tech	WCHA	25	11	7	2	1300	70	0	3.23	....	....	....	....	....	....	....
1996-97	Michigan Tech	WCHA	18	1	13	0	855	59	1	4.14	....	....	....	....	....	....	....
1997-98	Michigan Tech	WCHA	34	14	16	2	1911	119	1	3.74	....	....	....	....	....	....	....

WHITMORE, KAY NYR

Goaltender. Catches left. 5'11", 175 lbs. Born, Sudbury, Ont., April 10, 1967.
(Hartford's 2nd choice, 26th overall, in 1985 Entry Draft).

			Regular Season								Playoffs						
Season	Club	Lea	GP	W	L	T	Mins	GA	SO	Avg	GP	W	L	Mins	GA	SO	Avg
1983-84	Peterborough	OHL	29	17	8	0	1471	110	0	4.49	....	....	....	....	....	....	....
1984-85	Peterborough	OHL	*53	*35	16	2	*3077	172	*2	3.35	17	10	4	1020	58	0	3.41
1985-86	Peterborough	OHL	41	27	12	2	2467	114	*3	*2.77	14	8	5	837	40	0	2.87
1986-87	Peterborough	OHL	36	14	17	5	2159	118	1	3.28	7	3	3	366	17	1	2.79
1987-88	Binghamton	AHL	38	17	15	4	2137	121	*3	3.40	2	0	2	118	10	0	5.08
1988-89	**Hartford**	**NHL**	**3**	**2**	**1**	**0**	**180**	**10**	**0**	**3.33**	**2**	**0**	**2**	**135**	**10**	**0**	**4.44**
	Binghamton	AHL	*56	21	29	4	*3200	241	1	4.52	....	....	....	....	....	....	....
1989-90	**Hartford**	**NHL**	**9**	**4**	**2**	**1**	**442**	**26**	**0**	**3.53**	....	....	....	....	....	....	....
	Binghamton	AHL	24	3	19	2	1386	109	0	4.72	....	....	....	....	....	....	....
1990-91	**Hartford**	**NHL**	**18**	**3**	**9**	**3**	**850**	**52**	**0**	**3.67**	....	....	....	....	....	....	....
	Springfield	AHL	33	22	9	1	1916	98	1	3.07	*15	*11	4	*926	37	0	*2.40
1991-92	**Hartford**	**NHL**	**45**	**14**	**21**	**6**	**2567**	**155**	**3**	**3.62**	**1**	**0**	**0**	**19**	**1**	**0**	**3.16**
1992-93	**Vancouver**	**NHL**	**31**	**18**	**8**	**4**	**1817**	**94**	**1**	**3.10**	....	....	....	....	....	....	....
1993-94	**Vancouver**	**NHL**	**32**	**18**	**14**	**0**	**1921**	**113**	**0**	**3.53**	....	....	....	....	....	....	....
1994-95	**Vancouver**	**NHL**	**11**	**0**	**6**	**2**	**558**	**37**	**0**	**3.98**	**1**	**0**	**0**	**20**	**2**	**0**	**6.00**
1995-96	Detroit	IHL	10	3	5	0	501	33	0	3.95	....	....	....	....	....	....	....
	Los Angeles	IHL	30	10	9	7	1563	99	1	3.80	....	....	....	....	....	....	....
	Syracuse	AHL	11	6	4	1	663	37	0	3.35	....	....	....	....	....	....	....
	Binghamton	AHL	....	....	....	....	....	....	....	....	2	0	2	127	9	0	4.27
1996-97	Sodertalje	Sweden	25	....	....	....	1320	85	0	3.86	....	....	....	....	....	....	....
1997-98	Long Beach	IHL	46	28	12	3	2516	109	3	2.60	14	9	5	838	43	0	3.08
	NHL Totals		**149**	**59**	**61**	**16**	**8335**	**487**	**4**	**3.51**	**4**	**0**	**2**	**174**	**13**	**0**	**4.48**

OHL First All-Star Team (1986) • Won Jack A. Butterfield Trophy (Playoff MVP - AHL) (1991) • Shared James Norris Memorial Trophy (fewest goals against - IHL) with Mike Buzak (1998)

Traded to **Vancouver** by **Hartford** for Corrie D'Alessio and future considerations, October 1, 1992. Traded to **NY Rangers** by **Vancouver** for Joe Kocur, March 20, 1996. Signed as a free agent by **San Jose**, September 10, 1997. Traded to **Buffalo** by **San Jose** with Colorado's 2nd round choice (previously acquired, Buffalo selected Jaroslav Kristek) in 1998 Entry Draft and San Jose's 5th round choice in 2000 Entry Draft for Steve Shields and Buffalo's 4th round choice (Miroslav Zalesak) in 1998 Entry Draft, June 18, 1998. Signed as a free agent by **NY Rangers**, August 17, 1998.

WICKENHEISER, CHRIS (wih-KEHN-high-zehr) EDM.

Goaltender. Catches left. 6'1", 185 lbs. Born, Lethbridge, Alta., January 20, 1976.
(Edmonton's 12th choice, 179th overall, in 1994 Entry Draft).

			Regular Season								Playoffs						
Season	Club	Lea	GP	W	L	T	Mins	GA	SO	Avg	GP	W	L	Mins	GA	SO	Avg
1992-93	Lethbridge	AMHA	44	....	....	....	2532	118	4	2.80	....	....	....	....	....	....	....
1993-94	Red Deer	WHL	29	11	13	0	1356	114	0	5.04	....	....	....	....	....	....	....
1994-95	Red Deer	WHL	47	13	26	3	2429	181	1	4.47	....	....	....	....	....	....	....
1995-96	Red Deer	WHL	48	17	27	2	2666	183	1	4.12	10	3	6	550	34	1	3.71
1996-97	Red Deer	WHL	1	0	1	0	60	4	0	4.00	....	....	....	....	....	....	....
	Portland	WHL	40	24	13	3	2367	106	3	2.69	4	2	2	226	10	0	2.65
1997-98	Huntington	ECHL	32	16	10	3	1758	99	2	3.38	....	....	....	....	....	....	....
	Hamilton	AHL	2	0	0	0	20	1	0	2.96	....	....	....	....	....	....	....

WHL West Second All-Star Team (1997)

WILKINSON, DEREK T.B.

Goaltender. Catches left. 6', 170 lbs. Born, Lasalle, Ont., July 29, 1974.
(Tampa Bay's 7th choice, 145th overall, in 1992 Entry Draft).

			Regular Season								Playoffs						
Season	Club	Lea	GP	W	L	T	Mins	GA	SO	Avg	GP	W	L	Mins	GA	SO	Avg
1991-92	Detroit	OHL	38	16	17	1	1943	138	1	4.26	7	3	2	313	28	0	5.37
1992-93	Detroit	OHL	*4	1	2	1	*245	18	0	4.41	....	....	....	....	....	....	....
	Belleville	OHL	*59	21	24	11	*3370	237	0	4.22	7	3	4	434	29	0	4.01
1993-94	Belleville	OHL	*56	24	16	4	2860	179	*2	3.76	12	6	6	700	39	*1	3.34
1994-95	Atlanta	IHL	46	22	17	2	2414	121	1	3.01	4	2	1	197	8	0	2.43
1995-96	**Tampa Bay**	**NHL**	**4**	**0**	**3**	**0**	**200**	**15**	**0**	**4.50**	....	....	....	....	....	....	....
	Atlanta	IHL	28	11	11	2	1433	98	1	4.10	....	....	....	....	....	....	....
1996-97	**Tampa Bay**	**NHL**	**5**	**0**	**2**	**1**	**169**	**12**	**0**	**4.26**	....	....	....	....	....	....	....
	Cleveland	IHL	46	20	17	6	2595	138	1	3.19	14	8	6	893	44	0	2.95
1997-98	**Tampa Bay**	**NHL**	**8**	**2**	**4**	**1**	**311**	**17**	**0**	**3.28**	....	....	....	....	....	....	....
	Cleveland	IHL	25	9	12	2	1295	63	1	2.92	1	0	0	27	1	0	2.19
	NHL Totals		**17**	**2**	**9**	**2**	**680**	**44**	**0**	**3.88**	....	....	....	....	....	....	....

WILLIS, JORDAN

Goaltender. Catches left. 5'9", 155 lbs. Born, Kincardine, Ont., February 28, 1975.
(Dallas' 8th choice, 243rd overall, in 1993 Entry Draft).

			Regular Season								Playoffs						
Season	Club	Lea	GP	W	L	T	Mins	GA	SO	Avg	GP	W	L	Mins	GA	SO	Avg
1992-93	London	OHL	26	13	6	3	1428	101	1	4.24	7	2	4	355	19	0	3.21
1993-94	London	OHL	44	20	19	2	2428	158	1	3.90	1	0	0	8	1	0	7.50
1994-95	London	OHL	53	16	29	3	2824	202	0	4.29	3	0	3	165	15	0	5.45
1995-96	**Dallas**	**NHL**	**1**	**0**	**1**	**0**	**19**	**1**	**0**	**3.16**	....	....	....	....	....	....	....
	Michigan	IHL	38	17	9	9	2184	118	1	3.24	4	1	3	238	17	0	4.29
1996-97	Canada	Nat-Tm	15	7	4	2	804	42	....	3.13	....	....	....	....	....	....	....
	Daytona	ECHL	8	4	4	0	429	25	0	3.50	....	....	....	....	....	....	....
	Michigan	IHL	2	0	2	0	102	8	0	4.70	....	....	....	....	....	....	....
1997-98	Michigan	IHL	31	8	18	2	1584	93	1	3.52	....	....	....	....	....	....	....
	NHL Totals		**1**	**0**	**1**	**0**	**19**	**1**	**0**	**3.16**	....	....	....	....	....	....	....

WREGGET, KEN

(REHG-eht) **CGY.**

Goaltender. Catches left. 6'1", 201 lbs. Born, Brandon, Man., March 25, 1964.
(Toronto's 4th choice, 45th overall, in 1982 Entry Draft).

			Regular Season								Playoffs						
Season	**Club**	**Lea**	**GP**	**W**	**L**	**T**	**Mins**	**GA**	**SO**	**Avg**	**GP**	**W**	**L**	**Mins**	**GA**	**SO**	**Avg**
1981-82	Lethbridge	WHL	36	19	12	0	1713	118	0	4.13	3	2	0	84	3	0	2.14
1982-83	Lethbridge	WHL	48	26	17	1	2696	157	1	3.49	*20	14	5	*1154	58	*1	*3.02
1983-84	**Toronto**	**NHL**	**3**	**1**	**1**	**1**	**165**	**14**	**0**	**5.09**	....	....	....	....	....	....	....
	Lethbridge	WHL	53	32	20	0	3053	161	0	*3.16	4	1	3	210	18	0	5.14
1984-85	**Toronto**	**NHL**	**23**	**2**	**15**	**3**	**1278**	**103**	**0**	**4.84**	....	....	....	....	....	....	....
	St. Catharines	AHL	12	2	8	1	688	48	0	4.19	....	....	....	....	....	....	....
1985-86	**Toronto**	**NHL**	**30**	**9**	**13**	**4**	**1566**	**113**	**0**	**4.33**	**10**	**6**	**4**	**607**	**32**	***1**	**3.16**
	St. Catharines	AHL	18	8	9	0	1058	78	1	4.42	....	....	....	....	....	....	....
1986-87	**Toronto**	**NHL**	**56**	**22**	**28**	**3**	**3026**	**200**	**0**	**3.97**	**13**	**7**	**6**	**761**	**29**	**1**	**2.29**
1987-88	**Toronto**	**NHL**	**56**	**12**	**35**	**4**	**3000**	**222**	**2**	**4.44**	**2**	**0**	**1**	**108**	**11**	**0**	**6.11**
1988-89	**Toronto**	**NHL**	**32**	**9**	**20**	**2**	**1888**	**139**	**0**	**4.42**	....	....	....	....	....	....	....
	Philadelphia	**NHL**	**3**	**1**	**1**	**0**	**130**	**13**	**0**	**6.00**	**5**	**2**	**2**	**268**	**10**	**0**	**2.24**
1989-90	**Philadelphia**	**NHL**	**51**	**22**	**24**	**3**	**2961**	**169**	**0**	**3.42**	....	....	....	....	....	....	....
1990-91	**Philadelphia**	**NHL**	**30**	**10**	**14**	**3**	**1484**	**88**	**0**	**3.56**	....	....	....	....	....	....	....
1991-92	**Philadelphia**	**NHL**	**23**	**9**	**8**	**3**	**1259**	**75**	**0**	**3.57**	....	....	....	....	....	....	....
	Pittsburgh	**NHL**	**9**	**5**	**3**	**0**	**448**	**31**	**0**	**4.15**	**1**	**0**	**0**	**40**	**4**	**0**	**6.00** ♦
1992-93	**Pittsburgh**	**NHL**	**25**	**13**	**7**	**2**	**1368**	**78**	**0**	**3.42**	....	....	....	....	....	....	....
1993-94	**Pittsburgh**	**NHL**	**42**	**21**	**12**	**7**	**2456**	**138**	**1**	**3.37**	....	....	....	....	....	....	....
1994-95	**Pittsburgh**	**NHL**	**38**	***25**	**9**	**2**	**2208**	**118**	**0**	**3.21**	**11**	**5**	**6**	**661**	**33**	**1**	**3.00**
1995-96	**Pittsburgh**	**NHL**	**37**	**20**	**13**	**2**	**2132**	**115**	**3**	**3.24**	**9**	**7**	**2**	**599**	**23**	**0**	**2.30**
1996-97	**Pittsburgh**	**NHL**	**46**	**17**	**17**	**6**	**2514**	**136**	**2**	**3.25**	**5**	**1**	**4**	**297**	**18**	**0**	**3.64**
1997-98	**Pittsburgh**	**NHL**	**15**	**3**	**6**	**2**	**611**	**28**	**0**	**2.75**	....	....	....	....	....	....	....
	NHL Totals		**519**	**201**	**226**	**47**	**28494**	**1780**	**8**	**3.75**	**56**	**28**	**25**	**3341**	**160**	**3**	**2.87**

WHL East First All-Star Team (1984)

Traded to **Philadelphia** by **Toronto** for Philadelphia's 1st round choice (Rob Pearson) and Calgary's 1st round choice (previously acquired, Toronto selected Steve Bancroft) in 1989 Entry Draft, March 6, 1989. Traded to **Pittsburgh** by **Philadelphia** with Rick Tocchet, Kjell Samuelsson and Philadelphia's 3rd round choice (Dave Roche) in 1993 Entry Draft for Mark Recchi, Brian Benning and Los Angeles' 1st round choice (previously acquired, Philadelphia selected Jason Bowen) in 1992 Entry Draft, February 19, 1992. Traded to **Calgary** by **Pittsburgh** with Dave Roche for German Titov and Todd Hlushko, June 17, 1998.

YEREMEYEV, VITALI

(yehr-eh-MAY-ehv) **NYR**

Goaltender. Catches left. 5'10", 167 lbs. Born, Ust-Kamenogorsk, USSR, September 23, 1975.
(NY Rangers' 11th choice, 209th overall, in 1994 Entry Draft).

			Regular Season								Playoffs						
Season	**Club**	**Lea**	**GP**	**W**	**L**	**T**	**Mins**	**GA**	**SO**	**Avg**	**GP**	**W**	**L**	**Mins**	**GA**	**SO**	**Avg**
1993-94	Kamenogorsk	CIS	19	....	....	....	1015	38	....	2.24	....	....	....	....	....	....	....
1994-95	CSKA Moscow	CIS	49	....	....	....	2733	97	....	2.13	2	....	....	120	8	....	4.00
1995-96	CSKA Moscow	CIS	25	....	....	....	1339	37	5	1.66	3	....	....	179	7	....	2.34
1996-97	CSKA Moscow	Russia	14	....	....	....	635	35	0	3.31	1	....	....	59	3	0	3.05
1997-98	Yaroslavl	Russia	17	....	....	....	979	19	3	*1.16	....	....	....	....	....	....	....
	Kazakhstan	Olympics	*7	....	....	....	292	28	....	5.76	....	....	....	....	....	....	....

YOUNG, WENDELL

Goaltender. Catches left. 5'9", 181 lbs. Born, Halifax, N.S., August 1, 1963.
(Vancouver's 3rd choice, 73rd overall, in 1981 Entry Draft).

			Regular Season								Playoffs						
Season	**Club**	**Lea**	**GP**	**W**	**L**	**T**	**Mins**	**GA**	**SO**	**Avg**	**GP**	**W**	**L**	**Mins**	**GA**	**SO**	**Avg**
1980-81	Kitchener	OHA	42	19	15	0	2215	164	1	4.44	14	9	1	800	42	*1	3.15
1981-82	Kitchener	OHL	*60	*38	17	2	*3470	195	1	3.37	15	12	1	900	35	*1	*2.33
1982-83	Kitchener	OHL	61	*41	19	0	*3611	231	1	3.84	12	6	5	720	43	0	3.58
1983-84	Fredericton	AHL	11	7	3	0	569	39	1	4.11	....	....	....	....	....	....	....
	Milwaukee	IHL	6	4	1	1	339	17	0	3.01	....	....	....	....	....	....	....
	Salt Lake	CHL	20	11	6	0	1094	80	0	4.39	4	0	2	122	11	0	5.42
1984-85	Fredericton	AHL	22	7	11	3	1242	83	0	4.01	....	....	....	....	....	....	....
1985-86	**Vancouver**	**NHL**	**22**	**4**	**9**	**3**	**1023**	**61**	**0**	**3.58**	**1**	**0**	**1**	**60**	**5**	**0**	**5.00**
	Fredericton	AHL	24	12	8	4	1457	78	0	3.21	....	....	....	....	....	....	....
1986-87	**Vancouver**	**NHL**	**8**	**1**	**6**	**1**	**420**	**35**	**0**	**5.00**	....	....	....	....	....	....	....
	Fredericton	AHL	30	11	16	0	1676	118	0	4.22	....	....	....	....	....	....	....
1987-88	**Philadelphia**	**NHL**	**6**	**3**	**2**	**0**	**320**	**20**	**0**	**3.75**	....	....	....	....	....	....	....
	Hershey	AHL	51	*33	15	1	2922	135	1	2.77	12	*12	0	*767	28	*1	*2.19
1988-89	**Pittsburgh**	**NHL**	**22**	**12**	**9**	**0**	**1150**	**92**	**0**	**4.80**	**1**	**0**	**0**	**39**	**1**	**0**	**1.54**
	Muskegon	IHL	2	1	0	1	125	7	0	3.36	....	....	....	....	....	....	....
1989-90	**Pittsburgh**	**NHL**	**43**	**16**	**20**	**3**	**2318**	**161**	**1**	**4.17**	....	....	....	....	....	....	....
1990-91	**Pittsburgh**	**NHL**	**18**	**4**	**6**	**2**	**773**	**52**	**0**	**4.04**	....	....	....	....	....	....	.... ♦
1991-92	**Pittsburgh**	**NHL**	**18**	**7**	**6**	**0**	**838**	**53**	**0**	**3.79**	....	....	....	....	....	....	.... ♦
1992-93	**Tampa Bay**	**NHL**	**31**	**7**	**19**	**2**	**1591**	**97**	**0**	**3.66**	....	....	....	....	....	....	....
	Atlanta	IHL	3	3	0	0	183	8	0	2.62	....	....	....	....	....	....	....
1993-94	**Tampa Bay**	**NHL**	**9**	**2**	**3**	**1**	**480**	**20**	**1**	**2.50**	....	....	....	....	....	....	....
	Atlanta	IHL	2	2	0	0	120	6	0	3.00	....	....	....	....	....	....	....
1994-95	Chicago	IHL	37	14	11	7	1882	112	0	3.57	....	....	....	....	....	....	....
	Pittsburgh	**NHL**	**10**	**3**	**6**	**0**	**497**	**27**	**0**	**3.26**	....	....	....	....	....	....	....
1995-96	Chicago	IHL	61	30	20	6	3285	199	1	3.63	9	4	5	540	30	0	3.33
1996-97	Chicago	IHL	52	25	21	4	2931	170	1	3.48	4	1	3	256	13	0	3.04
1997-98	Chicago	IHL	51	31	14	3	2912	149	2	3.07	9	5	3	515	24	1	2.79
	NHL Totals		**187**	**59**	**86**	**12**	**9410**	**618**	**2**	**3.94**	**2**	**0**	**1**	**99**	**6**	**0**	**3.64**

AHL First All-Star Team (1988) • Won Baz Bastien Memorial Trophy (Top Goaltender - AHL) (1988) • Won Jack Butterfield Trophy (Playoff MVP - AHL) (1988)

Traded to **Philadelphia** by **Vancouver** with Vancouver's 3rd round choice (Kimbi Daniels) in 1990 Entry Draft for Darren Jensen and Daryl Stanley, August 28, 1987. Traded to **Pittsburgh** by **Philadelphia** with Philadelphia's 7th round choice (Mika Valila) in 1990 Entry Draft for Pittsburgh's 3rd round choice (Chris Therien) in 1990 Entry Draft, Steptember 1, 1988. Claimed by **Tampa Bay** from **Pittsburgh** in Expansion Draft, June 18, 1992. Traded to **Pittsburgh** by **Tampa Bay** for future considerations, February 16, 1995. • Only goaltender in hockey history to win Memorial Cup (1982), Calder Cup (1988), Stanley Cup (1991, 1992) and Turner Cup (1998).

Notes

Gerry Cheevers, right, was known for the stitches he painted on his mask to represent the injuries he might otherwise have sustained. Glenn Hall, bottom, and Harry Lumley, below, actually suffered many of those injuries while playing without masks. All are members of the Hockey Hall of Fame. Cheevers holds the NHL record for the longest undefeated streak by a goaltender, reeling off 24 wins and 8 ties for the Boston Bruins during the 1971-72 season. Lumley played for five of the "original six" teams, recording 71 shutouts from 1943-44 to 1959-60. He was 17 years old when he made his first NHL appearance. He passed away on September 13, 1998. Though Glenn Hall was beaten in this picture, Hall was a tower of strength for the Detroit Red Wings, Chicago Black Hawks and St. Louis Blues during his career. Hall never missed a game from the beginning of the 1952-53 season until 12 games into the 1962-63 campaign for an astonishing streak of 502 consecutive complete games.

Don Beaupre

Ed Giacomin

Clint Malarchuk

Les Binkley

George Hainsworth

Ron Scott

Turk Broda

Mark Laforest

Rogie Vachon

Tony Esposito

Mike Liut

Mike Veisor

Retired NHL Goaltender Index

Abbreviations: Teams/Cities: — **Ana.** – Anaheim; **Atl.** – Atlanta; **Bos.** – Boston, **Bro.** – Brooklyn; **Buf.** – Buffalo; **Cal.** – California; **Cgy.** – Calgary; **Cle.** – Cleveland; **Col.** – Colorado; **Dal.** – Dallas; **Det.** – Detroit; **Edm.** – Edmonton; **Fla.** – Florida; **Ham.** – Hamilton; **Hfd.** – Hartford; **K.C.** – Kansas City; **L.A.** – Los Angeles; **Min.** — Minnesota; **Mtl.** – Montreal; **Mtl. M.** – Montreal Maroons; **Mtl. W.** – Montreal Wanderers; **N.J.** – New Jersey; **NYA** – NY Americans; **NYI** – New York Islanders; **NYR** – New York Rangers; **Oak.** – Oakland; **Ott.** – Ottawa; **Phi.** – Philadelphia; **Pit.** – Pittsburgh; **Que.** – Quebec; **St. L.** – St. Louis; **S.J.** – San Jose; **T.B.** – Tampa Bay; **Tor.** – Toronto; **Van.** – Vancouver; **Wpg.** – Winnipeg; **Wsh.** – Washington.

Avg. – goals against per 60 minutes played; **GA** – goals against; **GP** – games played; **Mins** – minutes played; **SO** – shutouts.

• – deceased. § - Forward, defenseman or coach who appeared in goal. For complete career, see Retired Player Index.

			Regular Schedule								Playoffs										
Name	NHL Teams	NHL Seasons	GP	W	L	T	Mins	GA	SO	Avg	GP	W	L	T	Mins	GA	SO	Avg	NHL Cup Wins	First NHL Season	Last NHL Season
Abbott, George	Bos.	1	1	0	1	0	60	7	0	7.00	....	....	....	....	....	....	....	....		1943-44	1943-44
Adams, John	Bos., Wsh.	2	22	9	10	1	1180	85	1	4.32	....	....	....	....	....	....	....	....		1972-73	1974-75
Aiken, John	Mtl.	1	1	0	1	0	34	6	0	10.59	....	....	....	....	....	....	....	....		1957-58	1957-58
• Aikenhead, Andy	NYR	3	106	47	43	16	6570	257	11	2.35	10	6	2	2	608	15	3	1.48	1	1932-33	1934-35
Almas, Red	Det., Chi.	3	3	0	2	1	180	13	0	4.33	5	1	3	0	263	13	0	2.97		1946-47	1952-53
• Anderson, Lorne	NYR	1	3	1	2	0	180	18	0	6.00	....	....	....	....	....	....	....	....		1951-52	1951-52
Astrom, Hardy	NYR, Col.	3	83	17	44	12	4456	278	0	3.74	....	....	....	....	....	....	....	....		1977-78	1980-81
Baker, Steve	NYR	4	57	20	20	11	3081	190	3	3.70	14	7	7	0	826	55	0	4.00		1979-80	1982-83
Bannerman, Murray	Van., Chi.	8	289	116	125	33	16470	1051	8	3.83	40	20	18	0	2322	165	0	4.26		1977-78	1986-87
Baron, Marco	Bos., L.A., Edm.	6	86	34	39	9	4822	292	1	3.63	1	0	1	0	20	3	0	9.00		1979-80	1984-85
Bassen, Hank	Chi., Det., Pit.	9	157	46	66	31	8779	441	5	3.01	5	1	3	0	274	11	0	2.41		1954-55	1967-68
• Bastien, Baz	Tor.	1	5	0	4	1	300	20	0	4.00	....	....	....	....	....	....	....	....		1945-46	1945-46
Bauman, Gary	Mtl., Min.	3	35	6	18	6	1718	102	0	3.56	....	....	....	....	....	....	....	....		1966-67	1968-69
Beaupre, Don	Min., Wsh., Ott., Tor.	17	667	268	277	75	37396	2151	17	3.45	72	33	31	0	3943	220	3	3.35		1980-81	1996-97
Bedard, Jim	Wsh.	2	73	17	40	13	4232	278	1	3.94	....	....	....	....	....	....	....	....		1977-78	1978-79
Behrend, Marc	Wpg.	3	39	12	19	3	1991	160	1	4.82	7	1	3	0	312	19	0	3.65		1983-84	1985-86
Belanger, Yves	St.L., Atl., Bos.	6	78	29	33	6	4134	259	2	3.76	....	....	....	....	....	....	....	....		1974-75	1979-80
Belhumeur, Michel	Phi., Wsh.	3	65	9	36	7	3306	254	0	4.61	1	0	0	0	10	1	0	6.00		1972-73	1975-76
• Bell, Gordie	Tor., NYR	2	8	3	5	0	480	31	0	3.88	2	1	1	0	120	9	0	4.50		1945-46	1955-56
• Benedict, Clint	Ott., Mtl.M.	13	362	191	142	28	22360	858	58	2.30	48	25	18	5	2907	87	15	1.80	4	1917-18	1929-30
Bennett, Harvey	Bos.	1	25	10	12	2	1470	103	0	4.20	....	....	....	....	....	....	....	....		1944-45	1944-45
Bergeron, Jean-Claude	Mtl., T.B., L.A.	6	72	21	33	7	3772	232	1	3.69	....	....	....	....	....	....	....	....		1990-91	1996-97
Bernhardt, Tim	Cgy., Tor.	4	67	17	36	7	3748	267	0	4.27	....	....	....	....	....	....	....	....		1982-83	1986-87
Berthiaume, Daniel	Wpg., Min., L.A., Bos., Ott.	9	215	81	90	21	11662	714	5	3.67	14	5	9	0	807	50	0	3.72		1985-86	1993-94
Bester, Allan	Tor., Det., Dal.	10	219	73	99	17	11773	786	7	4.01	11	2	6	0	508	37	0	4.37		1983-84	1995-96
• Beveridge, Bill	Det., Ott., St.L., Mtl.M., NYR	9	297	87	166	42	18375	879	18	2.87	5	2	3	0	300	11	0	2.20		1929-30	1942-43
• Bibeault, Paul	Mtl., Tor., Bos., Chi.	7	214	81	107	25	12890	785	10	3.65	20	6	14	0	1237	71	2	3.44		1940-41	1946-47
Binette, Andre	Mtl.	1	1	1	0	0	60	4	0	4.00	....	....	....	....	....	....	....	....		1954-55	1954-55
Binkley, Les	Pit.	5	196	58	94	34	11046	575	11	3.12	7	5	2	0	428	15	0	2.10		1967-68	1971-72
Bittner, Richard	Bos.	1	1	0	0	1	60	3	0	3.00	....	....	....	....	....	....	....	....		1949-50	1949-50
Blake, Mike	L.A.	3	40	13	15	5	2117	150	0	4.25	....	....	....	....	....	....	....	....		1981-82	1983-84
Blue, John	Bos., Buf.	3	46	16	18	7	2521	126	1	3.00	2	0	1	0	96	5	0	3.13		1992-93	1995-96
Boisvert, Gilles	Det.	1	3	0	3	0	180	9	0	3.00	....	....	....	....	....	....	....	....		1959-60	1959-60
Bouchard, Dan	Atl., Cgy., Que., Wpg.	14	655	286	232	113	37919	2061	27	3.26	43	13	30	0	2549	147	1	3.46		1972-73	1985-86
• Bourque, Claude	Mtl., Det.	2	62	16	38	8	3830	193	4	3.02	3	1	2	0	188	8	1	2.55		1938-39	1939-40
Boutin, Rollie	Wsh.	3	22	7	10	1	1137	75	0	3.96	....	....	....	....	....	....	....	....		1978-79	1980-81
Bouvrette, Lionel	NYR	1	1	0	1	0	60	6	0	6.00	....	....	....	....	....	....	....	....		1942-43	1942-43
Bower, Johnny	NYR, Tor.	15	552	250	195	90	32016	1347	37	2.52	74	35	34	0	4378	184	5	2.52	4	1953-54	1969-70
§ • Branigan, Andy	NYA	1	1	0	0	0	7	0	0	0.00	....	....	....	....	....	....	....	....		1940-41	1940-41
Brimsek, Frank	Bos., Chi.	10	514	252	182	80	31210	1404	40	2.70	68	32	36	0	4394	186	2	2.54	2	1938-39	1949-50
• Broda, Turk	Tor.	14	629	302	224	101	38167	1609	62	2.53	101	60	39	0	6389	211	13	1.98	5	1936-37	1951-52
Broderick, Ken	Min., Bos.	3	27	11	12	1	1464	74	1	3.03	....	....	....	....	....	....	....	....		1969-70	1974-75
Broderick, Len	Mtl.	1	1	1	0	0	60	2	0	2.00	....	....	....	....	....	....	....	....		1957-58	1957-58
Brodeur, Richard	NYI, Van., Hfd.	9	385	131	176	62	21968	1410	6	3.85	33	13	20	0	2009	111	1	3.32		1979-80	1987-88
Bromley, Gary	Buf., Van.	6	136	54	44	28	7427	425	7	3.43	7	2	5	0	360	25	0	4.17		1973-74	1980-81
• Brooks, Arthur	Tor.	1	4	2	2	0	220	23	0	6.27	....	....	....	....	....	....	....	....		1917-18	1917-18
Brooks, Ross	Bos.	3	54	37	7	6	3047	134	4	2.64	1	0	0	0	20	3	0	9.00		1972-73	1974-75
• Brophy, Frank	Que.	1	21	3	18	0	1249	148	0	7.11	....	....	....	....	....	....	....	....		1919-20	1919-20
Brown, Andy	Det., Pit.	3	62	22	26	9	3373	213	1	3.79	....	....	....	....	....	....	....	....		1971-72	1973-74
Brown, Ken	Chi.	1	1	0	0	0	18	1	0	3.33	....	....	....	....	....	....	....	....		1970-71	1970-71
Brunetta, Mario	Que.	3	40	12	17	1	1967	128	0	3.90	....	....	....	....	....	....	....	....		1987-88	1989-90
Bullock, Bruce	Van.	3	16	3	9	3	927	74	0	4.79	....	....	....	....	....	....	....	....		1972-73	1976-77
Buzinski, Steve	NYR	1	9	2	6	1	560	55	0	5.89	....	....	....	....	....	....	....	....		1942-43	1942-43
Caley, Don	St.L.	1	1	0	0	0	30	3	0	6.00	....	....	....	....	....	....	....	....		1967-68	1967-68
Caprice, Frank	Van.	6	102	31	46	11	5589	391	1	4.20	....	....	....	....	....	....	....	....		1982-83	1987-88
Caron, Jacques	L.A., St.L., Van.	5	72	24	29	11	3846	211	2	3.29	12	4	7	0	639	34	0	3.19		1967-68	1973-74
Carter, Lyle	Cal.	1	15	4	7	0	721	50	0	4.16	....	....	....	....	....	....	....	....		1971-72	1971-72
• Chabot, Lorne	NYR, Tor., Mtl., Chi., Mtl.M., NYA	11	411	201	148	62	25307	860	73	2.04	37	13	17	6	2498	64	5	1.54	2	1926-27	1936-37
Chadwick, Ed	Tor., Bos.	6	184	57	92	35	11040	551	14	2.99	....	....	....	....	....	....	....	....		1955-56	1961-62
Champoux, Bob	Det., Cal.	2	17	2	11	3	923	80	0	5.20	1	1	0	0	55	4	0	4.36		1963-64	1973-74
Cheevers, Gerry	Tor., Bos.	13	418	230	102	74	24394	1175	26	2.89	88	53	34	0	5396	242	8	2.69	2	1961-62	1979-80
Chevrier, Alain	N.J., Wpg., Chi., Pit., Det.	6	234	91	100	14	12202	845	2	4.16	16	9	7	0	1013	44	0	2.61		1985-86	1990-91
§ • Clancy, King	Ott., Tor.	2	2	0	0	0	3	1	0	20.00	....	....	....	....	....	....	....	....		1924-25	1931-32
§ • Cleghorn, Odie	Pit.	1	1	1	0	0	60	2	0	2.00	....	....	....	....	....	....	....	....		1925-26	1925-26
§ • Cleghorn, Sprague	Ott., Mtl.	2	2	0	0	0	5	0	0	0.00	....	....	....	....	....	....	....	....		1918-19	1921-22
Clifford, Chris	Chi.	2	2	0	0	0	24	0	0	0.00	....	....	....	....	....	....	....	....		1984-85	1988-89
Cloutier, Jacques	Buf., Chi., Que.	12	255	82	102	24	12826	778	3	3.64	8	1	5	0	413	18	1	2.62		1981-82	1993-94
Colvin, Les	Bos.	1	1	0	1	0	60	4	0	4.00	....	....	....	....	....	....	....	....		1948-49	1948-49
§ • Conacher, Charlie	Tor., Det.	3	4	0	0	0	10	0	0	0.00	....	....	....	....	....	....	....	....		1932-33	1938-39
• Connell, Alex	Ott., Det., NYA, Mtl.M.	12	417	193	156	67	26050	830	81	1.91	21	8	5	8	1309	26	4	1.19	2	1924-25	1936-37
Corsi, Jim	Edm.	1	26	8	14	3	1366	83	0	3.65	....	....	....	....	....	....	....	....		1979-80	1979-80
Courteau, Maurice	Bos.	1	6	2	4	0	360	33	0	5.50	....	....	....	....	....	....	....	....		1943-44	1943-44
Cowley, Wayne	Edmonton	1	1	0	1	0	57	3	0	3.16	....	....	....	....	....	....	....	....		1993-94	1993-94
Cox, Abbie	Mtl.M., Det., NYA, Mtl.	3	5	1	1	2	263	11	0	2.51	....	....	....	....	....	....	....	....		1929-30	1935-36
Craig, Jim	Atl., Bos., Min.	3	30	11	10	7	1588	100	0	3.78	....	....	....	....	....	....	....	....		1979-80	1983-84
Crha, Jiri	Tor.	2	69	28	27	11	3942	261	0	3.97	5	0	4	0	186	21	0	6.77		1979-80	1980-81
• Crozier, Roger	Det., Buf., Wsh.	14	518	206	197	70	28567	1446	30	3.04	32	14	16	0	1789	82	1	2.75		1963-64	1976-77
• Cude, Wilf	Phi., Bos., Chi., Det., Mtl.	10	282	100	132	49	17586	798	24	2.72	19	7	11	1	1257	51	1	2.43		1930-31	1940-41
Cutts, Don	Edm.	1	6	1	2	1	269	16	0	3.57	....	....	....	....	....	....	....	....		1979-80	1979-80
• Cyr, Claude	Mtl.	1	1	0	0	0	20	1	0	3.00	....	....	....	....	....	....	....	....		1958-59	1958-59
Dadswell, Doug	Cgy.	2	27	8	8	3	1346	99	0	4.41	....	....	....	....	....	....	....	....		1986-87	1987-88
D'Alessio, Corrie	Hfd.	1	1	0	0	0	11	0	0	0.00	....	....	....	....	....	....	....	....		1992-93	1992-93
Daley, Joe	Pit., Buf., Det.	4	105	34	44	19	5836	326	3	3.35	....	....	....	....	....	....	....	....		1968-69	1971-72
Damore, Nick	Bos.	1	1	1	0	0	60	3	0	3.00	....	....	....	....	....	....	....	....		1941-42	1941-42
D'Amour, Marc	Cgy., Phi.	2	16	2	4	2	579	32	0	3.32	....	....	....	....	....	....	....	....		1985-86	1988-89
• Darragh, Jack		1	1	0	0	0	2	0	0	0.00	....	....	....	....	....	....	....	....			
Daskalakis, Cleon	Bos.	3	12	3	4	1	506	41	0	4.86	....	....	....	....	....	....	....	....		1984-85	1986-87
Davidson, John	St.L., NYR	10	301	123	124	39	17109	1004	7	3.52	31	16	14	0	1862	77	1	2.48		1973-74	1982-83
Decourcy, Robert	NYR	1	1	0	1	0	29	6	0	12.41	....	....	....	....	....	....	....	....		1947-48	1947-48
Defelice, Norman	Bos.	1	10	3	5	2	600	30	0	3.00	....	....	....	....	....	....	....	....		1956-57	1956-57
DeJordy, Denis	Chi., L.A., Mtl., Det.	11	316	124	128	51	17798	929	15	3.13	18	6	9	0	946	55	0	3.49		1962-63	1973-74
DelGuidice, Matt	Bos.	2	11	2	5	1	434	28	0	3.87	....	....	....	....	....	....	....	....		1990-91	1991-92
Desjardins, Gerry	L.A., Chi., NYI, Buf.	10	331	122	153	44	19014	1042	12	3.29	35	15	15	0	1874	108	0	3.46		1968-69	1977-78
• Dickie, Bill	Chi.	1	1	1	0	0	60	3	0	3.00	....	....	....	....	....	....	....	....		1941-42	1941-42
Dion, Connie	Det.	2	38	23	11	4	2280	119	1	3.13	5	1	4	0	300	17	0	3.40		1943-44	1944-45
Dion, Michel	Que., Wpg., Pit.	6	227	60	118	32	12695	898	2	4.24	5	2	3	0	304	22	0	4.34		1979-80	1984-85
Dolson, Dolly	Det.	3	93	35	41	17	5820	192	16	1.98	2	0	2	0	120	7	0	3.50		1928-29	1930-31
Dopson, Robert	Pit.	1	2	0	0	0	45	3	0	4.00	....	....	....	....	....	....	....	....		1993-94	1993-94
Dowie, Bruce	Tor.	1	2	0	1	0	72	4	0	3.33	....	....	....	....	....	....	....	....		1983-84	1983-84
Draper, Tom	Wpg., Buf., NYI, Wpg.	6	53	19	23	5	2807	173	1	3.70	7	3	4	0	433	19	1	2.63		1988-89	1995-96
Dryden, Dave	NYR, Chi., Buf., Edm.	9	203	66	76	31	10424	555	9	3.19	3	0	2	0	133	9	0	4.06		1961-62	1979-80

Name	NHL Teams	NHL Seasons	Regular Schedule GP	W	L	T	Mins	GA	SO	Avg	Playoffs GP	W	L	T	Mins	GA	SO	Avg	NHL Cup Wins	First NHL Season	Last NHL Season
Dryden, Ken	Mtl.	8	397	258	57	74	23352	870	46	2.24	112	80	32	0	6846	274	10	2.40	6	1970-71	1978-79
Duffus, Parris	Phx.	1	1	0	0	0	29	1	0	2.07	....	....	....	....	....	....	....	....		1996-97	1996-97
Dumas, Michel	Chi.	2	8	2	1	2	362	24	0	3.98	1	0	0	0	19	1	0	3.16		1974-75	1976-77
Dupuis, Bob	Edm.	1	1	0	1	0	60	4	0	4.00	....	....	....	....	....	....	....	....		1979-80	1979-80
• Durnan, Bill	Mtl.	7	383	208	112	62	22945	901	34	2.36	45	27	18	0	2871	99	2	2.07	2	1943-44	1949-50
Dyck, Ed	Van.	3	49	8	28	5	2453	178	1	4.35	....	....	....	....	....	....	....	....		1971-72	1973-74
Edwards, Don	Buf., Cgy., Tor.	10	459	208	155	74	26181	1449	16	3.32	42	16	21	0	2302	132	1	3.44		1976-77	1985-86
Edwards, Gary	St.L., L.A., Clev., Min., Edm., Pit.	13	286	88	125	51	16002	973	11	3.65	11	5	4	0	537	34	0	3.80		1968-69	1981-82
Edwards, Marv	Pit., Tor., Cal.	4	61	15	34	7	3467	218	2	3.77	....	....	....	....	....	....	....	....		1968-69	1973-74
Edwards, Roy	Det., Pit.	7	236	97	88	38	13109	637	12	2.92	4	0	3	0	206	11	0	3.20		1967-68	1973-74
Eliot, Darren	L.A., Det., Buf.	5	89	25	41	12	4931	377	1	4.59	1	0	0	0	40	7	0	10.50		1984-85	1988-89
Ellacott, Ken	Van.	1	12	2	3	4	555	41	0	4.43	....	....	....	....	....	....	....	....		1982-83	1982-83
Erickson, Chad	N.J.	1	2	1	1	0	120	9	0	4.50	....	....	....	....	....	....	....	....		1991-92	1991-92
Esposito, Tony	Mtl., Chi.	16	886	423	306	152	52585	2563	76	2.92	99	45	53	0	6017	308	6	3.07	1	1968-69	1983-84
• Evans, Claude	Mtl., Bos.	2	5	2	2	1	280	16	0	3.43	....	....	....	....	....	....	....	....		1954-55	1957-58
Exelby, Randy	Mtl., Edm.	2	2	0	1	0	63	5	0	4.76	....	....	....	....	....	....	....	....		1988-89	1989-90
Farr, Rocky	Buf.	3	19	2	6	3	722	42	0	3.49	....	....	....	....	....	....	....	....		1972-73	1974-75
Favell, Doug	Phi., Tor., Col.	12	373	123	153	69	20771	1096	18	3.17	21	5	16	0	1270	66	1	3.12		1967-68	1978-79
• Forbes, Jake	Tor., Ham., NYA, Phi.	13	210	85	113	11	12922	594	19	2.76	2	0	2	0	120	7	0	3.50		1919-20	1932-33
Ford, Brian	Que., Pit.	2	11	3	7	0	580	61	0	6.31	....	....	....	....	....	....	....	....		1983-84	1984-85
Foster, Norm	Bos., Edm.	2	13	7	4	0	623	34	0	3.27	....	....	....	....	....	....	....	....		1990-91	1991-92
Fowler, Hec	Bos.	1	7	1	6	0	420	43	0	6.14	....	....	....	....	....	....	....	....		1924-25	1924-25
Francis, Emile	Chi., NYR	6	95	31	52	11	5660	355	1	3.76	....	....	....	....	....	....	....	....		1946-47	1951-52
• Franks, Jim	Det., NYR, Bos.	4	42	12	23	7	2520	181	1	4.31	1	0	1	0	30	2	0	4.00	1	1936-37	1943-44
Frederick, Ray	Chi.	1	5	0	4	1	300	22	0	4.40	....	....	....	....	....	....	....	....		1954-55	1954-55
Friesen, Karl	N.J.	1	4	0	2	1	130	16	0	7.38	....	....	....	....	....	....	....	....		1986-87	1986-87
Froese, Bob	Phi., NYR	8	242	128	72	20	13451	694	13	3.10	18	3	9	0	830	55	0	3.98		1982-83	1989-90
Gage, Joaquin	Edm.	2	18	2	10	1	816	52	0	3.82	....	....	....	....	....	....	....	....		1994-95	1995-96
Gagnon, David	Det.	1	2	0	1	0	35	6	0	10.29	....	....	....	....	....	....	....	....		1990-91	1990-91
• Gamble, Bruce	NYR, Bos., Tor., Phi.	10	327	110	150	46	18442	992	22	3.23	5	0	4	0	206	25	0	7.28		1958-59	1971-72
Gamble, Troy	Van.	4	72	22	29	9	3804	229	1	3.61	4	1	3	0	249	16	0	3.86		1986-87	1991-92
Gardiner, Bert	NYR, Mtl., Chi., Bos.	6	144	49	68	27	8760	554	4	3.79	9	4	5	0	647	20	0	1.85		1935-36	1943-44
• Gardiner, Chuck	Chi.	7	316	112	152	52	19687	664	42	2.02	21	12	6	3	1472	35	5	1.43	1	1927-28	1933-34
Gardner, George	Det., Van.	5	66	16	30	6	3313	207	0	3.75	....	....	....	....	....	....	....	....		1965-66	1971-72
Garrett, John	Hfd., Que., Van.	6	207	68	91	37	11763	837	1	4.27	9	4	3	0	461	33	0	4.30		1979-80	1984-85
Gatherum, Dave	Det.	1	3	2	0	1	180	3	1	1.00	....	....	....	....	....	....	....	....		1953-54	1953-54
Gauthier, Paul	Mtl.	1	1	0	0	1	70	2	0	1.71	....	....	....	....	....	....	....	....		1937-38	1937-38
Gelineau, Jack	Bos., Chi.	4	143	46	64	33	8580	447	7	3.13	4	1	2	0	260	7	1	1.62		1948-49	1953-54
Giacomin, Ed	NYR, Det.	13	610	289	208	97	35693	1675	54	2.82	65	29	35	0	3834	180	1	2.82		1965-66	1977-78
Gilbert, Gilles	Min., Bos., Det.	14	416	192	143	60	23677	1290	18	3.27	32	17	15	0	1919	97	3	3.03		1969-70	1982-83
Gill, Andre	Bos.	1	5	3	2	0	270	13	1	2.89	....	....	....	....	....	....	....	....		1967-68	1967-68
• Goodman, Paul	Chi.	3	52	23	20	9	3240	117	6	2.17	3	0	3	0	187	10	0	3.21	1	1937-38	1940-41
Gordon, Scott	Que.	2	23	2	16	0	1082	101	0	5.60	....	....	....	....	....	....	....	....		1989-90	1990-91
Gosselin, Mario	Que., L.A., Hfd.	9	241	91	107	14	12857	801	6	3.74	32	16	15	0	1816	99	0	3.27		1983-84	1993-94
Goverde, David	L.A.	3	5	1	4	0	278	29	0	6.26	....	....	....	....	....	....	....	....		1991-92	1993-94
Grahame, Ron	Bos., L.A., Que.	4	114	50	43	15	6472	409	5	3.79	4	2	1	0	202	7	0	2.08		1977-78	1980-81
• Grant, Ben	Tor., NYA., Bos.	6	50	17	26	4	2990	187	4	3.75	....	....	....	....	....	....	....	....		1928-29	1943-44
Grant, Doug	Det., St.L.	7	77	27	34	8	4199	280	2	4.00	....	....	....	....	....	....	....	....		1973-74	1979-80
Gratton, Gilles	St.L., NYR	2	47	13	18	9	2299	154	0	4.02	....	....	....	....	....	....	....	....		1975-76	1976-77
Gray, Gerry	Det., NYI	2	8	1	5	1	440	35	0	4.77	....	....	....	....	....	....	....	....		1970-71	1972-73
Gray, Harrison	Det.	1	1	0	1	0	40	5	0	7.50	....	....	....	....	....	....	....	....		1963-64	1963-64
Greenlay, Mike	Edm.	1	2	0	0	0	20	4	0	12.00	....	....	....	....	....	....	....	....		1989-90	1989-90
Guenette, Steve	Pit., Cgy.	5	35	19	16	0	1958	122	1	3.74	....	....	....	....	....	....	....	....		1986-87	1990-91
• Hainsworth, George	Mtl., Tor.	11	465	246	145	74	29415	937	94	1.91	52	22	25	5	3486	112	8	1.93		1926-27	1936-37
Hall, Glenn	Det., Chi., St.L.	18	906	407	326	163	53484	2239	84	2.51	115	49	65	0	6899	321	6	2.79	1	1952-53	1970-71
Hamel, Pierre	Tor., Wpg.	4	69	13	41	7	3766	276	0	4.40	....	....	....	....	....	....	....	....		1974-75	1980-81
Hanlon, Glen	Van., St.L., NYR, Det.	14	477	167	202	61	26037	1561	13	3.60	35	11	15	0	1756	92	4	3.14		1977-78	1990-91
Harrison, Paul	Min., Tor., Pit., Buf.	7	109	28	59	9	5806	408	2	4.22	4	0	1	0	157	9	0	3.44		1975-76	1981-82
Hayward, Brian	Wpg., Mtl., Min., S.J.	11	357	143	156	37	20025	1242	8	3.72	37	11	18	0	1803	104	0	3.46		1982-83	1992-93
Head, Don	Bos.	1	38	9	26	3	2280	161	2	4.24	....	....	....	....	....	....	....	....	1	1961-62	1961-62
• Hebert, Sammy	Tor., Ott.	2	4	1	2	0	200	19	0	5.70	....	....	....	....	....	....	....	....		1917-18	1923-24
Heinz, Rick	St.L., Van.	5	49	14	19	5	2356	159	2	4.05	1	0	0	0	8	1	0	7.50		1980-81	1984-85
Henderson, John	Bos.	2	46	15	15	15	2688	113	5	2.52	2	0	2	0	120	8	0	4.00		1954-55	1955-56
• Henry, Gord	Bos.	4	3	1	2	0	180	5	1	1.67	5	0	4	0	283	21	0	4.45		1948-49	1952-53
Henry, Jim	NYR, Chi., Bos.	9	406	161	173	70	24355	1166	27	2.87	29	11	18	0	1741	81	2	2.79		1941-42	1954-55
Herron, Denis	Pit., K.C., Mtl.	14	462	146	203	76	25608	1579	10	3.70	15	5	10	0	901	50	0	3.33		1972-73	1985-86
Highton, Hec	Chi.	1	24	10	14	0	1440	108	0	4.50	....	....	....	....	....	....	....	....		1943-44	1943-44
§ • Himes, Normie	NYA	2	2	0	1	0	79	3	0	2.28	....	....	....	....	....	....	....	....		1927-28	1928-29
Hodge, Charlie	Mtl., Oak., Van.	13	358	152	124	60	20593	927	24	2.70	16	7	7	0	803	32	2	2.39	4	1954-55	1970-71
Hoffort, Bruce	Phi.	2	9	4	0	3	368	22	0	3.59	....	....	....	....	....	....	....	....		1989-90	1990-91
Hoganson, Paul	Pit.	1	2	0	1	0	57	7	0	7.37	....	....	....	....	....	....	....	....		1970-71	1970-71
Hogosta, Goran	NYI, Que.	2	22	5	12	3	1208	83	1	4.12	....	....	....	....	....	....	....	....		1977-78	1979-80
Holden, Mark	Mtl., Wpg.	4	8	2	2	1	372	25	0	4.03	....	....	....	....	....	....	....	....		1981-82	1984-85
Holland, Ken	Hfd., Det.	2	4	0	2	1	206	17	0	4.95	....	....	....	....	....	....	....	....		1980-81	1980-81
Holland, Robbie	Pit.	2	44	11	22	9	2513	171	1	4.08	....	....	....	....	....	....	....	....		1979-80	1980-81
• Holmes, Harry	Tor., Det.	4	103	39	54	10	6510	264	17	2.43	7	4	3	0	420	28	0	4.00		1917-18	1927-28
§ Horner, Red	Tor.	1	1	0	0	0	1	1	0	60.00	....	....	....	....	....	....	....	....		1931-32	1931-32
Hrivnak, Jim	Wsh., Wpg., St.L.	5	85	34	30	3	4217	262	0	3.73	....	....	....	....	....	....	....	....		1989-90	1993-94
Ing, Peter	Tor., Edm., Det.	4	74	20	37	9	3941	266	1	4.05	....	....	....	....	....	....	....	....		1989-90	1993-94
Inness, Gary	Pit., Phi., Wsh.	7	162	58	61	27	8710	494	2	3.40	9	5	4	0	540	24	0	2.67		1973-74	1980-81
Ireland, Randy	Buf.	1	2	0	0	0	30	3	0	6.00	....	....	....	....	....	....	....	....		1978-79	1978-79
Irons, Robbie	St.L.	1	1	0	0	0	3	0	0	0.00	....	....	....	....	....	....	....	....		1968-69	1968-69
• Ironstone, Joe	NYA, Tor.	2	2	0	0	1	110	3	1	1.64	....	....	....	....	....	....	....	....		1925-26	1927-28
Jackson, Doug	Chi.	1	6	2	3	1	360	42	0	7.00	....	....	....	....	....	....	....	....		1947-48	1947-48
Jackson, Percy	Bos., NYA, NYR	4	7	1	3	1	392	26	0	3.98	....	....	....	....	....	....	....	....		1931-32	1935-36
Jaks, Pauli	L.A.	1	1	0	0	0	40	2	0	3.00	....	....	....	....	....	....	....	....		1994-95	1994-95
Janaszak, Steve	Min., Col.	2	3	0	1	1	160	15	0	5.62	....	....	....	....	....	....	....	....		1979-80	1981-82
Janecyk, Bob	Chi., L.A.	6	110	43	47	13	6250	432	2	4.15	3	0	3	0	184	10	0	3.26		1983-84	1988-89
§ Jenkins, Roger	NYA	1	1	0	1	0	30	7	0	14.00	....	....	....	....	....	....	....	....		1938-39	1938-39
Jensen, Al	Det., Wsh., L.A.	7	179	95	53	18	9974	557	8	3.35	12	5	5	0	598	32	0	3.21		1980-81	1986-87
Jensen, Darren	Phi.	2	30	15	10	1	1496	95	2	3.81	....	....	....	....	....	....	....	....		1984-85	1985-86
Johnson, Bob	St.L., Pit.	2	24	9	9	1	1059	66	0	3.74	....	....	....	....	....	....	....	....		1972-73	1974-75
Johnston, Eddie	Bos., Tor., St.L., Chi.	16	592	234	257	81	34216	1855	32	3.25	18	7	10	0	1023	57	1	3.34	2	1962-63	1977-78
Junkin, Joe	Bos.	1	1	0	0	0	8	0	0	0.00	....	....	....	....	....	....	....	....		1968-69	1968-69
Kaarela, Jari	Col.	1	5	2	2	0	220	22	0	6.00	....	....	....	....	....	....	....	....		1980-81	1980-81
Kamppuri, Hannu	N.J.	1	13	1	10	1	645	54	0	5.02	....	....	....	....	....	....	....	....		1984-85	1984-85
• Karakas, Mike	Chi., Mtl.	8	336	114	169	53	20616	1002	28	2.92	23	11	12	0	1434	72	3	3.01	1	1935-36	1945-46
Keans, Doug	L.A., Bos.	9	210	96	64	26	11388	666	4	3.51	9	2	6	0	432	34	0	4.72		1979-80	1987-88
Keenan, Don	Bos.	1	1	0	1	0	60	4	0	4.00	....	....	....	....	....	....	....	....		1958-59	1958-59
• Kerr, Dave	Mtl.M., NYA, NYR	11	427	203	148	75	26639	954	51	2.15	40	18	19	3	2616	76	8	1.74	1	1930-31	1940-41
King, Scott	Det.	2	2	0	0	0	61	3	0	2.95	....	....	....	....	....	....	....	....		1990-91	1991-92
Kleisinger, Terry	NYR	1	4	0	2	0	191	14	0	4.40	....	....	....	....	....	....	....	....		1985-86	1985-86
Klymkiw, Julian	NYR	1	1	0	0	0	19	2	0	6.32	....	....	....	....	....	....	....	....		1958-59	1958-59
Knickle, Rick	L.A.	2	14	7	6	0	706	44	0	3.74	....	....	....	....	....	....	....	....		1992-93	1993-94
Kuntar, Les	Mtl.	1	6	2	2	0	302	16	0	3.18	....	....	....	....	....	....	....	....		1993-94	1993-94
Kurt, Gary	Cal.	1	16	1	7	5	838	60	0	4.30	....	....	....	....	....	....	....	....		1971-72	1971-72
Lacher, Blaine	Bos.	2	47	22	16	4	2636	123	4	2.80	5	1	4	0	283	12	0	2.54		1994-95	1995-96
Lacroix, Albert	Mtl.	1	5	1	4	0	280	15	0	3.21	....	....	....	....	....	....	....	....		1925-26	1925-26
LaFerriere, Rick	Col.	1	1	0	0	0	20	1	0	3.00	....	....	....	....	....	....	....	....		1981-82	1981-82
LaForest, Mark	Det., Phi., Tor., Ott.	6	103	25	54	4	5032	354	2	4.22	2	1	0	0	48	1	0	1.25		1985-86	1993-94
• Larocque, Michel	Mtl., Tor., Phi., St.L.	11	312	160	89	45	17615	978	17	3.33	14	6	6	0	759	37	1	2.92	4	1973-74	1983-84
Laskowski, Gary	L.A.	2	59	19	27	5	2942	228	0	4.65	....	....	....	....	....	....	....	....		1982-83	1983-84
Laxton, Gord	Pit.	4	17	4	9	0	800	74	0	5.55	....	....	....	....	....	....	....	....		1975-76	1978-79
LeBlanc, Raymond	Chi.	1	1	1	0	0	60	1	0	1.00	....	....	....	....	....	....	....	....		1991-92	1991-92
§ LeDuc, Albert	Mtl.	1	1	0	0	0	2	1	0	30.00	....	....	....	....	....	....	....	....		1931-32	1931-32

Name	NHL Teams	NHL Seasons	Regular Schedule GP	W	L	T	Mins	GA	SO	Avg	Playoffs GP	W	L	T	Mins	GA	SO	Avg	NHL Cup Wins	First NHL Season	Last NHL Season
Legris, Claude	Det.	2	4	0	1	1	91	4	0	2.64	....	....	....	....	....	....	....	....		1980-81	1981-82
• Lehman, Hugh	Chi.	2	48	20	24	4	3047	136	6	2.68	2	0	1	1	120	10	0	5.00		1926-27	1927-28
Lemelin, Reggie	Atl., Cgy., Bos.	15	507	236	162	63	28006	1613	12	3.46	59	23	25	0	3119	186	2	3.58		1978-79	1992-93
Lenarduzzi, Mike	Hfd.	2	4	1	1	1	189	10	0	3.17	....	....	....	....	....	....	....	....		1992-93	1993-94
Lessard, Mario	L.A.	6	240	92	97	39	13529	843	9	3.74	20	6	12	0	1136	83	0	4.38		1978-79	1983-84
Levasseur, Jean-Louis	Min.	1	1	0	1	0	60	7	0	7.00	....	....	....	....	....	....	....	....		1979-80	1979-80
§ • Levinsky, Alex	Tor.	1	1	0	0	0	1	1	0	60.00	....	....	....	....	....	....	....	....		1931-32	1931-32
• Lindbergh, Pelle	Phi.	5	157	87	49	15	9151	503	7	3.30	23	12	10	0	1214	63	3	3.11		1981-82	1985-86
• Lindsay, Bert	Mtl.W., Tor.	2	20	6	14	0	1238	118	0	5.72	....	....	....	....	....	....	....	....		1917-18	1918-19
Liut, Mike	St. L., Hfd., Wsh.	13	663	294	271	74	38155	2219	25	3.49	67	29	32	0	3814	215	2	3.38		1979-80	1991-92
Lockett, Ken	Van.	2	55	13	15	8	2348	131	2	3.35	1	0	1	0	60	6	0	6.00		1974-75	1975-76
• Lockhart, Howard	Tor., Que., Ham., Bos.	5	59	16	41	0	3413	287	1	5.05	....	....	....	....	....	....	....	....		1919-20	1924-25
LoPresti, Pete	Min., Edm.	6	175	43	102	20	9858	668	5	4.07	2	0	2	0	77	6	0	4.68		1974-75	1980-81
• LoPresti, Sam	Chi.	2	74	30	38	6	4530	236	4	3.13	8	3	5	0	530	17	1	1.92		1940-41	1941-42
Lorenz, Danny	NYI	3	8	1	5	0	357	25	0	4.20	....	....	....	....	....	....	....	....		1990-91	1992-93
Loustel, Ron	Wpg.	1	1	0	1	0	60	10	0	10.00	....	....	....	....	....	....	....	....		1980-81	1980-81
Low, Ron	Tor., Wsh., Det., Que., Edm., NJ	11	382	102	203	38	20502	1463	4	4.28	7	1	6	0	452	29	0	3.85		1972-73	1984-85
Lozinski, Larry	Det.	1	30	6	11	7	1459	105	0	4.32	....	....	....	....	....	....	....	....		1980-81	1980-81
Lumley, Harry	Det., NYR, Chi., Tor., Bos.	16	804	330	329	143	48104	2210	71	2.76	76	29	47	0	4777	199	7	2.50	1	1943-44	1959-60
MacKenzie, Shawn	N.J.	1	4	0	1	0	130	15	0	6.92	....	....	....	....	....	....	....	....		1982-83	1982-83
Madeley, Darrin	Ott.	3	39	4	23	5	1928	140	0	4.36	....	....	....	....	....	....	....	....		1992-93	1994-95
Malarchuk, Clint	Que., Wsh., Buf.	10	338	141	130	45	19030	1100	12	3.47	15	2	9	0	781	56	0	4.30		1981-82	1991-92
Maneluk, George	NYI	1	4	1	1	0	140	15	0	6.43	....	....	....	....	....	....	....	....		1990-91	1990-91
Maniago, Cesare	Tor., Mtl., NYR, Min., Van.	15	568	189	259	96	32570	1774	30	3.27	36	15	21	0	2245	100	3	2.67		1960-61	1977-78
Marois, Jean	Tor., Chi.	2	3	1	2	0	180	15	0	5.00	....	....	....	....	....	....	....	....		1943-44	1953-54
Martin, Seth	St.L.	1	30	8	10	7	1552	67	1	2.59	2	0	0	0	73	5	0	4.11		1967-68	1967-68
Mason, Bob	Wsh., Chi., Que., Van.	8	145	55	65	16	7988	500	1	3.76	5	2	3	0	369	12	1	1.95		1983-84	1990-91
Mattsson, Markus	Wpg., Min., L.A.	4	92	21	46	14	5007	343	6	4.11	....	....	....	....	....	....	....	....		1979-80	1983-84
May, Darrell	St. L.	2	6	1	5	0	364	31	0	5.11	....	....	....	....	....	....	....	....		1985-86	1987-88
Mayer, Gilles	Tor.	4	9	2	6	1	540	25	0	2.78	....	....	....	....	....	....	....	....		1949-50	1955-56
• McAuley, Ken	NYR	2	96	17	64	15	5740	537	1	5.61	....	....	....	....	....	....	....	....		1943-44	1944-45
McCartan, Jack	NYR	2	12	2	7	3	680	43	1	3.79	....	....	....	....	....	....	....	....		1959-60	1960-61
• McCool, Frank	Tor.	2	72	34	31	7	4320	242	4	3.36	13	8	5	0	807	30	4	2.23	1	1944-45	1945-46
McDuffe, Pete	St.L., NYR, K.C., Det.	5	57	11	36	6	3207	218	0	4.08	1	0	1	0	60	7	0	7.00		1971-72	1975-76
McGrattan, Tom	Det.	1	1	0	0	0	8	0	0	0.00	....	....	....	....	....	....	....	....		1947-48	1947-48
McKay, Ross	Hfd.	1	1	0	0	0	35	3	0	5.14	....	....	....	....	....	....	....	....		1990-91	1990-91
McKenzie, Bill	Det., K.C., Col.	6	91	18	49	13	4776	326	2	4.10	....	....	....	....	....	....	....	....		1973-74	1979-80
McKichan, Steve	Van.	1	1	0	0	0	20	2	0	6.00	....	....	....	....	....	....	....	....		1990-91	1990-91
McLachlan, Murray	Tor.	1	2	0	1	0	25	4	0	9.60	....	....	....	....	....	....	....	....		1970-71	1970-71
McLelland, Dave	Van.	1	2	1	1	0	120	10	0	5.00	....	....	....	....	....	....	....	....		1972-73	1972-73
McLeod, Don	Det., Phi.	2	18	3	10	1	879	74	0	5.05	....	....	....	....	....	....	....	....		1970-71	1971-72
McLeod, Jim	St.L.	1	16	6	6	4	880	44	0	3.00	....	....	....	....	....	....	....	....		1971-72	1971-72
McNamara, Gerry	Tor.	2	7	2	2	1	323	15	0	2.79	....	....	....	....	....	....	....	....		1960-61	1969-70
McNeil, Gerry	Mtl.	7	276	119	105	52	16535	650	28	2.36	35	17	18	0	2284	72	5	1.89	3	1947-48	1956-57
McRae, Gord	Tor.	5	71	30	22	10	3799	221	1	3.49	8	2	5	0	454	22	0	2.91		1972-73	1977-78
Melanson, Rollie	NYI, Min., L.A., N.J., Mtl.	11	291	129	106	33	16452	995	6	3.63	23	4	9	0	801	59	0	4.42	3	1980-81	1991-92
Meloche, Gilles	Chi., Cal., Cle., Min., Pit.	18	788	270	351	131	45401	2756	20	3.64	45	21	19	0	2464	143	2	3.48		1970-71	1987-88
Micalef, Corrado	Det.	5	113	26	59	15	5794	409	2	4.24	3	0	0	0	49	8	0	9.80		1981-82	1985-86
Middlebrook, Lindsay	Wpg., Min., N.J., Edm.	4	37	3	23	6	1845	152	0	4.94	....	....	....	....	....	....	....	....		1979-80	1982-83
• Millar, Al	Bos.	1	6	1	4	1	360	25	0	4.17	....	....	....	....	....	....	....	....		1957-58	1957-58
Millen, Greg	Pit., Hfd., St. L., Que., Chi., Det.	14	604	215	284	89	35377	2281	17	3.87	59	27	29	0	3383	193	0	3.42		1978-79	1991-92
• Miller, Joe	NYA, NYR, Pit., Phi.	4	127	24	87	16	7871	383	16	2.92	3	2	1	0	180	3	1	1.00	1	1927-28	1930-31
Mio, Eddie	Edm., NYR, Det.	7	192	64	73	30	10428	705	4	4.06	17	9	7	0	986	63	0	3.83		1979-80	1985-86
• Mitchell, Ivan	Tor.	3	22	10	9	0	1190	88	0	4.44	....	....	....	....	....	....	....	....		1919-20	1921-22
Moffat, Mike	Bos.	3	19	7	7	2	979	70	0	4.29	11	6	5	0	663	38	0	3.44		1981-82	1983-84
Moore, Alfie	NYA, Det., Chi.,	4	21	7	14	0	1290	81	1	3.77	3	1	2	0	180	7	0	2.33	1	1936-37	1939-40
Moore, Robbie	Phi., Wsh.	2	6	3	1	1	257	8	2	1.87	5	3	2	0	268	18	0	4.03		1978-79	1982-83
Morissette, Jean-Guy	Mtl.	1	1	0	1	0	36	4	0	6.67	....	....	....	....	....	....	....	....		1963-64	1963-64
• Mowers, Johnny	Det.	4	152	65	61	26	9350	399	15	2.56	32	19	13	0	2000	85	2	2.55	1	1940-41	1946-47
Mrazek, Jerome	Phi.	1	1	0	0	0	6	1	0	10.00	....	....	....	....	....	....	....	....		1975-76	1975-76
§ • Mummery, Harry	Que., Ham.	2	4	2	1	0	191	20	0	6.28	....	....	....	....	....	....	....	....		1919-20	1921-22
§ • Munro, Dunc	Mtl.	1	1	0	0	0	2	0	0	0.00	....	....	....	....	....	....	....	....		1924-25	1924-25
• Murphy, Hal	Mtl.	1	1	1	0	0	60	4	0	4.00	....	....	....	....	....	....	....	....		1952-53	1952-53
Murray, Mickey	Mtl.	1	1	0	1	0	60	4	0	4.00	....	....	....	....	....	....	....	....		1929-30	1929-30
Myllys, Jarmo	Min., S.J.	4	39	4	27	1	1846	161	0	5.23	....	....	....	....	....	....	....	....		1988-89	1991-92
Mylnikov, Sergei	Que.	1	10	1	7	2	568	47	0	4.96	....	....	....	....	....	....	....	....		1989-90	1989-90
Myre, Phil	Mtl., Atl., St.L., Phi., Col., Buf.	14	439	149	198	76	25220	1482	14	3.53	12	6	5	0	747	41	1	3.29		1969-70	1982-83
Newton, Cam	Pit.	2	16	4	7	1	814	51	0	3.76	....	....	....	....	....	....	....	....		1970-71	1972-73
Norris, Jack	Bos., Chi., L.A.	4	58	20	25	4	3119	202	2	3.89	....	....	....	....	....	....	....	....		1964-65	1970-71
Oleschuk, Bill	K.C., Col.	4	55	7	28	10	2835	188	1	3.98	....	....	....	....	....	....	....	....		1975-76	1979-80
• Olesevich, Dan	NYR	1	1	0	0	1	29	2	0	4.14	....	....	....	....	....	....	....	....		1961-62	1961-62
Ouimet, Ted	St.L.	1	1	0	1	0	60	2	0	2.00	....	....	....	....	....	....	....	....		1968-69	1968-69
Pageau, Paul	L.A.	1	1	0	1	0	60	8	0	8.00	....	....	....	....	....	....	....	....		1980-81	1980-81
Paille, Marcel	NYR	7	107	32	52	22	6342	362	2	3.42	....	....	....	....	....	....	....	....		1957-58	1964-65
Palmateer, Mike	Tor., Wsh.	8	356	149	138	52	20131	1183	17	3.53	29	12	17	0	1765	89	2	3.03		1976-77	1983-84
Pang, Darren	Chi.	3	81	27	35	7	4252	287	0	4.05	6	1	3	0	250	18	0	4.32		1984-85	1988-89
Parent, Bernie	Bos., Tor., Phi.	13	608	271	198	121	35136	1493	54	2.55	71	38	33	0	4302	174	6	2.43	2	1965-66	1978-79
Parent, Bob	Tor.	2	3	0	2	0	160	15	0	5.62	....	....	....	....	....	....	....	....		1981-82	1982-83
Parro, Dave	Wsh.	4	77	21	36	10	4015	274	2	4.09	....	....	....	....	....	....	....	....		1980-81	1983-84
§ • Patrick, Lester	NYR	1	....	....	....	....	....	....	....	....	1	1	0	0	46	1	0	1.30	1	1927-28	1927-28
Peeters, Pete	Phi., Bos., Wsh.	13	489	246	155	51	27699	1424	21	3.08	71	35	35	0	4200	232	2	3.31		1978-79	1990-91
Pelletier, Marcel	Chi., NYR	2	8	1	6	0	395	33	0	5.01	....	....	....	....	....	....	....	....		1950-51	1962-63
Penney, Steve	Mtl., Wpg.	5	91	35	38	12	5194	313	1	3.62	27	15	12	0	1604	72	4	2.69		1983-84	1987-88
• Perreault, Bob	Mtl., Det., Bos.	3	31	8	16	6	1827	106	3	3.48	....	....	....	....	....	....	....	....		1955-56	1962-63
Pettie, Jim	Bos.	3	21	9	7	2	1157	71	1	3.68	....	....	....	....	....	....	....	....		1976-77	1978-79
Pietrangelo, Frank	Pit., Hfd.	7	141	46	59	6	7141	490	1	4.12	12	7	5	0	713	34	1	2.86	1	1987-88	1993-94
• Plante, Jacques	Mtl., NYR, St.L., Tor., Bos.	18	837	434	247	146	49533	1965	82	2.38	112	71	37	0	6652	240	14	2.16	6	1952-53	1972-73
Plasse, Michel	St.L., Mtl., K.C., Pit., Col., Que.	12	299	92	136	54	16760	1058	2	3.79	4	1	2	0	195	9	1	2.77	1	1970-71	1981-82
§ Plaxton, Hugh	Mtl.M.	1	1	0	1	0	57	5	0	5.26	....	....	....	....	....	....	....	....		1932-33	1932-33
Pronovost, Claude	Bos., Mtl.	2	3	1	1	0	120	7	1	3.50	....	....	....	....	....	....	....	....		1955-56	1958-59
Pusey, Chris	Det.	1	1	0	0	0	40	3	0	4.50	....	....	....	....	....	....	....	....		1985-86	1985-86
Racicot, Andre	Mtl.	5	68	26	23	8	3357	196	2	3.50	4	0	1	0	31	4	0	7.74	1	1989-90	1993-94
Raymond, Alain	Wsh.	1	1	0	1	0	40	2	0	3.00	....	....	....	....	....	....	....	....		1987-88	1987-88
Rayner, Chuck	NYA, Bro., NYR	10	424	138	208	77	25491	1294	25	3.05	18	9	9	0	1135	46	1	2.43		1940-41	1952-53
Reaugh, Daryl	Edm., Hfd.	3	27	8	9	1	1246	72	1	3.47	....	....	....	....	....	....	....	....		1984-85	1990-91
Reddick, Pokey	Wpg., Edm., Fla.	6	132	46	58	16	7162	443	0	3.71	4	0	2	0	168	10	0	3.57	1	1986-87	1993-94
• Redding, George	Bos.	1	1	0	0	0	11	1	0	5.45	....	....	....	....	....	....	....	....		1924-25	1924-25
Redquest, Greg	Pit.	1	1	0	0	0	13	3	0	13.85	....	....	....	....	....	....	....	....		1977-78	1977-78
Reece, Dave	Bos.	1	14	7	5	2	777	43	2	3.32	....	....	....	....	....	....	....	....		1975-76	1975-76
Resch, Glenn	NYI, Col., N.J., Phi.	14	571	231	224	82	32279	1761	26	3.27	41	17	17	0	2044	85	2	2.50	1	1973-74	1986-87
Rheaume, Herb	Mtl.	1	31	10	20	1	1889	92	0	2.92	....	....	....	....	....	....	....	....		1925-26	1925-26
Ricci, Nick	Pit.	4	19	7	12	0	1087	79	0	4.36	....	....	....	....	....	....	....	....		1979-80	1982-83
Richardson, Terry	Det., St.L.	5	20	3	11	0	906	85	0	5.63	....	....	....	....	....	....	....	....		1973-74	1978-79
Ridley, Curt	NYR, Van., Tor.	6	104	27	47	16	5498	355	1	3.87	2	0	2	0	120	8	0	4.00		1974-75	1980-81
Riendeau, Vincent	Mtl., St.L., Det., Bos.	8	184	85	65	20	10423	573	5	3.30	25	11	12	0	1277	71	1	3.34		1987-88	1994-95
Riggin, Dennis	Det.	2	18	6	10	2	985	54	1	3.29	....	....	....	....	....	....	....	....		1959-60	1962-63
Riggin, Pat	Atl., Cgy., Wsh., Bos., Pit.	9	350	153	120	52	19872	1135	11	3.43	25	8	13	0	1336	72	0	3.23		1979-80	1987-88
Ring, Bob	Bos.	1	1	0	0	0	33	4	0	7.27	....	....	....	....	....	....	....	....		1965-66	1965-66
Rivard, Fern	Min.	4	55	9	26	11	2865	190	2	3.98	....	....	....	....	....	....	....	....		1968-69	1974-75
• Roach, John Ross	Tor., NYR, Det.	14	492	219	204	68	30444	1246	58	2.46	34	15	16	3	2206	69	8	1.88	1	1921-22	1934-35
• Roberts, Moe	Bos., NYA, Chi.	4	10	2	5	0	506	31	0	3.68	....	....	....	....	....	....	....	....		1925-26	1951-52
• Robertson, Earl	NYA, Bro., Det.	6	190	60	95	34	11820	575	16	2.92	15	7	7	0	995	29	2	1.75	1	1936-37	1941-42
• Rollins, Al	Tor., Chi., NYR	9	430	141	205	83	25723	1196	28	2.79	13	6	7	0	755	30	0	2.38	1	1949-50	1959-60
Romano, Roberto	Pit., Bos.	6	126	46	63	8	7111	471	4	3.97	....	....	....	....	....	....	....	....		1982-83	1993-94

Name	NHL Teams	NHL Seasons	Regular Schedule								Playoffs								NHL Cup Wins	First NHL Season	Last NHL Season
			GP	W	L	T	Mins	GA	SO	Avg	GP	W	L	T	Mins	GA	SO	Avg			
Rupp, Pat	Det.	1	1	0	1	0	60	4	0	4.00	....	....	....	....	....	....	....	....		1963-64	1963-64
Rutherford, Jim	Det., Pit., Tor., L.A.	13	457	151	227	59	25895	1576	14	3.65	8	2	5	0	440	28	0	3.82		1970-71	1982-83
Rutledge, Wayne	L.A.	3	82	28	37	9	4325	241	2	3.34	8	2	4	0	378	20	0	3.17		1967-68	1969-70
St. Croix, Rick	Phi., Tor.	8	129	49	54	18	7275	450	2	3.71	11	4	6	0	562	29	1	3.10		1977-78	1984-85
St. Laurent, Sam	N.J., Det.	5	34	7	12	4	1572	92	1	3.51	1	0	0	0	10	1	0	6.00		1985-86	1989-90
§ Sands, Charlie	Mtl.	1	1	0	0	0	25	5	0	12.00	....	....	....	....	....	....	....	....		1939-40	1939-40
Sands, Mike	Min.	2	6	0	5	0	302	26	0	5.17	....	....	....	....	....	....	....	....		1984-85	1986-87
Sauve, Bob	Buf., Det., Chi., N.J.	13	420	182	154	54	23711	1377	8	3.48	34	15	16	0	1850	95	4	3.08		1976-77	1987-88
• Sawchuk, Terry	Det., Bos., Tor., L.A., NYR	21	971	447	330	172	57228	2401	103	2.52	106	54	48	0	6290	267	12	2.55	4	1949-50	1969-70
Schaefer, Joe	NYR	2	2	0	2	0	86	8	0	5.58	....	....	....	....	....	....	....	....		1959-60	1960-61
Scott, Ron	NYR, L.A.	5	28	8	13	4	1450	91	0	3.77	1	0	0	0	32	4	0	7.50	1	1983-84	1989-90
Sevigny, Richard	Mtl., Que.	8	176	80	54	20	9485	507	5	3.21	4	0	3	0	208	13	0	3.75		1979-80	1986-87
Sharples, Scott	Cgy.	1	1	0	0	1	65	4	0	3.69	....	....	....	....	....	....	....	....		1991-92	1991-92
§ Shields, Al	NYA	1	2	0	0	0	41	9	0	13.17	....	....	....	....	....	....	....	....		1931-32	1931-32
Simmons, Don	Bos., Tor., NYR	11	247	101	100	40	14435	705	20	2.93	24	13	11	0	1436	64	3	2.67	2	1956-57	1968-69
Simmons, Gary	Cal., Clev., L.A.	4	107	30	57	15	6162	366	5	3.56	1	0	0	0	20	1	0	3.00		1974-75	1977-78
Skidmore, Paul	St.L.	1	2	1	1	0	120	6	0	3.00	....	....	....	....	....	....	....	....		1981-82	1981-82
Skorodenski, Warren	Chi., Edm.	5	35	12	11	4	1732	100	2	3.46	2	0	0	0	33	6	0	10.91		1981-82	1987-88
Smith, Al	Tor., Pit., Det., Buf., Hfd., Col.	10	233	74	99	36	12752	735	10	3.46	6	1	4	0	317	21	0	3.97		1965-66	1980-81
Smith, Billy	L.A., NYI	18	680	305	233	105	38431	2031	22	3.17	132	88	36	0	7645	348	5	2.73	4	1971-72	1988-89
Smith, Gary	Tor., Oak., Cal., Chi., Van., Min., Wsh., Wpg.	14	532	173	261	74	29619	1675	26	3.39	20	5	13	0	1153	62	1	3.23		1965-66	1979-80
• Smith, Norman	Mtl.M., Det.	8	199	81	83	35	12357	479	17	2.33	12	9	2	0	820	18	3	1.32	2	1931-32	1944-45
Sneddon, Bob	Cal.	1	5	0	2	0	225	21	0	5.60	....	....	....	....	....	....	....	....		1970-71	1970-71
Soetaert, Doug	NYR, Wpg., Mtl.	12	284	110	104	42	15583	1030	6	3.97	5	1	2	0	180	14	0	4.67	1	1975-76	1986-87
Soucy, Christian	Chi.	1	1	0	0	0	3	0	0	0.00	....	....	....	....	....	....	....	....		1993-94	1993-94
• Spooner, Red	Pit.	1	1	0	1	0	60	6	0	6.00	....	....	....	....	....	....	....	....		1929-30	1929-30
§ • Spring, Jesse	Ham.	1	1	0	0	0	2	0	0	0.00	....	....	....	....	....	....	....	....		1924-25	1924-25
Staniowski, Ed	St.L., Wpg., Hfd.	10	219	67	104	21	12075	818	2	4.06	8	1	6	0	428	28	0	3.93		1975-76	1984-85
§ Starr, Harold	Mtl.M.	1	1	0	0	0	3	0	0	0.00	....	....	....	....	....	....	....	....		1931-32	1931-32
Stefan, Greg	Det.	9	299	115	127	30	16333	1068	5	3.92	30	12	17	0	1681	99	1	3.53		1981-82	1989-90
Stein, Phil	Tor.	1	1	0	0	1	70	2	0	1.71	....	....	....	....	....	....	....	....		1939-40	1939-40
Stephenson, Wayne	St.L., Phi., Wsh.	10	328	146	103	49	18343	937	14	3.06	26	11	12	0	1522	79	2	3.11	1	1971-72	1980-81
Stevenson, Doug	NYR, Chi.	2	8	2	6	0	480	39	0	4.88	....	....	....	....	....	....	....	....		1944-45	1945-46
Stewart, Charles	Bos.	3	77	30	41	5	4742	194	10	2.45	....	....	....	....	....	....	....	....		1924-25	1926-27
Stewart, Jim	Bos.	1	1	0	1	0	20	5	0	15.00	....	....	....	....	....	....	....	....		1979-80	1979-80
Stuart, Herb	Det.	1	3	1	2	0	180	5	0	1.67	....	....	....	....	....	....	....	....		1926-27	1926-27
Sylvestri, Don	Bos.	1	3	0	0	2	102	6	0	3.53	....	....	....	....	....	....	....	....		1984-85	1984-85
Takko, Kari	Min., Edm.	6	142	37	71	14	7317	475	1	3.90	4	0	1	0	109	7	0	3.85		1985-86	1990-91
Tanner, John	Que.	3	21	2	11	5	1084	65	1	3.60	....	....	....	....	....	....	....	....		1989-90	1991-92
Tataryn, Dave	NYR	1	2	1	1	0	80	10	0	7.50	....	....	....	....	....	....	....	....		1976-77	1976-77
Taylor, Bobby	Phi., Pit.	5	46	15	17	6	2268	155	0	4.10	....	....	....	....	....	....	....	....	1	1971-72	1975-76
• Teno, Harvey	Det.	1	5	2	3	0	300	15	0	3.00	....	....	....	....	....	....	....	....		1938-39	1938-39
Thomas, Wayne	Mtl., Tor., NYR	8	243	103	93	34	13768	766	10	3.34	15	6	8	0	849	50	1	3.53		1972-73	1980-81
• Thompson, Tiny	Bos., Det.	12	553	284	194	75	34175	1183	81	2.08	44	20	24	0	2972	93	7	1.88	1	1928-29	1939-40
§ Toppazzini, Jerry	Bos.	1	1	0	0	0	1	0	0	0.00	....	....	....	....	....	....	....	....		1960-61	1960-61
Tremblay, Vince	Tor., Pit.	5	58	12	26	8	2785	223	1	4.80	....	....	....	....	....	....	....	....		1979-80	1983-84
Tucker, Ted	Cal.	1	5	1	1	1	177	10	0	3.39	....	....	....	....	....	....	....	....		1973-74	1973-74
• Turner, Joe	Det.	1	1	0	0	1	70	3	0	2.57	....	....	....	....	....	....	....	....		1941-42	1941-42
Vachon, Rogie	Mtl., L.A., Det., Bos.	16	795	355	291	127	46298	2310	51	2.99	48	23	23	0	2876	133	2	2.77	3	1966-67	1981-82
Veisor, Mike	Chi., Hfd., Wpg.	10	139	41	62	26	7806	532	5	4.09	4	0	2	0	180	15	0	5.00		1973-74	1983-84
• Vezina, Georges	Mtl.	9	190	103	81	5	11586	633	13	3.28	26	17	8	1	1596	74	4	2.78	2	1917-18	1925-26
Villemure, Gilles	NYR, Chi.	10	205	100	64	29	11581	542	13	2.81	14	5	5	0	656	32	0	2.93		1963-64	1976-77
Wakely, Ernie	Mtl., St.L.	5	113	41	42	17	6244	290	8	2.79	10	2	6	0	509	37	1	4.36		1962-63	1971-72
• Walsh, James	Mtl.M., NYA	7	108	48	43	16	6642	256	12	2.31	8	2	4	2	570	16	2	1.68		1926-27	1932-33
Wamsley, Rick	Mtl., St.L., Cgy., Tor.	13	407	204	131	46	23123	1287	12	3.34	27	7	18	0	1397	81	0	3.48	1	1980-81	1992-93
Watt, Jim	St.L.	1	1	0	0	0	20	2	0	6.00	....	....	....	....	....	....	....	....		1973-74	1973-74
Weeks, Steve	NYR, Hfd., Van., NYI, L.A., Ott.	13	290	111	119	33	15879	989	5	3.74	12	3	5	0	486	27	0	3.33		1980-81	1992-93
Wetzel, Carl	Det., Min.	2	7	1	3	1	301	22	0	4.39	....	....	....	....	....	....	....	....		1964-65	1967-68
Wilson, Dunc	Phi., Van., Tor., NYR, Pit.	10	287	80	150	33	15851	988	8	3.74	....	....	....	....	....	....	....	....		1969-70	1978-79
Wilson, Lefty	Det., Tor., Bos.	3	3	0	0	1	81	1	0	0.74	....	....	....	....	....	....	....	....		1953-54	1957-58
• Winkler, Hal	NYR, Bos.	2	75	35	26	14	4739	126	21	1.60	10	2	3	5	640	18	2	1.69		1926-27	1927-28
Wolfe, Bernie	Wsh.	4	120	20	61	21	6104	424	1	4.17	....	....	....	....	....	....	....	....		1975-76	1978-79
Wood, Alex	NYA	1	1	0	1	0	70	3	0	2.57	....	....	....	....	....	....	....	....		1936-37	1936-37
Worsley, Gump	NYR, Mtl., Min.	21	861	335	352	150	50183	2432	43	2.91	70	40	26	0	4081	192	5	2.82	4	1952-53	1973-74
• Worters, Roy	Pit., NYA, Mtl.	12	484	171	229	83	30175	1143	66	2.27	11	3	6	2	690	24	3	2.09		1925-26	1936-37
Worthy, Chris	Oak., Cal.	3	26	5	10	4	1326	98	0	4.43	....	....	....	....	....	....	....	....		1968-69	1970-71
§ Young, Doug	Det.	1	1	0	0	0	21	1	0	2.86	....	....	....	....	....	....	....	....		1933-34	1933-34
Zanier, Mike	Edm.	1	3	1	1	1	185	12	0	3.89	....	....	....	....	....	....	....	....		1984-85	1984-85

1997-98 Transactions

September 1997

28 – NHL Waiver Draft

Pos.	Player	Claimed By	Claimed From
C	**Tim Taylor**	Boston	Detroit
LW	**Tom Chorske**	NY Islanders	Ottawa
LW	**Mike Peluso**	Calgary	NY Rangers
C	**Robert Lang**	Boston	Pittsburgh
RW	**Mick Vukota**	Tampa Bay	NY Islanders
C	**Pascal Rheaume**	St. Louis	New Jersey
G	**Jimmy Waite**	Phoenix	Chicago
LW	**Brent Severyn**	Anaheim	Colorado
LW	**Scott Daniels**	New Jersey	Philadelphia

October 1997

10 – RW **Martin Gendron** and a sixth-round choice (G **Jonathan Pelletier**) in the 1998 Entry Draft traded to Chicago by Washington for Chicago's fifth-round choice (C **Erik Wendell**) in the 1998 Entry Draft.

15 – LW **Jason Bowen** traded to Edmonton by Philadelphia for RW **Brantt Myhres**.

21 – RW **Mike Maneluk** traded to Philadelphia by Ottawa for cash.

22 – C **Greg Johnson** traded to Chicago by Pittsburgh for D **Tuomas Gronman**.

November 1997

12 – G **Andrei Trefilov** traded to Chicago by Buffalo for future considerations.

14 – LW **Dave Lowry** and Florida's first-round choice (C **Vincent Lecavalier**) (traded to Tampa Bay) in the 1998 Entry Draft traded to San Jose by Florida for LW **Viktor Kozlov** and Florida's fifth-round choice (D **Jaroslav Spacek**) (previously acquired) in the 1998 Entry Draft.

14 – RW **Brad Smyth** traded to NY Rangers by Los Angeles for a conditional draft choice.

18 – D **Sean Hill** traded to Carolina by Ottawa for RW **Chris Murray**.

20 – C **Mike Ricci** and a second-round choice (traded to Buffalo) in the 1998 Entry Draft (RW **Jaroslav Krisnek**) traded to San Jose by Colorado for RW **Shean Donovan** and a first-round choice (C **Alex Tanguay**) in the 1998 Entry Draft.

December 1997

7 – RW **John MacLean** and D **Ken Sutton** traded to San Jose by New Jersey for D **Doug Bodger** and C **Dody Wood**.

30 – D **Bryan Marchment**, C **Steve Kelly** and C **Jason Bonsignore** traded to Tampa Bay by Edmonton for D **Roman Hamrlik** and the rights to C **Paul Comrie**.

January 1998

2 – D **Jeff Brown** traded to Toronto by Carolina for a conditional choice in the 1999 Entry Draft.

3 – G **Sean Burke**, D **Enrico Ciccone** and LW **Geoff Sanderson** traded to Vancouver by Carolina for G **Kirk McLean** and LW **Martin Gelinas**.

4 – RW **Bill Guerin** and LW **Valeri Zelepukin** traded to Edmonton by New Jersey for C **Jason Arnott** and D **Bryan Muir**.

8 – LW **Reid Simpson** traded to Chicago by New Jersey for a fourth-round choice (D **Mikko Jokela**) in the 1998 Entry Draft and future considerations.

9 – D **Bobby Dollas** traded to Edmonton by Anaheim for D **Drew Bannister**.

15 – RW **Stephane Richer**, C **Darcy Tucker** and D **David Wilkie** traded to Tampa Bay by Montreal for LW **Patrick Poulin**, RW **Mick Vukota** and D **Igor Ulanov**.

16 – RW **Dino Ciccarelli** and D **Jeff Norton** traded to Florida by Tampa Bay for G **Mark Fitzpatrick** and RW **Jody Hull**.

17 – C **Vaclav Prospal**, RW **Pat Falloon** and Dallas's second-round choice (LW **Chris Bala**) in the 1998 Entry Draft (previously acquired) traded to Ottawa by Philadelphia for RW **Alexandre Daigle**.

February 1998

1 – C **Valeri Bure** and a fourth-round choice (C **Shaun Sutter**) in the 1998 Entry Draft traded to Calgary by Montreal for RW **Jonas Hoglund** and D **Zarley Zalapski**.

4 – LW **Geoff Sanderson** traded to Buffalo by Vancouver for LW **Brad May** and Buffalo's third-round choice in the 1999 Entry Draft.

5 – C **Mike Sillinger** traded to Philadelphia by Vancouver for Philadelphia's fifth-round choice in the 1998 Entry Draft (C **Garret Prosofsky**) (traded back to Philadelphia).

5 – C **Peter Zezel** traded to Vancouver by New Jersey for Vancouver's fifth-round choice (RW **Anton But**) in the 1998 Entry Draft.

6 – C **Trevor Linden** traded to NY Islanders by Vancouver for D **Bryan McCabe**, LW **Todd Bertuzzi** and NY Islanders' third-round choice (LW **Jarkko Ruutu**) in the 1998 Entry Draft.

6 – C **Travis Green**, D **Doug Houda** and RW **Tony Tuzzolino** traded to Anaheim by NY Islanders for D **Jean-Jacques Daigneault**, C **Mark Janssens** and RW **Joe Sacco**.

March 1998

3 – D **Grant Ledyard** traded to Boston by Vancouver for Boston's eighth-round choice (LW **Curtis Valentine**) in the 1998 Entry Draft.

4 – D **Keith Carney** and RW **Jim Cummins** traded to Phoenix by Chicago for D **Jayson More** and C **Chad Kilger**.

4 – G **Sean Burke** traded to Philadelphia by Vancouver for G **Garth Snow**.

7 – RW **Lonny Bohonos** traded to Toronto by Vancouver for C **Brandon Convery**.

8 – LW **Esa Tikkanen** traded to Washington by Florida for LW **Dwayne Hay** and future considerations.

9 – D **Frank Musil** traded to Edmonton by Ottawa for D **Scott Ferguson**.

14 – D **Jamie Huscroft** traded to Vancouver by Tampa Bay for D **Enrico Ciccone**.

14 – RW **Martin Gendron** traded to Montreal by Chicago for RW **David Ling**.

17 – LW **Per Gustafsson** traded to Ottawa by Toronto for Ottawa's eighth-round choice (D **Dwight Wolfe**) in the 1998 Entry Draft.

23 – LW **Gino Odjick** traded to NY Islanders by Vancouver for D **Jason Strudwick**.

24 – D **Dave Babych** and Philadelphia's fifth-round choice (C **Garrett Prosofsky**) in the 1998 Entry Draft (previously acquired) traded to Philadelphia by Vancouver for Philadelphia's third-round choice (RW **Justin Morrison**) in the 1998 Entry Draft.

24 – D **Dmitri Mironov** traded to Detroit by Anaheim for D **Jamie Pushor** and Detroit's fourth-round choice (LW **Viktor Wallin**) in the 1998 Entry Draft.

24 – RW **Ray Sheppard** traded to Carolina by Florida for G **Kirk McLean**.

24 – D **Jeff Brown** traded to Washington by Toronto for D **Sylvain Cote**.

24 – LW **Jason Dawe** traded to NY Islanders by Buffalo for D **Jason Holland** and LW **Paul Kruse**.

24 – D **Dan McGillis** and Edmonton's second-round choice (D **Jason Beckett**) in the 1998 Entry Draft traded to Philadelphia by Edmonton for D **Janne Niinimaa**.

24 – D **Mark Janssens** traded to Phoenix by NY Islanders for Phoenix's ninth-round choice (RW **Jason Doyle**) in the 1998 Entry Draft.

24 – LW **Warren Rychel** and a conditional choice in the 1999 Entry Draft traded to Colorado by Anaheim for C **Josef Marha**.

24 – C **Sean Pronger** traded to Pittsburgh by Anaheim for the rights to G **Patrick Lalime**.

24 – D **Todd Gill** traded to St. Louis by San Jose for RW **Joe Murphy**.

24 – D **Bryan Marchment** and D **David Shaw** traded to San Jose by Tampa Bay for RW **Andrei Nazarov** and the option to acquire Florida's first-round choice (C **Vincent Lecavalier**) in the 1998 Entry Draft (previously acquired) in return for Tampa Bay's first-round choice in the 1998 Entry Draft (later traded to Nashville). Nashville selected David Legwand.

24 – C **Mike Eastwood** traded to St. Louis by NY Rangers for C **Harry York**.

24 – C **Mike Kennedy** traded to Dallas by Toronto for Dallas's eighth-round choice (RW **Mihail Travnicek**) in the 1998 Entry Draft.

24 – RW **Sandy McCarthy**, Calgary's third-round choice (LW **Brad Richards**) in the 1998 Entry Draft and their option of either their own fifth-round choice (D **Curtis Rich**) or Anaheim's fifth-round choice (previously acquired) in the 1998 Entry Draft traded to Tampa Bay by Calgary for C **Jason Wiemer**.

24 – RW **Todd Harvey**, LW **Bob Errey** and Dallas's fourth-round choice (LW **Boyd Kane**) in the 1998 Entry Draft traded to NY Rangers by Dallas for C **Brian Skrudland**, RW **Mike Keane** and either NY Rangers' sixth-round choice (LW **Pavel Patera**) in the 1998 Entry Draft.

24 – RW **Tom Fitzgerald** traded to Colorado by Florida for the rights to LW **Mark Parrish** and Anaheim's third-round choice (D **Lance Ward**) in the 1998 Entry Draft (previously acquired).

24 – G **Jason Muzzatti** traded to San Jose by NY Rangers for D **Rich Brennan**.

24 – D **Ryan Risidore** traded to NY Rangers by Chicago for RW **Ryan Vandenbussche**.

24 – D **Jamie Macoun** traded to Detroit by Toronto for Tampa Bay's fourth-round choice (LW **Alexei Ponikarovsky**) in the 1998 Entry Draft (previously acquired).

May 1998

29 – RW **Marian Cisar** traded to Nashville by Los Angeles for future considerations.

30 – LW **Dmitri Nabokov** traded to NY Islanders by Chicago for RW **Jean-Pierre Dumont** and NY Islanders' fifth-round choice in the 1998 Entry Draft (later traded to Philadelphia. Philadelphia selected **Francis Belanger**.)

June 1998

1 – G **Randy Petruk** traded to Carolina by Colorado for Carolina's fifth-round choice in the 1999 Entry Draft.

1 – LW **Colin Pepperall** traded to Chicago by NY Rangers for a conditional choice in the 1999 Entry Draft.

11 – C **Craig Janney** traded to Tampa Bay by Phoenix for LW **Louie DeBrusk** and Tampa Bay's fifth-round choice (D **Jay Leach**) in the 1998 Entry Draft.

16 – C **Josef Beranek** traded to Edmonton by Pittsburgh for D **Bobby Dollas** and C **Tony Hrkac**.

17 – G **Ken Wregget** and LW **Dave Roche** traded to Calgary by Pittsburgh for C **German Titov** and LW **Todd Hlushko**.

18 – D **Doug Bodger** traded to Los Angeles by New Jersey for Boston's fourth-round choice (LW **Pierre Dagenais**) in the 1998 Entry Draft (previously acquired).

18 – G **Bill Ranford** traded to Tampa Bay by Washington for Tampa Bay's third-round choice (C **Todd Hornung**) in the 1998 Entry Draft and second-round choice in the 1999 Entry Draft.

18 – G **Steve Shields** and Buffalo's fourth-round choice (RW **Miroslav Zalesak**) in the 1998 Entry Draft traded to San Jose by Buffalo for G **Kay Whitmore**, Colorado's second-round choice (RW **Jaroslav Kristek**) in the 1998 Entry Draft (previously acquired) and San Jose's fifth-round choice in the 2000 Entry Draft.

18 – LW **Jim McKenzie** traded to Anaheim by Phoenix for RW **Jean-Francois Jomphe**.

18 – G **Eric Fichaud** traded to Edmonton by NY Islanders for LW **Mike Watt**.

26 – C **Jim Dowd** traded to Nashville by Calgary for future considerations.

26 – G **Dominic Roussel** and D **Jeff Staples** traded to Nashville by Philadelphia for Nashville's seventh-round choice (G **Cam Ondrik**) in the 1998 Entry Draft.

26 – C **Sebastien Bordeleau** traded to Nashville by Montreal for future considerations.

26 – LW **Ville Peltonen** traded to Nashville by San Jose for Nashville's fifth-round choice in the 1998 Entry Draft (later traded to Phoenix. Phoenix selected G **Josh Blackburn**).

26 – D **Jan Vopat** and D **Kimmo Timonen** traded to Nashville by Los Angeles for future considerations.

26 – LW **Sergei Krivokrasov** traded to Nashville by Chicago for future considerations.

26 – C **Darren Turcotte** and future considerations traded to Nashville by St. Louis for future considerations.

27 – D **Paul Coffey** traded to Chicago by Philadelphia for Chicago's fifth-round choice (LW **Francis Belanger**) in the 1998 Entry Draft.

27 – Tampa Bay's first-round choice (C **David Legwand**) and New Jersey's third-round choice (LW **Geoff Koch**) in the 1998 Entry Draft (previously acquired) traded to Nashville by San Jose for Nashville's first-round choice (D **Brad Stuart**) and second-round choice (RW **Jonathan Cheechoo**) in the 1998 Entry Draft.

27 – Toronto's first-round choice (LW **Mark Bell**) and Toronto's fourth-round choice (C **Matthias Trattnig**) in the 1998 Entry Draft traded to Chicago by Toronto for Chicago's first-round choice (C **Nikolai Antropov**) and third-round choice (G **Jamie Hodson**) and Carolina's fifth-round choice (RW **Morgan Warren**) (previously acquired) in the 1998 Entry Draft.

27 – Dallas's first-round choice (C **Scott Gomez**) in the 1998 Entry Draft traded to New Jersey by Dallas for Carolina's second-round choice (D **John Erskine**) (previously acquired) and New Jersey's second-round choice (RW **Tyler Bouck**) in the 1998 Entry Draft.

27 – Nashville's fifth-round choice (G **Josh Blackburn**) in the 1998 Entry Draft (previously acquired) traded to Phoenix by San Jose for Phoenix's fifth-round choice in the 1999 Entry Draft.

30 – D **Peter Popovic** traded to NY Rangers by Montreal for LW **Sylvain Blouin** and a sixth-round choice in the 1999 Entry Draft.

30 – LW **Mike Sullivan** traded to Phoenix by Nashville for a seventh-round choice in the 1999 Entry Draft.

July 1998

2 – RW **Ladislav Kohn** traded to Toronto by Calgary for D **David Cooper**.

7 – RW **Vitali Yachmenev** traded to Nashville by Los Angeles for future considerations.

9 – C **Tony Hrkac** traded to Dallas by Nashville for future considerations.

14 – C **Bob Bassen** traded to Calgary by Dallas for C **Aaron Gavey**.

14 – RW **Doug Brown** traded back to Detroit by Nashville for C **Petr Sykora**, a third-round choice in the 1999 Entry Draft and future considerations.

14 – LW **Jorgen Jonsson** traded to NY Islanders by Calgary for LW **Jan Hlavac**.

17 – D **Michal Sykora** traded to Tampa Bay by Chicago for G **Mark Fitzpatrick** and a fourth-round choice in the 1999 Entry Draft.

31 – G **Manny Legace** traded to Los Angeles by Carolina for a conditional choice in the 1999 Entry Draft.

August, 1998

6 – G **Johan Hedberg** traded to San Jose by Philadelphia for San Jose's seventh-round choice in the 1999 Entry Draft.

7 – G **Rick Tabaracci** traded to Washington from Calgary for future considerations.

11 – LW **Stu Grimson** and D **Kevin Haller** traded to Anaheim from Carolina for D **David Karpa** and Anaheim's fourth-round choice in the 2000 Entry Draft.

19 – C **Jeff Nelson** traded to Nashville from Washington for future considerations.

21 – LW **Brian Felsner** traded to Ottawa from Chicago for D **Justin Hocking**.

25 – G **Chris Terreri** traded to New Jersey from Chicago for a conditional choice in the 1999 Entry Draft.

25 – D **Raymond Giroux** traded to NY Islanders from Philadelphia for NY Islander's sixth-round choice in the 2000 Entry Draft.

26 – D **Ken Sutton** traded to New Jersey from San Jose for future considerations.

Trades and free agent signings that occurred after September 1, 1998 are listed on page 258.

Notes

TOTAL
HOCKEY